Badger
STATE ANIMAL

Muskellunge
STATE FISH

Sugar Maple
STATE TREE

Wood Violet
STATE FLOWER

State Representative
Jeff Fitzgerald

State Capitol
Room 201 West

P.O. Box 8952
Madison, WI 53708-8952

(608) 266-2540
Rep.Fitzgerald@legis.wi.gov

SCOTT
FITZGERALD
WISCONSIN STATE SENATOR
SENATE REPUBLICAN LEADER

STATE CAPITOL: (608) 266-5660
P.O. BOX 7882 ▪ MADISON, WI 53707-7882

DISTRICT OFFICE: (920) 386-2218
N4692 MAPLE ROAD ▪ JUNEAU, WI 53039

WWW.SENATORFITZGERALD.COM
SEN.FITZGERALD@LEGIS.WI.GOV

State of Wisconsin
2009 - 2010
Blue Book

Compiled by the
Wisconsin Legislative Reference Bureau

**Wisconsin Legislative
Reference Bureau**

Sold and Distributed By:

Document Sales Unit
Department of Administration
202 South Thornton Avenue
P.O. Box 7840, Madison, WI 53707
Telephone: (608) 266-3358

*Published Biennially
In Odd-Numbered Years*

The following LRB staff members produced the *2009-2010 Wisconsin Blue Book*:

Lynn Lemanski, lead publications editor and co-editor
Kathleen Sitter, photo editor

Jason Anderson, legislative analyst
Kinnic Eagan, legislative analyst
Sam-Omar Hall, legislative analyst
Peter G. Herman, IT analyst
Lauren Jackson, legislative analyst
Michael J. Keane, senior legislative analyst
Robert A. Paolino, senior legislative analyst
Clark G. Radatz, senior legislative analyst
Daniel F. Ritsche, senior legislative analyst
Crystal L. Smith, publications editor

Lawrence S. Barish, editor

ISBN 978-0-9752820-3-8

JIM DOYLE
GOVERNOR
STATE OF WISCONSIN

July 2009

Dear Readers:

The State of Wisconsin has always celebrated many diverse qualities that make it such an excellent place to live, work and play. From the shores of Lake Michigan to the thousands of lakes many use for recreation, to Milwaukee's beautiful skyline and to the farms and forests spread throughout our state, Wisconsin is a state we are proud to call home.

Residents of Wisconsin have become accustomed to state leaders who fight for the best interests and rights for everyone, and strive to improve the overall quality of life in Wisconsin. As elected leaders of our state, we will continue to work hard for our constituents. We must ensure that as public leaders, Wisconsin's government lives up to its founding values: hard work, sense of community, concern for others and commitment to educating future generations.

I am proud to lead a state with such a progressive tradition, and will continue to work with state legislators to further these principles. The State of Wisconsin's Blue Book serves as an excellent resource for information of the current and past leadership of Wisconsin. This year, the Wisconsin Blue Book features even greater insight into one of Wisconsin's most intriguing and historic fields of study – astronomy.

Astronomy is one of the first fields of science studied at the University of Wisconsin, and continues to remain at the forefront in astronomical research. In "Wisconsin at the Frontiers of Astronomy: A History of Innovation and Exploration" (Page 100), you will see the contributions of Wisconsin go beyond the borders of our state – and our planet.

Whether gazing at a starry night sky or admiring the beautiful murals of the State Capitol dome, the Wisconsin Blue Book will serve as a helpful guide to our state's history and present.
As citizens of Wisconsin, I encourage you to remain active in state politics. If there is an issue you feel particularly passionate about – whether it be health care, taxes or the environment – use the Blue Book as a resource to contact your local politicians and express your views.

Thank you for picking up the 2009-2010 State of Wisconsin Blue Book. It will undoubtedly be a resource you will both use and enjoy.

Sincerely,

Jim Doyle

(signature)

P.O. BOX 7863, MADISON, WISCONSIN 53707-7863 • (608) 266-1212 • FAX: (608) 267-8983 •
WWW.WISGOV.STATE.WI.US

State of Wisconsin
LEGISLATIVE REFERENCE BUREAU

INTRODUCTION

Each edition of the *Wisconsin Blue Book* includes a main article which focuses on some aspect of Wisconsin government or history, or our physical, cultural, or social environment. These articles supplement the detailed statistical information about the organization and functions of state government and constitute an eclectic repository of knowledge about our state and its proud traditions. Prior articles have addressed such varied topics as the Wisconsin court system, the renovation of the State Capitol, the Wisconsin Idea, and most recently, a detailed roster of the names and background of those who have served in the Wisconsin Legislature since statehood.

The feature article in this, the *2009-2010 Wisconsin Blue Book* and 89th edition in the series, takes an entirely different direction. "Wisconsin at the Frontiers of Astronomy: A History of Innovation and Exploration" by Peter Susalla and James Lattis of the University of Wisconsin-Madison, provides a wide-ranging overview of the role that the University and state have played in advancing mankind's knowledge of the universe. Jim Lattis is a faculty associate in the UW-Madison Astronomy Department and cofounder and Director of UW Space Place, an education and public outreach center. Peter Susalla is a doctoral candidate in the History of Science Department of the UW-Madison and wrote his master's thesis on George Comstock and the early history of the Washburn Observatory. The article that they have produced plows new ground and tells a story of the contributions Wisconsin and its state university have made to the development of the science of astronomy. The authors cover a lot of ground – beginning with the evidence of interest in the cosmos left by the cultures that existed many thousands of years before the arrival of Europeans in what is now Wisconsin, to the establishment of the Washburn Observatory, to the contributions UW scientists have made to the Hubble Space Telescope and the International Space Station, and finally, to the groundbreaking research currently being conducted in places as far afield as the South Pole and South Africa.

The text is augmented by a generous number of photos and graphics, many in full color, which add visual interest and additional information. A striking poster, "Stardust Memories" highlights some of the cosmic phenomena studied by UW astronomers and is a colorful and informative adjunct to the article. The *Blue Book* editors are grateful to authors Lattis and Susalla and their colleagues in the UW Astronomy department for their efforts in producing this exceptional contribution to the *2009-2010 Blue Book*.

The feature article topic is particularly fitting in that the year 2009 has been designated as the International Year of Astronomy. 2009 marks the 400th anniversary of the discoveries made by Galileo who pointed a telescope skyward to peer into the cosmos. That was humankind's first magnified look at the moon and is considered to be the birth of the science of astronomy. In addition, in 2009 the UW's Washburn Observatory reopened after undergoing extensive restoration and remodeling.

The astronomical theme is continued throughout the book. LRB photo editor Kathleen Sitter, who designed the layout of the feature article, also chose the vivid photographs and graphics on each of the 12 chapter divider pages which organize the book.

Finally, the photographs appearing on the front and back covers deserve mention. The striking images of the moon, the State Capitol dome and the Madison skyline that appear on the front and back covers are not only dramatic but are an especially fitting complement to the astronomical theme. The photos are the work of John Rummel, a Madison school psychologist and an amateur astronomer and photographer of considerable talent. The photographs have not been digitally altered or manipulated in any manner and are the products of years of painstaking planning by John in his quest to photograph the capitol dome and Madison skyline framed by the rising and setting moon. Studying the movement of the moon and its relationship to the capitol and finding the appropriate location to take his photos required years of trial and error. Success also depended on the vagaries of the weather—a clear sky and the absence of ground haze were prerequisites. Working with a narrow window of opportunity, John ultimately succeeded in aligning the heavens and the earth, producing the dramatic images that we have reproduced here.

The cover photo of a rising moon, captured in stunning detail and seemingly floating just above the Madison skyline and adjacent to the State Capitol, is further enhanced by the sailboats bathed in the lights reflected off the tranquil waters of Lake Mendota. It was taken from the northwest shore of Lake Mendota near Governor Nelson State Park. The photo on the back cover is a fitting counterpoint to the cover photo. It was taken from the eastern shore of Lake Monona and is highlighted by the setting crescent moon in the twilight sky. The image also includes, in perfect alignment, the planets Saturn and Mars, and the star Regulus.

We are indebted to John Rummel for sharing his remarkable photos and generously allowing us to reprint them on the covers of the *2009-2010 Blue Book*.

As always, the *Blue Book* contains a wealth of information befitting its status as the Almanac of Wisconsin State Government. We hope that you find the latest edition to be an informative and useful resource and a worthy addition to the *Blue Book* series.

Lawrence S. Barish
Blue Book Editor
July 2009

TABLE OF CONTENTS

Biographies

Biographies and photos: Wisconsin constitutional executive officers, Supreme Court justices, members of the U.S. Congress from Wisconsin, and legislators (also includes congressional and legislative district maps)

The Earth and Moon

(NASA, JPL)

ALPHABETICAL INDEX TO BIOGRAPHIES

GOVERNOR

Jim Doyle (Dem.): Born Washington, D.C., November 23, 1945; married; 2 children. Graduate West H.S., Madison 1963; attended Stanford U. 1963-66; B.A. UW-Madison 1967; J.D. (*cum laude*) Harvard U. Law School 1972. Attorney. Former Madison law firm partner; lecturer, UW Law School; attorney for a federal legal services office on Navajo Indian Reservation in Chinle, AZ (1972-75). Served in Peace Corps. Member: Amer. Bar Assn., State Bar of Wis. and Arizona and Dane Co. Bar Assns. Dane Co. District Attorney 1977-83.

Elected governor 2002; reelected 2006. Member: State of Wisconsin Building Comn. (chp.); Public Records Board; Women's Council; Transportation Projects Comn. (chp.); Council of State Governments; National Governors' Assn.; Democratic Governor's Association; Council of Great Lakes Governors (chp.); Midwest Governors' Assn.; Education Comn. of the States.

Elected attorney general 1990; reelected 1994 and 1998. Member: State Board of Commissioners of Public Lands; State Board of Canvassers; State Council on Alcohol and Other Drug Abuse; Judicial Council; National Assn. of Attorneys General (president, 1997-98) and member of its committees on Antitrust, on Civil Rights, on Criminal Law, on Environment, and on Energy Consumer Protection (exec. com.), member of its task forces on Juvenile Justice, on Health Care Fraud and Elder Abuse, and on Youth Violence and School Safety, and member of its working groups on Indian Gaming, on the Internet, and on Utility Deregulation (chp.).

Telephone: Office: (608) 266-1212; Fax: (608) 267-8983.

E-mail: governor@wisconsin.gov

Mailing address: Office: P.O. Box 7863, Madison 53707-7863.

LIEUTENANT GOVERNOR

Barbara Lawton (Dem.): Born Milwaukee, July 5, 1951; married; 2 children, 4 grandchildren. Graduate Waterford Union H.S., Waterford; B.A. Lawrence University, Appleton 1987; M.A. University of Wisconsin-Madison 1991; Honorary Doctorate of Law, Lawrence U.; Honorary Doctorate of Fine Arts, Milwaukee Institute of Art and Design 2008. Member: Greater Green Bay Area Community Foundation (founding trustee); Advisory Board to Wisconsin Institute for Public Policy and Service; Democratic Party of Wis. Former member: Entrepreneurs of Color (advisory board); Latinos Unidos (founding director); Heffernan Commission on Clean Elections; Greater Green Bay Multicultural Center (adv. bd.); Northeast Wisconsin Technical College Educational Foundation (board of directors); Planned Parenthood Advocates of Wisconsin (director).

Elected lieutenant governor 2002; reelected 2006. Member: National Lieutenant Governors Association (chp.); Wisconsin State Arts Board (chp.); American Association of Colleges and Universities National Leadership Council; Task Force on Arts and Creativity in Education (chp.); Wisconsin United for Mental Health (chp.); Women Leaders Intercultural Forum; Democratic Lieutenant Governor's Assn.

Telephone: Office: (608) 266-3516; Fax: (608) 267-3571.

Internet address: www.ltgov.wisconsin.gov

E-mail: ltgov@wisconsin.gov

Mailing address: Office: P.O. Box 2043, Madison 53701-2043.

Governor
JIM DOYLE

SECRETARY OF STATE

Douglas J. La Follette (Dem.): Single. B.S. in chemistry Marietta College 1963; M.S. in chemistry Stanford U. 1964; Ph.D. in organic chemistry Columbia U. 1967. Former director of training and development with an energy marketing company; assistant professor, UW-Parkside; public affairs director, Union of Concerned Scientists; owner and operator of a small business; research associate, UW-Madison. Member: Amer. Solar Energy Society; Audubon Society; Friends of the Earth; Phi Beta Kappa. Former member: Council of Economic Priorities; Amer. Federation of Teachers; Federation of American Scientists; Lake Michigan Federation; Southeastern Wis. Coalition for Clean Air; Clean Wisconsin (formerly Wis. Environmental Decade, founder).

Elected secretary of state 1974 and 1982; reelected since 1986. Member: State Board of Commissioners of Public Lands (chp.).

Elected to Senate 1972.

Telephone: Office: (608) 266-8888; Fax: (608) 266-3159.

Mailing address: Office: 30 West Mifflin Street, 10th Floor, P.O. Box 7848, Madison 53707-7848.

STATE TREASURER

Dawn Marie Sass (Dem.): Born Milwaukee, September 18, 1959. Graduate Milwaukee St. Mary's Academy; B.A. in history and political science UW-Milwaukee 1994; post graduate work National-Louis University 2004-05. Former Milwaukee County juvenile justice probation/custody placement specialist. Member: Democratic Party; Emily's List; National Association of State Treasurers; UW-Milwaukee Alumni Association; Smithsonian; World Wildlife Fund; Nature Conservancy; Zoological Society; Aircraft Owners and Pilots Association (AOPA); Harley Owners Group - National and Kettle Moraine Chapter (HOG); Becoming an Outdoors Woman (BOW). Delegate to the Democratic National Convention 2004, 2000, 1996; member of credentials committee, Democratic National Convention 2008.

Elected state treasurer 2006. Member: State Board of Commissioners of Public Lands; State Depository Selection Board; Insurance Security Fund (bd. of dir.); State of Wisconsin Investment Board (treas.); Wisconsin Retirement Fund (treas.); MissingMoney.com task force through NAUPA/NAST.

Telephone: Office: (608) 266-1714; (800) 462-2814 (toll free); Fax: (608) 266-2647.

E-mail: dawn.sass@wisconsin.gov

Mailing address: Office: 1 South Pinckney Street, 3rd Floor, Suite 360, P.O. Box 7871, Madison 53707-7871.

ATTORNEY GENERAL

J.B. Van Hollen (Rep.): Born Rice Lake, February 19, 1966; married; 2 children. Graduate Ondossagon H.S. 1984; B.A. St. Olaf College (Northfield, MN) 1988; J.D. UW-Madison 1990. Attorney. Former U.S. Attorney, Western District of Wis. (2002-05); Bayfield County District Attorney (1999-2002); Ashland County District Attorney (1993-99). Former assistant U.S. attorney and former state public defender. Member: State Bar of Wis.; National Association of Attorneys General (exec. com. – Midwestern Region Chair of NAAG); Republican Attorneys General Association (exec. com); Republican Party of Wisconsin; Republican Party of Dane County; National Rifle Association; Living Water Lutheran Church; Free and Accepted Masons; George Washington Masonic National Memorial Assn. (bd. of dir.); National Bar Committees. Former member: Iron River Fire Department; Iron River EMS.

Elected attorney general 2006. Member: State Board of Commissioners of Public Lands.

Telephone: Office: (608) 266-1221; Fax: (608) 267-2779.

Mailing address: Office: Room 114 East, State Capitol, Madison 53702.

STATE SUPERINTENDENT OF PUBLIC INSTRUCTION

Elizabeth Burmaster (nonpartisan office): Born Baltimore, MD, July 26, 1954; married; 3 children. Graduate Governor Thomas Johnson H.S., Frederick, MD; B.M. UW-Madison 1976; M.S. UW-Madison 1984; honorary doctorates, Beloit College and Edgewood College 2004. Former music and drama teacher, district fine arts coordinator, and principal in Madison Metropolitan School District (Hawthorne Elementary and Madison West High School).

Elected state superintendent 2001; reelected 2005. Member: UW Board of Regents; Wisconsin Technical College System Board; Governor's Council on Workforce Investment; Council of Chief State School Officers (past pres.); National Center for Learning and Citizenship (past chp.); National Pre-K Now Advisory Bd.

Telephone: Office: (608) 266-1771; (800) 441-4563 (toll free).

E-mail: state.superintendent@dpi.state.wi.us

Mailing address: Office: 125 South Webster Street, P.O. Box 7841, Madison 53707-7841.

Tony Evers (nonpartisan office): Born Plymouth, November 5, 1951; married; 3 children. Graduate Plymouth H.S. 1969; B.S. UW-Madison 1973; M.S. UW-Madison 1976; Ph.D. UW-Madison 1986. Former teacher, technology coordinator, principal, Tomah; superintendent of schools, Oakfield, Verona; CESA 6 administrator, Oshkosh; deputy state superintendent of public instruction. Member: Council of Chief State School Officers (past pres., Deputies Leadership Comn.). Former member: Wis. Association of CESA Administrators; Wis. Association of School District Administrators.

Elected state superintendent 2009.

Telephone: Office: (608) 266-1771.

E-mail: state.superintendent@dpi.wi.gov

Mailing address: Office: 125 South Webster Street, P.O. Box 7841, Madison 53707-7841.

**Lieutenant Governor
LAWTON**

**Secretary of State
La FOLLETTE**

**State Treasurer
SASS**

**Attorney General
VAN HOLLEN**

**State Superintendent of
Public Instruction
BURMASTER**

**State Superintendent of
Public Instruction
EVERS**

SUPREME COURT JUSTICES

Mailing address: Supreme Court, P.O. Box 1688, Madison 53701-1688. Telephone: (608) 266-1298.

CHIEF JUSTICE

Shirley S. Abrahamson: Born New York City, December 17, 1933; married; 1 child. Graduate Hunter College H.S. 1950; B.A. N.Y.U. 1953; J.D. Indiana U. Law Sch. 1956; S.J.D. UW Law Sch. 1962; D.L. (honorary) Willamette U. 1978, Ripon College 1981, Beloit College 1982, Capital U. 1983, John Marshall Law Sch. 1984, Northeastern U. 1985, Indiana U. 1986, Northland College 1988, Hamline U. 1988, Notre Dame U. 1993, Suffolk U. 1994, DePaul U. 1996, Lawrence U. 1998, Marian College 1998, Roger Williams U. School of Law 2007. Member: American Philosophical Society (elected 1998); American Academy of Arts and Sciences (fellow 1997). Recipient: Wisconsin Counties Association *Friend of County Government Award* 2007; American Judicature Society *Dwight D. Opperman Award* 2004 and *Herbert Harley Award* 1999; ABA Commission on Women in the Profession *Margaret Brent Women Lawyers of Achievement Award* 1995; UW-Madison *Distinguished Alumni Award* 1994. Featured in *Great American Judges: An Encyclopedia* 2003.

Appointed to Supreme Court August 1976 to fill vacancy created by death of Chief Justice Horace W. Wilkie; elected to full term 1979; reelected 1989, 1999, and 2009. Became chief justice August 1, 1996, upon the retirement of Chief Justice Roland B. Day.

JUSTICES

(In Order of Seniority)

Ann Walsh Bradley: Born Richland Center, July 5, 1950; married; 4 children. Graduate Richland Center H.S.; B.A. Webster College (St. Louis, MO) 1972; J.D. UW-Madison (Knapp Scholar) 1976. Former high school teacher, practicing attorney, and Marathon Co. circuit court judge. Member: National Conference on Uniform Laws; Wisconsin Judicial Council; elected member of the American Law Institute; Wisconsin Bench Bar Committee; UW Law School Board of Visitors; Amer. Judicature Soc.; American Bar Assn.; State Bar of Wis.; Federal-State Judicial Council; elected fellow of the American Bar Foundation, Wisconsin Legal History Committee; Rotary International; lecturer for the ABA's Asian Law Initiative. Served on Wis. Task Force on Children in Need. Former member: Wis. Judicial College (associate dean and faculty); Wis. Rhodes Scholarship Com. (chp.); Wis. Equal Justice Task Force; Wis. Jud. Conference (chp. and legis. com.); Civil Law Com. (exec. com.); Task Force on Children and Families; Wis. State Public Defender Board (bd. of dir.); Com. on the Admin. of Courts. Recipient: American Judicature Society's *Herbert Harley Award* 2004; *Business and Professional Woman of the Year* 1993; *Business Woman of the Year Athena Award* 1990.

Elected to Supreme Court 1995; reelected 2005.

N. Patrick Crooks: Born Green Bay, May 16, 1938; married; 6 children. Graduate Green Bay Premontre H.S. 1956; B.A. (*magna cum laude*) St. Norbert Coll. 1960; J.D. U. of Notre Dame Law Sch. 1963; Army Judge Advocate General's School at U. of VA 1963-64; Natl. Jud. Coll. at U. of Nevada-Reno May 1984; Inst. of Jud. Admin. at N.Y.U. Law Sch. 1996. Former practicing attorney (1966-77); business law instructor, UW-Green Bay (1970-72); faculty, Wis. Jud. Coll.; attorney, Military Affairs Div., Army Judge Advocate General Office, Pentagon (1964-66); legal intern, Internal Security Div., U.S. Dept. of Justice (1962). Vietnam Era vet.; served in Army (capt.) 1963-66. Member: Amer. Bar Assn. and law school evaluator in its judicial division; Fellow of the American Bar Foundation; State Bar of Wis. and its Media and Law Relations Com.; Dane Co. Bar Assn.; Brown Co. Bar Assn. (pres. 1977); Assn. for Women Lawyers of Brown Co.; Notre Dame Law Assn. (bd. of dir.); Wis. Law Foundation (exec. com.). Former member: Wis. Judicial Council (1998-2002); Juvenile Justice Study Task Force (1994-95); United Way of Brown Co. (pres. 1976-78); East Central Criminal Justice Planning Coun. (1973-85); Brown Co. Legal Aid (chp. 1971-73); Fed. Bar Assn. (1964-65). Recipient: Notre Dame Academy *Distinguished Alumnus of the Year Award* 2002; Amer. Bd. of Trial Advocates *Trial Judge of the Year* 1994; St. Norbert Coll. *Alma Mater Award* 1992 and *Distinguished Achievement Award in Social Science* 1977; U. of Notre Dame *Award of the Year* 1978; Army Judge Advocate *General Commendation Medal* 1966. Author of works in *Notre Dame Lawyer* 1961-63; *Judges Bench Book-Juvenile*. Brown Co. Ct. judge 1977-78; Brown Co. Circuit Ct. judge 1978-96.

Elected to Supreme Court 1996; reelected 2006.

Justice
BRADLEY

Justice
CROOKS

Justice
PROSSER

Chief Justice
ABRAHAMSON

Justice
ROGGENSACK

Justice
ZIEGLER

Justice
GABLEMAN

David T. Prosser, Jr.: Born Chicago, IL, December 24, 1942; single. Graduate Appleton H.S.; B.A. DePauw Univ. 1965; J.D. UW-Madison Law School 1968. Former practicing attorney; admin. asst. to U.S. Congressman Harold V. Froehlich 1973-74; attorney-advisor, U.S. Dept. of Justice 1969-72; lecturer, Indiana U.-Indianapolis Law School 1968-69. Member: State Bar of Wis.; Dane Co., Milwaukee Co., and Outagamie Co. Bar Assns.; James E. Doyle American Inn of Court; Friends of the Fox; James Watrous Gallery Advisory Committee. Former member: Wis. Coun. on Criminal Justice 1980-83 (exec. com.); Judicial Coun. Com. on Prelim. Examinations 1981; Wis. Sentencing Comn. 1984-88 and 1994-95; Wis. Sesquicentennial Comn. 1993-99; National Conference of Commissioners on Uniform State Laws 1983-96, 2005-07. Outagamie Co. District Attorney 1977-78. Commissioner, Wis. Tax Appeals Comn. 1997-98.

Elected to Wisconsin Assembly 1978. Speaker of the Assembly 1995-96; Minority Leader 1989-94.

Appointed to Supreme Court September 1998 to fill vacancy created by resignation of Justice Janine P. Geske; elected to full term 2001. Supreme Court Planning and Policy Advisory Committee's Court Financing Subcommittee 2002-04; Judicial Council of Wis. 2002-06; Citation of Unpublished Opinions Committee (2009).

Patience Drake Roggensack: Born Joliet, IL, July 7, 1940; married; 3 children. Graduate Lockport Township H.S.; B.A. Drake University 1962; J.D. UW-Madison Law School 1980 (*cum laude*). Former practicing attorney. Member: State Bar of Wis.; American Judicature Soc.; American Bar Assn.; Dane Co. Bar Assn.; American Bar Foundation (fellow); American Judges Assn.; Legal Assn. of Women; Bar Assn. for the Western District of Wisconsin (past president). Board service on: YMCA; YWCA; Wisconsin Center for Academically Talented Youth; Olbrich Botanical Society; International Women's Forum (past president).

Court of Appeals Judge, District IV (1996-2003). Served on Judicial Conference (legislative liaison); Committee for Public Trust and Confidence in the Courts; Publication Committee for the Court of Appeals; State Court/Tribal Court Planning Committee (co-chair); Personnel Review Board (appeals court delegate).

Elected to Supreme Court 2003. Served on Personnel Review Board (supreme court delegate); 2005 Statewide Bench Bar Conference (co-chair).

Annette K. Ziegler: Born Grand Rapids, MI, March 6, 1964; married; 3 children. Graduate Forest Hills Central H.S.; B.A. in Business Administration and Psychology Hope College (Holland, MI) 1986; J.D. Marquette University Law School 1989.

Washington County Circuit Court Judge, Branch 2, 1997-2007.

Elected to Supreme Court 2007.

Michael J. Gableman: Born West Allis, September 18, 1966. Graduate New Berlin West H.S.; A.B. in History/Education Ripon College 1988; J.D. Hamline U. Law School 1993. Former practicing attorney; Deputy corporation counsel, Forest County 1997-99; Assistant District Attorney, Langlade County 1996-99; Assistant District Attorney, Marathon County 1998-99; District Attorney, Ashland County, appointed 1999, elected 2002; Administrative Law Judge, Department of Workforce Development 2002; Burnett County Circuit Court Judge, appointed 2002, elected 2003. Member: State Bar of Wis.; Grantsburg Rotary International; Siren Fraternal Order of Moose. Past member: Burnett County Republican Party (chairman); Ashland Knights of Columbus (Grand Knight); Ashland Masons; Milwaukee Teachers Assoc.; Burnett County Restorative Justice (chairman of the board); Burnett County Drug and Alcohol Court (founding and first presiding judge); Siren Rotary International.

Elected to Supreme Court 2008.

WISCONSIN MEMBERS OF THE 111th CONGRESS
2009-2010
MEMBERS OF THE U.S. SENATE

U.S. Senator
KOHL

Herbert H. Kohl (Dem.)

Born Milwaukee, February 7, 1935; single. Graduate Milwaukee Sherman Elementary School; Milwaukee Washington H.S.; B.A. in Business Administration, UW-Madison 1956; M.B.A. Harvard U. 1958; honorary L.L.D. Cardinal Stritch College 1986. Businessman; president of an investment company; owner of a professional basketball team; part owner of a professional baseball team. Former president of a business corporation. Served in Army Reserve 1958-64. Member: Democratic Party of Wisconsin (state chp. 1975-77). Recipient: Working Mother Magazine *Best of Congress Award* 2008; 2007 Inductee into the Wisconsin Athletic Hall of Fame; Madison Magazine *Best Corporate Citizen of 1997*; Pen and Mike Club *Wisconsin Sports Personality of the Year* 1985; Wisconsin Broadcasters Assn. *Joe Killeen Memorial Sportsman of the Year* 1985; Greater Milwaukee Convention and Visitors Bureau *Lamplighter Award* 1986; Wisconsin Parkinson Assn. *Humanitarian of the Year* 1986; Kiwanis *Milwaukee Award* 1987.

Elected to U.S. Senate 1988; reelected since 1994. Committee assignments: **111th Congress** — Appropriations Committee (since 103rd Congress) and its Subcommittees on Agriculture, Rural Development and FDA and Related Agencies (chp. since 110th Congress), on Commerce, Justice, Science and Related Agencies, on Defense, on Interior, Environment and Related Agencies, on Labor, Health, Human Services, Education and Related Agencies, on Transportation, Housing and Urban Development and Related Agencies; Banking, Housing and Urban Affairs Committee and its Subcommittees on Housing, Transportation and Community Development, on Financial Institutions, on Security and International Trade and Finance; Judiciary Committee (since 101st Congress) and its Subcommittee on Antitrust, Competition Policy and Consumer Rights (chp. since 110th Congress), on Crime and Drugs, on Terrorism and Homeland Security; Special Committee on Aging (chp. since 110th Congress, mbr. since 101st Congress). **102nd Congress** — Governmental Affairs Committee (also 101st Congress) and its Subcommittee on Government Information and Regulation (chp.); Select Committee on POW/MIA Affairs.

Telephones: Washington office: (202) 224-5653, TTY: (202) 224-4464; District offices: Appleton: (920) 738-1640; Eau Claire: (715) 832-8424; La Crosse: (608) 796-0045; Madison: (608) 264-5338; Milwaukee: (414) 297-4451; Toll free: (800) 247-5645.

Internet address: www.kohl.senate.gov

E-mail: www.kohl.senate.gov

Voting address: 929 North Astor, Milwaukee 53202.

Mailing addresses: Washington office: 330 Hart Senate Office Building, Washington, D.C. 20510-4903; District offices: 4321 West College Avenue, Suite 370, Appleton 54914; 402 Graham Avenue, Suite 206, Eau Claire 54701; 205 5th Avenue South, Room 216, La Crosse 54601; 14 West Mifflin Street, Suite 207, Madison 53703; 310 West Wisconsin Avenue, Suite 950, Milwaukee 53203.

U.S. Senator
FEINGOLD

Russell D. Feingold (Dem.)

Born Janesville, March 2, 1953; 2 children. Graduate Janesville Craig H.S. 1971; B.A. with honors (Phi Beta Kappa) UW-Madison 1975; B.A. in law with first-class honors Oxford U. (Rhodes Scholar, Magdalen Coll.) 1977; J.D. with honors Harvard U. Law Sch. 1979. Former practicing attorney 1979-85; visiting professor Beloit Coll. 1985. Member: Wis. and Dane Co. Democratic Parties; Amer. Bar Assn., State Bar of Wis., and Dane Co. Bar Assn.; Phi Beta Kappa; Amer. Assn. of Rhodes Scholars. Recipient: Wis. Dept. of Public Instruction *Friend of Education Award* 1992; ABATE of Wis., Inc.'s Award 1994-1996; Concord Coalition *Deficit Reduction Honor Roll* 1993-95, 1997-2004, and *Deficit Hawk Award* 1994 and 1997; Long Term Care Campaign *Claude Pepper Legislative Award* 1997; Milwaukee Minority Business and Development Center Award 1992; National Assn. of Police Organizations *Senator of the Year Award* 1997; National Fair Housing Alliance *Award for Excellence* 1996; John F. Kennedy Library Foundation *Profile in Courage Award* 1999; University of Illinois *Paul H. Douglas Ethics in Government Award* 2000; Taxpayers for Common Sense Action *Taxpayer Hero* 1997-98 and 2000-03; Wis. State Council of Vietnam Veterans of America *Distinguished Achievement Award* 1993 and *Legislator of the Year* 1997; Wis. Civil Liberties Union *William Gorham Rice Civil Libertarian of the Year Award* 2001; Panetta Institute *Jefferson-Lincoln Award* 2002; Consumer Federation of America *Philip Hart Public Service Award* 2003; Wis. Primary Health Care Assn. and National Assn. of Community Health Center, Inc. *Community Health Super Hero Award* 2002, 2007; Friends of Libraries *Public Service Award* 2004; National Association of Consumer Bankruptcy Attorneys *Champion of Consumer Rights* 2004; Rotary International *Polio Eradication Champion* 2004; National Farmers Union *Golden Triangle Award* 2004, 2006-08; National Guard Association of the United States *Charles Dick Medal of Merit* 2004; League of Conservation Voters *Environmental Champion* 2004; Wisconsin Democracy Campaign *Mr. Smith Award* 2005; National Assn. for Home Care and Hospice *Home Care and Hospice Hero* 2006; American-Arab Discrimination Committee *Courageous Legislator of the Year* 2006; Clean Water Network *Clean Water Champion Award* 2007; Fire Apparatus Manufacturers Association and Fire and Emergency Manufacturers and Service Association *Award of Appreciation* 2007; Coalition for Wisconsin Aging Groups *President's Award* 2007; American Library Association *James Madison Award* 2008.

State legislative service: Elected to Senate 1982-90 (served through 1/5/93).

Elected to U.S. Senate 1992; reelected since 1998. Committee assignments: **111th Congress** — Foreign Relations Committee and its Subcommittees on African Affairs (chp. since 110th Congress), on East Asian and Pacific Affairs, on International Operations and Terrorism; Budget Committee; Judiciary Committee and its Subcommittees on the Constitution (chp. since 110th Congress), on Administrative Oversight and the Courts, on Crime and Drugs; Senate Select Committee on Intelligence.

Congressional membership: Democracy Policy Committee, Deputy Democratic Whip.

Telephones: Washington office: (202) 224-5323, TTY: (202) 224-1280; District offices: Green Bay: (920) 465-7508; La Crosse: (608) 782-5585; Middleton: (608) 828-1200, TTY: (608) 828-1215; Milwaukee: (414) 276-7282; Wausau: (715) 848-5660.

Internet address: http://feingold.senate.gov; E-mail: Russ_Feingold@feingold.senate.gov

Voting address: Middleton 53562.

Mailing addresses: Washington office: 506 Hart Senate Office Building, Washington, D.C. 20510-4904; District offices: 1640 Main Street, Green Bay 54302; 425 State Street, Room 225, La Crosse 54601-3341; 1600 Aspen Commons, Room 100, Middleton 53562; 517 East Wisconsin Avenue, Room 408, Milwaukee 53202-4504; 401 5th Street, Room 410, Wausau 54403.

U.S. Representative
RYAN

U.S. Representative
BALDWIN

MEMBERS OF THE U.S. HOUSE OF REPRESENTATIVES

Paul Ryan (Rep.), 1st Congressional District

Born Janesville, 1970; married; 3 children. Graduate Janesville Craig H.S.; B.A. in economics and political science Miami U. of Ohio 1992. Former aide to U.S. Senator Robert Kasten and employed at family construction business. Member: Janesville Bowmen, Inc.; Ducks Unlimited; St. John Vianney's Parish.

Elected to U.S. House of Representatives 1998; reelected since 2000. Committee assignments: **111th Congress** — Ways and Means Committee (since 107th Congress) and its Subcommittees on Health, on Oversight; Budget Committee (ranking member since 110th Congress, mbr. since 108th Congress, also 106th Congress). **109th Congress** — Joint Economic Committee (also 108th and 106th Congresses). **106th Congress** — Banking Committee; Government Reform Committee.

Telephones: Washington office: (202) 225-3031; District offices: Janesville: (608) 752-4050; Kenosha: (262) 654-1901; Racine: (262) 637-0510; Toll free: (888) 909-7926.

Internet address: http://www.house.gov/ryan/

Voting address: Janesville 53545.

Mailing addresses: Washington office: 1113 Longworth House Office Building, Washington, D.C. 20515; District offices: 20 South Main Street, Suite 10, Janesville 53545; 5455 Sheridan Road, Suite 125, Kenosha 53140; 216 6th Street, Racine 53403.

1st Congressional District: Kenosha, Milwaukee (part), Racine, Rock (part), Walworth, and Waukesha (part) Counties. (For detailed description, see Section 3.11, Wisconsin Statutes.)

Tammy Baldwin (Dem.), 2nd Congressional District

Born Madison, February 11, 1962. Graduate Madison West H.S.; A.B. in mathematics and government, Smith College (MA) 1984; J.D. UW-Madison 1989. Former practicing attorney, 1989-92. Member: American Civil Liberties Union of Wisconsin; Democratic Parties of Dane County and Wisconsin; Madison NAACP; State Bar of Wisconsin. Madison City Council 1986; Dane Co. Board 1986-94.

State legislative service: Elected to Assembly, 78th District, 1992-96 (served until January 4, 1999).

Elected to U.S. House of Representatives 1998; reelected since 2000. Committee assignments: **111th Congress** — Energy and Commerce Committee (since 109th Congress) and its Subcommittees on Health, on Energy and Environment; Judiciary Committee and its Subcommittee on the Constitution, Civil Rights and Civil Liberties.

Telephones: Washington office: (202) 225-2906; District offices: Madison: (608) 258-9800; Beloit: (608) 362-2800.

Internet address: http://tammybaldwin.house.gov

Voting address: Madison 53703.

Mailing addresses: Washington office: 2446 Rayburn House Office Building, Washington, D.C. 20515-4902; District offices: 10 East Doty Street, Suite 405, Madison 53703; 400 E. Grand Avenue, Suite 402, Beloit 53511.

2nd Congressional District: Columbia, Dane, Green, Jefferson (part), Rock (part), Sauk (part), and Walworth (part) Counties. (For detailed description, see Section 3.12, Wisconsin Statutes.)

U.S. Representative   U.S. Representative
KIND   MOORE

Ron Kind (Dem.), 3rd Congressional District

Born La Crosse, March 16, 1963; married; 2 children. Graduate Logan H.S.; B.A. Harvard U. 1985; M.A. London School of Economics (England); J.D. U. of Minnesota Law School 1990. Attorney. Former La Crosse County assistant district attorney and State of Wisconsin special prosecutor. Member: U.S. Supreme Court Bar; State Bar of Wis. and La Crosse Co. Bar Assn.; Assn. of State Prosecutors; Democratic Party; Wis. Harvard Club (bd. of dir.); Boys and Girls Club of La Crosse (bd. of dir.); Coulee Council on Alcohol and Other Drug Abuse (bd. of dir.); Moose Club; Optimist Club.

Elected to U.S. House of Representatives 1996; reelected since 1998. Committee assignments: **111th Congress** — Natural Resources Committee (since 105th Congress) and its Subcommittees on Insular Affairs, Oceans and Wildlife, on National Parks, Forests and Public Lands; Ways and Means Committee (since 110th Congress) and its Subcommittees on Oversight, on Health, and on Social Security. Congressional memberships: New Democrat Coalition (co-chair); Upper Mississippi River Task Force (founder); Congressional Wildlife Refuge Caucus (founder); Rural Health Care Coalition; Congressional Sportsmen's Caucus (co-chair); Human Rights Caucus; Native American Caucus; Renewable Energy and Energy Efficiency Caucus. House Leadership: Regional Whip.

Telephones: Washington office: (202) 225-5506; District offices: Eau Claire: (715) 831-9214; La Crosse: (608) 782-2558; Toll free: (888) 442-8040; TTY: (888) 880-9180.

Internet address: http://www.house.gov/kind/

Voting address: La Crosse 54603.

Mailing addresses: Washington office: 1406 Longworth House Office Building, Washington, D.C. 20515-4906; District offices: 131 S. Barstow Street, Suite 301, Eau Claire 54701; 205 5th Avenue South, Suite 400, La Crosse 54601.

3rd Congressional District: Buffalo, Clark (part), Crawford, Dunn, Eau Claire, Grant, Iowa, Jackson, Juneau, La Crosse, Lafayette, Monroe, Pepin, Pierce, Richland, St. Croix, Sauk, Trempealeau, and Vernon Counties. (For detailed description, see Section 3.13, Wisconsin Statutes.)

Gwendolynne S. Moore (Dem.), 4th Congressional District

Born Racine, April 18, 1951; 3 children. Graduate North Division H.S. (Milwaukee); B.A. in political science, Marquette U. 1978; certification in credit union management, Milwaukee Area Technical College 1983. Former housing officer with Wisconsin Housing and Economic Development Authority; development specialist Milwaukee City Development; program and planning analyst with Wisconsin Departments of Employment Relations and Health and Social Services. Member: National Black Caucus of State Legislators; National Conference of State Legislatures' Host Committee, Milwaukee 1995; National Black Caucus of State Legislators – Host Committee (chair), 1997; Wisconsin Legislative Black and Hispanic Caucus (chair since 1997). State legislative service: Elected to Assembly 1988 and 1990; elected to Senate 1992, 1996, and 2000. Senate President Pro Tempore 1997, 1995 (eff. 7/15/96).

Elected to U.S. House of Representatives 2004; reelected since 2006. Committee assignments: **111th Congress** — Budget Committee; Financial Services Committee (since 109th Congress) and its Subcommittees on Capital Markets, Insurance, and Government Sponsored Enterprises, on International Monetary Policy and Trade, on Oversight and Investigations. **110th Congress** — Small Business Committee and its Subcommittees on Contracting and Technology, on Regulations, Healthcare and Trade, on Rural and Urban Entrepreneurship.

Telephones: Washington office: (202) 225-4572; District office: Milwaukee: (414) 297-1140.

Internet address: www.house.gov/gwenmoore

Voting address: 4043 North 19th Place, Milwaukee 53209.

Mailing addresses: Washington office: 1239 Longworth House Office Building, Washington, D.C. 20515-4904; District offices: 219 N. Milwaukee Street, Suite 3A, Milwaukee 53202-5818.

4th Congressional District: Milwaukee County (part): consisting of the Village of West Milwaukee; the Cities of Cudahy, Milwaukee, St. Francis, South Milwaukee, and West Allis (part). (For detailed description, see Section 3.14, Wisconsin Statutes.)

U.S. Representative
SENSENBRENNER

U.S. Representative
PETRI

F. James Sensenbrenner, Jr. (Rep.), 5th Congressional District

Born Chicago, June 14, 1943; married; 2 children. Graduate Milwaukee Country Day School 1961; A.B. Stanford U. 1965; J.D. UW-Madison Law School 1968. Attorney. Former assistant to State Senate Majority Leader Jerris Leonard and to U.S. Congressman Arthur Younger. Member: State Bar of Wis.; Friends of the Museum, Milwaukee County; Riveredge Nature Center; American Philatelic Society; Waukesha Co. Republican Party. Former member: Whitefish Bay Jaycees; Shorewood Men's Club.

State legislative service: Elected to Assembly 1968-74; elected to Senate in April 1975 special election and reelected 1976. Assistant Minority Leader 1977.

Elected to U.S. House of Representatives 1978; reelected since 1980. Committee assignments: **111th Congress** — Judiciary Committee (chp. 107th-109th Congress, mbr. since 97th Congress) and its Subcommittees on Constitution, Civil Rights and Civil Liberties (ranking mbr.), on Courts and Competition Policy; Science and Technology Committee (since 110th Congress) and its Subcommittee on Space and Aeronautics; Select Committee on Energy Independence and Global Warming (ranking mbr.). **106th Congress** — Science Committee (chp., also mbr. since 97th Congress). **103rd Congress** — House Select Committee on Narcotics Abuse and Control (since 100th Congress). **96th Congress** — Standards of Official Conduct Committee.

Telephones: Washington office: (202) 225-5101; District office: (262) 784-1111; Toll free: (800) 242-1119.

Internet address: http://sensenbrenner.house.gov/contactform

E-mail: www.house.gov/writerep

Voting address: N76 W14726 North Point Drive, P.O. Box 186, Menomonee Falls 53052-0186.

Mailing addresses: Washington office: 2449 Rayburn House Office Building, Washington, D.C. 20515-4905; District office: 120 Bishops Way, Room 154, Brookfield 53005-6294.

5th Congressional District: Jefferson (part), Ozaukee, Milwaukee (part) Counties: consisting of the Villages of Bayside (part), Brown Deer, Fox Point, River Hills, Shorewood, and Whitefish Bay; the Cities of Glendale, Wauwatosa, and West Allis (part); Washington and Waukesha (part) Counties. (For detailed description, see Section 3.15, Wisconsin Statutes.)

Thomas E. Petri (Rep.), 6th Congressional District

Born Marinette, May 28, 1940; married; 1 child. Graduate Goodrich H.S.; B.A. Harvard College 1962; J.D. Harvard Law School 1965. Attorney. Former Peace Corps volunteer; White House aide.

State legislative service: Elected to Senate 1972 and 1976.

Elected to U.S. House of Representatives in April 1979 special election; reelected since 1980. Committee assignments: **111th Congress** — Education and Labor (mbr. since 96th Congress) and its Subcommittee on Early Childhood, Elementary and Secondary Education; Transportation and Infrastructure Committee (mbr. since 98th Congress) and its Subcommittees on Aviation (ranking mbr.), on Highways and Transit, on Railroads, Pipelines, and Hazardous Materials.

Telephones: Washington office: (202) 225-2476; District offices: Fond du Lac: (920) 922-1180; Oshkosh: (920) 231-6333; Toll free: (800) 242-4883.

Internet address: http://www.house.gov/petri/welcome.htm

Voting address: (Town of Empire) N5329 DeNeveu Lane, Fond du Lac 54935.

Mailing addresses: Washington office: 2462 Rayburn House Office Building, Washington, D.C. 20515-4906; District offices: 490 West Rolling Meadows Drive, Suite B, Fond du Lac 54937; 2390 State Road 44, Suite B, Oshkosh 54904.

6th Congressional District: Adams, Calumet (part), Dodge, Fond du Lac, Green Lake, Jefferson (part), Manitowoc, Marquette, Outagamie (part), Sheboygan, Waushara, and Winnebago Counties. (For detailed description, see Section 3.16, Wisconsin Statutes.)

U.S. Representative
OBEY

U.S. Representative
KAGEN

David R. Obey (Dem.), 7th Congressional District

Born October 3, 1938; married. Graduate St. James Grade School; Wausau East H.S.; B.S. UW-Madison 1960; M.A. UW-Madison 1963. Former real estate broker; worker in family-owned supper club and motel.

State legislative service: Elected to Assembly 1962-68. Asst. Minority Leader 1967, 1969.

Elected to U.S. House of Representatives in April 1969 special election; reelected since 1970. Committee assignments: **111th Congress** — Appropriations Committee (chp., also 103rd Congress, mbr. since 91st Congress), *ex officio* mbr. of all its subcommittees and chp. of its Subcommittee on Labor, Health and Human Services, Education, and Related Agencies (since 110th Congress).

Telephones: Washington office: (202) 225-3365; District offices: Superior: (715) 398-4426; Wausau: (715) 842-5606.

Voting address: 1212 Grand Avenue, No. 32, Wausau 54403.

Mailing addresses: Washington office: 2314 Rayburn House Office Building, Washington, D.C. 20515-4907; District offices: 1401 Tower Avenue, Suite 307, Superior 54880-1553; Federal Building, 401 Fifth Street, Suite 406A,Wausau 54403-5468.

7th Congressional District: Ashland, Barron, Bayfield, Burnett, Chippewa, Clark (part), Douglas, Iron, Langlade (part), Lincoln, Marathon, Oneida (part), Polk, Portage, Price, Rusk, Sawyer, Taylor, Washburn, and Wood Counties. (For detailed description, see Section 3.17, Wisconsin Statutes.)

Steve Kagen (Dem.), 8th Congressional District

Born Appleton, December 12, 1949; married; 4 children. Graduate Appleton East H.S.; B.S. in molecular biology UW-Madison 1972; M.D. UW-Madison 1976. Physician; founder of the Kagen Allergy Clinics in the Fox Valley area.

Elected to U.S. House of Representatives 2006; reelected 2008. Committee assignments: **111th Congress** — Agriculture Committee (since 110th Congress) and its Subcommittees on Department Operations, Oversight, Nutrition and Forestry, on Livestock, Dairy and Poultry; Transportation and Infrastructure Committee (since 110th Congress) and its Subcommittees on Coast Guard and Maritime Transportation, on Highways and Transit, on Water Resources and Environment.

Telephones: Washington office: (202) 225-5665; District offices: Appleton: (920) 380-0061; Green Bay: (920) 437-1954.

Voting address: 1712 South Mason Street, Appleton 54914.

Mailing addresses: Washington office: 1232 Longworth House Office Building, Washington, D.C. 20515; District offices: 333 West College Avenue, Appleton 54911; 700 East Walnut Street, Green Bay 54301.

8th Congressional District: Brown, Calumet (part), Door, Florence, Forest, Kewaunee, Langlade (part), Marinette, Menominee, Oconto, Oneida (part), Outagamie (part), Shawano, Vilas, and Waupaca Counties. (For detailed description, see Section 3.18, Wisconsin Statutes.)

CONGRESSIONAL DISTRICTS
Enacted by 2001 Wisconsin Act 46

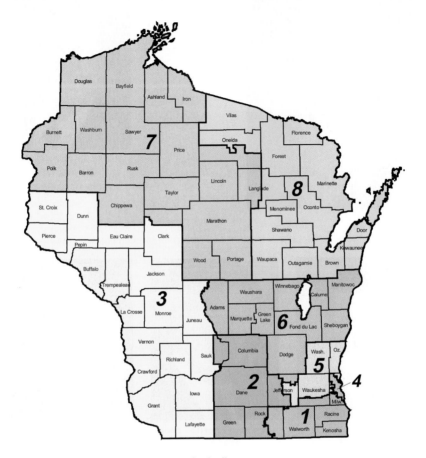

See Chapter 3, *2007-2008 Wisconsin Statutes,* for detail maps.

2000 POPULATION OF CONGRESSIONAL DISTRICTS

District	Population*	Deviation from Equal Population		Minority Population	
		Number	Percent	Hispanic	Other
Cong. Dist. 1	670,458	−1	−0.00	37,888	46,517
Cong. Dist. 2	670,457	−2	−0.00	22,644	51,078
Cong. Dist. 3	670,462	3	0.00	6,193	19,916
Cong. Dist. 4	670,458	−1	−0.00	75,285	257,364
Cong. Dist. 5	670,458	−1	−0.00	14,906	25,632
Cong. Dist. 6	670,459	0	0.00	15,410	24,227
Cong. Dist. 7	670,462	3	0.00	5,823	27,102
Cong. Dist. 8	670,461	2	0.00	14,772	37,288
TOTAL	5,363,675			192,921	489,124

*Wisconsin's 8 congressional districts were established by 2001 Wisconsin Act 46, based on the 2000 U.S. Census of Population. The ideal size of each district is 670,459.

Source: U.S. Department of Commerce, Census Bureau, P.L. 94-171 Redistricting File, March 2001.

18

President
RISSER

President Pro Tempore
KREITLOW

Majority Leader
DECKER

Assistant Majority Leader
HANSEN

Minority Leader
S. FITZGERALD

Assistant Minority Leader
GROTHMAN

Chief Clerk
MARCHANT

Sergeant at Arms
BLAZEL

2009 State Assembly Officers

Speaker
SHERIDAN

Speaker Pro Tempore
STASKUNAS

Majority Leader
NELSON

Assistant Majority Leader
SEIDEL

Minority Leader
J. FITZGERALD

Assistant Minority Leader
GOTTLIEB

Chief Clerk
FULLER

Sergeant at Arms
NAGY

1st SENATE DISTRICT

Senator
LASEE

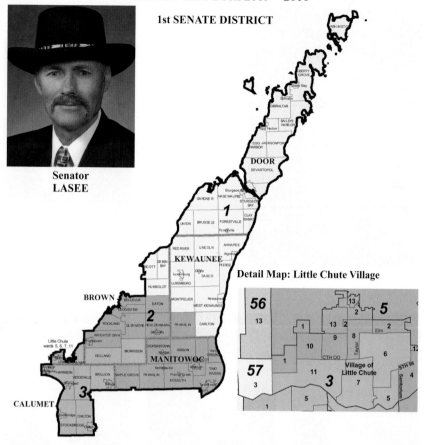

Detail Map: Little Chute Village

Alan J. Lasee (Rep.), 1st Senate District

Born Town of Rockland, Brown County, July 30, 1937; married; 6 children. Attended St. Norbert H.S. Raises exotic animals including llamas, camels, miniature donkeys, and fainting goats. Former dairy farmer. Member: Brown Co. Farm Bureau (bd. of dir. 1972-75); Way-Morr Lions (pres. 1991-92, dir. 1976); Brown Co. Republican Party; Wisconsin Towns Assn. Former Brown Co. 4-H leader (licensed gun safety instructor). Town of Rockland (Brown Co.) supervisor 1971-73; town chairman 1973-82, 1985-2000.

Elected to Assembly 1974; elected to Senate in May 1977 special election; reelected since 1978. President of the Senate 2005, 2003; President Pro Tempore 1995 (eff. 1/5/95 to 6/13/96), 1993 (eff. 4/20/93); Minority Caucus Chairperson 1987, 1981, and 1979. Biennial committee assignments: **2009** — Ethics Reform and Government Operations; Labor, Elections and Urban Affairs (also 2007). **2007** — Jt. Legislative Audit (also 1993, 1991); Jt. Legis. Council (co-chp. 2005, mbr. 2003, 1997 eff. 4/21/98). **2005** — Campaign Finance Reform and Ethics; Organization (eff. 5/9/01); Jt. Com. on Employment Relations (co-chp. and mbr. since 2003); Jt. Com. on Legislative Organization (co-chp., mbr. since 5/9/01); State and Federal Relations; Disability Bd.; Transportation Projects Commission (also 2003, 2001, 1997, vice chp. 1/93 to 6/96, mbr. 1987). **2001** — Insurance, Tourism, and Transportation; Labor and Agriculture. **1999** — Agriculture, Environmental Resources and Campaign Finance Reform; Insurance, Tourism, Transportation and Corrections. **1997** — Transportation, Agriculture and Rural Affairs (chp. eff. 4/21/98); State Government Operations and Corrections (eff. 4/21/98, also mbr. 1/95 to 6/96, also 1993); Agriculture and Environmental Resources (1/15/97 to 4/20/98); Human Resources, Labor, Tourism, Veterans and Military Affairs (eff. 4/21/98, also 1995, 1993); Council on Highway Safety (also 1995); Rustic Roads Bd. (eff. 4/21/98, also 1995, 1993). **1995** — Agriculture, Transportation, Utilities and Financial Institutions; Transportation, Agriculture and Local Affairs (chp. 1/95 to 6/96); State Capitol and Executive Residence Bd. (mbr. since 1983); Legis. Coun. and its Com. on Federally Tax-Exempt Lands. **1993** — Transportation, Agriculture, Local and Rural Affairs (mbr. and chp.); Transportation, Agriculture, Tourism and Veterans Affairs (mbr. and vice chp.).

Telephone: Office: (608) 266-3512; District: (920) 336-8830.

E-mail: Sen.Lasee@legis.wisconsin.gov

Voting address: (Town of Rockland) 2259 Lasee Road, De Pere 54115.

Mailing address: Office: Room 130 South, State Capitol, P.O. Box 7882, Madison 53707-7882.

| Representative | Representative | Representative |
| BIES | ZIGMUNT | A. OTT |

Garey Bies (Rep.), 1st Assembly District

Born Manitowoc, October 26, 1946; married; 4 children. Graduate Lincoln H.S., Manitowoc; Associate Degree Northeastern Technical College 1982. Full-time legislator. Former chief deputy sheriff, deputy sheriff, Door County Sheriff's Dept. 30 years, and project director for Door/Kewaunee Drug Task Force, 1990-2000. Navy veteran, 1964-69. Member: American Legion Post 527, 1970-present; Knights of Columbus, 1970-present; Northern Door Child Care (bd. dir.); St. Rosalia Catholic Church (former trustee and council member); Sturgeon Bay Rotary; volunteer guardian for disabled adults. Former member: Boy Scouts of America (cubmaster, scout master); Door/Kewaunee Selective Service Bd. (chp., vice chp.); Door Co. Highway Safety Com.; Door Co. Local Emergency Planning Com.; Help of Door County (bd. dir.); Comn. on Reducing Racial Disparities 2007.

Elected to Assembly 2000; reelected since 2002. Biennial committee assignments: **2009** — Public Safety; Tourism, Recreation and State Properties (also 2007); Transportation (vice chp. 2007). **2007** — Corrections and the Courts (chp. since 2003); Natural Resources (since 2003); Veterans and Military Affairs (also 2003); Legis. Coun. Spec. Com. on Placement of Sex Offenders (co-chp.). **2005** — Highway Safety (vice chp. since 2001); Veterans Affairs; Gov's Coun. on Highway Safety (since 2001); Wis. Sentencing Comn. (since 2003); Legis. Coun. Com. on State and Tribal Relations. **2003** — Speaker's Task Force on Technical College System (co-chp.).

Telephone: Office: (608) 266-5350; (888) 482-0001 (toll free); District: (920) 854-2811.

E-mail: Rep.Bies@legis.wisconsin.gov

Voting address: 2520 Settlement Road, Sister Bay 54234.

Mailing address: Office: Room 125 West, State Capitol, P.O. Box 8952, Madison 53708.

Ted Zigmunt (Dem.), 2nd Assembly District

Born Manitowoc, December 8, 1951; married. Graduate Mishicot H.S. 1970. Full-time legislator. Former radio announcer and salesperson. Member: Francis Creek Lions Club (bd. mbr., dir.); Francis Creek Volunteer Fire Dept. Village of Francis Creek president 2004-present; Manitowoc County Bd. 2004-2008.

Elected to Assembly 2008. Biennial committee assignments: **2009** — Transportation (vice chp.); Corrections and the Courts; Energy and Utilities.

Telephone: Office: (608) 266-9870; (888) 534-0002 (toll free); District: (920) 686-1060.

E-mail: Rep.Zigmunt@legis.wisconsin.gov

Voting address: 305 Oakwood Drive, Francis Creek 54214; P.O. Box 321, Francis Creek 54214.

Mailing address: Office: Room 420 North, State Capitol, P.O. Box 8953, Madison 53708.

Al Ott (Alvin R. Ott) (Rep.), 3rd Assembly District

Born Green Bay, June 19, 1949; married; 4 children, 6 grandchildren. Graduate Brillion H.S.; UW-Madison Farm and Industry Short Course 1968; 1st Class of Participants in WI Rural Leadership Program 1986. Former agri-business salesman, owner/operator of independent agri-business, tenant dairy farmer, and cash crop farmer. Member: Forest-Ever Ready 4-H Club (adult leader); Republican Party of Wis.; Calumet Co. Agricultural Assn.; Calumet Co. Farm Progress 1993 Exec. Com. (chm.). Calumet Co. Board 1973-92 (vice chp.), chp. of its Ag/Extension Educ. Com. and vice chp. of its Land Conservation and Planning/Zoning Coms.; Wis. Land Conservation Bd. 1984-88 (secy.).

Elected to Assembly since 1986. Biennial committee assignments: **2009** — Agriculture (chp. 1995-2007, mbr. 1989, 1987); Public Safety; Transportation (since 2003). **2007** — Rural Economic Development (vice chp. since 2003). **2005** — Natural Resources (mbr. since 1995); Rural Development (mbr. since 2003). **2001** — Energy and Utilities; Environment; World Dairy Center Authority (also 1999). **1999** — Conservation and Land Use; Consumer Affairs (also 1997); Utilities. **1993** — Agriculture, Forestry and Rural Affairs (ranking minority mbr.); Environmental Resources; Labor and Job Training; Legis. Coun. Com. on Protection of Rural Resources. **1991** — Agriculture, Aquaculture and Forestry.

Telephone: Office: (608) 266-5831; (888) 534-0003 (toll free); District: (920) 989-1240.

E-mail: Rep.Ott@legis.wisconsin.gov

Voting address: (Town of Brillion) W2168 Campground Road, Forest Junction 54123-0112.

Mailing address: Office: Room 323 North, State Capitol, P.O. Box 8953, Madison 53708; District: P.O. Box 112, Forest Junction 54123-0112.

2nd SENATE DISTRICT

Senator
COWLES

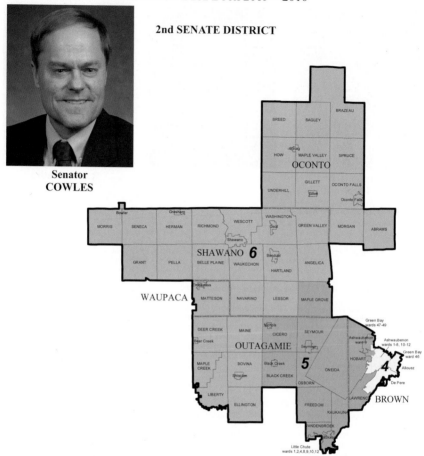

See Green Bay Area Detail Map on p. 96

Robert L. Cowles (Rep.), 2nd Senate District

Born Green Bay, July 31, 1950. B.S. UW-Green Bay 1975; graduate work UW-Green Bay. Full-time legislator. Former director of an alternative energy division for a communications construction company. Member: Allouez Kiwanis; Prevent Blindness Wisconsin – NE Wis. Chapter; Friends of the Fox River Trail; Salvation Army Volunteer.

Elected to Assembly 1982-86 (resigned 4/21/87); elected to Senate in April 1987 special election; reelected since 1988. Biennial Senate committee assignments: **2009** — Commerce, Utilities, Energy, and Rail; Joint Com. for Review of Administrative Rules (also 2001, 1987 to 4/20/93); Jt. Legis. Audit Com. (since 2003, also 1993); Jt. Com. on Information Policy and Technology. **2007** — Commerce, Utilities and Rail; Public Health, Senior Issues, Long-Term Care and Privacy. **2005** — Energy, Utilities and Information Technology (chp.); Jt. Com. on Finance (also 1993-99). **2003** — Energy and Utilities (chp.); Higher Education and Tourism; Building Comn. **2001** — Environmental Resources; Health, Utilities, Veterans and Military Affairs. **1999** — Jt. Survey Com. on Tax Exemptions; Joint Legislative Council (also 1997). **1997** — Environmental Education Bd. (since 1991). **1995** — Environment and Energy (chp. since 4/20/93). **1993** — Urban Affairs, Financial Institutions and Environmental Resources (mbr. and vice chp. to 4/20/93); Judiciary and Consumer Affairs (mbr. to 4/20/93); Legis. Coun. Com. on State Fire Programs (co-chp.). **1991** — Urban Affairs, Environmental Resources and Elections; Legis. Coun. Com. on Energy Resources; Gov.'s Council on Recycling. **1989** — Educational Financing, Higher Education and Tourism; Science, Technology, Communications and Energy; Legis. Coun. Com. on Nonpoint Source Pollution; Low-Level Radioactive Waste Council. **1987** — Economic Development, Financial Institutions and Fiscal Policies; Housing, Government Operations and Cultural Affairs. Assembly committee assignments: **1987** — Jt. Com. for Review of Administrative Rules (since 1983); Trade, Industry and Small Business. **1985** — Jt. Com. on Debt Management; Energy; Legis. Coun. Com. on Environmental Resource Management. **1983** — Energy and Utilities; Economic Development (eff. 10/25/83); Family and Economic Assistance; Revenue.

Telephone: Office: (608) 266-0484; (800) 334-1465 (toll free); District: (920) 448-5092; Fax: (920) 448-5093.
E-mail: Sen.Cowles@legis.wisconsin.gov
Voting address: 300 West St. Joseph Street, Green Bay 54301.
Mailing address: Office: Room 319 South, State Capitol, P.O. Box 7882, Madison 53707-7882.

  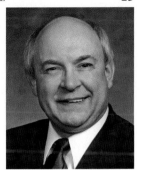

Representative
MONTGOMERY

Representative
NELSON

Representative
TAUCHEN

Phil Montgomery (Rep.), 4th Assembly District

Born Hammond, IN, July 7, 1957; married; 2 children. Graduate T.F. North H.S.; B.S. in Business and Commerce, U. of Houston-Downtown, Houston, TX 1988. Former systems engineer. Member: Leadership Green Bay Alumni; Ashwaubenon Optimist Club; Waterfront Study Com. (past chp.); Junior Achievement.

Elected to Assembly 1998; reelected since 2000. Biennial committee assignments: **2009** — Energy and Utilities (chp. 2007, 2005, mbr. since 2003); Jt. Com. on Finance. **2007** — Corrections and Courts (vice chp.); Elections and Constitutional Law; Insurance (since 2003, chp. 2003). **2005** — Jt. Survey Com. on Tax Exemptions (co-chp.); Housing; State-Federal Relations. **2003** — Financial Institutions (chp., vice chp. 2001, mbr. since 1999); Electronic Democracy and Government Reform; Health. **2001** — Jt. Com. on Information Policy and Technology; Information Policy and Technology; Personal Privacy (vice. chp.); Judiciary. **1999** — Campaigns and Elections; Family Law; Information Policy; Labor and Employment.

Telephone: Office: (608) 266-5840; District: (920) 496-5953; E-mail: Rep.Montgomery@legis.wisconsin.gov

Voting address: 1305 Oak Crest Drive, Ashwaubenon 54313.

Mailing address: Office: Room 129 West, State Capitol, P.O. Box 8953, Madison 53708.

Thomas M. Nelson (Dem.), 5th Assembly District

Born St. Paul, MN, March 3, 1976. Graduate Little Chute H.S. 1994; B.A. Carleton College (Northfield, MN) 1998; M.P.A. Princeton U. (Princeton, NJ) 2004. Full-time legislator. Member: Loaves and Fishes food pantry (bd. mbr.); Christ the King Lutheran Church, ELCA; Outagamie County Democratic Party; Nichols Historical Society; Seymour Historical Society.

Elected to Assembly 2004; reelected since 2006. Majority Leader 2009. Biennial committee assignments: **2009** — Rules (chp.); Assembly Organization (vice chp.); Jt. Com. on Employee Relations; Jt. Com. on Legislative Organization; Jt. Legislative Council (also 2007, eff. 11/16/07); Transportation Projects Commission. **2007** — Jt. Com. for Review of Administrative Rules; Financial Institutions; Labor and Industry; Rural Economic Development. **2005** — Health; Insurance; Rural Development; Transportation.

Telephone: Office: (608) 266-2418; (888) 534-0005 (toll free); District: (920) 759-7404.

E-mail: Rep.Nelson@legis.wisconsin.gov

Voting address: 1510 Orchard Drive, Kaukauna 54130.

Mailing address: Office: Room 215 West, State Capitol, P.O. Box 8953, Madison 53708.

Gary Tauchen (Rep.), 6th Assembly District

Born Rice Lake, November 23, 1953; single. Graduate Bonduel H.S. 1971; attended UW-Madison 1971-72; B.S. in Animal Science, UW-River Falls 1976. Dairy farmer. Member: Wis. Farm Bureau; Badger AgVest, LLC (dir.); Professional Dairy Producers of Wis. (fmr. dir.); Dairy Business Assn.; Wis. Livestock Identification Consortium (fmr. dir., fmr. chm.); Shawano, Oconto, Outagamie, Waupaca Co. Republican Party; Shawano Area Chamber of Commerce; Shawano Co. Dairy Promotions (fmr. dir.); Cooperative Resources International (fmr. vice chm.); AgSource Cooperative Services (fmr. chm.); National Dairy Herd Improvement Assn. (fmr. dir.); UW Center for Dairy Profitability (fmr. chm.); Shawano Rotary.

Elected to Assembly 2006; reelected 2008. Minority Caucus Sergeant at Arms 2009. Biennial committee assignments: **2009** — Agriculture (also 2007); Renewable Energy and Rural Affairs; Workforce Development. **2007** — Rural Affairs (vice chp.); Biofuels and Sustainable Energy; State Affairs.

Telephone: Office: (608) 266-3097; (888) 529-0006 (toll free); District: (715) 758-6181.

E-mail: Rep.Tauchen@legis.wisconsin.gov

Voting address: N3397 South Broadway Road, Bonduel 54107.

Mailing address: Office: Room 9 West, State Capitol, P.O. Box 8953, Madison 53708.

Senator   **3rd SENATE DISTRICT**
CARPENTER

See Milwaukee County Detail Map on pp. 92 & 93

Tim Carpenter (Dem.), 3rd Senate District

Born Milwaukee. Graduate Pulaski H.S.; B.A. UW-Milwaukee; M.A. UW-Madison La Follette Institute. Full-time legislator. Member: Sierra Club; Jackson Park Neighborhood Assn. Recipient: Wisconsin Public Health Association's *Champion of Public Health* 2008; Coalition of Wisconsin Aging Groups *Russ Feingold Award for Service to Seniors* 2007; Shepherd Express *Best State Legislator* 2008; Wisconsin League of Conservation Voters *Conservation Champion* 2008; Shepherd Express *Legislator of the Year* 2003; Wis. Professional Fire Fighters *Legislator of the Year* 2002; Environmental Decade *Clean 16 Awards*.

Elected to Assembly 1984-2000; elected to Senate 2002; reelected 2006. President Pro Tempore 2007; Speaker Pro Tempore 1993. Biennial Senate committee assignments: **2009** — Public Health, Senior Issues, Long-Term Care and Job Creation (chp.); Law Revision (co-chp., mbr. since 2005); Health, Health Insurance, Privacy, Property Tax Relief, and Revenue (vice chp.); Veterans and Military Affairs, Biotechnology and Financial Institutions (also 2007); Jt. Survey Com. on Retirement Systems. **2007** — Public Health, Senior Issues, Long-Term Care and Privacy (chp.); Small Business, Emergency Preparedness, Workforce Development, Technical Colleges and Consumer Protection (vice chp.); Health and Human Services (Health, Human Services, Insurance and Job Creation eff. 11/6/07); Jt. Legislative Council; Alcohol and Other Drug Abuse (since 2003). **2005** — Health, Children, Families, Aging and Long-Term Care (also 2003); Labor and Election Process Reform; State and Federal Relations. **2003** — Jt. Com. for Review of Administrative Rules (through 5/23/03); Administrative Rules (through 5/23/03); Judiciary, Corrections and Privacy; Council on Migrant Labor. Assembly committee assignments: **2001** — Aging and Long-Term Care (also 1997, 1995); Health (chp. 1991, mbr. since 1987); Public Health (also 1999); State and Local Finance. **1999** — Census and Redistricting; Urban and Local Affairs (also 1985). **1997** — Managed Care. **1995** — Legis. Coun. Com. to Review the Election Process. **1993** — Financial Institutions and Housing; Insurance, Securities and Corporate Policy; Joint Legislative Council and co-chp. of its Com. on Communication of Governmental Proceedings; Rules. **1991** — Elections and Constitutional Law (chp. 1989); Financial Institutions and Insurance (mbr. 1989, 1987, vice chp. 1985); Judiciary; Labor (since 1985); Public Health and Regulation; Special Com. on Reapportionment (vice chp.); Special Com. on Reform of Health Insurance; Legis. Coun. Com. on Campaign Financing. **1989** — Select Com. on the Census (co-chp.); Environmental Resources and Utilities; Legis. Coun. Coms. on Prenatal Care, on Privacy and Information Technology. **1987** — Elections (vice chp., also 1985); Housing and Securities; Legis. Coun. Com. on Solid Waste Management. **1985** — Economic Development; Transportation.

Telephone: Office: (608) 266-8535; (800) 249-8173 (toll free); Fax: (608) 282-3543; District: (414) 383-9161.

E-mail: Sen.Carpenter@legis.wisconsin.gov

Voting address: 2957 South 38th Street, Milwaukee 53215.

Mailing address: Office: Room 306 South, State Capitol, P.O. Box 7882, Madison 53707-7882.

| Representative | Representative | Representative |
| KRUSICK | COLÓN | ZEPNICK |

Peggy Krusick (Dem.), 7th Assembly District

Born Milwaukee, Oct. 26, 1956; married; 1 daughter and 1 son. Grad. Milwaukee Hamilton H.S. 1974; B.A. in political science with honors, certificate in law studies, UW-Milwaukee 1978. Full-time legislator. Former Assembly legislative aide; staff member Governor's Ombudsman Program for the Aging and Disabled. Member: UWM Alumni Association; Alliance for Attendance Truancy Abatement Task Force; Alzheimer's Association; Jackson Park Community Association; Fairview Neighborhood Association; St. Gregory the Great Church.

Elected to Assembly in June 1983 special election; reelected since 1984. Author of 2007 Emergency Organ Transport Act; 2006 Disabled Parking Accessibility Act; 2006 Unpaid Property Tax Collection Act; 2006 Stolen Goods Recovery Act; 2004 Child Protection and Clergy Abuse Reporting Act; 2004 Child Support Collection Act; 2004 Comprehensive Background Checks for School Bus Drivers Act; 2002 Senior Care Prescription Drug Benefit Program; 1998 Caregiver Criminal Background Checks and Abuse Prevention Act; 1998 Nursing Home Resident Protection Act; 1998 Child Abuse Prosecution Act; 1998 Truancy Reform Act; 1996 Anti-Graffiti Act; 1994 Fair Prescription Drug Pricing Act; 1994 Truancy Driver's License Suspension Act; 1993 Welfare Fugitive Arrest Act; 1990 Stolen Goods Recovery Act; 1989 Elder Abuse Fund; 1987 Nursing Home Reform Act; 1985 Youth Suicide Prevention Act. Biennial committee assignments: **2009** — Aging and Long-Term Care (chp., mbr. 2007); Education; Jobs, the Economy and Small Business. **2007** — Consumer Protection and Personal Privacy; Education Reform.

Telephone: Office: (608) 266-1733; District: (414) 543-0017; E-mail: Rep.Krusick@legis.wisconsin.gov

Voting address: 3426 South 69th Street, Milwaukee 53219.

Mailing address: Office: Room 128 North, State Capitol, P.O. Box 8952, Madison 53708.

Pedro Colón (Dem.), 8th Assembly District

Born Ponce, Puerto Rico, April 7, 1968; married; 2 daughters. Graduate Thomas More H.S. (Milwaukee); B.A. Marquette U. 1991; J.D. UW-Madison 1994. Attorney. Member: Wisconsin Hispanic Lawyers Association; State Bar of Wis.; National Association of Latino Elected Officials (NALEO) (bd. mbr.); Greater Milwaukee Boys & Girls Club (bd. of trustees); Milwaukee Metropolitan Sewerage District Commissioner.

Elected to Assembly 1998; reelected since 2000. Biennial committee assignments: **2009** — Judiciary and Ethics (vice chp.); Jt. Com. on Finance (vice chp., mbr. since 2005); Migrant Labor Council (chp., also 2007, mbr. since 1999). **2005** — Highway Safety. **2003** — Budget Review (eff. 5/13/03); Corrections and the Courts (also 2001); Criminal Justice (since 1999); Health (also 2001); Ways and Means (resigned 5/13/03); Workforce Development. **2001** — Judiciary. **1999** — Children and Families; Judiciary and Personal Privacy; Urban and Local Affairs.

Telephone: Office: (608) 267-7669; (888) 534-0008 (toll free).

E-mail: Rep.Colon@legis.wisconsin.gov

Voting address: 821 South 3rd Street, Milwaukee 53204.

Mailing address: Office: Room 306 East, State Capitol, P.O. Box 8952, Madison 53708.

Josh Zepnick (Dem.), 9th Assembly District

Born Milwaukee, March 21, 1968; married. Graduate Rufus King H.S. (Milwaukee); B.A. UW-Madison 1990; M.A. Univ. of Minnesota 1998. Full-time legislator. Former project consultant, Milwaukee Jobs Initiative, Milwaukee Community Service Corps, and Urban Economic Development Association of Wisconsin; research associate, Center for Democracy and Citizenship; aide to State Senator Bob Jauch and Congressman David R. Obey. Member: Jackson Park Neighborhood Assn.; Jackson Park Business Assn.; South Side Business Club. Former member: UFCW Local 1444.

Elected to Assembly 2002; reelected since 2004. Biennial committee assignments: **2009** — Jt. Com. for Review of Administrative Rules (co-chp.); Energy and Utilities (vice chp., mbr. since 2005); Financial Institutions (since 2003); Ways and Means; Workforce Development (also 2007, 2003). **2007** — Gov's Council on Workforce Investment (also 2005). **2005** — Government Operations and Spending Limitations (also 2003); Southeast Wisconsin Freeways; State-Federal Relations; Jt. Select Com. on Road to the Future. **2003** — Transportation.

Telephone: Office: (608) 266-1707; (888) 534-0009 (toll free); Home: (414) 727-0841.

E-mail: Rep.Zepnick@legis.wisconsin.gov

Voting address: 3173 South 49th Street, Milwaukee 53219.

Mailing address: Office: Room 219 North, State Capitol, P.O. Box 8953, Madison 53708.

4th SENATE DISTRICT

Senator
TAYLOR

See Milwaukee County Detail
Map on pp. 92 & 93

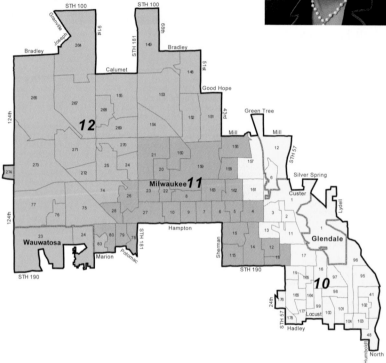

Lena C. Taylor (Dem.), 4th Senate District

Born Milwaukee, July 25, 1966; 1 child. Graduate Rufus King H.S. (Milwaukee) 1984; B.A. in english UW-Milwaukee 1990; J.D. SIU-Carbondale 1993. Attorney. Member: Democratic Party of Wisconsin (1st vice chr.); Democratic National Com.; UW-Milwaukee Alumni Assn. (bd. of trustees); Milwaukee Boy Scouts (advisory bd.); NAACP; Urban League of Milwaukee; Girl Scouts of Milwaukee Area; Unity Caucus.

Elected to Assembly in April 2003 special election; elected to Senate 2004; reelected 2008. Biennial Senate committee assignments: **2009** — Judiciary, Corrections, Insurance, Campaign Finance Reform, and Housing (chp.); Jt. Review Com. on Criminal Penalties (co-chp., mbr. since 2007); Jt. Com. on Finance (since 2005). **2007** — Judiciary and Corrections (chp., Judiciary, Corrections and Housing eff. 11/6/07); Health, Human Services, Insurance and Job Creation (eff. 11/6/07); Jt. Survey Com. on Retirement Systems; Wisconsin Housing and Economic Development Authority (also 2005); Judicial Council; Sentencing Commission. **2005** — Judiciary, Corrections and Privacy. Assembly committee assignments: **2003** — Criminal Justice; Economic Development; Financial Institutions; Tourism; Urban and Local Affairs.

Telephone: Office: (608) 266-5810; District: (414) 342-7176.

E-mail: Sen.Taylor@legis.wisconsin.gov

Voting address: Ward 17, City of Milwaukee.

Mailing address: Office: Room 415 South, State Capitol, P.O. Box 7882, Madison 53707-7882.

| Representative
A. WILLIAMS | Representative
FIELDS | Representative
KESSLER |

Annette P. Williams (Dem.), 10th Assembly District

Born Belzoni, MS, Jan. 10, 1937; 4 children. Grad. Milw. North Div. H.S.; attended Milw. Area Tech. College 1971-73; B.S. UW-Milwaukee 1975. Full-time legislator. Former mental health assistant, counselor, cashier/clerk, keypunch operator, typist. Lectured at Harvard, Yale, Marquette, Stanford, Johns Hopkins, and Minnesota Universities. Coordinated food, clothing, and fund drive for Hurricane Katrina survivors 2005. Appeared on CBS's 60 Minutes, NBC's Today, ABC's World News, and PBS's MacNeil-Lehrer Report. First African American and first female candidate for Milwaukee County Exec. 1992. State chair, Jesse Jackson presidential campaign 1988, 1984. Awards: Education Week *Faces of the 20th Century;* UW-Milwaukee *Lifetime Achievement Award* 1998; New York Times – one of 13 innovators who changed education in the 20th century; UW-Milwaukee Alumni Assn.'s *Distinguished Alumnus* 1994; National Black Caucus of State Legislators *President's Award for Distinguished Service* 1990. Received presidential invitation to White House Conference on Parental Choice, January 1989. Auckland Inst. of Technology 1993 Visiting Fellow, Auckland, New Zealand; Scholar in Residence, Natl. Alliance of Black School Educators 1996; Natl. Black Caucus of State Legislators (financial secy.). Presidential elector for Barack Obama 2008.

Elected to Assembly since 1980. Longest serving woman legislator in either house. Author of nation's first parents education choice legislation. Biennial committee assignments: **2009** — Education Reform (chp., mbr. since 1999); Aging and Long Term Care (vice chp.); Elections and Campaign Reform; Housing.

Telephone: Office: (608) 266-0960; (888) 534-0010 (toll free); District: (414) 374-7474.
E-mail: Rep.WilliamsA@legis.wisconsin.gov
Voting address: 3927 North 16th Street, Milwaukee 53206.
Mailing address: Office: Room 113 North, State Capitol, P.O. Box 8953, Madison 53708.

Jason M. Fields (Dem.), 11th Assembly District

Born Milwaukee, January 29, 1974; single. Graduate Milwaukee Lutheran H.S. 1992. Former stockbroker, financial advisor, banker. Member: Prince Hall Masonic Lodge No. 4; Alpha Phi Alpha Fraternity, Inc.; Milwaukee Urban League Young Professionals; National Association of Insurance and Financial Advisors; National Association of Black Accountants. Member: Democratic Party of Wisconsin (fmr. Chairman of 4th Congressional District); Milwaukee County Democrats (fmr. 2nd District vice chairman); YPM (Young Professionals of Milwaukee).

Elected to Assembly 2004; reelected since 2006. Biennial committee assignments: **2009** — Financial Institutions (chp.); Education Reform; Jobs, the Economy and Small Business; Transportation. **2007** — Jobs and the Economy; Small Business (also 2005); Ways and Means (also 2005); Workforce Development. **2005** — Economic Development; Financial Institutions; Urban and Local Affairs.

Telephone: Office: (608) 266-3756; (888) 534-0011 (toll free); District: (414) 466-1660.
E-mail: Rep.Fields@legis.wisconsin.gov
Voting address: 5686 North 60th Street, Milwaukee 53218.
Mailing address: Office: Room 221 North, State Capitol, P.O. Box 8952, Madison 53708.

Frederick P. Kessler (Dem.), 12th Assembly District

Born Milwaukee, January 11, 1940; married; 2 children. Graduate Milwaukee Lutheran H.S. and Capitol Page School 1957; B.A. U. of Wisconsin-Madison 1962; L.L.B. U. of Wisconsin-Madison 1966. Labor arbitrator. Member: Goethe House (vice pres., former pres.); Milwaukee Chap. ACLU (bd. mbr., former pres.); World Affairs Council of Milwaukee (bd. mbr.); Wis. Bar Assn.; Industrial Relations Research Assn. (advisory com. mbr.); Democratic Party; DANK (German-American National Congress), Milwaukee chap. (former vice pres.); Milwaukee Donauschwaben; Amnesty International Group 107 (former chairman); Milwaukee Turners; NAACP. Former member: City of Milwaukee Harbor Comn. Wisconsin ACLU *Eunice Edgar Lifetime Service Award* 2008. County court judge (Milw. Co.) 1972-78; Circuit court judge (Milw. Co.) 1978-81, 1986-88. On January 11, 1961, his 21st birthday, he became the youngest person, up to that time, ever to serve in the legislature.

Elected to Assembly 1960, 1964-70; reelected since 2004. Biennial committee assignments: **2009** — State Affairs and Homeland Security (chp.); Criminal Justice (vice chp., mbr. since 2007); Corrections and the Courts; Education Reform; Elections and Campaign Reform; Judiciary and Ethics (also 2007); Personal Privacy. **2007** — Elections and Constitutional Law; Ways and Means. **2005** — Campaigns and Elections; Criminal Justice and Homeland Security; Judiciary (also 1965-71); State-Federal Relations. **1971** — Elections (chp., mbr. 1969, 1965); Rules. **1961** — Education.

Telephone: Office: (608) 266-5813; (888) 534-0012 (toll free); District: (414) 535-0266.
E-mail: Rep.Kessler@legis.wisconsin.gov
Voting address: 11221 West Sanctuary Drive, Milwaukee 53224.
Mailing address: Office: Room 302 North, State Capitol, P.O. Box 8952, Madison 53708.

5th SENATE DISTRICT

Senator
SULLIVAN

See Milwaukee County Detail Map on pp. 92 & 93

See Waukesha County Detail Map on pp. 94 & 95

Jim Sullivan (Dem.), 5th Senate District

Born Astoria, OR, December 26, 1967; married; 2 children. Graduate Whitefish Bay H.S. 1986; B.A. in political science UW-Madison 1991; J.D. Marquette U. 2001. Attorney, small business owner. Former advertising sales representative. Member U.S. Naval Reserve, 1998-2006. Member: State Bar of Wisconsin; West Suburban Chamber of Commerce – Milwaukee; Christ King Parish; Democratic Party of Wisconsin. Former member: Wauwatosa Bd. of Health; Wauwatosa Senior Commission; Wauwatosa Economic Development Corp.; Wauwatosa Community Development Committee. Wauwatosa Common Council 2000-07.

Elected to Senate 2006. Biennial committee assignments: **2009** — Veterans and Military Affairs, Biotechnology and Financial Institutions (chp. since 2007); Judiciary, Corrections, Insurance, Campaign Finance Reform, and Housing (vice chp.); Transportation, Tourism, Forestry, and Natural Resources; State Fair Park Bd. (also 2007); Wisconsin Center District Bd. (also 2007).

Telephone: Office: (608) 266-2512; (866) 817-6061 (toll free).

E-mail: Sen.Sullivan@legis.wisconsin.gov

Voting address: 2650 North 72nd Street, Wauwatosa 53213.

Mailing address: Office: Room 15 South, State Capitol, P.O. Box 7882, Madison 53707-7882.

| Representative | Representative | Representative |
| CULLEN | VUKMIR | STASKUNAS |

David A. Cullen (Dem.), 13th Assembly District

Born Milwaukee, February 1, 1960; married; 2 children. Graduate John Marshall H.S.; B.S. in secondary ed. UW-Madison 1981; J.D. Marquette U. 1984. Attorney. Member: State Bar of Wis.; Democratic Party of Wisconsin. Awards: Wis. Environmental Decade *Clean 16 Award* 2003-04, 1999-2000, 1993-96; Wis. Maternal and Child Health Coalition *Outstanding Elected Official* 1997. Milwaukee School Board 1983-90 (pres. 1987-90).

Elected to Assembly in May 1990 special election; reelected since November 1990. Biennial committee assignments: **2009** — Insurance (chp., also mbr. since 2003, 1999); Jt. Survey Com. on Tax Exemptions (vice chp.); Colleges and Universities; Education Reform (also 1999-2003); Judiciary and Ethics; Public Safety. **2007** — Jt. Legis. Audit (since 1999); Consumer Protection and Personal Privacy; Sentencing Comn.; Comn. on Uniform State Laws (since 1999). **2005** — Family Law; Southeast Wisconsin Freeways. **2003** — Judiciary (also mbr. 1995, 1993, vice chp. 1991). **2001** — Economic Development. **1999** — Campaigns and Elections; Special Com. on the Renovation of Lambeau Field. **1997** — Campaign Finance Reform; Insurance, Securities and Corporate Policy (also 1995, vice chp. 1993); Law Revision Com. (also 1995); Legis. Coun. Com. on Discipline of Health Care Professionals.

Telephone: Office: (608) 267-9836; (888) 534-0013 (toll free); District: (414) 774-4115; Fax: (608) 282-3613.

E-mail: Rep.Cullen@legis.wisconsin.gov

Voting address: 2845 North 68th Street, Milwaukee 53210.

Mailing address: Office: Room 216 North, State Capitol, P.O. Box 8952, Madison 53708.

Leah Vukmir (Rep.), 14th Assembly District

Born Milwaukee, April 26, 1958; 2 children. Graduate Brookfield East H.S. 1976; B.S. in nursing Marquette U. 1980; M.S. in nursing UW-Madison 1983. Registered nurse; nationally certified pediatric nurse practitioner. Former research fellow, Wisconsin Policy Research Institute; Past Pres. and Co-founder of Parents Raising Educational Standards in Schools (PRESS). Member: Republican Party of Milwaukee Co., Republican Party of Waukesha Co., Wauwatosa Republican Club; West Allis Speedskating Club (former ASU Speedskating Referee). Former member: Standards and Assessments Subcommittee of Gov. Thompson's Task Force on Education and Learning; English/Language Arts Task Force of Gov. Thompson's Council on Model Academic Standards. Nationally recognized authority and speaker on education issues and educational standards. Recipient: Center for Education Reform's *Unsung Hero Award* 1998; Brookfield East High School *Alumni Achievement Award* 2002.

Elected to Assembly 2002; reelected since 2004. Biennial committee assignments: **2009** — Education (also 2007); Education Reform (chp. 2005, vice chp. 2003, mbr. since 2003); Health and Health Care Reform (chp. 2007); Public Health (vice chp. 2007). **2007** — Criminal Justice (also 2003). **2005** — Health (vice chp., mbr. 2003); Children and Families (since 2003); Criminal Justice and Homeland Security; Medicaid Reform. **2003** — Economic Development.

Telephone: Office: (608) 266-9180; District: (414) 453-0024; E-mail: Rep.Vukmir@legis.wisconsin.gov

Voting address: 2544 North 93rd Street, Wauwatosa 53226.

Mailing address: Office: Room 107 West, State Capitol, P.O. Box 8953, Madison 53708.

Anthony J. Staskunas (Dem.), 15th Assembly District

Born West Allis, January 3, 1961; married; 3 children. Graduate West Allis Nathan Hale H.S.; B.A. *cum laude* UW-Milwaukee (Phi Beta Kappa) 1983; J.D. UW-Madison 1986. Legislator and attorney. Member: WA/WM Chamber of Commerce (bd. of dir.); WA/WM Community Alliance Against Drugs; volunteer attorney to WA/WM Crimestoppers; Wis. Exposition Center (bd. dir.). Recipient: Wis. League of Conservation Voters *Conservation Champion* 2009; MADD *Public Policy Recognition Award* 2008; Wis. PTA *Friend of Education Award* 2004; WA/WM Education Assn. *Friend of Education Award* 2000; Wis. Right to Life *Leadership Award* 2000; Independent Business Assn. of Wis. *Freshman of the Session Award* 1997-98 session; WA/WM Alliance Against Drugs *Outstanding Community Involvement Award;* WMC *Working for Wisconsin Award* 2002, 2000; West Allis Chamber of Com. *Distinguished Service Award.* West Allis Bd. of Health (chm.). West Allis City Coun. 1988-97 (License and Health Com., chm.).

Elected to Assembly since 1996. Speaker Pro Tempore 2009; Minority Caucus Chairperson 2007. Biennial committee assignments: **2009** — Public Safety (chp.); Assembly Organization; Criminal Justice (also 2007, 2003, 2001); Energy and Utilities (since 2005); Personal Privacy; Rules (also 2007); Jt. Legislative Council. **2007** — Judiciary and Ethics; State Fair Park Bd. (since 2001). **2005** — Insurance; Judiciary (since 2001 and co-chp. of its 2001 Special Task Force on Identity Theft).

Telephone: Office: (608) 266-0620; (888) 534-0015 (toll free); District: (414) 541-9440.

E-mail: Rep.Staskunas@legis.wisconsin.gov

Voting address: 2010 South 103rd Court, West Allis 53227.

Mailing address: Room 212 North, State Capitol, P.O. Box 8953, Madison 53708.

6th SENATE DISTRICT

**See Milwaukee County Detail
Map on pp. 92 & 93**

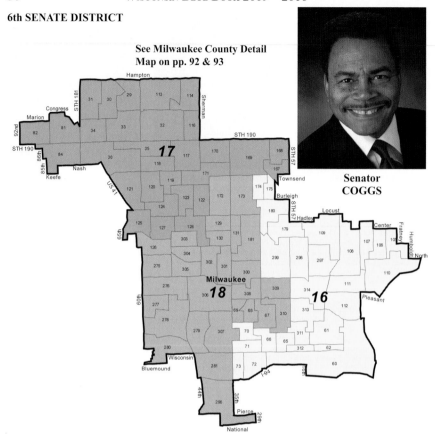

**Senator
COGGS**

Spencer Coggs (Dem.), 6th Senate District

Born Milwaukee, August 6, 1949; married; 2 children. Graduate Riverside H.S.; A.A. MATC (Milw.) 1975; B.S. UW-Milwaukee 1976. Full-time legislator. Former City of Milwaukee health officer, postal worker, and industrial printer. Member: NAACP; National Labor Caucus of State Legislators (pres.); Natl. Conference of State Legislatures (exec. com.); Natl. Black Caucus of State Legislators (exec. com.); African American Male Natl. Council (exec. bd.); AFSCME Local 1091 (former chief steward). Former member: Fed. of Black City Empl. (pres.); Isaac Coggs and MLK Community Health Centers Bd. (bd. chair). Governor's Business Opportunity Advisory Commission (co-chp.); Governor's Commission on Reducing Racial Disparities in Wisconsin's Criminal Justice System (co-chp.).

Elected to Assembly 1982-2002; elected to Senate in November 2003 special election; reelected since 2004. Majority Caucus Sergeant at Arms 2007; Majority Caucus Vice Chairperson 1989, 1987, 1985. Biennial Senate committee assignments: **2009** — Labor, Elections and Urban Affairs (chp.); Public Health, Senior Issues, Long-Term Care and Job Creation; Veterans and Military Affairs, Biotechnology and Financial Institutions (vice chp. 2007); Jt. Legislative Council (also 2007, 2003); Migrant Labor Council. **2007** — Public Health, Senior Issues, Long-Term Care and Privacy (vice chp.); Educational Communications Bd. (since 2003); Milwaukee Child Welfare Partnership Council (since 2003); Legis. Coun. Com. on State-Tribal Relations (since 2003, also 1999, 1993, 1985-89). **2005** — Housing and Financial Institutions; Judiciary, Corrections and Privacy (res. 4/1/05, also 2003 eff. 12/1/03, res. 7/26/04); Jt. Com. for Review of Criminal Penalties (also 2003 eff. 12/1/03). **2003** — Jt. Com. for the Review of Administrative Rules; Select Com. on Control of Health Care Costs. Assembly committee assignments: **2003** — Finance (also 2001); Jt. Com. on Finance (also 2001, 1993-97); Workforce Development. **2001** — Census and Redistricting; Children and Families (also 1999); Corrections and the Courts (also 1999); Public Health. **1999** — Government Operations. **1997** — Gang Violence Prevention Council. **1995** — Legis. Coun. Com. on Lead Poisoning Prevention and Control. **1993** — State Council on Alcohol and Other Drug Abuse; Speaker's Task Force on Gang Violence (chp., also 1991). **1991** — Urban and Local Affairs (chp. since 1985); Children and Human Services (since 1987); Colleges and Universities (since 1987); Urban Education (also 1989); Special Com. on Reapportionment. **1989** — Select Com. on the Census; State of Wis. Building Comn.

Telephone: Office: (608) 266-2500; (877) 474-2000 (toll free); District: (414) 442-0739.

E-mail: Sen.Coggs@legis.wisconsin.gov

Voting address: 7819 West Potomac Avenue, Milwaukee 53222.

Mailing address: Office: Room 123 South, State Capitol, P.O. Box 7882, Madison 53707-7882.

Representative
YOUNG

Representative
TOLES

Representative
GRIGSBY

Leon D. Young (Dem.), 16th Assembly District

Born Los Angeles, July 4, 1967; single. Graduate Rufus King H.S.; attended UW-Milwaukee. Full-time legislator. Former police aide and police officer. Member: Democratic Party; Harambee Ombudsman Project; Milwaukee Police Association; League of Martin; House of Peace (Love Committee); NAACP; Urban League; Social Development Commission Minority Male Forum on Corrections; National Black Caucus of State Legislators' Task Force on African American Males; 100 Black Men; Milwaukee Metropolitan Fair Housing; Boy Scouts of America (Urban Emphasis Com.); Martin Luther King Community Center (Revitalization Com.).

Elected to Assembly since 1992. Biennial committee assignments: **2009** — Housing (chp., mbr. since 2005); State Affairs and Homeland Security (vice chp.); Education Reform. **2007** — State Affairs (since 1993, vice chp. 1993); Tourism, Recreation and State Properties. **2005** — Highway Safety (since 1999); Tourism (also 2003 eff. 2/14/03). **2003** — Criminal Justice (since 1999); Ways and Means (eff. 5/13/03). **2001** — Council on Alcohol and Other Drug Abuse (also 1999). **1999** — Transportation. **1997** — Government Operations; Highways and Transportation (also 1995). **1995** — Urban Education (also 1993). **1993** — Children and Human Services; Small Business and Economic Development; Urban and Local Affairs; Speaker's Task Force on African American Males; Legis. Coun. Com. on Educational Communications Technology.

Telephone: Office: (608) 266-3786; (888) 534-0016 (toll free); District: (414) 374-7414.

E-mail: Rep.Young@legis.wisconsin.gov

Voting address: 2224 North 17th Street, Milwaukee 53205.

Mailing address: Office: Room 11 North, State Capitol, P.O. Box 8953, Madison 53708.

Barbara L. Toles (Dem.), 17th Assembly District

Born Milwaukee. Graduate West Division H.S. (Milwaukee) 1973; B.A. UW-Madison 1979; M.Ed. Marquette U. 1997. Full-time legislator. Former adjunct faculty, community outreach coordinator and advisor, Milwaukee Area Technical College. Member: American Federation of Teachers Local 212 (fmr. exec. bd. mbr.); League of Women Voters of Milwaukee County (past pres.); NAACP; Women in Government (state dir.); Wisconsin Donor Network Advisory Bd.; National Organization of Black Elected Legislative Women (corr. sec.); Women Legislators' Lobby (WILL) (bd. mbr.). Recipient: NAACP 2006 Theme Award, *Voting Our Values/Valuing Our Votes*.

Elected to Assembly in January 2004 special election; reelected since November 2004. Majority Caucus Vice Chairperson 2009. Biennial committee assignments: **2009** — Workforce Development (chp., mbr. since 2003, eff. 2/6/04); Jobs, the Economy and Small Business; Labor; Ways and Means (since 2005). **2007** — Jobs and the Economy; State Affairs (also 2005). **2005** — Economic Development. **2003** — Children and Families (eff. 2/6/04); Health (eff. 2/6/04).

Telephone: Office: (608) 266-5580; (888) 534-0017 (toll free); District: (414) 444-3810.

E-mail: Rep.Toles@legis.wisconsin.gov

Voting address: 3835 North 56th Street, Milwaukee 53216.

Mailing address: Office: Room 124 North, State Capitol, P.O. Box 8953, Madison 53708.

Tamara D. Grigsby (Dem.), 18th Assembly District

Born November 19, 1974; single. Graduate Madison Memorial H.S. 1993; B.A. Howard U. (Washington, D.C.) 1997; M.S.W. UW-Madison 2000. Former social worker; adjunct professor, Carroll College, UW-Milwaukee, Cardinal Stritch University; child advocate; family counselor. Member: NAACP; National Assn. of Social Workers; Democratic Party of Wisconsin; Milwaukee County W-2 Monitoring Task Force; Felmers Chaney Advisory Board; Midwest Progressive Elected Officials Network; Sherman Park Neighborhood Assn.; Justice 2000 (bd. of dir.); Milwaukee Fair Housing Council Advisory Bd.

Elected to Assembly 2004; reelected since 2006. Minority Caucus Vice Chairperson 2007. Biennial committee assignments: **2009** — Children and Families (chp., mbr. 2005); Jt. Com. on Finance; Milwaukee Child Welfare Partnership Council (since 2005); Interstate Adult Offender Supervision Board (since 2005). **2007** — Children and Family Law; Criminal Justice; Rules; Workforce Development. **2005** — Criminal Justice and Homeland Security; Public Health; Tourism.

Telephone: Office: (608) 266-0645; (888) 534-0018 (toll free); District: (414) 873-5557.

E-mail: Rep.Grigsby@legis.wisconsin.gov

Voting address: 2354 North 41st Street, Milwaukee 53210.

Mailing address: Office: Room 324 East, State Capitol, P.O. Box 8952, Madison 53708.

7th SENATE DISTRICT

Senator
PLALE

See Milwaukee County Detail Map on
pp. 92 & 93

Jeffrey T. Plale

(Dem.), 7th Senate District
Born South Milwaukee, May 31, 1968; 2
children. Graduate South Milwaukee H.S.;
B.A. in communications and public relations
Marquette U. 1990; M.A. in communica-
tions and public relations Marquette U. 1992.
Former investment agent. Member: Boy
Scouts of America Community Fund Raising
(former chp.); Marquette U. Alumni Assn.;
Ancient Order of Hibernians; Dem. Party of
Wis.; Democratic Leadership Coun.; South
Milwaukee Lions Club; American Legisla-
tive Exchange Coun.; Youth in Govt. (bd. of
governors); Center for Policy Alternatives
Flemming Fellowship. Recipient: Wis. Build-
ers Assn. *Friend of Housing Award* 2008;
Wis. Grocers Assn. *Friend of Grocers Award*
2008; Wis. State Telecommunications Assn.
Excellence in Legislative Leadership Award
2007-08; Wisconsin Elec. Cooperatives *En-
lightened Legislator of the Year* 2008; Wis.
Federation of Cooperatives *Friend of Coop-
eratives Award* 2008; Wis. Counties Assn.
Outstanding Legislator Award 2008; Stem
Cell Now *Voice of Courage* 2006; Dept. of
Veterans Affairs *Certificate of Commendation* 2006; WMC *Working for Wisconsin Award* 2004, 2002, 2000, 1998;
NFIB *Guardian of Small Business Award* 1998. South Milwaukee City Council 1993-96.

Elected to Assembly in March 1996 special election; reelected November 1996-2002 (resigned eff. 5/9/03); elected
to Senate in April 2003 special election; reelected 2006. Majority Caucus Vice Chairperson 2007; Minority Caucus
Chairperson 2005. Biennial Senate committee assignments: **2009** — Commerce, Utilities, Energy and Rail (chp.);
Agriculture and Higher Education (also 2007); Small Business, Emergency Preparedness, Technical Colleges and
Consumer Protection; Transportation, Tourism, Forestry, and Natural Resources. **2007** — Commerce, Utilities and
Rail (chp.); Transportation, Tourism and Insurance (vice chp.); Small Business, Emergency Preparedness, Workforce
Development, Technical Colleges and Consumer Protection. **2005** — Energy, Utilities and Information Technology;
Higher Education and Tourism; Housing and Financial Institutions. **2003** — Jt. Com. on Audit; Economic Develop-
ment, Job Creation and Housing. Assembly committee assignments: **2003** — Aging and Long-Term Care; Financial
Institutions (since 1997); Tourism; Workforce Development. **2001** — Jt. Survey Com. on Retirement Systems; Energy
and Utilities; Transportation; Forward Wisconsin, Inc. (since 1997); Building Com. **1999** — Insurance; Utilities;
Ways and Means; Speaker's Special Task Force on Abandoned Children (co-chp.). **1997** — Government Operations;
Insurance, Securities and Corporate Policy; Utilities Oversight; Legis. Coun. Coms. on Historic Building Code, on
Services for Visually Handicapped Students. **1995** — Jt. Com. for Review of Administrative Rules; Urban and Local
Affairs; Legis. Coun. Coms. on Adoption Laws, on Economics and Health of the Tavern Industry.

Telephone: Office: (608) 266-7505; (800) 361-5487 (toll free); District: (414) 744-1444.

E-mail: Sen.Plale@legis.wisconsin.gov

Voting address: 1404 18th Avenue, South Milwaukee 53172.

District office: 3195 South Superior Street, Milwaukee 53207.

Mailing address: Office: Room 313 South, State Capitol, P.O. Box 7882, Madison 53707-7882.

| Representative | Representative | Representative |
| RICHARDS | SINICKI | HONADEL |

Jon Richards (Dem.), 19th Assembly District

Born Waukesha, September 5, 1963; married. Graduate Waukesha North H.S.; B.A. Lawrence U. 1986; J.D. UW-Madison (Law Review) 1994; attended Keio University (Tokyo). Attorney. Former English teacher in Japan and former volunteer with Mother Teresa, Calcutta, India. Volunteer Big Brothers/Big Sisters. Member: New Brady Street Area Assn. (bd. mbr.); Bay View Historical Soc.; Amer. Coun. of Young Political Leaders; Natl. Caucus of Environmental Legislators; Milwaukee Co. Dem. Party; Bay View Lions Club; Bay View Neighborhood Assn.; Clean Wisconsin. Recipient: Environmental Decade *Clean 16 Award Winner* and *Conservation Honor Roll*; Center for Policy Alternatives Flemming Fellow; Planned Parenthood of Wis. *Voice for Choice Award Winner;* Wis. Family Planning and Reproductive Health Assn. *Legislator of the Year;* Wis. Farm Bureau *Friend of Agriculture* 2005-2006; Shepherd Express's *Milwaukee's Best Legislator* 2007, 2006, 2005, 2001.

Elected to Assembly 1998; reelected since 2000. Assistant Minority Leader 2003-2007. Biennial committee assignments: **2009** — Health and Healthcare Reform (chp); Energy and Utilities; Judiciary and Ethics; Rules (since 2003); Wisconsin Center District Bd. **2007** — Assembly Organization (since 2003); Financial Institutions (since 2001, ranking min. mbr. since 2003); Jt. Com. on Legislative Organization (since 2003). **2001** — Insurance; Tax and Spending Limitations; Transportation Projects Comn.

Telephone: Office: (608) 266-0650; (888) 534-0019 (toll free); District: (414) 270-9898.

E-mail: Rep.Richards@legis.wisconsin.gov

Internet address: www.jonrichards.org

Voting address: 1823 North Oakland Avenue, Milwaukee 53202.

Mailing address: Office: Room 118 North, State Capitol, P.O. Box 8953, Madison 53708.

Christine Sinicki (Dem.), 20th Assembly District

Born Milwaukee, March 28, 1960; married; 2 children. Graduate Bay View H.S. Former small business manager. Member: Delegate-U.S. Pres. Electoral College, 2000; Wis. Delegate to Democratic Natl. Convention, Los Angeles, 2000; Amer. Coun. of Young Political Leaders, Delegate to Israel and Palestine, 2001; Milwaukee Com. on Domestic Violence and Sexual Assault; Wis. Civil Air Patrol, Major; Wis. Congress of Parents and Teachers; Milwaukee City Coun. Parents and Teachers Assn.; Bay View Historical Soc.; Bay View Neighborhood Assn.; Fellow, Bowhay Institute, La Follette School, UW-Madison 2001; Founder, Conservatory of Lifelong Learning, Innovative School, Milwaukee Public School District; Flemming Fellow, Center for Policy Alternatives 2003. Awards: Wisconsin Environmental Decade *Clean 16 2000;* Wisconsin Ob/Gyn Physicians' *Legislator of the Year* 2000; Wisconsin Coalition Against Domestic Violence *DV Diva* 2003; Wis. Dept. of Veterans Affairs *Certificates of Commendation* 2006, 2005. Assembly Democratic Task Force on Working Families (chp.) 2003. State Assembly Milw. Caucus (chp. 2005, 2003). Dept. of Workforce Development State Minimum Wage Council (gov. appointee) 2005. Milw. School Board 1991-98.

Elected to Assembly 1998; reelected since 2000. Minority Caucus Secretary 2001. Biennial committee assignments: **2009** — Labor (chp., mbr. 2005, 2003); Education Reform (vice chp., mbr. 1999-2005); Children and Families (also 1999-2005); Education; Transportation; Veterans and Military Affairs (also 2003). **2007** — Consumer Protection and Personal Privacy; Homeland Security and State Preparedness; State Affairs.

Telephone: Office: (608) 266-8588; (888) 534-0020 (toll free); District: (414) 481-7667.

E-mail: Rep.Sinicki@legis.wisconsin.gov

Voting address: 3132 South Indiana Avenue, Milwaukee 53207.

Mailing address: Office: Room 114 North, State Capitol, P.O. Box 8953, Madison 53708.

Mark R. Honadel (Rep.), 21st Assembly District

Born Milwaukee, March 29, 1956; married; 3 children. Graduate Oak Creek H.S. 1974; attended Milwaukee Area Technical College and Marquette U. Independent businessman. Former professional metal fabricator, welding instructor, industrial manager. Member: South Milwaukee Street Scaping; Grant Park Garden Club; South Milwaukee Chamber of Commerce; South Milwaukee Lions. Former member: American Welding Society, V.I.C.A. welding judge.

Elected to Assembly in July 2003 special election; reelected since 2004. Majority Caucus Chairperson 2007. Biennial committee assignments: **2009** — Energy and Utilities (since 2003 eff. 8/23/03); Labor; Workforce Development. **2007** — Labor and Industry (chp.); Jobs and the Economy (vice chp.); Assembly Organization; Housing; Rules. **2005** — Southeast Wisconsin Freeways (chp.); Economic Development (also 2003 eff. 8/23/03). **2003** — Corrections and the Courts (eff. 8/28/03, res. 9/18/03); Insurance (eff. 9/18/03); Transportation (eff. 9/8/03).

Telephone: Office: (608) 266-0610; (888) 534-0021 (toll free); District: (414) 764-9921.

E-mail: Rep.Honadel@legis.wisconsin.gov

Voting address: 1219 Manitoba Avenue, South Milwaukee 53172.

Mailing address: Office: Room 113 West, State Capitol, P.O. Box 8952, Madison 53708.

8th SENATE DISTRICT

See Milwaukee County Detail
Map on pp. 92 & 93

See Waukesha County Detail
Map on pp. 94 & 95

Senator
DARLING

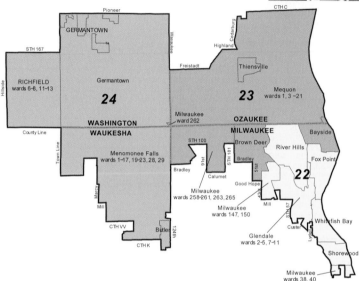

Alberta Darling (Rep.), 8th Senate District

Born Hammond, IN, April 28, 1944; married; 2 children. Graduate UW-Madison 1966; grad. work UW-Milwaukee 1972-74. Former teacher and marketing director. Member: North Shore Rotary; College Savings Program Bd. (Ed-Vest) (chp.); Junior League of Milwaukee (former pres.); YMCA (bd. mbr.); Tempo Professional Women's Organization. Former member: Next Door Foundation; Public Policy Forum; Wis. Strategic Planning Council for Economic Development; Greater Milwaukee Com.; Goals for Greater Milwaukee 2000 Project (exec. com.); United Way Bd. (chp., allocations com.); Future Milwaukee (pres.); Milwaukee Forum; Children's Service Soc. of Wis. (bd. of dir.); American Red Cross of Wis. (exec. com., bd. of dir.); League of Women Voters; Today's Girls/Tomorrow's Women/ Boys Girls Club (founder); NCSL Education Com. (chp.). Recipient: Coalition of Wisconsin Aging Groups *Tommy G. Thompson Award for Service;* Wis. Stem Cell Now *Courage Award;* Multiple Sclerosis (MS) *Advocate of the Year* 2006; 2006 Inductee into the National MS Hall of Fame; Wisconsin Manufacturers and Commerce *100% Pro-Business Legislator* 2006; Wis. Builders Assn. *Friend of Housing* 2008; Amer. Cancer Soc. *Legislative Champion* 2006; Fair Air Coalition *Friend of Education;* Metropolitan Milwaukee Assn. of Commerce *Champion of Commerce;* Wis. Head Start Directors Assn. *Award of Excellence;* National Assn. of Community Leadership *Leadership Award;* United Way *Gwen Jackson Leadership Award;* William Steiger *Award for Human Service;* St. Francis Children's Center *Children Service Award.*

Elected to Assembly in May 1990 special election; reelected November 1990; elected to Senate 1992; reelected since 1996. Biennial committee assignments: **2009** — Economic Development; Health, Health Insurance, Privacy, Property Tax Relief, and Revenue; Jt. Com. on Finance (co-chp. 2003, mbr. since 2001); Jt. Legislative Council (since 2001). **2007** — Economic Development; Job Creation, Family Prosperity and Housing; Milwaukee Child Welfare Partnership Council (since 1995). **2005** — Education; Health, Children, Families, Aging and Long-Term Care. **2003** — Jt. Legis. Audit; Jt. Com. on Employment Relations; Wis. Center District Board of Dir.; UW Hospitals and Clinics Authority Bd. **2001** — Education (also 1999, 1997, 1993). **1999** — Jt. Com. for Review of Administrative Rules (since 1993); Jt. Com. on Information Policy (also 1995); Judiciary and Consumer Affairs; Child Abuse and Neglect Prevention Bd. (since 1993). **1997** — Education and Financial Institutions (chp., eff. 4/21/98, also 1995); Business, Economic Development and Urban Affairs (eff. 4/21/98, also 1995); Judiciary (eff. 4/21/98, also 1995); Labor, Transportation and Financial Institutions; Education Comn. of the States (eff. 4/30/98, also 1995).

Telephone: Office: (608) 266-5830; E-mail: Sen.Darling@legis.wisconsin.gov

Voting address: 1325 West Dean Road, River Hills 53217.

Mailing address: Office: Room 131 South, State Capitol, P.O. Box 7882, Madison 53707-7882.

| Representative | Representative | Representative |
| PASCH | J. OTT | KNODL |

Sandy Pasch (Dem.), 22nd Assembly District

Born Milwaukee, May 19, 1954; married; 3 children. Graduate Bay View H.S. 1972; B.S. Nursing UW-Madison 1976; M.S. Psychiatric nursing U. of Rochester (NY) 1981; M.A. Bioethics Medical Coll. of Wisconsin 1999. Full-time legislator. Former assistant professor Columbia College of Nursing; clinical nurse specialist; community health nurse. Member: American Public Health Assn.; Wis. Nurses Assn.; National Alliance on Mental Illness (fmr. pres.); American Red Cross – Southeastern Wis.; Milw. Mental Health Task Force (steering com.); American Society for Bioethics and Humanities. Former member: Hope House (bd. mbr., secy.).

Elected to Assembly 2008. Biennial committee assignments: **2009** — Public Health (vice chp.); Corrections and the Courts; Criminal Justice; Health and Healthcare Reform; Housing.

Telephone: Office: (608) 266-7671; (888) 534-0022 (toll free); District: (414) 332-5843.

Voting address: 6301 North Berkeley Boulevard, Whitefish Bay 53217.

Mailing address: Office: Room 122 North, State Capitol, P.O. Box 8953, Madison 53708.

Jim Ott (Rep.), 23rd Assembly District

Born Milwaukee, June 5, 1947; married; 2 sons, 1 grandchild. Graduate Milwaukee Washington H.S. 1965; B.S. UW-Milwaukee 1970; M.S. UW-Milwaukee 1975; J.D. Marquette U. 2000. Full-time legislator. Former broadcast meteorologist and instructor at UW-Parkside. Served in U.S. Army, 1970-73; Vietnam veteran. Member: State Bar of Wisconsin; American Meteorological Society; Mequon/Thiensville Sunrise Rotary; Mequon/Thiensville Chamber of Commerce; American Legion; Ozaukee County Republican Party; North Shore Branch Milwaukee Co. Republican Party; Lumen Christi Catholic Church (past parish council pres.). Recipient: National Weather Service *Public Service Award* 2006; Archbishops Vatican II *Service Award* 1999; Vietnam Campaign Medal and Meritorious Unit Citation.

Elected to Assembly 2006; reelected 2008. Biennial committee assignments: **2009** — Education Reform (also 2007); Fish and Wildlife; Natural Resources (vice chp. 2007). **2007** — Elections and Constitutional Law; Workforce Development.

Telephone: Office: (608) 266-0486; (888) 534-0023 (toll free); District: (262) 240-0808.

E-mail: Rep.OttJ@legis.wisconsin.gov

Voting address: 11743 North Lake Shore Drive, Mequon 53092.

Mailing address: Office: Room 317 North, State Capitol, P.O. Box 8953, Madison 53708.

Dan Knodl (Rep.), 24th Assembly District

Born Milwaukee, December 14, 1958; 4 children. Graduate Menomonee Falls East H.S. 1977; attended UW-Madison. Resort owner. Member: Hartford Chamber of Commerce; Washington Co. Convention and Visitors Bureau; Ozaukee/Washington Land Trust; Pike Lake Sportsmans Club. Pike Lake Protection District 2000-present. Washington County Board 2006-08.

Elected to Assembly 2008. Biennial committee assignments: **2009** — Labor; State Affairs and Homeland Security; Ways and Means.

Telephone: Office: (608) 266-3796; (888) 529-0024 (toll free); District: (262) 502-0118.

Voting address: N101 W14475 Ridgefield Court, Germantown 53022.

Mailing address: Office: Room 4 West, State Capitol, P.O. Box 8952, Madison 53708.

9th SENATE DISTRICT

Senator
LEIBHAM

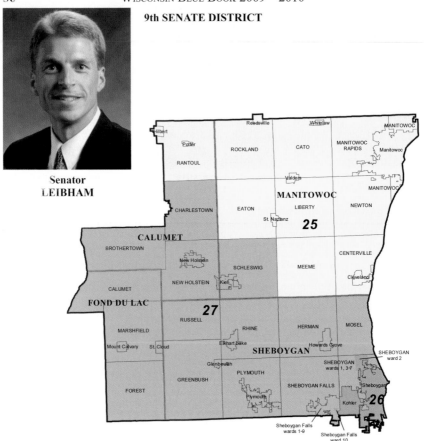

See Sheboygan Area Detail Map on p. 98

Joseph K. Leibham (Rep.), 9th Senate District

Born Sheboygan, June 6, 1969; married; two sons. Graduate Sheboygan Area Lutheran H.S.; B.A. UW-Madison 1991; attended UW-La Crosse 1987-89 and Ealing College (London, England) 1990. Former food service industry account executive and manager/membership development, Sheboygan County Chamber of Commerce. Member: Friends of Sheboygan Senior Center (vice pres.); Citizen's Police Academy (graduate); Boy Scouts of America (Eagle Scout); American Luther Assn.; Manitowoc County Vision 2011 Committee. Sheboygan City Council 1993-2000 (pres. 1995-96).

Elected to Assembly 1998-2000; elected to Senate 2002; reelected 2006. Minority Caucus Chairperson 2009; Assistant Minority Leader 2007; Majority Caucus Vice Chairperson 2003. Biennial Senate committee assignments: **2009** — Economic Development; Transportation, Tourism, Forestry, and Natural Resources; Veterans and Military Affairs, Biotechnology and Financial Institutions (also 2007); Jt. Com. on Information Policy and Technology. **2007** — Ethics Reform and Government Operations; Transportation, Tourism and Insurance; Jt. Com. on Legis. Org.; Jt. Com. for Review of Administrative Rules (co-chp. 2003). **2005** — Jt. Com. for Review of Criminal Penalties (co-chp.); Jt. Com. on Finance; Energy, Utilities and Information Technologies (through 6/13/05); Higher Education and Tourism (eff. 6/13/05). **2003** — Transportation and Information Infrastructure (chp.); Energy and Utilities. Assembly committee assignments: **2001** — Jt. Legis. Audit (co-chp.); Census and Redistricting (vice chp., also 1999); Tax and Spending Limitations (vice chp.); Energy and Utilities; State and Local Finance; Transportation (also 1999). **1999** — Utilities (vice chp.); Small Business and Economic Development; State Affairs.

Telephone: Office: (608) 266-2056; (888) 295-8750 (toll free); District: (920) 457-7367.

E-mail: Sen.Leibham@legis.wisconsin.gov

Internet address: leibhamsenate.com

Voting address: 3618 River Ridge Drive, Sheboygan 53083.

Mailing address: Office: Room 5 South, State Capitol, P.O. Box 7882, Madison 53707-7882

| Representative | Representative | Representative |
| ZIEGELBAUER | VAN AKKEREN | KESTELL |

Bob Ziegelbauer (Dem.), 25th Assembly District

Born Manitowoc, August 26, 1951; single. Graduate Manitowoc Roncalli H.S.; B.B.A. U. of Notre Dame; M.B.A. U. of Pennsylvania, Wharton School. Former small businessman, retail music store owner, City of Manitowoc finance director, and part-time instructor at Silver Lake College. Member: Manitowoc Co. Local Emergency Planning Committee; Manitowoc-Two Rivers YMCA (dir. 1989-95). Manitowoc City Council 1981-84; Manitowoc Co. Board 1982-88; Lakeshore Technical College Bd. 1987-88; Manitowoc Public Utilities Comn. 1990-2000; Manitowoc County Executive 2006-present.

Elected to Assembly since 1992. Biennial committee assignments: **2009** — Ways and Means (chp., mbr. since 1993); Public Safety (vice chp.); Insurance (also 2007, 1999); Urban and Local Affairs (also 1995, vice chp. 1993); Jt. Survey Com. on Retirement Systems (vice chp.). **2007** — Homeland Security and State Preparedness. **2005** — Agriculture; Education (since 1993); Government Operations and Spending Limitations; Tourism (also 2003). **2003** — Energy and Utilities (also member 2001 to 5/16/01); Rural Affairs. **2001** — State and Local Finance; Council on Workforce Excellence (also 1999). **1999** — Jt. Legis. Audit; Utilities; Special Com. on the Renovation of Lambeau Field; Law Revision; Gov.'s Blue Ribbon Comn. on State-Local Partnerships for the 21st Century. **1997** — Government Operations; Income Tax Review; Insurance, Securities and Corporate Policy (also 1995); Mandates (also 1995). **1995** — Financial Institutions; Forward Wisconsin, Inc.; Select Com. on Milwaukee Brewers Stadium; Legis. Coun. Coms. on Adoption Laws, on Economics and Health of the Tavern Industry, on Public School Open Enrollment.

Telephone: Office: (608) 266-0315; (888) 529-0025 (toll free); District: (920) 684-6783 (home); (920) 683-5107 (Manitowoc County Executive office); Fax: (608) 282-3625.

E-mail: Rep.Ziegelbauer@legis.wisconsin.gov; Internet address: www.bobziegelbauer.com

Voting address: 1213 South 8th Street, Manitowoc 54220.

Mailing address: Office: Room 207 North, State Capitol, P.O. Box 8953, Madison 53708; District: P.O. Box 325, Manitowoc 54221-0325.

Terry Van Akkeren (Dem.), 26th Assembly District

Born Sheboygan, March 10, 1954; married; 4 children. Graduate Sheboygan North H.S. 1972; Lakeshore Tech. College 1982. Engineering tech.; former tool and die maker. Member: BPO Elks, Sheboygan Lodge. Sheboygan alderman 1986-2003; Sheboygan County Supervisor 1990-92.

Elected to Assembly 2002; reelected since 2004. Biennial committee assignments: **2009** — Tourism, Recreation and State Properties (chp., mbr. 2007); Labor (vice chp., mbr. 2005, 2003); Urban and Local Affairs (vice chp.). **2007** — Education (since 2003); Labor and Industry. **2005** — Natural Resources; Tourism (also 2003). **2003** — Economic Development.

Telephone: Office: (608) 266-0656; (888) 529-0026 (toll free); District: (920) 458-8829.

E-mail: Rep.VanAkkeren@legis.wisconsin.gov

Voting address: 1612 South 7th Avenue, Sheboygan 53081.

Mailing address: Office: Room 220 North, State Capitol, P.O. Box 8953, Madison 53708.

Steve Kestell (Rep.), 27th Assembly District

Born Town of Lyndon, Sheboygan Co., June 15, 1955; married; 3 adult children. Graduate Plymouth H.S. Bowhay Institute of Legislative Leadership 2000. Full-time legislator. Former retail manager and regional sales manager. Member: Sheboygan Co. Republican Party; Family Resource Center of Sheboygan County (bd. mbr.). Former member: Gov.'s Council on Highway Safety; Howards Grove Jaycees; ADA Volunteer Firefighters; 4-H project leader; Junior Achievement instructor. Howards Grove School Bd. 1981-84, 1986-98 (pres. 1995-98).

Elected to Assembly 1998; reelected since 2000. Biennial committee assignments: **2009** — Children and Families (chp. 2001-2005, mbr. 1999); Corrections and the Courts; Workforce Development; Wis. Aerospace Auth. (also 2007); Wis. Historical Soc. Bd. of Curators (also 2007). **2007** — Jt. Com. on Finance; Legis. Coun. Spec. Com. on Strengthening Wis. Families (chp.). **2005** — Education (vice chp., mbr. since 1999); Family Law (vice chp. and mbr. since 2001); Rural Development (also 2003); Legis. Coun. Spec. Com. on Adoption and Termination of Parental Rights. **2003** — Agriculture (since 1999); Child Abuse and Neglect Prevention Bd. (since 4/7/2000). **2001** — Small Business and Consumer Affairs; Legis. Coun. Com. on Relative Caregivers (co-chp.). **1999** — Government Operations (vice chp.); Transportation; Legis. Coun. Spec. Com. on Navigable Waters Recodification.

Telephone: Office: (608) 266-8530; (888) 529-0027 (toll free); District: (920) 565-2044.

E-mail: Rep.Kestell@legis.wisconsin.gov

Voting address: (Town of Herman) W3829 State Highway 32, Elkhart Lake 53020.

Mailing address: Office: Room 15 West, State Capitol, P.O. Box 8952, Madison 53708.

10th SENATE DISTRICT

Senator
HARSDORF

Detail Map: Somerset Town

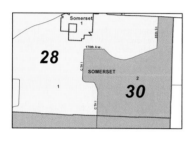

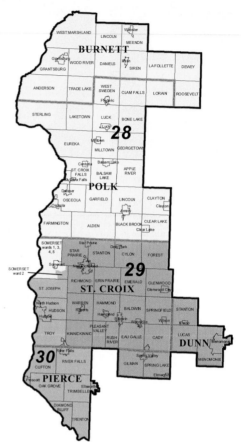

Sheila E. Harsdorf (Rep.), **10th Senate District**

Born St. Paul, MN, July 25, 1956; 1 child. Graduate River Falls H.S.; B.S. in animal science, U. of Minnesota 1978; Wis. Rural Leadership Program, grad. of 1st class (1986). Member: Pierce Co. Republican Party; Pierce Co. Farm Bureau (former dir. and treas.); Luther Memorial Church. Former member: Wis. State FFA Sponsors Bd. (chp.); Wis. Conservation Corps Bd. (secy.); Kinnickinnic River Land Trust Bd.; Pierce Co. Dairy Promotion Com. (past chm.); Wis. State ASCS Com.; Adv. Council on Small Business, Agriculture, Labor for Federal Reserve Bank of Minneapolis.

Elected to Assembly 1988-96; elected to Senate 2000; reelected since 2004. Minority Caucus Vice Chairperson 2009; Majority Caucus Sergeant at Arms 2005. Biennial Senate committee assignments: **2009** — Agriculture and Higher Education (also 2007); Commerce, Utilities, Energy, and Rail; Jt. Legislative Council (also 2007, 2003); Mississippi River Parkway Commission (since 2001); World Dairy Center Authority (since 2003). **2007** — Commerce, Utilities and Rail. **2005** — Higher Education and Tourism (chp., also 2003); Jt. Survey Com. on Tax Exemptions (co-chp., mbr. 2003); Education (also 2001); Housing and Financial Institutions. **2003** — Jt. Com. on Finance; Law Revision Com. (also 2001). **2001** — Jt. Com. on Information Policy and Technology; 2001-2003 Biennial Budget; Labor and Agriculture; Environmental Education Bd.; Ad. Bd. for Midwest Center for Agricultural Research, Education, and Disease and Injury Prevention; Jt. Legis. Council Special Com. on the Public Health System's Response to Terrorism and Public Health Emergencies. Assembly committee assignments: **1997** — Jt. Com. on Finance (also 1995). **1995** — Legis. Coun. Com. on Land Use Policies. **1993** — Agriculture, Forestry and Rural Affairs; Colleges and Universities (ranking minority mbr. since 1991); Natural Resources (since 1989); Veterans and Military Affairs (eff. 4/26/93); Educational Communications Bd. (since 1989); Legis. Coun. Com. on University and State Economic Development. **1991** — Agriculture, Aquaculture and Forestry; State Affairs (also 1989); Legis. Coun. Com. on Farm Safety. **1989** — Agriculture and its Subcom. on Aquaculture; Special Com. on Bonding for Clean Water; Legis. Coun. Com. to Review Sexual Assault Laws.

Telephone: Office: (608) 266-7745; (800) 862-1092 (toll free); Fax: (608) 267-0369.

E-mail: Sen.Harsdorf@legis.wisconsin.gov

Voting address: (Town of River Falls) N6627 County Road E, River Falls 54022.

Mailing address: Office: Room 19 South, P.O. Box 7882, Madison 53707-7882.

| Representative
HRAYCHUCK | Representative
MURTHA | Representative
RHOADES |

Ann Hraychuck (Dem.), 28th Assembly District

Born Amery, July 24, 1951; married; 2 stepchildren. Graduate Unity H.S. 1969. Former sheriff, investigator/deputy sheriff, jailer/dispatcher, secretary, and certified trainer for Wis. Dept. of Justice. Member: Wis. Sheriffs', Deputy Sheriffs' Assn.; Polk Co. Sportsmen's Club (fmr. pres.); Wis. Bear Hunter's Assn.; National Rifle Assn.; Wis. Bow Hunter's Assn.; National Wild Turkey Federation; Whitetails Unlimited; Polk Co. Democratic Party. Former member: Badger Sheriff's Assn.; Federal Nominating Commission; Wis. Radio Interoperability Homeland Security Coun.; Wis. Sentencing Guidelines Comn.; Violence Against Women Act Advisory Bd.; Polk Co Methamphetamine, Domestic Violence, Elder Abuse, and Child Abuse Task Forces (chm.). Recipient: *Medal of Valor* 1991; Unity H.S. *Wall of Honor* 2001. Polk Co. Sheriff 2001-06.

Elected to Assembly 2006; reelected 2008. Majority Caucus Secretary 2009; Minority Caucus Sergeant at Arms 2007. Biennial committee assignments: **2009** — Fish and Wildlife (chp.); Natural Resources (also 2007); Rural Economic Development; Tourism, Recreation and State Properties (also 2007).

Telephone: Office: (608) 267-2365; (888) 529-0028 (toll free); District: (715) 485-3362.

E-mail: Rep.Hraychuck@legis.wisconsin.gov

Voting address: P.O. Box 334, 1629 130th Street, Balsam Lake 54810.

Mailing address: Office: Room 6 North, State Capitol, P.O. Box 8952, Madison 53708.

John Murtha (Rep.), 29th Assembly District

Born Baldwin, August 8, 1951; married; 4 children. Graduate St. Croix Central H.S. (Hammond) 1969; Chippewa Valley Tech. (Eau Claire) wood tech. 1970. Self employed. Member: NRA; AOPA. Town of Eau Galle Board (St. Croix Co.) supervisor 1999-2003, chairman 2003-present.

Elected to Assembly 2006; reelected 2008. Biennial committee assignments: **2009** — Agriculture (also 2007); Housing; Rural Economic Development (also 2007). **2007** — Small Business (vice chp.); Labor and Industry.

Telephone: Office: (608) 266-7683; (888) 529-0029 (toll free).

E-mail: Rep.Murtha@legis.wisconsin.gov

Voting address: 2283 20th Avenue, Baldwin 54002.

Mailing address: Office: Room 304 North, State Capitol, P.O. Box 8953, Madison 53708.

Kitty Rhoades (Rep.), 30th Assembly District

Born Hudson, April 7, 1951; married; 3 children. Graduate Hudson H.S.; B.S. UW-River Falls 1973; M.A. Illinois State U. 1978. Consultant. Former educator, small business owner, and Chamber of Commerce pres. Member: St. Croix County Homemakers; Hudson Rotary (fmr. pres. and dist. officer). Former member: Forward Wisconsin (bd. of dir.); Chamber of Commerce Exec. Assn. (bd. of dir.); St. Croix River Regional Tourism Alliance (bd. of dir.); Governor's Council on Trails; Century College Pres. Adv. Council; UW-River Falls Alumni Foundation (bd. of dir.); Project Child Care (bd. of dir.).

Elected to Assembly 1998; reelected since 2000. Biennial committee assignments: **2009** — Aging and Long-Term Care (chp. 2001); Colleges and Universities (also 2001, vice chp. 1999); Health and Healthcare Reform. **2007** — Jt. Com. on Finance (co-chp., mbr. since 2003); Jt. Legislative Audit (vice chp.); Jt. Com. on Employment Relations; Jt. Legislative Council (co-chp. 2001); University of Wisconsin Hospitals and Clinics Authority Bd. **2001** — Education (also 1999); Financial Institutions (also 1999). **1999** — Conservation and Land Use; Rural Affairs and Forestry.

Telephone: Office: (608) 266-1526; (888) 529-0030 (toll free); District: (715) 386-0660.

E-mail: Rep.Rhoades@legis.wisconsin.gov

Voting address: 708 4th Street, Hudson 54016.

Mailing address: Office: Room 115 West, State Capitol, P.O. Box 8953, Madison 53708.

11th SENATE DISTRICT

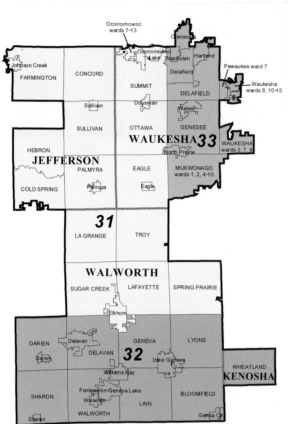

**Senator
KEDZIE**

See Waukesha County Detail
Map on pp. 94 & 95

Neal J. Kedzie (Rep.), 11th Senate District

Born Waukesha, January 27, 1956; married; 3 children. Graduate Oak Creek H.S.; B.S. UW-Whitewater 1978; graduate school UW-Whitewater. Full-time legislator. Former government relations representative. Member: American Legislative Exchange Council; National Conference of State Legislatures; Council of State Governments; Civil Air Patrol (rank of major); Walworth, Waukesha, and Jefferson Co. Republican Parties; Walworth Co. Farm Bureau; Walworth Co. Historical Society (*ex officio* mbr.); Walworth Co. Local Emergency Planning Committee; UW-Whitewater Communications Advisory Committee (2004-present). Former member: Lauderdale-La Grange Volunteer Fire Dept. (secy.). La Grange Town Board 1987-98 (chm. 1988-98); La Grange Planning and Zoning Comn. (chm.).

Elected to Assembly 1996-2000; elected to Senate 2002; reelected 2006. Assistant Senate Majority Leader 2005. Biennial Senate committee assignments: **2009** — Children and Families and Workforce Development; Commerce, Utilities, Energy, and Rail; Environment; Transportation, Tourism, Forestry, and Natural Resources; Wis. Environmental Education Bd. (since 1999). **2007** — Commerce, Utilities and Rail; Environment and Natural Resources (chp. 2003); Small Business, Emergency Preparedness, Workforce Development, Technical Colleges and Consumer Protection; Leg. Council Spec. Com. on Great Lakes Water Resources Compact (chp.). **2005** — Natural Resources and Transportation (chp.); Agriculture and Insurance; Campaign Finance Reform and Ethics; Energy, Utilities and Information Technology (eff. 6/13/05); Higher Education and Tourism (through 6/13/05); Organization; Jt. Com. on Legislative Organization; Gov.'s Council on Highway Safety (eff. 1/23/06); Wis. Rustic Roads Bd. **2003** — Agriculture, Financial Institutions and Insurance; Labor, Small Business Development and Consumer Affairs; Transportation and Information Infrastructure. Assembly committee assignments: **2001** — Environment (chp., also 1999, mbr. 1997); Aging and Long-Term Care; Financial Institutions (since 1997); Natural Resources (also 1999); Jt. Survey Com. on Tax Exemptions. **1999** — Conservation and Land Use (vice chp.); Housing (vice chp. 1997); Urban and Local Affairs. **1997** — Rural Affairs (vice chp.); State-Federal Relations; Legis. Coun. Com. on Utility Public Benefit Programs.

Telephone: Office: (608) 266-2635; (800) 578-1457 (toll free); District: (262) 742-2025.

E-mail: Sen.Kedzie@legis.wisconsin.gov

Voting address: (Town of La Grange) N7661 Highway 12, Elkhorn 53121.

Mailing address: Office: Room 126 South, State Capitol, P.O. Box 7882, Madison 53707-7882.

Representative	Representative	Representative
NASS	LOTHIAN	NEWCOMER

Stephen L. Nass (Rep.), 31st Assembly District

Born Whitewater, October 7, 1952; single. Graduate Whitewater H.S.; B.S. UW-Whitewater 1978; M.S. Ed. in school business management UW-Whitewater 1990. Former payroll benefits analyst and information analyst/negotiator. Member of Wis. Air National Guard (retired, 33 years of service), served in Middle East in Operations Desert Shield and Desert Storm. Member: American Legion; Veterans of Foreign Wars; Wis. State Assn. of Parliamentarians; Kiwanis. Whitewater City Council 1977-81; UW-Whitewater Bd. of Visitors 1979-89.

Elected to Assembly since 1990. Biennial committee assignments: **2009** — Colleges and Universities (chp. 2007, mbr. since 2003); Education (vice chp. 1995-2001, mbr. since 1991); Labor (chp. 2005, 2003); Ways and Means (vice chp. 2005, mbr. 2003). **2007** — Education Reform (vice chp., mbr. since 2003, chp. 2001, mbr. since 1999); Labor and Industry. **2005** — Property Rights and Land Management (vice chp.). **2001** — Labor and Workforce Development; Personal Privacy; Education Commission of the States (also 1999). **1999** — Government Operations; Labor and Employment (vice chp. 1997, mbr. 1995); Jt. Com. on Audit. **1997** — Mandates (chp.); Criminal Justice and Corrections; Rural Affairs; Legis. Coun. Com. on Services for Visually Handicapped Students.

Telephone: Office: (608) 266-5715; (888) 529-0031 (toll free); District: (262) 495-3424.

E-mail: Rep.Nass@legis.wisconsin.gov

Voting address: (Town of La Grange) N8330 Jackson Road, Whitewater 53190.

Mailing address: Office: Room 12 West, State Capitol, P.O. Box 8953, Madison 53708.

Thomas A. Lothian (Rep.), 32nd Assembly District

Born Cleveland, Ohio, December 14, 1928; 2 sons. Graduate Cleveland Heights H.S. 1947; B.A. in education Ohio State U. 1953; M.A. in chemistry Illinois Institute of Technology. Full-time legislator. Former assistant professor and administrator, U. of Illinois-Chicago. Member: Racine/Kenosha/Walworth Work Force Development Bd. (LEO); Geneva Lake Environmental Assn.; Geneva Lake Sailing School (fmr. treas.); Geneva Lake Assn.; Inland Lake Yacht Assn.; Skeeter Ice Boat Club (fmr. treas.); Wisconsin Counties Assn. (fmr. pres.); Walworth Co. Republican Party; National Republican Party; Williams Bay Master Plan Com.; Williams Bay Lions (fmr. pres.); Williams Bay United Church of Christ (trustee, deacon, fmr. moderator); Masonic Order (fmr. master); Shrine. Former member: Rock/Walworth Community Action, Inc. (dir.); American Chemical Society; U.S. Sailing; O'Hare Spacemen. Williams Bay village trustee 1974-82; Walworth Co. supervisor 1992-2003.

Elected to Assembly 2002; reelected since 2004. Biennial committee assignments: **2009** — Consumer Protection; Renewable Energy and Rural Affairs; Ways and Means (vice chp. 2007, mbr. since 2003). **2007** — Consumer Protection and Personal Privacy (chp.); Urban and Local Affairs (since 2003); Workforce Development (vice chp. 2005, mbr. since 2003); Jt. Survey Com. on Retirement Systems. **2005** — State-Federal Relations (chp.); Economic Development (also 2003).

Telephone: Office: (608) 266-1190; (888) 529-0032 (toll free); District: (262) 245-5901.

E-mail: Rep.Lothian@legis.wisconsin.gov

Voting address: 539 Park Ridge Road, Williams Bay 53191.

Mailing address: Office: Room 306 North, State Capitol, P.O. Box 8952, Madison 53708.

Scott Newcomer (Rep.), 33rd Assembly District

Born Waukesha, August 12, 1965; married; 3 children. Graduate Waukesha South H.S. 1983; B.S. UW-Madison 1989. Owner of capital restructuring firm for banks and credit unions and mortgage company. Former owner of a home inspection company, home inspection franchise system and nationwide home inspection training company. Member: Veritas Society; Pregnancy Support Network (bd. of advisors); Waukesha Co. Republican Party Leadership Council. Former member: Metropolitan Milwaukee and Waukesha Co. Assn. of Realtors (bd. of dir., political action com.); Boy Scouts of America Potawatomi Council (bd. of dir.); American Society of Home Inspectors (public relations com.); Sales and Marketing Executives of Metro Milwaukee; IBAW. Recipient: National Assn. of Home Inspectors *Spirit of NAHI Award* 2001.

Elected to Assembly in January 2006 special election; reelected since November 2006. Biennial committee assignments: **2009** — Financial Institutions (chp. 2007); Housing; Public Health. **2007** — Education (vice chp., mbr. 2005); Health and Health Care Reform; Labor and Industry; State Affairs (also 2005). **2005** — Labor (vice chp.); Medicaid Reform.

Telephone: Office: (608) 266-3007; (888) 529-0033 (toll free); District: (262) 646-3233.

Voting address: 1829 Nagawicka Road, Hartland 53029.

Mailing address: Office: Room 19 North, State Capitol, P.O. Box 8953, Madison 53708.

12th SENATE DISTRICT

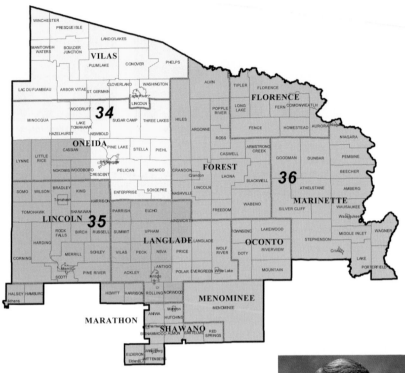

Jim Holperin (Dem.), **12th Senate District**
   Born Eagle River, December 18, 1950; married; 2 children. Graduate
Eagle River H.S. 1969; B.S. UW-Whitewater 1973. Full-time legislator.
Former executive director, Trees for Tomorrow Natural Resources Spe-
cialty School; director of aging programs, Vilas Co.; legislative analyst,
Wis. Assembly; business services coordinator, North Central Wis. Work-
force Development Bd. Member: Rotary International (pres. of Eagle
River club); Northwoods Land Trust (bd. mbr.); 1000 Friends of Wisconsin
(founding bd. mbr.); WXPR Public Radio (founding bd. mbr.). Former
member: Nicolet College Bd. of Trustees; Wisconsin Rural Leadership
Program (bd. mbr.); Governor's Forestry Council. Asst. Chief Clerk, Wis.
Senate 1977-79. Secretary, Wis. Dept. of Tourism 2003-07.
   Elected to Assembly 1982-1992; elected to Senate 2008. Majority
Caucus Sergeant at Arms 2009. Biennial committee assignments: **2009 —**
Transportation, Tourism, Forestry, and Natural Resources (chp.); Jt. Com.
for Review of Administrative Rules (co-chp.); Rural Issues, Biofuels, and
Information Technology; Small Business, Emergency Preparedness, Tech-
nical Colleges, and Consumer Protection.

**Senator
HOLPERIN**

   Telephone: Office: (608) 266-2509; District: (715) 891-1412.

   E-mail: Sen.Holperin@legis.wisconsin.gov

   Voting address: 3575 Monheim Road, Conover 54519.

   Mailing address: Office: Room 409 South, State Capitol, P.O. Box 7882, Madison 53707-7882; District: P.O. Box
1256, Eagle River 54521.

Representative   Representative   Representative
MEYER   FRISKE   MURSAU

Dan Meyer (Rep.), 34th Assembly District

Born Neenah, January 1, 1949; married; 2 children. Graduate Neenah H.S.; B.B.A. UW-Oshkosh 1978. Full-time legislator. Former executive director of Eagle River Chamber of Commerce and Visitors Center. Vietnam Era veteran; served in U.S. Army. Member: Vilas County Republican Party; American Legion Post 431. Mayor of Eagle River 1997 to April 2001.

Elected to Assembly 2000; reelected since 2002. Biennial committee assignments: **2009** — Consumer Protection; Rural Economic Development; Veterans and Military Affairs. **2007** — Jt. Com. on Finance (vice chp., mbr. since 2003). **2001** — Tourism and Recreation (vice chp.); Aging and Long-Term Care; Housing; Natural Resources; Small Business and Consumer Affairs; Urban and Local Affairs.

Telephone: Office: (608) 266-7141; (888) 534-0034 (toll free); District: (715) 479-6270.

E-mail: Rep.Meyer@legis.wisconsin.gov

Voting address: 1013 Walnut Street, Eagle River 54521.

Mailing address: Office: Room 308 North, State Capitol, P.O. Box 8953, Madison 53708.

Donald Friske (Rep.), 35th Assembly District

Born Tomahawk, November 9, 1961; married; 3 children. Graduate Tomahawk H.S. Full-time legislator. Former deputy sheriff. Veteran; served in Army November 1979 to 1985. Member: Amvets; Optimist Club; NRA. Former member: American Legion.

Elected to Assembly 2000; reelected since 2002. Biennial committee assignments: **2009** — Criminal Justice (vice chp. 2007, 2003); Forestry (chp. 2003-07); Jobs, the Economy and Small Business. **2007** — Jobs and the Economy; Judiciary and Ethics; Jt. Com. for Review of Administrative Rules (also 2005). **2005** — Criminal Justice and Homeland Security (vice chp.); Transportation (also 2003). **2003** — Energy and Utilities (mbr., vice chp. 2001); Family Law (also 2001). **2001** — Rural Affairs and Forestry (vice chp.); Corrections and the Courts; Small Business and Consumer Affairs; Tourism and Recreation.

Telephone: Office: (608) 266-7694; (888) 534-0035 (toll free); District: (715) 536-4515.

E-mail: Rep.Friske@legis.wisconsin.gov

Voting address: N2998 Highway K, Merrill 54452.

Mailing address: Office: Room 312 North, State Capitol, P.O. Box 8952, Madison 53708.

Jeffrey L. Mursau (Rep.), 36th Assembly District

Born Oconto Falls, June 12, 1954; married; 4 sons, 3 grandchildren. Graduate Coleman H.S. 1972; attended UW-Oshkosh. Small business owner; electrical contractor. Member: Crivitz Ski Cats waterski team (advisor, former pres.); Crivitz Lions Club; Crivitz, WI – Crivitz, Germany Sister City Organization (fmr. dir.); Wings over Wisconsin; St. Mary's Catholic Church; 4th Degree Knights of Columbus. Recipient: Crivitz Business Association *Citizen of the Year* 1994. Crivitz Village President 1991-2004.

Elected to Assembly 2004; reelected since 2006. Biennial committee assignments: **2009** — Forestry (vice chp. 2007, mbr. 2005); Natural Resources (since 2005); Workforce Development; Spec. Com. on State-Tribal Relations (vice chp., chp. 2007). **2007** — Rural Economic Development (chp.); Agriculture; Consumer Protection and Personal Privacy. **2005** — Tourism (vice chp.); Rural Development; Small Business.

Telephone: Office: (608) 266-3780; (888) 534-0036 (toll free).

Voting address: 4 Oak Street, Crivitz 54114.

Mailing address: Office: Room 18 North, State Capitol, P.O. Box 8953, Madison 53708.

13th SENATE DISTRICT

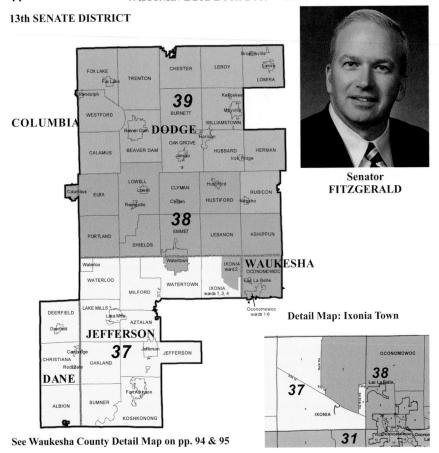

Senator
FITZGERALD

Detail Map: Ixonia Town

See Waukesha County Detail Map on pp. 94 & 95

Scott L. Fitzgerald (Rep.), **13th Senate District**

Born Chicago, IL, November 16, 1963; married; 3 children. Graduate Hustisford H.S. 1981; B.S. in journalism UW-Oshkosh 1985; U.S. Army Armor Officer Basic Course 1985; U.S. Army Command and General Staff College. Former associate newspaper publisher; member of the U.S. Army Reserve (rank of Lt. Colonel), Public Affairs Officer 84th ARRTC Ft. McCoy. Member: Dodge Co. Republican Party (chm. 1992-94); Juneau Lions Club; Reserve Officers Assn.; Knights of Columbus. Former member: Forward Wisconsin, Inc.

Elected to Senate 1994; reelected since 1998. Minority Leader 2009, 2007. Majority Leader 9/17/04 to 11/10/04. Biennial committee assignments: **2009** — Senate Org. (also 2007); Jt. Com. on Employment Relations (also 2007); Jt. Com. on Legis. Org. (also 2007); Jt. Legislative Council (since 2005). **2005** — Jt. Com. on Finance (co-chp., mbr. since 2003); Jt. Legis. Audit. **2003** — Jt. Com. for Review of Criminal Penalties (co-chp.); Education, Ethics and Elections; Homeland Security, Veterans and Military Affairs and Government Reform; Judiciary, Corrections and Privacy; Claims Bd. (eff. 12/5/03). **2001** — Health, Utilities, Veterans and Military Affairs; Judiciary, Consumer Affairs, and Campaign Finance Reform; Privacy, Electronic Commerce and Financial Institutions (also 1999); Wis. Housing and Economic Development Authority. **1999** — Economic Development, Housing and Government Operations (member to 2/24/99, also 1997); Rural Economic Development Bd. (also 1997). **1997** — State Government Operations and Corrections (chp., eff. 4/21/98); Education (eff. 1/7/98); Health, Human Services, Aging, Corrections, Veterans and Military Affairs (1/15/97 to 4/20/98); Government Effectiveness (eff. 4/21/98, also 1995); Human Resources, Labor, Tourism, Veterans and Military Affairs (eff. 4/21/98); Jt. Com. on Information Policy (eff. 4/21/98, also 1995); Legis. Coun. Coms. on Local Government Spending (vice chp.), on the School Calendar. **1995** — Business, Economic Development and Urban Affairs (member to 6/96); Agriculture, Transportation, Utilities and Financial Institutions; Legis. Coun. Coms. on Americans with Disabilities Act (co-chp.), on Recodification of Fish and Game Laws.

Telephone: Office: (608) 266-5660; District: (920) 386-2218; E-mail: Sen.Fitzgerald@legis.wisconsin.gov

Voting address: (Town of Clyman) N4692 Maple Road, Juneau 53039.

Mailing address: Office: Room 206 South, State Capitol, P.O. Box 7882, Madison 53707-7882.

Representative	Representative	Representative
JORGENSEN	KLEEFISCH	FITZGERALD

Andy Jorgensen (Dem.), 37th Assembly District

Born Berlin, September 10, 1967; married; 3 children. Graduate Omro H.S. 1986; Brown Institute (MN) 1987. Assembly line operator, General Motors, Janesville. Former morning radio personality, UAW shop steward, worked on family dairy farm. Member: UAW Local 95; UAW Local CAP; Cub Scout leader Pack 137; Jefferson Co. Labor Council; Rock Co. Labor Coalition; Jefferson Co. Farm Bureau; Jefferson Co. Agribusiness Club; Respite Care (bd. mbr.); Trinity Lutheran Church, Fort Atkinson (Sunday school teacher); UAW Public Relations Committee (chp.). Former member: Fort Atkinson FFA Alumni; Fort Fest, Inc. (chp. of exec. bd.).

Elected to Assembly 2006; reelected 2008. Biennial committee assignments: **2009** — Renewable Energy and Rural Affairs (chp.); Rural Economic Development (vice chp.); Jt. Legis. Audit (vice chp.); Agriculture (also 2007); Labor. **2007** — Biofuels and Sustainable Energy; Consumer Protection and Personal Privacy; Rural Affairs.

Telephone: Office: (608) 266-3790; (888) 534-0037 (toll free).

E-mail: Rep.Jorgensen@legis.wisconsin.gov

Voting address: 1424 Endl Boulevard, Fort Atkinson 53538.

Mailing address: Office: Room 320 West, State Capitol, P.O. Box 8952, Madison 53708.

Joel Kleefisch (Rep.), 38th Assembly District

Born Waukesha, June 8, 1971; married; 2 children. Graduate Waukesha North H.S. 1989; B.A. Pepperdine U. 1993. Small business owner. Former investigative television news reporter for WISN-TV; legislative policy advisor and constituent director. Member: Watertown Elks Club; Watertown Moose Club; Okauchee Lions Club; Musky Mike's fishing pro-staff; Lakewatch Volunteer Organization (founder).

Elected to Assembly 2004; reelected since 2006. Minority Caucus Vice Chairperson 2009. Biennial committee assignments: **2009** — Consumer Protection; Criminal Justice (chp. 2007); Rules; State Affairs and Homeland Security. **2007** — State Affairs (vice chp., also 2005); Children and Family Law; Colleges and Universities; Judiciary and Ethics. **2005** — Financial Institutions; Judiciary; State-Federal Relations.

Telephone: Office: (608) 266-8551; (888) 534-0038 (toll free).

E-mail: Rep.Kleefisch@legis.wisconsin.gov

Voting address: W357 N6189 Spinnaker Drive, Oconomowoc 53066.

Mailing address: Office: Room 8 West, State Capitol, P.O. Box 8952, Madison 53708; District: P.O. Box 273, Okauchee 53069.

Jeff Fitzgerald (Rep.), 39th Assembly District

Born Chicago, IL, October 12, 1966; married; 2 children. Graduate Hustisford H.S.; B.S. UW-Oshkosh. Former small business owner and former member Chicago Mercantile Exchange. Member: Dodge Co. Republican Party (former chm.); Beaver Dam Chamber of Commerce; Juneau Chamber of Commerce; Community Relations Board of Fox Lake Correctional Institution; American Legislative Exchange Council; Pheasants Forever; American Council of Young Political Leaders; State Legislative Leaders Foundation (bd. mbr.). Beaver Dam City Council 2000-July 2003.

Elected to Assembly 2000; reelected since 2002. Minority Leader 2009; Majority Leader 2007; Assistant Majority Leader 2005. Biennial committee assignments: **2009** — Assembly Organization (since 2005); Rules (chp. 2007, mbr. 2005); Jt. Com. on Employment Relations (also 2007); Jt. Com. on Legislative Organization (since 2005); Jt. Legis. Council (also 2007). **2007** — Wisconsin Center District Bd. **2005** — State Affairs (chp., also 2003); Financial Institutions (vice chp., mbr. since 2001); Labor (also 2003); State Building Comn. (also 2003). **2003** — Energy and Utilities. **2001** — Housing (vice chp.); Campaigns and Elections; Criminal Justice; Economic Development; Labor and Workforce Development; Speakers Task Force on Budget Review.

Telephone: Office: (608) 266-2540; District: (920) 485-0586.

E-mail: Rep.Fitzgerald@legis.wisconsin.gov

Voting address: 910 Sunset, Horicon 53032.

Mailing address: Office: Room 201 West, State Capitol, P.O. Box 8952, Madison 53708.

14th SENATE DISTRICT

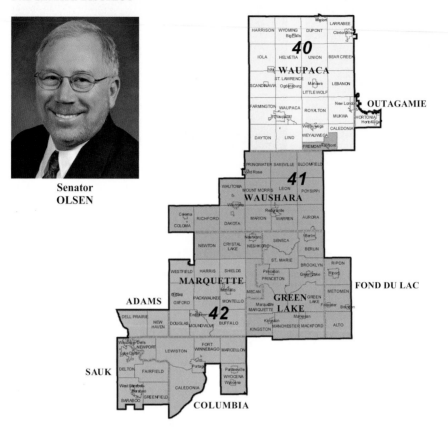

Senator
OLSEN

Luther S. Olsen (Rep.), **14th Senate District**

Born Berlin, February 26, 1951; married. Graduate Berlin H.S. 1969; B.S. UW-Madison 1973; Wis. Rural Leadership Program Group IV 1990-92. Partner in farm supply and grain dealerships. Member: Green Lake Co. Republican Party; Waushara Co. Republican Party; Education Commission of the States (bd. of dir.); Learning Point Associates (bd. of dir.). Former member: Waushara Co. Fair Bd. (dir.); Family Health/La Clinica director (1995-99); Berlin Area School Board 1976-97 (pres. 1986-95).

Elected to Assembly 1994-2002; elected to Senate 2004; reelected 2008. Biennial Senate committee assignments: **2009** — Education (chp. 2005, mbr. 2007); Environment; Jt. Com. on Finance (since 2005). **2007** — Jt. Survey Com. on Retirement Systems; Child Abuse and Neglect Prevention Bd. (also 2005); Educational Communications Board (also 2005); University of Wisconsin Hospitals and Clinics Authority Bd. (also 2005). **2005** — Agriculture and Insurance; Legis. Coun. Spec. Com. on School Aid Formula (chp.). Assembly committee assignments: **2003** — Education (chp. since 1997, mbr. 1995); Education Reform (since 1999, vice chp. 2001); Health (since 1997); Housing; Rural Affairs; Workforce Development. **2001** — Ways and Means; Migrant Labor Council (since 1995). **1999** — Tourism and Recreation; Legis. Coun. Coms. on Dental Care Access, on Navigable Waters Recodification. **1997** — Colleges and Universities; State-Federal Relations; Gov.'s Council on Model Academic Standards; Legis. Coun. Coms. on Services for Visually Handicapped Students (chp.), on Children at Risk Program, on the School Calendar. **1995** — Government Operations (vice chp.); Jt. Com. for Review of Administrative Rules; Agriculture; Mandates; State Supported Programs Study and Adv. Com.; Legis. Coun. Coms. on Public Libraries, on Public School Open Enrollment, on the School Aid Formula.

Telephone: Office: (608) 266-0751; District: (920) 229-4141; E-mail: Sen.Olsen@legis.wisconsin.gov

Voting address: 1023 Thomas Street, Ripon 54971.

Mailing address: Room 22 South, State Capitol, P.O. Box 7882, Madison 53707-7882.

Representative
PETERSEN

Representative
BALLWEG

Representative
CLARK

Kevin David Petersen (Rep.), 40th Assembly District

Born Waupaca, December 14, 1964; married; 2 children. Graduate Waupaca H.S. 1983; B.S.M.E. U. of New Mexico 1989. Co-owner family-run electronics corporation. Served in U.S. Navy sub service, 1983-94, Persian Gulf War veteran. Member U.S. Naval Reserve 1994-2008. Member: Waupaca Co. Republican Party; Outagamie Co. Republican Party; VFW Post 1037 (life member); Amvets Post 1887 (life member); American Legion Post 161; United States Submarine Veterans, Inc.; Waupaca Area Chamber of Commerce; New London Chamber of Commerce; Clintonville Chamber of Commerce; National Rifle Association. Town of Dayton Supervisor 2001-07.

Elected to Assembly 2006; reelected 2008. Biennial committee assignments: **2009** — Aging and Long-Term Care (also 2007); Energy and Utilities (vice chp. 2007); Veterans and Military Affairs (also 2007). **2007** — Homeland Security and State Preparedness.

Telephone: Office: (608) 266-3794; (888) 947-0040 (toll free).

E-mail: Rep.Petersen@legis.wisconsin.gov

Voting address: N1433 Drivas Road, Waupaca 54981.

Mailing address: Office: Room 109 West, State Capitol, P.O. Box 8953, Madison 53708.

Joan Ballweg (Rep.), 41st Assembly District

Born Milwaukee, March 16, 1952; married; 3 children. Graduate Nathan Hale H.S. (West Allis) 1970; attended UW-Waukesha; B.A. Elementary Education UW-Stevens Point 1974. Co-owner of farm equipment business. Former 1st grade teacher. Member: FEMA V Regional Advisory Council; Markesan Chamber of Commerce (former treas.); Waupun Chamber of Commerce; Green Lake County Farm Bureau; Waupun Memorial Hospital (bd. of dir., fmr. chp.); Agnesian HealthCare Enterprises, LLC management com. (fmr. secy.); volunteer, Markesan District Schools; Markesan PTA (fmr. pres.); Markesan AFS Chapter (hosting coordinator, pres., fmr. host family, liaison). Recipient: Markesan District Education Assn. *Friend of Education Award* 1990. Markesan City Council 1987-91; Mayor of Markesan 1991-97.

Elected to Assembly 2004; reelected since 2006. Biennial committee assignments: **2009** — Colleges and Universities (vice chp. 2007, 2005); Renewable Energy and Rural Affairs; State Affairs and Homeland Security; Leg. Coun. Spec. Com. on Emergency Management and Continuity of Government (vice chp.). **2007** — Homeland Security and State Preparedness (chp.); Insurance (also 2005); Public Health; Small Business (also 2005); Leg. Coun. Spec. Com. on Disaster Preparedness Planning (chp.). **2005** — Family Law; Rural Affairs and Renewable Energy.

Telephone: Office: (608) 266-8077; (888) 534-0041 (toll free); District: (920) 398-3708.

E-mail: Rep.Ballweg@legis.wisconsin.gov

Voting address: 170 West Summit Street, Markesan 53946.

Mailing address: Office: Room 10 West, State Capitol, P.O. Box 8952, Madison 53708.

Fred Clark (Dem.), 42nd Assembly District

Born Ann Arbor, MI, May 14, 1959; 1 child. Graduate Huron H.S. (Ann Arbor, MI) 1977; attended Michigan Tech. U.; B.S. in horticulture Michigan State U. 1985; M.S. in forest science UW-Madison 1992. Forester. Former consulting forester, small business owner, forestry contractor, arborist, WDNR service forester. Member: Society of American Foresters (chair, southwest Wis. chapter); Great Lakes Timber Professionals Assn.; Wis. League of Conservation Voters; The Forest Guild (membership and policy council); Pheasants Forever. Former member: Wis. Council on Forestry; Lower Wis. Riverway Bd.; Baraboo Range Preservation Assn. (vice pres.); The Nature Conservancy.

Elected to Assembly 2008. Biennial committee assignments: **2009** — Forestry (vice chp.); Tourism, Recreation and State Properties (vice chp.); Natural Resources; Rural Economic Development.

Telephone: Office: (608) 266-7746; (888) 534-0042 (toll free); District: (608) 356-3342.

Voting address: E12367 County Highway W, Baraboo 53913.

Mailing address: Room 418 North, State Capitol, P.O. Box 8952, Madison 53708.

15th SENATE DISTRICT

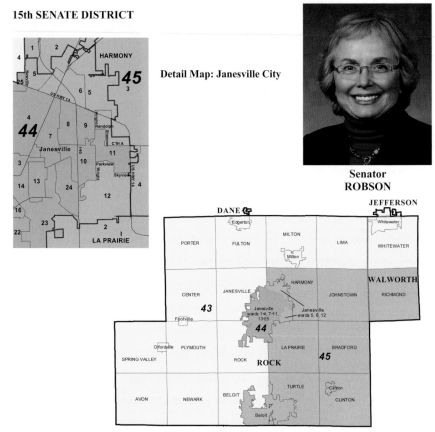

Detail Map: Janesville City

Senator ROBSON

Judith Biros Robson (Dem.), **15th Senate District**

Born Cleveland, OH; 3 children, 4 grandchildren. B.S.N. St. John College; M.S. UW-Madison. Registered Nurse, associate degree nursing instructor at Blackhawk Technical College and geriatric nurse practitioner. Member: League of Women Voters (past vice president); Who's Who In American Nursing; Sigma Theta Tau; Wis. Nurses Assn.; Zonta; AAUW; Beloit Bike and Ski Club.

Elected to Assembly in June 1987 special election; reelected 1988-96; elected to Senate since 1998. Senate Majority Leader 2007 (through 10/24/07); Senate Minority Leader 2005; Senate Majority Caucus Chairperson 2001, 1999. Assembly: Minority Caucus Vice Chairperson 1995; Majority Caucus Vice Chairperson 1993. Biennial Senate committee assignments: **2009** — Ethics Reform and Government Operations; Health, Health Insurance, Privacy, Property Tax Relief, and Revenue; Jt. Com. on Finance; Jt. Legislative Council (since 2005, also 2001, 1999); Jt. Leg. Coun. Spec. Com. on Regional Transportation Authority (chp.); State Capitol and Exec. Residence Bd. (also 2007); Women's Council. **2007** — Jt. Com. on Legislative Organization (also 2005). **2003** — Jt. Com. for Review of Administrative Rules (mbr., co-chp. 2001, 1999); Agriculture, Financial Institutions and Insurance (through 5/23/03); Education, Ethics and Elections; Health, Children, Families, Aging and Long Term Care. **2001** — Human Services and Aging (chp., also 1999); Jt. Com. on Audit (also 1999); Education (also 1999); Health, Utilities, Veterans and Military Affairs (also 1999); Jt. Legis. Coun. Spec. Coms. on the Public Health System's Response to Terrorism and Public Health Emergencies (co-chp.), on Improving Wisconsin's Fiscal Management; Migrant Labor Council. **1999** — Child Abuse and Neglect Prevention Bd.; Jt. Legis. Coun. Spec. Com. on Developmental Disabilities (co-chp.). Assembly committee assignments: **1997** — Environment; Health (chp. 1993, mbr. since 1987); Insurance, Securities and Corporate Policy (since 1993). **1995** — Environment and Utilities; Ways and Means (since 1989); Jt. Legis. Coun. Coms. on Prevention of Child Abuse and Neglect, on Teacher Preparation, Licensure and Regulation. **1993** — Environmental Resources; Rules; Trade, Science and Technology (eff. 4/26/93, also 1991); Legis. Coun. Com. on School Health Services. **1991** — Public Health and Regulation (chp.); Energy and Commerce (vice chp.); Task Force to Combat Controlled Substance Use by Pregnant Women and Women with Young Children (also 1989); Legis. Coun. Com. on Emergency Medical Services (chp.).

Telephone: Office: (608) 266-2253; (800) 334-1468 (toll free); District: (608) 365-6587.

E-mail: Sen.Robson@legis.wisconsin.gov; Internet address: http://www.legis.state.wi.us/senate/sen15/sen15.html

Voting address: 2411 East Ridge Road, Beloit 53511.

Mailing address: Office: Room 122 South, State Capitol, P.O. Box 7882, Madison 53707-7882.

Representative
HIXSON

Representative
SHERIDAN

Representative
BENEDICT

Kim Hixson (Dem.), 43rd Assembly District

Born Chattanooga, TN, July 26, 1957; married; 3 children. Graduate Chattanooga H.S.; A.A. in broadcasting Chattanooga State; B.A. in advertising and English U. of Tennessee-Chattanooga; M.A. in professional writing U. of Tennessee-Chattanooga; Ph.D. in Journalism Southern Illinois U. Associate professor UW-Whitewater. Member: American Academy of Advertising; Association for Education in Journalism and Mass Communication; International Association of Business Disciplines; TAUWP-AFT; First United Methodist Church, Whitewater. Recipient: UW-Whitewater College of Arts and Communication *Excellence Award for Service* 2005. City of Whitewater Common Council 2004-07; Council President 2005-06.

Elected to Assembly 2006; reelected 2008. Biennial committee assignments: **2009** — Colleges and Universities (chp.); Consumer Protection; Education (also 2007); Financial Institutions (also 2007); Workforce Development. **2007** — Aging and Long-Term Care; Rural Economic Development (eff. 3/20/07).

Telephone: Office: (608) 266-9650; (888) 534-0043 (toll free).

E-mail: Rep.Hixson@legis.wisconsin.gov

Voting address: 327 South Woodland Drive, Whitewater 53190.

Mailing address: Office: Room 109 North, State Capitol, P.O. Box 8952, Madison 53708.

Michael J. Sheridan (Dem.), 44th Assembly District

Born Janesville, September 17, 1958; married; 3 children, 2 grandchildren. Graduate Parker H.S. (Janesville) 1977; Associates degree UW-Rock County (Janesville) 2004. Former auto assembly worker; UAW president. Member: Janesville Performing Arts Center (bd. of dir.); Rock Co. Labor Coalition; NAACP; LCLAA; Boy Scouts of America. Former member: UAW WI CAP (chp.); United Way (bd. mbr.); Blackhawk Tech. Foundation (bd. mbr.); Leadership Development Academy (bd. of dir.); Boys and Girls Club (bd. of dir.); Janesville School District ATODA (com. mbr.); UAW Education Com.; Laborfest (treas.); UAW Veterans Com.

Elected to Assembly 2004; reelected since 2006. Speaker of the Assembly 2009. Biennial committee assignments: **2009** — Assembly Organization (chp.); Rules (vice chp.); Jt. Com. on Employment Relations (co-chp.); Jt. Com. on Legislative Organization (co-chp.); Jt. Legislative Council. **2007** — Jobs and the Economy; Labor and Industry; Transportation; Speaker's Task Force on State Information Technology Failures. **2005** — Insurance; Labor; Small Business; Workforce Development; Jt. Select Com. on Road to the Future.

Telephone: Office: (608) 266-3387; (888) 947-0044 (toll free); District: (608) 756-0788.

E-mail: Rep.Sheridan@legis.wisconsin.gov

Voting address: 1032 Nantucket Drive, Janesville 53546.

Mailing address: Office: Room 211 West, State Capitol, P.O. Box 8953, Madison 53708.

Chuck Benedict (Dem.), 45th Assembly District

Born Norwalk, CT, August 13, 1946. Graduate New Canaan H.S. (Conn.) 1964; A.B. Dartmouth Coll. 1968; M.A. Princeton U. 1970; attended Duke U.; M.D. U. of Conn. Medical School 1979. Full-time legislator. Retired physician (neurologist); former high school math and science teacher. Member: Wisconsin Medical Society; American Academy of Neurology; American Assoc. for Advancement of Science; Beloit Mem. Hospital Ethics Com. (co-founder); League of Conservation Voters; Physicians for Social Responsibility; Union of Concerned Scientists; Bowhay Institute for Legislative Leadership Development 2006.

Elected to Assembly 2004; reelected since 2006. Biennial committee assignments: **2009** — Public Health (chp., mbr. since 2005); Corrections and the Courts (vice chp.); Health and Health Care Reform (also 2007); Jobs, the Economy and Small Business. **2007** — Homeland Security and State Preparedness; State Affairs (also 2005). **2005** — Health; Medicaid Reform; Rural Affairs and Renewable Energy.

Telephone: Office: (608) 266-9967; District: (608) 362-7698.

E-mail: Rep.Benedict@legis.wisconsin.gov

Internet address: www.legis.state.wi.us/assembly/asm45/news

Voting address: 3639 Bee Lane, Beloit 53511.

Mailing address: Office: Room 306 West, State Capitol, P.O. Box 8952, Madison 53708.

16th SENATE DISTRICT

**Senator
MILLER**

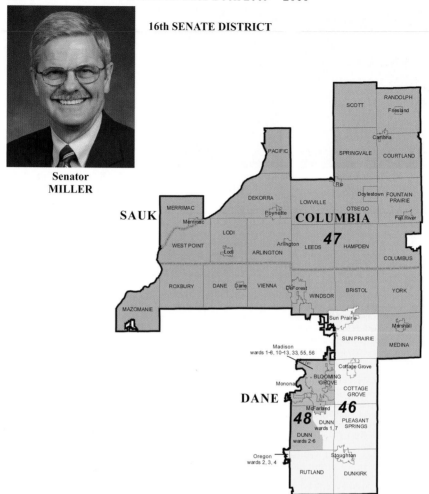

Mark Miller (Dem.), 16th Senate District

Born Boston, MA, February 1, 1943. Graduate Middleton H.S.; B.S. UW-Madison; Bowhay Institute for Legislative Leadership Development (BUILLD) 1999; Flemming Fellows Leadership Institute 2002. Former military pilot; Wis. Air National Guard, 1966-95 (ret., Lt. Colonel); former real estate property manager. Member: The Madison Institute; Research Education and Policy on Food Group (REAP) (founding mbr.); Environmental Action Teams (En-Act) (founding mbr.); Governor's Task Force to Improve Access to Oral Health 2005. Dane County Bd. of Health 1998-2004; Bd. of Health for Madison and Dane Co. 2004-07. Dane Co. Board of Supervisors 1996-2000.

Elected to Assembly 1998-2002; elected to Senate 2004; reelected 2008. Majority Caucus Chairperson 2007; Minority Caucus Vice Chairperson 2005. Biennial Senate committee assignments: **2009** — Environment (chp.); Jt. Com. on Finance (co-chp. since 11/5/07, mbr. 2007); Jt. Legis. Audit Com. (also 2005); Jt. Com. on Employment Relations; Jt. Com. on Information Policy and Technology; Jt. Legislative Council (since 2005). **2007** — Environment and Natural Resources (chp.); Ethics Reform and Government Operations (vice chp.). **2005** —Agriculture and Insurance; Campaign Finance Reform and Ethics; Jt. Com. for Review of Administrative Rules; Child Abuse and Neglect Prevention Bd. (also 2003). Assembly committee assignments: **2003** — Aging and Long-Term Care (eff. 5/13/03); Budget Review; Children and Families (since 1999); Health (since 1999); Natural Resources (also 2001); Veterans and Military Affairs; Environmental Education Bd. (also 2001). **2001** — Environment. **1999** — Campaigns and Elections; Consumer Affairs; Public Health; Law Revision Committee.

Telephone: Office: (608) 266-9170; District: (608) 221-2701.

E-mail: Sen.Miller@legis.wisconsin.gov

Voting address: 4903 Roigan Terrace, Monona 53716.

Mailing address: Office: Room 317 East, State Capitol, P.O. Box 7882, Madison 53707-7882.

Representative	Representative	Representative
HEBL	**RIPP**	**PARISI**

Gary Alan Hebl (Dem.), 46th Assembly District

Born Madison, May 15, 1951; married; 3 children. Graduate Sun Prairie H.S. 1969; B.A. Political Science UW-Madison 1973; Gonzaga U. Law School 1976. Bowhay Institute for Legislative Leadership Development 2008. Attorney and owner of a title insurance company. Member: Dane Co. Bar Assn.; Wis. Bar Assn.; Sun Prairie Optimist Club (youth coordinator, fmr. pres.); Sun Prairie Chamber of Commerce (fmr. pres.); U.W. Flying Club (chm., bd. of dir.); Dane Co. Pilots Assn.; Aircraft Owners Assn.; Experimental Aircraft Assn.; Knights of Columbus (4th deg. mbr.); Sun Prairie Cable Access Bd.; Sun Prairie Telecommunications Bd.; YMCA (bd. of dir., fmr. pres.); Sun Prairie Public Library Bd. of Trustees (fmr. pres.); Sacred Heart Parish Council (fmr. trustee); Sun Prairie Quarterback Club (fmr. pres.). Recipient: Pharmacy Society of Wis. *Legislator of the Year* 2009; Sun Prairie *Star* poll *Best Attorney in Sun Prairie* 2008, 2004, 2003, 2002; *James Reininger Award* 2008; Wis. Assn. of PEG Channels *Friend of Access Award* 2007; Wis. League of Conservation Voters *Conservation Champion* 2005-06; Madison Magazine *One of Madison's Best Real Estate Attorneys* 2002; Sun Prairie Exchange Club *Book of Golden Deeds Award* 2003; Chamber of Commerce *Judith Krivsky Business Person of the Year Award* 2002; Sun Prairie Business and Education Partnership *Outstanding Small Business of the Year* 2001.

Elected to Assembly 2004; reelected since 2006. Biennial committee assignments: **2009** — Judiciary and Ethics (chp.); Ways and Means (vice chp., mbr. since 2005); Insurance; Natural Resources (since 2005); Jt. Com. for Review of Administrative Rules. **2007** — Housing; Small Business (also 2005). **2005** — Property Rights and Land Management.

Telephone: Office: (608) 266-7678.

E-mail: Rep.Hebl@legis.wisconsin.gov

Voting address: 515 Scheuerell Lane, Sun Prairie 53590.

Mailing address: Office: Room 120 North, State Capitol, P.O. Box 8952, Madison 53708.

Keith Ripp (Rep.), 47th Assembly District

Born Madison, November 13, 1961; married; 3 children. Graduate Lodi H.S. 1980; UW-Madison farm and industry short course 1981. Farmer and small business owner. Member: Wis. Soybean Marketing Bd. (pres., fmr. vice pres.); Badger Agvest LLC (pres. and co-founder); Wis. Corn Growers Assn. (fmr. pres., vice pres.); Wis. Farm Bureau; Lodi FFA Alumni (fmr. pres., co-founder); Columbia and Dane Co. Republican Party; Yellow Thunder Snowmobile Club; Ducks Unlimited. Former member: Poynette Bowhunters Club. Town of Dane Supervisor 2006-present.

Elected to Assembly 2008. Biennial committee assignments: **2009** — Criminal Justice; Renewable Energy and Rural Affairs; Transportation.

Telephone: Office: (608) 266-3404; District: (608) 849-3596.

Voting address: 7113 County Road V, Lodi 53555.

Mailing address: Office: Room 3 North, State Capitol, P.O. Box 8953, Madison 53708.

Joseph T. Parisi (Dem.), 48th Assembly District

Born Madison, October 24, 1960; married; 2 children. Attended Middleton H.S.; Madison Area Technical College; B.A. in sociology UW-Madison. Former member: Operation Fresh Start (bd. of dir.); Atwood Community Center (bd. of dir.). Recipient: League of Conservation Voters *Conservation Champion* 2007-08, 2005-06; Wis. Counties Assn. *Outstanding Legislator Award* 2007-08. Dane County Clerk 1996-2004.

Elected to Assembly 2004; reelected since 2006. Biennial committee assignments: **2009** — Corrections and the Courts (chp., mbr. since 2005); Energy and Utilities; Insurance; Labor; Urban and Local Affairs (since 2005). **2007** — Jt. Legislative Audit; Insurance. **2005** — Aging and Long-Term Care; Agriculture; Budget Review.

Telephone: Office: (608) 266-5342; District: (608) 242-0575.

E-mail: Rep.Parisi@legis.wisconsin.gov

Voting address: 702 McLean Drive, Madison 53718.

Mailing address: Office: Room 126 North, State Capitol, P.O. Box 8953, Madison 53708.

Dale W. Schultz (Rep.), 17th Senate District

Born Madison, June 12, 1953; married; 2 children. Graduate Madison West H.S.; B.B.A. UW-Madison 1975. Farm manager and real estate broker. Member: Sauk Co. Farm Bureau; Masons; Shrine; Lions; Hillpoint Rod and Gun Club. Awards: Military Order of the Purple Heart *Legislator of the Year* 2002; Wisconsin Wetlands Association and Sierra Club *Conservation Award* 2002; Deer and Elk Farmers Association *Legislator of the Year* 2002; WMC *Outstanding Legislator Award* 2001; Tavern League of Wisconsin *Top Shelf Award* 2000; Neighborhood Housing Services *Legislative Leadership Award* 2000; *Excellence in Education Award* 2000; *Friend of Grocers Award* 2006, 2004; AFSCME Local 2748 *Appreciation Award* 1998; Wis. Sheriffs and Deputy Sheriffs Assn. *Commendation* 1997; Wis. Counties Assn. *Friend of County Government* 2004; Council of State Governments *Toll Fellow* 1996, 1995; Wis. Hospitals Assn. *Health Care Leadership Award* 2003; Wis. Farm Bureau Federation *Friend of Agriculture* 2006, 2004; Wis. Federation of Cooperatives *Friend of Cooperatives* 2003; Wis. Pharmacists Assn. *Outstanding Legislator;* Wis. Assn. of Health Underwriters *Insuring Freedom Award* 2004; Wis. Medical Society *Health Leadership Award* 2004; Wis. Ethanol Producers Assn. and Wis. Corn Growers Assn. *Legislator of the Year* 2006; Wis. Dept. of Veterans Affairs *Iron Mike Award* 2006; Wis. Community Action Program Assn. *William Steiger Human Services Award* 2008.

**Senator
SCHULTZ**

Elected to Assembly 1982-91 (resigned 10/7/91); elected to Senate in September 1991 special election; reelected since 1994. Majority Leader 2005. Biennial committee assignments: **2009** — Public Health, Senior Issues, Long-Term Care, and Job Creation; Jt. Legis. Coun. (also 2005); Jt. Survey Com. on Retirement Systems (co-chp. 2003); State Historical Soc. Bd. of Curators (since 2001). **2007** — Environment and Natural Resources; Public Health, Senior Issues, Long-Term Care and Privacy; Transportation, Tourism and Insurance. **2005** — Organization (chp.); Jt. Com. on Employment Relations; Jt. Com. on Legislative Organization; State and Federal Relations; State Capitol and Executive Residence Bd. (since 1999). **2003** — Agriculture, Financial Institutions and Insurance (chp.); Health, Children, Families, Aging and Long Term Care; Higher Education and Tourism; Transportation Projects Commission (also 2001).

Telephone: Office: (608) 266-0703; (800) 978-8008 (toll free); District: (608) 647-4614.

E-mail: Sen.Schultz@legis.wisconsin.gov

Voting address: 515 North Central Avenue, Richland Center 53581.

Mailing address: Office: Room 127 South, State Capitol, P.O. Box 7882, Madison 53707-7882.

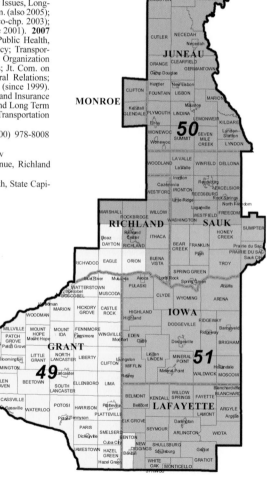

| Representative | Representative | Representative |
| GARTHWAITE | BROOKS | HILGENBERG |

Phil Garthwaite (Dem.), 49th Assembly District

Born Lancaster, October 6, 1972; single. Graduate West Grant H.S. (Patch Grove) 1991; attended UW-River Falls 1991-95; graduate Continental Auctioneers University (Mankato, MN) 1993; Madison Media Institute 1999. Farm radio broadcaster. Former farm radio director and broadcaster, farm manager.

Elected to Assembly 2006; reelected 2008. Biennial committee assignments: **2009** — Rural Economic Development (chp., mbr. 2007); Agriculture (also 2007); Financial Institutions; Renewable Energy and Rural Affairs; Transportation (also 2007). **2007** — Rural Affairs.

Telephone: Office: (608) 266-1170; (888) 872-0049 (toll free).

E-mail: Rep.Garthwaite@legis.wisconsin.gov

Voting address: 141 South Main Street, Dickeyville 53808.

Mailing address: Office: Room 304 West, State Capitol, P.O. Box 8952, Madison 53708.

Ed Brooks (Rep.), 50th Assembly District

Born Baraboo, July 1, 1942; married; 3 children. Graduate Webb H.S. (Reedsburg) 1960; B.S. agricultural economics UW-Madison 1965. Dairy producer. Former co. sup. f/USDA, FmHA, loan officer f/PCA Madison. Served in U.S. Army Reserve 1965-71. Member: Wis. Fed. of Co-ops (fmr. chairman); Wis. Farm Bureau. Former member: C.A.L.S. B.O.V.; Endeavor 4-H Club (leader); St. John Lutheran Church (past pres. church council). Recipient: *Friend of Education* 1998; *Friend of Extension*. Town supervisor 1979-1985; town chairman 1985-present.

Elected to Assembly 2008. Biennial committee assignments: **2009** — Agriculture; Corrections and the Courts; Criminal Justice.

Telephone: Office: (608) 266-8531; (877) 947-0050 (toll free); District: (608) 524-2406.

Voting address: S4311 Grote Hill Road, Reedsburg 53959.

Mailing address: Office: Room 20 North, State Capitol, P.O. Box 8952, Madison 53708.

Steve Hilgenberg (Dem.), 51st Assembly District

Born Appleton, November 26, 1944; married; 1 child. Graduate Kaukauna H.S. 1963; attended UW-Madison 1963-66; Madison Area Tech. College 1971-72. Offset press operator. Former owner/operator commercial printing business. Served in U.S. Army 1966-69; Vietnam Era veteran. Member: Head Start Policy Council; Dodgeville VFW Post 7345; Wis. Farmers Union; Iowa Co. Democratic Party. Dodgeville School Bd. 1988-95.

Elected to Assembly 2006; reelected 2008. Biennial committee assignments: **2009** — Veterans and Military Affairs (chp.); Renewable Energy and Rural Affairs (vice chp.); Education; Tourism, Recreation and State Properties. **2007** — Insurance; Rural Economic Development; Small Business.

Telephone: Office: (608) 266-7502; (888) 534-0051 (toll free); District: (608) 935-3509.

E-mail: Rep.Hilgenberg@legis.wisconsin.gov

Voting address: 3607 Evans Quarry Road, Dodgeville 53533.

Mailing address: Office: Room 5 North, State Capitol, P.O. Box 8952, Madison 53708.

18th SENATE DISTRICT

Senator
HOPPER

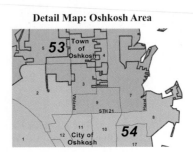

Detail Map: Oshkosh Area

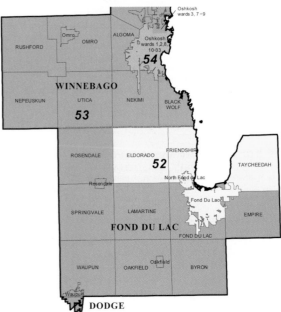

Randy Hopper (Rep.), 18th Senate District

Born Taylorville, IL, January 23, 1966; married; 2 children. Graduate The Hill School (Pottstown, PA) 1985; B.A. history Denison U. (Granville, OH) 1989; M.B.A. Northwestern U. Kellogg Business School 2002. Small business owner. Member: Fond du Lac YMCA (bd. mbr.); Fond du Lac Area Chamber of Commerce (bd. mbr.); Charles M. Boesel Foundation (bd. mbr.); Bertrand Hopper Memorial Foundation (bd. mbr.). Former member: Marian U. Bd. of Trustees; Fond du Lac Festivals (pres.); Fond du Lac Cops for Kids (founding bd. mbr.).

Elected to Senate 2008. Biennial committee assignments: **2009** — Children and Families and Workforce Development; Education; Judiciary, Corrections, Insurance, Campaign Finance Reform, and Housing; Small Business, Emergency Preparedness, Technical Colleges, and Consumer Protection; Jt. Review Com. on Criminal Penalties (eff. 7/6/09).

Telephone: Office: (608) 266-5300; (888) 736-8720 (toll free).

E-mail: Sen.Hopper@legis.wisconsin.gov

Voting address: W5192 Rienzi Road, Fond du Lac 54935.

Mailing address: Office: Room 108 South, State Capitol, P.O. Box 7882, Madison 53707-7882.

Representative
TOWNSEND

Representative
SPANBAUER

Representative
HINTZ

John F. Townsend (Rep.), 52nd Assembly District

Born St. Louis, MO, May 23, 1938; married; 2 children. Graduate Madison H.S. (Madison Heights, MI); B.S. Wayne State U. 1960; M.B.A. Wayne State U. 1967. Full-time legislator. Former partner in a small business and a corporate executive. Vietnam veteran; served in U.S. Navy and U.S. Naval Reserves; retired Captain U.S. Naval Reserves. Member: Fond du Lac Noon Rotary (former programs chm.); Fond du Lac Redevelopment Authority (bd. mbr. 1996-98); Fond du Lac Adult Literacy (bd. mbr.); Wisconsin Literacy (bd. mbr.); Fond du Lac Arts Council (adv. bd.); Fond du Lac Visiting Nurses Assn. (bd. mbr.); VFW Post 1904; American Legion Post 0075. Former member: Fond du Lac Salvation Army Adv. Bd. (1996-2006); Fond du Lac Public Library Bd. (1992-98). Fond du Lac County Economic Development Corp. (bd. mbr. 1992-96); Fond du Lac City Council 1992-98.

Elected to Assembly 1998; reelected since 2000. Biennial committee assignments: **2009** — Aging and Long-Term Care (chp. 2007, mbr. 2005); Colleges and Universities (vice chp. 2001, mbr. 1999); Education (since 2001); Veterans and Military Affairs (vice chp. 2007, 2003, mbr. 2001). **2007** — Consumer Protection and Personal Privacy; Financial Institutions (since 2003); Housing (vice chp. 2003-05); Small Business; Council on Alcohol and Other Drug Abuse (since 2001); Migrant Labor Council (since 2001). **2005** — Military Affairs; Public Health (also 1999); Veterans Affairs. **2003** — Electronic Democracy and Government Reform (chp.); Jt. Legislative Council. **2001** — Economic Development (chp.).

Telephone: Office: (608) 266-3156; (888) 529-0052 (toll free); District: (920) 923-0935.

E-mail: Rep.Townsend@legis.wisconsin.gov

Voting address: 297 Roosevelt Street, Fond du Lac 54935.

Mailing address: Office: Room 22 West, State Capitol, P.O. Box 8953, Madison 53708.

Richard J. Spanbauer (Rep.), 53rd Assembly District

Born New York, NY, March 5, 1946; married; 4 children. Graduate Oshkosh H.S. 1963; attended Fox Valley Tech. Full-time legislator. Former realtor, manufacturer. Served in U.S. Marine Corps Reserve 1963-68. Member: Winnebago Lakes Council; Butte des Morts Conservation Club; West Side Association. Former member: Marine Corps League. Town of Algoma Chairman 2001-09.

Elected to Assembly 2008. Biennial committee assignments: **2009** — Children and Families; Consumer Protection; Urban and Local Affairs.

Telephone: Office: (608) 267-7990; District: (920) 233-2656.

Voting address: 3040 Sheldon Drive, Oshkosh 54904.

Mailing address: Office: Room 121 West, State Capitol, P.O. Box 8953, Madison 53708.

Gordon Hintz (Dem.), 54th Assembly District

Born Oshkosh, November 29, 1973; single. Graduate Oshkosh North H.S. 1992; B.A. Hamline U. (St. Paul, MN) 1996; M.P.A. UW-Madison 2001. Municipal consultant. Former legislative staff assistant, U.S. Representative Jay Johnson, U.S. Senator Herb Kohl; management and budget analyst, City of Long Beach, CA; instructor, political science dept., UW-Oshkosh. Member: Oshkosh Rotary Club; Oshkosh Diversity Council; Propel; Oshkosh Chamber of Commerce; Winnebago Co. Democratic Party; 6th Congressional Dist. Democratic Party (chm.). Former member: International City/County Management Assn.

Elected to Assembly 2006; reelected 2008. Biennial committee assignments: **2009** — Consumer Protection (chp.); Workforce Development (vice chp.); Colleges and Universities (also 2007); Jobs, the Economy, and Small Business; Urban and Local Affairs (also 2007); Building Comn. **2007** — Aging and Long-Term Care; Judiciary and Ethics.

Telephone: Office: (608) 266-2254; (888) 534-0054 (toll free); District: (920) 232-0805.

E-mail: Rep.Hintz@legis.wisconsin.gov

Voting address: 1209 Waugoo Avenue, Oshkosh 54901.

Mailing address: Office: Room 322 West, State Capitol, P.O. Box 8952, Madison 53708.

19th SENATE DISTRICT

See Little Chute Village Map on p. 20
See Appleton Area map on p. 98

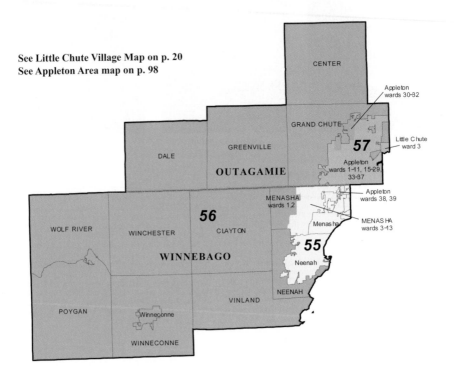

Michael G. Ellis (Rep.), 19th Senate District

Born Neenah, February 21, 1941; married. Graduate Neenah H.S.; B.S. in secondary education UW-Oshkosh 1965. Legislator and farmer. Neenah City Council 1969-75.

Elected to Assembly 1970-80; elected to Senate since 1982. Minority Leader 1999 (resigned 1/25/00), 1997 (1/15/97 to 4/20/98), 1995 (eff. 6/96); Majority Leader 1997 (eff. 4/21/98), 1995 (eff. 1/95 to 6/96), 1993 (eff. 4/20/93); Assistant Minority Leader 1987, 1985. Biennial committee assignments: **2009** — Ethics Reform and Government Operations (also 2007); Jt. Survey Com. on Tax Exemptions (co-chp. 2003, mbr. 2007, 2001). **2005** — Campaign Finance Reform and Ethics (chp.); Jt. Survey Com. on Tax Exemptions (co-chp. 2003, mbr. 2007, 2001). **2005** — Campaign Finance Reform and Ethics (chp.); Jt. Survey Com. on Tax Exemptions (co-chp. 2003, mbr. 2007, 2001). **2005** — Campaign Finance Reform and Ethics (chp.); State and Federal Relations (chp.). **2003** — Education, Ethics and Elections (chp.). **2001** — Jt. Survey Com. on Retirement Systems (also 1999); Retirement Research Com. (also 1999); Universities, Housing, and Government Operations. **1999** — Jt. Com. on Employment Relations (resigned 1/25/00, mbr. since 1989); Jt. Com. on Legislative Organization (resigned 1/25/00, mbr. since 1985); Senate Organization (resigned 1/25/00, chp. 1997, eff. 4/21/98, also 1/95 to 6/96, 1993, mbr. since 1985); Disability Bd. (resigned 1/25/00, mbr. since 1989); Jt. Legislative Council (resigned 1/25/00, mbr. since 1989). **1995** — Jt. Com. on Information Policy (resigned 12/5/95); Spec. Com. on State and Federal Relations (vice chp. eff. 6/96, chp. 1/95 to 6/96); School Funding Commission. **1993** — Senate Rules (mbr. 1987 to 4/20/93). **1991** — Legis. Coun. Coms. on Drainage District Laws, on Issues Relating to Hunger Prevention, on Oversight of Community Mental Health Services, on Private Forest Land Programs. **1987** — Urban Affairs, Energy, Environmental Resources and Elections; Housing, Government Operations and Cultural Affairs (resigned 4/21/87); Legis. Coun. Com. on Natural and Recreational Resources. **1985** — Energy and Environmental Resources (also 1983); Tourism, Revenue, Financial Institutions and Forestry; Child Labor Coun. **1983** — Transportation; Legis. Coun. Peace Officer Study Com.

Telephone: Office: (608) 266-0718; District: (920) 751-4801.

Voting address: 1752 County Road GG, Neenah 54956.

Mailing address: Office: Room 7 South, State Capitol, P.O. Box 7882, Madison 53707-7882; District: 429 South Commercial Street, Neenah 54956.

**Senator
ELLIS**

Representative
KAUFERT

Representative
ROTH

Representative
BERNARD SCHABER

Dean R. Kaufert (Rep.), 55th Assembly District

Born Outagamie County, May 23, 1957; married; 2 children, 2 grandchildren. Graduate Neenah H.S. Trophy and Awards store owner. Member: Winnebago Co. Republican Party; Neenah-Menasha Noon Optimists; Neenah-Menasha Elks Club; Fox Cities Chamber of Commerce; Governor's Council on Domestic Abuse 2001-07. Neenah City Council 1985-91.

Elected to Assembly since 1990. Majority Caucus Sergeant at Arms 1997, 1995; Minority Caucus Sergeant at Arms 1993. Biennial committee assignments: **2009** — Financial Institutions (vice chp. 2007, chp. 1995, mbr. 1993); Tourism, Recreation and State Properties (chp. 2007); Jt. Legislative Council (since 2003); State Building Comn. (also 2007); Governor's Council on Tourism. **2007** — Corrections and the Courts. **2005** — Jt. Com. on Finance (co-chp., also 2003, mbr. since 1997); Jt. Legis. Audit (vice chp., mbr. 2003); Jt. Com. on Employment Relations (also 2003). **1999** — Jt. Com. on Information Policy (also 1997). **1997** — Legis. Coun. Com. on Local Government Funding. **1995** — Housing (vice chp., mbr. 1993, 1991); Criminal Justice and Corrections; Mandates; Small Business and Economic Development (also 1993); Spec. Com. on Gambling Oversight (vice chp.). **1993** — Criminal Justice and Public Safety (also 1991). **1991** — Environmental Resources, Utilities and Mining; Small Business and Education or Training for Employment; Legis. Coun. Com. on Energy Resources; Task Force on Regulatory Barriers to Affordable Housing.

Telephone: Office: (608) 266-5719; (888) 534-0055 (toll free); District: (920) 729-0521.

E-mail: Rep.Kaufert@legis.wisconsin.gov

Voting address: 1360 Alpine Lane, Neenah 54956.

Mailing address: Office: Room 15 North, State Capitol, P.O. Box 8952, Madison 53708.

Roger Roth (Rep.), 56th Assembly District

Born Appleton, February 5, 1978; single. Graduate St. Mary Central H.S. (Menasha) 1996; B.A. in history UW-Oshkosh 2001; attended St. Mary's University (London, UK) 1998. Self-employed homebuilder. Member Wis. Air National Guard since 2003; Iraq War veteran. Member: Twin Cities Rod and Gun Club; NRA; NFIB; Valley Homebuilders Assn.; Winnebago Co. Republican Party; Outagamie Co. Republican Party; American Legion; AMVETS (life mbr.); VFW (life mbr.); Appleton Northside Business Assn.

Elected to Assembly 2006; reelected 2008. Biennial committee assignments: **2009** — Elections and Campaign Finance Reform; Housing (vice chp. 2007); Insurance; Jt. Leg. Coun. Spec. Com. on High-Risk Juvenile Offenders; Law Revision. **2007** — Financial Institutions; Jobs and the Economy; Workforce Development; State Capitol and Executive Residence Bd.

Telephone: Office: (608) 266-7500; District: (920) 734-6902.

Voting address: 2732 Glenpark Drive, Appleton 54914.

Mailing address: Office: Room 316 North, State Capitol, P.O. Box 8953, Madison 53708.

Penny Bernard Schaber (Dem.), 57th Assembly District

Born Mundelein, IL, November 5, 1953; married. Graduate Mundelein H.S. 1971; associate degree, physical therapist assistant, Southern Illinois U. 1973; B.S. physiology Southern Illinois U. 1977; B.S. physical therapy Northwestern U. 1980; associate degree, natural resources technology, Fox Valley Technical Coll. 1986. Full-time legislator. Retired physical therapist, last 10 years as a school physical therapist. Peace corps volunteer, Campino Grande Brazil 1977-78. Member: Historic Hearthstone (bd. of dir.); Fox Valley Sierra Group (former chp., membership chair); John Muir Chapter, Sierra Club (former chp., outings and membership chair); American Physical Therapy Assn.; Wis. Physical Therapy Assn. Former member: Master Gardener, Outagamie Co.

Elected to Assembly 2008. Biennial committee assignments: **2009** — Jobs, the Economy and Small Business (vice chp.); Health and Health Care Reform; Public Health; Transportation.

Telephone: Office: (608) 266-3070; (888) 534-0057 (toll free); District: (920) 739-6041.

E-mail: Rep.BernardSchaber@legis.wisconsin.gov

Voting address: 815 East Washington Street, Appleton 54911-5660.

Mailing address: Office: Room 412 North, State Capitol, P.O. Box 8952, Madison 53708.

20th SENATE DISTRICT

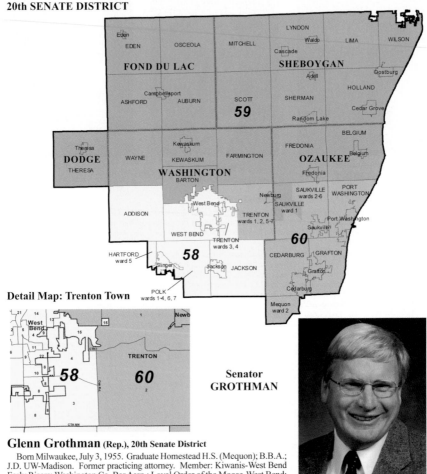

Detail Map: Trenton Town

Senator
GROTHMAN

Glenn Grothman (Rep.), 20th Senate District

Born Milwaukee, July 3, 1955. Graduate Homestead H.S. (Mequon); B.B.A.; J.D. UW-Madison. Former practicing attorney. Member: Kiwanis-West Bend Early Risers; Washington Co. Bar Assn.; Loyal Order of the Moose-West Bend; UW-Madison Alumni Assn. of Washington Co.; Kettle Moraine Symphony (bd. member). Recipient: Milwaukee Co. Rep. Party *Assembly Tax Cutter of the Year* 2002; Ind. Bus. Assn. *Legislator of the Year* 2000; Wis. Counties Assn. *Outstanding Legislator Award* 1997-98; Wis. Right to Life *Pro-Life Hero Award* 1996, *Sanctity of Life Award* 2004; Pro-Life Wis. *Legislator of the Year* 1995; Wis. Grocers Assn. *Friend of Grocers Award* 1997-2004; Wis. Farm Bureau *Friend of Agriculture Award* 1995-2007; Wis. Dairy Business Assn. *Milk Bottle Award* 2006, 2004; Wis. Curves for Women *Legislator of the Year Award* 2003; Wis. Builders Assn. *Friend of Housing Award* 2001-07, *Legislator of the Year* 2005; Apartment Assoc. *Legislator of the Year* 2000; Nat'l Fed. of Independent Businesses *Guardian of Small Business Award* 1999-2000, 2005-06; WMC *Working for Wisconsin Award* 1998-2006; Wis. Guild of Midwives *Legislator of the Year* 2006; Eagle Forum *Leadership Award* 2005.

Elected to Assembly in December 1993 special election; reelected 1994-2002; elected to Senate 2004; reelected 2008. Assistant Minority Leader 2009; Minority Caucus Chairperson 2007; Majority Caucus Vice Chairperson 2003, 2001, 1999. Biennial Senate committee assignments: **2009** — Education (since 2005); Judiciary, Corrections, Insurance, Campaign Finance Reform and Housing; Labor, Elections and Urban Affairs (also 2007); Senate Org.; Transportation, Tourism, Forestry, and Natural Resources; Jt. Com. for Review of Administrative Rules (co-chp. 2005, mbr. 2007); Jt. Com. on Leg. Org.; Jt. Review Com. on Criminal Penalties (through 7/6/09); WHEDA Bd. (also 2007). **2007** — Jt. Leg. Coun. Spec. Coms. on Affirmative Action (chp.) and Navigability and Drainage Ditches. **2005** — Jt. Survey Com. on Retirement Systems (co-chp.); Judiciary, Corrections and Privacy; Jt. Legislative Council. Assembly committee assignments: **2003** — Jt. Com. for Review of Administrative Rules (co-chp. since 1995); Campaigns and Elections; Judiciary (vice chp. 1997, also 1995, mbr. 1993); Labor; Rules (since 1999); Law Revision Com. (co-chp. since 1997, mbr. 1995). **2001** — Children and Families (also 1999); Education Reform (also 1999). **1999** — Legis. Coun. Com. on Use of Prescription Drugs for Children (co-chp.). **1997** — Income Tax Review. **1993** — Spec. Com. on Welfare Reform.

Telephone: Office: (608) 266-7513; (800) 662-1227 (toll free); District: (262) 338-8061.
E-mail: Sen.Grothman@legis.wisconsin.gov
Voting address: 111 South 6th Avenue, West Bend 53095.
Mailing address: Office: Room 20 South, State Capitol, P.O. Box 7882, Madison 53707-7882.

| Representative | Representative | Representative |
| STRACHOTA | LeMAHIEU | GOTTLIEB |

Pat Strachota (Rep.), 58th Assembly District

Born Cuyahoga Co., Ohio, June 29, 1955; married; 4 children. Graduate Glen Oak/Gimour Academy 1973; B.A. Government, minor in American History, certificate in Urban Planning, St. Mary's College (Notre Dame, IN) 1977. Full-time legislator. Member: West Bend Noon Rotary; Kettle Moraine YMCA (bd. mbr.); West Bend Chamber of Commerce; Washington Co. Ag. and Industry Society; Washington Co. Historical Society; Friend of West Bend Art Gallery; St. Frances Cabrini Parish. Former member: West Bend Economic Development Corp. (bd. mbr.); West Bend/Jackson Boys & Girls Club (bd. mbr.); Great Blue Heron Girl Scout Council (bd. mbr.). Washington Co. Board 1986-2002. Southeast Wisconsin Regional Planning Commission 1986-2002.

Elected to Assembly 2004; reelected since 2006. Majority Caucus Vice Chairperson 2007. Biennial committee assignments: **2009** — Health and Health Care Reform (also 2007); Jobs, the Economy and Small Business; Public Health. **2007** — Jobs and the Economy (chp.); Workforce Development (vice chp.); Aging and Long-Term Care (also 2005); Rules; Ways and Means (also 2005). **2005** — Medicaid Reform (vice chp.); Health; Southeast Wisconsin Freeways.

Telephone: Office: (608) 264-8486; District: (262) 338-3790.
E-mail: Rep.Strachota@legis.wisconsin.gov
Voting address: 639 Ridge Road, West Bend 53095.
Mailing address: Office: Room 13 West, State Capitol, P.O. Box 8953, Madison 53708.

Daniel R. LeMahieu (Rep.), 59th Assembly District

Born Sheboygan, November 5, 1946; married; 3 children. Graduate Oostburg H.S. 1964; attended UW-Sheboygan and UW-Milwaukee. Former publisher of Lakeshore Weekly. Vietnam Era veteran; served in Army, 1969-71. Member: Oostburg Business Association (past pres.); Oostburg Kiwanis Club (past pres.). Recipient: *Friend of Agriculture Award* 2005-06, 2003-04; Wis. Counties Assn. *Legislator of the Year* 2008, *Outstanding Legislator Award* 2005-06, 2003-04; Wis. Grocers Assn. *Friend of Grocers Award* 2007-08, 2003-04; *Friend of the Dairy Industry Award* 2005-06, 2003-04; Wis. Pro-Life *Legislator of the Year* 2005; Wis. Builders Assn. *Friend of the Housing Industry Award* 2009, 2008, 2007, 2006, 2005; Metropolitan Milwaukee Assn. of Commerce *Champion of Commerce Award* 2005-06; NFIB *Guardian of Small Business Award* 2007-08. Sheboygan Co. Bd. 1988-Dec. 2002 (chm. 2000-Dec. 2002).

Elected to Assembly 2002; reelected since 2004. Biennial committee assignments: **2009** — Corrections and the Courts (since 2005); Natural Resources (also 2007); Urban and Local Affairs (vice chp. 2007, 2003, chp. 2005); Jt. Com. for Review of Administrative Rules (co-chp. 2007, vice chp. 2005). **2007** — Aging and Long-Term Care (also 2003). **2003** — Rural Development; Small Business.

Telephone: Office: (608) 266-9175; (888) 534-0059 (toll free); District: (920) 528-8679.
E-mail: Rep.LeMahieu@legis.wisconsin.gov
Voting address: W6284 Lake Ellen Drive, P.O. Box 277, Cascade 53011.
Mailing address: Office: Room 17 North, State Capitol, P.O. Box 8952, Madison 53708.

Mark Gottlieb (Rep.), 60th Assembly District

Born Milwaukee, December 11, 1956; married; 4 children. Graduate James Madison H.S. (Milwaukee) 1974; B.S. UW-Milwaukee 1981; M. Engr. UW-Milwaukee 1984. Civil engineer. Vietnam Era veteran; served in Navy, 1974-78. Member: American Legion Post 82; Port Washington Chamber of Commerce; Cedarburg Chamber of Commerce; Grafton Chamber of Commerce; Port Washington Police and Fire Comn. Recipient: Wis. Co. Assn. *Outstanding Legislator* 2007-08, 2005-06, 2003-04; League of Wis. Munic. *Outstanding Legislator* 2007-08; MMAC *Champion of Commerce* 2007-08, 2005-06; Farm Bureau *Friend of Agriculture* 2005-06; Amer. Cancer Soc. *Excellence in Tobacco Control* 2006; Wis. Builders Assn. *Friend of Housing* 2009, 2008, 2007, 2006, 2005; Port Washington Chamber of Commerce *Citizen of the Year* 2002. City of Port Washington alderman 1991-97; Mayor of Port Washington 1997-2003.

Elected to Assembly 2002; reelected since 2004. Assistant Minority Leader 2009; Speaker Pro Tempore 2007; Majority Caucus Vice Chairperson 2005. Biennial committee assignments: **2009** — Assembly Organization (also 2007); Colleges and Universities (vice chp. 2003, mbr. 2007); Rules (since 2005); Urban and Local Affairs (chp. 2007, mbr. since 2003); Jt. Com. on Legislative Organization; Jt. Survey Com. on Retirement Systems; Transportation Projects Comn. (since 2005). **2007** —Labor and Industry (vice chp.); Transportation (also 2003); Jt. Legislative Coun. **2005** — Jt. Com. for Review of Administrative Rules (co-chp.); Southeast Wisconsin Freeways (vice chp.); Energy and Utilities (also 2003); Jt. Com. on Finance (eff. 3/22/06). **2003** — Veterans and Military Affairs.

Telephone: Office: (608) 267-2369; (888) 534-0060 (toll free).
E-mail: Rep.Gottlieb@legis.wisconsin.gov
Voting address: 1205 Noridge Trail, Port Washington 53074.
Mailing address: Office: Room 309 North, State Capitol, P.O. Box 8952, Madison 53708.

21st SENATE DISTRICT

Senator
LEHMAN

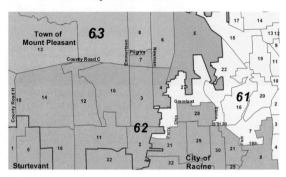

Detail Map: Racine Area

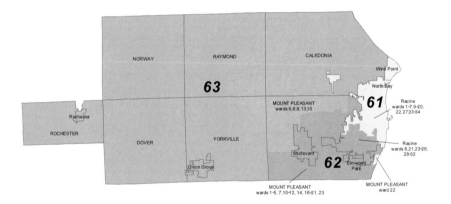

John W. Lehman (Dem.), 21st Senate District

Born Rhinelander, August 2, 1945; married; 3 daughters. Graduate Washington Park H.S. (Racine); B.A. Luther College 1967; M.Ed. Carthage College 1979; attended UW-Parkside and UW-Madison. Full-time legislator. Former high school history and economics teacher. Member: Racine Co. Democratic Party; Prader-Willi Syndrome Assn. of Wis.; Racine Heritage Museum; Friends of the Library, Racine Public Library; Clean Wisconsin; Sierra Club; Southeastern Wis. Educator Hall of Fame; Washington Park H.S. Hall of Fame. Former member: Racine Public Library Bd. (former pres.); Racine Sister City Planning Council; Racine Bd. of Health; Racine Education Association. Recipient: Luther College *Distinguished Service Award* 2007; Wis. League of Conservation Voters *Conservation Champion* 2007-08, 2005-06. Racine City Council 1988-2000 (former pres.).

Elected to Assembly 1996-2004; elected to Senate 2006. Majority Caucus Chairperson 2009. Biennial Senate committee assignments: **2009** — Education (chp., also 2007); Economic Development; Labor, Elections and Urban Affairs; Jt. Com. for Review of Admin. Rules (vice co-chp. 2007); Jt. Com. on Finance. **2007** — Economic Development, Job Creation, Family Prosperity and Housing (vice chp.). Assembly committee assignments: **2005** — Education (since 1997); Education Reform (since 2001); Insurance (also 2003); Workforce Development (also 2003). **2001** — Environment; Natural Resources (also 1999); Public Health (eff. 11/19/01); Small Business and Consumer Affairs; Legis. Coun. Spec. Com. on Mental Health Parity. **1999** — Family Law; Small Business and Economic Development (also 1997). **1997** — Urban and Local Affairs; Legis. Coun. Com. on the School Calendar.

Telephone: Office: (608) 266-1832; (866) 615-7510 (toll free); District: (262) 632-3330.

E-mail: Sen.Lehman@legis.wisconsin.gov

Voting address: 708 Orchard Street, Racine 53405-2354.

Mailing address: Office: Room 310 South, State Capitol, P.O. Box 7882, Madison 53707-7882.

Representative
TURNER

Representative
MASON

Representative
VOS

Robert L. Turner (Dem.), 61st Assembly District

Born Columbus, MS, September 14, 1947; married; 3 children. Graduate R.E. Hunt H.S., Columbus, MS; attended Dominican College 1972; B.S. in business administration UW-Parkside 1976. Vietnam veteran; served in Air Force 1967-70. Member: Big Brothers and Big Sisters (bd. of advisors); NAACP; Amer. Legion; Vietnam Veterans of Amer. (life mbr.); AMVETS; VFW Post 1391 (life mbr.); 33rd degree Mason; Urban League (bd. of dir., former pres.); I-94 NS Labor Advisory Com. 2006-present. Racine City Council 1976-2004; State Elections Board 1987-90 (chp. 1990).

Elected to Assembly since 1990. Minority Caucus Chairperson 2005, 2003; Minority Caucus Vice Chairperson 2001, 1999; Minority Caucus Sergeant at Arms 1997. Biennial committee assignments: **2009** — Criminal Justice (chp., mbr. 2007, 2003); Judiciary and Ethics; Housing; Veterans and Military Affairs (also 2007); Jt. Leg. Coun. Spec. Com. on Justice Reinvestment Initiative Oversight (vice chp.). **2007** — Urban and Local Affairs (also 2003 eff. 2/14/03). **2005** — Criminal Justice and Homeland Security; Judiciary; Rules (also 2003); Veterans Affairs. **2003** — State Affairs. **2001** — Jt. Com. for Review of Administrative Rules; Labor and Workforce Development; Tax and Spending Limitations; Ways and Means (since 1991). **1999** — Financial Institutions (also 1995); Labor and Employment (since 1995); Transportation (mbr., chp. 1993); State of Wis. Building Comn. (since 1991). **1997** — Highways and Transportation (also 1995). **1995** — Urban and Local Affairs; Governor's Clean Air Act Amendments Implementation Task Force (also 1993); Legis. Coun. Com. to Review the Election Process. **1993** —Elections, Constitutional Law and Corrections; Excise and Fees (also 1991); Highways (also 1991); Legis. Coun. Com. on Emergency Government Services.

Telephone: Office: (608) 266-0731; (888) 529-0061 (toll free); District: (262) 634-7371.

E-mail: Rep.Turner@legis.wisconsin.gov

Voting address: 36 McKinley Avenue, Racine 53404-3414.

Mailing address: Office: Room 223 North, State Capitol, P.O. Box 8953, Madison 53708.

Cory Mason (Dem.), 62nd Assembly District

Born Racine, January 25, 1973; married; 1 daughter. Graduate Case H.S. (Racine); B.A. in philosophy UW-Madison. Full-time legislator. Member: River Alliance of Wis. (bd. mbr.); Racine Rotary West; UW Center for Tobacco Research and Intervention (bd. mbr.); League of Conservation Voters; Racine Heritage Museum; Root River Council; I-94 Labor Development Com. (co-chp.); Wis. Coastal Management Bd. Redevelopment Authority of Racine 2005-present (commissioner).

Elected to Assembly 2006; reelected 2008. Biennial committee assignments: **2009** — Natural Resources (also 2007); Jt. Com. on Finance. **2007** — Education; Jobs and the Economy.

Telephone: Office: (608) 266-0634; District: (262) 638-2362.

Voting address: 3611 Kinzie Avenue, Racine 53405.

Mailing address: Office: Room 321 East, State Capitol, P.O. Box 8953, Madison 53708.

Robin J. Vos (Rep.), 63rd Assembly District

Born Burlington, July 5, 1968; married. Graduate Burlington H.S. 1986; UW-Whitewater 1991. Owner of several small businesses. Former congressional district director; former legislative assistant. Member: Rotary Club (past pres.); Ducks Unlimited; Racine/Kenosha Farm Bureau; Racine Zoological Soc.; Knights of Columbus; Racine Co. Rep. Party; Racine Area Manufacturers and Commerce; NFIB (leadership council mbr.); Union Grove Chamber of Commerce; Wind Lake Chamber of Commerce; Waterford Chamber of Commerce; Caledonia Historical Soc. Recipient: Wis. Associated Gen. Contractors of America *Legislator of the Year* 2008; National Federation of Independent Businesses *Small Business Champion Award* 2008; Wis. Builders Assn. *Friend of Housing* 2008; Goodwill Industries of SE Wis. *Legislative Appreciation Award* 2008; Republican Party of Wis. 1st Cong. Dist. *Alvan E. Bovay Award for Outstanding Service;* Rehabilitation for Wis., Inc. *Excellence Award* 2006; National Federation of Independent Businesses *Guardian of Small Business* 2005-06; Wis. Grocers Assn. *Friend of Wisconsin Grocers* 2005-06; Wis. Counties Assn. *Outstanding Legislator Award* 2005-06; Metropolitan Milwaukee Assn. of Commerce *Champion of Commerce* 2007-08, 2005-06. UW Board of Regents 1989-91. Racine Co. Board 1994-2004 (former chp. of Finance and Personnel Com.).

Elected to Assembly 2004; reelected since 2006. Biennial committee assignments: **2009** — Insurance; Jt. Com. on Finance (also 2007); Jt. Legislative Council. **2007** — Elections and Constitutional Law (vice chp. eff. 1/3/08); Jobs and the Economy (eff. 1/17/08).

Telephone: Office: (608) 266-9171; (888) 534-0063 (toll free); Fax: (608) 282-3663; District: (262) 631-7871.

E-mail: Rep.Vos@legis.wisconsin.gov

Voting address: 4710 Eastwood Ridge, Racine 53406.

Mailing address: Office: Room 105 West, State Capitol, P.O. Box 8953, Madison 53708.

22nd SENATE DISTRICT

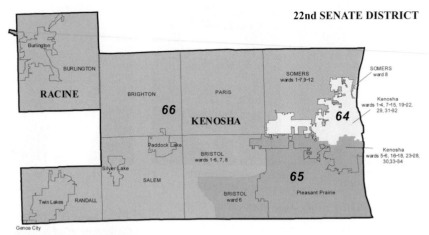

Detail Map: Kenosha City

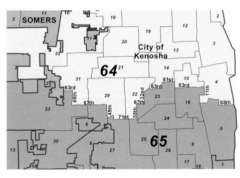

Senator
WIRCH

Robert W. Wirch (Dem.), 22nd Senate District

Born Kenosha, November 16, 1943; married; 2 children. Graduate Mary D. Bradford H.S.; B.A. UW-Parkside 1970. Full-time legislator. Former factory worker and liaison to JTPA programs. Served in Army Reserve 1965-71. Member: Polish Legion of American Veterans; Danish Brotherhood; Kenosha Sport Fishing and Conservation Assn.; Friends of the Museum; Kenosha Scout Leaders Rescue Squad Advisory Council; Senior Action Council; Kenosha Area Business Alliance; Democratic. Party of Wis. Former member: Kenosha Boys and Girls Club (bd. of dir.). Kenosha County supervisor 1986-94 (served on Health and Human Services Com., Welfare Bd., and Developmental Disabilities Bd.).

Elected to Assembly 1992; reelected 1994; elected to Senate since 1996. Minority Caucus Chairperson 2003. Biennial committee assignments: 2009 — Small Business, Emergency Preparedness, Technical Colleges, and Consumer Protection (chp.); Jt. Survey Com. on Retirement Systems (co-chp., also 2007, 2001, 1999, mbr. since 1997); Commerce, Utilities, Energy and Rail; Environment; Labor, Elections and Urban Affairs (vice chp. 2007); Jt. Legislative Council. 2007 — Small Business, Emergency Preparedness, Workforce Development, Technical Colleges and Consumer Protection (chp.); Commerce, Utilities and Rail; Environment and Natural Resources. 2005 — Energy, Utilities and Information Technology; Natural Resources and Transportation; Veterans, Homeland Security, Military Affairs, Small Business and Government Reform; Retirement Research Com. (since 1997). 2003 — Energy and Utilities; Environment and Natural Resources; Homeland Security, Veterans and Military Affairs and Government Reform. 2001 — Jt. Com. on Finance; Environmental Resources; Human Services and Aging (also 1999); Judiciary, Consumer Affairs, and Campaign Finance Reform. 1999 — Economic Development, Housing and Government Operations (chp.); Agriculture, Environmental Resources and Campaign Finance Reform; State of Wis. Building Comn.; Law Revision Com.; Transportation Projects Comn. 1997 — Jt. Legis. Audit (co-chp., eff. 1/15/97 to 4/20/98); Jt. Com. for Review of Administrative Rules (eff. 1/15/97 to 1/5/98, also 1995); Agriculture and Environmental Resources (eff. 1/15/97 to 4/20/98); Health, Family Services and Aging (eff. 4/21/98); Health, Human Services, Aging, Corrections, Veterans and Military Affairs (eff. 1/15/97 to 1/7/98); Judiciary, Campaign Finance Reform and Consumer Affairs (chp., eff. 1/5/98); Council on Workforce Excellence; Legis. Coun. Coms. on Conservation Laws Enforcement, on Disciplinary Procedures for Represented Police and Fire Personnel.

Telephone: Office: (608) 267-8979; District: (262) 694-7379; Office Hotline: (888) 769-4724.

E-mail: Sen.Wirch@legis.wisconsin.gov

Voting address: 3007 Springbrook Road, Pleasant Prairie 53158.

Mailing address: Office: Room 316 South, State Capitol, P.O. Box 7882, Madison 53707-7882.

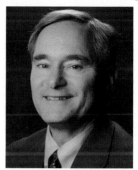  

| Representative | Representative | Representative |
| BARCA | STEINBRINK | KERKMAN |

Peter W. Barca (Dem.), 64th Assembly District

Born Kenosha, August 7, 1955; married; 2 children. Graduate Mary D. Bradford H.S. 1973; B.S. UW-Milwaukee 1977; attended Harvard U.; M.A. UW-Madison 1983. President, Aurora Assoc. International. Former CEO, North-pointe Resources; National Ombudsman, USSBA; Midwest Regional Administrator, USSBA. Member: Foundation Bd. of Dir., UW-Parkside; Society for ISCTR (co-founder); WISITALIA (past pres.). Former member: Lake County Econ. Dev. Com. on Small Business (chp.); Com. to Found the Boys and Girls Club of Kenosha (chp.); Lake County Partnership on Econ. Dev. (exec. com.); Small Business Forum of DNC (nat'l co-chair); Kenosha Family and Aging Soc. (bd. mbr.); Kenosha Incubator Assn. (chm.).

Elected to Assembly 1984-1992 (resigned 6/8/93 upon election to U.S. Congress); reelected 2008. Majority Caucus Chairperson 2009, 1993, 1991. Biennial committee assignments: **2009** — Jt. Legis. Audit Com. (co-chp.); Assembly Organization; Financial Institutions; Jobs, the Economy and Small Business; Rules.

Telephone: Office: (608) 266-5504; (888) 534-0064 (toll free).

E-mail: Rep.Barca@legis.wisconsin.gov

Voting address: 1339 38th Avenue, Kenosha 53144.

Mailing address: Office: Room 107 North, State Capitol, P.O. Box 8952, Madison 53708.

John P. Steinbrink (Dem.), 65th Assembly District

Born Kenosha, April 17, 1949; married; 3 children, 3 grandchildren. Graduate George Tremper H.S.; attended Carthage College and UW-Madison Farm and Industry Short Course. Grain farmer. Former dairy farmer. Member: Kenosha Co. Farm Bureau (former pres. and vice pres.); Rotary Club of Kenosha – West; Danish Brotherhood; Senior Action Council; Wis. League of Municipalities; Moose Lodge No. 286; Italian-American Society; Kenosha Area Busi-ness Alliance; St. Anne's Catholic Church. Former member: Wis. Electric Community Round Table; Conserv F.S.; Kenosha-Racine F.S.; Pleasant Prairie Police Auxiliary; Pleasant Prairie Planning Commission; Wisconsin Towns Assn. Pleasant Prairie Town Board 1985-89; Pleasant Prairie Village Board 1989-present (pres. 1995-present).

Elected to Assembly since 1996. Biennial committee assignments: **2009** — Transportation (chp., mbr. since 1999); Energy and Utilities (since 2003); Fish and Wildlife; Natural Resources (since 1999); Ways and Means (also 2007). **2007** — Coun. on Tourism (since 2003). **2005** — Agriculture (eff. 11/2/05, 2003 eff. 5/13/03, 1997-2001); Economic Development (also 2003). **2003** — Budget Review. **2001** — Government Operations (ranking minority mbr.); Tourism and Recreation (since 1997). **1997** — Highways and Transportation; Land Use.

Telephone: Office: (608) 266-0455; (888) 534-0065 (toll free); District: (262) 694-5863.

E-mail: Rep.Steinbrink@legis.wisconsin.gov

Voting address: 8640 88th Avenue, Pleasant Prairie 53158.

Mailing address: Office: Room 104 North, State Capitol, P.O. Box 8953, Madison 53708.

Samantha Kerkman (Rep.), 66th Assembly District

Born Burlington, March 6, 1974; married; 2 children. Graduate Wilmot H.S.; B.A. UW-Whitewater 1996. Full-time legislator. Former legislative aide. Member: Burlington Area Chamber of Commerce; Kenosha Area Business Alliance; Twin Lakes Chamber and Area Business Assn.; Twin Lakes American Legion Auxiliary Post 544; VFW Auxiliary, Bloomfield Center Post 5830; Powers Lake Sportsmen Club; St. Alphonsus Catholic Church.

Elected to Assembly 2000; reelected since 2002. Biennial committee assignments: **2009** — Judiciary and Ethics (also 2007); Ways and Means (chp. 2007, mbr. since 2001); Jt. Legis. Audit (since 2001). **2007** — Homeland Security and State Preparedness (vice chp.); Consumer Protection and Personal Privacy; Jobs and the Economy. **2005** — Budget Review (chp., also 2003); State-Federal Relations (vice chp.); Judiciary (since 2001); Southeast Wisconsin Freeways. **2003** — Financial Institutions (also 2001). **2001** — Urban and Local Affairs (vice chp.); Government Operations.

Telephone: Office: (608) 266-2530; (888) 534-0066 (toll free); District: (262) 279-1037.

E-mail: Rep.Kerkman@legis.wisconsin.gov

Internet: www.legis.state.wi.us/assembly/asm66/news/default.htm

Voting address: (Town of Randall) 40255 105th Street, Genoa City 53128.

Mailing address: Office: Room 103 West, State Capitol, P.O. Box 8952, Madison 53708; District: 40255 105th Street, Genoa City 53128.

23rd SENATE DISTRICT

See Eau Claire Area Detail Map on p. 97

Senator
KREITLOW

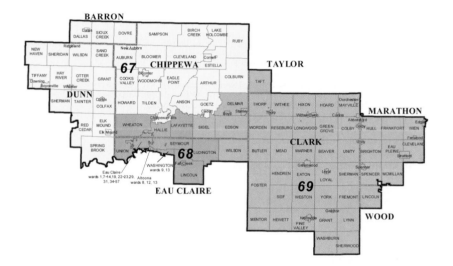

Pat Kreitlow (Dem.), 23rd Senate District

Born St. Paul, MN, July 3, 1964; married; 2 children. Graduate Apple Valley, MN H.S. 1982; B.A. in journalism UW-Eau Claire 1986. Full-time legislator. Former television and radio news anchor-reporter. Member: JCIPT (co-chp.); RED (bd. mbr.). Former member: Literacy Volunteers-Chippewa Valley (bd. of dir.); Western Wisconsin Press Club (pres.); Our Saviour's Lutheran Church, Chippewa Falls (trustee).

Elected to Senate 2006. President Pro Tempore 2009. Biennial committee assignments: **2009** — Rural Issues, Biofuels, and Information Technology (chp.); Jt. Com. on Information Policy and Technology (co-chp.); Agriculture and Higher Education; Commerce, Utilities, Energy, and Rail; Economic Development; Ethics Reform and Government Operations (also 2007); Jt. Legis. Council. **2007** — Campaign Finance Reform, Rural Issues and Information Technology (chp.); Economic Development, Job Creation, Family Prosperity and Housing; Education; Public Health, Senior Issues, Long-Term Care and Privacy; Jt. Com. for Review of Admin. Rules; Women's Council.

Telephone: Office: (608) 266-7511; (888) 437-9436 (toll free); District: (715) 726-0596.

E-mail: Sen.Kreitlow@legis.wisconsin.gov

Voting address: 15854 93rd Avenue, Chippewa Falls 54729.

Mailing address: Office: Room 10 South, State Capitol, P.O. Box 7882, Madison 53707-7882.

Representative	Representative	Representative
WOOD	DEXTER	SUDER

Jeffrey Wood (Ind.), 67th Assembly District

Born Juneau Co., September 12, 1969; married; 3 children. Graduate Chippewa Falls Senior H.S. 1987; attended UW-Eau Claire. Full-time legislator. Former small business owner and local government reporter. Served in U.S. Navy and U.S. Naval Reserve 1986-94. Member: American Legion; Farm Bureau; Chamber of Commerce. Former member: Libertarian Party of the Chippewa Valley.

Elected to Assembly 2002; reelected since 2004. Biennial committee assignments: **2009** — Renewable Energy and Rural Affairs; Rural Economic Development (also 2007); Ways and Means (chp. 2005, vice chp. 2003). **2007** — Workforce Development (chp., mbr. since 2003); Jt. Survey Com. on Tax Exemptions (co-chp.); Biofuels and Sustainable Energy (vice chp.); Education Reform (since 2003); Rural Affairs. **2005** — Campaigns and Elections (also 2003); Property Rights and Land Management (also 2003).

Telephone: Office: (608) 266-1194; (888) 534-0067 (toll free).

E-mail: Rep.WoodJ@legis.wisconsin.gov

Voting address: 559 Roland Street, Chippewa Falls 54729.

Mailing address: Office: Room 21 North, State Capitol, P.O. Box 8953, Madison 53708.

Kristen Dexter (Dem.), 68th Assembly District

Born Hallock, MN, July 20, 1961; married; 3 children. Graduate Hallock H.S. 1979; attended Moorehead State U., U. of Oregon, Lund U. (Lund, Sweden); B.S. liberal arts UW-River Falls 1988. Full-time legislator. Member: Eau Claire Chamber of Commerce; AAUW Wisconsin; Wis. Farmers Union; Beaver Creek Reserve. Former member: Wis. Assn. of School Boards; Girl Scouts of America (troop leader). Altoona Board of Education 2002-08.

Elected to Assembly 2008. Biennial committee assignments: **2009** — Education (vice chp.); Public Health; Renewable Energy and Rural Affairs; Rural Economic Development.

Telephone: Office: (608) 266-9172; (888) 534-0068 (toll free).

E-mail: Rep.Dexter@legis.wisconsin.gov

Voting address: 7410 Lakeview Drive, Eau Claire 54701.

Mailing address: Office: Room 9 North, State Capitol, P.O. Box 8952, Madison 53708.

Scott Suder (Rep.), 69th Assembly District

Born Medford, September 28, 1968. Graduate Abbotsford H.S.; B.A. UW-Eau Claire 1991. Former legislative aide. Member of Wis. Air National Guard, 2003-present; veteran of Operation Iraqi Freedom. Member: Abbotsford Sportsman Club; Loyal Sportsman's Club; NRA (lifetime mbr.); NRA-ILA; Natl. Assn. of Sportsmen Legislators; Lublin Amer. Legion-Sons of the Amer. Legion; Wis. Farm Bureau; ALEC Criminal Justice Task Force (chm. 2002-04); ALEC Homeland Security Task Force (since 2004); NWTF; Abbotsford Lions Club. Recipient: NCSL *Medal of Civic Honor* 2007; Wis. Council of the Blind and Visually Impaired *Outstanding Leadership Award* 2007; Am. Acad. of Pediatrics *Legislator of the Year* 2007; Wis. Bearhunters Assn. *Legislator of the Year* 2006; Wis. Coalition Against Sexual Assault *Voices of Courage Public Policy Award* 2006; Wis. Coalition Against Domestic Abuse *Partner in Social Justice Award* 2003; NWTF *Legislator of the Year* 2002; Amer. Police Hall of Fame *Distinguished Service Award;* NFIB *Guardian of Small Business Award; Friend of Wis. Grocers Award;* NRA *Defender of Freedom Award; Friend of Agriculture Award* 2000-04. Abbotsford City Coun. 1996-2001.

Elected to Assembly since 1998. Minority Caucus Chairperson 2009. Biennial committee assignments: **2009** — Assembly Organization; Fish and Wildlife; Insurance; Personal Privacy; Rules. **2007** — Jt. Com. on Finance; Rural Economic Development Bd. (since 2003). **2005** — Criminal Justice and Homeland Security (chp.); Rural Development (vice chp., also 2003); Agriculture (since 1999); Corrections and the Courts (vice chp. 1999-2001, mbr. 2003); Transportation (since 1999). **2003** — Criminal Justice (chp. and mbr. since 2001); Law Revision Com. (also 2001). **2001** — Census and Redistricting. **1999** — Campaigns and Elections (vice chp.); Highway Safety (eff. 10/12/99); Judiciary and Personal Privacy; Waste Cutters Task Force (chp.).

Telephone: Office: (608) 267-0280; (888) 534-0069 (toll free); District: (715) 223-6964.

E-mail: Rep.Suder@legis.wisconsin.gov

Voting address: 102 South Fourth Avenue, Abbotsford 54405.

Mailing address: Office: Room 315 North, State Capitol, P.O. Box 8953, Madison 53708.

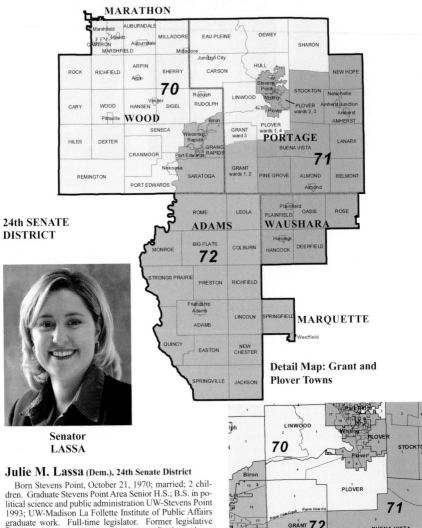

24th SENATE DISTRICT

Detail Map: Grant and Plover Towns

Senator LASSA

Julie M. Lassa (Dem.), 24th Senate District

Born Stevens Point, October 21, 1970; married; 2 children. Graduate Stevens Point Area Senior H.S.; B.S. in political science and public administration UW-Stevens Point 1993; UW-Madison La Follette Institute of Public Affairs graduate work. Full-time legislator. Former legislative aide and executive director, Plover Area Business Assn. Member: Heart of Wisconsin Business and Economic Alliance; Marshfield Area Chamber of Commerce and Industry; Portage Co. Democratic Party (former chp.); Portage Co. Business Council. Dewey Town Board 1993-94.

Elected to Assembly 1998-2002 (resigned eff. 5/9/03); elected to Senate in April 2003 special election; reelected since 2004. Minority Caucus Secretary 1999. Biennial Senate committee assignments: **2009** — Economic Development (chp.); Children and Families and Workforce Development; Health, Health Insurance, Privacy, Property Tax Relief, and Revenue; Jt. Com. on Finance; Child Abuse and Neglect Prevention Bd. (also 2007, 2003, 2001). **2007** — Economic Development, Job Creation, Family Prosperity and Housing (chp.); Agriculture and Higher Education (vice chp.); Campaign Finance Reform, Rural Issues and Information Technology; Jt. Legislative Audit (also 2005). **2005** — Housing and Financial Institutions; Job Creation, Economic Development and Consumer Affairs (ranking min. mbr.). **2003** — Agriculture, Financial Institutions and Insurance; Jt. Com. for Review of Administrative Rules. Assembly committee assignments: **2003** — Agriculture (since 1999); Budget Review (ranking min. mbr.); Economic Development (ranking minority mbr., 2001); Financial Institutions; Rural Affairs. **2001** — Colleges and Universities (also 1999); Labor and Workforce Development. **1999** — Small Business and Economic Development; Transportation; World Dairy Center Authority.

Telephone: Office: (608) 266-3123; (800) 925-7491 (toll free); District: (715) 342-3806.

E-mail: Sen.Lassa@legis.wisconsin.gov

Voting address: 4901 Beaver Dam Road, Stevens Point 54481.

Mailing address: Office: Room 323 South, State Capitol, P.O. Box 7882, Madison 53707-7882.

Representative	Representative	Representative
VRUWINK	**MOLEPSKE**	**SCHNEIDER**

Amy Sue Vruwink (Dem.), 70th Assembly District

Born Wisconsin Rapids, May 22, 1975; married. Graduate Auburndale H.S. 1993; B.S. Marian College (Fond du Lac) 1997. Full-time legislator. Former legislative aide to U.S. Representative David R. Obey and Area Program Director for the Minnesota Farm Bureau. Member: Marshfield Business and Professional Women; Marshfield Area Chamber of Commerce and Industry; Marshfield Eagles; Wood County Farm Bureau; National Rifle Association; Wisconsin Bear Hunters; Central Wisconsin Fair Association; New Visions Art Gallery.

Elected to Assembly 2002; reelected since 2004. Minority Caucus Secretary 2005, 2003. Biennial committee assignments: **2009** — Agriculture (chp., mbr. since 2003); Fish and Wildlife; Health and Health Care Reform (since 2007); Personal Privacy; Renewable Energy and Rural Affairs; Transportation (since 2003); Rural Economic Development Bd. (since 2005). **2007** — Transportation Projects Commission (since 2003). **2005** — Aging and Long-Term Care (also 2003); Health (also 2003); Rural Affairs and Renewable Energy.

Telephone: Office: (608) 266-8366; (888) 534-0070 (toll free); District: (715) 652-2909.

E-mail: Rep.Vruwink@legis.wisconsin.gov

Voting address: 9425 Flower Lane, Milladore 54454.

Mailing address: Office: Room 112 North, State Capitol, P.O. Box 8953, Madison 53708.

Louis John Molepske, Jr. (Dem.), 71st Assembly District

Born Stevens Point, January 6, 1974. Graduate Stevens Point Area H.S. 1993; B.A. political science with an emphasis in journalism UW-Madison 1997; J.D. Marquette 2001. Attorney. Former special prosecutor, Portage Co. D.A. office; assistant city attorney and mayoral assistant, City of Stevens Point. Member: Portage County Democratic Party; Portage County Bar Assn.; Wisconsin Bar Assn.; Knights of Columbus; Izaak Walton League (Bill Cook chapter); Portage County Big Brothers and Big Sisters; Wisconsin/Nicaragua Partners for the Americas; Lawyers Legislative Action Network; Wis. Bar Assn. Government Lawyers Division; UW-Stevens Point College of Natural Resources Advisory Bd.; Wis. Assn. of Health Underwriter's Foundation Bd.

Elected to Assembly in July 2003 special election; reelected since 2004. Biennial committee assignments: **2009** — Jobs, the Economy and Small Business (chp.); Insurance (vice chp., mbr. 2003); Agriculture (since 2003); Fish and Wildlife; Natural Resources (since 2005). **2007** — Biofuels and Sustainable Energy; Elections and Constitutional Law; Property Rights. **2005** — Colleges and Universities; Financial Institutions (also 2003); Transportation; Wis. Environmental Education Bd. **2003** — Education; Rural Affairs; Workforce Development.

Telephone: Office: (608) 267-9649; (888) 534-0071 (toll free).

E-mail: Rep.Molepske@legis.wisconsin.gov

Internet address: http://www.legis.state.wi.us/assembly/asm71/news

Voting address: 1557 Church Street, Stevens Point 54481.

Mailing address: Office: Room 214 North, State Capitol, P.O. Box 8953, Madison 53708.

Marlin D. Schneider (Dem.), 72nd Assembly District

Born La Crosse, November 16, 1942; married; 3 children. Graduate Longfellow Elem. Sch.; La Crosse Central H.S. 1960; B.S. WSU-La Crosse 1965; M.S.T. UW-Stevens Point 1976; M.S. UW-Madison 1979; certificate from Madison Area Technical College Police Academy 1982. Full-time legislator.

Elected to Assembly since 1970. Longest serving member in the history of the Wisconsin Assembly. Majority Caucus Sergeant at Arms 2009; Assistant Minority Leader 1999, 1997, 1995; Assistant Majority Leader 1989; Majority Caucus Vice Chairperson 1973-81. Biennial committee assignments: **2009** — Personal Privacy (chp., also 2007); Jt. Legislative Council (co-chp., also mbr. since 2003, 1985-99, vice chp. 1993, chp. 1991); Veterans and Military Affairs (vice chp., mbr. 2003, 2001); Tourism, Recreation and State Properties (also 2007 eff. 3/20/07). **2007** — Homeland Security and State Preparedness; Public Health; Rural Affairs; State Capitol and Executive Residence Bd. (also 2005); Educational Communications Bd. (also 2005). **2005** — Jt. Com. for Review of Administrative Rules; Colleges and Universities (also 2003); Military Affairs; Rural Affairs and Renewable Energy.

Telephone: Office: (608) 266-0215; (888) 529-0072 (toll free); Fax: (608) 282-3672 or (608) 266-8955; District: (715) 423-1223.

E-mail: Rep.Schneider@legis.wisconsin.gov

Voting address: 3820 Southbrook Lane, Wisconsin Rapids 54494.

Mailing address: Office: Room 204 North, State Capitol, P.O. Box 8953, Madison 53708.

25th SENATE DISTRICT

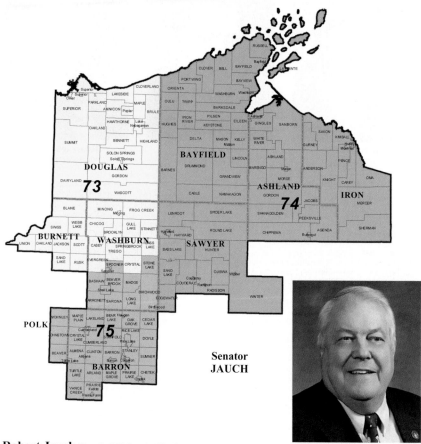

Senator
JAUCH

Robert Jauch (Dem.), 25th Senate District

Born Wheaton, IL, November 22, 1945; married; 2 children. Graduate Wheaton Central H.S.; attended UW-Eau Claire 1968-71, UW-Superior 1973. Full-time legislator. Former field rep. for Congressman David Obey. Veteran; served in Army 1964-68. Member: Hawthorne Lions; Vietnam Veterans of America; VFW; NCSL.

Elected to Assembly 1982, 1984; elected to Senate since 1986. Minority Leader 1995, 1993 (eff. 5/12/93). Biennial committee assignments: **2009** — Children and Families and Workforce Development (chp.); Education (vice chp., mbr. 2005, 1993-2001); Environment; Rural Issues, Biofuels, and Information Technology; Jt. Legis. Audit; Jt. Com. on Information Policy and Technology (also 2007, co-chp. 2001). **2007** — Tax Fairness and Family Prosperity (chp., eff. 11/5/07); Jt. Com. for Review of Administrative Rules (co-chp., mbr. 1987-1993); Environment and Natural Resources (vice chp.); Jt. Com. on Finance (also 1991-99). **2005** — Jt. Survey Com. on Tax Exemptions. **2003** — Education, Ethics and Elections; Health, Children, Families, Aging and Long Term Care. **2001** — 2001-03 Biennial Budget (chp.); Economic Development and Corrections (chp.); Privacy, Electronic Commerce and Financial Institutions (also 1999); Legis. Adv. Com. to the Minn.-Wis. Boundary Area Comn. (since 1997). **1999** — Jt. Com. on Information Policy (co-chp., also 1997, eff. 1/15/97 to 4/20/98, 1995). **1997** — Education and Financial Institutions (eff. 4/21/98); Insurance, Tourism and Rural Affairs (eff. 1/15/97 to 4/20/98); Jt. Legislative Council (also 1995); Education Comn. of the States (also 1995); Submerged Cultural Resources Council (also 1995); Midwestern Higher Education Comn.; Legis. Coun. Coms. on Children at Risk Program, on School Discipline and Safety. **1995** — Jt. Com. on Employment Relations (resigned 10/17/95, also 1993); Jt. Com. on Legislative Organization (resigned 10/17/95, also 1993); Insurance (eff. 12/95-6/96); Insurance, Tourism, Veterans and Military Affairs (eff. 6/96); Senate Organization (resigned 10/17/95, also 1993); School Funding Comn.; Spec. Com. on State and Federal Relations (vice chp., resigned 10/17/95); Council on Alcohol and Other Drug Abuse; Disability Bd.; Legis. Coun. Com. on Lead Poisoning and Control. **1993** — Student Readiness Study Com.; Jt. Survey Com. for Retirement Systems (mbr. and co-chp. 1987 to 4/20/93); Retirement Research Com. (mbr. and co-chp. 1987-4/20/93); Legis. Coun. Coms. on AISC, on Children in Need of Protection or Services, on State Fire Programs.

Telephone: Office: (608) 266-3510; (800) 469-6562 (toll free); District: (715) 364-2438.

E-mail: Sen.Jauch@legis.wisconsin.gov

Voting address: 5271 South Maple Drive, Poplar 54864-9126.

Mailing address: Office: Room 118 South, State Capitol, P.O. Box 7882, Madison 53707-7882.

Representative
MILROY

Representative
SHERMAN

Representative
HUBLER

Nick Milroy (Dem.), 73rd Assembly District
Born Duluth, MN, April 15, 1974; married; 1 child. Graduate Superior Senior H.S. 1992; B.S. UW-Superior 1998; attended UW-Eau Claire 1999-2000. Full-time legislator. Former fisheries biologist. Served in U.S. Navy 1992-94, U.S. Naval Reserve 1994-2000; deployed to Persian Gulf during Operation Southern Watch. Member: Douglas Co. Democratic Party (former secy.); Lake Superior Bi-national Forum. Former member: St. Louis River Watershed TMDL Partnership (bd. of dir.); Am. Fisheries Soc.; Duluth-Superior Metropolitan Interstate Council (policy bd. mbr.); Head of the Lakes Fair (bd. of dir.). Superior City Council 2005-09.

Elected to Assembly 2008. Biennial committee assignments: **2009** — Fish and Wildlife (vice chp.); Forestry; Natural Resources; Veterans and Military Affairs.

Telephone: Office: (608) 266-0640; (888) 534-0073 (toll free); District: (715) 392-8690.

E-mail: Rep.Milroy@legis.wisconsin.gov

Voting address: 2706 North 17th Street, Superior 54880.

Mailing address: Office: Room 8 North, State Capitol, P.O. Box 8953, Madison 53708.

Gary E. Sherman (Dem.), 74th Assembly District
Born Chicago, May 5, 1949; 2 children. Graduate A.G. Lane Technical H.S. (Chicago); B.A. in history and American institutions, UW-Madison 1970; J.D. *cum laude* UW-Madison 1973. Attorney. Served in Air Force 1973. Member: State Bar of Wis. (former pres.); Port Wing Fire Dept. (former chief); American Law Institute; Ashland-Bayfield Counties Bar Assn. (former pres.); Port Wing Baseball Club (fish boil); American Legion Post 531; Amvets Post 1998 (LCO); Red Cliff Bar; Wis. Assn. of Criminal Defense Lawyers. State Superintendent's Advisory Council on Rural Schools, Libraries and Communities; Group Insurance Board; Employee Trust Fund Bd.; Gov.'s Council on Military and State Relations; State Tribal Justice Forum.

Elected to Assembly since 1998. Minority Caucus Vice Chairperson 2005, 2003. Biennial committee assignments: **2009** — Forestry (chp., mbr. 2007); Jt. Com. on Finance; Claims Bd. **2007** — Transportation (since 1999); Veterans and Military Affairs (also 2003); Legis. Coun. Com. on State-Tribal Relations (since 1999). **2005** — Financial Institutions (also 2003); Rules; Veterans Affairs. **2003** — Education Reform; Gov.'s Council on Highway Safety. **2001** — Criminal Justice; Education (also 1999); Highway Safety. **1999** — Campaigns and Elections; Judiciary and Personal Privacy; Rural Affairs and Forestry; Legis. Coun. Com. on Dental Care Access.

Telephone: Office: (608) 266-7690; (888) 534-0074 (toll free); District: (715) 774-3691; Fax: (608) 282-3674.

E-mail: Rep.Sherman@legis.wisconsin.gov

Voting address: Town of Port Wing.

Mailing address: Office: Room 304 East, State Capitol, P.O. Box 8953, Madison 53708; District: P.O. Box 157, Port Wing 54865.

Mary Hubler (Dem.), 75th Assembly District
Born July 31, 1952. Graduate Rice Lake H.S.; B.S. UW-Superior 1973; J.D. UW-Madison 1980. Full-time legislator. Attorney, former teacher. Member: Wisconsin Farmers Union; Barron Co. Farm Bureau; Barron Co. Historical Society; State Bar of Wis.; Ducks Unlimited; Women of the Moose, Chapter 725; Barron County Home and Community Education; Rice Lake Elks Lodge No. 1441; Rocky Mountain Elk Foundation.

Elected to Assembly since 1984. Biennial committee assignments: **2009** — Jt. Survey Com. on Retirement Systems (co-chp., mbr. 2005, 2003); Jt. Survey Com. on Tax Exemptions (co-chp., mbr. since 2003); Veterans and Military Affairs (also 2007, 2003); Jt. Com. for Review of Administrative Rules. **2007** — Biofuels and Sustainable Energy; Forestry (since 2003). **2005** — Veterans Affairs. **2003** — Rural Development. **2001** — Agriculture (vice chp. 1987, mbr. 1985); Rural Affairs and Forestry (also 1999); Small Business and Consumer Affairs. **1999** — Natural Resources. **1997** — Judiciary (also 1987, 1985); Tourism and Recreation (also 1995); Joint Legislative Council (also 1995) and its Com. on Conservation Laws Enforcement (secy.). **1995** — Com. on Uniform State Laws (also 1993); Governor's Council on Recycling (also 1993); Legis. Coun. Com. on Federally Tax-Exempt Lands. **1993** — Jt. Com. on Finance (since 1989); Legis. Coun. Coms. on Law Revision (co-chp., also 1989, mbr. 1987), on Child Custody, Support and Visitation Laws. **1989** — Select Com. on Health Care Financing; Legis. Coun. Com. on Marital Property Implementation (also 1987).

Telephone: Office: (608) 266-2519; (888) 534-0075 (toll free); District: (715) 234-7421.

E-mail: Rep.Hubler@legis.wisconsin.gov

Voting address: 1966 21-7/8 Street (Hawthorne Lane), Rice Lake 54868.

Mailing address: Office: Room 119 North, State Capitol, P.O. Box 8952, Madison 53708; District: P.O. Box 544, Rice Lake 54868.

26th SENATE DISTRICT

Senator
RISSER

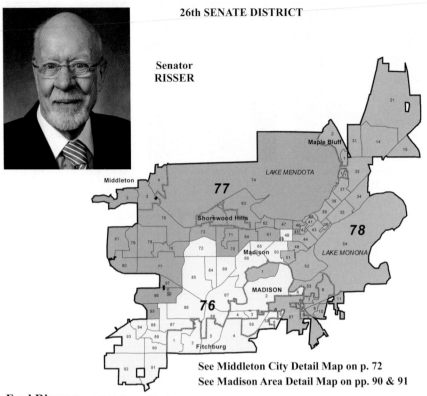

See Middleton City Detail Map on p. 72
See Madison Area Detail Map on pp. 90 & 91

Fred Risser (Dem.), 26th Senate District

Born Madison, May 5, 1927; married; 3 children. Attended Carleton College (MN), UW-Madison; B.A. U. of Oregon 1950; LL.B. U. of Oregon 1952. Attorney. World War II veteran; Navy. Member: State Bar of Wis. and Oregon and Dane Co. Bar Assns.; NCSL (past mbr. Natl. Exec. Com.); CSG (past mbr. Natl. Exec. Com., Midwestern Conf. chp. 1993, 1982). Presidential Elector 2008, 1964.

Elected to Assembly 1956-60; elected to Senate in 1962 special election; reelected since 1964. Longest serving legislator in Wisconsin history, currently, longest serving state legislator in U.S. President of the Senate 2009, 2007, 2001, 1999, 1997 (eff. 1/15/97 to 4/20/98), 1995 (eff. 7/9/96), also 1979 to 4/20/93; Co-Majority Leader 2001 (eff. 10/22/02); Assistant Minority Leader 1995 (eff. 1/5/95 to 7/12/96), 1993 (eff. 4/20/93, also 1965); Sen. Pres. Pro Tempore 1977, 1975; Minority Ldr. 1967-73. Biennial committee assignments: **2009** — Ethics Reform and Government Operations (chp., also 2007); Jt. Com. for Review of Admin. Rules; Joint Legislative Council (co-chp., also 2007, 2001, 1999, 1997, chp. 1987, 1983, 1971, mbr. since 1967); Jt. Com. on Legislative Organization (co-chp., also 2007, 2001, 1999, 1997, eff. 1/15/97 to 4/20/98, also 1977 to 4/20/93, mbr. 1967-2003); Jt. Com. on Employment Relations (co-chp., also 2007, 2001, 1999, 1997, eff. 1/6/97 to 4/20/98, also 1995, eff. 7/9/96, also 1979 to 4/20/93, mbr. since 1973); Senate Organization (chp. 1987 to 4/20/98, also chp. 1977-1981, mbr. 2007, 1967-2003); State of Wis. Building Comn. (vice chp., also 2007, 2001, 1999, 1971 to 5/19/93, mbr. since 1969); State Historical Society Bd. of Curators (since 1983); State Capitol and Executive Residence Bd. (chp. since 2003, co-chp. 1989 to 4/20/98, mbr. since 1983); Comn. on Uniform State Laws (also 2005). **2007** — Wis. Environmental Education Bd. (also 2005). **2005** — Campaign Finance Reform and Ethics; Judiciary, Corrections and Privacy (eff. 4/1/05); State and Federal Relations. **2003** — Environment and Natural Resources. **2001** — Judiciary, Consumer Affairs, and Campaign Finance Reform; Disability Bd. (since 1997). **1999** — Judiciary and Consumer Affairs. **1997** — Government Effectiveness (eff. 4/21/98); Judiciary (eff. 4/21/98); Judiciary, Campaign Finance Reform and Consumer Affairs; Wis. Sesquicentennial Comn. (also 1995). **1993** — Judiciary and Insurance; Senate Rules (since 1987). **1989** — Urban Affairs, Environmental Resources, Utilities and Elections (chp.); Jt. Com. on Debt Management (co-chp); Adv. Com. on the Capitol Master Plan (co-chp.). **1987** — Select Com. on the Regulation of Gambling; Com. on the Management of the Yahara Watershed. For earlier committee activities, see previous editions of the *Wisconsin Blue Book*.

Telephone: Office: (608) 266-1627; District: (608) 238-5008; E-mail: Sen.Risser@legis.wisconsin.gov

Voting address: 100 Wisconsin Avenue, #501, Madison 53703.

Mailing address: Office: Room 220 South, State Capitol, P.O. Box 7882, Madison 53707-7882.

Representative
BERCEAU

Representative
BLACK

Representative
POCAN

Terese Berceau (Dem.), 76th Assembly District

Born Green Bay, August 23, 1950. B.S. UW-Madison 1973; graduate studies in urban and regional planning UW-Madison. Staff, UW-Madison Robert M. La Follette School; staff, Wis. Counties Assn.; real estate sales; substitute teacher. Member: Dane Co. Dem. Party; Planned Parenthood Advocates of Wisconsin. Former member: Monona Terrace Community and Convention Center Bd.; Greater Madison Convention and Visitors Bureau Bd. Recipient: Wis. Women's Network *Stateswoman of the Year* 2006; Wis. League of Conservation Voters *Conservation Champion* 2005-06; Wis. Council of the Blind *Legislator of the Year* 2005; Wis. Coalition Against Sexual Assault *Voices of Courage Award* 2005; Wis. Alliance of Cities *Urban Families Recognition* 2004; Clean Wisconsin Action Fund *Clean Sixteen Award* 2003-04; Domestic Abuse Intervention Services *Certificate of Recognition* 2004; Wis. Coalition Against Domestic Violence *"DV Diva" Award* 2003; Domestic Abuse Intervention Service *Public Service Award* 2002; National Alliance for the Mentally Ill – Dane County *Community Action Citizen Award* 2003. City of Madison Community Development Authority (chp. 1989-92); Dane Co. Bd. of Supervisors 1992-2000.

Elected to Assembly since 1998. Biennial committee assignments: **2009** — Urban and Local Affairs (chp.); Children and Families; Colleges and Universities; Insurance; Public Safety; Jt. Legislative Council.

Telephone: Office: (608) 266-3784; District: (608) 225-8193; E-mail: Rep.Berceau@legis.wisconsin.gov
Internet address: http://www.terese.org
Voting address: 4326 Somerset Lane, Madison 53711.
Mailing address: Office: Room 208 North, State Capitol, P.O. Box 8952, Madison 53708.

Spencer Black (Dem.), 77th Assembly District

Born May 25, 1950; married; 1 son. B.A. in economics and history Stony Brook University 1972; M.S. in urban and regional planning UW-Madison 1980; M.A. in public policy and administration UW-Madison 1981. Former conservationist, Sierra Club; curator of education, State Historical Society of Wisconsin; high school teacher. Recipient: League of Conservation Voters *Environmental Champion* 2008; Wis. Federation of Teachers *Legislator of the Year* 1999; Clean Water Action Council *Environmental Advocate of the Year* 1993; Midwest Renewable Energy Association *Environmental Excellence Award* 1992; Wis. Community Action Programs Assn. *Gaylord Nelson Human Service Award* 1991; Audubon Society *Environmentalist of the Year Award* 1990; The Nature Conservancy *President's Public Service Award* 1989; Wis. Wildlife Fed. *Legislator of the Year Award* 1988; Common Cause *Leadership Award* 1985.

Elected to Assembly since 1984. Minority Leader 2001 (eff. 5/1/01); Assistant Minority Leader 2001 (1/3/01 to 5/1/01). Biennial committee assignments: **2009** — Natural Resources (chp., also 1987-93, mbr. since 2003, 1997, 1995); Colleges and Universities (since 2003); Jt. Legislative Council (also 2001); Building Comn. (also 2003). **2007** — Jt. Com. for Review of Administrative Rules (also 2005, 1999); Public Health.

Telephone: Office: (608) 266-7521; District: (608) 233-0317; E-mail: Rep.Black@legis.wisconsin.gov
Voting address: 5742 Elder Place, Madison 53705.
Mailing address: Office: Room 210 North, State Capitol, P.O. Box 8952, Madison 53708.

Mark Pocan (Dem.), 78th Assembly District

Born Kenosha, August 14, 1964; married. Graduate Mary D. Bradford H.S. (Kenosha); B.A. UW-Madison 1986. Small businessperson. Member: American Civil Liberties Union; Colombia Support Network/Apartadó Sister City Organization; Clean Wisconsin; Painters and Allied Trades Union (AFL-CIO); Sierra Club; Fair Wisconsin; Southern Poverty Law Center. Former member: Big Brothers-Big Sisters. Recipient: Wis. Library Assn. *Public Policy Award* 2008; Wis. Coalition Against Sexual Assault *Voices of Courage Public Policy Award* 2008; Professional Fire Fighters of Wis. *Legislator of the Year* 2008; Wis. League of Conservation Voters *Conservation Honor Roll* 2008; Wis. AIDS Fund *Educate, Prevent, Protect* 2007; Wis. League of Conservation Voters *Conservation Champion* 2006; Wis. Counties Assn. *Outstanding Legislator Award* 2008, 2006; Clean Wisconsin *Clean 16 Award* 2004, 2002, 2000; ACLU *Special Recognition Award* 2001; Wis. Federation of Teachers State Employees Council *Representative of the Year* 2003, 2002. Dane Co. Board 1991-96.

Elected to Assembly since 1998. Biennial committee assignments: **2009** — Jt. Com. on Finance (co-chp., mbr. since 2003); Jt. Legis. Audit (also 2003); Jt. Com. on Employment Relations; Jt. Legislative Council (since 2005). **2007** — Corrections and the Courts (also 1999-2003). **2003** — Campaigns and Elections (also 2001); Colleges and Universities; Criminal Justice. **2001** — Environment; Ways and Means. **1999** — Consumer Affairs; Education; Labor and Employment.

Telephone: Office: (608) 266-8570; District: (608) 256-6214; E-mail: Rep.Pocan@legis.wisconsin.gov
Voting address: 309 North Baldwin Street, Madison 53703.
Mailing address: Office: Room 309 East, State Capitol, P.O. Box 8953, Madison 53708.

27th SENATE DISTRICT

See Madison Area Detail Map on pp. 90 & 91

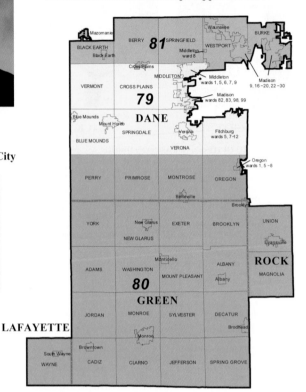

Senator
ERPENBACH

Detail Map: Middleton City

Jon B. Erpenbach (Dem.), 27th Senate District

Born Middleton, January 28, 1961; 2 children. Graduate Middleton H.S.; attended UW-Oshkosh 1979-81. Former communications director, legislative aide, radio personality, short order cook, meat packer, truck driver, and City of Middleton recreation instructor. Member: League of Women Voters; 1,000 Friends; NAACP; Wis. Farm Bureau; League of Conservation Voters; Monroe Optimists.

Elected to Senate 1998; reelected since 2002. Minority Leader 2003 session. Biennial committee assignments: **2009** — Health, Health Insurance, Privacy, Property Tax Relief, and Revenue (chp.); Jt. Survey Com. on Tax Exemptions (co-chp., also 2007); Commerce, Utilities, Energy, and Rail; Education (vice chp. 2007, mbr. 2005, 2001, 1999); Judiciary, Corrections, Insurance, Campaign Finance Reform, and Housing. **2007** — Health and Human Services (chp.); Campaign Finance Reform, Rural Issues and Information Technology (vice chp.); Transportation, Tourism and Insurance. **2005** — Agriculture and Insurance; Health, Children, Families, Aging and Long-Term Care. **2003** — Jt. Com. on Employment Relations; Jt. Com. on Legislative Organization; Senate Organization; Jt. Legis. Coun. (also 1999); Disability Bd.; Jt. Legis. Coun. Spec. Com. on Review of Open Records Law (co-chp. since 2001). **2001** — Privacy, Electronic Commerce and Financial Institutions (chp., also 1999); 2001-03 Biennial Budget; Health, Utilities, Veterans and Military Affairs (also 1999); Jt. Com. on Information Policy and Technology; Law Revision Committee (also 1999); Legis. Coun. Com. on Condominium Law Review (co-chp. since 1999). **1999** — Jt. Committee on Information Policy; Lambeau Field; Jt. Survey Committee on Retirement Systems; Census Education Bd.; Governor's Blue Ribbon Task Force on Passenger Rail.

Telephone: Office: (608) 266-6670; District: (888) 549-0027 (toll free).

E-mail: Sen.Erpenbach@legis.wisconsin.gov

Voting address: 6150 Briggs Road, Waunakee 53597.

Mailing address: Office: Room 8 South, State Capitol, P.O. Box 7882, Madison 53707-7882.

Representative	Representative	Representative
POPE-ROBERTS	**DAVIS**	**ROYS**

Sondy Pope-Roberts (Dem.), 79th Assembly District

Born Madison, April 27, 1950; widowed; one child. Graduate River Valley H.S.; attended Madison Area Technical College and Edgewood College. Former Associate Director of the Foundation for Madison's Public Schools. Member: Natl. Caucus of Environmental Legislators; Honorary Life Member, Wis. Congress of Parents and Teachers. Fellow, Bowhay Institute, La Follette School, UW-Madison 2003. Fellow, Flemming Institute, Center of Policy Alternatives 2007. Oakhill Correctional Institute Advisory Bd.; State Superintendent's Entrepreneurship Task Force (co-chp.).

Elected to Assembly 2002; reelected since 2004. Biennial committee assignments: **2009** — Education (chp., mbr. since 2003); Children and Families; Consumer Protection; Corrections and the Courts (since 2005); State Affairs and Homeland Security; Leg. Coun. Spec. Com. on School Safety. **2007** — Aging and Long-Term Care (since 2003); Education Reform. **2005** — Medicaid Reform. **2003** — Rural Affairs; Small Business.

Telephone: Office: (608) 266-3520; (888) 534-0079 (toll free); District: (608) 829-2750.

E-mail: Rep.Pope-Roberts@legis.wisconsin.gov

Voting address: 4793 Delmara Road, Middleton 53562.

Mailing address: Office: Room 209 North, State Capitol, P.O. Box 8953, Madison 53708.

Brett H. Davis (Rep.), 80th Assembly District

Born Oshkosh, December 5, 1975; married; 2 children. Graduate Monroe H.S. 1994; B.A. in business administration, UW-Oshkosh 1999. Former legislative aide to State Rep. Mike Powers, State Sen. Joe Leibham, and former Governor and U.S. Health and Human Services Secretary Tommy Thompson. Member: Oregon Area Chamber of Commerce (pres.); Oregon-Brooklyn Lions Club; Green Co. Local Emergency Planning Com.; Green Co. Conservation League; Friends of Cadiz Springs State Park; Monroe Noon Optimists; Monroe Kiwanis; Farm Bureau; Green, Rock, Dane Co. Republican Parties.

Elected to Assembly 2004; reelected since 2006. Biennial committee assignments: **2009** — Education (chp. 2007, mbr. 2005); Financial Institutions; Renewable Energy and Rural Affairs; Rural Economic Development. **2007** — Consumer Protection and Personal Privacy (vice chp.); Biofuels and Sustainable Energy; Energy and Utilities (vice chp. 2005); Transportation (also 2005). **2005** — Medicaid Reform.

Telephone: Office: (608) 266-1192; (888) 534-0080 (toll free); District: (608) 835-0939.

E-mail: Rep.Davis@legis.wisconsin.gov

Voting address: 1420 Ravenoaks Trail, Oregon 53575.

Mailing address: Office: Room 11 West, State Capitol, P.O. Box 8952, Madison 53708.

Kelda Helen Roys (Dem.), 81st Assembly District

Born Marshfield, June 24, 1979. Graduate Madison East H.S. 1997; B.A. *magna cum laude* NYU 2000; J.D. *magna cum laude* UW-Madison Law School 2004. Attorney. Former executive director NARAL Pro-Choice Wisconsin. Member TEMPO Madison; State Bar of Wisconsin; Legal Assn. for Women; Madison Repertory Theatre (bd. of dir.).

Elected to Assembly 2008. Biennial committee assignments: **2009** — Health and Healthcare Reform (vice chp.); Aging and Long-Term Care; Consumer Protection; Elections and Campaign Reform; State Affairs and Homeland Security.

Telephone: Office: (608) 266-5340; District: (608) 513-7697.

E-mail: Rep.Roys@legis.wisconsin.gov

Voting address: 2215 North Sherman Avenue, Madison 53704.

Mailing address: Office: 7 North, State Capitol, P.O. Box 8953, Madison 53708.

28th SENATE DISTRICT

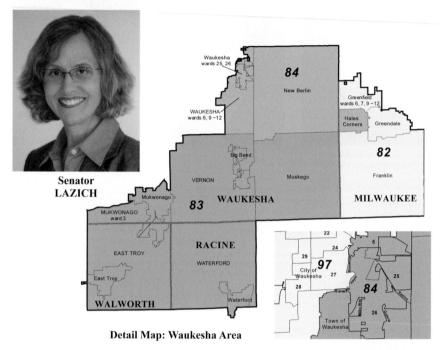

Senator LAZICH

Detail Map: Waukesha Area

See Milwaukee County Area Detail Map
on pp. 92 & 93

See Waukesha County Area Detail Map
on pp. 94 & 95

Mary A. Lazich (Rep.), **28th Senate District**

Born Loyal, October 3, 1952; married; 3 children. B.A. UW-Milwaukee, *summa cum laude*. Former county board supervisor and city council member. Member: Waukesha Co. Republican Party; Waukesha Co. Republican Women's Club; New Berlin Lioness; New Berlin Historical Society; Boy Scout Advisory Com., Potawatomi Area Council. Waukesha Co. Board supervisor 1990-93, and mbr. of its Legislative, Intergovernmental and Education Com., Health and Human Services Com., Transportation Com., and Community Development Block Grant Bd.; New Berlin City Council 1986-92 (former president, chm. of Finance Com., chm. of Board of Public Works, mbr. of Planning Commission and Crime Prevention Com.).

Elected to Assembly 1992-96 (resigned eff. 4/20/98); elected to Senate in April 1998 special election; reelected since 2000. Majority Caucus Chairperson 2003. Biennial Senate committee assignments: **2009** — Health, Health Insurance, Privacy, Property Tax Relief, and Revenue; Small Business, Emergency Preparedness, Technical Colleges, and Consumer Protection; Jt. Legis. Audit (also 2001, 1999, co-chp. 1997 eff. 4/21/98). **2007** — Education (also 2001, 1999); Health and Human Services; Judiciary and Corrections; Sentencing Comn. **2005** — Jt. Com. on Finance (also 2003); Labor and Election Process Reform; Women's Council (also 1999, 1997). **2003** — Jt. Com. on Administrative Rules; Energy and Utilities; Law Revision Com. (co-chp.). **2001** — Health, Utilities, Veterans and Military Affairs; Jt. Com. on Information Policy and Technology. **1999** — Council on Highway Safety. **1997** — Education and Financial Institutions; Government Effectiveness; State Government Operations and Corrections; Forward Wisconsin, Inc. Assembly committee assignments: **1997** — Jt. Legis. Audit (co-chp., also 1995); Working Families (vice chp.); Financial Institutions; Health (since 1993); Labor and Employment (also 1995). **1995** — Insurance, Securities and Corporate Policy; Urban Education (also 1993); Welfare Reform; Legis. Coun. Com. on Health Care Information. **1993** — Excise and Fees; Judiciary; Transportation; Legis. Coun. Com. on Child Care Economics.

Telephone: Office: (608) 266-5400; (800) 334-1442 (toll free); District: (414) 425-9452.

E-mail: Sen.Lazich@legis.wisconsin.gov

Voting address: 4405 South 129th Street, New Berlin 53151.

Mailing address: Office: Room 109 South, State Capitol, P.O. Box 7882, Madison 53707-7882.

| Representative | Representative | Representative |
| STONE | GUNDERSON | GUNDRUM |

Jeff Stone (Rep.), 82nd Assembly District

Born Topeka, KS, January 28, 1961; married. Graduate West Muskingum H.S. (Zanesville, OH); B.A. in political science and history, Washburn U. (Topeka) *magna cum laude* and Phi Kappa Phi 1983. Printing business owner. Member: Metro. Milwaukee Assn. of Commerce; Partners of Parks, Greenfield; Greenfield Chamber of Commerce (past secy.); Greendale Lions. Awards: Wis. Troopers Assn. *Legislator of the Year* 2007; Wis. Counties Assn. *Outstanding Legislator Award* 2005-06; TDA *Transportation Service Award* 2005; MMAC *Champion of Commerce* 2005-06; *Friend of YMCA of Metropolitan Milwaukee* 2006; Aggregate Producers of Wis. 2005; Wis. Builders Assn. *Friend of the Housing Industry* 2001-05; Milwaukee Co. Republican Party *Taxcutter of the Year* 2001; *Legislative Leadership National Com. Against Drunk Driving Award* 2000; Wisconsin Manufacturers and Commerce *Working for Wisconsin* 2004, 2002, 2000, 1998. Greenfield City Council 1994-98.

Elected to Assembly in April 1998 special election; reelected since November 1998. Biennial committee assignments: **2009** — Elections and Campaign Finance Reform; Health and Healthcare Reform; Transportation. **2007** — Jt. Com. on Finance (since 2003); Leg. Coun. Spec. Com. on Airport Authorities (chp.); Wis. Center District Bd. (eff 4/29/08). **2005** — University of Wis. Hospitals and Clinics Authority.

Telephone: Office: (608) 266-8590; (888) 534-0082 (toll free); District: (414) 529-1100.

E-mail: Rep.Stone@legis.wisconsin.gov

Voting address: 5535 Grandview Drive, Greendale 53129.

Mailing address: Office: Room 314 North, State Capitol, P.O. Box 8953, Madison 53708.

Scott L. Gunderson (Rep.), 83rd Assembly District

Born Burlington, October 24, 1956; married; 3 children. Graduate Waterford H.S. 1974. Small business owner and farmer. Member: Wind Lake Chamber of Commerce (past pres., vice pres.); Waterford Lions Club; Waterford FFA Alumni (past pres., vice pres.); St. Thomas Athletic Assn.; Wings Over Wis. (bd. mbr.); Ducks Unlimited (com. chairman); Pheasants Forever; Wis. Waterfowl Assn.; Racine Co. Farm Bureau; Racine Co. Fair (pres.). Former member: Waterford Chamber of Commerce (pres., vice pres.); Waterford Jaycees (pres., vice pres.); Waterford 4th of July Parade Com. Waterford Town Board 1991-95.

Elected to Assembly since 1994. Biennial committee assignments: **2009** — Fish and Wildlife; Natural Resources (chp. 2007, 2005, vice chp. 1999-2003, mbr. since 1995); Jt. Com. for Review of Administrative Rules (also 1995-2003). **2007** — Property Rights; Tourism, Recreation and State Properties; Urban and Local Affairs (also 2005, chp. 1997-2003); State Fair Park Bd. (since 2001). **2005** — Budget Review (vice chp., mbr. 2003); Tourism (also 2003). **2001** — Environment; Transportation; Wis. Coastal Management Council (since 1996). **1999** — Criminal Justice; Legis. Coun. Com. on Navigable Waters Recodification (co-chp.).

Telephone: Office: (608) 266-3363; (888) 534-0083 (toll free); District: (262) 534-2616.

E-mail: Rep.Gunderson@legis.wisconsin.gov

Voting address: 123 North 2nd Street, Waterford 53185.

Mailing address: Office: Room 7 West, State Capitol, P.O. Box 8952, Madison 53708; District: P.O. Box 7, Waterford 53185.

Mark Gundrum (Rep.), 84th Assembly District

Born Milwaukee, March 20, 1970; married; 6 children. Graduate Waukesha Catholic Memorial H.S. 1988; B.A. in economics and political science, graduated Phi Beta Kappa, UW-Madison 1992; J.D., Law Review, Moot Court, UW-Madison Law School 1994. Attorney. Judicial intern for Fed. Court of Appeals; prosecution intern for Outagamie Co. District Attorney's Office 1994; Staff attorney for Fed. District Judge, Eastern District of Wis. 1995-96; Army Officer Reserve Judge Advocate General Corps 2000-present. Member: State Bar of Wis.; Waukesha Co. Bar Assn. Hales Corners Village Board 1995-99.

Elected to Assembly since 1998. Assistant Majority Leader 2007; Majority Caucus Chairperson 2005. Biennial committee assignments: **2009** — Corrections and the Courts; Judiciary and Ethics (chp. 2007); Personal Privacy. **2007** — Elections and Constitutional Law; Assembly Organization; Rules; Jt. Com. on Legislative Organization; Uniform Law Comn. **2005** — Judiciary (chp.); Campaigns and Elections; Criminal Justice and Homeland Security; State Affairs; Jt. Legis. Coun. Spec. Com. on Sexually Violent Person Commitments; Criminal Justice Reforms Task Force (chp.). **2003** — Criminal Justice; Jt. Legis. Coun. Com. on Review of the Open Records Law (co-chp.).

Telephone: Office: (608) 267-5158; District: (414) 425-2556; E-mail: Rep.Gundrum@legis.wisconsin.gov

Internet address: www.legis.state.wi.us/assembly/asm84/news/

Voting address: 5239 South Guerin Pass, New Berlin 53151.

Mailing address: Office: Room 119 West, State Capitol, P.O. Box 8952, Madison 53708.

29th SENATE DISTRICT

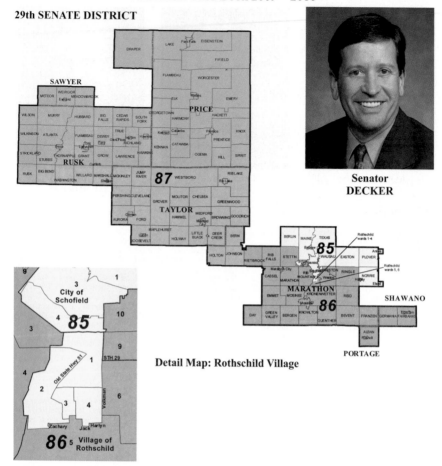

Senator
DECKER

Detail Map: Rothschild Village

Russell S. Decker (Dem.), **29th Senate District**

Born Athens, May 25, 1953. Graduate Athens H.S.; bricklayer apprenticeship graduate, Northcentral Technical College 1980. Full-time legislator and journeyman bricklayer. Member: Bricklayers Intl. Union; Marathon Co. Democratic Party; National Rifle Association; Friends of Rib Mountain; Rib Mountain Bowmen Archery Club. Former member: Central Wisconsin Building Trades (pres.); Boy Scouts of America (assistant Cub master); AFL-CIO Conservation Committee (secy./treas.); Bricklayers Joint Apprenticeship Committee.

Elected to Senate 1990; reelected since 1994. Majority Leader 2009, 2007 (eff. 10/24/07). Biennial committee assignments: **2009** — Senate Organization (also 2007 eff. 10/24/07); Jt. Legislative Council (since 2005); Jt. Com. on Employment Relations; Jt. Com. on Legislative Org. (also 2007 eff. 10/24/07); Jt. Survey Com. on Tax Exemptions (also 2007, 2003). **2007** — Jt. Com. on Finance (co-chp. through 11/5/07, mbr. 1995-11/5/07); Jt. Legis. Audit Com. **2005** — Job Creation, Economic Development and Consumer Affairs. **2003** — Labor, Small Business Development and Consumer Affairs. **2001** — Labor and Agriculture; Rural Economic Development Bd. (since 1991). **1999** — Labor. **1997** — Labor, Transportation and Financial Institutions (eff. 1/15/97 to 4/20/98); Human Resources, Labor, Tourism, Veterans and Military Affairs (eff. 4/21/98); Transportation, Agriculture and Rural Affairs (eff. 4/21/98).

Telephone: Office: (608) 266-2502; (877) 496-0472 (toll free); District: (715) 359-8739.

Voting address: (Village of Weston) 6803 Lora Lee Lane, Schofield 54476.

Mailing address: Office: Room 211 South, State Capitol, P.O. Box 7882, Madison 53707-7882.

Representative
SEIDEL

Representative
PETROWSKI

Representative
M. WILLIAMS

Donna J. Seidel (Dem.), 85th Assembly District

Born Neenah, August 6, 1950; married; 1 daughter, 2 stepchildren. Graduate Neenah H.S.; B.S. UW-Stevens Point 1972. Full-time legislator. Former clerk of courts; investigator for district attorney's office; police officer. Member: Marathon County Democratic Party; Wausau Noon Optimists Club. Former member: Northcentral Technical College (bd. of trustees); Wis. Assn. of Clerks of Circuit Court (legislative com. chair, past pres.); United Way of Marathon Co. (bd. of dir.); The Womens' Community (bd. of dir., pres.); YMCA (bd. of dir.). Recipient: Wis. County Treasurer's Assn. *Friend in the Legislature* 2008; Wis. Council of the Blind and Visually Impaired *Legislator of the Year* 2007; WCCO *Outstanding Legislator Award* 2008, 2006, *Legislator Rookie of the Year* 2005; Family Planning Health Services *Public Service Support of Reproductive Rights Award* 2006. Marathon Co. Clerk of Circuit Court 1989-2004.

Elected to Assembly 2004; reelected since 2006. Assistant Majority Leader 2009; Minority Caucus Secretary 2007. Biennial committee assignments: **2009** — Children and Families (vice chp.); Assembly Organization; Corrections and the Courts (since 2005); Health and Health Care Reform (also 2007); Rules; Workforce Development (also 2005); Jt. Com. on Legislative Organization; Child Abuse and Neglect Prevention Bd. (since 2005). **2007** — Children and Family Law; Legis. Coun. Spec. Com. on Strengthening Wisconsin Families. **2005** —Tourism.

Telephone: Office: (608) 266-0654; (888) 534-0085 (toll free); District: (715) 845-2988.
E-mail: Rep.Seidel@legis.wisconsin.gov
Voting address: 807 South 20th Street, Wausau 54403.
Mailing address: Office: Room 218 North, State Capitol, P.O. Box 8953, Madison 53708.

Jerry Petrowski (Rep.), 86th Assembly District

Born Wausau, June 16, 1950; married; 4 children. Graduate Newman H.S. (Wausau); attended UW-Marathon County and Northcentral Technical College. Former ginseng, dairy, and beef farmer. Served in Army Reserve 1968-74. Member: Marathon Co. and 7th District Republican Parties; Farm Bureau; Natl. Rifle Assn.; Friends of Rib Mountain; Marathon Lions. Former member: Wis. Rifle and Pistol Assn.; Internatl. Brotherhood of Electrical Workers Local #1791; Childcare Connection Bd.; DOT Law Enforcement Adv. Coun. Recipient: Wis. Housing Alliance *Outstanding Legislative Leader* 2006; UWSP Paper Science Foundation *Friends of the Foundation Award* 2005; Amer. Academy of Pediatrics *Childhood Legislator Advocate of the Year* 2005; Troopers Assn. *Legislator of the Year Award* 2003; Farm Bureau's *Friend of Agriculture Award* 2004; Wis. Vietnam Veterans' *Legislator of the Year Award* 2002.

Elected to Assembly since 1998. Majority Caucus Sergeant at Arms 2003-2007. Biennial committee assignments: **2009** — Renewable Energy and Rural Affairs; Transportation (chp. 2007, vice chp. 2001-05, mbr. 1999); Veterans and Military Affairs (also 2007, 1999-2003); **2007** — Rural Affairs; State Affairs (since 1999); Gov.'s Council on Highway Safety (since 2003). **2005** — Highway Safety (chp. since 2001); Agriculture (since 1999, vice chp. 1999); Military Affairs; Natural Resources. **2003** — Criminal Justice. **1999** — Small Business and Economic Development.

Telephone: Office: (608) 266-1182; (888) 534-0086 (toll free); District: (715) 845-6193.
E-mail: Rep.Petrowski@legis.wisconsin.gov
Voting address: (Town of Stettin) 720 North 136th Avenue, Marathon 54448-6193.
Mailing address: Office: Room 16 West, State Capitol, P.O. Box 8953, Madison 53708.

Mary Williams (Rep.), 87th Assembly District

Born Phillips, July 8, 1949; married; 3 children, 3 grandchildren. Graduate Phillips H.S. 1967; associate degree Taylor Co. Teachers Coll. 1969; B.S. elementary ed. UW-Stevens Point 1974. Restaurant owner. Former elementary teacher, Medford Area School Dist. Member: Farm Bureau; Dairy Promotion Com.; Dairy Breakfast Com.; Pri-Ru-Ta RC&D (pres.); Taylor Co. Safe & Stable Families; Wis. Restaurant Assn.; Natl. Fed. of Ind. Businesses; Chamber of Commerce; We Whittlesey Whizzers Snowmobile Club; Taylor Co. Local Emergency Planning Com. Former member: Big Brothers/Big Sisters of Taylor Co. (pres.); Restorative Justice of Taylor Co. (pres.); Intl. Trade, Business and Economic Development Council – Tourism Com. (chp.); Price Waterways Assn.; Taylor Co. Cooperative Youth Fair; WEAC; NEA. Recipient: Wis. Forestry Council *Distinguished Service Award* 2008; Wis. Bear Hunters *Hero Award;* Wis. Builders Assn. *Friend of Housing; Friend of Wis. Dairy Industry;* WCCO *Legislator of the Year* 2004, 2003; Natl. MS Society *Outstanding Volunteer Advocate* 2003. Taylor Co. Tourism Council. Taylor Co. Bd. 1992-96.

Elected to Assembly 2002; reelected since 2004. Minority Caucus Secretary 2009; Majority Caucus Secretary 2007. Biennial committee assignments: **2009** — Fish and Wildlife; Jobs, the Economy and Small Business; Personal Privacy; Rules (also 2007); Tourism, Recreation and State Properties (vice chp. 2007).

Telephone: Office: (608) 266-7506; (888) 534-0087 (toll free); District: (715) 748-5980.
E-mail: Rep.WilliamsM@legis.wisconsin.gov
Voting address: 542 Billings Avenue, Medford 54451.
Mailing address: Office: Room 17 West, State Capitol, P.O. Box 8953, Madison 53708.

30th SENATE DISTRICT

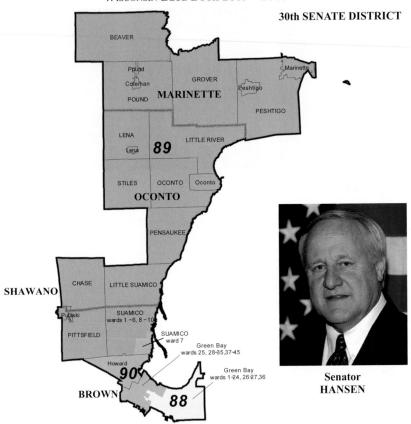

Senator
HANSEN

See Green Bay Area Detail Map on p. 96

Dave Hansen (Dem.), 30th Senate District

Born Green Bay, December 18, 1947; married; 3 children, 8 grandchildren. Graduate Green Bay West H.S.; B.S. UW-Green Bay 1971. Full-time legislator. Former teacher. Former truck driver for Green Bay Department of Public Works. Former Teamster's Union steward. Former member: Brown Co. Human Services Bd. (chp.); N.E.W. Zoo Advisory Bd.; Brown Co. Education and Recreation Com. (chp.); Great Lakes Compact Commission. Brown Co. Bd. Supervisor 1996-2002.

Elected to Senate 2000; reelected since 2004. Assistant Majority Leader 2009, 2007; Assistant Minority Leader 2005, 2003. Biennial committee assignments: **2009** — Education (since 2005); Senate Organization (since 2003); Transportation, Tourism, Forestry, and Natural Resources; Jt. Com. on Finance (vice co-chp. 2007); Jt. Com. on Legislative Organization (since 2003); Jt. Leg. Coun. Spec. Com. on State-Tribal Relations; Claims Bd.; Transportation Projects Commission (also 2001); Women's Council. **2007** — Commerce, Utilities and Rail; Transportation, Tourism and Insurance. **2005** — Agriculture and Insurance; Labor and Election Process Reform. **2003** — Jt. Legis. Audit (through 5/23/03); Agriculture; Financial Institutions and Insurance; Education, Ethics and Elections; Labor, Small Business Development and Consumer Affairs. **2001** — Labor and Agriculture (chp.); Jt. Com. for Review of Administrative Rules; Environmental Resources; Human Services and Aging; Universities, Housing, and Government Operations; Law Revision Committee; Unemployment Insurance Advisory Council (*ex officio* member).

Telephone: Office: (608) 266-5670; (866) 221-9395 (toll free); District: (920) 492-2200.

E-mail: Sen.Hansen@legis.wisconsin.gov

Voting address: 920 Coppens Road, Green Bay 54303.

Mailing address: Office: Room 18 South, State Capitol, P.O. Box 7882, Madison 53707-7882.

Representative
SOLETSKI

Representative
NYGREN

Representative
VAN ROY

Jim Soletski (Dem.), 88th Assembly District

Born Green Bay, October 7, 1948; 2 children. Graduate Preble H.S. (Green Bay) 1967; attended UW-Green Bay and UW-Stevens Point. Full-time legislator. Former nuclear utility industry worker. Member: Joshua. Former member: Parish council (vice pres. 2001-08); Parish school volunteer group; Parish board of education.

Elected to Assembly 2006; reelected 2008. Biennial committee assignments: **2009** — Energy and Utilities (chp., mbr. 2007); Consumer Protection (vice chp.); Elections and Campaign Reform (vice chp.); Colleges and Universities; Criminal Justice; Labor (eff. 4/13/09). **2007** — Small Business; Tourism, Recreation and State Properties.

Telephone: Office: (608) 266-0485; (888) 534-0088 (toll free); District: (920) 468-5921.

E-mail: Rep.Soletski@legis.wisconsin.gov

Voting address: 496 Menlo Park Road, Green Bay 54302.

Mailing address: Office: Room 307 West, State Capitol, P.O. Box 8953, Madison 53708.

John Nygren (Rep.), 89th Assembly District

Born Marinette, February 27, 1964; married; 3 children. Graduate Marinette H.S. 1982; attended UW-Marinette. Insurance and financial representative. Former restaurant owner and operator. Member: Jaycees (lifetime mbr., fmr. chapter, state, U.S. pres.); Marinette Kiwanis (fmr. pres.); Marinette Co. GOP (fmr. chm.). City of Marinette Recreation and Planning Bd. 2003-06.

Elected to Assembly 2006; reelected 2008. Biennial committee assignments: **2009** — Education (also 2007); Health and Health Care Reform (also 2007); Insurance (vice chp. 2007). **2007** — Jobs and the Economy.

Telephone: Office: (608) 266-2343; (888) 534-0089 (toll free); District: (715) 330-5402.

E-mail: Rep.Nygren@legis.wisconsin.gov

Voting address: 1224 Carney Boulevard, Marinette 54143.

Mailing address: Office: Room 127 West, State Capitol, P.O. Box 8953, Madison 53708.

Karl Van Roy (Rep.), 90th Assembly District

Born Green Bay, December 1, 1938. Graduate Premontre H.S. (Green Bay) 1957; B.A. in economics, St. Norbert Coll. (De Pere) 1961. Full-time legislator. Former restaurateur. Served in U.S. Army 1962-64. Member: Wis. Restaurant Assn. (bd. of dir., past pres.); Howard-Suamico Optimist Club (past pres. and Optimist International life member); Brown Co. Republican Party; N.E.W. Zoo Board; YMCA Partners in Youth. Former member: Howard-Suamico Business Assn.; Green Bay Chamber of Commerce; Brown Co. Corrections Bd. Recipient: Wis. Restaurant Assn. *Restaurateur of the Year* 1990.

Elected to Assembly 2002; reelected since 2004. Biennial committee assignments: **2009** — Corrections and the Courts; Jobs, the Economy and Small Business; Tourism, Recreation and State Properties (also 2007). **2007** — State Affairs (chp.); Insurance (since 2003); Small Business (chp. 2005, vice chp. 2003); Transportation (since 2003). **2005** — Highway Safety (also 2003); Tourism (also 2003).

Telephone: Office: (608) 266-0616; (888) 534-0090 (toll free); Fax: (608) 282-3690.

District: (920) 662-0804; Fax: (920) 662-0804.

E-mail: Rep.VanRoy@legis.wisconsin.gov

Voting address: 805 Riverview Drive, Green Bay 54303.

Mailing address: Office: Room 123 West, State Capitol, P.O. Box 8953, Madison 53708.

31st SENATE DISTRICT

Senator
VINEHOUT

See Eau Claire Area Detail Map on p. 97

Kathleen Vinehout (Dem.), 31st Senate District

Born Albany, NY, June 16, 1958; married; 1 child. B.S. with honors in education Southern Illinois U. 1980; M.P.H. St. Louis U. 1982; Ph.D. (health services research) St. Louis U. 1987; A.D. in agriculture, Lincolnland Community College 1992. Organic farmer. Former university professor, health care manager. Member: Wis. Farmers Union; Wis. Farm Bureau Federation (fmr. bd. mbr., Buffalo Co.); Alma Chamber of Commerce; Democratic Party of Buffalo Co. (chp.); Andrew Blackfoot American Legion Auxiliary Post 129. Former member: Buffalo Co. Agricultural Fair Assn. (bd. mbr.); American Federation of Teachers (treas., Local 4100); American Public Health Assn. Recipient: Wis. League of Conservation Voters *Conservation Champion* 2008; Wis. Assn. of PEG Channels *Friend of Access* 2008; Wis. Assn. of FFA *Honorary State FFA Degree* 2008; Pharmacy Soc. of Wis. *Legislator of the Year* 2008; Wis. Federation of Cooperatives *Friend of Cooperatives* 2008. Mississippi River Regional Planning Commission 2004-present.

Elected to Senate 2006. Majority Caucus Vice Chairperson 2009. Biennial committee assignments: **2009** — Agriculture and Higher Education (chp., also 2007); Jt. Legislative Audit Com. (co-chp.); Children, Families and Workforce Development; Economic Development; Public Health, Senior Issues, Long-Term Care, and Job Creation. **2007** — Health and Human Services (vice chp.); Economic Development, Job Creation, Family Prosperity and Housing; Judiciary and Corrections.

Telephone: Office: (608) 266-8546; (877) 763-6636 (toll free).

E-mail: Sen.Vinehout@legis.wisconsin.gov

Voting address: W1490 Cesler Valley Road, Alma 54610.

Mailing address: Office: Room 104 South, State Capitol, P.O. Box 7882, Madison 53707-7882.

| Representative | Representative | Representative |
| DANOU | RADCLIFFE | SMITH |

Chris Danou (Dem.), 91st Assembly District

Born Bloomington, IL, January 18, 1967; married; 2 children. Graduate Columbus H.S. (Marshfield) 1985; A.A. UW-Marshfield/Wood Co. 1987; B.A. with distinction UW-Madison 1989; M.A. international affairs The American U. (Washington, D.C.) 1991; M.S. natural resources UW-Stevens Point 1997. Full-time legislator. Former police officer, City of Onalaska. Member: Wis. Farm Bureau Fed.; Ducks Unlimited; National Farmers Union; Pheasants Forever; Trout Unlimited; The Nature Conservancy. Former member: Onalaska Professional Police Assn. (pres.); Wis. Professional Police Assn.

Elected to Assembly 2008. Biennial committee assignments: **2009** — Natural Resources (vice chp.); Agriculture; Fish and Wildlife; Renewable Energy and Rural Affairs.

Telephone: Office: (608) 266-7015; (888) 534-0091 (toll free); District: (608) 534-5016.

E-mail: Rep.Danou@legis.wisconsin.gov

Voting address: 23951 8th Street, Trempealeau 54661.

Mailing address: Office: Room 303 West, State Capitol, P.O. Box 8952, Madison 53708.

Mark A. Radcliffe (Dem.), 92nd Assembly District

Born Madison, June 20, 1971; married; 1 child. Graduate Black River Falls H.S. 1989; B.S. UW-Stevens Point 1993; J.D. Hamline U. School of Law 1997. Attorney. Village attorney, Alma Center 1999-present.

Elected to Assembly 2008. Biennial committee assignments: **2009** — Agriculture (vice chp.); Aging and Long Term Care; Education; Renewable Energy and Rural Affairs.

Telephone: Office: (608) 266-7461; (888) 534-0092 (toll free); District (715) 284-1234.

E-mail: Rep.Radcliffe@legis.wisconsin.gov

Voting address: 376 North 12th Street, Black River Falls 54615.

Mailing address: Office: Room 321 West, State Capitol, P.O. Box 8953, Madison 53708.

Jeff Smith (Dem.), 93rd Assembly District

Born Eau Claire, March 15, 1955; 2 children. Graduate Eau Claire North H.S. 1973. Owner of window cleaning business. Member: Kiwanis Club of Eau Claire; Eau Claire Area Chamber of Commerce; Eau Claire Parent Advisory Com. (fmr. chp.); Eau Claire Family Resource Center (bd. mbr.); UW Extension CPAG; Wis. Conservation Voters. Former member: Gov.'s Task Force for Educational Excellence; Wis. State PTA Bd.; Parent Leadership Corps, DPI; Wis. Alliance for Excellent Schools; Township Fire Dept. Bd. (vice pres.) 2001-07. Town of Brunswick chairperson 2001-07.

Elected to Assembly 2006; reelected 2008. Biennial committee assignments: **2009** — Elections and Campaign Reform (chp.); Colleges and Universities (vice chp., mbr. 2007); Financial Institutions (vice chp.); Education; Public Safety; Renewable Energy and Rural Affairs. **2007** — Rural Affairs.

Telephone: Office: (608) 266-0660; (888) 534-0093 (toll free).

E-mail: Rep.Smith@legis.wisconsin.gov

Voting address: S7747 Norrish Road, Eau Claire 54701.

Mailing address: Office: Room 111 North, State Capitol, P.O. Box 8953, Madison 53708; District: P.O. Box 8186, Eau Claire 54702-8186.

32nd SENATE DISTRICT

Senator
KAPANKE

Detail Map: Shelby Town

Daniel E. Kapanke (Rep.), 32nd Senate District

Born La Crosse, August 21, 1947; married; 4 children. Graduate Onalaska Luther H.S. 1965; B.S. UW-La Crosse 1975; M.E.P.D. UW-La Crosse 1987. Owner La Crosse Loggers baseball team. Former district sales manager Kaltenberg Seed Farms. Served in U.S. Marine Corps Reserve 1967-72; Wisconsin National Guard 1971-72, 1991-92. Former member: La Crosse Area Development Corporation (bd. mbr.); La Crosse Area Convention and Visitors Bureau (bd. mbr.); La Crosse Area Planning Committee (bd. mbr.). Town of Campbell Board 1981-87, 1997-2004.

Elected to Senate 2004; reelected 2008. Biennial committee assignments: **2009** — Agriculture and Higher Education (also 2007); Public Health, Senior Issues, Long-Term Care, and Job Creation; Rural Issues, Biofuels, and Information Technology. **2007** — Campaign Finance Reform, Rural Issues and Information Technology; Transportation, Tourism and Insurance. **2005** — Agriculture and Insurance (chp.); Energy, Utilities and Information Technology; Higher Education and Tourism; Natural Resources and Transportation; Jt. Legislative Council.

Telephone: Office: (608) 266-5490; (800) 385-3385 (toll free); District: (608) 782-3975.

E-mail: Sen.Kapanke@legis.wisconsin.gov

Voting address: 1610 Lakeshore Drive, La Crosse 54603.

Mailing address: Office: Room 3 South, State Capitol, P.O. Box 7882, Madison 53707-7882.

| Representative | Representative | Representative |
| HUEBSCH | SHILLING | NERISON |

Michael D. Huebsch (Rep.), 94th Assembly District

Born Milwaukee, July 19, 1964; married; 2 sons. Graduate Onalaska H.S. 1982; Oral Roberts U. 1982-87. Full-time legislator. Former marketing director and legislative assistant. Member: Onalaska Business Association; Greater La Crosse Area Chamber of Commerce; La Crosse Co. Republican Party (past treas.); UW-La Crosse Chancellor's Community Council; Holmen Rod and Gun Club. La Crosse Co. Board 1992-95.

Elected to Assembly since 1994. Speaker of the Assembly 2007; Majority Leader 2005. Biennial committee assignments: **2009** — Energy and Utilities; Financial Institutions (also 1999); Natural Resources. **2007** — Assembly Organization (chp., vice chp. 2005); Jt. Com. on Employment Relations (co-chp., mbr. 2005); Jt. Com. on Legislative Organization (co-chp., mbr. 2005); Rules (vice chp., chp. 2005); Jt. Legislative Council (also 2005). **2003** — Jt. Com. on Finance (since 2001). **2001** — Judicial Council (also 1999). **1999** — Judiciary and Personal Privacy (chp.); Family Law; Transportation; Ways and Means (since 1995); Special Com. on The Renovation of Lambeau Field; Child Abuse and Neglect Prevention Bd. (also 1997); Law Revision. **1997** — Children and Families (chp., mbr. 1995); Wis. Works Oversight (chp., eff. 12/19/97); Highways and Transportation; Legis. Adv. Com. to the Minn.-Wis. Boundary Area Comn. (also 1995). **1995** — Small Business and Economic Development; Welfare Reform.

Telephone: Office: (608) 266-0631; (888) 534-0094 (toll free); District: (608) 786-3512.

E-mail: Rep.Huebsch@legis.wisconsin.gov

Voting address: 419 West Franklin, West Salem 54669.

Mailing address: Office: Room 115 West, State Capitol, P.O. Box 8952, Madison 53708.

Jennifer Shilling (Dem.), 95th Assembly District

Born Oshkosh, July 4, 1969; married; 2 children. Graduate Buffalo Grove, IL H.S.; B.A. in political science and public administration, UW-La Crosse 1992. Former congressional aide and legislative aide. Member: UW-La Crosse Alumni Assn. (fmr. pres.); La Crosse Co. League of Women Voters; La Crosse Co. Democratic Party (former chp.); UW-La Crosse Chancellor's Community Council; Viterbo University Bd. of Advisors; Family and Children's Center Community Bd.; Wis. Technology Council; Riverfront La Crosse Community Advisory Bd. La Crosse Co. Bd. 1990-92.

Elected to Assembly 2000; reelected since 2002. Minority Caucus Sergeant at Arms 2005. Biennial committee assignments: **2009** — Health and Health Care Reform (also 2007); Rules; Jt. Com. on Finance. **2007** — Colleges and Universities (since 2003); Workforce Development; State of Wisconsin Building Commission (also 2005). **2005** — Financial Institutions (since 2001); Health (since 2001); Highway Safety (also 2003). **2003** — Insurance (also 2001). **2001** — Personal Privacy; Legis. Adv. Com. to the Minn.-Wis. Boundary Area Comn.

Telephone: Office: (608) 266-5780; (888) 534-0095 (toll free); District: (608) 788-9854.

E-mail: Rep.Shilling@legis.wisconsin.gov

Voting address: 2608 Main Street, La Crosse 54601.

Mailing address: Office: Room 320 East, State Capitol, P.O. Box 8953, Madison 53708.

Lee Nerison (Rep.), 96th Assembly District

Born La Crosse, July 31, 1952; married; 3 children. Graduate Viroqua H.S. 1970; UW-Madison Farm and Industry Short Course 1971. Farmer. Former dairy farmer. Member: Coon Valley Lions. Former member: Vernon Co-op Oil and Gas (bd. mbr., secretary); Viroqua FFA Alumni (reporter); Westby FFA Alumni; Church Council (vice pres., treasurer). Vernon Co. Board 1998-2006 (chairperson 2002-06).

Elected to Assembly 2004; reelected since 2006. Biennial committee assignments: **2009** — Agriculture (vice chp. 2007, mbr. 2005); Natural Resources (also 2007); Public Safety; Rural Economic Development. **2007** — Rural Affairs (chp.); Energy and Utilities (also 2005); Public Health. **2005** — Rural Affairs and Renewable Energy; Tourism.

Telephone: Office: (608) 266-3534; District: (608) 634-4562.

Voting address: S3035 County Road B, Westby 54667.

Mailing address: Office: Room 310 North, State Capitol, P.O. Box 8953, Madison 53708.

33rd SENATE DISTRICT

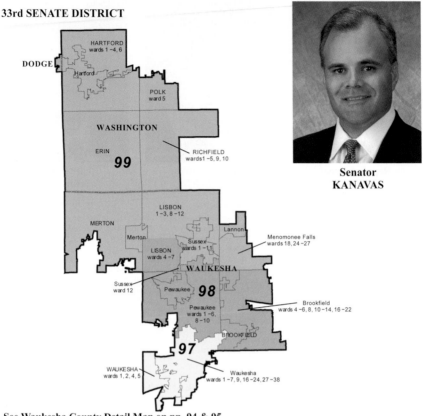

Senator
KANAVAS

See Waukesha County Detail Map on pp. 94 & 95

See Waukesha Area Detail Map on pp. 74 & 97

Theodore J. Kanavas (Rep.), 33rd Senate District

Born April 29, 1961; married; 3 children. Graduate Brookfield East H.S.; B.A. political science UW-Madison 1983; attended Pepperdine U. Law School. Co-founder, software company; senior software executive. Member: Orthodox Christian Charities of Wis. (bd. mbr.); Advisory Bd. for Entrepreneurship and Innovation in the College of Business at UW-Whitewater; Wis. Technology Council (bd. of dir.); Waukesha Co. Republican Party (former membership dir.); Washington Co. Republican Party; Order of Ahepa, Chap. 43 (scholarship com.); Annunciation Greek Orthodox Church; Elmbrook Historical Society; Greater Brookfield Chamber of Commerce; Hartford Area Chamber of Commerce; Multi-modal Transportation Review Com. 2006, 2004, 2002. Elmbrook School Board April 1999-2002.

Elected to Senate in July 2001 special election; reelected since 2002. Biennial committee assignments: **2009** — Economic Development; Health, Health Insurance, Privacy, Property Tax Relief, and Revenue; Rural Issues, Biofuels and Information Technology; Veterans and Military Affairs, Biotechnology and Financial Institutions (also 2007); Building Comn. (also 2007). **2007** — Campaign Finance Reform, Rural Issues and Information Technology; Economic Development, Job Creation, Family Prosperity and Housing; Health and Human Services; Jt. Leg. Coun. Spec. Com. on Charter Schools; State Fair Park Bd. (also 2003). **2005** — Job Creation, Economic Development and Consumer Affairs (chp.); Labor and Election Process Reform; Jt. Survey Com. on Tax Exemptions; Veterans, Homeland Security, Military Affairs, Small Business and Government Reform; Wis. Housing and Economic Development Authority; Jt. Leg. Council Spec. Com. on Wisconsin's Transportation Infrastructure (chp.). **2003** — Jt. Com. on Finance; Health, Children, Families, Aging and Long Term Care (vice chp.); Transportation and Information Infrastructure (vice chp.); Jt. Legislative Council Spec. Com. on Public and Private Broadband; Governor's Council on Highway Safety; Special Select Com. on Job Creation (co-chp.); Senate Select Com. on State and Local Government Relations; Statewide Multi-modal Improvement Program (proj. review com. mbr.). **2001** — Education; Privacy, Electronic Commerce and Financial Institutions; Human Services and Aging; Governor's Task Force on Financial Education; Governor's Council on Workforce Development.

Telephone: Office: (608) 266-9174; (800) 863-8883 (toll free).

E-mail: Sen.Kanavas@legis.wisconsin.gov

Voting address: 17570 Sierra Lane, Brookfield 53045.

Mailing address: Office: Room 106 South, State Capitol, P.O. Box 7882, Madison 53707-7882.

| Representative | Representative | Representative |
| KRAMER | ZIPPERER | PRIDEMORE |

Bill Kramer (Rep.), 97th Assembly District

Born Waukesha, January 21, 1965; single. Graduate Waukesha South H.S. 1983; B.B.A. in accounting, *magna cum laude,* UW-Whitewater 1987; J.D. Duke U. School of Law 1994. Certified financial planner, attorney, and certified public accountant. Member: Waukesha Elks; Free and Accepted Mason; Waukesha Chamber of Commerce; St. Mary's Parish; Waukesha Co. Republican Party. Waukesha Co. Board 1998-99, 2004-07.

Elected to Assembly 2006; reelected 2008. Biennial committee assignments: **2009** — Criminal Justice (also 2007); Financial Institutions (also 2007); Judiciary and Ethics (vice chp. 2007); Jt. Legis. Audit. **2007** — Aging and Long-Term Care; Elections and Constitutional Law; Insurance.

Telephone: Office: (608) 266-8580; District: (262) 546-4603.

Voting address: 2005 Cliff Alex Court South, #3, Waukesha 53189.

Mailing address: Office: Room 18 West, State Capitol, P.O. Box 8952, Madison 53708.

Rich Zipperer (Rep.), 98th Assembly District

Born Green Bay, April 16, 1974; married; 2 children. Graduate Reedsville Public H.S. 1992; B.A. St. Norbert College (De Pere) 1996; M.A. The George Washington University (Washington, D.C.) 2000; J.D. Georgetown University Law Center 2008. Attorney. Former deputy chief of staff to Cong. James Sensenbrenner. Member: Brookfield Optimists; Pewaukee Chamber of Commerce; State Bar of Wisconsin; Waukesha Co. Republican Party; Whitetails Unlimited; St. Anthony on the Lake Catholic Church.

Elected to Assembly 2006; reelected 2008. Biennial committee assignments: **2009** — Energy and Utilities; Jobs, the Economy and Small Business; Judiciary and Ethics; Jt. Survey Com. on Tax Exemptions. **2007** — Jt. Com. for Review of Administrative Rules (vice chp.); Colleges and Universities; Health and Health Care Reform; Workforce Development.

Telephone: Office: (608) 266-5120; District: (262) 695-8883.

E-mail: Rep.Zipperer@legis.wisconsin.gov

Voting address: N24 W26419 Bucks Island Court, Pewaukee 53072.

Mailing address: Office: Room 307 North, State Capitol, P.O. Box 8953, Madison 53708.

Don Pridemore (Rep.), 99th Assembly District

Born Milwaukee, October 20, 1946; married; 3 sons. Graduate Milwaukee Lutheran H.S. 1964; B.S.E.E. Marquette U. 1977. Full-time legislator. Former electronics research technician, electronics design engineer, senior electronics project engineer, and amateur ABATE chili judge. Vietnam Era veteran; served in U.S. Air Force 1965-69. Member: Hartford Lions; Hartford Area Taxpayers Assn. (com. mbr., fmr. pres.); Greater Hartford Optimists Club (charter bd. mbr.); Land-O-Hills Baseball League (commissioner); Erin Baseball Club (pres.); Washington and Waukesha Co. Republican Party; American Legion; VFW; NRA; Senior Friends (Hartford). Former member: IEEE; Wis. Citizens for Legal Reform (st. dir.); BSA Troop 741 (former ASM). Erin Park Bd. 1995-present.

Elected to Assembly 2004; reelected since 2006. Biennial committee assignments: **2009** — Children and Families; Education Reform (chp. 2007, mbr. 2005); Elections and Campaign Reform. **2007** — Children and Family Law (vice chp.); Judiciary and Ethics; Urban and Local Affairs (vice chp. 2005); Ways and Means (also 2005); Workforce Development (also 2005). **2005** — Budget Review.

Telephone: Office: (608) 267-2367; (888) 534-0099 (toll free); Fax: (608) 282-3699; District: (262) 670-0638.

E-mail: Rep.Pridemore@legis.wisconsin.gov

Voting address: 2277 Highway K, Hartford 53027.

Mailing address: Office: Room 318 North, State Capitol, P.O. Box 8953, Madison 53708.

Robert J. Marchant: Senate Chief Clerk

Born Green Bay, April 1, 1971; married; 2 children. Graduate East De Pere H.S. 1989; B.S. UW-Madison 1994; J.D. UW-Madison 1997. Chief clerk and director of operations, Wisconsin Senate. Former attorney Wis. Legislative Reference Bureau; Bender, Levi and Marchant S.C. Member: American Society of Legislative Clerks and Secretaries (secy./treas.); State Bar of Wisconsin.

Elected Senate Chief Clerk 1/20/04; reelected since 2005.

Telephone: Office: (608) 266-2517.

Voting address: City of Watertown.

Mailing address: Office: Room B20 Southeast, State Capitol, P.O. Box 7882, Madison 53707-7882.

Edward (Ted) A. Blazel: Senate Sergeant at Arms

Born Quincy, IL, June 14, 1972; married; 2 children. Graduate Quincy Senior H.S. 1990; B.A. St. Norbert College (De Pere) 1994; M.A. Marquette U. (Milwaukee) 1998. Former legislative aide. Member: National Legislative Service and Security Assn. (3rd trustee); Heritage Heights Community Assn. (pres.).

Elected Senate Sergeant at Arms 2003; reelected since 2005.

Telephone: Office: (608) 266-1801.

Voting address: 5301 Knightsbridge Road, Madison 53714.

Mailing address: Office: Room B35 South, State Capitol, P.O. Box 7882, Madison 53707-7882.

Patrick E. Fuller: Assembly Chief Clerk

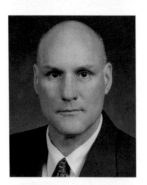

Born Toledo, OH, February 24, 1954; married; 1 child. Graduate St. Francis de Sales H.S. (Toledo) 1972; B.E. U. of Toledo 1980; M.B.A. Touro University International (Los Alamitos, CA) 2001. Former director Wisconsin Troops to Teachers Program, Wis. Dept. of Veterans Affairs 1998-2000. Vietnam Era and Operation Desert Storm veteran. Served in U.S. Marine Corps 1972-86; U.S. Army 1986-97. Member: NRA; Second Marine Division Assn.; Veterans of Foreign Wars; Disabled Veterans of America; American Legion; Force Recon Association; 75th Ranger Regiment Association.

Elected Assembly Chief Clerk 2003; reelected since 2005.

Telephone: Office: (608) 266-5811; E-mail address: Patrick.Fuller@legis.wisconsin.gov

Voting address: 214 Grove Street, Ridgeway 53582.

Mailing address: Office: Suite 401, 17 West Main Street, Risser Justice Center, Madison 53708-8952.

William M. Nagy: Assembly Sergeant at Arms

Born Plainfield, NJ, January 22, 1966; single. Graduate Altoona H.S. 1984; B.A. in Criminal Justice, UW-Eau Claire 1989. Former political consultant; analyst, Assembly Democratic Caucus; legislative assistant, Wis. Senate; automotive industry consultant; assistant fiscal, records, and journal clerk, Wis. Senate; messenger, Wis. Senate. Member: American Society of Legislative Clerks and Secretaries.

Elected Assembly Sergeant at Arms 2009.

Telephone: Office: (608) 266-1503.

E-mail address: bill.nagy@legis.wisconsin.gov

Voting address: 3139 South Seminole Highway, Fitchburg 53711.

Mailing address: Office: Room 411 West, State Capitol, P.O. Box 8953, Madison 53708.

SENATE DISTRICTS

Promulgated by the U.S. District Court
for the Eastern District of Wisconsin
May 30, 2002

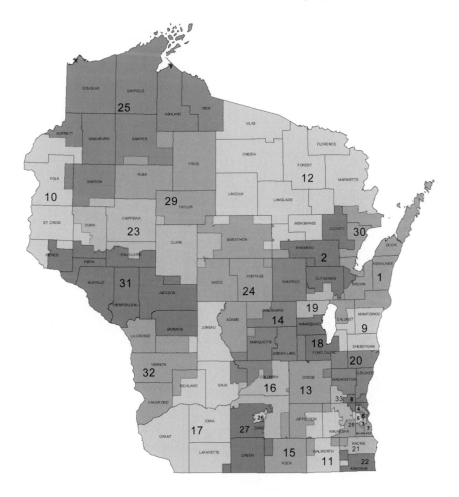

ASSEMBLY DISTRICTS

Promulgated by the U.S. District Court
for the Eastern District of Wisconsin
May 30, 2002

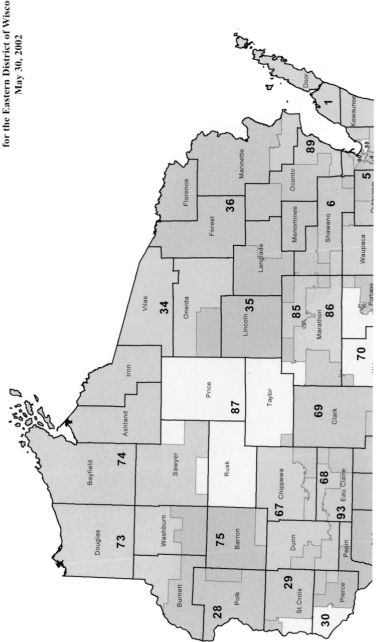

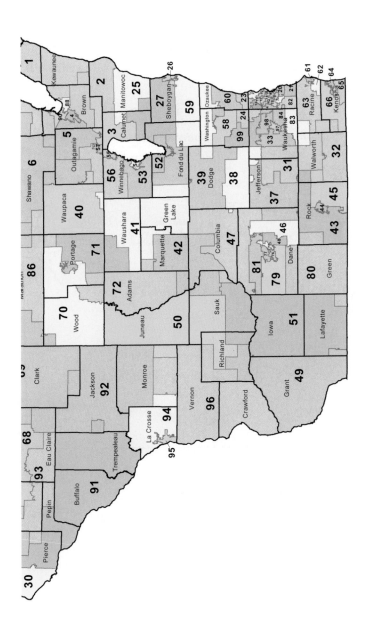

Detail Map: Madison Area

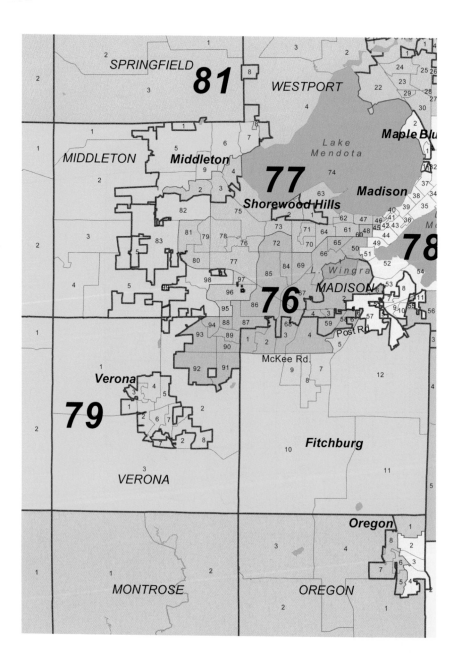

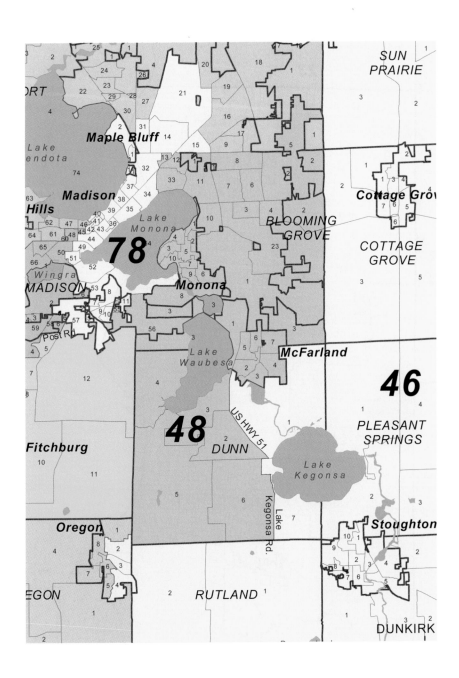

Detail Map: Milwaukee Area (North)

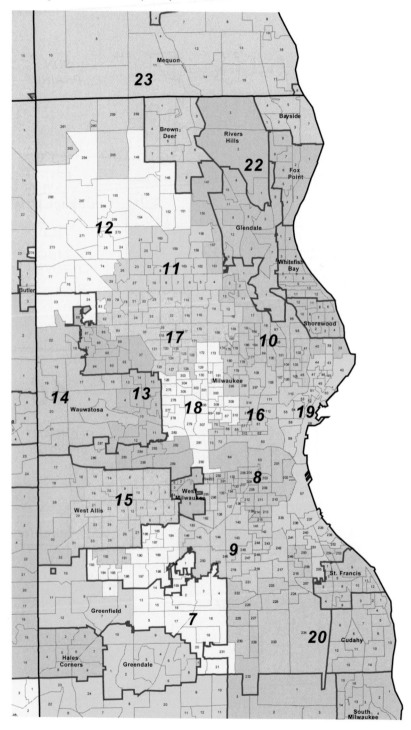

Detail Map: Milwaukee Area (South)

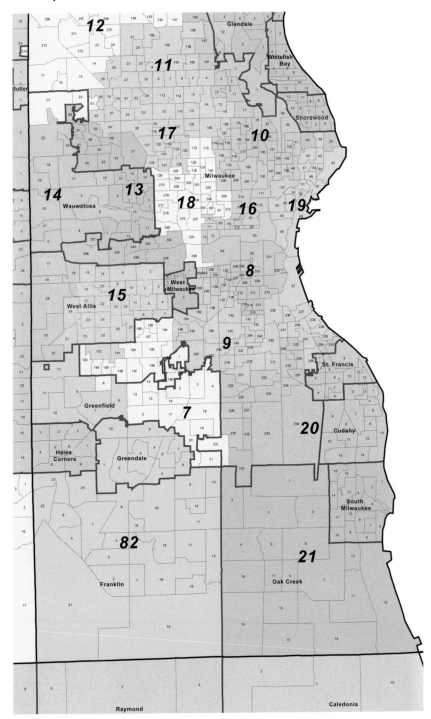

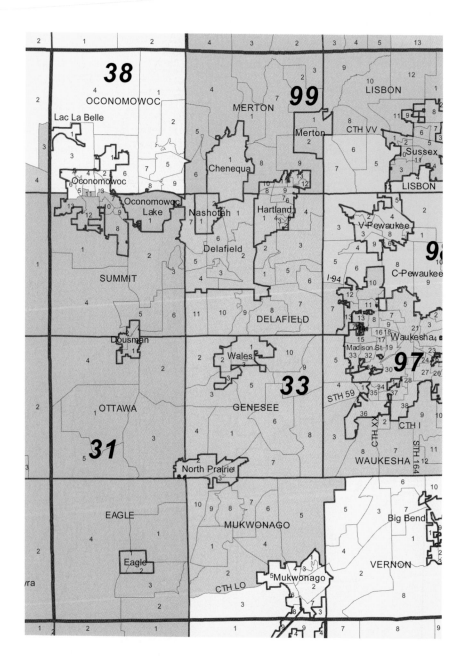

Detail Map: Waukesha County (East)

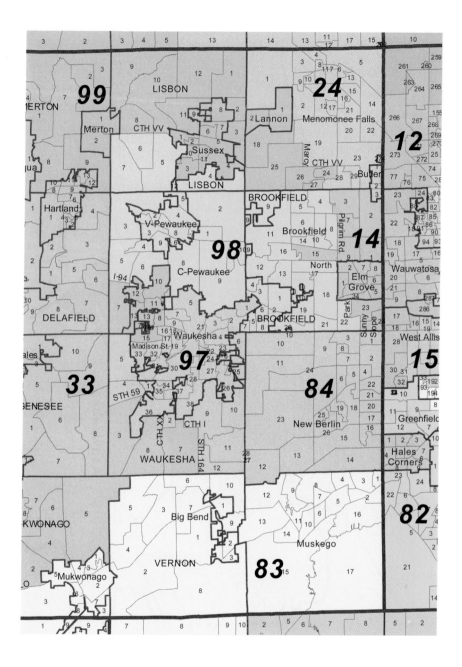

Detail Map: Green Bay Area

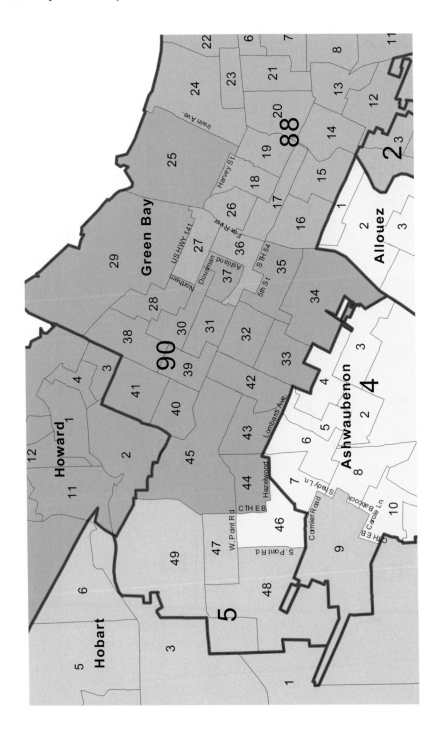

Detail Map: Eau Claire Area

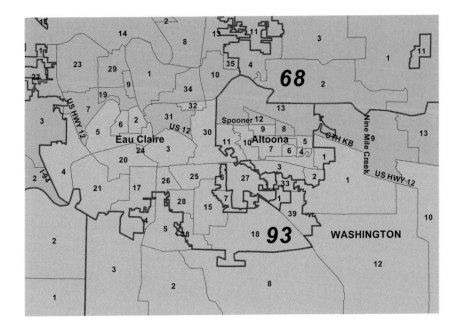

Detail Map: Waukesha Area

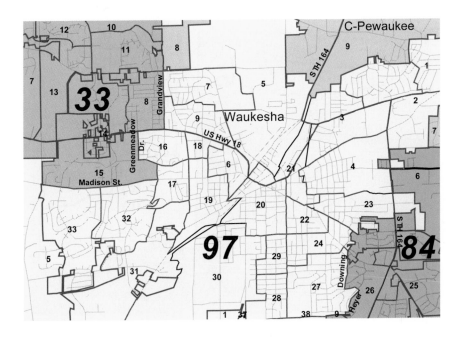

Detail Map: Sheboygan Area

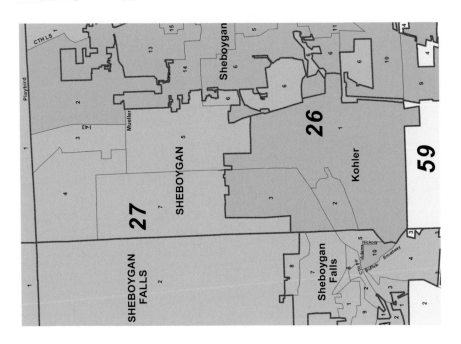

Detail Map: Appleton Area

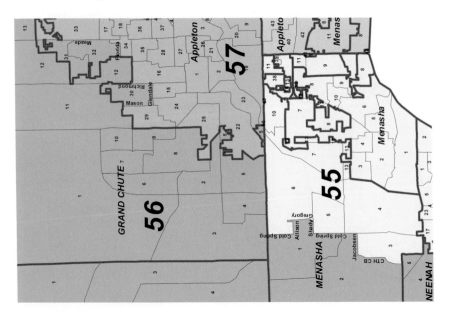

Feature
Article

Wisconsin at the Frontiers of Astronomy:
A History of Innovation and Exploration

Collage of NASA/Hubble Images

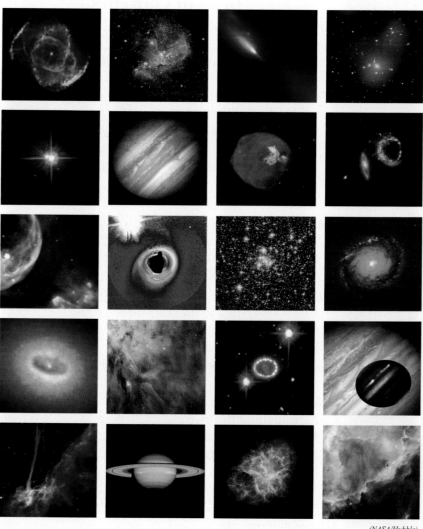

(NASA/Hubble)

Wisconsin at the Frontiers of Astronomy: A History of Innovation and Exploration

by Peter Susalla & James Lattis
University of Wisconsin-Madison

Graphic Design by Kathleen Sitter, LRB

Table of Contents

Wisconsin at the Frontiers of Astronomy: A History of Innovation and Exploration

Introduction

Few residents of Wisconsin know that their state ranks as one of the leaders in the world of astronomy today, and fewer still are aware that this was true 128 years ago as well. Astronomy was one of the earliest scientific fields in which the growth of the University of Wisconsin took root, with the result that it has blossomed into one of the world's leading research universities. Wisconsin astronomy is famous for historic telescopes, major astronomical discoveries, great technological developments, and as a place where talent is recognized, nurtured, and frequently transplanted to other parts of the world as our young researchers find other fields to plow. Wisconsin is one of the places where traditional astronomy gave birth to the modern science of astrophysics and was, as it still is, home to pivotal figures who create the scientific institutions that deliver the astronomy of the future.

This history of Wisconsin's astronomers and the early emergence of world-class astronomy in the American Midwest shows that excellence in academic research drives excellence in education, a truth that was recognized early by Cadwallader Washburn, former governor and observatory benefactor, and some of his forward-looking contemporaries who took it to heart and invested their hard won fortunes in it. They saw the novel concept of a "research university," which was showing considerable promise and success in Europe, as an important example for the young universities of the growing United States. Perhaps less apparent to them at the time, but well born out by the history of science in the late nineteenth and early twentieth centuries, is that academic research drives innovation in science, and new science is a powerful force in technological development, which in turn is a strong foundation for economic success. It is an admirable example of the real power of ideas. Astronomy played a major role in establishing Wisconsin as more than abundant forests, fertile farmland, and a staging area for long treks across the frontier of the American West. In fact, Wisconsin became a geographical fulcrum in the development of American astronomy, which as early as the 1890s was dominated by institutions on the two coasts. Connections between our own Washburn Observatory and California's Lick Observatory are only the most obvious of the connections made in Wisconsin that contributed greatly to the growth of astronomy in the U.S. and, especially after World War II, the global astronomical community.

This historical account of the contributions of our state to the development of astronomy is necessarily very selective. We have attempted to include the most important aspects that illuminate the development of astronomy in Wisconsin as well as the major contributions the state has made to the science and institutions of astronomy more generally. Although much of this study necessarily focuses on the University of Wisconsin, we have attempted to widen the scope enough to indicate that astronomy's story in Wisconsin extends from well before statehood and well beyond Madison. In fact, although created and operated by the University of Chicago, we claim the Yerkes Observatory in Williams Bay as also a Wisconsin institution and argue for Wisconsin's contribution to its worldwide fame and success. It is inevitable that many important and interesting stories will be passed over, and to this we can only respond with the hope that other authors will work to rectify our reluctant omissions. We have also attempted to convey the scientific content and significance of the history with a minimum of technical details. A fuller accounting would benefit from deeper exploration of the science at the root of these stories, but for the purposes here we refer the interested reader instead to the sources listed in the bibliography.

Early Days

American Indian Traditions and the Prehistory of Wisconsin Astronomy

The first human inhabitants of what is now Wisconsin were also the first to think about the cosmos and to make meaning out of what they saw in the sky. Unfortunately, little is known about the cultures that lived in present-day Wisconsin for over 11,000 years before the arrival of the first Europeans.

One American Indian culture, dubbed the Mississippian culture by archaeologists, flourished from around 1000 to 1400 A.D. along the Mississippi River in what is now southern Illinois with some settlements in modern Wisconsin. One of the best known Mississippian settlements is located in Wisconsin's Aztalan State Park, near Lake Mills between Madison and Milwaukee. The Mississippian culture may have practiced what looks to us like "astronomy" in the sense of building instruments to mark the motions of heavenly bodies. However, we must be very careful when assigning intent to a culture that existed centuries ago and left behind no written records. Near the Mississippians' largest settlement, the city now called Cahokia (in southwestern Illinois), the Mississippians constructed a number of structures that have been dubbed "woodhenges." These woodhenges consisted of a number of wooden posts set upright in the ground in the shape of a circle. When viewed from the center of this circle, the rising (or setting) sun appears to line up with one of these posts on particular days of the year. Archaeologists believe that these structures served as physical calendars to alert Mississippian priests about important ceremonial days, although there is no evidence that Mississippians used woodhenges to understand or to predict the motion of the sun systematically.

Related to the Mississippian culture was the succeeding Effigy Mound culture, which flourished almost entirely within present-day Wisconsin. The Effigy Mound culture was named for the thousands of elaborate and sometimes enormous mounds that were built in the shapes of animals, including lizards, panthers, bears, and birds. Many of these mounds contain human remains and thus likely served important ceremonial and funerary functions. However, the unique shapes of these

Bird-shaped effigy mound located near the Washburn Observatory on the UW-Madison campus. (UW-Madison Archives)

mounds have raised many questions about their exact purpose. Archaeologists and anthropologists speculate that the mounds may also have been offerings that reflected a desire for stability and renewal during a period of unsettling social change for the Mound Builders. The shapes of the mounds and the animals that they represent are thought to be related to important realms of the physical world and thus also form a picture of the Mound Builders' "universe:" lizard- and panther-shaped mounds were related to water and are frequently found along lakeshores and river-banks, bear mounds represent the land or the earth, while bird mounds, often found on hilltops or areas of higher elevation, represent air or the sky. If the builders were thinking of the sky while constructing some of these bird-shaped effigies, it is perhaps appropriate that a bird mound sits adjacent to the Washburn Observatory in Madison, the first permanent astronomical observatory of the Effigy Mound culture's European-descended successors. It is also painfully ironic that another mound was destroyed in the construction of this observatory.

As with the Mississippian woodhenges, some researchers have suggested that the effigy mounds show alignments with rising and setting points of the sun, moon, and certain stars. In addition to the animal-shaped mounds, there are also a large number of "linear" mounds across Wisconsin, the purpose or meaning of which is not understood. It is possible that these linear mounds had some relationship with particular astronomical phenomena. Nevertheless, without compelling evidence that effigy mounds served this supposed observational purpose, we should resist the temptation to see them as such. Instead, we should understand the mounds as their builders seem to have intended: important ceremonial sites and representations of key realms of their physical and spiritual world.

The sky also figures into the cultures of the American Indians who occupied Wisconsin when the first Europeans arrived, including the Ho-Chunk and Menominee tribes. Numerous stories survive from these cultures that incorporate the sun, moon, and stars, often in creation narratives that relate Earth, sky, humans, animals, and spirits. Consider this Ho-Chunk legend about the origin of the phases of the moon.

"The Moons"

A long, long time ago, the good spirits and the bad ones divided things among themselves, but sometimes they did not agree, for the evil spirits wanted too much; they were selfish. One day they all held a council to decide how long the seasons should be. The Wild Turkey strutted out before all the others, spreading his tail feathers. He said that the year should have as many moons in it as there were spots on his tail feathers.

But the councilors said that would be much too long. Then the Partridge strutted out as had the Turkey, and wanted as many moons, or months, as there were spots in his tail. But the spirits said that his tail was too large, also, and had too many spots.

Then the little Chipmunk ran out into a sunny spot among them … In his squeaky little voice he suggested that every year have as many moons as there are stripes on his back. There were, as you know, six yellowish-white stripes and six black ones. The councilors said they guessed that it would be about right to have 12 moons, or months, every year, and that the white stripes could be the winter months, and the black stripes the summer months …

When the moon is full, the evil spirits begin to nibble at it, to put out its light, for the evil spirits like the darkness best. Each night they eat away a part of the moon, until in two weeks it is gone. But the Great Spirit will not permit them to take advantage of the darkness to go about the world doing mischief, so he makes a new moon. He makes a little of it each night for the next two weeks until finally a big new moon hangs in the sky again. Then he rests, and the evil spirits begin all over again.

(Oliver La Mere and Harold B. Shinn, Winnebago Stories *(New York: Rand McNally, 1928): 91-99.)*

Tribes such as the Ho-Chunk continue to tell stories such as these today, and they remain an important part of Wisconsin culture as a whole. Although the rest of this article focuses on the history of the 150 years of astronomy as Wisconsin's European-descended occupants practiced it, we would do well to remember that inhabitants of Wisconsin have been thinking about the cosmos for millennia.

The European Tradition: Astronomy and Higher Education at the University of Wisconsin

Astronomy in the European tradition likely entered Wisconsin with the first French explorers in the seventeenth century, as a basic understanding of astronomy was essential to safe navigation. Astronomy in such practical forms continued to play an important role in the development of Wisconsin through the eighteenth and nineteenth centuries. For instance, surveyors used astronomical techniques to determine a given location's latitude and longitude. These skills were necessary for mapping and parceling the territory that had been added to the United States after the Revolutionary War. However, organized astronomical research was effectively absent from the Wisconsin Territory, developing only with the growth of the new university that was created after Wisconsin attained statehood in 1848.

The history of astronomy at the University of Wisconsin began almost immediately after the university's founding in 1849. Its first faculty member was John Sterling, who held the title Professor of Mathematics, Natural Philosophy, and Astronomy. By 1854, all UW undergraduates were required to complete at least one term of astronomy as part of a fixed curriculum that mixed the sciences with classical languages, philosophy, and literature. Although this "classical curriculum" is often portrayed as stodgy and outdated, UW graduates in the nineteenth century had a greater literacy in astronomy than an average student of today. However, for the first three decades of the university, astronomy remained a classroom exercise: UW possessed no astronomical instruments, nor did it have an observatory.

As expensive, elaborate, and highly visible sites of scientific research, observatories in the nineteenth century served not only as places for teaching and making new discoveries, but also as symbols of prestige for new colleges and universities in the expanding United States. The UW Regents believed from the beginning that an observatory would be essential to the school's educational mission. When the university

John W. Sterling
(UW-Madison Archives)

campus was designed in the early 1850s, plans called for a central building "surmounted by an observatory for astronomical observations." Because of a lack of funds, this observatory was never incorporated into the building known today as Bascom Hall. The Board of Regents continued to discuss the need for an observatory throughout the 1860s and 1870s, arguing in 1875 "[I]n this age, an astronomical observatory is one of the characteristic and essential features of every educational institution of this order. It is scarcely possible to conceive of a university worthy of the title, where professors and attendants are denied this necessary instrumentality in the promotion of the interesting and progressive study of astronomical science." Other nearby schools, such as the University of Michigan and the Old University of Chicago (which existed from 1857 to 1886 and was succeeded by another university of the same name) had recently acquired observatories with large telescopes, both of which wealthy private citizens had funded. The Wisconsin Regents were no doubt very aware of these facts and clearly believed that their university was lagging behind in a nationwide movement to develop the practice and teaching of science within higher education.

The Birth of the Washburn Observatory, 1877-1880

Funding for Wisconsin's first major observatory did not materialize until 1877. During the previous year, the Wisconsin Legislature passed a resolution providing a salary for a new professor of astronomy at the university provided that some wealthy patrons donate an observatory. This patron, who had in fact helped to craft the legislation behind the scenes, was Cadwallader C. Washburn. Washburn was a former U.S. Representative, Civil War general, and governor of Wisconsin from 1872 to 1874, and thus had a strong political presence. Washburn had made his fortune in the flour-milling industry; his Minneapolis-based mills served as the foundation for the company known today as General Mills. As Washburn never revealed any strong interest in astronomy, it is not clear why he chose to give the university an observatory, although he likely knew some basic astronomical skills from an early career as a land surveyor. It is most likely that Washburn was influenced by the trend of other wealthy individuals who were donating money to build large observatories across the United States. One such patron was James Lick, who bequeathed money in 1876 to build the world's largest observatory outside of San Jose, California. Lick's observatory was built both to further the practice of science in America and also as a monument to himself (Lick was later buried at the base of his observatory's main telescope).

In addition to the donation of an observatory building and instruments, the University of Wisconsin also received an endowment from Washburn's friend and business partner Cyrus Woodman to support an astronomical library. The Woodman Fund (which still exists despite being severely diminished during the Great Depression) was significant for several reasons. First, it provided the observatory with the essential texts and journals necessary for any effective scientific research institution of the era, a seemingly mundane yet very significant resource. Second, it allowed for the purchase of many old texts that strengthened the university's rare book collection in later years. Finally, and most important, the Woodman Library earned a

Cadwallader Colden Washburn (1818-1882), governor of Wisconsin (1872-1874) and founder of the Washburn Observatory. (UW-Madison Archives)

prestigious reputation among astronomers across the United States for the depth and quality of its holdings. The observatory became a node in an information exchange that connected it to other observatories and institutions not only across the U.S., but also around the world.

Construction of the new Washburn Observatory began in 1878 on a small hill, now appropriately known as Observatory Hill, west of campus and about a mile from the State Capitol. Flanked by brushy woodland on the north, sloping down to Lake Mendota, and by farmland and orchards on the south slopes, the observatory site was adequately remote from town and campus. Edward Holden, Washburn's second director, who edited the first volumes of the *Publications of Washburn Observatory,* provides many details of the observatory's design and construction. The hilltop was already occupied by a house owned by the university that served as the residence of the UW president. That house, only a few steps from the observatory site, was reassigned to be the residence of the observatory director. The directors of

Cyrus Woodman (1814-1889), Washburn's business partner and founder of the Woodman Astronomical Library. (UW Astronomy Dept.)

Washburn Observatory would keep their residence there until 1948, when Joel Stebbins retired and left Madison. His successor, Albert Whitford, elected not to move in. The building today is the home of the La Follette School of Public Affairs.

For its first observatory director, the university secured James Craig Watson, then the director of the Detroit Observatory at the University of Michigan. As one

The Washburn Observatory (Jeff Miller/UW-Madison)

James Craig Watson (1838-1880), first director of the Washburn Observatory, 1879-1880. (UW Astronomy Dept.)

historian of the observatory has noted, "to judge by contemporary newspaper accounts Watson was wooed by Wisconsin and Michigan with an ardor nowadays reserved for football coaches," an indication of Watson's prestige. He was likely lured by the better facilities that Washburn offered as well as an opportunity to develop a brand-new observatory in order to fit his own particular research interests. Watson was known at the time for his discovery of more than 20 aster-

oids, which had earned him considerable fame. However, he is perhaps best remembered today for his belief in the hypothetical planet "Vulcan." The orbit of the planet Mercury changes over time in a way that nineteenth-century astronomers found difficult to explain. Some astronomers suggested that the gravitational influence of an unseen planet between Mercury and the sun, dubbed "Vulcan," could explain Mercury's orbital anomalies. After all, such a technique had worked well to explain a similar problem with the orbit of Uranus, which had led to the discovery of Neptune in 1846. Watson had attempted to discover whether or not Vulcan actually existed by observing the sky near the sun during the few minutes of a total solar eclipse: the darkened sky might reveal the planet, which was thought to orbit very close to the sun and would otherwise be invisible because of the sun's brightness. Mercury itself is difficult to observe except at certain times of the year and then only under ideal conditions; Vulcan should have been even more difficult to see. After careful study of the sky near the sun during the total solar eclipse of July 29, 1878, Watson announced to a skeptical world that he had discovered Vulcan.

When he arrived in Madison, Watson began developing a new instrument that he believed would allow him to search for Vulcan any time that the sun was visible, not just during the rare moments of a total solar

THE DISCOVERY OF VULCAN.

PROF. WATSON, OF ANN ARBOR, GIVES DETAILS OF HIS OBSERVATIONS—HE IS CERTAIN THAT HIS CONCLUSIONS ARE CORRECT.

Special Dispatch to the New York Times.

DETROIT, Aug. 7.—The *Post and Tribune* will publish to-morrow a letter from Prof. James C. Watson, the astronomer, of Ann Arbor, giving the details of his discovery of the planet Vulcan during his observations of the recent total eclipse of the sun. After stating his conviction of

From an article in The New York Times, *August 8, 1878, announcing James Watson's claimed discovery of the planet "Vulcan." (© The New York Times)*

The campus of the University of Wisconsin in 1879, including an artist's conception of the Washburn Observatory (lower right sketch), then under construction. (SHSW WHi-32525)

eclipse. Watson based his technique on the ancient but erroneous idea that stars are visible during the daytime from the bottom of a very deep well or shaft. Watson personally funded the construction of a small "solar" observatory near the larger Washburn Observatory building. This solar observatory consisted of a long shaft that ran through the hillside: at the top was a movable mirror that directed light down the shaft, and at the bottom was a telescope to make observations.

While he was building his solar observatory, Watson also paid for additions to the main observatory building, funded a smaller observatory for students, and oversaw the installation of one of the observatory's main instruments. This instrument was a 15.6-inch diameter refracting telescope made by the Alvan Clark and Sons company of Cambridge, Massachusetts. (Refracting telescopes, usually called "refractors," use a glass lens to collect and focus light, whereas a reflecting telescope or "reflector" uses a glass or metal mirror to accomplish the same task.) By the late nineteenth century, Clark telescopes were considered among the best in the world, and the Clarks specialized in building the largest telescopes of the era. When it was completed, the Washburn 15.6-inch was the fourth-largest refractor in the world. However, it held this position only for a brief time as many larger instruments were made shortly thereafter. Most significant about the size of this telescope was that Washburn stipulated it be "equal or superior to" the 15-inch refractor at the Harvard College Observatory. Having a telescope slightly larger than that of Harvard suggested that the University of Wisconsin, as a young midwestern institution, was exceeding, even modestly, the scientific resources of one of the most prestigious East Coast colleges.

The Development of Astronomy and Scientific Research at the University of Wisconsin, 1881-1922

Watson never saw the completion of the observatory; he died in 1880 at age 42 after spending only two years in Madison. His claim to have discovered Vulcan was forgotten. (Mercury's orbit was eventually understood when Albert Einstein showed in 1916 that his theory of General Relativity predicted distortions of space near the sun that produce the observed effects.) Watson's successor was Edward S. Holden, who was then an astronomer at the U.S. Naval Observatory (USNO) in Washington, D.C. Holden proved to be a good administrator and worked hard to develop the Washburn Observatory into an effective research and teaching institution. Holden supervised the completion of the buildings and instruments, began observations, and started the *Publications of the Washburn Observatory*, which was the university's first research journal. Holden completed Watson's solar observatory, but found that he could not even observe bright stars – let alone a dim planet near the sun – in broad daylight.

Edward Singleton Holden (1846-1914), second director of the Washburn Observatory, 1881-1885. (UW Astronomy Dept.)

Although Washburn had supplied Wisconsin with an observatory, upon which Watson quickly found necessary to expand, he left no permanent endowment for staff or future development. As a result, the financial standing of the observatory for much of its early history was relatively weak. Although Holden and his successors did their best to secure additional funding from the state or from other patrons, the observatory remained a comparatively small institution and retained its original telescopes well into the twentieth century. This lack of finances placed severe restrictions on the types of research that UW astronomers could perform. At the same time, it also forced them to make the best use of the available instruments and to innovate by inventing entirely new ones. Washburn astronomers proved themselves capable of such innovation on numerous occasions.

One way that many nineteenth-century American observatories, including the Washburn Observatory, earned additional income was by selling accurate time signals to railroad companies and other businesses, such as jewelers and clock-makers. Although astronomically determined time was much too exact for daily use, it reflected an emphasis on punctuality that was popular during an industrial age that put a premium on precision and routine. At one point, selling time signals earned the Washburn Observatory at least 15% of its annual income, which helped to subsidize equipment costs and to pay salaries for assistants. The

Top: The Washburn Observatory viewed from the east in the 1880s. The 15.6-inch Clark refractor shows through the dome of the main building; the Students' Observatory stands at right. Left: Clock room of the Washburn Observatory. The master clock (in the cabinet, right of center) was used in astronomical observations and in setting other clocks around campus. (UW Astronomy Dept.)

observatory also controlled the clocks at the State Capitol as well as the clocks on campus, making the telegraph lines running to the observatory a frequent target for student vandals. Selling time at UW continued through the end of the nineteenth century; it eventually ceased owing in part to competition with national telegraph networks like Western Union, which supplied time signals much more cheaply.

The Washburn time service emphasizes how the practice of astronomy in the late nineteenth century still had some of the practical functions that had long been part of the history of the field. Newspaper reports from the early days of Washburn expressed hope that the observatory would not be an ivory tower institution of teaching and research, but would instead serve the state in more concrete ways. The time service fulfilled such a role, as did the observatory's function as a weather and seismological station. However, the public saw the observatory principally as a place to view the heavens. Interest in visiting the observatory was so high that Holden quickly made a bargain with the citizens of Wisconsin: he would open the observatory for public viewing on the first and third Wednesdays of each month; otherwise, he requested peace in order to carry out his research. Not that this deal pleased all parties, as a persistent reporter from the *Milwaukee Sentinel* wrote in 1882: "Gov. Washburn's munificent gift to the state of an astronomical observatory might as well have been located in the interior of a convent and be as accessible to the public as it now is. Your correspondent has tried, the Lord only knows how many times, to get inside of it, and never yet succeeded. The officer in charge is so absorbed in the discovery of 'new nebulae' that even the students are denied the privileges of the observatory, and a separate building for them has been erected. Only on two evenings in each month is permission given to examine any more than the outside walls." The observatory was a private gift to the UW, yet Holden himself was an employee of the university and thus the state. He was therefore beholden to the demands of an eager public, and his bargain reflects an attempt to strike a balance between private and public interests. With a few exceptions, such as the above, Holden's deal was successful and the tradition of opening the observatory to the public twice each month continues to the present.

Since Watson had died before he could begin observations with the new 15.6-inch telescope, Holden faced the task of inaugurating systematic astronomical research at the UW, which began in 1881. His own major observing project was the positional measurement of 300 "fundamental" stars – well known stars measured over many years to achieve very precise values. For this project Holden used the observatory's other principal instrument, a meridian circle made by the German firm Repsold. A meridian circle was a special kind of refracting telescope that could only pivot up and down, much like a cannon. As a trade-off for this lack of maneuverability, meridian circles could measure the positions of stars or other celestial objects to a very high degree of precision as the earth's rotation brought these objects into the telescope's field of view. Measuring the positions of stars, called astrometry, was a traditional astronomical practice that dates to antiquity. Precise stellar positions were important not only for navigation and for tracking orbiting bodies, but also provided clues about the distribution and motions of stars in space. This information thus provided some insight into the structure of the Milky

Way, our local system of stars. Although astrometry was an ancient practice, nineteenth-century astronomers used techniques and instruments that were very much state-of-the-art.

Holden did not make Madison his permanent home. He left Wisconsin to become president of the University of California at the end of 1885, and then took over the directorship of the newly completed Lick Observatory in 1887. Housing a 36-inch diameter Clark refracting telescope, the Lick was the world's largest observatory

Edward Holden with 4.8-inch Repsold meridian circle. (UW Astronomy Dept.)

and the first built atop a mountain. The success of the Lick Observatory and its excellent observing conditions demonstrated the value of building high-altitude observatories. Nearly all of the world's largest telescopes since then have been built on mountains. Holden was not the first UW astronomer to be involved with the Lick Observatory, as the trustees of Lick's bequest had consulted earlier with Watson while they were planning the observatory. A close association between the Washburn and Lick Observatories, and the sharing of both people and ideas, became very important throughout the histories of both institutions. So much interaction occurred between Wisconsin and West Coast astronomers that one historian has dubbed Washburn and another Wisconsin observatory, the Yerkes Observatory, as two endpoints of the "California-Wisconsin Axis" of American astronomy.

In the early 1880s, Holden was joined by Sherburne Wesley Burnham, a court reporter and amateur astronomer from Chicago who frequently spent weekends in Madison, taking advantage of the clearer and darker skies surrounding Observatory Hill. Burnham's career shows that the boundaries between "amateur" and "professional" astronomers were very fluid in the late nineteenth century. Indeed, Burnham was one of the most respected astronomers of his time. He possessed a 6-inch Clark refracting telescope, a very large and expensive instrument for a private individual to own, and he put this refractor to use in discovering hundreds of new double stars, that is, two stars that appear very close together. Burnham was known for having extremely keen eyesight, not to mention a telescope that could rival larger instruments in distinguishing close double stars. Burnham's observing expertise was trusted to the point

Sherburne Wesley Burnham (1838-1921). (Special Collections, University of California, Santa Cruz, Lick Observatory Records)

that he helped to select the sites for the Lick and Yerkes Observatories.

Burnham worked in Madison for a year before selling his Clark telescope to the UW and returning to Chicago and his court position (the objective lens for this telescope is still in use in a telescope atop UW's Sterling Hall). When Holden took over the directorship of the Lick Observatory, he hired Burnham as a member of the staff and gave him use of the 36-inch refractor. Burnham left California for Chicago in 1892, in large part because of a brewing controversy over Holden's troubled administration. In 1897, Burnham was given a nominal professorship at the University of Chicago and access to the Yerkes Observatory, and in 1902 he finally resigned his job at the court and devoted all of his time to astronomy. Burnham worked for 17 years at Yerkes, spending two nights each week observing and cataloging double stars with its great 40-inch refractor.

SATURN.
(1881, NOVEMBER 27.)

Left: Drawing of Saturn made by Edward Holden using the 15.6-inch Clark refractor in 1881. Below: The Clark refractor on its original mounting, which was replaced in the 1930s. (Washburn Observatory/UW Astronomy Dept.)

Remarkably, Burnham had earned this distinguished career with no formal education in astronomy or mathematics. In fact, the most important form of education for researchers in astronomy in the nineteenth century was at the eyepiece of a telescope. Very few "professional" astronomers held degrees higher than a bachelor's, including the first three directors of the Washburn Observatory. It was not until the early twentieth century that a doctoral degree was a prerequisite to a career in astronomy, although amateurs continue to make significant contributions to the field.

When Edward Holden departed Madison for California he left the Washburn Observatory without a director. The Regents spent almost two years finding his replacement, in large part because the office of the University President, a much more important position, was also vacant. Meanwhile, two of Holden's former assistants, Milton Updegraff and Alice Lamb, took charge of the observatory. They finished Holden's observations and performed other research on the positions of stars. In 1886, physics professor John Davies became Acting Director until a permanent director was found. Lamb and Updegraff, who

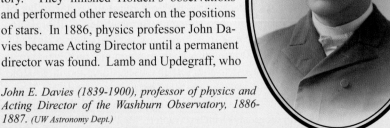

John E. Davies (1839-1900), professor of physics and Acting Director of the Washburn Observatory, 1886-1887. (UW Astronomy Dept.)

Alice Maxwell Lamb (1863-1952), Milton Updegraff (1861-1938); both assistants at the Washburn Observatory, 1884-1887. (UW Astronomy Dept.)

spent many long nights working together at the meridian circle, eventually fell in love and married, leaving the UW in 1887.

Although significantly fewer in number than their male counterparts, a small but increasing number of women performed research in astronomy during the late nineteenth century. Lamb, however, was notable, in that she was one of only a handful of women in the U.S. to carry out observational research at a coeducational institution like the UW. Most other women served as astronomy instructors or worked at observatories as "computers," that is, people who processed large amounts of astronomical data for relatively low pay. Lamb was given partial control over the observatory not out of direct choice by the university administration, but because of the delay in finding a director. Nevertheless, she used the opportunity to develop the necessary skills to carry out high-quality research. Lamb hoped to make a career in astronomy after her time in Madison, but found few opportunities worthy of her expertise. For instance, in 1886 she received an offer to teach mathematics and run a small observatory

Elizabeth Schofield (1859?-1919), assistant and "computer" at the Washburn Observatory, 1882-1883. (UW Astronomy Dept.)

at a woman's college in the Dakota Territory, but argued that she would "rather work in a true observatory than direct a toy one." Although Updegraff went on to a successful career as an astronomer for the U.S. Navy, Lamb appears to have given up astronomy after their marriage.

The UW found a permanent successor for Holden in another former Washburn Observatory assistant. George Cary Comstock, the third official Washburn director, was a Madison native and had studied under James Watson at the University of Michigan. Comstock returned to Wisconsin as Watson's assistant in 1879 and contemplated a career in law before deciding to devote his life to astronomy. Comstock remained at the observatory as an assistant until 1885, spending the summer of 1886 in California working with Holden at the Lick Observatory. Although Holden wanted to keep Comstock as a permanent staff member, Comstock felt ready to return to Madison and take control of an observatory of his own.

Comstock was called back to Wisconsin in 1887, but was not granted full control of the observatory. He was appointed Associate Director while USNO astronomer Asaph Hall was made Consulting Director. It is not fully clear why the UW made this complicated arrangement, which effectively gave the Washburn Observatory two directors. After Holden's departure in 1885, the UW Board of Regents offered the use of the Washburn Observatory to the USNO. The USNO was moving to a new location, which idled its observing staff and forced its astronomers to look elsewhere for telescope time. The UW Regents had also hoped that the USNO would aid the "reorganization" of the Washburn staff as they sought a new director, perhaps seeing the USNO as the ideal institution on which to model their own observatory. Hall was an experienced astronomer who was best known for discovering the two moons of the planet Mars in 1873; the Regents clearly

Above: George Gary Comstock (1855-1934), third director of the Washburn Observatory, 1889-1922. (UW Astronomy Dept.) Right: Asaph Hall (1829-1907), Consulting Director of the Washburn Observatory, 1887-1889. (U.S. Naval Observatory Library)

valued this expertise. However, Hall lived in Washington, D.C. and only visited Madison rarely. In the end, Hall seems to have given Comstock nearly full control of the observatory during this period and served mainly as a source of advice and funding for the young Associate Director. Comstock was made full director in 1889 when the UW's arrangement with the USNO ended.

Like Holden before him, Comstock's early research was based in the field of astrometry. His first major research project was the measurement of an important value called the constant of stellar aberration. Stellar aberration is a phenomenon that occurs because of the earth's motion around the sun. Because light travels at a finite speed, a star will appear to shift slightly toward the direction of the earth's motion at any given moment. This effect is similar to walking or running during a rainstorm: raindrops that are actually falling vertical will appear slanted, as if they were coming at an angle towards the observer and thus forcing a tip of the umbrella toward the direction of motion. The amount that stars appear to shift is called the constant of stellar aberration. This constant provides a measurement of the speed of the earth as it orbits the sun. Astronomers used the orbital speed of the earth, along with the value of the speed of light, to determine the distance from the sun to earth. This distance served as the baseline for most astronomical distance measurements in this period and was thus a value of critical importance. Even a small improvement in the value of the constant of aberration could affect a wide range of measurements, from the scale of the solar system to interstellar distances. Comstock measured stellar aberration using an unusual yet inventive apparatus that he attached to the end of Burnham's telescope, which was mounted in the Students' Observatory. His final results did not change the value of the constant of aberration significantly, but instead confirmed the accepted value by an accurate, alternative method. Although Comstock has often been portrayed as a member of the "old school" of positional astronomers, his research projects throughout his career show a willingness to think creatively and to use new instruments and methods to solve critical problems in the field. This project earned Comstock recognition within the American astronomical community and was a key factor to his election to the National Academy of Sciences. He was one of the first faculty members chosen for that distinguished body of scientists for research performed while at the UW.

While Comstock was performing this aberration research he also spent many years carrying out systematic observations of special kinds of stars. He measured the positions of double stars, the orbits of binary stars (stars bound together gravitationally), and the "proper" motions of very faint stars. Proper motion describes the motion that is intrinsic to an individual star as it travels through space, and not some apparent effect that is the result of the earth's motion around the sun. Comstock's studies of the distributions and motions of stars led him into important debates about the size and structure of the Milky Way at the turn of the twentieth century. He was an early proponent of the idea that interstellar space is filled with a diffuse medium that dimmed light and made stars appear more distant than they actually are. Although most astronomers rejected Comstock's value for the dimming effect of this proposed interstellar medium, his research contributed to one of the key problems of the period. The question of whether or not an interstellar medium existed took several decades to solve and became, as we will see, one of the central research areas in twentieth-century astronomy, especially at Washburn Observatory.

A third branch of Comstock's research was in the new and growing area of astrophysics. Although the work of figures like Isaac Newton showed how the laws of physics applied to the motions of heavenly bodies, in the mid-nineteenth century a new branch of astronomy developed that sought to examine directly the physical and chemical compositions of celestial objects. Called "astrophysics" after 1860, the key elements to this research field were three instruments: the photographic camera, the photometer (a device used to measure the intensity of light), and the spectroscope. A spectroscope is a device that passes light first through a narrow slit and then through a series of prisms (or reflected off of a metal or glass plate with very fine rulings on its surface, called a grating) to break up light into its constituent colors. Chemists and physicists discovered in the late 1850s that when a given chemical element or molecule is energized it radiates energy in a very specific array of colors, called an emission spectrum. An emission spectrum appears as a series of colored lines, each representing one particular wavelength of light. For instance, the visible light emission spectrum for the element hydrogen has bright lines in red, green, blue, and violet. Similarly, an element or molecule will absorb light in these same specific wavelengths. With this discovery, scientists could use a spectroscope to determine the chemical composition of nearly any object, no matter how remote. In the hands of astronomers, the spectroscope could show the chemical structures of stars and the atmospheres of planets, in addition to other physical parameters like temperature and pressure. One of the most important discoveries that astronomers made with spectroscopes was that most stars belong to roughly ten or so different categories or "classes" based on similarities in their spectra. Stellar classification was recognized in the nineteenth century as an important way of understanding how stars are different yet related to one another physically and how they might evolve over time.

Comstock's contributions to astrophysics demonstrate further his ability to push the boundaries of astronomical technique. His major astrophysical project was a study of what he called the "effective wavelength" of starlight, that is, the color in which a star radiates most of its energy. He measured effective wavelength by attaching a special screen to the lens-end of the 15.6-inch refractor. Comstock was interested in this question because he wanted to know how the color of starlight affected the apparent position of a star when viewed through Earth's atmosphere. Since air refracts (or bends) light of different colors by different amounts, light from a star that is mostly blue will bend differently than light from a star that is mostly red. Comstock sought to relate the effective wavelength of a star to its spectral class in order to improve his research on the positions and motions of stars, thus showing a mixture of older problems and newer approaches. His study did not draw much immediate attention. However, within a few years it helped to contribute to the work of the Danish astronomer Ejnar Hertzsprung, whose research on the relationship between stellar color and stellar luminosity, parallel with the American Henry Norris Russell, provided one of the keys to answering the question about the evolution of stars. This relationship, portrayed graphically as the "Hertzsprung-Russell Diagram," has been a central tool in astrophysics for nearly a century.

Comstock provided the stability in leadership that the early Washburn Observatory had lacked, remaining director until 1922. He was not only an active researcher but also an avid teacher and author. He frequently taught up to six courses each year and published textbooks on mathematics, astronomy, engineering, and navigation. He was devoted to the idea that astronomy ought to be not just an abstract science but one that retained some of its traditional, practical applications. Although the observatory grew little under Comstock's tenure, he also recognized that performing research from the center of a growing urban center was becoming increasingly difficult. Artificial lighting and air pollution became so troubling that Comstock inquired seriously about moving the observatory away from central Madison in the early 1910s. The observatory remains in its original location to this day, but Comstock had identified early on a problem that would trouble UW astronomers for decades to come.

The foundation of the Washburn Observatory and the directorships of Holden and Comstock were important developments in the establishment of a permanent

The former residence of the directors of the Washburn Observatory, now home to the La Follette School of Public Affairs. (*Jeff Miller/UW-Madison*)

scientific research culture at the UW and in Wisconsin as a whole. Although science formed an important part of the university's curriculum since its foundation, faculty were hired for their teaching skills and not for their ability to carry out scientific research. By the end of the nineteenth century, universities across the United States began placing a higher premium on original research among their faculty and on training their students for careers in science and industry. Associated with this new emphasis on research was the spread of scientific institutions, such as observatories and laboratories. As one of the earliest and most expensive scientific facilities at the UW in the nineteenth century, the Washburn Observatory was a prominent reminder of the growing value of science in higher education. Another key development in promoting scientific research at the UW was the founding of the Graduate School in 1904, of which Comstock was the first director and later its first dean. Although the UW awarded master's and Ph.D. degrees before 1904, Comstock and UW president Charles Van Hise developed a much more formal system of graduate education. This in turn gave science a more prominent place at the university, as original research is an important requirement for a graduate degree. It is somewhat ironic that although the size of the graduate program at the UW as a whole grew significantly under Comstock's tenure, he never developed a strong graduate program in astronomy during his tenure, supervising only one Ph.D. dissertation and a few master's theses.

The Growth of Astronomy Across Wisconsin, 1880-1932

Although Madison was home to the earliest organized astronomy research in the state, there were other important astronomical sites across Wisconsin. Several small observatories were built in the late nineteenth and early twentieth centuries, such as the Beloit College Observatory and the Underwood Observatory at Lawrence College in Appleton. These observatories principally aided the teaching missions of their associated schools. Private individuals and astronomy organizations also built a large number of small observatories across the state. Two of these observatories, one very small and one very large, demonstrate the range of astronomical research facilities operating in Wisconsin in the late nineteenth and early twentieth centuries.

Johann Georg Hagen, S.J. (1847-1930). (Special Collections, University of California, Santa Cruz, Lick Observatory Records)

The first of these observatories was located at the College of the Sacred Heart, once a Catholic academy in Prairie du Chien. In 1880, the school's astronomy instructor, an Austrian Jesuit named Johann Hagen, built a small observatory and equipped it with two three-inch refracting telescopes. Interested mainly in positional astronomy, Hagen collaborated with Edward Holden in Madison and reported on some of his work in the *Publications of the Washburn Observatory*. Although Hagen's research in Wisconsin amounted to only a few brief publications, he used his experience in Wisconsin as a springboard to a much more prestigious career. Hagen left Wisconsin when Sacred Heart closed in 1888 (it later reopened as Campion College), becoming the director of the observatory at Georgetown University in Washington, D.C. He later served the director of the Vatican Observatory in Rome. Hagen and his small observatory are reminders that most astronomical research was not performed at giant observatories with the largest telescopes. Individual astronomers like Hagen had to make do with what resources they had, and although observatories like the one at Sacred Heart are largely forgotten, they make up an important part of the landscape of astronomy in America in the nineteenth century.

By way of contrast, Wisconsin hosted what was in fact the largest observatory with the biggest telescope in the United States at the time. This institution, the Yerkes Observatory in Williams Bay, was a Wisconsin institution mainly by virtue of the fact that it was located in the state, although its roots were in the booming city of Chicago. In 1892, the astronomer George Ellery Hale (1868-1938) of the new University of Chicago convinced the wealthy streetcar magnate Charles Yerkes to finance the largest telescope in the world. This telescope had a 40-inch diameter lens figured by Alvan Clark and Sons and a 60-foot tube and mounting by the Warner and Swasey company of Cleveland, making it the largest operational refractor that has ever been built. Astronomers realized that refracting telescopes larger than this were impractical, both because of the difficulty of procuring large glass lenses that are almost perfectly transparent and uniform and because big refractor lenses tended to sag significantly under their own weight.

Hale knew that the virtues of this telescope would be wasted in a city like Chicago, which was filled with coal smoke, artificial light, and the vibrations of trains. Numerous offers came in from locations hoping to host the new observatory, and a site selection committee eventually settled on a hill overlooking Lake Geneva in Williams Bay, Wisconsin. This committee was aided in its choice by Burnham, then working full-time in Chicago in his job as a court reporter, who delivered a favorable report on the observing conditions near Lake Geneva. Williams Bay was considered an ideal site because it was relatively close to Chicago (about a one-hour train ride) and because of the fact that Lake Geneva was surrounded by resort communities: significant urbanization in the area seemed unlikely at the time.

The Yerkes Observatory opened in 1897 to considerable fanfare. It had the largest telescope in the world and was one of the first American observatories built

The Yerkes Observatory in Williams Bay, Wisconsin. (SHSW WHi-1811)

primarily with astrophysics in mind, containing laboratories and instrument shops designed for spectroscopy and photography. However, the research performed at Yerkes shows a mixture of astronomy old and new. In addition to Burnham and his work measuring double stars, Hale hired Edward Barnard, who had earned fame for discovering the fifth moon of Jupiter (the first since Galileo) while working at the Lick Observatory and who was also a pioneer of astronomical photography. Barnard's wide-angle photographs of the Milky Way showed curious dark patches, which Barnard believed were areas devoid of stars but what other astronomers argued were silhouettes of clouds of obscuring matter, perhaps further evidence in favor of the supposed interstellar medium. Hale himself studied the physics of the sun, including the nature of sunspots and the solar corona, the hot and diffuse outermost portion of the sun's atmosphere. Hale also hired Edwin Frost, who developed a program to measure the velocities of stars using spectroscopy.

A large number of the leading astronomers in the country attended the dedication ceremony of the Yerkes Observatory, and this gathering provided the inspiration to form a nationwide astronomical society. This organization, the Astronomical and Astrophysical Society of America (AASA) held its first meeting at Yerkes in 1899. The name of the society was chosen to reflect the importance of astrophysics, although many members found the name cumbersome and changed it to the simpler American Astronomical Society (AAS) in 1914. The society's first president was Simon Newcomb, one of the most respected figures in American science, with Hale as one of two vice-presidents and George Comstock as secretary. Comstock was a particularly active member in the early years of the AASA and drew on his legal background in writing the society's constitution. He served a decade as secretary, several terms as a vice-president, and three years as president following his retirement from the Washburn Observatory. In fact, a total of four Washburn directors to date (Comstock, Joel Stebbins, Albert Whitford, and Arthur Code) would serve as AAS president at some point in their careers.

Hale retired as Yerkes director in 1905, having already founded the Mt. Wilson Observatory near Pasadena, California. His successor was Edwin Frost, who remained director until retiring in 1932. Frost's directorship has been characterized as a period of stagnation for the observatory, owing in part to a loss of eyesight that prevented him from carrying out any research of his own after 1915. Frost also did little to change the scientific direction of Yerkes, hiring astronomers who continued the work of Burnham and Barnard instead of pursuing entirely new lines of research. Even though Yerkes under Frost may not have pursued the most innovative research, the observatory continued to make important contributions to the discipline as a whole. For nearly three decades Frost served as editor of the *Astrophysical Journal*, which Hale had founded in 1895 as the flagship American publication for astrophysical research. Furthermore, Yerkes in this period trained several astronomers who went on to have very influential careers. These students include Otto Struve, a refugee from the Russian Civil War for whom Frost had worked strenuously to bring to the United States and who became Frost's successor at Yerkes, and Edwin Hubble, one of the most important observational astronomers of the twentieth century.

The New Astronomy

The Electric Eye

In 1922, George Comstock retired as director of the Washburn Observatory and was succeeded by Joel Stebbins, who was then director of the observatory at the University of Illinois. Stebbins had studied with Comstock from 1900 to 1901 before earning a Ph.D. at the Lick Observatory. He was the first UW astronomer to have a Ph.D. While at Illinois, Stebbins became a pioneer in the field of photoelectric photometry, which was the application of sensitive electric detectors – what Stebbins called an "electric eye" – attached to the end of a telescope to measure the intensity of light from celestial objects. Astronomers used electric photometers to distinguish changes in brightness too small or rapid to measure with other methods: the naked eye is not sensitive enough to detect such changes and photographic plates were too slow and cumbersome to measure rapid changes in brightness. Stebbins first studied variable stars (a variable star is a star with a brightness that changes periodically over time), including groundbreaking research on the

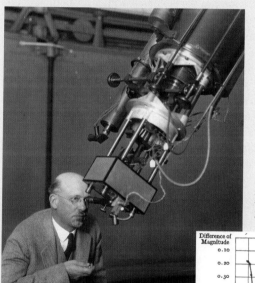

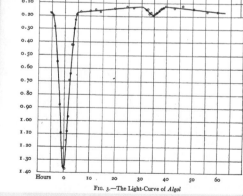

FIG. 3.—The Light-Curve of *Algol*

Above: Joel S. Stebbins (1878-1966), fourth director of the Washburn Observatory (1922-1948), observing with a photoelectric photometer on the 15.6-inch refractor. Right: The light-curve of the binary star Algol, from a paper published by Stebbins in The Astrophysical Journal *in 1910. This graph shows the brightness of the star system plotted vertically, and time (in hours) plotted horizontally. The first "dip" in brightness, about which astronomers had long known, is caused when the dimmer "secondary" star passes in front of the brighter "primary" star. Stebbins showed the existence of the smaller dip, which is caused when the secondary star passes behind the primary. (UW Astronomy Dept.)*

star Algol in 1910. Astronomers suspected that Algol was an eclipsing binary star, or two stars orbiting around and periodically passing in front of each other from our line of sight. When one star passes in front of the other the total amount of light from the binary star system appears to decrease. Stebbins used his early photometers to demonstrate that Algol was an eclipsing binary and determined its "light curve," a plot of the system's brightness over time, to an unprecedented degree of accuracy. This discovery not only earned Stebbins a reputation as a careful researcher, but also demonstrated the power and sensitivity of the new electric light detectors. The study of eclipsing binaries also provided important information about the sizes and masses of stars, which was key information in an era when astronomers and physicists were working hard to understand how stars produce energy and how they evolve over time.

Stebbins' first photometers were simply wires coated with a crystalline compound that contained the element selenium. When these selenium "cells" were exposed to light their electrical resistance changed, which a device called an ohmmeter could measure. However, Stebbins' first selenium photometers were very insensitive and were only able to detect changes in the brightness of the moon as it went through its monthly cycle of phases. Stebbins was able to increase the sensitivity of his selenium cells over time to the point where they could detect variations in bright stars, such as Algol. In the early 1910s, Stebbins teamed up with physicist Jakob Kunz at Illinois, who was making a new type of photocell. These cells took advantage of the photoelectric effect, a phenomenon whose physical properties Albert Einstein had described in 1905. The photoelectric effect occurs when light strikes a metallic surface, freeing electrons capable of producing

Meeting of the Astronomical and Astrophysical Society of America at Harvard University in 1910. George Comstock is in the back row, center. Joel Stebbins (wearing bowtie) is seated in the front row, center. (UW Astronomy Dept.)

a small electric current. Kunz's photoelectric cells proved considerably more sensitive than the older selenium cells, and Stebbins quickly made the switch to the new detectors.

When Stebbins came to Madison in 1922 to take over the directorship of the Washburn Observatory, he brought his array of photometers with him, establishing a research tradition in photometry at the UW that would continue into the space age. Stebbins did not perform all of his research in Wisconsin, but used the Washburn Observatory primarily as a testing ground for new instrumentation. He frequently took his instruments to observatories in California such as Lick or the new Mt. Wilson Observatory, which had better viewing conditions and much larger telescopes. (Mt. Wilson helped to make standard the use of large reflecting telescopes, installing a 60-inch reflector in 1908 and the 100-inch Hooker Telescope in 1917.) By moving back and

Stebbins-Whitford photoelectric photometer. At left: Kunz photoelectric cell (top) with vacuum tube amplifier (bottom). At right: vacuum chamber, which attaches to the end of a telescope. (UW Astronomy Dept.)

forth between Wisconsin and California, Stebbins could still make good use of the outdated Washburn telescope while also maintaining connections to the important research sites on the West Coast.

Photoelectric photometry was still in its infancy, and very few astronomers seemed willing to take the professional risk by moving into a completely new area of astronomical technology. As Stebbins wrote in 1928, "Perhaps a word of warning or of commiseration is due to those who may take up this kind of work. The photo-electric cell with its installation is a delicate piece of apparatus, and requires considerable patience to learn its idiosyncrasies. Nowadays, our photometer will work uniformly for months at a time, but occasionally some trouble arises, and perhaps once a year a new kind of 'tick' will turn up which is a real puzzle. The ordinary troubles from moisture, defective battery, dirty or poor contacts, etc., can be recognized by simple tests, but it is difficult to put down in black and white just what to do when things go wrong." Photoelectric photometry remained an experimental branch of the discipline before the Second World War, and Stebbins and his students and collaborators largely had a monopoly on photoelectric techniques during this period.

Stebbins spent most of the 1920s continuing his research on variable stars using Kunz's photoelectric cells. He also carried out an interesting study on whether or not the sun is a variable star. By studying the brightnesses of the planet Jupiter's four largest satellites, which shine because of light reflected from the sun, Stebbins argued that his photometers would detect any significant change in the sun's light output. Stebbins tested his theory at the Lick Observatory in the late 1920s, but found no variability.

What was perhaps the most significant research of Stebbins' career centered on understanding the nature of the newly discovered interstellar medium. In 1930, astronomer Robert Trumpler of the Lick Observatory argued conclusively that interstellar space was filled with a diffuse substance that both dimmed and reddened the light from celestial objects. Reddening is a result of the fact that objects like stars emit light in all parts of the electromagnetic spectrum, from radio waves to visible light to gamma rays. The interstellar medium scatters away some of the light from the bluer part of the visible portion of the spectrum, allowing the redder light to pass through unhindered and making the object appear redder (and dimmer) than it would if no interstellar medium existed. Stebbins explored this reddening effect by using his photometers to measuring the colors of bright stars that are intrinsically very blue. He found that stars located near the plane of the Milky Way showed the greatest degree of reddening, which provided further confirmation of Trumpler's discovery and support to the idea that our galaxy contained not only stars but also a significant amount of dust and gas.

A related discovery occurred when Stebbins turned his attention from bright stars to globular clusters. Globular clusters are dense balls of tens of thousands of stars that seem to crowd around the center of the Milky Way. In the late 1910s, the astronomer Harlow Shapley at the Mt. Wilson Observatory measured the distances to globular clusters and constructed a three-dimensional map of the Milky Way. He then used this map to estimate that our galaxy was about 250,000 light-years across, with the sun about 50,000 light-years from the center. (A light-year is the distance that light travels in one year, about 9.5 trillion kilometers or 5.9 trillion miles. The sun's nearest neighboring star, Alpha Centauri, is about 4.4 light-years distant.) Shapley believed that his results answered one of the outstanding questions in astronomy at the time: the nature of the thousands of mysterious "spiral" nebulae that populated the sky. Some astronomers believed that these nebulae, like the Great Andromeda Nebula (also known as Messier 31 or M31), were systems of billions of stars similar to but separate from the Milky Way, "island universes" or galaxies unto their own. Others believed that the spiral nebulae were part of the Milky Way and were places where material was condensing into relatively few new stars. Shapley argued that because of his large estimate for the size of the Milky Way, the spiral nebulae could not be external galaxies. In the mid-1920s, Edwin Hubble, also at Mt. Wilson, measured the distances to a few large nebulae (using a technique that Shapley himself had helped to develop) and found that the nearest, the Andromeda Nebula, was several hundred thousand light years away and so could not be part of our galaxy. Hubble had provided compelling evidence in favor of the island universe theory, but one question remained. The other spiral galaxies seemed to be only about half as big as the Milky Way, according to Shapley's measurement. Why should the Milky Way be so much larger? Was this discrepancy real, or were astronomers not accounting for something? Stebbins turned his attention to this question and showed that the effects of the interstellar medium had a significant effect on determining the distances to celestial objects. Stebbins measured the reddening of globular clusters and found that they were much closer to the sun – and therefore the Milky Way was much smaller – than Shapley

Charles Morse Huffer (1894-1981) with the 15.6-inch Washburn refractor, circa 1950. (UW Astronomy Dept.)

thought, once the effects of the interstellar medium were taken into account. Stebbins' estimate for the size of the Milky Way was about half of Shapley's and much closer to the estimated size of other spiral galaxies, like the Andromeda Galaxy.

One of Stebbins' most important collaborators at the UW was Charles Morse Huffer, who studied with Stebbins while an undergraduate at the University of Illinois. When Stebbins took over as director of Washburn he hired Huffer as an assistant, who then decided to earn a Ph.D. in astronomy. Huffer contributed to Stebbins' work on variable stars, which formed the basis for Huffer's dissertation. Huffer then worked with Stebbins on the latter's study of absorption and reddening, co-authoring several important papers with Stebbins. Huffer became a professor of astronomy and remained at UW until his retirement in 1961. Huffer continued and extended the early work by Stebbins on applying photometry to eclipsing binary stars, for which he used the 15.6-inch telescope into the mid-1950s. He was also a very active member of the astronomy community, serving as secretary of the AAS for over a decade.

In 1931, Albert Whitford, another of Stebbins' collaborators and his future successor, joined the Washburn Observatory staff while studying for a graduate degree in physics. Whitford, a native of Milton, Wisconsin and a graduate of Milton College, was looking for a job and Stebbins hired him to look after the electrical apparatus used in Stebbins' photometric research. Whitford was then experimenting with newly developed vacuum tubes, using them to amplify weak electric currents. Whitford attached his amplifiers to Stebbins' photoelectric photometers, which drastically increased the sensitivity of these instruments and reduced the amount of noise in the signal. Another, more practical effect of using these amplifiers was that Stebbins could switch from a relatively delicate and difficult-to-use current-measuring device called an electrometer to a far more robust instrument known as a galvanometer, which simplified observations considerably. These photometers were among the very first applications of electronics to astronomy. Whitford then took an additional step and placed the entire photometer and amplifier assembly within a vacuum chamber, which was then attached to the end of the telescope. Putting the detector in a vacuum increased the signal-to-noise ratio by reducing the effects of cosmic rays. When cosmic rays collide with air molecules they produce charged subatomic particles, which created additional interference within

Staff of the Washburn Observatory in 1936. Front row, from left: C. Morse Huffer, Elsie De-Noyer, Joel Stebbins. Back row: Edward Burnett, Gerald Kron, Albert Whitford. (UW Astronomy Dept.)

the photometer assembly. The robustness of Stebbins and Whitford's final instruments attracted the attention of other astronomers, such as the eminent Hale, who hoped to install such a system at his planned 200-inch telescope at the Mt. Palomar Observatory.

The introduction of electronic amplifiers into photoelectric photometry presaged another important technological development with which Stebbins and his students began to experiment in the late 1930s: photomultiplier tubes. These devices combined a light detector and a series of amplifiers, all contained within a small glass tube. Invented in the mid-1930s and perfected at RCA by a team working under Vladimir Zworykin, a central figure in the invention of television, photomultiplier tubes were compact, simple, and could amplify a signal over one million times. Stebbins corresponded with Zworykin about RCA's photomultipliers, hoping to apply them to his photometric research. However, key developments in the use of photomultipliers in astronomy came through the work of Gerald Kron, a UW engineering student who joined the Washburn Observatory in 1931. Along with Whitford, Kron first used photomultiplier tubes in helping to develop an innovative telescope guiding system for the Mt. Wilson Observatory. Most astronomical photographs at the time required very long exposures using specially coated glass plates. In order to produce a good image the telescope had to stay focused on the target object, say, a distant galaxy, for perhaps several hours or more. Otherwise, during that time the telescope would likely drift away from the object slightly, ruining the exposure. Astronomers avoided this problem by using a "guide" star that happened to be in the telescope's field of view: keeping this star steady on a pair of crosswires ensured a good image. The downside to this technique was that the astronomer had to stay at the telescope with his or her eye at the eyepiece until the exposure was complete, no matter how cold the evening air was. Kron and Whitford hoped that their experimental, photomultiplier-based guider would automatically correct for any off-course drifting and point the tele-scope back in the right direction. After World War II, Kron continued to work with photomultipliers as image detectors, and through his work and that of his contem-poraries the photomultiplier replaced the older photoelectric cell as the principle instrument for astronomical photometry.

Karl Jansky (1905-1950) was another UW student from the early days of vacu-um tube electronics who became part of astronomical history. Jansky, whose father was a UW Engineering professor, went to work for Bell Telephone Laboratories after graduating from the UW. He was assigned to investigate radio noise sources that might interfere with radio communications. To carry out the investigations, he designed and built a rotating antenna connected to radio receiving and recording equipment. In 1933, Jansky identified a major radio noise source coming from the direction of the constellation Sagittarius, the same direction in which the center of our Milky Way galaxy was suspected to lie. Jansky's work was the beginning of the field of radio astronomy, and although Jansky himself was not allowed to do further research in the field, others would eventually follow-up and expand upon his pioneering work.

During the 1940s, Stebbins, and Whitford, who was now a professor of as-tronomy, continued to study the nature of the interstellar medium, developing a system of photometry that measured light in six different colors in order to under-stand very precisely the effects of reddening. Stebbins' "law of interstellar redden-ing" became such a fundamental part of astronomical practice that Whitford later wrote, "the method that Stebbins introduced eventually came to be a routine step in determining the distances of all types of objects other than the nearest stars." Steb-bins' contributions to photometry, and to astronomy as a whole, were far-reaching indeed.

In his final years as director of the Washburn Observatory in the late 1940s, Stebbins turned his attention from stars to study the colors and brightnesses of galaxies. Once again, Stebbins' work brought him into the center of a major astro-nomical debate, this time concerning the origin and fate of the universe as a whole. In the late 1920s, after demonstrating that the spiral nebulae were objects outside of the Milky Way, Edwin Hubble then discovered an astounding fact about them: the light from nearly every galaxy that he examined was shifted toward the red end of the spectrum compared with what he expected. This effect, known as the cosmic redshift, is comparable to what physicists call a Doppler shift, which oc-curs when an object emitting light moves toward or away from an observer. Light from an object moving away from an observer is shifted toward the red end of the spectrum. Conversely, light from an object moving towards an observer is shifted towards the blue end of the spectrum. A galaxy whose spectrum is red-shifted thus appears to be moving away from us; Hubble found that all but the closest galaxies seemed to be receding from us at very high speeds in excess of hundreds or even thousands of kilometers per second (by way of comparison, the orbital speed of the earth around the sun is about 30 kilometers per second, while the orbital speed of the sun around the center of the Milky Way is about 220 kilometers per second). By combining his measurements of distance and redshift, Hubble discovered a

Artist's illustration of what one of the first galaxies in the universe may have looked like 750 million years after the Big Bang. (W. M. Keck Observatory, Artwork by Jon Lomberg)

striking correlation: there exists a direct relationship between the distance to a galaxy and its recessional speed. Astronomers and physicists quickly interpreted Hubble's data as evidence that the entire universe – space and everything in it – is expanding rapidly. But what did this expansion mean? Did it say anything about how the universe may have begun, or how it might develop over time?

By the late 1940s, cosmologists had put forward two important interpretations of the expanding universe. One idea, which built upon the research of physicists in the 1930s, was supported by George Gamow and his students at George Washington University. Gamow argued that if you imagine running the expansion of the universe backwards in time, like a movie played in reverse, then at a certain point in the past all space and matter must have been contained within an extraordinarily tiny, dense, and hot volume. Run time forward from this beginning point and space begins to expand – like a balloon blowing up – filled with primordial matter that cools off and condenses into galaxies and stars, from which planets and people would eventually evolve. A key consequence of this "big bang" theory was that the universe as we know it had a finite beginning in time and space, although it was not clear whether this expansion would continue forever, gradually slow down, or stop and reverse itself, compressing everything back together in a "big crunch."

The other key cosmology of the period opposed the idea of a beginning or an end to either time or space. According to this "steady-state" theory, of which Cambridge University astronomer Fred Hoyle was the leading promoter, the universe had always existed, had always been expanding, and was the same regardless of where one looked in the cosmos. Hoyle argued that as space expanded, a tiny, unobservable amount of new material (say, a hydrogen atom per year per cubic light-year of space) came into existence. Enough new matter would eventually accumulate to form into new galaxies, which would then fill the voids that the expansion of the universe created.

In the late 1940s and early 1950s, both of these theories drew supporters from within the scientific community, and astronomers and physicists mounted evidence hoping to prove one model over the other. Stebbins and Whitford entered the fray when they discovered that some of the distant galaxies that they were measuring were redder than galaxies that were nearer to us. They could not account for this reddening either through an interstellar or intergalactic medium, nor was it a result of Doppler shifting. Some scientists, including Gamow, argued that this "Stebbins-Whitford effect" meant perhaps that these more distant galaxies were simply intrinsically redder, perhaps because they were made of different, redder types of stars than the nearer galaxies. (Because light travels at a finite speed, when we observe an object in space we see it not as it is now but as it was when the light left the object. For example, light from the sun takes about eight minutes to travel to the earth, so we actually see the sun as it appeared eight minutes ago. The Andromeda Galaxy, which we now know to be about two million light-years away, appears to us now as it actually was two million years ago.) Thus, since the light from very distant galaxies takes longer to reach us than light from galaxies that are closer, the Stebbins-Whitford effect suggested that these more distant galaxies were at different points in their development and were perhaps older than the closer ones. However, according the steady-state theory, all galaxies should appear the same no matter how deep one peered into space; the Stebbins-Whitford effect seemed to contradict this basic premise. Their discovery caused a stir in the early 1950s as a plausible argument against the steady-state theory (even if it was not, as big bang proponents hoped, a necessary argument in favor of their own theory). Stebbins and Whitford, as a result of a critical analysis by UW astronomer Arthur Code, eventually revisited their observations and withdrew their claim about the reddening of distant galaxies.

Stebbins retired as director of the Washburn Observatory in 1948, but maintained an active career in astronomical research. He became a research associate at the Lick Observatory, where he continued to develop his system of six-color photometry and studied "pulsating" variable stars. (Pulsating variables change in brightness because the stars grow and shrink in size periodically.) Shapley and Hubble had used these types of stars in measuring the scale of the Milky Way and the distances to other galaxies, and so Stebbins' final work had continuing relevance to questions about the scale of the universe.

From World War II and Into the Space Age

From its very beginning, Washburn Observatory's status, in effect its place on the university's organizational chart, was as a research institute, independent of any department or college, whose director reported to the UW president. This arrangement was consistent with its original role in establishing the University of Wisconsin as a research university, but teaching was always part of the astronomer's duties as well. Watson, Holden, Comstock, and Stebbins all taught traditional introductory astronomy courses, and student accounts of the Stebbins era mention exercises in surveying and celestial navigation on the lake – typical activities for astronomy classes before World War II. Comstock, as already noted, was an energetic teacher and prolific textbook author.

Astronomy teaching became a more pressing issue as undergraduate enrollment in astronomy courses grew steadily, especially during and after World War II. Also, the independent status of the observatory introduced difficulties into the routine offering of advanced courses and awarding of degrees at just the time when the nation's post-war research growth demanded more technical training in all fields, including astronomy. Up until the early 1960s, Washburn Observatory had produced only four Ph.D. astronomers: Stephan Hadley, who worked with Comstock; Charles Morse Huffer, who worked with Stebbins for many years; Olin J. Eggin, who left Madison to do important photometric research; and Theodore E. "Ted" Houck, who would be an important figure in Wisconsin's early space astronomy efforts.

Stebbins perceived the need to reorganize astronomy research and education at the university to meet the needs of post-war education; as early as 1946 he began petitioning the UW administration for restructuring. In September 1948, only a few months after Stebbins retired, the Board of Regents approved the observatory's transformation into the Department of Astronomy within the College of Letters and Science. The university conducted a nationwide search among top young astronomers to find a new observatory director and, in the end, followed Stebbins' forceful recommendation to President E. B. Fred that any choice but Whitford "would not make sense." Thus it fell to Whitford to implement the new department's development in both curriculum and facilities.

As Stebbins foresaw, the growing program of instruction and the increasingly complex instrumental work involved in research could no longer fit in the old building on Observatory Hill, but finding new space on campus for telescopes and laboratories is never simple. In the early 1950s, the astronomers considered expanding the old building to the south, but the steep slope down the southern face of Observatory Hill presented too many difficulties. Such planning was also complicated by the question of whether to relocate the old Clark 15.6-inch refractor to a better site. The solution appeared on the horizon when the Board of Regents approved, in 1955, the addition of an eastward extension to Sterling Hall to be funded by gifts from the Wisconsin Alumni Research Foundation (WARF), which eventually amounted to $1.2 million. Originally planned to be four floors, the new wing would house physics laboratories as well as the new Army Mathematics Research Center. By 1957, before the project was complete, two additional floors had been added to the plans so that the Astronomy Department could be accommodated on the sixth floor with additional space on the roof. The roof would support the dome of the modest planetarium, used for astronomy instruction, which had previously been housed inconveniently across campus in Journalism Hall (near the present site of Helen C. White Hall). In addition, provision was made for rooftop observatory domes to house smaller telescopes (including Burnham's 6-inch Clark refractor formerly in the Student Observatory on Observatory Hill) for instructional use. So, under Whitford's leadership, the astronomers vacated the hallowed but long-outgrown halls of Washburn Observatory itself. By mid-year 1959, the astronomers were moving into the newly completed east wing of Sterling Hall with a machine shop, library, laboratories, office spaces, and classrooms providing a new level of research and teaching support. Thus, Wisconsin astronomers were finally equipped for the new level of activity then developing for both space and ground-based astronomy.

The 15.6-inch Clark refractor remained behind on Observatory Hill because, being an antique of minimal use for modern research, relocating it made no sense. The original Student Observatory on the hill was donated to Madison Astronomical Society (MAS), the local amateur astronomy club, to which Professor C. M. Huffer had close ties, on the condition that they relocate it at their expense to a new site, which they did. (After many years of use by MAS, the building was donated to the town of Fitchburg, which maintains it as a landmark that stands prominently above Fish Hatchery Road to this day.) After the astronomers moved out, the Washburn Observatory building's first floor and basement were remodeled extensively to provide a home for the Institute for Research in the Humanities. Until 2008, Washburn Observatory would be the home to advanced scholars, many visiting Madison from around the globe, doing research and writing in history, classics, philosophy, and other fields. The 15.6-inch telescope and its dome were almost all that remained of astronomy on Observatory Hill, but they remained fully functional and in use for classroom instruction and public viewing (on the traditional first and third Wednesday nights of each month) while the scholars labored on the floors below. (As of Spring 2009, the historic Washburn Observatory building nears the completion of another remodeling accompanied by extensive historical restoration. When the remodeling is complete, the building will become the home of the Honors Program of the UW-Madison College of Letters and Science. The telescope and dome will remain essentially unchanged and continue to be available to visitors.)

Access to a modern research telescope remained a problem even after the move to Sterling Hall. The 15.6-inch refractor, having been remounted (the original Clark mounting was removed and replaced with one made by Warner & Swasey) and improved in 1933, remained fully functional, but the often cloudy Wisconsin skies, increasing light pollution from city and campus, and especially competition from ever larger reflecting telescopes, rendered the venerable refractor increasingly unsuitable for competitive research. Huffer was able to continue his highly specialized photometric work on eclipsing binary stars using the

Albert E. Whitford (1906-2002), fifth director of the Washburn Observatory (1948-1958), left, and C. Morse Huffer, right, inspect the mirror blank for the 36-inch Pine Bluff Observatory telescope, circa 1952. (UW Astronomy Dept.)

15.6-inch up until the new instruments at Pine Bluff Observatory became available in the late 50s – a remarkable testament to the utility of such a classic telescope. Other, much larger refractors, like the giants of Yerkes and Lick Observatories continued to find roles in research, but it was rare even then to find a relatively small instrument like Washburn's still active in research. Most cutting-edge research projects required greater light-collecting power. Stebbins, often accompanied by Whitford, had repeatedly managed to get access to larger instruments, notably at Mt. Wilson, in order to keep his research program competitive. But relying on the indulgence of large, distant observatories for telescope access was a significant handicap for research, instrument development, and training of graduate students. With his usual prescience, Stebbins had initiated discussion after the war of a larger "country" telescope, but issues of funding and a suitable site stalled any action.

Whitford, like his mentor, recognized a new telescope as a priority, and by early 1955 he was making the case for the new instrument to UW's President Fred. By late 1955, the WARF Trustees had approved funding and by late 1956

The Pine Bluff Observatory, circa 1960. (UW Astronomy Dept.)

the Board of Regents had endorsed Wisconsin's first new research telescope project since Washburn Observatory opened in 1881. Whitford saw to the acquisition of a 36-inch reflecting telescope from Boller & Chivens taking advantage of the fact that Yerkes Observatory wanted a similar instrument for their photometric work at McDonald Observatory, which they operated in partnership with the University of Texas. It made sense to let one design serve for two telescopes with very similar missions, namely to serve as "light buckets" for photometric measurements rather than more complex systems for refined astrophotography. The Yerkes optical shop made both telescope mirrors. Whitford also oversaw the construction of a new observatory to house and support the work of the new telescope. The new observatory took shape about 20 miles west of Madison on a high ridge above the little town of Pine Bluff, Wisconsin. Arthur Code, Whitford's eventual successor, but then a young faculty member who helped with the site search, recalls that they expected that urban development (and hence light pollution) would take place mostly in the directions of Middleton and Verona, so they hoped the Pine Bluff site might retain its dark sky longer than sites to the north and south. Pine Bluff Observatory (PBO), with a research-grade telescope and dark skies, was a major

Pointing out through an open dome slit at Pine Bluff Observatory, a spectropolarimeter coupled to a 36-inch telescope records data from a distant target in the sky. (Jeff Miller/UW-Madison)

enhancement to the capabilities of UW astronomers. PBO opened in 1958 and has since been the site of many research programs and instrument development programs and also hosts astronomical instruments constructed and operated by the UW Physics Department. A modern research telescope under their direct control was a major advantage for the entire department, including graduate students, who would otherwise have a difficult time winning access to instruments belonging to other institutions.

By the time he left UW in 1958 to become director of California's Lick Observatory (following in the footsteps of his nineteenth-century predecessor Edward Holden), Whitford had radically transformed UW astronomy by shaping an academic department, guiding the relocation to modern facilities, and acquiring a powerful new research instrument. Whitford, more than any other single director, established the foundations that would allow Washburn Observatory to adapt to the new opportunities and challenges of the nascent Space Age and flourish in it.

Wisconsin was well known already to the astronomical world before Whitford, as the careers of Watson, Holden, Comstock, and Stebbins show. As we have seen, the University of Chicago had chosen Williams Bay, on the shore of Lake Geneva, in southern Wisconsin, as the site of their new Yerkes Observatory and home of the largest refracting telescope ever used for research. Thus, Williams Bay was, as of the observatory's opening in 1897, immediately on the astronomical map of the world. The astronomical community at Yerkes became integrated into the Williams Bay community: the Yerkes staff to this day own homes, serve on school and town boards, pay their taxes, raise their families, and find well deserved retirement in southern Wisconsin. Well known Yerkes astronomer W. W. Morgan, for example, was elected to the Williams Bay Village Board from 1943 to 1951, serving as chair (and de facto mayor) the last four of those years.

Under director Otto Struve (director 1932-1948), Williams Bay became the training ground, work place, and often the home of many talented astrophysicists from around the world including Struve himself, Subrahmanyan Chandrasekhar, Gerard Kuiper, Bengt Strömgren, as well as later Washburn director Arthur D. Code. Yerkes also attracted world-famous visitors to southern Wisconsin, famously including Albert Einstein, but also a variety of foreign delegations and many who came for longer periods to collaborate on shared research interests.

Albert Einstein (eighth from the right) with the staff of the Yerkes Observatory in 1921. Yerkes director Edwin Frost is directly to the left of Einstein. (Barnett Harris, AIP Emilio Segre Visual Archives, Physics Today Collection)

The reputation of Wisconsin astronomy can be measured by the fact that after World War II, in 1946, the International Astronomical Union convened a meeting in Copenhagen to attempt to restart European astronomical research devastated by the war. The three U.S. representatives to that meeting were Harlow Shapley of Harvard, Otto Struve of Williams Bay, and Joel Stebbins of Madison.

Shortly after World War II, Struve attempted to lure Albert Whitford away from the University of Wisconsin in order to establish a Yerkes expertise in photoelectric photometry, but Whitford preferred to remain in Madison. Yerkes astronomers were well aware of the developing photometric technology in Madison and were among the first to request a Washburn photoelectric photometer so that they could begin to assess the new methods for themselves.

Wisconsin's astronomers shaped national and international astronomy in other ways too. As noted earlier, George Comstock was one of the founding members of the American Astronomical Society and, like Stebbins, Whitford, and Code after him, served in various roles including president of the society. Most important in this respect was Whitford, who, while still at Madison, helped create one of the most influential forces in modern science, the idea of a national observatory.

A National Observatory

Scientific research and development programs organized on a national scale had proved to be very effective, perhaps even crucial in the successful outcome of World War II. From the invention

of fluorescent lights to radar, jet engines to the atomic bomb, "national" laboratories demonstrated the potential of federally funded development efforts to marshal the nation's technical talents toward even the most challenging of goals. Certain military planners realized this immediately after the war and found ways to support pure scientific research. The Office of Naval Research (ONR), for example, was very supportive of astronomers, and sig-

Replica of Sputnik I, *the world's first artificial satellite. (NS-SDC/NASA)*

nificant ONR funding came to Washburn Observatory to support Whitford's work. Fueling the engines of scientific research was a major part of the motivation for the establishment of the National Science Foundation (NSF) in 1950. Starting just after the war, developments in rocketry for both military and scientific ends were pointing to the exploration of space, which would become an international obsession after the October 1957 launch of Sputnik, the first artificial satellite, by the Soviet Union. Astronomers like Whitford saw the coming demands on the scientific research establishment and realized the inadequacy of a "system" in which a handful of major research universities and private institutions controlled access to the nation's largest telescopes. Whitford's own work had benefited from Stebbins' connections at Mt. Wilson, which secured the Wisconsin astronomers access to the Carnegie Institution's 100-inch reflector. But without such connections, how could even the most energetic and ingenious astronomers ever get a chance to visit the astronomical frontiers?

In early 1953, Whitford, along with Otto Struve, Ira Bowen (Mt. Wilson Observatory), and Robert McMath (University of Michigan) were appointed by the NSF to consider the possibility of a national observatory that would be open to all qualified astronomers subject only to the scientific merit of their proposals. The goal was to build a large mountain-top telescope where the sky was dark and clear most of the time. Whitford, who was at the hub of these organizing efforts, envisioned that the national observatory would be run by a consortium of academic astronomy departments funded in part by their universities and in part by NSF. The first result, in 1959, was the creation of the Association of Universities for Research in Astronomy (AURA), in which the University of Wisconsin was a founding member. The second result was the construction of Kitt Peak National Observatory west of Tucson, Arizona, where UW astronomers have now

Aerial view of the Kitt Peak National Observatory as it appeared in 2003. In the foreground is the McMath-Pierce solar facility, the largest solar telescope in the world. At far right is the dome housing the 4-meter Mayall telescope, with the two domes of the WIYN Observatory at far left. (NOAO/AURA/NSF)

pursued research goals for a half century. AURA was soon running observatories beyond Kitt Peak, including the National Solar Observatory, the National Radio Astronomy Observatory, and eventually the Space Telescope Science Institute (the founding director of which in 1980 would be Art Code, Whitford's successor as Washburn director).

To the Stars

Joel Stebbins could not have known in the 1920s that his work would set later generations of Wisconsin astronomers on a path to the stars that would open wide after Sputnik's dramatic voyage. The world had been preparing to enter space for some time: one of the scientific goals for the International Geophysical Year 1957-1958 was to place an artificial satellite in orbit around the earth to probe its space environment. But Sputnik shifted the idea of space exploration from a purely scientific endeavor to a political-military competition and a symbol of Cold War tensions. The imperative for both sides to demonstrate scientific and technological strength as proof of their ideological superiority resulted in astronauts, orbiting laboratories, Moon landings, and robots racing to planets and other extra-terrestrial destinations. Part of the U.S. response was the founding of the National Aeronautics and Space Administration (NASA), almost exactly one year after the launch of Sputnik, as the primary and nominally civilian agency for space science and exploration. NASA's missions included human exploration of space as well as unmanned exploration of the distant universe, and Wisconsin has produced astronauts, space scientists, and spacecraft in answer to the call.

NASA's program to gain experience with human spaceflight began with Project Mercury (1959-1963), and the first group of Mercury astronauts, the "Mercury Seven," included Donald K. "Deke" Slayton, a native of Sparta, Wisconsin. Like many of the other early astronauts, Slayton was a veteran combat pilot (he served in World War II) and had, by the mid-1950s, become a test pilot. Slayton

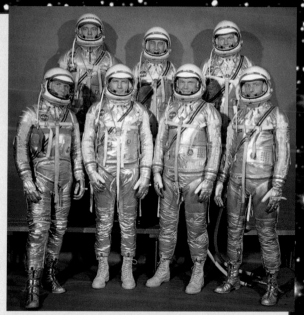

The Mercury 7, NASA's first class of astronauts. Front row, from left: Walter M. "Wally" Schirra (1923-2007), Donald K. "Deke" Slayton (1924-1993), John H. Glenn (b. 1921), M. Scott Carpenter (b. 1925). Back row: Alan B. Shepard (1923-1998), Virgil I. "Gus" Grissom (1926-1967), L. Gordon "Gordo" Cooper (1927-2004). (NASA)

never flew in the Mercury Program owing to a heart condition, discovered after his original selection, which disqualified him for space flight owing to the extremely conservative protocols of those early days. Despite being removed from the flight rosters, Slayton continued with NASA as a manager of astronaut crews until he was re-qualified for flight in 1972. He finally flew on the crew of the Apollo-Soyuz Test Project, in June 1975, in which U.S. and Soviet astronauts conducted successful orbital rendezvous and docking maneuvers bearing both technical significance and strong political overtones. The Deke Slayton Museum in Sparta memorializes his Wisconsin roots.

James A. Lovell is a veteran astronaut of many flights, but most famously the ill-fated Apollo 13, the story of which has been told in books (including one by Lovell himself), film, and television. Lovell is an alumnus of the University of Wisconsin and married Marilyn Gerlach of Milwaukee. His personal ties to Wisconsin are recognized in both the street and museum in Milwaukee bearing his name. Another Apollo astronaut, Harrison H. Schmitt, was the first and only Ph.D. scientist to walk the moon during the Apollo program. A native of New Mexico with doctorate in Geology from Harvard, Schmitt joined the faculty of UW-Madison in 1994 as an Adjunct Professor of Engineering. Astronaut Robert A. Parker was an astronomy professor at the UW when he was selected for the astronaut program in 1967, while Brewster Shaw received B.S. and M.S. degrees in Engineering Mechanics from the UW in 1968 and 1969 before entering NASA's

Viroqua native Mark Lee exits the Space Shuttle Discovery *in the first untethered space walk in ten years on October 2, 2001. (NASA)*

astronaut corps. Another astronomy professor, Kenneth Nordsieck (b. 1946), was in the astronaut corps from 1984 to 1990. Wisconsin natives who have served as astronauts include Mark Lee, a native of Viroqua, Leroy Chiao, from Milwaukee, and Jeffrey Williams of Superior. Last but not least, Wisconsin can claim Dr. Laurel Salton Clark, who died with the rest of the crew of Space Shuttle Columbia on February 1, 2003, at the end of her first mission. She was a veteran flight physician who grew up in Racine and was an alumna of UW-Madison, receiving degrees in Zoology and Medicine in 1983 and 1987, respectively.

Wisconsin became a major player early in the Space Age by virtue of the innovative thought and work of a few university scientists. When Sputnik and its successor satellites showed the feasibility of operating scientific instruments in orbit, scientists of many fields began to consider how satellite-based instruments might open up new ways to understand nature. A prime example is that of meteorologist Professor Verner E. Suomi, who as early as 1963 recognized the scientific potential

of satellites to track weather systems and began searching for practical approaches. Early weather satellites occupied relatively low orbits, which could survey only a small fraction of Earth's surface at a given time, with a field of view that changed constantly. When planning began for geosynchronous satellites, which orbit at an altitude of 22,000 miles, Suomi recognized that a camera on such a satellite could take in a view of an entire hemisphere. Geosynchronous satellites orbit in the same period that the earth rotates, so they appear to hang motionless above a fixed point on the surface and can thus continuously track the atmospheric activity below them. Suomi began working with Electrical Engineering Professor Robert Parent in 1964 to develop a "spin-scan" camera in which the rotation of the satellite itself would sweep the camera's field of view across a strip of the earth. By tipping the camera slightly from one scan to the next, an image of the entire hemisphere could be built up.

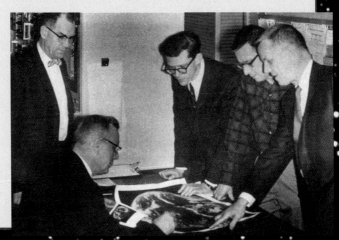

Robert Parent, left, Verner Suomi (1915-1995), seated, and NASA colleagues examine early ATS-I spin-scan camera images. (SSEC)

ATS-I spin-camera image from December 11, 1966. (SSEC)

With funding from NASA and NSF, Suomi and Parent started the Space Science and Engineering Center (SSEC) on the UW-Madison campus in 1965. Their purpose was to develop a spin-scan camera to fly on the ATS-1 satellite, which was eventually launched in 1966 and was very successful. Development of the camera technology continued at SSEC. Cameras on later satellites were sensitive to specific spectral bands that made possible color, moisture, and temperature measuring capabilities. These instruments dramatically advanced our understanding of Earth's atmosphere and weather systems that affect us. Recording, reducing, and analyzing the huge amount of data generated by the instruments was a challenge in itself ("drinking from a firehose" as Suomi liked to put it), so SSEC developed computer processing and data visualization tools that have become widely used. Their expertise in satellite remote sensing instruments was soon applied to planets other than Earth. SSEC supplied Wisconsin-designed and built instruments for interplanetary spacecraft including the Pioneer Venus mission and the Galileo mission to Jupiter. SSEC's expertise in comparative atmospheric science uses images from the Hubble Space Telescope, for example, to study even the dynamic atmosphere of distant Neptune.

Ad astra pro astris (To the stars for the stars)

The UW's entry into space astronomy had its roots in the photoelectric photometry developed by Stebbins and Whitford in the years before World War II. Unlike photographic film, which was what most astronomers used to measure and record light before the 1980s, electronic instruments could be readily adapted to space because radio signals can be used to control them remotely and the results of their measurements can be transmitted back to Earth the same way. In addition, the electronic photometers were sensitive to ultraviolet (UV) light. Astronomers are very interested in UV light from stars, galaxies, comets, planets, etc., but such studies are almost impossible from Earth's surface because our atmosphere blocks nearly all UV from space. So the possibility of building an ultraviolet instrument that would operate on a satellite was no less than the opening of an entirely new field of astronomical research. Astronomers were ignorant, for example, of how much light stars emit in the UV part of the spectrum. Theories of how stars work made predictions of how stellar spectra behaved in the UV, but there was no way to check those theories. UV photometry offered promise of further understanding the physics of interstellar matter – the stuff out of which stars and planets form – just as visual photometry had established its existence and distribution. It was precisely because of the technical expertise and scientific accomplishments of the Stebbins-Whitford era that Arthur D. Code, a young astronomy professor at California Institute of Technology when Sputnik was launched, saw Wisconsin as the place to establish and explore the astronomy of the ultraviolet universe.

SAL Logo

Code knew Wisconsin's astronomical community personally because he had done his graduate work at Yerkes Observatory with Subrahmanyan Chandrasekhar, one of the giants of twentieth-century astrophysics. Soon after Code earned his Ph.D., Whitford recruited him to come to Washburn Observatory to work on photoelectric photometry, which he did from 1951 until 1956, when Code was lured away by Caltech. Soon afterward, in 1958, Whitford, then at the peak of his career, accepted the directorship of California's Lick Observatory. Whitford was intrigued no doubt by the challenge of bringing Lick's new 120-inch telescope to its full potential. But also, despite being the principal architect of the transformations (new department, new building, and new observatory) of the Washburn Observatory, he might have felt that organizing the rapidly expanding programs of undergraduate and graduate instruction was not where his talents were best employed. Thus in the summer of 1958, Art Code accepted the position of director of the Washburn Observatory with the intention of establishing a space astronomy program as well as expanding faculty and graduate programs. In doing so he gave up a tenured position at Caltech with access to major research telescopes and other facilities

Professor Arthur D. Code, astronomer, sixth director of Washburn Observatory, founder of Space Astronomy Laboratory, leader of UW OAO team and leader of WUPPE team. (UW Astronomy Dept.)

in return for the opportunity to take astronomy in the completely new direction he envisioned. In order to attract Code, the UW agreed to a further expansion of the Astronomy Department, and Code convinced his Caltech colleague, Donald E. Osterbrock to accept a new faculty position and relocate to Madison. The department further expanded by hiring a theoretician, Professor John S. Mathis. This rapid expansion was simultaneously building a base for more ambitious research programs and making possible an expanded graduate studies program.

Meanwhile, recognition of the importance of space science was growing at the national level: NASA was formed to develop the nation's aerospace capacities, and the National Academy of Sciences created a Space Science Board (SSB) to identify and evaluate the myriad new scientific possibilities. One of the first actions by the SSB, in summer 1958, was to send telegrams to selected U.S. astronomers requesting their ideas for satellite experiments. Art Code, newly arrived at Washburn, was one of those astronomers, and he had clear ideas about how to respond to the opportunity. His concept envisioned a 100-pound satellite containing a single reflecting telescope feeding light to a UV-sensitive photoelectric photometer accompanied by the necessary electronics for control, data collection, and telemetry. Although there were a great many suggestions for astronomical satellite experiments, relatively few astronomers were willing to commit to the formal studies and proposals that would be required for actual project development. The most committed of these constituted a group convened by NASA in early 1959 called the Space Science Working Group (SSWG) whose members began receiving NASA funds to explore techniques and methods. Code's commitment to the still unproven potential of space astronomy, which many scientists saw as too risky to build a career on, quickly made him one of the leaders in the SSWG planning.

At the local level, Code prepared for the effort that would be needed to succeed in space astronomy. Working with Assistant Professor Ted Houck, Code set up the Space Astronomy Laboratory (SAL) within the Astronomy Department to support the new level of technical development and operational capabilities of a space astronomy program. Houck (who had earned his Ph.D. with Whitford at Madison) would remain a key figure in the work of SAL for the rest of his abbreviated career. Robert Bless had come to Washburn as a post-doctoral fellow in 1958, after finishing his Astronomy Ph.D. at the University of Michigan, to work on a project started by Whitford with funding from the Office of Naval Research and later the National Science Foundation. The project, continued under Code, was to investigate the absolute energy distributions in stellar spectra, a

Professor Robert C. Bless (b. 1927), astronomer, leading member of UW OAO team, and leader of the High Speed Photometer project. (UW Astronomy Dept.)

problem directly related to the local expertise in photoelectric photometry. Bless, who joined the UW astronomy faculty as Assistant Professor in 1961, also joined SAL at its founding. John McNall, UW Ph.D. in electrical engineering and computer science in 1960, joined the SAL astronomers that same year. With their first NASA funding, the close-knit SAL group began testing small instruments capable of becoming flying scientific payloads. They recognized the need to proceed in small steps in order to master the techniques of instrument design, building, and control, along with data acquisition and processing. Code used his NASA funding efficiently, in part by adding talented, dedicated graduate students to the group. Code's management style was to keep the team small, to minimize bureaucracy, and to keep equipment and instruments as simple as possible. This management style, although at times attracting the suspicion of NASA, was an important element in their success.

SAL's first flying instrument, consisting of a photometer two-thirds the size of a shoebox, was launched in June 1961. It took flight over Lake Mendota on a weather balloon, was tracked by radio from a ground station, and eventually landed in a farmer's field in Illinois. Code recognized another incremental step toward true satellite operation was offered by NASA's X-15 rocket plane. The X-15 could fly high enough to make some UV measurements possible and ensured that the instrument payload would be recovered after the flight. NASA funded SAL's X-15 instrument as a test not only of UV instruments but as an experiment in human control (in this case by the X-15's pilot) of scientific payloads. The X-15 program yielded several successful sets of observations between 1963 and 1966, but technical advances in rocketry offered a new and much more capable instrument platform. This next incremental step forward came with SAL's development of instruments to fly on so-called "sounding" rockets. These are smaller rockets that do not reach orbit (hence also called "suborbital" rockets), but fall back to the ground after reaching altitudes well in excess of 100 miles. Earlier suborbital rocket flights were not designed to recover the payload (which fell back into the ocean), but that had changed by the early 1960s. When all goes according to plan, a parachute opens upon re-entry

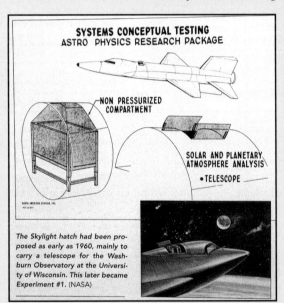

The Skylight hatch had been proposed as early as 1960, mainly to carry a telescope for the Washburn Observatory at the University of Wisconsin. This later became Experiment #1. (NASA)

An illustration from North American Aviation Inc. showing the SAL experiment in the instrument bay of the X-15. (UW Astronomy Dept.)

Aerobee suborbital rocket being assembled for launch. (UW Astronomy Dept.)

enabling the payload to survive landing in the desert of White Sands, New Mexico. Although the time spent in space is limited to a few minutes, suborbital rocket instruments can be much cheaper than satellite instruments, so they were a perfect testbed for SAL experimentation. The first flights, beginning in 1962, served as a step on the way to a satellite mission, but suborbital rocket experiments proved so cost effective and scientifically productive that they have remained a specialty of Wisconsin astronomers and physicists since those test flights of the early 1960s.

Orbiting Astronomical Observatory

All of this early SAL development was leading to the goal of a true UV observatory in space, which NASA called the Orbiting Astronomical Observatory (OAO) program. NASA decided early on that the common requirements (pointing accuracy and stability, programmable command and control, electrical power, communications, etc.) of the various proposed space astronomy instruments made it logical to design a standard OAO spacecraft able to carry and support a variety of payloads. The proposed spacecraft design was a hexagonal column about 10 feet tall and 7 feet wide. Winglike solar panels stretched more than 20 feet from the sides. The hollow center of the spacecraft enclosed a 4 feet diameter tube running through the center to accommodate instruments that would look out the ends. Able to encompass instruments much larger than Code's original 100-pound photometer satellite, the design of the SAL instrument (called the Wisconsin Experiment Package, or WEP) grew more ambitious and sophisticated while still guided by the SAL design mantra of simplicity. (Note: A full-scale OAO prototype spacecraft with prototype WEP is on public display at UW Space Place in Madison.) WEP would consist of one central reflecting telescope with a 16-inch mirror delivering light to a UV photometer, four 8-inch telescopes, each with its own UV photometer package, and two low-resolution scanning spectro-photometers. Each of these instruments was a descendant of the Stebbins-Whitford instruments.

Since its founding, SAL had moved to several locations, finally setting up shop in the summer of 1960 in an empty warehouse at 35 N. Park Street, about a fifteen minute walk from the Astronomy Department in Sterling Hall. With laboratories and machine shop in operation there, most of SAL's early payloads took shape on that site, including WEP's components. Fabrication of these instruments involved a number of technical challenges. For example, the UV filters required were not available anywhere, so the techniques for depositing multilayer thin films on glass to make the needed filters had to be developed by SAL's Dan Schroeder (who, after finishing his Ph.D., became a physics professor at Beloit College and later an im-

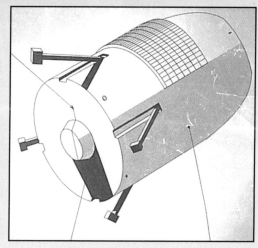

Sketch of Code's early "100-pound" UV satellite concept, which eventually developed into the Wisconsin Experiment Package. (UW Astronomy Dept.)

portant member of the Hubble Space Telescope project). Manufacture of these filters continued under Tim Fairchild and were a specialty of SAL for the next 20 years. Although the actual building of the WEP electronics was done by SAL in Madison, the detailed design and testing of the instrument package and its associated electronics required the resources of an experienced aerospace contractor. The bids submitted included some from major aerospace contractors, but the winning bid came from a much smaller and closer Chicago area firm, Cook Technological Center. Code and his team were pleased with this outcome reasoning that a smaller firm would work better with the SAL management style. Also, being relatively nearby, it would be easier for the SAL team to work with Cook on such a complex project than with any firm on the east or west coast.

By late 1961, SAL was at work with Cook to produce prototype instruments suitable for tests on suborbital rocket flights scheduled for late 1961 and 1964, with still others to follow. SAL scientists Ted Houck and John McNall handled the majority of the seemingly endless meetings and reviews that keep large, complex projects on track. It must have felt auspicious and encouraging that the September 1964 SAL suborbital mission produced a major scientific result: Wisconsin's UV astronomers solved a puzzle first posed by a Goddard Spaceflight Center measurement, which seemed to show some stars to be oddly dim in the UV. But, in fact, the expected UV light was there, thus eliminating the need for theories to explain why the light was disappearing. Such a result hinted at the scientific potential promised by the OAO project. Unlike the few earlier attempts at space astronomy, which were mostly specialized suborbital experiments, OAO would be highly flexible and able to conduct a wide variety of observations. NASA designed the OAO spacecraft to be capable of pointing its instruments anywhere in the sky to an accuracy of one arc minute (one-sixtieth of a degree) and maintain that orientation

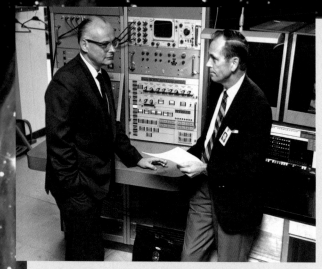

Professor Theodore E. "Ted" Houck (on the left) (1926-1974), astronomer and leading member of the UW OAO team. (UW Astronomy Dept.)

to an accuracy of one arc second (one-sixtieth of a minute). Two instrument packages, back-to-back in the central corridor of the satellite, looked out in diametrically opposite directions on the sky. (Code and Bless both recall that this arrangement, first suggested by the Wisconsin team, was first met with resistance from the NASA engineers, but quickly became a "feature" of the spacecraft design.) The OAO program was thus a huge step forward from small limited experiments to a 4,600 pound spacecraft in a 500 mile high orbit.

WEP was completed, tested, delivered to NASA, and installed in the first OAO spacecraft in time for a launch in Spring of 1966. WEP's companion instrument, looking out the other end of the satellite, was a set of gamma-ray and x-ray instruments designed at MIT by a team including William Kraushaar, with his MIT colleague Frank Scherb, both of whom would later join the faculty of UW-Madison's Physics Department. After a series of launch delays, bringing the teams to near exhaustion because of the constant replanning of post-launch orbital operations, which had to be redone after every delay, the launch took place on April 8, 1966. To everyone's relief, the Atlas-Agena rocket delivered the OAO-1 satellite successfully into orbit. Art Code and Bob Bless liked to joke that their first WEP instrument performed flawlessly: the WEP was turned off before launch, commanded to stay off, and it did so. The mission was a total disaster. As soon as ground

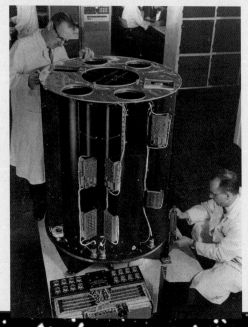

The Wisconsin Experiment Package (WEP), before installation in the spacecraft, being checked by Cook Technology Center engineers. The WEP controller is visible below. (UW Astronomy Dept.)

The launch of the highly successful OAO-2 mission on December 7, 1968. (UW Astronomy Dept.)

controllers turned on electrical power to some of the spacecraft systems, big trouble appeared. No one knows exactly what happened, but the failures are consistent with electrical discharges – sparks and arcs – when the high voltage power supplies were turned on. The electrical surges and interruptions caused other systems to malfunction and fail, and radio contact with the satellite was lost. Soon after, ground-based radar indicated several pieces where OAO-1 should have been. One theory is that the batteries overcharged and exploded. In any case, by Easter Sunday 1966, SAL's first satellite mission was over before it had started.

In reviewing the huge loss, NASA concluded that they could fix things well enough to try again with a new OAO, and they proved themselves correct in that. Other experiments were awaiting their chance to fly in the OAO series, and complex negotiations ensued, but in the end NASA wanted to know: Would SAL be willing to build a second WEP identical with the one lost on OAO-1? Code concluded that the effort already invested in design and testing, not to mention the scientific work that still awaited, was justification enough to try again. A second WEP was built by SAL and Cook, tested, and delivered to NASA, which launched OAO-2 on December 7, 1968. This time WEP's companion instrument was a set of UV imaging cameras from the Smithsonian Astrophysical Observatory. Tensions were, of course, high in the first hours of the mission, but the spacecraft and its systems were energized without incident and operations began. Bless recalls that actual satellite operation was much more complex than they had anticipated, so the team members had to work very hard in the first weeks to understand the quirks in the OAO pointing system, the disturbances caused by anomalies in Earth's magnetic field, technical limitations in the instrument electronics, and the like. John McNall and his graduate student Curt Heacox wrote sophisticated software to handle the intricate process of scheduling scientific observations, which had to take into account available target objects, spacecraft pointing motions and limitations, contact opportunities with ground control stations, orbital night and day, terrestrial magnetic field disturbances, and instrument setup (such as filter selections, exposure time, etc.). The software then generated a set of commands that was transmitted to the OAO to control its operations for the planned observing period. With OAO-2 operational as the first space observatory, scientific investigations could begin in earnest.

WEP was such a scientific success that the OAO-2 mission, originally scheduled to last one year, was extended by NASA several times. By the time OAO-2 operations were forced to end (by failure of the WEP power supply) in January 1973, WEP had observed about 1,200 different objects, including seven planets, two comets, hundreds of stars, a bright nova (a stellar explosion), and a variety of nebulae and galaxies. All this observing activity produced an impressive list of scientific results. The scientific results were published in a number of places, but were largely summarized in a NASA symposium publication edited by Code and published in 1972. Art Code has stated that in his view the catalog of UV stellar spectra compiled was the most important scientific product of the OAO-2 mission. Of great importance to astronomers was the first real understanding of the "interstellar extinction" in the UV, that is, how interstellar dust blocks and scatters starlight as a function of the wavelength of the light. (This, again, was a logical extension of the studies of interstellar matter and extinction in visible light that had begun with Steb-

bins and Whitford.) Among many other scientific results, WEP observations of Nova Serpentis 1970 (an explosive stellar outburst that occurred during the OAO-2 mission) showed that UV brightness of the nova increased even as the visual bright-

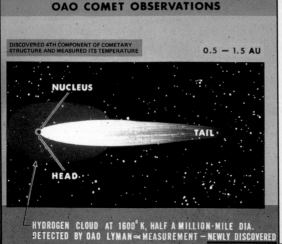

OAO COMET OBSERVATIONS

DISCOVERED 4TH COMPONENT OF COMETARY STRUCTURE AND MEASURED ITS TEMPERATURE   0.5 — 1.5 AU

NUCLEUS

TAIL

HEAD

HYDROGEN CLOUD AT 1600°K, HALF A MILLION-MILE DIA. DETECTED BY OAO LYMAN-∝ MEASUREMENT — NEWLY DISCOVERED

Above: UW-Madison Astronomy Department personnel, circa 1970. Front row from left: Arthur Code, Bea Ersland, Donald Osterbrock. Back row: Jack Forbes, John McNall, Lowell Doherty, Robert Bless, Chris Anderson, John Mathis, Blair Savage. Left: Diagram prepared by Grumman Corp. illustrating the discovery of a new component of the structure of comets by WEP instruments. UV observations revealed a huge cloud of hydrogen surrounding the head of Comet Bennett, observed in 1970, which indicated breakdown of water molecules contained in the comet. (UW Astronomy Dept.)

This old warehouse at 35 N. Park St. was home to the Space Astronomy Laboratory during much of the OAO project. (UW Astronomy Dept.)

ness decreased. This finding brought about a new understanding of the behavior of the expanding shell of luminous matter ejected by this kind of stellar explosion. Another highly influential result came from the discovery of huge clouds of hydrogen, detectable by its UV emission, surrounding the nuclei of two comets that appeared in 1970. The hydrogen was identified as a breakdown product of water, thus showing that water is a common and plentiful constituent of comets and hence would have been plentiful in the formation of the planets early in the development of the solar system. In the final analysis, Bob Bless observes, perhaps the greatest impact of the OAO-2 mission was to demonstrate conclusively that UV astronomy was as important as they had thought it might be and that first-class space astronomy research was within the means of current technology. Had either of these factors come out in the negative, finding support for subsequent UV work, and perhaps any other space astronomy projects, like the Hubble Space Telescope, would have been much more difficult.

In nearly every respect, OAO-2 represented a tremendous step forward. OAO-2 was the largest scientific satellite to date, enabling it to carry a versatile suite of instruments and to provide the power, thermal control, communications, pointing abilities and the like needed by the instruments. It could carry out automatic observing programs, store the resulting data, and relay it to Earth. It was capable of long-term operations, yet available to take advantage of unforeseeable opportunities, such as comets and novas. It was controlled from Earth by a team of astronomers who sought to maximize the scientific value of the program and knew their machine well enough to do just that. OAO-2 was, in fact, the first true general purpose space observatory, and it set the standard for success in the many incremental stages that followed, leading eventually to the Hubble Space Telescope.

The prominent success of OAO-2 and WEP set the stage for two major projects that came to dominate SAL activity in the 1980s. One was an instrument designed to fly on the Hubble Space Telescope, the other was to be part of a series of astronomical space shuttle missions. Both were direct descendants of WEP,

From left, Professors Art Code, Ted Houck, John McNall (1930-1978), and Bob Bless examining one of the 8-inch photometric telescopes that were part of the WEP. (UW Astronomy Dept.)

and many members of SAL's WEP team were key to the new projects. After OAO-2, NASA launched two more in the OAO series (one was a serious failure; the other, renamed Copernicus, a notable success). The idea of a much larger general-purpose space observatory, a "Large Space Telescope," had been in various stages of planning for many years. Wisconsin's astronomers, largely as a result of the success of OAO-2, were deeply involved in the Space Telescope from the beginning. Bless, Houck, and McNall served on various NASA panels helping to define scientific goals and instruments for the project. Late in the project but before launch as delays became a serious concern to the astronomical community, NASA chose Bless to chair an oversight committee to monitor progress and make assessment reports to NASA. Code chaired a committee charged with considering the organizational possibilities for creating and operating the new space observatory and later guided the efforts of AURA, which won the contract to create and operate the Space Telescope Science Institute, of which he was the acting director in its formative stages. Wisconsin astronomers also served on several of the instrument teams other than SAL's own: Code worked on the Wide Field/Planetary Camera project, as did Professor John Hoessel, and Professor Blair Savage worked on the team that produced the High Resolution Spectrograph.

By 1978, the project, eventually named the Hubble Space Telescope, had been designed to be a remotely operated general purpose facility launched in the cargo bay of the Space Shuttle – a decision that placed significant constraints on many aspects of size and operations. It was unique in being designed to be serviced and upgraded in orbit by astronauts. (This would prove to be the salvation of the entire project.) The Space Shuttle was to have other scientific missions as well, including acting as an orbiting platform for temporary specialized astronomical instruments that could be operated by astronaut astronomers in real time. These two types of operation – remotely operated space observatory and shuttle-based, manned astronomy experiments – would give rise to the next two major initiatives for UW-Madison's Space Astronomy Laboratory, the High Speed Photometer and the Wisconsin Ultraviolet Photo-Polarimeter Experiment (WUPPE).

UW Astronomy and the Hubble Space Telescope

The High Speed Photometer (HSP) grew out of a simpler idea in response to a unique opportunity in much the same way that WEP had come about. NASA requested ideas from the community of astronomers for instruments to become part of the new space telescope. To Wisconsin's astronomers, for whom photometry was a familiar and powerful technique, it made sense that the new space telescope should have photometric capabilities. But in the SAL tradition of keeping things as simple as possible, Bless's team proposed a small instrument with no moving parts and very simple operations. The space photometer would operate much like a ground-based model, but would take advantage of being behind a big telescope high above our atmosphere to try something new: making measurements as rapidly as 100,000 times per second; hence a "high speed" photometer. On Earth's surface this is nearly impossible to do because our restless atmosphere constantly distorts images, making them blur and shimmer. (This is what makes stars twinkle.) Hence, in high speed photometry from the ground, it is hard to distinguish atmospheric effects from those in the object. High time-resolution measurements could reveal, for example, the details of incandescent matter falling into black holes, the vagaries of rapidly rotating neutron stars, the structure in planetary ring systems, behavior of stellar eruptions, and so on, all of which are observations limited by our fluctuating atmosphere. And in space, of course, there is access to the UV and infrared parts of the spectrum. Measurement of the polarization of starlight would add a further dimension. HSP would once again take Wisconsin's photometry tradition in an

The Hubble Space Telescope in orbit. It initially carried five primary science instruments, one of which was the UW Space Astronomy Laboratory's High Speed Photometer. (NASA)

The Crab Nebula, consisting of remnants of a star that exploded over 1,000 years ago, contains a rapidly spinning neutron star (not visible here), called a pulsar. HSP made the first ultraviolet observations of the pulsar's flashes. (NASA/ESA/J. Hester and A. Loll (Arizona State University))

entirely new direction. NASA found the scientific possibilities compelling enough that instead of the small auxiliary instrument originally proposed by SAL, they wanted HSP to be enhanced in abilities and promoted to one of the five primary science instruments to be launched with Hubble. Despite the expanded scale and capacity, HSP remained the simplest and least expensive of the Hubble's science instruments, capable of a vast variety of observing modes and filter combinations yet without a single moving part.

Bless decided that SAL did not have adequate facilities, such as clean rooms and technical shops, to handle the construction of HSP, especially since WUPPE, the shuttle-based instrument, was also being built at SAL. Bless discussed the project with the UW-Madison Space Science and Engineering Center (SSEC), only one block away from SAL's home base in Chamberlin Hall. SSEC collaborated

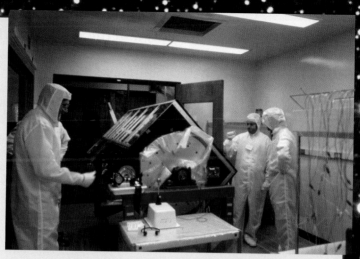

The High Speed Photometer under construction around 1985 in the clean room at UW's Space Science and Engineering Center. On the left is Principal Investigator Robert Bless, on the right facing the camera is Project Manager Evan Richards. (UW Astronomy Dept.)

in the final proposal to NASA and, after SAL won the award, SSEC received the subcontract for the construction and testing program of the new instrument. Thus, in addition to being the simplest and least expensive of the Hubble science instruments, it was the only one constructed entirely on a university campus. In addition, quite a few UW students, both graduate and undergraduates, were employed in various aspects of the project. SAL delivered the instrument to NASA on schedule for acceptance testing in 1983 and launch in 1990. HSP operated perfectly for its entire mission, but it was not a happy ending.

The dramatic story of the Hubble Space Telescope's flawed mirror, a complex tragedy of poor management by the Perkin-Elmer Corporation and NASA, has been often told. Less well known is that HSP was the final victim of the story. The flawed mirror produced distorted star images instead of the sharp spots of light that all the science instruments needed for their best work. HSP's performance was particularly hurt by the optical problem, which made the star images even bigger than the smaller apertures of HSP's photometers. This considerably reduced the efficiency of the instrument and prevented much of the planned observations. Moreover, during most of the time that HSP was in the Hubble telescope, the telescope systems had a pointing instability that made it very difficult to keep the light, poorly focused as it was, centered on the entrance apertures of HSP's photometers. Despite these handicaps, the HSP team completed a number of successful observing programs with published results including the most precise visible light pulse profile and the first ever UV pulse profile of the pulsar in the heart of the Crab Nebula. NASA engineers eventually fixed the Hubble Space Telescope on the first space shuttle servicing mission in December 1993. The plan was to remove one of the science instruments and use that space to install corrective optics that would restore the near perfect images that the telescope was designed to deliver. The instrument chosen for that sacrifice was HSP, which returned to Earth after a flawless mission but with disappointing results; the Hubble observatory's mission and reputation were salvaged by that painful compromise.

UW Astronomy and the Space Shuttle

The Hubble Space Telescope was delivered to Earth orbit by the space shuttle and then left there to operate under ground control. But NASA also planned a series of missions in which the shuttle would be loaded with a specially designed space astronomy observatory designed to work in the shuttle bay under the active control of astronomer-astronauts. The so-called "Astro" missions would be dedicated to the already highly productive programs of UV astronomy, of which OAO-2 had been the pioneer. SAL saw a new opportunity in an instrument called a spectro-polarimeter, which measures the amount and direction of polarized light received from an astronomical object. Polarization can convey information about shapes and sizes of stars and the disks of matter that often surround them (which, in many cases, hold nascent systems of planets). Polarization can also be used to probe the nature and distribution of the interstellar matter of our galaxy. Study of interstellar matter had been a major activity of the Stebbins-Whitford era and had become a strength of the Washburn astronomers at both the theoretical and observational levels through the work, for example, of Professors John Mathis and Don Osterbrock. Extending spectro-polarimetry into the UV would be valuable research and could be done with a polarimetric instrument invented by Professor Ken Nordsieck, but it could only be done from space like most UV observing. So Professor Nordsieck's instrument became the heart of the Wisconsin Ultraviolet Photo-Polarimeter Experiment (WUPPE), which would accomplish the first ever polarimetry at wavelengths invisible on Earth's surface. But the timing was awkward because the HSP and WUPPE opportunities came along at the same time. Art Code recalled that his philosophy of conflicting opportunities has always been "If you come to a fork in the road, go both ways." So SAL wrote both proposals, one for the space telescope and the other for the space shuttle program, expecting that they would be lucky to land even one of them given the stiff competition for major NASA projects, and little expecting that both, as it turned out, would be accepted. Code led the WUPPE team with Bless as co-leader, Bless led the HSP team with Code as his co-leader. As HSP took form in the facilities of SSEC, WUPPE

Astronauts Story Musgrave and Jeffrey Hoffman working on the Hubble Space Telescope, temporarily docked in the space shuttle cargo bay, during the first servicing mission in December 1993. The astronaut on the left maneuvers the corrective optics package, which replaced HSP, into the telescope's science instrument section. (NASA)

came together on the sixth floor of Chamberlin Hall. One of the ideas behind the Astro missions was that instruments under active control from the shuttle itself could be operated more like ground-based instruments, e.g., responding rapidly to changing conditions, adapting to unexpected results, and seizing unforeseen opportunities. Toward that end, NASA recruited astronomers to enter the astronaut program as "payload specialist" astronauts, a path Ken Nordsieck followed in 1984. He ultimately left the

UW-Madison's Kenneth Nordsieck (b. 1946) in a zero-gravity simulation flight during his astronaut training. (NASA)

astronaut corps in 1990 without flying a space mission and directed his efforts to the flight of Astro-2 and other projects.

WUPPE (invariably pronounced "whoopee") coupled Nordsieck's polarimeter instrument to a 0.5 meter reflecting telescope along with all the necessary control and support equipment. WUPPE would fly as one member of a suite of UV instruments built by other groups to accomplish tasks such as imaging and spectrometry all mounted on a common pointing platform in the cargo bay of a space shuttle. WUPPE and its companion instruments could be controlled, and their data examined, from inside the shuttle itself or from the ground. Although WUPPE was the largest and most complex instrument program ever undertaken by SAL, it was delivered to NASA on time for its integration into the shuttle and eventual launch on the mission called "Astro-1," which was originally scheduled for February of 1986 aboard the space shuttle Columbia. Astro-1 was to be the first of six such astronomical spaceflights, but that plan changed in January 1986. WUPPE and the Astro-1 payload were already at Kennedy Space Center being loaded into Columbia, and Nordsieck and his fellow Astro payload specialists were preparing at KSC, when the space shuttle Challenger exploded during launch on January 29, 1986. Challenger's entire crew and payload were lost, and WUPPE was stranded on the ground.

No shuttles would fly for a several years as NASA's inquiries into the explosion proceeded and the agency re-evaluated their operations. Payload instruments that were ready to fly, like WUPPE, went into storage for the duration. Besides the long delay, the Challenger disaster resulted in, among other things, a large shift in NASA's priorities for shuttle missions. In particular, science-specific missions were reduced in number, and the scheduled Astro missions were reduced to two. WUPPE did eventually fly after NASA resumed shuttle operations. The Astro-1

From left, Kenneth Nordsieck, Arthur Code, and Professor Christopher Anderson with WUPPE in the background. (UW Astronomy Dept.)

flight was finally launched aboard Shuttle Columbia on December 2, 1990, and flew for nine days. Nordsieck, as alternate payload specialist for that mission, was the chief ground-to-air communicator, which proved to be a very challenging job. The mission's science was plagued with problems, mostly in the shuttle's payload interface and control systems. The control system problems considerably slowed and limited the observations, although with a great deal of trouble-shooting and replanning, the orbital and ground-based teams did eventually develop new methods that made possible some successful scientific work. The Astro-2 flight aboard Shuttle Endeavor flew a record-breaking 17-day mission March 2-18, 1995. Astronomical observations on this mission went smoothly and were very productive. WUPPE observed a wide variety of objects, using the first UV spectro-polarimetry to investigate solar system objects, distant galaxies, and unusual and exploding stars. WUPPE's success encouraged further development of UV polarimeters sensitive to diffuse objects

WUPPE and the Astro payload viewed through the space shuttle's payload bay windows with the constellation Orion in the background. WUPPE is the right-most of the instruments in the cluster with its dark, rectangular sunshade near the top. (UW Astronomy Dept.)

and higher spectral resolution spectro-polarimeters going farther into the ultraviolet. During its missions WUPPE made UV spectro-polarimetric observations of 121 objects and collected spectra for 65 objects resulting in more than 100 scientific publications. WUPPE's observations provided insights into the distribution and effects of interstellar dust and improved our understanding of stars surrounded by disks of dust and gas, making possible better models of these systems where new planets might be forming.

Pine Bluff Observatory played an import role in WUPPE's scientific work by hosting a ground-based counterpart. A spectro-polarimeter for the visible spectrum was designed and built to be used on PBO's 36-inch telescope. Before, during, and after the Astro missions, it observed the same stars that WUPPE observed, sometimes, when possible, at the same time that WUPPE was observing in orbit. This provided the possibility of obtaining polarimetry data on any given object encompassing both visual and UV parts of the spectrum. Scientific results included better understanding of the structure and composition of interstellar matter, investigations of the nature of rapidly rotating stars, and the discovery of new features in the complex systems of interacting binary stars.

Space Physics

Innovative research in astronomy and space science have not been the exclusive domain of any one department, or indeed any one campus in the University of Wisconsin system. UW-Milwaukee, for example, today hosts a Center for Gravitation and Cosmology, and UW-Green Bay is the headquarters of the NASA-funded Wisconsin Space Grant Consortium. There are far too many examples to list, but the pattern is clear. Federally funded research, especially from NASA and NSF, has opened opportunities for a great many space science programs, from Engineering to Plant Pathology to Medicine, along more or less the same pattern that emerged in the early days of space astronomy, namely the federal agency identifies and prioritizes areas of inquiry that deserve serious investigation, then talented scientists and other academic experts of Wisconsin's universities turn their attention to those inquiries, thus exploring the universe while simultaneously enriching teaching on our campuses and building them into stronger institutions of learning. Another excellent example of this kind of synergy is the development of x-ray astronomy at Madison, which came about through NASA-funded research in the UW Physics Department.

Like UV light, x-ray energy (which is also a form of electromagnetic radiation, like visible and UV light but with much higher energy) cannot penetrate Earth's atmosphere, so investigating x-rays from astronomical sources can only be done from space. The same is true of the even higher energy gamma-rays. At the same time that NASA was encouraging Wisconsin's astronomers to invent UV astronomy, researchers elsewhere were working on the earliest x-ray experiments. As mentioned earlier, WEP's companion instrument on the ill-fated OAO-1 was a package of x-ray instruments designed and built by a team at MIT led by William Kraushaar. The OAO-1 payload was, of course, lost with the entire mission.

(On OAO-2, the second WEP's companion payload was not an x-ray payload but a suite of UV cameras designed by a team at the Smithsonian Astrophysical Observatory.) Kraushaar at MIT had built the first space-based gamma-ray detectors before starting on x-ray astronomy. He joined the faculty of the UW Physics Department in 1965, where he continued his work in developing instruments for x-ray astronomy and inventing new methods for x-ray spectroscopy in space. Like his astronomical colleagues in Madison, Kraushaar and his laboratory built and launched instruments on suborbital rockets.

Portrait of Professor William Kraushaar (1920-2008), physicist and pioneer of x-ray and gamma-ray astronomy. (UW-Madison Archives)

Their experiments showed, among other things, that our local galactic neighborhood resides within a "bubble" of gas at a temperature of about one million degrees, contradicting earlier results that located this x-ray source outside of our galaxy. Kraushaar's work, like that of Stebbins, Whitford, Code, Suomi, and so many others, added a completely new dimension not only to our understanding of the universe, but to instruction, research, and graduate training at the UW.   A second generation of researchers

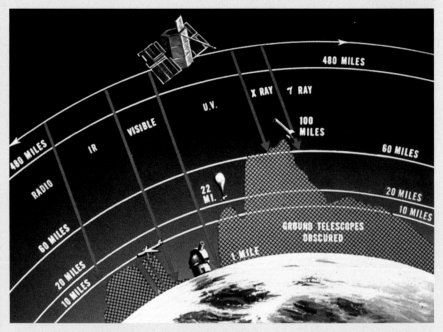

Diagram prepared by Grumman Aerospace Co. for the OAO program showing how Earth's atmosphere at various altitudes blocks radiation in the different parts of the electromagnetic spectrum. (UW Astronomy Dept.)

who began work with Kraushaar, continues today to extend and improve the research programs that he started. A team led by Dr. Wilt Sanders, of the UW-Madison Physics Department, in partnership with SSEC, built an instrument called the Diffuse X-ray Spectrometer (DSX), which flew on the space shuttle in January 1993, to study the million degree hot gas in our neighborhood of the galaxy. This extremely hot "bubble" was presumably caused by a local supernova

UW-Madison's Diffuse X-ray Spectrometer operating in the cargo bay of the space shuttle. The two halves of DXS are visible at the left and right edges of the cargo bay. (UW Astronomy Dept.)

10,000 years or more in the past. Also following in Wisconsin's long tradition of technical innovation, Physics Professor Dan McCammon has invented a completely new kind of x-ray spectrometer, which uses cryogenic micro-calorimeters, for studying astronomical x-ray sources from satellites and suborbital rockets. The strengths in orbital and suborbital instruments, along with the theoretical studies that complement them, have established UW-Madison's astrophysicists as one of the world's pre-eminent x-ray research groups.

Astronomy growing out of the Physics Department is not a new phenomenon at (nor is it unique to) UW-Madison. Albert Whitford was a graduate of the UW Physics Department, which gave him the background he needed to help Joel Stebbins invent astronomical photoelectric photometry. Whitford had worked with UW physicist Professor Julian Mack, an expert in spectroscopy. Mack's work included development of a specialized spectrometer using a series of Fabry-Perot interferometers. A Fabry-Perot can be thought of as a very selective filter that passes light of only a very narrow range of wavelengths. Mack's high-resolution spectrometer (called PEPSIOS) has some very interesting capabilities. First, it is a wide-field instrument, which means, for example, that the whole disk of a planet or a galaxy can be analyzed at once. Second, it can be "scanned" or "tuned," meaning that the part of the spectrum that it allows to pass can be shifted, by varying the pressure of the gas filling the interferometer chambers. UW Physics Professor Fred Roesler, a student of Mack's, developed scanning spectrographs that could be applied to astronomical photometry and with which he discovered optical evidence that Jupiter is surrounded by a torus (a doughnut-shaped region) of ionized sulfur – an important clue to the understanding of the high energy environment of

WHAM newly installed in March 2009, at Cerro Tololo, Chile, with team members (from left) Greg Madsen, Kurt Jaehnig, Matt Haffner, and Alex Hill. (UW Astronomy Dept.)

the rapidly spinning giant planet. Professor Frank Scherb and his student Professor Ron Reynolds combined the scanning Fabry-Perot techniques with photometry and later CCD imagers (the solid state descendants of Stebbins' early photoelectric tubes) to detect and map the optical emission of interstellar hydrogen in our galaxy. This work led to the Wisconsin Hydrogen-Alpha Mapper (WHAM), which was tested at PBO, then sent to a dark sky site at Kitt Peak National Observatory in Arizona, where it went to work (under remote control from Madison) mapping the Milky Way. As of early 2009, WHAM has mapped the distribution of ionized hydrogen gas throughout most of our Milky Way. WHAM has been moved to Cerro Tololo, Chile, where it will have access to more of the southern sky, so that it can complete its maps of the single most common element in our galaxy. This will be a fundamental contribution to our understanding of the workings of the galaxy in which we live. Traditions of innovative and productive research, like this one reaching nearly 80 years from Julian Mack to WHAM, are typical of Wisconsin's University.

Today's Frontiers

Astronomy of the Invisible

There is a sense in which, in science at least, we are always on the verge of entering a new era. No sooner have we crossed yesterday's frontier of knowledge than we find ourselves confronting a new one. But in retrospect, some moments of history are particularly compelling. Galileo's first use of the telescope some 400 years ago is one such moment. Galileo, in 1609 a poorly paid professor at the University of Padua, heard about simple telescopes being sold as toys in northern Europe. After making one himself, he recognized the many possibilities in an improved version, which he proceeded to create. Turning his instrument on the sky, seeing, analyzing, and publishing his findings, Galileo launched observational astronomy into its modern orbit. Did his contemporaries appreciate the epochal events being wrought by this obscure college professor? We don't know if he told his classroom students about his experiments, but it is fascinating to imagine being one of them and perhaps hearing about his experimental devices and gaining some inkling of the new era then dawning. Such historical moments are rare, but when we gain a new ability to investigate the previously invisible, chances are that such a moment is imminent. And that is exactly what is happening with a project based at UW-Madison where a new kind of observational astronomy, the astronomy of neutrinos, is taking shape.

Well before Galileo, all observational astronomy was based on light. The telescope made it possible to amplify the powers of the human eye, making a vast universe perceivable. Access to space made possible the measurement of the light, such as UV and x-rays, that does not penetrate our atmosphere. But it is still light in one form or another, which includes radio and microwave energy, infrared, visible light, and the rest. Why is light so useful? Why not, for example, observe the electrons that reach us from celestial objects? The answer is that light, like electrons, is abundant, but unlike electrons, light typically travels through space in straight lines. Electrons, which carry an electric charge, swerve and spiral in the magnetic fields that pervade the universe. An electron detector would find plenty of them, but an image from an "electron telescope" looking in any direction would reveal only a blur of electrons swarming from everywhere with no possibility of distinguishing those coming from the sun from others originating in some distant galaxy. It would be as useful as using a telescope in a thick fog bank.

Any alternative to light as a means to cosmic exploration would have to be an abundant energy or particle that travels in more or less straight lines from its source to us so we can identify its origins. One theoretical possibility opened by modern physics is the gravity wave, and although known to exist, they have not yet been unambiguously detected in a laboratory. Nevertheless there are a number of projects underway to open that new door to the universe, including participation of a group at the Center for Gravitation and Cosmology in the Physics Department at UW-Milwaukee. What about something that we know how to detect? The neutrino is just such a particle. Predicted by theory in 1930, the neutrino was first detected in the laboratory in 1956. Neutrinos are created in interactions between high energy particles and in the nuclei of atoms. Neutrinos fly away from their origin at nearly the speed of light and, having no electric charge, are undeflected by magnetic fields and pass easily through even very massive objects. Unlike light, neutrinos fly straight out of the core of the sun, for example. So for studying the core of the sun, neutrinos would be better than light. We are today in the position of Galileo's students, witnessing the beginnings of completely new kinds of observational astronomy, and some of the first neutrino telescopes, the counterpart of Galileo's first optical telescopes, come from UW-Madison.

Making a neutrino telescope is more challenging than an optical telescope for several reasons, but the first is that collecting neutrinos is tricky. Galileo could make a telescope with a lens the size of a half-dollar because light interacts strongly enough with matter that a piece of glass that size can form an image that the eye can see. But neutrinos hardly interact with matter at all. The space around us is alive with neutrinos, most of them from deep inside the sun. In fact, in every tick of the clock, trillions of solar neutrinos are passing through the page you are reading, but unlike the countless photons of visible light that reach the page and then reflect toward your eyes, the neutrinos pass right through with almost no effect. To have a realistic chance of catching a neutrino, it has to pass through a lot of matter, so neutrino detectors must be very big. One early attempt, in which UW-Madison Physics Professor Robert March was deeply involved, would have taken the form of an array of detectors distributed through a region of deep water in the Pacific Ocean. This Deep Underwater Muon And Neutrino Detector (DUMAND) proved not to be practical, but another approach using expanses of Antarctic ice is proving more productive.

UW-Madison physicists, led by Professors Francis Halzen (b. 1944), Robert Morse, and many collaborators, with funding from NSF and WARF, began with their Antarctic Muon And Neutrino Detector Array (AMANDA) in the late 1980s. Most of AMANDA (in its most advanced form) was incorporated into a much larger project, now in progress, called IceCube. UW-Madison's IceCube partners include WARF, as well as participants in Germany, Sweden, Belgium, Japan, New Zealand, and the Netherlands. Why Antarctic ice? The vast majority of neutrinos that reach Earth pass right on through without interacting with matter at all. Detecting the few high energy neutrinos that do interact takes advantage of the fact that the interaction produces an energetic particle called a muon, which flies off in approximately the same direction as the original neutrino was traveling. As the muon moves through the ice at nearly the speed of light, it produces a characteristic bluish light (called Cherenkov radiation), which can be measured with photodetectors. The propagation of the

Diagram of IceCube neutrino telescope. The array of detectors is defined by the strings that run vertically from the ice surface at the top, through the ice, to nearly the continental surface shown at the bottom. The comparison to the Eiffel Tower indicates the vast scale of the detector array. The blue line from lower left indicates the path of an incoming neutrino, which produces a muon, which in turn produces the blue cone of light seen by the detectors. (IceCube/NSF)

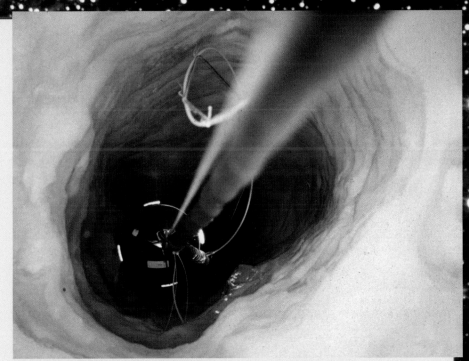

Scientists are melting holes in the bottom of the world. Astronomers with the Antarctic Muon And Neutrino Detector Array (AMANDA) lower into each vertical lake a string knotted with basketball-sized light detectors. Analyses of data have recently been used to create the first map of the high-energy neutrino sky. (NASA)

light through the ice traces the path of the muon and reveals the direction of origin of the neutrino. Many high energy particles produce light traces in the ice. Ice-Cube looks for the traces of neutrinos coming through the bulk of the earth from the north, that is to say, those that are coming upwards at the South Pole having passed through the Earth's interior. So by using the earth as a huge filter, in effect, to screen out all but neutrinos, IceCube can survey the northern sky for neutrino sources.

Accomplishing this kind of observation requires a lot of ice and many detectors. And the photo-detectors can only do their work if they are very deep in the ice, where the pressure makes the ice quite transparent to light so the faint bluish flashes are visible in the darkness. So IceCube, like AMANDA before it, is built by "drilling" into the ice with jets of hot water, which melts a column of ice into a column of water as deep as 2.4 kilometers (nearly 1.5 miles). A set of 60 detectors, each contained in a sphere of thick glass, are arranged like pearls on a necklace attached to a long cable, which is lowered into the watery hole, and then the ice refreezes around them. There will be 86 such strings arranged so that the detectors form an array whose top begins nearly a mile below the surface of the ice. (Six of those strings will be extraordinary "deep-core" strings extending into the deepest, clearest ice.) When complete, IceCube's detector array will comprise

Composite optical, radio, and x-ray image of active galaxy Centaurus A. Extremely energetic jets emanating from the galaxy are produced by a super-massive black hole at the center. Neutrinos emitted by monster black holes will allow IceCube to investigate the otherwise invisible depths of such objects. (ESO/WFI (Optical); MPIfR/ESO/APEX/A. Weiss et al. (Submillimetre); NASA/CXC/ CfA/R. Kraft et al. (X-ray))

5,160 detectors distributed through a cubic kilometer of ice. This will be the largest telescope ever made, and, as Halzen likes to note, the cheapest as well: about 25 cents per ton!

Building IceCube at the South Pole is a major challenge: simply getting people and complex equipment to the South Pole station is a very long journey, requiring typically 72 hours or more of travel from the northern hemisphere; working conditions at the pole, at an altitude of 10,000 feet and where the record high temperature is less than 8°F, are a challenge under the best of conditions; and the working season is limited by the austral summer to three months per year. Much of the specialized equipment needed for IceCube has been supplied by the UW-

Madison's Physical Sciences Laboratory (PSL) in Stoughton. PSL has built the glass-encased detector modules, which are the pearls along the strings that are lowered into the ice to form the eyes of IceCube. These devices must withstand the cold and pressure below the ice while they digitize and transmit their observations up the cable to the IceCube Lab on the surface. Hot water drilling into the ice required the design and construction of a unique suite of equipment, which PSL also fabricated. A giant hot water heater feeds a spool containing over 2.5 kilometers of high-pressure hose, which is in turn handled by a hot water drilling rig that stands over the hole location. This equipment can make a hole ready to receive a detector string in a less than two days. Construction of IceCube began in January 2005, and is projected to be completed on time in 2011. At the end of the austral summer 2008-2009 construction season, 59 strings comprising 3,540 detector modules had been installed in the ice. It is estimated that from 2002 to 2009, the IceCube project has brought $77 million, distributed among at least 22 counties, into the Wisconsin economy.

Even the partially complete IceCube should begin producing scientific results in 2009. IceCube's mission is to identify high-energy neutrino sources in the universe and use the elusive neutrinos to learn more about them. The ability of neutrinos to escape highly dense regions that are opaque to light offer the possibility to understand a number of exotic celestial objects. Such objects will include the super-massive black holes at the centers of galaxies and the super-hot remnants of supernova explosions. IceCube should also be able to detect sudden neutrino outbursts from deep inside collapsing stars, offering insight into how supernovas develop. Similarly, IceCube should detect the core collapse of very massive "hypernova" stars, the explosions of which produce gamma-ray bursts – the most energetic explosions in the universe. IceCube will also look for wide-field neutrino background emissions and investigate the distribution compared, for example, to the Milky Way and the entire sky. These are examples from among the possibilities we can anticipate, but as Francis Halzen writes, "We don't know what we will find, but experience tells us that with a new window we can expect new discoveries."

Beyond Light Buckets

It is in the nature of science that our understanding moves from the more familiar to the less familiar. After a biologist has studied and begun to understand the flora and fauna in, for example, lake waters within about 20 feet of the surface, it may become evident that conditions in deeper and less accessible waters are important for understanding the upper layers. Studying the deeper waters will require new and more sophisticated tools and techniques, but once those are available and the scientists have begun to use them, it will inevitably come about that yet a new depth of investigation is required. New research will demand new technology, and new technology will open avenues for new research. And thus will we pursue the study of nature to the ocean's depths, to the mountain's tops, and beyond. This is as true for astronomers as it is for limnologists. The most advanced research will nearly always imply the most advanced research tools, and for observational astronomers that means larger telescopes.

The 36-inch telescope at PBO was in its day a big step beyond the classic 15.6-inch refractor. As had been true with the 15.6-inch, innovative instruments helped keep the PBO telescope productive. But as research questions become more refined, astronomers require higher quality data to sift and winnow the competing theories, and higher quality data will usually mean larger telescopes. The emergence in the 1960s of the national observatories operated by AURA helped widen telescope access considerably by making telescope time available on a competitive basis. But there are never sufficient resources in the national observatory system to support all of the worthy research programs that are proposed at any given time. So it is a big advantage to an ambitious astronomy department to have alternate access to a large telescope. Thus, Wisconsin needed a bigger telescope than was available at PBO.

In the early 1970s, Wisconsin astronomers participated in a number of attempts to form a consortium of midwestern universities with the goal of building a telescope with a mirror in the 3-meter diameter or greater range located at a dark sky site, probably on a mountain top in the southwestern U.S. They explored possibilities with other Big 10 universities, discussed plans with the University of Chicago/Yerkes, and considered a partnership with the University of California. These efforts eventually came to nothing, partly for lack of funding (this would be an expensive telescope), but also partly for lack of finding a good site that was agreeable to all parties.

Nearly 20 years would pass until a workable consortium did develop. The fortuitous result of the delay was that the designers of the new telescope could take advantage of technologies to make it one of the finest telescopes in the world. University of Wisconsin-Madison, Indiana University, and the National Optical Astronomy Organization (NOAO), joined soon after by Yale University, collaborated to create the WIYN telescope.

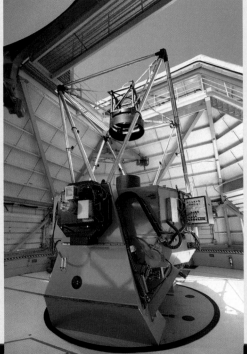

The WIYN 3.5-meter telescope inside its dome at Kitt Peak. The telescope's primary mirror resides in the blue base between the blue fork arms, one of which faces the camera. The secondary mirror is in the black housing atop the trusswork. (NOAO/AURA/NSF)

Aerial view of the WIYN telescopes on a promontory at KPNO. Upper left, in the silvery dome, is the 3.5-meter telescope. At lower right, in the larger white dome, is the WIYN 0.9-meter telescope. The smaller dome in the middle houses a 16-inch telescope operated by Kitt Peak. (NOAO/AURA/NSF)

The three universities contributed to the capital costs of the telescope itself, while NOAO (which operates three major observatories, including Kitt Peak National Observatory) provided the site and operational support. The WIYN telescope, which went into operation in 1994, is a 3.5-meter telescope and the second largest at Kitt Peak after the 4-meter Mayall telescope. The two telescopes, with nearly the same size mirrors, are a study in contrasts that illustrate the advanced design of the 3.5-meter. The Mayall telescope, opened in 1973, has a massive mirror with relatively long focal length and a huge equatorial mounting. This type of telescope design became common with the first large reflecting telescopes in the early twentieth century, and being successful, the design was steadily scaled up as mirrors grew larger. As a result, the Mayall is a telescope weighing in at 375 tons and housed in a huge dome surmounting a six-story structure. In contrast, the 3.5-meter mirror was made by an advanced "spin-casting" technique, perfected by the University of Arizona Mirror Laboratory that allows it to be of short focal length and relatively light weight. Shorter focal length and lighter weight in the mirror mean a shorter, lighter telescope structure overall. In addition, the advent of computerized guidance systems means that it is possible to dispense with the heavy equatorial mounting system used by the Mayall, and instead use a much simpler, lighter, and more compact "altitude-azimuth" mounting. The result of these design advances is that the WIYN 3.5-meter comes in at a svelte 46 tons. The entire 3.5-meter housing is very compact, a small fraction of the Mayall's structure, and designed from the beginning to control temperatures so that the building and telescope are always very close to the temperature of the ambient air. The much lower mass of mirror,

telescope, and building helps a great deal with temperature management. The mirror has its own temperature control system as well. The detailed attention to temperature management is because temperature differences cause air currents, and air currents bend and distort the images of celestial objects, producing what astronomers call bad "seeing." Seeing was also a major consideration in the selection of the site of the 3.5-meter on Kitt Peak, which has proved to be a good one. Finally, the 3.5-meter mirror includes actuators on its rear surface that make fine adjustments to the shape of the mirror that help optimize the image produced by the telescope.

The result is that the 3.5-meter telescope produces some of the sharpest images of any telescope in the world at a very low expense for a research telescope – about $14 million. If built today, a conventional telescope like the Mayall would cost many times that of the 3.5-meter. An array of advanced instruments takes advantage of this optical perfection. Several different fiber optics assemblies can channel the light from many specific sites in the image plane in order to produce spectra of many objects simultaneously, or of various points within a single object, for example across the disk of a galaxy. A variety of CCD cameras provide imaging capabilities taking advantage of the 3.5-meter telescope's wide field and high image quality. In development is the One Degree Imager, which will achieve a one-gigapixel image filling the telescope's one-degree field of view. These and other capabilities make the WIYN 3.5-meter a world-class research telescope. The fact that UW-Madison is a consortium member means that UW-Madison's astronomers receive a fixed fraction of the observing time, so that proposals for allocating the UW share of telescope time can be evaluated and assigned locally. This is a major advantage for Madison-based research, both by faculty, staff scientists, and graduate students. The 3.5-meter's remote operations capability, designed and implemented by SAL's Dr. Jeffrey Percival, is also a major advantage to Madison-based astronomers because many observing runs that would once have required a trip to Arizona by the astronomer can now be accomplished from a control center locally.

The WIYN consortium acquired a second, smaller telescope by accepting a refurbished 0.9-meter (36-inch, the same aperture as the largest PBO telescope) reflector from Kitt Peak. This smaller telescope is ideal for many photometric purposes and makes additional telescope time at the dark mountain-top site available for Wisconsin's astronomers. Of the nine consortium partners that run the 0.9-meter, five are based in Wisconsin: the UW System campuses of Madison, Oshkosh, Stevens Point, and Whitewater, and the Wisconsin Space Grant Consortium in Green Bay. The 0.9-meter has operated under WIYN consortium management since 2001.

WIYN 3.5-meter image of spiral galaxy NGC 891 by UW-Madison astronomers Chris Howk and Blair Savage. The exquisite optical quality of WIYN 3.5-meter images is evident in the fine filaments stretching away from the dusty central plane of the galaxy, which we view edge-on. (C. Howk (JHU), B. Savage (UW), N. A. Sharp (NOAO/WIYN/NOAO/NSF))

Southern African Large Telescope

Stars could not form immediately after the Big Bang, the explosive event in which the universe as we know it began. It took many millions of years before gravity could gather and compress the primordial gas of the universe to the point where hydrogen nuclei began fusing into helium, producing in the process the energy we see as starlight amid the vast islands we call galaxies. What did those first galaxies look like? How did they form? What were those early stars like? How did the rich chemistry of which we are made develop out of the barren expanses of hydrogen and helium produced in the Big Bang? Looking to the future, how will the expansion of the universe evolve? What forces drive and shape the expansion? What kind of universe will the minds of the distant future see? These cosmological questions are fascinating and very important ones, but until recently they were almost purely academic. It is remarkable testimony to the progress of modern science that astronomers are bringing answers within our grasp. Those answers will come in part from new space-based instruments, descendants of the ones built by UW's astronomers. But for the immediate future, the vast majority of telescope time available for cosmological inquiries will come from ground-based telescopes in the 10-meter class and beyond. As powerful as the WIYN and other 4-meter class telescopes are, astronomers need still larger telescopes to push the envelope of current

Star trails above the Pine Bluff Observatory. (Jeff Miller/UW-Madison)

research. To pursue such topics as galaxy evolution, UW-Madison astronomers are now partners in one of the world's largest telescopes, the Southern African Large Telescope, or SALT.

UW's astronomical connections to South Africa actually go back more than half a century. In 1952-1953, when Art Code was first on the faculty at Washburn Observatory, he collaborated with W. W. Morgan of Yerkes in a program to measure the distances to certain bright star clusters in order to trace the spiral arms of our Milky Way galaxy. To do this, photometric data from Washburn's 15.6-inch telescope was combined with spectroscopy obtained with the Yerkes 40-inch. But from Wisconsin it was impossible to survey the entire Milky Way, so the project needed to be completed with observations from a site in the southern hemisphere. For that reason, in 1953 Code and Ted Houck (then still a graduate student) spent most of the year in South Africa. Code worked on the spectroscopic part of the project at the Radcliffe Observatory (then outside of Pretoria), while Houck worked on the photometry at the Cape Observatory. Code also used an extremely wide-field (140°) camera, which had been developed during the war by Yerkes astronomers, to record wide field images of the Milky Way and map the broad distributions of luminous and obscuring matter. (This was probably the only major research project at Washburn Observatory ever to employ photography.) Code had made a series of Milky Way images in Wisconsin in both visible and infrared light and followed that with a set from South Africa as well. These images of the southern Milky Way were some of the best available for many years and were widely reproduced.

Fifty years later, UW-Madison is again deeply involved with South Africa as a member of the SALT consortium, running a world-class cosmological telescope, and the largest in the southern hemisphere. This giant telescope is a 10-meter class instrument – its hexagonal mirror measures 11 meters across at its widest dimensions. Like some other 10-meter class telescopes, such as the Keck telescopes, the large mirror is composed of smaller identical hexagonal spherical mirrors, in SALT's case each 1 meter across, which are tiled together to make a single large spherical mirror. Unlike all but one other, SALT embodies a new design for giant telescopes that reduces construction costs dramatically. SALT follows a design first employed in the McDonald Observatory's Hobby-Eberly Telescope (HET) in Texas. This new kind of optical telescope makes use of an optical trick to simplify the telescope mounting, which is a large fraction of the total cost of a telescope. As Earth's rotation carries a star or other object across the sky, a typical telescope follows the object by moving the entire telescope so that the light from the target object falls into the center of the field of view, where the camera or other instruments are normally located. If the telescope does not track, then the image of the object drifts across the field of the telescope. In the HET design, the instruments are designed to move on a special structure at the front of the telescope, so that as the image drifts, the instruments follow it. This requires a complex truss at the front of the telescope to allow the motion of the instrument platform to be precisely controlled. It also requires some extra optics to correct an error, called spherical aberration,

that is inherent to a spherical mirror design. But on the other hand, the massive mounting of the telescope can be much simpler than a fully steerable mounting. A further simplification is achieved by mounting the telescope at a fixed angle inclined to the vertical. The

Above: View of the SALT 10-meter mirror through the telescope trusswork with the closed dome aperture visible above. The orange crane is installing the last of the 1-meter mirror segments into the main mirror assembly. Left: The telescope's trusswork is reflected in the mirror's surface. (UW Astronomy Dept./SALT)

telescope can rotate about the vertical axis, but does not tip up or down. Consequently, it cannot point just anywhere in the sky, like a typical telescope can; but the angle of the mounting is carefully chosen so that the region of the sky that the telescope can see includes the targets of greatest scientific interest.

The SALT design follows the HET, but with elements such as an improved spherical aberration corrector. The design innovations make possible the construction of a cosmological telescope at a fraction of the cost of a fully pointable instrument. SALT's construction costs much less than one of the similarly sized Keck telescopes, which have mosaic mirrors but are also fully pointable and so need a much more complex mounting. The mosaic mirror design itself entails some sophisticated engineering. Each single mirror of the 90 that tile together to form the large surface must be independently adjustable so that the edges and angles match up, and the entire ensemble performs as one. This alignment must be done frequently, which is the reason for the prominent collimation tower adjacent to the telescope's dome. Operators point the telescope at the top of the tower, where a set of lasers and optics measures the reflected laser light and sends signals to the actuators that move each mirror segment to bring it into ideal alignment. A benefit of the mosaic mirror is that the individual segments can be removed one at a time for cleaning, recoating, or replacement.

UW-Madison is a member of SALT's international consortium. In fact, UW-Madison is the largest non-governmental partner in a long list that includes the South African National Research Foundation, the South African Astrophysical Observatory (SAAO), a consortium of UK universities, and other institutions in Germany, Poland, India, and the U.S. Since "first light" in September 2005, SALT has been in the "commissioning" phase as it is completed and brought up to full operation and its instrumentation finished and installed. SALT will have three primary instruments: a large array CCD camera built by SAAO, a fiber-optic fed very high resolution spectrograph built by the

Installation of RSS (Robert Stobie Spectrograph, named for a prominent South African astronomer) atop the SALT truss-work. Formerly known as PFIS (Prime-Focus Imaging Spectrograph), RSS is one of SALT's most important science instruments. When complete it will be capable of imaging spectroscopy and polarimetry from the near UV through the near IR parts of the spectrum. (UW Astronomy Dept./SALT)

SALT's "first light" image of spiral galaxy NCG 6744. (UW Astronomy Dept./SALT)

University of Durham Center for Advanced Instrumentation, and the Robert Stobie Spectrograph (RSS). The RSS was designed by Ken Nordsieck and built by SAL in Madison. RSS is a highly versatile and complex instrument, which must operate at the telescope's prime focus, high above the mirror. RSS is capable of high and medium resolution spectroscopy in visible and near UV light, Fabry-Perot imaging spectroscopy, and spectro-polarimetry. RSS was designed to accommodate an infrared instrument as well, and thanks to recent funding from WARF, it is now under development. The Near InfraRed (NIR) addition to RSS, under the direction of Professor Andrew Scheinis, will extend RSS capabilities to span the spectrum of light, from near UV to near IR, accessible at Earth's surface.

New Directions

We get a direct glimpse into the research now in progress in the UW-Madison Astronomy Department by looking at the ground-breaking science already done and in planning for SALT, WIYN, space observatories, and other facilities. Much of today's work grows out of the traditional strengths of UW's astronomy accomplishments and follows it, on both observational and theoretical levels, to the very frontiers of modern knowledge.

Early studies of the interstellar medium, which Stebbins and Whitford helped define, have bloomed today into a more integrated field involving the complex interactions of magnetic fields and matter from stars to the largest structures in the universe: How do magnetic forces shape stars themselves and affect the processes inside? How do the complex environments inside and surrounding galaxies affect and respond to star formation, supernovas, and other events? What is the composition and behavior of the intergalactic medium? How are clusters of galaxies affected by the scorching energy beams from supermassive black holes? SALT will acquire spectra of distant galaxies that we see in very early stages of their formation, providing insights into both the evolution of galaxies as well as the earliest star formation. SALT's location in the southern hemisphere means that it has access to our two neighborhood galaxies, the Large and Small Magellanic Clouds. They are the only examples we have of galaxies close enough for us to see and count even their smallest stars, and SALT is the only telescope able to do the job. The new wide-field imaging capability of WIYN will allow surveys of early star formation. Massive stars are major sources of UV light, which is why UW's historical expertise in massive stars developed along with UV astronomy. Study of massive stars continues as a research specialty of the department and dovetails with the chemical evolution of galaxies of which massive stars are very important drivers. Indeed, the structure and environment of "local" galaxies, which are mature galaxies more like our own home galaxy, constitutes another research strength of UW-Madison and leads to yet another part of the spectrum, namely radio astronomy, where Wisconsin's astronomers also work. International radio telescope projects, such as the nascent Square Kilometer Array, will soon become important tools for that research. UW astronomers also use space-based instruments, of course, including the Hubble Space Telescope and Chandra, NASA's orbiting x-ray observatory. UW-Madison is the lead institution in a major survey of the Milky Way galaxy using the Spitzer Space Telescope, an infrared observatory in space. Professor Ed Churchwell leads this project, called GLIMPSE (Galactic Legacy Infrared Mid-Plane Survey Extraordinaire). GLIMPSE exploits the power of IR radiation to penetrate interstellar dust clouds and has begun to lay bare the spiral structure of

The Large Magellanic Cloud, visible in southern skies, is a nearby dwarf galaxy. Close enough for detailed studies, it will be an important scientific target for SALT. (Yuri Beletsky, European Southern Observatory)

our own galaxy at a level of detail far beyond the work that Code, Houck, and Morgan were able to do in the 1950s. SAL continues a long history of technological development in support of astronomical research in two directions. Ground-based instrumentation projects for SALT like RSS and NIR, as well as instrument development for WIYN, represent the newer, shorter branch. The longer branch, SAL's traditional expertise in space instrumentation, continues as well. Sub-orbital rocketry has been the most consistently active category of space instrumentation, including a very successful and versatile descendant of WUPPE named WISP (Wide-field Imaging Spectro-Polarim-

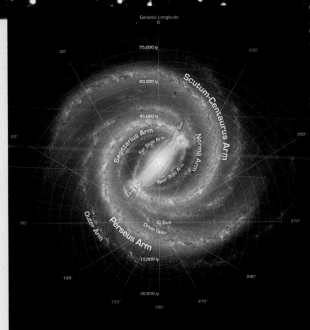

Annotated Roadmap to the Milky Way
(artist's concept)

NASA / JPL-Caltech / R. Hurt (SSC-Caltech)   ssc2008-10b

A new view of the structure of our Milky Way galaxy based on GLIMPSE observations. The GLIMPSE survey of the Milky Way, making use of the penetrating power of Spitzer Space Telescope's IR capabilities, demonstrates that our galaxy possesses a central "bar" structure and maps the spiral arms in unprecedented detail. (GLIMPSE/NASA)

eter) designed by Ken Nordsieck for UV studies. WISP's career is a prime example of the value of suborbital rocket research. Not only are suborbital instruments much cheaper to develop and build than a comparable satellite-based instrument, but they are retrieved after each flight so that they are available for post-flight calibration, refitting, and reflying. During its five rocket missions, WISP studied UV light from dust scattering in the Pleiades star cluster and detected diffuse UV light from the Large Magellanic Cloud, leading to a three-dimensional model of that dwarf galaxy. One WISP flight was to study Comet Hale-Bopp. In addition to enhancing our knowledge of comets, WISP's mission illustrates another advantage of suborbital rocket research, which is that it can be planned and launched on relatively short notice. WISP was not built specifically to study Comet Hale-Bopp, but when the previously unknown comet appeared in 1995, WISP was "on the shelf," and a flight to study it could be rapidly organized. A satellite instrument would have taken years to prepare, by which time the comet would have been far beyond reach. Suborbital rocket research is very important from another vital aspect: it is a low cost, quick turn-around training ground for the young scientists who will imagine, build, and launch future generations of spacecraft.

Comet Hale-Bopp, which appeared in our skies for much of 1997, was the scientific target of one of the suborbital rocket flights of WISP. (Thomas A. Ferch)

Inventing the technology that will support those future research projects is another category of important SAL work. The best example of this is a remarkable device named Star Tracker 5000 (ST5000). Almost all astronomical instruments (although IceCube is an exception to this) need to be pointed to particular places in the sky. In ground-based telescopes this has traditionally meant elaborate mountings, and with spacecraft the solutions often involve complex systems of gyroscopes, momentum wheels, rocket thrusters, and

A Terrier-Black Brant suborbital rocket ready to launch an experiment controlled by SAL's Star Tracker 5000. ST5000 team members Kurt Jaehnig (left) and Jeffrey Percival are visible near top center just below the tail of the rocket. (UW Astronomy Dept.)

imaging devices. SAL astronomer Dr. Jeffrey Percival and his team have created ST5000 to replace the elaborate and expensive devices conventionally used for this job with a smart, compact, and cheap tracking system that adds new capabilities. ST5000 locates itself in space by recognizing star patterns, in something like the way a boy or girl scout recognizes the Big Dipper and knows which way is north. But ST5000 is better and faster at that task than the typical scout because it can look in a random direction in the sky, recognize the star patterns, and within seconds can report exactly which direction in space it is pointed – information that the payload controller can then use to issue tracking commands. Using a patented image compression technique, ST5000 can transmit images of the star field (or other images) many times faster than usual techniques allow. With a number of successful flights now accomplished, ST5000 is in a position to enhance a range of research projects while lowering their costs and complexity. ST5000 constitutes a perfect example of how academic research creates a cycle: scientific questions demand new problem solving and new technologies, which lead to technical development and research results, which in turn produce valuable products and new research questions. This cycle has been at work in UW astronomy and countless other programs in the University of Wisconsin's schools for well over a century.

Taking Astronomy Home

When Washburn Observatory was dedicated in October 1881, there was considerable public notice and interest in Madison. In recognition of this interest, Edward Holden, who had succeeded James Watson as director, established a policy that the observatory would be opened to the public for night sky viewing on the first and third Wednesday evenings of each month. Whatever his mix of motivations, Holden created a public astronomy outreach program that has lasted for 128 years. Unless the weather precludes it, or equipment or the building is under repair, Washburn's astronomers have shared their work with the public since the observatory's opening. There are older observatories, but few if any can claim a constant heritage of public outreach with such longevity.

In a report to UW President Fred in 1948, Albert Whitford reaffirmed the commitment of Wisconsin's astronomers to public outreach in the language and vision of that era:

> The third activity [after teaching and research] which the
> University tries to supply to the people of the State ... would in
> our case mean helping amateur astronomers and adult education
> groups. Dr. Huffer is already doing far more in that line than
> is the case at any other university I know about. It should be
> continued.

It has been continued, and greatly expanded over the years. During the busiest days of the HSP and WUPPE programs, press and public requests for information grew rapidly: school teachers requested that astronomers visit their classrooms and requested help teaching about the new science taking shape in our state; community groups asked for talks by astronomers; groups requested tours of SAL and SSEC so they could see the famous instruments being developed. It was difficult to respond adequately to public interest, and especially difficult to accommodate requests to visit campus laboratories. Art Code and Bob Bless, the heads of the WUPPE and HSP programs, respectively, and Kathy Stittleburg, SAL's energetic and creative associate director, began searching for a place that the public and schools could visit to learn more about space science work at UW-Madison. She located an available commercial building on South Park Street in Madison and set up UW Space Place, which opened in July 1990 with a series of talks by UW-Madison scientists about astronomy. Space Place, located well away from the complications of parking and scheduling that burden campus sites, and soon furnished with displays and exhibits, quickly became a place for presentations to school groups, a base for science teaching workshops for teachers, a source for information about the progress of SAL's projects, and a gathering place for local astronomy enthusiasts on the occasions of lunar eclipses, comets, and other astronomical events. The great response during the first year convinced the three founders to continue their experiment in education and outreach. Capabilities increased as a result of NASA funding, from the HSP and WUPPE projects, for educational equipment and materials, and demand for programs, especially from school teachers, continued to grow. The SALT project brought the opportunity to extend in-service teacher training to groups of South African teachers, who, because of the importance of the SALT project in their home country, visited Madison in preparation for adding astronomy to their classroom lessons. In autumn of 2005, with support from UW-Madison Chancellor John Wiley, UW Space Place relocated and expanded at 2300 South Park Street. Among other exhibits available to

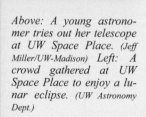

Above: A young astronomer tries out her telescope at UW Space Place. (Jeff Miller/UW-Madison) Left: A crowd gathered at UW Space Place to enjoy a lunar eclipse. (UW Astronomy Dept.)

the public are some of the most important pieces of spaceflight hardware from SAL's history: a full scale engineering model of OAO-2, space shuttle veterans DXS and WUPPE, the rocket instrument WISP, and many items from Washburn Observatory's history.

A signature astronomy outreach element from UW-Madison is the statewide Universe in the Park (UitP) program. UitP was started by astronomer Dr. Karen Bjorkman (at that time a member of the WUPPE team) in the summer of 1996 with funding from NASA and has been continued and expanded by Professor Eric Wilcots with partial support from NSF. UitP events take place at state parks during the late spring, summer, and early fall recreational seasons. One or more astronomers, often graduate students, take a portable

UW Space Place director Jim Lattis (in the background) leads a group of student visitors as they view the 15.6-inch refractor (in service since 1881) in the Washburn Observatory. (Jeff Miller/UW-Madison)

telescope to the park, present an evening talk to park visitors, and then follow up with a sky-viewing session. The sessions are very popular. At the height of the season there will typically be three events each weekend at Wisconsin parks. Since the program began, UitP has visited every state park in Wisconsin at least once, and most parks have hosted repeated visits. As this program shows, the UW-Madison Astronomy Department and Space Astronomy Laboratory take outreach and science education for Wisconsin's residents very seriously – the number and quality of outreach programs is far out of proportion to the relatively small size of the department. The fascination we all have with the heavens runs as strongly today as it did in 1881, which is why astronomy is such an effective motivator of science education. Astronomers are acutely aware of this and have been among the most active faculty members in the movement to make public outreach experience and commitment a significant part of graduate student professional development. Like Holden, Whitford, Huffer, Code, and others, Wisconsin's astronomers today remain committed to astronomy outreach for our state and beyond.

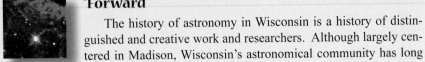

"Forward"

The history of astronomy in Wisconsin is a history of distinguished and creative work and researchers. Although largely centered in Madison, Wisconsin's astronomical community has long included Yerkes Observatory as well and now extends to several UW System campuses. Between them they have made Wisconsin a state well known in the international astronomical community for the past century. As we have seen, Wisconsin's astronomers were leaders in the emergence of modern astrophysics as well as the development of space astronomy. That heritage continues today with active research programs distributed across several groups working at the leading edges of their fields. In addition, the graduate training programs are among the best in the world and attract the most promising future scientists to Madison. Active and innovative outreach programs directly serve the residents of the state and seek to inspire new generations to build on the accomplishments of their predecessors.

Astronomy is vital to progress in the modern world. Not only does astronomical research help drive innovation that leads to technical and economic development, but astronomy is also a "gateway" science. For many generations astronomy has been the subject that first inspires talented people to take a serious interest in scientific and technical careers. Astronomy presents itself to all who take the moment to ponder the night sky and to reflect on humanity's place within

The Einstein Memorial on the grounds of the National Academy of Sciences in Washington, D.C. The photographer staged the photo on the 50th anniversary of Einstein's death in 2005. The placement of the small telescope next to the bronze statue was to symbolize the importance of Einstein's work which revolutionized our understanding of the universe. (Greg Piepol)

Observatory domes on the roof of Sterling Hall. (Jeff Miller/UW-Madison)

the universe and our relationship to it. A glimpse of a planet through a telescope, the solemn beauty of an eclipse, the dream of exploring a distant world, all these and more motivate questions about how we understand the world around us and how we can learn more.

Astronomy is part of modern culture but with deep roots in the ancient quest to understand nature. Modern science is one of human culture's most recent, valuable, and remarkable developments. Science teaches us to value empirical evidence and careful reasoning over preconception and authority. Scientists insist that in understanding the natural world, nothing is above examination, criticism, and confrontation with evidence. No scientific theory, regardless how venerable, is permanent; so all are subject to revision and perhaps rejection. As a result of adhering to rigorous standards and methodologies, scientists have provided amazing technical advances, improvements in quality of life, and deeper understanding of the nature of our universe and how it came to be. Astronomy is deeply important to modern culture, and has been important in nearly every historical culture we know (although often for very different reasons).

Both as an inspiration to the future and as an object lesson from history on the value of science, the study and advancement of astronomy is truly an investment for posterity. But astronomy is, like other academic research, also a stimulus for and investment in a vigorous economy for Wisconsin and beyond. Projects like IceCube and RSS result in employment of talented scientists and engineers. Development of new technologies, like those that make ST5000 possible, create products and help open new markets for them. The history of astronomy in Wisconsin teaches that these and other benefits emerge from continuity and commitment to long-term stability. Talented scientists with innovative ideas and a willingness to devote their careers to them, like Art Code with his vision of space astronomy in

UW-Madison's Washburn Observatory, viewed from Lake Mendota, underwent historical restoration and remodeling in 2008-2009 to become home to the Honors Program of the College of Letters and Science. The telescope remains fully operational. (Jeff Miller/UW-Madison)

1957, need consistent support to explore possibilities, identify opportunities, recruit other talent, and attract further support for the projects that can change the world. The great successes of Wisconsin's space astronomy and physics programs and SSEC's space meteorology and remote sensing programs (only a few of many possible examples) show how talented visionaries with initial support from sources like WARF can turn ideas into jobs, buildings, and a wide open future. This is clear testimony to the power of ideas, and great universities are in the idea business. The Wisconsin Idea states that the boundaries of the University are the boundaries of the state. The Wisconsin Idea is itself an idea, but of a unique type, because it amplifies, transforms, and launches other ideas out from the University and into the world. In the modern era, returning the benefits of the University to the citizens of Wisconsin means connecting Wisconsin's academic research across the globe. Wisconsin's astronomers accomplish this in many ways, from the large scale, like international projects such as SALT and IceCube, to the small scale building of telescopes with South African school teachers, and extending even to the elegant simplicity of pointing out stars and planets to families in the dark skies of our state parks.

Acknowledgments

Thanks to Bob Bless, Dan Bull, Sam Gabelt, Daniel Huffman, Evelyn Malkus, Jordan Marchè, David Null, Jeff Percival, Jean Phillips, Bernie Schermetzler, and Barb Whitney. Much of the material on Washburn Observatory from the 1940s to the 1970s and on the Space Astronomy Laboratory is based on oral history interviews conducted by UW Archivists and James Lattis.

In Memoriam

Arthur Dodd Code
(1923-2009)

Sixth Director of Washburn Observatory

Professor of Astronomy, University of Wisconsin-Madison

Pioneer of space astronomy and founder of UW Space Astronomy Laboratory

Founding director of the Hubble Space Telescope Science Institute

Aurora Over Wisconsin (Chris VenHaus)

Informational Web Sites

Astronomy Department, UW-Madison: http://www.astro.wisc.edu
Chandra X-ray Observatory: http://chandra.harvard.edu
Deke Slayton Museum: http://www.dekeslayton.com
DXS: http://www.ssec.wisc.edu/dxs
GLIMPSE: http://www.astro.wisc.edu/sirtf
Hubble Space Telescope: http://hubblesite.org
IceCube: http://icecube.wisc.edu
Physics Department, UW-Madison: http://www.physics.wisc.edu
SALT: http://www.salt.ac.za
Space Astronomy Laboratory, UW-Madison: http://www.sal.wisc.edu
Space Science and Engineering Center, UW-Madison: http://www.ssec.wisc.edu
Square Kilometer Array: http://www.skatelescope.org
UW Space Place: http://spaceplace.wisc.edu
WIYN: http://www.noao.edu/wiyn
Yerkes Observatory: http://astro.uchicago.edu/yerkes

Planet Earth - Courtesy of Apollo 17 Crew (NASA)

Selected Bibliography and Further Reading

Baum, Richard and William Sheehan. *In Search of Planet Vulcan: The Ghost in Newton's Clockwork Universe.* Cambridge, MA: Basic Books, 1997.

Birmingham, Robert A. and Leslie E. Eisenberg. *Indian Mounds of Wisconsin.* Madison: University of Wisconsin Press, 2000.

Bless, R. C., et al. "The Hubble Space Telescope's High-Speed Photometer." *Publications of the Astronomical Society of the Pacific*, 111 (1999), 364.

Code, Arthur D., ed. *The Scientific Results from the Orbiting Astronomical Observatory (OAO-2).* NASA SP-310. NASA Scientific and Technical Information Office, Washington, D.C., 1972.

Halzen, Francis. "Astronomy and astrophysics with neutrinos." *Physics Today.* May 2008, 29-35.

Hearnshaw, J. B. *The Measurement of Starlight: Two Centuries of Astronomical Photometry.* Cambridge: Cambridge University Press, 1996.

Hirsh, Richard F. *Glimpsing an Invisible Universe: The Emergence of X-ray Astronomy.* Cambridge: Cambridge University Press, 1983.

Judson, Katharine B., ed. *Native American Legends of the Great Lakes and the Mississippi Valley.* Dekalb, Illinois: Northern Illinois University Press, 2000.

Liebl, David S. & Christopher Fluke. "Investigations of the interstellar medium at Washburn Observatory, 1930-58." *Journal of Astronomical History and Heritage*, 7 (2004), 85-94.

Lovell, Jim & Jeffrey Kluger. *Lost Moon: The Perilous Voyage of Apollo 13.* Boston: Houghton-Mifflin, 1994.

March, Robert. "Physics at the University of Wisconsin: A History." *Physics in Perspective,* 5 (2003), 130-149.

Marché, Jordan D., II. "The Wisconsin Experiment Package (WEP) aboard the Orbiting Astronomical Observatory (OAO-2)." *Journal of Astronomical History & Heritage*, 9 no.2 (2006), 185-199.

Osterbrock, Donald. "The California-Wisconsin Axis in American Astronomy." *Journal of Astronomical History and Heritage*, 6 (2003), 120-136.

Osterbrock, Donald. *Yerkes Observatory, 1892 – 1950. The Birth, Near Death, and Resurrection of a Scientific Research Institution.* Chicago: Chicago University Press, 1997.

Smith, Robert. *The Space Telescope.* Cambridge: Cambridge University Press, 1989.

SPECIAL ARTICLES IN PRIOR BLUE BOOKS, 1970 to 2007

For 1919 to 1933 *Blue Books:* see 1954 *Blue Book,* pp. 177-182.

For 1935 to 1962 *Blue Books:* see 1964 *Blue Book,* pp. 227-232.

For 1964 to 1968 *Blue Books:* see 2007-2008 *Blue Book,* pp. 192-193.

Commerce and Culture

The Indians of Wisconsin, by William H. Hodge, 1975 *Blue Book,* pp. 95-192.

Wisconsin Business and Industry, by James J. Brzycki, Paul E. Hassett, Joyce Munz Hach, Kenneth S. Kinney, and Robert H. Milbourne, 1987-1988 *Blue Book,* pp. 99-165.

Wisconsin Writers, by John O. [Jack] Stark, 1977 *Blue Book,* pp. 95-185.

Wisconsin's People: A Portrait of Wisconsin's Population on the Threshold of the 21st Century, by Paul R. Voss, Daniel L. Veroff, and David D. Long, 2003-2004 *Blue Book,* pp. 99-174.

Education

Education for Employment: 70 Years of Vocational, Technical and Adult Education in Wisconsin, by Kathleen A. Paris, 1981-1982 *Blue Book,* pp. 95-212.

The Wisconsin Idea: The University's Service to the State, by Jack Stark, 1995-1996 *Blue Book,* pp. 99-179.

The Wisconsin Idea for the 21st Century, by Alan B. Knox and Joe Corry, 1995-1996 *Blue Book,* pp. 180-192.

Environment

Exploring Wisconsin's Waterways, by Margaret Beattie Bogue, 1989-1990 *Blue Book,* pp. 99-297.

Protecting Wisconsin's Environment, by Selma Parker, 1973 *Blue Book,* pp. 97-161.

Wisconsin's Troubled Waters, by Selma Parker, 1973 *Blue Book,* pp. 102-136.

Government

The Changing World of Wisconsin Local Government, by Susan C. Paddock, 1997-1998 *Blue Book,* pp. 99-172.

Equal Representation: A Study of Legislative and Congressional Apportionment in Wisconsin, by Dr. H. Rupert Theobald, 1970 *Blue Book,* pp. 70-260.

The Legislative Process in Wisconsin, by Richard L. Roe, Pamela J. Kahler, Robin N. Kite, and Robert P. Nelson, 1993-1994 *Blue Book,* pp. 99-194.

Local Government in Wisconsin, by James R. Donoghue, 1979-1980 *Blue Book,* pp. 95-218.

Rules and Rulings: Parliamentary Procedure from the Wisconsin Perspective, by H. Rupert Theobald, 1985-1986 *Blue Book,* pp. 99-215.

The Wisconsin Court System: Demystifying the Judicial Branch, by Robin Ryan and Amanda Todd, 2005-2006 *Blue Book,* pp. 99-184.

History

Capitals and Capitols in Early Wisconsin, by Stanley H. Cravens, 1983-1984 *Blue Book,* pp. 99-167.

A History of the Property Tax and Property Tax Relief in Wisconsin, by Jack Stark, 1991-1992 *Blue Book,* pp. 99-165.

Restoring the Vision: The First Century of Wisconsin's Capitol, by Michael J. Keane, 2001-2002 *Blue Book,* pp. 99-188.

Ten Events That Shaped Wisconsin's History, by Norman K. Risjord, 1999-2000 *Blue Book,* pp. 99-146.

Those Who Served: Wisconsin Legislators 1848-2007, by Michael J. Keane, 2007-2008 *Blue Book,* pp. 99-191.

Wisconsin at 150 Years, by Michael J. Keane and Daniel F. Ritsche, 1997-1998 *Blue Book,* color supplement.

Wisconsin Celebrates 150 Years of Statehood: A Photographic Review, 1999-2000 *Blue Book,* color supplement.

Capitol Visitor's Guide

Hours:
Building open daily 8 a.m. - 6 p.m.
The Capitol closes at 4 p.m. weekends and holidays.

Information Desk
Located in the rotunda, ground floor.

Tours
Daily Monday - Saturday at 9, 10, and 11 a.m., 1, 2, and 3 p.m.; Sundays at 1, 2, and 3 p.m. A 4 p.m. tour is offered weekdays between Memorial Day and Labor Day. Tours start at the Information Desk in the rotunda and last 45 to 55 minutes. Reservations are required for groups of 10 or more. Call (608) 266-0382 7:30 a.m. - 4:30 p.m. Monday - Friday, or visit the Web site at www. wisconsin.gov/state/capfacts/tour_select.html.

Observation Deck
6th Floor, accessible from 4th floor via NW or W stairways. Open daily from Memorial Day to Labor Day. There is a small museum devoted to the Capitol at the entrance to the observation deck.

Souvenirs
Available at the Information Desk, include books,
postcards, miniatures, and tour videos.

Capitol Police
Room B2 North.

Handicapped Entrances
At Martin Luther King Jr. Blvd., East Washington Avenue,
Wisconsin Avenue, and West Washington Avenue.

Parking
Limited parking (meters) on the Capitol Square.
Several public ramps are located within two blocks of the Capitol.

Food
Vending machines in rotunda basement.

Senate Chamber
South wing, 2nd floor; visitors gallery, 3rd floor.

Assembly Chamber
West wing, 2nd floor; visitors gallery, 3rd floor.

Supreme Court Hearing Room
East wing, 2nd floor.

Governor's Office & Conference Rm
East wing, 1st floor.

Lieutenant Governor's Office
East wing, ground floor.

Attorney General's Office
East wing, 1st floor.

Legislative Offices
To find a specific office, check one of the Capitol Directories located in the rotunda and on the ground floor of each wing.

Hearings
Information about the time and location of public hearings is posted at the entrance to each legislative chamber.

Hearing Rooms
North Hearing Room, North wing, 2nd floor.
Grand Army of the Republic Hall, Room 417 North.
Joint Committee on Finance, Room 412 East.
Senate Hearing Room, Room 411 South.
Additional hearing rooms are located on the 2nd and 3rd floors.

Capitol Facts & Figures

Construction Chronology
West wing: 1906 – 1909
East wing: 1908 – 1910
Central portion: 1910 – 1913
South wing: 1909 – 1913
North wing: 1914 – 1917
First meeting of legislature in building: 1909
Dedication: July 8, 1965
Renovation: 1990 – 2001

Statistics
Height of each wing: 61 feet
Height of observation deck: 92 feet
Height of dome mural: 184 feet, 3 inches
Height of dome (to top of statue): 284 feet, 9 inches
Length of building from N to S & E to W:
483 feet, 9 inches
Floor space: 448,297 square feet
Volume: 8,369,665 cubic feet
Original cost: $7,203,826.35
(including grounds, furnishings, and
power plant)

Wisconsin Constitution

3

Wisconsin Constitution: text as amended through June 2009 and votes on constitutional amendments and statewide referenda submitted to the people

The Seahorse of the Large Magellanic Cloud

(NASA, ESA, and M. Livio (STScI))

WISCONSIN CONSTITUTION
As amended through June 30, 2009 *

TABLE OF CONTENTS

WISCONSIN CONSTITUTION

As amended through June 30, 2009 *

Preamble

We, the people of Wisconsin, grateful to Almighty God for our freedom, in order to secure its blessings, form a more perfect government, insure domestic tranquility and promote the general welfare, do establish this constitution.

Article I.
Declaration of Rights

Equality; inherent rights. Section 1. [*As amended April 1986*] All people are born equally free and independent, and have certain inherent rights; among these are life, liberty and the pursuit of happiness; to secure these rights, governments are instituted, deriving their just powers from the consent of the governed. [*1983 AJR-9; 1985 AJR-9*]

Equality; inherent rights. Section 1. [*As amended November 1982*] All people are born equally free and independent, and have certain inherent rights; among these are life, liberty and the pursuit of happiness; to serve these rights, governments are instituted, deriving their just powers from the consent of the governed. [*1979 AJR-76; 1981 AJR-35; submit: May'82 Spec.Sess. AJR-1*]

Equality; inherent rights. Section 1. [*Original form*] All men are born equally free and independent, and have certain inherent rights; among these are life, liberty and the pursuit of happiness; to secure these rights, governments are instituted among men, deriving their just powers from the consent of the governed.

Slavery prohibited. Section 2. There shall be neither slavery, nor involuntary servitude in this state, otherwise than for the punishment of crime, whereof the party shall have been duly convicted.

Free speech; libel. Section 3. Every person may freely speak, write and publish his sentiments on all subjects, being responsible for the abuse of that right, and no laws shall be passed to restrain or abridge the liberty of speech or of the press. In all criminal prosecutions or indictments for libel, the truth may be given in evidence, and if it shall appear to the jury that the matter charged as libelous be true, and was published with good motives and for justifiable ends, the party shall be acquitted; and the jury shall have the right to determine the law and the fact.

Right to assemble and petition. Section 4. The right of the people peaceably to assemble, to consult for the common good, and to petition the government, or any department thereof, shall never be abridged.

Trial by jury; verdict in civil cases. Section 5. [*As amended November 1922*] The right of trial by jury shall remain inviolate, and shall extend to all cases at law without regard to the amount in controversy; but a jury trial may be waived by the parties in all cases in the manner prescribed by law. Provided, however, that the legislature may, from time to time, by statute provide that a valid verdict, in civil cases, may be based on the votes of a specified number of the jury, not less than five-sixths thereof. [*1919 AJR-26; 1921 AJR-14; 1921 c. 504*]

Trial by jury. Section 5. [*Original form*] The right of trial by jury shall remain inviolate; and shall extend to all cases at law, without regard to the amount in controversy; but a jury trial may be waived by the parties in all cases, in the manner prescribed by law.

Excessive bail; cruel punishments. Section 6. Excessive bail shall not be required, nor shall excessive fines be imposed, nor cruel and unusual punishments inflicted.

---

* Current provisions of the constitution are printed the full width of the page, and previous wordings (if any) follow each active provision in double-column format. Any section not indicated as having been amended and not followed by two-column text still exists as ratified by the people of Wisconsin when they adopted the Wisconsin Constitution on March 13, 1848.

Rights of accused. SECTION 7. In all criminal prosecutions the accused shall enjoy the right to be heard by himself and counsel; to demand the nature and cause of the accusation against him; to meet the witnesses face to face; to have compulsory process to compel the attendance of witnesses in his behalf; and in prosecutions by indictment, or information, to a speedy public trial by an impartial jury of the county or district wherein the offense shall have been committed; which county or district shall have been previously ascertained by law.

Prosecutions; double jeopardy; self-incrimination; bail; habeas corpus. SECTION 8. [*As amended per certification of the Board of State Canvassers dated April 7, 1982*] (1) No person may be held to answer for a criminal offense without due process of law, and no person for the same offense may be put twice in jeopardy of punishment, nor may be compelled in any criminal case to be a witness against himself or herself.

(2) All persons, before conviction, shall be eligible for release under reasonable conditions designed to assure their appearance in court, protect members of the community from serious bodily harm or prevent the intimidation of witnesses. Monetary conditions of release may be imposed at or after the initial appearance only upon a finding that there is a reasonable basis to believe that the conditions are necessary to assure appearance in court. The legislature may authorize, by law, courts to revoke a person's release for a violation of a condition of release.

(3) The legislature may by law authorize, but may not require, circuit courts to deny release for a period not to exceed 10 days prior to the hearing required under this subsection to a person who is accused of committing a murder punishable by life imprisonment or a sexual assault punishable by a maximum imprisonment of 20 years, or who is accused of committing or attempting to commit a felony involving serious bodily harm to another or the threat of serious bodily harm to another and who has a previous conviction for committing or attempting to commit a felony involving serious bodily harm to another or the threat of serious bodily harm to another. The legislature may authorize by law, but may not require, circuit courts to continue to deny release to those accused persons for an additional period not to exceed 60 days following the hearing required under this subsection, if there is a requirement that there be a finding by the court based on clear and convincing evidence presented at a hearing that the accused committed the felony and a requirement that there be a finding by the court that available conditions of release will not adequately protect members of the community from serious bodily harm or prevent intimidation of witnesses. Any law enacted under this subsection shall be specific, limited and reasonable. In determining the 10-day and 60-day periods, the court shall omit any period of time found by the court to result from a delay caused by the defendant or a continuance granted which was initiated by the defendant.

(4) The privilege of the writ of habeas corpus shall not be suspended unless, in cases of rebellion or invasion, the public safety requires it. [*June 1980 Spec.Sess. AJR-9; 1981 AJR-5*]

Prosecutions; second jeopardy; self-incrimination; bail; habeas corpus. SECTION 8. [*As amended November 1870*] No person shall be held to answer for a criminal offense without due process of law, and no person for the same offense may be put twice in jeopardy of punishment, nor shall be compelled in any criminal case to be a witness against himself. All persons shall, before conviction, be bailable by sufficient sureties, except for capital offenses when the proof is evident or the presumption great; and the privilege of the writ of habeas corpus shall not be suspended unless when, in cases of rebellion or invasion, the public safety may require it. [*1869 AJR-6; 1870 SJR-3; 1870 c. 118*]

Criminal procedure. SECTION 8. [*Original form*] No person shall be held to answer for a criminal offense, unless on the presentment, or indictment of a grand jury, except in cases of impeachment, or in cases cognizable by justices of the peace, or arising in the army or navy, or in the militia when in actual service in time of war, or public danger; and no person for the same offence shall be put twice in jeopardy of punishment, nor shall be compelled in any criminal case to be a witness against himself; all persons shall, before conviction, be bailable by sufficient sureties except for capital offences when the proof is evident, or the presumption great; and the privilege of the writ of habeas corpus shall not be suspended unless when, in cases of rebellion, or invasion, the public safety may require.

Remedy for wrongs. SECTION 9. Every person is entitled to a certain remedy in the laws for all injuries, or wrongs which he may receive in his person, property, or character; he ought to obtain justice freely, and without being obliged to purchase it, completely and without denial, promptly and without delay, conformably to the laws.

Victims of crime. SECTION 9m. [*As created April 1993*] This state shall treat crime victims, as defined by law, with fairness, dignity and respect for their privacy. This state shall ensure that crime victims have all of the following privileges and protections as provided by law: timely disposition of the case; the opportunity to attend court proceedings unless the trial court finds sequestration is necessary to a fair trial for the defendant; reasonable protection from the accused throughout the criminal justice process; notification of court proceedings; the opportunity to confer with the prosecution; the opportunity to make a statement to the court at disposition; restitution; compensation; and information about the outcome of the case and the release of the accused. The legislature shall provide remedies for the violation of this section. Nothing in this section, or in any statute enacted pursuant to this section, shall limit any right of the accused which may be provided by law. [*1991 SJR-41; 1993 SJR-3*]

Treason. SECTION 10. Treason against the state shall consist only in levying war against the same, or in adhering to its enemies, giving them aid and comfort. No person shall be convicted of treason unless on the testimony of two witnesses to the same overt act, or on confession in open court.

Searches and seizures. SECTION 11. The right of the people to be secure in their persons, houses, papers, and effects against unreasonable searches and seizures shall not be violated; and no warrant shall issue but upon probable cause, supported by oath or affirmation, and particularly describing the place to be searched and the persons or things to be seized.

Attainder; ex post facto; contracts. SECTION 12. No bill of attainder, ex post facto law, nor any law impairing the obligation of contracts, shall ever be passed, and no conviction shall work corruption of blood or forfeiture of estate.

Private property for public use. SECTION 13. The property of no person shall be taken for public use without just compensation therefor.

Feudal tenures; leases; alienation. SECTION 14. All lands within the state are declared to be allodial, and feudal tenures are prohibited. Leases and grants of agricultural land for a longer term than fifteen years in which rent or service of any kind shall be reserved, and all fines and like restraints upon alienation reserved in any grant of land, hereafter made, are declared to be void.

Equal property rights for aliens and citizens. SECTION 15. No distinction shall ever be made by law between resident aliens and citizens, in reference to the possession, enjoyment or descent of property.

Imprisonment for debt. SECTION 16. No person shall be imprisoned for debt arising out of or founded on a contract, expressed or implied.

Exemption of property of debtors. SECTION 17. The privilege of the debtor to enjoy the necessary comforts of life shall be recognized by wholesome laws, exempting a reasonable amount of property from seizure or sale for the payment of any debt or liability hereafter contracted.

Freedom of worship; liberty of conscience; state religion; public funds. SECTION 18. [*As amended November 1982*] The right of every person to worship Almighty God according to the dictates of conscience shall never be infringed; nor shall any person be compelled to attend, erect or support any place of worship, or to maintain any ministry, without consent; nor shall any control of, or interference with, the rights of conscience be permitted, or any preference be given by law to any religious establishments or modes of worship; nor shall any money be drawn from the treasury for the benefit of religious societies, or religious or theological seminaries. [*1979 AJR-76; 1981 AJR-35; submit: May '82 Spec.Sess. AJR-1*]

Freedom of worship; liberty of conscience; state religion; public funds. SECTION 18. [*Original form*] The right of every man to worship Almighty God according to the dictates of his own conscience shall never be infringed; nor shall any man be compelled to attend, erect or support any place of worship, or to maintain any ministry, against his consent; nor shall any control of, or interference with, the rights of conscience be permitted, or any preference be given by law to any religious establishments or modes of worship; nor shall any money be drawn from the treasury for the benefit of religious societies, or religious or theological seminaries.

Religious tests prohibited. SECTION 19. No religious tests shall ever be required as a qualification for any office of public trust under the state, and no person shall be rendered incompetent to give evidence in any court of law or equity in consequence of his opinions on the subject of religion.

Military subordinate to civil power. SECTION 20. The military shall be in strict subordination to the civil power.

Rights of suitors. SECTION 21. [*As amended April 1977*] (1) Writs of error shall never be prohibited, and shall be issued by such courts as the legislature designates by law.

(2) In any court of this state, any suitor may prosecute or defend his suit either in his own proper person or by an attorney of the suitor's choice. [*1975 AJR-11; 1977 SJR-9*]

Writs of error. SECTION 21. [*Original form*] Writs of error shall never be prohibited by law.

Maintenance of free government. SECTION 22. The blessings of a free government can only be maintained by a firm adherence to justice, moderation, temperance, frugality and virtue, and by frequent recurrence to fundamental principles.

Transportation of school children. SECTION 23. [*As created April 1967*] Nothing in this constitution shall prohibit the legislature from providing for the safety and welfare of children by providing for the transportation of children to and from any parochial or private school or institution of learning. [*1965 AJR-70; 1967 AJR-7*]

Use of school buildings. SECTION 24. [*As created April 1972*] Nothing in this constitution shall prohibit the legislature from authorizing, by law, the use of public school buildings by civic, religious or charitable organizations during nonschool hours upon payment by the organization to the school district of reasonable compensation for such use. [*1969 AJR-74; 1971 AJR-10*]

Right to keep and bear arms. SECTION 25. [*As created November 1998*] The people have the right to keep and bear arms for security, defense, hunting, recreation or any other lawful purpose. [*1995 AJR-53; 1997 AJR-11*]

Right to fish, hunt, trap, and take game. SECTION 26. [*As created April 2003*] The people have the right to fish, hunt, trap, and take game subject only to reasonable restrictions as prescribed by law. [*2001 SJR-2; 2003 AJR-1*]

ARTICLE II.
BOUNDARIES

State boundary. SECTION 1. It is hereby ordained and declared that the state of Wisconsin doth consent and accept of the boundaries prescribed in the act of congress entitled "An act to enable the people of Wisconsin territory to form a constitution and state government, and for the admission of such state into the Union," approved August sixth, one thousand eight hundred and forty-six, to wit: Beginning at the northeast corner of the state of Illinois - that is to say, at a point in the center of Lake Michigan where the line of forty-two degrees and thirty minutes of north latitude crosses the same; thence running with the boundary line of the state of Michigan, through Lake Michigan, Green Bay, to the mouth of the Menominee river; thence up the channel of the said river to the Brule river; thence up said last-mentioned river to Lake Brule; thence along the southern shore of Lake Brule in a direct line to the center of the channel between Middle and South Islands, in the Lake of the Desert; thence in a direct line to the head waters of the Montreal river, as marked upon the survey made by Captain Cram; thence down the main channel of the Montreal river to the middle of Lake Superior; thence through the center of Lake Superior to the mouth of the St. Louis river; thence up the main channel of said river to the first rapids in the same, above the Indian village, according to Nicollet's map; thence due south to the main branch of the river St. Croix; thence down the main channel of said river to the Mississippi; thence down the center of the main channel of that river to the northwest corner of the state of Illinois; thence due east with the northern boundary of the state of Illinois to the place of beginning, as established by "An act to enable the people of the Illinois territory to form a constitution and state government, and for the admission of such state into the Union on an equal footing with the original states," approved April 18th, 1818.

Alternate boundary. [*An additional paragraph, adopted by the convention as part of Art. II, sec. 1, was rejected by the act which admitted Wisconsin into the Union (9 U.S. Stat. Ch. L, pp. 233-235)*]: Provided, however, that the following alteration of the foresaid boundary be, and hereby is proposed to the congress of the United States as the preference of the state of Wisconsin, and if the same shall be assented and agreed to by the congress of the United States, then the same shall be and forever remain obligatory on the state of Wisconsin, viz.: Leaving the aforesaid boundary line at the foot of the rapids of the St. Louis river; thence in a direct line, bearing south-westerly, to the mouth of the Iskodewabo, or Rum river, where the same empties into the Mississippi river, thence down the main channel of said Mississippi river as prescribed in the aforesaid boundary.

Enabling act accepted. SECTION 2. [*As amended April 1951*] The propositions contained in the act of congress are hereby accepted, ratified and confirmed, and shall remain irrevocable without the consent of the United States; and it is hereby ordained that this state shall never interfere with the primary disposal of the soil within the same by the United States, nor with any regulations congress may find necessary for securing the title in such soil to bona fide purchasers thereof; and in no case shall nonresident proprietors be taxed higher than residents. Provided, that nothing in this constitution, or in the act of congress aforesaid, shall in any manner prejudice or affect the right of the state of Wisconsin to 500,000 acres of land granted to said state, and to be hereafter selected and located by and under the act of congress entitled "An act to appropriate the proceeds of the sales of the public lands, and grant pre-emption rights," approved September fourth, one thousand eight hundred and forty-one. [*1949 AJR-64; 1951 AJR-7*]

Enabling act accepted. SECTION 2. [*Original form*] The propositions contained in the act of congress are hereby accepted, ratified and confirmed, and shall remain irrevocable without the consent of the United States; and it is hereby ordained that this state shall never interfere with the primary disposal of the soil within the same by the United States, nor with any regulations congress may find necessary for securing the title in such soil to bona fide purchasers thereof; and no tax shall be imposed on land the property of the United States; and in no case shall nonresident proprietors be taxed higher than residents. Provided, that nothing in this constitution, or in the act of congress aforesaid, shall in any manner prejudice or affect the right of the state of Wisconsin to five hundred thousand acres of land granted to said state, and to be hereafter selected and located by and under the act of congress entitled "An act to appropriate the proceeds of the sales of the public lands, and grant pre-emption rights," approved September fourth, one thousand eight hundred and forty-one.

ARTICLE III.

SUFFRAGE

Electors. SECTION 1. [*As created April 1986*] Every United States citizen age 18 or older who is a resident of an election district in this state is a qualified elector of that district. [*1983 AJR-33; 1985 AJR-3*]

Implementation. SECTION 2. [*As created April 1986*] Laws may be enacted:

(1) Defining residency.

(2) Providing for registration of electors.

(3) Providing for absentee voting.

(4) Excluding from the right of suffrage persons:

(a) Convicted of a felony, unless restored to civil rights.

(b) Adjudged by a court to be incompetent or partially incompetent, unless the judgment specifies that the person is capable of understanding the objective of the elective process or the judgment is set aside.

(5) Subject to ratification by the people at a general election, extending the right of suffrage to additional classes. [*1983 AJR-33; 1985 AJR-3*]

Secret ballot. SECTION 3. [*As created April 1986*] All votes shall be by secret ballot. [*1983 AJR-33; 1985 AJR-3*]

Revision of Article III. The original 6 sections of Article III of the constitution were repealed in April 1986 when the wording of the article was reorganized into the 3 new sections shown above.

Electors. SECTION 1. [*As amended November 1934*] Every person, of the age of twenty-one years or upwards, belonging to either of the following classes, who shall have resided in the state for one year next preceding any election, and in the election district where he offers to vote such time as may be prescribed by the legislature, not exceeding thirty days, shall be deemed a qualified elector at such election: (1) Citizens of the United States.

(2) Persons of Indian blood, who have once been declared by law of congress to be citizens of the United States, any subsequent law of congress to the contrary notwithstanding.

(3) The legislature may at any time extend, by law, the right of suffrage to persons not herein enumerated; but no such law shall be in force until the same shall have been submitted to a vote of the people at a general election, and approved by a majority of all the votes cast on that question at such election; and provided further, that the legislature may provide for the registration of electors, and prescribe proper rules and regulations therefor. [*1931 AJR-52; 1933 SJR-74*]

Termination of voting by resident aliens. [*Subdivision* 2 (of the text adopted in 1882), *as amended November*

1908] 2. Persons of foreign birth who, prior to the first day of December, A.D. 1908, shall have declared their intentions to become citizens conformable to the laws of the United States on the subject of naturalization, provided that the rights hereby granted to such persons shall cease on the first day of December, A.D. 1912. [*1905 AJR-16; 1907 AJR-47; 1907 c. 661*]

Qualifications of electors. SECTION 1. [*As amended November 1882*] Every male person of the age of twenty-one years or upwards, belonging to either of the following classes, who shall have resided in the state for one year next preceding any election, and in the election district where he offers to vote such time as may be prescribed by the legislature not exceeding thirty days shall be deemed a qualified elector at such election. 1. Citizens of the United States. 2. Persons of foreign birth who shall have declared their intention to become citizens, conformably to the laws of the United States on the subject of naturalization. 3. Persons of Indian blood who have once been declared by law of congress to be citizens of the United States, any subsequent law of congress to the contrary notwithstanding. 4. Civilized persons of Indian descent not members of any tribe; provided that the legislature may at any time extend, by law, the right of suffrage to persons not herein enumerated, but no such law shall be in force until the same shall have been submitted to a vote of the people at a general election, and approved by a majority of all the votes cast at such election; and provided further, that in incorporated cities and villages, the legislature may provide for the registration of electors and prescribe proper rules and regulations therefor. [*1881 AJR-26; 1882 SJR-18; 1882 c. 272*]

Equal suffrage to colored persons. In *Gillespie v. Palmer*, 20 Wis. (1866) 544, the Wisconsin Supreme Court ruled that Chapter 137, Laws of 1849, extending *equal suffrage to colored persons*, was approved by the voters on November 6, 1849.

Qualifications of electors. SECTION 1. [*Original form*] Every male person of the age of twenty-one years or upwards belonging to either of the following classes, who shall have resided in the state for one year next preceding any election, shall be deemed a qualified elector at such election:

[*First.*] White citizens of the United States.

[*Second.*] White persons of foreign birth who shall have declared their intention to become citizens, conformably to the laws of the United States on the subject of naturalization.

[*Third.*] Persons of Indian blood who have once been declared by law of congress to be citizens of the United States, any subsequent law of congress to the contrary notwithstanding.

[*Fourth.*] Civilized persons of Indian descent, not members of any tribe. Provided, that the legislature may at any time extend, by law, the right of suffrage to persons not herein enumerated, but no such law shall be in force until

the same shall have been submitted to a vote of the people at a general election, and approved by a majority of all the votes cast at such election.

Who not electors. SECTION 2. [*Original form*] No person under guardianship, non compos mentis or insane shall be qualified to vote at any election; nor shall any person convicted of treason or felony be qualified to vote at any election unless restored to civil rights.

Votes to be by ballot. SECTION 3. [*Original form*] All votes shall be given by ballot except for such township officers as may by law be directed or allowed to be otherwise chosen.

Residence saved. SECTION 4. [*Original form*] No person shall be deemed to have lost his residence in this state by reason of his absence on business of the United States or of this state.

Military stationing does not confer residence. SECTION 5. [*Original form*] No soldier, seaman or marine in the army or navy of the United States shall be deemed a resident of this state in consequence of being stationed within the same.

Exclusion from suffrage. SECTION 6. [*Original form*] Laws may be passed excluding from the right of suffrage all persons who have been or may be convicted of bribery or larceny, or of any infamous crime, and depriving every person who shall make or become directly or indirectly interested in any bet or wager depending upon the result of any election from the right to vote at such election.

ARTICLE IV.
LEGISLATIVE

Legislative power. SECTION 1. The legislative power shall be vested in a senate and assembly.

Legislature, how constituted. SECTION 2. The number of the members of the assembly shall never be less than fifty-four nor more than one hundred. The senate shall consist of a number not more than one-third nor less than one-fourth of the number of the members of the assembly.

Apportionment. SECTION 3. [*As amended November 1982*] At its first session after each enumeration made by the authority of the United States, the legislature shall apportion and district anew the members of the senate and assembly, according to the number of inhabitants. [*1979 AJR-76; 1981 AJR-35; submit: May '82 Spec.Sess. AJR-1*]

Apportionment. SECTION 3. [*As amended November 1962*] At their first session after each enumeration made by the authority of the United States, the legislature shall apportion and district anew the members of the senate and assembly, according to the number of inhabitants, excluding soldiers, and officers of the United States army and navy. [*1959 SJR-12; 1961 SJR-11*]

Senate district area factor. SECTIONS 3, 4 AND 5. [*Approved by voters April 1953*] An amendment to Art. IV, secs. 3, 4, 5, relating to senate apportionment based on area and population, was approved by 1951 SJR-50 and 1953 AJR-7. However, the Supreme Court held the amendment not validly submitted to the voters in State ex rel. Thomson v. Zimmerman, 264 W. 644, 60 NW (2d) 416.

Apportionment. SECTION 3. [*As amended November 1910*] At their first session after each enumeration made

by the authority of the United States, the legislature shall apportion and district anew the members of the senate and assembly, according to the number of inhabitants, excluding Indians not taxed, soldiers, and officers of the United States army and navy. [*1907 SJR-18; 1909 SJR-35; 1909 c. 478*]

Census and apportionment. SECTION 3. [*Original form*] The legislature shall provide by law for an enumeration of the inhabitants of the state in the year one thousand eight hundred and fifty-five, and at the end of every ten years thereafter; and at their first session after such enumeration, and also after each enumeration made by the authority of the United States, the legislature shall apportion and district anew the members of the senate and assembly, according to the number of inhabitants, excluding Indians not taxed, and soldiers and officers of the United States army and navy.

Representatives to the assembly, how chosen. SECTION 4. [*As amended November 1982*] The members of the assembly shall be chosen biennially, by single districts, on the Tuesday succeeding the first Monday of November in even-numbered years, by the qualified electors of the several districts, such districts to be bounded by county, precinct, town or ward lines, to consist of contiguous territory and be in as compact form as practicable. [*1979 AJR-76; 1981 AJR-35; submit: May '82 Spec.Sess. AJR-1*]

Representatives to the assembly, how chosen. SECTION 4. [*As amended November 1881*] The members of the assembly shall be chosen biennially, by single districts, on the Tuesday succeeding the first Monday of November after the adoption of this amendment, by the qualified electors of the several districts, such districts to be bounded by county,

precinct, town or ward lines, to consist of contiguous territory and be in as compact form as practicable. [*1880 SJR-9; 1881 AJR-7; 1881 c. 262*]

Assemblymen, how chosen. SECTION 4. [*Original form*] The members of the assembly shall be chosen annually by single districts, on the Tuesday succeeding the first Monday of November, by the qualified electors of the several districts. Such districts to be bounded by county, precinct,

town, or ward lines, to consist of contiguous territory, and be in as compact form as practicable.

Senators, how chosen. SECTION 5. [*As amended November 1982*] The senators shall be elected by single districts of convenient contiguous territory, at the same time and in the same manner as members of the assembly are required to be chosen; and no assembly district shall be divided in the formation of a senate district. The senate districts shall be numbered in the regular series, and the senators shall be chosen alternately from the odd and even-numbered districts for the term of 4 years. [*1979 AJR-76; 1981 AJR-35; submit: May '82 Spec.Sess. AJR-1*]

Senators, how chosen. SECTION 5. [*As amended November 1881*] The senators shall be elected by single districts of convenient contiguous territory, at the same time and in the same manner as members of the assembly are required to be chosen, and no assembly district shall be divided in the formation of a senate district. The senate districts shall be numbered in the regular series, and the senators shall be chosen alternately from the odd and even-numbered districts. The senators chosen or holding over at the time of the adoption of this amendment shall continue in office till their successors are duly elected and qualified; and after the adoption of this amendment all senators shall be chosen for the term of four years. [*1880 SJR-9; 1881 AJR-7; 1881 c. 262*]

Senators, how chosen. SECTION 5. [*Original form*] The senators shall be chosen by single districts of convenient contiguous territory, at the same time and in the same manner as members of the assembly are required to be chosen, and no assembly district shall be divided in the formation of a senate district. The senate districts shall be numbered in regular series, and the senators chosen by the odd-numbered districts shall go out of office at the expiration of the first year, and the senators chosen by the even-numbered districts shall go out of office at the expiration of the second year, and thereafter the senators shall be chosen for the term of two years.

Qualifications of legislators. SECTION 6. No person shall be eligible to the legislature who shall not have resided one year within the state, and be a qualified elector in the district which he may be chosen to represent.

Organization of legislature; quorum; compulsory attendance. SECTION 7. Each house shall be the judge of the elections, returns and qualifications of its own members; and a majority of each shall constitute a quorum to do business, but a smaller number may adjourn from day to day, and may compel the attendance of absent members in such manner and under such penalties as each house may provide.

Rules; contempts; expulsion. SECTION 8. Each house may determine the rules of its own proceedings, punish for contempt and disorderly behavior, and with the concurrence of two-thirds of all the members elected, expel a member; but no member shall be expelled a second time for the same cause.

Officers. SECTION 9. [*As amended April 1979*] Each house shall choose its presiding officers from its own members. [*1977 SJR-51; 1979 SJR-1*]

Officers. SECTION 9. [*Original form*] Each house shall choose its own officers, and the senate shall choose a

temporary president when the lieutenant governor shall not attend as president, or shall act as governor.

Journals; open doors; adjournments. SECTION 10. Each house shall keep a journal of its proceedings and publish the same, except such parts as require secrecy. The doors of each house shall be kept open except when the public welfare shall require secrecy. Neither house shall, without consent of the other, adjourn for more than three days.

Meeting of legislature. SECTION 11. [*As amended April 1968*] The legislature shall meet at the seat of government at such time as shall be provided by law, unless convened by the governor in special session, and when so convened no business shall be transacted except as shall be necessary to accomplish the special purposes for which it was convened. [*1965 AJR-5; 1967 AJR-15*]

Meeting of legislature. SECTION 11. [*As amended November 1881*] The legislature shall meet at the seat of government at such time as shall be provided by law, once in two years, and no oftener, unless convened by the governor, in special session, and when so convened no business shall be transacted except as shall be necessary to

accomplish the special purposes for which it was convened. [*1880 SJR-9; 1881 AJR-7; 1881 c. 262*]

Place and time of meeting. SECTION 11. [*Original form*] The legislature shall meet at the seat of government, at such time as shall be provided by law, once in each year and not oftener, unless convened by the governor.

Ineligibility of legislators to office. SECTION 12. No member of the legislature shall, during the term for which he was elected, be appointed or elected to any civil office in the state, which shall have been created, or the emoluments of which shall have been increased, during the term for which he was elected.

Ineligibility of federal officers. SECTION 13. [*As amended April 1966*] No person being a member of congress, or holding any military or civil office under the United States, shall be eligible to a seat in the legislature; and if any person shall, after his election as a member of the legislature, be elected to congress, or be appointed to any office, civil or military, under the government of the United States, his acceptance thereof shall vacate his seat. This restriction shall not prohibit a legislator from accepting short periods of active duty as a member of the reserve or from serving in the armed forces during any emergency declared by the executive. [*1963 SJR-24; 1965 SJR-15*]

Ineligibility of federal officers. SECTION 13. [*Original form*] No person being a member of congress, or holding any military or civil office under the United States, shall be eligible to a seat in the legislature; and if any person shall,

after his election as a member of the legislature, be elected to congress, or be appointed to any office, civil or military, under the government of the United States, his acceptance thereof shall vacate his seat.

Filling vacancies. SECTION 14. The governor shall issue writs of election to fill such vacancies as may occur in either house of the legislature.

Exemption from arrest and civil process. SECTION 15. Members of the legislature shall in all cases, except treason, felony and breach of the peace, be privileged from arrest; nor shall they be subject to any civil process, during the session of the legislature, nor for fifteen days next before the commencement and after the termination of each session.

Privilege in debate. SECTION 16. No member of the legislature shall be liable in any civil action, or criminal prosecution whatever, for words spoken in debate.

Enactment of laws. SECTION 17. [*As amended April 1977*] (1) The style of all laws of the state shall be "The people of the state of Wisconsin, represented in senate and assembly, do enact as follows:".

(2) No law shall be enacted except by bill. No law shall be in force until published.

(3) The legislature shall provide by law for the speedy publication of all laws. [*1975 AJR-11; 1977 SJR-9*]

Style of laws; bills. SECTION 17. [*Original form*] The style of the laws of the state shall be "The people of the state of Wisconsin, represented in senate and assembly, do

enact as follows:" and no law shall be enacted except by bill.

Title of private bills. SECTION 18. No private or local bill which may be passed by the legislature shall embrace more than one subject, and that shall be expressed in the title.

Origin of bills. SECTION 19. Any bill may originate in either house of the legislature, and a bill passed by one house may be amended by the other.

Yeas and nays. SECTION 20. The yeas and nays of the members of either house on any question shall, at the request of one-sixth of those present, be entered on the journal.

SECTION 21. [*Repealed. 1927 SJR-61; 1929 SJR-7; vote April 1929*]

Compensation of members. SECTION 21. [*As amended November 1881*] Each member of the legislature shall receive for his services, for and during a regular session, the sum of five hundred dollars, and ten cents for every mile he shall travel in going to and returning from the place of meeting of the legislature on the most usual route. In case of an extra session of the legislature, no additional compensation shall be allowed to any member thereof, either directly or indirectly, except for mileage to be computed at the same rate as for a regular session. No stationery, newspapers, postage or other perquisite except the salary and mileage above provided, shall be received from the state by any member of the legislature for his services, or in any other manner as such member. [*1880 SJR-9; 1881 AJR-7; 1881 c. 262*]

Compensation of members. SECTION 21. [*As amended November 1867*] Each member of the legislature shall receive for his services three hundred and fifty dollars per annum and ten cents for every mile he shall travel in going to and returning from the place of the meeting of the legislature on the most usual route. In case of an extra session of the legislature no additional compensation shall be allowed to any member thereof either directly or indirectly. [*1865 SJR-26; 1866 SJR-16; 1867 c. 25*]

Compensation of members. SECTION 21. [*Original form*] Each member of the legislature shall receive for his services two dollars and fifty cents for each day's attendance during the session, and ten cents for every mile he shall travel in going to and returning from the place of meeting of the legislature, on the most usual route.

Powers of county boards. SECTION 22. The legislature may confer upon the boards of supervisors of the several counties of the state such powers of a local, legislative and administrative character as they shall from time to time prescribe.

Town and county government. SECTION 23. [*As amended April 1972*] The legislature shall establish but one system of town government, which shall be as nearly uniform as practicable; but the legislature may provide for the election at large once in every 4 years of a chief executive officer in any county with such powers of an administrative character as they may from time to time prescribe in accordance with this section and shall establish one or more systems of county government. [*1969 SJR-58; 1971 SJR-4*]

Uniform town and county government. SECTION 23. [*As amended April 1969*] The legislature shall establish but one system of town and county government, which shall be as nearly uniform as practicable, except that the requirement of uniformity shall not apply to the administrative means of exercising powers of a local legislative character conferred by section 22 upon the boards of supervisors of the several counties; but the legislature may provide for the election at large once in every 4 years of a chief executive officer in any county with such powers of an administrative character as they may from time to time prescribe in accordance with this section. [*1967 AJR-18; 1969 SJR-8*]

Uniform town and county government. SECTION 23. [*As amended November 1962*] The legislature shall establish but one system of town and county government, which shall be as nearly uniform as practicable; but the legislature may provide for the election at large once in every four years of a chief executive officer in any county having a population of five hundred thousand or more with such powers of an administrative character as they may from time to time prescribe in accordance with this section. [*1959 AJR-121; 1961 AJR-61*]

Uniform town and county government. SECTION 23. [*Original form*] The legislature shall establish but one system of town and county government, which shall be as nearly uniform as practicable.

Chief executive officer to approve or veto resolutions or ordinances; proceedings on veto. SECTION 23a. [*As amended April 1969*] Every resolution or ordinance passed by the county board in any county shall, before it becomes effective, be presented to the chief executive officer. If he approves, he shall sign it; if not, he shall return it with his objections, which objections shall be entered at large upon the journal and the board shall proceed to reconsider the matter. Appropriations may be approved in whole or in part by the chief executive officer and the part approved shall become law, and the part objected to shall be returned in the same manner as provided for in other resolutions or ordinances. If, after such reconsideration, two-thirds of the members-elect of the county board agree to pass the resolution or ordinance or the part of the resolution or ordinance objected to, it shall become effective on the date prescribed but not earlier than the date of passage following reconsideration. In all such cases, the votes of the members of the county board shall be determined by ayes and noes and the names of the members voting for or against the resolution or ordinance or the part thereof objected to shall be entered on the journal. If any resolution or ordinance is not returned by the chief executive officer to the county board at its first meeting occurring not less than 6 days, Sundays excepted, after it has been presented to him, it shall become effective unless the county board has recessed or adjourned for a period in excess of 60 days, in which case it shall not be effective without his approval. [*1967 AJR-18; 1969 SJR-8*]

Chief executive officer to approve or veto resolutions or ordinances; proceedings on veto. SECTION 23A. [*Created November 1962*] Every resolution or ordinance passed by the county board in any county having a population of five hundred thousand or more shall, before it becomes effective, be presented to the chief executive officer. If he approves, he shall sign it; if not, he shall return it with his objections, which objections shall be entered at large upon the journal and the board shall proceed to reconsider the matter. Appropriations may be approved in whole or in part by the chief executive officer and the part approved shall become law, and the part objected to shall be returned in the same manner as provided for in other resolutions or ordinances. If, after such reconsideration, two-thirds of the members-elect of the county board agree to pass the resolution or ordinance or the part of the resolution or ordinance objected to, it shall become effective on the date prescribed but not earlier than the date of passage following reconsideration. In all such cases, the votes of the members of the county board shall be determined by ayes and nays and the names of the members voting for or against the resolution or ordinance or the part thereof objected to shall be entered on the journal. If any resolution or ordinance is not returned by the chief executive officer to the county board at its first meeting occurring not less than six days, Sundays excepted, after it has been presented to him, it shall become effective unless the county board has recessed or adjourned for a period in excess of sixty days, in which case it shall not be effective without his approval. [*1959 AJR-121; 1961 AJR-61*]

Gambling. SECTION 24. [*As amended April 1993*] (1) Except as provided in this section, the legislature may not authorize gambling in any form.

(2) Except as otherwise provided by law, the following activities do not constitute consideration as an element of gambling:

(a) To listen to or watch a television or radio program.

(b) To fill out a coupon or entry blank, whether or not proof of purchase is required.

(c) To visit a mercantile establishment or other place without being required to make a purchase or pay an admittance fee.

(3) [*As amended April 1999*] The legislature may authorize the following bingo games licensed by the state, but all profits shall accrue to the licensed organization and no salaries, fees or profits may be paid to any other organization or person: bingo games operated by religious, charitable, service, fraternal or veterans' organizations or those to which contributions are deductible for federal or state income tax purposes. All moneys received by the state that are attributable to bingo games shall be used for property tax relief for residents of this state as provided by law. The distribution of moneys that are attributable to bingo games may not vary based on the income or age of the person provided the property tax relief. The distribution of moneys that

are attributable to bingo games shall not be subject to the uniformity requirement of section 1 of article VIII. In this subsection, the distribution of all moneys attributable to bingo games shall include any earnings on the moneys received by the state that are attributable to bingo games, but shall not include any moneys used for the regulation of, and enforcement of law relating to, bingo games. [1997 AJR-80; 1999 AJR-2]

(3) The legislature may authorize the following bingo games licensed by the state, but all profits shall accrue to the licensed organization and no salaries, fees or profits may be paid to any other organization or person: bingo games operated by religious, charitable, service, fraternal or veterans' organizations or those to which contributions are deductible for federal or state income tax purposes.

(4) The legislature may authorize the following raffle games licensed by the state, but all profits shall accrue to the licensed local organization and no salaries, fees or profits may be paid to any other organization or person: raffle games operated by local religious, charitable, service, fraternal or veterans' organizations or those to which contributions are deductible for federal or state income tax purposes. The legislature shall limit the number of raffles conducted by any such organization.

(5) [*As amended April 1999*] This section shall not prohibit pari-mutuel on-track betting as provided by law. The state may not own or operate any facility or enterprise for pari-mutuel betting, or lease any state-owned land to any other owner or operator for such purposes. All moneys received by the state that are attributable to pari-mutuel on-track betting shall be used for property tax relief for residents of this state as provided by law. The distribution of moneys that are attributable to pari-mutuel on-track betting may not vary based on the income or age of the person provided the property tax relief. The distribution of moneys that are attributable to pari-mutuel on-track betting shall not be subject to the uniformity requirement of section 1 of article VIII. In this subsection, the distribution of all moneys attributable to pari-mutuel on-track betting shall include any earnings on the moneys received by the state that are attributable to pari-mutuel on-track betting, but shall not include any moneys used for the regulation of, and enforcement of law relating to, pari-mutuel on-track betting. [*1997 AJR-80; 1999 AJR-2*]

(5) This section shall not prohibit pari-mutuel on-track betting as provided by law. The state may not own or operate any facility or enterprise for pari-mutuel betting, or lease any state-owned land to any other owner or operator for such purposes.

(6) (a) [*As amended April 1999*] The legislature may authorize the creation of a lottery to be operated by the state as provided by law. The expenditure of public funds or of revenues derived from lottery operations to engage in promotional advertising of the Wisconsin state lottery is prohibited. Any advertising of the state lottery shall indicate the odds of a specific lottery ticket to be selected as the winning ticket for each prize amount offered. The net proceeds of the state lottery shall be deposited in the treasury of the state, to be used for property tax relief for residents of this state as provided by law. The distribution of the net proceeds of the state lottery may not vary based on the income or age of the person provided the property tax relief. The distribution of the net proceeds of the state lottery shall not be subject to the uniformity requirement of section 1 of article VIII. In this paragraph, the distribution of the net proceeds of the state lottery shall include any earnings on the net proceeds of the state lottery. [*1997 AJR-80; 1999 AJR-2*]

(6) (a) The legislature may authorize the creation of a lottery to be operated by the state as provided by law. The expenditure of public funds or of revenues derived from lottery operations to engage in promotional advertising of the Wisconsin state lottery is prohibited. Any advertising of the state lottery shall indicate the odds of a specific lottery ticket to be selected as the winning ticket for each prize amount offered. The net proceeds of the state lottery shall be deposited in the treasury of the state, to be used for property tax relief as provided by law.

(b) The lottery authorized under par. (a) shall be an enterprise that entitles the player, by purchasing a ticket, to participate in a game of chance if: 1) the winning tickets are randomly predetermined and the player reveals preprinted numbers or symbols from which it can be immediately determined whether the ticket is a winning ticket entitling the player to win a prize as prescribed in the features and procedures for the game, including an opportunity to win a prize in a secondary or subsequent chance drawing or game; or 2) the ticket is evidence of the numbers or symbols selected by the player or, at the player's option, selected by a computer, and the player becomes entitled to a prize as prescribed in the features and procedures for the game, including an opportunity to win a prize in a secondary or subsequent chance drawing or game if some or all of the player's symbols or numbers are selected in a chance drawing or game, if the player's ticket is randomly selected by the computer at the time of purchase or if the ticket is selected in a chance drawing.

(c) Notwithstanding the authorization of a state lottery under par. (a), the following games, or games simulating any of the following games, may not be conducted by the state as a lottery: 1) any game in which winners are selected based on the results of a race or sporting event; 2) any banking card game, including blackjack, baccarat or chemin de fer; 3) poker; 4) roulette; 5) craps or any other game that involves rolling dice; 6) keno; 7) bingo 21, bingo jack, bingolet or bingo craps; 8) any game of chance that is placed on a slot machine or any mechanical, electromechanical or electronic device that is generally available to be played at a gambling casino; 9) any game or device that is commonly known as a video game of chance or a video gaming machine or that is commonly considered to be a video gambling machine, unless such machine is a video device operated by the state in a game authorized under par. (a) to permit the sale of tickets through retail outlets under contract with the state and the device does not determine or indicate whether the player has won a prize, other than by verifying that the player's ticket or some or all of the player's symbols or numbers on the player's ticket have been selected in a chance drawing, or by verifying that the player's ticket has been randomly selected by a central system computer at the time of purchase; 10) any game that is similar to a game listed in this paragraph; or 11) any other game that is commonly considered to be a form of gambling and is not, or is not substantially similar to, a game conducted by the state under par. (a). No game conducted by the state under par. (a) may permit a player of the game to purchase a ticket, or to otherwise participate in the game, from a residence by using a computer, telephone or other form of electronic, telecommunication, video or technological aid. *[(1), (2)(intro.) amended; (6) (b), (c) created; June 1992 AJR-1; 1993 SJR-2]*

Lotteries and divorces. SECTION 24. [*As amended April 1987*] (1) Except as provided in this section, the legislature shall never authorize any lottery or grant any divorce.

(2) Except as otherwise provided by law, the following activities do not constitute consideration as an element of a lottery:

(a) To listen to or watch a television or radio program.

(b) To fill out a coupon or entry blank, whether or not proof of purchase is required.

(c) To visit a mercantile establishment or other place without being required to make a purchase or pay an admittance fee.

(3) The legislature may authorize the following bingo games licensed by the state, but all profits shall accrue to the licensed organization and no salaries, fees or profits may be paid to any other organization or person: bingo games operated by religious, charitable, service, fraternal or veterans' organizations or those to which contributions are deductible for federal or state income tax purposes.

(4) The legislature may authorize the following raffle games licensed by the state, but all profits shall accrue to the licensed organization and no salaries, fees or profits may be paid to any other organization or person: raffle games operated by local religious, charitable, service, fraternal or veterans' organizations or those to which contributions are deductible for federal or state income tax purposes. The legislature shall limit the number of raffles conducted by any such organization.

(5) This section shall not prohibit pari-mutuel on-track betting as provided by law. The state may not own or operate any facility or enterprise for pari-mutuel betting, or lease any state-owned land to any other owner or operator for such purposes.

(6) The legislature may authorize the creation of a lottery to be operated by the state as provided by law. The expenditure of public funds or of revenues derived from lottery operations to engage in promotional advertising of the Wisconsin state lottery is prohibited. Any advertising of the state lottery shall indicate the odds of a specific lottery ticket to be selected as the winning ticket for each prize amount offered. The net proceeds of the state lottery shall be deposited in the treasury of the state, to be used for property tax relief as provided by law. [*Pari-mutuel: 1985 AJR-45; 1987 AJR-2. State lottery: 1985 SJR-1; 1987 AJR-3.*]

Lotteries and divorces. SECTION 24. [*As amended April 1977*] The legislature shall never authorize any lottery or grant any divorce. (1) The legislature may authorize bingo

games licensed by the state, and operated by religious, charitable, service, fraternal or veterans' organizations or those to which contributions are deductible for federal or state income tax purposes. All profits must inure to the licensed organization and no salaries, fees or profits shall be paid to any other organization or person. (2) The legislature may authorize raffle games licensed by the state, and operated by local religious, charitable, service, fraternal or veterans' organizations or those to which contributions are deductible for federal or state income tax purposes. The legislature shall limit the number of raffles conducted by any such organization. All profits must inure to the licensed local organization and no salaries, fees or profits shall be paid to any other organization or person. (3) Except as the legislature may provide otherwise, the following activities do not constitute consideration as an element of a lottery: (a) To listen to or watch a television or radio program. (b) To fill out a coupon or entry blank, whether or not proof of purchase is required. (c) To visit a mercantile establishment or other place without being required to make a purchase or pay an admittance fee. [*1975 AJR-43; 1977 AJR-10*]

Lotteries and divorces. SECTION 24. [*As amended April 1973*] The legislature shall never authorize any lottery, or grant any divorce, but may authorize bingo games licensed by the state, and operated by religious, charitable, service, fraternal or veterans' organizations or those to which contributions are deductible for federal or state income tax purposes. All profits must inure to the licensed organization and no salaries, fees or profits shall be paid to any other organization or person. Except as the legislature may provide otherwise, to listen to or watch a television or radio program, to fill out a coupon or entry blank, whether or not proof of purchase is required, or to visit a mercantile establishment or other place without being required to make a purchase or pay an admittance fee does not constitute consideration as an element of a lottery. [*1971 SJR-13; 1973 AJR-6*]

Lotteries and divorces. SECTION 24. [*As amended April 1965*] The legislature shall never authorize any lottery, or grant any divorce. Except as the legislature may provide otherwise, to listen to or watch a television or radio program, to fill out a coupon or entry blank, whether or not proof of purchase is required, or to visit a mercantile establishment or other place without being required to make a purchase or pay an admittance fee does not constitute consideration as an element of a lottery. [*1963 SJR-42; 1965 SJR-13*]

Lotteries and divorces. SECTION 24. [*Original form*] The legislature shall never authorize any lottery, or grant any divorce.

Stationery and printing. SECTION 25. The legislature shall provide by law that all stationery required for the use of the state, and all printing authorized and required by them to be done for their use, or for the state, shall be let by contract to the lowest bidder, but the legislature may establish a maximum price; no member of the legislature or other state officer shall be interested, either directly or indirectly, in any such contract.

Extra compensation; salary change. SECTION 26. [*As amended April 1992*] (1) The legislature may not grant any extra compensation to a public officer, agent, servant or contractor after the services have been rendered or the contract has been entered into.

(2) Except as provided in this subsection, the compensation of a public officer may not be increased or diminished during the term of office:

(a) When any increase or decrease in the compensation of justices of the supreme court or judges of any court of record becomes effective as to any such justice or judge, it shall be effective from such date as to every such justice or judge.

(b) Any increase in the compensation of members of the legislature shall take effect, for all senators and representatives to the assembly, after the next general election beginning with the new assembly term.

(3) Subsection (1) shall not apply to increased benefits for persons who have been or shall be granted benefits of any kind under a retirement system when such increased benefits are provided by a legislative act passed on a call of ayes and noes by a three-fourths vote of all the members elected to both houses of the legislature and such act provides for sufficient state funds to cover the costs of the increased benefits. [*1989 AJR-47; 1991 AJR-16*]

Extra compensation; salary change. SECTION 26. [*As amended April 1977*] The legislature shall never grant any extra compensation to any public officer, agent, servant or contractor, after the services shall have been rendered or the contract entered into; nor shall the compensation of any public officer be increased or diminished during his term of office except that when any increase or decrease provided by the legislature in the compensation of the justices of the supreme court or judges of any court of record shall become effective as to any such justice or judge, it shall be effective from such date as to each of such justices or judges. This section shall not apply to increased benefits for persons who have been or shall be granted benefits of any kind under a retirement system when such increased benefits are provided by a legislative act passed on a call of ayes and noes by a three-fourths vote of all the members elected to both houses of the legislature, which act shall provide for sufficient state funds to cover the costs of the increased benefits. [*1975 AJR-11; 1977 SJR-9*]

Extra compensation; salary change. SECTION 26. [*As amended April 1974*] The legislature shall never grant any extra compensation to any public officer, agent, servant or contractor, after the services shall have been rendered or the contract entered into; nor shall the compensation of any public officer be increased or diminished during his term of office except that when any increase or decrease provided by the legislature in the compensation of the justices of the supreme court, or judges of the circuit court shall become effective as to any such justice or judge, it shall become effective from such date as to each of such justices or judges. This section shall not apply to increased benefits for persons who have been or shall be granted benefits of any kind under a retirement system when such increased benefits are provided by a legislative act passed on a call of yeas and nays by a three-fourths vote of all the members elected to both houses of the legislature, which act shall provide for sufficient state funds to cover the costs of the increased benefits. [*1971 SJR-3; 1973 SJR-15*]

Extra compensation; salary change. SECTION 26. [*As amended April 1967*] The legislature shall never grant any extra compensation to any public officer, agent, servant or contractor, after the services shall have been rendered or the contract entered into; nor shall the compensation of any public officer be increased or diminished during his term of office except that when any increase or decrease provided by the legislature in the compensation of the justices of the supreme court, or judges of the circuit court shall become effective as to any such justice or judge, it shall be effective from such date as to each of such justices or judges. This section shall not apply to increased benefits for teachers under a teachers' retirement system when such increased benefits are provided by a legislative act passed on a call of yeas and nays by a three-fourths vote of all the members elected to both houses of the legislature. [*1965 AJR-162; 1967 AJR-17*]

Extra compensation; salary change. SECTION 26. [*As amended April 1956*] The legislature shall never grant any extra compensation to any public officer, agent, servant or contractor, after the services have been rendered or the contract entered into; nor shall the compensation of any public officer be increased or diminished during his term of office. This section shall not apply to increased benefits for teachers under a teachers' retirement system when such increased benefits are provided by a legislative act passed on a call of yeas and nays by a three-fourths vote of all the members elected to both houses of the legislature. [*1953 SJR-21; 1955 SJR-8*]

Extra compensation; salary change. SECTION 26. [*Original form*] The legislature shall never grant any extra compensation to any public officer, agent, servant or contractor after the services shall have been rendered or the contract entered into; nor shall the compensation of any public officer be increased or diminished during his term of office.

Suits against state. SECTION 27. The legislature shall direct by law in what manner and in what courts suits may be brought against the state.

Oath of office. SECTION 28. Members of the legislature, and all officers, executive and judicial, except such inferior officers as may be by law exempted, shall before they enter upon the duties of their respective offices, take and subscribe an oath or affirmation to support the constitution of the United States and the constitution of the state of Wisconsin, and faithfully to discharge the duties of their respective offices to the best of their ability.

Militia. SECTION 29. The legislature shall determine what persons shall constitute the militia of the state, and may provide for organizing and disciplining the same in such manner as shall be prescribed by law.

Elections by legislature. SECTION 30. [*As amended November 1982*] All elections made by the legislature shall be by roll call vote entered in the journals. [*1979 AJR-76; 1981 AJR-35; submit: May'82 Spec.Sess. AJR-1*]

Elections by legislature. SECTION 30. [*Original form*] In all elections to be made by the legislature the members thereof shall vote viva voce, and their votes shall be entered on the journal.

Special and private laws prohibited. SECTION 31. [*As amended April 1993*] The legislature is prohibited from enacting any special or private laws in the following cases:

(1) For changing the names of persons, constituting one person the heir at law of another or granting any divorce.

(2) For laying out, opening or altering highways, except in cases of state roads extending into more than one county, and military roads to aid in the construction of which lands may be granted by congress.

(3) For authorizing persons to keep ferries across streams at points wholly within this state.

(4) For authorizing the sale or mortgage of real or personal property of minors or others under disability.

(5) For locating or changing any county seat.

(6) For assessment or collection of taxes or for extending the time for the collection thereof.

(7) For granting corporate powers or privileges, except to cities.

(8) For authorizing the apportionment of any part of the school fund.

(9) For incorporating any city, town or village, or to amend the charter thereof. [*(1) amended; June 1992 AJR-1; 1993 SJR-2*]

Special and private laws prohibited. SECTION 31. [*As amended November 1892*] The legislature is prohibited from enacting any special or private laws in the following cases:

1st. For changing the name of persons or constituting one person the heir at law of another.

2d. For laying out, opening or altering highways, except in cases of state roads extending into more than one county, and military roads to aid in the construction of which lands may be granted by congress.

3d. For authorizing persons to keep ferries across streams at points wholly within this state.

4th. For authorizing the sale or mortgage of real or personal property of minors or others under disability.

5th. For locating or changing any county seat.

6th. For assessment or collection of taxes or for extending the time for the collection thereof.

7th. For granting corporate powers or privileges, except to cities.

8th. For authorizing the apportionment of any part of the school fund.

9th. For incorporating any city, town or village, or to amend the charter thereof. [*1889 SJR-13; 1891 SJR-13; 1891 c. 362*]

Special or private laws. SECTION 31. [*Created November 1871*] The legislature is prohibited from enacting any special or private laws in the following cases:

1st. For changing the name of persons or constituting one person the heir at law of another.

2d. For laying out, opening or altering highways, except in cases of state roads extending into more than one county, and military roads to aid in the construction of which lands may be granted by congress.

3d. For authorizing persons to keep ferries across streams at points wholly within this state.

4th. For authorizing the sale or mortgage of real or personal property of minors or others under disability.

5th. For locating or changing any county seat.

6th. For assessment or collection of taxes or for extending the time for the collection thereof.

7th. For granting corporate powers or privileges, except to cities.

8th. For authorizing the apportionment of any part of the school fund.

9th. For incorporating any town or village or to amend the charter thereof. [*1870 SJR-14; 1871 AJR-29; 1871 c. 122*]

General laws on enumerated subjects. SECTION 32. [*As amended April 1993*] The legislature may provide by general law for the treatment of any subject for which lawmaking is prohibited by section 31 of this article. Subject to reasonable classifications, such laws shall be uniform in their operation throughout the state. [*June 1992 AJR-1; 1993 SJR-2*]

General laws on enumerated subjects. SECTION 32. [*Created November 1871*] The legislature shall provide general laws for the transaction of any business that may be prohibited by section thirty-one of this article, and all such laws shall be uniform in their operation throughout the state. [*1870 SJR-14; 1871 AJR-29; 1871 c. 122*]

Auditing of state accounts. SECTION 33. [*Created November 1946*] The legislature shall provide for the auditing of state accounts and may establish such offices and prescribe such duties for the same as it shall deem necessary. [*1943 SJR-35; 1945 SJR-24*]

Continuity of civil government. SECTION 34. [*Created April 1961*] The legislature, in order to ensure continuity of state and local governmental operations in periods of emergency resulting from enemy action in the form of an attack, shall (1) forthwith provide for prompt and temporary succession to the powers and duties of public offices, of whatever nature and whether filled by election or appointment, the incumbents of which may become unavailable for carrying on the powers and duties of such offices, and (2) adopt such other measures as may be necessary and proper for attaining the objectives of this section. [*1959 AJR-48; 1961 SJR-1*]

ARTICLE V.
EXECUTIVE

Governor; lieutenant governor; term. SECTION 1. [*As amended April 1979*] The executive power shall be vested in a governor who shall hold office for 4 years; a lieutenant governor shall be elected at the same time and for the same term. [*1977 SJR-51; 1979 SJR-1*]

Governor; lieutenant governor; term. SECTION 1. [*Original form*] The executive power shall be vested in a governor, who shall hold his office for two years; a lieutenant governor shall be elected at the same time, and for the same term.

SECTION 1m. [*Repealed. 1977 SJR-51; 1979 SJR-1; vote April 1979*]

Governor; 4-year term. SECTION 1M. [*Created April 1967*] Notwithstanding section 1, beginning with the general election in 1970 and every four years thereafter, there shall be elected a governor to hold office for a term of four years. [*1965 AJR-4; 1967 AJR-9 and SJR-12*]

SECTION 1n. [*Repealed. 1977 SJR-51; 1979 SJR-1; vote April 1979*]

Lieutenant governor; 4-year term. SECTION 1N. [*Created April 1967*] Notwithstanding section 1, beginning with the general election in 1970 and every four years thereafter, there shall be elected a lieutenant governor to hold office for a term of four years. [*1965 AJR-4; 1967 AJR-9 and SJR-12*]

Eligibility. SECTION 2. No person except a citizen of the United States and a qualified elector of the state shall be eligible to the office of governor or lieutenant governor.

Election. SECTION 3. [*As amended April 1967*] The governor and lieutenant governor shall be elected by the qualified electors of the state at the times and places of choosing members of the legislature. They shall be chosen jointly, by the casting by each voter of a single vote applicable to both offices beginning with the general election in 1970. The persons respectively having the highest number of votes cast jointly for them for governor and lieutenant governor shall be elected; but in case two or more slates shall have an equal and the highest number of votes for governor and lieutenant governor, the two houses of the legislature, at its next annual session shall forthwith, by joint ballot, choose one of the slates so having an equal and the highest number of votes for governor and lieutenant governor. The returns of election for governor and lieutenant governor shall be made in such manner as shall be provided by law. [*1965 AJR-3; 1967 AJR-8 and SJR-11*]

Election. SECTION 3. [*Original form*] The governor and lieutenant governor shall be elected by the qualified electors of the state at the times and places of choosing members of the legislature. The persons respectively having the highest number of votes for governor and lieutenant governor shall be elected; but in case two or more shall have an equal and the highest number of votes for governor, or lieutenant governor, the two houses of the legislature, at its next annual session shall forthwith, by joint ballot, choose one of the persons so having an equal and the highest number of votes for governor, or lieutenant governor. The returns of election for governor and lieutenant governor shall be made in such manner as shall be provided by law.

Powers and duties. SECTION 4. The governor shall be commander in chief of the military and naval forces of the state. He shall have power to convene the legislature on extraordinary occasions, and in case of invasion, or danger from the prevalence of contagious disease at the seat of government, he may convene them at any other suitable place within the state. He shall communicate to the legislature, at every session, the condition of the state, and recommend such matters to them for their consideration as he may deem expedient. He shall transact all necessary business with the officers of the government, civil and military. He shall expedite all such measures as may be resolved upon by the legislature, and shall take care that the laws be faithfully executed.

SECTION 5. [*Repealed. 1929 SJR-81; 1931 SJR-6; vote November 1932*]

Compensation of governor. SECTION 5. [*As amended November 1926*] The governor shall receive, during his continuance in office, an annual compensation of not less than five thousand dollars, to be fixed by law, which shall be in full for all traveling or other expenses incident to his duties. The compensation prescribed for governor immediately prior to the adoption of this amendment shall continue in force until changed by the legislature in a manner consistent with the other provisions of this constitution. [*1923 AJR-88; 1925 AJR-50; 1925 c. 413*]

Compensation of governor. SECTION 5. [*As amended November 1869*] The governor shall receive during his continuance in office, an annual compensation of five thousand dollars which shall be in full for all traveling or other expenses incident to his duties. [*1868 AJR-13; 1869 SJR-6; 1869 c. 186*]

Compensation of governor. SECTION 5. [*Original form*] The governor shall receive during his continuance in office, an annual compensation of one thousand two hundred and fifty dollars.

Pardoning power. SECTION 6. The governor shall have power to grant reprieves, commutations and pardons, after conviction, for all offenses, except treason and cases of impeachment, upon such conditions and with such restrictions and limitations as he may think proper, subject to such regulations as may be provided by law relative to the manner of applying for pardons. Upon conviction for treason he shall have the power to suspend the execution of the sentence until the case shall be reported to the legislature at its next meeting, when the legislature shall either pardon, or commute the sentence, direct the execution of the sentence, or grant a further reprieve. He shall annually communicate to the legislature each case of reprieve, commutation or pardon granted, stating the name of the convict, the crime of which he was convicted, the sentence and its date, and the date of the commutation, pardon or reprieve, with his reasons for granting the same.

Lieutenant governor, when governor. SECTION 7. [*As amended April 1979*] (1) Upon the governor's death, resignation or removal from office, the lieutenant governor shall become governor for the balance of the unexpired term.

(2) If the governor is absent from this state, impeached, or from mental or physical disease, becomes incapable of performing the duties of the office, the lieutenant governor shall serve as acting governor for the balance of the unexpired term or until the governor returns, the disability ceases or the impeachment is vacated. But when the governor, with the consent of the legislature, shall be out of this state in time of war at the head of the state's military force, the governor shall continue as commander in chief of the military force. [*1977 SJR-51; 1979 SJR-1*]

Lieutenant governor, when governor. SECTION 7. [*Original form*] In case of the impeachment of the governor, or his removal from office, death, inability from mental or physical disease, resignation, or absence from the state, the powers and duties of the office shall devolve upon the lieutenant governor for the residue of the term or until the governor, absent or impeached, shall have returned, or the disability shall cease. But when the governor shall, with the consent of the legislature, be out of the state in time of war, at the head of the military force thereof, he shall continue commander in chief of the military force of the state.

Secretary of state, when governor. SECTION 8. [*As amended April 1979*] (1) If there is a vacancy in the office of lieutenant governor and the governor dies, resigns or is removed from office, the secretary of state shall become governor for the balance of the unexpired term.

(2) If there is a vacancy in the office of lieutenant governor and the governor is absent from this state, impeached, or from mental or physical disease becomes incapable of performing the duties of the office, the secretary of state shall serve as acting governor for the balance of the unexpired term or until the governor returns, the disability ceases or the impeachment is vacated. [*1977 SJR-51; 1979 SJR-1*]

Lieutenant governor president of senate; when secretary of state to be governor. SECTION 8. [*Original form*] The lieutenant governor shall be president of the senate, but shall have only a casting vote therein. If, during a vacancy in the office of the governor, the lieutenant governor shall be impeached, displaced, resign, die, or from mental or physical disease become incapable of performing the duties of his office, or be absent from the state, the secretary of state shall act as governor until the vacancy shall be filled or the disability shall cease.

SECTION 9. [*Repealed. 1929 SJR-82; 1931 SJR-7; vote November 1932*]

Compensation of lieutenant governor. SECTION 9. [*As amended November 1869*] The lieutenant governor shall receive during his continuance in office an annual compensation of one thousand dollars. [*1868 AJR-13; 1869 SJR-6; 1869 c. 186*]

Compensation of lieutenant governor. SECTION 9. [*Original form*] The lieutenant governor shall receive double the per diem allowance of members of the senate, for every day's attendance as president of the senate, and the same mileage as shall be allowed to members of the legislature.

Governor to approve or veto bills; proceedings on veto. SECTION 10. [*As amended April 1990; April 2008*] (1) (a) Every bill which shall have passed the legislature shall, before it becomes a law, be presented to the governor.

(b) If the governor approves and signs the bill, the bill shall become law. Appropriation bills may be approved in whole or in part by the governor, and the part approved shall become law.

(c) In approving an appropriation bill in part, the governor may not create a new word by rejecting individual letters in the words of the enrolled bill, and may not create a new sentence by combining parts of 2 or more sentences of the enrolled bill. [*2005 SJR-33; 2007 SJR-5*]

Governor to approve or veto bills; proceedings on veto. Section 10. [*As amended April 1990*] (c) In approving an appropriation bill in part, the governor may not create a new word by rejecting individual letters in the words of the enrolled bill.

(2) (a) If the governor rejects the bill, the governor shall return the bill, together with the objections in writing, to the house in which the bill originated. The house of origin shall enter the objections at large upon the journal and proceed to reconsider the bill. If, after such reconsideration, two-thirds of the members present agree to pass the bill notwithstanding the objections of the governor, it shall be sent, together with the objections, to the other house, by which it shall likewise be reconsidered, and if approved by two-thirds of the members present it shall become law.

(b) The rejected part of an appropriation bill, together with the governor's objections in writing, shall be returned to the house in which the bill originated. The house of origin shall enter the objections at large upon the journal and proceed to reconsider the rejected part of the appropriation bill. If, after such reconsideration, two-thirds of the members present agree to approve the rejected part notwithstanding the objections of the governor, it shall be sent, together with the objections, to the other house, by which it shall likewise be reconsidered, and if approved by two-thirds of the members present the rejected part shall become law.

(c) In all such cases the votes of both houses shall be determined by ayes and noes, and the names of the members voting for or against passage of the bill or the rejected part of the bill notwithstanding the objections of the governor shall be entered on the journal of each house respectively.

(3) Any bill not returned by the governor within 6 days (Sundays excepted) after it shall have been presented to the governor shall be law unless the legislature, by final adjournment, prevents the bill's return, in which case it shall not be law. [*1987 AJR-71; 1989 SJR-11*]

Governor to approve or veto bills; proceedings on veto. Section 10. [*As amended November 1930*] Every bill which shall have passed the legislature shall, before it becomes a law, be presented to the governor; if he approve, he shall sign it, but if not, he shall return it, with his objections, to that house in which it shall have originated, who shall enter the objections at large upon the journal and proceed to reconsider it. Appropriation bills may be approved in whole or in part by the governor, and the part approved shall become law, and the part objected to shall be returned in the same manner as provided for other bills. If, after such reconsideration, two-thirds of the members present shall agree to pass the bill, or the part of the bill objected to, it shall be sent, together with the objections, to the other house, by which it shall likewise be reconsidered, and if approved by two-thirds of the members present it shall become a law. But in all such cases the votes of both houses shall be determined by yeas and nays, and the names of the members voting for or against the bill or the part of the bill objected to, shall be entered on the journal of each house respectively. If any bill shall not be returned by the governor within six days (Sundays excepted) after it shall have been presented to him, the same shall be a law unless the legislature shall, by their adjournment, prevent its return, in which case it shall not be a law. [*1927 SJR-35; 1929 SJR-40*]

Approval of bills. Section 10. [*As amended November 1908*] Every bill which shall have passed the legislature shall, before it becomes a law, be presented to the governor; if he approve, he shall sign it, but if not, he shall return it, with his objections, to that house in which it shall have originated, who shall enter the objections at large upon the journal and proceed to reconsider it. If, after such reconsideration, two-thirds of the members present shall agree to pass the bill, it shall be sent, together with the objections to the other house, by which it shall likewise be reconsidered, and if approved by two-thirds of the members present it shall become a law. But in all such cases the votes of both houses shall be determined by yeas and nays, and the names of the members voting for or against the bill shall be entered on the journal of each house respectively. If any bill shall not be returned by the governor within six days (Sundays excepted) after it shall have been presented to him, the same shall be a law unless the legislature shall, by their adjournment, prevent its return, in which case it shall not be a law. [*1905 AJR-45; 1907 AJR-46; 1907 c. 661*]

Approval of bills. Section 10. [*Original form*] Every bill which shall have passed the legislature shall, before it becomes a law, be presented to the governor; if he approve, he shall sign it, but if not, he shall return it, with his objections, to that house in which it shall have originated, who shall enter the objections at large upon the journal, and proceed to reconsider it. If, after such reconsideration two-thirds of the members present shall agree to pass the bill, it shall be sent, together with the objections, to the other house, by which it shall likewise be reconsidered, and if approved by two-thirds of the members present, it shall become a law. But in all such cases the votes of both houses shall be determined by yeas and nays, and the names of the members voting for or against the bill, shall be entered on the journal of each house respectively. If any bill shall not be returned by the governor within three days (Sundays excepted) after it shall have been presented to him, the same shall be a law, unless the legislature shall, by their adjournment, prevent its return, in which case it shall not be a law.

ARTICLE VI.
ADMINISTRATIVE

Election of secretary of state, treasurer and attorney general; term. Section 1. [*As amended April 1979*] The qualified electors of this state, at the times and places of choosing the members of the legislature, shall in 1970 and every 4 years thereafter elect a secretary of state, treasurer and attorney general who shall hold their offices for 4 years. [*1977 SJR-51; 1979 SJR-1*]

Election of secretary of state, treasurer and attorney-general; term. SECTION 1. [*Original form*] There shall be chosen by the qualified electors of the state, at the times and places of choosing the members of the legislature, a secretary of state, treasurer and attorney-general, who shall severally hold their offices for the term of two years.

SECTION 1m. [*Repealed. 1977 SJR-51; 1979 SJR-1; vote April 1979*]

Secretary of state; 4-year term. SECTION 1M. [*Created April 1967*] Notwithstanding section 1, beginning with the general election in 1970 and every four years thereafter, there shall be chosen a secretary of state to hold office for a term of four years. [*1965 AJR-4; 1967 AJR-9 and SJR-12*]

SECTION 1n. [*Repealed. 1977 SJR-51; 1979 SJR-1; vote April 1979*]

Treasurer; 4-year term. SECTION 1N. [*Created April 1967*] Notwithstanding section 1, beginning with the general election in 1970 and every four years thereafter, there shall be chosen a treasurer to hold office for a term of four years. [*1965 AJR-4; 1967 AJR-9 and SJR-12*]

SECTION 1p. [*Repealed. 1977 SJR-51; 1979 SJR-1; vote April 1979*]

Attorney general; 4-year term. SECTION 1P. [*Created April 1967*] Notwithstanding section 1, beginning with the general election in 1970 and every four years thereafter, there shall be chosen an attorney general to hold office for a term of four years. [*1965 AJR-4; 1967 AJR-9 and SJR-12*]

Secretary of state; duties, compensation. SECTION 2. [*As amended November 1946*] The secretary of state shall keep a fair record of the official acts of the legislature and executive department of the state, and shall, when required, lay the same and all matters relative thereto before either branch of the legislature. He shall perform such other duties as shall be assigned him by law. He shall receive as a compensation for his services yearly such sum as shall be provided by law, and shall keep his office at the seat of government. [*1943 SJR-35; 1945 SJR-24*]

Secretary of state. SECTION 2. [*Original form*] The secretary of state shall keep a fair record of the official acts of the legislature and executive department of the state, and shall, when required, lay the same and all matters relative thereto, before either branch of the legislature. He shall be ex officio auditor, and shall perform such other duties as shall be assigned him by law. He shall receive as a compensation for his services yearly, such sum as shall be provided by law, and shall keep his office at the seat of government.

Treasurer and attorney general; duties, compensation. SECTION 3. The powers, duties and compensation of the treasurer and attorney general shall be prescribed by law.

County officers; election, terms, removal; vacancies. SECTION 4. [*As amended April 2005*] (1) (a) Except as provided in pars. (b) and (c) and sub. (2), coroners, registers of deeds, district attorneys, and all other elected county officers, except judicial officers, sheriffs, and chief executive officers, shall be chosen by the electors of the respective counties once in every 2 years.

(b) Beginning with the first general election at which the governor is elected which occurs after the ratification of this paragraph, sheriffs shall be chosen by the electors of the respective counties, or by the electors of all of the respective counties comprising each combination of counties combined by the legislature for that purpose, for the term of 4 years and coroners in counties in which there is a coroner shall be chosen by the electors of the respective counties, or by the electors of all of the respective counties comprising each combination of counties combined by the legislature for that purpose, for the term of 4 years.

(c) Beginning with the first general election at which the president is elected which occurs after the ratification of this paragraph, district attorneys, registers of deeds, county clerks, and treasurers shall be chosen by the electors of the respective counties, or by the electors of all of the respective counties comprising each combination of counties combined by the legislature for that purpose, for the term of 4 years and surveyors in counties in which the office of surveyor is filled by election shall be chosen by the electors of the respective counties, or by the electors of all of the respective counties comprising each combination of counties combined by the legislature for that purpose, for the term of 4 years.

(2) The offices of coroner and surveyor in counties having a population of 500,000 or more are abolished. Counties not having a population of 500,000 shall have the option of retaining the elective office of coroner or instituting a medical examiner system. Two or more counties may institute a joint medical examiner system.

(3) (a) Sheriffs may not hold any other partisan office.

(b) Sheriffs may be required by law to renew their security from time to time, and in default of giving such new security their office shall be deemed vacant.

(4) The governor may remove any elected county officer mentioned in this section except a county clerk, treasurer, or surveyor, giving to the officer a copy of the charges and an opportunity of being heard.

(5) All vacancies in the offices of coroner, register of deeds or district attorney shall be filled by appointment. The person appointed to fill a vacancy shall hold office only for the unexpired portion of the term to which appointed and until a successor shall be elected and qualified.

(6) When a vacancy occurs in the office of sheriff, the vacancy shall be filled by appointment of the governor, and the person appointed shall serve until his or her successor is elected and qualified. [*2003 AJR-10; 2005 SJR-2*]

County officers; election, terms, removal; vacancies. SECTION 4. [*As amended November 1998*] (1) Except as provided in sub. (2), coroners, registers of deeds, district attorneys, and all other elected county officers except judicial officers, sheriffs and chief executive officers, shall be chosen by the electors of the respective counties once in every 2 years.

(2) The offices of coroner and surveyor in counties having a population of 500,000 or more are abolished. Counties not having a population of 500,000 shall have the option of retaining the elective office of coroner or instituting a medical examiner system. Two or more counties may institute a joint medical examiner system.

(3) (a) Sheriffs may not hold any other partisan office.

(b) Sheriffs may be required by law to renew their security from time to time, and in default of giving such new security their office shall be deemed vacant.

(c) Beginning with the first general election at which the governor is elected which occurs after the ratification of this paragraph, sheriffs shall be chosen by the electors of the respective counties once in every 4 years.

(4) The governor may remove any elected county officer mentioned in this section, giving to the officer a copy of the charges and an opportunity of being heard.

(5) All vacancies in the offices of coroner, register of deeds or district attorney shall be filled by appointment. The person appointed to fill a vacancy shall hold office only for the unexpired portion of the term to which appointed and until a successor shall be elected and qualified.

(6) When a vacancy occurs in the office of sheriff, the vacancy shall be filled by appointment of the governor, and the person appointed shall serve until his or her successor is elected and qualified. [*1995 AJR-37; 1997 SJR-43*]

County officers; election, terms, removal; vacancies. SECTION 4. [*As amended April 1982*] (1) Sheriffs, coroners, registers of deeds, district attorneys, and all other elected county officers except judicial officers and chief executive officers, shall be chosen by the electors of the respective counties once in every 2 years.

(2) The offices of coroner and surveyor in counties having a population of 500,000 or more are abolished. Counties not having a population of 500,000 shall have the option of retaining the elective office of coroner or instituting a medical examiner system. Two or more counties may institute a joint medical examiner system.

(3) Sheriffs shall hold no other office. Sheriffs may be required by law to renew their security from time to time, and in default of giving such new security their office shall be deemed vacant.

(4) The governor may remove any elected county officer mentioned in this section, giving to the officer a copy of the charges and an opportunity of being heard.

(5) All vacancies in the offices of sheriff, coroner, register of deeds or district attorney shall be filled by appointment. The person appointed to fill a vacancy shall hold office only for the unexpired portion of the term to which appointed and until a successor shall be elected and qualified. [*1979 AJR-99; 1981 AJR-7*]

County officers; election, terms, removal; vacancies. SECTION 4. [*As amended April 1972*] Sheriffs, coroners, register of deeds, district attorneys, and all other county officers except judicial officers and chief executive officers, shall be chosen by the electors of the respective

counties once in every two years. The offices of coroner and surveyor in counties having a population of 500,000 or more are abolished. Counties not having a population of 500,000 shall have the option of retaining the elective office of coroner or instituting a medical examiner system. Two or more counties may institute a joint medical examiner system. Sheriffs shall hold no other office; they may be required by law to renew their security from time to time, and in default of giving such new security their office shall be deemed vacant, but the county shall never be made responsible for the acts of the sheriff. The governor may remove any officer in this section mentioned, giving to such a copy of the charges against him and an opportunity of being heard in his defense. All vacancies shall be filled by appointment, and the person appointed to fill a vacancy shall hold only for the unexpired portion of the term to which he shall be appointed and until his successor shall be elected and qualified. [*1969 SJR-63; 1971 SJR-38*]

County officers; election, terms, removal; vacancies. SECTION 4. [*As amended April 1967*] Sheriffs, coroners, registers of deeds, district attorneys, and all other county officers except judicial officers and chief executive officers, shall be chosen by the electors of the respective counties once in every two years. The offices of coroner and surveyor in counties having a population of 500,000 or more are abolished at the conclusion of the terms of office during which this amendment is adopted. Sheriffs shall hold no other office; they may be required by law to renew their security from time to time, and in default of giving such new security their office shall be deemed vacant, but the county shall never be made responsible for the acts of the sheriff. The governor may remove any officer in this section mentioned, giving to such a copy of the charges against him and an opportunity of being heard in his defense. All vacancies shall be filled by appointment, and the person appointed to fill a vacancy shall hold only for the unexpired portion of the term to which he shall be appointed and until his successor shall be elected and qualified. [*1965 AJR-72; 1967 SJR-7*]

County officers; election, terms, removal; vacancies. SECTION 4. [*As amended April 1965*] Sheriffs, coroners, register of deeds, district attorneys, and all other county officers except judicial officers and chief executive officers, shall be chosen by the electors of the respective counties once in every two years. The offices of coroner and surveyor in counties having a population of 500,000 or more are abolished at the conclusion of the terms of office during which this amendment is adopted. Sheriffs shallhold no other office, and shall not serve more than two terms or parts thereof in succession; they may be required by law to renew their security from time to time, and in default of giving such new security their office shall be deemed vacant, but the county shall never be made responsible for the acts of the sheriff. The governor may remove any officer in this section mentioned, giving to such a copy of the charges against him and an opportunity of being heard in his defense. All vacancies shall be filled by appointment, and the person appointed to fill a vacancy shall hold only for the unexpired portion of the term to which he shall be appointed and until his successor shall be elected and qualified. [*1963 AJR-14; 1965 SJR-17*] County officers; election, terms, removal; vacancies. Section 4. [As amended November 1962] Sheriffs, coroners, registers of deeds, district attorneys, and all other county officers except judicial officers and chief executive officers, shall be chosen by the electors of the respective counties once in every two years. Sheriffs shall hold no other office, and shall not serve more than two terms or parts thereof in succession; they may be required by law to renew their security from time to time, and in default of giving such new security their office shall be deemed vacant, but the county shall never be made responsible for the acts of the sheriff. The governor may remove any officer in this section mentioned, giving to such a copy of the charges against him and an opportunity of being heard in his defense. All vacancies shall be filled by appointment, and the person appointed to fill a vacancy shall hold only for the unexpired portion of the term to which he shall be appointed and until his successor shall be elected and qualified. [1959 AJR-121; 1961 AJR-61]

County officers; election, terms, removal; vacancies. SECTION 4. [*As amended April 1929*] Sheriffs, coroners, registers of deeds, district attorneys, and all other county officers except judicial officers, shall be chosen by the electors of the respective counties once in every two years. Sheriffs shall hold no other office, and shall not serve more than two terms or parts thereof in succession; they may be required by law to renew their security from time to time, and in default of giving such new security their office shall be deemed vacant, but the county shall never be made responsible for the acts of the sheriff. The governor may remove any officer in this section mentioned, giving to such a copy of the charges against him and an opportunity of being heard in his defense. All vacancies shall be filled by appointment, and the person appointed to fill a vacancy shall hold only for the unexpired portion of the term to which he shall be appointed and until his successor shall be elected and qualified. [*1927 AJR-8; 1929 AJR-8*]

County officers. SECTION 4. [*As amended November 1882*] Sheriffs, coroners, registers of deeds, district attorneys, and all other county officers, except judicial officers shall be chosen by the electors of the respective counties, once in every two years. Sheriffs shall hold no other office and be ineligible for two years next succeeding the termination of their offices; they may be required by law to renew their security from time to time, and in default of giving such new security their office shall be deemed vacant, but the county shall never be made responsible for the acts of the sheriff. The governor may remove any officer in this section mentioned, giving to such a copy of the charges against him and an opportunity of being heard in his defense. All vacancies shall be filled by appointment and the person appointed to fill a vacancy shall hold only for the unexpired portion of the term to which he shall be appointed, and until his successor shall be elected and qualified. [*1881 AJR-16; 1882 SJR-20; 1882 c. 290*]

County officers. SECTION 4. [*Original form*] Sheriffs, coroners, registers of deeds and district attorneys shall be chosen by the electors of the respective counties, once in every two years, and as often as vacancies shall happen; sheriffs shall hold no other office, and be ineligible for two years next succeeding the termination of their offices. They may be required by law, to renew their security from time to time; and in default of giving such new security, their offices shall be deemed vacant. But the county shall never be made responsible for the acts of the sheriff. The governor may remove any officer in this section mentioned, giving to such officer a copy of the charges against him, and an opportunity of being heard in his defence.

ARTICLE VII.
JUDICIARY

Impeachment; trial. SECTION 1. [*As amended November 1932*] The court for the trial of impeachments shall be composed of the senate. The assembly shall have the power of impeaching all civil officers of this state for corrupt conduct in office, or for crimes and misdemeanors; but a majority of all the members elected shall concur in an impeachment. On the trial of an impeachment against the governor, the lieutenant governor shall not act as a member of the court. No judicial officer shall exercise his office, after he shall have been impeached, until his acquittal. Before the trial of an impeachment the members of the court shall take an oath or affirmation truly and impartially to try the impeachment according to evidence; and no person shall be convicted without the concurrence of two-thirds of the members present. Judgment in cases of impeachment shall not extend further than to removal from office, or removal from office and disqualification to hold any office of honor, profit or trust under the state; but the party impeached shall be liable to indictment, trial and punishment according to law. [*1929 SJR-103; 1931 SJR-8*]

Impeachments. SECTION 1. [*Original form*] The court for the trial of impeachments shall be composed of the senate. The house of representatives shall have the power of impeaching all civil officers of this state, for corrupt conduct in office, or for crimes and misdemeanors; but a majority of all the members elected shall concur in an impeachment. On the trial of an impeachment against the governor, the lieutenant governor shall not act as a member of the court. No judicial officer shall exercise his office, after he shall have been impeached, until his acquittal. Before the trial of an impeachment, the members of the court shall take an oath or affirmation, truly and impartially to try the impeachment according to evidence; and no person shall be convicted without the concurrence of two-thirds of the members present. Judgment in cases of impeachment shall not extend further than to removal from office, or removal from office and disqualification to hold any office of honor, profit or trust under the state; but the party impeached shall be liable to indictment, trial and punishment according to law.

Court system. SECTION 2. [*As amended April 1977*] The judicial power of this state shall be vested in a unified court system consisting of one supreme court, a court of appeals, a circuit court, such trial courts of general uniform statewide jurisdiction as the legislature may create by law, and a municipal court if authorized by the legislature under section 14. [*1975 AJR-11; 1977 SJR-9*]

Judicial power, where vested. SECTION 2. [*As amended April 1966*] The judicial power of this state, both as to matters of law and equity, shall be vested in a supreme court, circuit courts, and courts of probate. The legislature may also vest such jurisdiction as shall be deemed necessary in municipal courts, and may authorize the establishment of inferior courts in the several counties, cities, villages or towns, with limited civil and criminal jurisdiction. Provided, that the jurisdiction which may be vested in municipal courts shall not exceed in their respective municipalities that of circuit courts in their respective circuits as prescribed in this constitution; and that the legislature shall provide as well for the election of judges of the municipal courts as of the judges of inferior courts, by the qualified electors of the respective jurisdictions. The term of office of the judges of the said municipal and inferior courts shall not be longer than that of the judges of the circuit courts. [*1963 SJR-32; 1965 SJR-26*]

Judicial power, where vested. Section 2. [*Original form*] The judicial power of this state, both as to matters of law and equity, shall be vested in a supreme court, circuit courts, courts of probate, and in justices of the peace. The legislature may also vest such jurisdiction as shall be deemed necessary in municipal courts, and shall have power to establish inferior courts in the several counties, with limited civil and criminal jurisdiction. Provided, that the jurisdiction which may be vested in municipal courts shall not exceed in their respective municipalities that of circuit courts in their respective circuits as prescribed in this constitution; and that the legislature shall provide as well for the election of judges of the municipal courts as of the judges of inferior courts, by the qualified electors of the respective jurisdictions. The term of office of the judges of the said municipal and inferior courts shall not be longer than that of the judges of the circuit courts.

Supreme court: jurisdiction. Section 3. [*As amended April 1977*] (1) The supreme court shall have superintending and administrative authority over all courts.

(2) The supreme court has appellate jurisdiction over all courts and may hear original actions and proceedings. The supreme court may issue all writs necessary in aid of its jurisdiction.

(3) The supreme court may review judgments and orders of the court of appeals, may remove cases from the court of appeals and may accept cases on certification by the court of appeals. [*1975 AJR-11; 1977 SJR-9*]

Supreme court, jurisdiction. Section 3. [*Original form*] The supreme court, except in cases otherwise provided in this constitution, shall have appellate jurisdiction only, which shall be coextensive with the state; but in no case removed to the supreme court shall a trial by jury be allowed. The supreme court shall have a general superintending control over all inferior courts; it shall have power to issue writs of habeas corpus, mandamus, injunction, quo warranto, certiorari, and other original and remedial writs, and to hear and determine the same.

Supreme court: election, chief justice, court system administration. Section 4. [*As amended April 1977*] (1) The supreme court shall have 7 members who shall be known as justices of the supreme court. Justices shall be elected for 10-year terms of office commencing with the August 1 next succeeding the election. Only one justice may be elected in any year. Any 4 justices shall constitute a quorum for the conduct of the court's business.

(2) The justice having been longest a continuous member of said court, or in case 2 or more such justices shall have served for the same length of time, the justice whose term first expires, shall be the chief justice. The justice so designated as chief justice may, irrevocably, decline to serve as chief justice or resign as chief justice but continue to serve as a justice of the supreme court.

(3) The chief justice of the supreme court shall be the administrative head of the judicial system and shall exercise this administrative authority pursuant to procedures adopted by the supreme court. The chief justice may assign any judge of a court of record to aid in the proper disposition of judicial business in any court of record except the supreme court. [*1975 AJR-11; 1977 SJR-9*]

Supreme court justices; term; election; quorum. Section 1 [4]. [*As amended April 1903*] The chief justice and associate justices of the supreme court shall be severally known as the justices of said court, with the same terms of office of ten years respectively as now provided. The supreme court shall consist of seven justices, any four of whom shall be a quorum, to be elected as now provided, not more than one each year. The justice having been longest a continuous member of said court, or in case two or more such senior justices shall have served for the same length of time, then the one whose commission first expires shall be ex officio, the chief justice. [*1901 AJR-33; 1903 AJR-5; 1903 c. 10*]

Supreme court, how constituted. Section 1 [4]. [*As amended April 1889*] The chief justice and associate justices of the supreme court shall be severally known as justices of said court with the same terms of office, respectively, as now provided. The supreme court shall consist of five justices (any three of whom shall be a quorum), to be elected as now provided. The justice having been longest a continuous member of the court (or in case two or more of such senior justices having served for the same length of time, then the one whose commission first expires), shall be ex officio the chief justice. [*1887 SJR-19; 1889 AJR-7; 1889 c. 22*]

Supreme court, how constituted. Section 4. [*As amended November 1877*] The supreme court shall consist of one chief justice and four associate justices, to be elected by the qualified electors of the state. The legislature shall at its first session after the adoption of this amendment provide by law for the election of two associate justices of said court to hold their offices respectively for terms ending two and four years respectively after the end of the term of the justice of the said court, then last to expire. And thereafter the chief justice and associate justices of the said court shall be elected and hold their offices respectively for the term of ten years. [*1876 SJR-16; 1877 SJR-2; 1877 c. 48*]

Supreme court, how constituted. Section 4. [*Original form*] For the term of five years, and thereafter until the legislature shall otherwise provide, the judges of the several circuit courts, shall be judges of the supreme court, four of whom shall constitute a quorum, and the concurrence of a majority of the judges present shall be necessary to a decision. The legislature shall have power, if they should think it expedient and necessary to provide by law, for the organization of a separate supreme court, with the jurisdiction and powers prescribed in this constitution, to consist of one chief justice, and two associate justices, to be elected by the qualified electors of the state, at such time and in such manner as the legislature may provide. The separate supreme court when so organized, shall not be changed or discontinued by the legislature; the judges thereof shall be so classified that but one of them shall go out of office at the same time; and their term of office shall be the same as is provided for the judges of the circuit court. And whenever the legislature may consider it necessary to establish a separate supreme court, they shall have power to reduce the number of circuit court judges to four, and subdivide the judicial circuits, but no such subdivision or reduction shall take effect until after the expiration of the term of some one of said judges, or till a vacancy occur by some other means.

SECTION 5. [*Repealed. 1975 AJR-11; 1977 SJR-9; vote April 1977*]

Judicial circuits. SECTION 5. [*Original form*] The state shall be divided into five judicial circuits, to be composed as follows: The first circuit shall comprise the counties of Racine, Walworth, Rock and Green; the second circuit, the counties of Milwaukee, Waukesha, Jefferson and Dane; the third circuit, the counties of Washington, Dodge, Columbia, Marquette, Sauk and Portage; the fourth circuit, the counties of Brown, Manitowoc, Sheboygan, Fond du Lac, Winnebago and Calumet; and the fifth circuit shall comprise the counties of Iowa, LaFayette, Grant, Crawford and St. Croix; and the county of Richland shall be attached to Iowa, the county of Chippewa to the county of Crawford, and the county of La Pointe to the county of St. Croix, for judicial purposes, until otherwise provided by the legislature.

Court of appeals. SECTION 5. [*Created April 1977*] (1) The legislature shall by law combine the judicial circuits of the state into one or more districts for the court of appeals and shall designate in each district the locations where the appeals court shall sit for the convenience of litigants.

(2) For each district of the appeals court there shall be chosen by the qualified electors of the district one or more appeals judges as prescribed by law, who shall sit as prescribed by law. Appeals judges shall be elected for 6-year terms and shall reside in the district from which elected. No alteration of district or circuit boundaries shall have the effect of removing an appeals judge from office during the judge's term. In case of an increase in the number of appeals judges, the first judge or judges shall be elected for full terms unless the legislature prescribes a shorter initial term for staggering of terms.

(3) The appeals court shall have such appellate jurisdiction in the district, including jurisdiction to review administrative proceedings, as the legislature may provide by law, but shall have no original jurisdiction other than by prerogative writ. The appeals court may issue all writs necessary in aid of its jurisdiction and shall have supervisory authority over all actions and proceedings in the courts in the district. [*1975 AJR-11; 1977 SJR-9*] Circuit court: boundaries. Section 6. [As amended April 1977] The legislature shall prescribe by law the number of judicial circuits, making them as compact and convenient as practicable, and bounding them by county lines. No alteration of circuit boundaries shall have the effect of removing a circuit judge from office during the judge's term. In case of an increase of circuits, the first judge or judges shall be elected. [1975 AJR-11; 1977 SJR-9]

Alteration of circuits. SECTION 6. [*Original form*] The legislature may alter the limits or increase the number of circuits, making them as compact and convenient as practicable, and bounding them by county lines; but no such alteration or increase shall have the effect to remove a judge from office. In case of an increase of circuits, the judge or judges shall be elected as provided in this constitution and receive a salary of not less than that herein provided for judges of the circuit court.

Circuit court: election. SECTION 7. [*As amended April 1977*] For each circuit there shall be chosen by the qualified electors thereof one or more circuit judges as prescribed by law. Circuit judges shall be elected for 6-year terms and shall reside in the circuit from which elected. [*1975 AJR-11; 1977 SJR-9*]

Circuit judges; election, eligibility, term, salary. SECTION 7. [*As amended November 1924*] For each circuit there shall be chosen by the qualified electors thereof one circuit judge, except that in any circuit in which there is a county that had a population in excess of eighty-five thousand, according to the last state or United States census, the legislature may, from time to time, authorize additional circuit judges to be chosen. Every circuit judge shall reside in the circuit from which he is elected, and shall hold his office for such term and receive such compensation as the legislature shall prescribe. [*1921 SJR-24; 1923 SJR-27; 1923 c. 408*]

Circuit judges, election. SECTION 7. [*As amended April 1897*] For each circuit there shall be chosen by the qualified electors thereof, one circuit judge, except that in any circuit composed of one county only, which county shall contain a population, according to the last state or United States census, of one hundred thousand inhabitants or over, the legislature may from time to time authorize additional circuit judges to be chosen. Every circuit judge shall reside in the circuit from which he is elected and shall hold his office for such term and receive such compensation as the legislature shall prescribe. [*1895 SJR-9; 1897 SJR-10; 1897 c. 69*]

Circuit judges, election. SECTION 7. [*Original form*] For each circuit there shall be a judge chosen by the qualified electors therein, who shall hold his office as is provided in this constitution, and until his successor shall be chosen and qualified; and after he shall have been elected, he shall reside in the circuit for which he was elected. One of said judges shall be designated as chief justice in such manner as the legislature shall provide. And the legislature shall at its first session provide by law as well for the election of, as for classifying the judges of the circuit court to be elected under this constitution, in such manner that one of said judges shall go out of office in two years, one in three years, one in four years, one in five years and one in six years, and thereafter the judge elected to fill the office shall hold the same for six years.

Circuit court: jurisdiction. SECTION 8. [*As amended April 1977*] Except as otherwise provided by law, the circuit court shall have original jurisdiction in all matters civil and criminal within this state and such appellate jurisdiction in the circuit as the legislature may prescribe by law. The circuit court may issue all writs necessary in aid of its jurisdiction. [*1975 AJR-11; 1977 SJR-9*]

Circuit court, jurisdiction. SECTION 8. [*Original form*] The circuit courts shall have original jurisdiction in all matters civil and criminal within this state, not excepted in this constitution, and not hereafter prohibited by law; and appellate jurisdiction from all inferior courts and tribunals, and a supervisory control over the same. They shall also have the power to issue writs of habeas corpus, mandamus, injunction, quo warranto, certiorari, and all other writs necessary to carry into effect their orders, judgments and decrees, and give them a general control over inferior courts and jurisdictions.

Judicial elections, vacancies. SECTION 9. [*As amended April 1977*] When a vacancy occurs in the office of justice of the supreme court or judge of any court of record, the vacancy shall be filled by appointment by the governor, which shall continue until a successor is elected and qualified. There shall be no election for a justice or judge at the partisan general election for state or county officers, nor within 30 days either before or after such election. [*1975 AJR-11; 1977 SJR-9*]

Vacancies; judicial elections. SECTION 9. [*As amended April 1953*] When a vacancy shall happen in the office of judge of the supreme or circuit courts, such vacancy shall be filled by an appointment of the governor, which shall continue until a successor is elected and qualified; and a supreme court justice when so elected shall hold his office for a term of 10 years and a circuit judge when so elected shall hold his office for such term as the legislature prescribes for circuit judges elected under section seven of this article. There shall be no election for a judge or judges at any general election for state or county officers, nor within 30 days either before or after such election. [*1951 SJR-3; 1953 SJR-5*]

Vacancies; judicial elections. SECTION 9. [*Original form*] When a vacancy shall happen in the office of judge of the supreme or circuit courts, such vacancy shall be filled by an appointment of the governor, which shall continue until a successor is elected and qualified; and when elected such successor shall hold his office the residue of the unexpired term. There shall be no election for a judge or judges at any general election for state or county officers, nor within thirty days either before or after such election.

Judges: eligibility to office. SECTION 10. [*As amended April 1977*] (1) No justice of the supreme court or judge of any court of record shall hold any other office of public trust, except a judicial office, during the term for which elected. No person shall be eligible to the office of judge who shall not, at the time of election or appointment, be a qualified elector within the jurisdiction for which chosen.

(2) Justices of the supreme court and judges of the courts of record shall receive such compensation as the legislature may authorize by law, but may not receive fees of office. [*1975 AJR-11; 1977 SJR-9*]

Compensation and qualifications of judges. SECTION 10. [*As amended November 1912*] Each of the judges of the supreme and circuit courts shall receive a salary, payable at such time as the legislature shall fix, of not less than one thousand five hundred dollars annually; they shall receive no fees of office, or other compensation than their salary; they shall hold no office of public trust, except a judicial office, during the term for which they are respectively elected, and all votes for either of them for any office, except a judicial office, given by the legislature or the people, shall be void. No person shall be eligible to the office of judge who shall not, at the time of his election, be a citizen of the United States and have attained the age of twenty-five years, and be a qualified elector within the jurisdiction for which he may be chosen. [*1909 AJR-36; 1911 AJR-26; 1911 c. 665*]

Compensation and qualifications of judges. SECTION 10. [*Original form*] Each of the judges of the supreme and circuit courts shall receive a salary, payable quarterly, of not less than one thousand five hundred dollars annually; they shall receive no fees of office, or other compensation than their salaries; they shall hold no office of public trust, except a judicial office, during the term for which they are respectively elected, and all votes for either of them for any office, except a judicial office, given by the legislature or the people, shall be void. No person shall be eligible to the office of judge, who shall not, at the time of his election, be a citizen of the United States, and have attained the age of twenty-five years, and be a qualified elector within the jurisdiction for which he may be chosen.

SECTION 11. [*Repealed. 1975 AJR-11; 1977 SJR-9; vote April 1977*]

Terms of courts; change of judges. SECTION 11. [*Original form*] The supreme court shall hold at least one term annually, at the seat of government of the state, at such time as shall be provided by law. And the legislature may provide for holding other terms and at other places when they may deem it necessary. A circuit court shall be held at least twice in each year in each county of this state rganized for judicial purposes. The judges of the circuit court may hold courts for each other, and shall do so when required by law.

Disciplinary proceedings. SECTION 11. [*Created April 1977*] Each justice or judge shall be subject to reprimand, censure, suspension, removal for cause or for disability, by the supreme court pursuant to procedures established by the legislature by law. No justice or judge removed for cause shall be eligible for reappointment or temporary service. This section is alternative to, and cumulative with, the methods of removal provided in sections 1 and 13 of this article and section 12 of article XIII. [*1975 AJR-11; 1977 SJR-9*]

Clerks of circuit and supreme courts. SECTION 12. [*As amended April 2005*] (1) There shall be a clerk of circuit court chosen in each county organized for judicial purposes by the qualified electors thereof, who, except as provided in sub. (2), shall hold office for two years, subject to removal as provided by law.

(2) Beginning with the first general election at which the governor is elected which occurs after the ratification of this subsection, a clerk of circuit court shall be chosen by the electors of each county, for the term of 4 years, subject to removal as provided by law.

(3) In case of a vacancy, the judge of the circuit court may appoint a clerk until the vacancy is filled by an election.

(4) The clerk of circuit court shall give such security as the legislature requires by law.

(5) The supreme court shall appoint its own clerk, and may appoint a clerk of circuit court to be the clerk of the supreme court. [*2003 AJR-10; 2005 SJR-2*]

Clerks of circuit and supreme courts. Section 12. [*As amended November 1882*] There shall be a clerk of the circuit court chosen in each county organized for judicial purposes by the qualified electors thereof, who shall hold his office for two years, subject to removal as shall be provided by law; in case of a vacancy, the judge of the circuit court shall have power to appoint a clerk until the vacancy shall be filled by an election; the clerk thus elected or appointed shall give such security as the legislature may require. The supreme court shall appoint its own clerk, and a clerk of the circuit court may be appointed a clerk of the supreme court. [*1881 AJR-16; 1882 SJR-20; 1882 c. 290*]

Clerks of courts. Section 12. [*Original form*] There shall be a clerk of the circuit court chosen in each county organized for judicial purposes, by the qualified electors thereof, who shall hold his office for two years, subject to removal, as shall be provided by law. In case of a vacancy, the judge of the circuit court shall have the power to appoint a clerk until the vacancy shall be filled by an election. The clerk thus elected or appointed shall give such security as the legislature may require; and when elected shall hold his office for a full term. The supreme court shall appoint its own clerk, and the clerk of a circuit court may be appointed clerk of the supreme court.

Justices and judges: removal by address. Section 13. [*As amended April 1977*] Any justice or judge may be removed from office by address of both houses of the legislature, if two-thirds of all the members elected to each house concur therein, but no removal shall be made by virtue of this section unless the justice or judge complained of is served with a copy of the charges, as the ground of address, and has had an opportunity of being heard. On the question of removal, the ayes and noes shall be entered on the journals. [*1975 AJR-11; 1977 SJR-9*]

Removal of judges. Section 13. [*As amended April 1974*] Any judge of the supreme, circuit, county or municipal court may be removed from office by address of both houses of the legislature, if two-thirds of all the members elected to each house concur therein, but no removal shall be made by virtue of this section unless the judge complained of shall have been served with a copy of the charges against him, as the ground of address, and shall have had an opportunity of being heard in his defense. On the question of removal, the ayes and noes shall be entered on the journals. [*1971 AJR-31; 1973 AJR-55*]

Removal of judges. Section 13. [*Original form*] Any judge of the supreme or circuit court may be removed from office by address of both houses of the legislature, if two-thirds of all the members elected to each house concur therein, but no removal shall be made by virtue of this section unless the judge complained of shall have been served with a copy of the charges against him, as the ground of address, and shall have had an opportunity of being heard in his defense. On the question of removal, the ayes and noes shall be entered on the journals.

Municipal court. Section 14. [*As amended April 1977*] The legislature by law may authorize each city, village and town to establish a municipal court. All municipal courts shall have uniform jurisdiction limited to actions and proceedings arising under ordinances of the municipality in which established. Judges of municipal courts may receive such compensation as provided by the municipality in which established, but may not receive fees of office. [*1975 AJR-11; 1977 SJR-9*]

Judges of probate. Section 14. [*Original form*] There shall be chosen in each county, by the qualified electors thereof, a judge of probate, who shall hold his office for two years and until his successor shall be elected and qualified, and whose jurisdiction, powers and duties shall be prescribed by law. Provided, however, that the legislature shall have power to abolish the office of judge of probate in any county, and to confer probate powers upon such inferior courts as may be established in said county.

Section 15. [*Repealed. 1963 SJR-32; 1965 SJR-26; vote April 1966*]

Justices of the peace. Section 15. [*As amended April 1945*] The electors of the several towns at their annual town meeting, and the electors of cities and villages at their charter elections except in cities of the first class, shall, in such manner as the legislature may direct, elect justices of the peace, whose term of office shall be for 2 years and until their successors in office shall be elected and qualified. In case of an election to fill a vacancy occurring before the expiration of a full term, the justice elected shall hold for the residue of the unexpired term. Their number and classification shall be regulated by law. And the tenure of 2 years shall in no wise interfere with the classification in the first instance. The justices thus elected shall have such civil and criminal jurisdiction as shall be prescribed by law. [*1943 SJR-9; 1945 SJR-6*]

Justices of the peace. Section 15. [*Original form*] The electors of the several towns, at their annual town meeting, and the electors of cities and villages, at their charter elections, shall in such manner as the legislature may direct, elect justices of the peace, whose term of office shall be for two years, and until their successors in office shall be elected and qualified. In case of an election to fill a vacancy, occurring before the expiration of a full term, the justice elected shall hold for the residue of the unexpired term. Their number and classification shall be regulated by law. And the tenure of two years shall in no wise interfere with the classification in the first instance. The justices, thus elected, shall have such civil and criminal jurisdiction as shall be prescribed by law.

SECTION 16. [*Repealed. 1975 AJR-11; 1977 SJR-9; vote April 1977*]

Tribunals of conciliation. SECTION 16. [*Original form*] The legislature shall pass laws for the regulation of tribunals of conciliation, defining their powers and duties. Such tribunals may be established in and for any township, and shall have power to render judgment to be obligatory on the parties when they shall voluntarily submit their matter in difference to arbitration, and agree to abide the judgment or assent thereto in writing.

SECTION 17. [*Repealed. 1975 AJR-11; 1977 SJR-9; vote April 1977*]

Style of writs; indictments. SECTION 17. [*Original form*] The style of all writs and process shall be, "The state of Wisconsin;" all criminal prosecutions shall be carried on in the name and by the authority of the same, and all indictments shall conclude against the peace and dignity of the state.

SECTION 18. [*Repealed. 1975 AJR-11; 1977 SJR-9; vote April 1977*]

Suit tax. SECTION 18. [*Original form*] The legislature shall impose a tax on all civil suits commenced or prosecuted in the municipal, inferior or circuit courts, which shall constitute a fund to be applied toward the payment of the salary of judges.

SECTION 19. [*Repealed. 1975 AJR-11; 1977 SJR-9; vote April 1977*]

Testimony in equity suits; master in chancery. SECTION 19. [*Original form*] The testimony in causes in equity shall be taken in like manner as in cases at law, and the office of master in chancery is hereby prohibited.

SECTION 20. [*Repealed. 1975 AJR-11; 1977 SJR-9; vote April 1977*] See Art. 1, sec. 21.

Rights of suitors. SECTION 20. [*Original form*] Any suitor, in any court of this state, shall have the right to prosecute or defend his suit either in his own proper person, or by an attorney or agent of his choice.

SECTION 21. [*Repealed. 1975 AJR-11; 1977 SJR-9; vote April 1977*] See Art. IV, sec. 17.

Publication of laws and decisions. SECTION 21. [*Original form*] The legislature shall provide by law for the speedy publication of all statute laws, and of such judicial decisions, made within the state, as may be deemed expedient. And no general law shall be in force until published.

SECTION 22. [*Repealed. 1975 AJR-11; 1977 SJR-9; vote April 1977*]

Commissioners to revise code of practice. SECTION 22. [*Original form*] The legislature, at its first session after the adoption of this constitution, shall provide for the appointment of three commissioners, whose duty it shall be to inquire into, revise and simplify the rules of practice, pleadings, forms and proceedings, and arrange a system adapted to the courts of record of this state, and report the same to the legislature, subject to their modification and adoption; and such commission shall terminate upon the rendering of the report, unless otherwise provided by law.

SECTION 23. [*Repealed. 1975 AJR-11; 1977 SJR-9; vote April 1977*]

Court commissioners. SECTION 23. [*Original form*] The legislature may provide for the appointment of one or more persons in each organized county, and may vest in such persons such judicial powers as shall be prescribed by law. Provided, that said power shall not exceed that of a judge of a circuit court at chambers.

Justices and judges: eligibility for office; retirement. SECTION 24. [*As amended April 1977*] (1) To be eligible for the office of supreme court justice or judge of any court of record, a person must be an attorney licensed to practice law in this state and have been so licensed for 5 years immediately prior to election or appointment.

(2) Unless assigned temporary service under subsection (3), no person may serve as a supreme court justice or judge of a court of record beyond the July 31 following the date on which such person attains that age, of not less than 70 years, which the legislature shall prescribe by law.

(3) A person who has served as a supreme court justice or judge of a court of record may, as provided by law, serve as a judge of any court of record except the supreme court on a temporary basis if assigned by the chief justice of the supreme court. [*1975 AJR-11; 1977 SJR-9*]

Retirement and eligibility for office of justices and circuit judges. SECTION 24. [*As amended April 1968*] No person seventy years of age or over may take office as a supreme court justice or circuit judge. No person may take or hold such office unless he is licensed to practice law in this state and has been so licensed for five years immediately prior to his election or appointment. No supreme court justice or circuit judge may serve beyond the July 31 following the date on which he attains the age of seventy. A person who has served eight or more years as a supreme court justice or circuit judge may serve temporarily, on appointment by the chief justice of the supreme court or by any associate justice designated by the supreme court, as a judge of a circuit court, under such general laws as the legislature may enact. [*1965 SJR-36; 1967 SJR-96*]

Retirement and eligibility for office of justices and circuit judges. SECTION 24. [*Created April 1955*] No person seventy years of age or over may take office as a supreme court justice or circuit judge. No person may take or hold such office unless he is licensed to practice law in this state and has been so licensed for five years immediately prior to his election or appointment. No supreme court justice or circuit judge may serve beyond the end of the month in which he attains the age of seventy, but any such justice or judge may complete the term in which he is serving or to which he has been elected when this section takes effect. Any person retired under the provisions of this section may, at the request of the chief justice of the supreme court, serve temporarily as a circuit judge and shall be compensated as the legislature provides. This section shall take effect on July first following the referendum at which it is approved. [*1953 SJR-6; 1955 SJR-10*]

ARTICLE VIII.
FINANCE

Rule of taxation uniform; income, privilege and occupation taxes. SECTION 1. [*As amended April 1974*] The rule of taxation shall be uniform but the legislature may empower cities, villages or towns to collect and return taxes on real estate located therein by optional methods. Taxes shall be levied upon such property with such classifications as to forests and minerals including or separate or severed from the land, as the legislature shall prescribe. Taxation of agricultural land and undeveloped land, both as defined by law, need not be uniform with the taxation of each other nor with the taxation of other real property. Taxation of merchants' stock-in-trade, manufacturers' materials and finished products, and livestock need not be uniform with the taxation of real property and other personal property, but the taxation of all such merchants' stock-in-trade, manufacturers' materials and finished products and livestock shall be uniform, except that the legislature may provide that the value thereof shall be determined on an average basis. Taxes may also be imposed on incomes, privileges and occupations, which taxes may be graduated and progressive, and reasonable exemptions may be provided. [*1971 AJR-2; 1973 AJR-1*]

Rule of taxation uniform; income, privilege and occupation taxes. SECTION 1. [*As amended April 1961*] The rule of taxation shall be uniform but the legislature may empower cities, villages or towns to collect and return taxes on real estate located therein by optional methods. Taxes shall be levied upon such property with such classifications as to forests and minerals including or separate or severed from the land, as the legislature shall prescribe. Taxation of merchants' stock-in-trade, manufacturers' materials and finished products, and livestock need not be uniform with the taxation of real property and other personal property, but the taxation of all such merchants' stock-in-trade, manufacturers' materials and finished products and livestock shall be uniform, except that the legislature may provide that the value thereof shall be determined on an average basis. Taxes may also be imposed on incomes; privileges and occupations, which taxes may be graduated and progressive, and reasonable exemptions may be provided. [*1959 AJR-120; 1961 SJR-34*]

Rule of taxation uniform; income, privilege and occupation taxes. SECTION 1. [*As amended April 1941*]. The rule of taxation shall be uniform but the legislature may empower cities, villages or towns to collect and return taxes on real estate located therein by optional methods. Taxes shall be levied upon such property with such classifications as to forests and minerals including or separate or severed from the land, as the legislature shall prescribe. Taxes may

also be imposed on incomes, privileges and occupations, which taxes may be graduated and progressive, and reasonable exemptions may be provided. [*1939 AJR-37; 1941 AJR-15*]

Rules of taxation; income taxes. SECTION 1. [*As amended April 1927*] The rule of taxation shall be uniform, and taxes shall be levied upon such property with such classifications as to forests and minerals, including or separate or severed from the land, as the legislature shall prescribe. Taxes may also be imposed on incomes, privileges and occupations, which taxes may be graduated and progressive, and reasonable exemptions may be provided. [*1925 AJR-51; 1927 AJR-3*]

Uniform rule of taxation; income tax. SECTION 1. [*As amended November 1908*] The rule of taxation shall be uniform, and taxes shall be levied upon such property as the legislature shall prescribe. Taxes may also be imposed on incomes, privileges and occupations, which taxes may be graduated and progressive, and reasonable exemptions may be provided. [*1905 AJR-12; 1907 SJR-19; 1907 c. 661*]

Uniform rule of taxation. SECTION 1. [*Original form*] The rule of taxation shall be uniform, and taxes shall be levied upon such property as the legislature shall prescribe.

Appropriations; limitation. SECTION 2. [*As amended November 1877*] No money shall be paid out of the treasury except in pursuance of an appropriation by law. No appropriation shall be made for the payment of any claim against the state except claims of the United States and judgments, unless filed within six years after the claim accrued. [*1876 SJR-14; 1877 SJR-5; 1877 c. 158*]

Appropriations. SECTION 2. [*Original form*] No money shall be paid out of the treasury, except in pursuance of an appropriation by law.

Credit of state. SECTION 3. [*As amended April 1975*] Except as provided in s. 7 (2) (a), the credit of the state shall never be given, or loaned, in aid of any individual, association or corporation. [*1973 AJR-145; 1975 AJR-1*]

Credit of state. SECTION 3. [*Original form*] The credit of the state shall never be given, or loaned, in aid of any individual, association or corporation.

Contracting state debts. SECTION 4. The state shall never contract any public debt except in the cases and manner herein provided.

Annual tax levy to equal expenses. SECTION 5. The legislature shall provide for an annual tax sufficient to defray the estimated expenses of the state for each year; and whenever the expenses of any year shall exceed the income, the legislature shall provide for levying a tax for the ensuing year, sufficient, with other sources of income, to pay the deficiency as well as the estimated expenses of such ensuing year.

Public debt for extraordinary expense; taxation. SECTION 6. For the purpose of defraying extraordinary expenditures the state may contract public debts (but such debts shall never in the aggregate exceed one hundred thousand dollars). Every such debt shall be authorized by law, for some purpose or purposes to be distinctly specified therein; and the vote of a majority of all the members elected to each house, to be taken by yeas and nays, shall be necessary to the passage of such law; and every such law shall provide for levying an annual tax sufficient to pay the annual interest of such debt and the principal within five years from the passage of such law, and shall specially appropriate the proceeds of such taxes to the payment of such principal and interest; and such appropriation shall not be repealed, nor the taxes postponed or diminished, until the principal and interest of such debt shall have been wholly paid.

Public debt for public defense; bonding for public purposes. SECTION 7. [*As amended April 1992*] (1) The legislature may also borrow money to repel invasion, suppress insurrection, or defend the state in time of war; but the money thus raised shall be applied exclusively to the object for which the loan was authorized, or to the repayment of the debt thereby created.

(2) Any other provision of this constitution to the contrary notwithstanding:

(a) The state may contract public debt and pledges to the payment thereof its full faith, credit and taxing power:

1. To acquire, construct, develop, extend, enlarge or improve land, waters, property, highways, railways, buildings, equipment or facilities for public purposes.

2. To make funds available for veterans' housing loans.

(b) The aggregate public debt contracted by the state in any calendar year pursuant to paragraph (a) shall not exceed an amount equal to the lesser of:

1. Three-fourths of one per centum of the aggregate value of all taxable property in the state; or

2. Five per centum of the aggregate value of all taxable property in the state less the sum of: a. the aggregate public debt of the state contracted pursuant to this section outstanding as of January 1 of such calendar year after subtracting therefrom the amount of sinking funds on hand on January 1 of such calendar year which are applicable exclusively to repayment of such outstanding public debt and, b. the outstanding indebtedness as of January 1 of such calendar year of any entity of the type described in paragraph (d) to the extent that such indebtedness is supported by or payable from payments out of the treasury of the state.

(c) The state may contract public debt, without limit, to fund or refund the whole or any part of any public debt contracted pursuant to paragraph (a), including any premium payable with respect thereto and any interest to accrue thereon, or to fund or refund the whole or any part of any indebtedness incurred prior to January 1, 1972, by any entity of the type described in paragraph (d), including any premium payable with respect thereto and any interest to accrue thereon.

(d) No money shall be paid out of the treasury, with respect to any lease, sublease or other agreement entered into after January 1, 1971, to the Wisconsin State Agencies Building Corporation, Wisconsin State Colleges Building Corporation, Wisconsin State Public Building Corporation, Wisconsin University Building Corporation or any similar entity existing or operating for similar purposes pursuant to which such nonprofit corporation or such other entity undertakes to finance or provide a facility for use or occupancy by the state or an agency, department or instrumentality thereof.

(e) The legislature shall prescribe all matters relating to the contracting of public debt pursuant to paragraph (a), including: the public purposes for which public debt may be contracted; by vote of a majority of the members elected to each of the 2 houses of the legislature, the amount of public debt which may be contracted for any class of such purposes; the public debt or other indebtedness which may be funded or refunded; the kinds of notes, bonds or other evidence of public debt which may be issued by the state; and the manner in which the aggregate value of all taxable property in the state shall be determined.

(f) The full faith, credit and taxing power of the state are pledged to the payment of all public debt created on behalf of the state pursuant to this section and the legislature shall provide by appropriation for the payment of the interest upon and instalments of principal of all such public debt as the same falls due, but, in any event, suit may be brought against the state to compel such payment.

(g) At any time after January 1, 1972, by vote of a majority of the members elected to each of the 2 houses of the legislature, the legislature may declare that an emergency exists and submit to the people a proposal to authorize the state to contract a specific amount of public debt for a purpose specified in such proposal, without regard to the limit provided in paragraph (b). Any such authorization shall be effective if approved by a majority of the electors voting thereon. Public debt contracted pursuant to such authorization shall thereafter be deemed to have been contracted pursuant to paragraph (a), but neither such public debt nor any public debt contracted to fund or refund such public debt shall be considered in computing the debt limit provided in paragraph (b). Not more than one such authorization shall be thus made in any 2-year period. [*1989 SJR-76; 1991 SJR-30*]

Public debt for public defense; bonding for public purposes. SECTION 7. [*As amended April 1975*] (1) The legislature may also borrow money to repel invasion, suppress insurrection, or defend the state in time of war; but the money thus raised shall be applied exclusively to the object for which the loan was authorized, or to the repayment of the debt thereby created.

(2) Any other provision of this constitution to the contrary notwithstanding:

(a) The state may contract public debt and pledges to the payment thereof its full faith, credit and taxing power:

1. To acquire, construct, develop, extend, enlarge or improve land, waters, property, highways, buildings, equipment or facilities for public purposes.

2. To make funds available for veterans' housing loans.

(b) The aggregate public debt contracted by the state in any calendar year pursuant to paragraph (a) shall not exceed an amount equal to the lesser of:

1. Three-fourths of one per centum of the aggregate value of all taxable property in the state; or

2. Five per centum of the aggregate value of all taxable property in the state less the sum of: a. the aggregate public debt of the state contracted pursuant to this section outstanding as of January 1 of such calendar year after subtracting therefrom the amount of sinking funds on hand on January 1 of such calendar year which are applicable exclusively to repayment of such outstanding public debt and, b. the outstanding indebtedness as of January 1 of such calendar year of any entity of the type described in paragraph (d) to the extent that such indebtedness is supported by or payable from payments out of the treasury of the state.

(c) The state may contract public debt, without limit, to fund or refund the whole or any part of any public debt contracted pursuant to paragraph (a), including any premium payable with respect thereto and any interest to accrue thereon, or to fund or refund the whole or any part of any indebtedness incurred prior to January 1, 1972, by any entity of the type described in paragraph (d), including any premium payable with respect thereto and any interest to accrue thereon.

(d) No money shall be paid out of the treasury, with respect to any lease, sublease or other agreement entered into after January 1, 1971, to the Wisconsin State Agencies Building Corporation, Wisconsin State Colleges Building Corporation, Wisconsin State Public Building Corporation, Wisconsin University Building Corporation or any similar entity existing or operating for similar purposes pursuant to which such nonprofit corporation or such other entity undertakes to finance or provide a facility for use or occupancy by the state or an agency, department or instrumentality thereof.

(e) The legislature shall prescribe all matters relating to the contracting of public debt pursuant to paragraph (a), including: the public purposes for which public debt may

be contracted; by vote of a majority of the members elected to each of the 2 houses of the legislature, the amount of public debt which may be contracted for any class of such purposes; the public debt or other indebtedness which may be funded or refunded; the kinds of notes, bonds or other evidence of public debt which may be issued by the state; and the manner in which the aggregate value of all taxable property in the state shall be determined.

(f) The full faith, credit and taxing power of the state are pledged to the payment of all public debt created on behalf of the state pursuant to this section and the legislature shall provide by appropriation for the payment of the interest upon and instalments of principal of all such public debt as the same falls due, but, in any event, suit may be brought against the state to compel such payment.

(g) At any time after January 1, 1972, by vote of a majority of the members elected to each of the 2 houses of the legislature, the legislature may declare that an emergency exists and submit to the people a proposal to authorize the state to contract a specific amount of public debt for a purpose specified in such proposal, without regard to the limit provided in paragraph (b). Any such authorization shall be effective if approved by a majority of the electors voting thereon. Public debt contracted pursuant to such authorization shall thereafter be deemed to have been contracted pursuant to paragraph (a), but neither such public debt nor any public debt contracted to fund or refund such public debt shall be considered in computing the debt limit provided in paragraph (b). Not more than one such authorization shall be thus made in any 2-year period. [*1973 AJR-145; 1975 AJR-1*]

Public debt for public defense; bonding for public purposes. SECTION 7. [*As amended April 1969*] (1) The legislature may also borrow money to repel invasion, suppress insurrection, or defend the state in time of war; but the money thus raised shall be applied exclusively to the object for which the loan was authorized, or to the repayment of the debt thereby created.

(2) Any other provision of this constitution to the contrary notwithstanding:

(a) The state may contract public debt and pledges to the payment thereof its full faith, credit and taxing power to acquire, construct, develop, extend, enlarge or improve land, waters, property, highways, buildings, equipment or facilities for public purposes.

(b) The aggregate public debt contracted by the state in any calendar year pursuant to paragraph (a) shall not exceed an amount equal to the lesser of:

1. Three-fourths of one per centum of the aggregate value of all taxable property in the state; or

2. Five per centum of the aggregate value of all taxable property in the state less the sum of: a. the aggregate public debt of the state contracted pursuant to this section outstanding as of January 1 of such calendar year after subtracting therefrom the amount of sinking funds on hand on January 1 of such calendar year which are applicable

exclusively to repayment of such outstanding public debt and, b. the outstanding indebtedness as of January 1 of such calendar year of any entity of the type described in paragraph (d) to the extent that such indebtedness is supported by or payable from payments out of the treasury of the state.

(c) The state may contract public debt, without limit, to fund or refund the whole or any part of any public debt contracted pursuant to paragraph (a), including any premium payable with respect thereto and any interest to accrue thereon, or to fund or refund the whole or any part of any indebtedness incurred prior to January 1, 1972, by any entity of the type described in paragraph (d), including any premium payable with respect thereto and any interest to accrue thereon.

(d) No money shall be paid out of the treasury, with respect to any lease, sublease or other agreement entered into after January 1, 1971, to the Wisconsin State Agencies Building Corporation, Wisconsin State Colleges Building Corporation, Wisconsin State Public Building Corporation, Wisconsin University Building Corporation or any similar entity existing or operating for similar purposes pursuant to which such nonprofit corporation or such other entity undertakes to finance or provide a facility for use or occupancy by the state or an agency, department or instrumentality thereof.

(e) The legislature shall prescribe all matters relating to the contracting of public debt pursuant to paragraph (a), including: the public purposes for which public debt may be contracted; by vote of a majority of the members elected to each of the 2 houses of the legislature, the amount of public debt which may be contracted for any class of such purposes; the public debt or other indebtedness which may

be funded or refunded; the kinds of notes, bonds or other evidence of public debt which may be issued by the state; and the manner in which the aggregate value of all taxable property in the state shall be determined.

(f) The full faith, credit and taxing power of the state are pledged to the payment of all public debt created on behalf of the state pursuant to this section and the legislature shall provide by appropriation for the payment of the interest upon and instalments of principal of all such public debt as the same falls due, but, in any event, suit may be brought against the state to compel such payment.

(g) At any time after January 1, 1972, by vote of a majority of the members elected to each of the 2 houses of the legislature, the legislature may declare that an emergency exists and submit to the people a proposal to authorize the state to contract a specific amount of public debt for a purpose specified in such proposal, without regard to the limit provided in paragraph (b). Any such authorization shall be effective if approved by a majority of the electors voting thereon. Public debt contracted pursuant to such authorization shall thereafter be deemed to have been contracted pursuant to paragraph (a), but neither such public debt nor any public debt contracted to fund or refund such public debt shall be considered in computing the debt limit provided in paragraph (b). Not more than one such authorization shall be thus made in any 2-year period. [*1967 AJR-1; 1969 AJR-1*]

Public debt for public defense. SECTION 7. [*Original form*] The legislature may also borrow money to repel invasion, suppress insurrection, or defend the state in time of war; but the money thus raised shall be applied exclusively to the object for which the loan was authorized, or to the repayment of the debt thereby created.

Vote on fiscal bills; quorum. SECTION 8. On the passage in either house of the legislature of any law which imposes, continues or renews a tax, or creates a debt or charge, or makes, continues or renews an appropriation of public or trust money, or releases, discharges or commutes a claim or demand of the state, the question shall be taken by yeas and nays, which shall be duly entered on the journal; and three-fifths of all the members elected to such house shall in all such cases be required to constitute a quorum therein.

Evidences of public debt. SECTION 9. No scrip, certificate, or other evidence of state debt, whatsoever, shall be issued, except for such debts as are authorized by the sixth and seventh sections of this article.

Internal improvements. SECTION 10. [*As amended April 1992*] Except as further provided in this section, the state may never contract any debt for works of internal improvement, or be a party in carrying on such works.

(1) Whenever grants of land or other property shall have been made to the state, especially dedicated by the grant to particular works of internal improvement, the state may carry on such particular works and shall devote thereto the avails of such grants, and may pledge or appropriate the revenues derived from such works in aid of their completion.

(2) The state may appropriate money in the treasury or to be thereafter raised by taxation for: (a) The construction or improvement of public highways. (b) The development, improvement and construction of airports or other aeronautical projects.

(c) The acquisition, improvement or construction of veterans' housing.

(d) The improvement of port facilities.

(e) The acquisition, development, improvement or construction of railways and other railroad facilities.

(3) The state may appropriate moneys for the purpose of acquiring, preserving and developing the forests of the state. Of the moneys appropriated under the authority of this subsection in any one year an amount not to exceed two-tenths of one mill of the taxable property of the state as determined by the last preceding state assessment may be raised by a tax on property. [*1989 SJR-76; 1991 SJR-30*]

Internal improvements. SECTION 10. [*As amended April 1968*] The state shall never contract any debt for works of internal improvement, or be a party in carrying on

such works; but whenever grants of land or other property shall have been made to the state, especially dedicated by the grant to particular works of internal improvement, the state may carry on such particular works and shall devote thereto the avails of such grants, and may pledge or appropriate the revenues derived from such works in aid of their completion. Provided, that the state may appropriate money in the treasury or to be thereafter raised by taxation for the construction or improvement of public highways or the development, improvement and construction of airports or other aeronautical projects or the acquisition, improvement or construction of veterans' housing or the improvement of port facilities. Provided, that the state may appropriate moneys for the purpose of acquiring, preserving and developing the forests of the state; but of the moneys appropriated under the authority of this section in any one year an amount not to exceed two-tenths of one mill of the taxable property of the state as determined by the last preceding state assessment may be raised by a tax on property. [*1965 SJR-28; 1967 SJR-18*]

Internal improvements. SECTION 10. [*As amended April 1960*] The state shall never contract any debt for works of internal improvement, or be a party in carrying on such works; but whenever grants of land or other property shall have been made to the state, especially dedicated by the grant to particular works of internal improvement, the state may carry on such particular works and shall devote thereto the avails of such grants, and may pledge or appropriate the revenues derived from such works in aid of their completion. Provided, that the state may appropriate money in the treasury or to be thereafter raised by taxation for the construction or improvement of public highways or the development, improvement and construction of airports or other aeronautical projects or the acquisition, improvement or construction of veterans' housing or the improvement of port facilities. Provided, that the state may appropriate moneys for the purpose of acquiring, preserving and developing the forests of the state; but there shall not be appropriated under the authority of this section in any one year an amount to exceed two-tenths of one mill of the taxable property of the state as determined by the last preceding state assessment. [*1957 AJR-39; 1959 SJR-20*]

Internal improvements. SECTION 10. [*As amended April 1949*] The state shall never contract any debt for works of internal improvement, or be a party in carrying on such works; but whenever grants of land or other property shall have been made to the state, especially dedicated by the grant to particular works of internal improvement, the state may carry on such particular works and shall devote thereto the avails of such grants, and may pledge or appropriate the revenues derived from such works in aid of their completion. Provided, that the state may appropriate money in the treasury or to be thereafter raised by taxation for the construction or improvement of public highways or the development, improvement and construction of airports or other aeronautical projects or the acquisition, improvement or construction of veterans' housing. Provided, that the state may appropriate moneys for the purpose of acquiring, preserving and developing the forests of the state; but there shall not be appropriated under the authority of this section in any one year an amount to exceed two-tenths of one mill of the taxable property of the state as determined by the last preceding state assessment. [*1948 Spec.Sess. SJR-2; 1949 SJR-5*]

Internal improvements. SECTION 10. [*As amended April 1945*] The state shall never contract any debt for works of internal improvement, or be a party in carrying on

such works; but whenever grants of land or other property shall have been made to the state, especially dedicated by the grant to particular works of internal improvement, the state may carry on such particular works, and shall devote thereto the avails of such grants, and may pledge or appropriate the revenues derived from such works in aid of their completion. Provided, that the state may appropriate money in the treasury or to be thereafter raised by taxation for the construction or improvement of public highways or the development, improvement and construction of airports or other aeronautical projects. Provided, that the state may appropriate moneys for the purpose of acquiring, preserving and developing the forests of the state; but there shall not be appropriated under the authority of this section in any one year an amount to exceed two-tenths of one mill of the taxable property of the state as determined by the last preceding state assessment. [*1943 SJR-16; 1945 SJR-7*]

Internal improvements. SECTION 10. [*As amended November 1924*] The state shall never contract any debt for works of internal improvement, or be a party in carrying on such works; but whenever grants of land or other property shall have been made to the state, especially dedicated by the grant to particular works of internal improvement, the state may carry on such particular works, and shall devote thereto the avails of such grants, and may pledge or appropriate the revenues derived from such works in aid of their completion. Provided, that the state may appropriate money in the treasury or to be thereafter raised by taxation for the construction or improvement of public highways. Provided, that the state may appropriate moneys for the purpose of acquiring, preserving and developing the forests of the state; but there shall not be appropriated under the authority of this section in any one year an amount to exceed two-tenths of one mill of the taxable property of the state as determined by the last preceding state assessment. [*1921 SJR-30; 1923 AJR-70; 1923 c. 289*]

Water power and forests. SECTION 10. [*Approved by voters November 1910*] An amendment to Art. VIII, sec. 10, authorizing a state property tax of two-tenths of one mill to finance appropriations for acquisition and development of water power and forests was approved by 1907 SJR-43. There was no "second consideration" resolution but 1909 SB\553 enacted the proposal into law as Chap. 514, Laws of 1909. The procedure was declared invalid by the Supreme Court in *State ex rel. Owen v. Donald*, 160 W 21, 151 NW 331.

Public highways. [*As amended November 1908, a new sentence was added at the end of the section*] Provided, that the state may appropriate money in the treasury or to be thereafter raised by taxation for the construction or improvement of public highways. [*1905 SJR-14; 1907 SJR-22; 1907 c. 238*]

Internal improvements. SECTION 10. [*Original form*] The state shall never contract any debt for works of internal improvement, or be a party in carrying on such works, but whenever grants of land or other property shall have been made to the state, especially dedicated by the grant to particular works of internal improvements, the state may carry on such particular works, and shall devote thereto the avails of such grants, and may pledge or appropriate the revenues derived from such works in aid of their completion.

ARTICLE IX.
EMINENT DOMAIN AND PROPERTY OF THE STATE

Jurisdiction on rivers and lakes; navigable waters. SECTION 1. The state shall have concurrent jurisdiction on all rivers and lakes bordering on this state so far as such rivers or lakes shall form a common boundary to the state and any other state or territory now or hereafter to be formed, and bounded by the same; and the river Mississippi and the navigable waters leading into the Mississippi and St. Lawrence, and the carrying places between the same, shall be common highways and forever free, as well to the inhabitants of the state as to the citizens of the United States, without any tax, impost or duty therefor.

Territorial property. SECTION 2. The title to all lands and other property which have accrued to the territory of Wisconsin by grant, gift, purchase, forfeiture, escheat or otherwise shall vest in the state of Wisconsin.

Ultimate property in lands; escheats. SECTION 3. The people of the state, in their right of sovereignty, are declared to possess the ultimate property, in and to all lands within the jurisdiction of the state; and all lands the title to which shall fail from a defect of heirs shall revert or escheat to the people.

ARTICLE X.
EDUCATION

Superintendent of public instruction. SECTION 1. [*As amended November 1982*] The supervision of public instruction shall be vested in a state superintendent and such other officers as the legislature shall direct; and their qualifications, powers, duties and compensation shall be prescribed by law. The state superintendent shall be chosen by the qualified electors of the state at the same time and in the same manner as members of the supreme court, and shall hold office for 4 years from the succeeding first Monday in July. The term of office, time and manner of electing or appointing all other officers of supervision of public instruction shall be fixed by law. [*1979 AJR-76; 1981 AJR-35; submit: May'82 Spec.Sess. AJR-1*]

Superintendent of public instruction. SECTION 1. [*As amended November 1902*] The supervision of public instruction shall be vested in a state superintendent and such other officers as the legislature shall direct; and their qualifications, powers, duties and compensation shall be prescribed by law. The state superintendent shall be chosen by the qualified electors of the state at the same time and in the same manner as members of the supreme court, and shall hold his office for four years from the succeeding first Monday in July. The state superintendent chosen at the general election in November, 1902, shall hold and continue in his office until the first Monday in July, 1905, and his successor shall be chosen at the time of the judicial election in April, 1905. The term of office, time and manner of electing or appointing all other officers of supervision of public instruction shall be fixed by law. [*1899 SJR-21; 1901 SJR-24; 1901 c. 258*]

Superintendent of public instruction. SECTION 1. [*Original form*] The supervision of public instruction shall be vested in a state superintendent, and such other officers as the legislature shall direct. The state superintendent shall be chosen by the qualified electors of the state, in such manner as the legislature shall provide; his powers, duties and compensation shall be prescribed by law. Provided, that his compensation shall not exceed the sum of twelve hundred dollars annually.

School fund created; income applied. SECTION 2. [*As amended November 1982*] The proceeds of all lands that have been or hereafter may be granted by the United States to this state for educational purposes (except the lands heretofore granted for the purposes of a university) and all moneys and the clear proceeds of all property that may accrue to the state by forfeiture or escheat; and the clear proceeds of all fines collected in the several counties for any breach of the penal laws, and all moneys arising from any grant to the state where the purposes of such grant are not specified, and the 500,000 acres of land to which the state is entitled by the provisions of an act of congress, entitled "An act to appropriate the proceeds of the sales of the public lands and to grant pre-emption rights," approved September 4, 1841; and also the 5 percent of the net proceeds of the public lands to which the state shall become entitled on admission into the union (if congress shall consent to such appropriation of the 2 grants last mentioned) shall be set apart as a separate fund to be called "the school fund," the interest of which and all other revenues derived from the school lands shall be exclusively applied to the following objects, to wit:

(1) To the support and maintenance of common schools, in each school district, and the purchase of suitable libraries and apparatus therefor.

(2) The residue shall be appropriated to the support and maintenance of academies and normal schools, and suitable libraries and apparatus therefor. [*1979 AJR-76; 1981 AJR-35; submit: May'82 Spec.Sess. AJR-1*]

School fund created; income applied. SECTION 2. [*Original form*] The proceeds of all lands that have been or hereafter may be granted by the United States to this state for educational purposes (except the lands heretofore granted for the purpose of a university) and all moneys and the clear proceeds of all property that may accrue to the state by forfeiture or escheat, and all moneys which may be paid as an equivalent for exemption from military duty; and the clear proceeds of all fines collected in the several counties for any breach of the penal laws, and all moneys arising from any grant to the state where the purposes of such grant are not specified, and the five hundred thousand acres of land to which the state is entitled by the provisions of an act of congress, entitled "An act to appropriate the proceeds of the sales of the public lands and to grant pre-emption rights," approved the fourth day of September, one thousand eight hundred and forty-one; and also the five per centum of the net proceeds of the public lands to which the state shall become entitled on her admission into the union (if congress shall consent to such appropriation of the two grants last mentioned) shall be set apart as a separate fund to be called "the school fund," the interest of which and all other revenues derived from the school lands shall be exclusively applied to the following objects, to wit: 1. To the support and maintenance of common schools, in each school district, and the purchase of suitable libraries and apparatus therefor.

2. The residue shall be appropriated to the support and maintenance of academies and normal schools, and suitable libraries and apparatus therefor.

District schools; tuition; sectarian instruction; released time. SECTION 3. [*As amended April 1972*] The legislature shall provide by law for the establishment of district schools, which shall be as nearly uniform as practicable; and such schools shall be free and without charge for tuition to all children between the ages of 4 and 20 years; and no sectarian instruction shall be allowed therein; but the legislature by law may, for the purpose of religious instruction outside the district schools, authorize the release of students during regular school hours. [*1969 AJR-41; 1971 AJR-17*]

District schools; tuition; sectarian instruction. SECTION 3. [*Original form*] The legislature shall provide by law for the establishment of district schools, which shall be as nearly uniform as practicable; and such schools shall be free and without charge for tuition to all children between the ages of four and twenty years; and no sectarian instruction shall be allowed therein.

Annual school tax. SECTION 4. Each town and city shall be required to raise by tax, annually, for the support of common schools therein, a sum not less than one-half the amount received by such town or city respectively for school purposes from the income of the school fund.

Income of school fund. SECTION 5. Provision shall be made by law for the distribution of the income of the school fund among the several towns and cities of the state for the support of common schools therein, in some just proportion to the number of children and youth resident therein between the ages of four and twenty years, and no appropriation shall be made from the school fund to any city or town for the year in which said city or town shall fail to raise such tax; nor to any school district for the year in which a school shall not be maintained at least three months.

State university; support. SECTION 6. Provision shall be made by law for the establishment of a state university at or near the seat of state government, and for connecting with the same, from time to time, such colleges in different parts of the state as the interests of education may require. The proceeds of all lands that have been or may hereafter be granted by the United States to the state for the support of a university shall be and remain a perpetual fund to be called "the university fund," the interest of which shall be appropriated to the support of the state university, and no sectarian instruction shall be allowed in such university.

Commissioners of public lands. SECTION 7. The secretary of state, treasurer and attorney general, shall constitute a board of commissioners for the sale of the school and university lands and for the investment of the funds arising therefrom. Any two of said commissioners shall be a quorum for the transaction of all business pertaining to the duties of their office.

Sale of public lands. SECTION 8. Provision shall be made by law for the sale of all school and university lands after they shall have been appraised; and when any portion of such lands shall be sold and the purchase money shall not be paid at the time of the sale, the commissioners shall take security by mortgage upon the lands sold for the sum remaining unpaid, with seven per cent interest thereon, payable annually at the office of the treasurer. The commissioners shall be authorized to execute a good and sufficient conveyance to all purchasers of such lands, and to discharge any mortgages taken as security, when the sum due thereon shall have been paid. The commissioners shall have power to withhold from sale any portion of such lands when they shall deem it expedient, and shall invest all moneys arising from the sale of such lands, as well as all other university and school funds, in such manner as the legislature shall provide, and shall give such security for the faithful performance of their duties as may be required by law.

ARTICLE XI.

CORPORATIONS

Corporations; how formed. SECTION 1. [*As amended April 1981*] Corporations without banking powers or privileges may be formed under general laws, but shall not be created by special act, except for municipal purposes. All general laws or special acts enacted under the provisions of this section may be altered or repealed by the legislature at any time after their passage. [*1979 AJR-53; 1981 AJR-13*]

Corporations; how formed. SECTION 1. [*Original form*] Corporations without banking powers or privileges may be formed under general laws, but shall not be created by special act, except for municipal purposes, and in cases where, in the judgment of the legislature, the objects of the corporation cannot be attained under general laws. All general laws or special acts enacted under the provisions of this section may be altered or repealed by the legislature at any time after their passage.

Property taken by municipality. SECTION 2. [*As amended April 1961*] No municipal corporation shall take private property for public use, against the consent of the owner, without the necessity thereof being first established in the manner prescribed by the legislature. [*1959 AJR-22; 1961 SJR-8*]

Property taken by municipality. SECTION 2. [*Original form*] No municipal corporation shall take private property for public use, against the consent of the owner, without the necessity thereof being first established by the verdict of a jury.

Municipal home rule; debt limit; tax to pay debt. SECTION 3. [*As amended April 1981*]

(1) Cities and villages organized pursuant to state law may determine their local affairs and government, subject only to this constitution and to such enactments of the legislature of statewide concern as with uniformity shall affect every city or every village. The method of such determination shall be prescribed by the legislature.

(2) No county, city, town, village, school district, sewerage district or other municipal corporation may become indebted in an amount that exceeds an allowable percentage of the taxable property located therein equalized for state purposes as provided by the legislature. In all cases the allowable percentage shall be 5 percent except as specified in pars. (a) and (b):

(a) For any city authorized to issue bonds for school purposes, an additional 10 percent shall be permitted for school purposes only, and in such cases the territory attached to the city for school purposes shall be included in the total taxable property supporting the bonds issued for school purposes.

(b) For any school district which offers no less than grades one to 12 and which at the time of incurring such debt is eligible for the highest level of school aids, 10 percent shall be permitted.

(3) Any county, city, town, village, school district, sewerage district or other municipal corporation incurring any indebtedness under sub. (2) shall, before or at the time of doing so, provide for the collection of a direct annual tax sufficient to pay the interest on such debt as it falls due, and also to pay and discharge the principal thereof within 20 years from the time of contracting the same.

(4) When indebtedness under sub. (2) is incurred in the acquisition of lands by cities, or by counties or sewerage districts having a population of 150,000 or over, for public, municipal purposes, or for the permanent improvement thereof, or to purchase, acquire, construct, extend, add to or improve a sewage collection or treatment system which services all or a part of such city or county, the city, county or sewerage district incurring the indebtedness shall, before or at the time of so doing, provide for the collection of a direct annual tax sufficient to pay the interest on such debt as it falls due, and also to pay and discharge the principal thereof within a period not exceeding 50 years from the time of contracting the same.

(5) An indebtedness created for the purpose of purchasing, acquiring, leasing, constructing, extending, adding to, improving, conducting, controlling, operating or managing a public utility of a town, village, city or special district, and secured solely by the property or income of such public utility, and whereby no municipal liability is created, shall not be considered an indebtedness of such town, village, city or special district, and shall not be included in arriving at the debt limitation under sub. (2). [*1979 SJR-28; 1981 SJR-5*]

Municipal home rule; debt limit; tax to pay debt. SECTION 3. [*As amended April 1966*] Cities and villages organized pursuant to state law are hereby empowered, to determine their local affairs and government, subject only to this constitution and to such enactments of the legislature of statewide concern as shall with uniformity affect every city or every village. The method of such determination shall be prescribed by the legislature. No county, city, town, village, school district or other municipal corporation may become indebted in an amount that exceeds an allowable percentage of the taxable property located therein equalized for state purposes as provided by the legislature. In all cases the allowable percentage shall be five per centum except as follows: (a) For any city authorized to issue bonds for school purposes, an additional ten per centum shall be permitted for school purposes only, and in such cases the territory attached to the city for school purposes shall be included in the total taxable property supporting the bonds issued for school purposes. (b) For any school district which offers no less than grades one to twelve and which at the time of incurring such debt is eligible for the highest level of school aids, ten per centum shall be permitted. Any county, city, town, village, school district, or other municipal corporation incurring any indebtedness as aforesaid, shall before or at the time of doing so, provide for the collection of a direct annual tax sufficient to pay the interest on such debt as it falls due, and also to pay and discharge the principal thereof within twenty years from the time of contracting the same; except that when such indebtedness is incurred in the acquisition of lands by cities, or by counties having a population of one hundred fifty thousand or over, for public, municipal purposes, or for the permanent improvement thereof, the city or county incurring the same shall, before or at the time of so doing, provide for the collection of a direct annual tax sufficient to pay the interest on such debt as it falls due, and also to pay and discharge the principal thereof within a period not exceeding fifty years from the time of contracting the same. An indebtedness created for the purpose of purchasing, acquiring, leasing, constructing, extending, adding to, improving, conducting, controlling, operating or managing a public utility of a town, village, city or special district, and secured solely by the property or income of such public utility, and whereby no municipal liability is created, shall not be considered an indebtedness of such town, village, city or special district, and shall not be included in arriving at such debt limitation. [*1963 SJR-59; 1965 AJR-10*]

Municipal home rule; debt limit; tax to pay debt. SECTION 3. [*As amended April 1963*] Cities and villages organized pursuant to state law are hereby empowered, to determine their local affairs and government, subject only to this constitution and to such enactments of the legislature of state-wide concern as shall with uniformity affect every city or every village. The method of such determination shall be prescribed by the legislature. No county, city, town, village, school district or other municipal corporation may become indebted in an amount that exceeds an allowable percentage of the taxable property located therein equalized for state purposes as provided by the legislature. In all cases the allowable percentage shall be five per centum except as follows: (a) For any city authorized to issue bonds for school purposes, an additional ten per centum shall be permitted for school purposes only, and in such cases the territory attached to the city for school purposes shall be included in the total taxable property supporting the bonds issued for school purposes. (b) For any school district which offers no less than grades one to twelve and which at the time of incurring such debt is eligible for the highest level of school aids, ten per centum shall be permitted. Any county, city, town, village, school district, or other municipal corporation incurring any indebtedness as aforesaid, shall before or at the time of doing so, provide for the collection of a direct annual tax sufficient to pay the interest on such debt as it falls due, and also to pay and discharge the principal thereof within twenty years from the time of contracting the same; except that when such indebtedness is incurred in the acquisition of lands by cities, or by counties having a population of one hundred fifty thousand or over, for public, municipal purposes, or for the permanent improvement thereof, the city or county incurring the same shall, before or at the time of so doing, provide for the collection of a direct annual tax sufficient to pay the interest on such debt as it falls due, and also to pay and discharge the principal thereof within a period not exceeding fifty years from the time of contracting the same. An indebtedness created for the purpose of purchasing, acquiring, leasing, constructing, extending, adding to, improving, conducting, controlling, operating or managing a public utility of a town, village or city, and secured solely by the property or income of such public utility, and whereby no municipal liability is created, shall not be considered an indebtedness of such town, village or city, and shall not be included in arriving at such five or eight per centum debt limitation. [*1961 AJR-92; 1963 AJR-19*]

Municipal home rule; debt limit; tax to pay debt. SECTION 3. [*As amended April 1961*] Cities and villages organized pursuant to state law are hereby empowered, to determine their local affairs and government, subject only to this constitution and to such enactments of the legislature of state-wide concern as shall with uniformity affect every city or every village. The method of such determination shall be prescribed by the legislature. No county, city, town, village, school district, or other municipal corporation shall be allowed to become indebted in any manner or for any purpose to any amount, including existing indebtedness, in

the aggregate exceeding five per centum on the value of the taxable property therein, to be ascertained, other than for school districts and counties having a population of 500,000 or over, by the last assessment for state and county taxes previous to the incurring of such indebtedness and for school districts and counties having a population of 500,000 or over by the value of such property as equalized for state purposes; except that for any city which is authorized to issue bonds for school purposes the total indebtedness of such city shall not exceed in the aggregate eight per centum of the value of such property as equalized for state purposes and except that for any school district offering no less than grades one to twelve and which is at the time of incurring such debt eligible for the highest level of school aids, the total indebtedness of such school district shall not exceed ten per centum of the value of such property as equalized for state purposes; the manner and method of determining such equalization for state purposes to be provided by the legislature. Any county, city, town, village, school district, or other municipal corporation incurring any indebtedness as aforesaid, shall, before or at the time of doing so, provide for the collection of a direct annual tax sufficient to pay the interest on such debt as it falls due, and also to pay and discharge the principal thereof within twenty years from the time of contracting the same; except that when such indebtedness is incurred in the acquisition of lands by cities, or by counties having a population of one hundred fifty thousand or over, for public, municipal purposes, or for the permanent improvement thereof, the city or county incurring the same shall, before or at the time of so doing, provide for the collection of a direct annual tax sufficient to pay the interest on such debt as it falls due, and also to pay and discharge the principal thereof within a period not exceeding fifty years from the time of contracting the same. An indebtedness created for the purpose of purchasing, acquiring, leasing, constructing, extending, adding to, improving, conducting, controlling, operating or managing a public utility of a town, village or city, and secured solely by the property or income of such public utility, and whereby no municipal liability is created, shall not be considered an indebtedness of such town, village or city, and shall not be included in arriving at such five or eight per centum debt limitation. [*1959 SJR-6; 1961 AJR-1*]

Municipal home rule; debt limit; tax to pay debt. SECTION 3. [*As amended November 1960*] Cities and villages organized pursuant to state law are hereby empowered, to determine their local affairs and government, subject only to this constitution and to such enactments of the legislature of state-wide concern as shall with uniformity affect every city or every village. The method of such determination shall be prescribed by the legislature. No county, city, town, village, school district, or other municipal corporation shall be allowed to become indebted in any manner or for any purpose to any amount, including existing indebtedness, in the aggregate exceeding five per centum on the value of the taxable property therein, to be ascertained, other than for school districts and counties having a population of 500,000 or over, by the last assessment for state and county taxes previous to the incurring of such indebtedness and for school districts and counties having a population of 500,000 or over by the value of such property as equalized for state purposes; except that for any city which is authorized to issue bonds for school purposes the total indebtedness of such city shall not exceed in the aggregate eight per centum of the value of such property as equalized for state purposes; the manner and method of determining such equalization for state purposes to be provided by the legislature. Any county, city, town, village, school district, or other municipal corporation incurring any indebtedness as aforesaid, shall, before or at the time of doing so, provide for the collection of a direct annual tax sufficient to pay the interest on such debt as it falls due, and also to pay and discharge the principal thereof within twenty years from the time of contracting the same; except that when such indebtedness is incurred in the acquisition of lands by cities, or by counties having a population of one hundred fifty thousand or over, for public, municipal purposes, or for the permanent improvement thereof, the city or county incurring the same shall, before or at the time of so doing, provide for the collection of a direct annual tax sufficient to pay the interest on such debt as it falls due, and also to pay and discharge the principal thereof within a period not exceeding fifty years from the time of contracting the same. Providing, that an indebtedness created for the purpose of purchasing, acquiring, leasing, constructing, extending, adding to, improving, conducting, controlling, operating or managing a public utility of a town, village or city, and secured solely by the property or income of such public utility, and whereby no municipal liability is created, shall not be considered an indebtedness of such town, village or city, and shall not be included in arriving at such five or eight per centum debt limitation. [*1957 SJR-47; 1959 SJR-53*]

Municipal home rule; debt limit; tax to pay debt.
SECTION 3. [*As amended April 1955*] Cities and villages organized pursuant to state law are hereby empowered, to determine their local affairs and government, subject only to this constitution and to such enactments of the legislature of state-wide concern as shall with uniformity affect every city or every village. The method of such determination shall be prescribed by the legislature. No county, city, town, village, school district, or other municipal corporation shall be allowed to become indebted in any manner or for any purpose to any amount, including existing indebtedness, in the aggregate exceeding five per centum on the value of the taxable property therein, to be ascertained, other than for school district, by the last assessment for state and county taxes previous to the incurring of such indebtedness and for school districts by the value of such property as equalized for state purposes; except that for any city which is authorized to issue bonds for school purposes the total indebtedness of such city shall not exceed in the aggregate eight per centum of the value of such property as equalized for state purposes; the manner and method of determining such equalization for state purposes to be provided by the legislature. Any county, city, town, village, school district, or other municipal corporation incurring any indebtedness as aforesaid, shall, before or at the time of doing so, provide for the collection of a direct annual tax sufficient to pay the interest on such debt as it falls due, and also to pay and discharge the principal thereof within twenty years from the time of contracting the same; except that when such indebtedness is incurred in the acquisition of lands by cities, or by counties having a population of one hundred fifty thousand or over, for public, municipal purposes, or for the permanent improvement thereof, the city or county incurring the same shall, before or at the time of so doing, provide for the collection of a direct annual tax sufficient to pay the interest on such debt as it falls due, and also to pay and discharge the principal thereof within a period not exceeding fifty years from the time of contracting the same. Providing, that an indebtedness created for the purpose of purchasing, acquiring, leasing, constructing, extending, adding to, improving, conducting, con- trolling, operating or managing a public utility of a town, village or city, and secured solely by the property or income of such public utility, and whereby no municipal liability is created, shall not be considered an indebtedness of such town, village or city, and shall not be included in arriving at such five or eight per centum debt limitation. [*1953 SJR-17; 1955 AJR-18*]

Municipal home rule; debt limit; tax to pay debt.
SECTION 3. [*As amended April 1951*] Cities and villages organized pursuant to state law are hereby empowered, to determine their local affairs and government, subject only to this constitution and to such enactments of the legislature of state-wide concern as shall with uniformity affect every city or every village. The method of such determination shall be prescribed by the legislature. No county, city, town, village, school district, or other municipal corporation shall be allowed to become indebted in any manner or for any purpose to any amount, including existing indebtedness, in the aggregate exceeding 5 per centum on the value of the taxable property therein, to be ascertained by the last assessment for state and county taxes previous to the incurring of such indebtedness; except that for any city which is authorized to issue bonds for school purposes the total indebtedness of such city shall not exceed in the aggregate 8 per centum of the value of such property. Any county, city, town, village, school district, or other municipal corporation incurring any indebtedness as aforesaid, shall, before or at the time of

doing so, provide for the collection of a direct annual tax sufficient to pay the interest on such debt as it falls due, and also to pay and discharge the principal thereof within 20 years from the time of contracting the same; except that when such indebtedness is incurred in the acquisition of lands by cities, or by counties having a population of 150,000 or over, for public, municipal purposes, or for the permanent improvement thereof, the city or county incurring the same shall, before or at the time of so doing, provide for the collection of a direct annual tax sufficient to pay the interest on such debt as it falls due, and also to pay and discharge the principal thereof within a period not exceeding 50 years from the time of contracting the same. Providing, that an indebtedness created for the purpose of purchasing, acquiring, leasing, constructing, extending, adding to, improving, conducting, controlling, operating or managing a public utility of a town, village or city, and secured solely by the property or income of such public utility, and whereby no municipal liability is created, shall not be considered an indebtedness of such town, village or city, and shall not be included in arriving at such 5 or 8 per centum debt limitation. [*1949 SJR-11; 1951 SJR-9*]

Municipal home rule; debt limit; tax to pay debt.
SECTION 3. [*As amended November 1932*] Cities and villages organized pursuant to state law are hereby empowered, to determine their local affairs and government, subject only to this constitution and to such enactments of the legislature of state-wide concern as shall with uniformity affect every city or every village. The method of such determination shall be prescribed by the legislature. No county, city, town, village, school district, or other municipal corporation shall be allowed to become indebted in any manner or for any purpose to any amount, including existing indebtedness, in the aggregate exceeding five per centum on the value of the taxable property therein, to be ascertained by the last assessment for state and county taxes previous to the incurring of such indebtedness. Any county, city, town, village, school district, or other municipal corporation incurring any indebtedness as aforesaid, shall, before or at the time of doing so, provide for the collection of a direct annual tax sufficient to pay the interest on such debt as it falls due, and also to pay and discharge the principal thereof within twenty years from the time of contracting the same; except that when such indebtedness is incurred in the acquisition of lands by cities, or by counties having a population of one hundred fifty thousand or over, for public, municipal purposes, or for the permanent improvement thereof, the city or county incurring the same shall, before or at the time of so doing, provide for the collection of a direct annual tax sufficient to pay the interest on such debt as it falls due, and also to pay and discharge the principal thereof within a period not exceeding fifty years from the time of contracting the same. Providing, that an indebtedness created for the purpose of purchasing, acquiring, leasing, constructing, extending, adding to, improving, conducting, controlling, operating or managing a public utility of a town, village or city, and secured solely by the property or income of such public utility, and whereby no municipal liability is created, shall not be considered an indebtedness of such town, village or city, and shall not be included in arriving at such five per centum debt limitation. [*1929 AJR-61; 1931 AJR-14*]

Municipal home rule; debt limit; tax to pay debt.
SECTION 3. [*As amended November 1924*] Cities and villages organized pursuant to state law are hereby empowered, to determine their local affairs and government, subject only to this constitution and to such enactments of the legislature of state-wide concern as shall with uniformity affect every city or every village. The method of such determination shall be prescribed by the legislature. No county, city, town, village, school district, or other municipal corporation shall be allowed to become indebted in any manner or for any purpose to any amount, including existing indebtedness, in the aggregate exceeding five per centum on the value of the taxable property therein, to be ascertained by the last assessment for state and county taxes previous to the incurring of such indebtedness. Any county, city, town, village, school district, or other municipal corporation incurring any indebtedness as aforesaid, shall, before or at the time of doing so, provide for the collection of a direct annual tax sufficient to pay the interest on such debt

as it falls due, and also to pay and discharge the principal thereof within twenty years from the time of contracting the same; except that when such indebtedness is incurred in the acquisition of lands by cities, or by counties having a population of one hundred fifty thousand or over, for public, municipal purposes, or for the permanent improvement thereof, the city or county incurring the same shall, before or at the time of so doing, provide for the collection of a direct annual tax sufficient to pay the interest on such debt as it falls due, and also to pay and discharge the principal thereof within a period not exceeding fifty years from the time of contracting the same. [*1921 SJR-5; 1923 SJR-18; 1923 c. 203*]

Organization of cities and villages. SECTION 3. [*As amended November 1912*] It shall be the duty of the legislature, and they are hereby empowered to provide for the organization of cities and incorporated villages, and to restrict their power of taxation, assessment, borrowing money, contracting debts, and loaning their credit, so as to prevent abuses in assessments and taxation, and in contracting debts by such municipal corporations. No county, city, town, village, school district, or other municipal corporation shall be allowed to become indebted in any manner or for any purpose to any amount, including existing indebtedness, in the aggregate exceeding five per centum on the value of the taxable property therein, to be ascertained by the last assessment for state and county taxes previous to the incurring of such indebtedness. Any county, city, town, village, school district, or other municipal corporation incurring any indebtedness as aforesaid, shall, before or at the time of doing so, provide for the collection of a direct annual tax sufficient to pay the interest on such debt as it falls due, and also to pay and discharge the principal thereof within twenty years from the time of contracting the same; except that when

such indebtedness is incurred in the acquisition of lands by cities, or by counties having a population of one hundred fifty thousand or over, for public, municipal purposes, or for the permanent improvement thereof, the city or county incurring the same shall, before or at the time of so doing, provide for the collection of a direct annual tax sufficient to pay the interest on such debt as it falls due, and also to pay and discharge the principal thereof within a period not exceeding fifty years from the time of contracting the same. [*1909 SJR-32; 1911 SJR-26; 1911 c. 665*]

Municipal debt limit. [*An amendment approved by the voters in November 1874 added two new paragraphs at the end of the section*] No county, city, town, village, school district, or other municipal corporation shall be allowed to become indebted in any manner or for any purpose to any amount including existing indebtedness, in the aggregate exceeding five per centum on the value of the taxable property therein to be ascertained by the last assessment for state and county taxes previous to the incurring of such indebtedness. Any county, city, town, village, school district or other municipal corporation incurring any indebtedness as aforesaid, shall before or at the time of doing so provide for the collection of a direct annual tax sufficient to pay the interest on said debt as it falls due, and also to pay and discharge the principal thereof within twenty years from the time of contracting the same. [*1872 AJR-17; 1873 SJR-6; 1874 c. 3*]

Organization of cities and villages. SECTION 3. [*Original form*] It shall be the duty of the legislature, and they are hereby empowered, to provide for the organization of cities and incorporated villages, and to restrict their power of taxation, assessment, borrowing money, contracting debts and loaning their credit, so as to prevent abuses in assessments and taxation, and in contracting debts by such municipal corporations.

Acquisition of lands by state and subdivisions; sale of excess. SECTION 3a. [*As amended April 3, 1956*] The state or any of its counties, cities, towns or villages may acquire by gift, dedication, purchase, or condemnation lands for establishing, laying out, widening, enlarging, extending, and maintaining memorial grounds, streets, highways, squares, parkways, boulevards, parks, playgrounds, sites for public buildings, and reservations in and about and along and leading to any or all of the same; and after the establishment, layout, and completion of such improvements, may convey any such real estate thus acquired and not necessary for such improvements, with reservations concerning the future use and occupation of such real estate, so as to protect such public works and improvements, and their environs, and to preserve the view, appearance, light, air, and usefulness of such public works. If the governing body of a county, city, town or village elects to accept a gift or dedication of land made on condition that the land be devoted to a special purpose and the condition subsequently becomes impossible or impracticable, such governing body may by resolution or ordinance enacted by a two-thirds vote of its members elect either to grant the land back to the donor or dedicator or his heirs or accept from the donor or dedicator or his heirs a grant relieving the county, city, town or village of the condition; however, if the donor or dedicator or his heirs are unknown or cannot be found, such resolution or ordinance may provide for the commencement of proceedings in the manner and in the courts as the legislature shall designate for the purpose of relieving the county, city, town or village from the condition of the gift or dedication. [*1953 SJR-29; 1955 SJR-9*]

Acquisition of lands by state and cities; sale of excess. SECTION 3a. [*Created November 1912*] The state or any of its cities may acquire by gift, purchase, or condemnation lands for establishing, laying out, widening, enlarging, extending, and maintaining memorial grounds, streets, squares, parkways, boulevards, parks, playgrounds, sites for public buildings, and reservations in and about and along and leading to any or all of the same; and

after the establishment, layout, and completion of such improvements, may convey any such real estate thus acquired and not necessary for such improvements, with reservations concerning the future use and occupation of such real estate, so as to protect such public works and improvements, and their environs, and to preserve the view, appearance, light, air, and usefulness of such public works. [*1909 SJR-63; 1911 SJR-25; 1911 c. 665*]

General banking law. SECTION 4. [*As amended April 1981*] The legislature may enact a general banking law for the creation of banks, and for the regulation and supervision of the banking business. [*1979 AJR-53; 1981 AJR-13*]

General banking law. SECTION 4. [*Created November 1902. This section was adopted to replace original sections 4 and 5 of this article*] The legislature shall have power to

enact a general banking law for the creation of banks, and for the regulation and supervision of the banking business, provided that the vote of two-thirds of all the members elected to each house, to be taken by yeas and nays, be in favor of the passage of such law. *[P1899 AJR-16; 1901 SJR-25; 1901 c. 73]*

Legislature prohibited from incorporating banks. SECTION 4. *[Original form, repealed November 1902. 1899 AJR-16; 1901 SJR-25; 1901 c. 73]* The legislature shall not have power to create, authorize or incorporate, by any general, or special law, any bank, or banking power or privilege, or any institution or corporation having any banking power or privilege whatever, except as provided in this article.

Referendum on banking laws. SECTION 5. *[Original form, repealed November 1902. 1899 AJR-16; 1901 SJR-*

25; 1901 c. 73] The legislature may submit to the voters, at any general election, the question of "bank," or "no bank," and if at any such election a number of votes equal to a majority of all the votes cast at such election on that subject shall be in favor of banks, then the legislature shall have power to grant bank charters, or to pass a general banking law, with such restrictions and under such regulations as they may deem expedient and proper for the security of the bill holders. Provided, that no such grant or law shall have any force or effect until the same shall have been submitted to a vote of the electors of the state, at some general election, and been approved by a majority of the votes cast on that subject at such election.

ARTICLE XII.
AMENDMENTS

Constitutional amendments. SECTION 1. Any amendment or amendments to this constitution may be proposed in either house of the legislature, and if the same shall be agreed to by a majority of the members elected to each of the two houses, such proposed amendment or amendments shall be entered on their journals, with the yeas and nays taken thereon, and referred to the legislature to be chosen at the next general election, and shall be published for three months previous to the time of holding such election; and if, in the legislature so next chosen, such proposed amendment or amendments shall be agreed to by a majority of all the members elected to each house, then it shall be the duty of the legislature to submit such proposed amendment or amendments to the people in such manner and at such time as the legislature shall prescribe; and if the people shall approve and ratify such amendment or amendments by a majority of the electors voting thereon, such amendment or amendments shall become part of the constitution; provided, that if more than one amendment be submitted, they shall be submitted in such manner that the people may vote for or against such amendments separately.

Constitutional conventions. SECTION 2. If at any time a majority of the senate and assembly shall deem it necessary to call a convention to revise or change this constitution, they shall recommend to the electors to vote for or against a convention at the next election for members of the legislature. And if it shall appear that a majority of the electors voting thereon have voted for a convention, the legislature shall, at its next session, provide for calling such convention.

ARTICLE XIII.
MISCELLANEOUS PROVISIONS

Political year; elections. SECTION 1. *[As amended April 1986]* The political year for this state shall commence on the first Monday of January in each year, and the general election shall be held on the Tuesday next succeeding the first Monday of November in even-numbered years. *[1983 AJR-33; 1985 AJR-3]*

Political year; elections. SECTION 1. *[As amended November 1884]* The political year for the state of Wisconsin shall commence on the first Monday in January in each year, and the general election shall be holden on the Tuesday next succeeding the first Monday in November. The first general election for all state and county officers, except judicial officers, after the adoption of this amendment, shall be holden in the year A.D. 1884, and thereafter the general election shall be held biennially. All state, county or other officers elected at the general

election in the year 1881, and whose term of office would otherwise expire on the first Monday of January in the year 1884, shall hold and continue in such offices respectively until the first Monday in January in the year 1885. *[1881 AJR-16; 1882 SJR-20; 1882 c. 290]*

Political year; general election. SECTION 1. *[Original form]* The political year for the state of Wisconsin shall commence on the first Monday in January in each year, and the general election shall be holden on the Tuesday succeeding the first Monday in November in each year.

SECTION 2. *[Repealed. 1973 SJR-6; 1975 SJR-4; vote April 1975]*

Dueling. SECTION 2. *[Original form]* Any inhabitant of this state who may hereafter be engaged, either directly or indirectly, in a duel, either as principal or accessory, shall forever be disqualified as an elector, and from holding any

office under the constitution and laws of this state, and may be punished in such other manner as shall be prescribed by law.

Eligibility to office. SECTION 3. *[As amended November 1996]* (1) No member of congress and no person holding any office of profit or trust under the United States except postmaster, or under any foreign power, shall be eligible to any office of trust, profit or honor in this state.

(2) No person convicted of a felony, in any court within the United States, no person convicted in federal court of a crime designated, at the time of commission, under federal law

as a misdemeanor involving a violation of public trust and no person convicted, in a court of a state, of a crime designated, at the time of commission, under the law of the state as a misdemeanor involving a violation of public trust shall be eligible to any office of trust, profit or honor in this state unless pardoned of the conviction.

(3) No person may seek to have placed on any ballot for a state or local elective office in this state the name of a person convicted of a felony, in any court within the United States, the name of a person convicted in federal court of a crime designated, at the time of commission, under federal law as a misdemeanor involving a violation of public trust or the name of a person convicted, in a court of a state, of a crime designated, at the time of commission, under the law of the state as a misdemeanor involving a violation of public trust, unless the person named for the ballot has been pardoned of the conviction. [*1993 AJR-3; 1995 AJR-16*]

Eligibility to office. SECTION 3. [*Original form*] No member of congress, nor any person holding any office of profit or trust under the United States (postmasters excepted) or under any foreign power; no person convicted of any infamous crime in any court within the United States; and no person being a defaulter to the United States or to this state, or to any county or town therein, or to any state or territory within the United States, shall be eligible to any office of trust, profit or honor in this state.

Great seal. SECTION 4. It shall be the duty of the legislature to provide a great seal for the state, which shall be kept by the secretary of state, and all official acts of the governor, his approbation of the laws excepted, shall be thereby authenticated.

SECTION 5. [*Repealed. 1983 AJR-33; 1985 SJR-3; vote April 1986*]

Residents on Indian lands, where to vote. SECTION 5. [*Original form*] All persons residing upon Indian lands, within any county of the state, and qualified to exercise the right of suffrage under the constitution, shall be entitled to vote at the polls which may be held nearest their residence, for state, United States or county officers. Provided, that no person shall vote for county officers out of the county in which he resides.

Legislative officers. SECTION 6. The elective officers of the legislature, other than the presiding officers, shall be a chief clerk and a sergeant at arms, to be elected by each house.

Division of counties. SECTION 7. No county with an area of nine hundred square miles or less shall be divided or have any part stricken therefrom, without submitting the question to a vote of the people of the county, nor unless a majority of all the legal voters of the county voting on the question shall vote for the same.

Removal of county seats. SECTION 8. No county seat shall be removed until the point to which it is proposed to be removed shall be fixed by law, and a majority of the voters of the county voting on the question shall have voted in favor of its removal to such point.

Election or appointment of statutory officers. SECTION 9. All county officers whose election or appointment is not provided for by this constitution shall be elected by the electors of the respective counties, or appointed by the boards of supervisors, or other county authorities, as the legislature shall direct. All city, town and village officers whose election or appointment is not provided for by this constitution shall be elected by the electors of such cities, towns and villages, or of some division thereof, or appointed by such authorities thereof as the legislature shall designate for that purpose. All other officers whose election or appointment is not provided for by this constitution, and all officers whose offices may hereafter be created by law, shall be elected by the people or appointed, as the legislature may direct.

Vacancies in office. SECTION 10. [*As amended April 1979*] (1) The legislature may declare the cases in which any office shall be deemed vacant, and also the manner of filling the vacancy, where no provision is made for that purpose in this constitution.

(2) Whenever there is a vacancy in the office of lieutenant governor, the governor shall nominate a successor to serve for the balance of the unexpired term, who shall take office after confirmation by the senate and by the assembly. [*1977 SJR-51; 1979 SJR-1*]

Vacancies in office. SECTION 10. [*Original form*] The legislature may declare the cases in which any office shall be deemed vacant, and also the manner of filling the vacancy, where no provision is made for that purpose in this constitution.

Passes, franks and privileges. SECTION 11. [*As amended November 1936*] No person, association, copartnership, or corporation, shall promise, offer or give, for any purpose, to any political committee, or any member or employe thereof, to any candidate for, or incumbent of any office or position under the constitution or laws, or under any ordinance of any town or municipality, of this state, or to any person at the request or for the advantage of all or any of them, any free pass or frank, or any privilege withheld from any person, for the traveling accommodation or transportation of any person or property, or the transmission of any message or communication.

No political committee, and no member or employe thereof, no candidate for and no incumbent of any office or position under the constitution or laws, or under any ordinance of any town or municipality of this state, shall ask for, or accept, from any person, association, copartnership, or corporation, or use, in any manner, or for any purpose, any free pass or frank, or any privilege withheld from any person, for the traveling accommodation or transportation of any person or property, or the transmission of any message or communication.

Any violation of any of the above provisions shall be bribery and punished as provided by law, and if any officer or any member of the legislature be guilty thereof, his office shall become vacant.

No person within the purview of this act shall be privileged from testifying in relation to anything therein prohibited; and no person having so testified shall be liable to any prosecution or punishment for any offense concerning which he was required to give his testimony or produce any documentary evidence.

Notaries public and regular employes of a railroad or other public utilities who are candidates for or hold public offices for which the annual compensation is not more than three hundred dollars to whom no passes or privileges are extended beyond those which are extended to other regular employes of such corporations are excepted from the provisions of this section. [*1933 AJR-50; 1935 AJR-67*]

Free passes forbidden. Section 11. [*Created November 1902*] No person, association, co-partnership, or corporation, shall promise, offer or give, for any purpose, to any political committee, or any member or employee thereof, to any candidate for, or incumbent of any office or position under the constitution or laws, or under any ordinance of any town or municipality, of this state, or to any person at the request or for the advantage of all or any of them, any free pass or frank, or any privilege withheld from any person, for the traveling accommodation or transportation of any message or communication.

No political committee, and no member or employee thereof, no candidate for and no incumbent of any office or position under the constitution or laws, or under any ordinance of any town or municipality of this state, shall ask for, or accept, from any person, association, co-partnership, or corporation, or use, in any manner, or for any purpose, any free pass or frank, or any privilege withheld from any person, for the traveling accommodation or transportation of any person or property, or the transmission of any message or communication.

Any violation of any of the above provisions shall be bribery and punished as provided by law, and if any officer or any member of the legislature be guilty thereof, his office shall become vacant.

No person within the purview of this act shall be privileged from testifying in relation to anything therein prohibited; and no person having so testified shall be liable to any prosecution or punishment for any offense concerning which he was required to give his testimony or produce any documentary evidence.

The railroad commissioner and his deputy in the discharge of duty are excepted from the provisions of this amendment. [*1899 SJR-12; 1901 AJR-8; 1901 c. 437*]

Recall of elective officers. Section 12. [*As amended April 1981*] The qualified electors of the state, of any congressional, judicial or legislative district or of any county may petition for the recall of any incumbent elective officer after the first year of the term for which the incumbent was elected, by filing a petition with the filing officer with whom the nomination petition to the office in the primary is filed, demanding the recall of the incumbent.

(1) The recall petition shall be signed by electors equaling at least twenty-five percent of the vote cast for the office of governor at the last preceding election, in the state, county or district which the incumbent represents.

(2) The filing officer with whom the recall petition is filed shall call a recall election for the Tuesday of the 6th week after the date of filing the petition or, if that Tuesday is a legal holiday, on the first day after that Tuesday which is not a legal holiday.

(3) The incumbent shall continue to perform the duties of the office until the recall election results are officially declared.

(4) Unless the incumbent declines within 10 days after the filing of the petition, the incumbent shall without filing be deemed to have filed for the recall election. Other candidates may file for the office in the manner provided by law for special elections. For the purpose of conducting elections under this section:

(a) When more than 2 persons compete for a nonpartisan office, a recall primary shall be held. The 2 persons receiving the highest number of votes in the recall primary shall be the 2 candidates in the recall election, except that if any candidate receives a majority of the total number of votes cast in the recall primary, that candidate shall assume the office for the remainder of the term and a recall election shall not be held.

(b) For any partisan office, a recall primary shall be held for each political party which is by law entitled to a separate ballot and from which more than one candidate competes for the party's nomination in the recall election. The person receiving the highest number of votes in the recall primary for each political party shall be that party's candidate in the recall election. Independent candidates and candidates representing political parties not entitled by law to a separate ballot shall be shown on the ballot for the recall election only.

(c) When a recall primary is required, the date specified under sub. (2) shall be the date of the recall primary and the recall election shall be held on the Tuesday of the 4th week after the recall primary or, if that Tuesday is a legal holiday, on the first day after that Tuesday which is not a legal holiday.

(5) The person who receives the highest number of votes in the recall election shall be elected for the remainder of the term.

(6) After one such petition and recall election, no further recall petition shall be filed against the same officer during the term for which he was elected.

(7) This section shall be self-executing and mandatory. Laws may be enacted to facilitate its operation but no law shall be enacted to hamper, restrict or impair the right of recall. [*1979 SJR-5; 1981 SJR-2*]

Recall of elective officers. SECTION 12. [*Created November 1926*] The qualified electors of the state or of any county or of any congressional, judicial or legislative district may petition for the recall of any elective officer after the first year of the term for which he was elected, by filing a petition with the officer with whom the petition for nomination to such office in the primary election is filed, demanding the recall of such officer. Such petition shall be signed by electors equal in number to at least twenty-five per cent of the vote cast for the office of governor at the last preceding election, in the state, county or district from which such officer is to be recalled. The officer with whom such petition is filed shall call a special election to be held not less than forty nor more than forty-five days from the filing of such petition. The officer against whom such petition has been filed shall continue to perform the duties of his office until the result of such special election shall have been officially declared. Other candidates for such office may be nominated in the manner as is provided by law in primary elections. The candidate who shall receive the highest number of votes shall be deemed elected for the remainder of the term. The name of the candidate against whom the recall petition is filed shall go on the ticket unless he resigns within ten days after the filing of the petition. After one such petition and special election, no further recall petition shall be filed against the same officer during the term for which he was elected. This article shall be self-executing and all of its provisions shall be treated as mandatory. Laws may be enacted to facilitate its operation, but no law shall be enacted to hamper, restrict or impair the right of recall. [*1923 SJR-39; 1925 SJR-12; 1925 c. 270*]

Marriage. SECTION 13. [*Created November 2006*] Only a marriage between one man and one woman shall be valid or recognized as a marriage in this state. A legal status identical or substantially similar to that of marriage for unmarried individuals shall not be valid or recognized in this state. [*2003 AJR-66; 2005 SJR-53*]

ARTICLE XIV.
SCHEDULE

Effect of change from territory to state. SECTION 1. That no inconvenience may arise by reason of a change from a territorial to a permanent state government, it is declared that all rights, actions, prosecutions, judgments, claims and contracts, as well of individuals as of bodies corporate, shall continue as if no such change had taken place; and all process which may be issued under the authority of the territory of Wisconsin previous to its admission into the union of the United States shall be as valid as if issued in the name of the state.

Territorial laws continued. SECTION 2. All laws now in force in the territory of Wisconsin which are not repugnant to this constitution shall remain in force until they expire by their own limitation or be altered or repealed by the legislature.

SECTION 3. [*Repealed. 1979 AJR-76; 1981 AJR-35; submit: May'82 Spec.Sess. AJR-1; vote November 1982*]

Territorial fines accrue to state. SECTION 3. [*Original form*] All fines, penalties, or forfeitures accruing to the territory of Wisconsin shall enure to the use of the state.

SECTION 4. [*Repealed. 1979 AJR-76; 1981 AJR-35; submit: May'82 Spec.Sess. AJR-1; vote November 1982*]

Rights of action and prosecution saved. SECTION 4. [*Original form*] All recognizances heretofore taken, or which may be taken before the change from territorial to a permanent state government, shall remain valid, and shall pass to and may be prosecuted in the name of the state; and all bonds executed to the governor of the territory, or to any other officer or court in his or their official capacity, shall pass to the governor or state authority and their successors in office, for the uses therein respectively expressed, and may be sued for and recovered accordingly; and all the estate, or property, real, personal or mixed, and all judgments, bonds, specialties, choses in action and claims or debts of whatsoever description of the territory of Wisconsin, shall enure to and vest in the state of Wisconsin, and may be sued for and recovered in the same manner and to the same extent by the state of Wisconsin as the same could have been by the territory of Wisconsin. All criminal prosecutions and penal actions which may have arisen, or which may arise before the change from a territorial to a state government, and which shall then be pending, shall be prosecuted to judgment and execution in the name of the state. All offenses committed against the laws of the territory of Wisconsin before the change from a territorial to a state government, and which shall not be prosecuted before such change, may be prosecuted in the name and by the authority of the state of Wisconsin with like effect as though such change had not taken place; and all penalties incurred shall remain the same as if this constitution had not been adopted. All actions at law and suits in equity which may be pending in any of the courts of the territory of Wisconsin at the time of the change from a territorial to a state government may be continued and transferred to any court of the state which shall have jurisdiction of the subject matter thereof.

SECTION 5. [*Repealed. 1979 AJR-76; 1981 AJR-35; submit: May '82 Spec.Sess. AJR-1; vote November 1982*]

Existing officers hold over. SECTION 5. [*Original form*] All officers, civil and military, now holding their offices under the authority of the United States or of the territory of Wisconsin shall continue to hold and exercise their respective offices until they shall be superseded by the authority of the state.

SECTION 6. [*Repealed. 1979 AJR-76; 1981 AJR-35; submit: May '82 Spec.Sess. AJR-1; vote November 1982*]

Seat of government. SECTION 6. [*Original form*] The first session of the legislature of the state of Wisconsin shall commence on the first Monday in June next, and shall be held at the village of Madison, which shall be and remain the seat of government until otherwise provided by law.

SECTION 7. [*Repealed. 1979 AJR-76; 1981 AJR-35; submit: May '82 Spec.Sess. AJR-1; vote November 1982*]

Local officers hold over. SECTION 7. [*Original form*] All county, precinct, and township officers shall continue to hold their respective offices, unless removed by the competent authority, until the legislature shall, in conformity with the provisions of this constitution, provide for the holding of elections to fill such offices respectively.

SECTION 8. [*Repealed. 1979 AJR-76; 1981 AJR-35; submit: May '82 Spec.Sess. AJR-1; vote November 1982*]

Copy of constitution for president. SECTION 8. [*Original form*] The president of this convention shall, immediately after its adjournment, cause a fair copy of this constitution, together with a copy of the act of the legislature of this territory, entitled "An act in relation to the formation of a state government in Wisconsin, and to change the time of holding the annual session of the legislature," approved October 27, 1847, providing for the calling of this convention, and also a copy of so much of the last census of this territory as exhibits the number of its inhabitants, to be forwarded to the president of the United States to be laid before the congress of the United States at its present session.

SECTION 9. [*Repealed. 1979 AJR-76; 1981 AJR-35; submit: May '82 Spec.Sess. AJR-1; vote November 1982*]

Ratification of constitution; election of officers. SECTION 9. [*Original form*] This constitution shall be submitted at an election to be held on the second Monday in March next, for ratification or rejection, to all white male persons of the age of twenty-one years or upwards, who shall then be residents of this territory and citizens of the United States, or shall have declared their intention to become such in conformity with the laws of congress on the subject of naturalization; and all persons having such qualifications shall be entitled to vote for or against the adoption of this constitution, and for all officers first elected under it. And if the constitution be ratified by the said electors it shall become the constitution of the state of Wisconsin. On such of the ballots as are for the constitution shall be written or printed the word "yes," and on such as are against the constitution the word "no." The election shall be conducted in the manner now prescribed by law, and the returns made by the clerks of the boards of supervisors or county commissioners (as the case may be) to the governor of the territory at any time before the tenth day of April next. And in the event of the ratification of this constitution by a majority of all the votes given, it shall be the duty of the governor of this territory to make proclamation of the same, and to transmit a digest of the returns to the senate and assembly of the state on the first day of their session. An election shall be held for governor, lieutenant governor, treasurer, attorney-general, members of the state legislature, and members of congress, on the second Monday of May next; and no other for further notice of such election shall be required.

SECTION 10. [*Repealed. 1979 AJR-76; 1981 AJR-35; submit: May '82 Spec.Sess. AJR-1; vote November 1982*]

Congressional apportionment. SECTION 10. [*Original form*] Two members of congress shall also be elected on the second Monday of May next; and until otherwise provided by law, the counties of Milwaukee, Waukesha, Jefferson, Racine, Walworth, Rock and Green, shall constitute the first congressional district, and elect one member; and the counties of Washington, Sheboygan, Manitowoc, Calumet, Brown, Winnebago, Fond du Lac, Marquette, Sauk, Portage, Columbia, Dodge, Dane, Iowa, LaFayette, Grant, Richland, Crawford, Chippewa, St. Croix and La Pointe, shall constitute the second congressional district, and shall elect one member.

SECTION 11. [*Repealed. 1979 AJR-76; 1981 AJR-35; submit: May '82 Spec.Sess. AJR-1; vote November 1982*]

First elections. Section 11. [*Original form*] The several elections provided for in this article shall be conducted according to the existing laws of the territory; provided, that no elector shall be entitled to vote except in the town, ward or precinct where he resides. The returns of election for senators and members of assembly shall be transmitted to the clerk of the board of supervisors or county commissioners, as the case may be; and the votes shall be canvassed and certificates of election issued as now provided by law. In the first senatorial district the returns of the election for senator shall be made to the proper officer in the county of Brown; in the second senatorial district to the proper officer in the county of Columbia; in the third senatorial district to the proper officer in the county of Crawford; in the fourth senatorial district to the proper officer in the county of Fond du Lac; and in the fifth senatorial district to the proper officer in the county of Iowa. The returns of election for state officers and members of congress shall be certified and transmitted to the speaker of the assembly, at the seat of government, in the same manner as the vote for delegate to congress are required to be certified and returned by the laws of the territory of Wisconsin, to the secretary of said territory, and in such time that they may be received on the first Monday in June next; and as soon as the legislature shall be organized the speaker of the assembly and the president of the senate shall, in the presence of both houses, examine the returns and declare who are duly elected to fill the several offices hereinbefore mentioned, and give to each of the persons elected a certificate of his election.

Section 12. [*Repealed. 1979 AJR-76; 1981 AJR-35; submit: May'82 Spec.Sess. AJR-1; vote November 1982*]

Legislative apportionment. Section 12. [*Original form*] Until there shall be a new apportionment, the senators and members of the assembly shall be apportioned among the several districts, as hereinafter mentioned, and each district shall be entitled to elect one senator or member of the assembly, as the case may be. [*Enumeration of districts omitted as obsolete: see R.S. 1849 pp. 40-43; R.S. 1858 pp. 49-53*]

Common law continued in force. Section 13. Such parts of the common law as are now in force in the territory of Wisconsin, not inconsistent with this constitution, shall be and continue part of the law of this state until altered or suspended by the legislature.

Section 14. [*Repealed. 1979 AJR-76; 1981 AJR-35; submit: May'82 Spec.Sess. AJR-1; vote November 1982*]

Officers, when to enter on duties. Section 14. [*Original form*] The senators first elected in the even-numbered senate districts, the governor, lieutenant governor and other state officers first elected under this constitution, shall enter upon the duties of their respective offices on the first Monday of June next, and shall continue in office for one year from the first Monday of January next; the senators first elected in the odd-numbered senate districts, and the members of the assembly first elected, shall enter upon their duties respectively on the first Monday of June next, and shall continue in office until the first Monday in January next.

Section 15. [*Repealed. 1979 AJR-76; 1981 AJR-35; submit: May'82 Spec.Sess. AJR-1; vote November 1982*]

Oath of office. Section 15. [*Original form*] The oath of office may be administered by any judge or justice of the peace until the legislature shall otherwise direct.

Implementing revised structure of judicial branch. Section 16. [*As affected November 1982*] (1), (2), (3) and (5) [*Repealed*]

(4) [*Amended*] The terms of office of justices of the supreme court serving on August 1, 1978, shall expire on the July 31 next preceding the first Monday in January on which such terms would otherwise have expired, but such advancement of the date of term expiration shall not impair any retirement rights vested in any such justice if the term had expired on the first Monday in January. [*1979 AJR-76; 1981 AJR-35; submit: May'82 Spec.Sess. AJR-1*]

Implementing revised structure of judicial branch. Section 16. [*Created April 1977*] (1) The 1975/1977 amendment relating to a revised structure of the judicial branch shall take effect on August 1 of the year following the year of ratification by the voters.

(2) All county courts and the branches thereof in existence on the effective date of this amendment shall, as trial courts of general uniform statewide jurisdiction, continue after such effective date with the same jurisdiction, powers and duties conferred by law upon such courts and the branches and judges thereof until the legislature by law alters or abolishes such county courts and their jurisdiction, powers and duties.

(3) Subject to the jurisdiction established in section 14 of article VII, municipal courts and municipal court judges shall continue after the effective date of this amendment with the same jurisdiction, powers and duties as conferred upon suc h courts and judges as of the effective date until the legislature acts under sections 2 and 14 of article VII to alter or abolish such municipal courts and their jurisdiction, powers and duties.

(4) The terms of office of justices of the supreme court serving on the effective date shall expire on the July 31 next preceding the first Monday in January on which such terms would otherwise have expired, but such advancement of the date of term expiration shall not impair any retirement rights vested in any such justice if the term had expired on the first Monday in January.

(5) Prior to the effective date of this amendment the legislature shall by law establish one or more appeals court districts, provide for the election of appeals judges in such districts, and determine the jurisdiction of the court of appeals under section 21 of article I and section 5 of article VII as affected by this amendment, so that the court of appeals shall become operative on the effective date. [*1975 AJR-11; 1977 SJR-9*]

Note: Attached resolutions and signatures appear at the end of the constitution as printed in the *Revised Statutes* of 1849 and 1858.

HISTORY OF CONSTITUTIONAL AMENDMENTS
April 1, 2008

Art.	Sec.	Subject	First Approval	Second Approval	Submission to People	Date of Election	Vote For	Vote Against	Total Vote for Governor
IV	4	Assemblymen, 2-year terms	Ch.95 / 1853	Ch.89 / 1854	Ch.89 / 1854	Nov. 1854	6,549	11,580	
IV	5	Senators, 4-year terms	"	"	"	"	6,348	11,885	"
IV	11	Biennial legislative sessions	"	"	"	"	6,752	11,589	"
V	5	Governor's salary, changed from $1,250 to $2,500 a year	SJR 35 / JR 4 / 1861	SJR 15 / JR 6 / 1862	Ch.202 / 1862	Nov. 1862	14,519	32,612	142,522
IV	21	*Change legislators' pay to $350 a year	SJR 26 / JR 9 / 1865	SJR 16 / JR 3 / 1866	Ch.25 / 1867	Nov. 1867	58,363	24,418	130,781
V	5	*Change governor's salary from $1,250 to $5,000 a year	AJR 13 / JR 9 / 1868	SJR 6 / JR 2 / 1869	Ch.186 / 1869	Nov. 1869	47,353	41,764	"
V	9	*Change lieutenant governor's salary to $1,000 a year	"	"	Ch.118 / 1870	Nov. 1870	48,894	18,606	146,953[2]
L	8	*Grand jury system modified	AJR 6 / JR 7 / 1869	SJR 3 / JR 3 / 1870	Ch.122 / 1871	Nov. 1871	54,087	3,675	147,274
IV	31,32	*Private and local laws, prohibited on 9 subjects	SJR 14 / JR 13 / 1870	AJR 29 / JR 1 / 1871	Ch.111 / 1872	Nov. 1872	16,272	29,755	"
VII	4	*Supreme court, 1 chief and 4 associate justices	SJR 12 / JR 2 / 1871	AJR 16 / JR 8 / 1872	Ch.37 / 1874	Nov. 1874	66,061	1,509	178,122
XI	3	*Indebtedness of municipalities limited to 5%	AJR 17 / JR 11 / 1872	SJR 6 / JR 4 / 1873	Ch.48 / 1877	Nov. 1877	79,140	16,763	"
VII	4	*Supreme court, 1 chief and 4 associate justices	SJR 16 / JR 10 / 1876	SJR 2 / JR 1 / 1877	Ch.158 / 1877	"	33,046	3,371	171,856
VIII	2	*Claims against state, 6-year limit	SJR 14 / JR 7 / 1876	SJR 5 / JR 4 / 1877	Ch.262 / 1881	Nov. 1881	53,532	13,936	"
IV	4,5,11	*Biennial sessions; assemblymen 2-year, senators 4-year terms	SJR 9 / 1880	AJR 7 / none[3] / 1881					
IV	21	*Change legislators' pay to $500 a year	AJR 26 / none[3] / 1881	SJR 18 / JR 5 / 1882					
III	1	*Voting residence 30 days; in municipalities voter registration	AJR 16 / none[3] / 1881	SJR 20 / JR 3 / 1882					
VI	4	*County officers except judicial, vacancies filled by appointment	AJR 16 / JR 34 / 1885	AJR 2 / JR 4 / 1887	Ch.272 / 1887				
VII	12	*Clerk of court, full term election	SJR 19 / JR 5 / 1887	AJR 3 / JR 3 / 1889	Ch.290 / 1889				
XIII	1	*Political year; biennial elections	SJR 13 / JR 4 / 1889	SJR 13 / JR 4 / 1891	Ch.357 / 1887	Nov. 1882	36,223	5,347	"
X	1	State superintendent, qualifications and pay fixed by legislature	AJR 16 / JR 34 / 1885	AJR 2 / JR 4 / 1887	Ch.22 / 1889	Nov. 1882	60,091	8,089	"
VII	4	*Supreme court, composed of 5 justices of supreme court	SJR 19 / JR 5 / 1887	AJR 3 / JR 3 / 1889	Ch.362 / 1891	Nov. 1888	12,967	18,342	354,714
IV	31	*Cities incorporated by general law	SJR 13 / JR 4 / 1889	SJR 13 / JR 4 / 1891	Ch.177 / 1895	Apr. 1889	125,759	14,712	211,111[4]
X	1	State superintendent, pay fixed by law	AJR 15 / JR 10 / 1893	SJR 7 / JR 2 / 1895	Ch.69 / 1897	Nov. 1892	15,718	9,015	371,559
VIII	7	*Circuit judges, additional in populous counties	SJR 9 / JR 8 / 1895	SJR 10 / JR 9 / 1897	Ch.258 / 1901	Nov. 1896	38,752	56,506	444,110
X	1	*State superintendent, nonpartisan 4-year term, pay fixed by law	SJR 21 / JR 16 / 1899	SJR 24 / JR 3 / 1901	Ch.73 / 1901	Apr. 1897	45,823	41,513	119,572[4]
XI	4	*General banking law authorized	AJR 16 / JR 13 / 1899	SJR 25 / JR 2 / 1901	Ch.437 / 1901	Nov. 1902	71,550	57,411	365,676
XI	5	*Banking law referenda requirement repealed	SJR 12 / 1899	AJR 8 / JR 9	Ch.10	"	64,836	44,620	"
XIII	11	*Free passes prohibited	AJR 33 / 1901	AJR 5 / JR 7	Ch.661	"	67,781	40,697	"
VII	4	*Supreme court, 7 justices, 10-year terms	AJR 16 / 1905	AJR 47 / JR 25	"	"	51,377	39,857	"
III	1	*Suffrage for full citizens only	AJR 45 / 1905	AJR 46 / JR 13	"	Apr. 1903	85,838	36,733	114,468[4]
V	10	*Governor's approval of bills in 6 days	AJR 14 / 1905	SJR 19 / JR 29	Ch.238	Nov. 1908	85,958	27,270	449,656
VIII	1	*Income tax	SJR 14 / 1905	SJR 22 / JR18	Ch.478	"	85,696	37,729	"
VIII	10	*Highways, appropriations for	SJR 18 / 1907	SJR 35 / JR 55	Ch.508	"	116,421	46,739	"
IV	3	*Apportionment after each federal census	AJR 8 / 1907	AJR 33 / JR 7	Ch.514	"	54,932	52,634	"
IV	21	Change legislators' pay to $1,000 a year	SJR 43 / 1907	Ch.514	Ch.508	Nov. 1910	44,153	76,278	319,522
IV	21	Water power and forests, appropriations for[5]	AJR 36 / 1909	AJR 26 / JR 24	Ch.514	"	62,468[5]	45,924[5]	"
VII	10	*Judges' salaries, time of payment	AJR 36 / 1909	AJR 26 / JR 24	Ch.665	Nov. 1912	44,855	34,865	393,849

HISTORY OF CONSTITUTIONAL AMENDMENTS
April 1, 2008–Continued

Art.	Sec.	Subject	First Approval	Second Approval	Submission to People	Date of Election	For	Against	Total Vote for Governor
XI	3	*City or county debt for lands, discharge within 50 years	SJR 32 1909	SJR 26 JR 42 1911	"	"	46,369	34,975	"
XI	3a	*Public parks, playgrounds, etc.	SJR 63 1909	SJR 25 JR 48 1911	"	"	48,424	33,931	"
IV	1	Initiative and referendum	AJR 36 1911	AJR 4 JR 22 1913	1913	Nov. 1914	84,934	148,536	325,430
IV	21	Change legislators' pay to $600 a year, 2 cents a mile for additional round trips	AJR 78 1911	AJR 8 JR 24 1913	"	"	68,907	157,202	"
VII	6,7	Judicial circuits, decreased number, additional judges	AJR 134 1911	AJR 11 JR 26 1913	Ch.770 1913	Nov. 1914	63,311	154,827	325,430
VIII	new	State annuity insurance	SJR 72 1911	AJR 38 JR 35 1913	Ch. 770 1913	"	59,909	170,338	"
VIII	new	State insurance	AJR 119 1911	AJR 9 JR 12 1913	"	"	58,490	165,966	"
XI	new	Home rule of cities and villages	SJR 31 1911	SJR 19 JR 21 1913	"	"	86,020	141,472	"
XI	new	Municipal power of condemnation	AJR 104 1911	AJR 10 JR 25 1913	"	"	61,122	154,945	"
XII	1	Constitutional amendments, submission after 3/5 approval by one legislature	SJR 57 1911	SJR 22 JR 22 1913	"	"	71,734	160,761	"
XII	new	Constitution amended upon petition	AJR 36 1911	AJR 4 JR 22 1913	"	"	68,435	150,215	"
XIII	new	Recall of civil officers	SJR 9 1911	SJR 18 JR 15 1913	"	"	81,628	144,386	"
IV	21	Legislators' pay fixed by law	AJR 16 1917	AJR 13 JR 37 1919	Ch.480 1919	Apr. 1920	126,243	132,258	"
VII	6,7	Judicial circuits, decreased number, additional judges	AJR 74 1917	SJR 100 JR 92 1919	Ch.604 1919	"	113,786	116,436	"
I	5	*Jury verdict, 5/6 in civil cases	AJR 26 1919	AJR 14 JR 17 1921	Ch.504 1921	Nov. 1922	171,433	156,820	481,828
VII	4	Sheriffs, no limit on successive terms	AJR 38 1919	AJR 39 JR 36 1921	Ch.437 1921	"	161,832	207,594	"
XI	new	Municipal indebtedness for public utilities	AJR 22 1919	AJR 16 JR 37 1921	Ch.566 1921	"	105,234	219,639	"
IV	21	Change legislators' pay to $750 a year	AJR 21 1921	SJR 5 JR 18 1923	Ch.241 1923	Apr. 1924	189,635	250,236	344,137[4]
VII	7	*Circuit judges, additional in populous counties	SJR 28 1921	SJR 27 JR 64 1923	Ch.408 1923	Nov. 1924	240,207	226,562	796,432
VIII	10	*Forestry, appropriations for	SJR 24 1921	AJR 70 JR 57 1923	Ch.289 1923	"	336,360	173,563	"
XI	3	*Home rule for cities and villages	SJR 30 1921	SJR 18 JR 34 1923	Ch.203 1923	"	299,792	190,165	"
V	5	*Governor's salary fixed by law	AJR 88 1923	AJR 50 JR 52 1925	Ch.413 1925	Nov. 1926	202,156	188,302	552,912
XIII	12	*Recall of elective officials	SJR 39 1923	SJR 12 JR 16 1925	Ch.270 1925	"	205,868	201,125	"

Note: JR 41 of 1925, which became Joint Rule 16 of the Wisconsin Legislature, established a new procedure to incorporate the "submission to the people" clause into the proposal at second approval.

Art.	Sec.	Subject	First Approval	Second Approval	Date of Election	For	Against	Total Vote for Governor
IV	21	Change legislators' pay to $1,000 for session	AJR 16 JR 33 1925	AJR 2 JR 12 1927	Apr. 1927	151,786	199,260	308,885[4]
VIII	1	*Severance tax: forests, minerals	AJR 51 JR 61 1925	AJR 3 JR 13 1927	"	179,217	141,888	"
IV	21	*Legislators' salary repealed; to be fixed by law	SJR 61 JR 57 1927	SJR 7 JR 6 1929	Apr. 1929	237,250	212,846	397,912[2]
IV	4	*Sheriffs succeeding themselves for 2 terms	AJR 8 JR 24 1927	AJR 8 JR 13 1929	"	259,881	210,964	"
VI	10	*Item veto on appropriation bills	SJR 35 JR 37 1927	SJR 40 JR 43 1929	"	252,655	153,703	"
V	5	*Governor's salary provision repealed; fixed by law	SJR 81 JR 69 1929	SJR 6 JR 52 1931	Nov. 1930	452,605	275,175	606,825
V	9	*Lieutenant governor's salary repealed; fixed by law	SJR 82 JR 70 1929	SJR 7 JR 53 1931	Nov. 1932	427,768	267,120	1,124,502

Art.	Sec.	Subject	First Approval			Second Approval			Date of Election	Vote For	Vote Against	Total Vote for Governor
VII	1	*Wording of section corrected	SJR 103	JR 72	1929	SJR 8	JR 58	1931	"	436,113	221,563	"
XI	3	*Municipal indebtedness for public utilities	AJR 61	JR 74	1929	AJR 14	JR 71	1931	"	401,194	279,631	"
III	1	*Women's suffrage	AJR 52	JR 91	1931	SJR 74	JR 76	1933	Nov. 1934	411,088	166,745	953,797
XIII	11	*Free passes, permitted as specified	AJR 50	JR 63	1933	AJR 67	JR 98	1935	Nov. 1936	365,971	361,799	1,237,095
VIII	1	*Installment payment of real estate taxes	AJR 37	JR 88	1939	AJR 15	JR 18	1941	Apr. 1941	330,971	134,808	547,213[2]
VII	15	*Justice of peace, abolish office in first class cities	SJR 9	JR 27	1943	SJR 6	JR 2	1945	Apr. 1945	160,965	113,408	381,192[4]
VIII	10	*Aeronautical program	SJR 16	JR 37	1943	SJR 7	JR 3	1945	"	187,111	101,169	"
VI	4	*Sheriffs, no limit on successive terms	AJR 6	JR 36	1943	AJR 10	JR 47	1945	Apr. 1946	121,144	170,131	306,354[4]
IV	33	*Auditing of state accounts	SJR 35	JR 60	1943	SJR 24	JR 73	1945	Nov. 1946	480,938	308,072	1,040,444
VI	2	*Auditing (part of same proposal)	SJR 35	JR 60	1943	SJR 24	JR 73	1945	"			"
X	3	Public transportation of school children to any school	SJR 48	JR 73	1943	SJR 19	JR 78	1945	"	437,817	545,475	"
XI	2	Repeal; relating to exercise of eminent domain by municipalities	SJR 30	JR 89	1945	SJR 15	JR 48	1947	Nov. 1948	210,086	807,318	1,266,139
II	2	Prohibition on taxing federal lands repealed	AJR 26	JR 33	1947	SJR 6	JR 2	1949	Apr. 1949	245,412	297,237	633,606[4]
VIII	10	*Allow internal improvement debt for veterans' housing	SJR 2	JR 1	SS'48[6]	SJR 5	JR 7	1949	"	311,576	290,736	"
II	2	*Prohibition on taxing federal lands repealed	AJR 64	JR 11	1949	AJR 7	JR 7	1951	Apr. 1951	305,612	186,284	515,822[4]
XI	3	*City debt limit 8% for combined city and school purposes	SJR 11	JR 12	1949	SJR 9	JR 6	1951	Apr. 1951	313,739	191,897	515,822[4]
IV	3,4,5	Apportionment based on area and population[7]	SJR 50	JR 59	1951	AJR 7	JR 9	1951	Apr. 1953	433,043[3]	406,133	735,860[4]
VII	9	*Judicial elections to full terms	SJR 3	JR 41	1951	SJR 5	JR 5	1953	"	386,972	345,094	"
VII	24	*Judges: qualifications, retirement	SJR 6	JR 46	1953	SJR 10	JR 14	1955	Apr. 1955	380,214	177,929	520,554[4]
XI	3	*School debt limit, equalized value	SJR 17	JR 47	1953	AJR 18	JR 12	1955	"	320,376	228,641	"
IV	26	*Teachers' retirement benefits	SJR 21	JR 41	1953	SJR 8	JR 17	1955	Apr. 1956	365,560	255,284	740,411[4]
VI	4	*Sheriffs, no limit on successive terms	AJR 13	JR 23	1953	AJR 22	JR 53	1955	"	269,722	328,603	"
VI	3a	*Municipal acquisition of land for public purposes	SJR 29	JR 35	1953	SJR 9	JR 36	1955	"	376,692	193,544	"
XIII	11	Free passes, not for public use	AJR 12	JR 61	1953	AJR 47	JR 47	1955	"	188,715	380,207	"
VIII	10	*Port development	AJR 39	JR 58	1957	SJR 20	JR 15	1959	Apr. 1960	472,177	451,045	1,182,160[8]
XI	3	*Debt limit in populous counties, 5% of equalized valuation	SJR 47	JR 59	1957	SJR 53	JR 32	1959	Nov. 1960	686,104	529,467	1,728,009
IV	26	Salary increases during term for various public officers	SJR 21	JR 29	1959	SJR 6	JR 11	1961	Apr. 1961	297,066	307,575	765,807[4]
IV	34	*Continuity of civil government	AJR 48	JR 50	1959	SJR 1	JR 10	1961	"	498,869	132,728	"
VI	4	Sheriffs, no limit on successive terms	AJR 31	JR 48	1959	AJR 7	JR 9	1961	"	283,495	388,238	"
VIII	1	*Personal property classified for tax purposes	AJR 120	JR 77	1959	SJR 34	JR 13	1961	"	381,881	220,434	"
XI	2	*Municipal eminent domain, abolished jury verdict of necessity	AJR 22	JR 47	1959	SJR 8	JR 12	1961	"	348,406	259,566	"
XI	3	*Debt limit 10% of equalized valuation for integrated aid school district	SJR 6	JR 35	1959	AJR 1	JR 8	1961	"	409,963	224,783	"
IV	3	*"Indians not taxed" exclusion removed from apportionment formula	SJR 12	JR 30	1959	SJR 11	JR 32	1961	Nov. 1962	631,296	259,577	1,265,900
IV	23	*County executive: 4-year term	AJR 121	JR 68	1961	AJR 61	JR 64	1961	"	527,075	331,393	"
IV	4	*County executive: 2-year terms							"	524,240	319,378	"
IV	23a	*County executive veto power							"			"
IV	3	Time for apportionment of seats in the state legislature	AJR 162	JR 96	1961	AJR 23	JR 9	1963	Apr. 1963	232,851	277,014	635,510[4]
IV	26	Salary increases during term for justices and judges	SJR 76	JR 68	1961	SJR 4	JR 7	1963	"	216,205	335,774	"
XI	3	*Equalized value debt limit	AJR 92	JR 71	1961	AJR 19	JR 8	1963	"	285,296	231,702	"
VIII	10	Maximum state appropriation for forestry increased	AJR 133	JR 90	1961	AJR 73	JR 32	1963	Apr. 1964	440,978	536,724	1,046,801[4]
XI	3	Property valuation for debt limit adjusted	AJR 134	JR 91	1961	AJR 74	JR 33	1963	"	336,994	572,276	"

HISTORY OF CONSTITUTIONAL AMENDMENTS
April 1, 2008 – Continued

Art.	Sec.	Subject	First Approval (bill)	First Approval (enr. JR)	First Approval (year)	Second Approval (bill)	Second Approval (enr. JR)	Second Approval (year)	Date of Election	For	Against	Total Vote for Governor
XII	1	Constitutional amendments, submission of related items in a single proposition	SJR 15	JR 30	1961	SJR 1	JR 1	SS'63[6]	"	317,676	582,045	"
VI	4	*Coroner and surveyor abolished in counties of 500,000	AJR 14	JR 30	1963	SJR 17	JR 5	1965	Apr. 1965	380,059	215,169	738,831[4]
IV	24	*Lotteries, definition revised	SJR 42	JR 35	1963	SJR 13	JR 13	1965	"	454,390	194,327	"
IV	13	*Legislators on active duty in armed forces	SJR 24	JR 34	1963	SJR 15	JR 14	1965	Apr. 1966	362,935	189,641	564,132[4]
VII	2	*Establishment of inferior courts	SJR 32	JR 48	1963	SJR 26	JR 50	1965	"	321,434	216,341	"
VII	15	*Justices of the peace abolished	"	"	"	"	"	"	"	"	"	"
XI	3	*Special district public utility debt limit	SJR 59	JR 44	1963	SJR 11	JR 51	1965	"	307,502	199,919	"
						AJR 10	JR 58	1965				
I	23	*Transportation of children to private schools	AJR 70	JR 46	1965	AJR 7	JR 13	1967	Apr. 1967	494,236	377,107	856,650[4]
IV	26	*Judicial salary increased during term	AJR 162	JR 96	1965	AJR 17	JR 17	1967	"	489,989	328,292	"
V	1m,1n	*4-year term for governor and lieutenant governor	AJR 4	JR 80	1965	SJR 12	JR 10	1967	"	534,368	310,478	"
V	3	*Joint election of governor and lieutenant governor	AJR 3	JR 45	1965	SJR 11	JR 11	1967	"	507,339	312,267	"
						AJR 8	JR 14	1967				
VI	1m	*4-year term for secretary of state	AJR 4	JR 80	1965	SJR 12	JR 10	1967	"	520,326	311,974	"
VI	1n	*4-year term for state treasurer	AJR 4	JR 80	1965	SJR 12	JR 10	1967	"	514,280	314,873	"
VI	1p	*4-year term for attorney general	AJR 4	JR 80	1965	SJR 12	JR 10	1967	"	515,962	311,603	"
VI	4	*Sheriffs, no limit on successive terms	AJR 72	JR 61	1965	SJR 7	JR 12	1967	"	508,242	324,544	856,650[4]
IV	11	*Legislative sessions, more than one permitted in biennium	AJR 5	JR 57	1965	AJR 15	JR 48	1967	Apr. 1968	670,757	267,997	884,996[4]
VII	24	*Uniform retirement date for justices and circuit judges	SJR 36	JR 101	1965	SJR 96	JR 56	1967	"	734,046	215,455	"
VII	24	*Temporary appointment of justices and circuit judges	SJR 36	JR 101	1965	SJR 96	JR 56	1967	"	678,249	245,807	"
VIII	10	*Forestry appropriation from sources other than property tax	SJR 28	JR 43	1965	SJR 18	JR 25	1967	"	652,705	286,512	"
IV	23	*Uniform county government modified	AJR 18	JR 49	1967	SJR 8	JR 2	1969	Apr. 1969	326,445	321,851	706,324[2]
IV	23a	*County executive to have veto power	"	"	"	"	"	"	"	"	"	"
VII	7	*State public debt for specified purposes allowed	AJR 1	JR 58	1967	AJR 1	JR 3	1969	Apr. 1972	411,062	258,366	"
I	24	*Private use of school buildings	AJR 74	JR 38	1969	AJR 10	JR 27	1971	"	871,707	298,016	"
IV	23	*County government systems authorized	SJR 58	JR 32	1969	SJR 4	JR 13	1971	"	571,285	515,255	"
VI	4	*Coroner/medical examiner option	SJR 63	JR 33	1969	SJR 38	JR 21	1971	"	795,497	323,930	"
X	3	*Released time for religious instruction	AJR 41	JR 37	1969	AJR 17	JR 28	1971	Apr. 1973	595,075	585,511	1,008,553[2]
I	25	Equality of the sexes	AJR 140	JR 44	1971	AJR 21	JR 5	1973	"	447,240	520,936	"
IV	24	*Charitable bingo authorized	SJR 13	JR 31	1971	AJR 6	JR 3	1973	Apr. 1974	645,544	391,499	758,587[4]
IV	26	*Increased benefits for retired public employes	SJR 3	JR 12	1971	SJR 15	JR 15	1973	"	396,051	315,545	"
VII	13	*Removal of judges by 2/3 vote of legislature for cause	AJR 31	JR 32	1971	AJR 55	JR 25	1973	Apr. 1975	493,496	193,867	699,043[4]
VIII	1	*Taxation of agricultural lands	AJR 1	JR 39	1971	AJR 1	JR 29	1973	"	353,377	340,518	"
VIII	3,7	*Public debt for veterans' housing	AJR 145	JR 38	1973	AJR 1	JR 3	1975	"	385,915	300,232	"
VIII	7,10	Internal improvements for transportation facilities[9]	AJR 133	JR 37	1973	AJR 2	JR 2	1975	"	342,396[9]	341,291[9]	"
XI	3	*Exclusion of certain debt from municipal debt limit	SJR 44	JR 32	1971	SJR 55	JR 133	1973	"	310,434	337,925	"
XIII	2	*Dueling: repeal of disenfranchisement	SJR 6	JR 10	1973	SJR 4	JR 4	1975	"	395,616	282,726	"

Art.	Sec.	Subject	First Approval	Second Approval	Date of Election	Vote For	Vote Against	Total Vote for Governor
XI	3	Municipal indebtedness increased up to 10% of equalized valuation	AJR 58 JR 35 1973	AJR 6 JR 6 1975	Apr. 1976	328,097	715,420	1,168,606[4]
VIII	7(2)(a),10	Internal improvements for transportation facilities[9]	AJR 133 JR 37 1973	AJR 2 JR 2 1975	Nov. 1976[9]	722,658	935,152	1,332,220[8]
IV	24	*Charitable raffle games authorized	AJR 43 JR 19 1975	AJR 10 JR 6 1977	Apr. 1977	483,518	300,473	775,490[4]
VII	2	*Unified court system [also changed I-21; IV-17 and 26; VII-3 to 11, 14, 16 to 23; XIV-16(1) to (4)]	AJR 11 JR 13 1975	SJR 9 JR 7 1977	"	490,437	215,939	"
VII	5	*Court of appeals created [also changed I-21(1); VII-2 and 3(3); XIV-16(5)]	"	"	"	455,350	229,316	"
VII	11,13	*Court system disciplinary proceedings	"	"	"	565,087	151,418	"
VII	24	*Retirement age for justices and judges set by law	"	"	"	506,207	244,170	"
IV	23	Town government uniformity	"	"	"	179,011	383,395	"
V	7,8	*Gubernatorial succession	AJR 22 JR 15 1975	AJR 20 JR 18 1977	Apr. 1978	538,959	187,440	840,166[4]
XIII	10	*Lieutenant governor vacancy	SJR 51 JR 32 1977	SJR 1 JR 3 1979	Apr. 1979	540,186	181,497	"
IV	9	*Senate presiding officer [also changed 5-8]	"	"	"	372,734	327,008	"
V	1	*4-year constitutional officer terms (improved wording) [also changed V-1m and 1n; VI-1, 1m, 1n and 1p]	"	"	"	533,620	164,768	"
I	8	*Right to bail[10]	AJR 9 JR 76 SS*80[10]	AJR 5 JR 8 1981	Apr. 1981	505,092[10]	185,405[10]	"
XI	1,4	*Obsolete corporation and banking provisions	AJR 53 JR 21 1979	AJR 13 JR 9 1981	"	418,997	186,898	"
XI	3	*Indebtedness period for sewage collection or treatment systems	SJR 28 JR 43 1979	SJR 5 JR 7 1981	"	386,792	250,866	"
XIII	12	*Primaries in recall elections	SJR 5 JR 41 1979	SJR 2 JR 6 1981	"	366,635	259,820	"
VI	4	*Counties responsible for acts of sheriff	AJR 99 JR 38 1979	AJR 7 JR 15 1981	Apr. 1982	316,156	219,752	1,580,344
I	1,18	*Gender-neutral wording (also changed X-1 and 2)	AJR 76 JR 36 1979	AJR 35 JR 29 1981	Nov. 1982	771,267	479,053	"
IV	3	*Military personnel treatment in redistricting	"	"	"	834,188	321,331	"
IV	4,5	*Obsolete 1881 amendment reference	AJR 76 JR 36 1979	AJR 35 JR 29 1981	Nov. 1982	919,349	238,884	1,580,340
IV	30	*Elections by legislature	"	"	"	977,438	193,679	"
X	1	*Obsolete reference to election and term of superintendent of public instruction	AJR 76 JR 36 1979	AJR 35 JR 29 1981	Nov. 1982	934,236	215,961	"
X	2	*Obsolete reference to military draft exemption purchase; school fund	"	"	"	887,488	295,693	"
XIV	3	*Obsolete transition from territory to statehood (also changed XIV-4 to 12; XIV-14, 15)	"	"	"	926,875	223,213	"
XIV	16(1)	*Obsolete transitional provisions of 1977 court reorganization [also changed XIV-16(2), (3), (5)]	"	"	"	882,091	237,698	"
XIV	16(4)	*Terms on supreme court effective date provision	AJR 9 JR 40 1983	AJR 9 JR 21 1985	Apr. 1986	960,540	190,366	"
I	1	*Rewording to parallel Declaration of Independence	AJR 33 JR 30 1983	AJR 3 JR 14 1985	"	419,699	65,418	461,118[4]
III	1-6	*Revision of suffrage defined by general law	"	"	"	401,911	83,183	"
XIII	1	*Modernizing constitutional text	"	"	"	404,273	82,512	"
XIII	5	*Obsolete suffrage right on Indian land	"	"	"	381,339	102,090	"
IV	24(5)	*Permitting pari-mutuel on-track betting	AJR 45 JR 36 1985	AJR 2 JR 3 1987	Apr. 1987	580,089	529,729	837,747[4]
IV	24(6)	*Authorizing the creation of a state lottery	SJR 1 JR 35 1985	AJR 3 JR 4 1987	Apr. 1987	739,181	391,942	"
VIII	1	Authorizing income tax credits or refunds for property or sales taxes	AJR 117 JR 74 1987	SJR 9 JR 39 1989	Apr. 1989	405,765	406,863	882,784[4]
V	10	*Redefining the partial veto power of the governor	SJR 71 JR 76 1987	SJR 11 JR 29 1989	Apr. 1990	387,068	252,481	685,878[4]
VIII	10	Providing housing for persons of low or moderate income	AJR 101 JR 55 1989	AJR 7 JR 2 1991	Apr. 1991	295,823	402,921	"
VIII	7(2)(a)1	*Railways and other railroad facilities (also created VIII-10)	SJR76 JR 52 1989	SJR 30 JR 9 1991	Apr. 1991	650,592	457,690	"
IV	26	*Legislative and judiciary compensation, effective date	AJR 47 JR54 1989	AJR 16 JR 13 1991	Apr. 1992	736,832	348,645	"

HISTORY OF CONSTITUTIONAL AMENDMENTS
April 1, 2008 – Continued

Art.	Sec.	Subject	First Approval			Second Approval			Date of Election	Vote For	Against	Total Vote for Governor
VIII		Residential property tax reduction	AJR 81	JR 76	1989	SJR 12	JR 14	1991	Nov. 1992	675,876	1,536,975	2,531,114[8]
I	9m	*Crime victims	SJR 41	JR 17	1991	SJR 3	JR 2	1993	Apr. 1993	861,405	163,087	1,075,386[2]
IV	24	*Gambling, limiting "lottery"; divorce under general law (also amended IV-31,32)	AJR 1	JR 27	SS'92	SJR 2	JR 3	1993	"	623,987	435,180	"
I	3	*Removal of unnecessary references to masculine gender [also amended I-3, 7, 9, 19, 21(2); IV-6, 12, 13, 23a; V-4, 6; VI-2; VII-1, 12; XI-3a; XIII-4, 11, 12(6)]	AJR 121	JR 21	1993	AJR 12	JR 3	1995	Apr. 1995	412,032	498,801	939,676[4]
IV	24(6)(a)	Authorizing sports lottery dedicated to athletic facilities	SJR 49	JR 27	1993	SJR 3	JR 2	1995	Apr. 1995	348,818	618,377	"
VII	10(1)	Removal of restriction on judges holding nonjudicial public office after resignation during the judicial term	AJR 81	JR 20	1993	AJR 15	JR 4	1995	Apr. 1995	390,744	503,239	"
XIII	3	*Eligibility to seek or hold public office if convicted of a felony or a misdemeanor involving violation of a public trust	AJR 3	JR 19	1993	AJR 16	JR 28	1995	Nov. 1996	1,292,934	543,516	2,196,169[8]
I	25	*Guaranteeing the right to keep and bear arms	AJR 53	JR 27	1995	AJR 11	JR 21	1997	Nov. 1998	1,205,873	425,052	1,756,014
VI	4(1)(3) (5)(6)	*4-year term for sheriff; sheriffs permitted to hold nonpartisan office; allowed legislature to provide for election to fill vacancy during term	AJR 37	JR 23	1995	SJR 43	JR 18	1997	Nov. 1998	1,161,942	412,508	"
IV	24(3) (5)(6)	*Distributing state lottery, bingo and pari-mutuel proceeds for property tax	AJR 80	JR 19	1997	AJR 2	JR 2	1999	Apr. 1999	648,903	105,976	758,965[4]
I	(26)	*Right to fish, hunt, trap, and take game	SJR 2	JR 16	2001	AJR 1	JR 8	2003	Apr. 2003	668,459	146,182	800,785[4]
VI	4(1)(3) (4)	*4-year term for county clerks, treasurers, clerks of circuit court, district attorneys, coroners, elected surveyors, and registers of deeds (also amended VII-12)	AJR 10	JR 12	2003	SJR 2	JR 2	2005	Apr. 2005	534,742	177,037	552,790[4]
XIII	13	*Marriage between one man and one woman	AJR 66	JR 29	2003	SJR 53	JR 30	2005	Nov. 2006	1,264,310	862,924	2,161,700
V	10(1)(c)	*Gubernatorial partial veto power	SJR 33	JR 46	2005	SJR 5	JR 26	2007	Apr. 2008	575,582	239,613	830,450[8]

*Ratified.

[1]No election for statewide office. [2]Total vote for State Superintendent. [3]Total vote for Justice of Supreme Court. [4]Ratified but declared invalid by Supreme Court in State ex rel. Owen v. Donald, 160 Wis. 21 (1915). [5]Special session: July 1948, December 1964, June 1980, and August 1992. [6]Ratified but declared invalid by Supreme Court in State ex rel. Thomson v. Zimmerman, 264 Wis. 644 (1953). [7]Total vote for presidential delegate election. [8]Recount resulted in rejection (342,132 to 342,309). However, the Dane County Circuit Court ruled the recount invalid due to election irregularities and required that the referendum be resubmitted to the electorate. Resubmitted November 1976 by the 1975 Wisconsin Legislature through Ch. 224, s.145r, Laws of 1975. [10]As a result of a Dane County Circuit Court injunction, vote totals were certified April 7, 1982, by the Board of State Canvassers.

Sources: Official records of the Government Accountability Board; Laws of Wisconsin, 2007 and previous volumes.

SUMMARY – CHANGING THE WISCONSIN CONSTITUTION

To amend the Wisconsin Constitution, it is necessary for two consecutive Wisconsin Legislatures to adopt an identical amendment (known as "first consideration" and "second consideration") and for a majority of the electorate to ratify the amendment at a subsequent election. See Art. XII, Sec. 1.

Since the adoption of the Wisconsin Constitution in 1848, the electorate has voted 142 out of 192 times to amend a total of 126 sections of the constitution (excluding the same vote for more than one item but including a vote that was later resubmitted by the legislature and two votes declared invalid by the courts). The Wisconsin Legislature adopted 156 acts or joint resolutions to submit these changes to the electorate.

STATEWIDE REFERENDA ELECTIONS OTHER THAN CONSTITUTIONAL AMENDMENTS

Question	Law Submitting	(year)	Date of Election	Vote For	Vote Against
Territorial					
*Formation of a state government[2]	Territorial Laws 1846, page 5 (Jan.31)		Apr. 1846	12,334	2,487
*Ratification of first constitution	Art. XIX, Sec. 9 of 1846 Constitution		Apr. 1847	14,119	20,231
*Extend suffrage to colored persons[1]	Supl. resolution to 1846 Constitution		Apr. 1847	7,664	14,615
*Ratification of second constitution	Art. XIV, Sec. 9 of 1848 Constitution		Mar. 1848	16,799	6,384
State					
*Extend suffrage to colored persons[2]	Ch.137	1849	Nov. 1849	5,265	4,075
*State banks; advisory referendum	Ch.143	1851	Nov. 1851	31,289	9,126
*General banking law	Ch.479	1852	Nov. 1852	32,826	8,711
*Liquor prohibition; advisory referendum	Ch.101	1853	Nov. 1853	27,519	24,109
*Extend suffrage to colored persons	Ch.44	1857	Nov. 1857	28,235	41,345
*Amend general banking law; redemption of bank notes	Ch.98	1857	Nov. 1857	27,267	2,837
*Amend general banking law; circulation of bank notes	Ch.242	1858	Nov. 1858	57,646	2,515
*Amend general banking law; interest rate 7% per year	Ch.203	1861	Nov. 1861	46,269	7,794
*Extend suffrage to colored persons[2]	Ch.414	1862	Nov. 1862	46,588	55,591
*Amend general banking law; taxing shareholders	Ch.102	1865	Nov. 1865	49,714	19,151
*Abolish office of bank comptroller	JR12	1866	Nov. 1866	15,499	1,948
*Incorporation of savings banks and savings societies	Ch.28	1867	Nov. 1868	4,029	3,069
*Women's suffrage upon school matters	Ch.384	1885	Nov. 1886	43,581	38,998
*Revise 1897 banking law; banking department under commission	Ch.211	1897	Nov. 1898	86,872	92,607
*Primary election law	Ch.303	1903	Nov. 1904	130,366	80,102
*Pocket ballots and coupon voting systems	Ch.451	1905	Apr. 1906	45,958	111,139
*Women's suffrage	Ch.522	1911	Nov. 1912	135,545	227,024
*Soldiers' bonus financed by 3-mill property tax and income tax	Ch.227	1919	Sept. 1919	165,762	57,324
*U.S. prohibition act (Volstead Act); memorializing Congress to amend	Ch.667	1919	Nov. 1920	419,309	199,876
*Wisconsin prohibition enforcement act	Ch.556	1919	Nov. 1920	349,443	177,603
*Repeal of Wisconsin prohibition enforcement act; advisory referendum	JR47	1925	Nov. 1926	350,337	196,402
*Modification of Wisconsin prohibition enforcement act; advisory referendum	SJR42	1929	Apr. 1929	321,688	200,545
County distribution of auto licenses; advisory referendum	SJR14	1931	Apr. 1931	183,716	368,674
*Sunday blue law repeal; advisory referendum	SJR26	1931	Apr. 1931	396,436	271,786
*Old-age pensions; advisory referendum	AJR116	SS'33	Apr. 1934	531,915	154,729
*Teacher tenure law repeal; advisory referendum	AJR42	1939	Apr. 1940	403,782	372,524
Property tax levy for high school aid; 2 mills of assessed valuation	Ch.525	1943	Apr. 1944	131,004	410,315
Daylight saving time; advisory referendum	JR4	1947	Apr. 1947	313,091	379,740
3% retail sales tax for veterans bonus; advisory referendum	JR62	1947	Nov. 1948	258,497	825,990
4-year term for constitutional officers; advisory referendum	JR13	1951	Apr. 1951	210,821	328,613
Apportionment of legislature by area and population; advisory referendum	Ch.728	1951	Nov. 1952	689,615	753,092
*New residents entitled to vote for president and vice president	Ch.76	1953	Nov. 1954	550,056	414,680

STATEWIDE REFERENDA ELECTIONS OTHER THAN CONSTITUTIONAL AMENDMENTS-Continued

Question	Law Submitting		Date of Election	Vote For	Vote Against
Statewide educational television tax-supported; advisory referendum	AJR74	JR66 1953	Nov. 1954	308,385	697,262
*Daylight saving time		Ch.6 1957	Apr. 1957	578,661	480,656
*Ex-residents entitled to vote for president and vice president		Ch.512 1961	Nov. 1962	627,279	229,375
Gasoline tax increase for highway construction; advisory referendum	AJR3	JR3 SS'63	Apr. 1964	150,769	889,364
*New residents entitled to vote after 6 months		Chs.88,89 1965	Nov. 1966	582,389	256,246
State control and funding of vocational education; advisory referendum	AJR12	JR4 1969	Apr. 1969	292,560	409,789
*Recreational lands bonding; advisory referendum	AJR17	JR5 1969	Apr. 1969	361,630	322,882
*Water pollution abatement bonding	"	" "	"	446,763	246,968
*New residents entitled to vote after 10 days		Ch.85 1975	Nov. 1976	1,017,887	660,875
*Presidential voting revised		Ch.394 1977	Nov. 1978	782,181	424,386
*Overseas voting revised		" "	"	658,289	524,029
*Public inland lake protection and rehabilitation districts		Ch.299 1979	Nov. 1980	1,210,452	355,024
*Nuclear weapons moratorium and reduction; advisory referendum	AJR99	JR38 1981	Sept. 1982	641,514	205,018
*Nuclear waste site locating; advisory referendum	AJR5	JR5 1983	Apr. 1983	78,327	628,414
*Gambling casinos on excursion vessels; advisory referendum		WisAct 321 1991	Apr. 1993	465,432	604,289
*Gambling casino restrictions; advisory referendum		" "	"	646,827	416,722
*Video poker and other forms of video gambling allowed; advisory referendum		" "	"	358,045	702,864
*Pari-mutuel on-track betting continuation; advisory referendum		" "	"	548,580	507,403
*State-operated lottery continuation; advisory referendum		" "	"	773,306	287,585
*Extended suffrage in federal elections to adult children of U.S. citizens living abroad	SJR5	WisAct 182 1999	Nov. 2000	1,293,458	792,975
*Death penalty; advisory referendum		JR58 2005	Nov. 2006	1,166,571	934,508

*Ratified.

[1] For text of resolution, see Wisconsin State Historical Society, Constitutional Series, Volume II, *The Convention of 1846*, edited by Milo M. Quaife, p. 755.

[2] In *Gillespie v. Palmer*, 20 Wis. 544 (1866), the Wisconsin Supreme Court ruled that Chapter 137, Laws of 1849, extending suffrage to colored persons, was ratified November 6, 1849.

Sources: Official records of the Government Accountability Board; *Laws of Wisconsin*, 2005 and previous volumes.

SUMMARY – STATEWIDE REFERENDA ELECTIONS

Statewide referendum questions are submitted to the electorate by the Wisconsin Legislature: 1) to ratify a law extending the right of suffrage (as required by the state constitution); 2) to ratify a law that has been passed contingent on voter approval; or 3) to seek voter opinion through an advisory referendum. Since 1848, the Wisconsin Legislature has presented 53 referendum questions to the Wisconsin electorate; 41 were ratified. During territorial times, the territorial legislature sent 4 questions to the electorate. Two of these passed: one to ratify the state constitution and one to allow the formation of a state government.

Framework of Government

4

The framework of Wisconsin government: an overall view of Wisconsin government, a chart of its organization, and a map of state agencies

Hot Galactic Halo

(X-ray: NASA/UMass/D.Wang et al.; Optical: NASA/HST/D.Wang et al.)

LOCATION OF STATE AGENCIES IN MADISON
June 15, 2009

State Agency	Street Address	Map Locator Number
Administration, Department of	101 E. Wilson St.	14
Agriculture, Trade and Consumer Protection, Department of	2811 Agriculture Dr.	—
Attorney General, Office of the	State Capitol, Rm. 114 East	1
Children and Families, Department of	201 E. Washington Ave.	10
Commerce, Department of	201 W. Washington Ave.	17
Corrections, Department of	3099 E. Washington Ave.	—
Educational Approval Board	30 W. Mifflin St., 9th Floor	9
Educational Communications Board	3319 W. Beltline Hwy.	—
Emergency Management, Wisconsin	2400 Wright St.	—
Employee Trust Funds, Department of	801 W. Badger Rd.	—
Financial Institutions, Department of	345 W. Washington Ave.	18
Government Accountability Board	212 E. Washington Ave.	19
Governor, Office of the	State Capitol, Rm. 115 East	1
Health Services, Department of	1 W. Wilson St.	15
Higher Educational Aids Board	131 W. Wilson St., Suite 902	16
Housing and Economic Development Authority	201 W. Washington Ave., Suite 700	17
Insurance, Commissioner of	125 S. Webster St.	12
Investment Board	121 E. Wilson St.	13
Justice, Department of	17 W. Main St.	6
Legislative Audit Bureau	22 E. Mifflin St., Suite 500	2
Legislative Council	1 E. Main St., Suite 401	5
Legislative Fiscal Bureau	1 E. Main St., Suite 301	5
Legislative Reference Bureau	1 E. Main St., Suite 200	5
Legislative Technology Services Bureau	17 W. Main St., Suite 200	6
Lieutenant Governor, Office of the	State Capitol, Rm. 19 East	1
Military Affairs, Department of	2400 Wright St.	—
Natural Resources, Department of	101 S. Webster St.	11
Privacy Protection, Office of	2811 Agriculture Dr.	—
Public Instruction, Department of	125 S. Webster St.	12
Public Service Commission	610 N. Whitney Way	—
Railroads, Office of the Commissioner	610 N. Whitney Way, Rm. 110	—
Regulation and Licensing, Department of	1400 E. Washington Ave., Rm. 112	—
Revenue, Department of	2135 Rimrock Rd.	—
Secretary of State, Office of the	30 W. Mifflin St., 10th Floor.	9
State Courts, Director of	State Capitol, Rm. 16 East	1
State Employment Relations, Office of	101 E. Wilson St., 4th Floor.	14
State Law Library	120 Martin Luther King, Jr. Blvd.	6
State Historical Society Museum	30 N. Carroll St.	8
State Historical Society of Wisconsin	816 State St.	—
State Public Defender, Office of the	315 N. Henry St.	7
State Treasurer, Office of the	1 S. Pinckney St., Suite 360	4
Supreme Court	State Capitol, Rm. 16 East	1
Technical College System	4622 University Ave.	—
Tourism, Department of	201 W. Washington Ave.	17
Transportation, Department of	4802 Sheboygan Ave.	—
University of Wisconsin System	1220 Linden Dr.	—
Veterans Affairs, Department of	30 W. Mifflin St.	9
Wisconsin Homeland Security	2400 Wright St.	—
Wisconsin Veterans Museum	30 W. Mifflin St.	9
Workforce Development, Department of	201 E. Washington Ave.	10

Sources: List of State Agencies, at: http://www.wisconsin.gov/state/core/agency_index.html [June 2009].

CENTRAL MADISON LOCATOR MAP

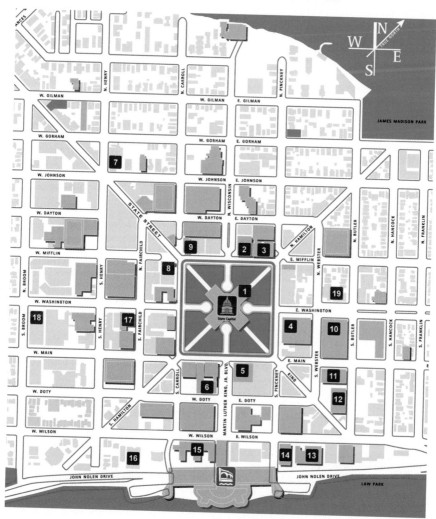

Base map: City of Madison, Planning Division.

THE FRAMEWORK OF WISCONSIN GOVERNMENT

Government at a Glance

Wisconsin state government is divided into three branches: legislative, executive, and judicial. The legislative branch includes the Wisconsin Legislature, which is composed of the senate and the assembly, and the service agencies and staff that assist the legislators. The executive branch, headed by the governor, includes five other elected constitutional officers, as well as 18 departments and 11 independent agencies created by statute. The judicial branch consists of the Wisconsin Supreme Court, the Court of Appeals, circuit courts, and municipal courts, as well as the staff and advisory groups that assist the courts. Each of the three branches is described in detail in its respective section of the *Blue Book.*

Local units of government in Wisconsin include 72 counties, 190 cities, 403 villages, 1,258 towns, and several hundred special districts.

Origins of the 30th State

Wisconsin's original residents were Native American hunters who arrived here about 14,000 years ago. The area's first farmers appear to have been the Hopewell people who raised corn, squash, and pumpkins about 2,000 years ago. They also were hunters and fishers, and their trade routes stretched to the Atlantic Coast and the Gulf of Mexico. Later arrivals included the Chippewa, Ho-Chunk (Winnebago), Mahican/Munsee, Menominee, Oneida, Potawatomi, and Sioux.

From Wilderness to Statehood. The first Europeans to reach Wisconsin were French explorers, fur trappers, and missionaries. Wisconsin was included in the French sphere of influence from the 1630s until the signing of the 1763 Treaty of Paris, which concluded the French and Indian War and ceded the land encompassing Wisconsin to Great Britain. At the end of the Revolutionary War, 20 years later, the British ceded the vast, unsettled territory west of the Appalachian Mountains to the new United States of America. (Actual British control of the area did not end, however, until 1814 at the conclusion of the War of 1812.)

As a U.S. territory, Wisconsin was initially governed by the Northwest Ordinance of 1787, and then sequentially by the laws of the Indiana Territory, the Illinois Territory, the Michigan Territory and, finally in 1836, the Wisconsin Territory.

On August 6, 1846, the Congress of the United States authorized the people living in what was then called the Territory of Wisconsin "to form a constitution and State government, for the purpose of being admitted into the Union". Based on this enabling act, the people of the territory called a constitutional convention in Madison to draft a fundamental law for governing the new state. The first proposal for a constitution was drafted in 1846 and submitted to the people on April 6, 1847, but the voters rejected it on a 20,231-to-14,119 vote because of several controversial provisions involving banking, voting rights, property rights of married women, and homesteading.

On March 13, 1848, a second convention submitted its draft, which was ratified by a vote of 16,799 to 6,384. The constitution then adopted remains in force to this day, although it has been amended on numerous occasions.

On May 29, 1848, Wisconsin became the 30th state admitted to the Union.

State Powers and Prohibitions. The enabling act passed by the U.S. Congress in 1846 declared that the Territory of Wisconsin was authorized to form a constitution and state government "on an equal footing with the original States in all respects whatsoever". From the moment of its birth, like the original states, the State of Wisconsin, its people, its lawmaking bodies, its administrative machinery, and its courts were subject to the U.S. Constitution.

In ratifying the U.S. Constitution, the 13 original states specifically delegated a number of powers to the U.S. Congress. Wisconsin agreed to this delegation when joining the Union. Congress is given the authority to regulate interstate and foreign commerce, maintain armed forces, declare war, coin money, establish a postal system, and grant patents and copyrights. Congress also has power to "make all laws which shall be necessary and proper" for carrying out its responsibilities.

The Tenth Amendment to the U.S. Constitution specifies: "The powers not delegated to the United States by the constitution, nor prohibited by it to the States, are reserved to the States, respectively, or to the people." Although the powers delegated to the federal government and the powers reserved to the states might appear to be neatly delineated, government responsibilities and activities have not been that clear-cut. In fact, many powers are exercised concurrently by the federal government and the states. Through judicial interpretation and laws enacted in response to changing societal needs, the powers exercised by Congress have been greatly expanded to include many activities once considered reserved to the states, as well as new authority not even imagined by the drafters, such as regulation of television and radio or development of a space exploration program. Likewise, the states have broadened their functions as society and technology have evolved.

The Many Sources of State Law

On April 20, 1836, the U.S. Congress passed the Organic Law establishing the Wisconsin Territory, as of July 3, 1836. It prescribed that the existing laws of the Territory of Michigan, to which Wisconsin had belonged, were to be "extended over the said territory . . . subject, nevertheless, to be altered, modified or repealed, by the governor and legislative assembly".

The Wisconsin Constitution continued the laws of the Territory of Wisconsin, by providing in Section 2 of Article XIV: "All laws now in force in the territory of Wisconsin which are not repugnant to this constitution shall remain in force until they expire by their own limitation or be altered or repealed by the legislature."

In addition to the provisions of the U.S. and Wisconsin Constitutions, the citizens of this state are governed by the wide-ranging laws contained in more than 6,400 pages of the Wisconsin Statutes. Even this body of law is not detailed enough. The Wisconsin Legislature has found that some areas are so technically complex that implementation of legislative policy must be left to certain state agencies with the power to issue administrative rules that have the effect of state law.

Notwithstanding the detailed wording of statutory law and administrative rules, there will still be specific provisions that are subject to various interpretations. In these cases, formal law is further defined by courts or administrative commissions authorized to interpret state law.

Making State Government Work

According to the general division of state government powers, the legislative branch enacts the laws; the executive branch carries them out (or *executes* them); and the judicial branch interprets them. This very simple description of state government tells only part of the story. Actually, all three branches play a part in establishing public policy, determining the meaning of the law, and ensuring that the laws are faithfully administered.

When most people think of "the law", they tend to regard it as something restrictive – a rule prohibiting certain actions. Although this may be one outcome, the real reason for the existence of law in a democratic system is to give the greatest benefit to the greatest number of people while protecting the individual rights prescribed by the federal and state constitutions. The only manner in which this can be achieved is by establishing a specific set of rules that attempt to prescribe for all citizens the limits of their rights and obligations.

Developing Public Policy. Policy cannot become law without legislative action. Each member of the legislature may introduce bills proposing new laws, joint resolutions proposing constitutional amendments, or simple and joint resolutions dealing with other matters, and each may offer amendments to proposals introduced by other members.

The governor also plays a major role in the development of formal public policy. The Wisconsin Constitution requires the governor to "communicate to the legislature, at every session, the condition of the state, and recommend such matters . . . for their consideration as he may deem expedient." This is done in the State of the State message, the budget message, and in special messages focusing on particular matters. In cases where a specific problem needs immediate legislative attention, the governor may call the legislature into a special session focusing on the matter. Before a bill becomes law, it must be passed by the legislature and signed by the governor. If the governor vetoes the bill instead of signing it, it can only become law if it is approved a second time by a two-thirds vote in each house of the legislature. In the case of appropriation bills that authorize spending, such as a budget, the governor can use the "partial veto" and veto only parts of the bill rather than the whole proposal. The veto power gives the governor a great deal of control over the content of any new law.

Once a new proposal is enacted, the governor, as the chief executive officer of the state, takes an active part in implementing the policy through oversight of the agencies involved in day-to-day administration of the law. According to the constitution, the governor "shall expedite all such measures as may be resolved upon by the legislature, and shall take care that the laws be faithfully executed."

The judicial branch also has an official role to play in the development of public policy. Although courts are not involved in the enactment of new laws, they do resolve conflicts about existing law – that is, they interpret the law. A court decision may occasionally result in an interpretation of a law that has quite a different effect from what the legislature originally intended. The legislature can redraft and clarify that law if it disagrees with the interpretation.

The opinions and concerns voiced by citizens of Wisconsin constitute the major source of ideas for new legislation. New policy proposals often result from everyday situations citizens encounter in their own communities. If they think that greater property tax relief is needed or that health insurance is unaffordable or that the business climate could be improved, they may determine "there ought to be a law". An individual may decide to write a letter to the editor of a newspaper, contact a legislator, or tell the governor about it. An association to which the person belongs may hire a spokesperson, called a "lobbyist", to recommend legislation or appear at legislative hearings.

State agencies are another primary source of public policy ideas. While administering current programs, departments are in a natural position to see how policies are working and whether they need to be changed, expanded, or abolished. Department heads have opportunities to discuss their insights with the governor, especially during development of the biennial budget, and they may be invited to contribute expert testimony at legislative hearings.

Increasing Services. In 1848, when Wisconsin became a state, government services were relatively simple. In his annual report of 1849, the secretary of state reported payments to only 14 people within the state's executive branch, and that included the constitutional officers. In 2009, full- and part-time state employees totaled 74,491.

This growth is primarily the result of the increasing size and complexity of today's society. At one time, many Wisconsin residents had little opportunity for formal schooling; in 2008, the University of Wisconsin System enrolled 175,056 students and public elementary and secondary enrollments totaled 873,586. In 2007, the Technical College System served 390,272 students. Once, the wooden Watertown Plank Road constituted an unequaled technological advancement over the muddy wagon trails of the day; by 2008, Wisconsin had 114,705 miles of highways and streets, more than 78% of them paved, and 98 publicly owned airports. In 1900, the average U.S. life expectancy at birth was 47.3 years; by 2006, it had reached 77.7 years (75.1 for males and 80.2 for females). As Wisconsin's population increases in numbers and lives longer, the state faces many challenges, including improving education, renovating mature industries, developing the economy, protecting the environment, and improving transportation and health care.

Local Units of Government

In order to carry out its numerous responsibilities, every state has created subordinate units of local government. In most cases, these are legal, rather than constitutional, creations. This means the legislature may abolish them, change them, or give them increased or decreased powers and duties, as it chooses. In Wisconsin, the local units of government consist of counties, cities, villages, towns, and school districts. Special districts may be formed to handle regional concerns. Within the limits of statutory law, each unit has the power to tax and to make legally binding rules governing its own affairs.

Counties. Wisconsin has 72 counties. Together, they cover the entire territory of the state. The government offices for each county are located in a municipality within the county designated as the "county seat". The governing body of the county is the board of supervisors. The number of supervisors may vary from county to county, but within a particular county each supervisor must represent, as nearly as practicable, an equal number of inhabitants. County supervisors are elected in the spring nonpartisan elections for 2-year terms, with the exception of the members of the Milwaukee County Board of Supervisors who serve 4-year terms. Other county officials, all of whom are elected in the fall partisan elections for 4-year terms, include the sheriff, the district attorney, clerk, treasurer, coroner, register of deeds, and clerk of circuit courts. As permitted by law, counties may employ a registered land surveyor in lieu of electing a surveyor, and the majority do. An appointed county medical examiner system may be substituted for an elected coroner. (Milwaukee County must appoint a medical examiner and a registered land surveyor.)

Since January 1, 1987, counties have been required to have a central administrative officer. Counties with a population of 500,000 or more (currently only Milwaukee County) must elect a "county executive", who is chosen for a 4-year term in the spring nonpartisan elections. Counties with a population of less than 500,000 may choose to have a "county administrator" appointed by the county board. If the county has neither an executive nor an administrator, the board must designate an elected or appointed official to serve as "administrative coordinator" for the county. The county board chairperson often is chosen for this post. There are 11 counties with elected executives; 20 have appointed administrators; and 41 have an appointed administrative coordinator.

Cities and Villages. Wisconsin's 190 cities and 403 villages are incorporated under general law. Based on a constitutional amendment ratified in 1924, they have "home rule" powers to determine their local affairs. In general, minimum population for incorporation as a village is 150 residents for an isolated village and 2,500 for a metropolitan village located in a more densely populated area. For cities, the minimums are 1,000 and 5,000, respectively, but an existing village that exceeds 1,000 population may opt for city status. Depending on population, a city qualifies to be in one of four classes. However, an increase or decrease in population does not automatically move a city to a different classification. In order to move from one class to another, a city whose population makes it eligible to be in a different class may initiate the action by making the required changes in governmental structure and by the mayor publishing a proclamation to that effect. For example, Milwaukee currently is the only "first class" city. Although Madison meets the population requirements to change from "second class" to "first class", it has not chosen to do so.

Wisconsin cities currently use two forms of executive organization. The vast majority elect a mayor and a city common council, but 10 operate under a council-manager system, in which the elected council selects the manager to serve as chief executive. In those cities with the mayor-council form of government, 95 have also appointed full- or part-time city administrators. City alderpersons are elected for 2-year terms in the spring nonpartisan elections, except in Milwaukee, where alderpersons serve 4-year terms.

In most villages, executive power is vested in the village president, who presides over the village board of trustees and votes as an *ex officio* trustee, but 10 villages use a village manager form of government with the manager chosen by the elected board. An additional 88 have created full- or part-time village administrators. Village trustees are elected for 2-year terms in the spring nonpartisan elections.

Towns. Town governments govern those areas of Wisconsin that are not included inside the corporate boundaries of either a city or a village. Wisconsin has 1,258 towns, including the entire County of Menominee, which is designated as a town. Towns have only those powers granted by the Wisconsin Statutes. In addition to their traditional responsibility for local road maintenance, town governments carry out a variety of functions and, in some instances, even undertake urban-type services. The town board is usually composed of 3 supervisors, but if a board is authorized to exercise village powers or if the town population is 2,500 or more it may have up to 5 members. (Menominee County has 7 town board members, who also serve as the county board of supervisors.) Town supervisors are elected for 2-year terms in the spring nonpartisan election. They perform a number of administrative functions, and the town board chairperson has certain executive powers and duties. A town board may also create the position of town administrator.

Supervisors are expected to carry out the policies set at the annual town meeting. The annual meeting is held on the second Tuesday of April (or another date set by the electors), and during the meeting all qualified voters of the town are entitled to discuss and vote on matters specified by state law.

School Districts. There are 426 school districts in Wisconsin. These are special units of government organized to carry out a single function, the operation of the public schools. Each district is run by an elected school board, which appoints the district administrators.

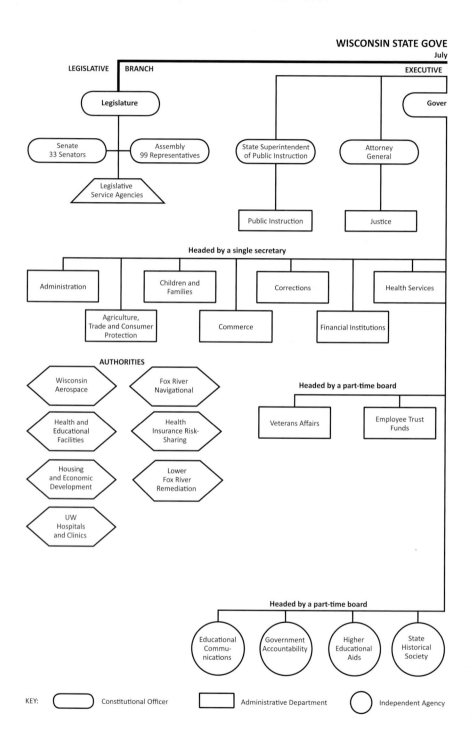

WISCONSIN STATE GOVE
July

LEGISLATIVE BRANCH | EXECUTIVE

Legislature

Senate
33 Senators

Assembly
99 Representatives

Legislative
Service Agencies

State Superintendent
of Public Instruction

Attorney
General

Gover

Public Instruction

Justice

Headed by a single secretary

Administration

Children and
Families

Corrections

Health Services

Agriculture,
Trade and Consumer
Protection

Commerce

Financial Institutions

AUTHORITIES

Wisconsin
Aerospace

Fox River
Navigational

Headed by a part-time board

Health and
Educational
Facilities

Health
Insurance Risk-
Sharing

Veterans Affairs

Employee Trust
Funds

Housing
and Economic
Development

Lower
Fox River
Remediation

UW
Hospitals
and Clinics

Headed by a part-time board

Educational
Commu-
nications

Government
Accountability

Higher
Educational
Aids

State
Historical
Society

KEY: Constitutional Officer   Administrative Department   Independent Agency

RNMENT ORGANIZATION
2009

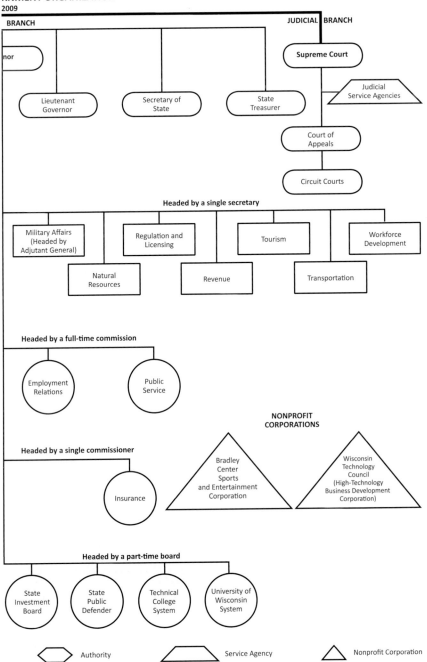

BRANCH

JUDICIAL BRANCH

nor

Supreme Court

Judicial Service Agencies

Lieutenant Governor

Secretary of State

State Treasurer

Court of Appeals

Circuit Courts

Headed by a single secretary

Military Affairs (Headed by Adjutant General)

Regulation and Licensing

Tourism

Workforce Development

Natural Resources

Revenue

Transportation

Headed by a full-time commission

Employment Relations

Public Service

NONPROFIT CORPORATIONS

Headed by a single commissioner

Insurance

Bradley Center Sports and Entertainment Corporation

Wisconsin Technology Council (High-Technology Business Development Corporation)

Headed by a part-time board

State Investment Board

State Public Defender

Technical College System

University of Wisconsin System

Authority

Service Agency

Nonprofit Corporation

Units of state government not shown on the chart are listed on following page.

Units of State Government Not Shown on Organization Chart

The following units of state government are independent entities, which are attached to the agencies indicated for administrative purposes under Section 15.03 of the statutes.

Boards

Board on Aging and Long-Term Care (DOA)

Arts Board (Tourism)

Building Inspector Review Board (Commerce)

Burial Sites Preservation Board (State Historical Society)

Child Abuse and Neglect Prevention Board (DCF)

Claims Board (DOA)

College Savings Program Board (Treasurer)

Crime Victims Rights Board (DOJ)

Depository Selection Board (DOA)

Development Finance Board (Commerce)

Disability Board (Governor)

Educational Approval Board (Technical College System)

Emergency Medical Services Board (DHS)

Environmental Education Board (UW)

Historic Preservation Review Board (State Historical Society)

Incorporation Review Board (DOA)

Information Technology Management Board (DOA)

Interstate Adult Offender Supervision Board (DOC)

State Board for Interstate Juvenile Supervision (DOC)

Investment and Local Impact Fund Board (DOR)

Kickapoo Reserve Management Board (Tourism)

Lake Michigan Commercial Fishing Board (DNR)

Lake Superior Commercial Fishing Board (DNR)

Land and Water Conservation Board (DATCP)

Law Enforcement Standards Board (DOJ)

Livestock Facility Siting Review Board (DATCP)

Lower Wisconsin State Riverway Board (Tourism)

Minority Business Development Board (Commerce)

National and Community Service Board (DOA)

Board for People with Developmental Disabilities (DOA)

Prison Industries Board (DOC)

Public Records Board (DOA)

Rural Economic Development Board (Commerce)

Small Business Regulatory Review Board (Commerce)

State Capitol and Executive Residence Board (DOA)

State Fair Park Board (Tourism)

State Use Board (DOA)

Veterinary Diagnostic Laboratory Board (UW)

Volunteer Fire Fighter and Emergency Medical Technician Service Award Board (DOA)

Waste Facility Siting Board (DOA)

Commissions

Labor and Industry Review Commission (DWD)

Tax Appeals Commission (DOA)

Wisconsin Waterways Commission (DNR)

Councils

Electronic Recording Council (DOA)

Groundwater Coordinating Council (DNR)

Interoperability Council (DOA)

Invasive Species Council (DNR)

Milwaukee Child Welfare Partnership Council (DCF)

Council on Physical Disabilities (DHS)

Council on Recycling (DNR)

Council on Utility Public Benefits (DOA)

Women's Council (DOA)

Divisions

Division of Hearings and Appeals (DOA)

Division of Trust Lands and Investments (DOA)

Offices

Office of Credit Unions (DFI)

Office of Justice Assistance (DOA)

Office of the Commissioner of Railroads (PSC)

Office of State Employment Relations (DOA)

Legislative Branch

5

The legislative branch: profile of the legislative branch, description of the legislative process, summary of 2007-08 legislation, and description of legislative committees and service agencies

Orion Nebula: The Hubble View

(NASA, ESA, M. Robberto (STScI/ESA) et al.)

OFFICERS OF THE 2009 LEGISLATURE

SENATE

President . . . . Senator Fred Risser

President pro tempore . . . . .Senator Pat Kreitlow

Chief clerk . . . . .Honorable Robert J. Marchant

Sergeant at arms . . . . Honorable Edward A. Blazel

Majority Party Officers	**Minority Party Officers**
Leader . . . . Senator Russell S. Decker	Senator Scott L. Fitzgerald
Assistant leader . . . . . Senator Dave Hansen	Senator Glenn Grothman
Caucus chairperson . . . Senator John W. Lehman	Senator Joseph K. Leibham
Caucus vice chairperson . Senator Kathleen Vinehout	Senator Sheila E. Harsdorf
Caucus sergeant at arms . Senator Jim Holperin	None

Chief Clerk: Mailing Address: P.O. Box 7882, Madison 53707-7882; Location: B20 South East, State Capitol; Telephone: (608) 266-2517.

Sergeant at Arms: Mailing Address: P.O. Box 7882, Madison 53707-7882; Location: B35 South, State Capitol; Telephone: (608) 266-1801.

ASSEMBLY

Speaker. . . . . .Representative Michael J. Sheridan

Speaker pro tempore . . . . Representative Anthony J. Staskunas

Chief clerk . . . . Honorable Patrick E. Fuller

Sergeant at arms . . . . Honorable William Nagy

Majority Party Officers	**Minority Party Officers**
Leader . . . . Representative Thomas M. Nelson	Representative Jeff Fitzgerald
Assistant leader . . . . . Representative Donna J. Seidel	Representative Mark Gottlieb
Caucus chairperson . . . Representative Peter W. Barca	Representative Scott Suder
Caucus vice chairperson . Representative Barbara L. Toles	Representative Joel Kleefisch
Caucus secretary . . . . . Representative Ann Hraychuck	Representative Mary Williams
Caucus sergeant at arms . Representative Marlin D. Schneider	Representative Gary Tauchen

Chief Clerk: Mailing Address: P.O. Box 8952, Madison 53708-8952; Location: 17 West Main Street, Suite 401; Telephone: (608) 266-1501.

Sergeant at Arms: Mailing Address: P.O. Box 8952, Madison 53708-8952; Location: 411 West, State Capitol; Telephone: (608) 267-9808.

LEGISLATIVE HOTLINE: Monday-Friday, 8:15 a.m.-4:45 p.m.; Telephone: Madison Area: 266-9960; Outside Madison Area: (800) 362-9472.

LEGISLATIVE INTERNET ADDRESS: http://www.legis.wisconsin.gov

LEGISLATIVE
BRANCH

A PROFILE OF THE LEGISLATIVE BRANCH

The legislative branch consists of the bicameral Wisconsin Legislature, made up of the senate with 33 members and the assembly with 99 members, together with the service agencies created by the legislature and the staff employed by each house. The legislature's main responsibility is to make policy by enacting state laws. Its service agencies assist it by performing fiscal analysis, research, bill drafting, auditing, statute editing, and information technology functions.

A new legislature is sworn into office in January of each odd-numbered year, and it meets in continuous biennial session until its successor is sworn in. The 2009 Legislature is the 99th Wisconsin Legislature. It convened on January 5, 2009, and will continue until January 3, 2011.

U.S. and Wisconsin Constitutions Grant Broad Legislative Powers. The power to determine the state's policies and programs lies primarily in the legislative branch of state government. According to the Wisconsin Constitution: "The legislative power shall be vested in a senate and assembly." This power is quite extensive, but certain limitations are imposed by the U.S. Constitution and the Wisconsin Constitution. In addition, the legislature's power is restricted by the governor's authority to veto legislation, but a veto may be overridden by a two-thirds vote in both houses of the legislature.

All actions taken by the legislature must conform with the U.S. Constitution. For example, the U.S. Congress has exclusive powers to regulate foreign affairs and coin money, and states are denied the power to make treaties with foreign countries. In addition, state legislation may not abridge the rights guaranteed in the U.S. Bill of Rights. Powers that are not granted exclusively to the U.S. Congress or denied the states are considered to be reserved for the individual states.

In addition to the boundaries set by the U.S. Constitution, the legislature's authority is also limited by the state constitution. For instance, the Wisconsin Constitution requires the legislature to establish as uniform a system of town government as practicable, prevents it from enacting private or special laws on certain subjects, and prohibits laws that would infringe on the rights of Wisconsin citizens, as protected by the Declaration of Rights of the Wisconsin Constitution.

Biennial Sessions: 4-Year Senate Terms; 2-Year Assembly Terms. Originally, members of the assembly served for one year, while senators served for 2 years. An 1881 constitutional amendment doubled the respective terms to the current 2 and 4 years and converted the legislature from annual to biennial sessions.

Since its adoption on March 13, 1848, the Wisconsin Constitution has provided that the membership of the assembly shall be not less than 54 nor more than 100, and the membership of the senate shall consist of not more than one-third nor less than one-fourth of the number of assembly members. The first legislature had 85 members – 19 senators and 66 assemblymen. (Assembly members were renamed "representatives to the assembly" in 1969.) The number increased several times until the legislature became a 133-member body in 1862, with the constitutionally permitted maximums of 33 in the senate and 100 in the assembly. Over a century later, membership dropped to 132 in the 1973 Legislature, when the number of representatives was reduced to 99 so that each of the 33 senate districts would encompass 3 assembly districts. This is the current number and structure.

THE WISCONSIN LEGISLATURE

Number of Positions 2009 Legislature: Senate: 33 members, 203 employees; Assembly: 99 members, 317 employees.

Total Budget 2007-09: $142,945,500 (including service agencies).

Constitutional Reference: Article IV.

Statutory Reference: Chapter 13, Subchapter I.

Election of Legislators. All members of the legislature are elected from single-member districts. At the general election on the first Tuesday after the first Monday in November of even-numbered years, the voters of Wisconsin elect all members of the assembly and approximately one-half of the senators. These legislators-elect assume office in January of the following odd-numbered year when they convene to open the new legislative session at the State Capitol, together with the "holdover" senators who still have 2 years remaining of their 4-year terms. When a midterm vacancy occurs in any legislative office, it is filled through a special election called by the governor.

The 33 senators are elected for 4-year terms from districts numbered 1 through 33. The 16 senators representing even-numbered districts are elected in the years in which a presidential election occurs. The 17 senators who represent odd-numbered districts are elected in the years in which a gubernatorial election is held.

Since statehood in 1848, the Wisconsin Constitution has required the legislature, after each U.S. decennial census, to redraw the districts for both houses "according to the number of inhabitants". Thus, Wisconsin was following this practice long before the U.S. Supreme Court decided in 1962 that all states must redistrict according to the "one person, one vote" principle.

Under the campaign finance reporting law enacted by the 1973 Legislature, candidates for the legislature, as well as for other public offices, are required to make full, detailed disclosure of their campaign contributions and expenditures. Candidates must make this disclosure to the Elections Division of the Government Accountability Board. Limits are placed on the amounts of contributions received from individuals and various committees. State law also requires legislators and candidates for legislative office to file a statement of their economic interests with the Ethics and Accountability Division of the Government Accountability Board. A 1977 law authorized candidates for legislative office and statewide executive and judicial offices to receive public campaign funding from state revenues, funded by a $1 check-off on state individual income tax returns.

Political Parties in the Legislative Process. Partisan political organizations play an important role in the Wisconsin legislative process. Since 1949, all legislators, with rare exceptions, have been affiliated with either the Democratic Party or the Republican Party. The strongest representation of other parties was between 1911 and 1937, when there were one or more Socialists in the legislature, and between 1933 and 1947, when the Progressives maintained an independent party. In fact, in 1937 the Progressive Party had a plurality in both houses.

Party organization in the legislature is based on the party group called the "caucus". In each house, all members of a particular political party form that party's caucus. Thus, there are four caucuses related to the party divisions in the two houses. The primary purpose of a caucus is to help party members maintain a unified position on critical issues. Party leaders, however, do not expect to secure party uniformity on every measure under consideration.

Caucus meetings may be held at regular intervals or whenever convened by party leaders, and occasionally the senate and assembly caucuses of the same party meet in joint caucus. A caucus meeting is scheduled shortly after the general election and before the opening of the session to select candidates for the various leadership positions in each house. Although each party caucus nominates a slate of officers, the positions are usually won by the nominees of the majority party when a vote is taken in the full house.

Legislative Officers and Leadership. The Wisconsin Constitution originally required the lieutenant governor to serve as president of the senate. As a result of an April 1979 constitutional amendment, the senate now selects its own president from among its members. When the

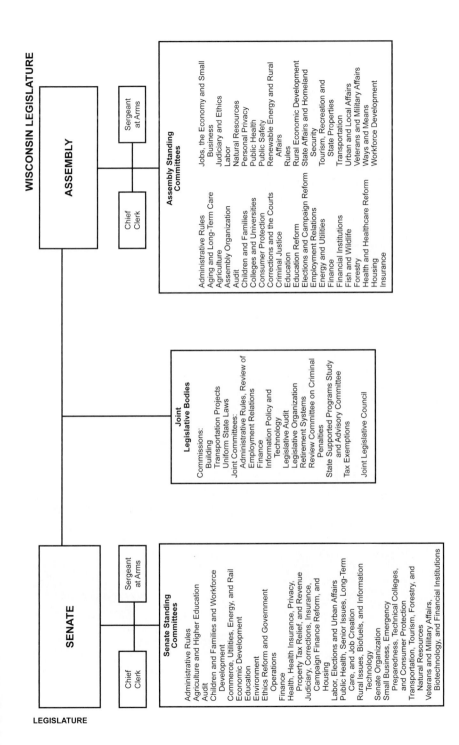

WISCONSIN LEGISLATURE

LEGISLATURE

SENATE

Chief Clerk

Sergeant at Arms

Senate Standing Committees

Administrative Rules
Agriculture and Higher Education
Audit
Children and Families and Workforce Development
Commerce, Utilities, Energy, and Rail
Economic Development
Education
Environment
Ethics Reform and Government Operations
Finance
Health, Health Insurance, Privacy, Property Tax Relief, and Revenue
Judiciary, Corrections, Insurance, Campaign Finance Reform, and Housing
Labor, Elections and Urban Affairs
Public Health, Senior Issues, Long-Term Care, and Job Creation
Rural Issues, Biofuels, and Information Technology
Senate Organization
Small Business, Emergency Preparedness, Technical Colleges, and Consumer Protection
Transportation, Tourism, Forestry, and Natural Resources
Veterans and Military Affairs, Biotechnology, and Financial Institutions

Joint Legislative Bodies

Commissions:
Building
Transportation Projects
Uniform State Laws
Joint Committees:
Administrative Rules, Review of
Employment Relations
Finance
Information Policy and Technology
Legislative Audit
Legislative Organization
Retirement Systems
Review Committee on Criminal Penalties
State Supported Programs Study and Advisory Committee
Tax Exemptions
Joint Legislative Council

ASSEMBLY

Chief Clerk

Sergeant at Arms

Assembly Standing Committees

Administrative Rules
Aging and Long-Term Care
Agriculture
Assembly Organization
Audit
Children and Families
Colleges and Universities
Consumer Protection
Corrections and the Courts
Criminal Justice
Education
Education Reform
Elections and Campaign Reform
Employment Relations
Energy and Utilities
Finance
Financial Institutions
Fish and Wildlife
Forestry
Health and Healthcare Reform
Housing
Insurance
Jobs, the Economy and Small Business
Judiciary and Ethics
Labor
Natural Resources
Personal Privacy
Public Health
Public Safety
Renewable Energy and Rural Affairs
Rules
Rural Economic Development
State Affairs and Homeland Security
Tourism, Recreation and State Properties
Transportation
Urban and Local Affairs
Veterans and Military Affairs
Ways and Means
Workforce Development

Representative Michael Sheridan, Speaker of the Assembly for the 2009 Session, gavels the Assembly to order. The Democratic Party assumed control of that body for the first time since the 1993 Session. (Brent Nicastro, Legislative Photographer)

president of the senate is absent or unable to preside, the president pro tempore, elected from the membership, may preside as substitute president.

The presiding officer of the assembly is the speaker, who is elected by majority vote of the assembly membership. The speaker supervises all other officers of the chamber and appoints committees. When the speaker is absent or unable to preside, the speaker pro tempore, who is also elected from the membership, may substitute.

Each party in each house elects floor leaders, respectively known as the majority leader and assistant majority leader and the minority leader and assistant minority leader. To varying degrees, these party officers play powerful roles in directing and coordinating legislative activities.

Each house has a chief clerk and a sergeant at arms, who are elected by, but are not themselves members of, the legislature. The chief clerk serves as the clerk of the house when it is in session and supervises the preparation of legislative records. In conjunction with the presiding officers, the chief clerks supervise personnel and administrative functions for their respective houses. The sergeants at arms maintain order in and about the chambers and supervise the messengers.

Legislative Compensation. When the 2009 Legislature convened on January 5, 2009, all members were eligible for a salary of $49,943 per year. The process for setting legislative salaries requires the Director of the Office of State Employment Relations to submit proposed changes as part of the state compensation plan to the legislature's Joint Committee on Employment Relations. If the committee approves the plan, the new salary goes into effect for all legislators at the next inauguration. The committee also sets the salaries of the chief clerks and the sergeants at arms of the two houses within a range established under civil service procedures.

Members of the legislature, the chief clerks, and the sergeants at arms are entitled to an allowance not to exceed $88 per day ("per diem") for living expenses for each day spent in Madison on legislative business if they certify by affidavit that they have established temporary residence at the state capital. Those who choose not to establish temporary residence are entitled to half that amount. All members are reimbursed for one weekly round trip from the capital to their homes. They also are reimbursed for expenses incurred while serving as legislative members of a state or interstate agency or when specifically authorized to attend meetings of such agencies as nonmembers. The Speaker of the Assembly also receives a stipend, currently $25 per month.

Legislators receive allowances for their office and mailing expenses while attending legislative sessions. If the legislature is in session three or fewer days in a particular month, legislative leadership may authorize an interim expense allowance to cover postage and clerical assistance ($25 for representatives and $75 for senators).

Legislative Sessions. Members of each new legislature convene in the State Capitol at 2 p.m. on the first Monday in January of each odd-numbered year to take the oath of office, select officers, and organize for business. The initial meeting occurs on January 3 if the first Monday falls on January 1 or 2. The previous legislature usually holds its adjournment meeting on the same day, just prior to the convening of the new legislature. Thus, there is almost no interim between the two.

Originally, the constitution required the legislature to meet once during each annual session. An 1881 amendment restricted the body to one meeting in the two years comprising the biennial session. As a result, the legislature scheduled its meetings in a continuing biennial session with periodic recesses. It would meet in regular session from January through June of the odd-numbered year and then recess after completing the major portion of its work. It then might reconvene from time to time in the remainder of the year, as needed. When a legislature had completed its work for the biennium, it adjourned *sine die,* meaning it did not set a date to reconvene. At that point, the session was over even though only a portion of its two-year term had elapsed, and the legislature could not return unless called into special session by the governor.

In 1968, the state constitution was amended to permit the legislature to determine its own meeting schedule for the biennium. Beginning with the 1971 Legislature, annual sessions were formally initiated by law with the requirement that regular sessions begin in January of each year. Early in each biennium, the Joint Committee on Legislative Organization develops a work schedule for the 2-year period and submits it to the legislature in the form of a joint resolution.

2009-2010 SESSION SCHEDULE

January 5, 2009	2009 Inauguration
January 13, 2009	Floorperiod
January 27 to February 10, 2009	Floorperiod
February 24 to 26, 2009	Floorperiod
March 24 to 26, 2009	Floorperiod
April 9, 2009	Deadline for sending bills to governor
April 21 to 30, 2009	Floorperiod
May 12 to 21, 2009	Floorperiod
June 9 to 30, 2009 (or until passage of budget)	Floorperiod
August 6, 2009	Deadline for sending nonbudget bills to governor
August 6, 2009 (or later)	Deadline for sending budget bill to governor*
September 15 to 24, 2009	Floorperiod
October 20 to November 5, 2009	Floorperiod
December 10, 2009	Deadline for sending bills to governor
January 19 to 28, 2010	Floorperiod
February 16 to March 4, 2010	Floorperiod
March 25, 2010	Deadline for sending bills to governor
April 13 to 22, 2010	Last general-business floorperiod
May 4 to 6, 2010	Limited-business floorperiod
May 13, 2010	Deadline for sending bills to governor
May 25 and 26, 2010	Veto review floorperiod
May 27, 2010, to January 3, 2011	Interim committee work
June 9, 2010	Deadline for sending bills to governor
January 3, 2011	2011 Inauguration

Any floorperiod may be convened earlier or extended beyond its scheduled dates by majority action of the membership or the organization committees of the two houses. The Committee on Senate Organization may schedule sessions outside floorperiods for senate action on gubernatorial nominations, but the assembly does not have to hold skeleton sessions during these appointment reviews. The legislature may call itself into extraordinary session or the governor may call a special session during a floorperiod or on any intervening day.

*Deadline for budget bill will depend on bill's passage.

Source: 2009 Senate Joint Resolution 1.

The 2009-2010 session schedule, for example, is structured around 14 floorperiods, with periods of committee work interspersed throughout the biennium.

Meetings of the respective houses of the legislature are held in the senate and assembly chambers in the State Capitol. Usually, the legislature meets Tuesday through Thursday of each week. Toward the end of many floorperiods, however, the houses may meet continuously during the day Tuesday through Friday and hold evening sessions. Unless otherwise ordered, daily sessions begin at 10 a.m. for the senate and 9 a.m. for the assembly (10 a.m. on the first legislative day of the week). Daily sessions usually extend beyond noon, especially later in the legislative session. If business permits, afternoons may be devoted to committee hearings or a combination of hearings and late afternoon sessions.

As illustrated in the foregoing description, the word "session" has several meanings. The "legislative session" usually refers to the 2-year period that comprises a particular legislature. If the legislature is "not in session", that may mean it is in an interim period between floorperiods. Saying that either the senate or assembly is "not in session", however, may mean that the house has adjourned for the day or that it has recessed until a later hour of the same day.

Extraordinary and Special Sessions. Beginning in 1962, the legislature adopted procedures that would permit it to reassemble through a petition signed by a majority of the members of each house. An amendment to the 1977 Joint Rules codified this procedure by allowing the legislature to call itself into an "extraordinary session". The legislature may convene in extraordinary session or extend a floorperiod at the direction of the majority of the members of the organization committee in each house, by passage of a joint resolution, or by a joint petition signed by the majority of members of each house.

In addition, the governor has the authority to call a "special session", in which the legislature can act only upon matters specifically mentioned in the governor's call. As of the adjournment of the 2007 Legislature, there had been 86 special sessions since Wisconsin became a state in 1848. It is possible for a regular session and a special session to be scheduled at different times during a week or even on the same day. Because special sessions may occur at any time during the legislative biennium, enactments resulting from a special session are now numbered within the regular sequence of biennial laws.

Session Records. Each house of the legislature keeps a record of its actions known as the daily journal. This record differs from the federal *Congressional Record* in that it does not provide a transcript or abbreviated account of speeches made on the floor. It is, instead, an outline record of the business before the house, including procedural actions taken on all measures considered on that particular day, roll call votes, communications received from the governor or the other house, special committee reports, and miscellaneous items.

The *Bulletin of the Proceedings of the Wisconsin Legislature* is issued periodically during the legislative session as needed. Each issue contains a cumulative record of actions taken on bills, joint resolutions, and resolutions by both houses, listed by bill or resolution number. It includes a subject and author index to legislation; a subject index to the legislative journals; a subject index to new laws and enrolled bills and joint resolutions; a numeric listing of statute sections affected by these laws; changes made to statutory court rules by supreme court orders; and the complete text of constitutional amendments ratified since the most recent publication of the *Wisconsin Statutes*. Another part indexes and reports action on administrative rule changes. The final edition of the *Bulletin* at the end of each biennium also includes a directory of lobbying organizations, licensed lobbyists, and legislative liaisons from state agencies.

Each week during the session, the chief clerks jointly issue a *Weekly Schedule of Committee Activities,* listing the business scheduled by the various committees for the coming week, together with the time and place of each hearing and advanced notices on hearings deemed to be of special interest. Each house also issues a daily calendar indicating the business to be taken up on the floor that day.

Complete texts of bills, amendments, and resolutions; bill histories; a subject index to legislation; hearing notices and calendars; and other information on the legislature are available on the Internet at www.legis.state.wi.us. Reference copies of all these legislative documents are available at the Legislative Reference Bureau, and numerous libraries throughout the state also

The legislative session begins with Inauguration Day in January. Senators elected to new terms in 2008 were sworn in on January 5, 2009. (Brent Nicastro, Legislative Photographer)

The Wisconsin Constitution requires the governor to "communicate to the legislature, at every session, the condition of the state, and recommend such matters to them for their consideration as he may deem expedient." Governor Jim Doyle fulfilled that obligation with his State of the State Address on January 28, 2009. (Brent Nicastro, Legislative Photographer)

receive them. Individuals and organizations may subscribe to receive printed versions of legislative documents. (See the table on Legislative Service in this section for fees and details.)

Standing Committees. To a large extent, the legislature does its work in committees. In the 2009 Legislature, the senate has 19 standing committees, the assembly 39, and there are 10 joint standing committees, composed of members from both houses. Joint standing committees are created in the statutes and membership is determined by law. Regular standing committees are created under the rules of their respective houses.

The standing committees in the individual houses consist of legislators only and operate throughout the biennium. Each committee is concerned with one or more broad subject areas related to government functions. It may hold public hearings on measures introduced in the legislature, conduct studies and investigations, and generally review matters within its area of concern. Legislative committees may also appoint subcommittees or study groups.

Senate rules require that each senator serve on at least one standing committee, and the Committee on Senate Organization sets the number of members on each committee. Usually the two major political parties are represented on the committees in proportion to their membership in the senate. The chairperson of the organization committee, who is also the majority leader, makes the appointments to committees. Committee nominations for individual members of the minority party are proposed by that party. An exception to the general method of appointment is the Committee on Senate Organization. It is an *ex officio* committee, consisting of members in leadership positions: the president, the majority and minority leaders, and the assistant leaders.

In the assembly, the speaker determines the number of members of each committee and the division of membership between the majority and minority parties. Under assembly rules, the speaker appoints majority party committee members directly and minority party committee members upon nomination by the assembly minority leader. Customarily, every member serves

NEWS MEDIA CORRESPONDENTS
ACCREDITED TO THE 2009 LEGISLATURE
January 5, 2009

Organization	Correspondents	Telephone
Newspaper and Wire Services		
Appleton Post-Crescent	Ben Jones	255-9256
Associated Press	Scott Bauer, Ryan Foley, Todd Richmond	255-3679
Badger Herald	Alicia Yager	257-4712
Capital Times	Judith Davidoff, Steve Elbow	252-6438/252-6430
Capitol News Service	Stan Milam	(608) 774-8584
Isthmus	Bill Lueders	251-5627
Milwaukee Journal Sentinel	Stacy Forster, Patrick Marley, Steve Walters	258-2262/258-2274
Wheeler News Service	Thom Gerresten	(715) 389-2373
Wheeler Reports	George Coburn, Gwyn Guenther, Dick Wheeler	287-0130
Wisconsin Catholic Newspapers	John Huebscher	257-0004
Wisconsin State Journal	Mark Pitsch, Jason Stein	252-6145/206-0219/ 252-6129
Radio and Television		
WIBA-AM and FM (Madison)	John Colbert	251-1978/274-2995/ (608) 438-6853
WISC-TV (Madison)	Jessica Arp, Colin Benedict	277-5249
WKOW-TV (Madison)	Judy Frankel	273-2727
WMTV-TV (Madison)	Ryan Lobenstein, Zac Schultz	274-1500
WNWC-FM (Madison)	Greg Walters	271-1025
WOLX-FM (Madison)	Adam Elliot	826-0077
WTDY-AM (Madison)	Tara Arnold, Erik Greenfield, Dustin Weis	271-1301
Wisconsin Public Radio	Shawn Johnson, Michael Leland, Shamane Mills	263-4358/263-7985
Wisconsin Public Television	Kathy Bissen, Frederica Freyberg, Art Hackett, Andy Moore	263-2121/263-8496/ 265-6646/263-8585/ 263-5628
Wisconsin Radio Network	Andrew Beckett, Bob Hague, Jackie Johnson, Brian Moon	251-3900
Internet News Service		
Wispolitics.com	Greg Bump, J.R. Ross, Andy Szal	441-8418

Sources: Assembly Sergeant at Arms and information from various news organizations.

THE LEGISLATURE ON THE INTERNET

Legislative Information

The Wisconsin Legislature's Internet home page at **http://www.legis.state.wi.us** provides extensive information regarding the legislature and the legislative process. Follow the links under **Legislative Activity** to access basic information on current legislative activity. **Request text and history of legislative proposals** allows users to access legislative documents by bill or act number. The **Spotlight** link provides a weekly update on recent actions in the legislature. In addition, the legislative **service agencies** have individual home pages where many of their publications are available.

The nxt search engine enables users to search for specific acts, bills, or statutes from 1995 to date. It also offers access to a variety of other legislative documents and indexes, which can also be searched by word. **Searchable Infobases** offers access to nxt on the legislature's Web site.

The legislature's home page links to individual legislator's home pages, which include e-mail addresses, district maps, committee assignments, and biographical information. Some legislators also provide brief audio clips and personally designed pages to communicate with their constituents.

Live Video and Audio – WisconsinEye

WisconsinEye, a private, nonprofit public affairs network, began offering exclusive live video and audio of legislative floor sessions and certain other legislative activities in May 2007. Links to live video and audio, as well as archives of past activity, are available at **http://wisconsineye.org**.

Legislative Notification Service

This service allows citizens to track legislation by creating a profile of items of interest. Profiles may include specific proposals identified by author, committee, or subject matter and may specify activity occurring at various stages of the legislative process. After a profile is filed on the Web site **http://notify.legis.state.wisconsin.gov**, users will receive daily or weekly e-mails of relevant activities.

on at least one committee, although the rules are silent on the distribution of committee assignments. The speaker may appoint himself or herself to one or more standing committees and is a nonvoting member of all others. By rule, the Committee on Assembly Organization is composed of the speaker, the speaker pro tempore, the majority and minority leaders, the assistant leaders, and the caucus chairpersons. The Committee on Rules includes all members of the organization committee plus one majority and one minority party member appointed by the speaker.

Temporary Special Committees. In addition to the standing committees, special committees may be appointed during a legislative session to study specific problems or conduct designated investigations and report to the legislature before the conclusion of the session.

Prior to 1947, the legislature created interim committees to investigate particular subjects. They functioned between legislative sessions and reported their findings and recommendations to the next legislature. Since 1947, almost all interim studies have been referred to the Joint Legislative Council, which coordinates a program of study and investigation after deciding which topics it will consider. The council usually appoints separate committees to study specific matters, and these committees include nonlegislative members.

Employees of the Legislature. Each house of the legislature provides staff services, which are managed by the respective chief clerk and sergeant at arms under the supervision of the Committee on Senate Organization or the speaker of the assembly. Although senate and assembly employees are not part of the classified service, they are paid in accordance with the compensation and classification plan established for employees in the classified service and within pay ranges approved by the Joint Committee on Legislative Organization.

The legislature is assisted by five service agencies responsible for financial and program audits, fiscal information and analysis, bill drafting, research services, statutory revision, legal counsel and policy assistance, and computer and telecommunications services.

The Assembly Rules Committee, comprised of leadership from each party, controls which bills come to the floor of the Assembly. The committee met in the Assembly Parlor in March 2009. (Brent Nicastro, Legislative Photographer)

HOW A BILL BECOMES A LAW

The legislature decides policy by passing bills. A bill must pass both houses of the legislature and be signed by the governor before it becomes law. Other proposals introduced in the legislature also support the body's policy making function. Joint resolutions, which must pass both houses, may propose constitutional amendments, develop a session schedule, or modify the rules that govern both houses. They do not require the governor's signature. Simple resolutions, which are adopted by only one house, may organize the house at the beginning of the session, propose changes to house rules, or ask the attorney general for a legal opinion on a bill.

Introducing a Bill. A bill that proposes to change existing law will usually amend, create, repeal, renumber, renumber and amend, or repeal and recreate one or more sections of the *Wisconsin Statutes*. After the Legislative Reference Bureau (LRB) drafts a bill, it is ready for introduction in one of the legislative houses. Each measure must go through regular procedures and be passed by the house of origin before it can go to the other house, where the process is repeated.

No one but individual legislators or legislative committees may introduce a bill. However, the statutes direct the Joint Committee on Finance to introduce the governor's executive budget bill without change. The legislator who introduces a bill is its "author"; others in the house of origin who support the bill may sign on as "coauthors". The measure may also list "cosponsors" from the second house.

When passing laws, legislators act as the representatives of the people. Therefore, the constitution requires that every bill introduced in the legislature begin with the words: "The people of the state of Wisconsin, represented in senate and assembly, do enact as follows:".

Fiscal Estimates and Bill Analyses. Fiscal estimates put a price tag on legislation. In 1953, Wisconsin pioneered fiscal estimates, often called "fiscal notes", and many other states have copied this important legislative tool. Every measure that increases or decreases state or general local government revenues or expenditures must be accompanied by a reliable estimate of its short-range and long-range fiscal effects. Agencies that would ultimately administer the proposed program or be affected by the measure, should it be enacted, prepare most fiscal notes. In the highly technical area of public retirement systems, the Joint Survey Committee on Retirement Systems prepares fiscal estimates with the assistance of Legislative Council staff. In these cases, the note must evaluate not only the fiscal effect of a proposal but also its legality under state and federal law and its desirability as a matter of public policy.

Since 1967, the LRB has prepared an analysis of each bill introduced in the legislature, explaining in plain language the existing law and how it will change if the bill becomes law. The analysis is printed in the bill immediately following the title. As a general rule, analyses are not updated to reflect amendments approved during the legislative process, so they usually describe only the content of the bill at introduction.

Introduction, First Reading, and Referral to Committee. A bill is introduced when the chief clerk of the author's house assigns it a number and records the introduction for the house journal. Traditionally, the "first reading" took place when the clerk read that part of the proposal's title known as the "relating clause" – the clause that briefly describes the subject matter of the bill, e.g., "relating to the powers and duties of state traffic patrol officers and motor vehicle inspectors" when the house was meeting. In recent times, the clerk usually distributes a report showing the numbers and relating clauses of proposals offered for introduction which takes the place of an actual reading. After first reading, the presiding officer usually refers the proposal to the appropriate standing committee for review. Generally bills that appropriate money, provide for revenue, or relate to taxation are referred to the Joint Committee on Finance before they can be enacted into law.

Committee Hearings. All committee proceedings are open to the general public. Neither assembly nor senate rules require a chairperson to schedule a hearing. If a hearing is held, anyone may speak to the committee to support or oppose a measure or merely to present information to the committee without taking a position. Persons may also register for or against a proposal or submit written comments or petitions without making an oral presentation.

Committees do not keep verbatim transcripts of their hearings, but they do maintain appearance records listing persons who testify or register at the hearing, together with any printed information those parties submit relative to bills and resolutions before the committee. Records for the current legislative session are filed in the office of the committee chairperson. Copies of appearance records for prior sessions, beginning with the 1951 session, are filed in the LRB. Records from 1997 to the present are available on the legislature's Web site.

The chairperson of a committee decides whether or not to take action on a particular proposal. If the decision is to act, the chairperson will call an "executive session" of the committee. In the session, committee members discuss the bill and may ask questions of persons in attendance, but no further public testimony is taken. At the close of the executive session, the committee decides whether to recommend passage of the bill as originally introduced, passage with amendments, or rejection. If the result is a tie vote, the committee can report the bill without recommendation. A committee's decision is contained in a brief report to the house. (Bills that receive a negative recommendation are almost never reported to the floor.)

The following is an example of a committee report to the senate from the *Senate Journal,* May 12, 2009:

The committee on **Health, Health Insurance, Privacy, Property Tax Relief, and Revenue** reports and recommends:

Senate Bill 181

Relating to: prohibiting smoking in indoor areas, in sports arenas, in public conveyances, and at certain outdoor locations and providing a penalty.

Adoption of Senate Substitute Amendment 1:

Ayes, 6 – Senators Erpenbach, Robson, Lassa, Lazich, Kanavas and Darling.

Noes, 1 – Senator Carpenter.

Passage as amended.

Ayes, 5 – Senators Erpenbach, Robson, Lassa, Kanavas and Darling.

Noes, 2 – Senators Carpenter and Lazich.

Jon Erpenbach

Chairperson

Committee chairpersons determine the scheduling of committee hearings. A committee is allowed a reasonable period of time to consider matters referred to it. A majority of the members of the assembly may withdraw a bill not reported by an assembly committee 21 days after the date of referral by motion or petition. In the senate, a majority may vote to withdraw a bill from a committee at any time but not during the 7 days preceding any scheduled committee hearing nor the 7 days following the date on which the hearing was held. In both houses, when an attempt is unsuccessful, all subsequent motions to withdraw the same proposal require at least a two-thirds vote of the members. In practice, bills are very rarely withdrawn from committees without a committee report.

Scheduling Debate. Both the senate and assembly make use of a daily calendar to schedule proposals for consideration. In the 2009 Legislature, all proposals reported by senate standing committees are referred to the Committee on Senate Organization; in the assembly, they are referred to the Committee on Rules. These committees schedule business for floor debate.

Parliamentary Procedure. The rules of parliamentary procedure, which are guides for each house, facilitate the legislative process and are printed in pamphlets, titled "Senate Rules" and "Assembly Rules". Each house may create new rules and amend or repeal its current rules by passage of a simple resolution. "Joint Rules" deal with the relations between the houses and with administrative proceedings common to both. Changes in joint rules require the passage of a joint resolution.

Parliamentary process may seem unduly cumbersome to the onlooker, but it helps the houses operate in an organized fashion. The process is designed to protect the minority in its right to be heard and to promote careful deliberation and orderly consideration of all legislation. For particularly difficult procedural questions, the presiding officer of each house has access to such standard sources as *Mason's Manual of Legislative Procedure, Jefferson's Manual,* and *Rulings of the Chair.*

Second Reading. Once a bill is scheduled for house action, the clerk gives it a second reading by title. The purpose of a second reading is to consider amendments. An amendment may be a "simple" amendment, which makes changes within the bill, or a "substitute amendment", which completely replaces the original bill. Members may offer, debate, and vote upon amendments at any time prior to a vote to "engross" the measure and read it a third time. Engrossment of a bill incorporates all adopted amendments and all approved technical corrections into a proposal in its house of origin. The rules of both houses require a formal delay after the proposal is engrossed, which gives legislators time to reconsider the issues raised by the bill. In many cases, however, the rules are suspended by unanimous consent or a two-thirds vote so that second and third readings can occur on the same legislative day.

Third Reading. The purpose of the third reading is to make a final decision on a proposal itself. After a third reading, the proposal is put to the house for a vote with the following questions: "This bill having been read 3 separate times, the question is, 'Shall the bill pass?'" (for the senate) or "Shall the bill be passed?" (for the assembly). Members can debate the bill's contents at this point, but it is not subject to amendment. When all members finish speaking they vote. A bill may pass on a voice vote, unless a roll call vote is required by the state constitution, by law or legislative rule, or by request of a prescribed number of members.

Majority Leader Russell Decker directs the agenda of the majority party in the Senate. Decker addressed his colleagues on the Senate floor in May 2009. (Jay Salvo, Legislative Photographer)

Action in the Second House. If the bill passes, it is "messaged" (sent) to the other house, where it goes through substantially the same procedure as in the first house. In the second house, however, the bill may be referred directly to the daily calendar without referral to a standing committee. When the second house concurs in the bill, whether with or without additional amendments, the measure is messaged back to the house of origin.

If the second house amends the bill before concurring, the house of origin must vote upon those amendments. If the original house rejects amendments or further amends the bill, the resulting proposal may be sent back to the second house or to a conference committee made up of members representing both houses, where attempts are made to iron out the differences between the 2 versions. The compromise version, drawn up by the conference committee, cannot be amended in either house when it is brought to a vote. When both houses have agreed on identical wording of a bill, the LRB "enrolls" it in its final form, incorporating any amendments and corrections approved by both houses, and the measure is forwarded for the governor's signature.

On average about 1,600 bills were introduced in each of the past 10 legislatures, but only about 20% of those passed. Bills fail for many reasons: the house of origin may vote to "indefinitely postpone" or "table" a bill and then never take it up again; the second house may vote to "nonconcur" or may concur but with amendments unacceptable to the house of origin; or the proposal may "die in committee" and never be reported back to the house. An unsuccessful proposal does not carry over to the following legislature. A member must reintroduce it as a new bill.

Action of the Governor. The governor has 6 days (excluding Sundays) in which to act on the bill by: 1) signing it, in which case it becomes law; 2) vetoing it in whole or, if an appropriation bill, in part; or 3) failing to sign it within 6 days, in which case it becomes law without the governor's signature. Partial veto of words or numbers within a bill is permitted in the case of bills which contain an appropriation. If the governor signs the bill but vetoes part of it, the portion not vetoed becomes law.

Bills are not sent to the office of the governor immediately following passage but are presented when the governor calls for them. The legislative session schedule, however, provides deadlines after each floorperiod when all bills not yet called for must be sent to the governor. It also provides a specific floorperiod for final legislative review of the governor's vetoes.

If the governor vetoes a bill, in whole or part, the vetoed parts must be returned to the house of origin with the governor's written objections. A vetoed bill or part of a bill can become law despite the governor's objections, but it requires a two-thirds vote in each house to override the veto. If either house fails to muster the sufficient number of votes, the governor's veto is sustained, and the vetoed bill or portion dies.

Session Laws. Each new law is numbered as a Wisconsin Act, based on the year of the legislative session and its order of enactment, e.g., 2009 Wisconsin Act 1. The date of enactment is the date the governor approves the act, the date it becomes a law without the governor's signature, or the date the legislature votes to override the governor's veto. The secretary of state assigns the new law a date of publication. On or before that date, copies of the act in pamphlet form, called a "slip law", must be available for public distribution. The secretary of state must publish the act's number, title, and original bill number within 10 working days after the date of enactment in the newspaper designated as the official state paper for publication of legal notices (currently the *Wisconsin State Journal*). The notice contains the date of enactment and date of publication and states the act is available for public distribution. The act takes effect the day after its assigned publication date, unless another effective date is specified in the law itself.

Ultimately, the LRB combines all the laws enacted during the biennium into bound volumes, called the "Laws of Wisconsin". The LRB incorporates any portions of these laws that make changes in the statutes into the edition of the "Wisconsin Statutes" dated for that legislative biennium. Thus, the edition identified as the *2007-2008 Wisconsin Statutes* includes all statutory changes resulting from laws enacted by the 2007 Legislature.

The Budget Bill. The budget bill is the longest and most complex bill of the session. Because Wisconsin's budget covers a 2-year period from July 1 of one odd-numbered year through June 30 of the next, its development involves a chain of events stretching over almost a year. In the fall of every even-numbered year, state agencies must submit funding requests to the Department of Administration. Their funding requests include estimates of the cost of existing services over the next 2 years and may propose changes they hope are made in their programs. The Department of Administration's state budget office then compiles the data for review by the governor or governor-elect. While developing the budget, the governor may hold a hearing on any department's budget request to get additional input.

State law requires the governor to deliver the budget message to the new legislature on or before the last Tuesday in January, although the legislature may extend the deadline at the governor's request. The state budget report and the biennial executive budget bill or bills accompany the message.

In the legislature, the Joint Committee on Finance holds hearings on the departmental requests and governor's program initiatives. When these are completed, it reports the budget bill to the house of the legislature in which it was introduced. The committee's report takes the form of a substitute amendment. The bill then follows the normal legislative procedure through both houses of the legislature and is submitted for the governor's approval. The governor may sign the budget bill, veto it in its entirety (which would be unlikely), or use partial vetoes, as is usually the case. To meet the state's budgetary cycle, the new budget law should be effective by July 1 of the odd-numbered year, but there sometimes is a delay of several days, or even weeks or months, during which state agencies continue to operate at their levels of appropriation from the preceding budget.

Further Reading. The preceding section has provided a brief description of how a bill becomes a law in Wisconsin. In practice, legislative procedure is more complex than explained here. The feature article in the *1993-1994 Wisconsin Blue Book* contains a more detailed description and uses a case study approach to further illustrate the legislative process. It may be accessed via the *Wisconsin Blue Book* link on the Legislative Reference Bureau's Web site: www.legis.state.wi.us/lrb/pubs.

Assembly Minority Leader Jeff Fitzgerald, Horicon, Assistant Minority Leader Mark Gottlieb, Port Washington, and Representative Joel Kleefisch, Oconomowoc, contemplate an address by the speaker just before the final vote on the 2009-2011 budget on June 26, 2009. (Brent Nicastro, Legislative Photographer)

2009-2010 LEGISLATIVE SERVICE

The complete 2009-2010 Legislative Service consists of 6 parts, which may be ordered by subscription from the Document Sales office:

Bills, resolutions, and amendments (complete text of each as introduced).

Acts are the laws enacted in bill form by the legislature and signed by the governor or passed over the governor's veto. The acts are distributed separately as "slip laws".

Journals are a daily record of the business conducted in each house, but they are not verbatim accounts. The service provides preliminary editions of the journals (published on the morning after the legislative day on yellow paper for senate journals and green paper for assembly journals) and the final corrected editions (printed on white paper and distributed two or three weeks later).

The **Bulletin of Proceedings** contains a numerical listing of all bills and other measures introduced in each house of the legislature and a cumulative record of actions taken on each. It includes a subject index to all measures introduced and to all acts, a list of proposals introduced by each legislator, and a numerical listing of statutory sections affected by acts and enrolled bills. It is issued as needed during the biennial session.

The **Weekly Schedule of Committee Activities** lists the time and place of legislative committee hearings for the coming week and advanced notices for hearings on issues of special interest.

Administrative Rules lists the administrative rules submitted by executive branch agencies by clearinghouse rule number. It includes a subject index, a list of agency contacts, and a cumulative record of actions taken on each proposal.

To obtain all or part of the legislative service, contact Document Sales, Wisconsin Department of Administration, 202 S. Thornton Avenue, P.O. Box 7840, Madison 53707-7840 or call (608) 266-3358, TTY (608) 264-8499, or (800) 362-7253 for an order form. Any part may be ordered separately. Prepayment is required on all orders. Faxed orders are accepted at (608) 261-8150 when paying with a credit card. Subscribers receive their documents through the mail. All subscriptions to the 2009-2010 Legislative Service will expire on December 31, 2010.

SERVICE	Interdepartmental Delivery*	United Parcel Service (UPS) and U.S. Postal Service*
Complete service, including daily calendars . . .	$500	$845
Bills, resolutions, and amendments	160	335
Acts (slip laws)	20	85
Journals	55	145
Bulletin of Proceedings	200	350
Weekly Schedule of Committee Activities . . .	15	85
Administrative Rules	65	95

*All sales are subject to the 5% state sales tax, 0.5% county sales tax, and 0.5% or 0.1% stadium tax, where applicable.

Senate President Fred Risser of Madison is the longest-serving state legislator in the United States, with a continuous tenure dating from 1957. (Brent Nicastro, Legislative Photographer)

EXECUTIVE VETOES, 1931 – 2007 SESSIONS

Session	Bills Vetoed in Entirety			Bills Partially Vetoed			Partial Vetoes Contained in Biennial Budget Bills	
	Number Vetoed	Vetoes Sustained	Vetoes Overridden	Number Partially Vetoed	All Partial Vetoes Sustained	One or More Partial Vetoes Overridden	Number of Partial Vetoes[1]	Vetoes Overridden
1931	58	58	—	2	2	—	12	0
1933	15	15	—	1	1	—	12	0
1935	27	27	—	4	4	—	0	0
1937	10	10	—	1	1	—	0	0
1939	22[2]	22	—	4	4	—	1	0
1941	17	17	—	1	1	—	1	0
1943	39	19	20	1	—	1	0	0
1945	30	25	5	2	1	1	1	0
1947	10	9	1	1	1	—	2	0
1949	17	15	2	2	1	1	0	0
1951	18	18	—	2	2	—	0	0
1953	31	28	3	4[3]	4	—	2	0
1955	38	38	—	—	—	—	0	0
1957	35	34	1	3	3	—	2	0
1959	36	32	4	1	1	—	0	0
1961	70	68	2	3	3	—	2	0
1963	72	68	4	1	1	—	0	0
1965	24	23	1	4	4	—	1	0
1967	18	18	—	5	5	—	0	0
1969	34	33	1	11	11	—	27	0
1971	32	29	3	8	8	—	12	0
1973	13	13	—	18	15	3	38	2
1975	37	31	6	22	18	4	42	5
1977	21	17	4	16	13	3	67	21
1979	19	16	3	9	7	2	45	1
1981	11	9	2	11	10	1	121[4]	0
1983	3	3	—	11	10	1	70	6
1985	7	7	—	7	6	1	78	2
1987	38	38	—	20	20	—	290	0
1989	35	35	—	28	28	—	203	0
1991	33	33	—	13	13	—	457	0
1993	8	8	—	24	24	—	78	0
1995	4	4	—	21	21	—	112	0
1997	3	3	—	8	8	—	152	0
1999	5	5	—	9	9	—	255	0
2001	—	—	—	3	3	—	315	0
2003	54	54	—	10	10	—	131	0
2005	47	47	—	2	2	—	139	0
2007	1	1	—	4	4	—	33	0

Note: The legislature is not required to act on vetoes. Any veto not acted upon is counted as sustained, including pocket vetoes. "Vetoes sustained" includes the following pocket vetoes: 1931 (20); 1937 (5); 1941 (12); 1943 (4); 1951 (14); 1955 (10); 1957 (1); 1973 (1). A "pocket veto" resulted if the governor took no action on a bill after the legislature had adjourned *sine die*. (*Sine die*, from the Latin for "without a day", means the legislature adjourns without setting a date to reconvene.) With this type of adjournment, the legislature concluded all its business for the biennium, and there was no opportunity for it to sustain or override the veto (see Article V, Section 10, *Wisconsin Constitution*). Under current legislative session schedules, in which the legislature usually adjourns on the final day of its existence, just hours before the newly elected legislature is seated, the pocket veto is unlikely.

[1]The number of individual veto statements in the governor's veto message.

[2]Attorney general ruled veto of 1939 SB-43 was void and it became law (see Vol. 28, *Opinions of the Attorney General*, p. 423).

[3]1953 AB-141, partially vetoed in two separate sections by separate veto messages, is counted as one.

[4]Attorney general ruled several vetoes "ineffective" because the governor failed to express his objections (see Vol. 70, *Opinions of the Attorney General*, p. 189).

Source: Compiled by Wisconsin Legislative Reference Bureau from the *Bulletin of the Proceedings of the Wisconsin Legislature* and the Assembly and Senate *Journals*.

POLITICAL COMPOSITION OF THE
WISCONSIN LEGISLATURE
1885 – 2009

Legislative Session[1]	Senate							Assembly						
	D	R	P	S	SD	M[3]	Vacant	D	R	P	S	SD	M[4]	Vacant
1885	13	20	—	—	—	—	—	39	61	—	—	—	—	—
1887	6	25	—	—	—	2	—	30	57	—	—	—	13	—
1889	6	24	—	—	—	3	—	29	71	—	—	—	—	—
1891	19	14	—	—	—	—	—	66	33	—	—	—	1	—
1893	26	7	—	—	—	—	—	56	44	—	—	—	—	—
1895	13	20	—	—	—	—	—	19	81	—	—	—	—	—
1897	4	29	—	—	—	—	—	8	91	—	—	—	1	—
1899	2	31	—	—	—	—	—	19	81	—	—	—	—	—
1901	2	31	—	—	—	—	—	18	82	—	—	—	—	—
1903	3	30	—	—	—	—	—	25	75	—	—	—	—	—
1905	4	28	—	—	1	—	—	11	85	—	—	4	—	—
1907	5	27	—	—	1	—	—	19	76	—	—	5	—	—
1909	4	28	—	—	1	—	—	17	80	—	—	3	—	—
1911	4	27	—	—	2	—	—	29	59	—	—	12	—	—
1913	9	23	—	—	1	—	—	37	57	—	—	6	—	—
1915	11	21	—	—	1	—	—	29	63	—	—	8	—	—
1917	6	24	—	3	—	—	—	14	79	—	7	—	—	—
1919	2	27	—	4	—	—	—	5	79	—	16	—	—	—
1921	2	27	—	4	—	—	—	2	92	—	6	—	—	—
1923	—	30	—	3	—	—	—	1	89	—	10	—	—	—
1925	—	30	—	3	—	—	—	1	92	—	7	—	—	—
1927	—	31	—	2	—	—	—	3	89	—	8	—	—	—
1929	—	31	—	2	—	—	—	6	90	—	3	—	1	—
1931	1	30	—	2	—	—	—	2	89	—	9	—	—	—
1933	9	23	—	1	—	—	—	59	13	24	3	—	1	—
1935	13	6	14	—	—	—	—	35	17	45	3	—	—	—
1937	9	8	16	—	—	—	—	31	21	46	2	—	—	—
1939	6	16	11	—	—	—	—	15	53	32	—	—	—	—
1941	3	24	6	—	—	—	—	15	60	25	—	—	—	—
1943	4	23	6	—	—	—	—	14	73	13	—	—	—	—
1945	6	22	5	—	—	—	—	19	75	6	—	—	—	—
1947	5	27	1	—	—	—	—	11	88	—	—	—	—	1
1949	3	27	—	—	—	—	3	26	74	—	—	—	—	—
1951	7	26	—	—	—	—	—	24	75	—	—	—	—	1
1953	7	26	—	—	—	—	—	25	75	—	—	—	—	—
1955	8	24	—	—	—	—	1	36	64	—	—	—	—	—
1957	10	23	—	—	—	—	—	33	67	—	—	—	—	—
1959	12	20	—	—	—	—	1	55	45	—	—	—	—	—
1961	13	20	—	—	—	—	—	45	55	—	—	—	—	—
1963	11	22	—	—	—	—	—	46	53	—	—	—	—	1
1965	12	20	—	—	—	—	1	52	48	—	—	—	—	—
1967	12	21	—	—	—	—	—	47	53	—	—	—	—	—
1969	10	23	—	—	—	—	—	48	52	—	—	—	—	—
1971	12	20	—	—	—	—	1	67	33	—	—	—	—	—
1973	15	18	—	—	—	—	—	62	37	—	—	—	—	—
1975	18	13	—	—	—	—	2	63	36	—	—	—	—	—
1977	23	10	—	—	—	—	—	66	33	—	—	—	—	—
1979	21	10	—	—	—	—	2	60	39	—	—	—	—	—
1981	19	14	—	—	—	—	—	59	39	—	—	—	—	1
1983	17	14	—	—	—	—	2	59	40	—	—	—	—	—
1985	19	14	—	—	—	—	—	52	47	—	—	—	—	—
1987	19	11	—	—	—	—	3	54	45	—	—	—	—	—
1989	20	13	—	—	—	—	—	56	43	—	—	—	—	—
1991	19	14	—	—	—	—	—	58	41	—	—	—	—	—
1993[2]	15	15	—	—	—	—	3	52	47	—	—	—	—	—
1995[2]	16	17	—	—	—	—	—	48	51	—	—	—	—	—
1997[2]	17	16	—	—	—	—	—	47	52	—	—	—	—	—
1999	17	16	—	—	—	—	—	44	55	—	—	—	—	—
2001	18	15	—	—	—	—	—	43	56	—	—	—	—	—
2003	15	18	—	—	—	—	—	41	58	—	—	—	—	—
2005	14	19	—	—	—	—	—	39	60	—	—	—	—	—
2007	18	15	—	—	—	—	—	47	52	—	—	—	—	—
2009	18	15	—	—	—	—	—	52	46	—	—	—	1	—

Note: The number of assembly districts was reduced from 100 to 99 beginning in 1973.

Key: Democrat (D); Progressive (P); Republican (R); Socialist (S); Social Democrat (SD); Miscellaneous (M).

[1]Political composition at inauguration.

[2]In the 1993, 1995, and 1997 Legislatures, majority control of the senate shifted during the session. On 4/20/93, vacancies were filled resulting in a total of 16 Democrats and 17 Republicans; on 6/16/96, there were 17 Democrats and 16 Republicans; and on 4/19/98, there were 16 Democrats and 17 Republicans.

[3]Miscellaneous = one Independent and one People's (1887); one Independent and 2 Union Labor (1889).

[4]Miscellaneous = 3 Independent, 4 Independent Democrat, and 6 People's (1887); one Union Labor (1891); one Fusion (1897); one Independent (1929); one Independent Republican (1933); one Independent (2009).

Sources: Pre-1943 data is taken from the Secretary of State, *Officers of Wisconsin: U.S., State, Judicial, Congressional, Legislative and County Officers*, 1943 and earlier editions, and the *Wisconsin Blue Book*, various editions. Later data compiled from Wisconsin Legislative Reference Bureau sources.

STATUTES, SESSION LAWS, AND ADMINISTRATIVE CODE

Printed Materials

The printed state documents listed below are available from Document Sales, 202 S. Thornton Avenue, P.O. Box 7840, Madison 53707-7840; telephone (608) 266-3358; TTY (608) 264-8499; Fax: (608) 261-8150.

Prices listed do not reflect 5% state sales tax and, where applicable, 0.5% county sales tax and/or 0.5% or 0.1% stadium tax. Taxes must be included with payment. Prepayment is required for all orders. Make check or money order payable to Wisconsin Department of Administration. For MasterCard or Visa orders, call (608) 264-9419 or (800) 362-7253.

Wisconsin Statutes 2007-2008:

Hardcover 5-volume set – $70 (picked up); $76 (shipped)

Softcover 5-volume set – $54 (picked up); $60 (shipped)

2007 Laws of Wisconsin: Hardcover 2-volume set – $28.35 (picked up); $32.50 (shipped)

Wisconsin Administrative Code, including loose-leaf *Administrative Register.* Subscriptions are available for the entire code or individual code books. Contact Document Sales at (608) 266-3358 for current pricing information.

Machine-Readable Data

WisLaw, the computer-searchable CD-ROM, contains the Wisconsin Statutes and Annotations, plus the Wisconsin and U.S. Constitutions, Supreme Court Rules, Wisconsin Acts, recent Opinions of the Attorney General, the Administrative Code and Register, executive orders, town law forms, and the Wisconsin Code of Military Justice.

WisLaw is continuously updated and is available only by annual subscription. (The number of CD updates released in any 12-month period may vary.) The CD will only be delivered upon receipt of a signed end-user license, subscription form, and full payment. Subscription forms and *WisLaw* end-user licenses are available at Document Sales (see address above) or through the Legislative Reference Bureau home page at **http://www.legis.state. wi.us/rsb/cdinfo.html**

Sources: Wisconsin Department of Administration, *Document Sales Catalog,* and Legislative Reference Bureau.

Senate Minority Leader Scott Fitzgerald of Juneau advocates for his party's position during the budget debate at a conference committee meeting. (Jay Salvo, Legislative Photographer)

STANDING COMMITTEES
OF THE 2009 WISCONSIN LEGISLATURE

All standing committees of the 2009 Wisconsin Legislature are described in this section. The standing committees of the senate are created by the Committee on Senate Organization while standing committees of the assembly are enumerated in Assembly Rule 9. In the case of each standing committee listed below, the names of committee officers are followed by those of the majority party and minority party, separated by a semicolon. An * indicates the ranking minority member.

SENATE STANDING COMMITTEES

Administrative Rules — HOLPERIN, *chairperson;* LEHMAN, RISSER; GROTHMAN*, COWLES.

Agriculture and Higher Education — VINEHOUT, *chairperson;* KREITLOW, PLALE; HARSDORF*, KAPANKE.

Audit — VINEHOUT, *chairperson;* JAUCH, MILLER; COWLES*, LAZICH.

During an executive session, committee members decide whether or not to recommend a bill for passage. Senator Joseph Leibham of Sheboygan is a member of the Senate Committee on Transportation, Tourism, Forestry and Natural Resources. (Jay Salvo, Legislative Photographer)

Children and Families and Workforce Development — JAUCH, *chairperson;* LASSA, VINEHOUT; KEDZIE*, HOPPER.

Commerce, Utilities, Energy, and Rail — PLALE, *chairperson;* WIRCH, ERPENBACH, KREITLOW; COWLES*, HARSDORF, KEDZIE.

Economic Development — LASSA, *chairperson;* LEHMAN, VINEHOUT, KREITLOW; KANAVAS*, DARLING, LEIBHAM.

Education — LEHMAN, *chairperson;* JAUCH, *vice chairperson;* ERPENBACH, HANSEN; OLSEN*, GROTHMAN, HOPPER.

Environment — MILLER, *chairperson;* JAUCH, WIRCH; KEDZIE*, OLSEN.

Ethics Reform and Government Operations — RISSER, *chairperson;* ROBSON, KREITLOW; ELLIS*, LASEE.

Finance — MILLER, *chairperson;* HANSEN, TAYLOR, LEHMAN, ROBSON, LASSA; DARLING*, OLSEN.

Health, Health Insurance, Privacy, Property Tax Relief, and Revenue — ERPENBACH, *chairperson;* CARPENTER, *vice chairperson;* ROBSON, LASSA; LAZICH*, KANAVAS, DARLING.

Judiciary, Corrections, Insurance, Campaign Finance Reform, and Housing — TAYLOR, *chairperson;* SULLIVAN, *vice chairperson;* ERPENBACH; GROTHMAN*, HOPPER.

Labor, Elections and Urban Affairs — COGGS, *chairperson;* WIRCH, LEHMAN; LASEE*, GROTHMAN.

Public Health, Senior Issues, Long-Term Care, and Job Creation — CARPENTER, *chairperson;* COGGS, VINEHOUT; SCHULTZ*, KAPANKE.

Rural Issues, Biofuels, and Information Technology — KREITLOW, *chairperson;* JAUCH, HOLPERIN; KAPANKE*, KANAVAS.

Senate Organization — DECKER, *chairperson;* RISSER, HANSEN; S. FITZGERALD*, GROTHMAN.

Small Business, Emergency Preparedness, Technical Colleges, and Consumer Protection — WIRCH, *chairperson;* PLALE, HOLPERIN; HOPPER*, LAZICH.

Transportation, Tourism, Forestry, and Natural Resources — HOLPERIN, *chairperson;* SULLIVAN, PLALE, HANSEN; LEIBHAM*, KEDZIE, GROTHMAN.

Veterans and Military Affairs, Biotechnology, and Financial Institutions — SULLIVAN, *chairperson;* COGGS, CARPENTER; LEIBHAM*, KANAVAS.

ASSEMBLY STANDING COMMITTEES

Administrative Rules — ZEPNICK, *chairperson;* HUBLER, *vice chairperson;* HEBL; LEMAHIEU*, GUNDERSON.

Aging and Long-Term Care — KRUSICK, *chairperson;* A. WILLIAMS, *vice chairperson;* ROYS, RADCLIFFE; RHOADES*, TOWNSEND, PETERSEN.

Agriculture — VRUWINK, *chairperson;* RADCLIFFE, *vice chairperson;* GARTHWAITE, JORGENSEN, MOLEPSKE, DANOU; A. OTT*, NERISON, MURTHA, TAUCHEN, BROOKS.

Assembly Organization — SHERIDAN, *chairperson;* NELSON, SEIDEL, STASKUNAS, BARCA; J. FITZGERALD*, GOTTLIEB, SUDER.

Audit — BARCA, *chairperson;* JORGENSEN, *vice chairperson;* POCAN; KRAMER*, KERKMAN.

Children and Families — GRIGSBY, *chairperson;* SEIDEL, *vice chairperson;* POPE-ROBERTS, SINICKI, BERCEAU; KESTELL*, PRIDEMORE, SPANBAUER.

Colleges and Universities — HIXSON, *chairperson;* SMITH, *vice chairperson;* BLACK, CULLEN, SOLETSKI, HINTZ, BERCEAU; NASS*, RHOADES, TOWNSEND, GOTTLIEB, BALLWEG.

Consumer Protection — HINTZ, *chairperson;* SOLETSKI, *vice chairperson;* HIXSON, POPE-ROBERTS, ROYS; LOTHIAN*, KLEEFISCH, SPANBAUER, MEYER.

Corrections and the Courts — PARISI, *chairperson;* BENEDICT, *vice chairperson;* SEIDEL, KESSLER, POPE-ROBERTS, ZIGMUNT, PASCH; VAN ROY*, GUNDRUM, KESTELL, LEMAHIEU, BROOKS.

Criminal Justice — TURNER, *chairperson;* KESSLER, *vice chairperson;* STASKUNAS, HRAYCHUCK, SOLETSKI, PASCH; KLEEFISCH*, FRISKE, KRAMER, BROOKS, RIPP.

Education — POPE-ROBERTS, *chairperson;* DEXTER, *vice chairperson;* HILGENBERG, SINICKI, HIXSON, SMITH, KRUSICK, RADCLIFFE; DAVIS*, NASS, TOWNSEND, VUKMIR, NYGREN.

Education Reform — A. WILLIAMS, *chairperson;* SINICKI, *vice chairperson;* FIELDS, CULLEN, YOUNG, KESSLER; PRIDEMORE*, VUKMIR, J. OTT.

Elections and Campaign Reform — SMITH, *chairperson;* SOLETSKI, *vice chairperson;* KESSLER, A. WILLIAMS, ROYS; STONE*, PRIDEMORE, ROTH.

Employment Relations — SHERIDAN, *chairperson;* NELSON, POCAN; J. FITZGERALD*.

Energy and Utilities — Soletski, *chairperson;* Zepnick, *vice chairperson;* Staskunas, Richards, Steinbrink, Parisi, Zigmunt; Huebsch*, Montgomery, Honadel, Petersen, Zipperer.

Finance — Pocan, *chairperson;* Colón, *vice chairperson;* Mason, Shilling, Sherman, Grigsby; Vos*, Montgomery.

Financial Institutions — Fields, *chairperson;* Smith, *vice chairperson;* Barca, Zepnick, Hixson, Garthwaite; Newcomer*, Kaufert, Huebsch, Davis, Kramer.

Fish and Wildlife — Hraychuck, *chairperson;* Milroy, *vice chairperson;* Molepske, Steinbrink, Danou, Vruwink; Gunderson*, Suder, M. Williams, J. Ott.

Forestry — Sherman, *chairperson;* Clark, *vice chairperson;* Milroy; Friske*, Mursau.

Health and Healthcare Reform — Richards, *chairperson;* Roys, *vice chairperson;* Benedict, Shilling, Vruwink, Seidel, Pasch, Bernard Schaber; Vukmir*, Rhoades, Stone, Strachota, Nygren.

Housing — Young, *chairperson;* A. Williams, *vice chairperson;* Turner, Pasch; Roth*, Newcomer, Murtha.

Insurance — Cullen, *chairperson;* Molepske, *vice chairperson;* Ziegelbauer, Parisi, Berceau, Hebl; Nygren*, Suder, Vos, Roth.

Jobs, the Economy and Small Business — Molepske, *chairperson;* Bernard Schaber, *vice chairperson;* Fields, Hintz, Barca, Krusick, Benedict, Toles; Zipperer*, Friske, Van Roy, M. Williams, Strachota.

Judiciary and Ethics — Hebl, *chairperson;* Colón, *vice chairperson;* Kessler, Cullen, Richards, Turner; Gundrum*, Kerkman, Kramer, Zipperer.

Labor — Sinicki, *chairperson;* Van Akkeren, *vice chairperson;* Jorgensen, Parisi, Toles, Soletski (eff. 4/13/09); Honadel*, Nass, Knodl.

Natural Resources — Black, *chairperson;* Danou, *vice chairperson;* Molepske, Steinbrink, Hraychuck, Hebl, Mason, Milroy, Clark; J. Ott*, Gunderson, Huebsch, LeMahieu, Mursau, Nerison.

Personal Privacy — Schneider, *chairperson;* Vruwink, *vice chairperson;* Kessler, Staskunas; Suder*, Gundrum, M. Williams.

   Subcommittee on AB 29 RFID Sale of Consumer Goods — M. Williams, *chairperson;* Gundrum, Kessler, Schneider.

   Subcommittee on AB 30 Monitoring of Electronic Mail Usage — Vruwink, *chairperson;* Kessler, Suder, M. Williams.

   Subcommittee on AB 137 Real ID — Suder, *chairperson;* M. Williams, Vruwink, Schneider.

   Subcommittee on AB 171 Unlawful Use of Global Position Device — Kessler, *chairperson;* Staskunas, Suder, Gundrum.

Public Health — Benedict, *chairperson;* Pasch, *vice chairperson;* Dexter, Bernard Schaber; Strachota*, Vukmir, Newcomer.

Public Safety — Staskunas, *chairperson;* Ziegelbauer, *vice chairperson;* Cullen, Smith, Berceau; Bies*, A. Ott, Nerison.

Renewable Energy and Rural Affairs — Jorgensen, *chairperson;* Hilgenberg, *vice chairperson;* Radcliffe, Garthwaite, Smith, Dexter, Danou, Vruwink; Wood; Tauchen*, Petrowski, Lothian, Ballweg, Davis, Ripp.

Rules — Nelson, *chairperson;* Sheridan, *vice chairperson;* Staskunas, Seidel, Barca, Richards, Shilling; J. Fitzgerald*, Gottlieb, Suder, Kleefisch, M. Williams.

Rural Economic Development — Garthwaite, *chairperson;* Jorgensen, *vice chairperson;* Hraychuck, Clark, Dexter; Wood; Meyer*, Davis, Nerison, Murtha.

State Affairs and Homeland Security — Kessler, *chairperson;* Young, *vice chairperson;* Pope-Roberts, Roys, Black; Ballweg*, Kleefisch, Knodl.

Tourism, Recreation and State Properties — VAN AKKEREN, *chairperson;* CLARK, *vice chairperson;* SCHNEIDER, HRAYCHUCK, HILGENBERG; KAUFERT*, BIES, VAN ROY, M. WILLIAMS.

Transportation — STEINBRINK, *chairperson;* ZIGMUNT, *vice chairperson;* VRUWINK, GARTHWAITE, FIELDS, BERNARD SCHABER, SINICKI; PETROWSKI*, A. OTT, STONE, BIES, RIPP.

Urban and Local Affairs — BERCEAU, *chairperson;* VAN AKKEREN, *vice chairperson;* ZIEGELBAUER, HINTZ, PARISI; LEMAHIEU*, GOTTLIEB, SPANBAUER.

Veterans and Military Affairs — HILGENBERG, *chairperson;* SCHNEIDER, *vice chairperson;* TURNER, HUBLER, SINICKI, MILROY; PETERSEN*, PETROWSKI, TOWNSEND, MEYER.

Ways and Means — ZIEGELBAUER, *chairperson;* HEBL, *vice chairperson;* STEINBRINK, ZEPNICK, TOLES; WOOD; KERKMAN*, NASS, LOTHIAN, KNODL.

Workforce Development — TOLES, *chairperson;* HINTZ, *vice chairperson;* SEIDEL, ZEPNICK, HIXSON; MURSAU*, KESTELL, HONADEL, TAUCHEN.

Representative Peggy Krusick of Milwaukee, a veteran of 14 legislative sessions, is a passionate advocate for her district. As a member of the Assembly Committee on Jobs, the Economy and Small Business, she deals with issues that affect the well-being of all residents of the state. (Brent Nicastro, Legislative Photographer)

PERSONAL DATA ON WISCONSIN LEGISLATORS
1999 – 2009 Sessions

	1999 Sen.	1999 Rep.	2001 Sen.	2001 Rep.	2003 Sen.	2003 Rep.	2005 Sen.	2005 Rep.	2007 Sen.	2007 Rep.	2009 Sen.	2009 Rep.*
Party affiliation												
Democrat	17	44	18	43	15	41	14	39	18	47	18	52
Republican	16	55	15	56	18	58	19	60	15	52	15	46
Number with previous legislative service												
In senate	30	0	30	0	27	0	28	0	29	0	31	0
In assembly	23	78	24	89	22	84	23	81	23	82	23	86
Highest number of prior sessions in same house	18	14	19	15	20	16	21	17	22	18	23	19
Occupations												
Full-time legislator	14	38	15	40	13	39	11	39	12	38	11	39
Attorney	5	10	5	10	3	8	2	11	3	11	3	12
Farmer	1	12	1	13	3	9	3	9	3	5	3	5
Other	13	39	12	36	14	43	17	40	15	45	16	43
Education												
High school only	2	12	2	13	4	12	4	9	2	7	1	7
Beyond high school	31	87	31	86	29	87	29	90	31	92	32	92
Bachelor's or associate degree	26	67	28	67	25	67	26	70	28	69	29	69
Advanced degree	8	29	8	31	7	32	8	34	10	37	11	35
Number with experience on local governing body												
County board	4	19	4	18	4	19	4	18	4	17	4	15
Municipal board	6	31	5	36	8	35	10	28	12	25	12	30
Age												
Oldest	71	69	73	71	75	75	77	77	79	79	81	80
Youngest	35	27	37	26	33	27	34	28	36	28	38	29
Average	50	46	52	47	51	49	52	50	54	50	55	50
Veterans	4	14	4	15	4	13	4	13	2	16	2	16
Marital status												
Single	6	23	5	23	5	17	10	25	8	25	9	24
Married	27	74	28	76	28	80	23	70	25	69	24	71
Widowed	0	2	0	0	0	2	0	4	0	5	0	4
Number of women	11	19	11	22	8	27	8	26	8	22	7	22

*Includes one Independent.

Sen. – Senators; Rep. – Representatives.

Note: Most data are recorded as of the date on which the legislature first convened; ages are determined as of January 1.

Sources: *Wisconsin Blue Book*, various issues, and data collected by the Wisconsin Legislative Reference Bureau, January 2009.

JOINT LEGISLATIVE COMMITTEES AND COMMISSIONS

Joint committees and commissions are created by statute and include members from both houses. Three joint committees include nonlegislative members. Names of committee officers are followed by those of the majority and minority party, separated by a semicolon. The ranking minority member is indicated by an *. Commissions also include gubernatorial appointees and, in 2 cases, the governor. All telephone numbers that do not include an area code are Madison numbers, area code 608.

JOINT COMMITTEE FOR REVIEW OF ADMINISTRATIVE RULES

Members: SENATOR HOLPERIN, REPRESENTATIVE ZEPNICK, *cochairpersons;* SENATORS LEHMAN, RISSER; GROTHMAN*, COWLES; REPRESENTATIVES HUBLER, HEBL; LEMAHIEU*, GUNDERSON.

Mailing Addresses: Senator Holperin, Room 409 South, State Capitol, P.O. Box 7882, Madison 53707-7882; Representative Zepnick, Room 219 North, State Capitol, P.O. Box 8953, Madison 53708-8953.

Telephones: Senator Holperin, 266-2509; Representative Zepnick, 266-1707.

E-mail: sen.holperin@legis.wisconsin.gov; rep.zepnick@legis.wisconsin.gov

Statutory References: Sections 13.56, 227.19, 227.24, 227.26, 227.40 (5), and 806.04 (11).

Agency Responsibility: The Joint Committee for Review of Administrative Rules must review proposed rules when standing committees object to them. It also may suspend rules that have been promulgated; suspend or extend the effective period of all or part of emergency rules; and order an agency to put unwritten policies in rule form.

When a standing committee objects to a proposed rule or portion of a rule, it must be referred to the joint committee. The joint committee then has 30 days to review the rule, but that period may be extended for an additional 30 days. The joint committee may uphold or reverse the standing committee's action. If it concurs with the objection, it introduces bills concurrently in both houses to prevent promulgation of the rule. If either bill is enacted, the agency may not adopt the rule unless specifically authorized to do so by subsequent legislative action. If the joint committee disagrees with the objection, it may overrule the standing committee and allow the agency to adopt the rule or it may request the agency to modify the rule.

The joint committee may suspend a rule after holding a public hearing, but suspension must be based on one or more of the following reasons: absence of statutory authority; an emergency related to public health or welfare; failure to comply with legislative intent; conflict with existing state law; a change in circumstances since passage of the law that authorized the rule; or a rule that is arbitrary or capricious or imposes undue hardship. Within 30 days following the suspension, the committee must introduce bills concurrently in both houses to repeal the suspended rule. If either bill is enacted, the rule is repealed and the agency may not promulgate it again unless authorized by the legislature. If both bills fail to pass, the rule remains in effect and may not be suspended again.

The joint committee receives notice of any action in the circuit court of Dane County for declaratory judgments about the validity of a rule and may intervene in the action with the consent of the Joint Committee on Legislative Organization.

Organization: The joint committee consists of 5 senators and 5 representatives, and the membership from each house must include representatives of both the majority and minority parties.

History: The Joint Committee for Review of Administrative Rules was one of the first of its kind in the country, and it has served as a model widely copied by other states. Chapter 221, Laws of 1955, revised administrative rules procedures and created the committee with "advisory powers only". It could investigate complaints about rules and recommend changes to rule-making agencies but could not directly affect the rule-making process. Chapter 659, Laws of 1965, granted the committee authority to suspend a rule based on testimony at a public hearing. With enactment of Chapter 34, Laws of 1979, the joint committee acquired the power to review

Former Speaker Pro Tempore Mark Gottlieb (right) of Port Washington, confers with current Speaker Pro Tempore Anthony Staskunas, of West Allis. The Speaker Pro Tempore, an office filled by a member of the majority party, usually presides over Assembly floor sessions. Staskunas was elected to the office when the Democrats took control of the Assembly. (Jay Salvo, Legislative Photographer)

proposed rules based on the objections of a legislative standing committee. Further modifications occurred when 1985 Wisconsin Act 182 authorized the joint committee to extend its 30-day review period and allowed it to negotiate with agencies to modify existing rules.

State of Wisconsin
BUILDING COMMISSION

Members: Governor Doyle, *chairperson;* Senator Risser (through 1/5/10), *vice chairperson;* Senators Kreitlow (eff. 1/6/10), Plale; Kanavas; Representatives Black, Hintz; Kaufert; Terry McGuire (citizen member appointed by governor). Nonvoting advisory members from Department of Administration: Michael Morgan (departmental secretary), Adel Tabrizi (chief engineer), David Haley (chief architect).

Secretary: David Helbach, *administrator,* Division of State Facilities, Department of Administration.

Mailing Address: P.O. Box 7866, Madison 53707-7866.

Location: 101 East Wilson Street, 7th Floor, Madison.

Telephone: 266-1031.

Fax: 267-2710.

Total Budget 2007-09: $82,462,000*.

*Total budget includes bond revenues, building trust fund expenditures, and debt service payments for state office buildings, the State Capitol, and the Executive Residence.

Statutory Reference: Section 13.48.

Agency Responsibility: The State of Wisconsin Building Commission coordinates the state building program and establishes long-range plans for development of the state's physical plant.

The commission determines the projects to be incorporated into the long-range program and recommends a biennial building program to the legislature, including the amount to be appropriated in the biennial budget. It oversees all state construction, except highway development. In addition, the commission may authorize expenditures from the State Building Trust Fund for construction, remodeling, maintenance, and planning of future development. The commission is the only state body that can authorize the contracting of state debt. All transactions for the sale of instruments that result in a state debt liability must be approved by official resolution of the commission.

Organization: The 11-member commission includes 6 legislators. Both the majority and minority parties in each house must be represented, and one legislator from each house must also be a member of the State Supported Programs Study and Advisory Committee. The governor serves as chairperson; one citizen member serves at the pleasure of the governor. Three officials from the Department of Administration – the secretary, the head of the engineering function, and the ranking architect – serve as nonvoting, advisory members.

History: The State of Wisconsin Building Commission was created by Chapter 563, Laws of 1949, to establish a long-range public building program. Another 1949 law (Chapter 604) gave the commission authority to organize the quasi-public Wisconsin State Public Building Corporation. This legal device, familiarly known as a "dummy building corporation", was used to finance public buildings to house state agencies because the Wisconsin Constitution prevented direct borrowing by the state for such projects. The quasi-public corporation was first used in 1925, when the University Building Corporation was developed to permit construction of revenue-producing facilities on the Madison campus, including dormitories and athletic buildings. The State Agencies Building Corporation, a similar entity, was formed in 1958 (Chapter 593, Laws of 1957) to finance nonrevenue-producing buildings, such as classroom facilities, and Chapter 267, Laws of 1961, extended the corporation's authority to the financing of public welfare buildings.

In 1969, voters amended the constitution, and the legislature passed Chapter 259, which provided for direct state borrowing and ended the use of the various building corporations. The law enlarged the powers of the commission to finance capital facilities for all state agencies.

A separate State Bond Board, including 4 members of the Building Commission, was established by Chapter 259 to supervise the contracting of state debt. Chapter 90, Laws of 1973, abolished the bond board and returned its duties and responsibilities to the Building Commission.

Joint Review Committee on
CRIMINAL PENALTIES

Members: SENATOR TAYLOR, vacancy; REPRESENTATIVE STASKUNAS, vacancy; J.B. VAN HOLLEN (attorney general); RICK RAEMISCH (secretary of corrections); NICHOLAS CHIARKAS (state public defender); JAMES T. BAYORGEON, DAVID G. DEININGER (reserve judges appointed by supreme court); BRADLEY GEHRING, ALLAN KEHL (public members appointed by governor).

Mailing Address: Senator Taylor, Room 415 South, State Capitol, P.O. Box 7882, Madison 53707-7882.

Telephone: Senator Taylor, 266-5810.

E-mail: sen.taylor@legis.wisconsin.gov

Statutory Reference: Section 13.525.

Agency Responsibility: The Joint Review Committee on Criminal Penalties, created by 2001 Wisconsin Act 109, reviews any bill that creates a new crime or revises a penalty for an existing crime when requested to do so by a chairperson of a standing committee in the house of origin to which the bill was referred. The presiding officer in the house of origin may also request a report from the joint committee if the bill is not referred to a standing committee.

Committee reports on bills submitted for its review concern the costs or savings to public agencies; the consistency of proposed penalties with existing penalties; whether alternative language is needed to conform the proposed penalties to existing penalties; and whether any acts prohibited by the bill are already prohibited under existing law.

Once a report is requested for a bill, a standing committee may not vote on the bill and the house of origin may not pass the bill before the joint committee submits its report or before the 30th day after the request is made, whichever is earlier.

Organization: Legislative members include one majority and one minority party member from each house. One reserve judge must reside somewhere within judicial administrative districts one through 5, and the other in districts 6 through 10. Public members must include an individual with law enforcement experience and one who is an elected county official.

Joint Committee on
EMPLOYMENT RELATIONS

SENATOR RISSER (senate president), REPRESENTATIVE SHERIDAN (assembly speaker), SENATORS DECKER (majority leader), S. FITZGERALD (minority leader); REPRESENTATIVES NELSON (majority leader), J. FITZGERALD (minority leader); SENATOR MILLER, REPRESENTATIVE POCAN (joint finance committee cochairpersons).

Mailing Address: Legislative Council Staff, P.O. Box 2536, Madison 53701-2536.

Location: 1 East Main Street, Suite 401, Madison.

Telephone: 266-1304.

Statutory References: Sections 13.111, 20.923, and 230.12; Chapter 111, Subchapter V.

Agency Responsibility: The Joint Committee on Employment Relations approves all changes to the collective bargaining agreements that cover state employees represented by unions, and the compensation plans for nonrepresented state employees. These plans and agreements include pay adjustments; fringe benefits; performance awards; pay equity adjustments; and other items related to wages, hours, and conditions of employment. The committee also approves the assignment of unclassified positions to the executive salary group ranges.

In the case of unionized employees, the Office of State Employment Relations submits tentative agreements negotiated between it and certified labor organizations to the committee. If the committee disapproves an agreement, it is returned to the bargaining parties for renegotiation.

When the committee approves an agreement for unionized employees, it introduces those portions requiring legislative approval in bill form and recommends passage without change. If the legislature fails to pass the bill, the agreement is returned to the bargaining parties for renegotiation.

The Office of State Employment Relations also submits the compensation plans for nonrepresented employees to the committee. One plan covers all nonrepresented classified employees and certain officials outside the classified service, including legislators, justices of the supreme court, court of appeals judges, circuit court judges, constitutional officers, district attorneys, heads of executive agencies, division administrators, and others designated by law. The faculty and academic staff of the UW System are covered by a separate compensation plan, which is based on recommendations made by the UW Board of Regents.

After public hearings on the nonrepresented employee plans, the committee may modify the office's recommendations, but the committee's modifications may be disapproved by the governor. The committee may set aside the governor's disapproval by a vote of 6 committee members.

Organization: The committee, which was established by Chapter 270, Laws of 1971, is a permanent joint legislative committee comprised of 8 members. It is assisted in its work by the Legislative Council Staff and the Legislative Fiscal Bureau.

A Conference Committee is organized when the Senate and Assembly cannot agree on identical versions of a bill. Senate members Russell Decker, Mark Miller, and Scott Fitzgerald negotiate changes to reconcile differences in versions of Assembly Bill 75, the biennial budget. (Jay Salvo, Legislative Photographer)

Joint Committee on
FINANCE

SENATOR MILLER, REPRESENTATIVE POCAN, SENATORS HANSEN, TAYLOR, LEHMAN, ROBSON, LASSA; DARLING*, OLSEN; REPRESENTATIVES COLÓN, MASON, SHILLING, SHERMAN, GRIGSBY; VOS*, MONTGOMERY.

Mailing Addresses: Senator Miller, Room 317 East, State Capitol, P.O. Box 7882, Madison 53707-7882; Representative Pocan, Room 309 East, State Capitol, P.O. Box 8953, Madison 53708-8953.

Telephones: Senator Miller, 266-9170; Representative Pocan, 266-8570.

E-mail: sen.miller@legis.wisconsin.gov; rep.pocan@legis.wisconsin.gov

Statutory References: Sections 13.09-13.11, 16.505, 16.515, and 20.865 (4).

Agency Responsibility: The Joint Committee on Finance examines all legislation that deals with state income and spending. It also gives final approval to a wide variety of state payments and assessments. Any bill introduced in the legislature that appropriates money, provides for revenue, or relates to taxation must be referred to the joint committee.

The joint committee introduces the biennial budget as recommended by the governor. After holding a series of public hearings and executive sessions, it submits its own version of the budget as a substitute amendment to the governor's budget bill for consideration by the legislature.

At regularly scheduled quarterly meetings, the joint committee considers agency requests to adjust their budgets. It may approve a request for emergency funds if it finds that the legislature has authorized the activities for which the appropriation is sought. It may also transfer funds between existing appropriations and change the number of positions authorized to an agency in the budget process.

When required, the joint committee introduces legislation to pay claims against the state, resolve shortages in funds, and restore capital reserve funds of the Wisconsin Housing and Economic Development Authority to the required level. As an emergency measure, it may reduce certain state agency appropriations when there is a decrease in state revenues.

The joint committee gives final approval for a variety of fiscal operations including: disposition of federal block grant funds and private gifts, grants, and bequests; changes in supplemental security income payment levels if approved by the governor; plans to deal with shortfalls in state agency fund accounts; disposition of oil overcharge funds; expenditure plans for federal low-income assistance funds; and oversight and review of expenditure of funds received from the American Recovery and Reinvestment Act (ARRA). In addition, the committee may inquire into the operations of any state agency for the purpose of improving agency efficiency.

Organization: The committee is a joint standing committee composed of the 8 senators on the Senate Finance Committee and the 8 representatives on the Assembly Finance Committee. It generally includes members of the majority and minority party in each house. Cochairpersons of the joint committee are appointed in the same manner as are standing committees of their respective houses.

History: The use of a joint standing committee to consider appropriation bills dates back to 1857 when the legislature created the Joint Committee on Claims. In 1911 (Chapter 6), the Joint Committee on Finance replaced the claims committee and was given the responsibility to consider all bills related to revenue and taxation. Chapter 609, Laws of 1915, authorized the governor, secretary of state, and state treasurer to approve emergency appropriations when the legislature was not in session to permit departments with insufficient funds to carry out their normal duties. Chapter 97, Laws of 1929, transferred this function to a new Emergency Board, which consisted of the governor and the cochairpersons of the joint finance committee. The power to approve supplemental appropriations, transfer funds between appropriations, and handle other interim fiscal matters was given to a joint legislative committee called the Board on Government Operations (BOGO) by Chapter 228, Laws of 1959. BOGO's functions were transferred to the Joint Committee on Finance by Chapter 39, Laws of 1975.

Speaker Michael Sheridan (left) and Minority Leader Jeff Fitzgerald lead their respective parties in the Assembly. (Jay Salvo, Legislative Photographer)

Joint Committee on
INFORMATION POLICY AND TECHNOLOGY

Members: SENATORS KREITLOW, JAUCH, MILLER; COWLES, LEIBHAM; 5 vacancies (representatives).
Statutory Reference: Section 13.58.

Agency Responsibility: The Joint Committee on Information Policy and Technology reviews information management practices of state and local units of government to ensure economic and efficient service, maintain data security and integrity, and protect the privacy of individuals who are subjects of the databases. It studies the effects of proposals by the state to expand existing information technology or implement new technologies. With concurrence of the Joint Committee on Finance, it may direct the Department of Administration to report on any information technology system project that could cost $1 million or more in the current or succeeding biennium. The committee may direct the Department of Administration to prepare reports or conduct studies and may make recommendations to the governor, the legislature, state agencies, or local governments based on this information. The University of Wisconsin Board of Regents is required to submit a report to the committee twice annually, detailing each information technology project in the University of Wisconsin System costing more than $1 million or deemed "high-risk" by the board. The committee may make recommendations on the identified projects to the governor and the legislature. The committee is composed of 3 majority and 2 minority party members from each house of the legislature. It was created by 1991 Wisconsin Act 317 and its membership was revised by 1999 Wisconsin Act 29.

Joint
LEGISLATIVE AUDIT COMMITTEE

Members: SENATOR VINEHOUT, REPRESENTATIVE BARCA, *cochairpersons;* SENATOR MILLER, REPRESENTATIVE POCAN (joint finance committee cochairpersons); SENATORS JAUCH; COWLES*, LAZICH; REPRESENTATIVES JORGENSEN; KRAMER*, KERKMAN.

Mailing Addresses: Senator Vinehout, Room 104 South, State Capitol, P.O. Box 7882, Madison 53707-7882; Representative Barca, Room 107 North, State Capitol, P.O. Box 8952, Madison 53708-8952.

Telephones: Senator Vinehout, 266-8546; Representative Barca, 266-5504.

E-mail: sen.vinehout@legis.wisconsin.gov; rep.barca@legis.wisconsin.gov

Statutory Reference: Section 13.53.

Agency Responsibility: The Joint Legislative Audit Committee, which was created by Chapter 224, Laws of 1975, advises the Legislative Audit Bureau, subject to general supervision of the Joint Committee on Legislative Organization. Its members include the cochairpersons of the Joint Committee on Finance, plus 2 majority and 2 minority party members from each house of the legislature. The committee evaluates candidates for the office of state auditor and makes recommendations to the Joint Committee on Legislative Organization, which selects the auditor.

The committee may direct the state auditor to undertake specific audits and review requests for special audits from individual legislators or standing committees, but no legislator or standing committee may interfere with the auditor in the conduct of an audit.

The committee reviews each report of the Legislative Audit Bureau and then confers with the state auditor, other legislative committees, and the audited agencies on the report's findings. It may propose corrective action and direct that followup reports be submitted to it.

The committee may hold hearings on audit reports, ask the Joint Committee on Legislative Organization to investigate any matter within the scope of the audit, and request investigation of any matter relative to the fiscal and performance responsibilities of a state agency. If an audit report cites financial deficiencies, the head of the agency must report to the Joint Legislative Audit Committee on remedial actions taken. Should the agency head fail to report, the committee may refer the matter to the Joint Committee on Legislative Organization and the appropriate standing committees.

When the committee determines that legislative action is needed, it may refer the necessary information to the legislature or a standing committee. It can also request information from a committee on action taken or seek advice of a standing committee on program portions of an audit. The committee may introduce legislation to address issues covered in audit reports.

JOINT LEGISLATIVE COUNCIL

Members: SENATOR RISSER (senate president), REPRESENTATIVE SCHNEIDER (designated by assembly speaker), *cochairpersons;* SENATORS KREITLOW (president pro tempore), DECKER (majority leader), S. FITZGERALD (minority leader), MILLER (cochairperson, Joint Committee on Finance), DARLING (ranking minority member, Joint Committee on Finance), COGGS, ROBSON, WIRCH, HARSDORF, SCHULTZ; REPRESENTATIVES SHERIDAN (assembly speaker), STASKUNAS (speaker pro tempore), NELSON (majority leader), J. FITZGERALD (minority leader), POCAN (cochairperson, Joint Committee on Finance), VOS (ranking minority member, Joint Committee on Finance), BERCEAU, BLACK, BALLWEG, KAUFERT. (Members designated by title serve *ex officio.*)

Director of Legislative Council Staff: TERRY C. ANDERSON, terry.anderson@legis.wisconsin.gov

Deputy Director: LAURA D. ROSE, laura.rose@legis.wisconsin.gov

Legislative Council Rules Clearinghouse: RONALD SKLANSKY, *director,* ronald.sklansky@legis.wisconsin.gov; RICHARD SWEET, *assistant director,* richard.sweet@legis.wisconsin.gov

Mailing Address: P.O. Box 2536, Madison 53701-2536.

Location: 1 East Main Street, Suite 401, Madison.

Telephone: 266–1304.

Fax: 266–3830.

Internet Address: http://www.legis.state.wi.us/lc

Publications: General Report of the Joint Legislative Council to the Legislature; State Agency Staff Members With Responsibilities Related to the Legislature; Wisconsin Legislator Briefing Book; Directory of Joint Legislative Council Committees; rules clearinghouse reports; staff briefs; information memoranda on substantive issues considered by council committees; staff memoranda; amendment and act memoranda.

Number of Employees: 34.17.

Total Budget 2007-09: $7,501,000.

Statutory References: Sections 13.81–13.83, 13.91, and 227.15.

Agency Responsibility: The Joint Legislative Council creates special committees made up of legislators and interested citizens to study various problems of state and local government. Study topics are selected from requests presented to the council by law, joint resolution, individual legislators, and others. After research and public hearings, the study committees draft proposals and submit them to the council, which must approve those drafts it wants introduced in the legislature as council bills.

The council is assisted in its work by the Legislative Council staff, a bureau created in Section 13.91, Wisconsin Statutes. The staff provides legal counsel and scientific and policy research assistance to all of the legislature's substantive standing committees and joint statutory committees (except the Joint Committee on Finance) and assists individual legislators on request. The staff operates the rules clearinghouse to review proposed administrative rules and assists standing committees in their oversight of rulemaking. The staff also assists the legislature in identifying and responding to issues relating to the Wisconsin Retirement System.

By law, the Legislative Council staff must be "strictly nonpartisan" and must observe the confidential nature of the research and drafting requests received by it. The law requires that state agencies and local governmental units cooperate fully with the council staff in its carrying out of its statutory duties.

All sides of an issue may be aired during floor debate. Here Senator Neal Kedzie of Elkhorn listens respectfully to his colleagues' point of view. (Jay Salvo, Legislative Photographer)

Organization: The council consists of 22 legislators. The majority of them serve *ex officio,* and the remainder are appointed as are members of standing committees. The president of the senate and the speaker of the assembly serve as cochairpersons of the council, but each may designate another member to assume that office. The council operates two permanent statutory committees and various special committees appointed to study selected subjects. The Legislative Council staff director is appointed from outside the classified service by the Joint Committee on Legislative Organization, and the director makes staff appointments from outside the service.

History: Chapter 444, Laws of 1947, created the council to conduct interim studies on subjects affecting the general welfare of the state. The first council was organized later that year with 12 members. In 1967, the council began to appoint staff members to provide legal counsel and technical assistance to legislative standing committees. The 1979 executive budget (Chapter 34) assigned the administrative rules clearinghouse function to the council. 1993 Wisconsin Act 52 made a number of reorganizational changes. The act renamed the council the Joint Legislative Council and designated the president of the senate and the speaker of the assembly (or their designees) cochairpersons. Under Act 52, the council was directed to reorganize at the beginning of the biennial session, instead of May 1 of the odd–numbered year, and its support agency was officially named the Legislative Council Staff. 2005 Wisconsin Act 316 transferred the functions of the retirement research director to the council staff, making the staff responsible for supporting the Joint Survey Committee on Retirement Systems and the legislature regarding legislation involving the Wisconsin Retirement System.

PERMANENT STATUTORY COMMITTEES

Special Committee on State-Tribal Relations

Members: SENATOR COGGS, *chairperson;* REPRESENTATIVE MURSAU, *vice chairperson;* SENATORS S. FITZGERALD, JAUCH, HANSEN; REPRESENTATIVES SHERMAN, SOLETSKI; AGNES FLEMING (Lac Courte Oreilles Band of Lake Superior Chippewa Indians), DEE ANN MAYO (Lac du Flambeau Band of Lake Superior Chippewa Indians), MARK MONTANO (Red Cliff Band of

Lake Superior Chippewas), ANDREW ADAMS III (St. Croix Band of Chippewa Indians), DANIEL BROWN (Ho-Chunk Nation), KEN FISH (Menominee Indian Tribe of Wisconsin), GREGG DUFFEK (Stockbridge-Munsee Band of Mohican Indians), PATRICIA NINHAM HOEFT (Oneida Tribe of Indians of Wisconsin), PHILIP SHOPODOCK (Forest County Potawatomi Community).

The Special Committee on State-Tribal Relations is appointed by the Joint Legislative Council each biennium to study issues related to American Indians and the Indian tribes and bands in this state and develop specific recommendations and legislative proposals relating to such issues. Legislative membership includes not fewer than 6 nor more than 12 members with at least one member of the majority and the minority party from each house. The council appoints no fewer than 6 and no more than 11 members from names submitted by federally recognized Wisconsin Indian tribes or bands or the Great Lakes Inter-Tribal Council. The council may not appoint more than one member recommended by any one tribe or band or the Great Lakes Inter-Tribal Council. The committee has its origins in the Menominee Indians Committee, created in 1955 to study the governmental status of the Menominee Indian Tribe at that time. Chapter 39, Laws of 1975, replaced that committee with the more broadly focused Native American Study Committee. Its name was changed to the American Indian Study Committee in 1982. 1999 Wisconsin Act 60 gave it its current name and revised the membership. The committee's composition and duties are prescribed in Section 13.83 (3) of the statutes.

. . .Technical Advisory Committee

Members: vacancy (Department of Children and Families), JIM WEBER (Department of Health Services), TOM BELLAVIA (Department of Justice), MICHAEL LUTZ (Department of Natural Resources), J.P. LEARY (Department of Public Instruction), TOM OURADA (Department of Revenue), GWEN CARR (Department of Transportation), RACHELLE ASHLEY (DEPARTMENT OF WORKFORCE DEVELOPMENT).

JOINT LEGISLATIVE COUNCIL

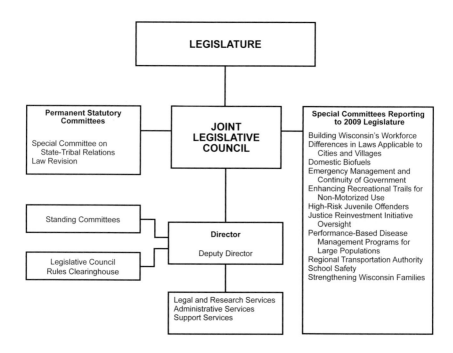

The Joint Legislative Council is responsible for creating special study committees that meet throughout the biennium. Council cochairs Marlin Schneider and Fred Risser meet with council staff, including, from Risser's left, Terry Anderson, director, Wendy Ulrich and Kelly Mautz, administrative assistants, and Anne Sappenfield and Melissa Schmidt, staff attorneys. At the far left is legislative aide Terry Tuschen. (Kathleen Sitter, LRB)

Under Section 13.83 (3) (f), Wisconsin Statutes, as created by Chapter 39, Laws of 1975, the Technical Advisory Committee, consisting of representatives of 8 major executive agencies, assists the Special Committee on State-Tribal Relations.

Law Revision Committee

Members: SENATOR CARPENTER, REPRESENTATIVE SUDER, *cochairpersons;* SENATORS GROTHMAN, SULLIVAN; REPRESENTATIVES HUBLER, ROTH.

The Law Revision Committee is appointed each biennium by the Joint Legislative Council. The membership of the committee is not specified, but it must include majority and minority party representation from each house. The committee reviews minor nonsubstantive remedial changes to the statutes as proposed by state agencies, in attorney general's opinions, or in court decisions declaring a Wisconsin statute unconstitutional, ambiguous, or otherwise in need of revision. It considers proposals by the Legislative Reference Bureau to correct statutory language and session laws that conflict or need revision, and it may submit recommendations for major law revision projects to the Joint Legislative Council. It serves as the repository for interstate compacts and agreements and makes recommendations to the legislature regarding revision of such agreements. The committee was created by Chapter 204, Laws of 1979, as a combination of the Judiciary Committee, which had its origins in a 1951 mandate to prepare a criminal code, and the Remedial Legislation Committee, created in 1959. Its composition and duties are prescribed in Section 13.83 (1) of the statutes.

SPECIAL COMMITTEES REPORTING IN 2009

Special Committee on Building Wisconsin's Workforce

Members: REPRESENTATIVE STRACHOTA, *chairperson;* SENATOR WIRCH, *vice chairperson;* SENATORS DARLING, JAUCH; REPRESENTATIVES HINTZ, HONADEL; JIM GOLEMBESKI, JOHN KECKHAVER, MARK KESSENICH, STEVE MERCAITIS, PETER THILLMAN, CAROL WAGENSON, JUDY WARMUTH.

The special committee is directed to study and make recommendations regarding the coordination of existing resources of K-12 educational institutions, technical colleges, universities, government agencies, and private organizations to: 1) meet the future workforce needs of the health care, skilled trades, construction, advanced manufacturing, and technology fields; 2) retain workers in the health care, skilled trades, construction, advanced manufacturing, and technology fields; and 3) retrain and update the skills and education of workers in the health care, skilled trades, construction, advanced manufacturing, and technology fields.

Special Committee on Differences in Laws Applicable to Cities and Villages

Members: REPRESENTATIVE GOTTLIEB, *chairperson;* SENATOR PLALE, *vice chairperson;* REPRESENTATIVES BALLWEG, JESKEWITZ; PATRICK CANNON, DAN MAHONEY, MIKE MAY, JERRY MENNE, MIKE MORSE, CURT WITYNSKI.

The special committee is directed to review laws relating to cities and villages, other than those laws that relate to the fundamental organizational structure that distinguishes cities and villages; to determine discrepancies and inconsistencies in the application of those laws to each type of municipality; and recommend, when appropriate and advantageous, rectifying those discrepancies and inconsistencies that exist for no apparent policy rationale.

Special Committee on Domestic Biofuels

Members: SENATOR KREITLOW, *chairperson;* REPRESENTATIVE SUDER, *vice chairperson;* SENATORS COWLES, JAUCH; REPRESENTATIVES FRISKE, SHERIDAN; MARY BLANCHARD, HOWARD BOHL, STEVE CHRISTENSEN, T. RANDALL FORTENBERY, JENNIFER GIEGERICH, JEREMY GOODFELLOW, STEVE GRAHAM, DON GUAY, BILL JOHNSON, STEVE LOEHR, JOHN SALDEN, PETER TAGLIA, PETER TOMASI.

The special committee is directed to: 1) evaluate the economic and environmental costs and benefits of domestically produced fuels derived from biomass; 2) review state and federal policies to promote the development of the industry and infrastructure for the production and distribution of such fuels; 3) recommend state policies to address any deficiencies in existing policies; and 4) recommend state policies to encourage minimum targets for ethanol-blended transportation fuel sales.

Brothers Scott and Jeff Fitzgerald are the minority leaders of the Senate and Assembly, respectively. They coordinate the policy positions of legislative Republicans. Representative Jim Ott of Mequon, Senator Robert Cowles of Green Bay, and Representative John Murtha of Baldwin joined the Fitzgeralds at a press conference to announce a new initiative. (Jay Salvo, Legislative Photographer)

Special Committee on Emergency Management and Continuity of Government

Members: SENATOR JAUCH, *chairperson;* REPRESENTATIVE BALLWEG, *vice chairperson;* REPRESENTATIVES KERKMAN, SCHNEIDER; GARY DALTON, AZITA HAMEDANI, KEN HARTJE, DOUGLAS HOLTON, KEITH KESLER, ROBERT RITGER, DEAN ROLAND, JOHNNIE SMITH.

The special committee is directed to: 1) conduct a recodification of Chapter 166, Wisconsin Statutes, relating to emergency management, to include reorganizing the chapter in a logical manner, renumbering and retitling sections, consolidating related provisions, modernizing language, resolving ambiguities in language, and making other necessary changes; 2) make recommendations on issues relating to continuity of legislative operations during emergencies, including but not limited to lines of succession, alternate seat of state government for the legislature, suspension of legislative quorum requirements, and participation by legislators through alternative means from remote locations; and 3) review the Uniform Emergency Volunteer Health Practitioners Act for consideration and introduction in the next legislative biennium.

Special Committee on Enhancing Recreational Trails for Non-Motorized Use

Members: SENATOR SULLIVAN, *chairperson;* REPRESENTATIVE J. OTT, *vice chairperson;* REPRESENTATIVES BLACK, KAUFERT; MIKE CARLSON, CHARLIE DEE, CHRIS FORTUNE, JACK HIRT, MARY MOTIFF, JOEL PATENAUDE, DAVID PHILLIPS, HARRY WOZNIAK.

The special committee is directed to review safety issues regarding conflicts between motorized and non-motorized uses, ways to avoid conflicts among trail uses, education programs to provide information about how to avoid trail use conflicts, and increased enforcement by Department of Natural Resources wardens regarding safety, noise, and operational issues. The special committee will also review the availability of private land for non-motorized recreation and address ways to increase that availability.

Special Committee on High-Risk Juvenile Offenders

Members: SENATOR CARPENTER, *chairperson;* REPRESENTATIVE ZIPPERER, *vice chairperson;* REPRESENTATIVES GRIGSBY, ROTH; WALTER DICKEY, BARBARA FRANKS, CRAIG HASTING, WENDY HENDERSON, DEVON LEE, MICHAEL MALMSTADT, MARK MERTENS, MIKE MOORE, BRAD SCHIMEL.

The special committee is directed to study high-risk juvenile offenders and best practices for decreasing the risk of recidivism among high-risk offenders. Specifically, the committee shall study current law relating to the Serious Juvenile Offender Program, waiver of juveniles to adult court, original adult court jurisdiction over juvenile offenders, and placement of juveniles in juvenile correctional institutions and adult prisons. The special committee shall also review successful practices relating to juvenile justice in Wisconsin and other states, including the State of Missouri.

Special Committee on Justice Reinvestment Initiative Oversight

Members: SENATOR TAYLOR, *chairperson;* REPRESENTATIVE TURNER, *vice chairperson;* SENATORS KAPANKE, OLSEN; REPRESENTATIVES GRIGSBY, KLEEFISCH, SUDER; NICHOLAS CHIARKAS, JOHN CHISHOLM, RICHARD DUFOUR, JAMES DWYER, DAVE GRAVES, FRANK HUMPHREY, KIT MCNALLY, LISA STARK, TONY STREVELER, A. JOHN VOELKER, MAXINE WHITE, NOBLE WRAY.

The special committee is directed to serve as the entity to which the Council of State Governments (CSG) Justice Center reports. The study committee process creates a unique forum in which legislators will receive data from the Justice Center along with public members who work directly in different aspects of the corrections and criminal justice systems. The CSG Justice Center will provide technical assistance relating to corrections costs. Specifically, the technical assistance will include: 1) mapping of specific neighborhoods where large numbers of offenders are released from prison to identify how to improve coordination of services, correctional supervision, and law enforcement; 2) analyzing the prison population to determine what is driving its growth and to identify which categories of offenders are at high risk of reoffending; 3) developing policy options, based upon the data collected, to increase public safety and decrease corrections spending; and 4) projecting the fiscal impact of any policy options identified.

The recent economic downturn necessitated quick action on the part of the legislature in 2009. During a February debate on Senate Bill 62, Representative Kitty Rhoades of Hudson discussed the proposal to alleviate the state's financial shortfall. (Brent Nicastro, Legislative Photographer)

Special Committee on Performance-Based Disease Management Programs for Large Populations

Members: Senator Lassa, *chairperson;* Representative Benedict; Alexandra Adams, Cinthia S. Christensen, Mikki Duran, Marilyn Follen, Jo Musser, Susan A. Nitzke, Kenneth Schellhase, Deborah Wubben, Steve Wieckert.

The special committee is directed to: 1) examine the role of disease management programs in assisting to address the state's health care needs; 2) review best practice disease management programs from around the nation; 3) review current practices of the State of Wisconsin's programs; 4) review state-of-the-art procedures for measuring performance of disease management programs; 5) make recommendations on ways to more effectively measure disease management results; and 6) focus on group settings for children, primarily schools, preschool, and day care settings and the laws, rules, and policies related to nutrition and physical activities in those settings, especially in regard to childhood obesity.

Special Committee on Regional Transportation Authority

Members: Senator Robson, *chairperson;* Senator Lehman; Representatives A. Ott, Stone, Toles, Vos; Larry Arft, Len Brandrup, Gerald Derr, Brett Geboy, Dick Granchalek, Anita Gulotta-Connelly, Tim Hanna, Richard Johnson, Chuck Kamp, Scott McDonell, Delora Newton, Brian Ohm, Fritz Ruf, Dick Wagner, Tom Walker.

The special committee is directed to review and provide recommendations on how to create a statutory framework enabling counties, cities, villages, and towns to create regional transportation authorities (RTA) to promote regional cooperation on transportation issues, including: the funding mechanisms to be used to support an RTA; the method of creation of an RTA, the representation and participation of member units of government on an RTA; the types of transportation services that an RTA could be authorized to administer; and the scope and limits of other RTA authority.

Special Committee on School Safety

Members: SENATOR LEHMAN, *chairperson;* REPRESENTATIVE PRIDEMORE, *vice chairperson;* SENATOR OLSEN; REPRESENTATIVE POPE-ROBERTS; VINCENT FLORES, BETSY GEORG, TOM GROGAN, TERRY MILFRED, GARY MYRAH, ROBERT ROSCH, LUKE VALITCHKA, LAURA VERNON, LUIS YUDICE.

The special committee is directed to review means by which school safety can be improved by examining the relationship between maintaining a safe and secure physical environment and fostering a safe and secure learning environment. The special committee is directed to focus on best practices relating to school discipline, including suspension and expulsion; programs for disciplined students; creation and implementation of bullying prevention and other school conduct enforcement measures; and interagency coordination with mental health, law enforcement, and other relevant agencies. The committee may also review means by which information can be disseminated and assistance can be provided.

Special Committee on Strengthening Wisconsin Families

Members: SENATOR TAYLOR, REPRESENTATIVE KESTELL, *cochairpersons;* SENATOR SCHULTZ; REPRESENTATIVE GRIGSBY; SHERYL ALBERS, JON ANGELI, JOHN BURGESS, GARY ERDMANN, DEBRA FIELDS, UNDRAYE HOWARD, WANDA MONTGOMERY, TERENCE RAY, LUCILLE ROSENBERG, MARY JO TITTL, JACK WESTMAN.

The Special Committee on Strengthening Wisconsin Families is appointed each biennium to study issues relating to strengthening Wisconsin families and to develop specific recommendations and legislative proposals relating to that topic. In the 2009-10 legislative biennium, the council has directed the special committee to develop recommendations to advise the new Department of Children and Families on the administration of programs administered by the new department, to promote the integration of family services formerly administered by multiple departments.

The special committee is to have no fewer than 4 nor more than 12 legislative members, and no fewer than 6 nor more than 11 nonlegislative members. The composition and duties of the special committee are prescribed in Section 13.83 (4) of the statutes.

The special committee was created by 2005 Wisconsin Act 467, and is scheduled to sunset on December 31, 2010.

Joint Committee on
LEGISLATIVE ORGANIZATION

Members: SENATOR RISSER (senate president), REPRESENTATIVE SHERIDAN (assembly speaker), *cochairpersons;* SENATORS DECKER (majority leader), S. FITZGERALD (minority leader), HANSEN (assistant majority leader), GROTHMAN (assistant minority leader); REPRESENTATIVES NELSON (majority leader), J. FITZGERALD (minority leader), SEIDEL (assistant majority leader), GOTTLIEB (assistant minority leader).

Mailing Address: Legislative Council Staff, P.O. Box 2536, Madison 53701-2536.

Location: 1 East Main Street, Suite 401, Madison.

Telephone: 266-1304.

Statutory References: Sections 13.80 and 13.90.

Agency Responsibility: The Joint Committee on Legislative Organization is the policy-making body for the legislative service bureaus: the Legislative Audit Bureau, the Legislative Fiscal Bureau, the Legislative Reference Bureau, and the Legislative Technology Services Bureau. In this capacity, it assigns tasks to each bureau, approves bureau budgets, and sets the salary of bureau heads. The joint committee selects the four bureau heads, but it acts on the recommendation of the Joint Legislative Audit Committee when appointing the state auditor. The joint committee also selects the director of the Legislative Council Staff.

The committee may inquire into misconduct by members and employees of the legislature. It oversees a variety of operations, including the work schedule for the legislative session, computer use, space allocation for legislative offices and legislative service agencies, parking on the State Capitol Park grounds, and sale and distribution of legislative documents. The joint committee recommends which newspaper should serve as the official state newspaper for publication of state legal notices. It advises the Government Accountability Board on its operations and, upon recommendation of the Joint Legislative Audit Committee, may investigate any problems the Legislative Audit Bureau finds during its audits. The committee may employ outside consultants to study ways to improve legislative staff services and organization.

Organization: The 10-member joint committee is a permanent body, consisting of the presiding officers and party leadership of both houses. The committee has established a Subcommittee on Legislative Services to advise it on matters pertaining to the legislative institution, including the review of computer technology purchases. The Legislative Council Staff provides staff assistance to the committee.

History: The joint committee was created by Chapter 149, Laws of 1963, as part of a legislative reorganization proposed by the Committee on Legislative Organization and Procedure under the authority of Chapter 686, Laws of 1961. The 1963 law also transferred the Legislative Reference Bureau and the Statutory Revision Bureau to the legislative branch and placed them under the supervision of the joint committee. The three other service agencies were placed under the committee's authority by later legislation: the Legislative Audit Bureau in Chapter 659, Laws of 1965; the Legislative Fiscal Bureau in Chapter 215, Laws of 1971; and the Legislative Technology Services Bureau in 1997 Wisconsin Act 27. 2007 Wisconsin Act 20 eliminated the Revisor of Statutes Bureau and transferred its duties to the Legislative Reference Bureau.

In 1966, the joint committee was empowered to investigate misconduct by legislators and legislative staff. Actions by subsequent legislatures expanded the joint committee's supervision of legislative operations to include legislative office space, legislative computer operations, and publication of notices and documents.

Representative Tom Nelson (left) of Kaukauna, conferring with Speaker Sheridan on the Assembly floor, is the youngest Assembly Majority Leader since the 1970s. (Brent Nicastro, Legislative Photographer)

Joint Survey Committee on
RETIREMENT SYSTEMS

Members: SENATOR WIRCH, REPRESENTATIVE HUBLER, *cochairpersons;* SENATORS CARPENTER; SCHULTZ; REPRESENTATIVES ZIEGELBAUER; GOTTLIEB; CHARLOTTE GIBSON (assistant attorney general appointed by attorney general), *secretary;* DAVID STELLA (designated by secretary of employee trust funds), SEAN DILWEG (insurance commissioner); MICHAEL R. LUTTIG (public member appointed by governor).

Mailing Address: Legislative Council Staff, P.O. Box 2536, Madison 53701-2536.

Telephone: 266-1304.

Statutory Reference: Section 13.50.

Agency Responsibility: The Joint Survey Committee on Retirement Systems makes recommendations on legislation that affects retirement and pension plans for public officers and employees, and its recommendations must be attached as an appendix to each retirement bill. Neither house of the legislature may consider such a bill until the joint survey committee submits a written report that describes the proposal's purpose, probable costs, actuarial effect, and desirability as a matter of public policy.

Organization: The 10-member joint survey committee includes majority and minority party representation from each legislative house. An experienced actuary from the Office of the Commissioner of Insurance may be designated to serve in the commissioner's place on the committee. The public member cannot be a participant in any public retirement system in the state and is expected to "represent the interests of the taxpayers". Appointed members serve 4-year terms unless they lose the status upon which the appointment was based. The joint survey committee is assisted by the Joint Legislative Council staff in the performance of its duties, but may contract for actuarial assistance outside the classified service.

Joint Legislative
STATE SUPPORTED PROGRAMS
STUDY AND ADVISORY COMMITTEE

Members: SENATOR OLSEN, 4 vacancies; 6 vacancies (representatives).

Statutory Reference: Section 13.47.

Agency Responsibility: Members of the Joint Legislative State Supported Programs Study and Advisory Committee visit and inspect the State Capitol and all institutions and office buildings owned or leased by the state. They are granted free and full access to all parts of the buildings, the surrounding grounds, and all persons associated with the buildings. The committee may also examine any institution, program, or organization that receives direct or indirect state financial support.

Organization: The committee consists of 5 senators and 6 representatives. Members appointed from each house must represent the two major political parties, and one legislator from each house must also be a member of the State of Wisconsin Building Commission. Assistance to the committee is provided by the Legislative Council Staff.

History: The use of a legislative committee to visit and supervise the use of state institutions and property dates back to 1881. The current joint committee was created by Chapter 266, Laws of 1973. It replaced the Committee to Visit State Properties, which had combined the functions of the Committee to Visit State Institutions, created in 1947 to inspect state property and state institutions, and the Committee on Physical Plant Maintenance, created in 1957 to manage the State Capitol and the single state office building then in existence.

Joint Survey Committee on
TAX EXEMPTIONS

Members: SENATOR ERPENBACH, REPRESENTATIVE HUBLER, *cochairpersons;* SENATORS DECKER, ELLIS*; REPRESENTATIVES CULLEN, ZIPPERER*; ROGER M. ERVIN (secretary of revenue); F. THOMAS CREERON (Department of Justice representative appointed by attorney general); KATHRYN DUNN (public member appointed by governor).

Mailing Address: Legislative Council Staff, P.O. Box 2536, Madison 53701-2536.

Telephone: 266-1304.

Statutory Reference: Section 13.52.

Agency Responsibility: The Joint Survey Committee on Tax Exemptions, created by Chapter 153, Laws of 1963, considers all legislation related to the exemption of persons or property from state or local taxes. It is assisted by the Legislative Council Staff.

Any legislative proposal that affects tax exemptions must be referred to the committee immediately upon introduction. Budget bills containing tax exemptions are referred simultaneously to the joint survey committee and the Joint Committee on Finance. The joint survey committee must report within 60 days on the tax exemptions contained within a budget bill. Neither house of the legislature may consider tax exemption proposals until the joint survey committee has issued its report, attached as an appendix to the bill, describing the proposal's legality, desirability as public policy, and fiscal effect. In the course of its review, the committee is authorized to conduct investigations, hold hearings, and subpoena witnesses.

Organization: The 9-member committee includes representation from each house of the legislature with 2 members from the majority party and one from the minority party. The public member must be familiar with the tax problems of local government. Members' terms expire on January 15 of odd-numbered years.

TRANSPORTATION PROJECTS COMMISSION

Members: GOVERNOR DOYLE, *chairperson;* SENATORS DECKER, HOLPERIN, HANSEN; LASEE, GROTHMAN; REPRESENTATIVES 5 vacancies; LEE MEYERHOFER, MICHAEL R. RYAN, LEONARD SOBCZAK (citizen members appointed by governor). Nonvoting member: FRANK BUSALACCHI (secretary of transportation).

Commission Secretary: JENNIFER CANCHOLA, jennifer.canchola@dot.wi.gov

Mailing Address: P.O. Box 7913, Madison 53707-7913.

Location: Hill Farms State Transportation Building, 4802 Sheboygan Avenue, Room 901, Madison.

Telephone: 266-5408.

Fax: 267-1856.

Statutory Reference: Section 13.489.

Agency Responsibility: The Transportation Projects Commission, created by 1983 Wisconsin Act 27, includes representation from each house of the legislature with 3 members from the majority party and 2 from the minority party. The commission reviews Department of Transportation recommendations for major highway projects. The department must report its recommendations to the commission by September 15 of each even-numbered year, and the commission, in turn, reports its recommendations to the governor or governor-elect, the legislature, and the Joint Committee on Finance before December 15 of each even-numbered year. The department must also provide the commission with a status report on major transportation projects every 6 months. The commission also approves the preparation of environmental impact or assessment statements for potential major highway projects.

Commission on
UNIFORM STATE LAWS

Members: JOANNE HUELSMAN, *chairperson;* RICHARD A. CHAMPAGNE (designated by chief,
Legislative Reference Bureau), *secretary;* SENATOR RISSER; REPRESENTATIVES CULLEN, GUNDRUM;
TERRY ANDERSON (director, Legislative Council Staff); JUSTICE ANN WALSH BRADLEY, MICHAEL
WEIDEN (public members appointed by governor).

Mailing Address: 1 East Main Street, Suite 200, Madison 53701-2037.

Telephone: 266-9930.

Fax: 264-6948.

Statutory Reference: Section 13.55.

Agency Responsibility: The Commission on Uniform State Laws advises the legislature on
uniform laws and model laws. It examines subjects on which interstate uniformity is desirable
and the best methods for achieving it, cooperates with the National Conference of Commissioners on Uniform State Laws in preparing uniform acts, and prepares bills adapting the uniform
acts to Wisconsin. The commission reports biennially to the Law Revision Committee of the
Joint Legislative Council.

*The Capitol is open to all citizens of Wisconsin. Senator Kathleen Vinehout of Alma meets with
representatives of her district's agricultural community.* (Brent Nicastro, Legislative Photographer)

Organization: The commission consists of 8 members, including 2 public members appointed by the governor for 4-year terms. Legislative members serve 2-year terms, must represent the
2 major political parties, and must be state bar association members. A legislative seat may be
filled by a former legislator if no current legislator meets the criteria, or if no eligible legislator
is willing or able to accept the appointment.

History: The commission was originally created by Chapter 83, Laws of 1893, which autho-
rized the governor to appoint 3 members to serve as the Commissioners for the Promotion of
Uniformity of Legislation in the United States. In 1931, Chapter 67 designated the Revisor of
Statutes as the sole Wisconsin commissioner. Chapter 173, Laws of 1941, added the chief of the
Legislative Reference Library as a commissioner. The commission was created in its present

form by Chapter 312, Laws of 1957, and its membership was expanded to include 2 members of the State Bar appointed by the governor. Chapter 135, Laws of 1959, added the director (then called the executive secretary) of the Legislative Council Staff as a member. Chapter 294, Laws of 1979, added 4 legislative members and deleted the requirement that public members appointed by the governor be members of the State Bar. 2003 Wisconsin Act 2 added a requirement that legislative members must be state bar association members. 2007 Wisconsin Act 20 eliminated the Revisor of Statutes, reducing the total membership to 8.

LEGISLATIVE SERVICE AGENCIES

LEGISLATIVE AUDIT BUREAU

State Auditor: JANICE L. MUELLER, janice.mueller@

Deputy State Auditor for Financial Audit: BRYAN NAAB, bryan.naab@

Deputy State Auditor for Program Evaluation: PAUL STUIBER, paul.stuiber@

Special Assistant to the State Auditor: JOE CHRISMAN, james.chrisman@

Audit Directors: DIANN L. ALLSEN, diann.allsen@; CAROLYN STITTLEBURG, carolyn.stittleburg@; DEAN SWENSON, dean.swenson@; KATE WADE, kate.wade@

Mailing Address: 22 East Mifflin Street, Suite 500, Madison 53703-2512.

Telephones: 266-2818; Fraud, waste, and mismanagement hotline: (877) FRAUD-17.

Fax: 267-0410.

Internet Address: http://www.legis.wisconsin.gov/lab

Legislative service agencies play an important role in the legislative process. State Auditor Janice Mueller (left) heads the Legislative Audit Bureau, which is responsible for assisting the legislature in its oversight role. Mueller and Kate Wade, Program Evaluation Director, testified on a proposed audit of the Wisconsin Shares program. (*Kristyna Wentz-Graff*/Milwaukee Journal Sentinel)

E-mail Address: Leg.Audit.Info@legis.wisconsin.gov

Address e-mail by combining the user ID and the state extender: userid@**legis.wisconsin.gov**

Publications: Audit reports of individual state agencies and programs; biennial reports.

Number of Employees: 86.80.

Total Budget 2007-09: $15,454,100.

Statutory Reference: Section 13.94.

Agency Responsibility: The Legislative Audit Bureau is responsible for conducting financial and program audits to assist the legislature in its oversight function. The bureau performs financial audits to determine whether agencies have conducted and reported their financial transactions legally and properly. It undertakes program audits to analyze whether agencies have managed their programs efficiently and effectively and have carried out the policies prescribed by law.

The bureau's authority extends to executive, legislative, and judicial agencies; authorities created by the legislature; special districts or zones; and certain service providers that receive state funds. The bureau may audit any county, city, village, town, or school district at the request of the Joint Legislative Audit Committee.

The bureau audits and reports on the financial transactions and records of every state agency at least once every 5 years. Agencies or funds audited more frequently include the State of Wisconsin Investment Board, the Department of Employee Trust Funds, State Fair Park, the state lottery, and various state insurance funds. The bureau maintains a toll-free number (1-877-FRAUD-17) to receive reports of fraud, waste, and mismanagement in state government. In addition, the bureau provides an annual audit opinion on the state's comprehensive financial statements, which are prepared by the Department of Administration.

Typically, the bureau's program audits are conducted at the request of the Joint Legislative Audit Committee, initiated by bureau staff, or required by legislation. The reports are reviewed by the Joint Legislative Audit Committee, which may hold hearings on them and may introduce legislation in response to audit recommendations.

Organization: The director of the bureau is the State Auditor, who is appointed by the Joint Committee on Legislative Organization upon the recommendation of the Joint Legislative Audit Committee. Both the State Auditor and the bureau's staff are appointed from outside the classified service.

History: The bureau was created as a legislative service agency under the jurisdiction of the Joint Committee on Legislative Organization by Chapter 659, Laws of 1965. It replaced the Department of State Audit, which was created by Chapter 9, Laws of 1947, as an executive agency. This followed a 1946 constitutional amendment that removed auditing powers from the secretary of state and authorized the legislature to provide for state audits by law.

Statutory Advisory Council

Municipal Best Practices Reviews Advisory Council: CRAIG KNUTSON, ADAM PAYNE (representing the Wisconsin Counties Association); ANTHONY ROACH (representing the League of Wisconsin Municipalities); EDWARD HUCK (representing the Wisconsin Alliance of Cities); DONNA VOGEL (representing the Wisconsin Towns Association). (All are appointed by the State Auditor.)

The 5-member Municipal Best Practices Reviews Advisory Council advises the State Auditor on the selection of county and municipal service delivery practices to be reviewed by the State Auditor. The auditor is required to conduct periodic reviews of procedures and practices used by local governments in the delivery of governmental services; identify variations in costs and effectiveness of such services between counties and municipalities; and recommend practices to save money or provide more effective service delivery. Council members are chosen from candidates submitted by the organizations represented. The council was created by 1999 Wisconsin Act 9 in Section 13.94 (8), Wisconsin Statutes, and succeeds the council created by 1995 Wisconsin Act 27.

LEGISLATIVE COUNCIL STAFF

See Joint Legislative Council pp. 286-287

LEGISLATIVE FISCAL BUREAU

Director: ROBERT WM. LANG.

Program Supervisors: FRED AMMERMAN, JERE BAUER, DARYL HINZ, DAVID LOPPNOW, CHARLES MORGAN, ROB REINHARDT.

Administrative Assistant: VICKI HOLTEN.

Mailing Address: 1 East Main Street, Suite 301, Madison 53703.

Telephone: 266-3847.

Fax: 267-6873.

Internet Address: www.legis.state.wi.us/lfb

E-mail Address: fiscal.bureau@legis.wisconsin.gov

Publications: Biennial budget and budget adjustment: summaries of state agency budget requests; cumulative and comparative summaries of the governor's proposals, Joint Committee on Finance provisions and legislative amendments, and separate summaries of legislative amendments when necessary; summary of governor's partial vetoes. Informational reports, budget issue papers on various state programs, and revenue estimates. (Reports and papers available on the Internet or upon request.)

Number of Employees: 35.00.

Total Budget 2007-09: $7,431,400.

Statutory Reference: Section 13.95.

Agency Responsibility: The Legislative Fiscal Bureau develops fiscal information for the legislature, and its services must be impartial and nonpartisan. One of the bureau's principal duties is to staff the Joint Committee on Finance and assist its members. As part of this responsibility, the bureau studies the state budget and its long-range implications, reviews state revenues and expenditures, and suggests alternatives to the committee and the legislature. In addition, the bureau provides information on all other bills before the joint committee and analyzes agency requests for new positions and appropriation supplements outside of the budget process.

The bureau provides fiscal information to any legislative committee or legislator upon request. On its own initiative, or at legislative direction, the bureau may conduct studies of any financial issue affecting the state. To aid the bureau in performing its duties, the director or designated employees are granted access, with or without notice, to all state departments and to any records maintained by the agencies relating to their expenditures, revenues, operations, and structure.

Organization: The Joint Committee on Legislative Organization is the policy-making body for the Legislative Fiscal Bureau, and it selects the bureau's director. The director is assisted by program supervisors responsible for broadly defined subject areas of government budgeting and fiscal operations. The director and all bureau staff are chosen outside the classified service.

History: The bureau was created by Chapter 154, Laws of 1969. It evolved from the legislative improvement study that was initiated by Chapter 686, Laws of 1961, using a Ford Foundation grant and state funding. Through the improvement program, the legislature developed its own fiscal staff, known as the Legislative Budget Staff, under the supervision of the Legislative Programs Study Committee. In February 1968, the study committee renamed the budget staff the Legislative Fiscal Bureau and specified its functions. Chapter 215, Laws of 1971, transferred responsibility for the bureau's supervision to the Joint Committee on Legislative Organization.

LEGISLATIVE REFERENCE BUREAU

Chief: STEPHEN R. MILLER, 267-2175, steve.miller@legis.wisconsin.gov

Administrative Services: CATHLENE M. HANAMAN, *deputy chief,* 267-9810, cathlene.hanaman@legis.wisconsin.gov

Information and Research Services: LAWRENCE S. BARISH, *research manager,* 266-0344, larry.barish@legis.wisconsin.gov

Legal Services: PETER R. GRANT, JEFFREY T. KUESEL, MARC E. SHOVERS, REBECCA C. TRADEWELL, *managing attorneys.*

Library Services: MARIAN G. ROGERS, *managing librarian,* 266-2824, marian.rogers@legis.wisconsin.gov

Mailing Address: P.O. Box 2037, Madison 53701-2037.

Location: 1 East Main Street, Suite 200.

Telephones: Legal: 266-3561; Research: 266-0341; Library Circulation: 266-7040.

Fax: Legal: 264-6948; Research and Library: 266-5648.

Internet Address: http://www.legis.wisconsin.gov/lrb

Publications: *Wisconsin Blue Book; Capitol Headlines;* Laws of Wisconsin; *Selective List of Recent Acquisitions;* various sections of the *Bulletin of the Proceedings of the Wisconsin Legislature;* Wisconsin Statutes and Annotations; Wisconsin Administrative Code and Register; Wisconsin Town Law Forms; *WisLaw* on compact disc; informational reports on various subjects. (All informational reports and the *Blue Book* are also available on the Internet.)

Number of Employees: 60.00.

Total Budget 2007-09: $11,738,500.

Representative Pat Strachota of West Bend, in her third term in the Assembly, discusses policy with Representative Ed Brooks of Reedsburg, who is serving his first term in the legislature. *(Jay Salvo, Legislative Photographer)*

LEGISLATIVE SERVICE AGENCIES

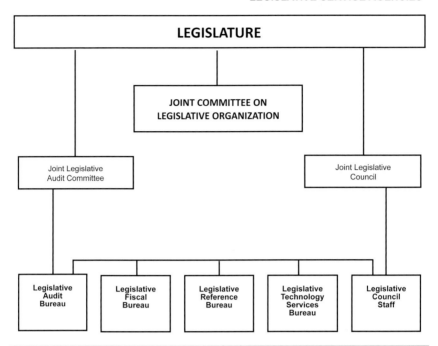

Statutory Reference: Section 13.92.

Agency Responsibility: The Legislative Reference Bureau provides nonpartisan, professional, confidential bill drafting, research, and library services to the legislature. Although it is primarily a legislative service agency, the bureau also serves public officials, students of government, and citizens.

By statute, the bureau is responsible for drafting all legislative proposals and amendments for introduction in the legislature. Legislative attorneys also prepare plain language analyses that are printed with all bills and most resolutions. A significant portion of the work of the legislative attorneys involves the drafting of the state's biennial budget.

The bureau enrolls the final text of all bills that have passed both houses before the bills are submitted for the governor's action. The bureau also publishes each act and produces the bound volumes of all session laws enacted during the biennial legislative session.

The bureau incorporates newly enacted laws into the existing statutes. The bureau prints updated Wisconsin Statutes and Annotations every two years when the legislature completes its session and publishes quarterly updated versions of the statutes on its Internet site and on compact disc.

As part of its statutory revision duties, the bureau prepares corrections bills to correct errors or resolve conflicts arising from the enactment of laws and systematically examines the statutes and session laws for similar defects and proposes revision bills to the Law Revision Committee.

The bureau edits and publishes the Wisconsin Administrative Code, the compilation of all current administrative rules that is updated monthly, and the semimonthly Wisconsin Administrative Register, which contains rule hearing and publication notices and summaries of emergency rules. It also prepares the Wisconsin Town Law Forms distributed to town officials to aid them in administering town government.

The reference and library sections provide a broad range of information to aid legislators and other government officials in the performance of their duties. The reference section publishes reports on subjects of legislative concern and, in the odd-numbered years, it publishes the *Wisconsin Blue Book*, the official almanac of Wisconsin government. The reference desk responds to inquiries about the work of the legislature and state government in general. The bureau also offers seminars on legislative procedure to students and civic groups.

The Dr. H. Rupert Theobald Legislative Library contains the bureau's extensive collection of material pertaining to government helps and public policy issues. The library staff prepares the *Index to the Bulletin of the Proceedings of the Wisconsin Legislature* which includes a subject index to legislation, author indexes, and subject indexes to legislative journals, administrative rules, and Wisconsin acts.

State law requires the bureau to maintain the drafting records of all legislation introduced and to use those records to provide information on legislative intent. Drafting records, beginning with the 1927 session, are available to the public as part of the bureau's noncirculating reference collection.

Organization: The Joint Committee on Legislative Organization is the policy-making body for the bureau, and it selects the bureau chief. The bureau chief and staff members are not included in the classified service.

History: The creation of the Legislative Reference Bureau, originally the Legislative Reference Library, by Chapter 168, Laws of 1901, was the first organized effort in the nation to provide a state legislature with professional staff assistance. Initially under the governance of the Free Library Commission, the bureau soon began providing bill drafting services to the legislature, a task officially assigned by Chapter 508, Laws of 1907. The bureau acquired the duty of editing the *Wisconsin Blue Book* in 1929 (Chapter 194). In 1963, the legislature renamed the agency the Legislative Reference Bureau and placed it under the direction of the Joint Committee on Legislative Organization. In 2008, the legislature transferred statutory revision duties to the bureau.

The Assistant Minority Leader helps define his party's position on legislation. Senator Glenn Grothman of West Bend makes that position known to his colleague Spencer Coggs of Milwaukee, a member of the majority Democrats. (Brent Nicastro, Legislative Photographer)

LEGISLATIVE TECHNOLOGY SERVICES BUREAU

Director: JEFF YLVISAKER.
Administration Manager: PAM BENISCH.
Enterprise Operations Manager: MATT HARNED.
Graphical Information Systems Manager: TONY VAN DER WIELEN.
Software Development Manager: DOUG DeMUTH.
Technical Support Manager: PHIL SCHWARZ.
Mailing Address: 17 West Main Street, Suite 200, Madison 53703.
Telephone: 264-8582.
Fax: 267-6763.
Internet Address: http://www.legis.wisconsin.gov/ltsb
Publications: *Wisconsin Legislative Biennial Strategic Technology Plan,* 2009-2010.
Number of Employees: 43.00.
Total Budget 2007-09: $7,351,300.
Statutory Reference: Section 13.96.

Agency Responsibility: The Legislative Technology Services Bureau (LTSB) provides confidential, nonpartisan information technology services and support to the Wisconsin Legislature. These services include legislative office automation, e-mail, web publishing, training, project management, custom software creation, and management of the information technology infrastructure.

LTSB creates, maintains, and enhances specialized software used for bill drafting, production of the *Wisconsin Statutes* and *Administrative Code,* and publication of the *Wisconsin Blue Book.* It supports the publication of legislative documents including bills and amendments, house journals, daily calendars, and the Bulletin of the Proceedings.

The bureau also maintains network infrastructure, data center operations, electronic communications, desktop computers, laptops, printers, and other technology devices. It keeps an inventory of computer hardware and software assets and manages technology replacement schedules. It provides redistricting services following each decennial U.S. Census and mapping services throughout the decade.

LTSB also provides specialized software for managing constituent interactions, delivers audio and video services, supports the legislature during floor sessions including the voting systems, manages the technology for the Wisconsin Legislature's Internet site, and offers training services for legislators and staff in the use of information technology.

Organization: The Joint Committee on Legislative Organization is the policy-making body for the bureau. It selects the director and is specifically responsible for reviewing and approving all information technology proposals. The director appoints bureau staff. Both the director and the staff serve outside the classified service.

History: The bureau was statutorily created by 1997 Wisconsin Act 27 as the Integrated Legislative Information Staff and was renamed by 1997 Wisconsin Act 237.

Representative Pedro Colón of Milwaukee, a member of the Joint Committee on Finance since 2005, confers with Speaker Michael Sheridan on the Assembly floor. Sheridan is the first Assembly Speaker from Janesville since 1877. (Jay Salvo, Legislative Photographer)

SUMMARY OF SIGNIFICANT LEGISLATION
ENACTED BY THE 2007 LEGISLATURE

This section highlights significant legislation enacted by the 2007 Wisconsin Legislature in the biennial session that began January 3, 2007, and concluded January 5, 2009. The legislation is categorized by subject matter and in cases when an act affects more than one area of state law, such as 2007 Wisconsin Act 20 (the budget act), significant provisions are separately described under multiple subject headings. The section concludes with a summary of major proposals that failed to be enacted or adopted.

The following table summarizes activity in recent legislative sessions:

	Legislative Session				
	1999-2000	2001-02	2003-04	2005-06	2007-08
Total Drafting Requests	9,774	10,192	9,560	10,134	7,919
Bills Introduced	1,503	1,440	1,568	1,971	1,581
Assembly Bills.	973	941	998	1,232	988
Senate Bills	530	499	570	739	593
Acts	198	109	327	491	242
Percentage of Bills Enacted . . .	13.2%	7.6%	20.9%	24.9%	15.3%
Bills Totally Vetoed	5	0	54	47	1
Bills Partially Vetoed	10	3	10	2	4

SIGNIFICANT 2007-2008 LEGISLATION

Agriculture

Act 20 (*SB-40*) creates the Buy Local, Buy Wisconsin Program under which the Department of Agriculture, Trade and Consumer Protection (DATCP) promotes, through grants and other activities, local consumption of agricultural products produced in Wisconsin.

Floor action is the final hurdle for legislation – the point at which a bill's merits are debated before it is voted on by the entire body. Representative Leah Vukmir of Wauwatosa, a veteran of four legislative sessions, addresses her colleagues on April 29, 2009. (Jay Salvo, Legislative Photographer)

Act 37 (*AB-52*) provides that a police dog who bites a person while performing law enforcement functions is not required to be quarantined under the rabies control law if the dog is immunized against rabies.

Alcoholic Beverages

Act 3 (*SB-52*) provides that on the Sunday that daylight saving time begins, certain beer and liquor retailers, including taverns, may remain open until 3:30 a.m.

Act 9 (*AB-122*) allows certain beer retailers, including grocery and liquor stores, to provide free samples of beer to customers.

Act 20 (*SB-40*) creates a brewpub permit for an applicant that makes 10,000 barrels of beer or less each year, operates a restaurant on the premises at which the sale of alcohol beverages is less than 60 percent of the restaurant's gross receipts, holds a retail beer license for the restaurant, and sells beer other than its own in the restaurant. A brewpub permit-holder may annually make up to 10,000 barrels of beer on the premises, bottle the beer, transport the beer to other brewpub or retail premises, sell and deliver the beer to wholesalers, annually sell at wholesale and deliver to retailers up to 1,000 barrels of the beer, and sell alcohol beverages at retail at the brewpub under the brewpub's retail license.

Act 85 (*SB-485*) makes numerous changes to laws related to wine distribution and production, and to distribution and sale of other alcohol beverages, including the following:

- Eliminates the reciprocal agreement system for authorizing interstate wine shipments directly to consumers in this state and replaces it with a new permit system available for both interstate and intrastate wine.
- Eliminates the authority of wineries, manufacturers, and rectifiers to sell wine at wholesale to retailers and eliminates the authority of rectifiers to sell liquor, other than wine, directly to retailers. The act eliminates the authority of a person holding an out-of-state shipper's permit to ship liquor to any person in Wisconsin other than a wholesaler or, under certain circumstances, to a manufacturer, rectifier, or winery.

Buildings and Safety

Act 11 (*SB-7*) changes terminology in the laws governing mobile homes, manufactured homes, and the mobile and manufactured housing industry, including standardizing the use of the terms "mobile home" and "manufactured home." The act clarifies the applicability of certain vehicle regulations to recreational vehicles and increases from two to three the minimum number of mobile or manufactured homes needed to qualify as a manufactured and mobile home community, which is subject to municipal regulation.

Act 14 (*AB-227*) requires an applicant for a building permit to complete at least 12 hours of continuing education every two years instead of six hours annually, as under former law.

Act 63 (*SB-167*) changes the standards for electrical wiring, and for inspection of electrical wiring, and the regulation of electricians. The act:

- Expands the scope of state and local standards for wiring and regulation of electrical inspections to include all buildings.
- Requires, with certain exceptions, that any person doing electrical work be licensed.
- Prohibits municipalities and counties from licensing electrical contractors and electricians.
- Expands the scope of state and local regulation of electrical inspections to include all buildings versus just public buildings and places of employment, as under former law.

Act 225 (*AB-717*) requires all cigarettes to be manufactured so that they extinguish when they are left burning without being smoked and requires cigarette manufacturers to mark packaging to show that the cigarettes meet the requirement.

Business and Consumer Law

Act 15 (*SB-133*) prohibits advertising or conducting a live musical performance using a false or deceptive connection between the performing group and a group that released a commercial recording.

Act 42 (*AB-207*) prohibits persons from providing video programming service, including cable television service, without a video service franchise granted by the Department of Financial Institutions, except that the act does not apply to video programming provided via satellite, broadcast television, wireless telecommunications, or Internet access. The act also provides requirements for persons granted video service franchises, including paying specific fees and maintaining certain service and privacy requirements, and regulation abilities of municipalities.

Act 125 (*AB-741*) directs the Legislative Audit Bureau to audit the economic development programs administered by the Department of Commerce (Commerce), the UW System, DATCP, the Department of Natural Resources (DNR), the Wisconsin Housing and Economic Development Authority (WHEDA), the Department of Tourism, the Technical College System, and the Department of Transportation (DOT) by July 1, 2012, and makes the following changes:

- Eliminates a number of unfunded, inactive, or duplicative economic development programs administered by Commerce, DATCP, or WHEDA.
- Consolidates several minority business grant and loan programs administered by Commerce.
- Consolidates several gaming economic development grant and loan programs administered by Commerce.
- Requires Commerce and other state entities to annually prepare comprehensive reports assessing economic development programs.
- Requires various state entities that administer economic development programs to establish goals and policies to improve the transparency and accountability of the economic development programs.

Act 226 (*March 2008 Special Session AB-1*) authorizes the addition of certain cell phone numbers to the "Do Not Call" directory maintained by DATCP.

Children

Act 20 (*SB-40*) makes the following changes to the laws relating to children:

- Creates the Department of Children and Families (DCF) on July 1, 2008; transfers from the Department of Health and Family Services (DHFS) to DCF the duty to provide or oversee county provision of various services to assist children and families, including services for children in need of protection or services and their families, adoption services, licensing of facilities that provide care for children, background investigations of caregivers of children, and child abuse and neglect investigations; and transfers from the Department of Workforce Development (DWD) to DCF administration of Wisconsin Works (W-2), including the child care subsidy program, child support enforcement and paternity establishment, and programs related to temporary assistance for needy families (TANF).
- Requires a juvenile court, when ordering a child to be placed outside the home under the supervision of a county or DHFS (DCF effective on July 1, 2008), and requires a circuit court, when transferring to a county or DHFS legal custody of a child found to be in need of protection or services in a divorce proceeding or other action affecting the family, to order the child into the placement and care of the county or DHFS and to assign the county or DHFS primary responsibility for providing services to the child. The act also requires a circuit court to include in an order transferring legal custody of a child certain findings, including a finding that continued placement of the child in the home would be contrary to the welfare of the child.

Act 104 (*SB-142*) requires day care center, group home, and shelter care facility staff who provide care for children to be proficient in the use of an automated external defibrillator, requires residential care centers for children and youth to have in each building that houses residents at

The majority party controls the agenda in a legislative body. Leaders of the Assembly Democrats discuss strategy during a recess of the March 24, 2009, floor session. (Brent Nicastro, Legislative Photographer)

least one staff member who has that proficiency, and requires shelter care facilities to have on the premises a staff member or other person who has that proficiency.

Constitutional Amendment

Enrolled Joint Resolution 26 (*Senate Joint Resolution 5*), approved by the 2007 Legislature on second consideration, prohibits the governor, in exercising his or her partial veto authority, from creating a new sentence by combining parts of two or more sentences of an enrolled bill. The electors ratified this amendment on April 1, 2008.

Correctional System

Act 20 (*SB-40*) makes the following changes relating to the correctional system:
- Expands the type of sex offenders required to be tracked using a global positioning system tracking device to include persons on lifetime supervision, persons about whom a special bulletin notification has been issued, and sex offenders whose results of a risk assessment test administered by the Department of Corrections (DOC) indicate that tracking is appropriate.
- Allows DOC and DHFS to provide substance abuse treatment programs to inmates who are eligible to earn early release to parole or to extended supervision.

Courts and Civil Actions

Act 20 (*SB-40*) creates the Judicial Council as an independent agency and authorizes the council to hire a staff attorney.

Act 179 (*AB-248*) allows part-time court commissioners to conduct preliminary examinations and arraignments and, with the consent of all parties, accept guilty pleas.

Crime and Criminal Procedure

Act 116 (*SB-292*) creates specific felonies of human trafficking and trafficking of a child. A business entity that engages in or benefits from trafficking may be dissolved or have its authorization to conduct business revoked.

Act 118 (*AB-8*) prohibits taking, exhibiting, or sending a depiction of a person in a locker room who is nude or partially nude without that person's consent. The act requires all owners or operators of a locker room to adopt a written locker room policy that meets requirements specified in the act.

Act 127 (*SB-260*) makes it a felony to intentionally impede the normal breathing or blood circulation of another person by applying pressure on the person's throat or neck or by blocking the person's nose or mouth.

Act 181 (*AB-597*) makes it a felony to interfere with a signal transmitted by a global positioning system tracking device.

All members have an opportunity to be heard by their colleagues on the Assembly floor. Representative Kristen Dexter of Eau Claire, serving her first term in the Assembly, addressed the body on February 24, 2009. (Brent Nicastro, Legislative Photographer)

Education

Higher Education

Act 20 (*SB-40*) makes the following changes to the laws governing higher education:

- Creates the Wisconsin Covenant Scholars Program to award grants, beginning in the 2011-12 academic year, to resident students who are enrolled as undergraduates in institutions of higher education in this state. Requires the Higher Educational Aids Board to reimburse the Board of Regents of the UW System and each Technical College System district board for all tuition and fees remitted for a veteran or for a spouse, surviving spouse, or child of a veteran.
- Creates the following information technology (IT) requirements for the UW System: a) requires the submission of annual IT strategic plans and quarterly reports on open-ended IT contracts to the Board of Regents; b) requires the Board of Regents to adopt written policies for certain IT projects and to establish requirements for certain high-risk IT projects and commercially available IT

products; c) imposes contract requirements for certain high-risk or high-cost IT projects; and d) requires the Board of Regents to report to the Joint Committee on Information Policy and Technology regarding certain high-risk or high-cost IT projects and allows that committee to review such projects.

- Requires the Board of Regents to make available information regarding segregated fees on the Internet Web site of each institution or campus of the UW System and that a student's bills for tuition or academic fees separately list tuition, academic fees, and segregated fees.

Primary and Secondary Education

Act 20 (*SB-40*) makes the following changes to the laws governing primary and secondary education:

- Awards grants to school districts to implement four-year-old kindergarten programs.
- Awards grants to school districts for school district consolidation studies.

Act 34 (*SB-214*) requires a public library to disclose to a law enforcement officer, at the officer's request, all library records pertinent to the alleged criminal conduct being investigated by the officer that were produced by a surveillance device under the library's control.

Act 40 (*SB-249*) provides that a school district may use federal, state, local, or private funds to pay the costs of advanced placement examinations taken by pupils enrolled in the school district who are eligible for a free or reduced-price lunch under the federal School Lunch Program.

Act 222 (*SB-396*) authorizes school districts to establish virtual charter schools, in which all or a portion of the instruction is provided via the Internet and the teachers and pupils are geographically remote from each other, and to accept pupils for attendance at virtual charter schools through the Open Enrollment Program. The act limits to 5,250 the total enrollment of all virtual charter schools beginning in the 2009-10 school year. The act requires instructional staff of virtual charter schools to hold teacher licenses issued by DPI and directs the Legislative Audit Bureau to conduct a financial and performance evaluation audit of virtual charter schools.

Act 226 (*March 2008 Special Session AB-1*) requires any school district that offers a four-year-old kindergarten program to make the program available to all eligible pupils.

Elections

Act 52 (*AB-295*) makes voter registration numbers publicly accessible.

Act 56 (*AB-82*) permits the electors of a town sanitary district to recall elective town sanitary district commissioners.

Employment

Act 7 (*AB-123*) permits volunteer fire fighters and emergency medical technicians to be paid semiannually or annually. Generally, employees must be paid no later than 31 days after the wages are earned.

Act 159 (*AB-32*) prohibits employment discrimination based on military service. However, under the act, an employer may refuse to employ for a particular job an individual who has been less than honorably discharged if the circumstances of the discharge substantially relate to the duties of the particular job.

Environment

Act 20 (*SB-40*) creates the Lower Fox River Remediation Authority to issue bonds to pay the costs of cleaning up environmental contamination caused by discharges of pollutants into the Fox River, from Lake Winnebago to Green Bay. The act provides reimbursement for a portion of the costs of out-of-state disposal of sediments contaminated with high levels of polychlorinated biphenyls (PCBs). Act 20 also raises fees, called tipping fees, imposed on the disposal of solid waste in landfills, increasing revenues for the recycling fund and the environmental fund.

Act 227 (*April 2008 Special Session SB-1*) ratifies the Great Lakes-St. Lawrence River Basin Water Resources Compact (the compact). The compact took effect on December 8, 2008, after being ratified by the eight Great Lakes states, approved by the U.S. Congress, and signed by President Bush. The compact requires the states to enact laws relating to the withdrawal and use of surface water and groundwater from the Great Lakes basin (the basin) that are at least as restrictive as requirements in the compact.

The compact generally prohibits new and increased diversions of water out of the basin. There are exceptions for new and increased diversions to provide water to the public in communities that are partly within the basin and partly outside of the basin (straddling communities), if certain requirements are satisfied, and for new or increased diversions to provide water to the public in communities that are entirely outside of the basin but within counties that are partly within the basin (communities within straddling counties), if more stringent requirements are satisfied.

The compact requires each state to regulate new and increased withdrawals of water from the basin by applying a decision-making standard, specified in the compact, to those withdrawals.

Under the act, DNR administers the requirements that apply to diversions and to water withdrawals in the basin through a permitting program. The act also requires reporting of large water withdrawals throughout the state to DNR. Finally, the act requires DNR to promote water conservation statewide, but generally DNR may not impose water conservation requirements outside of the basin.

Financial Institutions

Act 196 (*SB-483*) recreates the Wisconsin Uniform Securities Law to conform generally to the Uniform Securities Act of 2002. The act retains the general structure and substance of preexisting law with respect to securities registration and regulation of securities professionals and securities transactions, but makes numerous changes in definitions, requirements, enforcement, and administration related to the state's securities laws.

Act 211 (*SB-517*) alters the scope of the state's mortgage banking law by changing the definition of "loan" for purposes related to the regulation of mortgage bankers, mortgage brokers, and loan originators. The act narrows the definition of "loan" to apply only to loans for personal, family, or household purposes and only if the real property securing the lender's interest is located in this state.

Health and Social Services

Health

Act 102 (*AB-377*) requires a hospital that provides emergency services to an alleged victim of sexual assault to provide her with written and oral emergency contraception information and, if she is not pregnant and so requests, emergency contraception.

Act 106 (*SB-310*) changes laws governing donation of organs and other body parts to conform to the Revised Uniform Anatomical Gift Act of 2006. The changes include:

- Allowing a person who is 15 and one-half years old to make a donation that is effective upon death, subject to revocation of the donation by the donor's parent.
- Allowing new methods for making a donation, including using an organ donor sticker without other documentation or submitting a request for inclusion on a donor registry.
- Granting additional people the authority to make donations on behalf of another.

Medical Assistance

Act 20 (*SB-40*) required DHFS to request from the federal government the approval to implement a Medical Assistance (MA) program called BadgerCare Plus (BC+) that would provide health care benefits for eligible individuals. The request was granted, and BC+ began operating on February 1, 2008. BC+ replaces all of Badger Care and part of MA, so that certain persons eligible for MA will receive their health care coverage under BC+ instead. Generally, all of the following are eligible for BC+: a pregnant woman whose family income does not exceed 300 percent of the federal poverty level; a child under one year of age whose mother had coverage under MA or BC+ when the child was born; a child, including an unborn child, whose family income does not exceed 300 percent of the poverty level; a parent or caretaker of a child whose family income does not exceed 200 percent of the poverty level; and an individual, regardless of family income, who is under 21 years of age and who was in foster care on his or her eighteenth birthday. Additionally, a child whose family income exceeds 300 percent of the poverty level may purchase coverage under BC+.

Public Assistance

Act 20 (*SB-40*) creates a two-year "real work, real pay" pilot project in W-2, under which DWD pays an employer a monthly wage subsidy for employing an individual who is eligible for a W-2 employment position. An employer must make a good faith effort to retain the employee as a permanent unsubsidized employee after the employee's participation in the pilot projects ends.

Insurance

Act 20 (*SB-40*) transfers $200 million over the 2007-09 biennium to the Medical Assistance trust fund from the Injured Patients and Families Compensation Fund (fund); appropriates moneys to cover any claims, up to $100 million, that the fund is unable to pay because of insufficient moneys; and requires the board of governors of the fund to take the appropriation into account when setting health care provider assessments to be paid into the fund.

Local Law

Act 43 (*AB-254*) creates procedures for resolving boundary disputes between municipalities, for establishing common municipal boundaries, and for using alternative dispute resolution in municipal boundary, annexation, and land use disputes.

Act 49 (*SB-280*) authorizes an elective member of a political subdivision's governing body to refuse his or her salary.

Act 114 (*SB-176*) denies salary and wages to a suspended or discharged member of the Milwaukee police force pending an appeal to the Board of Fire and Police Commissioners if criminal charges are pending against the officer and the charges arose out of the same conduct that resulted in the discharge or suspension. The act also allows the board to grant to either party, only for cause, an adjournment of a trial or investigation before the board.

Legislators often advocate for their proposals at public hearings. Representatives Mark Gundrum of New Berlin and Scott Newcomer of Hartland testified before the Assembly Committee on Public Safety regarding 2009 Assembly Bill 130, which would require certain drunken driving suspects to pay for the costs of blood tests if convicted. (Jay Salvo, Legislative Photographer)

The front row of the Assembly Chamber is assigned to leadership. This group of veteran Republicans assembled there for an impromptu strategy session on March 24, 2009. (Brent Nicastro, Legislative Photographer)

Act 184 (*SB-269*) prohibits a political subdivision from imposing a fee for a call for certain law enforcement services related to domestic abuse, sexual assault, or stalking.

Natural Resources

Conservation, Forestry, and Stewardship

Act 20 (*SB-40*) extends the Warren Knowles-Gaylord Nelson Stewardship 2000 program to fiscal year 2019-20 and increases the overall funding from $803 million to $1,663 million.

Fish and Game

Act 23 (*AB-130*) requires DNR to issue resident fish and game licenses, stamps, and other such approvals to members of the Wisconsin national guard who apply, regardless of their residency. This requirement allows the members to pay lower fees.

Act 51 (*AB-296*) allows the following persons to be considered residents for the purpose of receiving Wisconsin hunting, trapping, and fishing licenses, resulting in lower fees:

- Members of the armed forces reserve units that are located in this state.
- Members of the armed forces who are in active service and who are no longer Wisconsin residents but who resided in Wisconsin when they entered active service.

Act 119 (*AB-334*) requires DNR to designate wild swine and feral swine as harmful wild animals.

Navigable Waters

Act 204 (*AB-297*) makes various changes to the laws regulating piers, wharves, and similar structures, including the following:

- Exempts from permitting requirements certain piers and wharves that were put in place on or before February 6, 2004.
- Prohibits DNR from taking enforcement action against a riparian owner for the improper placement of a pier, a wharf, or certain other structures if the owner obtained authorization for that pier, wharf, or structure on or before February 6, 2004.
- Allows a pier or wharf that is exempt from permit requirements to be relocated

or reconfigured if the owner previously registered the pier or wharf with DNR and, before relocating or reconfiguring the pier or wharf, registers it again with DNR.

Act 226 (*March 2008 Special Session AB-1*) prohibits most people from possessing invasive fish species of a type specified by DNR. The act also prohibits a person from transporting a boat or boating equipment upon a highway if the boat or equipment has any nonindigenous species attached that is of a type that causes economic or environmental harm, or harm to human health.

Parks and Recreation

Act 29 (*AB-526*) imposes a speed limit of 55 miles per hour on snowmobiles operated during the night through the winter of 2009-10.

Act 35 (*SB-161*) names the state trail system the Aldo Leopold Legacy Trail System.

Occupational Regulation

Act 20 (*SB-40*) establishes new licensure and regulatory requirements for prescription drug wholesale distributors, including restrictions on the transfer of wholesale prescription drugs and requirements for prescription drug pedigrees that detail the movement of prescription drugs through the distribution chain.

Act 31 (*AB-153*) requires dentists to complete 30 hours of continuing education every two years as a condition of license renewal.

Act 202 (*SB-409*) authorizes the Pharmacy Examining Board to create exceptions to the general requirement that pharmacists dispense prescription drugs only at licensed pharmacies by authorizing a pharmacist to dispense prescription drugs at any of the following locations: 1) a health care facility; 2) the office or clinic of a person authorized to prescribe and administer drugs; 3) a county jail, rehabilitation facility, state prison, or county house of correction; and 4) specified correctional, detention, and residential care facilities for children and youth.

Real Estate

Act 44 (*AB-341*) allows a political subdivision to impose a charge to fund the acquisition or initial improvement of land for public parks as a condition for subdivision approval and specifies the conditions under which the dedication of lands for storm water facilities is accepted by a municipality.

Act 184 (*SB-269*) allows a tenant to terminate his or her tenancy if the tenant or the tenant's child faces an imminent threat of serious physical harm from another person by remaining on the premises and if the tenant provides the landlord with notice and a certified copy of any of the following: certain injunctions protecting the tenant or child from the other person; a condition of release ordering the person not to contact the tenant; a criminal complaint alleging that the person sexually assaulted or stalked the child or tenant; or a criminal complaint filed as a result of the person's arrest for domestic abuse against the tenant. The act allows a landlord to terminate the tenancy of a tenant who causes an imminent threat of serious physical harm to another tenant or tenant's child if the tenant causing the threat is the named offender against the other tenant or child in a threat or harm-prevention document.

State Government

Act 1 (*January 2007 Special Session SB-1*) creates a nonpartisan Government Accountability Board that replaces the Elections Board and the Ethics Board. The act prescribes procedures for the board's investigation and enforcement of elections, ethics, and lobbying laws.

Act 5 (*SB-39*) authorizes 31 positions at the Department of Justice for the analysis of deoxyribonucleic acid (DNA).

Act 20 (*SB-40*) makes the following changes to the laws governing executive branch agency information technology (IT) projects:

- Requires the Department of Administration (DOA) to adopt written policies for executive branch IT projects that are included in the annual strategic plans for each executive branch agency and that either exceed $1 million or are vital to agency functions.
- Requires executive branch agencies to review commercially available products before initiating a customized IT development project and to justify to DOA the

development of a customized product.

- Requires DOA to submit, for each executive branch agency, detailed reports about high-risk and high-cost IT projects to the Joint Committee on Information Policy and Technology, including the original and updated costs, completion dates, and funding sources for the projects.

Act 20 also creates an Office of Energy Independence in DOA, which must work on initiatives for generating at least 25 percent of this state's power and transportation fuels from renewable resources, capturing at least 10 percent of the national emerging bioindustry and renewable energy markets, and ensuring that Wisconsin is a national leader in alternative energy research.

Act 20 also eliminates the Revisor of Statutes Bureau and transfers its functions to the Legislative Reference Bureau.

Act 166 (*AB-450*) requires that a United States flag that is displayed at a government building, structure, or facility be manufactured in the United States.

Act 217 (*AB-212*) designates the Wisconsin state tartan.

Act 226 (*March 2008 Special Session AB-1*) authorizes the secretary of administration to repurchase the state's right to receive any of the payments under the tobacco settlement agreement. The tobacco settlement agreement resulted from a settlement of lawsuits brought against U.S. tobacco product manufacturers. In 2001, the secretary sold the state's right to receive payments under the tobacco settlement agreement. The act further requires that all proceeds from the repurchase be deposited into the permanent endowment fund.

Taxation

Act 19 (*SB-122*) exempts from the property tax certain property used to treat waste or air contaminants.

Act 20 (*SB-40*) makes the following changes in the laws related to taxation:

- Creates income and franchise tax credits for all of the following: amounts paid by a health care provider for information technology hardware and software that maintains electronic medical records; amounts paid to install or retrofit service station pumps that dispense motor vehicle fuel consisting of at least 85 percent ethanol or at least 20 percent biodiesel; amounts paid for dairy manufacturing modernization or expansion; amounts paid to a community rehabilitation program to perform work for the taxpayer's business; and an amount equal to 10 cents per gallon for each gallon of biodiesel fuel produced by the taxpayer.
- Increases the excise tax on cigarettes from 77 cents per pack to $1.77 per pack.
- Increases the excise tax on tobacco products from 25 percent to 50 percent of the manufacturer's list price.
- Lowers from $25,000 to $5,000 the threshold amount that requires DOR to post on the Internet the identities of persons with delinquent tax accounts.

Act 190 (*AB-77*) distributes school levy and lottery and gaming property tax credits to counties rather than to municipalities.

Transportation

Act 20 (*SB-40*) does the following:

- Incorporates into state law requirements of the federal REAL ID Act of 2005 necessary for federal agencies to recognize for an "official purpose" state driver's licenses and identification cards. The act requires DOT to verify certain information about applicants for driver's licenses and identification cards, including the applicant's identity, date of birth, and proof of citizenship or legal presence in the United States (as under preexisting law). DOT must retain for at least ten years a copy of any documentation verifying information. For certain noncitizen applicants, any driver's licenses or identification cards must identify the license or card as temporary. DOT must also cancel a driver's license or identification card if it receives notice that the person's presence in the United States is no longer authorized. Every driver's license and identification card must include a digital color photograph of the applicant. DOT must provide electronic access to DOT's driver's license and identification card records to the driver licensing agencies of other states. These changes generally do not become effective until the later of May 11, 2008, or the date specified in a notice provided by DOT after DOT has determined that it is ready to fully implement the provisions of the act.

- Creates an additional federal fee of $10 that must be paid to DOT for issuance, renewal, or reinstatement of a driver's license or identification card. The act doubles the valid period for an identification card, from four years to eight years, and doubles the identification card fee, from $9 to $18.

Act 94 (*SB-369*) restricts a person with an occupational driver's license to vehicles equipped with an ignition interlock device if the person has two or more violations relating to operating a motor vehicle while intoxicated and a court requires the person to use an ignition interlock device.

Act 111 (*SB-116*) changes the criminal penalties for repeat drunken driving offenses. A fifth or sixth offense is a Class H felony; a seventh, eighth, or ninth offense is a Class G felony; and a tenth or subsequent offense is a Class F felony.

Act 117 (*SB-72*) provides for the state to join the Midwest Interstate Passenger Rail Compact, which promotes and facilitates intercity passenger rail service in the Midwest and coordinates interstate passenger rail service. The compact creates a Midwest Interstate Passenger Rail Commission, the duties of which include funding and authorizing passenger rail improvements in the Midwest, seeking partnerships to improve passenger rail service, and seeking a long-term, interstate plan for high-speed passenger rail service.

Veterans and Military Affairs

Act 20 (*SB-40*) makes a number of changes in the laws regarding veterans and military affairs. The act:

- Requires the Department of Veterans Affairs to establish a voluntary statewide registry of information regarding veteran's health issues, including post-traumatic stress disorder and Gulf War syndrome.

One of the most high-profile bills of the early part of the 2009 session was Senate Bill 4, popularly known as Melinda's Law, which regulates traveling sales crews. Speaker Sheridan, a cosponsor of the bill, advocated its passage. (Brent Nicastro, Legislative Photographer)

- Increases from $2,000 to $3,000 the maximum amount available for subsistence aid to a veteran under the Veterans Assistance Program during a 12-month period and increases from $5,000 to $7,500 the total amount available to a veteran.
- Expands eligibility for burial at a veterans cemetery to include veterans who died while on active duty and deceased resident veterans who were released from active duty under conditions other than dishonorable.
- Provides funding to the city of Milwaukee for the housing costs of homeless veterans and their families.

The proposal to ban smoking in many public areas of the state was a hotly contested issue. Assembly Democrats discussed the issue prior to the floor debate on the bill on May 13, 2009. (Brent Nicastro, Legislative Photographer)

MAJOR PROPOSALS THAT FAILED ENACTMENT OR ADOPTION

Children

Assembly Bill 746 and *Senate Bill 401* would have raised from 17 to 18 the age at which an adult criminal court, rather than the juvenile court, has jurisdiction over a person who violates a criminal law.

Constitutional Amendments

Assembly Joint Resolution 17 would have required a photographic identification issued by this state or the federal government in order for a person to vote, or register to vote, at the polls on election day.

Assembly Joint Resolution 106 would have established the right of the people to contract privately for health care services and would have prohibited mandatory participation in a state-sponsored health care system or plan.

Courts and Civil Actions

Senate Bill 343 would have allowed creators of video programs, such as the Big Ten Network and the NFL Network, to seek arbitration regarding their attempts to broadcast their programs on certain cable and satellite television systems.

Assembly Bill 418 would have restricted access to the Consolidated Court Automation Programs (CCAP), the circuit court online database of civil and criminal cases, to judges and court officials, law enforcement personnel, attorneys, accredited journalists, persons who regularly review court documents as one of their job duties, and persons who have submitted a written application for access to the clerk of courts or district attorney and have shown a reasonable purpose for accessing CCAP.

Crime and Criminal Procedure

Assembly Bill 695 and *Senate Bill 537* would have modified the John Doe statute, which permits a person to file a complaint with a judge if the person believes a crime may have been committed and requires a judge who receives such a complaint to commence a proceeding to determine if a crime has been committed. Assembly Bill 695 would have prohibited a John Doe complaint if the victim of the alleged crime was in custody, if the alleged crime occurred on property of DOC, DHFS, or a county jail, or if the crime was alleged to have been committed by certain DOC, DHFS, or law enforcement employees. Under Senate Bill 537, a judge who received a John Doe complaint but determined that a hearing was not necessary could have disregarded the complaint.

Employment

Assembly Bill 208 and *Senate Bill 80* would have required employers of traveling sales crews to register with DWD; imposed certain bonding, disclosure, safety, insurance, and other requirements on those employers; and prohibited certain employment practices by those employers.

Financial Institutions

Assembly Bill 218 would have adopted the Uniform Debt-Management Services Act, which was approved by the National Conference of Commissioners on Uniform State Laws in 2005.

Health and Social Services

Senate Bill 40 would have devoted certain cigarette tax and tobacco products tax revenues, an increased annual assessment on hospital gross revenues, tobacco settlement moneys, and moneys transferred from the injured patients and families compensation fund. The fund would have supported a board, an authority, and certain health care programs, including MA, that are currently funded from general purpose revenues.

Senate Bill 490 would have increased the annual assessment on gross revenues of hospitals to support certain MA provider reimbursements and would have transferred moneys to the Injured Patients and Families Compensation Fund.

Senate Bill 562 would have created the Healthy Wisconsin health care plan, funded through assessments paid by employers and persons employed in this state, to provide to all residents of the state who are under 65 years of age and not eligible for MA or for federal health care coverage the health care benefits that are provided under the state's health care plan for state employees.

Assembly Bill 216 would have required the Department of Justice, when conducting a background check on a prospective handgun purchaser, to check whether a court had determined that the person's mental health rendered him or her ineligible to possess a firearm under federal law.

Assembly Bill 834 and *Senate Bill 150* would have banned smoking inside all restaurants, taverns, and almost all other places of employment.

Insurance

Senate Bill 178 would have required health insurance policies to cover treatment for autism spectrum disorders.

Public Utilities

Assembly Bill 346 would have eliminated limits on the PSC's authorization of the construction of nuclear power plants.

State Government

Senate Bill 12 and *December 2007 Special Session Senate Bill 1* would have made extensive changes to campaign finance and related laws.

Assembly Bill 250 and *Senate Bill 171* would have provided for public financing of campaigns for the office of justice of the supreme court.

Assembly Bill 272, Assembly Bill 355, and *Assembly Bill 704* and *Senate Bill 77, Senate Bill 182,* and *Senate Bill 463* would have expressly specified that the campaign finance law regulates certain communications that do not urge a vote for or against a candidate ("issue ads").

Senate President Fred Risser of Madison reacts joyously upon the signing of the state smoking ban, the culmination of decades of advocacy. (Brent Nicastro, Legislative Photographer)

Executive
Branch

6

The executive branch: profile of the executive branch and descriptions of constitutional offices, departments, independent agencies, state authorities, regional agencies, and interstate agencies and compacts

An Infrared View of Saturn

(Erich Karkoschka (University of Arizona), and NASA)

ELECTIVE CONSTITUTIONAL EXECUTIVE STATE OFFICERS

Office	Officer/Party	Residence[1]	Term Expires	Annual Salary[2]
Governor	Jim Doyle (Democrat)	Madison	January 3, 2011	$137,092
Lieutenant Governor	Barbara Lawton (Democrat)	Green Bay	January 3, 2011	72,394
Secretary of State	Douglas J. La Follette (Democrat)	Kenosha	January 3, 2011	65,079
State Treasurer	Dawn Marie Sass (Democrat)	Milwaukee	January 3, 2011	65,079
Attorney General.	J.B. Van Hollen (Republican)	Waunakee	January 3, 2011	133,033
Superintendent of Public Instruction	Elizabeth Burmaster (nonpartisan office)	Madison	July 6, 2009	109,587
Superintendent of Public Instruction	Tony Evers (nonpartisan office)	Madison	July 1, 2013	122,516

[1]Residence when originally elected.

[2]Annual salary as established for term of office by the Wisconsin Legislature. Constitutional officers may not receive a pay raise during their term of office. Effective January 2009, the annual salaries for newly elected or reelected officers is: Governor: – $144,423; Lt. Governor – $76,261: Secretary of State – $68,556; State Treasurer – $68,556; Attorney General – $140,147; Superintendent of Public Instruction – $122,516.

Sources: 2007-2008 Wisconsin Statutes; Wisconsin Legislative Reference Bureau, Wisconsin Brief 08-13, *Salaries of State Elected Officials*, December 2008.

Summer Storm (Rick Langer)

EXECUTIVE BRANCH

A PROFILE OF THE EXECUTIVE BRANCH

Structure of the Executive Branch

The structure of Wisconsin state government is based on a separation of powers among the legislative, executive, and judicial branches. The legislative branch sets broad policy objectives and establishes the general structures and regulations for carrying them out. The executive branch supervises the day-to-day administration of the programs and policies, while the judicial branch is responsible for adjudicating any conflicts that may arise from the interpretation or application of the laws.

Constitutional Officers. The executive branch includes the state's six constitutional officers – the governor, lieutenant governor, secretary of state, state treasurer, attorney general, and state superintendent of public instruction. Originally, the term of office for all constitutional officers was two years, but since the 1970 elections, their terms have been four years. All, except the state superintendent, are elected on partisan ballots in the fall elections of the even-numbered years at the midpoint between presidential elections. Though originally a partisan officer, the superintendent is now elected on a nonpartisan ballot in the April election.

The governor, as head of the executive branch, is constitutionally required to "take care that the laws be faithfully executed". In Article V of the state constitution, as ratified in 1848, the people of Wisconsin provided for the election of a governor and a lieutenant governor who would become "acting governor" in the event of a vacancy in the governor's office. Originally, the lieutenant governor was also the presiding officer of the senate. (By subsequent amendments, the lieutenant governor was relieved of senate duties and now assumes the full title of "governor" if the office is vacated.)

In Article VI, the constitution provided for three additional elected officers to assist in administering the laws of the new state. The first session of the legislature in 1848 authorized the secretary of state to keep official records, including enrolled laws and various state papers, and to act as state auditor by examining the treasurer's books and preparing budget projections for the legislature. The state treasurer was given responsibility for receiving all money and tax collections and paying out only those amounts authorized by the legislature for the operation of state government. The attorney general was to provide legal advice to the legislature and other constitutional officers and represent the state in legal matters tried in the courts of this state, other states, and the federal government.

The sixth officer, created by Article X of the constitution, was the state superintendent of public instruction. The first legislature gave the superintendent very specific duties, including the mandate to travel throughout the state inspecting common schools and advocating good public schools. The superintendent was to recommend texts, take a census of school age children, collect statistics on existing schools, and determine the apportionment of school aids.

The simplicity of administering state government in the early years is illustrated by the fact that total expenditures for 1848 government operations were only $13,472, which included the expenses of the legislature and circuit courts. As prescribed by the constitution and state law, the salaries of all six constitutional officers totaled $5,050 that year. (The lieutenant governor did not receive a salary, but he was given a double legislative per diem.) The state's annual budget totaled $26.5 billion in 2007-2009, and many of the duties first assigned to the constitutional officers are now carried out by specialized state agencies.

1967 Reorganization. Over a century later, the Wisconsin Committee on the Reorganization of the Executive Branch, in its report to the 1967 Legislature, concluded that state government could no longer be neatly divided into precise legislative, executive, and judicial domains. In many instances the subjects of legislation had become so technically complex that the legislature found it necessary to grant rule-making authority to the administrative agencies. The courts had also encountered a staggering load of technical detail and had come to depend on administrative agencies to use their quasi-judicial powers to assist the judicial branch.

Although the Wisconsin Constitution delegated ultimate responsibility for state administration to the governor, the proliferation of agencies over the years had made it increasingly difficult for one official to exercise effective executive control. The committee identified 85 state agencies within the executive branch of Wisconsin state government, many of which had no direct relationship to the governor. Chapter 75, Laws of 1967, attempted to integrate agencies by function and make them responsive to the elected chief executive, by drastically reducing the number of executive agencies from 85 to 32. Like everything else, state government does not remain static, however. Since the 1967 reorganization, the legislature has created new state agencies, while abolishing or consolidating others. In addition, there have been numerous changes to the duties and responsibilities of the various agencies. The following sections describe the current organization of the executive branch.

Departments. The term "department" is used to designate a principal administrative agency within the executive branch. Within a department, the major subunit is the division, which is headed by an administrator. Each division, in turn, is divided into bureaus, headed by directors. Bureaus may include sections, headed by chiefs, and smaller units, headed by supervisors. There currently are 18 departments in the executive branch.

Wisconsin Administrative Departments

Administration	Military Affairs
Agriculture, Trade and Consumer Protection	Natural Resources
Children and Families	Public Instruction
Commerce	Regulation and Licensing
Corrections	Revenue
Employee Trust Funds	Tourism
Financial Institutions	Transportation
Health Services	Veterans Affairs
Justice	Workforce Development

In the majority of cases, the departments are headed by a secretary appointed by the governor with the advice and consent of the senate. Only the Department of Employee Trust Funds and the Department of Veterans Affairs are headed by boards that select the secretary. When administrators are personally chosen by and serve at the pleasure of the governor, they usually work in close cooperation with the chief executive.

Debate about whether the governor should directly appoint department heads continues. Public administration theory has long held that a governor can be the chief executive only if he or she has the authority to hold department heads directly accountable. On the other hand, the original purpose of a board was to insulate a department from politics, thereby enabling its head and staff to develop expertise and a sense of professionalism.

Independent Agencies. In addition to constitutional offices and administrative departments, there are 11 units of the executive branch that have been specifically designated as independent agencies.

Independent Executive Agencies

Educational Communications Board	State Historical Society of Wisconsin
Employment Relations Commission	State Investment Board
Government Accountability Board	State Public Defender Board
Higher Educational Aids Board	Technical College System
Office of the Commissioner of Insurance	University of Wisconsin System
Public Service Commission	

Although the independent agencies are usually headed by part-time boards or multiple commissioners, the governor appoints most of these officials, with advice and consent of the senate, which serves to strengthen executive control of these units.

Authorities. In some instances, the legislature has decided to create corporate public bodies, known as "authorities", to handle specific functions. Although they are agencies of the state, the authorities operate outside the regular government structure and are intended to be financially self-sufficient. Currently, there are 8 authorities provided for by Wisconsin law, 7 of which are active – the Wisconsin Aerospace Authority (WAA), the Fox River Navigational System Authority, the Lower Fox River Remediation Authority, the Wisconsin Health and Educational Facilities Authority (WHEFA), the Health Insurance Risk-Sharing Plan Authority, the Wisconsin Housing and Economic Development Authority (WHEDA), and the University of Wisconsin Hospitals and Clinics Authority. WAA, the Lower Fox River Remediation Authority, WHEDA, WHEFA, and UW Hospitals and Clinics Authority are authorized to issue bonds to finance their respective activities. Most authority members are appointed by the governor with advice and consent of the senate, but some are chosen from the legislature or serve as *ex officio* members.

Nonprofit Corporations. In 1985, the legislature created the Bradley Center Sports and Entertainment Corporation, a public, nonprofit corporation, which operates the Bradley Center in Milwaukee, the home of the Milwaukee Bucks, the Milwaukee Admirals hockey team, and the Marquette University basketball team. The corporation is headed by a board of directors appointed by the governor.

1999 Wisconsin Act 105 created the Wisconsin Technology Council, referenced in the statutes as the High-Technology Business Development Corporation. It supports the creation, development, and retention of science-based and technology-based businesses in the state.

Special Districts. The legislature may create special districts that serve "a statewide public purpose." These districts oversee the management of facilities for exposition centers, sports teams, and the cultural arts. Members of the governing boards are appointed by public officials. Currently, the Wisconsin Center, Miller Park, Lambeau Field, and the Madison Overture Center operate as special districts.

Boards, Councils, and Committees. Many departments and agencies have subordinate part-time boards, councils, and committees that carry out specific tasks or act in an advisory capacity. Boards may function as policy-making units, and some are granted policy-making or quasi-judicial powers. Examining boards set the standards of professional competence and conduct for the professions they supervise, and they are authorized to examine new practitioners, grant

Governor Doyle signed the 2009-2011 biennial budget bill on June 29, 2009. It was the earliest completion of the budget process since 1979. (Brent Nicastro, Legislative Photographer)

licenses, and investigate complaints of alleged unprofessional conduct. Councils function on a continuing basis to study and recommend solutions for problems arising in a specified functional area of state government. Committees usually are short-term bodies, appointed to study a specific problem and to recommend solutions or policy alternatives.

Boards are always created by statute. Councils are usually created by statute, but committees, because of their temporary nature, are created by session law rather than being written into the statutes. In addition, agency heads may create and appoint their own councils or committees as needed. The *Blue Book* describes only those units created by statute.

Attached Units. Under the 1967 reorganization, certain boards, commissions, and councils were attached to departments or independent agencies for administrative purposes only. These units are sometimes referred to as "15.03 units" because of the statutory section number that defines them. The larger agencies are expected to provide various services, such as budgeting and program coordination, but the 15.03 units exercise their statutory powers independently of the department or agency to which they are attached.

Government Employment

Classified Service. An important feature of Wisconsin state government employment is the merit system. Wisconsin's civil service, which is called "classified service", is designed to ensure that the most qualified person is hired for the job, based on test results and experience, rather than political affiliation. In 1905, Wisconsin was one of the first states to adopt such a system, and the Wisconsin classified service was considered one of the strongest because it encompassed the major portion of state personnel.

Since the 1967 reorganization of the executive branch, the trend has been to make top agency positions, including deputy secretaries, executive assistants, and division administrators, unclassified appointments. Despite this change at the top levels, most state employees, with the principal exception of legislative staff and the University of Wisconsin faculty and academic appointments, are hired and promoted through the classified service on the basis of merit.

Salaries. All positions in the classified service are categorized so that those involving similar duties, responsibilities, and qualifications are paid on the same basis. The Office of State Employment Relations (OSER) is directed to apply the principle of equal pay for equivalent skills and responsibilities when assigning a classification to a pay range.

State employees, with some exceptions, may join labor unions and engage in collective bargaining, but they are prohibited by state law from striking. Collective bargaining agreements, negotiated between OSER and labor organizations, are submitted to the Joint Committee on Employment Relations. The committee forwards its recommendations to the legislature in bill form for approval of salaries, fringe benefits, and other changes in the law. If the committee or legislature does not approve the proposed agreement, it is returned for renegotiation.

Each biennium, OSER establishes the compensation plan of classifications and related salary ranges for those classified employees not covered by collective bargaining agreements, subject to modification by the Joint Committee on Employment Relations. The governor may veto the committee's actions, although the vote of six committee members can override a veto. Some provisions of the compensation plan, as approved by the committee, may require changes in existing law, in which case they must be presented in bill form to the legislature for enactment.

Number of State Employees. The increasing size and complexity of state government is reflected in the number of employees. To illustrate this, a total of 1,924 people worked for Wisconsin state government in 1906. By contrast, according to the Department of Administration's State Budget Office, 74,491 full- and part-time employees were working for the state in January 2009, which corresponds to 68,821 full-time equivalent employees.

Housing State Government

The first capitol in Madison was built during the Wisconsin Territory days at a cost of more than $60,000. Construction began in 1837 but was not completed until 1845. The building, which served as the first state capitol, was demolished in 1863 to make way for a larger second capitol, which was completed in 1866. When the second state capitol was extensively damaged by fire in 1904, construction of the current capitol began. The present capitol, which was completed in 1917 for $7,203,826.35, has undergone extensive restoration and renovation, costing more than $140 million, completed in 2001.

Today, the agencies of state government in Madison are housed in the capitol and various state-owned office buildings, with additional space leased from private landlords. There are also state office buildings in Eau Claire, Green Bay, La Crosse, Milwaukee, Waukesha, and Wisconsin Rapids, plus district offices maintained throughout the state for the field units of many of the operating departments.

Besides its office buildings, the state owns or maintains a variety of educational, correctional, and mental health institutions across Wisconsin. The University of Wisconsin System operates 13 degree-granting institutions and 13 two-year colleges that feature freshman-sophomore instruction.

The state's adult corrections program, under the direction of the Department of Corrections, currently operates 5 maximum security prisons, 11 medium security prisons, 2 minimum security institutions, a prison for women, and 16 correctional centers. The department's juvenile corrections program operates Ethan Allen School at Wales and Lincoln Hills School at Irma for male juveniles and Southern Oaks Girls School at Union Grove.

Through the Department of Health Services, the state operates 4 mental health institutions at Madison, Mauston, and Winnebago, and 3 centers for the developmentally disabled at Madison, Chippewa Falls, and Union Grove. The department also operates the Mendota Juvenile Treatment Center, a secure juvenile correctional facility in an inpatient mental hospital setting.

The Department of Public Instruction maintains a school that offers special training for blind and visually impaired students at Janesville and a similar school for the deaf and hard-of-hearing at Delavan. The Wisconsin Veterans Homes at King in Waupaca County and Union Grove in Racine County are operated by the state to serve eligible Wisconsin veterans and qualifying spouses.

Functions of the Executive Branch

Governor and Lieutenant Governor. The governor, as Wisconsin's chief executive officer, represents all the people of the state. Because of this, the Office of the Governor is the focal point for receiving suggestions and complaints about state affairs. Administratively, the governor exercises authority through the power of appointment, consultation with department heads, and execution of the executive budget after its enactment by the legislature. The governor plays a key role in the legislative process through drafting the initial version of the biennial budget, which is submitted to the legislature in the form of a bill. Other opportunities to influence legislative action arise in the chief executive's state of the state message and special messages to the legislature about topics of concern. The governor also shapes the legislative process through the power to veto bills, call special sessions of the legislature, and appoint committees or task forces to study state problems and make recommendations for changes in the law.

Based on a 1979 amendment, the constitution provides that if the incumbent governor dies, resigns, or is removed from office, the lieutenant governor becomes governor for the unexpired term. The lieutenant governor serves temporarily as "acting governor" when the governor is impeached, incapacitated, or absent from the state.

Commerce. While the U.S. Constitution specifically delegates to Congress the regulation of interstate commerce, each state regulates intrastate commerce within its borders. The definitions of interstate and intrastate commerce overlap at times, and over the years the U.S. Supreme Court has greatly broadened the meaning of the "commerce clause" in the federal constitution. Despite this broad interpretation, the states continue to exercise considerable authority over commerce.

Commerce involves goods, services, and commercial documents, as well as transportation and communication, so the state's involvement in regulating commerce is broad. The state's primary objective is to protect the public as consumers and as participants in financial transactions. Wisconsin state government is also interested in maintaining a stable, orderly market for carrying out commercial activities and for promoting the state's economic development.

One aspect of consumer protection is the inspection of farm products and the conditions under which they are produced. The state inspects cattle for infectious diseases, conducts research in animal and plant diseases, regulates the use of pesticides, grades fruits and vegetables for marketing, and sets standards for processed food. Explicit standards are set by law or in the administrative rules promulgated by the Department of Agriculture, Trade and Consumer Protection. The department is concerned not only with the conditions of growing and processing food but also with fair trade practices in its sale.

Another important aspect of consumer protection is the licensing of various trades and professions. Individuals working in certain professions must achieve state-mandated levels of training and proficiency before they can offer their services to the public. Examples include professions affecting public health, such as doctors and nurses, or public safety, such as architects and engineers. The Department of Regulation and Licensing assists a variety of examining boards associated with various trades and professions and directly regulates certain types of professional activity.

The state protects consumers by maintaining an orderly market in which the public can conduct business. State activities include specifying methods of fair competition, regulating rates for public utilities, setting standards for the operation of financial institutions, regulating gambling, and regulating the sale of securities and insurance. The Department of Financial Institutions regulates banks, savings institutions, credit unions, and the sale of securities. It also registers trademarks, corporations, and other organizations and files Uniform Commercial Code documents. The Office of the Commissioner of Insurance regulates the sale of insurance. The Public Service Commission regulates public utility rates and services. The Gaming Division in the Department of Administration regulates racing and charitable gambling and oversees gaming compacts between Indian tribes and the state. The Department of Revenue administers the Wisconsin Lottery.

The state is concerned with promoting economic development. The Department of Commerce provides assistance to communities and small businesses, promotes international trade, and recommends private and public sector programs to further long-term growth. Through the Wisconsin Development Fund and other programs, it awards grants or loans to fund technical research, labor training programs, and other major economic development projects that promise to create jobs and increase capital investment. The Department of Tourism promotes travel to Wisconsin's scenic, historic, artistic, educational, and recreational sites. It stimulates the development of private commercial tourist facilities and encourages local tourist-related businesses.

In the interests of public safety and welfare, the state enforces laws that regulate public and private buildings. The Department of Commerce enforces dwelling codes, reviews construction plans for new buildings, inspects subsystems that serve buildings, and performs training and consulting services for the building industry.

Education. Wisconsin officially recognized the importance of education within a democratic society at statehood in 1848 when it provided for the establishment of local schools in the state constitution and required that education be free to all children. The constitution further directed the legislature to establish a state university at Madison and colleges throughout the state as needed.

Wisconsin's public educational institutions now enroll over one million students each year. In fall 2008, there were 873,586 pupils in the public elementary (589,418) and secondary (284,168) schools and 175,056 students enrolled in the University of Wisconsin System. The Technical College System enrolled 117,722 students in its associate degree programs for the 2007-08 school year and 264,218 in its vocational, technical diploma, and college transfer classes.

Wisconsin relies on 426 local school districts to administer its elementary and secondary programs. Twelve cooperative educational service agencies (CESAs) furnish support activities to the local districts on a regional basis, and the Department of Public Instruction, headed by the State Superintendent of Public Instruction, a nonpartisan constitutional officer, provides supervision and consultation for the districts.

In 1970 the state was divided into 16 vocational, technical, and adult education districts. These districts, renamed technical college districts, are each supervised by a district board that has taxing power. At the state level, the Technical College System Board supervises the districts.

At the collegiate level, all state-financed institutions of higher education are integrated into a single University of Wisconsin System. The system's two largest campuses at Madison and Milwaukee offer programs leading to doctoral degrees. Eleven other degree-granting institutions provide 4-year courses of baccalaureate study, and 13 UW Colleges provide 2-year courses of college-level study. State funding also supports Wisconsin residents enrolled at the Medical College of Wisconsin, Inc.

Three other state agencies perform educational functions. The Higher Educational Aids Board administers federal and state student financial assistance programs. The Educational Communications Board operates the state's networks for educational radio and educational television. The State Historical Society of Wisconsin maintains the state historical library, museum, and various historic sites.

Environmental Resources and Transportation. From a wilderness inhabited by 305,391 people in 1850, the state has evolved into a complex society with an estimated January 1, 2008 population of 5,675,156. Most of Wisconsin is not densely populated, and the state has a comparatively large amount of open space. However, population growth, higher levels of consumption, and industrial development have increased environmental pollution.

Once pioneers could come to a wilderness, cut the forests, clear the land, and hunt and fish with little thought of damage to the soil, streams, or wildlife. Now these resources must be protected from destruction, depletion, or extinction. The Department of Natural Resources administers numerous programs that control water quality, air pollution, and solid waste disposal. Under state regulations, municipalities and industries cannot dump untreated sewage or industrial wastes into surface waters; smokestacks and automobiles must meet air pollution limits; farmers are encouraged to preserve soil and groundwater quality; and solid waste disposal facilities must meet construction and operation standards. The department regulates hunting and fishing to protect fish and wildlife resources and manages other programs designed to conserve and restore endangered and threatened species. It also promotes recreational and educational opportunities through state parks, forests, trails, and natural areas.

The Department of Transportation administers a variety of programs related to environmental resources. The highways that crisscross the state have a major impact on land use and people's lifestyles. Urban freeways and interstate highways greatly affect the use and development of surrounding land. They determine where people live, work, and play. When state government plans the location and financing of highways and roads, it must carefully consider both short- and long-range consequences.

The state's highway system consists of interstate highways, state highways, county trunk highways, town roads, city and village streets, and park and forest roads. The state is concerned not only with building and maintaining adequate roads to meet demands, but also with providing for the safety of travelers using those roads. In 2007, more than 5.4 million vehicles were registered in Wisconsin, and approximately 4.1 million residents were licensed to drive. With 659 traffic fatalities in 2006, and 655 in 2007, traffic safety is a constant concern.

The department must ensure that licensed drivers know the laws, are physically fit to drive, and have the required driving skills. It keeps track of drivers' records and can suspend the licenses of those who prove hazardous to themselves or others. It oversees highway construction and maintenance, highway patrol, and enforcement of driver and vehicle standards. The department is also involved in developing aviation and airports in Wisconsin and with promoting mass transit and passenger rail transportation.

Human Relations and Resources. Besides protecting the environment, the state must also protect its citizens directly. Population growth that affects the quality of land, water, and air resources has an increasingly complex effect on people themselves and their relationships to each other and their government. The inhabitants of a state are its prime resource, and government must ensure their general welfare. Records of birth, marriage, divorce, and death are collected and used to identify trends and potential problems.

In the state's early days, public health was primarily concerned with preventing the spread of communicable diseases. Today, the work of the Department of Health Services includes protection from biological terrorist attacks, disease prevention and detection, health education programs, and maintenance of institutions for the care and treatment of the mentally handicapped or mentally ill. The department is also responsible for a broad range of social services for the aged, the handicapped, and children.

A wide range of work-related issues are subject to state regulation. Minimum wages and maximum hours are set by law. If a worker is injured on the job, state worker's compensation may be available; unemployment compensation helps many workers faced with loss of a job. If a worker is seeking a job, the state (in partnership with the federal government) provides a job service to help the individual find work or to acquire the skills necessary for employment. If a worker suspects job discrimination because of age, race, creed, color, handicap, marital status, sex, national origin, ancestry, sexual orientation, or arrest or conviction record, the state may investigate the matter. The Department of Workforce Development is responsible for protecting and assisting workers and provides employment and assistance to rehabilitate the handicapped. The Department of Children and Families provides training and other services to help welfare recipients join the labor market under the state's Wisconsin Works (W-2) program. The Employment Relations Commission mediates or arbitrates labor disputes between workers and their employers.

The Department of Veterans Affairs has grant and loan programs to help eligible veterans acquire a home, business, or education, and it provides personal and medical care for eligible elderly veterans and their spouses at the Wisconsin Veterans Homes at King and Union Grove.

The state also protects its citizens from society's lawless elements by maintaining stability and order. Law enforcement is largely a local matter, but the Department of Corrections is responsible for segregating convicted adult and juvenile offenders in its penal institutions and rehabilitating them for eventual return to society. The Office of the State Public Defender represents indigents in trial and postconviction legal proceedings. The Department of Justice furnishes legal services to state agencies and technical assistance and training to local law enforcement agencies. It also enforces state laws against gambling, arson, child pornography, and narcotic drugs.

The state maintains an armed military force, the Wisconsin National Guard, to protect the populace in times of state or national emergency, whether natural or human caused, and to supplement the federal armed forces in time of war. These activities come under the jurisdiction of the Department of Military Affairs.

General Executive Functions. The services described so far are direct services to the public. In order for the state to perform these functions, it must also perform certain "staff" functions. The state requires general departments that oversee the hiring of agency personnel and provide space, equipment, salaries, and a retirement system for them. It must levy and collect taxes to support its activities, manage these state funds, and ensure that they are spent according to law. It also evaluates agency operations to assure that the various departments are performing their assigned tasks and preparing for future needs.

Some agencies are designed to perform staff functions almost exclusively. The Department of Administration, for example, is called the state's "housekeeping" department. Its duties include state budgeting, preauditing, engineering and facilities management, state planning, and data processing. The Office of State Employment Relations operates the state's classified service system. The Department of Revenue collects taxes levied by state law, distributes part of that revenue to local units of government, and calculates the equalized value of the property that has been assessed by local government.

The Department of Employee Trust Funds manages the state's retirement systems and the employee insurance programs that cover state and local government workers. At any one time, the state must have large sums of money in its employee trust funds to meet its obligations. The Investment Board invests these funds in stocks, bonds, and real estate in order to earn the maximum amount of interest possible until the funds are needed. The Office of the State Treasurer processes the receipt and disbursement of these and other state moneys.

Marjorie Ehle, Administrator of the Government Records Division in the Office of the Secretary of State, consults the 1880 edition of the Wisconsin Blue Book. *The Secretary of State was responsible for compiling the* Blue Book *from 1866 through 1901. (Kathleen Sitter, LRB)*

The Office of the Secretary of State handles general executive duties, such as keeping various state records and affixing the state seal on certain records. The Government Accountability Board oversees the state's election processes, monitors campaign expenditures, keeps election records, administers a code of ethics for state public officials and regulates lobbyists and their employers.

This introduction illustrates how state government both benefits and regulates dozens of aspects of life in Wisconsin. The following sections describe in detail the agencies that make up the executive branch of state government and the numerous services they perform each day.

Total Budget, under each agency's entry, reflects the dollars budgeted during the 2007-08 legislative session for the 2007-09 fiscal biennium (July 1, 2007 to June 30, 2009). These figures are based on the final published appropriation schedule under Chapter 20, Wisconsin Statutes, and do not include statutorily-directed funding modifications or supplemental funding adjustments.

Number of Employees are the number of full-time equivalent positions authorized in the agency's 2008-09 "adjusted base", which is the set of figures each agency uses to begin budgeting for the next biennium.

Budget and employee data provided by the Legislative Fiscal Bureau. Telephone numbers listed without an area code are Madison numbers in area code 608.

OFFICE OF THE GOVERNOR

Governor: JAMES E. DOYLE.

Chief of Staff: Susan Goodwin.

Deputy Chief of Staff: Katie Boyce.

Chief Legal Counsel: Chandra Miller Fienen.

Deputy Legal Counsel: Mindy Dumermuth.

Communications Director: Carol Andrews.

Deputy Communications Director: Lee Sensenbrenner.

Senior Policy Director: Tim Casper.

Policy Advisors: Coral Butson, Nina Carlson, Andy Feldman.

Office of Recovery and Reinvestment Director: Christopher Patton.

Legislative Director: Dan Kanninen.

External Relations Director: Larry Martin.

Deputy External Relations Director: Nathan Franklin.

Appointments Director: Libby Gerds.

Director of Constituent Services: Rich West.

Correspondence Administrator: Donna O'Connell.

Scheduling Director: Rachel Allen Larrivee.

Administrative Operations Director: Teri Devine.

Director of Milwaukee Office: Tim Mahone, 819 North 6th Street, Room 560, Milwaukee 53203, (414) 227-4344.

Director of Northern Office: Bryce Luchterhand, 400 4th Avenue South, Park Falls 54552, (715) 762-5900.

Director of Wisconsin Office in Washington, D.C.: Tanya Bjork, (202) 624-5870; Aaron McCann, *deputy director,* (202) 624-5997; 444 North Capitol Street NW, Suite 613, Washington, D.C. 20001.

Mailing Address: P.O. Box 7863, Madison 53707-7863.

Location: 115 East, State Capitol, Madison.

Telephone: 266-1212.

Office E-mail: governor@wisconsin.gov

Fax: General: 267-8983; Press office: 266-3970; Policy: 261-6804; Appointments: 267-7888.

Internet Address: www.wisgov.state.wi.us/

Number of Employees: 37.25.

Total Budget 2007-09: $8,095,600.

Constitutional Reference: Article V.

Statutory Reference: Chapter 14, Subchapter I.

    Agency Responsibility: As the state's chief executive, the governor represents all the people and is responsible for safeguarding the public interest. The constitution sets certain limits on the governor's powers, but the increased size and complexity of state government have given the governor's office many more responsibilities than it originally had.

    The governor gives policy direction to the state and plays an important role in the legislative process. Through the biennial budget, developed and administered in conjunction with the Department of Administration and various agency heads, the governor ultimately reviews and directs the activities of all administrative agencies. Major policy changes are highlighted in the governor's annual state of the state message and other special messages to the legislature.

    The governor has other specialized powers related to the legislative process. The chief executive may call a special legislative session to deal with specific legislation, may veto an entire bill, or may veto parts of appropriation bills. In the case of either whole or partial vetoes, a two-thirds vote of the members present in each house of the legislature is required to override the governor's action.

Although various administrators direct the day-to-day operations of state agencies, the governor is considered the head of the executive branch. For the most part, the individuals, commissions, or part-time boards that head the major administrative departments are appointed by, and serve at the pleasure of the governor, although many of these appointments require senate confirmation.

As the state's chief administrative officer, the governor must approve federal aid expenditures; state land purchases; highway and airport construction; land or building leases for state use; and numerous state contracts, including compacts negotiated with Indian gaming authorities. The governor may request the attorney general to protect the public interest in various legal actions.

The statutes authorize the governor to create special advisory committees or task forces to conduct studies and make recommendations. These committees frequently attract experienced citizens from many fields, who donate their time and expertise as a public service. The governor also appoints over 1,000 persons to various councils and boards, which are created by law to advise and serve state government, and personally serves on selected bodies, such as the State of Wisconsin Building Commission.

If a vacancy occurs in the state senate or assembly, state law directs the governor to call a special election. Vacancies in elective county offices and judicial positions can be filled by gubernatorial appointment for the unexpired terms or until a successor is elected. The governor may dismiss sheriffs, district attorneys, coroners, or registers of deeds for proven malfeasance.

The governor serves as commander in chief of the Wisconsin National Guard when it is called into state service during emergencies, such as natural disasters and civil disturbances. (When National Guard units perform national service, they are under command of the U.S. President.)

Governor Jim Doyle and First Lady Jessica Doyle join Alice in Dairyland Jill Makovec and Bucky Badger in welcoming children to the Executive Residence as part of Earth Day festivities. The event featured educational activities promoting environmentalism and conservation. (Office of the Governor)

The chief executive has sole power to extradite a person charged with a criminal offense and to exercise executive clemency by granting a pardon, reprieve, or sentence commutation to a convicted criminal offender. The nonstatutory Pardon Advisory Board, which was created by executive order in 1980 to expedite the pardon process, reviews applications for executive clemency and makes recommendations to the governor.

History: Before Wisconsin entered the Union, the U.S. President appointed the territorial governor, but the state constitution, adopted in 1848, gave executive powers to an elected governor. Debate during the constitutional conventions revealed reluctance to change the duties traditionally performed by the chief executive. Questions regarding the post of governor concentrated instead on the amount of salary, length of term, location of residence and, above all, veto power. An effort to divest the governor of veto power failed, as did attempts to vest pardoning power in the legislature and to deny the governor power to remove county officials from office for cause.

There have been several constitutional amendments adopted over the years affecting the authority of the governor. A 1967 amendment lengthened the governor's term from 2 to 4 years, effective 1971. A constitutional amendment, ratified in 1930, empowered the governor to approve appropriation bills in part, thereby creating the partial veto. Another amendment, ratified in 1990, restricted the partial veto power by forbidding the governor to create new words by striking individual letters within words. An amendment ratified in 2008 further restricted the partial veto power by forbidding the governor from creating a new sentence by combining parts of two or more sentences.

Statutory Councils

State Council on Alcohol and Other Drug Abuse: CORAL BUTSON (designated to represent governor), SENATORS CARPENTER, vacancy; REPRESENTATIVES TOWNSEND, HILGENBERG; MICHAEL MYSZEWSKI (attorney general designee), STEVE FERNAN (superintendent of public instruction designee), KEVIN HAYDEN (secretary of health services designee), EILEEN MALLOW (commissioner of insurance designee), SALLY TESS (secretary of corrections designee), DAVE COLLINS (secretary of transportation designee), PAMELA PHILLIPS (chairperson of Pharmacy Examining Board designee), DOUG ENGLEBERT (Controlled Substances Board representative), vacancy (Governor's Commission on Law Enforcement and Crime representative), SANDY HARDIE (consumer of AODA services representing public), MICHAEL WAUPOOSE (service provider representative), MARK SEIDL (nominated by Wisconsin County Human Service Association, Inc.); LINDA MAYFIELD, JOYCE O'DONNELL, MATT RASMUSSEN, DUNCAN SHROUT, SCOTT STOKES (public members). (All except *ex officio* members or their designees are appointed by governor.)

The State Council on Alcohol and Other Drug Abuse recommends, coordinates, and reviews the efforts of state agencies to control and prevent alcohol and drug abuse. It evaluates program effectiveness, recommends improved programming, issues reports to educate people about the dangers of drug abuse, and allocates responsibility for various alcohol and drug abuse programs among state agencies. The council also recommends legislation, cooperates with federal agencies, and receives federal funds.

The 22-member council includes 6 members with a professional, research, or personal interest in alcohol and other drug abuse problems, appointed for 4-year terms, and one of them must be a consumer representing the public. It was created by Chapter 384, Laws of 1969, as the Drug Abuse Control Commission. Chapter 219, Laws of 1971, changed its name to the Council on Drug Abuse and placed the council in the executive office. It was renamed the Council on Alcohol and Other Drug Abuse by Chapter 370, Laws of 1975, and the State Council on Alcohol and Other Drug Abuse by Chapter 221, Laws of 1979. Its composition and duties are prescribed in Sections 14.017 (2) and 14.24 of the statutes.

Council on Military and State Relations: LARRY OLSON (representative of the department of military affairs); LINDA FOURNIER (representative of Fort McCoy, Monroe County); SENATOR SULLIVAN (appointed by senate majority leader); SENATOR HOPPER (appointed by senate minority leader); vacancy (appointed by assembly speaker); vacancy (appointed by assembly minority leader); JAMIE AULIK (representative of the governor). (All except legislative members appointed by the governor.)

The 7-member Council on Military and State Relations assists the governor by working with the state's military installations, commands and communities, state agencies, and economic development professionals to develop and implement strategies designed to enhance those installations. It advises and assists the governor on issues related to the location of military installations and assists and cooperates with state agencies to determine how those agencies can better serve military communities and families. It also assists the efforts of military families and their support groups regarding quality-of-life issues for service members and their families. The council was created by 2005 Wisconsin Act 26 and its composition and duties are prescribed in Section 14.017 (4) of the statutes.

Standards Development Council: Inactive.

The 7-member Standards Development Council, created by 1997 Wisconsin Act 27, was directed to submit to the governor, by November 14, 1997, recommendations relating to pupil academic standards in mathematics, science, reading and writing, geography, and history. The act provided that if the governor approved the standards, he or she was authorized to issue them as an executive order. The council is directed to periodically review the standards and recommend changes to the governor. The composition and duties of the council are prescribed in Sections 14.017 (3) and 14.23 of the statutes.

INDEPENDENT UNIT ATTACHED FOR BUDGETING, PROGRAM COORDINATION, AND RELATED MANAGEMENT FUNCTIONS BY SECTION 15.03 OF THE STATUTES

DISABILITY BOARD

Disability Board: GOVERNOR JAMES E. DOYLE, CHIEF JUSTICE SHIRLEY ABRAHAMSON, SENATOR RISSER (senate president), SENATOR S. FITZGERALD (senate minority leader), REPRESENTATIVE SHERIDAN (assembly speaker), REPRESENTATIVE J. FITZGERALD (assembly minority leader), ROBERT GOLDEN (dean, UW Medical School).

Statutory References: Sections 14.015 (1) and 17.025.

Agency Responsibility: The Disability Board is authorized by law to determine when a temporary disability exists in any of the constitutional offices because the incumbent is incapacitated due to illness or injury, and it may fill a temporary vacancy. The board, which was created by Chapter 422, Laws of 1969, originally had similar powers for supreme court justices and circuit court judges, but these were repealed by Chapter 449, Laws of 1977, and Chapter 332, Laws of 1975, respectively.

GOVERNOR'S APPOINTMENTS TO MISCELLANEOUS COMMITTEES AND ORGANIZATIONS

Wisconsin Humanities Council

Members: Gubernatorial appointees: JOYCE ERICKSON, MARY C. KNAPP, CONNIE LODEN. (The governor appoints 6 members to the council. Other members are elected by the council.)

Executive Director: DENA WORTZEL.

Address: 222 South Bedford Street, Suite F, Madison 53703-3688.

Telephone: (608) 262-0706.

Fax: (608) 263-7970.

E-mail Address: contact@wisconsinhumanities.org

Internet Address: www.wisconsinhumanities.org

Publications: Grant guidelines, speakers bureau catalogs, and an online newsletter.

The Wisconsin Humanities Council, an independent, nonprofit organization, was established in 1972 under the provisions of federal Public Law 89-209. Members of the council include civic leaders; representatives of business, government, labor, professional, cultural, and educational institutions; and scholars and teachers in the humanities. The council receives annual funding from the National Endowment for the Humanities, the State of Wisconsin, and other sources. It makes grants to support projects that promote the use, understanding, and appreciation of the humanities among Wisconsin citizens. Any nonprofit organization or institution may apply to the council for project support. In planning and presenting public programs, applicant organizations must ordinarily involve scholars with graduate degrees in the humanities.

The Medical College of Wisconsin, Inc.

Board of Trustees: Gubernatorial appointees: CHRISTOPHER ABELE, CURT S. CULVER, TIMOTHY T. FLAHERTY, TIMOTHY E. HOEKSEMA, JEFFREY A. JOERRES, NATALIE BLACK KOHLER, SHELDON B. LUBAR, LINDA T. MELLOWES, CORY L. NETTLES, EDWARD J. ZORE. (The governor appoints one-third of the board with senate consent.)

President: T. MICHAEL BOLGER.

Mailing Address: 8701 Watertown Plank Road, P.O. Box 26509, Milwaukee 53226-0509.

Telephone: (414) 456-8225.

Fax: (414) 456-6560.

State Appropriation 2007-09: $14,507,100.

Publications: *Alumni News,* annual reports, directory of physician consultants, *Facts, Medical College of Wisconsin News, World.*

Statutory Reference: Sections 13.106, 39.15, and 39.155.

The Medical College of Wisconsin, Inc., is a private nonprofit educational corporation located in Milwaukee. The college receives a specified sum under the "student capitation" program for each Wisconsin resident it enrolls. The Higher Educational Aids Board determines whether applicants qualify as state residents. The college also receives state funds for its family medicine residency program.

The governor appoints one-third of the college's board of trustees for 6-year terms. The college is required to fulfill certain reporting requirements, and the Legislative Audit Bureau conducts biennial postaudits of expenditures made under state appropriations.

In September 1967, Marquette University terminated its sponsorship of the college, then known as the Marquette School of Medicine, Inc. To increase the supply of physicians in Wisconsin, the legislature enacted Chapter 3, Laws of 1969, which appropriated funds to the school provided Wisconsin residents received first preference for admission. The legislature made a token appropriation to test the law's constitutionality, and the Wisconsin Supreme Court ruled the law constitutional in *State ex rel. Warren v. Rueter,* 44 Wis. 2d 201 (1969). Chapter 185, Laws of 1969, fully funded state support for the college. In 1970, the college's name was changed to The Medical College of Wisconsin, Inc.

GOVERNOR'S SPECIAL COMMITTEES
June 30, 2009

The committees described in this section include those Governor Jim Doyle created or continued. Most of the committees were created under Section 14.019, Wisconsin Statutes, which provides that "the governor may, by executive order, create nonstatutory committees in such number and with such membership as desired, to conduct such studies and to advise the governor in such matters as directed." Committee members serve at the pleasure of the governor.

Unless terminated sooner, a special committee expires automatically on the fourth Monday of January of the year in which a new gubernatorial term begins. The governor may, however, provide for its continued existence by executive order. In that event, existing members continue to serve unless they resign or until the governor replaces them.

The law also provides that the governor may designate an employee of the Office of the Governor or of the Department of Administration to coordinate the activities of nonstatutory committees. In some cases, the governor has ordered other state agencies to staff and financially support committees.

When a new gubernatorial term begins, each committee is required to submit a final report to the governor or governor-elect prior to the new term. Copies of each final report and any other report a special committee prepared must be submitted to the Reference and Loan Library in the Department of Public Instruction for distribution under Section 35.83 (3), Wisconsin Statutes.

Section 20.505 (1) (ka), Wisconsin Statutes, provides for the expenses of special committees created by executive order. In addition, certain committees receive specific state appropriations, and some receive federal funds because they are established in response to federal program requirements.

The special committees are listed in alphabetical order by the key word in each committee name.

Autism Advisory Council

Members: NISSAN BAR-LEV, TERRI ENTERS, VIVIAN HAZELL, ROSALIA HELMS, JOAN KETTERMAN, MILANA MILLAN, GLEN SALLOWS, PAM STOIKA, BRADLEY THOMPSON, MICHAEL WILLIAMS.

Contact person: ANGELA RUSSELL.

Address: Office of the Governor, Room 115 East, State Capitol, Madison 53707.

Telephone: 266-1212.

Fax: 261-6804.

Governor Jim Doyle created the council in Executive Order 94, April 5, 2005, to meet quarterly and advise the Department of Health Services on strategies for implementing statewide supports and services for children with autism. Of the maximum 15 members appointed by the governor to the council, at least a majority must be parents of children with autism or autism spectrum disorders. The remaining members may be providers of services to children with autism, local government officials, persons who are knowledgeable of autism issues, or simply members of the general public.

Bicycle Coordinating Council

Members: SENATOR COWLES (appointed by senate minority leader), SENATOR SULLIVAN (appointed by senate majority leader); REPRESENTATIVE DAVIS (appointed by assembly speaker), REPRESENTATIVE BLACK (appointed by assembly minority leader); WILLIAM CHRISTIANSON (designated by secretary of tourism); THOMAS HUBER (designated by secretary of transportation); LARRY CORSI (designated by director, Department of Transportation, Bureau of Transportation Safety); BRIGIT BROWN (designated by secretary of natural resources); DOUGLAS WHITE (designated by state superintendent of public instruction); JON MORGAN (designated by secretary of health services); PETER A. FLUCKE, CHRISTOPHER S. FORTUNE, KEVIN HARDMAN, CRAIG A. HEYWOOD, SHARON KAMINEKI, KRYSTYNA KORNILOWICZ, BRENDA MAXWELL (public members).

Contact person: TOM HUBER, thomas.huber@dot.state.wi.us

Address: Department of Transportation, P.O. Box 7913, Madison 53707-7913.

Telephone: 267-7757.

Fax: 267-0294.

Governor Tommy G. Thompson created the council in Executive Order 122, June 24, 1991, and Governor Jim Doyle most recently recreated it in Executive Order 182, January 18, 2007. A similar council was originally created by Governor Patrick J. Lucey in June 1977 under Executive Order 43, and it has been recreated several times since. The council consists of not more than 17 members. The council considers all matters relating to: efforts of state agencies to encourage the use of the bicycle as an alternative means of transportation; promoting bicycle safety and education; promoting safe bicycling to school; promoting bicycling as a recreational and tourist activity; and disseminating information on state and federal funding for bicycle programs. The council also reviews the bicycle programs of state agencies, issues reports to the governor and the legislature, and makes recommendations concerning pertinent legislation.

Governor's Business Council

Members: GOVERNOR JIM DOYLE, *chairperson;* RICHARD J. LEINENKUGEL (department of commerce secretary); MICHAEL MORGAN (department of administration secretary); ROBERTA GASSMAN (department of workforce development secretary); JENNIFER ALEXANDER, LINDA CLARK, JERRY MURPHY, TIM SHEEHY, JULIA TAYLOR, WILLIAM TEHAN (Qualified Regional Economic Development Association Staff Member); *Rotating members* (Senior Business Executives and Members of Qualified Regional Economic Development Associations).

Contact person: ZACH BRANDON, *executive assistant.*

Address: 201 West Washington Avenue, 6th Floor, P.O. Box 7970, Madison 53707-7970.

Telephone: 266-8976.

Fax: 266-3447.

Governor Jim Doyle created the council in Executive Order 193, April 17, 2007, to collaborate on regional and statewide development priorities, share best practices, and identify concrete ways that the state can support regional and statewide economic development. The council consists of the governor, serving as the chairperson, and the secretaries of the departments of administration, commerce, and workforce development. The council must also include at least 2 staff members of a qualified regional economic development association and at least 3 rotating senior executives from the business community, who are members of a qualified economic development association. A "qualified regional economic development association" is defined as representing at least 5 adjacent counties, having a board consisting of at least 50% private business/industry representatives, and operating under a budget comprised of at least 65% private funding. The council is appointed by and serves at the pleasure of the governor.

State of Wisconsin Citizen Corps Council

Members: vacancy (local law enforcement representative); TERRY DRYDEN (sheriff representative); vacancy (fire chief representative); MICHAEL EGAN (firefighter representative); TERRENCE TIMMERMAN (emergency medical services representative); WILLIAM STOLTE (emergency management representative); STEVE HERMAN (crime prevention representative); TERRI LEECE, DOREEN MARTINEZ (charitable organization representatives); PETER FOX, ROGER WEBER, BETSY WILCOX (nongovernmental representatives); JASON BISONETTE (tribal representative).

Contact person: DAVID STEINGRABER.

Address: Office of Justice Assistance, 1 South Pinckney Street, Suite 600, Madison 53702-0001.

Telephone: 266-3323.

Fax: 266-6676.

Governor Jim Doyle created the council in Executive Order 67, September 8, 2004, and recreated it on January 18, 2007, in Executive Order 182, to act as a statewide advisory council to encourage community participation in domestic preparedness through public education, training, and volunteer service. The council provides information and recommendations to the governor, the legislature, and the public regarding the operation, program priorities, and allocation of funds for the Wisconsin Citizen Corps initiative. Members of the council, which consists of up to 20 members, are appointed by the governor, including chairperson and vice chairperson. Membership consists of at least one representative from local law enforcement, a county sheriff, a local fire chief, a local firefighter, a local emergency medical services professional, an emergency management professional, representatives from charitable organizations with a focus on disaster readiness and volunteer mobilization, a member from an existing local or county Citizens Corps Council, and nongovernmental citizen members.

Wisconsin Coastal Management Council

Members: LARRY MACDONALD, *chairperson;* vacancy, *vice chairperson;* SENATOR WIRCH; REPRESENTATIVE MASON; JAMES P. HURLEY (UW System representative), BRIAN VIGUE (designated by secretary of administration), TODD L. AMBS (designated by secretary of natural resources), LAWRENCE KIECK (designated by secretary of transportation); ERVIN SOULIER (tribal government representative); ROBERT D. BROWNE, SHARON COOK (City of Milwaukee representatives); PATRICIA HOEFT, KENNETH L. LEINBACH, WILLIAM SCHUSTER.

Contact person: MIKE FRIIS.

Address: Wisconsin Coastal Management Program, Department of Administration, 101 East Wilson Street, 10th Floor, P.O. Box 8944, Madison 53708-8944.

Telephone: 267-7982.

Fax: 267-6917.

Internet Address: http://coastal.wisconsin.gov

Acting Governor Martin J. Schreiber established the council in Executive Order 49, October 7, 1977. It has been recreated or revised several times, and was continued most recently by Governor Jim Doyle in Executive Order 182, January 18, 2007. It succeeded the Coastal Coordinating and Advisory Council appointed by Governor Patrick J. Lucey in 1974. The 1977 council was created to comply with provisions of the federal Coastal Zone Management Act of 1972 and to implement Wisconsin's official Coastal Management Program, which received federal approval on May 22, 1978. The council advises the governor on issues pertaining to the Great Lakes coasts and assists in providing policy direction for Wisconsin's coastal management efforts. Members represent the legislature, state agencies, units of local government, tribal governments, and citizens. To provide opportunities for full participation in the program, the governor encouraged the council to establish citizens' committees to advise the council on key issues affecting the coasts. The council endorsed "Wisconsin Coastal Management Program: Needs Assessment and Multi-Year Strategy, 2006-2010" in January 2006. Annually since 2002, the program has produced the *Wisconsin Great Lakes Chronicle.* Archived copies are available from the Wisconsin Coastal Management Program's Web site.

Governor's Committee for People With Disabilities

Members: JOSEPH MIELCZAREK, JR., *chairperson;* JEFF FOX (Council on Physical Disabilities), *vice chairperson;* JOANNE STEPHENS (Council on Mental Health); JACKIE WENKMAN (Council on Developmental Disabilities); ALEX H. SLAPPEY (Council for the Deaf and Hard of Hearing); MARK JANOWIAK (Council on Blindness); vacancy (State Council on Alcohol and Other Drug Abuse); WAYNE COREY, THOMAS FELL, DANIEL LAATSCH, NANCY LEIPZIG, JOHN W. OLSON, SANDRA POPP (at-large members). Nonvoting *ex officio* member: LT. GOVERNOR LAWTON.

Contact person: MOLLY MICHELS.

Address: 1 West Wilson Street, Room 437, Madison 53703-7851.

Telephone: 266-7816.

Fax: 266-3386.

The Wisconsin Governor's Committee for People with Disabilities in its present form was established in March of 1976 by Governor Patrick J. Lucey, and has been reauthorized through executive order by every governor since that time. It was most recently recreated by Governor Doyle's Executive Order 182 on January 18, 2007. The original executive order provided initial guidance for the committee to advise the governor's office on a broad range of issues affecting people with disabilities. The committee's mission, "to enhance the health and general well-being of disabled citizens in Wisconsin", was created out of a realization that state government lacked a process of systematically communicating the needs of people with disabilities to responsible state and local officials. In an effort to enhance the value of the committee, the executive order was rewritten in 2004 to support a focus on issues, policies, and programs that will encourage involvement in the workforce.

The committee consists of the Lieutenant Governor as a nonvoting, *ex officio* member, and not more than 20 members, appointed by the governor to serve at his pleasure. The committee as a whole includes Wisconsin residents with disabilities and individuals that have demonstrated interest in the concerns of all disability groups. All serve as unpaid volunteers. Six of the committee members represent specific disability constituencies: 1) Council on Blindness; 2) Wisconsin Council for the Deaf and Hard of Hearing; 3) Wisconsin Council on Developmental Disabilities; 4) Wisconsin Council on Mental Health; 5) State Council on Alcohol and Other Drug Abuse; and 6) Council on Physical Disabilities.

The committee meets quarterly, usually in March, June, September, and December. In addition to the Executive Committee, the Governor's Committee also has two subcommittees: the Business Leadership Network Subcommittee and the Youth Leadership Forum Subcommittee.

Early Childhood Advisory Council

Members: REGGIE BICHA (department of children and families secretary), TONY EVERS (state superintendent of public instruction), *cochairpersons;* THERESE AHLERS, NANCY ARMBRUST, JOHN ASHLEY, MARY BELL, MIKE BURKE, DAN BURKHALTER, DANIEL CLANCY, SHELLEY COUSIN, LINDA DAVIS, DAVE EDIE, DELORES GOKEE-RINDAL, RICK GROBSCHMIDT, DAN HARRIS, PETER KELLY, LAURA KLINGELHOETS, VILUCK KUE, KIA LA BRACKE, LINDA LEONHART, GENNIENE LOVELACE-MICHEL, LUPE MARTINEZ, RICK RAEMISCH, KEVIN REILLY, BROOKE ROETTGER, RICHARD SCHLIMM, RUTH SCHMIDT, MARY ANN SNYDER, CAROLYN STANFORD TAYLOR, JON STELLMACHER, ANN TERRELL, KAREN TIMBERLAKE, PHONG VANG, JUDGE WALL.

Governor Jim Doyle created the council in Executive Order 269 on October 30, 2008, in accordance with Federal Public Law 110-134. The council makes recommendations to the governor regarding development of a comprehensive statewide early childhood system. Responsibilities of the council include the following: conducting needs assessments; identifying barriers to collaboration between federal and state programs; developing recommendations for increasing participation of children in early childhood services; developing recommendations for a unified data collection system; supporting professional development; assessing the capacity of higher education to support the development of early childhood professionals; and making recommendations to improve early learning standards.

Early Intervention Interagency Coordinating Council

Members: SANDRA L. BUTTS, *chairperson;* NORMA J. VRIEZE, *vice chairperson;* vacancy (state legislator); JULIE WALSH (designated by commissioner of insurance), LINDA HUFFER (Department of Health Services, Division of Long-Term Care designee), SHARON FLEISCHFRESSER (Department of Health Services, Division of Public Health designee), LAURA SATERFIELD (State Office of Child Care designee), JILL HAGLUND (Department of Public Instruction designee); vacancy (Council on Developmental Disabilities designee); WILLIAM BARREAU, JONELLE BROM, TONI DAKINS, VICTORIA DEER, GREGORY DIMICELI, CYNTHIA S. FLAUGER, LINDA LEONHART, MARY MARONEK, NANCY MARZ, JILL SOLTAU, LINDA TUCHMAN, THERESA VINCENT.

Contact person: CAROL NODDINGS EICHINGER, carol.eichinger@wisconsin.gov

Address: Department of Health Services, 1 West Wilson Street, Room B-138, P.O. Box 7851, Madison 53707-7851.

Telephone: 267-3270.

Fax: 261-6752.

Governor Tommy G. Thompson first established the council in Executive Order 17, June 26, 1987, and recreated it in Executive Order 334, May 21, 1998. Governor Jim Doyle continued it in Executive Order 1, January 27, 2003 and recreated it in Executive Order 182, January 18, 2007. Often called the "Birth to Three" Council, it was created to comply with the federal Individuals With Disabilities Education Act of 1986 and recreated to comply with the federal Individuals With Disabilities Education Act of 1997. The council advises and assists the Department of Health Services in the development and administration of early intervention services for infants and toddlers with developmental delays and their families. It consists of at least 15 members and is directed by the governor to include at least 4 parents of infants, toddlers, or children aged 12 or younger with disabilities; at least 4 private or public providers of early intervention services; at least one state legislator; at least one member involved in personnel training; at least one representative of a Head Start agency or program; and other members representing state agencies that provide services or payment for early intervention services to infants and toddlers and their families. Members, other than those serving *ex officio,* serve 3-year terms. Administrative and support services are provided to the council by the Department of Health Services. The council issues an annual report for each federal fiscal year.

eHealth Care Quality and Patient Safety Board

Members: KAREN TIMBERLAKE (department of health services secretary), *chairperson;* PEGGY SMELSER (employer purchaser representative); LON SPRECHER (HMO representative); GARY BEZUCHA, CATHERINE HANSEN, DEBRA RISLOW (hospital representatives); EDWARD BARTHELL, JUSTIN STARREN (physician representatives); JOHN TOUSSAINT (health care representative); CHRISTOPHER ALBAN, RAVI KALLA, HUGH ZETTEL (IT representatives); BEVAN BAKER (local public health department); CANDICE OWLEY (union representative); DONALD LAYDEN (business representative); PATRICIA FLATLEY BRENNAN (education representative); JOSEPH KACHELSKI, KIM PEMBLE (public members); DAN SCHOOFF (department of administration deputy secretary); DAVE STELLA (department of employee trust funds secretary).

Contact person: DENISE B. WEBB, *eHealth Program Manager.*

Address: Department of Health Services, 1 West Wilson Street, Madison 53707.

Telephone: 267-6767.

Fax: 267-0358.

E-mail Address: ehealthboard@dhs.wisconsin.gov

Internet Address: http://ehealthboard.dhs.wisconsin.gov.

Governor Jim Doyle created the board in Executive Order 129, November 2, 2005, and recreated it on January 18, 2007 through Executive Order 182, to review issues surrounding the creation of an electronic health information infrastructure in Wisconsin. In response to the executive order, the board worked intensively to development the eHealth Action Plan, providing a roadmap for public-private partnerships to advance adoption of electronic health records and the exchange of health information in Wisconsin. The report is available at the board's Web site. The board is appointed by and serves at the pleasure of the governor.

Governor's Council on Financial Literacy

Members: JESSICA DOYLE, *honorary chairperson;* LORRIE KEATING HEINEMANN, *chairperson;* WILLIAM WILCOX, *vice chairperson;* WENDY BAUMANN, DEBORAH BLANKS, SEAN DILWEG, WILLIAM DUDDLESTON, ROGER ERVIN, TONY EVERS, ROBERTA GASSMAN, DAVID HACKWORTHY, DAVID MANCL, MERIDEE MAYNARD, KEVIN MCKINLEY, ANN PEGGS, ANTONIO RILEY, MARK SCHUG, CATHERINE TIERNEY, DOUG TIMMERMAN, ALEJO TORRES.

Contact person: DAVID MANCL, *executive director.*

Address: 345 West Washington Avenue, Fifth Floor, Madison 53708.

Telephone: 261-9540.

Fax: 261-4334.

Governor Jim Doyle created the council in Executive Order 92, March 30, 2005, and recreated it in Executive Order 182, January 18, 2007, to work with existing state agencies, private entities, and nonprofit associations in improving the financial literacy of Wisconsin citizens. The council was directed to develop a unified strategy, establish benchmarks, promote best practices, catalog existing materials, and create a financial literacy Web site. The council has not more than 20 members, with an honorary chairperson, chairperson, and vice chairperson selected from within the group. The Secretary of the Department of Financial Institutions has submitted semiannual progress reports to the governor since December 31, 2005.

State Historical Records Advisory Board

Members: Menzi L. Behrnd-Klodt, Clayborn Benson, Matthew Blessing, Anita T. Doering, Maria Escalante, Peter Gottlieb, Laura McCoy, Jane M. Pederson, Rick Pifer, Kenneth J. Wirth.

Coordinator: Peter Gottlieb, peter.gottlieb@wisconsinhistory.org

Address: 816 State Street, Madison 53706.

Telephone: 264-6480.

Governor Patrick J. Lucey created the advisory board on April 4, 1977. It was most recently continued by Governor Jim Doyle in Executive Order 182, January 18, 2007. That action enables the state to participate in the grants program of the National Historical Publications and Records Commission, which coordinates the preservation of historic records in the United States and approves federal grants to qualified Wisconsin institutions and to the state advisory board. The board promotes the availability and use of historical records as keys to improved understanding of our cultural heritage. Members serve staggered 3-year terms.

Wisconsin Homeland Security Council

Members: Brigadier General Donald P. Dunbar, *chairperson;* Oskar Anderson, David Collins, Edward Flynn, Seth Foldy, Martin Henert, Douglas Holton, David Mahoney, Mike Myszewski, Johnnie Smith, David Steingraber, Charles Tubbs, vacancy.

Contact persons: Randi Milsap, randi.milsap@wisconsin.gov; Lori Getter, lori.getter@wisconsin.gov

Address: 2400 Wright Street, P.O. Box 14587, Madison 53708.

Telephones: 242-3072 or 242-3239.

Fax: 242-3082.

Internet Address: http://homelandsecurity.wi.gov

Governor Jim Doyle created the council in Executive Order 7, March 18, 2003, to advise the governor and to coordinate the efforts of state and local agencies regarding the prevention of, and response to, potential threats to the homeland security of the state. Council members are appointed by and serve at the pleasure of the governor. The council works with federal, state, and local agencies, nonprofit organizations, and private industry to prevent and respond to any threat of terrorism, promote personal preparedness, and make recommendations to the governor on additional steps to further enhance Wisconsin's homeland security. Executive Order 143, issued on March 14, 2006, increased the council to nine members, all appointed by the governor. The council was recreated in Executive Order 182, January 18, 2007. Executive Order 268, September 16, 2008, expanded the council to 13 members.

Statewide Independent Living Council

Members: Kathleen Knoble-Iverson (director of a center for independent living); Charles A. Benner, Bruce Huseboe, Patricia Lerch (representatives of the directors of Native American Vocational Rehabilitation programs); Benjamin Barrett, Molly Cisco, Karen Foxgrover, Christine Honkavaara, Tamara Jandorwski, Ron Jansen, August Krieser, Theodore Pyke, Lewis Tyler, vacancy. Nonvoting members: Charlene Dwyer (representing Department of Workforce Development, Division of Vocational Rehabilitation), John Reiser (representing Department of Health Services), Bobbi Beson-Crone (representing Department of Transportation), vacancy (representing Department of Commerce).

Contact person: Mike Bachhuber.

Address: 201 West Washington Avenue, Suite 110, Madison 53703.

Telephones: 256-9257; (866) 656-4010 (toll free); TTY: 256-9316 or (866) 656-4011 (toll free).

Fax: 256-9301.

Internet Address: www.ilcw.org

Governor Tommy G. Thompson created the council in Executive Order 212, February 10, 1994, to comply with the 1992 amendments to the federal Rehabilitation Act of 1973. In 2004,

Governor Jim Doyle issued Executive Order 65, which outlines the current membership and established the council as a nonprofit entity. Governor Doyle most recently recreated the council in Executive Order 182, January 18, 2007. In coordination with the Division of Vocational Rehabilitation, the council has the responsibility to develop and submit the state plan for independent living services for the severely disabled to state and federal agencies; monitor, review, and evaluate the state plan; and submit reports to the U.S. Commissioner of the Rehabilitation Services Administration as requested.

The council currently consists of 14 voting members and 4 *ex officio* members representing the Department of Workforce Development, the Department of Health Services, the Department of Transportation, and the Department of Commerce's Bureau of Housing. The majority of members must be persons with disabilities who do not work for a center for independent living or the State of Wisconsin. At least one member must be a director of a center for independent living chosen by centers for independent living, and at least one representative of the directors of Native American vocational rehabilitation programs. Voting members of the council serve staggered 3-year terms and may serve no more than two consecutive terms.

International Trade Council

Members: ROGER AXTELL, DAVID D. BASKERVILLE, DAN CLANCY, JANE DAUFFENBACH, CRISS DAVIS, THOMAS P. GEHL, JAMES HALL, JAMES S. HANEY, JOE HEIL, PAUL HSU, KIM KINDSCHI, PAULINE KLAFFENBOECK, RICHARD MARTENS, REBECCA MARTIN, RICK MICKSCHL, SUSAN HUBER MILLER, FREDERICK MONIQUE, ROD NILSESTUEN, MARTY PAYNE, KAILAS RAO, TIM A. RIEMENSCHNEIDER, JOHN S. SKILTON, ANDREW SEABORG, KATHI P. SEIFERT, KENNETH SHAPIRO, BILL STEPHEN, STEVE WASSER, ROLF WEGENKE.

Contact person: MARY REGEL.

Address: Division of Business Development, Department of Commerce, 201 West Washington Avenue, Madison 53702.

Telephone: 266-1767.

Governor Tommy G. Thompson created the council in Executive Order 301, November 19, 1996, as amended in Executive Order 319, October 28, 1997, and Governor Jim Doyle continued it most recently in Executive Order 182, January 18, 2007, to advise the governor and the secretaries for the Department of Commerce and the Department of Agriculture, Trade and Consumer Protection on the state's role in the development of international trade. The council is directed to study the impact of national policies on Wisconsin business; state policies that could increase incentives for international trade; and trade services that are now provided and those that need to be further developed. The governor instructed the council to: develop procedures to integrate public and private export services into a system that is easy to use; develop an annual International Trade Development Plan that would include specific benchmarks and evaluation criteria for trade development services; target markets for trade development; and encourage public and private cooperative trade services and programs. The council is directed to develop educational programs on international trade for all levels of schooling and is required to create grant programs to support expansion of foreign trade by Wisconsin businesses. The council consists of not more than 35 members, and the governor appoints the chair from the voting membership. The chair may designate individuals with specialized knowledge in international trade to serve as nonvoting associate members of the council.

Governor's Advisory Council on Judicial Selection

Members: SUSAN STEINGASS, *chairperson;* MICHELLE BEHNKE, FRANK DAILY, STAN DAVIS, TOM EAGON, JON FURLOW, JAMES JOHNSON, ED MANYDEEDS, CHRISTINE BREMER MUGGLI.

Contact person: CHANDRA MILLER FIENEN, *governor's legal counsel.*

Address: Office of the Governor, Room 115 East, State Capitol, P.O. Box 7863, Madison 53707-7863.

Telephone: 266-1212.

Governor Anthony Earl established the council in Executive Order 1, January 6, 1983. Governor Tommy G. Thompson recreated and restructured the council in Executive Order 2, January 28, 1987, and Governor Scott McCallum recreated and restructured it in Executive Order 6, April 27, 2001. Governor Jim Doyle most recently recreated the council in Executive Order 182, January 18, 2007. The council makes recommendations to the governor on filling vacancies in the state court system. It is expected to provide the governor with a list of at least 3, but not more than 5, qualified persons, no later than 6 weeks after notification that the vacancy exists. The council consists of permanent members and up to 2 temporary members, who are selected according to the particular type of vacancy and serve only until the council makes its recommendations. For a supreme court vacancy, the governor appoints up to 2 temporary members. For a court of appeals vacancy, the governor appoints up to 2 temporary members who must reside in the district in which the vacancy occurs. In the case of circuit courts, the chairperson appoints up to 2 temporary members who must reside in the circuit.

Governor's Juvenile Justice Commission

Members: DEIRDRE WILSON GARTON, *chairperson;* TASHA JENKINS, *vice chairperson;* SEYMOUR ADLER, JENNIFER BIAS, MARGARET CARPENTER, ANNETTE CROWDER, PATRICIA DAVENPORT, GUS DOYLE, TERRANCE C. ERICKSON, BARBARA FRANKS, MARC HAMMER, EDDIE M. JACKSON, KENN JOHNSON, DAVID MADDEN, ADAM MCGESHICK, CATHERINE MORGAN, DARIUS PARKS, JANET PROCTOR, JOSE R. RAMOS, LUCY ROWLEY, JOHN SWEENEY, CAROLYN STANFORD TAYLOR, CHARLES A. TUBBS, MANEE VONGPHAKDY, POLLY WOLNER.

Contact person: DAVID STEINGRABER.

Address: Office of Justice Assistance, 1 South Pinckney Street, Suite 600, Madison 53702-0001.

Telephone: 266-3323.

Fax: 266-6676.

Governor Tommy G. Thompson created the commission as the Juvenile Justice Advisory Group in Executive Order 55, January 30, 1989, repealed and recreated it as the Governor's Juvenile Justice Commission in Executive Order 110, February 6, 1991, and Governor Jim Doyle continued it most recently in Executive Order 182, January 18, 2007. The commission awards funds received by the state under the federal Juvenile Justice and Delinquency Prevention Act, the Juvenile Accountability Block Grant, and other state and federal programs. It also advises the governor and the legislature on juvenile justice issues. The Office of Justice Assistance provides staff and pays the expenses of the commission.

Wisconsin Lincoln Bicentennial Commission

Members: MICHAEL MORAN (senate majority leader designee); JOHN SCHULZE (senate minority leader designee); ERROLL KINDSCHY (assembly speaker designee); ELLSWORTH BROWN (director, state historical society); TONY EVERS (superintendent of public instruction); JOHN SKILTON (attorney representative); DAVID EICHER, DANIEL NETTESHEIM (Civil War Roundtable representatives); KATHLEEN WOIT (foundation representative); CLAYBORN BENSON, MAURICE MONTGOMERY, DAVID SIMMONS, PAULA TOUHEY (historical representatives); STEVEN ROGSTAD, PETER SKELLY (Lincoln Fellowship representatives); RALPH CAGLE, JOHN COOPER, VALERIA DAVIS, STEPHEN KANTROWITZ, ABIGAIL MARKWYN, JAMES MARTEN, JERALD PODAIR (university representatives); BOB DRANE, CARL GULBRANDSEN, DAVID HECKER, JAMES HOYT, JOSEPH RANNEY, MAXINE WHITE (public members).

Internet Address: http://lincoln200.wisconsin.gov

Governor Jim Doyle created the commission in Executive Order 245, April 7, 2008. The commission is charged with planning and carrying out bicentennial tributes to President Abraham Lincoln, born on February 12, 1809. The commission consists of not more than 31 members, in addition to honorary members, all appointed and to serve at the pleasure of the governor. The commission will dissolve when its final report is accepted by the governor.

Pardon Advisory Board

Members: CHANDRA MILLER FIENEN (governor's legal counsel), *chairperson;* WILLIAM RANKIN (representing secretary of corrections); CINDY L. O'DONNELL (representing attorney general); JENNIFER BIAS, SEAN DUFFY, HAROLD MOORE, SHANNON YOUNG.

Address: Office of the Governor, Room 115 East, State Capitol, P.O. Box 7863, Madison 53707-7863.

Telephone: 266-7603.

Governor Lee Sherman Dreyfus originally created the Pardon Advisory Board in Executive Order 39, March 6, 1980. Governor Tommy G. Thompson recreated and restructured the board in Executive Order 121, June 3, 1991, and Governor Scott McCallum recreated the board in Executive Order 24, September 12, 2001, as amended by Executive Order 50, July 18, 2002. Governor Jim Doyle most recently continued it in Executive Order 182, January 18, 2007. The board consists of 7 members appointed by the governor and specifies the application process. One member represents the secretary of corrections and another represents the attorney general. The governor's legal counsel or his/her designee is a voting member and chairs the board. Four members constitute a quorum for executive action by the board. The board reviews applications for executive clemency and makes recommendations to the governor on each request. As part of its review procedure, it may hold a public hearing on each qualifying application and hear from the applicant. After a hearing is concluded, the board makes a recommendation to grant, deny, or defer each application. The factors the board considers in making its decision include, but are not limited to, the severity of the offense, time passed since discharge or conviction, the applicant's need for clemency, and the applicant's activities and conduct since committing the offense.

Governor's Council on Physical Fitness and Health

Members: ALEXANDRA ADAMS, SUSAN BIETILA, AARON CARREL, PAUL COSTANZO, AMY DELONG, TERRY ERICKSON, MARY FELDT, WALLY GRAFFEN, YVONNE D. GREER, LINDA LEE, KAREN ORDINANS, JENNIFER QUADRACCI, LARRY REED, MICHELE STELLRECHT, MARY JO TUCKWELL, JOHN WEINSHEIM, 3 vacancies.

Contact persons: AMY MEINEN, Department of Health Services; CORAL BUTSON, policy advisor, Office of the Governor.

Address: Department of Health Services, 1 West Wilson Street, Room 243, P.O. Box 2659, Madison 53701-2659.

Telephones: 267-9194, 266-1212.

Governor Anthony Earl established the council in Executive Order 10, April 19, 1983, and Governor Jim Doyle most recently continued it in Executive Order 182, January 18, 2007. The council makes recommendations to the governor concerning programs and policy development related to fitness, nutrition, and health. It develops cooperative relationships among state agencies, educational institutions, businesses, associations, and foundations in order to improve the availability of fitness and health activities to all citizens. Most recently, the council established the Governor's School Health Award. The award is intended to motivate and empower schools as they create and maintain healthy school environments through policy change and improved infrastructure and programs. Furthermore, the council established the Healthy Wisconsin Worksite Wellness Project to maximize partnerships with business and industry to promote and support healthy lifestyles in the workplace.

Governor's Poet Laureate Commission

Members: JANE HAMBLEN, CHARLES RIES, *cochairpersons;* STORM ELSER, CHARLOTTTE MEYER, DAVID SCHELER, CHERENE SHERRARD-JOHNSON, MARY WEHNER.

Contact person: CHARLES RIES.

Address: 5821 West Trenton Place, Milwaukee 53213.

Telephone: (414) 313-7366.

Internet Address: http://wipoetlaureate.wi.gov

Poet Laureate: MARILYN TAYLOR.

Governor Tommy G. Thompson created the commission in Executive Order 404, July 31, 2000, and was most recently continued by Governor Jim Doyle in Executive Order 182, January 18, 2007. The commission's purpose is to recommend 3 candidates for the poet laureate of Wisconsin, define the responsibilities of the poet laureate, and assist that individual in performing official duties that will contribute to the growth of poetry in this state. The 7 members are appointed to 4-year terms. Each of 5 organizations recommends one person for membership: the Council for Wisconsin Writers, the Wisconsin Fellowship of Poets, the Wisconsin Regional Writers Association, the Wisconsin Humanities Council, and the Wisconsin Arts Board. Two citizens-at-large are appointed to the membership as well. Subject to commission approval, the poet laureate is required to plan and attend at least 4 statewide literacy events each year; and perform in at least 4 government, state, or civic events as requested by the governor's office, school systems, or nonprofit organizations. The first poet laureate was Ellen Kort of Appleton, the second was Denise Sweet of Green Bay. Governor Doyle appointed Marilyn Taylor of Milwaukee to a 2-year term in November 2008.

Racial Disparities Oversight Commission

Members: NOBLE WRAY (Police Chief, City of Madison), *chairperson;* JENNIFER BIAS (deputy director, State Public Defender Trial Division), JOHN CHISHOLM (District Attorney, Milwaukee County), JAMES MARTIN (Circuit Court Judge, Dane County).

Contact person: LINDSEY D. DRAPER, Office of Justice Assistance,
    lindsey.draper@wisconsin.gov

Address: 1 South Pinckney Street, Suite 600, Madison 53702.

Telephones: 266-7639, (414) 550-9731.

Fax: 266-6676.

Governor Jim Doyle created the commission in Executive Order 251, May 13, 2008. He directed the commission to exercise oversight and advocacy concerning programs and policies to reduce disparate treatment of people of color across the spectrum of the criminal justice system. The council is composed of no more than 4 members, including representatives from law enforcement, the legal profession, the judiciary, and the criminal justice system. All members are appointed by the governor and serve at the pleasure of the governor. The commission is required to meet not less than two times each year.

Reentry Task Force

Members: appointments pending.

Governor Jim Doyle created the task force in Executive Order 279, April 17, 2009. The task force was created to help establish a more systematic and coordinated approach to implementing strategies for prisoners to reenter communities after their release. The governor specifically directed the task force to provide coordination at the executive level of reentry initiatives across the state and ensure eligibility for federal Second Chance Act Grant opportunities; identify methods to improve collaboration and coordination of offender transition services among state agencies; establish a means to share data research and measurement resources in relation to reentry initiatives; identify funding areas that should be coordinated to maximize the delivery of state and community-based services; promote areas of research and program evaluation that can be coordinated across agencies with an emphasis on applying evidence-based practices to support treatment and intervention programs for offenders; and conduct a review of existing policies and practices and make specific recommendations to the governor on how the system and state laws may be improved in order to reduce recidivism. The task force consists of no more than nine members, including the Secretary of the Department of Corrections, who also serves as the chairperson; the secretaries of the Departments of Health Services, Children and Families, Workforce Development, and Commerce; the State Superintendent of Public Instruction; a representative from the Department of Justice to represent crime victims; a representative from county or local law enforcement; and a representative from county or local behavioral health departments. The task force must meet at least four times a year and is staffed by the Department of Corrections.

State Rehabilitation Council

Members: LINDA VEGOE (client assistance programs), *chairperson;* ROBERT BUETTNER (disability advocacy groups), *vice chairperson;* ASHLEY MARSHALL (disability advocacy groups), *treasurer;* JILL GONZALEZ (parent training and information center); ALVIN HILL (community rehabilitation program service provider); RONALD JANSEN (Statewide Independent Living Council); CAROL ANN SCHAUFEL (vocational rehabilitation counselor); BEN ANDERSON, JAMES DOBRINSKA, ROXAN PEREZ, DANIEL SIPPL (business, industry and labor representatives); JODI HANNA, MONICA KAMALROSSA, GAIL KOLVENBACH, VIVIAN LARKIN, JOHN W. LUI, WILLIAM MALONE, CINDI PICHLER (disability advocacy groups); KEN KLUEVER, PETER G. LUCAS (vocational rehabilitation recipients); PATRICIA LERCH (American Indian vocational rehabilitation); STEVEN GILLES (Department of Public Instruction). Nonvoting member: CHARLENE DWYER (administrator, Division of Vocational Rehabilitation).

Contact person: PATRICIA SEVERT.

Address: Division of Vocational Rehabilitation, 201 East Washington Avenue, P.O. Box 7852, Madison 53707-7852.

Telephone: 261-0090.

Governor Tommy G. Thompson created the council in Executive Order 363, January 30, 1999, to advise the Department of Workforce Development on the statewide vocational rehabilitation plan for disabled individuals required under 29 U.S. Code Section 720, *et seq.* Governor Jim Doyle most recently continued the council in Executive Order 182, January 18, 2007. The council is similar to one established in Executive Order 196, July 1, 1993, as the State Rehabilitation Advisory Council. Council members serve 3-year terms. A majority must be individuals with disabilities not employed by the Department of Workforce Development, Division of Vocational Rehabilitation Services. The administrator of that division is a nonvoting *ex officio* member of the council. The council issued its "Annual Report" in 2006.

Telecommunications Relay Service Council

Members: THOMAS E. HARBISON, *chairperson;* RONALD E. BYINGTON, MARGARET CALTEAUX, JILL COLLINS, CHERI FRENCH, DAVID FRIGEN, KAREN E. JORGENSEN, TOM MEITNER, HELEN RIZZI, vacancy.

Contact person: JACK R. CASSELL, jack.cassell@wisconsin.gov

Address: Division of Enterprise Technology, Department of Administration, 101 East Wilson Street, 8th Floor, P.O. Box 7844, Madison 53707-7844.

Telephones: (800) 901-8389; TTY: 267-6934.

Fax: 266-2164.

Governor Tommy G. Thompson created the council in Executive Order 95, June 19, 1990, recreated it in Executive Order 131, October 2, 1991, and Governor Jim Doyle continued it most recently in Executive Order 182, January 18, 2007. The council was directed to advise the Bureau of Telecommunications Management in the Department of Administration on the feasibility or desirability of: establishing requirements and procedures for a telecommunications relay service; requiring the service to be available 24 hours a day, 7 days a week; requiring users to pay rates that are no greater than rates for functionally equivalent voice telecommunications service; prohibiting relay service operators from refusing or limiting the length of calls; prohibiting relay service operators from disclosing the contents of calls, keeping records of their contents beyond the duration of the calls, and intentionally altering the content of a call; requiring relay service operators to take training on the problems faced by hearing-impaired and speech-impaired persons using the service; and authorizing the establishment by contract of a statewide telecommunications relay service. The council consists of not more than 11 members, 4 of whom must use a telecommunications relay service. These must include one speech-impaired person, one hearing-impaired person, one speech- and hearing-impaired person, and one person not having a speech or hearing impairment. Five of the members must include one representative each from the Wisconsin Association of the Deaf, Wisconsin Telecommunications, Inc., Wisconsin State Telephone Association, a local exchange telecommunications utility, and an interexchange telecommunications utility doing business in this state.

Governor's Commission on the United Nations

Members: WOLFGANG A. SCHMIDT, *chairperson;* CAROL EDLER BAUMANN, JEAN PIERRE BIAGUI, ROBERT CHASE, SAMUEL DUNLOP, JOSEPH W. ELDER, TAMERIN HAYWARD, KATHARINE P. MARRS,

SUSAN MCGOVERN, JENNIFER LABORDE MONROE, THAO N. NUON, JASON RAE, GARETH A. SHELLMAN, JOHN N. SMART, JOSEPH TULLBANE.

Contact person: GARETH A. SHELLMAN.

Address: 1060 West Theresa Lane, Glendale 53209.

Telephone: (414) 228-1854.

Originally created in 1959, the commission was continued most recently by Governor Jim Doyle in Executive Order 182, January 18, 2007. The commission is responsible for sponsoring statewide educational programs about the United Nations, coordinating Wisconsin's official participation in the annual observance of United Nations Day and anniversary of the Universal Declaration of Human Rights, expressing its views on issues affecting the UN, and communicating its views to public officials and the news media. The membership of the commission is drawn from various civic, religious, labor, business, and educational organizations.

Governor's Council on Workforce Investment

Members: TIM SULLIVAN, *chairperson;* LYLE BALISTRERI, THOMAS BRIEN, PHILLIP L. NEUENFELDT, MARK REIHL (labor representatives); COLLEEN BATES (local government representative); LEE RASCH, JOEL ROGERS, JOAN WILK (public education representatives); DANIEL ANDRIST, THOMAS L. BURSE, SHARON CANTER, WILLIAM CHAUDOIR, JEWEL CURRIE, KATHLEEN DRENGLER, KATHRYN DUNN, BARBARA FLEISNER, JAMES S. HANEY, SUSAN H. HATCH, JOHN HEYER, JAMES P. HILL, CELESTINE KOEHN, GAYLE KUGLER, DON MADELUNG, A. KENT OLSON, DONALD J. ROUSE, CHRISTOPHER A. RUUD, HARRY SANDERS, JR., JEFF STEREN, JULIA TAYLOR, DEAN WELCH (private sector representatives); ROBERT BORREMANS (nonprofit representative). REGGIE BICHA, DANIEL CLANCY, GOVERNOR JIM DOYLE, TONY EVERS, ROBERTA GASSMAN, KIM KINDSCHI, RICHARD J. LEINENKUGEL, RICK RAEMISCH, JOHN A. SCOCOS, KAREN TIMBERLAKE (state agency representatives); SENATORS COGGS, LEIBHAM, REPRESENTATIVE ZEPNICK (state legislative representatives).

Contact person: RON DANOWSKI.

Address: Department of Workforce Development, P.O. Box 7972, Madison 53707-7972.

Telephone: 266-3485.

Governor Tommy G. Thompson created the council in Executive Order 385, November 17, 1999, and Governor Jim Doyle most recently continued it in Executive Order 182, January 18, 2007, to qualify the state to receive federal funds allotted under the Workforce Investment Act (WIA) of 1998. The council consists of members appointed in accordance with federal law and additional members the governor may designate. As specified by law, the majority of members are from the private sector. The governor directed the council to carry out the duties and functions prescribed in WIA, Public Law 105-220; to advise the governor on workforce development strategy and policy, and undertake research and other activities to assist the governor in enhancing the operation and performance of workforce programs in the state; and to provide direction and guidance for the Wisconsin Forward Award to advance high performance workplaces, and advance other initiatives to support a skilled workforce. The governor further directed that all appropriate state agencies work together on the council and at the local level to develop a strong, skilled workforce for Wisconsin's future.

STATE OFFICERS APPOINTED BY THE GOVERNOR
AS REQUIRED BY STATUTE
June 30, 2009

Officers[1]	Name	Home Address[2]	Term Expires[3]	Salary or Per Diem[4]
*Accounting Examining Board Secs. 15.08, 15.405 (1)	Lucretia Mattson	Eau Claire	July 1, 2007	$25 per day
	Steve Corbeille	Crivitz	July 1, 2009	$25 per day
	Thomas J. Kilkenny	Brookfield	July 1, 2009	$25 per day
	Kim Tredinnick[5]	DeForest	July 1, 2010	$25 per day
	Marian Wozniak[5]	Edgerton	July 1, 2010	$25 per day
	Karla Blair	Kaukauna	July 1, 2012	$25 per day
	vacancy			
Adjutant General Sec. 15.31	Brig. Gen Donald P. Dunbar		Sept. 1, 2012	Group 4
*Administration, Dept. of, Secy. Secs. 15.05 (1) (a), 15.10	Michael Morgan	Madison	Pleasure of Gov.	Group 8
Adult Offender Supervision Board, Interstate Sec. 15.145 (3)	Nate Zolik	Madison	May 1, 2007	None
	Gregory Potter	Wisconsin Rapids	May 1, 2009	None
	William Rankin	Janesville	May 1, 2009	None
	Tamara Grigsby	Milwaukee	May 1, 2011	None
	Ann Gustafson	River Falls	May 1, 2011	None
Adult Offender Supervision Board, Interstate Compact Administrator Sec. 304.16 (2)(d)	William Rankin	Janesville	Pleas. of Gov.	None None None None
*Aerospace Authority, Wis. Sec. 114.61	Mark Hanna	Sheboygan	June 30, 2009	None
	Mark Lee	Middleton	June 30, 2009	None
	Thomas Crabb	Middleton	June 30, 2010	None
	Judith Schieble	Sheboygan	June 30, 2010	None
	Thomas Mullooly	Wauwatosa	June 30, 2011	None
	Edward Wagner	Marshfield	June 30, 2011	None
Affirmative Action, Council on Secs. 15.09 (1)(a), 15.105 (29)(d)	David Dunham	Madison	July 1, 2008	None
	Sandra Ryan	Sun Prairie	July 1, 2008	None
	Yolanda Santos Adams	Kenosha	July 1, 2009	None
	Thresessa Childs	Milwaukee	July 1, 2009	None
	Janice Hughes	Madison	July 1, 2009	None
	John Magerus	Racine	July 1, 2009	None
	James R. Parker	La Crosse	July 1, 2009	None
	Santiago Rosas	Madison	July 1, 2009	None
	Lakshmi Bharadwaj	Shorewood	July 1, 2010	None
	Ronald Shaheed	Milwaukee	July 1, 2011	None
	Nancy Vue	Madison	July 1, 2011	None
*Aging and Long-Term Care, Board on Secs. 15.07 (1)(b) 9, 15.105 (10)	Dale Taylor	Eau Claire	May 1, 2010	None
	Terry Lynch	Racine	May 1, 2011	None
	Eva Arnold	Beloit	May 1, 2012	None
	Tanya Meyer	Gleason	May 1, 2012	None
	Barbara Thoni	Madison	May 1, 2012	None
	Patricia Finder-Stone	De Pere	May 1, 2013	None
	James Surprise[5]	Wautoma	May 1, 2013	None
*Agriculture, Trade and Consumer Protection, Board of Secs. 15.07 (1)(a), 15.07 (5)(d),15.13	Richard L. Cates	Spring Green	May 1, 2009	Not exc. $35 per day nor $1,000 per yr.
	Michael Dummer	Holmen	May 1, 2009	Not exc. $35 per day nor $1,000 per yr.
	Shelly A. Mayer	Slinger	May 1, 2009	Not exc. $35 per day nor $1,000 per yr.
	Andrew Diercks	Coloma	May 1, 2011	Not exc. $35 per day nor $1,000 per yr.
	Michael Krutza	Wausau	May 1, 2011	Not exc. $35 per day nor $1,000 per yr.
	Brian Rude	Coon Valley	May 1, 2011	Not exc. $35 per day nor $1,000 per yr.
	Cynthia Brown	Menomonie	May 1, 2013	Not exc. $35 per day nor $1,000 per yr.
	Enrique Figueroa	Milwaukee	May 1, 2013	Not exc. $35 per day nor $1,000 per yr.
	Margaret Krome	Madison	May 1, 2013	Not exc. $35 per day nor $1,000 per yr.
*Agriculture, Trade and Consumer Protection, Dept. of, Secy. Secs. 15.05 (1)(d), 15.07 (1)	Rod Nilsestuen	Madison	Pleas. of Gov.	Group 6
Alcohol and Other Drug Abuse, State Council on Secs. 14.017 (2), 15.09	Mark C. Seidl	Algoma	Pleas. of Gov.	None
	Michael Waupoose	Madison	Pleas. of Gov.	None
	Sandy Hardie	Eden	July 1, 2007	None
	Linda Mayfield	Milwaukee	July 1, 2007	None
	Joyce O'Donnell	West Allis	July 1, 2009	None
	Mary Rasmussen	Boyceville	July 1, 2009	None
	Scott Stokes	Bonduel	July 1, 2009	None
	Duncan Shrout	Milwaukee	July 1, 2011	None

Officers[1]	Name	Home Address[2]	Term Expires[3]	Salary or Per Diem[4]
*Architects, Landscape Architects, Professional Engineers, Designers and Land Surveyors, Board of Secs. 15.08, 15.405 (2)	Bernie Abrahamson	Black River Falls	July 1, 2006	$25 per day
	James E. Rusch	New Richmond	July 1, 2006	$25 per day
	Thomas Gasperetti	Milwaukee	July 1, 2009	$25 per day
	Martin Hanson	Eau Claire	July 1, 2009	$25 per day
	Ryan Klippel	Sun Prairie	July 1, 2009	$25 per day
	Charles Kopplin	Milwaukee	July 1, 2009	$25 per day
	Steven Nielsen	Luck	July 1, 2009	$25 per day
	Lawrence Schnuck	Whitefish Bay	July 1, 2009	$25 per day
	Rosheen Styczinski	Milwaukee	July 1, 2009	$25 per day
	Steven Tweed	Marshall	July 1, 2009	$25 per day
	Rick Van Goethem	Green Bay	July 1, 2009	$25 per day
	Steven Hook	Milwaukee	July 1, 2010	$25 per day
	James Mickowski	Stoughton	July 1, 2010	$25 per day
	Daniel Sheldon	Waukesha	July 1, 2010	$25 per day
	Wayne Tlusty	Rib Lake	July 1, 2011	$25 per day
	Walter Wilson[5]	Milwaukee	July 1, 2010	$25 per day
	Scott Berg	Appleton	July 1, 2011	$25 per day
	Julia DeCicco	Milwaukee	July 1, 2011	$25 per day
	Gary Gust	Menomonie	July 1, 2011	$25 per day
	Matthew Janiak	Mondovi	July 1, 2011	$25 per day
	Ruth Johnson	Madison	July 1, 2011	$25 per day
	Michael Kinney	River Falls	July 1, 2012	$25 per day
	Gary Kohlenberg	Oconomowoc	July 1, 2012	$25 per day
	Nancy Ragland	Madison	July 1, 2012	$25 per day
	4 vacancies			
*Artistic Endowment Foundation Chap. 247	Inactive			
Arts Board Sec. 15.445 (1)	Robert A. Wagner	Milwaukee	May 1, 2006	None
	Glenda Noel-Ney	Madison	May 1, 2008	None
	James Hall	Milwaukee	May 1, 2009	None
	Helen Klebesadel	Madison	May 1, 2009	None
	Michael Reyes	Glendale	May 1, 2009	None
	Linda L. Ware	Wausau	May 1, 2009	None
	Bruce Bernberg	Racine	May 1, 2010	None
	Jerry Hembd	Superior	May 1, 2010	None
	Gerald Kember	La Crosse	May 1, 2010	None
	Barbara Lawton	Madison	May 1, 2010	None
	Sharon Stewart	Washburn	May 1, 2010	None
	Storm Elser	Hartland	May 1, 2011	None
	Paul Meinke	Green Bay	May 1, 2011	None
	Nick Meyer	Eau Claire	May 1, 2011	None
	Barbara Munson	Mosinee	May 1, 2011	None
Athletic Trainers Affiliated Credentialing Board Sec. 15.406 (4)	John Sybeldon	Wausau	July 1, 2006	$25 per day
	Jodi Pelegrin	Green Bay	July 1, 2008	$25 per day
	Ryan Berry	Madison	July 1, 2009	$25 per day
	James Nesbit	Phillips	July 1, 2010	$25 per day
	Jeanne Brown	Eau Claire	July 1, 2011	$25 per day
	Steven Nass	Lake Mills	July 1, 2012	$25 per day
*Auctioneer Board Sec. 15.504 (3)	Jay N. Clarke	Ripon	May 1, 2006	$25 per day
	Byron Krueger	Melrose	May 1, 2007	$25 per day
	Carl Theorin[5]	Wausau	May 1, 2008	$25 per day
	Alan S. Hager	Lena	May 1, 2009	$25 per day
	Patrick McNamara[5]	Lancaster	May 1, 2010	$25 per day
	Kathryn Daley	Green Bay	May 1, 2011	$25 per day
	Timothy Sweeney	Green Lake	May 1, 2012	$25 per day
*Banking Review Board Secs. 15.07 (1)(b) 1, 15.185 (1), 15.555 (1)	Debra R. Lins	Prairie du Sac	May 1, 2009	$25 per day, not exc. $1,500 per yr.
	Ralph Tenuta	Kenosha	May 1, 2010	$25 per day, not exc. $1,500 per yr.
	Thomas Spitz	Sun Prairie	May 1, 2011	$25 per day, not exc. $1,500 per yr.
	Douglas Farmer	La Crosse	May 1, 2012	$25 per day, not exc. $1,500 per yr.
	Amelia Macareno	Milwaukee	May 1, 2013	$25 per day, not exc. $1,500 per yr.
*Barbering and Cosmetology Examining Board Secs. 15.08, 15.405 (17)	Jeannie Bush	La Crosse	July 1, 2010	$25 per day
	Susan Kolve	La Crosse	July 1, 2010	$25 per day
	Tina Rettler	Madison	July 1, 2010	$25 per day
	Janice Boeck	Racine	July 1, 2011	$25 per day
	Cheryl Pearse	La Crosse	July 1, 2011	$25 per day
	Laura Ruiz	Milwaukee	July 1, 2012	$25 per day
	Eugene Gottfredsen	Beloit	July 1, 2012	$25 per day
	Jeffrey Patterson	Madison	July 1, 2012	$25 per day
	Howard Twait	Wisconsin Rapids	July 1, 2012	$25 per day
*Bradley Center Sports and Entertainment Corporation, Bd. of Directors of the Sec. 232.03	Gail A. Lione	Milwaukee	July 1, 2006	None
	Virgis W. Colbert	Mequon	July 1, 2009	None
	Ulice Payne, Jr.	Greenfield	July 1, 2009	None
	Gary Sweeney	Fox Point	July 1, 2009	None
	Ned W. Bechthold	Elm Grove	July 1, 2011	None
	Douglas G. Kiel	Milwaukee	July 1, 2011	None
	Michael F. Hart	Mequon	July 1, 2011	None
	Marc Marotta	Mequon	July 1, 2013	None
	Rolen L. Womack	Brown Deer	July 1, 2013	None

Officers[1]	Name	Home Address[2]	Term Expires[3]	Salary or Per Diem[4]
Building Commission Sec. 13.48 (2)	Terry McGuire	Beloit	Pleas. of Gov.	None
Building Inspector Review Board Sec. 15.155 (6)	Jack Van Der Weele	Sheboygan	May 1, 2010	None
	Martin Rifken	Madison	May 1, 2013	None
*Burial Sites Preservation Board Secs. 15.07 (5)(o), 15.705 (1)	David Grignon	Keshena	July 1, 2008	$25 per day
	Roseanne Meer	Pardeeville	July 1, 2009	$25 per day
	Robert Powless	Odanah	July 1, 2009	$25 per day
	Kathryn Egan-Bruhy[5]	Minocqua	July 1, 2010	$25 per day
	Corina Williams	Oneida	July 1, 2010	$25 per day
	Robert Boszhardt	La Crosse	July 1, 2011	$25 per day
*Cemetery Board Sec. 15.405 (3m)	Ed Greenfield	Green Bay	July 1, 2010	$25 per day
	Mary Lehman	Appleton	July 1, 2010	$25 per day
	Tim Stanley	Monona	July 1, 2011	$25 per day
	Kathleen Cantu	Madison	July 1, 2012	$25 per day
	E. Glen Porter III	New Berlin	July 1, 2012	$25 per day
	Cecelia Timmons[5]	Madison	July 1, 2012	$25 per day
Child Abuse and Neglect Prevention Board Secs. 15.07 (1)(a), 15.195 (4)	Anne Arnesen	Madison	May 1, 2008	None
	Florence Ninham	Gresham	May 1, 2008	None
	Reginald Bicha	River Falls	May 1, 2009	None
	Cyrus Behroozi	Milwaukee	May 1, 2010	None
	Barbara Knox	Cross Plains	May 1, 2010	None
	Richard Schlimm	Madison	May 1, 2010	None
	Nancy Armbrust	Green Bay	May 1, 2011	None
	Stephen Gilbertson	Milwaukee	May 1, 2011	None
	James Leonhart	Madison	May 1, 2011	None
	Sandra McCormick	La Crosse	May 1, 2012	None
	Coral Butson 2 vacancies	Madison	Pleas. of Gov.	None
*Children and Families, Dept. of, Secy. Secs. 15.20	Reggie Bicha	Eau Claire	Pleas. of Gov.	Group 6
*Chiropractic Examining Board Secs. 15.08, 15.405 (5)	Wendy M. Henrichs	Rhinelander	July 1, 2007	$25 per day
	Steven Silverman	Merrill	July 1, 2007	$25 per day
	Steven Conway	Athens	July 1, 2009	$25 per day
	James Koshick	New Berlin	July 1, 2009	$25 per day
	Mania Moore	New Richmond	July 1, 2009	$25 per day
	Kathleen Schneider	Minocqua	July 1, 2012	$25 per day
Circus World Museum Foundation Secs. 44.16 (2)	David Hoffman	Black River Falls	Pleas. of Gov.	None
Claims Board Secs. 15.07 (2)(e), 15.105 (2)	Chandra Miller Fienen	Madison	Pleas. of Gov.	None
*College Savings Program Board Sec. 14.57	Paul Adamski	Stevens Point	May 1, 2009	None
	Alberta Darling	River Hills	May 1, 2009	None
	Patrick Sheehy	Mequon	May 1, 2009	None
	Mary Cook	Mount Horeb	May 1, 2011	None
	William Oemichen	New Glarus	May 1, 2011	None
	Jeff Plale	South Milwaukee	May 1, 2011	None
*Commerce, Dept. of, Secy. Secs. 15.05 (1)(a), 15.15	Richard Leinenkugel	Menomonee Falls	Pleas. of Gov.	Group 6
Controlled Substances Board Sec. 15.405 (5g)	Cecilia Hillard	Milwaukee	July 1, 2011	None
	Darold Treffert	Fond du Lac	July 1, 2011	None
Conveyance Safety Code Council Sec. 15.157 (14)(a)	Andrew Ziekle	Madison	July 1, 2007	None
	Jesse Kaysen	Madison	July 1, 2009	None
	Kevin Kraemer	Plain	July 1, 2009	None
	Paul Rosenberg	Mequon	July 1, 2010	None
	Calvin King	Onalaska	July 1, 2011	None
	Kelvin Nord	Slinger	July 1, 2011	None
	George Semenak	Green Bay	July 1, 2011	None
*Corrections, Dept. of, Secy. Secs. 15.05 (1)(a), 15.14	Richard Raemisch	Waunakee	Pleas. of Gov.	Group 6
*Credit Union Review Board Secs. 15.07 (1)(b) 3, 15.07 (5)(s), 15.185 (7)(b)	Quirin E. Braam	New Berlin	May 1, 2008	$25 per day, not exc. $1,500 per yr.
	Dennis Degenhardt	Fitchburg	May 1, 2009	$25 per day, not exc. $1,500 per yr.
	Carla Altepeter	Oshkosh	May 1, 2010	$25 per day, not exc. $1,500 per yr.
	Gregory Lentz	Menomonie	May 1, 2011	$25 per day, not exc $1,500 per yr.
	Lisa Greco	Brookfield	May 1, 2012	$25 per day, not exc. $1,500 per yr.
*Credit Unions, Office of, Director Sec. 15.185 (7)(a)	Suzanne T. Cowan	Oregon	Pleas. of Gov.	Group 3
Crematory Authority Council Sec. 15.407 (8)	Paul Haubrich	Bayside	July 1, 2008	None
	Gary Langendorf	Racine	July 1, 2008	None
	Scott Brainard	Wausau	July 1, 2009	None
	Adam Casper	West Salem	July 1, 2009	None
	Kelly Coleman-Kohorn	Germantown	July 1, 2010	None
	William Cress	Stoughton	July 1, 2010	None
	Linda Reid	Whitewater	July 1, 2011	None

Officers[1]	Name	Home Address[2]	Term Expires[3]	Salary or Per Diem[4]
Crime Victims Rights Bd. Sec. 15.255 (2)	Angela Sutkiewicz	Sheboygan	May 1, 2011	None
Criminal Penalties, Joint Review Committee on Sec. 13.525 (1)	Bradley Gehring	Appleton	Pleas. of Gov.	None
	David Mahoney	Madison	Pleas. of Gov.	None
Deaf and Hard of Hearing, Council for the Secs. 15.09 (1)(a), 15.197 (8)	Margaret Bossman	Woodville	July 1, 2009	None
	Mary Griffin	Eau Claire	July 1, 2009	None
	Terri Matenaer	Franksville	July 1, 2009	None
	Harry W. Mauldin, Jr.	Madison	July 1, 2009	None
	Thomas Meitner	Watertown	July 1, 2009	None
	Eloise Schwarz	Wauwatosa	July 1, 2009	None
	Jennifer Evans	Neenah	July 1, 2011	None
	Daniel Houlihan	Milwaukee	July 1, 2011	None
	Stefanie Saltern	Fitchburg	July 1, 2011	None
*Deferred Compensation Board Secs. 15.07 (1)(b) 14, 15.07 (5)(f), 15.165 (4)	Edward Main	Madison	July 1, 2004	None
	John F. Nelson	Middleton	July 1, 2005	None
	Martin Beil	Madison	July 1, 2009	None
	Gail Hanson	Delafield	July 1, 2010	None
	Michael Drury	Merrill	July 1, 2011	None
*Dentistry Examining Board Secs. 15.08, 15.405 (6)	Anne N. Taylor	Milwaukee	July 1, 2008	$25 per day
	John Grignon	New Berlin	July 1, 2009	None
	Adriana Jaramillo	Madison	July 1, 2009	$25 per day
	Kirk Ritchie	Rhinelander	July 1, 2009	$25 per day
	Lori Barbeau	New Berlin	July 1, 2010	$25 per day
	Blane Christman	Ladysmith	July 1, 2010	$25 per day
	Carol Howard	Shorewood	July 1, 2010	$25 per day
	Sandra Linhart	La Crosse	July 1, 2010	$25 per day
	Nancy Rublee	Phillips	July 1, 2010	$25 per day
	William Stempski	Green Bay	July 1, 2011	$25 per day
	Linda Bohacek	Eau Claire	July 1, 2012	$25 per day
Development Finance Board Secs. 15.07 (1) (cm), 15.155 (1)	Mickey Judkins	Eau Claire	May 1, 2008	None
	Margaret Henningsen	Milwaukee	May 1, 2009	None
	Ralph Kauten	Madison	May 1, 2009	None
	Kenneth Wanek	Milwaukee	May 1, 2009	None
	Mark Reihl	Madison	May 1, 2010	None
	vacancy			
Developmental Disabilities, Bd. for People with Secs. 15.09 (1)(a), 15.105 (8)	Debra Glover	Milwaukee	July 1, 2007	None
	Susan Kay Nutter	La Crosse	July 1, 2007	None
	Roxanne M. Price	La Crosse	July 1, 2007	None
	Cindy Zellner-Ehlers	Sturgeon Bay	July 1, 2007	None
	Daniel Remick	Madison	July 1, 2008	None
	Shu Cheng	Eau Claire	July 1, 2009	None
	Mari Frederick	Wautoma	July 1, 2009	None
	Ashley Hesse	Oshkosh	July 1, 2009	None
	Barbara Katz	Madison	July 1, 2009	None
	Barbara Sorensen	Washburn	July 1, 2009	None
	Maureen Arcand	Madison	July 1, 2010	None
	Cynthia Bentley	Glendale	July 1, 2010	None
	Kristin C. Berg	Eau Claire	July 1, 2010	None
	Gerald Born	Madison	July 1, 2010	None
	Jackie Wenkman	Jefferson	July 1, 2010	None
	Joan Burns	Madison	July 1, 2011	None
	Kevin Fech	Cudahy	July 1, 2011	None
	Jonathan Donnelly	Madison	July 1, 2012	None
	Ruth Gullerud	Eau Claire	July 1, 2012	None
	Katherine Maloney Perhach	Whitefish Bay	July 1, 2012	None
	L. Lynn Stansberry-Brusnahan	Shorewood	July 1, 2012	None
*Dietitians Affiliated Credentialing Board Sec. 15.406 (2)	Diane Johnson	Hazelhurst	July 1, 2010	$25 per day
	Patricia Roblee	Oshkosh	July 1, 2010	$25 per day
	Virginia Jordan	Eau Claire	July 1, 2011	$25 per day
	Gail Underbakke	Madison	July 1, 2011	$25 per day
*Domestic Abuse, Council on Secs. 15.09 (1)(a), 15.197 (16)	Lisa Stewart-Boettcher	Columbus	July 1, 2006	None
	Stormy M. Walker-Mercadel[5]	Milwaukee	July 1, 2007	None
	Marilyn Lensert Harris	Beloit	July 1, 2009	None
	Gene Redhail[5]	Green Bay	July 1, 2009	None
	Terese Berceau[5]	Madison	July 1, 2010	None
	Peter Helein	Appleton	July 1, 2010	None
	Rachel Rodriguez	Waunakee	July 1, 2010	None
	Maytong Chang	Milwaukee	July 1, 2011	None
	L. Kevin Hamberger	Franklin	July 1, 2011	None
	Justine Schmidt	Milwaukee	July 1, 2011	None
	Mariana Rodriguez	Milwaukee	July 1, 2011	None
	Beth Schnorr	Appleton	July 1, 2011	None
	Gerald Wilkie	Eau Claire	July 1, 2011	None
Dry Cleaner Environmental Response Council Sec. 15.347 (2)	Brett Donaldson	Menasha	July 1, 2009	None
	Jeanne Tarvin	Slinger	July 1, 2009	None
	Jim Fitzgerald	Mequon	July 1, 2010	None
	Richard Klinke	Cottage Grove	July 1, 2010	None
	Kevin Braden	Brookfield	July 1, 2011	None
	Jill Fitzgerald	Muskego	July 1, 2011	

Officers[1]	Name	Home Address[2]	Term Expires[3]	Salary or Per Diem[4]
Dwelling Code Council Secs. 15.09 (1)(a), 15.157 (3)	Thomas Doleschy	Muskego	July 1, 2007	None
	William Turner	Hayward	July 1, 2007	None
	Robert Jakel	Kaukauna	July 1, 2008	None
	Kathleen Stadtherr	Green Bay	July 1, 2008	None
	Brian Juarez	Fort Atkinson	July 1, 2009	None
	Steven Levine	Madison	July 1, 2009	None
	Frank Opatik	Wausau	July 1, 2009	None
	Gary Ruhl	Oshkosh	July 1, 2009	None
	Mary Schroeder	Brookfield	July 1, 2009	None
	Dennis Bauer	McFarland	July 1, 2010	None
	Michael Mueller	Greendale	July 1, 2010	None
	Thomas Palecek	Marshfield	July 1, 2010	None
	Robert Premo	Hartland	July 1, 2010	None
	John Vande Castle	Fond du Lac	July 1, 2010	None
	Michael Wallace	New Richmond	July 1, 2010	None
	Jeffrey Bechard	Eau Claire	July 1, 2011	None
	David Dolan-Wallace	Green Bay	July 1, 2011	None
	Dan Gorski	McFarland	July 1, 2011	None
Education Commission of the States Sec. 39.76	Jessica Doyle	Madison	Pleas. of Gov.	None
	Bette Lang	Beloit	Pleas. of Gov.	None
	Luther Olsen	Ripon	Pleas. of Gov.	None
Educational Approval Board Sec. 15.945 (1)	Christy L. Brown	Bayside	Pleas. of Gov.	$25 per day
	Michael J. Cooney	Oshkosh	Pleas. of Gov.	$25 per day
	Terrance L. Craney	Baraboo	Pleas. of Gov.	$25 per day
	Joe Heim	La Crosse	Pleas. of Gov.	$25 per day
	Jo Oyama-Miller	Monona	Pleas. of Gov.	$25 per day
	Richard F. Raemisch	Waunakee	Pleas. of Gov.	$25 per day
	Monica Williams	Appleton	Pleas. of Gov.	$25 per day
*Educational Communications Board Secs. 15.07 (1)(a) 5, 15.57	Thomas Basting	Madison	May 1, 2009	None
	Diane Everson	Edgerton	May 1, 2009	None
	June Anderson	Oshkosh	May 1, 2011	None
	Rolf Wegenke	Sun Prairie	May 1, 2011	None
	Eileen Littig	Green Bay	Pleas. of Gov.	None
*Electronic Recording Council Sec. 15.107 (6)	Marvel Lemke[5]	Medford	July 1, 2008	None
	Cathy Williquette[5]	Green Bay	July 1, 2008	None
	Craig Haskins	Franklin	July 1, 2009	None
	Jane Licht[5]	Dunn	July 1, 2009	None
	Cynthia Wisinski[5]	Stevens Point	July 1, 2009	None
	Steven Hansen[5]	Middleton	July 1, 2010	None
	Hal Karas[5]	Milwaukee	July 1, 2010	None
*Emergency Management Div., Administrator of Sec. 15.313 (1)	Johnnie Smith	Sun Prairie	Pleas. of Gov.	Group 1
Emergency Medical Services Board Sec. 15.195 (8)	Thomas B. Brazelton III	Madison	May 1, 2008	None
	Steven Bane	West Allis	May 1, 2009	None
	Kenneth Johnson	Greenleaf	May 1, 2009	None
	Travis Teesch	Kaukauna	May 1, 2009	None
	James Austad	Oshkosh	May 1, 2010	None
	Troy Haase	Fond du Lac	May 1, 2010	None
	Melinda Allen	Monroe	May 1, 2011	None
	Mark Fredrickson	Hilbert	May 1, 2011	None
	Cal Lintz	Green Bay	May 1, 2011	None
	Gloria Murawsky	Milwaukee	May 1, 2011	None
*Employee Trust Funds Board Secs. 15.07 (1)(a) 3, 15.07 (5)(f), 15.16 (1) (c)	Rosemary Finora[5]	Pewaukee	May 1, 2009	$25 per day
	Gary Sherman	Port Wing	Pleas. of Gov.	None
*Employment Relations, Office of, Dir. Sec. 15.105 (29)	Jennifer Donnelly[5]	Verona	Pleas. of Gov.	Group 7
*Employment Relations Comn. Secs. 15.06 (1), 15.58	Paul P. Gordon	Chippewa Falls	March 1, 2009	Group 5
	Susan Bauman	Madison	March 1, 2011	Group 5
	Judith Neumann	Madison	March 1, 2013	Group 5
Federal-State Relations Office, Director Sec. 16.548 (1)	Jen Jinks	Washington, D.C.	Pleas. of Gov.	Group 3
*Financial Institutions, Dept. of Secy. of Secs. 15.05 (1)(a), 15.18	Lorrie Keating Heinemann	Madison	Pleas. of Gov.	Group 6

Officers[1]	Name	Home Address[2]	Term Expires[3]	Salary or Per Diem[4]
Forestry, Council on	Michael Bolton.	Plover	Pleas. of Gov.	None
Sec. 15.347 (19)	Dennis G. Brown	Rhinelander	Pleas. of Gov.	None
	Troy Brown	Antigo	Pleas. of Gov.	None
	Leon A. Church	Appleton	Pleas. of Gov.	None
	Fred A. Clark.	Baraboo	Pleas. of Gov.	None
	Paul J. DeLong.	Madison	Pleas. of Gov.	None
	Donald Friske	Merrill	Pleas. of Gov.	None
	James Heerey	New Auburn	Pleas. of Gov.	None
	Jeanne Higgins.	Chequamegon	Pleas. of Gov.	None
	James Hoppe.	Rhinelander	Pleas. of Gov.	None
	William J. Horvath.	Stevens Point	Pleas. of Gov.	None
	Mary Hubler	Rice Lake	Pleas. of Gov.	None
	Mary J. Huston.	Madison	Pleas. of Gov.	None
	Bob Jauch	Poplar	Pleas. of Gov.	None
	Kenneth A. Ottman	Milwaukee	Pleas. of Gov.	None
	Robert Rogers	Custer	Pleas. of Gov.	None
	Jane Severt.	Tomahawk	Pleas. of Gov.	None
	Frederic J. Souba, Jr..	Wisconsin Rapids	Pleas. of Gov.	None
	Jeffrey C. Stier.	Madison	Pleas. of Gov.	None
	Kathleen Vinehout	Alma	Pleas. of Gov.	None
*Fox River Navigational	Jack Nelson	Oshkosh	July 1, 2010	None
System Authority	Will Stark	De Pere	July 1, 2010	None
Sec. 237.02	Celestine Jeffreys	Green Bay	July 1, 2011	None
	William Raaths.	Menasha	July 1, 2011	None
	S. Timothy Rose	Appleton	July 1, 2011	None
	Ron Van De Hey	Kaukauna	July 1, 2011	None
*Funeral Directors	Michele Moore.	La Crosse	July 1, 2009	$25 per day
Examining Board	Rosalie Murphy	Lena	July 1, 2009	$25 per day
Secs. 15.08, 15.405 (16)	J.C. Frazier.	Milwaukee	July 1, 2010	$25 per day
	Connie Ryan	Madison	July 1, 2010	$25 per day
	David Olsen	Jefferson	July 1, 2011	$25 per day
	Patricia Thornton.	Grand View	July 1, 2012	$25 per day
*Geologists, Hydrologists and	Stephen V. Donohue	De Pere	July 1, 2006	$25 per day
Soil Scientists, Examining	Jon H. Gumtow	Random Lake	July 1, 2006	$25 per day
Board of Professional	John Hahn	Elm Grove	July 1, 2007	$25 per day
Secs. 15.08, 15.405 (2m)	Sue Bridson	Madison	July 1, 2009	$25 per day
	Bryant Browne.	Stevens Point	July 1, 2009	$25 per day
	William Mode	Neenah	July 1, 2009	$25 per day
	Patricia Trochlell.	Blue Mounds	July 1, 2009	$25 per day
	Ruth Johnson[5]	Madison	July 1, 2010	$25 per day
	James Robertson[5]	Madison	July 1, 2010	$25 per day
	Brenda Halminiak	Rhinelander	July 1, 2012	$25 per day
	Randall Hunt.	Cross Plains	July 1, 2012	$25 per day
	Frederick Madison.	Lodi	July 1, 2012	$25 per day
*Government Accountability	William Eich.	Madison	May 1, 2010	None
Board	Gordon Myse[5]	Appleton	May 1, 2011	None
Secs. 15.07 (1)(a) 2, 15.60	Gerald Nichol	Madison	May 1, 2012	None
	Thomas Cane	Wausau	May 1, 2013	None
	Michael Brennan.	Marshfield	May 1, 2014	None
	Thomas Barland[5].	Eau Claire	May 1, 2015	None
Great Lakes Comn.	Todd Ambs.	Madison	July 1, 2009	None
Sec. 14.78 (1)	Dave Hansen.	Green Bay	July 1, 2009	None
	Fred Schnook	De Pere	July 1, 2012	None
Great Lakes Protection Fund	Todd Ambs.	Madison	Oct. 11, 2009	None
Sec. 14.84	Alan Fish.	Madison	Oct. 11, 2010	None
Groundwater Coordinating	George Kraft.	Amherst	July 1, 2007	None
Council				
Secs. 15.09 (5)(f), 15.347 (13)				
Group Insurance Board	Robert Baird	Waukesha	May 1, 2009	$25 per day
Secs. 15.07 (1)(b),	Martin Beil.	Mazomanie	May 1, 2009	$25 per day
15.07 (5)(f), 15.165 (2)	Janis Doleschal.	Milwaukee	May 1, 2009	$25 per day
	Stephen Frankel	Mequon	May 1, 2009	$25 per day
	Esther Olson	Belleville	May 1, 2009	$25 per day
	Gary Sherman	Port Wing	Pleas. of Gov.	None
	vacancy			
*Health and Educational	John Noreiko.	Madison	June 30, 2010	None
Facilities Authority, Wis.	Tim K. Size	Sauk City	July 1, 2011	None
Sec. 231.02 (1)	Beth Gillis	Shawano	June 30, 2012	None
	Ken Thompson.	Milwaukee	June 30, 2013	None
	Bruce Colburn	Milwaukee	July 1, 2014	None
	Richard Canter.	Milwaukee	July 1, 2015	None
	Kevin Flaherty	Milwaukee	Pleas. of Gov.	None
*Health Services,	Karen Timberlake	Madison	Pleas. of Gov.	Group 9
Dept. of, Secy.				
Secs. 15.05 (1)(a), 15.19				
Health Care Liability	Scott Froehlke	Montello	May 1, 2008	None
Insurance Plan/Injured Patients	Reid Olson	Middleton	May 1, 2009	None
and Families Compensation	Dennis Conta.	Milwaukee	May 1, 2010	None
Fund Bd. of Governors	Stan Davis	Sun Prairie	May 1, 2010	None
Sec. 619.04 (3), 655.27 (2)				

Officers[1]	Name	Home Address[2]	Term Expires[3]	Salary or Per Diem[4]
*Health Insurance Risk-Sharing Plan Authority Sec. 149.41 (1)	Michelle Bachhuber	Marshfield	May 1, 2009	None
	Deborah Severson	Eau Claire	May 1, 2009	None
	Dennis Conta	Milwaukee	May 1, 2010	None
	Joseph Kachelski	Verona	May 1, 2010	None
	Wayne MacArdy	New Lisbon	May 1, 2010	None
	Annette Stebbins	Madison	May 1, 2010	None
	Larry Zanoni	Middleton	May 1, 2010	None
	Michael Gifford	Milwaukee	May 1, 2011	None
	Dianne Greenley	Madison	May 1, 2011	None
	Carol Peirick	Madison	May 1, 2011	None
	Larry Rambo[5]	Waukesha	May 1, 2011	None
	Luann Simpson	Racine	May 1, 2011	None
	vacancy			
*Hearing and Speech Examining Board Secs. 15.08, 15.405 (6m)	Terrence M. Greenleaf	Whitewater	July 1, 2007	$25 per day
	Katie Lepak	Milwaukee	July 1, 2007	$25 per day
	Marilyn S. Workinger	Marshfield	July 1, 2007	$25 per day
	Bruce Baier	Brown Deer	July 1, 2008	$25 per day
	Thomas E. Fisher	Wausau	July 1, 2008	$25 per day
	Okie Allen	Eau Claire	July 1, 2009	$25 per day
	David Friedland	Menomonee Falls	July 1, 2009	$25 per day
	Edward Korabic	Shorewood	July 1, 2009	$25 per day
	Peter Zellmer	Appleton	July 1, 2009	$25 per day
	Alma Peters	Mequon	July 1, 2010	$25 per day
Higher Educational Aids Board Secs. 15.07 (1)(a) 1, 15.67 (1)	Maria Flores	Cudahy	May 1, 2009	None
	Mary Jo Green	Nekoosa	May 1, 2009	None
	Ann Greenheck	Lone Rock	May 1, 2009	None
	James Palmer	Madison	May 1, 2009	None
	Teresa Rutherford	Rice Lake	May 1, 2009	None
	Alan Stager	Greendale	May 1, 2009	None
	Debra McKinney	Allenton	May 1, 2010	None
	Elizabeth Tucker	Platteville	May 1, 2010	None
	Jeffrey Bartell	Middleton	May 1, 2011	None
	Jerry Curren	Madison	May 1, 2011	None
Higher Educational Aids Board, Exec. Secy. Sec. 39.29	Connie Hutchison	McFarland	Pleas. of Gov.	Group 3
Highway Safety, Council on Secs. 15.09 (1)(a), 15.467 (3)	Sherrick Anderson	Beloit	July 1, 2009	None
	Dave Collins	Madison	July 1, 2009	None
	John Corbin	Brookfield	July 1, 2009	None
	Kari K. Kinnard	Appleton	July 1, 2009	None
	Patrick Becker	Rice Lake	July 1, 2010	None
	Dennis Kocken	Green Bay	July 1, 2010	None
	LaVerne Hermann	Milwaukee	July 1, 2011	None
	Randall Thiel	Madison	July 1, 2011	None
	Roger Breske	Eland	Pleas. of Gov.	None
Historic Preservation Review Board Sec. 15.705 (2)	Shawn K. Graff	Slinger	July 1, 2009	None
	Carol McChesney Johnson	Black Earth	July 1, 2009	None
	William Laatsch	Sturgeon Bay	July 1, 2009	None
	David V. Mollenhoff	Madison	July 1, 2009	None
	Sissel Schroeder	Madison	July 1, 2009	None
	Anne Biebel	Cross Plains	July 1, 2009	None
	Bruce Block	Bayside	July 1, 2010	None
	Robert Gough	Eau Claire	July 1, 2010	None
	Kelly Jackson-Golly	Lac du Flambeau	July 1, 2010	None
	Kubet Luchterhand	Ellison Bay	July 1, 2010	None
	Carlen Hatala	Milwaukee	July 1, 2011	None
	Daniel Joyce	Kenosha	July 1, 2011	None
	Valentine Schute	La Crosse	July 1, 2011	None
	Daniel Stephans	Madison	July 1, 2011	None
	Donna Zimmerman	Amherst Junction	July 1, 2011	None
Historical Society Endowment Fund Council Secs. 15.09 (1)(a), 15.707 (3)	Inactive			
*Housing and Economic Development Authority, Wis. Sec. 234.02 (1)	Cheryll A. Olson-Collins	DeForest	Jan. 1, 2008	None
	Linda Stewart	Milwaukee	Jan. 1, 2008	None
	Perry Armstrong	Mount Horeb	Jan. 1, 2010	None
	Geoff Hurtado	Milwaukee	Jan. 1, 2010	None
	Daniel Lee	Waunakee	Jan. 1, 2011	None
	Paul Senty	Verona	Jan. 1, 2011	None
*Housing and Economic Development Authority, Wis., Executive Director Sec. 234.02 (3)	Antonio Riley	Milwaukee	Feb. 1, 2007	Group 6
Information Technology Management Board Sec. 15.215 (1)	Gina Frank	Madison	May 1, 2009	None
	Carla Cross	Milwaukee	May 1, 2011	None
	Sean Dilweg	Madison	Pleas. of Gov.	None
	Lorrie Heinemann	Madison	Pleas. of Gov.	None
*Insurance, Commissioner of Secs. 15.06 (1) (b), (3)(a) 1, 15.06 (3)(b), 15.73	Sean Dilweg	Madison	Pleas. of Gov.	Group 5

Officers[1]	Name	Home Address[2]	Term Expires[3]	Salary or Per Diem[4]
Invasive Species Council Sec. 15.347 (18)	Charles Henriksen	Baileys Harbor	July 1, 2007	None
	Gregory Long	New Berlin	July 1, 2007	None
	Peter T. Murray	Madison	July 1, 2007	None
	Rick Yedica	Luxemburg	July 1, 2008	None
	Patricia Morton	Whitewater	July 1, 2009	None
	James Reinartz	Saukville	July 1, 2010	None
	Paul Schumacher	Fredonia	July 1, 2012	None
	Kenneth F. Raffa	Madison	July 1, 2013	None
Investment and Local Impact Fund Board Sec. 15.435	Richard L. Gurnoe	Bayfield	May 1, 2001	None
	Sidney Bjorkman	Amery	May 1, 2003	None
	Erhard Huettl	Wabeno	May 1, 2003	None
	Daniel B. Merriam	Ladysmith	May 1, 2003	None
	Roger O. Day, Jr.	Rhinelander	May 1, 2004	None
	Elizabeth M. Sorensen	Bruce	May 1, 2004	None
	Michael S. Brandner	Medford	May 1, 2005	None
	Ronald E. Henkel	Laona	May 1, 2006	None
	vacancy			
*Investment Board, State of Wis. Secs. 15.07 (1)(a) 4, 15.07 (2)(a), 15.07 (5)(a), 15.76	David M. Geertsen	Racine	May 1, 2011	$50 per day
	David Kruger	Verona	May 1, 2011	$50 per day
	James Senty	La Crosse	May 1, 2011	$50 per day
	Thomas Boldt[5]	Appleton	May 1, 2015	$50 per day
	Bruce Colburn	Milwaukee	May 1, 2015	$50 per day
	William H. Levit, Jr.[5]	Milwaukee	May 1, 2015	$50 per day
*Judicial Commission Sec. 757.83	Bill Vander Loop	Kaukauna	Aug. 1, 2009	$25 per day
	Ginger Alden	Wausau	Aug. 1, 2011	$25 per day
	James M. Haney	Plover	Aug. 1, 2011	$25 per day
	Cynthia Herber	Glendale	Aug. 1, 2011	$25 per day
	Michael Miller	West Bend	Aug. 1, 2011	$25 per day
Judicial Council Secs. 15.09 (1)(a), 758.13 (1)	Michael Christopher	Madison	July 1, 2007	None
	Al Foeckler	Oak Creek	July 1, 2009	None
	Kathleen Pakes	Ladysmith	Pleas. of Gov.	None
Justice Assistance, Office of Exec. Staff Director Sec. 15.105 (19)	David Steingraber	Oregon	Pleas. of Gov.	Group 2
*Kickapoo Reserve Management Board Secs. 15.07 (1) (b) 20, 15.07 (5) (y), 15.445 (2)	Senn Brown	Madison	May 1, 2009	$25 per day
	Gail Frei	Viroqua	May 1, 2009	$25 per day
	Tamara Riddle	La Farge	May 1, 2009	$25 per day
	Richard Wallin	Viroqua	May 1, 2009	$25 per day
	Rebecca Zahm	La Farge	May 1, 2009	$25 per day
	Susan Cushing	La Farge	May 1, 2010	$25 per day
	Adlai Mann	Black River Falls	May 1, 2010	$25 per day
	Jack Robinson	Ontario	May 1, 2010	$25 per day
	Ronald Johnson	La Farge	May 1, 2011	$25 per day
	William Quackenbush	Black River Falls	May 1, 2011	$25 per day
	vacancy			
*Labor and Industry Review Commission Secs. 15.06 (2)(a), 15.225 (1)	Robert Glaser	Brown Deer	March 1, 2009	Group 5
	James Flynn	Madison	March 1, 2011	Group 5
	Ann Crump	Mukwonago	March 1, 2013	Group 5
Labor and Management Council Secs. 15.09 (1)(a), 15.227 (17)	Inactive			
Laboratory of Hygiene Bd. Sec. 15.915 (2)	Michael Russell	Arena	May 1, 2009	None
	David Taylor	Verona	May 1, 2009	None
	Darryll Farmer	Eau Claire	May 1, 2010	None
	Bernard Poeschel	Eleva	May 1, 2010	None
	Michael Ricker	De Pere	May 1, 2010	None
	John Stanley	DeForest	May 1, 2010	None
	vacancy			
Lake Michigan Commercial Fishing Board Sec. 15.345 (3)	Charles W. Henriksen	Baileys Harbor	Pleas. of Gov.	None
	Richard R. Johnson	Ellison Bay	Pleas. of Gov.	None
	Michael Le Clair	Two Rivers	Pleas. of Gov.	None
	Mark Maricque	Green Bay	Pleas. of Gov.	None
	Dan Pawlitzke	Two Rivers	Pleas. of Gov.	None
	Neil A. Schwarz	Sheboygan	Pleas. of Gov.	None
	Dean Swaer	Oconto	Pleas. of Gov.	None
Lake States Wood Utilization Consortium Sec. 26.37 (1)	Inactive			
Lake Superior Commercial Fishing Board Sec. 15.345 (2)	Jeff Bodin	Bayfield	Pleas. of Gov.	None
	Bill Damberg	Bayfield	Pleas. of Gov.	None
	Maurine Halvorson	Bayfield	Pleas. of Gov.	None
	Craig Hoopman	Bayfield	Pleas. of Gov.	None
	vacancy			
Land and Water Conservation Bd. Secs. 15.07 (1)(b) 10, 15.07 (1)(cm), 15.07 (5)(h), 15.135 (4)(am)	Robin Leary	Eau Claire	May 1, 2009	$25 per day
	Dennis Caneff	Madison	May 1, 2010	$25 per day
	Sandi Cihlar	Mosinee	May 1, 2011	$25 per day
	Marc Cupp	Blue River	May 1, 2012	$25 per day
	vacancy			

Officers[1]	Name	Home Address[2]	Term Expires[3]	Salary or Per Diem[4]
Law Enforcement Standards Board Sec. 15.255 (1)	Timothy Baxter	Wauzeka	May 1, 2009	None
	Scott Pedley	Darlington	May 1, 2009	None
	Teresa Smoczyk	Rhinelander	May 1, 2010	None
	Donnie Snow	Racine	May 1, 2010	None
	Dale Marsolek	Galesville	May 1, 2011	None
	Floyd Peters	Poplar	May 1, 2011	None
	Michael Serpe	Egg Harbor	May 1, 2011	None
	Timothy Goke	Waupaca	May 1, 2012	None
	Patricia Seger	Madison	May 1, 2012	None
	vacancy			
Library and Network Development, Council on Secs. 15.09 (1)(a), 15.377 (6)	Barbara Arnold	Madison	July 1, 2009	None
	Donald Bulley	South Milwaukee	July 1, 2009	None
	Catherine Hansen	Shorewood	July 1, 2009	None
	Lisa Jewell	Rice Lake	July 1, 2009	None
	Douglas Lay	Mosinee	July 1, 2009	None
	John Nichols	Oshkosh	July 1, 2009	None
	Cal Potter	Sheboygan Falls	July 1, 2009	None
	Michael Bahr	Germantown	July 1, 2010	None
	Bob Koechley	Madison	July 1, 2010	None
	Sandra Lockett	Milwaukee	July 1, 2010	None
	Kathy L. Pletcher	Denmark	July 1, 2010	None
	Annette Smith	Milton	July 1, 2010	None
	Kris Wendt	Rhinelander	July 1, 2010	None
	Kristi A. Williams	Cottage Grove	July 1, 2010	None
	Mary Bayorgeon	Appleton	July 1, 2011	None
	Francis Cherney	Milladore	July 1, 2011	None
	Miriam Erickson	Fish Creek	July 1, 2011	None
	Susan Reynolds	Hayward	July 1, 2011	None
	Lisa Sterrett	Viroqua	July 1, 2011	None
*Lower Fox River Remediation Authority Secs. 279.02	Tripp Ahern	Fond du Lac	June 30, 2009	None
	David Stegeman	Mequon	June 30, 2009	None
	James Wall	Green Bay	June 30, 2009	None
	Gregory B. Conway	De Pere	June 30, 2011	None
	Patrick Schillinger	De Pere	June 30, 2011	None
	Robert Cowles	Green Bay	June 30, 2013	None
	Dave Hansen	Green Bay	June 30, 2013	None
*Lower Wisconsin State Riverway Board Secs. 15.07 (1)(b) 15, 15.07 (5)(w), 15.445 (3)	Don Greenwood	Spring Green	May 1, 2008	$25 per day
	Ritchie Brown[5]	Black River Falls	May 1, 2009	$25 per day
	Melody Moore	Mazomanie	May 1, 2009	$25 per day
	L.B. Nice	Boscobel	May 1, 2009	$25 per day
	Gerald Dorscheid	Arena	May 1, 2010	$25 per day
	Greg Greenheck	Lone Rock	May 1, 2010	$25 per day
	Frederick Madison	Lodi	May 1, 2010	$25 per day
	Ronald Leys	Gays Mills	May 1, 2011	$25 per day
	William Lundberg	Wisconsin Rapids	May 1, 2011	$25 per day
Madison Cultural Arts District Board Secs. 71.05 (1) (c) 6, 229.842	Susan Cook	Madison	July 1, 2008	None
	Carol Toussaint	Madison	July 1, 2010	None
	Deirdre Wilson Garton	Madison	Pleas. of Gov.	None
	vacancy			
Main Street Programs, Council on Secs. 15.09 (1)(a), 15.157 (7)	Timothy L. Anderson	Madison	July 1, 2007	None
	Virginia Haske	Algoma	July 1, 2007	None
	Judith Wall	Prairie du Chien	July 1, 2007	None
	Darryl Johnson	Milwaukee	July 1, 2008	None
	Thomas Meiklejohn	Fond du Lac	July 1, 2008	None
	Gerald White	Beloit	July 1, 2008	None
	Dick Best	Menomonie	July 1, 2009	None
	John Gardner	Stevens Point	July 1, 2009	None
	Shawn Graff	Slinger	July 1, 2009	None
	Michael Iwinski	Green Bay	July 1, 2009	None
	Lisa Kuss	Clintonville	July 1, 2009	None
	Dawn Rog	Rhinelander	July 1, 2009	None
	Paul Knuth	Rhinelander	July 1, 2011	None
Managed Forest Land Board Sec. 15.345 (6)	Eugene Roark	Madison	May 1, 2009	None
	Neil Paulson	Drummond	May 1, 2010	None
	Kevin Koth	Tomahawk	May 1, 2011	None
	Elroy Zemke	Rothschild	May 1, 2011	None
*Marriage and Family Therapy, Professional Counseling, and Social Work, Examining Board of Secs. 15.08 (7), 15.405 (7c)	LaMarr J. Franklin	Glendale	July 1, 2007	$25 per day
	George Kamps	Green Bay	July 1, 2009	$25 per day
	Leslie Mirkin	Madison	July 1, 2009	$25 per day
	Abe Rabinowitz	Middleton	July 1, 2009	$25 per day
	Evelyn Pumphrey[5]	Milwaukee	July 1, 2010	$25 per day
	Ann Marie Starr[5]	Shorewood	July 1, 2010	$25 per day
	Bruce Kuehl	Menomonie	July 1, 2011	$25 per day
	Mary Jo Walsh	Mukwonago	July 1, 2011	$25 per day
	Arlie Albrecht	Green Bay	July 1, 2012	$25 per day
	Eric Alvin	Madison	July 1, 2012	$25 per day
	Charles Lindsey	Sun Prairie	July 1, 2012	$25 per day
	Darryl Wood	La Crosse	July 1, 2012	$25 per day
	vacancy			

Officers[1]	Name	Home Address[2]	Term Expires[3]	Salary or Per Diem[4]
Massage Therapy and Body Work Council Sec. 15.407 (7)	June Motzer	Hudson	July 1, 2009	None
	Lillian Pounds	Milwaukee	July 1, 2009	None
	Amy Remillard	Waukesha	July 1, 2010	None
	Carie Martin	Eau Claire	July 1, 2011	None
	Amy Connell	Madison	July 1, 2012	None
	Claude Gagnon	Milwaukee	July 1, 2012	None
	Xiping Zhou	Madison	July 1, 2012	None
*Medical College of Wis., Inc., Board of Trustees of the Sec. 39.15	Jeffrey E. Joerres	Milwaukee	May 1, 2008	None
	Timothy Flaherty	Neenah	May 1, 2009	None
	Natalie Black Kohler	Kohler	May 1, 2009	None
	Linda Mellowes	Milwaukee	May 1, 2009	None
	Curt S. Culver	Nashotah	May 1, 2010	None
	Sheldon Lubar	Milwaukee	May 1, 2011	None
	Chris Abele	Milwaukee	May 1, 2012	None
	Timothy Hoeksema[5]	Nashotah	May 1, 2013	None
	Cory Nettles	Milwaukee	May 1, 2013	None
	Edward Zore[5]	Milwaukee	May 1, 2014	None
Medical Education Review Committee Sec. 39.16	Inactive (7 members)			
*Medical Examining Board Secs. 15.08, 15.405 (7)	Carolyn Bronston	Wausau	July 1, 2008	$25 per day
	Bhupinder Saini	Cudahy	July 1, 2008	$25 per day
	Jack M. Lockhart	La Crosse	July 1, 2009	$25 per day
	Gene Musser	Middleton	July 1, 2009	$25 per day
	Sheldon Wasserman	Milwaukee	July 1, 2009	$25 per day
	Jude Genereaux	Sturgeon Bay	July 1, 2010	$25 per day
	Jerold Harter	Stevens Point	July 1, 2010	$25 per day
	Ramond Mager	Bayside	July 1, 2010	$25 per day
	Suresh Misra	Milwaukee	July 1, 2011	$25 per day
	Ian Munro	Green Bay	July 1, 2011	$25 per day
	Sujatha Kailas	Fond du Lac	July 1, 2012	$25 per day
	Sandra Osborn	Verona	July 1, 2012	$25 per day
	vacancy			
Mental Health, Council on Secs. 15.09 (1)(a), 15.197 (1)	Michael J. Bachhuber	Madison	July 1, 2009	None
	Martha Rasmus	Waterford	July 1, 2009	None
	Judy Wilcox	Madison	July 1, 2009	None
	Lynn Boreson	Madison	July 1, 2010	None
	Corrie Briggs	Hudson	July 1, 2010	None
	Amy Parker	Fort Atkinson	July 1, 2010	None
	John Quaal	Pewaukee	July 1, 2010	None
	Donna Wrenn	Madison	July 1, 2010	None
	John Easterday	Madison	July 1, 2011	None
	Donald Hands	Madison	July 1, 2001	None
	Mary Neubauer	Cudahy	July 1, 2011	None
	Joann Stephens	Westfield	July 1, 2011	None
	Katharine Swanson	Ashland	July 1, 2011	None
	Leslie Mirkin	Madison	July 1, 2012	None
	Ann Catherine Veierstahler	Milwaukee	July 1, 2013	None
	Benita Walker	Madison	July 1, 2013	None
	Jackie Baldwin	St. Germain	July 1, 2012	None
	Kathy Roetter	Nekoosa	July 1, 2012	None
*Merit Recruitment and Selection Administrator, Division of (OSER) Sec. 15.173 (1) (b)	John R. Lawton	Madison	March 26, 2014	Group 3
*Midwest Interstate Low-Level Radioactive Waste Comn., Wis. Commissioner Sec. 14.81 (1)	Stanley York	Middleton	Pleas. of Gov.	None
Midwest Interstate Passenger Rail Commission Sec. 14.86 (1)	Karl Ostby	Kenosha	Jan. 3, 2011	None
	Frank Busalacchi	Brookfield	Pleas. of Gov.	None
Midwestern Higher Educ. Comn. Sec. 14.90 (1)	Judith VanderMeulen Crain	Green Bay	July 1, 2010	None
	Rolf Wegenke	Sun Prairie	July 1, 2010	None
	John E. Kerrigan	Dubuque, IA	Pleas. of Gov.	None
Migrant Labor, Council on Secs. 15.09 (1)(a), 15.227 (8)	John F. Ebbott	Milwaukee	July 1, 2004	None
	Liliana Parodi	Clinton	July 1, 2007	None
	Rachel Rodriguez	Waunakee	July 1, 2007	None
	Steve Ziobro	Reeseville	July 1, 2007	None
	Enrique Figueroa	Milwaukee	July 1, 2009	None
	James Kern	Eau Claire	July 1, 2009	None
	Lupe Martinez	Milwaukee	July 1, 2009	None
	Richard Okray	Plover	July 1, 2009	None
	John Bauknect	Cross Plains	July 1, 2011	None
	Jennifer Cloute	Pardeeville	July 1, 2011	None
	2 vacancies			
Military and State Relations, Council on Sec. 14.017 (4)	Jamie Aulik	Manitowoc	Pleas. of Gov.	None
	Linda Fournier	Sparta	Pleas. of Gov.	None
	Larry Olson	Madison	Pleas. of Gov.	None

Officers[1]	Name	Home Address[2]	Term Expires[3]	Salary or Per Diem[4]
Milwaukee Child Welfare Partnership Council Secs. 15.09 (1)(a), 15.197 (24)	Peggy West.	Milwaukee	July 1, 2006	None
	Willie Johnson, Jr.	Milwaukee	July 1, 2007	None
	Elisa Castellon	Shorewood	July 1, 2008	None
	Toni Clark	Milwaukee	July 1, 2008	None
	Leonor Rosas	Milwaukee	July 1, 2008	None
	Bregetta Wilson	Milwaukee	July 1, 2008	None
	Linda Davis	Mequon	July 1, 2009	None
	David Hoffman	Milwaukee	July 1, 2009	None
	Earnestine Willis.	Milwaukee	July 1, 2009	None
	Julius Agara	Milwaukee	July 1, 2010	None
	Archie Ivy	Milwaukee	July 1, 2010	None
	Michael Skwierawski	Milwaukee	July 1, 2010	None
	Mary Triggiano	Milwaukee	July 1, 2010	None
	Deborah Blanks	Milwaukee	July 1, 2011	None
	vacancy			
Milwaukee River Revitalization Council Secs. 15.09 (1)(a), 15.347 (15)	Richard Flood	Cedarburg	July 1, 2008	None
	Jon Richards	Milwaukee	July 1, 2009	None
	Dan Small	Belgium	July 1, 2009	None
	Christopher Svoboda.	Milwaukee	July 1, 2009	None
	Cheryl Brickman.	Mequon	July 1, 2010	None
	Raymond Krueger	Milwaukee	July 1, 2010	None
	Christine Nuernberg	Mequon	July 1, 2010	None
	Nancy Frank	Elkhorn	July 1, 2011	None
	Ronald Stadler	Cedarburg	July 1, 2011	None
	Caroline Icks Torinus	West Bend	July 1, 2011	None
	vacancy			
Minority Business Development Board Sec. 15.155 (3)	Winnifred Thomas	Seymour	May 1, 2007	None
	John Cadotte	Hayward	May 1, 2009	None
	Willie Johnson	Milwaukee	May 1, 2009	None
	Steven Little	Middleton	May 1, 2009	None
	Katherine Marks	Kenosha	May 1, 2009	None
	Aaron Olver	Madison	May ,1 2009	None
	Charles V. Vang	Brookfield	May 1, 2009	None
Mississippi River Parkway Commission Sec. 14.85 (1)(a)	Barbara Gronemus	Whitehall	Feb. 1, 2008	None
	Sheila Harsdorf	River Falls	Feb. 1, 2008	None
	Pat Kreitlow	Chippewa Falls	Feb. 1, 2008	None
	Lee Nerison	Westby	Feb. 1, 2008	None
	Mark Clements.	Genoa	Feb. 1, 2012	None
	Dennis Donath	Prescott	Feb. 1, 2012	None
	Frank Fiorenza	Potosi	Feb. 1, 2012	None
	Jean Galasinski.	Trempealeau	Feb. 1, 2012	None
	Al Lorenz	La Crosse	Feb. 1, 2012	None
	Robert Miller.	Alma	Feb. 1, 2012	None
	Sherry Quamme	Ferryville	Feb. 1, 2012	None
	Bruce Quinton	Pepin	Feb. 1, 2012	None
Multifamily Dwelling Code Council Secs. 15.09 (1)(a), 15.157 (12)	Emory Budzinski	Mosinee	July 1, 2007	None
	Korinne Schneider	Milwaukee	July 1, 2007	None
	Keviin Wipperfurth	McFarland	July 1, 2007	None
	Edward Gray	Kenosha	July 1, 2008	None
	Greta Hansen.	Edgerton	July 1, 2008	None
	Michael Morey.	Madison	July 1, 2008	None
	Nicholas Rivecca	Hartland	July 1, 2008	None
	Jeffery Brohmer	La Crosse	July 1, 2009	None
	Beth Gonnering	Kenosha	July 1, 2009	None
	David Nitz	Berlin	July 1, 2009	None
	Mark Scott	Pewaukee	July 1, 2009	None
	James Klett.	Milwaukee	July 1, 2010	None
	Kraig Biefeld.	Ixonia	July 1, 2011	None
	Richard Paur	Milwaukee	July 1, 2011	None
National and Community Service Board Sec. 15.105 (24)	Larry Kleinsteiber	Madison	May 1, 2008	None
	Elizabeth Burmaster	Madison	May 1, 2009	None
	Kathleen Groat.	Appleton	May 1, 2009	None
	Bob Guenther	Brown Deer	May 1, 2009	None
	Joel Haubrich	Milwaukee	May 1, 2009	None
	Robert Hawley	Baileys Harbor	May 1, 2009	None
	Anthony Hallman	Three Lakes	May 1, 2010	None
	Sondra LeGrand	La Crosse	May 1, 2010	None
	Kyle O'Brien.	La Crosse	May 1, 2010	None
	Yia Thao	Green Bay	May 1, 2010	None
	Marguita Fox.	Middleton	May 1, 2011	None
	Mark Mueller	Sun Prairie	May 1, 2011	None
	Andrew Russell	Madison	May 1, 2011	None
	Marilynn Pelky.	Racine	May 1, 2011	None
	3 vacancies			
*Natural Resources, Dept. of, Secy. Sec. 15.05 (1)(c)	Matt Frank	Middleton	Pleas. of Gov.	Group 7
*Natural Resources Board Secs. 15.07 (1)(a), 15.34	Christine Thomas	Plover	May 1, 2009	None
	Jane Wiley	Wausau	May 1, 2009	None
	Jonathan Ela[5].	Madison	May 1, 2011	None
	Gary Rohde	River Falls	May 1, 2011	None
	John W. Welter	Eau Claire	May 1, 2011	None
	David Clausen	Amery	May 1, 2013	None
	Preston Cole	Milwaukee	May 1, 2013	None

Officers[1]	Name	Home Address[2]	Term Expires[3]	Salary or Per Diem[4]
*Nursing, Board of	June A. Bahr	Fond du Lac	July 1, 2006	$25 per day
Secs. 15.01 (6), 15.08,	Evelyn Merriett	Milwaukee	July 1, 2007	$25 per day
15.405 (7g)	Margaret Wood	La Crosse	July 1, 2007	$25 per day
	Margaret Heine	Janesville	July 1, 2009	$25 per day
	Gretchen Lowe	Madison	July 1, 2009	$25 per day
	Marilyn Kaufmann	Manitowoc	July 1, 2010	$25 per day
	Julia Nelson	Boscobel	July 1, 2010	$25 per day
	Kathleen Sullivan	Madison	July 1, 2011	$25 per day
	Lou Ann Weix	Green Bay	July 1, 2012	$25 per day
*Nursing Home Administrator	Loreli Dickinson	Oconto	July 1, 2007	$25 per day
Examining Board	David Egan	Kenosha	July 1, 2007	$25 per day
Secs. 15.08, 15.405 (7m)	Mary Ann Clark	Cumberland	July 1, 2009	$25 per day
	Susan Kinast-Porter	Monroe	July 1, 2009	$25 per day
	Kenneth Arneson	Oshkosh	July 1, 2010	$25 per day
	Heather Sheehan	Hayward	July 1, 2010	$25 per day
	Mary Lease	Oregon	July 1, 2011	$25 per day
	Mary Pike	Madison	July 1, 2011	$25 per day
	vacancy			
*Occupational Therapists	David Cooper	Slinger	July 1, 2007	$25 per day
Affiliated Credentialing	Brian Holmquist	Madison	July 1, 2009	$25 per day
Board	Corliss Rice	Milwaukee	July 1, 2009	$25 per day
Sec. 15.406 (5)	Mylinda Barisas-Matula	Sheboygan	July 1, 2010	$25 per day
	Deborah McKernan-Ace	Stoughton	July 1, 2010	$25 per day
	Dorothy Olson	Appleton	July 1, 2011	$25 per day
	Gail Slaughter	Two Rivers	July 1, 2011	$25 per day
	vacancy			
*Optometry Examining Bd.	Raymond Heiser	Wausau	July 1, 2008	$25 per day
Secs. 15.08, 15.405 (8)	Linda Foley	Lake Mills	July 1, 2009	$25 per day
	Gregory Foster	Neillsville	July 1, 2009	$25 per day
	Swaminat Balachandran	Verona	July 1, 2010	$25 per day
	Ann Meier Carli	Green Bay	July 1, 2010	$25 per day
	Richard Wright	Sun Prairie	July 1, 2011	$25 per day
	Kathi Leach	Junction City	July 1, 2012	$25 per day
*Parole Commission Chairperson	Alfonso Graham	Brookfield	March 1, 2009	Group 2
Sec. 15.145 (1)				
Perfusionists Examining Council	David Cobb	Madison	July 1, 2010	$25 per day
Sec. 15.407 (2m)				
*Pharmacy Examining Board	Jeanne Severson	Cottage Grove	July 1, 2009	$25 per day
Secs. 15.08, 15.405 (9)	Jason Walker-Crawford	Stoughton	July 1, 2009	$25 per day
	Pamela Phillips	Green Bay	July 1, 2010	$25 per day
	Gregory Weber	Brown Deer	July 1, 2010	$25 per day
	Amy Mattila	Washburn	July 1, 2011	$25 per day
	Tim Boehmer	Neenah	July 1, 2012	$25 per day
	Suzette Renwick	La Crosse	July 1, 2012	$25 per day
Physical Disabilities,	Jon Baltmanis	Waupaca	July 1, 2009	None
Council on	Marge Liberski-Aznoe	Green Bay	July 1, 2009	None
Secs. 15.09 (1)(a), 15.197 (4)	John Meissner	Little Chute	July 1, 2009	None
	Benjamin Barrett	Trego	July 1, 2010	None
	JorJan Borlin	Dodgeville	July 1, 2010	None
	Karen Secor	Montreal	July 1, 2010	None
	Sandra Stokes	Green Bay	July 1, 2010	None
	Lewis Tyler	Brookfield	July 1, 2010	None
	Charles Vandenplas	Clintonville	July 1, 2010	None
	Joanne Zimmerman	Bayside	July 1, 2010	None
	Claire Draeger	Madison	July 1, 2011	None
	Christine Duranceau	Rothschild	July 1, 2011	None
	Jeffrey Fox	Gordon	July 1, 2011	None
	Coral Butson	Madison	Pleas. of Gov.	None
*Physical Therapists	Otto Cordero	Sauk City	July 1, 2007	$25 per day
Affiliated Credentialing Bd.	Larry Nosse	Wauwatosa	July 1, 2009	$25 per day
Sec. 15.406 (1)	Enid Mistele	Sparta	July 1, 2010	$25 per day
	Mark Shropshire	Appleton	July 1, 2012	$25 per day
	Jane Stroede	Wisconsin Dells	July 1, 2013	$25 per day
Physician's Assistants,	Mary Pangman Schmitt[5]	Waterford	July 1, 2008	None
Council on				
Secs. 15.08, 15.407 (2)				
*Podiatrists Affiliated	Melanie Berg	Hudson	July 1, 2008	$25 per day
Credentialing Board	Ian Furness	Fond du Lac	July 1, 2009	$25 per day
Secs. 15.08, 15.406 (3)	Gary Brown	Kenosha	July 1, 2010	$25 per day
	Rene Settle-Robinson	Milwaukee	July 1, 2011	$25 per day
*Prison Industries Board	Lyle Balistreri	Wauwatosa	May 1, 2008	None
Secs. 15.07 (1)(b) 12,	Richard Raemisch	Waunakee	May 1, 2008	None
15.145 (2)	Jose Carrillo	Janesville	May 1, 2010	None
	Corey Odom	Milwaukee	May 1, 2010	None
	James Langdon	DeForest	May 1, 2011	None
	Debra Pickett	Darlington	May 1, 2011	None
	Bill G. Smith	Madison	May 1, 2011	None
	Bill Holley[5]	Middleton	May 1, 2012	None
	vacancy			

Officers[1]	Name	Home Address[2]	Term Expires[3]	Salary or Per Diem[4]
*Private Employer Health Care Coverage Board Sec. 15.165 (5)	Inactive			
*Psychology Examining Board Secs. 15.08, 15.405 (10m)	Don Crowder.	Lake Geneva	July 1, 2009	$25 per day
	Cynthia Bagley.	Clinton	July 1, 2010	$25 per day
	Bruce Erdmann	Madison	July 1, 2010	$25 per day
	Gerald Hollander.	Milwaukee	July 1, 2010	$25 per day
	Erica Serlin.	Madison	July 1, 2011	$25 per day
	Teresa Rose	Hazelhurst	July 1, 2012	$25 per day
*Public Defender Board Secs. 15.07 (1)(a), 15.78	William Drengler	Wausau	May 1, 2009	None
	Joe Morales	Racine	May 1, 2009	None
	Mai Neng Xiong	Wausau	May 1, 2009	None
	James Brennan	Milwaukee	May 1, 2010	None
	Regina Dunkin	Beloit	May 1, 2010	None
	Ellen Thorn	West Salem	May 1, 2010	None
	Daniel Berkos	Mauston	May 1, 2011	None
	John Hogan	Hazelhurst	May 1, 2011	None
	Nancy Wettersten	Madison	May 1, 2011	None
Public Health Council Sec. 15.197 (13)	Jeanan Yasiri	Madison	July 1, 2008	None
	Bevan Baker	Milwaukee	July 1, 2009	None
	John Bartkowski	Glendale	July 1, 2009	None
	Bridget Clementi.	Waukesha	July 1, 2009	None
	Terri Kramolis	Ashland	July 1, 2009	None
	Charles LaRoque.	Spooner	July 1, 2009	None
	Douglas Nelson	Milwaukee	July 1, 2009	None
	Thai Vue	Onalaska	July 1, 2009	None
	Amy Bremel	Fish Creek	July 1, 2010	None
	Susan Garcia Franz	Neenah	July 1, 2010	None
	Corazon Loteyro	Mercer	July 1, 2010	None
	John Meurer	Elm Grove	July 1, 2010	None
	James Sanders	Milwaukee	July 1, 2010	None
	Lynn Sheets	Sussex	July 1, 2010	None
	Mary Jo Baisch	Milwaukee	July 1, 2011	None
	Catherine Frey	Madison	July 1, 2011	None
	Gary Gilmore	La Crosse	July 1, 2011	None
	Deborah Miller.	Dorchester	July 1, 2011	None
	A. Charles Post.	Milwaukee	July 1, 2011	None
	Ayaz Samadani.	Beaver Dam	July 1, 2011	None
	Julie Willems Van Dijk	Wausau	July 1, 2011	None
	Mark Villalpando	Sturtevant	July 1, 2011	None
	vacancy			
Public Records Board Sec. 15.105 (4)	Carol Hemersbach	Greenwood	Pleas. of Gov.	None
	Melanie Swank.	Milwaukee	Pleas. of Gov.	None
	2 vacancies			
*Public Service Commission Secs. 15.06 (1), 15.79	Mark Meyer	La Crosse	March 1, 2011	Group 5
	Lauren Azar	Madison	March 1, 2013	Group 5
	Eric Callisto	Madison	March 1, 2015	Group 5
*Railroads, Commissioner of Secs. 15.06 (1)(ar), 15.795 (1)	Roger Breske.	Eland	March 1, 2011	Group 5
*Real Estate Appraisers Board Secs. 15.07 (1)(b) 17, 15.07 (1)(cm), 15.07 (5)(x), 15.405 (10r)	Mark P. Kowbel	Racine	May 1, 2004	$25 per day
	Sharon R. Fiedler	Neenah	May 1, 2006	$25 per day
	Henry F. Simon	Middleton	May 1, 2009	$25 per day
	Karen Scott[5]	Madison	May 1, 2010	$25 per day
	Nikhil Bagadia	Milwaukee	May 1, 2011	$25 per day
	Marla Britton.	Westby	May 1, 2011	$25 per day
	Micquel Hoffmann.	Hartford	May 1, 2012	$25 per day
*Real Estate Board Secs. 15.07 (1)(b) 8, 15.07 (1)(cm), 15.07 (5)(r), 15.405 (11)	Robert Dueholm	Luck	July 1, 2009	$25 per day
	Dennis Pierce	Kenosha	July 1, 2009	$25 per day
	Stephen Beers	Fontana	July 1, 2010	$25 per day
	Ryan Schroeder	Delavan	July 1, 2010	$25 per day
	Peter Sveum[5].	Stoughton	July 1, 2010	$25 per day
	J. Kenneth Lee	River Falls	July 1, 2011	$25 per day
	Lisabeth Weirich	Middleton	July 1, 2011	$25 per day
Real Estate Curriculum and Examinations, Council on Secs. 15.09 (1)(a), 15.407 (5)	Susan E. Hamer	Green Bay	July 1, 2004	None
	Lawrence Sager	Madison	July 1, 2004	None
	Paul G. Hoffman.	Waukesha	July 1, 2006	None
	Peter Sveum	Stoughton	July 1, 2006	None
	Richard Hinsman	Racine	July 1, 2007	None
	Peggy Lovejoy.	West Salem	July 1, 2007	None
	Barbara McGill	Waukesha	July 1, 2010	None
Recycling, Council on Secs. 15.09 (1)(b), 15.347 (17)	Greg David.	Watertown	Jan. 7, 2011	None
	Jeffrey Fielkow	Bayside	Jan. 7, 2011	None
	Rick Meyers	Milwaukee	Jan. 7, 2011	None
	Neil Peters-Michaud	Middleton	Jan. 7, 2011	None
	John Reindl	Madison	Jan. 7, 2011	None
	Charlotte R. Zieve	Elkhart Lake	Jan. 7, 2011	None
	vacancy			
Regional Transit Authority Sec. 59.58 (6)	Julia Taylor.	Milwaukee	Pleas. of Gov.	None
*Regulation and Licensing, Dept. of, Secy. Secs. 15.05 (1)(a), 15.40	Celia M. Jackson.	Madison	Pleas. of Gov.	Group 4

Officers[1]	Name	Home Address[2]	Term Expires[3]	Salary or Per Diem[4]
Respiratory Care Practitioners Examining Council Secs. 15.08, 15.407 (1m)	vacancy			
Retirement Board, Wis. Secs. 15.07 (1)(a), 15.165 (3)(b)	Marilyn J. Wigdahl	La Crosse	May 1, 1999	None
	John David	Watertown	May 1, 2008	$25 per day
	Wayne E. Koessl	Kenosha	May 1, 2009	$25 per day
	Michael Woodzicka	Hortonville	May 1, 2011	$25 per day
	Herbert Stinski	Milton	May 1, 2012	$25 per day
	Jamie Aulik	Manitowoc	May 1, 2013	$25 per day
	Mary Von Ruden	Sparta	May 1, 2013	$25 per day
	vacancy			
Retirement Systems, Jt. Survey Com. on Sec. 13.50 (1)(c)	Michael R. Luttig	Madison	July 1, 2003	None
*Revenue, Dept. of, Secy. Secs. 15.05 (1)(a), 15.43	Roger Ervin	Madison	Pleas. of Gov.	Group 7
Rural Economic Development Board Secs. 15.155 (4)(a) 5	Connie Seefeldt	Coleman	May 1, 2008	None
	Michael Krutza	Wausau	May 1, 2009	None
	Richard Martin	Fox Lake	May 1, 2010	None
*Rural Health Development Council Secs. 15.09 (1)(a), 15.157 (8)	Blane Christman	Ladysmith	July 1, 2007	None
	Byron J. Crouse	Fitchburg	July 1, 2007	None
	Tim K. Size	Sauk City	July 1, 2008	None
	BeckySue Wolf[5]	Abrams	July 1, 2008	None
	Erica Hoven	Westby	July 1, 2009	None
	Linda L. McFarlin	Friendship	July 1, 2009	None
	James O'Keefe	Mauston	July 1, 2011	None
	Leslie Patterson[5]	Greenfield	July 1, 2011	None
	4 vacancies			
*Savings Institutions Review Board Sec. 15.185 (3)	George E. Gary	Milwaukee	May 1, 2009	$10 per day
	Robert Holmes	Tomah	May 1, 2009	$10 per day
	James K. Olson	Appleton	May 1, 2009	$10 per day
	Paul Adamski	Stevens Point	May 1, 2012	$10 per day
	vacancy			
Small Business Environmental Council Secs. 15.09 (1)(a), 15.157 (10)	Michael Simpson	Milwaukee	July 1, 2009	None
	Jeanne Whitish	Cross Plains	July 1, 2010	None
	Gerald Jones	Kohler	July 1, 2011	None
Small Business Regulatory Review Board Sec. 15.155 (5)	Randy Meffert	Waunakee	May 1, 2008	None
	Minoo Seifoddini	Glendale	May 1, 2009	None
	Karen Vernal	Wauwatosa	May 1, 2009	None
	Guy Wood	New Auburn	May 1, 2009	None
	Rick Petershack	Madison	May 1, 2011	None
	Bonnie Schwid	Mequon	May 1, 2011	None
*Snowmobile Recreational Council Secs. 15.09 (1)(a), 15.347 (7)	Larry D. Erickson	Hurley	July 1, 2006	None
	Thomas Chwala	Lake Mills	July 1, 2009	None
	Richard Steimel	Dane	July 1, 2009	None
	Donna White	Cambria	July 1, 2009	None
	Karen Carlson	Frederic	July 1, 2010	None
	Mike J. Cerny	Sharon	July 1, 2010	None
	Beverly Dittmar	Eagle River	July 1, 2010	None
	John Schweitzer	Black River Falls	July 1, 2010	None
	Michael Willman	Merrill	July 1, 2010	None
	Jerry Green	Black River Falls	July 1, 2011	None
	Samuel Landes	Dane	July 1, 2011	None
	Robert Lang	Cable	July 1, 2011	None
	Andrew Malecki	Green Bay	July 1, 2011	None
	Thomas Thornton	Grand View	July 1, 2011	None
	vacancy			
*Southeast Wis. Professional Baseball Park Dist. Board Sec. 229.66 (2)	Robert Henzl	Racine	July 1, 2009	None
	Christine Nuernberg	Mequon	July 1, 2009	None
	Jay Williams	Hartland	July 1, 2009	None
	Martin Greenberg[5]	Milwaukee	July 1, 2011	None
	Michael Miller	West Bend	July 1, 2011	None
	Gregory M. Wesley	Milwaukee	July 1, 2011	None
Speech-Language Pathology and Audiology, Council on Secs. 15.08, 15.407 (4)	Debra McLauchlin	Milwaukee	July 1, 2006	None
	Shannon Theis	Monona	July 1, 2007	None
	John Knox	New Berlin	July 1, 2008	None
	Gregory Wiersema	Fond du Lac	July 1, 2008	None
	Michael Collins	Middleton	July 1, 2010	None
State Capitol and Executive Residence Board Sec. 15.105 (5)	Robert Lewcock	Oconomowoc	May 1, 2007	None
	Anthony A. Puttnam	Madison	May 1, 2007	None
	John J. Fernholz	Holmen	May 1, 2009	None
	Arlan K. Kay	Madison	May 1, 2009	None
	Sally Basting	Madison	May 1, 2011	None
	Eugene Potente, Jr.	Pleasant Prairie	May 1, 2011	None
	Debra Woodward	Middleton	May 1, 2013	None
State Employees Suggestion Board Sec. 15.105 (29)(c) 1.	Gene Dalhoff	Baraboo	May 1, 2009	None
	Sandy Drew	Madison	May 1, 2009	None
	David M. Vriezen	Waterloo	May 1, 2011	None

Officers[1]	Name	Home Address[2]	Term Expires[3]	Salary or Per Diem[4]
*State Fair Park Board Secs. 15.07 (1)(b), 15 15.07 (5)(j), 15.445 (4)	Dan Devine	Milwaukee	May 1, 2009	$10 per day, not exc. $600 per year
	Bennie Joyner	Milwaukee	May 1, 2009	$10 per day, not exc. $600 per year
	Michelle Nettles	Shorewood	May 1, 2010	$10 per day, not exc. $600 per year
	Rebecca Wickhem-House	Milwaukee	May 1, 2011	$10 per day, not exc. $600 per year
	Sue Rupnow	Wausau	May 1, 2012	$10 per day, not exc. $600 per year
	Scott Gunderson	Waterford	Jan. 1, 2012	None
	Ted Kanavas	Brookfield	Jan. 1, 2012	None
	Anthony Staskunas	West Allis	Jan. 1, 2012	None
	Jim Sullivan	Wauwatosa	Jan. 1, 2012	None
	Sue Crane	Burlington	May 1, 2013	$10 per day, not exc. $600 per year
	vacancy			
*State Historical Society of Wisconsin Board of Curators Sec. 15.70	Elizabeth Adelman	Mukwonago	July 1, 2007	None
	Victor Ferrall	Orfordville	July 1, 2008	None
	Linda Clifford	Madison	July 1, 2009	None
	Helen Laird	Marshfield	Pleas. of Gov.	None
State Interoperability Council Sec. 15.107 (18)	Melinda Allen	Juda	May 1, 2009	None
	Neil Cameron	Appleton	May 1, 2009	None
	Thomas Czaja	Mequon	May 1, 2009	None
	David Mahoney	Madison	May 1, 2011	None
	Larry Nelson	Waukesha	May 1, 2011	None
	Sue Riseling	Stoughton	May 1, 2011	None
	Ben Schliesman	Kenosha	May 1, 2011	None
	Frank Taylor	Milltown	May 1, 2012	None
	Martin Antone	Green Bay	Pleas. of Gov.	None
	Thomas Richie	Rice lake	Pleas. of Gov.	None
State Trails Council Secs. 15.09 (1)(a), 15.347 (16)	Thomas Huber	Madison	July 1, 2007	None
	Michael P. McFadzen	Plymouth	July 1, 2009	None
	David Phillips	Madison	July 1, 2009	None
	Robbie Webber	Madison	July 1, 2009	None
	Ken Carpenter	Fort Atkinson	July 1, 2011	None
	Randy Harden	Sheboygan	July 1, 2011	None
	Jim Joque	Mosinee	July 1, 2011	None
	Thomas Thornton	Grand View	July 1, 2011	None
	vacancy			
State Use Board Secs. 15.07 (1)(b), 15.105 (22)	Nickolas C. George, Jr.	Madison	May 1, 2003	None
	Bill G. Smith	Middleton	May 1, 2003	None
	Marie Danforth	Madison	May 1, 2009	None
	Joseph D'Costa	Madison	May 1, 2009	None
	David Dumke	Brule	May 1, 2009	None
	Andrew Moyer	Madison	May 1, 2009	None
	Michael Casey	Bloomington	May 1, 2011	None
	Jean Zweifel	Albany	May 1, 2011	None
*Tax Appeals Commission Secs. 15.01 (2), 15.06 (1)(a), 15.06 (3)(a) 2, 15.105 (1)	David Swanson	Milwaukee	March 1, 2011	Group 4
	Thomas McAdams	Greendale	March 1, 2013	Group 4
	Roger LeGrand	La Crosse	March 1, 2015	Group 4
Tax Exemptions, Jt. Survey Com. on Sec. 13.52 (1) (d)	Kathryn Dunn	Greendale	Jan. 15, 2007	None
Teachers Retirement Board Secs. 15.07 (5)(f), 15.165 (3)(a)	Sandra Claflin-Chalton	Menomonie	May 1, 2012	$25 per day
	Daniel Nerad	Madison	May 1, 2013	$25 per day
	Roberta Rasmus	Chippewa Falls	May 1, 2013	None
	Susan Harrison	Menomonie	May 1, 2014	$25 per day
*Technical College System Board Secs. 15.07 (1)(a), 15.07 (5)(e), 15.94	Ann Greenheck	Lone Rock	May 1, 2009	$100 per year
	Vanessa Pickar	West Salem	May 1, 2009	$100 per year
	Terrance Erickson	La Crosse	May 1, 2011	$100 per year
	Michael Rosen	Milwaukee	May 1, 2011	$100 per year
	Brent Smith	La Crosse	May 1, 2011	$100 per year
	Mary Cuene	Green Bay	May 1, 2013	$100 per year
	Phillip Neuenfeldt	Milwaukee	May 1, 2013	$100 per year
	S. Mark Tyler	Woodville	May 1, 2013	$100 per year
	Stan Davis	Sun Prairie	May 1, 2015	$100 per year
	vacancy			
Tourism, Council on Secs. 15.09 (1)(a), 15.447 (1)	David Holtze	La Crosse	July 1, 2009	None
	Doug Neilson	Whitefish Bay	July 1, 2009	None
	Linda Adler	Eau Claire	July 1, 2010	None
	Brian Kelsey	Fish Creek	July 1, 2010	None
	David Olsen	Jefferson	July 1, 2010	None
	Lola Roeh	Elkhart	July 1, 2010	None
	Omar Shaikh	Brookfield	July 1, 2010	None
	Gerald Danforth	Oneida	July 1, 2011	None
	Joe Klimczak	Blue Mounds	July 1, 2011	None
	Romy Snyder	Sun Prairie	July 1, 2011	None
	Kari Johnson Zambon	Rhinelander	July 1, 2011	None
	Deborah Archer	Madison	July 1, 2012	None
	Ruth Goetz	Ashland	July 1, 2012	None
	vacancy			
*Tourism, Dept. of, Secy. Secs. 15.05 (1)(a), 15.44	Kelli Trumble	Wisconsin Dells	Pleas. of Gov.	Group 6

Officers[1]	Name	Home Address[2]	Term Expires[3]	Salary or Per Diem[4]
*Transportation, Dept. of, Secy. Secs. 15.05 (1)(a), 15.46	Frank Busalacchi.	Brookfield	Pleas. of Gov.	Group 7
Transportation Projects Commission Sec. 13.489 (1)	Lee Meyerhofer . . . . Michael R. Ryan . . . . Leonard Sobczak.	Kaukauna Waunakee Racine	Pleas. of Gov. Pleas. of Gov. Pleas. of Gov.	None None None
Uniform State Laws, Commission on Sec. 13.55 (1)	Mike Weiden. . . . . Ann Walsh Bradley	Madison Wausau	May 1, 2009 May 1, 2011	None None
*Univ. of Wis. Hospitals and Clinics Authority Sec. 15.96, 233.02	Carol L. Booth . . . . Richard W. Choudoir . . . . . . Patrick Boyle. . . . . Dian Palmer . . . . Roger Axtell . . . . Humberto Vidaillet. . . . . . . Mike Weiden. . . . . Pablo Sanchez	Madison Columbus Madison Brookfield Janesville Marshfield Madison Madison	Pleas. of Gov. Pleas. of Gov. July 1, 2008 July 1, 2009 July 1, 2010 July 1, 2010 July 1, 2011 July 1, 2012	None None None None None None None None
*Univ. of Wis. System, Bd. of Regents of the Secs. 15.07 (1)(a), 15.91	Mark Bradley . . . . Jose Vasquez . . . . Eileen Connolly-Keesler. . . . . Kevin Opgenorth[5] . . . . Danae Davis[5]. . . . . Thomas Loftus . . . . Aaron Wingad . . . . Judith VanderMeulen Crain . . . Michael Spector . . . . Jeffrey Bartell . . . . Brent Smith . . . . John Drew[5]. . . . . Betty Womack[5]. . . . . Michael Falbo[5]. . . . . David Walsh[5]. . . . . Chuck Pruitt[5].	Wausau Milwaukee Neenah Platteville Milwaukee Sun Prairie Eau Claire Green Bay Shorewood Middleton La Crosse Milwaukee Milwaukee Franklin Madison Milwaukee	May 1, 2007 May 1, 2009 May 1, 2010 May 1, 2010 May 1, 2011 May 1, 2011 May 1, 2011 May 1, 2012 May 1, 2012 May 1, 2013 May 1, 2013 May 1, 2014 May 1, 2014 May 1, 2015 May 1, 2015 May 1, 2016	None None None None None None None None None None None None None None None None
Utility Public Benefits Council on Sec. 15.107 (17)	Janis Ringhand. . . . . James Boullion.	Evansville Madison	July 1, 2007 July 1, 2008	None None
*Veterans Affairs, Board of Secs. 15.07 (1)(a), 15.49	Marvin J. Freedman . . . . Peter J. Moran . . . . Rodney Moen . . . . Marcia Anderson. . . . . Jackie Guthrie . . . . Daniel Naylor . . . . vacancy	Middleton Superior Whitehall Verona Sun Prairie Waupaca	May 1, 2009 May 1, 2009 May 1, 2011 May 1, 2013 May 1, 2013 May 1, 2013	None None None None None None
Veterinary Diagnostic Laboratory Board Sec. 15.915 (1)	Tod Fleming . . . . Brian McCulloh . . . . Jay Bailey . . . . Robert Weigle . . . . Linda Hodorff	Baraboo Viroqua Kiel Shawano Eden	May 1, 2009 May 1, 2009 May 1, 2010 May 1, 2010 May 1, 2011	None None None None None
*Veterinary Examining Bd. Secs. 15.08, 15.405 (12)	Donald J. Peterson . . . . William Rice . . . . Robert R. Spencer[5]. . . . . . . Wesley Elford . . . . JoAnn Kleman[5] . . . . Joan Wywialowski . . . . Marthina Greer. . . . . Theresa Waage[5]	Barron Whitefish Bay La Crosse Mayville Mosinee Phillips Lomira Argyle	July 1, 2008 July 1, 2009 July 1, 2009 July 1, 2010 July 1, 2010 July 1, 2010 July 1, 2011 July 1, 2012	$25 per day $25 per day $25 per day $25 per day $25 per day $25 per day $25 per day $25 per day
Volunteer Fire Fighter and Emergency Medical Technician Service Award Board Sec.15.105 (26)	Robert H. Seitz. . . . . Carl Stolte . . . . Kenneth Bartz . . . . Kristen Halverson . . . . Allen Schraeder . . . . Melinda Allen . . . . John Scherer	Monticello Reedsburg Mount Horeb Monona Ripon Madison Middleton	May 1, 2005 May 1, 2007 May 1, 2009 May 1, 2009 May 1, 2009 May 1, 2010 May 1, 2010	None None None None None None None
*Waste Facility Siting Board Secs. 15.07 (1)(b) 11, 15.07 (5)(t), 15.105 (12)	Allan Jansen . . . . James Schuerman . . . . Dale Shaver	Hazel Green Wisconsin Rapids Waukesha	May 1, 2009 May 1, 2010 May 1, 2011	$35 per day $35 per day $35 per day
*Waterways Commission, Wis. Secs. 15.01 (2), 15.06 (1)(ag), 15.06 (3)(a) 3, 15.345 (1)	Maureer Kinney . . . . James F. Rooney . . . . Kurt Koeppler . . . . David Kedrowski . . . . Roger Walsh	La Crosse Racine Oshkosh Washburn Wauwatosa	March 1, 2009 March 1, 2009 March 1, 2010 March 1, 2011 March 1, 2013	None None None None None
Wisconsin Center District Board of Directors Sec. 229.42 (4)(e)	Franklyn Gimbel. . . . . Michael Morgan . . . . Stephen Marcus . . . . Jacob Weissberger	Milwaukee Madison River Falls Hartland	May 1, 2009 May 1, 2009 May 1, 2010 May 1, 2010	None None None None
Women's Council Secs. 15.09 (1)(a), 15.107 (11)	Kris Martinsek . . . . Ann Peggs . . . . Renee Boldt . . . . Nicole Bowman-Farrell . . . . . Jane Clark . . . . Arlene Siss . . . . Joan Prince.	Milwaukee Oconto Appleton Shawano Madison Platteville Milwaukee	July 1, 2008 July 1, 2008 July 1, 2009 July 1, 2009 July 1, 2009 July 1, 2009 July 1, 2011	None None None None None None None
Worker's Compensation Rating Committee Sec. 626.31 (1)(b)	Daniel Burazin. . . . . John C Metcalf.	Waterford Madison	Pleas. of Gov. Pleas. of Gov.	None None

Officers[1]	Name	Home Address[2]	Term Expires[3]	Salary or Per Diem[4]
*Workforce Development, Dept. of, Secy. Secs. 15.05 (1)(a), 15.22	Roberta Gassman	Madison	Pleas. of Gov.	Group 6
World Dairy Center Authority Sec. 235.02	Inactive			

*Nominated by the governor and appointed with the advice and consent of the senate. Senate confirmation is required for secretaries of departments, members of commissions and commissioners, governing boards, examining boards, and other boards as designated by statute.

[1]List includes *only* appointments made by the governor. Additional members frequently serve *ex officio* or are appointed by other means. The governor also appoints members of intrastate regional agencies and nonstatutory committees and makes temporary appointments under statute Chapter 17 to elected state and county offices when vacancies occur. For complete membership list of unit, including officers, see full description elsewhere in the *Blue Book*. Section numbers under each entry refer to statute sections authorizing appointment by the governor. Statute Section 21.18 provides for the governor's military staff.

[2]Home address is the municipality from which the officer was appointed to a full-time office or the current address of part-time officials.

[3]Terms are specified by the following statute sections or as otherwise provided by law: Sec. 15.05 (1) - secretaries; Sec. 15.06 (1) - commissioners; Sec. 15.07 (1) - governing boards and attached boards; Sec. 15.08 (1) - examining boards and councils; Sec. 15.09 (1) - councils.

[4]Members of boards and councils are reimbursed for actual and necessary expenses incurred in performing their duties. In addition, examining board members receive $25 per day for days worked, and members of certain other boards under statute Section 15.07 (5) receive a per diem as noted in the table. Statute Section 20.923 places state officials in one of 10 executive salary groups (ESG) for which salary ranges have been established. Group salary ranges for the period July 6, 2008 through July 4, 2009, are: Group 1: $59,406-$92,081; Group 2: $64,160-$99,449; Group 3: $69,294-$107,407; Group 4: $74,838-$116,001; Group 5: $80,826-$125,282; Group 6: $87,293-$135,304; Group 7: $94,277-$146,131; Group 8: $101,821-$157,824; Group 9: $109,969-$170,452; Group 10: $118,768-$184,091.

[5]Nominated by governor but not yet confirmed by senate.

Source: Appointment lists maintained by governor's office and received by the Legislative Reference Bureau on or before June 30, 2009.

Lieutenant Governor Barbara Lawton announces her new Guide for Penny Pinchers Web site at a service station in Onalaska in September 2008. The Web site is a comprehensive resource to help Wisconsin consumers save money on gasoline, prescription drugs, home energy, health care, and other family expenses. (Office of the Lieutenant Governor)

OFFICE OF THE LIEUTENANT GOVERNOR

Lieutenant Governor: BARBARA LAWTON.

Chief of Staff: BENJAMIN NUCKELS.

Policy and Community Relations Director: MATTHEW DULAK.

Operations Manager: SHANNON DONNICK.

Mailing Address: P.O. Box 2043, Madison 53702-2043.

Location: Room 19 East, State Capitol, Madison.

Telephone: 266-3516.

Fax: 267-3571.

Agency E-mail Address: ltgov@wisconsin.gov

Internet Address: www.ltgov.wisconsin.gov

Number of Employees: 4.00.

Total Budget 2007-09: $816,400.

Constitutional References: Article V, Sections 1, 2, 3, 7, and 8; Article XIII, Section 10.

Statutory Reference: Chapter 14, Subchapter II.

Agency Responsibility: The lieutenant governor is the state's second-ranking executive officer, a position comparable to that of the Vice President of the United States. If the incumbent governor dies, resigns, or is removed from office, the lieutenant governor becomes governor for the balance of the unexpired term. (Prior to a constitutional amendment in April 1979, the lieutenant governor was considered only "acting governor" in those circumstances.) The lieutenant governor serves as acting governor when the governor is temporarily unable to perform the duties of the office due to impeachment, incapacitation, or absence from the state. If the lieutenant governor becomes governor, he or she must nominate a new lieutenant governor and the successor must be confirmed by the senate and the assembly.

The governor may designate the lieutenant governor to represent the governor's office on any statutory board, commission, or committee on which the governor is entitled to membership. Under such designation, the lieutenant governor has all the authority and responsibility granted by law to the governor. The governor may also designate the lieutenant governor to represent the chief executive's office on any nonstatutory committee or intergovernmental body created to maintain relationships with federal, state, and local governments or regional agencies. The lieutenant governor participates in national organizations of lieutenant governors and may be asked by the governor to coordinate specific state services and programs.

Organization: From 1848 until 1970, the lieutenant governor was elected for a 2-year term on a separate ballot in the November general election of even-numbered years. Since 1970, following amendment of the Wisconsin Constitution, voters have elected the governor and lieutenant governor on a joint ballot to a 4-year term. Candidates are nominated independently in the September primary, but voters cast a combined ballot for the two offices in the November election.

History: The Territory of Wisconsin had no lieutenant governor, but the secretary of the territory was authorized to act as governor in the event of the governor's death or absence. The Wisconsin Constitution of 1848 provided for the post of lieutenant governor after considerable debate. Some delegates to the convention argued that the president of the senate, chosen from the membership of that body, should succeed the governor, with the secretary of state second in line of succession. The convention delegates who objected to a person's becoming governor without being elected on a statewide basis prevailed, however, and the post of lieutenant governor was included in the constitution.

Originally, the lieutenant governor was also the president of the senate and could cast a deciding vote in case of a tie. In 1979, the voters ratified a constitutional amendment enabling the senate to choose its own presiding officer from among its members, beginning in 1981.

Department of
ADMINISTRATION

Secretary of Administration: MICHAEL L. MORGAN, 266-1741, michael.morgan@

Deputy Secretary: DAN SCHOOFF, 266-1741, dan.schooff@

Executive Assistant: ANDREW MOYER, 266-1741, andrew.moyer@

Legal Counsel: CARI ANNE RENLUND, 267-0202, carianne.renlund@

Mailing Address: P.O. Box 7864, Madison 53707-7864.

Location: State Administration Building, 101 East Wilson Street, Madison.

Telephone: (608) 266-1741.

Fax: (608) 267-3842.

Internet Address: www.doa.state.wi.us

Number of Employees: 935.68.

Total Budget 2007-09: $1,567,351,300.

Statutory References: Sections 15.10 and 15.103; Chapter 16.

Address e-mail by combining the user ID and the state extender: userid@**wisconsin.gov**

Administrative Services, Division of: THOMAS HERMAN, *acting administrator,* 266-0239, tom.herman@; THOMAS HERMAN, *deputy administrator,* 266-0239, tom.herman@; Fax: 264-9500; P.O. Box 7869, Madison 53707-7869.

 Financial Management, Bureau of: MARTHA KERNER, *director,* 266-1359, martha.kerner@

 Personnel, Bureau of: PETER OLSON, *director,* 266-2308, peter.olson@

 State Prosecutors Office: PHILIP WERNER, *director,* 267-2700, phil.werner@

Capitol Police, Division of: CHARLES TUBBS, *police chief and administrator,* 266-7546, charles.tubbs@; Fax: 267-9343; B2N State Capitol, Madison 53702.

Energy Services, Division of: SHEREE DALLAS BRANCH, *administrator,* 261-6357, sheree.dallas@; SUSAN S. BROWN, *deputy administrator,* 266-2035, susan.brown@; Fax: 267-6931; P.O. Box 7868, Madison 53707-7868.

 Planning and Development, Bureau of: vacancy, *director,* 261-6609.

 Quality Assurance, Bureau of: GARY GORLEN, *director,* 266-8870, gary.gorlen@

Enterprise Operations, Division of: RON HERMES, *administrator,* 266-0779, ron.hermes@; JAMES M. LANGDON, *deputy administrator,* 267-2715, james.langdon@; Fax: 267-0600; P.O. Box 7867, Madison 53707-7867.

 Enterprise Fleet, Bureau of: JOHN MARX, *director,* 267-7693, john.marx@

 Procurement, Bureau of: HELEN MCCAIN, *director,* 267-9634, helen.mccain@

 State Risk Management, Bureau of: ROLLIE BOEDING, *director,* 266-1866, rollie.boeding@; Fax: 264-8250.

 State Minority Business Program: vacancy, *director,* 261-2436.

Enterprise Technology, Division of: OSKAR ANDERSON, *administrator and state chief information officer,* 264-9502, oskar.anderson@; DIANE KOHN, *deputy administrator,* 267-0614, diane.kohn@; Fax: 267-0626; P.O. Box 7844, Madison 53707-7844.

 Business Application Services, Bureau of: HERB THOMPSON, *director,* 261-9570, herb.thompson@

 Business Services, Bureau of: ROBERT STUESSY, *director,* 264-6186, robert.stuessy@

 Business Planning, Bureau of: PATRICIA CARLSON, *director,* 261-7750, patricia.carlson@

 District Attorneys Information Technology, Bureau of: LAURA RADKE, *director,* 261-6614, laura.radke@

 Infrastructure Support, Bureau of: JIM SCHMOLESKY, *director,* 266-1952, jim.schmolesky@

DEPARTMENT OF ADMINISTRATION

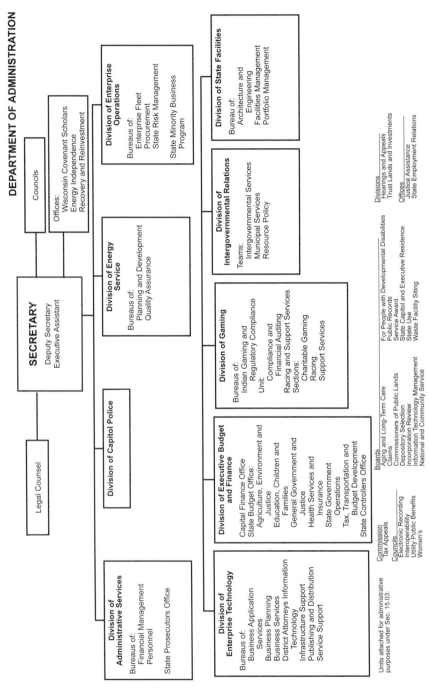

Legal Counsel

SECRETARY
Deputy Secretary
Executive Assistant

Councils

Offices:
Wisconsin Covenant Scholars
Energy Independence
Recovery and Reinvestment

Division of Administrative Services
Bureaus of:
Financial Management
Personnel

State Prosecutors Office

Division of Capitol Police

Division of Energy Service
Bureaus of:
Planning and Development
Quality Assurance

Division of Enterprise Operations
Bureaus of:
Enterprise Fleet
Procurement
State Risk Management

State Minority Business Program

Division of State Facilities
Bureau of:
Architecture and Engineering
Facilities Management
Portfolio Management

Division of Enterprise Technology
Bureaus of:
Business Application Services
Business Planning
Business Services
District Attorneys Information Technology
Infrastructure Support
Publishing and Distribution
Service Support

Division of Executive Budget and Finance
Capital Finance Office
State Budget Office:
Agriculture, Environment and Justice
Education, Children and Families
General Government and Justice
Health Services and Insurance
State Government Operations
Tax, Transportation and Budget Development
State Controllers Office

Division of Gaming
Bureaus of:
Indian Gaming and Regulatory Compliance
Unit:
Compliance and Financial Auditing
Racing and Support Services
Sections:
Charitable Gaming
Racing
Support Services

Division of Intergovernmental Relations
Teams:
Intergovernmental Services
Municipal Services
Resource Policy

Units attached for administrative purposes under Sec. 15.03:

Commission
Tax Appeals
Councils
Electronic Recording
Interoperability
Utility Public Benefits
Women's

Boards
Aging and Long-Term Care
Claims
Commissioners of Public Lands
Depository Selection
Incorporation Review
Information Technology Management
National and Community Service

For People with Developmental Disabilities
Public Records
Service Award
State Capitol and Executive Residence
State Use
Waste Facility Siting

Divisions
Hearings and Appeals
Trust Lands and Investments
Offices
Justice Assistance
State Employment Relations

ADMINISTRATION

Publishing and Distribution, Bureau of: TIMOTHY SMITH, *director,* 266-5800, timothy.smith@

Service Support, Bureau of: JUDITH HEIL, *director,* 261-8402, judith.heil@

Executive Budget and Finance, Division of: DAVID SCHMIEDICKE, *administrator,* 266-1035, david.schmiedicke@; JENNIFER KRAUS, *deputy administrator,* 266-1353, jennifer.kraus@; Fax: 267-0372; P.O. Box 7864, Madison 53707-7864.

   Capital Finance Office: FRANK HOADLEY, *director,* 266-2305, frank.hoadley@

   State Budget Office:

      Agriculture, Environment and Justice: JANA STEINMETZ, *team leader,* 266-2081, jana.steinmetz@

      Education, Children and Families: ROBERT HANLE, *team leader,* 266-1037, bob.hanle@

      General Government and Justice: JANE PAWASARAT, *team leader,* 267-6921, jane.pawasarat@

      Health Services and Insurance: MICHELLE GAUGER, *team leader,* 266-3420, michelle.gauger@

      State Government Operations: SCOTT THORNTON, *team leader,* 266-5051, scott.thornton@

      Tax, Transportation and Budget Development: KIRSTEN GRINDE, *team leader,* 266-1040, kirsten.grinde@

   State Controller's Office: STEPHEN J. CENSKY, *state controller,* 266-1694, steve.censky@; P.O. Box 7932, Madison 53707-7932.

Gaming, Division of: BOB SLOEY, *administrator,* 270-2555, robert.sloey@; Fax: 270-2564; 3319 West Beltline Highway, First Floor, P.O. Box 8979, Madison 53708-8979; Internet Address: www.doa.state.wi.us/gaming

   Indian Gaming and Regulatory Compliance, Bureau of: JOHN DILLETT, *director,* 270-2533, john.dillett@.

      Compliance and Financial Auditing Unit: JESSICA DUSHEK, *supervisor,* 270-2547, jessica.dushek@

   Racing and Support Services, Bureau of: vacancy, *director,* 270-2546.

      Charitable Gaming Section: BRIAN WHITTOW, *supervisor,* 270-2545, brian.whittow@

      Racing Section: DAN SUBACH, *supervisor,* 270-2539, dan.subach@

      Support Services Section: RACHEL MEEK, *supervisor,* 270-2535, rachel.meek@

Intergovernmental Relations, Division of: BRIAN VIGUE, *administrator,* 267-1824, brian.vigue@; HARALD JORDAHL, *deputy administrator,* 261-7520, harald.jordahl@; Fax: 267-6917; P.O. Box 8944, Madison 53707-8944; Internet Address: www.doa.state.wi.us/dhir

   Intergovernmental Services Team: DAWN VICK, *team leader,* 266-7043, dawn.vick@

   Municipal Services Team: DONALD R. HARRIER, JR., *team leader,* 267-2705, don.harrier@

   Resource Policy Team: MIKE FRIIS, *team leader,* 267-7982, mike.friis@

State Facilities, Division of: DAVID HELBACH, *administrator,* 266-1031, david.helbach@; GIL FUNK, *deputy administrator,* 266-7066, gil.funk@; Fax: 267-2710; P.O. Box 7866, Madison 53707-7866; Internet Address: www.doa.state.wi.us/index.asp?locid=4

   Architecture and Engineering, Bureau of: ADEL TABRIZI, *director and state chief engineer,* 266-3850, adel.tabrizi@

   Facilities Management, Bureau of: KEITH BECK, *director,* 266-3783, keith.beck@

   Portfolio Management, Bureau of: PETER MATERNOWSKI, *director,* 266-5565, peter.maternowski@

Wisconsin Covenant, Office of the: AMY S. BECHTUM, *director,* 267-9389, amy.bechtum@; Office toll-free: (866) 967-9389; Fax: 264-9500; P.O. Box 7869, Madison 53707-7869; Office e-mail: wisconsincovenant@; Office Web site: www.wisconsincovenant.wi.gov

Energy Independence, Office of: JUDY K. ZIEWACZ, *executive director,* judy.ziewacz@; Office: 261-6609; Fax: 261-8427; 17 West Main Street, Suite 429, Madison 53703; Office E-mail: oei@wisconsin.gov; Office Internet Address: www.energyindependence.wi.gov

Recovery and Reinvestment, Office of: CHRISTOPHER PATTON, *director;* Office 266-7871; Fax: 261-6804; P.O. Box 7863, Madison 53707; Office E-mail: govrecovery@wisconsin.gov; Office Internet Address: www.recovery.wisconsin.gov

Publications: Agency Budget Requests and Revenue Estimates; Annual Fiscal Report; Biennial Report; Budget in Brief; Budget Message; Capital Budget Recommendations; Comprehensive Annual Financial Report; Continuing Disclosure Annual Report; Decisions of Tax Appeals Commission; Executive Budget; Summary of Tax Exemption Devices; Wisconsin Energy Statistics; Wisconsin Population Estimates.

Agency Responsibility: One of the chief duties of the Department of Administration (DOA) is to provide the governor with fiscal management information and the policy alternatives required for preparation of Wisconsin's biennial budget. It analyzes administrative and fiscal issues facing the state and recommends solutions. The department also coordinates telecommunications, energy, and land use planning and community development. It regulates racing, charitable gaming, and Indian gaming. It is responsible for providing a wide range of support services to other state agencies and manages the state's buildings and leased office space. The department maintains a federal-state relations office in Washington, D.C.

Organization: The department is administered by a secretary appointed by the governor with the advice and consent of the senate. The secretary must be appointed "on the basis of recognized interest, administrative and executive ability, training and experience in and knowledge of problems and needs in the field of administration." The secretary appoints the department's division administrators from outside the classified service.

Unit Functions: The *Division of Administrative Services* provides numerous support services to the department and agencies attached for administrative support, including personnel, records and forms, space and property management, financial management, mail, printing, business recovery, and management planning. Other major functions are to prepare and administer the departmental budget, advise the secretary on policies and procedures, and perform internal audits. It pays the salaries and any associated fringe benefits for all district attorneys and their staff attorneys. It also reviews and pays the compensation of special prosecutors for the 71 district attorneys' offices. (Menominee and Shawano Counties share a district attorney.)

The *Division of Capitol Police* uses officers working in Madison and Milwaukee to provide a wide range of investigative, security, and related public safety services to state agencies, employees, and others. It protects state facilities; conducts criminal investigations, including the use of sophisticated surveillance and alarm devices used to detect criminal activity; and provides protective services to the governor and visiting dignitaries. The division's uniformed patrol officers detect and complete preliminary investigations of crimes, traffic accidents, and traffic violations. They also protect lives and property in department-managed facilities. The Capitol Police are also responsible for monitoring and managing other potential safety threats, such as hazardous material spills, injury accidents, and other situations impacting the safety of employees and visitors. The division also maintains bike and horse patrols to enhance public contact with officers and to meet other needs.

The *Division of Energy Services* administers statewide low-income household energy assistance programs involving conservation, weatherization, and bill payment.

The *Division of Enterprise Operations* manages state procurement policies and contracts, auto and air fleet transportation, and risk management. The division handles statewide contracts, DOA and consolidated agency purchasing, municipal cooperative purchasing, work center contracting, federal and state surplus property disposition, state agency recycling and waste reduction programs, and minority business contracting. It oversees fleet policies, records management, interdepartmental mail, and state agency document sales and distribution. It also manages the state's self-funded programs for liability, property, and worker's compensation, and assists agencies in controlling and reducing losses.

The *Division of Enterprise Technology* manages the state's information technology (IT) assets and uses technology to improve government efficiency and service delivery. It provides computer services to state agencies and operates the statewide voice data and video telecommunications network. In consultation with business and IT managers from state agencies and local governments, the division develops strategies, policies, and standards for cross-agency and multijurisdictional use of IT resources. The division provides centralized security training, research, and print and mail services to other state agencies and provides statewide computer systems for district attorneys. Through the Geographic Information Office, the division coordinates Wisconsin's geospatial information activities and provides geographic information systems (GIS) services to state agencies, service organizations, and local governments.

The *Division of Executive Budget and Finance* provides fiscal and policy analysis to the governor for development of executive budget proposals and assists agencies in the technical preparation of budget requests. It reviews legislation and coordinates the fiscal estimates that accompany all expenditure bills. It also advises the State of Wisconsin Building Commission and the governor on the issuance of state debt and administers finances for the clean water revolving loan fund program. The division provides program and management evaluation and maintains the management information system for authorized state employee positions. It establishes accounting policies and procedures, maintains the state's central payroll and accounting systems, monitors agency internal control procedures, and produces the state's annual fiscal and financial reports.

The *Division of Gaming* regulates racing, pari-mutuel on-track wagering and simulcasting, bingo, raffles, crane games, and Class III Indian gaming pursuant to state/tribal gaming compacts. The division licenses and performs compliance audits of racetrack operations and supervises racetrack operations including animal drug testing, monitoring and collection of taxes, and ensuring humane treatment of animals and sponsors the "Adopt-a-Greyhound" program for retired racing dogs. The division licenses and regulates bingo games and raffles conducted by

David Schmiedicke is the administrator of the Division of Executive Budget and Finance in the Department of Administration. As State Budget Director, he plays an important role in the budget process and is shown here addressing the Conference Committee that reached agreement on the 2009-2011 biennial budget. (Jay Salvo, Legislative Photographer)

nonprofit, charitable, religious, fraternal, and service organizations. It conducts tribal gaming compliance audits and certifies vendors to conduct gaming business in accordance with state/tribal compacts and federal law.

The *Division of Intergovernmental Relations* provides a variety of services to the public and state, local, and tribal governments. It advises the department and the governor on state, local ,and tribal relationships and coordinates the state's federal agenda by reviewing federal legislation and directing state lobbying efforts at the federal level (through the Office of Federal-State Relations in Washington, D.C.). It manages the Coastal Management Program, which focuses on environmental and economic issues related to Lakes Michigan and Superior and adjoining counties. The division provides annual population estimates for both state and municipal use, prepares population projections, develops demographic research on the state's changing population, and is responsible for coordinating and distributing census information.

The division administers the Comprehensive Planning and Land Information Grants. Working with the Incorporation Review Board, the division reviews and issues determinations on petitions to incorporate towns into villages or cities. It oversees the Municipal Boundary Review Program, which examines changes in local government boundaries, and issues advisory opinions on municipal annexations. It administers the Plat Review Program, which coordinates state agency and county planning agency subdivision plat review, and examines land subdivision plats and assessors' plats to ensure compliance with state surveying, mapping, and minimum layout standards. It administers the municipal service payment program which reimburses local governments for providing police, fire, and solid waste services to state facilities.

The *Division of State Facilities* develops and administers the state building program under the direction of the State of Wisconsin Building Commission. Its functions include statewide facilities planning and evaluation, real estate acquisition, architectural and engineering design, technology, consultation, management, and supervision of construction projects, energy conservation, power plant fuel management, fuels procurement, administration of state building contracts, and ensuring access for people with disabilities to state buildings. The division operates and maintains 30 major buildings in 7 cities throughout the state, including the State Capitol, the Executive Residence, and state office buildings in Madison. The division is responsible for all state real estate leasing, planning of office space, and building engineering services.

The *Office of the Wisconsin Covenant* administers the Wisconsin Covenant Program, which is designed to improve college planning and preparedness in collaboration with its partners: the Office of the Governor, the Higher Educational Aids Board, the Department of Public Instruction, the University of Wisconsin System, the Wisconsin Technical College System, and the Wisconsin Association of Independent Colleges and Universities. The office coordinates statewide efforts with Wisconsin K-12 schools, post-secondary institutions, and community organizations to promote college attendance, increase financial aid availability, and reduce barriers to higher education. The office was created by 2007 Wisconsin Act 20 and is officially designated the Office of the Wisconsin Covenant Scholars Program in Section 15.105 (31), Wisconsin Statutes.

The *Office of Energy Independence* facilitates implementation of Wisconsin's energy independence initiatives. The office is federally funded and is the official state energy office. It administers federal funds received from the U.S. Department of Energy under the State Energy Program Strategic Plan and various federal laws. It serves as the single point of contact to assist businesses, local units of government, and nongovernmental organizations that are pursuing biodevelopment, energy efficiency, and energy independence. It develops policy options for consideration by the governor and state agencies, coordinates activities with other state agencies, identifies federal funding opportunities and facilitates applications for funding by state and local governments and private entities, and performs duties necessary to maintain federal designation and funding.

The office was created by Governor Doyle in Executive Order 192 on April 5, 2007, and codified by 2007 Wisconsin Act 20. Its composition and duties are prescribed in Sections 15.105 (30) and 16.956, Wisconsin Statutes.

The *Office of Recovery and Reinvestment* was created by Governor Doyle in Executive Order 274, January 23, 2009, to coordinate and implement state activities under the federal American Recovery and Reinvestment Act of 2009 and other federal economic stimulus legislation. Under

Sections 14.019 and 15.02 (3), Wisconsin Statutes, the governor directed that the office be established within the Department of Administration and for the department to provide appropriate staff support.

History: The legislature created the Department of Administration in Chapter 228, Laws of 1959, and authorized it to provide centralized staff services to the governor, to assume common administrative functions for other executive agencies, and to coordinate the state's business affairs. Chapter 228 also abolished the Bureaus of Engineering, Personnel, and Purchases; the Department of Budget and Accounts; and the Division of Departmental Research in the Office of the Governor. Their functions and personnel were transferred to the new department.

Since its creation, the department has assumed additional duties. State comprehensive planning responsibilities and population estimation were added in 1967 and 1972, respectively. 1976 Executive Order 36 moved the Office of Emergency Energy Assistance from the Office of the Governor to the department's State Planning Office and broadened its responsibilities to include energy policy planning and program management. The 1989 executive budget created the Division of Housing (subsequently repealed in 2003) and gave the department responsibility for grant and loan programs for low- and moderate-income housing. The 1991 executive budget created the Division of Information Technology Services to consolidate and manage the state's computer and telecommunications resources.

Other functions assigned to the department have included the Coastal Management Program (1981), low-income weatherization assistance (1991), low-income energy assistance (1995), a college tuition prepayment program (1995) (transferred to the Office of the State Treasurer by 1999 Wisconsin Act 9), municipal boundary and plat review (1997), and the Wisconsin Fresh Start Program (1998).

Over the years, legislation has transferred various functions out of the department. Chapter 645, Laws of 1961, created a separate Personnel Board to review departmental decisions. Chapter 196, Laws of 1977, transferred the administration of civil service, collective bargaining, and classification and compensation to the newly created Department of Employment Relations. The Division of Emergency Government, which became part of the department in 1979, was moved to the Department of Military Affairs by 1989 Wisconsin Act 31. Regulation of mobile home dealers and mobile parks was transferred to the Department of Commerce by 1999 Wisconsin Act 9. With the repeal of the Division of Housing, 2003 Wisconsin Act 33 transferred grant and loan programs for low- and moderate-income housing to the Department of Commerce.

Gaming Regulation. 1997 Wisconsin Act 27 repealed the Wisconsin Gaming Board and created the Division of Gaming in the department to monitor gaming on Indian lands and regulate pari-mutuel wagering, racing, and charitable gaming.

Originally, the Wisconsin Constitution stated: "The legislature shall never authorize any lottery." This provision was interpreted as prohibiting all forms of gambling. Following a 1973 constitutional amendment to allow charitable bingo, the legislature enacted Chapter 156, Laws of 1973, to permit bingo games and create the Bingo Control Board in the Department of Regulation and Licensing. Charitable raffles were permitted by a 1977 constitutional amendment, and the legislature assigned their regulation to the Bingo Control Board in Chapter 426, Laws of 1977.

Pari-mutuel on-track wagering and the state lottery were permitted by constitutional amendments in 1987. The legislature created the Racing Board to regulate the sport in 1987 Wisconsin Act 354. The Wisconsin Lottery, originally operated by the Lottery Board, was created by 1987 Wisconsin Act 119.

The Wisconsin Gaming Commission, created by 1991 Wisconsin Act 269, replaced the Lottery Board and the Racing Board and also assumed responsibility for Indian gaming, charitable gaming (bingo and raffles), and crane games. The Wisconsin Gaming Board, created by 1995 Wisconsin Act 27, replaced the Gaming Commission. (That act also transferred responsibility for management of the Wisconsin Lottery to the Department of Revenue.) 1997 Wisconsin Act 27 transferred gaming duties, except for lottery regulation, to the Department of Administration.

Statutory Councils

Acid Deposition Research Council: Inactive.

The 7-member Acid Deposition Research Council makes recommendations on types and levels of funding for acid deposition research and reviews "acid rain" research. The council was created by 1985 Wisconsin Act 296, and its composition and duties are prescribed in Sections 15.107 (5) and 16.02 of the statutes.

Certification Standards Review Council: DAVID KLIBER (commercial laboratory representative), *chairperson;* SUSAN HILL (appointed by UW-Madison chancellor to represent Laboratory of Hygiene), *vice chairperson;* STEVE JOSSART (industrial laboratory representative), *secretary;* RANDALL THATER (large municipal wastewater plant representative); JUDY THOLEN (small municipal wastewater plant representative); KIRSTI SORSA (public water utility representative); vacancy (solid and hazardous waste disposal facility representative); CHRIS GROH (demonstrated interest in laboratory certification); vacancy (livestock farmer). (Unless otherwise designated, all are appointed by secretary of administration.)

The 9-member Certification Standards Review Council reviews the Department of Natural Resources laboratory certification and registration program and makes recommendations to the department about its programs for testing water, wastewater, waste material, soil, and hazardous waste. The council's members serve 3-year terms, and no member may serve more than two consecutive terms. The council was created by 1983 Wisconsin Act 410, and its composition and duties are prescribed in Sections 15.107 (12) and 299.11 (3) of the statutes.

Small Business, Veteran-Owned Business and Minority Business Opportunities, Council on: DAVID W. ARAGON, *chairperson;* AGGO AKYEA, CRAIG A. ANDERSON, NORMAN BARRIENTOS, WILLIAM BECKETT, TINA CHANG, MOHAMMED HASHIM, WILLIAM JOHNSON, JR., BRIAN MITCHELL, HENRY SANDERS, JR., ALLEN R. SCHRAEDER, 2 vacancies. (All are appointed by secretary of administration.) Nonvoting secretary: RON HERMES (Department of Administration designee).

The 13-member Council on Small Business, Veteran-Owned Business and Minority Business Opportunities advises the department on the participation of its constituent groups in state purchasing. Its members are appointed for 3-year terms and may not serve more than two consecutive full terms. The law prescribes minimum membership numbers for the types of businesses represented on the council: racial minority-owned (2); owned by handicapped person (1); nonprofit for rehabilitation of disabled (1); and veteran-owned (2). At least one member must represent the Department of Commerce and one must be a consumer member. The council was created by Chapter 419, Laws of 1977, and its name and membership were amended by 1991 Wisconsin Act 170 to include veteran-owned business. Its composition and duties are prescribed in Sections 15.107 (2) and 16.755 of the statutes.

INDEPENDENT UNITS ATTACHED FOR BUDGETING, PROGRAM COORDINATION, AND RELATED MANAGEMENT FUNCTIONS BY SECTION 15.03 OF THE STATUTES

BOARD ON AGING AND LONG-TERM CARE

Members: EVA ARNOLD, PATRICIA A. FINDER-STONE, TERRY LYNCH, TANYA L. MEYER, JAMES SURPRISE, DALE TAYLOR, BARBARA THONI (appointed by governor with senate consent).

Executive Director: HEATHER A. BRUEMMER, (608) 246-7014,
heather.bruemmer@wisconsin.gov

Mailing Address: 1402 Pankratz Street, Suite 111, Madison 53704.

Telephones: (608) 246-7013; Ombudsman Program: (800) 815-0015; Medigap Helpline: (800) 242-1060.

Fax: (608) 246-7001.

E-mail Address: boaltc@wisconsin.gov

Publications: Biennial Report.

Number of Employees: 34.00.

Total Budget 2007-09: $4,812,200.

Statutory References: Sections 15.07 (1)(b) 9., 15.105 (10), and 16.009.

Agency Responsibility: The 7-member Board on Aging and Long-Term Care reports biennially to the governor and the legislature on long-term care for the aged and disabled; state involvement in long-term care; program recommendations; and actions taken by state agencies to carry out the board's recommendations. The board monitors the development and implementation of federal, state, and local laws and regulations related to long-term care facilities. The board's ombudsman service investigates complaints from persons receiving long-term care concerning improper treatment or noncompliance with federal or state law and serves as mediator or advocate to resolve disputes between patients and institutions.

The board operates the Medigap Helpline, which provides information and counseling on various types of insurance, including health, hospital indemnity, cancer, nursing home, and long-term care and nursing home policies designed to supplement Medicare. Helpline information also covers the Health Insurance Risk-Sharing Plan (HIRSP), group insurance continuation and conversion rights, and health maintenance organization plans for Medicare beneficiaries.

The board members, who serve staggered 5-year terms, must have demonstrated a continuing interest in the problems of providing long-term care for the aged and disabled. At least four must be public members with no interest in or affiliation with any nursing home. The board appoints the executive director from the classified service.

The board was created by Chapter 20, Laws of 1981, which merged the Board on Aging and the Governor's Ombudsman Program for the Aging and Disabled, as the result of a legislative study. Predecessor agencies included the State Commission on Aging, created by Chapter 581, Laws of 1961, followed in 1967 (Chapters 75 and 327) by the Council on Aging in the Department of Health and Social Services, which was subsequently renamed the Board on Aging in Chapter 332, Laws of 1971.

CLAIMS BOARD

Members: STEVE MEANS (Department of Justice representative designated by attorney general), *chairperson;* vacancy (Department of Administration representative designated by secretary of administration); SENATOR HANSEN (chairperson, Senate Committee on Finance), REPRESENTATIVE SHERMAN (designated by chairperson, Assembly Committee on Finance); CHANDRA MILLER FIENEN (representative of the Office of the Governor designated by governor).

Secretary: CARI ANNE RENLUND.

Mailing Address: P.O. Box 7864, Madison 53707-7864.

Location: State Administration Building, 101 East Wilson Street, 10th Floor, Madison.

Telephone: (608) 264-9595.

Fax: (608) 267-3842.

E-mail Address: patricia.reardon@wisconsin.gov

Number of Employees: 0.00.

Total Budget 2007-09: $140,900.

Statutory References: Sections 15.07 (2)(e), 15.105 (2), and 16.007.

Agency Responsibility: The 5-member Claims Board investigates and pays, denies, or makes recommendations on all money claims against the state of $10 or more, when such claims are referred to it by the Department of Administration. The findings and recommendations of the board are reported to the legislature and no claim may be considered by the legislature until the board has made its recommendation.

Originally, the statutory procedure for making claims against the state was to file the claim with the Director of Budget and Accounts or to have a legislator introduce it as a bill. The legislature created the Claims Commission in Chapter 669, Laws of 1955, to handle these matters. Under the 1967 executive branch reorganization, the commission was renamed the Claims Board, and it absorbed the Commission for the Relief of Innocent Persons and the Judgment Debtor Relief Commission.

DEPOSITORY SELECTION BOARD

Members: DAWN MARIE SASS (state treasurer), MICHAEL L. MORGAN (secretary of administration), ROGER M. ERVIN (secretary of revenue).

Statutory References: Sections 15.105 (3) and 34.045.

Agency Responsibility: The 3-member Depository Selection Board, as created by Chapter 418, Laws of 1977, establishes procedures to be used by state agencies in the selection of depositories for public funds and in contracting for their banking services. The board's *ex officio* members may designate others to serve in their place. The secretary of revenue replaced the executive director of the investment board as a member as a result of 2001 Wisconsin Act 16.

ELECTRONIC RECORDING COUNCIL

Members: JANE LICHT (register of deeds), *chairperson;* STEVEN E. HANSON (representing an association of bankers), *vice chairperson;* MARVEL A. LEMKE, CATHY WILLOQUETTE, CYNTHIA WISINSKI (registers of deeds); CRAIG HASKINS (representing an association of title insurance); HAL KARAS (representing attorneys who practice real property law). (All members are appointed by governor).

Agency Responsibility: The 7-member Electronic Recording Council recommends standards regarding the electronic recording of real estate documents for adoption by rules promulgated by the Department of Administration. The council was created by 2005 Wisconsin Act 421, and its composition and duties are prescribed in Sections 15.107 (6) and 706.25 (4) of the statutes.

DIVISION OF HEARINGS AND APPEALS

Administrator: DAVID H. SCHWARZ, david.schwarz@wisconsin.gov

Mailing Address: 5005 University Avenue, Suite 201, Madison 53705-5400.

Telephone: (608) 266-8007.

Fax: Madison: (608) 264-9885; Milwaukee: (414) 227-3818; Eau Claire: (715) 831-3235.

E-mail Address: dhamail@wisconsin.gov

Internet Address: http://dha.state.wi.us

Number of Employees: 51.50.

Total Budget 2007-09: $11,302,200.

Statutory References: Sections 15.103 (1), 50.04 (4)(e), 227.43, 301.035, and 949.11.

Publications: Probation and Parole Digest.

Agency Responsibility: The Division of Hearings and Appeals conducts quasi-judicial hearings for several state agencies. It must decide contested administrative proceedings for the Department of Natural Resources, cases arising under the Department of Justice's Crime Victim Compensation Program, and appeals related to actions of the Departments of Health Services, Children and Family Services, Regulation and Licensing, and Agriculture, Trade and Consumer Protection. It also hears appeals from the Department of Transportation, including those related to motor vehicle dealer licenses, highway signs, motor carrier regulation, and disputes arising between motor vehicle dealers and manufacturers. The division conducts hearings for the Department of Corrections regarding probation, parole, and extended supervision revocation and juvenile aftercare supervision. It also handles contested cases for the Department of Public Instruction, the Department of Employee Trust Funds, and the Low-Income Home Energy Assistance Program of the Department of Administration. Other agencies may contract with the division for hearing services.

The secretary of administration appoints the division's administrator from the classified service. By law, the division operates independently of the department except for certain budgeting and management functions. 1983 Wisconsin Act 27 created the division by combining the Division of Natural Resources Hearings and the Division of Nursing Home Forfeiture Appeals, both originating with the 1977 Legislature. In 1986, the division received jurisdiction over crime victim compensation hearings and cases involving protection of human burial sites. With the creation of the Department of Corrections in 1990, the legislature transferred a portion of the Office of Administrative Hearings from the Departments of Health and Social Services to the division, making the division responsible for parole, probation, and juvenile aftercare revocation. When the Office of the Commissioner of Transportation was abolished in 1993, the legislature transferred many Department of Transportation hearing functions to the division. Contested administrative hearings for the Department of Health and Family Services and the Department of Workforce Development were transferred to the division by 1995 Wisconsin Act 370.

INCORPORATION REVIEW BOARD

Members: BRIAN VIGUE (designated by secretary of administration); TERRENCE J. MCMAHON, LONNIE MULLER (appointed by Wisconsin Towns Association); JEFF SPEAKER (appointed by League of Wisconsin Municipalities); RICH EGGELSTON (appointed by Wisconsin Alliance of Cities).

Contact person: ERICH SCHMIDTKE, Planning Analyst, Division of Intergovernmental Relations.

Mailing Address: 101 East Wilson Street, 10th Floor, Madison 53702.

Telephone: (608) 264-6102.

Statutory References: Sections 15.07 (2)(m), 15.105 (23), 16.53 (4), 66.0203, and 66.0207.

The 5-member Incorporation Review Board reviews petitions to incorporate territory as a city or village to determine whether the petition meets certain public interest statutory standards. These standards may include characteristics of the proposed municipality's territory, that part of the territory beyond its most densely populated core, its ability to provide services and generate revenue, and its impact on neighboring jurisdictions. The board is also charged with prescribing and collecting an incorporation review fee. The board must present its findings to the Division of Intergovernmental Relations within 180 days after receipt of referral from a circuit court unless the court sets a different time limit or all parties agree to a stay to allow time for an alternative dispute resolution of any disagreements. Any board member who owns property in, or resides in the town that is the subject of the incorporation petition, or a contiguous city or village, must be replaced for purposes of reviewing that petition. Members serve at the pleasure of the appointing authority and, with the exception of the DOA representative, serve only in an advisory capacity. The board was created by 2003 Wisconsin Act 171.

INFORMATION TECHNOLOGY MANAGEMENT BOARD

Members: Inactive.

Agency Responsibility: The Information Technology Management Board advises the Department of Administration on strategic information technology plans submitted by state agencies, the management of the state's information technology assets, and progress made on agency projects. The board may review the department's decisions on appeal from other state agencies. The board's membership includes the governor, the cochairpersons of the legislature's Joint Committee on Information Policy and Technology or their designees, a member of the minority party from the senate and the assembly, the secretary of administration or designee, 2 heads of departments or independent agencies appointed by the governor, and 2 other members appointed by the governor to 4-year terms. The board was created by 2001 Wisconsin Act 16 and attached to the Department of Administration by 2003 Wisconsin Act 33. Its composition and duties are prescribed in Sections 15.105 (28) and 16.978 of the statutes.

INTEROPERABILITY COUNCIL

Members: DAVID STEINGRABER (executive director of the office of justice assistance), *chairperson;* SUE RISELING (person with experience or expertise in interoperable communications), *vice chairperson;* ROB RUDE (adjutant general designee); RANDY STARK (secretary of natural resources designee); DAVID COLLINS (secretary of transportation designee); MARKLEY WAHL (department of administration information technology representative); TOM CZAJA (chief of police); DAVID MAHONEY (sheriff); NEIL CAMERON (fire chief); MINDY ALLEN (emergency medical services director); LARRY NELSON (local government elected official); BEN SCHLIESMAN (local government emergency management director); vacancy (American Indian tribe or band representative); vacancy (hospital representative); vacancy (local health department representative).

Agency Responsibility: The 15-member Interoperability Council recommends goals, standards, timelines, guidelines, and procedures for achieving a statewide public safety interoperable communication system. The system will enable the exchange of voice, data, and video communications among public safety agencies and associated resources including public works and transportation agencies, hospitals, and volunteer emergency services agencies. It assists the Office of Justice Assistance in obtaining and allocating funding, including for homeland security. The council, which receives staff support from the Office of Justice Assistance, was created by 2007 Wisconsin 79, and its composition and duties are prescribed in Sections 15.107 (28) and 15.9645 of the statutes.

OFFICE OF JUSTICE ASSISTANCE

Executive Director: DAVID STEINGRABER.

Mailing Address: 1 South Pinckney Street, Suite 600, Madison 53702.

Telephone: (608) 266-3323.

Fax: (608) 266-6676.

Publications: Annual Tribal Action Plan; Anti-Drug Abuse Strategy; Building Safer Communities Report; Crime and Arrests in Wisconsin; Drug Arrests in Wisconsin; Jail Population Trends; Juvenile Justice Improvement Plan; Sexual Assaults in Wisconsin; Violence Against Women Plan; Wisconsin Homeland Security Strategic Plan.

Number of Employees: 33.00.

Total Budget 2007-09: $127,112,100.

Statutory References: Sections 15.105 (19) and 16.964.

Agency Responsibility: The Office of Justice Assistance (OJA) is an independent state agency with an executive director appointed by the governor. OJA is almost entirely federally funded. OJA administers a variety of public safety programs including state and federal grant programs related to criminal justice and homeland security. Specific federal formula grant programs include the Juvenile Justice and Delinquency Prevention Act, the Anti-Drug Abuse Act, the Byrne Memorial Justice Assistance Grant, the Juvenile Accountability Incentive Block Grant Program, the Violence Against Women Act, and Homeland Security funding which includes Interoperable Emergency Communication Grant Program, Public Safety Interoperable Communications; Citizen Corps, the Urban Area Security Initiative, Emergency Operations Center, Buffer Zone Protection, and Rail and Transit Security. Federal discretionary grant programs include Grants to Encourage Arrests, the National Criminal History Repository Improvement Program, and Project Safe Neighborhoods. State funded grant programs include Beat Patrol; Treatment Alternatives and Diversion; Assess, Inform and Measure; Child Advocacy Center grants; and Digital Recording of Custodial Interviews grants.

The office also manages several programs that serve the public safety and justice communities. The Statistical Analysis Center administers the State Uniform Crime Reporting System and Incident-Based Reporting programs, conducts policy-related research, and publishes annual reports on statewide crime statistics. The Wisconsin Justice Information Sharing (WIJIS) initiative designed, implemented, and manages the Justice Gateway, an online sharing information tool for law enforcement and other justice agencies as well as other replicable technologies to improve justice system operations. The Sex Offender Apprehensive and Felony Enforcement (SAFE) locates and apprehends noncompliant sex offenders required to maintain registration with the state. The office supports the Governor's Juvenile Justice Commission, the Governor's Racial Disparities Oversight Commission, the Wisconsin State Citizen Corps Council, the WIJIS Policy Advisory Group, the State Interoperability Council, and numerous other advisory groups related to program responsibilities.

The Office of Justice Assistance originally was known as the Wisconsin Council on Criminal Justice, created by executive order in 1969 in the Department of Justice as the state planning body required by the federal Law Enforcement Assistance Administration. In 1971, the council was transferred by executive order to the governor's office. Chapter 418, Laws of 1977, created the council as a statutory agency in the governor's office. 1983 Wisconsin Act 27 created the council as an independent statutory body and attached it to the Department of Administration. The council was repealed and recreated under its current name by 1987 Wisconsin Act 27.

NATIONAL AND COMMUNITY SERVICE BOARD

Members: Kathleen Groat (private, nonprofit organization representative), *president;* Joel M. Haubrich (business representative), *vice president;* vacancy (youth education and training representative); Marguita Fox (older adult volunteer representative); Richard Grobschmidt (superintendent of public instruction designee); Sheree Dallas Branch (secretary of administration designee); vacancy (local government representative); Robert Guenther (organized labor representative); vacancy (national service youth representative); Marilynn Pelky (national service program representative); Anthony Hallman, Robert Hawley, Sondra LeGrand, Mark Mueller, Kyle O'Brien, Andrew Russell, Yia Thao (public members). Nonvoting members: Linda Sunde (Corporation for National and Community Service); Larry Kleinsteiber (Department of Veterans Affairs), Amy McDowell (Department of Health Services), Larry Olson (Department of Military Affairs), Jennifer Ortiz (Department of Workforce Development). (All except *ex officio* members are appointed by governor.)

Executive Director: Thomas H. Devine.

Mailing Address: 1 West Wilson Street, Room 456, Madison 53703.

Telephones: (608) 261-6716; (800) 620-8307 (toll free).

Fax: (608) 266-9313.

Internet Address: www.servewisconsin.org

Number of Employees: 5.00.

Total Budget 2007-09: $7,662,200.

Statutory References: Sections 15.105 (24) and 16.22.

Agency Responsibility: The National and Community Service Board, created by 1993 Wisconsin Act 437, in accordance with the federal National and Community Trust Act of 1993, oversees the planning and implementation of community service programs in Wisconsin that meet previously unmet human, public safety, educational, environmental, and homeland security needs. The board is authorized to receive and distribute funds from governmental and private sources, and it acts as an intermediary between the Corporation for National and Community Service (CNCS) and local agencies providing funding for AmeriCorps State programs.

The board oversees 18 AmeriCorps programs consisting of 800 AmeriCorps members serving in over 300 placement sites statewide. After completing a successful year of service, AmeriCorps members in Wisconsin are eligible for Federal Education Awards that can be used to pay tuition or pay back student loans.

The board's voting members, who must number at least 16, are appointed to serve 3-year terms. No more than 4 of them may be state officers and employees, and no more than 9 may be members from the same political party. To the extent practicable, membership should be diverse in terms of race, national origin, age, sex, and disability. Nonvoting members appointed by the governor must include the state representative of the CNCS and may include representatives of state agencies providing community social services.

BOARD FOR PEOPLE WITH DEVELOPMENTAL DISABILITIES

Members: Craig Wehner (designated by secretary of workforce development); Fredi Bove (designated by secretary of health services); Carolyn Stanford Taylor (designated by state superintendent of public instruction); Dan Bier (designated by UW Waisman Center Director); Jeffrey Spitzer-Resnick (designated by Disability Rights Wisconsin); Maureen Arcand, Cindy Bentley, Kristin Berg, Joan Burns, Shu-Chuan Cheng, John Donnelly, Mari Frederick, Debra Glover, Ruth Gullerud, Barbara Katz, Denise Konicki, Sue Nutter, Katherine Maloney Perhach, Roxanne Price, Barbara Sorensen, L. Lynn Stansberry-Brusnahan, Jacquelyn Wenkman, Cindy Zellner-Ehlers (all appointed by governor).

Executive Director: Jennifer Ondrejka.

Mailing Address and Location: 201 West Washington Avenue, Suite 110, Madison 53703-2796.

Telephones: 266-7826; TTY: 266-6660.

Fax: 267-3906.

Internet Address: www.wcdd.org
E-mail Address: help@wcdd.org
Number of Employees: 7.75.
Total Budget 2007-09: $2,556,400.
Statutory References: Sections 15.09 (1)(a), 15.105 (8), and 51.437 (14r).

Agency Responsibility: The board, formerly the Council on Developmental Disabilities, advises the Department of Administration, other state agencies, the legislature, and the governor on matters related to developmental disabilities. The statutes do not specify the exact number of board members, but all who serve are appointed to staggered 4-year terms, must be state residents, represent all geographic areas of the state, and the state's diversity with respect to race and ethnicity. The public members appointed by the governor must include representatives of public and private nonprofit agencies that provide direct services at the local level to persons with developmental disabilities. At least 60% of the board's members must be persons who have developmental disabilities or are the parents, relatives, or guardians of such individuals, but these members may not be associated with public or private agencies that receive federal funding. The members appointed by agency heads represent the relevant agencies of the state that administer federal funds related to individual with disabilities. The Council on Developmental Disabilities was created within the Department of Health and Family Services by Chapter 322, Laws of 1971, and made an independent unit by Chapter 29, Laws of 1977. 2007 Wisconsin Act 20 renamed it the Board for People with Developmental Disabilities, renumbered it from s. 15.197 (11n), and attached it to the Department of Administration under s. 15.03.

———

BOARD OF COMMISSIONERS OF PUBLIC LANDS

Commissioners: DOUGLAS J. LA FOLLETTE (secretary of state), DAWN MARIE SASS (state treasurer), J.B. VAN HOLLEN (attorney general). (All serve as *ex officio* members.)

DIVISION OF TRUST LANDS AND INVESTMENTS

Executive Secretary: TIA NELSON, 266-8369, tia.nelson@bcpl.state.wi.us; TOM GERMAN, *deputy secretary,* 267-2233, tom.german@bcpl.state.wi.us

Mailing Address: P.O. Box 8943, Madison 53708-8943.

Location: 125 South Webster Street, Suite 200, Madison.

Telephone: (608) 266-1370.

Fax: (608) 267-2787.

Internet Address: http://bcpl.state.wi.us

District Office: MICHAEL PAUS, *administrator,* michael.paus@bcpl.state.wi.us, P.O. Box 277, 7271 Main Street, Lake Tomahawk 54539-0277, (715) 277-3366; Fax: (715) 277-3363.

Publications: Biennial Report; State Trust Fund Loan Program Brochure.

Number of Employees: 8.50.

Total Budget 2007-09: $3,114,200.

Constitutional Reference: Article X, Sections 2, 7, and 8.

Statutory References: Section 15.103 (4) and Chapter 24.

Agency Responsibility and History: The Board of Commissioners of Public Lands and its Division of Trust Lands and Investments manage the state's remaining trust lands, manage trust funds primarily for the benefit of public education, and maintain the state's original 19th century land survey and land sales records.

The board was created in 1848 by Article X of the Wisconsin Constitution to manage and sell lands that were granted to the state by the federal government for the purposes of supporting public education and developing the state's infrastructure. Nearly all of the approximately 3.6 million acres from federal land grants that were placed into trust for the benefit of public education have been sold. The agency still holds title to about 78,000 acres of trust lands which are managed for sustainable forestry, natural areas preservation, and public use.

The constitution established "a board of commissioners for the sale of school and university lands and for the investment of funds arising therefrom" consisting of the Secretary of State, State Treasurer, and Attorney General. The Revised Statutes of 1849 created the Board of Commissioners of the School and University Lands. In 1878, the board was renamed the Board of Commissioners of Public Lands. Chapter 75, Laws of 1967, created the Division of Trust Lands and Investments, under the supervision of the board, to serve as the board's operating agency. The board appoints an executive secretary outside the classified service to administer the division. The division was originally attached to the Department of Natural Resources. Since then, the legislature has successively attached the division to the Department of Justice (Chapter 34, Laws of 1979), the Department of Administration (1993 Wisconsin Act 16), the Office of the State Treasurer (1995 Wisconsin Act 27), and again to the Department of Administration (1997 Wisconsin Act 27).

The agency manages four "trust funds", the largest of which is the Common School Fund. The principal of this fund continues to grow through the collection of fees, fines, and forfeitures that accrue to the state. Most of the trust fund assets are invested in loans to Wisconsin municipalities and school districts through the State Trust Fund Loan Program. The loans finance a wide variety of public purpose projects statewide while providing the trust funds with a reasonable rate of return at low risk. Over the last five years, Wisconsin citizens have benefited from nearly $600 million in trust fund loans used to support community, public safety, economic development, and school projects. The board received a record number of loan applications in 2008-2009 due to the credit crisis affecting the financial markets. Trust assets that are not invested in trust fund loans are invested in state bonds and the State Investment Fund.

The net earnings of the Common School Fund are distributed annually by the Department of Public Instruction to all Wisconsin public school districts. In 2009, $35.3 million of earn-

The Board of Commissioners of Public Lands presents a check representing $35.3 million to the Department of Public Instruction (DPI). The net earnings of the Common School Fund, managed by the board, are distributed through DPI to all Wisconsin public school districts. (Pictured from left to right: the 3 commissioners – State Treasurer Dawn Marie Sass, Attorney General J.B. Van Hollen, Secretary of State Douglas La Follette; and Rick Grobschmidt, Assistant State Superintendent of Public Instruction.) (Board of Commissioners of Public Lands)

ings were distributed from the Common School Fund, which marked six consecutive years of increased distributions. The other small trust funds are used to support the University of Wisconsin and the state's general fund. 2005 Wisconsin Act 352 directed the board to use the proceeds of the sale of trust lands which it sells to the state under the Warren Knowles-Gaylord Nelson Stewardship Program to purchase other trust lands to be managed by the board which will improve timberland management, address forest fragmentation, or increase public access to existing land holdings.

PUBLIC RECORDS BOARD

Members: PETER GOTTLIEB (representing the director, state historical society), *chairperson;* CAROL HEMERSBACH (designee of governor), *vice chairperson;* RUSS WHITESEL (representing the joint legislative council staff director), *secretary;* LEWIS W. BEILIN (designee of attorney general); BRYAN NAAB (designee of state auditor); vacancy (small business representative); vacancy (representative of school board or governing body of a municipality); vacancy (public member). (Representatives are appointed by the respective officers or the governor.)

Executive Secretary: HAROLD COLTHARP, harold.coltharp@wisconsin.gov

Mailing Address: 4622 University Avenue, Room 10A, Madison 53702.

Telephone: (608) 266-2770.

Fax: (608) 266-5050.

Internet Address: www.doa.state.wi.us/section_detail.asp?linkcatid=231&linkid=49&locid=2

Publications: Biennial Report; General Schedules for Records Common to State Agencies and Local Units of Government; Registry of State Agency Record Series Containing Personally Identifiable Information.

Statutory References: Sections 15.105 (4) and 16.61.

Agency Responsibility: The Public Records Board is responsible for the preservation of important state records, the cost-effective management of records by state agencies, and the orderly disposition of state records that have become obsolete. State agencies must have written approval from the board to dispose of records they generate or receive.

1991 Wisconsin Acts 39 and 269 directed the board to create a registry of those record series that contain personally identifiable information and made it the repository for general information about state computer matching programs.

Originally created by Chapter 316, Laws of 1947, as the Committee on Public Records and placed under the State Historical Society, the agency was transferred to the governor's office by Chapter 547, Laws of 1957. The committee was renamed the Public Records Board and attached to the Department of Administration by Chapter 75, Laws of 1967. Chapter 350, Laws of 1981, changed the board's name to the Public Records and Forms Board and added forms management to its duties. In 1995, Wisconsin Act 27 designated the board's current name and removed its forms management duties.

STATE CAPITOL AND EXECUTIVE RESIDENCE BOARD

Members: DAVID HELBACH (designated by secretary of administration); JAMES SEWELL (designated by director, state historical society); DAVID HALEY (engineer employed by the Department of Administration and appointed by secretary); SENATORS LASEE, RISSER, vacancy; REPRESENTATIVES ROTH, SCHNEIDER, vacancy; ARLAN K. KAY, vacancy (architects); JOHN J. FERNHOLZ (landscape architect); DEBRA ALTON, EUGENE POTENTE, JR., vacancy (interior designers); SALLY C. BASTING (citizen member or architect, landscape architect, or interior designer). (All except *ex officio* members and their designees are appointed by governor.)

Statutory References: Sections 15.105 (5) and 16.83.

Agency Responsibility: The 16-member State Capitol and Executive Residence Board, created by Chapter 183, Laws of 1967, includes 7 citizen members with specified expertise, appointed by the governor to serve staggered 6-year terms. The purpose of the board is to direct the continuing and consistent maintenance of the property, decorative furniture, and furnishings of the capitol and executive residence. No renovations, repairs (except of an emergency nature), installation of fixtures, decorative items, or furnishings for the ground and buildings of the capitol or executive residence may be performed by or become the property of the state by purchase wholly or in part from state funds, or by gift, loan or otherwise, until approved by the board as to design, structure, composition, and appropriateness.

Office of State
EMPLOYMENT RELATIONS

Director: JENNIFER DONNELLY.

Executive Assistant: YER VANG, 266-9820, yer.vang@

Legal Counsel: DAVID J. VERGERONT, 266-0047, david.vergeront@

State Employee Suggestion Program: ROBERT TOOMEY, *coordinator,* (608) 266-0664, robert.toomey@; Program e-mail: wiemployeesuggestionprogram@; Program Internet address: http://suggest.wi.gov

Affirmative Action and Workforce Planning, Division of: ALPHONSO COOPER, *administrator,* 266-3017, alphonso.cooper@

Compensation, Classification and Labor Relations, Division of: JAMES A. PANKRATZ, *administrator,* 266-1860, jim.pankratz@

  Compensation, Bureau of: PAUL HANKES, *director,* 266-1729, paul.hankes@

  Labor Relations, Bureau of: MARK WILD, *director,* 266-9564, mark.wild@

Merit Recruitment and Selection, Division of: JOHN R. LAWTON, *administrator,* 266-1499, jack1lawton@

  Agency Services, Bureau of: LINDA BRENNAN, *director,* 267-0344, linda.brennan@

  Outreach Services, Bureau of: JENNIFER GEBERT, *director,* 267-2155, jennifer.gebert@

Address e-mail by combining the user ID and the state extender: userid@**wisconsin.gov**

Mailing Address: P.O. Box 7855, Madison 53707-7855.

Location: 101 East Wilson Street, 4th Floor, Madison.

Telephones: General: (608) 266-9820, State job information: (608) 266-1731.

Fax: (608) 267-1020.

Internet Address: http://oser.state.wi.us

Publications: Council on Affirmative Action Report; Wisc.Jobs Bulletin; Veterans Employment Report; W-2 Hiring Report; Workforce Planning and Fact Book; Written Hiring Reasons Report.

Number of Employees: 55.50.

Total Budget 2007-09: $12,735,400.

Statutory References: Sections 15.105 (29); Chapter 111, Subchapter V, and Chapter 230.

  Agency Responsibility: The Office of State Employment Relations is responsible for personnel and employment relations policies and programs for state government employees. The office administers the state's classified service, which is designed to staff state governmental agencies with employees chosen on the basis of merit. It evaluates job categories, determines employee performance and training needs, and assists managers in their supervisory duties. The office sets standards for and ensures compliance with affirmative action plans and provides training on human resource programs to supervisors, managers, human resource staff, and other state employees. It represents the executive branch in its role as an employer under the state's employment relations statutes.

  A director, appointed by the governor, administers the office. The director appoints the administrators of the Division of Affirmative Action and Workforce Planning and the Division of Compensation, Classification and Labor Relations from outside the classified service. The governor appoints the administrator of the Division of Merit Recruitment and Selection to a 5-year term, with the advice and consent of the senate, based on a competitive examination. The governor may appoint the administrator for subsequent 5-year terms with the senate's consent.

Unit Functions: The *Division of Affirmative Action and Workforce Planning* administers the state's equal employment opportunity/affirmative action program and reports annually to the governor and legislature about the affirmative action accomplishments of state agencies. It develops standards for executive agencies, the UW System, and legislative service agencies and provides staff support to the Council on Affirmative Action. The division provides technical assistance to agencies in the development and implementation of affirmative action and workforce plans, trains new supervisors, and monitors agency programs.

The *Division of Compensation, Classification and Labor Relations* administers the state's compensation plan and leave statutes and policies. It also assists in state agency compliance with the federal and state family and medical leave acts. The division represents the state as employer in negotiating wages, benefits, and working conditions with the 19 labor unions that represent state employees, but the legislature must ratify all contracts. The division also serves the state in arbitration proceedings, conducts labor relations training programs for state management representatives, and coordinates the Labor-Management Cooperation Program. The division also allocates positions to classifications, assigns nonrepresented classifications to pay ranges, and assigns represented classifications to pay ranges as part of the collective bargaining process. It administers the state's performance evaluation program and assists in state agency compliance with protective occupation determinations and the federal Fair Labor Standards Act.

The *Division of Merit Recruitment and Selection,* created in Section 15.105 (29)(b) in 2003 Wisconsin Act 33, administers the state's civil service system by coordinating the recruiting, testing, evaluating, and hiring of applicants. The division administers layoffs, transfers, and reinstatements of nonrepresented classified employees. It operates Wisconsin Personnel Partners, which provides personnel services to local government units and Wisconsin Certification Examination Services, which provides licensure examination services to agencies on a fee bases. The division also oversees the administration of employee assistance programs in all state agencies, under which state employees and their families receive assistance with personal or work-related problems.

History: An office that administers state employment procedures dates back to the creation of a State Civil Service Commission in Chapter 363, Laws of 1905. The law declared that appointments to and promotions in the civil service would be made only according to merit. Chapter 456, Laws of 1929, reconstituted the commission as the Personnel Board within the newly created Bureau of Personnel. This structure continued for 30 years until the legislature placed the board and bureau in the new Department of Administration, created in Chapter 228, Laws of 1959.

In 1972, Governor Patrick Lucey issued an executive order creating an affirmative action unit in the Bureau of Personnel. The order also directed the head of every state agency to encourage women and minorities to apply for promotions and to designate an affirmative action officer responsible for developing an affirmative action plan.

Chapter 196, Laws of 1977, created the Department of Employment Relations and transferred to it from the Department of Administration the organizational units and functions of the Employee Relations Division, including affirmative action, personnel, collective bargaining, and human resources services.

The legislature reorganized personnel functions in 1983 Wisconsin Act 27 by assigning classification and compensation responsibility to the secretary and recruitment and examination responsibility to a statutorily created Division of Merit Recruitment and Selection. The same law created the Personnel Board as an independent agency to review civil service rules and investigate and report on their impact. 1989 Wisconsin Act 31 abolished the Personnel Board and transferred its functions to the department. The 2003-05 biennial budget, Act 33, abolished the department and created the Office of State Employment Relations attached to the Department of Administration.

Statutory Council and Board

Affirmative Action, Council on: JAMES PARKER (appointed by governor), *chairperson;* CHRISTOPHER ZENCHENKO (appointed by senate president); ROGER L. PULLIAM (appointed by assembly speaker); vacancy (appointed by senate minority leader), ADELENE GREENE (appointed by assembly minority leader); YOLANDA SANTOS ADAMS, LAKSHMI BHARADWAJ, THRESESSA CHILDS, DAVID DUNHAM, JANICE K. HUGHES, JOHN MAGERUS, SANDRA RYAN, RONALD SHAHEED, NANCY VUE, vacancy (appointed by governor).

Contact person: ALPHONSO COOPER, *administrator,* Division of Affirmative Action and Workforce Planning, 266-3017.

The 15-member Council on Affirmative Action advises the director of state employment relations, evaluates affirmative action programs throughout the classified service, seeks compliance with state and federal regulations, and recommends improvements in the state's affirmative action efforts. The council must report annually to the legislature and governor. It may recommend legislation, consult with agency personnel and other interested groups, and conduct hearings. Council members serve 3-year terms. A majority of them must be public members, and a majority must represent minority persons, women, and people with disabilities. The council was created by Chapter 196, Laws of 1977, in the Department of Employment Relations and is located in the Office of State Employment Relations (2003 Wisconsin Act 33). Its composition and duties are prescribed in Sections 15.105 (29)(d) and 230.46 of the statutes.

State Employees Suggestion Board: SANDY DREW, *chairperson;* GENE DALHOFF, DAVID M. VRIEZEN (all appointed by governor).

Internet Address: http://suggest.wi.gov

The 3-member State Employees Suggestion Board administers an awards program to encourage unusual and meritorious suggestions and accomplishments by state employees that promote economy and efficiency in government services. Board members are appointed for 4-year terms, and at least one of them must be a state officer or employee. The board was created by Chapter 278, Laws of 1953, as the Wisconsin State Employees Merit Award Board and renamed in 1987 Wisconsin Act 142. It has been successively located in the Bureau of Personnel, the Department of Administration, the Department of Employment Relations (1989 Wisconsin Act 31), and the Office of State Employment Relations (2003 Wisconsin Act 33). Its composition and duties are prescribed in Sections 15.105 (29)(c) and 230.48 of the statutes.

STATE USE BOARD

Members: DAVID M. DUMKE (public member), *chairperson;* MICHAEL CASEY (public member); MARIE DANFORTH (mental health services representative, Department of Health Services); JOSEPH D'COSTA (vocational rehabilitation representative, Department of Workforce Development); NICKOLAS C. GEORGE, JR. (private business representative); RON HERMES (Department of Administration representative); BILL G. SMITH (small business representative); JEAN ZWEIFEL (work center representative). (All are appointed by governor.)

Mailing Address: Bureau of Procurement, Division of Enterprise Operations, P.O. Box 7867, Madison 53707-7867.

Telephone: (608) 266-5462.

Fax: (608) 267-0600.

Publication: Annual Report to the Secretary.

Number of Employees: 1.50

Total Budget 2007-09: $252,000.

Statutory References: Sections 15.105 (22) and 16.752.

Agency Responsibility: The 8-member State Use Board was created by 1989 Wisconsin Act 345. Its members, who serve 4-year terms, oversee state purchases from work centers certified by the board. To be certified, centers must meet certain conditions: 1) the work center must make a product or provide a service the state needs; 2) it must offer these goods or services at a fair market price; and 3) it must employ individuals with severe disabilities for at least 75% of the direct labor used in providing the goods or services.

TAX APPEALS COMMISSION

Commissioners: DAVID C. SWANSON, *chairperson;* ROGER W. LEGRAND, THOMAS J. MCADAMS (appointed by governor with senate consent).

Legal Assistant: NANCY BATZ, 266-9754, nancy.batz@wisconsin.gov

Mailing Address: 5005 University Avenue, Suite 110, Madison 53705.

Telephone: (608) 266-1391.

Fax: (608) 261-7060.

Number of Employees: 5.00.

Total Budget 2007-09: $1,105,600.

Statutory References: Sections 15.01 (2), 15.06 (1), 15.105 (1), and 73.01.

Publications: Decisions are at: www.wisbar.org (under Legal Research).

Agency Responsibility: The 3-member Tax Appeals Commission hears and decides appeals of persons and entities of assessments of the Department of Revenue involving all major state-imposed taxes, including individual and corporate income taxes, homestead and farmland preservation tax credits, real estate transfer fees, and sales and use taxes, as well as appeals of state assessments of manufacturing property. The commission also decides disputes between persons or entities and the Department of Transportation regarding certain motor vehicle taxes and fees. The commission's decisions may be appealed to circuit court.

Commissioners serve staggered 6-year terms and must be experienced in tax matters. The chairperson, who is designated by the governor to serve a 2-year term, must not serve on or under any committee of a political party. Employees of the commission are appointed by the chairperson from the classified service.

The Tax Appeals Commission was created as the Board of Tax Appeals by Chapter 412, Laws of 1939. Before 1939, individuals took appeals of income and property taxes to the local county board of review with appeal permitted to the state Tax Commission. Corporations took their appeals to the Commissioner of Taxation with appeal to the circuit court. The board was renamed the Tax Appeals Commission by Chapter 75, Laws of 1967. 1985 Wisconsin Act 29 provided that the commission include a small claims division.

COUNCIL ON UTILITY PUBLIC BENEFITS

Members: Inactive

The 11-member Council on Utility Public Benefits advises the Department of Administration on issues related to energy efficiency, conservation programs, and energy assistance to low-income households, including weatherization, payment of energy bills, and early identification and prevention of energy crises. Services are provided through community action agencies, nonprofit corporations, or local governments. Grants are also awarded to nonprofit corporations for energy conservation and efficiency services, renewable resources in the least competitive sectors of the energy conservation market, and programs that promote environmental protection, electric system reliability, or rural economic development. The council was created by 1999 Wisconsin Act 9, and its composition and duties are prescribed in Sections 15.107 (17) and 16.957 if the statutes.

VOLUNTEER FIRE FIGHTER AND EMERGENCY MEDICAL TECHNICIAN SERVICE AWARD BOARD

Members: ROBERT H. SEITZ (fire chiefs statewide organization representative), *chairperson;* MELINDA R. ALLEN (volunteer emergency medical service technician), KENNETH A. BARTZ (volunteer fire fighters statewide organization representative), KRISTEN HALVERSON, ALLEN R. SCHRAEDER, vacancy (representatives of municipalities using volunteer fire fighters), RON HERMES (secretary of administration designee), JOHN SCHERER (individual experienced in financial planning). (All but *ex officio* members are appointed by governor.)

Contact person: TERRI LENZ, 261-2298.

Mailing Address: 101 East Wilson Street, 6th Floor, Madison 53703.

Telephone: (608) 261-6580.

Number of Employees: 0.00

Total Budget 2007-09: $3,467,800.

Statutory References: Sections 15.105 (26) and 16.25.

The Service Award Program operates under the direction of an 8-member Volunteer Fire Fighter and Emergency Medical Technician Service Award Board appointed by the governor. It establishes by rule a tax-deferred benefit program for volunteer fire fighters, emergency medical technicians, and first responders based on their length of service to a community. The program is designed to assist municipalities in retaining volunteers. The board contracts with qualified organizations to provide investment plans and administrative services to municipalities that choose to participate in the service awards program, and the communities make payments directly to the plan providers. In appointing the board members, who serve 3-year terms, the governor must seek representatives from different regions of the state and from municipalities of different sizes. Representatives of the fire chiefs and volunteer fire fighters organizations must be volunteer fire fighters themselves. The board was created by 1999 Wisconsin Act 105.

WASTE FACILITY SITING BOARD

Members: JAMES SCHUERMAN (town official), *chairperson;* ALLEN JANSEN (town official), *vice chairperson;* PATRICIA TRAINER (designated by secretary of transportation), *secretary;* DAVID JELINSKI (designated by secretary of agriculture, trade and consumer protection), JAMES M. FRYMARK (designated by secretary of commerce); DALE SHAVER (county official). (Town and county officials are appointed by governor with senate consent.)

Executive Director: DAVID H. SCHWARZ.

Mailing Address: 5005 University Avenue, Suite 201, Madison 53705-5400.

E-mail Address: dhamail@wisconsin.gov

Internet Address: http://dha.state.wi.us

Telephone: (608) 261-6339.

Fax: (608) 264-9885

Number of Employees: 0.00.

Total Budget 2007-09: $107,800.

Statutory References: Sections 15.07 (1)(b) 11., 15.105 (12), 289.33, and 289.64.

Agency Responsibility: The 6-member Waste Facility Siting Board supervises a mandated negotiation-arbitration procedure between applicants for new or expanded solid or hazardous waste facility licenses and local committees composed of representatives from the municipalities affected by proposed facilities. It is authorized to make final awards in arbitration hearings and can enforce legal deadlines and other obligations of applicants and local committees during the process.

Town and county officials serve staggered 3-year terms, and the governor, when making these appointments, must consider timely recommendations of the Wisconsin Towns Association and the Wisconsin Counties Association. The board appoints an executive director who is authorized to request assistance from any state agency in helping the board fulfill its duties. The board is funded by a fee on each ton of waste disposed of in a licensed solid or hazardous waste facility. The board was created by Chapter 374, Laws of 1981.

WOMEN'S COUNCIL

Members: KRISTINE MARTINSEK (public member appointed by governor), *chairperson;* SENATORS HANSEN, ROBSON (appointed by senate majority leader); REPRESENTATIVES PASCH, ROYS (appointed by assembly speaker); JOAN M. PRINCE (designated by governor); SARAH BRIGANTI, MARY ANN GERRARD (public members appointed by senate president); MARY JO BAAS, HEIDI GREEN (public members appointed by assembly speaker); RENEE BOLDT, NICOLE BOWMAN-FARRELL, JANE D. CLARK, ANN PEGGS, ARLENE C. SISS (public members appointed by governor).

Executive Director: CHRISTINE LIDBURY.

Mailing Address: 101 East Wilson Street, 8th Floor, Madison 53702.

Telephone: (608) 266-2219.

Fax: (608) 267-0626.

Internet Address: http://womenscouncil.wi.gov

Publications: Numerous publications related to the council's mission.

Number of Employees: 1.00.

Total Budget 2007-09: $288,400.

Statutory References: Sections 15.107 (11) and 16.01.

Agency Responsibility: The 15-member Women's Council is charged with identifying barriers that prevent women in Wisconsin from participating fully and equally in all aspects of life. The council promotes public and private sector initiatives that empower women through educational opportunity; provides a clearinghouse for information relating to women's issues; works in cooperation with related groups and organizations; and promotes opportunities for partnerships with various organizations to address issues affecting Wisconsin women. The council advises state agencies about the impact upon women of current and emerging state policies, laws, and rules; recommends changes to the public and private sectors and initiates legislation to further women's economic and social equality and improve this state's tax base and economy; and disseminates information on the status of women in this state.

The governor or governor's designee serves a 4-year term on the council; all other members serve 2-year terms. The governor appoints 6 public members, one of whom the governor designates as chairperson. The Women's Council was created by 1983 Wisconsin Act 27. It was preceded by a nonstatutory commission, the Governor's Commission on the Status of Women, which was created in 1964 and abolished in 1979.

Department of
AGRICULTURE, TRADE AND CONSUMER PROTECTION

Board of Agriculture, Trade and Consumer Protection: CYNTHIA BROWN, RICHARD CATES, ANDREW DIERCKS, MICHAEL DUMMER, ENRIQUE FIGUEROA, MICHAEL KRUTZA, SHELLY MAYER (agricultural representatives); MARGARET KROME, BRIAN RUDE (consumer representatives) (appointed by governor with senate consent).

Secretary of Agriculture, Trade and Consumer Protection: RODNEY J. NILSESTUEN, 224-5015.

Deputy Secretary: RANDALL ROMANSKI, 224-5001.

Executive Assistant: MARTIN M. HENERT, 224-5035.

Wisconsin Agricultural Statistics Service: ROBERT J. BATTAGLIA, *state agricultural statistician,* 224-4838, robert.battaglia@

Legal Counsel, Office of: JAMES K. MATSON, *chief counsel,* 224-5022, james.matson@

Budget Director: WILLIAM D. WALKER, 224-4353, williamd.walker@

For e-mail by combine the user ID and the state extender: userid@**wisconsin.gov**

Mailing Address: P.O. Box 8911, Madison 53708-8911.

Location: 2811 Agriculture Drive, Madison.

Telephones: Consumer Protection Hotline: (800) 422-7128; Farm and Rural Services Hotline: (800) 942-2474; Wisconsin Telemarketing No-Call List sign-up: (866) 966-2255.

Fax: Office of the Secretary: 224-5045; Division of Agricultural Development: 224-5110; Division of Agricultural Resource Management: 224-4656; Division of Animal Health: 224-4871; Division of Food Safety: 224-4710; Division of Management Services: 224-4737; Division of Trade and Consumer Protection: 224-4963.

Internet Address: www.datcp.state.wi.us

Departmental E-mail Address: datcp_web@wisconsin.gov

Agricultural Development, Division of: WILL H. HUGHES, *administrator,* 224-5142, will.hughes@

    Agricultural Business and Sector Development Bureau: PERRY L. BROWN, *director,* 224-5114, perry.brown@

DEPARTMENT OF AGRICULTURE, TRADE AND CONSUMER PROTECTION

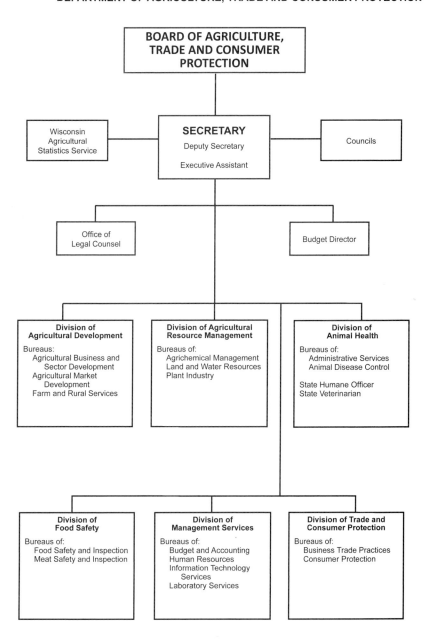

BOARD OF AGRICULTURE, TRADE AND CONSUMER PROTECTION

Wisconsin Agricultural Statistics Service

SECRETARY

Deputy Secretary

Executive Assistant

Councils

Office of Legal Counsel

Budget Director

Division of Agricultural Development

Bureaus:
Agricultural Business and Sector Development
Agricultural Market Development
Farm and Rural Services

Division of Agricultural Resource Management

Bureaus of:
Agrichemical Management
Land and Water Resources
Plant Industry

Division of Animal Health

Bureaus of:
Administrative Services
Animal Disease Control

State Humane Officer
State Veterinarian

Division of Food Safety

Bureaus of:
Food Safety and Inspection
Meat Safety and Inspection

Division of Management Services

Bureaus of:
Budget and Accounting
Human Resources
Information Technology Services
Laboratory Services

Division of Trade and Consumer Protection

Bureaus of:
Business Trade Practices
Consumer Protection

Units attached for administrative purposes under Sec. 15.03: Land and Water Conservation Board
Livestock Facility Siting Review Board

Agricultural Market Development Bureau: LORA J. KLENKE, *director,* 224-5119, lora.klenke@

Farm and Rural Services Bureau: PAUL DIETMANN, *director,* 224-5038, paul.dietmann@

Agricultural Resource Management, Division of: KATHY F. PIELSTICKER, *administrator,* 224-4567, kathy.pielsticker@

   Agrichemical Management, Bureau of: LORI BOWMAN, *director,* 224-4550, lori.bowman@

   Land and Water Resources, Bureau of: J. DAVID JELINSKI, *director,* 224-4621, dave.jelinski@

   Plant Industry, Bureau of: BRIAN KUHN, *director and assistant division administrator,* 224-4590, brian.kuhn@

Animal Health, Division of: ROBERT G. EHLENFELDT, *state veterinarian, administrator,* 224-4880, robert.ehlenfeldt@

   Administrative Services, Bureau of: vacancy, *director.*

   Animal Disease Control, Bureau of: PAUL J. MCGRAW, *assistant state veterinarian, assistant division administrator, director,* 224-4884, paul.mcgraw@

   State Humane Officer: YVONNE M. BELLAY, 224-4888, yvonne.bellay@

Food Safety, Division of: STEVEN C. INGHAM, *administrator,* 224-4701, steven.ingham@

   Food Safety and Inspection, Bureau of: CHARLES T. LEITZKE, *director,* 224-4711, tom.leitzke@

   Meat Safety and Inspection, Bureau of: JAMES LARSON, *director,* 224-4729, james.larson@

Management Services, Division of: SUSAN J. BUROKER, *administrator,* 224-4740, susan.buroker@

   Budget and Accounting, Bureau of: KAREN VAN SCHOONHOVEN, *director,* 224-4800, karen.vanschoonhoven@

   Human Resources, Bureau of: SUSAN J. BUROKER, *acting director and assistant division administrator,* 224-4740, susan.buroker@

   Information Technology Services, Bureau of: RAYNOLD W. ANDERSON, *director,* 224-4777, raynold.anderson@

   Laboratory Services, Bureau of: STEVEN M. SOBEK, *director,* 267-3500, steve.sobek@

Trade and Consumer Protection, Division of: JANET A. JENKINS, *administrator,* 224-4920, janet.jenkins@

   Business Trade Practices, Bureau of: JEREMY S. MCPHERSON, *director,* 224-4922, jeremy.mcpherson@

   Consumer Protection, Bureau of: JIM L. RABBITT, *director and assistant division administrator,* 224-4965, jim.rabbitt@

Publications: Agricultural Land Sales; *Chloroacetanilide Herbicide Metabolites in Wisconsin Groundwater;* Complaint Guide for the Wisconsin Consumer; Farm Transfers in Wisconsin – A Guide for Farmers; *Groundwater Protection: An Evaluation of Wisconsin's Atrazine Rule; Groundwater Quality – Agricultural Chemicals in Wisconsin Groundwater May 2002;* Guide to Wisconsin Cheese Factory Outlets and Tours; *Landlord and Tenants: The Wisconsin Way; Livestock Guidance: Local Planning for Livestock Operations in Wisconsin; Planning for Agriculture in Wisconsin: A Guide for Communities; Preventing Senior Citizen Rip-offs;* Wisconsin Agricultural Statistics; Wisconsin Dairy Plant Directory; Wisconsin Nursery Directory; Wisconsin Pest Bulletin.

Number of Employees: 582.37.

Total Budget 2007-09: $188,765,200.

Statutory References: Sections 15.13, 15.135, and 15.137; Chapters 88, 91-100, 127, and 136.

   Agency Responsibility: The Department of Agriculture, Trade and Consumer Protection regulates agriculture, trade, and commercial activity in Wisconsin for the protection of the state's

Food Scientist Thomas Starich checks refrigeration temperatures at a retail store as part of the statewide food safety testing program administered by the Department of Agriculture, Trade and Consumer Protection. (Department of Agriculture, Trade and Consumer Protection)

citizens. It enforces the state's primary consumer protection laws, including those relating to deceptive advertising, unfair business practices, and consumer product safety. The department oversees enforcement of Wisconsin's animal health and disease control laws and conducts a variety of programs to conserve and protect the state's vital land, water, and plant resources.

The department administers financial security programs to protect agricultural producers, facilitates the marketing of Wisconsin agricultural products in interstate and international markets, and promotes agricultural development and diversification.

Organization: The 9 members of the Board of Agriculture, Trade and Consumer Protection serve staggered 6-year terms. Of the board members, 2 must be consumer representatives and 7 must have an agricultural background. Appointments to the board must be made "without regard to party affiliation, residence or interest in any special organized group". The board directs and supervises the department, which is administered by a secretary appointed by the governor with the advice and consent of the senate. The secretary appoints the division administrators from outside the classified service.

Unit Functions: The *Division of Agricultural Development* provides services to assist producers, agribusinesses, and organizations to develop local, state, national, and international markets for Wisconsin agricultural products and to foster agricultural development and diversification in the state. It also provides counseling and mediation services to farmers, administers a rural electric power service program with the Public Service Commission, and oversees the operation of producer-elected marketing boards that assess fees within their respective groups for promotion, research, and education related to their commodities. The division also administers Agricultural Development and Diversification grants, a federal-state market news program, the "Something Special from Wisconsin" and Alice in Dairyland marketing programs, as well as the state aid programs for county and district fairs, the Livestock Breeders Association, and World Dairy Expo.

The *Division of Agricultural Resource Management* administers programs designed to protect the state's agricultural resources, as well as public health and the environment. It works to prevent agricultural practices that contaminate surface water and groundwater and jointly administers a nonpoint source pollution control program with the Department of Natural Resources. It directs programs related to farmland preservation and soil and land conservation, agricultural chemical cleanup, drainage districts, and agricultural impact statements. It regulates the sale and use of pesticides, animal feed, fertilizers, seed, and soil and plant additives and conducts programs to prevent and control plant pests, such as the gypsy moth.

The *Division of Animal Health* works closely with agricultural producers and veterinarians to diagnose, prevent, and control serious domestic animal diseases that threaten public health and the food chain. It licenses and inspects animal dealers and markets, regulates the import and export of animals across state lines, acts to prevent the spread of animal diseases, and assists in the enforcement of state humane laws. Through the Premises Identification Program, it registers persons who keep livestock and assigns an identification code to each place at which livestock are kept to facilitate animal disease control. It also regulates emerging industries, such as aquaculture and farm-raised deer.

The *Division of Food Safety* protects the state's food supply. From production through processing, packaging, distribution, and retail sale, the division works to ensure safe and wholesome food and to prevent fraud and misbranding in food sales. It licenses and inspects dairy plants, food and beverage processing establishments, meat slaughter and processing facilities, food warehouses, grocery stores, and other food establishments. The division inspects all dairy farms; inspects and samples food products; oversees food grading; and regulates the advertising, packaging, and labeling of food products.

The *Division of Management Services* provides administrative services to the department, including budget and accounting; facilities and fleet management; shipping, mailing, and printing; human resource management; and information technology services. The division also operates a general laboratory that provides analytical support to departmental inspection and sampling programs.

The *Division of Trade and Consumer Protection* enforces a wide range of consumer protection laws and handles nearly 200,000 consumer complaints and inquiries annually. It promulgates and enforces rules pertaining to deceptive advertising, consumer fraud, consumer product safety, landlord-tenant practices, home improvement, telecommunications, telemarketing, motor vehicle repair, fair packaging and labeling, weights and measures, and many other aspects of marketing. To promote fair and open competition in the marketplace, the division investigates and regulates unfair and anticompetitive business practices. It monitors the financial condition and business practices of dairy plants, grain warehouses, food processing plants, and public storage warehouses in order to protect agricultural producers and depositors. It also administers the state's Telemarketing No-Call List.

History: The present form of the Department of Agriculture, Trade and Consumer Protection is largely the result of the consolidation of several related agencies in 1929, but the department traces its lineage and responsibilities back to pre-statehood days.

From its beginnings, Wisconsin has been concerned with agriculture; food quality, safety, and labeling; plant and animal health; unfair business and trade practices; and consumer protection, and has taken steps to protect the public. The 1839 territorial legislature provided for the inspection of certain food and other products and established a program to regulate weights and measures. County inspectors were responsible for certifying the grade, wholesomeness, quantity, and proper packaging of food and distilled spirits, with county treasurers charged with enforcing the weights and measures standards. The 1867 Legislature, in Chapter 176, authorized the governor to appoint a treasury agent to enforce the laws relating to itinerant sales by "hawkers and peddlers". The 1889 Legislature, in Chapter 452, created the Office of the Dairy and Food Commissioner to enforce food safety, food labeling, and weights and measures laws. Other legislation over the years created various related functions such as the State Veterinarian, the State Board of Agriculture, the Inspector of Apiaries, the State Orchard and Nursery Inspector, the State Supervisor of Illuminating Oils, and the State Humane Agent.

The Department of Agriculture was created by Chapter 413, Laws of 1915, which combined the functions of several prior entities including the Board of Agriculture, Livestock Sanitary Board, State Veterinarian, Inspector of Apiaries, and Orchard and Nursery Inspector. Under the control and supervision of a Commissioner of Agriculture appointed by the governor with senate consent, the department had the responsibility to promote the interests of agriculture, dairying, horticulture, manufactures, and the domestic arts. It collected and published farm crop, livestock, and other statistics relating to state resources and regulated the practice of veterinary medicine. Through its own informational publications and paid advertisements in print media both inside the country and in foreign lands, it also sought to further the "development and enrichment" of the state by attracting "desirable immigrants" and "capital seeking profitable investment". These efforts were intended to promote the advantages and opportunities offered by the state "to the farmer, the merchant, the manufacturer, the home seeker, and the summer visitor".

The Division of Markets was created within the Department of Agriculture by Chapter 670, Laws of 1919. The duty of the division was to promote, in the interest of the producer, distributor, and consuming public, the economical and efficient distribution of farm products. Responsibilities included devising systems for marketing, grading, standardization, and storage of farm products; preventing deceptive practices; maintaining a market news service for collecting and reporting information on the supply, demand, prices, and commercial movement of farm products; and designing copyrighted trademarks, labels, and brands for Wisconsin farm products. A separate Department of Markets was created by Chapter 571, Laws of 1921, under the direction of a commissioner of markets appointed by the governor with senate consent. The department retained most of the duties of the former division, but was allowed to give assistance to cooperative associations and was specifically charged with regulating unfair methods of competition in business and unfair trade practices.

The modern department had its inception when Chapter 479, Laws of 1929, created the Department of Agriculture and Markets by consolidation of the Department of Agriculture, the

Department of Agriculture, Trade and Consumer Protection employees, Hans Gudyeron and Frank Schemberger, check an ash tree sample for evidence of emerald ash borer beetle larvae at Nagawaukee Park in Waukesha County. The emerald ash borer is an invasive insect from Asia which has killed millions of ash trees since its discovery in North America in 2002 and its first appearance in Wisconsin in 2008. (Department of Agriculture, Trade and Consumer Protection)

Department of Markets, the Dairy and Food Commissioner, the State Treasury Agent, the State Supervisor of Inspectors of Illuminating Oils, and the State Humane Agent. The department, which was under the control of three commissioners appointed by the governor with senate consent, assumed all duties performed by the component agencies. The department was reorganized and renamed the Department of Agriculture by Chapter 85, Laws of 1939, but its basic mission and authority was not changed. The department was overseen by a 7-member State Board of Agriculture, whose members, appointed by the governor with senate consent, in turn appointed the department's director. All members of the board were required to be persons experienced in farming.

The department's name was changed to the current Department of Agriculture, Trade and Consumer Protection by Chapter 29, Laws of 1977. This law also specified that one of the 7 board members must be a consumer representative.

1995 Wisconsin Act 27 directed the governor, rather than the board, to appoint the department secretary with senate consent, and expanded the board's membership to 8, including 2 consumer representatives. The board continues to set policy for the agency. Act 27 also consolidated the administration of most consumer protection activities within the department by transferring some staff and functions from the Department of Justice. However, the Department of Justice cooperates in the enforcement of consumer protection laws by providing legal services such as civil litigation. 1997 Wisconsin Act 95 added a ninth board member to represent agriculture.

In recent decades, the legislature has expanded the department's responsibilities related to land and water resources, including the areas of soil conservation, drainage districts, groundwater protection, nonpoint source pollution abatement, pesticides, animal disease control, and agricultural chemical storage and cleanup. It has allowed the department to create marketing boards for agricultural commodities, to promote agricultural development and diversification, and promote the state's agricultural products in interstate and international markets. The department also conducts programs for protecting producers against catastrophic financial defaults, farmland preservation, and farm mediation.

Statutory Councils

Agricultural Education and Workforce Development Council: PAUL DIETMAN (secretary of agriculture, trade and consumer protection designee); ELIZABETH BURMASTER (state superintendent of public instruction); MIKE GRECO (secretary of workforce development designee); RICHARD J. LEINENKUGEL (secretary of commerce); CARRIE MICKELSON (secretary of natural resources designee); JOHN SHUTSKE (president of the University of Wisconsin System designee); DAN CLANCY (director of the technical college system); DAVID WILLIAMS (chancellor of the University of Wisconsin-Extension designee); DUANE FORD (member chosen jointly by deans of specified UW System colleges and UW-Madison School of Veterinary School); KAREN KNOX (technical college system director appointed by director of the technical college system); WILLIAM BRENDEL (technical college dean with authority over agricultural programs appointed by director of technical college system); vacancy (chairperson of a senate standing committee concerned with education); REPRESENTATIVE DAVIS (chairperson of an assembly standing committee concerned with education); vacancy (chairperson of a senate standing committee concerned with agriculture); REPRESENTATIVE AL OTT (chairperson of an assembly standing committee concerned with agriculture); PAUL LARSON (Wisconsin Association of Agricultural Educators representative); DARLENE ARNESON, CONNIE SEEFELDT (general agriculture representatives); SAM SKEMP, DOUG WILSON (agribusiness representatives); GERRY MICH (representative environmental stewardship); vacancy (representative of businesses related to natural resources); JOHN PETTY (representative of businesses related to plant agriculture); BLISS NICHOLSON (representative of landscaping, golf course, greenhouse, floral, and related businesses); MARK MACPHAIL (representative of food product and food processing businesses); KATHY MUTH (representative of businesses related to animal agriculture); CAL DALTON (representative of businesses related to renewable energy); PAM JAHNKE (representative of agricultural communication interests); AL HERMAN (representative of businesses providing engineering, mechanical, electronic, and power services relating to agriculture); SHELLY MAYER (board of agriculture, trade and consumer protection representative); DAVID GLINIECKI (teacher of science, vocational technology, business, math, or a similar field, appointed by superintendent of public instruction); CHARLES HANSEN (school guidance counselor, appointed by superintendent of public instruction); RICHARD AUSTIN (school board member, appointed by superintendent of public instruction); GREGORY PEYER (school district administrator, appointed by superintendent of public instruction) (all except *ex officio* members, legislators, and those appointed by the superintendent of public instruction are appointed by the secretary of agriculture, trade and consumer protection).

The mission of the 34-member Agricultural Education and Workforce Development Council is to recommend policies and other changes to improve the efficiency of the development and provision of agricultural education across educational systems and to support employment in industries related to agriculture, food, and natural resources by seeking to increase the hiring and retention of well-qualified employees and promote the coordination of educational systems to develop, train, and retrain employees for current and future careers. It also advises state agencies on matters relating to integrating agricultural education and workforce development systems. All except *ex officio* members and legislators are appointed for staggered 3-year terms and may not serve more than 2 consecutive terms. The council was created by 2007 Wisconsin Act 223 and its composition and duties are prescribed in Sections 15.137 (2) and 93.33 of the statutes.

Agricultural Producer Security Council: DOUG CARUSO (Farmer's Educational and Cooperative Union of America, Wisconsin Division, representative), NICHOLAS GEORGE (Midwest Food Processor's Association, Inc., representative), RON STATZ (National Farmer's Organization, Inc., representative), JOHN PETTY (Wisconsin Agri-Service Association, Inc., representative), JIM UMHOEFER (Wisconsin Cheese Makers Association representative), JIM ZIMMERMAN (representative of both the Wisconsin Corn Growers Association, Inc. and the Wisconsin Soybean Association, Inc.), ED WELCH (Wisconsin Dairy Products Association, Inc., representative), DAVE DANIELS (Wisconsin Farm Bureau Federation representative), JOHN MANSKE (Wisconsin Federation of Cooperatives representative), DUANE MAATZ (Wisconsin Potato and Vegetable Growers Association, Inc., representative) (appointed by the secretary of agriculture, trade and consumer protection).

The 10-member Agricultural Producer Security Council advises the Department of Agriculture, Trade and Consumer Protection (DATCP) on the administration and enforcement of agricultural producer security programs. All members are appointed by the secretary of DATCP for 3-year terms. The council was created by 2001 Wisconsin Act 16 and its composition and duties are prescribed in Sections 15.137 (1) and 126.90 of the statutes.

Fertilizer Research Council: Voting members: MIKE MLEZIVA, JEFF SOMMERS, vacancy (industry representatives nominated by fertilizer industry); TOM CRAVE, RANDY VOLLRATH, vacancy (crop producing farmer representatives); ANDREW CRAIG (water quality expert appointed by secretary of natural resources). (All except the water quality expert are appointed jointly by secretary of agriculture, trade and consumer protection and dean of UW-Madison College of Agricultural and Life Sciences.) Nonvoting members: ROD NILSESTUEN (secretary of agriculture, trade and consumer protection), MATT FRANK (secretary of natural resources), MOLLY JAHN (dean, UW-Madison College of Agricultural and Life Sciences).

Mailing Address: P.O. Box 8911, Madison 53708-8911.

Telephone: 224-4614.

The 10-member Fertilizer Research Council meets annually to review and recommend projects involving research on soil management, soil fertility, plant nutrition, and for research on surface and groundwater problems related to fertilizer use. The secretary of agriculture, trade and consumer protection grants final approval for project funding. These research projects are granted to the UW System and are financed through funds generated from the sale of fertilizer and soil or plant additives in Wisconsin. The council's voting members are appointed for 3-year terms and may not serve more than 2 consecutive terms. The council was created by Chapter 418, Laws of 1977, and its composition and duties are prescribed in Sections 15.137 (5) and 94.64 (8m) of the statutes.

INDEPENDENT UNITS ATTACHED FOR BUDGETING, PROGRAM COORDINATION, AND RELATED MANAGEMENT FUNCTIONS BY SECTION 15.03 OF THE STATUTES

LAND AND WATER CONSERVATION BOARD

Members: JANA STEINMETZ (secretary of administration designee), MATTHEW FRANK (secretary of natural resources), KATHY PIELSTICKER (secretary of agriculture, trade and consumer protection designee); TOM RUDOLPH, THOMAS W. TRAXLER, JR., CHARLES WAGNER (county land conservation committee members); vacancy (public member); ROBIN LEARY (resident of city of 50,000 or more); MARK E. CUPP (representing governmental unit involved in river management); SANDI CIHLAR (farmer); DENNIS CANEFF (representing charitable natural resources organization). (All except *ex officio* members or designees are appointed by governor with senate consent.)

Advisory Members: PATRICIA LEAVENWORTH (U.S. Department of Agriculture, Natural Resources Conservation Service); BEN BRANCEL (U.S. Department of Agriculture, Farm Service Agency); FRED MADISON (designated by dean of the UW-Madison College of Agricultural and Life Sciences); KEN GENSKOW (appointed by director of UW-Extension); JULIANA ZELAZNY (designated by staff of county land conservation committees).

Statutory References: Sections 15.135 (4), 91.06, and 92.04.

Agency Responsibility: The 11-member Land and Water Conservation Board advises the secretary and department regarding soil and water conservation, animal waste management, and farmland preservation. As part of its farmland preservation duties, the board certifies agricultural preservation plans and zoning ordinances. It reviews and makes recommendations to the department on county land and water resource plans, local livestock regulations, agricultural shoreland management ordinances, and funding allocations to county land conservation committees. The board also advises the UW System annually about needed research and education programs related to soil and water conservation. In addition, it assists the Department of Natural Resources with issues related to runoff from agriculture and other rural sources of pollution.

The board's 3 county land conservation committee members are chosen by the Wisconsin Land and Water Conservation Association, Inc., to serve 2-year terms. The 4 members who must fulfill statutorily defined categories serve staggered 4-year terms. The undesignated member serves a 2-year term. In addition, the board must invite the appointment of advisory members from agencies or organizations specified by statute.

The board was originally created as the Land Conservation Board by Chapter 346, Laws of 1981, which also abolished the Agricultural Lands Preservation Board and transferred its functions to the new board. Chapter 346 also transferred administration of the state's soil and water conservation program from the UW System to the department but continued the university's responsibility for soil and water conservation research and educational programs. 1993 Wisconsin Act 16 changed the name of the board to the Land and Water Conservation Board.

LIVESTOCK FACILITY SITING REVIEW BOARD

Members: LEE ENGELBRECHT (representing towns); ANDY JOHNSON (representing counties); BOB SELK (representing environmental interests); JIM HOLTE (representing livestock farming interests); FRAN BYERLY, JEROME GASKA, BOB TOPEL (public members). (All nominated by the secretary of agriculture, trade and consumer protection and appointed by the governor with senate consent.)

Telephone: 224-4500.

The 7-member Livestock Facility Siting Review Board may review certain decisions made by political subdivisions relating to the siting or expansion of livestock facilities, such as feedlots. An aggrieved person may challenge the decision of a city, village, town, or county government approving or disapproving the siting or expansion of a livestock facility by requesting the board to review the decision. If the board determines that a challenge is valid, it shall reverse the decision of the governmental body. The decision of the board is binding on the political subdivision, but either party may appeal the board's decision in circuit court. All members are appointed for 5-year terms. The four members representing specific interests are selected from lists of names submitted by the Wisconsin Towns Association, Wisconsin Counties Association, environmental organizations, and statewide agricultural organizations, respectively. The board was created by 2003 Wisconsin Act 235 and its composition and duties are prescribed in Sections 15.135 (1) and 93.90 of the statutes.

Department of
CHILDREN AND FAMILIES

Secretary of Children and Families: REGGIE BICHA, 266-8684.

Deputy Secretary: HENRY WILDE, 266-8684, henry.wilde@

Executive Assistant: ANGELA RUSSELL, 266-8684, angela.russell@

Communications: ERIKA MONROE-KANE, 266-8684, erika.monroe-kane@

Legal Counsel: NANCY WETTERSTEN, 266-8684, nancy.wettersten@

Legislative Liaison: KIMMIE COLLINS, 266-8684, kimmie.collins@

Performance and Quality Assurance, Office of: NIKKI HATCH, *director,* 264-8734, nikki.hatch@

Community and Family Outreach: JANEL HINES, *director,* (414) 220-7082, janel.hines@

Mailing Address: P.O. Box 8916, Madison 53708-8916.

Location: 201 East Washington Avenue, Second Floor, Madison.

Telephone: 266-8684.

Fax: 261-6972.

Internet Address: www.dcf.wi.gov

Department E-mail Address: dcfweb@wisconsin.gov

Publications: Annual fiscal reports; Biennial reports; Reports and informational brochures (available through divisions).

Number of Employees: 635.89.

Total Budget 2007-09: $1,105,565,200.

Statutory References: Section 15.20; Chapter 46.

Address e-mail by combining the user ID and the state extender: userid@**wisconsin.gov**

Early Child Care and Education, Division of: DAN HARRIS, *administrator,* 266-8702, dan.harris@

  Early Care and Regulation, Bureau of: JILL CHASE, *director,* 266-8842, jill.chase@

  Early Childhood Education, Bureau of: LAURA SATTERFIELD, *director,* 266-3059, laura.satterfield@

  Head Start Collaboration: LINDA LEONHART, *director,* 261-2137, linda.leonhart@

Enterprise Solutions, Division of: RON HUNT, *administrator,* 266-9718, ron.hunt@

  Finance, Bureau of: MARGARET ERICKSON, *director,* 266-5712, margaret.erickson@

  Human Resources, Bureau of: LYNN WIESER, *director,* 266-9936, lynn.wieser@

  Information Technology, Bureau of: MAYTEE ASPURO, *director,* 264-9831, maytee.aspuro@

Family and Economic Security, Division of: JULIE KERKSICK, *administrator,* 266-8719, julie.kerksick@

  Child Support, Bureau of: SUE PFEIFFER, *director,* 267-8978, sue.pfeiffer@

  Working Families, Bureau of: JANICE PETERS, *director,* 267-0513, janice.peters@

Prevention and Service Integration, Division of: LISA PATRICK, *administrator,* (414) 227-1741, lisa.patrick@

  Milwaukee Family Service Integration Office: BRENDA BELL-WHITE, *director,* (414) 227-4202, brenda.bellwhite@

  Prevention Initiatives: vacancy, *director,* 267-3874.

Safety and Permanence, Division of: CYRUS BEHROOZI, *administrator,* 266-8717, cyrus.behroozi@; JOHN TUOHY, *deputy administrator,* 267-7932, john.tuohy@

DEPARTMENT OF CHILDREN AND FAMILIES

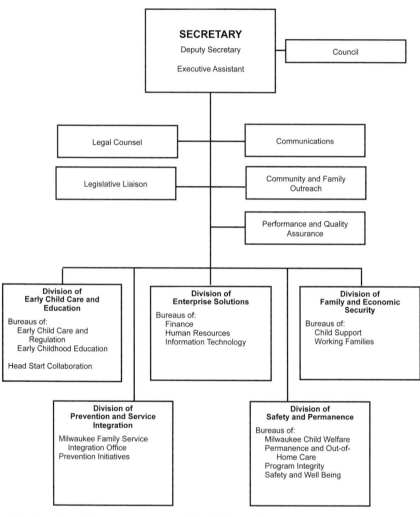

Units attached for administrative purposes under Sec. 15.03:   Child Abuse and Neglect Prevention Board
Milwaukee Child Welfare Partnership Council

Milwaukee Child Welfare, Bureau of: vacancy, *director,* (414) 220-7063.

Permanence and Out-of-Home Care, Bureau of: vacancy, *director,* 266-9293.

Program Integrity, Bureau of: vacancy, *director,* 267-3850.

Safety and Well Being, Bureau of: MARK CAMPBELL, *director,* 266-3784, mark.campbell@

Agency Responsibility: The Department of Children and Families provides or oversees county provision of various services to assist children and families, including services for children in need of protection or services for their families, adoption and foster care services, licensing of facilities that care for children, background investigations of child caregivers, and child abuse and neglect investigations. It administers the Wisconsin Works (W-2) program, including the child care subsidy program, child support enforcement and paternity establishment, and programs related to the Temporary Assistance to Needy Families (TANF) income support program. The department works to ensure families have access to high quality and affordable early care and education and also administers the licensing and regulation of day care centers.

Organization: The department is administered by a secretary who is appointed by the governor with the advice and consent of the senate. The secretary appoints the division administrators from outside the classified service.

Unit Functions: The *Office of Performance and Quality Assurance,* located within the secretary's office, works to build a culture that values outcomes over process; performance over minimum compliance; and uses data and analysis to drive decision making. The Office of Performance and Quality Assurance includes the department's budget office. The office analyzes, researches, and evaluates the performance of programs serving children and families and furthers the department's goal of aiding children to be healthy, safe, and ready for success.

The *Division of Early Child Care and Education* is responsible for the licensing, quality, and reimbursement of early child care and education providers and programs.

The *Division of Enterprise Solutions* oversees financial management, information systems and technology, personnel and employment relations, affirmative action and civil rights compliance, purchasing and contract administration, facilities management, project management, and other administrative services. It handles billing and collection of client debts and bills Medical Assistance and Medicare claims to the federal government. It oversees the department's regional offices and is responsible for oversight of county human service programs.

The *Division of Family and Economic Security* is responsible for the W-2 and child support programs. The division is focused on helping clients achieve economic security for their families.

The *Division of Prevention and Service Integration* focuses on enhancing prevention, early intervention, and service integration activities across the Department of Children and Families.

The *Division of Safety and Permanence* incorporates the Bureau of Milwaukee Child Welfare and oversight of child welfare services throughout the state and has the goal of having all children be in safe, permanent families that love, nurture, protect, and guide them.

History: By the time the federal government entered the field of public welfare during the Great Depression of the 1930s, Wisconsin had already pioneered a number of programs, including aid to children and pensions for the elderly (enacted in 1931). The Wisconsin Children's Code, enacted by Chapter 439, Laws of 1929, was one of the most comprehensive in the nation. The state's initial response to federal funding was to establish separate departments to administer social security funds and other public welfare programs. After several attempts at reorganization and a series of studies, the legislature established the State Department of Public Welfare in Chapter 435, Laws of 1939, to provide unified administration of all existing welfare functions. Public health and care for the aged were delegated to separate agencies.

The executive branch reorganization act of 1967 created the Department of Health and Social Services. The Board of Health and Social Services, appointed by the governor, directed the new department and appointed the departmental secretary to administer the agency, whose responsibilities included public welfare. In Chapter 39, Laws of 1975, the legislature abolished the board and replaced it with a secretary appointed by the governor with the advice and consent of the senate. That same law called for a reorganization of the department, which was completed by July 1977. The Department of Health and Social Services was renamed the Department of Health and Family Services (DHFS), effective July 1, 1996.

The decades of the 1960s and 1970s saw an expansion of public welfare and health services at both the federal and state levels. Especially notable were programs for medical care for the needy and aged (Medical Assistance and Medicare), drug treatment programs, food stamps, and Aid to Families with Dependent Children Program (AFDC). DHFS was assigned additional duties during the 1980s in the areas of child support, child abuse and neglect, and welfare reform.

1995 Wisconsin Act 27 revised AFDC and transferred it and other income support programs including Medical Assistance eligibility and food stamps to the Department of Workforce Development (DWD). (Wisconsin Works, known as W-2, replaced AFDC in 1995 Wisconsin Act

289.) Existing welfare reform programs, including Job Opportunities and Basic Skills (JOBS), Learnfare, Parental Responsibility, and Work-Not-Welfare, were also transferred to DWD, along with child and spousal support, the Children First Program, Older American Community Service Employment, refugee assistance programs, and vocational rehabilitation functions. Health care facilities plan review was transferred from the Department of Industry, Labor and Human Relations to DHFS by 1995 Wisconsin Act 27. Act 27 also transferred laboratory certification to the Department of Agriculture, Trade and Consumer Protection and low-income energy assistance to the Department of Administration.

As a result of 1995 Wisconsin Act 303, DHFS assumed responsibility for direct administration and operation of Milwaukee County child welfare services. 2001 Wisconsin Act 16 transferred the Medical Assistance Eligibility Program and the Food Stamp Program to DHFS from the Department of Workforce Development.

2007 Wisconsin Act 20 created the Department of Children and Families (DCF), beginning July 1, 2008. It also changed the name of DHFS to the Department of Health Services and split the responsibilities of DHFS between the two departments. Act 20 transferred from DHFS to DCF the duty to provide or oversee county supervision of various services to assist children and families, including services for children in need of protection or services and their families, adoption services, licensing of facilities that provide care for children, child caregiver background investigations, and child abuse and neglect investigations. The act also transferred from

Governor Jim Doyle meets with youngsters in Milwaukee on June 30, 2008, as part of his announcement of the launch of the Department of Children and Families. The newly established cabinet agency focuses on promoting the safety and economic and social well-being of Wisconsin children and families. (Office of the Governor)

DWD to DCF administration of Wisconsin Works, including the child care subsidy program, child support enforcement and paternity establishment, and programs related to temporary assistance for needy families (TANF).

Statutory Council

Domestic Abuse, Council on: LISA STEWART BOETTCHER (designated by assembly speaker), STORMY WALKER MERCADEL (designated by assembly minority leader), MARILYN LENSERT HARRIS (designated by senate majority leader), BETH SCHNORR (designated senate minority leader); MAYTONG CHANG, L. KEVIN HAMBERGER, PETER HELEIN, DEAN KAUFERT, GENE REDHAIL, MARIANA RODRIGUEZ, RACHEL RODRIGUEZ, JUSTINE SCHMIDT, GERALD WILKIE (members not designated by legislative leadership are nominated and appointed by governor with senate consent.)

The 13-member Council on Domestic Abuse makes recommendations to the secretary on domestic abuse, reviews grant applications, advises the department and legislature on domestic abuse policy, and, in conjunction with the Judicial Conference, develops forms for filing petitions for domestic abuse restraining orders and injunctions. Members are appointed for staggered 3-year terms. Members designated by legislative leadership do not have to be legislators. The council was created by Chapter 111, Laws of 1979, and it was transferred from the Department of Health and Family Services to the Department of Children and Families by 2007 Wisconsin Act 20. Its composition and duties are prescribed in Sections 15.207 (16) and 49.165 (3) of the statutes.

INDEPENDENT UNITS ATTACHED FOR BUDGETING, PROGRAM COORDINATION, AND RELATED MANAGEMENT FUNCTIONS BY SECTION 15.03 OF THE STATUTES

CHILD ABUSE AND NEGLECT PREVENTION BOARD

Members: RICHARD SCHLIMM (public member), *chairperson;* BARBARA KNOX (public member), *vice chairperson;* CORAL BUTSON (designated by governor), JANICE CUMMINGS (designed by attorney general), REA HOLMES (designated by secretary of health services), NIC DIBBLE (designated by state superintendent of public instruction), ISMAEL OZANNE (designated by secretary of corrections), LISA PATRICK (designated by secretary of children and families); REPRESENTATIVE KLEEFISCH (representative to the assembly appointed by speaker), REPRESENTATIVE SEIDEL (representative to the assembly appointed by assembly minority leader), SENATOR OLSEN (senator appointed by president of senate), SENATOR LASSA (senator appointed by senate minority leader); NANCY ARMBRUST, ANNE ARNESEN, STEVE GILBERTSON, JAMES LEONHART, SANDRA MCCORMICK, FLORENCE NINHAM, 2 vacancies (public members appointed by governor).

Executive Director: MARY ANNE SNYDER, maryanne.snyder@wisconsin.gov

Mailing Address: 110 East Main Street, Suite 810, Madison 53703-3316.

Telephone: 266-6871; (866) 640-3936 (toll free).

Fax: 266-3792.

Internet Address: http://wctf.state.wi.us

Publications: Child Sexual Abuse Prevention: Tips for Parents; Positive Parenting: Tips on Discipline; Positive Parenting: Tips on Fathering; Shaken Baby Syndrome Prevention materials; and the Blue Ribbons for KIDS Campaign.

Number of Employees: 7.00.

Total Budget 2007-09: $7,272,800.

Statutory References: Sections 15.205 (4) and 48.982.

Agency Responsibility: The 20-member Child Abuse and Neglect Prevention Board administers the Children's Trust Fund. The board recommends policies to the legislature, governor, and state agencies to protect children and support prevention activities. The board supports, funds, and evaluates evidence-informed and innovative strategies that are effective in helping Wisconsin communities prevent child maltreatment through culturally competent, family-centered, coordinated approaches to the delivery of support services that strengthen families. The board also implements consumer education and social marketing campaigns and provides education on prevention and positive parenting through printed materials and informational seminars. Funding is derived through charges on duplicate birth certificates, federal matching funds, and private contributions. In 2001, the board created a nonprofit corporation, the Celebrate Children Foundation with funds from the sale of the Celebrate Children special license plates to raise additional money for improving the lives of children and families in Wisconsin.

The board's 10 public members serve staggered 3-year terms. The board appoints the executive director and staff from the classified service. It was created by 1983 Wisconsin Act 27, and it was transferred from the Department of Health and Family Services to the Department of Children and Families by 2007 Wisconsin Act 20.

MILWAUKEE CHILD WELFARE PARTNERSHIP COUNCIL

Members: ARCHIE IVY (public member), *chairperson;* WILLIE JOHNSON, JR., 2 vacancies (Milwaukee County board members nominated by Milwaukee County Executive), REPRESENTATIVE GRIGSBY (representative to the assembly appointed by assembly speaker), vacancy (representative to the assembly appointed by assembly minority leader), SENATOR COGGS (senator appointed by senate president), SENATOR DARLING (senator appointed by senate minority leader); JULIUS F. AGARA, LINDA DAVIS, DAVID HOFFMAN, MICHAEL SKWIERAWSKI, MARY TRIGGIANO, EARNESTINE WILLIS, 3 vacancies (public members); DEBORAH BLANKS, vacancy (children's services network nominees). (All but legislators are appointed by governor.)

Contact Person: JANEL HINES.

Mailing Address: 1555 North Rivercenter Drive, Suite 220, Milwaukee 53212.

Telephone: (414) 220-7029.

Statutory References: Sections 15.207 (24) and 46.562.

Agency Responsibility: The 19-member Milwaukee Child Welfare Partnership Council makes recommendations to the Department of Children and Families and the legislature regarding policies and plans to improve the child welfare system in Milwaukee County, including a neighborhood-based system for delivery of services. It may also recommend funding priorities and identify innovative public and private funding opportunities. The 15 nonlegislative members are appointed to 3-year terms, and the governor designates one of the public members as chairperson. At least 6 public members must be residents of Milwaukee County. The council was created by 1995 Wisconsin Act 303, and it was transferred from the Department of Health and Family Services to the Department of Children and Families by 2007 Wisconsin Act 20.

Department of
COMMERCE

Secretary of Commerce: RICHARD J. LEINENKUGEL, 266-7088, dick.leinenkugel@

Deputy Secretary: AARON D. OLVER, 267-0754, aaron.olver@

Executive Assistant: ZACH BRANDON, 266-2125, zach.brandon@

General Counsel: JOSEPH THOMAS, 261-5402, joseph.thomas@

Office of Communications: TONY HOZENY, *director,* 267-9661, tony.hozeny@

Mailing Address: P.O. Box 7970, Madison 53707-7970.

Location: 201 West Washington Avenue, Madison.

Telephones: 266-1018; Business hotline: (800) 435-7287.

Fax: Business: 267-2829; Eau Claire: (715) 836-2510; Green Bay: (920) 498-6313; Milwaukee: (414) 382-1754; Milwaukee Center-City Initiative: (414) 227-4064; Stevens Point: (715) 346-4277.

Publications: A variety of reports are available upon request.

Internet Address: http://commerce.wi.gov

DEPARTMENT OF COMMERCE

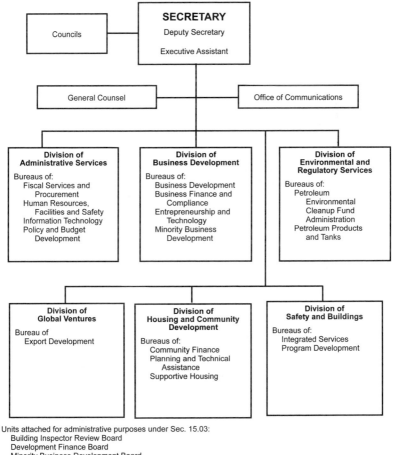

Units attached for administrative purposes under Sec. 15.03:
Building Inspector Review Board
Development Finance Board
Minority Business Development Board
Rural Economic Development Board
Small Business Regulatory Review Board

Number of Employees: 394.70.

Total Budget 2007-09: $387,061,200.

Statutory References: Section 15.15; Chapter 560.

For e-mail: firstname.lastname@wisconsin.gov

Administrative Services, Division of: TERRY CRANEY, *administrator,* 266-3494, terry.craney@; Division Fax: 266-0182.

    Fiscal Services and Procurement, Bureau of: AUDREY CHASE, *director,* 267-7200, audrey.chase@

    Human Resources, Facilities and Safety, Bureau of: BARRY WANNER, *director,* 264-7836, barry.wanner@

    Information Technology, Bureau of: GREG BEACH, *director,* 266-7404, gregory.beach@

Policy and Budget Development, Bureau of: LOUIS CORNELIUS, *director,* 266-8629, louie.cornelius@

Business Development, Division of: JIM O'KEEFE, *administrator,* 264-7837, jim.okeefe@; Division Fax: 267-2829.

   Business Development, Bureau of: JOHN STRICKER, *director,* 261-7710, john.stricker@

   Business Finance and Compliance, Bureau of: MARY GAGE, *director,* 266-2766, mary.gage@

   Entrepreneurship and Technology, Bureau of: vacancy, *director,* 267-9834.

   Minority Business Development, Bureau of: AGGO AKYEA, *director,* 261-7729, aggo.akyea@; Fax: 267-9550.

Environmental and Regulatory Services, Division of: BERNICE A. MATTSSON, *administrator,* 266-9403, berni.mattsson@; Division Fax: 267-1381.

   Petroleum Environmental Cleanup Fund Administration (PECFA) Bureau: OSCAR HERRERA, *director,* 266-7605, oscar.herrera@; Claim Review: P.O. Box 7838, Madison 53707-7838, 267-1381; Site Review: P.O. Box 8044, Madison 53708-8044, 266-8516.

   Petroleum Products and Tanks, Bureau of: MIKE FEHRENBACH, *director,* 266-8076, mike.fehrenbach@; P.O. Box 7839, Madison 53707-7839.

Global Ventures, Division of: MICKEY JUDKINS, *administrator,* 266-6675, mickey.judkins@; Division Fax: 266-5551.

   Export Development, Bureau of: MARY REGEL, *director,* 266-1767, mary.regel@

Housing and Community Development, Division of: JIM O'KEEFE, *administrator,* 264-7837, jim.okeefe@; Division Fax: 266-8969.

   Community Finance, Bureau of: JAMES FRYMARK, *director,* 266-2742, jim.frymark@

   Planning and Technical Assistance, Bureau of: JAMES ENGLE, *director,* 267-0766, james.engle@

   Supportive Housing, Bureau of: MARTY EVANSON, *director,* 267-2713, marty.evanson@

Safety and Buildings, Division of: GREGORY C. JONES, *administrator,* 266-1816, gregory.jones@; Division Fax: 267-9566; Regional Fax: Chippewa Falls: (715) 726-2549; Green Bay: (920) 492-5604; Hayward: (715) 634-5150; La Crosse: (608) 785-9330; Shawano: (715) 524-3633; Stevens Point: (715) 345-5269; Waukesha: (262) 548-8614.

   Integrated Services, Bureau of: RANDALL V. BALDWIN, *director,* 267-9152, randy.baldwin@

   Program Development, Bureau of: ROBERT G. DUPONT, *director,* 266-8984, robert.dupont@

Agency Responsibility: The Department of Commerce administers the state's economic development programs and policies. It provides consultation, technical assistance, and other services for industrial and commercial expansion. The department promotes the development or relocation of new businesses within the state and the retention of existing firms, especially small or minority-owned enterprises. In addition, it encourages job creation, particularly in economically depressed areas, and helps communities draw up development plans. The agency administers federal economic assistance programs that affect local governments and businesses. It also provides financial assistance for foreign trade development and reports on state economic trends, business aid programs, and long-term development strategies. Businesses and communities may use the department's information clearinghouse for help in dealing with other state and federal agencies. The department administers and enforces laws to assure safe and sanitary conditions in public and private buildings. It also administers the relocation assistance program and regulates petroleum products and petroleum storage tank systems. The agency provides housing assistance to benefit low- and moderate-income households.

Organization: The department is directed by a secretary, who is appointed by the governor with the advice and consent of the senate. The secretary appoints the division administrators from outside the classified service.

Unit Functions: The *Office of the Secretary* coordinates economic development programs in conjunction with other state agencies and private corporations. The secretary advises the governor and legislature on state economic growth and community development.

The *Division of Administrative Services* provides internal management services to the department in the areas of information technology, telecommunications, personnel, payroll, employee development, affirmative action, policy and budget development, procurement and printing, fiscal management, health and safety, property and space management, and mail services.

The *Division of Business Development* administers statewide business economic development programs and provides a wide array of technical assistance to local municipalities and businesses interested in starting or expanding operations in Wisconsin. The division also administers many of the state's economic development financing programs, including the Wisconsin Development Fund and the Forward Innovation Fund, which makes grants or loans to businesses, governments, and nonprofit organizations with an economic or community development mission; the Rural Economic Development Program; the Gaming Economic Development Diversification Program; the economic development component of the federally funded Community Development Block Grant Program for small cities, the tax credit programs; the Industrial Revenue Bond Program; and the Technology Commercialization Grant and Loan Program. The Development Zone Program encourages private sector investment in economically depressed areas by providing tax incentives to develop employment opportunities for the unemployed and persons facing barriers to employment.

The division helps Wisconsin companies access foreign markets through counseling and technical assistance, as well as through the new Global Partnership Services initiative. This initiative leverages state and local resources to train local communities, universities, technical colleges, economic development organizations and service organizations in the basics of exporting, to enable them to help companies in their respective areas succeed in the international markets. The division also provides information on resources for business start-ups, public and private financing programs, and government permits. It helps small businesses understand and comply in a cost-effective manner with clean air regulations through the Small Business Clean Air Assistance Program and advocates the interests of small businesses through its Small Business Ombudsman Program.

The *Division of Environmental and Regulatory Services,* created in Section 15.153 (3), Wisconsin Statutes, by 1995 Wisconsin Act 27, is responsible for sampling and testing petroleum products. It inspects existing tank systems at terminals, bulk plants, and retail and nonretail sites. It registers, reviews plans, and issues permits for new underground and aboveground storage tank systems. The division also cooperates with the Department of Natural Resources in administering the state's Petroleum Storage Environmental Cleanup Fund Act (PECFA) program for sites environmentally damaged through petroleum contamination and supervises the remediation of low and medium priority sites.

The *Division of Global Ventures* fosters strategic alliances between Wisconsin firms that have research and development capabilities with firms outside the state which are looking to invest in Wisconsin.

The *Division of Housing and Community Development* administers a variety of programs to help Wisconsin communities be desirable places for families to live and businesses to thrive. The Main Street Program assists selected communities in revitalizing their downtown areas. Other programs provide assistance in management, marketing, and financial analysis to entrepreneurs and small businesses in smaller communities. The Brownfields Initiative provides assistance and funding to persons, businesses, development organizations, and municipalities for redevelopment and environmental remediation activities for contaminated sites where the owner cannot be located or cannot meet the cleanup costs. The division also administers programs that provide financial assistance to communities for infrastructure improvements, blight elimination, and community facilities through the public facilities portion of the federally funded Community Development Block Grant Program for small cities. In addition, it provides technical assistance and approves relocation payment plans and assistance service plans under the state's eminent domain law.

Department of Commerce Secretary Richard Leinenkugel admires a student group's "mini-chopper" project on an April 2009 visit to the Industrial Arts program at Lincoln Hills High School in Manitowoc. (Department of Commerce)

To provide housing assistance to low- and moderate-income households, the division administers funding through the Local Housing Organization Grant Program for local organizations that offer housing opportunities and services. It awards grants under the Fresh Start Program that helps young people gain construction work experience particularly for high school dropouts and other young people-at-risk. The division channels federal funding to local organizations through various programs, including the Home Investment Partnerships and Community Block Grant Programs. It administers state and federal funds to provide immediate shelter for the homeless and support transitional and permanent housing, as well. To meet federal and state requirements, the division prepares the state consolidated housing plan that addresses housing and community development needs.

The *Division of Safety and Buildings* promotes public safety, health, and welfare by administering state laws pertaining to commercial buildings, dwellings, structures, amusement rides, ski lifts, mines, and the subsystems that serve buildings, such as plumbing, boilers, private sewage, electrical service, fire sprinklers, heating, and elevators. It oversees the housing design and construction requirements of the Fair Housing Law. The division develops and enforces health and safety-related administrative rules, reviews plans for proposed construction, makes initial and follow-up inspections, issues credentials, and provides training and consulting services. Finally, the division administers the Fire Dues Program. The program provides support and direction for municipal fire protection and is funded by a percentage of fire-related insurance premiums, which are paid to the Office of the Commissioner of Insurance by insurers providing fire coverage.

History: The state's promotion of business and economic development originated with the Division of Industrial Development, established in the governor's office by Chapter 271, Laws of 1955. The division was transferred to the newly created Department of Resource Development in 1959 and renamed the Division of Economic Development. Chapter 614, Laws of

1965, returned it to the governor's office. While in the executive office, it absorbed the Office of Economic Opportunity (1966), which had been created in the Department of Resource Development to administer the federal antipoverty programs enacted in 1964. Under the 1967 executive branch reorganization, the division became part of the Department of Local Affairs and Development, and local and regional planning functions were integrated into it.

Chapter 125, Laws of 1971, elevated the division to departmental status as the Department of Business Development. The department absorbed the Division of Tourism from the Department of Natural Resources in 1975. Under Chapter 361, Laws of 1979, the Department of Business Development was reunited with the Department of Local Affairs and Development to form the Department of Development, subsequently renamed the Department of Commerce by 1995 Wisconsin Act 27.

The department's responsibility for state tourism promotion ended with creation of the Department of Tourism by 1995 Wisconsin Act 27. Act 27 also transferred the PECFA program and the safety and buildings functions from the Department of Industry, Labor and Human Relations to the Department of Commerce. In 2003, Wisconsin Act 33 transferred housing programs to the department from the Department of Administration.

Wisconsin was a pioneer in the use of administrative law for safety and building regulation. The 1911 Legislature created the Industrial Commission in Chapter 485 to set standards for a safe place of employment. This "safe place" statute was extended in Chapter 588, Laws of 1913, to include public buildings, defined as "any structure used in whole or in part as a place of resort, assemblage, lodging, trade, traffic, occupancy, or use by the public, or by three or more tenants." The commission adopted its first building code in 1914. Programs added over the years include plumbing, heating, ventilation, air conditioning, energy conservation, private on-site waste treatment systems, accessibility for people with disabilities, and electrical inspection and certification.

Other programs absorbed by the department, as a result of 1995 Wisconsin Act 27, include plat review from the Department of Agriculture, Trade and Consumer Protection; municipal boundary review from the Department of Administration; and relocation assistance under eminent domain law from the Department of Industry, Labor and Human Relations. Plat review and municipal boundary review were transferred to the Department of Administration in 1997 Wisconsin Act 27.

Since 1999, functions related to manufactured homes have been transferred to the department. Regulation of manufactured home dealers and manufactured home parks was transferred to the department from the Department of Administration by 1999 Wisconsin Act 9. Act 9 also transferred titling of manufacturing homes from the Department of Transportation. Regulation of manufactured home park utilities was transferred from the Public Service Commission by 2001 Wisconsin Act 16.

2009 Wisconsin Act 2 deleted five existing zone programs, including the Enterprise Development Zones, the Community Development Zones, the Agricultural Development Zones, the Technology Development Zones, and the Airport Development Zones, and created a new consolidated tax credit program to promote job creation, capital investment, employee training, and job retention in Wisconsin. Act 2 also increased substantially the amount of angel and early-stage seed investment tax credits available annually for high-technology, biotechnology, and nanotechnology start-up companies which had been initiated by 2003 Wisconsin Act 255.

Statutory Councils

Automatic Fire Sprinkler System Contractors and Journeymen Council: JAMES SMITH (department employee); DAN DRIEBLE, CHRIS SCHOENBECK (licensed journeymen automatic fire sprinkler fitters); JEFF BATEMAN, GREG HINTZ (representing licensed automatic fire sprinkler contractors) (all appointed by secretary of commerce).

Mailing Address: P.O. Box 2689, Madison 53701-2689.

Telephone: 266-0251.

The 5-member Automatic Fire Sprinkler System Contractors and Journeymen Council reviews the content of examinations and advises the department on related matters. Journeymen and contractor members serve staggered 4-year terms. The council was created as an examining council in the Department of Health and Social Services by Chapter 255, Laws of 1971; transferred to the Department of Industry, Labor and Human Relations by Chapter 221, Laws of 1979; and transferred to the Department of Commerce by 1995 Wisconsin Act 27. The council's duties and composition are prescribed in Sections 15.157 (9) and 145.17 (2) of the statutes.

Contractor Certification Council: CRAIG RAKOWSKI (building contractor representing Wisconsin Builders Association), JAY STATZ (building contractor representing National Association of Remodeling Contractors), JOSEPH WELCH (building contractor representing Wisconsin State Council of Carpenters) (all appointed by secretary of commerce).

Mailing Address: P.O. Box 2689, Madison 53701-2689.

Telephone: 266-9292.

The 3-member Contractor Certification Council recommends rules for promulgation by the department for certifying the financial responsibility of contractors. It also recommends courses that meet continuing education requirements and advises the department on the development of course examinations. Council members serve 3-year terms, and must be building contractors holding certificates of financial responsibility who are involved in, or have demonstrated an interest in, continuing education for building contractors. The council was created by 2005 Wisconsin Act 200, and its composition and duties are prescribed in Sections 15.157 (5) and 101.625 of the statutes. It assumes some of the duties of the Contractor Financial Responsibility Council, which was repealed by 2005 Wisconsin Act 200.

Conveyance Safety Code Council: ANDREW ZIEKLE (representative of a manufacturer of elevators); vacancy (representative of an elevator servicing business); PAUL ROSENBERG (representative of an architectural design or elevator consulting profession); KELVIN NORD (representative of a labor organization involved in elevator installation, maintenance, and repair); CALVIN KING (representative of a city, village, town, or county); GEORGE SEMENAK (representative of an owner or manager of a building containing an elevator); JESSE KAYSEN (public member); KEVIN KRAEMER (commercial construction building contractor involved in construction or installation of conveyances); LARRY SWAZIEK (secretary of commerce designee); DAN MENEGUIN (department employee who is familiar with commercial building inspectors designated by secretary of commerce to serve as nonvoting secretary). (Except as indicated, all members appointed by governor.)

Mailing Address: P.O. Box 2689, Madison 53701-2689.

Telephone: 267-7701.

The 10-member Conveyance Safety Code Council recommends a statewide conveyance safety code for promulgation by the department and makes recommendations pertaining to enforcement of rules, the granting of variances, administrative appeal procedures, fees, and other relevant matters. Under the law, a "conveyance" includes devices such as an elevator, escalator, dumbwaiter, belt manlift, moving walkway, platform lift, personnel or material hoist, stairway chair lift, and any similar device, such as an automated people mover, used to elevate or move people or things. The council, which is required to meet at least twice a year, was created by 2005 Wisconsin Act 456, and its composition and duties are prescribed in Sections 15.157 (14) and 101.986 of the statutes.

Dwelling Code Council: JEFFREY D. BECHARD, THOMAS DOLESCHY, MICHAEL MUELLER, GARY RUHL (building trade labor organization representatives); BRIAN JUAREZ, ROBERT PREMO, KATHLEEN STADTHERR, MICHAEL WALLACE (certified building inspectors employed by local government); DAN GORSKI, MARY L. SCHROEDER (representatives of on-site housing contractors); FRANK OPATIK, TOM PALECEK (manufactured housing representatives); DAVID DOLAN-WALLACE (architect, engineer, or designer); WILLIAM TURNER, JOHN VANDE CASTLE (construction material supply representatives); DENNIS BAUER (one- and 2-family house remodeling contractor representative); ROBERT JAKEL, STEVEN LEVINE (public members) (all appointed by governor). Nonvoting secretary: LARRY SWAZIEK (department employee appointed by secretary of commerce).

Mailing Address: P.O. Box 2689, Madison 53701-2689.

Telephone: 267-7701.

The 18-member Dwelling Code Council reviews the rules and standards for one- and 2-family dwellings and manufactured housing. Members are appointed to 3-year terms. One public member must represent persons with disabilities. The council was created by Chapter 404, Laws of 1975, in the Department of Industry, Labor and Human Relations and transferred to the Department of Commerce by 1995 Wisconsin Act 27. Its composition and duties are prescribed in Sections 15.157 (3), 101.62, and 101.72 of the statutes.

Main Street Programs, Council on: JIM O'KEEFE (designated by secretary of commerce); vacancy (director, state historical society or designee); TIM ANDERSON (Wisconsin Downtown Action Council representative); DICK BEST (local chamber of commerce representative); SHAWN K. GRAFF (Wisconsin Trust for Historic Preservation representative); VIRGINIA HASKE (city, village, or town representative); JOHN GARDNER (planning profession representative); TOM MEIKLEJOHN (architectural profession representative); GERRY WHITE (financial community representative); PAUL KNUTH, DAWN ROG (business community representatives); MICHAEL IWINSKI, DARRYL JOHNSON, LISA KUSS, JUDITH WALL (members with expertise in downtown revitalization). (All except *ex officio* members or their designees are appointed by governor.) Nonvoting secretary: JAMES ENGLE (department employee designated by secretary of commerce).

Mailing Address: P.O. Box 7970, Madison 53701-7970.

Telephone: 267-0766.

The 15-member Council on Main Street Programs helps develop the state's Main Street Program for revitalization of business areas, reviews the program's effectiveness, and recommends municipalities for participation. Members are appointed for 3-year terms, and representative members must provide geographic diversity. At least 3 members must own or operate a business in a business area that has requested services under the Main Street Program. At least 5 members must have experience in business area revitalization combined with historical preservation. In addition, the secretary designates a department employee to serve as secretary. The council was created by 1987 Wisconsin Act 109, and its composition and duties are prescribed in Sections 15.157 (7), 560.081, and 560.082 of the statutes.

Manufactured Housing Code Council: STEVE ANDRESKE, JOHN GEISE (representing manufacturers of manufactured homes); BART HUNTINGTON, MARK THEIDE (representing manufactured home dealers); RON MIDDLETON, JIM REITZNER (representing owners of manufactured home communities); AL RHINERSON, AL SCHWOERER (representing installers of manufactured homes); ROSS KINZLER (representing an industry association in Wisconsin); BOB KLUWIN (representing suppliers of materials or services); KRISTEN ZEHNER (representative of the public); HARRY KREUSER (representative of labor); DAN CURRAN (representative of inspectors of manufactured homes); LARRY SWAZIEK (employee of department serving as nonvoting secretary) (all appointed by the secretary of commerce).

Mailing Address: P.O. Box 2689, Madison 53701-2689.

Telephone: 267-7701.

The 13-member Manufactured Housing Code Council recommends a statewide manufactured housing code for promulgation by the department. It also makes recommendations regarding licensure and professional discipline of manufacturers of manufactured homes and manufactured home dealers, salespersons, and installers; and regarding consumer protection applicable to consumers of manufactured homes. Members are appointed for 3-year terms, and the council is required to meet at least twice a year. In addition, the secretary designates a department employee to serve as secretary. The council was created by 2005 Wisconsin Act 45 and its composition and duties are prescribed in Sections 15.157 (13) and 101.933 of the statutes.

Multifamily Dwelling Code Council: EDWARD R. GRAY, MARK SCOTT (skilled building trades labor representatives); DAVID A. NITZ (municipal inspector from county less than 50,000 population); RICHARD P. PAUR (municipal inspector from county over 50,000 population); KRAIG BIELFELD, JEFFREY BROHMER (fire service workers); BETH A. GONNERING, MICHAEL MOREY (multifamily dwelling contractors and developers); EMORY BUDZINSKI, NICHOLAS RIVECCA, KEVIN WIPPERFURTH (representing materials manufacturers and finished product suppliers); JAMES R. KLETT (representing architects, engineers, and designers of multifamily housing);

GRETA HANSEN, KORINNE SCHNEIDER (public members) (all appointed by governor). Nonvoting secretary: JAMES SMITH (department employee member).

Mailing Address: P.O. Box 2689, Madison 53701-2689.

Telephone: 266-9292.

The 14-member Multifamily Dwelling Code Council advises the department on rules for multifamily dwelling construction. Members are appointed to 3-year terms. Those representing designated businesses and professions must be actively engaged in their work. At least one of the fire services representatives must be a fire chief. At least one of the public members must be a fair housing advocate. The council was created by 1991 Wisconsin Act 39 in the Department of Industry, Labor and Human Relations and transferred to the Department of Commerce by 1995 Wisconsin Act 27. Its composition and duties are prescribed in Sections 15.157 (12) and 101.972 of the statutes.

Plumbers Council: LYNITA DOCKEN (department employee), *secretary;* DAVE JONES (master plumber), SCOTT HAMILTON (journeyman plumber) (all appointed by secretary of commerce).

Mailing Address: 4003 North Kinney Coulee Road, La Crosse 54650.

Telephone: (608) 785-9349.

The 3-member Plumbers Council advises the department about the testing and licensing of plumbers. The 2 plumber members are appointed for 2-year terms. The council was created by Chapter 327, Laws of 1967, as an examining council in the Department of Health and Social Services; renamed and moved to the Department of Industry, Labor and Human Relations by Chapter 221, Laws of 1979; and transferred to the Department of Commerce by 1995 Wisconsin Act 27. Its composition and duties are prescribed in Sections 15.157 (6) and 145.02 (4) of the statutes.

Rural Health Development Council: JAMES FRYMARK (designated by secretary of commerce), vacancy (designated by secretary of health services); BYRON J. CROUSE (UW Medical School representative); LESLIE PATTERSON (Medical College of Wisconsin, Inc., representative); TIM SIZE (Wisconsin Health and Educational Facilities Authority representative); vacancy (Farmers Home Administration representative); ERICA HOVEN, vacancy (private rural lender representatives); JIM O'KEEFE, vacancy (rural health care facility representatives); vacancy (physician practicing in rural area); BLANE CHRISTMAN (dentist practicing in rural area); BECKY WOLF (nurse practicing in rural area); vacancy (dental hygienist practicing in rural area); LINDA MCFARLIN (public health services representative). (All except *ex officio* members or their designees are appointed by governor with senate consent.)

Mailing Address: Wisconsin Office of Rural Health, UW School of Medicine and Public Health, 310 N. Midvale Boulevard, Suite 301, Madison 53705.

Telephone: 261-1883, (800) 385-0005 (toll free).

The 15-member Rural Health Development Council advises the department regarding administration of the health professions loan assistance program, delivery of health care and improvement of facilities in rural areas, and coordination of state and federal programs available to assist rural health facilities. Appointed members serve 5-year terms. The council was created by 1989 Wisconsin Act 317, and its composition and duties are prescribed in Sections 15.157 (8) and 560.185 of the statutes.

Small Business Environmental Council: STEVE ALDRIDGE (appointed by senate president); CARL KOMASSA (appointed by senate minority leader); vacancy (appointed by assembly speaker); DAN MARTINO II (appointed by assembly minority leader); vacancy (appointed by secretary of commerce); MARK W. MCDERMID (appointed by secretary of natural resources); GERALD JONES, MICHAEL H. SIMPSON, JEANNE WHITISH (representing general public and appointed by governor).

Mailing Address: P.O. Box 7970, Madison 53707-7970.

Telephone: 267-9214.

The 9-member Small Business Environmental Council advises the Department of Commerce on the effectiveness of assistance programs to small businesses that enable them to comply with the federal Clean Air Act. It also advises on the fairness and effectiveness of air pollution rules promulgated by the Department of Natural Resources and the U.S. Environmental Protection Agency regarding the impact on small businesses. Members are appointed to 3-year terms. The 4 members appointed by legislative officers must own or represent owners of small business stationary air pollution sources. The 3 members appointed by the governor may not own or represent small business stationary sources. The council was created by 1991 Wisconsin Act 302, and its composition and duties are prescribed in Sections 15.157 (10) and 560.11 of the statutes.

INDEPENDENT UNITS ATTACHED FOR BUDGETING, PROGRAM COORDINATION, AND RELATED MANAGEMENT FUNCTIONS BY SECTION 15.03 OF THE STATUTES

BUILDING INSPECTOR REVIEW BOARD

Members: vacancy (senate majority leader designee); vacancy (speaker of assembly designee); vacancy (secretary of commerce or designee); MARTIN RIFKEN (representing building contractors and building developers); JACK VAN DER WEELE (certified building inspector) (except as indicated, all members appointed by governor with senate consent).

Statutory References: Sections 15.155 (6) and 101.596.

Agency Responsibility: The 5-member Building Inspector Review Board reviews complaints received from holders of building permits concerning possible incompetent, negligent, or unethical conduct by building inspectors. The board may revoke the certification of an inspector for cause and may modify or reverse erroneous decisions made by building inspectors. The board was created by 2005 Wisconsin Act 457.

DEVELOPMENT FINANCE BOARD

Members: AARON OLVER (designated by secretary of commerce), ROBERTA GASSMAN (secretary of workforce development), DAN CLANCY (director, Technical College System Board); RALPH KAUTEN (representing scientific community); KENNETH WANEK (representing technical community); MARK REIHL (representing labor community); vacancy (representing small business community); vacancy (minority business community); MARGARET HENNINGSEN (representing financial community); vacancy (appointed by assembly speaker); vacancy (appointed by senate majority leader). (All except *ex officio* members are appointed by governor.)

Statutory References: Section 15.155 (1); Chapter 560, Subchapter V.

Agency Responsibility: The 11-member Development Finance Board awards grants and loans from the Wisconsin Development Fund. Its 6 appointed members serve 2-year terms and are nominated by the governor and appointed with senate consent. The members appointed by legislative leaders need not be legislators. The board may make technology grants or loans to consortiums to support research to develop new products or improve existing products or processes. Businesses may obtain customized labor training grants or loans to provide state residents with job training in new technology and industrial skills if the training is not available through existing federal, state, or local resources. Funds are available for major economic development projects that cannot secure other financing and for activities that do not fit into existing programs. Through Employee Ownership Assistance Loans, the board approves funding for feasibility studies by employee groups considering the purchase of existing businesses as an alternative to plant closings. The board was created by 1987 Wisconsin Act 27 and its membership was revised by 2007 Wisconsin Act 20.

MINORITY BUSINESS DEVELOPMENT BOARD

Members: J. WILLIAM CADOTTE, WILLIE JOHNSON, JR., STEVEN C. LITTLE, KATHERINE MARKS, AARON OLVER, WINNIFRED THOMAS, CHARLES V. VANG (all appointed by governor).

Statutory References: Section 15.155 (3); Chapter 560, Subchapter VII.

Agency Responsibility: The Minority Business Development Board may award grants or loans to minority group members, minority businesses, or local development corporations for projects to plan a new business (early planning projects) or projects to start a new business or expand an existing business (development projects). Recipients must finance a portion of the project's cost from private funds. Department of Commerce rules governing the administration of the programs are subject to board review. Board members serve 2-year terms; the number and qualifications of members are not specified by law. The board was created by 1989 Wisconsin Act 31.

RURAL ECONOMIC DEVELOPMENT BOARD

Members: WILL HUGHES (designated by secretary of agriculture, trade and consumer protection), AARON OLVER (designated by secretary of commerce); SENATORS KAPANKE, vacancy; REPRESENTATIVES 2 vacancies; MICHAEL R. KRUTZA, RICHARD MARTIN, CONNIE SEEFELDT (other members). (All except *ex officio* members or designees are appointed by governor.)

Statutory References: Sections 15.155 (4) and 560.17.

Agency Responsibility: The 9-member Rural Economic Development Board awards grants or loans to rural businesses with fewer than 50 employees to assist in starting or expanding their operations. The board includes 4 legislative members who represent the majority and minority parties in each house and must be from rural districts. The 3 members appointed by the governor serve 3-year terms. Each of them must have experience operating a business located in a rural municipality, and at least one must have operated a cooperative. The board was created by 1989 Wisconsin Act 31.

SMALL BUSINESS REGULATORY REVIEW BOARD

Members: ANDREW MOYER (Department of Administration representative), CHERYL DANIELS (Department of Agriculture, Trade and Consumer Protection representative), vacancy (Department of Children and Families representative), ZACH BRANDON (Department of Commerce representative), PAT COOPER (Department of Health Services representative), AL SHEA (Department of Natural Resources representative), vacancy (Department of Regulation and Licensing representative), AMY BOMKAMP (Department of Revenue representative), HAL BERGAN (Department of Workforce Development representative), vacancy (senate small business committee chairperson), vacancy (assembly small business committee chairperson); RANDY MEFFERT, RICHARD PETERSHACK, BONNIE SCHWID, MINOO SEIFODDINI, KAREN VERNAL, GUY WOOD (appointed by governor).

Statutory References: Sections 15.07 (1)(b), 15.155 (5), 227.24 (3), and 227.30.

Agency Responsibility: The 17-member Small Business Regulatory Review Board may determine that a newly filed emergency rule would have a significant fiscal impact on small businesses, defined as ones that employ 25 or fewer full-time employees or have gross annual sales of less than $5 million. The board may further determine whether the issuing agency has complied with statutory provisions that seek to reduce the impact of rules on small businesses and whether the data used to propose a rule is accurate. If the board finds an agency has not complied with the law, it may request compliance from that agency, and, in addition, suggest changes to the proposed rule. The board may also review state agency rules and guidelines to determine whether they place an unnecessary burden on small businesses. If the board determines a rule or guideline does place an undue burden on small businesses, it submits a report and recommendations to the Joint Committee for Review of Administrative Rules.

The department secretaries appoint department representatives. The 6 members the governor appoints represent small business and serve 3-year terms. The senate majority leader and assembly speaker each appoint one chairperson from standing committees concerned with small business. The board was created by 2003 Wisconsin Act 145 and its membership was revised by 2007 Wisconsin Act 20.

Department of
CORRECTIONS

Secretary of Corrections: RICK RAEMISCH, 240-5055, rick.raemisch@

Deputy Secretary: AMY SMITH, 240-5055, amy.smith@

Executive Assistant: ISMAEL OZANNE, 240-5055, ismael.ozanne@

Office of Legal Counsel: KATHRYN ANDERSON, *chief,* 240-5049, kathryn.anderson@

Legislative Liaison: ROBERT MARGOLIES, 240-5056, robert.margolies@

Public Information Director: JOHN DIPKO, 240-5060, john.dipko@

Detention Facilities, Office of: MARTIN J. ORDINANS, *director,* 240-5052, martin.ordinans@; Milwaukee: (414) 227-5199.

Victim Services, Office of: COLLEEN JO WINSTON, *director,* 240-5888, colleen.winston@

Reentry Director: MARY KAY KOLLAT, 240-5015, marykay.kollat@; KRISTI DIETZ, *project manager,* 240-5010, kristi.dietz@

Mailing Address: P.O. Box 7925, Madison 53707-7925.

Location: 3099 East Washington Avenue, Madison 53704.

Telephone: 240-5000.

Fax: 240-3300.

Internet Address: www.wi-doc.com

Number of Employees: 10,394.87.

Total Budget 2007-09: $2,431,555,900.

Statutory References: Section 15.14; Chapter 301.

For e-mail: firstname.lastname@wisconsin.gov

Adult Institutions, Division of: WILLIAM GROSSHANS, *administrator,* 240-5100, william.grosshans@; DENISE SYMDON, *assistant administrator,* 240-5103, denise.symdon@; RICHARD SCHNEITER, *assistant administrator,* 240-5102, richard.schneiter@; DAN WESTFIELD, *security chief,* 240-5105, daniel.westfield@; Division Fax: 240-3310.

> *Correctional Enterprises, Bureau of:* TIM PETERSON, *director,* 240-5201, timothy.peterson@; Fax: 240-3320.

> *Health Services, Bureau of:* JAMES GREER, *director,* 240-5122, james.greer@; Fax: 240-3311.

> *Offender Classification and Movement, Bureau of:* MARK HEISE, *director,* 240-5800, mark.heise@; Fax: 240-3350.

> *Program Service, Bureau of:* JULIE WURL-KOTH, *director,* 240-5160, julianne.wurlkoth@; Fax: 340-3310.

> *Planning and Operations Unit:* JEFF WYDEVEN, *director,* 240-5180, jeffrey.wydeven@; Fax: 240-3310.

PRISONS

Maximum Security:

> *Columbia Correctional Institution:* GREG GRAMS, *warden,* P.O. Box 950, Portage 53901-0950, (608) 742-9100; Fax: (608) 742-9111.

> *Dodge Correctional Institution:* TIMOTHY LUNDQUIST, *warden,* P.O. Box 661, Waupun 53963-0661, (920) 324-5577; Fax: (920) 324-6297.

> *Green Bay Correctional Institution:* WILLIAM POLLARD, *warden,* P.O. Box 19033, Green Bay 54307-9033, (920) 432-4877; Fax: (920) 448-6545.

> *Waupun Correctional Institution:* MIKE THURMER, *warden,* P.O. Box 351, Waupun 53963-0351, (920) 324-5571; Fax: (920) 324-7250.

> *Wisconsin Secure Program Facility:* PETE HUIBREGTSE, *warden,* P.O. Box 1000, Boscobel 53805-0900, (608) 375-5656; Fax: (608) 375-5434.

Medium Security:

> *Fox Lake Correctional Institution:* JODINE DEPPISCH, *warden,* P.O. Box 147, Fox Lake 53933-0147, (920) 928-3151; Fax: (920) 928-6981.

> *Jackson Correctional Institution:* RANDY HEPP, *warden,* P.O. Box 232, Black River Falls 54615-0232, (715) 284-4550; Fax: (715) 284-7335.

DEPARTMENT OF CORRECTIONS

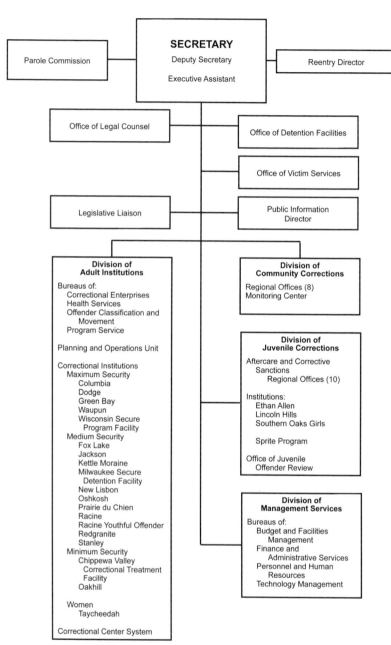

Units attached for administrative purposes under Sec. 15.03:   Interstate Adult Offender Supervision Board
Prison Industries Board
State Board for Interstate Juvenile Supervision

Kettle Moraine Correctional Institution: MICHAEL DITTMANN, *warden,* P.O. Box 31, Plymouth 53073-0031, (920) 526-3244; Fax: (920) 526-9320.

Milwaukee Secure Detention Facility: JOHN HUSZ, *warden,* 1015 North 10th Street, P.O. Box 05740, Milwaukee 53205-0740, (414) 212-3535; Fax: (414) 212-6811.

New Lisbon Correctional Institution: ANA BOATWRIGHT, *warden,* P.O. Box 2000, New Lisbon 53950-2000, (608) 562-6400; Fax (608) 562-6410.

Oshkosh Correctional Institution: JUDY SMITH, *warden,* P.O. Box 3530, Oshkosh 54903-3530, (920) 231-4010; Fax: (920) 236-2615/2626.

Prairie du Chien Correctional Facility: JOHN PAQUIN, *warden,* P.O. Box 6000, Prairie du Chien 53821, (608) 326-7828; Fax: (608) 326-5960.

Racine Correctional Institution: ROBERT HUMPHREYS, *warden,* 2019 Wisconsin Street, Sturtevant 53177-1829, (262) 886-3214; Fax: (262) 886-3514.

Racine Youthful Offender Correctional Institution: FLOYD MITCHELL, *warden,* P.O. Box 2200, Racine 53404-2713, (262) 638-1999; Fax: (262) 638-1777.

Redgranite Correctional Institution: LARRY L. JENKINS, *warden,* 1006 County Road EE, P.O. Box 900, Redgranite 54970-0925, (920) 566-2600; Fax: (920) 566-2610.

Stanley Correctional Institution: BRAD HOMPE, *warden,* 100 Corrections Drive, Stanley 54768-6500, (715) 644-2960; Fax (715) 644-2966.

Minimum Security:

Chippewa Valley Correctional Treatment Facility: PAMELA WALLACE, *warden,* 2909 East Park Avenue, Chippewa Falls 54729, (715) 720-2850; Fax (715) 720-2859.

Oakhill Correctional Institution: DEIRDRE MORGAN, *warden,* P.O. Box 140, Oregon 53575-0140, (608) 835-3101; Fax: (608) 835-9196.

Women:

Taycheedah Correctional Institution: CATHY A. JESS, *warden,* 751 County Road K, P.O. Box 1947, Fond du Lac 54936-1947, (920) 929-3800; Fax: (920) 929-2946.

CENTER SYSTEM

MICKEY McCASH, *warden, Wisconsin Correctional Center System,* 8500 Rainbow Road, Lake Tomahawk 54539-9588, (715) 277-2445; Fax: (715) 277-2293.

Black River Correctional Center: DAVID ANDRASKA, superintendent, W6898 East Staffon Road, Route #5, Black River Falls 54615-6426, (715) 333-5681; Fax: (715) 333-2708.

John C. Burke Correctional Center: CHRIS KRUEGER, *superintendent,* 900 South Madison Street, P.O. Box 900, Waupun 53963-0900, (920) 324-3460; Fax: (920) 324-4575.

Felmers Chaney Correctional Center: MICHAEL COCKROFT, *superintendent,* 2825 North 30th Street, Milwaukee 53210, (414) 874-1600; Fax: (414) 874-1695.

Drug Abuse Correctional Center: PATRICK MELMAN, *superintendent,* Kempster Hall/Winnebago Mental Health Institute, 1305 North Drive, P.O. Box 36, Winnebago 54985-0036, (920) 236-2700; Fax: (920) 426-5601.

Robert E. Ellsworth Correctional Center: SUZANNE SCHMITT, *superintendent,* 21425-A Spring Street, Union Grove 53182-9408, (262) 878-6000; Fax: (262) 878-6015.

Flambeau Correctional Center: JOHN CLARK, *superintendent,* N671 County Road M, Hawkins 54530-9400, (715) 585-6394; Fax: (715) 585-6563.

Gordon Correctional Center: TIM NELSON, *superintendent,* 10401 East County Road G, Gordon 54838, (715) 376-2680; Fax: (715) 376-4361.

Kenosha Correctional Center: ANN KRUEGER, *superintendent,* 6353 14th Avenue, Kenosha 53143, (262) 653-7099; Fax: (262) 653-7241.

McNaughton Correctional Center: MOLLY SULLIVAN OLSON, *superintendent,* 8500 Rainbow Road, Lake Tomahawk 54539-9558, (715) 277-2484; Fax: (715) 277-2293.

Milwaukee Women's Correctional Center: DEB CHAMBERS, *superintendent,* 615 West Keefe Avenue, Milwaukee 53212, (414) 267-6101; Fax: (414) 267-6130.

Oregon Correctional Center: JEFF PUGH, *superintendent,* 5140 Highway M, P.O. Box 25, Oregon 53575-0025, (608) 835-3233; Fax: (608) 835-3145.

Sanger B. Powers Correctional Center: JOHN A. RICHARDS, *superintendent,* N8375 County Line Road, Oneida 54155-9300, (920) 869-1095; Fax: (920) 869-2650.

St. Croix Correctional Center: JO SKALSKI, *superintendent,* 1859 North 4th Street, P.O. Box 36, New Richmond 54017-0036, (715) 246-6971; Fax: (715) 246-3680.

Marshall E. Sherrer Correctional Center: JEFF RADCLIFFE, *superintendent,* 1318 North 14th Street, Milwaukee 53205-2596, (414) 343-5000; Fax: (414) 343-5039.

Thompson Correctional Center: TROY HERMANS, *superintendent,* 434 State Farm Road, Deerfield 53531-9562, (608) 423-3415; Fax: (608) 423-9852.

Winnebago Correctional Center: SUSAN ROSS, *superintendent,* 4300 Sherman Road, P.O. Box 128, Winnebago 54985-0128, (920) 424-0402; Fax: (920) 424-0430.

Community Corrections, Division of: QUALA CHAMPAGNE, *administrator,* 240-5300; SHARON WILLIAMS, *assistant administrator, business and records;* Fax: 240-3330.

Region 1: ART THURMER, *chief,* 3099 East Washington Avenue, Madison 53704, 246-1960; Fax: 246-1900.

Region 2: LISA YEATES, *chief,* 9531 Rayne Road, Suite 2, Sturtevant 53177-1833, (262) 884-3780; Fax: (262) 884-3799.

Region 3: vacancy, *chief,* 4160 North Port Washington Road, Milwaukee 53212, (414) 229-0600; Fax: (414) 229-0584.

Region 4: ROSE SNYDER-SPAAR, *chief,* 1360 American Drive, Neenah 54956, (920) 751-4623; Fax: (920) 751-4601.

Region 5: GENA JARR, *chief,* 718 West Clairemont Avenue, Room 130, Eau Claire 54701-6143, (715) 836-5242; Fax: (715) 836-2331.

Region 6: ROBERT GRUSNICK, *chief,* 2187 North Stevens Street, Suite B, Rhinelander 54501-0497, (715) 365-2587; Fax: (715) 369-5255.

Region 7: SALLY TESS, *chief,* 141 Northwest Barstow Street, Room 126, Waukesha 53188-3756, (262) 521-5157; Fax: (262) 548-8697.

Region 8: RON KALMUS, *chief,* 427 East Tower Drive, Suite 200, Wautoma 54982-6927, (920) 787-5500; Fax: (920) 787-5589.

Monitoring Center: DOUGLAS MILSAP, *director,* 3309 East Washington Avenue, Madison 53704, 240-3948.

Juvenile Corrections, Division of: MARGARET CARPENTER, *administrator,* 240-5901, margaret.carpenter@; SILVIA JACKSON, *assistant administrator,* 240-5902, silvia.jackson@; 3099 East Washington Avenue, Madison 53704; Division Fax: 240-3370.

Aftercare and Corrective Sanctions:

Appleton: 2107 Spencer Street, Appleton 54914-4638, (920) 997-3870.

Eau Claire: 718 West Clairemont Avenue, Room 140, Eau Claire 54701-6143, (715) 836-6683.

Green Bay: 200 North Jefferson Street, Suite 134, Green Bay 54301, (920) 448-6548.

Madison: 2909 Landmark Place, Suite 104, Madison 53713, 288-3350.

Milwaukee: 4200 North Holton Street, Suite 120, Milwaukee 53212, (414) 229-0701.

Neenah: 1356 American Drive, Neenah 54956, (920) 729-3900.

Schofield: 1699 Schofield Avenue, Suite 120, Schofield 54476-1021, (715) 241-8890.

Sheboygan: 3422 Wilgus Avenue, Sheboygan 53081, (920) 456-6548.

Sparta: 820 Industrial Drive, Suite 6, Sparta 54656, (608) 269-1921.

Sturtevant: 9531 Rayne Road, Suite 3, Sturtevant 53177-1833, (262) 884-3748.

Institutions:

Ethan Allen School: KYLE K. DAVIDSON, *superintendent,* P.O. Box 900, Wales 53183-0900, (262) 646-3341; Fax: (262) 646-3761, kyle.davidson@

Lincoln Hills School: PAUL J. WESTERHAUS, *superintendent,* W4380 Copper Lake Road, Irma 54442-9720, (715) 536-8386; Fax (715) 536-8236, paul.westerhaus@

Southern Oaks Girls School: JANE DIER-ZIMMEL, *superintendent,* 21425B Spring Street, Union Grove 53182-9707, (262) 878-6500; Fax: (262) 878-6520, jane.dierzimmel@

Sprite Program: JOANN MERCURIO, *program director,* Highway M, Fire No. 4986, Oregon 53575, (608) 835-7131; Fax: (608) 835-2749.

Juvenile Offender Review, Office of: SHELLEY HAGAN, *director,* 240-5918; Fax: 240-3370, shelley.hagan@

Management Services, Division of: EARL FISCHER, *administrator,* 240-5400, earl.fischer@; STACEY ROLSTON, *assistant administrator,* 240-5470, stacey.rolston@; Division Fax: 240-3342.

Budget and Facilities Management, Bureau of: ROLAND COUEY, *director,* 240-5405, roland.couey@

Finance and Administrative Services, Bureau of: JERRY SALVO, *director,* 240-5420, jerry.salvo@

Personnel and Human Resources, Bureau of: JEAN NICHOLS, *director,* 240-5496, jean.nichols@

Technology Management, Bureau of: ANN SCHWARTZ, *director,* 240-5646, ann.schwartz@

Agency Responsibility: The Department of Corrections administers Wisconsin's state prisons, community correctional centers, and juvenile corrections programs. It supervises the custody and discipline of all prisoners in order to protect the public and seeks to rehabilitate offenders and reintegrate them into society. The department currently operates 19 correctional facilities and 16 community correctional centers for adults, and 3 facilities for juveniles. It also supervises prisoners on probation and parole; monitors compliance with deferred prosecution programs; and may make recommendations for pardons or commutations of sentence when requested by the governor. The department maintains a register of sex offenders who are required to report by law.

Organization: The department is headed by a secretary who is appointed by the governor with the advice and consent of the senate. The secretary appoints the division administrators from outside the classified service.

Unit Functions: The *Office of Detention Facilities,* in the office of the secretary, is responsible for the inspection and evaluation of all local detention facilities, including jails, houses of correction, secure juvenile detention centers, and municipal lockups. It provides technical assistance and training on various detention issues.

The *Division of Adult Institutions* supervises adult inmates in a variety of correctional settings. It assigns inmates to one of 6 security classifications, based on their records, backgrounds, and the risk they may pose to the public, correctional officers, and other inmates.

Security classifications include 2 levels each of maximum, medium, and minimum security. These levels determine how closely inmates are guarded, how restricted their movements are within the institution, and the programs in which they may participate. Although prisons are classified by the highest level of security for which the facility is built and administered, an individual facility may contain several security levels.

The prison program is designed to offer offenders opportunities to develop skills necessary to lead law-abiding lives upon release. Services include evaluation of an offender's background and needs and the provision of programs to meet those needs. Programs include academic and vocational education, alcohol and other drug abuse treatment, other clinical treatment, work, and religious observance. The division offers job training for inmates through Badger State Industries, which produces various items, including furniture, textiles and linens, license plates, and signs, and performs such services as printing, computer recycling, and wheelchair refurbishing.

The division also administers 16 minimum security correctional centers across the state. Center staff work closely with probation and parole agents to assist the transition of inmates back into the community. Center programming includes basic education, alcohol and drug counseling, work experience, and work release. The division operates the Milwaukee Secure Detention Facility, which confines offenders who have violated conditions of community supervision as well as those participating in alcohol and other drug abuse inpatient programs.

The *Division of Community Corrections* supervises persons released on parole or sentenced to probation or extended supervision. The supervision is community-based to strengthen family and community ties, encourage lawful behavior, and provide local treatment programs. Probation and parole agents hold offenders accountable for their behavior, provide direct services, and refer their clients to community service agencies. They also provide investigative services to the courts, the Division of Adult Institutions, and the Parole Commission to aid in sentencing, institutional programming, and parole planning. Under limited circumstances, agents supervise juveniles released to aftercare programs and persons conditionally released from mental health facilities.

The *Division of Juvenile Corrections,* created in Section 301.025, Wisconsin Statutes, by 1995 Wisconsin Act 27, administers programs to treat and rehabilitate delinquent youth and protect the public. It operates the state's juvenile corrections institutions and community corrections programs. Through its Juvenile Offender Review Program, the division determines whether offenders in the institutions are eligible for release, oversees the aftercare services of those who are released, and selects the participants for intensive surveillance under the Corrective Sanctions Program. The division also administers the Community Youth and Family Aids Program, which offers financial incentives to counties to divert juveniles from state institutions and into less restrictive community rehabilitation programs, and it awards grants to counties that participate in the Intensive Aftercare Program, which offers a wide range of social, educational, and employment assistance.

The *Division of Management Services* provides budgeting, data processing, personnel, and telecommunications services and oversees accounting, procurement, and facilities management.

The front yard of Waupun Correctional Institution, depicted prior to 1916. Waupun, the oldest prison in the state, was established in 1852. Besides the addition of administrative facilities and the removal of the central tower, the scene remains little changed since this photograph was taken. (Department of Corrections)

History: In Chapter 288, Laws of 1851, the legislature established a commission to locate and supervise the building and administration of a state prison. The commissioners chose Waupun as the site, and the facility was opened in 1852. Waupun housed both male and female offenders until 1933 when the Wisconsin Prison for Women opened in Taycheedah.

From 1853 to 1874 an elected state prison commissioner ran the prison. Beginning in 1874, the governor appointed three state prison commissioners to hire a warden and direct state prison operation. In 1881, prisons and other public welfare functions were placed under the supervision of the State Board of Supervision of Wisconsin Charitable, Reformatory and Penal Institutions, subsequently renamed the State Board of Control of the Wisconsin Reformatory, Charitable and Penal Institutions in 1891. Both adult and juvenile facilities came under the board's control.

By 1939, the Division of Corrections within the newly created Department of Public Welfare had assumed supervision of prisons, juvenile institutions, and parole and probation. Under the 1967 executive branch reorganization, the division became part of the Department of Health and Social Services. The division was reorganized as a separate Department of Corrections in 1989 Wisconsin Act 31, but responsibility for juvenile offenders remained with the Department of Health and Social Services until 1995 Wisconsin Act 27 transferred juvenile corrections and related services to the Department of Corrections.

Waupun was the state's only prison until 1898, when the Wisconsin State Reformatory for prisoners from 16 to 30 years-of-age opened at Green Bay. The age limitation was repealed in 1966 and the facility was renamed the Green Bay Correctional Institution in 1978. A separate facility for women, the Industrial Home for Women, began operations in Taycheedah in 1921. The Wisconsin Prison for Women at Taycheedah opened in 1933. Fox Lake Correctional Institution opened in 1962. Further expansion of the state prison system occurred when Kettle Moraine Boys School was converted to an adult institution in 1975, followed by the conversion of Oregon School for Girls to a minimum security prison (Oakhill) in 1977. The Dodge Correctional Institution, which serves as reception and evaluation center for all adult male felons sentenced by Wisconsin courts, opened in 1978. Rapid growth of the prison population led to the opening of the Columbia and the Oshkosh Correctional Institutions in 1986, the Racine Correctional Institution in 1991, the Jackson Correctional Institution in 1996, a super maximum security prison, located in Boscobel, in 1999, the Redgranite Correctional Institution in 2001, the Stanley Correctional Institution in 2003, and the New Lisbon Correctional Institution in 2004. The department opened a minimum security facility to serve the needs of inmates with alcohol and other drug abuse problems in Chippewa Falls in 2004.

While the capacity of Wisconsin prisons had grown considerably since 1986, the number of prisoners confined to adult institutions grew from just over 6,000 in 1989 to more than 15,000 in 1995. As a result, 1995 Wisconsin Act 344 authorized the department to contract with other states to house Wisconsin prisoners. 1997 Wisconsin Act 27 authorized housing state prisoners in private prisons in other states. By the end of 2002, out-of-state prisons housed more than 3,400 Wisconsin inmates. Near the end of 2004, fewer than 300 inmates were located out-of-state, due to new institutions, an increased number of beds at existing prisons, expanded contracting with county sheriffs to house inmates in county jails, and expanded noninstitutionalization options created in 2003 Wisconsin Act 33.

Wisconsin's first juvenile institution for boys opened in 1860 at Waukesha and was replaced by Kettle Moraine at Plymouth in 1963. A second facility, Wisconsin School for Boys, which was subsequently renamed the Ethan Allen School, opened at Wales in 1959. Lincoln Hills School for Boys began operations in 1970. (It was opened to girls in 1976 and the school was renamed.) The first juvenile institution for girls was established in 1875 in Milwaukee as a private agency that received state aid. The Wisconsin School for Girls, later renamed the Oregon School for Girls, opened in 1931 and closed in 1976. Girls were then sent to Lincoln Hills. In response to concerns about overcrowding at Lincoln Hills and the need for treatment programs for girls, the legislature authorized a separate facility, which opened as Southern Oaks Girls School at Union Grove in 1994. Another juvenile facility was opened in Prairie du Chien in 1997, but it has been converted into a medium security adult prison.

Probation and parole were unknown in the early years of statehood. Criminal sentences were for definite periods of time and to be fully served. Until 1860, executive pardons were the only means for early release. Chapter 324, Laws of 1860, established early releases for good behavior, known as "good time". Calculations of good time ended with the adoption of mandatory release dates for crimes committed after May 31, 1984. Parole was first enacted in 1889, but was apparently invalidated by the Wisconsin Supreme Court. New parole provisions were enacted in 1897 for the Green Bay Reformatory and for the Waupun State Prison in Chapter 110, Laws of 1907. That law allowed the State Board of Control to parole prisoners with the governor's approval, but the approval requirement was removed in 1947. The State Board of Control was also given supervisory responsibility for prisoners placed on probation in 1909. Currently, the Parole Commission, created in 1989, has final authority in granting discretionary paroles. Under 1997 Wisconsin Act 283, a person who is convicted of a felony committed on or after December 31, 1999, and sentenced to prison must serve a specified time in prison followed by a specified period of "extended supervision" in the community. Persons given this "bifurcated sentence" are not eligible for parole.

Statutory Commission

Parole Commission: ALFONSO J. GRAHAM (appointed by governor with senate consent), *chairperson;* JAYNE HACKBARTH, JAMES HART, DANIELLE LACOST, STEVEN LANDREMAN, DAVID WHITE, 2 vacancies (appointed by chairperson from classified service).

Address: 3099 East Washington Avenue, P.O. Box 7960, Madison 53707-7960.

Telephone: 240-7280.

Fax: 240-7299.

E-mail Address: parole.commission@wisconsin.gov

The 8-member Parole Commission is the final authority for granting discretionary paroles for prisoners who committed felonies before December 31, 1999. (Parole is not an option in the case of felonies committed on or after that date.) The commission conducts regularly scheduled interviews to consider the parole of inmates confined in a state correctional institution, a contracted facility, or a county house of corrections or inmates transferred to mental health institutions. The governor appoints the commission's chairperson for a 2-year term.

The commission's statutory predecessor, the Parole Board, was created by Chapter 221, Laws of 1979, to advise the secretary of health and social services, and its members were appointed by the secretary. The commission was created by 1989 Wisconsin Act 107. Its composition and duties are prescribed in Sections 15.145 (1) and 304.01 of the statutes.

INDEPENDENT UNITS ATTACHED FOR BUDGETING, PROGRAM COORDINATION, AND RELATED MANAGEMENT FUNCTIONS BY SECTION 15.03 OF THE STATUTES

INTERSTATE ADULT OFFENDER SUPERVISION BOARD

Members: WILLIAM RANKIN (compact administrator); TAMARA GRIGSBY (legislative branch representative); GREGORY J. POTTER (judicial branch representative); CHANDRA MILLER FIENEN (executive branch representative); ANN GUSTAFSON (victims' group representative). (All are appointed by governor).

Statutory References: Sections 15.145 (3) and 304.16 (4).

Agency Responsibility: The 5-member Interstate Adult Offender Supervision Board officially appoints the Wisconsin representative to the national commission. The board advises the department on its participation in the compact and on the operation of the compact within this state. The representatives serve 4-year terms while the compact administrator serves at the pleasure of the governor. It was created by 2001 Wisconsin Act 96.

PRISON INDUSTRIES BOARD

Members: DEBRA M. PICKETT, BILL HOLLEY, BILL G. SMITH (private business and industry representatives); LYLE A. BALISTRERI, JOSE CARILLO, vacancy (private labor organization representatives); COREY F. ODOM, JR. (Technical College System representative); RICK RAEMISCH (Department of Corrections representative); JIM LANGDON (Department of Administration representative). (All are appointed by governor.)

Statutory References: Sections 15.145 (2) and 303.015.

Agency Responsibility: The 9-member Prison Industries Board advises Prison Industries. It develops a plan for the manufacturing and marketing of prison industry products, the provision of prison industry services, and research and development activities. No prison industry may be established or permanently closed without board approval. The board reviews the department's budget request for Prison Industries and may make recommendations to the governor for changes. The board gives prior approval for Prison Industries purchases exceeding $250,000. Members are appointed for 4-year terms. It was created by 1983 Wisconsin Act 27.

STATE BOARD FOR INTERSTATE JUVENILE SUPERVISION

Members: vacancy (administrator of Interstate Compact for Juveniles); vacancy (deputy compact administrator or designee); vacancy (representative(s) of legislative branch); vacancy (representative(s) of judicial branch); vacancy (representative(s) of executive branch); vacancy (representative of victims groups) (all appointed by governor).

Statutory References: Sections 15.145 (4) and 938.999 (9).

Agency Responsibility: The members of the State Board for Interstate Juvenile Supervision are appointed by the governor for 3-year terms to advise and exercise oversight and advocacy concerning the state's participation in activities of the Interstate Compact for Juveniles and may exercise any other statutorily authorized duties including the development of policy concerning the operations and procedures of the compact within the state. The board consists of at least six members, as more than one member may be appointed to represent the legislative, judicial, and executive branches of the state. The board was created by 2005 Wisconsin Act 234.

EDUCATIONAL COMMUNICATIONS BOARD

Board Members: ROLF WEGENKE (private schools representative), *chairperson;* TONY EVERS (superintendent of public instruction), *vice chairperson;* SENATORS COGGS, OLSEN; REPRESENTATIVES NEWCOMER, SCHNEIDER; MICHAEL MORGAN (secretary of administration), KEVIN P. REILLY (president, UW System), DAN CLANCY (director, Technical College System), THOMAS J. BASTING, SR., EILEEN LITTIG (public members); JUNE ANDERSON (public schools representative), JUDITH CRAIN (appointed by UW System Board of Regents), ELLEN ROSEWALL (president, Wisconsin Public Radio Association), DIANE EVERSON (educational TV coverage area representative), ELLIS BROMBERG (appointed by Technical College System Board). (Public members and representatives of public and private schools are appointed by governor.)

Executive Director: GENE PURCELL, 264-9666, gpurcell@ecb.state.wi.us

Deputy Director: vacancy.

Education, Division of: LIN HANSON, *administrator,* 264-9688, Fax: 264-9622, lhanson@ecb.state.wi.us

Engineering Services, Division of: TERRENCE BAUN, *administrator,* 264-9746, Fax: 264-9664, tbaun@ecb.state.wi.us

Public Radio, Division of: PHIL CORRIVEAU, *director,* 821 University Avenue, Madison 53706, 263-4199, Fax: 263-9763, phil.corriveau@wpr.org

Public Television, Division of: JAMES STEINBACH, *director,* 821 University Avenue, Madison 53706, 263-1232, Fax: 263-9763, james.steinbach@wpt.org

Mailing Address: 3319 West Beltline Highway, Madison 53713-4296.

Telephone: (608) 264-9600.

Fax: (608) 264-9664.

Internet Address: www.ecb.org

Publications: Biennial report; Interconnect Newsletter; Parade of Programs (Instructional multimedia schedule for elementary/secondary schools); Television Program Guide; WPR Annual Report; WPT Annual Report; teachers' manuals and guides for instructional multimedia programs.

Number of Employees: 62.18.

Total Budget 2007-09: $35,952,100.

Statutory References: Section 15.57; Chapter 39, Subchapter I.

Agency Responsibility: The Educational Communications Board oversees the statewide public broadcasting system, its instructional telecommunications programming, and public service media for the cultural and educational needs of the state's citizens. The board plans, constructs, and operates the state's public radio and television networks, and it is the licensee for the state's 17 public radio stations and 5 public television stations. The board operates the Emergency Alert System, the Amber Alert System, National Weather Service Transmitters, a telecommunication operations center, satellite facilities, and an educational broadband system/ instructional television fixed service system (EBS/ITFS).

The board shares responsibility for public broadcasting with the University of Wisconsin Board of Regents. Programming is produced through UW facilities or acquired from national, regional, state, and local sources. The board also is affiliated with public television stations licensed to Milwaukee Area Technical College, television station WSDE in Duluth, and several public radio stations.

Educational services include selection, acquisition or production, implementation, and evaluation of instructional multimedia programming and accompanying materials (CD-ROMs, manuals, and software) in cooperation with teachers in public and private schools, the Cooperative Educational Service Agencies, the Department of Public Instruction, the Technical College System, and the UW System.

Organization: The board includes 16 members. Those appointed by the governor, the UW Board of Regents, and the Technical College System Board serve 4-year terms. Legislative members must represent the majority and minority party in each house. The board appoints an executive director from outside the classified service. Division administrators are appointed by the executive director and may be from outside the classified service.

Unit Functions: The *Division of Education* provides public service media, instructional multimedia programming along with field services, online assistance, and other instructional services for public and private PK-12 schools and higher education. It offers professional development opportunities for professional educators through the use of all technologies.

The *Division of Engineering Services* develops, operates, and maintains the statewide telecommunication systems used to receive and deliver instructional, educational, and cultural programming. It coordinates broadcasting of the Emergency Alert System, the National Weather Service, and the Amber Alert System.

The *Division of Public Radio* operates the statewide Wisconsin Public Radio service in partnership with the UW Board of Regents (through UW-Colleges and UW-Extension). Wisconsin Public Radio service includes three networks: 1) the News and Classical Music Network, 2) the Wisconsin Ideas Network, and 3) an HD-2 Classical Network – all of which offer national, regional, and local programming.

The *Division of Public Television* operates the statewide Wisconsin Public Television service in partnership with the UW Board of Regents (through UW-Colleges and UW-Extension). Daytime broadcast hours are devoted to children's and instructional programming and evening hours to cultural, informational, and entertainment programs. Wisconsin Public Television delivers national programming from the Public Broadcasting Service and focuses on producing local programs on topics of regional and state interest.

History: Wisconsin's history in educational broadcasting dates back to the oldest public radio station in the nation. The University of Wisconsin's research in "wireless" communication led to the beginning of scheduled radio broadcasting in 1917 on Station 9XM, which was renamed WHA-AM in 1922. Wisconsin made a commitment to statewide educational broadcasting in 1945. Chapter 570, Laws of 1945, created the State Radio Council to plan, produce, and transmit educational, cultural, and service programs over a statewide FM radio network. Over the next two decades, the council constructed and activated 10 radio transmitters. In Chapter 360, Laws of 1953, the council also assumed responsibility for research in educational television.

The 1967 executive branch reorganization renamed the council the Educational Broadcasting Board, created the Educational Broadcasting Division under its supervision, and attached the board and the division to the Coordinating Council for Higher Education. The name was changed to the Educational Communications Board in Chapter 276, Laws of 1969. With the demise of the Coordinating Council, the Educational Communications Board became an independent agency in Chapter 100, Laws of 1971. In 1971, the board began to extend educational television to the entire state, and it had constructed 5 UHF television stations by 1977. Signal translator facilities erected in the 1980s extended service to areas of the state beyond the reach of regular transmitters. Most recently, the Educational Communications Board has completed the statewide transition to digital broadcasting, in accordance with the FCC mandate to convert to the digital format. The board has worked cooperatively with the UW Board of Regents to enhance public broadcasting service for the state's citizens.

Department of
EMPLOYEE TRUST FUNDS

Employee Trust Funds Board: MARILYN WIGDAHL (Wisconsin Retirement Board member), *chairperson;* WAYNE KOESSL (Wisconsin Retirement Board member), *vice chairperson;* ROBERT M. NIENDORF (Teachers Retirement Board member), *secretary;* GARY E. SHERMAN (governor's designee on Group Insurance Board); JENNIFER DONNELLY (Director, Office of State Employment Relations); MICHAEL LANGYEL, WAYNE MCCAFFERY, DAN NERAD (Teachers Retirement Board members); DAVID JOHN, MARY VON RUDEN (Wisconsin Retirement Board members); ROSEMARY FINORA (appointed by governor to represent taxpayers), THERON FISHER (annuitant, elected by annuitants), KATHLEEN KREUL (Technical College or educational support personnel employee). (Board representatives are appointed by their respective boards; the annuitant member and the technical college or public school educational support employee are elected by the constituency groups.)

Secretary of Employee Trust Funds: DAVID A. STELLA, 266-0301, david.stella@

Deputy Secretary: BOB CONLIN, 261-7940, bob.conlin@

Executive Assistant: RHONDA L. DUNN, 266-9854, rhonda.dunn@

Deferred Compensation, Office of: SHELLEY SCHUELLER, *director,* 266-6661, shelley.schueller@

Internal Audit, Office of: JOHN VINCENT, *director,* 261-7942, john.vincent@

Insurance Services, Division of: THOMAS KORPADY, *administrator,* 266-0207, tom.korpady@; LISA ELLINGER, *deputy administrator,* 264-6627, lisa.ellinger@

Legislative Affairs, Communications and Quality Assurance, Office of: MATT STOHR, *director,* 266-3641, matthew.stohr@

Chief Information Officer: JOANNE CULLEN, 266-3960, joanne.cullen@

Legal Services, Office of: DAVID NISPEL, *general counsel,* 264-6936, david.nispel@

Management Services, Division of: PAM HENNING, *administrator,* 267-2929, pamela.henning@

Retirement Services, Division of: JEAN GILDING, *administrator,* 266-1210, jean.gilding@

Budget and Trust Finance, Office of: JON KRANZ, *director,* 267-0908, jon.kranz@

Address e-mail by combining the user ID and the state extender: userid**@etf.state.wi.us**

Mailing Address: P.O. Box 7931, Madison 53707-7931.

Location: 801 West Badger Road, Madison.

Waukesha Branch Office: 141 N.W. Barstow Street, Room 411, Waukesha 53186 (appointment required). To make an appointment: (877) 533-5020.

Telephones: Member services: (608) 266-3285 (Madison) or (877) 533-5020; Appointments (608) 266-5717; Telephone message center: (800) 991-5540; Self-service line: (877) 383-1888; Wisconsin Relay Service 7-1-1 or (800) 947-3529 (English) or (800) 833-7813 (Spanish).

Internet Address: http://etf.wi.gov (includes e-mail inquiry form).

Publications: *Comprehensive Annual Financial Report; Employer Bulletin; It's Your Benefit; Trust Fund News;* and various employer manuals and employee brochures on the Wisconsin

Retirement System, the group insurance plans, the deferred compensation program, and the employee reimbursement account program.

Number of Employees: 220.80.

Total Budget 2007-09: $54,683,100.

Statutory References: Sections 15.16 and Chapter 40.

Agency Responsibility: The Department of Employee Trust Funds administers various employee benefit programs, including the retirement, group insurance, disability, and deferred compensation programs and employee reimbursement and commuter benefits accounts. It serves all state employees and teachers and most municipal employees, with the notable exceptions of employees of the City and County of Milwaukee.

Organization: The 13-member Employee Trust Funds Board provides direction and supervision to the department and the Wisconsin Retirement System (WRS). Board membership includes 2 *ex officio* members and 11 members who are appointed or elected for 4-year terms to represent employers, employees, taxpayers, and annuitants. The member appointed by the governor to represent taxpayers must have specific professional experience and cannot be a WRS participant. The board approves all administrative rules; authorizes payment of all retirement annuities, except those for disability; and hears appeals of benefit determinations. It appoints the secretary from outside the classified service, and the secretary selects the deputy from outside the service. Division and office heads are appointed from within the classified service by the secretary.

Unit Functions: The *Division of Insurance Services* is responsible for policy development and implementation of health, life, disability, and long-term care insurance; accumulated sick leave conversion credit; and the employee reimbursement and commuter benefits accounts.

The *Division of Management Services* provides support services for human resources, payroll, information technology, facility management, capital budget and inventory, records management, document design, mail and supplies, word processing, library, and telecommunications.

The *Division of Retirement Services* develops and implements retirement policies and services for the members of the retirement system, including calculation and payment of retirement and related benefits. The division monitors and interprets related state and federal legislation.

History: The 1891 Legislature initiated pension coverage for local government employees when it required Milwaukee to create a pension fund for retired and disabled police and fire fighters in Chapter 287. Sixteen years later, the legislature extended pension coverage to protective service employees of smaller cities through Chapter 671, Laws of 1907. The 1909 Legislature authorized a pension system for City of Milwaukee teachers in Chapter 510; and Chapter 323, Laws of 1911, created a retirement system for those school districts throughout the rest of the state that wished to enroll their teachers. With enactment of Chapter 459, Laws of 1921, Wisconsin established a mandatory, joint contributory, statewide teachers' pension system, covering virtually all teachers in public schools (outside of Milwaukee), normal schools, and the University of Wisconsin.

The legislature first provided retirement plans for general municipal employees outside of Milwaukee in Chapter 175, Laws of 1943. In the same session, a retirement system was created for general employees by Chapter 176, Laws of 1943. Local fire and police pension funds were closed to new members by Chapter 206, Laws of 1947, and these employees have since been covered with the general employees. Chapter 60, Laws of 1951, created the Public Employees Social Security Fund, making Wisconsin the first state in the nation to permit some state and local government employees to be covered by Social Security.

Chapter 211, Laws of 1959, created group life and group health insurance programs for state employees, a group life insurance program for municipal employees, and the Group Insurance Board to monitor the administration of the programs. The 1967 executive branch reorganization created the Department of Employee Trust Funds to administer the various retirement funds, and the Group Insurance Board was attached to it.

Chapter 280, Laws of 1975, initiated the merger of the existing, separate retirement funds that covered all publicly employed teachers in the state and all state and local public employees, except employees of the City of Milwaukee and Milwaukee County who have their own systems.

The legislature transferred local police and fire pension funds to the overall general employee system in Chapter 182, Laws of 1977. The implementation of the merged Wisconsin Retirement System was completed, effective January 1, 1982, by Chapter 96, Laws of 1981.

Statutory Boards

Deferred Compensation Board: EDWARD D. MAIN, *chairperson;* JOHN NELSON, *vice chairperson;* MARTIN BEIL, *secretary;* MICHAEL DRURY, GAIL HANSON (appointed by governor with senate consent).

The 5-member Deferred Compensation Board establishes rules for offering deferred compensation plans to state and local employees and contracts with deferred compensation plan providers. Its members are appointed for 4-year terms. The board was created by 1989 Wisconsin Act 31, and its composition and duties are prescribed in Sections 15.165 (4) and 40.80 of the statutes.

Group Insurance Board: CINDY O'DONNELL (designated by attorney general), *chairperson;* EILEEN MALLOW (designated by commissioner of insurance), *vice chairperson;* ESTHER M. OLSON (WRS-insured teacher participant), *secretary;* GARY SHERMAN (designated by governor); DAVID SCHMIEDICKE (designated by secretary of administration); JENNIFER DONNELLY (Director of the Office of State Employment Relations); MARTIN BEIL (WRS-insured nonteacher participant); JANIS DOLESCHAL (retired WRS-insured participant); ROBERT BAIRD (WRS-insured local government participant); vacancy (chief executive or member of local government participating in WRS); vacancy (public member). (All except *ex officio* members are appointed by governor.)

The 11-member Group Insurance Board oversees the group health, life, income continuation, and other insurance programs offered to state employees, covered local employees, and retirees. The board's 5 appointed members serve 2-year terms. The board was created by Chapter 211, Laws of 1959, and its composition and duties are prescribed in Sections 15.165 (2) and 40.03 (6) of the statutes.

Private Employer Health Care Coverage Board: Inactive.

The 13-member Private Employer Health Care Coverage Board was created by 1999 Wisconsin Act 9 to oversee the Private Employer Health Care Purchasing Alliance Program. Its composition and duties are prescribed in Sections 15.07 (1) (b) 22. and 15.165 (5). The board is scheduled to sunset on January 1, 2010.

Teachers Retirement Board: LON L. MISHLER (teacher annuitant), *chairperson;* MICHAEL LANGYEL (Milwaukee teacher), *vice chairperson;* ROBIN STARCK (public school teacher), *secretary;* BETSY M. KIPPERS, MARY JO MEIER, PATRICK PHAIR, STEVEN SCHEIBLE, DAVID WILTGEN (public school teachers); R. THOMAS PEDERSEN (technical college teacher); DAN NERAD (public school administrator appointed by governor); SANDRA CLAFLIN-CHALTON, SUSAN HARRISON (UW System teacher representatives appointed by governor); ROBERTA RASMUS (school board member appointed by governor). (Members not appointed by governor are elected by their constituent groups.)

The 13-member Teachers Retirement Board advises the Employee Trust Funds Board about retirement matters related to teachers, recommends and approves or rejects administrative rules, authorizes payment of disability annuities for teachers, and hears appeals of staff determinations of disability. Board members serve staggered 5-year terms; the 2 UW System representatives may not be from the same campus. The board was created by Chapter 204, Laws of 1953, and its composition and duties are prescribed in Sections 15.165 (3) (a) and 40.03 (7) of the statutes.

Wisconsin Retirement Board: MARILYN J. WIGDAHL (participating state employee), *chairperson;* WAYNE E. KOESSL (county or town governing body member), *vice chairperson;* MARY VON RUDEN (participating employee of local employer other than city or village), *secretary;* DAVID JOHN (city or village chief executive or governing board member); HERBERT STINSKI (participating city or village finance officer); MICHAEL WOODZICKA (participating city or village employee); JAMIE AULIK (county clerk or deputy); vacancy (nonparticipant representing taxpayers); SEAN DILWEG (commissioner of insurance). (All, except insurance commissioner or designee, are appointed by governor.)

The 9-member Wisconsin Retirement Board advises the Employee Trust Funds Board about retirement matters related to state and local general and protective employees and performs the same functions for these employees as the Teachers Retirement Board does for teachers. The board's appointed members serve staggered 5-year terms, and the municipal official and county board member are nominated by their respective statewide associations. The board was created by Chapter 96, Laws of 1981, and its composition and duties are prescribed in Sections 15.165 (3) (b) and 40.03 (8) of the statutes.

EMPLOYMENT RELATIONS COMMISSION

Commissioners: JUDITH M. NEUMANN, *chairperson,* 266-0166, judy.neumann@; PAUL GORDON, paul.gordon@; SUSAN J.M. BAUMAN, susan.bauman@ (appointed by governor with senate consent).

General Counsel: PETER G. DAVIS, 266-2993, peter.davis@

Team Leaders: MARSHALL L. GRATZ, (414) 963-4695, marshall.gratz@; WILLIAM C. HOULIHAN, 266-0147, william.houlihan@; GEORGANN KRAMER, 266-9287, georgann.kramer@

Mailing Address: P.O. Box 7870, Madison 53707-7870.

Location: 1457 East Washington Avenue, Suite 101, Madison.

Telephone: (608) 266-1381.

Fax: (608) 266-6930.

Agency E-mail Address: werc@werc.state.wi.us

Address e-mail by combining the user ID and the state extender: userid@**wisconsin.gov**

Internet Address: http://werc.wi.gov

Publications: Biennial reports; complaint procedures manual; agency decisions.

Number of Employees: 24.00.

Total Budget 2007-09: $6,331,300.

Statutory References: Sections 15.58, 230.44, and 230.45; Chapter 111.

Agency Responsibility: The Employment Relations Commission promotes collective bargaining and peaceful labor relations in the private and public sectors. It processes various types of labor relations cases, including elections, bargaining unit clarifications, union security referenda, mediations, interest arbitrations, grievance arbitrations, prohibited or unfair labor practices, and declaratory rulings. The commission also issues decisions arising from state employee civil service appeals, including appeals relating to certain classification, examination, and appointment issues, disciplinary actions, hazardous employment injury benefits, and noncontractual grievances. The commission's decisions are subject to review in state court. In addition to mediating labor disputes, the commission provides training and assistance to parties interested in labor/management cooperation and a consensus approach to resolving labor relations issues.

Organization: The 3 full-time commissioners are chosen for staggered 6-year terms, and the governor designates one commissioner to serve as chairperson for a 2-year term. The chairperson functions as the agency administrator and is assisted by supervisors who head teams of attorney/mediators and their support staff. The general counsel reviews all complaint appeals and declaratory ruling records; prepares draft decisions for commission consideration; and serves as liaison to the legislature and to the attorney general, who represents the commission in court.

History: Chapter 51, Laws of 1937, created the Wisconsin Labor Relations Board as an independent agency in the executive branch. Chapter 57, Laws of 1939, replaced the board with the Employment Relations Board and amended state laws governing labor relations. The 1967 Legislature renamed the board the Employment Relations Commission and continued it as an independent agency.

Over the years, the legislature has expanded the rights of public employees and the duties of the commission in the area of public employment labor relations. Chapter 509, Laws of 1959, authorized municipal employees to organize and be represented by labor organizations in negotiating wages, hours, and conditions of employment. Chapter 124, Laws of 1971, gave municipal employees the right to bargain collectively and made a municipal employer's refusal to bargain a prohibited practice. Chapters 246 and 247, Laws of 1971, established compulsory interest arbitration for police and firefighters in Milwaukee and other municipalities. Chapter 270, Laws of 1971, gave state employees the right to bargain collectively. 2003 Wisconsin Act 33 abolished the Personnel Commission and transferred to the Employment Relations Commission responsibility for various appeals related to state employment.

Department of
FINANCIAL INSTITUTIONS

Secretary of Financial Institutions: LORRIE KEATING HEINEMANN, 264-7800, lorrie.heinemann@; Fax: 261-4334.

Deputy Secretary: JOHN COLLINS, 264-7800, john.collins@

Executive Assistant: CATHERINE HABERLAND, 267-1719, catherine.haberland@

Financial Literacy, Office of: DAVID D. MANCL, *director,* 261-9540, david.mancl@; Fax: 261-4334.

General Counsel: CHRISTOPHER GREEN, 266-7968, chris.green@; Fax: 261-4334.

Mailing Address: P.O. Box 8861, Madison 53708-8861.

Location: 345 West Washington Avenue, 5th Floor, Madison.

Telephones: 261-9555; TDY: 266-8818.

Fax: 261-4334.

Internet Address: www.wdfi.org

Number of Employees: 119.24.

Total Budget 2007-09: $30,280,000.

Address e-mail by combining the user ID and the state extender: userid@**wisconsin.gov**

Statutory References: Sections 15.18 and 182.01; Chapters 224, Subchapter II, and 421-427.

Administrative Services and Technology, Division of: WILLIAM J. MORRISSEY, *administrator,* 267-1707, william.morrissey@; P.O. Box 7876, Madison 53707-7876; Division Fax: 261-7200.

    Budget and Fiscal Services, Bureau of: SUSAN J. DIETZEL, *director,* 267-0399, susan.dietzel@

    Information Technology, Bureau of: JOHN AMUNDSON, *director,* 267-1714, john.amundson@

Banking, Division of: MICHAEL MACH, *administrator,* 266-0451, mike.mach@; P.O. Box 7876, Madison 53707-7876; Division Fax: 267-6889.

    Licensed Financial Services Bureau: JEAN PLALE, *director,* 266-0447, jean.plale@

    Mortgage Banking Bureau: JEAN PLALE, *director,* 266-0447, jean.plale@

Corporate and Consumer Services, Division of: CHERYLL A. OLSON-COLLINS, *administrator,* 266-6810, cheryll.olsoncollins@; P.O. Box 7846, Madison 53707-7846; Division Fax: 267-6813.

    Consumer Affairs, Bureau of: PAUL EGIDE, *director,* 267-3518, paul.egide@; Consumer Act inquiries: 264-7969, (800) 452-3328 in Wisconsin; P.O. Box 8041, Madison 53708-8041.

    Video Franchising: RAY ALLEN, *deputy division administrator,* 264-7950, ray.allen@; P.O. Box 8041, Madison 53707-8041.

Securities, Division of: PATRICIA D. STRUCK, *administrator,* 266-3432, patricia.struck@; P.O. Box 1768, Madison 53701-1768; Division Fax: 256-1259.

    Legal Counsel: RANDALL E. SCHUMANN, 266-3414, randall.schumann@

    Licensing and Compliance, Bureau of: KENNETH L. HOJNACKI, *director,* 266-7824, kenneth.hojnacki@

DEPARTMENT OF FINANCIAL INSTITUTIONS

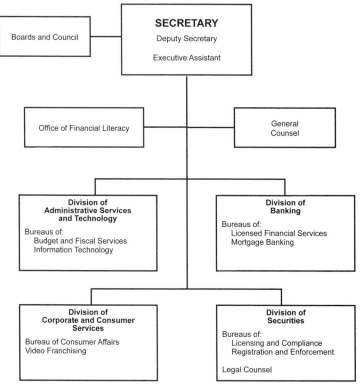

	SECRETARY
Boards and Council	Deputy Secretary
	Executive Assistant

Office of Financial Literacy

General Counsel

Division of Administrative Services and Technology
Bureaus of:
Budget and Fiscal Services
Information Technology

Division of Banking
Bureaus of:
Licensed Financial Services
Mortgage Banking

Division of Corporate and Consumer Services
Bureau of Consumer Affairs
Video Franchising

Division of Securities
Bureaus of:
Licensing and Compliance
Registration and Enforcement

Legal Counsel

Unit attached for administrative purposes under Sec. 15.03: Office of Credit Unions

Registration and Enforcement, Bureau of: LESLIE VAN BUSKIRK, *supervising attorney,* 266-1603, leslie.vanbuskirk@

Publications: Annual Report; Annual Report on Condition of Wisconsin Banks; Annual Report on Condition of Wisconsin Savings and Loan Associations and Savings Banks; Quarterly Report on Condition of Wisconsin Banks; Securities Bulletin; credit and consumer protection information; industry bulletins, newsletters, and forms. (All publications are available only online.)

Agency Responsibility: The Department of Financial Institutions regulates state-chartered banks, savings and loans associations, and savings banks, as well as various operations of the securities industry. It examines and files charters and other documents of businesses and organizations and registers and regulates the mortgage banking industry and other financial service providers. It oversees Uniform Commercial Code filings. It also administers the Wisconsin Consumer Act and registers merchants who extend credit. The department is self-supporting through program revenue derived from fees and assessments paid by regulated entities and individuals.

Organization: The department is administered by a secretary, who is appointed by the governor with the advice and consent of the senate. The secretary appoints the administrators for 3 of the 4 divisions from outside the classified service and the administrator of the Division of Administrative Services and Technology from the classified service.

Unit Functions: The *Office of Financial Literacy* (OFL), in the office of the secretary, promotes financial literacy to the public as a vital life skill. It emphasizes financial and economic literacy for Wisconsin's youth. The OFL works closely with the Governor's Council on Financial Literacy (GCFL) in a statewide effort to improve the financial literacy of students, employees, and families, with special attention to fraud prevention and encouraging the "unbanked" to take advantage of the important services offered by financial institutions. The OFL takes the lead role in producing the GCFL's Money Smart Week Wisconsin (MSWW) campaign in conjunction with the Federal Reserve Bank of Chicago. MSWW is the nation's first ever financial literacy campaign to focus on an entire state. The OFL also has a lead role in the National Institute of Financial and Economic Literacy, a nationally recognized, graduate-level, teacher-training program consisting of three week-long programs each summer. It has been designated "a best practice for teacher training" by the U.S. Department of the Treasury.

The *Division of Administrative Services and Technology* provides support services to the department through its administration of the agency's budget, personnel, procurement, and information technology services.

The *Division of Banking,* created in Section 15.183 (1), Wisconsin Statutes, by 1995 Wisconsin Act 27, is advised by the Banking Review Board. It regulates and supervises state-chartered banks and consumer financial service industries under statutory Chapters 220 through 224. In addition to chartering and regularly examining state banks, the division licenses loan companies, mortgage bankers, mortgage brokers, loan originators, collection agencies, community currency exchanges, sales finance companies, adjustment service companies, sellers of checks, insurance premium finance companies, and credit services organizations. It also regulates auto dealers' installment sales contracts. The division investigates applications for expanded banking powers, new financial products, and interstate bank acquisitions and mergers. It may conduct joint examinations with Federal Reserve System examiners and with the Federal Deposit Insurance Corporation. With Banking Review Board approval, the administrator may establish uniform rules for savings programs and fiduciary operations.

The division supervises state-chartered savings and loan associations and savings banks and enforces the laws governing them under statutory Chapters 214 and 215 with the advice of the Savings Institutions Review Board. It works to resolve consumer complaints and reviews and approves applications for acquisitions, new branches and other offices, and the organization of mutual holding companies. It may rule on interstate mergers or acquisitions. It also conducts joint examinations of associations with the federal Office of Thrift Institutions and may examine savings banks with the Federal Deposit Insurance Corporation.

The *Division of Corporate and Consumer Services* is responsible for examining and filing business records for corporations and other organizations. It examines charters, documents that affect mergers, consolidations, and dissolutions, and reviews the annual reports of various businesses, including partnerships, corporations, limited liability companies, cooperatives, and foreign corporations. It also examines and files documents under the Uniform Commercial Code, including statements of business indebtedness, consignments, terminations, and financing statements and maintains the statewide Uniform Commercial Code lien system. The division prepares certified copies of the records in its custody and responds to inquiries about corporations and other business entities and organizations for which it has records.

The division administers the Wisconsin Consumer Act, which resolves consumer complaints and advises consumers and lenders regarding their rights and responsibilities under consumer law. The division also is responsible for the issuance of state video franchise authority certificates.

The *Division of Securities,* created in Section 15.183 (3), Wisconsin Statutes, by 1995 Wisconsin Act 27, regulates the sale of investment securities and franchises under statutory Chapters 551, 552, and 553. It examines and registers the offerings and may bar them from registration in this state. The division licenses and monitors the activities of broker-dealers, securities agents, investment advisers, and investment adviser representatives. It conducts field audits and investigates complaints. When violations are detected, it initiates the appropriate administrative, injunctive, or criminal action. The division also regulates corporate takeovers.

History: The Department of Financial Institutions (DFI) was created in 1995 Wisconsin Act 27. The act reorganized formerly independent offices of the commissioners of banking, savings and loan, and securities as divisions and transferred them to the department. In addition, Act 27 transferred the responsibility for business organization filings and the Uniform Commercial Code lien information filings to the department from the Office of the Secretary of State. The same act transferred the regulation of mortgage bankers and loan originators and solicitors to the department from the Department of Regulation and Licensing. 2007 Wisconsin Act 42 replaced cable television franchises granted by municipalities with statewide video service franchises granted by DFI.

Banking. For the first five years of statehood, no regular commercial banks existed in Wisconsin. Prior to amendment in 1902, Article XI of the Wisconsin Constitution required that any banking law must be approved in a statewide referendum. Bank regulation began when the legislature created the Office of Bank Comptroller in Chapter 479, Laws of 1852, and the voters approved the law in 1853. That law allowed any group meeting state requirements to go into the banking business. It was designed primarily to regulate the issuance of bank notes. Bank supervision was transferred to the state treasurer in 1868 and remained with that office until 1903.

The 1902 constitutional amendment gave the legislature the power to enact general banking laws without a referendum. In Chapter 234, Laws of 1903, the legislature created the State Banking Department. The department also supervised savings and loan associations until 1947 and credit unions until 1972. Under the 1967 executive branch reorganization, the department continued as an independent agency and was renamed the Office of the Commissioner of Banking. 1995 Wisconsin Act 27 reorganized the agency as the Division of Banking and transferred it to the Department of Financial Institutions.

Savings Institutions. Attempts to register and examine savings and loan associations date back to the 1850s in Wisconsin, but there are no records of any associations incorporating under these laws. In 1876, the legislature passed Chapter 384 to require that savings banks and savings societies register with the county registers of deeds and the secretary of state. Voters approved the law in November 1876. Several associations incorporated shortly afterward. Beginning with Chapter 368, Laws of 1897, building and loan associations were regulated by the bank examiner in the state treasurer's office.

In 1903, responsibility for regulating savings and loan associations was transferred to the State Banking Department. Chapter 411, Laws of 1947, moved regulation from that department to the newly created Savings and Loan Association Department. The law also created the forerunner of the current Savings Institutions Review Board. In 1967, the executive branch reorganization act renamed the department the Office of the Commissioner of Savings and Loan. In 1991 Wisconsin Act 221, the office assumed responsibility for chartering, regulating, and examining savings banks. The same law created the Savings Bank Review Board. 1995 Wisconsin Act 27 reorganized the agency as the Division of Savings and Loan and transferred it to the Department of Financial Institutions. It was renamed the Division of Savings Institutions in 1999 and repealed in 2003 Wisconsin Act 33. Its duties were transferred to the Division of Banking.

Securities. Laws enacted by states to protect the public against securities fraud are commonly referred to as "blue sky" laws. (The term "blue sky" is believed to have originated when a judge ruled that a particular stock had about the same value as a patch of blue sky.) Wisconsin's first "blue sky" law was Chapter 756, Laws of 1913. This law was revised successively in 1919, 1933, 1941, and 1969. The current Wisconsin Uniform Securities Law was enacted as Chapter 71, Laws of 1969, and it is based upon the model Uniform Securities Act, which has been adopted in most states. From 1913 until 1939, the regulation of securities came under the jurisdiction first of the Railroad Commission (and its successor the Public Service Commission) and later the State Banking Department. The Department of Securities was created by Chapter 68, Laws of 1939, to regulate the sale of stocks, bonds, and other forms of business ownership or debt. It was renamed the Office of the Commissioner of Securities by Chapter 75, Laws of 1967. 1995 Wisconsin Act 27, reorganized the agency as the Division of Securities and transferred it to the Department of Financial Institutions.

Statutory Boards and Council

Banking Review Board: RALPH J. TENUTA, *chairperson;* DOUGLAS L. FARMER, DEBRA R. LINS, AMELIA E. MACARENO, THOMAS E. SPITZ (appointed by governor with senate consent).

The 5-member Banking Review Board advises the Division of Banking regarding the banking industry in Wisconsin and reviews the division's administrative actions. Members are appointed for staggered 5-year terms, and at least 3 of them must each have at least 5 years' banking experience. No member may act in any matter involving a bank of which the member is an officer, director, or stockholder or to which that person is indebted. The board was created by Chapter 10, Laws of Special Session 1931-32, under the State Banking Department (renamed the Office of the Commissioner of Banking in 1967), and transferred to the Department of Financial Institutions by 1995 Wisconsin Act 27. Its composition and duties are prescribed in Sections 15.185 (1) and 220.035 of the statutes.

Mortgage Loan Originator Council: BRIAN FAUST, STEVE JACOBSON, RICHARD PARINS, vacancy (loan originators); DIRK TODD (mortgage broker agent); MARIE JONES (mortgage banker agent) (all appointed by secretary of financial institutions); CATHERINE HABERLAND (designated by secretary of financial institutions).

The 7-member Mortgage Loan Originator Council approves examination standards in the law of mortgage banking and brokering proposed by the Division of Banking for applicants who either register or renew a certificate of registration as loan originators and loan solicitors. The council also approves the standards of curriculum for required course work taken by loan originators and loan solicitors that covers primary and subordinate mortgage finance transactions. The appointed members serve 4-year terms. The council was created in 2003 Wisconsin Act 260 as the Loan Originator Review Council. 2009 Wisconsin Act 2 changed the council's name to the Mortgage Loan Originator Council and changed its membership. Its composition and duties are prescribed in Sections 15.187 (1), 224.72 (3) (b), (7) (d), and 224.79 of the statutes.

Savings Institutions Review Board: PAUL C. ADAMSKI, GEORGE E. GARY, ROBERT W. HOLMES, JAMES K. OLSON, vacancy (appointed by governor with senate consent).

The 5-member Savings Institutions Review Board advises the Division of Banking on matters impacting savings and loan associations and savings banks in Wisconsin. It reviews division orders and determinations, hears appeals on certain actions taken by the division, and may act on any matter submitted by the division. Members serve 5-year terms. At least 3 of them must each have a minimum of 5 years' experience in the savings and loan or savings bank business in this state. Chapter 441, Laws of 1974, created the board as the Savings and Loan Review Board in the Savings and Loan Association Department (renamed the Office of the Commissioner of Savings and Loan in 1967) and 1995 Wisconsin Act 27 transferred it to the Department of Financial Institutions. In 2003, Act 33 renamed the board and eliminated the Savings Bank Review Board. Its composition and duties are prescribed in Sections 15.185 (3) and 215.04 of the statutes.

INDEPENDENT UNIT ATTACHED FOR BUDGETING, PROGRAM COORDINATION, AND RELATED MANAGEMENT FUNCTIONS BY SECTION 15.03 OF THE STATUTES

OFFICE OF CREDIT UNIONS

Director: SUZANNE COWAN, 267-2609, Fax: 267-0479.

Mailing Address: P.O. Box 14137, Madison 53708-0137.

Location: 345 West Washington Avenue, 3rd Floor, Madison.

Telephone: 261-9543.

Fax: 267-0479.

Internet Address: www.wdfi.org

Publications: Quarterly Credit Union Bulletin.

Number of Employees: 19.80.

Total Budget 2007-09: $3,859,800.

Statutory References: Section 15.185 (7) (a); Chapter 186.

Agency Responsibility: The Office of Credit Unions regulates credit unions chartered to do business in Wisconsin. It charters new credit unions, examines credit union records and assets, consents to consolidation of credit unions within the state and, in cooperation with similar agencies in neighboring states, approves interstate mergers. If a credit union is not in compliance with state law, the office may remove its officers, suspend operations, or take possession of the credit union's business. The director is appointed by the governor and must have at least 3 years' experience either in the operation of a credit union or in a credit union supervisory agency or a combination of both. All personnel and budget requests by the office must be processed and forwarded without change by the department, unless the office requests or concurs in a change.

History: Regulation of credit unions began in 1913 (Chapter 733) when the legislature passed a law that required "cooperative credit associations" to obtain their charters from the State Banking Department. That law was repealed by Chapter 334, Laws of 1923, which required the department to charter and regulate "credit unions". The Office of the Commissioner of Credit Unions was created in Chapter 193, Laws of 1971, as a separate agency by removing the credit union division and its advisory board from the Office of the Commissioner of Banking and giving it expanded powers. 1995 Wisconsin Act 27 created the Office of Credit Unions and attached it to the Department of Financial Institutions under Section 15.03, Wisconsin Statutes.

Statutory Board

Credit Union Review Board: Carla Altepeter, Quirin Braam, Dennis Degenhardt, Lisa Greco, Gregory Lentz (appointed by governor with senate consent).

The 5-member Credit Union Review Board advises the Office of Credit Unions regarding credit unions in Wisconsin. It reviews rules and regulations issued by the office, acts as an appeals board for persons aggrieved by any act of the office, and may require the office to submit its actions for approval. Members serve staggered 5-year terms and each must have at least 5 years' experience in credit union operations. The board was created within the State Banking Department by Chapter 411, Laws of 1947, then transferred to the Office of the Commissioner of Credit Unions in 1971, and later made part of the Office of Credit Unions in 1995 Wisconsin Act 27. Its composition and duties are prescribed in Sections 15.185 (7) (b) and 186.015 of the statutes.

GOVERNMENT ACCOUNTABILITY BOARD

Members: Michael Brennan, *chairperson;* William Eich, *vice chairperson;* Gerald Nichol, *secretary;* Thomas Cane, Thomas Barland*, Gordon Myse. (All members are former judges appointed to staggered terms by the governor, and confirmed by two-thirds vote of the senate.) (*Thomas Barland was appointed to succeed Victor Manian on May 20, 2009, pending senate confirmation.)

Director and General Counsel: KEVIN J. KENNEDY, 266-8005, kevin.kennedy@

Address e-mail by combining the user ID and the state extender: userid@**wisconsin.gov**

Mailing Address: P.O. Box 7984, Madison 53707-7984.

Location: 212 East Washington Avenue, Third Floor, Madison.

Telephones: Elections: 266-8005; Campaign Finance, Ethics, and Lobbying: 266-8005.

Fax: 267-0500.

E-Mail Address: gab@wi.gov

Internet Address: http://gab.wi.gov

Elections Division: Nathaniel E. Robinson, *administrator,* 267-0715, nathaniel.robinson@

Ethics and Accountability Division: Jonathan Becker, *administrator,* 266-8123, jonathan.becker@

Number of Employees: 17.75.

Total Budget 2007-09: $10,543,100.

Statutory References: Chapters 5-12, Subchapter III of Chapter 13, and Subchapter III of Chapter 19.

Agency Responsibility: The Government Accountability Board (GAB) administers the state's campaign finance, elections, ethics, and lobby laws, investigates alleged violations of those laws, and brings civil actions to collect forfeitures. It may subpoena records and notify the district attorney or attorney general of any grounds for civil or criminal prosecution. The GAB issues advisory opinions to officials, local governments, and others asking about their own conduct; promulgates administrative rules; and conducts training for local election officials, campaign and lobby registrants, and state public officials.

The GAB administers the campaign finance registration and reporting system which limits and requires full disclosure of contributions and disbursements made on behalf of every candidate for public office. The statutes specify which candidates, individuals, political parties, and groups must register and file detailed financial statements. Registration and reporting are required for nonresident committees that make contributions and for all individuals who make independent disbursements. The GAB administers the electronic filing of campaign finance reports of all registrants that receive contributions in excess of $20,000 in a campaign period for candidate committees or in excess of $20,000 in a biennium for other registrants.

The GAB also administers the Wisconsin Election Campaign Fund, created by Chapter 207, Laws of 1977, to provide publicly funded grants to eligible candidates for statewide and legislative office. Candidates who apply for the grants must, with some exceptions, agree to abide by spending limits. Funding for the grants is provided through a $1 checkoff on the state income tax form that does not affect the taxpayer's liability.

The GAB administers the state elections code along with implementing the federal Help America Vote Act of 2002 that establishes certain election requirements regarding the conduct of federal elections in the state. The director and general counsel serves as the chief state election official. The GAB is responsible for the design and maintenance of the Statewide Voter Registration System (SVRS) which is required to be used by all municipalities in the state to administer federal, state, and local elections.

The GAB also has compliance review authority over local election officials' actions relating to ballot preparation, candidate nomination, voter qualifications, recall, conduct of elections, and election administration. The GAB holds information and training meetings with local election officials to promote uniform election procedures. The GAB is responsible for the training and certification of all municipal clerks and chief election inspectors in the state.

The GAB administers the Code of Ethics for State Public Officials and Wisconsin's lobbying law. The intent of the ethics code is to forbid a state official from using a public position to obtain anything of value for the personal benefit of the official, the official's family, or the official's private business. Wisconsin's lobbying law prohibits lobbyists and the organizations that employ them from furnishing anything of value to a state official or employee except in a limited number of well-defined circumstances. The GAB collects and makes available information about the financial interests of state officials, candidates, and nominees; and compiles and disseminates on its Web sites information about organizations' efforts to influence legislation and administrative rules as well as the time and money spent by those organizations in lobbying activities.

Organization: The 6 members of the board, each of whom must have formerly been elected to and served as a judge of a court of record in Wisconsin, are appointed to 6-year terms by the governor from nominations submitted by a nominating committee called the Governmental Accountability Candidate Committee. The committee consists of one court of appeals judge from each of the court of appeals districts, chosen by lot by the chief justice of the supreme court in the presence of the other justices.

Board members may not be involved in partisan political activities and may not hold another state office or position except that of reserve judge of a circuit court or court of appeals. The board appoints a legal counsel outside the classified service as agency head to perform legal and administrative functions for the board. The board includes an Elections Division and an Ethics and Accountability Division, each of which is under the direction and supervision of an administrator appointed by the board. The board designates an employee to serve as the chief election officer of the state.

History: The Government Accountability Board was created by 2007 Wisconsin Act 1. Act 1 abolished the State Ethics and Elections Boards and their functions were merged into the new agency, effective after January 10, 2008.

The Elections Board was created as an independent agency by Chapter 334, Laws of 1973, which transferred administration of the state's election laws from the secretary of state and created the campaign finance registration and reporting system.

The Ethics Board was created by Chapter 90, Laws of 1973, to administer the ethics code applicable to public officials and employees created by the act. Lobbying has been regulated in Wisconsin since 1858. The secretary of state was made responsible for the enforcement of lobbying laws by Chapter 278, Laws of 1977, and this regulation was transferred to the Elections Board by 1989 Wisconsin Act 338.

Statutory Council

Election Administration Council: LISA WEINER (Milwaukee County Board of Election Commissioners); SUE EDMAN (City of Milwaukee Board of Election Commissioners); SUE ERTMER (Winnebago County Clerk); NAN KOTTKE (Marathon County Clerk); KATHY NICKOLAUS (Waukesha County Clerk); MARILYN K. BHEND (Johnson Town Clerk); JULEE HELT (Waunakee Village Clerk); DIANE HERMANN-BROWN (Sun Prairie City Clerk); MIKE HOPPENRATH (Watertown City Clerk); MARCIA KELLY (Dale Town Clerk); SUE PECK (Marshall Village Clerk); AUDREY RUE (Brigham Town Clerk); JOHN FRITZ (President, National Federation of the Blind of Wisconsin); HOWARD SEIFERT (Board for People with Developmental Disabilities); ALICIA M. BOEHME (Disability Rights Wisconsin); MAUREEN RYAN (Wisconsin Coalition of Independent Living Centers, Inc.); ANDREA KAMINSKI (Executive Director, League of Women Voters of Wisconsin); SANDI WESOLOWSKI (Clerk, City of Franklin); ANITA JOHNSON (Election Administration Advocate, Citizen Action of Wisconsin, Milwaukee).

The Election Administration Council assists the Government Accountability Board in preparing and revising, as necessary, a state plan that meets the requirements of Public Law 107-252, the federal "Help America Vote Act of 2002", which will enable participation by the state in federal financial assistance programs authorized under that law. The members of the council are appointed by the GAB elections division administrator. The membership must include the clerk or executive director of the board of election commissioners of the two counties or municipalities having the largest population, one or more election officials of other counties or municipalities, representatives of organizations that advocate for the interests of the voting public, and other electors of Wisconsin. The council was created by 2003 Wisconsin Act 265 in the Elections Board, and was attached to the GAB by 2007 Wisconsin Act 1. The composition and duties of the council are specified in Sections 5.05 (10), 5.68 (3m), and 15.607 (1) of the statutes.

Department of
HEALTH SERVICES

Secretary of Health Services: KAREN TIMBERLAKE, 266-9622, karen.timberlake@

Deputy Secretary: MARK THOMAS, 266-9622, mark.thomas@

Executive Assistant: REA HOLMES, 266-9622, rea.holmes@

Communications Director: SETH BOFFELI, 266-5862, seth.boffeli@

Legislative Liaison: RACHEL CURANS-SHEEHAN, 266-3262, rachel.curranssheehan@

Legal Counsel, Office of: DIANE WELSH, *chief legal counsel,* 266-1404, diane.welsh@

Policy Initiatives and Budget, Office of: vacancy, *director,* 266-2907; Fax: 267-0358.

Mailing Address: P.O. Box 7850, Madison 53707-7850.

Location: Wilson Street State Human Services Building, 1 West Wilson Street, Madison.

Telephone: 266-1865.

DEPARTMENT OF HEALTH SERVICES

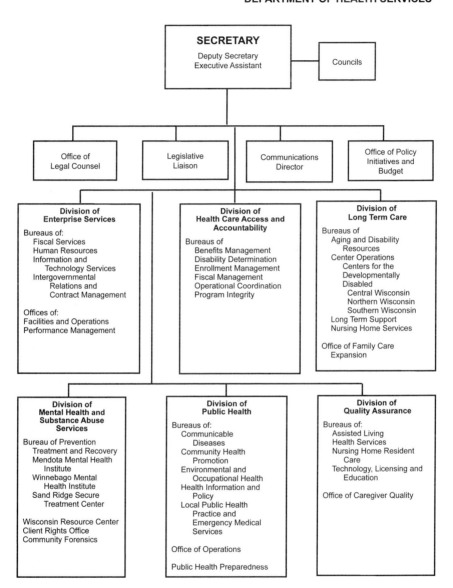

SECRETARY
Deputy Secretary
Executive Assistant

Councils

Office of
Legal Counsel

Legislative
Liaison

Communications
Director

Office of Policy
Initiatives and
Budget

**Division of
Enterprise Services**

Bureaus of:
Fiscal Services
Human Resources
Information and
Technology Services
Intergovernmental
Relations and
Contract Management

Offices of:
Facilities and Operations
Performance Management

**Division of
Health Care Access and
Accountability**

Bureaus of
Benefits Management
Disability Determination
Enrollment Management
Fiscal Management
Operational Coordination
Program Integrity

**Division of
Long Term Care**

Bureaus of
Aging and Disability
Resources
Center Operations
Centers for the
Developmentally
Disabled
Central Wisconsin
Northern Wisconsin
Southern Wisconsin
Long Term Support
Nursing Home Services

Office of Family Care
Expansion

**Division of
Mental Health and
Substance Abuse
Services**

Bureau of Prevention
Treatment and Recovery
Mendota Mental Health
Institute
Winnebago Mental
Health Institute
Sand Ridge Secure
Treatment Center

Wisconsin Resource Center
Client Rights Office
Community Forensics

**Division of
Public Health**

Bureaus of:
Communicable
Diseases
Community Health
Promotion
Environmental and
Occupational Health
Health Information and
Policy
Local Public Health
Practice and
Emergency Medical
Services

Office of Operations

Public Health Preparedness

**Division of
Quality Assurance**

Bureaus of:
Assisted Living
Health Services
Nursing Home Resident
Care
Technology, Licensing and
Education

Office of Caregiver Quality

Units attached for administrative purposes under Sec. 15.03:
Emergency Medical Services Board
Council on Physical Disabilities

Internet Address: http://dhs.wisconsin.gov

Publications: Annual fiscal reports; Biennial reports; Reports and informational brochures (available through divisions).

Number of Employees: 5,510.88.

Total Budget 2007-09: $13,605,438,200.

Statutory References: Section 15.19; Chapter 46.

| Address e-mail by combining the user ID and the state extender: userid@**dhs.wisconsin.gov** |

Enterprise Services, Division of: REGINA FRANK, *administrator,* 261-6837, regina.frank@; PATRICK COOPER, *deputy administrator,* 267-2846, patrick.cooper@; Fax: 267-6749.

  Fiscal Services, Bureau of: CHERYL JOHNSON, *director,* 266-5869, cheryl.johnson@

  Human Resources, Bureau of: CHERYL L. ANDERSON, *director,* 266-9862, cheryl.anderson@

  Information and Technology Services, Bureau of: ROBERT MARTIN, *director,* 266-0125, roberth.martin@

  Intergovernmental Relations and Contract Management, Bureau of: CHUCK WILHELM, *director,* 267-9326, charles.wilhelm@

  Facilities and Operations, Office of: RITA PRIGIONI, *director,* 266-8472, rita.prigioni@

  Performance Management, Office of: vacancy, *director.*

Health Care Access and Accountability, Division of: JASON A. HELGERSON, *administrator,* 266-8922, jasona.helgerson@; JIM JONES, *deputy administrator,* 266-8922, james.jones@; P.O. Box 309, Madison 53701-0309, Fax: 266-6786.

  Benefits Management, Bureau of: JAMES VAVRA, *director,* 261-7838, james.vavra@

  Disability Determination, Bureau of: AUDREY KOEHN, *acting director,* 266-1988, audrey.koehn@

  Enrollment Management, Bureau of: ANGELA DOMBROWICKI, *director,* 266-1935, angela.dombrowicki@

  Fiscal Management, Bureau of: JAMES JOHNSTON, *director,* 267-7283, james.johnston@

  Operational Coordination, Bureau of: ELIAS SOTO, *director,* 266-0203, eliasn.soto@

  Program Integrity, Bureau of: ALAN WHITE, *director,* 266-7436, alan.white@

Long Term Care, Division of: FREDI BOVE, *acting administrator,* 261-5987, frediellen.bove@; FREDI BOVE, *deputy administrator,* 261-5987, frediellen.bove@

  Family Care Expansion, Office of: JUDITH FRYE, *director,* 266-5156, judith.frye@

  Aging and Disability Resources, Bureau of: DONNA MCDOWELL, *director,* 266-3840, donna.mcdowell@

  Center Operations, Bureau of: THEODORE BUNCK, *director,* 301-9200, theodore.bunck@

    Central Wisconsin Center for the Developmentally Disabled: THEODORE BUNCK, *director,* 317 Knutson Drive, Madison 53704-1197, 301-9200, Fax: 301-1390, theodore.bunck@

    Northern Wisconsin Center for the Developmentally Disabled: LOUISE RAMSEIER, *interim director,* 2820 East Park Avenue, P.O. Box 340, Chippewa Falls 54729-0340, (715) 723-5542, Fax: (715) 723-5841, louise.ramseier@

    Southern Wisconsin Center for the Developmentally Disabled: JIM HENKES, *director,* 2415 Spring Street, P.O. Box 100, Union Grove 53182-0100, (262) 878-2411, Fax: (262) 878-2922, james.henkes@

  Long Term Support, Bureau of: BETH WROBLESKI, *director,* 266-7469, beth.wrobleski@

  Nursing Home Services, Bureau of: FREDI BOVE, *interim director,* 261-5987, frediellen.bove@

Mental Health and Substance Abuse Services, Division of: JOHN EASTERDAY, *administrator,* 266-2000, john.easterday@; LINDA HARRIS, *deputy administrator,* 267-7909; linda.harris@

Client Rights Office: JAMES YEADON, *supervisor,* 266-5525, james.yeadon@

Community Forensics: RODNEY MILLER, *supervisor,* 266-2715, rodney.miller@

Prevention Treatment and Recovery, Bureau of: JOYCE ALLEN, *director,* 266-2717, joyce.allen@

  Mendota Mental Health Institute: GREGORY VAN RYBROEK, *director,* 301 Troy Drive, Madison 53704-1599, 301-1000, Fax: 301-1390, gregory.vanrybroek@

  Winnebago Mental Health Institute: ROBERT KNEEPKENS, *director,* P.O. Box 9, Winnebago 54985-0009, (920) 235-4910, Fax: (920) 237-2043, robert.kneepkens@

  Sand Ridge Secure Treatment Center: STEVEN WATTERS, *director,* 1111 North Road, Mauston 53948, (608) 847-4438, Fax: (608) 847-1790, steven.watters@

  Wisconsin Resource Center: BYRAN BARTOW, *director,* 1505 North Street, P.O. Box 16, Winnebago 54985-0016, (920) 426-4310, Fax: (920) 231-6353, byran.bartow@

Public Health, Division of: SETH FOLDY, *administrator and State Health Officer,* (414) 227-4997, seth.foldy@; TOM SIEGER, *deputy administrator,* 266-9780, thomas.sieger@; P.O. Box 2659, Madison 53701-2659, Fax: 267-6988, TTY: (888) 701-1253.

  Operations, Office of: CYNTHIA DAGGETT, *director,* 261-9434, cynthia.daggett@

  Communicable Diseases, Bureau of: SANDRA BREITBORDE, *director,* 267-9863, sandra.breitborde@

  Community Health Promotion, Bureau of: SUSAN UTTECH, *director,* 267-3561, susan.uttech@

  Environmental and Occupational Health, Bureau of: CHARLES WARZECHA, *director,* 264-9880, charles.warzecha@

  Health Information and Policy, Bureau of: PATRICIA GUHLEMAN, *director,* 266-1347, patricia.guhleman@

  Local Public Health Practice and Emergency Medical Services, Bureau of: LARRY GILBERTSON, *director,* 266-8154, larry.gilbertson@

  Public Health Preparedness: DIANE CHRISTEN, *director,* 266-6770, diane.christen@

Quality Assurance, Division of: OTIS WOODS, *administrator,* 267-7185, otis.woods@; JANE WALTERS, *deputy administrator,* 266-7952, jane.walters@; Milwaukee office: 819 North Sixth Street, Milwaukee 53203, (414) 227-5000.

  Caregiver Quality, Office of: SHARI BUSSE, *director,* 264-9876, shari.busse@

  Assisted Living, Bureau of: KEVIN COUGHLIN, *director,* (920) 448-5255, kevin.coughlin@

  Health Services, Bureau of: CREMEAR MIMS, *director,* (414) 227-4556, cremear.mims@

  Nursing Home Resident Care, Bureau of: PAUL PESHEK, *director,* 267-0351, paul.peshek@

  Technology, Licensing and Education, Bureau of: ALFRED JOHNSON, *director,* 266-2055, alfred.johnson@

Agency Responsibility: The Department of Health Services administers a wide range of services to clients in the community and at state institutions, regulates certain care providers, and supervises and consults with local public and voluntary agencies. Its responsibilities span public health; mental health and substance abuse; long-term support and care; services to people who have a disability, medical assistance, and children's services; aging programs; physical and developmental disability services; sensory disability programs; operation of care and treatment facilities; quality assurance programs; nutrition supplementation programs; medical assistance; and health care for low-income families, elderly, and disabled persons.

Organization: The department is administered by a secretary who is appointed by the governor with the advice and consent of the senate. The secretary appoints the division administrators from outside the classified service.

Unit Functions: The *Division of Enterprise Services* oversees financial management, information systems and technology, personnel and employment relations, affirmative action and civil rights compliance, purchasing and contract administration, facilities management, project management, and other administrative services. It handles billing, collection, and related accounting for state institutions. It oversees the department's regional offices and is responsible for oversight of county human service programs.

The *Division of Health Care Access and Accountability* provides access to health care for low-income persons, the elderly, and people with disabilities. It administers the Medical Assistance (Medicaid), BadgerCare Plus, SeniorCare, Chronic Disease Aids, General Relief, and FoodShare programs.

The *Division of Long Term Care* administers a variety of programs that provide long-term support for the elderly and people with disabilities. These programs include Family Care, Aging and Disability Resource Centers, Community Relocation Initiative, Community Integration Initiative, Pathways to Independence, and the Community Options Program. The division manages nursing home funding, nursing home policies, and reimbursement and auditing services. It also operates three state centers for persons with developmental disabilities: Northern Wisconsin Center (Chippewa Falls), Central Wisconsin Center (Madison), and Southern Wisconsin Center (Union Grove).

The *Division of Mental Health and Substance Abuse Services* administers programs to meet mental health and substance abuse prevention, diagnosis, early intervention, and treatment needs. It also administers the state's institutional programs for persons whose mental needs or developmental disabilities cannot be met in a community setting. The two mental health institutes, Mendota Mental Health Institute and Winnebago Mental Health Institute, provide treatment for persons with mental health problems who are in need of hospitalization including medical, psychological, social, and rehabilitative services. Mendota Mental Health Institute also houses a secure correctional facility to meet the mental health needs of male adolescents from Department of Corrections juvenile institutions. The division operates the Wisconsin Resource Center as a medium security facility for mentally ill prison inmates whose treatment needs cannot be met by the Department of Corrections. It also provides treatment at the Sand Ridge Secure Treatment Center for individuals civilly committed under the sexually violent persons law, and provides services for persons placed on supervised release.

The *Division of Public Health* promotes and protects public health in Wisconsin through various services and regulations. It administers programs that address environmental and occupational health, family and community health, chronic and communicable disease prevention and control, and programs relating to maternal and child health, including the Women, Infants and Children (WIC) Supplemental Food Program. It licenses emergency medical service providers and technicians and approves and supervises their training. The division is also responsible for inspecting restaurants, hotels and motels, bed and breakfast establishments, camps and campgrounds, food vendors, and swimming pools. The division performs vital recordkeeping functions including providing birth, death, marriage, and divorce certificates and the gathering, analysis and publishing of statistical information related to the health of the state's population. The division conducts formal statutory reviews of all local health departments every five years.

The *Division of Quality Assurance* licenses and regulates over 40 different programs and facilities that provide health, long-term care, and mental health and substance abuse services including assisted living facilities, nursing homes, community-based residential facilities home health agencies, and facilities serving people with developmental disabilities. It also performs caregiver background checks and investigations.

History: The Department of Health Services combines supervision of many state and local functions that had developed separately in the 1800s. For more than two decades after statehood, Wisconsin created separate governing boards and institutions for the care of prisoners; juveniles; and blind, deaf, and mentally ill persons. By 1871, there were six such institutions. The first attempt to institute overall supervision of these services came when the legislature passed Chapter 136, Laws of 1871, creating the State Board of Charities and Reform. Its duties included examination of the operations of state institutions and their boards and investigation of practices in local asylums, jails, and schools for the blind and deaf.

In Chapter 298, Laws of 1881, the legislature abolished the separate institutional boards and combined their functions under the State Board of Supervision of Wisconsin Charitable, Reformatory and Penal Institutions. The State Board of Charities and Reform continued to operate until 1891. In that year, the two boards were combined as the State Board of Control of the

Wisconsin Reformatory, Charitable and Penal Institutions in Chapter 221, Laws of 1891, thus completing the consolidation of public welfare activities.

In the early days of statehood, public health was primarily a function of local governments. In Chapter 366, Laws of 1876, the legislature established the State Board of Health to "study the vital statistics of this state, and endeavor to make intelligent and profitable use of the collected records of death and sickness among the people." The board was directed to "make sanitary investigations and inquiries respecting the causes of disease, and especially of epidemics; the causes of mortality, and the effects of localities, employments, conditions, ingesta, habits and circumstances on the health of the people." This directive defines much of the work still done in public health. Later legislation required the board to take responsibility for tuberculosis care (1905), to direct its efforts toward preventing blindness in infants (1909), and to inspect water and sewerage systems to prevent typhoid and dysentery (1919). In addition, at various times, the board licensed restaurants, health facilities, barbers, embalmers, and funeral directors.

By the time the federal government entered the field of public welfare during the Great Depression of the 1930s, Wisconsin had already pioneered a number of programs, including aid to children and pensions for the elderly (enacted in 1931). The Wisconsin Children's Code, enacted by Chapter 439, Laws of 1929, was one of the most comprehensive in the nation. The state's initial response to federal funding was to establish separate departments to administer social security funds and other public welfare programs. After several attempts at reorganization and a series of studies, the legislature established the State Department of Public Welfare in Chapter 435, Laws of 1939, to provide unified administration of all existing welfare functions. Public health and care for the aged were delegated to separate agencies.

The executive branch reorganization act of 1967 created the Department of Health and Social Services. The Board of Health and Social Services, appointed by the governor, directed the new department and appointed the departmental secretary to administer the agency. In addition to combining public welfare, public health, and care for the aged in the reorganization act, the 1967 Legislature added the Division of Vocational Rehabilitation in Chapter 43. In Chapter 39, Laws of 1975, the legislature abolished the board and replaced it with a secretary appointed by the governor with the advice and consent of the senate. That same law called for a reorganization of the department, which was completed by July 1977. The Department of Health and Social Services was renamed the Department of Health and Family Services (DHFS), effective July 1, 1996.

The decades of the 1960s and 1970s saw an expansion of public welfare and health services at both the federal and state levels. Especially notable were programs for medical care for the needy and aged (Medical Assistance and Medicare), drug treatment programs, food stamps, Aid to Families with Dependent Children Program (AFDC), and increased regulation of hospitals and nursing homes.

While continuing to administer its established programs, the department was assigned additional duties during the 1980s in the areas of child support, child abuse and neglect, programs for the handicapped, and welfare reform. However, 1989 Wisconsin Acts 31 and 107 created a separate Department of Corrections to administer adult corrections institutions and programs, and 1995 Wisconsin Act 27 transferred responsibility for juvenile offenders to that department.

1995 Wisconsin Act 27 revised AFDC and transferred it and other income support programs including Medical Assistance eligibility and food stamps to the Department of Workforce Development (DWD). (Wisconsin Works, known as W-2, replaced AFDC in 1995 Wisconsin Act 289.) Existing welfare reform programs, including Job Opportunities and Basic Skills (JOBS), Learnfare, Parental Responsibility, and Work-Not-Welfare, were also transferred to DWD, along with child and spousal support, the Children First Program, Older American Community Service Employment, refugee assistance programs, and vocational rehabilitation functions. Health care facilities plan review was transferred from the Department of Industry, Labor and Human Relations to DHFS by 1995 Wisconsin Act 27. Act 27 also transferred laboratory certification to the Department of Agriculture, Trade and Consumer Protection and low-income energy assistance to the Department of Administration.

As a result of 1995 Wisconsin Act 303, the department assumed responsibility for direct administration and operation of Milwaukee County child welfare services. Primary responsibility for the Health Insurance Risk-Sharing Program (HIRSP) was transferred to the department from the Office of the Commissioner of Insurance by 1997 Wisconsin Act 27. 2001 Wisconsin Act 16 transferred the Medical Assistance Eligibility Program and the Food Stamp Program to DHFS from the Department of Workforce Development.

2007 Wisconsin Act 20 changed the name of the department to the Department of Health Services beginning July 1, 2008. Act 20 also created a separate Department of Children and Families and split the responsibilities of DHFS between the two departments.

Statutory Councils

Birth Defect Prevention and Surveillance, Council on: LINDSAY ZETZSCHE (UW Medical School representative), WILLIAM RHEAD (Medical College of Wisconsin, Inc., representative), vacancy (pediatric nurse representative), Statewide Genetic Counselor/Consultant (children and youth with special health care needs DHS program representative), CAROL NODDINGS-EICHINGER (early intervention services DHS program representative), ANN SPOONER (health statistics research and analysis DHS representative), PHILIP GIAMPIETRO (State Medical Society representative), vacancy (Wisconsin Health and Hospital Association representative), KERRY BALDWIN JEDELE (Wisconsin Chapter, American Academy of Pediatrics representative), vacancy (Council on Developmental Disabilities representative), MIR BASIR (nonprofit organization representative), LISA B. NELSON (parent/guardian of child with a birth defect), CYNTHIA DESTEFFEN (local health department representative) (appointed by secretary of health services).

Contact Person: PEGGY HELM-QUEST, 267-2945, peggy.helmquist@

The 13-member Council on Birth Defect Prevention and Surveillance makes recommendations to the department regarding the administration of the Wisconsin Birth Defects Registry. The registry documents diagnoses and counts the number of birth defects for children up to age two. The council advises what birth defects are to be reported; the content, format, and procedures for reporting; and the contents of the aggregated reports. Members are appointed by the secretary of health services to 4-year terms. The UW Medical School and Medical College of Wisconsin, Inc., representatives must have expertise in birth defects epidemiology. Nurse representatives must specialize in pediatrics or have expertise in birth defects. The program representatives are from the appropriate subunits in the department. The nonprofit representative must be from an organization whose primary purpose is birth defect prevention and which does not promote abortion as a method of prevention. The department has added a nonstatutory council member to represent parents or guardians of children born with birth defects. The council was created by 1999 Wisconsin Act 114. Its duties and composition are prescribed in Sections 15.197 (12) and 253.12 (4) of the statutes.

Blindness, Council on: WILLIAM HYDE, *chairperson;* ELEANOR LOOMANS, *vice chairperson;* EDWARD H. WEISS, *secretary;* MARK JANOWIAK, DENNIS L. NIELSON, BRUCE PARKINSON, CAROLYN SPAIN, RHONDA STAATS, JOAN J. WUCHERER (appointed by secretary of health services).

The 9-member Council on Blindness makes recommendations to the department and other state agencies on policies, procedures, services, programs, and research that affect blind or visually impaired people. Members are appointed by the secretary of health services for staggered 3-year terms, and 7 of them must be blind or visually impaired. Originally, the council was created by Chapter 305, Laws of 1947, as the Advisory Committee of the Blind to advise the Board of Public Welfare and the State Superintendent of Public Instruction. The current council was created in the Department of Health and Social Services by Chapter 366, Laws of 1969. Its composition and duties are prescribed in Sections 15.197 (2) and 47.03 (9) of the statutes.

Deaf and Hard of Hearing, Council for the: JENNIFER EVANS, MARY JANE GRIFFIN, DAN HOULIHAN, TERRI MATENAER, BILLY MAULDIN, TOM MEITNER, STEFANIE SALTERN, ELOISE SCHWARZ, ALEX SLAPPEY (all appointed by governor).

The 9-member Council for the Deaf and Hard of Hearing advises the department on the provision of effective services to deaf, hard-of-hearing, late-deafened, and deaf-blind people. Members are appointed by the governor for staggered 4-year terms. The council was created by Chapter 34, Laws of 1979, as the Council for the Hearing Impaired and renamed by 1995

Wisconsin Act 27. Its duties and composition are prescribed in Sections 15.09 (5) and 15.197 (8) of the statutes.

Mental Health, Council on: MICHAEL BACHHUBER, *chairperson;* JACKY BALDWIN, *vice chairperson;* LYNN BORESON, CORRIE BRIGGS, JOHN EASTERDAY, KIM EITHUN-HARSNER, DONALD HANDS, LESLIE MIRKIN, MARY NEUBAUER, AMY PARKER, JOHN QUAAL, MARTHA RASMUS, KATHY ROETTER, KATHARINE SWANSON, JOANN T. STEPHENS, BENITA WALKER, JUDY WILCOX, DONNA WREN.

The Council on Mental Health is composed of not less than 21 nor more than 25 members nominated by the secretary of health services and appointed by the governor for 3-year terms. Persons appointed shall include representatives of groups and a proportion of members as specified in 42 USC 300x-3 (c), as amended to April 2, 2008. The council advises the department, governor, and legislature on mental health programs; provides recommendations on the expenditure of federal mental health block grants; reviews the department's plans for mental health services; and serves as an advocate for the mentally ill. The council was created by 1983 Wisconsin Act 439, and its membership was amended by 2007 Wisconsin Act 20. Its composition and duties are prescribed in Sections 15.197 (1) and 51.02 of the statutes.

Public Health Council: JOHN BARTKOWSKI, CATHERINE FREY, CORAZON LOTEYRO, DOUGLAS NELSON, THAI VUE (consumer representatives); MARY JO BAISCH, SUSAN GARCIA FRANZ, JOHN MEUER, DEBORAH MILLER, A. CHARLES POST, AYAZ SAMADANI, JAMES SANDERS (provider representatives); BRIDGET CLEMENTI, GARY GILMORE, LYNN SHEETS (health professionals educator representatives); BEVAN BAKER, TERRI KRAMOLIS, JULIE WILLEMS VAN DIJK (local health representatives); MARK VILLALPANDO (public safety representative); vacancy (tribal representative); 3 vacancies.

The 23-member Public Health Council advises the department, the governor, the legislature, and the public on progress made in the implementation of the department's 10-year public health plan and coordination of responses to public health emergencies. Members are nominated by the secretary of health services and appointed by the governor to serve 3-year terms and must include representatives of health care consumers, health care providers, health professions educators, local health departments and boards, federally recognized American Indian tribes or bands in this state, public safety agencies, and, if established by the secretary of health services, the Public Health Advisory Committee. 2003 Wisconsin Act 186 created the council and its composition and duties are prescribed in Sections 15.197 (13) and 250.07 (1m) of the statutes.

Trauma Advisory Council: RAYMOND GEORGEN, DAVID GOURLAY, GABY ISKANDER, MATTHEW MOORMAN (physicians); CECILE D'HUYVETTER, CHERYL PAAR (registered nurses); KAVIN KAMINSKI (emergency medical service provider); JAMES AUSTAD (emergency medical service provider representing a municipality); MERRILLEE CARLSON, SCOTT CARPENTER (rural hospital representatives); KAREN BRASEL, JOHN FOLSTAD (urban hospital representatives); BRENDA FELLENZ (EMS Board representative). Additional members identified by the secretary: NIRAV PATEL (physician), JEFF GRIMM (aero medical representative).

State Trauma Care System Coordinator: CONNIE RIGDON, 266-0601, connie.rigdon@dhs.state.wi.us

The 13-member Trauma Advisory Council, all appointed by the secretary of health services, advises the department on developing and implementing a statewide trauma care system. Membership must include physicians, registered nurses, prehospital emergency medical service providers, urban and rural hospital personnel, and the medical services board. They must represent "all geographical areas of the state". Physician appointees must represent urban and rural areas, and one of the prehospital emergency medical service providers must represent a municipality. The council was created by 1997 Wisconsin Act 154 and its composition and duties are prescribed in Sections 15.197 (25) and 146.56 (1) of the statutes.

INDEPENDENT UNITS ATTACHED FOR BUDGETING, PROGRAM COORDINATION, AND RELATED MANAGEMENT FUNCTIONS BY SECTION 15.03 OF THE STATUTES

EMERGENCY MEDICAL SERVICES BOARD

Members: CAL LINTZ, *chairperson;* STEVE BANE, *vice chairperson;* MINDY ALLEN, JIM AUSTAD, BRENDA FELLENZ, MARK FREDRICKSON, TROY HAASE, KENNETH JOHNSON, GLORIA MURAWSKY, TRAVIS TEESCH, vacancy (voting members appointed by governor). *Ex officio* nonvoting members: BRIAN LITZA (designated by secretary of health services), DON HAGEN (designated by secretary of transportation), TIMOTHY WEIR (designated by state director, Technical College System Board), MICHAEL KIM (state medical director for emergency medical services).

Mailing Address: P.O. Box 2659, Madison 53701-2659.

Telephone: 266-1568.

Statutory References: Sections 15.195 (8) and 146.55 (3).

Agency Responsibility: The 15-member Emergency Medical Services Board appoints an advisory committee of physicians to advise the department on the selection of the state medical director for emergency medical services and to review that person's performance. It also advises the director on medical issues; reviews emergency medical service statutes and rules concerning the transportation of patients; and recommends changes to the Department of Health Services and the Department of Transportation. The board includes personnel from the appropriate state agencies and related emergency services in its deliberations.

The board includes 11 voting members, appointed by the governor for 3-year terms, who must "represent the various geographical areas of the state" and various types of emergency medical service providers. The board, which was created by 1993 Wisconsin Act 16, replaced the Emergency Medical Services Assistance Board, created by 1989 Wisconsin Act 102.

COUNCIL ON PHYSICAL DISABILITIES

Members: JEFF FOX, *vice chairperson;* JOANNE ZIMMERMAN, *secretary;* DONNA WONG (designated by governor), MARGE LIBERSKI AZNOE, JON BALTMANIS, JORJAN BORLIN, CHRISTINE DURANCEAU, PATRICIA LERCH, VIRGINIA LUKKEN, JOHN MEISSNER, KAREN SECOR, JACKIE STENBERG, LEWIS TYLER, PAMELA WILSON (all members are appointed by governor).

Contact Person: DAN JOHNSON.

Mailing Address: P.O. Box 7851, Madison 53707-7851.

Location: 1 West Wilson Street, Room 1150, Madison.

Telephones: 266-9582; TTY 267-9880.

Fax: 267-3208.

E-mail Address: dan.johnson@

Statutory References: Sections 15.197 (4) and 46.29.

Agency Responsibility: The 14-member Council on Physical Disabilities develops and modifies the state plan for services to persons with physical disabilities. It advises the secretary of health services, recommends legislation, encourages public understanding of the needs of persons with physical disabilities, and promotes programs to prevent physical disability. The 13 appointed members are appointed by the governor to serve 3-year terms and must be state residents. At least 6 members must be persons with physical disabilities; 2 may be parents, guardians, or relatives of persons with physical disabilities; and at least one must be a service provider. The council must include equitable representation for sex, race, and urban and rural areas. The council was created by 1989 Wisconsin Act 202.

HIGHER EDUCATIONAL AIDS BOARD

Members: JEFFREY BARTELL (UW System Board of Regents member); ANN GREENHECK (Technical College System Board member); ELIZABETH TUCKER (UW System financial aids administrator); MARY JO GREEN (Technical College System financial aids administrator);

ALAN STAGER (UW System student representative); TERESA RUTHERFORD (Technical College System student representative); JERRY CURREN (independent colleges and universities board of trustees representative); DEBRA MCKINNEY (independent colleges and universities financial aid administrator); MIKE BORMETT (designated by superintendent of public instruction); MARIA FLORES (independent colleges and universities student representative); JAMES PALMER (public member); VERNA FOWLER (nonstatutory nonvoting representative of tribal higher educational institutions). (All members, except *ex officio* member and tribal representative, are appointed by governor.)

Executive Secretary: CONNIE HUTCHISON, (608) 264-6181, connie.hutchison@wisconsin.gov
Mailing Address: P.O. Box 7885, Madison 53707-7885.
Location: 131 West Wilson Street, Suite 902, Madison.
Telephone: (608) 267-2206.
Fax: (608) 267-2808.
Agency E-mail Address: HEABmail@wisconsin.gov
Internet Address: http://heab.wi.gov
Publications: Biennial report; Report on Financial Aid Programs; various board reports.
Number of Employees: 10.50.
Total Budget 2007-09: $251,942,900.
Statutory References: Section 15.67; Chapter 39, Subchapter III.

Agency Responsibility: The Higher Educational Aids Board is responsible for the management and oversight of the state's student financial aid system for Wisconsin residents attending institutions of higher education. It also enters into interstate agreements and performs student loan collection services.

The board establishes policies for the state's student financial aid programs, including academic excellence scholarships, Wisconsin tuition grants, Wisconsin higher education grants, talent incentive grants, handicapped student grants, Indian student grants, minority student grants (private sector and Technical College System), teacher education loans, minority teacher loans, nursing loans, and interstate reciprocity. It administers the contracts for medical and dental education services and the Wisconsin Health Education Loan Program and approves the participants in the Medical College of Wisconsin, Inc., per capita grant program.

Organization: The 11 statutory members of the board include the superintendent of public instruction or designee, 7 members who serve 3-year terms, and 3 student members who serve 2-year terms. The students must be at least 18 years old, residents of this state, enrolled at least half-time, and in good academic standing. The UW and private nonprofit institution students must be undergraduates. The governor appoints the board's executive secretary. In 2005, the board added a nonstatutory nonvoting member to represent tribal institutions of higher education.

History: The Higher Educational Aids Board originated as the State Commission for Academic Facilities. It was created by Chapter 573, Laws of 1963, to administer Title I of the Federal Higher Education Facilities Act of 1963, which funded grants for university and college building programs in Wisconsin. Chapter 264, Laws of 1965, gave the commission student financial aid responsibilities and changed its name to the State Commission for Higher Educational Aids. Chapter 313, Laws of 1967, authorized the commission to organize the Wisconsin Higher Education Corporation to administer the federal Guaranteed Student Loan Program. The corporation was given an independent board of directors as a private nonstock corporation in 1984. Chapter 276, Laws of 1969, renamed the commission the Higher Educational Aids Board. The Higher Educational Aids Board was inadvertently repealed by 1995 Wisconsin Act 27, but was continued as the Higher Educational Aids Council by Executive Order 283. The legislature recreated the board in 1997 Wisconsin Act 27.

STATE HISTORICAL SOCIETY OF WISCONSIN

Board of Curators: JUDY NAGEL, *president;* ELLEN D. LANGILL, *president-elect;* HELEN LAIRD (designated by governor); vacancy (designated by assembly speaker); SENATOR RISSER (senate president), SENATOR SCHULTZ (minority party senator), vacancy (minority party representative to the assembly); Elizabeth Adelman, Linda Clifford, Victor E. Ferrall (appointed by governor with senate consent); Angela Bartell, Murray D. Beckford, Bruce T. Block, Mary F. Buestrin, William J. Cronon, Craig C. Culver, Laurie Davidson, George Dionisopoulos, Mark J. Gajewski, Conrad Goodkind, Beverly A. Harrington, Chuck Hatfield, Betty Havlik, Norbert Hill, Jr., John O. Holzhueter, Carol McChesney Johnson, John E. Kerrigan, Jerry Phillips, Brian Rude, Michael Schmudlach, John Schroeder, Carlyle H. Whipple. (Unless otherwise indicated, curators are elected by the membership of the state historical society or serve *ex officio*.)

Board Secretary: Ellsworth H. Brown.

Director: ELLSWORTH H. BROWN, 264-6440, ellsworth.brown@

Associate Director: vacancy

    Information Technology: Paul E. Hedges, *coordinator,* 264-6451, paul.hedges@

    Special Assistant: Betsy B. Trane, 264-6589, betsy.trane@

    Public Information: Robert L. Granflaten, *coordinator,* 264-6586, bob.granflaten@

For e-mail combine the user ID and the state extender: userid@**wisconsinhistory.org**

Administrative Services, Division of: Greg T. Parkinson, *administrator,* 264-6581, greg.parkinson@

    Facility Maintenance: John D. Kees, *coordinator,* 264-6431, john.kees@

    Financial Services: Greg T. Parkinson, 264-6581, greg.parkinson@

    Human Resources: Alice L. Jackson, *coordinator,* 264-6448, alice.jackson@

Historic Preservation – Public History, Division of: Michael E. Stevens, *administrator and State Historic Preservation Officer,* 264-6464, michael.stevens@

    Historic Preservation Section: James R. Draeger, *section chief,* 264-6511, james.draeger@; *state archaeologist:* John H. Broihahn, 264-6496, john.broihahn@

    School and Local Assistance Section: vacancy, *section chief.*

    Society Press: Kathryn Borkowski, *editorial director and state historian,* 264-6461, kathy.borkowski@

Historic Sites, Division of: Alicia L. Goehring, *administrator,* 264-6515, alicia.goehring@; Cheryl E. Sullivan, *deputy administrator,* 264-6434, cheryl.sullivan@

    First Capitol: Allen L. Schroeder, *site director,* (608) 987-2122; Highway G, Belmont 53510; allen.schroeder@

    H.H. Bennett Studio: Dale B. Williams, *site director,* (608) 253-3523; 215 Broadway, P.O. Box 147, Wisconsin Dells 53965; dale.williams@

    Madeline Island Museum: Steve R. Cotherman, *site director,* (715) 747-2415; La Pointe 54850; steve.cotherman@

    Old World Wisconsin: Dawn St. George, *site director,* (262) 594-6302; S103 W37890 Highway 67, Eagle 53119; dawn.stgeorge@

    Pendarvis: Allen L. Schroeder, *site director,* (608) 987-2122; 114 Shake Rag Street, Mineral Point 53565; allen.schroeder@

    Reed School: Dale B. Williams, *site director,* (608) 253-3523; U.S. Highway 10 and Cardinal Avenue, Neillsville 54456; reedschool@

    Stonefield: Allen L. Schroeder, *site director,* (608) 725-5210; P.O. Box 125, Cassville 53806; allen.schroeder@

    Villa Louis: Michael P. Douglass, *site director,* (608) 326-2721; P.O. Box 65, Prairie du Chien 53821; michael.douglass@

    Wade House: David M. Simmons, *site director,* (920) 526-3271; P.O. Box 34, Greenbush 53026; david.simmons@

Library – Archives, Division of: Peter Gottlieb, *state archivist,* 264-6480, peter.gottlieb@; Michael I. Edmonds, *deputy administrator,* 264-6538, michael.edmonds@

STATE HISTORICAL SOCIETY

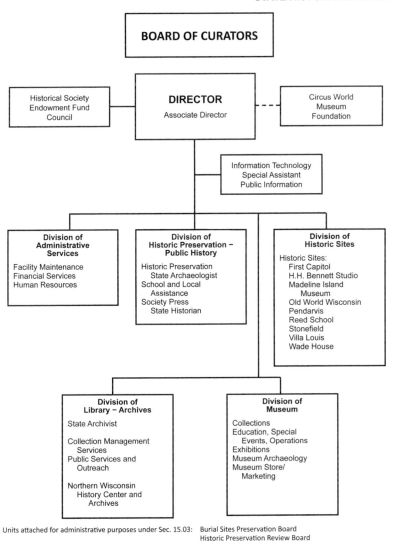

BOARD OF CURATORS

Historical Society
Endowment Fund
Council

DIRECTOR
Associate Director

Circus World
Museum
Foundation

Information Technology
Special Assistant
Public Information

**Division of
Administrative
Services**

Facility Maintenance
Financial Services
Human Resources

**Division of
Historic Preservation –
Public History**

Historic Preservation
State Archaeologist
School and Local
Assistance
Society Press
State Historian

**Division of
Historic Sites**

Historic Sites:
First Capitol
H.H. Bennett Studio
Madeline Island
Museum
Old World Wisconsin
Pendarvis
Reed School
Stonefield
Villa Louis
Wade House

**Division of
Library – Archives**

State Archivist

Collection Management
Services
Public Services and
Outreach

Northern Wisconsin
History Center and
Archives

**Division of
Museum**

Collections
Education, Special
Events, Operations
Exhibitions
Museum Archaeology
Museum Store/
Marketing

Units attached for administrative purposes under Sec. 15.03: Burial Sites Preservation Board
Historic Preservation Review Board

Collection Management Services: vacancy, *coordinator,* 264-6456.

Public Services and Outreach: RICHARD L. PIFER, *coordinator,* 264-6477, rick.pifer@

Northern Wisconsin History Center and Archives at the Northern Great Lakes Visitor Center: LINDA L. MITTLESTADT, *archivist,* (715) 685-2649; 29270 County Highway G, Ashland 54806; linda.mittlestadt@

Museum, Division of: ANN L. KOSKI, *administrator,* 261-9359, ann.koski@; JENNIFER L. KOLB, *deputy administrator,* 261-2461, jennifer.kolb@

Collections: PAUL G. BOURCIER, *chief curator,* 264-6573, paul.bourcier@

Education, Special Events, Operations: JENNIFER L. KOLB, *deputy administrator,* 261-2461, jennifer.kolb@

Exhibitions: DOUGLAS GRIFFIN, *curator of exhibits,* 264-6561, douglas.griffin@

Museum Archaeology: KELLY E. HAMILTON, *coordinator,* 264-6560, kelly.hamilton@

Museum Store/Marketing: JOHN W. LEMKE, *store manager,* 264-6550, john.lemke@

Main Information Desk: (608) 264-6400.

Mailing Address: 816 State Street, Madison 53706-1417.

Archives and Library Location: 816 State Street, Madison.

Archives Telephone: 264-6460; Archives Fax: 264-6472; Library Telephone: 264-6534; Library Fax: 264-6520.

Museum Location: 30 North Carroll Street, Madison 53703-2707.

Museum Information: 264-6555; Museum Tours: 264-6557; Museum Fax: 264-6575.

Internet Address: www.wisconsinhistory.org

Publications: *Columns; Wisconsin Magazine of History.* The society also publishes books, research guides, and miscellaneous brochures. Recent publications include *Fill'er Up: The Glory Days of Wisconsin Gas Stations; On the Hunt: The History of Deer Hunting in Wisconsin; Wisconsin: Our State, Our Story.*

Number of Employees: 143.54.

Total Budget 2007-09: $44,185,200.

Statutory References: Section 15.70; Chapter 44, Subchapters I and II.

Agency Responsibility: The mission of the State Historical Society of Wisconsin, known informally as the Wisconsin Historical Society, is to help connect people to the past. The society has a statutory duty to collect and preserve historical and cultural resources related to Wisconsin and to make them available to the public. To meet these objectives, the society maintains a major history research collection in Madison and in 14 area research centers; operates a museum, 9 historic sites, an office at the Northern Great Lakes Visitor Center, a field services office in Eau Claire, and statewide school services programs. It owns Circus World Museum, which is managed by the Circus World Museum Foundation. It provides public history programming such as National History Day and collaborates with other agencies such as Wisconsin Public Television to deliver history programming to the public. It provides technical services and advice to about 375 affiliated local historical societies throughout the state. It conducts, publishes, and disseminates research on Wisconsin and U.S. history, and serves as the state's historic preservation office, which regulates the designation of historic structures and archaeological sites by administering the state and national registers of historic places. The society is also responsible for implementation of the state's Burial Sites Preservation Law.

Organization: The state historical society is both a state agency and a membership organization. The society's Board of Curators includes 8 statutory appointments and up to 30 members who are elected according to the society's constitution and bylaws. The 3 members appointed by the governor with senate consent serve staggered 3-year terms. The board selects the society's director, who serves as administrative head and as secretary to the board.

Unit Functions: The *Division of Administrative Services* provides management and program support in the areas of financial services, budgeting, human resources, purchasing, and facility maintenance of the society's headquarters building.

The *Division of Historic Preservation – Public History* helps make the history of Wisconsin more accessible to state residents and awards historic designations to places of historic value. It administers Wisconsin's portion of the National Register of Historic Places in partnership with the National Park Service and manages the State Register of Historic Places. It nominates places of architectural, historic, and archaeological significance to the registers. It reviews federal, state, and local projects for their effect on historic and archaeological properties. The division certifies historic building rehabilitation projects for state and federal income tax credits, archaeological sites for property tax exemptions, and historic buildings as eligible for the state historic building code. The division administers the historical markers program, identifies and promotes underwater archaeological sites, and administers the state's burial sites preservation program. The division, through the Wisconsin Historical Society Press, edits and publishes most of the materials issued by the society, including books and a quarterly magazine of history. The division offers instructional materials and programs to schools and teachers to assist them in teaching the history of Wisconsin, coordinates the state's National History Day program, and provides technical assistance to local historical societies affiliated with the society through the Wisconsin Council for Local History. It also operates a field services office in Eau Claire to serve northern Wisconsin.

The *Division of Historic Sites* operates 9 historic sites and outdoor museums: First Capitol, H.H. Bennett Studio, Madeline Island Museum, Old World Wisconsin, Pendarvis, Reed School, Stonefield, Villa Louis, and Wade House. These sites contain historic structures and visitor service buildings that reflect major themes of Wisconsin history, such as ethnic pioneer settlement, mining, farming, fur trade, exploration, transportation, rural life, and town development.

The society owns an additional historic site in Baraboo, Circus World, which is operated by the Circus World Museum Foundation. This museum offers an extensive collection of circus memorabilia, unique circus wagons, and it operates a circus in Baraboo during the summer months.

The *Division of Library – Archives* maintains notable collections in Wisconsin and North American history including areas such as genealogy; labor; business and industry; social action, including civil rights, antiwar movements, and reproductive rights issues; mass communications; and dramatic arts, including theater, motion pictures, and television. The library and archives serve as the North American history research collection for the UW-Madison. The library acts as regional depository for U.S. government publications and official depository for Wisconsin state government publications. The archives program acquires, catalogs, preserves, and makes available primary source materials, including manuscripts, maps, newspapers, photographs, sound recordings, films, videos, and other records pertaining to Wisconsin history and selected fields of U.S. history. It serves as the state archives, collecting and providing access

After exhaustive research, the Wisconsin Historical Society has undertaken a project to restore the grandeur of the Library Reading Room, one of the great architectural spaces in the state. When completed, the reading room will also meet the needs of modern researchers. (State Historical Society of Wisconsin)

to permanent records of state and local government. In partnership with several other institutions, the archives operates 14 Area Research Centers throughout Wisconsin to bring its archival holdings on regional history closer to the public. It also makes available the collections of the Wisconsin Center for Film and Theater Research, which is administered jointly by the society and the UW-Madison.

The *Division of Museum* collects and preserves the material culture of Wisconsin and interprets the state's history and prehistory for the public. It operates the Wisconsin Historical Museum, supervises the preservation and development of artifact collections, and operates an archaeology program under a cooperative agreement with the Department of Transportation and the Department of Natural Resources. The division fulfills its educational role through exhibitions, tours, and a variety of public programs conducted at the museum in Madison and other venues throughout the state.

History: The State Historical Society of Wisconsin was originally founded as a private association, the Wisconsin Historical Society, in 1846, two years before statehood. It was chartered by the Wisconsin Legislature in Chapter 17, Laws of 1853, which made the society responsible for the preservation and care of all records, articles, and other materials of historic interest to the state. The society has received state funding since 1854 (Chapter 16) – longer than any other state historical society in the nation.

The legislature expanded the state's historic preservation program in Chapter 29, Laws of 1977, by making the society responsible for preservation activities associated with the designation, restoration, and repair of historic properties. Chapter 341, Laws of 1981, provided statutory support for local ordinances designed to preserve historic buildings. It set up a framework for a state historic building code with alternative standards for the preservation or restoration of historic structures. 1987 Wisconsin Act 395 strengthened the state's historic preservation laws by creating the State Register of Historic Places to protect historic and prehistoric properties. This law and 1987 Wisconsin Act 399 provided state tax credits and exemptions for owners of certain historic and archaeological properties.

1985 Wisconsin Act 29 formalized the practice of allowing the historical society to enter into a lease agreement with a nonprofit corporation, now called the Circus World Museum Foundation, for the purpose of operating the Circus World Museum.

Statutory Council

Historical Society Endowment Fund Council: Inactive.

The Historical Society Endowment Fund Council advises the state historical society regarding the raising and disbursement of funds used to support the society's historical and cultural preservation services and educational activities. The 10-member council must include representation from the Wisconsin Arts Board, the State Historical Society of Wisconsin, the Wisconsin Academy of Science, Arts and Letters, the Wisconsin Humanities Council, Wisconsin Public Radio and Wisconsin Public Television, and 4 public members, all appointed by the governor. The council was created by 1997 Wisconsin Act 27 and its composition and duties are prescribed in Section 15.707 (3) of the statutes.

Independent Units Attached for Budgeting, Program Coordination, and Related Management Functions by Section 15.03 of the Statutes

BURIAL SITES PRESERVATION BOARD

Burial Sites Preservation Board: Ellsworth H. Brown (state historical society director); Robert F. Boszhardt, Katherine C. Egan-Bruhy, Roseanne M. Meer (nominated by Wisconsin Archaeological Survey); Corina Burke, David J. Grignon, Robert D. Powless, Sr. (nominated by the Great Lakes Inter-Tribal Council, Inc., and the Menominee Tribe). Nonvoting members: Michael E. Stevens (state historic preservation officer), John H. Broihahn (state archaeologist). (All except *ex officio* members are appointed by governor.)

Mailing Address: 816 State Street, Madison 53706-1417.

Telephones: (608) 264-6505; (800) 342-7834 (within Wisconsin).

Statutory References: Section 15.705 (1); Chapter 157, Subchapter III.

Agency Responsibility: The Burial Sites Preservation Board was created to protect all the interests related to human burial sites and to ensure equal treatment and respect for all human burials, regardless of ethnic origin, cultural background, or religious affiliation. The board develops detailed policies to implement the burial sites preservation program; reviews decisions of the director or the administrative hearing examiner concerning applications for permits to disturb cataloged burial sites; and reviews the director's decisions regarding the disposition of human remains and burial objects removed from a burial site. This program was created by 1985 Wisconsin Act 316.

Organization: The 9-member board includes 3 members with professional qualifications in archaeology, physical anthropology, or history and 3 members of federally recognized Indian nations in Wisconsin who have a knowledge of tribal preservation planning, history, or archaeology or who serve as elders, traditional persons, or spiritual leaders of a tribe. The 6 appointed members serve 3-year terms.

HISTORIC PRESERVATION REVIEW BOARD

Historic Preservation Review Board: ANNE E. BIEBEL, BRUCE T. BLOCK, ROBERT J. GOUGH, SHAWN K. GRAFF, CARLEN HATALA, KELLY S. JACKSON-GOLLY, CAROL MCCHESNEY JOHNSON, DAN J. JOYCE, WILLIAM G. LAATSCH, KUBET LUCHTERHAND, DAVID V. MOLLENHOFF, SISSEL SCHROEDER, VALENTINE J. SCHUTE, JR., DANIEL J. STEPHANS, DONNA ZIMMERMAN (all appointed by governor).

State Historic Preservation Officer: MICHAEL E. STEVENS, 264-6464.

Mailing Address: 816 State Street, Madison 53706-1417.

Telephone: (608) 264-6498.

Statutory References: Section 15.705 (2); Chapter 44, Subchapter II.

Agency Responsibility: The Historic Preservation Review Board approves nominations to the Wisconsin State Register of Historic Places and the National Register of Historic Places upon recommendation of the State Historic Preservation Officer. (By statute, the director of the State Historical Society serves as the state officer or designates someone to do so.) The board approves the distribution of federal grants-in-aid for preservation; advises the state historical society; and requests comments from planning departments of affected municipalities, local landmark commissions, and local historical societies regarding properties being considered for nomination to the state and national registers. The board was created by Chapter 29, Laws of 1977.

Organization: The board consists of 15 members appointed by the governor to staggered 3-year terms. At least 9 must be professionally qualified in the areas of architecture, archaeology, art history, and history. Up to 6 members may be qualified in related fields, such as landscape architecture, urban and regional planning, law, or real estate.

Office of the Commissioner of INSURANCE

Commissioner: SEAN DILWEG, 267-3782, sean.dilweg@

Deputy Commissioner: KIMBERLY SHAUL, 267-1233, kimberly.shaul@

Assistant Deputy Commissioner: EILEEN K. MALLOW, 266-7843, eileen.mallow@

Insurance Administrator for Funds and Program Management: JOHN C. MONTGOMERY, 264-8113, john.montgomery@

Legal Counsel: FRED NEPPLE, 266-7726, fred.nepple@

Regulation and Enforcement, Division of: GUENTHER RUCH, *administrator,* 266-0295, guenther.ruch@

    Financial Analysis and Examinations, Bureau of: ROGER PETERSON, *director,* 267-4384, roger.peterson@

    Market Regulation, Bureau of: SUSAN EZALARAB, *director,* 266-8885, sue.ezalarab@

Mailing Address: P.O. Box 7873, Madison 53707-7873.

Location: 125 South Webster Street, Madison 53702.

Telephones: General: 266-3585; Agent licensing: 266-8699; Insurance complaint hotline: (800) 236-8517; Local Government Property Insurance Fund: (877) 229-0009 (Wisconsin only); State Life Insurance Fund: (800) 562-5558.

Fax: 266-9935.

Internet Address: http://oci.wi.gov

Address e-mail by combining the user ID and the state extender: userid@**oci.state.wi.us**

Publications: Annual reports; *Wisconsin Insurance News;* various pamphlets and materials for consumers, insurance companies, and agents. (Contact the Office of the Commissioner of Insurance.)

Number of Employees: 133.00.

Total Budget 2007-09: $207,901,900.

Statutory References: Section 15.73; Chapter 601.

Agency Responsibility: The Office of the Commissioner of Insurance supervises the insurance industry in Wisconsin. The office is responsible for examining insurance industry financial practices and market conduct, licensing insurance agents, reviewing policy forms for compliance with state insurance statutes and regulations, investigating consumer complaints, and providing consumer information. Its goals are to ensure the financial soundness of insurers doing business in Wisconsin; secure fair treatment by insurance companies and agents of policyholders and claimants; encourage industry self-regulation; emphasize loss prevention as part of good insurance practice; and educate the public on insurance issues.

The office administers two segregated insurance funds. The State Life Insurance Fund offers up to $10,000 of low-cost life insurance protection to any Wisconsin resident who meets prescribed risk standards. The Local Government Property Insurance Fund provides mandatory coverage for local governments against fire loss, as well as optional coverage for certain property damage they may incur.

The agency oversees activities of the Health Care Liability Insurance Plan, which provides liability coverage for hospitals, physicians, and other health care providers in Wisconsin, and the Injured Patients and Families Compensation Fund, which provides medical malpractice coverage for qualified health care providers on claims in excess of a provider's underlying coverage.

Organization: The commissioner of insurance is appointed by the governor with the advice and consent of the senate. The commissioner cannot be a candidate for public office and there are stringent restrictions on the commissioner's political activities. The commissioner appoints the deputy commissioner from outside the classified service and the division administrators from the classified service.

Unit Functions: The *Funds and Program Management Organizational Unit* contains the Management Analysis and Planning Section, the Information Technology Section, the Local Government Property Insurance Fund, and the State Life Insurance Fund. The first two sections are responsible for providing a variety of administrative services in support of all agency programs and employees. These services include budget, finance and accounting, receivables, certain procurement tasks, training and employee development, project management, and all IT services including help desk, applications development and support, security, e-mail, and network management. The two funds operate state programs providing property insurance for local units of government in Wisconsin, and basic life insurance for Wisconsin residents, respectively.

The *Division of Regulation and Enforcement* conducts field reviews of insurer underwriting, rating, claim handling, and marketing practices. It investigates insurance agent activities, prepares enforcement proceedings, and, in conjunction with the legal unit, prosecutes offenders. It helps consumers resolve problems with insurers and agents, and carries out the agency's consumer education program. Other duties include review of premium rates and insurance policy forms and contracts filed with the office to ensure their compliance with state law; review of insurer advertising files; and licensing and testing of insurance agents.

The division also conducts field examinations of the financial condition of insurers domiciled in Wisconsin and monitors the financial condition of insurers doing business in the state. It oversees insurer rehabilitations and liquidations, and audits and collects insurer taxes and fees. It incorporates the formation of new insurers and is responsible for the licensing of nondomestic insurers that want to do business in the state. It reviews and approves, as appropriate, transactions that result in the change of control or financial structure of domestic insurers. It also administers the fire department dues program in cooperation with the Department of Commerce and the state treasurer, whereby dues paid by insurers who provide fire coverage are disbursed to municipalities for fire protection and the fire fighters' pension and disability funds.

History: State regulation of insurance dates back to 1870 when Chapter 56 created a Department of Insurance in the secretary of state's office to license agents and, upon complaint, examine the books of fire and inland navigation insurance companies. In 1878 (Chapter 214), the legislature created a separate Department of Insurance, headed by a commissioner appointed by the governor, to perform these functions. From 1881 to 1911, based on Chapter 300, Laws of 1881, an elected commissioner administered the insurance department. With the enactment of Chapter 484, Laws of 1911, the insurance commissioner was again made an appointee. The 1967 executive branch reorganization act renamed the department the Office of the Commissioner of Insurance and continued it as an independent regulatory agency.

Other highlights include the development of the standard fire insurance contract in Chapter 195, Laws of 1891, and stricter regulation of the life insurance industry in 1907 to prevent fraud and misrepresentation. In 1911 and 1913, Wisconsin added coverage of local governments' property and buildings under the State Insurance Fund.

Wisconsin became the only state to establish a state life insurance fund for its residents under Chapter 577, Laws of 1911, which authorized the Department of Insurance to issue life insurance and annuity contracts. Since 1947 (Chapters 487 and 521), the office's responsibilities have included the review of all insurance policy forms and the filing of most premium rates. Wisconsin's current insurance laws are largely the result of a recodification developed between 1967 and 1979 by the Legislative Council and they have served as a basis for the model acts adopted by the National Association of Insurance Commissioners (an association of state insurance regulators).

Statutory Boards and Council

Insurance Security Fund, Board of Directors of the: SEAN DILWEG (insurance commissioner), J.B. VAN HOLLEN (attorney general), DAWN MARIE SASS (state treasurer); MARK J. BACKE, JOHN F. CLEARY, JAMES E. CRIST, DAVID G. DIERCKS, PETER C. FARROW, J. STANLEY HOFFERT, WILLIAM M. O'REILLY, SCOTT SEYMOUR, JAMES P. THOMAS, TOD J. ZACHARIAS (insurance industry representatives appointed by commissioner).

The Board of Directors of the Insurance Security Fund administers a fund that protects certain insurance policyholders and claimants from excessive delay and loss in the event of insurer liquidation. The fund consists of life, allocated annuity, health, HMO, property and casualty, and administrative accounts. The fund supports continuation of coverage under many life, annuity, and health policies. It is financed by assessments paid by most insurers in this state. The board may consist of 12 to 14 members but must include the attorney general, state treasurer, and insurance commissioner or their designees. The industry members must be chosen from representatives of insurers who are subject to the security fund law, and one member must be a representative of a service insurance corporation. The board's advice and recommendations to the commissioner are not subject to the state's open records law. The board was originally created in Chapter 144, Laws of 1969, with substantial revisions in Chapter 109, Laws of 1979, and its composition and duties are prescribed in Sections 646.12 and 646.13 of the statutes.

Injured Patients and Families Compensation Fund/Wisconsin Health Care Liability Insurance Plan, Board of Governors of the: SEAN DILWEG (insurance commissioner), *chairperson;* RANDY BLUMER, ERIK HUTH, CHRISTOPHER SPENCER (insurance industry representatives appointed by commissioner); JOHN WALSH (named by State Bar of Wisconsin);

JAMES JANSEN (named by Wisconsin Association for Justice); ROBERT JAEGER, SUSAN TURNEY (named by State Medical Society of Wisconsin); MARILU BINTZ (named by Wisconsin Hospital Association); DENNIS CONTA, STAN DAVIS, SCOTT FROEHLKE, REID OLSON (public members appointed by governor).

The 13-member Board of Governors of the Injured Patients and Families Compensation Fund/Wisconsin Health Care Liability Insurance Plan oversees the health care liability plans for licensed physicians and nurse anesthetists, medical partnerships and corporations, cooperative sickness care associations, ambulatory surgery centers, hospitals, some nursing homes, and certain other health care providers. The board also supervises the Injured Patients and Families Compensation Fund, which pays medical malpractice claims in excess of a provider's underlying coverage. The 4 public members serve staggered 3-year terms, and at least 2 of them must not be attorneys or physicians nor be professionally affiliated with any hospital or insurance company. The insurance commissioner or the commissioner's designee, who must be an employee of the office of the commissioner, serves as chairperson. The board was created by the medical malpractice law, Chapter 37, Laws of 1975, and its composition and duties are prescribed in Sections 619.04 (3) and 655.27 of the statutes.

Injured Patients and Families Compensation Fund Peer Review Council: JOHN KELLY, *chairperson;* MICHAEL GILMAN, SANDRA OSBORN (physicians); TOM KIRSCHBAUM, JEFF RENIER (public members).

The 5-member Injured Patients and Families Compensation Fund Peer Review Council reviews within one year of the first payment on a claim each claim for damages arising out of medical care provided by a health care provider or provider's employee, if the claim is paid by any of the following: the Patients Compensation Fund, a mandatory health care risk-sharing plan, a private health care liability insurer, or a self-insurer. The council can recommend adjustments in fees paid to the Injured Patients and Families Compensation Fund and the Wisconsin Health Care Liability Insurance Plan or premiums paid to private insurers, if requested by the insurer. The Board of Governors of the Injured Patients and Families Compensation Fund/Wisconsin Health Care Liability Insurance Plan appoints the council and designates its officers and the terms of the members. Not more than 3 members may be physicians. The chairperson must be a physician, who also serves as an *ex officio* nonvoting member of the Medical Examining Board. The council was created by 1985 Wisconsin Act 340, and its composition and duties are prescribed in Section 655.275 of the statutes.

State of Wisconsin
INVESTMENT BOARD

Members: MICHAEL MORGAN (secretary of administration); DAVID GEERTSEN (representing Local Government Pooled-Investment Fund participants); WAYNE D. MCCAFFERY (teacher participant appointed by Teachers Retirement Board); DAVID A. STELLA (nonteacher participant appointed by Wisconsin Retirement Board); THOMAS BOLDT, DAVID KRUGER, WILLIAM H. LEVIT, JR., JAMES A. SENTY, DELORIS SIMS. (Except as noted, the governor appoints the members with senate consent.)

Executive Director: KEITH S. BOZARTH, 266-9451.

Deputy/Assistant Executive Director: GAIL HANSON, 261-0187.

Chief Investment Officer: DAVID VILLA, 266-9734.

Chief Operating Officer: KEN JOHNSON, 267-0221.

Internal Auditor: BRANDON DUCK, 261-2417.

Chief Legal Counsel: JANE HAMBLEN, 266-8824.

Public Information Officer: VICKI HEARING, 261-2415.

Legislative and Beneficiary Liaison: SANDY DREW, 261-0182.

Mailing Address: P.O. Box 7842, Madison 53707-7842.

Location: 121 East Wilson Street, Madison.

Telephone: (608) 266-2381; Toll-Free Beneficiary Hotline: (800) 424-7942.

Fax: (608) 266-2436.

Internet Address: www.swib.state.wi.us

Agency E-mail Address: info@swib.state.wi.us

Publications: Annual Report; Schedule of Investments.

Number of Employees: 113.50.

Total Budget 2007-09: $44,949,400.

Statutory References: Section 15.76; Chapter 25.

Agency Responsibility: The State of Wisconsin Investment Board is responsible for investing the assets of the Wisconsin Retirement System, the State Life Insurance Fund, the Local Government Property Insurance Fund, the State Historical Society of Wisconsin Endowment Trust Fund, the Injured Patients and Families Compensation Fund, the Tuition Trust Fund, Ed-Vest, and the State Investment Fund.

For purposes of investment, the retirement system's assets are divided into two funds. The Core Retirement Investment Trust is a broadly diversified portfolio of domestic and international common stocks, corporate and government bonds, corporate loans, and private markets that include real estate holdings and private debt and equity. The Variable Retirement Investment Trust is invested primarily in common stocks. On December 31, 2008, Wisconsin Retirement System trust funds constituted 91% of the $67.8 billion managed by the Investment Board.

The State Investment Fund invests the commingled cash balances of various state and local government funds in short-term investments with earnings and losses distributed on a pro rata basis to the individual component funds. The fund encompasses the cash balance of the state's general fund and over 50 separate state funds, including the Children's Trust Fund, the Lottery Fund, the Recycling Fund, the Tuition Trust Fund, and the Wisconsin Election Campaign Fund, as well as various state agency accounts. Authorized local governments may participate by depositing moneys in the Local Government Pooled-Investment Fund, which is a separate fund within the State Investment Fund.

Organization: Except for the secretary of administration, appointments to the 9-member board, which is a corporate body with power to sue and be sued, are for 6-year terms. The secretary of administration is an *ex officio* member. At least 4 of the 5 general members must have a minimum of 10 years investment experience, and none may have a financial interest in or be employed by a dealer or broker in securities, mortgages, or real estate investments. The sixth member appointed by the governor must have 10 years of financial experience and be an employee of a government that participates in the Local Government Pooled-Investment Fund.

The board appoints the executive director and the internal auditor from outside the classified service. The executive director, with the participation of the board, appoints the deputy executive director, chief investment officer, and the managing and investment directors from outside the classified service. All other professional employees are also appointed by the executive director from outside the classified service. Board employees may not have any direct or indirect financial interest in any firm engaged in the sale or marketing of real estate or investments or give paid investment advice to others.

Unit Functions: The *Chief Investment Officer,* operating under the supervision of the executive director, monitors and directs the activities of the investment directors and portfolio managers for compliance with board investment policies, guidelines, and reporting procedures. The position of chief investment officer was created by 1995 Wisconsin Act 274.

The *Chief Operating Officer* is responsible for administering the agency's budget, legislative liaison, policy analysis, human resources, information technology, financial operations and accounting, communications, and general administrative services.

The *Internal Audit* unit, directed by the internal auditor, may review any activity of the board and has access to records of the board and any external party under contract with the board. The auditor plans and conducts audits under the direction of the board; assists with external audits and reviews of the board; and monitors the board's contractual agreements with financial institutions, investment advisers, and any other external party providing investment services. The internal audit function was also created by 1995 Wisconsin Act 274.

History: Chapter 459, Laws of 1921, created a mandatory pension system for teachers and three separate boards to invest the annuity funds of public school, normal school, and university teachers. The 1929 Legislature created the State Annuity and Investment Board and made it responsible for investing the assets of the teachers' pension funds and other state funds, except the school funds that remained under control of the Commissioners of Public Lands (Chapter 491). The board also assumed oversight and asset management of funds for the newly created state employee pension system as the result of Chapter 176, Laws of 1943.

Chapter 511, Laws of 1951, replaced the three teacher retirement boards and the Annuity and Investment Board with the State Teachers Retirement Board and the State Investment Board, which was responsible for investing the assets of all non-Milwaukee teachers. Chapter 511 also granted the State Investment Board authority to invest the assets of the nonteaching, non-Milwaukee public employees who were covered under the Wisconsin Retirement Fund. Chapter 430, Laws of 1957, brought the funds of the Milwaukee teachers under the control of the State Investment Board. Chapter 96, Laws of 1981, consolidated all public employee retirement plans, with the exception of the City and County of Milwaukee, into the Wisconsin Retirement System (WRS), and the State Investment Board has continued to invest the funds for the WRS. As a result of the consolidation, the WRS is the ninth largest public pension fund in the U.S. and the 24th largest public or private pension fund worldwide.

Chapter 449, Laws of 1925, created a State Board of Deposits to insure state funds on deposit in state banks through a deposit fund, managed by the state treasurer under the direction of the board. The board's duties were to designate the banks in which state funds could be deposited and to specify the maximum amount of state funds each could receive. Participating banks paid into the deposit fund, which was designed to reimburse any losses incurred through bank failure.

Chapter 511, Laws of 1951, authorized the State Investment Board to invest the state's operating funds and directed it to carry out the investment functions of the State Board of Deposits. Although state funds had been invested since 1911, the 1951 reorganization increased the types of investments the board could consider for the funds it managed. Previously, the state's operating funds had been placed in noninterest bearing accounts. In 1957, the legislature created the State Investment Fund, which merged all state funds except for a handful that are reported separately. The Local Government Pooled-Investment Fund, created in 1976, allows local governments to invest their idle cash at competitive rates of return and withdraw it on a two-day notice with no penalty.

2007 Wisconsin Act 212 made the prudent investor standard the prevailing standard with respect to assets of the Wisconsin Retirement System, thereby overriding other provisions in law that had previously constrained the board's investment authority.

Department of
JUSTICE

Attorney General: J.B. VAN HOLLEN, 266-1221.

Deputy Attorney General: RAYMOND P. TAFFORA, 266-1221.

Special Assistant Attorney General: KEVIN M. ST. JOHN, 266-1221.

Executive Assistant: DEAN F. STENSBERG, 266-1221.

Scheduler: DONNA J. SAROW, 266-1221.

Communications, Office of: WILLIAM A. COSH, 266-1221.

Legislative Liaison, Office of: MARK RINEHART, 266-1221.

Policy Advisor: CINDY M. POLZIN, 266-1221.

Mailing Address: P.O. Box 7857, Madison 53707-7857.

Location: Attorney General's Office, 114 East, State Capitol; Department of Justice, 17 West Main Street, Madison.

Telephones: General: 266-1221; Arson Tip Line: (800) 362-3005; Office of Crime Victim Services: (800) 446-6564; Drug Tip Helpline: (800) 622-DRUG (622-3784); Amber Alert Hotline: (866) 65AMBER (652-6237).

Fax: 267-2779.

Internet Address: www.doj.state.wi.us

Number of Employees: 578.99.

Total Budget 2007-09: $181,796,600.

Constitutional References: Article VI, Sections 1 and 3.

Statutory References: Section 15.25; Chapter 165.

DEPARTMENT OF JUSTICE

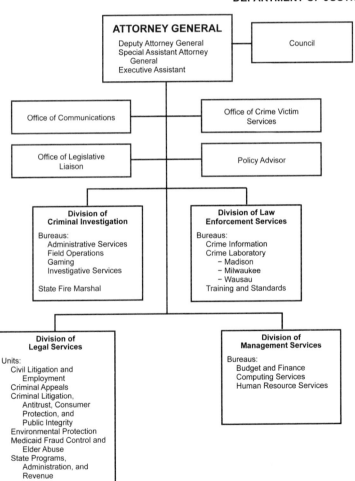

Units attached for administrative purposes under Sec. 15.03: Crime Victims Rights Board
Law Enforcement Standards Board

Crime Victim Services, Office of: Janice Cummings, *executive director,* 266-0109; Fax: 267-1938.

Criminal Investigation, Division of: Michael G. Myszewski, *administrator,* 266-1671; Fax: 267-2777.

    Administrative Services Bureau: Tina R. Virgil, *director,* 266-1671.

    Field Operations Bureau: David Spakowicz, *director,* 266-1671.

    Gaming Bureau: Robbie Lowery, *director,* 266-1671.

    Investigative Services Bureau: Craig S. Klyve, *director,* 266-1671.

    State Fire Marshal: Tina R. Virgil, 266-1671.

Law Enforcement Services, Division of: Gary H. Hamblin, *administrator,* 266-7052; Fax: 266-1656.

    Crime Information Bureau: Walter M. Neverman, *director,* 264-6207.

    Crime Laboratory Bureau-Madison: Jerome A. Geurts, *director,* 266-2031, 4626 University Avenue, Madison 53705-2174.

    Crime Laboratory Bureau-Milwaukee: Jana L. Champion, *director,* (414) 382-7500, 1578 South 11th Street, Milwaukee 53204-2860.

    Crime Laboratory Bureau-Wausau: Michael A. Haas, *director,* (715) 845-8626, 7100 West Stewart Avenue, Wausau 54401.

    Training and Standards Bureau: Kenneth Hammond, *director,* 266-9606.

Legal Services, Division of: Kevin C. Potter, *administrator,* 266-0332; Steven P. Means, *deputy administrator,* 266-3860; Fax: 266-1656.

    Civil Litigation and Employment Unit: Corey Finkelmeyer, *director,* 266-7906.

    Criminal Appeals Unit: Gregory Weber, *director,* 267-2167.

    Criminal Litigation, Antitrust, Consumer Protection, and Public Integrity Unit: Roy Korte, *director,* 266-1447.

    Environmental Protection Unit: Thomas Dawson, *director,* 266-8912.

    Medicaid Fraud Control and Elder Abuse Unit: Thomas Storm, *director,* 266-9222.

    State Programs, Administration, and Revenue Unit: Sandy Tarver, *director,* 266-3952.

Management Services, Division of: Cindy O'Donnell, *administrator,* 267-1300; Fax: 266-1656.

    Budget and Finance, Bureau of: Bonnie Anderson, *director,* 267-6714.

    Computing Services, Bureau of: Frank Ace, *director,* 266-7076.

    Human Resource Services, Bureau of: Gary Martinelli, *director,* 266-0461.

Publications: Opinions of the Attorney General; Annual Report; Criminal Investigation and Physical Evidence Handbook; Domestic Abuse Incident Report; Law Enforcement Bulletin; Safe Schools Legal Resource Manual; *When Crime Strikes: Injured Victims Can Get Help;* Wisconsin Law Enforcement Film Catalog; *Wisconsin Open Meetings Law: A Citizen's Guide; Wisconsin Open Meetings Law: A Compliance Guide; Wisconsin Public Records Law;* Wisconsin Prosecutor's Newsletter; Wisconsin Resource Directory for Crime Victims.

Agency Responsibility: The Department of Justice provides legal advice and representation, criminal investigation, and various law enforcement services for the state. It represents the state in civil cases and handles criminal cases that reach the Wisconsin Court of Appeals or the Wisconsin Supreme Court. It also represents the state in criminal cases on appeal in federal courts and participates with other states in federal cases that are important to Wisconsin. The department provides legal representation in lower courts when expressly authorized by law or requested by the governor, either house of the legislature, or a state agency head. It also represents state agencies in court reviews of their administrative decisions.

Organization: The Department of Justice is supervised by the attorney general, a constitutional officer who is elected on a partisan ballot to a 4-year term. The attorney general appoints the deputy attorney general, the executive assistant, the department's division administrators,

Attorney General J.B. Van Hollen speaks at the Law Enforcement Memorial ceremony on the State Capitol grounds, on May 8, 2009. (Department of Justice)

and the director of the Office of Crime Victim Services. With the exception of the administrator of the Division of Criminal Investigation, which is a classified position, all of these positions serve at the pleasure of the attorney general.

Unit Functions: The *Office of Crime Victim Services* administers state and federal funding to programs that assist victims of crime. Three programs receive full or partial funding from surcharges assessed against convicted criminals: the Crime Victim Compensation Program reimburses eligible victims and their dependents for medical and other qualifying expenses; the Sexual Assault Victim Services (SAVS) Program provides grants to nonprofit organizations that offer services to sexual assault victims; and the Victim/Witness Assistance Program partially reimburses counties for their costs of providing services to crime victims and witnesses. Federal funding supports four programs: the Wisconsin Victim Resource Center, which mediates victims reports of rights violations; the Victims of Crime Act (VOCA) Program that provides grants to programs to provide direct services to innocent victims of crime; the Children's Justice Act, which supports improved investigation, prosecution, and judicial handling of child abuse and neglect; and the Crime Victim Compensation Program.

The *Division of Criminal Investigation,* created in Section 15.253 (2), Wisconsin Statutes, by 1991 Wisconsin Act 269, investigates crimes that are statewide in nature. Special agents work closely with local law enforcement officials and prosecuting attorneys to investigate and prosecute arson, explosions of suspected criminal origin, high level drug trafficking, illegal gaming, child pornography, Internet crimes against children, conducting computer and forensic analysis, antitrust violations, organized crime, financial crimes, and public corruption. Upon request, the division assists local law enforcement agencies on cases, such as homicide and multijurisdictional theft or fraud.

The *Division of Law Enforcement Services* provides advanced technical services, information, and training to state and local law enforcement agencies and jails. It maintains central fingerprint identification records and computerized criminal history information, operates the Handgun Hotline, and provides criminal history background check services. The statewide telecommunications system links Wisconsin police agencies to national, state, and local crime files and databases. Three state crime laboratories, located in Madison, Milwaukee, and Wausau, analyze forensic evidence for the Wisconsin criminal justice system and provide crime scene response in major cases.

The division ensures that all officers at the municipal, county, and state levels meet the mandatory recruitment and training qualifications established by the Law Enforcement Standards Board. Regional academies are certified by the board to offer basic training for law enforcement recruits, jail officers, or security detention officers or to provide the annual recertification classes required for all officers. Training resources and instructors are also provided to local law enforcement organizations.

The *Division of Legal Services* provides legal representation and advice to the governor, legislature, other state officers and agencies, district attorneys, and county corporation counsels. It also provides training and education to all district attorneys and assistant district attorneys. It enforces state environmental, antitrust, employment, consumer protection, and Medicaid fraud laws. It also prosecutes economic crimes and represents the state in all felony appeals and litigation brought by prison inmates. At the request of district attorneys, the division provides special prosecutors in complex homicide, drug, and white collar and other criminal cases. It defends the state in civil lawsuits filed against the state or its officers and employees and handles matters related to public records, Indian law, and fair housing.

The *Division of Management Services* prepares the agency budget; manages agency personnel, finances, and facilities; and provides information technology services.

History: When Wisconsin became a territory in 1836, the U.S. President appointed the attorney general. In 1839, a territorial act gave the governor the power to appoint the attorney general with the consent of the Legislative Council (the upper house of the territorial legislature) to a term of 3 years. The Wisconsin Constitution, as adopted in 1848, provided for an elected attorney general with a 2-year term. A constitutional amendment ratified in 1967 increased the term to 4 years, effective in 1971.

Chapter 75, Laws of 1967, named the agency headed by the attorney general the Department of Justice and transferred to its control the State Crime Laboratory, the arson investigation program from the Commissioner of Insurance, and the criminal investigation functions of the Beverage and Cigarette Tax Division of the Department of Revenue. The 1975 Legislature returned alcohol and tobacco tax enforcement to the Department of Revenue.

The 1969 Legislature added enforcement of certain laws related to dangerous drugs, narcotics, and organized crime to the duties of the department and created the public intervenor to intervene in or initiate proceedings to protect public rights in water and other natural resources. In Chapter 189, Laws of 1979, the legislature transferred the crime victims program from the Department of Industry, Labor and Human Relations to the Department of Justice. 1995 Wisconsin Act 27 transferred the public intervenor to the Department of Natural Resources and consumer protection functions to the Department of Agriculture, Trade and Consumer Protection.

Statutory Council

Crime Victims Council: MICHELLE G. ARROWOOD, ARMENTIE J. MOORE-HAMMONDS (victim services representatives); KURT D. HEUER (law enforcement representative); THOMAS J. COATY (district attorney representative); SCOTT L. HORNE (judicial representative); AVE M. BIE, NICHOLAS J. BREAZEAU, JR., DEBORAH H. JORDAHL, MARGARET R. KENDRIGAN, JENNIFER L. NOYES, MALLORY E. O'BRIEN, MICHAEL S. ROGOWSKI, ANNA M. RUZINSKI, PETER M. TEMPELIS, vacancy (citizen members). (All are appointed by attorney general.)

The 15-member Crime Victims Council provides advice and recommendations on victims' rights issues and legislation. Members are appointed for staggered 3-year terms, and the 10 citizen members must have demonstrated sensitivity and concern for crime victims. The council was created by Chapter 189, Laws of 1979, as the Crime Victims Compensation Council. It was renamed in Chapter 20, Laws of 1981, and its duties and composition are prescribed in Sections 15.09 (5) and 15.257 (2) of the statutes.

INDEPENDENT UNITS ATTACHED FOR BUDGETING, PROGRAM COORDINATION, AND RELATED MANAGEMENT FUNCTIONS BY SECTION 15.03 OF THE STATUTES

CRIME VICTIMS RIGHTS BOARD

Members: KEN KRATZ (district attorney appointed by Wisconsin District Attorneys' Association); KEITH GOVIER (local law enforcement representative appointed by the attorney general); TRISHA ANDERSON (county provider of victim and witness services appointed by attorney general); CHRIS NOLAN (citizen member appointed by the Crime Victims Council); ANGELA SUTKIEWICZ (citizen member appointed by governor).

Statutory References: Sections 15.255 (2) and 950.09.

The 5-member Crime Victims Rights Board may review and investigate complaints filed by victims of crime regarding their rights. The board is an independent agency. The Department of Justice provides staff to help administer the duties of the board, but actions of the board are not subject to approval or review by the attorney general. The board may issue a private or public reprimand against a public official or agency that violates a crime victim's rights; refer a possible violation of a victim's rights by a judge to the judicial commission; seek appropriate relief on behalf of a crime victim necessary to protect that person's rights; or seek a forfeiture up to $1,000 against a public officer or agency for intentional violations. The board can also issue reports and recommendations regarding victims' rights and service provision.

Members serve 4-year terms. The 2 citizen members may not be employed in law enforcement, by a district attorney, or by a county board to provide crime victim's services. The board was created by 1997 Wisconsin Act 181.

LAW ENFORCEMENT STANDARDS BOARD

Members: SCOTT E. PEDLEY (law enforcement representative), *chairperson;* TIMOTHY GOKE, DALE MARSOLEK, FLOYD PETERS, TERRI SMOCZYK, vacancy (law enforcement representatives); TIMOTHY BAXTER (district attorney); MICHAEL J. SERPE, DONNIE SNOW (local government representatives); PATRICIA SEGER (public member); DAVID COLLINS (designated by secretary of transportation); GARY HAMBLIN (designated by attorney general); DAVID O. STEINGRABER (executive director, Office of Justice Assistance), RANDY STARK (designated by secretary of natural resources). Nonvoting member: RICHARD RUMINSKI (special agent in charge, Milwaukee FBI Office). (All except *ex officio* members are appointed by governor.)

Secretary: GARY H. HAMBLIN, *administrator,* Division of Law Enforcement Services, P.O. Box 7857, Madison 53707-7857.

Statutory References: Sections 15.255 and 165.85.

Agency Responsibility: The 15-member Law Enforcement Standards Board sets minimum employment, education, and training standards for law enforcement, tribal law enforcement, and jail and secure detention officers. It certifies persons who meet the standards as qualified to be officers. The board consults with other government agencies regarding the development of training schools and courses, conducts research to improve law enforcement and jail administration and performance, and evaluates governmental units' compliance with standards. Its appointed members serve staggered 4-year terms. The law enforcement representatives must include at least one sheriff and one chief of police. The public member cannot be employed in law enforcement. Chapter 466, Laws of 1969, created the board.

Curriculum Advisory Committee: TONY BARTHULY, DANIEL BURGESS, MICHAEL KING, ROGER LEQUE, RICHARD OLIVA, MICHAEL STEFFES (police chiefs); DARRELL BERGLIN, RON CRAMER, DAVID GRAVES, DAVID PETERSON, TERRY VOGEL, RANDY WRIGHT (sheriffs); SANDRA HUXTABLE (training director, Wisconsin State Patrol) (appointed by Law Enforcement Standards Board).

The 13-member Curriculum Advisory Committee advises the Law Enforcement Standards Board on the establishment of curriculum requirements for training of law enforcement and jail and secure detention officers. The board may appoint no more than one sheriff and one police chief from any one of the state's 8 administrative districts. The statutes do not stipulate length of terms. Chapter 466, Laws of 1969, created the committee and its composition and duties are prescribed in Section 165.85 (3) (d) of the statutes.

Department of
MILITARY AFFAIRS

Commander in Chief: Governor Jim Doyle.

Adjutant General: BRIGADIER GENERAL DONALD P. DUNBAR, 242-3001,
donald.p.dunbar@us.army.mil

Assistant Adjutant General for Army: Brig. Gen. Mark E. Anderson, 242-3010,
mark.e.anderson2@us.army.mil

Assistant Adjutant General for Air: Brig. Gen. John E. McCoy, 242-3020,
john.mccoy@wimadi.ang.af.mil

Division of Emergency Management: Johnnie L. Smith, *administrator,* 242-3210,
johnnie.smith@wisconsin.gov

Executive Assistant: Larry L. Olson, 242-3009, larry.l.olson@us.army.mil

Mailing Address: P.O. Box 8111, Madison 53708-8111.

Location: 2400 Wright Street, Madison 53704-2572.

Telephones: General: 242-3000; Division of Emergency Management: 242-3232; 24-hour
hotline for emergencies and hazardous materials spills: (800) 943-0003.

Fax: 242-3111; Division of Emergency Management: 242-3247.

Internet Address: Department of Military Affairs and Wisconsin National Guard:
http://dma.wi.gov; Wisconsin Emergency Management:
http://emergencymanagement.wi.gov; Wisconsin Homeland Security:
http://homelandsecurity.wi.gov

Number of State Employees: 432.11.

Total State Budget 2007-09: $151,563,100.

Total Federal Budget: Approximately $306 million annually.

Constitutional References: Article IV, Section 29; Article V, Section 4.

Statutory References: Sections 15.31 and 15.313; Chapters 21 and 166.

Adjutant General Staff:

   Assistant Adjutant General – Readiness and Training: Brig. Gen. Dominic A. Cariello.

   U.S. Property and Fiscal Officer: Col. Peter E. Seaholm, Camp Williams, Camp Douglas,
      (608) 427-7266, peter.seaholm@us.army.mil

   Inspector General: Col. Donna Williams, 242-3086, donna.williams@us.army.mil

   Director of Public Affairs: Lt. Col. Jackie Guthrie, 242-3050,
      jacqueline.guthrie@us.army.mil

   Staff Judge Advocate: Col. Julio R. Barron, 242-3077, julio.barron2@us.army.mil

   Legal Counsel: Randi Wind Milsap, 242-3072, randi.milsap@wisconsin.gov

   State Budget and Finance Officer: Brett Coomber, 242-3155,
      brett.coomber@wisconsin.gov

   State Human Resources Officer: Lynn E. Boodry, 242-3163, lynn.boodry@wisconsin.gov

   Wisconsin National Guard Challenge Academy (Fort McCoy): Col. (Ret.) M.G. MacLaren,
      director, (608) 269-9000, director@challenge.dma.state.wi.us

Joint Staff:

   Director, Joint Staff: Brig. Gen. Scott D. Legwold, 242-3006, scott.legwold@us.army.mil

   Human Resources (J1), Director of Manpower and Personnel: Col. Kenneth A. Koon, 242-
      3700, kenneth.koon@us.army.mil

   Intelligence (J2), Director of Security and Intelligence: Lt. Col. Chris J. Charney.

   Operations (J3), Director of Operations: Col. Gunther H. Neumann, 242-3540,
      gunther.h.neumann@ng.army.mil.

Facilities (J4), Director of Installation Management: Col. Jeffrey J. Liethen, 242-3365, jeffrey.liethen@wisconsin.gov

Strategic Plans (J5/J7), Director of Strategic Plans and Policy: Lt. Col. Steven Sherrod, 242-3036, steven.g.sherrod@us.army.mil

Information Systems (J6), Director of Information Systems: Col. Steven Lewis, 242-3650, steven.lewis2@us.army.mil

Resource Management (J8), Director of Property and Fiscal Operations: Col. John Van de Loop, (608) 427-7212, john.vandeloop@us.army.mil

Director of Counterdrug Division: Col. Paul F. Russell, 242-3540, paul.f.russell@wimadi.ang.af.mil

Commander, 54th Civil Support Team (CST): Maj. Timothy Covington, 245-8431, timothy.covington@us.army.mil

Wisconsin Army National Guard: Brig. Gen. Mark E. Anderson, *commander,* 242-3010, mark.e.anderson2@us.army.mil

State Command Sergeant Major: Command Sgt. Maj. George E. Stopper, 242-3012, george.stopper@us.army.mil

Army National Guard Staff:

Chief of Staff, Army Staff: Col. Kevin J. Greenwood, 242-3030, kevin.j.greenwood@us.army.mil

Deputy Chief of Staff for Personnel (G1): Col. Mark W. Bruns, 242-3444, mark.bruns@us.army.mil

Deputy Chief of Staff for Operations (G3): Col. Tim Lawson, 242-3500, tim-lawson@us.army.mil

Deputy Chief of Staff for Logistics (G4): Col. John Schroeder, 242-3552, john.schroeder@us.army.mil

Deputy Chief of Staff for Aviation and Safety: Col. Jeffrey D. Paulson, 242-3140, jeffrey.paulson2@us.army.mil

Recruiting and Retention Command: Lt. Col. Russell Sweet, 242-3804, russell.j.sweet@us.army.mil

State Surface Maintenance Manager: Lt. Col. Galen D. White, (608) 427-7223, galen.white@us.army.mil

State Surgeon: Col. Kenneth K. Lee, 242-3443, kenneth.k.lee@us.army.mil

Army National Guard Units (major commands):

32nd Infantry Brigade Combat Team (Camp Douglas): Col. Steve Bensend, *commander;* Lt. Col. Mark R. Greenwood, *administrative officer,* (608) 427-7349, mark.greenwood@us.army.mil

157th Maneuver Enhancement Brigade (Milwaukee): Col. Mark Michie, *commander;* Maj. Eric J. Leckel, *administrative officer,* (414) 961-8682, eric.leckel@us.army.mil

64th Troop Command (Madison): Col. Darrel Feucht, *commander;* Lt. Col. Ricky Kappus, *administrative officer,* 242-3840, ricky.kappus@us.army.mil

426th Regiment (Wisconsin Military Academy) (Fort McCoy): Col. Kenneth A. Koon, *commander;* Maj. Gary Thompson, *administrative officer,* (608) 388-9990, gary.r.thompson1@us.army.mil

Wisconsin Air National Guard: Brig. Gen. John E. McCoy, 242-3020, john.mccoy@wimadi.ang.af.mil

Command Chief Master Sergeant: Command Chief Master Sgt. James F. Chisholm.

Air National Guard Staff:

Chief of Staff, Air Staff: Brig. Gen. Margaret H. Bair.

Director of Staff: Col. Murry Mitten, 242-3120, murry.mitten@wimadi.ang.af.mil

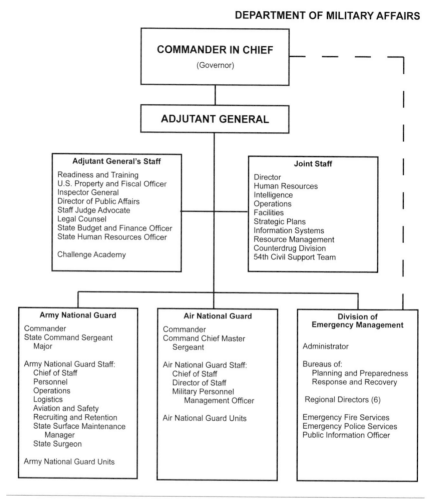

DEPARTMENT OF MILITARY AFFAIRS

COMMANDER IN CHIEF
(Governor)

ADJUTANT GENERAL

Adjutant General's Staff

Readiness and Training
U.S. Property and Fiscal Officer
Inspector General
Director of Public Affairs
Staff Judge Advocate
Legal Counsel
State Budget and Finance Officer
State Human Resources Officer

Challenge Academy

Joint Staff

Director
Human Resources
Intelligence
Operations
Facilities
Strategic Plans
Information Systems
Resource Management
Counterdrug Division
54th Civil Support Team

Army National Guard

Commander
State Command Sergeant
 Major

Army National Guard Staff:
 Chief of Staff
 Personnel
 Operations
 Logistics
 Aviation and Safety
 Recruiting and Retention
 State Surface Maintenance
  Manager
 State Surgeon

Army National Guard Units

Air National Guard

Commander
Command Chief Master
 Sergeant

Air National Guard Staff:
 Chief of Staff
 Director of Staff
 Military Personnel
  Management Officer

Air National Guard Units

**Division of
Emergency Management**

Administrator

Bureaus of:
 Planning and Preparedness
 Response and Recovery

Regional Directors (6)

Emergency Fire Services
Emergency Police Services
Public Information Officer

Military Personnel Management Officer: Lt. Col. Brian S. Buhler, 242-3122, brian.buhler@wimadi.ang.af.mil

Air National Guard Units (major commands):

115th Fighter Wing (Madison): Col. Joseph J. Brandemuehl, *commander,* 245-4501, joe.brandemuehl@wimadi.ang.af.mil

128th Air Refueling Wing (Milwaukee): Col. Edward E. Metzgar, *commander,* (414) 944-8333, edward.metzgar@wimilw.ang.af.mil

Volk Field Combat Readiness Training Center (Camp Douglas): Col. Gary L. Ebben, *commander,* (608) 427-1200, gary.ebben@ang.af.mil

128th Air Control Squadron (Volk Field): Lt. Col. Herbert T. Dannenberg, *commander,* (608) 427-1295, herb.dannenberg@wicrtc.ang.af.mil

Emergency Management, Division of: Johnnie L. Smith, *administrator,* 242-3210, johnnie.smith@wisconsin.gov

Planning and Preparedness, Bureau of: Steve Peterson, *director,* 242-3206, steve.peterson@wisconsin.gov

Lt. Col. Glen Messner, 115th Fighter Wing, flies a Wisconsin Air National Guard F-16 Fighting Falcon past the State Capitol in Madison. (Wisconsin Air National Guard photo by Master Sgt. Paul Gorman)

Response and Recovery, Bureau of: LAWRENCE C. REED III, *director,* 242-3203, larry.reed@wisconsin.gov

Public Information Officer: LORI GETTER, 242-3239, lori.getter@wisconsin.gov

Southwest Regional Office (Madison): PATRICK O'CONNOR, *director and response section supervisor,* 242-3336, patrick.oconnor@wisconsin.gov

East Central Regional Office (Fond du Lac): DAN DAHLKE, *director,* (920) 929-3730, dan.dahlke@wisconsin.gov

Northeast Regional Office (Wausau): ROB RUDE, *director,* (715) 845-9517, rob.rude@wisconsin.gov

Northwest Regional Office (Spooner): RHONDA REYNOLDS, *director,* (715) 635-8704, rhonda.reynolds@wisconsin.gov

Southeast Regional Office (Waukesha): PAUL FRANCE, *director,* (262) 782-1515, paul.france@wisconsin.gov

West Central Regional Office (Eau Claire): LOIS RISTOW, *director,* (715) 839-3825, lois.ristow@wisconsin.gov

Emergency Fire Services: KEITH TVEIT, *coordinator,* (608) 220-6049, keith.tveit@wisconsin.gov

Emergency Police Services: DALLAS NEVILLE, *coordinator,* (608) 444-0003, dallas.neville@wisconsin.gov

Publications: *At Ease;* Biennial Report; Wisconsin Emergency Management *Digest;* Wisconsin Homeland Security *Homefront.*

Agency Responsibility: The Department of Military Affairs provides an armed military force through the Wisconsin National Guard, which is organized, trained, equipped, and available for deployment under official orders in state and national emergencies. The federal mission of the National Guard is to provide trained units to the U.S. Army and U.S. Air Force in time of war or national emergency. Its state mission is to help civil authorities protect life and property and preserve peace, order, and public safety in times of natural or human-caused emergencies.

The *Division of Emergency Management* is headed by a division administrator appointed by the governor with the advice and consent of the senate. It coordinates the development and implementation of the state emergency operations plan; provides assistance to local jurisdictions in the development of their programs and plans; administers private and federal disaster and emergency relief funds; administers the Wisconsin Disaster Fund; and maintains the state's 24-hour duty officer reporting and response system. The division also conducts training programs in emergency planning for businesses and state and local officials, as well as educational programs for the general public. Under Title III of the federal 1986 Superfund Amendments and Reauthorization Act and 1987 Wisconsin Act 342, the division requires public and private entities that possess hazardous substances to file reports on these substances. It establishes local emergency response committees and oversees implementation of their plans and corresponding state plans. The division administers emergency planning performance grants that assist local emergency planning committees in complying with state and federal law. In addition, the division contracts with regional hazardous materials response teams which respond to the most dangerous levels of hazardous substance releases. It also coordinates planning and training for off-site radiological emergencies at nuclear power plants in and near Wisconsin. The Emergency Police Services (EPS) program provides support to law enforcement in times of crisis. The program coordinates state law enforcement response to emergencies, including coordination of mutual aid for law enforcement assistance in natural disasters, prison disturbances, and other emergencies. The Emergency Fire Services Coordinator enhances fire service emergency response throughout the state and coordinates intrastate mutual aid through the Mutual Aid Box Alarm System (MABAS).

A key resource within Wisconsin Emergency Management (WEM) is its system of 6 regional offices located throughout the state. The regional offices are co-located with the Wisconsin State Patrol regional posts in Waukesha, Fond du Lac, Eau Claire, Spooner, and Wausau, and at WEM's central office in Madison. Each office is assigned to work with a group of 8 to 14 counties. Regional directors are knowledgeable in each of the division's programs, and support both municipal and county programs in planning, training, exercising, response and recovery activities, as well as the coordination of administrative activities between the division and local governments. When disasters and emergencies strike, regional directors are the division's initial responders, serving as field liaisons for the State Emergency Operations Center.

The *Wisconsin Homeland Security Council* was created in March 2003 (Executive Order 7) to advise the governor and coordinate the efforts of state and local officials regarding the prevention of, and response to, potential threats to the homeland security of the state. Council members are appointed by and serve at the pleasure of the governor with the adjutant general serving as the chairperson. The council works with federal, state, and local agencies, nongovernment organizations, and private industry to prevent and respond to any threat of terrorism, promote personal preparedness, and make recommendations to the governor on what additional steps are needed to further enhance Wisconsin's homeland security.

Organization: The Wisconsin Constitution designates the governor as the commander in chief of the Wisconsin National Guard. The department is directed by the adjutant general, who is appointed by the governor for a 5-year term and may serve successive terms. The adjutant general must be an officer actively serving in the Army or Air National Guard of Wisconsin who has attained at least the rank of colonel and is fully qualified to hold the rank of major general in either the Army or Air National Guard.

In addition to state support, the Wisconsin National Guard is also funded and maintained by the federal government, and when it is called up in an active federal duty status, the president of the United States becomes its commander in chief. The federal government provides arms and ammunition, equipment and uniforms, major outdoor training facilities, pay for military and support personnel, and training and supervision. The state provides personnel; conducts training as required under the National Defense Act; and shares the cost of constructing, maintaining, and operating armories and other military facilities. The composition of Wisconsin Army and Air National Guard units is authorized by the U.S. secretary of defense through the National

Guard Bureau. All officers and enlisted personnel must meet the same physical, education, and other eligibility requirements as members of the active-duty U.S. Army or U.S. Air Force.

History: Until the 20th century, the United States relied heavily on military units organized by the states to fight its wars. Known as "minutemen" in the American Revolution, state militias, which could be called up on brief notice, provided soldiers for the Revolutionary War, the Mexican War, the Civil War, and the Spanish-American War.

In 1792, the U.S. Congress passed a law that required all able-bodied men between 18 and 45 years of age to serve in local militia units, a provision that was incorporated into the territorial statutes of Wisconsin. The Wisconsin Constitution, as adopted in 1848, authorized the legislature to determine the composition, organization, and discipline of the state militia.

The 1849 Wisconsin Statutes specified the procedure for the organization of locally controlled "uniform companies". Each uniform company included 30 men who had to equip themselves with arms and uniforms.

By 1858 (Chapter 87), the legislature provided for the organization of the state militia, which ultimately replaced the uniform companies. As commander in chief of the militia, the governor appointed the adjutant general and the general officers and issued commissions to the elected officers of uniform companies. The governor could provide arms for the officers, but they were required to supply their own uniforms and horses. Not until 1873 (Chapter 202) was money appropriated from the general fund to help support militia companies. Chapter 208, Laws of 1879, changed the militia's name to the Wisconsin National Guard.

Federal supervision of and financial responsibility for the National Guard came with Congressional passage of the Dick Act in 1903. Congress passed the law in response to the lack of uniformity among state units, which became evident during the Spanish-American War and subsequent occupation of the Philippines. The act set standards for Guard units, granted federal aid, and provided for inspections by regular U.S. Army officers.

The National Defense Act of 1933 formally created the National Guard of the United States, a reserve component of the U.S. Army. The act allowed the mobilization of intact National

Wisconsin National Guard soldiers and airmen fire a ceremonial howitzer at the 2008 Rhythm and Booms Independence Day fireworks celebration at Warner Park, Madison, June 28, 2008. (Wisconsin National Guard photo by Officer Candidate Emily Yttri)

Guard units through their simultaneous dual enlistment as state and federal military forces. This permitted Guard personnel to mobilize for federal duty directly from state status in event of a federal emergency, rather than being discharged to enlist in the federal forces, as was done in World War I. A 1990 U.S. Supreme Court case upheld the authority of the U.S. Congress to send Army National Guard units (under U.S. Army command) out of the country to train for their federal mission.

Wisconsin National Guard troops fought in the Civil War, the Spanish-American War, World War I, and World War II. Wisconsin troops from the "Iron Brigade" gained national recognition in the Civil War, and the 32nd "Red Arrow" Infantry Division won fame for its combat record in both World Wars. The Wisconsin Air National Guard became a separate service in 1947, and members of the Wisconsin Air Guard served in the Korean War. Over the past 50 years, Wisconsin units have been called to active federal service on numerous occasions. In 1961, the 32nd Division was activated during the Berlin Crisis. More than 1,400 Guard members from Wisconsin were sent to the Persian Gulf to participate in Operations Desert Shield and Desert Storm in 1990-91. Beginning in 1996, units were called to support peacekeeping efforts in the Balkans. Wisconsin Air National Guard units were deployed to enforce U.N. no-fly zones in Southwest Asia in the 1990s, and two units were called to support Operation Allied Force, the NATO air operations over Kosovo in 1999.

Within hours of the September 11, 2001, terrorist attacks on America, the Wisconsin National Guard began yet another period of extensive support to U.S. military operations. Air National Guard units in Wisconsin have provided fighter aircraft to patrol the skies over major U.S. cities and critical national infrastructure, tanker aircraft to refuel patrolling fighters and U.S. military aircraft overseas, and critical radar support to North American Aerospace Defense Command and the Federal Aviation Administration.

Wisconsin Army National Guard units began mobilizing into active federal service in December 2001. Since then, nearly every unit in the Wisconsin Army and Air National Guard has been ordered to active duty in support of operations in Afghanistan (Operation Enduring Freedom) and Iraq (Operation Iraqi Freedom), as well as homeland defense missions in the United States (Operation Noble Eagle) and continuing operations in the Balkans. In 2009, nearly 4,000 Wisconsin Guard members will deploy in support of the Global War on Terror including 3,200 members of the 32nd Infantry Brigade Combat Team who are conducting the largest operational deployment since World War II.

However, while the soldiers and airmen of the state's militia continue to deploy overseas and serve in harm's way when America calls, they remain available to answering the call to service in Wisconsin and throughout the nation when a natural disaster strikes or in response to domestic emergencies.

The **Division of Emergency Management** originated as the Office of Civil Defense, which was developed to administer emergency programs in case of enemy attack and was located in the governor's office under Chapter 443, Laws of 1951. Its predecessors include the Wisconsin Council of Defense, organized by executive order of Governor Julius P. Heil in 1940, and the State Council on Civil Defense, created in the governor's office by Chapter 9, Laws of 1943. The 1943 council was abolished in 1945 and its functions transferred to the adjutant general, who was appointed director of the Office of Civil Defense by the governor, as permitted in the 1951 law.

Chapter 628, Laws of 1959, renamed the office the Bureau of Civil Defense and added responsibilities for natural and human-caused disasters. The 1967 executive branch reorganization transferred the bureau to the Department of Local Affairs and Development as the Division of Emergency Government. In Chapter 361, Laws of 1979, the division was transferred to the Department of Administration. The division became part of the Department of Military Affairs in 1989 Wisconsin Act 31 and was renamed by 1995 Wisconsin Act 247. When 1997 Wisconsin Act 27 abolished the State Emergency Response Board, the division assumed the board's responsibilities pertaining to hazardous chemical substances and spills and the contracts with regional hazardous materials response teams. Since 1997, Wisconsin Emergency Management has coordinated the state's terrorism preparedness efforts by working to deter, prevent, respond to, and recover from terrorist attacks. In March 2003 (Executive Order 7), Governor Doyle created the Governor's Homeland Security Council to advise the governor and coordinate the efforts of state and local officials regarding the prevention of, and response to, potential threats to the homeland security of the state. The council works with federal, state, and local agencies, nonprofit organizations, and private industry to prevent and respond to any threat of terrorism, to promote personal preparedness, and to make recommendations to the governor on what additional steps are needed to further enhance Wisconsin's homeland security.

Department of
NATURAL RESOURCES

Natural Resources Board: CHRISTINE L. THOMAS (southern member), *chairperson;* JONATHAN P. ELA (southern member), *vice chairperson;* JOHN W. WELTER (northern member), *secretary;* DAVID CLAUSEN, JANE WILEY (northern members); PRESTON D. COLE (southern member); GARY E. RHODE (member-at-large). (All are appointed by governor with senate consent.)

Secretary of Natural Resources: MATTHEW J. FRANK, 266-7556, DNR.Secretary.Frank@

Deputy Secretary: PATRICK HENDERSON, 264-6266, patrick.henderson@

Executive Assistant: MARY ELLEN VOLLBRECHT, 267-9521, mary.vollbrecht@

Legislative and Policy Advisor: PAUL HEINEN, 266-2120, paul.heinen@

Legal Services, Bureau of: vacancy, *director.*

Management and Budget, Bureau of: JOSEPH P. POLASEK, JR., *director,* 266-2794, joseph.polasekjr@

Diversity Affairs, Office of: RUDOLPH F. BENTLEY, *director,* 267-9481, rudolph.bentley@

Mailing Address: P.O. Box 7921, Madison 53707-7921.

Location: State Natural Resources Building (GEF 2), 101 South Webster Street, Madison.

Telephones: Customer and General Information: (888) WDNRINFo (936-7463) or (608) 266-2621; Violation Hotline (to confidentially report suspected wildlife, recreational, and environmental violations): (800) TIP-WDNR (847-9367) or #367 by cellular phone; Hazardous Substance Spill Line: (800) 943-0003; Outdoor Report (recorded message): (608) 266-2277; Daily Air Quality: (866) 324-5924; Gypsy Moth: (800) 642-6684; Emerald Ash Borer: (800) 462-2803; Firewood: (877) 303-9663; Burning Permits (888) WIS-BURN (947-2876).

Fax: (608) 261-4380.

TTY: (608) 267-6897.

Internet Address: dnr.wi.gov

Address e-mail by combining the user ID and the state extender: userid@**wisconsin.gov**

Air and Waste, Division of: ALLEN K. SHEA, *administrator,* 266-5896, allen.shea@; SUZANNE A. BANGERT, *deputy administrator,* 266-0014, suzanne.bangert@

   Air Management, Bureau of: JOHN H. MELBY, JR., *director,* 264-8884, john.melbyjr@

   Cooperative Environmental Assistance, Bureau of: MARK MCDERMID, *director,* 267-3125, mark.mcdermid@

   Remediation and Redevelopment, Bureau of: MARK F. GIESFELDT, *director,* 267-7562, mark.giesfeldt@

   Waste and Materials Management, Bureau of: vacancy, *director.*

Customer and Employee Services, Division of: VANCE RAYBURN, *administrator,* 266-2241, vance.rayburn@

   Community Financial Assistance, Bureau of: vacancy, *director.*

   Customer Service and Licensing, Bureau of: DIANE L. BROOKBANK, *director,* 267-7799, diane.brookbank@

DEPARTMENT OF NATURAL RESOURCES

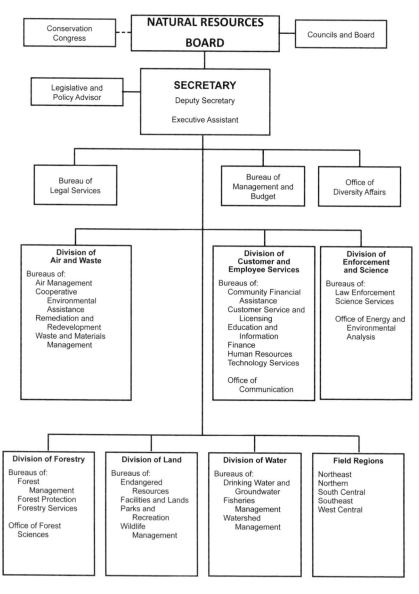

Units attached for administrative purposes under Sec. 15.03: Groundwater Coordinating Council
Invasive Species Council
Lake Michigan Commercial Fishing Board
Lake Superior Commercial Fishing Board
Council on Recycling
Wisconsin Waterways Commission

Education and Information, Bureau of: JEFFREY SMOLLER, *director,* 266-2747, jeffrey.smoller@

Finance, Bureau of: MICHELE A. YOUNG, *director,* 266-7566, michele.young@

Human Resources, Bureau of: vacancy, *director.*

Technology Services, Bureau of: ARTHUR K. PRZYBYL, *director,* 266-7547, arthur.przybyl@

Communication, Office of: LAUREL J. STEFFES, *director,* 266-8109, laurel.steffes@

Enforcement and Science, Division of: vacancy, *administrator.*

   Law Enforcement, Bureau of: RANDALL J. STARK, *director,* 266-1115, randall.stark@

   Science Services, Bureau of: JOHN R. SULLIVAN, *director,* 267-9753, john.r.sullivan@

   Energy and Environmental Analysis, Office of: DAVID R. SIEBERT, *director,* 264-6048, david.siebert@

Forestry, Division of: PAUL DELONG, *administrator and State Forester,* 264-9224, paul.delong@; vacancy, *deputy administrator.*

   Forest Management, Bureau of: ROBERT J. MATHER, *director,* 266-1727, robert.mather@

   Forest Protection, Bureau of: TRENT L. MARTY, *director,* 266-7978, trent.marty@

   Forestry Services, Bureau of: WENDY M. MCCOWN, *director,* 266-7510, wendy.mccown@

   Forest Sciences, Office of: DARRELL E. ZASTROW, *director,* 266-0290, darrell.zastrow@

Land, Division of: LAURIE OSTERNDORF, *administrator,* 267-7552, laurie.osterndorf@; vacancy, *deputy administrator.*

   Endangered Resources, Bureau of: SIGNE L. HOLTZ, *director,* 264-9210, signe.holtz@

   Facilities and Lands, Bureau of: STEVEN W. MILLER, *director,* 266-5782, steven.miller@

   Parks and Recreation, Bureau of: DANIEL J. SCHULLER, *director,* 266-2185, daniel.schuller@

   Wildlife Management, Bureau of: THOMAS M. HAUGE, *director,* 266-2193, thomas.hauge@

Water, Division of: TODD L. AMBS, *administrator,* 264-6278, todd.ambs@; BRUCE J. BAKER, *deputy administrator,* 266-1902, bruce.baker@

   Drinking Water and Groundwater, Bureau of: JILL D. JONAS, *director,* 267-7545, jill.jonas@

   Fisheries Management, Bureau of: MICHAEL D. STAGGS, *director,* 267-0796, mike.staggs@

   Watershed Management, Bureau of: RUSSELL A. RASMUSSEN, *director,* 267-7651, russell.rasmussen@

Field Regions:

   Northeast: RONALD KAZMIERCZAK, *director,* (920) 662-5115, 2984 Shawano Avenue, Green Bay 54313-6727, ronald.kazmierczak@

   Northern: JOHN F. GOZDZIALSKI, *director,* (715) 635-4002, 810 West Maple Street, Spooner 54801; Co-regional office: (715) 369-8900, 107 Sutliff Avenue, Rhinelander 54501, john.gozdzialski@

   South Central: LLOYD EAGAN, *director,* (608) 275-3206, 3911 Fish Hatchery Road, Fitchburg 53711, lloyd.eagan@

   Southeast: GLORIA L. MCCUTCHEON, *director,* (414) 263-8510, 2300 North Dr. Martin Luther King Jr. Drive, Milwaukee 53212, gloria.mccutcheon@

   West Central: SCOTT HUMRICKHOUSE, *director,* (715) 839-3711, 1300 West Clairemont Avenue, P.O. Box 4001, Eau Claire 54702-4001, scott.humrickhouse@

Publications: *Wisconsin Natural Resources* (bimonthly magazine by subscription – call (608) 267-7410 or (800) 678-9472); *Wisconsin State Parks – Explore and Enjoy;* parks newspapers and visitor guides; hunting, fishing, trapping, snowmobiling, ATV, and boating regulations; various brochures, fact sheets, and reports (lists available). Teachers may write to the Bureau of Education and Information for a list of publications. Individuals may subscribe to receive weekly e-mail links to the DNR Weekly News, DNR Outdoor Report, and other topics at: dnr.wi.gov/newsletters.

Number of Employees: 2,745.53.

Total Budget 2007-09: $1,143,299,200.

Statutory References: Sections 15.05 (1) (c), 15.34, and 15.343; Chapters 23, 26-33, 87, 88, and 160.

Agency Responsibility: The Department of Natural Resources (DNR) is responsible for implementing state and federal laws that protect and enhance Wisconsin's natural resources, including its air, land, water, forests, wildlife, fish, and plants. It coordinates the many state-administered programs that protect the environment and provides a full range of outdoor recreational opportunities for Wisconsin residents and visitors.

Organization: The 7 members of the Natural Resources Board serve staggered 6-year terms. At least 3 of them must be from the northern part of the state and at least 3 from the southern part. Board members are subject to restrictions on holding DNR permits or depending on permit holders for a significant portion of their income. The board directs and supervises the department and acts as a formal point of contact for citizens.

The department is administered by a secretary appointed by the governor with the advice and consent of the senate. The secretary appoints the department's division administrators from outside the classified service. The regional directors, who are appointed from the classified service, manage all of the agency's field operations for their respective areas and report directly to the secretary.

Unit Functions: The *Division of Air and Waste* protects the state's air quality and general environmental health through air pollution control and solid and hazardous waste management in cooperation with the federal Environmental Protection Agency, international agencies, local governments, private industry, and citizens. It develops air quality implementation plans, monitors air quality, conducts inspections, operates a permit program, and initiates compliance actions in accordance with state and federal requirements. The division's waste and materials management program oversees plan review, licensing, inspection, and compliance actions, relating to the generation, transportation, treatment, storage, reuse, and disposal of solid and hazardous waste materials. It reviews and approves local recycling programs and provides technical and marketing assistance and public outreach in support of recycling efforts and expertise for businesses regarding pollution prevention and waste reduction. It also regulates metallic mining activities and oversees the statewide implementation of county and local nonmetallic mining reclamation programs. The division's remediation and redevelopment program is responsible for the cleanup of contaminated sites that fall under the following legislation: the hazardous substances spills law, the environmental repair law, the abandoned container law, the federal Superfund and Brownfields laws, the state land recycling law, and the Resource Conservation and Recovery Act. The division's Cooperative Environmental Assistance Program promotes Wisconsin as a model "green" state through Green Tier and other environmental programs designed to enhance business performance.

The *Division of Customer and Employee Services* provides a variety of customer services including the sale of hunting and fishing licenses, boat, ATV, and snowmobile registration, environmental education programs, and public information. It oversees distribution of financial aids for environmental programs that benefit local governments and nonprofit conservation organizations, such as the Clean Water Fund and the Stewardship Fund, and acts as liaison to federal and state agencies. The division also provides a variety of management services for the department, including budgetary and financial services, personnel and human resource management, computer and information technology support, affirmative action, employee assistance, training, and telecommunication services.

The *Division of Enforcement and Science* is responsible for enforcing the state's conservation, hunting, fishing, environmental, and recreational safety laws, for providing scientific research and environmental analyses to inform agency policy and operational decisions on natural resource issues, for providing interagency coordination of the review of transportation infrastructure projects, and for providing a central point of contact for the regulated community on energy-related projects. The division's wardens and environmental staff promote safety and compliance with the law through enforcement and educational outreach programs, such as classes in hunting, boating, snowmobile, and all-terrain vehicle safety, and community involvement programs such as the Learn to Hunt Program. The division reviews major public and private proposals under the federal and state Environmental Policy Acts, and certifies laboratories and laboratory operators for wastewater treatment systems, water supply systems, incinerators, sanitary landfills, and septage services. The division is also responsible for provision of agency laboratory services (analytical chemistry and biological) through the Wisconsin State Laboratory of Hygiene and other private contract laboratories as necessary. The division also conducts biological and social science research, provides technical writing, editing, and publication of research results, and provides expertise to assist other divisions and guide the department in policy formation. The Office of Energy and Environmental Analysis is also housed in the division, and is responsible for coordinating the regulatory review for all energy and transportation projects statewide. The office also serves all DNR programs coordinating the environmental review of complex projects under the Wisconsin Environmental Policy Act.

The *Division of Forestry,* created by 1999 Wisconsin Act 9, is responsible for the administration and implementation of programs that protect and manage the state's forest resources in a sustainable manner so as to provide economic, ecological, social, recreational, and cultural benefits. The division is involved with the management of about 16 million acres of public and private forest land and millions of urban trees in the state. All of the 500,000 acres of state forest land were certified in 2004 as sustainably managed by third party auditors from the Forest Stewardship Council and Sustainable Forestry Initiative. More than 2 million acres of county forest lands, which DNR works in partnership with 29 counties to manage, were certified in 2005, as were over 2 million acres of private lands managed under the Managed Forest Law pro-

Department of Natural Resources forest fire control staff work with county and tribal law enforcement agencies during a forest fire near Hayward. The DNR fire captain coordinated successful operations to evacuate residents from threatened areas and contain and suppress the fire. (Department of Natural Resources)

gram. Foresters provide assistance to private woodlot owners; offer expertise in urban forestry; manage and monitor forest insects and diseases; operate three tree nurseries; provide public education and awareness activities; and work in partnership with local governments, the timber industry, environmental groups, and recreation interests. The division administers grants and loans to county forests, urban forestry grants to communities, forest landowner grants to woodland owners, and forest fire protection grants to fire departments. The fire management program is responsible for forest fire protection on 18 million acres of forest, brush, and grassland and coordinates with local fire departments to prevent and control forest fires.

The *Division of Land* has major responsibility for protecting and conserving the state's biological diversity and providing nature-based recreational opportunities. The division administers programs related to wildlife; state lands, parks, trails, southern forests, and recreation areas; rare and endangered animal and plant species, and natural communities; and outdoor recreational resources. The division operates educational programs and helps private landowners manage their lands for the benefit of wildlife and rare resources. It manages wildlife and habitats on about 1.5 million acres of land owned or leased by the state and works with federal, county, and other local government authorities to protect and manage the resources on an additional 3.6 million acres of public lands, including national and county forests. The wildlife program manages populations such as deer, bear, furbearers, waterfowl and birds, and maintains and restores habitats such as wetlands, grasslands, and prairies. The endangered resources program conserves Wisconsin's rare and declining species and natural communities through the State Natural Areas program and the Nongame and Endangered Species program work that is supported primarily by funds derived from voluntary contributions designated by taxpayers on their state income tax returns and through purchase of the Endangered Resources license plate. The Endangered Resources program also supports ecosystem management decision-making in the department through the Citizen-Based Monitoring Program, the Natural Heritage Inventory Program, and the Aquatic and Terrestrial Resources inventory. Parks personnel manage the state's extensive parks, southern forests, recreation areas, and trails systems, including the Ice Age and North Country National Scenic Trails, which are designed for the conservation of natural resources and a wide variety of recreational activities including biking, hiking, snowmobiling, and camping. The division is also responsible for land acquisition for parks, trails, southern forests, recreation areas, wildlife areas, fishery areas, natural areas, and other state wildlife-related recreation lands, as well as property planning and the development of public use facilities on state lands. It coordinates the Stewardship Program, which provides grants for the purchase of lands for natural and recreational areas, wildlife habitats, urban green spaces, local parks, trails, and riverways.

The *Division of Water* works with many partners to protect public health and safety, and the quality and quantity of Wisconsin's groundwater, surface water, and aquatic ecosystems. The division is responsible for implementing the Clean Water Act in order to achieve the goal of fishable and swimmable waters throughout Wisconsin. Division staff work to prevent or regulate water pollution from industries, municipal sewage treatment facilities, construction sites, farms, and urban areas. The division monitors compliance, sets water quality standards, and provides financial and technical assistance. Division programs protect drinking water and groundwater resources for both human and ecosystem health, and ensure the safety and security of the state's drinking water systems and private wells. The division strives to enhance and restore outstanding fisheries in Wisconsin's waters. It regulates sport and commercial fishing through licensing and provides fish hatchery services, fish stocking and surveying, aquatic habit improvement, angler education, and public access programs. The division helps protect the waters of the state that are held in trust for all the people of the state through the Public Trust Doctrine. Division staff oversee the placement of structures in state waters, wetland management and restoration, shoreland zoning, and floodplain management. The division helps local government units to protect lives and property through floodplain management and dam safety inspections. The division cooperates with many states and Canada to protect the water quality, quantity, and ecosystems of the Mississippi River and Great Lakes basins.

The *Field Regions* enable the department to make its programs accessible to the general public. Each of the 5 regions is divided into 4 to 6 geographic management units whose boundaries are principally based on major river basins. Most DNR field staff work within these units, although some, such as conservation wardens, are assigned to counties within units. This structure combines employees with different types of expertise into interdisciplinary teams responsible for assessing natural resource and environmental needs from a broader perspective.

History: Today, the Department of Natural Resources has dual responsibility for both traditional conservation duties and environmental protection. Its history and structure reflect more than a century of government and citizen involvement with these concerns. Wisconsin's earliest conservation legislation focused on fish, game, and forests. Chapter 253, Laws of 1874, created a Board of Fish Commissioners charged with hatching fish eggs received from the federal government and distributing the fry to Wisconsin waters. The governor was authorized in 1885 by Chapter 455 to appoint 3 fish wardens to enforce fishing regulations and collect statistics from commercial fishermen. Chapter 456, Laws of 1887, directed the governor to appoint 4 game wardens to enforce all laws protecting fish and game.

Chapter 229, Laws of 1897, established a 3-member commission to develop legislation creating a forestry department. The commission was directed to devise ways to use the state's forest resources without harming the climate or water supplies and to preserve forest resources without retarding the state's economic development. The report of this commission led to Chapter 450, Laws of 1903, which established a Department of State Forestry with a superintendent appointed by the Board of State Forest Commissioners. Chapter 495, Laws of 1907, created a State Park Board with authority to acquire and manage land for park purposes.

Chapter 406, Laws of 1915, consolidated all park and conservation functions under a 3-member Conservation Commission of Wisconsin, appointed by the governor with senate approval. From then until 1995, the management and conservation of Wisconsin's natural resources was directed by a part-time commission or board, except for the period 1923 to 1927, when a single full-time commissioner was created by Chapter 118, Laws of 1923, to head the Department of Conservation. Since the enactment of 1995 Wisconsin Act 27, which provided that the secretary would be appointed by the governor with senate consent rather than appointed by the board, the current board's role has been an advisory one.

The 1960s saw major changes in conservation legislation. Chapter 427, Laws of 1961, created a committee charged with developing a long-range plan for acquiring and improving outdoor recreation areas. It initiated the Outdoor Recreation Act Program (ORAP) to fund land acquisitions. In 1969, Chapter 353 expanded ORAP and authorized the state to incur debt up to $56 million between 1969 and 1981 for the purpose of providing outdoor recreation opportunities. With enactment of 1989 Wisconsin Act 31, the legislature created the Stewardship Program, which authorized up to $250 million in state debt to acquire and develop land for recreational uses, wildlife habitats, fisheries, and natural areas.

Wisconsin's antipollution efforts date back to Chapter 412, Laws of 1911, when the legislature gave the State Board of Health investigative powers in water pollution cases. Prior to that, such investigations were primarily the responsibility of local government. In Chapter 264, Laws of 1927, the legislature created a committee to supervise the water pollution control activities carried out by several state agencies, including the Conservation Commission. The Department of Resource Development, which had been created by Chapter 442, Laws of 1959, assumed water pollution control duties under Chapter 614, Laws of 1965, and statewide air pollution regulation with Chapter 83, Laws of 1967.

In the 1967 executive branch reorganization, the legislature created the Department of Natural Resources by combining the Department of Conservation and the Department of Resource Development. The new department was given authority to regulate air and water quality, as well as solid waste disposal, and directed to develop an integrated program to protect air, land, and water resources.

Chapter 274, Laws of 1971, required all state agencies to report on the environmental impacts of proposed actions that could significantly affect environmental quality. Chapter 275, Laws of 1971, provided for state protection of endangered fish and wildlife, and Chapter 370, Laws of 1977, placed nongame species and endangered wild plants under state protection. A program protecting surface waters from nonpoint source pollution was created by Chapter 418, Laws of 1977, and a groundwater protection program, based on numerical standards for polluting sub-

Department of Natural Resources Conservation Wardens Shawna Stringham and Mike Cross practice responding to emergencies in their patrol boat on the Mississippi River. (Burt Walters)

stances, was created by 1983 Wisconsin Act 410. In Wisconsin Act 335, the 1989 Legislature made major changes in the laws governing recycling, source reduction, and disposal of solid wastes.

Statutory Board and Councils

Dry Cleaner Environmental Response Council: JILL C. FITZGERALD (small dry cleaning operation); BRETT DONALDSON, RICHARD W. KLINKE (large dry cleaning operation); KEVIN BRADEN (wholesale distributor of dry cleaning solvent); JEANNE TARVIN (engineer, professional geologist, hydrologist, or soil scientist); JIM FITZGERALD (manufacturer or seller of dry cleaning equipment) (appointed by governor).

The 6-member Dry Cleaner Environmental Response Council advises the department on matters related to the Dry Cleaner Environmental Response Program, which is administered by DNR and provides awards to dry cleaning establishments for assistance in the investigation and cleanup of environmental contamination. Council members are appointed for staggered 3-year terms. The council, which is scheduled to sunset on June 30, 2032, was created by 1997 Wisconsin Act 27, as amended by 1997 Wisconsin Act 300. Its composition and duties are prescribed in Sections 15.347 (2) and 292.65 (13) of the statutes.

Council on Forestry: PAUL DeLONG (chief state forester); SENATORS JAUCH, VINEHOUT; REPRESENTATIVES FRISKE, HUBLER; FREDERIC SOUBA, JR. (forest products company which owns and manages large forest land tracts representative); WILLIAM HORVATH (owners of nonindustrial, private forest land representative); JANE SEVERT (counties containing county forests representative); JIM HOPPE (paper and pulp industry representative); TROY BROWN (lumber industry representative); MARY JEAN HUSTON (nonprofit conservation organization representative); FRED CLARK (forester who provides consultation services); JEFFREY STIER (school of forestry representative); JAMES HEEREY (conservation education representative); MICHAEL BOLTON (forestry-affiliated labor union representative); KEN OTTMAN (urban and community forestry representative); BOB ROGERS (Society of American Foresters representative); DENNIS BROWN (timber producer organization representative); LEON CHURCH (secondary wood industry representative); JEANNE HIGGINS (nonvoting member, U.S. Forest Service employee).

The 20-member Council on Forestry advises the governor, the legislature, the Departments of Natural Resources and Commerce, and other state agencies on topics relating to forestry in Wisconsin including: protection from fire, insects, and disease; sustainable forestry; reforestation and forestry genetics; management and protection of urban forests; increasing the public's knowledge and awareness of forestry issues; forestry research; economic development and marketing of forestry products; legislation affecting forestry; and staff and funding needs for forestry programs. The council shall submit a biennial report on the status of the state's forestry resources and industry to the governor and the appropriate standing committees of the legislature by June 1 of each odd-numbered year. All members are appointed by the governor. Lengths of terms are not specified by law. The council was created by 2001 Wisconsin Act 109. Its composition and duties are prescribed in Sections 15.347 (19) and 26.02 of the statutes.

Managed Forest Land Board: PAUL DELONG (chief state forester); NEAL PAULSON (nominated by Wisconsin Counties Association); KEVIN KOTH (nominated by Wisconsin Towns Association); ELROY ZEMKE (nominated by association representing counties with county forests); EUGENE ROARK (nominated by Council on Forestry). (All except *ex officio* members are appointed by governor.)

The 5-member Managed Forest Land Board administers the program established by the Department of Natural Resources to award grants to nonprofit conservation organizations, to local governmental units, and to the department to acquire land, including conservations easements on land, to be used for hunting, fishing, hiking, sightseeing, and cross-country skiing. The department consults with the board to promulgate administrative rules establishing requirements for awarding grants. Appointed board members serve 3-year terms. The board was created by 2007 Wisconsin Act 20, and its composition and duties are prescribed in Sections 15.345 (6) and 77.895 of the statutes.

Metallic Mining Council: Inactive.

The 9-member Metallic Mining Council advises the department on matters relating to the reclamation of mined land. Its members are appointed by the secretary of natural resources for staggered 3-year terms, and they are expected to represent "a variety and balance of economic, scientific, and environmental viewpoints." The council was created by Chapter 377, Laws of 1977, and its composition and duties are prescribed in Sections 15.347 (12) and 144.448 of the statutes.

Milwaukee River Revitalization Council: RAYMOND R. KRUEGER, *chairperson;* SHARON GAYAN (designated by secretary of natural resources), KIT SORENSON (designated by secretary of tourism); CHERYL BRICKMAN, NANCY FRANK, CHRISTINE NUERNBERG, JON RICHARDS, DAN SMALL, RON STADLER, CHRIS SVOBODA, CAROLINE TORINUS, 2 vacancies. (All except *ex officio* members are appointed by governor.)

The 13-member Milwaukee River Revitalization Council advises the legislature, governor, and department on matters related to environmental, recreational, and economic revitalization of the Milwaukee River Basin, and it assists local governments in planning and implementing projects. It is also responsible for developing and implementing a plan that encourages multiple recreational, entrepreneurial, and cultural activities along the streams of the Milwaukee River Basin. Its 11 appointed members serve 3-year terms. Each of the priority watersheds in the basin must be represented by at least one council member. The council was created by 1987 Wisconsin Act 399, and its composition and duties are prescribed in Sections 15.347 (15) and 23.18 of the statutes.

Natural Areas Preservation Council: CHARLES LUTHIN (appointed by council of the Wisconsin Academy of Sciences, Arts and Letters), *chairperson;* SUSAN E. LEWIS (appointed by council of the Wisconsin Academy of Sciences, Arts and Letters), *vice chairperson;* SIGNE HOLTZ (representing Department of Natural Resources, appointed by the board of natural resources), *secretary;* KIMBERLY WRIGHT (representing Department of Natural Resources, appointed by the board of natural resources); EVELYN HOWELL, PATRICK ROBINSON, JOY ZEDLER, vacancy (representing University of Wisconsin System, appointed by board of regents); MICHAEL

STRIGEL (appointed by council of the Wisconsin Academy of Sciences, Arts and Letters); DENNIS YOCKERS (representing the Department of Public Instruction, appointed by the secretary of public instruction); SUSAN BORKIN (representing Milwaukee Public Museum, appointed by MPM board of directors).

The 11-member Natural Areas Preservation Council advises the department on matters pertaining to the protection of natural areas that contain native biotic communities and habitats for rare species. It also makes recommendations about gifts or purchases for the state natural areas system. The council was created by Chapter 566, Laws of 1951, as the State Board for Preservation of Scientific Areas. It was renamed the Scientific Areas Preservation Council in Chapter 327, Laws of 1961, and given its current name in 1985 Wisconsin Act 29. One of the appointments from the Wisconsin Academy of Sciences, Arts and Letters must represent private colleges in the state. Its composition and duties are prescribed in Sections 15.347 (4) and 23.26 of the statutes.

Snowmobile Recreational Council: KAREN CARLSON, BEVERLY DITTMAR, LARRY ERICKSON, ROBERT LANG, ANDREW MALECKI, THOMAS THORNTON, MICHAEL WILLMAN (northern representatives); MIKE CERNY, THOMAS CHWALA, JERRY GREEN, SAMUEL LANDES, JON SCHWEITZER, RICHARD STEIMEL, DONNA WHITE, vacancy (southern representatives). (All are appointed by governor with senate consent.)

The 15-member Snowmobile Recreational Council carries out studies and makes recommendations to the governor, the legislature, and the Department of Natural Resources and the Department of Transportation regarding all matters affecting snowmobiling. Council members are appointed for staggered 3-year terms. At least 5 must represent the northern part of the state, and at least 5 must represent the southern part. The council was created by Chapter 277, Laws of 1971, and its composition and duties are prescribed in Sections 15.347 (7) and 350.14 of the statutes.

State Trails Council: RANDY HARDEN, *chairperson;* KEN L. CARPENTER, *vice chairperson;* ROBBIE WEBBER, *secretary;* TOM HUBER, JAMES JOQUE, MIKE MCFADZEN, DAVID W. PHILLIPS, THOMAS J. THORNTON, vacancy (appointed by governor).

The 9-member State Trails Council advises the department about the planning, acquisition, development, and management of state trails. Its members are appointed for 4-year terms. It was created by 1989 Wisconsin Act 31, and its composition and duties are prescribed in Sections 15.347 (16) and 23.175 (2) (c) of the statutes.

Independent Organization — Conservation Congress

Conservation Congress Executive Council: RICHARD KIRCHMEYER, JOE WEISS (District 1); ALLAN BROWN, RAYMOND SMITH (District 2); MIKE RIGGLE, ROGER SABOTA (District 3); WADE JESKE, ARNOLD NINNEMAN (District 4); MARK NOLL, MARC SCHULTZ (District 5); DAVID PUHL, FRANK REITH (District 6); RICHARD KOERNER, DALE MAAS (District 7); JOHN EDELBLUTE, EDGAR HARVEY, JR. (District 8); LARRIE HAZEN, MIKE ROGERS (District 9); AL PHELAN, KEN RISLEY (District 10); ROBERT BOHMANN, ALLEN SHOOK (District 11); JO ANN KUHARSKE, JAMES WROLSTAD (District 12).

The Conservation Congress is a 360-member publicly elected citizen advisory group, and its 24-member executive council advises the Natural Resources Board on all matters under the board's jurisdiction. The Conservation Congress is organized into 12 districts statewide. Each district elects 2 members to one-year terms on the executive council. The congress originated in 1934 and received statutory recognition in Chapter 179, Laws of 1971. Its duties are prescribed in Section 15.348 of the statutes.

INDEPENDENT UNITS ATTACHED FOR BUDGETING, PROGRAM COORDINATION, AND RELATED MANAGEMENT FUNCTIONS BY SECTION 15.03 OF THE STATUTES

GROUNDWATER COORDINATING COUNCIL

Groundwater Coordinating Council: TODD AMBS (designated by secretary of natural resources), *chairperson;* BERNI MATTSSON (designated by secretary of commerce), KATHY PIELSTICKER (designated by secretary of agriculture, trade and consumer protection), HENRY

ANDERSON (designated by secretary of health services), DAN SCUDDER (designated by secretary of transportation), ANDERS ANDREN (designated by president, UW System), JAMES ROBERTSON (state geologist), GEORGE KRAFT (representing governor).

Statutory References: Sections 15.347 (13) and 160.50.

Agency Responsibility: The 8-member Groundwater Coordinating Council advises state agencies on the coordination of nonregulatory programs related to groundwater management. Member agencies exchange information regarding groundwater monitoring, budgets for groundwater programs, data management, public information efforts, laboratory analyses, research, and state appropriations for research. The council reports annually to the legislature, governor, and agencies represented regarding the council's activities and recommendations and its assessment of the current state of groundwater resources and related management programs. Persons designated to serve on behalf of their agency heads must be agency employees with "sufficient authority to deploy agency resources and directly influence agency decision making." The governor's representative serves a 4-year term. The council was created by 1983 Wisconsin Act 410.

INVASIVE SPECIES COUNCIL

Invasive Species Council: LAURIE OSTERNDORF (designated by secretary of natural resources); HARALD JORDAHL (designated by secretary of administration); BRIAN KUHN (designated by secretary of agriculture, trade and consumer protection); RENEE BASHEL (designated by secretary of commerce); WILL CHRISTIANSON (designated by secretary of tourism); JOHN KINAR (designated by secretary of transportation); CHARLES HENRIKSEN, GREGORY LONG, PATRICIA MORTON, PETER MURRAY, KENNETH RAFFA, JAMES REINARTZ, PAUL SCHUMACHER (appointed by governor).

The 13-member Invasive Species Council conducts studies related to controlling invasive species and makes recommendations to the Department of Natural Resources regarding a system for classifying invasive species under the department's statewide invasive species control program and procedures for awarding grants to public and private agencies engaged in projects to control invasive species. All except *ex officio* members or their designees are appointed by the governor to 5-year terms to represent public and private interests affected by the presence of invasive species in the state. The council was created by 2001 Wisconsin Act 109. Its composition and duties are prescribed in Sections 15.347 (18) and 23.22 of the statutes.

LAKE MICHIGAN COMMERCIAL FISHING BOARD

Lake Michigan Commercial Fishing Board: CHARLES W. HENRIKSEN, RICHARD R. JOHNSON, MICHAEL LECLAIR, MARK MARICQUE, DEAN SWAER (licensed, active commercial fishers); NEIL A. SCHWARZ (licensed, active wholesale fish dealer); DAN PAWLITZKE (state citizen). (All are appointed by governor.)

Statutory References: Sections 15.345 (3) and 29.33 (7).

Agency Responsibility: The 7-member Lake Michigan Commercial Fishing Board was created by Chapter 418, Laws of 1977. Its members must live in counties contiguous to Lake Michigan. The 5 commercial fishers must represent fisheries in specific geographic areas. The board reviews applications for transfers of commercial fishing licenses between individuals, establishes criteria for allotting catch quotas to individual licensees, assigns catch quotas when the department establishes special harvest limits, and assists the department in establishing criteria for identifying inactive license holders.

LAKE SUPERIOR COMMERCIAL FISHING BOARD

Lake Superior Commercial Fishing Board: MAURINE HALVORSON, CRAIG HOOPMAN, vacancy (licensed, active commercial fishers); JEFF BODIN (licensed, active wholesale fish dealer); vacancy (state citizen). (All are appointed by governor.)

Statutory References: Sections 15.345 (2) and 29.33 (7).

Agency Responsibility: The 5-member Lake Superior Commercial Fishing Board was created by Chapter 418, Laws of 1977. Its members must live in counties contiguous to Lake Superior. The board reviews applications for transfers of commercial fishing licenses between individuals, establishes criteria for allotting catch quotas to individual licensees, assigns catch quotas when the department establishes special harvest limits, and assists the department in establishing criteria for identifying inactive license holders.

COUNCIL ON RECYCLING

Council on Recycling: GREG DAVID, JEFFREY A. FIELKOW, RICK MEYERS, NEIL PETERS-MICHAUD, JOHN REINDL, CHARLOTTE R. ZIEVE, vacancy (appointed by governor).

Statutory References: Sections 15.347 (17) and 159.22.

Agency Responsibility: The 7 members of the Council on Recycling are appointed to 4-year terms that coincide with that of the governor. The council, which was created by 1989 Wisconsin Act 335, promotes implementation of the state's solid waste reduction, recovery, and recycling programs; helps public agencies coordinate programs and exchange information; advises state agencies about creating administrative rules and establishing priorities for market development; and advises the DNR and the UW System about education and research related to solid waste recycling. The council also promotes a regional and interstate marketing system for recycled materials and reports to the legislature about market development and research to encourage recycling. The council advises the department about statewide public information activities and advises the governor and the legislature.

WISCONSIN WATERWAYS COMMISSION

Wisconsin Waterways Commission: JAMES F. ROONEY (Lake Michigan area), *chairperson;* ROGER WALSH (inland area), *vice chairperson;* DAVID KEDROWSKI (Lake Superior area), MAUREEN KINNEY (Mississippi River area), KURT KOEPPLER (Lake Winnebago watershed). (All are appointed by governor with senate consent.)

Mailing Address: P.O. Box 7921, Madison 53707.

Location: State Natural Resources Building (GEF 2), 101 South Webster Street, Madison.

Telephone: (715) 822-8583.

Statutory References: Sections 15.345 (1) and 30.92.

Agency Responsibility: The 5-member Wisconsin Waterways Commission was created by Chapter 274, Laws of 1977. Its members serve staggered 5-year terms, and each must represent a specific geographic area and be knowledgeable about that area's recreational water use problems. The commission may have studies conducted to determine the need for recreational boating facilities; approve financial aid to local governments for development of recreational boating projects, including the acquisition of weed harvesters; and recommend administrative rules for the recreational facilities boating program.

Office of the
STATE PUBLIC DEFENDER

Public Defender Board: DANIEL M. BERKOS, *chairperson;* JOSEPH G. MORALES (public member), *vice chairperson;* NANCY C. WETTERSTEN, *secretary;* JAMES M. BRENNAN, WILLIAM DRENGLER, JOHN HOGAN, ELLEN THORN (State Bar members); REGINA DUNKIN, MAI NENG XIONG (public members). (Except as indicated, all are state bar members. All are appointed by governor with senate consent.)

State Public Defender: NICHOLAS L. CHIARKAS, 266-0087, chiarkasn@

Deputy State Public Defender: KELLI THOMPSON, 266-5480, thompsonk@

Executive Assistant/Legislative Liaison: KRISTA GINGER, 264-8572, gingerk@

Budget Director: MEGAN CHRISTIANSEN, 267-0311, christiansenm@

Communications Director: RANDY KRAFT, 267-3587, kraftr@

Information Technology Director: GAIL ZAUCHA, 261-0621, zauchag@

Training and Development Office: GINA PRUSKI, *director,* 266-6782, pruskig@

Administrative Services Division: ARLENE F. BANOUL, *director,* 266-9447, banoula@

Appellate Division: MARLA J. STEPHENS, *director,* Madison: 264-8573; Milwaukee: (414) 227-4891; stephensm@

Assigned Counsel Division: DEBORAH M. SMITH, *director,* 261-8856, smithd@

Trial Division: MICHAEL TOBIN, *director,* 266-8259, tobinm@; JENNIFER BIAS, *deputy director and affirmative action officer,* Madison: 261-7981; Milwaukee: (414) 227-4028; biasj@

For e-mail combine the user ID and the state extender: userid**@opd.wi.gov**

Mailing Address: P.O. Box 7923, Madison 53707-7923.

Location: 315 North Henry Street, 2nd Floor, Madison.

Telephone: 266-0087.

Fax: 267-0584.

Internet Address: www.wisspd.org

Number of Employees: 535.45.

Total Budget 2007-09: $161,804,100.

Statutory References: Section 15.78; Chapter 977.

Agency Responsibility: The Office of the State Public Defender makes determinations of indigence and provides legal representation for specified defendants who are unable to afford a private attorney. The state public defender, who must be a member of the state bar, serves at the pleasure of the Public Defender Board.

Organization: The 9-member Public Defender Board appoints the state public defender, promulgates rules for determining indigence, and establishes procedures for certifying lists of private attorneys who can be assigned as counsel. Board members are appointed for staggered 3-year terms, and at least 5 of these must be members of the State Bar of Wisconsin. Members may not be or be employed by a judicial or law enforcement officer, a district attorney, a corporation counsel, or the state public defender.

Unit Functions: The *Administrative Services Division* oversees purchasing, payroll services, budget preparation, case management, and fiscal analysis.

The *Appellate Division* uses both program staff and private attorneys to provide appellate assistance to indigents in all counties. It represents indigents involved in post-conviction or post-commitment proceedings in certain state and federal courts. It also acts upon certain cases relating to persons confined to state correctional and mental health institutions.

The *Assigned Counsel Division* oversees a variety of functions related to appointment of private attorneys to represent indigent clients in cases not handled by staff, including certification and training, logistical support, and payment of fees.

The *Trial Division* provides legal representation at the trial level to indigent persons who have been charged with adult felony crimes or misdemeanors punishable by imprisonment. It also represents minors charged with juvenile offenses, persons petitioned mentally ill, or individuals involved in termination of parental rights.

History: Both the United States Constitution (Sixth and Fourteenth Amendments) and the Wisconsin Constitution (Article I, Section 7), as interpreted by the U.S. and Wisconsin Supreme Courts, guarantee the right to publicly-provided counsel for poor people charged with crimes or facing potential deprivations of liberty. In 1859, the Wisconsin Supreme Court ruled, in *Carpenter and Sprague vs. the County of Dane* (9 Wis. 274), that a county is liable to pay for an attorney provided by the court in a criminal case to represent an indigent defendant who cannot otherwise afford representation.

The position of state public defender was created in 1966 by Chapter 479, Laws of 1965, under the supervision of the Wisconsin Supreme Court and funded, in part, by a private grant from the Ford Foundation. The duties of the office were originally confined to appellate defense, and its mission was to pursue post-conviction appeals for indigents before the appropriate court, including the U.S. Supreme Court. Defense of indigents at the trial court level remained a county responsibility, dependent upon court-appointed private counsel paid by the county or privately funded public defender services.

Chapter 29, Laws of 1977, transferred the state public defender from the judicial branch to the executive branch as an independent agency under the Public Defender Board, which was authorized to appoint the defender to a 5-year renewable term with removal only for cause. (Chapter 356, Laws of 1979, later provided that the public defender serve at the pleasure of the board.) Chapter 29 also transferred the responsibility for defense of indigents at the trial level from the counties to the public defender's office, but representation by the defender's staff was limited, based on funding and statutory criteria. Trial duties were, and continue to be, divided between state attorneys and private counsel paid by the state.

Chapter 29, Laws of 1977, directed the public defender to determine the percentage of cases that private counsel would handle in each county. Chapter 356, Laws of 1979, established those percentages by law with the public defender staff assuming various portions of the caseloads in 47 counties and private counsel responsible for all cases in the remaining 25 counties. 1985 Wisconsin Act 29 expanded the use of public defender staff attorneys to all 72 counties and repealed the sunset provision enacted in 1979, which would have abolished the agency, effective November 15, 1985.

1995 Wisconsin Act 27 directed the public defender to enter into annual fixed fee contracts with private counsel and limited the number of trial-level cases assigned to private attorneys to one-third of all cases handled. It also eliminated public defender representation in some cases, including certain matters related to prison and jail conditions, sentence modifications, probation and parole revocations, child support, and parents of children in need of protection or services (CHIPS).

Department of
PUBLIC INSTRUCTION

State Superintendent: TONY EVERS, 266-1771, anthony.evers@

Deputy State Superintendent: MIKE THOMPSON, 266-1771, michael.thompson@

Executive Assistant: SUE GRADY, 266-1771, sue.grady@

Special Assistant: BURTON S. JONES, 266-1771, burton.jones@

Legal Services, Office of: SHEILA ELLEFSON, *chief legal counsel,* 266-9353, sheila.ellefson@

Education Information Services: JOHN JOHNSON, *director,* 266-1098, john.johnson@

Mailing Address: P.O. Box 7841, Madison 53707-7841.

Location: State Education Building (GEF 3), 125 South Webster Street, Madison.

Telephones: 266-3390; (800) 441-4563; TDD: 267-2427.

Fax: 267-1052.

Internet Addresses: Departmental: www.dpi.wi.gov
BadgerLink: www.badgerlink.net

Address e-mail by combining the user ID and the state extender: userid@**dpi.wi.gov**

Number of Employees: 631.50.

Total Budget 2007-09: $12,586,851,700.

Constitutional Reference: Article X, Section 1.

Statutory References: Section 15.37; Chapters 43 and 115-121.

Academic Excellence, Division for: DEBORAH MAHAFFEY, *assistant superintendent,* 266-3361, deborah.mahaffey@; Division Fax: 266-1965.

   Career and Technical Education: SHARON WENDT, *director,* 267-9251, sharon.wendt@

   Content and Learning: vacancy, *director,* 266-2364.

   Teacher Education, Professional Development, and Licensing: JUDY PEPPARD, *director,* 266-0986, judith.peppard@

DEPARTMENT OF PUBLIC INSTRUCTION

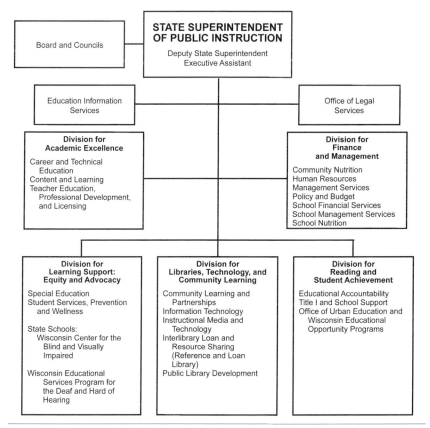

Finance and Management, Division for: BRIAN PAHNKE, *assistant superintendent,* 267-9124, brian.pahnke@; Division Fax: 266-3644.

  Community Nutrition Programs: DAVID DEES, *director,* 267-9123, david.dees@

  Human Resources: KATHY KNUDSON, *director,* 267-9200, katherine.knudson@

  Management Services: SUE LINTON, *director,* 266-3320, suzanne.linton@

  Policy and Budget: MICHAEL BORMETT, *director,* 266-2804, michael.bormett@

  School Financial Services: DAVID CARLSON, *director,* 266-6968, david.carlson@

  School Management Services: ROBERT SOLDNER, *director,* 266-7475, robert.soldner@

  School Nutrition Programs: JUNE PAUL, *director,* 267-9121, june.paul@

Learning Support: Equity and Advocacy, Division for: CAROLYN STANFORD TAYLOR, *assistant superintendent,* 266-1649, carolyn.stanford.taylor@; Division Fax: 267-3746, Division TTY: 267-2427.

  Special Education: STEPHANIE PETSKA, *director,* 266-1781, stephanie.petska@

  Student Services, Prevention and Wellness: DOUGLAS WHITE, *director,* 266-5198, douglas.white@

  Wisconsin Center for the Blind and Visually Impaired: DAN WENZEL, *director,* 1700 West State Street, Janesville 53546-5399, (608) 758-6100, (800) 832-9784, Fax: (608) 758-6161, dan.wenzel@wcbvi.k12.wi.us

Wisconsin Educational Services Program for the Deaf and Hard of Hearing: ALEX SLAPPEY, *director,* 309 West Walworth Avenue, Delavan 53115-1099, (262) 740-2066, voice: (877) 973-3323, TTY: (877) 973-3324, Fax: (262) 728-7160, alex.slappey@

Libraries, Technology, and Community Learning, Division for: RICHARD GROBSCHMIDT, *assistant superintendent,* 266-2205, richard.grobschmidt@; Division Fax: 266-8770.

Division Internet Address: www.dpi.wi.gov/dltcl

> *Community Learning and Partnerships:* JANE GRINDE, *director,* 266-9356, jane.grinde@
>
> *Information Technology:* RODNEY PACKARD, *director,* 266-7049, rodney.packard@
>
> *Instructional Media and Technology:* STEPHEN SANDERS, *director,* 266-3856, stephen.sanders@
>
> *Interlibrary Loan and Resource Sharing (Reference and Loan Library):* SALLY DREW, *director,* 224-6161, sally.drew@
>
> *Public Library Development:* MICHAEL CROSS, *director,* 267-9225, michael.cross@

Reading and Student Achievement, Division for: JENNIFER THAYER, *assistant superintendent,* 266-5450, jennifer.thayer@; Division Fax: 264-9553.

> *Educational Accountability, Office of:* LYNETTE RUSSELL, *director,* 267-1072, lynette.russell@
>
> *Title I and School Support:* MARY KLEUSCH, *director,* 267-3163, mary.kleusch@
>
> *Urban Education, Office of* and *Wisconsin Educational Opportunity Programs:* KEVIN INGRAM, *director,* (414) 227-4413, kevin.ingram@

Publications: Biennial Report; *Channel;* Directory of Wisconsin Public/Private Schools; various curriculum, instruction, library and student services publications and research studies. SEAchange, School Performance Report, Wisconsin Information Network for Successful Schools (WINSS), and electronic publications are available at the department's Internet site.

Agency Responsibility: The Department of Public Instruction provides direction and technical assistance for public elementary and secondary education in Wisconsin. The department offers a broad range of programs and professional services to local school administrators and staff. It distributes state school aids and administers federal aids to supplement local tax resources, improves curriculum and school operations, ensures education for children with disabilities, offers professional guidance and counseling, and develops school and public library resources.

Organization: The department is headed by the State Superintendent of Public Instruction, a constitutional officer who is elected on the nonpartisan spring ballot for a term of 4 years. The state superintendent appoints a deputy state superintendent and assistant state superintendents from outside the classified service. The assistant superintendents are responsible for administering the operating divisions of the department. The superintendent also appoints the director of the Office of Educational Accountability, which was created in Section 15.374 (1), Wisconsin Statutes, by 1993 Wisconsin Act 16.

Unit Functions: The *Division for Academic Excellence* offers assistance with curriculum development, developing and implementing academic and technical skills standards, instructional methods and strategies, including web-based education programs and professional development. The division reviews college and university teacher and administrator training programs and licenses public school teachers, pupil services personnel, administrators, and library professionals, as well as private school teachers and administrators upon request. It monitors school district compliance with state curriculum standards, required days and hours of instruction, American Indian Education, and compliance with U.S. Office of Civil Rights laws and regulations.

The division administers a variety of programs that provide assistance, scholarships, and grants to public school students and teachers on the basis of merit and need. These programs include the Presidential Awards for Mathematics and Science Teaching; U.S. Senate Youth Program; talent search and talent incentive grants; the federal Robert C. Byrd Honors Scholarships; the Kohl Teacher Fellowship, Kohl Student Excellence Scholarship, and Kohl Student Initiative Scholarship Programs; and international exchanges with Germany, Japan, Thailand, and France.

It conducts youth options and technical preparation programs, the high school equivalency/ general educational development (HSED/GED) program for state residents who have not completed high school, and provides state grants to school districts to support induction programs for new educators. It administers state and federal programs that provide grants for world language assistance, student advanced placement, and alternative education. The division also administers funds for school districts under the Carl D. Perkins Career and Technical Education Improvement Act of 2006, to enhance and improve career and technical educational programs. It administers the state and federally funded Bilingual/English as a Second Language Program, as well as the federally funded Title IIB Mathematics-Science Partnership grant and Title IIA grant programs to support highly qualified teacher requirements.

The *Division for Finance and Management* distributes state and federal school aids and grants; administers school district revenue limits; monitors the Milwaukee Parental Choice Program and the interdistrict open enrollment program; prescribes school financial accounting methods; consults with school districts on their budgets; and collects, analyzes, and publishes school finance data. Consulting services are provided to assist districts and charter schools with management and planning, school district reorganization, pupil transportation, private school relations, school board elections and duties, and finance and asset management. The division is responsible for both state and federally funded school food and nutrition services, nonschool child care food services, and elderly nutrition programs. It also provides support services to the department for financial management, human resources, budget preparation, educational policy and administrative rule development, and legislative analysis.

The *Division for Learning Support: Equity and Advocacy,* created in Section 15.373 (1), Wisconsin Statutes, as the Division for Handicapped Children by Chapter 327, Laws of 1967, and most recently renamed in 1993 Wisconsin Act 335, provides technical assistance, leadership, advocacy, staff development, training, and education to help meet the diverse cultural, emotional, social, health, and educational needs of Wisconsin's youth. The mission is met through collaboration with federal, state, and local groups. The division, through the state centers, Wisconsin School for the Deaf and Wisconsin School for the Visually Handicapped, provides direct instruction to students and technical assistance through outreach to local educational agencies, communities, and families statewide. The division manages state and federal resources, monitors and evaluates programs and practices, and facilitates school-district and community efforts to meet specific needs of students. The division administers programs involving school nursing, social work, and psychological services; guidance and counseling services; alcohol, tobacco, and other drug abuse; suicide prevention; mental health; alcohol and traffic safety; school-age parents; school violence; prevention of HIV and other sexually transmitted diseases; pregnancy prevention; health education; physical activity; comprehensive school health programs; compulsory school attendance; and after-school programs.

The division offers technical assistance and financial support to help school districts provide a better education for students with disabilities, combat educational discrimination, and train professional staff. It is responsible for special educational programs and services for students with disabilities. It must ensure that all students with disabilities are identified, evaluated, and provided appropriate education and services. It supervises all special education programs and checks their compliance with departmental standards and state and federal law. The division provides consultation for and supervision of the Pupil Nondiscrimination Program.

The division administers the Wisconsin Educational Services Program for the Deaf and Hard of Hearing (WESP-DHH) and the Wisconsin Center for the Blind and Visually Impaired (WCBVI). Each program operates a residential school for state residents ages 3 to 21, who are determined to need placement at these schools by their Individualized Education Plan (IEP) committee. Both schools provide academic and vocational education on site. Both programs also offer instructional and technical assistance, teaching materials, and evaluations of pupils to local school districts and other agencies. WCBVI also provides summer programs for students and adults and administers the Federal Quota Funds for student materials.

The *Division for Libraries, Technology, and Community Learning,* created as the Division for Library Services in Section 15.373 (2), Wisconsin Statutes, by Chapter 327, Laws of 1967, and most recently renamed in 2001 Wisconsin Act 48, provides assistance for the development

Tony Evers was elected the State's Superintendent of Public Instruction in April 2009, and took office in July 2009. Evers formerly served as Deputy State Superintendent, CESA administrator, district superintendent, and principal. (Department of Public Instruction)

and improvement of public and school libraries; fosters interlibrary cooperation and resource sharing; and promotes information and instructional technology in libraries. The division administers the state aid program for Wisconsin's 17 public library systems. It also administers the federal Library Services and Technology Act and the federal Enhancing Education Through Technology grants. The division provides interlibrary loan and reference services to the state's libraries, maintains electronic union and virtual catalogs of statewide library holdings (WIS-CAT), administers BadgerLink (www.badgerlink.net), the statewide full-text database project that allows access to thousands of magazines, newsletters, newspapers, pamphlets, and historical documents, provides statewide virtual reference services (AskAway) (http://dpi.wi.gov/rll/gp_form.html), and maintains the Wisconsin Document Depository Program and Digital Archive of Wisconsin government publications. It operates a professional library for department staff, state educators, and librarians. The division directs the public librarian certification program, the summer library reading program, and programs that foster family and community involvement and quality early childhood programs (including four-year-old kindergarten) in schools, libraries, and communities. With grants from the Corporation for National and Community Service, the division administers the school-based Learn and Serve grant, and multisite, statewide VISTA (Volunteers In Service To America) and AmeriCorps grants. The grants enable the Department of Public Instruction to promote service learning and partnerships to close the achievement gap. Other grants enable the division to develop and enhance early childhood collaboration, nutrition education, and civic learning. The division also administers a grant from the U.S. Department of Education to develop a Longitudinal Data System and oversee the department's information technology support and data processing, as well as school and library data collections and records management. Information and resources for and about schools are provided through WINSS (Wisconsin Information Network for Successful Schools) (http://dpi.wi.gov/sig), and other department resources.

The *Division for Reading and Student Achievement* is responsible for ensuring that all children attain proficiency in meeting the Wisconsin Model Academic Standards. The three teams in this division, Educational Accountability, Title I and School Support, and Wisconsin Educational Opportunity Programs and Urban Education, have as a major focus closing the achievement gap that exists among children of color, the economically disadvantaged, and their peers.

The Office of Educational Accountability provides assessment results through statewide tests that measure student proficiency related to the Wisconsin Model Academic Standards. These data assist district and school personnel in evaluating and making decisions related to educational planning and programming. This team provides accountability outcomes related to state and federal legislation and gives technical assistance in evaluating results and developing balanced assessment systems for schools and districts.

The Title I and School Support Team provides a multitude of resources to districts and schools that include a number of programs under the federal Elementary and Secondary Education Act of 1965 and the No Child Left Behind Act of 2001, including programs under Title I-Part A, Reading First, Even Start, Migrant Education, Neglected and Delinquent Youth, Comprehensive School Reform, Innovative Programs, McKinney-Vento Homeless Assistance Act, and the state class size reduction program Student Achievement Guarantee in Education (SAGE).

The Wisconsin Educational Opportunity Programs and Urban Education Team focuses on improving high school graduation rates, reducing dropouts and encourages nontraditional, minority, disadvantaged, and low-income students with college potential to pursue postsecondary education. Programs to achieve team objectives include state and federal Talent Search, Talent Incentive Program, Early Identification Program, Pre-College Scholarship Program, Gear Up, and Upward Bound. The Urban Education program was established in 1995 to provide services to urban areas including Beloit, Kenosha, Milwaukee, and Racine to facilitate cooperative efforts to address the challenges and equity needs facing families, children, and educators in an urban setting. The Preschool to Grade 5 (P-5) program was created to provide for the special needs of this population.

History: The Wisconsin Constitution, as adopted in 1848, required the state legislature to provide by law for the establishment of district schools that would be free to all children between the ages of 4 and 20 years. It also created a State Superintendent of Public Instruction to supervise public education. Under the 1849 Wisconsin Statutes, the superintendent was ordered to visit schools in all the counties, recommend textbooks and courses of instruction, and distribute state money for public schools to the counties.

Originally, the superintendent was elected to a 2-year term at the partisan general election in November. With the adoption of a constitutional amendment in 1902, the superintendent was placed on the nonpartisan April ballot and given a 4-year term of office.

In the early years of statehood, the hiring of teachers was entirely a local matter. In 1861, the legislature created county superintendents of schools with the power to license teachers beginning in 1862. The state superintendent was also given licensing authority in 1868 (Chapter 169). Local districts and county superintendents continued to license teachers until 1939, when the legislature gave that power exclusively to the Department of Public Instruction.

For a number of years, state support of public education consisted of money derived principally from the sale of public lands that the federal government had granted to the state. In Chapter 287, Laws of 1885, the legislature levied a one-mill (one-tenth of a cent) state property tax to be collected by the state and distributed to counties for school support. The state's first attempt to equalize tax support for schools in property-poor districts was the Wisconsin Elementary Equalization Law of 1927 (Chapter 536). It was promoted by State Superintendent John Callahan, who also urged a 40% level of state support for local school costs – a figure not reached until after 1970. The 1995 Legislature enacted a law to ensure that state aids and school levy tax credits would cover two-thirds of local school revenues, but subsequently repealed that requirement in 2003.

Originally, Wisconsin only required tax support for elementary schools. Individual cities, such as Racine and Kenosha, funded their own high schools. The legislature enacted public support for high schools in 1875 (Chapter 323). Kindergarten originated in 1856 when Margarethe Schurz started a German-speaking program for children 2 through 5 years of age in Watertown, Wisconsin. The first public school kindergarten opened in Manitowoc in 1873 for 4- and 5-year-old children. The program continued to spread until, in 1973, the legislature required school districts to provide a 5-year-old kindergarten. In the 1990s, an increasing number of school districts offered full-day programs for 5-year-old children and kindergarten programs for 4-year-olds.

Although state law had contained some curriculum requirements as early as 1849, the legislature did not establish high school graduation requirements until 1983. In 1985, it prescribed a detailed set of standards local districts must meet to be eligible for state aid. The 1997 Legislature mandated that school boards adopt pupil academic standards in certain subjects, a series of examinations to measure pupil achievement in 4th, 8th, and 10th grades, and a high school graduation examination. The 2003 Legislature eliminated the high school graduation examination.

State concern for special education began with the establishment of the Wisconsin Institute for Education of the Blind in Janesville in 1850 and a school for the deaf in Delavan in 1852. These schools were administered by public welfare agencies until transferred to the Department of Public Instruction in 1947. The 1927 Legislature enacted laws to provide aid for special classes for "crippled children" and increased aid for districts to educate mentally handicapped children. Funding for education of all handicapped children was enacted in 1973 to comply with federal law.

While state administration of school libraries fell under the jurisdiction of the superintendent, the Free Library Commission set standards for public libraries. In 1965, the legislature transferred this function to the department.

Statutory Board and Councils

Alcohol and Other Drug Abuse Programs, Council on: TASHA JENKINS, *chairperson;* GARY ALBRECHT, *vice chairperson;* KARLA VINCI, *secretary;* EDWARD COYLE, DOROTHY CRUST, CLAUDE GILMORE, LISA HESCH, BARBARA HICKMAN, BOB KOVAR, PAT NEUDECKER, CINDY PAGEL, GEORGE THATTAKARA, SANDRA THURMAN, KATHRYN WOLF, 4 vacancies (appointed by state superintendent).

The Council on Alcohol and Other Drug Abuse Programs advises the state superintendent about programs to prevent or reduce alcohol, tobacco, and other drug abuse by minors. The council consists of 18 members (by administrative rule) who serve at the pleasure of the state superintendent. The council was created by Chapter 331, Laws of 1979, and its duties are prescribed in Section 115.36 of the statutes.

Blind and Visual Impairment Education Council: NISSAN BAR-LEV (special education director), *chairperson;* JAKE LICHOSIK, VICKI LICHOSIK, ERIN RANDALL-CLARK (parents of visually impaired children); DIANE NOBLITT, CHERYL ORGAS, CHRIS ZENCHENKO (members of organizations affiliated with visually impaired); DAWN SOTO (licensed teacher of visually impaired); SADIQUA WHITE-HARPER (licensed teacher of orientation and mobility); vacancy (licensed general education teacher); NANCY THOMPSON (school board member); RON DAYTON (school district administrator); FRED WOLLENBURG (CESA representative); JANE SIERACKE (higher education representative); MARY ANN DAMM, SUE KOKKO, vacancy (other members) (all appointed by superintendent).

The 17-member Blind and Visual Impairment Education Council advises the state superintendent on statewide activities that will benefit visually impaired pupils; makes recommendations for improvements in services provided by the Wisconsin Center for the Blind and Visually Impaired; and proposes ways to improve the preparation of teachers and staff and coordination between the department and other agencies that offer services to the visually impaired. Members serve 3-year terms. At least one must be certified by the Library of Congress as a Braille transcriber. The higher education representative must either have experience as an educator of the visually impaired or an educator of teachers of the visually impaired. At least one of the three remaining members must be visually impaired. The council was created as the Council on the Blind by Chapter 276, Laws of 1969, renamed as the Council on the Education of the Blind in Chapter 292, Laws of 1971, and renamed and substantially revised by 1999 Wisconsin Act 9. Its composition and duties are prescribed in Sections 15.377 (1) and 115.37 of the statutes.

Deaf and Hard-of-Hearing Education Council: DAVID COLLINS, MICHELLE KIHNTOPF (parents of hearing impaired children); POLLY ANN WILLIAMS-SLAPPEY (teacher of hearing impaired pupils); KRISTA SHERIN (licensed speech-language pathologist); BRIAN ANDERSON (school district special education director); ANNE BLAYLOCK (licensed audiologist with expertise in educational audiology); AMY OTIS-WILBORN (educator of hearing impaired teachers); PAM CONINE (technical college interpreter training instructor); JAMIE AMACCI (educational interpreter); ROBIN BARNES, CATHERINE FRANKLIN, ALICE SYKORA (other members) (all appointed by state superintendent).

The Deaf and Hard-of-Hearing Education Council advises the state superintendent on issues related to pupils who are hearing impaired. It informs the superintendent on services, programs, and research that could benefit those students. The council makes recommendations for improving services provided by the Wisconsin Educational Services Program for the Deaf and Hard of Hearing; reviews and makes recommendations on the level of quality and services available to hearing-impaired pupils; proposes ways to improve the preparation of teachers and other staff who provide services to the hearing impaired; and proposes ways to improve coordination between the department and providers of services to the hearing impaired. The council's 12 members serve 3-year terms. It was created by 2001 Wisconsin Act 57, and its composition and duties are prescribed in Sections 15.377 (2) and 115.372 of the statutes.

Library and Network Development, Council on: KATHY PLETCHER (professional member), *chairperson;* SANDRA MELCHER (professional member), *vice chairperson;* MICHAEL BAHR (public member), *secretary;* BARBARA ARNOLD, MARY M. BAYORGEON, CATHERINE HANSEN, LISA JEWELL, ANNETTE SMITH, LISA STERRETT, KRIS ADAMS WENDT (professional members); DONALD BULLEY, FRANCIS CHERNEY, MIRIAM ERICKSON, ROBERT KOECHLEY, DOUGLAS H. LAY, JOHN NICHOLS, CALVIN POTTER, SUSAN REYNOLDS, KRISTI A. WILLIAMS (public members) (appointed by governor).

The 19-member Council on Library and Network Development advises the state superintendent and the administrator of the Division for Libraries, Technology, and Community Learning on the performance of their duties regarding library service. Members serve 3-year terms. The professional members represent various types of libraries and information services. The public members must demonstrate an interest in libraries and other types of information services. The council was created by Chapter 347, Laws of 1979, and its composition and duties are prescribed in Sections 15.377 (6) and 43.07 of the statutes.

Professional Standards Council for Teachers: LINDA HELF (public school teacher), *chairperson;* RYAN CHAMPEAU (public school principal), *vice chairperson;* ANN CATTAU (public school pupil services professional), *secretary;* LISA BENZ, PAULA HASE, THOMAS MULLIGAN, AL PYATSKOWIT, TERRY SCHOESSOW (public school teachers); KAY STAFF (public school pupil service professional); STEPHANIE ARMSTRONG (public school special education teacher); ALAN BITTER (private school teacher); JOHN GAIER (public school district administrator); JEFFREY BARNETT, DWIGHT WATSON (UW System educational faculty members); JAMES JUERGENSEN (private college education faculty member); FRANCES BOHON, JEFF MCCABE (public school board members); MICHAEL CASTANEDA (parent of public school child); JAMIE TOMEI (student enrolled in teacher preparatory program) (appointed by state superintendent with senate consent).

The 19-member Professional Standards Council for Teachers advises the state superintendent regarding licensing and evaluating teachers; evaluation and approval of teacher education programs; the status of teaching in Wisconsin; school board practices to develop effective teaching; peer mentoring; evaluation systems; and alternative dismissal procedures.

Members serve 3-year terms, except the student member, who serves for 2 years. Public school teachers and pupil service professionals are recommended by the largest statewide labor organization representing teachers. The private school teacher is recommended by the Wisconsin Council of Religious and Independent Schools. The public school administrator and principal are recommended by their statewide organizations. Faculty members are recommended by the UW System president and the Wisconsin Association of Independent Colleges and Universities. The council was created by 1997 Wisconsin Act 298, and its composition and duties are prescribed in Sections 15.377 (8) and 115.425 of the statutes.

School District Boundary Appeal Board: vacancy (superintendent of public instruction or designee); DAVID AMUNDSON, PATRICK DORIN, RICHARD ELORANTA, MARY KATHLEEN MALONEY, JOHN OSTERTAG, STEVEN PATE, SPENCER ROTZER, PETER SEVERSON, PATRICIA SILVER, THERESE TRAVIA, ARNOLD WIDDES, vacancy (appointed by state superintendent).

The 13-member School District Boundary Appeal Board hears appeals from persons aggrieved by actions taken under Chapter 117, Wisconsin Statutes, providing for school district reorganization. The appointed members include 4 each from large, medium, and small district school boards, who are appointed for staggered 2-year terms. No two members may live within the boundaries of the same CESA. The board was created by 1983 Wisconsin Act 27, and its composition and duties are prescribed in Sections 15.375 (2) and 117.05 of the statutes.

Special Education, Council on: GARY MYRAH, *chairperson;* HOLLY HART, *vice chairperson;* GLENDA CARTER, RENEE DERCKS-ENGELS, CAROL NODDINGS EICHINGER, CHERYL FUNMAKER, JILL GONZALEZ, JENNIFER GRENKE, KIM HENDERSON, ANNE KNAPP, JULIE LIDBURY, MICHAEL LINAK, DON NIELSEN, JUNE PAUL, QYLA PERSON, MARY SOBCZAK, WAYNE SWANGER, BONNIE VANDER MEULEN, LISA WING, PATRICIA YAHLE (appointed by state superintendent).

The Council on Special Education advises the state superintendent on programs for children with disabilities. It assists in developing evaluations, and reporting data to the U.S. Department of Education, developing policies, and advising the state superintendent regarding the needs of children with disabilities. The number of council members is unspecified, but the following categories must be represented: regular and special education teachers; institutions of higher education that train special education personnel; state and local education officials; administrators of programs for children with disabilities; agencies involved in financing or delivery of related services; private schools and charter schools; a vocational, community, or business organization that provides transitional services; the Department of Corrections; parents of children with disabilities; and individuals with disabilities. Council members are appointed for 3-year terms, and the majority must be individuals with disabilities or parents of children with disabilities. The council was created as the Council on Exceptional Education by Chapter 89, Laws of 1973, and renamed and revised by 1997 Wisconsin Act 164. Its composition and duties are prescribed in Section 15.377 (4) of the statutes.

PUBLIC SERVICE COMMISSION

Commissioners: ERIC CALLISTO, 267-7897, eric.callisto@, *chairperson;* LAUREN AZAR, 267-7899, lauren.azar@; MARK MEYER, 267-7898, mark.meyer@ (appointed by governor with senate consent).

Executive Assistant to the Chairperson: NATHAN ZOLIK, 267-7897, nathan.zolik@

Secretary to the Commission: SANDRA PASKE, 266-1265, sandra.paske@

Administrative Law Judge, Office of: MICHAEL NEWMARK, *acting administrative law judge,* 261-8523, michael.newmark@

Governmental and Public Affairs, Office of: TIM LEMONDS, *director,* 267-0912, timothy.lemonds@

General Counsel: JENNIFER NASHOLD, 266-1264, jennifer.nashold@

Legislative Liaison: LORI SAKK, 266-1383, lori.sakk@

Administrative Services, Division of: SARAH KLEIN, *administrator,* 266-3587, sarah.klein@

Gas and Energy Division: ROBERT NORCROSS, *administrator,* 266-0699, robert.norcross@

Telecommunications Division: GARY EVENSON, *administrator,* 266-6744, gary.evenson@

Water, Compliance and Consumer Affairs, Division of: AMELIA RAMIREZ, *administrator,* 267-7829, amelia.ramirez@

Address e-mail by combining the user ID and the state extender: userid@**psc.state.wi.us**

Mailing Address: P.O. Box 7854, Madison 53707-7854.

Location: Public Service Commission Building, 610 North Whitney Way, Madison.

Telephones: General inquiries: (888) 816-3831 (in-state only) or 266-5481; Complaints: (800) 225-7729 (in-state only) or 266-2001; Media relations: 266-9600; TTY: (800) 251-8345 (in-state only) or 267-1479.

Fax: 266-3957.

E-mail Address: pscrecs@psc.state.wi.us

Internet Address: http://psc.wi.gov

Publications: Biennial report; strategic energy assessment; various statistics on electric utilities, gas utilities, and telephone companies and guides for utility customers, including publications for consumers related to electricity, natural gas, water, and telephone services.

Number of Employees: 157.00.

Total Budget 2007-09: $53,870,800.

Statutory References: Sections 15.06 and 15.79; Chapter 196.

Agency Responsibility: The Public Service Commission (PSC) is responsible for regulating Wisconsin's public utilities and ensuring that utility services are provided to customers at prices reasonable to both ratepayers and utility owners. The commission regulates the rates and services of electric, gas distribution, heating, water, combined water and sewer utilities, and certain telecommunications providers. In most instances, its jurisdiction does not extend to the activities of electric cooperatives, wireless telephone providers, cable television, or Internet service.

Responsibilities of the commission include setting utility rates, determining levels for adequate and safe service, and utility bond sales and stock offerings. It confirms or rejects utility applications for major construction projects, such as power plants, transmission lines, and wind farms. In addition to ensuring utility compliance with statutes, administrative codes, and record-keeping requirements, the commission's staff investigates and mediates thousands of consumer complaints annually. During the complaint process, commission staff reviews all pertinent information to make certain that the utility's handling of the complaint is in compliance with the applicable rules. The commission also rules on proposed mergers between utility companies.

Organization: The governor appoints the 3 full-time commissioners, with senate approval, to serve staggered 6-year terms, but an individual commissioner holds office until a successor is appointed and qualified. No commissioner may have a financial interest in a railroad or public utility or water carrier or serve on or under a political party committee. By work rule, no employee or immediate family member may own stock in a utility or any entity regulated by the commission. The governor designates a chairperson who, in turn, may appoint division administrators from outside the classified service.

Unit Functions: The *Division of Administrative Services* provides business management services to the commission, including budget development, revenue collections, intervenor financing coordination, and procurement. The division is also responsible for managing the PSC's data and information, including data processing services and maintenance of central records.

The *Gas and Energy Division* is responsible for all aspects of regulating electric utilities and the provision of natural gas service. PSC approval is required for utilities to change rates, build power plants, or construct major transmission lines. The division looks at need, alternatives, costs, and environmental impacts for construction cases and reviews finances, corporate structure, and affiliated interests in rate cases. It also provides the commissioners with information they need in order to make decisions regarding construction and rate cases.

The *Telecommunications Division* is responsible for overseeing the telecommunication industry in Wisconsin and regulating those services that are within PSC jurisdiction. The PSC promotes competition in the state's telecommunications markets in order to ensure access to modern and affordable service throughout the state. The division oversees price regulation and alternative plans of telecommunication utilities, earnings and rate levels, service quality, tariffs and contracts, and deployment of telecommunication infrastructure. The PSC also works to resolve interconnection disputes between service providers, administers universal service programs, manages the wireless 911 (E-911) program, and advises the Federal Communications Commission on matters pertaining to Wisconsin's interests in federal telecommunications policy.

The *Division of Water, Compliance and Consumer Affairs* is responsible for regulating water and sewer public utilities in Wisconsin and ensuring utility compliance with the consumer sections of the state administrative code and statutes. The division offers assistance to all of the state's utilities for compliance with the statutes, code, and record-keeping requirements and the development of consumer affairs policies. The division also coordinates consumer information and mediates resolutions to consumer complaints.

History: Public utility regulation in Wisconsin followed and was closely related to railroad regulation. Railroads were the first modern enterprise to have their rates regulated, and Wisconsin became one of the first states to pass such laws. Chapter 273, Laws of 1874, established a railroad rate structure and provided for 3 appointed railroad commissioners to supervise rail freight operations. Two years later in Chapter 57, Laws of 1876, the legislature repealed much of the 1874 law and established a single appointed commissioner of railroads. The commissioner was made an elected official in 1881 (Chapter 300).

The forerunner of today's commission dates from Chapter 362, Laws of 1905, which created an appointed 3-member Railroad Commission to supervise rail operations, appraise railroad property, and set rates. With the enactment of Chapter 499, Laws of 1907, which extended the powers of the Railroad Commission, Wisconsin became the first state to regulate all public utilities.

Chapter 183, Laws of 1931, renamed the agency the Public Service Commission of Wisconsin and made it responsible for comprehensive motor carrier regulation in 1933 (Chapter 488). The 1967 executive branch reorganization continued the commission as an independent agency. Chapter 29, Laws of 1977, transferred the commission's railroad and motor carrier regulatory functions to the Transportation Commission (recreated in 1982 as the now defunct Office of the Commissioner of Transportation). Railroad regulation was assigned to the newly created Office of the Commissioner of Railroads by 1993 Wisconsin Act 123.

Laws passed in 1985 provided for a partial deregulation of public utility holding companies and telecommunications service, and 1993 Wisconsin Act 496 established a new regulatory framework for telecommunications utilities, which authorizes the commission to regulate the prices utilities charge rather than limiting their total earnings.

Statutory Councils

Telecommunications Privacy Council: Inactive.

The Telecommunications Privacy Council advises the commission on guidelines designed to protect the privacy of users of telecommunications services. The number of members on the council is not specified, but all must represent telecommunications providers or consumers. The council was created by 1993 Wisconsin Act 496 and its composition and duties are prescribed in Section 196.209 of the statutes.

Universal Service Fund Council: RICHARD SCHLIMM, *chairperson;* JILL COLLINS, PAUL FUGLIE, STEPHANIE HARRISON, PAM HOLMES, GWEN JACKSON, ROBERT KELLERMAN, JEAN PAUK, GARY RADLOFF, CHERYL RUE, PAMELA SHERWOOD, PAULETTE WATFORD (appointed by Public Service Commission).

Universal Service Fund Manager: ANITA SPRENGER, Public Service Commission, P.O. Box 7854, Madison 53707-7854; Telephone: 266-3843; Fax: 266-3957; TTY: (800) 251-8345 (in-state only) or 267-1479; anita.sprenger@

The Universal Service Fund Council advises the commission on the administration of the Universal Service Fund, which assists low-income customers, disabled customers, and customers in areas where telecommunication service costs are relatively high, in obtaining affordable access to basic telecommunication services. The Universal Service Fund manager acts as liaison between the commission and the council. The number of members on the council is not specified. All must represent telecommunication service providers or consumers, but the majority of members must be consumers. The council was created by 1993 Wisconsin Act 496 and its composition and duties are prescribed in Section 196.218 (6) of the statutes.

INDEPENDENT UNIT ATTACHED FOR BUDGETING, PROGRAM COORDINATION, AND RELATED MANAGEMENT FUNCTIONS BY SECTION 15.03 OF THE STATUTES

OFFICE OF THE COMMISSIONER OF RAILROADS

Commissioner of Railroads: ROGER BRESKE, 266-0276, roger.breske@psc.state.wi.us

Legal Counsel: DOUGLAS S. WOOD, 266-9536, doug.wood@psc.state.wi.us

Agency Liaison: ELIZABETH PILIOURAS, 266-0276, elizabeth.piliouras@psc.state.wi.us

Rail Safety Analyst: TOM RUNNING, 266-7607, tom.running@psc.state.wi.us

Mailing Address: P.O. Box 7854, Madison 53707-7854.

Location: 610 North Whitney Way, Suite 110, Madison.

Telephone: 266-0276.

Fax: 261-8220.

Internet Address: http://psc.wi.gov

Number of Employees: 5.00.

Total Budget 2007-09: $953,400.

Statutory References: Sections 15.06 (1) (a) and 15.795 (1); Chapters 189-192 and 195.

Agency Responsibility: The Office of the Commissioner of Railroads enforces regulations related to railway safety and determines the safety of highway crossings including the adequacy of railroad warning devices. The office also regulates water carriers. The office is funded by assessments on railroads.

The governor appoints the commissioner with senate consent to a 6-year term and holds office until a successor is appointed. The commissioner may not have a financial interest in railroads or water carriers and may not serve on or under any committee of a political party. The office was created by 1993 Wisconsin Act 123 as an independent regulatory agency to assume the functions relating to railroad regulation that 1993 Wisconsin Act 16 had transferred to the Public Service Commission when the Office of the Commissioner of Transportation was eliminated. The responsibility for regulating water carriers was added by 2005 Wisconsin Act 179.

Department of
REGULATION AND LICENSING

Secretary of Regulation and Licensing: CELIA M. JACKSON, 266-1352,
celia.jackson@wisconsin.gov

Deputy Secretary: BARBARA WYATT SIBLEY, 267-2435, barbara.wyattsibley@wisconsin.gov

Executive Assistant/Legislative Liaison: HECTOR COLON, 266-8608,
hector.colon@wisconsin.gov

General Counsel: MICHAEL BERNDT, 266-0011, michael.berndt@wisconsin.gov

Mailing Address: P.O. Box 8935, Madison 53708-8935.

Location: 1400 East Washington Avenue, Madison.

Telephones: 266-2112 (for operator, select menu option "6"); TTY: 267-2416.

Internet Address: http://drl.wi.gov

Fax: 267-0644.

Number of Employees: 114.32.

Total Budget 2007-09: $25,458,200.

Statutory References: Sections 15.08, 15.085, 15.40, and 15.405-15.407; Chapters 440-460, 470, and 480.

Enforcement, Division of: MARVIN ROBINSON, *administrator,* 266-3445,
marvin.robinson@wisconsin.gov

Management Services, Division of: MARTHA ZYDOWSKY, *administrator,* 261-2392,
martha.zydowsky@wisconsin.gov

Professional Credential Processing, Division of: CATHERINE POND, *administrator,* 266-0557, cathy.pond@wisconsin.gov

Education and Examinations, Office of: JILL REMY, *program manager,* 266-7703, jill.remy@wisconsin.gov

Board Services, Division of: GAIL SUMI, *administrator,* 261-2393, gail.sumi@wisconsin.gov

Bureau Assignments: GAIL SUMI, *administrator;* MICHAEL BERNDT, *legal counsel.*

Medical Examining Board (266-2112): GENE MUSSER, *chairperson;* SUJATHA KAILAS, *vice chairperson;* IAN J. MUNRO, *secretary;* JEROLD J. HARTER, JACK M. LOCKHART, RAYMOND P. MAGER, SURESH K. MISRA, SANDRA L. OSBORN, BHUPINDER S. SAINI, SHELDON WASSERMAN (physicians), CAROLYN H. BRONSTON*, JUDE GENEREAUX*, vacancy*. Nonvoting member: vacancy (Patient Compensation Fund Peer Review Council).

Athletic Trainers Affiliated Credentialing Board (266-2112): STEVEN J. NASS, *chairperson;* RYAN A. BERRY, *vice chairperson;* JEANNE M. BROWN, *secretary;* JAMES W. NESBIT, vacancy (physician member), JOHN M. SYBELDON*.

Dietitians Affiliated Credentialing Board (266-2112): DIANE L. JOHNSON, *vice chairperson;* VIRGINIA A. JORDAN, *secretary;* GAIL L. UNDERBAKKE, PATRICIA M. ROBLEE*, vacancy.

Occupational Therapists Affiliated Credentialing Board (266-2112): GAIL C. SLAUGHTER (occupational therapist), *chairperson;* BRIAN B. HOLMQUIST (occupational therapist), *vice chairperson;* DAVID COOPER*, *secretary;* MYLINDA BARISAS-MATULA (occupational therapist), DEBORAH A. MCKERNAN-ACE, DOROTHY J. OLSON (occupational therapist assistants), CORLISS A. RICE*.

Perfusionists Examining Council (266-2112): MATTHEW J. HIETPAS, *chairperson;* DAVID B. HELLENBRAND, *vice chairperson;* GARY R. HAWKINS, JR., *secretary;* vacancy (physician); DAVID F. COBB*. (Medical Examining Board appoints the perfusionist members. Governor appoints the public member.)

Physical Therapists Affiliated Credentialing Board (266-2112): MARK W. SHROPSHIRE (physical therapist), *chairperson;* LARRY J. NOSSE (physical therapist), *vice chairperson;* JANE L. STROEDE (physical therapist assistant), *secretary;* OTTO A. CORDERO (physical therapists); ENID MISTELE*.

Physician Assistants, Council on (266-2112): ANNE B. HLETKO (physician assistant), *chairperson;* ERIC L. GARLAND (physician assistant), *vice chairperson;* JERRY NOACK (designated by vice chancellor for health sciences of UW-Madison), *secretary;* RICHARD L. FAUST (physician assistant), MARY PANGMAN SCHMITT*. (Medical Examining Board appoints the physician assistant members. Governor appoints the public member.)

Podiatrists Affiliated Credentialing Board (266-2112): IAN C. FURNESS, *chairperson;* MELANIE L. BERG, *vice chairperson;* GARY BROWN*, *secretary;* RENE F. SETTLE-ROBINSON.

Respiratory Care Practitioners Examining Council (266-2112): ANN M. JOHNSON, *chairperson;* ANN M. MEICHER, *vice chairperson;* vacancy, *secretary;* WILLIAM D. ROSANDICK, EDWARD R. WINGA (physician); vacancy*. (Medical Examining Board appoints respiratory care practitioners. Governor appoints the public member.)

Nursing Home Administrator Examining Board (266-2112): DAVID M. EGAN, *chairperson;* MARY ANN CLARK, *vice chairperson;* MARY K. LEASE (registered nurse), *secretary;* KENNETH D. ARNESON, SUSAN KINAST-PORTER (physician), HEATHER L. SHEEHAN, vacancy, LORELI DICKINSON*, MARY F. PIKE*. Nonvoting member: PAUL PESHEK (designee of secretary of health services); COLLEEN BAIRD, *legal counsel.*

Bureau Director: YOLANDA MCGOWAN, 261-4486, yolanda.mcgowan@wisconsin.gov; PEGGY WICHMANN, *legal counsel.*

Accounting Examining Board (266-2112): THOMAS J. KILKENNY, *chairperson;* KARLA E. PLAIR, *vice chairperson;* LUCRETIA S. MATTSON, *secretary;* KIM L. TREDINNICK, MARION R. WOZNIAK, STEVEN A. CORBEILLE*.

Architects, Landscape Architects, Professional Engineers, Designers and Land Surveyors, Examining Board of (266-2112).

DEPARTMENT OF REGULATION AND LICENSING

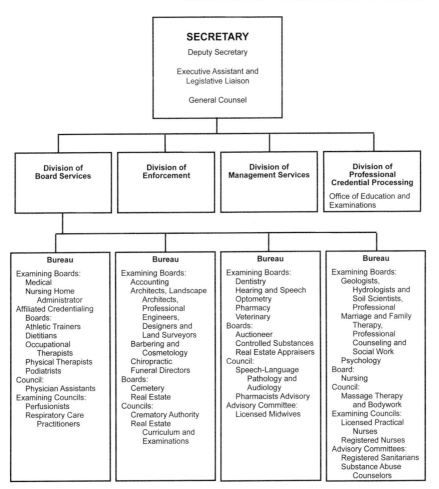

Under Section 440.042, Wisconsin Statutes, the secretary of the department of regulation and licensing may appoint advisory committees to advise the department and its boards on matters relating to the regulation of credential holders. Professions for which an advisory committee may be created are as follows: acupuncture; athletic agent; boxing; charitable organizations; firearms certifier and permits; home inspector; interior designer; licensed midwife; music, art and dance therapy; peddler; private detective; private security person; professional fund raiser; professional fund raising council; real estate contractual forms; real estate appraisers application; real estate appraisers education and experience; registered sanitarian; substance abuse counselor.

The 5 professional sections listed below comprise the examining board for a total of 15 professional members and 10 public members. Examining board officers: Martin J. Hanson, *chairperson;* Rosheen Styczinski, *vice chairperson;* James E. Rusch, *secretary.*

Architect Section: Walter L. Wilson, *chairperson;* Gary A. Gust, *vice chairperson;* Julia A. DeCicco*, *secretary;* Lawrence J. Schnuck, Gary Kohlenberg*.

Designer Section: SCOTT B. BERG, *chairperson;* THOMAS J. GASPERETTI*, *vice chairperson;* JAMES F. MICKOWSKI, *secretary;* STEVEN T. TWEED, vacancy*.

Engineer Section: MARTIN J. HANSON, *chairperson;* CHARLES W. KOPPLIN, *vice chairperson;* DANIEL J. SHELDON, *secretary;* STEVEN J. HOOK*, RYAN W. KLIPPEL*.

Landscape Architect Section: ROSHEEN M. STYCZINSKI, *chairperson;* WAYNE G. TLUSTY, *vice chairperson;* NANCY T. RAGLAND, *secretary;* BERNIE A. ABRAHAMSON*, MICHAEL J. KINNEY*.

Land Surveyor Section: RICK A. VAN GOETHEM, *chairperson;* STEVEN NIELSEN*, *vice chairperson;* MATTHEW J. JANIAK, *secretary;* RUTH G. JOHNSON*, JAMES E. RUSCH.

Barbering and Cosmetology Examining Board (266-2112): JEANNIE M. BUSH (electrologist), *chairperson;* JEFFREY A. PATTERSON, *vice chairperson;* JANICE M. BOECK (public school of barbering or cosmetology representative), *secretary;* E. ROD GOTTFREDSEN, SUSAN KOLVE-FEEHAN (private school of barbering or cosmetology representatives), LAURA E. RUIZ (aesthetician), HOWARD TWAIT, CHERYL A. PEARSE*, TINA M. RETTLER*.

Cemetery Board (266-2112): E. GLEN PORTER III, *chairperson;* W. E. GREENFIELD, *vice chairperson;* MARY B. LEHMAN, *secretary;* TIMOTHY J. STANLEY, KATHLEEN M. CANTU*, CECELIA L. TIMMONS*.

Chiropractic Examining Board (266-2112): WENDY M. HENRICHS, *chairperson;* STEVEN J. SILVERMAN, *vice chairperson;* JAMES P. KOSHICK, *secretary;* STEVEN R. CONWAY, MANIA F. MOORE*, KATHLEEN A. SCHNEIDER*.

Crematory Authority Council (266-2112): SCOTT K. BRAINARD, WILLIAM R. CRESS, GARY A. LANGENDORF (funeral director/crematory); ADAM J. CASPER, KELLY L. COLEMAN-KOHORN, PAUL A. HAUBRICH (cemetery/crematory); LINDA A. REID*. (Senate confirmation is not required for council members.)

Funeral Directors Examining Board (266-2112): DAVID E. OLSEN, *chairperson;* ROSALIE A. MURPHY*, *vice chairperson;* CONNIE C. RYAN, *secretary;* J.C. FRAZIER, MICHELE M. MOORE, PATRICIA THORNTON*.

Real Estate Board (266-2112): PETER A. SVEUM, *chairperson;* LISABETH R. WEIRICH, *vice chairperson;* DENNIS M. PIERCE*, *secretary;* STEPHEN P. BEERS, J. KENNETH LEE, ROBERT DUEHOLM*, RYAN J. SCHROEDER*.

Real Estate Curriculum and Examinations, Council on (266-2112): LISABETH R. WEIRICH (real estate board designee); SUSAN E. HAMER, RICHARD E. HINSMAN, PEGGY A. LOVEJOY, BARBARA MCGILL, PAUL G. HOFFMAN*, LAWRENCE SAGER*. (Senate confirmation is not required for council members.)

Bureau Director: THOMAS RYAN, 266-8098, thomas.ryan@wisconsin.gov; RUBY JEFFERSON-MOORE, *legal counsel.*

Auctioneer Board (266-2112): PATRICK J. MCNAMARA, *chairperson;* TIMOTHY D. SWEENY, *vice chairperson;* KATHRYN A. DALEY* *secretary;* JAY N. CLARKE, vacancy (auctioneer/auction company representative), ALAN S. HAGER*, vacancy*.

Controlled Substances Board (266-2112): DAROLD A. TREFFERT (psychiatrist), *chairperson;* ROBERT BLOCK (designated by attorney general), *vice chairperson;* YVONNE M. BELLAY (designated by secretary of agriculture, trade and consumer protection), *secretary;* TIMOTHY J. BOEHMER (designated by pharmacy examining board), DOUG ENGLEBERT (designated by secretary of health services); CECILIA J. HILLARD (pharmacologist).

Dentistry Examining Board (266-2112): LORI R. BARBEAU (dentist), *chairperson;* BLANE R. CHRISTMAN (dentist), *vice chairperson;* LINDA BOHACEK (dental hygienist), *secretary;* JOHN W. GRIGNON (dentist), ADRIANA JARAMILLO (dentist), SANDRA E. LINHART (dental hygienist), KIRK R. RITCHIE (dentist); NANCY J. RUBLEE (dental hygienist); WILLIAM J. STEMPSKI (dentist), CAROL L. HOWARD*, vacancy.

Hearing and Speech Examining Board (266-2112): OKIE E. ALLEN (hearing instrument specialist), *chairperson;* PETER J. ZELLMER (hearing instrument specialist), *vice chairperson;* EDWARD W. KORABIC (audiologist), *secretary;* THOMAS E. FISHER (audiologist), DAVID R.

FRIEDLAND (otolaryngologist), TERRENCE M. GREENLEAF (hearing instrument specialist), ALMA D. PETERS, MARLIYN S. WORKINGER (speech-language pathologists); vacancy* (hearing aid user), BRUCE BAIER*.

Speech-Language Pathology and Audiology, Council on: (Inactive).

Licensed Midwives Advisory Committee (266-2112): INGRID S. ANDERSSON (license nurse-midwife), JANE C. PETERSON, ERIC E. STADER (physicians), DEBRA J. STUDEY, GLORIA TARRER*. (Appointed by secretary of regulation and licensing.)

Optometry Examining Board (266-2112): GREGORY A. FOSTER, *chairperson;* RICHARD T. WRIGHT, *vice chairperson;* KATHI L. LEACH, *secretary;* ANN MEIER M. CARLI, LINDA M. FOLEY, SWAMINAT BALACHANDRAN*, vacancy*.

Pharmacy Examining Board (266-2112): GREGORY C. WEBER, *chairperson;* JEANNE M. SEVERSON, *vice chairperson;* SUZETTE RENWICK*, *secretary;* TIMOTHY J. BOEHMER, AMY MATTILA, JASON WALKER-CRAWFORD, PAMELA J. PHILLIPS*.

Pharmacist Advisory Council: (Inactive).

Real Estate Appraisers Board (266-2112): MARLA L. BRITTON (assessor), *chairperson;* SHARON R. FIEDLER (certified residential appraiser and licensed appraiser), *vice chairperson;* vacancy, *secretary;* MARK P. KOWBEL (certified residential appraiser and licensed appraiser), KAREN SCOTT (certified general appraiser and licensed appraiser), MICQUEL H. HOFFMANN*, HENRY F. SIMON*, vacancy*.

Veterinary Examining Board (266-2112): ROBERT R. SPENCER, *chairperson;* MARTHINA L. GREER, *vice chairperson;* JoANN M. KLEMAN (veterinary technician), *secretary;* WESLEY G. ELFORD, DONALD J. PETERSON, WILLIAM S. RICE, THERESA L. WAAGE*, JOAN WYWIALOWSKI*.

Bureau Director: JEFF SCANLAN, 267-7223, jeff.scanlan@wisconsin.gov; COLLEEN BAIRD, *legal counsel.*

Geologists, Hydrologists and Soil Scientists, Examining Board of Professional (266-2112). The 3 professional sections listed below comprise the examining board for a total of 9 professional members and 3 public members. Examining board officers: RANDALL J. HUNT (hydrologist), *chairperson;* WILLIAM N. MODE (geologist), *vice chairperson;* FREDERICK W. MADISON (soil scientist), *secretary.*

Geologist Section: WILLIAM N. MODE, *chairperson;* BRENDA S. HALMINIAK, *vice chairperson;* SUE E. BRIDSON*, *secretary;* JAMES M. ROBERTSON.

Hydrologist Section: STEPHEN V. DONOHUE, *chairperson;* vacancy, *vice chairperson;* RUTH G. JOHNSON*, *secretary;* BRYANT A. BROWNE, RANDALL J. HUNT.

Soil Scientist Section: FREDERICK W. MADISON, *chairperson;* PATRICIA A. TROCHLELL, *vice chairperson;* JOHN A. HAHN*, *secretary;* vacancy.

Marriage and Family Therapy, Professional Counseling and Social Work Examining Board (266-2112). The following 3 sections comprise the examining board, for a total of 10 professional members and 3 public members. Examining board officers: MARY J. WALSH, *chairperson;* LESLIE D. MIRKIN, *vice chairperson;* ARLIE J. ALBRECHT, *secretary.*

Marriage and Family Therapist Section: BRUCE P. KUEHL, *chairperson;* ABE RABINOWITZ*, *vice chairperson;* ARLIE J. ALBRECHT, *secretary;* ANN MARIE STARR.

Professional Counselor Section: LESLIE D. MIRKIN, *chairperson;* EVELYN PUMPHREY, *vice chairperson;* SUSAN M. PUTRA, *secretary;* LaMARR J. FRANKLIN*.

Social Worker Section: GEORGE J. KAMPS (clinical social worker), *chairperson;* ERIC M. ALVIN (government social worker), *vice chairperson;* DARYL D. WOOD*, *secretary;* MARY JO WALSH (advanced practice social worker), vacancy (independent social worker).

Massage Therapy and Bodywork Council: CLAUDE J. GAGNON, *chairperson;* CARIE A. MARTIN, *vice chairperson;* LILLIAN C. POUNDS, *secretary;* AMY C. CONNELL, JUNE M. MOTZER, AMY C. REMILLARD, XIPING ZHOU. (Senate confirmation is not required.)

Nursing, Board of (266-2112): MARILYN A. KAUFMANN (registered nurse), *chairperson;*

KATHLEEN L. SULLIVAN (registered nurse), *vice chairperson;* JULIA NELSON (registered nurse), *secretary;* JUNE A. BAHR (licensed practical nurse), EVELYN N. MERRIETT (registered nurse), LOU ANN M. WEIX (registered nurse), vacancy (licensed practical nurse), GRETCHEN R. LOWE*, MARGARET WOOD*.

Licensed Practical Nurses, Examining Council on: (Inactive).

Registered Nurses, Examining Council on: (Inactive).

Psychology Examining Board (266-2112): DON L. CROWDER, *chairperson;* ERICA R. SERLIN, *vice chairperson;* TERESA H. ROSE*, *secretary;* BRUCE R. ERDMANN, GERALD W. HOLLANDER, CYNTHIA B. BAGLEY*.

Registered Sanitarians Advisory Committee (266-2112): DOUGLAS GIERYN, ROBERT HARRIS, NICOLE HUNGER, BRIAN JINDRA, ROMAN KAMINSKI, JEFFERY KINDRAI, MICHELE WILLIAMS. (Appointed by the secretary of regulation and licensing.)

Substance Abuse Counselors Advisory Committee (266-2112): VALERIE L. ALLEN, FREDERICKA L. DECOTEAU, LORIE A. GOESER, SHERYL L. GRAEBER, GAIL B. KINNEY, STERLON R. WHITE, KATHERYN L. WOLF. (Appointed by secretary of regulation and licensing.)

---

*Asterisk indicates public member. Other members represent the profession regulated, unless otherwise noted. The governor appoints all examining board and council members with the advice and consent of the senate, unless otherwise indicated.

Visit the DRL Web site at http://drl.wi.gov for the latest information on board memberships

Publications: Biennial reports; Consumer Complaints; Other Resources; The Impaired Professionals Procedure; Information About Your Hearing; Wisconsin Directory of Accredited Schools of Nursing; plus informational bulletins for credential holders, monthly disciplinary reports, and statute/rules codebooks.

Boards and Councils within the Department of Regulation and Licensing

Unit	Statutory Citation	Session Laws Creating or Amending	Duties Specified in Wisconsin Statutes
Accounting Examining Board	S. 15.405 (1)	Ch. 337, L. 1913; Ch. 327, L. 1967; Ch. 356, L. 1981	Ch. 442
Architects, Landscape Architects, Professional Engineers, Designers and Land Surveyors, Examining Board of	S. 15.405 (2)	Ch. 644, L. 1917; Ch. 486, L. 1931; Ch. 547, L. 1955; Ch. 446, L. 1969; 1993 WisActs 463 and 465, 1997 WisAct 300	Ch. 443
Auctioneer Board	S. 15.405 (3)	1993 WisAct 102	Ch. 480
Barbering and Cosmetology Examining Board	S. 15.405 (17)	Ch. 221, L. 1915 (Committee of Examiners in Barbering); Ch. 431, L. 1939 (Board of Examiners in Cosmetology); 1987 WisAct 265 (combined the 2); 2005 WisAct 314	Ch. 454
Cemetery Board	S. 15.405 (3m)	2005 WisAct 25	Ch. 440, Subchap.VIII
Chiropractic Examining Board	S. 15.405 (5)	Ch. 408, L. 1925	Ch. 446
Controlled Substances Board	S. 15.405 (5g)	Ch. 384, L. 1969; Ch. 219, L. 1971; 1995 WisAct 305	Ch. 961
Crematory Authority Council	S. 15.407 (8)	2005 WisAct 31	S. 15.09 (5)
Dentistry Examining Board	S. 15.405 (6)	Ch. 129, L. 1885; 1997 WisAct 96	Ch. 447
Funeral Directors Examining Board	S. 15.405 (16)	Ch. 420, L. 1905; Ch. 39, L. 1975; 1983 WisAct 485	Ch. 445
Geologists, Hydrologists and Soil Scientists, Examining Board of Professional	S. 15.405 (2m)	1997 WisAct 300	Ch. 470
Hearing and Speech Examining Board	S. 15.405 (6m)	Ch. 300, L. 1969; 1989 WisAct 316; 2003 WisAct 270	Ch. 459
Council on Speech-Language Pathology and Audiology	S. 15.407 (4)	1989 WisAct 316	S. 459.23

Boards and Councils within the Department of Regulation and Licensing–Continued

Unit	Statutory Citation	Session Laws Creating or Amending	Duties Specified in Wisconsin Statutes
Marriage and Family Therapy, Professional Counseling and Social Work Examining Board	S. 15.405 (7c)	1991 WisAct 160, 2001 WisAct 80	Ch. 457
Massage Therapy and Bodywork Council	S. 15.407 (7)	2001 WisAct 74	Ch. 460
Medical Examining Board	S. 15.405 (7)	Ch. 264, L. 1897; Ch. 426, L. 1903; Ch. 325, L. 1953; 1985 WisAct 340; 1993 WisAct 16	Ch. 448, Subchap.II
Athletic Trainers Affiliated Credentialing Board	S. 15.406 (4)	1999 WisAct 9	Ch. 448, Subchap.VI
Dietitians Affiliated Credentialing Board	S. 15.406 (2)	1993 WisAct 443, 1997 WisAct 75	Ch. 448, Subchap.V
Occupational Therapists Affiliated Credentialing Board	S. 15.406 (5)	1999 WisAct 180	Ch. 448, Subchap.VII
Perfusionists Examining Council	S. 15.407 (2m)	2001 WisAct 89	S. 448.40 (2)
Physical Therapists Affiliated Credentialing Board	S. 15.406 (1)	Ch. 327, L. 1967; 1993 WisAct 107, 2001 WisAct 70	Ch. 448, Subchap.III
Physician Assistants, Council on	S. 15.407 (2)	Ch. 149, L. 1973; Ch. 418, L. 1977	S. 448.20
Podiatrists Affiliated Credentialing Board	S. 15.406 (3)	1997 WisAct 175	Ch. 448, Subchap.IV
Respiratory Care Practitioners Examining Council	S. 15.407 (1m)	1989 WisAct 229	S. 15.407 (1m)
Midwives Advisory Committee	S. 440.987	2005 WisAct 292	Ch. 440, Subchap.XII
Nursing, Board of	S. 15.405 (7g)	Ch. 346, L. 1911; Ch. 327, L. 1967	Ch. 441, Subchap.I
Registered Nurses, Examining Council on	S. 15.407 (3)(a)	Ch. 365, L. 1921	S. 441.05
Licensed Practical Nurses, Examining Council on	S. 15.407 (3)(b)	Ch. 402, L. 1949	S. 441.10
Nursing Home Administrator Examining Board	S. 15.405 (7m)	Ch. 478, L. 1969	Ch. 456
Optometry Examining Board	S. 15.405 (8)	Ch. 488, L. 1915	Ch. 449
Pharmacy Examining Board	S. 15.405 (9)	Ch. 167, L. 1882	Ch. 450
Pharmacist Advisory Council	S. 15.407 (6)	1997 WisAct 68	S. 450.025
Psychology Examining Board	S. 15.405 (10m)	Ch. 290, L. 1969	Ch. 455
Real Estate Appraisers Board	S. 15.405 (10r)	1989 WisAct 340, 1991 WisAct 78	Ch. 458
Real Estate Board	S. 15.405 (11)	Ch. 656, L. 1919; Ch. 94, L. 1981	Ch. 452
Real Estate Curriculum and Examinations, Council on	S. 15.407 (5)	1989 WisAct 341, 1989 WisAct 359	S. 452.06 (2)
Veterinary Examining Board	S. 15.405 (12)	Ch. 294, L. 1961; 1995 WisAct 321	Ch. 453

Agency Responsibility: The Department of Regulation and Licensing is responsible for en-suring the safe and competent practice of licensed professionals in Wisconsin. It provides ad-ministrative services to the state occupational regulatory authorities responsible for regulation of occupations and offers policy assistance in such areas as evaluating and establishing new professional licensing programs, creating routine procedures for legal proceedings, and adjust-ing policies in response to public needs. Currently, the department and regulatory authorities are responsible for regulating about 350,000 credential holders and 132 types of credentials.

The department investigates and prosecutes complaints against credential holders and assists with drafting statutes and administrative rules. Through the Office of Impaired Professional Procedures, it enforces participation agreements with credential holders who are chemically im-paired, allowing them to retain their professional credentials if they comply with requirements, including treatment for chemical dependency.

The department provides direct regulation and licensing of certain occupations and activi-ties. Numerous boards and regulatory authorities attached to the department have independent responsibility for the regulation of specific professions in the public interest. Within statutory limits, they determine the education and experience required for credentialing, develop and evaluate examinations, and establish standards for professional conduct. These standards are set by administrative rule and enforced through legal action upon complaints from the public. The regulatory authorities may reprimand a credential holder; limit, suspend, or revoke the credential of a practitioner who violates laws or board rules; and, in some cases, impose forfeitures.

Regulatory authority members must be state residents, and they cannot serve more than two consecutive terms. No member may be an officer, director, or employee of a private organization that promotes or furthers the profession or occupation regulated by that board.

Organization: The governor appoints the secretary of the department with the advice and consent of the senate. The secretary appoints a deputy secretary, an executive assistant, and the heads of various subunits from outside the classified service.

The boards and councils attached to the department consist primarily of members of the professions and occupations they regulate. In 1975, the legislature mandated that at least one public member serve on each board. In 1984, it required an additional public member on most boards. Public members are prohibited from having ties to the profession they regulate. In most cases, the governor appoints all members of the licensing and regulatory boards with the advice and consent of the senate. However, in some cases, council members are appointed by the governor without senate confirmation, by the secretary of the department, or by their related examining boards.

Unit Functions: The *Division of Board Services* provides professional, legal, and administrative support to 64 regulatory boards, councils, and committees. This includes: preparing agendas, transcribing meeting minutes, and researching and analyzing issues related to the regulated professions. The division also facilitates the drafting and implementation of new laws, rules, and policies. It provides legal advice, counsel, and assistance throughout the agency and to the boards. Legal counsel researches and responds to practice questions, drafts administrative rules, and analyzes legislation.

The *Division of Enforcement* investigates complaints against credential holders and initiates formal disciplinary actions, where appropriate. The division also inspects business establishments of credential holders and has authority to audit specific trust accounts and financial records.

The *Division of Management Services* provides administrative and technical support assistance to the department and boards, including information technology, budget and fiscal services, and administrative support services.

The *Division of Professional Credential Processing* receives applications for licenses and permits, creates applicant records, and determines whether credential criteria have been met.

History: Chapter 75, Laws of 1967, created the Department of Regulation and Licensing and attached to it 14 separate examining boards that had been independent agencies. The 1967 reorganization also transferred to the department some direct licensing and registration functions not handled by boards, including those for private detectives and detective agencies, charitable organizations, and professional fund-raisers and solicitors.

The department's responsibilities have changed significantly since its creation. Initially, it performed routine housekeeping functions for the examining boards, which continued to function as independent agencies. Subsequently, a series of laws required the department to assume various substantive administrative functions previously performed by the boards and to provide direct regulation of several professions.

Department of
REVENUE

Secretary of Revenue: ROGER M. ERVIN, 266-6466, roger.ervin@; Fax: 266-5718.

Deputy Secretary: WENDY WINK, 266-6466, wendy.wink@; Fax: 266-5718.

Executive Assistant: CARRIE TEMPLETON, 266-6466, carrie.templeton@; Fax: 266-5718.

General Counsel, Office of: DANA J. ERLANDSEN, *chief counsel,* 266-3974, dana.erlandsen@; Fax: 266-9949.

Public Information Officer: JESSICA IVERSON, 266-2300, jessica.iverson@; Fax: 266-5718.

Address e-mail by combining the user ID and the state extender: userid@**revenue.wi.gov**

Enterprise Services Division: KIRBIE G. MACK, *administrator,* 264-8175, kirbie.mack@

  Budget and Strategic Services Bureau: ANTHONY TIMMONS, *director,* 266-3347, anthony.timmons@

  Financial Management Services Bureau: BLANCA RIVERA, *director,* 266-8469, blanca.rivera@

  Human Resource Services Bureau: vacancy, *director,* 264-8175.

Income, Sales and Excise Tax Division: DIANE L. HARDT, *administrator,* 266-2772, diane.hardt@; LILI BEST CRANE, *deputy administrator,* 266-2772, lili.crane@; Division Fax: 261-6240.

  Audit Bureau: VICKI GIBBONS, *director,* 266-3612, vicki.gibbons@

  Compliance Bureau: CATHERINE BINK, *director,* 266-9635, catherine.bink@

  Customer Service Bureau: FRANK HUMPHREY, *director,* 266-2772, frank.humphrey@

  Tax Operations Bureau: NANCY CHRISTENSEN, *director,* 266-2772, nancy.christensen@

Lottery Division: MICHAEL J. EDMONDS, *administrator,* 261-8800, michael.edmonds@; Division Fax: 264-6644.

  Administrative Services Bureau: RICH GRADE, *director,* 264-6651, richard.grade@

  Operations Bureau: ANDREW BOHAGE, *director,* 264-6604, andrew.bohage@

  Product Development Bureau: SAVERIO MAGLIO, *director,* 267-4817, saverio.maglio@

  Retailer Relations Bureau: BOB HAYD, *director,* 267-7180, robert.hayd@

Research and Policy Division: JOHN KOSKINEN, *administrator,* 267-8973, john.koskinen@; Division Fax: 266-6240.

  Income Tax Policy and Economic Team: REBECCA BOLDT, *leader,* 266-6785, rebecca.boldt@

  Legislation and Planning Team: SHERRIE GATES-HENDRIX, *leader,* 267-1262, sherrie.gateshendrix@

  Sales and Property Tax Policy Team: PAUL ZIEGLER, *leader,* 266-5773, paul.ziegler@

State and Local Finance Division: CAROL ROESSLER, *administrator,* 266-0939, carol.roessler@; JEAN ADLER, *deputy administrator,* 266-9759, jean.adler@; Division Fax: 264-6887.

  Assessment Practices Bureau: JIM MURPHY, *director,* 261-5275, james.murphy@

  Property Tax Bureau: DANIEL DAVIS, *director,* 261-5350, daniel.davis@

Technology Services Division: PAT LASHORE, *administrator,* 266-9751, patricia.lashore@; Division Fax: 266-9923.

  Application Environment Support Bureau: RICHARD OFFENBECHER, *director,* 261-2276, richard.offenbecher@

  Application Services Bureau: vacancy, *director,* 264-6879.

  Business Intelligence Services Bureau: JANNA BAGANZ, *director,* 261-5357, janna.baganz@

  Customer Service Bureau: LAWRENCE LOWDEN, *director,* 267-8951, lawrence.lowden@

Mailing Address: P.O. Box 8933, Madison 53713-8933.

Locations: 2135 Rimrock Road, Madison, and district and branch offices throughout the state.

Telephones: (608) 266-2772 – individuals; (608) 266-2776 – businesses; Wisconsin Relay System: (800) 947-6644, for Spanish: (800) 833-7813.

Fax: (608) 267-0834.

Internet Address: www.revenue.wi.gov

DEPARTMENT OF REVENUE

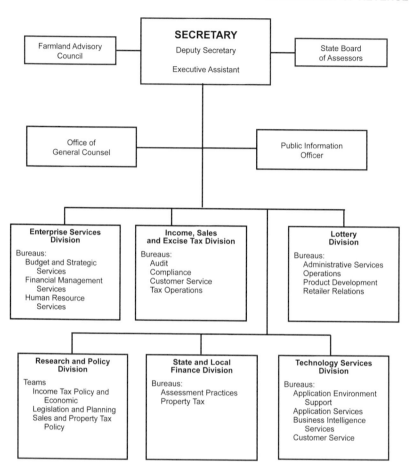

Unit attached for administrative purposes under Sec. 15.03:   Investment and Local Impact Fund Board

Publications: *Agricultural Assessment Guide;* biennial report; *County and Municipal Revenues and Expenditures;* A Guide for Property Owners; *Quarterly Economic Outlook;* Summary of Tax Exemption Devices; *Town, Village, and City Taxes; Wisconsin Tax Bulletin;* and various brochures and publications on specific issues.

Number of Employees: 1,119.83.

Total Budget 2007-09: $353,400,600.

Statutory References: Sections 15.43 and 15.435; Chapters 70-79, 125, and 139.

Agency Responsibility: The Department of Revenue administers all major state tax laws (except the insurance premiums tax) and enforces the state's alcohol beverage and tobacco laws. It estimates state revenues, forecasts state economic activity, helps formulate tax policy, and administers the Wisconsin Lottery. It also determines equalized value of taxable property and assesses manufacturing property. It administers local financial assistance programs and assists local governments in their property assessments and financial management.

Organization: The department is administered by a secretary who is appointed by the governor with the advice and consent of the senate. The secretary appoints the administrators of the Income, Sales and Excise Tax Division and the Technology Services Division from the classified service and the other division administrators from outside the classified service.

Unit Functions: The *Office of General Counsel* provides legal counsel and opinions; drafts and reviews tax legislation and administrative rules; represents the department in all cases brought before the Tax Appeals Commission; and represents the department in nontax cases before administrative agencies. It also is responsible for providing a prompt and impartial review of all assessments appealed by individuals, partnerships, trusts, and corporations relating to income, franchise, sales, use, withholding, and gift taxes and the homestead tax credit.

The *Enterprise Services Division* provides to the department support services in the areas of administration, budget and financial management, business services and business planning and annual performance evaluations and measurement, printing, records management, personnel, affirmative action, and equal opportunity, employee development, employment relations, and other management services.

The *Income, Sales and Excise Tax Division* administers various tax laws relating to individual income, employee withholding, corporate franchise and income, state and county sales and use, excise, alcohol beverages, tobacco products, motor vehicles, alternate and aviation fuels, recycling, local exposition districts, premier resort areas, and others. It also administers the homestead credit, farmland preservation, earned income, and other tax credit programs. The division drafts and reviews tax legislation and administrative rules, tax forms/instructions and publications, and provides technical assistance to taxpayers. The division audits returns, collects delinquent taxes, and conducts criminal investigations.

The *Lottery Division* administers the Wisconsin Lottery. It manages the design, distribution, and sale of lottery products; conducts lottery game drawings; handles media relations; assists retailers with marketing lottery products; makes payment on winning tickets; provides product information through informational advertisements and its Web site (www.wilottery.com); and answers players' questions.

The *Research and Policy Division* provides detailed analyses of fiscal and economic policies to the departmental secretary, the governor, and other state officials. It assesses the impact of current and proposed tax laws, prepares official general fund tax collection estimates used to develop the state budget, issues quarterly forecasts of the state's economy, and develops statistical reports. The division represents the department with the legislature, coordinates the department's tax policy agenda, coordinates the department's administrative rules, and responds to legislative inquiries.

The *State and Local Finance Division* establishes the state's equalized values; assesses all manufacturing and telecommunications company property for property tax purposes; and assess and collects taxes on utilities, railroads, airlines, mining, and other special properties, and provides financial management and technical assistance to municipal and county governments. It administers the state shared revenue program, property tax relief for municipal services, the lottery credit program, and tax incremental financing programs. It provides property assessment administration and certifies assessment personnel.

The *Technology Services Division* administers technology services for all parts of the department, including data administration, applications development, workstation support, data collection, and technology planning.

History: The antecedents of the Department of Revenue date back at least to Chapter 130, Laws of 1868, which created a State Board of Assessors, composed of the secretary of state and the entire state senate, to perform the state's taxing functions. At that time, the property tax was the state's primary source of revenue.

Chapter 235, Laws of 1873, changed the board's composition to the secretary of state, state treasurer, and attorney general. The 1899 Legislature created the Office of Tax Commissioner (Chapter 206) to supervise the state's taxation system and made the commissioner a member and presiding officer of the State Board of Assessors.

The composition of the State Board of Assessors was changed again in Chapter 237, Laws of 1901, when the legislature replaced the constitutional officers with two assistant commissioners. The 1905 Legislature abolished the State Board of Assessors (Chapter 380) and assigned its functions to a 3-member Tax Commission, appointed by the governor with the advice and consent of the senate. This structure lasted until Chapter 412, Laws of 1939, created the Department of Taxation, headed by a single commissioner. Chapter 75, Laws of 1967, renamed the agency the Department of Revenue and the commissioner became the secretary.

Throughout the years, certain tax-related functions have been moved from one agency or level of government to another. For example, local officials originally assessed manufacturing property, but the 1973 Legislature gave the department responsibility for assessing all manufacturing property in the state.

Similarly, the 1939 Legislature made the Department of Taxation responsible for performing audits upon the request of local governmental units. After assignment to several other agencies, the legislature returned this function to the Department of Revenue in 1971. In 1983, the legislature repealed the department's mandatory municipal audit functions but left intact its discretionary oversight of municipal accounting.

The department currently is responsible for administration of the Wisconsin State Lottery. The lottery was originally created by 1987 Wisconsin Act 119 and administered by the Lottery Board. It was later managed by the Wisconsin Gaming Commission. 1995 Wisconsin Act 27, which transferred the State Lottery to the Department of Revenue, also repealed the commission and created the Gaming Board. The Gaming Board was repealed in 1997 Wisconsin Act 27.

Statutory Board and Council

State Board of Assessors: WILLIAM B. WARDWELL, *chairperson;* TIM DRASCIC, KURT KELLER, STEVE LARRABEE, JULIE MATHES (Department of Revenue employees appointed by secretary).

The State Board of Assessors investigates objections to the amount, valuation, or taxability of real or personal manufacturing property, as well as objections to the penalties issued for late filing or nonfiling of required manufacturing property report forms. The number of board members is determined by the secretary, but all must be department employees. The board was created by Chapter 90, Laws of 1973, and its composition and duties are prescribed in Section 70.995 (8) of the statutes.

Farmland Advisory Council: ROGER M. ERVIN (secretary of revenue), *chairperson;* vacancy (agribusiness), CARL AXNESS (knowledgeable about agricultural lending practices), BRUCE JONES (UW System agricultural economist), TIM HANNA (mayor of a city of 40,000 or more population), LINDA BOCHERT (environmental expert), vacancy (representing nonagricultural business), STEPHEN HINTZ (urban studies professor), HERB TAUCHEN (farmer) (all appointed by secretary of revenue); MELVIN RAATZ (assessor) (appointed by secretary of revenue as an advisor to council).

Contact: ROGER M. ERVIN, 266-6466.

Agency Responsibility: The 9-member Farmland Advisory Council advises the Department of Revenue on implementing use-value assessment of agricultural land and reducing urban sprawl. It is required to report annually to the legislature on the usefulness of use-value assessment as a way to preserve farmland, discourage urban sprawl, and reduce the conversion of farmland to other uses. It also recommends changes to the shared revenue formula to compensate local governments adversely affected by use-value assessment. In carrying out its duties, it cooperates with the Wisconsin Strategic Growth Task Force of the State Interagency Land Use Council. The council was created by 1995 Wisconsin Act 27, and its composition and duties are prescribed in Section 73.03 (49) of the statutes.

INDEPENDENT BOARD ATTACHED FOR BUDGETING, PROGRAM COORDINATION, AND RELATED MANAGEMENT FUNCTIONS BY SECTION 15.03 OF THE STATUTES

INVESTMENT AND LOCAL IMPACT FUND BOARD ("Mining Board")

Investment and Local Impact Fund Board: Inactive.

The 11-member Investment and Local Impact Fund Board administers the Investment and Local Impact Fund, created to help municipalities alleviate costs associated with social, educational, environmental, and economic impacts of metalliferous mineral mining. The board certifies to the Department of Administration the amount of the payments to be distributed to municipalities from the fund. It also provides guidance and funding to local governments throughout the development of a mining project.

In addition to the secretary of commerce and the secretary of revenue, or their designees, the board's 9 appointed members serve staggered 4-year terms. They include 3 public members; the 5 local officials recommended by: the League of Wisconsin Municipalities (1), the Wisconsin Towns Association (1), the Wisconsin Association of School Boards (1), and the Wisconsin Counties Association (2); and a Native American member is recommended by the Great Lakes Inter-Tribal Council, Inc. Certain board members must meet qualifications based on residence in or adjacent to a county or municipality with a metallic minerals ore body or mineral development. The board was created by Chapter 31, Laws of 1977, and its composition and duties are specified in Sections 15.435 (1) and 70.395 (2), Wisconsin Statutes.

Currently, there are no operating or proposed metalliferous mines in the state, and the board is inactive.

Office of the
SECRETARY OF STATE

Secretary of State: DOUGLAS La FOLLETTE, 266-8888.

Deputy Secretaries of State: SUSAN CHURCHILL, SHARON RICKORDS, 266-3470.

Administrative Services Division: HASMUKH RAJANI, *administrator,* 267-6810.

Government Records Division: MARJORIE H. EHLE, *administrator,* 266-1437.

Mailing Address: P.O. Box 7848, Madison 53707-7848.

Location: 30 West Mifflin Street, 10th Floor, Madison 53703.

Telephone: (608) 266-8888.

Fax: (608) 266-3159.

Internet Address: www.sos.state.wi.us

E-mail Address: statesec@wi.gov

Publications: Notary Public Information Brochure.

Number of Employees: 7.50.

Total Budget 2007-09: $1,526,800.

Constitutional References: Article VI, Sections 1 and 2.

Statutory Reference: Chapter 14, Subchapter III.

Agency Responsibility: The Office of the Secretary of State performs a variety of services for state government and Wisconsin municipalities. Wisconsin's Constitution requires the secretary of state to maintain the official acts of the legislature and governor, and to keep the Great Seal of the State of Wisconsin and affix it to all official acts of the governor.

Organization: The secretary of state, a constitutional officer elected on a partisan ballot in the November general election, heads the Office of the Secretary of State.

Unit Functions: The *Administrative Services Division* maintains revenue and expenditure accounting systems and provides administrative support for the agency.

The *Government Records Division* keeps the Great Seal of the State of Wisconsin and affixes it to all official acts of the governor, issues notary public commissions, registers trade names and trademarks, coordinates the publication of state laws with the Legislative Reference Bureau, records official acts of the legislature and the governor, and files oaths of office. It also files deeds for state lands and buildings, issues notary authentications and apostilles (a form of international authentication of notaries public), preserves the original copies of all enrolled laws and resolutions, and files annexations, charter ordinances, and incorporation papers for villages and cities. Municipal records and deeds, registered trademarks, and information about notaries commissioned in Wisconsin can be accessed via the agency Web site.

History: The 1836 congressional act that organized the Territory of Wisconsin provided for a secretary of the territory to be appointed by the President of the United States. This office was the forerunner of the post of secretary of state created by the Wisconsin Constitution. Delegates to the constitutional conventions of 1846 and 1848 determined that the secretary of state would be a constitutional officer. From the beginning of statehood until 1970, the secretary of state was elected for a 2-year term. Pursuant to a constitutional amendment ratified in 1967 and effective since the 1970 election, the term was extended to 4 years.

In the early days of statehood, the secretary of state personally performed a broad range of duties that are now delegated to the specialized departments of the executive branch. Chapter 276, Laws of 1969, created the Office of the Secretary of State to assist the secretary.

Office of the
STATE TREASURER

State Treasurer: DAWN MARIE SASS, 266-1714, dawn.sass@wisconsin.gov

Deputy State Treasurer: JOHN LEASE, 266-7982, john.lease@wisconsin.gov

Executive Assistant: CHRISTINE LEE, 266-3712, christine.lee@wisconsin.gov

Mailing Address: P.O. Box 7871, Madison 53707-7871.

Location: One South Pinckney Street, Suite 360, Madison.

Telephones: (608) 266-1714, Toll-free (800) 462-2814; Unclaimed property: (608) 267-7977, Toll-free (877) 699-9211; EdVest College Savings Program: (888) 338-3789; Local Government Investment Pool: (877) 947-7665.

Fax: (608) 266-2647.

Internet Address: www.statetreasury.wisconsin.gov

Publications: Monthly report on the Local Government Investment Pool (LGIP); periodic newsletter for local clerks and treasurers; semiannual classified listing of unclaimed property owners; annual report for Wisconsin's "529" college savings program; and reports to investors in the EdVest program.

Number of Employees: 14.70.

Total Budget 2007-09: $12,523,600.

Constitutional References: Article VI, Sections 1 and 3.

Statutory Reference: Chapter 14, Subchapter IV.

Agency Responsibility: The Office of the State Treasurer serves citizens and local government by providing for receipt, custody, oversight, and disbursement of unclaimed property reported to the state. The office also administers the state's Section 529 college savings program and the state's Local Government Investment Pool.

Organization: The state treasurer, a constitutional officer elected for a 4-year term by partisan ballot in the November general election, heads the Office of the State Treasurer and is the fiscal trustee for the State of Wisconsin.

Functions: The state treasurer administers the Local Government Pooled-Investment Fund. The state treasurer serves as custodian of unclaimed and escheated property that is transferred to the state when owners and heirs cannot be found and conducts outreach programs to locate rightful owners. The state treasurer also administers EdVest and Tomorrow's Scholar, the state's $2 billion Section 529 college savings program.

History: The territorial treasurer, an office created in 1839, was appointed by the governor, but the Wisconsin Constitution, adopted in 1848, made the office an elective partisan position. From 1848 through 1968, the state treasurer was elected to a 2-year term in the November general election. Since 1970, following ratification of a constitutional amendment in April 1967, the state treasurer has been elected to a 4-year term. Chapter 276, Laws of 1969, created the Office of the State Treasurer to assist the treasurer.

INDEPENDENT UNIT ATTACHED FOR BUDGETING, PROGRAM COORDINATION, AND RELATED MANAGEMENT FUNCTIONS BY SECTION 15.03 OF THE STATUTES

COLLEGE SAVINGS PROGRAM BOARD

Members: ALBERTA DARLING, *chairperson;* DAWN MARIE SASS (state treasurer); DEBORAH DURCAN (designated by UW Board of Regents president); ROLF WEGENKE (president of the Wisconsin Association of Independent Colleges and Universities); KEN JOHNSON (designated by the chairperson of the Investment Board); MICHAEL ROSEN (designated by the president of the Technical College System Board); PAUL C. ADAMSKI, MARY COOK, WILLIAM OEMICHEN, JEFF PLALE, PATRICK SHEEHY. (All except *ex officio* members are appointed by the governor with senate consent.)

Mailing Address: P.O. Box 7871, Madison 53707-7871.

Telephone: 264-7899.

Fax: 266-2647.

E-mail Address: edvest@wisconsin.gov

Internet Address: www.edvest.com

Statutory References: Sections 14.57, 14.64, and 15.07 (1) (b) 2.

Agency Responsibility: The 11-member College Savings Program Board was created by 1999 Wisconsin Act 44 and its members serve 4-year terms. It administers the EdVest and Tomorrow's Scholar college savings program that provides for tax-sheltered investment accounts held in a trust fund to cover future higher education expenses.

TECHNICAL COLLEGE SYSTEM

Technical College System Board: BRENT SMITH (public member), *president;* STAN DAVIS (public member), *vice president;* ROBERTA GASSMAN (secretary of workforce development), *secretary;* ANTHONY EVERS (superintendent of public instruction), JOSE VASQUEZ (designated by UW System Board of Regents President); PHILLIP L. NEUENFELDT (employee member); TERRY ERICKSON (employer member); ANN GREENHECK (farmer member); VANESSA PICKAR (student member); MARY QUINNETTE CUENE, MICHAEL ROSEN, S. MARK TYLER, vacancy (public members). (All except *ex officio* members are appointed by governor.)

President and State Director: DANIEL CLANCY, 266-7983, daniel.clancy@

Executive Assistant: MORNA FOY, 266-2449, morna.foy@

    Policy and Government Relations, Office of: vacancy, *associate vice president,* 266-2017.

Finance, Division of: JAMES ZYLSTRA, *vice president,* 266-1739, james.zylstra@

    Management Services, Office of: NORMAN KENNEY, *associate vice president,* 266-1766, norman.kenney@

    System Finance and Administration, Office of: KELLY SHISLER, *associate vice president,* 266-2947, kelly.shisler@

Teaching and Learning, Division of: KATHLEEN CULLEN, *vice president,* 266-9399, kathleen.cullen@

    Instruction, Office of: ANNETTE SEVERSON, *associate vice president,* 267-9064, annette.severson@

    Student Development and Assessment, Office of: WILLA PANZER, *associate vice president,* 267-9065, willa.panzer@

Address e-mail by combining the user ID and the state extender: userid@**wtcsystem.edu**

Mailing Address: P.O. Box 7874, Madison 53707-7874.

Location: 4622 University Avenue, Madison.

Telephone: 266-1207.

Fax: 266-1690.

Internet Address: www.wtcsystem.edu

Publications: *Wisconsin Technical Colleges;* Technical College Facts; annual and biennial reports; annual evaluation reports of technical college offerings and services; cost allocation summaries; employer satisfaction reports; graduate follow-up reports.

Number of Employees: 77.30.

Total Budget 2007-09: $366,831,400.

Statutory References: Section 15.94; Chapter 38.

Agency Responsibility: The Technical College System Board is the coordinating agency for the Technical College System. The board establishes statewide policies and standards for the educational programs and services provided by the 16 technical college districts that cover the state. The district boards, in turn, are responsible for the direct operation of their respective schools and programs. They are empowered to levy property taxes, provide for facilities and equipment, employ staff, and contract for services. The districts set academic and grading standards, appoint the district directors, hire instructional and other staff, and manage the district budget.

The system board supervises district operations through reporting and audit requirements and consultation, coordination, and support services. It sets standards for building new schools and adding to current facilities. It also provides assistance to districts in meeting the needs of target groups, including services for the disadvantaged, the disabled, women, dislocated workers, the incarcerated, and minorities.

The board administers state and federal aids. It works with the Department of Public Instruction to coordinate secondary and postsecondary vocational and technical programs. It also cooperates with the University of Wisconsin System to establish coordinated programming to make the services of the two agencies fully available to state residents. The board cooperates with the Department of Workforce Development to provide training for apprentices.

Organization: The 13-member Technical College System Board includes 9 members appointed by the governor to serve staggered 6-year terms and a technical college student appoint-

Wisconsin's Technical College System coordinates and promotes vocational education and training. The system includes 16 districts and 47 campuses. (Technical College System)

ed for a 2-year term. The student must be 18 years of age and a state resident who is enrolled at least half-time and in good academic standing. The governor may not appoint a student member from the same technical college in any two consecutive terms. No person may serve as board president for more than two successive annual terms. A 1971 opinion of the attorney general held that a member of a technical college district board could not serve concurrently on the state board (60 *OAG* 178). The board appoints a director, called the "system president", from outside the classified service to serve at its pleasure, and the system president selects the executive assistant and division administrators from outside the classified service.

The 16 technical college districts encompass 47 campuses. Each district is headed by a board of 9 members who serve staggered 3-year terms. District boards include 2 employers, 2 employees, a school district administrator, a state or local elected official, and 3 additional members as defined by statute. A district appointment committee, composed of county board chairpersons or school board presidents, appoints the board members, subject to approval of the state system board. Each district is administered by a director, called a "president", appointed by the district board.

Unit Functions: The *Office of Policy and Government Relations* provides leadership for systemwide policy analysis and development, public outreach, and federal and state government relations. It is responsible for coordination of systemwide budgeting and planning; research; labor market information; personnel certification; and coordination of state and federal grant programs.

The *Division of Finance* has oversight responsibility for internal operations including accounting, budgeting, procurement, payroll, human resources, facilities, and information technology. In addition, the division provides guidance to the technical colleges in developing financial policies and standards, distributes state aid, and assists the board in determining student fees and tuition rates and approving district facility development projects. The division is also responsible for management information and oversight of district budgets and enrollments.

The *Division of Teaching and Learning* has responsibility for program definition, approval, evaluation, and review. It focuses on programs in agriculture, office services, marketing, home economics (including family and consumer education), health occupations, trade and industry (including apprenticeship, fire service, law enforcement, safety, and technical and vocational training), general education, adult basic education, and environmental education.

The division is responsible for student financial aid, federal projects for the disabled and disadvantaged, adult and continuing education outreach, and Workforce Investment Act projects. It serves as liaison to business, industry, and secondary schools.

History: Laws passed in 1907 permitted cities to operate trade schools for persons age 16 or older as part of the public school system (Chapter 122), and allowed them to establish technical schools or colleges, under the control of either the school board or a special board (Chapter 344). In Chapter 616, Laws of 1911, Wisconsin was the first state to establish a system of state aid and support for industrial education. The law required every community with a population of 5,000 or more to establish an industrial education board, which was authorized to levy a property tax. It created the State Board of Industrial Education and an assistant for industrial education in the office of the State Superintendent of Public Instruction.

In the Laws of 1911, Wisconsin was the first state to set up apprenticeship agreements (Chapter 347) and require employers to release 14- to 16-year-olds for part-time attendance in continuation schools for apprentices, if such schooling was available (Chapter 505). Hours in class were to count as part of the total paid work hours. The schools, established through the work of Charles McCarthy, first director of the present-day Legislative Reference Bureau, emphasized general cultural and vocational education, as well as trade skills.

Due in part to the efforts of McCarthy, the U.S. Congress passed the Smith-Hughes Act in 1917, the first federal legislation specifically designed to promote vocational education, which it modeled on Wisconsin's vocational training programs. The act offered financial aid to states to help pay teachers' and administrators' salaries and provided funds for teacher training.

Chapter 494, Laws of 1917, changed the name of the State Board of Industrial Education to the State Board of Vocational Education, authorized it to employ a state director, and designated it as the sole agency to work with the newly created federal board.

During the Great Depression, Wisconsin tightened its compulsory school attendance laws, which resulted in more 14- to 18-year-olds attending vocational school. The demand for adult education also increased, as recognized by Chapter 349, Laws of 1937, which renamed the board the State Board of Vocational and Adult Education. During that same period, the vocational school in Milwaukee began to offer college transfer courses.

Events of the 1960s transformed the Wisconsin vocational-technical system into the post-secondary system of today. Federal vocational school legislation affected business education and emphasized training for the unemployed. The federal Vocational Education Act, passed in 1963, helped the local boards build new facilities. Chapter 51, Laws of 1961, authorized the state board to offer associate degrees for 2-year technical courses. The 1965 Legislature passed Chapter 292, which required a system of vocational, technical and adult education (VTAE) districts covering the entire state by 1970 and changed the board's name to the State Board of Vocational, Technical and Adult Education. (Chapter 327, Laws of 1967, dropped "State" from the name.) College transfer programs were authorized in Madison, Milwaukee, and Rhinelander.

As a result of federal and state legislative changes in the 1960s, VTAE enrollments more than doubled to 466,000 between 1967 and 1982. The 1970s also saw significant increases in the number of associate degree programs. Other major statutory changes included the requirement that VTAE schools charge tuition and that they improve cooperation and coordination with the University of Wisconsin System. More recently, a greater emphasis has been placed on services to 16- to 18-year-old students.

In the past two decades, the system has increased its focus on lifelong learning; education for economic development; and services for groups that formerly had less access to education, including people in rural areas, women, and minorities. The system has placed special emphasis on assisting the unemployed, displaced homemakers, and those with literacy problems.

1993 Wisconsin Act 399 renamed the VTAE system, changing the name to the Technical College System, and designated the state board as the Technical College System Board. District VTAE schools became "technical colleges".

Independent Board Attached for Budgeting, Program Coordination, and Related Management Functions by Section 15.03 of the Statutes

EDUCATIONAL APPROVAL BOARD

Members: Michael Cooney, *chairperson;* Christy L. Brown, Terry Craney, Joseph Heim, Jo Oyama-Miller, Richard F. Raemisch, Monica Williams (appointed by governor).

Executive Secretary: David C. Dies, 267-7733.

Mailing Address: 30 West Mifflin Street, Madison 53703.

Telephone: (608) 266-1996.

Fax: (608) 264-8477.

Publications: EAB Quarterly; A Guide to the EAB; School and Program Approval Guide; Wisconsin Directory of Private Postsecondary Schools.

Number of Employees: 5.00.

Total Budget 2007-09: $1,162,400.

Statutory References: Sections 15.945 (1) and 38.50.

Agency Responsibility: The Educational Approval Board is an independent state agency responsible for protecting Wisconsin's consumers and supporting quality educational options, by regulating and evaluating for-profit postsecondary business, trade, or distance learning schools; out-of-state, nonprofit colleges and universities; and in-state, nonprofit institutions incorporated after 1991. The board currently oversees more than 150 schools serving more than 45,000 adults in 800+ degree and nondegree programs.

The board consists of not more than 7 members who serve at the pleasure of the governor and represent state agencies and others interested in educational programs. It employs the executive secretary and other staff from the classified service. Originally formed by order of the governor in 1944, the legislature created the agency in Chapter 137, Laws of 1953, as the Governor's Educational Advisory Committee to approve and supervise schools and educational courses that trained veterans under various federal laws. A 1957 law (Chapter 438) directed the committee to certify those private vocational schools that offered adequate courses and to prevent fraud and misrepresentation. Chapter 568, Laws of 1963, gave the committee responsibility for licensing agents of private vocational schools, and Chapter 595, Laws of 1965, renamed it the Educational Approval Council. It was renamed the Educational Approval Board and administratively attached to the Department of Public Instruction by Chapter 214, Laws of 1967. The board was attached to the Board of Vocational, Technical and Adult Education by Chapter 125, Laws of 1971.

The Educational Approval Board was repealed by 1995 Wisconsin Act 27, as part of an initiative to create a state Department of Education. The Wisconsin Supreme Court ruled the measure unconstitutional and the agency's functions were continued under Executive Orders 283 and 287 which created the Educational Approval Council. The legislature recreated the board in 1997 Wisconsin Act 27 and attached it to the Higher Educational Aids Board. In 1999 Wisconsin Act 9, the board was attached to the Department of Veterans Affairs. 2001 Wisconsin Act 16 repealed statutory language which specifically made the board responsible for approving schools and courses of instruction for veterans and war orphans. The board was attached to the Wisconsin Technical College System Board (WTCSB) by 2005 Wisconsin Act 25. Under EAB's administrative attachment, budgeting, program operations, and related management functions are conducted with the help of the WTCSB. However, the EAB is treated as a distinct unit of government that exercises its powers, duties, and functions prescribed by law, including rule making, licensing and regulation, and operational planning independently of the WTCSB.

Department of
TOURISM

Secretary of Tourism: KELLI A. TRUMBLE, 266-2345, ktrumble@

Deputy Secretary: MARK RICHARDSON, 266-8773, mrichardson@

Mailing Address: P.O. Box 8690, Madison 53708-8690.

Location: 201 West Washington Avenue, 2nd Floor, Madison.

Telephones: 266-2161; Personalized trip planning and publications: (800) 432-8747; Travel Information M-F 8:00 a.m.-4:30 p.m.: (800) 372-2737.

Fax: 266-3403.

Tourism Information Internet Address: www.travelwisconsin.com

Industry Internet Address: http://industry.travelwisconsin.com

| For e-mail combine the user ID and the state extender: userid@**travelwisconsin.com** |

Communications and Marketing, Bureau of: JANET DESCHENES, *director,* 266-7018, jdeschenes@

Information Technology and Customer Services, Bureau of: FREYA REEVES, *director,* 261-8767, freeves@

Number of Employees: 38.40.

Total Budget 2007-09: $30,290,400.

Statutory References: Section 15.44; Chapter 41.

Publications: *Rustic Roads; Wisconsin Heritage Traveler;* Wisconsin State Parks Visitor Guide; Wisconsin Snowmobile Map; *Wisconsin Travel Guide;* guides for biking, birding, and seasonal events and recreation.

Agency Responsibility: The Department of Tourism promotes travel to Wisconsin's scenic, historic, artistic, educational, and recreational sites. Travel sectors targeted by the department include leisure, meetings and conventions, sports, group tour, and international. Through planning, research, and assistance it provides guidance to the tourism and recreation industry to aid in the development of facilities. It also assists cooperative projects between profit and nonprofit tourist ventures. The department encourages local tourist development through the Joint Effort Marketing Program and the "Ready, Set, Go" Sports Marketing Grant Program.

Organization: The governor appoints the secretary, with the advice and consent of the senate, to direct the department. The secretary appoints the bureau directors from the classified service.

Unit Functions: The Secretary's Office provides administrative support to the department and to its attached boards, including budget, policy planning and analysis, and accounting. Reporting to the secretary's office is the Industry Services Team, which is deployed by geographic regions within the state. The team's tourism development specialists consult with tourism professionals and organizations to promote tourism efforts.

The *Bureau of Communications and Marketing* promotes and advertises Wisconsin as "the Midwest's premier travel destination". Through market research, coordinated advertising, promotional campaigns and programs, grant programs, and publications targeted to travelers' interests, the bureau works to attract in-state and out-of-state tourists and associated travel dollars. It assists in the production of commercials, advertisements, educational materials, and the annual Governor's Conference on Tourism. It produces a consumer show program that provides information at exhibitions focusing on hunting, fishing, boating, golf, sports, and other outdoor activities. The Communications team works with the new media worldwide to develop positive stories about Wisconsin as a travel destination.

The *Bureau of Information Technology and Customer Services* delivers Wisconsin travel information to visitors through various channels, including publication distribution, telephone travel assistance, and travelwisconsin.com, the official travel and tourism Web site for the State of Wisconsin. The bureau coordinates several programs to collect local travel information from destination marketing organizations around the state, and makes the details on more than 13,000 attractions, restaurants, accommodations, and events readily available to potential visitors.

History: State tourism promotion originated in the Department of Natural Resources to encourage travel to state parks and commercial recreational sites. Chapter 39, Laws of 1975, transferred tourism functions to the Department of Business Development and created the Division of Tourism as a statutory entity within the department. Chapter 361, Laws of 1979, created the Department of Development, which absorbed the division, through a merger of the Department of Business Development and the Department of Local Affairs and Development. 1995 Wisconsin Act 27 reorganized the division as the Department of Tourism, effective January 1, 1996.

Statutory Council

Tourism, Council on: DEBORAH T. ARCHER, *chairperson;* LINDA ADLER, JERRY DANFORTH, RUTH GOETZ, DAVID HOLTZE, BRIAN KELSEY, JOE KLIMCZAK, DOUG A. NIELSON, DAVID OLSEN, LOLA L. ROEH, OMAR SHAIKH, ROMY SNYDER, KARI ZAMBON, vacancy; KELLI A. TRUMBLE (secretary of tourism); SENATORS HOLPERIN, S. FITZGERALD; REPRESENTATIVES CLARK, KAUFERT; GEORGE TZOUGROS (executive director, Arts Board); ELLSWORTH BROWN (director, state historical society). (All except *ex officio* members are appointed by governor.)

The 21-member Council on Tourism advises the secretary about tourism and encourages Wisconsin private companies to promote the state in their advertisements. The 14 appointed members serve 3-year terms and assist the secretary in formulating a statewide marketing plan. Nominations for public member appointments must be sought from (but are not limited to) multicounty regional associations engaged in promoting tourism; statewide associations of businesses related to tourism; area visitor and convention bureaus; arts organizations; the Great Lakes Inter-Tribal Council, Inc., and other agencies with knowledge of American Indian tourism; and persons engaged in businesses catering to tourists. Nominees must have experience in marketing and promotion strategy and must represent the different geographical areas of the state and the diversity of the tourism industry. The council was created by 1987 Wisconsin Act

1 in the Department of Development and transferred to the Department of Tourism by 1995 Wisconsin Act 27. Its composition and duties are prescribed in Sections 15.447 (1) and 41.12 of the statutes.

Independent Units Attached for Budgeting, Program Coordination, and Related Management Functions by Section 15.03 of the Statutes

ARTS BOARD

Members: Barbara Lawton, *chairperson;* Bruce Bernberg, *vice chairperson;* Paul Meinke, *secretary;* Storm Elser, James Hall, Jerry Hembd, Gerald Kember, Helen R. Klebesadel, Nick Meyer, Barbara E. Munson, Glenda P. Noel-Ney, Michael Reyes, Sharon Stewart, Robert A. Wagner, Linda L. Ware (appointed by governor).

Executive Director: George Tzougros, 267-2006, george.tzougros@arts.state.wi.us

Mailing Address: State Administration Building, 101 East Wilson Street, 1st Floor, Madison 53702.

Telephones: 266-0190; TTY: 267-9629.

Fax: 267-0380.

E-mail Address: artsboard@arts.state.wi.us

Internet Address: www.arts.state.wi.us

Publications: Print and Internet: Basic Record Keeping Procedures Handbook for Grant Applications; Wisconsin Art and Craft Fairs Directory; Wisconsin Art Museums and Gallery Guide; Wisconsin Performing Arts Presenters Network Guide; Wisconsin Touring and Arts in Education Artist Directory. Internet only: Annual Report; Guide to Programs and Services; Statewide Arts Service Organization Directory; grant applications (all programs).

Number of Employees: 10.00.

Total Budget 2007-09: $7,299,600.

Statutory References: Section 15.445 (1); Chapter 44, Subchapter III.

Wisconsin offers abundant waterways for the enjoyment of its citizens and visitors to the state. These canoeists chose a trip down the Black River. (Department of Tourism)

Agency Responsibility: The legislature directs the Arts Board to study and assist artistic and cultural activities in the state, assist communities in developing their own arts programs, and plan and implement funding programs for groups or individuals engaged in the arts.

As a funding agency, the board assists arts organizations and individual artists through a variety of programs designed to provide broad public access to the arts, strengthen the state's artistic resources, and create opportunities for individuals of exceptional talent. Financial support programs for individuals and organizations include apprenticeships, artists-in-education programs, challenge grants, community activities, fellowships, opportunity grants, program assistance and support, and programs for presenters. The board also provides matching grants to local arts agencies and municipalities through the Wisconsin Regranting Program.

The board aids Wisconsin's artistic community through an information program that includes workshops, conferences, research projects, and publications. The board regularly produces and distributes materials on local, state, and national arts activities for both the arts community and the general public. It arranges for the governor's official portrait, and it selects the artwork placed in state buildings as required by law.

The 15 board members serve staggered 3-year terms and must be state residents with a concern for the arts. Each geographic quadrant of the state must be represented by at least 2 members. The board selects the executive director from outside the classified service. Chapter 90, Laws of 1973, created the board and attached it to the Department of Administration to succeed the Governor's Council on the Arts, which Governor Gaylord Nelson had established in 1963. 1995 Wisconsin Act 27 attached the board to the Department of Tourism.

KICKAPOO RESERVE MANAGEMENT BOARD

Members: SUSAN C. CUSHING, RONALD M. JOHNSON, JACK H. ROBINSON, REBECCA E. ZAHM (residents of specified municipalities and school districts within watershed); GAIL A. FREI, RICHARD T. WALLIN (watershed residents outside specified units); WILLIAM L. QUACKENBUSH (nonresident environmental advocate); SENN R. BROWN (nonresident education representative); vacancy (nonresident recreation and tourism representative); ADLAI J. MANN, TAMARA S. RIDDLE (members with knowledge of watershed's cultural resources, nominated by Ho-Chunk Nation) (appointed by governor).

Executive Director: MARCY WEST, marcy.west@wisconsin.gov

Mailing Address: S 3661 State Highway 131, La Farge 54639.

Telephone: (608) 625-2960.

Fax: (608) 625-2962.

E-mail Address: kickapoo.reserve@krm.state.wi.us

Internet Address: http://kvr.state.wi.us

Publications: Kickapoo Valley Reserve Visitors' Guide.

Number of Employees: 3.00.

Total Budget 2007-09: $1,741,400.

Statutory References: Sections 15.07 (1) (b) 20., 15.445 (2), 41.40, and 41.41.

Agency Responsibility: The 11-member Kickapoo Reserve Management Board manages 8,569 acres in the Kickapoo Valley Reserve to preserve and enhance the area's environmental, scenic, and cultural features; provides facilities for the use and enjoyment of visitors; and promotes the reserve as a destination for vacationing and recreation. Subject to the approval of the governor, the board may purchase land for inclusion in the reserve and trade land in the reserve under certain conditions. The Kickapoo Valley Reserve Visitor Center offers meetings and classrooms, interactive exhibits, educational programs, and tourist information.

The board also may lease land for purposes consistent with the management of the reserve or for agricultural purposes; authorize, license, regulate, and collect and spend revenue from private concessions in the reserve; accept gifts, grants, and bequests; and cooperate with and provide matching funds to nonprofit groups organized to provide assistance to the reserve.

The board may not authorize mining in the reserve or on any land acquired by the board and may not sell land that is in the reserve. It has authority to promulgate rules about use of the

Fond du Lac's Lookout Lighthouse, built in 1932, is located on Lake Winnebago, Wisconsin's largest lake, at 137,708 acres. (Department of Tourism)

waters, land, and facilities under its jurisdiction, and the Department of Tourism is responsible for enforcement of state laws and rules relating to the reserve.

The governor appoints board members for staggered 3-year terms. Four members must be residents of villages, towns, and school districts in the immediate vicinity of the reserve; 2 must be residents of the Kickapoo River watershed outside of the immediate vicinity of the reserve; and 3 members who are not residents of the watershed are appointed by the governor to represent education, environment, and tourism issues. In addition, 2 members are nominated by the Ho-Chunk Nation who have an interest in and knowledge of the cultural resources within the watershed. Various state agencies must appoint nonmember liaisons to the board, and the board may request that any federally recognized American Indian tribe or band in this state, other than the Ho-Chunk Nation, appoint a nonmember liaison. The board appoints the executive director from outside the classified service. The board was created as the Kickapoo Valley Governing Board by 1993 Wisconsin Act 349 and attached to the Department of Administration. 1995 Wisconsin Act 27 attached the board to the Department of Tourism, and it was renamed by 1995 Wisconsin Act 216. The board's membership was revised by 2005 Wisconsin Act 396.

LOWER WISCONSIN STATE RIVERWAY BOARD

Members: RONALD LEYS (Crawford County), MELODY K. MOORE (Dane County), LLOYD B. NICE (Grant County), GERALD DORSCHEID (Iowa County), GREG GREENHECK (Richland County), DONALD GREENWOOD (Sauk County); RITCHIE J. BROWN, WILLIAM S. LUNDBERG, FRED MADISON. (County representatives are nominated by respective county boards and appointed by governor; recreational user groups' representative appointed by governor with senate consent.)

Executive Director: MARK E. CUPP, 202 North Wisconsin Avenue, P.O. Box 187, Muscoda 53573-0187, mark.cupp@wisconsin.gov

Telephones: (608) 739-3188; (800) 221-3792.

Fax: (608) 739-4263.

Internet Address: http://lwr.state.wi.us

Publications: Summary of regulations, Strategic Plan, Biennial Report.

Number of Employees: 2.00.

Total Budget 2007-09: $373,800.

Statutory References: Section 15.445 (3); Chapter 30, Subchapter IV.

Agency Responsibility: The Lower Wisconsin State Riverway Board is responsible for protecting and preserving the scenic beauty and natural character of the riverway. The board reviews permit applications for buildings, walkways, timber harvests, utility facilities, bridges, and other structures in the riverway and issues permits for activities that meet established standards.

The 9 board members serve staggered 3-year terms. Each of the 6 county representatives must be either an elected official or a resident of a city or village that abuts the Lower Wisconsin State Riverway or of a town located at least in part in the riverway. The 3 members representing recreational user groups may not reside in any of the 6 specified counties. The board was created by 1989 Wisconsin Act 31 and attached to the Department of Natural Resources. 1995 Wisconsin Act 27 attached the board to the Department of Tourism.

STATE FAIR PARK BOARD

Members: SUSAN CRANE (business agricultural experience), *chairperson;* SENATORS KANAVAS, SULLIVAN; REPRESENTATIVES GUNDERSON, STASKUNAS (legislative members recommended by party leadership and appointed by governor); MICHELLE NETTLES, REBECCA WICKHEM-HOUSE, vacancy (general business experience); BENNIE JOYNER, JR. (business technology experience); DAN DEVINE (West Allis resident); SUE RUPNOW (state resident); ROD NILSESTUEN (secretary of agriculture, trade and consumer protection); KELLI A. TRUMBLE (secretary of tourism). (All are appointed by governor with senate consent.)

Executive Director: vacancy, (414) 266-7020.

Executive Assistant: MARIAN SANTIAGO-LLOYD, (414) 266-7021.

Mailing Address: 640 South 84th Street, West Allis 53214.

Telephones: (414) 266-7000; (414) 266-7100 (ticket office); (800) 884-FAIR (recorded announcement of events).

Fax: (414) 266-7007.

E-mail Address: wsfp@sfp.state.wi.us

Internet Address: www.wistatefair.com

Publications: *A Brief History of the Wisconsin State Fair;* WSFP Update (semi-annual); cook book (semi-annual); annual non-fair events schedule; monthly non-fair events schedule; fair brochures, daily events schedule, and premium books.

Number of Employees: 29.40.

Total Budget 2007-09: $40,589,800.

Statutory References: Section 15.445 (4); Chapter 42.

Agency Responsibility: The State Fair Park Board manages the State Fair Park and supervises its use for fairs, exhibits, or promotional events for agricultural, commercial, educational, and recreational purposes. It also leases or licenses the property at reasonable rates for other uses when not needed for public purposes. The board is directed to develop new facilities at State Fair Park and to provide a permanent location for an annual Wisconsin State Fair, major sports events, agricultural and industrial expositions, and other programs of civic interest.

Organization: The State Fair Park Board consists of 13 members. Legislative members, who represent the majority and minority parties, are nominated by party leadership and appointed by the governor. The 7 citizen members serve staggered 5-year terms. The board appoints the park director from outside the classified service.

History: Beginning with the first Wisconsin State Fair at Janesville in October 1851, the event has served as a showcase for Wisconsin agriculture and commerce. The State Agricultural Society, which sponsored the first fair, continued to operate it through 1897. In that year, Chapter 301 created the Wisconsin State Board of Agriculture and placed operation of the fair under its control. When the Department of Agriculture was created in 1915, the state fair became part of the new department.

In Chapter 149, Laws of 1961, the independent Wisconsin Exposition Department, headed by a 7-member board, was created to manage the fair and the park's year-round operation. Under the 1967 executive branch reorganization, the Exposition Department became the Wisconsin Exposition Council in the Department of Local Affairs and Development.

Chapter 125, Laws of 1971, created a 3-member State Fair Park Board, appointed by the governor and attached to the Department of Agriculture for administrative purposes. In 1985 Wisconsin Act 20, the legislature increased board membership to 5, specified 5-year terms of service, and required senate confirmation of the governor's nominees.

In 1990, as provided by 1989 Wisconsin Act 219, the State Fair Park Board became an independent body. 1995 Wisconsin Act 27 attached the board to the Department of Tourism, and 1999 Wisconsin Act 197 revised and increased board membership.

Over the years, the location of the state fair was debated and even its continued existence was in doubt. At various times between 1851 and 1885, Fond du Lac, Janesville, Madison, Milwaukee, and Watertown hosted the fair. Milwaukee was chosen as the state fair site from 1886 through 1891, and the fairs held there were so successful that a permanent site was purchased in what is now West Allis, a Milwaukee suburb. That site, first used for the 1892 fair, is included in the state fair's location today.

Several studies published during the 1960s recommended that the fair be moved to a larger site in the Milwaukee area. Chapter 125, Laws of 1971, decided the fair would remain at its site (partially in West Allis, partially in Milwaukee), with updated or new facilities being funded through self-amortizing state bonds. Fair operations have been self-financed since 1935. 1999 Wisconsin Act 9 provided funding for substantial construction and renovation of park facilities. 1999 Wisconsin Act 197 authorized the board to create a nonprofit corporation to raise funds and provide support and contract with that same corporation for operation and development of the park. Act 197 also authorized the park board to permit private individuals to construct facilities on fair grounds under a lease agreement with the board.

Today, State Fair Park draws more than 2 million visitors to its events and activities each year, and the Wisconsin State Fair, with attendance of more than 900,000, remains the state's oldest and largest annual event.

Department of
TRANSPORTATION

Secretary of Transportation: FRANK BUSALACCHI, 266-1114, frank.busalacchi@

Deputy Secretary: Ruben Anthony, Jr., 266-1114, ruben.anthonyjr@

Executive Assistant: Christopher P. Klein, 266-1114, christopher.klein@

General Counsel, Office of: Robert Jambois, *director,* 266-8807, robert.jambois@

Policy, Budget and Finance, Office of: Kenneth Newman, *director,* 267-9618, kenneth.newman@

Public Affairs, Office of: Peg Schmitt, *director,* 266-7744, peg.schmitt@, Fax: 266-7186.

Mailing Address: P.O. Box 7910, Madison 53707-7910.

Location: Hill Farms State Transportation Building, 4802 Sheboygan Avenue, Madison.

Internet Address: www.dot.wisconsin.gov

Number of Employees: 3,448.78.

Total Budget 2007-09: $5,435,309,700.

Statutory References: Sections 15.46, 15.465, and 15.467; Chapters 80, 84-86, 110, 114, and 340-351.

Address e-mail by combining the user ID and the state extender: userid@**dot.wi.gov**

Business Management, Division of: Brenda Brown, *administrator,* 266-2090, brenda.brown@

   Business Services, Bureau of: James D. McDonnell, *director,* 264-7700, james.mcdonnell@

   Human Resource Services, Bureau of: Jack Lawton, *director,* 261-5897, jack.lawton@; TTY: 267-0259 (for affirmative action/equal employment opportunity).

   Information Technology Services, Bureau of: Mary Bates, *director,* 266-0033, mary.bates@

Motor Vehicles, Division of: Lynne B. Judd, *administrator,* 266-2234, lynne.judd@; Patrick Fernan, *operations manager,* 261-8605, patrick.fernan@

   Driver Services, Bureau of: Taqwanya Smith, *director,* 266-9890, taqwanya.smith@

   Field Services, Bureau of: Kristina Boardman, *director,* 266-2743, kristina.boardman@

   Vehicle Services, Bureau of: Anna Biermeier, *director,* 267-5121, anna.biermeier@

      Vehicle Emission Testing (Southeast Wisconsin): (800) 242-7510; Milwaukee/Waukesha area: (414) 266-1080.

   Motor Vehicle Regional Managers:

      North Central Region: Jill Hjelsand, (715) 355-4613, 5301 Rib Mountain Drive, Wausau 54401, jill.hjelsand@

      Northeast Region: Joyce Abrego, (920) 492-5731, 942 Vanderperren Way, Green Bay 54304-5344, joyce.abrego@

      Northwest Region: Patricia Nelson, (715) 234-3773, 735 West Avenue, Rice Lake 54868-1359, patricia.nelson@

      Southeast Region: Sandra Brisco, (414) 266-1109, 1150 North Alois Street, Milwaukee 53208, sandra.brisco@

      Southwest Region: Donald Reincke, (608) 789-4630, 9477 Highway 16 East, Onalaska 54650-9903, donald.reincke@

DEPARTMENT OF TRANSPORTATION

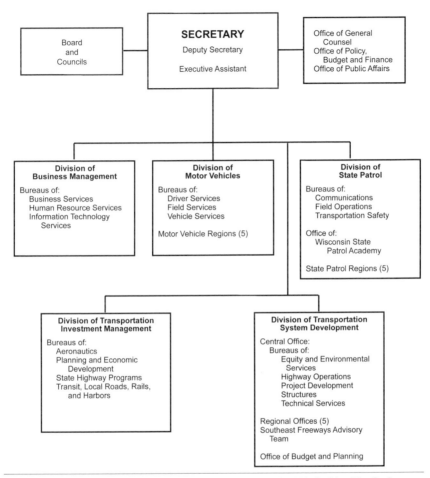

State Patrol, Division of: DAVID L. COLLINS, *superintendent,* 266-0454, david.collins@; COLONEL BEN H. MENDEZ, 266-3908, benjamin.mendez@

Division Mailing Address: P.O. Box 7912, Madison 53707-7912.

Telephones: General: (608) 266-3212; Road Condition Reports: Madison: (608) 246-7580; Milwaukee: (414) 785-7140; elsewhere in Wisconsin: (800) 762-3947.

Fax: 267-4495.

Communications, Bureau of: vacancy, *director,* 266-0184.

Field Operations, Bureau of: MAJOR DARREN C. PRICE, 267-9522, darren.price@

Transportation Safety, Bureau of: MAJOR DANIEL W. LONSDORF, 266-3048, daniel.lonsdorf@

Wisconsin State Patrol Academy, Office of: MAJOR SANDRA K. HUXTABLE, *director of training,* (608) 269-2500, sandra.huxtable@; Fax: (608) 269-5681; 95 South 10th Avenue, Fort McCoy 54656-5168.

State Patrol Region Captains/Executive Officers:

North Central Region:

Wausau Post: Jeffrey J. Frenette, *captain,* (715) 845-1143, jeffrey.frenette@; Timothy L. Carnahan, *executive officer,* (715) 845-1143, timothy.carnahan@; Fax: (715) 848-9255; 2805 Martin Avenue, Wausau 54401-7172.

Northeast Region:

Fond du Lac Post: David J. Pichette, *captain,* (920) 929-3700, david.pichette@; Nicholas Scorcio, Jr., *executive officer,* (920) 929-3700, nick.scorcio@; Fax: (920) 929-7666; 851 South Rolling Meadows Drive, P.O. Box 984, Fond du Lac 54936-0984.

Northwest Region:

Eau Claire Post: Douglas M. Notbohm, *captain,* (715) 839-3800, douglas.notbohm@; Fax: (715) 839-3841; Jeffrey D. Lorentz, *executive officer,* (715) 839-3800, jeffrey.lorentz@; Fax: (715) 839-3873; 5005 Highway 53 South, Eau Claire 54701-8846.

Spooner Post: Nicholas R. Wanink, *executive officer,* (715) 635-2141, nicholas.wanink@; Fax: (715) 635-6373; W7102 Green Valley Road, Spooner 54801.

Southeast Region:

Waukesha Post: Varla J. Bishop, *captain,* (262) 785-4700, varla.bishop@; Ted Meagher, *executive officer,* (262) 785-4700, ted.meagher@; Fax: (262) 785-4722; 21115 Highway 18, Waukesha 53186-2985.

Southwest Region:

DeForest Post: Charles R. Teasdale, *captain,* (608) 846-8500, charles.teasdale@; Brad Altman, *executive officer,* (608) 846-8500, brad.altman@; Fax: (608) 846-8536; 911 West North Street, DeForest 53532-1971.

Tomah Post: James D. Lind, *executive officer,* (608) 374-0513, james.lind@; Fax: (608) 374-0599; 23928 Lester McMullin Drive, Tomah 54660-5376.

Transportation Investment Management, Division of: Mark Wolfgram, *administrator,* 266-5791, mark.wolfgram@; Fax: 266-0686; P.O. Box 7913, Madison 53707-7913.

Aeronautics, Bureau of: David Greene, *director,* 266-2480, david.greene@

Planning and Economic Development, Bureau of: Sandra Beaupré, *director,* 266-7575, sandra.beaupre@

State Highway Programs, Bureau of: Joseph Nestler, *director,* 266-9495, joseph.nestler@

Transit, Local Roads, Rails, and Harbors, Bureau of: Rod Clark, *director,* 266-2963, rod.clark@

Transportation System Development, Division of: Kevin Chesnik, *administrator,* 267-7111, kevin.chesnik@; Division Fax: 264-6667.

Division Mailing Address: 4802 Sheboygan Avenue, Room 451, P.O. Box 7965, Madison 53707-7965.

Division E-mail Address: division-office.dtsd@dot.wi.gov

Statewide Bureaus Operations Director: Rory Rhinesmith, 266-2392, rory.rhinesmith@; Fax: 264-6667.

Equity and Environmental Services, Bureau of: Eugene S. Johnson, *director,* 267-9527, eugene.johnson@; Fax: 266-7818.

Highway Operations, Bureau of: David I. Vieth, *director,* 267-8999, david.vieth@; Fax: 267-7856; John M. Corbin, *state traffic engineer,* 266-0459, john.corbin@; Fax: 261-6295.

Project Development, Bureau of: Donald J. Miller, *director,* 266-3707, donald.miller@; Fax: 266-8459.

Structures, Bureau of: Beth Cannestra, *director,* 266-0075, beth.cannestra@; Fax: 261-6277.

Technical Services, Bureau of: Daniel K. McGuire, *director,* 246-5399, daniel.mcguire@; Fax: 267-0307.

Budget and Planning, Office of: vacancy, *chief.*

Regional Operation Director: Paul Trombino, 264-6677, paul.trombino@; Fax: 264-6667.

North Central Region, Rhinelander: Daniel Grasser, *director,* (715) 365-3490, daniel.grasser@; Fax: (715) 365-5780; TTY: (715) 365-5719; 510 Hanson Lake Road, P.O. Box 777, Rhinelander 54501-0777; Rebecca Burkel, *operations manager,* (715) 421-8300, rebecca.burkel@; Fax: (715) 423-0334; 2610 Industrial Street, P.O. Box 8021, Wisconsin Rapids 54495-8021.

Northeast Region, Green Bay: Michael Berg, *director,* (715) 421-8300, michael.berg@; Will Dorsey, *operations manager,* (920) 492-5643, will.dorsey@; Fax: (920) 492-5640; TTY: (920) 492-5673; 944 Vanderperren Way, P.O. Box 28080, Green Bay 54324-0080.

Northwest Region, Eau Claire: Donald Gutkowski, *director,* (715) 836-2891, donald.gutkowski@; Fax: (715) 836-2807; TTY: (715) 836-6578; 718 West Clairemont Avenue, Eau Claire 54701-5108; Jerald Mentzel, *operations manager,* (715) 392-7925, jerald.mentzel@; Fax: (715) 392-7863; TTY Relay Service: (800) 947-3529; 1701 North Fourth Street, Superior 54880-1068.

Southeast Region, Waukesha: Dewayne Johnson, *director,* (262) 548-5884, dewayne.johnson@; Fax: (414) 548-5662; TTY: (414) 548-8801; 141 Northwest Barstow Street, Waukesha 53187-0798; Reggie Newson, *operations manager,* (262) 548-5884, reggie.newson@; Fax: (414) 548-5662; 151 Northwest Barstow Street, Waukesha 53187-0798.

Southwest Region, La Crosse: Joseph Olson, *director,* (608) 785-9022, joseph.olson@; Fax: (608) 785-9969; TTY: (608) 789-7862; 3550 Mormon Coulee Road, La Crosse 54601-6767; Rose Phetteplace, *operations manager,* (608) 246-3801, rose.phetteplace@; Fax: (608) 246-7996; TTY: (608) 246-5385; 2101 Wright Street, Madison 53704-2583.

Southeast Freeways Advisory Team: Donna Brown, *chief,* (262) 548-8713, donna.brown@

Publications: Biennial Report; Connections 2030; Five-Year Airport Improvement Program (annual); Motorcyclist Handbook for Wisconsin; *Rustic Roads;* Six-Year Highway Improvement Program; Traffic Safety Reporter; *Trucking Wisconsin Style;* Wisconsin Aeronautical Chart (annual); Wisconsin Airport Directory (odd-numbered years); Wisconsin Alcohol Traffic Facts; Wisconsin Aviation Bulletin (even-numbered years); Wisconsin Commercial Drivers' Manual; Wisconsin Drivers' Book; Wisconsin Highway Map; Wisconsin Motorcycle Crash Facts; Wisconsin Motorists' Handbook and Study Guide; Wisconsin Traffic Crash Facts (annual).

Agency Responsibility: The Department of Transportation is responsible for the planning, promotion, and protection of all transportation systems in the state. Its major responsibilities involve highways, motor vehicles, motor carriers, traffic law enforcement, railroads, waterways, mass transit, and aeronautics.

The department works with several federal agencies in the administration of federal transportation aids. It also cooperates with departments at the state level in travel promotion, consumer protection, environmental analysis, and transportation services for elderly and handicapped persons.

Organization: The secretary is appointed by the governor with the advice and consent of the senate and has overall management responsibility for the department. The secretary appoints the deputy secretary, executive assistant, and all division administrators from outside the classified service.

Unit Functions: The *Division of Business Management* plans and administers the department's programs for accounting and auditing, information technology, human resources, purchasing, vehicle fleet, facilities, and management services.

The *Division of Motor Vehicles* issues vehicle titles and registrations, individual identification cards, and handicapped parking permits; examines and licenses drivers, commercial driving instructors, and vehicle salespersons; certifies commercial driver examiners; licenses motor carriers, commercial driving schools, vehicle dealers, manufacturers, and distributors; and investigates consumer complaints about vehicle sales and trade practices. It keeps the records of drivers' traffic violations and demerit points. It is responsible for the vehicle emissions inspection program, and it administers reciprocal trucking agreements with other states and the Canadian provinces and provides traffic accident data to law enforcement officials, highway engineers, and traffic safety and media representatives. The division operates 5 district offices and 89 customer service centers to support the state's approximately 4.1 million licensed drivers and over 5.4 million registered vehicles.

The *Division of State Patrol* promotes highway safety by enforcing state traffic laws regarding motor vehicles and motor carriers. The State Patrol also has criminal law enforcement powers and can assist local law enforcement agencies by providing emergency police services. It operates the statewide mobile data communications network, which is available to local law enforcement agencies, and it makes annual inspections of Wisconsin's school buses and ambulances. The division oversees 5 regional offices and a law enforcement training academy open to all federal, state, county, local, and tribal law enforcement officers.

The *Division of Transportation Investment Management* performs statewide planning for highways, railroads, harbors, airports, and mass transit and promotes a multimodal transportation system to best serve state citizens and businesses. The division directs data collection; provides service to local governments and planning agencies; and manages state road aids, highway finance, and other transportation assistance programs. The division is responsible for uniform statewide direction in the planning, design, construction, maintenance, and operation of Wisconsin's airports, harbors, highways, and railroads. The division is involved with the state's 132 public use airports, 3,400 miles of railroad tracks, 15 commercial water ports, and

Wisconsin State Patrol inspectors examine large trucks and other commercial motor vehicles traveling through the state to ensure their brakes, lights, and other safety equipment meet stringent requirements. (Department of Transportation)

the approximately 12,000 miles of roads and streets in the STH system, including 640 miles of Interstate highways within the state. The division administers all state and federal funding for airport, railroad, and harbor development projects in Wisconsin.

The *Division of Transportation System Development* performs development, maintenance, and operations functions related to the State Trunk Highway (STH) system. The division is split into two basic areas: Statewide Bureaus and Regional Operations. It provides uniform direction in planning, design, and construction phases of project delivery as well as improving the safety and efficiency of the STH system. The division also provides leadership in the protection of public interests and resources through public and local interactions.

The five state statewide bureaus include: 1) Equity and Environmental Services, 2) Highway Operations, 3) Project Development, 4) Structures, and 5) Technical Services. These statewide bureaus advise the regional offices as well as other divisions regarding engineering, economic, environmental, and social standards and practices. The division also monitors the quality and efficiency of the department's various programs and assures compliance with federal and state laws and regulations. The five regional offices manage the operation and development of state highways and participate in the development, management, and implementation of local road and nonhighway transportation projects. They also maintain working relationships with local units of government, represent the department in local and regional planning efforts, and represent local and regional needs in departmental processes.

History: The history of the Department of Transportation mirrors the evolution of twentieth century transportation. The Highway Commission was created when Chapter 337, Laws of 1911, authorized state aid for public highways. Later, Chapter 410, Laws of 1939, consolidated registration, licensing, inspection, enforcement, and highway safety promotion in the Motor Vehicle Department. The legislature established the Aeronautics Commission in Chapter 513, Laws of 1945, and directed it to cooperate with the federal government and other states to "prepare for the generally expected extensive expansion of aviation following the termination of World War II."

The Department of Transportation was created by Chapter 75, Laws of 1967, which merged the Highway Commission, the Aeronautics Commission, and the Motor Vehicle Department. Chapter 500, Laws of 1969, required three divisions within the department: aeronautics, highways, and motor vehicles. The department was strengthened by Chapter 29, Laws of 1977, which vested accountability at the departmental, instead of divisional, level and gave the secretary, rather than the governor, the authority to appoint division heads. The secretary was also allowed to reorganize the department with the governor's approval.

Statutory Board and Councils

Highway Safety, Council on: RANDALL R. THIEL (state officer), *chairperson;* KARI K. KINNARD (citizen member), *vice chairperson;* SENATOR LEIBHAM, vacancy; REPRESENTATIVES 3 vacancies; ROGER BRESKE, DAVID L. COLLINS, JOHN CORBIN, ANDREW FELDMAN (state officers); SHERRICK ANDERSON, PATRICK BECKER, LAVERNE E. HERMANN, DENNIS KOCKEN (citizen members). (All except legislators are appointed by governor.)

The 15-member Council on Highway Safety advises the secretary about highway safety matters. The council includes 2 senators and 3 assembly representatives who serve on standing committees that deal with transportation matters. The other 10 members, who serve staggered 3-year terms, include 5 state officers with transportation and highway safety duties and 5 citizen members. The council was originally created in the Office of the Governor by Chapter 276, Laws of 1969, and was moved to the Department of Transportation by Chapter 34, Laws of 1979. Its composition and duties are prescribed in Sections 15.467 (3) and 85.07 (2) of the statutes.

Rustic Roads Board: MARION FLOOD, *chairperson;* DANIEL FEDDERLY, *vice chairperson;* SENATOR HOLPERIN; REPRESENTATIVE STEINBRINK; RAYMOND DEHAHN, ROBERT HANSEN, BRUCE LINDGREN, ALAN LORENZ, CHARLES RAYALA, THOMAS SOLHEIM. (Nonlegislative members are appointed by secretary of transportation.)

The 10-member Rustic Roads Board oversees the application and selection process of locally-nominated county highways and local roads for inclusion in the Rustic Roads network. Established in 1973, the Rustic Roads Program is a partnership between local officials and state government to showcase some of Wisconsin's most picturesque and lightly-traveled roadways for the leisurely enjoyment of hikers, bikers, and motorists. The board includes the chairpersons of the senate and assembly committees with jurisdiction over transportation matters. Its 8 non-legislative members serve staggered 4-year terms, and at least 4 of them must be nominees of the Wisconsin Counties Association. The board was created by Chapter 142, Laws of 1973, and its composition and duties are prescribed in Sections 15.465 (2) and 83.42 of the statutes.

Uniformity of Traffic Citations and Complaints, Council on.

The 10-member Council on Uniformity of Traffic Citations and Complaints recommends forms used for traffic violations. The council was created by Chapter 292, Laws of 1967, as the Uniform Traffic Citation and Complaint Committee and renamed by 1985 Wisconsin Act 145. Its composition and duties are prescribed in Sections 15.467 (4) and 345.11 of the statutes.

The council meets on an as-needed basis, and members are designated when required. Members include the secretary of transportation or designee, a member of the Department of Transportation responsible for law enforcement, a member designated by the Director of State Courts, and members designated by the presidents of the following: the Wisconsin Sheriffs and Deputy Sheriffs Association, the County Traffic Patrol Association, the Chiefs of Police Association, the State Bar of Wisconsin, the Wisconsin Council of Safety, the Wisconsin District Attorneys Association, and the Judicial Conference.

UNIVERSITY OF WISCONSIN SYSTEM

Board of Regents: CHARLES PRUITT, *president;* MICHAEL J. SPECTOR, *vice president;* ANTHONY EVERS (superintendent of public instruction), MARY QUINETTE CUENE (president, Technical College System Board); JEFFREY BARTELL, MARK J. BRADLEY, EILEEN CONNOLLY-KEESLER, JUDITH VANDERMUELEN CRAIN, DANAE D. DAVIS, JOHN DREW, MICHAEL J. FALBO, THOMAS LOFTUS, BRENT SMITH, JOSE VASQUEZ, DAVID G. WALSH, BETTY WOMACK; KEVIN OPGENORTH, AARON WINGAD (students). (All except *ex officio* members are appointed by governor with senate consent.)

Secretary to the Board: JUDITH A. TEMBY, 1860 Van Hise Hall, 1220 Linden Drive, Madison 53706-1557, (608) 262-2324.

Mailing Address: Central administrative offices for the UW System and the UW Colleges are located in Madison. Individual universities and 2-year UW Colleges can be reached by contacting them directly. Administrative offices for UW-Extension are in Madison; Extension representatives are located at each county seat.

Publications: administrative directory; biennial and annual reports; *Fact Book; Introduction to the University of Wisconsin System;* unit bulletins, catalogs, reports, circulars; periodicals and books.

Number of Employees: 31,972.95.

Total Budget 2007-09: $8,942,605,000.

Constitutional Reference: Article X, Section 6.

Statutory References: Section 15.91; Chapter 36.

System Administration

1220 Linden Drive, Madison 53706-1559
General Telephone: (608) 262-2321
Internet Address: www.wisconsin.edu

President of the University of Wisconsin System: KEVIN P. REILLY, 1720 Van Hise Hall, 1220 Linden Drive, Madison 53706-1559, (608) 262-2321.

Senior Vice President for Administration and Fiscal Affairs: THOMAS K. ANDERES, 1752 Van Hise Hall, 262-4048.

Senior Vice President for Academic Affairs: REBECCA R. MARTIN, 1730 Van Hise Hall, 262-3826.

A bird's-eye view of the Marquette Interchange in downtown Milwaukee. The interchange is a key hub of the state's interstate highway system, carrying more than 300,000 vehicles per day. Reconstruction of the interchange began in 2004 and was completed in 2008 ahead of schedule and under the $810 million budget. (Department of Transportation)

UNIVERSITY OF WISCONSIN SYSTEM

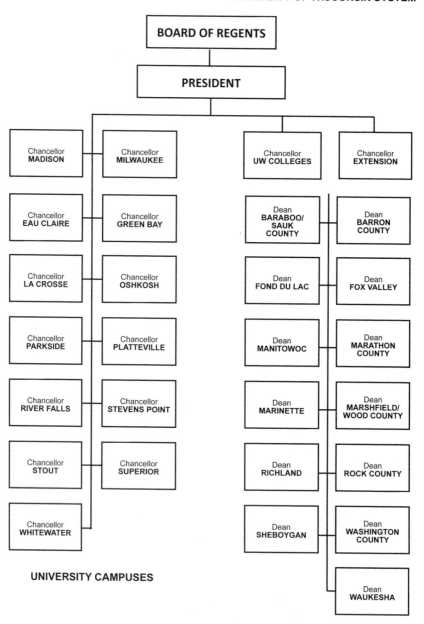

BOARD OF REGENTS

PRESIDENT

Chancellor **MADISON**

Chancellor **MILWAUKEE**

Chancellor **UW COLLEGES**

Chancellor **EXTENSION**

Chancellor **EAU CLAIRE**

Chancellor **GREEN BAY**

Dean **BARABOO/ SAUK COUNTY**

Dean **BARRON COUNTY**

Chancellor **LA CROSSE**

Chancellor **OSHKOSH**

Dean **FOND DU LAC**

Dean **FOX VALLEY**

Chancellor **PARKSIDE**

Chancellor **PLATTEVILLE**

Dean **MANITOWOC**

Dean **MARATHON COUNTY**

Chancellor **RIVER FALLS**

Chancellor **STEVENS POINT**

Dean **MARINETTE**

Dean **MARSHFIELD/ WOOD COUNTY**

Chancellor **STOUT**

Chancellor **SUPERIOR**

Dean **RICHLAND**

Dean **ROCK COUNTY**

Chancellor **WHITEWATER**

Dean **SHEBOYGAN**

Dean **WASHINGTON COUNTY**

Dean **WAUKESHA**

UNIVERSITY CAMPUSES

TWO-YEAR COLLEGES

Units attached for administrative purposes under Sec. 15.03:
Environmental Education Board
Veterinary Diagnostic Laboratory Board

Vice President for Finance: DEBORAH A. DURCAN, 1624 Van Hise Hall, 262-1311.

General Counsel: PATRICIA A. BRADY, 1856 Van Hise Hall, 262-6497.

UW-Madison
161 Bascom Hall, 500 Lincoln Drive, Madison 53706
General Telephone: (608) 262-1234
Internet Address: www.wisc.edu

Chancellor: CAROLYN A. "BIDDY" MARTIN, 161 Bascom Hall, 500 Lincoln Drive, Madison 53706, 262-9946.

Provost and Vice Chancellor for Academic Affairs: PAUL M. DELUCA, JR., 150 Bascom Hall, 262-1304.

Vice Chancellor for Administration: DARRELL BAZZELL, 100 Bascom Hall, 263-2467.

Director of the Office of Administrative Legal Services: LISA RUTHERFORD, 361 Bascom Hall, 263-7400.

Vice Chancellor for Medical Affairs: ROBERT GOLDEN, 4129 Health Sciences Learning Center, 750 Highland Avenue, 263-4910.

Dean of Agricultural and Life Sciences: MOLLY JAHN, 140 Agricultural Hall, 262-4930.

Dean of Business: MICHAEL KNETTER, 4339 Grainger Hall, 262-1758.

Interim Dean of Education: ADAM GAMORAN, 310 Lathrop Hall, 262-6137.

Dean of Engineering: PAUL PEERCY, 2610 Engineering Hall, 262-3482.

Dean of the Graduate School: MARTIN CADWALLADER, 333 Bascom Hall, 262-1044.

Dean of Human Ecology: ROBIN DOUTHITT, 141 Human Ecology Building, 262-4847.

Dean of International Studies and Programs: GILLES BOUSQUET, 268 Bascom Hall, 262-9833.

Dean of Law: KENNETH DAVIS, JR., 5211 Law Building, 262-0618.

Dean of Letters and Science: GARY SANDEFUR, 105 South Hall, 263-2303.

Director of Libraries: KENNETH FRAZIER, 372 Memorial Library, 262-2600.

Dean of Medicine and Public Health: ROBERT GOLDEN, 4129 Health Sciences Learning Center, 750 Highland Avenue, 263-4910.

Dean of Nursing: KATHARYN MAY, BX2455 Clinical Science Center-Module K6, 263-5155.

Dean of Pharmacy: JEANETTE ROBERTS, 1126B Rennebohm Hall, 262-1414.

Dean of Veterinary Medicine: DARYL BUSS, 2015 Linden Drive West, 263-6716.

Dean of Students: LORI BERQUAM, 75 Bascom Hall, 263-5702.

Interim Dean of Continuing Studies and Associate Vice Chancellor: MARVIN VAN KEKERIX, Room 305, 1305 Linden Drive, 262-5821.

Secretary of the Academic Staff: DONNA SILVER, 270 Bascom Hall, 263-2985.

Secretary of the Faculty: DAVID MUSOLF, 133 Bascom Hall, 262-3956.

Director of Admissions and Visitor and Information Programs: STEVE AMUNDSON, 140 Armory and Gymnasium, 716 Langdon Street, 265-9501.

Vice Provost of Enrollment Management and Registrar: JOANNE BERG, Room 7223, 21 North Park Street, 262-3964.

UW-Milwaukee
P.O. Box 413, Milwaukee 53201-0413
General Telephone: (414) 229-1122
Internet Address: www.uwm.edu

Chancellor: CARLOS E. SANTIAGO, 202 Chapman Hall, P.O. Box 413, Milwaukee 53201, 229-4331.

Provost/Vice Chancellor: RITA CHENG, 215 Chapman Hall, 229-4501.

Vice Chancellor, Finance and Administrative Affairs: CHRISTY BROWN, 310 Chapman Hall, 229-4461.

Vice Chancellor for Research and Dean of the Graduate School: COLIN SCANES, 335 Chapman Hall, 229-2591.

Vice Chancellor for Student Affairs: HELEN MAMARCHEV, 132 Chapman Hall, 229-4038.

Vice Chancellor, University Relations and Communications: THOMAS LULJAK, 180A Chapman Hall, 229-4035.

Dean, College of Engineering and Applied Science: MICHAEL LOVELL, 524 Engineering and Mathematical Sciences Building, 229-4126.

Dean, College of Letters and Science: G. RICHARD MEADOWS, 218A Holton Hall, 229-5895.

Interim Dean, College of Health Sciences: JOHANNES BRITZ, 897 Enderis Hall, 229-4712.

Dean, School of Architecture and Urban Planning: ROBERT C. GREENSTREET, 241 Architecture and Urban Planning Building, 229-4016.

Dean, Peck School of the Arts: WADE HOBGOOD, 284 Arts Building, 229-4762.

Dean, School of Business Administration: KANTI PRASAD, N425 Business Administration Building, 229-6256.

Dean, School of Education: ALFONZO THURMAN, 595 Enderis Hall, 229-4181.

Dean, School of Library and Information Science: JOHANNES BRITZ, 1193 Enderis Hall, 229-4709.

Dean, School of Nursing: SALLY LUNDEEN, 767B Cunningham Hall, 229-4189.

Dean, School of Social Welfare: STAN STOJKOVIC, 1095 Enderis Hall, 229-4400.

Interim Dean, Outreach and Continuing Education Extension: PATRICIA ARREDONDO, 161 West Wisconsin Avenue, 53203, 227-3326.

Director of Admissions: BETH L. WECKMUELLER, 222 Mellencamp Hall, 229-6164.

Secretary of the University: TRUDY TURNER, 225 Mitchell Hall, 229-5989.

UW-Eau Claire

Park and Garfield Avenues, P.O. Box 4004, Eau Claire 54702-4004
General Telephone: (715) 836-2637
Internet Address: www.uwec.edu

Chancellor: BRIAN L. LEVIN-STANKEVICH, 836-2327.

Provost and Vice Chancellor, Academic Affairs: PATRICIA KLEINE, 836-2320.

Assistant Chancellor for Budget and Finance: DAVID GESSNER, 836-5182.

Vice Chancellor for Student Affairs and Dean of Students: BETH HELLWIG, 836-5992.

Dean, College of Arts and Sciences: MARTY WOOD, 836-2542.

Dean, College of Education and Human Sciences: GAIL P. SCUKANEC, 836-3264.

Dean, College of Business: V. THOMAS DOCK, 836-5509.

Interim Dean, College of Nursing and Health Sciences: MARY ZWYGART-STAUFFACHER, 836-5287.

Executive Director, Enrollment Services and Admissions: KRISTINA C. ANDERSON, 836-5415.

Registrar: SUE E. MOORE, 836-3887.

UW-Green Bay

2420 Nicolet Drive, Green Bay 54311-7001
General Telephone: (920) 465-2000
Internet Address: www.uwgb.edu

Chancellor: THOMAS K. HARDEN, 465-2207.

Interim Provost and Vice Chancellor for Academic Affairs: WILLIAM G. LAATSCH, 465-5161.

Associate Provost for Student Services/Dean of Students: SUE KEIHN, 465-2152.

Vice Chancellor, Business and Finance: THOMAS MAKI, 465-2210.
Interim Assistant Chancellor for University Advancement: DAN SPIELMANN, 465-2074.
Dean, Liberal Arts and Sciences: SCOTT FURLONG, 465-2336.
Dean, Professional and Graduate Studies: FRITZ ERICKSON, 465-2050.
Communications Director: CHRISTOPHER SAMPSON, 465-2527.
Media Relations Coordinator: MIKE HEINE, 465-2526.
Registrar: MICHAEL HERRITY, 465-2155.

UW-La Crosse
1725 State Street, La Crosse 54601-9959
General Telephone: (608) 785-8000
Internet Address: www.uwlax.edu

Chancellor: JOE GOW, 785-8004.
Provost/Vice Chancellor: KATHLEEN ENZ FINKEN, 785-8042.
Vice Chancellor, Administration and Finance: BOB HETZEL, 785-8021.
Interim President, UW-L Foundation: ALLEN TRAPP, 785-8489.
Affirmative Action Officer: CARMEN WILSON, 785-8043.
Associate Dean, Diversity: BARBARA STEWART, 785-5092.
Associate Vice Chancellor for Academic Affairs: VIJENDRA AGARWAL, 785-8007.
Executive Director, Human Resources: JENNIFER WILSON, 785-8013.
Executive Director, Facilities Planning and Management: MATTHEW N. LEWIS, 785-8019.
Chief Information Officer: JOHN P. TILLMAN, 785-8662.
Assistant Chancellor and Dean of Students: PAULA M. KNUDSON, 785-8150.
Dean, College of Business Administration: WILLIAM G. COLCLOUGH III, 785-8095.
Dean, College of Liberal Studies: RUTHANN E. BENSON, 785-8116.
Interim Dean, College of Science and Health: BRUCE V. RILEY, 785-8218.
Director, Admissions: KATHRYN C. KIEFER, 785-8939.
Registrar: CHRISTINE S. BAKKUM, 785-8953.

UW-Oshkosh
800 Algoma Boulevard, Oshkosh 54901-8617
General Telephone: (920) 424-1234
Internet Address: www.uwosh.edu

Chancellor: RICHARD H. WELLS, 424-0200.
Chancellor's Assistant for Strategic Planning and Office Communications: SUSAN NUERNBERG, 424-0424.
Provost/Vice Chancellor: LANE EARNS, 424-0300.
Vice Chancellor, Student Affairs: PETRA M. ROTER, 424-4000.
Assistant Vice Chancellor, Academic Support: vacancy, 424-3080.
Director, Graduate Studies: GREGORY B. WYPISZYNSKI, 424-0007.
Vice Chancellor, Administrative Services: THOMAS G. SONNLEITNER, 424-3030.
Assistant Vice Chancellor, Administrative Services: LORI WORM, 424-3033.
Dean, College of Business: BURK TOWER, 424-1424.
Dean, College of Education and Human Services: FREDERICK L. YEO, 424-3322.
Dean, College of Letters and Science: JOHN J. KOKER, 424-1210.
Dean, College of Nursing: ROSEMARY SMITH, 424-3089.
Dean of Students: JAMES M. CHITWOOD, 424-3100.
Director, Admissions: JILL M. ENDRIES, 424-0228.
Registrar: LISA M. DANIELSON, 424-3007.

UW-Parkside

P.O. Box 2000, Kenosha 53141-2000
General Telephone: (262) 595-2345
Internet Address: www.uwp.edu

Chancellor: DEBORAH L. FORD, 595-2211.
Interim Provost/Vice Chancellor: GERALD GREENFIELD, 595-2144.
Interim Associate Provost: DOUG DEVINNY, 595-2261.
Vice Chancellor, Administrative and Fiscal Affairs: WILLIAM W. STREETER, 595-2141.
Vice Chancellor for Student Services/Dean of Students: STEPHEN MCLAUGHLIN, 595-2598.
Vice Chancellor for University Relations and Advancement: LENNY KLAVER, 595-2591.
Dean, College of Arts and Sciences: DONALD CRESS, 595-2188.
Dean, School of Business and Technology: FRED EBEID, 595-2243.
Dean, Community Engagement and Civic Learning: JOHN SKALBECK, 595-3340.
Director of Admissions: MATTHEW JENSEN, 595-2355.
Registrar: RHONDA KIMMEL, 595-2237.
Assistant to the Chancellor for Equity and Diversity: EUGENE FUJIMOTO, 595-2369.

UW-Platteville

1 University Plaza, Platteville 53818-3099
General Telephone: (608) 342-1491
Internet Address: www.uwplatt.edu

Chancellor: DAVID J. MARKEE, 342-1234.
Provost and Vice Chancellor for Academic Affairs: CAROL SUE BUTTS, 342-1261.
Associate Vice Chancellor: DAVID VAN BUREN, 342-1262.
Assistant Chancellor for Administrative Services: ROBERT G. CRAMER, 342-1226.
Assistant Chancellor for Student Affairs: MICHAEL VINEY, 342-1854.
Director of Admissions and Enrollment Services: ANGELA UDELHOFEN, 342-1125.
Dean, College of Business, Industry, Life Science and Agriculture: DUANE M. FORD, 342-1547.
Dean, College of Engineering, Mathematics, and Science: RICHARD SHULTZ, 342-1561.
Dean, College of Liberal Arts and Education: MITTIE J. NIMOCKS, 342-1151.
Dean, School of Graduate Studies: DAVID VAN BUREN, 342-1262.
Registrar: DAVID KIECKHAFER, 342-1321.

UW-River Falls

410 South Third Street, River Falls 54022-5001
General Telephone: (715) 425-3911
Internet Address: www.uwrf.edu

Chancellor: DEAN VAN GALEN, 425-3201.
Provost/Vice Chancellor for Academic Affairs: FERNANDO DELGADO, 425-3700.
Interim Vice Chancellor, Administration and Finance: LISA WHEELER, 425-3737.
Dean, College of Agriculture, Food and Environmental Sciences: DALE GALLENBERG, 425-3841.
Dean, College of Arts and Sciences: TERRY BROWN, 425-3777.
Interim Dean, College of Education and Professional Studies: FAYE PERKINS, 425-3774.
Dean, College of Business and Economics: GLENN POTTS, 425-3335.
Associate Vice Chancellor for Student Affairs: GREGG HEINSELMAN, 425-4444.
Associate Vice Chancellor for Enrollment Services: ALAN TUCHTENHAGEN, 425-3500.
Interim Associate Vice Chancellor for Academic Affairs: DOUGLAS JOHNSON, 425-0699.
Registrar: DAN VANDE YACHT, 425-3342.

UW-Stevens Point

Room 213 Old Main, 2100 Main Street, Stevens Point 54481-3897
General Telephone: (715) 346-0123
Internet Address: www.uwsp.edu

Interim Chancellor: MARK NOOK, 346-2123.
Interim Provost/Vice Chancellor, Academic Affairs: JEFFREY MORIN, 346-4686.
Vice Chancellor, Business Affairs: GREGORY DIEMER, 346-2641.
Vice Chancellor, Student Affairs: ROBERT TOMLINSON, 346-2481.
Associate Vice Chancellor, Personnel, Budget, Grants, and Summer Session: MICHAEL VEUM, 346-3710.
Associate Vice Chancellor, Teaching, Learning and Academic Programs: GREGORY SUMMERS, 346-4446.
Chief Information Officer, Information Technology: DAVID DUMKE, 346-3612.
Interim Coordinator, UWSP Continuing Education: JOHN BIRRENKOTT, 346-4568.
Interim Dean, College of Fine Arts and Communication: JAMES HANEY, 346-4920.
Dean, College of Letters and Science: CHRISTOPHER CIRMO, 346-4224.
Dean, College of Natural Resources: CHRISTINE THOMAS, 346-4185.
Dean, College of Professional Studies: JOAN NORTH, 346-3169.
Director, Admissions and High School Relations/Registrar: CATHY GLENNON, 346-2441; Registration and Records: DANIEL KELLOGG, 346-4301.
Director of International Programs: ERIC YONKE, 346-3693.

UW-Stout

P.O. Box 790, Menomonie 54751-0790
General Telephone: (715) 232-1431
Internet Address: www.uwstout.edu

Chancellor: CHARLES W. SORENSEN, 232-2441.
Provost/Vice Chancellor, Academic and Student Affairs: JULIE FURST-BOWE, 232-2421.
Vice Chancellor, Administrative and Student Life Services: DIANE MOEN, 232-1683.
Vice Chancellor, University Advancement: DAVID WILLIAMS, 232-1151.
Associate Vice Chancellor, Academic and Student Affairs: JANICE COKER, 232-2421.
Dean, College of Arts, Humanities and Social Sciences: JOHN MURPHY, 232-2596.
Dean, College of Education, Health and Human Sciences: MARY HOPKINS-BEST, 232-1088.
Interim Dean, College of Management: CAROL MOONEY, 232-1444.
Interim Dean, College of Science, Technology, Engineering and Mathematics: RICHARD ROTHAUPT, 232-5021.
Dean of Students: JOAN THOMAS, 232-1181.
Executive Director of Enrollment Services: CYNTHIA GILBERTS, 232-2639.
Interim Registrar: LARRY GRAVES, 232-1233.

UW-Superior

Belknap and Catlin Streets, P.O. Box 2000, Superior 54880-4500
General Telephone: (715) 394-8101
Internet Address: www.uwsuper.edu

Chancellor: JULIUS E. ERLENBACH, 394-8221.
Provost: CHRISTOPHER L. MARKWOOD, 394-8449.
Vice Chancellor for Administration and Finance: JANET K. HANSON, 394-8014.
Vice Chancellor for Campus Life/Dean of Students: VICKI HAJEWSKI, 394-8241.
Assistant Chancellor, University Advancement: JILL SCHOER, 394-8598.
Assistant to the Chancellor for EO/AA and Diversity: MICHAEL MCDONALD, 394-8141.

Assistant Vice Chancellor for Enrollment Management: JANE BIRKHOLZ, 394-8306.
Dean of Faculties: CHRISTOPHER L. MARKWOOD, 394-8449.
Registrar: BARBARA A. ERICKSON, 394-8218.

UW-Whitewater
Hyer Hall, 800 West Main Street, Whitewater 53190-1790
General Telephone: (262) 472-1234
Internet Address: www.uww.edu

Chancellor: RICHARD J. TELFER, 472-1918.
Interim Provost/Vice Chancellor for Academic Affairs: CHRISTINE CLEMENTS, 472-1672.
Vice Chancellor, Administrative Affairs: RANDY D. MARNOCHA, 472-1922.
Assistant Chancellor for Student Affairs: THOMAS R. RIOS, 472-1172.
Associate Vice Chancellor for Academic Affairs: BARBARA S. MONFILS, 472-1055.
Interim Dean, College of Arts and Communication: RICHARD HAVEN, 472-1221.
Interim Dean, College of Business and Economics: LOIS J. SMITH, 472-1343.
Dean, College of Education: KATHARINA E. HEYNING, 472-1101.
Dean, College of Letters and Sciences: MARY A. PINKERTON, 472-1712.
Dean, Graduate School, Continuing Education and Summer Session: JOHN F. STONE, 472-1006.
Interim Director of Admissions: JODI M. HARE, 472-1512.
Interim Registrar: JODI M. HARE, 472-1570.

UW Colleges and UW-Extension
432 North Lake Street, Madison 53706-1498
General Telephone: (608) 262-3786

Chancellor: DAVID WILSON, (608) 262-3786.
Assistant to the Chancellor: BARB SANDRIDGE, 262-3786.

UW Colleges
Internet Address: www.uwc.edu/
Provost/Vice Chancellor: GREG LAMPE, (608) 263-1794.
Vice Chancellor, Administrative and Financial Services: STEVEN WILDECK, (608) 265-3040.
Interim Associate Vice Chancellor for Academic Affairs: LISA SEALE, (608) 263-7217.
Interim Associate Vice Chancellor for Student Services and Enrollment Management: PATTI WISE, 265-0476.
Assistant Vice Chancellor for Information Technology: MARSHA HENFER, (608) 263-6012.
Registrar: CHERIE HATLEM, (608) 262-9652.
Baraboo/Sauk County: 1006 Connie Road, Baraboo 53913-1098, (608) 355-5200, www.baraboo.uwc.edu
  Dean: TOM PLEGER.
Barron County: 1800 College Drive, Rice Lake 54868-2497, (715) 234-8176, www.barron.uwc.edu
  Dean: PAUL CHASE.
Fond du Lac: 400 University Drive, Fond du Lac 54935-2998, (920) 929-1100, www.fdl.uwc.edu
  Interim Dean: JUDY GOLDSMITH.
Fox Valley: 1478 Midway Road, Menasha 54952-1297, (920) 832-2600, www.fox.uwc.edu
  Dean: JAMES PERRY.

Manitowoc: 705 Viebahn Street, Manitowoc 54220-6699, (920) 683-4700, www.manitowoc.uwc.edu

Dean: DANIEL CAMPAGNA.

Marathon County: 518 South 7th Avenue, Wausau 54401-5396, (715) 261-6100, www.uwmc.uwc.edu

Dean: SANDRA SMITH.

Marinette: 750 West Bay Shore Street, Marinette 54143-4299, (715) 735-4300, www.marinette.uwc.edu

Dean: PAULA LANGTEAU.

Marshfield/Wood County: 2000 West 5th Street, Marshfield 54449-0150, (715) 389-6500, www.marshfield.uwc.edu

Dean: ANDREW KEOGH.

Richland: 1200 Highway 14 West, Richland Center 53581-1399, (608) 647-6186, www.richland.uwc.edu

Interim Dean: DEBORAH CURETON.

Rock County: 2909 Kellogg Avenue, Janesville 53546-5699, (608) 758-6565, www.rock.uwc.edu

Dean: DIANE PILLARD.

Sheboygan: One University Drive, Sheboygan 53081-4789, (920) 459-6600, www.sheboygan.uwc.edu

Dean: AL HARDERSEN.

Washington County: 400 University Drive, West Bend 53095-3699, (262) 335-5200, www.washington.uwc.edu

Dean: DAVID NIXON.

Waukesha: 1500 North University Drive, Waukesha 53188-2799, (262) 521-5200, www.waukesha.uwc.edu

Dean: PATRICK SCHMITT.

UW-Extension

Internet Address: www.uwex.edu

Vice Chancellor/Provost: CHRISTINE QUINN, 262-6151.

Dean, Outreach and E-Learning Extension: DAVID SCHEJBAL, 262-1034.

Dean and Director, Cooperative Extension: RICK KLEMME, 263-2775.

Associate Vice Chancellor for Administrative and Financial Services: SUE SCHYMANSKI, 263-6470.

Director, Broadcasting and Media Innovations: MALCOLM BRETT, 263-2129.

Executive Director, Entrepreneurship and Economic Development: KIM KINDSCHI, 263-7794.

Assistant Vice Chancellor for Information Technology: MARSHA HENFER, 263-6012.

Secretary of the Faculty/Academic Staff: RAYMOND SCHULTZ, 262-4387.

Officers and Units Required by Statute

State Cartographer: TED KOCH, (608) 262-6852, 384 Science Hall, 550 North Park Street, Madison 53706-1491.

State Geologist: JAMES ROBERTSON, (608) 263-7384, Geological and Natural History Survey, 3817 Mineral Point Road, Madison 53705-5100.

Agricultural Safety and Health Center: CHERYL SKJOLAAS, *acting director,* (608) 265-0568, 230 Agricultural Engineering Building, 460 Henry Mall, Madison 53706.

Center for Environmental Education: RANDY CHAMPEAU, *director,* (715) 346-4973, 110 College of Natural Resources, 403 Learning Resources Center, Stevens Point 54481.

Geological and Natural History Survey: JAMES ROBERTSON, *state geologist,* (608) 262-1705, 3817 Mineral Point Road, Madison 53705-5100.

Area Health Education Center: NANCY SUGDEN, *director,* (608) 263-4927, 203 Bradley Memorial, 1300 University Avenue, Madison 53706.

Wisconsin State Herbarium: KENNETH CAMERON, *director,* (608) 262-2792, Department of Botany, Room 160, Birge Hall, Madison 53706-1381.

Psychiatric Research Institute: NED KALIN, *director,* (608) 263-6079, 6001 Research Park Boulevard, Madison 53719.

Robert M. La Follette Institute of Public Affairs: CAROLYN HEINRICH, *director,* (608) 262-5443, 1225 Observatory Drive, Madison 53706.

State Soils and Plant Analysis Laboratory: JOHN PETERS, *director,* (608) 262-4364, 8452 Mineral Point Road, Madison 53705.

Institute for Excellence in Urban Education: GAIL SCHNEIDER, *associate dean for academic affairs,* (414) 229-5253, School of Education, P.O. Box 413, UW-Milwaukee, Milwaukee 53201.

James A. Graaskamp Center for Real Estate: vacancy, *director,* (608) 262-5800, 975 University Avenue, Room 5262, Grainger Hall, Madison 53706.

School of Veterinary Medicine: DARYL BUSS, *dean,* (608) 263-6716, 2015 Linden Drive West, Madison 53706-1102.

Agency Responsibility: The prime responsibilities of the University of Wisconsin System are teaching, public service, and research. The system provides postsecondary academic education for more than 173,000 students, including 131,000 full-time equivalent undergraduates.

Organization: The UW System consists of 13 four-year universities, 13 two-year colleges, and statewide extension programs. UW-Madison and UW-Milwaukee offer bachelor's, master's, doctoral, and professional degrees. Eleven other universities in the UW System offer associate, bachelor's, and master's degree programs: UW-Eau Claire, UW-Green Bay, UW-La Crosse,

The UW-Oshkosh Student Recreation and Wellness Center was built in 2007. It encompasses several indoor courts, a cyber cafe, and exercise equipment. It also offers childcare and wellness programs. (University of Wisconsin-Oshkosh)

UW-Oshkosh, UW-Parkside, UW-Platteville, UW-River Falls, UW-Stevens Point, UW-Stout, UW-Superior, and UW-Whitewater.

The two-year UW Colleges serve local and commuter students by providing freshman-sophomore university course work that is transferable to other campuses. In addition, the colleges offer general education associate degrees. While UW colleges faculty and staff are employed by the UW System, municipalities and/or counties own the campuses and buildings in which the UW Colleges are located.

UW-Extension provides noncredit and for-credit classroom and distance learning courses, as well as continuing education and a wide range of public service programs.

The 18-member Board of Regents of the University of Wisconsin System establishes policies to govern the system and plans for the future of public higher education in Wisconsin. Two members serve *ex officio;* the student members serve staggered 2-year terms; and the other 14 members serve staggered 7-year terms. The governor may not appoint a student member from the same institution in any 2 consecutive terms.

The board appoints the president of the UW System, the chancellors of the 13 universities, the chancellor of UW-Extension and the UW Colleges, and the deans of the 13 UW Colleges. All appointees serve at the pleasure of the board. The board also sets admission standards, reviews and approves university budgets, and establishes the regulatory framework within which the individual units operate.

Unit Functions: The president of the University of Wisconsin System has full executive responsibility for system operation and management. This officer carries out the duties prescribed by statute; implements the policies established by the Board of Regents; manages and coordinates the system's administrative offices; and exercises fiscal control through budget development, management-planning programs, and coordination and evaluation of the academic programs on all campuses.

Each chancellor serves as executive head of a particular campus or program, administers board policies under the direction of the system's president, and is accountable to the board of regents. Subject to board policy, the chancellors, in consultation with their faculties, design curricula and set degree requirements; determine academic standards and establish grading systems; define and administer institutional standards for faculty peer evaluation; screen candidates for appointment, promotion, and tenure; administer auxiliary services; and control all funds allocated to or generated by their respective programs. One chancellor administers both UW Colleges and UW-Extension.

History: Today's UW System is the product of the 1971 merger of two existing university boards – the Board of Regents of the University of Wisconsin and the Board of Regents of the State Universities – and the institutions they governed.

From earliest times, Wisconsin lawmakers recognized the need for a tax-supported university. The territorial legislature passed laws in 1836, 1838, and 1839 regarding establishment and location of a university, and Article X, Section 6, of the state constitution ratified in 1848, provided for a state university at or near the seat of state government. Chapter 20, Laws of 1848, which implemented the constitutional provision, delegated university administration to a board of regents and classes began in 1849. Critical to the university's early development was Chapter 114, Laws of 1866, which reorganized the board of regents, expanded its authority, and authorized the governor to appoint the regents. The 1866 reorganization provided for instruction in agriculture on the Madison campus and an experimental farm, thereby making the university eligible, as Wisconsin's land-grant institution, to receive the proceeds derived from sale of lands granted by the federal government to support agricultural education and research.

The State Universities originated with Chapter 82, Laws of 1857, which provided funds for a system of 2-year normal schools to train teachers and created the Board of Regents of Normal Schools. The first normal school opened at Platteville in 1866 and the ninth 50 years later at Eau Claire. In 1929, the 9 normal schools became "state teachers colleges" and were authorized to offer baccalaureate degree programs. They were renamed state colleges in 1951 and state universities in 1964. Chapter 75, Laws of 1967, renamed the governing body, designating it the Board of Regents of State Universities.

The Hoeschler Clocktower, erected in the 1990s, stands at the center of the UW-La Crosse campus. La Crosse is one of 13 universities in the UW System. (University of Wisconsin-La Crosse)

Chapter 100, Laws of 1971, mandated the merger of Wisconsin's two systems of public higher education to form the University of Wisconsin System. Chapter 335, Laws of 1973, recreated Chapter 36 of the statutes and provided a single statutory charter to govern public higher education in Wisconsin. The University of Wisconsin Colleges, which were previously called UW Centers, were renamed by 1997 Wisconsin Act 237.

ORGANIZATION CREATED BY STATUTE
WITHIN THE UNIVERSITY OF WISCONSIN SYSTEM

LABORATORY OF HYGIENE

Laboratory of Hygiene Board: DARRELL BAZZELL (designated by chancellor of UW-Madison), SETH FOLDY (designated by secretary of health services), JACK SULLIVAN (designated by secretary of natural resources), SUSAN BUROKER (designated by secretary of agriculture, trade and consumer protection); ROBERT BAGLEY (local health department representative); BERNARD POESCHEL (physician representing clinical laboratories); MICHAEL RICKER (representing private environmental testing laboratories); MICHAEL RUSSELL (representing occupational health laboratories); JOHN STANLEY (medical examiner or coroner); DAVID TAYLOR, vacancy (public members). Nonvoting member: CHARLES D. BROKOPP (director, Laboratory of Hygiene). (All except *ex officio* officers or designees are appointed by governor.)

Director: CHARLES D. BROKOPP.

Medical Director: DANIEL F. KURTYCZ.

Associate Director: SHERRY GEHL.

Mailing Address: 465 Henry Mall, Madison 53706-1578; 2601 Agriculture Drive, Madison 53707-7996 (Environmental Health Division).

Telephones: (608) 262-1293; Customer service: (800) 442-4618; Administrative office: (608) 262-3911; Wisconsin Occupational Health Laboratory: (608) 224-6210, (800) 446-0403; Proficiency Testing Program: (608) 890-1800, (800) 462-5261; Environmental Health Division: (608) 224-6202, (800) 442-4618.

Internet Address: www.slh.wisc.edu

Division Fax: (608) 262-3257; Environmental Health Division Fax: (608) 224-6213.

Publications: Newborn Screening Newsletter; Occupational Health Newsletter; reference manual; annual report; research annual report, fee schedules; assorted special publications.

Number of Employees: 309.75.

Total Budget 2007-09: $66,188,600.

Statutory References: Sections 15.07 (1), 15.915 (2), and 36.25 (11).

Agency Responsibility: The Laboratory of Hygiene, headed by a director appointed by the UW Board of Regents, provides complete laboratory services for appropriate state agencies and local health departments in the areas of water quality, air quality, public health, and contagious diseases. It performs laboratory tests and consultation for physicians, health officers, local agencies, private citizens, and resource management officials to prevent and control diseases and environmental hazards. As part of the UW-Madison, the laboratory provides facilities for teaching and research in the fields of public health and environmental protection.

The laboratory operates under the direction and supervision of the Laboratory of Hygiene Board, composed of 11 members, 7 of whom are appointed by the governor to serve 3-year terms.

History: Chapter 344, Laws of 1903, created the Laboratory of Hygiene at the University of Wisconsin to examine water supplies, investigate contagious and infectious diseases, and function as the official laboratory of the State Board of Health. The executive branch reorganization act of 1967 extended the laboratory's services to the Department of Natural Resources.

Independent Units Attached for Budgeting, Program Coordination, and Related Management Functions by Section 15.03 of the Statutes

ENVIRONMENTAL EDUCATION BOARD

Environmental Education Board: Okho Bohm Hagedorn (energy representative), *chairperson;* Senators Kedzie, Risser; Representatives Friske, Molepske; Shelley Lee (designated by superintendent of public instruction), Vance Rayburn (designated by secretary of natural resources), Robin Harris (designated by president, UW System), Randy Zogbaum (designated by president, Technical College System Board); Debra McRae (nature centers, museums, zoos representative), Mike Krysiak (business and industry representative), William Neuhaus (labor representative), Gerry Mich (forestry representative), Scott Ashmann (higher education institutions faculty representative), Kathe Crowley Conn (environmental educators representative), David D. Wisnefske (conservation and environmental organizations representative), Darlene Arneson (agricultural representative). (Unless otherwise designated, members are appointed by president of UW System.)

Mailing Address: 110B College of Natural Resources, UW-Stevens Point, Stevens Point 54481.

Telephone: (715) 346-3805.

Internet Address: www.uwsp.edu/cnr/weeb

Statutory References: Sections 15.915 (6) and 115.375.

Agency Responsibility: The Environmental Education Board awards matching grants to public agencies and nonprofit corporations to develop and distribute environmental education programs. The board consults with the state's educational agencies, the Department of Natural Resources, and other state agencies to identify needs and establish priorities for environmental education. Its 17 members include 9 representatives of educational institutions and nongovernmental interest groups who are appointed to serve 3-year terms. The senate and assembly members must represent the majority and the minority parties in their respective houses. The board was created by 1989 Wisconsin Act 299 and was transferred from the Department of Public Instruction to the UW System by 1997 Wisconsin Act 27.

VETERINARY DIAGNOSTIC LABORATORY BOARD

Veterinary Diagnostic Laboratory Board: Linda Hodorff (livestock producer), *chairperson;* Robert Ehlenfeldt (designated by secretary of agriculture, trade and consumer protection), Darrell Bazzell (designated by chancellor of UW-Madison), Daryl Buss (dean of the UW-Madison School of Veterinary Medicine), vacancy (veterinarian employed by the federal government); Berwyn Cadman, Lloyd Sorenson (veterinarians); Brian McCulloh (livestock producer); Tod Fleming (animal agriculture industry representative); Thomas McKenna (laboratory director) (nonvoting member). (All except *ex officio* members are appointed by governor.)

Mailing Address: 445 Easterday Lane, Madison 53706.

Telephone: (608) 262-5432.

Fax: (847) 574-8085.

Statutory References: Sections 15.915 (1) and 36.58.

Agency Responsibility: The Veterinary Diagnostic Laboratory Board oversees the Veterinary Diagnostic Laboratory, which provides animal health testing and diagnostic services on a statewide basis for all types of animals. The board has 10 members, 6 of whom are appointed by the governor to serve staggered 3-year terms. The board prescribes policies for the laboratory's operation, develops its biennial budget, and sets fees for laboratory services. It also consults with the UW-Madison chancellor on the appointment of the laboratory director.

History: Both the board and the laboratory were created by 1999 Wisconsin Act 107, which transferred the laboratory's facilities and employees from the Department of Agriculture, Trade and Consumer Protection to the UW System, effective July 1, 2000.

Department of
VETERANS AFFAIRS

Board of Veterans Affairs: MARVIN J. FREEDMAN, *chairperson;* MARCIA M. ANDERSON, *vice chairperson;* JACQUELINE A. GUTHRIE, *secretary;* RODNEY C. MOEN, PETER J. MORAN, DANIEL J. NAYLOR, vacancy. (All are veterans appointed by governor with senate consent.)

Secretary of Veterans Affairs: JOHN A. SCOCOS, 266-1315, john.scocos@

Deputy Secretary: KENNETH B. BLACK, 266-1315, ken.black@

Executive Assistant: vacancy, 266-1315.

Legal Counsel: JAMES STEWART, 266-3733, jimmy.stewart@

Policy, Planning and Budget, Office of: KEN ABRAHAMSEN, *director,* 266-0117, ken.abrahamsen@

Public Affairs, Office of: ANDREW M. SCHUSTER, *director,* 266-1315, andrew.schuster@

Mailing Address: P.O. Box 7843, Madison 53707-7843.

Location: 30 West Mifflin Street, Madison.

Telephone: (608) 266-1311, toll free: 1-800-WIS-VETS (800-947-8387).

Fax: (608) 264-7616.

Address e-mail by combining the user ID and the state extender: userid@**dva.state.wi.us**

Internet Address: www.dva.state.wi.us

Number of Employees: 1,079.90.

Total Budget 2007-09: $288,960,700.

Statutory References: Section 15.49; Chapter 45.

Administration, Division of: TONY CAPPOZZO, *administrator,* 267-2707, tony.cappozzo@; Fax: 264-6089.

> *Administrative Services, Bureau of:* AMY FRANKE, *director,* 266-3344, amy.franke@; Fax (608) 266-5414.

> *Fiscal Services, Bureau of:* RANDALL L. KRUEGER, *director,* 267-1789, randy.krueger@

> *Information Systems, Bureau of:* CHRIS APFELBECK, *director,* 267-1794, chris.apfelbeck@

Veterans Benefits, Division of: SETH PERELMAN, *administrator,* 266-0644, seth.perelman@; Fax: (608) 267-0403.

> *Veterans Benefits, Bureau of:* CHRIS SCHULDES, *director,* 266-6783, chris.schuldes@

> *Veterans Cemeteries, Bureau of:* MARK MATHWIG, *director,* 261-0179, mark.mathwig@

>> *Military Funeral Honors Program:* (877) 944-6667, Fax: (866) 454-0356.

Veterans Homes, Division of: THOMAS RHATICAN, *administrator,* (608) 264-7619, tom.rhatican@

> Wisconsin Veterans Home, King 54946-0600, Fax: (715) 258-5736; JOHN WILLIAM CROWLEY, *commandant,* (715) 258-4241, bill.crowley@; JACKIE MOORE, *deputy commandant,* (715) 258-4251, jackie.moore@; STEVEN D'AMANDA, *adjutant,* (715) 258-4249, steven.damanda@; *Public Information/Volunteer Coordinator:* LAURA MAYS, (715) 258-4247, laura.mays@

>> *Admissions and Discharges, Bureau of:* MARGE MARONEY, *director,* (715) 258-4252, marge.maroney@

>> *Dietary Services, Bureau of:* JENNIFER HANLON, *director,* (715) 258-1679, jennifer.hanlon@

>> *Engineering/Physical Plant, Bureau of:* GEORGE KONKOL, *director,* (715) 258-4253, george.konkol@

>> *Financial Services, Bureau of:* STEVE STEAD, *director,* (715) 258-4248, steve.stead@

>> *Materials Management, Bureau of:* NANCY J. O'CONNELL, *director,* (715) 258-4245, nancy.oconnell@

DEPARTMENT OF VETERANS AFFAIRS

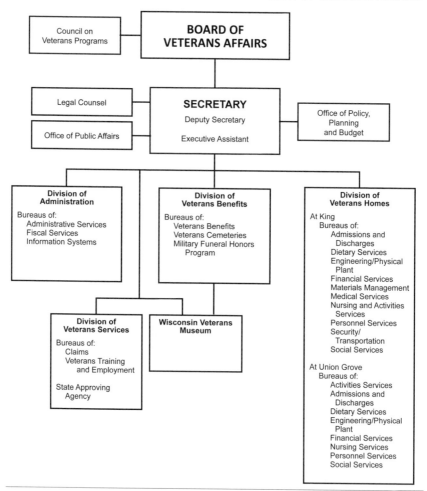

Medical Services, Bureau of: MARK LOCHNER, *director,* (715) 258-4240, mark.lochner@

Nursing and Activities Services, Bureau of: DONNA WARZYNSKI, *director,* (715) 256-3238, donna.warzynski@

Personnel Services, Bureau of: NEAL SPRANGER, *director,* (715) 258-4244, neal.spranger@

Security/Transportation, Bureau of: RON WOODS, *director,* (715) 258-1485, ron.woods@

Social Services, Bureau of: CATE GITTER, *director,* (715) 258-1660, cate.gitter@

Wisconsin Veterans Home, Union Grove, 21425D Spring Street, Union Grove 53182; RANDY NITSCHKE, *commandant,* (262) 878-6752, randy.nitschke@; PATRICK SHAUGHNESSY, *deputy commandant,* (262) 878-6724, patrick.shaughnessy@; GARY WISTROM, *adjutant,* (262) 878-6770, gary.wistrom@

Activities Services, Bureau of: DEB CANAK, *director,* (262) 878-6725, deb.canak@

Admissions and Discharges, Bureau of: JOAN CLARK, *director,* (262) 878-6749, joan.clark@

Dietary Services, Bureau of: GARY BEBLER, *director,* (262) 878-5803, gary.bebler@

Engineering/Physical Plant, Bureau of: DAVE CARROLL, *director,* (262) 878-6783, dave.carroll@.

Financial Services, Bureau of: KENNETH WIBERG, *director,* (262) 878-6797, kenneth.wiberg@

Nursing Services, Bureau of: MARIE MAGUIRE, *director,* (262) 878-6788, marie.maguire@

Personnel Services, Bureau of: RACHAEL HARRIS, *director,* (262) 878-6792, rachael.harris@

Social Services, Bureau of: KATHY MOEN, *director,* (262) 878-6729, kathy.moen@

Veterans Services, Division of: vacancy, *administrator,* 266-1311.

Claims, Bureau of: DENNIS BOHEN, *director,* VA Regional Office, 5400 West National Avenue, BM 157, Milwaukee 53214, (414) 902-5763, dennis.bohen@; Fax: (414) 902-9421.

Veterans Training and Employment, Bureau of: vacancy, *manager,* 267-7329.

State Approving Agency: JOE BERTALAN, *manager,* 267-7329, joe.bertalan@

Wisconsin Veterans Museum: TONY CAPPOZZO, *acting director,* 267-7207, tony.cappozzo@

Publications: *The Bugle; The Courier; Old Abe the War Eagle; USS Wisconsin; ForwardVETERANS, WDVA Update; Wisconsin in the Civil War; Wisconsin's Warriors;* brochures on the state veterans' programs and services for Wisconsin veterans, Wisconsin Veterans Museum (Madison), the Wisconsin Veterans Home (King), the Wisconsin Veterans Home (Union Grove), and Wisconsin's veterans memorial cemeteries.

Agency Responsibility: The Department of Veterans Affairs provides educational and economic assistance to eligible veterans of the U.S. Armed Forces and their dependents through loan and grant programs. It also operates the Wisconsin veterans homes at King and Union Grove, the Wisconsin Veterans Museum in Madison, the Southern Wisconsin Veterans Memorial Cemetery at Union Grove, the Northern Wisconsin Veterans Memorial Cemetery near Spooner, and the Central Wisconsin Veterans Memorial Cemetery at King.

The department currently serves an estimated 470,000 veterans living in Wisconsin, including approximately 76,200 veterans of the World War II era, 65,200 from the Korean War era, 150,000 from the Vietnam War era, and 66,000 from the Gulf War era.

Organization: The department is headed by a board of 7 members who serve staggered 6-year terms. All board members must be veterans, as defined by statute, and at least 2 must be Vietnam War veterans. Administrative powers and duties are exercised by the department secretary, who is appointed by the board.

Unit Functions: The *Division of Administration* administers data processing and fiscal management, systems analysis, human resources, personnel benefits and training, procurement, verification and processing of veterans' eligibility applications, and veterans' disability and pension claims.

The *Division of Veterans Benefits* administers loan and emergency grant programs offered by the state, state veteran cemeteries, and the state military funeral honors program.

The department offers 30-year fixed rate home loans as well as home improvement loans with terms up to 15 years. These loan programs are funded through self-amortizing general obligation bonds. The division's property management section maintains properties reclaimed by foreclosure due to loan defaults and arranges to sell them at fair market value to recoup loan expenses.

The department also offers through the division of veterans benefits, personal loans to qualified veterans. These loans can be used for any purpose. Personal loans under this program are funded through the veterans trust fund. Revenue from these loans funds veteran benefits and department operating costs.

The Northern Wisconsin Veterans Memorial Cemetery, near Spooner, opened in 2000. The Department of Veterans Affairs also operates cemeteries, at which eligible veterans and family members may be interred, at Union Grove and King. (Department of Veterans Affairs)

Emergency grants are available to qualified veterans to provide subsistence aid for veterans who have experienced a loss of income due to illness or disability, and veterans who require health care that cannot be obtained through other means. These grants have strict income and asset limits.

The division provides administration for the veterans memorial cemeteries. These cemeteries provide burial space for veterans, their spouses, and eligible family members. Veterans can be buried free of charge; non-veteran spouses and family members are charged a burial fee.

The division administers the military funeral honors program, coordinating the efforts of veterans service organizations, the active duty military and reserve forces, as well as the Wisconsin National Guard. The division provides training of veteran organizations and military units who provide military funeral honors requested by the family. The division has limited capability to provide military funeral honors teams with departmental staff.

The *Division of Veterans Homes* administers the state's facilities for eligible veterans who are permanently incapacitated from performing any substantially gainful employment due to age or physical disability and who may be admitted if they meet service and residency criteria. Applicants must apply their income and resources to the cost of their care as required by Medicaid eligibility standards. The spouses of eligible veterans may also be admitted.

The Wisconsin Veterans Home at King serves approximately 740 members. It includes licensed skilled nursing care buildings, cottages for married couples, and the Central Wisconsin Veterans Memorial Cemetery. Residents receive complete medical and nursing care, along with therapeutic treatments and social services. Veterans and spouses or surviving spouses may be admitted at King.

The Wisconsin Veterans Home at Union Grove is capable of serving 240 members by providing three assisted living residences and a 120-bed skilled nursing facility. This continuum of care is available to veterans and their spouses and offers assistance with health care, daily living needs, memory care, short-term rehabilitation, and long-term care.

The *Division of Veterans Services* administers education and employment services programs, claims services, and transition assistance programs.

As part of the Bureau of Veterans Training and Employment, the Veterans Assistance Program operates veterans assistance centers in Tomah, King, and Union Grove. Through the centers, homeless veterans and veterans at risk of becoming homeless receive education, job training, and rehabilitative services to enable them to obtain steady employment and affordable housing. The program is a joint effort with the U.S. Department of Veterans Affairs and community-based agencies and is supplemented by service delivery support and outreach to veterans service organizations, veterans health care facilities, and correctional institutions. The bureau also provides an array of employment and educational services to include transition assistance, grants, job referrals, academic credit for military experience programs, and assistance in obtaining teaching credentials through the Troops to Teachers Program.

The State Approving Agency coordinates programs and approves schools to assist veterans to effectively use their GI Bill benefits.

The *Wisconsin Veterans Museum* in Madison is dedicated to Wisconsin veterans of all wars. It houses and exhibits artifacts related to Wisconsin's participation in U.S. military actions from the Civil War to the present and offers programs to the public on the history of Wisconsin's war efforts. It also houses exhibits and archives documenting the history of the Wisconsin National Guard and operates the Wisconsin National Guard Museum at Camp Douglas.

History: Legislation to benefit Wisconsin veterans dates back to the post-Civil War era. Most of the enactments between the Civil War and World War I were concerned with providing relief for destitute veterans and their families. In 1887, the Grand Army of the Republic (GAR), the prominent Civil War veterans' organization, founded the Grand Army Home at King, supported by private donations and federal and state subsidies. Now called the Wisconsin Veterans Home, the institution was first operated by the GAR and later by a state board and the adjutant general's office. Further recognition of Civil War veterans came in 1901, when the legislature established a Grand Army of the Republic headquarters and museum in the State Capitol. In 1993, the state opened the Wisconsin Veterans Museum in a separate building on the Capitol Square. The Southern Wisconsin Veterans Home at Union Grove, authorized in 1999 Wisconsin Act 9, opened in 2001.

After World War I, the 1919 Legislature granted a cash bonus, or alternatively an education bonus, to soldiers who fought in the war. It also created a fund for the relief of sick, wounded, or disabled veterans, administered by the Service Recognition Board and later its successor, the Soldiers' Rehabilitation Board. Other legislation between World Wars I and II provided funds for hospitalization, memorials, and free courses through the University of Wisconsin-Extension.

Chapter 443, Laws of 1943, created the Veterans Recognition Board to provide medical, hospital, educational, and economic assistance to returning Wisconsin veterans of World War II and their dependents.

The creation of the Department of Veterans Affairs by Chapter 580, Laws of 1945, brought all veterans programs under a single agency. The department absorbed the Grand Army Home, the GAR Memorial Hall, the veterans claim services, and the Soldiers' Rehabilitation Board. The department was assigned the economic aid, hospital care, and education grants programs. It also took over three segregated veterans funds that were combined into the Veterans Trust Fund in 1961.

Two major new programs relating to housing and education were implemented after World War II. Beginning with legislation in 1947, programs were established to help veterans finance home loans through a trust fund. The state supreme court declared earmarking liquor tax moneys for the fund unconstitutional under the internal improvements clause, but a constitutional amendment, approved by the voters in 1949, resolved the problem. Chapter 627, Laws of 1949, authorized loans to qualified veterans for a portion of the value of their housing. The legislature converted this program to a second mortgage home loan program in 1973, when it established the Primary Home Loan Program that is financed with general obligation bonds. The state's use of general obligation bonding to offer home loans to veterans raised constitutional concerns. The legislature responded by proposing an amendment to the Wisconsin Constitution, which the voters ratified in April 1975.

1997 Wisconsin Act 27 expanded eligibility for state veterans benefits to any person who has served on active duty in the U.S. armed forces for two continuous years or the full period of the individual's initial service obligation, whichever is less, regardless of when or where the service occurred, including during peacetime. Previously, to be considered a "veteran" for the purposes of state benefits, a person must generally have performed active service for 90 days or more during a designated war period or a period of duty during specified conflicts or peacekeeping operations.

1999 Wisconsin Act 136 required the department to administer a program to coordinate the provision of military funeral honors to eligible deceased veterans. 2003 Wisconsin Act 102 authorized the department to develop and operate residential, treatment, and nursing care facilities in northwestern Wisconsin, on surplus land located at the Northern Wisconsin Center for the Developmentally Disabled in Chippewa Falls.

Statutory Council

Council on Veterans Programs: JOHN MARGOWSKI (Vietnam Veterans of America), *chairperson;* RICK CHERONE (Military Order of the Purple Heart), *vice chairperson;* RUSS ALSTEEN (Navy Club of the U.S.A.), *secretary;* CHARLES ROLOFF (American Legion), CLARENCE STOEL (Disabled American Veterans), STEVE LAWRENCE (Veterans of Foreign Wars), MARK GRAMS (Marine Corps League), TIMOTHY THIERS (AMVETS), WALTER PETERSON (American Ex-Prisoners of War), MARK FOREMAN (Vietnam Veterans Against the War), JESSE HARO (Catholic War Veterans of the U.S.A.), PAUL WEPRINSKY (Jewish War Veterans of the U.S.A.), JERRY RABETSKY (Polish Legion of American Veterans), WILLIAM SIMS (National Association for Black Veterans, Inc.), PAUL FINE (Army and Navy Union of the United States of America), CLIFTON SORENSON (Wisconsin Association of Concerned Veterans Organizations), CONNIE ALLORD (United Women Veterans, Inc.), CLEON BROWN (U.S. Submarine Veterans of World War II), WILLIAM HUSTAD (Wisconsin Vietnam Veterans, Inc.), MAX OLESON (American Red Cross), KEN BROWN (County Veterans Service Officers Association), JACK STONE (Wisconsin Chapter of the Paralyzed Veterans of America), ROGER FETTERLY (Wisconsin Council of the Military Officers Association of America), RICK LANGAN (Retired Enlisted Association). (All are appointed by their respective organizations.)

The Council on Veterans Programs studies and presents policy alternatives and recommendations to the Board of Veterans Affairs. It is comprised of representatives appointed for one-year terms by organizations that have a direct interest in veterans' affairs. The council was created by Chapter 443, Laws of 1943, and its composition and duties are prescribed in Sections 15.497 and 45.35 (3d) of the statutes.

Department of
WORKFORCE DEVELOPMENT

Secretary of Workforce Development: ROBERTA GASSMAN, 267-1410,
  roberta.gassman@

Deputy Secretary: JOANNA RICHARD, 267-3200, joanna.richard@

Executive Assistant: JESSICA ERICKSON, 266-6753, jessica.erickson@

Legal Counsel: HOWARD BERNSTEIN, 266-9427, howard.bernstein@

Chief Information Officer (information technology): ROSE LYNCH, 261-2131, rose.lynch@

Communications Director: vacancy.

Office of Economic Advisors: DENNIS WINTERS, 267-3262, dennis.winters@

Office of Policy and Budget: vacancy.

Tribal Liaison: RACHELLE ASHLEY, 261-4883, rachelle.ashley@

Mailing Address: P.O. Box 7946, Madison 53707-7946.

Location: 201 East Washington Avenue, Madison.

Telephone: (608) 266-3131.

Fax: (608) 266-1784.

Internet Address: www.dwd.state.wi.us

Publications: Contact individual divisions for publications.

Number of Employees: 1,639.96.

Total Budget 2007-09: $1,335,025,500.

Statutory References: Sections 15.22, 15.223, 15.225, and 15.227; Chapters 49, 102-106, 108, 109, and 111.

Address e-mail by combining the user ID and the state extender: userid@**dwd.wisconsin.gov**

Administrative Services Division: SUSAN D. CANTY, *administrator,* 261-4599, susan.canty@; GREGORY R. SMITH, *assistant administrator,* 261-2138, gregoryr.smith@

> *Finance, Bureau of:* TAMI MOE, *acting director and controller,* 261-4582, tami.moe@
>
> *General Services, Bureau of:* JOHN WALKER, *director,* 266-1777, john.walker@
>
> *Human Resource Services, Bureau of:* GERALD GUENTHER, *director,* 266-6496, gerald.guenther@
>
> *Information Technology Services, Bureau of:* VINNIE THOUSAND, *director,* 266-5588, vinnie.thousand@

Employment and Training, Division of: RON DANOWSKI, *administrator,* 266-3485, ron.danowski@; JAMES BOND, *deputy administrator,* 266-3623, james.bond@

> *Apprenticeship Standards, Bureau of:* KAREN P. MORGAN, *director,* 266-3133, karen.morgan@
>
> *Job Service, Bureau of:* BRIAN SOLOMON, *director,* 267-7514, brian.solomon@
>
> *Migrant, Refugee and Labor Services, Bureau of:* JUAN JOSE LOPEZ, *director,* 266-0002, juan.lopez@
>
> *Program Management and IT Coordination, Bureau of:* JOAN LARSEN, *director,* 266-6721, joan.larson@
>
> *Workforce Trainings, Bureau of:* GARY DENIS *director,* 266-6886, gary.denis@
>
> *Regional Offices:*
>
>> *Ashland:* 411 Ellis Avenue, P.O. Box 72, Ashland 54806-0072, (715) 682-7285.
>>
>> *Eau Claire:* 221 West Madison Street, Suite 218, Eau Claire 54703-4404, (715) 836-2177.
>>
>> *Green Bay:* 701 Cherry Street, Green Bay 54301, (920) 448-6760.
>>
>> *Madison:* 3319 West Beltline Highway, Room E234, Madison 53713-2834, (608) 243-2404.
>>
>> *Milwaukee:* 819 North 6th Street, 8th Floor, Milwaukee 53203-1697, (414) 227-4836.
>>
>> *Rhinelander:* P.O. Box 697, 100 West Keenan Street, Rhinelander 54501, (715) 365-2568.
>>
>> *Waukesha:* 141 NW Barstow Street, Room 157, Waukesha 53188-3789, (262) 521-5303.

Equal Rights Division: JENNIFER ORTIZ, *administrator,* 266-0946, jennifer.ortiz@; Division TTY: 264-8752.

> *Civil Rights, Bureau of:* LEANNA WARE, *director,* 266-1997, leanna.ware@
>
> *Labor Standards, Bureau of:* ROBERT ANDERSON, *director,* 266-3345, bob.anderson@
>
> *Support Services, Office of:* LYNN HENDRICKSON, *manager,* 266-7560, lynn.hendrickson@

DEPARTMENT OF WORKFORCE DEVELOPMENT

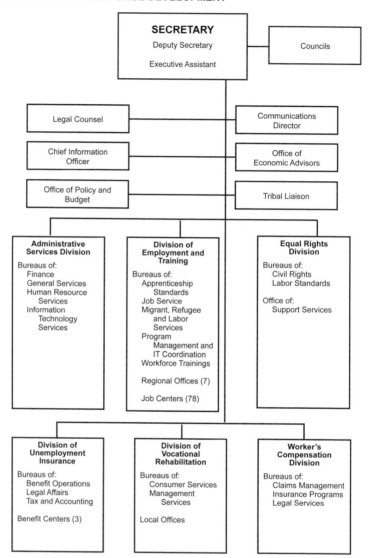

Unit attached for administrative purposes under Sec. 15.03:   Labor and Industry Review Commission

Unemployment Insurance, Division of: HAL BERGAN, *administrator,* 266-8533, hal.bergan@;
  ANDREA REID, *deputy administrator,* 266-7192, andrea.reid@

  Benefit Operations, Bureau of: LUTFI SHAHRANI, *director,* 266-8211, lutfi.shahrani@

  Legal Affairs, Bureau of: DANIEL J. LAROCQUE, *director,* 267-1406, daniel.larocque@

  Tax and Accounting, Bureau of: THOMAS MCHUGH, *director,* 266-3130, thomas.mchugh@

Benefit Centers:

Madison: Initial claims: (608) 232-0678; Employee inquiries: (608) 232-0824; Employer inquiries: (608) 232-0633.

Milwaukee: Initial claims: (414) 438-7700; Employee inquiries: (414) 438-7713; Employer inquiries: (414) 438-7705.

Statewide: Initial claims: (800) 822-5246; Employee inquiries: (800) 494-4944; Employer inquiries: (800) 247-1744.

Vocational Rehabilitation, Division of: Charlene Dwyer, *administrator,* (608) 261-2126, charlene.dwyer@; Manuel Lugo, *deputy administrator,* (608) 261-0074, manuel.lugo@; Division TTY: (608) 243-5601.

Consumer Services, Bureau of: Michael Greco, *director,* 261-4576, michael.greco@

Management Services, Bureau of: Joseph D'Costa, *director,* 261-0073, joseph.dcosta@

Local Offices: To contact a local DVR office, call (800) 442-3477 or visit http://dwd.wisconsin.gov/dvr/locations/default.htm

Worker's Compensation Division: Frances Huntley-Cooper, *administrator,* 266-6841, frances.huntley-cooper@; John Conway, *deputy administrator,* 266-0337, john.conway@

Claims Management, Bureau of: Tracy Aiello, *director,* 267-9407, tracy.aiello@

Insurance Programs, Bureau of: Brian Krueger, *director,* 267-4415, brian.krueger@

Legal Services, Bureau of: Jim O'Malley, *director,* 267-6704, jim.omalley@

Agency Responsibility: The Department of Workforce Development conducts a variety of work-related programs designed to connect people with employment opportunities in Wisconsin. It has major responsibility for the state's employment and training services; job centers; job training and placement services provided in cooperation with private sector employers; apprenticeship programs; and employment-related services for people with disabilities. It oversees the unemployment insurance and worker's compensation programs and is also responsible for adjudicating cases involving employment discrimination, housing discrimination, and labor law.

Organization: The department is administered by a secretary who is appointed by the governor with the advice and consent of the senate. The secretary appoints the division administrators from outside the classified service.

Unit Functions: The *Administrative Services Division* provides management and program support to the other divisions, including facilities, finance, human resources, and information technology services.

The *Division of Employment and Training* oversees all workforce services administered by the department including the state labor exchange system; analyzes and distributes labor market information; monitors migrant worker services; and operates the state apprenticeship program. The division also administers a comprehensive interdepartmental employment and training system through public-private partnerships and a statewide network of 78 job centers.

The *Equal Rights Division,* created by Chapter 327, Laws of 1967, enforces state laws that protect citizens from discrimination in employment, housing, and public accommodations. It also administers the enforcement of family and medical leave laws and the labor laws relating to hours, conditions of work, minimum wage standards, and timely payment of wages. It determines prevailing wage rates and enforces them for state and municipal public works projects not including highway projects. The division also enforces child labor laws and plant closing laws.

The *Division of Unemployment Insurance* administers programs to pay benefits to unemployed workers, collect employer taxes, resolve contested benefit claims and employer tax issues, detect unemployment insurance fraud, and collect unemployment insurance overpayments and delinquent taxes. The division also collects wage information for national and Wisconsin New Hire Directory databases.

The *Division of Vocational Rehabilitation* provides employment services to individuals who have significant physical and mental disabilities that create barriers in obtaining, maintaining, or improving employment. Each person is counseled and may receive medical, psychological, and vocational evaluations and training services. Employment programs, which are supported through state and federal funding, include vocational rehabilitation for eligible persons with disabilities; supported employment, including job coaching for individuals with severe disabilities; and the Business Enterprise Program, which establishes business or vending stand locations for individuals who are legally blind.

The *Worker's Compensation Division* administers programs designed to ensure that injured workers receive required benefits from insurers or self-insured employers; encourage rehabilitation and reemployment for injured workers; and promote the reduction of work-related injuries, illnesses, and deaths.

History: In response to the state's industrialization, which began in the 1880s, Wisconsin took the lead nationally in adjusting labor laws to modern industrial conditions. Based on European models, the legislature adopted social insurance, whereby the costs of correcting labor problems, such as worker injuries and unemployment, were imposed on employers as an inducement to prevent the problems.

Wisconsin's laws, enacted during the early part of the 20th century, dealt with minimum wages, conditions of employment for women and children, worker's compensation, free public employment offices, apprenticeship standards, and job safety regulations. Many of these programs served as models for legislation in other states. Wisconsin's original worker's compensation act (Chapter 50, Laws of 1911) was the first state law of its kind in the nation. In the 1930s, Wisconsin led in developing the unemployment compensation system (Chapter 20, Laws of Special Session 1931) and issued the first benefit check in the nation in 1936.

Since World War II, Wisconsin has enacted legislation prohibiting discrimination in employment on the basis of race, sex, creed, national origin, marital status, ancestry, arrest or conviction record, off-duty use of lawful products, membership in military reserve, sexual orientation, age, and disability. Similar laws now protect access to housing and public accommodations.

Early in the 20th century, the state delegated labor law administration to a politically independent body of experts, the State Industrial Commission, and its advisory committees. The commission was encouraged to solve problems through administrative decision making and the development of administrative rules to supplement the laws. A close tie between state government and the University of Wisconsin enabled the governor and legislature to translate reforms conceived in the academic arena into law. This cooperative meshing of academic research and government action came to be known as "The Wisconsin Idea".

The Department of Workforce Development evolved from the Wisconsin Bureau of Labor Statistics, which was created in 1883. The bureau was succeeded by the State Industrial Commission in 1911. Following the 1967 executive branch reorganization, the commission directed the new Department of Industry, Labor and Human Relations (DILHR) and was renamed the Industry, Labor and Human Relations Commission by Chapter 276, Laws of 1969. The commission was replaced by a secretary in Chapter 29, Laws of 1977.

Effective July 1, 1996, the Department of Industry, Labor and Human Relations was renamed the Department of Industry, Labor and Job Development by 1995 Wisconsin Act 29, but the department was given the option of using the name Department of Workforce Development in 1995 Wisconsin Act 289. It formally chose to exercise that option beginning July 1, 1996, and the legislature officially recognized the name choice in 1997 Wisconsin Act 3.

The department was significantly altered by 1995 Wisconsin Act 27. It assumed many duties formerly performed by other agencies, in particular supervision of welfare and income maintenance programs and vocational rehabilitation services, which were transferred from the former Department of Health and Social Services. At the same time, the Division of Safety and Buildings was transferred out of the department to the new Department of Commerce. 1997 Wisconsin Act 191 assigned the department primary responsibility for establishing and operating a statewide system for enforcing child, family, and spousal support obligations, including expanded authority to deny, revoke, or suspend various licenses, permits, and credentials of delinquent payors.

The statutes provide that the minimum wage is set through the administrative rules process, which includes legislative review. In January 2004, the secretary established the Minimum

Wage Advisory Council to recommend an appropriate increase in the minimum wage. The council was comprised of representatives from business, labor organizations, the university system, and the legislature, and issued its final report on May 1, 2004.

2007 Wisconsin Act 20 created the Department of Children and Families (DCF), beginning July 1, 2008. It also changed the name of the Department of Health and Family Services (DHFS) to the Department of Health Services and split the responsibilities of DHFS between the two departments. Act 20 also transferred from the Department of Workforce Development to DCF administration of Wisconsin Works, including the child care subsidy program, child support enforcement and paternity establishment, and programs related to temporary assistance to needy families (TANF).

Statutory Councils

Wisconsin Apprenticeship Council: WAYNE BELANGER, EARL BUFORD, GERT GROHMANN, TERRY HAYDEN, HENRY HURT, BRENT KINDRED, MIKE LEWIN, MARCI MARQUARDT, JOHN METCALF, JAMES MOORE, DAVID NEWBY, JAMES NOWAK, ROBERT RIBERICH, BENITO RODRIGUEZ, SUSAN SCAFFIDI, TOM SCHOENBERGER, RON SPLAN, CLAY TSCHILLARD, DANIEL VANDEN BUSH, MARJORIE WOOD. (All are appointed by the Labor and Industry Review Commission.)

Mailing Address: P.O. Box 7972, Madison 53707-7972.

Telephone: (608) 266-3133.

The Wisconsin Apprenticeship Council advises the department on matters pertaining to Wisconsin's apprenticeship system. The statutes do not stipulate the number of council members. The council was created by Chapter 29, Laws of 1977, and its duties and composition are prescribed in Sections 15.09 (5) and 15.227 (13) of the statutes.

Labor and Management Council: Inactive.

The 21-member Labor and Management Council provides a forum for labor, management, and public sector representatives to discuss issues that affect the state's economy and to foster positive labor-management relations in the workplace. Council members serve 5-year terms. The council was created by 1987 Wisconsin Act 27, and its composition and duties are prescribed in Section 15.227 (17) of the statutes.

Migrant Labor, Council on: REPRESENTATIVE COLÓN, *chairperson;* LUPE MARTINEZ (migrant representative), *vice chairperson;* JENNIFER A. CLOUTE (migrant employer representative), *secretary;* SENATORS KAPANKE, WIRCH; REPRESENTATIVE TOWNSEND; JOHN I. BAUKNECHT, JOHN F. EBBOTT, ENRIQUE FIGUEROA, RACHEL RODRIGUEZ, vacancy (migrant representatives); JAMES KERN, RICHARD W. OKRAY, LILIANA PARODI, STEVE ZIOBRO, vacancy (migrant employer representatives). (All except legislative members are appointed by governor.)

The 16-member Council on Migrant Labor advises the department and other state officials about matters affecting migrant workers. The council's 4 legislator members represent the two major political parties and are appointed "to act as representatives of the public". The nonlegislative members serve 3-year terms. The council was created by Chapter 17, Laws of 1977, and its composition and duties are prescribed in Sections 15.227 (8), 103.967, and 103.968 of the statutes.

Self-Insurers Council: MICHAEL FONTAINE, KEITH W. GARRETT, JILL E. JOSWIAK, RICK KANTE, CHRISTINE MCKINZIE (appointed by secretary of workforce development).

The 5-member Self-Insurers Council advises the department about matters related to companies that cover their own worker's compensation losses rather than insuring them with an insurance carrier. Members are appointed for 3-year terms by the secretary of the department. The council was created by Chapter 29, Laws of 1977, and its duties and composition are prescribed in Sections 15.09 (5) and 15.227 (11) of the statutes.

Unemployment Insurance, Council on: DANIEL J. LAROQUE (permanent classified employee of department) (nonvoting member), *chairperson;* JAMES BUCHEN, EARL GUSTAFSON, SUSAN FRICANO HAINE, DANIEL PETERSEN (employer representatives); ED LUMP (employer representative, small business owner or representing small business association); SALLY FEISTEL, PHILLIP NEUENFELDT, DENNIS PENKALSKI, ANTHONY RAINEY, PATRICIA L. YUNK (employee representatives). (All are appointed by secretary of workforce development.)

The 11-member Council on Unemployment Insurance advises the legislature and the department about unemployment compensation matters. It includes 5 employers and 5 labor representatives who are appointed for 6-year terms, plus a permanent, classified employee of the department who acts as the council's nonvoting chairperson. In making council appointments, the secretary must consider "balanced representation of the industrial, commercial, construction, nonprofit and public sectors of the state's economy." One employer representative must be a small business owner or represent a small business association. The council was created as the Council on Unemployment Compensation by Chapter 327, Laws of 1967. Its name was changed by 1997 Wisconsin Act 39. Its composition and duties are prescribed in Sections 15.227 (3) and 108.14 (5) of the statutes.

Worker's Compensation, Council on: FRANCES HUNTLEY-COOPER (nonvoting member), *chairperson;* JEFFREY J. BEIRIGER, JEFFREY BRAND, JAMES A. BUCHEN, MARY NUGENT (employer representatives); CHRISTINE PEHLER (employer representative, small business owner or representing small business association); RON KENT, DAVID NEWBY, SCOTT REDMAN, BRAD SCHWANDA, CAROL VETTER (employee representatives); DAVID COLLINGWOOD, JODI CONNORS, BRUCE OLSON (nonvoting insurance company representatives). (All are appointed by secretary of workforce development.)

The 14-member Council on Worker's Compensation is appointed by the secretary of the department to advise the legislature and the department about worker's compensation and related matters. The council was created by Chapter 281, Laws of 1963, as the Advisory Committee on Workmen's Compensation, appointed by the Industrial Commission. It was given its current name and located in the Department of Industry, Labor and Human Relations by Chapter 327, Laws of 1967. The council includes three nonvoting representatives of insurers authorized to do worker's compensation insurance business in Wisconsin and a department employee acting as chairperson. The council's composition and duties are prescribed in Sections 15.227 (4) and 102.14 (2) of the statutes.

Health Care Provider Advisory Committee: FRANCES HUNTLEY-COOPER (administrator, worker's compensation division), *chairperson;* DAVID BRYCE, GINA BUONO, MARY JO CAPODICE, MAJA JURISIC, STEVEN KIRKHORN, MIKE LISCHAK (medical doctors); JEFF LYNE, PETER SCHUBBE (chiropractors); AMANDA GILLILAND, TIMOTHY WALDOCH (hospital representatives); BARB JANUSIAK (registered nurse); JENNIFER POLLAK (physical therapist); RON H. STARK, SRI VASUDEVAN (at-large members). (All are appointed pursuant to Section DWD 81.14 (1), Wisconsin Administrative Code.)

The Health Care Provider Advisory Committee advises the department and the Council on Worker's Compensation on guidelines related to the modification of standards of medical treatment of employees with compensable worker's compensation injuries. Section 102.15 (2m) (g), created by 2005 Wisconsin Act 172, directs the department to establish the committee, but does not specify its membership. Section DWD 81.14 (1), Wisconsin Administrative Code, created in the Wisconsin Administrative Register of October 2007, Number 622, provides that the committee is to be composed of the administrator of the worker's compensation division as chairperson, and 14 other members: 6 doctors of different specialties, 2 chiropractors, 2 hospital representatives, 1 registered nurse, 1 physical therapist, and 2 at-large members. All except the chairperson must be licensed and practicing in Wisconsin, and provide treatment under Section 102.42. Appointments are made by the department from a consensus list of 24 names submitted by the Wisconsin Medical Society, the Wisconsin Chiropractic Association, and the Wisconsin Hospital Association, with the exception of the 2 at-large members selected by the department.

INDEPENDENT UNIT ATTACHED FOR PROGRAM COORDINATION AND RELATED MANAGEMENT FUNCTIONS BY SECTION 15.03 OF THE STATUTES

LABOR AND INDUSTRY REVIEW COMMISSION

Labor and Industry Review Commission: JAMES T. FLYNN, *chairperson;* ANN CRUMP, ROBERT GLASER (appointed by governor with senate consent).

General Counsel: JAMES L. PFLASTERER, james.pflasterer@dwd.wisconsin.gov

Mailing Address: P.O. Box 8126, Madison 53708-8126.

Location: Public Broadcasting Building, 3319 West Beltline Highway, Madison.

Telephone: (608) 266-9850.

Fax: (608) 267-4409.

E-mail Address: lirc@dwd.wisconsin.gov

Internet Address: http://dwd.wisconsin.gov/lirc

Publications: Informational brochure.

Number of Employees: 25.68.

Total Budget 2007-09: $6,504,800.

Statutory References: Sections 15.225, 15.227, and 103.04.

Agency Responsibility: The 3-member Labor and Industry Review Commission is a quasi-judicial body, created by Chapter 29, Laws of 1977, which handles petitions seeking review of the decisions of the Department of Workforce Development related to unemployment insurance, worker's compensation, fair employment, and public accommodations. It also hears appeals about discrimination in postsecondary education involving a person's physical condition or developmental disability. Commission decisions may be appealed to the circuit court. Commission decisions are enforced by the Department of Justice or the commission's legal staff. Commission members serve full-time for staggered 6-year terms, and they select a chairperson from their membership to serve for a 2-year period. By law, the commission's budget must be transmitted to the governor by the department without modification, unless the commission agrees to the change.

Signing of the first workmen's compensation check in 1911. (State Historical Society #WHi (X3) 22668)

STATE AUTHORITIES

Authorities are public, corporate bodies created for specific purposes.

WISCONSIN AEROSPACE AUTHORITY

Members: THOMAS CRABB (public member), *chairperson;* MARK HANNA (public member), *vice chairperson;* THOMAS MULLOOLY (public member), *secretary-treasurer;* SENATOR LEIBHAM (appointed by senate president); REPRESENTATIVE KESTELL (appointed by assembly speaker); R. AILEEN YINGST (Wisconsin Space Grant Consortium director); MARK LEE, JUDITH SCHIEBLE, EDWARD WAGNER (public members).

Executive Director: vacancy.

Statutory References: Sections 114.60-114.78.

Agency Responsibility: The Wisconsin Aerospace Authority is directed to promote the state's aerospace industry by developing a business plan in cooperation with the Wisconsin Space Grant Consortium, securing adequate funding for spaceport facilities and services, sponsoring events to attract space-related businesses, advertising the use of spaceports to the public, and establishing a safety program. As the central clearinghouse, the authority will coordinate access to information and services related to the aerospace industry in Wisconsin. The authority will also analyze the aerospace industry, recommend actions to be taken by the state, and issue annual reports.

Organization: The authority is a public corporation consisting of the director of the Wisconsin Space Grant Consortium and 8 members serving 3-year terms. One member is a state senator appointed by the president of the senate and one member is a state representative appointed by the speaker of the assembly. The 6 public members are nominated by the governor with the consent of the senate and must be Wisconsin residents with experience in the commercial space industry, education, finance, or some other significant experience related to the functions of the authority.

The authority was created by 2005 Wisconsin Act 335.

FOX RIVER NAVIGATIONAL SYSTEM AUTHORITY

Board of Directors: RONALD VAN DE HEY (Outagamie County representative), *chairperson;* BILL RAATHS (Winnebago County representative), *vice chairperson/treasurer;* WILL STARK (Brown County representative), *secretary;* TIMOTHY ROSE (Outagamie County representative); JACK NELSON (Winnebago County representative); CELESTINE JEFFREYS (Brown County representative); CHARLES VERHOEVEN (designated by secretary of natural resources); WILL DORSEY (designated by secretary of transportation); JIM DRAEGER (designated by director, state historical society) (county residents are appointed by the governor).

Chief Executive Officer: HARLAN P. KIESOW.

Telephone: (920) 759-9833.

Number of Employees: 10.50 (not state funded).

Total Budget 2007-09: $352,600.

Statutory References: Chapter 237.

Agency Responsibility: The Fox River Navigational System Authority will rehabilitate, repair, and manage the navigation system on or near the Fox River in 3 counties, once the federal government transfers the ownership of the navigational system to the State of Wisconsin and the authority enters into a lease agreement with the Department of Administration (DOA). The authority may enter into contracts with third parties to replace, repair, rehabilitate, and operate the system. It may not sublease all or any part of the navigational system without DOA approval. It may enter into contracts with nonprofit organizations to raise funds. The authority may charge fees for services provided to watercraft owners and users of navigational facilities. While the authority may contract debt, it may not issue bonds. It must submit a management plan to DOA that addresses the costs of operating the navigational system and how it will manage its funds. In addition, it must submit an audited financial statement annually.

Organization: The Fox River Navigational System Authority is a public corporation consisting of 9 members. The 6 members the governor appoints serve 3-year terms. At least one member from each of the 3 counties must be a resident of a city, village, or town in which a navigational system lock is located. The board appoints the chief executive officer to serve at its pleasure. The authority was created by 2001 Wisconsin Act 16.

HEALTH INSURANCE RISK-SHARING PLAN AUTHORITY

Board of Directors: DENNIS CONTA, *chairperson;* CAROL PEIRICK, LARRY RAMBO, LARRY ZANONI, vacancy (represent insurers participating in the plan); MICHELLE BACHHUBER (Wisconsin Medical Society representative); JOE KACHELSKI (Wisconsin Hospital Association, Inc., representative); WAYNE MACARDY (Pharmacy Society of Wisconsin representative); MICHAEL GIFFORD (health care providers representative); DEBORAH SEVERSON (small business representative); DIANNE GREENLEY (professional consumer advocate); LUANN SIMPSON, ANNETTE STEBBINS (persons with coverage under plan). Nonvoting member: EILEEN MALLOW (designated by commissioner of insurance).

Executive Director: AMIE GOLDMAN.

Mailing Address: 33 East Main Street, Suite 230, Madison 53703.

Telephone: (608) 441-5777.

Fax: (608) 441-5667.

Agency E-mail Address: info@hirsp.org

Internet Address: www.hirsp.org

Publications: Quarterly Newsletter "News from the HIRSP Authority"; Monthly "Financial and Policyholder Activity Report".

Number of Employees: 4.00.

Statutory References: Sections 149.41-149.53.

Agency Responsibility: The Health Insurance Risk-Sharing Plan Authority is responsible for the operation of the Health Insurance Risk-Sharing Plan (HIRSP), which provides health insurance to Wisconsin residents who are unable to find adequate coverage in the private market due to their medical conditions or who have lost their employer-sponsored group health insurance. The authority can adopt policies for the operation of the plan, enter into contracts for the plan's administration, and pay the operating and administrative expenses from a designated fund. The authority is also tasked with maintaining the plan as a state pharmacy assistance program and reporting annually to both the legislature and the governor on the operation of the plan.

Organization: The authority is a public corporation consisting of a 13-member board of directors appointed by the governor, with the advice and consent of the senate, who serve for 3-year terms. Four of the members must represent participating insurers, 4 must represent certain health care providers, and 5 other members must include one small business representative, one professional consumer advocate, and at least 2 who have HIRSP coverage. The Commissioner of Insurance (or his or her designee) serves as a nonvoting member of the board. Annually, the governor appoints one of the voting members as the chairperson. The authority's board of directors can elect officers and appoint a nonboard member as the executive director. The authority was created by 2005 Wisconsin Act 74.

LOWER FOX RIVER REMEDIATION AUTHORITY

Members: TRIPP AHERN, GREGORY CONWAY, ROBERT COWLES, DAVE HANSEN, PATRICK SCHILLINGER, DAVID STEGEMAN, JAMES WALL (all appointed by governor with advice and consent of the senate).

Executive Director: vacancy.

Statutory References: Chapter 279.

Agency Responsibility: The authority is authorized to issue assessment bonds for eligible waterway improvement costs, which generally include environmental investigation and remediation of the Fox River extending from Lake Winnebago to the mouth of the river in Lake Michigan, and including any portion of Green Bay in Lake Michigan containing sediments discharged from the river, as described in an administrative or judicial order or decree or an administrative or judicially approved agreement. A consenting landowner may submit an application to the authority to request it to issue bonds for eligible waterway improvement costs. The consenting landowner making application must agree to the levy of an assessment against affected property owned by the landowner for the bond repayment costs, costs of financing and associated administrative costs, fees, and reserves. The authority calculates the amount of the assessment and levies the assessment on the consenting landowner. The landowner pays the assessment to the authority. The authority uses the assessment to repay the bonds and associated costs. The state is not liable for the authority's bonds, and the bonds are not a debt of the state.

Organization: The authority is a public corporation consisting of 7 members appointed by the governor with the advice and consent of the senate, for 7-year terms. Members of the board must be Wisconsin residents and no more than 4 members may be from the same political party. The term of each member expires on June 30 or until a successor is appointed. Annually the governor appoints one member as the chairperson; the board selects the vice chairperson. The executive director is appointed by the board and serves at the pleasure of the board. The board may also appoint an associate executive director.

The authority was created by 2007 Wisconsin Act 20.

UNIVERSITY OF WISCONSIN HOSPITALS AND CLINICS AUTHORITY

Board of Directors: DAVID WALSH (UW Board of Regents member appointed by board president), *chairperson;* PATRICK G. BOYLE (appointed by governor with senate consent), *vice chairperson;* SENATOR ERPENBACH (designated by senate cochairperson, Joint Committee on Finance), REPRESENTATIVE MASON (designated by assembly cochairperson, Joint Committee on Finance); ROGER AXTELL, DIAN PALMER, PABLO SANCHEZ, HUMBERTO VIDAILLET, MICHAEL WEIDEN (appointed by governor with senate consent); JUDITH CRAIN, MICHAEL SPECTOR (UW Board of Regents members appointed by board president); CAROLYN MARTIN (chancellor, UW-Madison); ROBERT GOLDEN (dean, UW-Madison Medical School); GEORGE WILDING (departmental chairperson, UW-Madison Medical School, appointed by UW-Madison chancellor), KATHARYN MAY (UW health professions faculty, other than UW Medical School, appointed by UW-Madison chancellor); MICHAEL MORGAN (secretary of administration). Nonvoting members: CAROL L. BOOTH, RICHARD W. CHOUDOIR (labor representatives appointed by governor).

President and Chief Executive Officer: DONNA KATEN-BAHENSKY.

Mailing Address: 600 Highland Avenue, Room H4/810, Madison 53792-8350.

Location: 600 Highland Avenue, Madison.

Telephone: (608) 263-8025.

Fax: (608) 263-9830.

Publications: @ *UW Health; Kids Connections; Level One; Medical Directions.*

Number of Employees: 7,518 (not state funded).

Total Budget 2007-09: $1,790,700,000 (not state funded).

Statutory References: Section 15.96; Chapter 233.

Agency Responsibility: The University of Wisconsin Hospitals and Clinics Authority operates the UW Hospital and Clinics, including the American Family Children's Hospital. Through the UW Hospital and Clinics and its other programs it delivers health care, including care for the indigent; provides an environment for instruction of physicians, nurses, and other health-related disciplines; sponsors and supports health care research; and assists health care programs and personnel throughout the state. Subject to approval by its board of directors, the authority may issue bonds to support its operations and may seek financing from the Wisconsin Health and Educational Facilities Authority.

A parallel state agency named the University of Wisconsin Hospitals and Clinics Board was created by Section 15.96, Wisconsin Statutes, to employ some of the hospital's employees. The employees of this state agency are included in the 7,518 hospital employees. The governing body of this state agency has the same composition as the board of directors of the authority. The authority is responsible for the payroll of this state agency.

Organization: The authority is a public corporation, which is self-financing. It derives much of its income from charges for clinical and hospital services. The 18-member board of directors includes 2 nonvoting members from two separate bargaining units that represent authority employees. The governor's appointees serve 5-year terms. The board elects a chairperson annually and appoints the chief executive officer for the authority. The authority was created by 1995 Wisconsin Act 27, which separated UW Hospital and Clinics and their related services from the UW System, effective July 1, 1996.

WISCONSIN HEALTH AND EDUCATIONAL FACILITIES AUTHORITY

Members: JOHN A. NOREIKA, *chairperson;* TIMOTHY K. SIZE, *vice chairperson;* RICHARD CANTER, BRUCE COLBURN, KEVIN FLAHERTY, BETH L. GILLIS, KEN THOMPSON (appointed by governor with senate consent).

Executive Director: LAWRENCE R. NINES.

Mailing Address: 18000 West Sarah Lane, Suite 300, Brookfield 53045-5841.

Telephone: (262) 792-0466.

Fax: (262) 792-0649.

Agency E-mail Address: info@whefa.com

Internet Address: www.whefa.com

Publications: Annual Report; WHEFA Capital Comments Newsletter.

Number of Employees: 4.00 (not state funded).

Statutory Reference: Chapter 231.

Agency Responsibility: The Wisconsin Health and Educational Facilities Authority (WHEFA) issues bonds on behalf of qualifying tax-exempt health care and educational facilities to help them finance their capital costs. Since interest earned on the bonds is exempt from federal income taxation, they can be marketed at lower interest rates, which reduces the cost of borrowing. WHEFA has no taxing power and receives no general appropriations from the state; it supports its operations by imposing fees on participating institutions. WHEFA's bonds and notes are funded solely through loan repayments from the borrowing institution or sponsor. Technically, they are not a debt, liability, or obligation of the State of Wisconsin or any of its subdivisions.

WHEFA may issue bonds to finance any qualifying capital project, including new construction, remodeling, and renovation; expansion of current facilities; and purchase of new equipment or furnishings. WHEFA may also issue bonds to refinance outstanding debt of qualifying health care and educational institutions. Certain health care institutions qualify only when the Department of Health Services certifies that refinancing will lead to interest savings on the debt.

Organization: WHEFA is a public corporation. Its 7 members are appointed by the governor with consent of the senate for staggered 7-year terms, and no more than 4 may be members of the same political party. Each member's appointment remains in effect until a successor is appointed. The governor annually appoints one member as chairperson, and the members appoint the vice chairperson and executive director. The executive director and staff are employed outside the classified service and are not paid by state funds. The members receive no compensation.

History: WHEFA was created as the Wisconsin Health Facilities Authority by Chapter 304, Laws of 1973. Operations began in September 1979, after the Wisconsin Supreme Court found the law constitutional in *State ex rel. Wisconsin Health Facilities Authority v. Lindner,* 91 Wis. 2d 145 (1979), when it ruled that assistance to a religiously affiliated hospital does not advance religion or foster unnecessary entanglement between church and state. WHEFA issued its first debt in December 1979.

1987 Wisconsin Act 27 expanded the scope of WHEFA to include assistance to private, tax-exempt colleges and universities and continuing care retirement communities and changed its name to reflect the broader responsibilities. 1993 Wisconsin Act 438 added not-for-profit institutions that have health education as their primary purpose. 2003 Wisconsin Act 109 further expanded the scope of WHEFA to include the issuance of bonds for the benefit of private, tax-exempt elementary or secondary educational institutions.

WISCONSIN HOUSING AND ECONOMIC DEVELOPMENT AUTHORITY

Members: PERRY ARMSTRONG, *chairperson;* DANIEL F. LEE, *vice chairperson;* GEOFFREY HURTADO, *secretary;* CHERYLL A. OLSON-COLLINS, *treasurer;* SENATORS GROTHMAN, TAYLOR; REPRESENTATIVES YOUNG, vacancy; RICHARD J. LEINENKUGEL (secretary of commerce), MICHAEL MORGAN (secretary of administration); PAUL SENTY, vacancy. (All except legislative and *ex officio* members are appointed by governor with senate consent.)

Executive Director: ANTONIO RILEY, 266-2893, antonio.riley@

Deputy Executive Director: NELSON FLYNN, 266-2748, nelson.flynn@

Executive Assistant: CHRIS GUNST, 261-5930, chris.gunst@

Executive Secretary: MAUREEN BRUNKER, 266-7354, maureen.brunker@

Mailing Address: P.O. Box 1728, Madison 53701-1728; Milwaukee Office: Suite 200, 140 South 1st Street, Milwaukee 53204.

Location: Suite 700, 201 West Washington Avenue, Madison.

Telephones: Madison: (608) 266-7884; Milwaukee: (414) 227-4039; Hotline: (800) 334-6873.

Fax: Madison: (608) 267-1099; Milwaukee: (414) 227-4704.

Internet Address: www.wheda.com

Address e-mail by combining the user ID and the state extender: userid@**wheda.com**

Communications: KATE VENNE, *director,* 266-8655, kate.venne@

Community Development: JOHN SCHULTZ, *director,* (414) 227-2292, john.schultz@

Economic Development: FARSHAD MALTES, *director,* 266-2027, farshad.maltes@

Financial Services: LAURA B. MORRIS, *chief financial officer,* 266-1640, laura.morris@

General Counsel: NELSON FLYNN, 266-2748, nelson.flynn@

Human Resources and Administration: vacancy, *director.*

Information Technology: JAMES SIEBERS, *director,* 266-3183, jim.siebers@

Multifamily: RAE ELLEN PACKARD, *director,* 266-6622, rae_ellen.packard@

Single Family: GEOFFREY COOPER, *director,* 266-2184, geoffrey.cooper@

Publications: Annual Report; Dividends for Wisconsin; Inventory of Federally Assisted Rental Housing – State of Wisconsin; Wisconsin Housing Authorities Directory.

Number of Employees: 178.00 (not state funded).

Total Budget 2007-09: $18,200,000 (not state funded).

Statutory Reference: Chapter 234.

Agency Responsibility: The Wisconsin Housing and Economic Development Authority (WHEDA) provides loans for low- and moderate-income housing, as well as small business and agricultural development projects. The authority finances most of its programs through the sale of bonds that technically are not an obligation of the State of Wisconsin. Since interest earned on the bonds is exempt from federal income taxation, they can be marketed at lower interest rates, which reduces the cost of borrowing.

In October 2008, WHEDA was forced to temporarily suspend its single family lending program due to unrest in the capital markets. As of press time, WHEDA's bond program had not resumed lending. However, WHEDA has brought to market a new, niche mortgage loan, the Wisconsin Neighborhood Advantage. This loan features an affordable 30-year fixed interest rate and can be used to purchase foreclosed and vacant properties in Brown, Dane, Kenosha, Milwaukee, Racine, Rock, and Waukesha counties. WHEDA has also developed and launched an outreach Web site, WisconsinForeclosureResource.com to help troubled homeowners. The initiative included capacity building for foreclosure counselors across Wisconsin and created a network of resources to help people facing foreclosure.

Both federally taxable and tax-exempt bonds are used to finance multifamily housing programs, which include homeless and special needs housing initiatives and loans to help with predevelopment of rental housing projects. In addition, the authority administers the federal Affordable Housing Tax Credit Program for developers of affordable rental housing.

WHEDA acts for the state in administering federally funded housing programs in coordination with the U.S. Department of Housing and Urban Development. Foremost among these are the Section 8 programs of the federal Housing and Community Development Act of 1979, which fund construction and rehabilitation of rental housing through rent subsidies to owners.

A companion organization, the WHEDA Foundation, makes grants to nonprofit organizations and local governments for housing projects that benefit persons-in-crisis. Grants are made to acquire and/or rehabilitate existing housing or construct new housing. The foundation also receives grant money on behalf of WHEDA.

WHEDA administers several economic development programs that encourage job creation and economic growth. These include the Credit Relief Outreach Program (CROP), a loan guarantee program for Wisconsin farmers, and the Linked Deposit Loan Program, which provides an interest rate subsidy for loans to businesses owned and controlled by women and minorities.

The authority administers a variety of loan guarantee programs: the Agribusiness Fund for businesses that utilize Wisconsin agricultural commodities; the Farm Assets Reinvestment Management Loan Program that assists qualified farmers in acquiring equipment, facilities, land, or livestock or improving facilities or land; and the WHEDA Small Business Guarantee for the expansion of businesses with 50 or fewer employees. It administers the Beginning Farmer Bond Program to help new farmers finance their first farm through tax-exempt bonds.

Organization: WHEDA is a public corporation consisting of 12 members. In addition to the secretary of administration and the secretary of commerce, or their designees, there are 4 legislative members who must represent the majority and minority party in each house. The 6 public members serve staggered 4-year terms, and the governor selects one to serve as chairperson for a one-year term. The governor appoints WHEDA's executive director with the advice and consent of the senate for a 2-year term. Staff members are employed outside the classified service and are not paid from state funds.

History: WHEDA was created as the Wisconsin Housing Finance Authority by Chapter 287, Laws of 1971. Program operations began in July 1973, after the Wisconsin Supreme Court declared the Housing Finance Authority constitutional in *State ex rel. Warren v. Nusbaum*, 59 Wis. 2d 391 (1973). The authority issued its first debt instruments in March 1974. In 1983, Wisconsin Act 81 broadened the authority's mission to include financing for economic development projects and changed the name to the Wisconsin Housing and Economic Development Authority. In 1985 Wisconsin Acts 9 and 153 and 1987 Wisconsin Act 421, the legislature expanded WHEDA's powers to include the insuring and subsidizing of farm operating loans, drought assistance loan guarantees, and interest rate reductions. The legislature added loan guarantee programs for agricultural development and small businesses (1989 Wisconsin Act 31), recycling (1989 Wisconsin Act 335), tourism businesses (1989 Wisconsin Act 336), and businesses located in targeted areas of the state (1991 Wisconsin Act 39). 1993 Wisconsin Act 16 transferred the property tax deferral loan program to WHEDA from the Department of Administration. In 2005, WHEDA's Modernization Bill (2005 Wisconsin Act 75) was passed, representing the first comprehensive enhancement of WHEDA's programs in over 30 years. This legislation has increased WHEDA's financing capacity for rental housing, small businesses, and single mortgages to first-time home buyers. WHEDA estimates that this Modernization Bill will generate nearly $500 million in economic impact throughout Wisconsin over the next several years.

WORLD DAIRY CENTER AUTHORITY

Members: Inactive.

Statutory Reference: Chapter 235.

Agency Responsibility: The World Dairy Center Authority is directed to establish a center for the development of dairying in Wisconsin, the United States, and the world. The authority, which is supported by private funding, analyzes worldwide trends in the dairy industry and recommends actions to be taken by Wisconsin to compete in the global dairy market. It coordinates access to commercial, technical, and general dairy information; promotes Wisconsin and U.S. dairy cattle, technology, products, and services in the global dairy market; and develops new markets for dairy and dairy-related products in cooperation with the Department of Agriculture, Trade and Consumer Protection.

Organization: The authority is a public corporation consisting of 23 members, including 12 who are appointed by the governor to serve 4-year terms. The governor also appoints an additional public member to serve as chairperson for one year and the executive director to serve a 2-year term.

History: The authority was created by 1991 Wisconsin Act 39.

NONPROFIT CORPORATIONS

A public nonprofit corporation is created by the legislature for a specific purpose.

BRADLEY CENTER SPORTS AND ENTERTAINMENT CORPORATION

Board of Directors: ULICE PAYNE, JR., *chairperson;* VIRGIS W. COLBERT, DOUGLAS G. KIEL, GAIL A. LIONE (nominated by Bradley Family Foundation); NED W. BECHTHOLD, MICHAEL F. HART, MARC MAROTTA, GARY SWEENEY, ROLEN L. WOMACK, JR. (All are appointed by governor.)

Mailing Address: 1001 North Fourth Street, Milwaukee 53203-1314.

Telephone: (414) 227-0400.

Fax: (414) 227-0497.

E-mail Address: sac@bcsec.com

Internet Address: www.bradleycenter.com

Statutory Reference: Chapter 232.

Agency Responsibility: The Bradley Center Sports and Entertainment Corporation is a public nonprofit corporation, created by 1985 Wisconsin Act 26 as an instrumentality of the state to receive the donation of the Bradley Center, a sports and entertainment facility located in Milwaukee County, from the Bradley Center Corporation. Its responsibility is to own and operate the center for the economic and recreational benefit of the citizens of Wisconsin. The center is the home of the Milwaukee Bucks basketball team, the Milwaukee Admirals hockey team, the Marquette University men's basketball team, and the Milwaukee Iron arena football team. Other tenants are family entertainment shows and concerts. The state and its political subdivisions are not liable for any debt or obligation of the corporation. The corporation may not divest itself of the center, nor may it dissolve unless the legislature directs it to do so by law. If the corporation is dissolved, all of its assets become state property.

State law exempts the corporation from most open records and open meeting laws applicable to state agencies, but the board must submit an annual financial statement to the governor and the legislature.

Organization: The corporation's board of directors is made up of 9 members appointed by the governor, serving staggered 7-year terms. Six members require senate consent, must "represent the diverse interests of the people of this state", and must be state residents. Three of those 6 must have executive and managerial business experience. The remaining 3 directors are nominated by the Bradley Family Foundation, Inc. No director may be an elected public official; the board selects it chairperson annually.

WISCONSIN ARTISTIC ENDOWMENT FOUNDATION

Members: Inactive.

Statutory Reference: Chapter 247.

Agency Responsibility: The Wisconsin Artistic Endowment Foundation is a nonprofit corporation that supports the arts by converting donated property and art objects into cash and distributing these and other moneys to the arts board for programs that provide operating support to arts organizations. The foundation also directly funds various arts programs, which are reviewed biennially with the advice of the arts board and statewide arts organizations.

Organization: Of the 14 board members, 2 come from the arts board, the chairperson of the arts board (or designee) and the executive secretary of the arts board (nonvoting member), while 4 are appointed by legislative officers: majority leader of the senate, minority leader of the senate, speaker of the assembly, and minority leader of the assembly. The governor appoints the remaining 8 nominees for 7-year terms, but they must represent diverse artistic interests and each of the geographic regions of the state, with one member knowledgeable in marketing and fundraising. The foundation was created by 2001 Wisconsin Act 16 and can only be dissolved by the legislature.

WISCONSIN TECHNOLOGY COUNCIL (HIGH-TECHNOLOGY BUSINESS DEVELOPMENT CORPORATION)

Directors: MARK D. BUGHER, *chairperson;* RICHARD J. LEINENKUGEL (secretary of commerce); KEVIN REILLY (president, UW System); DAN CLANCY (state director, Technical College System Board); ROLF WEGENKE (executive director, Wisconsin Association of Independent Colleges and Universities); BILL BEREZOWITZ, ROBERT W. BRENNAN, NEIL BRETL, ROBERT CARLSON, SUJEET CHAND, KRISTEN COGSWELL, DAN COLLINS, KEVIN CONROY, DERON CURLISS, JIM DAHLBERG, TREVOR D'SOUZA, JAN EDDY, MARK EHRMANN, FRED EVERT, GREGG FERGUS, E. KELLY FITZSIMMONS, MICHAEL FLANAGAN, WILLIAM D. GREGORY, TERRY GROSENHEIDER, CARL E. GULBRANDSEN, JAMES HANEY, LORRIE KEATING HEINEMANN, WILLIAM HICKEY, JOE HILL, CHARLES HOSLET, DAVE KIEFER, KIM KINDSCHI, ROCHELLE KLASKIN, TOD P. LINSTROTH, WILLIAM LINTON, KEVIN MCFARLING, MARK MILLER, JON P. NEIS, PAUL S. PEERCY, ALEXANDER T. PENDLETON, CHERYL PERKINS, FREDERICK T. RIKKERS, MARK SHERRY, JENNIFER SHILLING, BRUCE SIEBOLD, TONI SIKES, JIM SULLIVAN, MICHAEL R. SUSSMAN, BRIAN THOMPSON, DAVID G. WALSH (all except *ex officio* members are appointed by corporation).

President: TOM STILL, tstill@wisconsintechnologycouncil.com

Telephone: (608) 442-7557.

Fax: (608) 231-6877.

Internet Address: www.wisconsintechnologycouncil.com

Statutory Reference: Section 560.27.

Agency Responsibility: The Wisconsin Technology Council, referenced in the statutes as the High-Technology Business Development Corporation, supports the creation, development, and retention of science-based and technology-based businesses in Wisconsin. Created in 1999 Wisconsin Act 106, the corporation is a nonstock, nonprofit entity under Chapter 181, Wisconsin Statutes. The Department of Commerce may make core annual grants to the corporation if the corporation: 1) submits an expenditure plan that the secretary of commerce approves; 2) provides 50% of the funding for the project from other sources; 3) provides information requested by the department related to funds received from private sources; and 4) enters into a written agreement with the department related to the use of grants. Core department grants may not exceed $250,000 in any fiscal year. In addition, the corporation may accept funding grants from other public or private sources. The state does not guarantee any obligations of the corporation. The corporation is required to submit an annual report on its activities to the governor and the legislature.

Organization: The board of directors consists of 4 *ex officio* members and at least 11 other members who are appointed by the board of directors. The appointed members must include one or more individuals from each of the following categories: entrepreneurs, high-technology businesses, the venture capital industry, the investment banking industry, local governments, the business development community, and professionals who have experience providing services to persons in those categories. Members are appointed to 5-year terms.

REGIONAL AGENCIES

The following agencies were created by state law to function in one specific area of the state, usually an area composed of more than one county.

REGIONAL PLANNING COMMISSIONS

Regional planning commissions advise local units of government on the planning and delivery of public services to the citizens of a defined region, and they prepare and adopt master plans for the physical development of the region they serve. Regional planning provides a way to address problems that transcend local government boundaries, and offers joint solutions for intergovernmental cooperation.

The commissions may conduct research studies; make and adopt plans for the physical, social, and economic development of the region; assist in grant writing for financial assistance; provide advisory services to local governmental units and other public and private agencies; and coordinate local programs that relate to their objectives. Many commissions serve as a one-stop source of statistical information for the local governments of their area.

Currently, there are nine regional planning commissions, serving all but five of the state's 72 counties. Their boundaries are based on such considerations as common topographical and geographical features; the extent of urban development; existence of special or acute agricultural, forestry, or other rural problems; or regional physical, social, and economic characteristics.

Among the many categories of projects developed or assisted by regional planning commissions are rail and air transportation, waste disposal and recycling, highways, air and water quality, farmland preservation and zoning, land conservation and reclamation, outdoor recreation, parking and lakefront studies, and land records modernization.

Chapter 466, Laws of 1955, created the statute that governs the state's regional planning commissions (Section 66.0309, Wisconsin Statutes) and authorized the governor (or a state agency designated by the governor) to create a regional planning commission upon petition by the local governing bodies.

Membership of regional planning commissions varies according to conditions defined by statute. Unless otherwise specified by a region's local governments, the term of office for a commissioner is six years. The commissions are funded through state and federal planning grants, contracts with local governments for special planning services, and a statutorily authorized levy of up to .003% of equalized real estate value charged to each local governmental unit.

As authorized by state law, Wisconsin's regional planning commissions have established the Association of Wisconsin Regional Planning Commissions. The association's purposes include assisting the study of common problems and serving as an information clearinghouse.

Bay-Lake Regional Planning Commission

Region: Brown, Door, Florence, Kewaunee, Manitowoc, Marinette, Oconto, and Sheboygan Counties.

Members: JAMES E. GILLIGAN (Sheboygan), *chairperson;* CHERYL R. MAXWELL (Marinette), *vice chairperson;* LOIS L. TREVER (Oconto), *secretary-treasurer;* WILLIAM CLANCY, TONI LOCH, CHRIS SWAN (Brown); PAUL DEWITT, MARIAH GOODE, vacancy (Door); EDWIN A. KELLEY, BRUCE OSTERBERG, YVONNE VANPEMBROOK (Florence); MARY HANRAHAN, BRIAN PAPLHAM, CHARLES R. WAGNER (Kewaunee); DONALD C. MARKWARDT, VALERIE MELLON, NYIALONG VANG (Manitowoc); ALICE BAUMGARTEN, MARY G. MEYER (Marinette); DONALD A. GLYNN, THOMAS D. KUSSOW (Oconto); MICHAEL HOTZ, RON MCDONALD (Sheboygan).

Executive Director: MARK A. WALTER.

Mailing Address: 441 South Jackson Street, Green Bay 54301.

Telephone: (920) 448-2820; Fax: (920) 448-2823.

Internet Address: www.baylakerpc.org; E-mail Address: mwalter@baylakerpc.org

Capital Area Regional Planning Commission

Region: Dane County.

Members: Jeff Miller (Dane County Cities and Villages Association appointee), *chairperson;* Kristine Euclide (Dane County Executive appointee), *vice chairperson;* Martha Gibson, Sally Kefer (Dane County Executive appointees); John Murray, Kurt Sonnentag (Dane County Cities and Villages Association appointees); Carlton Hamre, Harold Krantz, Phil Van Kampen (Dane County Towns Association appointees); Zachariah B. Brandon, Curt Brink, Steve Hiniker, Larry Palm (Mayor of Madison appointees).

Executive Director: vacancy.

Deputy Director: Kamran Mesbah.

Mailing Address: City-County Building, 210 Martin Luther King Jr. Boulevard, Room 362, Madison 53703.

Telephone: 266-4137; Fax: 266-9117.

Internet Address: www.CapitalAreaRPC.org; E-mail Address: info@CapitalAreaRPC.org

East Central Wisconsin Regional Planning Commission

Region: Calumet, Fond du Lac*, Green Lake*, Marquette*, Menominee, Outagamie, Shawano, Waupaca, Waushara, and Winnebago Counties. *Inactive members.

Members: Merlin Gentz (Calumet), *chairperson;* Brian Kowalkowski (Menominee), *vice chairperson;* Patrick Laughrin, Clarence Wolf (Calumet); Elizabeth Moses, Ruth M. Winter (Menominee); Tim Hanna, Paul Hirte, Bob Lamers, Helen Nagler, Robert Paltzer, Clifford Sanderfoot (Outagamie); Ken Capelle, Marshall Giese, M. Eugene Zeuske (Shawano); Duane Brown, Duwayne Federwitz, Dick Koeppen, Brian Smith (Waupaca); Yvonne Feavel, Neal Strehlow, Norman Weiss (Waushara); David Albrecht, Ernie Bellin, Mark Harris, Ken Robl, Frank Tower (Richard Wollangk, alternate), vacancy (Winnebago).

Executive Director: Eric W. Fowle.

Mailing Address: 400 Ahnaip Street, Suite 100, Menasha 54952.

Telephone: (920) 751-4770; Fax: (920) 751-4771.

Internet Address: www.eastcentralrpc.org; E-mail Address: efowle@eastcentralrpc.org

Mississippi River Regional Planning Commission

Region: Buffalo, Crawford, Jackson, La Crosse, Monroe, Pepin, Pierce, Trempealeau, and Vernon Counties.

Members: Eugene Savage (Jackson), *chairperson;* vacancy, *vice chairperson;* Vicki Burke (La Crosse), *secretary-treasurer;* Bergie Ritscher, James Scholmeier, Kathleen Vinehout (Buffalo); Virgil Butteris, Gerald F. Krachey, Ronald Leys (Crawford); Ron Carney, James E. Christenson (Jackson); James E. Ehrsam, Tara Johnson (La Crosse); George Baker, James Kuhn, Cedric A. Schnitzler (Monroe); George T. Dupre, Norman Murray, David Smith (Pepin); Richard E. Purdy, William Schroeder, vacancy (Pierce); Margaret M. Baecker, Jerold O. Nysven, Barb Semb (Trempealeau); Gail Frie, Jo Ann Nickelatti, Eldon D. Warren (Vernon).

Executive Director: Gregory D. Flogstad.

Mailing Address: 1707 Main Street, Suite 435, La Crosse 54601-3227.

Telephone: (608) 785-9396; Fax: (608) 785-9394.

Internet Address: www.mrrpc.com; E-mail Address: plan@mrrpc.com

North Central Wisconsin Regional Planning Commission

Region: Adams, Forest, Juneau, Langlade, Lincoln, Marathon, Oneida, Portage, Vilas, and Wood Counties.

Members: Erhard Huettl (Forest), *chairperson;* Bettye Nall (Marathon), *vice chairperson;* Maurice Mathews (Wood), *secretary-treasurer;* Ron Jacobson, Donald E. Krahn, Glenn Licitar (Adams); Paul Millan, vacancy (Forest); Helmi Mehus, Edmund Wafle, vacancy

(Juneau); George Bornemann, Ronald Nye, Paul Schuman (Langlade); Robert Lussow, Tom Rick, Douglas Williams (Lincoln); Marilyn Bhend, vacancy (Marathon); Wilbur Petroskey, Thomas Rudolph, vacancy (Oneida); 3 vacancies (Portage); 3 vacancies (Vilas); Fred Camacho, Tom Haferman (Wood).

Executive Director: Dennis L. Lawrence.

Mailing Address: 210 McClellan Street, Suite 210, Wausau 54403.

Telephone: (715) 849-5510; Fax: (715) 849-5110.

Internet Address: www.ncwrpc.org; E-mail Address: staff@ncwrpc.org

Northwest Regional Planning Commission

Region: Ashland, Bayfield, Burnett, Douglas, Iron, Price, Rusk, Sawyer, Taylor, and Washburn Counties and the Tribal Nations of Bad River, Lac Courte Oreilles, Lac du Flambeau, Red Cliff, and St. Croix.

Members: Douglas Finn (Douglas), *chairperson;* John Blahnik (Bayfield), *vice chairperson;* Harold Helwig (Sawyer), *secretary-treasurer;* Peg Kurilla, Edward Monroe, Richard Pufall (Ashland); William Kacvinsky, vacancy (Bayfield); Philip Lindeman, Ed Peterson (Burnett); Karen Livingston, Larry Quam, David Ross (Douglas); Dennis DeRosso, Jim Kichak (Iron); Richard Kelnhofer, Robert Kopisch, Thomas Ratzlaff (Price); Dan Gudis, Eldon Skogen, Randy Tatur (Rusk); Jean Laier (Sawyer); Allen Beadles, Jim Metz, George Southworth, Michael Wellner (Taylor); Michael Bobin, Gary Cuskey, Tom Mackie (Washburn); Ray DePerry (Northwest Tribal nations representative); Joe Maday (Bad River Tribal Council); Carl Edwards (Lac du Flambeau Tribal Council); Rose Soulier (Red Cliff Tribal Council); Louis Taylor (Lac Courte Oreilles Tribal Council); David Merrill (St. Croix Tribal Council).

Executive Director: Myron Schuster.

Mailing Address: 1400 South River Street, Spooner 54801-1390.

Telephone: (715) 635-2197; Fax: (715) 635-7262.

Internet Address: www.nwrpc.com; E-mail Address: mschuster@nwrpc.com

Southeastern Wisconsin Regional Planning Commission

Region: Kenosha, Milwaukee, Ozaukee, Racine, Walworth, Washington, and Waukesha Counties.

Members: David L. Stroik (Washington), *chairperson;* Richard A. Hansen (Walworth), *vice chairperson;* Adelene Greene (Kenosha), *secretary;* William R. Drew (Milwaukee), *treasurer;* Anita M. Faraone, Robert W. Pitts (Kenosha); Brian Dranzik, John F. Weishan (Milwaukee); Thomas H. Buestrin, William E. Johnson, Gustav V. Wirth (Ozaukee); Susan Greenfield, Mary A. Kacmarcik, Michael J. Miklasevich (Racine); Gregory L. Holden, Nancy Russell (Walworth); John M. Jung, Daniel S. Schmidt (Washington); James T. Dwyer, Anselmo Villarreal, Paul G. Vrakas (Waukesha).

Executive Director: Kenneth R. Yunker.

Mailing Address: W239 N1812 Rockwood Drive, P.O. Box 1607, Waukesha 53187-1607.

Telephone: (262) 547-6721; Fax: (262) 547-1103.

Internet Address: www.sewrpc.org; E-mail Address: sewrpc@sewrpc.org

Southwestern Wisconsin Regional Planning Commission

Region: Grant, Green, Iowa, Lafayette, and Richland Counties.

Members: Mark Masters (Iowa), *chairperson;* John Patcle (Grant), *vice chairperson;* Timothy McGettigan (Lafayette), *secretary-treasurer;* Eileen Nickels, Richard Rogers (Grant); Arthur Carter, Nathan Klassy, John Waelti (Green); Bradley Glass, Susan Hollett (Iowa); Lance McNaughton, Jack Sauer (Lafayette); Ann Greenheck, Robert Smith, Bruce Wunnicke (Richland).

Executive Director: Lawrence T. Ward.

Mailing Address: Room 719 Pioneer Tower, 1 University Plaza, UW-Platteville, Platteville 53818.

Telephone: (608) 342-1214; Fax: (608) 342-1220.

Internet Address: www.swwrpc.org; E-mail Address: wardla@uwplatt.edu

West Central Wisconsin Regional Planning Commission

Region: Barron, Chippewa, Clark, Dunn, Eau Claire, Polk, and St. Croix Counties.

Members: JESS MILLER (Barron), *chairperson;* ROGER HAHN (Eau Claire), *vice chairperson;* RICHARD CREASER (Dunn), *secretary-treasurer;* JOHN HARDIN, PETER OLSON (Barron); RICHARD PECHA, JR., EUGENE RINECK, EMERY SEDLACEK (Chippewa); STEVE AMACHER, CHARLES HARWICK, CHARLES RUETH (Clark); DAN FEDDERLY, PHILIP SAWIN (Dunn); JOHN L. FRANK, GERALD WILKIE (Eau Claire); KATHY KIENHOLZ, KEITH REDISKE, KEN SAMPLE (Polk); JOE HURTGEN, LINDA LUCKEY, LARRY WEISENBECK (St. Croix).

Director: JERRY L. CHASTEEN.

Mailing Address: 800 Wisconsin Street, Mail Box 9, Eau Claire 54703-3606.

Telephone: (715) 836-2918; Fax: (715) 836-2886.

Internet Address: www.wcwrpc.org; E-mail Address: wcwrpc@wcwrpc.org

REGIONAL PLANNING COMMISSION AREAS

Not part of a planning region

Map by Wisconsin Legislative Technology Services Bureau.

MADISON CULTURAL ARTS DISTRICT BOARD

District Board Members: LINDA BALDWIN O'HERN (appointed by City of Madison Mayor), *chairperson;* BRIAN E. BUTLER (appointed by Dane County Executive), *vice chairperson;* JAMES K. RUHLY (appointed by City of Madison Mayor), *secretary;* DANA CHABOT (designated by City of Madison Mayor), *treasurer;* SUSAN COOK (UW Board of Regents nominee appointed by governor); DEIRDRE GARTON (designated by governor); CAROL T. TOUSSAINT, vacancy (appointed by governor); WILLIAM C. KEYS (Madison School Board nominee appointed by City of Madison Mayor); ANTHONY AMATO, JED SANBORN, MICHAEL E. VERVEER (appointed by City of Madison Mayor); DIANE CHRISTIANSEN (designated by Dane County Executive).

Staff: TOM CARTO.

Mailing Address: 201 State Street, Madison 53703.

Telephone: 258-4177.

Internet Address: www.ci.madison.wi.us/mayor/301650.html

Statutory Reference: Chapter 229, Subchapter V.

Agency Responsibility: The Madison Cultural Arts District Board manages the Overture Center for the Arts, which is owned by the Overture Development Corporation. The center is organized for the performance of cultural arts, the development of resident arts organizations, and the dissemination of the arts throughout the community. The Madison Board is organized as a local cultural arts district. Arts districts are public corporations that may acquire, construct, operate, and manage cultural arts facilities. A local district may issue revenue bonds, invest funds, set standards for the use of facilities, and establish and collect fees for usage.

The 10 appointed members serve staggered 4-year terms. At least one of the governor's appointees must demonstrate an interest in the cultural arts. The Madison Common Council must approve the 6 members appointed by the mayor. At least 2 members appointed by the mayor must exhibit an interest in the cultural arts and not more than 3 may be elected public officials. The member appointed by the Dane County Executive may not be a county official. Local arts districts were authorized by 1999 Wisconsin Act 65.

REGIONAL TRANSIT AUTHORITY

Members: KARL J. OSTBY (Kenosha County), *chairperson;* JULIA H. TAYLOR (appointed by governor), *vice chairperson;* DAVID EBERLE (Racine County), *secretary;* JODY F. KARLS (City of Racine), *treasurer;* LEN BRANDRUP (City of Kenosha); SHARON D. ROBINSON (City of Milwaukee); BRIAN DRANZIK (Milwaukee County).

Region: Kenosha, Milwaukee, and Racine Counties.

Executive Director: KENNETH R. YUNKER.

Mailing Address: W239 N1812 Rockwood Drive, P.O. Box 1607, Waukesha 53187-1607.

Telephone: (262) 547-6721.

Fax: (262) 547-1103.

E-mail Address: rta@sewrpc.org

Internet Address: www.sewisrta.org

Statutory Reference: Section 59.58 (6).

The Regional Transit Authority was originally created as the Regional Transportation Authority by 1991 Wisconsin Act 39 as an 11-member authority serving a 7-county region, but by 1995 the authority had become inactive. The 7-member Regional Transit Authority was created by 2005 Wisconsin Act 25 to address transit activities in a 3-county region in southeastern Wisconsin. The authority submitted its report as required to the governor and the legislature on November 15, 2008, addressing how best to improve the funding, provision, and coordination of mass transit, commuter rail, and passenger rail services in the region.

The authority is being staffed on an interim basis by the Southeastern Wisconsin Regional Planning Commission.

SOUTHEAST WISCONSIN PROFESSIONAL BASEBALL PARK DISTRICT

District Board Members: JAY B. WILLIAMS (Waukesha County, appointed by governor), *chairperson;* DANIEL McKEITHAN, JR. (Milwaukee County, appointed by chief executive officer), *vice chairperson;* MARK THOMSEN (City of Milwaukee representative appointed by mayor), *secretary;* KAREN MAKOUTZ (Ozaukee County, appointed by chief executive officer), *treasurer;* GREGORY WESLEY (Milwaukee County, appointed by governor), *assistant secretary;* CHRISTINE NUERNBERG (Ozaukee County), ROBERT HENZL (Racine County), MICHAEL MILLER (Washington County) (county members appointed by governor); MARTIN GREENBERG (at-large member, appointed by governor); PERFECTO RIVERA (Milwaukee County), DOUGLAS STANSIL (Racine County), MARK McCUNE (Washington County), vacancy (Waukesha County) (members appointed by county's chief executive officer).

Executive Director: MICHAEL R. DUCKETT.

Mailing Address: Miller Park, One Brewers Way, Milwaukee 53214.

Telephone: (414) 902-4040.

Fax: (414) 902-4033.

Statutory Reference: Chapter 229, Subchapter III.

Agency Responsibility: The Southeast Wisconsin Professional Baseball Park District is majority owner of Miller Park, the home of the Milwaukee Brewers baseball club. It is a public corporation that may acquire, construct, maintain, improve, operate, and manage baseball park facilities which include parking lots, garages, restaurants, parks, concession facilities, entertainment facilities, and other related structures. The district may impose a sales tax and a use tax at a rate not to exceed 0.1%.

The district is also authorized to issue bonds for certain purposes related to baseball park facilities. A city or county within the district's jurisdiction may make loans or grants to the district, expend funds to subsidize the district, borrow money for baseball park facilities, or grant property to the state dedicated for use by a professional baseball park.

The district, which was created by 1995 Wisconsin Act 56, includes Milwaukee, Ozaukee, Racine, Washington, and Waukesha Counties. The district board consists of 13 members, 6 appointed by the governor, 6 appointed by the chief executive officers of each county in the district (2 from the most populous county), and one appointed by the mayor of Milwaukee. The governor appoints the chairperson. Members appointed by the governor must be confirmed by the senate. Members appointed by county executive officers or the mayor of Milwaukee must be confirmed by their respective county boards or the city council.

PROFESSIONAL FOOTBALL STADIUM DISTRICT

Board Members: ANN PATTESON, *chairperson;* MARGARET JENSEN, *vice chairperson;* RON ANTONNEAU, *secretary;* GILES TASSOUL, *treasurer;* MARK ANDERSON, KEN GOLOMSKI, vacancy.

Statutory Reference: Chapter 229, Subchapter IV.

Agency Responsibility: The Professional Football Stadium District is responsible for the renovation of Lambeau Field, the designated home of the Green Bay Packers football team. It is a public corporation that may acquire, construct, equip, maintain, improve, operate, and manage football stadium facilities or hire others to do the same. The district issued bonds for the redevelopment of Lambeau Field, which was substantially completed on July 31, 2003. Maintenance and operation of the stadium is governed by provisions of the Lambeau Field Lease Agreement by and among the district, Green Bay Packers, Inc., and the City of Green Bay. The district currently imposes a 0.5% sales and use tax approved by Brown County voters in a referendum. Proceeds from the tax must first be used to pay current debt service on the district's bonds. Remaining amounts can be used for district administrative expenses, maintenance, and operating costs of stadium facilities and related purposes consistent with statutory limitations and lease provisions. The district was created by 1999 Wisconsin Act 167.

WISCONSIN CENTER DISTRICT

Board of Directors: FRANKLYN M. GIMBEL (private sector representative appointed by governor), *chairperson;* JACOB WEISSBERGER (private sector representative appointed by governor), *vice chairperson;* WILLIE L. HINES, JR. (Milwaukee Common Council President), *secretary;* W. MARTIN MORICS (City of Milwaukee comptroller), *treasurer;* SENATOR SULLIVAN (designated by senate cochairperson, Joint Committee on Finance), REPRESENTATIVE RICHARDS (designated by assembly cochairperson, Joint Committee on Finance); MICHAEL MORGAN (secretary of administration); STEPHEN H. MARCUS (private sector representative appointed by governor); JOHN J. BURKE, JR., JAMES VILLA (private sector representatives appointed by Milwaukee County Executive); JILL DIDIER (mayor of city that contributes room taxes appointed by Milwaukee County Executive); ALDERMEN HAMILTON, WITKOWSKI (public sector representatives appointed by Milwaukee Common Council President); JOEL BRENNAN, JAMES C. KAMINSKI (private sector representatives appointed by Mayor of City of Milwaukee).

President: RICHARD A. GEYER, (414) 908-6050, rgeyer@wcd.org

Mailing Address: 400 West Wisconsin Avenue, Milwaukee 53203.

Telephone: (414) 908-6000.

Fax: (414) 908-6010.

Internet Addresses: www.wcd.org, www.midwestairlinescenter.com, www.milwaukeetheatre.org, www.uscellulararena.com

Statutory Reference: Chapter 229, Subchapter II.

Agency Responsibility: The Wisconsin Center District (WCD) owns and operates the U.S. Cellular Arena, the Milwaukee Theatre, and the Midwest Airlines Center. The district is not supported by property taxes or state subsidies. It is funded by operating revenue and special sales taxes on hotel rooms, restaurant food and beverages, and car rentals within its taxing boundaries (Milwaukee County). The WCD is classified by law as a local exposition district that may acquire, construct, and operate an exposition center and related facilities; enter into contracts and grant concessions; mortgage district property and issue bonds; and invest funds as the district board considers appropriate. Local exposition districts are public corporations. Interest income on exposition district bonds is tax-exempt, and the district is exempt from state income and franchise taxes.

The board has 15 members, 13 of whom serve 3-year terms. Legislative members serve for terms concurrent with their term of office. Public officials can no longer serve after their term of office expires. Public sector representatives appointed by the Milwaukee Common Council President must be city residents. The 2 private sector representatives the Mayor of Milwaukee appoints must reside in the city. The private sector representatives the county executive appoints must live outside the City of Milwaukee. Of the 4 gubernatorial appointees, 2 must live in Milwaukee County but not in the City of Milwaukee. The governor's appointees must include the secretary of the state Department of Administration (or designee), a member who has significant involvement with the lodging industry, and a member who has significant involvement with the food and beverage industry. Local exposition districts were authorized by 1993 Wisconsin Act 263.

INTERSTATE AGENCIES AND COMPACTS

Wisconsin is party to a variety of interstate compacts. These agreements are binding on two or more states, and they establish uniform guidelines or procedures for agencies within the signatory states. The following section lists agencies created by enactment of enabling legislation in all of the participating states or by interstate agreement of their respective governors. It also describes interstate compacts that are expressly ratified in the Wisconsin Statutes but do not require appointment of delegates.

EDUCATION COMMISSION OF THE STATES

Wisconsin Delegates: GOVERNOR DOYLE, *chairperson;* ANTHONY EVERS (superintendent of public instruction); SENATOR LEHMAN; REPRESENTATIVE PRIDEMORE; JESSICA DOYLE, BETTE LANG, LUTHER OLSEN (public members appointed by governor).

Mailing Addresses: Wisconsin delegation: Secretary of the Department of Administration, 101 East Wilson Street, P.O. Box 7864, Madison 53707-7864. National commission: Education Commission of the States, 700 Broadway, Suite 1200, Denver, Colorado 80203.

Telephones: Wisconsin: 266-1741; National Commission: (303) 299-3600.

Internet Address: www.ecs.org

Statutory References: Sections 39.75 and 39.76.

Agency Responsibility: The Education Commission of the States was established to foster national cooperation among executive, legislative, educational, and lay leaders of the various states. It offers a forum for discussing policy alternatives in the education field; provides an information clearinghouse about educational problems and their various solutions throughout the nation; and facilitates the improvement of state and local educational systems. The governor designates the chairperson of the 7-member delegation, and the Department of Administration provides staff services. Wisconsin's participation in the commission originated in Chapter 641, Laws of 1965, which established an interstate compact for education and specified the composition of the Wisconsin delegation.

GREAT LAKES COMMISSION

Wisconsin Members: TODD L. AMBS (state officer member), *secretary;* DAVE HANSEN, FRED SCHNOOK (all appointed by governor).

Mailing Address: Great Lakes Commission: Thomas Eder, *executive director,* 2805 South Industrial Highway, Suite 100, Ann Arbor, Michigan 48104.

Telephones: Wisconsin Delegation Secretary: (608) 264-6278; Great Lakes Commission: (734) 971-9135.

Commission Fax: (734) 971-9150.

Internet Address: www.glc.org

Publications of the Great Lakes Commission: *Advisor; ANS Update;* annual reports; special reports.

Statutory Reference: Section 14.78.

Agency Responsibility: A 3-member delegation represents Wisconsin on the 8-state Great Lakes Commission. The interstate commission promotes orderly development of the water resources of the Great Lakes Basin; offers advice on balancing industrial, commercial, agricultural, water supply, and residential and recreational uses of the lakes' water resources; and enables basin residents to benefit from public works, such as navigational aids.

Commissioners from the states of Illinois, Indiana, Michigan, Minnesota, New York, Ohio, Pennsylvania, and Wisconsin share information and coordinate state positions on issues of regional concern.

Organization: The governor appoints the 3 Wisconsin delegates to the Great Lakes Commission. The delegates are chosen on the basis of their knowledge of and interest in Great Lakes Basin problems. One commissioner, who must be a state officer or employee, is appointed to an indefinite term and serves as secretary of Wisconsin's compact commission and as a member of the executive committee of the interstate commission. Wisconsin's other commissioners serve 4-year terms.

History: The Great Lakes Commission was established in 1955 following enactment of enabling legislation by a majority of the Great Lakes states. It replaced the Deep Waterways Commission, established to promote the St. Lawrence Seaway project. With enactment of Chapter 275, Laws of 1955, Wisconsin ratified the Great Lakes Basin Compact and created the Wisconsin Great Lakes Compact Commission, consisting of the state members of the Great Lakes Commission. Congress recognized the Great Lakes Basin Compact in P.L. 90-419 on July 24, 1968.

GREAT LAKES PROTECTION FUND

Wisconsin Representatives: TODD L. AMBS, ALAN FISH (appointed by governor with senate consent).

Mailing Addresses and Telephones: 101 South Webster Street, Madison 53703, (608) 264-6278; 610 Walnut Street, Madison 53726. Great Lakes Protection Fund: Russ Van Herick, *executive director,* 1560 Sherman Avenue, Suite 880, Evanston, Illinois 60201, (847) 425-8150, Fax: (847) 424-9832.

Statutory Reference: Section 14.84.

Agency Responsibility: The Great Lakes Protection Fund was created by the Council of Great Lakes Governors to finance projects for the protection and cleanup of the Great Lakes. Priorities include the prevention of toxic pollution, the identification of effective clean-up approaches, the demonstration of natural resource stewardship, and the classification of health effects of toxic pollution.

In 1989, the governors of Illinois, Michigan, Minnesota, New York, Ohio, Pennsylvania, and Wisconsin signed the formal agreement creating the Great Lakes Protection Fund, and the Wisconsin Legislature approved the state's participation in 1989 Wisconsin Act 31. The fund was incorporated as a not-for-profit corporation, managed by a board of directors composed of 2 representatives from each member state. Each state's contribution to the original $100 million endowment was determined by estimating its proportion of Great Lakes water consumption. Wisconsin's share was $12 million.

GREAT LAKES-ST. LAWRENCE RIVER BASIN
WATER RESOURCES COUNCIL

Wisconsin Members: GOVERNOR DOYLE, *chair;* MATT FRANK (secretary of department of natural resources), *alternate.*

Contact: TODD L. AMBS, *Wisconsin advisor,* todd.ambs@wisconsin.gov

Mailing Addresses: Great Lakes-St. Lawrence River Basin Water Resources Council, c/o Council of Great Lakes Governors: DAVID NAFTZGER, *executive director*, 35 East Wacker Drive, Suite 1850, Chicago, Illinois 60601.

Telephones: Wisconsin advisor Todd Ambs: (608) 264-6278; Secretariat, Council of Great Lakes Governors: (312) 407-0177.

Secretariat, Council of Great Lakes Governors Fax: (312) 407-0038.

Secretariat, Council of Great Lakes Governors E-mail: dnaftzger@cglg.org

Secretariat, Council of Great Lakes Governors Internet Address: www.cglg.org (temporary).

Statutory References: Sections 14.95, 281.343.

Agency Responsibility: The governor serves as Wisconsin's representative on the council, and is the chair of the council until December 8, 2009. The council is charged with aiding and promoting the coordination of the activities and programs of the Great Lakes states concerned with water resources management in the Great Lakes basin. The council may promulgate and enforce rules and regulations as may be necessary for the implementation and enforcement of the Great Lakes-St. Lawrence River Basin Water Resources Compact. The compact governs withdrawals, consumptive uses, conservation and efficient use, and diversions of basin water resources.

Under the compact, the governors from the states of Illinois, Indiana, Michigan, Minnesota, New York, Ohio, Pennsylvania, and Wisconsin, jointly pursue intergovernmental cooperation and consultation to protect, conserve, restore, improve, and effectively manage the waters and water dependent natural resources of the basin.

Organization: The governors of all participating states are *ex officio* members of the council. The governor may designate the secretary of natural resources as his alternate to attend and vote at all meetings. Any other alternate must be nominated by the governor with the advice and consent of the senate. The alternate serves at the pleasure of the governor. The governor may also appoint an advisor to attend all meetings of the council. If the governor does appoint an advisor, that person must have knowledge of and experience with Great Lakes water management issues.

History: The council was created by the ratification of the Great Lakes-St. Lawrence River Basin Water Resources Compact. Wisconsin joined the compact with the passage and signing of 2007 Wisconsin Act 227. Congress ratified the compact in Public Law 110-342. The compact became effective as state and federal law on December 8, 2008.

GREAT LAKES-ST. LAWRENCE RIVER
WATER RESOURCES REGIONAL BODY

Wisconsin Members: Governor Doyle; Matt Frank (secretary of department of natural resources), *designee.*

Contact: Todd L. Ambs, *Wisconsin advisor,* todd.ambs@wisconsin.gov

Mailing Addresses: Great Lakes-St. Lawrence River Water Resources Regional Body, c/o Council of Great Lakes Governors: David Naftzger, *executive director*, 35 East Wacker Drive, Suite 1850, Chicago, Illinois 60601.

Telephones: Wisconsin advisor Todd Ambs: (608) 264-6278; Secretariat, Council of Great Lakes Governors: (312) 407-0177.

Secretariat, Council of Great Lakes Governors Fax: (312) 407-0038.

E-mail Address: secretariat@glslregionalbody.org

Internet Address: www.glslregionalbody.org

Statutory Reference: Section 281.343.

Agency Responsibility: The governor serves as Wisconsin's representative on the regional body. The regional body is charged with aiding and promoting the coordination of the activities and programs of the Great Lakes states and provinces concerned with water resources management in the Great Lakes basin. The regional body may develop procedures for implementation of the Great Lakes-St. Lawrence River Basin Water Resources Sustainable Water Resources Agreement. The agreement is a good-faith agreement between Great Lakes states and provinces that governs withdrawals, consumptive uses, conservation and efficient use, and diversions of basin water resources.

Governors from the states of Illinois, Indiana, Michigan, Minnesota, New York, Ohio, Pennsylvania, and Wisconsin, and the premiers of Ontario and Quebec jointly pursue intergovernmental cooperation and consultation to protect, conserve, restore, improve, and manage the waters and water dependent natural resources of the basin.

Organization: The governors and premiers of all participating states are *ex officio* members of the regional body. The governor may designate an alternate to attend and vote at all meetings. The designee serves at the pleasure of the governor.

History: The regional body was created by Great Lakes governors and premiers by signing the Great Lakes-St. Lawrence River Basin Sustainable Water Resources Agreement on December 13, 2005. Parts of the agreement entered into force on the day the agreement was signed. Other parts will enter into force once all of the parties have enacted the necessary state or provincial measures.

INTERSTATE INSURANCE PRODUCT REGULATION COMMISSION

Wisconsin Member: SEAN DILWEG (commissioner of insurance).

Mailing Address: Commission: 444 North Capitol Street NW, Hall of the States, Suite 701, Washington, D.C. 20001-1509.

Telephone: Commission: (202) 471-3962.

Commission Fax: (816) 460-7476.

Internet Address: www.insurancecompact.org

Statutory References: Sections 14.82 and 601.58.

Agency Responsibility: The Interstate Insurance Product Regulation Commission is made up of the member states of the Interstate Insurance Product Regulation Compact. The compact's purposes are to develop uniform standards for life, annuity, disability income, and long-term care insurance products, create a central clearinghouse to provide prompt review of insurance products, approve product filings, long-term care advertisements and disability income and long-term care rate filings that satisfy uniform standards, and improve coordination of regulatory resources and expertise between state insurance departments. The commission establishes reasonable uniform standards for insurance products covered under the compact. As of May 1, 2009, 35 states were members of the compact.

Organization: Wisconsin is represented on the commission by the state's commissioner of insurance or his or her designee. Each state member is entitled to one vote.

History: The commission reached its operational threshold in 2006. Wisconsin joined the commission with the signing of 2007 Wisconsin Act 168 in March 2008.

INTERSTATE COMMISSION FOR JUVENILES

Wisconsin Member: MARGARET CARPENTER, *administrator,* Division of Juvenile Corrections, Wisconsin Department of Corrections.

Mailing Address: Council of State Governments, 2760 Research Park Drive, P.O. Box 11910, Lexington, Kentucky 40578-1910.

Telephone: (859) 244-8000.

Statutory References: Sections 14.92 and 938.999.

Agency Responsibility: The Interstate Commission for Juveniles is designed to oversee, supervise, and coordinate the interstate movement of certain juveniles, delinquents, and run-away offenders. The commission has the authority to promulgate rules, which have the effect of statutory law, and enforce compliance with the Interstate Compact for Juveniles, including through judicial means. The commission is directed to resolve disputes between states regarding the compact, levy assessments against compacting states to cover its costs, and report annually on its activities. The commission is also directed to collect standardized data concerning the interstate movement of juveniles. The commission came into existence when 35 states ratified the Interstate Compact for Juveniles in August 2008.

Organization: The commission is composed of one commissioner from each of the compacting states. Each compacting state has one vote on the interstate commission. The commission will meet at least once per year. The Council of State Governments provides organizational support to the commission.

INTERSTATE WILDLIFE VIOLATOR COMPACT ADMINISTRATORS BOARD

Wisconsin Administrator: KRISTIN TURNER, kristin.turner@wisconsin.gov

Mailing Address: Wisconsin Department of Natural Resources, P.O. Box 7921, Madison, Wisconsin 53707-7921.

Telephone: (608) 267-5151.

Statutory Reference: Section 29.03.

Agency Responsibility: The Interstate Wildlife Violator Compact establishes a process whereby wildlife law violations by a nonresident while in a member state may be handled as if the person were a resident in the state where the violation took place, meaning personal recognizance may be permitted instead of arrest, booking, and bonding. The process is aimed at increasing the efficiency of conservation wardens by allowing more time for enforcement duties rather than violator processing. The compact requires each member state to recognize the revocations and suspensions of individuals hunting, fishing, and trapping privileges from other member states that result from a wildlife related violation. The compact also requires each member state to revoke or suspend the hunting, fishing, and trapping licenses of any resident of that state who violates a wildlife related law in another member state and fails to resolve the matter by payment of the penalty or appearance in court. The board of compact administrators was established to serve as the governing body for the resolution of all matters relating to the operation of the compact.

Organization: The board is composed of one representative from each participating state. The Wisconsin representative is appointed by the secretary of natural resources. Each member of the board has one vote. As of May 2009, 31 states are members of the compact.

History: Wisconsin was authorized to develop administrative rules for Wisconsin's role in the Wildlife Violator Compact and apply to become a member of the compact with the signing of 2005 Wisconsin Act 282 in April 2006. Once the administrative rules were adopted and in effect, Wisconsin applied to become a member of the Wildlife Violator Compact and was accepted effective April 15, 2008.

LOWER ST. CROIX MANAGEMENT COMMISSION

Wisconsin Member: SCOTT HUMRICKHOUSE (designated by secretary of natural resources).

Telephone and Mailing Address: Department of Natural Resources, West Central Region, P.O. Box 4001, Eau Claire 54702-4001, (715) 839-3700.

Agency Responsibility: The Lower St. Croix Management Commission was created to provide a forum for discussion of problems and programs associated with the Lower St. Croix National Scenic Riverway. It coordinates planning, development, protection, and management of the riverway for Wisconsin, Minnesota, and the U.S. government.

The commission was created by a cooperative agreement signed in 1973 by the National Park Service and the governors of Wisconsin and Minnesota. It consists of one member each from the National Park Service and the natural resources departments of the two states.

MIDWEST INTERSTATE LOW-LEVEL
RADIOACTIVE WASTE COMMISSION

Wisconsin Member: STANLEY YORK (appointed by governor with senate consent).

Mailing Address: Chair and Executive Director Stanley York, Midwest Interstate Low-Level Radioactive Waste Commission, P.O. Box 2659, Madison 53701-2659.

Telephones: Wisconsin member: 831-5434; Commission: 267-4793.

E-Mail Address: Wisconsin member: stan.york@tds.net

Commission Fax: 267-4799.

Statutory References: Sections 14.81 and 16.11.

Agency Responsibility: The Midwest Interstate Low-Level Radioactive Waste Commission is responsible for the disposal of low-level radioactive wastes. Based on the Midwest Interstate Low-Level Radioactive Waste Compact, it may negotiate agreements for disposal of waste at facilities within or outside the region; appear as an intervenor before any court, board, or commission in any matter related to waste management; and review the emergency closure of a regional facility. The commission is directed to settle disputes between party states regarding the compact and adopt a regional management plan designating host states for the establishment of needed regional facilities.

Wisconsin's commission member must promote Wisconsin's interest in an equitable distribution of responsibilities among compact member states, encourage public access and participation in the commission's proceedings, and notify the governor and legislature if the commission proposes to designate a disposal facility site in this state.

Organization: The commission represents Indiana, Iowa, Minnesota, Missouri, Ohio, and Wisconsin, each of which has one voting member.

History: 1983 Wisconsin Act 393 ratified the Midwest Interstate Low-Level Radioactive Waste Compact, which provided for formation of the Midwest Low-Level Radioactive Waste Commission. The U.S. Congress encouraged the development of such compacts by enacting the Low-Level Radioactive Waste Policy Act in 1980, as amended by the Low-Level Radioactive Waste Policy Amendments Act of 1985.

MIDWEST INTERSTATE PASSENGER RAIL COMMISSION

Wisconsin Representatives: FRANK BUSALACCHI (designated by governor); REPRESENTATIVE GOTTLIEB (appointed by assembly speaker); SENATOR RISSER (appointed by senate president); KARL OSTBY (private sector representative).

Mailing Address: Commission: Laura Kliewer, *director,* 701 East 22nd Street, Suite 110, Lombard, Illinois 60148.

Telephone: Commission: (630) 925-1922.

Commission Fax: (630) 925-1930.

Internet Address: www.miprc.org

Statutory References: Sections 14.86 and 85.067.

Agency Responsibility: The commission brings together state leaders from the members of the Midwest Interstate Passenger Rail Compact to advocate for the funding and authorization necessary to make passenger rail improvements. It also seeks to develop a long-term interstate plan for high-speed passenger rail service implementation. The current members are Illinois, Indiana, Iowa, Michigan, Minnesota, Missouri, Nebraska, North Dakota, Ohio, and Wisconsin. The commission is empowered to work with local and federal officials, to educate the public on the advantages of passenger rail, and to make recommendations to member states.

Organization: Wisconsin is represented by 4 members on the commission. Those members must be the governor or his or her designee; one assembly member appointed by the assembly speaker for a 2-year term; one senate member appointed by the senate president for a 2-year term; and one member representing the private sector, who serves for the governor's term of office. The members serve without compensation.

History: The Midwest Interstate Passenger Rail Compact became operational in 2000 when three states, Indiana, Minnesota, and Missouri, approved it. Wisconsin joined the compact and gained commission membership with the signing of 2007 Wisconsin Act 117 in April 2008.

MIDWESTERN HIGHER EDUCATION COMMISSION

Wisconsin Members: JOHN KERRIGAN (designated by governor); SENATOR SULLIVAN (appointed by senate president); REPRESENTATIVE NASS (appointed by assembly speaker); JUDITH CRAIN, ROLF WEGENKE; THOMAS ANDERES, DANIEL CLANCY (alternates) (appointed by governor).

Mailing Address: 1300 South Second Street, Suite 130, Minneapolis, Minnesota 55454-1079.

Telephone: (612) 626-8286.

Statutory References: Sections 14.90 and 39.80.

Agency Responsibility: The Midwestern Higher Education Commission was organized to further higher educational opportunities for residents of states participating in the Midwest Higher Education Compact. The commission may enter into agreements with member and non-member states, or their universities and colleges, to provide programs and services for students, including student exchanges and improved access. The commission also studies the effects of the compact on higher education and the needs and resources for programs in member states. The compact's three core functions are cost-savings initiatives, student access, and policy research and analysis.

Organization: The compact currently includes Illinois, Indiana, Iowa, Kansas, Michigan, Minnesota, Missouri, Nebraska, North Dakota, Ohio, South Dakota, and Wisconsin. Each state appoints 5 members to the governing commission, including the governor (or governor's designee) and 2 legislators, who serve 2-year terms. The 2 at-large members appointed by the governor serve 4-year terms, and must be selected from the field of higher education. Any member state may withdraw from the compact 2 years after the passage of a law authorizing withdrawal.

History: Wisconsin ratified the Midwestern Higher Education Compact in 1993 Wisconsin Act 358, effective July 1, 1994.

MISSISSIPPI RIVER PARKWAY COMMISSION

Wisconsin Commissioners: ALAN L. LORENZ (La Crosse County), *chairperson;* ROBERT MILLER (Buffalo County), *treasurer;* SENATORS HARSDORF, KREITLOW; REPRESENTATIVE NERISON, vacancy; SHERRY QUAMME (Crawford County); vacancy (Grant County); DENNIS DONATH (Pierce County); BRUCE QUINTON (Pepin County); JEAN GALASINSKI (Trempealeau County); MARK CLEMENTS (Vernon County). (Legislators are nominated by presiding officer and appointed by governor. County representatives are appointed by governor.) Nonvoting members: RICHARD J. LEINENKUGEL (secretary of commerce), MATT FRANK (secretary of natural resources), FRANK BUSALACCHI (secretary of transportation), ELLSWORTH BROWN (director, state historical society), KELLI A. TRUMBLE (secretary of tourism).

Contact: ALAN L. LORENZ, alanlorenz@centurytel.net

Mailing Address: W4927 Hoeth Street, La Crosse 54601.

Telephone: (608) 788-8264.

Statutory Reference: Section 14.85.

Agency Responsibility: The Mississippi River Parkway Commission coordinates development and preservation of Wisconsin's portion of the Great River Road corridor along the Mississippi River. It assists and advises state and local agencies about maintaining and enhancing the scenic, historic, economic, and recreational assets within the corridor and cooperates with

Ice collects on the shore of Lake Michigan in front of the Algoma Pierhead Light near Algoma in Kewaunee County. The tower was built in 1908 to a height of 26 feet, with a Fifth Order Fresnel lens. In 1932, the tower was raised to 42 feet by adding a wider base. The light is still an active aid to navigation. (Timothy Ditzman)

similar commissions in other Mississippi River states and the Province of Ontario. On June 15, 2000, the U.S. Secretary of Transportation designated the entire 250-mile length of the Wisconsin Great River Road as a National Scenic Byway, thereby recognizing it as an outstanding example of America's scenic beauty. It is Wisconsin's only National Scenic Byway.

Organization: The 17-member Wisconsin commission includes 12 voting members, appointed to 4-year terms, and 5 nonvoting *ex officio* members. The 4 legislative members represent the two major political parties in each house.

The commission selects its own chairperson who is Wisconsin's sole voting representative at national meetings of the Mississippi River Parkway Commission.

History: The Wisconsin commission is part of the Mississippi River Parkway Commission, which was given statutory recognition by Chapter 482, Laws of 1961. It dates back to 1939 when Wisconsin Governor Julius P. Heil appointed a 10-member committee to cooperate with agencies from other Mississippi River states in planning the Great River Road. This scenic route extends from the Gulf of Mexico to the Mississippi River's headwaters at Lake Itasca, Minnesota. North of Lake Itasca, the route connects with the Trans-Canada Highway and terminates at Minaki, Ontario.

The Federal Highway Aid Acts of 1973, 1976, and 1978 provided Wisconsin approximately $21 million in Great River Road funding. While categorical funding is no longer available, the Wisconsin Department of Transportation has continued improvements to Wisconsin's portion of the Great River Road, including pedestrian and bicycle trails, landscaping, preservation of historic sites, and other programs. Wisconsin has also received more than $5 million in discretionary grants from the National Scenic Byways Program from 2000 through 2008. These grants were matched with 20% state and local government funds. The commission also boasts an active Promotions Committee, comprised of volunteers and commissioners who are active in the Wisconsin tourism industry.

UPPER MISSISSIPPI RIVER BASIN ASSOCIATION

Wisconsin Representative: TODD L. AMBS (appointed by governor).

Mailing Addresses: Wisconsin representative: 101 South Webster Street, Madison 53703. Upper Mississippi River Basin Association: Holly Stoerker, *executive director,* 415 Hamm Building, 408 St. Peter Street, St. Paul, Minnesota 55102.

Madison Location: 115 East, State Capitol, Madison.

Telephones: Wisconsin: (608) 264-6278; Minnesota: (612) 224-2880.

Agency Responsibility: The Upper Mississippi River Basin Association is a nonprofit organization created by Illinois, Iowa, Minnesota, Missouri, and Wisconsin to facilitate cooperative action regarding the basin's water and related land resources. It sponsors studies of river-related issues, cooperative planning for use of the region's resources, and an information exchange. It also enables the member states to develop regional positions on resource issues and to advocate the basin states' collective interests before the U.S. Congress and federal agencies. The association has placed major emphasis on its Environmental Management Program, a partnership among the U.S. Army Corps of Engineers, the U.S. Fish and Wildlife Service, and the five states. This program, which was approved by the federal Water Resources Development Act of 1986, authorized habitat rehabilitation projects, resource inventory and analysis, recreation projects, and river traffic monitoring.

Organization: The association consists of one representative from each member state. The members annually elect one of their number to serve as chairperson. Five federal agencies with major water resources responsibilities serve as advisory members: the Environmental Protection Agency and the U.S. Departments of Agriculture, Army, Interior, and Transportation.

History: The Upper Mississippi River Basin Association was formed on December 2, 1981, when the articles of association were signed by representatives of the member states. In late 1983 and early 1984, executive orders were issued by four of the five governors reaffirming membership in the association.

INTERSTATE COMPACTS

Interstate Compact on Adoption and Medical Assistance

The compact authorizes the Department of Children and Families, on behalf of this state, to enter into interstate agreements, including the interstate compact on adoption and medical assistance, with other states that enter into adoption assistance agreements. In these agreements, other states must provide Medical Assistance (MA) benefits, under its own laws, to children who were adopted as residents of Wisconsin, and Wisconsin must provide the same benefits to children who were adopted as residents of other states. Any interstate agreement is revocable upon written notice to the other state but remains in effect for one year after the date of the notice. Benefits already granted continue even if the agreement is revoked. The compact has been adopted by 49 states and the District of Columbia. (1985 Wisconsin Act 302)

Statutory Reference: Section 48.9985.

Administrator: Department of Children and Families.

Interstate Compact for Adult Offender Supervision

The compact creates cooperative procedures for individuals placed on parole, probation, or extended supervision in one state to be supervised in another state if certain conditions are met. The compact has been adopted by all 50 states, the District of Columbia, U.S. Virgin Islands, and Puerto Rico. (2001 Wisconsin Act 96)

Statutory Reference: Section 304.16.

Administrator: William Rankin, Department of Corrections (appointed by governor).

Corrections Compact

The compact allows Wisconsin to enter into contracts with states that are party to the compact to confine Wisconsin's inmates in the other state's correctional facilities or receive inmates from other states. The contract provides for inmate upkeep and special services. The compact has been adopted by 40 states and the District of Columbia. (Chapter 20, Laws of 1981)

Statutory Reference: Sections 302.25-302.26.

Administrator: Department of Corrections.

Agreement on Detainers

The agreement is designed to clear up indictments or complaints that serve as a basis for a detainer lodged against a prisoner incarcerated in one jurisdiction and wanted in another. The agreement allows the state making the request to obtain temporary custody of the prisoner to conduct a trial on outstanding charges. The agreement has been adopted by 48 states and the District of Columbia. (Chapter 255, Laws of 1969)

Statutory Reference: Sections 976.05 and 976.06.

Emergency Management Assistance Compact

The compact authorizes states that are members to provide mutual assistance to other member states in an emergency or disaster declared by the governor of the affected state. Under the compact, member states cooperate in emergency-related training and formulate plans for interstate cooperation in responding to a disaster. All 50 states now belong to the compact. (1999 Wisconsin Act 26)

Statutory Reference: Section 166.30.

Administrator: Division of Emergency Management, Department of Military Affairs.

Interstate Compact on Mental Health

The compact facilitates the proper and expeditious treatment of persons with mental illness or mental retardation by the cooperative action of the party states, to the benefit of the person, their families, and society. The compact (and enacting laws) provides for this to be done irrespective of the legal residence and citizenship status of the person. The compact has been adopted in 45 states and the District of Columbia. (Chapter 611, Laws of 1965)

Statutory Reference: Sections 51.75-51.80.

Administrator: Department of Health Services.

Nurse Licensure Compact

The compact allows a nurse licensed by a party state to practice nursing in any other party state without obtaining a license. It requires each party state to participate in a database of all licensed nurses. The compact has been adopted by Arizona, Arkansas, Colorado, Delaware, Idaho, Iowa, Kentucky, Maine, Maryland, Mississippi, Nebraska, New Hampshire, New Mexico, North Carolina, North Dakota, Rhode Island, South Carolina, South Dakota, Tennessee, Texas, Utah, Virginia, and Wisconsin. (1999 Wisconsin Act 22)

Statutory Reference: Section 441.50.

Administrator: Department of Regulation and Licensing.

Interstate Compact on Placement of Children

The compact provides a legal framework to administer the compact law among the party states to ensure protection and services when a child is placed across state lines when under the jurisdiction of that state and the most suitable placement is in a different state. It requires notice and proof of appropriateness and safety before a placement is made; allocates legal and administrative responsibilities by the sending state for the duration of placement; provides a basis for enforcement of rights; and authorizes joint actions to improve operations and services. All states have adopted the compact. (Chapter 354, Laws of 1977)

Statutory Reference: Sections 48.988 and 48.989.

Administrator: Department of Children and Families.

Interstate Agreement on Qualification of Educational Personnel

The agreement authorizes the State Superintendent of Public Instruction to enter into contracts with party states to accept their educational personnel. These agreements allow Wisconsin to offer initial licenses to teachers from contracting states and allows other states to accept Wisconsin-trained teachers on the same basis. The agreement has been adopted by 35 states and the District of Columbia. (Chapter 42, Laws of 1969)

Statutory Reference: Sections 115.46-115.48.

Administrator: State Superintendent of Public Instruction.

Judicial Branch

7

The judicial branch: profile of the judicial branch, summary of recent significant supreme court decisions, and descriptions of the supreme court, court system, and judicial service agencies

First Quarter Moon

(Brian Lockett, Goleta Air & Space Museum)

WISCONSIN SUPREME COURT

Justice	First Assumed Office	Began First Elected Term	Current Term Expires July 31
Shirley S. Abrahamson, Chief Justice	1976*	August 1979	2009**
Ann Walsh Bradley	1995	August 1995	2015
N. Patrick Crooks	1996	August 1996	2016
David T. Prosser, Jr.	1998*	August 2001	2011
Patience Drake Roggensack	2003	August 2003	2013
Annette K. Ziegler	2007	August 2007	2017
Michael J. Gableman	2008	August 2008	2018

*Initially appointed by the governor.
**Chief Justice Abrahamson was reelected to a new term beginning August 1, 2009 and expiring July 31, 2019.
Source: Director of State Courts, departmental data, April 2009.

The justices of the Supreme Court typically hear cases in the East Wing of the State Capitol. The room is decorated with four murals depicting the evolution of Wisconsin law. Above the justices is Albert Herter's depiction of the signing of the U.S. Constitution. Seated, from left to right, are Justice Annette K. Ziegler, Justice David T. Prosser, Jr., Justice Ann Walsh Bradley, Chief Justice Shirley S. Abrahamson, Justice N. Patrick Crooks, Justice Patience D. Roggensack, and Justice Michael J. Gableman. (Wisconsin Supreme Court)

JUDICIAL BRANCH

A PROFILE OF THE JUDICIAL BRANCH

Introducing the Court System. The judicial branch and its system of various courts may appear very complex to the nonlawyer. It is well-known that the courts are required to try persons accused of violating criminal law and that conviction in the trial court may result in punishment by fine or imprisonment or both. The courts also decide civil matters between private citizens, ranging from landlord-tenant disputes to adjudication of corporate liability involving many millions of dollars and months of costly litigation. In addition, the courts act as referees between citizens and their government by determining the permissible limits of governmental power and the extent of an individual's rights and responsibilities.

A court system that strives for fairness and justice must settle disputes on the basis of appropriate rules of law. These rules are derived from a variety of sources, including the state and federal constitutions, legislative acts and administrative rules, as well as the "common law", which reflects society's customs and experience as expressed in previous court decisions. This body of law is constantly changing to meet the needs of an increasingly complex world. The courts have the task of seeking the delicate balance between the flexibility and the stability needed to protect the fundamental principles of the constitutional system of the United States.

The Supreme Court. The judicial branch is headed by the Wisconsin Supreme Court of 7 justices, each elected statewide to a 10-year term. The supreme court is primarily an appellate court and serves as Wisconsin's "court of last resort". It also exercises original jurisdiction in a small number of cases of statewide concern. There are no appeals to the supreme court as a matter of right. Instead, the court has discretion to determine which appeals it will hear.

In addition to hearing cases on appeal from the court of appeals, there also are three instances in which the supreme court, at its discretion, may decide to bypass the appeals court. First, the supreme court may review a case on its own initiative. Second, it may decide to review a matter without an appellate decision based on a petition by one of the parties. Finally, the supreme court may take jurisdiction in a case if the appeals court finds it needs guidance on a legal question and requests supreme court review under a procedure known as "certification".

The Court of Appeals. The Court of Appeals, created August 1, 1978, is divided into 4 appellate districts covering the state, and there are 16 appellate judges, each elected to a 6-year term. The "court chambers", or principal offices for the districts, are located in Madison (5 judges), Milwaukee (4 judges), Waukesha (4 judges), and Wausau (3 judges).

In the appeals court, 3-judge panels hear all cases, except small claims actions, municipal ordinance violations, traffic violations, and mental health, juvenile, and misdemeanor cases. These exceptions may be heard by a single judge unless a panel is requested.

Circuit Courts. Following a 1977-78 reorganization of the Wisconsin court system, the circuit court became the "single level" trial court for the state. Circuit court boundaries were revised so that, except for 3 combined-county circuits (Buffalo-Pepin, Florence-Forest, and Menominee-Shawano), each county became a circuit, resulting in a total of 69 circuits.

In the more populous counties, a circuit may have several branches with one judge assigned to each branch. As of August 1, 2009, Wisconsin had a combined total of 248 circuits or circuit branches and the same number of circuit judgeships, with each judge elected to a 6-year term. For administrative purposes, the circuit court system is divided into 10 judicial administrative districts, each headed by a chief judge appointed by the supreme court. The circuit courts are funded with a combination of state and county money. For example, state funds are used to pay the salaries of judges, and counties are responsible for most court operating costs.

A final judgment by the circuit court can be appealed to the Wisconsin Court of Appeals, but a decision by the appeals court can be reviewed only if the Wisconsin Supreme Court grants a petition for review.

Municipal Courts. Individually or jointly, cities, villages, and towns may create municipal courts with jurisdiction over municipal ordinance violations that have monetary penalties. There are more than 200 municipal courts in Wisconsin. These courts are not courts of record, and they have limited jurisdiction. Usually, municipal judgeships are not full-time positions.

Selection and Qualification of Judges. In Wisconsin, all justices and judges are elected on a nonpartisan ballot in April. The Wisconsin Constitution provides that supreme court justices and appellate and circuit judges must have been licensed to practice law in Wisconsin for at least 5 years prior to election or appointment. While state law does not require that municipal judges be attorneys, municipalities may impose such a qualification in their jurisdictions.

Supreme court justices are elected on a statewide basis; appeals court and circuit court judges are elected in their respective districts. The governor may make an appointment to fill a vacancy in the office of justice or judge to serve until a successor is elected. When the election is held, the candidate elected assumes the office for a full term.

Since 1955, Wisconsin has permitted retired justices and judges to serve as "reserve" judges. At the request of the chief justice of the supreme court, reserve judges fill vacancies temporarily or help to relieve congested calendars. They exercise all the powers of the court to which they are assigned.

Judicial Agencies Assisting the Courts. Numerous state agencies assist the courts. The Wisconsin Supreme Court appoints the Director of State Courts, the State Law Librarian and staff, the Board of Bar Examiners, the director of the Office of Lawyer Regulation, and the Judicial Education Committee. Other agencies that assist the judicial branch include the Judicial Commission, Judicial Council, and the State Bar of Wisconsin.

The shared concern of these agencies is to improve the organization, operation, administration, and procedures of the state judicial system. They also function to promote professional standards, judicial ethics, and legal research and reform.

Court Process in Wisconsin. Both state and federal courts have jurisdiction over Wisconsin citizens. State courts generally adjudicate cases pertaining to state laws, but the federal government may give state courts jurisdiction over specified federal questions. Courts handle two types of cases – civil and criminal.

Civil Cases. Generally, civil actions involve individual claims in which a person seeks a remedy for some wrong done by another. For example, if a person has been injured in an automobile accident, the complaining party (plaintiff) may sue the offending party (defendant) to compel payment for the injuries.

In a typical civil case, the plaintiff brings an action by filing a summons and a complaint with the circuit court. The defendant is served with copies of these documents, and the summons directs the defendant to respond to the plaintiff's attorney. Various pretrial proceedings, such as pleadings, motions, pretrial conferences, and discovery, may be required. If no settlement is reached, the matter goes to trial. The U.S. and Wisconsin Constitutions guarantee trial by jury, except in cases involving an equitable action, such as a divorce action. In civil actions, unless a party demands a jury trial and pays the required fee, the trial may be conducted by the court without a jury. The jury in a civil case consists of 6 persons unless a greater number, not to exceed 12, is requested. Five-sixths of the jurors must agree on the verdict. Based on the verdict, the court enters a judgment for the plaintiff or defendant.

Wisconsin law provides for small claims actions that are streamlined and informal. These actions typically involve the collection of small personal or commercial debts and are limited to questions of $5,000 or less. Small claims cases are decided by the circuit court judge, unless a jury trial is requested. Attorneys commonly are not used.

Criminal Cases. Under Wisconsin law, criminal conduct is an act prohibited by state law and punishable by a fine or imprisonment or both. There are two types of crime – felonies and misdemeanors. A felony is punishable by confinement in a state prison for one year or more; all other crimes are misdemeanors punishable by imprisonment in a county jail. Misdemeanors have a maximum sentence of 12 months unless the violator is a "repeater" as defined in the statutes.

Because a crime is an offense against the state, the state, rather than the crime victim, brings action against the defendant. A typical criminal action begins when the district attorney, an elected official, files a criminal complaint in the circuit court stating the essential facts concerning the offense charged. The defendant may or may not be arrested at that time. If the defendant has not yet been arrested, generally the judge or a court commissioner then issues an "arrest warrant" in the case of a felony or a "summons" in the case of a misdemeanor. A law enforcement officer then must serve a copy of the warrant or summons on an individual and, in the case of a warrant, make an arrest.

Once in custody, the defendant is taken before a circuit judge or court commissioner, informed of the charges, and given the opportunity to be represented by a lawyer at public expense if he or she cannot afford to hire one. Bail is usually set at this time. In the case of a misdemeanor, a trial date is set. In felony cases, the defendant has a right to a preliminary examination, which is a hearing before the court to determine whether the state has probable cause to charge the individual.

If the preliminary examination is waived, or if it is held and probable cause found, the district attorney files an information (a sworn accusation on which the indictment is based) with the court. The arraignment is then held before the circuit court judge, and the defendant enters a plea ("guilty", "not guilty", "no contest subject to the approval of the court", or "not guilty by reason of mental disease or defect").

Following further pretrial proceedings, if a plea agreement is not reached, the case goes to trial in circuit court. Criminal cases are tried by a jury of 12, unless the defendant waives a jury trial or there is agreement for fewer jurors. The jury considers the evidence presented at the trial, determines the facts and renders a verdict of guilty or not guilty based on instructions given by the circuit judge. If the jury issues a verdict of guilty, a judgment of conviction is entered and the court determines the sentence. In a felony case the court may order a presentence investigation before pronouncing sentence.

In a criminal case, the jury's verdict to convict the defendant must be unanimous. If not, the defendant is acquitted (cleared of the charge) or, if the jury is unable to reach a unanimous verdict, the court may declare a mistrial and the prosecutor may seek a new trial. Once acquitted, a person cannot be tried again in criminal court for the same charge, based on provisions in both the federal and state constitutions that prevent double jeopardy. Aggrieved parties may, however, bring a civil action against the individual for damages, based on the incident.

History of the Court System. The basic powers and framework of the court system were established by Article VII of the state constitution when Wisconsin gained statehood in 1848. At that time, judicial power was vested in a supreme court, circuit courts, courts of probate, and justices of the peace. Subject to certain limitations, the legislature was granted power to establish inferior courts and municipal courts and determine their jurisdiction.

The constitution originally divided the state into five judicial circuit districts. The five judges who presided over those circuit courts were to meet at least once a year at Madison as a "Supreme Court" until the legislature established a separate court. The Wisconsin Supreme Court was instituted in 1853 with 3 members chosen in statewide elections – one was elected as chief justice and the other 2 as associate justices. In 1877, a constitutional amendment increased the number of associate justices to 4. An 1889 amendment prescribed the current practice under which all court members are elected as justices. The justice with the longest continuous service presides as chief justice, unless that person declines, in which case the office passes to the next justice in terms of seniority. Since 1903, the constitution has required a court of 7 members.

Over the years, the legislature created a large number of courts with varying types of jurisdiction. As a result of numerous special laws, there was no uniformity among the counties. Different types of courts in a single county had overlapping jurisdiction, and procedure in the various courts was not the same. A number of special courts sprang up in heavily urbanized areas, such as Milwaukee County, where the judicial burden was the greatest. In addition, many municipalities established police justice courts for enforcement of local ordinances, and there were some 1,800 justices of the peace.

The 1959 Legislature enacted Chapter 315, effective January 1, 1962, which provided for the initial reorganization of the court system. The most significant feature of the reorganization was the abolition of special statutory courts (municipal, district, superior, civil, and small claims). In addition, a uniform system of jurisdiction and procedure was established for all county courts.

The 1959 law also created the machinery for smoother administration of the court system. One problem under the old system was the imbalance of caseloads from one jurisdiction to another. In some cases, the workload was not evenly distributed among the judges within the same jurisdiction. To correct this, the chief justice of the supreme court was authorized to assign circuit and county judges to serve temporarily as needed in either type of court. The 1961 Legislature took another step to assist the chief justice in these assignments by creating the post of Administrative Director of Courts. This position has since been redefined by the supreme court and renamed the Director of State Courts. In recent years, the director has been given added administrative duties and increased staff to perform them.

The last step in the 1959 reorganization effort was the April 1966 ratification of two constitutional amendments that abolished the justices of the peace and permitted municipal courts. At this point the Wisconsin system of courts consisted of the supreme court, circuit courts, county courts, and municipal courts.

In April 1977, the court of appeals was authorized when the voters ratified an amendment to Article VII, Section 2, of the Wisconsin Constitution, which outlined the current structure of the state courts:

> The judicial power of this state shall be vested in a unified court system consisting of one supreme court, a court of appeals, a circuit court, such trial courts of general uniform statewide jurisdiction as the legislature may create by law, and a municipal court if authorized by the legislature under section 14.

In June 1978, the legislature implemented the constitutional amendment by enacting Chapter 449, Laws of 1977, which added the court of appeals to the system and eliminated county courts.

SUPREME COURT

Chief Justice: **SHIRLEY S. ABRAHAMSON**
Justices: ANN WALSH BRADLEY
                       N. PATRICK CROOKS
                       DAVID T. PROSSER, JR.
                       PATIENCE DRAKE ROGGENSACK
                       ANNETTE K. ZIEGLER
                       MICHAEL J. GABLEMAN

Mailing Address: Supreme Court and Clerk: P.O. Box 1688, Madison 53701-1688.

Locations: Supreme Court: Room 16 East, State Capitol, Madison; Clerk: 110 East Main Street, Madison.

Telephone: 266-1298.

Fax: 261-8299.

Internet Address: www.wicourts.gov

Clerk of Supreme Court: DAVID R. SCHANKER, 266-1880, Fax: 267-0640.

Court Commissioners: COLEEN KENNEDY, NANCY KOPP, JULIE RICH, DAVID RUNKE; 266-7442.

Number of Positions: 38.50.

Total Budget 2007-09: $9,731,800.

Constitutional References: Article VII, Sections 2-4, 9-13, and 24.

Statutory Reference: Chapter 751.

Responsibility: The Wisconsin Supreme Court is the final authority on matters pertaining to the Wisconsin Constitution and the highest tribunal for all actions begun in the state, except those involving federal issues appealable to the U.S. Supreme Court. The court decides which cases it will hear, usually on the basis of whether the questions raised are of statewide importance. It exercises "appellate jurisdiction" if 3 or more justices grant a petition to review a decision of a lower court. It exercises "original jurisdiction" as the first court to hear a case if 4 or more justices approve a petition requesting it to do so. Although the majority of cases advance from the circuit court to the court of appeals before reaching the supreme court, the high court may decide to bypass the court of appeals. The supreme court can do this on its own motion or at the request of the parties; in addition, the court of appeals may certify a case to the supreme court, asking the high court to take the case directly from the circuit court.

The supreme court does not take testimony. Instead, it decides cases on the basis of written briefs and oral argument. It is required by statute to deliver its decisions in writing, and it may publish them in the *Wisconsin Reports* as it deems appropriate.

The supreme court sets procedural rules for all courts in the state, and the chief justice serves as administrative head of the state's judicial system. With the assistance of the director of state courts, the chief justice monitors the status of judicial business in Wisconsin's courts. When a calendar is congested or a vacancy occurs in a circuit or appellate court, the chief justice may assign an active judge or reserve judge to serve temporarily as a judge of either type of court.

Organization: The supreme court consists of 7 justices elected to 10-year terms. They are chosen in statewide elections on the nonpartisan April ballot and take office on the following August 1. The Wisconsin Constitution provides that only one justice can be elected in any single year, so supreme court vacancies are sometimes filled by gubernatorial appointees who serve until a successor can be elected. The authorized salary for supreme court justices for 2009 is $144,495. The chief justice receives $152,495.

The justice with the most seniority on the court serves as chief justice unless he or she declines the position. In that event, the justice with the next longest seniority serves as chief justice. Any 4 justices constitute a quorum for conducting court business.

The court staff is appointed from outside the classified service. It includes the director of state courts who assists the court in its administrative functions; 4 commissioners who are attorneys and assist the court in its judicial functions; a clerk who keeps the court's records; and a marshal who performs a variety of duties. Each justice has a secretary and one law clerk.

WISCONSIN COURT SYSTEM – ADMINISTRATIVE STRUCTURE

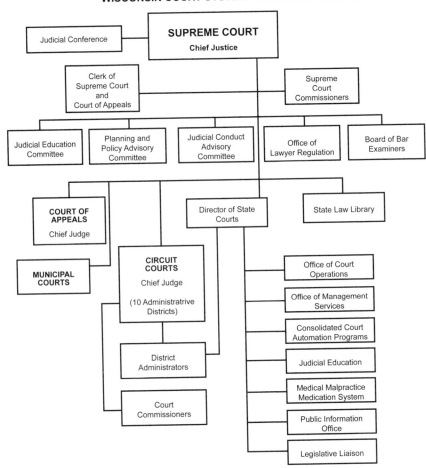

Independent Bodies: Judicial Commission; Judicial Council
Associated unit: State Bar of Wisconsin

COURT OF APPEALS

Judges: *District I:*   KITTY B. BRENNAN (2015)
                         PATRICIA S. CURLEY* (2014)
                         RALPH ADAM FINE (2012)
                         JOAN F. KESSLER (2010)

         District II: DANIEL P. ANDERSON* (2013)
                         RICHARD S. BROWN** (2012)
                         LISA S. NEUBAUER (2014)
                         HARRY G. SNYDER (2010)

         District III: EDWARD R. BRUNNER (2013)
                         MICHAEL W. HOOVER* (2015)
                         GREGORY PETERSON (2011)

         District IV: BURNIE BRIDGE (2014)
                         CHARLES P. DYKMAN (2010)
                         PAUL B. HIGGINBOTHAM* (2011)
                         PAUL LUNDSTEN (2013)
                         MARGARET J. VERGERONT (2012)

Note: *Indicates the presiding judge of the district. **Indicates chief judge of the court of appeals. The judges' current terms expire on July 31 of the year shown.

Court of Appeals Clerk: DAVID R. SCHANKER, P.O. Box 1688, Madison 53701-1688; Location: 110 East Main Street, Suite 215, Madison, 266-1880, Fax: 267-0640.

Staff Attorneys: 10 East Doty Street, 7th Floor, Madison 53703, 266-9320.

Internet Address: www.wicourts.gov/about/organization/appeals/index.htm

Number of Positions: 75.50.

Total Budget 2007-09: $19,264,000.

Constitutional Reference: Article VII, Section 5.

Statutory Reference: Chapter 752.

Organization: A constitutional amendment ratified on April 5, 1977, mandated the Court of Appeals, and Chapter 187, Laws of 1977, implemented the amendment. The court consists of 16 judges serving in 4 districts (4 judges each in Districts I and II, 3 judges in District III, and 5 judges in District IV). The Wisconsin Supreme Court appoints a chief judge of the court of appeals to serve as administrative head of the court for a 3-year term, and the clerk of the supreme court serves as the clerk for the court.

Appellate judges are elected for 6-year terms in the nonpartisan April election and begin their terms of office on the following August 1. They must reside in the district from which they are chosen. Only one court of appeals judge may be elected in a district in any one year. The authorized salary for appeals court judges for 2009 is $136,316.

Functions: The court of appeals has both appellate and supervisory jurisdiction, as well as original jurisdiction to issue prerogative writs. The final judgments and orders of a circuit court may be appealed to the court of appeals as a matter of right. Other judgments or orders may be appealed upon leave of the appellate court.

The court usually sits as a 3-judge panel to dispose of cases on their merits. However, a single judge may decide certain categories of cases, including juvenile cases; small claims; municipal ordinance and traffic violations; and mental health and misdemeanor cases. No testimony is taken in the appellate court. The court relies on the trial court record and written briefs in deciding a case, and it prescreens all cases to determine whether oral argument is needed. Both oral argument and "briefs only" cases are placed on a regularly issued calendar. The court gives criminal cases preference on the calendar when it is possible to do so without undue delay of civil cases. Staff attorneys, judicial assistants, and law clerks assist the judges.

Decisions of the appellate court are delivered in writing, and the court's publication committee determines which decisions will be published in the *Wisconsin Reports.* Only published opinions have precedential value and may be cited as controlling law in Wisconsin. Unpublished opinions that are authored by a judge and issued after July 1, 2009, may be cited for their persuasive value.

District I: 633 West Wisconsin Avenue, Suite 1400, Milwaukee 53203-1908. Telephone: (414) 227-4680.

District II: 2727 North Grandview Boulevard, Suite 300, Waukesha 53188-1672. Telephone: (262) 521-5230.

District III: 2100 Stewart Avenue, Suite 310, Wausau 54401. Telephone: (715) 848-1421.

District IV: 10 East Doty Street, Suite 700, Madison 53703-3397. Telephone: (608) 266-9250.

COURT OF APPEALS DISTRICTS

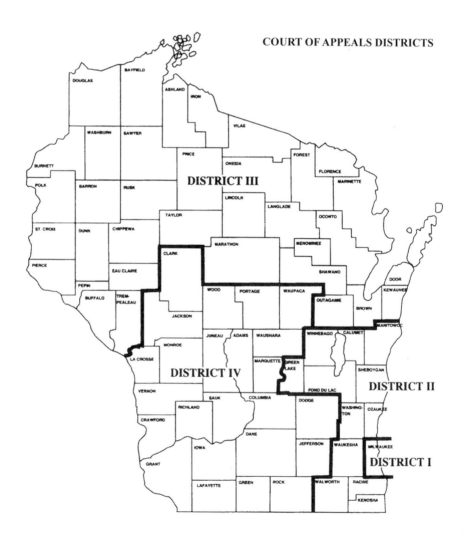

CIRCUIT COURTS

District 1: Milwaukee County Courthouse, 901 North 9th Street, Room 609, Milwaukee 53233-1425. Telephone: (414) 278-5113; Fax: (414) 223-1264.
Chief Judge: JEFFREY KREMERS.
Administrator: BRUCE HARVEY.

District 2: Racine County Courthouse, 730 Wisconsin Avenue, Racine 53403-1274. Telephone: (262) 636-3133; Fax: (262) 636-3437.
Chief Judge: MARY K. WAGNER.
Administrator: vacancy.

District 3: Waukesha County Courthouse, 515 West Moreland Boulevard, Room 359, Waukesha 53188-2428. Telephone: (262) 548-7209; Fax: (262) 548-7815.
Chief Judge: J. MAC DAVIS.
Administrator: MICHAEL NEIMON.

District 4: 404 North Main Street, Suite 105, Oshkosh 54901-4901. Telephone: (920) 424-0028; Fax: (920) 424-0096.
Chief Judge: DARRYL W. DEETS.
Administrator: JERRY LANG.

District 5: Dane County Courthouse, 215 South Hamilton Street, Madison 53703-3290. Telephone: 267-8820; Fax: 267-4151.
Chief Judge: C. WILLIAM FOUST.
Administrator: GAIL RICHARDSON.

District 6: 3317 Business Park Drive, Suite A, Stevens Point 54481-8834. Telephone: (715) 345-5295; Fax: (715) 345-5297.
Chief Judge: JOHN STORCK.
Administrator: RON LEDFORD.

District 7: La Crosse County Law Enforcement Center, 333 Vine Street, Room 3504, La Crosse 54601-3296. Telephone: (608) 785-9546; Fax: (608) 785-5530.
Chief Judge: WILLIAM DYKE.
Administrator: PATRICK BRUMMOND.

District 8: 414 East Walnut Street, Suite 221, Green Bay 54301-5020. Telephone: (920) 448-4281; Fax: (920) 448-4336.
Chief Judge: SUE BISCHEL.
Administrator: H. BRITT BEASLEY.

District 9: 2100 Stewart Avenue, Suite 310, Wausau 54401. Telephone: (715) 842-3872; Fax: (715) 845-4523.
Chief Judge: GREGORY GRAU.
Administrator: SUSAN BYRNES.

District 10: 4410 Golf Terrace, Suite 150, Eau Claire 54701-3606. Telephone: (715) 839-4826; Fax: (715) 839-4891.
Chief Judge: BENJAMIN PROCTOR.
Administrator: SCOTT JOHNSON.

Internet Address: www.wicourts.gov/about/organization/circuit/index.htm

State-Funded Positions: 521.00.

Total Budget 2007-09: $178,758,300.

Constitutional References: Article VII, Sections 2, 6-13.

Statutory Reference: Chapter 753.

Responsibility: The circuit court is the trial court of general jurisdiction in Wisconsin. It has original jurisdiction in both civil and criminal matters unless exclusive jurisdiction is given to another court. It also reviews state agency decisions and hears appeals from municipal courts. Jury trials are conducted only in circuit courts.

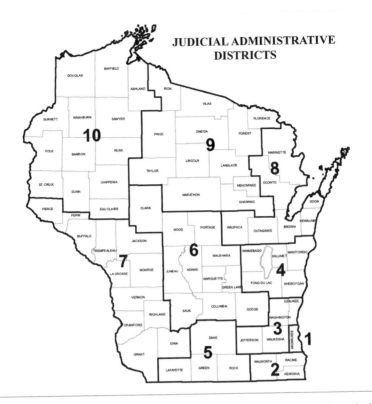

JUDICIAL ADMINISTRATIVE DISTRICTS

The constitution requires that a circuit be bounded by county lines. As a result, each circuit consists of a single county, except for 3 two-county circuits (Buffalo-Pepin, Florence-Forest, and Menominee-Shawano). Where judicial caseloads are heavy, a circuit may have several branches, each with an elected judge. Statewide, 39 of the state's 69 judicial circuits had multiple branches as of August 1, 2008, for a total of 246 circuit judgeships, and effective August 1, 2009, 40 of the circuits have multiple branches for a total of 248 circuit judgeships.

Organization: Circuit judges, who serve 6-year terms, are elected on a nonpartisan basis in the county in which they serve in the April election and take office the following August 1. The governor may fill circuit court vacancies by appointment, and the appointees serve until a successor is elected. The authorized salary for circuit court judges for 2009 is $128,600. The state pays the salaries of circuit judges and court reporters. It also covers some of the expenses for interpreters, guardians ad litem, judicial assistants, court-appointed witnesses, and jury per diems. Counties bear the remaining expenses for operating the circuit courts.

Administrative Districts. Circuit courts are divided into 10 administrative districts, each supervised by a chief judge, appointed by the supreme court from the district's circuit judges. A judge usually cannot serve more than 3 successive 2-year terms as chief judge. The chief judge has authority to assign judges, manage caseflow, supervise personnel, and conduct financial planning.

The chief judge in each district appoints a district court administrator from a list of candidates supplied by the director of state courts. The administrator manages the nonjudicial business of the district at the direction of the chief judge.

Circuit Court Commissioners are appointed by the circuit court to assist the court, and they must be attorneys licensed to practice law in Wisconsin. They may be authorized by the court to conduct various civil, criminal, family, small claims, juvenile, and probate court proceedings.

Their duties include issuing summonses, arrest warrants, or search warrants; conducting initial appearances; setting bail; conducting preliminary examinations and arraignments; imposing monetary penalties in certain traffic cases; conducting certain family, juvenile, and small claims court proceedings; hearing petitions for mental commitments; and conducting uncontested probate proceedings. On their own authority, court commissioners may perform marriages, administer oaths, take depositions, and issue subpoenas and certain writs.

The statutes require Milwaukee County to have full-time family, small claims, and probate court commissioners. All other counties must have a family court commissioner, and they may employ other full- or part-time court commissioners as deemed necessary.

Dodge County Circuit Court Judge John R. Storck, right, discusses appellate court procedure with District IV Court of Appeals Judges Margaret J. Vergeront and Paul Lundsten. Storck, chief judge of the Sixth Judicial Administrative District, temporarily sat on the District IV bench as part of the Supreme Court's Judicial Exchange Program. Established by Wisconsin Supreme Court Chief Justice Shirley S. Abrahamson in 1996, the Judicial Exchange offers judges the opportunity to better understand each others' roles. (Tom Sheehan, Court Information Officer)

JUDGES OF CIRCUIT COURT
June 1, 2009

County Circuits	Court Location	Judges	Term Expires July 31
Adams	Friendship	Charles A. Pollex[1]	2009
Ashland	Ashland	Robert E. Eaton	2012
Barron			
Branch 1	Barron	James C. Babler	2010
Branch 2	Barron	Timothy M. Doyle	2014
Branch 3	Barron	James D. Babbitt	2014
Bayfield	Washburn	John P. Anderson[1]	2009
Brown			
Branch 1	Green Bay	Donald R. Zuidmulder[1]	2009
Branch 2	Green Bay	Mark A. Warpinski	2012
Branch 3	Green Bay	Susan Bischel	2010
Branch 4	Green Bay	Kendall M. Kelley[1]	2009
Branch 5	Green Bay	Marc A. Hammer[1,2]	2009
Branch 6	Green Bay	John D. McKay[1]	2009
Branch 7	Green Bay	Timothy A. Hinkfuss	2013
Branch 8	Green Bay	William M. Atkinson[1]	2009
Buffalo-Pepin	Alma	James J. Duvall	2012
Burnett	Siren	Kenneth Kutz[1,2]	2009
Calumet	Chilton	Donald A. Poppy	2010
Chippewa			
Branch 1	Chippewa Falls	Roderick A. Cameron	2014
Branch 2	Chippewa Falls	vacancy[3]	—
Branch 3	Chippewa Falls	Steven R. Cray	2014
Clark	Neillsville	Jon M. Counsell	2012
Columbia			
Branch 1	Portage	Daniel S. George[1]	2009
Branch 2	Portage	James O. Miller	2011
Branch 3	Portage	Alan White	2013
Crawford	Prairie du Chien	Michael T. Kirchman	2013
Dane			
Branch 1	Madison	John Markson	2014
Branch 2	Madison	Maryann Sumi	2011
Branch 3	Madison	John C. Albert	2012
Branch 4	Madison	Steven D. Ebert	2010
Branch 5	Madison	Diane M. Nicks	2013
Branch 6	Madison	Shelley J. Gaylord[1]	2009
Branch 7	Madison	William E. Hanrahan	2014
Branch 8	Madison	Patrick J. Fiedler	2012
Branch 9	Madison	Richard Niess	2011
Branch 10	Madison	Juan B. Colas[1,2]	2009
Branch 11	Madison	Daniel R. Moeser[1]	2009
Branch 12	Madison	David T. Flanagan	2012
Branch 13	Madison	Michael Nowakowski[4]	2009
Branch 14	Madison	C. William Foust	2010
Branch 15	Madison	Stuart A. Schwartz	2010
Branch 16	Madison	Sarah B. O'Brien	2010
Branch 17	Madison	James L. Martin	2010
Dodge			
Branch 1	Juneau	Brian A. Pfitzinger	2014
Branch 2	Juneau	John R. Storck	2013
Branch 3	Juneau	Andrew P. Bissonnette	2013
Branch 4	Juneau	Steven Bauer	2014
Door			
Branch 1	Sturgeon Bay	D. Todd Ehlers	2012
Branch 2	Sturgeon Bay	Peter C. Diltz	2012
Douglas			
Branch 1	Superior	Michael T. Lucci[5]	2009
Branch 2	Superior	George L. Glonek[1]	2009
Dunn			
Branch 1	Menomonie	William C. Stewart, Jr.	2010
Branch 2	Menomonie	Rod W. Smeltzer[1]	2009
Eau Claire			
Branch 1	Eau Claire	Lisa K. Stark	2012
Branch 2	Eau Claire	Michael Schumacher	2014
Branch 3	Eau Claire	William M. Gabler	2012
Branch 4	Eau Claire	Benjamin D. Proctor	2012
Branch 5	Eau Claire	Paul J. Lenz	2012
Florence-Forest	Crandon	Leon D. Stenz	2014
Fond du Lac			
Branch 1	Fond du Lac	Dale L. English	2014
Branch 2	Fond du Lac	Peter L. Grimm	2010
Branch 3	Fond du Lac	Richard J. Nuss[1]	2009
Branch 4	Fond du Lac	Steven W. Weinke	2010
Branch 5	Fond du Lac	Robert J. Wirtz	2011
Forest (see *Florence-Forest*)			
Grant			
Branch 1	Lancaster	Robert P. VanDeHey	2011
Branch 2	Lancaster	George S. Curry[6]	2009
Green			
Branch 1	Monroe	Jim Beer[1]	2009
Branch 2	Monroe	newly created branch[7]	—
Green Lake	Green Lake	William M. McMonigal	2011
Iowa	Dodgeville	William D. Dyke	2010

JUDGES OF CIRCUIT COURT
June 1, 2009–Continued

County Circuits	Court Location	Judges	Term Expires July 31
Iron.	Hurley	Patrick John Madden.	2011
Jackson.	Black River Falls.	Thomas Lister[1,2]	2009
Jefferson			
Branch 1.	Jefferson	John M. Ullsvik[8]	2009
Branch 2.	Jefferson	William F. Hue.	2013
Branch 3.	Jefferson	Jacqueline R. Erwin[1]	2009
Branch 4.	Jefferson	Randy R. Koschnick.	2011
Juneau			
Branch 1.	Mauston	John Pier Roemer	2010
Branch 2.	Mauston	Paul S. Curran	2014
Kenosha			
Branch 1.	Kenosha	David Mark Bastianelli[1]	2009
Branch 2.	Kenosha	Barbara A. Kluka	2013
Branch 3.	Kenosha	Bruce E. Schroeder	2014
Branch 4.	Kenosha	Anthony Milisauskas	2011
Branch 5.	Kenosha	Wilbur W. Warren III[1]	2009
Branch 6.	Kenosha	Mary K. Wagner[1].	2009
Branch 7.	Kenosha	S. Michael Wilk.	2012
Branch 8.	Kenosha	newly created branch[9]	—
Kewaunee	Kewaunee	Dennis J. Mleziva	2010
La Crosse			
Branch 1.	La Crosse	Ramona A. Gonzalez	2013
Branch 2.	La Crosse	Elliott Levine	2013
Branch 3.	La Crosse	Todd Bjerke	2013
Branch 4.	La Crosse	Scott L. Horne	2013
Branch 5.	La Crosse	Dale T. Pasell	2011
Lafayette.	Darlington	William D. Johnston[1]	2009
Langlade.	Antigo	Fred W. Kawalski	2011
Lincoln			
Branch 1.	Merrill	Jay R. Tlusty.	2010
Branch 2.	Merrill	Glenn H. Hartley.	2011
Manitowoc			
Branch 1.	Manitowoc	Patrick L. Willis	2010
Branch 2.	Manitowoc	Darryl W. Deets	2013
Branch 3.	Manitowoc	Jerome L. Fox	2011
Marathon			
Branch 1.	Wausau.	vacancy[10]	—
Branch 2.	Wausau.	Gregory Huber.	2010
Branch 3.	Wausau.	Vincent K. Howard	2014
Branch 4.	Wausau.	Gregory Grau	2013
Branch 5.	Wausau.	Patrick Brady	2011
Marinette			
Branch 1.	Marinette.	David G. Miron	2014
Branch 2.	Marinette.	Tim A. Duket.	2014
Marquette	Montello	Richard O. Wright	2013
Menominee-Shawano			
Branch 1.	Shawano	James R. Habeck.	2014
Branch 2.	Shawano	Thomas G. Grover.	2013
Milwaukee			
Branch 1.	Milwaukee	Maxine Aldridge White	2011
Branch 2.	Milwaukee	Joe Donald[1]	2009
Branch 3.	Milwaukee	Clare L. Fiorenza[1]	2009
Branch 4.	Milwaukee	Mel Flanagan	2012
Branch 5.	Milwaukee	Mary Kuhnmuench	2010
Branch 6.	Milwaukee	Ellen Brostrom[11]	2009
Branch 7.	Milwaukee	Jean W. DiMotto[1]	2009
Branch 8.	Milwaukee	William Sosnay	2012
Branch 9.	Milwaukee	Paul R. Van Grunsven	2011
Branch 10.	Milwaukee	Timothy G. Dugan.	2011
Branch 11.	Milwaukee	Dominic S. Amato.	2013
Branch 12.	Milwaukee	David L. Borowski[1]	2009
Branch 13.	Milwaukee	Mary Triggiano	2011
Branch 14.	Milwaukee	Christopher R. Foley.	2010
Branch 15.	Milwaukee	J.D. Watts[11].	2009
Branch 16.	Milwaukee	Michael J. Dwyer[1].	2009
Branch 17.	Milwaukee	Francis Wasielewski	2014
Branch 18.	Milwaukee	Patricia D. McMahon	2011
Branch 19.	Milwaukee	Dennis R. Cimpl.	2011
Branch 20.	Milwaukee	Dennis P. Moroney.	2012
Branch 21.	Milwaukee	William Brash III	2014
Branch 22.	Milwaukee	Timothy M. Witkowiak[1].	2009
Branch 23.	Milwaukee	Elsa C. Lamelas	2012
Branch 24.	Milwaukee	Charles F. Kahn, Jr.	2010
Branch 25.	Milwaukee	Stephanie Rothstein[2]	2010
Branch 26.	Milwaukee	William Pocan	2013
Branch 27.	Milwaukee	Kevin E. Martens	2014
Branch 28.	Milwaukee	Thomas R. Cooper.	2012
Branch 29.	Milwaukee	Richard J. Sankovitz[1].	2009
Branch 30.	Milwaukee	Jeffrey A. Conen[1].	2009
Branch 31.	Milwaukee	Daniel A. Noonan.	2014
Branch 32.	Milwaukee	Michael D. Guolee.	2014
Branch 33.	Milwaukee	Carl Ashley.	2011
Branch 34.	Milwaukee	Glen H. Yamahiro	2010

JUDGES OF CIRCUIT COURT
June 1, 2009–Continued

County Circuits	Court Location	Judges	Term Expires July 31
Branch 35	Milwaukee	Frederick C. Rosa	2011
Branch 36	Milwaukee	Jeffrey A. Kremers	2011
Branch 37	Milwaukee	Karen Christenson	2010
Branch 38	Milwaukee	Jeffrey A. Wagner	2012
Branch 39	Milwaukee	Jane Carroll	2012
Branch 40	Milwaukee	Rebecca Dallett	2014
Branch 41	Milwaukee	John J. DiMotto	2014
Branch 42	Milwaukee	David A. Hansher[1]	2009
Branch 43	Milwaukee	Marshall B. Murray	2012
Branch 44	Milwaukee	Daniel L. Konkol	2010
Branch 45	Milwaukee	Thomas P. Donegan	2010
Branch 46	Milwaukee	Bonnie L. Gordon	2012
Branch 47	Milwaukee	John Siefert	2011
Monroe			
Branch 1	Sparta	Todd L. Ziegler	2013
Branch 2	Sparta	Michael J. McAlpine	2010
Oconto			
Branch 1	Oconto	Michael T. Judge	2011
Branch 2	Oconto	Richard D. Delforge	2010
Oneida			
Branch 1	Rhinelander	Patrick F.O'Melia	2014
Branch 2	Rhinelander	Mark A. Mangerson	2012
Outagamie			
Branch 1	Appleton	Mark McGinnis	2011
Branch 2	Appleton	Nancy J. Krueger	2014
Branch 3	Appleton	Mitchell J. Metropulos	2014
Branch 4	Appleton	Harold V. Froehlich	2012
Branch 5	Appleton	Michael W. Gage[1]	2009
Branch 6	Appleton	Dee R. Dyer	2012
Branch 7	Appleton	John A. Des Jardins	2012
Ozaukee			
Branch 1	Port Washington	Paul V. Malloy[1]	2009
Branch 2	Port Washington	Thomas R. Wolfgram	2013
Branch 3	Port Washington	Sandy A. Williams[11]	2009
Pepin (see *Buffalo-Pepin*)			
Pierce	Ellsworth	Robert W. Wing	2010
Polk			
Branch 1	Balsam Lake	Molly E. GaleWyrick	2014
Branch 2	Balsam Lake	Robert H. Rasmussen[1]	2009
Portage			
Branch 1	Stevens Point	Frederic W. Fleishauer	2011
Branch 2	Stevens Point	John V. Finn	2013
Branch 3	Stevens Point	Thomas T. Flugaur	2012
Price	Phillips	Douglas T. Fox	2014
Racine			
Branch 1	Racine	Gerald P. Ptacek	2013
Branch 2	Racine	Stephen A. Simanek	2010
Branch 3	Racine	Emily S. Mueller	2011
Branch 4	Racine	John S. Jude	2010
Branch 5	Racine	Dennis J. Barry	2011
Branch 6	Racine	Wayne J. Marik[1]	2009
Branch 7	Racine	Charles H. Constantine	2014
Branch 8	Racine	Faye M. Flancher[1]	2009
Branch 9	Racine	Allan B. Torhorst[1]	2009
Branch 10	Racine	Richard J. Kreul	2012
Richland	Richland Center	Edward E. Leineweber[1]	2009
Rock			
Branch 1	Janesville	James P. Daley	2014
Branch 2	Janesville	Alan Bates	2010
Branch 3	Janesville	Michael Fitzpatrick[1,2]	2009
Branch 4	Beloit	Daniel T. Dillon	2013
Branch 5	Beloit	Kenneth Forbeck[1,2]	2009
Branch 6	Janesville	Richard T. Werner[1]	2009
Branch 7	Beloit	James E. Welker	2012
Rusk	Ladysmith	Frederick A. Henderson	2010
St. Croix			
Branch 1	Hudson	Eric J. Lundell	2014
Branch 2	Hudson	Edward F. Vlack III	2013
Branch 3	Hudson	Scott R. Needham	2012
Branch 4	Hudson	Howard Cameron	2014
Sauk			
Branch 1	Baraboo	Patrick J. Taggart	2012
Branch 2	Baraboo	James Evenson	2010
Branch 3	Baraboo	Guy D. Reynolds	2012
Sawyer	Hayward	Norman L. Yackel[12]	2009
Shawano-Menominee (see *Menominee-Shawano*)			
Sheboygan			
Branch 1	Sheboygan	L. Edward Stengel[1]	2009
Branch 2	Sheboygan	Timothy M. Van Akkeren	2013
Branch 3	Sheboygan	Gary J. Langhoff	2011
Branch 4	Sheboygan	Terence T. Bourke[1]	2009
Branch 5	Sheboygan	James J. Bolgert	2012
Taylor	Medford	Ann Knox-Bauer[1,2]	2009

JUDGES OF CIRCUIT COURT
June 1, 2009–Continued

County Circuits	Court Location	Judges	Term Expires July 31
Trempealeau	Whitehall	John A. Damon	2013
Vernon	Viroqua	Michael J. Rosborough	2011
Vilas	Eagle River	Neal A. Nielsen	2010
Walworth			
Branch 1	Elkhorn	Robert J. Kennedy	2012
Branch 2	Elkhorn	James L. Carlson	2010
Branch 3	Elkhorn	John R. Race[1]	2009
Branch 4	Elkhorn	Michael S. Gibbs	2010
Washburn	Shell Lake	Eugene D. Harrington[1]	2009
Washington			
Branch 1	West Bend	Patrick J. Faragher	2013
Branch 2	West Bend	James K. Muehlbauer	2014
Branch 3	West Bend	David C. Resheske	2012
Branch 4	West Bend	Andrew T. Gonring	2012
Waukesha			
Branch 1	Waukesha	Michael O. Bohren	2013
Branch 2	Waukesha	Richard Congdon[2]	2010
Branch 3	Waukesha	Ralph M. Ramirez	2011
Branch 4	Waukesha	Paul F. Reilly[1]	2009
Branch 5	Waukesha	Lee Sherman Dreyfus, Jr.	2014
Branch 6	Waukesha	Patrick C. Haughney	2014
Branch 7	Waukesha	J. Mac Davis[1]	2009
Branch 8	Waukesha	James R. Kieffer[1]	2009
Branch 9	Waukesha	Donald J. Hassin, Jr.	2013
Branch 10	Waukesha	Linda M. Van De Water[1]	2009
Branch 11	Waukesha	Robert G. Mawdsley	2012
Branch 12	Waukesha	Kathryn W. Foster	2012
Waupaca			
Branch 1	Waupaca	Philip M. Kirk	2011
Branch 2	Waupaca	John P. Hoffmann	2010
Branch 3	Waupaca	Raymond S. Huber	2012
Waushara	Wautoma	Guy Dutcher	2011
Winnebago			
Branch 1	Oshkosh	Thomas J. Gritton	2012
Branch 2	Oshkosh	Scott C. Woldt	2011
Branch 3	Oshkosh	Barbara Hart Key	2010
Branch 4	Oshkosh	Karen L. Seifert	2012
Branch 5	Oshkosh	William H. Carver	2010
Branch 6	Oshkosh	Bruce K. Schmidt[1]	2009
Wood			
Branch 1	Wisconsin Rapids	Gregory J. Potter	2014
Branch 2	Wisconsin Rapids	James M. Mason	2010
Branch 3	Wisconsin Rapids	Edward F. Zappen, Jr.[13]	2009

[1]Reelected on April 7, 2009, for a 6-year term to commence on August 1, 2009.
[2]Appointed by the governor.
[3]James Isaacson was newly elected on April 7, 2009, for a 6-year term to commence on August 1, 2009.
[4]Julie Genovese was newly elected on April 7, 2009, for a 6-year term to commence on August 1, 2009.
[5]Kelly J. Thimm was newly elected on April 7, 2009, for a 6-year term to commence on August 1, 2009.
[6]Craig R. Day was newly elected on April 7, 2009, for a 6-year term to commence on August 1, 2009.
[7]Thomas J. Vale was newly elected on April 7, 2009, for a 6-year term to commence on August 1, 2009.
[8]Jennifer L. Weston was newly elected on April 7, 2009, for a 6-year term to commence on August 1, 2009.
[9]Chad G. Kerkman was newly elected on April 7, 2009, for a 6-year term to commence on August 1, 2009.
[10]Jill N. Falstad was newly elected on April 7, 2009, for a 6-year term to commence on August 1, 2009, then appointed by governor to begin term early.
[11]Newly elected on April 7, 2009, for a 6-year term to commence on August 1, 2009, then appointed by governor to begin term early.
[12]Jerry Wright was newly elected on April 7, 2009, for a 6-year term to commence on August 1, 2009.
[13]Todd P. Wolf was newly elected on April 7, 2009, for a 6-year term to commence on August 1, 2009.
Sources: *2007-2008 Wisconsin Statutes*; Government Accountability Board, departmental data, May 2009; Director of State Courts, departmental data, April 2009; governor's appointment notices.

MUNICIPAL COURTS

Constitutional References: Article VII, Sections 2 and 14.

Statutory References: Chapters 755 and 800.

Internet Address: www.wicourts.gov/about/organization/municipal/index.htm

Responsibility: The Wisconsin Legislature authorizes cities, villages, and towns to establish municipal courts to exercise jurisdiction over municipal ordinance violations that have monetary penalties. In addition, the Wisconsin Supreme Court ruled in 1991 (*City of Milwaukee v. Wroten,* 160 Wis. 2d 107) that municipal courts have authority to rule on the constitutionality of municipal ordinances.

As of May 1, 2009, there were 253 municipal courts with 255 municipal judges. Courts may have multiple branches; the City of Milwaukee's municipal court, for example, has 3 branches. (Milwaukee County, which is the only county authorized to appoint municipal court commissioners, had 3 part-time commissioners as of May 2009.) Two or more municipalities may agree to form a joint court, and there are 46 joint courts, serving up to 15 municipalities each. Besides Milwaukee, Madison is the only city with a full-time municipal court.

Upon convicting a defendant, the municipal court may order payment of a forfeiture plus costs and surcharges, or, if the defendant agrees, it may require community service in lieu of a forfeiture. In general, municipal courts may also order restitution up to $4,000. Where local ordinances conform to state drunk driving laws, a municipal judge may suspend or revoke a driver's license.

If a defendant fails to pay a forfeiture or make restitution, the municipal court may suspend the driver's license or commit the defendant to jail. Municipal court decisions may be appealed to the circuit court of the county where the offense occurred.

Organization: Municipal judges are elected at the nonpartisan April election and take office May 1. The local governing body fixes the term of office at 2 to 4 years and determines the position's salary. There is no state requirement that the office be filled by an attorney, but a municipality may enact such a qualification by ordinance.

If a municipal judge is ill, disqualified, or unavailable, the chief judge of the judicial administrative district containing the municipality may transfer the case to another municipal judge in the district. If none is available, the case will be heard in circuit court.

History: Chapter 276, Laws of 1967, authorized cities, villages, and towns to establish municipal courts after the forerunner of municipal courts (the office of the justice of the peace) was eliminated by a constitutional amendment, ratified in April 1966. A constitutional amendment ratified in April 1977, which reorganized the state's court system, officially granted the legislature the power to authorize municipal courts.

STATEWIDE JUDICIAL AGENCIES

A number of statewide administrative and support agencies have been created by supreme court order or legislative enactment to assist the Wisconsin Supreme Court in its supervision of the Wisconsin judicial system.

DIRECTOR OF STATE COURTS

Director of State Courts: A. JOHN VOELKER, 266-6828, john.voelker@

Deputy Director for Court Operations: SHERYL GERVASI, 266-3121, sheryl.gervasi@

Deputy Director for Management Services: PAM RADLOFF, 266-8914, pam.radloff@

Consolidated Court Automation Programs: JEAN BOUSQUET, *director,* 267-0678, jean.bousquet@

Fiscal Officer: BRIAN LAMPRECH, 266-6865, brian.lamprech@

Judicial Education: DAVID H. HASS, *director,* 266-7807, david.hass@

Medical Malpractice Mediation System: RANDY SPROULE, *director,* 266-7711, randy.sproule@

Public Information Officers: AMANDA TODD, 264-6256, amanda.todd@; TOM SHEEHAN, 261-6640, tom.sheehan@

Legislative Liaison: NANCY ROTTIER, 267-9733, nancy.rottier@

Address e-mail by combining the user ID and the state extender: userid@**wicourts.gov**

Mailing Address: Director of State Courts: P.O. Box 1688, Madison 53701-1688; Staff: 110 East Main Street, Madison 53703.

Location: Director of State Courts: Room 16 East, State Capitol, Madison; Staff: 110 East Main Street, Madison.

Fax: 267-0980.

Internet Address: www.wicourts.gov

Number of Employees: 132.25.

Total Budget 2007-09: $37,242,400.

References: Wisconsin Statutes, Chapter 655, Subchapter VI, and Section 758.19; Supreme Court Rules 70.01-70.08.

Responsibility: The Director of State Courts administers the nonjudicial business of the Wisconsin court system and informs the chief justice and the supreme court about the status of judicial business. The director is responsible for supervising state-level court personnel; developing the court system's budget; and directing the courts' work on legislation, public information, and information systems. This office also controls expenditures; allocates space and equipment; supervises judicial education, interdistrict assignment of active and reserve judges, and planning and research; and administers the medical malpractice mediation system.

The director is appointed by the supreme court from outside the classified service. The position was created by the supreme court in orders, dated October 30, 1978, and February 19, 1979. It replaced the administrative director of courts, which had been created by Chapter 261, Laws of 1961.

STATE LAW LIBRARY

State Law Librarian: JANE COLWIN, 261-2340, jane.colwin@wicourts.gov

Deputy Law Librarian: JULIE TESSMER, 261-7557, julie.tessmer@wicourts.gov

Mailing Address: P.O. Box 7881, Madison 53707-7881.

Location: 120 Martin Luther King, Jr. Blvd., 2nd Floor, Madison.

Telephones: General Information and Circulation: 266-1600; Reference Assistance: 267-9696; (800) 322-9755 (toll-free).

Fax: 267-2319.

Internet Address: http://wilawlibrary.gov
Reference E-mail Address: wsll.ref@wicourts.gov
Publications: *WSLL @ Your Service* (e-newsletter), at: http://wilawlibrary.gov/newsletter/index.html
Number of Employees: 16.50.
Total Budget 2007-09: $5,508,000.
References: Wisconsin Statutes, Section 758.01; Supreme Court Rule 82.01.
Responsibility: The State Law Library is a public library open to all citizens of Wisconsin. It serves as the primary legal resource center for the Wisconsin Supreme Court and Court of Appeals, the Department of Justice, the Wisconsin Legislature, the Office of the Governor, executive agencies, and members of the State Bar of Wisconsin. The library is administered by the supreme court, which appoints the library staff and determines the rules governing library use. The library acts as a consultant and resource for county law libraries throughout the state. Milwaukee County and Dane County contract with the State Law Library for management and operation of their courthouse libraries (the Milwaukee Legal Resource Center and the Dane County Legal Resource Center).

The library's 150,000-volume collection features session laws, statutory codes, court reports, administrative rules, legal indexes, and case law digests of the U.S. government, all 50 states and U.S. territories. It also includes selected documents of the federal government, legal and bar periodicals, legal treatises, and legal encyclopedias. The library also offers reference, basic legal research, and document delivery services. The collection circulates to judges, attorneys, legislators, and government personnel.

OFFICE OF LAWYER REGULATION

Board of Administrative Oversight: TERRY ROSE (lawyer), *chairperson;* STEVE KOSZAREK (nonlaywer), *vice chairperson;* BARRETT J. CORNEILLE, MARK A. PETERSON, SCOTT ROBERTS, ALICE A. RUDEBUSCH, THOMAS S. SLEIK, HARVEY WENDEL, vacancy (lawyers); DEANNA M. HOSIN, CLAUDE GILMORE, vacancy (nonlawyers). (All members are appointed by the supreme court.)

Preliminary Review Committee: MICHAEL ANDERSON (lawyer), *chairperson;* GREGORY STACKER (lawyer), *vice chairperson;* ROBERT J. ASTI, TERENCE BOURESSA, JOHN W. CAMPION, DONALD CHRISTL, MICHAEL COHEN, EDWARD HANNAN, JAMES R. SMITH (lawyers); PATRICIA EVANS, CLAIRE FOWLER, MAJID SARMADI, JERRY SAUVE, vacancy (nonlawyers). (All members are appointed by the supreme court.)

Special Preliminary Review Panel: LORI S. KORNBLUM, RUDOLPH L. OLDESCHULTE, MICHAEL S. WEIDEN, JOSEPH J. WELCENBACH (lawyers); JOHN DRIESSEN, LAWRENCE J. QUAM, vacancy (nonlawyers). (All members are appointed by the supreme court.)

Sixteen District Committees (all members are appointed by the supreme court):

District 1 Committee (serves Jefferson, Kenosha, and Walworth Counties): JOHN HIGGENS (lawyer), *chairperson;* PATRICK ANDERSON, F. MARK BROMLEY, WILLIAM BRYDGES, ROBERT I. DUMEZ, TIMOTHY GERAGHTY, RAYMOND KREK, MATTHEW S. VIGNALI (lawyers); JOHN G. BRAIG, JEFFREY CASSITY, RANDALL HAMMETT, JEROME HONORE, GERALD PELISHEK (nonlawyers).

District 2 Committee (serves Milwaukee County): THOMAS CABUSH (lawyer), *chairperson;* JULIE A. O'HALLORAN (lawyer), *vice chairperson;* JAMES L. ADASHEK, COLLEEN D. BALL, PATRICIA KLING BALLMAN, ELIOT BERNSTEIN, REBECCA BLEMBERG, MARGARDETTE M. DEMET, ANNELIESE M. DICKMAN, ROBIN DORMAN, JOHN FERNANDES, BRADLEY FOLEY, MICHELE FORD, IRVING D. GAINES, JAMES GEHRKE, JAMES GREER, KENAN J. KERSTEN, R. JEFFREY KRILL, ROBERT C. MENARD, THOMAS MERKLE, ELLEN NOWAK, KEITH O'DONNELL, RAYMOND E.H. SCHRANK, DAVID W. SIMON, FRANK TERSCHAN, KATHERINE WILLIAMS (lawyers); J. STEPHEN ANDERSON, NEILAND COHEN, DONALD G. DORO, PATRICK DOYLE, SHEL GENDELMAN, JEFFREY HANEWALL, BARBARA J. JANUSIAK, ERICA MILLS, HOLLY PAZER, DEEDEE RONGSTAD, WILLIAM WARD (nonlawyers).

District 3 Committee (serves Fond du Lac, Green Lake, and Winnebago Counties): STEVEN R. SORENSON (lawyer), *chairperson;* PETER CULP, KENNARD N. FRIEDMAN, KRISTI L. FRY, SAM KAUFMAN, ELIZABETH J. NEVITT, BETH OSOWSKI, DAVID J. SCHULTZ, TIMOTHY R. YOUNG, JOHN S. ZARBANO (lawyers); SUSAN J. ANDREWS, KRISTY BRADISH, JOHN FAIRHURST, MARY JO KEATING, GARY KNOKE, ELLEN C. SORENSEN, SUSAN T. VETTE (nonlawyers).

District 4 Committee (serves Calumet, Door, Kewaunee, Manitowoc, and Sheboygan Counties): MARK JINKINS (lawyer), *chairperson;* MARY LYNN DONOHUE, ROBERTA A. HECKES, ROBERT LANDRY, SUSAN H. SCHLEISNER, NATASHA TORRY-ABATE (lawyers); ROBERT A. DOBBS, SUSAN M. MCANINCH, DONALD A. SCHWOBE, ALAN WHITE, RICHARD YORK (nonlawyers).

District 5 Committee (serves Buffalo, Clark, Crawford, Jackson, La Crosse, Monroe, Pepin, Richland, Trempealeau, and Vernon Counties): RICHARD A. RADCLIFFE (lawyer), *chairperson;* MICHAEL C. ABLAN, BRUCE J. BROVOLD, JAMES P. CZAJKOWSKI, MARVIN H. DAVIS, STEPHANIE HOPKINS, PAUL B. MILLIS, GEORGE PARKE III, J. DAVID RICE, JON D. SEIFERT (lawyers); ELVIN E. FLEMING, JAMES W. GEISSNER, RICHARD KYTE, PAUL R. LORENZ, DIANE MORRISON, JOHN PARKYN, REED POMEROY, LINDA LEE SONDREAL, LARRY D. WYMAN (nonlawyers).

District 6 Committee (serves Waukesha County): GARY KUPHALL (lawyer), *chairperson;* MARK P. ANDRINGA, COLLEEN MERRILL BROWN, MARTIN DITKOF, JAMES GENDE, ROSEMARY JUNE GORETA, LANCE S. GRADY, MICHAEL JASSAK, ANTHONY J. MENTING, DANIEL MURRAY, ROBYN A. SCHUCHARDT (lawyers); MICHAEL BRANKS, CARLA FRIEDRICH, ROBERT HAMILTON, RAYMOND KLITZKE, SARAH KRUEGER, JOHN SCHATZMAN (nonlawyers).

District 7 Committee (serves Adams, Columbia, Juneau, Marquette, Portage, Sauk, Waupaca, Waushara, and Wood Counties): THOMAS M. KUBASTA (lawyer), *chairperson;* KAYE ANDERSON, KENNETH W. GORSKI, CYNTHIA KIEPER, JOHN KRUSE, LEON SCHMIDT (lawyers); LAVINDA CARLSON, ELLEN M. DAHL, LEO J. GRILL, DAVID A. KORTH, DOROTHY E. MANSAVAGE, LINDA L. REDFIELD, JAMES E. STRASSER (nonlawyers).

District 8 Committee (serves Dunn, Eau Claire, Pierce, and St. Croix Counties): DOUGLAS M. JOHNSON (lawyer), *chairperson;* JAY E. HEIT, ROBERT L. LOBERG, CAROL N. SKINNER, PHILLIP M. STEANS, DENNIS M. SULLIVAN, TRACY N. TOOL, MICHAEL P. WAGNER, R. MICHAEL WATERMAN (lawyers); DAVID CRONK, JOHN DEROSIER, EDWARD HASS, SHARON NORTON-BAUMAN, WILLIAM O'GARA, PAUL W. SCHOMMER (nonlawyers).

District 9 Committee (serves Dane County): MEREDITH J. ROSS (lawyer), *chairperson;* LEE ATTERBURY, WILLIAM F. BAUER, ANNE M. BLOOD, ANDREW CLARKOWSKI, BRUCE F. EHLKE, MAUREEN MCGLYNN FLANAGAN, JESUS G.Q. GARZA, AARON HALSTEAD, PETER E. HANS, THOMAS HORNIG, JAMES R. JANSEN, ROBERT KASIETA, WILLIAM F. MUNDT, JENNIFER E. NASHOLD, JUDITH OLINGY, LAWRENCE P. PETERSON, BRUCE AL. SCHULTZ, THOMAS W. SHELLANDER (lawyers); PETER ANDERSON, NINA PETROVICH BARTELL, CHARLES A. BUNGE, PATRICK DELMORE, DAVID CHARLES DIES, R.C. HECHT, ROBERT C. HODGE, JUDITH A. MILLER, LARRY NESPER, THERON E. PARSONS, CONSUELO LOPEZ SPRINGFIELD, RODNEY TAPP, DAVID G. UTLEY, KENNETH YUSKA (nonlawyers).

District 10 Committee (serves Marinette, Menominee, Oconto, Outagamie, and Shawano Counties): JANE KIRKEIDE (lawyer), *chairperson;* GALE MATTISON, GERALD WILSON (lawyers); GUY T. GOODING, JOHN W. HILL, STEPHEN C. WARE (nonlawyer).

District 11 Committee (serves Ashland, Barron, Bayfield, Burnett, Chippewa, Douglas, Iron, Polk, Price, Rusk, Sawyer, Taylor, and Washburn Counties): KATHLEEN PAKES (lawyer), *chairperson;* MICHAEL O. ERSPAMER, CRAIG HAUKAAS, TIMOTHY T. SEMPF (lawyers); GENE ANDERSON, ELIZABETH ESSER, DIANE FJELSTAD, MARY ANN KING, MARGARET KOLBEK, JOHN M. MIZERKA (nonlawyers).

District 12 Committee (serves Grant, Green, Iowa, Lafayette, and Rock Counties): PATRICK K. MCDONALD (lawyer), *chairperson;* JAMES A. CARNEY, JODY L. COOPER, THOMAS H. GEYER, DERRICK A. GRUBB, WILLIAM T. HENDERSON, GAYLE BRANAUGH JEBBIA, ERIC D. REINICKE (lawyers); DENNIS L. EVERSON, MICHAEL FURGAL, LAURA MCBAIN, MICHAEL F. METZ, KATHLEEN J. ROELLI, JOHN SIMONSON, CLINTON A. WRUCK (nonlawyers).

District 13 Committee (serves Dodge, Ozaukee, and Washington Counties): WILLIAM BUCHHOLZ (lawyer), *chairperson;* GERALD H. ANTOINE, JOSEPH G. DOHERTY, CHRISTINE EISENMANN KNUDTSON (lawyers); MARK L. BORN, DEBORAH L. LUKOVICH, ALAN MARTENS, BONNIE L. SCHWID, DANIEL L. VANDE SANDE (nonlawyers).

District 14 Committee (serves Brown County): SANDRA L. HUPFER (lawyer), *chairperson;* BRUCE R. BACHHUBER, LAURA J. BECK, TERRY GERBERS, MARK A. PENNOW, BETH RAHMIG PLESS, THOMAS V. ROHAN (lawyers); RICHARD ALLCOX, DEBRA L. BURSIK, GREGORY L. GRAF, GERALD C. LORITZ, KIM E. NIELSEN, FAYE WILSON-GORRING (nonlawyers).

District 15 Committee (serves Racine County): MARK F. NIELSEN (lawyer), *chairperson;* JOHN J. BUCHAKLIAM, JAMES DRUMMOND, STEVEN G. GABRIEL, MARK R. HINKSTON, SALLY HOELZEL, ROBERT W. KELLER, MARK LUKOFF (lawyers); JOHN P. CRIMMINGS, THOMAS CHRYST, RAYMOND G. FEEST, MARK GLEASON, PATRICIA HOFFMAN, PETER SMET (nonlawyers).

District 16 Committee (serves Forest, Florence, Langlade, Lincoln, Marathon, Oneida, and Vilas Counties): WILLIAM D. MANSELL (lawyer), *chairperson;* DAVID J. CONDON, DOUGLAS KLINGBERG, DAWN R. LEMKE, GINGER MURRAY, BRENDA K. SUNBY, JESSICA TLUSTY (lawyers); THOMAS E. BURG, JUDY A. FRYMARK, ARNO WM. HAERING, TOM LONSDORF, DIANNE M. WEILER, BERNICE WISNEWSKI (nonlawyers).

Office of Lawyer Regulation: KEITH L. SELLEN, *director;* keith.sellen@wicourts.gov; JOHN O'CONNELL, *deputy director,* john.o'connell@wicourts.gov; ELIZABETH ESTES, *deputy director,* elizabeth.estes@wicourts.gov

Telephone: 267-7274; Central Intake toll-free (877) 315-6941.

Fax: 267-1959.

Mailing Address: 110 East Main Street, Suite 315, Madison 53703-3383.

Number of Employees: 27.50.

Total Budget 2007-09: $5,049,400.

References: Supreme Court Rules, Chapters 21 and 22.

Responsibility: The Office of Lawyer Regulation was created by order of the supreme court, effective October 1, 2000, to assist the court in fulfilling its constitutional responsibility to supervise the practice of law and protect the public from professional misconduct by members of the State Bar of Wisconsin. This agency assumed the attorney disciplinary functions that had previously been performed by the Board of Attorneys Professional Responsibility and, prior to January 1, 1978, by the Board of State Bar Commissioners.

The director of the Office of Lawyer Regulation is appointed by the supreme court and must be admitted to the practice of law in Wisconsin no later than six months following appointment. The Board of Administrative Oversight and the Preliminary Review Committee perform oversight and adjudicative responsibilities under the supervision of the supreme court.

The Board of Administrative Oversight consists of 12 members, 8 lawyers and 4 public members. Board members are appointed by the supreme court to staggered 3-year terms and may not serve more than two consecutive terms. The board monitors the overall system for regulating lawyers but does not handle actions regarding individual complaints or grievances. It reviews the "fairness, productivity, effectiveness and efficiency" of the system and reports its findings to the supreme court. After consultation with the director, it proposes the annual budget for the agency to the supreme court.

The Office of Lawyer Regulation receives and evaluates all complaints, inquiries, and grievances related to attorney misconduct or medical incapacity. The director is required to investigate any grievance that appears to support an allegation of possible attorney misconduct, and the attorney in question must cooperate with the investigation. District investigative committees are appointed in the 16 State Bar districts by the supreme court to aid the director in disciplinary investigations, forward matters to the director for review, and provide assistance when grievances can be settled at the district level.

After investigation, the director decides whether the matter should be forwarded to a panel of the Preliminary Review Committee, be dismissed, or be diverted for alternative action. This

14-member committee consists of 9 lawyers and 5 public members, who are appointed by the supreme court to staggered 3-year terms and may not serve more than two consecutive terms.

If a panel of the Preliminary Review Committee determines there is cause to proceed, the director may seek disciplinary action, ranging from private reprimand to filing a formal complaint with the supreme court that requests public reprimand, license suspension or revocation, monetary payment, or imposing conditions on the continued practice of law. An attorney may be offered alternatives to formal disciplinary action, including mediation, fee arbitration, law office management assistance, evaluation and treatment for alcohol and other substance abuse, psychological evaluation and treatment, monitoring of the attorney's practice or trust account procedures, continuing legal education, ethics school, or the multistate professional responsibility examination.

Formal disciplinary actions for attorney misconduct are filed by the director with the supreme court, which appoints a referee from a permanent panel of attorneys and reserve judges to hear discipline cases, make disciplinary recommendations to the court, and to approve the issuance of certain private and public reprimands. Referees conduct hearings on complaints of attorney misconduct, petitions alleging attorney medical incapacity, and petitions for reinstatement. They make findings, conclusions, and recommendations and submit them to the supreme court for review and appropriate action. Only the supreme court has the authority to suspend or revoke a lawyer's license to practice law in the State of Wisconsin.

Allegations of misconduct against the director, a lawyer member of staff, retained counsel, a lawyer member of a district committee, a lawyer member of the preliminary review committee, a lawyer member of the board of administrative oversight, or a referee are assigned by the director for investigation by a special investigator. The special investigator may close a matter if there is not enough information to support an allegation of possible misconduct. If there is enough information to support an allegation of possible misconduct an investigation is commenced. The investigator can then dismiss the matter after investigation or submit an investigative report to the special preliminary review panel which will ultimately decide whether or not there is cause to proceed. The special preliminary review panel consists of seven members, four lawyers and three public members appointed by the supreme court who serve staggered 3-year terms and may not serve more than two consecutive terms. If cause is found, the special investigator can proceed to file a complaint with the supreme court and prosecute the matter personally or may assign that responsibility to counsel retained by the director for such purposes.

BOARD OF BAR EXAMINERS

Board of Bar Examiners: JAMES A. MORRISON (State Bar member), *chairperson;* JAMES L. HUSTON (State Bar member), *vice chairperson;* CHARLES H. CONSTANTINE (circuit court judge); THOMAS M. BOYKOFF, KURT D. DYKSTRA, MARY BETH KEPPEL (State Bar members); DANIEL D. BLINKA (Marquette University Law School faculty); JOHN A. PRAY (UW Law School faculty); MARK J. BAKER, JAMES A. COTTER, LINDA HOSKINS (public members). (All members are appointed by the supreme court.)

Director: JOHN E. KOSOBUCKI, 266-9760; Fax: 266-1196.

Mailing Address: 110 East Main Street, Suite 715, P.O. Box 2748, Madison 53701-2748.

E-mail Address: bbe@wicourts.gov

Internet Address: www.wicourts.gov/about/organization/offices/bbe.htm

Number of Employees: 8.00.

Total Budget 2007-09: $1,409,800.

References: Supreme Court Rules, Chapters 30, 31, and 40.

Responsibility: The 11-member Board of Bar Examiners manages all bar admissions by examination or by motion on proof of practice; conducts character and fitness investigations of all candidates for admission to the bar, including diploma privilege graduates; and administers the Wisconsin mandatory continuing legal education requirement for attorneys.

The board was formed from two Supreme Court Boards: the Board of Continuing Legal Education and the Board of Bar Commissioners. The Board of Continuing Legal Education was created effective January 1, 1976, to administer the Wisconsin Supreme Court's mandatory continuing legal education requirements for lawyers. Effective January 1, 1978, the Board of Continuing Legal Education was renamed the Board of Attorneys Professional Competence and continued to be charged with administering mandatory continuing legal education.

The Board of Bar Commissioners was charged with administering bar admission and compliance with the Code of Professional Responsibility. Effective January 1, 1978, the Board of Bar Commissioners' duties with respect to bar admission were transferred to the Board of Attorneys Professional Competence. Effective January 1, 1991, the Board of Attorneys Professional Competence was renamed the Board of Bar Examiners.

Members are appointed for staggered 3-year terms, but no member may serve more than two consecutive full terms. The number of public members was increased from one to 3 by a supreme court order, effective January 1, 2001.

JUDICIAL CONDUCT ADVISORY COMMITTEE

Judicial Conduct Advisory Committee: vacancy (circuit court or reserve judge serving in a rural area); J. MAC DAVIS (judicial administrative district chief judge); vacancy (court of appeals judge); vacancy (circuit court or reserve judge serving in an urban area); BRUCE GOODNOUGH (municipal court judge); vacancy (reserve judge); SANDRA J. MARCUS (circuit court commissioner); FRANK R. TERSCHAN (State Bar member); vacancy (public member). (All members are selected by the supreme court.)

Mailing Address: P.O. Box 1688, Madison 53701-1688.

Internet Address: www.wicourts.gov/about/committees/judicialconduct.htm

Telephone: 266-6828.

Fax: 267-0980.

Reference: Supreme Court Rules, Chapter 60 Appendix.

Responsibility: The Wisconsin Supreme Court established the Judicial Conduct Advisory Committee as part of its 1997 update to the Code of Judicial Conduct. The 9-member committee gives formal advisory opinions and informal advice regarding whether actions judges are contemplating comply with the code. It also makes recommendations to the supreme court for amendment to the Code of Judicial Conduct or the rules governing the committee.

JUDICIAL CONFERENCE

Members: All supreme court justices, court of appeals judges, circuit court judges, reserve judges, 3 municipal court judges (designated by the Wisconsin Municipal Judges Association), 3 judicial representatives of tribal courts (designated by the Wisconsin Tribal Judges Association), one circuit court commissioner designated by the Family Court Commissioner Association, and one circuit court commissioner designated by the Judicial Court Commissioner Association.

Internet Address: www.wicourts.gov/about/committees/judicialconf.htm

References: Sections 758.171-758.18, Wisconsin Statutes; Supreme Court Rule 70.15.

Responsibility: The Judicial Conference, which was created by the Wisconsin Supreme Court, meets at least once a year to recommend improvements in administration of the justice system, conduct educational programs for its members, adopt the revised uniform traffic deposit and misdemeanor bail schedules, and adopt forms necessary for the administration of certain court proceedings. Since its initial meeting in January 1979, the conference has devoted sessions to family and children's law, probate, mental health, appellate practice and procedures, civil law, criminal law, truth-in-sentencing, and traffic law.

Judicial Conference bylaws have created a Nominating Committee and five standing committees. Committee members are elected by the Judicial Conference. The standing committees include: the Civil Jury Instructions Committee, the Criminal Jury Instructions Committee, the Juvenile Jury Instructions Committee, the Legislative Committee, and the Uniform Bond Committee. Chairpersons of each standing committee are selected annually by the committee members. The Nominating Committee is made up of the judges who chair the standing committees and the secretary of the Judicial Conference.

The Judicial Conference may create study committees to examine particular topics. These study committees must report their findings and recommendations to the next annual meeting of the Judicial Conference. Study committees usually work for one year, unless extended by the Judicial Conference.

JUDICIAL EDUCATION COMMITTEE

Judicial Education Committee: SHIRLEY S. ABRAHAMSON (supreme court chief justice); MICHAEL W. HOOVER (designated by appeals court chief judge); A. JOHN VOELKER (director of state courts); JUAN B. COLAS, JEROME L. FOX, NANCY J. KRUEGER, PAUL LENZ, 4 vacancies (circuit court judges appointed by supreme court); JASON J. HANSON, WILLIAM H. HONRATH (circuit court commissioners appointed by supreme court); JINI M. RABAS (designated by dean, UW Law School); THOMAS HAMMER (designated by dean, Marquette University Law School). *Ex officio* member: ROBERT G. MAWDSLEY (dean, Wisconsin Judicial College).

Office of Judicial Education: DAVID H. HASS, *director,* david.hass@wicourts.gov

Mailing Address: Office of Judicial Education, 110 East Main Street, Room 200, Madison 53703.

Telephone: 266-7807.

Fax: 261-6650.

E-mail Address: JED@wicourts.gov

Internet Address: www.wicourts.gov/about/committees/judicialed.htm

Reference: Supreme Court Rules, Chapters 32, 33, and 75.05.

Responsibility: The 16-member Judicial Education Committee approves educational programs for judges and court personnel. The 8 circuit court judges and 2 circuit court commissioners on the committee serve staggered 2-year terms and may not serve more than two consecutive terms. The dean of the Wisconsin Judicial College is an *ex officio* member of the committee and has voting privileges.

In 1976, the supreme court issued Chapter 32 of the Supreme Court Rules, which established a mandatory program of continuing education for the Wisconsin judiciary, effective January 1, 1977. This program applies to all supreme court justices and commissioners, appeals court judges and staff attorneys, circuit court judges, and reserve judges. Each person subject to the rule must obtain a specified number of credit hours of continuing education within a 6-year period. The Office of Judicial Education, which the supreme court established in 1971, administers the program. It also sponsors initial and continuing educational programs for municipal judges and circuit court clerks.

PLANNING AND POLICY ADVISORY COMMITTEE

Planning and Policy Advisory Committee: SHIRLEY S. ABRAHAMSON (supreme court chief justice), *chairperson;* CARL ASHLEY (circuit court judge), *vice chairperson;* JOAN KESSLER (appeals court judge selected by court); RICHARD BATES, TIMOTHY DUGAN, BONNIE GORDON, WILLIAM JOHNSTON, EDWARD LEINEWEBER, PAT MADDEN, WAYNE MARIK, J.D. MCKAY, RICHARD NUSS, GREGORY POTTER, BILL STEWART, LINDA VAN DE WATER (circuit court judges elected by judicial administrative districts); DANIEL KOVAL (municipal judge elected by Wisconsin Municipal Judges Association); JOHN WALSH, MARY WOLVERTON (selected by State Bar Board of Governors); JAMES DWYER (nonlawyer, elected county official); OSCAR BOLDT, LINDA HOSKINS (nonlawyers); MICHAEL TOBIN (public defender); GAIL RICHARDSON (court administrator);

Adam Gerol (prosecutor); Kris Deiss (circuit court clerk); Darcy McManus (circuit court commissioner). (Unless indicated otherwise, members are appointed by the chief justice.) Nonvoting associates: William Foust (chief judge liaison), A. John Voelker (director of state courts).

Planning Subcommittee: Barbara Kluka (circuit court judge), *chairperson;* Lisa Neubauer (appeals court judge); Jeffrey Kremers, J.D. McKay, Michael Rosborough (circuit court judges); Gail Richardson (court administrator); Sheila Reiff (circuit court clerk); Darcy McManus (circuit court commissioner); Diane Treis-Rusk (public member). *Ex officio* members: Shirley S. Abrahamson (supreme court chief justice), Carl Ashley (circuit court judge, vice chairperson of Planning and Policy Advisory Committee), A. John Voelker (director of state courts).

Staff Policy Analyst: Michelle Cyrulik, michelle.cyrulik@wicourts.gov

Mailing Address: 110 East Main Street, Room 410, Madison 53703.

Telephone: 266-8861.

Fax: 267-0911.

Internet Address: www.wicourts.gov/about/committees/ppac.htm

Reference: Supreme Court Rule 70.14.

Responsibility: The 26-member Planning and Policy Advisory Committee advises the Wisconsin Supreme Court and the Director of State Courts on planning and policy and assists in a continuing evaluation of the administrative structure of the court system. It participates in the budget process of the Wisconsin judiciary and appoints a subcommittee to review the budget of the court system. The committee meets at least quarterly, and the supreme court meets with the committee annually. The Director of State Courts participates in committee deliberations, with full floor and advocacy privileges, but is not a member of the committee and does not have a vote.

This committee was created in 1978 as the Administrative Committee of the Courts and renamed the Planning and Policy Advisory Committee in December 1990.

WISCONSIN JUDICIAL SYSTEM — INDEPENDENT BODIES

JUDICIAL COMMISSION

Members: Donald Leo Bach, John R. Dawson (State Bar members); Ginger Alden, James M. Haney, Cynthia Herber, Michael R. Miller, William Vander Loop (nonlawyers); David Hansher (circuit court judge); Gregory Peterson (appeals court judge). (Judges and State Bar members appointed by supreme court. Nonlawyers are appointed by governor with senate consent.)

Executive Director: James C. Alexander.

Administrative Assistant: Laury Bussan.

Mailing Address: 110 East Main Street, Suite 700, Madison 53703-3328.

Telephone: 266-7637.

Fax: 266-8647.

Agency E-mail: judcmm@wicourts.gov

Internet Address: www.wicourts.gov/judcom

Publication: Annual Report.

Number of Employees: 2.00.

Total Budget 2007-09: $478,200.

Statutory References: Sections 757.81-757.99.

Responsibility: The 9-member Judicial Commission conducts investigations for review and action by the supreme court regarding allegations of misconduct or permanent disability of a judge or court commissioner. Members are appointed for 3-year terms but cannot serve more than two consecutive full terms.

The commission's investigations are confidential. If an investigation results in a finding of probable cause that a judge or court commissioner has engaged in misconduct or is disabled, the commission must file a formal complaint of misconduct or a petition regarding disability with the supreme court. Prior to filing a complaint or petition, the commission may request a jury hearing of its findings before a single appellate judge. If it does not request a jury hearing, the chief judge of the court of appeals selects a 3-judge panel to hear the complaint or petition.

The commission is responsible for prosecution of a case. After the case is heard by a jury or panel, the supreme court reviews the findings of fact, conclusions of law, and recommended disposition. It has ultimate responsibility for determining appropriate discipline in cases of misconduct or appropriate action in cases of permanent disability.

History: In 1972, the Wisconsin Supreme Court created a 9-member commission to implement the Code of Judicial Ethics it had adopted. The code enumerated standards of personal and official conduct and identified conduct that would result in disciplinary action. Subject to supreme court review, the commission had authority to reprimand or censure a judge.

A constitutional amendment approved by the voters in 1977 empowered the supreme court, using procedures developed by the legislature, to reprimand, censure, suspend, or remove any judge for misconduct or disability. With enactment of Chapter 449, Laws of 1977, the legislature created the Judicial Commission and prescribed its procedures. The supreme court abolished its own commission in 1978.

JUDICIAL COUNCIL

Members: Ann Walsh Bradley (justice designated by supreme court); Patricia S. Curley (judge designated by court of appeals); A. John Voelker (director of state courts); George S. Curry, Edward E. Leineweber, Mary K. Wagner, Maxine A. White (circuit court judges designated by Judicial Conference); Senator Taylor (chairperson, senate judicial committee); Representative Hebl (chairperson, assembly judicial committee); Greg M. Weber (designated by attorney general); Stephen R. Miller (Legislative Reference Bureau Chief); David E. Schultz (faculty member, UW Law School, designated by dean); Jay Grenig (faculty member, Marquette University Law School, designated by dean); Marla J. Stephens (designated by state public defender); William C. Gleisner (State Bar member, designated by president-elect); Beth E. Hanan, Catherine A. La Fleur, Robert L. McCracken (State Bar members selected by State Bar); Kathleen Anne Pakes (district attorney appointed by governor); Michael R. Christopher, Allan M. Foeckler (public members appointed by governor).

Mailing Address: 110 East Main Street, Suite 822, Madison 53703.

Telephone: 261-8290.

Fax: 261-8289.

Number of Employees: 1.00.

Total Budget 2007-09: $201,200.

Statutory References: Section 758.13.

Responsibility: The Judicial Council, created by Chapter 392, Laws of 1951, assumed the functions of the Advisory Committee on Rules of Pleading, Practice and Procedure, created by the 1929 Legislature. The 21-member council is authorized to advise the supreme court, the governor, and the legislature on any matter affecting the administration of justice in Wisconsin, and it may recommend legislation to change the procedure, jurisdiction, or organization of the courts. The council studies the rules of pleading, practice, and procedure and advises the supreme court about changes that will simplify procedure and promote efficiency.

Several council members serve at the pleasure of their appointing authorities. The 4 circuit judges selected by the Judicial Conference serve 4-year terms. The 3 members selected by the State Bar and the 2 citizen members appointed by the governor serve 3-year terms. The council is supported by one staff attorney.

Fifth Grader Holden Bradfield reads his winning essay to Supreme Court justices before oral arguments during a Justice on Wheels visit during October 2008 in Oshkosh. As part of the Justice on Wheels outreach program, the Supreme Court holds oral arguments outside Madison. The Oshkosh visit marked the 20th Justice on Wheels visit. (Joe Sienkiewicz/Oshkosh Northwestern)

WISCONSIN JUDICIAL SYSTEM — ASSOCIATED UNIT

STATE BAR OF WISCONSIN

Board of Governors (effective July 1, 2009): *Officers:* DOUGLAS W. KAMMER, *president;* JAMES C. BOLL, JR., *president-elect;* DIANE S. DIEL, *past president;* MARK A. PENNOW, *secretary;* MARGARET W. HICKEY, *treasurer;* JAMES M. BRENNAN, *chair of the board. District members:* SAMUEL W. BENEDICT, JAMES A. CARNEY, DONALD J. CHEWNING, SUSAN L. COLLINS, WILLIAM T. CURRAN, WILLIAM J. DOMINA, JAMES R. DUCHEMIN, ROBERT R. GOEPEL, CATHERINE R. GROGAN, KIMBERLY K. HAINES, CHARLES E. HANSON, ARTHUR J. HARRINGTON, DAVID A. HART III, FREDERICK B. KAFTAN, KEVIN G. KLEIN, LYNN R. LAUFENBERG, ATHENEÉ P. LUCAS, MARSHA M. MANSFIELD, KELLY C. NICKEL, CARMEN M. ORTIZ-BABILONIA, KEVIN J. PALMERSHEIM, THEODORE PERLICK-MOLINARI, FRANK D. REMINGTON, THOMAS L. SCHOBER, JOHN T. SCHOMISCH, JR., MARLA J. STEPHENS, ROBERT H. STORM, PATRICIA D. STRUCK, PAUL G. SWANSON, JAMES S. THIEL, JESSICA J. TLUSTY, AMY E. WOCHOS, NICHOLAS C. ZALES, JEFFREY R. ZIRGIBEL. *Young Lawyers Division:* JESSICA J. KING. *Government Lawyers Division:* CHARLES M. KERNATS. *Nonresident Lawyers Division:* W.D. CALVERT, DONNA M. JONES, GORDON G. KIRSTEN, STEVEN H. SCHUSTER, ALBERT E. WEHDE. *Senior Lawyers Division:* MARGADETTE DEMET. *Nonlawyer members:* TOM HEINE, EDWARD KONDRACKI, CATHERINE ZIMMERMAN. *Minority Bar Liaisons:* STEVEN M. DEVOUGAS, JO DEEN B. LOWE, CARLOS A. PABELLON, ARMAN S. ROUF (nonvoting members).

Executive Director: GEORGE C. BROWN.

Mailing Address: P.O. Box 7158, Madison 53707-7158.

Location: 5302 Eastpark Boulevard, Madison.

Internet Address: www.wisbar.org; Consumer site: www.legalexplorer.com

Telephones: General: 257-3838; Lawyer Referral and Information Service: (800) 362-9082.

Agency E-mail: lroys@wisbar.org

Publications: *WisBar InsideTrack; Wisconsin Lawyer Directory; Wisconsin Lawyer Magazine; Wisconsin News Reporter's Legal Handbook;* various legal practice handbooks and resources; various consumer pamphlets and videotapes, including *A Gift to Your Family: Planning Ahead for Future Health Care Needs.*

References: Supreme Court Rules, Chapters 10 and 11.

Responsibility: The State Bar of Wisconsin is an association of persons authorized to practice law in Wisconsin. It works to raise professional standards, improve the administration of justice and the delivery of legal services, and provide continuing legal education to lawyers. The State Bar conducts legal research in substantive law, practice, and procedure and develops related reports and recommendations. It also maintains the roll of attorneys, collects mandatory assessments imposed by the supreme court for supreme court boards and to fund civil legal services for the poor, and performs other administrative services for the judicial system.

Attorneys may be admitted to the State Bar by the full Wisconsin Supreme Court or by a single justice. Members are subject to the rules of ethical conduct prescribed by the supreme court, whether they practice before a court, an administrative body, or in consultation with clients whose interests do not require court appearances.

Organization: Subject to rules prescribed by the Wisconsin Supreme Court, the State Bar is governed by a board of governors, of not fewer than 52 members, consisting of the board's 6 officers, not fewer than 35 members selected by State Bar members from the association's 16 districts, 8 members selected by divisions of the State Bar, and 3 nonlawyers appointed by the supreme court. The board of governors selects the executive director, the executive committee, and the chairperson of the board.

History: In 1956, the Wisconsin Supreme Court ordered the organization of the State Bar of Wisconsin, effective January 1, 1957, to replace the formerly voluntary Wisconsin Bar Association, organized in 1877. All judges and attorneys entitled to practice before Wisconsin courts were required to join the State Bar. Beginning July 1, 1988, the Wisconsin Supreme Court suspended its mandatory membership rule, and the State Bar temporarily became a voluntary membership association, pending the disposition of a lawsuit in the U.S. Supreme Court. The Supreme Court ruled in *Keller v. State Bar of California*, 496 U.S. 1 (1990) that it is permissible to mandate membership provided certain restrictions are placed on the political activities of the mandatory State Bar. Effective July 1, 1992, the Wisconsin Supreme Court reinstated the mandatory membership rule upon petition from the State Bar Board of Governors.

SUMMARY OF SIGNIFICANT DECISIONS OF THE WISCONSIN SUPREME COURT AND COURT OF APPEALS

July 2007 – June 2009

Robin Ryan, Mary Gibson-Glass, and Robert Nelson
Legislative Reference Bureau

CONSTITUTIONAL LAW

Free Speech and Identify Theft

A city employee logged onto his supervisor's e-mail account without the supervisor's consent and forwarded to community members e-mail messages regarding the supervisor's extramarital affair, with the result that it appeared that the supervisor had sent the forwarded messages. In *Wisconsin v. Baron*, 2009 WI 58 (2009) (to be published), the employee was charged with the crime of identity theft. The law prohibits using an individual's personal identifying information without the individual's consent or authorization, by representing that one is the individual, for any of several specified purposes. One of the specified purposes is harming the reputation of the individual.

The employee argued that applying the criminal prohibition to his actions violated his First Amendment free speech right to defame a public official. The threshold question for the supreme court was whether charging the employee with identity theft implicated the First Amendment. The First Amendment is implicated if a statute regulates speech or expressive conduct as opposed to regulating only conduct. Five of the 6 justices who decided the case concluded that the statute, as applied in this case, regulated speech because the content of the e-mails was critical to the issue of harming the supervisor's reputation. The court concluded that the statute prohibited "the combination of the use of the individual's personal identifying information with the intent to harm the reputation of the individual."

The court next addressed whether the regulation of speech was content based or content neutral. A regulation that is content based is subject to greater scrutiny. A statute that distinguishes favored speech from disfavored speech on the basis of the ideas or views expressed is content based. A statute that confers benefits or imposes burdens on speech without reference to the ideas or views expressed is content neutral. The court determined that the identify theft statute as applied to the employee's actions was content based because whether the employee's conduct was prohibited depended entirely on whether the content of the e-mail messages was intended to harm the supervisor's reputation.

A regulation that is content based is constitutional if it serves a compelling state interest and is narrowly tailored to achieve that interest. The parties did not disagree that the state has a compelling interest in preventing identity theft; however, the employee argued that the identify theft statute was not narrowly tailored because it eliminates his First Amendment right to defame a public official with true information. The court determined that the statute is narrowly tailored because it only applies when a person steals another's personal identifying information. Further, the statute did not prevent the employee from revealing information that harmed the supervisor's reputation, it just prevented the employee from doing so while pretending to be the supervisor.

CRIMINAL LAW

Admission of Secret Tape Recording Made on School Bus

In *State v. Duchow*, 2008 WI 57, 310 Wis. 2d 1, 749 N.W.2d 913 (2008), the court determined that Wisconsin's Electronic Surveillance Control Law does not prohibit the trial court from admitting into evidence a surreptitiously made tape recording of a bus driver abusing a child on a public school bus. The parents of a nine-year old boy who suffers from Downs Syndrome and Attention Deficit Disorder became concerned that their son's school bus driver was abusing the boy. The concern stemmed from the boy's behavioral changes: he resisted boarding the bus in the morning, cried at school as the time to get on the bus neared, punched toys, began to kick at the family dog, and allegedly spit at the bus driver.

The boy was the first student picked up in the morning. The parents placed a voice-activated tape recorder in the boy's backpack. Upon his return home from school, the parents listened to the tape which revealed abusive statements by the driver, including: "Stop before I beat the living hell out of you"; "Do I have to tape your mouth shut because you know I will"; and "Do you want me to come back there and smack you?" The recording also included a sound that the parents believed was a slap.

At criminal trial for physical abuse of a child, the driver asked the trial court to suppress the tape, arguing that the tape was made in violation of the Electronic Surveillance Control Law. The Electronic Surveillance Control Law prohibits recording oral communications without consent, provides some exceptions to the prohibitions, and establishes a process by which law enforcement agencies may obtain court permission to record communications. The trial court determined that the Electronic Surveillance Control Law does not prohibit admitting the recording of the bus driver at trial because the driver's communication is not "oral communication" that is protected by the Electronic Surveillance Control Law.

The law defines "oral communication," in part, as "any oral communication uttered by a person exhibiting an expectation that the communication is not subject to interception under circumstances justifying the expectation." The supreme court determined that the appropriate test of whether a statement is protected by the Electronic Surveillance Control Law is whether it is spoken under circumstances in which the speaker has a reasonable expectation of privacy. A person has a reasonable expectation of privacy if he or she has both 1) an actual subjective expectation of privacy in the communication, and 2) the expectation is one that society is willing to recognize as reasonable. There was no question that the bus driver had an expectation of privacy, so the court focused on whether the driver's expectation was reasonable. In determining reasonableness the court reviewed a variety of factors including the volume of the driver's statements, the proximity of other individuals to the driver and the potential for others to overhear the driver, the potential for the driver's communications to be reported, the actions taken by the driver to ensure privacy, the place where the communication was made, and whether there was a need to employ technological enhancements to hear the statements. In determining that the driver did not have a reasonable expectation of privacy, the court focused on the fact that the driver was speaking on a public school bus used to transport public school students, and that the driver's statements were likely to be reported because they were threats to injure the person to whom they were spoken.

Suppression of Evidence as an Appropriate Remedy

In *State v. Popenhagen*, 2008 WI 55, 309 Wis. 2d 601, 749 N.W.2d 611 (2008), the court determined that when an invalid subpoena is used to obtain documents, suppression of the documents, as well as incriminating statements made by the defendant when confronted with the documents, was an appropriate remedy. A store owner suspected that one of his employees was stealing money from the store and reported his suspicion to the police. In the course of the police investigation, the district attorney obtained subpoenas, signed by the circuit court judge, requiring the bank to produce the defendant's bank records. However, the district attorney used the wrong form of subpoena. And, even though the police had completed two affidavits supplying probable cause for the subpoenas, the district attorney did not attach them to the subpoenas, and the circuit court did not make findings of probable cause for the subpoenas. The bank complied with the invalid subpoenas by supplying the defendant's bank records to the police. Those records showed deposits to the defendant's bank account equal to the amounts stolen from the store. When confronted with the bank records, the defendant made incriminating statements.

The court was asked to determine whether suppression of evidence obtained with an invalid subpoena is an appropriate remedy when the statute does not specify suppression as a remedy.

The applicable statute concerning subpoenas for documents provides that, upon the request of the attorney general or a district attorney, and upon a showing of probable cause, a court shall issue a subpoena requiring the production of documents. The only reference in the statute to a remedy for a violation of the statute is as follows: "Motions to the court, including, but not limited to motions to quash or limit the subpoena, shall be addressed to the court which issued the subpoena." The court read this sentence as an incomplete list of remedies, which contemplates additional remedies, including suppression. In addition, the court found the remedy of suppression consistent with the strict requirements for issuing a subpoena for documents, namely that only the attorney general or district attorney may request a subpoena; it must be signed by a judge; the judge must find probable cause; and that the subpoena may be quashed or limited. The court determined that denying suppression as a remedy would emasculate the clear directives of the statute and render the safeguards of the statute meaningless.

The court rejected the state's argument that prior court opinions allow suppression of evidence only when the evidence is obtained in violation of a defendants constitutional rights or when a statute expressly provides for suppression as a remedy. Instead, the court states that the proper reading of prior opinions is that, "Suppression of evidence obtained in violation of the requirements of a statute is permissible at the discretion of the circuit court when a statute does not specifically require suppression."

The Mayhem Statute

In *State v. Quintana,* 2008 WI 33, 308 Wis. 2d 615, 748 N.W.2d 447 (2008), the court was asked to determine whether intentionally disabling or disfiguring another person's forehead may constitute the crime of mayhem. The court found that it may. The mayhem statutes provides that, "Whoever, with intent to disable or disfigure another, cuts or mutilates the tongue, eye, ear, nose, lip, limb or other bodily member of another is guilty of a Class C felony."

The defendant hit his ex-wife in the head with a hammer, lacerating her forehead, fracturing her skull, and causing intracranial injury. The prosecutor charged the defendant with first-degree reckless injury and aggravated battery, in addition to mayhem, but neither of those crimes has as great a penalty as mayhem.

In reviewing the history of the mayhem statute, the court explained that under early English common law, mayhem prohibited disabling a part of the body important for fighting. After Sir John Coventry was slit on the nose for uttering obnoxious words in Parliament, the English adopted the Coventry Act, which prohibited cutting out or disabling the tongue, putting out an eye, slitting the nose, cutting off a nose or lip, or cutting off or disabling any limb or member of another person with intent to maim or disfigure the person. From before statehood through 1955, Wisconsin had a crime of "maiming and disfiguring" that was similar to the Coventry Act. The court explained that the legislature nearly consolidated mayhem with assault as part of the 1955 revision of the criminal code that produced the current mayhem statute. Ultimately, the legislature retained mayhem as a separate crime to distinguish, and punish more severely, incidents in which a person has specific intent to disable or disfigure.

In determining what "other bodily member" covers in the mayhem statute, the court attempted to apply a rule of statutory interpretation providing that when general words follow specific words, the general word encompasses only things of the same type as the specific words. However, the court determined that the specific body parts listed in the mayhem statute do not form a class. The court rejected the defendant's argument that they constitute a class of parts of the body that have function in and of themselves, and without which a person may survive. Instead the court determined that "other bodily member" encompasses all bodily parts.

Subpoenas, Discovery, and the Right to View Police Records

In *State v. Schaefer,* 2008 WI 25, 308 Wis. 2d 279, 746 N.W.2d 457 (2008), the court determined that a defendant does not have a right to subpoena police records of an investigation before a preliminary examination. The defendant was charged with sexual assault of a child for events that had occurred 16 years earlier. The defendant issued a subpoena to the chief of police, or his designee, to appear before the court and bring all records related to the police investigation of the defendant in connection with the sexual assault charge. The defendant issued the subpoena before his preliminary examination. A preliminary examination is a pre-trial hearing at which the court determines whether there is probable cause to believe that the defendant committed a felony.

The defendant argued that the statutes authorizing subpoenas provide a basis for subpoenaing the police chief and the police investigation records. The defendant further argued that the rights to compulsory process for obtaining witnesses and to effective assistance of counsel under the U.S. and Wisconsin Constitutions authorize the subpoena. The majority of justices treated the defendant's subpoena as a request for discovery. Discovery is a statutory process under which the parties in a case are required to provide various information to the opposing party upon request. The majority concluded that discovery does not apply before a preliminary examination. Three justices concurred in the decision of the court but rejected the majority's treatment of the subpoena as a discovery request. Instead, the concurring justices simply found that the subpoena statutes do not provide a right to obtain police investigation report before the preliminary examination. All the justices determined that the constitutional rights to compulsory process and effective assistance of counsel do not support the subpoena.

The Office of the State Public Defender and the Wisconsin Innocence Project filed amicus briefs requesting that court exercise its superintending power over the courts to adopt a rule granting criminal defendants access to police records before the preliminary hearing. They argued, among other points, that such a rule would lead to fewer wrongful prosecutions and make preliminary hearings more fair. They also noted that several district attorneys in Wisconsin already permit defendants access to police records before the preliminary examination. The court declined to use this case to make such a rule.

Removal of Judge's Relative from Jury

State v. Tody, 2009 WI 31 (2009) (to be published), addresses whether a judge's mother may serve as a juror in a criminal trial over which the judge presides. The defendant was tried for taking and driving a car without the owner's consent. During questioning of potential jurors for the trial, it became apparent that the judge's mother was among the potential jurors. When questioned by the district attorney and the defense attorney regarding her ability to be fair and impartial, she said she could be. The defense requested that the judge strike his mother from the pool of potential jurors for cause, arguing that the close relationship between the judge and the potential juror was *per se* a prejudicial matter. The district attorney opposed the request. The judge reluctantly denied the request to strike for cause, stating that he had no legal basis for removing his mother from the pool of potential jurors. Neither the district attorney nor the defense attorney used a peremptory challenge to remove the judge's mother. The jury convicted the defendant.

Six of the seven supreme court justices participated in this case. The six agreed that the trial judge should not have presided over a trial in which his mother was a juror, and that the defendant is entitled to a new trial. They also agreed that a trial judge should err on the side of dismissing a potential juror when the juror's presence may create bias or an appearance of bias, because dismissal saves judicial time and resources over the long run.

Three of the justices determined that the judge's mother was "objectively biased." A juror is objectively biased when a reasonable person in the juror's position could not be impartial. As these three justices further explained, a juror is objectively biased if he or she could not avoid basing his or her verdict upon considerations extraneous to evidence put before the jury at trial.

The other three justices determined that this is not a case of juror bias. They described the situation of the mother serving as a trial juror as "problem waiting to happen" and a "recipe for disaster" and concluded that the trial judge should have exercised his inherent authority to administer justice to either remove his mother for cause or recuse himself from the trial.

Sexual Assault of a Corpse

In *State v. Grunke,* 2008 WI 82, 311 Wis. 2d 439, 752 N.W.2d 769 (2008), the court determined that the crime of third-degree sexual assault may apply if the victim is already dead and the defendant did not cause the death of the victim. In this case, the three defendants attempted to remove a corpse from a grave for the purpose of having sexual intercourse. After the preliminary hearing, the circuit court determined that the crime of third-degree sexual assault did not apply to the facts. The state appealed the circuit court's decision.

The statutes prohibit four degrees of sexual assault. First-degree sexual assault applies to cases of sexual intercourse without consent of the victim that are committed by threat or use of a weapon, committed by more than one person by threat of force, or that result in pregnancy or great bodily harm. A person who has who has sexual intercourse with a person without the consent of that person is guilty of third-degree sexual assault. Consent is defined as words or overt actions indicating a freely given agreement to have sexual intercourse. The statutes expressly provide that consent is not an issue for certain types of sexual assault, including if the victim is unconscious or intoxicated, or if the perpetrator is an employee of certain types of facilities and the victim is a ward of the facility. In addition, the statutes provide that the prohibition against sexual assault, which includes all degrees of sexual assault, applies whether the victim is dead or alive.

The defense argued that the statute on sexual assault is ambiguous, with respect to whether it applies when the victim is already dead, and therefore the court should look to the legislative intent in enacting the provision stating that sexual assault applies whether the victim is dead or alive. The defense argued ambiguity for two reasons. First, the requirement for lack of consent is superfluous when applied in a case where the victim is dead. As applied to sexual intercourse with a victim who is dead, the sexual assault statute becomes a general prohibition against necrophilia. Second, it is absurd to apply the graduated penalties for first- to fourth-degree sexual assault in cases where the victim is dead, because the differences in the elements are irrelevant. The defense argued that the legislature enacted the provision that sexual assault applies whether the victim is dead or alive to address the difficulty of proving that the victim was alive when a sexual assault occurs in cases where a defendant sexually assaults and murders the victim. It is not meant to apply, they argued, in cases where the defendant does not cause the death of the victim.

The court concluded that the statute is not ambiguous and that third-degree sexual assault may apply to a case where the victim is dead and the defendant did not cause the death. It found that even though it may be simple for the prosecution to prove lack of consent, it is still an element of the crime. The court further acknowledged that first- and second-degree sexual assault cannot apply when the victim is dead because the facts cannot correspond with the elements of first or second degree sexual assault. Therefore the statute does not provide an absurd result of penalizing necrophilia under a graduated penalty scheme. Although the court found that the sexual assault statute was clear on its face, it also addressed the legislative history of the statute. The court said that even if one accepts that the legislative intent was to apply the crime of sexual assault of a dead victim only in cases where the defendant caused the victim's death, the applicability of the statute is not limited to the legislature's intent.

CIVIL LAW

The Designation of Indian Trust Land

The Wisconsin Statutes provide that the state shall refund to an Indian tribe 70% of taxes collected on cigarettes sold on the tribe's reservation or trust land provided that certain conditions are met, including that the land was designated as reservation or trust land on or before January 1, 1983. In *Ho-Chunk Nation v. Wisconsin Department of Revenue*, 2009 WI 48 (2009) (to be published), the supreme court determined that the Ho-Chunk Nation is not entitled to a refund of taxes collected on sales of cigarettes sold on the DeJope land in Dane County.

There is no question that the DeJope land is currently trust land. The critical issue in this case was whether the DeJope land was "designated" as trust land before January 1, 1983. The Ho-Chunk Nation argued that an August 1982 memo from the Bureau of Indian Affairs (BIA) office in Washington, D.C., that authorized the BIA regional office in Minneapolis to accept conveyance of the DeJope land to the United States in trust, shows that the land was designated as trust land in 1982. The Department of Revenue argued that the land was not designated as trust land until the Secretary of the U.S. Department of the Interior signed the deed of conveyance on January 31, 1983.

The majority determined that even though there are two plausible readings of the word "designate" the statute is not ambiguous, and the meaning of the tax refund statute may be interpreted from the context in which the word is used. The majority noted that the first sentence of the cigarette refund provision refers to taxes collected on sales of cigarettes on "reservations or trust lands of an Indian tribe." The majority reasoned that the subsequent use of the words "reservation or trust land" in the condition establishing the January 1, 1983 cut-off date, must refer to the same lands – lands that are already reservation or trust land, not lands in the process of becoming reservation or trust land. The majority further noted that the word "designated" applies to both reservation and trust land. The majority reasoned that since there is no indication that federal law recognizes an official status for land preliminarily approved as reservation land, there is no basis for reading the tax refund statute to apply to land that has received only preliminary informal approval. The majority concluded that "designated" is used to refer to the variety of ways in which land may become reservation or trust land.

The dissenting justices concluded that the statute is ambiguous. They argued that the majority's interpretation of the statute renders the word "designated" superfluous. One dissenting justice examined the legislative history of the tax refund statute and concluded that it was impossible that parties involved in crafting the legislation intended to exclude the DeJope trust land from the cigarette tax refund.

Reasonable Accommodation of an Employee's Disability

In *Stoughton Trailers, Inc. v. LIRC,* 2007 WI 105, 303 Wis. 2d 514, 735 N.W.2d 477 (2007), Geen, an employee of Stoughton Trailers, developed severe headaches in December 1996, and was absent from work for 3 weeks. Geen's physician prescribed medicine for migraine headaches and depression. That period of absence was counted as one occurrence under Stoughton Trailers' no-fault attendance policy because Geen did not complete the state and federal family and medical leave act (FMLA) form. Under the policy, an employee would be fired if he or she had 6 occurrences of unapproved absences. Geen also missed work on January 24, 27, and 28, 1997, for the same reason. He never submitted the FMLA form. Geen was told to complete the FMLA form and obtain a note from his physician saying he was unable to work but that he could return to work without any restrictions. He obtained a note regarding the absences of the 27th and 28th, and stating that he could continue to work, but did not obtain a note for the January 24 absence. On January 31 Geen was told he was being discharged because he had accrued an "occurrence" on January 24, which brought his total to 6.5 occurrences.

Geen filed a disability discrimination complaint with the Department of Workforce Development. A hearing examiner ruled in Geen's favor, saying that Stoughton Trailers terminated Geen's employment in part because of the disability, and that it had failed to reasonably accommodate Geen's disability. Stoughton Trailers appealed to the Labor and Industry Review Commission (LIRC), which reversed the examiner's decision. The circuit court reversed the LIRC decision and, on appeal, the court of appeals remanded the case back to LIRC. LIRC then held that Geen was terminated because of his disability and that Stoughton Trailers did not reasonably accommodate his disability.

The supreme court opinion, written by Justice Louis Butler, determined that the primary disputed issues before the court were whether Stoughton Trailers terminated Geen because of his disability and whether it took adequate steps to accommodate Geen's disability.

The court reviewed the LIRC holding that because two of Geen's "occurrences" were related to his migraines, the termination was because of Geen's disability, in violation of state law. Instead of adopting that holding, the court concluded that Stoughton Trailers gave Geen only two days from the date it provided him with the FMLA form to submit the completed form, in violation of their own policy, which provided for a 15-day period to submit the form. By not waiting the full 15 days, the court said Stoughton Trailers terminated Geen after only 5.5 occurrences, and such a termination was invalid under Stoughton Trailers' policy. This fact, said the court, supported LIRC's conclusion that Stoughton Trailers terminated Geen because of his disability.

The court agreed with LIRC that Stoughton Trailers' provision of the FMLA form to Geen to complete and submit in order to avoid being assessed an "occurrence" for the second migraine-related absence was not a reasonable accommodation because Geen was not allowed sufficient time to submit the form. The supreme court also agreed that Stoughton Trailers failed to temporarily accommodate Geen's disability while Geen was seeking medical intervention to resolve his problem, citing an earlier LIRC interpretation that "reasonable accommodation" includes forbearing from enforcing a rule while an employee is undergoing treatment for the disability-related medical problem. The court held:

> LIRC's conclusion was consistent with [Wisconsin Statute Section] 111.34 (1) (b), and is in harmony with both the express purpose of the WFEA [Wisconsin Fair Employment Act] to "encourage and foster to the fullest extent practicable the employment of all qualified individuals" regardless of disability or other protective status, and its directive that its provisions "be liberally construed for the accomplishment of this purpose." (p. 550)

The supreme court then discussed the disputed issue of the remedy provided by LIRC, the reinstatement of Geen and back pay, and concluded that LIRC properly exercised it discretion in determining the award.

Justice David Prosser dissented, saying the court failed to answer the specific questions raised by this extensively litigated case, including whether an employer may apply a neutral no-fault attendance policy to terminate an employee when some of the employee's absences are caused by a disability, and whether an employer has not reasonably accommodated an employee's disability when that employer has promised to disregard disability-related absences if the employee submits the appropriate FMLA form, but the employee fails to submit that form.

The Economic Loss Doctrine and Property Representations

Below v. Norton, 2008 WI 77, 310 Wis. 2d 713, 751 N.W.2d 351 (2008), involved the sale of a home by sellers who represented that they were not aware of any defect in the house's plumbing system. However, the buyer learned after moving into the house that the sewer line between the house and the street was broken. The buyer sued, alleging a number of claims, including intentional misrepresentation, negligent misrepresentation, misrepresentation in violation of the false advertising law, and misrepresentation in violation of the criminal statute prohibiting the taking of a title to property by intentional false representation and its related civil statute. The buyer later attempted to amend the complaint to add a breach of contract claim, but because of a procedural error, that claim was not before the court. The circuit court dismissed the case, saying the economic loss doctrine barred the common law misrepresentation claims and that the false advertising and criminal misrepresentation claims did not apply.

The court of appeals reversed the circuit court ruling, saying the economic loss doctrine does not bar the plaintiff's action under the false advertising misrepresentation claim, and ordered that the case be returned to the circuit court for further action. The supreme court was asked to decide if the economic loss doctrine bars common law intentional misrepresentation claims arising from a residential real estate transaction.

The supreme court decision, written by Justice N. Patrick Crooks, discussed previous decisions concerning the economic loss doctrine. That court-created doctrine prevents a person from recovering in an action based on a tort claim if there was a claim for the same damages under contract law. The policy reason for the economic loss doctrine, said the court, is to preserve the distinction between tort and contract law by protecting the parties' freedom to allocate economic risk by contract and by encouraging the party best situated to assess the risk of economic loss to assume, allocate or insure against that risk. The court noted that previous decisions applied the economic loss doctrine to bar negligence and strict liability claims in the context of consumer goods. In other cited cases, the court barred tort claims against subcontractors who had helped construct the plaintiff's home and the court held that if the tort claim was extraneous to, rather than interwoven with, a contract regarding land, the economic loss doctrine would not bar recovery for that tort claim. The latter case, said the court, held that the economic loss doctrine is applicable to real estate transactions.

In this case, said the court, the plaintiffs may have a breach of contract claim if the defendants knew of the defect in the sewer line and failed to disclose that fact in the property condition report that the defendants were required by law to provide to the plaintiffs. Based on the previous cases and the facts of this case, the court held that the economic loss doctrine does bar the plaintiff's claim based on the tort of intentional misrepresentation arising out of the purchase of residential real estate.

The dissent, written by Justice Ann Walsh Bradley, said that this state is the only state that has expanded the economic loss doctrine, which originally was narrowly applied to commercial transactions involving products under warranty, to prevent homeowners from recovering damages in tort based on misrepresentations by fraudulent sellers. The dissent argued that the court's interpretation of the early cases was in error because none of those cases involved residential real estate transactions.

Liability of the Catholic Diocese for Sexual Abuse by Priests

In *Doe v. Archdiocese of Milwaukee*, 2007 WI 95, 303 Wis. 2d 34, 734 N.W.2d 827 (2007), the plaintiffs alleged that when they were minors they were sexually molested by a priest of the Milwaukee Archdiocese. The plaintiffs brought an action against the archdiocese for negligent supervision of the priest and for fraud. The last alleged molestation occurred about 23 years before the plaintiffs commenced this action. The priest involved had been convicted of sexually molesting another child and the archdiocese, knowing of that conviction, moved the priest to the parish where the plaintiffs were molested. The trial court and court of appeals dismissed the case because the action was barred by the statute of limitations, which is generally 3 years from the act that resulted in the injury.

The supreme court decision, written by Justice Patience Drake Roggensack, considered the two separate claims made by the plaintiffs, one for negligent supervision of the priest and one for fraud for not informing the parishioners of the priest's former behavior and conviction. Each claim involved a separate statute of limitations, said the court, but both involved the "discovery rule", which requires a plaintiff to bring an action within the statutory time limit after the plaintiff knew of, or in the exercise of reasonable diligence, should have discovered the injury and the cause of the injury. In this case, the time limit was within one year after becoming 18 years of age.

To prove the claim of negligent supervision, the court said that the plaintiffs must prove that the employer had a duty of care toward the plaintiffs, that the employer breached that duty, that a wrongful act of the employee caused the injury, and that the employer's wrongful act caused the wrongful act of the employee. The court reviewed the policy behind the statute of limitations, which is to allow plaintiffs a fair opportunity to enforce legitimate claims while protecting defendants from defending against a claim after so much time has passed that witnesses and evidence may be unavailable. The court concluded that the plaintiffs should have discovered their injury by the time of the last incident of assault. The court dismissed the plaintiffs' argument that they repressed the memory of the assaults and therefore did not know of their injury until recently. Citing previous decisions, the court held that the claim of negligent supervision was derived directly from the claim against the priest for sexual molestation, so the claim of negligent supervision was also barred because this action was not commenced until long after the statutory time limit.

The court went on to review the claim of fraud made against the archdiocese. To prove fraud, said the court, the plaintiffs must prove that the defendant made an untrue factual representation knowing the representation was untrue and with intent to defraud the plaintiffs and induce them to act on that representation; and that the plaintiffs believed the representation to be true and relied on it to their detriment. The court discussed the issue of the archdiocese making an untrue factual representation and held that a representation may be in the form of speech or acts. In this case, said the court, the complaint alleges that the archdiocese placed the priest in the parish where he had unsupervised access to children and their families, and this placement represented to those children and families that the archdiocese did not know that the priest had a history of molesting children or that the priest was a danger to the children. Because this case was before the court on a motion to dismiss the action, the court said it could not conclude that the acts described in the complaint were not sufficient to maintain the action, and therefore the question of whether the statute of limitations barred the action had to be considered.

In discussing the statute of limitations, in contrast to the claim of negligent supervision, which the court said was derivative of the action of molestation by the priest, the court held that the claim of fraud was independent of the priest's behavior. Therefore, said the court, the issue becomes when the plaintiffs discovered the injury and the cause of the injury. The court noted that, unlike other cases, the plaintiffs had no way of knowing or suspecting that the archdiocese knew that the priest had a prior history of sexual molestation of children. Nothing in the pleadings suggests that the plaintiffs should have, before the end of the year after they became 18 years old, investigated whether the archdiocese knew of the priest's former behavior. The court held that the date of accrual of the fraud claim cannot be resolved by a motion to dismiss, and remanded the case back to the circuit court for that determination.

Chief Justice Shirley Abrahamson, dissenting in part, argued that the claim of negligent supervision, which the court said was derivative of the action of molestation by the priest, was not derived from that action but was independent of the priest's behavior.

In *Hornback v. Archdiocese of Milwaukee,* 2008 WI 98, 313 Wis. 2d 294, 752 N.W.2d 862 (2008), a priest had been involved in a pattern of sexual abuse of children while a member of the Archdiocese of Milwaukee and the Diocese of Madison, then left the area and became a parish priest in Louisville, Kentucky, where the sexual abuse continued. The plaintiffs alleged that they were sexually abused by the priest in Kentucky, and that the archdiocese and diocese were negligent for failing to take steps to prevent his future sexual abuse and for failing to warn of the priest's propensity for sexual abuse. Allegedly, the archdiocese knew of the priest's behavior, promised affected parents in Milwaukee that the priest would receive treatment, then told the priest to leave the Milwaukee Archdiocese quietly, without receiving any treatment. The circuit court and court of appeals granted the defendant's motions to dismiss on the grounds that the 32-year-old claims were barred by the statute of limitations.

The supreme court decision, written by Justice Butler, discusses the issue of whether the archdiocese is negligent and whether, based on public policy grounds, the negligence results in a finding that the plaintiffs have the right to receive damages for their injuries. The court said that negligence and liability are two distinct concepts, and even if negligence is found, liability may be restricted based on public policy concerns. To reach the issues presented in the case, the court first discussed the sufficiency of the negligence claim. The plaintiff's claim, said the court, was that the archdiocese failed to warn unforeseeable third parties of the priest's propensity for sexual abuse of children. Reviewing cases regarding employer's duties to disclose information regarding their former employees, the court concluded that the "failure to warn" claims recognized in this state do not include the type of "failure to warn" claimed by the plaintiffs. In this case there was no direct contact between the past employer and the injured party, and the specific victims are unforeseeable, said the court. The plaintiffs had virtually no relationship with the defendants, being separated both in distance and time, so the court held that the plaintiffs did not state a claim for negligence.

The court went on to address the public policy concerns generated by the case. Even if negligence was proved, the court said, creating liability in a case like this one would allow recovery where there is no sensible or just stopping point, because it would create a precedent requiring employers to search out and disclose all potential employers, individuals who may be subject to the priest's behavior, as well as a broad and undefined category of parents of unforeseen victims.

The court was equally divided on whether to affirm or reverse the decision of the court of appeals dismissing the plaintiff's complaint, with Justice Prosser recusing himself, so the court affirmed the court of appeals ruling.

Liability and Immunity in School Sports Injuries

Noffke v. Bakke, 2009 WI 10, ___ Wis. 2d, ___, 760 N.W.2d 156 (2009) (to be published), concerns the liability or immunity resulting from a cheerleading stunt. The cheerleaders were performing a stunt that involved one girl standing on the shoulders of other cheerleaders. In this case, a cheerleader was assigned to assist with the stunt (called a spotter), which included standing behind the cheerleaders doing the stunt. There were no mats in use during the stunt, and the cheerleading coach was instructing another group of cheerleaders nearby at the time. The spotter-cheerleader, by mistake, stood in front of the cheerleaders involved in the stunt, so when the cheerleader fell backwards, the spotter was not there to catch plaintiff and as a result she was injured. She brought an action against the spotter-cheerleader and the school district for negligence. The circuit court granted summary judgment for the defendants, saying they were immune from liability. The court of appeals upheld the circuit court decision regarding the school district but said the spotter-cheerleader was not immune from liability.

The supreme court decision, written by Justice Annette Ziegler, interprets the recreational immunity statute, Section 895.525, which provides immunity to certain parties who provide or are involved in recreational activities, and Section 895.80, which provides immunity to certain public agencies and employees. The recreational immunity statute, said the court, provides immunity to participants in a recreation activity that involves physical contact between persons in a sport involving amateur teams. Based on the dictionary definition of "physical contact," and the manual describing rules related to cheerleading, the court found that cheerleading involves a significant amount of physical contact between the participants.

The court discussed the plaintiff's assertion that there must be more than incidental physical contact to be immune from liability because the title of the subsection involved, "Liability of contact sports participants," means there must aggressive sports involving teams, such as football, hockey, or boxing. But, said the court, the title is not determinate and the statute does not restrict its application to aggressive sports. In addition, applying an "incidental" contact exception to that statute would be difficult to apply and would create uncertainty in the law. The plaintiff's argument that the immunity should only apply to competitive sports was not persuasive, said the court, because no competitive requirement exists in the language of the statute and in some circumstances cheerleaders are involved in competitions and at other times they are not, and football players during practices are not involved in competition.

Discussing the spotter-cheerleader's immunity, the court said that immunity applies if he was not acting in a reckless manner. Recklessness, said the court, involves a reckless disregard for the safety of another, when the person knows that his or her behavior creates a high risk of physical harm to another and proceeds in conscious disregard to that risk. From the facts of the case, the spotter-cheerleader was told to take the appropriate position behind the cheerleaders, but he failed to do so fast enough to prevent the injury. The behavior in this case, said the court, was inadvertence and simple negligence, not recklessness. Therefore, the court held that he was immune from liability.

The court reviewed the issues regarding the immunity of the school district, which was based on statutory language providing immunity to public agencies and employees for acts done in the exercise of a legislative, quasi-legislative, judicial, or quasi-judicial function. The court held that to be liable for acts in performance of ministerial duties the actor must have no discretion. The court said a ministerial duty must be imposed by law; there must be a known and compelling danger that gave rise to a ministerial duty; the act must involved medical discretion; or the act must involve malicious, willful, or intentional behavior. In this case, said the court, the written procedures for practicing cheerleading stunts did not impose a ministerial duty because the coach had discretion as to how to practice the skills necessary to learn the stunt. The written procedures themselves, said the court, noted that they were guidelines that had been developed to serve as a useful reminder of basic procedures. The court also found that the cheerleaders were performing a stunt that was less difficult than those they had performed in the past, and they had a spotter assigned to the stunt who had been instructed on how to act, so the court concluded that the danger was not so known and compelling that it gave rise to a ministerial duty.

Power of Attorney and Violation of Fiduciary Relationship

In *Russ v. Russ*, 2007 WI 83, 302 Wis. 2d 264, 734 N.W.2d 874 (2007), an elderly woman with some health problems lived with her son and daughter-in-law. The woman received a social security check, a pension, and some oil royalties, which she agreed to deposit in a joint checking account with her son. The son provided his mother with a place to stay and treated her as part of his family. A few years after opening the joint checking account, the woman, without the assistance of an attorney, executed a durable power of attorney (POA) for finances and property, naming her son as her agent. The POA authorized the son to pay her bills and manage her bank accounts, but did not authorize him to make gifts or be compensated for his services. The son did not deposit any of his own money into the joint checking account, but withdrew most of the money for his own use. The elderly mother became ill, was admitted to a hospital and then transferred to a nursing home. The circuit court declared her incompetent and appointed a guardian for her, and terminated the POA. The appointed guardian sued, saying the son had violated his fiduciary relationship under the POA by using money in the joint account for his own use. The circuit court determined that the son had assumed the fiduciary duty to care for his mother and had not breached that duty. The court of appeals certified the case to the supreme court.

The supreme court decision, written by Justice Crooks, discusses the relationship between the POA and the agreement of the son and mother to have a joint checking account. The POA, said the court, does produce a fiduciary duty upon the son, including the duty to not engage in actions that help the agent son (self-dealing) and are to the detriment of the principal, his mother. The POA, as written, did not provide the son with any authority to make gifts or to engage in self-dealing. However, the court noted, the establishment of the joint checking account, which predated the POA, gave each joint owner authority to use all of the account's money for his or her own use. This conflict between the presumptions under the joint checking account and the POA had to be resolved in this case, the court said, and mentioned that it would have preferred that the POA had clarified the intentions between the parties regarding this conflict.

The court discussed cases that involved agents who used POA authority to benefit themselves and cited the rule that an attorney-in-fact may not make a gift to himself or herself unless there is specific intent in writing from the principal allowing the gift. The court rejected the plaintiff's argument that the POA is clear and convincing evidence that it overrides the presumption of the son's use of the joint checking account unless the POA specifically addresses that issue, and decided that the establishment of joint checking account before the signing of the POA creates a presumption of intent to allow any member of the joint account to use the funds in the account for his or her own use. The court also decided that an agent under a POA who transfers funds deposited by a principal into a joint checking account for the agent's use is presumed to be committing fraud. In this case, said the court, the circuit court did make a number of findings that support the dismissal of the guardian's suit, including findings regarding the care, housing, clothing, and food provided to the mother, the provision of a paid caretaker for the mother while in the son's home, and the mother's wishes that there not be a dispute or litigation over the expenditure of her money. Based on these findings, the court dismissed the action.

Arbitrary and Capricious Termination of Insurance Coverage

Summers v. Touchpoint Health Plan, Inc., 2008 WI 45, 309 Wis. 2d 78, 749 N.W.2d 182 (2008), involves a decision by Touchpoint, a health care maintenance organization (HMO), to refuse to provide benefits to a child who had a cancerous brain tumor removed and needed additional health care services. After removal of the tumor, which Touchpoint paid for, the child was referred to a pediatric oncologist, who decided on a treatment plan that involved high-dose chemotherapy with stem cell rescue because it had a higher success rate than other treatments. The doctor attempted to enroll the child in a clinical trial providing that treatment, but Touchpoint refused to provide coverage because their medical director determined the treatment was the subject of an on-going Phase I or II clinical trial and was therefore experimental. Upon appeal, an independent review organization upheld the denial, although it determined that the treatment was medically necessary. In response, the child was removed from the clinical trial and the doctor proposed providing the same treatment outside of the clinical trial, but Touchpoint rejected that request. The family continued the treatment but appealed Touchpoint's decision, and the circuit court granted summary judgment to Touchpoint, saying the HMO's decision was reasonable and based on language that unambiguously excluded coverage that was the subject of Phase II clinical trials. The court of appeals reversed, saying Touchpoint's letter rejecting the request for coverage was arbitrary and capricious, in violation of federal law and regulations regarding claims under the Employee Retirement Income Security Act (ERISA).

The supreme court decision, written by Justice Crooks, had to determine if Touchpoint's decision violated federal law by being arbitrary and capricious, and if so, what the remedy was. The court decided that the decision of Touchpoint was a termination of benefits, not a denial of benefits, because the child had undergone surgery for the removal of the cancerous tumor and was seeking additional treatment that was necessary to cure the child of the cancer. The distinction was important, because the court said that standard for review of a termination of benefits depends on the insurance plan's language regarding terminations; if the plan reserves the discretion to terminate benefits to the plan administrator as in this case, the termination of benefits is reversed only if it was arbitrary and capricious.

The court discussed the Touchpoint letter stating that it would not provide coverage even though the child was no longer being treated as part of a clinical trial. The court said that the letter, in order to satisfy ERISA requirements and not be arbitrary and capricious, must provide adequate reasoning to explain the decision so that the beneficiary has a clear and precise understanding of the decision. The decision, said the court, must provide adequate notice in writing to the beneficiary setting forth the specific reasons for the denial, must be written in way that the beneficiary could understand, and must provide references to the specific plan provisions on which the denial is based. The court found that the letter of denial did not meet these requirements but merely made reference to an exclusion of coverage and referenced a broad, nonspecific segment of the policy. In addition, the court held that the termination letter did not contain the required explanation of the scientific or clinical judgment for the determination.

The court also found that Touchpoint was arbitrary and capricious in its position on what it would cover under the terms of the plan, citing testimony of an attorney and the medical director's statements that were inconsistent with their decision. The court noted that the external review agency upheld the termination while finding that the treatment was the standard of care and medically necessary for that cancer, again showing that Touchpoint was arbitrary and capricious in its position.

The court, when discussing the appropriate remedy for Touchpoint's decision, restated that because surgery had occurred and some follow-up care had been provided and paid for by Touchpoint, this was a termination case and two remedies were available. If the beneficiary had not yet undergone the treatments, the court said the appropriate remedy was for the beneficiary to be provided with a benefit application process that was not arbitrary and capricious. However, if the beneficiary has undergone treatments and then coverage is terminated, the appropriate remedy was retroactive reinstatement of benefits. This case involved a failure on the part of Touchpoint to communicate specific reasons for its termination, thus, held the court, the appropriate remedy is retroactive reinstatement of benefits.

The dissent, written by Justice Roggensack, stated that the majority failed to follow federal court precedents interpreting ERISA that have concluded that covered plans must state the basis for the payment of benefits and that the administrator must administer the plan in accord with the plan's terms, which the administrator did in this case by denying benefits for a treatment that was the subject of an ongoing Phase I or II clinical trial. The dissent also stated that this was a denial of benefits, not a termination, and that the correct standard of review is whether the administrator's interpretation of the plan was reasonable.

Liability of Property Owners for a Minor's Actions

Nichols v. Progressive Northern Insurance Company, 2008 WI 20, 308 Wis. 2d 17, 746 N.W.2d 220 (2008), concerns the liability of property owners for the injury caused by a minor operating a vehicle while under the influence of alcohol consumed on that property. The property owners did not purchase the alcohol, provide the alcohol to the minor, or encourage the consumption of the alcohol on their property although they were aware of the alcohol consumption. Shortly after leaving the property, the minor struck the vehicle in which Nichols was riding, causing severe injuries. The circuit court dismissed the claim for common-law negligence and the court of appeals reversed the circuit court ruling.

The supreme court decision, written by Justice Crooks, first discussed the elements of negligence and how those elements apply to the facts of this case. The court said that the plaintiff must establish negligence on the part of the defendants, and to establish that, they must show that there was a duty of care on the part of the defendants, that the defendants breached that duty, that there is a causal connection between the duty of care and the plaintiff's injury, and finally that the plaintiff suffered actual damages that resulted from the breach of that duty. If negligence was determined, the court said the final decision as to imposing liability would be based on policy factors that the court must consider.

In this case, because the action was decided on a motion to dismiss, the court accepted the alleged facts and inferences in the complaint as true, and would dismiss the action only if it was clear that there were no conditions under which the plaintiffs could recover. The court reviewed the four factors of negligence and assumed, without deciding, that the court of appeals was correct in holding that the plaintiffs had established the four factors in their complaint. The court mentioned and rejected the following public policy factors for precluding liability: the injury being too remote from the negligence, the injury being too wholly out of proportion to the defendants' culpability, it being too highly extraordinary that the negligence should have brought about the harm, the allowance of recovery would place too unreasonable a burden on the defendants, and the allowance of recovery would be too likely to open the way to fraudulent claims.

However, the court did determine that the defendants were not liable in this case based on the public policy factor that allowing recovery would have no sensible or just stopping point. If the claim was allowed, said the court, liability might also apply to parents who allegedly should have known that drinking would occur on their property while they were absent, knowing the behavior of teenagers. In addition, the court said it would only be a short step away from imposing strict liability upon property owners for any underage drinking that occurs on property under their control. The court went on to say that the expansion of liability to this type of case should be made by the legislature, not by the court.

Constitutionality of Permitted Use Ordinance

In *Town of Rhine v. Bizzell,* 2008 WI 76, 311 Wis. 2d 1, 751 N.W.2d 780 (2008), the supreme court found a zoning ordinance enacted by the Town of Bizzell (Town) to be unconstitutional. Land subject to the ordinance was owned by the Manitowoc Area Off Highway Vehicle Club (Club). At the time the Club took ownership the land was zoned for "B-2 Commercial, Manufacturing or Processing". Under this classification, no permitted use for the land existed, that is, the ordinance did not automatically permit the land to be used for any purpose. In order to use the land, a conditional-use permit had to be issued by the Town.

A second issue before the court was whether the activities being conducted on the land by the Club were a public nuisance. After purchasing the property, the Club used the property for all-terrain vehicle riding and hunting. Upon becoming aware that the Town required a conditional-use permit in order to use the land, the Club applied for a permit. The permit was denied because the conditional use would not be one of the manufacturing or commercial purposes for which such a permit could be issued under the ordinance. The Club also applied for the land to be rezoned and was denied. Subsequently the local police issued citations to six club members for violating the Town's public nuisance ordinance. The municipal court dismissed the citations for insufficient evidence.

The Town then filed a civil complaint in circuit court on both the zoning and the public nuisance issues. The circuit court invalidated the zoning ordinance because it prohibited all uses. The circuit court found this prohibition "unreasonable" and "confiscatory in nature," resulting in the ordinance being unconstitutional. As to the public nuisance claim, the circuit court found that for the activities on the land to be a public nuisance, the land had to be a "public place" and the nuisance had to affect the entire community.

On the zoning issue, the supreme court affirmed the lower court ruling. (The court of appeals, instead of hearing the case, certified it directly to the supreme court.) The supreme court agreed with the circuit court, dismissing the arguments made by the Town. The Town had argued that the B-2 classification did allow some uses, albeit only conditional ones for which Town approval must be sought, and that other municipalities have similar ordinances.

In finding the ordinance unconstitutional, the supreme court noted that an ordinance permitting no automatic uses of land could be constitutionally valid if the restriction bears a substantial relation to the public health, safety, morals or general welfare. The court stated that an example of a valid ordinance would be one that banned any permitted uses in a floodplain.

As to the nuisance claim, the supreme court reversed the circuit court's decision, stating that it erred in not applying the definition of "public nuisance" found in the Town's ordinance. The court therefore sent this issue back to the circuit court for a new hearing.

Jail Confinement for Tubercular Patient

In *City of Milwaukee v. Washington,* 2007 WI 104, 304 Wis. 2d 98, 735 N.W.2d 111 (2007), the supreme court held the City of Milwaukee (City) could confine to jail a person with noninfectious tuberculosis who is at a high risk of developing the infectious version of the disease and who fails to comply with the prescribed treatment. The Wisconsin statute establishing public health procedures to prevent the spread of tuberculosis allows a person with noninfectious tuberculosis to be "confined" if there is no other alternative that is less restrictive. The statute does not specifically authorize or prohibit the use of a jail or other correctional facility for the purpose of confining the person.

At the time Washington was diagnosed with noninfectious tuberculosis she was living in a shelter. The staff of a city tuberculosis clinic at which she was diagnosed gave Washington bus tickets so that she would come to the clinic as prescribed to receive her medication under the observation of clinic staff. She failed to make two of these medication appointments, so the City health department issued treatment and isolation orders to be served on Washington as soon as she was found. The department found her in a hospital where she had been admitted to give birth to a baby. The department served her with the orders and asked that she remain in the hospital. When Washington threatened to leave the hospital, the City petitioned the circuit court for enforcement of its orders. An agreement was made between Washington and the City that Washington would remain in the hospital for approximately a month until there could be a hearing on the City's petition. At that hearing, the City noted that Washington's condition had progressed to the point that the department believed Washington no longer needed to be confined. She was released but was required to report to the tuberculosis clinic at regular intervals to receive her medication under observation, and to stay with her sister. Washington failed to comply with these requirements and was reported missing by her sister two days after being released. She was discovered that day in a store parking lot, was detained by police, was taken to the hospitable for a medical assessment, and was then transported to the county jail. The City then filed a motion requesting that Washington be confined in jail for violation of the treatment and isolation orders.

Two days before the scheduled hearing on the motion, Washington was mistakenly released from jail. She was found a few days later, detained by the police, and appeared in court that afternoon. At the hearing, the circuit court confined Washington to jail with a review in six months; the court noted, however, that if an alternative place of confinement could be found then it would entertain that proposal. The court of appeals unanimously affirmed the circuit court's decision.

In her appeal to the supreme court, Washington did not challenge the fact that she should be confined but argued that the circuit court could have confined her to a hospital with surveillance as opposed to a jail. She first argued that a jail was not a facility within the meaning of the statute. She also argued that the statute would have to specifically authorize a jail as a possible place of confinement because the purpose of the statute was to protect public health and not to impose punitive measures. The supreme court rejected these arguments reasoning that a facility, by its dictionary definition, may include a jail; that the use of the word confine, instead of quarantine or isolate, suggests a jail setting; and that confinement is the last resort since it is allowed only when there is no less restrictive place available.

Washington also argued that the lower courts erred in saying that relative costs of confinement could be a factor in determining the place of confinement. The supreme court rejected this argument, saying that costs could be a factor if there were two or more places, such as a hospital and a jail, where treatment could be provided and the spread of the disease could be prevented. In conclusion, the court held that the applicable statute authorizes confinement to a jail for a person with noninfectious tuberculosis with a high risk of developing the infectious version. The court, in a footnote, noted that this decision was limited to only the noninfectious version of the disease. The court stated it would be doubtful that the jail would be an appropriate place for a person with infectious tuberculosis to be confined because such a placement would almost certainly increase the chances of the disease being transmitted to other inmates.

Assessing Property at Fair Market Value

Walgreen Co. v. City of Madison, 2008 WI 80, 311 Wis. 2d 158, 752 N.W.2d 687 (2008), involves a dispute between the Walgreen Corporation (Walgreens) and the City of Madison (City) as to the proper way to assess the value of two buildings which house Walgreens stores on the east side of the City. Walgreens has a business model which it uses in operating its stores. Instead of owning a store outright or simply leasing space, Walgreens works with developers who find prime store sites and who buy out the existing businesses on the site. The developer then rebuilds or remodels the property especially to suit Walgreens' needs. Walgreens then leases the property from the developer and pays back the developer for the development of the site by entering into a lease under which the rental payments are higher than what they would be at the regular market rate. The lease requires Walgreens to pay the property taxes. The lease has a term of 60 years, but may be ended after 20 years.

For the years 2003 and 2004, the City assessed these properties for property tax purposes basing the assessment on the fair market value of the property, but enhanced by the fact that the developer was receiving rental payments at above fair market value. This resulted in the amount of property tax being higher than it would have been if there had not been rental payment above market value. Walgreens tried to appeal these assessments to the Madison Board of Review but was unsuccessful. Walgreens then filed suit in circuit court, seeking a refund in the amount that, according to Walgreens, was paid in excess. Walgreens lost both in circuit court and in the court of appeals. Throughout the litigation, Walgreens argued that the City could not use the fact that the rental payments were above market value as a factor in determining value for property tax purposes.

In this decision, the supreme court found that the legislature had the power to determine the appropriate way to assess municipal property taxes, and that it had done so by requiring the use of a property assessment manual (manual) prepared by the state Department of Revenue. Statutory law requires that the manual "discuss and illustrate accepted assessment methods, techniques and practices with a view to more nearly uniform and more consistent assessments of property at the local level" and requires that the manual be amended to reflect advances in these methods and any court decisions concerning assessment issues. The supreme court goes on to describe the three methods presented in the manual for assessing real property: the sales comparison approach, the cost approach, and the income approach. The manual states that for leased properties, the income approach is often the most reliable. The court accepts the income approach as the appropriate one, but states that the Madison Board of Review and the lower courts did not apply it properly. The court noted that under the manual, the rent that could be received on the open market (market rent), as opposed to the actual amount of rent in the lease (lease rent), must be used, unless the market rent would be lower than the lease rent. With the Walgreens leases, however, the lease rent was higher, so the exception presented in the manual was inapplicable. The City argued, and the lower courts agreed, that the approach specified by the manual should be disregarded, taking the position that using the manual's approach does not result in assessing the "full value" at sale, which is what is required by statute. The City argued that previous court decisions supported their position. The supreme court rejected this, finding that the use of the manual was required under statutory law, and that prior case law and the manual were not in conflict. The court stated that the City was in effect taxing a business effort as opposed to the actual real property and that artificially increased sales or rental prices caused by unusual financing arrangements may not be used to determine property assessments. If such an arrangement is used, the court stated that the City would be assessing financial arrangements entered into a lease agreement as opposed to the value of the actual property that is being leased.

Statistics

8

Statistical information about Wisconsin: agriculture, associations, commerce and industry, conservation and recreation, education, employment and income, geography and climate, history, local and state government, military and veterans affairs, news media, population and vital statistics, post offices, social services, state and local finance, and transportation

A Piece of Interplanetary Dust

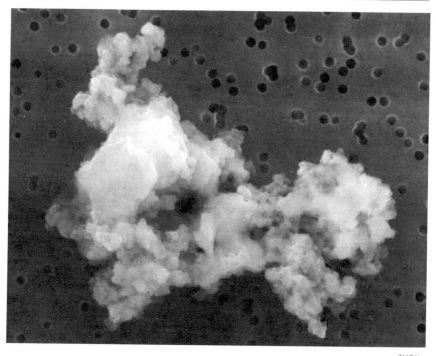

(NASA)

WISCONSIN STATE DOCUMENT DEPOSITORY LIBRARIES

Most of the data presented in the statistical section of the *Wisconsin Blue Book* are based on publications issued by the federal government and Wisconsin state agencies. Persons wishing to consult the original sources for further information may find them at one of following depository libraries or may borrow many of them from libraries throughout the state on interlibrary loan. State depository libraries are designated to receive copies of all collected publications. Regional depository libraries receive approximately three-quarters of all collected publications, and selective depository libraries receive two-thirds.

City	Library	Street Address
STATE LEVEL DEPOSITORY		
Madison	Dr. H. Rupert Theobald Library, Legislative Reference Bureau	1 E. Main Street, Suite 200
Madison	State Historical Society of Wisconsin	816 State Street
Madison	Reference and Loan Library, Department of Public Instruction	2109 S. Stoughton Road
REGIONAL DEPOSITORY		
Appleton	Appleton Public Library	225 N. Oneida Street
Eau Claire	William D. McIntyre Library, UW-Eau Claire	105 Garfield Avenue
Green Bay	Cofrin Library, UW-Green Bay	2420 Nicolet Drive
La Crosse	La Crosse Public Library	800 Main Street
Milwaukee	Milwaukee Public Library	814 W. Wisconsin Avenue
Platteville	Elton S. Karrmann Library, UW-Platteville	1 University Plaza
Racine	Racine Public Library	75 Seventh Street
River Falls	Chalmer Davee Library, UW-River Falls	410 S. Third Street
Stevens Point	UW-Stevens Point Library	900 Reserve Street
Superior	Superior Public Library	1530 Tower Avenue
SELECTIVE DEPOSITORY		
Appleton	Seeley G. Mudd Library, Lawrence University	113 S. Lawe Street
Baraboo	T.N. Savides Library, UW College-Baraboo/Sauk County	1006 Connie Road
Beaver Dam	Beaver Dam Community Library	311 N. Spring Street
Beloit	Morse Library, Beloit College Library	731 College Street
Eau Claire	L.E. Phillips Memorial Public Library	400 Eau Claire Street
Fond du Lac	Fond du Lac Public Library	32 Sheboygan Street
Green Bay	Brown County Library	515 Pine Street
Hayward	Lac Courte Oreilles Ojibwa College Community Library	13466 W. Trepania Road
Janesville	Gary J. Lenox Library, UW College-Rock County	2909 Kellogg Avenue
Kenosha	UW-Parkside Library	900 Wood Road
La Crosse	Murphy Library, UW-La Crosse	1631 Pine Street
Madison	Madison Public Library	201 W. Mifflin Street
Manitowoc	Manitowoc Public Library	707 Quay Street
Marshfield	Hamilton Roddis Library, UW College-Marshfield/Wood County	2000 W. Fifth Street
Menomonie	Library Learning Center, UW-Stout Library	315 Tenth Avenue
Milwaukee	Golda Meir Library, UW-Milwaukee	2311 E. Hartford Avenue
Oshkosh	Forrest R. Polk Library, UW-Oshkosh	800 Algoma Boulevard
Oshkosh	Oshkosh Public Library	106 Washington Avenue
Portage	Portage Public Library	253 W. Edgewater Street
Rhinelander	Richard J. Brown Library, Nicolet Area Technical College	5364 College Drive
Ripon	Lane Library, Ripon College	300 Seward Street
Shawano	Shawano City-County Library	128 S. Sawyer Street
Superior	Jim Dan Hill Library, UW-Superior	Belknap and Catlin Streets
Two Rivers	Lester Public Library	1001 Adams Street
Waukesha	UW College-Waukesha County Library	1500 University Drive
Waukesha	Waukesha Public Library	321 Wisconsin Avenue
Wausau	Marathon County Public Library	300 N. First Street
Wauwatosa	Wauwatosa Public Library	7635 W. North Avenue
West Bend	UW College-Washington County Library	400 University Drive
Whitewater	Harold G. Andersen Library, UW-Whitewater	800 W. Main Street
Wisconsin Rapids . . .	McMillan Memorial Library	490 E. Grand Avenue

Source: Wisconsin Department of Public Instruction, Reference and Loan Library, *Wisconsin Document Depository Program State Depository Libraries,* at: http://dpi.wi.gov/rll/liblist.html [February 27, 2009].

HIGHLIGHTS OF AGRICULTURE IN WISCONSIN

Farm Production — In 2007, Wisconsin ranked first nationally in the production of cheese (including leading the nation with 39% of domestic Muenster production and 20% of American production) and dry whey products and second to California in the production of milk and butter. In crop production, it ranked first in cranberries and snap beans for processing. It was among the top five producers of corn for silage, oats, forage, potatoes, tart cherries, maple syrup, mint for oil, carrots for processing, sweet corn for processing, green peas for processing, and cucumbers for pickles. Wisconsin is also the leading producer of mink pelts and milk goats in the country. As befits the state known as "America's Dairyland", Wisconsin had more milk cows than any other state in the nation except California, with over 1.24 million head, about 14% of the nation's total.

Cash Receipts and Income — Total net Wisconsin farm income was $2.65 billion in 2007, an increase of $912 million from 2005. Wisconsin ranked 8th nationally in total net farm income in 2007, up from 15th in 2005. California led the nation in farm income for 2007 with about $12.75 billion, while Alaska, with $11.4 million, ranked last.

Total cash receipts for Wisconsin farm products marketed in 2007 amounted to almost $8.9 billion. California led the nation that year in total cash receipts from farm marketings at $36.6 billion. Dairy products accounted for 51.9% of Wisconsin's cash receipts from farm marketings in 2007, with food grains and feed and oil crops providing 19.7% and meat animals 11.6%.

Number and Size of Farms — From 2002 to 2007, the number of farms in the nation increased by 75,810 to 2,204,792; in Wisconsin, the number increased from about 77,100 to 78,500. Until the 1990s, the number of Wisconsin's farms had decreased fairly steadily from a peak of 199,877 in 1935, but the decline slowed in recent years, and has now begun to reverse itself. Wisconsin farmland decreased from 23.5 million acres to 15.2 million acres between 1935 and 2007, and the average farm size increased from 117 acres to 194 acres over the same period.

Dane and Grant Counties had the largest number of farms in Wisconsin in 2007. Dane County had 3,331 farms, 444 more than in 2002, and Grant County had 2,866 farms, an increase of 376. Grant County had the most farmland in 2007 with 610,914 acres. Adams County had the largest average farm size at 283 acres. Smallest were the Milwaukee County farms, averaging 57 acres.

Value of Farms and Farmland — Land and buildings on Wisconsin farms were valued at about $57.8 billion in 2007, an increase of $8.8 billion or 18% from 2006. The average value per farm increased from $644,211 in 2006 to $735,796 in 2007. The average value per acre in 2007 was $3,800, an increase of $600 over 2006.

The average price for agricultural land sold in Wisconsin during 2007 was $4,365 per acre, a $346 decrease from the $4,711 average selling price in 2006. Land continuing in agricultural use after sale sold for a statewide average of $3,518 per acre in 2007; agricultural land that sold for other uses was purchased for an average price of $10,125 per acre.

Farm Assets and Debts — Wisconsin farms recorded assets of $802,653 per farm in 2007 and debt of $96,059 per farm for a debt-to-asset ratio of 12%.

Farm Ownership — In 2007, about 68.5% of the farms in Wisconsin were operated by full owners, and about 27% were operated by part owners. Only about 4% of Wisconsin farms were run by tenants. The vast majority of Wisconsin farms (86.8%) were individually run or operated by family organizations or partnerships, while only a small number were organized as family or nonfamily corporations.

The following tables present selected data. Consult footnoted sources for more detailed information on agriculture.

NUMBER, SIZE AND VALUE OF FARMS IN WISCONSIN
1935 – 2007

Year	Number of Farms	Land in Farms (acres)	Average Size of Farm (acres)	Total (in millions)	Average per Farm	Average per Acre
				Value of Land and Buildings		
1935	200,000	23,500,000	117	$1,246	$6,228	$53
1940	187,000	22,900,000	123	1,191	6,368	52
1945	178,000	23,600,000	133	1,440	8,088	61
1950	174,000	23,600,000	136	2,100	12,071	89
1955	155,000	23,200,000	150	2,343	15,117	101
1960	138,000	22,200,000	161	2,953	21,396	133
1965	124,000	21,400,000	173	3,317	26,750	155
1970	110,000	20,100,000	183	4,663	42,393	232
1975	100,000	19,300,000	193	8,376	83,762	434
1980	93,000	18,600,000	200	18,674	200,800	1,004
1985	83,000	17,900,000	216	16,898	203,586	944
1990	80,000	17,600,000	220	14,098	176,220	801
1995	80,000	16,800,000	210	17,472	218,400	1,040
1996	79,000	16,600,000	210	18,758	237,443	1,130
1997	79,000	16,500,000	209	19,305	244,367	1,170
1998	78,000	16,300,000	209	20,212	259,128	1,240
1999	78,000	16,200,000	208	23,490	301,154	1,450
2000	77,500	16,000,000	206	27,200	350,968	1,700
2001	77,000	15,800,000	205	30,810	400,130	1,950
2002	77,000	15,700,000	204	33,755	438,377	2,150
2003	76,500	15,600,000	204	35,880	469,020	2,300
2004	76,500	15,500,000	203	38,750	507,500	2,500
2005	76,500	15,400,000	201	43,890	573,725	2,850
2006	76,000	15,300,000	201	48,960	644,211	3,200
2007	78,500	15,200,000	194	57,760	735,796	3,800

Notes: "Farm" is currently defined as a place that sells, or would normally sell, at least $1,000 of agricultural products during the year. The actual number of farms in Wisconsin peaked at 199,877 in 1935. Average value per farm amounts calculated by Wisconsin Legislative Reference Bureau. Prior year's numbers have been revised to reflect updated source data.

Sources: U.S. Department of Agriculture, National Agricultural Statistics Service, "Farms, Land in Farms, and Livestock Operations 2008 Summary", February 2009, and "Land Values and Cash Rents 2008 Summary", August 2008.

2007 WISCONSIN CASH RECEIPTS FROM FARM MARKETINGS
(Percent of All Commodities)

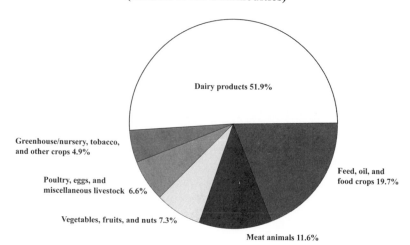

Dairy products 51.9%

Greenhouse/nursery, tobacco, and other crops 4.9%

Poultry, eggs, and miscellaneous livestock 6.6%

Vegetables, fruits, and nuts 7.3%

Feed, oil, and food crops 19.7%

Meat animals 11.6%

WISCONSIN CASH RECEIPTS FROM FARM MARKETINGS
By Commodity, 2003 – 2007
(In Thousands)

Commodity	2003	2004	2005	2006	2007
ALL COMMODITIES	**$5,895,708**	**$6,855,643**	**$6,799,841**	**$6,920,894**	**$8,858,242**
LIVESTOCK, DAIRY, AND POULTRY . .	**4,093,530**	**5,093,564**	**5,011,615**	**4,648,981**	**6,203,752**
Meat animals	**823,624**	**938,107**	**1,004,478**	**1,047,307**	**1,025,669**
Cattle and calves.	711,340	813,166	877,971	932,442	908,691
Hogs	105,936	118,619	120,073	109,697	111,262
Sheep and lambs	6,348	6,323	6,434	5,168	5,716
Dairy products	**2,838,258**	**3,687,242**	**3,527,784**	**3,075,492**	**4,593,207**
Poultry and eggs	**249,312**	**279,018**	**281,739**	**316,804**	**399,344**
Broilers.	54,180	68,445	70,268	62,345	86,895
Farm chickens	179	171	162	266	235
Chicken eggs.	55,579	56,679	39,702	45,323	89,263
Other poultry.	51,475	51,555	51,650	51,840	52,890
Miscellaneous livestock.	**182,336**	**189,197**	**197,614**	**209,378**	**185,532**
Honey	8,376	6,959	6,321	6,785	5,796
Wool	120	150	147	140	204
Aquaculture.	**6,769**	**6,865**	**6,973**	**6,973**	**39,490**
Trout	1,369	1,465	1,573	1,573	1,625
Other aquaculture	5,400	5,400	5,400	5,400	37,865
Other livestock.	167,071	175,223	184,173	195,480	140,042
Mink pelts	20,961	28,323	36,173	47,380	42,042
All other livestock*	146,110	146,900	148,000	148,100	98,000
CROPS	**1,802,178**	**1,762,079**	**1,788,226**	**2,271,913**	**2,654,490**
Food grains	**38,567**	**43,609**	**34,336**	**65,926**	**106,424**
Wheat	38,215	43,069	33,460	64,802	105,530
Feed crops.	**745,656**	**734,354**	**702,373**	**1,025,374**	**1,314,898**
Barley	1,012	841	748	837	898
Corn	669,176	646,462	562,306	924,003	1,228,334
Hay.	68,471	78,773	127,848	91,239	73,531
Oats	6,997	8,278	11,471	9,294	12,135
Tobacco	**6,680**	**7,430**	**6,197**	**0**	**0**
Oil crops.	**227,411**	**219,988**	**255,402**	**278,603**	**321,716**
Soybeans	227,018	219,617	255,042	278,169	320,937
Vegetables	**384,348**	**349,399**	**339,602**	**418,519**	**432,654**
Beans, dry	2,923	3,790	3,725	3,124	3,268
Potatoes, fall	185,803	165,655	163,260	231,115	198,196
Beans, snap, processing	30,389	37,095	28,629	36,641	31,297
Cabbage	9,593	6,111	6,519	8,282	17,323
Carrots	6,300	5,087	5,373	6,261	5,140
Corn, sweet	56,938	46,292	56,913	54,995	64,577
Cucumbers, processing	6,422	4,738	5,774	6,490	9,217
Onions, storage	7,740	4,510	4,900	7,021	6,671
Peas, green, processing	17,373	14,655	15,939	15,587	18,739
Miscellaneous vegetables	59,500	60,500	47,500	47,000	76,850
Fruits and nuts	**143,911**	**137,202**	**157,571**	**185,338**	**213,226**
Apples	9,294	19,010	19,026	22,061	25,756
Cherries, tart	5,239	2,513	2,196	1,365	2,842
Cranberries.	122,463	108,954	129,246	154,550	176,360
Strawberries, spring	5,265	5,125	5,453	5,762	5,848
Other berries	1,200	1,150	1,200	1,150	1,700
Miscellaneous fruits and nuts	450	450	450	450	720
All other crops	**255,605**	**270,097**	**292,745**	**298,153**	**265,572**
Maple products.	2,212	3,230	1,620	3,120	2,678
Mint	3,145	3,131	2,962	4,385	3,961
Greenhouse/nursery	237,048	238,685	244,029	245,000	172,800
Floriculture.	81,548	82,785	86,529	NA	NA
Christmas trees.	29,500	29,400	29,500	29,500	27,300

Note: Bold figures indicate category totals of the commodities immediately following and indicate categories included in next higher level of aggregation. Category totals may include amounts for specific commodities not listed separately or that are not listed to provide confidentiality to large producers in concentrated industries. Prior year's entries have been revised to reflect updated source data.

NA – Not available.

*Horses and mules are included in "all other livestock."

Source: U.S. Department of Agriculture, Economic Research Service, "Farm Cash Receipts, 2000-2007," at: http://www.ers.usda.gov/Data/FarmIncome/FinfidmuXls.htm#receipts [March 4, 2009].

CASH RECEIPTS AND INCOME FROM FARMING
By State, 2007
(In Thousands)

State	Cash Receipts Livestock and Products	Crops	Total	Government Payments[1]	Income Gross	Net	Rank[2]
Alabama	$3,370,617	$795,638	$4,166,255	$181,232	$5,229,540	$1,437,811	26
Alaska	6,925	26,260	33,185	4,073	45,814	11,410	50
Arizona.	1,577,007	1,843,487	3,420,494	92,862	4,150,979	1,158,470	28
Arkansas	4,100,483	3,037,967	7,138,450	484,176	8,304,083	2,161,147	13
California	10,734,914	25,839,936	36,574,850	478,766	39,571,855	12,746,767	1
Colorado	4,270,914	2,019,199	6,290,113	198,837	7,523,531	1,535,364	23
Connecticut	202,427	361,425	563,852	10,768	682,858	208,174	42
Delaware	795,450	209,084	1,004,534	18,119	1,163,981	353,180	38
Florida	1,462,619	6,183,421	7,646,040	121,297	8,619,852	1,911,182	19
Georgia.	4,361,765	2,451,775	6,813,540	373,246	8,531,873	2,635,111	9
Hawaii	75,755	457,395	533,150	5,452	611,156	76,755	46
Idaho	3,269,314	2,412,564	5,681,878	122,361	6,467,127	1,784,635	20
ILLINOIS	2,073,464	9,605,145	11,678,609	600,976	13,882,179	3,244,075	6
Indiana	2,564,580	5,211,162	7,775,742	302,688	9,165,326	2,314,587	11
IOWA	8,857,013	10,179,840	19,036,853	775,891	21,930,872	5,333,999	3
Kansas	7,211,504	4,517,824	11,729,328	520,325	14,085,712	2,155,737	14
Kentucky	2,957,627	1,474,781	4,432,408	338,100	5,670,036	1,505,849	24
Louisiana.	941,322	1,768,902	2,710,224	286,004	3,431,613	949,018	30
Maine	344,642	339,855	684,497	11,213	767,592	262,296	41
Maryland.	1,144,377	827,872	1,972,249	44,410	2,426,697	730,346	34
Massachusetts	99,880	350,267	450,147	8,409	611,457	143,117	43
MICHIGAN	2,366,949	3,374,555	5,741,504	141,081	6,789,858	1,538,048	22
MINNESOTA	5,628,604	6,909,825	12,538,429	479,598	14,376,213	3,439,435	4
Mississippi.	2,753,775	1,588,182	4,341,957	591,152	5,797,096	1,434,187	27
Missouri	3,450,649	3,469,029	6,919,678	382,440	8,665,617	2,027,103	16
Montana	1,157,251	1,237,053	2,394,304	258,041	3,629,920	760,589	33
Nebraska	8,358,073	6,197,747	14,555,820	441,301	16,584,622	3,391,521	5
Nevada	337,312	215,616	552,928	25,256	634,518	127,698	44
New Hampshire	79,750	104,714	184,464	42,483	246,536	66,471	47
New Jersey	176,987	768,939	945,926	13,458	1,131,966	312,383	39
New Mexico	2,358,193	699,707	3,057,900	53,064	3,361,125	821,754	31
New York	2,723,237	1,723,580	4,446,817	48,070	5,027,179	1,608,718	21
North Carolina	5,767,500	2,923,599	8,691,099	569,943	11,138,769	2,806,927	7
North Dakota.	956,702	4,533,636	5,490,338	389,645	6,734,539	1,991,905	17
Ohio	2,526,041	4,371,576	6,897,617	268,671	8,705,300	1,949,739	18
Oklahoma	3,977,191	1,180,498	5,157,689	249,015	6,711,194	1,069,479	29
Oregon	1,066,542	3,298,399	4,364,941	124,010	5,526,049	1,482,646	25
Pennsylvania	3,831,302	1,929,113	5,760,415	77,192	6,802,748	2,154,517	15
Rhode Island	11,185	58,612	69,797	10,736	99,545	37,905	49
South Carolina	1,242,303	785,224	2,027,527	164,529	2,541,469	534,902	35
South Dakota.	2,705,201	3,029,088	5,734,289	317,068	7,529,197	2,301,661	12
Tennessee	1,399,484	1,341,663	2,741,147	306,741	3,577,137	375,241	37
Texas	11,386,493	7,688,334	19,074,827	1,345,851	25,199,218	7,181,007	2
Utah	950,732	388,947	1,339,679	37,041	1,867,758	399,738	36
Vermont	581,038	92,997	674,035	13,510	771,428	263,248	40
Virginia.	2,063,683	886,698	2,950,381	132,517	3,923,720	799,790	32
Washington.	2,126,501	5,323,189	7,449,690	185,127	8,395,195	2,449,182	10
West Virginia.	398,865	81,016	479,881	12,600	703,137	49,104	48
WISCONSIN	6,203,752	2,654,490	8,858,242	207,973	10,520,562	2,653,787	8
Wyoming.	881,554	184,378	1,065,932	34,695	1,282,722	90,016	45
UNITED STATES[3]. . . .	$137,889,448	$146,954,202	$284,843,650	$11,902,013	$341,148,471	$86,777,732	

[1]Includes both cash payments and payments-in-kind (PIK).

[2]Ranking of net income calculated by Wisconsin Legislative Reference Bureau.

[3]Detail may not add due to rounding.

Source: U.S. Department of Agriculture, Economic Research Service, Income and Production Expenses, at: http://www.ers.usda.gov/Data/FarmIncome/FinfidmuXls.htm [March 4, 2009].

WISCONSIN'S RANK IN AGRICULTURE, 2007

Commodity	Unit	United States (000s)	Wisconsin (000s)	Wisconsin Percent of U.S.	Rank in U.S.	Leading State in U.S.
CASH RECEIPTS						
ALL COMMODITIES		$284,843,650	$8,858,242	3.1%	8	California
Livestock and livestock products . .		137,889,448	6,203,752	4.5	6	Texas
Crops.		146,954,202	2,654,490	1.8	19	California
PRODUCTION						
DAIRY						
Milk production	Lbs	185,602,000	24,080,000	13.0	2	California
Butter.	Lbs	1,532,890	373,027	24.3	2	California
Cheese (excluding cottage cheese)	Lbs	9,700,499	2,450,760	25.3	1	**Wisconsin**
American.	Lbs	3,877,827	771,853	19.9	1	**Wisconsin**
Muenster.	Lbs	103,485	40,250	38.9	1	**Wisconsin**
Mozzarella.	Lbs	3,303,305	853,080	25.8	2	California
Italian	Lbs	4,134,230	1,166,903	28.2	2	California
Dry whey, human food.	Lbs	1,072,553	311,160	29.0	1	**Wisconsin**
LIVESTOCK AND POULTRY						
Cattle and calves, all[1]	Head	97,003	3,400	3.5	9	Texas
Milk cows[1].	Head	9,158	1,247	13.6	2	California
Hogs and pigs, all[2]	Head	65,110	430	0.7	18	Iowa
Sheep[1]	Head	6,055	90	1.5	18	Texas
Milk goats	Head	305	33	10.8	1	**Wisconsin**
Chickens[2].	Head	454,902	5,697	1.3	21	Iowa
Broilers.	Head	8,898,200	47,100	0.5	18	Georgia
Trout, sold 12" or longer.	Lbs	69,343	441	0.6	8	Idaho
Mink pelts	Pelts	2,828	914	32.3	1	**Wisconsin**
Honey	Lbs	148,482	5,040	3.4	8	North Dakota
Eggs	Eggs	90,581,000	1,370,000	1.5	18	Iowa
CROPS						
Corn for grain	Bu	13,073,893	442,800	3.4	10	Iowa
Corn for silage	Tons	106,328	11,920	11.2	2	California
Oats	Bu	91,599	10,720	11.7	3	North Dakota
Soybeans.	Bu	2,585,207	51,870	2.0	14	Iowa
Wheat, all	Bu	2,066,722	18,910	0.9	21	North Dakota
Barley	Bu	211,825	1,311	0.6	16	North Dakota
Forage (dry equivalent), all	Tons	107,124	9,035	8.4	3	Texas
Hay (dry only), all	Tons	150,304	4,515	3.0	13	Texas
Potatoes, all	Cwt	449,156	28,160	6.3	3	Idaho
Dry edible beans	Cwt	25,371	92	0.4	17	North Dakota
Cherries, tart	Lbs	248,700	10,000	0.4	5	Michigan
Apples	Lbs	9,113,900	59,000	0.6	9	Washington
Strawberries	Cwt	24,994	43	0.2	8	California
Maple syrup	Gals	1,258	75	6.0	3	Vermont
Cranberries.	Bbl	6,554	3,830	58.4	1	**Wisconsin**
Mint for oil.	Lbs	9,173	281	3.1	5	Washington
Onions	Cwt	79,413	666	0.8	11	California
Cabbage for fresh market	Cwt	25,824	1,025	4.0	8[3]	California
Sweet corn for fresh market	Cwt	28,234	570	2.0	13	Florida
Carrots for processing	Tons	345	81	23.5	2	Washington
Sweet corn for processing	Tons	2,897	579	20.0	3	Washington
Green peas for processing	Tons	436	81	18.6	3	Washington
Snap beans for processing	Tons	768	265	34.5	1	**Wisconsin**
Cucumbers for pickles	Tons	508	49	9.7	3	Michigan

Abbreviations: Bbl = barrels, Bu = bushels, Cwt = hundredweight, Gals = gallons, Lbs = pounds.

Note: Wisconsin is also a leading state in the production of turkeys, ducks, and ginseng; Wisconsin's rank is not available for these commodities.

[1] January 1, 2008 inventory. [2] December 1, 2007 inventory. [3] Tied with Ohio.

Sources: U.S. Department of Agriculture, National Agricultural Statistics Service, "Wisconsin's Rank in the Nation's Agriculture, 2007", at: http://www.nass.usda.gov/Statistics_by_State/Wisconsin/Publications/Miscellaneous/rankwi. pdf [March 4, 2009]; U.S. Department of Agriculture, Economic Research Service, "All Commodities," "Livestock and Products," and "All Crops," in States Rankings for Cash Receipts, 2007, at: http://www.ers.usda.gov/Data/FarmIncome/ firkdmu.htm [March 4, 2009].

NUMBER AND SIZE OF FARMS IN WISCONSIN
By County, 2002 and 2007

| | 2002 | | | | 2007 | | | |
County	No. of Farms	Avg. Size of Farms in Acres	Land in Farms Acres	Rank	No. of Farms	Avg. Size of Farms in Acres	Land in Farms Acres	Rank
Adams	414	298	123,539	53	408	283	115,343	53
Ashland	227	259	58,746	64	203	273	55,370	64
Barron	1,647	214	351,930	12	1,484	218	324,196	16
Bayfield	468	239	111,851	54	383	233	89,284	58
Brown	1,117	176	196,859	37	1,053	178	187,167	38
Buffalo	1,128	280	316,132	18	1,229	250	307,035	19
Burnett	451	218	98,271	59	531	181	96,168	57
Calumet	733	205	150,316	45	732	207	151,659	44
Chippewa	1,621	231	374,103	8	1,575	224	353,491	10
Clark	2,200	210	461,353	4	2,170	203	440,376	4
Columbia.	1,526	228	348,369	14	1,585	199	316,193	17
Crawford.	1,278	199	254,755	30	1,347	177	238,225	31
Dane	2,887	179	515,475	3	3,331	161	535,756	2
Dodge	1,968	205	404,054	5	1,979	209	412,949	5
Door	877	154	135,128	50	854	157	134,472	49
Douglas	391	217	84,858	62	333	218	72,686	62
Dunn	1,683	237	398,768	6	1,690	226	382,545	6
Eau Claire	1,174	174	204,298	36	1,223	168	205,375	36
Florence	121	177	21,360	68	115	176	20,264	68
Fond du Lac	1,634	211	344,286	15	1,643	204	335,745	15
Forest.	164	205	33,630	67	173	195	33,805	67
Grant.	2,490	243	605,836	1	2,866	213	610,914	1
Green.	1,490	206	306,946	20	1,534	200	306,859	20
Green Lake.	670	221	147,916	47	723	197	142,757	47
Iowa	1,686	218	367,373	10	1,813	201	364,970	7
Iron.	62	206	12,741	69	54	187	10,110	69
Jackson.	914	282	258,152	26	945	253	238,978	30
Jefferson	1,421	174	247,914	31	1,434	170	244,238	28
Juneau	805	224	179,959	40	797	227	181,046	39
Kenosha	466	190	88,708	61	460	183	84,345	61
Kewaunee	915	190	174,212	42	893	196	175,449	40
La Crosse	868	201	174,213	41	845	196	165,368	41
Lafayette	1,205	284	342,800	17	1,342	255	342,617	13
Langlade	542	260	141,088	49	487	252	122,895	51
Lincoln.	593	166	98,168	60	575	151	86,770	59
Manitowoc	1,469	175	257,111	29	1,444	172	248,238	26
Marathon.	2,898	183	531,263	2	2,545	193	490,628	3
Marinette.	729	204	148,777	46	746	193	144,303	46
Marquette	624	233	145,552	48	626	217	135,914	48
Menominee	4	89	354	72	4	80	318	72
Milwaukee	78	72	5,579	71	96	57	5,458	71
Monroe.	1,938	182	351,775	13	2,115	166	351,306	11
Oconto	1,132	193	218,887	35	1,244	166	205,924	35
Oneida	183	279	51,006	66	179	219	39,172	66
Outagamie	1,430	184	263,485	25	1,362	182	247,482	27
Ozaukee	533	142	75,467	63	513	138	70,689	63
Pepin	501	222	111,313	55	503	216	108,426	54
Pierce.	1,510	177	267,311	24	1,531	177	271,178	24
Polk	1,659	177	292,860	21	1,582	183	288,994	21
Portage	1,197	244	292,109	22	1,066	264	281,575	22
Price	477	218	103,957	57	545	188	102,407	55
Racine	631	197	124,201	52	652	185	120,459	52
Richland	1,358	190	257,807	27	1,545	164	253,776	25
Rock	1,529	225	343,763	16	1,556	221	344,361	12
Rusk	715	242	173,310	43	651	247	160,534	43
St. Croix	1,864	166	310,178	19	1,808	171	308,275	18
Sauk	1,673	211	353,104	11	1,923	187	358,919	8
Sawyer	230	235	54,056	65	231	204	47,093	65
Shawano	1,465	185	270,534	23	1,450	187	271,718	23
Sheboygan	1,116	175	195,248	38	1,059	181	191,719	37
Taylor	1,056	244	257,143	28	1,208	201	242,932	29
Trempealeau	1,744	211	367,830	9	1,721	198	341,370	14
Vernon	2,230	171	382,218	7	2,492	143	357,090	9
Vilas	71	137	9,721	70	71	140	9,942	70
Walworth.	988	222	219,502	34	1,000	218	217,593	34
Washburn	471	224	105,432	56	558	183	101,862	56
Washington.	844	154	129,807	51	831	156	129,790	50
Waukesha	762	129	98,404	58	675	128	86,602	60
Waupaca	1,398	177	247,351	32	1,330	176	234,392	32
Waushara.	717	269	192,576	39	677	220	148,969	45
Winnebago	963	177	170,404	44	1,001	164	164,014	42
Wood	1,108	206	228,050	33	1,114	199	221,962	33
STATE*	77,131	204	15,741,552		78,463	194	15,190,804	

Notes: Rank calculated by Wisconsin Legislative Reference Bureau. "Farm" is currently defined as a place that sells, or would normally sell, at least $1,000 of agricultural products during the year. USDA Census of Agriculture data may differ from USDA estimates in other tables.

*State totals as recorded by source document.

Source: U.S. Department of Agriculture, National Agricultural Statistics Service, "2007 Census of Agriculture, Volume 1, Chapter 2: Wisconsin County Level Data, Table 8", February 2009, at: http://www.agcensus.usda.gov/Publications/2007/ Full_Report/Volume_1,_Chapter_2_County_Level/Wisconsin/st55_2_008_008.pdf [March 12, 2009].

NUMBER AND ACREAGE OF FARMS
By State, 2002 and 2007

State	Number of Farms 2002	2007	Farm Acreage (in thousands) 2002	2007	Average Farm Size (acres) 2002	2007
Alabama	45,126	48,753	8,904	9,034	197	185
Alaska	609	686	901	882	1,479	1,285
Arizona.	7,294	15,637	26,587	26,118	3,645	1,670
Arkansas	47,483	49,346	14,503	13,873	305	281
California	79,631	81,033	27,589	25,365	346	313
Colorado	31,369	37,054	31,093	31,605	991	853
Connecticut	4,191	4,916	357	406	85	83
Delaware	2,391	2,546	540	510	226	200
Florida	44,081	47,463	10,415	9,232	236	195
Georgia.	49,311	47,846	10,744	10,151	218	212
Hawaii	5,398	7,521	1,300	1,121	241	149
Idaho	25,017	25,349	11,767	11,497	470	454
ILLINOIS	73,027	76,860	27,311	26,775	374	348
Indiana	60,296	60,938	15,059	14,773	250	242
IOWA	90,655	92,856	31,729	30,748	350	331
Kansas	64,414	65,531	47,228	46,346	733	707
Kentucky.	86,541	85,260	13,844	13,993	160	164
Louisiana.	27,413	30,106	7,831	8,110	286	269
Maine	7,196	8,136	1,370	1,348	190	166
Maryland.	12,198	12,834	2,078	2,052	170	160
Massachusetts	6,075	7,691	519	518	85	67
MICHIGAN	53,315	56,014	10,143	10,032	190	179
MINNESOTA	80,839	80,992	27,512	26,918	340	332
Mississippi.	42,186	41,959	11,098	11,456	263	273
Missouri	106,797	107,825	29,946	29,027	280	269
Montana	27,870	29,524	59,612	61,388	2,139	2,079
Nebraska	49,355	47,712	45,903	45,480	930	953
Nevada	2,989	3,131	6,331	5,865	2,118	1,873
New Hampshire	3,363	4,166	445	472	132	113
New Jersey.	9,924	10,327	806	733	81	71
New Mexico	15,170	20,930	44,810	43,238	2,954	2,066
New York	37,255	36,352	7,661	7,175	206	197
North Carolina	53,930	52,913	9,079	8,475	168	160
North Dakota.	30,619	31,970	39,295	39,675	1,283	1,241
Ohio	77,797	75,861	14,583	13,957	187	184
Oklahoma	83,300	86,565	33,662	35,087	404	405
Oregon	40,033	38,553	17,080	16,400	427	425
Pennsylvania.	58,105	63,163	7,745	7,809	133	124
Rhode Island	858	1,219	61	68	71	56
South Carolina	24,541	25,867	4,846	4,889	197	189
South Dakota.	31,736	31,169	43,785	43,666	1,380	1,401
Tennessee	87,595	79,280	11,682	10,970	133	138
Texas.	228,926	247,437	129,878	130,399	567	527
Utah	15,282	16,700	11,731	11,095	768	664
Vermont	6,571	6,984	1,245	1,233	189	177
Virginia.	47,606	47,383	8,625	8,104	181	171
Washington.	35,939	39,284	15,318	14,973	426	381
West Virginia.	20,812	23,618	3,585	3,698	172	157
WISCONSIN	77,131	78,463	15,742	15,191	204	194
Wyoming.	9,422	11,069	34,403	30,170	3,651	2,726
UNITED STATES	2,128,982	2,204,792	938,279	922,096	441	418

Notes: "Farm" is currently defined as a place that sells, or would normally sell, at least $1,000 of agricultural products during the year.

Source: U.S. Department of Agriculture, National Agricultural Statistics Service, "2007 Census of Agriculture, Volume 1, Table 8", February 2009, at: http://www.agcensus.usda.gov/Publications/2007/Full_Report/Volume_1,_Chapter_2_US_State_Level/st99_2_008_008.pdf [March 12, 2009].

WISCONSIN FARM OPERATORS
By County, 2007

County	Total Farms	Tenure of Operator			Type of Organization				
		Full Owners	Part Owners	Tenants	Individual or Family	Partnership	Family-held Corporation	Corporation Other than Family-held	Other*
Adams	408	291	104	13	348	33	17	5	5
Ashland	203	137	63	3	190	7	5	—	1
Barron	1,484	934	511	39	1,361	62	59	—	2
Bayfield	383	234	136	13	325	26	25	—	7
Brown	1,053	615	383	55	915	99	27	6	6
Buffalo	1,229	901	292	36	1,068	101	49	1	10
Burnett	531	374	150	7	485	32	12	—	2
Calumet	732	396	301	35	634	57	37	4	—
Chippewa	1,575	1,090	442	43	1,401	119	48	4	3
Clark	2,170	1,310	724	136	1,980	140	47	1	2
Columbia.	1,585	1,067	443	75	1,374	141	50	6	14
Crawford.	1,347	1,035	260	52	1,177	124	29	6	11
Dane	3,331	2,384	775	172	2,786	347	148	14	36
Dodge	1,979	1,265	621	93	1,684	195	86	6	8
Door	854	585	242	27	749	57	33	4	11
Douglas	333	235	93	5	300	20	10	2	1
Dunn	1,690	1,255	396	39	1,534	100	47	3	6
Eau Claire	1,223	903	275	45	1,105	84	30	—	4
Florence	115	79	35	1	99	12	4	—	—
Fond du Lac	1,643	1,028	529	86	1,391	171	66	6	9
Forest.	173	126	42	5	161	7	2	—	3
Grant	2,866	2,111	607	148	2,428	307	83	10	38
Green.	1,534	1,085	381	68	1,352	120	40	3	19
Green Lake.	723	502	191	30	605	78	27	6	7
Iowa	1,813	1,403	356	54	1,539	182	59	6	27
Iron.	54	27	21	6	52	—	2	—	—
Jackson.	945	692	234	19	798	79	51	4	13
Jefferson	1,434	946	403	85	1,227	114	67	6	20
Juneau	797	561	206	30	692	78	13	4	10
Kenosha	460	302	119	39	351	42	54	4	9
Kewaunee	893	575	298	20	761	100	23	6	3
La Crosse	845	582	227	36	740	81	12	4	8
Lafayette	1,342	911	350	81	1,143	145	37	3	14
Langlade	487	317	159	11	403	39	41	3	1
Lincoln.	575	414	141	20	508	39	25	2	1
Manitowoc.	1,444	911	466	67	1,280	106	44	8	6
Marathon.	2,545	1,567	857	121	2,215	195	129	5	1
Marinette.	746	552	182	12	673	45	24	3	1
Marquette	626	450	157	19	535	59	25	1	6
Menominee	4	3	1	—	2	1	—	—	1
Milwaukee	96	55	24	17	69	4	19	2	2
Monroe.	2,115	1,572	468	75	1,881	146	70	5	13
Oconto	1,244	879	329	36	1,095	96	47	—	6
Oneida	179	155	22	2	145	11	14	1	8
Outagamie	1,362	864	433	65	1,180	110	62	6	4
Ozaukee	513	340	142	31	405	37	56	5	10
Pepin	503	352	138	13	448	33	18	—	4
Pierce.	1,531	1,114	378	39	1,336	102	64	6	23
Polk	1,582	1,138	417	27	1,407	106	56	4	9
Portage	1,066	660	357	49	904	96	56	7	3
Price	545	375	160	10	509	30	5	1	—
Racine	652	403	196	53	516	77	47	2	10
Richland	1,545	1,182	324	39	1,341	138	43	6	17
Rock	1,556	1,033	413	110	1,319	124	93	7	13
Rusk	651	420	210	21	594	38	17	1	1
St. Croix	1,808	1,360	401	47	1,580	121	75	11	21
Sauk	1,923	1,364	461	98	1,649	164	92	12	6
Sawyer	231	159	61	11	198	14	13	2	4
Shawano	1,450	882	533	35	1,248	131	51	6	14
Sheboygan	1,059	615	393	51	924	71	55	4	5
Taylor	1,208	815	372	21	1,130	59	16	1	2
Trempealeau	1,721	1,318	362	41	1,513	148	39	5	16
Vernon	2,492	1,844	569	79	2,264	182	26	2	18
Vilas	71	59	12	—	51	8	9	—	3
Walworth.	1,000	625	282	93	764	104	97	15	20
Washburn	558	388	154	16	504	40	9	1	4
Washington.	831	495	271	65	668	86	60	11	6
Waukesha	675	478	146	51	557	46	57	5	10
Waupaca	1,330	850	438	42	1,179	102	37	2	10
Waushara	677	450	202	25	575	62	34	1	5
Winnebago	1,001	643	314	44	845	83	57	5	11
Wood	1,114	741	346	27	969	73	55	15	2
STATE	78,463	53,783	21,501	3,179	68,138	6,386	3,036	297	606

*Includes cooperative, estate or trust, institutional, etc.

Source: U.S. Department of Agriculture, National Agricultural Statistics Service, *2007 Census of Agriculture,* Volume 1, Chapter 2: Wisconsin County Level Data, February 2009, at: http://www.agcensus.usda.gov/Publications/2007/Full_Report/ Volume_1,_Chapter_2_County_Level/Wisconsin/index.asp [March 13, 2009].

WISCONSIN AGRICULTURAL LAND SALES
By County, 2006 and 2007

County[1]	Total Agricultural Land Sales[2]				Land Continuing in Agricultural Use		Agricultural Land Diverted to Other Uses	
	Number		Dollar Avg. per Acre		Dollar Avg. per Acre		Dollar Avg. per Acre	
	2006	2007	2006	2007	2006	2007	2006	2007
Adams	19	18	$1,909	$2,919	$1,857	$2,901	$3,661	$4,300
Ashland	8	6	1,783	1,494	1,354	1,392	3,864	1,786
Barron	65	49	2,363	2,455	2,250	2,444	3,128	2,501
Bayfield	19	11	1,750	2,599	1,183	2,696	3,597	2,050
Brown	18	17	16,005	5,644	4,374	5,069	19,437	13,231
Buffalo	15	15	3,319	3,318	3,346	3,235	2,390	3,636
Burnett	5	9	2,499	2,178	2,432	2,178	2,735	—
Calumet	26	15	4,165	4,781	3,683	4,494	14,141	12,952
Chippewa	33	51	1,983	2,150	1,838	2,084	2,718	4,590
Clark	89	92	2,292	2,346	2,201	2,285	4,174	4,019
Columbia	26	42	5,499	5,864	4,832	5,216	9,252	10,751
Crawford	36	24	2,410	3,290	2,377	2,957	2,499	4,571
Dane	46	39	15,754	11,430	9,029	8,218	18,974	23,896
Dodge	32	39	4,755	5,016	4,674	4,654	9,000	6,716
Door	10	12	4,849	4,741	3,548	4,335	10,666	7,645
Douglas	7	5	1,338	1,648	1,307	1,648	1,469	—
Dunn	34	33	2,494	2,339	2,409	2,311	2,777	2,670
Eau Claire	32	36	3,412	2,921	3,398	2,719	3,600	4,091
Florence	1	—	2,068	—	2,068	—	—	—
Fond du Lac	33	37	3,455	4,991	2,770	3,975	9,994	9,531
Forest	3	1	1,720	1,000	1,520	1,000	2,081	—
Grant	63	69	3,193	3,674	3,209	3,603	3,028	4,520
Green	50	34	3,816	3,698	3,566	3,763	5,294	2,761
Green Lake	20	24	4,649	4,035	4,126	4,030	8,530	4,233
Iowa	39	32	3,725	3,995	3,641	3,981	6,161	4,236
Iron	—	—	—	—	—	—	—	—
Jackson	24	20	2,396	2,389	2,396	2,390	—	2,248
Jefferson	28	31	8,143	8,020	6,623	5,380	12,764	17,517
Juneau	24	29	2,616	3,114	2,720	3,125	2,075	2,045
Kenosha	23	16	17,993	30,193	14,700	12,254	21,222	37,130
Kewaunee	26	21	3,217	3,376	3,217	3,320	—	5,080
La Crosse	11	8	5,670	3,200	4,069	2,944	8,212	3,681
Lafayette	47	56	3,623	4,171	3,673	4,086	2,117	5,890
Langlade	15	24	2,152	1,793	2,226	1,828	1,717	1,751
Lincoln	16	22	3,580	2,205	2,532	2,205	6,247	—
Manitowoc	29	44	3,556	3,467	3,556	3,358	—	7,050
Marathon	76	61	2,932	2,705	2,282	2,571	5,992	3,414
Marinette	9	9	3,332	3,264	3,206	2,727	5,289	5,902
Marquette	15	14	3,070	2,909	2,958	2,909	5,928	—
Milwaukee	3	1	14,700	80,000	—	—	14,700	80,000
Monroe	45	39	3,367	3,041	3,116	2,897	5,788	3,353
Oconto	12	33	2,860	2,967	2,743	2,917	3,789	6,912
Oneida	3	4	1,814	2,625	1,814	2,625	—	—
Outagamie	21	16	5,750	9,029	4,270	4,345	7,407	12,698
Ozaukee	12	11	11,412	15,366	6,199	7,531	22,675	31,749
Pepin	7	11	4,587	3,157	4,161	3,157	6,774	—
Pierce	28	33	6,483	4,333	4,183	4,223	9,550	5,580
Polk	26	21	3,258	4,001	3,327	4,001	2,481	—
Portage	17	27	2,247	2,730	2,105	2,633	2,970	3,520
Price	25	18	2,744	2,083	2,717	2,083	4,245	—
Racine	12	7	19,280	16,220	20,847	9,430	18,991	22,914
Richland	60	67	2,782	3,057	2,719	2,953	3,664	3,386
Rock	32	46	5,162	5,865	4,567	5,074	8,248	17,145
Rusk	27	34	1,608	1,667	1,627	1,667	1,545	1,664
St. Croix	37	34	8,912	4,577	7,092	3,752	11,157	6,811
Sauk	41	47	3,943	4,206	3,571	3,610	13,624	7,836
Sawyer	4	5	2,313	1,784	2,746	1,820	1,839	1,370
Shawano	52	33	3,136	3,685	3,232	3,752	2,932	2,801
Sheboygan	31	20	8,732	6,654	4,979	4,539	16,594	23,141
Taylor	40	43	1,515	1,698	1,311	1,713	2,399	1,570
Trempealeau	37	39	2,378	2,297	2,177	2,297	5,647	2,463
Vernon	65	55	3,158	3,239	3,037	3,121	4,552	4,073
Vilas	2	1	7,739	3,025	—	—	7,739	3,025
Walworth	44	24	11,980	10,353	7,324	7,195	17,785	15,817
Washburn	10	8	1,573	2,378	1,547	2,408	2,000	2,295
Washington	17	16	15,257	12,470	6,840	11,069	17,283	19,725
Waukesha	16	10	16,492	26,653	12,393	15,878	17,743	31,804
Waupaca	26	33	3,765	3,297	3,510	3,190	6,062	4,673
Waushara	18	22	3,627	3,386	3,617	3,001	3,769	12,331
Winnebago	20	15	10,954	6,619	5,116	3,195	15,935	14,928
Wood	36	21	1,975	2,703	2,009	2,271	1,730	4,101
STATE	1,898	1,859	$4,711	$4,365	$3,366	$3,518	$10,681	$10,125

[1]Menominee County had no agricultural sales in years shown.
[2]Includes land with and without buildings and other improvements.

Sources: U.S. Department of Agriculture, National Agricultural Statistics Service, "Agricultural Land Sales: Total Agricultural Land, Wisconsin, 2006", at http://www.nass.usda.gov/Statistics_by_State/Wisconsin/Publications/Land_Sales/total06.pdf [March 17, 2009], and "Agricultural Land Sales: Total Agricultural Land, Wisconsin, 2007", at: http://www.nass.usda.gov/Statistics_by_State/Wisconsin/Publications/Land_Sales/total07.pdf [March 17, 2009].

WISCONSIN NET FARM INCOME, 2003 – 2007

	2003	2004	2005	2006	2007
Number of farms.	76,500	76,500	76,500	76,000	78,500
Average net farm income per farm (dollars).	$21,982	$24,280	$21,946	$18,079	$33,806
			Income (in thousands)		
Value of crop production.	$1,681,377	$1,844,258	$1,932,466	$2,131,394	$2,658,331
Value of livestock production	4,100,943	5,106,771	5,092,558	4,668,096	6,217,173
Revenues from services and forestry	1,078,193	1,143,464	1,206,010	1,327,548	1,437,085
VALUE OF AGRICULTURAL SECTOR OUTPUT[1].	$6,860,512	$8,094,493	$8,231,034	$8,127,037	$10,312,589
Less: Purchased inputs[2]	3,158,934	3,865,300	4,298,875	4,212,125	4,793,450
Less: Motor vehicle registration and licensing	8,702	9,730	9,845	10,934	13,775
Less: Property taxes	290,000	300,000	320,000	340,000	380,000
Plus: Direct government payments	488,810	298,217	585,758	414,250	207,973
GROSS VALUE ADDED	$3,891,686	$4,217,679	$4,188,073	$3,978,229	$5,333,337
Less: Capital consumption (depreciation).	997,264	1,071,043	1,149,159	1,201,356	1,241,284
NET VALUE ADDED[3]	$2,894,422	$3,146,636	$3,038,914	$2,776,873	$4,092,053
Less: Payments to stakeholders[4].	1,212,792	1,289,213	1,360,059	1,402,858	1,438,266
NET FARM INCOME[5]	$1,681,630	$1,857,423	$1,678,855	$1,374,015	$2,653,787

Note: Average net farm income calculated by Wisconsin Legislative Reference Bureau. Prior year's numbers have been revised to reflect updated source data.

[1]Value of agricultural sector output is the gross value of the commodities and services produced within a year.

[2]Includes purchases of feed, livestock, poultry, and seed; outlays for fertilizers and lime, pesticides, fuel and electricity; capital repair and maintenance; and marketing, storage, transportation, contract labor, and other expenses.

[3]Net value added is the sector's contribution to the national economy and is the sum of the income from production earned by all factors of production, regardless of ownership.

[4]Includes compensation for hired labor, net rent received by nonoperator landlords, and interest payments.

[5]Net farm income is the farm operators' share of income from the sector's production activities.

Sources: U.S. Department of Agriculture, Economic Research Service, "Number of Farms, U.S. and states, 2000 – 2008", and "Value added to the U.S. economy by the agricultural sector via the production of goods and services, 2000-2007, Wisconsin", at: http://www.ers.usda.gov/Data/FarmIncome/FinfidmuXls.htm [March 5, 2009].

FARM ASSETS AND LIABILITIES
By Leading Agricultural States, 2007

State	Number of Farms[1]	Average Assets Per Farm[2]	Average Liability Per Farm[2]	Average Equity Per Farm[2]	Debt as Percentage of Assets[3]
Arkansas	46,501	$618,919	$62,407	$556,513	10.1%
California	75,002	1,974,702	163,966	1,810,736	8.3
Florida	40,000	1,530,367	78,101	1,452,266	5.1
Georgia.	47,500	788,238	53,701	734,537	6.8
ILLINOIS	72,501	1,140,947	99,117	1,041,830	8.7
Indiana	58,801	772,905	73,133	699,772	9.5
IOWA	88,401	1,103,313	112,974	990,340	10.2
Kansas	63,800	671,541	86,883	584,658	12.9
MINNESOTA	79,001	1,007,128	91,482	915,646	9.1
Missouri	104,502	680,710	46,333	634,378	6.8
Nebraska	47,302	1,023,250	138,269	884,981	13.5
North Carolina	48,002	675,707	41,871	633,836	6.2
Texas	229,000	689,409	37,414	651,995	5.4
Washington.	33,001	924,142	70,018	854,125	7.6
WISCONSIN	76,001	802,653	96,059	706,594	12.0

[1]"Farm" is currently defined as a place that sells, or would normally sell, at least $1,000 of agricultural products during the year.

[2]Dollar amounts represent farm businesses, excluding household assets and debts.

[3]Debt does not include all financial obligations that are contained in the liabilities column.

Source: U.S. Department of Agriculture, Economic Research Service, "Farm Business and Household Survey Data: Customized Data Summaries From ARMS", at: http://www.ers.usda.gov/Data/ARMS/app/Farm.aspx [June 29, 2009]

STATEWIDE ASSOCIATIONS OF WISCONSIN
Listed by Key Word

AAA Wisconsin, Inc.
Tom Frymark, Regional Pres.
P.O. Box 33, Madison 53701-0033
(608) 836-6555 www.aaa.com

Academic Staff Public Representative Org.
Bill Steffenhagen, Pres.
10 E. Doty St., Suite 403, Madison 53703
(608) 286-9599 aspro@aspro.net www.aspro.net

Academy of Sciences, Arts and Letters, Wis.
Margaret Lewis, Exec. Dir.
1922 University Ave., Madison 53726
(608) 263-1692 mlewis@wisconsinacademy.org
www.wisconsinacademy.org

Accountants, Wis. Inst. of Certified Public
Dennis Tomorsky, CEO
235 N. Executive Dr., Suite 200, Brookfield 53005
(262) 785-0445 dennis@wicpa.org www.wicpa.org

ACOG (American College of Obstetricians and
   Gynecologists), Wis. Section
Dawn M. Maerker, Exec. Dir.
P.O. Box 636,N44 W25940 Lindsay Rd.,
Pewaukee 53072-0636
(262) 695-7411 dmman@wi.rr.com
www.acog.com/acog_sections

Activity Professionals, Wis. Representatives of (WRAP)
Debbie R. Bera, Pres.
825 Whiting Ave., Stevens Point 54481
(715) 346-1613 berad@co.portage.wi.us

AFL-CIO Women's Committee, Wis. State
Paula Dorsey, Chairperson
6333 Bluemound Rd. West, Milwaukee 53213
(414) 771-0700 solidarity@wisaflcio.org

AFT – Wisconsin (Federation of Teachers)
Bryan Kennedy, Pres.
6602 Normandy Ln., Madison 53719
(608) 662-1444 kennedy@aft-wisconsin.org
www.aft-wisconsin.org

Aging Groups, Coalition of Wis.
Grant Nyhammer, Legal Dir.
2850 Dairy Dr., Suite 100, Madison 53718
(608) 224-0606 gnyhammer@cwag.org www.cwag.org

Agribusiness Council, Wis.
Ferron Havens, Pres./CEO
P.O. Box 46100, Madison 53744
(608) 235-1799 fhavenswac@mhtc.net wisagri.com

Agricultural Educators, Wis. Assn. Of
Bridgett Neu, Exec. Dir.
1172 Hummingbird Ln., Plymouth 53073
(262) 224-7553 bridgett@waae.com www.waae.com

Agriculture, Wis. Women for
Victoria Coughlin, Pres.
N 901 Welsh Rd., Watertown 53098
(920) 261-1777

Agri-Service Assn., Inc., Wis.
John Petty, Exec. Dir.
6000 Gisholt Dr., Suite 208, Madison 53713-4816
(608) 223-1111 info@wasa.org www.wasa.org

Agronomy, Amer. Soc. of
Ellen Bergfeld, CEO
677 S. Segoe Rd., Madison 53711
(608) 273-8080 www.agronomy.org

Alcohol Problems Council of Wis.
Jim Cotter, Secy.
222 S. Dickason Blvd., Columbus 53925
(920) 623-3625 jcotter@wisconsinumc.org
alcoholproblemswi.org

American Fed. Of State, County and Municipal Employees,
   AFL-CIO
Debbie Garcia, Area Field Serv. Dir.
8033 Excelsior Dr., Suite A, Madison 53717-1903
(608) 836-6666 dgarcia@afscme.org

American Legion Aux. (Dept. of Wis.)
Kathy Wollmer, Secy./Treas.
P.O. Box 140,2930 American Legion Dr.,
Portage 53901-0124
(608) 745-0124 alawi@amlegionauxwi.org

American Legion, Dept. of Wis.
Jim Reigel, Cmdr.
2930 American Legion Dr., P.O. Box 388,
Portage 53901-0388-0388
(608) 745-1090 info@wilegion.org www.wilegion.org

Amusement and Music Operators, Wis.
Maxine D. O'Brien, Exec. Dir.
P.O. Box 620830, Middleton 53562
(608) 836-6090 wamomax@aol.com www.wamo.net

Amvets (Dept. of Wis.)
Michael H. Mahoney, Exec. Dir.
750 N. Lincoln Memorial Dr., Rm. 306,
War Memorial Center, Milwaukee 53202
(414) 273-5288 amvetswi@yahoo.com
www.amvets-wi.org

Amvets Ladies Aux., Dept. of Wis.
Georgette Sampo, Pres.
2600 E. Main St., Lot 88, Merrill 54452
(715) 536-4102 glsampo@verizon.net

Anesthetists, Wis. Assn. of Nurse, Inc.
Shelley L. Ekblad, Pres.
3610 Parkside Circle East, Eau Claire 54701
(715) 828-8977 president@wiana.com wiana.com

Animals, Alliance for
Lynn Pauly, Exec. Dir.
P.O. Box 1632, Madison 53701-1632
(608) 257-6333 Alliance@AllAnimals.org
www.allanimals.org

Animals, Citizens United for
Kim Fisher-Isaacs, Pres.
P.O. Box 07176, Milwaukee 53207
(414) 659-2832 cufa@sbcglobal.net cufa-wi.org

Annuitants, Wis. Coalition of
Edwin Kehl, Pres.
318 Karen Ct., Madison 53705
(608) 233-6737 wcoaemk@charter.net

Apartment Assn., Wis.
Kristy Weinke, Admin. Asst.
627 Bayshore Dr., Oshkosh 54901
(920) 230-9221 waa@ntd.net www.waaonline.org

Apple Growers Assn., Wis.
Anna M. Maenner, Exec. Dir.
211 Canal Rd., Waterloo 53594
(920) 478-4277 acminc@verizon.net

Aquaculture Assn., Inc., Wis.
Cindy Johnson, Secy.
P.O. Box 1408, Bayfield 54814
(715) 373-2990 cindy@wisconsinaquaculture.com
www.wisconsinaquaculture.com

Arabian Horse Assn., Wis.
Jessica Cole, Pres.
E 14058 Hein Road, Baraboo 53913
(262) 672-9742 jcts@jvlnet.com
www.wisconsinarabian.com/

Arborist Assn., Wis.
Jeff Treu, Legis. Chair
7301 W. Calumet Rd., WE Energies, Milwaukee 53223
(414) 362-5143 jeffrey.treu@we-energies.com
www.waa-isa.org/index.htm

Arc – Wisconsin, Disability Assoc. Inc., The
James Hoegemeier, Exec. Dir.
2800 Royal Ave., #209, Madison 53713
(608) 222-8907 arcw@att.net www.arc-wisconsin.org

Architects, Wis. Society of
William Babcock, Exec. Dir.
321 S. Hamilton St., Madison 53703-4000
(608) 257-8477 aiaw@aiaw.org www.aiaw.org

Army and Navy Union
Howard Cole, Cmdr.
5000 W. National Ave, Bldg 70 C-7, Milwaukee 53295
(414) 384-2000, ext. 46420

Art Therapy Association, Wis.
Jeanne Zilske, Pres.
P.O. Box 1765, Milwaukee 53201-1765
info@wiarttherapy.org www.wiarttherapy.org

Arthritis Foundation, Wis. Chapter
Judy Haugsland, Pres./CEO
1650 S. 108th St., West Allis 53214
(414) 321-3933 or (800) 242-9945 info.wi@arthritis.org
www.arthritis.org

Artists Assn., Wis. Regional
Leslee Nelson, Advisor
21 N. Park St., Rm. 7356, Madison 53715-1218
(608) 263-7814 lnelson@dcs.wisc.edu
www.wraawrap.com

Asphalt Pavement Assn., Wis., Inc.
Scot Schwandt, Exec. Dir.
4600 American Parkway, Suite 206, Madison 53718
(608) 255-3114 scot@wispave.org www.wispave.org

Auctioneers Assn., Inc., Wis.
Maxine O'Brien, Exec. Dir.
P.O. Box 620830, Middleton 53562
(608) 836-6542 waamaxine@aol.com
www.wisconsinauctioneers.org

Automatic Merchandising Council, Wis.
David Kwarciany, Jr., Govt. Affairs Chm.
16300 W. Silver Spring Dr., Menomonee Falls 53051
(262) 781-8507

Automobile and Truck Dealers Assn., Inc., Wis.
William Sepic, Pres.
P.O. Box 5345, Madison 53705-0345
(608) 251-5577 wsepic@watda.org www.watda.org

Automotive Aftermarket Association, Wis.
Gary Manke, Exec. Dir.
5330 Wall St., Suite 100, Madison 53718-7929
(608) 240-2065 gmanke@medaassn.com www.waaa.info

Automotive Historians, Soc. of (Wis. Ch.)
Kenneth E. Nimocks, Pres.
3765 Spring Green Rd., Green Bay 54313-7565
(920) 865-4004 knimocks@netnet.net

Automotive Parts Assn., Inc., Wis.
Gary W. Manke, CAE, Exec. Dir.
5330 Wall St., Suite 100, Madison 53718-7929
(608) 240-2066 gmanke@medaassn.com
www.wapaonline.com

Bandmasters' Assn., Inc., Wis.
Donna Wirth, Exec. Secy.
14544 Squire Ln., Kiel 53042
(920) 894-3991 wbasec@dotnet.com

Bankers Assn., Wis.
Kurt R. Bauer, Pres./CEO
P.O. Box 8880, Madison 53708
(608) 441-1200 bauer@wisbank.com www.wisbank.com

Bankers Assn., Wis. Mortgage
Barbara A. Schwarz, Assn. Manager
P.O. Box 1606, Madison 53701-1606
(608) 255-4180 bschwarz@wimba.org www.wimba.org

Bankers of Wis., Community
Daryll J. Lund, Pres. & CEO
455 Cty Rd. M., Suite 101, Madison 53719
(608) 833-4229 daryll@communitybankers.org
www.communitybankers.org

Beef Council, Inc., Wis.
John W. Freitag, Exec. Dir.
632 Grand Canyon Dr., Madison 53719
(608) 833-7177 jwf@beeftips.com beeftips.com

Beer Distributors Assn., Inc., Wis.
Eric Jensen, Exec. Dir.
16 N. Carroll St., Suite 950, Madison 53703
(608) 255-6464 ericj@chorus.net

Berry Growers Assn., Wis.
Anna Maenner, Exec. Dir.
211 Canal Rd., Waterloo 53594
(920) 478-3852 acminc@verizon.net

Beverage Assn., Wis.
Kelly McDowell, Exec. Secy.
7 N. Pinckney Street, Suite 300, Madison 53703
(608) 259-1212, ext. 2 kelly@martinschreiber.com

Bicycle Federation of Wisconsin Action Coalition
Jack Hirt, Exec. Dir.
1845 N. Farwell St., Suite 100, Milwaukee 53202
(414) 271-9685 jack@bfw.org www.bfw.org

Biomedical Research and Education, Wis. Assn. for
Norman Holman, Exec. Dir.
P.O. Box 390, Milwaukee 53201-0390
(608) 443-6654 wabre@charter.net

Blind and Visually Impaired, Inc., Badger Assn. of the
Patrick Brown, Exec. Dir.
912 N. Hawley Rd., Milwaukee 53213-3292
(877) 258-9200 or (414) 258-9200 info@badgerassoc.org
www.badgerassoc.org

Blind and Visually Impaired, Inc., Wis. Council of the
Karen V. Majkrzak, Exec. Dir.
754 Williamson St., Madison 53703
(608) 255-1166 or (800) 783-5213 karen@wcblind.org
www.wcblind.org

Botanical Club of Wis.
Theodore S. Cochrane, Secy.
Room 251 Birge Hall, 430 Lincoln Dr.
UW-Madison Herbarium, Madison 53706-1381
(608) 262-2792 tscochra@wisc.edu
wisplants.uwsp.edu/BCW

Bowhunters Assn., Wis., Inc.
Wright Allen, Pres.
P.O. Box 240, Clintonville 54929
(715) 823-4670 office@wisconsinbowhunters.org
www.wisconsinbowhunters.org

Bowling Assn., Wis. State USBC
Phillip A. LaPorte, Assn. Mgr.
N104 W16275 Hedge Way, Germantown 53022
(262) 532-0623 plaporte@wibowl.com

Bowling Proprietors Assn. of Wis.
Gary Hartel, Exec. Dir.
21140 Capitol Dr., Suite 5, Pewaukee 53072
(262) 783-4292 bcaw@bowlwi.com www.bowlwi.com

Brain Injury Assn. of Wis., Inc.
Mark Warhus, Exec. Dir.
21100 W. Capitol Dr., Suite 5, Pewaukee 53072
(262) 790-9660 admin@biaw.org www.biaw.org

Breeders Assn., Wis. Brown Swiss
Barbara Muenzenberger, Secy.-Treas.
W561 Muenzenberger Rd., Coon Valley 54623
(608) 486-2297 bovalleyswiss@aol.com
www.allbreedaccess.com/wibrownswiss

Breeders Assn., Wis. Chester White
Bruce Hashieder
Sauk City 53583

Breeders Assn., Wis. Draft Horse
Mrs. Richard Lee, Secy.
W5072 Faro Springs Rd., Hilbert 54129
(920) 989-1131

Breeders Assn., Wis. Guernsey
Deb Lakey, Secy.-Treas.
W23375 11th St., Trempealeau 54661
(608) 534-6010 wisgba@yahoo.com
www.wiguernsey.com

Breeders Assn., Wis. Livestock
Jill Alf, Exec. Dir.
7811 N Consolidated School Rd., Edgerton 53534
(608) 868-2505 wlba@centurytel.net

Breeder's Assn., Wis. Shorthorn
Ann Jennings, Secy.
W3876 Old B Rd., Rio 53960-9767
(920) 992-5515

Brewers Assn., Wis. State
Martin J. Schreiber
2700 S. Shore Dr., Suite A, Milwaukee 53207-2300
(414) 482-1214 martin@martinschreiber.com

Broadcasters Assn., Wis.
Michelle Vetterkind, Pres.
44 E. Mifflin St., Suite 900, Madison 53703-2800
(608) 255-2600 mvetterkind@wi-broadcasters.org
www.wi-broadcasters.org

Buck and Bear Club, Inc., Wis.
Steve Ashley, Dir. Of Records
3051 110th Ave., Glenwood City 54013
(877) 273-6408 sashley@wi-buck-bear.org
www.wi-buck-bear.org

Builders and Contractors of Wis., Inc., Associated
Stephen L. Stone, Pres.
5330 Wall St., Madison 53718
(608) 244-5883 sstone@abcwi.org www.abcwi.org

Builders Assn. of Wis., Master
John Topp, CEO
17100 W. Bluemound Rd., Suite 102, Brookfield 53005
(262) 785-1430 john@buildacea.org www.buildacea.org

Builders Assn., Wis.
Exec. Vice Pres.
4868 High Crossing Blvd., Madison 53704-7403
(608) 242-5151 info@wisbuild.org www.wisbuild.org

Burial Vault Assn., Wis.
Mark Lipscomb, Jr., Exec. Dir.
2602 W. Silver Spring Dr., Glendale 53209
(414) 276-5763 marklipscombjr@sbcglobal.net

Business Assn. of Wis., Independent
Daniel J. Schwartzer, Exec. Dir.
4600 American Pkwy., Suite 208, Madison 53718
(608) 251-5546 iba@ibaw.com www.ibaw.com

Business, Natl. Federation of Independent (Wis. Ch.)
Bill G. Smith, State Director
10 E. Doty St., Suite 519, Madison 53703
(608) 255-6083 Bill.Smith@nfib.com/wi www.nfib.com/wi

Businesses, Inc., Wis. Independent
Thomas Dohm, Pres.
P.O. Box 2135, Madison 53701-2135
(608) 255-0373 tdohm@wibiz.org www.wibiz.org

Cable Communications Assn., Wis.
Thomas E. Moore, Exec. Dir.
22 E. Mifflin St., Suite 1010, Madison 53703
(608) 256-1683 www.wicable.tv

Camp Assn., American, Wis.
Kim Rathsack, Section Exec.
N9659 Hopfensperger Rd., Appleton 54915
(920) 716-4133 acawisconsin@sbcglobal.net
www.acawisconsin.org

Campground Owners, Wis. Assn. of
Lori Severson, Exec. Dir.
P.O. Box 130, Galesville 54630
(608) 582-2092 or (800) 843-1821
director@wisconsincampgrounds.com
wisconsincampgrounds.com

Cancer Soc., Amer. (Midwest Div.)
Jari Allen, CEO
P.O. Box 902, Pewaukee 53072-0902
(262) 523-5500 www.cancer.org

Carpenters, Wis. State Council of
Mark S. Reihl, Exec. Dir.
115 W. Main St., Madison 53703
(608) 256-1206 mreihl@sbcglobal.net

Cast Metals Assn., Wis.
Brian L. Mitchell, Exec. Dir.
P.O. Box 247,405 East Forest Street, Oconomowoc 53066
(262) 244-0045 blm@mitchellgov.com wicastmetals.com

Cattlemen's Assn., Wis.
Jessica Miller, Exec. Asst.
2 E. Mifflin Street, Suite 601, Madison 53703
(608) 848-8080 wisbeef@yahoo.com
www.wisconsincattlemen.com

Cattlewomen's Council, Wis.
Kathy Miller, Pres.
8434 198th Ave., Bristol 53104
(262) 857-7168 millersmagnum@aol.com
www.wisconsincattlemen.com

Cemetery Assn., Wisconsin
William Hoffmann, Treas.
6401 N. 43rd St., Milwaukee 53209
(414) 353-8850 bhoffmann@choiceonemail.com
www.wicemeteries.org

Cemetery Soc., Wis. State Old
Beverly Silldorff, Pres.
6100 West Mequon Rd., Mequon 53092
(262) 242-3290 bevjdorf@execpc.com

Charter Schools Assn., Wis.
John Gee, Exec. Dir.
P.O. Box 1704, Madison 53701-1704
(608) 261-1120 info@wicharterschools.org
www.wicharterschools.org

Children and Families, Inc., Wis. Council on
Charity Eleson, Exec. Dir.
555 W. Washington Ave., Suite 200, Madison 53703
(608) 284-0580 celeson@wccf.org www.wccf.org

Children of the American Revolution, Wis. St. Soc.
Mrs. Ivan Niedling, Honorary Sr. State Pres.
700 3rd St., Plover 54467
(715) 341-1996

Children with Behavioral Disorders, Inc., Wis. Assn. for
Debbie Brent, Prog. Chair
P.O. Box 1993, Waukesha 53187-1993
(262) 370-2434 brentde@wauwatosa.k12.wi.us
www.wiccbd.com

Children's Service Soc. of Wis.
Kenneth Munson, CEO
620 S. 76th Street, Suite 120, Milwaukee 53214
(414) 453-1400 www.cssw.org

Chiropractic Assn., Wis.
Russell A. Leonard, Exec. Dir.
521 E. Washington Ave., Madison 53703
(608) 256-7023 rleonard@aol.com
www.wisconsinchiropractic.com

Christmas Tree Producers Assn., Inc., Wis.
Cheryl Nicholson, Exec. Secy.
W9833 Hogan Rd., Portage 53901-9279
(608) 742-8663 info@christmastrees-wi.org
www.christmastrees-wi.org

Churches, Wis. Council of
Scott Anderson, Exec. Dir.
750 Windsor St., Suite 301, Sun Prairie 53590-2149
(608) 837-3108 sanderson@wichurches.org
www.wichurches.org

Cities, Wis. Alliance of
Ed Huck, Exec. Dir.
122 W. Washington Ave., #300, Madison 53703
(608) 257-5881 ed@wiscities.org www.wiscities.org

City/County Management Assn., Wis.
Ed Henschel, Exec. Dir.
3919 Oakmont Tr., Waukesha 53188
(414) 303-4554 ehenschel@wcma-wi.org
www.wcma-wi.org

Civil Air Patrol, Wis. Wing
Col. Donald J. Haffner, Commander
2400 Wright St., Madison 53704
(608) 242-3067 terry.norby@dma.state.wi.us wiwgcap.org

Civil Liberties Union of Wis., Inc., American
Christopher Ahmuty, Exec. Dir.
207 E. Buffalo St., No. 325, Milwaukee 53202-5774
(414) 272-4032 liberty@aclu-wi.org www.aclu-wi.org

Civil Trial Counsel of Wis.
Jane Svinicki, CAE, Exec. Dir.
6737 W. Washington St., Suite 1300, Milwaukee 53214
(414) 276-1881 ctcw@ctcw.org www.ctcw.org

Clerks of Circuit Court Assn., Wis.
Karen Hepfler, Pres.
711 N. Bridge St., Chippewa Falls 54729
(715) 726-7758 karen.hepfler@wicourts.gov

Collectors Assn., Inc., Wis.
Cheryl A. Donohue, Exec. Secy.
P.O. Box 399, Janesville 53547-0399
(608) 563-4345 cdonohue-wca@charter.net
www.acainternational.org/wi

Colleges and Universities, Wis. Assn. of Independent
Rolf Wegenke, Pres.
122 W. Washington Ave., Suite 700, Madison 53703-2718
(608) 256-7761 mail@waicu.org www.waicu.org

Colleges, Inc., Wis. Foundation for Independent
Christy Miller, Vice Pres. – Operations
4425 N. Port Washington Rd., #402, Milwaukee 53212
(414) 273-5980 cmiller@wficweb.org www.wficweb.org

Colonial Wars in the State of Wis., Society of
Jerry P. Hill, Gov.
5677 N. Consaul Pl., Milwaukee 53217-4818
(414) 332-9479 jerryp@execpc.com

Common Cause in Wis.
Jay Heck, Exec. Dir.
P.O. Box 2597, Madison 53701-2597
(608) 256-2686 ccwisjwh@itis.com

Communication, International Training In
Priscilla W. Bartoloth, Chair
8728 Jackson Park Blvd., Wauwatosa 53226-2710
(414) 774-6812 pbartoloth@wi.rr.com

Community Action Program Assn., Wis.
Richard Schlimm, Exec. Dir.
1310 Mendota St., Suite 107, Madison 53714-1039
(608) 244-4422 rschlimm@wiscap.org wiscap.org

Concrete Assn., Wis. Pre-Cast
Ann Gryphan, Assn. Manager
Essie Kammer Group
16 N. Carroll St., Suite 900, Madison 53703
(608) 256-7701 agryphan@ekgmail.com
www.wiprecast.org

Concrete Assn., Wis. Ready Mixed
Patrick Essie, Exec. Dir.
Essie Kammer Group
16 N. Carroll St., Suite 925, Madison 53703
(608) 250-6304 info@wrmca.com www.wrmca.com

Concrete Masonry Assn., Wis.
Jane Svinicki, Exec. Dir.
6737 W. Washington St., Suite 1300, Milwaukee 53214
(414) 276-0667 info@concretemasonry.org
www.concretemasonry.org

Concrete Paving Assn., Wis.
Kevin McMullen, Pres.
2423 American Ln., Suite 2, Madison 53704
(608) 240-1020 kmcmullen@wisconcrete.org
www.wisconcrete.org

Construction Employers Assn., Inc., Allied
John Topp, Exec. Chief Officer
17100 W. Bluemound Rd., Suite 102, Brookfield 53005
(262) 785-1430 john@buildacea.org www.buildacea.org

Contractors Assn. of Wis., Mechanical
David Seitz, Exec. Vice Pres.
3315 N. Ballard, Suite D, Appleton 54911
(920) 734-3148 david@omswi.com

Contractors Assn., Inc., Wis. Underground
Richard W. Wanta, Exec. Dir.
2835 N. Mayfair Rd., Suite 22, Milwaukee 53222-4405
(414) 778-1050 rwanta@wuca.org www.wuca.org

Cooperative Network
William Oemichen, Pres./CEO
131 W. Wilson St., Suite 400, Madison 53703-3269
(608) 258-4400 bill.oemichen@cooperativenetwork.coop
cooperativenetwork.coop

Corn Promotion Board, Inc., Wis.
Bob Oleson, Exec. Dir.
W1360 Hwy 106, Palmyra 53156
(262) 495-2232 wicorn@centurytel.net www.wicorn.org

Counties Assn., Wis.
Mark D. O'Connell, Exec. Dir.
22 E. Mifflin St., Suite 900, Madison 53703
(608) 663-7188 mail@wicounties.org www.wicounties.org

Counties Mineral Resources Assn., Inc., Wis.
Erhard Huettl, Chm.
6116 Evergreen Ln., Wabeno 54566-9631
(715) 473-5314

Counties Utility Tax Assn., Wis.
Alice O'Connor, Exec. Dir.
P.O. Box 2038, Madison 53701-2038
(608) 257-7181

County Agricultural Agents, Wis. Assn.
Ken Williams, Pres.
209 S. St. Marie, Wautoma 54982
(920) 787-0416 ken.williams@ces.uwex.edu
www.uwex.edu/ces/wacaa

County and Municipal Employees, Wis. Council 40
AFSCME, AFL-CIO
Rick Badger, Exec. Dir.
8033 Excelsior Dr., Suite B, Madison 53717
(608) 836-4040 www.afscmecouncil40.org

County Clerk's Assn., Wis.
Kimberly Bushey, Pres.
P.O. Box 1001, Elkhorn 53121
(262) 241-4245 kbushey@co.walworth.wi.us

County Code Administrators, Wis.
Mary G. Greenman, Secy./Treas.
330 Court St., Eagle River 54521
(715) 479-3621 www.wccadm.com

County Constitutional Officers Assn., Inc., Wis.
Jay Zahn
421 Nebraska, Door County Treasurer, Sturgeon Bay 54235
(920) 746-2286

County Executives and Administrators Assn., Wis.
Adam Payne, Pres.
615 N. 6th St., Room 311, Sheboygan 53081
(920) 459-3103 www.co.sheboygan.wi.us

County Forests Assn., Inc., Wis.
Jane Severt, Exec. Dir.
518 W. Somo Ave., Tomahawk 54487
(715) 453-6741 wcfa@verizon.net
www.wisconsincountyforests.com

County Officers, Wis. Assn. of
Donna Hanson, Treas.
400 4th St. N., Rm. 1290,Administrative Center,
La Crosse 54601-3200
(608) 785-9712 hanson.donna@co.la-crosse.wi.us

County Personnel Directors, Wis. Assn. of
John Becker, Pres.
51 S. Main Street, Janesville 53545
(608) 757-5520 beckerj@co.rock.wi.us www.wacpd.org/

County Planning Directors Assn., Wis.
Scott Godfrey, Pres.
Iowa County Courthouse, 222 N. Iowa St., Dodgeville 53555
(608) 935-0398 scott.godfrey@iowacounty.org

County Police Assn. Ltd., Wis.
Bob Wierenga, Exec. Dir.
P.O. Box 764, Delavan 53115
(262) 728-2233 info@wcpawi.com www.wcpawi.com

County Surveyors Assn., Inc., Wis.
Kathleen E. Swingle, Secy.
5251 County Rd. C, Danbury 54830
(715) 866-8420

County Treasurers Assn., Wis.
Marilynn Sheahan, Pres.
P.O. Box 28, Alma 54610
(608) 685-6215 marilynn.sheahan@buffalocounty.com
www.co.ozaukee.wi.us/wcta

County Veterans Service Officers Assn. of Wis.
Mark Baldwin, Jr., Secy.-Treas.
432 E. Washington St., West Bend 53095
(262) 335-4457 vetmark@co.washington.wi.us

Court Reporters Assn., Wis.
Christine J. Willette, Pres.
2113 County Road XX, Rothschild 54474
(715) 355-4384 cwillette@wicourtreporters.org
www.wicourtreporters.org

Credit Union League, Wis.
Tom Liebe, Vice Pres.
N25 W23131 Paul Rd., Pewaukee 53072
(262) 549-0200, ext. 6016 tliebe@theleague.coop
www.theleague.coop

Crop Improvement Assn., Inc., Wis.
Jack Kaltenberg, Pres.
1575 Linden Dr.,554 Moore Hall, UW-Madison,
Madison 53706-1514
(608) 262-1341 wcia@mailplus.wisc.edu
www.wisc.edu/wcia

Crop Production Assn., Wis.
Michael Turner, Exec. Dir.
2317 International Ln., Suite 102, Madison 53704
(608) 249-4070 wcpa@tds.net www.wicrops.org

Crop Science Society of America
Ellen Bergfeld, CEO
677 S. Segoe Rd., Madison 53711-1086
(608) 273-8080 www.crops.org

Dahlia Soc., Badger State
Monique Volden, Secy.
1167 State Rd. 78, Mt. Horeb 53572
(608) 437-6846

Dairy Products Assn., Inc., Wis.
Brad Legreid, Exec. Dir.
8383 Greenway Blvd., Middleton 53562-3506
(608) 836-3336 info@wdpa.net www.wdpa.net

Dance Council, Wis.
Jo Jean Janus, Pres.
P.O. Box 707, Madison 53701-0707
(608) 831-1383 wisconsindancecouncil.org

Deferred Deposit Assn., Wis.
Patrick Essie, Exec. Dir.
Essie Kammer Group
16 N. Carroll St., Suite 900, Madison 53703
(608) 256-7701

Democratic Party of Wis.
Mike Tate, Chair
110 King St., Suite 230, Madison 53703
(608) 255-5172 party@wisdems.org www.wisdems.org

Diabetes Assn., Amer. (Wis. Area)
John Quinette, Exec. Dir.
375 Bishops Way, Suite 220, Brookfield 53005-6200
(888) 342-2383 jquinette@diabetes.org www.diabetes.org

Dietetic Assn., Inc., Wis.
Lynn Edwards, Exec. Coor.
1411 W. Montgomery St., Sparta 54656-1003
(888) 232-8631 wda@centurytel.net www.eatrightwisc.org

Disability Rights Wisconsin
Lynn Breedlove, Exec. Dir.
131 W. Wilson St., Suite 700, Madison 53703-2716
(608) 267-0214 lynnb@drwi.org
www.disabilityrightswi.org

Domestic Violence, Wis. Coalition Against
Patti Seger, Exec. Dir.
307 S. Paterson St., Suite 1, Madison 53703
(608) 255-0539 wcadv@wcadv.org www.wcadv.org

Driver and Traffic Safety Education Assn., Wis.
Karen Sorenson, Pres.
P.O. Box 192, Spooner 54801
(715) 635-7042 kmsoren@charter.net
www.adtsea.org/wisconsin

Eagle Forum of Wis.
Dottie Feder, Pres.
17305 Oak Park Row, Brookfield 53045
(262) 786-6200 eagles@eagleforumofwisconsin.org
www.eagleforumofwisconsin.org

Easter Seals Wisconsin, Inc.
Christine Fessler, Pres./CEO
101 Nob Hill Rd., Suite 301, Madison 53713-3969
(608) 277-8288 info@wi.easterseals.com
www.eastersealswisconsin.com

Economic Development Assn., Wis.
Daniel J. Schwartzer, Exec. Dir.
4600 American Parkway, Suite 208, Madison 53718
(608) 255-5666 weda@weda.org www.weda.org

Economic Education, Inc., Wis. Council on
James R. Guenther, Pres.
7635 W. Bluemound Rd., Suite 106, Milwaukee 53213
(414) 221-9400 econed@economicswisconsin.org
www.economicswisconsin.org

Education Assn., Council, Wis.
Bob Burke, Dir. Gov. Rel.
P.O. Box 8003, Madison 53708-8003
(608) 276-7711 www.weac.org

Education Association, Creation
Eugene A. Sattler, Dir.
W2228 Badger Ave., Pine River 54965-9640
(920) 987-5979

Educators' Assn., Inc., Wis. Retired
Jane Elmer, Exec. Dir.
2564 Branch St., Middleton 53562
(608) 831-5115 jelmer@wrea.net www.wrea.net

Egg Producers Assn., Wis.
N9416 Tamarack Rd., Whitewater 53190
(414) 495-6220

Electric Cooperative Assn., Wis.
Share Brandt, Mgr.
131 W. Wilson St., Suite 400, Madison 53703-3269
(608) 258-4400 share.brand@cooperativenetwork.coop
www.weca.coop

Electric Utilities of Wis., Municipal
David J. Benforado, Exec. Dir.
725 Lois Drive, Sun Prairie 53590
(608) 837-2263 dbenforado@meuw.org www.meuw.org

Electrical Contractors Assn., Inc., National (Wis. Chap.)
Loyal O'Leary, Exec. Vice-Pres.
2200 Kilgust Rd., Madison 53713
(608) 221-4650 loyal@wisneca.com www.wisneca.com

Electronic Service Assn., Wis.
Larry Neuens, Pres.
P.O. Box 125, Sussex 53089-0125
(262) 246-6495 neuens@execpc.com www.wesa.org

EMS Assn., Wis.
Don Hunjadi, Exec. Dir.
21332 W. 7 Mile Rd., Franksville 53126-9769
(800) 793-6820 WEMSA@wisconsinems.com
www.wisconsinems.com

Engineering Assn., State
Mark Klipstein, Pres.
4510 Regent St., Madison 53705-4963
(608) 233-4696 wisea@wisea.org wisea.org

Engineering Companies of Wis., Amer. Coun. Of
Carol Godiksen, Exec. Dir.
3 S. Pinckney St., Suite 800, Madison 53703
(608) 257-9223 acecwi@acecwi.org www.acecwi.org

Environment Wis., Inc.
John Minnich, Treas.
222 S. Hamilton St., No. 1, Madison 53703-3201
johnmaudubon@yahoo.com

Environmental Education, Inc., Wis. Assn. for
Carol Weston, Admin. Asst.
8 Nelson Hall, UW Stevens Point, Stevens Point 54481
(715) 346-2796 waee@uwsp.edu www.uwsp.edu/waee

Environmental Technologists, Federation of, Inc. (FET)
Barbara Hurula, Exec. Dir.
9451 N. 107th St., Milwaukee 53224
(414) 354-0070 info@fetinc.org www.fetinc.org

Equipment Dealers Assn., Midwest
Gary W. Manke, CAE, CEO
5330 Wall St., Suite 100, Madison 53718-7929
(608) 240-4700 gmanke@medaassn.com
www.medaassn.com

Ex-POWS, American
Shirley Wittenberg, Adj.
1329 Lauderdale Pl., Onalaska 54650
(608) 783-2127

Fabricare Institute, Wis.
Brian Swingle, Exec. Dir.
12342 W. Layton Ave., Greenfield 53228
(414) 529-4707 bswingle@toriiphillips.com
www.wiscleaners.com

Fairs, Wis. Assn. of
Jayme Buttke, Exec. Secy.
6097 Pinion Pine Way, Fitchburg 53719
(608) 274-6228 wifairs@sbcglobal.net www.wifairs.com

Families Against Mandatory Minimums (Wis. Chap.)
Carla Widener, Wis. Coord.
6828 W. Wisconsin Ave., Wauwatosa 53213-3816
(414) 476-4599

Family and Children's Agencies, Wis. Assn. of
Linda A. Hall, Exec. Dir.
131 W. Wilson St., Suite 901, Madison 53703
(608) 257-5939 lhall@wafca.org www.wafca.org

Family Council, Inc., Wis.
Julaine K. Appling, CEO
P.O. Box 2075, Madison 53701-2075
(608) 256-3228 info@wifamilycouncil.org
wifamilycouncil.org

Family Court Commissioners Assn., Inc., Wis.
Michael Bruch, Exec. Secy.
901 N. 9th St., Room 707, Milwaukee County Courthouse,
Milwaukee 53233
(414) 278-5288 michael.bruch@wicourts.gov

Family Ties, Inc., Wis.
Hugh Davis, Exec. Dir.
16 N. Carroll St., Suite 640, Madison 53703
(608) 267-6888 info@wifamilyties.org
www.wifamilyties.org

Farm Bureau Federation, Cooperative, Wis.
Roger Cliff, CAO
P.O. Box 5550,1241 John Q. Hammons Dr.,
Madison 53705-0550
(608) 828-5703 www.wfbf.com

Farm Bureau Service Cooperative, Wis.
Debbi Raemisch, Manager
P.O. Box 5550, Madison 53705-0550
(608) 828-5712 draemisch.fbcenter@wfbf.com
www.wfbf.com

Farmers Union, Wis.
Sue Beitlich, Pres.
117 W. Spring St., Chippewa Falls 54729-2359
(715) 723-5561 wfusueb@charter.net
wisconsinfarmersunion.com

Fathers for Children and Families, Wis.
Steve Blake, Pres.
P.O. Box 1742, Madison 53701-1742
(608) 255-3237 wisconsinfathers.org

FFA, Wis. Assn. of
Jeff Hicken, State Advisor
P.O. Box 7841, Madison 53707-7841
(608) 267-9255 jeffrey.hicken@dpi.wi.gov
dpi.wi.gov/ffa/ffa.html

Financial Services Assn., Wis.
Thomas Hanson, Exec. Dir.
22 E. Mifflin St., Suite 1010, Madison 53703
(608) 256-6413

Financial Services Assn., Wis. Alliance of
Patrick Essie, Exec. Dir.
Essie Kammer Group
16 N. Carroll St., Suite 900, Madison 53703
(608) 256-7701

Fire Fighters of Wis., Inc., Professional
Rick Gale, State Pres.
7 N. Pinckney St., Suite 200, Madison 53703-2840
(608) 251-5832 pffwpres@aol.com www.pffw.org

Firefighters Assn., Inc., Wis. State
Larry Plumer, Pres.
P.O. Box 126, Durand 54736-0126
(715) 279-8010 plumer@wi-state-fighters.org
www.wi-state-firefighters.org

First Freedoms Foundation, Inc.
Michael D. Dean, Gen. Counsel
20975 Swanson Dr., Suite 125, Waukesha 53186
info@firstfreedomsfoundation.org
www.firstfreedomsfoundation.org

Fisheries Soc., Amer. (Wis. Chap.)
Ted Treska, Secy./Treas.
P.O. Box 1846, Madison 53701
(608) 267-7659 ted.treska@wi.gov www.wi-afs.org

Food Processors Assn., Inc., Midwest
Nicholas C. George, Jr., Pres.
4600 American Parkway, Suite 110, Madison 53718
(608) 255-9946 info@mwfpa.org www.mwfpa.org

Food Protection, Wis. Assn. For
Randall Daggs, Secy.
P.O. Box 329, Sun Prairie 53590-0329
(608) 837-2087 rdaggs@juno.com

Forest History Association of Wis., Inc.
Sara Connor, Pres.
P.O. Box 424, Two Rivers 54241-0424
http://chipsandsawdust.com

Forest Industry Safety and Training Alliance, Inc.
Lynn Woodford, Admin.
3243 Golf Course Rd., Rhinelander 54501
(800) 551-2656 info@fistausa.org

Foresters, Inc., Assn. of Consulting, Wis. Chap.
Robert L. Karl, Chm.
856 N. Fourth St., Steigerwaldt Land Services, Inc.,
Tomahawk 54487
(715) 453-3274 bobk@slstomahawk.com
www.acf-foresters.org

Forty (40) Hommes et 8 Chevaux, La Societe des
Thomas J. Orval, Grand Corres.
312 Hillside Circle, Johnson Creek 53038
(920) 699-5676 fortyandeight.org

Fresh Market Vegetable Growers Assn., Wis.
Anna Maenner, Exec. Dir.
211 Canal Rd., Waterloo 53594
(920) 478-3852 office@wisconsinfreshproduce.org

Funeral Directors Assn., Wis.
Scott W. Peterson, Exec. Dir.
22 E. Mifflin St., Suite 1010, Madison 53703
(608) 256-1757 info@wfda.org www.wfda.org

Funeral Services and Cremation Alliance of Wis.
Erin Krueger, Exec. Dir.
Essie Kammer Group
16 N. Carroll St., Suite 900, Madison 53703
(608) 251-8044 info@fsawisconsin.com
www.fsawisconsin.org

Genealogical Society, Inc., Wis. State
Mary Rieder, Pres.
P.O. Box 5106, Madison 53705-0106
(608) 833-4327 wsgs@tds.net www.wsgs.org

Ginseng Board of Wisconsin
Rachel Tate, Exec. Asst.
555 N. 72nd Ave., Suite 2, Wausau 54401
(715) 845-7300 ginseng@ginsengboard.com
www.ginsengboard.com

Gold Star Wives of America, Inc.
Crystal Wenum, Pres.
692 Baker Rd., Hudson 54016-7946
(715) 386-8615

Golf Assn., Inc., Wis. State
Thomas J. Schmidt, Exec. Dir.
11350 W. Theo Trecker Way, West Allis 53214
(414) 443-3560 info@wsga.org www.wsga.org

Golf Course Supts. Assn., Inc., Wis.
Brian M. Zimmerman
9480 W. Watertown Plank Rd., Wauwatosa 53226-3560
(414) 333-7623 www.wgcsa.com

Grandparents Rights of Wis., Inc.
Sherry Galonski, Pres.
P.O. Box 341015, Milwaukee 53234
(414) 535-1218 or (920) 989-1869

Grange, Wis. State
Alan Arner, Master
25 S. Martin Rd., Janesville 53545-2658
(608) 756-0545 wisgrange@charter.net

Green Industry Federation, Wis.
Brian Swingle, Exec. Dir.
12342 W. Layton Ave., Greenfield 53228
(414) 529-4705 bswingle@toriiphillips.com www.wgif.net

Grocers Assn., Inc., Wis.
Brandon Scholz, Pres.
1 South Pinckney, Suite 504, Madison 53703
(608) 244-7150 brandon@wisconsingrocers.com
wisconsingrocers.com

Hazardous Materials Responders, Inc., Wis. Assn.
Doug Rohn, Pres.
6517 Bettys Lane, Madison 53711
(608) 274-3949 madinstr@tds.net www.wahmr.com

Head Start Assn., Wis.
Shelley Cousin, Exec. Dir.
122 E. Olin Ave., Suite 110, Madison 53713
(608) 442-6879 cousin@whsaonline.org
www.whsaonline.org

Health Care Assn., Wis.
James McGinn, Dir. Of Govt. Rel.
121 E. Wilson St., Suite L200, Madison 53703
(608) 257-0125 jim@whca.com

Health Care Assn., Wis. Primary
Stephanie Harrison, Exec. Dir.
4600 American Pkwy, #204, Madison 53718
(608) 277-7477 wphca@wphca.org www.wphca.org

Health Charities of Wis., Community
Jane Wood, Pres.
6737 W. Washington St., Suite 2253, West Allis 53214
(414) 918-9100 or (800) 783-0242
jwood@healthcharities.org
www.healthcharities.org/wisconsin

Health Information Management Assn., Wis.
Cassandra Bissen, Exec. Dir.
2350 South Ave., Suite 107, La Crosse 54601-6272
(608) 787-0168 whima@whima.org whima.org

Health Plans, Wis. Assn. of
Nancy J. Wenzel, CEO
10 E. Doty St., Suite 503, Madison 53703
(608) 255-8599 nancy@wihealthplans.org
www.wihealthplans.org

Health Underwriters, Wis. Assn. of
Daniel J. Schwartzer, Exec. Vice Pres.
4600 American Pkwy., Suite 208, Madison 53718
(608) 268-0200 dan@ewahu www.ewahu.org

Health, Physical Education, Recreation and Dance, Wis.
Assn. for
Keith Bakken, Exec. Dir.
1725 State St., 24 Mitchell Hall, UW-La Crosse,
La Crosse 54601
(608) 785-8175 wahperd@uwlax.edu www.wahperd.org

Hearing Professionals, Wis. Alliance of
Doug Johnson, Exec. Dir.
123 W. Washington Ave., Suite 201, Madison 53703-2558
(608) 257-2979 dqj@jjassociates.com

Heart Assn., American (Greater Midwest Affiliate)
Luke Rollins, Dir. Of State Advocacy
2850 Dairy Dr., Suite 300, Madison 53718-6751
(608) 221-8866, ext. 2 luke.rollins@heart.org
www.americanheart.org

Hereford Assn., Wis. Polled
Ruth Espenscheid, Secy.
12044 Hwy 78, Argyle 53504-0296
(608) 543-3788 wlbaosf@mhtc.net

History, Wis. Council for Local
Betty Havlik, Pres.
739 Hill Ave., No. 11, Hillsboro 54634-9026
(608) 489-3192 bettyhavlik@hotmail.com
wisconsinhistory.com

Holstein Assn., Wis.
Christianne Williams, Dir. Of Operations
902 Eighth Ave., Baraboo 53913
(800) 223-4269 or (608) 356-2114
chrisw@wisholsteins.com www.wisholsteins.com

Home Health United/Visiting Nurse Service, Inc.
Rick Bourne, Pres./CEO
4801 Hayes Rd., Madison 53704
(608) 242-1516 rbourne@hhuvns.org
homehealthunited.org

Homecare Organization, Wis.
Russell King, Exec. Dir.
5610 Medical Cir., Suite 33, Madison 53719
(608) 278-1115 wishomecare@earthlink.net
www.wishomecare.org

Honey Producers Assn., Wis.
Tom Fulton, Pres.
3308 4th St., Kenosha 53140
(262) 553-5510 tfulton.whpa@sbcglobal.net
www.wihoney.com

Horse Club, Inc., Wis. Morgan
Gary Shipshock, Pres.
W5359 Old 60 Rd., Juneau 53039-9676
(920) 349-3623 lazycreek.farm2@verizon.net
www.wisconsinmorganhorseclub.org

Horse Council, Wis. State, Inc.
Pam Pritchard, Adm. Asst.
121 S. Ludington St., Columbus 53925
(920) 623-0393 pam@wisconsinstatehorsecouncil.org
www.wisconsinstatehorsecouncil.org

Horse Trail Assn., Inc., Glacial Drumlin
Ken Carpenter, Pres.
P.O. Box 82, Deerfield 53531-0082
(608) 576-4104 witrails@yahoo.com
www.madison.com/communities/gdhta

Hospice Organization and Palliative Experts of Wis. (HOPE)
Melanie G. Ramey, Exec. Dir.
3240 University Ave., Suite 2, Madison 53705-3570
(608) 233-7166 MELR217@aol.com
www.wisconsinhospice.org

Hospital Assn., Inc., Wis.
Steve Brenton, Pres.
P.O. Box 259038, Madison 53725-9038
(608) 274-1820 www.wha.org

Housing Alliance, Wis.
Ross Kinzler, Exec. Dir.
301 N. Broom St., Suite 101, Madison 53703
(608) 255-3131 ross@housingalliance.us
www.housingalliance.us

Humane Societies, Inc., Wis. Federated
Debby Lewis, Pres.
N115 Two Mile Rd., Appleton 54914
(920) 733-1717, ext. 101 deb.lewis@foxvalleypets.org
wifedhs.org

Humanities Council, Wis.
Dena Wortzel, Exec. Dir.
222 S. Bedford St., Suite F, Madison 53703-3688
(608) 262-0706 contact@wisconsinhumanities.org
wisconsinhumanities.org

Innkeepers Assn., Wis.
Trisha A. Pugal, Pres., CEO
1025 S. Moorland Rd., Suite 200, Brookfield 53005
(262) 782-2851 pugal@wisconsinlodging.info
www.wisconsinlodging.info

Insulation Contractors Assn., Inc., Wis.
Deborah Wanta, Exec. Secy.
P.O. Box 26797, Milwaukee 53226-0797
(414) 282-5758 debbiewanta@hotmail.com

Insurance Agents of Wis., Inc., Professional
Ronald Von Haden, Exec. Vice-Pres.
6401 Odana Rd., Madison 53719-1126
(608) 274-8188 rvonhaden@piaw.org www.piaw.org

Insurance Agents of Wisconsin, Independent
Robert C. Jartz, Exec. Vice-Pres.
725 John Nolen Dr., Madison 53713-1421
(608) 256-4429 iiaw@aol.com

Insurance Alliance, Wis.
Andrew J. Franken, Pres.
44 E. Mifflin St., Suite 201, Madison 53703
(608) 255-1749 contact@wial.com wial.com

Insurance Companies, Wis. Assn. of Mutual
James Tlusty, Pres.
P.O. Box 14106, Madison 53708-0106
(608) 246-2552 wamic@chorus.net www.wamic.org

International Institute of Wis., Inc.
Alexander P. Durtka, Jr., Dir.
1110 N. Old World 3rd St., Milwaukee 53203-1117
(414) 225-6220 iiw@execpc.com

Interscholastic Athletic Assn., Wis.
Douglas E. Chickering, Exec. Dir.
P.O. Box 267, Stevens Point 54481
(715) 344-8580 dchickering@wiaawi.org www.wiaawi.org

Japan-America Soc. of Wis., Inc.
Alexander P. Durtka, Jr., Pres.
1110 W. 3rd St., Suite 420, Milwaukee 53203-1117
(414) 225-6220 jasw@execpc.com

Jaycees, Inc., Wis.
Steve Moddie, Exec. Vice Pres.
P.O. Box 1547, Appleton 54912-1547
(920) 731-7681 evp@wijaycees.org

Jewish Learning, Inc., Wis. Soc. For
Gwen Rivkin, Pres.
5225 N. Ironwood Rd., Suite 120, Milwaukee 53217-4909
(414) 963-4135 wsjl@wsjl.org www.wsjl.org

Judges Assn., Wis. Municipal
Jodi A. Sanfelippo, Secy.-Treas.
710 N. Plankinton Ave., Suite 335, Milwaukee 53203
(414) 287-9875 secretary-treasurer@wmja.net
www.wmja.net

Kidney Foundation of Wis., Inc., Natl.
Cynthia A. Huber, CEO
16655 W. Bluemound Rd., Suite 240,
Brookfield 53005-5935
(262) 821-0705 or (800) 543-6393 nkfw@kidneywi.org
www.kidneywi.org

Labor and Employment Relations Assn. (Wis. Ch.)
Irving Gottschalk, Pres.
310 W. Wisconsin Ave., Suite 700, Milwaukee 53203
(414) 297-3875 irving.gottschalk@nlrb.gov

Labor History Society, Wis.
Ken Germanson, Pres.
6333 W. Blue Mound Rd., Milwaukee 53213
(414) 771-0700, ext. 20 info@wisconsinlaborhistory.org
www.wisconsinlaborhistory.org

Laborers' Dist. Council, Wis.
Thomas E. Fisher, Pres. and Bus. Mgr.
4633 Liuna Way, Suite 101, DeForest 53532
(608) 846-8242 tfisher@wilaborers.org
www.wilaborers.org

Lakes, Inc., Wis. Assn. Of
Karen von Huene, Exec. Dir.
4513 Vernon Blvd., Suite 101, Madison 53705
(608) 661-4313 info@wisconsinlakes.org
www.wisconsinlakes.org

Land and Water Conservation Assn., Inc., Wis.
Julian Zelazny, Exec. Dir.
702 E. Johnson St., Madison 53703-1533
(608) 441-2677 julian@wlwca.org www.wlwca.org

Language Teachers, Wis. Assn. For (WAFLT)
Marge Draheim, Pres.
2137 W. Seneca Dr., Appleton 54914
(920) 731-3924 draheim@aol.com www.waflt.org

Law Librarians Assn. of Wis., Inc.
James Mumm, Pres.
P.O. Box 3137, Marquette University Law Library,
Milwaukee 53201-3137
(414) 288-5351 jim.mumm@marquette.edu
www.aallnet.org/chapter/llaw

Lawns of Wisconsin Network (LAWN)
Lou Wierichs, Past Pres.
1635 W. Haskel St., Appleton 54914
(920) 734-5615

Lawyers Assistance Program, Wis.
Linda Albert, Coord.
5302 E. Park Blvd., Madison 53718
(608) 250-6172 lalbert@wisbar.org www.wisbar.org/wislap

Lawyers, Assn. for Women
Margo Kirchner, Pres.
3322 N. 92nd St., Milwaukee 53222
(414) 463-0758 dana@barefoot-marketing.com

Lawyers, Wis. Assn. for Justice
Jane E. Garrott
44 E. Mifflin St., Suite 402, Madison 53703-2897
(608) 257-5741 jgarrott@wisjustice.org
www.wisjustice.org

League of Women Voters of Wis., Inc.
Andrea Kaminski, Exec. Dir.
122 State St., Suite 201A, Madison 53703-2500
(608) 256-0827 lwvwisconsin@lwvwi.org www.lwvwi.org

Learning Disabilities Assn. of Wis.
Diane Sixel, Pres.
7625 Lechler Ln., Kiel 53042
(866) 532-9472 ifo@ldawisconsin.com ldawisconsin.com

Legal Assn. for Women
Carrie Benedon, Pres.
740 Regent St., Madison 53715
(608) 257-7766 cbenedon@lahtropclark.com
www.wisbar.org

Letter Carriers' Assn., Wis. Rural
c/o Secretary's Office
5857 Prill Rd., Eau Claire 54701
(715) 836-9612 karenschauer@wirlca.org wirlca.org

Leukemia and Lymphoma Soc. (Wis. Chap.)
Bede Barth Potter, Exec. Dir.
200 S. Executive Dr., Suite 203, Brookfield 53005
(262) 790-4701 bede.barthpotter@lls.org www.lls.org

Libertarian Party of Wisconsin
Jim Maas Rothschild, Chair
P.O. Box 20815, Greenfield 53220-0815
(800) 236-9236 chairman@lpwi.org www.lpwi.org/

Lions Clubs Internatl. (MD. 27 - Wis.)
Mary Lee Wiza, State Secy.
2809 Post Road, Stevens Point 54481
(715) 341-2277 lionstat@sbcglobal.net wisconsinlions.org

Liquid Waste Carriers Assn., Wis.
Ann Gryphan
Essie Kammer Group
16 N. Carroll St., Suite 900, Madison 53703
(608) 255-2770 agryphan@ekgmail.com www.wlwca.org

Livestock and Meat Council, Wis.
Daniel Vogel, Marketing Division
2811 Agriculture Dr., Madison 53704-6777
(608) 224-5113 dan.vogel@datcp.state.wi.us

Lobbyists, Inc., Assn. of Wis.
Mary Kaja, Exec. Dir.
P.O. Box 1604, Madison 53701
(608) 257-3541 awl@wisconsinlobbyists.com
www.wisconsinlobbyists.com

LSLA Education, Inc.
Tim Kassis, Pres.
P.O. Box 160, Antigo 54409
(715) 623-5410 lsla@lakestateslumber.com

Lumber Assoc., Inc., Wis. Retail
David L. Rosenmeier
W175 N11086 Stonewood Dr., Germantown 53022
(262) 250-1835 wrla@wrlamsi.com www.wrlamsi.com

Lung Assn. of Wis., Amer.
Dona Wininsky, Dir. Of Public Policy and Comm.
13100 W. Lisbon Rd., Suite 700, Brookfield 53005
(262) 703-4840 dwininsky@lungwisconsin.org
www.lungwi.org

Lupus Foundation of Amer., Inc., Wis. Chap.
Sandra Hofstetter, Exec. Dir.
2600 N. Mayfair Rd., Suite 320, Milwaukee 53226
(414) 443-6400 lupuswi@lupuswi.org www.lupuswi.org

Make-A-Wish Foundation of Wis.
Patti Gorsky, Pres.
13195 W. Hampton Ave., Butler 53007
(262) 781-4445 info@wisconsin.wish.org
www.wisconsin.wish.org

Manufacturers' Agents, Inc., Wis. Assn. of
C.J. Bluem, Exec. Dir.
1504 N. 68th St., Milwaukee 53213-2806
(414) 778-0640 wama@wama.org wama.org

Manufacturers and Commerce, Wis.
James S. Haney, Pres.
P.O. Box 352, Madison 53701-0352
(608) 258-3400 wmc@wmc.org

Map Society, Ltd., Wis.
Virginia Schwartz, Secy.-Treas.
814 W. Wisconsin Ave., c/o Milwaukee Public Library,
Milwaukee 53233-2387
(414) 286-3216 vschwa@mpl.org

Maple Syrup Producers Assoc., Wis.
Gretchen Grape, Exec. Dir.
33186 Cty Hwy W, Holcombe 54745
(715) 447-5758 gretchen_grape@yahoo.com
www.wismaple.org

Marine Corps League Auxiliary
Diane Solberg, Pres.
1415 Ohio St., Racine 53405-3119
(262) 633-4070

Marine Corps League, Dept. of Wis.
Vernon Riedle, Commandant
322 Paul Dr., Kimberly 54136-1222
(920) 364-0169 vpriedle@yahoo.com

Marketing and Management Assn., Wis.
Mae Laatsch, State Dir.
130 Keyes, P.O. Box 85, Lake Mills 53551
(920) 648-5965 mlaatsch@matcmadison.edu
wideltaepsilonchi.org

Matchcover Club, Badger State
Marilyn Reese, Editor
3201 S. 72nd St., Milwaukee 53219-3969

Mayflower Descendants, Wis., Soc. of
Mrs. Robert R. Pekowsky, Historian
1629 North Golf Glen, Unit D, Madison 53704-7074
(608) 467-6646 martell135@charter.net
www.mayflowerwi.org

Meat Processors, Inc., Wis. Assn. of
Peter Drone, Exec. Secy.
P.O. Box 331, Bloomington 53804
(608) 994-2559 peter@wi-amp.com www.wi-amp.com

Medical Society of Wis., State
Susan Turney, Exec. Vice-Pres./CEO
P.O. Box 1109, Madison 53701-1109
(608) 442-3800 communications@wismed.org
www.wisconsinmedicalsociety.org

Military Officers Assn. of America
Donald T. Ford, Pres.
5044 Hearthside Ln., Racine 53402
(262) 639-5821

Milk Marketing Board, Wis.
James Robson, CEO
8418 Excelsior Dr., Madison 53717
(608) 836-8820 www.wisdairy.com

Mining Impact Coalition of Wis., Inc.
David Blouin, Coord.
3918 Paunack Ave., Madison 53711
(608) 233-8455 burroak15@charter.net

Mortgage Professionals Assn., Wis.
Patrick Essie, Exec. Dir.
Essie Kammer Group
16 N. Carroll St., Suite 900, Madison 53703
(608) 259-9262 info@wmpa.info www.wmpa.info

Mothers Against Drunk Driving (MADD)
Kari Kinnard, Exec. Dir.
1845 N. Farwell Ave., Suite 310, Milwaukee 53202
(414) 727-7505 maddwi@tds.net maddwisconsin.org

Motor Carriers Assn., Wis.
Thomas Howells, Pres.
562 Grand Canyon Dr., Madison 53719-1033
(608) 833-8200 thowells@witruck.org

Movers Assn., Wis.
Cherie Tuhus, Division Admin.
562 Grand Canyon Dr., Madison 53719-1033
(608) 833-8200 ctuhus@witruck.org www.wismovers.org

MRA – The Management Assn., Inc.
Susan M. Fronk, Pres.
N19 W24400 Riverwood Dr., Waukesha 53188
(262) 523-9090 www.mranet.org

Muck Farmers Assn., Wis.
Rod Gumz, Pres.
N570 6th Ct., Endeavor 53930
(608) 981-2488 gumz@mwwb.net

Multiple Sclerosis Soc., Natl. (Wis. Chap.)
Colleen G. Kalt, Pres.
1120 James Dr., Suite A, Hartland 53029
(262) 369-4400 colleen.kalt@wisms.org
www.nationalmssociety.org/wig/home

Municipalities, League of Wis.
Dan Thompson, Exec. Dir.
122 W. Washington Ave., Suite 300, Madison 53703
(608) 267-2380 league@lwm-info.org www.lwm-info.org

Music Educators Assn., Inc., Wis.
Robert W. Kase, Exec. Dir.
1005 Quinn Dr., Waunakee 53597
(608) 850-3566 rkase@wsmamusic.org

Music Heritage Soc., Inc., Wis.
Howard Kanetzke
6333 Masthead Dr., Madison 53705-4325
(608) 238-6567

Myasthenia Gravis Foundation of Amer. (Wis. Chapter)
Lindsay Knudsen, Chp.
2474 S. 96th St., West Allis 53227
(262) 938-9800 wiscmg@yahoo.com myasthenia.org

NAIFA Wisconsin
Susan K. Linck, Exec. Vice Pres.
2702 International Ln., No. 207, Madison 53704
(608) 244-3131 www.naifa.org

NAMI Wisconsin, Inc.
Terence Schnapp, Exec. Dir.
4233 W. Beltline Hwy, Madison 53711
(608) 268-6000 nami@namiwisconsin.org
www.namiwisconsin.org

National Farmers Organization, Wis.
Don Hamm, State Pres.
955 17th St., Prairie du Sac 53578
(608) 643-3341, Ext. 222 dhamm@nfo.org

National Guard Assn., Inc., Wis.
Ronald R. Wagner, Exec. Dir.
2400 Wright St., Rm. 208, Madison 53704-2572
(608) 242-3114 wingainc@att.net www.winga.org

National Guard Enlisted Assn., Inc., Wis.
Robert Serrahn, Exec. Dir.
2400 Wright St., Madison 53704-2572
(608) 242-3112 wngea@yahoo.com wngea.org

Natural Food Associates, Inc., Wis.
Michael Hittner, Pres.
910 W. Grand Ave., Wisconsin Rapids 54495
(715) 421-2061 wisconsinnaturalfoods.org

Nature Conservancy, Wis. Chap.
Mary Jean Huston, State Dir.
633 W. Main St., Madison 53703
(608) 251-8140 wisconsin@tnc.org

Navy Club of USA
Harry Alvey, Cmdr.
400 River Dr., #385, Wausau 54403-5469
(715) 848-0384 hea264@juno.com

Newspaper Assn., Inc., Wis.
Peter D. Fox, Exec. Dir.
P.O. Box 259837, Madison 53705
(608) 283-7620 peter.fox@WNAnews.com
www.wnanews.com

Nursery Assn., Wis.
Brian Swingle, Exec. Dir.
12342 W. Layton Ave., Greenfield 53228
(414) 529-4705 bswingle@toriiphillips.com www.wgif.net

Nurses Assn., Wis.
Gina Dennik-Champion, Exec. Dir.
6117 Monona Dr., Suite 1, Madison 53716-3995
(608) 221-0383 gina@wisconsinnurses.org
www.wisconsinnurses.org

Nurses, Wis. Assn. of Licensed Practical
JoAnn Shaw, Pres.
22 E. Mifflin St., Suite 1010, Madison 53703
(608) 256-5299 jslpn@sbcglobal.net

Nursing Home Social Workers Assn., Wis.
Jeff McCabe, Pres.
3300 W. Brewster St., c/o Brewster Village, Appleton 54914
(920) 225-1985 mccabeja@co.outagamie.wi.us
wnhswa.org

Nursing, Inc., Wis. League for
Marilyn Frenn, Pres.
2121 E. Newport Ave., Milwaukee 53211
(888) 755-3329 wln@wisconsinwln.org
www.wisconsinwln.org

Occupational Therapy Assn., Inc., Wis.
Linda Anderson, Pres.
122 E. Olin Ave., Suite 165, Madison 53713
(608) 287-1606 wota@execpc.com www.wota.net/online

Ophthalmology, Wis. Academy of
Richard H. Paul, Exec. Dir.
10 W. Phillip Rd., Suite 120, Vernon Hills, IL 60061
(800) 780-4312 richardpaul@dls.net

Orchid Soc., Wis.
Bruce Efflandt
3518 North 98th St., Milwaukee 53222
(262) 327-9373 berniesfloral@mail.com
www.wisconsinorchidsociety.com

Ornithology, Inc., Wis. Soc. for
Christine Reel, Treas.
2022 Sherryl Ln., Waukesha 53188-3142
(262) 547-6128 wso1939@hotmail.com www.wsobirds.org

Orthodontists, Wis. Soc. of
Dr. Jane Bentz, Pres.
1845 E. Main St., Onalaska 54650
(608) 783-8333

Otolaryngology - Head and Neck Surgery, Wis Soc. of
David R. Friedland, Secy.-Treas.
MCW Clinic at Froedtert Hospital,
Dept. of Otolaryngology,
9200 W. Wisconsin Ave., Milwaukee 53226
(414) 805-5625 dfriedla@mcw.edu

Outdoor Advertising Assoc. of Wis.
Janet Swandby, Exec. Dir.
10 E. Doty St., Suite 403, Madison 53703
(608) 286-0764 swandby@swandby.com www.oaaw.org

Paper Council, Wis.
Jeffrey G. Landin, Pres.
P.O. Box 718, Neenah 54957-0718
(920) 722-1500 landin@wipapercouncil.org
www.wisconsinpapercouncil.org

Paratransit Provider, Wis. Rural and
Judy Lindholm, Pres.
222 N. Iowa St., Suite 110, Dodgeville 53533
(608) 935-0324 judy.lindholm@iowacounty.org
www.witransportation.com

Parents and Teachers Inc., Wis. Congress of
Roxanne Starks, Pres.
4797 Hayes Rd., Suite 102, Madison 53704-3288
(608) 244-1455 wi_office@pta.org www.wisconsinpta.org

Park and Recreation Assn., Inc., Wis.
Steven J. Thompson, Exec. Dir.
6601-C Northway, Greendale 53129
(414) 423-1210 sthompson@wpraweb.org

Pathologists, Wis. Soc. of
Dawn M. Maerker, Exec. Secy.
N44 W25940 Lindsay Rd., P.O. Box 636, Pewaukee 53072
(262) 695-7411 dmman@wi.rr.com
www.wisconsinpathologistsociety.com

Pawn Brokers Assn., Wis.
Patrick Essie, Exec. Dir.
Essie Kammer Group
16 N. Carroll St., Suite 900, Madison 53703
(608) 256-7701

Peace and Justice, Wis. Network for
Judy Miner, Off. Coor.
122 State St., No. 402, Madison 53703-2500
(608) 250-9240 info@wnpj.org www.wnpj.org

Pediatric Dentists, Wis. Soc. of
Brian Hodgson, DDS, Pres.
Marquette University School of Dentistry,
1801 W. Wisconsin Ave., Milwaukee 53233
(414) 288-1566 brian.hodgson@mu.edu

Perinatal Care, Wis. Assn. for
Ann E. Conway, Exec. Dir.
McConnell Hall, 1010 Mound St., Madison 53715
(608) 417-6060 wapc@perinatalweb.org
www.perinatalweb.org

Perinatal Foundation
Ann E. Conway, Exec. Dir.
McConnell Hall, 1010 Mound St., Madison 53715
(608) 417-6200 foundation@perinatalweb.org
www.perinatalweb.org

Petroleum Council, Wis. (Div. of Amer. Petroleum Institute)
Erin T. Roth, Exec. Dir.
10 E. Doty St., Suite 500, Madison 53703
rothe@api.org api.org

Petroleum Marketers & Convenience Store Assn., Wis.
Matthew C. Hauser, Pres.
121 S. Pinckney St., Suite 300, Madison 53703
(608) 256-7555 hauser@wpmca.org www.wpmca.org

Pharmacy Soc. Of Wis.
Christopher Decker, Exec. Vice Pres.
701 Heartland Tr., Madison 53717
(608) 827-9200 cdecker@pswi.org www.pswi.org

PHCC/Master Plumbers - Wis. Assn.
Jeffrey J. Beiriger, Exec. Dir.
660 E. Mason St., Milwaukee 53202
(414) 227-1230 beiriger@cf.law.com
www.wisconsinsbestplumbers.com

Phenological Soc., Wis.
Mark Schwartz, Pres.
Department of Geography, UW-Milwaukee,
P.O. Box 413, Milwaukee 53201
(414) 229-3740 mds@uwm.edu
www.naturenet.com/alnc/wps

Physical Medicine and Rehabilitation, Wis. Soc. of
James W. Leonard, D.O., Secy./Treas.
6630 University Ave., Middleton 53562
(608) 263-8632 jleonard@uwhealth.org www.wispmr.org

Physical Therapy Assn., Wis.
Karen Oshman, Exec. Dir.
4781 Hayes Rd., Suite 201, Madison 53704
(608) 221-9191 wpta@wpta.org www.wpta.org

Physician Assistants, Wis. Academy of
Jim Ginter
702 Eisenhower Dr., Suite A, Kimberly 54136
(800) 762-8965 wapa@wapa.org wapa.org

Physicians, Inc., Am. College of Emergency (Wis. Ch.)
Richard H. Paul, Exec. Dir.
10 W. Phillip Rd., Suite 120, Vernon Hills, IL 60061-1330
(800) 798-4911 richardpaul@dls.net
www.wisconsinacep.org

Physicians, Wis. Academy of Family
Larry Pheifer, Exec. Dir.
210 Green Bay Rd., Thiensville 53092
(262) 512-0606 academy@wafp.org www.wafp.org

Pipe Welding Bureau, Natl. Certified (Wis. Chap.)
Marcie M. Marquardt, Chap. Exec.
5940 Seminole Centre Ct., Suite 102, Madison 53711
(608) 288-1414 OrganServ@aol.com

Podiatric Medicine, Wis. Soc. of
Steven Frydman, Exec. Dir.
7929 N. 76th St., Milwaukee 53223
(414) 371-2468 wspm@aol.com
www.wisconsinpodiatrists.com

Police Assn., Wis. Chiefs of
Donald Thaves, Exec. Dir.
River Ridge - 1141 South Main St., Shawano 54166
(715) 524-8283 dthaves@frontiernet.net www.wichiefs.org

Police Assn., Wis. Professional
James L. Palmer, Exec. Dir.
340 Coyier Ln., Madison 53713
(608) 273-3840 palmer@wppa.com www.wppa.com

Polygraph Assn., Wis.
Anthony O'Neill, Pres.
346 S. Emery St., Peshtigo 54157
(715) 923-8381 wispoly@new.rr.com

Pork Assn., Wis. Cooperative
Tammy Vaassen, Dir. Of Operations
9185 Old Potosi Rd., Lancaster 53813-0327
(608) 723-7551 wppa@wppa.com www.wppa.org

Postal History Soc., Wis.
Frank Moertl, Pres.
N95 W32259 County Line Rd., Hartland 53029-9735
(262) 966-7096

Postsecondary Agricultural Students
Paul Cutting, State Director
1800 Bronson Blvd., Fennimore 53809
(800) 362-3322, Ext. 2467
pcutting@swtc.edu www.wipas.org

Potato and Vegetable Growers Assn., Wis.
T.J. Kennedy, Pres.
P.O. Box 327, Antigo 54409-0327
(715) 623-7683 www.wisconsinpotatoes.com

Potato Growers Aux., Inc., Wis.
Lynn Isherwood, Pres.
P.O. Box 327, Antigo 54409-0327
(715) 623-7683

Potato Improvement Assn., Wis. Seed
John Hein, Pres.
P.O. Box 173, Antigo 54409-0173
(715) 623-7683 www.potatoseed.org

Preferred Provider Assn., Wis. (WPPO)
Daniel J. Schwartzer, Exec. Dir.
4600 American Pkwy., Suite 208, Madison 53719
(608) 243-1007 dan@smgltd.org www.wisconsinppo.org

Prevent Blindness Wis., Inc.
Robert P. Goldstein, Pres./CEO
759 N. Milwaukee St., Milwaukee 53202-3714
(414) 765-0505 bobg@preventblindnesswisconsin.org
www.preventblindness.org/wi

Preventive Medicine, Wis., Soc. for
Henry A. Anderson, M.D., Pres.
200 Lakewood Blvd., Madison 53704-5916
(608) 266-1253 anderha@sbcglobal.net

Printing Industries of Wis., Inc.
N. Niall Power, Pres.
800 Main St., Pewaukee 53072
(262) 695-6250 info@piw.org piw.org

Psychological Assn., Wis.
Sarah Bowen, Exec. Dir.
126 S. Franklin St., Madison 53703
(608) 251-1450 wispsych@execpc.com

Purple Heart, Military Order of the (Dept. of Wis.)
John O'Brien, Dept. Adjutant
26570 Fiddlers Green Rd., Richland Center 53581
(608) 647-8491 irishi48@countryspeed.com

Purple Heart, Military Order of the (Dept. of Wis.), Aux.
Marge Reinders, Pres.
7517 County Rd. T, Oshkosh 54904

Quality, Amer. Soc. For
Paul E. Borawski, Exec. Dir.
600 N. Plankinton Ave., Milwaukee 53203
(414) 272-8575 cs@asq.org www.asq.org

Radiologic Technologists, Wis. Soc. of
Marnet Zimmer, Pres.
3801 Spring St., Racine 53405
(262) 687-4579 marnet.zimmer@wfhc.org www.wsrt.net

Radiological Soc., Wis.
Jane Svinicki, Exec. Dir.
6737 W. Washington St., Suite 1300, Milwaukee 53214
(414) 755-6293 jane@svinicki.com www.wi-rad.org

Railroad Passengers, Wis. Assn. of
Mark Weitenbeck, Treas.
3385 S. 119th St., West Allis 53227-3943
(414) 541-1112 wisarp@hotmail.com www.wisarp.org

Reading Assn., Wis. State
Sue Bradley, Admin. Asst.
N7902 E. Friesland Rd., Randolph 53956
(920) 326-6280 wsra@wsra.org www.wsra.org

Real Property Listers Assn., Wis.
Jeremiah Erickson, Pres.
202 S. K St., Room 3, Sparta 54656
(608) 269-8623 jerickson@co.monroe.wi.us
www.wrpla.org

Red Cross, Amer.
Tracey Sparrow, Reg. Chapter Exec.
2600 W. Wisconsin Ave., Milwaukee 53233
(414) 342-8680 www.redcross.org

Register of Deeds Assn., Wis.
Rose Ottum, Pres.
36245 Main St., Whitelaw 54773
(715) 538-2311 www.wrdaonline.org

Rehabilitation For Wisconsin, Inc.
C. Thomas Cook, Exec. Dir.
1302 Mendota St., Suite 200, Madison 53714
(608) 244-5310 tcook@rfw.org www.rfw.org

Republican Party of Wis.
Mark Jefferson, Exec. Dir.
148 E. Johnson St., Madison 53703
(608) 257-4765 info@wisgop.org www.wisgop.org

Reserve Officers Assn. of the U.S. (Dept. of Wis.)
LTC Timothy Lubinsky, Exec. Secy.
728 Newbury St., Ripon 54971
(920) 748-2308 timothy.lubinsky@wisconsin.gov
www.roa.org

Residential Services Association of Wis.
Jennifer Rzepka, Exec. Dir.
6737 W. Washington St., Suite 1300, Milwaukee 53214
(414) 276-9273 info@rsawisconsin.org
www.rsawisconsin.org

Restaurant Assn., Wis.
Edward J. Lump, Pres./CEO
2801 Fish Hatchery Rd., Madison 53713
(608) 270-9950 elump@wirestaurant.org
www.wirestaurant.org

Retarded, Inc., Wis. Parents Coalition for the
Kevin Underwood, Pres.
669 McCarthy Dr. North, Hartford 53027
(920) 474-4129

Retired Enlisted Assn., The
Holly Hoppe, Pres.
Courthouse, 301 Washington St., Oconto 54153
(920) 834-6817 holly.hoppe@co.oconto.wi.us
www.trea.org

RID (Remove Intoxicated Drivers)
Mardy Meacham, Coord.
122 Eagle Lake Ave., Mukwonago 53149
(262) 363-5554 christysmom15@aim.com
www.rid-usa.org

Right to Life, Inc., Wis.
Barbara L. Lyons, Exec. Dir.
10625 W. North Ave., Suite LL, Milwaukee 53226-2331
(877) 855-5007 admin@wrtl.org www.wrtl.org

Runaway Services, Wis. Assn. for
Patricia Balke, Exec. Dir.
2318 E. Dayton St., Madison 53704
(608) 241-2649 pbalke@sbcglobal.net wahrs.org

Saddlebred Assn. of Wis., Amer.
Shelagh Roell, Pres.
19140 Edmonton Dr., Brookfield 53045
(262) 784-3554 wiasb@yahoo.com www.asaw.org

Safety Patrols Inc., Wis.
Jeremy McGilligan-Bentin, Exec. Dir.
P.O. Box 796, Elkhorn 53121
(608) 332-5480 wisconsinsafetypatrols@gmail.com

St. Francis Children's Center, Inc.
Gerald Coon, Exec. Dir.
6700 N. Port Washington Rd., Milwaukee 53217-3919
(414) 351-0450 gcoon@sfcckids.org

Sanitary Engineering, Amer. Soc. of (Wis. Chap.)
Ervin Mirr, Secy.
4610 Raven Ct., Brookfield 53005-1242
(262) 781-4725

School Administrators, Assn. of Wis.
Jim Lynch, Exec. Dir.
4797 Hayes Rd., Suite 103, Madison 53704-3288
(608) 241-0300 jimlynch@awsa.org www.awsa.org

School Attorneys Assn., Wis.
John Ashley, Secy.
122 W. Washington Ave., Suite 400, Madison 53703
(608) 257-2622 jashley@wasb.org

School Boards, Inc., Wis. Assn. of
John Ashley, Exec. Dir.
122 W. Washington Ave., Suite 400, Madison 53703
(608) 257-2622 jashley@wasb.org www.wasb.org

School Bus Assn., Wis.
Robert W. Christian, Exec. Dir.
P.O. Box 168, Sheboygan 53082-0168
(920) 457-7008 dirbob@dirwsba.com

School Music Assn., Inc., Wis.
Robert W. Kase, Exec. Dir.
1005 Quinn Dr., Waunakee 53597
(608) 850-3566 rkase@wsmamusic.org

School Music, Wis. Foundation for
Robert W. Kase, Exec. Dir.
1005 Quinn Dr., Waunakee 53597
(608) 850-3566 rkase@wsmamusic.org

Schools Accreditation, Religious and Independent, Inc., Wis.
Beatrice Weiland, Exec. Dir.
P.O. Box 685, Muskego 53150
(262) 895-3679 wrisa@wrisa.net www.wrisa.net

Schools, Wis. Assn. of Christian
Matt Williams, Exec. Dir.
W10085 Pike Plains Rd., Dunbar 54119
(715) 324-6900, Ext. 1651 mwilliams@nbbc.edu
www.wiacs.org

Seasonal Residents Assn.
Nick Kaufmann
P.O. Box 46108, Madison 53744
(800) 880-9944 info@wisra.org www.wisra.org

Seniors of Wis., Inc., United
Dorothy Seeley, Pres.
4515 W. Forest Home Ave., Milwaukee 53219-4837
(414) 321-0220

Settlement Companies, Assoc. of
Ann Marie French, Exec. Dir.
Essie Kammer Group
16 N. Carroll St., Suite 900, Madison 53703
(888) 657-8272 afrench@tascsite.org www.tascsite.org

Sexual Assault, Wis. Coalition Against
Jeanie Kurka Reimer, Exec. Dir.
600 Williamson St., Suite N2, Madison 53703
(608) 257-1516 wcasa@wcasa.org www.wcasa.org

Sheet Metal and Air Conditioning Contractors Assn. of
Wis., Inc.
Peter Lentz, Exec. Vice Pres.
10427 W. Lincoln Ave., Suite 1600, Milwaukee 53227
(414) 543-7622

Sheriffs and Deputy Sheriffs Assn., Wis.
James Cardinal, Exec. Dir.
P.O. Box 145, Chippewa Falls 54729-0145
(715) 723-7173 jcardinal@wsdsa.org www.wsdsa.org

Sheriff's Assn., Badger State
Sheriff David A. Graves, Pres.
P.O. Box 1004, Elkhorn 53121-1004
(262) 741-4400 dgraves@co.walworth.wi.us

Sign Assn., Wis.
Christopher Ruditys, Exec. Dir.
11801 W. Silver Spring Dr., #200, Milwaukee 53225
(414) 271-9277 ruditys@wamllc.net

Sister Relationships, Inc., Wis.
Alexander P. Durtka, Jr., Pres.
1110 N. Old World Third St., Milwaukee 53203-1102
(414) 225-6220 wisci@execpc.com

Skills USA-VICA (Post Secondary)
Dale A. Drees, State Dir.
1825 N. Bluemound Dr., Fox Valley Technical College,
Appleton 54912
(920) 735-2489 drees@fvtc.edu

Soccer Assn., Inc., Wis.
Richard Williams, Pres.
10708 W. Hayes Ave., West Allis 53227
(414) 545-7227 richkaren123@msn.com
www.wisoccer.org

Social Workers, Inc., Natl. Assn. of (Wis. Chap.)
Marc Herstand, Exec. Dir.
16 N. Carroll St., Suite 220, Madison 53703
(608) 257-6334 naswwi@tds.net www.naswwi.org

Socialist Party of Wis.
Paul J. Cigler, State Chm.
1001 E. Keefe Ave., Milwaukee 53212
(414) 332-0654 info@spwi.org www.spwi.org

Sod Producers Assn., Wis.
Gina Halter, Exec. Secy.
22920 Hanson Rd., Union Grove 53182
(262) 895-6820

Soil Science Soc. of America
Ellen Bergfeld, CEO
677 S. Segoe Rd., Madison 53711
(608) 273-8080 www.soils.org

Sons of the Amer. Revolution, Wis. Soc. of the
Thomas Cochran, Pres.
P.O. Box 139, Black Creek 54106
(920) 858-1025 foxvalley@charter.net

Soybean Assn., Wis.
R. Karls, Exec. Dir.
2976 Triverton Pike Dr., Madison 53711-5840

Specialized Medical Vehicle Association of Wisconsin
Jim Brown, Pres.
2703 Industrial St., Wisconsin Rapids 54495
(800) 423-7818 woi_rcc@wctc.net

Speech-Language Pathology and Audiology Assn., Wis.
Dawn Merth-Johnson, Pres.
1360 Regent St., #154, Madison 53715
(800) 545-0640 wsha@wisha.org www.wisha.org

Spinal Cord Injury Assn., Natl. (Wis. Chapter)
John Dziewa, Pres.
1545 S. Layton Blvd., Rm. 320, Milwaukee 53215-1924
(414) 384-4022 office@nsciasew.org www.nsciasew.org

Stamp Clubs, Inc., Wis. Federation of
Charles Green, Treas.
5199 Bittersweet Ln., Oshkosh 54901
(920) 426-1066 bgreen9001@yahoo.com
www.wfscstamps.org

State Employees Union, Wis. (AFSCME Council 24,
AFL-CIO)
Marty Beil, Exec. Dir.
8033 Excelsior Dr., Suite C, Madison 53717-1903
(608) 836-0024 mbeil@wseu-24.org wseu-24.org

Student Financial Aid Administrators, Wis. Assn. of
Lloyd Mueller, Pres.
273 E. Erie St., Milwaukee Institute of Art and Design,
Milwaukee 53202
(414) 291-3272 llmueller@miad.edu www.wasfaa.net/

Students, Inc., United Council of UW
Nicolet Juan, Exec. Dir.
14 W. Mifflin St., Suite 212, Madison 53703
(608) 263-3422 ed@unitedcouncil.net.
www.unitedcouncil.net

Surgeons, Wis. Soc. of Oral and Maxillofacial
Mary Grote
301 A South Roosevelt Dr., Beaver Dam 53916
(920) 887-8423

Surgeons, Wis. Soc. of Plastic
Michelle Bonness, Pres.
20611 Watertown Rd., Suite D, Waukesha 53186
(262) 782-7021

Surveyors, Inc., Wis. Soc. of Land
Francis R. Thousand, Exec. Dir.
5113 Spaanem Ave., Madison 53716
(608) 770-9759 fthousant@charter.net www.wsls.org

Taxicab Owners, Wis. Assn. of
Richard Running, Pres.
520 E. Decker St., Viroqua 54665
(608) 637-2599 richard@runninginc.net

Taxpayers Alliance, Wis.
Todd A. Berry, Pres.
401 North Lawn Ave., Madison 53704-5033
(608) 241-9789 wistax@wistax.org www.wistax.org

Taxpayers Assn., Inc., Wis. Property
Thomas Dohm, Pres.
P.O. Box 1493, Madison 53701-1493
(608) 255-7473 wptonline.org

Teachers, American Assn. of Physics (Wis. Section)
Erik Hendrickson, Secy.-Treas.
UW-Eau Claire, Dept. of Physics and Astronomy,
Eau Claire 54702-4004
(715) 836-5834 hendrije@uwec.edu www.wapt.org

Teamsters Joint Council No.39, Wis.
Paul G. Lovinus, Secy.-Treas.
10020 W. Greenfield Ave., Milwaukee 53214
(414) 258-4545 local344.org

Telecommunications Assn., Wis. State
William C. Esbeck, Exec. Dir.
121 E. Wilson St., Suite 102, Madison 53703
(608) 256-8866 bill.esbeck@wsta.info www.wsta.info

Telemedia Council, Inc., Natl.
Marieli Rowe, Exec. Dir.
1922 University Ave., Madison 53726
(608) 218-1182 ntelemedia@aol.com

Textile Services, Wis. Assn. of
Brian Swingle, Exec. Dir.
12342 W. Layton Ave., Greenfield 53228
(414) 529-4703 bswingle@toriiphillips.com

Theatre Owners of Wis., Natl. Assn. of
Paul J. Rogers, Pres.
W168 N8936 Appleton Ave., Menomonee Falls 53051
(262) 532-0017 nato@natoofwiup.org
www.natoofwiup.org

Timber Professionals Assn., Inc., Great Lakes
Henry Schienebeck, Exec. Dir.
P.O. Box 1278, Rhinelander 54501-1278
(715) 282-5828 henry@newnorth.net www.timberpa.com

Timber, Inc., Lakes States Women in
Jean Peters, Secy.
P.O. Box 10, Long Lake 54542
(715) 767-5185 jh2522@newnorth.net www.lswit.org

Title Assn., Inc., Wis. Land
Karen E. Gilster, Exec. Off.
P.O. Box 873, West Salem 54669
(608) 786-2336 kgilster@wlta.org www.wlta.org

Tool Die and Machining Association of Wis.
Rebecca Fisher, Exec. Secy
W175 N11117 Stonewood Dr., Suite 204,
Germantown 53022
(262) 532-2440 info@tdmaw.org www.tdmaw.org

Tourism Federation, Wis.
Julia Hertel
P.O. Box 393, Sun Prairie 53590
(608) 286-9599 info@witourismfederation.org
www.witourismfederation.org

Towing Assoc., Wis.
Mike DeHaan, Field Services Dir.
P.O. Box 44849, Madison 53744-4849
(608) 833-8200 mdehaan@witruck.org www.witow.org

Towns Assn., Wis.
Richard J. Stadelman, Exec. Dir.
W7686 County Rd. MMM, Shawano 54166
(715) 526-3157 wtowns@frontiernet.net
www.wisctowns.com

Translators and Interpreters Guild, AFL-CIO (Wis. Chap.)
Rick Kissell
P.O. Box 1101, Milwaukee 53201-1101
(414) 617-8039 rick@kissell.org www.ttig.org

Transportation Builders Assn., Wis.
Pat Goss, Exec. Dir.
1 South Pinckney St., Suite 300, Madison 53703
(608) 256-6891 pgoss@wtba.org www.wtba.org

Transportation Development Assn. of Wis., Inc.
Craig Thompson, Exec. Dir.
131 W. Wilson St., Suite 302, Madison 53703
(608) 256-7044 craig.thompson@tdawisconsin.org
www.tdawisconsin.org

Transportation Union, United
Timothy S. Deneen, State Dir.
7 N. Pinckney St., Suite 320, Madison 53703-4262
(608) 251-4120 utulo56@gmail.com

Tree Farm Com., Wis.
Randy Sthokal
PO Box 285, Stevens Point 54481
(715) 252-2001 wtfc@athenet.net www.witreefarm.org

Trees For Tomorrow, Inc.
Maggie Bishop, Exec. Dir.
P.O. Box 609, Eagle River 54521-0609
(800) 838-9472 learning@treesfortomorrow.com
www.treesfortomorrow.com

United Professionals for Quality Care/SEIU District 1199W
Dian Palmer, Pres.
2001 W. Beltline Hwy, Suite 201, Madison 53713-2366
(608) 277-1199 dianp@1199wup.org www.seiu1199wi.org

University of Wis. Foundation
Andrew A. Wilcox, Pres.
1848 University Ave., Madison 53726
(608) 263-4545 www.uwfoundation.wisc.edu

Utilities Assn., Wis.
William R. Skewes, Exec. Dir.
44 E. Mifflin St., Suite 202, Madison 53703
(608) 257-3151 kwilcox@wisconsinutilities.com
www.wiutilities.org

Utility Investors, Inc., Wis.
Robert Seitz, Exec. Dir.
10 E. Doty St., Suite 500, Madison 53703-3397
(608) 663-5813 contact@wuiinc.org www.wuiinc.org

Utility Tax Assn., Wis.
Marge Pearce, Rec. Secy.
4809 Moenning Rd., Sheboygan 53081
(920) 458-2000 margep@powercom.net

Veteran Organizations, Wis. Assn. of Concerned
Bob Buhr, Contact Person
510 3rd St., Clear Lake 54005
(715) 263-3357 bobbuhr@cltcomm.net www.wacvo.org

Veterans Against the War, Vietnam
John Zutz, Coord.
2922 N. Booth St., Milwaukee 53212-2537
www.vvaw.org

Veterans Assn., WAC (Women's Army Corps)
Naomi Horwitz, Pres.
6101 N. Lovers Lane Rd., Apt. D, Milwaukee 53225-3701
(414) 464-2765

Veterans' Memorial, Clear Lake
Douglas Cahow, Pres.
P.O. Box 450, Clear Lake 54005
(612) 716-7478 teachdoug@aol.com
www.clvetsmemorial.com

Veterans of Amer., Vietnam
Mike Demske, Pres.
928 N. 16th St., Manitowoc 54220
(920) 684-1624 mikedemske@co.manitowoc.wi.us

Veterans of America, Wis. Paralyzed
Gus Sorenson, Govt. Rel. Dir.
2311 S. 108th St., West Allis 53227-1901
(414) 328-8910 gsorenson@wisconsinpva.org
www.wisconsinpva.org

Veterans of Foreign Wars (Auxiliary)
Diane Hogan, Secy.
8930 W. Highland Park, #120, Franklin 53132
(414) 425-6123 whogan4@wi.rr.com www.vfwofwi.com

Veterans of Foreign Wars (Dept. of Wis.)
Steve Lawrence, Adj/Qm
P.O. Box 1623, Madison 53701-1623
(608) 255-6655 wivfw@att.net
www.vfwwebcom.org/wisconsin

Veterans of World War I
Carla Kleinheinz
8088 136th St., Chippewa Falls 54729

Veterans, Catholic War (Wis. Dept.)
Ray Wozniak, Dept. Cmdr.
418 Forest Ave., Fond du Lac 54935
(920) 922-3636 rayperv@charter.net

Veterans, Catholic War, Aux. (Wis. Dept.)
Susan Jane Schwartz, Rep.
645 W. Scott St., #102, Fond du Lac 54937
(920) 251-0210

Veterans, Disabled Amer. (Dept. of Wis.)
Roger F. Dorman, Cmdr.
P.O. Box 1000, Poynette 53955

Veterans, Disabled Amer., Aux. (Dept. of Wis.)
Patty Davis, St. Adj
455 W. Sunnyview Dr., #104, Oak Creek 53154
(414) 232-6670 pdadjdava05@hotmail.com
www.davwi.org/dava.html

Veterans, Jewish War – Dept. of Wis.
Ronald Laux, Cmdr.
3628 N. 97th Place, Milwaukee 53222-2633
(414) 464-1386

Veterans, Natl. Assoc. for Black (Wis. Chap.)
William Sims, State Pres.
P.O. Box 11432, Milwaukee 53211-0432
(800) 842-4597 nabvets@nabvets.com

Veterans, Polish Legion of American
Margaret Wojcehowicz, Cmdr.
4902 7th Ave., Kenosha 53140-3343
(262) 657-0758

Veterans, Polish Legion of American, Ladies Aux. (Dept. of Wis.)
Michelle Ewald, St. Pres.
3441 Burrell St., Milwaukee 53207
(414) 708-1165 mewald4@wi.rr.com

Veterans, U.S. Submarine of WWII
Owen Williams, Secy./Treas.
309 Gibson St., Apt. N, Mukwonago 53149-1354
(262) 363-7330 barbss220@yahoo.com

Veterans, United Spanish War, Aux.
Peggy Schaefer, Pres.
7500 W. Dean Rd., Suite 100, Milwaukee 53223-2638
(414) 371-7423

Veterans, Wis. Vietnam
William F. Hustad, Pres.
W4489 Exeter Crossing Rd., Monticello 53570
(608) 527-2942 wfhus1@tds.net www.wivietnamvets.org

Veterinary Medical Assn., Wis.
Kim Brown Pokorny, Exec. Dir.
301 N. Broom St., Madison 53703
(608) 257-3665 wvma@wvma.org www.wvma.org

Water Recycling Assn., Wis. Onsite
Ann Gryphan, Assn. Manager
Essie Kammer Group
16 N. Carroll Street, Suite 900, Madison 53703
(800) 377-6672 agryphan@ekgmail.com www.wowra.com

Water Well Assoc., Inc., Wis.
Keith Meyers, Pres.
P.O. Box 565, Prairie du Chien 53821
(608) 875-2062 www.wisconsinwaterwell.com

WEA Credit Union
Mark Schrimpf, Pres.
P.O. Box 8003, Madison 53708-8003
(608) 274-9828 www.weacu.com

Wetlands Assn., Wis.
Becky Abel, Exec. Dir.
222 S. Hamilton St., Suite 1, Madison 53703
(608) 250-9971 becky.abel@wisconsinwetlands.org
www.wisconsinwetlands.org

Wildlife Society, Wis. Chapter
Harvey Halvorsen, Pres.
890 Spruce St., Baldwin 54002
(715) 684-2914 ext.113 harvey.halvorsen@wisconsin.gov
www.witws.org

Wine and Spirit Inst., Wis.
Eric Petersen, Exec. Dir.
22 N. Carroll St., Suite 200, Madison 53703
(608) 256-5223

Wisconsin AIRS, Inc.
Matricia Patterson, Pres.
6737 W. Washington St., West Allis 53214
(414) 302-6626 mpatterson@impactinc.org
www.wisconsinairs.org

Wisconsin Information Network (WIN)
Dottie Feder, Pres.
17305 Oak Park Row, Brookfield 53045
(262) 786-6200 dottiebrkf@sbcglobal.net

Wisconsin Intercollegiate Athletic Conference
Gary F. Karner, Commissioner
780 Regent St., Madison 53715
(608) 263-4402 gkarner@uwsa.edu www.wiacsports.com

Women Highway Safety Leaders, Inc., Wis. Assn. of
LaVerne Hoerig, National Rep.
1321 Clara Ave., Sheboygan 53081-5261
(920) 452-0905

Women Veterans, United
Vera Roddy, Pres.
2256 N. 60th St., Milwaukee 53208-1044
(414) 443-6453 vroddy@milwol.com

Women, Wis. National Organization for
Sheila Evanoff, Pres.
122 State St., Suite 403, Madison 53703
(608) 255-3911 admin@winow.org winow.org

Women's Network, Wis.
Administrator
122 State St., Suite 201B, Madison 53703-2500
(608) 255-9809 wiwomen@execpc.com
wiwomensnetwork.org

Woodland Owners Assn., Inc., Wis.
Nancy C. Bozek, Exec. Dir.
P.O. Box 285, Stevens Point 54481-0285
(715) 346-4798 wwoa@uwsp.edu
www.wisconsinwoodlands.org

Writers, Inc., Council for Wis.
Ted Hertel, Pres.
12249 N. Lake Shore Dr., Mequon 53092
(262) 243-6144 thertel@execpc.com
www.wisconsinwriters.org

WWOA Foundation, Inc. (Wisconsin Woodland Owners Assn)
Charles Haubrich, Pres.
3606 Dyer Lake Rd., Burlington 53105
(262) 539-3222 senocenter@senocenter.org
www.senocenter.org

Youth Development Initiative, Inc., Wis. Positive
Paul Vidas, Chair
919 S. Fidelis, Appleton 54915
(920) 731-0145

Source: This list was compiled from a questionnaire mailed to known statewide associations in Fall 2008.

NOTE

If you know of any additional PERMANENT, STATEWIDE, NONPROFIT associations – other than religious or fraternal – please send the information to the Blue Book Editor, Legislative Reference Bureau, P.O. Box 2037, Madison, Wisconsin 53701-2037. New associations which meet the stated criteria will be included in the next edition of the *Wisconsin Blue Book*.

HIGHLIGHTS OF COMMERCE AND INDUSTRY IN WISCONSIN

Manufacturing — Value added by manufacture in Wisconsin totaled $71.9 billion in 2006, an increase of $10.4 billion since 2002. The industry groups with the highest value added in 2006 were food, $8.6 billion; machinery, $8.2 billion; computer and electronic products, $7.3 billion; fabricated metal products, $7 billion; and paper, $6.8 billion.

Wisconsin ranked 10th among the states in value added by manufacture in 2006. Leaders in this category were California, $237.8 billion; Texas, $194.8 billion; and Ohio, $124.9 billion. The national total for value added was $2.286 trillion in 2006, an increase of $398 billion since 2002.

Energy Consumption — In 2007, Wisconsin's total energy use per capita reached 313.9 million Btu, about 10.7% higher than the usage rate in 1990 and more than 20.7% higher than in 1970. Seen from a national perspective, Wisconsin has gone from consuming energy at about 85% of the U.S. average in 1970 to about 1% more than the national average in 2007. Compared to various national averages, Wisconsin places a much heavier reliance on coal for its energy usage, but uses less petroleum, natural gas, nuclear power, and renewable energy. As energy consumption has increased, Wisconsin, which was an exporter of electricity in the 1970s, has increasingly become a net importer. Of the petroleum consumed in Wisconsin in 2007, the largest portion, about 83.5%, was used for transportation, followed by residential (6.7%), industrial (3.8%), and agricultural (3.7%) usage.

Gasoline Usage and Tax — In 2006, each automobile in Wisconsin was driven an average of 13,794 miles. This is 1,367 miles, or about 10.4%, more than the national average of 12,427 miles per year. Wisconsin automobiles averaged 22.5 miles per gallon of gasoline, nearly the same as the national average of 22.4 mpg. These mileage and fuel economy statistics pertain to standard passenger cars and do not include data for minivans, pickup trucks, or sport utility vehicles.

The state motor fuel tax was indexed annually prior to April 1, 2006. Since indexing began on April 1, 1985, the average annual adjustment in state tax was typically between 0.4 and 0.8 cents. After April 1, 2006, the state motor fuel tax can only be changed by legislative action. The current tax has not increased since then, when it was indexed to a total of 30.9 cents per gallon. The federal government's gasoline tax has also remained at 18.4 cents per gallon since that date, for a total of 49.3 cents per gallon in federal and state taxes.

Exports and Markets — In 2008, Wisconsin's leading exports were industrial machinery, including computers, $6.9 billion; electric machinery, $2.4 billion; and scientific and medical instruments, $2.1 billion. The leading market for Wisconsin exports in 2008 was Canada ($6.5 billion), followed by Mexico ($1.8 billion), and China ($1.2 billion). The total of all exports from Wisconsin to all markets in 2008 was $20.6 billion.

Financial Institutions — The number of banks operating in Wisconsin has decreased from the post-Depression high of 647 in 1982 to 254 in 2008. Over the same period, deposits increased from $22.5 billion to $99.9 billion. In 2008, Wisconsin's 35 state and federally chartered savings institutions had total deposits of $14.9 billion.

In 2008, Wisconsin had 250 state-chartered credit unions with over 2.1 million members and $18.2 billion in assets.

Corporations — In 2008, a total of 2,900 foreign corporations were licensed in Wisconsin, a 106% increase from 1,408 in 1990. Incorporation and licensing fees collected by the state in 2008 totaled $18.5 million.

The following tables present selected data. Consult footnoted sources for more detailed information about commerce and industry.

WISCONSIN USE OF PETROLEUM 1970 – 2007
(In Trillions of Btu)

Year	Total[1]	Transportation	Residential	Industrial	Agricultural	Commercial	Electric Utility
1970	457.7	271.2	107.9	21.1	18.1	31.5	7.9
1975	475.0	314.0	87.6	19.3	18.8	27.5	7.8
1980	454.4	329.2	71.2	13.2	21.4	14.6	4.8
1985	412.0	314.3	51.7	9.4	19.2	16.0	1.4
1990	444.4	347.7	42.6	22.1	16.0	15.0	1.0
1995	473.3	384.2	40.8	18.5	15.6	13.4	0.8
1996	488.6	393.2	43.5	20.9	15.9	14.2	0.9
1997	492.7	401.5	40.5	20.8	15.3	13.1	1.5
1998	491.4	411.3	33.9	19.1	14.5	10.8	1.8
1999	508.6	422.2	36.6	21.2	15.0	11.6	2.0
2000	507.2	419.8	38.8	20.5	14.4	12.1	1.6
2001	509.4	420.9	36.7	25.0	14.0	11.5	1.3
2002	519.2	433.7	38.0	19.2	14.4	11.8	2.1
2003	522.4	434.4	39.6	20.4	14.6	12.2	1.2
2004	532.1	442.8	38.3	23.5	14.3	11.7	1.5
2005	516.9	427.4	37.6	25.5	13.1	11.5	1.8
2006	514.2	425.8	35.1	24.0	17.4	10.6	1.4
2007[2]	515.9	430.6	34.7	19.5	19.1	10.3	1.7

Note: The numbers for 2000 to the present have been revised to reflect updated source data.

[1]Detail may not add to total due to rounding.

[2]Preliminary estimates.

Source: Wisconsin Office of Energy Independence, *Wisconsin Energy Statistics, 2008*, "Wisconsin Petroleum Use, by Economic Sector, 1970-2007", at: http://energyindependence.wi.gov/subcategory.asp?linksubcatid=2825&linkcatid=2847&linkid=1451&locid=160 [March 24, 2009].

WISCONSIN AND U.S. ENERGY CONSUMPTION BY RESOURCE 1970 – 2007
(In Millions of Btu per Capita)

Energy Resource	1970	1975	1980	1985	1990	1995	2000	2005	2006	2007[1]
Petroleum										
U.S.	127.0	133.0	128.0	113.0	114.0	112.0	116.0	115.9	113.4	111.6
Wisconsin	103.6	104.0	96.6	86.8	90.8	92.2	93.8	94.2	92.7	92.1
Wisconsin as % of U.S. per capita .	82.0%	78.0	75.0	77.0	80.0	82.3	80.9	81.3	81.8	82.5
Natural Gas										
U.S.	106.0	93.0	90.0	75.0	77.0	85.6	84.8	77.2	74.3	78.2
Wisconsin	74.7	80.0	73.2	64.3	62.6	74.2	73.1	74.4	67.2	70.7
Wisconsin as % of U.S. per capita .	70.0%	86.0	82.0	86.0	81.0	86.8	86.2	96.4	90.5	90.4
Coal										
U.S.	60.0	59.0	68.0	74.0	76.0	75.4	80.0	77.0	75.3	75.6
Wisconsin	80.4	57.4	69.0	78.9	84.1	90.3	96.8	96.0	92.6	92.1
Wisconsin as % of U.S. per capita .	123.4%	89.8	99.4	106.1	121.3	139.4	141.4	152.8	141.2	150.1
Nuclear										
U.S.	1.0	9.0	12.0	17.0	25.0	26.6	28.9	27.5	27.5	27.8
Wisconsin	0.4	24.3	22.7	25.0	24.8	23.1	23.2	14.8	23.8	23.4
Wisconsin as % of U.S. per capita .	33.0%	276.0	189.0	143.0	100.0	86.9	83.2	53.7	86.6	84.1
Renewable[2]										
U.S.	13.5	13.5	17.5	18.9	17.4	18.0	15.9	15.3	17.8	17.0
Wisconsin	7.4	7.9	12.3	13.5	13.1	13.4	12.7	14.3	14.2	14.2
Wisconsin as % of U.S. per capita .	54.7%	58.6	70.2	71.5	75.2	74.9	79.4	81.4	69.3	80.0
Electric Imports[3]										
Wisconsin	–6.4	–4.5	–1.4	–0.4	8.1	14.9	16.3	21.6	13.8	21.3
Total Resource Use										
U.S.	307.5	307.5	315.5	297.9	309.4	317.5	324.6	312.9	308.3	310.3
Wisconsin	260.1	269.2	272.4	268.1	283.5	308.1	315.9	315.4	304.3	313.9
Wisconsin as % of U.S. per capita .	84.6%	87.6	86.3	90.0	91.6	97.0	97.3	100.3	98.2	101.1

Note: Previous years' numbers have been updated to reflect revisions in source.

[1]Preliminary data.

[2]Includes wood, waste, alcohol, and other biomass energy; hydroelectric; geothermal; solar; and wind.

[3]Import of electricity reflects estimated resource energy used in other states or Canada to produce electricity imported into Wisconsin. This resource energy is estimated assuming 11,300 Btu per kWh imported into Wisconsin. A negative number indicates energy used in Wisconsin to produce electricity exported out of state.

Source: Wisconsin Office of Energy Independence, *Wisconsin Energy Statistics, 2008*, at: http://energyindependence.wi.gov/subcategory.asp?linksubcatid=2825&linkcatid=2847&linkid=1451&locid=160. Percentages calculated by Division of Energy.

AUTOMOBILE USAGE AND GASOLINE MILEAGE
Wisconsin and United States, 1980 – 2006

	Average Miles Driven Per Auto		Average Auto Miles Per Gallon of Gasoline	
Year	Wisconsin	U.S.	Wisconsin	U.S.
1980	9,782	8,813	16.1	16.0
1985	10,455	9,419	17.6	17.5
1990	11,659	10,504	20.3	30.2
1995	12,435	11,203	21.2	21.1
2000	13,293	11,976	22.0	21.9
2001	13,132	11,831	22.2	22.1
2002	13,544	12,202	22.1	22.0
2003	13,681	12,325	22.3	22.2
2004	13,831	12,460	22.6	22.5
2005	13,886	12,510	22.2	22.1
2006*	13,794	12,427	22.5	22.4

Note: This table does not include data for minivans, pickup trucks, or sport utility vehicles. Wisconsin and U.S. figures are derived from different sources and may not be strictly comparable.

*Preliminary data.

Source: Wisconsin Office of Energy Independence, *Wisconsin Energy Statistics 2008,* "Energy Efficiency Indices", at: http://energyindependence.wi.gov/subcategory.asp?linksubcatid=2825&linkcatid=2847&linkid=1451&locid=160.

WISCONSIN MOTOR VEHICLE FUEL TAX
1925 – 2009

	Gasoline Tax	Change	
Date of Change	Per Gallon[1]	Amount	Percent
April 1, 1925	2.0¢	2.0¢	—
April 1, 1931	4.0	2.0	100.0%
July 1, 1955	6.0	2.0	50.0
July 1, 1966	7.0	1.0	16.7
May 1, 1980	9.0	2.0	28.6
August 1, 1981	13.0	4.0	44.4
August 1, 1983	15.0	2.0	15.4
July 1, 1984	16.0	1.0	6.7
April 1, 1985[2]	16.5	0.5	3.1
April 1, 1986	17.5	1.0	6.1
April 1, 1987	18.0	0.5	2.9
August 1, 1987[3]	20.0	2.0	11.1
April 1, 1988	20.9	0.9	4.5
April 1, 1989	20.8	(0.1)	(0.5)
April 1, 1990	21.5	0.7	3.4
April 1, 1991	22.2	0.7	3.3
April 1, 1993[4]	23.2	1.0	4.5
April 1, 1994	23.1	(0.1)	(0.4)
April 1, 1995[5]	23.4	0.3	1.3
April 1, 1996[5]	23.7	0.3	1.3
April 1, 1997	23.8	0.1	0.4
November 1, 1997[6]	24.8	1.0	4.2
April 1, 2000	26.4	0.6	2.3
April 1, 2001	27.3	0.9	3.4
April 1, 2002	28.1	0.8	2.9
April 1, 2003	28.5	0.4	1.4
April 1, 2004	29.1	0.6	2.1
April 1, 2005	29.9	0.8	2.7
April 1, 2006[7]	30.9	1.0	3.3
April 1, 2007	30.9	0.0	0.0
April 1, 2008	30.9	0.0	0.0
April 1, 2009	30.9	0.0	0.0

[1]Tax rates for some alternate fuels are based on energy density. The rates effective April 1, 2005, are 21.9 cents for LPG (liquified petroleum gas) and 23.9 cents for CNG (compressed natural gas). E85 (85% fuel ethanol) is taxed at the same rate as gasoline.

[2]Beginning in April 1985, the state motor fuel tax was indexed (1983 Wisconsin Act 27) to take into account fuel consumption and inflation. By law, the tax increase or decrease is automatically calculated annually, based on the inflation rate from the National Highway Maintenance and Operations Cost Index and the percentage change in motor fuel consumption. (The federal gasoline tax has been 18.4 cents per gallon since October 1, 1993.)

[3]Statutory adjustment (1987 Wisconsin Act 27).

[4]1991 Wisconsin Act 119 postponed further fuel tax indexing until April 1, 1993.

[5]1993 Wisconsin Act 16 set aside the calculation of the consumption factor for 1995 and 1996 and provided fixed consumption factors for each year.

[6]1997 Wisconsin Act 27 increased the motor fuel tax rate and modified the indexing formula to take into account only the change to the cost index.

[7]2005 Wisconsin Act 85 ended annual motor fuel tax indexing as of April 1, 2006.

Sources: Session laws of the Wisconsin Legislature; Wisconsin Department of Revenue, *Motor Vehicle Fuel Tax Information,* April 2005 and previous years, and Motor Vehicle Fuel Tax FAQ, at: http://www.dor.state.wi.us/faqs/ise/mofuel.html [April 2009].

VALUE ADDED BY MANUFACTURING
By State, 2002 and 2006
(In Thousands)

State	Value Added 2002	Value Added 2006	2006 State Rank	State	Value Added 2002	Value Added 2006	2006 State Rank
Alabama	$28,641,670	$40,508,374	23	Montana	$1,673,980	$3,473,829	47
Alaska	1,283,586	1,591,723	50	Nebraska	11,469,004	15,442,084	35
Arizona	25,976,992	27,434,381	27	Nevada	4,654,748	7,461,470	42
Arkansas	21,965,415	27,227,220	28	New Hampshire	8,527,926	9,184,912	38
California	197,574,490	237,839,913	1	New Jersey	51,602,288	51,717,072	14
Colorado	17,798,062	20,827,682	32	New Mexico	5,990,566	9,556,167	37
Connecticut	27,673,466	32,714,281	26	New York	83,874,558	92,045,545	7
Delaware	5,063,899	8,861,847	39	North Carolina	87,355,207	106,995,548	6
District of Columbia	163,118	170,703	51	North Dakota	2,679,559	3,874,006	46
Florida	41,912,600	50,783,649	15	Ohio	113,243,351	124,940,967	3
Georgia	59,651,286	61,846,157	13	Oklahoma	17,005,404	23,845,537	30
Hawaii	1,217,728	2,049,067	49	Oregon	26,440,699	39,460,642	24
Idaho	7,440,111	7,241,625	43	Pennsylvania	92,319,195	108,927,106	4
ILLINOIS	91,825,126	107,367,302	5	Rhode Island	6,148,634	7,829,237	40
Indiana	78,023,817	90,202,790	8	South Carolina	38,611,266	38,048,632	25
IOWA	31,394,257	40,930,701	22	South Dakota	5,176,605	5,385,977	44
Kansas	21,347,336	26,021,290	29	Tennessee	49,811,004	62,013,449	12
Kentucky	34,075,367	42,967,301	21	Texas	124,462,554	194,846,489	2
Louisiana	28,404,879	64,354,626	11	Utah	12,158,925	17,667,739	34
Maine	7,122,274	7,746,705	41	Vermont	5,163,905	5,079,245	45
Maryland	19,265,920	22,807,831	31	Virginia	48,261,833	50,648,560	16
Massachusetts	44,508,791	48,427,263	19	Washington	35,398,551	48,861,784	18
MICHIGAN	97,575,395	88,161,261	9	West Virginia	7,983,845	10,467,886	36
MINNESOTA	39,610,449	48,943,285	17	WISCONSIN	61,501,462	71,864,921	10
Mississippi	16,126,629	20,697,706	33	Wyoming	1,430,036	3,417,945	48
Missouri	41,528,244	45,147,536	20	UNITED STATES	$1,887,792,650	$2,285,928,967	

Note: State amounts may not sum to United States total due to rounding.

Source: U.S. Census Bureau, *2002 Economic Census* and *Annual Survey of Manufactures, Geographic Area Statistics*, 2006. Rank calculated by Wisconsin Legislative Reference Bureau.

VALUE ADDED BY MANUFACTURING IN WISCONSIN
By Industry Group, 2002 – 2006
(In Thousands)

Industry Group	2002	2003	2004	2005	2006
Food	$7,856,243	$7,696,824	$8,295,053	$8,863,075	$8,646,704
Machinery	6,522,392	6,307,282	7,028,494	7,312,531	8,164,613
Computer and electronic products	2,549,497	2,541,931	3,354,889	5,631,022	7,255,171
Fabricated metal products	5,631,624	5,937,123	6,341,911	6,363,020	6,989,573
Paper	7,406,066	7,089,579	6,409,695	6,659,988	6,843,929
Transportation equipment	8,273,374	11,846,678	9,084,964	5,787,996	6,531,169
Chemicals	4,006,783	3,657,681	4,205,862	4,778,424	4,617,007
Electrical equipment, appliances, and components .	3,298,215	3,947,480	3,899,155	3,550,389	4,006,418
Printing and related support activities	3,007,917	3,115,369	3,040,360	3,187,552	3,416,351
Plastics and rubber products	2,958,241	2,822,125	2,845,889	3,227,285	3,283,212
Primary metal industries	2,212,845	2,179,272	2,426,148	2,394,146	2,535,149
Wood products	1,939,575	2,082,629	2,358,708	2,343,922	2,220,368
Miscellaneous manufacturing	1,845,029	1,997,699	1,820,029	1,869,395	2,011,878
Nonmetallic mineral products	1,456,767	1,634,848	1,685,123	1,838,041	1,907,558
Furniture and related products	1,262,327	1,307,566	1,358,089	1,380,842	1,442,194
Beverage and tobacco products	616,601	601,729	861,875	935,488	916,413
Textile mills	170,123	161,892	159,432	162,400	312,817
Textile products	102,224	95,195	124,650	150,257	159,648
Apparel	82,315	79,317	96,652	96,122	101,287
Leather and allied products	183,675	166,253	112,434	107,123	100,373
TOTAL*	$61,478,322	$65,354,715	$65,693,306	$66,964,978	$71,864,921

*Total may not add due to the exclusion in this table of certain manufacturing categories that have very little presence in the state.

Source: U.S. Census Bureau, *Annual Survey of Manufactures, Geographic Area Statistics*, 2006, and previous editions.

WISCONSIN EXPORTS
By Leading Export, 2004 – 2008 (In Thousands)

Export*	2008	2007	2006	2005	2004
Industrial machinery	$6,864,229	$6,152,767	$5,520,286	$5,137,562	$4,462,483
Electrical machinery	2,425,965	2,745,656	2,597,357	1,830,517	1,288,475
Scientific and medical instruments . . .	2,098,800	2,062,089	2,063,929	2,000,260	1,633,554
Vehicles (not including railway)	1,990,879	1,738,268	1,467,583	1,003,120	967,982
Paper and paperboard	793,484	831,604	799,986	781,939	686,630
Plastic	670,406	612,632	569,465	524,400	496,808
Iron and steel products	372,792	293,267	241,854	225,021	171,304
Books and newspapers	270,734	261,307	253,952	214,597	169,694
Furniture and bedding	267,534	218,921	216,665	163,892	134,065
Cereals	230,370	502,526	258,686	250,420	216,597
Aircraft and spacecraft	225,076	129,327	161,400	105,641	83,706
Dairy, eggs, honey, etc.	212,707	195,851	84,731	76,561	42,715
Miscellaneous chemical products	206,515	165,986	142,858	142,080	126,980
Ores, slag, and ash	182,436	57,189	50,250	23,354	33,743
Baking related	173,507	148,102	118,771	117,568	98,654
Wood	168,226	164,517	132,238	130,819	102,720
Miscellaneous food	162,266	117,607	93,489	92,048	84,060
Iron and steel	145,918	72,828	74,959	76,906	58,934
Beverages	140,499	111,916	87,344	103,502	77,956
Pharmaceutical products	124,052	83,807	80,967	74,547	52,795
Total of Leading Exports	$17,726,396	$16,666,167	$15,016,771	$13,074,756	$10,989,854
Total of All Exports	$20,552,773	$19,185,670	$17,169,113	$14,923,487	$12,706,343

*Export categories based on U.S. Census Bureau, Foreign Trade Division, 2004 Schedule B commodity codes.

Source: Wisconsin Department of Commerce, Wisconsin Export Data by Product, at:
    http://commerce.wi.gov/IE/docs/IE-WIExportsByProduct.xls [March 31, 2009].

WISCONSIN EXPORTS
By Leading Market, 2004 – 2008 (In Thousands)

Market	2008	2007	2006	2005	2004
Canada	$6,497,735	$5,845,788	$5,446,925	$5,237,728	$4,856,674
Mexico	1,761,700	1,890,879	1,854,465	1,333,043	1,064,414
China	1,231,218	1,178,516	870,287	673,767	583,303
Germany	790,365	660,820	582,727	549,555	460,588
Japan	724,430	655,118	738,809	695,965	624,627
United Kingdom	683,135	722,780	686,452	642,836	517,304
Australia	583,454	563,687	466,617	424,739	325,525
Saudi Arabia	556,285	475,566	505,112	167,531	91,955
France	517,860	441,932	467,838	414,631	364,565
Brazil	420,055	326,535	248,450	246,424	158,117
Belgium	414,084	422,929	383,760	375,618	330,803
Netherlands	365,876	388,160	339,797	263,956	228,291
Korean Republic	344,051	344,593	342,519	307,939	273,018
Chile	307,705	188,210	120,797	120,825	147,010
Italy	307,343	329,252	292,924	305,366	229,446
Hong Kong	278,439	312,773	288,255	214,638	193,697
United Arab Emirates	262,734	205,014	120,865	86,569	54,772
Taiwan	249,720	219,040	259,508	198,450	188,689
Thailand	247,802	187,886	75,910	66,066	61,974
India	241,086	217,589	168,582	138,415	115,344
Total of Leading Markets	$16,785,077	$15,577,075	$14,260,599	$12,464,061	$10,870,116
Total of All Markets*	$20,552,773	$19,185,670	$17,169,113	$14,923,487	$12,706,343

*Includes markets not individually identified in this table.

Source: Wisconsin Department of Commerce, Wisconsin Export Data by Destination, at:
    http://commerce.wi.gov/IE/docs/IE-WIExportsByCountry.xls [March 31, 2009].

BASIC DATA ON WISCONSIN CORPORATIONS
1905 – 2008

	Transactions[1]			Fees			
	Domestic						
	Articles of	Amdts. and	Foreign	Fees for	Fees for	Other	
	Incorporation	Restated	Corporations	Articles of	Foreign	Corporation	Total Fees
Year[2]	Filed[3]	Articles	Licensed[3]	Incorporation	Corporation[4]	Fees[5]	Collected
Calendar							
1905	98	—	95	—	—	—	$69,312
1915	1,043	382	112	$28,287	$3,743	$89,695	121,725
1925	1,438	896	198	57,614	11,139	78,153	146,906
1935	1,272	439	176	30,839	8,956	41,631	81,426
1945	1,120	680	131	31,823	4,826	113,963	150,612
1955	2,537	874	287	89,951	31,146	175,973	297,070
1965	4,063	1,320	401	344,906	120,506	193,844	659,256
Fiscal							
1975	5,976	1,483	663	361,013	386,061	594,498	1,341,572
1980	7,334	1,978	753	373,220	753,461	788,204	1,914,885
1985	7,605	2,359	1,018	485,835	1,142,129	1,371,476	2,999,440
1990	8,387	2,525	1,408	546,550	2,368,900	1,491,104	4,406,554
1995	10,031	2,716	1,507	829,555	4,208,178	2,538,521	7,576,254
1996	10,196	2,592	1,476	843,645	3,707,643	2,735,822	7,287,110
1997	14,599	2,616	1,950	1,446,285	3,928,923	3,137,473	8,512,681
1998	15,352	2,761	2,218	1,581,395	4,621,261	3,644,146	9,846,802
1999	18,641	3,082	2,358	1,943,935	4,830,592	3,524,182	10,298,709
2000	21,133	3,088	2,464	2,265,455	6,403,447	3,548,264	12,217,166
2001	20,461	3,064	2,394	2,631,375	6,901,290	3,257,622	12,790,287
2002	22,734	3,145	2,314	2,735,390	6,330,109	3,408,267	12,473,766
2003	26,629	3,057	2,436	3,223,455	7,379,300	5,262,635	15,865,390
2004	31,440	3,644	2,566	3,820,735	6,253,800	6,406,280	16,480,815
2005	33,589	3,595	2,787	4,092,782	6,043,400	5,509,178	15,645,000
2006	33,829	3,711	3,010	4,084,800	8,693,800	4,149,400	16,928,000
2007	32,555	3,596	3,067	1,525,538	5,406,350	6,208,548	17,113,116
2008	31,943	3,401	2,900	1,488,312	5,871,084	7,264,855	18,534,351

[1]Includes only those corporate entities for which the reporting agency is the office of record.

[2]Since 1975, data is computed on a fiscal year basis, ending June 30 of year shown.

[3]Beginning in 1997, includes limited liability companies.

[4]Since 1975, totals include fees for foreign corporation annual reports.

[5]Includes fees for filing annual reports and corporation charter documents other than articles of incorporation.

Sources: Wisconsin Department of Financial Institutions, departmental data for 1997-2008, April 2009; previous data from the Office of the Wisconsin Secretary of State.

FINANCIAL INSTITUTIONS OPERATING IN WISCONSIN
Number and Deposits, 1900 – 2008

Year*	Number	Total Deposits (in thousands)	Year*	Number	Total Deposits (in thousands)
1900	349	$124,892	1995	449	$59,918,000
1910	630	268,766	2000	365	75,379,000
1920	976	767,534	2001	337	78,567,000
1930	936	935,006	2002	328	83,602,000
1940	574	993,155	2003	319	95,909,000
1950	556	2,965,580	2004	322	96,111,000
1960	561	4,385,838	2005	318	100,643,000
1970	602	8,750,823	2006	320	103,511,000
1980	634	24,763,910	2007	316	109,734,000
1990	504	37,588,879	2008	307	114,838,000

*Beginning in 1994, data includes federal charter savings associations and state-chartered savings associations, supervised by the U.S. Office of Thrift Supervision, and institutions operating in Wisconsin but headquartered outside the state. Deposits for these years are rounded to nearest thousands of dollars.

Sources: **1950 and earlier:** Board of Governors of the Federal Reserve System, *All-Bank Statistics, U.S.,* 1959; **1960:** Wisconsin Commissioner of Banks, agency data, December 1965; **1970:** Federal Deposit Insurance Corporation, *Assets and Liabilities – Commercial and Mutual Savings Banks,* June 1971; **1980:** Federal Deposit Insurance Corporation, corporate data; **1981-93:** Federal Deposit Insurance Corporation, *Data Book: Operating Banks and Branches,* Book 3, June 30, 1993, and previous issues; **1994 to date:** *Federal Deposit Insurance Corporation, Summary of Deposits,* "State Totals by Charter Class for All Institution Deposits, Deposits of All FDIC-Insured Institutions Operating in Wisconsin", June 30, 2008, and previous issues.

FDIC-INSURED INSTITUTIONS OPERATING IN WISCONSIN
By County, June 30, 2008

County	Commercial Banks			Savings Institutions		
	Number of		Deposits	Number of		Deposits
	Institutions	Offices	(in millions)	Institutions	Offices	(in millions)
Adams	5	6	$194	1	1	$1
Ashland	4	9	271	0	0	0
Barron	10	20	721	3	4	119
Bayfield	6	11	193	0	0	0
Brown	18	75	5,176	4	20	520
Buffalo	4	10	266	1	1	10
Burnett	3	8	203	0	0	0
Calumet	8	14	499	2	3	58
Chippewa	10	20	575	3	8	183
Clark	8	16	414	2	3	64
Columbia	11	27	887	2	2	86
Crawford	6	11	343	1	1	61
Dane	37	157	9,119	7	40	2,871
Dodge	17	35	946	5	6	190
Door	4	15	621	2	4	108
Douglas	7	12	564	1	3	54
Dunn	8	23	368	2	3	43
Eau Claire	12	29	1,117	3	9	298
Florence	2	5	74	0	0	0
Fond du Lac	13	33	1,369	4	5	270
Forest	2	6	131	0	0	0
Grant	13	37	1,031	1	3	116
Green	11	17	773	1	2	81
Green Lake	9	12	470	2	2	45
Iowa	7	13	326	1	1	44
Iron	1	2	72	0	0	0
Jackson	3	9	271	1	1	1
Jefferson	14	30	1,031	0	0	0
Juneau	7	15	372	0	0	0
Kenosha	12	40	1,947	3	4	30
Kewaunee	5	14	367	0	0	0
La Crosse	14	43	1,767	0	0	0
Lafayette	9	15	324	0	0	0
Langlade	5	6	157	0	0	0
Lincoln	5	10	315	2	2	94
Manitowoc	12	27	1,436	1	1	28
Marathon	21	57	2,336	3	6	181
Marinette	11	21	650	1	4	104
Marquette	6	9	205	0	0	0
Milwaukee	22	212	27,298	16	90	3,815
Monroe	11	18	640	0	0	0
Oconto	7	17	333	0	0	0
Oneida	9	18	716	0	0	0
Outagamie	22	50	2,201	6	18	697
Ozaukee	11	36	1,824	3	9	184
Pepin	3	3	201	0	0	0
Pierce	7	14	451	2	2	50
Polk	8	14	590	2	7	95
Portage	13	24	1,003	1	2	156
Price	5	8	150	1	1	83
Racine	13	57	3,089	5	14	286
Richland	7	8	236	1	1	33
Rock	16	43	1,731	3	5	204
Rusk	5	8	182	1	1	28
St. Croix	15	29	834	2	5	145
Sauk	14	34	1,335	1	1	1
Sawyer	6	10	421	1	1	26
Shawano	10	18	485	1	1	39
Sheboygan	13	40	1,647	3	7	60
Taylor	4	8	311	1	1	129
Trempealeau	10	19	520	0	0	0
Vernon	9	17	392	1	1	22
Vilas	10	15	420	0	0	0
Walworth	16	42	1,619	2	3	58
Washburn	5	9	197	1	1	21
Washington	13	34	1,646	6	27	702
Waukesha	27	152	7,546	13	51	1,640
Waupaca	9	26	967	1	1	28
Waushara	11	16	286	1	1	26
Winnebago	13	34	1,524	4	10	305
Wood	12	30	1,222	4	7	426
TOTAL*	268	1,982	$99,920	39	407	$14,918

*Total number of institutions is an unduplicated total for institutions operating in more than one county. Deposit figures do not add to state totals due to rounding.

Note: Menominee County did not report separately.

Source: Federal Deposit Insurance Corporation, "Deposits of all FDIC-Insured Institutions Operating in Wisconsin: State Totals by County, as of June 30, 2008", at: http://www2.fdic.gov/sod/SODSummary2.asp [April 24, 2009].

WISCONSIN FINANCIAL INSTITUTIONS
June 30, 2008

Type of Institution or Branch	Insured Commercial Banks and Trust Companies				Insured Savings Institutions		
			State Charter			Federal	State
		National	Federal Reserve System			Federal	State
	Total	Charter	Member	Nonmember	Total	Charter	Charter
Headquartered in state	254	37	27	190	35	19	16
Headquartered outside of state. . . .	14	7	2	5	4	4	0
Total institutions	268	44	29	195	39	23	16
Total offices	1,982	787	405	790	407	335	72
Total deposits (in millions)	$99,920	$40,945	$31,076	$27,900	$14,918	$11,729	$3,189

Source: Federal Deposit Insurance Corporation, Summary of Deposits, June 30, 2008, "Individual State Tables – Charter Class", at: http://www2.fdic.gov/sod/sodSummary.asp?barItem=3 [June 24, 2009].

WISCONSIN STATE-CHARTERED CREDIT UNIONS
Number, Members, and Assets
1930 – 2008

Year	Credit Unions	Membership		Assets	
		Total Members	Annual % Change	Total Assets (in millions)	Annual % Change
1930	22	4,659	—	$0.5	—
1935	383	57,847	—	2.9	—
1940	592	153,849	—	11.2	—
1945	536	144,524	—	19.1	—
1950	542	193,296	—	42.9	—
1955	696	292,552	—	120.6	—
1960	733	363,444	—	206.4	—
1965	781	493,399	—	346.6	—
1970	766	628,543	—	480.4	—
1975	673	805,123	—	875.5	—
1980	618	1,060,292	—	1,403.8	—
1985	550	1,261,407	—	2,831.4	—
1990	440	1,485,109	4.3%	4,148.8	8.6%
1991	427	1,596,547	7.5	4,495.6	8.4
1992	418	1,608,412	0.7	4,991.5	11.0
1993	406	1,646,847	2.4	5,360.1	7.4
1994	394	1,714,182	4.1	5,755.1	7.4
1995	384	1,744,696	1.8	6,179.2	7.4
1996	375	1,773,611	1.7	6,569.9	6.3
1997	369	1,803,529	1.7	7,175.4	9.2
1998	358	1,834,944	1.7	8,192.4	14.2
1999	350	1,887,429	2.9	8,737.3	6.7
2000	340	1,918,729	1.7	9,425.9	7.9
2001	326	1,883,387	-1.8	10,439.4	10.8
2002	308	1,937,867	2.9	11,665.6	11.7
2003	298	1,966,929	1.5	12,772.5	9.5
2004	287	1,992,238	1.3	13,684.4	7.1
2005	280	2,047,031	2.8	14,805.3	8.2
2006	267	2,086,700	1.9	15,656.2	5.7
2007	260	2,083,319	-0.2	16,543.3	5.7
2008	250	2,118,505	1.7	18,182.3	9.9

Note: Annual percentage increase not available for years preceding 1990.

Source: Wisconsin Department of Financial Institutions, Office of Credit Unions, *Year-End 2008 Bulletin*, at: http://www.wdfi.org/_resources/indexed/site/fi/cu/EndOfYear2007CUBulletin.pdf [April 2009] and previous editions. Percentages calculated by Wisconsin Legislative Reference Bureau.

HIGHLIGHTS OF CONSERVATION AND RECREATION IN WISCONSIN

Recreation — Wisconsin's recreational assets include more than 14,000 lakes, 2,000 miles of trout streams, almost 6,000 state-owned campsites, and 6 million acres of hunting land. Wisconsin currently operates 48 state parks, 13 state forests, and 5 recreation areas. The parks range in size from Devil's Lake with 18,275 acres to Lakeshore with 22 acres. The largest single state recreational facility is the Northern Highland-American Legion Forest with 223,283 acres. A total of 36 state trails are open to the public.

Visitors to Wisconsin's state parks, forests, trails, and recreation areas numbered nearly 13.5 million in 2008.

Hunting and fishing are major recreational activities. Recently, approximately 33.6 million fish and 3.5 million game animals of various species have been taken annually. Over 649,000 resident annual fishing licenses were sold in 2007. In addition, resident husband and wife fishing licenses totaled over 229,000, and nonresident annual and family annual fishing licenses totaled approximately 157,000. Over 555,000 boats were registered in 2007.

Land Acquisition — Three land acquisition programs have been established to acquire land for recreational purposes. From fiscal year 1990, when the legislature created the current Warren Knowles-Gaylord Nelson Stewardship Program, through fiscal year 1999, the stewardship fund has spent over $124 million to acquire an additional 167,000 acres. From fiscal year 2000 through 2009, the Stewardship 2000 Fund acquired over 292,000 acres and spent over $328 million.

Natural Resources Funding and Expenditures — The Department of Natural Resources spent almost $565 million on conservation and recreation programs in fiscal year 2007-08, up from $544 million in fiscal year 2006-07. Funding comes from the state's general fund and segregated funds, including registration and licensing fees, park stickers, and federal aids.

The following tables present selected data. Consult footnoted sources for more detailed information about conservation and recreation.

FISH AND GAME HARVESTED AND STOCKED

Catch and Harvest Data for Wisconsin Fish, 2007-2008[1]

	Catch	Harvest		Harvest
All fish species	88,000,000	33,000,000		
Great Lakes trout (2007)	—	119,539		
Great Lakes salmon (2007)	—	525,820		

Harvest Estimate, 2007-2008

Wild turkey	—	64,438	Raccoon	224,357
Pheasant[2]	—	360,207	Red fox	15,158
Ruffed grouse[2]	—	493,637	Gray fox	6,957
Gray partridge[2]	—	1,091	Coyotes	54,181
Bobwhite quail[2]	—	1,545	Deer (with guns)	402,563
Woodcock[2]	—	48,027	Deer (with bows)	116,010
Squirrels[2]	—	371,750	Bear	2,797
Cottontail rabbit[2]	—	275,858	Ducks[3]	431,200
Snowshoe hare[2]	—	30,540	Canada geese	81,852
Doves[3]	—	202,000		

Furbearer Harvest, 2007-2008

Muskrats	—	255,499	Bobcat	477
Mink	—	19,243	Opossum	25,066
Beaver	—	29,924	Skunk	8,179
River otter	—	990	Fisher	1,385
Total value of all pelts purchased by licensed Wisconsin fur buyers				$6,624,364

Fish and Wildlife Stocked

Game farm pheasants released (2007)	56,730
Warmwater fish, produced and distributed (2007-08)	2,145,383
Warmwater fish fry, produced and distributed (2007-08)	
Coldwater fish (2007-08)	5,575,357

[1]Harvest is the actual number of fish caught and kept; catch is the estimate of all fish caught, including those released. Estimated by angler mail survey.

[2]Estimates based on hunter surveys.

[3]Harvest data from U.S. Fish and Wildlife Service, Division of Migratory Bird Management.

Source: Wisconsin Department of Natural Resources, departmental data, April 2009.

FISH AND GAME LICENSES AND RECREATION PERMITS
Number Issued, 2002 – 2007

	2002	2003	2004	2005	2006	2007
Boats registered	619,124	610,800	602,515	628,119	626,740	555,232
Snowmobiles registered	209,128	220,652	221,419	213,787	178,195	219,688
All terrain vehicles registered	176,146	200,515	215,417	227,546	272,773	277,113
Annual park admission stickers for motor vehicles	185,371	184,806	NA	NA	NA	NA
Daily park admission for motor vehicles	168,076	168,915	NA	NA	NA	NA
Deer hunting and license tags including nonresident	462,022	491,403	493,344	487,906	505,620	508,854
Small game hunting license tags including nonresident	132,000	139,109	125,600	117,967	127,216	137,012
Resident annual fishing licenses*	637,288	657,997	649,986	652,642	638,171	649,662
Resident husband and wife fishing licenses	211,835	215,260	209,980	213,218	221,925	229,513
Nonresident annual fishing licenses	106,324	107,617	101,983	101,400	94,810	92,084
Nonresident family annual fishing licenses	63,726	63,286	61,681	63,555	61,998	64,825
15-day nonresident family fishing licenses	33,049	32,158	29,811	32,983	16,414	18,270
15-day nonresident fishing licenses	42,061	40,245	31,296	31,733	33,232	35,197
4-day nonresident fishing licenses	118,551	118,419	128,722	114,942	109,855	98,329
Resident sports licenses	75,123	72,541	82,144	81,701	75,811	72,057
Nonresident sports licenses	277	313	4,502	2,451	3,400	3,748
2-day Great Lakes fishing licenses	31,021	31,667	29,035	31,257	32,158	34,278
Resident archer's licenses	138,011	158,650	170,298	173,127	189,331	193,339
Nonresident archer's licenses	6,691	7,449	7,482	7,521	8,285	8,797
Guide licenses (residents only)	1,511	1,492	1,549	1,482	1,457	1,452
Conservation patron licenses	81,896	81,074	74,430	69,859	59,914	56,559
Nonresident patron licenses	38	38	392	551	864	957

NA: not available from licensing data; see Wisconsin State Forest, Parks, Trails, and Recreation Areas table for visitor numbers.

*Includes senior and junior fishing licenses.

Source: Wisconsin Department of Natural Resources, departmental data, April 2009.

Wisconsin State Parks, Forests, and Trails

▲ State Parks & Recreation Areas

■ State Forests

— State Trails

★ Ice Age National Scientific Reserve Unit

⎯ Ice Age National and State Scenic Trail

• • • • North Country National Scenic and State Trail

▲ Park/Forest under development
Please see our website for development and progress updates.

Source: Wisconsin Department of Natural Resources, April 2009.

WISCONSIN STATE PARKS, TRAILS, AND RECREATION AREAS

Name	Location	Dominant Features	Established	Acres	Number of Visitors[1]				
					1995	2000	2006	2007	2008
NORTHERN FORESTS[2]									
Black River	SE of Black River Falls US 12, STH 27 & 54	Abundance of wildlife and scenery	1957	67,070	238,311	195,579	3,488	3,424	3,536
Brule River	S of Brule, STH 27	Excellent fishing and canoeing	1907	40,882	141,113	125,339	1,801	1,916	2,003
Flambeau River	23 mi. W of Phillips CTH W	Outstanding canoeing river	1931	90,147	154,685	162,665	1,470	1,129	1,165
Governor Knowles	1 mi. W of Grantsburg STH 70	River scenery	1970	19,753	73,755	89,714	578	758	710
Northern Highland- American Legion	SE Iron, WC Vilas, NC Oneida Counties	Scenic lakes and forests	1925	223,283	1,796,734	2,050,151	47,163	46,849	49,414
Peshtigo River	.5 mi. W of Crivitz, N of CTH W	Diverse natural communities and rivers	2001	9,200	NA	NA	NA	1,460	1,592
TOTAL				450,335	2,404,598	2,623,448	54,500	55,536	58,420
SOUTHERN FORESTS									
Havenwoods	Milwaukee, N. Hopkins St.	A nature preserve in the city	1978	237	60,461	49,581	51,829	49,230	38,561
Kettle Moraine North	N of Kewaskum, STH 45, 23 & 67	Glacial formations	1936	29,498	921,634	620,903	664,455	590,737	578,436
Kettle Moraine South	Whitewater US 12, STH 59/67	Glacial topography	1936	21,241	1,225,384	1,230,519	893,991	985,908	1,025,840
Lapham Peak	S of Delafield, CTH C	Highest point in county, glacial formations	1985	1,006	200,033	250,681	256,600	313,304	332,416
Loew Lake	10 mi. W of Menomonee Falls, CTH Q	Kettle lake, glacial valley	1987	1,086	NA	NA	NA	NA	NA
Pike Lake	2 mi. E of Hartford STH 60	Glacial lake	1960	678	154,890	156,325	164,659	164,496	161,737
Point Beach	4 mi. N of Two Rivers STH 42	Sand beach, natural history	1938	2,903	360,119	407,066	383,350	388,045	378,850
TOTAL				56,648	2,922,521	2,715,075	2,414,884	2,491,720	2,515,840
STATE PARKS									
Amnicon Falls	10 mi. SE of Superior US 2	Scenic waterfalls, covered bridge	1961	825	74,389	84,773	81,787	83,516	84,022
Aztalan	4 mi. E of Lake Mills CTH Q	Ancient Native American village	1947	172	49,150	60,565	69,121	50,136	48,535
Belmont Mound[3]	2 mi. N of Belmont CTH G & B	Wide vista from hilltop tower	1961	254	7,500	8,484	31,045	NA	NA
Big Bay	On Madeline Island in Lake Superior	Sand beach, natural history	1963	2,418	125,772	108,365	128,384	140,048	138,910
Big Foot Beach	1 mi. S of Lake Geneva STH 12 & 120	A beach park	1949	271	161,457	177,963	180,911	161,355	176,060
Blue Mound	1 mi. NW of Blue Mounds STH 18 & 151	Highest point in southern Wisconsin	1959	1,153	157,349	154,128	355,149	145,579	150,260
Brunet Island	1 mi. Northwest of Cornell	River island park	1936	1,225	244,720	178,962	152,622	154,998	151,355
Buckhorn	13 mi. N of Mauston STH 58, CTH G	River scenery	1971	2,637	84,549	107,590	125,942	149,838	130,262
Capital Springs	.5 mi. SE of Madison on Lake Farm Rd.	Shoreline and trails	2000	323	NA	NA	NA	165,938	125,936
Copper Culture[3]	.5 mi. W of Oconto on N. River Rd.	Archaeological site	1959	42	NA	NA	NA	NA	NA
Copper Falls	4 mi. N of Mellen STH 13 & 169	River gorge, waterfalls	1929	2,716	140,773	125,080	129,119	107,983	90,667
Council Grounds	1 mi. NW of Merrill STH 107	River scenery	1938	509	205,806	213,411	224,504	223,011	223,877
Devil's Lake	3 mi. S of Baraboo STH 123	Bluffs, mountain scenery	1911	18,275	1,117,887	1,317,275	1,128,070	1,170,532	923,640
Governor Dodge	3 mi. N of Dodgeville STH 23	Rocky promontories	1948	5,149	417,934	407,629	437,989	339,424	519,647
Governor Nelson	5 mi. E of Middleton CTH M	Wooded lakeshore, effigy mounds	1975	422	183,830	218,015	163,145	183,122	175,335
Governor Thompson	25 miles northwest of Crivitz	Lakeshore and trout streams	2000	2,450	NA	NA	50,494	43,688	60,558
Harrington Beach	10 mi. N of Port Washington 143, CTH D	Lake Michigan shoreline	1966	637	115,064	114,912	124,258	126,963	137,000
Hartman Creek	6 mi. W of Waupaca STH 54	Lake scenery, pine plantation	1962	1,417	224,388	239,539	156,317	148,688	135,108
Heritage Hill[3]	S Green Bay STH 57	Restored early American buildings	1973	55	NA	36,528	NA	NA	NA
High Cliff	9 mi. E of Menasha STH 114	Wooded bluffs, Lake Winnebago	1954	1,145	687,253	820,560	883,900	898,900	2,052,400
Interstate	St. Croix Falls US 8	River gorge, rocky bluffs, glacial features	1900	1,330	320,649	354,715	279,272	267,469	261,757
Kinnickinnic	6 mi. W of River Falls CTH F	River scenery	1972	1,239	211,800	207,900	213,600	213,600	203,600
Kohler-Andrae	4 mi. S of Sheboygan STH 141	Lake Michigan sand dunes	1928	1,848	330,471	378,483	395,083	385,339	355,160
Lake Kegonsa	3 mi. N of Stoughton CTH N	Prairie and lakeshore	1962	343	180,218	187,782	156,958	175,164	158,780

WISCONSIN STATE PARKS, TRAILS, AND RECREATION AREAS—Continued

Name	Location	Dominant Features	Established	Acres	Number of Visitors[1]				
					1995	2000	2006	2007	2008
Lake Wissota	5 mi. NE of Chippewa Falls STH 29, CTH K & O	Lake scenery	1962	1,062	118,707	108,222	NA	103,005	104,531
Lakeshore	Milwaukee, N. Harbor Dr.	Urban oasis, marina, Lake Michigan	1998	22	NA	NA	NA	NA	157,050
Merrick	1 mi. N of fountain City STH 35	Mississippi River, birds	1932	322	81,024	101,609	82,215	85,162	84,169
Mill Bluff	4 mi. W of Camp Douglas US 12/16	Rocky bluffs	1936	1,337	30,350	49,541	56,590	55,898	52,375
Mirror Lake	1 mi. S of Lake Delton	Lake scenery	1962	2,200	260,113	341,452	316,788	337,923	356,154
Natural Bridge	15 mi. NW of Sauk City CTH C	Natural rock bridge	1972	530	27,314	57,454	27,016	26,024	3,837
Nelson Dewey	1 mi. N of Cassville CTH VV	Home of first governor, river bluffs	1935	756	43,722	51,456	28,691	53,313	22,519
New Glarus Woods	1 mi. S of New Glarus STH 69 & CTH NN	Wooded valleys, natural oak woods	1934	415	27,711	48,276	84,983	81,864	66,646
Newport	2 mi. SE of Gills Rock, STH 42	Lake scenery, forests	1964	2,373	204,466	177,194	128,432	138,727	129,868
Pattison	10 mi. S of Superior STH 35	Highest waterfall in Wisconsin	1920	1,436	140,583	167,221	192,444	193,569	192,657
Peninsula	N of Fish Creek STH 42	Green Bay, limestone bluffs	1910	3,777	944,655	1,105,651	1,003,371	1,000,091	1,002,948
Perrot	1 mi. N of Trempealeau STH 35	River scenery, wooded bluffs	1918	1,270	309,449	208,537	285,280	240,341	220,761
Potawatomi	2 mi. NW of Sturgeon Bay STH 42	Limestone bluffs	1928	1,221	233,139	228,909	198,787	201,673	193,559
Rib Mountain	4 mi. SW of Wausau CTH N	State's 3rd highest place, spectacular views	1927	1,503	214,205	208,670	229,349	239,590	256,160
Roche-A-Cri	2 mi. NW of Friendship STH 13	Woodlands, 300-foot-high rock outcropping	1948	492	93,569	72,232	48,361	98,025	93,313
Rock Island	Ferry (no vehicles) from Washington Island	Island scenery, historic stone buildings	1965	912	16,201	16,998	16,179	16,777	17,845
Rocky Arbor	1 mi. NW of Wisconsin Dells US 12	Rocky ledges, wooded valleys	1932	244	66,117	57,545	86,394	72,652	50,245
Straight Lake	5 mi. NE of Luck via SH 35 & 270th Ave.	Wooded wilderness and lake	2002	NA	NA	NA	NA	NA	NA
Tower Hill	3 mi. S of Spring Green STH 23 & CTH C	Historic shot tower, panoramic views	1922	77	61,492	51,031	23,898	21,391	12,525
Whitefish Dunes	10 mi. NE of Sturgeon Bay STH 57	Lake Michigan, sand dunes	1967	864	264,523	189,778	159,782	167,161	171,784
Wildcat Mountain	3 mi. S of Ontario STH 33	Bluff lands, Kickapoo River	1948	3,628	150,200	173,100	187,061	189,673	177,644
Willow River	NE of Hudson CTH A	River scenery, waterfalls, lake	1967	2,854	231,118	354,470	338,972	345,939	353,200
Wyalusing	12 mi. S of Prairie du Chien US 18 & CTH C & X	Junction of Wisconsin & Mississippi rivers	1917	2,628	184,116	173,439	164,639	171,551	168,731
Yellowstone Lake	7 mi. NW of Argyle CTH N	Lake scenery, wooded valleys	1970	890	228,551	260,981	239,131	273,924	235,380
TOTAL				77,665	8,972,284	9,706,425	9,455,483	9,449,564	10,426,770

STATE TRAILS[2]

Name	Location	Dominant Features	Established	Acres	1995	2000	2006	2007	2008
"400"	Reedsburg STH 23/33 to Elroy STH 80/82	22 miles of trail, bluffs	1988	410	24,494	35,125	41,925	44,775	34,205
Ahnapee[3]	Sturgeon Bay STH 42/57 to E of Luxemburg CTH A	18.6-mile trail, river scenery	1970	571	NA	NA	NA	NA	NA
Badger	Madison to Freeport, IL, STH 69	40 miles of trail, former railroad grade	2000	—	—	—	NA	NA	NA
Bearskin-Hiawatha	Minocqua to CH K & Heatford Jct. to Tomahawk	24.6 miles of trail, forests	1973	516	39,835	115,200	142,050	154,550	176,653
Buffalo River	Fairchild to Mondovi, US 10	36.4 miles of trail, rural scenery	1976	454	28,960	39,280	38,307	38,307	38,307
Capital City[3]	Madison, Dempsey Rd. to US 18/151 Frontage Rd.	Asphalt path through woods, fields, and city	2001	405	—	—	NA	NA	NA
Cattail[3]	Amery STH 46 to Almena CTH P	17.8-mi. trail, forests, farms, wetlands	1999	273	—	NA	NA	NA	NA
Chippewa River	Eau Claire SW to Red Cedar Trail, STH 85	20 miles of trail, river scenery	1990	642	171,899	334,607	115,880	96,450	96,450
Elroy-Sparta	Elroy STH 80/82 to Sparta STH 71	32.5 miles of trail, hills, valleys, tunnels	1965	298	59,250	60,075	57,870	60,620	60,560
Fox River[3]	Trailhead at Porlier and Adams Sts. Green Bay	Fox River bridge, 14-mi. trail along river	1991	8	NA	—	NA	NA	NA
Friendship[3]	Brillion – Forest Junction parallel to US 10	6 miles of trail, former farms and woods	2000	810	NA	NA	NA	NA	NA
Gandy Dancer[3]	St. Croix Falls US 8 to S of Superior CTH C	66 miles of trail, forests, connects to MN	1989	651	109,239	177,939	231,180	226,690	224,617
Glacial Drumlin	Waukesha CTH X to NE of Jefferson CTH Y	49 miles of trail, views of Ice Age features	1984	256	23,200	65,572	68,631	73,449	80,208
Great River[3]	Onalaska US 53 to NW of Trempealeau STH 35/54	24 miles of trail, Mississippi River, bluffs	1986	0	NA	NA	NA	NA	NA
Green Circle[3]	Circles Stevens Point area	River scenery	1992	0	—	NA	NA	NA	NA
Hank Aaron	Milwaukee, Menomonee River Valley	Menomonee River Valley	1996	66	NA	NA	NA	NA	NA
Hillsboro[3]	Union Center to Hillsboro STH 33/82	4.2 miles of trail, rural scenery	1988	66	NA	NA	NA	NA	NA
Ice Age Trail[5]	Sturgeon Bay to St. Croix Falls	Moraines and other glacial features	1988	5,097	NA	NA	NA	NA	NA

WISCONSIN STATE PARKS, TRAILS, AND RECREATION AREAS–Continued

Name	Location	Dominant Features	Established	Acres	Number of Visitors[1]				
					1995	2000	2006	2007	2008
La Crosse River	Sparta STH 16 to NE of La Crosse	24.5-mile trail, broad river valley	1978	360	27,750	37,150	45,485	48,325	51,925
Mascoutin Valley[3]	Ripon to Berlin STH 49	19-mi. trail, farms, woods, and wetlands	1996	45	—	NA	NA	NA	NA
Military Ridge	Madison US 18/151 to Dodgeville STH 23	39.6 miles of trail, most on crest of ridge	1981	516	60,073	67,224	121,015	134,740	145,575
Mountain-Bay[3]	Wausau CTH SS to Green Bay CTH HS	80.5-mile trail, varied landscape	1993	1,083	NA	NA	NA	NA	NA
Nicolet[1]	Gillett to Townsend STH 32	Forests, streams	1999	1,171	—	—	NA	NA	NA
North Country[5]	Douglas, Bayfield, Ashland & Iron Counties	Footpath across Northern Wisconsin	2000	546	—	—	NA	NA	NA
Oconto River[3]	Oconto US 41 to Stiles Junction US 141	8-mi. trail along Oconto River	1997	91	—	NA	NA	NA	NA
Old Abe	NE of Chippewa Falls CTH S to Cornell STH 27/64	17-mile trail, Chippewa River	1990	243	NA	NA	NA	NA	NA
Pecatonica3	Belmont E to Calamine, CTH G	10 miles of trail, stream	1974	242	NA	NA	NA	NA	NA
Red Cedar	Menomonie STH 29 S to Chippewa River Trail	14.5 miles of trail, river, bluffs	1973	427	38,490	45,760	47,600	47,430	54,370
Saunders[3]	S of Superior CTH C SW to MN border	8.4 miles of trail, wet words	1991	207	NA	NA	NA	NA	NA
Sugar River	New Glarus STH 39/69 to Brodhead STH 11	23.5 miles of trail, farms, prairies, woods	1972	265	42,275	45,362	51,696	49,044	45,110
Tomorrow River[3]	Plover to Portage-Waupaca County line	15 miles of trail, glacial terrain	1996	389	NA	NA	NA	NA	NA
Tuscobia	Park Falls CTH B to Rice Lake CTH SS	74 miles of trail, forests	1966	1,073	45,250	44,150	47,906	49,911	36,057
White River[3]	Elkhorn CTH H to Racine County, Spring Valley Rd.	10-mile trail, farmlands and historic town	1999	247	—	NA	NA	NA	NA
Wild Goose[3]	Fond du Lac US 41/151 to STH 60 S of Juneau	32 miles of trail, Horicon Marsh	1986	418	NA	NA	NA	NA	NA
Wild Rivers[3]	Solon Springs CTH A to Rice Lake	63.5 miles of trail, woods	1993	1,139	NA	NA	NA	NA	NA
Wiouwash[3]	Oshkosh-Hortonville, Split Rock-Aniwa	51.6 miles of trail, prairies, woods	1992	283	NA	NA	NA	NA	NA
TOTAL				19,201	670,715	1,067,444	1,009,545	1,024,291	1,210,937
RECREATION AREAS									
Richard Bong	.8 mi. SE of Burlington STH 142	Small lakes, open space, varied recreation	1963	4,537	544,090	462,274	217,600	378,824	440,724
Browntown-Cadiz Springs	.6 mi. W of Monroe STH 11	Spring-fed lakes	1970	644	97,379	99,191	63,363	62,336	46,622
Chippewa Moraine Ice Age	.6 mi. E of New Auburn CTH M	Kettle lakes, other glacial features	1974	3,224	12,125	17,737	22,095	23,960	23,330
Fischer Creek[3]	.1 mi. N of Cleveland on Lakeshore Rd.	L. Michigan shoreline, scenic bluffs	1991	124	NA	NA	NA	NA	NA
Hoffman Hills	.8 mi. NE of Menomonie CTH B or E	Wooded hills	1980	707	23,330	32,460	28,630	21,589	21,889
TOTAL				9,235	676,924	622,662	331,688	486,709	532,565

Abbreviations: US – U.S. highway; STH – state trunk highway; CTH – county trunk highway; NA – not available.

[1]Visitor numbers are estimates.
[2]Norther Forests figures for 2005-2006 are camping attendance only.
[3]Operated locally or by county; no attendance information available.
[4]Not accessible by vehicle.
[5]Various owners and operators (National Scenic Trails).

Source: Wisconsin Department of Natural Resources, Bureau of Parks and Recreation, departmental data, April 2009.

DEPARTMENT OF NATURAL RESOURCES SOURCES OF FUNDING
Fiscal Years 2003-04 – 2007-08
(In Thousands)

Source of Funding	2003-04	2004-05	2005-06	2006-07	2007-08
Segregated funds					
All-terrain vehicle registration fees	$1,739	$3,058	$3,247	$3,834	$4,698
Boat registration fees	5,114	5,046	5,095	5,355	5,442
Dry cleaner fund	707	1,788	1,924	2,162	717
Endangered resources voluntary payments	1,896	1,481	1,368	1,050	826
Environmental improvement fund	1,951	2,161	2,200	2,294	2,368
Environmental management account	13,920	12,706	16,970	17,219	17,637
Federal aids	34,058	39,342	42,006	37,613	48,989
Fishing, hunting licenses and permits	63,607	64,139	64,263	70,453	76,173
Forestry mill tax	79,182	81,280	90,090	107,102	96,145
Gifts and donations	126	131	136	254	338
Heritage State Parks and Forests Trust Fund	32	32	33	30	36
Motorcycle account	98	30	26	7	0
Nonpoint source account.	4,108	5,221	4,394	4,233	3,887
Park stickers and fees	10,748	10,695	10,299	12,293	13,418
Petroleum storage environmental cleanup fund . . .	4,310	4,305	4,192	4,598	5,358
Program revenue.	17,750	19,050	29,521	33,822	33,506
Recycling fund.	28,229	28,312	28,722	28,703	35,334
Snowmobile registration fees	3,295	3,336	3,806	3,458	4,231
Waste management fund.	14	13	133	35	116
Water resources account	11,685	15,651	14,358	13,855	13,490
Wisconsin Natural Resources Magazine.	848	844	827	724	891
TOTAL.	$283,417	$298,621	$323,610	$349,095	$363,601
General funds					
General purpose revenue.	$91,894	$135,493	$135,833	$132,176	$141,250
Program revenues	21,012	20,970	20,512	22,369	21,913
Program revenue – services	11,013	12,305	9,960	12,064	12,318
Federal aids	26,309	27,258	29,285	28,596	25,952
TOTAL.	$150,228	$196,026	$195,590	$195,205	$201,432
GRAND TOTAL.	$433,645	$494,647	$519,200	$544,301	$565,033

Source: Wisconsin Department of Natural Resources, departmental data, April 2009.

DEPARTMENT OF NATURAL RESOURCES EXPENDITURES
Fiscal Years 2003-04 – 2007-08
(In Thousands)

Program	2003-04	2004-05	2005-06	2006-07	2007-08
Land Management	**$91,975***	**$94,580***	**$97,980***	**$111,127***	**$114,512***
Wildlife management	15,358	16,097	16,896	20,626	21,344
Forestry	44,393	45,208	47,835	52,320	53,693
Southern forests	4,831	4,853	5,096	5,733	5,599
Parks	15,598	15,392	15,122	16,938	17,892
Endangered resources	3,290	3,768	4,290	4,979	5,023
Facilities and lands	8,038	8,229	8,233	9,409	9,968
Lands program management	466	1,034	508	1,122	992
Air and Waste Management	**$36,134***	**$36,041***	**$36,701***	**$37,187***	**$36,191***
Air management	15,632	16,040	15,939	16,080	15,893
Cooperative environmental assistance[1]	—	—	1,003	959	875
Remediation and redevelopment	11,618	11,622	10,953	11,705	11,184
Waste management	7,885	7,282	7,596	7,174	7,405
Air/waste program management	998	1,096	1,210	1,268	834
Enforcement and Science	**$34,706***	**$34,758***	**$35,840***	**$39,922***	**$41,793***
Law enforcement	23,490	24,013	25,682	28,423	30,871
Integrated science services	10,550	9,871	9,156	10,478	10,102
Enforcement/science program management	666	874	1,002	1,021	820
Water Management	**$62,381***	**$62,719***	**$66,435***	**$73,243***	**$80,781***
Fisheries management and habitat protection	27,102	27,335	29,037	24,687	28,344
Watershed management	22,594	22,957	23,647	35,430	39,002
Drinking and groundwater	9,071	8,893	10,096	11,474	12,338
Water program management	3,614	3,533	3,655	1,652	1,096
Conservation Aids	**$33,751***	**$40,435***	**$43,750***	**$43,446***	**$43,483***
Fish and wildlife aids	856	849	2,119	685	1,568
Forestry aids	8,407	8,747	9,525	10,937	10,265
Recreational aids	11,930	17,655	18,032	16,222	16,092
Aids in lieu of taxes	6,126	7,926	8,817	9,986	10,944
Enforcement aids	1,722	1,947	1,951	1,916	2,020
Wildlife damage aids	4,709	3,311	3,307	3,699	2,594
Environmental Aids	**$35,980***	**$38,694***	**$38,403***	**$38,436***	**$42,831***
Water quality aids	3,408	3,858	3,621	4,048	3,544
Solid and hazardous waste aids	28,410	28,020	29,014	28,657	35,337
Environmental aids	603	1,659	1,868	2,168	822
Environmental planning aids	381	291	488	363	302
Nonpoint aids	3,179	4,867	3,413	3,198	2,826
Debt Service	**$62,169***	**$112,309***	**$120,221***	**$125,610***	**$124,833***
Resource	19,038	34,163	40,169	45,431	48,071
Environmental	1,601	2,182	3,007	3,216	3,531
Water quality	39,731	73,853	74,427	73,914	69,456
Administrative facility	1,799	2,111	2,618	3,049	3,775
Acquisition and Development	**$10,205***	**$12,740***	**$10,910***	**$10,004***	**$11,937***
Wildlife	575	1,771	1,175	1,833	795
Fish	1,233	1,657	1,083	1,326	3,359
Forestry	1,044	906	3,060	2,785	2,558
Southern forests	474	249	241	629	497
Parks	3,389	5,809	3,128	1,939	2,539
Endangered resources	1,422	937	1,014	733	917
Facilities and lands	2,051	1,396	1,202	703	1,159
CAES (Customer and Employee Services)	18	14	8	25	72
Water resources	—	—	—	32	42
Law enforcement	—	1	—	—	—
Mississippi/Lower St. Croix	—	—	—	—	—
Administration and Technology	**$42,730***	**$39,567***	**$27,389***	**$22,532***	**$25,816***
Administration	1,144	975	965	1,038	1,563
Administrative and field services	5,816	3,909	—	—	—
Enterprise and technology	9,752	9,458	—	—	—
Finance	6,337	5,988	—	—	—
Personnel and human services	2,413	2,292	—	—	—
Legal services	2,553	2,419	2,241	2,365	2,353
Management and budget	841	774	706	770	770
Facility rental	5,774	5,320	4,864	4,471	6,564
Nonbudget accounts	8,101	8,430	18,613	13,888	14,567
Customer and Employee Services (CAES)	**$23,611***	**$21,917***	**$41,259***	**$42,796***	**$42,856***
Administrative and field services[2]	—	—	683	720	—
Enterprise and technology[2]	—	—	7,519	8,722	9,051
Finance[2]	—	—	5,979	5,984	6,011
Personnel and human services[2]	—	—	3,434	3,650	3,694
Communication and education strategy	3,672	3,490	3,609	3,438	3,561
Community financial assistance	5,782	5,137	4,814	4,769	5,201
Cooperative environmental assistance	1,240	1,139	—	—	—
Customer service and licensing	11,103	10,189	11,719	11,919	12,114
CAES program management	1,815	1,962	3,500	3,595	3,224
TOTAL	**$433,643**	**$493,760**	**$518,888**	**$544,301**	**$565,033**

*Total of detail immediately following. Totals do not add due to rounding.

[1]Moved from Customer and Employee Services (CAES) to Air/Waste Management in fiscal year 2006.

[2]Moved from Administration and Technology to the CAES division in fiscal year 2006.

Source: Wisconsin Department of Natural Resources, departmental data, April 2009.

NATURAL RESOURCES LAND ACQUISITIONS
Fiscal Years 1990 – 2009*

Fiscal Year	Fisheries Mgmnt.	Northern Forests	Parks	Natural Areas	Southern Forests	Wildlife Mgmnt.	Wild Rivers	Other	Total
				ACRES ACQUIRED					
			WARREN KNOWLES-GAYLORD NELSON STEWARDSHIP PROGRAM						
1990	2,322	975	683	1,278	283	4,269	2,490	10	12,311
1991	1,671	930	1,352	4,745	1,567	5,997	11,832	61	28,155
1992	1,787	791	362	3,176	157	3,940	15,067	226	25,506
1993	1,475	721	624	3,166	298	5,160	4,328	245	16,018
1994	2,879	396	1,820	3,288	306	3,137	3,191	563	15,580
1995	8,093	373	271	1,985	370	5,052	835	633	17,612
1996	2,344	977	1,248	5,830	398	3,566	2,012	368	16,743
1997	1,548	213	884	2,038	161	2,929	2,003	332	10,110
1998	1,133	278	107	1,467	81	4,045	9,944	317	17,372
1999	600	815	641	1,904	513	2,501	775	209	7,957
			STEWARDSHIP 2000 PROGRAM						
2000	2,808	496	3,705	3,301	110	11,800	16,135	136	38,489
2001	2,773	149	4,295	1,063	194	5,191	3,558	683	17,905
2002	1,595	5,525	1,349	3,174	208	4,997	607	258	17,713
2003	1,880	35,464	2,029	5,801	0	3,765	2,406	86	51,432
2004	1,177	4,132	3,060	1,747	159	7,513	2,132	156	20,076
2005	2,511	6,673	3,845	5,161	475	5,390	10,692	329	35,075
2006	957	18,799	1,823	2,474	103	6,024	767	414	31,360
2007	1,018	45,073	673	2,555	171	3,247	8,793	192	61,721
2008	937	6,188	1,639	1,925	12	3,625	2,397	102	16,825
2009	277	404	303	142	41	483	347	135	2,133
TOTAL. . . .	39,786	129,370	30,716	56,219	5,605	92,632	100,312	5,455	460,095
				COST TO ACQUIRE (in thousands)					
			WARREN KNOWLES-GAYLORD NELSON STEWARDSHIP PROGRAM						
1990	$1,951	$395	$727	$610	$490	$1,880	$2,216	$1	$8,269
1991	1,498	385	384	2,133	1,675	3,027	6,245	1,557	16,902
1992	1,530	416	461	1,195	398	2,735	5,537	48	12,320
1993	1,359	547	547	1,473	249	1,636	1,950	31	7,791
1994	2,315	178	902	724	793	2,118	1,843	148	9,021
1995	3,688	640	762	3,472	1,315	3,872	1,120	219	15,087
1996	2,596	542	2,758	3,108	1,036	2,832	1,413	441	14,726
1997	1,757	378	1,168	589	617	2,439	1,321	80	8,349
1998	1,513	137	337	2,077	293	4,331	11,005	1,307	21,001
1999	1,534	941	1,548	1,075	1,170	3,693	580	336	10,878
			STEWARDSHIP 2000 PROGRAM						
2000	$2,861	$550	$2,734	$3,472	$403	$9,061	$12,633	$352	$32,066
2001	5,247	533	8,605	2,156	873	4,251	739	420	22,824
2002	4,156	13,575	3,244	2,955	1,105	5,635	1,095	3,822	35,587
2003	3,976	7,680	4,105	3,603	0	3,908	3,807	117	27,196
2004	3,054	13,474	5,727	2,770	579	8,490	4,629	130	38,853
2005	5,421	7,263	16,693	4,993	3,050	8,781	3,591	401	50,194
2006	3,965	9,852	3,247	3,463	1,220	5,574	1,526	81	28,927
2007	3,522	20,447	6,460	4,039	1,081	7,227	15,864	254	58,894
2008	2,527	7,034	3,190	2,213	246	6,770	5,433	135	27,548
2009	627	2,218	750	389	84	1,246	1,239	102	6,655
TOTAL. . . .	$55,097	$87,184	$64,349	$46,510	$16,675	$89,506	$83,785	$9,982	$453,088

*The Warren Knowles-Gaylord Nelson Stewardship Program replaced the Outdoor Recreation Act Program (ORAP) in 1990.
Source: Wisconsin Department of Natural Resources, Bureau of Facilities and Lands, departmental data, March 2009.

CONSERVATION AND RECREATION LAND IN WISCONSIN
Acres By Ownership

County[1]	Forests	Wild Rivers	Natural Areas	Parks	Fisheries	Wildlife	Other	Total DNR	U.S. Forest Service 2008[2]	Total
Adams	—	—	6,281	492	1,508	7,311	640	16,231	—	16,231
Ashland	756	—	5,812	324	6,763	122	13,777	182,166	195,943
Barron	60	—	—	343	1,185	6,173	47	7,807	—	7,807
Bayfield	49	—	11,577	—	10,790	952	214	23,583	272,770	296,353
Brown	—	—	170	509	143	2,410	90	3,322	—	3,322
Buffalo	—	—	417	399	22	13,166	—	14,003	—	14,003
Burnett	15,257	—	—	239	3,834	51,662	222	71,214	—	71,214
Calumet	—	—	34	1,237	14	10,569	18	11,872	—	11,872
Chippewa . . .	—	—	—	6,809	1,897	2,579	85	11,370	—	11,370
Clark	224	—	—	—	163	495	1	882	—	882
Columbia. . . .	—	116	648	419	1,776	19,329	12	22,300	—	22,300
Crawford. . . .	—	7,977	3,095	—	984	7,113	275	19,444	—	19,444
Dane	—	4,385	889	2,589	5,095	10,333	264	23,554	39	23,593
Dodge	—	—	—	220	654	24,379	292	25,545	—	25,545
Door	—	—	2,869	9,349	161	3,493	119	15,991	—	15,991
Douglas	47,173	—	223	4,059	6,804	994	500	59,752	—	59,752
Dunn	—	—	2,119	1,278	849	11,873	—	16,118	—	16,118
Eau Claire . . .	—	—	433	145	475	2,103	50	3,207	—	3,207
Florence	36,323	11,455	8,427	177	86	40	45	56,553	85,175	141,728
Fond du Lac . .	10,697	—	99	408	51	17,098	112	28,465	—	28,465
Forest.	6,231	—	—	525	269	3,769	2	10,796	345,824	356,620
Grant	619	13,848	567	3,410	1,590	—	303	20,337	—	20,337
Green.	—	—	230	1,324	127	4,022	—	5,703	—	5,703
Green Lake. . .	—	—	429	—	750	17,407	—	18,586	—	18,586
Iowa	85	10,023	680	6,601	2,551	2,037	146	22,124	—	22,124
Iron.	35,901	35,102	2,896	63	1	10,775	172	84,910	—	84,910
Jackson.	67,763	—	605	113	4,740	3,254	166	76,641	—	76,641
Jefferson	3,580	—	85	464	173	16,010	4	20,315	—	20,315
Juneau	—	—	1,481	4,504	536	5,140	53	11,714	—	11,714
Kenosha	—	—	435	4,537	192	1,977	26	7,167	—	7,167
Kewaunee . . .	—	—	—	493	1	2,707	—	3,201	—	3,201
La Crosse . . .	2,972	55	61	371	619	3,692	—	7,771	—	7,771
Lafayette	—	—	226	1,418	725	4,048	—	6,416	—	6,416
Langlade	18,515	—	326	307	14,074	2,830	212	36,263	32,727	68,990
Lincoln.	20,149	2,354	80	2,816	2,927	4,641	236	33,203	—	33,203
Manitowoc . . .	2,943	—	296	335	11	6,568	827	10,979	—	10,979
Marathon. . . .	1,724	—	—	2,682	2,505	21,592	9	28,512	—	28,512
Marinette. . . .	12,931	6,644	1,956	2,687	1,679	8,542	1,013	35,452	—	35,452
Marquette . . .	—	—	1,293	—	—	4,483	6,507	2	12,285	—	12,285
Menominee[1] . .	—	—	—	—	—	—	16	16	—	16
Milwaukee . . .	304	—	—	107	—	3	66	479	—	479
Monroe.	—	—	—	1,607	4,064	361	98	6,129	—	6,129
Oconto	632	—	270	760	1,117	4,303	204	7,285	141,705	148,990
Oneida	66,048	27,982	6,636	586	714	7,770	196	109,932	11,312	121,244
Outagamie . . .	—	—	1,503	326	328	9,392	42	11,591	—	11,591
Ozaukee	—	—	1,714	637	85	846	50	3,332	—	3,332
Pepin	—	—	1,815	—	17	3,663	—	5,495	—	5,495
Pierce.	—	—	410	1,445	500	1,069	883	4,306	—	4,306
Polk	5,399	—	—	3,777	1,924	13,078	104	24,282	—	24,282
Portage.	—	—	306	796	5,280	24,751	205	31,338	—	31,338
Price	9,066	—	—	263	321	9,645	20	19,315	151,587	170,902
Racine	—	—	10	99	531	3,034	37	3,711	—	3,711
Richland	—	6,832	2	—	2,339	3,083	—	12,256	—	12,256
Rock	—	—	529	1	339	7,278	112	8,260	—	8,260
Rusk	15,289	—	—	—	446	2,989	148	18,872	—	18,872
St. Croix	—	—	128	2,889	990	6,863	713	11,583	—	11,583
Sauk	—	5,544	4,710	14,722	1,408	3,555	1,142	31,080	—	31,080
Sawyer	65,221	14,182	—	658	2,534	6,684	345	89,624	129,055	218,679
Shawano	—	—	231	957	281	13,913	91	15,472	—	15,472
Sheboygan . . .	15,979	—	53	964	1,968	3,142	59	22,164	—	22,164
Taylor	—	—	249	17	225	8,064	81	8,636	125,116	133,752
Trempealeau . .	58	—	—	1,618	1,140	4,343	43	7,203	—	7,203
Vernon	52	—	452	3,726	2,107	221	877	7,435	—	7,435
Vilas	140,247	—	3,708	—	542	7,188	82	151,766	54,568	206,334
Walworth. . . .	6,989	—	1,604	522	525	5,675	105	15,420	—	15,420
Washburn . . .	155	—	442	501	3,496	2,496	158	7249	—	7,249
Washington. . .	4,934	—	—	629	378	7,116	82	13,139	—	13,139
Waukesha . . .	11,786	—	282	357	291	5,035	66	17,818	—	17,818
Waupaca	—	—	645	1,274	5,511	3,527	90	11,047	—	11,047
Waushara. . . .	—	—	535	743	12,456	5,432	259	19,424	—	19,424
Winnebago. . .	—	—	402	5	80	12,868	126	13,480	—	13,480
Wood.	173	—	14	—	513	15,115	44	15,858	—	15,858
STATE . . .	626,284	146,500	75,579	107,116	127,213	526,851	12,821	1,628,260	1,531,233	3,159,493

[1]Land in Menominee County that is not privately owned is held by the Menominee Nation.

[2]Federal lands controlled by the U.S. Forest Service as of November 18, 2008.

Sources: U.S. Forest Service, "Land Areas as of September 30, 2008", March 2009; Wisconsin Department of Natural Resources, departmental data, March 2009.

HIGHLIGHTS OF EDUCATION IN WISCONSIN

Universities and Colleges — A total of 175,056 students enrolled in the University of Wisconsin System for the 2008 fall semester. The system's 2008 summer school enrollment was 49,910, and the enrollments in UW-Extension's credit outreach enrolled 40,649 in the 2007-08 fiscal year.

Wisconsin's private institutions of higher education encompass a broad range of schools, including 7 universities, 11 colleges, 6 technical and professional schools, 3 theological seminaries, and 2 tribal colleges. Over the past five years, enrollments in private institutions have grown from 60,985 in the 2004-05 school year to 64,632 in 2008-09.

Technical Colleges — Wisconsin's Technical College System had a total enrollment of 390,272 students in the 2007-08 school year. Enrollments for individual institutions that year ranged from 8,898 at Nicolet Technical College in Rhinelander to 47,100 at Fox Valley Technical College in Appleton.

Elementary and Secondary Schools — Following a peak enrollment of 999,921 for the 1971-72 school year, public school registrations declined to a low of 767,542 in 1984-85. In the last 10 years, enrollments have remained midway between those levels, with a total of 873,586 for 2008-09.

In the 2008-09 school year, 130,800 students, or 13% of Wisconsin's more than 1 million elementary and secondary pupils, were enrolled in private schools. Over the last 10 years, private school enrollments have steadily decreased by more than 16,000 students.

Teachers — Of Wisconsin's 59,309 public school teachers employed in the 2008-09 school year, 40,508 taught in elementary grades and 18,801 were secondary teachers. In the 2008-09 school year, Wisconsin's average salary for all teachers was $50,424. Nationally, Wisconsin ranked 21st for the 2007-08 school year. California had the highest average salary that year at an estimated $64,424. South Dakota's average salary was the lowest at $36,674.

Educational Alternatives — In the past 10 years, reported enrollment in Wisconsin home-based private education programs increased from 18,503 in the 1998-99 school year to a peak of 21,288 students during 2002-03, and has since steadily declined to 19,725 in 2007-08. In the 2007-08 school year, Wisconsin charter school enrollments totaled 35,572 students with 232 charter schools operating in 47 counties.

Educational Expenditures — State and local expenditures for education in Wisconsin for the 2007-08 fiscal year totaled $15.4 billion, or $2,719 per capita, based on Wisconsin's estimated population. Wisconsin ranked 15th in the nation with total expenditures per pupil of $10,367 in the 2006-07 fiscal year, while New Jersey was first ($16,163) and Utah was 50th ($5,706). In fiscal year 2008-09, school costs in Wisconsin totaled $10.7 billion ($5.5 billion in state school aid and $4.3 billion from the gross school levy). The 2008-09 cost per pupil was $12,471.

Educational Attainment — In the 2006-07 school year, Wisconsin schools conferred 1,113 doctoral degrees, 8,686 master's degrees, and 32,646 bachelor's degrees. In the same year, it awarded 64,120 public high school diplomas.

The following tables present selected data. Consult footnoted sources for more detailed information about education.

UNIVERSITY OF WISCONSIN SYSTEM
Fall Enrollment, 2003 – 2008

Institution	2003-04	2004-05	2005-06	2006-07	2007-08	2008-09	2008-09 Detail Female	Male
Universities*	**153,567**	**153,746**	**155,907**	**157,067**	**160,364**	**161,781**	**87,617**	**74,164**
Eau Claire	10,719	10,689	10,726	10,766	10,854	11,140	6,576	4,564
Green Bay	5,804	5,728	5,820	5,690	6,110	6,286	4,060	2,226
La Crosse	9,595	9,060	9,421	9,849	9,994	9,880	5,832	4,048
Madison*	41,184	40,750	41,106	41,028	41,563	41,620	21,636	19,984
Undergraduate*	29,850	29,372	29,751	29,639	30,166	30,362	15,860	14,502
Agricultural and Life Sciences . .	2,220	2,235	2,262	2,254	2,301	2,365	1,351	1,014
Business	1,261	1,253	1,237	1,266	1,321	1,403	546	857
Education	2,293	2,234	2,148	1,944	1,902	1,861	1,382	479
Engineering	3,460	3,331	3,171	3,164	3,156	3,396	631	2,765
Human Ecology	983	905	844	885	874	991	800	191
Letters and Science	17,265	17,096	17,592	17,608	18,032	17,843	9,563	8,280
Medicine	201	226	235	215	239	211	143	68
Nursing	514	548	607	721	714	691	609	82
Pharmacy	20	24	30	26	22	16	6	10
University Special†	1,633	1,520	1,625	1,556	1,605	1,585	829	756
Graduate	8,912	8,929	8,828	8,814	8,844	8,696	4,332	4,364
Audiology	—	—	29	29	32	37	32	5
Law	843	859	867	888	871	830	385	445
Medical	711	746	785	801	819	863	484	379
Pharmacy	551	529	532	535	518	519	298	221
Veterinary Medicine	317	315	314	322	313	313	245	68
Milwaukee*	25,811	27,248	27,978	28,309	29,338	29,215	15,611	13,604
Undergraduate*	21,379	22,673	23,326	23,595	24,395	24,299	12,592	11,707
Architecture and Urban Planning .	620	648	636	633	702	707	202	505
Arts	1,671	1,752	1,847	1,920	1,944	2,017	1,085	932
Business Administration	3,249	3,354	3,622	3,750	3,957	3,990	1,508	2,482
Education	1,878	1,802	1,853	1,869	1,794	1,747	1,266	481
Engineering and Applied Science .	1,561	1,557	1,484	1,496	1,451	1,454	123	1,331
Health Sciences	992	1,123	1,265	1,366	1,556	1,635	1,147	488
Letters and Science	6,411	7,073	7,295	7,602	7,845	7,857	4,158	3,699
Information Studies	152	161	143	156	168	178	68	110
Nursing	1,295	1,408	1,276	1,036	1,062	983	873	110
Social Welfare	722	857	967	967	982	942	548	394
Academic Opportunity Center . . .	1,248	1,151	1,230	1,176	1,332	1,223	623	600
Global Studies Interdisciplinary . .	2	48	63	95	144	176	124	52
University Special†	1,578	1,739	1,645	1,529	1,458	1,390	867	523
Graduate	4,432	4,575	4,652	4,714	4,943	4,916	3,019	1,897
Oshkosh	12,530	12,473	12,485	12,530	12,772	12,753	7,725	5,028
Parkside	5,097	5,074	5,018	5,007	5,010	5,167	2,818	2,349
Platteville	6,156	6,196	6,518	6,813	7,189	7,512	2,913	4,599
River Falls	5,905	5,959	6,126	6,229	6,452	6,555	3,906	2,649
Stevens Point	9,034	8,996	8,837	9,048	9,115	9,163	4,971	4,192
Stout	8,019	7,750	8,227	8,372	8,477	8,839	4,466	4,373
Superior	2,871	2,868	2,876	2,924	2,753	2,689	1,577	1,112
Whitewater	10,842	10,955	10,769	10,502	10,737	10,962	5,526	5,436
Colleges*	**12,614**	**12,499**	**12,597**	**12,639**	**13,029**	**13,275**	**7,085**	**6,190**
Baraboo/Sauk County	651	640	616	616	666	679	328	351
Barron County	647	625	575	587	606	627	333	294
Fond du Lac	719	692	772	763	751	736	370	366
Fox Valley	1,737	1,690	1,742	1,730	1,745	1,650	841	809
Manitowoc	636	655	642	584	594	543	280	263
Marathon County	1,300	1,334	1,296	1,315	1,368	1,364	682	682
Marinette	514	497	523	466	459	469	260	209
Marshfield/Wood County	631	667	657	592	636	628	365	263
Richland	521	516	467	450	449	474	271	203
Rock County	918	893	888	929	912	1,058	586	472
Sheboygan	798	753	731	691	725	782	416	366
Washington County	961	987	955	968	1,018	1,018	508	510
Waukesha	2,215	2,026	2,060	2,014	2,038	2,035	990	1,045
Online	366	524	673	934	1,062	1,212	855	357
SYSTEM TOTAL	166,181	166,245	168,504	169,706	173,393	175,056	94,702	80,354

*Total of detail immediately following.

†"University Special" designates students at UW-Madison and UW-Milwaukee who are allowed to take courses without having to qualify as degree candidates.

Source: University of Wisconsin System, Office of Policy Analysis and Research.

UNIVERSITY OF WISCONSIN SYSTEM
Summer Session Enrollment, 2003 – 2008

Institution	2003	2004	2005	2006	2007	2008	2008 Detail Female	2008 Detail Male
Universities*	48,438	46,709	45,431	45,162	45,650	46,030	27,440	18,590
Eau Claire	2,792	2,816	2,463	2,561	2,524	2,464	1,585	879
Green Bay	1,445	1,440	1,809	1,547	1,615	1,887	1,368	519
La Crosse	2,662	2,660	2,556	2,638	2,888	2,931	1,987	944
Madison*	13,583	13,342	12,945	12,579	12,540	12,123	6,397	5,726
Undergraduate*	8,587	8,186	7,804	7,408	7,464	7,118	4,002	3,116
Agricultural and Life Sciences	584	609	583	574	536	578	315	263
Business	387	368	357	324	322	345	148	197
Education	533	545	490	434	441	379	289	90
Engineering	757	781	701	665	684	666	134	532
Human Ecology	388	304	292	307	385	385	306	79
Letters and Science	3,732	3,409	3,431	3,371	3,427	3,292	1,833	1,459
Medicine	98	114	108	107	112	109	74	35
Nursing	87	86	86	84	85	73	66	7
Pharmacy	3	4	4	3	4	2	0	2
University Special†	2,018	1,966	1,752	1,539	1,468	1,289	837	452
Graduate	4,434	4,600	4,567	4,580	4,510	4,411	2,050	2,361
Audiology	—	—	—	—	—	24	21	3
Law	227	234	229	216	182	171	77	94
Medical	101	115	131	151	159	198	119	79
Pharmacy	157	137	138	148	145	129	70	59
Veterinary Medicine	77	70	76	76	80	72	58	14
Milwaukee*	9,772	9,403	8,855	8,662	8,707	9,072	5,449	3,623
Undergraduate*	7,485	7,254	6,793	6,543	6,563	6,849	3,901	2,948
Architecture and Urban Planning	96	61	70	62	79	78	27	51
Arts	392	370	356	328	315	367	225	142
Business Administration	1,143	1,079	1,097	1,075	1,188	1,243	544	699
Education	668	584	533	506	485	466	373	93
Engineering and Applied Science	441	445	343	345	358	382	36	346
Health Sciences	362	356	402	401	477	507	380	127
Letters and Science	1,577	1,662	1,630	1,648	1,670	1,787	1,008	779
Information Studies	66	66	54	38	47	52	15	37
Nursing	430	425	421	305	248	282	243	39
Social Welfare	202	239	265	268	261	254	168	86
Academic Opportunity Center	289	264	175	149	155	144	63	81
Global Studies Interdisciplinary	—	6	9	16	33	41	27	14
University Special†	1,819	1,697	1,438	1,402	1,247	1,246	792	454
Graduate	2,287	2,149	2,062	2,119	2,144	2,223	1,548	675
Oshkosh	2,092	1,927	2,158	2,096	2,309	2,292	1,575	717
Parkside	1,427	1,452	1,426	1,453	1,342	1,362	790	572
Platteville	2,137	1,739	1,690	1,798	1,792	1,854	972	882
River Falls	1,981	1,914	1,842	1,955	1,849	1,798	1,124	674
Stevens Point	3,118	2,913	2,960	3,243	3,447	3,673	2,172	1,501
Stout	2,992	2,784	2,595	2,537	2,587	2,494	1,505	989
Superior	818	789	759	775	796	691	472	219
Whitewater	3,619	3,530	3,373	3,318	3,254	3,389	2,044	1,345
Colleges*	4,213	4,072	3,470	3,513	3,769	3,880	2,494	1,386
Baraboo/Sauk County	143	142	107	98	107	111	40	71
Barron	81	78	52	47	59	61	38	23
Fond du Lac	330	294	226	218	191	167	101	66
Fox Valley	586	578	420	444	355	379	222	157
Manitowoc	184	200	168	146	147	109	76	33
Marathon County	340	317	284	271	178	242	144	98
Marinette	128	97	84	66	77	69	45	24
Marshfield/Wood County	171	121	77	78	147	134	93	41
Richland	90	67	59	57	76	24	11	13
Rock County	349	305	211	202	179	157	92	65
Sheboygan	254	228	136	77	109	132	77	55
Washington County	183	219	245	209	221	178	132	46
Waukesha	1,050	938	756	793	860	778	504	274
Online Courses	324	488	645	807	1,063	1,339	919	420
SYSTEM TOTAL	52,651	50,781	48,901	48,675	49,419	49,910	29,934	19,976

*Total of detail immediately following.

†"University Special" designates students at UW-Madison and UW-Milwaukee who are allowed to take courses without having to qualify as degree candidates.

Source: University of Wisconsin System, Office of Policy Analysis and Research.

UNIVERSITY OF WISCONSIN – EXTENSION PROGRAMS
2003-04 – 2007-08

Program type	2003-04	2004-05	2005-06	2006-07	2007-08
Broadcasting and Media Innovations[1]					
Wisconsin Public Radio (listeners per week)	414,600	411,600	383,400	407,800	424,000
Wisconsin Public Television (viewers per week)	574,000	574,000	538,000	539,000	527,560
Wisconsin Public Television telecourses (enrollments)	3,711	3,092	1,345	477[2]	250[2]
Interactive conferencing hours.	159,298	107,781	175,029	194,447	203,766
Continuing Education, Outreach and E-Learning					
Online courses.	244	261	269	301	301
Online certificate and degree programs	16	18	17	19	16
Online enrollments.	4,359	3,514	3,339	4,561	3,891
Number of enrollments[3]	37,492	44,531	45,734	39,330	40,649
Noncredit programs	5,729	4,697	5,631	4,719	5,664
Noncredit enrollments	167,284	139,615	198,252	133,196	146,097
UW HELP contacts	32,001	32,050	34,180	30,501	32,900
Learner Support Services contacts.	65,026	29,344	34,526	99,367	144,929
Online applications to UW System campuses.	104,738	116,330	127,767	141,640	151,000
Independent Learning enrollments	3,247	2,882	2,339	2,295	2,551[4]
Cooperative Extension Teaching Contacts[5]					
Agriculture/Agribusiness	108,796	301,838	290,142	240,958	274,013
Community, Natural Resources and Economic Development. .	114,747	111,853	90,704	83,251	113,856
Family Living Programs.	418,082	437,954	425,751	417,484	431,633
4-H/Youth Development.	244,690	249,323	263,829	242,671	274,715
Wisconsin Geological and Natural History Survey	22,330	21,860	20,842	15,178	15,228
Entrepreneurship and Economic Development[6]					
Counseling and technical assistance clients	2,384	2,086	2,242	3,147	2,951
Business Answerline-assisted clients	3,254	3,638	3,594	3,073	2,668
Counseling and technical assistance hours	22,331	18,910	18,192	21,374	23,942
Training programs	515	1,043	1,021	1,239	1,261
Training program participants	10,587	19,252	20,797	20,339	17,337
Extension Conference Centers					
J.F. Friedrick Center[7]**, The Lowell Center, The Pyle Center**					
Conference participants	85,508	84,600	80,297	81,512	74,816
Conference days	146,715	151,800	164,390	152,294	139,844
Events	2,342	2,400	2,138	2,058	2,024
Event days	3,927	4,500	3,919	3,854	4,025

[1]Wisconsin Public Radio and Wisconsin Public Television are cooperative services of the University of Wisconsin-Extension and the Wisconsin Educational Communications Board.

[2]Number represents telecourse hours.

[3]Undergraduate and graduate enrollments combined.

[4]Adjusted for student withdrawals.

[5]Cooperative Extension data are for the calendar year. In addition, its faculty and staff offer contacts through publications, telephone, mass media, and the World Wide Web.

[6]Formerly called Business and Manufacturing Extension.

[7]The J.F. Friedrick Center closed June 22, 2008.

Source: The University of Wisconsin-Extension, *2008 Annual Report,* at: www.uwex.edu/publications/annualreport [February 6, 2009], and previous editions.

ENROLLMENT IN WISCONSIN TECHNICAL COLLEGE SYSTEM
Annual Enrollment Summary, 1998-99 – 2007-08

School Year	Total[1]	College Parallel	Associate Degree	Technical Diploma	Vocational Adult	Non-Post Secondary[2]	Community Services
1998-99	442,274	17,218	102,590	35,658	253,764	80,256	15,619
1999-2000	453,668	16,850	104,262	34,878	264,320	79,258	16,011
2000-01	439,934	16,760	106,248	35,631	248,976	80,032	14,870
2001-02	451,271	17,953	108,921	38,038	255,888	82,993	14,675
2002-03	429,355	19,064	113,253	40,098	232,766	81,860	13,277
2003-04	416,857	19,282	115,675	41,125	221,283	79,265	12,156
2004-05	406,323	20,181	115,422	39,291	214,948	76,870	10,817
2005-06	409,380	20,242	117,408	38,305	219,584	74,556	10,631
2006-07	400,057	21,053	117,028	39,045	210,396	72,951	10,206
2007-08	390,272	22,142	117,722	38,583	203,493	70,585	9,113

[1]Unduplicated student headcount.
[2]Includes basic education.
Source: Wisconsin Technical College System, *Fact Book 2009*, at: www.wtcsystem.edu/reports/data/factbook/index.htm, and previous issues.

Annual Enrollment Summary, By Technical College, 2007-08

Technical College	Total[1]	College Parallel	Associate Degree	Technical Diploma	Vocational Adult	Non-Post Secondary[2]	Community Services
Blackhawk	11,250	—	2,836	1,041	6,810	1,880	65
Chippewa Valley.	19,462	457	7,034	2,396	10,076	3,100	—
Fox Valley	47,100	—	12,396	3,535	30,483	4,660	839
Gateway	22,789	—	9,087	2,073	8,599	6,456	—
Lakeshore	15,204	—	3,257	1,265	9,560	2,613	176
Madison Area	41,848	8,813	12,910	4,649	16,291	5,680	2,475
Mid-State.	10,053	—	3,581	1,320	5,099	1,793	97
Milwaukee Area	46,638	12,065	18,668	4,044	11,304	22,052	41
Moraine Park.	20,020	—	7,901	2,560	8,638	3,789	8
Nicolet Area	8,898	807	1,234	533	5,438	830	1,685
Northcentral	22,318	—	5,001	1,475	14,027	4,455	—
Northeast Wisconsin	41,527	—	13,584	4,699	25,540	3,165	363
Southwest Wisconsin . . .	11,401	—	3,456	1,166	7,281	2,181	—
Waukesha County	27,767	—	6,987	3,624	15,414	3,516	2,335
Western.	19,229	—	5,600	1,930	11,000	2,544	513
Wisconsin Indianhead . . .	24,768	—	4,190	2,273	17,933	1,871	516
TOTAL.	390,272	22,142	117,722	38,583	203,493	70,585	9,113

[1]Unduplicated student headcount.
[2]Includes basic education.
Source: Wisconsin Technical College System, *Fact Book 2009*, at: www.wtcsystem.edu/reports/data/factbook/index.htm, and previous issues.

WISCONSIN PRIVATE INSTITUTIONS OF HIGHER EDUCATION
Fall Enrollment, 2004-05 – 2008-09

Institution (Location)	2004-05	2005-06	2006-07	2007-08	2008-09
Universities and Colleges					
Alverno College (Milwaukee)	2,241	2,372	2,480	2,654	2,782
Beloit College (Beloit)	1,370	1,385	1,420	1,366	1,388
Cardinal Stritch University (Milwaukee)	6,672	6,471	6,000	6,277	6,242
Carroll University (Waukesha)	3,003	3,123	3,292	3,325	3,318
Carthage College (Kenosha)	2,679	2,699	2,757	2,778	2,816
Concordia University Wisconsin (Mequon)	5,395	5,418	5,574	5,933	6,549
Edgewood College (Madison)	2,454	2,646	2,550	2,582	2,544
Lakeland College (Sheboygan)	4,013	4,021	4,047	3,695	3,744
Lawrence University (Appleton)	1,380	1,450	1,480	1,433	1,496
Marian University (Fond du Lac)	2,918	2,975	3,040	2,957	2,891
Marquette University (Milwaukee)	11,510	11,594	11,548	11,516	11,633
Mount Mary College (Milwaukee)	1,632	1,684	1,732	1,681	1,862
Northland College (Ashland)	721	751	692	687	695
Ripon College (Ripon)	929	979	977	1,000	1,057
Saint Norbert College (De Pere)	2,103	2,050	2,072	2,169	2,137
Silver Lake College (Manitowoc)	1,034	913	939	832	853
Viterbo University (La Crosse)	2,690	2,554	2,991	3,088	2,944
Wisconsin Lutheran College (Milwaukee)	697	691	741	706	753
Technical and Professional					
Bellin College of Nursing (Green Bay)	216	247	240	304	289
Herzing University[1] (Madison)	751	1,082	826	1,803	1,902
Medical College of Wisconsin (Milwaukee)	1,359	1,365	1,281	1,235	1,228
Milwaukee Institute of Art & Design (Milwaukee)	636	645	646	636	675
Milwaukee School of Engineering (Milwaukee)	2,363	2,315	2,427	2,516	2,621
Wisconsin School of Professional Psychology (Milwaukee)	57	54	62	60	75
Theological Seminaries					
Maranatha Baptist Bible College (Watertown)	904	863	866	897	866
Nashotah House (Nashotah)	69	72	75	98	107
Sacred Heart School of Theology (Hales Corners)	155	154	175	170	175
Saint Francis Seminary[2] (Milwaukee)	67	68	66	—	—
Tribal Colleges					
College of the Menominee Nation (Keshena)	507	532	513	505	512
Lac Courte Oreilles Ojibwa Community College (Hayward)	460	505	574	574	478
TOTAL	60,985	61,678	62,083	63,477	64,632

[1]For-profit institution.

[2]Began academic collaboration with Sacred Heart School of Theology in 2006.

Sources: National Center for Education Statistics, Integrated Postsecondary Education Data System, Peer Analysis System, at: http://nces.ed.gov/ipedspas; U.S. Department of Education, Office of Postsecondary Education, Database of Accredited Postsecondary Institutions and Programs, accredited by the Higher Learning Commission of the North Central Association of Colleges and Schools, at: http://ope.ed.gov/accreditation/; individual school registrars.

DIPLOMAS AND EARNED DEGREES
by State, 2006-07

State	High School Diplomas Private[1]	Public[2]	Associate Degree	Bachelor's Degree	Master's Degree	Higher Education Doctorate Degree (Ph.D., Ed.D., etc.)	First Professional Degree (M.D., J.D., etc.)
Alabama	4,576	38,060	8,265	21,981	9,757	728	1,126
Alaska	198	7,930	1,039	1,512	716	33	0
Arizona	2,593	69,060	25,780	36,605	27,831	1,098	906
Arkansas	1,379	27,920	5,721	11,479	3,257	218	512
California	34,878	375,930	95,797	153,312	56,797	7,124	8,899
Colorado	2,524	46,890	8,999	28,865	11,672	1,031	1,086
Connecticut	7,993	37,450	5,069	18,290	8,405	828	956
Delaware	1,797	7,080	1,396	5,113	2,292	283	291
District of Columbia	1,665	3,400	1,083	10,261	9,610	628	2,855
Florida	18,583	150,280	63,080	73,874	25,573	3,338	4,531
Georgia	7,574	76,550	13,098	37,418	12,337	1,625	2,178
Hawaii	2,385	10,680	3,254	5,695	1,922	186	171
Idaho	908	16,360	2,945	7,996	1,609	161	171
ILLINOIS	15,105	130,080	35,180	69,946	37,828	3,028	4,853
Indiana	4,788	61,060	14,110	38,533	11,832	1,472	1,807
IOWA	2,261	35,480	14,368	22,388	4,544	878	1,780
Kansas	2,378	29,550	7,845	17,065	5,830	503	837
Kentucky	4,028	38,850	9,976	19,079	7,322	578	1,093
Louisiana	7,531	31,690	4,974	21,671	6,335	601	1,622
Maine	2,618	13,390	2,463	6,900	1,614	59	201
Maryland	9,454	57,080	10,421	25,694	14,169	1,370	1,140
Massachusetts	10,435	62,460	10,691	47,885	27,802	3,325	4,503
MICHIGAN	8,522	106,750	25,191	53,280	21,090	1,960	3,350
MINNESOTA	4,930	59,640	15,817	29,618	16,387	1,968	1,919
Mississippi	3,355	24,540	8,623	12,052	3,949	437	590
Missouri	7,330	59,680	13,994	35,755	17,368	1,573	2,802
Montana	1,703	10,130	1,598	5,217	1,159	133	136
Nebraska	2,156	19,860	4,918	12,332	3,551	450	870
Nevada	695	17,450	3,695	6,390	2,059	157	399
New Hampshire	2,294	14,240	3,346	8,306	3,017	198	198
New Jersey	13,344	95,590	15,848	32,727	12,736	1,245	1,774
New Mexico	1,495	17,430	4,845	7,839	3,105	278	293
New York	29,891	158,850	57,775	114,081	64,365	4,661	8,572
North Carolina	5,594	81,080	19,690	41,263	12,921	1,492	2,083
North Dakota	NA	7,220	2,310	5,543	1,317	182	208
Ohio	13,057	119,710	24,175	59,025	20,409	2,195	3,516
Oklahoma	2,033	36,860	9,801	18,892	5,386	462	1,149
Oregon	2,814	32,020	8,130	17,906	6,054	554	1,191
Pennsylvania	17,477	129,890	26,317	81,042	28,876	3,515	4,847
Rhode Island	1,582	10,180	3,822	9,982	2,230	279	353
South Carolina	3,211	38,080	7,791	19,484	5,112	483	843
South Dakota	556	8,240	2,268	4,965	1,191	91	183
Tennessee	5,889	50,830	10,592	27,272	9,031	1,040	1,450
Texas	11,923	255,830	44,701	95,747	32,802	3,619	5,325
Utah	1,351	31,480	9,835	20,922	4,465	510	426
Vermont	1,759	7,140	1,275	5,101	1,951	60	282
Virginia	6,913	78,710	16,946	39,744	13,833	1,643	2,626
Washington	4,565	65,050	20,923	29,160	8,778	934	1,342
West Virginia	605	17,260	3,742	11,105	3,302	228	542
WISCONSIN	5,426	64,120	11,787	32,646	8,686	1,113	1,159
Wyoming	NA	5,380	2,805	1,691	423	61	118
UNITED STATES	306,605	2,950,450	728,114	1,524,092[3]	604,607	60,616	90,064

NA – Not available.

[1]Estimated. Private high school diploma detail may not add to total due to rounding.

[2]Projected.

[3]Total includes U.S. Service schools: 3,443 Bachelor's Degrees granted.

Sources: U.S. Department of Education, Institute of Education Sciences, National Center for Education Statistics, *Digest of Education Statistics 2008,* March 2009, at: http://nces.ed.gov/pubs2009/2009020.pdf; U.S. Department of Education, National Center for Education Statistics, *Characteristics of Private Schools in the United States: Results From the 2007-08 Private School Universe Survey,* March 2009, at:http://nces.ed.gov/pubs2009/2009313.pdf.

WISCONSIN SCHOOL DISTRICT FINANCIAL DATA
1985-86 – 2008-09

	State School Aid		Gross School Levy		Total School Costs[1]		Cost Per Pupil	
Fiscal Year	Amount[2] (in millions)	Percent Change	Amount[2] (in millions)	Percent Change	Amount[2] (in millions)	Percent Change	Amount	Percent Change
1985-86	$1,299.2	—	$1,583.3	—	$3,154.5	—	$4,106	—
1986-87	1,358.1	4.5%	1,709.5	8.0%	3,344.9	6.0%	4,356	6.1%
1987-88	1,481.6	9.1	1,840.4	7.7	3,590.9	7.4	4,649	6.7
1988-89	1,572.4	6.1	1,989.9	8.1	3,848.4	7.2	4,967	6.8
1989-90	1,693.2	7.7	2,158.5	8.5	4,142.1	7.6	5,291	6.5
1990-91	1,857.4	9.7	2,356.4	9.2	4,555.7	10.0	5,712	8.0
1991-92	1,950.4	5.0	2,568.0	9.0	4,877.1	7.1	5,987	4.8
1992-93	2,046.0	4.9	2,843.8	10.7	5,287.9	8.4	6,375	6.5
1993-94	2,186.6	6.9	2,988.1	5.1	5,527.1	4.5	6,549	2.7
1994-95	2,462.0	12.6	2,995.7	0.3	5,848.2	5.8	6,796	3.8
1995-96	2,705.2	9.9	3,023.6	0.9	6,150.2	5.2	7,068	4.0
1996-97	3,566.1	31.8	2,528.1	–16.4	6,546.8	6.4	7,447	5.4
1997-98	3,804.7	6.7	2,590.4	2.5	6,939.0	6.0	7,874	5.7
1998-99	3,989.4	4.9	2,735.8	5.6	7,250.7	4.5	8,244	4.7
1999-2000	4,226.3	5.9	2,794.9	2.2	7,546.9	4.1	8,376	1.6
2000-01	4,463.3	5.6	2,928.1	4.8	7,899.5	4.7	8,765	4.6
2001-02	4,602.4	3.1	3,071.8	4.9	8,347.5	5.7	9,571	5.7
2002-03	4,775.2	3.8	3,192.0	3.9	8,749.9	4.8	10,023	9.2
2003-04	4,806.4	0.7	3,367.6	5.5	8,911.2	1.8	10,229	2.1
2004-05	4,858.0	1.1	3,610.7	7.2	9,216.2	3.4	10,605	3.7
2005-06	5,159.2	6.2	3,592.3	–0.5	9,539.4	3.5	10,989	3.6
2006-07	5,294.4	2.6	3,787.8	5.4	9,902.9	3.8	11,413	3.9
2007-08	5,340.3	0.9	4,066.6	7.4	10,265.1	3.7	11,894	4.2
2008-09	5,462.5	2.3	4,279.0	5.2	10,732.2[3]	4.6	12,471[3]	4.9

[1]Includes the gross costs of general operations, special projects, debt service, and food service; the net cost of capital projects; and the costs of CESA and County Children with Disabilities Education Board operations.

[2]1996-97 through 2008-09 are appropriated amounts.

[3]2008-09 amounts are unaudited.

Sources: Wisconsin Department of Public Instruction, School Financial Services, departmental data, April 2009 and previous years; Wisconsin Legislative Fiscal Bureau, *2007-09 Summary of Budget Provisions,* December 2007.

WISCONSIN SCHOOL DISTRICT ENROLLMENT LEVELS

Number of Districts by Total Enrollment Level, 2003-04 – 2008-09

	Number of Districts					
Enrollment Level[1]	2003-04	2004-05[2]	2005-06	2006-07	2007-08	2008-09
1-499	101	111	111	104	113	113
500-999	128	125	130	130	128	124
1,000-1,999	106	100	100	101	100	101
2,000-2,999	42	41	39	40	37	39
3,000-3,999	24	25	25	25	25	25
4,000-4,999	13	12	13	11	12	11
5,000-9,999	17	17	18	20	20	20
10,000 and above	11	11	11	11	11	11
TOTAL	442	442	447	442	446	444

[1]Enrollment data includes nondistrict-sponsored charter schools.

[2]Major changes were implemented for data collection in 2004-05. Data from 2004-05 is not comprehensive.

Number of Districts by 9-12 Enrollment Level, 2003-04 – 2008-09

	Number of Districts					
Enrollment Level[1]	2003-04	2004-05[3]	2005-06	2006-07	2007-08	2008-09
0[2]	58	58	61	57	59	59
1-299	152	164	164	163	165	163
300-499	79	68	70	71	71	73
500-999	80	80	79	71	73	71
1,000-1,999	51	51	51	58	55	55
2,000 and above	22	21	22	22	23	23
TOTAL	442	442	447	442	446	444

[1]Enrollment data includes nondistrict-sponsored charter schools.

[2]This group includes the K3-8 districts, which do not have secondary level students.

[3]Major changes were implemented for data collection in 2004-05. Data from 2004-05 is not comprehensive.

Source: Wisconsin Department of Public Instruction, "Public School Enrollment Data – Public Enrollment by District and Grade", at: http://dpi.wi.gov/lbstat/pubdata2.html

ENROLLMENT IN WISCONSIN PUBLIC AND PRIVATE ELEMENTARY AND SECONDARY SCHOOLS

Public Schools, 1998-99 – 2008-09

Grade Level	1998-99	1999-2000	2000-01	2001-02	2002-03	2003-04	2004-05*	2005-06	2006-07	2007-08	2008-09
Pre-kindergarten	20,090	20,814	23,751	24,673	26,092	26,668	27,444	31,218	33,821	37,773	43,153
Kindergarten	59,610	58,536	56,507	57,469	57,670	59,372	58,724	60,382	60,408	59,590	60,373
1	62,656	61,413	59,962	58,174	58,538	58,368	58,521	59,593	60,696	60,474	59,779
2	63,501	62,260	61,205	60,059	58,628	58,877	57,807	58,978	59,703	60,000	60,486
3	64,312	63,680	62,810	61,655	60,819	59,196	58,874	58,664	59,554	60,000	60,969
4	64,255	64,914	64,455	63,509	62,436	61,744	59,267	59,984	59,356	59,995	60,308
5	63,969	64,950	65,570	65,101	64,213	62,970	61,493	60,304	60,261	59,581	60,222
6	65,786	64,977	66,163	67,208	66,925	65,762	62,557	62,737	61,257	60,827	60,235
7	67,996	67,107	66,367	67,398	68,631	68,192	66,095	65,153	63,938	62,030	61,588
8	68,475	67,880	67,950	66,558	67,751	68,663	67,168	66,985	65,606	64,135	62,305
9	76,664	78,953	78,140	77,802	77,508	77,798	76,173	76,674	75,282	73,746	71,662
10	71,277	70,913	73,796	73,512	73,022	72,043	71,196	73,409	72,425	70,788	69,395
11	67,148	67,301	67,605	70,297	70,284	70,989	69,928	71,428	73,694	72,507	71,326
12	63,725	64,015	65,195	65,946	68,714	69,389	69,510	69,665	70,699	72,380	71,785
TOTAL	879,464	877,713	879,476	879,361	881,231	880,031	864,757	875,174	876,700	874,633	873,586

Private Schools, 1998-99 – 2008-09

Grade Level	1998-99	1999-2000	2000-01	2001-02	2002-03	2003-04	2004-05	2005-06	2006-07	2007-08	2008-09
Pre-kindergarten	12,114	12,728	12,901	12,866	13,487	13,604	14,434	14,431	14,662	15,008	14,814
Kindergarten	12,866	12,660	13,012	12,625	11,736	11,191	11,517	11,440	10,890	10,663	10,483
1	13,118	12,896	12,694	12,468	12,021	11,201	10,950	10,896	11,017	10,714	10,306
2	12,847	12,797	12,696	12,337	11,888	11,460	10,970	10,756	10,629	10,764	10,376
3	13,000	12,705	12,605	12,467	11,807	11,412	11,187	10,698	10,466	10,484	10,481
4	12,599	12,922	12,478	12,369	11,896	11,304	11,114	10,866	10,522	10,338	10,187
5	12,255	12,513	12,655	12,201	11,865	11,309	11,047	10,800	10,641	10,412	10,078
6	11,921	12,078	12,042	12,116	11,286	10,994	10,824	10,564	10,325	10,368	9,961
7	10,963	11,332	11,185	11,192	11,193	10,408	10,420	10,164	9,984	9,952	9,775
8	11,052	10,858	10,959	10,938	10,682	10,683	10,247	10,092	9,841	9,876	9,563
9	6,105	6,747	6,574	6,372	6,414	6,112	6,332	6,300	6,306	6,414	6,287
10	6,054	6,062	6,461	6,273	6,076	6,214	5,950	6,275	6,134	6,153	6,072
11	5,637	5,873	5,698	6,005	5,949	5,880	5,925	5,825	5,936	5,923	5,857
12	5,497	5,426	5,450	5,397	6,073	5,750	5,665	5,616	5,559	5,599	5,555
Ungraded Elementary and Secondary	1,125	769	926	519	246	330	210	310	507	938	1,005
TOTAL	147,153	148,366	148,336	146,145	142,619	137,852	136,792	135,033	133,419	133,606	130,800

Note: Discrepancies between these statistics and those shown in earlier Blue Books reflect revised data in the source.

*Major changes were implemented for data collection in 2004-05. Data from 2004-05 is not comprehensive.

Sources: Wisconsin Department of Public Instruction, *Basic Facts About Wisconsin Elementary and Secondary Schools, 2003-2004*, and previous issues; departmental data, April 2005; Non-Public (Private) School Enrollment Data, at: www.dpi.wi.gov/lbstat/pubdata2.html [February 11, 2009].

WISCONSIN PUBLIC HIGH SCHOOL COMPLETION RATES
By CESA District and Race, 2006-07

							Student Detail by Race				
						Am. Indian/ Alaskan	Asian/ Pacific				Combined/ Small
		Total Students and Rates									
CESA[1]	Total[2]	Rate	Female	Rate	Male	Rate	Native	Islander	Black	Hispanic	White	Groups[3]
1	18,031	86.2%	9,198	88.2%	8,833	84.2%	56	466	3,485	1,321	12,299	407
2	10,652	91.1	5,240	92.5	5,412	89.8	9	217	465	271	8,401	1,289
3	1,821	96.7	913	97.6	908	95.7	0	0	1	2	893	925
4	2,790	95.4	1,450	96.7	1,395	94.2	36	91	19	8	1,809	882
5	4,413	95.3	2,145	96.4	2,304	94.2	13	76	0	33	3,111	1,216
6	7,754	93.7	3,894	95.9	3,860	91.7	6	212	38	96	5,849	1,553
7	6,556	90.5	3,256	92.3	3,300	88.8	73	315	54	167	4,495	1,452
8	1,792	90.7	897	93.1	894	88.6	71	0	2	0	968	770
9	3,096	94.8	1,517	96.1	1,592	93.6	34	238	11	0	2,311	515
10.	2,924	95.9	1,387	96.4	1,537	95.5	12	78	19	10	1,464	1,341
11.	3,756	95.4	1,889	97.1	1,867	93.8	12	51	0	12	2,264	1,417
12.	1,295	92.3	645	93.9	644	90.8	35	0	0	0	775	507
TOTAL.	64,880	91.1%	32,431	92.8%	32,546	89.6%	357	1,744	4,094	1,920	44,639	12,274

Note: Percent completion calculated by number of graduates divided by number of students expected to complete high school. Rates calculated by the Wisconsin Legislative Reference Bureau.

[1]Cooperative Educational Service Agency.

[2]Includes students who have earned certificates, HSED, and regular diplomas. Details may not sum to total because of privacy rules on identifying small groups.

[3]This group includes members of racial and ethnic and/or gender groups not identified as such because of privacy rules.

Source: Department of Public Instruction's WINSS Web site, at: www.dpi.wi.gov/sig/index.html.

WISCONSIN CHARTER SCHOOL ENROLLMENTS
By CESA District and Race, 2007-08

CESA	Number of Charter Schools	Total Students			American Indian	Asian	Black	Hispanic	White
		Total	Female	Male					
1	83	22,564	11,257	11,307	169	965	10,711	4,407	6,312
2	28	2,550	1,198	1,352	21	69	309	317	1,834
3	2	21	11	10	1	0	0	1	19
4	11	847	409	438	11	39	19	34	744
5	18	2,485	1,245	1,240	29	172	49	90	2,145
6	30	4,100	2,024	2,076	34	329	134	118	3,485
7	17	1,186	614	572	12	199	42	139	794
8	6	166	72	94	24	1	1	5	135
9	7	361	159	202	4	7	7	4	339
10.	8	388	186	202	7	9	9	9	354
11.	13	800	385	415	17	14	34	14	721
12.	9	104	63	41	29	0	0	2	73
TOTAL. . .	232	35,572	17,623	17,949	358	1,804	11,315	5,140	16,955

Note: There are 232 charter schools operated in 47 counties under Section 118.40, Wisconsin Statutes.

Sources: Wisconsin Department of Public Instruction's WINSS Web site, at: http://dpi.wi.gov/sig/index.html, and departmental data.

Wisconsin Cooperative Educational Service Agency (CESA) Districts

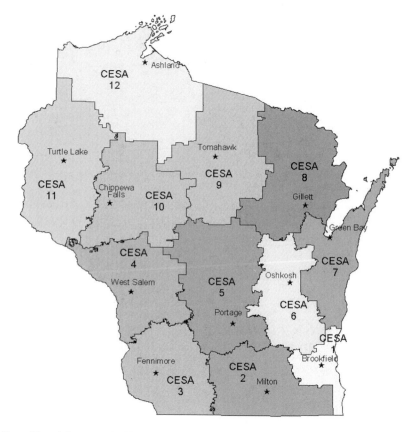

Source: Wisconsin Department of Public Instruction.

WISCONSIN PUBLIC SCHOOL SALARIES
Instructional Staff Employment and Average Salaries 2004-05 to 2008-09

			Instructional Staff			
		Avg. Salary		Non-		Avg. Salary
Year	Total	of Total	Principals	supervisory	Teachers	of Teachers
2004-05	66,357	$47,631	2,472	3,758	60,127	$44,299
2005-06	65,614	50,497	2,443	3,619	59,552	46,390
2006-07	65,292	52,116	2,431	3,570	59,291	47,901
2007-08	65,083	53,339	2,430	3,555	59,098	49,051
2008-09	65,130	54,747	2,386	3,435	59,309	50,424

Detail: Elementary and Secondary Teachers 2004-05 to 2008-09

	Elementary			Secondary		
			Avg.			Avg.
Year	Men	Women	Salary	Men	Women	Salary
2004-05	7,809	33,462	$44,128	8,979	9,877	$44,672
2005-06	7,607	33,177	46,409	8,825	9,943	46,350
2006-07	7,432	33,152	47,988	8,723	9,984	47,712
2007-08	7,314	33,161	49,159	8,610	10,013	48,817
2008-09	7,320	33,188	50,424	8,692	10,109	50,424

Sources: National Education Association, *Rankings of the States 2008 and Estimates of School Statistics 2009,* at: www.nea.org/assets/docs/02rankings08.pdf, December 2008, and previous issues.

AVERAGE SALARIES OF PUBLIC SCHOOL TEACHERS
by State, 2007-08

State	Average Salary	State Rank	State	Average Salary	State Rank
Alabama	$46,604	32	Montana	$42,874	46
Alaska	56,758	10	Nebraska	42,885	45
Arizona.	45,772	36	Nevada	47,710	23
Arkansas	45,773*	35	New Hampshire	47,609*	24
California	64,424*	1	New Jersey.	61,277*	4
Colorado	47,248	26	New Mexico	45,112	39
Connecticut	61,976	3	New York	62,332	2
Delaware.	55,994	12	North Carolina	47,354	25
District of Columbia	60,628*	5	North Dakota.	40,279	50
Florida	46,930	29	Ohio	53,410	14
Georgia.	51,560	18	Oklahoma	43,551	42
Hawaii	53,400	15	Oregon	51,811	17
Idaho	44,099	41	Pennsylvania	55,833*	13
ILLINOIS	60,474	6	Rhode Island	57,168*	9
Indiana	48,508	22	South Carolina	45,758	37
IOWA	46,664	31	South Dakota.	36,674	51
Kansas	45,136	38	Tennessee	45,030*	40
Kentucky.	47,207	27	Texas.	46,179	34
Louisiana	46,964	28	Utah	41,615*	49
Maine	43,397	43	Vermont	46,593*	33
Maryland.	60,069*	8	Virginia.	46,796*	30
Massachusetts	60,471	7	Washington.	49,884	20
MICHIGAN	56,096*	11	West Virginia.	42,529	47
MINNESOTA	50,582*	19	**WISCONSIN**	49,051	21
Mississippi	42,403*	48	Wyoming.	53,074	16
Missouri	43,206	44	UNITED STATES	$52,308*	

*Data estimated.

Source: National Education Association, *Rankings and Estimates: Rankings of the States 2008 and Estimates of School Statistics 2009,* at: www.nea.org/assets/docs/02rankings08.pdf, December 2008.

STATE AND LOCAL EDUCATION PAYROLLS
Instructional Employees, By State, March 2007

State	Kindergarten-12 FTE Employees* Number	Rank	Payroll (in thousands)	Rank	Higher Education FTE Employees* Number	Rank	Payroll (in thousands)	Rank
Alabama	69,198	23	$235,638	25	9,032	21	$58,176	19
Alaska	11,596	47	50,794	44	1,118	50	7,960	50
Arizona	74,370	19	277,541	21	8,995	22	57,216	21
Arkansas	46,045	32	152,578	32	6,370	30	33,656	33
California	379,234	2	2,221,785	1	41,874	1	328,397	1
Colorado	61,955	26	238,367	24	9,353	20	64,527	16
Connecticut	63,513	25	304,729	18	4,384	34	30,411	34
Delaware	10,454	48	47,063	46	1,524	47	10,450	42
District of Columbia	5,934	51	27,536	51	215	51	1,461	51
Florida	198,309	4	761,779	6	20,654	5	142,283	3
Georgia	157,035	8	591,810	9	12,596	12	75,241	13
Hawaii	19,140	42	74,734	42	2,717	38	16,842	37
Idaho	21,502	41	69,699	43	2,521	39	12,002	40
ILLINOIS	190,164	5	810,878	5	16,575	8	102,764	9
Indiana	86,327	16	336,799	15	17,345	7	92,101	11
IOWA	47,865	31	163,085	30	5,475	33	39,364	28
Kansas	53,226	29	174,442	29	6,563	29	41,761	27
Kentucky	69,944	22	217,311	26	9,390	19	58,140	20
Louisiana	65,469	24	207,413	27	7,255	27	45,023	26
Maine	25,620	40	83,663	41	1,731	44	9,139	47
Maryland	79,712	17	400,560	14	9,404	18	60,919	17
Massachusetts	107,110	13	481,048	13	6,064	31	36,942	32
MICHIGAN	121,744	12	574,084	10	20,790	4	137,760	4
MINNESOTA	71,155	20	299,917	20	10,773	15	58,847	18
Mississippi	49,474	30	149,105	33	7,930	26	38,799	29
Missouri	90,245	14	303,289	19	9,446	17	51,350	22
Montana	14,713	44	46,536	47	1,748	43	10,914	41
Nebraska	30,556	36	103,322	37	3,704	36	20,342	35
Nevada	27,794	37	112,576	34	2,234	40	15,621	39
New Hampshire	26,087	39	91,653	39	1,477	48	9,882	46
New Jersey	161,603	7	905,172	4	9,668	16	87,390	12
New Mexico	33,779	34	108,071	36	4,012	35	16,468	38
New York	324,925	3	1,671,610	2	23,307	3	136,328	5
North Carolina	147,738	10	508,866	12	20,173	6	112,014	7
North Dakota	9,307	50	38,268	50	1,976	41	10,164	43
Ohio	154,525	9	656,717	8	16,478	9	112,786	6
Oklahoma	60,647	27	186,723	28	6,602	28	38,118	31
Oregon	39,123	33	152,809	31	8,891	23	47,094	24
Pennsylvania	165,428	6	730,110	7	16,384	10	110,764	8
Rhode Island	16,258	43	84,142	40	1,780	42	10,109	45
South Carolina	70,284	21	238,412	23	8,518	24	48,320	23
South Dakota	12,926	46	38,387	49	1,688	46	10,136	44
Tennessee	86,671	15	307,638	17	8,090	25	46,086	25
Texas	431,550	1	1,495,858	3	34,527	2	234,274	2
Utah	30,815	35	112,419	35	5,913	32	38,651	30
Vermont	13,670	45	47,420	45	1,296	49	8,326	49
Virginia	128,070	11	516,549	11	14,379	11	96,418	10
Washington	57,863	28	273,219	22	12,065	13	68,202	15
West Virginia	26,939	38	95,067	38	3,328	37	18,714	36
WISCONSIN	79,487	18	317,205	16	11,672	14	73,320	14
Wyoming	10,369	49	42,081	48	1,705	45	8,428	48
UNITED STATES	4,337,467		$18,136,478		471,709		$3,000,400	

Note: State payroll detail may not sum to U.S. total due to rounding.

*FTE – Full-time equivalent employees.

Source: U.S. Department of Commerce, Bureau of the Census, *State and Local Government Employment and Payroll, March 2007*, at: www.census.gov/govs/www/apesstl07.html [February 2009]. Rank calculated by Wisconsin Legislative Reference Bureau.

EXPENDITURES PER PUPIL
By State and Source
2003-04 – 2006-07

	Expenditures per Pupil				Revenue Sources for 2006-07 Pupil Expenditure		
State	2003-04	2004-05	2005-06	2006-07	2006-07 State Rank	Federal	State	Local
Alabama	$6,581	$7,073	$7,683	$8,398	37	10.1%	57.3%	32.5%
Alaska	10,116	10,847	11,476	12,324	8	15.0	60.4	24.6
Arizona.	5,991	6,184	6,515	7,338	47	11.2	51.4	37.4
Arkansas	6,842	7,659	8,030	8,391	38	11.2	57.3	31.5
California	7,673[1]	7,905[1]	8,301[1]	8,952[1]	28	9.6	61.5	28.9
Colorado	7,478	7,826	8,166	8,286	39	7.0	43.1	49.9
Connecticut	11,436	12,263	13,072	13,659	3	4.6	38.8	56.6
Delaware	10,212	10,911	11,621	11,760	10	7.5	63.1	29.4
District of Columbia . . .	12,959	13,348	13,752	15,511	—	12.1	—	87.9
Florida	6,793	7,215	7,812	8,567	34	9.3	40.7	50.1
Georgia.	7,742	8,065	8,595	9,102	25	8.5	44.8	46.6
Hawaii	8,533	8,997	9,876	11,060	12	8.6	89.7	1.7
Idaho	6,168	6,319	6,469	6,648	49	10.3	67.2	22.5
ILLINOIS	8,606	8,896	9,113	9,596	21	7.8	30.5	61.8
Indiana	8,431	8,919	8,929	9,080	26	8.0	53.2	38.8
IOWA	7,626	7,962	8,355	8,791	32	8.0	45.5	46.5
Kansas	7,776	7,926	8,644	9,243	23	8.5	56.7	34.9
Kentucky.	6,861	7,132	7,668	7,940[1]	41	11.2	56.7	32.1
Louisiana.	7,271	7,669	8,486	8,937	29	17.3	42.6	40.1
Maine	9,746	10,342	10,841	11,644	11	9.1	45.2	45.6
Maryland.	9,433	10,031	10,909	11,975	9	5.8	40.3	53.8
Massachusetts	11,015	11,642	12,564	12,857	7	5.4	46.8	47.8
MICHIGAN	9,094	9,340	9,577	9,922	19	8.0	58.6	33.3
MINNESOTA	8,405	8,718	9,159	9,589	22	6.1	66.8	27.2
Mississippi.	6,199	6,548	7,173	7,459	45	17.1	53.3	29.6
Missouri	7,542[2]	7,858[2]	8,273	8,848	31	8.4	33.3	58.3
Montana	7,825	8,133	8,626	9,191	24	13.1	48.1	38.8
Nebraska	8,452	8,794	9,324	10,068	17	9.4	31.7	58.9
Nevada	6,410	6,804	7,177	7,806	44	7.0	26.9	66.1
New Hampshire	9,161	9,771	10,396	11,037	13	5.5	37.5	57.0
New Jersey.	13,338	14,117	14,954	16,163	1	4.4	42.1	53.5
New Mexico	7,572	7,834	8,354	8,849	30	14.0	71.6	14.4
New York	12,638	13,703	14,615	15,546	2	6.7	43.5	49.8
North Carolina.	6,613	6,904	7,396	7,878	42	10.0	63.5	26.5
North Dakota.	7,297	7,829	8,728	8,671	33	15.1	35.5	49.4
Ohio	9,029	9,330	9,692	9,940	18	7.1	44.5	48.4
Oklahoma	6,154	6,610	6,941	7,430	46	12.4	53.9	33.7
Oregon	7,618	8,071	8,645	8,958	27	9.7	51.4	39.0
Pennsylvania	9,708	10,235	10,723	10,905	14	7.3	36.2	56.5
Rhode Island	11,078	11,667	12,609	13,453	5	8.1	40.3	51.6
South Carolina	7,177	7,549	8,120	8,566	35	9.8	44.1	46.0
South Dakota.	7,068	7,464	7,775	8,064	40	15.6	32.9	51.6
Tennessee	6,466[1]	6,850[2]	7,004[2]	7,129[2]	48	10.7	43.4	45.9
Texas	7,151	7,246	7,480	7,850	43	10.3	37.8	51.9
Utah	4,991	5,216	5,464	5,706	50	8.9	55.7	35.4
Vermont	11,211	11,972	12,805	13,629	4	6.7	85.9	7.3
Virginia.	8,219	8,886	9,445	10,214	16	6.4	41.6	52.0
Washington.	7,391[2]	7,717[2]	7,984[2]	8,524[2]	36	8.3	61.1	30.6
West Virginia.	8,588	9,024	9,440	9,727	20	11.7	59.5	28.8
WISCONSIN	9,240	9,755	9,993	10,367	15	5.7	51.6	42.6
Wyoming.	9,308	10,190	11,437	13,266	6	7.5	48.9	43.6
UNITED STATES . .	$8,310[1,2]	$8,701[1,2]	$9,154[1,2]	$9,683[1,2]		8.5%	47.6%	43.9%

[1]Pre-kindergarten students imputed, affecting total student count and per pupil expenditure calculation.

[2]Value affected by redistribution of reported expenditure values to correct for missing data items.

Source: U.S. Department of Education, Institute of Education Sciences, National Center for Education Statistics, *Revenues and Expenditures for Public Elementary and Secondary Education: School Year 2006-07 (Fiscal Year 2007)*, February 2009, and previous NCES publications. Rank calculated by Wisconsin Legislative Reference Bureau. Detail may not add to total due to rounding.

STATE AND LOCAL PER CAPITA EDUCATION EXPENDITURES
By State, Fiscal Year 2005-06

State	All Education Amount	All Education Rank	Elementary and Secondary Amount	Elementary and Secondary Rank	Higher Education Amount	Higher Education Rank	Other Education* Amount	Other Education* Rank
Alabama	$2,372	28	$1,425	40	$814	13	$134	17
Alaska	3,666	1	2,682	1	864	10	120	21†
Arizona	1,914	50	1,255	49	580	35	79	42
Arkansas	2,271	36	1,470	35	678	25	123	20
California	2,534	17	1,759	11	668	26†	107	28
Colorado	2,301	32	1,561	27	668	26†	72	45
Connecticut	2,833	7	2,085	6	606	34	142	16
Delaware	3,100	5	1,894	8	1,011	3	196	4
District of Columbia	2,541	15	2,348	4	193	51	—	—
Florida	1,954	49	1,438	36	412	50	104	30†
Georgia	2,274	35	1,645	20	484	47	145	15
Hawaii	2,266	38	1,507	31	728	19	31	50
Idaho	1,961	48	1,266	48	607	33	87	38†
ILLINOIS	2,295	33	1,612	22†	578	37	104	30†
Indiana	2,357	29	1,548	28	685	24	124	19
IOWA	2,609	11†	1,563	26	927	7	118	23
Kansas	2,437	24	1,490	34	875	9	73	44
Kentucky	2,069	44	1,232	50	654	30	183	7
Louisiana	2,129	43	1,391	42†	572	38	166	8†
Maine	2,269	37	1,612	22†	541	43	117	24
Maryland	2,563	14	1,731	15	721	20	110	25†
Massachusetts	2,645	9	1,803	10	551	42	291	1
MICHIGAN	2,609	11†	1,707	18	822	11	80	41
MINNESOTA	2,527	18†	1,722	16	658	29	146	14
Mississippi	2,209	42	1,373	44	732	18	104	30†
Missouri	2,043	46	1,426	39	529	45	88	37
Montana	2,287	34	1,431	38	708	21	148	11
Nebraska	2,459	22	1,541	29	821	12	98	36
Nevada	2,055	45	1,526	30	470	49	60	49
New Hampshire	2,386	26	1,739	13	579	36	67	46†
New Jersey	3,185	4	2,512	2	562	39	110	25†
New Mexico	2,669	8	1,564	25	958	4	147	12†
New York	2,962	6	2,354	3	506	46	102	34
North Carolina	2,254	39	1,299	45	888	8	67	46†
North Dakota	2,619	10	1,492	32†	1,041	2	86	40
Ohio	2,505	21	1,732	14	621	32	153	10
Oklahoma	2,243	41	1,402	41	735	17	106	29
Oregon	2,253	40	1,391	42†	796	15	66	48
Pennsylvania	2,527	18†	1,744	12	534	44	249	2
Rhode Island	2,538	16	1,833	9	559	40	147	12†
South Carolina	2,445	23	1,606	24	649	31	190	6
South Dakota	1,968	47	1,293	46	555	41	120	21†
Tennessee	1,805	51	1,224	51	472	48	78	43
Texas	2,384	27	1,641	21	665	28	103	33
Utah	2,328	31	1,290	47	935	6	191	5
Vermont	3,252	3	1,995	7	1,066	1	100	35
Virginia	2,518	20	1,721	17	697	22	166	8†
Washington	2,400	25	1,492	32†	742	16	230	3
West Virginia	2,354	30	1,432	37	692	23	87	38†
WISCONSIN	2,580	13	1,680	19	813	14	125	18
Wyoming	3,287	2	2,207	5	956	5		
UNITED STATES	$2,431		$1,672		$640		$119	

Note: Per capita amounts are based on population as of July 2006.

*Includes assistance and subsidies to individuals and private elementary and secondary schools, and colleges and universities, as well as miscellaneous education expenditures.

†Tied.

Source: U.S. Department of Education, Institute of Education Sciences, National Center for Education Statistics, *Digest of Education Statistics 2008,* March 2009, at: http://nces.ed.gov/pubs2009/2009020.pdf. Rank calculated by Wisconsin Legislative Reference Bureau. Detail may not add to total due to rounding.

EDUCATION EXPENDITURES
BY STATE AND LOCAL GOVERNMENTS
By State, Fiscal Year 2005-06
(In Millions)

State	Total Expenditures[1]	Higher Education	Elem. & Secondary Schools	State	Total Expenditures[1]	Higher Education	Elem. & Secondary Schools
Alabama – State	$4,358	$3,743	—	Montana – State	777	637	—
Local	6,552	—	$6,552	Local	1,383	32	1,351
Alaska – State	965	558	326	Nebraska – State	1,379	1,206	—
Local	1,491	20	1,471	Local	2,969	245	2,724
Arizona – State.	3,067	2,579	—	Nevada – State	1,320	1,172	—
Local	8,733	995	7,738	Local	3,809	—	3,809
Arkansas – State	2,252	1,906	—	New Hampshire – State .	850	762	—
Local	4,131	—	4,131	Local	2,287	—	2,287
California – State	20,169	15,894	361	New Jersey – State. . . .	7,013	3,880	2,169
Local	72,202	8,442	63,760	Local	20,774	1,027	19,748
Colorado – State	3,438	3,093	0+	New Mexico – State . . .	1,896	1,608	0+
Local	7,501	83	7,418	Local	3,320	264	3,056
Connecticut – State . . .	2,621	2,124	0+	New York – State	9,394	7,425	—
Delaware – State	1,068	862	39	Local	47,796	2,345	45,451
Local	1,578	—	1,578	North Carolina – State . .	7,271	6,426	249
Florida – State	6,885	5,008	—	Local	12,693	1,440	11,253
Local	28,460	2,438	26,022	North Dakota – State. . .	720	662	3
Georgia – State.	5,865	4,509	1	Local	946	—	946
Local	15,427	23	15,405	Ohio – State	8,392	6,632	—
Hawaii – State	2,913	936	1,937	Local	20,366	490	19,876
Local	—	—	—	Oklahoma – State	3,018	2,630	7
Idaho – State	901	773	—	Local	5,011	—	5,011
Local	1,974	118	1,857	Oregon – State	2,440	2,194	—
ILLINOIS – State	6,732	5,396	—	Local	5,899	752	5,147
Local	22,713	2,024	20,689	Pennsylvania – State. . .	8,932	5,831	0+
Indiana – State	5,107	4,323	—	Local	22,503	810	21,692
Local	9,774	1	9,774	Rhode Island – State . . .	801	596	48
IOWA – State	2,479	2,126	—	Local	1,909	—	1,909
Local	5,300	638	4,662	South Carolina – State . .	3,793	2,805	167
Kansas – State	2,005	1,803	—	Local	6,772	—	6,772
Local	4,732	614	4,117	South Dakota – State. . .	481	387	—
Kentucky – State.	3,517	2,749	—	Local	1,058	47	1,011
Local	5,183	—	5,183	Tennessee – State	3,507	2,847	—
Louisiana – State.	3,168	2,454	—	Local	7,393	—	7,393
Local	5,963	—	5,963	Texas – State	14,431	12,575	18
Maine – State	883	715	14	Local	41,608	3,060	38,548
Local	2,116	—	2,116	Utah – State	2,647	2,385	—
Maryland – State.	3,800	3,182	0+	Local	3,291	—	3,291
Local	10,592	869	9,723	Vermont – State	784	665	—
Massachusetts – State . .	5,377	3,492	9	Local	1,245	—	1,245
Local	11,652	53	11,600	Virginia – State.	5,987	5,191	32
MICHIGAN – State . . .	8,313	6,864	645	Local	13,255	136	13,120
Local	18,023	1,434	16,588	Washington – State. . . .	5,806	4,746	0+
MINNESOTA – State . .	4,157	3,402	—	Local	9,545	—	9,545
Local	8,899	—	8,899	West Virginia – State. . .	1,677	1,259	—
Mississippi – State	1,886	1,584	—	Local	2,604	—	2,604
Local	4,544	548	3,997	**WISCONSIN** – State . .	3,944	3,459	—
Missouri – State	2,917	2,404	—	Local	10,393	1,056	9,337
Local	9,017	687	8,330	Wyoming – State.	372	307	0+
				Local	1,321	185	1,136
				U.S. TOTAL – State . .	$202,474	$160,769	$6,025
				Local[2]	$525,493	$30,990	$494,503

Notes: State payments to local governments for education aids appear as local government expenditures.

[1]"Total expenditures" includes "other education" expenditures not reported separately here. Figures may not add to total due to rounding by Wisconsin Legislative Reference Bureau.

[2]Includes District of Columbia expenditures: Total = $1,478; Higher Ed. = $112; Elem & Sec. = $1,365 (in millions).

Source: U.S. Department of Commerce, Bureau of the Census, "State and Local Government Finances by Level of Government and by State: 2005-2006", at: www.census.gov/govs/www/estimate06.html [September 2008].

STATE AND LOCAL EXPENDITURES FOR
PUBLIC EDUCATION IN WISCONSIN
2003-04 – 2007-08
(In Millions)

Agency/Program	2003-04	2004-05	2005-06	2006-07	2007-08
Public elementary and secondary schools[1]	$8,911.2	$9,216.2	$9,539.4	$9,902.9	$10,265.1
Department of Public Instruction	82.9	88.1	93.6	93.9	95.6
University of Wisconsin System	3,647.9	3,853.7	3,955.2	4,203.5	4,438.1
Wisconsin Technical College System Board	175.8	176.2	175.4	175.5	175.2
Public libraries (local expenditures)[2]	189.8	194.4	203.0	210.4	216.0
Other:					
Arts Board (Department of Tourism)	3.1	3.4	3.6	3.9	4.0
Educational Communications Board	13.2	15.5	15.3	15.8	16.0
Higher Educational Aids Board	80.7	92.5	107.5	100.6	120.7
Medical College of Wisconsin, Inc. (state funding)	5.5	5.6	5.6	6.2	6.6
State Historical Society	16.8	17.5	18.4	19.3	20.0
TOTAL	$13,126.9	$13,663.1	$14,117.0	$14,732.0	$15,357.3
Per capita expenditures[3]	$2,391	$2,469	$2,530	$2,622	$2,719

[1]Includes the gross costs of general operations, special projects, debt service, and food service; the net cost of capital projects; and the costs of CESA and County Children with Disabilities Education Board operations.

[2]Expenditures are for calendar year ending in the fiscal year shown.

[3]Based on total state population. Wisconsin population estimate for January 1, 2006: 5,617,744; for January 1, 2007 5,648,124.

Sources: Wisconsin Department of Administration, *Annual Fiscal Report, Appendix (Budgetary Basis) 2007-08,* 2008 and previous issues; Wisconsin Department of Administration, Demographic Services Center, *Time Series of the Final Official Population Estimates and Census Counts for Wisconsin Counties* [April 15, 2009]; Wisconsin Department of Public Instruction, Library Service Data, 2007 and previous data; Wisconsin Department of Public Instruction, departmental data. Per capita data calculated by Wisconsin Legislative Reference Bureau.

WISCONSIN HOME-BASED PRIVATE EDUCATIONAL PROGRAMS
1998-99 to 2007-08 Enrollments

Grade Level	1998-99	1999-2000	2000-01	2001-02	2002-03	2003-04	2004-05	2005-06	2006-07	2007-08
1	1,372	1,424	1,481	1,524	1,473	1,403	1,423	1,428	1,375	1,356
2	1,404	1,450	1,377	1,446	1,489	1,377	1,415	1,368	1,352	1,317
3	1,414	1,428	1,453	1,414	1,514	1,522	1,402	1,338	1,350	1,376
4	1,297	1,446	1,410	1,496	1,408	1,453	1,476	1,369	1,389	1,349
5	1,292	1,382	1,468	1,468	1,503	1,427	1,446	1,417	1,320	1,383
6	1,331	1,421	1,396	1,549	1,452	1,457	1,360	1,430	1,447	1,332
7	1,409	1,445	1,438	1,423	1,528	1,487	1,482	1,387	1,376	1,424
8	1,335	1,496	1,487	1,466	1,511	1,512	1,475	1,427	1,393	1,314
9	1,482	1,589	1,683	1,710	1,532	1,488	1,516	1,428	1,422	1,273
10	1,596	1,726	1,678	1,792	1,729	1,616	1,446	1,507	1,538	1,375
11	1,564	1,681	1,637	1,699	1,657	1,592	1,551	1,370	1,453	1,397
12	1,016	1,150	1,188	1,154	1,245	1,241	1,233	1,212	1,036	1,134
Ungraded	1,991	2,199	2,686	2,945	3,247	3,459	3,518	3,642	3,706	3,695
TOTAL	18,503	19,837	20,382	21,013	21,288	21,034	20,743	20,323	20,157	19,725

Note: A home-based private educational program is a program of educational instruction provided to a child by a child's parent or guardian or by a person designated by the parent or guardian. These programs must provide at least 875 hours of instruction each school year and must offer a sequentially progressive curriculum of fundamental instruction in reading, language arts, mathematics, social studies, science, and health.

Source: Wisconsin Department of Public Instruction, "Home-Based Private Educational Program Enrollment Trends: Enrollment by Grade", at: www.dpi.wi.gov/sms/hbstats.html [September 2008].

WISCONSIN PUBLIC LIBRARY SYSTEMS, 2007

Library System	Resource Library	Address	Counties or Cities Served	2007 Total Service Population	Circulation	State Aid for 2007
Arrowhead	Hedberg Public Library (608) 758-6600	316 S. Main Street Janesville, WI 53545-3971	Rock	159,507	1,961,503	$474,629
Eastern Shores	Mead Public Library (920) 459-3400 Ext. 3414	710 N. 8th Street Sheboygan, WI 53081-4563	Ozaukee, Sheboygan	203,552	2,369,865	612,269
Indianhead Federated . . .	L.E. Phillips Memorial Public Library (715) 839-5001	400 Eau Claire Street Eau Claire, WI 54701-3799	Barron, Chippewa, Dunn, Eau Claire, Pepin, Pierce, Polk, Price, Rusk, St. Croix	454,556	5,026,439	1,526,247
Kenosha County	Kenosha Public Library (262) 564-6324	812 56th Street P.O. Box 1414 Kenosha, WI 53141-1414	Kenosha	161,362	1,308,268	451,711
Lakeshores	Racine Public Library (262) 636-9252	75 Seventh Street Racine, WI 53403-1200	Racine, Walworth	284,541	2,042,598	718,542
Manitowoc-Calumet.	Manitowoc Public Library (920) 683-4863 Ext. 337	707 Quay Street Manitowoc, WI 54220-5439	Calumet, Manitowoc	117,885	1,150,642	467,431
Mid-Wisconsin Federated .	West Bend Community Memorial Library (262) 335-5151	630 Poplar Street West Bend, WI 53095-3246	Dodge, Jefferson, Washington, City of Whitewater	314,004	3,150,094	1,098,496
Milwaukee County Federated	Milwaukee Public Library (414) 286-3020	814 W. Wisconsin Avenue Milwaukee, WI 53233-2385	Milwaukee	937,429	7,441,915	3,239,633
Nicolet Federated	Brown County Library (920) 448-4400 Ext. 351	515 Pine Street Green Bay, WI 54301-5194	Brown, Door, Florence, Kewaunee, Marinette, Menominee, Oconto, Shawano	433,903	3,690,018	1,146,252
Northern Waters Library Service . .	Superior Public Library (715) 394-8860	1530 Tower Avenue Superior, WI 54880-2563	Ashland, Bayfield, Burnett, Douglas, Iron, Sawyer, Vilas, Washburn	158,206	1,275,995	574,559
Outagamie Waupaca	Appleton Public Library (920) 832-6170	225 N. Oneida Street Appleton, WI 54911-4780	Outagamie, Waupaca	237,720	2,918,152	640,317
South Central	Madison Public Library (608) 266-6363	201 W. Mifflin Street Madison, WI 53703-2597	Adams, Columbia, Dane, Green, Portage, Sauk, Wood	791,655	12,339,201	2,129,104
Southwest Wisconsin	Platteville Public Library (608) 348-7441	65 S. Elm Street Platteville, WI 53818-3139	Crawford, Grant, Iowa, Lafayette, Richland	127,366	990,623	539,669
Waukesha County Federated. .	Waukesha Public Library (262) 524-3681	321 Wisconsin Avenue Waukesha, WI 53186-4786	Waukesha	381,695	4,877,997	991,080
Winding Rivers	La Crosse Public Library (608) 789-7123	800 Main Street La Crosse, WI 54601-4122	Buffalo, Jackson, Juneau, La Crosse, Monroe, Trempealeau, Vernon	274,621	2,610,823	836,024
Winnefox.	Oshkosh Public Library (920) 236-5210	106 Washington Avenue Oshkosh, WI 54901-4985	Fond du Lac, Green Lake, Marquette, Waushara, Winnebago	323,119	4,319,469	1,627,964
Wisconsin Valley Library Service . .	Marathon County Public Library (715) 261-7211	300 N. First Street Wausau, WI 54403-5405	Clark, Forest, Langlade, Lincoln, Marathon, Oneida, Taylor	287,003	2,409,412	917,667
TOTAL.				5,648,124	59,883,014	$17,991,594

Sources: Wisconsin Department of Public Instruction, Public Library Statistics, "Statistics at the State and System Level, 2007: 2007 Wisconsin Public Library Service Data", at: www.dpi.wi.gov/pld/dm-lib-stat.html, and *Wisconsin Public Library Directory, 2008* [November 2008], at: www.dpi.wi.gov/pld/pdf/wipldir.pdf.

HIGHLIGHTS OF EMPLOYMENT AND INCOME IN WISCONSIN

Labor Force — An average of about 2,937,900 workers were employed in Wisconsin in 2008. Another 146,300 were part of the available workforce but were unemployed, resulting in an average unemployment rate of 4.7% for 2008. Since 1970, Wisconsin's labor force has increased by over 1.1 million workers from 1,941,700 to 3,048,100 in 2008. Based on January figures, the state's highest unemployment rate for that period occurred in 1983 when it reached 11.7%.

Employment by Industry — An average of 2.88 million Wisconsin workers were engaged in nonfarm employment in 2007. The greatest number worked in trade, transportation, and utilities (547,000); and manufacturing (501,000).

Nationally, 137.6 million were employed in nonfarm work in 2007. Trade, transportations, and utilities, with 26.6 million workers; and government, with 22.2 million, were the largest segments.

In March 2006, manufacturing and retail trade together accounted for more than one-third of the number of employees in Wisconsin. The majority (84.5%) of the more than 145,836 business establishments in the state had fewer than 20 employees in March 2006. Manufacturing accounted for the greatest number of large-sized firms, 408 out of 1,179 establishments with 250 or more employees.

Income by Industry — Earned income, which consists of wages and salaries, labor income, and proprietor's income, totaled $154.1 billion in Wisconsin in 2008. Service industries provided the greatest percentage of Wisconsin's earned income during that year, about 30.8%, with manufacturing at 22.2%. Government (all levels) and government enterprises were a distant third at 14.4%.

Personal Income — Personal income in Wisconsin totaled $210 billion in 2008. Wisconsin's per capita personal income of $37,314 lags behind the national average of $39,751, ranking Wisconsin 28th among the states. Connecticut had the highest per capita personal income ($56,248 in 2008, or about 141.5% of the national average). Mississippi had the lowest per capita personal income in 2008 at $29,569, about 74.4% of the national average.

Wisconsin's total adjusted gross income (total income reported for tax purposes) in 2007 was about $137.7 billion, or $42,474 per tax return. Ozaukee County had the highest per return AGI in 2007 at $89,593, followed by Waukesha County at $75,958. Trempealeau County is third ($60,573), and St. Croix County is fourth ($58,028). Rusk County ($31,584), Forest County ($29,563), and Menominee County ($16,442) had the lowest per return adjusted gross incomes.

Unemployment Benefits — In an average month in 2008, Wisconsin reported that 88,200 persons (about 57% of the 154,000 unemployed) received unemployment compensation. Nationally, 3.3 million people, or 37.5% of the 8.9 million unemployed, received benefits during an average month. The average weekly benefit in Wisconsin was $273.11, less than the national average of $297.09. The highest average weekly benefit of $413.07 was paid in Hawaii, followed by Massachusetts ($390.69), and New Jersey ($377.48). Lowest in the nation were Alabama ($202.16), Alabama ($196.23), and Mississippi ($182.74).

The following tables present selected data. Consult footnoted sources for more detailed information about employment and income.

EMPLOYMENT IN WISCONSIN, BY INDUSTRY
Annual Average, 2004 – 2008
(In Thousands)

	2004	2005	2006	2007	2008
Civilian Labor Force.	3,020.4	3,031.8	3,070.5	3,093.8	3,084.1
Unemployed	152.0	145.3	143.2	145.6	146.3
Percentage of labor force unemployed . .	5.0%	4.8%	4.7%	4.7%	4.7%
Employed	2,868.4	2,886.6	2,927.3	2,948.1	2,937.9
Total nonfarm	2,807.1	2,842.1	2,886.4	2,884.4	2,870.2
Service providing	2,173.8	2,205.7	2,229.3	2,253.5	2,256.2
Goods producing.	633.3	636.4	637.2	630.9	614.0
Trade, transportation, and utilities. . . .	538.9	543.2	544.5	547.1	539.7
Manufacturing	502.7	504.9	505.8	501.3	492.6
Educational and health services	374.9	383.3	392.0	398.7	405.5
Local government	281.2	284.1	282.8	283.4	287.2
Professional and business services. . . .	253.0	263.1	270.9	278.9	279.3
Leisure and hospitality.	250.8	255.2	259.5	262.0	258.3
Financial activities.	158.8	159.8	161.8	163.1	163.5
Other services, except public services . .	135.3	136.0	136.0	137.6	139.2
Construction	126.8	127.5	127.5	125.9	118.0
State government	101.4	102.0	103.2	103.4	103.6
Information	49.9	49.7	49.3	50.2	50.2
Federal government	29.6	29.2	29.2	29.2	29.6
Natural resources and mining	3.8	4.0	3.9	3.6	3.4

Note: Industry classifications in this table are defined by the North American Industry Classification System (NAICS), and are not directly comparable to the Standard Industrial Classification (SIC) codes used previously.

Source: Wisconsin Department of Workforce Development, Bureau of Workforce Information, Labor Market Information, "Local Area Unemployment Statistics (LAUS) Program Data", 2008 and previous years, at: http://worknet.wisconsin.gov/worknet/dalaus.aspx?menuselection=da [April 28, 2009], and "Current Employment Statistics (CES) Program Data", 2008 and previous years, at: http://worknet.wisconsin.gov/worknet/daces.aspx?menuselection=da [April 28, 2009].

MANUFACTURING EMPLOYMENT IN WISCONSIN
by Industry Group, 2001 – 2006

Industry Group	2001	2002	2003	2004	2005	2006
Fabricated metal products	72,537	66,302	61,620	61,357	63,841	65,529
Machinery	77,784	67,314	61,301	60,008	60,602	61,331
Food	60,833	62,140	58,103	59,637	60,397	57,187
Transportation equipment	40,601	34,498	37,022	35,770	36,591	33,980
Printing and related support activities	38,231	35,057	35,041	33,650	33,752	32,925
Paper.	38,865	37,436	35,406	33,694	32,965	32,283
Wood products	29,024	28,714	29,230	30,121	30,537	28,981
Plastics and rubber products	35,480	30,297	29,751	26,213	26,851	26,305
Electrical equipment, appliances, and components . .	30,028	26,701	27,043	26,524	25,254	25,494
Primary metal industries.	24,511	22,229	22,323	20,048	20,001	20,344
Computer and electronic products.	22,931	20,516	16,234	20,263	19,723	19,785
Miscellaneous manufacturing	17,742	16,697	20,199	18,136	17,925	18,063
Furniture and related products	18,321	17,036	15,796	17,918	12,775	15,891
Chemicals	13,806	13,147	12,150	11,750	11,731	13,125
Nonmetallic mineral products	10,006	9,971	10,346	10,670	10,814	10,593
Beverage and tobacco products	2,497	—[3]	2,873	2,459	2,360	2,691
Textile products	2,359	2,057	1,810	1,849	1,952	1,844
Textile mills	2,214	2,202	1,694	1,458	1,297	1,481
Leather and allied products	2,957	2,176	2,117	1,494	1,381	1,418
Apparel.	2,382	—[2]	1,318	1,526	1,402	1,369
Petroleum and coal products.	422	—[3]	—[4]	—[4]	—[4]	—[4]
TOTAL.	543,531	499,518	481,862	475,432	473,012	471,262

Note: Some industries have reported number of employees as an employment-size class rather than a specific number.

[1] 2,500 to 4,999 employment-size class.

[2] 1,000 to 2,499 employment-size class.

[3] 250 to 499 employment-size class.

[4] Industries with fewer than 950 employees not individually reported after 2002.

Source: U.S. Census Bureau, "2006 Annual Survey of Manufactures, Geographic Area Statistics" and prior years.

EMPLOYMENT TRENDS IN WISCONSIN
January 1990 – January 2009 (In Thousands)

Month and Year	Civilian Labor Force[1]	Employed	Unemployed	Unemployment Rate	Total Nonfarm Employment	Service Producing	Goods Producing	Manufacturing	Trade, Transportation, and Utilities
Jan. 1990	2,567.2	2,437.8	129.4	5.0%	2,206.7	1,615.2	591.5	513.7	448.0
Jan. 1991	2,592.1	2,441.7	150.4	5.8	2,232.9	1,650.1	582.8	505.9	454.4
Jan. 1992	2,621.2	2,476.4	144.8	5.5	2,269.0	1,684.2	584.8	504.0	456.2
Jan. 1993	2,677.2	2,536.6	140.7	5.3	2,324.9	1,726.8	598.1	513.5	459.8
Jan. 1994	2,777.0	2,630.0	147.1	5.3	2,383.8	1,772.9	610.9	523.1	473.4
Jan. 1995	2,830.6	2,711.3	119.3	4.2	2,476.9	1,828.9	648.0	556.5	489.7
Jan. 1996	2,862.5	2,736.8	125.7	4.4	2,523.8	1,873.7	650.1	555.9	500.2
Jan. 1997	2,909.8	2,785.2	124.6	4.3	2,559.9	1,900.6	659.3	559.9	504.2
Jan. 1998	2,937.8	2,825.9	111.9	3.8	2,625.2	1,941.6	683.6	583.2	512.5
Jan. 1999	2,951.4	2,839.3	112.1	3.8	2,686.4	1,993.0	693.4	586.5	526.7
Jan. 2000	2,960.9	2,856.6	104.3	3.5	2,748.9	2,047.6	701.3	590.2	541.4
Jan. 2001	3,003.3	2,877.0	126.2	4.2	2,770.7	2,081.2	689.5	577.0	549.2
Jan. 2002	3,009.8	2,832.0	177.8	5.9	2,719.4	2,075.9	643.5	531.6	533.0
Jan. 2003	3,038.7	2,851.4	187.3	6.2	2,717.6	2,082.7	634.9	526.0	524.7
Jan. 2004	3,050.4	2,919.2	178.5	5.9	2,718.1	2,111.1	607.0	493.5	529.5
Jan. 2005	2,996.6	2,831.3	165.4	5.5	2,757.2	2,145.2	612.0	496.6	532.0
Jan. 2006	3,019.7	2,865.9	153.8	5.1	2,790.0	2,171.2	618.8	501.1	536.0
Jan. 2007	3,074.7	2,908.3	166.4	5.4	2,814.4	2,200.0	614.4	498.7	541.3
Jan. 2008	3,065.5	2,914.8	150.7	4.9	2,828.3	2,221.5	606.8	495.8	539.9
Feb. 2008	3,063.1	2,905.6	157.5	5.1	2,824.0	2,222.3	601.7	493.9	531.4
Mar. 2008	3,065.6	2,911.8	153.8	5.0	2,836.9	2,233.3	603.6	493.8	533.2
Apr. 2008	3,062.2	2,933.6	128.6	4.2	2,863.3	2,253.2	610.1	493.4	536.1
May 2008	3,067.3	2,939.8	127.5	4.2	2,903.7	2,283.1	620.6	493.7	542.6
June 2008	3,133.5	2,986.9	146.6	4.7	2,923.2	2,290.3	632.9	501.8	545.8
July 2008	3,126.2	2,983.7	142.5	4.6	2,886.7	2,254.4	632.3	499.9	540.4
Aug. 2008	3,102.8	2,960.2	142.6	4.6	2,884.6	2,253.8	630.8	498.7	540.8
Sept. 2008	3,077.9	2,947.5	130.4	4.2	2,878.0	2,257.6	620.4	492.0	537.2
Oct. 2008	3,083.0	2,947.2	135.8	4.4	2,892.1	2,275.8	616.3	489.0	540.3
Nov. 2008	3,082.2	2,923.1	159.1	5.2	2,877.9	2,274.3	603.6	481.8	545.5
Dec. 2008	3,080.1	2,900.1	180.0	5.8	2,843.5	2,254.8	588.7	477.6	543.7
Jan. 2009[2]	3,076.4	2,840.0	236.4	7.7	2,753.8	2,190.1	563.7	464.7	522.4

[1]Civilian labor force includes both employed and unemployed persons, age 16 and over, and excludes current military personnel and other institutionalized individuals.

[2]January 2009 numbers are based on preliminary data and are subject to change.

Sources: Wisconsin Department of Workforce Development, "Current Employment Statistics, 2008 Monthly Reports", "Local Area Unemployment Statistics, 2008 Monthly Reports", and previous editions, at: http://worknet.wisconsin.gov/worknet/datablelist.aspx?menuselection=da [April 29, 2009].

WISCONSIN PERSONAL EARNED INCOME
By Source, 2003 – 2007 (In Millions)

Industry	2003	2004	2005	2006	2007
Services*	$36,179	$38,285	$40,169	$42,897	$45,443
Manufacturing	29,481	30,774	31,464	31,941	32,262
Government and government enterprises	19,244	19,990	20,698	21,108	21,710
Finance and insurance	8,243	8,643	8,908	9,530	9,981
Retail trade	8,683	8,867	8,990	9,187	9,344
Construction	7,944	8,461	8,955	9,110	9,184
Wholesale trade	6,522	7,049	7,549	8,005	8,241
Transportation and warehousing	4,535	4,797	5,069	5,219	5,407
Information	2,740	3,020	3,119	3,185	3,433
Real estate and rental and leasing	1,721	1,889	2,035	1,856	1,822
Farm earnings	1,323	1,328	1,165	929	1,768
Utilities	1,042	1,129	1,154	1,166	1,214
Agricultural services, forestry, and fishing	347	346	349	356	375
Mining	214	251	271	268	275
TOTAL	$128,217	$135,080	$140,151	$144,756	$150,459

Note: Total may not add due to rounding.

*Services includes the following NAICS classification categories: Professional, scientific, and technical services; Management of companies and enterprises; Administrative and waste services; Educational services; Health care and social assistance; Arts, entertainment, and recreation; Accommodation and food services; and Other services except public administration.

Source: U.S. Department of Commerce, Bureau of Economic Analysis, Income and employment tables by NAICS industry, 2006 and 2007, *Table SA05N: Personal Income and Detailed Earnings by Industry – Wisconsin*, at: http://www.bea.gov/regional/spi/default.cfm?selTable=SA05N&selSeries=NAICS [May 5, 2009].

DISTRIBUTION OF WISCONSIN BUSINESS ESTABLISHMENTS
By Number of Employees and Establishments, March 2006

Industry[1]	Total Employees[2]	Total	1 to 19	20 to 49	50 to 99	100 to 249	250 to 499	500 or more
			Number of Establishments by Employment Size					
Forestry, fishing, hunting and agricultural support . . .	3,299	542	523	11	4	2	1	1
Mining	3,857	157	123	23	4	5	1	1
Utilities	13,946	293	181	52	28	22	6	4
Construction	120,114	17,032	15,862	838	225	83	18	6
Manufacturing	492,822	9,670	5,964	1,611	942	745	261	147
Food, beverage, and tobacco products[3]	63,524	1,044	583	195	106	101	39	20
Textiles, textile products, apparel and leather and allied products[4]	6,053	289	232	27	12	15	3	0
Wood products	30,320	661	411	127	51	51	12	9
Paper	33,338	243	66	45	42	52	21	17
Printing and related support activities	33,227	906	660	107	70	46	14	9
Petroleum and coal products	756	22	12	6	2	2	0	0
Chemicals	14,019	349	216	62	49	16	1	5
Plastics and rubber products	29,881	486	203	112	78	69	21	3
Nonmetallic mineral products	10,731	408	303	66	14	18	6	1
Primary metal	22,286	185	64	30	33	32	18	8
Fabricated metal products	68,095	1,976	1,270	358	180	127	32	9
Machinery	61,796	1,123	649	207	135	84	29	19
Computer and electronic products	23,193	259	134	44	35	32	4	10
Electrical equipment, appliances, and components . .	25,523	186	72	38	17	23	22	14
Transportation equipment	37,006	283	142	42	29	27	25	18
Furniture and related products	16,175	558	418	66	48	17	6	3
Miscellaneous manufacturing	16,899	692	529	79	41	33	8	2
Wholesale trade	114,530	7,241	5,901	869	288	145	30	8
Durable goods	70,852	4,364	3,492	593	183	76	14	6
Nondurable goods	38,854	2,032	1,604	249	99	63	15	2
Retail trade	321,788	21,102	17,792	1,969	711	549	75	6
Motor vehicles and parts	40,022	2,780	2,262	332	141	42	3	0
Furniture and home furnishings	10,994	1,240	1,111	108	13	8	0	0
Electronics and appliances	9,170	866	792	31	25	17	1	0
Building materials and garden supplies	32,204	2,091	1,735	225	57	73	0	1
Food and beverages	57,067	2,221	1,617	234	177	182	11	0
Health and personal care	19,781	1,395	1,078	224	89	4	0	0
Gasoline stations	24,232	2,605	2,390	196	17	2	0	0
Clothing and clothing accessories	21,722	2,257	2,006	190	54	7	0	0
Sporting goods, hobbies, books and music	12,997	1,308	1,154	114	33	6	1	0
General merchandise	60,048	866	474	59	80	196	57	0
Miscellaneous retail	16,663	2,416	2,227	179	9	0	0	1
Nonstore retailers (including online)	16,888	1,057	946	77	16	12	2	4
Transportation and warehousing	103,047	5,577	4,652	554	204	118	29	20
Truck transportation	56,659	3,845	3,357	302	110	48	17	11
Couriers and messengers	10,049	251	173	38	13	24	1	2
Transit and ground passenger service	14,287	537	349	112	50	23	2	1
Warehousing and storage	11,471	295	217	37	19	13	6	3
Information	57,154	2,254	1,743	308	101	60	28	14
Publishing	19,955	580	408	103	34	21	9	5
Motion Pictures and sound recording	3,454	296	236	47	12	1	0	0
Broadcasting	5,170	178	114	36	15	12	1	0
Internet Publishing and broadcasting	205	32	30	1	1	0	0	0
Telecommunications	16,897	836	698	88	23	14	10	3
Internet service providers and data processing	11,217	305	233	32	14	12	8	6
Other Information Services	256	27	24	1	2	0	0	0
Finance and insurance	139,953	9,488	8,522	612	196	102	25	31
Real estate and rental and leasing	28,004	5,159	4,931	167	43	17	1	0
Professional, scientific, and technical services	102,240	11,586	10,623	646	196	93	21	7
Management of companies and enterprises	59,305	1,019	671	151	84	52	36	25
Administrative support and waste management	136,788	6,699	5,566	555	279	200	65	34
Educational services	48,747	1,429	1,053	244	80	29	6	17
Health care and social assistance	358,027	14,260	11,771	1,359	510	424	102	94
Ambulatory health care	118,221	7,969	6,977	611	215	107	36	23
Hospitals	108,436	144	3	1	7	41	30	62
Nursing and residential care	72,444	2,324	1,652	284	171	186	25	6
Social assistance	58,926	3,823	3,139	463	117	90	11	3
Arts, entertainment, and recreation	37,843	2,633	2,232	270	68	47	13	3
Accommodations and food services	225,445	14,120	10,531	2,695	745	121	21	7
Accommodations	35,064	1,529	1,165	248	58	35	16	7
Food services and drinking places	190,381	12,591	9,366	2,447	687	86	5	0
Other services (except public administration)	114,970	15,134	14,079	823	147	70	12	3
Repair and maintenance	23,325	4,426	4,264	135	19	7	1	0
Personal and laundry services	27,884	4,327	4,105	176	27	19	0	0
Religious, grantmaking, civic, professional, and like organizations	63,761	6,381	5,710	512	101	44	11	3
Unclassified establishments	402	441	440	1	0	0	0	0
TOTAL	2,482,281	145,836	123,160	13,758	4,855	2,884	751	428

[1]Industry categories and the total include subcategories not reported separately.

[2]Number of employees for the week including March 12, 2006. Excludes most government and railroad employees and self-employed persons.

[3]Beverage and tobacco product manufacturers report number of employees using employment-size class of 2,500 to 4,999, which is not included in industry group total.

[4]Apparel manufacturers report number of employees using employment-size class of 1,000 to 2,499, which is not included in industry group total.

Source: U.S. Census Bureau, "County Business Patterns, Wisconsin: 2006", at: http://www.census.gov/econ/cbp/index.html [May 12, 2009].

EMPLOYEES IN NONAGRICULTURAL
Average by
(In

State	Total[1]	Other Services	Professional and Business Services	Education and Health Services	Manu- facturing	Finance, Insurance, and Real Estate
Alabama	2,006	81	221	209	297	100
Alaska	318	12	25	37	13	15
Arizona	2,666	97	402	304	182	184
Arkansas	1,204	45	117	154	189	53
California	15,163	514	2,263	1,664	1,463	907
Colorado	2,330	93	348	240	146	160
Connecticut	1,698	64	206	288	191	145
Delaware	437	20	60	58	33	45
District of Columbia	695	63	154	98	2	29
Florida	8,041	344	1,329	1,007	389	542
Georgia	4,147	161	560	456	431	231
Hawaii	624	27	76	73	15	30
Idaho	656	19	83	74	66	33
ILLINOIS	5,981	262	869	779	676	405
Indiana	2,988	112	290	396	550	139
IOWA	1,517	58	121	203	230	103
Kansas	1,379	52	144	171	186	74
Kentucky	1,869	76	182	241	256	93
Louisiana	1,921	69	201	247	158	97
Maine	617	20	54	116	59	33
Maryland	2,610	118	397	374	132	158
Massachusetts	3,277	120	482	624	295	225
MICHIGAN	4,262	177	573	595	617	211
MINNESOTA	2,771	117	329	428	341	179
Mississippi	1,152	37	95	126	170	47
Missouri	2,796	121	338	384	300	167
Montana	443	17	41	59	20	22
Nebraska	963	35	104	132	101	69
Nevada	1,292	37	158	92	51	65
New Hampshire	649	22	66	103	78	39
New Jersey	4,074	164	608	580	313	275
New Mexico	843	30	109	111	37	35
New York	8,738	363	1,137	1,602	554	731
North Carolina	4,146	180	500	514	539	211
North Dakota	358	15	30	51	26	20
Ohio	5,424	222	666	790	773	301
Oklahoma	1,566	63	181	193	150	84
Oregon	1,732	60	198	212	204	107
Pennsylvania	5,796	257	704	1,074	658	332
Rhode Island	493	23	56	99	51	35
South Carolina	1,950	74	227	201	250	106
South Dakota	406	16	28	60	42	31
Tennessee	2,797	103	322	350	381	144
Texas	10,359	354	1,291	1,255	935	644
Utah	1,252	36	161	140	128	75
Vermont	308	10	22	57	36	13
Virginia	3,761	185	644	417	279	194
Washington	2,932	105	345	348	293	155
West Virginia	757	56	61	114	59	30
WISCONSIN	2,882	138	277	399	501	163
Wyoming	288	12	18	23	10	11
UNITED STATES[3]	137,623	5,491	17,962	18,327	13,884	8,308

[1]Includes natural resources and mining, not shown separately.

[2]Construction includes natural resources and mining for Delaware, District of Columbia, Hawaii, Maryland, Nebraska, South Dakota, and Tennessee.

[3]State totals do not sum to U.S. totals because of differing methodologies.

Source: U.S. Census Bureau, "Statistical Abstract of the United States: 2009, Table 611. Employees in Nonfarm Establishments – States: 2007", at: http://www.census.gov/compendia/statab/tables/09s0611.pdf [June 3, 2009].

ESTABLISHMENTS
State, 2007
Thousands)

Trade, Transportation, and Utilities	Construction[2]	Government	Leisure and Hospitality	Information	State
396	113	376	174	28	. . . . Alabama
64	18	82	32	7	. . . . Alaska
525	224	423	273	43	. . . . .Arizona
250	56	210	99	20	. . . . Arkansas
2,911	892	2,497	1,553	473	. . . . .California
430	167	375	270	76	. . . . Colorado
311	69	249	136	39	. . . . .Connecticut
83	28	61	41	7	. . . . Delaware
28	13	232	55	22	. . . . . District of Columbia
1,611	598	1,124	929	161	. . . . Florida
888	222	676	397	115	. . . . .Georgia
121	739	122	110	11	. . . . Hawaii
132	53	118	63	11	. . . . Idaho
1,212	271	851	531	116	. . . . ILLINOIS
588	151	432	284	40	. . . . Indiana
309	73	250	137	34	. . . . .IOWA
264	65	258	116	41	. . . . .Kansas
387	85	325	173	30	. . . . .Kentucky
383	134	359	194	28	. . . . .Louisiana
126	31	104	60	11	. . . . .Maine
477	191	479	235	51	. . . . .Maryland
571	137	433	302	88	. . . . Massachusetts
788	166	657	405	66	. . . . MICHIGAN
530	121	415	248	58	. . . . MINNESOTA
227	58	244	126	13	. . . . Mississippi
549	148	440	281	63	. . . . Missouri
92	33	85	58	8	. . . . Montana
205	51	164	82	19	. . . . Nebraska
232	134	157	339	16	. . . . Nevada
142	28	94	64	12	. . . . New Hampshire
876	172	648	340	98	. . . . New Jersey
144	59	195	88	16	. . . . New Mexico
1,526	351	1,504	699	265	. . . . .New York
778	255	695	394	73	. . . . North Carolina
76	19	76	33	8	. . . . North Dakota
1,051	225	798	500	88	. . . . Ohio
288	71	321	140	29	. . . . Oklahoma
340	104	290	172	36	. . . . Oregon
1,135	263	744	500	107	. . . . Pennsylvania
80	22	65	51	11	. . . . Rhode Island
377	128	338	218	28	. . . . South Carolina
82	23	76	43	7	. . . . South Dakota
611	138	421	276	50	. . . . Tennessee
2,104	642	1,728	980	221	. . . . Texas
246	104	207	113	32	. . . . Utah
59	17	54	33	6	. . . . Vermont
668	241	686	346	91	. . . . .Virginia
553	208	533	281	103	. . . . .Washington
143	39	145	71	11	. . . . .West Virginia
547	126	416	262	50	. . . . **WISCONSIN**
55	26	67	34	4	. . . . Wyoming
26,608	7,614	22,203	13,474	3,029	. . . . . . UNITED STATES[3]

UNEMPLOYMENT, UNEMPLOYMENT RATES, AND UNEMPLOYMENT INSURANCE BENEFITS
By State, 2008

State	Rate[1]	Unemployment Persons (in millions) Total	Unemployment Persons (in millions) Insured[2]	Insured as % of Total	Unemployment Insurance Benefits Average Weekly	Unemployment Insurance Benefits Total Paid (in thousands)
Alabama	4.9%	107.7	37.7	35.0%	$196.23	$321,598
Alaska	6.9	24.6	11.2	45.5	202.16	108,737
Arizona.	5.1	159.2	48.2	30.3	217.72	437,849
Arkansas	5.1	70.7	34.7	49.1	264.86	342,044
California	7.2	1,333.5	509.0	38.2	307.12	6,818,097
Colorado	5.1	139.3	30.7	22.0	340.72	412,583
Connecticut	5.8	109.5	47.8	43.7	321.97	743,014
Delaware	4.6	20.4	10.3	50.5	256.89	128,133
District of Columbia	6.9	23.0	5.2	22.6	290.83	140,949
Florida	6.0	559.7	179.0	32.0	238.41	1,827,610
Georgia.	6.1	298.4	85.4	28.6	272.78	950,464
Hawaii	4.0	26.4	11.9	45.1	413.07	220,811
Idaho	4.2	31.6	19.4	61.4	272.18	219,190
ILLINOIS	6.6	442.7	161.6	36.5	312.09	2,317,087
Indiana	5.9	190.7	74.8	39.2	297.73	971,681
IOWA	4.0	67.4	29.5	43.8	302.14	421,486
Kansas	4.5	66.9	22.3	33.3	316.03	326,284
Kentucky.	6.4	130.8	40.7	31.1	299.68	562,853
Louisiana.	4.6	93.0	26.9	28.9	209.12	213,748
Maine	5.5	38.9	12.7	32.6	264.78	143,038
Maryland.	4.3	129.7	50.5	38.9	304.93	633,490
Massachusetts	5.1	174.8	97.2	55.6	390.69	1,708,944
MICHIGAN	8.4	418.0	165.0	39.5	299.58	2,225,042
MINNESOTA	5.5	162.4	60.1	37.0	346.93	907,708
Mississippi.	7.0	92.5	25.6	27.7	182.74	176,292
Missouri	6.1	185.2	59.5	32.1	244.10	580,571
Montana	4.2	21.2	9.9	46.7	255.19	101,297
Nebraska	3.4	33.4	10.9	32.6	241.25	103,415
Nevada	6.8	94.4	40.2	42.6	292.32	536,744
New Hampshire	4.0	29.7	10.2	34.3	272.03	117,220
New Jersey.	5.5	249.5	134.6	53.9	377.48	2,380,001
New Mexico	4.0	38.1	14.3	37.5	278.07	165,762
New York	5.4	520.4	211.5	40.6	306.54	2,769,461
North Carolina	6.4	290.7	109.7	37.7	287.32	1,289,143
North Dakota.	3.3	12.3	3.7	30.1	286.21	45,233
Ohio	6.6	395.5	128.3	32.4	302.69	1,586,561
Oklahoma	3.9	67.5	17.0	25.2	272.43	191,935
Oregon	6.3	124.0	62.7	50.6	301.69	810,473
Pennsylvania.	5.5	350.1	196.3	56.1	335.40	2,850,183
Rhode Island	7.8	44.4	15.9	35.8	370.46	272,607
South Carolina	7.0	150.0	53.8	35.9	239.81	484,358
South Dakota.	3.0	13.4	2.4	17.9	238.82	22,046
Tennessee	6.4	194.5	54.2	27.9	220.98	561,656
Texas.	4.9	568.5	123.0	21.6	302.94	1,591,044
Utah	3.4	47.4	15.0	31.6	311.60	194,448
Vermont	4.9	17.5	8.0	45.7	293.62	112,868
Virginia.	4.2	172.1	44.3	25.7	281.86	504,608
Washington.	5.5	192.0	69.1	36.0	355.33	1,028,074
West Virginia.	4.7	37.9	15.0	39.6	241.52	150,577
WISCONSIN	5.0	154.0	88.2	57.3	273.11	1,051,394
Wyoming.	3.2	9.2	2.9	31.5	307.52	40,776
UNITED STATES[3]. . .	5.8%	8,924.0	3,343.6	37.5%	$297.09	$43,054,822

Note: Unemployment and unemployment insurance data include Puerto Rico and U.S. Virgin Islands, not listed separately. "Insured as percent of total" calculated by Wisconsin Legislative Reference Bureau.

[1]Total unemployed as a percentage of civilian workforce in the state.

[2]Insured unemployed are unemployed persons receiving unemployment benefits.

[3]Because of separate processing and weighting procedures, U.S. totals may differ from the sum of state data.

Source: U.S. Department of Labor, Employment and Training Administration, "Unemployment Insurance Data Summary – 4th Quarter 2008", at: http://www.ows.doleta.gov/unemploy/content/data_stats/datasum08/DataSum_2008_4.pdf [May 11, 2009].

WISCONSIN ADJUSTED GROSS INCOME
By County, 2003 – 2007

County	2007 AGI[1]	Per Return AGI					2007 Rank
		2003	2004	2005	2006	2007	
Adams	$301,840,407	$28,767	$29,379	$32,059	$33,494	$33,264	69
Ashland	265,880,125	27,997	28,848	30,473	32,442	33,352	66
Barron	862,101,847	32,608	32,665	34,423	34,787	36,654	54
Bayfield	319,288,432	32,059	33,223	34,819	36,976	41,841	33
Brown	6,231,526,196	44,572	46,749	47,855	50,658	50,773	9
Buffalo	255,769,474	31,401	32,379	33,601	35,835	36,696	53
Burnett	260,675,588	30,912	31,543	32,373	34,916	33,279	68
Calumet	1,143,678,469	45,709	47,565	49,417	52,469	53,155	7
Chippewa	1,219,642,357	34,654	35,575	37,556	38,343	41,857	32
Clark	571,939,145	29,166	32,116	32,169	33,850	37,165	50
Columbia	1,315,077,417	39,656	41,051	42,966	44,851	45,434	21
Crawford	278,536,586	28,853	30,107	31,427	32,187	33,799	64
Dane	14,204,844,971	49,928	50,911	53,570	55,792	57,270	5
Dodge	1,884,537,459	38,134	40,041	40,551	42,947	43,922	27
Door	695,134,547	36,518	38,336	40,671	43,748	44,934	23
Douglas	837,199,062	34,043	34,510	35,324	37,817	39,143	45
Dunn	766,837,518	34,979	36,044	37,633	39,198	40,826	39
Eau Claire	2,115,296,015	66,817	53,566	41,592	74,282	44,499	24
Florence	81,745,276	32,805	32,577	35,729	35,169	36,526	55
Fond du Lac	2,354,788,269	39,415	41,247	42,789	45,292	46,302	18
Forest	136,847,556	25,990	27,398	28,113	29,718	29,563	71
Grant	855,884,054	31,793	32,548	35,083	35,435	37,098	51
Green	825,989,997	37,519	39,424	41,810	43,822	44,415	25
Green Lake	409,169,378	34,148	36,110	37,579	39,398	41,778	34
Iowa	513,714,682	37,825	37,906	40,191	41,618	43,126	30
Iron	111,410,166	28,117	29,010	31,044	31,589	33,376	65
Jackson	378,085,067	29,962	31,254	32,793	35,681	38,978	46
Jefferson	1,818,281,436	38,864	39,812	41,637	43,850	45,137	22
Juneau	446,716,711	30,478	31,546	33,593	33,663	34,796	63
Kenosha	3,577,634,928	41,392	42,088	43,525	45,641	46,273	19
Kewaunee	433,720,516	35,776	38,007	38,795	40,743	41,926	31
La Crosse	2,579,913,967	43,383	43,932	45,783	46,115	47,334	15
Lafayette	289,253,964	29,618	31,499	32,626	33,830	35,570	61
Langlade	364,746,903	30,390	31,436	33,333	35,430	35,163	62
Lincoln	604,785,365	35,154	36,288	38,061	40,884	40,332	42
Manitowoc	1,849,217,486	37,252	38,562	40,385	42,325	44,076	26
Marathon	3,177,376,178	41,625	42,641	44,672	46,221	47,695	13
Marinette	778,111,220	31,812	33,035	34,778	35,357	36,077	59
Marquette	293,589,747	31,323	31,344	33,508	34,630	36,703	52
Menominee	22,492,235	16,065	17,054	16,683	16,806	16,442	72
Milwaukee	20,249,038,364	37,459	38,350	40,244	42,296	43,390	29
Monroe	772,033,314	32,223	33,203	34,401	35,926	36,288	57
Oconto	747,303,929	34,716	35,938	37,591	38,609	40,145	43
Oneida	822,410,179	36,481	37,594	39,647	42,145	41,605	35
Outagamie	4,565,549,279	44,027	45,445	47,065	49,484	50,774	8
Ozaukee	3,960,707,636	71,800	75,435	81,365	85,546	89,593	1
Pepin	151,531,348	32,765	35,133	37,264	38,712	40,582	40
Pierce	916,319,676	44,095	44,745	47,180	49,525	50,450	10
Polk	890,996,675	36,961	37,544	38,915	40,377	41,332	37
Portage	1,497,415,558	39,138	40,085	42,448	43,665	45,844	20
Price	274,549,208	28,159	29,753	31,333	34,989	36,441	56
Racine	4,803,106,791	43,124	44,568	45,928	48,154	49,266	12
Richland	346,933,669	31,595	34,032	34,903	35,888	40,487	41
Rock	3,712,273,483	40,696	41,038	41,906	44,393	46,611	17
Rusk	222,571,868	27,459	27,801	28,994	30,600	31,584	70
St. Croix	2,297,862,290	50,451	51,810	54,381	56,937	58,028	4
Sauk	1,362,874,392	37,413	38,433	40,150	40,906	41,573	36
Sawyer	281,746,300	29,373	29,926	31,917	33,108	33,280	67
Shawano	752,294,946	31,659	33,032	34,495	35,689	37,435	48
Sheboygan	2,797,212,872	41,786	42,972	44,381	46,824	47,428	14
Taylor	373,218,345	33,745	33,675	33,932	36,296	39,179	44
Trempealeau	901,749,725	39,688	43,134	48,256	53,012	60,573	3
Vernon	484,402,752	30,148	31,116	32,909	34,279	36,088	58
Vilas	443,592,079	33,562	33,515	35,978	39,223	38,704	47
Walworth	2,284,594,297	41,355	42,019	44,742	46,485	47,237	16
Washburn	308,321,274	30,585	32,809	36,625	36,435	35,822	60
Washington	3,741,881,374	49,449	51,283	54,089	55,966	56,652	6
Waukesha	15,077,154,751	61,987	64,012	67,954	72,581	75,958	2
Waupaca	1,083,158,430	36,194	38,162	40,107	40,514	41,063	38
Waushara	429,918,743	30,560	31,972	33,530	35,354	37,261	49
Winnebago	3,980,184,024	42,904	44,761	46,101	47,960	49,459	11
Wood	1,703,250,844	38,515	39,463	40,197	41,871	43,726	28
STATE[2]	$137,669,439,131	$42,474	$43,512	$45,357	$48,107	$48,985	

Note: This table previously reported AGI on a per capita, rather than per return, basis. The change to a per return basis should result in more useful data because it will reflect the AGI of each taxpayer, rather than the AGI of the entire population, many of whom pay no taxes.

[1]"Wisconsin adjusted gross income" (AGI) is Wisconsin income as reported to the Wisconsin Department of Revenue for income tax purposes and is based on the federal income tax definition of gross income as modified by certain additions and subtractions required by state law.

[2]State totals and state per return figures include amounts not allocated to a particular county.

Source: Wisconsin Department of Revenue, "Wisconsin Municipal Income Per Return Report, 2007" and earlier volumes, at: http://www.dor.state.wi.us/report/i.html#income [May 28, 2009]. Rankings calculated by Wisconsin Legislative Reference Bureau.

EARNED INCOME BY INDUSTRY,
(In

State	Earned Income Total[1]	Rank per Capita[2]	Farm Earnings	Agricultural Services, Forestry, Fishing, and Other[3]	Mining	Utilities	Construction	Manufacturing
Alabama	$111,184.2	43	$850.2	$578.1	$1,281.1	$1,579.9	$6,656.9	$18,475.9
Alaska	23,822.8	6	–3.5	191.0	2,080.0	223.2	1,740.9	803.4
Arizona.	155,423.1	42	589.8	419.9	1,512.7	1,488.0	11,711.8	14,391.7
Arkansas	61,821.9	49	1,425.6	532.9	917.8	691.9	3,285.2	9,274.2
California	1,188,737.9	14	8,277.1	6,985.7	5,263.4	12,442.9	67,287.2	132,865.8
Colorado	166,903.7	8	590.2	238.0	5,777.8	1,156.6	11,826.3	11,782.6
Connecticut	143,727.6	2	136.5	47.2	290.6	1,366.0	6,514.4	19,444.8
Delaware	29,169.7	11	216.2	22.7	39.4	274.8	1,735.6	2,873.5
District of Columbia	76,475.4	1	0.0	964.1	12.7	306.4	935.8	178.3
Florida	446,953.7	41	1,596.3	1,858.2	870.5	3,282.0	30,484.8	26,223.4
Georgia.	255,648.9	34	1,308.1	770.7	582.3	3,476.0	13,798.9	26,945.2
Hawaii	40,763.1	17	180.7	58.9	62.0	325.4	3,156.4	1,012.4
Idaho	34,374.4	47	958.1	402.7	249.1	310.0	2,551.9	4,227.5
ILLINOIS	416,319.6	15	3,593.2	424.1	3,768.5	3,539.4	22,944.7	53,436.7
Indiana	161,702.2	38	1,807.9	221.0	1,016.6	1,881.4	9,920.7	39,018.4
IOWA	83,747.2	25	5,167.7	299.1	185.8	867.6	4,914.5	14,849.3
Kansas	80,959.7	23	948.6	263.4	1,869.9	861.1	4,148.4	13,770.2
Kentucky.	101,288.5	44	932.4	421.6	2,474.9	655.3	5,356.5	16,305.7
Louisiana.	115,510.4	36	699.1	517.7	7,809.5	1,257.9	9,118.0	12,162.8
Maine	32,156.7	40	161.6	362.1	23.0	248.5	1,928.2	3,937.0
Maryland.	187,202.3	12	293.1	121.8	195.8	3,493.2	13,538.7	11,184.9
Massachusetts	258,563.6	3	77.6	537.2	451.4	1,900.9	12,637.4	26,709.5
MICHIGAN	262,654.5	35	1,196.4	349.4	1,251.5	3,310.5	11,965.5	51,269.6
MINNESOTA	174,690.1	10	3,490.9	357.4	676.9	1,616.0	8,730.6	24,782.9
Mississippi	58,409.0	51	931.8	488.3	1,129.1	692.2	3,781.3	8,452.9
Missouri	158,666.4	29	1,231.3	332.0	552.5	1,387.6	9,926.6	19,728.7
Montana	22,944.8	45	192.0	210.6	925.1	463.3	1,779.7	1,297.5
Nebraska	52,110.0	22	1,955.9	228.3	253.8	1,350.7	2,998.8	5,704.2
Nevada	77,261.2	20	104.6	48.9	1,288.2	557.3	9,027.9	3,458.0
New Hampshire . . .	40,661.5	19	37.5	116.5	59.1	366.4	2,356.8	6,256.0
New Jersey.	311,770.2	5	225.0	139.3	357.7	2,271.2	15,358.3	32,635.4
New Mexico	46,086.3	46	503.7	139.1	2,263.4	449.9	3,187.9	2,553.2
New York	753,472.2	4	1,014.8	1,299.6	2,456.5	6,672.4	30,091.7	46,448.1
North Carolina	237,095.1	37	1,852.6	651.8	377.0	1,558.8	13,850.6	34,470.9
North Dakota.	20,847.9	13	2,413.1	110.9	669.0	426.5	1,329.4	1,631.0
Ohio	305,553.0	32	1,428.5	269.9	1,931.8	2,623.4	14,741.7	54,155.5
Oklahoma	98,146.6	28	–157.9	190.0	10,525.6	1,830.4	4,587.5	15,341.3
Oregon	100,893.3	31	1,014.5	1,420.2	237.6	738.3	6,257.2	14,411.4
Pennsylvania.	367,058.0	21	1,416.4	473.4	3,164.2	4,039.7	20,243.7	49,176.4
Rhode Island.	29,403.6	24	15.4	31.9	29.0	311.6	1,538.6	3,265.5
South Carolina	100,186.8	48	225.6	362.0	119.4	1,330.8	6,351.8	15,863.9
South Dakota.	21,523.7	30	1,691.8	112.5	94.5	270.4	1,248.0	2,354.3
Tennessee	165,273.6	33	–149.8	337.9	463.0	421.2	8,968.9	25,516.0
Texas	768,203.1	18	2,074.3	1,586.3	66,369.8	15,134.8	48,907.7	94,022.3
Utah	68,660.5	39	81.9	68.4	1,354.7	486.5	5,132.5	8,332.3
Vermont	16,893.7	27	166.7	74.2	61.0	248.0	1,029.8	2,482.1
Virginia.	260,124.4	9	328.1	323.4	1,492.9	2,264.1	14,606.2	17,679.0
Washington.	209,330.3	16	1,656.5	2,118.3	344.1	795.0	14,902.2	24,933.7
West Virginia.	38,297.2	50	–134.5	111.3	3,410.4	635.2	2,453.2	3,919.2
WISCONSIN	154,138.5	26	1,588.6	389.5	292.7	1,314.1	8,772.6	32,617.2
Wyoming.	18,014.2	7	–10.0	46.5	3,510.4	257.2	1,895.9	761.8
UNITED STATES	$9,110,826.4		$56,192.0	$28,626.1	$142,395.8	$95,452.0	$522,215.7	$1,063,393.3

Note: Wisconsin's top five income earning industries, and the percent of total state income that they represent, are: Services (30.8%), Manufacturing (21.2%), Finance and Insurance (6.9%), Retail (6.1%), and Construction (5.7%).

[1]Includes wages and salaries, other labor income, and proprietor's income.

[2]Per capita rank calculated by the Wisconsin Legislative Reference Bureau.

[3]"Other" consists of income of U.S. residents employed by international organizations and foreign embassies and consulates in the United States.

[4]"Services" consists of the following NAICS industry categories: Professional and technical services; Management of companies and enterprises; Administrative and waste services; Educational services; Health care and social assistance; Arts, entertainment, and recreation; Accommodation and food services, and Other services, except public administration.

Source: U.S. Department of Commerce, Bureau of Economic Analysis, Regional Economic Accounts, 2008, Table SA05N, at: http://www.bea.gov/regional/spi/default.cfm?selTable=SA05N&selSeries=NAICS [July 1, 2009].

BY STATE – 2008
Millions)

Wholesale Trade	Retail Trade	Trans-portation	Infor-mation	Finance and Insurance	Real Estate and Rentals	Services[4]	Government and Government Enterprises	State
$5,687.4	$7,680.5	$3,537.5	$1,769.7	$5,709.6	$1,604.1	$31,880.8	$23,892.3	. . . . Alabama
448.0	1,413.2	1,552.5	534.2	745.7	368.6	5,957.4	7,768.0	. . . . Alaska
8,467.8	12,057.0	4,669.9	3,299.4	9,923.7	4,990.5	54,581.8	27,319.1	. . . . .Arizona
3,245.7	4,104.9	3,411.3	1,859.4	2,472.5	884.4	17,991.7	11,724.4	. . . . Arkansas
60,496.9	72,412.4	32,268.0	62,766.4	77,154.5	31,397.2	419,040.2	200,080.3	. . . . . . California
8,667.4	9,105.8	4,257.0	13,292.8	11,491.7	4,705.3	57,432.3	26,579.8	. . . . . . Colorado
7,057.7	8,106.9	2,736.1	4,261.3	24,139.4	2,545.7	48,586.2	18,494.6	. . . . Connecticut
1,322.5	1,772.8	616.1	590.5	3,982.8	479.2	10,923.7	4,319.8	. . . . . . Delaware
594.1	678.8	348.8	2,899.6	2,612.4	1,144.3	35,198.9	30,601.1	. District of Columbia
26,383.7	34,108.5	14,058.1	14,670.7	31,239.4	12,616.8	173,615.9	75,945.5	. . . . Florida
17,923.8	15,712.1	10,771.2	14,002.1	16,098.1	5,683.4	82,327.7	46,249.2	. . . . .Georgia
1,201.4	2,540.0	1,513.5	744.2	1,320.2	970.9	13,999.9	13,677.4	. . . . Hawaii
1,676.6	2,847.3	1,047.6	602.5	1,538.9	508.3	11,089.3	6,364.8	. . . . Idaho
26,869.0	21,634.5	15,872.0	12,178.5	38,468.2	8,780.0	149,899.0	54,911.7	. . . . . ILLINOIS
8,592.4	9,816.9	6,677.1	2,634.9	7,197.5	2,403.7	47,737.4	22,776.4	. . . . Indiana
4,581.6	5,328.5	3,151.3	1,937.6	7,295.8	873.6	20,938.6	13,356.2	. . . . IOWA
4,520.6	4,780.3	2,770.0	3,730.3	4,367.8	1,037.9	22,627.5	15,263.7	. . . . Kansas
5,310.0	6,560.4	5,353.1	1,726.7	5,235.3	1,155.4	28,991.5	20,809.5	. . . . . Kentucky
5,286.9	7,400.7	5,788.0	2,083.5	4,382.2	2,277.4	34,786.6	21,940.2	. . . . . .Louisiana
1,334.0	2,758.0	822.1	673.5	1,848.2	498.8	11,403.0	6,158.7	. . . . Maine
8,073.9	10,456.7	4,042.7	5,481.9	10,842.6	4,331.9	69,634.3	45,510.9	. . . . . .Maryland
13,570.1	12,623.6	4,390.6	9,956.1	30,400.8	4,925.3	110,129.3	30,253.8	. . . . Massachusetts
13,615.6	15,824.8	7,259.2	4,983.8	13,261.0	5,619.0	93,196.7	39,551.4	. . . . MICHIGAN
11,818.2	9,539.9	5,287.7	4,722.7	14,559.9	3,126.8	62,086.2	23,894.2	. . . . MINNESOTA
2,378.9	4,252.1	2,265.7	888.5	2,170.5	684.8	16,111.1	14,175.8	. . . . .Mississippi
9,148.8	10,241.7	5,865.8	5,797.1	9,510.0	2,398.2	56,829.4	25,716.8	. . . . . . Missouri
998.7	1,932.7	869.0	434.6	1,035.6	581.1	7,206.7	5,018.1	. . . . . . Montana
2,785.1	3,167.3	3,545.5	1,357.1	3,789.1	553.7	15,457.9	8,962.5	. . . . . Nebraska
3,031.2	5,206.9	2,690.9	1,257.9	3,898.6	2,104.1	32,851.8	11,734.9	. . . . Nevada
2,564.2	3,598.4	708.9	1,218.0	2,922.7	766.3	14,622.4	5,068.3	. . . New Hampshire
22,377.8	19,107.1	10,707.1	12,801.9	28,995.6	6,741.7	114,690.5	45,361.7	. . . . .New Jersey
1,497.8	3,244.9	1,257.0	956.9	1,631.7	695.5	15,521.7	12,183.5	. . . . New Mexico
32,433.9	35,081.4	14,614.4	44,958.8	147,543.5	16,195.5	266,967.4	107,694.2	. . . . . New York
13,184.9	15,443.6	6,486.3	6,320.0	14,873.5	3,827.7	75,262.2	48,935.1	. . . North Carolina
1,259.2	1,316.9	806.3	485.7	974.8	228.3	5,116.5	4,080.3	. . . . .North Dakota
17,533.0	18,531.9	11,432.6	6,275.0	17,909.6	4,530.5	106,323.4	47,866.3	. . . . Ohio
4,013.5	5,944.5	3,524.3	2,248.4	3,768.5	1,435.6	25,254.3	19,640.5	. . . . . . Oklahoma
6,504.0	6,758.9	3,425.5	3,008.3	4,911.0	1,842.0	33,324.5	17,039.9	. . . . Oregon
19,667.9	21,795.4	13,187.2	11,107.2	26,084.3	6,361.7	142,957.8	47,382.8	. . . .Pennsylvania
1,373.0	1,749.9	493.3	956.7	2,348.2	468.3	11,405.8	5,416.3	. . . .Rhode Island
4,956.2	7,606.0	2,750.0	1,985.6	4,967.3	1,900.0	29,730.2	22,038.1	. . . South Carolina
1,159.6	1,531.4	676.1	438.5	1,565.2	311.4	6,129.0	3,941.0	. . . .South Dakota
9,761.3	12,019.4	8,951.1	3,695.8	10,123.5	3,203.5	57,841.6	24,120.3	. . . . . Tennessee
46,053.5	42,934.0	32,742.4	23,392.7	46,272.5	17,482.2	220,647.2	110,583.4	. . . . Texas
3,314.7	5,104.3	2,748.6	1,879.2	3,953.7	1,341.9	22,276.3	12,585.5	. . . . Utah
689.1	1,374.0	394.7	354.9	825.3	216.0	5,858.0	3,120.0	. . . . Vermont
9,750.4	13,668.2	6,315.9	9,754.5	13,176.0	5,283.5	100,692.0	64,790.0	. . . . Virginia
10,523.6	13,552.0	6,365.7	15,247.2	11,475.9	4,018.3	63,619.2	39,778.6	. . . . .Washington
1,512.9	2,720.3	1,354.1	677.6	1,212.7	406.5	11,320.2	8,698.1	. . . . West Virginia
8,606.1	9,385.6	5,396.0	3,622.1	10,572.4	1,808.0	47,501.1	22,272.7	. . . **WISCONSIN**
655.3	1,063.7	904.5	210.7	557.8	406.8	3,812.6	3,940.7	. . . . . . .Wyoming
$484,479.7	$547,597.0	$292,680.4	$332,733.2	$703,357.7	$188,721.9	$3,123,393.1	$1,529,588.5	UNITED STATES

PERSONAL INCOME IN WISCONSIN
1929 – 2008

| | | | | | | Per Capita Personal Income | | | | | |
| | | Wisconsin | | | | | United States | | | | |
Year	Wisconsin Personal Income (in millions)[1]	Per Capita Amount	Annual % Change	State Rank	As % of National Average	Per Capita Amount	High[2]	State	Low	State
1929	$1,975	$673	—	18	96%	$700	$1,152	New York	$271	S.C.
1930	1,733	588	—	18	95	620	1,035	New York	202	Miss.
1935	1,416	461	—	19	97	474	722	Delaware	177	Miss.
1940	1,720	547	—	21	92	595	1,027	New York	215	Miss.
1945	3,499	1,182	—	22	96	1,237	1,644	Delaware	629	Miss.
1950	5,178	1,506	—	24	100	1,510	2,075	Nevada	770	Miss.
1955	6,899	1,875	—	21	98	1,911	2,527	Conn.	1,045	Miss.
1960	8,948	2,258	—	20	99	2,276	2,926	Conn.	1,237	Miss.
1965	11,803	2,789	—	22	98	2,859	3,583	Conn.	1,688	Miss.
1970	17,609	3,979	—	21	97	4,085	5,263	Alaska	2,617	Miss.
1975	27,810	6,086	—	25	99	6,172	10,683	Alaska	4,203	Miss.
1980	47,623	10,107	—	20	100	10,114	14,866	Alaska	7,007	Miss.
1985	65,709	13,840	—	28	94	14,758	20,321	Alaska	9,892	Miss.
1990	88,635	18,072	—	24	93	19,477	26,504	Conn.	13,089	Miss.
1991	92,124	18,557	2.7%	25	93	19,892	26,512	Conn.	13,702	Miss.
1992	98,917	19,683	6.1	24	94	20,854	28,362	Conn.	14,559	Miss.
1993	103,379	20,331	3.3	23	95	21,346	28,975	Conn.	15,290	Miss.
1994	109,927	21,413	5.3	23	97	22,172	29,693	Conn.	16,291	Miss.
1995	115,180	22,215	3.7	24	96	23,076	31,045	Conn.	16,885	Miss.
1996	121,718	23,273	4.8	25	96	24,175	32,424	Conn.	17,702	Miss.
1997	129,099	24,514	5.3	22	97	25,334	34,375	Conn.	18,550	Miss.
1998	138,667	26,175	6.8	20	97	26,883	36,822	Conn.	19,545	Miss.
1999	144,702	27,135	3.7	20	97	27,939	38,332	Conn.	20,053	Miss.
2000	153,548	28,570	5.3	20	96	29,845	41,489	Conn.	21,005	Miss.
2001	158,888	29,392	2.9	21	96	30,575	42,920	Conn.	21,950	Miss.
2002	162,866	29,937	1.9	21	97	30,804	42,521	Conn.	22,511	Miss.
2003	167,979	30,685	2.5	22	97	31,472	42,972	Conn.	23,466	Miss.
2004	177,154	32,157	4.8	22	98	32,937	45,398	Conn.	24,650	Miss.
2005	183,948	33,278	3.5	21	97	34,471	47,388	Conn.	24,664	Louis.
2006	192,818	34,701	4.3	22	96	36,276	49,852	Conn.	26,535	Miss.
2007	203,084	36,272	4.5	26	94	38,615	54,981	Conn.	28,541	Miss.
2008	209,999	37,314	2.9	28	94	39,751	56,248	Conn.	29,569	Miss.

Note: Alaska and Hawaii were not included in U.S. totals before 1950.

[1]Personal income includes all forms of income received by persons from business establishments; federal, state, and local governments; households and institutions; and foreign countries. Allowance is made for "in kind" income not received as cash.

[2]High shown is for the 50 states. In the following years, jurisdictions other than states had higher per capita personal income: 1950: Alaska (prestatehood) – $2,400, District of Columbia – $2,228; 1991: District of Columbia – $27,567; 1992: District of Columbia – $28,916; 1993: District of Columbia – $29,996; 1994: District of Columbia – $30,835; 1995: District of Columbia – $31,266; 1996: District of Columbia – $32,786; 1997: District of Columbia – $34,488; 2001: District of Columbia – $44,827; 2002: District of Columbia – $46,407; 2003: District of Columbia – $48,446; 2004: District of Columbia – $51,803; 2005: District of Columbia – $52,811; 2006: District of Columbia – $55,755; 2007: District of Columbia – $62,484; 2008: District of Columbia – $64,991.

Source: U.S. Department of Commerce, Bureau of Economic Analysis, Regional Accounts Data, "Annual State Personal Income", 2008 and previous editions, at: http://www.bea.gov/regional/spi/ [May 29, 2009].

HIGHLIGHTS OF GEOGRAPHY AND CLIMATE IN WISCONSIN

Land and Water Area — Wisconsin encompasses 34.8 million acres, not including those parts of the Mississippi River and Great Lakes located within the boundaries of the state. Its inland lakes, covering more than 982,000 acres, make up almost 3% of the state's total surface area. Based on land area, the largest county in the state is Marathon with 988,774 acres; the smallest is Ozaukee with 148,448 acres. The geographic center of the state is located in Wood County about 9 miles southeast of Marshfield.

Lakes — The largest lake in Wisconsin is Lake Winnebago (137,708 acres), which covers parts of three counties; the deepest natural lake is Green Lake in Green Lake County with a maximum depth of 236 feet. Most of Wisconsin's largest lakes are concentrated in the northern two-thirds of the state, and they include artificial bodies of water created by dams. Wisconsin has 15,057 lakes (6,040 named). Green County has only five lakes while Vilas County has 1,318.

High Points — The state's highest recorded elevation is Timms Hill in Price County, at 1,952 feet. There are also other recorded elevations of at least 1,900 feet in Forest, Langlade, Lincoln, and Marathon Counties.

Temperature — In 2007, the annual statewide average temperature was 44.7° Fahrenheit. Across the state, normal regional temperatures vary from 42.1° in the north central area to 47.7° in the southeast. Normal temperatures are the averages for the period 1971-2000, based on computations by the State Climatology Office.

Precipitation — In 2007, the total statewide average rainfall was 33.96 inches. Regional precipitation averages varied from a high of 41.68 inches in the south central area to a low of 26.91 inches in the northeast area. Normal precipitation correspond to the averages for the period 1971-2000, according to the State Climatology Office.

The following tables present selected data. Consult footnoted sources for more detailed information about geography and climate.

WISCONSIN'S LARGEST WATER AREAS

Name	County[1]	Area in Acres
Lake Winnebago	Winnebago (also Calumet and Fond du Lac)	137,708
Lake Pepin[2]	Pepin	—
Lake Petenwell	Juneau (also Adams and Wood)	23,040
Lake Chippewa (Chippewa Flowage)	Sawyer	15,300
Poygan Lake	Winnebago (also Waushara)	14,102
Castle Rock Lake	Juneau (also Adams)	13,955
Turtle-Flambeau Flowage	Iron	13,545
Lake Koshkonong	Rock (also Dane and Jefferson)	10,460
Lake Mendota	Dane	9,842
Lake Wisconsin	Sauk (also Columbia)	9,000
Lake Butte des Morts	Winnebago	8,857
Lake Onalaska	La Crosse	7,688
Green Lake (Big Green Lake)[3]	Green Lake	7,346
Big Eau Pleine Reservoir	Marathon	6,830
Lake Du Bay	Portage (also Marathon)	6,700
Beaver Dam Lake	Dodge	6,542
Lake Wissota	Chippewa	6,300
Shawano Lake	Shawano	6,063
Geneva Lake	Walworth	5,262
Lake Winneshiek	Crawford	5,250
Puckaway Lake	Green Lake (also Marquette)	5,039
Lac Courte Oreilles	Sawyer	5,039
Lake St. Croix	St. Croix (also Pierce)	4,668
Lake Winneconne	Winnebago	4,507
Willow Flowage	Oneida	4,217
Holcombe Flowage	Chippewa (also Rusk)	3,890
Trout Lake	Vilas	3,864
Pelican Lake	Oneida	3,545
Fence Lake	Vilas	3,483
Tomahawk Lake	Oneida	3,462
Gile Flowage	Iron	3,384
Long Lake	Washburn	3,290
Lake Monona	Dane	3,274
Namekagon Lake	Bayfield	3,227
Lake Kegonsa	Dane	3,209
Grindstone Lake	Sawyer	3,111
Rush Lake	Fond du Lac (also Winnebago)	3,070
Round Lake (Big Round)	Sawyer	3,054

[1]County listed first contains the water's source of origin. Other counties covered by the water area are shown in parentheses.

[2]Lake Pepin is part of Mississippi River backwaters. Definite area cannot be determined because of fluctuations in water levels.

[3]Green Lake, at a maximum depth of 236 feet, is Wisconsin's deepest natural lake.

Sources: Wisconsin Department of Natural Resources, *Wisconsin Lakes, 2005* (Revised January 18, 2007), and DNR departmental data, at: http://www.dnr.state.wi.us [October 17, 2008].

LAND AND INLAND LAKE AREA OF WISCONSIN COUNTIES

County	Total Land Area Acres	Inland Lakes Number	Inland Lakes Acres	County	Total Land Area Acres	Inland Lakes Number	Inland Lakes Acres
Adams	414,554	47	2,309	Marinette. . . .	897,126	442	13,735
Ashland	668,045	157	5,936	Marquette . . .	291,514	93	5,736
Barron	552,218	369	17,748	Menominee . .	229,094	128	4,044
Bayfield	944,800	962	22,629	Milwaukee . . .	154,598	41	197
Brown	338,355	22	170	Monroe.	576,493	120	3,437
Buffalo	438,061	8	196	Oconto	638,701	378	11,053
Burnett	525,773	509	31,258	Oneida	719,680	1,129	68,447
Calumet	204,698	8	98	Outagamie . . .	409,818	33	213
Chippewa . . .	646,675	449	20,027	Ozaukee	148,448	39	709
Clark	778,010	32	1,076	Pepin	148,659	29	278
Columbia. . . .	495,226	56	3,095	Pierce.	368,954	38	6,016
Crawford. . . .	366,522	77	6,243	Polk	587,053	437	20,900
Dane	769,210	36	21,520	Portage	516,038	136	12,203
Dodge	564,659	29	13,246	Price	801,638	389	15,129
Door	308,941	25	3,254	Racine	213,184	21	3,919
Douglas	837,843	431	14,113	Richland	375,168	9	251
Dunn	545,299	21	3,963	Rock	461,101	76	11,174
Eau Claire . . .	408,090	20	2,838	Rusk	584,403	250	7,854
Florence	312,339	259	7,259	St. Croix	461,965	64	3,667
Fond du Lac . .	462,662	42	1,655	Sauk	536,083	28	11,004
Forest.	648,992	824	22,531	Sawyer	804,109	496	56,183
Grant	734,624	33	1,569	Shawano	571,206	134	8,912
Green.	373,754	5	350	Sheboygan . . .	328,723	72	2,111
Green Lake. . .	226,739	36	17,120	Taylor	623,910	284	6,183
Iowa	488,109	15	685	Trempealeau . .	469,811	26	409
Iron.	484,627	494	29,368	Vernon	508,717	57	256
Jackson.	631,885	135	5,004	Vilas	559,181	1,318	93,889
Jefferson	356,486	35	3,770	Walworth	355,398	37	12,798
Juneau	491,270	57	45,950	Washburn . . .	518,195	964	31,265
Kenosha	174,611	33	3,674	Washington. . .	275,725	54	3,080
Kewaunee . . .	219,290	15	251	Waukesha . . .	355,571	118	15,156
La Crosse . . .	289,754	19	8,568	Waupaca	480,698	240	7,169
Lafayette	405,485	8	565	Waushara. . . .	400,659	138	4,623
Langlade	558,509	841	9,122	Winnebago . . .	280,691	30	169,755
Lincoln.	565,312	727	15,741	Wood.	507,379	78	6,245
Manitowoc. . .	378,579	101	1,492	STATE	34,758,464	15,057	982,155
Marathon. . . .	988,774	194	19,762				

Note: Land area statistics from the U.S. Census Bureau; lake statistics from Wisconsin Department of Natural Resources. Lake Superior and Lake Michigan are not included in totals.

Sources: Wisconsin Department of Natural Resources, *Wisconsin Lakes, 2005* (Revised January 18, 2007), at: http://dnr.wi.gov/org/water/fhp/lakes; U.S. Department of Commerce, Census Bureau, 2000 Census of Population and Housing, *Summary Population and Housing Characteristics, Wisconsin,* Table 16.

SELECTED HIGH POINTS IN WISCONSIN*

Site	County	Location by Section, Township, Range	Elevation in Feet
Friendship Mound	Adams	SW. 32, T. 18N., R. 6E.	1,290
Mt. Whittlesey	Ashland	SE. 9, T. 44N., R. 2W.	1,872
Blue Hills	Barron	W. 25, T. 35N., R. 10W.	1,630
Mount Telemark	Bayfield	NW. 28, T. 43N., R. 7W.	1,700
Morrison Hill	Brown	NW. 24, T. 21N., R. 20E.	1,020
Montana Ridge	Buffalo	2,3,11, T. 22N., R. 10W.	1,360
Flambeau Ridge	Chippewa	SE. 3, T. 32N., R. 7W.	1,530
Baraboo Range	Columbia	SE. 6, T. 11N., R. 8E.	1,480
Rising Sun Ridge	Crawford	NW. 22, T. 11N., R. 5W.	1,322
East Blue Mound	Dane	5,6, T. 6N., R. 6E.	1,489
Summit Hill	Douglas	21, T. 45N., R. 14W.	1,369
Dunnewa Hill	Dunn	NE. 24, T. 30N., R. 11W.	1,354
Kettle Moraine	Fond du Lac	SE. 2, T. 14N., R. 18E.	1,270
Sugarbush Hill	Forest	SW. 36, T. 36N., R. 13E.	1,939
Military Ridge	Grant	31, T. 7N., R. 2W.	1,240
West Blue Mound	Iowa	NW. 1, T. 6N., R. 5E.	1,719
Penokee Range	Iron	NE. 6, T. 44N., R. 1W.	1,860
Saddle Mound	Jackson	NE. 33, T. 22N., R. 1W.	1,409
Kettle Moraine	Jefferson	NE. 26, T. 5N., R. 16E.	1,062
Johnson Hill	Juneau	NW. 11, T. 15N., R. 2E.	1,380
Cherneyville Hill	Kewaunee	NE. 32, T. 23N., R. 23E.	1,020
Wadels Hill	La Crosse	NE. 24, SE. 14, T. 18N., R. 5W.	1,400
North Platte Mound	Lafayette	SE. 31, T. 4N., R. 1E.	1,440
Kent Tower Hill	Langlade	NW. 21, T. 32N., R. 13E.	1,903
Lookout Mountain	Lincoln	SW. 27, T. 34N., R. 8E.	1,920
Rib Mountain	Marathon	SE. 8, T. 28N., R. 7E.	1,924
Greenfield Hill	Monroe	SW. 9, T. 18N., R. 2W.	1,450
Carter Hills	Oconto	NW. 6, T. 33N., R. 15E.	1,781
Rohrscheib Hill	Pepin	SW. 22, T. 25N., R. 11W.	1,300
Frederic Tower Hill	Polk	NW. 1, T. 36N., R. 17W.	1,410
Timms Hill	Price	N. 11, T. 34N., R. 2E.	1,952
Pleasant Ridge	Richland	NE. 19, T. 12N., R. 1W.	1,300
Blue Hills	Rusk	27, T. 35N., R. 9W.	1,750
Sauk Point	Sauk	SW. 15, T. 11N., R. 7E.	1,593
Meteor Hill	Sawyer	SW. 17, T. 37N., R. 8W.	1,801
Parnell Hill	Sheboygan	NE. 10, T. 14N., R. 20E.	1,312
Irish Ridge	Vernon	2-4, 11-12, T. 14N., R. 3W.	1,360
Holy Hill	Washington	NE. 14, T. 9N., R. 18E.	1,332
Lapham Peak	Waukesha	SE. 29, T. 7N., R. 18E.	1,230
Powers Bluff	Wood	SE. 30, T. 24N., R. 4E.	1,481

*This list is based on data compiled by the State Cartographer's Office and includes the highest named point in each county having an elevation of at least 1,020 feet. The listing is not a ranking of all of the highest points in the state because 1) it includes only named features; 2) it includes only one high point per county; and 3) there may be others of comparable height that are unrecorded. Many elevations are approximations.

Source: Wisconsin State Cartographer's Office, *Individual High Points for WI Counties*, at:
http://www.sco.wisc.edu/maps/cntyelevation.php [October 17, 2008].

WISCONSIN TEMPERATURES AND PRECIPITATION,
By Region and Month, 2007

	Jan.	Feb.	Mar.	Apr.	May	June	July	Aug.	Sept.	Oct.	Nov.	Dec.	Annual[1]
Statewide													
2007 Temperature (°F) . .	20.5	11.7	34.6	42.6	58.7	66.7	69.4	68.4	60.9	52.4	33.2	17.4	44.7
Normal Temperature[2] . . .	13.2	19.0	30.1	43.2	55.5	64.5	69.1	66.9	58.1	46.7	32.4	19.0	43.1
2007 Precipitation (inches)	1.02	1.21	2.29	2.61	2.61	2.93	3.09	7.08	3.25	4.85	0.32	2.70	33.96
Normal Precipitation[2] . . .	1.22	1.00	1.96	2.86	3.37	4.02	4.07	4.27	3.74	2.50	2.29	1.34	32.63
Regions[3]													
Northwest													
2007 Temperature	16.8	9.0	32.6	41.4	57.5	65.3	68.9	66.9	59.0	50.0	32.0	14.3	42.8
Normal Temperature. . . .	9.5	16.2	28.0	41.7	54.4	63.1	68.1	65.9	56.6	45.1	29.8	15.4	41.2
2007 Precipitation	0.79	0.74	2.10	1.87	2.80	2.22	2.75	3.70	5.16	6.51	0.16	2.03	30.83
Normal Precipitation. . . .	1.12	0.83	1.78	2.39	3.29	4.19	4.29	4.44	3.89	2.57	2.16	1.09	32.04
North Central													
2007 Temperature	17.3	8.8	31.5	40.0	56.6	64.7	67.4	65.9	58.4	49.5	30.3	14.9	42.1
Normal Temperature. . . .	10.3	16.0	26.8	40.4	53.2	61.8	66.4	64.2	55.3	44.0	29.8	16.1	40.4
2007 Precipitation	1.13	0.68	2.06	2.18	2.98	2.93	2.57	2.89	3.63	5.74	0.64	2.42	29.85
Normal Precipitation. . . .	1.25	0.92	1.78	2.40	3.31	4.01	4.06	4.36	4.03	2.73	2.27	1.32	32.44
Northeast													
2007 Temperature	19.5	11.7	31.8	41.2	56.3	65.4	67.3	66.9	60.1	51.1	31.8	17.4	43.4
Normal Temperature. . . .	12.5	17.5	28.1	41.3	53.6	62.5	67.0	64.8	56.0	44.8	31.3	18.4	41.5
2007 Precipitation	0.99	1.02	2.24	2.00	1.79	3.15	3.68	2.11	1.85	5.65	0.37	2.06	26.91
Normal Precipitation. . . .	1.31	0.98	1.98	2.65	3.29	3.69	3.70	3.81	3.74	2.52	2.33	1.47	31.47
West Central													
2007 Temperature	20.3	11.8	36.5	44.4	61.3	68.7	71.3	69.3	62.0	53.3	33.3	16.6	45.7
Normal Temperature. . . .	12.7	19.3	31.2	45.2	57.4	66.4	70.8	68.3	59.3	47.6	32.3	18.5	44.1
2007 Precipitation	0.81	1.39	2.48	1.67	3.81	3.08	2.95	10.01	3.96	4.52	0.15	2.09	36.92
Normal Precipitation. . . .	1.06	0.87	1.93	3.05	3.69	4.24	4.45	4.54	3.82	2.36	2.19	1.14	33.34
Central													
2007 Temperature	22.6	13.4	35.7	43.7	59.8	67.5	69.9	69.0	61.4	53.3	33.7	18.2	45.7
Normal Temperature. . . .	14.5	20.2	31.2	44.5	56.7	65.8	70.2	67.7	59.0	47.5	33.2	20.1	44.2
2007 Precipitation	1.25	1.38	2.15	2.61	2.80	2.17	3.46	7.91	2.88	3.65	0.16	3.09	33.51
Normal Precipitation. . . .	1.15	1.01	2.07	3.02	3.52	3.88	4.13	4.22	3.72	2.36	2.29	1.31	32.68
East Central													
2007 Temperature	24.2	15.0	35.2	43.0	57.1	66.5	69.1	69.6	62.4	54.1	35.4	21.5	46.1
Normal Temperature. . . .	17.0	21.4	31.2	42.8	54.6	64.1	69.5	67.9	59.8	48.3	35.2	22.8	44.6
2007 Precipitation	1.07	1.36	2.59	2.18	2.21	3.10	3.12	4.09	2.11	3.63	0.33	2.67	28.46
Normal Precipitation. . . .	1.44	1.14	2.09	2.81	2.95	3.51	3.38	3.86	3.42	2.43	2.38	1.60	31.01
Southwest													
2007 Temperature	23.3	13.3	37.5	45.1	61.6	68.3	71.1	70.7	63.1	55.0	35.1	19.2	46.9
Normal Temperature. . . .	15.7	21.9	33.4	46.1	57.9	67.2	71.4	69.0	60.5	48.9	34.5	21.5	45.7
2007 Precipitation	1.13	1.81	2.35	4.31	2.18	3.49	3.79	16.66	2.96	4.81	0.28	3.67	47.44
Normal Precipitation. . . .	1.07	1.08	2.09	3.55	3.60	4.35	4.33	4.46	3.42	2.34	2.34	1.29	33.92
South Central													
2007 Temperature	24.3	14.2	38.0	44.8	61.8	68.8	71.2	71.1	63.4	55.6	35.6	20.2	47.4
Normal Temperature. . . .	16.8	22.3	33.5	45.8	57.8	67.2	71.3	68.9	60.6	49.0	35.4	22.5	45.9
2007 Precipitation	1.01	1.88	2.54	4.72	1.77	3.53	2.89	13.74	2.13	2.90	0.32	4.25	41.68
Normal Precipitation. . . .	1.28	1.25	2.20	3.47	3.40	4.19	4.07	4.24	3.51	2.48	2.41	1.61	34.11
Southeast													
2007 Temperature	26.2	15.7	38.5	43.8	59.2	67.6	70.3	71.0	63.7	55.9	37.3	23.1	47.7
Normal Temperature. . . .	18.9	24.0	34.0	45.0	56.3	66.0	71.2	69.4	61.4	49.9	37.0	24.7	46.5
2007 Precipitation	1.20	1.80	2.65	4.21	1.97	3.59	3.32	10.20	1.70	2.70	0.40	3.72	37.46
Normal Precipitation. . . .	1.56	1.32	2.19	3.48	3.13	3.76	3.82	4.22	3.48	2.51	2.55	1.91	33.93

[1]Annual temperature reflects the average of the monthly figures; annual precipitation is the total for the year.

[2]Normal temperatures and normal precipitation are the averages for the period 1971-2000, based on data computed by the State Climatologist Office.

[3]The counties in each region are:

Northwest — Barron, Bayfield, Burnett, Chippewa, Douglas, Polk, Rusk, Sawyer, and Washburn.

North Central — Ashland, Clark, Iron, Lincoln, Marathon, Oneida, Price, Taylor, and Vilas.

Northeast — Florence, Forest, Langlade, Marinette, Menominee, Oconto, and Shawano.

West Central — Buffalo, Dunn, Eau Claire, Jackson, La Crosse, Monroe, Pepin, Pierce, St. Croix, and Trempealeau.

Central — Adams, Green Lake, Juneau, Marquette, Portage, Waupaca, Waushara, and Wood.

East Central — Brown, Calumet, Door, Fond du Lac, Kewaunee, Manitowoc, Outagamie, Sheboygan, and Winnebago.

Southwest — Crawford, Grant, Iowa, Lafayette, Richland, Sauk, and Vernon.

South Central — Columbia, Dane, Dodge, Green, Jefferson, and Rock.

Southeast — Kenosha, Milwaukee, Ozaukee, Racine, Walworth, Washington, and Waukesha.

Source: National Agricultural Statistics Service, *2008 Wisconsin Agricultural Statistics Bulletin,* at:
http://www.nass.usda.gov/Statistics_by_State

HIGHLIGHTS OF HISTORY IN WISCONSIN

History — On May 29, 1848, Wisconsin became the 30th state in the Union, but the state's written history dates back more than 300 years to the time when the French first encountered the diverse Native Americans who lived here. In 1634, the French explorer Jean Nicolet landed at Green Bay, reportedly becoming the first European to visit Wisconsin. The French ceded the area to Great Britain in 1763, and it became part of the United States in 1783. First organized under the Northwest Ordinance, the area was part of various territories until creation of the Wisconsin Territory in 1836.

Since statehood, Wisconsin has been a wheat farming area, a lumbering frontier, and a preeminent dairy state. Tourism has grown in importance, and industry has concentrated in the eastern and southeastern part of the state.

Politically, the state has enjoyed a reputation for honest, efficient government. It is known as the birthplace of the Republican Party and the home of Robert M. La Follette, Sr., founder of the progressive movement.

Political Balance — After being primarily a one-party state for most of its existence, with the Republican and Progressive Parties dominating during portions of the state's first century, Wisconsin has become a politically competitive state in recent decades. The Republicans gained majority control in both houses in the 1995 Legislature, an advantage they last held during the 1969 session. Since then, control of the senate has changed several times. In 2009, the Democrats gained control of both houses for the first time since 1993.

Governor Jim Doyle is only the second Democrat to serve since 1979. In the last 50 years, Wisconsin's two main urban areas – Milwaukee and Madison – have provided over half of the state's constitutional officers. During this period, 10 women have served as constitutional officers: two as lieutenant governor, one as attorney general, two as secretary of state, three as state treasurer, and two as superintendent of public instruction.

National Office — Although the Democratic candidate has carried Wisconsin six times in a row, presidential elections in the state tend to be close. In fact, Barack Obama became the first candidate to win a majority (56%) of the presidential vote since 1988. This has resulted in Wisconsin being regarded as a hotly contested "swing state" in many recent presidential elections.

Wisconsin voters tend to retain their U.S. Senators in office for long periods of time. Since 1900, seven senators have served three terms or more, topped by Senator William Proxmire's 32 years in office. Democrats have held both of Wisconsin's U.S. Senate seats over the past 40 years, except for the 12 years served by Republican Senator Robert W. Kasten, Jr.

Currently, five Democrats and three Republicans represent Wisconsin in the U.S. House of Representatives, and three of the current members have been elected 15 or more times in regular elections. Democrats held the majority of seats from 1973 to 1991. The Republicans held the majority from 1991 to 1997, but lost it to the Democrats again in 1997. The Congressional delegation was evenly divided from 2003 to 2007. Democrats regained the majority in 2007. Certain congressional districts have traditionally been represented by one party or the other with little relationship to statewide politics.

Voter Turnout — Turnout in presidential and gubernatorial elections may vary as much as a half million votes from election to election. Although individual elections have been up and down, the trend has been upward. Nearly 3 million votes were cast in the each of the last two presidential elections.

Supreme Court — Although justices of the Wisconsin Supreme Court are elected officials, they sometimes are first named to the court by gubernatorial appointment to fill a vacancy. Subsequently, the appointees must be elected to the office if they wish to stay on the court; most have been successful. Among the current seven justices, two came to the court by the appointment route. The first woman justice to serve the court, Shirley S. Abrahamson, was appointed in 1976. She was elected in 1979 and became chief justice in 1996.

SIGNIFICANT EVENTS IN WISCONSIN HISTORY

Under the Flag of France

Although American Indians lived in the area of present-day Wisconsin for several thousand years before the arrival of the French – numbering about 20,000 when the French arrived – the written history of the state began with the accounts of French explorers. The French explored the state, named places and established trading posts, but left relatively little mark on it. They were interested in the fur trade, rather than agricultural settlement, and were never present in large numbers.

1634 — Jean Nicolet: First known European to reach Wisconsin. Sought Northwest Passage.

1654-59 — Pierre Esprit Radisson and Medart Chouart des Groseilliers: First of the fur traders in Wisconsin.

1661 — Father Rene Menard: First missionary to Wisconsin Indians.

1665 — Father Claude Allouez founded mission at La Pointe.

1666 — Nicholas Perrot opened fur trade with Wisconsin Indians.

1672 — Father Allouez and Father Louis

The early years of European contact in Wisconsin are commemorated by this statue on the grounds of the Brown County Courthouse in Green Bay. It depicts a Menominee Indian, Fr. Claude Allouez, and Nicholas Perrot. (Kathleen Sitter, LRB)

Andre built St. Francois Xavier mission at De Pere.

1673 — Louis Jolliet and Father Jacques Marquette discovered Mississippi River.

1678 — Daniel Greysolon Sieur du Lhut (Duluth) explored western end of Lake Superior.

1685 — Perrot made Commandant of the West.

1690 — Perrot discovered lead mines in Wisconsin and Iowa.

1701-38 — Fox Indian Wars.

1755 — Wisconsin Indians, under Charles Langlade, helped defeat British General Braddock.

1763 — Treaty of Paris. Wisconsin became part of British colonial territory.

Under the Flag of England

Wisconsin experienced few changes under British control. It remained the western edge of European penetration into the American continent, important only because of the fur trade. French traders worked in the state and British and colonial traders began to appear, but Europeans continued to be visitors rather than settlers.

1761 — Fort at Green Bay accepted by English.

1763 — Conspiracy of Pontiac. Two Englishmen killed by Indians at Muscoda.

1764 — Charles Langlade settled at Green Bay. First permanent settlement.

1766 — Jonathan Carver visited Wisconsin seeking Northwest Passage.

1774 — Quebec Act made Wisconsin a part of Province of Quebec.

1781 — Traditional date of settlement at Prairie du Chien.

1783 — Second Treaty of Paris. Wisconsin became United States territory.

Achieving Territorial Status

In spite of the Treaty of Paris, Wisconsin remained British in all but title until after the War of 1812. In 1815, the American army established control. Gradually, Indian title to the southeastern half of the state was extinguished. Lead mining brought the first heavy influx of settlers and ended the dominance of the fur trade in the economy of the area. The lead mining period ran from about 1824 to

1861. Almost half of the 11,683 people who lived in the territory in 1836 were residents of the lead mining district in the southwestern corner of the state.

1787 — Under the Northwest Ordinance of 1787, Wisconsin was made part of the Northwest Territory. The governing units for the Wisconsin area prior to statehood were:

1787-1800 — Northwest Territory.
1800-1809 — Indiana Territory.
1809-1818 — Illinois Territory.
1818-1836 — Michigan Territory.
1836-1848 — Wisconsin Territory.

1795 — Jacques Vieau established trading posts at Kewaunee, Manitowoc, and Sheboygan. Made headquarters at Milwaukee.

1804 — William Henry Harrison's treaty with Indians at St. Louis. United States extinguished Indian title to lead region (a cause of Black Hawk War).

1814 — Fort Shelby built at Prairie du Chien. Captured by English and name changed to Fort McKay.

1815 — War with England concluded. Fort McKay abandoned by British.

1816 — Fort Shelby rebuilt at Prairie du Chien (renamed Fort Crawford). Astor's American Fur Company began operations in Wisconsin.

1818 — Solomon Juneau bought trading post of Jacques Vieau at Milwaukee.

1820 — Rev. Jedediah Morse preached first Protestant sermon in Wisconsin at Fort Howard (Green Bay) July 9. Henry Schoolcraft, James Duane Doty, Lewis Cass made exploration trip through Wisconsin.

1822 — New York Indians (Oneida, Stockbridge, Munsee, and Brothertown) moved to Wisconsin. First mining leases in southwest Wisconsin.

1825 — Indian Treaty established tribal boundaries.

1826-27 — Winnebago Indian War. Surrender of Chief Red Bird.

1828 — Fort Winnebago begun at Portage.

1832 — Black Hawk War.

1833 — Land treaty with Indians cleared southern Wisconsin land titles. First newspaper, *Green Bay Intelligencer,* established.

1834 — Land offices established at Green Bay and Mineral Point. First public road laid out.

1835 — First steamboat arrived at Milwaukee. First bank in Wisconsin opened at Green Bay.

1836 — Act creating Territory of Wisconsin signed April 20 by President Andrew Jackson. (Provisions of Ordinance of 1787 made part of the act.)

Wisconsin Territory

Wisconsin's population reached 305,000 by 1850. About half of the new immigrants were from New York and New England. The rest were principally from England, Scotland, Ireland, Germany, and Scandinavia. New York's Erie Canal gave Wisconsin a water outlet to the Atlantic Ocean and a route for new settlers. Wheat was the primary cash crop for most of the newcomers.

State politics revolved around factions headed by James Doty and Henry Dodge. As political parties developed, the Democrats proved dominant throughout the period.

1836 — Capital located at Belmont – Henry Dodge appointed governor, July 4, by President Andrew Jackson. First session of legislature. Madison chosen as permanent capital.

1837 — Madison surveyed and platted. First Capitol begun. Panic of 1837 – all territorial banks failed. Winnebago Indians ceded all claims to land in Wisconsin. Imprisonment for debt abolished.

1838 — Territorial legislature met in Madison. Milwaukee and Rock River Canal Company chartered.

1840 — First school taxes authorized and levied.

1841 — James D. Doty appointed governor by President John Tyler.

1842 — C.C. Arndt shot and killed in legislature by James R. Vineyard.

1844 — Nathaniel P. Tallmadge appointed governor. Wisconsin Phalanx (a utopian colony) established at Ceresco (Ripon).

1845 — Dodge reappointed governor. Mormon settlement at Voree (Burlington). Swiss colony came to New Glarus.

1846 — Congress passed enabling act for admission of Wisconsin as state. First Constitutional Convention met in Madison.

1847 — Census population 210,546. First Constitution rejected by people. Second Constitutional Convention.

1848 — Second Constitution adopted. President James K. Polk signed bill on May 29 making Wisconsin a state.

Early Statehood

Heavy immigration continued after statehood. The state remained largely agricultural with wheat the primary crop. Slavery, banking laws, and temperance were the major issues of the period. Despite the number of foreign immigrants and a shift from Democratic control to Republican control, most political leaders continued to have ties to the northeastern United States. New York state laws and institutions provided models for much of the activity of the early legislative sessions.

1848 — Legislature met June 5. Governor Nelson Dewey inaugurated June 7. State university incorporated. First telegram reached Milwaukee. Large scale German immigration began.

1849 — School code adopted. First free, tax-supported, graded school with high school at Kenosha.

1850 — Bond Law for controlling sale of liquor passed. State opened the Wisconsin Institute for Education of the Blind at Janesville.

1851 — First railroad train – Milwaukee to Waukesha. First state fair at Janesville.

1852 — School for deaf opened at Delavan. Prison construction begun at Waupun.

1853 — Impeachment of Judge Levi Hubbell. Capital punishment abolished (third state to take action).

1854 — Republican Party named at a meeting in Ripon. First class graduated at state university. Joshua Glover, fugitive slave, arrested in Racine, and the Wisconsin Supreme Court, in related matter, declared Fugitive Slave Law of 1850 unconstitutional. Milwaukee and Mississippi Railroad reached Madison.

1856 — Bashford-Barstow election scandal. Legislative report on maladministration of school funds.

1857 — Railroad completed to Prairie du Chien. First high school class graduated at Racine. Industrial School for Boys opened at Waukesha.

1858 — Legislative investigation of bribery in 1856 Legislature.

1859 — Abraham Lincoln spoke at state fair in Milwaukee.

1861 — Beginning of Civil War. Governor called for volunteers for military service. Bank riot in Milwaukee. Office of county superintendent of schools created.

1862 — Governor Louis P. Harvey drowned. Draft riots. Edward G. Ryan's address at Democratic Convention criticized Lincoln's conduct of war.

1864 — Cheese factory started at Ladoga, Fond du Lac County, by Chester Hazen.

1865 — 96,000 Wisconsin soldiers served in Civil War; losses were 12,216.

The Maturing Commonwealth

After the Civil War Wisconsin matured into a modern political and economic entity. Heavy immigration continued throughout the period. The mix of immigrants remained similar to that prior to the Civil War until the end of the century, when Poles began to appear in large numbers.

The Republican Party remained in control of state government throughout the period, but was challenged by Grangers, Populists, Socialists, and Temperance candidates in addition to the Democratic Party and dissidents within the Republican Party. Temperance, the

The principles of Wisconsin's State University, as restated by the Board of Regents in 1894, are commemorated by this plaque affixed to Bascom Hall.

use of foreign languages in schools, railroad regulation, and currency reform were major issues in the state throughout the period.

Wheat culture gradually declined in importance in Wisconsin as more fertile wheatlands were opened to cultivation in the north and west. In the 1880s and 1890s, dairying gradually became the primary agricultural pursuit in the state. The agricultural school at the university developed into a national leader in the field of dairy science. From the 1870s through the 1890s, lumbering prospered in the northern half of the state. At its peak from 1888 to 1893, it accounted for one-fourth of all wages paid in the state. By the end of the period, Milwaukee and the southeastern half of the state had developed a thriving heavy machinery industry. The paper industry was established in the Fox River Valley by the end of the century. The tanning and the brewing industries were also prominent.

1866 — First state normal school opened at Platteville. Agricultural College at university reorganized under Morrill Act.

1871 — Peshtigo fire burned over much of 6 counties in northeast Wisconsin, resulting in over 1,000 deaths.

1872 — Wisconsin Dairymen's Association organized at Watertown.

1873 — Invention of typewriter by C. Latham Sholes. The Patrons of Husbandry, an agricultural organization nicknamed the Grangers, elected Governor William R. Taylor.

1874 — Potter Law limiting railroad rates passed.

1875 — Free high school law passed; women eligible for election to school boards. State Industrial School for Girls established at Milwaukee. Republicans defeated Grangers. Oshkosh almost destroyed by fire.

1876 — Potter Law repealed. Hazel Green cyclone.

1877 — John T. Appleby patented knotter for twine binders.

1882 — Constitution amended to make legislative sessions biennial. First hydroelectric plant established at Appleton.

1883 — Major hotel fire at the Newhall House in Milwaukee killed 71. South wing of Capitol extension collapsed; 7 killed. Agricultural Experiment Station established at university.

1885 — Gogebic iron range discoveries made

Ashland a major shipping port.

1886 — Strikes related to the 8-hour work day movement at Milwaukee culminate in confrontation with militia at Bay View; 5 killed. Agricultural Short Course established at university.

1887 — Marshfield almost destroyed by fire.

1889 — Bennett Law, requiring classroom instruction in English, passed. Wisconsin Supreme Court in the "Edgerton Bible case", prohibited reading and prayers from the King James Bible in public schools. Arbor Day authorized. Former Governor Jeremiah Rusk became first U.S. Secretary of Agriculture.

1890 — Stephen M. Babcock invented quick, easy, accurate test for milk butterfat content.

1891 — Bennett Law repealed after bitter opposition from German Protestants and Catholics.

1893 — Wisconsin Supreme Court ordered state treasurer to refund to the state interest on state deposits, which had customarily been retained by treasurers.

1894 — Forest fires in northern and central Wisconsin.

1897 — Corrupt practice act passed.

1898 — Wisconsin sent 5,469 men to fight in Spanish-American War; losses were 134.

1899 — Antipass law prohibited railroads from giving public officials free rides. Tax commission created. New Richmond tornado.

The Progressive Era

The state's prominent role in the reform movements which swept the country at the beginning of the century gave Wisconsin national fame and its first presidential candidate. Republicans dominated the state legislature, but Progressive and Stalwart factions fought continually for control of the party. Milwaukee consistently returned a strong Socialist contingent to the legislature.

Large-scale European immigration ended during this period, but ethnic groups retained strong individual identities and remained a significant force in the politics and culture of the state. Important social issues were reflected in the calendar of progressive legislation enacted during the period. The 2 world wars caused great stress because of the large German population of the state.

Heavy machinery manufacturing, paper products and dairying consolidated their position as the leading economic activities. As the last virgin forests in the northern half of the state were cut over, lumbering faded in importance. Brewing temporarily disappeared with the advent of Prohibition.

1900 — Wisconsin's first state park, Interstate near St. Croix Falls, established.

1901 — First Wisconsin-born Governor, Robert M. La Follette, inaugurated. Teaching of agriculture introduced into rural schools. Legislative Reference Library, which served as a model for other states and the Library of Congress, established – later renamed the Legislative Reference Bureau.

1904 — Primary election law approved by referendum vote. State Capitol burned.

1905 — State civil service established; auto license law passed; tuberculosis sanitoria authorized. Forestry Board created. Railroad Commission, regulating railroads and subsequently utilities, created.

1907 — Current Capitol begun.

1908 — Income tax amendment adopted.

1910 — Milwaukee elected Emil Seidel first Socialist mayor. Eau Claire first Wisconsin city to adopt commission form of government.

1911 — First income tax law; teachers' pension act; vocational schools authorized;

Industrial and Highway Commissions created; workmen's compensation act enacted.

1913 — Direct election of Wisconsin's U.S. senators approved.

1915 — Conservation Commission, State Board of Agriculture, and State Board of Education created.

1917 — Capitol completed, cost $7,258,763. 120,000 Wisconsin soldiers served in World War I; losses were 3,932. Wisconsin first state to meet draft requirements; 584,559 registrations.

1919 — Eighteenth Amendment (Prohibition) ratified.

1920 — Nineteenth Amendment (women's suffrage) ratified; first state to deliver ratification to Washington.

1921 — Equal rights for women and prohibition laws enacted.

1923 — Military training made optional at university.

1924 — La Follette won Wisconsin's vote for president as Progressive Party candidate. Reforestation amendment to state constitution adopted.

1925 — Senator La Follette died on June 18.

1929 — Professor Harry Steenbock of University of Wisconsin patented radiation of Vitamin D. Legislature repealed all Wisconsin laws for state enforcement of

Wisconsin's contribution to World War I was not entirely "over there". Liberty Loan drives such as this one were also important. (State Historical Society, #WHi (X3) 34890)

Prohibition.

1932 — Forest Products Laboratory erected at Madison.

1933 — Dairy farmers undertook milk strike to protest low prices. Wisconsin voted for repeal of 18th Amendment (Prohibition) to U.S. Constitution.

1934 — Wisconsin Progressive Party formed.

1942 — Governor-elect Loomis died; Supreme Court decided Lieutenant Governor Goodland to serve as acting governor.

1941-45 — Wisconsin enrolled 375,000 for World War II; casualties 7,980.

1946 — Wisconsin Progressive Party dissolved and rejoined Republican Party.

The Middle Years of the Twentieth Century

After the demise of the Progressives, the Democratic Party began a gradual resurgence and, by the late 1950s, became strongly competitive for the first time in over a century. With the decline in foreign immigration, the traditional ethnic differences became muted, but significant numbers of blacks appeared in the urban areas of the state for the first time. Discrimination in housing and employment became matters of concern. Other important issues included the growth in the size of state government, radicalism on the university campuses, welfare programs and environmental questions. Tourism emerged as a major industry during this period.

1948 — Centennial Year.

1949 — Legislature enacted new formula for distribution of state educational aids and classified school districts for this purpose.

1950 — Wisconsin enrolled 132,000 for the Korean Conflict; 800 casualties.

1951 — First major legislative reapportionment since 1892.

1957 — Legislation prohibited lobbyists from giving anything of value to a state employee.

1958 — Professor Joshua Lederberg, UW geneticist, Nobel prize winner in medicine.

1959 — Gaylord Nelson, first Democratic governor since 1933, inaugurated. Circus World Museum established at Baraboo. Frank Lloyd Wright, architect, died.

1960 — Mrs. Dena Smith elected state treasurer, first woman elected to statewide office in Wisconsin.

1961 — Legislation enacted to initiate long-range program of acquisition and improvement of state recreation facilities (ORAP program). Federal supervision of Menominee Indian tribe terminated on April 29; reservation became 72nd county.

1962 — Selective sales tax and income tax withholding enacted. Kohler Company strike, which began in 1954, settled.

1963 — John Gronouski, state tax commissioner, appointed U.S. Postmaster

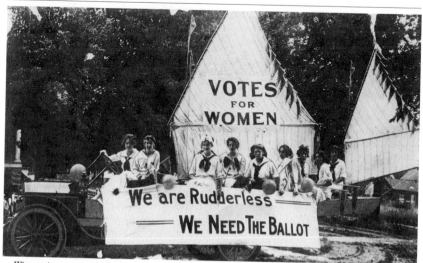

Wisconsin was among the first states to ratify the 19th Amendment to the U.S. Constitution, guaranteeing the right of women to vote. (State Historical Society, #WHi (X3) 18424)

General. State expenditures from all funds for 1963-64 fiscal year top $1 billion for first time.

1964 — Wisconsin Supreme Court redistricted legislature after legislature and governor failed to agree on a plan. Two National Farmers Organization members killed in demonstration at Bonduel stockyard. Legislature enacted property tax relief for aged. The office of county superintendent of schools abolished, but Cooperative Educational Service Agencies (CESAs) created to provide regional services.

1965 — School compulsory attendance age raised to 18. All parts of state placed into vocational school districts. County boards reapportioned on population basis. State law prevented discrimination in housing. The State Capitol, in use since 1917, officially dedicated, after extensive remodeling and cleaning.

1966 — 1965 Legislature held first full even-year regular session since 1882. Governor Warren P. Knowles called out National Guard to keep order during civil rights demonstrations in Wauwatosa. Wisconsin Supreme Court upheld Milwaukee Braves baseball team move to Atlanta. Grand jury investigation of illegal lobbying activities in the legislature resulted in 13 indictments.

1967 — Executive branch reorganized along functional lines. Ban on colored oleomargarine repealed. Racial rioting in Milwaukee in July-August. Marathon marches demonstrate for Milwaukee open housing ordinance. Antiwar protests at the University of Wisconsin in Madison culminate in riot with injuries.

1968 — Constitutional amendment permitted the legislature to meet as provided by law rather than once a biennium, resulting in annual sessions. Ninety black students expelled from Wisconsin State University-Oshkosh when December demonstration damaged the administration building. Wisconsin's first heart transplant performed at St. Luke's Hospital in Milwaukee; first successful bone marrow transplant performed by team of scientists and surgeons at the University of Wisconsin in Madison.

1969 — Selective sales tax became general sales tax. On opening day of special legislative session on welfare and urban aids, welfare mothers and UW-Madison students,

led by Father James Groppi, took over the Assembly Chamber; National Guard called to protect Capitol. Groppi cited for contempt and jailed; contempt charge upheld by Wisconsin Supreme Court. Student strikes at UW in Madison demanded Black studies department; National Guard activated to restore order. Congressman Melvin R. Laird appointed U.S. Secretary of Defense. Wisconsin's portion of Interstate Highway System completed.

1970 — Army Mathematics Research Building at the UW in Madison bombed by antiwar protestors, resulting in one death. "Old Main" at Wisconsin State University-Whitewater burned down in apparent arson. First elections to 4-year terms in Wisconsin history for all constitutional officers, based on constitutional amendment ratified in 1967. UW scientists, headed by Dr. Har Gobind Khorana, succeeded in the first total synthesis of a gene.

Wisconsin's role as America's Dairyland was official state policy by the 1930s, when the Department of Agriculture and Markets erected billboards extolling the virtues of butter and cheese across the state and beyond. (1937 Wisconsin Blue Book)

1971 — The legislature, now meeting in regular session throughout the biennium, enacted major shared tax redistribution, merger of University of Wisconsin and State University systems, revision of municipal employee relations laws.

1972 — Legislature enacted comprehensive consumer protection act, lowered the age of majority from 21 to 18, required environmental impact statement for all legislation affecting the environment, repealed railroad full crew law, and ratified the unsuccessful "equal rights" amendment to U.S. Constitution. Record highway death toll, 1,168.

1973 — State constitutional amendment permitting bingo adopted. Barbara Thompson first woman to hold the elective office of State Superintendent of Public Instruction. The 1954 Menominee Termination Act repealed by Congress. Legislature enacted state ethics code, repealed oleomargarine tax, funded programs for the education of all handicapped children, and established procedures for informal probate of simple estates.

1974 — Legislature enacted comprehensive campaign finance act and strengthened open meetings law. Democrats swept all constitutional offices and gained control of both houses of the 1975 Legislature for first time since 1893. Kathryn Morrison first woman elected to the state senate. Striking teachers fired in Hortonville.

1964-1975 — 165,400 Wisconsinites served in Vietnam; 1,239 were killed.

The Late Twentieth Century

Democrats lost control of the senate in 1993 for the first time since 1974, and in 1995 they lost control of the assembly for the first time since 1970. Control of the senate has changed several times since then. Women began to be widely represented in the legislature for the first time in the 90s.

Health care reform, restructuring welfare, the business climate in the state, taxation, education, and prisons were the chief concerns of policymakers in the 90s.

California challenged Wisconsin's dominance of the dairy industry. After an economic downturn in the 80s, the 90s saw a robust economy throughout most of the state with Madison leading the entire country in employment for several months. The farm sector and brewing industry continued to experience difficulties, however.

Litigation and demonstrations over off-reservation resource rights of the Chippewa Indians continued throughout the 80s to be replaced by controversy over Indian gaming in the 90s and into the new century.

1975 — Menominee Indians occupied Alexian Brothers Novitiate. Legislature made voter registration easier, established property tax levy limits on local governments, and eliminated statutory distinctions based on sex. UW-Madison scientist, Dr. Howard Temin, shared 1975 Nobel Prize in physiology-medicine.

1976 — U.S. District Court ordered integration of Milwaukee public schools. Ice storm damage reached $50.4 million. Wisconsin Legislature established a system for compensating crime victims. Exxon discovered sulfide zinc and copper deposits in Forest County. Shirley S. Abrahamson was appointed first woman on the Wisconsin Supreme Court. Wisconsin Supreme Court declared negative school aids law unconstitutional.

1977 — Governor Patrick J. Lucey appointed Ambassador to Mexico, and Lieutenant Governor Martin Schreiber became "acting governor". First state employees union strike lasted 15 days; National Guard ran prisons. Constitutional amendments authorized raffle games and revised the structure of the court system by creating a Court of Appeals. Legislation enacted included public support of elections campaigns, no-fault divorce, and implied consent law for drunk driving.

1978 — Wisconsin Supreme Court allowed cameras in state courtrooms. Vel Phillips elected secretary of state, first black constitutional officer. Laws enacted included a hazardous waste management program.

1979 — Constitutional amendment removed lieutenant governor from serving as president of the senate. Moratorium on tax collections gave state taxpayers a 3-month "vacation" from taxes. Shirley S. Abrahamson, became the first woman elected to Wisconsin Supreme Court after serving by appointment for 3 years. Legislature established school of veterinary medicine at the UW-Madison.

1980 — Eric Heiden of Madison won five Olympic gold medals for ice speed skating, named winner of the Sullivan Award as best amateur athlete in the country. 15,000 Cuban refugees housed for the summer at Fort McCoy. Former Governor Lucey ran as independent candidate for U.S. Vice President. State revenue shortfall led to 4.4 percent cuts in state spending. Laws enacted included specific rights for victims and witnesses of crimes, and mental patient commitment revisions.

1981 — U.S. Supreme Court ruled against Wisconsin's historic open primary. Laws enacted included stronger penalties for drunk driving and changes in mining taxes.

1982 — State unemployment hit highest levels since the Great Depression. Voters endorsed first statewide referendum in nation calling for a freeze on nuclear weapons. Laws enacted included extensions in the fair employment law, an "employees' right-to-know" law pertaining to toxic substances in the workplace, a new public records law, and a historic preservation law. Jos. Schlitz Brewing Co. acquired by Stroh Brewing Co. of Detroit, all Milwaukee operations closed.

1983 — Continued recession forced adoption of budget including a 10 percent tax surcharge and a pay freeze for state employees. Law raising minimum drinking age to 19 passed (effective 7/1/85). In one-day uprising, inmates at Waupun State Prison took 15 hostages, but released them uninjured. Laws enacted included a "lemon law" on motor vehicle warranties, changes in child support collection procedures and levels. UW-Madison School of Veterinary Medicine enrolled its first class.

1984 — Most powerful U.S. tornado of 1984 destroyed Barneveld; 9 dead. Democratic party chose presidential convention delegates in caucuses rather than by presidential preference primary as a result of the Democratic National Committee rules changes. Indian treaty rights to fish and hunt caused controversy. First liver transplants in Wisconsin conducted at UW Hospital. Laws enacted included a marital property reform act, groundwater protection act, establishment of high school graduation requirements, a "right-to-die" act, prohibition of smoking in public areas. Economic conditions began to improve from the low-point of the previous 2 years.

1985 — Milwaukee air crash killed 31. Major consolidation of state banks by large holding companies. Laws enacted included authorization for public utilities to form holding companies, comparable worth, and teen pregnancy prevention measures. First state tax amnesty program.

1986 — Farm land values dropped across the state. Exxon dropped plans to develop copper mine near Crandon. Laws enacted allowed regional banking, set sulfur dioxide emission limits, raised the drinking age to 21, and limited damages payable in malpractice actions.

1987 — Voters approved constitutional amendments allowing pari-mutuel betting and a state lottery. Laws enacted included a mandatory seatbelt law, antitakeover legislation, gradual end to the inheritance and gift taxes, and a "learnfare" program designed to keep in school the children of families receiving Aid to Families With Dependent Children (AFDC). G. Heileman Brewing Company taken over by Alan Bond.

1988 — Driest summer since the 1930s. The first state lottery games began. Chrysler Corporation's automobile assembly plant in Kenosha, the nation's oldest car plant, closed. Laws enacted included mandatory family leave for employees.

1989 — Laws enacted included creation of Department of Corrections, the Lower Wisconsin State Riverway, and a statewide land stewardship program.

1990 — More than 1,400 Wisconsin National Guard and Reserve soldiers were called to active duty in Persian Gulf crisis, 11 casualties. The number of Milwaukee murders set a new record, raising demands for crime and drug controls. Laws enacted included a major recycling law and Milwaukee Parental Choice voucher program for public and nonsectarian private schools.

1991 — The price of raw milk hit lowest point since 1978. First Indian gambling compacts signed. Governor Tommy G. Thompson vetoed a record 457 items in the state budget.

1992 — Train derailment caused major spill of toxic chemicals and evacuation of over 22,000 people in Superior. Thousands of opponents, including children, staged protests at 6 abortion clinics in Milwaukee throughout the summer. Laws enacted included parental consent for abortion, health care reform, and creation of a 3-member Gaming Commission.

1993 — Wisconsin Congressman Les Aspin and UW-Madison President Donna Shalala named President Bill Clinton's Secretary of Defense and Secretary of Health and Human Services, respectively. Thousands in Milwaukee became ill as a result of cryptosporidium in the water supply. California passed Wisconsin in milk production. Republicans won control of state senate for the first time since 1974. Laws enacted included a 1999 sunset for traditional welfare programs, a cap on school spending, and permission to organize limited liability companies.

1994 — Laws enacted included removal of about $1 billion in public school operating taxes from property tax by 1997, a new regulatory framework for Public Service Commission regulation of telecommunication utilities, and granting towns most of the same powers exercised by cities and villages.

1995 — Republicans won control of state assembly for the first time since 1970. Elk reintroduced in northern Wisconsin. July heat wave contributed to 172 deaths.

1996 — Governor Thompson's new welfare reform plan, known as Wisconsin Works (W-2), received national attention. Train derailment forced evacuation of Weyauwega. Pabst Brewing closed 152-year-old brewery in Milwaukee. Senator George Petak was removed from office in the first successful legislative recall election in state history.

1997 — Groundbreaking for controversial new Miller Park, future home of the Milwaukee Brewers baseball team.

1998 — Tammy Baldwin became first Wisconsin woman elected to the U.S. Congress. U.S. Supreme Court upheld constitutionality of extension of Milwaukee Parental Choice school vouchers to religious schools. Second state tax amnesty program. Laws enacted included a mining moratorium, new penalties for failure to pay child support, truth-in-sentencing, and protection of fetuses.

1999 — Governor Tommy Thompson began record fourth term. Laws enacted included "smart growth", graduated drivers licensing, a sales tax rebate. Supermax, the state's high security prison, opened at Boscobel. Record low unemployment.

2000 — Legislature approved a local sales tax and revenue bonds for renovation of Lambeau Field, home of the Green Bay Packers.

Recent Years

2001 — Governor Thompson ended a record 14 years in office and assumed post of U.S. Secretary of Health and Human Services. Lt. Governor Scott McCallum became governor and appointed State Senator Margaret Farrow as the first woman to serve as lieutenant governor. Chronic Wasting Disease discovered in the state's deer herd. Extensive Mississippi River flooding. Miller Park opened. Laws enacted included telemarketing "no call" list, wetland protection, and the "senior care" prescription drug assistance plan.

2002 — Barbara Lawton became the first woman elected lieutenant governor and Peggy A. Lautenschlager became first woman elected attorney general. Deadliest single traffic accident in state history killed 10 and injured 40 near Sheboygan. Investigation into legislative caucus staffs resulted in criminal charges against five legislators. Seven Milwaukee County board members recalled over pension scandal.

2003 — Jim Doyle became first Democratic governor in 16 years. The Crandon mine issue was apparently resolved when local Indian tribes purchased the ore deposits. The renovated Lambeau Field opened. Senator Gary George became the second legislator in Wisconsin history to be recalled. A number of Wisconsin Guard and Reserve units were activated for service in the Iraq war. Wisconsin held its first mourning dove hunt.

2004 — Louis Butler, Jr., became the first black member of the Wisconsin Supreme Court. State government began to reduce its automobile fleet after allegations of misuse. Significant legislation included a livestock facility siting law and revision to clean air and water laws intended to spur job creation. Voter turnout in the fall election was 73%, the highest in many years.

2005 — The state minimum wage was increased. Wisconsin experienced a record 62 tornadoes during the year, including a record 27 in one day – August 18, when tornadoes hit Viola, Stoughton, and other communities resulting in one death, 27 injuries, and $40 million in damage. Several current and former members of the legislature were convicted of illegal campaign activities.

2006 — Continued participation in the Iraq War by Wisconsin National Guard and Reserve units was a potent issue, as was immigration reform. The legislature limited the use of condemnation power for the benefit of private individuals. Voters approved a constitutional amendment limiting marriage to persons of the opposite gender in November. An advisory referendum in favor of the death penalty was also approved by the voters.

2007 — Ethics laws and elections regulation procedures were modified. Milwaukee-based Miller Brewing merged with Denver's Coors brewery. The state budget did not pass until late October, one of the latest budgets in state history.

2008 — Brett Favre ended his memorable 16-year career with the Green Bay Packers. Louis Butler became the first sitting Supreme Court justice to be defeated at the polls in 40 years, losing to Michael Gableman. Severe flooding hit southern Wisconsin in June. Failure of an embankment caused Lake Delton to drain, destroying three homes.

The Great Lakes Compact received state and federal approval, regulating the use of Great Lakes water outside their watershed. A sharp downturn in the economy caused a rise in unemployment and the closing of the General Motors plant in Janesville, closing a chapter in Wisconsin's 100-year involvement in auto assembly.

2009 — Democrats opened the 99th Legislature with control of the governor's office and both houses of the legislature for the first time since the 1985 session. The ongoing economic crisis resulted in a projected budget deficit of $6 billion for the next biennium. In the largest activation since the Berlin Crisis of 1961, 3,000 soldiers of the Wisconsin National Guard prepared for mobilization to Iraq.

Sources: State Historical Society, *The Thirtieth Star, 1948; The 1958 Compton Yearbook* and succeeding editions; *The Americana Annual – 1967;* Robert C. Nesbit, *Wisconsin, A History;* Wisconsin Legislative Reference Bureau, *Clippings: Wisconsin History.*

A chapter of Wisconsin's history was brought to life when the movie Public Enemies *was filmed at a number of Wisconsin locations in 2008, including the State Capitol (above) and Little Bohemia in Vilas County, site of a real life shoot-out between John Dillinger and federal authorities in 1934.* (Brent Nicastro, Legislative Photographer)

FAMOUS CITIZENS OF WISCONSIN

Edward P. Allis (1824-1889), industrialist — developed the steel rolling mill.

Don Ameche* (1908-1993), actor — began career in radio, appeared in 56 movies; won Academy Award for *Cocoon*.

Roy Chapman Andrews* (1884-1960), explorer — found first dinosaur egg in the Gobi Desert.

Les Aspin* (1938-1995), political leader — President Clinton's first secretary of defense, January 1993 – December 1993; served 22 years in the U.S. Congress.

Stephen M. Babcock (1843-1931), chemist — devised butterfat content test.

John Bardeen* (1908-1991), physicist — twice winner of the Nobel Prize for development of the transistor and for the theory of superconductivity.

John Bascom (1827-1911), educator — president, University of Wisconsin 1874-1887; leader in upgrading the university to a nationally recognized institution.

Aaron Bohrod (1907-1992), painter — twice winner of the Guggenheim Fellowship; artist-in-residence at the University of Wisconsin-Madison.

Richard Ira "Dick" Bong* (1920-1945), aviator — leading World War II pilot; shot down 40 enemy planes to become America's "all time ace"; awarded Congressional Medal of Honor.

Olympia Brown (1835-1926), minister and publisher — first ordained woman minister in U.S.; key figure in women's rights movement.

Jerome I. Case (1819-1891), manufacturer — leader in mechanization of agriculture.

Carrie Chapman Catt* (1859-1947), suffragist — President of the National American Woman Suffrage Association, which she reorganized as the League of Women Voters with 2 million members after passage of the 19th amendment guaranteed women the vote.

Bernard J. Cigrand* (1866-1932), activist — leader in the movement to celebrate Flag Day.

Laurel Blair Salton Clark* (1961-2003), astronaut and naval flight surgeon — mission specialist died in crash of space shuttle Columbia.

John R. Commons (1862-1945), economist — drafted Wisconsin civil service law.

Seymour Cray* (1925-1996), computer scientist — called the "father of the supercomputer".

Leo T. Crowley (1889-1972), banker — structured the Federal Deposit Insurance Corporation as its chairperson, 1934-1945.

Patrick Cudahy (1849-1919), businessman — founder of a leading meat-packing company.

August Derleth* (1909-1971), author — noted for many contributions to literature about Wisconsin.

Ole Evinrude (1877-1934), inventor — developed the first outboard motor designed for mass production.

Edna Ferber (1885-1968), author — received 1925 Pulitzer Prize for the novel, *So Big.*

Lynn Fontanne (1887-1983) and **Alfred Lunt***, acting couple — appeared in theater, motion pictures, and television; jointly awarded Presidential Medal of Freedom in 1964.

Zona Gale* (1874-1938), author — recipient of 1921 Pulitzer Prize in drama for the play, *Miss Lulu Bett.*

Hamlin Garland* (1860-1940), author — received 1922 Pulitzer Prize for the novel, *A Daughter of the Middle Border.*

Ezekiel Gillespie (1818-1892), activist — plaintiff in 1866 Wisconsin Supreme Court case which resulted in extension of suffrage to Wisconsin Blacks; one of the founders of the first African Methodist Episcopal church in Wisconsin.

William T. Green (1863-1911), activist — first Black attorney in Wisconsin; active in securing the 1895 passage of the first civil rights law in the state.

Owen J. Gromme* (1896-1991), painter — wildlife artist, author of *Birds of Wisconsin,* and painter of the 1945 federal duck stamp.

John A. Gronouski* (1919-1996), political leader — postmaster general under Presidents Kennedy and Johnson; one of the architects of the modern Democratic Party in Wisconsin.

Mildred Fish Harnack* (1902-1943), war hero — while instructor at the University of Berlin, organized resistance group and transmitted intelligence to Allies; executed by Nazis.

Cordelia Harvey (1824-1895), humanitarian — instrumental in establishing military hospitals in the North during the Civil War.

Woodrow Charles "Woody" Herman (1913-1987), musician — jazz clarinetist and one of the outstanding "big band" leaders.

William Dempster Hoard (1836-1918), farmer and governor — introduced the French version of the silo and the subearth vault for curing cheese.

Harry Houdini (1874-1926), magician — world-renowned escape artist.

J. Willard Hurst (1911-1997), legal scholar — University of Wisconsin-Madison professor of law; nationally recognized expert in legal history.

Samuel C. Johnson (1833-1919), industrialist — founded wax products firm.

George F. Kennan* (1904-2005), diplomat, scholar and statesman — architect of Cold War "containment policy".

Walter J. Kohler, Sr.* (1875-1940), industrialist and governor — founded plumbing equipment company.

Julius Frank Anthony "Pee Wee King" Kuczynski* (1914-2000), musician — member of the Country Music Hall of Fame; author of over 400 songs including "Tennessee Waltz", one of the state songs of the State of Tennessee.

Belle Case La Follette* (1859-1931), lawyer and editor — first woman to graduate from the University of Wisconsin Law School; leader in support of the rights of women and African Americans.

Robert M. La Follette, Sr.* (1855-1925), political leader — progressive reformer as governor and U.S. Senator.

Carl Laemmle (1867-1939), business executive — major figure in the growth of the motion picture industry; built Universal City Studios.

Earl L. "Curly" Lambeau (1898-1965), professional football coach — founder and coach of the Green Bay Packers; instrumental in establishing the National Football League.

Mary Lasker* (1901-1994), philanthropist — her financial donations and influence supported vast expansion of cancer research; awarded Presidential Medal of Freedom in 1969.

William D. Leahy* (1875-1959), fleet admiral U.S. Navy — Chief of Naval Operations and President Roosevelt's chief of staff during World War II; the only Wisconsinite to wear the 5 stars of fleet admiral.

Aldo Leopold (1887-1948), teacher and author — University of Wisconsin professor and prominent ecologist; wrote *Sand County Almanac*.

Wladziu Valentino Liberace* (1919-1986), musician — world famous pianist-singer; known for his showmanship.

Vince Lombardi (1913-1970), professional football coach — 1959-1968 coach of the Green Bay Packers, the first NFL team to win 3 consecutive championships.

Alfred Lunt* (1893-1977) and **Lynn Fontanne**, acting couple — appeared in theater, motion pictures, and television; jointly awarded Presidential Medal of Freedom in 1964.

Douglas MacArthur (1880-1964), general — served in World Wars I and II, noted for his Philippine campaign, led post-war occupation of Japan, commander of UN forces in Korea.

Frederic March* (1897-1975), actor — won Academy Awards for *Dr. Jekyll and Mr. Hyde* and *Best Years of Our Lives*.

Helen Farnsworth Mears* (1872-1916), sculptor — created the Frances Willard statue in Statuary Hall of the U.S. Capitol and "The Genius of Wisconsin" in the Wisconsin Capitol.

Charles McCarthy (1873-1921), government innovator — established and directed first legislative reference library in the nation (forerunner of the Legislative Reference Bureau); wrote *The Wisconsin Idea*; advocate of vocational schools.

Golda Meir (1898-1978), political leader — prime minister of Israel (1969-1974); was educated and taught school in Milwaukee.

William "Billy" Mitchell (1879-1936), brigadier general, U.S. Army — fervent advocate of a strong air force.

John Muir (1838-1914), naturalist — promoted the national parks system.

Gaylord Nelson* (1916-2005), state legislator, governor, and U.S. Senator — founder of Earth Day.

Lorine Niedecker* (1903-1970), poet — author of several books of poetry; featured in most anthologies of 20th century American poetry.

Albert Ochsner* (1858-1925), surgeon — pioneer in radium cancer treatment.

Georgia O'Keeffe* (1887-1986), artist — innovative painter of flowers and landscapes, awarded Presidential Medal of Freedom in 1977.

George C. Poage (1880-1962), athlete — first Black athlete to compete in the modern Olympics; won bronze medals in the 200 and 400 meter hurdles in the 1904 Olympics at St. Louis.

William Proxmire (1915-2005), U.S. Senator — noted for his "Golden Fleece Award" condemning government waste.

Mitchel Red Cloud, Jr.* (1925-1950), Winnebago war hero — posthumously awarded Congressional Medal of Honor for service in Korea; first member of a Wisconsin tribe so honored.

William H. Rehnquist* (1924-2005), jurist — Chief Justice of the U.S. Supreme Court 1986-2005; Associate Justice 1972-1986.

Albert Ringling (1852-1916), circus promoter — merged Ringling Brothers Circus with Barnum and Bailey Circus to become the "Greatest Show On Earth".

Jeremiah Rusk (1830-1893), soldier, governor, and congressman — brigadier general in Union army, first U.S. Secretary of Agriculture.

Carl Schurz (1829-1906), political activist — German immigrant to Wisconsin and national supporter of German-American interests; served as brigadier general in Union army, U.S. Secretary of the Interior, U.S. Senator from Missouri, ambassador to Spain, newspaper owner, and writer.

Margaretha Meyer Schurz (1833-1876), educator — opened the first U.S. kindergarten in Watertown in 1856, married to Carl Schurz.

C. Latham Sholes (1819-1890), inventor and journalist — developed first practical typewriter.

Donald Kent "Deke" Slayton* (1924-1993), astronaut — flew the first joint U.S.-Soviet space mission; awarded NASA Distinguished Service Medal in 1965.

Walter W. "Red" Smith* (1905-1982), sports columnist and commentator — first sportswriter to receive the Pulitzer Prize (1976) for distinguished criticism as a reporter with the *New York Times*.

Tom Snyder* (1936-2007), broadcaster — hosted national late-night television talk shows.

Harry Steenbock* (1886-1967), biochemist — produced Vitamin D in food by irradiation with ultraviolet light.

Brooks Stevens* (1911-1995), industrial designer — one of the founders of the Industrial Designers Society of America; designer of many notable automobiles and other items including trains, motorcycles, and appliances.

Howard Temin (1934-1994), scientist — winner of 1975 Nobel Prize in physiology for work on the relationship between viruses and cancer.

Spencer Tracy* (1900-1967), actor — won Academy Award for *Boys Town* and *Captains Courageous*.

Frederick Jackson Turner* (1861-1932), historian — developed noted theories regarding the American frontier; won 1933 Pulitzer Prize for history.

Charles Van Hise* (1857-1929), educator — president, University of Wisconsin 1903-1918; promoted the expansion of the university into many new fields, influenced the organization of graduate study as a separate division, and saw university enrollment double.

Thorstein Veblen* (1857-1929), economist — wrote *The Theory of the Leisure Class*.

William Vilas (1840-1908), political leader — served as U.S. Postmaster General, Secretary of Interior, and U.S. Senator; organized the Rural Free Delivery (RFD) mail system.

Cadwallader C. Washburn (1818-1882), multimillionaire businessman, congressman, and governor — had extensive flour, rail, and lumber business interests.

Orson Welles* (1915-1986), actor and director — performed in theater, radio, television, and motion pictures; directed and starred in the highly acclaimed movie, *Citizen Kane.*

Laura Ingalls Wilder* (1867-1957), author of children's books — wrote a series of books, including *Little House on the Prairie*, based on her life growing up in the Midwest.

Thornton N. Wilder* (1897-1975), playwright and novelist — received Pulitzer Prize for the novel *The Bridge of San Luis Rey* (1928) and the plays *Our Town* (1938) and *The Skin of Our Teeth* (1942).

Frances Willard (1839-1898), social reformer — organized the Woman's Christian Temperance Union.

Daniel Hale Williams (1856-1931), doctor — first physician to perform open heart surgery; only African American fellow in the original American College of Surgeons; began study of medicine in Janesville.

Laura Ross Wolcott (1834-1915), physician and suffragist — first woman physician in Wisconsin; active in organizing and first president of the Wisconsin Woman's Suffrage Association.

Frank Lloyd Wright* (1867-1959), architect — internationally known innovative designer.

Note: Only deceased Wisconsin citizens are included in this list.

*Born in Wisconsin.

Sources: Encyclopedias, books, newspaper, and periodical accounts.

HISTORIC SITES IN WISCONSIN

Site	Location	Attendance[1] 2004-05	2005-06	2006-07	2007-08	2007-08 Revenue[2]
Bennett Studios	Wisconsin Dells	3,460	2,757	3,107	2,889	$58,847
Madeline Island	La Pointe	11,394	11,987	13,791	13,987	123,940
Old World Wisconsin	Eagle	54,299	52,013	48,491	46,950	889,558
Pendarvis.	Mineral Point	5,080	4,651	4,672	4,707	53,734
Stonefield	Cassville	4,178	3,859	3,613	4,349	29,240
Villa Louis	Prairie du Chien	14,399	13,689	12,242	11,974	116,275
Wade House	Greenbush	15,221	12,682	13,709	15,917	151,576
TOTAL.		108,031	101,638	99,625	100,773	$1,423,170
Circus World Museum[3]	Baraboo	44,037	36,416	41,085	34,879	$657,425

[1]Sites are generally open from May to October, with the exception of Circus World, which is open all year. For current information: http://www.wisconsinhistory.org/sitesmuseum.asp.

[2]Revenue from admissions and inside sales (such as gift shop sales, restaurant sales, and tram rides).

[3]Statistics are for calendar year. Owned by the State Historical Society of Wisconsin, but operated by a private, nonprofit foundation.

Source: State Historical Society of Wisconsin, departmental data, June 2009.

OFFICIAL HISTORICAL MARKERS IN WISCONSIN
August 2008

County	Location/Nearest Community	Subject
Adams	At the Park, Hwy 13, 3 miles north of Friendship.	Roche-a-Cri State Park
Adams	S. Arkdale Cemetery, 1801 Cypress Ave., Town of	Site of First Norwegian Evangelical
	Strongs Prairie	Lutheran Church of Roche-a-Cri
Ashland	Bay View Park, Hwy 2, Ashland.	Fleet Admiral William D. Leahy
Ashland	Northland College campus, Ellis Avenue, Ashland	Northland College
Ashland	In park on Hwy 2 at western limits of Ashland	Radisson-Groseilliers Fort
Ashland	La Pointe, Madeline Island	Madeline Island
Ashland	Hwy 13, 10 miles south of Mellen.	Great Divide
Ashland	Hwy 2, Odanah	The Bad River
Barron	Rest Area #34, westbound Hwy 53, 2 mi. south of Chetek . .	Pine Was King (Pineries)
Barron	2411-23 Street, Rice Lake	Our Lady of Lourdes Catholic Church
Bayfield	Hwy 13, 0.5 mile east of Cornucopia	Tragedy of the Siskiwit
Bayfield	Hwy 13, Port Wing	School Consolidation
Bayfield	Hwy 13, 2.3 miles north of Washburn	Madeline Island
Brown	Denmark War Memorial Pk., Wisconsin Ave. (CTH KB) . . .	Denmark
Brown	In park at corner of Broadway and George Sts., De Pere . .	Marquette-Jolliet Expedition
Brown	In Voyageur Park, De Pere.	Rapides des Peres – Voyageur Park
Brown	403 North Broadway, De Pere	White Pillars
Brown	222 South Baird Street, Green Bay	Cnesses Israel Synagogue
Brown	Outside Packer Hall of Fame, Green Bay	Green Bay Packers
Brown	1008 South Monroe Avenue, Green Bay	Hazelwood
Brown	2640 South Webster Avenue, Green Bay	Heritage Hill State Park
Brown	Hwy 57, 5 miles northeast of Green Bay	Red Banks
Brown	Holy Apostles Church Cemetery, 2937 Freedom Rd., Oneida	Revolutionary War Veteran (Powlis)
Buffalo	Hwy 35, 0.5 mile north of Alma	Beef Slough
Burnett	Crex Meadows Wildlife Area, off Hwy F, N. of Grantsburg .	Crex Meadows
Calumet	Wayside #4, intersection of Hwys 55 and 151, Brothertown	
	Town	Brothertown Indians of Wisconsin
Calumet	City Hall, 2110 Washington Street, New Holstein.	New Holstein
Calumet	Stockbridge Harbor, CTH E, Village of Stockbridge	Stockbridge Harbor
Chippewa . . .	Hwy 124, 3 miles north of Chippewa Falls	Nation's First Cooperative Generating
		Station
Chippewa . . .	2820 East Park Avenue, Chippewa Falls	Northern WI Center for the Developmentally
		Disabled
Chippewa . . .	Fairgrounds, 308 Jefferson Ave., Chippewa Falls	Northern Wisconsin State Fair
Chippewa . . .	Cornell Mill Yard Park and Bridge St., Cornell	Cornell Pulpwood Stacker
Chippewa . . .	West side of Hwy 178, near Hwy T	Cobban Bridge
Chippewa . . .	Hwy 178, 0.5 mile north of Jim Falls	Old Abe, the War Eagle
Clark	2 blocks west of Hwy 13, Colby.	Colby Cheese
Columbia. . . .	Rest Area #12, westbound I90-94, E. of WI River	The Circus
Columbia. . . .	711 West James Street, Columbus	Governor James Taylor Lewis
Columbia. . . .	Hwy 113 at Wisconsin River crossing	Merrimac Ferry
Columbia. . . .	120 N. Main Street, Pardeeville	Historic Pardeeville
Columbia. . . .	Hwy 33, 0.5 mile east of Portage	Fort Winnebago
Columbia. . . .	West Wisconsin and Crook Streets, Portage.	Frederick Jackson Turner
Columbia. . . .	Across from sheriff's office, Cook Street, Portage	Ketchum's Point
Columbia. . . .	Hwy 33, 0.5 mile east of Portage	Marquette
Columbia. . . .	Hwy CM, 5 miles northeast of Portage	Potters' Emigration Society
Columbia. . . .	Museum at The Portage, 804 MacFarlane Rd., Portage . . .	Society Hill Historic District
Columbia. . . .	Commerce Plaza Park, 301 West Wisconsin St., Portage . .	Zona Gale
Columbia. . . .	Rest Area #11, eastbound I90-94, 0.5 mi. E. of WI River. .	Rest Areas on the I-Roads
Columbia. . . .	Hwy 51, 0.5 mile south of Poynette	John Muir View

OFFICIAL HISTORICAL MARKERS IN WISCONSIN
August 2008–Continued

County	Location/Nearest Community	Subject
Columbia	Hwy 16, 4 miles east of Wisconsin Dells	Kingsley Bend Indian Mounds
Columbia	314 Broadway, Wisconsin Dells	Stroud Bank
Columbia	Village Park, 150 Lovers Lane, Wyocena	Major Elbert Dickason/Dickason's "Hotel"
Crawford	Hwy 171, 0.5 mile east of Gays Mills	Gays Mills Apple Orchards
Crawford	Hwy 35, 1.2 miles south of Lynxville	Rafting on the Mississippi
Crawford	Cornelius Family Park, 211 S. Main St., Prairie du Chien	Black Hawk's Surrender
Crawford	Fort Crawford Museum, 717 S. Beaumont Rd., Prairie du Chien	Fort Crawford
Crawford	Mississippi River Bridge, Prairie du Chien	Pere Marquette and Sieur Jolliet
Crawford	Beaumont and Rice Streets, Prairie du Chien	Museum of Medical Progress
Crawford	Mississippi River Bridge, Prairie du Chien	Prairie du Chien
Crawford	At entrance, Villa Louis Road, Prairie du Chien	Villa Louis
Crawford	521 N. Villa Road, Prairie du Chien	Villa Louis
Crawford	In lawn west of the Villa, Villa Louis, Prairie du Chien	War of 1812
Crawford	Hwy 61, 0.5 mile south of Soldiers Grove	James Davidson
Crawford	Soldiers Grove Park, Mill and Main Sts., Soldiers Grove	Soldiers Grove Origin
Dane	In park off Hwy A, Albion	Albion Academy
Dane	8770 Ridge Drive, Belleville	Primrose Lutheran Church
Dane	1 mile northeast of Blue Mounds, Hwy F	Brigham Park
Dane	Quivey's Grove, 6261 Nesbitt Road, Fitchburg	Mann House
Dane	2915 Syene Rd., Fitchburg	McCoy House
Dane	Camp Randall Memorial Park, UW-Madison campus	Camp Randall
Dane	8-12 N. Blount St., Madison	Ceramic Art Studio of Madison
Dane	4718 Monona Dr., Madison	Nathaniel Dean, Dean House
Dane	Vilas Communication Hall, UW-Madison campus	9XM-WHA
Dane	Bascom Hill, UW-Madison campus	North Hall
Dane	GEF III, 125 S. Webster St., Madison	Peck Cabin
Dane	Resurrection Cemetery, 2705 Regent St., Madison	Site of Former Greenbush Cemetery Burials
Dane	Olbrich Park, 3330 Atwood Ave., Madison	Third Lake Passage
Dane	415 E. Wilson St., Madison	Tragedy of War
Dane	816 State Street, Madison	State Historical Society
Dane	501 South Thornton Avenue, Madison	Yahara River Parkway
Dane	Indian Lake County Park, Hwy 19, 1 mi. E. of Marxville	Indian Lake Passage
Dane	Village Park, 39 Brodhead Street, Mazomanie	Historic Mazomanie
Dane	Branch Creek Conservancy Pk, Pleasant Branch Rd., Middleton	Pheasant Branch Encampment
Dane	Indian Mound Pk., 6200 Bl. of Ridgewood Ave., Monona	Outlet Mound
Dane	2455 West Broadway, Monona	Royal Airport/Charles Lindbergh
Dane	Entrance to Prairie Mound Cemetery, CTH M, Vil. of Oregon	Revolutionary War Veteran
Dane	Hwy 51, east shore of Lake Waubesa	Stephen Moulton Babcock (1843-1931)
Dane	Yahara River Bridge, W. Main St., 381 E. Main St., Stoughton	Main Street Historic District
Dane	La Follette County Park, 3 miles north of Stoughton	Robert Marion La Follette, Sr. (1855-1925)
Dane	300 E. Main Street, Sun Prairie	Georgia O'Keeffe
Dodge	214-216 Front St., Beaver Dam	Frederick Douglas
Dodge	Adams Spring Park, Spring Street, Fox Lake	Bernard "Bunny" Berigan (1908-1942)
Dodge	Addie Joss Park, Juneau	Adrian "Addie" Joss
Dodge	105 N. River St., Lowell	Lowell Women Firefighters
Dodge	Rest Area #64, northbound Hwy 41	World War II
Dodge	Hwys 28 and 67, on Main Street, Mayville	Wisconsin's First Iron Smelter
Dodge	Hwy 175, Theresa	Solomon Juneau House
Dodge	Jct. Hwys 26 and 67, Waupun	Auto Race – Green Bay to Madison
Door	12171 Garrett Bay Rd., Ellison Bay	The Clearing
Door	Noble Square, 4167 Main Street, Fish Creek	The Alexander Noble House
Door	Namur, Hwy 57	Belgian Settlement in Wisconsin
Door	6145 Cave Point Drive, Town of Jacksonport	Jacksonport United Methodist Church
Door	Olde Stone Quarry Park, CTH B, Town of Sevastopol	Leathem and Smith Quarry
Door	3434 CTH V, Sturgeon Bay	The Episcopal Church of the Holy Nativity
Door	Hwy 42, 0.5 mile north of junction with Hwy 57	The Orchards of Door County
Douglas	Hwy 2, Brule	Brule River
Douglas	Hwys F and B, Lake Nebagamon	Evergreen Park Cottage Sanatorium
Douglas	Hwy 2, Poplar	Major "Dick" Bong
Douglas	Hwy 53, 1.5 miles south of Solon Springs	Brule-St. Croix Portage
Douglas	Allouez (Superior), along Hwys 2, 13, and 53	Burlington Northern Ore Docks
Douglas	Rest Area #23, Hwys 2 & 53, southern limits of Superior	Northwest Portal of Wisconsin
Douglas	Memorial Park, Superior	Old Stockade Site
Douglas	Whaleback Museum, Barker's Island, Superior	S. S. Meteor, last of the Whalebacks
Douglas	Superior Central High School, 1015 Belknap St., Superior	Summer White House – 1928
Douglas	Harbor Entry, Wisconsin Point Road, Superior	The Superior Entry
Douglas	Between McCaskill and Holden Bldgs., UW-Superior	University of Wisconsin-Superior
Douglas	Tourist Information Center, City Park, Hwy 2, Superior	Wartime Shipbuilding
Dunn	Caddie Woodlawn Park, Hwy 25, Menomonie	Caddie Woodlawn
Dunn	Rest Area #61, eastbound I94, Menomonie	Chippewa Valley White Pine
Dunn	Evergreen Cemetery, Menomonie	Dr. Stephen Tainter – Revolutionary War Veteran
Dunn	205 Main Street, Menomonie	Mabel Tainter Memorial
Dunn	Rest Area #62, I94	World War I
Eau Claire	Dells Mills Museum, N. of Augusta on STH 27, Augusta	Dells Mills
Eau Claire	Wayside #4, Hwy 85, 0.5 mi. west of Hwy 37, Eau Claire	Silver Mine Ski Jump
Fond du Lac	Fond du Lac Co. Park, W11413 CTH TC, Brandon	The Raube Road Site
Fond du Lac	Hwy 151, 6 miles north of Fond du Lac	Edward S. Bragg
Fond du Lac	Rolling Meadows Golf Course, 560 W. Rolling Meadows Dr., Fond du Lac	County Home Cemetery Fond du Lac

OFFICIAL HISTORICAL MARKERS IN WISCONSIN
August 2008–Continued

County	Location/Nearest Community	Subject
Fond du Lac	Main Street and Forest Avenue, Fond du Lac	Military Road
Fond du Lac	30 East 2nd Street, Fond du Lac	Wisconsin Progressive Party
Fond du Lac	St. John the Baptist Church, Hwy W, Johnsburg	Father Caspar Rehrl
Fond du Lac	Southeast corner of Blackburn and Blossom Sts., Ripon	Birthplace of Republican Party
Fond du Lac	Pedrick Wayside, Hwy 23, Ripon	Carrie Chapman Catt
Fond du Lac	In park on Union Street, 1 block south of Hwy 23, Ripon	Ceresco
Fond du Lac	Ripon College campus, Ripon	Ripon College
Fond du Lac	Taycheedah Correctional Institution, Tn. of Taycheedah	Home of Governor James Duane Doty
Fond du Lac	Hwy 49, 4 miles east of Waupun	Horicon Marsh
Forest	Hwy 8, 1.8 miles east of Crandon	Northern Highland
Forest	Hwy 32, 1 mile south of Laona	Laona School Forest
Forest	Hwy 55, 0.5 mile north of Mole Lake	Battle of Mole Lake
Grant	Hwy 61, 0.3 miles south of Boscobel	The Gideons
Grant	Cassville	Village of Cassville
Grant	117 East Front Street, Cassville	Old Denniston House
Grant	620 Lincoln Avenue, Fennimore	The "Dinky"
Grant	Hwy 80 at the WI-IL state line, south of Hazel Green	Point of Beginning (Survey Point)
Grant	Cemetery, 1 block west of Hwys 61, 35, and 81, Lancaster	Nelson Dewey
Grant	Highway 35 and Slabtown Rd., 5 miles west of Lancaster	Pleasant Ridge
Grant	Rountree Hall, UW-Platteville	First State Normal School
Grant	114-108 South Main St., Potosi	Village of Potosi
Green	English Settlement Cemetery, 300 North Main St., Albany	English Settlement Cemetery
Green	Monroe Arts Center, 1315 11th St., Monroe	First Methodist Episcopal Church
Green	Monticello Monument Wayside, Hwy 69, Monticello	Nickolaus Gerber
Green	Village Park, 300 Blk of 2nd St., Hwy O, New Glarus	Herbert Kubly
Green	Hwy 69, New Glarus	New Glarus
Green Lake	Nathan Strong Park, East Huron St. (Hwy 116), Berlin	Lucy Smith Morris
Green Lake	Riverside Park, Berlin	Upper Fox River
Iowa	Hwy 14, 3 miles east of Arena	Village of Dover
Iowa	CTH Y, 3 mi. S. of Dodgeville	Dodge's Grove and Fort Union
Iowa	Courthouse lawn, Hwy 151, Dodgeville	Iowa County Courthouse
Iowa	Hwy YZ, 4 miles east of Dodgeville	Old Military Road
Iowa	Water Tower Park, Hwy 151, Mineral Point	Historic Mineral Point
Iowa	Iowa Co. Fairgrounds, 900 Fair St., Mineral Point	Laurence F. Graber, "Mr. Alfalfa"
Iowa	114 Shake Rag Street, Mineral Point	Shake Rag
Iowa	Library Park, Mineral Point	Wisconsin Territory
Iowa	9 Fountain St., Mineral Point	Site of Fort Jackson
Iowa	Frank Lloyd Wright Visitor Ctr., CTH C, Spring Green	Military Route Crossing
Iowa	Hwy 14, east of Wisconsin River, near Spring Green	Frank Lloyd Wright
Iowa	Tower Hill State Park, Hwy C, south of Hwy 14	Shot Tower
Iron	Hwy 2, 10 miles west of Hurley	Gogebic Iron Range
Iron	Wayside WI Info. Ctr., Hwy 51, 1 mile north of Hurley	Iron Mining in Wisconsin
Jackson	Hwys 121 and 95, 1.5 mile west of Alma Center	Silver Mound
Jackson	Bell Mound Scenic Overlook, 5 mi. S. of Black River Falls	Black River Valley Scenic Outlook
Jackson	Hwy 54, 5 miles east of Black River Falls	Mitchell Red Cloud, Jr. (1925-1950)
Jackson	Rest Area #8, westbound I94, 15 mi. SE Black River Falls	The Passenger Pigeon
Jackson	Rest Area #7, eastbound I94, 15 mi. SE Black River Falls	Sphagnum Moss
Jackson	Rest Area #6, westbound I94	Highground Veterans Memorial
Jackson	Hwy 27, 6 miles south of Black River Falls	Martin W. Torkelson
Jefferson	Aztalan Museum, N6284 Hwy Q, Tn. of Aztalan	Princess Burial Mound
Jefferson	In park, north off Hwy 12, just east of Cambridge	Lake Ripley – Ole Evinrude
Jefferson	Burnt Village Co. Park, Hwy N, 2 mi. SE of Ft. Atkinson	Black Hawk War Encampment "Burnt Village"
Jefferson	400 block of Milwaukee Avenue East, Fort Atkinson	Fort Koshkonong
Jefferson	Koshkonong Mounds Road, near Fort Atkinson	Lake Koshkonong Effigy Mounds
Jefferson	Blackhawk Island Road, Town of Sumner	Lorine Niedecker
Jefferson	Hwy 106, western city limits of Fort Atkinson	Panther Intaglio
Jefferson	Iola Mills, 300 North Main St., Iola	Iola Mills
Jefferson	Rest Area #14, westbound I94	In Service to Their Country
Jefferson	3 miles east of Lake Mills on Hwy B, south on Hwy Q	Aztalan State Park
Jefferson	Rest Area #13, eastbound I94, 1 mile east of Lake Mills	Drumlins
Jefferson	Bald Bluff Overlook, CTH H, 1 1/2 mi. S. of Palmyra	Black Hawk War Encampment
Jefferson	919 Charles St., Watertown	First Kindergarten
Jefferson	7 miles southeast of Watertown, Hwy 16	Highway Marking
Jefferson	Milwaukee Street at the Rock River, Watertown	Milwaukee Street Bridge
Jefferson	919 Charles Street, Watertown	Octagon House
Jefferson	One Main St. (at bridge), Watertown	Trail Discovery
Juneau	Hwy C, 0.5 mile east of Camp Douglas	Castle Rock
Juneau	Camp Williams, off I94	Wisconsin Military Reservation
Juneau	On the trail at the western edge of Elroy	Elroy-Sparta State Trail
Juneau	In village park, Hwy HH, Lyndon Station	Hop Raising
Juneau	Rest Area #10, westbound I90-94	The Sand Counties – Aldo Leopold Territory
Juneau	Rest Area #9, eastbound I90-94, near Mauston	The Wisconsin River
Juneau	Rest Area #9, eastbound I90-94, near Mauston	The Iron Brigade
Kenosha	Rest Area #126, I94	Cordelia A.P. Harvey
Kenosha	24th Ave. & 56th St., Kenosha	Auto Production in Kenosha
Kenosha	Hwy 31 eastbound at 95th St., Kenosha	Green Bay Ethnic Trail
Kenosha	Green Ridge Cemetery, 6604 Seventh Ave., Kenosha	John McCaffery Burial Site
Kenosha	6501 3rd Avenue, Kenosha	Kemper Hall
Kenosha	5117 – 4th Ave., Kenosha	Kenosha (Southport) Lighthouse
Kenosha	Library Park, Kenosha	Reuben Deming
Kenosha	Green Ridge Cemetery, 6604 Seventh Avenue, Kenosha	Revolutionary War Veterans
Kenosha	15620 12th St., Kenosha	Schaefer Mammoth Site
Kenosha	Hwy 32 at the southern edge of Kenosha	32nd Division Memorial Highway

OFFICIAL HISTORICAL MARKERS IN WISCONSIN
August 2008–Continued

County	Location/Nearest Community	Subject
Kenosha	Rest Area-Tourist Info. Ctr. #26, westbound I94, N of I11	The Name "Wisconsin"
Kenosha	SE corner of STHs 50, 75, and 83, Town of Salem	Brass Ball Corners
Kewaunee	Ferry yard, Kewaunee	Car-Ferry Service
La Crosse	Rest Area #15, eastbound I90	The Driftless Area
La Crosse	McGilvray Rd. Access, Van Loon State Wildlife Area	The McGilvray "Seven Bridges Road"
La Crosse	Halfway Creek Lutheran Church, 2.5 mi. E. of Holmen	Luther College
La Crosse	Bishop's View Overlook, Hwy 33, 5 mi. E. of La Crosse	The Coulee Region
La Crosse	Rest Area #31, I94, French Island, La Crosse	Major General C.C. Washburn
La Crosse	La Crosse	Red Cloud Park
La Crosse	Corner of Front and State Streets, La Crosse	Spence Park
La Crosse	Rest Area-Tourist Info. Ctr. #31, I90, La Crosse	Upper Mississippi
La Crosse	Hwy 16 Valley View Mall entrance, just N. of Medary	Valley View Site
La Crosse	Neshonoc Cemetery, West Salem	Hamlin Garland
La Crosse	Swarthout Lakeside Park, Hwy 16, West Salem.	Village of Neshonoc
Lafayette	First Capitol State Park, Hwy G, 4 mi. northwest of Belmont	Belmont-Wisconsin Territory 1836
Lafayette	First Capitol State Park, Hwy G, 4 mi. northwest of Belmont	Gov. Tommy G. Thompson's 1998 Address at Wisconsin's First Capitol
Lafayette	First Capitol State Park, Hwy G, 4 mi. northwest of Belmont	1998 Wisconsin Assembly (Sesquicentennial Marker)
Lafayette	Hwy 11, 1 mile west of Benton	Father Samuel Mazzuchelli
Lafayette	Intersection of Hwys F, 78, & Madison St., Blanchardville.	Zarahemia – Predecessor of Blanchardville
Lafayette	101 S. Main St., Blanchardville	Zenas Gurley
Lafayette	Hwy 23, 5 miles south of Mineral Point.	Fort Defiance
Lafayette	Hwy 11, 1 mile west of Shullsburg	Wisconsin Lead Region
Langlade	Hwy 52, near junction with Hwy 64.	Antigo Silt Loam, State Soil of Wisconsin
Langlade	Wayside, Hwy 45, 3 miles south of Antigo	Langlade County Forest, Wisconsin's First County Forest
Langlade	Junction of Hwys 55 and 64, Langlade	De Langlade
Langlade	Hwy 55, 3.5 miles north of Lily at Wolf River	Old Military Road
Lincoln	715 E. 2nd St., Merrill	Merrill City Hall
Lincoln	Hwy 64 over the Prairie River – 200 W. First St., Merrill.	Three Arch Stone Bridge
Manitowoc	CTH R, 1/2 mile N. of Schley Rd.	Rock Mill
Manitowoc	Rest Area #51, southbound I43, S. of Brown County line.	Wisconsin's Dairy Industry
Manitowoc	Rest Area #52, northbound I43, S. of Brown County line.	Wisconsin's Maritime Industries
Manitowoc	Lake Michigan Carferry Dock, 700 S. Lakeview Dr., Manitowoc	*S. S. Badger*/Manitowoc and the Car Ferries
Manitowoc	Mariner's Park, S. 8th St., at the Manitowoc River	Manitowoc's Maritime Heritage
Manitowoc	Manitowoc Maritime Museum, 75 Maritime Drive	Manitowoc Submarines
Manitowoc	Silver Lake Park, Hwy 151, west of Manitowoc	Winnebago Trail
Manitowoc	924 Pinecrest Lane, Manitowoc Rapids	Collins Road Bridge Span
Manitowoc	Pioneer Rd. and CTH XX, Meeme	Meeme Poll House
Manitowoc	St. Nazianz Village Hall, 228 W. Main St., St. Nazianz.	George Washington School
Manitowoc	108 W. Birch, St. Nazianz	St. Nazianz
Manitowoc	Central Park, Two Rivers	Ice Cream Sundae
Manitowoc	Point Beach State Park, N. of Two Rivers on County O	Rawley Point Lighthouse
Manitowoc	Valders Memorial Park, Hwy J, Valders.	Thorstein Veblen
Marathon	Rothschild Pk., Grand Ave., Park & Kort Sts., Rothschild	Wisconsin's 1st Home-Built Flying Machine
Marathon	UW-Marathon County campus, Wausau.	The First Teachers' Training School in Wisconsin
Marathon	Wayside, northbound Hwy 51, 1 mile south of Hwy 153	First Workers Compensation Policy
Marinette	Peshtigo Cemetery, Oconto Avenue, Peshtigo.	Peshtigo Fire Cemetery
Marinette	N2155 USH 141, Town of Pound	Lena Road Schoolhouse
Marinette	W2349 County JJ, Wausaukee.	McAllister State Graded School
Marquette	Hwy 22, 8 miles south of Montello	John Muir Country
Marquette	Rest Area #82, Hwy 51, 4 miles north of Westfield	Korean War
Marquette	Westfield Town Hall, W 7703 Ember Ave. at 4th	Russell Flats
Menominee	Hwys 47 and 55, 5 miles north of Shawano	Menominee Reservation
Menominee	Hwy, 55, 2.5 miles north of Keshena	Spirit Rock
Milwaukee	8801 West Grange Avenue, Greendale.	Wisconsin's Lime Industry
Milwaukee	8685 West Grange Avenue, Greendale.	Jeremiah Curtin House
Milwaukee	6500 Northway, Greendale	Village of Greendale
Milwaukee	92nd and Forest Home Ave., Greenfield.	Janesville Plank Road
Milwaukee	7325 W. Forest Home Ave., Greenfield	Town of Greenfield
Milwaukee	Zillman Park, S. Kinnickinnic Ave., Milwaukee	Bay View's Immigrants
Milwaukee	South Superior Street and East Russell Ave., Milwaukee	Bay View's Rolling Mill
Milwaukee	2000 West Wisconsin Avenue, Milwaukee	Captain Frederick Pabst
Milwaukee	Zeidler Park, 300 block of West Michigan St., Milwaukee	Carl Frederick Zeidler
Milwaukee	East Hartford & North Maryland Aves., UW-Milwaukee	Carl Sandburg Hall
Milwaukee	1756 North Prospect Avenue, Milwaukee	Civil War Camp
Milwaukee	Lobby, 700 West Virginia Street, Milwaukee	The Cream City
Milwaukee	Grounds of VA Hospital, Wood (Milwaukee)	Erastus B. Wolcott, M.D.
Milwaukee	Fourth Street and Kilbourn Avenue, Milwaukee	First African-American Church Built in Wisconsin
Milwaukee	Foot of East Michigan Street, Milwaukee	First Milwaukee Cargo Pier
Milwaukee	Layton Avenue, Milwaukee	General Mitchell Field
Milwaukee	Golda Meir Library on UW-Milwaukee campus	Golda Meir
Milwaukee	4th and State Streets, Milwaukee	Invention of the Typewriter
Milwaukee	Marquette Law School, 1103 W. WI Ave., Milwaukee	Mabel Wanda Raimey
Milwaukee	Civic Center, Milwaukee	MacArthur Square
Milwaukee	Merrill Park, 461 North 35th St., Milwaukee	Merrill Park
Milwaukee	Currie Park, Wauwatosa	Milwaukee County's First Airport
Milwaukee	East Hartford and North Downer Avenues, Milwaukee	Milwaukee-Downer College
Milwaukee	231 West Michigan Street, Milwaukee	Milwaukee Interurban Terminal, 1905-1951
Milwaukee	Zablocki VA Medical Center, Hwy 59.	National Soldiers Home

OFFICIAL HISTORICAL MARKERS IN WISCONSIN
August 2008–Continued

County	Location/Nearest Community	Subject
Milwaukee	At the lighthouse in Lake Park, Milwaukee	North Point Lighthouse
Milwaukee	East North Avenue, Milwaukee	Old North Point Water Tower
Milwaukee	Wells and Edison Streets, Milwaukee	Oneida Street Station, T.M.E.R. and L. Co.
Milwaukee	144 East Wells Street, Milwaukee	Pabst Theater
Milwaukee	Cathedral Square Park, northeast corner, Milwaukee	Rescue of Joshua Glover
Milwaukee	North Avenue and Lake Drive, Milwaukee	Saint John's Infirmary
Milwaukee	North Lake Drive, Milwaukee	St. Mary's School of Nursing
Milwaukee	North Water and East Erie Streets, Milwaukee	Sinking of the *Lady Elgin*
Milwaukee	200 North Broadway, Milwaukee	Third Ward Fire
Milwaukee	Mitchell Hall, UW-Milwaukee, North Downer Avenue	The University of Wisconsin-Milwaukee
Milwaukee	Miller Brewing Company, Milwaukee	Watertown Plank Road
Milwaukee	100 East Wisconsin Avenue, Milwaukee	Wisconsin's Oldest Newspaper: The *Milwaukee Sentinel*
Milwaukee	3500 block on N. Oakland Ave., Shorewood	Lueddeman's On-the-River
Milwaukee	4145 N. Oakland Ave., Shorewood	Shorewood Armory
Milwaukee	1701 E. Capitol Drive, Shorewood	Shorewood High School
Milwaukee	3930 N. Murray Ave., Shorewood	Shorewood Village Hall
Milwaukee	909 Menomonee Ave., South Milwaukee	Lawson Airplane Company
Milwaukee	Wauwatosa Cemetery, 2405-2485 Wauwatosa Ave., Wauwatosa	Revolutionary War Veteran (Morgan)
Milwaukee	State Fair Park, Main Gate, West Allis	Camp Harvey
Milwaukee	In triangle at 57th, Hayes, and Fillmore, West Allis	Meadowmere
Milwaukee	State Fair Park, Main Gate, West Allis	Wisconsin State Fair Park
Monroe	Hwy 12, 4 miles west of Camp Douglas	Mesas and Buttes
Monroe	Rest Area #16, westbound I90, 5 miles east of Bangor	Coulee Country
Monroe	At the Kendall Depot, North Railroad Street, Kendall	Elroy-Sparta State Trail
Monroe	200 West Main Street, Sparta	Masonic Lodge
Monroe	112 South Court Street, Sparta	Monroe County Courthouse
Monroe	124 West Main Street, Sparta	Sparta Free Library
Monroe	123 West Main Street, Sparta	U.S. Post Office
Monroe	In park on Hwy 12, Tomah	Tomah
Oconto	Hwy F, 1.5 miles east of Lakewood	The Holt and Balcom Logging Camp No. 1
Oconto	Chicago and Main Streets, Oconto	First Church of Christ Scientist
Oconto	On Oconto River at Brazeau Avenue, Oconto	Mission of St. Francois Xavier
Oconto	Copper Culture State Park, Oconto	Old Copper Culture Cemetery
Oneida	Oneida County Courthouse grounds, Rhinelander	First Rural Zoning Ordinance
Oneida	Hodag Park, Rhinelander	The Hodag
Oneida	W. edge of National Forest, off Hwy 32 E. of Three Lakes	Nicolet National Forest
Outagamie	807 South Oneida Street, Appleton	First Electric Street Railway
Outagamie	600 Vulcan Street, Appleton	World's First Hydroelectric Central Station
Outagamie	North of jct. Hwys BB and 45, 4 miles west of Appleton	South Greenville Grange No. 225
Outagamie	Thelen Park, Kaukauna	Revolutionary War Veterans
Outagamie	Hwy 96, 0.1 mile west of Little Chute	Treaty of the Cedars
Outagamie	Beacon Avenue and Division Street, New London	Birthplace of the American Water Spaniel
Ozaukee	Intersection of CTHs R & C, Belgium	Wisconsin's Luxembourgers
Ozaukee	Columbia Rd. and Mequon Ave., Cedarburg	Cedar Creek
Ozaukee	City Hall, Washington Avenue, Cedarburg	Historic Cedarburg
Ozaukee	W62 N646 Washington Ave., Cedarburg	Interurban Bridge
Ozaukee	Doctor's Park, Washington Ave. and Mill St., Cedarburg	Washington Avenue Historic District
Ozaukee	Covered Bridge Road, 1 mile north of Five Corners	Last Covered Bridge
Ozaukee	Mequon City Hall, 11333 North Cedarburg Rd., Mequon	Wisconsin's German Settlers
Ozaukee	108 N. Lake St., Port Washington	The Wisconsin Chair Company Fire
Ozaukee	Triangle Park and Green Bay Rd., Saukville	The Saukville Trails
Ozaukee	Entrance Wall, 250 S. Main St., Thiensville	Historic Thiensville
Ozaukee	Junction of Hwys F and M, 3 miles west of Thiensville	The Oldest Lutheran Church in Wisconsin
Ozaukee	Hwy I, 0.5 mile east of Waubeka	Birthplace of Flag Day
Pepin	Washington Square, Durand	Pepin County Courthouse
Pepin	Hwy 35, 1 mile north of Stockholm	Maiden Rock
Pepin	Hwy 35, Pepin Park	Laura Ingalls Wilder
Pepin	Hwy 35, 3 miles northwest of Pepin	Site of Fort St. Antoine
Pierce	Hwy 35, 1 mile south of Hwy 63, southeast of Hager City	"Bow and Arrow"
Pierce	Hwy 35, 3 miles west of Maiden Rock	Lake Pepin
Pierce	Spring Pond Park, East Mill Rd., Plum City	Historic Plum City
Pierce	Hwy 65, 3 miles south of I94	Edgar Wilson Nye
Polk	Hwy 35, Luck	Danish Cooperative Company
Polk	City Park, St. Croix Falls	The Battle of St. Croix Falls
Polk	Interstate Park, St. Croix Falls	Gaylord Nelson
Polk	Interstate Park, Hwy 8, St. Croix Falls	State Park Movement in Wisconsin
Polk	Overlook Park, N. Washington (Main) St., St. Croix Falls	Where Are the Falls of the St. Croix?
Portage	County W, Buena Vista Marsh Wildlife Area	Wisconsin's Greater Prairie Chicken
Portage	Portage County Park, Hwy E, 3 miles south of Knowlton	Du Bay Trading Post
Portage	1700 block of Monroe St., Stevens Point	The Historic Southside Railroad Complex of Stevens Point
Price	Movrich Park, Willow Avenue, Town of Fifield	Historic Fifield
Price	Hwy 13, Phillips City Park, Phillips	Phillips Fire
Racine	Weimhoff-Jucker Park, Burlington	Mormons in Early Wisconsin
Racine	Hwy 31 at 5 Mile Rd., Town of Caledonia	Bohemian School House
Racine	Zoological Gardens, 2131 N. Main St., Racine	Northside Historic District of Cream Brick Cottages
Racine	Graceland and Mound Cemeteries, 1147 West Blvd., Racine	Soldiers of the American Revolution
Racine	Simonsen Park, Main & Fourteenth Sts., Racine	Southside Historic District
Racine	Hwy 11, western limits of Racine	The Spark
Racine	Racine Village Park, 4725 Lighthouse Dr., Racine	The Wind Point Lighthouse
Racine	1407 71st Drive, Union Grove	Revolutionary War Veteran

OFFICIAL HISTORICAL MARKERS IN WISCONSIN
August 2008–Continued

County	Location/Nearest Community	Subject
Racine	Heg Park Road, Waterford	Old Muskego
Richland	Boaz Park, Hwy 171, Boaz	Ocooch Mountains
Richland	Boaz Park, Hwy 171, Boaz	Richard M. Brewer
Richland	Wayside, Hwy 14, 1 mi. E. Gotham, Town of Buena Vista	The Pursuit West
Richland	Krouskop Park, 400 W. 6th St. (Hwy 14), Richland Center	Ada James
Richland	Krouskop Park, 400 W. 6th St. (Hwy 14), Richland Center	Birthplace of General Telephone and Electronics Corporation (GTE)
Richland	Hwy 14, 5 miles west of Richland Center	Boaz Mastodon
Richland	Pier County Park, Hwy 80, Rockbridge	Rockbridge
Richland	5 miles west of Richland Center on Hwy 14	Rural Electrification
Richland	Pier Co. Park, Hwy 80, Rockbridge	Troop Encampment
Rock	Beloit College campus, Beloit	Beloit College
Rock	Rock River Heritage Wky., Public Ave. & State St., Beloit	Black Hawk at Turtle Village
Rock	Tourist Info. Ctr. #22, westbound I90, south of Beloit	Black Hawk War
Rock	Rest Area-Tourist Information Center, westbound I90	Medal of Honor
Rock	I43 at I90, Beloit	Wisconsin's First Aviator
Rock	Hwy 140, 4 miles south of Clinton	Jefferson Prairie Settlement
Rock	11204 N. Church St., Cooksville	Historic Cooksville/Historic Waucoma
Rock	Mt. Philip Cemetery, west of Darien	Soldier of the American Revolution
Rock	Hwy 51, 0.5 miles south of Edgerton	Wisconsin's Tobacco Land
Rock	Blackhawk Golf Course Clubhouse, 2100 Palmer, Janesville	The Black Hawk War/Black Hawk's Grove
Rock	NW corner of Delavan Dr. and Beloit Ave., Janesville	Burr Robins Circus
Rock	In Courthouse Park on S. Atwood Ave., Janesville	First State Fair, October 1-2, 1851
Rock	Rock County Historical Society, 10 S. High St., Janesville	Janesville Tank Company
Rock	Rest Area #17, eastbound I90	Rock River Industry
Rock	Hwy 51, 3.8 miles south of Janesville	Route of Abraham Lincoln 1832 and 1859
Rock	18 South Janesville Street, Hwy 26, Milton	Milton House
Rock	On southwest bank of Storr's Lake, off Hwy 26, Milton	Storr's Lake, Milton
Rock	Beckman Mill Co. Park, Co. Rd. H, Town of Newark	How-Beckman Mill
Rock	Hwy J, Shopiere	Home of Governor Harvey
Rusk	Appolonia Cong. Church, Hwy 8 & Cemetery Rd., Bruce	Appolonia
Rusk	Hwy 8, Weyerhauser	Chippewa River and Menomonie Railway
St. Croix	Rest Area-Tourist Info. Ctr. #25, I94 east of Hudson	Brule-St. Croix Waterway
St. Croix	Hwy 35, 4.7 miles north of Hudson	St. Croix River
St. Croix	Campus Drive, Outlot #3, New Richmond	New Richmond Cyclone
Sauk	Devil's Lake State Park, S5975 Park Rd., Baraboo	Civilian Conservation Corps
Sauk	Hwy 33 at County U, 5 miles east of Baraboo	Lower Narrows
Sauk	Hwy 12, 1.5 miles south of Baraboo	Ringling Brothers Circus
Sauk	E8948 Diamond Hill Rd., North Freedom	Mid-Continent Railway Historical Society
Sauk	Reedsburg Area Historical Park, 3 mi. E. of Reedsburg	Clare A. Briggs, Cartoonist
Sauk	State Hwy 136, 0.75 mi. N of STH 154, Rock Springs	Van Hise Rock
Sauk	Derleth Park, Water Street, Sauk City	August W. Derleth
Sauk	Hwy 12, 5 miles northwest of Sauk City	The Baraboo Range
Sauk	Lower WI Riverway, Hwy 78, 2 mi. N. of Sauk City	Battle of Wisconsin Heights
Sauk	Lower WI Riverway, Hwy 60, 2 mi. E. of Spring Green	Western Escape
Sauk	Hwy A, 1.5 miles south of Wisconsin Dells	Dawn Manor – Site of Lost City of Newport
Sauk	Hwy 16, 0.1 mile west of Wisconsin Dells	Wisconsin Dells
Sawyer	Hwys 70 and 27, Couderay	Court Oreilles
Sawyer	Hwys 27 and 70, 7 miles west of Couderay	Radisson-Groseilliers
Sawyer	Hermans Landing, Cty Rd CC, at bridge, Hayward	The Chippewa Flowage
Sawyer	Lac Courte Oreilles Reservation, 13891 W. Mission Rd.	St. Francis Solanus Indian Mission
Sawyer	Hwy 27, 5.5 miles south of Hayward	Namekagon-Court Oreilles Portage
Sawyer	Hwy W, 6.75 miles southeast of Winter	John Deitz, "Battle of Cameron Dam"
Shawano	Hwy 22, 3.5 miles east of Shawano	Shawano
Shawano	Hwy 45 at city limits of Wittenberg	Homme Homes
Sheboygan	50 South Main Street, Cedar Grove	Early Dutch Settlers in Wisconsin
Sheboygan	Lake Street Café Beer Garden, N. of Vil. of Elkhart Lake	Elkhart Lake – Road Race Circuits
Sheboygan	Hwy 23, in the Park at Greenbush, 6 mi. W. of Plymouth	Old Wade House State Park
Sheboygan	Memorial Park, Cedar Grove, 3 miles south of Oostburg	Dutch Settlement
Sheboygan	Heritage House Triangle Pk., Ctr. & N. 10th Sts., Oostburg	Historic Oostburg
Sheboygan	Greenleaf Historic Park, 900 Short Street, Random Lake	Nowack House
Sheboygan	Sheboygan North Point Park, North Point Dr., Sheboygan	The Phoenix Tragedy
Sheboygan	Wildwood Cemetery, 2026 New Jersey Ave., Sheboygan	Revolutionary War Veteran (David Waldo)
Sheboygan	Center Avenue and North Water Street, Sheboygan	Seils-Sterling Circus
Sheboygan	9th Street and Panther Avenue, Sheboygan	Sheboygan Indian Mound Park
Sheboygan	Rochester Inn, 504 Water St., Sheboygan Falls	Cole Historic District
Sheboygan	Sheboygan River Dam, Broadway St., Sheboygan Falls	Downtown Sheboygan Falls Historic District
Taylor	Hwy 102, Rib Lake	Rib Lake Lumber Company
Taylor	Hwy 102, 5 miles northeast of Rib Lake	Rustic Road
Trempealeau	Hwy 53, 1.5 miles southeast of Galesville	Decorah Peak
Trempealeau	Rest Area #5, eastbound I94, 2 miles southeast of Osseo	Winnebago Indians
Trempealeau	Great River State Tr., Hwy 35, 0.5 mi. E. of Trempealeau	The Mississippi River Parkway: First Project
Trempealeau	Perrot State Park	Brady's Bluff
Trempealeau	Perrot State Park, off Hwy 93	Perrot's Post
Vernon	Hwy 14, 0.5 mile west of Coon Valley	Nation's First Watershed Project
Vernon	Hwy 35, 2.5 miles north of De Soto	Battle of Bad Axe
Vernon	Hwy 35, 2 miles north of De Soto	Chief Win-no-shik, the Elder
Vernon	Hwy 35, Genoa	Dams on the Mississippi
Vernon	In power plant parking lot, west side of Hwy 35, Genoa	Wisconsin's First Nuclear-Fueled Generating Station
Vernon	Hwy 33, 0.1 mile west of Hillsboro	Admiral Marc A. Mitscher
Vernon	Hillsboro Lake Park, 300 Water Ave. at Hwys 80, 82, 33, Hillsboro	African American Settlers of the Cheyenne Valley
Vernon	Hwy 14, 0.5 mile north of Viroqua	Governor Rusk

OFFICIAL HISTORICAL MARKERS IN WISCONSIN
August 2008–Continued

County	Location/Nearest Community	Subject
Vernon	City Hall, 202 N. Main St., Viroqua	Viroqua's First Settler
Vilas	Hwy M, 6 miles south of Boulder Junction	First Forest Patrol Flight
Vilas	Trout Lake Nursery, Hwy M.	Forest Restoration – The Beginning
Vilas	Hwy 47, Flambeau Lake.	Lac du Flambeau
Vilas	Lac Vieux Desert Park, West Shore Dr. near Land O'Lakes	Lac Vieux Desert
Vilas	Hwys 32 and 45, 0.5 mile south of Land O'Lakes	32nd Division Memorial Highway
Vilas	Hwy 45, 1.5 miles south of Land O'Lakes	Wisconsin River Headwaters
Vilas	Sayner Park, Sayner	Snowmobile
Walworth	Village Park, Allen Grove, on Hwy X, 3 mi. SW of Darien	Allen Family
Walworth	City of Delavan Parking Lot, 218 South 7th St., Delavan	Birthplace of "The Greatest Show on Earth"
Walworth	Horton Park, Hwy 11 in Delavan	Delavan's Circus Colony
Walworth	Tower Park, Walworth Ave., Delavan	Delavan's Historic Brick Street
Walworth	Grounds of State School for the Deaf, Hwy 11, Delavan	Wisconsin's First School for Deaf
Walworth	300 Church Street, East Troy	East Troy Railroad
Walworth	Veterans Memorial Park, Hwy 12, Genoa City	First Swedish Settlers in Wisconsin
Walworth	Hwy BB, 3.5 miles south of Lake Geneva	Wisconsin's First 4-H Club
Walworth	Oak Grove Cemetery, East Main Street, Whitewater	Revolutionary War Veterans
Walworth	Hwy 67 Industrial Park, N3440 STH 67 Williams Bay	755 Aircraft Control and Warning Squadron
Washburn	Hwy 70, 0.5 mile east of Spooner	Yellow River
Washburn	Junction of Hwys 53 and 63, Trego	Namekagon River
Washington	Dheinsville Park, Holy Hill Rd., Germantown	Dheinsville Settlement
Washington	Chandelier Ballroom, 700 South Main Street, Hartford	The Schwartz Ballroom
Washington	Hwy 83, Hartford	"Kissel"
Washington	South side of Hwy 33, 550 feet west of jct. with Hwy 144	Great Divide
Washington	At the park, Hwy A, E. of Hwy 114, NW of West Bend	Lizard Mound County Park
Waukesha	408 Main St., Delafield	Delafield Fish Hatchery
Waukesha	Southern Kettle Moraine State Forest, County C, Delafield	Lapham Peak
Waukesha	Mission Road at Mill Road, west of Delafield	Nashotah Mission
Waukesha	1101 North Genesee Street, Delafield	St. John's Northwestern Military Academy
Waukesha	Hwy 18, near Dousman	Masonic Home
Waukesha	Main Street, Lannon	Lannon Stone
Waukesha	N51 W34922 Wisconsin Ave., Okauchee	Historic Okauchee
Waukesha	Carroll College campus, Waukesha	Carroll College
Waupaca	Municipal Airport, Clintonville	Birthplace of an Airline
Waupaca	Walter Olen Park, Clintonville	Four-Wheel Drive
Waupaca	Marden Memorial Center, WI Veterans Home, King	General Charles King
Waupaca	Marden Memorial Center, WI Veterans Home, King	Grand Army Home
Waupaca	Triangle Park, Jct. of Hwy 22 with 110 and Hwy B, Manawa	Melvin O. Handrich – Medal of Honor Recipient
Waushara	Hwy 110, 3.5 miles south of Marion	Chief Waupaca
Waushara	County J, 2 miles south of Almond	Sir Henry Wellcome
Waushara	State Hwy 49, Auroraville	The Auroraville Fountain
Waushara	6th Ave., Town of Hancock	Whistler Mound Group and Enclosure
Winnebago	9088 Clayton Avenue, Town of Menasha	Fox-Irish Cemetery
Winnebago	Menasha Hotel, Main and Mills Streets, Menasha	Wisconsin Central Railroad
Winnebago	Fritsie Park, Menasha	Butte des Morts
Winnebago	Interior walkway, 135 W. Wisconsin Ave., Neenah	Wisconsin Avenue Commercial Historic District
Winnebago	Scott Park, 515 E. Main St., Omro	Historic Omro
Winnebago	1619 Oshkosh Avenue, Oshkosh	Coles Bashford House
Winnebago	Oshkosh Public Museum, 1331 Algoma Blvd., Oshkosh	Edgar Sawyer House
Winnebago	Rainbow Park, Oshkosh	Knaggs Ferry
Winnebago	Wittman Field Airport, 20th Street Road, Oshkosh	S.J. Wittman
Winnebago	UW-Oshkosh campus, Oshkosh	University of Wisconsin-Oshkosh
Winnebago	Town of Winchester Cemetery, 1 mi. SW of Winchester	Samuel N. Rogers, Sr., American Revolutionary Soldier
Winnebago	Hwy B, west of Winneconne	Poygan Paygrounds
Wood	Wayside #4, junction of Hwys 10 and 13	Prisoners of War
Wood	West 100 Block of North Central Ave., Marshfield	Founder's Square
Wood	Riverside Park, Hwys 54 and 73, Nekoosa	Point Basse
Wood	Hwy 54, 5 miles west of Port Edwards	Cranberry Culture
Wood	Hwys 54 and 73, southern city limits of Wisconsin Rapids	Centralia Pulp and Paper Mill

Sources: State Historical Society of Wisconsin, Historical Markers Council, *A Guide to Wisconsin Historical Markers,* 1982; Division of Historic Preservation, departmental data, June 2009.

WISCONSIN VOTE IN PRESIDENTIAL ELECTIONS
1848 – 2008

Key:

A – American (Know Nothing)	LR – Liberal Republican	Soc – Socialist
AFC – America First Coalition	NA – New Alliance	SocUSA – Socialist Party USA
Cit – Citizens	Nat – National	SoD – Southern Democrat
Com – Communist	ND – National Democrat	SPW – Socialist Party of Wis.
Con – Constitution	NER – National Economic Recovery	SW – Socialist Worker
CU – Constitutional Union	NL – Natural Law	Tax – U.S. Taxpayers
D – Democrat	People's – People's (Populist)	TBL – The Better Life
ER – Independents for Economic Recovery	Pop – Populist	3rd – Third Party
FS – Free Soil	PP – People's Progressive	U – Union
G – Greenback	Prog – Progressive	UL – Union Labor
Gr – Grassroots	Proh – Prohibition	USL – U.S. Labor
Ind – Independent	R – Republican	W – Whig
IP – Ind. Progressive	Rfm – Reform	WG – Wisconsin Greens
IS – Ind. Socialist	SD – Social Democrat	WIA – Wis. Independent Alliance
ISL – Ind. Socialist Labor	SL – Socialist Labor	Workers – Workers
ISW – Ind. Socialist Worker	S&L – Party for Socialism and	WtP – We, the People
LF – Labor–Farm/Laborista-Agrario	Liberation	WW – Worker's World
Lib – Libertarian		

Note: The party designation listed for a candidate is taken from the Congressional Quarterly *Guide to U.S. Elections.* A candidate whose party did not receive 1% of the vote for a statewide office in the previous election or who failed to meet the alternative requirement of Section 5.62, Wisconsin Statutes, must be listed on the Wisconsin ballot as "independent". In this listing, candidates whose party affiliations appear as "Ind", followed by a party designation, were identified on the ballot simply as "independent" although they also provided a party designation or statement of principle.

Under the Electoral College system, each state is entitled to electoral votes equal in number to its total congressional delegation of U.S. Senators and U.S. Representatives.

1848 (4 electoral votes)

Lewis Cass (D)	15,001
Zachary Taylor (W)	13,747
Martin Van Buren (FS)	10,418
TOTAL	39,166

1852 (5 electoral votes)

Franklin Pierce (D)	33,658
Winfield Scott (W)	22,210
John P. Hale (FS)	8,814
TOTAL	64,682

1856 (5 electoral votes)

John C. Fremont (R)	66,090
James Buchanan (D)	52,843
Millard Fillmore (A)	579
TOTAL	119,512

1860 (5 electoral votes)

Abraham Lincoln (R)	86,113
Stephen A. Douglas (D)	65,021
John C. Breckinridge (SoD)	888
John Bell (CU)	161
TOTAL	152,183

1864 (8 electoral votes)

Abraham Lincoln (R)	83,458
George B. McClellan (D)	65,884
TOTAL	149,342

1868 (8 electoral votes)

Ulysses S. Grant (R)	108,857
Horatio Seymour (D)	84,707
TOTAL	193,564

1872 (10 electoral votes)

Ulysses S. Grant (R)	104,994
Horace Greeley (D & LR)	86,477
Charles O'Conor (D)	834
TOTAL	192,305

1876 (10 electoral votes)

Rutherford B. Hayes (R)	130,668
Samuel J. Tilden (D)	123,927
Peter Cooper (G)	1,509
Green Clay Smith (Proh)	27
TOTAL	256,131

1880 (10 electoral votes)

James A. Garfield (R)	144,398
Winfield S. Hancock (D)	114,644
James B. Weaver (G)	7,986
John W. Phelps (A)	91
Neal Dow (Proh)	68
TOTAL	267,187

1884 (11 electoral votes)

James G. Blaine (R)	161,157
Grover Cleveland (D)	146,477
John P. St. John (Proh)	7,656
Benjamin F. Butler (G)	4,598
TOTAL	319,888

1888 (11 electoral votes)

Benjamin Harrison (R)	176,553
Grover Cleveland (D)	155,232
Clinton B. Fisk (Proh)	14,277
Alson J. Streeter (UL)	8,552
TOTAL	354,614

1892 (12 electoral votes)

Grover Cleveland (D)	177,325
Benjamin Harrison (R)	171,101
John Bidwell (Proh)	13,136
James B. Weaver (People's)	10,019
TOTAL	371,581

1896 (12 electoral votes)

William McKinley (R)	268,135
William J. Bryan (D)	165,523
Joshua Levering (Proh)	7,507
John M. Palmer (ND)	4,584
Charles H. Matchett (SL)	1,314
Charles E. Bentley (Nat)	346
TOTAL	447,409

1900 (12 electoral votes)

William McKinley (R)	265,760
William J. Bryan (D)	159,163
John G. Wooley (Proh)	10,027
Eugene V. Debs (SD)	7,048
Joseph F. Malloney (SL)	503
TOTAL	442,501

1904 (13 electoral votes)

Theodore Roosevelt (R)	280,164
Alton B. Parker (D)	124,107
Eugene V. Debs (SD)	28,220
Silas C. Swallow (Proh)	9,770
Thomas E. Watson (People's)	530
Charles H. Corregan (SL)	223
TOTAL	443,014

1908 (13 electoral votes)

William H. Taft (R)	247,747
William J. Bryan (D)	166,632
Eugene V. Debs (SD)	28,164
Eugene W. Chafin (Proh)	11,564
August Gillhaus (SL)	314
TOTAL	454,421

WISCONSIN VOTE IN PRESIDENTIAL ELECTIONS
1848 – 2008–Continued

1912 (13 electoral votes)

Woodrow Wilson (D)	164,230
William H. Taft (R)	130,596
Theodore Roosevelt (Prog)	62,448
Eugene V. Debs (SD)	33,476
Eugene W. Chafin (Proh)	8,584
Arthur E. Reimer (SL)	632
TOTAL	399,966

1916 (13 electoral votes)

Charles E. Hughes (R)	220,822
Woodrow Wilson (D)	191,363
Allan Benson (Soc)	27,631
J. Frank Hanly (Proh)	7,318
TOTAL	447,134

1920 (13 electoral votes)

Warren G. Harding (R)	498,576
James M. Cox (D)	113,422
Eugene V. Debs (Soc)	80,635
Aaron S. Watkins (Proh)	8,647
TOTAL	701,280

1924 (13 electoral votes)

Robert M. La Follette (Prog)	453,678
Calvin Coolidge (R)	311,614
John W. Davis (D)	68,096
William Z. Foster (Workers)	3,834
Herman P. Faris (Proh)	2,918
TOTAL	840,140

1928 (13 electoral votes)

Herbert Hoover (R)	544,205
Alfred E. Smith (D)	450,259
Norman Thomas (Soc)	18,213
William F. Varney (Proh)	2,245
William Z. Foster (Workers)	1,528
Verne L. Reynolds (SL)	381
TOTAL	1,016,831

1932 (12 electoral votes)

Franklin D. Roosevelt (D)	707,410
Herbert Hoover (R)	347,741
Norman Thomas (Soc)	53,379
William Z. Foster (Com)	3,112
William D. Upshaw (Proh)	2,672
Verne L. Reynolds (SL)	494
TOTAL	1,114,808

1936 (12 electoral votes)

Franklin D. Roosevelt (D)	802,984
Alfred M. Landon (R)	380,828
William Lemke (U)	60,297
Norman Thomas (Soc)	10,626
Earl Browder (Com)	2,197
David L. Calvin (Proh)	1,071
John W. Aiken (SL)	557
TOTAL	1,258,560

1940 (12 electoral votes)

Franklin D. Roosevelt (D)	704,821
Wendell Willkie (R)	679,206
Norman Thomas (Soc)	15,071
Earl Browder (Com)	2,394
Roger Babson (Proh)	2,148
John W. Aiken (SL)	1,882
TOTAL	1,405,522

1944 (12 electoral votes)

Thomas Dewey (R)	674,532
Franklin D. Roosevelt (D)	650,413
Norman Thomas (Soc)	13,205
Edward Teichert (Ind)	1,002
TOTAL	1,339,152

1948 (12 electoral votes)

Harry S Truman (D)	647,310
Thomas Dewey (R)	590,959
Henry Wallace (PP)	25,282
Norman Thomas (Soc)	12,547
Edward Teichert (Ind)	399
Farrell Dobbs (ISW)	303
TOTAL	1,276,800

1952 (12 electoral votes)

Dwight D. Eisenhower (R)	979,744
Adlai E. Stevenson (D)	622,175
Vincent Hallinan (IP)	2,174
Farrell Dobbs (ISW)	1,350
Darlington Hoopes (IS)	1,157
Eric Hass (ISL)	770
TOTAL	1,607,370

1956 (12 electoral votes)

Dwight D. Eisenhower (R)	954,844
Adlai E. Stevenson (D)	586,768
T. Coleman Andrews (Ind Con)	6,918
Darlington Hoopes (Ind Soc)	754
Eric Hass (Ind SL)	710
Farrell Dobbs (Ind SW)	564
TOTAL	1,550,558

1960 (12 electoral votes)

Richard M. Nixon (R)	895,175
John F. Kennedy (D)	830,805
Farrell Dobbs (Ind SW)	1,792
Eric Hass (Ind SL)	1,310
TOTAL	1,729,082

1964 (12 electoral votes)

Lyndon B. Johnson (D)	1,050,424
Barry M. Goldwater (R)	638,495
Clifton DeBerry (Ind SW)	1,692
Eric Hass (Ind SL)	1,204
TOTAL	1,691,815

1968 (12 electoral votes)

Richard M. Nixon (R)	809,997
Hubert H. Humphrey (D)	748,804
George C. Wallace (Ind A)	127,835
Henning A. Blomen (Ind SL)	1,338
Frederick W. Halstead (Ind SW)	1,222
TOTAL	1,689,196

1972 (11 electoral votes)

Richard M. Nixon (R)	989,430
George S. McGovern (D)	810,174
John G. Schmitz (A)	47,525
Benjamin M. Spock (Ind Pop)	2,701
Louis Fisher (Ind SL)	998
Gus Hall (Ind Com)	663
Evelyn Reed (Ind SW)	506
TOTAL	1,851,997

1976 (11 electoral votes)

Jimmy Carter (D)	1,040,232
Gerald R. Ford (R)	1,004,987
Eugene J. McCarthy (Ind)	34,943
Lester Maddox (A)	8,552
Frank P. Zeidler (Ind Soc)	4,298
Roger L. MacBride (Ind Lib)	3,814
Peter Camejo (Ind SW)	1,691
Margaret Wright (Ind Pop)	943
Gus Hall (Ind Com)	749
Lyndon H. LaRouche, Jr. (Ind USL)	738
Jules Levin (Ind SL)	389
TOTAL	2,104,175

WISCONSIN VOTE IN PRESIDENTIAL ELECTIONS
1848 – 2008–Continued

1980 (11 electoral votes)

Ronald Reagan (R).	1,088,845
Jimmy Carter (D)	981,584
John Anderson (Ind)	160,657
Ed Clark (Ind Lib)	29,135
Barry Commoner (Ind Cit).	7,767
John Rarick (Ind Con)	1,519
David McReynolds (Ind Soc)	808
Gus Hall (Ind Com)	772
Deidre Griswold (Ind WW)	414
Clifton DeBerry (Ind SW)	383
TOTAL	2,273,221

1984 (11 electoral votes)

Ronald Reagan (R).	1,198,800
Walter F. Mondale (D).	995,847
David Bergland (Lib)	4,884
Bob Richards (Con)	3,864
Lyndon H. LaRouche, Jr. (Ind)	3,791
Sonia Johnson (Ind Cit)	1,456
Dennis L. Serrette (Ind WIA)	1,007
Larry Holmes (Ind WW)	619
Gus Hall (Ind Com)	597
Melvin T. Mason (Ind SW)	445
TOTAL	2,212,018

1988 (11 electoral votes)

Michael S. Dukakis (D)	1,126,794
George Bush (R).	1,047,499
Ronald Paul (Ind Lib)	5,157
David E. Duke (Ind Pop)	3,056
James Warren (Ind SW)	2,574
Lyndon H. LaRouche, Jr. (Ind NER)	2,302
Lenora B. Fulani (Ind NA).	1,953
TOTAL	2,191,612

1992 (11 electoral votes)

Bill Clinton (D)	1,041,066
George Bush (R).	930,855
Ross Perot (Ind)	544,479
Andre Marrou (Lib)	2,877
James Gritz (Ind AFC).	2,311
Ron Daniels (LF)	1,883
Howard Phillips (Ind Tax)	1,772
J. Quinn Brisben (Ind Soc).	1,211
John Hagelin (NL).	1,070
Lenora B. Fulani (Ind NA).	654
Lyndon H. LaRouche, Jr. (Ind ER)	633
Jack Herer (Ind Gr)	547
Eugene A. Hem (3rd)	405
James Warren (Ind SW)	390
TOTAL	2,531,114

1996 (11 electoral votes)

Bill Clinton (D)	1,071,971
Bob Dole (R).	845,029
Ross Perot (Rfm).	227,339
Ralph Nader (Ind WG).	28,723
Howard Phillips (Tax)	8,811
Harry Browne (Lib)	7,929
John Hagelin (Ind NL).	1,379
Monica Mooerhead (Ind WW).	1,333
Mary Cal Hollis (Ind Soc)	848
James E. Harris (Ind SW)	483
TOTAL	2,196,169

2000 (11 electoral votes)

Al Gore (D)	1,242,987
George W. Bush (R)	1,237,279
Ralph Nader (WG).	94,070
Pat Buchanan (Ind Rfm).	11,446
Harry Browne (Lib)	6,640
Howard Phillips (Con).	2,042
Monica G. Moorehead (Ind WW)	1,063
John Hagelin (Ind Rfm)	878
James Harris (Ind SW).	306
TOTAL	2,598,607

2004 (10 electoral votes)

John F. Kerry (D)	1,489,504
George W. Bush (R)	1,478,120
Ralph Nader (Ind TBL)	16,390
Michael Badnarik (Lib)	6,464
David Cobb (WG)	2,661
Walter F. Brown (Ind SPW)	471
James Harris (Ind SW).	411
TOTAL	2,997,007

2008 (10 electoral votes)

Barack Obama (D).	1,677,211
John McCain (R).	1,262,393
Ralph Nader (Ind)	17,605
Bob Barr (Lib)	8,858
Chuck Baldwin (Ind Con)	5,072
Cynthia McKinney (WG)	4,216
Jeffrey J. Wamboldt (Ind WtP)	764
Brian Moore (Ind Soc USA).	540
Gloria LaRiva (Ind S&L)	237
TOTAL	2,983,417

Note: Some totals include scattered votes for other candidates.

Sources: Official records of the Government Accountability Board, Elections Division and Congressional Quarterly, *Guide to U.S. Elections*, 1994.

VOTE FOR GOVERNOR IN GENERAL ELECTIONS
1848 – 2006

Key:
A – American
C – Conservative
Com – Communist
Con – Constitution
D – Democrat
DS – Democratic Socialist
G – Greenback
Ind – Independent
IC – Independent Communist
ID – Independent Democrat
IL – Independent Labor
IP – Independent Prohibition

IPR – Independent Prohibition Republic
ISL – Independent Socialist Labor
ISW – Independent Socialist Worker
IW – Independent Worker
L – Labor
LF – Labor-Farm/Laborista-Agrario
Nat – National
NR – National Republic
People's – People's (Populist)
PLS – Progressive Labor Socialist
PP – People's Progressive

Prog – Progressive
Proh – Prohibition
R – Republican
Soc – Socialist
SD – Social Democrat
SDA – Social Democrat of America
SL – Socialist Labor
SW – Socialist Worker
Tax – U.S. Taxpayers
U – Union
UL – Union Labor
W – Whig

Note: A candidate whose party did not receive 1% of the vote for a statewide office in the previous election or who failed to meet the alternative requirement of Section 5.62, Wisconsin Statutes, is listed on the Wisconsin ballot as "independent". When a candidate's party affiliation is listed as "independent" and a party designation is shown in italics, "independent" was the official ballot listing, but a party designation was found by the Wisconsin Legislative Reference Bureau in newspaper reports.

1848	
Nelson Dewey (D)[1]	19,875
John Hubbard Tweedy (W)[1]	14,621
Charles Durkee (Ind)[1]	1,134
TOTAL	35,309

1849	
Nelson Dewey (D)	16,649
Alexander L. Collins (W)	11,317
Warren Chase (Ind)	3,761
TOTAL	31,759

1851	
Leonard James Farwell (W)	22,319
Don Alonzo Joshua Upham (D)	21,812
TOTAL	44,190

1853	
William Augustus Barstow (D)	30,405
Edward Dwight Holton (R)	21,886
Henry Samuel Baird (W)	3,304
TOTAL	55,683

1855	
William Augustus Barstow (D)[2]	36,355
Coles Bashford (R)	36,198
TOTAL	72,598

1857	
Alexander William Randall (R)	44,693
James B. Cross (D)	44,239
TOTAL	90,058

1859	
Alexander William Randall (R)	59,999
Harrison Carroll Hobart (D)	52,539
TOTAL	112,755

1861	
Louis Powell Harvey (R)	53,777
Benjamin Ferguson (D)	45,456
TOTAL	99,258

1863	
James Taylor Lewis (R)	72,717
Henry L. Palmer (D)	49,053
TOTAL	122,029

1865	
Lucius Fairchild (R)	58,332
Harrison Carroll Hobart (D)	48,330
TOTAL	106,674

1867	
Lucius Fairchild (R)	73,637
John J. Tallmadge (D)	68,873
TOTAL	142,522

1869	
Lucius Fairchild (R)	69,502
Charles D. Robinson (D)	61,239
TOTAL	130,781

1871	
Cadwallader Colden Washburn (R)	78,301
James Rood Doolittle (D)	68,910
TOTAL	147,274

1873	
William Robert Taylor (D)	81,599
Cadwallader Colden Washburn (R)	66,224
TOTAL	147,856

1875	
Harrison Ludington (R)	85,155
William Robert Taylor (D)	84,314
TOTAL	170,070

1877	
William E. Smith (R)	78,759
James A. Mallory (D)	70,486
Edward Phelps Allis (G)	26,216
Collin M. Campbell (Soc)	2,176
TOTAL	178,122

1879	
William E. Smith (R)	100,535
James G. Jenkins (D)	75,030
Reuben May (G)	12,996
TOTAL	189,005

1881	
Jeremiah McLain Rusk (R)	81,754
N.D. Fratt (D)	69,797
T.D. Kanouse (Proh)	13,225
Edward Phelps Allis (G)	7,002
TOTAL	171,856

1884	
Jeremiah McLain Rusk (R)	163,214
N.D. Fratt (D)	143,945
Samuel Dexter Hastings (Proh)	8,545
William L. Utley (G)	4,274
TOTAL	319,997

1886	
Jeremiah McLain Rusk (R)	133,247
Gilbert Motier Woodward (D)	114,529
John Cochrane (People's)	21,467
John Myers Olin (Proh)	17,089
TOTAL	286,368

1888	
William Dempster Hoard (R)	175,696
James Morgan (D)	155,423
E.G. Durant (Proh)	14,373
D. Frank Powell (L)	9,196
TOTAL	354,714

1890	
George Wilbur Peck (D)	160,388
William Dempster Hoard (R)	132,068
Charles Alexander (Proh)	11,246
Reuben May (UL)	5,447
TOTAL	309,254

1892	
George Wilbur Peck (D)	178,095
John Coit Spooner (R)	170,497
Thomas C. Richmond (Proh)	13,185
C.M. Butt (People's)	9,638
TOTAL	371,559

1894	
William H. Upham (R)	196,150
George Wilbur Peck (D)	142,250
D. Frank Powell (People's)	25,604
John F. Cleghorn (Proh)	11,240
TOTAL	375,449

1896	
Edward Scofield (R)	264,981
Willis C. Silverthorn (D)	169,257
Joshua H. Berkey (Proh)	8,140
Christ Tuttrop (SL)	1,306
Robert Henderson (Nat)	407
TOTAL	444,110

VOTE FOR GOVERNOR IN GENERAL ELECTIONS
1848 – 2006–Continued

1898

Edward Scofield (R)	173,137
Hiram Wilson Sawyer (D)	135,353
Albinus A. Worsley (People's)	8,518
Eugene Wilder Chafin (Proh)	8,078
Howard Tuttle (SDA)	2,544
Henry Riese (SL)	1,473
TOTAL	329,430

1900

Robert Marion La Follette (R)	264,419
Louis G. Bomrich (D)	160,674
J. Burritt Smith (Proh)	9,707
Howard Tuttle (SD)	6,590
Frank R. Wilke (SL)	509
TOTAL	441,900

1902

Robert Marion La Follette (R)	193,417
David Stuart Rose (D)	145,818
Emil Seidel (SD)	15,970
Edwin W. Drake (Proh)	9,647
Henry E.D. Puck (SL)	791
TOTAL	365,676

1904

Robert Marion La Follette (R)	227,253
George Wilbur Peck (D)	176,301
William A. Arnold (SD)	24,857
Edward Scofield (NR)	12,136
William H. Clark (Proh)	8,764
Charles M. Minkley (SL)	249
TOTAL	449,570

1906

James O. Davidson (R)	183,558
John A. Aylward (D)	103,311
Winfield R. Gaylord (SD)	24,437
Ephraim L. Eaton (Proh)	8,211
Ole T. Rosaas (SL)	455
TOTAL	320,003

1908

James O. Davidson (R)	242,935
John A. Aylward (D)	165,977
H.D. Brown (SD)	28,583
Winfred D. Cox (Proh)	11,760
Herman Bottema (SL)	393
TOTAL	449,656

1910

Francis Edward McGovern (R)	161,619
Adolph H. Schmitz (D)	110,442
William A. Jacobs (SD)	39,547
Byron E. Van Keuren (Proh)	7,450
Fred G. Kremer (SL)	430
TOTAL	319,522

1912

Francis Edward McGovern (R)	179,360
John C. Karel (D)	167,316
Carl D. Thompson (SD)	34,468
Charles Lewis Hill (Proh)	9,433
William H. Curtis (SL)	3,253
TOTAL	393,849

1914

Emanuel Lorenz Philipp (R)	140,787
John C. Karel (D)	119,509
John James Blaine (Ind)	32,560
Oscar Ameringer (SD)	25,917
David W. Emerson (Proh)	6,279
John Vierthaler (Ind)	352
TOTAL	325,430

1916

Emanuel Lorenz Philipp (R)	229,889
Burt Williams (D)	164,555
Rae Weaver (Soc)	30,649
George McKerrow (Proh)	9,193
TOTAL	434,340

1918

Emanuel Lorenz Philipp (R)	155,799
Henry A. Moehlenpah (D)	112,576
Emil Seidel (SD)	57,523
William C. Dean (Proh)	5,296
TOTAL	331,582

1920

John James Blaine (R)	366,247
Robert McCoy (D)	247,746
William Coleman (Soc)	71,126
Henry H. Tubbs (Proh)	6,047
TOTAL	691,294

1922

John James Blaine (R)	367,929
Arthur A. Bentley (ID)	51,061
Louis A. Arnold (Soc)	39,570
M.L. Welles (Proh)	21,438
Arthur A. Dietrich (ISL)	1,444
TOTAL	481,828

1924

John James Blaine (R)	412,255
Martin L. Lueck (D)	317,550
William F. Quick (Soc)	45,268
Adolph R. Bucknam (Proh)	11,516
Severi Alanne (IW)	4,107
Farrand K. Shuttleworth (IPR)	4,079
Jose Snover (SL)	1,452
TOTAL	796,432

1926

Fred R. Zimmerman (R)	350,927
Charles Perry (Ind)	76,507
Virgil H. Cady (D)	72,627
Herman O. Kent (Soc)	40,293
David W. Emerson (Proh)	7,333
Alex Gorden (SL)	4,593
TOTAL	552,912

1928

Walter Jodok Kohler, Sr. (R)	547,738
Albert George Schmedeman (D)	394,368
Otto R. Hauser (Soc)	36,924
Adolph R. Bucknam (Proh)	6,477
Joseph Ehrhardt (IL)	1,938
Alvar J. Hayes (IW)	1,420
TOTAL	989,143

1930

Philip Fox La Follette (R)	392,958
Charles E. Hammersley (D)	170,020
Frank B. Metcalfe (Soc)	25,607
Alfred B. Taynton (Proh)	14,818
Fred Bassett Blair (IC)	2,998
TOTAL	606,825

1932

Albert George Schmedeman (D)	590,114
Walter Jodok Kohler, Sr. (R)	470,805
Frank B. Metcalfe (Soc)	56,965
William C. Dean (Proh)	3,148
Fred Bassett Blair (Com)	2,926
Joe Ehrhardt (SL)	398
TOTAL	1,124,502

1934

Philip Fox La Follette (Prog)	373,093
Albert George Schmedeman (D)	359,467
Howard Greene (R)	172,980
George A. Nelson (Soc)	44,589
Morris Childs (IC)	2,454
Thomas W. North (PR)	857
Joe Ehrhardt (ISL)	332
TOTAL	953,797

1936

Philip Fox La Follette (Prog)	573,724
Alexander Wiley (R)	363,973
Arthur W. Lueck (D)	268,530
Joseph F. Walsh (U)	27,934
Joseph Ehrhardt (SL)	1,738
August E. Fehlandt (Proh)	1,008
TOTAL	1,237,095

1938

Julius Peter Heil (R)	543,675
Philip Fox La Follette (Prog)	353,381
Harry Wilbur Bolens (D)	78,446
Frank W. Smith (U)	4,564
John Schleier, Jr. (ISL)	1,459
TOTAL	981,560

1940

Julius Peter Heil (R)	558,678
Orland Steen Loomis (Prog)	546,436
Francis Edward McGovern (D)	264,985
Fred Bassett Blair (Com)	2,340
Louis Fisher (SL)	1,158
TOTAL	1,373,754

VOTE FOR GOVERNOR IN GENERAL ELECTIONS
1848 – 2006–Continued

1942	
Orland Steen Loomis (Prog)	397,664
Julius Peter Heil (R)	291,945
William C. Sullivan (D)	98,153
Frank P. Zeidler (Soc)	11,295
Fred Bassett Blair (IC)	1,092
Georgia Cozzini (ISL)	490
TOTAL	800,985
1946	
Walter Samuel Goodland (R)	621,970
Daniel W. Hoan (D)	406,499
Walter H. Uphoff (Soc)	8,996
Sigmund G. Eisenscher (IC)	1,857
Jerry R. Kenyon (ISL)	959
TOTAL	1,040,444
1948	
Oscar Rennebohm (R)	684,839
Carl W. Thompson (D)	558,497
Henry J. Berquist (PP)	12,928
Walter H. Uphoff (Soc)	9,149
James E. Boulton (ISW)	356
Georgia Cozzini (ISL)	328
TOTAL	1,266,139
1950	
Walter Jodok Kohler, Jr. (R)	605,649
Carl W. Thompson (D)	525,319
M. Michael Essin (PP)	3,735
William O. Hart (Soc)	3,384
TOTAL	1,138,148
1952	
Walter Jodok Kohler, Jr. (R)	1,009,171
William Proxmire (D)	601,844
M. Michael Essin (Ind)	3,706
TOTAL	1,615,214
1954	
Walter Jodok Kohler, Jr. (R)	596,158
William Proxmire (D)	560,747
Arthur Wepfer (Ind)	1,722
TOTAL	1,158,666
1956	
Vernon W. Thomson (R)	808,273
William Proxmire (D)	749,421
TOTAL	1,557,788
1958	
Gaylord Anton Nelson (D)	644,296
Vernon W. Thomson (R)	556,391
Wayne Leverenz (Ind)	1,485
TOTAL	1,202,219
1960	
Gaylord Anton Nelson (D)	890,868
Philip G. Kuehn (R)	837,123
TOTAL	1,728,009
1962	
John W. Reynolds (D)	637,491
Philip G. Kuehn (R)	625,536
Adolf Wiggert (Ind)	2,477
TOTAL	1,265,900
1964	
Warren P. Knowles (R)	856,779
John W. Reynolds (D)	837,901
TOTAL	1,694,887
1966	
Warren P. Knowles (R)	626,041
Patrick J. Lucey (D)	539,258
Adolf Wiggert (Ind)	4,745
TOTAL	1,170,173
1968	
Warren P. Knowles (R)	893,463
Bronson C. La Follette (D)	791,100
Adolf Wiggert (Ind)	3,225
Robert Wilkinson (Ind)	1,813
TOTAL	1,689,738

1970	
Patrick J. Lucey (D)	728,403
Jack B. Olson (R)	602,617
Leo James McDonald (A)	9,035
Georgia Cozzini (Ind–SL)	1,287
Samuel K. Hunt (Ind–SW)	888
Myrtle Kastner (Ind–PLS)	628
TOTAL	1,343,160
1974	
Patrick J. Lucey (D)	628,639
William D. Dyke (R)	497,189
William H. Upham (A)	33,528
Crazy Jim[3] (Ind)	12,107
William Hart (Ind–DS)	5,113
Fred Blair (Ind–C)	3,617
Georgia Cozzini (Ind–SL)	1,492
TOTAL	1,181,685
1978	
Lee Sherman Dreyfus (R)	816,056
Martin J. Schreiber (D)	673,813
Eugene R. Zimmerman (C)	6,355
John C. Doherty (Ind)	2,183
Adrienne Kaplan (Ind–SW)	1,548
Henry A. Ochsner (Ind–SL)	849
TOTAL	1,500,996
1982	
Anthony S. Earl (D)	896,872
Terry J. Kohler (R)	662,738
Larry Smiley (Lib)	9,734
James P. Wickstrom (Con)	7,721
Peter Seidman (Ind–SW)	3,025
TOTAL	1,580,344
1986	
Tommy G. Thompson (R)	805,090
Anthony S. Earl (D)	705,578
Kathryn A. Christensen (LF)	10,323
Darold E. Wall (Ind)	3,913
Sanford Knapp (Ind)	1,668
TOTAL	1,526,573
1990	
Tommy G. Thompson (R)	802,321
Thomas A. Loftus (D)	576,280
TOTAL	1,379,727
1994	
Tommy G. Thompson (R)	1,051,326
Charles J.Chvala (D)	482,850
David S. Harmon (Lib)	11,639
Edward J. Frami (Tax)	9,188
Michael J. Mangan (Ind)	8,150
TOTAL	1,563,835
1998	
Tommy G. Thompson (R)	1,047,716
Ed Garvey (D)	679,553
Jim Mueller (Lib)	11,071
Edward J. Frami (Tax)	10,269
Mike Mangan (Ind)	4,985
A-Ja-mu Muhammad (Ind)	1,604
Jeffrey L. Smith (WG)	14
TOTAL	1,756,014
2002	
Jim Doyle (D)	800,515
Scott McCallum (R)	734,779
Ed Thompson (Lib)	185,455
Jim Young (R)	44,111
Alan D. Eisenberg (Ind)	2,847
Ty A. Bollerud (Ind)	2,637
Mike Mangan (Ind)	1,710
Aneb Jah Rasta Sensas-Utcha Nefer-I (Ind)	929
TOTAL	1,775,349
2006	
Jim Doyle (D)	1,139,115
Mark Green (R)	979,427
Nelson Eisman (WG)	40,709
TOTAL	2,161,700

[1]Votes for Dewey and Tweedy are from *1874 Blue Book;* Durkee vote is based on county returns, as filed in the Office of the Secretary of State, but returns from Manitowoc and Winnebago Counties were missing. Without these 2 counties, Dewey had 19,605 votes and Tweedy had 14,514 votes.

[2]Barstow's plurality was set aside in *Atty. Gen. ex rel. Bashford v. Barstow,* 4 Wis. 567 (1855) because of irregularities in the election returns.

[3]Legal name.

Source: Elections Board records. Totals include scattered votes for other candidates.

WISCONSIN GOVERNORS SINCE 1848

	Governor[1]	Political Party	Service As Governor[2] Began	Ended	Born	Birthplace	Died	Burial Place
1	Nelson Dewey	Democrat	6-7-1848	1-5-1852	12-19-1813	Lebanon, Conn.	7-21-1889	Lancaster, Wis.
2	Leonard James Farwell	Whig	1-5-1852	1-2-1854	1-5-1819	Watertown, N.Y.	4-11-1889	Grant City, Mo.
3	William Augustus Barstow	Democrat	1-2-1854	3-21-1856	9-13-1813	Plainfield, Conn.	12-13-1865	Cleveland, Ohio
4	Arthur MacArthur[3]	Democrat	3-21-1856	3-25-1856	1-26-1815	Glasgow, Scotland	8-26-1896	Washington, D.C.
5	Coles Bashford	Republican	3-25-1856	1-4-1858	1-24-1816	Putnam Co., N.Y.	4-25-1878	Oakland, Cal.
6	Alexander William Randall	Republican	1-4-1858	1-6-1862	10-31-1819	Ames, N.Y.	7-26-1872	Elmira, N.Y.
7	Louis Powell Harvey[4]	Republican	1-6-1862	4-19-1862	7-22-1820	East Haddam, Conn.	4-19-1862	Madison, Wis.
8	Edward Salomon[4]	Republican	4-19-1862	1-4-1864	8-11-1828	Stroebeck, Prussia	4-21-1909	Frankfurt, Germany
9	James Taylor Lewis	Republican	1-4-1864	1-1-1866	10-30-1819	Clarendon, N.Y.	8-4-1904	Columbus, Wis.
10	Lucius Fairchild	Republican	1-1-1866	1-1-1872	12-27-1831	Kent, Ohio	5-23-1896	Madison, Wis.
11	Cadwallader Colden Washburn	Republican	1-1-1872	1-5-1874	4-22-1818	Livermore, Me.	5-23-1882	La Crosse, Wis.
12	William Robert Taylor	Democrat	1-5-1874	1-3-1876	7-10-1820	Woodbury, Conn.	3-17-1909	Madison, Wis.
13	Harrison Ludington	Republican	1-3-1876	1-7-1878	7-30-1812	Ludingtonville, N.Y.	6-17-1891	Milwaukee, Wis.
14	William E. Smith	Republican	1-7-1878	1-2-1882	6-18-1824	Near Inverness, Scotland	2-13-1883	Milwaukee, Wis.
15	Jeremiah McLain Rusk	Republican	1-2-1882	1-5-1889	6-17-1830	Morgan Co., Ohio	11-21-1893	Viroqua, Wis.
16	William Dempster Hoard	Republican	1-5-1889	1-5-1891	10-10-1836	Stockbridge, N.Y.	11-22-1918	Ft. Atkinson, Wis.
17	George Wilbur Peck	Democrat	1-5-1891	1-7-1895	9-28-1840	Henderson, N.Y.	4-16-1916	Milwaukee, Wis.
18	William Henry Upham	Republican	1-7-1895	1-4-1897	5-3-1841	Westminster, Mass.	7-2-1924	Marshfield, Wis.
19	Edward Scofield	Republican	1-4-1897	1-7-1901	3-28-1842	Clearfield, Pa.	2-3-1925	Oconto, Wis.
20	Robert Marion La Follette, Sr.[5]	Republican	1-7-1901	1-1-1906	6-14-1855	Primrose, Dane Co., Wis.	6-18-1925	Madison, Wis.
21	James O. Davidson[5]	Republican	1-1-1906	1-2-1911	2-10-1854	Sogn, Norway	12-16-1922	Madison, Wis.
22	Francis Edward McGovern	Republican	1-2-1911	1-4-1915	1-21-1866	Elkhart Lake, Wis.	5-16-1946	Milwaukee, Wis.
23	Emanuel Lorenz Philipp	Republican	1-4-1915	1-3-1921	3-25-1861	Honey Creek, Sauk Co., Wis.	6-15-1925	Milwaukee, Wis.
24	John James Blaine	Republican	1-3-1921	1-7-1929	5-4-1875	Wingville, Grant Co., Wis.	4-18-1934	Boscobel, Wis.
25	Fred R. Zimmerman	Republican	1-7-1927	1-7-1929	11-20-1880	Milwaukee, Wis.	12-14-1954	Milwaukee, Wis.
26	Walter Jodok Kohler, Sr.	Republican	1-7-1929	1-5-1931	3-3-1875	Sheboygan, Wis.	4-21-1940	Kohler, Wis.
27	Philip Fox La Follette	Republican	1-5-1931	1-2-1933	5-8-1897	Madison, Wis.	8-18-1965	Madison, Wis.
28	Albert George Schmedeman	Democrat	1-2-1933	1-7-1935	11-25-1864	Madison, Wis.	11-26-1946	Madison, Wis.
29	Philip Fox La Follette	Progressive	1-7-1935	1-2-1939	5-8-1897	Madison, Wis.	8-18-1965	Madison, Wis.
30	Julius Peter Heil	Republican	1-2-1939	1-4-1943	7-24-1876	Duesmond, Germany	11-30-1949	Milwaukee, Wis.
31	Orland Steen Loomis[6]	Progressive	Died prior to inauguration		11-2-1893	Mauston, Wis.	12-7-1942	Mauston, Wis
32	Walter Samuel Goodland[6,7]	Republican	1-4-1943	3-12-1947	12-22-1862	Sharon, Wis.	3-12-1947	Racine, Wis.
33	Oscar Rennebohm[7]	Republican	3-12-1947	1-1-1951	5-25-1889	Leeds, Columbia Co., Wis.	10-15-1968	Madison, Wis.
34	Walter Jodok Kohler, Jr.	Republican	1-1-1951	1-7-1957	4-4-1904	Sheboygan, Wis.	3-10-1976	Kohler, Wis.
35	Vernon Wallace Thomson	Republican	1-7-1957	1-5-1959	11-5-1905	Richland Center, Wis.	4-2-1988	Richland Center, Wis.
36	Gaylord Anton Nelson	Democrat	1-5-1959	1-7-1963	6-4-1916	Clear Lake, Wis.	7-3-2005	Clear Lake, Wis.
37	John W. Reynolds	Democrat	1-7-1963	1-4-1965	4-4-1921	Green Bay, Wis.	1-6-2002	Door County, Wis.
38	Warren Perley Knowles	Republican	1-4-1965	1-4-1971	8-19-1908	River Falls, Wis.	4-1-1993	River Falls, Wis.
39	Patrick Joseph Lucey[8]	Democrat	1-4-1971	7-6-1977	3-21-1918	La Crosse, Wis.		
40	Martin James Schreiber[8]	Democrat	7-6-1977	1-1-1979	4-8-1939	Milwaukee, Wis.		
41	Lee Sherman Dreyfus	Republican	1-1-1979	1-3-1983	6-20-1926	Milwaukee, Wis.	1-2-2008	Waukesha, Wis.
42	Anthony Scully Earl	Democrat	1-3-1983	1-5-1987	4-12-1936	Lansing, Mich.		
43	Tommy George Thompson[9]	Republican	1-5-1987	2-1-2001	11-19-1941	Elroy, Wis.		
44	Scott McCallum[9]	Republican	2-1-2001	1-6-2003	5-2-1950	Fond du Lac, Wis.		
44	James Edward Doyle, Jr.	Democrat	1-6-2003		11-23-1945	Washington, D.C.		

[1]Includes those serving as acting governor when office is vacated. Administrations are numbered. [2]Article XIII, Section 1 of the Wisconsin Constitution was amended in November 1884 so that the term of office of all state and county officers began in January of odd-numbered years, rather than January of even-numbered years. [3]Served as acting governor during dispute over who won gubernatorial election. [4]Salomon became acting governor on death of Harvey on 4/19/62. [5]Davidson served as acting governor from La Follette's resignation until beginning the terms to which he was elected on 1/7/07. [6]Goodland became acting governor on death of Governor-elect Loomis and served entire 1943-44 term. [7]Rennebohm became acting governor on the death of Goodland on 3/12/47. [8]Schreiber became acting governor when Lucey resigned to become U.S. ambassador to Mexico. [9]McCallum became governor when Thompson resigned to become U.S. Secretary of Health and Human Services.

Sources: "Wisconsin's Former Governors"; *1960 Wisconsin Blue Book*, pp. 69-206; Blue Book biographies.

WISCONSIN CONSTITUTIONAL OFFICERS, 1848 – 2009

Name	Term[1]	Residence
Governor		
(See separate table)		
Lieutenant Governors		
John E. Holmes (D)	1848-1850	Jefferson
Samuel W. Beall (D)	1850-1852	Taycheedah
Timothy Burns (D)	1852-1854	La Crosse
James T. Lewis (R)	1854-1856	Columbus
Arthur McArthur (D)[2]	1856-1858	Milwaukee
Erasmus D. Campbell (D)	1858-1860	La Crosse
Butler G. Noble (R)	1860-1862	Whitewater
Edward Salomon (R)[3]	1862-1864	Milwaukee
Wyman Spooner (R)	1864-1870	Elkhorn
Thaddeus C. Pound (R)	1870-1872	Chippewa Falls
Milton H. Pettit (R)[4]	1872-3/23/73	Kenosha
Charles D. Parker (D)	1874-1878	Pleasant Valley
James M. Bingham (R)	1878-1882	Chippewa Falls
Sam S. Fifield (R)	1882-1887	Ashland
George W. Ryland (R)	1887-1891	Lancaster
Charles Jonas (D)	1891-1895	Racine
Emil Baensch (R)	1895-1899	Manitowoc
Jesse Stone (R)	1899-1903	Watertown
James O. Davidson (R)[5]	1903-1907	Soldiers Grove
William D. Connor (R)	1907-1909	Marshfield
John Strange (R)	1909-1911	Oshkosh
Thomas Morris (R)	1911-1915	La Crosse
Edward F. Dithmar (R)	1915-1921	Baraboo
George F. Comings (R)	1921-1925	Eau Claire
Henry A. Huber (R)	1925-1933	Stoughton
Thomas J. O'Malley (D)	1933-1937	Milwaukee
Henry A. Gunderson (Prog)[6]	1937-10/16/37	Portage
Herman L. Ekern (Prog)[6]	5/16/1938-1939	Madison
Walter S. Goodland (R)[7]	1939-1945	Racine
Oscar Rennebohm (R)[8]	1945-1949	Madison
George M. Smith (R)	1949-1955	Milwaukee
Warren P. Knowles (R)	1955-1959	New Richmond
Philleo Nash (D)	1959-1961	Wisconsin Rapids
Warren P. Knowles (R)	1961-1963	New Richmond
Jack Olson (R)	1963-1965	Wisconsin Dells
Patrick J. Lucey (D)	1965-1967	Madison
Jack Olson (R)	1967-1971	Wisconsin Dells
Martin J. Schreiber (D)[9]	1971-1979	Milwaukee
Russell A. Olson (R)	1979-1983	Randall
James T. Flynn (D)	1983-1987	West Allis
Scott McCallum (R)[10]	1987-2001	Fond du Lac
Margaret A. Farrow (R)[10]	2001-2003	Pewaukee
Barbara Lawton (D)	2003-	Green Bay
Secretaries of State		
Thomas McHugh (D)	1848-1850	Delavan
William A. Barstow (D)	1850-1852	Waukesha
Charles D. Robinson (D)	1852-1854	Green Bay
Alexander T. Gray (D)	1854-1856	Janesville
David W. Jones (D)	1856-1860	Belmont
Lewis P. Harvey (R)	1860-1862	Shopiere
James T. Lewis (R)	1862-1864	Columbus
Lucius Fairchild (R)	1864-1866	Madison
Thomas S. Allen (R)	1866-1870	Mineral Point
Llywelyn Breese (R)	1870-1874	Portage
Peter Doyle (D)	1874-1878	Prairie du Chien
Hans B. Warner (R)	1878-1882	Ellsworth
Ernst G. Timme (R)	1882-1891	Kenosha
Thomas J. Cunningham (D)	1891-1895	Chippewa Falls
Henry Casson (R)	1895-1899	Viroqua
William H. Froehlich (R)	1899-1903	Jackson
Walter L. Houser (R)	1903-1907	Mondovi
James A. Frear (R)	1907-1913	Hudson
John S. Donald (R)	1913-1917	Mt. Horeb
Merlin Hull (R)	1917-1921	Black River Falls
Elmer S. Hall (R)	1921-1923	Green Bay
Fred R. Zimmerman (R)	1923-1927	Milwaukee
Theodore Dammann (R)	1927-1935	Milwaukee
Theodore Dammann (Prog)	1935-1939	Milwaukee
Fred R. Zimmerman (R)[11]	1939-12/14/54	Milwaukee
Louis Allis (R)[11]	12/16/54-1/3/55	Milwaukee
Mrs. Glenn M. Wise (R)[11]	1/3/55-1957	Madison
Robert C. Zimmerman (R)	1957-1975	Madison
Douglas J. La Follette (D)	1975-1979	Kenosha
Mrs. Vel R. Phillips (D)	1979-1983	Milwaukee
Douglas J. La Follette (D)	1983-	Madison

WISCONSIN CONSTITUTIONAL OFFICERS, 1848 – 2009–Continued

Name	Term[1]	Residence
State Treasurers		
Jarius C. Fairchild (D)	1848-1852	Madison
Edward H. Janssen (D)	1852-1856	Cedarburg
Charles Kuehn (D)	1856-1858	Manitowoc
Samuel D. Hastings (R)	1858-1866	Trempealeau
William E. Smith (R)	1866-1870	Fox Lake
Henry Baetz (R)	1870-1874	Manitowoc
Ferdinand Kuehn (D)	1874-1878	Milwaukee
Richard Guenther (R)	1878-1882	Oshkosh
Edward C. McFetridge (R)	1882-1887	Beaver Dam
Henry B. Harshaw (R)	1887-1891	Oshkosh
John Hunner (D)	1891-1895	Eau Claire
Sewell A. Peterson (R)	1895-1899	Rice Lake
James O. Davidson (R)	1899-1903	Soldiers Grove
John J. Kempf (R)[12]	1903-7/30/04	Milwaukee
Thomas M. Purtell (R)[12]	7/30/04-1905	Cumberland
John J. Kempf (R)	1905-1907	Milwaukee
Andrew H. Dahl (R)	1907-1913	Westby
Henry Johnson (R)	1913-1923	Suring
Solomon Levitan (R)	1923-1933	Madison
Robert K. Henry (D)	1933-1937	Jefferson
Solomon Levitan (Prog)	1937-1939	Madison
John M. Smith (R)[4]	1939-8/17/47	Shell Lake
John L. Sonderegger (R)[13]	8/19/47-9/30/48	Madison
Clyde M. Johnston (appointed from staff)[13]	10/1/48-1949	Madison
Warren R. Smith (R)[4]	1949-12/4/57	Milwaukee
Mrs. Dena A. Smith (R)[13]	12/5/57-1959	Milwaukee
Eugene M. Lamb (D)	1959-1961	Milwaukee
Mrs. Dena A. Smith (R)[4]	1961-2/20/68	Milwaukee
Harold W. Clemens (R)[13]	2/21/68-1971	Oconomowoc
Charles P. Smith (D)	1971-1991	Madison
Cathy S. Zeuske (R)	1991-1995	Shawano
Jack C. Voight (R)	1995-2007	Appleton
Dawn Marie Sass (D)	2007-	Milwaukee
Attorneys General		
James S. Brown (D)	1848-1850	Milwaukee
S. Park Coon (D)	1850-1852	Milwaukee
Experience Estabrook (D)	1852-1854	Geneva
George B. Smith (D)	1854-1856	Madison
William R. Smith (D)	1856-1858	Mineral Point
Gabriel Bouck (D)	1858-1860	Oshkosh
James H. Howe (R)[14]	1860-1862	Green Bay
Winfield Smith (R)[14]	1862-1866	Milwaukee
Charles R. Gill (R)	1866-1870	Watertown
Stephen Steele Barlow (R)	1870-1874	Dellona
Andrew Scott Sloan (R)	1874-1878	Beaver Dam
Alexander Wilson (R)	1878-1882	Mineral Point
Leander F. Frisby (R)	1882-1887	West Bend
Charles E. Estabrook (R)	1887-1891	Manitowoc
James L. O'Connor (D)	1891-1895	Madison
William H. Mylrea (R)	1895-1899	Wausau
Emmett R. Hicks (R)	1899-1903	Oshkosh
Lafayette M. Sturdevant (R)	1903-1907	Neillsville
Frank L. Gilbert (R)	1907-1911	Madison
Levi H. Bancroft (R)	1911-1913	Richland Center
Walter C. Owen (R)[15]	1913-1918	Maiden Rock
Spencer Haven (R)[15]	1918-1919	Hudson
John J. Blaine (R)	1919-1921	Boscobel
William J. Morgan (R)	1921-1923	Milwaukee
Herman L. Ekern (R)	1923-1927	Madison
John W. Reynolds (R)	1927-1933	Green Bay
James E. Finnegan (D)	1933-1937	Milwaukee
Orlando S. Loomis (Prog)	1937-1939	Mauston
John E. Martin (R)[16]	1939-6/1/48	Madison
Grover L. Broadfoot (R)[16]	6/5/48-11/12/48	Mondovi
Thomas E. Fairchild (D)[16]	11/12/48-1951	Verona
Vernon W. Thomson (R)	1951-1957	Richland Center
Stewart G. Honeck (R)	1957-1959	Madison
John W. Reynolds (R)	1959-1963	Green Bay
George Thompson (R)	1963-1965	Madison
Bronson C. La Follette (D)	1965-1969	Madison
Robert W. Warren (R)[17]	1969-10/8/74	Green Bay
Victor A. Miller (D)[17]	10/8/74-11/25/74	St. Nazianz
Bronson C. La Follette (D)[17]	11/25/74-1987	Madison
Donald J. Hanaway (R)	1987-1991	Green Bay
James E. Doyle (D)	1991-2003	Madison
Peggy A. Lautenschlager (D)	2003-2007	Fond du Lac
J.B. Van Hollen (R)	2007-	Waunakee

WISCONSIN CONSTITUTIONAL OFFICERS, 1848 – 2009–Continued

Name	Term[1]	Residence
Superintendents of Public Instruction[18]		
Eleazer Root	1849-1852	Waukesha
Azel P. Ladd	1852-1854	Shullsburg
Hiram A. Wright	1854-1855	Prairie du Chien
A. Constantine Barry	1855-1858	Racine
Lyman C. Draper	1858-1860	Madison
Josiah L. Pickard	1860-1864	Platteville
John G. McMynn	1864-1868	Racine
Alexander J. Craig	1868-1870	Madison
Samuel Fallows	1870-1874	Milwaukee
Edward Searing	1874-1878	Milton
William Clarke Whitford	1878-1882	Milton
Robert Graham	1882-1887	Oshkosh
Jesse B. Thayer	1887-1891	River Falls
Oliver Elwin Wells	1891-1895	Appleton
John Q. Emery	1895-1899	Albion
Lorenzo D. Harvey	1899-1903	Milwaukee
Charles P. Cary	1903-1921	Delavan
John Callahan	1921-1949	Madison
George Earl Watson	1949-1961	Wauwatosa
Angus B. Rothwell[19]	1961-7/1/66	Manitowoc
William C. Kahl[19]	7/1/66-1973	Madison
Barbara Thompson	1973-1981	Madison
Herbert J. Grover[20]	1981-4/9/93	Cottage Grove
John T. Benson	1993-2001	Marshall
Elizabeth Burmaster	2001-2009	Madison
Tony Evers	2009-	Madison

[1]Article XIII, Section 1 of the Wisconsin Constitution was amended in 1884, to provide the terms for all partisan state officers would begin in odd-numbered, rather than even-numbered, years. The section was further amended in 1968 to change the term from 2-years to 4-years, effective with the November 1970 elections.

[2]Served as acting governor 3/21/1856 to 3/25/1856 during dispute over outcome of gubernatorial election.

[3]Became acting governor on the death of Governor Louis P. Harvey on 4/19/1862.

[4]Died in office.

[5]Became acting governor on 1/1/1906 when Robert M. La Follette, Sr., resigned to become U.S. Senator.

[6]Resigned to accept appointment to the State Tax Commission. Ekern appointed by Governor Philip La Follette to fill the unexpired term. Appointment ruled valid in *State ex rel. Martin v. Ekern*, 228 Wis. 645 (1937).

[7]Goodland reelected lieutenant governor, November 1942; became acting governor on 1/1/1943 for the term of deceased Governor-elect Orlando Loomis.

[8]Became acting governor on the death of Goodland on 3/12/1947.

[9]Became acting governor when Lucey resigned on 7/6/1977 to accept appointment as U.S. ambassador to Mexico.

[10]McCallum became governor on 2/1/2001 when Governor Tommy Thompson resigned to become U.S. Secretary of Health and Social Services. Farrow was appointed lieutenant governor on 5/9/2001.

[11]Died 12/14/1954 after being elected to a new 2-year term. Allis was appointed to fill the unexpired term. Wise was appointed to fill the full 2-year term.

[12]Appointed 7/30/1904 to fill a vacancy caused by the failure of Kempf to give the required bond.

[13]Appointed.

[14]Resigned in October 1862 to join the Union Army. Smith was appointed 10/7/1862 to replace him.

[15]Resigned 1/7/1918 after being elected to the Wisconsin Supreme Court. Haven was appointed to fill the unexpired term.

[16]Resigned to accept appointment to the Wisconsin Supreme Court. Broadfoot was appointed to fill the unexpired term. Broadfoot resigned to accept appointment to the Wisconsin Supreme Court, and Attorney General-elect Fairchild was appointed to fill the unexpired term.

[17]Resigned to accept appointment as U.S. District Judge for the Eastern District of Wisconsin. Miller appointed to fill the unexpired term. Bronson La Follette was elected to a full term and Miller resigned so that La Follette could be appointed to fill the rest of Warren's unexpired term.

[18]Prior to 1902, the state superintendent was elected on a partisan ballot in November, and the term began the first Monday in January. A constitutional amendment moved the election to the nonpartisan April ballot and the beginning of the term to the first Monday in July beginning in July 1905.

[19]Resigned to accept appointment to the Coordinating Committee for Higher Education. Kahl was appointed to fill the unexpired term.

[20]Resigned 4/9/1993. Lee Sherman Dreyfus was appointed to serve as "interim superintendent" for remainder of the unexpired term but did not officially become superintendent.

Source: Wisconsin Legislative Reference Bureau, *Wisconsin Blue Books,* various editions, and bureau records.

JUSTICES OF THE SUPREME COURT
1836 – 2009

Name	Term	Residence[1]
Judges During the Territorial Period		
Charles Dunn (Chief Justice)[2]	1836-1848	
William C. Frazier	1836-1838	
David Irvin	1836-1838	
Andrew G. Miller	1836-1848	
Circuit Judges Who Served as Justices 1848-53[3]		
Alexander W. Stow	1848-1851 (C.J.)	Fond du Lac
Levi Hubbell	1848-1853 (C.J. 1851)	Milwaukee
Edward V. Whiton	1848-1853 (C.J. 1852-53)	Janesville
Charles H. Larrabee	1848-1853	Horicon
Mortimer M. Jackson	1848-1853	Mineral Point
Wiram Knowlton	1850-1853	Prairie du Chien
Timothy O. Howe	1851-1853	Green Bay
Justices Since 1853		
Edward V. Whiton	1853-1859 (C.J.)	Janesville
Samuel Crawford	1853-1855	New Diggings
Abram D. Smith	1853-1859	Milwaukee
Orsamus Cole	1855-1892 (C.J. 1880-92)	Potosi
Luther S. Dixon[4]	1859-1874 (C.J.)	Portage
Byron Paine[4]	1859-1864, 1867-71	Milwaukee
Jason Downer[4]	1864-1867	Milwaukee
William P. Lyon[4]	1871-1894 (C.J. 1892-94)	Racine
Edward G. Ryan[4]	1874-1880 (C.J.)	Racine
David Taylor	1878-1891	Sheboygan
Harlow S. Orton	1878-1895 (C.J. 1894-95)	Madison
John B. Cassoday[4]	1880-1907 (C.J. 1895-07)	Janesville
John B. Winslow[4]	1891-1920 (C.J. 1907-20)	Racine
Silas U. Pinney	1892-1898	Madison
Alfred W. Newman	1894-1898	Trempealeau
Roujet D. Marshall[4]	1895-1918	Chippewa Falls
Charles V. Bardeen[4]	1898-1903	Wausau
Joshua Eric Dodge[4]	1898-1910	Milwaukee
Robert G. Siebecker[5]	1903-1922 (C.J. 1920-22)	Madison
James C. Kerwin	1905-1921	Neenah
William H. Timlin	1907-1916	Milwaukee
Robert M. Bashford[4]	Jan.-June 1908	Madison
John Barnes	1908-1916	Rhinelander
Aad J. Vinje[4]	1910-1929 (C.J. 1922-29)	Superior
Marvin B. Rosenberry[4]	1916-1950 (C.J. 1929-50)	Wausau
Franz C. Eschweiler[4]	1916-1929	Milwaukee
Walter C. Owen	1918-1934	Maiden Rock
Burr W. Jones[4]	1920-1926	Madison
Christian Doerfler[4]	1921-1929	Milwaukee
Charles H. Crownhart[4]	1922-1930	Madison
E. Ray Stevens	1926-1930	Madison
Chester A. Fowler[4]	1929-1948	Fond du Lac
Oscar M. Fritz[4]	1929-1954 (C.J. 1950-54)	Milwaukee
Edward T. Fairchild[4]	1929-1957 (C.J. 1954-57)	Milwaukee
John D. Wickhem[4]	1930-1949	Madison
George B. Nelson[4]	1930-1942	Stevens Point
Theodore G. Lewis[4]	Nov. 15-Dec. 5, 1934	Madison
Joseph Martin[4]	1934-1946	Green Bay
Elmer E. Barlow[4]	1942-1948	Arcadia
James Ward Rector[4]	1946-1947	Madison
Henry P. Hughes	1948-1951	Oshkosh
John E. Martin[4]	1948-1962 (C.J. 1957-62)	Green Bay
Grover L. Broadfoot[4]	1948-1962 (C.J. Jan.-May 1962)	Mondovi
Timothy Brown[4]	1949-1964 (C.J. 1962-64)	Madison
Edward J. Gehl	1950-1956	Hartford
George R. Currie[4]	1951-1968 (C.J. 1964-68)	Sheboygan
Roland J. Steinle[4]	1954-1958	Milwaukee
Emmert L. Wingert[4]	1956-1959	Madison
Thomas E. Fairchild	1957-1966	Verona
E. Harold Hallows[4]	1958-1974 (C.J. 1968-74)	Milwaukee
William H. Dieterich	1959-1964	Milwaukee
Myron L. Gordon	1962-1967	Milwaukee
Horace W. Wilkie[4]	1962-1976 (C.J. 1974-76)	Madison
Bruce F. Beilfuss	1964-1983 (C.J. 1976-83)	Neillsville
Nathan S. Heffernan[4]	1964-1995 (C.J. 1983-95)	Sheboygan
Leo B. Hanley[4]	1966-1978	Milwaukee
Connor T. Hansen[4]	1967-1980	Eau Claire
Robert W. Hansen	1968-1978	Milwaukee
Roland B. Day[4]	1974-1996 (C.J. 1995-96)	Madison

JUSTICES OF THE SUPREME COURT
1836 – 2009–Continued

Name	Term		Residence[1]
Shirley S. Abrahamson[4]	1976-	(C.J. 1996-)	Madison
William G. Callow	1978-1992		Waukesha
John L. Coffey	1978-1982		Milwaukee
Donald W. Steinmetz	1980-1999		Milwaukee
Louis J. Ceci[4]	1982-1993		Milwaukee
William A. Bablitch	1983-2003		Stevens Point
Jon P. Wilcox[4]	1992-2007		Wautoma
Janine P. Geske[4]	1993-1998		Milwaukee
Ann Walsh Bradley	1995-		Wausau
N. Patrick Crooks	1996-		Green Bay
David T. Prosser, Jr.[4]	1998-		Appleton
Diane S. Sykes[4]	1999-2004		Milwaukee
Patience D. Roggensack	2003-		Madison
Louis B. Butler, Jr.[4]	2004-2008		Milwaukee
Annette K. Ziegler	2007-		West Bend
Michael J. Gableman	2008-		Webster

Note: The structure of the Wisconsin Supreme Court has varied. There were 3 justices during the territorial period. From 1848 to 1853, circuit judges acted as supreme court judges (5 from 1848 to 1850 and 6 from 1850 to 1853). From 1853 to 1877, there were 3 elected justices. The number was increased to 5 by constitutional amendment in 1877. In 1903 the constitution was amended to raise the number to 7.

[1]Home address is the municipality from which the justice was originally appointed or elected.

[2]As a result of a constitutional amendment adopted in April 1889, the most senior justice serves as chief justice. Previously, the chief justice was elected or appointed to that position.

[3]Circuit judges acted as Supreme Court justices 1848-1853.

[4]Initially appointed to the court.

[5]Siebecker was elected April 7, 1903, but prior to inauguration for his elected term was appointed April 9, 1903, to fill the vacancy caused by the death of Justice Bardeen.

Sources: Wisconsin Legislative Reference Bureau, *Wisconsin Blue Books,* 1935, 1944, 1977; Government Accountability Board, Elections Division records; Wisconsin Supreme Court, *Wisconsin Reports,* various volumes.

SENATE PRESIDENTS PRO TEMPORE, SENATE PRESIDENTS
AND ASSEMBLY SPEAKERS, 1848 – 2009

Legislative Session	Senate Presidents Pro Tempore or Presidents[1]	Residence	Assembly Speakers	Residence
1848	No permanent president pro tempore	—	Ninian E. Whiteside (D)	Lafayette County
1849	No permanent president pro tempore	—	Harrison C. Hobart (D)	Sheboygan
1850	No record	—	Moses M. Strong (D)	Mineral Point
1851	No record	—	Frederick W. Horn (D)	Cedarburg
1852	E.B. Dean, Jr. (D)	Madison	James M. Shafter (W)	Sheboygan
1853	Duncan C. Reed (D)	Milwaukee	Henry L. Palmer (D)	Milwaukee
1854	Benjamin Allen (D)	Hudson	Frederick W. Horn (D)	Cedarburg
1855	Eleazor Wakeley (D)	Whitewater	Charles C. Sholes (R)	Kenosha
1856	Louis Powell Harvey (R)	Shopiere	William Hull (D)	Grant County
1857	No permanent president pro tempore	—	Wyman Spooner (R)	Elkhorn
1858	Hiram H. Giles (R)	Stoughton	Frederick S. Lovell (R)	Kenosha County
1859	Dennison Worthington (R)	Summit	William P. Lyon (R)	Racine
1860	Moses M. Davis (R)	Portage	William P. Lyon (R)	Racine
1861	Alden I. Bennett (R)	Beloit	Amasa Cobb (R)	Mineral Point
1862	Frederick O. Thorp (D)	West Bend	James W. Beardsley (UD)	Prescott
1863	Wyman Spooner (R)	Elkhorn	J. Allen Barber (R)	Lancaster
1864	Smith S. Wilkinson (R)	Prairie du Sac	William W. Field (U)	Fennimore
1865	Willard H. Chandler (U)	Windsor	William W. Field (U)	Fennimore
1866	Willard H. Chandler (U)	Windsor	Henry D. Barron (U)	St. Croix Falls
1867	George F. Wheeler (U)	Nanuapa	Angus Cameron (U)	La Crosse
1868	Newton M. Littlejohn (R)	Whitewater	Alexander M. Thomson (R)	Janesville
1869	George C. Hazelton (R)	Boscobel	Alexander M. Thomson (R)	Janesville
1870	David Taylor (R)	Sheboygan	James M. Bingham (R)	Palmyra
1871	Charles G. Williams (R)	Janesville	William E. Smith (R)	Fox Lake
1872	Charles G. Williams (R)	Janesville	Daniel Hall (R)	Watertown
1873	Henry L. Eaton (R)	Lone Rock	Henry D. Barron (R)	St. Croix Falls
1874	John C. Holloway (R)	Lancaster	Gabriel Bouck (D)	Oshkosh
1875	Henry D. Barron (R)	St. Croix Falls	Frederick W. Horn (R)	Cedarburg
1876	Robert L.D. Potter (R)	Wautoma	Sam S. Fifield (R)	Ashland
1877	William H. Hiner (R)	Fond du Lac	John B. Cassoday (R)	Janesville
1878	Levi W. Barden (R)	Portage	Augustus R. Barrows (GB)	Chippewa Falls
1879	William T. Price (R)	Black River Falls	David M. Kelly (R)	Green Bay
1880	Thomas B. Scott (R)	Grand Rapids	Alexander A. Arnold (R)	Galesville
1881	Thomas B. Scott (R)	Grand Rapids	Ira B. Bradford (R)	Augusta
1882	George B. Burrows (R)	Madison	Franklin L. Gilson (R)	Ellsworth
1883	George W. Ryland (R)	Lancaster	Earl P. Finch (D)	Oshkosh
1885	Edward S. Minor (R)	Sturgeon Bay	Hiram O. Fairchild (R)	Marinette
1887	Charles K. Erwin (R)	Tomah	Thomas B. Mills (R)	Millston
1889	Thomas A. Dyson (R)	La Crosse	Thomas B. Mills (R)	Millston
1891	Frederick W. Horn (R)	Cedarburg	James J. Hogan (D)	La Crosse
1893	Robert J. MacBride (D)	Neillsville	Edward Keogh (D)	Milwaukee
1895	Thompson D. Weeks (R)	Whitewater	George B. Burrows (R)	Madison
1897	Lyman W. Thayer (R)	Ripon	George A. Buckstaff (R)	Oshkosh
1899	Lyman W. Thayer (R)	Ripon	George H. Ray (R)	La Crosse
1901	James J. McGillivray (R)	Black River Falls	George H. Ray (R)	La Crosse
1903-05	James J. McGillivray (R)	Black River Falls	Irvine L. Lenroot (R)	West Superior
1907	James H. Stout (R)	Menomonie	Herman L. Ekern (R)	Whitehall
1909	James H. Stout (R)	Menomonie	Levi H. Bancroft (R)	Richland Center
1911	Harry C. Martin (R)	Darlington	C.A. Ingram (R)	Durand
1913	Harry C. Martin (R)	Darlington	Merlin Hull (R)	Black River Falls
1915	Edward T. Fairchild (R)	Milwaukee	Lawrence C. Whittet (R)	Edgerton
1917	Timothy Burke (R)	Green Bay	Lawrence C. Whittet (R)	Edgerton
1919	Willard T. Stevens (R)	Rhinelander	Riley S. Young (R)	Darien
1921	Timothy Burke (R)	Green Bay	Riley S. Young (R)	Darien
1923	Henry A. Huber (R)	Stoughton	John L. Dahl (R)	Rice Lake
1925	Howard Teasdale (R)	Sparta	Herman Sachtjen (R)[2]	Madison
	Howard Teasdale (R)	Sparta	George A. Nelson (R)[2]	Milltown
1927	William L. Smith (R)	Neillsville	John W. Eber (R)	Milwaukee
1929	Oscar H. Morris (R)	Milwaukee	Charles B. Perry (R)	Wauwatosa
1931	Herman J. Severson (P)	Iola	Charles B. Perry (R)	Wauwatosa
1933	Orland S. Loomis (R)	Mauston	Cornelius T. Young (D)	Milwaukee
1935	Harry W. Bolens (D)	Port Washington	Jorge W. Carow (P)	Ladysmith
1937	Walter J. Rush (P)	Neillsville	Paul R. Alfonsi (P)	Pence
1939	Edward J. Roethe (R)	Fennimore	Vernon W. Thomson (R)	Richland Center
1941-43	Conrad Shearer (R)	Kenosha	Vernon W. Thomson (R)	Richland Center
1945	Conrad Shearer (R)	Kenosha	Donald C. McDowell (R)	Soldiers Grove

SENATE PRESIDENTS PRO TEMPORE, SENATE PRESIDENTS AND ASSEMBLY SPEAKERS, 1848 – 2009–Continued

Legislative Session	Senate Presidents Pro Tempore or Presidents[1]	Residence	Assembly Speakers	Residence
1947	Frank E. Panzer (R)	Brownsville	Donald C. McDowell (R)	Soldiers Grove
1949	Frank E. Panzer (R)	Brownsville	Alex L. Nicol (R)	Sparta
1951-53 . .	Frank E. Panzer (R)	Brownsville	Ora R. Rice (R)	Delavan
1955	Frank E. Panzer (R)	Brownsville	Mark Catlin, Jr. (R)	Appleton
1957	Frank E. Panzer (R)	Brownsville	Robert G. Marotz (R)	Shawano
1959	Frank E. Panzer (R)	Brownsville	George Molinaro (D)	Kenosha
1961	Frank E. Panzer (R)	Brownsville	David J. Blanchard (R)	Edgerton
1963	Frank E. Panzer (R)	Brownsville	Robert D. Haase (R)	Marinette
1965	Frank E. Panzer (R)	Brownsville	Robert T. Huber (D)	West Allis
1967-69 . .	Robert P. Knowles (R)	New Richmond	Harold V. Froehlich (R)	Appleton
1971	Robert P. Knowles (R)	New Richmond	Robert T. Huber (D)[3]	West Allis
	Robert P. Knowles (R)	New Richmond	Norman C. Anderson (D)[3]	Madison
1973	Robert P. Knowles (R)	New Richmond	Norman C. Anderson (D)	Madison
1975	Fred A. Risser (D)	Madison	Norman C. Anderson (D)	Madison
1977-81 . .	Fred A. Risser (D)[1]	Madison	Edward G. Jackamonis (D)	Waukesha
1983-89 . .	Fred A. Risser (D)	Madison	Thomas A. Loftus (D)	Sun Prairie
1991	Fred A. Risser (D)	Madison	Walter J. Kunicki (D)	Milwaukee
1993	Fred A. Risser (D)[4]	Madison	Walter J. Kunicki (D)	Milwaukee
	Brian D. Rude (R)[4]	Coon Valley	Walter J. Kunicki (D)	Milwaukee
1995	Brian D. Rude (R)[5]	Coon Valley	David T. Prosser, Jr. (R)	Appleton
	Fred A. Risser (D)[5]	Madison	David T. Prosser, Jr. (R)	Appleton
1997	Fred A. Risser (D)[6]	Madison	Ben Brancel (R)[7]	Endeavor
	Brian D. Rude (R)[6]	Coon Valley	Scott R. Jensen (R)[7]	Waukesha
1999	Fred A. Risser (D)	Madison	Scott R. Jensen (R)	Waukesha
2001	Fred A. Risser (D)	Madison	Scott R. Jensen (R)	Waukesha
2003-05 . .	Alan J. Lasee (R)	De Pere	John Gard (R)	Peshtigo
2007	Fred A. Risser (D)	Madison	Michael D. Huebsch (R)	West Salem
2009	Fred A. Risser (D)	Madison	Michael J. Sheridan (D)	Janesville

Note: Political party indicated is for session elected and is obtained from newspaper accounts for some early legislators.
Key: D-Democrat; GB-Greenback; P-Progressive; R-Republican; U-Union; UD-Union Democrat; W-Whig.
[1]Table lists the ranking legislator in each house, not the presiding officer. The "president pro tempore" is listed until May 1, 1979; "president of the senate" is listed after that date when the lieutenant governor's function as president was eliminated by a constitutional amendment adopted in April 1979. See separate table for a list of lieutenant governors.
[2]George A. Nelson (R), Polk County, was elected to serve at special session, 4/15/26 to 4/16/26, following the resignation of Herman Sachtjen after the regular session to accept circuit judge appointment.
[3]Anderson was elected speaker 1/18/72 to succeed Huber who resigned 12/13/71 to accept appointment as chairman of the Highway Commission.
[4]A new president was elected on 4/20/93 after a change in party control following two special elections.
[5]A new president was elected on 7/9/96 after a change in party control following a recall election.
[6]A new president was elected on 4/21/98 after a change in party control following a special election.
[7]Jensen was elected speaker 11/4/97 to succeed Brancel who resigned to become Wisconsin Secretary of Agriculture, Trade and Consumer Protection.
Sources: Senate and Assembly Journals; Wisconsin Legislative Reference Bureau records.

MAJORITY AND MINORITY LEADERS OF THE WISCONSIN SENATE AND ASSEMBLY, 1937 – 2009

	Senate		Assembly	
Session	Majority	Minority	Majority	Minority
1937	Maurice P. Coakley (R)	NA	NA	NA
1939	Maurice P. Coakley (R)	Philip E. Nelson (P)	NA	Paul R. Alfonsi (P)
1941	Maurice P. Coakley (R)	Cornelius T. Young (D)	Mark S. Catlin, Jr. (R)	Andrew J. Biemiller (P)
				Robert E. Tehan (P)
1943	Warren P. Knowles (R)[1]	NA	Mark S. Catlin, Jr. (R)	Elmer L. Genzmer (D)
	John W. Byrnes (R)[1]			Lyall T. Beggs (P)
1945	Warren P. Knowles (R)	Anthony P. Gawronski (D)	Vernon W. Thomson (R)	Lyall T. Beggs (P)
				Leland S. McParland (D)
1947	Warren P. Knowles (R)	Robert E. Tehan (D)	Vernon W. Thomson (R)	Leland S. McParland (D)
1949	Warren P. Knowles (R)	NA	Vernon W. Thomson (R)	Leland S. McParland (D)
1951	Warren P. Knowles (R)	Gaylord Nelson (D)	Arthur O. Mockrud (R)	George Molinaro (D)
1953	Warren P. Knowles (R)	Henry W. Maier (D)	Mark S. Catlin, Jr. (R)	George Molinaro (D)
1955	Paul J. Rogan (R)[2]	Henry W. Maier (D)	Robert G. Marotz (R)	Robert T. Huber (D)
1957	Robert Travis (R)	Henry W. Maier (D)	Warren A. Grady (R)	Robert T. Huber (D)
1959	Robert Travis (R)	Henry W. Maier (D)[3]	Keith Hardie (D)	David J. Blanchard (R)
1961	Robert Travis (R)	William R. Moser (D)[3]	Robert D. Haase (R)	Robert T. Huber (D)
1963	Robert P. Knowles (R)	Richard J. Zaborski (D)	Paul R. Alfonsi (R)	Robert T. Huber (D)
1965	Robert P. Knowles (R)	Richard J. Zaborski (D)	Frank L. Nikolay (D)	Robert D. Haase (R)[4]
				Paul J. Alfonsi (R)[4]
1967	Jerris Leonard (R)	Fred A. Risser (D)	J. Curtis McKay (R)	Robert T. Huber (D)

MAJORITY AND MINORITY LEADERS OF THE
WISCONSIN SENATE AND ASSEMBLY, 1937 – 2009–Continued

	Senate		Assembly	
Session	Majority	Minority	Majority	Minority
1969 . . . .Ernest C. Keppler (R)		Fred A. Risser (D)	Paul R. Alfonsi (R)	Robert T. Huber (D)
1971 . . . .Ernest C. Keppler (R)		Fred A. Risser (D)	Norman C. Anderson (D)[5]	Harold V. Froehlich (R)
			Anthony S. Earl (D)[5]	
1973 . . . .Raymond C. Johnson (R)		Fred A. Risser (D)	Anthony S. Earl (D)	John C. Shabaz (R)
1975 . . . .Wayne F. Whittow (D)[6]		Clifford W. Krueger (R)	Terry A. Willkom (D)	John C. Shabaz (R)
William A. Bablitch (D)[6]				
1977 . . . .William A. Bablitch (D)		Clifford W. Krueger (R)	James W. Wahner (D)	John C. Shabaz (R)
1979 . . . .William A. Bablitch (D)		Clifford W. Krueger (R)	James W. Wahner (D)[7]	John C. Shabaz (R)
			Gary K. Johnson (D)[7]	
1981 . . . .William A. Bablitch (D)[9]		Walter J. Chilsen (R)	Thomas A. Loftus (D)	John C. Shabaz (R)[8]
Timothy F. Cullen (D)[9]				Tommy G. Thompson (R)[8]
1983 . . . .Timothy F. Cullen (D)		James E. Harsdorf (R)	Gary K. Johnson (D)	Tommy G. Thompson (R)
1985 . . . .Timothy F. Cullen (D)		Susan S. Engeleiter (R)	Dismas Becker (D)	Tommy G. Thompson (R)
1987 . . . .Joseph A. Strohl (D)		Susan S. Engeleiter (R)	Thomas A. Hauke (D)	Betty Jo Nelsen (R)
1989 . . . .Joseph A. Strohl (D)		Michael G. Ellis (R)	Thomas A. Hauke (D)	David T. Prosser (R)
1991 . . . .David W. Helbach (D)		Michael G. Ellis (R)	David M. Travis (D)	David T. Prosser (R)
1993 . . . .David W. Helbach (D)[10]		Michael G. Ellis (R)[10]	David M. Travis (D)	David T. Prosser (R)
Michael G. Ellis (R)[10]		David W. Helbach (D)[10,11]		
		Robert Jauch (D)[11]		
1995 . . . .Michael G. Ellis (R)[13]		Robert Jauch (D)[12]	Scott R. Jensen (R)	Walter J. Kunicki (D)
		Charles Chvala (D)[12,13]		
Charles Chvala (D)[13]		Michael G. Ellis (R)[13]		
1997 . . . .Charles Chvala (D)[14]		Michael G. Ellis (R)[14]	Steven M. Foti (R)	Walter J. Kunicki (D)[15]
Michael G. Ellis (R)[14]		Charles Chvala (D)[14]		Shirley Krug (D)[15]
1999 . . . .Charles Chvala (D)		Michael G. Ellis (R)[16]	Steven M. Foti (R)	Shirley Krug (D)
		Mary E. Panzer (R)[16]		
2001 . . . .Charles Chvala (D)		Mary E. Panzer (R)	Steven M. Foti (R)	Shirley Krug (D)
Russell S. Decker (D)[17]				Spencer Black (D)[18]
Fred A. Risser (D)[17]				
Jon B. Erpenbach (D)[17]				
2003 . . . .Mary E. Panzer (R)[19]		Jon B. Erpenbach (D)	Steven M. Foti (R)	James E. Kreuser (D)
Scott Fitzgerald (R)[19]				
Dale W. Schultz (R)[20]		Judith Biros Robson (D)[20]		
2005 . . . .Dale W. Schultz (R)		Judith Biros Robson (D)	Michael D. Huebsch (R)	James E. Kreuser (D)
2007 . . . .Judith Biros Robson (D)		Scott Fitzgerald (R)	Jeff Fitzgerald (R)	James E. Kreuser (D)
Russell S. Decker (D)[21]				
2009 . . . .Russell S. Decker (D)		Scott Fitzgerald (R)	Thomas M. Nelson (D)	Jeff Fitzgerald (R)

Note: Majority and minority leaders, who are chosen by the party caucuses in each house, were first recognized officially in the senate and assembly rules in 1963. Prior to the 1977 session, these positions were also referred to as "floor leader".

Key: (D) – Democrat; (P) – Progressive; (R) – Republican.

NA – Not available.

[1]Knowles granted leave of absence to return to active duty in U.S. Navy; Byrnes chosen to succeed him on 4/30/1943.

[2]Resigned after sine die adjournment.

[3]Resigned 1/30/1962.

[4]Haase resigned 9/15/1965; Alfonsi elected 10/4/1965.

[5]Earl elected 1/18/1972 to succeed Anderson who became Assembly Speaker.

[6]Whittow resigned 4/30/1976; Bablitch elected 5/17/1976.

[7]Wahner resigned 1/28/1980; Johnson elected 1/28/1980.

[8]Shabaz resigned 12/18/1981; Thompson elected 12/21/1981.

[9]Bablitch resigned 5/26/1982; Cullen elected 5/26/1982.

[10]Democrats controlled senate from 1/4/1993 to 4/20/1993 when Republicans assumed control after a special election.

[11]Helbach resigned 5/12/1993; Jauch elected 5/12/1993.

[12]Jauch resigned 10/17/1995; Chvala elected 10/24/1995.

[13]Republicans controlled senate from 1/5/1995 to 6/13/1996 when Democrats assumed control after a recall election.

[14]Democrats controlled the senate from 1/6/1997 to 4/21/1998 when Republicans assumed control after a special election.

[15]Kunicki resigned 6/3/1998; Krug elected 6/3/1998.

[16]Ellis resigned 1/25/2000; Panzer elected 1/25/2000.

[17]Decker and Risser elected co-leaders 10/22/2002. Erpenbach elected leader 12/4/2002.

[18]Black elected 5/1/2001.

[19]Panzer resigned 9/17/2004; Fitzgerald elected 9/17/2004.

[20]Schultz elected 11/9/2004; Robson elected 11/9/2004.

[21]Decker elected 10/24/2007.

Sources: *Wisconsin Blue Book,* various editions; newspaper accounts.

SENATE AND ASSEMBLY CHIEF CLERKS
AND SERGEANTS AT ARMS, 1848 – 2009

Legislative	Senate		Assembly	
Session	Chief Clerk	Sergeant at Arms	Chief Clerk	Sergeant at Arms
1848 . . . . .Henry G. Abbey		Lyman H. Seaver	Daniel N. Johnson	John Mullanphy
1849 . . . . .William R. Smith		F. W. Shollner	Robert L. Ream	Felix McLinden
1850 . . . . .William R. Smith		James Hanrahan	Alex T. Gray	E. R. Hugunin
1851 . . . . .William Hull		E. D. Masters	Alex T. Gray	C. M. Kingsbury
1852 . . . . .John K. Williams		Patrick Cosgrove	Alex T. Gray	Elisha Starr
1853 . . . . .John K. Williams		Thomas Hood	Thomas McHugh	Richard F. Wilson
1854 . . . . .Samuel G. Bugh		J. M. Sherwood	Thomas McHugh	William H. Gleason
1855 . . . . .Samuel G. Bugh		William H. Gleason	David Atwood	William Blake
1856 . . . . .Byron Paine		Joseph Baker	James Armstrong	Egbert Mosely
1857 . . . . .William Henry Brisbane	Alanson Filer	William C. Webb	William C. Rogers
1858 . . . . .John L. V. Thomas		Nathaniel L. Stout	L. H. D. Crane	Francis Massing
1859 . . . . .Hiram Bowen		Asa Kinney	L. H. D. Crane	Emmanual Munk
1860 . . . . .J. H. Warren		Asa Kinney	L. H. D. Crane	Joseph Gates
1861 . . . . .J. H. Warren		J. A. Hadley	L. H. D. Crane	Craig B. Peebe
1862 . . . . .J. H. Warren		B. U. Caswell	John S. Dean	A. A. Huntington
1863 . . . . .Frank M. Stewart		Luther Bashford	John S. Dean	A. M. Thompson
1864 . . . . .Frank M. Stewart		Nelson Williams	John S. Dean	A. M. Thompson
1865 . . . . .Frank M. Stewart		Nelson Williams	John S. Dean	Alonzo Wilcox
1866 . . . . .Frank M. Stewart		Nelson Williams	E. W. Young	L. M. Hammond
1867 . . . . .Leander B. Hills		Asa Kinney	E. W. Young	Daniel Webster
1868 . . . . .Leander B. Hills		W. H. Hamilton	E. W. Young	C. L. Harris
1869 . . . . .Leander B. Hills		W. H. Hamilton	E. W. Young	Rolin C. Kelly
1870 . . . . .Leander B. Hills		E. M. Rogers	E. W. Young	Ole C. Johnson
1871 . . . . .O. R. Smith		W. W. Baker	E. W. Young	Sam S. Fifield
1872 . . . . .J. H. Waggoner		W. D. Hoard	E. W. Young	Sam S. Fifield
1873 . . . . .J. H. Waggoner		Albert Emonson	E. W. Young	O. C. Bissel
1874 . . . . .J. H. Waggoner		O. U. Aiken	George W. Peck	Joseph Deuster
1875 . . . . .Fred A. Dennett		O. U. Aiken	R. M. Strong	J. W. Brackett
1876 . . . . .A. J. Turner		E. T. Gardner	R. M. Strong	Elisha Starr
1877 . . . . .A. J. Turner		C. E. Bullard	W. A. Nowell	Thomas B. Reid
1878 . . . . .A. J. Turner¹		L. J. Brayton	Jabez R. Hunter	Anton Klaus
	Charles E. Bross¹			
1879 . . . . .Charles E. Bross		Chalmers Ingersoll	John E. Eldred	Miletus Knight
1880 . . . . .Charles E. Bross		Chalmers Ingersoll	John E. Eldred	D. H. Pulcifer
1881 . . . . .Charles E. Bross		W. W. Baker	John E. Eldred	G. W. Church
1882 . . . . .Charles E. Bross		A. T. Glaze	E. D. Coe	D. E. Welch
1883 . . . . .Charles E. Bross		A. D. Thorp	I. T. Carr	Thomas Kennedy
1885 . . . . .Charles E. Bross		Hubert Wolcott	E. D. Coe	John M. Ewing
1887 . . . . .Charles E. Bross		T. J. George	E. D. Coe	William A. Adamson
1889 . . . . .Charles E. Bross		T .J. George	E. D. Coe	F. E. Parsons
1891 . . . . .J. P. Hume		John A. Barney	George W. Porth	Patrick Whelan
1893 . . . . .Sam J. Shafer		John B. Becker	George W. Porth	Theodore Knapstein
1895 . . . . .Walter L. Houser		Charles Pettibone	W. A. Nowell	B. F. Millard
1897 . . . . .Walter L. Houser		Charles Pettibone	W. A. Nowell	C. M. Hambright
1889 . . . . .Walter L. Houser		Charles Pettibone	W. A. Nowell	James H. Agen
1901 . . . . .Walter L. Houser		Charles Pettibone	W. A. Nowell	A. M. Anderson
1903 . . . . .Theodore W. Goldin		Sanfield McDonald	C. O. Marsh	A. M. Anderson
1905 . . . . .L .K. Eaton		R. C. Falconer	C. O. Marsh	Nicholas Streveler
1907 . . . . .A. R. Emerson		R. C. Falconer	C. E. Shaffer	W. S. Irvine
1909 . . . . .F. E. Andrews		R. C. Falconer	C. E. Shaffer	W. S. Irvine
1911-13 . . . . . .F. M. Wylie		C. A. Leicht	C. E. Shaffer	W. S. Irvine
1915 . . . . .O. G. Munson		F. E. Andrews	C. E. Shaffer	W. S. Irvine
1917 . . . . .O. G. Munson		F. E. Andrews	C. E. Shaffer	T. G. Cretney
1919 . . . . .O. G. Munson		John Turner	C. E. Shaffer	T. G. Cretney
1921 . . . . .O. G. Munson		Vincent Kielpinski	C. E. Shaffer	T. G. Cretney
1923 . . . . .F. W. Schoenfeld		C. A. Leicht	C. E. Shaffer	T. W. Bartingale
1925 . . . . .F. W. Schoenfeld		C. A. Leicht	C. E. Shaffer	C. E. Hanson
1927-29 . . . . . .O. G. Munson		George W. Rickeman	C. E. Shaffer	C. F. Moulton
1931 . . . . .R. A. Cobban		Emil A. Hartman	C. E. Shaffer	Gustave Rheingans
1933 . . . . .R. A. Cobban		Emil A. Hartman	John J. Slocum	George C. Faust
1935-37 . . . . . .Lawrence R. Larsen		Emil A. Hartman	Lester R. Johnson	Gustave Rheingans
1939 . . . . .Lawrence R. Larsen		Emil A. Hartman	John J. Slocum	Robert A. Merrill
1941-43 . . . . . .Lawrence R. Larsen		Emil A. Hartman	Arthur L. May	Norris J. Kellman
1945 . . . . .Lawrence R. Larsen		Harold E. Damon	Arthur L. May	Norris J. Kellman
1947-53 . . . . . .Thomas M. Donahue		Harold E. Damon	Arthur L. May	Norris J. Kellman
1955-57 . . . . . .Lawrence R. Larsen		Harold E. Damon	Arthur L. May	Norris J. Kellman

SENATE AND ASSEMBLY CHIEF CLERKS
AND SERGEANTS AT ARMS, 1848 – 2009–Continued

Legislative	Senate		Assembly	
Session	Chief Clerk	Sergeant at Arms	Chief Clerk	Sergeant at Arms
1959	Lawrence R. Larsen	Harold E. Damon	Norman C. Anderson	Thomas H. Browne
1961	Lawrence R. Larsen	Harold E. Damon	Robert G. Marotz	Norris J. Kellman
1963	Lawrence R. Larsen	Harold E. Damon	Kenneth E. Priebe	Norris J. Kellman
1965	Lawrence R. Larsen[2]	Harold E. Damon	James P. Buckley	Thomas H. Browne
	William P. Nugent[2]			
1967	William P. Nugent	Harry O. Levander	Arnold W. F. Langner[3]	Louis C. Romell
			Wilmer H. Struebing[3]	
1969	William P. Nugent	Kenneth Nicholson	Wilmer H. Struebing	Louis C. Romell
1971	William P. Nugent	Kenneth Nicholson	Thomas P. Fox	William F. Quick
1973	William P. Nugent	Kenneth Nicholson	Thomas S. Hanson	William F. Quick
1975	Glenn E. Bultman	Robert M. Thompson	Everett E. Bolle	Raymond J. Tobiasz
1977	Donald J. Schneider	Robert M. Thompson	Everett E. Bolle	Joseph E. Jones
1979	Donald J. Schneider	Daniel B. Fields	Marcel Dandeneau	Joseph E. Jones
1981	Donald J. Schneider	Daniel B. Fields	David R. Kedrowski	Lewis T. Mittness
1983	Donald J. Schneider	Daniel B. Fields	Joanne M. Duren	Lewis T. Mittness
1985	Donald J. Schneider	Daniel B. Fields	Joanne M. Duren	Patrick Essie
1987	Donald J. Schneider	Daniel B. Fields	Thomas T. Melvin	Patrick Essie
1989-91	Donald J. Schneider	Daniel B. Fields	Thomas T. Melvin	Robert G. Johnston
1993	Donald J. Schneider	Daniel B. Fields[4]	Thomas T. Melvin	Robert G. Johnston
		Jon H. Hochkammer[4]		
1995	Donald J. Schneider	Jon H. Hochkammer	Thomas T. Melvin[5]	John A. Scocos
			Charles R. Sanders[5]	
1997	Donald J. Schneider	Jon H. Hochkammer	Charles R. Sanders	John A. Scocos[6]
				Denise L. Solie[6]
1999	Donald J. Schneider	Jon H. Hochkammer	Charles R. Sanders	Denise L. Solie
2001	Donald J. Schneider	Jon H. Hochkammer[7]	John A. Scocos[7]	Denise L. Solie
2003	Donald J. Schneider[8]	Edward A. Blazel	Patrick E. Fuller	Richard A. Skindrud
	Robert J. Marchant[8]			
2005-07	Robert J. Marchant	Edward A. Blazel	Patrick E. Fuller	Richard A. Skindrud
2009	Robert J. Marchant	Edward A. Blazel	Patrick E. Fuller	William M. Nagy

[1]Bross elected 2/6/78; Turner resigned 2/7/78.
[2]Larsen died 3/2/65; Nugent elected 3/31/65.
[3]Langner resigned 5/2/67; Struebing elected 5/16/67.
[4]Fields served until 8/2/93. Randall Radtke served as Acting Sergeant from 8/3/93 to 11/3/93. Hochkammer was elected 1/25/94.
[5]Melvin retired 1/31/95; Sanders elected 5/24/95.
[6]Scocos resigned 9/25/97; Solie elected 1/15/98.
[7]Scocos resigned 2/25/02. Hochkammer resigned 9/2/02. No replacement was elected for either.
[8]Schneider resigned 7/4/03; Marchant elected 1/20/04.
Sources: Wisconsin Legislative Reference Bureau, *Wisconsin Blue Book*, various editions; journals and organizing resolutions of each house.

MEMBERS OF THE WISCONSIN LEGISLATURE, 1848 – 2007
See *2007-2008 Blue Book* Feature Article
"Those Who Served: Wisconsin Legislators 1848 – 2007," pp. 99-191.

WISCONSIN LEGISLATIVE SESSIONS, 1848 – 2007

Session	Opening and Adjournment Dates	Calendar Days[2]	Meeting Days[3] (S)	(A)	Bills	Jt. Res.	Res.	Bills Vetoed	Over-ridden	Laws Enacted
1848	6/5-8/21	78	58	59	217	0	0	0	0	155
1849	1/10-4/2	83	69	65	428	0	0	1	1	220
1850	1/9-2/11	34	29	29	438	0	0	1	0	284
1851	1/8-3/17	69	59	59	707	0	0	9	0	407
1852	1/14-4/19	97	78	78	813	0	0	2	1	504
1853	1/12-4/4; 6/6-7/13	153	100	104	1,145	0	0	3	0	521
1854	1/11-4/3	83	66	66	880	0	0	2	0	437
1855	1/10-4/2	83	79	79	955	0	0	6	0	500
1856	1/9-3/31; 9/3-10/14	125	94	103	1,242	0	0	1	0	688
1857	1/14-3/9	55	46	46	895	0	0	0	0	517
1858	1/13-3/31; 4/10-5/17	116	95	97	1,364	157	342	28	0	436
1859	1/12-3/21	69	58	57	986	113	143	9	0	680
1860	1/11-4/2	83	66	67	1,024	69	246	2	0	489
1861	1/9-4/17	99	81	80	857	100	235	2	0	387
1861SS[4]	5/15-5/27	13	11	11	28	24	34	0	0	15
1862	1/8-4/7; 6/3-6/17	105	86	88	1,008	125	207	27	8	514
1862SS	9/10-9/26	17	15	15	43	25	37	0	0	17
1863	1/14-4/2	79	65	67	895	101	157	7	1	383
1864	1/13-4/4	83	68	69	835	66	141	0	0	509
1865	1/11-4/10	90	73	72	1,132	82	190	2	0	565
1866	1/10-4/2	83	75	74	1,107	64	208	5	0	733
1867	1/9-4/11	93	71	72	1,161	97	161	2	0	790
1868	1/8-3/6	59	46	45	987	73	119	2	0	692
1869	1/13-3/11	58	40	43	887	52	81	12	1	657
1870	1/12-3/17	65	51	51	1,043	54	89	2	0	666
1871	1/11-3/25	74	58	60	1,066	55	82	4	0	671
1872	1/10-3/26	77	61	60	709	79	124	2	0	322
1873	1/8-3/20	72	49	55	611	62	122	4	0	308
1874	1/14-3/12	58	50	49	688	91	111	2	0	349
1875	1/13-3/6	53	44	42	637	39	93	2	0	344
1876	1/12-3/14	63	50	50	715	57	115	2	0	415
1877	1/10-3/8	58	41	41	720	59	95	4	0	384
1878	1/9-3/21	72	55	55	735	79	134	2	0	342
1878SS	6/4-6/7	4	4	4	6	14	10	0	0	5
1879	1/8-3/5	57	43	43	610	49	105	0	0	256
1880	1/14-3/17	64	50	49	669	58	93	3	0	323
1881	1/12-4/14	93	63	64	780	104	100	3	0	334
1882	1/11-3/31	80	57	57	728	57	90	6	0	330
1883	1/10-4/4	85	57	67	705	75	100	2	0	360
1885	1/14-4/13	90	65	66	963	97	108	8	0	471
1887	1/12-4/15	94	69	68	1,293	114	60	10	0	553
1889	1/9-4/19	101	64	64	1,355	136	82	5	1	529
1891	1/14-4/25	102	68	69	1,216	137	91	8	1	483
1892SS	6/28-7/1	4	4	4	4	7	16	0	0	1
1892SS	10/17-10/27	11	9	9	8	6	14	0	0	2
1893	1/11-4/21	101	62	62	1,124	135	86	6	0	312
1895	1/9-4/20	102	70	70	1,154	139	88	0	0	387
1896SS	2/18-2/28	11	8	8	3	11	15	0	0	1
1897	1/13-4/21; 8/17-8/20	103	75	76	1,077	155	39	11	0	381
1899	1/11-5/4	114	78	77	910	113	40	4	0	357
1901	1/9-5/15	127	89	89	1,091	81	39	22	0	470
1903	1/14-5/23	130	87	89	1,115	65	81	23	0	451
1905	1/11-6/21	162	114	117	1,357	134	101	19	0	523
1905SS	12/4-12/19	16	12	14	24	15	26	0	0	17
1907	1/9-7/16	189	114	123	1,685	205	84	26	1	677
1909	1/13-6/18	157	100	101	1,567	213	49	24	0	550
1911	1/11-7/15	186	137	138	1,710	267	37	15	0	665
1912SS	4/30-5/6	7	6	6	41	7	6	0	0	22
1913	1/8-8/9	214	138	147	1,847	175	79	23	0	778
1915	1/13-8/24	224	147	148	1,560	220	79	15	0	637
1916SS	10/10-10/11	2	2	2	2	8	4	0	0	2
1917	1/10-7/16	188	130	133	1,439	229	115	18	0	679
1918SS	2/19-3/9	19	14	14	27	22	28	2	0	16
1918SS	9/24-9/25	2	2	2	2	6	9	0	0	2
1919	1/8-7/30	204	107	106	1,350	268	100	40	0	703
1919SS	9/4-9/8	5	4	3	7	4	6	0	0	7
1920SS	5/25-6/4	11	7	7	46	10	22	2	0	32
1921	1/12-7/14	184	116	116	1,199	207	93	41	1	591
1922SS	3/22-3/28	7	4	4	10	7	12	1	0	4
1923	1/10-7/14	186	114	120	1,247	215	93	52	0	449
1925	1/14-6/29	167	103	107	1,144	200	115	73	0	454
1926SS	4/15-4/16	2	2	2	1	8	12	0	0	1
1927	1/12-8/13	214	121	128	1,341	235	167	88	2	542
1928SS	1/24-2/4	12	9	8	20	35	23	0	0	5
1928SS	3/6-3/13	8	6	6	13	9	17	0	0	2
1929	1/9-9/20	255	137	135	1,366	278	185	44	0	530
1931	1/14-6/27	165	98	104	1,429	291	160	36	0	487

WISCONSIN LEGISLATIVE SESSIONS, 1848 – 2007–Continued

Session	Opening and Adjournment Dates	Length of Session Calendar Days[2]	Meeting Days[3] (S)	(A)	Measures Introduced Bills	Jt. Res.	Res.	Vetoes[1] Bills Vetoed	Over-ridden	Laws Enacted
1931SS. . . .	11/24/31-2/5/32	74	48	42	99	93	83	2	0	31
1933	1/11-7/25	196	111	121	1,411	324	157	15	0	496
1933SS. . . .	12/11/33-2/3/34	55	30	34	45	160	53	0	0	20
1935	1/9-9/27	262	153	156	1,662	346	190	27	0	556
1937	1/13-7/2	171	97	114	1,404	228	127	10	0	432
1937SS. . . .	9/15-10/16	32	23	23	28	18	23	0	0	15
1939	1/11-10/6	269	154	154	1,559	268	133	22	0	535
1941	1/8-6/6	150	90	93	1,368	160	109	17	0	333
1943	1/13-8/3;	375	105	104	1,153	202	136	39	20	577
	(1944: 1/12-1/22)									
1945	1/10-6/20; 9/5-9/6	240	97	93	1,156	208	109	31	5	590
1946SS. . . .	7/29-7/30	2	2	2	2	6	14	0	0	2
1947	1/8-7/19; 9/9-9/11	247	114	114	1,220	195	97	10	1	615
1948SS. . . .	7/19-7/20	2	2	2	0	5	11	0	0	0
1949	1/12-7/9; 9/12-9/13	245	105	106	1,432	188	86	17	2	643
1951	1/10-6/14	156	91	90	1,559	157	73	18	0	735
1953	1/14-6/12; 10/26-11/6	297	97	98	1,593	175	70	31	3	687
1955	1/12-6/24; 10/3-10/21	283	111	114	1,503	256	74	38	0	696
1957	1/9-6/28; 9/23-9/27	262	107	108	1,512	246	71	39	1	706
1958SS. . . .	6/11-6/13	3	3	3	3	7	13	0	0	3
1959	1/14/59-5/27/60	500	159	163	1,769	272	84	36	4	696
	(1959: 1/14-7/25, 11/3-12/23;									
	1960: 1/6-1/22, 5/16-5/27)									
1961	1/11/61-1/9/63	729	184	185	1,592	295	68	73	2	689
	(1961: 1/11-8/12, 10/30-12/22;									
	1962: 1/8-1/12, 6/18-7/31, 12/27-12/29;									
	1963: 1/9)									
1963	1/9/63-1/13/65	736	150	142	1,619	241	110	72	4	580
	(1963: 1/9-8/6, 11/4-11/21;									
	1964: 4/13-4/29, 11/9-11/11;									
	1965: 1/13)									
1963SS. . . .	12/10-12/12	3	3	3	9	10	10	0	0	3
1965[5]	1/13/65-1/2/67	720	161	157	1,818	293	86	24	1	666
	(1965: 1/13-7/30, 10/4-11/4;									
	1966: 5/2-6/10;									
	1967: 1/2)									
1967	1/11/67-1/6/69	727	122	126	1,700	215	61	18	0	355
	(1967: 1/11-3/9, 4/4-7/28, 10/17-11/16,									
	12/5-12/16;									
	1968: none;									
	1969: 1/6)									
1969	1/6/69-1/4/71	729	165	165	2,014	232	101	34	1	501
	(1969: 1/6, 1/21-11/15;									
	1970: 1/5-1/16;									
	1971: 1/4)									
1969SS[6]. . . .	9/29/69-1/17/70	111	28	18	5	5	8	0	0	1
1970SS. . . .	12/22/70	1	1	1	0	1	5	0	0	0
1971	1/4/71-1/1/73	729	179	180	2,568	291	121	32	3	336
	(1971: 1/4, 1/19-10/28;									
	1972: 1/18-3/10, 7/13-7/15;									
	1973: 1/1)									
1972SS. . . .	4/19-4/28	10	5	6	9	4	4	0	0	6
1973	1/1/73-1/6/75	736	150	150	2,501	277	126	13	0	341
	(1973: 1/1, 1/16-2/15, 3/13-7/26,									
	10/2-10/26;									
	1974: 1/29-3/29, 11/19-11/20;									
	1975: 1/6)									
1973SS. . . .	12/17-12/21	5	5	5	3	2	6	0	0	2
1974SS. . . .	4/29-6/13	46	17	21	12	1	4	0	0	6
1974SS[7] . . .	11/19-11/20	2	2	1	2	0	0	0	0	1
1975	1/6/75-1/3/77	729	124	125	2,325	169	88	36	6	414
	(1975: 1/6, 1/1-2/20, 4/1-7/16, 9/2-9/26;									
	1976: 1/28-3/26, 6/15-6/17;									
	1977: 1/3)									
1975SS. . . .	12/9-12/11	3	3	3	13	1	2	0	0	7
1976SS. . . .	5/18	1	1	1	2	2	3	0	0	1
1976SS[7] . . .	6/15-6/17	3	3	3	13	4	3	0	0	8
1976SS. . . .	9/8	1	1	1	4	1	1	0	0	2
1977	1/3/77-1/1/79	729	84	112	2,053	182	48	21	4	442
	(1977: 1/3, 1/11-2/18, 3/29-7/1, 9/6-9/30;									
	1978: 1/24-1/26, 1/31-3/31, 6/13-6/15;									
	1979: 1/3)									
1977SS. . . .	6/30	1	1	1	0	1	2	0	0	0
1977SS. . . .	11/7-11/11	5	5	5	6	4	2	0	0	5
1978SS[7] . . .	6/13-6/15	3	3	3	2	5	2	0	0	2
1978SS. . . .	12/20	1	1	1	2	4	2	0	0	2
1979	1/3/79-1/5/81	734	85	99	1,920	203	40	19	3	350

WISCONSIN LEGISLATIVE SESSIONS, 1848 – 2007–Continued

Session	Opening and Adjournment Dates	Calendar Days[2]	Meeting Days[3] (S)	Meeting Days[3] (A)	Bills	Jt. Res.	Res.	Bills Vetoed	Over-ridden	Laws Enacted
	1979: 1/3, 1/9, 1/23-3/2, 4/17-6/29, 10/2-11/2;									
	1980: 1/29-4/2, 5/28-5/30;									
	1981: 1/5)									
1979SS....	9/5	1	1	1	10	3	2	0	0	5
1980SS[8]...	1/22-1/25	4	2	4	8	3	2	0	0	0
1980SS....	6/3- 7/3	31	13	12	20	14	2	0	0	7
1981	1/5/81-1/3/83	729	121	130	1,987	176	70	10	2	381
	(1981: 1/5, 1/13, 1/27-2/20, 4/7-7/17, 9/30-10/30, 12/15-12/17;									
	1982: 1/20-6/14;									
	1983: 1/3)									
1981SS[9] ...	11/4-11/17	14	8	7	6	3	2	0	0	3
1982SS[9] ...	4/6-4/30, 5/5-5/20	45	18	21	4	2	2	1	0	1
1982SS[10] ...	5/26-5/28	3	3	3	13	7	2	0	0	9
1983	1/3/83-1/7/85	736	72	80	1,902	173	50	3	0	521
	(1983: 1/3, 1/25-1/28, 2/8-2/18, 4/12-6/30, 10/4-10/28;									
	1984: 1/31-4/6, 5/22-5/24;									
	1985: 1/7)									
1983SS....	1/4-1/6	3	3	1	2	2	1	0	0	2
1983SS....	4/12-4/14	3	3	3	1	1	0	0	0	1
1983SS....	7/11-7/14	4	4	4	5	3	1	0	0	4
1983SS....	10/18-10/28	11	8	7	12	1	0	0	0	11
1984SS....	2/2-4/4	63	18	13	2	1	0	0	0	0
1984SS....	5/22-5/24	3	3	2	12	5	1	0	0	11
1985	1/7/85-1/7/87	331	68	66	1,624	171	41	7	0	293
	(1985: 1/7, 1/15, 1/29-2/8, 3/19-3/21, 4/23-6/29, 9/24-10/18;									
	1986: 1/28-3/26, 5/20-5/22;									
	1987: 1/5)									
1985SS....	3/19-3/21	3	2	2	6	1	0	0	0	3
1985SS....	9/24-10/19	26	11	7	21	1	0	0	0	17
1985SS....	10/31	1	1	1	1	3	0	0	0	1
1985SS....	11/20	1	1	1	24	2	0	0	0	12
1986SS....	1/27-5/30	124	34	27	1	4	0	0	0	1
1986SS....	3/24-3/26	3	3	3	1	1	0	0	0	1
1986SS....	5/20-5/29	10	6	4	44	3	0	0	0	12
1986SS....	7/15	1	1	1	3	1	0	0	0	2
1987[10]	1/5/87-1/3/89	730	60	73	1,628	199	21	35	0	412
	(1987: 1/5, 1/13, 1/27-2/6, 3/17-3/19, 4/21-7/2, 10/6-10/30;									
	1988: 1/26-3/25, 5/17-5/19;									
	1989: 1/3)									
1987SS....	9/15-9/16	2	2	2	2	1	0	0	0	2
1987SS....	11/18/87-6/7/88	203	9	11	19	3	0	3	0	5
1988SS....	6/30	1	1	1	5	1	3	0	0	3
1989	1/3/89-1/7/91	735	68	70	1,557	244	45	35	0	361
	(1989: 1/3, 1/4-1/9, 1/10, 1/11-1/23, 1/24-2/3, 2/6-3/13, 3/14-3/16, 3/17-4/24, 4/25-4/27, 4/28-5/15, 5/16-6/30, 10/3-11/10, 11/13-12/31;									
	1990: 1/1-1/22, 1/23-3/23, 3/26-5/14, 5/15-5/17, 5/18-12/31;									
	1991: 1/1-1/4, 1/7)									
1989SS....	10/10/89-3/22/90	164	52	49	52	6	0	0	0	7
1990SS....	5/15/90	1	1	1	7	1	0	0	0	0
1991	1/7/91-1/4/93	729	102	100	1,676	244	32	33	0	318
	(1991: 1/7, 1/15, 1/29-3/14, 4/16-5/16, 6/4-7/3, 10/1-11/8;									
	1992: 1/28-3/27, 5/19-5/21;									
	1993: 1/4)									
1991SS....	1/29-7/4	157	49	52	16	1	0	0	0	2
1991SS....	10/15/91-5/21/92	220	50	47	9	2	0	0	0	1
1992SS[8] ...	4/14-6/4	52	20	17	7	1	2	0	0	2
1992SS....	6/1	1	1	1	0	2	0	0	0	0
1992SS....	8/25-9/15	22	7	7	1	1	2	0	0	1
1993	1/4/93-1/3/95	730	91	86	2,147	207	47	8	0	491
	(1993: 1/4, 1/26-3/11, 4/20-7/16, 10/5-10/28;									
	1994: 1/25-3/25, 5/17;									
	1995: 1/3)									
1994SS....	5/18-5/19	2	2	2	6	1	0	0	0	3
1994SS[11] ...	6/7-6/23	17	8	8	3	4	0	0	0	3
1995	1/3/95-1/6/97	735	78	90	1,780	163	38	4	0	467
	(1995: 1/3-1/5, 1/17-2/2, 2/14-3/9, 4/4-4/6, 5/16-6/29,									

WISCONSIN LEGISLATIVE SESSIONS, 1848 – 2007–Continued

Session	Opening and Adjournment Dates	Length of Session Calendar Days²	Meeting Days³ (S)	(A)	Measures Introduced Bills	Jt. Res.	Res.	Vetoes¹ Bills Vetoed	Over-ridden	Laws Enacted
	9/19-10/12; 11/7-11/16;									
	1996: 1/9-2/1, 3/5-3/28, 5/7-5/14, 7/9;									
	1997: 1/6)									
1995SS....	1/4	1	1	1	1	1	0	0	0	1
1995SS....	9/5-10/12	36	12	13	1	1	0	0	0	1
1997	1/6/97-1/4/99	729	87	92	1,508	183	30	3	0	333
	(1997: 1/6, 1/14, 1/28-1/30, 2/12, 2/25-2/26, 3/4-3/20, 5/13-5/29, 6/10-9/30, 11/4-11/6, 11/18-11/20;									
	1998: 1/13-1/22, 2/3-2/12, 3/10-3/26, 4/21-5/13;									
	1999: 1/4)									
1998SS¹²...	4/21-5/21	31	13	12	13	2	2	0	0	5
1999¹³	1/4/99-1/3/01	731	97	101	1,498	168	52	5	0	196
	(1999: 1/4, 1/14, 1/26-1/28, 2/16-2/18, 3/2-3/4, 3/16-3/25, 5/11-10/6, 10/26-11/11;									
	2000: 1/25-2/10, 3/7-3/30, 5/2-5/4, 5/23-5/24;									
	2001: 1/3)									
1999SS⁷ ...	10/27-11/11	16	7	8	3	1	0	0	0	1
2000SS....	5/4-5/9	8	3	3	2	2	1	0	0	1
2001	1/3/01-1/6/03	734	62	63	1,436	174	75	0	0	106
	(2001: 1/3, 1/30-2/1, 2/13-2/15, 3/6-3/22, 5/1-5/10, 6/5-7/26, 10/2-10/4, 10/16-11/8;									
	2002: 1/22-2/7, 2/26-3/14, 4/30-5/2, 5/14-5/15;									
	2003: 1/6)									
2001SS⁷ ...	5/1-5/3	3	1	2	1	0	0	0	0	1
2002SS⁷ ...	1/22-7/8	168	59	52	1	2	7	0	0	1
2002SS⁷ ...	5/13-5/15	3	3	2	2	0	0	0	0	1
2003¹⁴	1/6/03-1/3/05	729	104	94	1,567	164	78	54	0	326
	(2003: 1/6-1/7, 1/28-1/30, 2/18-2/20, 3/3-3/20, 4/29-5/8, 5/28-6/25, 9/23-10/2, 10/28-11/13;									
	2004: 1/20-2/5, 2/24-3/11, 4/27, 5/11-5/19;									
	2005: 1/3)									
2003SS....	1/30-2/20	22	7	7	1	0	0	0	0	1
2005¹⁵	1/3/05-1/3/07	731	69	72	1,967	196	76	47	0	489
	(2005: 1/3, 1/11-1/27, 2/8, 2/15-2/24, 3/8-3/16, 4/5-4/12, 5/3-5/12, 5/31-6/30, 7/5, 7/20, 9/20-9/28, 10/25-11/9, 12/6-12/15;									
	2006: 1/17-2/2, 2/21-3/9, 4/25-5/17, 5/30-5/31, 7/12;									
	2007: 1/3)									
2005SS....	1/12-1/20	9	4	1	2	0	0	0	0	1
2006SS....	2/14-3/7	22	7	6	2	0	0	0	0	1
2007	1/3/07-1/5/09	733	91	89	1,574	230	50	1	0	239
	(2007: 1/3, 1/9, 1/30-2/1, 2/13, 2/20-3/1, 3/13-3/15, 4/17-4/26, 5/8-5/16, 5/29-11/8, 12/11;									
	2008: 1/15-1/31, 2/19-3/13, 5/6-5/8, 5/27-5/28;									
	2009: 1/5)									
2007SS....	1/11-2/1	22	7	6	2	1	0	0	0	1
2007SS....	10/15-10/23	9	5	3	2	0	0	0	0	0
2007SS....	12/11/07, 1/15-5/14/08	156	38	39	1	1	0	0	0	0
2008SS....	3/12-4/15	65	22	22	1	4	2	0	0	1
2008SS....	4/17-5/15	29	11	11	1	4	2	0	0	1

Note: For 1836-1847 territorial sessions, see *1873 Blue Book*, p. 205.

[1]Partial vetoes not included. See Executive Vetoes table. [2]Number of calendar days from session opening date to final adjournment. [3]Number of days senate or assembly met, including "skeleton sessions" (those days on which the senate or assembly leadership calls the house in session *in absentia* to fulfill a procedural requirement). [4]SS denotes special session. Regular and special sessions may run concurrently with meetings held on the same day. Each is counted as a separate meeting day. [5]Although 1965 Legislature adjourned to 1/11/67, terms automatically expired on 1/2/67. [6]Senate adjourned the special session 11/15/69; assembly, 1/17/70. [7]Special session met concurrently with regular session. [8]1979 Legislature met concurrently in extraordinary and special session, 1/22/80 – 1/25/80. [9]Legislature met concurrently in special session and extended floorperiod. [10]Extraordinary sessions held in September 1987, and April, May and June 1988. May 1988 extraordinary session ran concurrently with May 1988 veto review period and also with June 1988 extraordinary session. [11]Extraordinary session held, 6/15/94 – 6/23/94. [12]Extraordinary session held in April 1998. [13]Extraordinary session held in April and May 2000. [14]Extraordinary sessions held in February, July, and August 2003; December 2003-February 2004; March 2004; May 2004; and July 2004. [15]Extraordinary sessions were held in July 2005 and April 2006.

Sources: *Bulletin of the Proceedings of the Wisconsin Legislature,* various editions; and senate and assembly journals.

WISCONSIN MEMBERS, U.S. HOUSE OF REPRESENTATIVES
1848 – 2009

Name	Party	Residence	District	Term
Adams, Henry C	Rep.	Madison	2	1903-1906
Amlie, Thomas R	Rep., Prog.	Elkhorn	1	1931-1933; 1935-1939
Aspin, Les	Dem.	East Troy	1	1971-1993
Atwood, David	Rep.	Madison	2	1870-1871
Babbitt, Clinton	Dem.	Beloit	1	1891-1893
Babcock, Joseph W	Rep.	Necedah	3	1893-1907
Baldus, Alvin	Dem.	Menomonie	3	1975-1981
Baldwin, Tammy	Dem.	Madison	2	1999-
Barber, J. Allen	Rep.	Lancaster	3	1871-1875
Barca, Peter W	Dem.	Kenosha	1	1993-1995
Barnes, Lyman E	Dem.	Appleton	8	1893-1895
Barney, Samuel S	Rep.	West Bend	5	1895-1903
Barrett, Thomas M	Dem.	Milwaukee	5	1993-2003
Barwig, Charles	Dem.	Mayville	2	1889-1895
Beck, Joseph D	Rep.	Viroqua	7	1921-1929
Berger, Victor L	Soc.	Milwaukee	5	1911-1913; 1919; 1923-1929
Biemiller, Andrew J	Dem.	Milwaukee	5	1945-1947; 1949-1951
Billinghurst, Charles	Rep.	Juneau	3	1855-1859
Blanchard, George W	Rep.	Edgerton	1	1933-1935
Boileau, Gerald J	Rep., Prog.	Wausau	8,7	1931-1939
Bolles, Stephen	Rep.	Janesville	1	1939-1941
Bouck, Gabriel	Dem.	Oshkosh	6	1877-1881
Bragg, Edward S	Dem.	Fond du Lac	5,2	1877-1883; 1885-1887
Brickner, George H	Dem.	Sheboygan Falls	5	1889-1895
Brophy, John C	Rep.	Milwaukee	4	1947-1949
Brown, James S	Dem.	Milwaukee	1	1863-1865
Brown, Webster E	Rep.	Rhinelander	9,10	1901-1907
Browne, Edward E	Rep.	Waupaca	8	1913-1931
Burchard, Samuel D	Dem.	Beaver Dam	5	1875-1877
Burke, Michael E	Dem.	Beaver Dam	6,2	1911-1917
Bushnell, Allen R	Dem.	Madison	3	1891-1893
Byrnes, John W	Rep.	Green Bay	8	1945-1973
Cannon, Raymond J	Dem.	Milwaukee	4	1933-1939
Cary, William J	Rep.	Milwaukee	4	1907-1919
Caswell, Lucien B	Rep.	Fort Atkinson	2,1	1875-1883; 1885-1891
Cate, George W	Reform	Stevens Point	8	1875-1877
Clark, Charles B	Rep.	Neenah	6	1887-1891
Classon, David G	Rep.	Oconto	9	1917-1923
Cobb, Amasa	Rep.	Mineral Point	3	1863-1871
Coburn, Frank P	Dem.	West Salem	7	1891-1893
Cole, Orasmus	Whig	Potosi	2	1849-1851
Cook, Samuel A	Rep.	Neenah	6	1895-1897
Cooper, Henry Allen	Rep.	Racine	1	1893-1919; 1921-1931
Cornell, Robert J	Dem.	De Pere	8	1975-1979
Dahle, Herman B	Rep.	Mount Horeb	2	1899-1903
Darling, Mason C	Dem.	Fond du Lac	2	1848-1849
Davidson, James H.	Rep.	Oshkosh	6,8	1897-1913; 1917-1918
Davis, Glenn R.	Rep.	Waukesha	2,9	1947-1957; 1965-1975
Deuster, Peter V	Dem.	Milwaukee	4	1879-1885
Dilweg, La Vern R	Dem.	Green Bay	8	1943-1945
Doty, James D	Dem.	Neenah	3	1849-1853
Durkee, Charles	Free Soil	Kenosha	1	1849-1853
Eastman, Ben C	Dem.	Platteville	2	1851-1855
Eldredge, Charles A	Dem.	Fond du Lac	4,5	1863-1875
Esch, John Jacob	Rep.	La Crosse	7	1899-1921
Flynn, Gerald T	Dem.	Racine	1	1959-1961
Frear, James A	Rep.	Hudson	10,9	1913-1935
Froehlich, Harold V	Rep.	Appleton	8	1973-1975
Gehrmann, Bernard J	Prog.	Mellen	10	1935-1943
Green, Mark A.	Rep.	Green Bay	8	1999-2007
Griffin, Michael	Rep.	Eau Claire	7	1894-1899
Griswold, Harry W.	Rep.	West Salem	3	1939-1941
Guenther, Richard W.	Rep.	Oshkosh	6,2	1881-1889
Gunderson, Steven	Rep.	Osseo	3	1981-1997
Hanchett, Luther	Rep.	Plover	2	1861-1862
Haugen, Nils P	Rep.	Black River Falls	8,10	1887-1895
Hawkes, Charles, Jr	Rep.	Horicon	2	1939-1941
Hazelton, George C	Rep.	Boscobel	3	1877-1883
Hazelton, Gerry W.	Rep.	Columbus	2	1871-1875
Henney, Charles W.	Dem.	Portage	2	1933-1935
Henry, Robert K	Rep.	Jefferson	2	1945-1947
Hopkins, Benjamin F	Rep.	Madison	2	1867-1870
Hudd, Thomas R	Dem.	Green Bay	5	1886-1889
Hughes, James	Dem.	De Pere	8	1933-1935
Hull, Merlin	Prog.	Black River Falls	7,9	1929-1931; 1935-1953
Humphrey, Herman L	Rep.	Hudson	7	1877-1883
Jenkins, John J	Rep.	Chippewa Falls	10,11	1895-1909
Johns, Joshua L	Rep.	Appleton	8	1939-1943
Johnson, Jay	Dem.	New Franken	8	1997-1999
Johnson, Lester R	Dem.	Black River Falls	9	1953-1965
Jones, Burr W	Dem.	Madison	3	1883-1885
Kading, Charles A	Rep.	Watertown	2	1927-1933
Kagen, Steve	Dem.	Appleton	8	2007-
Kasten, Robert W., Jr	Rep.	Waukesha	9	1975-1979
Kastenmeier, Robert W	Dem.	Sun Prairie	2	1959-1991
Keefe, Frank B	Rep.	Oshkosh	6	1939-1951
Kersten, Charles J	Rep.	Whitefish Bay	5	1947-1949; 1951-1955
Kimball, Alanson M	Rep.	Waushara	6	1875-1877
Kind, Ron	Dem.	La Crosse	3	1997-
Kleczka, Gerald D	Dem.	Milwaukee	4	1984-2005
Kleczka, John C	Rep.	Milwaukee	4	1919-1923

WISCONSIN MEMBERS, U.S. HOUSE OF REPRESENTATIVES
1848 – 2009–Continued

Name	Party	Residence	District	Term
Klug, Scott L.	Rep.	Madison	2	1991-1999
Konop, Thomas F	Dem.	Kewaunee	9	1911-1917
Kopp, Arthur W	Rep.	Platteville	3	1909-1913
Kustermann, Gustav	Rep.	Green Bay	9	1907-1911
La Follette, Robert M., Sr	Rep.	Madison	3	1885-1891
Laird, Melvin R	Rep.	Marshfield	7	1953-1969
Lampert, Florian	Rep.	Oshkosh	6	1918-1930
Larrabee, Charles H	Dem.	Horicon	3	1859-1861
Lenroot, Irvine L.	Rep.	Superior	11	1909-1918
Lynch, Thomas.	Dem.	Antigo	9	1891-1895
Lynde, William Pitt	Dem.	Milwaukee	1,4	1848-1849; 1875-1879
Macy, John B	Dem.	Fond du Lac	3	1853-1855
Magoon, Henry S	Rep.	Darlington	3	1875-1877
McCord, Myron H	Rep.	Merrill	9	1889-1891
McDill, Alexander S	Rep.	Plover	8	1873-1875
McIndoe, Walter D.	Rep.	Wausau	6	1863-1867
McMurray, Howard J	Dem.	Milwaukee	5	1943-1945
Miller, Lucas M	Dem.	Oshkosh	6	1891-1893
Minor, Edward S.	Rep.	Sturgeon Bay	8,9	1895-1907
Mitchell, Alexander	Dem.	Milwaukee	1,4	1871-1875
Mitchell, John L	Dem.	Milwaukee	4	1891-1893
Monahan, James G.	Rep.	Darlington	3	1919-1921
Moody, James P	Dem.	Milwaukee	5	1983-1993
Moore, Gwen	Dem.	Milwaukee	4	2005-
Morse, Elmer A	Rep.	Antigo	10	1907-1913
Murphy, James W	Dem.	Platteville	3	1907-1909
Murray, Reid F.	Rep.	Ogdensburg	7	1939-1953
Nelson, Adolphus P	Rep.	Grantsburg	11	1918-1923
Nelson, John Mandt	Rep.	Madison	2,3	1906-1919; 1921-1933
Neumann, Mark W.	Rep.	Janesville	1	1995-1999
Obey, David R	Dem.	Wausau	7	1969-
O'Konski, Alvin E	Rep.	Mercer	10	1943-1973
O'Malley, Thomas D. P	Dem.	Milwaukee	5	1933-1939
Otjen, Theobald	Rep.	Milwaukee	4	1895-1907
Paine, Halbert E	Rep.	Milwaukee	1	1865-1871
Peavey, Hubert H	Rep.	Washburn	11,10	1923-1935
Petri, Thomas E	Rep.	Fond du Lac	6	1979-
Potter, John F	Rep.	East Troy	1	1857-1863
Pound, Thaddeus C	Rep.	Chippewa Falls	8	1877-1883
Price, Hugh H	Rep.	Black River Falls	8	1887
Price, William T	Rep.	Black River Falls	8	1883-1886
Race, John A	Dem.	Fond du Lac	6	1965-1967
Randall, Clifford E.	Rep.	Kenosha	1	1919-1921
Rankin, Joseph	Dem.	Manitowoc	5	1883-1886
Reilly, Michael K	Dem.	Fond du Lac	6	1913-1917; 1930-1939
Reuss, Henry S.	Dem.	Milwaukee	5	1955-1983
Roth, Toby	Rep.	Appleton	8	1979-1997
Rusk, Jeremiah M	Rep.	Viroqua	6,7	1871-1877
Ryan, Paul	Rep.	Janesville	1	1999-
Sauerhering, Edward.	Rep.	Mayville	2	1895-1899
Sauthoff, Harry.	Prog.	Madison	2	1935-1939; 1941-1945
Sawyer, Philetus	Rep.	Oshkosh	5,6	1865-1875
Schadeberg, Henry C	Rep.	Burlington	1	1961-1965; 1967-1971
Schafer, John C	Rep.	Milwaukee	4	1923-1933; 1939-1941
Schneider, George J	Rep., Prog.	Appleton	9,8	1923-1933; 1935-1939
Sensenbrenner, F. James, Jr	Rep.	Menomonee Falls	9,5	1979-
Shaw, George B	Rep.	Eau Claire	7	1893-1894
Sloan, A. Scott	Rep.	Beaver Dam	3	1861-1863
Sloan, Ithamar C.	Rep.	Janesville	2	1863-1867
Smith, Henry.	Union Labor	Milwaukee	4	1887-1889
Smith, Lawrence H	Rep.	Racine	1	1941-1959
Somers, Peter J.	Dem.	Milwaukee	4	1893-1895
Stafford, William H	Rep.	Milwaukee	5	1903-1911; 1913-1919; 1921-1923; 1929-1933
Stalbaum, Lynn E	Dem.	Racine	1	1965-1967
Steiger, William A	Rep.	Oshkosh	6	1967-1978
Stephenson, Isaac	Rep.	Marinette	9	1883-1889
Stevenson, William H	Rep.	La Crosse	3	1941-1949
Stewart, Alexander.	Rep.	Wausau	9	1895-1901
Sumner, Daniel H	Dem.	Waukesha	2	1883-1885
Tewes, Donald E.	Rep.	Waukesha	2	1957-1959
Thill, Lewis D	Rep.	Milwaukee	5	1939-1943
Thomas, Ormsby B	Rep.	Prairie du Chien	7	1885-1891
Thomson, Vernon W.	Rep.	Richland Center	3	1961-1975
Van Pelt, William K	Rep.	Fond du Lac	6	1951-1963
Van Schaick, Isaac W	Rep.	Milwaukee	4	1885-1887; 1889-1891
Voigt, Edward	Rep.	Sheboygan	2	1917-1927
Washburn, Cadwallader C	Rep.	Mineral Point, La Crosse	2 6	1855-1861; 1867-1871
Wasielewski, Thaddeus F	Dem.	Milwaukee	4	1941-1947
Weisse, Charles H	Dem.	Sheboygan Falls	6	1903-1911
Wells, Daniel, Jr	Dem.	Milwaukee	1	1853-1857
Wells, Owen A.	Dem.	Fond du Lac	6	1893-1895
Wheeler, Ezra	Dem.	Berlin	5	1863-1865
Williams, Charles G	Rep.	Janesville	1	1873-1883
Winans, John.	Dem.	Janesville	1	1883-1885
Withrow, Gardner R	Rep., Prog.	La Crosse	7,3	1931-1939; 1949-1961
Woodward, Gilbert M	Dem.	La Crosse	7	1883-1885
Zablocki, Clement J	Dem.	Milwaukee	4	1949-1983

Sources: Wisconsin Legislative Reference Bureau, *Wisconsin Blue Book,* various editions; Congressional Quarterly, *Guide to U.S. Elections,* 1985; and official election records.

WISCONSIN MEMBERS, U.S. HOUSE OF REPRESENTATIVES
By District, 1943 – 2009

District	Name	Service	Party	Residence	Alphabetical Listing	
1st	Lawrence H. Smith	1941-59	Rep.	Racine	Aspin	1st
	Gerald T. Flynn	1959-61	Dem.	Racine	Baldus	3rd
	Henry C. Schadeberg	1961-65; 1967-71	Rep.	Burlington	Baldwin	2nd
	Lynn E. Stalbaum	1965-67	Dem.	Racine	Barca	1st
	Les Aspin[1]	1971-93	Dem.	East Troy	Barrett	5th
	Peter W. Barca[1]	1993-95	Dem.	Kenosha	Biemiller	5th
	Mark W. Neumann	1995-99	Rep.	Janesville	Brophy	4th
	Paul Ryan	1999-	Rep.	Janesville	Byrnes	8th
					Cornell	8th
2nd	Harry Sauthoff	1941-45	Prog.	Madison	Davis	2nd, 9th
	Robert K. Henry	1945-47	Rep.	Jefferson	Dilweg	8th
	Glenn R. Davis	1947-57	Rep.	Waukesha	Flynn	1st
	Donald E. Tewes	1957-59	Rep.	Waukesha	Froehlich	8th
	Robert W. Kastenmeier	1959-91	Dem.	Sun Prairie	Green	8th
	Scott L. Klug	1991-99	Rep.	Madison	Gunderson	3rd
	Tammy Baldwin	1999-	Dem.	Madison	Henry	2nd
					Hull	9th
3rd	William H. Stevenson	1941-49	Rep.	La Crosse	Johnson, J.	8th
	Gardner R. Withrow	1949-61	Rep.	La Crosse	Johnson, L.	9th
	Vernon W. Thomson	1961-75	Rep.	Richland Center	Kagen	8th
	Alvin Baldus	1975-81	Dem.	Menomonie	Kasten	9th
	Steven Gunderson	1981-97	Rep.	Osseo	Kastenmeier	2nd
	Ron Kind	1997-	Dem.	La Crosse	Keefe	6th
					Kersten	5th
4th	Thaddeus F. Wasielewski	1941-47	Dem.	Milwaukee	Kind	3rd
	John C. Brophy	1947-49	Rep.	Milwaukee	Kleczka	4th
	Clement J. Zablocki[2]	1949-83	Dem.	Milwaukee	Klug	2nd
	Gerald D. Kleczka[2]	1984-2005	Dem.	Milwaukee	Laird	7th
	Gwen Moore	2005-	Dem.	Milwaukee	McMurray	5th
					Moody	5th
5th[3]	Howard J. McMurray	1943-45	Dem.	Milwaukee	Moore	4th
	Andrew J. Biemiller	1945-47; 1949-51	Dem.	Milwaukee	Murray	7th
	Charles J. Kersten	1947-49; 1951-55	Rep.	Whitefish Bay	Neumann	1st
	Henry S. Reuss	1955-83	Dem.	Milwaukee	Obey	7th
	James P. Moody	1983-93	Dem.	Milwaukee	O'Konski	10th
	Thomas M. Barrett	1993-2003	Dem.	Milwaukee	Petri	6th
	F. James Sensenbrenner, Jr.	2003-	Rep.	Menomonee Falls	Race	6th
					Reuss	5th
6th	Frank B. Keefe	1939-51	Rep.	Oshkosh	Roth	8th
	William K. Van Pelt	1951-65	Rep.	Fond du Lac	Ryan	1st
	John A. Race	1965-67	Dem.	Fond du Lac	Sauthoff	2nd
	William A. Steiger[4]	1967-78	Rep.	Oshkosh	Schadeberg	1st
	Thomas E. Petri[4]	1979-	Rep.	Fond du Lac	Sensenbrenner	9th, 5th
					Smith	1st
7th	Reid F. Murray	1939-53	Rep.	Ogdensburg	Stalbaum	1st
	Melvin R. Laird[5]	1953-69	Rep.	Marshfield	Steiger	6th
	David R. Obey[5]	1969-	Dem.	Wausau	Stevenson	3rd
					Tewes	2nd
8th	La Vern R. Dilweg	1943-45	Dem.	Green Bay	Thomson	3rd
	John R. Byrnes	1945-73	Rep.	Green Bay	Van Pelt	6th
	Harold V. Froehlich	1973-75	Rep.	Appleton	Wasielewski	4th
	Robert J. Cornell	1975-79	Dem.	De Pere	Withrow	3rd
	Toby Roth	1979-97	Rep.	Appleton	Zablocki	4th
	Jay Johnson	1997-99	Dem.	New Franken		
	Mark A. Green	1999-2007	Rep.	Green Bay		
	Steve Kagen	2007-	Dem.	Appleton		
9th[3,6]	Merlin Hull	1935-53	Prog.	Black River Falls		
	Lester R. Johnson	1953-65	Dem.	Black River Falls		
	Glenn R. Davis	1965-75	Rep.	Waukesha		
	Robert W. Kasten	1975-79	Rep.	Thiensville		
	F. James Sensenbrenner, Jr.	1979-2003	Rep.	Menomonee Falls		
10th[7]	Alvin E. O'Konski	1943-73	Rep.	Rhinelander		

[1]Aspin resigned 1/20/1993, to become U.S. Secretary of Defense. Barca was elected in a special election, 5/4/1993.

[2]Zablocki died 12/3/1983. Kleczka was elected in a special election, 4/3/1984.

[3]In the congressional reapportionment following the 2000 Census, Wisconsin's delegation was reduced from 9 to 8 members. The previous 4th, 5th, and 9th were reconfigured into the new 4th and 5th.

[4]Steiger died 12/4/1978, following his November 1978 election. Petri was elected in a special election, 4/3/1979.

[5]Laird resigned 1/21/1969, to become U.S. Secretary of Defense. Obey was elected in a special election, 4/1/1969.

[6]In the congressional redistricting based on the results of the 1960 Census of Population, the previous 9th District in western Wisconsin ceased to exist and a new 9th District was created in the Waukesha-Milwaukee metropolitan area.

[7]In the congressional reapportionment based on the results of the 1970 Census of Population, Wisconsin's delegation was reduced from 10 members to 9 members.

Sources: *1944 Wisconsin Blue Book* and Wisconsin Legislative Reference Bureau data.

U.S. SENATORS FROM WISCONSIN, 1848 – 2009

Class 1		Class 3	
Name	Service	Name	Service
Henry Dodge (D)	1848-1857	Isaac P. Walker (D).	1848-1855
James R. Doolittle (R)	1857-1869	Charles Durkee (UR)	1855-1861
Matthew H. Carpenter (R)	1869-1875	Timothy O. Howe (UR)	1861-1879
Angus Cameron (R)[1]	1875-1881	Matthew H. Carpenter (R)	1879-1881
Philetus Sawyer (R)	1881-1893	Angus Cameron (R)[1]	1881-1885
John Lendrum Mitchell (D)	1893-1899	John C. Spooner (R)	1885-1891
Joseph Very Quarles (R)	1899-1905	William F. Vilas (D)	1891-1897
Robert M. La Follette, Sr. (R)[2]	1906-1925	John C. Spooner (R)	1897-1907
Robert M. La Follette, Jr. (R)[3]	1925-1935	Isaac Stephenson (R)[5]	1907-1915
Robert M. La Follette, Jr. (P)	1935-1947	Paul O. Husting (D)	1915-1917
Joseph R. McCarthy (R)	1947-1957	Irvine L. Lenroot (R)[6]	1918-1927
William Proxmire (D)[4]	1957-1989	John J. Blaine (R)	1927-1933
Herbert H. Kohl (D)	1989-	F. Ryan Duffy (D)	1933-1939
		Alexander Wiley (R).	1939-1963
		Gaylord A. Nelson (D).	1963-1981
		Robert W. Kasten, Jr. (R)	1981-1993
		Russell D. Feingold (D)	1993-

Note: Each state has two U.S. Senators, and each serves a 6-year term. They were elected by their respective state legislatures until passage of the 17th Amendment to the U.S. Constitution on April 8, 1913, which provided for popular election. Article I, Section 3, Clause 2, of the U.S. Constitution divides senators into three classes so that one-third of the senate is elected every two years. Wisconsin's seats were assigned to Class 1 and Class 3 at statehood.

Key: Democrat (D); Progressive (P); Republican (R); Union Republican (UR)

[1] Not a candidate for reelection to Class 1 seat, but elected 3/10/1881 to fill vacancy caused by death of Class 3 Senator Carpenter on 2/24/1881.

[2] Elected 1/25/1905 but continued to serve as governor until 1/1/1906.

[3] Elected 9/29/1925 to fill vacancy caused by death of Robert La Follette, Sr., on 6/18/1925.

[4] Elected 8/27/1957 to fill vacancy caused by death of McCarthy on 5/2/1957.

[5] Elected 5/17/1907 to fill vacancy caused by resignation of Spooner on 4/30/1907.

[6] Elected 5/2/1918 to fill vacancy caused by death of Husting on 10/21/1917.

Source: Wisconsin Legislative Reference Bureau records.

HIGHLIGHTS OF LOCAL AND STATE GOVERNMENT IN WISCONSIN

Employment and Earnings — In March 2007, Wisconsin ranked 21st among the states in full-time equivalent (FTE) state and local government employees with 281,645. The State of Wisconsin employed 68,714 workers, while local government employed 212,931.

In March 2007, Wisconsin ranked 19th in average total payroll for state and local government employees with $1,084,206,586. California ranked first with a payroll of $9,506,913,690 and South Dakota ranked 50th with $130,606,979.

Units of Local Government — As of January 1, 2008, Wisconsin had 1,923 general units of local government – 72 counties, 190 cities, 403 villages, and 1,258 towns.

Counties varied in 2008 population from Milwaukee at 938,490 to Menominee with 4,630. These two counties were also highest and lowest in 2007 full value property assessments at $67.1 billion and $285.6 million, respectively. As determined by the U.S. Bureau of the Census in 2000, Marathon County is the largest in land area with 1,545 square miles and Ozaukee County the smallest with 232 square miles.

Based on the 2000 census, Wisconsin's city residents totaled 2,994,433 in 2000, a 5.2% increase from the 1990 census; village population was 687,007, a 19.7% increase; and town population was 1,668,306, a 13.3% increase. As of January 1, 2008, a total of 86 Wisconsin municipalities had populations of 10,000 or more. The City of Milwaukee ranked first at 590,870, and the Village of Sussex, with 10,045 residents, was smallest in the group.

Administration — Wisconsin cities may adopt a mayor, manager, or commission form of government. Of 190 cities, 10 have a city manager and 180 have a mayor. Currently, no city uses the commission form of government. Villages may use a president or manager form of government. Of 403 villages, only 10 have an appointed manager. Currently, 95 cities and 88 villages employ an administrator in a full-time or combined position.

Each county board is headed by a chairperson chosen by the board. In addition, 11 counties have an elected county executive, 20 have an appointed county administrator, and 40 have an appointed administrative coordinator.

The following tables present selected data. Consult footnoted sources for more detailed information about local and state government.

WISCONSIN STATE GOVERNMENT EMPLOYEES
By Status and Funding, 1998 – 2008

Employee Status[1]	1998	2003	2008	Type of Funding for Authorized Positions[3]	1998	2003	2008
Classified	37,558	41,112	40,094	State appropriations . . .	32,458	35,835	35,089
Unclassified	20,018	22,589	21,509	User fees	17,303	17,917	19,063
Limited Term . . .	7,930	6,650	5,935	Federal appropriations . .	8,045	9,342	9,837
Project	619	643	491	Segregated funds.	5,398	5,570	5,162
Seasonal	154	99	68	TOTAL[4]	63,204	68,665	69,151
Other[2]	5,553	6,518	6,805				
TOTAL[4]	71,832	77,611	74,901				

[1]Headcount of employees working on a full- or part-time basis as of June 30.

[2]Includes UW System graduate assistants.

[3]Full-time equivalent positions authorized by legislature or under procedures authorized by the legislature as of June 30.

[4]Detail may not add to total due to rounding.

Sources: Wisconsin Department of Administration, Division of Executive Budget and Finance, *State Employment Report,* June 2008 and previous issues.

WISCONSIN STATE CLASSIFIED SERVICE PROFILE
1996 – 2006

| | 1996 | | 2001 | | 2006 | |
| | Number | Percent of Work Force | Number | Percent of Work Force | Number | Percent of Work Force |
Category						
Permanent Classified Employees . . .	40,175	100.0	40,513	100.0	39,085	100.0
Persons with Disabilities.	3,762	9.4	3,217	7.9	2,420	6.2
Persons with Severe Disabilities. .	425	1.1	461	1.1	326	0.8
Women	21,090	52.5	20,750	51.2	19,985	51.1
Racial/ethnic minorities	2,625	6.5	3,338	8.2	3,606	9.2
Black	1,382	3.4	1,769	4.4	1,762	4.5
Hispanic	524	1.3	684	1.7	868	2.2
Asian	402	1.0	557	1.4	690	1.8
American Indian	317	0.8	328	0.8	286	0.7

Source: Wisconsin State Office of Employment Relations, *28th Affirmative Action Report for Wisconsin State Government 2005-2006,* and Wisconsin Department of Employment Relations for previous issues.

WISCONSIN STATE AND LOCAL GOVERNMENT
EMPLOYMENT AND PAYROLLS
Employees and Payrolls by Function, March 2007

| | Number of Employees | | | |
	Full-time	Part-time	Full-time Equivalent (FTE)*	Total Payroll for FTE (in thousands)
Education	135,550	87,448	167,398	$635,323
Elementary and secondary	(101,759)	(39,611)	(119,559)	(426,057)
Higher education institutions	(31,207)	(44,415)	(43,950)	(196,262)
Libraries (local)	(1,631)	(3,047)	(2,814)	(7,989)
Other	(953)	(375)	(1,075)	(5,015)
Government administration (including courts)	14,720	14,269	17,408	71,235
Police protection	15,072	3,079	15,912	69,878
Public welfare and social insurance administration . .	12,205	4,195	14,567	49,282
Health and hospitals	10,182	5,109	12,577	47,123
Streets and highways.	9,721	1,537	10,165	40,082
Corrections	12,885	1,460	13,704	52,951
Fire protection	4,259	6,705	4,873	23,592
Natural resources	2,845	1,198	3,343	12,376
Parks and recreation	2,552	3,012	3,219	10,203
Sewerage (local)	1,870	818	1,997	8,149
Transit	1,646	114	1,715	5,019
Utilities (electric and water supply)	2,200	228	2,263	9,659
Housing and community development	1,020	385	1,150	3,813
Solid waste management (local)	1,590	903	1,660	5,903
Other	8,257	4,605	9,273	38,048
TOTAL	236,574	135,065	281,224	$1,082,363

*Full-time Equivalent (FTE) is a derived statistic that provides an estimate of a government's total full-time employment by converting part-time employees to a full-time amount.
Source: U.S. Census Bureau, Governments Division, *2007 Public Employment Data: State and Local Governments,* at: http://ftp2.census.gov/govs/apes/07stlwi.txt [January 2009].

Employment and Payrolls, 1990 – 2007

| | Employees (full-time equivalents) | | | Monthly Payroll (in thousands)* | | |
Year	State	Local	Total	State	Local	Total
1990	66,541	183,318	249,859	$152,660	$409,907	$562,567
1997	64,709	201,633	266,342	204,267	569,193	773,460
1998	64,703	211,790	276,493	207,996	625,686	833,681
1999	63,185	207,587	270,772	214,684	628,043	842,727
2000	63,697	219,793	283,490	230,570	662,358	892,928
2001	69,428	218,824	288,252	257,605	676,935	934,540
2002	70,962	218,982	288,543	261,095	719,434	977,410
2003	71,040	217,004	288,044	268,249	739,031	1,007,280
2004	69,834	217,422	287,256	275,465	749,415	1,024,880
2005	70,189	223,523	293,712	275,824	809,593	1,085,417
2006	68,143	219,930	288,073	283,681	813,141	1,096,822
2007	68,714	212,931	281,645	295,616	788,590	1,084,207

*Prior to 1997, annual data reflected October payrolls. Beginning with the 1997 Annual Survey of Government Employment and Payroll, data reflects March payrolls.
Source: U.S. Census Bureau, Governments Division, Federal, State, and Local Governments Public Employment and Payroll Data, March 2007 and previous years, at: http://www.census.gov/govs/www/apes.html [March 3, 2009].

STATE AND LOCAL GOVERNMENT EMPLOYEES
Number and Earnings by State
March 2007 Payroll

State	Full-time Equivalent Employees Number Total	State	Local	Earnings March Payroll Total	State	Local
Alabama	284,680	88,617	196,063	$909,020,919	$324,869,078	$584,151,841
Alaska	52,173	25,653	26,520	227,334,367	114,168,093	113,166,274
Arizona.	300,564	68,224	232,340	1,170,637,986	259,356,616	911,281,370
Arkansas	165,666	59,386	106,280	480,819,382	191,038,911	289,780,471
California	1,835,452	387,168	1,448,284	9,506,913,690	2,118,772,912	7,388,140,778
Colorado	262,424	67,784	194,640	1,029,817,142	301,750,774	728,066,368
Connecticut	187,545	61,823	125,722	857,954,479	308,093,898	549,860,581
Delaware	51,612	26,148	25,464	199,416,349	105,524,288	93,892,061
District of Columbia . . .	47,116	—	47,116	238,889,611	—	238,889,611
Florida	890,834	188,772	702,062	3,282,667,383	691,311,981	2,591,355,402
Georgia.	519,684	126,420	393,264	1,704,034,921	441,675,105	1,262,359,816
Hawaii	71,503	57,210	14,293	287,914,727	224,849,191	63,065,536
Idaho	80,585	22,190	58,395	257,764,467	83,181,635	174,582,832
ILLINOIS	645,306	125,015	520,291	2,590,289,613	556,183,840	2,034,105,773
Indiana	339,787	89,558	250,229	1,122,673,004	317,084,743	805,588,261
IOWA	182,356	53,427	128,929	648,531,991	239,302,959	409,229,032
Kansas	187,953	45,098	142,855	600,359,404	163,014,180	437,345,224
Kentucky.	246,837	80,307	166,530	737,895,733	282,497,459	455,398,274
Louisiana.	264,622	84,593	180,029	812,084,656	300,928,942	511,155,714
Maine	76,382	22,870	53,512	252,412,763	87,021,568	165,391,195
Maryland.	300,723	90,333	210,390	1,321,002,767	391,121,219	929,881,548
Massachusetts	334,715	96,109	238,606	1,460,337,777	450,308,816	1,010,028,961
MICHIGAN	493,466	144,807	348,659	1,986,463,858	627,823,540	1,358,640,318
MINNESOTA	280,783	78,266	202,517	1,126,366,622	352,923,171	773,443,451
Mississippi	189,188	55,824	133,364	541,311,862	176,865,361	364,446,501
Missouri	327,622	89,532	238,090	1,012,282,085	277,543,779	734,738,306
Montana	55,982	20,017	35,965	177,644,397	72,476,477	105,167,920
Nebraska	113,600	32,465	81,135	383,361,802	105,465,727	277,896,075
Nevada	110,317	28,506	81,811	493,913,797	128,939,233	364,974,564
New Hampshire	72,175	19,588	52,587	252,298,298	74,983,175	177,315,123
New Jersey.	513,111	155,685	357,426	2,507,613,397	811,663,283	1,695,950,114
New Mexico	133,660	52,255	81,405	414,263,901	179,110,247	235,153,654
New York	1,232,744	253,354	979,390	5,691,115,824	1,225,581,201	4,465,534,623
North Carolina	542,180	142,985	399,195	1,812,939,180	520,114,675	1,292,824,505
North Dakota.	41,431	17,918	23,513	136,849,163	58,489,402	78,359,761
Ohio	613,581	143,206	470,375	2,290,602,532	597,895,507	1,692,707,025
Oklahoma	215,723	69,961	145,762	651,119,409	243,245,766	407,873,643
Oregon	190,197	59,619	130,578	736,211,972	238,803,487	497,408,485
Pennsylvania	594,225	160,177	434,048	2,271,721,046	656,086,050	1,615,634,996
Rhode Island	53,798	20,435	33,363	239,107,259	94,855,397	144,251,862
South Carolina	254,272	76,213	178,059	790,011,402	252,164,498	537,846,904
South Dakota.	43,421	13,897	29,524	130,606,979	46,523,763	84,083,216
Tennessee	324,520	84,875	239,645	1,040,062,268	290,745,896	749,316,372
Texas	1,344,442	290,451	1,053,991	4,496,981,089	1,099,481,849	3,397,499,240
Utah	132,073	51,001	81,072	461,962,640	193,190,905	268,771,735
Vermont	39,792	14,759	25,033	142,421,924	60,864,041	81,557,883
Virginia.	441,928	124,536	317,392	1,623,383,487	486,558,571	1,136,824,916
Washington.	340,052	119,970	220,082	1,494,733,963	503,731,436	991,002,527
West Virginia.	101,073	38,060	63,013	303,080,799	119,944,289	183,136,510
WISCONSIN	281,645	68,714	212,931	1,084,206,586	295,616,184	788,590,402
Wyoming.	48,050	12,842	35,208	165,079,021	45,001,676	120,077,345
UNITED STATES . . .	16,453,570	4,306,623	12,146,947	$64,156,489,693	$17,788,744,794	$46,367,744,899

Source: U.S. Department of Commerce, Bureau of the Census, 2007 Public Employment and Payroll Data, at:
http://www.census.gov/govs/www/apes.html [April 9, 2009].

LOCAL UNITS OF GOVERNMENT BY STATE AND TYPE – 2007

	Total Units	Counties[1]	Municipalities[2]	Towns or Townships[3]	Special Districts	School Districts[4]
Alabama	1,185	67	458	—	529	131
Alaska	177	14	148	—	15	—
Arizona.	645	15	90	—	301	239
Arkansas	1,548	75	502	—	724	247
California	4,344	57	478	—	2,765	1,044
Colorado	2,416	62	270	—	1,904	180
Connecticut	649	—	30	149	453	17
Delaware	338	3	57	—	259	19
District of Columbia	2	—	1	—	1	—
Florida	1,623	66	411	—	1,051	95
Georgia	1,439	154	535	—	570	180
Hawaii	19	3	1	—	15	—
Idaho	1,240	44	200	—	880	116
ILLINOIS	6,994	102	1,299	1,432	3,249	912
Indiana	3,231	91	567	1,008	1,272	293
IOWA	1,954	99	947	—	528	380
Kansas	3,931	104	627	1,353	1,531	316
Kentucky.	1,346	118	419	—	634	175
Louisiana.	526	60	303	—	95	68
Maine	850	16	22	466	248	98
Maryland	256	23	157	—	76	—
Massachusetts	861	5	45	306	423	82
MICHIGAN	2,893	83	533	1,242	456	579
MINNESOTA	3,526	87	854	1,788	456	341
Mississippi	1,000	82	296	—	458	164
Missouri	3,723	114	952	312	1,809	536
Montana	1,273	54	129	—	758	332
Nebraska	2,659	93	530	454	1,294	288
Nevada	198	16	19	—	146	17
New Hampshire	545	10	13	221	137	164
New Jersey.	1,383	21	324	242	247	549
New Mexico	863	33	101	—	633	96
New York	3,403	57	618	929	1,119	680
North Carolina	963	100	548	—	315	—
North Dakota.	2,699	53	357	1,320	771	198
Ohio	3,702	88	938	1,308	700	668
Oklahoma	1,880	77	594	—	642	567
Oregon	1,546	36	242	—	1,034	234
Pennsylvania	4,871	66	1,016	1,546	1,728	515
Rhode Island	134	—	8	31	91	4
South Carolina	698	46	268	—	299	85
South Dakota.	1,983	66	309	916	526	166
Tennessee	928	92	347	—	475	14
Texas	4,835	254	1,209	—	2,291	1,081
Utah	599	29	242	—	288	40
Vermont	733	14	45	237	144	293
Virginia.	511	95	229	—	186	1
Washington.	1,845	39	281	—	1,229	296
West Virginia.	663	55	232	—	321	55
WISCONSIN[5]	3,120	72	592	1,259	756	441
Wyoming.	726	23	99	—	549	55
UNITED STATES	89,476	3,033	19,492	16,519	37,381	13,051

[1]Excludes areas corresponding to counties that have no organized government.

[2]"Municipalities" include cities, villages, boroughs (except in Alaska), and towns (except in Connecticut, Maine, Massachusetts, Minnesota, New Hampshire, New York, Rhode Island, Vermont, and Wisconsin).

[3]Includes both "townships" and "town" governments in the case of those states listed in footnote 2.

[4]Excludes systems operated as part of a state, county, municipal, or town government.

[5]Corrected figures from Wisconsin Department of Administration, Demographic Services Center, and the Wisconsin Department of Public Instruction. State and U.S. totals have not been adjusted.

Source: U.S. Census Bureau, Governments Division, *2007 Census of Governments, Local Governments and Public School Systems by Type and State: 2007*, March 2009.

BASIC DATA ON WISCONSIN COUNTIES

County (year created)[1]	County Seat	Full Value 2007 Assessment (in millions)[2]	Population 2008 Estimate	Pct. Change[3]	2008 Rank	Land Area in Sq. Miles[4]	2008 Density per Sq. Mile[5]
Adams (1848)	Friendship	$2,825,672	21,836	9.6%	50	647.7	33.7
Ashland (1860)	Ashland	1,272,195	16,929	0.4	60	1,043.8	16.2
Barron (1859)	Barron	3,935,742	47,727	6.1	29	862.8	55.3
Bayfield (1845)	Washburn	2,612,674	16,160	7.6	63	1,476.3	10.9
Brown (1818)	Green Bay	18,388,879	245,168	8.2	4	528.7	463.7
Buffalo (1853)	Alma	938,069	14,200	2.9	67	684.5	20.7
Burnett (1856)	Meenon[6]	2,920,021	16,791	7.1	61	821.5	20.4
Calumet (1836)	Chilton	3,258,816	46,292	13.9	30	319.8	144.8
Chippewa (1845)	Chippewa Falls	4,297,207	61,872	12.1	24	1,010.4	61.2
Clark (1853)	Neillsville	1,679,531	34,589	3.1	41	1,215.6	28.5
Columbia (1846)	Portage	5,088,615	56,130	7.0	26	773.8	72.5
Crawford (1818)	Prairie du Chien	1,083,223	17,629	2.2	59	572.7	30.8
Dane (1836)	Madison	50,114,198	471,559	10.6	2	1,201.9	392.3
Dodge (1836)	Juneau	6,094,769	89,810	4.6	17	882.3	101.8
Door (1851)	Sturgeon Bay	7,185,362	30,303	8.4	43	482.7	62.8
Douglas (1854)	Superior	3,292,212	44,326	2.4	33	1,309.1	33.9
Dunn (1854)	Menomonie	2,806,515	43,292	8.6	35	852.0	50.8
Eau Claire (1856)	Eau Claire	6,454,280	98,302	5.5	16	637.6	154.2
Florence (1881)	Florence	576,648	5,317	4.5	71	488.0	10.9
Fond du Lac (1836)	Fond du Lac	6,733,229	101,740	4.6	14	722.9	140.7
Forest (1885)	Crandon	1,135,240	10,393	3.7	68	1,014.1	10.2
Grant (1836)	Lancaster	2,598,571	51,290	3.4	28	1,147.9	44.7
Green (1836)	Monroe	2,612,647	36,493	8.5	40	584.0	62.5
Green Lake (1858)	Green Lake	2,297,614	19,416	1.6	55	354.3	54.8
Iowa (1829)	Dodgeville	1,828,318	24,196	6.2	48	762.7	31.7
Iron (1893)	Hurley	973,139	7,048	2.7	70	757.2	9.3
Jackson (1853)	Black River Falls	1,302,415	20,140	5.4	53	987.3	20.4
Jefferson (1836)	Jefferson	6,676,844	81,022	6.9	20	557.0	145.5
Juneau (1856)	Mauston	2,052,224	27,359	12.5	46	767.6	35.6
Kenosha (1850)	Kenosha	14,640,280	162,094	8.4	8	272.8	594.2
Kewaunee (1852)	Kewaunee	1,410,394	21,358	5.8	52	342.6	62.3
La Crosse (1851)	La Crosse	7,642,785	112,758	5.3	13	452.7	249.1
Lafayette (1846)	Darlington	886,239	16,468	2.1	62	633.6	26.0
Langlade (1879)	Antigo	1,677,863	21,680	4.5	51	872.7	24.8
Lincoln (1874)	Merrill	2,304,073	30,681	3.5	42	883.3	34.7
Manitowoc (1836)	Manitowoc	5,079,421	84,830	2.3	19	591.5	143.4
Marathon (1850)	Wausau	9,495,030	135,190	7.4	10	1,545.0	87.5
Marinette (1879)	Marinette	3,701,537	44,823	3.3	32	1,401.8	32.0
Marquette (1836)	Montello	1,533,892	15,423	6.0	66	455.5	33.9
Menominee (1961)	Keshena	285,551	4,630	1.5	72	358.0	12.9
Milwaukee (1834)	Milwaukee	67,119,284	938,490	–0.2	1	241.6	3,884.5
Monroe (1854)	Sparta	2,469,779	44,170	8.0	34	900.8	49.0
Oconto (1851)	Oconto	3,528,607	39,261	10.1	38	998.0	39.3
Oneida (1885)	Rhinelander	7,285,470	38,903	5.8	39	1,124.5	34.6
Outagamie (1851)	Appleton	12,846,627	174,778	8.5	6	640.3	273.0
Ozaukee (1853)	Port Washington	11,298,571	87,008	5.7	18	232.0	375.0
Pepin (1858)	Durand	541,885	7,743	7.3	69	232.3	33.3
Pierce (1853)	Ellsworth	3,213,432	40,523	10.1	37	576.5	70.3
Polk (1853)	Balsam Lake	4,989,036	45,892	11.1	31	917.3	50.0
Portage (1836)	Stevens Point	4,738,654	70,506	4.9	23	806.3	87.4
Price (1879)	Phillips	1,461,100	16,088	1.7	64	1,252.6	12.8
Racine (1836)	Racine	15,659,760	196,321	4.0	5	333.1	589.4
Richland (1842)	Richland Center	1,073,360	18,317	2.2	56	586.2	31.2
Rock (1836)	Janesville	10,165,219	160,477	5.4	9	720.5	222.7
Rusk (1901)	Ladysmith	1,166,267	15,657	2.0	65	913.1	17.1
St. Croix (1840)	Hudson	8,604,072	79,702	26.2	21	721.8	110.4
Sauk (1840)	Baraboo	6,759,982	61,086	10.6	25	837.6	72.9
Sawyer (1883)	Hayward	3,827,417	17,753	9.6	57	1,256.4	14.1
Shawano (1853)	Shawano	2,899,082	42,602	4.8	36	892.5	47.7
Sheboygan (1836)	Sheboygan	8,917,701	117,472	4.3	12	513.6	228.7
Taylor (1875)	Medford	1,278,609	20,065	2.0	54	974.9	20.6
Trempealeau (1854)	Whitehall	1,659,036	28,278	4.7	45	734.1	38.5
Vernon (1851)	Viroqua	1,668,825	29,719	5.9	44	794.9	37.4
Vilas (1893)	Eagle River	7,686,161	23,044	9.6	49	873.7	26.4
Walworth (1836)	Elkhorn	14,599,872	101,315	10.1	15	555.3	182.5
Washburn (1883)	Shell Lake	2,665,558	17,646	10.0	58	809.7	21.8
Washington (1836)	West Bend	13,661,989	130,493	11.1	11	430.8	302.9
Waukesha (1846)	Waukesha	51,988,144	382,697	6.1	3	555.6	688.8
Waupaca (1851)	Waupaca	3,803,180	54,157	4.5	27	751.1	72.1
Waushara (1851)	Wautoma	2,489,838	25,322	9.8	47	626.0	40.5
Winnebago (1840)	Oshkosh	11,601,105	165,358	5.5	7	438.6	377.0
Wood (1856)	Wisconsin Rapids	4,560,801	77,049	2.0	22	792.8	97.2
State Total		$497,920,349	5,675,156	5.8%		54,310.1	104.5

[1]Counties are created by legislative act. Depending on the date, Wisconsin counties were created by the Michigan Territorial Legislature (1818-1836), the Wisconsin Territorial Legislature (1836-1848), or the Wisconsin State Legislature (after 1848). [2]Reflects actual market value of all taxable general property, including personal property and real estate, as determined by the Wisconsin Department of Revenue. [3]Change from 2000 U.S. Census. [4]Determined by 2000 Census. [5]2008 density calculated by Wisconsin Legislative Reference Bureau. [6]Town of Siren is used as a mailing address for county offices.

Sources: Wisconsin Department of Revenue, Division of State and Local Finance, *Town, Village, and City Taxes 2007: Taxes Levied 2007 – Collected 2008*, 2009; Wisconsin Department of Administration, *Final Population Estimates for Wisconsin Counties*, April 2009.

COUNTY OFFICERS IN WISCONSIN
June 30, 2009

County	Number of Supervisors[1]	County Board Chairperson	Administrator, Executive, or Administrative Coordinator[2]
Adams	20	Al Sebastiani	Barb Petkovsek (AC)
Ashland	21	Margaret Kurilla	Jeff Beirl (CA)
Barron	29	Jess Miller	Duane Hebert (CA)
Bayfield	13	William Kacvinsky	Mark Abeles-Allison (CA)
Brown	26	Guy Zima	Tom Hinz (CE)
Buffalo	16	Del D. Twidt	Del D. Twidt (AC)
Burnett	21	Phillip J. Lindeman	Candace Fitzgerald (CA)
Calumet	21	Bill Barribeau	Jay Shambeau (CA)
Chippewa	29	Richard Schoch	William H. Reynolds (CA)
Clark	29	Wayne Hendrickson	Wayne Hendrickson (AC)
Columbia	31	Debra L.H. Wopat	Susan Moll (AC)
Crawford	17	Ron Leys	Ron Leys (AC)
Dane	37	Scott McDonell	Kathleen Falk (CE)
Dodge	37	Russell Kottke	James Mielke (CA)
Door	21	Leo W. Zipperer	Michael Serpe (CA)
Douglas	28	Douglas G. Finn	Steve Koszarek (CA)
Dunn	29	Steven Rasmussen	Eugene Smith (CA)
Eau Claire	29	Gregg A. Moore	J. Thomas McCarty (CA)
Florence	12	Jeanette Bomberg	Jerri Meyer (AC)
Fond du Lac	18	Martin F. Farrell	Allen J. Buechel (CE)
Forest	21	Erhard E. Huettl, Sr.	Erhard E. Huettl, Sr. (AC)
Grant	31	John Patcle	John Patcle (AC)
Green	31	Arthur F. Carter	Michael J. Doyle (AC)
Green Lake	19	Orrin W. Helmer	Margaret R. Bostelmann (AC)
Iowa	21	Mark Masters	Randy Terronez (CA)
Iron	15	Dennis DeRosso	Dennis DeRosso (AC)
Jackson	19	Dennis Eberhardt	Kyle Deno (AC)
Jefferson	30	Sharon L. Schmeling	Gary R. Petre (CA)
Juneau	21	Alan K. Peterson	Alan K. Peterson (CA)
Kenosha	28	Joseph Clark	James Kreuser (CE)
Kewaunee	20	Robert A. Weidner	Edward J. Dorner (CA)
La Crosse	35	Steven P. Doyle	Steve O'Malley (CA)
Lafayette	16	Jack Sauer	Jack Sauer (AC)
Langlade	21	Michael P. Klimoski	Michael P. Klimoski (AC)
Lincoln	22	Robert Lussow	John Mulder (AC)
Manitowoc	25	James N. Brey	Robert Ziegelbauer (CE)
Marathon	38	Keith Langenhahn	Brad Karger (CA)
Marinette	30	George A. Bousley	Steven L. Corbeille (CA)
Marquette	17	Howard Zellmer	Brent Miller (AC)
Menominee	7	Elizabeth Moses	Ronald Corn, Sr. (AC)
Milwaukee	19	Lee Holloway	Scott Walker (CE)
Monroe	24	Dennis Hubbard	Dennis Hubbard (AC)
Oconto	31	Leland T. Rymer	Kevin Hamann (AC)
Oneida	21	Andrew Smith	Andrew Smith (AC)
Outagamie	36	Clifford Sanderfoot	Robert Toby Paltzer, Jr. (CE)
Ozaukee	31	Robert A. Brooks	Thomas W. Meaux (CA)
Pepin	12	Peter Adler	Lawrence J. Krcmar (AC)
Pierce	17	Paul K. Barkla	Paul K. Barkla (Interim AC)
Polk	23	Bryan Beseker	Bryan Beseker (AC)
Portage	29	O. Philip Idsvoog	Mark Maslowski (CE)
Price	13	Robert Kopisch	Robert Kopisch (AC)
Racine	23	Peter L. Hansen	William L. McReynolds (CE)
Richland	21	Ann M. Greenheck	Victor V. Vlasak (AC)
Rock	29	J. Russell Podzilni	Craig Knutson (CA)
Rusk	21	Randy Tatur	Denise Wetzel (AC)
St. Croix	31	Roger Rebholz	Charles Whiting (CA)
Sauk	31	Marty Krueger	Kathryn Schauf (AC)
Sawyer	15	Hal Helwig	Hal Helwig (AC)
Shawano	30	Marshal Giese	Frank Pascarella (AC)
Sheboygan	34	Michael J. Vandersteen	Adam N. Payne (AC)
Taylor	17	Jim Metz	Jim Metz (AC)
Trempealeau	17	Barbara Semb	Barbara Semb (AC)
Vernon	29	Thomas Spenner	Ronald Hoff (AC)
Vilas	21	Stephen Favorite	None
Walworth	11	Nancy Russell	David Bretl (CA)
Washburn	21	Michael Bobin	Michael Keefe (AC)
Washington	30	Herbert J. Tennies	Douglas Johnson (AC)
Waukesha	25	James Dwyer	Daniel Vrakas (CE)
Waupaca	27	Dick Koeppen	Mary A. Robbins (AC)
Waushara	11	Norman Weiss	Debra Behringer (AC)
Winnebago	36	David Albrecht	Mark Harris (CE)
Wood	19	Lance Pliml	Lance Pliml (AC)

COUNTY OFFICERS IN WISCONSIN
June 30, 2009–Continued

County	Clerk	County Clerk Office Address
Adams	Cindy Phillippi (D)	1917 Thomas Av., Friendship 53934
Ashland	Patricia Somppi (D)	201 W. Main St., Ashland 54806
Barron	DeeAnn Cook (R)	330 E. LaSalle Av., #2130, Barron 54812
Bayfield	Scott S. Fibert (D)	P.O. Box 878, Washburn 54891
Brown	Darlene K. Marcelle (R)	P.O. Box 23600, Green Bay 54305-3600
Buffalo	Roxann M. Halverson (D)	P.O. Box 58, Alma 54610-0058
Burnett	Wanda Hinrichs (D)	7410 County Road K, #105, Siren 54872
Calumet	Beth A. Hauser (R)	206 Court St., Chilton 53014
Chippewa	Kathleen M. Bernier (R)	711 N. Bridge St., Chippewa Falls 54729
Clark	Christina M. Jensen (R)	517 Court St., Rm. 301, Neillsville 54456
Columbia	Susan Moll (R)	400 DeWitt St., Portage 53901
Crawford	Janet L. Geisler (R)	225 N. Beaumont Rd., Suite 210, Prairie du Chien 53821
Dane	Robert Ohlsen (D)	210 Martin Luther King Jr. Blvd., Madison 53703
Dodge	Karen J. Gibson (R)	127 E. Oak St., Juneau 53039
Door	Jill M. Lau (R)	421 Nebraska St., Sturgeon Bay 54235
Douglas	Susan T. Sandvick (D)	1313 Belknap St., Superior 54880
Dunn	Marilyn Hoyt (D)	800 Wilson Av., Rm. 147, Menomonie 54751
Eau Claire	Janet K. Loomis (D)	721 Oxford Av., Eau Claire 54703
Florence	Jerri Meyer (R)	P.O. Box 410, Florence 54121
Fond du Lac	Lisa Freiberg (R)	P.O. Box 1557, Fond du Lac 54936-1557
Forest	Ann Mihalko (D)	200 E. Madison St., Crandon 54520
Grant	Linda K. Gebhard (R)	111 S. Jefferson St., Lancaster 53813
Green	Michael J. Doyle (R)	1016 16th Av., Monroe 53566
Green Lake	Margaret R. Bostelmann (R)	P.O. Box 3188, Green Lake 54941-3188
Iowa	Gregory T. Klusendorf (R)	222 N. Iowa St., Dodgeville 53533
Iron	Michael Saari (R)	300 Taconite St., Suite 101, Hurley 54534
Jackson	Kyle Deno (R)	307 Main St., Black River Falls 54615
Jefferson	Barbara A. Frank (R)	320 S. Main St., Rm. 109, Jefferson 53549
Juneau	Kathleen Kobylski (R)	220 E. State St., Mauston 53948
Kenosha	Mary Schuch-Krebs (D)	1010 56th St., Kenosha 53140
Kewaunee	Linda J. Teske (D)	810 Lincoln St., Kewaunee 54216
La Crosse	Linda Stone (R)	400 4th St. N, Rm. 1210, La Crosse 54601
Lafayette	Linda Bawden (R)	626 Main St., Darlington 53530
Langlade	Kathryn Jacob (D)	800 Clermont St., Antigo 54409
Lincoln	Robert Kunkel (R)	801 N. Sales St., Suite 201, Merrill 54452-1632
Manitowoc	Jamie J. Aulik (R)	1010 S. 8th St., Manitowoc 54220
Marathon	Nan Kottke (D)	500 Forest St., Wausau 54403
Marinette	Kathy Brandt (R)	1926 Hall Av., Marinette 54143-1717
Marquette	Donna J. Seddon (D)	77 W. Park St., P.O. Box 186, Montello 53949
Menominee	Ruth Waupoose (D)	P.O. Box 279, Keshena 54135
Milwaukee	Joseph Czarnezki (D)	901 N. 9th St., Rm. 105, Milwaukee 53233
Monroe	Shelley Bohl (R)	202 S. K St., Rm. 1, Sparta 54656
Oconto	Kim Pytleski (R)	301 Washington St., Oconto 54153-1699
Oneida	Robert Bruso (D)	P.O. Box 400, Rhinelander 54501-0400
Outagamie	Nancy J. Christensen (R)	410 S. Walnut St., Appleton 54911
Ozaukee	Julianne B. Winkelhorst (R)	121 W. Main St., Port Washington 53074-0994
Pepin	Marcia R. Bauer (D)	740 7th Av. W., P.O. Box 39, Durand 54736
Pierce	Jamie R. Feuerhelm (D)	414 W. Main St., P.O. Box 119, Ellsworth 54011
Polk	Carole T. Wondra (D)	100 Polk County Plaza, Ste. 110, Balsam Lake 54810
Portage	Shirley M. Simonis (D)	1516 Church St., Stevens Point 54481
Price	Jean Gottwald (D)	126 Cherry St., Rm. 106, Phillips 54555
Racine	Wendy M. Christensen (R)	730 Wisconsin Av., Racine 53403
Richland	Victor J. Vlasak (R)	P.O. Box 310, Richland Center 53581
Rock	Lori Stottler (D)	51 S. Main St., Janesville 53545
Rusk	Denise Wetzel (D)	311 E. Miner Av., Suite C150, Ladysmith 54848
St. Croix	Cindy Campbell (D)	1101 Carmichael Rd., Hudson 54016
Sauk	Beverly J. Mielke (R)	505 Broadway, Rm. 144, Baraboo 53913
Sawyer	Kris Mayberry (R)	P.O. Box 836, Hayward 54843
Shawano	Rosemary Bohm (R)	311 N. Main St., Shawano 54166
Sheboygan	Julie Glancey (D)	508 New York Av., Sheboygan 53081-4126
Taylor	Bruce P. Strama (D)	224 S. 2nd St., Medford 54451
Trempealeau	Paul L. Syverson (D)	36245 Main St., Whitehall 54773
Vernon	Ronald Hoff (R)	Courthouse Annex, Rm. 108, Viroqua 54665
Vilas	David R. Alleman (R)	330 Court St., Eagle River 54521
Walworth	Kimberly S. Bushey (R)	100 W. Walworth, Elkhorn 53121
Washburn	Lynn K. Hoeppner (R)	P.O. Box 639, Shell Lake 54871
Washington	Brenda Jaszewski (R)	432 E. Washington St., West Bend 53095-7986
Waukesha	Kathy Nickolaus (R)	515 W. Moreland Blvd., Waukesha 53188
Waupaca	Mary A. Robbins (R)	811 Harding St., Waupaca 54981
Waushara	John Benz (R)	P.O. Box 488, Wautoma 54982-0488
Winnebago	Susan Ertmer (R)	415 Jackson St., Oshkosh 54901
Wood	Cynthia Cepress (D)	P.O. Box 8095, Wisconsin Rapids 54495-8095

COUNTY OFFICERS IN WISCONSIN
June 30, 2009–Continued

County	Treasurer	Register of Deeds	Clerk of Circuit Court
Adams	Mary Ann Bays (R)	Jodi Helgeson (R)	Dianna Helmrick (D)
Ashland	Tracey A. Hoglund (R)	Karen M. Miller (D)	Kathleen R. Colgrove (R)
Barron	Yvonne K. Ritchie (R)	Joyce Kaseno (D)	Judith Espeseth (R)
Bayfield	Daniel Anderson (D)	Patricia Olson (D)	Kay Cederberg (D)
Brown	Kerry M. Blaney (D)	Cathy A. Williquette (D)	Lisa Wilson (D)
Buffalo	Marilynn Sheahan (R)	Carol Burmeister (D)	Roselle Urness (R)
Burnett	Joanne Pahl (D)	Jeanine Chell (D)	Trudy Schmidt (D)
Calumet	Michael V. Schlaak (R)	Shirley Gregory (R)	Barbara Van Akkeren (R)
Chippewa	Patricia Schimmel (D)	Marge L. Geissler (D)	Karen J. Hepfler (D)
Clark	Kathryn M. Brugger (D)	Lois Hagedorn (D)	Gail Walker (D)
Columbia	Deborah A. Raimer (R)	Lisa Walker (R)	Susan Raimer (R)
Crawford	Martin E. Sprosty (D)	Melissa Nagel (D)	Donna M. Steiner (D)
Dane	David Worzala (D)	Kristi Chlebowski (D)	Carlo Esqueda (D)
Dodge	Patti Hilker (R)	Chris Planasch (R)	Lynn Hron (R)
Door	Jay Zahn (R)	Carey Petersilka (R)	Nancy Robillard (R)
Douglas	Sandra J. Petzold (D)	Gayle Wahner (D)	Joan Osty (D)
Dunn	Mary Erpenbach (R)	James Mrdutt (D)	Clara D. Minor (D)
Eau Claire	Larry C. Lokken (D)	Mary L. Kaiser (R)	Kristina L. Aschenbrenner (R)
Florence	JoAnne Friberg (R)	Pattie Gehlhoff (R)	Paula Coraggio (R)
Fond du Lac	Judeen V. Damm (R)	Patricia Kraus (R)	Mary L. Karst (R)
Forest	Amy T. Krause (D)	Paul Aschenbrenner (D)	Penny Carter (D)
Grant	Louise F. Ketterer (R)	Marilyn Pierce (R)	Diane Perkins (R)
Green	Sherri Hawkins (R)	Cynthia A. Meudt (R)	Carol Thompson (R)
Green Lake	Kathleen A. Morris (R)	Leone Seaman (R)	Susan J. Krueger (R)
Iowa	Jolene M. Millard (R)	Dixie L. Edge (R)	Carolyn K. Olson (R)
Iron	Mark Beaupré (D)	Robert Traczyk (D)	Karen Ransanici (D)
Jackson	Carol Bue (D)	Shari Marg (R)	Claudia Singleton (D)
Jefferson	John E. Jensen (R)	Staci M. Hoffman (R)	Carla J. Robinson (R)
Juneau	Denise Giebel (R)	Christie L. Bender (R)	Louise Schulz (R)
Kenosha	Teri Jacobsen (D)	Louise Principe (D)	Rebecca Matoska-Mentink (D)
Kewaunee	Michelle M. Dax (R)	Janet L. Wolf (D)	Rebecca A. Deterville (D)
La Crosse	Donna M. Hanson (R)	Cheryl A. McBride (R)	Pamela Radtke (R)
Lafayette	Rebecca Taylor (R)	Joseph Boll (R)	Catherine McGowan (R)
Langlade	Ann Meyer (D)	Sandra M. Fischer (D)	Victoria Adamski (D)
Lincoln	Jan Lemmer (D)	Sarah Koss (R)	Cindy Kimmons (R)
Manitowoc	Cheryl M. Duchow (D)	Preston F. Jones (D)	Lynn Zigmunt (D)
Marathon	Lorraine I. Beyersdorff (R)	Michael J. Sydow (D)	Diane L. Sennholz (D)
Marinette	Cris Faucett (R)	Melanie I. Huempfner (R)	Linda L. Dumke-Marquardt (R)
Marquette	Diana Campbell (R)	Bette L. Krueger (R)	Shari Rudolph (R)
Menominee	Nanette Corn (D)	Nanette Corn (D)	Pamela Frechette (D)
Milwaukee	Daniel Diliberti (D)	John La Fave (D)	John Barrett (D)
Monroe	Annette M. Erickson (R)	John D. Burke (R)	Carol Thorsen (R)
Oconto	Victoria Coopman (R)	Loralee Lasley (R)	Michael C. Hodkiewicz (R)
Oneida	Kris Ostermann (D)	Thomas H. Leighton (R)	Kenneth J. Gardner (R)
Outagamie	Dina Mumford (R)	Janice Flenz (R)	Lonnie Wolf (R)
Ozaukee	Karen L. Makoutz (R)	Ronald A. Voigt (R)	Jeffrey S. Schmidt (R)
Pepin	Nancy Richardson (R)	Monica J. Bauer (R)	Audrey Lieffring (R)
Pierce	Phyllis J. Beastrom (D)	Vicki J. Nelson (R)	Peg M. Feuerhelm (D)
Polk	Amanda Nissen (D)	Laurie Anderson (D)	Lois Hoff (R)
Portage	Stephanie Stokes (D)	Cynthia A. Wisinski (D)	Bernadette Flatoff (D)
Price	Lynn M. Neeck (D)	Judith Chizek (D)	Chris Cress (D)
Racine	Elizabeth A. Majeski (R)	James A. Ladwig (R)	Roseanne Lee (D)
Richland	Julie Keller (R)	Susan Triggs (R)	Stacy Kleist (R)
Rock	Vicki Brown (D)	Randy Leyes (R)	Eldred Mielke (D)
Rusk	Joanne Phetteplace (R)	Linda Ann Effertz (D)	Renae Baxter (D)
St. Croix	Cheryl A. Slind (R)	Beth Pabst (D)	Lori Meyer (R)
Sauk	Elizabeth Geoghegan (R)	Brent Bailey (R)	Vicki Meister (R)
Sawyer	Dianne M. Ince (R)	Paula Chisser (R)	Ricki Briggs (R)
Shawano	Kay Schroeder (R)	Amy Dillenburg (R)	Susan M. Krueger (R)
Sheboygan	Laura Henning-Lorenz (D)	Ellen Schleicher (D)	Nan Todd (D)
Taylor	Deb Wiinamaki (R)	Marvel Lemke (D)	Margaret M. Gebauer (R)
Trempealeau	Laurie Halama (D)	Rose Ottum (D)	Angeline J. Sylla (R)
Vernon	Rachel Hanson (R)	Konna Spaeth (R)	Kathy Buros (R)
Vilas	Jerri Radtke (R)	Joan Hansen (R)	Jean Numrich (R)
Walworth	Kathy DuBois (R)	Connie Woolever (R)	Sheila Reiff (R)
Washburn	Janet L. Ullom (R)	Diane M. Poach (R)	Karen Nord (D)
Washington	Janice Gettelman (R)	Sharon Martin (R)	Kristine Deiss (R)
Waukesha	Pamela Reeves (R)	Jim Behrend (R)	Kathy Madden (R)
Waupaca	Clyde Tellock (R)	Michael Mazemke (R)	Terrie Tews-Liebe (R)
Waushara	Elaine Wedell (R)	Barbara Struzynski (R)	Jane Putskey (R)
Winnebago	Mary Krueger (R)	Julie Pagel (D)	Diane Fremgen (D)
Wood	Karen Kubisiak (D)	René Krause (D)	Cindy Joosten (R)

COUNTY OFFICERS IN WISCONSIN
June 30, 2009–Continued

County	District Attorney	Sheriff	Coroner/Medical Examiner
Adams	Mark Thibodeau (D)	Darrell Renner (D)	Terry Scheel (D)
Ashland	Sean P. Duffy (R)	John Kovach (D)	Barbara Beeksma (D)
Barron	Angela Beranek (D)	Chris Fitzgerald (D)	Tom Aydt (ME)
Bayfield	Craig Haukaas (R)	Robert Follis (D)	Gary Victorson (D)
Brown	John Zakowski (R)	Dennis Kocken (R)	Al Klimek (ME)
Buffalo	Thomas Clark (D)	Mike Schmidtknecht (R)	Peter Samb (R)
Burnett	William Norine (I)	Dean Roland (R)	Michael Maloney (ME)
Calumet	Kenneth Kratz (R)	Jerry Pagel (R)	Michael Klaeser (ME)
Chippewa	Jon M. Theisen (R)	James Kowalczyk (D)	Katherine Gerrits (D)
Clark	Darwin Zwieg (D)	Louis Rosandich (R)	Richard Schleifer (R)
Columbia	Jane E. Kohlwey (R)	Dennis Richards (R)	Angela Hinze (ME)
Crawford	Timothy Baxter (D)	Jerry Moran (D)	Joe Morovits (D)
Dane	Brian Blanchard (D)	David Mahoney (D)	John Stanley (D)
Dodge	William Bedker (R)	Todd Nehls (R)	Patrick Schoebel (ME)
Door	Raymond L. Pelrine (R)	Terry J. Vogel (R)	None
Douglas	Daniel Blank (D)	Thomas Dalbec (D)	Darrell Witt (ME)
Dunn	James M. Peterson (R)	Dennis Smith (D)	None
Eau Claire	Rich White (D)	Ron D. Cramer (R)	Thomas Thelen (ME)
Florence	Douglas Drexler (R)	Jeffery Rickaby (R)	Mary T. Johnson (R)
Fond du Lac	Daniel Kaminsky (R)	Mylan C. Fink, Jr. (R)	P. Douglas Kelley (ME)
Forest	Chuck Simono (D)	Keith VanCleve (D)	Traci England (ME)
Grant	Lisa A. Riniker (R)	Keith Govier (R)	Ronald A. Sturmer (R)
Green	Gary L. Luhman (R)	Randy Roderick (R)	Jan Perry (R)
Green Lake	Winn Collins (R)	Mark A. Podoll (R)	Darlene Strey (R)
Iowa	Larry Nelson (D)	Steven R. Michek (R)	William Finley (D)
Iron	Martin Lipske (D)	Robert Bruneau (D)	Diane Simonich (D)
Jackson	Gerald Fox (D)	Duane Waldera (D)	Michael Quinn (D)
Jefferson	Susan Happ (D)	Paul Milbrath (R)	Patrick J. Theder (R)
Juneau	Scott Southworth (R)	Brent H. Oleson (R)	Howard T. Fischer (R)
Kenosha	Robert Zapf (D)	David Beth (R)	Mark Witeck (ME)
Kewaunee	Andrew P. Naze (D)	Matthew J. Joski (R)	David G. Hudson (R)
La Crosse	Tim Gruenke (D)	Steven J. Helgeson (R)	John W. Steers (ME)
Lafayette	Charlotte Doherty (D)	Scott Pedley (R)	A. Virginia Douglas (D)
Langlade	Ralph M. Uttke (D)	William Greening (D)	Larry E. Shadick (R)
Lincoln	Don Dunphy (R)	Jeff Jaeger (R)	Paul Proulx (R)
Manitowoc	Mark Rohrer (D)	Robert Hermann (D)	Curtis Green (D)
Marathon	Jill Falstad (D)	Randy Hoenisch (D)	John Larson (ME)
Marinette	Allen R. Brey (D)	James J. Kanikula (R)	George F. Smith (R)
Marquette	Richard Dufour (R)	Kim Gaffney (R)	Thomas G. Wastart II (R)
Menominee	Gregory Parker (R)[3]	Robert Butch Summers (D)	Roderick Boivin (D)
Milwaukee	John Chisholm (D)	David Clarke, Jr. (D)	Christopher Happy (ME)
Monroe	Dan Cary (R)	Dennis A. Pedersen (R)	Toni Eddy (ME)
Oconto	Jay Conley (R)	Michael R. Jansen (R)	Al Klimek (ME)
Oneida	Michael H. Bloom (R)	Jeffrey Hoffman (D)	Traci England (ME)
Outagamie	Carrie Schneider (R)	Bradley Gehring (R)	Ruth Wulgaert (R)
Ozaukee	Adam Gerol (R)	Maury A. Straub (R)	John R. Holicek (R)
Pepin	Jon D. Seifert (D)	John Andrews (D)	Duane A. Sinz (D)
Pierce	John M. O'Boyle (D)	Nancy Hove (D)	Susan Dzubay (ME)
Polk	Daniel P. Steffen (D)	Timothy Moore (D)	Jonn Dinnies (ME)
Portage	Thomas Eagon (D)	John Charewicz (D)	Scott W. Rifleman (R)
Price	Mark T. Fuhr (D)	Wallace Krenzke (D)	James Dalbesio III (D)
Racine	Michael E. Nieskes (R)	Robert D. Carlson (D)	Thomas A. Terry (ME)
Richland	Wm. Andrew Sharp (R)	Darrell Berglin (R)	Ralph W. Shireman (R)
Rock	David O'Leary (D)	Robert Spoden (D)	Jenifer Keach (D)
Rusk	Kathleen Pakes (D)	David Kaminski (D)	Annette Grotzinger (I)
St. Croix	Eric Johnson (R)	Dennis Hillstead (R)	Casey Swetlik (ME)
Sauk	Patricia A. Barrett (R)	Randy Stammen (R)	Betty A. Hinze (R)
Sawyer	Thomas Van Roy (R)	James Meier (R)	John Ryan (R)
Shawano	Gregory Parker (R)[3]	Randall Wright (R)	Marcus Jesse (R)
Sheboygan	Joe DeCecco (D)	Michael Helmke (D)	David J. Leffin (D)
Taylor	Karl Kelz (R)	Bruce A. Daniels (D)	Scott Perrin (ME)
Trempealeau	Jeri Marsolek (D)	Richard A. Anderson (D)	Bonnie Kindschy (D)
Vernon	Timothy Gaskell (R)	Gene Cary (R)	Janet Reed (R)
Vilas	Albert Moustakis (R)	John Niebuhr (R)	Paul Tirpe (R)
Walworth	Phillip Koss (R)	David Graves (R)	John Griebel (R)
Washburn	J. Michael Bitney (R)	Terry C. Dryden (R)	Karen L. Baker (R)
Washington	Todd Martens (R)	Dale Schmidt (R)	Kelly McAndrews (ME)
Waukesha	Brad Schimel (R)	Daniel Trawicki (R)	Lynda Biedrzycki (ME)
Waupaca	John P. Snider (R)	Brad Hardel (R)	Barry Tomaras (R)
Waushara	Scott Blader (R)	David R. Peterson (R)	Roland Handel, Sr. (R)
Winnebago	Christian Gossett (R)	Michael Brooks (R)	Barry Busby (R)
Wood	vacancy	Thomas Reichert (D)	Garry Kronstedt (R)

COUNTY OFFICERS IN WISCONSIN
June 30, 2009–Continued

County	Surveyor[4]	County	Surveyor[4]
Adams	Gregory Rhinehart	Marathon	Chester Nowaczyk
Ashland	David Carlson	Marinette	None
Barron	Mark Netterlund	Marquette	Jerol Smart
Bayfield	None	Menominee	None
Brown	None	Milwaukee	None
Buffalo	None	Monroe	Gary Sime
Burnett	Jason Towne	Oconto	Mark Teuteberg[5]
Calumet	Peter Hatas	Oneida	None
Chippewa	Steven Johnson	Outagamie	James Hebert
Clark	Wade Pettit	Ozaukee	None
Columbia	Jim Grothman	Pepin	Ron Jasperson
Crawford	Rich Marx	Pierce	Bob Lannan
Dane	Dan Frick	Polk	Steve Geiger
Dodge	Jerry Thomasen	Portage	Joseph S. Glodowski
Door	None	Price	Alfred Schneider
Douglas	Ben Klitzke	Racine	None
Dunn	None	Richland	Michael Goebel
Eau Claire	Matt Janiak	Rock	Donald Barnes
Florence	None	Rusk	David Kaiser
Fond du Lac	Peter Kuen	St. Croix	Brian Halling
Forest	None	Sauk	Patrick Dederich
Grant	None	Sawyer	Daniel Ploeger
Green	None	Shawano	Van Horn & Van Horn LLC
Green Lake	Alan Shute	Sheboygan	Edgar Harvey, Jr.
Iowa	Bruce D. Bowden	Taylor	Robert Meyer
Iron	None	Trempealeau	Joe Nelson
Jackson	Tim Jeatran	Vernon	None
Jefferson	Thomas R. Wollin	Vilas	Thomas Boettcher
Juneau	Gary Dechant	Walworth	SEWRPC[6]
Kenosha	None	Washburn	Steven Waak
Kewaunee	None	Washington	Scott Schmidt
La Crosse	Bryan Meyer	Waukesha	None
Lafayette	Larry Schmit	Waupaca	Joseph Glodowski
Langlade	David Tlusty	Waushara	Michael Moe
Lincoln	Tony Dallman	Winnebago	None
Manitowoc	None	Wood	Kevin Boyer

Key: AC – Administrative Coordinator; CA – County Administrator; CE – County Executive; D – Democrat; I – Independent; R – Republican; ME – Medical Examiner.

Note: All officers are elected countywide with the exception of the county board chairperson, county administrator, administrative coordinator, and medical examiner, who are elected or appointed by the county board. Elected county officers serve 2-year terms, except county executives who serve 4-year terms. Beginning 2003, sheriffs serve 4-year terms per constitutional amendment ratified 11/3/98. Reflecting a constitutional amendment ratified 4/5/2005, beginning 2006, clerks of circuit court and coroners serve 4-year terms; beginning 2008, all remaining county officers serve 4-year terms.

[1]2005 Wisconsin Act 100 allowed counties, by petition and referendum, to decrease the size of their county board once prior to November 15, 2010, pursuant to Section 59.10 (3)(cm), Wisconsin Statutes.

[2]Counties with a population of 500,000 or more are statutorily required to establish the office of county executive. Smaller counties may establish the office of county executive or name a county administrator. In counties without a county executive or county administrator, the county board must designate an elected or appointed official to serve as administrative coordinator.

[3]Menominee and Shawano County share a District Attorney.

[4]County boards are permitted to designate any registered land surveyor to perform the duties of the county surveyor.

[5]Surveyor/Land Information Systems Administrator.

[6]Southeastern Wisconsin Regional Planning Commission.

Source: Data collected from county clerks by Wisconsin Legislative Reference Bureau, February 2009, and governor's appointment notices.

WISCONSIN CITIES
January 1, 2008

City (Year Incorporated)[1]	County	2000 Census	2008 Estimate	Percent Change	2000 Nonwhite[5]	2000 Hispanic or Latino Origin[6]
First Class Cities (150,000 or more) — 1 City						
Milwaukee (1846)	Milwaukee, Washington, Waukesha	596,974	590,870	−1.0	254,339	71,646
Second Class Cities (39,000 to 149,999) — 16 Cities						
Appleton (1857)	Calumet, Outagamie, Winnebago	70,087	72,297	3.2	5,063	1,775
Brookfield (1954)	Waukesha	38,649	39,780	2.9	2,145	453
Eau Claire (1872)[2]	Chippewa, Eau Claire	61,704	65,362	5.9	3,777	619
Fond du Lac (1852)[2]	Fond du Lac	42,203	43,460	3.0	2,065	1,232
Green Bay (1854)	Brown	102,767	103,950	1.2	9,885	7,294
Janesville (1853)[2]	Rock	60,200	63,540	5.5	2,089	1,569
Kenosha (1850)[3]	Kenosha	90,352	95,910	6.2	9,663	9,003
La Crosse (1856)	La Crosse	51,818	51,840	0.0	4,068	592
Madison (1856)	Dane	208,054	226,650	8.9	29,033	8,512
Oshkosh (1853)[2]	Winnebago	62,916	65,920	4.8	4,105	1,062
Racine (1848)[3]	Racine	81,855	80,320	−1.9	18,471	11,422
Sheboygan (1853)	Sheboygan	50,792	50,580	−0.4	4,569	3,034
Superior (1858)	Douglas	27,368	27,170	−0.7	1,465	226
Waukesha (1895)[3]	Waukesha	64,825	68,030	4.9	3,071	5,563
Wauwatosa (1897)[3]	Milwaukee	47,271	45,880	−2.9	2,523	813
West Allis (1906)[3]	Milwaukee	61,254	60,370	−1.4	2,667	2,155
Third Class Cities (10,000 to 38,999) — 30 Cities						
Baraboo (1882)[3]	Sauk	10,711	11,755	9.7	243	168
Beloit (1857)[2]	Rock	35,775	37,110	3.7	6,786	3,257
Cedarburg (1885)[3]	Ozaukee	11,102	11,435	3.0	185	94
Chippewa Falls (1869)[3]	Chippewa	12,925	13,410	3.8	264	82
Cudahy (1906)	Milwaukee	18,429	18,620	1.0	743	872
De Pere (1883)[3]	Brown	20,559	22,645	10.1	619	202
Franklin (1956)	Milwaukee	29,494	33,550	13.8	2,427	780
Glendale (1950)[3]	Milwaukee	13,367	12,990	−2.8	1,672	236
Greenfield (1957)	Milwaukee	35,476	36,270	2.2	1,588	1,376
Hartford (1883)[3]	Dodge, Washington	10,905	13,700	25.6	188	326
Kaukauna (1885)	Outagamie	12,983	14,925	15.0	537	103
Manitowoc (1870)	Manitowoc	34,053	34,670	1.8	1,941	859
Marinette (1887)	Marinette	11,749	11,365	−3.3	252	123
Marshfield (1883)[3]	Marathon, Wood	18,800	19,454	3.5	496	146
Menasha (1874)	Calumet, Winnebago	16,331	17,408	6.6	570	590
Middleton (1963)[3]	Dane	15,770	16,960	7.5	1,018	444
Muskego (1964)[3]	Waukesha	21,397	23,075	7.8	306	281
Neenah (1873)	Winnebago	24,507	25,560	4.3	717	495
New Berlin (1959)	Waukesha	38,220	39,500	3.3	1,360	595
Oak Creek (1955)[3]	Milwaukee	28,456	32,470	14.1	1,675	1,267
Oconomowoc (1875)[3]	Waukesha	12,382	14,300	15.5	203	204
Pewaukee (1999)[3]	Waukesha	11,783	12,645	7.3	261	153
River Falls (1875)[3]	Pierce, St. Croix	12,560	14,228	13.3	378	119
Stevens Point (1858)	Portage	24,551	26,050	6.1	1,677	395
Sun Prairie (1958)[3]	Dane	20,369	25,810	26.7	1,243	555
Two Rivers (1878)[2]	Manitowoc	12,639	12,540	−0.8	458	170
Watertown (1853)	Dodge, Jefferson	21,598	23,163	7.2	409	1,067
Wausau (1872)	Marathon	38,428	40,360	5.0	5,226	398
West Bend (1885)[3]	Washington	28,152	30,320	7.7	554	519
Wisconsin Rapids (1869)	Wood	18,435	18,480	0.2	998	242
Fourth Class Cities (Under 10,000) — 143 Cities						
Abbotsford (1965)	Clark, Marathon	1,956	1,982	1.3	15	39
Adams (1926)[3]	Adams	1,831	1,879	2.6	30	37
Algoma (1879)[3]	Kewaunee	3,357	3,372	0.4	29	33
Alma (1885)	Buffalo	942	934	−0.8	26	8
Altoona (1887)[3]	Eau Claire	6,698	6,793	1.4	245	49
Amery (1919)[3]	Polk	2,845	2,919	2.6	49	27
Antigo (1885)[3]	Langlade	8,560	8,637	0.9	203	103
Arcadia (1925)	Trempealeau	2,402	2,416	0.6	21	74
Ashland (1887)[3]	Ashland, Bayfield	8,620	8,508	−1.3	779	118
Augusta (1885)	Eau Claire	1,460	1,476	1.1	46	19
Barron (1887)	Barron	3,248	3,321	2.2	60	61
Bayfield (1913)	Bayfield	611	616	0.8	139	3
Beaver Dam (1856)	Dodge	15,169	15,740	3.8	292	640

WISCONSIN CITIES
January 1, 2008–Continued

City (Year Incorporated)[1]	County	Population[4]				
		2000 Census	2008 Estimate	Percent Change	2000 Nonwhite[5]	2000 Hispanic or Latino Origin[6]
Berlin (1857)[3]	Green Lake, Waushara	5,305	5,302	−0.1	95	242
Black River Falls (1883). .	Jackson.	3,618	3,583	−1.0	214	42
Blair (1949)	Trempealeau	1,273	1,292	1.5	9	17
Bloomer (1920)	Chippewa	3,347	3,473	3.8	29	11
Boscobel (1873)[3].	Grant	3,047	3,334	9.4	146	36
Brillion (1944)[3]	Calumet	2,937	2,989	1.8	34	15
Brodhead (1891).	Green, Rock	3,180	3,233	1.7	44	31
Buffalo City (1859) . . .	Buffalo	1,040	1,055	1.4	14	6
Burlington (1900)[3]. . . .	Racine, Walworth	9,936	10,490	5.6	177	462
Chetek (1891)	Barron	2,180	2,259	3.6	24	21
Chilton (1877)	Calumet	3,708	3,776	1.8	46	32
Clintonville (1887)[3] . . .	Waupaca	4,736	4,641	−2.0	82	102
Colby (1891).	Clark, Marathon	1,616	1,751	8.4	25	62
Columbus (1874)[3]	Columbia, Dodge	4,479	4,866	8.6	63	44
Cornell (1956)[3].	Chippewa	1,466	1,449	−1.2	20	5
Crandon (1898)	Forest.	1,961	1,984	1.2	165	18
Cuba City (1925).	Grant, Lafayette	2,156	2,126	−1.4	10	2
Cumberland (1885) . . .	Barron	2,280	2,399	5.2	53	17
Darlington (1877)	Lafayette	2,418	2,406	−0.5	15	27
Delafield (1959)[3].	Waukesha	6,472	6,934	7.1	109	95
Delavan (1897)[3]	Walworth.	7,956	8,440	6.1	271	1,690
Dodgeville (1889)	Iowa	4,220	4,607	9.2	75	18
Durand (1887)[3].	Pepin	1,968	1,962	−0.3	19	4
Eagle River (1937)[3] . . .	Vilas	1,443	1,641	13.7	55	12
Edgerton (1883)[3]	Dane, Rock.	4,898	5,312	8.5	104	188
Elkhorn (1897)[3]	Walworth.	7,305	8,953	22.6	140	448
Elroy (1885)[3].	Juneau	1,578	1,541	−2.3	16	20
Evansville (1896)[3]	Rock	4,039	4,947	22.5	62	72
Fennimore (1919)	Grant	2,387	2,335	−2.2	12	18
Fitchburg (1983)[3]	Dane	20,501	23,420	14.2	2,863	1,329
Fort Atkinson (1878)[2] . .	Jefferson.	11,621	12,130	4.4	209	508
Fountain City (1889). . .	Buffalo	983	1,011	2.8	5	1
Fox Lake (1938)[3].	Dodge	1,454	1,509	3.8	24	51
Galesville (1942)	Trempealeau	1,427	1,479	3.6	12	6
Gillett (1944).	Oconto	1,262	1,214	−3.8	34	11
Glenwood City (1895). . .	St. Croix	1,183	1,218	3.0	11	2
Green Lake (1962).	Green Lake.	1,100	1,160	5.5	9	10
Greenwood (1891).	Clark	1,079	1,077	−0.2	5	12
Hayward (1915).	Sawyer	2,129	2,321	9.0	216	18
Hillsboro (1885)[3].	Vernon	1,302	1,310	0.6	8	9
Horicon (1897).	Dodge	3,775	3,702	−1.9	49	79
Hudson (1857)[3]	St. Croix	8,775	11,865	35.2	151	91
Hurley (1918)	Iron.	1,818	1,756	−3.4	42	16
Independence (1942) . . .	Trempealeau	1,244	1,257	1.0	7	20
Jefferson (1878)[3]	Jefferson.	7,208	7,777	7.9	154	498
Juneau (1887)	Dodge	2,485	2,686	8.1	19	63
Kewaunee (1883)[3].	Kewaunee	2,806	2,906	3.6	43	16
Kiel (1920)[3]	Calumet, Manitowoc.	3,450	3,658	6.0	37	25
Ladysmith (1905)[3]. . . .	Rusk	3,932	3,648	−7.2	135	30
Lake Geneva (1883)[3]. . .	Walworth.	7,148	7,661	7.2	186	1,054
Lake Mills (1905)[2]	Jefferson	4,843	5,389	11.3	83	113
Lancaster (1878)[3]	Grant	4,070	4,018	−1.3	27	17
Lodi (1941)	Columbia.	2,882	3,007	4.3	32	29
Loyal (1948)	Clark	1,308	1,276	−2.4	14	10
Manawa (1954)	Waupaca	1,330	1,313	−1.3	12	18
Marion (1898)	Shawano, Waupaca	1,297	1,241	−4.3	8	1
Markesan (1959).	Green Lake.	1,396	1,357	−2.8	6	44
Mauston (1883)[3]	Juneau	3,740	4,293	14.8	100	79

WISCONSIN CITIES
January 1, 2008–Continued

		Population[4]				
City (Year Incorporated)[1]	County	2000 Census	2008 Estimate	Percent Change	2000 Nonwhite[5]	2000 Hispanic or Latino Origin[6]
Mayville (1885)	Dodge	4,902	5,242	6.9	40	71
Medford (1889)[3]	Taylor	4,350	4,275	−1.7	55	25
Mellen (1907)	Ashland	845	799	−5.4	24	8
Menomonie (1882)[3]	Dunn	14,937	15,950	6.8	828	170
Mequon (1957)[3]	Ozaukee	22,643	23,670	4.5	1,202	261
Merrill (1883)[3]	Lincoln	10,146	10,130	−0.2	173	104
Milton (1969)[3]	Rock	5,132	5,667	10.4	64	47
Mineral Point (1857)	Iowa	2,617	2,653	1.4	24	11
Mondovi (1889)[3]	Buffalo	2,634	2,706	2.7	33	12
Monona (1969)[3]	Dane	8,018	8,194	2.2	384	256
Monroe (1882)[3]	Green	10,843	10,965	1.1	168	158
Montello (1938)	Marquette	1,397	1,479	5.9	34	33
Montreal (1924)	Iron	838	834	−0.5	10	6
Mosinee (1931)[3]	Marathon	4,063	4,220	3.9	35	28
Neillsville (1882)	Clark	2,731	2,648	−3.0	81	26
Nekoosa (1926)	Wood	2,590	2,620	1.2	52	47
New Holstein (1926)	Calumet	3,301	3,347	1.4	38	19
New Lisbon (1889)[3]	Juneau	1,436	2,381	65.8	28	20
New London (1877)[3]	Outagamie, Waupaca	7,085	7,204	1.7	135	174
New Richmond (1885)[3]	St. Croix	6,310	7,981	26.5	93	49
Niagara (1992)[3]	Marinette	1,880	1,831	−2.6	9	14
Oconto (1869)[3]	Oconto	4,708	4,756	1.0	89	37
Oconto Falls (1919)[3]	Oconto	2,843	2,917	2.6	49	12
Omro (1944)[3]	Winnebago	3,177	3,421	7.7	32	88
Onalaska (1887)	La Crosse	14,839	16,660	12.3	658	141
Osseo (1941)	Trempealeau	1,669	1,660	−0.5	12	6
Owen (1925)	Clark	936	920	−1.7	12	4
Park Falls (1912)	Price	2,793	2,617	−6.3	53	30
Peshtigo (1903)	Marinette	3,474	3,496	0.6	61	25
Phillips (1891)	Price	1,675	1,625	−3.0	49	6
Pittsville (1887)	Wood	866	908	4.8	8	2
Platteville (1876)[2]	Grant	9,989	10,575	5.9	348	88
Plymouth (1877)	Sheboygan	7,781	8,420	8.2	95	86
Port Washington (1882)[3]	Ozaukee	10,467	11,185	6.9	243	168
Portage (1854)[3]	Columbia	9,728	10,120	4.0	575	330
Prairie du Chien (1872)[3]	Crawford	6,018	6,045	0.4	287	53
Prescott (1857)[3]	Pierce	3,764	4,056	7.8	56	46
Princeton (1920)[3]	Green Lake	1,504	1,462	−2.8	16	12
Reedsburg (1887)[3]	Sauk	7,827	9,118	16.5	135	124
Rhinelander (1894)[3]	Oneida	7,735	8,223	6.3	215	56
Rice Lake (1887)[3]	Barron	8,312	8,664	4.2	187	125
Richland Center (1887)[3]	Richland	5,114	5,167	1.0	72	47
Ripon (1858)[3]	Fond du Lac	7,450	7,659	2.8	88	151
St. Croix Falls (1958)[3]	Polk	2,033	2,184	7.4	19	27
St. Francis (1951)[3]	Milwaukee	8,662	8,952	3.3	356	392
Schofield (1951)	Marathon	2,117	2,310	9.1	76	28
Seymour (1879)	Outagamie	3,335	3,463	3.8	126	40
Shawano (1874)[3]	Shawano	8,298	8,754	5.5	818	134
Sheboygan Falls (1913)	Sheboygan	6,772	7,501	10.8	108	58
Shell Lake (1961)[3]	Washburn	1,309	1,392	6.3	16	13
Shullsburg (1889)	Lafayette	1,246	1,205	−3.3	6	0
South Milwaukee (1897)[3]	Milwaukee	21,256	21,310	0.3	722	852
Sparta (1883)[3]	Monroe	8,648	9,198	6.4	196	157
Spooner (1909)[3]	Washburn	2,653	2,684	1.2	85	32
Stanley (1898)	Chippewa, Clark	1,898	3,381	78.1	16	24
Stoughton (1882)	Dane	12,354	12,865	4.1	347	153
Sturgeon Bay (1883)[3]	Door	9,437	9,778	3.6	195	121
Thorp (1948)[3]	Clark	1,536	1,535	−0.1	7	9
Tomah (1883)[3]	Monroe	8,419	9,075	7.8	368	119
Tomahawk (1891)	Lincoln	3,770	3,829	1.6	67	29
Verona (1977)[3]	Dane	7,052	10,240	45.2	161	50
Viroqua (1885)[3]	Vernon	4,335	4,404	1.6	48	30

WISCONSIN CITIES
January 1, 2008–Continued

		Population[4]				
City (Year Incorporated)[1]	County	2000 Census	2008 Estimate	Percent Change	2000 Nonwhite[5]	2000 Hispanic or Latino Origin[6]
Washburn (1904)[3] . . . . . Bayfield		2,280	2,247	–1.4	176	15
Waterloo (1962) . . . . Jefferson		3,259	3,352	2.9	50	240
Waupaca (1875)[3] . . . . . . Waupaca		5,676	6,028	6.2	113	194
Waupun (1878)[3] . . . . . . Dodge, Fond du Lac		10,944	11,034	0.8	1,427	304
Wautoma (1901) . . . . Waushara.		1,998	2,101	5.2	58	144
Westby (1920) . . . . Vernon		2,045	2,191	7.1	6	19
Weyauwega (1939)[3] . . . . Waupaca		1,806	1,885	4.4	31	17
Whitehall (1941)[3] . . . . . Trempealeau		1,651	1,666	0.9	5	5
Whitewater (1885)[2] . . . . Jefferson, Walworth		13,437	14,110	5.0	632	873
Wisconsin Dells (1925) . . Adams, Columbia, Juneau, Sauk . .		2,418	2,474	2.3	47	41

Note: A city is not automatically reclassified based on changes in population but must take action to initiate a reclassification. Under Section 62.05(2), Wisconsin Statutes, to change from one class to another a city must: 1) meet the required population size according to the last federal census; 2) fulfill required governmental changes; and 3) publish a mayoral proclamation.

[1] There are 190 cities in Wisconsin as of January 1, 2008.

[2] One of 10 cities with a city manager.

[3] One of 95 cities with a city administrator holding a full-time or combined position.

[4] Population estimates are based on the corrected totals. Race and ethnicity data have not been adjusted.

[5] In the 2000 U.S. Census, respondents were allowed to choose more than one race. The column "nonwhite" includes all who chose at least one race other than white.

[6] "Hispanic or Latino Origin" represents ethnicity and includes people of Cuban, Mexican, Puerto Rican, South or Central American, or other Spanish culture or origin, regardless of race.

Sources: Wisconsin Department of Administration, Demographic Services Center, *Municipality Final 2008 Population Estimates, January 1, 2008,* March 2009; League of Wisconsin Municipalities, *2008 Directory of Wisconsin City and Village Officials,* July 2008; and data compiled by Wisconsin Legislative Reference Bureau.

WISCONSIN VILLAGES
January 1, 2008

			Population			
Village (Year Incorporated)[1]	County	2000 Census	2008 Final Estimate	Percent Change	2000 Nonwhite	2000 Hispanic or Latino Origin[2]
Adell (1918).	Sheboygan	517	517	0.0%	11	12
Albany (1883)	Green.	1,191	1,146	3.8	12	14
Allouez (1986)[3]	Brown	15,443	15,470	0.2	1,105	199
Alma Center (1902)	Jackson.	446	457	2.5	5	7
Almena (1945).	Barron	720	751	4.3	15	11
Almond (1905).	Portage.	459	431	−6.1	2	33
Amherst (1899)	Portage.	964	1,052	9.1	8	5
Amherst Junction (1912).	Portage.	305	339	11.1	0	0
Aniwa (1899)	Shawano	272	268	−1.5	8	3
Arena (1923).	Iowa	685	845	23.4	10	5
Argyle (1903)	Lafayette.	823	815	−1.0	1	6
Arlington (1945)[3]	Columbia.	484	633	30.8	2	3
Arpin (1978)	Wood	337	332	1.5	4	4
Ashwaubenon (1977)[3]	Brown	17,634	17,730	0.5	763	202
Athens (1901)	Marathon.	1,095	1,120	2.3	8	23
Auburndale (1881).	Wood	738	773	4.7	0	0
Avoca (1870).	Iowa	608	617	1.5	10	3
Bagley (1919).	Grant	339	340	0.3	9	5
Baldwin (1875)[3]	St. Croix	2,667	3,568	33.8	38	11
Balsam Lake (1905)	Polk	950	1,075	13.2	37	4
Bangor (1899)	La Crosse	1,400	1,420	1.4	25	9
Barneveld (1906)	Iowa	1,088	1,249	14.8	14	1
Bay City (1909)	Pierce.	491	491	0.0	4	0
Bayside (1953)[4]	Milwaukee, Ozaukee. .	4,518	4,172	−7.7	241	77
Bear Creek (1902)	Outagamie	415	409	−1.4	4	45
Belgium (1922)	Ozaukee	1,678	2,053	22.3	31	69
Bell Center (1901)	Crawford.	116	113	−2.6	1	0
Belleville (1892)[3]	Dane, Green	1,908	2,202	15.4	27	15
Bellevue (2003)[3, 5]	Brown	11,828	14,965	26.5	374	310
Belmont (1894)	Lafayette.	871	906	4.0	3	1
Benton (1892)	Lafayette.	976	1,002	2.7	16	0
Big Bend (1928)	Waukesha	1,278	1,313	2.7	26	23
Big Falls (1925)	Waupaca	85	82	−3.5	1	0
Birchwood (1921)	Washburn	518	561	8.3	15	12
Birnamwood (1895)	Marathon, Shawano . .	795	813	2.3	19	1
Biron (1910)	Wood	915	868	−5.1	18	16
Black Creek (1904)	Outagamie	1,192	1,265	6.1	20	13
Black Earth (1901).	Dane	1,320	1,341	1.6	33	16
Blanchardville (1890)	Iowa, Lafayette	806	786	−2.5	5	3
Bloomington (1880)	Grant	701	678	−3.3	2	0
Blue Mounds (1912)	Dane	708	755	6.6	12	7
Blue River (1916)	Grant	429	418	−2.6	1	1
Boaz (1939)	Richland	137	133	−2.9	1	0
Bonduel (1916)	Shawano	1,416	1,436	1.4	25	27
Bowler (1923)	Shawano	343	341	−0.6	75	0
Boyceville (1922)	Dunn	1,043	1,088	4.3	15	4
Boyd (1891)	Chippewa	680	625	−8.1	2	1
Brandon (1881)	Fond du Lac	912	914	0.2	1	7
Brokaw (1903).	Marathon.	107	204	90.7	1	2
Brooklyn (1905)	Dane, Green	916	1,278	39.5	12	13
Brown Deer (1955)[4]	Milwaukee	12,170	11,705	−3.8	2,088	260
Brownsville (1952)	Dodge	570	568	−0.4	3	2
Browntown (1890).	Green.	252	263	4.4	0	6
Bruce (1901).	Rusk	787	758	−3.7	7	2
Butler (1913)[3]	Waukesha	1,881	1,799	−4.4	48	16
Butternut (1903)	Ashland	407	393	−3.4	7	1
Cadott (1895)	Chippewa	1,345	1,391	3.4	15	2
Caledonia (2005)[3, 5]	Racine	23,614	25,110	6.3	1,086	736
Cambria (1866)	Columbia.	792	781	−1.4	10	51
Cambridge (1891)	Dane, Jefferson. . . .	1,101	1,271	15.4	10	11
Cameron (1894)	Barron	1,546	1,749	13.1	28	28
Camp Douglas (1893)	Juneau.	592	550	−7.1	10	10
Campbellsport (1902)	Fond du Lac	1,913	1,995	4.3	20	8
Cascade (1914).	Sheboygan	681	707	3.8	8	11
Casco (1920).	Kewaunee	572	580	1.4	9	5
Cashton (1901).	Monroe.	1,005	1,081	7.6	6	16
Cassville (1882)[4].	Grant	1,085	1,034	−4.7	8	4
Catawba (1922)	Price	149	133	−10.7	1	0
Cazenovia (1902)	Richland, Sauk. . . .	326	356	9.2	2	1
Cecil (1905)	Shawano	466	572	22.7	21	3
Cedar Grove (1899)	Sheboygan	1,887	2,052	8.7	24	50
Centuria (1904)	Polk	865	939	8.6	25	13
Chaseburg (1922)	Vernon	306	294	−3.9	0	0
Chenequa (1928)[3]	Waukesha	583	592	1.5	13	5
Clayton (1909).	Polk	507	572	12.8	11	0
Clear Lake (1894)	Polk	1,051	1,143	8.8	5	33
Cleveland (1958).	Manitowoc	1,361	1,415	4.0	16	20
Clinton (1882)[3].	Rock	2,162	2,218	2.6	38	69

WISCONSIN VILLAGES
January 1, 2008–Continued

Village (Year Incorporated)[1]	County	2000 Census	2008 Final Estimate	Percent Change	2000 Nonwhite	2000 Hispanic or Latino Origin[2]
Clyman (1924)	Dodge	388	385	–0.8	10	18
Cobb (1902)	Iowa	442	441	–0.2	3	2
Cochrane (1910)	Buffalo	435	416	–4.4	2	4
Coleman (1903)	Marinette	716	700	–2.2	3	2
Colfax (1904)	Dunn	1,136	1,166	2.6	9	15
Coloma (1939)	Waushara	461	475	3.0	1	14
Combined Locks (1920)[3]	Outagamie	2,422	3,036	25.4	29	30
Conrath (1915)	Rusk	98	105	7.1	3	0
Coon Valley (1907)	Vernon	714	717	0.4	3	2
Cottage Grove (1924)[3]	Dane	4,059	5,525	36.1	150	73
Couderay (1922)	Sawyer	96	95	–1.0	19	1
Crivitz (1974)	Marinette	998	1,035	3.7	21	11
Cross Plains (1920)[3]	Dane	3,084	3,486	13.0	31	13
Curtiss (1917)	Clark	198	207	4.5	3	68
Dallas (1903)	Barron	356	369	3.7	8	5
Dane (1899)	Dane	799	958	19.9	29	15
Darien (1951)	Walworth	1,572	1,640	4.3	27	222
De Soto (1886)	Crawford, Vernon	366	440	20.2	17	6
Deer Park (1913)	St. Croix	227	222	–2.2	0	0
Deerfield (1891)[3]	Dane	1,971	2,240	13.6	87	43
DeForest (1903)[3]	Dane	7,368	8,492	15.3	272	161
Denmark (1915)[3]	Brown	1,958	2,132	8.9	41	6
Dickeyville (1947)	Grant	1,043	1,067	2.3	5	3
Dorchester (1901)	Clark, Marathon	827	858	3.7	8	19
Dousman (1917)	Waukesha	1,584	1,873	18.2	32	37
Downing (1909)	Dunn	257	249	–3.1	4	3
Doylestown (1907)	Columbia	328	342	4.3	3	14
Dresser (1919)	Polk	732	875	19.5	12	4
Eagle (1899)	Waukesha	1,707	1,846	8.1	26	52
East Troy (1900)[3]	Walworth	3,564	4,172	17.1	55	105
Eastman (1909)	Crawford	437	450	3.0	4	8
Eden (1912)	Fond du Lac	687	783	14.0	1	29
Edgar (1898)[3]	Marathon	1,386	1,491	7.6	13	2
Egg Harbor (1964)[3]	Door	250	279	11.6	3	0
Eland (1905)	Shawano	251	230	–8.4	17	3
Elderon (1917)	Marathon	189	181	–4.2	0	9
Eleva (1902)	Trempealeau	635	658	3.6	10	0
Elk Mound (1909)	Dunn	785	809	3.1	26	5
Elkhart Lake (1894)	Sheboygan	1,021	1,207	18.2	4	11
Ellsworth (1887)	Pierce	2,909	3,179	9.3	28	33
Elm Grove (1955)[4]	Waukesha	6,249	6,146	–1.6	153	75
Elmwood (1905)	Pierce	841	832	–1.1	6	12
Elmwood Park (1960)	Racine	474	439	–7.4	16	6
Embarrass (1895)	Waupaca	487	467	–4.1	0	3
Endeavor (1946)	Marquette	440	452	2.7	11	3
Ephraim (1919)[3]	Door	353	356	0.8	3	1
Ettrick (1948)	Trempealeau	521	516	–1.0	7	0
Exeland (1920)	Sawyer	212	208	–1.9	23	3
Fairchild (1880)	Eau Claire	564	524	–7.1	8	10
Fairwater (1921)	Fond du Lac	350	364	4.0	2	0
Fall Creek (1906)	Eau Claire	1,236	1,322	7.0	16	0
Fall River (1903)	Columbia	1,097	1,515	38.1	15	6
Fenwood (1904)	Marathon	174	153	–12.1	0	0
Ferryville (1912)	Crawford	174	186	6.9	2	0
Fontana-on-Geneva Lake (1924)[3]	Walworth	1,754	1,874	6.8	23	19
Footville (1918)	Rock	788	763	–3.2	12	1
Forestville (1960)	Door	429	426	–0.7	4	0
Fox Point (1926)[4]	Milwaukee	7,012	6,818	–2.8	297	74
Francis Creek (1960)	Manitowoc	681	699	2.6	0	6
Frederic (1903)[3]	Polk	1,262	1,239	–1.8	26	5
Fredonia (1922)	Ozaukee	1,934	2,143	10.8	48	27
Fremont (1882)	Waupaca	666	725	8.9	7	7
Friendship (1907)	Adams	781	796	1.9	36	8
Friesland (1946)	Columbia	298	310	4.0	2	0
Gays Mills (1900)[3]	Crawford	625	611	–2.2	2	3
Genoa (1935)	Vernon	263	252	–4.2	5	0
Genoa City (1901)	Kenosha, Walworth	1,949	2,766	41.9	38	63
Germantown (1927)[3]	Washington	18,260	19,895	9.0	680	205
Gilman (1914)	Taylor	474	454	–4.2	3	8
Glen Flora (1915)	Rusk	93	94	1.1	4	0
Glenbeulah (1913)	Sheboygan	378	438	15.9	1	2
Grafton (1896)[3]	Ozaukee	10,464	11,450	9.4	193	165
Granton (1916)	Clark	406	396	–2.5	8	1
Grantsburg (1887)	Burnett	1,369	1,460	6.6	39	16
Gratiot (1891)	Lafayette	252	237	–6.0	2	0
Greendale (1939)[4]	Milwaukee	14,405	13,995	–2.8	458	340

WISCONSIN VILLAGES
January 1, 2008–Continued

Village (Year Incorporated)[1]	County	2000 Census	2008 Final Estimate	Percent Change	2000 Nonwhite	2000 Hispanic or Latino Origin[2]
Gresham (1908)	Shawano	575	593	3.1	169	12
Hales Corners (1952)[3]	Milwaukee	7,765	7,646	−1.5	162	162
Hammond (1880)	St. Croix	1,153	1,638	42.1	14	3
Hancock (1902)	Waushara	463	443	−4.3	15	40
Hartland (1891)[3]	Waukesha	7,905	8,486	7.3	132	119
Hatley (1912)	Marathon	476	514	8.0	12	0
Haugen (1918)	Barron	287	296	3.1	0	2
Hawkins (1922)	Rusk	317	333	5.0	6	0
Hazel Green (1867)	Grant, Lafayette	1,183	1,186	0.3	5	4
Hewitt (1973)	Wood	670	764	14.0	2	2
Highland (1873)	Iowa	855	859	0.5	0	3
Hilbert (1898)	Calumet	1,089	1,109	1.8	11	16
Hixton (1920)	Jackson	446	455	2.0	6	1
Hobart (2003)[3,5]	Brown	5,090	5,875	15.4	956	44
Hollandale (1910)	Iowa	283	279	−1.4	1	1
Holmen (1946)[3]	La Crosse	6,200	7,899	27.4	265	56
Hortonville (1894)[3]	Outagamie	2,357	2,723	15.5	66	15
Howard (1959)[3]	Brown, Outagamie	13,546	15,965	17.9	461	147
Howards Grove (1967)	Sheboygan	2,792	3,095	10.9	24	21
Hustisford (1870)	Dodge	1,135	1,151	1.4	5	14
Hustler (1914)	Juneau	113	116	2.7	0	0
Ingram (1907)	Rusk	76	72	−5.3	0	0
Iola (1892)	Waupaca	1,298	1,352	4.2	17	17
Iron Ridge (1913)	Dodge	998	1,023	2.5	5	10
Ironton (1914)	Sauk	250	248	−0.8	6	4
Jackson (1912)[3]	Washington	4,938	6,309	27.8	51	61
Johnson Creek (1903)[3]	Jefferson	1,581	2,122	34.2	30	63
Junction City (1911)	Portage	440	429	−2.5	12	19
Kekoskee (1958)	Dodge	169	168	−0.6	9	3
Kellnersville (1971)	Manitowoc	374	361	−3.5	5	0
Kendall (1894)	Monroe	482	475	−1.5	1	3
Kennan (1903)	Price	171	167	−2.3	0	3
Kewaskum (1895)[3]	Fond du Lac, Washington . .	3,277	4,209	28.4	52	30
Kimberly (1910)[3]	Outagamie	6,146	6,451	5.0	138	46
Kingston (1923)	Green Lake	288	294	2.1	4	1
Knapp (1905)	Dunn	421	462	9.7	4	4
Kohler (1912)	Sheboygan	1,926	2,045	6.2	47	16
Kronenwetter (2002)[3,5]	Marathon	5,369	6,378	18.8	86	28
La Farge (1899)	Vernon	775	783	1.0	16	5
La Valle (1883)	Sauk	326	324	−0.6	1	7
Lac La Belle (1931)	Waukesha	329	338	2.7	0	1
Lake Delton (1954)	Sauk	1,982	2,770	39.8	79	33
Lake Hallie (2003)[5]	Chippewa	4,703	6,320	34.4	117	42
Lake Nebagamon (1907)	Douglas	1,015	1,045	3.0	13	8
Lannon (1930)	Waukesha	1,009	1,055	4.6	18	16
Lena (1921)	Oconto	529	505	−4.5	3	5
Lime Ridge (1910)	Sauk	169	163	−3.6	0	1
Linden (1900)	Iowa	615	604	−1.8	6	0
Little Chute (1899)[3]	Outagamie	10,476	11,035	5.3	203	175
Livingston (1914)	Grant, Iowa	597	592	−0.8	0	2
Loganville (1917)	Sauk	276	273	−1.1	0	1
Lohrville (1910)	Waushara	408	413	1.2	8	9
Lomira (1899)	Dodge	2,233	2,488	11.4	21	57
Lone Rock (1886)	Richland	929	907	−2.4	12	14
Lowell (1894)	Dodge	366	371	1.4	8	12
Lublin (1915)	Taylor	110	100	−9.1	0	0
Luck (1905)	Polk	1,210	1,226	1.3	20	12
Luxemburg (1908)	Kewaunee	1,935	2,354	21.7	19	9
Lyndon Station (1903)	Juneau	458	469	2.4	17	7
Lynxville (1899)	Crawford	176	180	2.3	2	3
Maiden Rock (1887)	Pierce	121	123	1.7	1	1
Maple Bluff (1930)[3]	Dane	1,358	1,378	1.5	31	9
Marathon City (1884)[3]	Marathon	1,640	1,626	−0.9	24	5
Maribel (1963)	Manitowoc	284	277	−2.5	9	1
Marquette (1958)	Green Lake	169	163	−3.6	1	1
Marshall (1905)	Dane	3,432	3,682	7.3	83	138
Mason (1925)	Bayfield	72	82	13.9	9	0
Mattoon (1901)	Shawano	466	447	−4.1	21	2
Mazomanie (1885)	Dane	1,485	1,624	9.4	35	29
McFarland (1920)[5]	Dane	6,416	7,359	14.7	143	73
Melrose (1914)	Jackson	529	513	−3.0	5	4
Melvina (1922)	Monroe	93	90	−3.2	2	0
Menomonee Falls (1892)[4]	Waukesha	32,647	34,600	6.0	1,045	377
Merrillan (1881)	Jackson	585	576	−1.5	24	4

WISCONSIN VILLAGES
January 1, 2008–Continued

Village (Year Incorporated)[1]	County	2000 Census	2008 Final Estimate	Percent Change	2000 Nonwhite	2000 Hispanic or Latino Origin[2]
Merrimac (1899)[3]	Sauk	416	457	9.9	8	6
Merton (1922)[3]	Waukesha	1,926	2,618	35.9	25	14
Milladore (1933)	Portage, Wood	268	271	1.1	3	0
Milltown (1910)	Polk	888	914	2.9	18	7
Minong (1915)	Washburn	531	566	6.6	14	4
Mishicot (1950)	Manitowoc	1,422	1,444	1.5	13	4
Montfort (1893)	Grant, Iowa	663	668	0.8	5	0
Monticello (1891)	Green	1,146	1,166	1.7	8	12
Mount Calvary (1962)	Fond du Lac	956	934	–2.3	79	80
Mount Hope (1919)	Grant	186	183	–1.6	0	3
Mount Horeb (1899)[3]	Dane	5,860	6,697	14.3	81	34
Mount Pleasant (2003)[3, 5]	Racine	23,142	26,040	12.5	1,989	1,149
Mount Sterling (1936)	Crawford	215	205	–4.7	2	0
Mukwonago (1905)	Walworth, Waukesha	6,162	6,953	12.8	83	117
Muscoda (1894)[3]	Grant, Iowa	1,453	1,393	–4.1	14	19
Nashotah (1957)	Waukesha	1,266	1,360	7.4	14	13
Necedah (1870)[3]	Juneau	888	883	–0.6	15	6
Nelson (1978)	Buffalo	395	398	0.8	3	1
Nelsonville (1913)	Portage	191	181	–5.2	5	0
Neosho (1902)	Dodge	593	581	–2.0	6	3
Neshkoro (1906)	Marquette	453	448	–1.1	3	3
New Auburn (1902)	Barron, Chippewa	562	577	2.7	4	2
New Glarus (1901)[3]	Green	2,111	2,108	–0.1	23	27
Newburg (1973)	Ozaukee, Washington	1,119	1,191	6.4	26	20
Nichols (1967)	Outagamie	307	276	–10.1	23	4
North Bay (1951)	Racine	260	244	–6.2	17	15
North Fond du Lac (1903)[3]	Fond du Lac	4,557	4,982	9.3	76	52
North Freedom (1893)	Sauk	649	629	–3.1	11	7
North Hudson (1912)[3]	St. Croix	3,463	3,700	6.8	94	17
North Prairie (1919)	Waukesha	1,571	1,955	24.4	12	17
Norwalk (1894)	Monroe	653	630	–3.5	4	209
Oakdale (1988)	Monroe	297	321	8.1	4	1
Oakfield (1903)	Fond du Lac	1,012	1,036	2.4	9	29
Oconomowoc Lake (1959)[3]	Waukesha	564	633	12.2	8	4
Ogdensburg (1912)	Waupaca	224	213	–4.9	0	0
Oliver (1917)	Douglas	358	437	22.1	10	0
Ontario (1890)	Vernon	476	467	–1.9	6	23
Oostburg (1909)	Sheboygan	2,660	2,905	9.2	18	33
Oregon (1883)[3]	Dane	7,514	8,764	16.6	162	50
Orfordville (1900)	Rock	1,272	1,407	10.6	17	29
Osceola (1886)[3]	Polk	2,421	2,732	12.8	53	22
Oxford (1912)	Marquette	536	564	5.2	16	10
Paddock Lake (1960)[3]	Kenosha	3,012	3,092	2.7	62	135
Palmyra (1866)	Jefferson	1,766	1,782	0.9	24	115
Pardeeville (1894)	Columbia	1,982	2,102	6.1	28	43
Park Ridge (1938)	Portage	488	469	–3.9	11	4
Patch Grove (1921)	Grant	166	150	–9.6	0	3
Pepin (1860)	Pepin	878	953	8.5	15	0
Pewaukee (1876)[3]	Waukesha	8,170	8,934	9.4	284	99
Pigeon Falls (1956)	Trempealeau	388	390	0.5	4	0
Plain (1912)	Sauk	792	803	1.4	8	7
Plainfield (1882)	Waushara	899	886	–1.4	14	161
Pleasant Prairie (1989)[3]	Kenosha	16,136	19,565	21.3	730	544
Plover (1971)[3]	Portage	10,520	11,850	12.6	274	142
Plum City (1909)	Pierce	574	596	3.8	1	1
Poplar (1917)	Douglas	552	630	14.1	9	2
Port Edwards (1902)[3]	Wood	1,944	1,893	–2.6	122	18
Potosi (1887)	Grant	711	724	1.8	6	7
Potter (1980)	Calumet	252	291	15.5	6	0
Pound (1914)	Marinette	355	331	–6.8	2	0
Poynette (1892)[3]	Columbia	2,266	2,534	11.8	39	33
Prairie du Sac (1885)[3]	Sauk	3,231	3,735	15.6	42	66
Prairie Farm (1901)	Barron	508	531	4.5	3	16
Prentice (1899)	Price	626	634	1.3	10	13
Pulaski (1910)[3]	Brown, Oconto, Shawano	3,060	3,463	13.2	67	29
Radisson (1953)	Sawyer	222	216	–2.7	21	6
Randolph (1870)	Columbia, Dodge	1,869	1,716	–8.2	17	27
Random Lake (1907)	Sheboygan	1,551	1,659	7.0	27	25
Readstown (1898)	Vernon	395	391	–1.0	0	0
Redgranite (1904)	Waushara	1,040	2,087	100.7	44	32
Reedsville (1892)	Manitowoc	1,187	1,192	0.4	19	10
Reeseville (1899)	Dodge	703	713	1.4	7	8
Rewey (1902)	Iowa	311	304	–2.3	11	1
Rib Lake (1902)	Taylor	878	860	–2.1	8	3
Richfield (2008)[5]	Washington	10,373	11,440	10.3	154	73
Ridgeland (1921)	Dunn	265	259	–2.3	1	1

WISCONSIN VILLAGES
January 1, 2008–Continued

Village (Year Incorporated)[1]	County	2000 Census	2008 Final Estimate	Percent Change	2000 Nonwhite	2000 Hispanic or Latino Origin[2]
Ridgeway (1902)	Iowa	689	698	1.3	12	0
Rio (1887)	Columbia	938	988	5.3	15	16
River Hills (1930)[4]	Milwaukee	1,631	1,641	0.6	229	34
Roberts (1945)	St. Croix	969	1,554	60.4	17	9
Rochester (1912)	Racine	1,149	1,192	3.7	17	40
Rock Springs (1894)	Sauk	425	406	–4.5	3	5
Rockdale (1914)	Dane	214	193	–9.8	1	1
Rockland (1919)	La Crosse	625	651	4.2	10	1
Rosendale (1915)	Fond du Lac	923	992	7.5	3	3
Rosholt (1907)	Portage	518	497	–4.1	3	11
Rothschild (1917)	Marathon	4,970	5,336	7.4	187	14
Rudolph (1960)	Wood	423	433	2.4	21	6
St. Cloud (1909)	Fond du Lac	497	519	4.4	2	4
St. Nazianz (1956)	Manitowoc	749	752	0.4	16	17
Sauk City (1854)[3]	Sauk	3,109	3,300	6.1	41	117
Saukville (1915)[3]	Ozaukee	4,068	4,358	7.1	83	89
Scandinavia (1894)	Waupaca	349	374	7.2	5	0
Sharon (1892)	Walworth	1,549	1,535	–0.9	44	113
Sheldon (1917)	Rusk	256	245	–4.3	1	0
Sherwood (1968)[3]	Calumet	1,550	2,499	61.2	22	15
Shiocton (1903)	Outagamie	954	955	0.1	4	64
Shorewood (1900)[4]	Milwaukee	13,763	13,425	–2.5	1,053	345
Shorewood Hills (1927)[3]	Dane	1,732	1,699	–1.9	112	55
Silver Lake (1926)	Kenosha	2,341	2,493	6.5	38	72
Siren (1948)[3]	Burnett	988	947	–4.1	40	1
Sister Bay (1912)[3]	Door	886	990	11.7	10	6
Slinger (1869)[3]	Washington	3,901	4,742	21.6	57	54
Soldiers Grove (1888)	Crawford	653	617	–5.5	6	3
Solon Springs (1920)	Douglas	576	576	0.0	30	3
Somerset (1915)	St. Croix	1,556	2,300	47.8	39	18
South Wayne (1911)	Lafayette	484	474	–2.1	2	0
Spencer (1902)	Marathon	1,932	1,960	1.4	11	18
Spring Green (1869)	Sauk	1,444	1,513	4.8	10	2
Spring Valley (1895)[3]	Pierce, St. Croix	1,189	1,319	10.9	10	7
Star Prairie (1900)	St. Croix	574	645	12.4	13	1
Stetsonville (1949)	Taylor	563	551	–2.1	6	4
Steuben (1900)	Crawford	177	160	–9.6	1	1
Stockbridge (1908)	Calumet	649	678	4.5	7	1
Stockholm (1903)	Pepin	97	95	–2.1	0	0
Stoddard (1911)[3]	Vernon	815	825	1.2	7	1
Stratford (1910)	Marathon	1,523	1,573	3.3	27	15
Strum (1948)[3]	Trempealeau	1,001	1,045	4.4	5	14
Sturtevant (1907)[3]	Racine	5,287	6,354	20.2	959	303
Suamico (2003)[3,5]	Brown	8,686	10,945	26.0	155	54
Sullivan (1915)	Jefferson	688	670	–2.6	6	1
Superior (1949)	Douglas	500	610	22.0	15	1
Suring (1914)	Oconto	605	564	–6.8	11	1
Sussex (1924)[3]	Waukesha	8,828	10,045	13.8	220	147
Taylor (1919)	Jackson	513	498	–2.9	14	0
Tennyson (1940)	Grant	370	361	–2.4	0	2
Theresa (1898)	Dodge	1,252	1,325	5.8	12	24
Thiensville (1910)[3]	Ozaukee	3,254	3,329	2.3	100	34
Tigerton (1896)	Shawano	764	726	–5.0	20	8
Tony (1911)	Rusk	105	99	–5.7	0	1
Trempealeau (1867)[3]	Trempealeau	1,319	1,456	10.4	17	8
Turtle Lake (1898)[3]	Barron, Polk	1,065	1,164	9.3	60	11
Twin Lakes (1937)[3]	Kenosha	5,124	5,609	9.5	95	127
Union Center (1913)	Juneau	214	219	2.3	1	3
Union Grove (1893)[3]	Racine	4,322	4,530	4.8	86	102
Unity (1903)	Clark, Marathon	368	353	–4.1	0	2
Valders (1919)	Manitowoc	948	993	4.7	6	5
Vesper (1948)	Wood	541	531	–1.8	6	4
Viola (1899)[3]	Richland, Vernon	667	694	4.0	6	8
Waldo (1922)	Sheboygan	450	480	6.7	11	0
Wales (1922)	Waukesha	2,523	2,655	5.2	27	26
Walworth (1901)	Walworth	2,304	2,640	14.6	37	165
Warrens (1973)	Monroe	286	360	25.9	8	2
Waterford (1906)[3]	Racine	4,048	4,848	19.8	57	76
Waunakee (1893)[3]	Dane	8,995	11,105	23.5	140	86
Wausaukee (1924)	Marinette	572	550	–3.8	17	5
Wauzeka (1890)	Crawford	768	815	6.1	14	5
Webster (1916)	Burnett	653	685	4.9	60	7
West Baraboo (1956)	Sauk	1,248	1,288	3.2	42	20
West Milwaukee (1906)[3]	Milwaukee	4,201	4,047	–3.7	384	504
West Salem (1893)[3]	La Crosse	4,738	4,852	2.4	84	27

WISCONSIN VILLAGES
January 1, 2008–Continued

Village (Year Incorporated)[1]	County	2000 Census	2008 Final Estimate	Percent Change	2000 Nonwhite	2000 Hispanic or Latino Origin[2]
Westfield (1902)	Marquette	1,217	1,221	0.3	24	43
Weston (1996)[3]	Marathon	12,079	14,040	16.2	793	84
Weyerhaeuser (1906)	Rusk	353	329	–6.8	2	1
Wheeler (1922)	Dunn	317	323	1.9	2	3
White Lake (1926)	Langlade	329	345	4.9	5	7
Whitefish Bay (1892)[4]	Milwaukee	14,163	13,875	–2.0	656	221
Whitelaw (1958)	Manitowoc	730	739	1.2	5	4
Whiting (1947)	Portage	1,760	1,671	–5.1	72	20
Wild Rose (1904)	Waushara	765	728	–4.8	11	17
Williams Bay (1919)[3]	Walworth	2,415	2,688	11.3	25	90
Wilson (1911)	St. Croix	176	205	16.5	8	2
Wilton (1890)	Monroe	519	550	6.0	6	44
Wind Point (1954)	Racine	1,853	1,810	–2.3	93	24
Winneconne (1887)[3]	Winnebago	2,401	2,520	5.0	22	15
Winter (1973)	Sawyer	344	333	–3.2	9	5
Withee (1901)	Clark	508	492	–3.1	6	2
Wittenberg (1893)	Shawano	1,177	1,113	–5.4	40	3
Wonewoc (1878)[5]	Juneau	834	805	–3.5	9	3
Woodman (1917)	Grant	96	94	–2.1	0	0
Woodville (1911)	St. Croix	1,104	1,328	20.3	18	8
Wrightstown (1901)[3]	Brown, Outagamie	1,934	2,667	37.9	41	34
Wyeville (1923)	Monroe	146	134	–8.2	5	4
Wyocena (1909)	Columbia	668	734	9.9	13	8
Yuba (1935)	Richland	92	85	–7.6	0	0

[1]There are 403 villages in Wisconsin as of January 1, 2008.

[2]"Hispanic or Latino Origin" represents ethnicity and includes people of Cuban, Mexican, Puerto Rican, South or Central American, or other Spanish culture or origin, regardless of race.

[3]One of 88 villages with an administrator, holding either a full-time or combination position.

[4]One of 10 villages operating under the manager form of government, holding either a full-time or combination position.

[5]2000 Census population reflects prior status as a town.

Sources: Wisconsin Department of Administration, Demographic Services Center, *Municipality Final 2008 Population Estimates, January 1, 2008,* March 2009; League of Wisconsin Municipalities, *2008 Directory of Wisconsin City and Village Officials,* July 2008; and data compiled by Wisconsin Legislative Reference Bureau.

WISCONSIN CITIES AND VILLAGES
OVER 10,000 POPULATION

City or Village (County)	Census 2000	2008 Estimate	Percent Change	2008 Rank	2000 All Other Races[2]	2000 Hispanic or Latino Origin[3]
Cities						
Appleton (Calumet, Outagamie, Winnebago)	70,087	72,297	3.2%	6	5,063	1,775
Baraboo (Sauk)	10,711	11,755	9.7	69	243	168
Beaver Dam (Dodge)	15,169	15,740	3.8	49	292	640
Beloit (Rock)	35,775	37,110	3.7	19	6,786	3,257
Brookfield (Waukesha)	38,649	39,780	2.9	17	2,145	453
Burlington (Racine, Walworth)	9,936	10,490	5.6	82	177	462
Cedarburg (Ozaukee)	11,102	11,435	3.0	73	185	94
Chippewa Falls (Chippewa)	12,925	13,410	3.8	61	264	82
Cudahy (Milwaukee)	18,429	18,620	1.0	41	743	872
De Pere (Brown)	20,559	22,645	10.1	36	619	202
Eau Claire (Chippewa, Eau Claire)	61,704	65,362	5.9	9	3,777	619
Fitchburg (Dane)	20,501	23,420	14.2	33	2,863	1,329
Fond du Lac (Fond du Lac)	42,203	43,460	3.0	15	2,065	1,232
Fort Atkinson (Jefferson)	11,621	12,130	4.4	66	209	508
Franklin (Milwaukee)	29,494	33,550	13.8	23	2,427	780
Glendale (Milwaukee)	13,367	12,990	−2.8	62	1,672	236
Green Bay (Brown)	102,767	103,950	1.2	3	9,885	7,294
Greenfield (Milwaukee)	35,476	36,270	2.2	20	1,588	1,376
Hartford (Dodge, Washington)	10,905	13,700	25.6	59	188	326
Hudson (St. Croix)	8,775	11,865	35.2	67	151	91
Janesville (Rock)	60,200	63,540	5.5	10	2,089	1,569
Kaukauna (Outagamie)	12,983	14,925	15.0	52	537	103
Kenosha (Kenosha)	90,352	95,910	6.2	4	9,663	9,003
La Crosse (La Crosse)	51,818	51,840	0.0	12	4,068	592
Madison (Dane)	208,054	226,650	8.9	2	29,033	8,512
Manitowoc (Manitowoc)	34,053	34,670	1.8	21	1,941	859
Marinette (Marinette)	11,749	11,365	−3.3	74	252	123
Marshfield (Marathon, Wood)	18,800	19,454	3.5	40	496	146
Menasha (Calumet, Winnebago)	16,331	17,408	6.6	44	570	590
Menomonie (Dunn)	14,937	15,950	6.8	48	828	170
Mequon (Ozaukee)	22,643	23,670	4.5	32	1,202	261
Merrill (Lincoln)	10,146	10,130	−0.2	84	173	104
Middleton (Dane)	15,770	16,960	7.5	45	1,018	444
Milwaukee (Milwaukee, Washington, Waukesha)	596,974	590,870	−1.0	1	254,339	71,646
Monroe (Green)	10,843	10,965	1.1	79	168	158
Muskego (Waukesha)	21,397	23,075	7.8	35	306	281
Neenah (Winnebago)	24,507	25,560	4.3	30	717	495
New Berlin (Waukesha)	38,220	39,500	3.3	18	1,360	595
Oak Creek (Milwaukee)	28,456	32,470	14.1	24	1,675	1,267
Oconomowoc (Waukesha)	12,382	14,300	15.5	53	203	204
Onalaska (La Crosse)	14,839	16,660	12.3	46	658	141
Oshkosh (Winnebago)	62,916	65,920	4.8	8	4,105	1,062
Pewaukee (Waukesha)	11,783	12,645	7.3	64	261	153
Platteville (Grant)	9,989	10,575	5.9	81	348	88
Port Washington (Ozaukee)	10,467	11,185	6.9	75	243	168
Portage (Columbia)	9,728	10,120	4.0	85	575	330
Racine (Racine)	81,855	80,320	−1.9	5	18,471	11,422
River Falls (Pierce, St. Croix)	12,560	14,228	13.3	54	378	119
Sheboygan (Sheboygan)	50,792	50,580	−0.4	13	4,569	3,034
South Milwaukee (Milwaukee)	21,256	21,310	0.3	37	722	852
Stevents Point (Portage)	24,551	26,050	6.1	27	1677	395
Stoughton (Dane)	12,354	12,865	4.1	63	347	153
Sun Prairie (Dane)	20,369	25,810	26.7	29	1,243	555
Superior (Douglas)	27,368	27,170	−0.7	26	1,465	226
Two Rivers (Manitowoc)	12,639	12,540	−0.8	65	458	170
Verona (Dane)	7,052	10,240	45.2	83	161	50
Watertown (Dodge, Jefferson)	21,598	23,163	7.2	34	409	1,067
Waukesha (Waukesha)	64,825	68,030	4.9	7	3,071	5,563
Waupun (Dodge, Fond du Lac)	10,944	11,034	0.8	78	1,427	304
Wausau (Marathon)	38,426	40,360	5.0	16	5,226	398
Wauwatosa (Milwaukee)	47,271	45,880	−2.9	14	2,523	813
West Allis (Milwaukee)	61,254	60,370	−1.4	11	2,667	2,155
West Bend (Washington)	28,152	30,320	7.7	25	554	519
Whitewater (Jefferson, Walworth)	13,437	14,110	5.0	55	632	873
Wisconsin Rapids (Wood)	18,435	18,480	0.2	42	998	242

WISCONSIN CITIES AND VILLAGES
OVER 10,000 POPULATION–Continued

City or Village (County)	Census 2000	2008 Estimate	Percent Change	2008 Rank	2000 All Other Races[2]	2000 Hispanic or Latino Origin[3]
Villages						
Allouez (Brown)	15,443	15,470	0.2	50	1,105	199
Ashwaubenon (Brown)	17,634	17,730	0.5	43	763	202
Bellevue (Brown)	11,828	14,965	26.5	51	374	310
Brown Deer (Milwaukee)	12,170	11,705	–3.8	70	2,088	260
Caledonia (Racine)	23,614	25,110	6.3	31	1,086	736
Germantown (Washington)	18,260	19,895	9.0	38	680	205
Grafton (Ozaukee)	10,464	11,450	9.4	71	193	165
Greendale (Milwaukee)	14,405	13,995	–2.8	57	458	340
Howard (Brown, Outagamie)	13,546	15,965	17.9	47	461	147
Little Chute (Outagamie)	10,476	11,035	5.3	77	203	175
Menomonee Falls (Waukesha)	32,647	34,600	6.0	22	1,045	377
Mount Pleasant (Racine)	23,142	26,040	12.5	28	1,989	1,149
Pleasant Prairie (Kenosha)	16,136	19,565	21.3	39	730	544
Plover (Portage)	10,520	11,850	12.6	68	274	142
Richfield (Washington)	10,373	11,440	10.3	72	154	73
Shorewood (Milwaukee)	13,763	13,425	–2.5	60	1,053	345
Suamico (Brown)	8,686	10,945	26.0	80	155	54
Sussex (Waukesha)	8,828	10,045	13.8	86	220	147
Waunakee (Dane)	8,995	11,105	23.5	76	140	86
Weston (Marathon)	12,079	14,040	16.2	56	793	84
Whitefish Bay (Milwaukee)	14,163	13,875	–2.0	58	656	221

[1]Race and ethnicity data have not been adjusted since the 2000 Census. Population estimates are based on the corrected 2000 Census totals.

[2]"All Other Races" includes those who chose any race other than "White". In the 2000 U.S. Census, respondents were allowed to choose more than one race.

[3]"Hispanic or Latino Origin" represents ethnicity and includes people of Cuban, Mexican, Puerto Rican, South or Central American, or other Spanish culture or origin, regardless of race.

Source: Wisconsin Department of Administration, Demographic Services Center, *Municipality Final 2008 Population Estimates, January 1, 2008,* March 2009.

WISCONSIN TOWNS OVER 2,500 POPULATION
2000 U.S. Census and 2008 Estimate

Town (County)	2000 Census*	2008 Estimate	Percent Change	Town (County)	2000 Census*	2008 Estimate	Percent Change
Addison (Washington)	3,341	3,570	6.9%	Menasha (Winnebago)	15,858	17,375	9.6%
Alden (Polk)	2,615	2,927	11.9	Menominee (Menominee)	4,562	4,630	1.5
Algoma (Winnebago)	5,702	6,423	12.6	Menomonie (Dunn)	3,174	3,475	9.5
Arbor Vitae (Vilas)	3,153	3,371	6.9	Merrill (Lincoln)	2,979	3,149	5.7
Barton (Washington)	2,546	2,651	4.1	Merton (Waukesha)	7,988	8,458	5.9
Beaver Dam (Dodge)	3,440	3,918	13.9	Middleton (Dane)	4,594	5,622	22.4
Beloit (Rock)	7,038	7,445	5.8	Milton (Rock)	2,844	3,005	5.7
Bloomfield (Walworth)	5,537	6,357	14.8	Minocqua (Oneida)	4,859	5,347	10.0
Bradley (Lincoln)	2,573	2,747	6.8	Mukwa (Waupaca)	2,773	3,053	10.1
Bristol (Dane)	2,698	3,408	26.3	Mukwonago (Waukesha)	6,868	7,558	10.0
Bristol (Kenosha)	4,538	4,863	7.2	Neenah (Winnebago)	2,657	2,917	9.8
Brockway (Jackson)	2,580	2,704	4.8	Newbold (Oneida)	2,710	2,927	8.0
Brookfield (Waukesha)	6,390	6,377	–0.2	Norway (Racine)	7,600	8,061	6.1
Buchanan (Outagamie)	5,827	6,708	15.1	Oakland (Jefferson)	3,135	3,354	7.0
Burke (Dane)	2,990	3,119	4.3	Oconomowoc (Waukesha)	7,451	8,217	10.3
Burlington (Racine)	6,384	6,491	1.7	Onalaska (La Crosse)	5,210	5,524	6.0
Campbell (La Crosse)	4,410	4,413	0.1	Oneida (Outagamie)	4,147	4,320	4.2
Cedarburg (Ozaukee)	5,550	5,789	4.3	Oregon (Dane)	3,148	3,372	7.1
Center (Outagamie)	3,163	3,412	7.9	Osceola (Polk)	2,085	2,793	34.0
Chase (Oconto)	2,082	2,822	35.5	Oshkosh (Winnebago)	3,234	2,823	–12.7
Clayton (Winnebago)	2,974	3,579	20.3	Ottawa (Waukesha)	3,758	3,807	1.3
Cottage Grove (Dane)	3,839	3,941	2.7	Pacific (Columbia)	2,518	2,764	9.8
Dale (Outagamie)	2,288	2,599	13.6	Pelican (Oneida)	2,902	2,661	–8.3
Dayton (Waupaca)	2,734	2,956	8.1	Peshtigo (Marinette)	3,702	4,008	8.3
Delafield (Waukesha)	7,820	8,331	6.5	Pine Lake (Oneida)	2,720	2,872	5.6
Delavan (Walworth)	4,559	4,887	7.2	Pittsfield (Brown)	2,433	2,685	10.4
Dover (Racine)	3,908	4,105	5.0	Pleasant Springs (Dane)	3,053	3,166	3.7
Dunn (Dane)	5,270	5,255	–0.3	Pleasant Valley (Eau Claire)	2,681	3,077	14.8
Eagle (Waukesha)	3,117	3,571	14.6	Plymouth (Sheboygan)	3,115	3,296	5.8
Eagle Point (Chippewa)	3,049	3,257	6.8	Polk (Washington)	3,938	4,023	2.2
East Troy (Walworth)	3,830	3,953	3.2	Randall (Kenosha)	2,929	3,180	8.6
Ellington (Outagamie)	2,535	2,806	10.7	Raymond (Racine)	3,516	3,797	8.0
Empire (Fond du Lac)	2,620	2,855	9.0	Rib Mountain (Marathon)	7,556	7,658	1.3
Erin (Washington)	3,664	3,911	6.7	Rice Lake (Barron)	3,026	3,171	4.8
Farmington (Washington)	3,239	3,560	9.9	Richmond (St. Croix)	1,556	2,883	85.3
Farmington (Waupaca)	4,148	4,247	2.4	Rochester (Racine)	2,254	2,539	12.6
Fond du Lac (Fond du Lac)	2,027	2,506	23.6	Rock (Rock)	3,338	3,277	–1.8
Fox Lake (Dodge)	2,402	2,691	12.0	Rome (Adams)	2,656	3,190	20.1
Freedom (Outagamie)	5,241	5,714	9.0	St. Joseph (St. Croix)	3,436	3,884	13.0
Friendship (Fond du Lac)	2,406	2,575	7.0	Salem (Kenosha)	9,871	11,420	15.7
Fulton (Rock)	3,158	3,291	4.2	Saratoga (Wood)	5,383	5,548	3.1
Genesee (Waukesha)	7,284	7,556	3.7	Scott (Brown)	3,138	3,553	13.2
Geneva (Walworth)	4,642	5,159	11.1	Sevastopol (Door)	2,667	2,871	7.6
Grafton (Ozaukee)	3,980	4,130	3.8	Seymour (Eau Claire)	2,978	3,154	5.9
Grand Chute (Outagamie)	18,392	20,520	11.6	Sheboygan (Sheboygan)	5,874	7,195	22.5
Grand Rapids (Wood)	7,801	7,998	2.5	Shelby (La Crosse)	4,687	4,824	2.9
Greenbush (Sheboygan)	2,619	2,616	–0.1	Somers (Kenosha)	9,059	9,452	4.3
Greenville (Outagamie)	6,844	9,401	37.4	Somerset (St. Croix)	2,644	3,447	30.4
Harrison (Calumet)	5,756	8,677	50.7	Sparta (Monroe)	2,753	3,054	10.9
Hartford (Washington)	4,031	3,992	–1.0	Springfield (Dane)	2,762	2,891	4.7
Hayward (Sawyer)	3,279	3,574	9.0	Star Prairie (St. Croix)	2,944	3,544	20.4
Holland (La Crosse)	3,042	3,406	12.0	Stephenson (Marinette)	3,065	3,517	14.7
Hudson (St. Croix)	6,213	7,931	27.7	Stockton (Portage)	2,896	3,062	5.7
Hull (Portage)	5,493	5,638	2.6	Sugar Creek (Walworth)	3,331	3,802	14.1
Ixonia (Jefferson)	2,902	3,580	23.4	Summit (Waukesha)	4,999	5,162	3.3
Jackson (Washington)	3,516	3,910	11.2	Taycheedah (Fond du Lac)	3,666	3,993	8.9
Janesville (Rock)	3,048	3,416	12.1	Trenton (Washington)	4,440	4,855	9.3
Koshkonong (Jefferson)	3,395	3,622	6.7	Troy (St. Croix)	3,661	4,534	23.8
La Grange (Walworth)	2,444	2,587	5.9	Union (Eau Claire)	2,402	2,572	7.1
Lac du Flambeau (Vilas)	3,004	3,299	9.8	Vernon (Waukesha)	7,227	7,450	3.1
Lafayette (Chippewa)	5,199	5,935	14.2	Washington (Eau Claire)	6,995	7,312	4.5
Lawrence (Brown)	1,548	3,075	98.6	Waterford (Racine)	5,938	6,566	10.6
Ledgeview (Brown)	3,363	5,407	60.8	Waukesha (Waukesha)	8,596	8,940	4.0
Lima (Sheboygan)	2,948	2,963	0.5	Wescott (Shawano)	3,653	3,780	3.5
Lincoln (Vilas)	2,579	2,810	9.0	West Bend (Washington)	4,834	4,875	0.8
Lisbon (Waukesha)	9,359	9,863	5.4	Westport (Dane)	3,586	3,825	6.7
Little Suamico (Oconto)	3,877	4,856	25.3	Wheatland (Kenosha)	3,292	3,440	4.5
Lodi (Columbia)	2,791	3,139	12.5	Wheaton (Chippewa)	2,366	2,677	13.1
Lyons (Walworth)	3,440	3,743	8.8	Wilson (Sheboygan)	3,227	3,537	9.6
Madison (Dane)	7,005	6,033	–13.9	Windsor (Dane)	5,286	5,861	10.9
Manitowoc Rapids (Manitowoc)	2,520	2,543	0.9	Yorkville (Racine)	3,291	3,385	2.9

*2000 Census population reflects corrected totals.

Source: Wisconsin Department of Administration, Demographic Services Center, *Municipality Final 2008 Population Estimates, January 1, 2008*, March 2009.

WISCONSIN POPULATION
BY COUNTY AND MUNCIPALITY
April 1, 2000 and January 1, 2008

County and Municipality	2000 Census	2008 Estimate	Percent Change	County and Municipality	2000 Census	2008 Estimate	Percent Change
ADAMS COUNTY	19,920	21,836	9.6%	Barnes, town	610	706	15.7
Adams, city	1,831	1,879	2.6	Bayfield, city	611	616	0.8
Adams, town	1,267	1,317	3.9	Bayfield, town	625	813	30.1
Big Flats, town	946	1,045	10.5	Bayview, town	491	538	9.6
Colburn, town	181	193	6.6	Bell, town	230	263	14.3
Dell Prairie, town	1,415	1,580	11.7	Cable, town	836	864	3.3
Easton, town	1,194	1,293	8.3	Clover, town	211	243	15.2
Friendship, village	781	796	1.9	Delta, town	235	261	11.1
Jackson, town	926	1,002	8.2	Drummond, town	541	572	5.7
Leola, town	265	285	7.5	Eileen, town	640	650	1.6
Lincoln, town	311	312	0.3	Grand View, town	483	551	14.1
Monroe, town	363	473	30.3	Hughes, town	408	448	9.8
New Chester, town	2,141	2,263	5.7	Iron River, town	1,059	1,187	12.1
New Haven, town	657	707	7.6	Kelly, town	377	458	21.5
Preston, town	1,360	1,494	9.9	Keystone, town	369	376	1.9
Quincy, town	1,181	1,333	12.9	Lincoln, town	293	304	3.8
Richfield, town	144	151	4.9	Mason, town	326	326	0.0
Rome, town	2,656	3,190	20.1	Mason, village	72	82	13.9
Springville, town	1,167	1,281	9.8	Namakagon, town	285	318	11.6
Strongs Prairie, town	1,115	1,216	9.1	Orienta, town	101	98	−3.0
Wisconsin Dells (part), city	19	26	36.8	Oulu, town	540	542	0.4
				Pilsen, town	203	221	8.9
ASHLAND COUNTY	16,866	16,929	0.4	Port Wing, town	420	434	3.3
Agenda, town	513	508	−1.0	Russell, town	1,216	1,420	16.8
Ashland (part), city	8,620	8,508	−1.3	Tripp, town	209	223	6.7
Ashland, town	603	614	1.8	Washburn, city	2,280	2,247	−1.4
Butternut, village	407	393	−3.4	Washburn, town	541	568	5.0
Chippewa, town	433	440	1.6				
Gingles, town	640	751	17.3	BROWN COUNTY	226,658	245,168	8.2
Gordon, town	357	366	2.5	Allouez, village	15,443	15,470	0.2
Jacobs, town	835	830	−0.6	Ashwaubenon, village	17,634	17,730	0.5
La Pointe, town	246	287	16.7	¹Bellevue, village	11,828	14,965	26.5
Marengo, town	362	383	5.8	De Pere, city	20,559	22,645	10.1
Mellen, city	845	799	−5.4	Denmark, village	1,958	2,132	8.9
Morse, town	515	541	5.0	Eaton, town	1,414	1,582	11.9
Peeksville, town	176	174	−1.1	Glenmore, town	1,187	1,274	7.3
Sanborn, town	1,272	1,231	−3.2	Green Bay, city	102,767	103,950	1.2
Shanagolden, town	150	148	−1.3	Green Bay, town	1,772	1,959	10.6
White River, town	892	956	7.2	²Hobart, village	5,090	5,875	15.4
				Holland, town	1,339	1,500	12.0
BARRON COUNTY	44,963	47,727	6.1	Howard (part), village	13,546	15,965	17.9
Almena, town	910	991	8.9	Humboldt, town	1,338	1,441	7.7
Almena, village	720	751	4.3	Lawrence, town	1,548	3,075	98.6
Arland, town	670	710	6.0	Ledgeview, town	3,363	5,407	60.8
Barron, city	3,248	3,321	2.2	Morrison, town	1,651	1,717	4.0
Barron, town	1,014	998	−1.6	New Denmark, town	1,482	1,551	4.7
Bear Lake, town	587	646	10.1	Pittsfield, town	2,433	2,685	10.4
Cameron, village	1,546	1,749	13.1	Pulaski (part), village	3,013	3,311	9.9
Cedar Lake, town	944	1,120	18.6	Rockland, town	1,522	1,648	8.3
Chetek, city	2,180	2,259	3.6	Scott, town	3,138	3,553	13.2
Chetek, town	1,686	1,786	5.9	Suamico, village	8,686	10,945	26.0
Clinton, town	920	1,015	10.3	Wrightstown, town	2,013	2,283	13.4
Crystal Lake, town	778	810	4.1	Wrightstown (part), village	1,934	2,505	29.5
Cumberland, city	2,280	2,399	5.2				
Cumberland, town	942	959	1.8	BUFFALO COUNTY	13,804	14,200	2.9
Dallas, town	604	608	0.7	Alma, city	942	934	−0.8
Dallas, village	356	369	3.7	Alma, town	377	387	2.7
Dovre, town	680	798	17.4	Belvidere, town	442	451	2.0
Doyle, town	498	540	8.4	Buffalo, city	1,040	1,055	1.4
Haugen, village	287	296	3.1	Buffalo, town	667	714	7.0
Lakeland, town	963	1,022	6.1	Canton, town	304	308	1.3
Maple Grove, town	968	1,004	3.7	Cochrane, village	435	416	−4.4
Maple Plain, town	876	946	8.0	Cross, town	366	416	13.7
New Auburn (part), village	15	23	53.3	Dover, town	484	509	5.2
Oak Grove, town	911	949	4.2	Fountain City, city	983	1,011	2.8
Prairie Farm, town	603	616	2.2	Gilmanton, town	470	475	1.1
Prairie Farm, village	508	531	4.5	Glencoe, town	478	503	5.2
Prairie Lake, town	1,369	1,584	15.7	Lincoln, town	187	182	−2.7
Rice Lake, city	8,312	8,664	4.2	Maxville, town	325	338	4.0
Rice Lake, town	3,026	3,171	4.8	Milton, town	517	547	5.8
Sioux Creek, town	689	756	9.7	Modena, town	318	311	−2.2
Stanfold, town	669	721	7.8	Mondovi, city	2,634	2,706	2.7
Stanley, town	2,237	2,464	10.1	Mondovi, town	449	470	4.7
Sumner, town	598	692	15.7	Montana, town	306	312	2.0
Turtle Lake, town	622	650	4.5	Naples, town	584	621	6.3
Turtle Lake (part), village	1,000	1,011	1.1	Nelson, town	586	611	4.3
Vance Creek, town	747	798	6.8	Nelson, village	395	398	0.8
				Waumandee, town	515	525	1.9
BAYFIELD COUNTY	15,013	16,160	7.6				
Ashland (part), city	0	0	0.0	BURNETT COUNTY	15,674	16,791	7.1
Barksdale, town	801	831	3.7	Anderson, town	372	402	8.1

WISCONSIN POPULATION
BY COUNTY AND MUNCIPALITY
April 1, 2000 and January 1, 2008–Continued

County and Municipality	2000 Census	2008 Estimate	Percent Change	County and Municipality	2000 Census	2008 Estimate	Percent Change
Blaine, town	224	229	2.2	Beaver, town	854	915	7.1
Daniels, town	665	713	7.2	Butler, town	88	91	3.4
Dewey, town	565	605	7.1	Colby (part), city	1,156	1,238	7.1
Grantsburg, town	967	1,139	17.8	Colby, town	908	937	3.2
Grantsburg, village	1,369	1,460	6.6	Curtiss, village	198	207	4.5
Jackson, town	765	860	12.4	Dewhurst, town	321	386	20.2
La Follette, town	511	517	1.2	Dorchester (part), village	823	854	3.8
Lincoln, town	286	310	8.4	Eaton, town	665	697	4.8
Meenon, town	1,172	1,257	7.3	Foster, town	95	99	4.2
Oakland, town	778	895	15.0	Fremont, town	1,190	1,301	9.3
Roosevelt, town	197	204	3.6	Grant, town	920	977	6.2
Rusk, town	420	405	–3.6	Granton, village	406	396	–2.5
Sand Lake, town	556	567	2.0	Green Grove, town	675	685	1.5
Scott, town	590	648	9.8	Greenwood, city	1,079	1,077	–0.2
Siren, town	873	920	5.4	Hendren, town	513	520	1.4
Siren, village	988	947	–4.1	Hewett, town	314	314	0.0
Swiss, town	815	871	6.9	Hixon, town	740	767	3.6
Trade Lake, town	871	970	11.4	Hoard, town	821	855	4.1
Union, town	351	346	–1.4	Levis, town	504	544	7.9
Webb Lake, town	381	421	10.5	Longwood, town	698	746	6.9
Webster, village	653	685	4.9	Loyal, city	1,308	1,276	–2.4
West Marshland, town	331	388	17.2	Loyal, town	787	801	1.8
Wood River, town	974	1,032	6.0	Lynn, town	834	841	0.8
				Mayville, town	919	951	3.5
CALUMET COUNTY	40,631	46,292	13.9	Mead, town	290	311	7.2
Appleton (part), city	10,974	11,195	2.0	Mentor, town	570	608	6.7
Brillion, city	2,937	2,989	1.8	Neillsville, city	2,731	2,648	–3.0
Brillion, town	1,438	1,548	7.6	Owen, city	936	920	–1.7
Brothertown, town	1,404	1,445	2.9	Pine Valley, town	1,121	1,265	12.8
Charlestown, town	789	780	–1.1	Reseburg, town	740	742	0.3
Chilton, city	3,708	3,776	1.8	Seif, town	212	201	–5.2
Chilton, town	1,130	1,188	5.1	Sherman, town	831	881	6.0
Harrison, town	5,756	8,677	50.7	Sherwood, town	252	262	4.0
Hilbert, village	1,089	1,109	1.8	Stanley (part), city	0	7	0.0
Kiel (part), city	321	313	–2.5	Thorp, city	1,536	1,535	–0.1
Menasha (part), city	688	1,633	137.4	Thorp, town	730	751	2.9
New Holstein, city	3,301	3,347	1.4	Unity, town	745	778	4.4
New Holstein, town	1,457	1,561	7.1	Unity (part), village	163	161	–1.2
Potter, village	252	291	15.5	Warner, town	627	668	6.5
Rantoul, town	812	847	4.3	Washburn, town	304	301	–1.0
Sherwood, village	1,550	2,499	61.2	Weston, town	638	674	5.6
Stockbridge, town	1,383	1,475	6.7	Withee, town	885	929	5.0
Stockbridge, village	649	678	4.5	Withee, village	508	492	–3.1
Woodville, town	993	941	–5.2	Worden, town	657	718	9.3
				York, town	853	885	3.8
CHIPPEWA COUNTY	55,195	61,872	12.1				
Anson, town	1,881	2,114	12.4	COLUMBIA COUNTY	52,468	56,130	7.0
Arthur, town	710	758	6.8	Arlington, town	848	876	3.3
Auburn, town	580	717	23.6	Arlington, village	484	633	30.8
Birch Creek, town	520	533	2.5	Caledonia, town	1,171	1,306	11.5
Bloomer, city	3,347	3,473	3.8	Cambria, village	792	781	–1.4
Bloomer, town	926	1,028	11.0	Columbus (part), city	4,443	4,866	9.5
Boyd, village	680	625	–8.1	Columbus, town	711	712	0.1
Cadott, village	1,345	1,391	3.4	Courtland, town	463	474	2.4
Chippewa Falls, city	12,925	13,410	3.8	Dekorra, town	2,350	2,462	4.8
Cleveland, town	900	1,027	14.1	Doylestown, village	328	342	4.3
Colburn, town	727	792	8.9	Fall River, village	1,097	1,515	38.1
Cooks Valley, town	632	699	10.6	Fort Winnebago, town	855	858	0.4
Cornell, city	1,466	1,449	–1.2	Fountain Prairie, town	810	871	7.5
Delmar, town	941	972	3.3	Friesland, village	298	310	4.0
Eagle Point, town	3,049	3,257	6.8	Hampden, town	563	571	1.4
Eau Claire (part), city	1,910	2,002	4.8	Leeds, town	813	830	2.1
Edson, town	966	1,094	13.3	Lewiston, town	1,187	1,261	6.2
Estella, town	469	498	6.2	Lodi, city	2,882	3,007	4.3
Goetz, town	695	753	8.3	Lodi, town	2,791	3,139	12.5
³Hallie, town	4,703	160	–96.6	Lowville, town	987	1,028	4.2
Howard, town	648	693	6.9	Marcellon, town	1,024	1,082	5.7
Lafayette, town	5,199	5,935	14.2	Newport, town	681	689	1.2
³Lake Hallie, village	0	6,320	0.0	Otsego, town	757	770	1.7
Lake Holcombe, town	1,010	1,126	11.5	Pacific, town	2,518	2,764	9.8
New Auburn (part), village	547	554	1.3	Pardeeville, village	1,982	2,102	6.1
Ruby, town	446	471	5.6	Portage, city	9,728	10,120	4.0
Sampson, town	816	930	14.0	Poynette, village	2,266	2,534	11.8
Sigel, town	825	842	2.1	Randolph, town	699	762	9.0
Stanley (part), city	1,898	3,374	77.8	Randolph (part), village	523	497	–5.0
Tilden, town	1,185	1,343	13.3	Rio, village	938	988	5.3
Wheaton, town	2,366	2,677	13.1	Scott, town	791	868	9.7
Woodmohr, town	883	855	–3.2	Springvale, town	550	563	2.4
				West Point, town	1,634	1,818	11.3
CLARK COUNTY	33,557	34,589	3.1	Wisconsin Dells (part), city	2,293	2,335	1.8
Abbotsford (part), city	1,412	1,377	–2.5	Wyocena, town	1,543	1,662	7.7

WISCONSIN POPULATION
BY COUNTY AND MUNCIPALITY
April 1, 2000 and January 1, 2008–Continued

County and Municipality	2000 Census	2008 Estimate	Percent Change	County and Municipality	2000 Census	2008 Estimate	Percent Change
Wyocena, village.	668	734	9.9	Verona, city	7,052	10,240	45.2
				Verona, town.	2,153	2,040	–5.2
CRAWFORD COUNTY. . . .	17,243	17,629	2.2	Vienna, town.	1,294	1,401	8.3
Bell Center, village.	116	113	–2.6	Waunakee, village	8,995	11,105	23.5
Bridgeport, town	946	1,018	7.6	Westport, town.	3,586	3,825	6.7
Clayton, town	956	923	–3.5	Windsor, town	5,286	5,861	10.9
De Soto (part), village . . .	118	182	54.2	York, town	703	705	0.3
Eastman, town	790	802	1.5				
Eastman, village	437	450	3.0	DODGE COUNTY	85,897	89,810	4.6
Ferryville, village	174	186	6.9	Ashippun, town	2,308	2,497	8.2
Freeman, town	719	766	6.5	Beaver Dam, city	15,169	15,740	3.8
Gays Mills, village.	625	611	–2.2	Beaver Dam, town.	3,440	3,918	13.9
Haney, town	330	342	3.6	Brownsville, village	570	568	–0.4
Lynxville, village	176	180	2.3	Burnett, town.	919	928	1.0
Marietta, town	510	539	5.7	Calamus, town	1,005	1,076	7.1
Mount Sterling, village . . .	215	205	–4.7	Chester, town.	734	719	–2.0
Prairie du Chien, city . . .	6,018	6,045	0.4	Clyman, town	849	868	2.2
Prairie du Chien, town . . .	1,076	1,139	5.9	Clyman, village	388	385	–0.8
Scott, town	503	538	7.0	Columbus (part), city . . .	36	0	—
Seneca, town	893	944	5.7	Elba, town	1,086	1,106	1.8
Soldiers Grove, village. . .	653	617	–5.5	Emmet, town.	1,221	1,422	16.5
Steuben, village	177	160	–9.6	Fox Lake, city	1,454	1,509	3.8
Utica, town.	674	703	4.3	Fox Lake, town	2,402	2,691	12.0
Wauzeka, town.	369	351	–4.9	Hartford (part), city	10	0	—
Wauzeka, village.	768	815	6.1	Herman, town.	1,207	1,242	2.9
				Horicon, city.	3,775	3,702	–1.9
DANE COUNTY	426,526	471,559	10.6	Hubbard, town	1,643	1,811	10.2
Albion, town	1,858	1,931	3.9	Hustisford, town	1,379	1,464	6.2
Belleville (part), village . .	1,795	1,882	4.8	Hustisford, village	1,135	1,151	1.4
Berry, town.	1,084	1,164	7.4	Iron Ridge, village	998	1,023	2.5
Black Earth, town	449	485	8.0	Juneau, city	2,485	2,686	8.1
Black Earth, village	1,320	1,341	1.6	Kekoskee, village	169	168	–0.6
Blooming Grove, town. . .	1,768	1,741	–1.5	Lebanon, town	1,664	1,743	4.7
Blue Mounds, town	842	912	8.3	Leroy, town	1,116	1,094	–2.0
Blue Mounds, village . . .	708	755	6.6	Lomira, town.	1,228	1,256	2.3
Bristol, town	2,698	3,408	26.3	Lomira, village.	2,233	2,488	11.4
Brooklyn (part), village . .	502	808	61.0	Lowell, town	1,169	1,197	2.4
Burke, town	2,990	3,119	4.3	Lowell, village.	366	371	1.4
Cambridge (part), village .	1,014	1,162	14.6	Mayville, city	4,902	5,242	6.9
Christiana, town	1,313	1,347	2.6	Neosho, village	593	581	–2.0
Cottage Grove, town. . . .	3,839	3,941	2.7	Oak Grove, town.	1,126	1,113	–1.2
Cottage Grove, village. . .	4,059	5,525	36.1	Portland, town	1,106	1,156	4.5
Cross Plains, town	1,419	1,489	4.9	Randolph (part), village . .	1,346	1,219	–9.4
Cross Plains, village	3,084	3,486	13.0	Reeseville, village	703	713	1.4
Dane, town.	968	998	3.1	Rubicon, town	2,005	2,257	12.6
Dane, village.	799	958	19.9	Shields, town.	554	577	4.2
Deerfield, town.	1,470	1,573	7.0	Theresa, town	1,080	1,127	4.4
Deerfield, village.	1,971	2,240	13.6	Theresa, village	1,252	1,325	5.8
DeForest, village	7,368	8,492	15.3	Trenton, town	1,301	1,313	0.9
Dunkirk, town	2,053	2,028	–1.2	Watertown (part), city . . .	8,063	8,578	6.4
Dunn, town.	5,270	5,255	–0.3	Waupun (part), city	7,662	7,663	0.0
Edgerton (part), city	7	26	271.4	Westford, town.	1,400	1,443	3.1
Fitchburg, city	20,501	23,420	14.2	Williamstown, town	646	680	5.3
Madison, city.	208,054	226,650	8.9				
Madison, town	7,005	6,033	–13.9	DOOR COUNTY	27,961	30,303	8.4
Maple Bluff, village	1,358	1,378	1.5	Baileys Harbor, town . . .	1,003	1,210	20.6
Marshall, village	3,432	3,682	7.3	Brussels, town	1,112	1,168	5.0
Mazomanie, town	1,185	1,231	3.9	Clay Banks, town	410	420	2.4
Mazomanie, village	1,485	1,624	9.4	Egg Harbor, town	1,194	1,454	21.8
McFarland, village.	6,416	7,359	14.7	Egg Harbor, village	250	279	11.6
Medina, town	1,235	1,305	5.7	Ephraim, village	353	356	0.8
Middleton, city.	15,770	16,960	7.5	Forestville, town	1,086	1,163	7.1
Middleton, town	4,594	5,622	22.4	Forestville, village	429	426	–0.7
Monona, city.	8,018	8,194	2.2	Gardner, town	1,197	1,294	8.1
Montrose, town	1,134	1,162	2.5	Gibraltar, town	1,063	1,374	29.3
Mount Horeb, village . . .	5,860	6,697	14.3	Jacksonport, town	738	810	9.8
Oregon, town.	3,148	3,372	7.1	Liberty Grove, town	1,858	2,170	16.8
Oregon, village.	7,514	8,764	16.6	Nasewaupee, town	1,873	1,992	6.4
Perry, town.	670	690	3.0	Sevastopol, town	2,667	2,871	7.6
Pleasant Springs, town. . .	3,053	3,166	3.7	Sister Bay, village	886	990	11.7
Primrose, town	682	727	6.6	Sturgeon Bay, city	9,437	9,778	3.6
Rockdale, village.	214	193	–9.8	Sturgeon Bay, town	865	890	2.9
Roxbury, town	1,700	1,757	3.4	Union, town	880	940	6.8
Rutland, town	1,887	1,997	5.8	Washington, town	660	718	8.8
Shorewood Hills, village. .	1,732	1,699	–1.9				
Springdale, town.	1,530	1,792	17.1	DOUGLAS COUNTY	43,287	44,326	2.4
Springfield, town.	2,762	2,891	4.7	Amnicon, town.	1,074	1,180	9.9
Stoughton, city	12,354	12,865	4.1	Bennett, town	622	644	3.5
Sun Prairie, city	20,369	25,810	26.7	Brule, town	591	638	8.0
Sun Prairie, town.	2,308	2,390	3.6	Cloverland, town.	247	244	–1.2
Vermont, town	839	886	5.6	Dairyland, town	186	200	7.5

WISCONSIN POPULATION
BY COUNTY AND MUNCIPALITY
April 1, 2000 and January 1, 2008–Continued

County and Municipality	2000 Census	2008 Estimate	Percent Change	County and Municipality	2000 Census	2008 Estimate	Percent Change
Gordon, town	645	738	14.4	FOND DU LAC COUNTY	97,296	101,740	4.6
Hawthorne, town	1,045	1,039	–0.6	Alto, town	1,103	1,118	1.4
Highland, town	245	273	11.4	Ashford, town	1,773	1,865	5.2
Lake Nebagamon, village	1,015	1,045	3.0	Auburn, town	2,075	2,315	11.6
Lakeside, town	609	662	8.7	Brandon, village	912	914	0.2
Maple, town	649	667	2.8	Byron, town	1,550	1,657	6.9
Oakland, town	1,144	1,214	6.1	Calumet, town	1,514	1,553	2.6
Oliver, village	358	437	22.1	Campbellsport, village	1,913	1,995	4.3
Parkland, town	1,240	1,322	6.6	Eden, town	979	1,004	2.6
Poplar, village	552	630	14.1	Eden, village	687	783	14.0
Solon Springs, town	807	910	12.8	Eldorado, town	1,447	1,488	2.8
Solon Springs, village	576	576	0.0	Empire, town	2,620	2,855	9.0
Summit, town	1,042	1,069	2.6	Fairwater, village	350	364	4.0
Superior, city	27,368	27,170	–0.7	Fond du Lac, city	42,203	43,460	3.0
Superior, town	2,058	2,264	10.0	Fond du Lac, town	2,027	2,506	23.6
Superior, village	500	610	22.0	Forest, town	1,108	1,152	4.0
Wascott, town	714	794	11.2	Friendship, town	2,406	2,575	7.0
				Kewaskum (part), village	0	0	0.0
DUNN COUNTY	39,858	43,292	8.6	Lamartine, town	1,616	1,762	9.0
Boyceville, village	1,043	1,088	4.3	Marshfield, town	1,118	1,153	3.1
Colfax, town	909	1,070	17.7	Metomen, town	709	731	3.1
Colfax, village	1,136	1,166	2.6	Mount Calvary, village	956	934	–2.3
Downing, village	257	249	–3.1	North Fond du Lac, village	4,557	4,982	9.3
Dunn, town	1,492	1,592	6.7	Oakfield, town	767	789	2.9
Eau Galle, town	797	799	0.3	Oakfield, village	1,012	1,036	2.4
Elk Mound, town	1,121	1,399	24.8	Osceola, town	1,802	1,873	3.9
Elk Mound, village	785	809	3.1	Ripon, city	7,450	7,659	2.8
Grant, town	426	432	1.4	Ripon, town	1,379	1,417	2.8
Hay River, town	546	644	17.9	Rosendale, town	783	770	–1.7
Knapp, village	421	462	9.7	Rosendale, village	923	992	7.5
Lucas, town	658	728	10.6	St. Cloud, village	497	519	4.4
Menomonie, city	14,937	15,950	6.8	Springvale, town	727	735	1.1
Menomonie, town	3,174	3,475	9.5	Taycheedah, town	3,666	3,993	8.9
New Haven, town	656	718	9.5	Waupun (part), city	3,282	3,371	2.7
Otter Creek, town	474	534	12.7	Waupun, town	1,385	1,420	2.5
Peru, town	247	266	7.7				
Red Cedar, town	1,673	1,965	17.5	FOREST COUNTY	10,024	10,393	3.7
Ridgeland, village	265	259	–2.3	Alvin, town	186	206	10.8
Rock Creek, town	793	828	4.4	Argonne, town	532	552	3.8
Sand Creek, town	586	628	7.2	Armstrong Creek, town	463	491	6.0
Sheridan, town	483	495	2.5	Blackwell, town	347	370	6.6
Sherman, town	748	856	14.4	Caswell, town	102	101	–1.0
Spring Brook, town	1,320	1,528	15.8	Crandon, city	1,961	1,984	1.2
Stanton, town	715	860	20.3	Crandon, town	614	615	0.2
Tainter, town	2,116	2,379	12.4	Freedom, town	376	398	5.9
Tiffany, town	633	654	3.3	Hiles, town	404	419	3.7
Weston, town	630	630	0.0	Laona, town	1,367	1,401	2.5
Wheeler, village	317	323	1.9	Lincoln, town	1,005	1,051	4.6
Wilson, town	500	506	1.2	Nashville, town	1,157	1,238	7.0
				Popple River, town	79	97	22.8
EAU CLAIRE COUNTY	93,142	98,302	5.5	Ross, town	167	169	1.2
Altoona, city	6,698	6,793	1.4	Wabeno, town	1,264	1,301	2.9
Augusta, city	1,460	1,476	1.1				
Bridge Creek, town	1,844	1,853	0.5	GRANT COUNTY	49,597	51,290	3.4
Brunswick, town	1,598	1,670	4.5	Bagley, village	339	340	0.3
Clear Creek, town	712	774	8.7	Beetown, town	734	817	11.3
Drammen, town	800	828	3.5	Bloomington, town	399	405	1.5
Eau Claire (part), city	59,794	63,360	6.0	Bloomington, village	701	678	–3.3
Fairchild, town	351	379	8.0	Blue River, village	429	418	–2.6
Fairchild, village	564	524	–7.1	Boscobel, city	3,047	3,334	9.4
Fall Creek, village	1,236	1,322	7.0	Boscobel, town	433	424	–2.1
Lincoln, town	1,080	1,156	7.0	Cassville, town	487	472	–3.1
Ludington, town	998	1,074	7.6	Cassville, village	1,085	1,034	–4.7
Otter Creek, town	531	536	0.9	Castle Rock, town	314	334	6.4
Pleasant Valley, town	2,681	3,077	14.8	Clifton, town	304	336	10.5
Seymour, town	2,978	3,154	5.9	Cuba City (part), city	1,945	1,916	–1.5
Union, town	2,402	2,572	7.1	Dickeyville, village	1,043	1,067	2.3
Washington, town	6,995	7,312	4.5	Ellenboro, town	608	618	1.6
Wilson, town	420	442	5.2	Fennimore, city	2,387	2,335	–2.2
				Fennimore, town	599	636	6.2
FLORENCE COUNTY	5,088	5,317	4.5	Glen Haven, town	490	471	–3.9
Aurora, town	1,186	1,223	3.1	Harrison, town	497	521	4.8
Commonwealth, town	419	425	1.4	Hazel Green, town	1,043	1,129	8.2
Fence, town	231	240	3.9	Hazel Green (part), village	1,171	1,171	0.0
Fern, town	153	165	7.8	Hickory Grove, town	443	508	14.7
Florence, town	2,319	2,425	4.6	Jamestown, town	2,077	2,164	4.2
Homestead, town	378	392	3.7	Lancaster, city	4,070	4,018	–1.3
Long Lake, town	197	211	7.1	Liberty, town	552	562	1.8
Tipler, town	205	236	15.1	Lima, town	721	797	10.5
				Little Grant, town	257	255	–0.8
				Livingston (part), village	584	586	0.3

WISCONSIN POPULATION
BY COUNTY AND MUNCIPALITY
April 1, 2000 and January 1, 2008–Continued

County and Municipality	2000 Census	2008 Estimate	Percent Change	County and Municipality	2000 Census	2008 Estimate	Percent Change
Marion, town	517	593	14.7	Dodgeville, town	1,407	1,657	17.8
Millville, town	147	158	7.5	Eden, town	397	404	1.8
Montfort (part), village	603	613	1.7	Highland, town	797	835	4.8
Mount Hope, town	225	234	4.0	Highland, village	855	859	0.5
Mount Hope, village	186	183	–1.6	Hollandale, village	283	279	–1.4
Mount Ida, town	523	543	3.8	Linden, town	873	887	1.6
Muscoda, town	674	746	10.7	Linden, village	615	604	–1.8
Muscoda (part), village	1,357	1,313	–3.2	Livingston (part), village	13	6	–53.8
North Lancaster, town	515	545	5.8	Mifflin, town	617	641	3.9
Paris, town	754	751	–0.4	Mineral Point, city	2,617	2,653	1.4
Patch Grove, town	390	404	3.6	Mineral Point, town	867	934	7.7
Patch Grove, village	166	150	–9.6	Montfort (part), village	60	55	–8.3
Platteville, city	9,989	10,575	5.9	Moscow, town	594	639	7.6
Platteville, town	1,343	1,443	7.4	Muscoda (part), village	96	80	–16.7
Potosi, town	831	836	0.6	Pulaski, town	381	397	4.2
Potosi, village	711	724	1.8	Rewey, village	311	304	–2.3
Smelser, town	756	794	5.0	Ridgeway, town	581	633	9.0
South Lancaster, town	808	916	13.4	Ridgeway, village	689	698	1.3
Tennyson, village	370	361	–2.4	Waldwick, town	500	526	5.2
Waterloo, town	557	593	6.5	Wyoming, town	364	388	6.6
Watterstown, town	362	364	0.6				
Wingville, town	394	417	5.8	IRON COUNTY	6,861	7,048	2.7
Woodman, town	194	198	2.1	Anderson, town	61	63	3.3
Woodman, village	96	94	–2.1	Carey, town	191	197	3.1
Wyalusing, town	370	396	7.0	Gurney, town	158	171	8.2
				Hurley, city	1,818	1,756	–3.4
GREEN COUNTY	33,647	36,493	8.5	Kimball, town	540	560	3.7
Adams, town	464	504	8.6	Knight, town	284	275	–3.2
Albany, town	775	1,028	32.6	Mercer, town	1,732	1,893	9.3
Albany, village	1,191	1,146	–3.8	Montreal, city	838	834	–0.5
Belleville (part), village	113	320	183.2	Oma, town	355	404	13.8
Brodhead (part), city	3,180	3,183	0.1	Pence, town	198	194	–2.0
Brooklyn, town	944	1,035	9.6	Saxon, town	350	343	–2.0
Brooklyn (part), village	414	470	13.5	Sherman, town	336	358	6.5
Browntown, village	252	263	4.4				
Cadiz, town	863	870	0.8	JACKSON COUNTY	19,100	20,140	5.4
Clarno, town	1,079	1,166	8.1	Adams, town	1,208	1,407	16.5
Decatur, town	1,688	1,946	15.3	Albion, town	1,093	1,185	8.4
Exeter, town	1,261	1,832	45.3	Alma, town	983	1,076	9.5
Jefferson, town	1,212	1,255	3.5	Alma Center, village	446	457	2.5
Jordon, town	577	639	10.7	Bear Bluff, town	128	112	–12.5
Monroe, city	10,843	10,965	1.1	Black River Falls, city	3,618	3,583	–1.0
Monroe, town	1,142	1,281	12.2	Brockway, town	2,580	2,704	4.8
Monticello, village	1,146	1,166	1.7	City Point, town	189	190	0.5
Mount Pleasant, town	547	600	9.7	Cleveland, town	438	476	8.7
New Glarus, town	943	1,300	37.9	Curran, town	366	379	3.6
New Glarus, village	2,111	2,108	–0.1	Franklin, town	325	365	12.3
Spring Grove, town	861	919	6.7	Garden Valley, town	406	415	2.2
Sylvester, town	809	908	12.2	Garfield, town	529	660	24.8
Washington, town	627	794	26.6	Hixton, town	611	645	5.6
York, town	605	795	31.4	Hixton, village	446	455	2.0
				Irving, town	602	705	17.1
GREEN LAKE COUNTY	19,105	19,416	1.6	Knapp, town	275	313	13.8
Berlin (part), city	5,222	5,227	0.1	Komensky, town	462	480	3.9
Berlin, town	1,145	1,171	2.3	Manchester, town	680	749	10.1
Brooklyn, town	1,904	1,969	3.4	Melrose, town	402	439	9.2
Green Lake, city	1,100	1,160	5.5	Melrose, village	529	513	–3.0
Green Lake, town	1,258	1,287	2.3	Merrillan, village	585	576	–1.5
Kingston, town	900	943	4.8	Millston, town	136	134	–1.5
Kingston, village	288	294	2.1	North Bend, town	397	435	9.6
Mackford, town	585	592	1.2	Northfield, town	586	571	–2.6
Manchester, town	848	892	5.2	Springfield, town	567	618	9.0
Markesan, city	1,396	1,357	–2.8	Taylor, village	513	498	–2.9
Marquette, town	481	496	3.1				
Marquette, village	169	163	–3.6	JEFFERSON COUNTY	75,767	81,022	6.9
Princeton, city	1,504	1,462	–2.8	Aztalan, town	1,447	1,468	1.5
Princeton, town	1,540	1,608	4.4	Cambridge (part), village	87	109	25.3
St. Marie, town	341	364	6.7	Cold Spring, town	766	785	2.5
Seneca, town	424	431	1.7	Concord, town	2,023	2,138	5.7
				Farmington, town	1,498	1,533	2.3
IOWA COUNTY	22,780	24,196	6.2	Fort Atkinson, city	11,621	12,130	4.4
Arena, town	1,444	1,507	4.4	Hebron, town	1,135	1,161	2.3
Arena, village	685	845	23.4	4Ixonia, town	2,902	3,580	23.4
Avoca, village	608	617	1.5	Jefferson, city	7,208	7,777	7.9
Barneveld, village	1,088	1,249	14.8	Jefferson, town	2,395	2,187	–8.7
Blanchardville (part), village	146	145	–0.7	Johnson Creek, village	1,581	2,122	34.2
Brigham, town	908	979	7.8	Koshkonong, town	3,395	3,622	6.7
Clyde, town	322	327	1.6	4Lac La Belle (part), village	0	2	0.0
Cobb, village	442	441	–0.2	Lake Mills, city	4,843	5,389	11.3
Dodgeville, city	4,220	4,607	9.2	Lake Mills, town	1,936	2,059	6.4

WISCONSIN POPULATION
BY COUNTY AND MUNCIPALITY
April 1, 2000 and January 1, 2008–Continued

County and Municipality	2000 Census	2008 Estimate	Percent Change	County and Municipality	2000 Census	2008 Estimate	Percent Change
Milford, town	1,055	1,082	2.6	Greenfield, town	1,538	1,759	14.4
Oakland, town	3,135	3,354	7.0	Hamilton, town	2,103	2,446	16.3
Palmyra, town	1,145	1,211	5.8	Holland, town	3,042	3,406	12.0
Palmyra, village	1,766	1,782	0.9	Holmen, village	6,200	7,899	27.4
Sullivan, town	2,124	2,244	5.6	La Crosse, city	51,818	51,840	0.0
Sullivan, village	688	670	-2.6	Medary, town	1,463	1,565	7.0
Sumner, town	904	906	0.2	Onalaska, city	14,839	16,660	12.3
Waterloo, city	3,259	3,352	2.9	Onalaska, town	5,210	5,524	6.0
Waterloo, town	832	962	15.6	Rockland, village	625	651	4.2
Watertown (part), city	13,535	14,585	7.8	Shelby, town	4,687	4,824	2.9
Watertown, town	1,876	1,962	4.6	Washington, town	738	747	1.2
Whitewater (part), city	2,611	2,850	9.2	West Salem, village	4,738	4,852	2.4
JUNEAU COUNTY	24,316	27,359	12.5	LAFAYETTE COUNTY	16,137	16,468	2.1
Armenia, town	707	894	26.4	Argyle, town	479	495	3.3
Camp Douglas, village	592	550	-7.1	Argyle, village	823	815	-1.0
Clearfield, town	737	798	8.3	Belmont, town	676	736	8.9
Cutler, town	282	299	6.0	Belmont, village	871	906	4.0
Elroy, city	1,578	1,541	-2.3	Benton, town	469	506	7.9
Finley, town	84	89	6.0	Benton, village	976	1,002	2.7
Fountain, town	582	628	7.9	Blanchard, town	261	285	9.2
Germantown, town	1,174	1,513	28.9	Blanchardville (part),			
Hustler, village	113	116	2.7	village	660	641	-2.9
Kildare, town	557	635	14.0	Cuba City (part), city	211	210	-0.5
Kingston, town	58	52	-10.3	Darlington, city	2,418	2,406	-0.5
Lemonweir, town	1,763	1,831	3.9	Darlington, town	757	830	9.6
Lindina, town	730	752	3.0	Elk Grove, town	463	491	6.0
Lisbon, town	1,020	1,043	2.3	Fayette, town	366	376	2.7
Lyndon, town	1,217	1,437	18.1	Gratiot, town	653	650	-0.5
Lyndon Station, village	458	469	2.4	Gratiot, village	252	237	-6.0
Marion, town	433	481	11.1	Hazel Green (part), village	12	15	25.0
Mauston, city	3,740	4,293	14.8	Kendall, town	320	344	7.5
Necedah, town	2,156	2,491	15.5	Lamont, town	267	291	9.0
Necedah, village	888	883	-0.6	Monticello, town	148	140	-5.4
New Lisbon, city	1,436	2,381	65.8	New Diggings, town	473	483	2.1
Orange, town	549	578	5.3	Seymour, town	363	378	4.1
Plymouth, town	639	678	6.1	Shullsburg, city	1,246	1,205	-3.3
Seven Mile Creek, town	369	407	10.3	Shullsburg, town	364	357	-1.9
Summit, town	623	683	9.6	South Wayne, village	484	474	-2.1
Union Center, village	214	219	2.3	Wayne, town	496	487	-1.8
Wonewoc, town	783	813	3.8	White Oak Springs, town	97	102	5.2
Wonewoc, village	834	805	-3.5	Willow Springs, town	632	695	10.0
				Wiota, town	900	911	1.2
KENOSHA COUNTY	149,577	162,094	8.4				
Brighton, town	1,450	1,526	5.2	LANGLADE COUNTY	20,740	21,680	4.5
Bristol, town	4,538	4,863	7.2	Ackley, town	510	538	5.5
Genoa City (part), village	0	8	0.0	Ainsworth, town	571	629	10.2
Kenosha, city	90,352	95,910	6.2	Antigo, city	8,560	8,637	0.9
Paddock Lake, village	3,012	3,092	2.7	Antigo, town	1,487	1,515	1.9
Paris, town	1,473	1,536	4.3	Elcho, town	1,317	1,403	6.5
Pleasant Prairie, village	16,136	19,565	21.3	Evergreen, town	468	495	5.8
Randall, town	2,929	3,180	8.6	Langlade, town	472	506	7.2
Salem, town	9,871	11,420	15.7	Neva, town	994	1,062	6.8
Silver Lake, village	2,341	2,493	6.5	Norwood, town	918	995	8.4
Somers, town	9,059	9,452	4.3	Parrish, town	108	134	24.1
Twin Lakes, village	5,124	5,609	9.5	Peck, town	354	372	5.1
Wheatland, town	3,292	3,440	4.5	Polar, town	995	1,040	4.5
				Price, town	243	256	5.3
KEWAUNEE COUNTY	20,187	21,358	5.8	Rolling, town	1,452	1,588	9.4
Ahnapee, town	977	1,014	3.8	Summit, town	168	192	14.3
Algoma, city	3,357	3,372	0.4	Upham, town	689	743	7.8
Carlton, town	1,000	1,061	6.1	Vilas, town	249	251	0.8
Casco, town	1,153	1,257	9.0	White Lake, village	329	345	4.9
Casco, village	572	580	1.4	Wolf River, town	856	979	14.4
Franklin, town	997	1,065	6.8				
Kewaunee, city	2,806	2,906	3.6	LINCOLN COUNTY	29,641	30,681	3.5
Lincoln, town	957	1,010	5.5	Birch, town	801	693	-13.5
Luxemburg, town	1,402	1,482	5.7	Bradley, town	2,573	2,747	6.8
Luxemburg, village	1,935	2,354	21.7	Corning, town	826	874	5.8
Montpelier, town	1,371	1,440	5.0	Harding, town	334	354	6.0
Pierce, town	897	929	3.6	Harrison, town	793	915	15.4
Red River, town	1,476	1,552	5.1	King, town	842	900	6.9
West Kewaunee, town	1,287	1,336	3.8	Merrill, city	10,146	10,130	-0.2
				Merrill, town	2,979	3,149	5.7
LA CROSSE COUNTY	107,120	112,758	5.3	Pine River, town	1,877	1,983	5.6
Bangor, town	583	595	2.1	Rock Falls, town	598	663	10.9
Bangor, village	1,400	1,420	1.4	Russell, town	693	726	4.8
Barre, town	1,014	1,190	17.4	Schley, town	909	967	6.4
Burns, town	979	1,028	5.0	Scott, town	1,287	1,381	7.3
Campbell, town	4,410	4,413	0.1	Skanawan, town	354	393	11.0
Farmington, town	1,733	1,939	11.9	Somo, town	121	153	26.4

WISCONSIN POPULATION
BY COUNTY AND MUNCIPALITY
April 1, 2000 and January 1, 2008–Continued

County and Municipality	2000 Census	2008 Estimate	Percent Change	County and Municipality	2000 Census	2008 Estimate	Percent Change
Tomahawk, city	3,770	3,829	1.6	Reid, town	1,191	1,273	6.9
Tomahawk, town	439	493	12.3	Rib Falls, town	907	991	9.3
Wilson, town	299	331	10.7	Rib Mountain, town	7,556	7,658	1.3
				Rietbrock, town	927	1,004	8.3
MANITOWOC COUNTY	82,893	84,830	2.3	Ringle, town	1,408	1,585	12.6
Cato, town	1,616	1,691	4.6	Rothschild, village	4,970	5,336	7.4
Centerville, town	713	723	1.4	Schofield, city	2,117	2,310	9.1
Cleveland, village	1,361	1,415	4.0	Spencer, town	1,341	1,560	16.3
Cooperstown, town	1,389	1,415	1.9	Spencer, village	1,932	1,960	1.4
Eaton, town	761	845	11.0	Stettin, town	2,191	2,365	7.9
Francis Creek, village	681	699	2.6	Stratford, village	1,523	1,573	3.3
Franklin, town	1,293	1,350	4.4	Texas, town	1,703	1,758	3.2
Gibson, town	1,352	1,445	6.9	Unity (part), village	205	192	–6.3
Kellnersville, village	374	361	–3.5	Wausau, city	38,426	40,360	5.0
Kiel (part), city	3,129	3,345	6.9	Wausau, town	2,214	2,252	1.7
Kossuth, town	2,033	2,115	4.0	Weston, town	514	600	16.7
Liberty, town	1,287	1,372	6.6	Weston, village	12,079	14,040	16.2
Manitowoc, city	34,053	34,670	1.8	Wien, town	712	807	13.3
Manitowoc, town	1,073	1,158	7.9				
Manitowoc Rapids, town	2,520	2,543	0.9	MARINETTE COUNTY	43,384	44,823	3.3
Maple Grove, town	852	882	3.5	Amberg, town	854	868	1.6
Maribel, village	284	277	–2.5	Athelstane, town	601	629	4.7
Meeme, town	1,538	1,554	1.0	Beaver, town	1,123	1,205	7.3
Mishicot, town	1,409	1,444	2.5	Beecher, town	783	848	8.3
Mishicot, village	1,422	1,444	1.5	Coleman, village	716	700	–2.2
Newton, town	2,241	2,358	5.2	Crivitz, village	998	1,035	3.7
Reedsville, village	1,187	1,192	0.4	Dunbar, town	1,303	1,252	–3.9
Rockland, town	896	969	8.1	Goodman, town	820	858	4.6
St. Nazianz, village	749	752	0.4	Grover, town	1,729	1,846	6.8
Schleswig, town	1,900	2,073	9.1	Lake, town	1,064	1,189	11.7
Two Creeks, town	551	552	0.2	Marinette, city	11,749	11,365	–3.3
Two Rivers, city	12,639	12,540	–0.8	Middle Inlet, town	831	900	8.3
Two Rivers, town	1,912	1,914	0.1	Niagara, city	1,880	1,831	–2.6
Valders, village	948	993	4.7	Niagara, town	924	957	3.6
Whitelaw, village	730	739	1.2	Pembine, town	1,036	1,126	8.7
				Peshtigo, city	3,474	3,496	0.6
MARATHON COUNTY	125,834	135,190	7.4	Peshtigo, town	3,702	4,008	8.3
Abbotsford (part), city	544	605	11.2	Porterfield, town	1,991	2,109	5.9
Athens, village	1,095	1,120	2.3	Pound, town	1,367	1,417	3.7
Bergen, town	615	665	8.1	Pound, village	355	331	–6.8
Berlin, town	887	967	9.0	Silver Cliff, town	529	606	14.6
Bern, town	562	596	6.0	Stephenson, town	3,065	3,517	14.7
Bevent, town	1,126	1,218	8.2	Wagner, town	722	831	15.1
Birnamwood (part), village	10	16	60.0	Wausaukee, town	1,196	1,349	12.8
Brighton, town	611	616	0.8	Wausaukee, village	572	550	–3.8
Brokaw, village	107	204	90.7				
Cassel, town	847	922	8.9	MARQUETTE COUNTY	14,555	15,423	6.0
Cleveland, town	1,160	1,336	15.2	Buffalo, town	1,085	1,236	13.9
Colby (part), city	460	513	11.5	Crystal Lake, town	513	544	6.0
Day, town	1,023	1,110	8.5	Douglas, town	768	812	5.7
Dorchester (part), village	4	4	0.0	Endeavor, village	440	452	2.7
Easton, town	1,062	1,132	6.6	Harris, town	729	795	9.1
Eau Pleine, town	750	783	4.4	Mecan, town	726	776	6.9
Edgar, village	1,386	1,491	7.6	Montello, city	1,397	1,479	5.9
Elderon, town	567	590	4.1	Montello, town	1,043	1,060	1.6
Elderon, village	189	181	–4.2	Moundville, town	574	595	3.7
Emmet, town	842	928	10.2	Neshkoro, town	595	614	3.2
Fenwood, village	174	153	–12.1	Neshkoro, village	453	448	–1.1
Frankfort, town	651	692	6.3	Newton, town	550	564	2.5
Franzen, town	505	524	3.8	Oxford, town	859	975	13.5
Green Valley, town	514	555	8.0	Oxford, village	536	564	5.2
Guenther, town	302	337	11.6	Packwaukee, town	1,297	1,298	0.1
Halsey, town	645	685	6.2	Shields, town	456	505	10.7
Hamburg, town	910	968	6.4	Springfield, town	628	687	9.4
Harrison, town	418	445	6.5	Westfield, town	689	798	15.8
Hatley, village	476	514	8.0	Westfield, village	1,217	1,221	0.3
Hewitt, town	545	617	13.2				
Holton, town	907	924	1.9	MENOMINEE COUNTY	4,562	4,630	1.5
Hull, town	773	760	–1.7	Menominee, town	4,562	4,630	1.5
Johnson, town	993	1,034	4.1				
Knowlton, town	1,688	1,897	12.4	MILWAUKEE COUNTY	940,164	938,490	–0.2
[5]Kronenwetter, village	5,369	6,378	18.8	Bayside (part), village	4,415	4,056	–8.1
Maine, town	2,407	2,460	2.2	Brown Deer, village	12,170	11,705	–3.8
Marathon, town	1,085	1,113	2.6	Cudahy, city	18,429	18,620	1.0
Marathon City, village	1,640	1,626	–0.9	Fox Point, village	7,012	6,828	–2.6
Marshfield (part), city	417	654	56.8	Franklin, city	29,494	33,550	13.8
McMillan, town	1,790	1,933	8.0	Glendale, city	13,367	12,990	–2.8
Mosinee, city	4,063	4,220	3.9	Greendale, village	14,405	13,995	–2.8
Mosinee, town	2,146	2,303	7.3	Greenfield, city	35,476	36,270	2.2
Norrie, town	967	1,051	8.7	Hales Corners, village	7,765	7,646	–1.5
Plover, town	686	726	5.8	Milwaukee (part), city	596,974	590,870	–1.0

WISCONSIN POPULATION
BY COUNTY AND MUNCIPALITY
April 1, 2000 and January 1, 2008–Continued

County and Municipality	2000 Census	2008 Estimate	Percent Change	County and Municipality	2000 Census	2008 Estimate	Percent Change
Oak Creek, city	28,456	32,470	14.1	Hazelhurst, town	1,267	1,382	9.1
River Hills, village.	1,631	1,641	0.6	Lake Tomahawk, town. . .	1,160	1,221	5.3
St. Francis, city	8,662	8,952	3.3	Little Rice, town	314	315	0.3
Shorewood, village	13,763	13,425	-2.5	Lynne, town	210	206	-1.9
South Milwaukee, city. . .	21,256	21,310	0.3	Minocqua, town	4,859	5,347	10.0
Wauwatosa, city	47,271	45,880	-2.9	Monico, town	364	372	2.2
West Allis, city.	61,254	60,370	-1.4	Newbold, town	2,710	2,927	8.0
West Milwaukee, village. .	4,201	4,047	-3.7	Nokomis, town.	1,363	1,474	8.1
Whitefish Bay, village . . .	14,163	13,875	-2.0	Pelican, town.	2,902	2,661	-8.3
				Piehl, town.	93	101	8.6
MONROE COUNTY	40,896	44,170	8.0	Pine Lake, town	2,720	2,872	5.6
Adrian, town	682	785	15.1	Rhinelander, city	7,735	8,223	6.3
Angelo, town.	1,268	1,309	3.2	Schoepke, town	352	354	0.6
Byron, town	1,394	1,462	4.9	Stella, town	633	690	9.0
Cashton, village	1,005	1,081	7.6	Sugar Camp, town	1,781	1,934	8.6
Clifton, town.	693	740	6.8	Three Lakes, town	2,339	2,460	5.2
Glendale, town.	563	628	11.5	Woodboro, town	685	727	6.1
Grant, town	483	509	5.4	Woodruff, town	1,982	2,169	9.4
Greenfield, town	626	672	7.3				
Jefferson, town	800	827	3.4	OUTAGAMIE COUNTY . . .	161,091	174,778	8.5
Kendall, village	482	475	-1.5	Appleton (part), city	58,301	60,170	3.2
La Grange, town	1,761	1,859	5.6	Bear Creek, village.	415	409	-1.4
Lafayette, town	318	339	6.6	Black Creek, town	1,268	1,286	1.4
Leon, town	858	1,052	22.6	Black Creek, village	1,192	1,265	6.1
Lincoln, town	827	892	7.9	Bovina, town.	1,130	1,233	9.1
Little Falls, town	1,334	1,539	15.4	Buchanan, town	5,827	6,708	15.1
Melvina, village	93	90	-3.2	Center, town	3,163	3,412	7.9
New Lyme, town.	141	157	11.3	Cicero, town	1,092	1,122	2.7
Norwalk, village	653	630	-3.5	Combined Locks, village .	2,422	3,036	25.4
Oakdale, town	679	813	19.7	Dale, town	2,288	2,599	13.6
Oakdale, village	297	321	8.1	Deer Creek, town	682	679	-0.4
Portland, town	686	716	4.4	Ellington, town.	2,535	2,806	10.7
Ridgeville, town	491	583	18.7	Freedom, town	5,241	5,714	9.0
Scott, town	117	120	2.6	Grand Chute, town.	18,392	20,520	11.6
Sheldon, town	682	706	3.5	Greenville, town	6,844	9,401	37.4
Sparta, city	8,648	9,198	6.4	Hortonia, town.	1,063	1,090	2.5
Sparta, town	2,753	3,054	10.9	Hortonville, village	2,357	2,723	15.5
Tomah, city.	8,419	9,075	7.8	Howard (part), village . . .	0	0	0.0
Tomah, town	1,194	1,308	9.5	Kaukauna, city	12,983	14,925	15.0
Warrens, village	286	360	25.9	[6]Kaukauna, town.	1,116	1,226	9.9
Wellington, town.	544	600	10.3	Kimberly, village.	6,146	6,451	5.0
Wells, town.	529	599	13.2	Liberty, town.	834	900	7.9
Wilton, town	925	987	6.7	Little Chute, village	10,476	11,035	5.3
Wilton, village	519	550	6.0	Maine, town	831	932	12.2
Wyeville, village	146	134	-8.2	Maple Creek, town.	687	675	-1.7
				New London (part), city . .	1,467	1,491	1.6
OCONTO COUNTY	35,652	39,261	10.1	Nichols, village	307	276	-10.1
Abrams, town	1,757	1,944	10.6	Oneida, town.	4,147	4,320	4.2
Bagley, town	333	347	4.2	Osborn, town.	1,029	1,157	12.4
Brazeau, town	1,408	1,491	5.9	Seymour, city	3,335	3,463	3.8
Breed, town	657	780	18.7	Seymour, town	1,216	1,266	4.1
Chase, town	2,082	2,822	35.5	Shiocton, village	954	955	0.1
Doty, town	249	286	14.9	Vandenbroek, town	1,351	1,371	1.5
Gillett, city	1,262	1,214	-3.8	[6]Wrightstown (part), village	0	162	0.0
Gillett, town	1,090	1,110	1.8				
How, town	563	583	3.6	OZAUKEE COUNTY	82,317	87,008	5.7
Lakewood, town	875	980	12.0	Bayside (part), village . . .	103	116	12.6
Lena, town	757	772	2.0	Belgium, town	1,513	1,617	6.9
Lena, village	529	505	-4.5	Belgium, village	1,678	2,053	22.3
Little River, town	1,065	1,121	5.3	Cedarburg, city.	11,102	11,435	3.0
Little Suamico, town. . . .	3,877	4,856	25.3	Cedarburg, town	5,550	5,789	4.3
Maple Valley, town	670	729	8.8	Fredonia, town	2,083	2,159	3.6
Morgan, town	882	1,016	15.2	Fredonia, village	1,934	2,143	10.8
Mountain, town	860	913	6.2	Grafton, town	3,980	4,130	3.8
Oconto, city	4,708	4,756	1.0	Grafton, village	10,464	11,450	9.4
Oconto, town.	1,251	1,439	15.0	Mequon, city.	22,643	23,670	4.5
Oconto Falls, city	2,843	2,917	2.6	Newburg (part), village . .	92	84	-8.7
Oconto Falls, town.	1,139	1,256	10.3	Port Washington, city . . .	10,467	11,185	6.9
Pensaukee, town	1,214	1,407	15.9	Port Washington, town. . .	1,631	1,685	3.3
Pulaski (part), village . . .	2	0	—	Saukville, town	1,755	1,805	2.8
Riverview, town	829	912	10.0	Saukville, village.	4,068	4,358	7.1
Spruce, town	871	956	9.8	Thiensville, village.	3,254	3,329	2.3
Stiles, town.	1,465	1,589	8.5				
Suring, village	605	564	-6.8	PEPIN COUNTY	7,213	7,743	7.3
Townsend, town	963	1,099	14.1	Albany, town.	620	736	18.7
Underhill, town	846	897	6.0	Durand, city	1,968	1,962	-0.3
				Durand, town	694	726	4.6
ONEIDA COUNTY	36,776	38,903	5.8	Frankfort, town	362	381	5.2
Cassian, town	962	1,041	8.2	Lima, town.	716	757	5.7
Crescent, town	2,071	2,144	3.5	Pepin, town	580	666	14.8
Enterprise, town	274	283	3.3	Pepin, village.	878	953	8.5

WISCONSIN POPULATION
BY COUNTY AND MUNCIPALITY
April 1, 2000 and January 1, 2008–Continued

County and Municipality	2000 Census	2008 Estimate	Percent Change	County and Municipality	2000 Census	2008 Estimate	Percent Change
Stockholm, town	75	175	133.3	Eau Pleine, town	931	985	5.8
Stockholm, village	97	95	–2.1	Grant, town	2,020	2,105	4.2
Waterville, town	859	887	3.3	Hull, town	5,493	5,638	2.6
Waubeek, town	364	405	11.3	Junction City, village	440	429	–2.5
				Lanark, town	1,449	1,597	10.2
PIERCE COUNTY	36,804	40,523	10.1	Linwood, town	1,111	1,170	5.3
Bay City, village	491	491	0.0	Milladore (part), village	0	9	0.0
Clifton, town	1,657	1,996	20.5	Nelsonville, village	191	181	–5.2
Diamond Bluff, town	479	511	6.7	New Hope, town	736	758	3.0
El Paso, town	690	775	12.3	Park Ridge, village	488	469	–3.9
Ellsworth, town	1,064	1,147	7.8	Pine Grove, town	904	921	1.9
Ellsworth, village	2,909	3,179	9.3	Plover, town	2,415	1,910	–20.9
Elmwood, village	841	832	–1.1	Plover, village	10,520	11,850	12.6
Gilman, town	772	922	19.4	Rosholt, village	518	497	–4.1
Hartland, town	814	855	5.0	Sharon, town	1,936	2,040	5.4
Isabelle, town	289	307	6.2	Stevens Point, city	24,551	26,050	6.1
Maiden Rock, town	589	629	6.8	Stockton, town	2,896	3,062	5.7
Maiden Rock, village	121	123	1.7	Whiting, village	1,760	1,671	–5.1
Martell, town	1,070	1,182	10.5				
Oak Grove, town	1,522	1,978	30.0	PRICE COUNTY	15,822	16,088	1.7
Plum City, village	574	596	3.8	Catawba, town	283	310	9.5
Prescott, city	3,764	4,056	7.8	Catawba, village	149	133	–10.7
River Falls (part), city	10,242	11,385	11.2	Eisenstein, town	669	684	2.2
River Falls, town	2,304	2,397	4.0	Elk, town	1,183	1,226	3.6
Rock Elm, town	504	531	5.4	Emery, town	325	332	2.2
Salem, town	505	532	5.3	Fifield, town	989	1,002	1.3
Spring Lake, town	550	597	8.5	Flambeau, town	535	583	9.0
Spring Valley (part), village	1,187	1,315	10.8	Georgetown, town	164	176	7.3
Trenton, town	1,737	1,896	9.2	Hackett, town	202	207	2.5
Trimbelle, town	1,511	1,671	10.6	Harmony, town	211	216	2.4
Union, town	618	620	0.3	Hill, town	364	419	15.1
				Kennan, town	378	399	5.6
POLK COUNTY	41,319	45,892	11.1	Kennan, village	171	167	–2.3
Alden, town	2,615	2,927	11.9	Knox, town	399	408	2.3
Amery, city	2,845	2,919	2.6	Lake, town	1,319	1,407	6.7
Apple River, town	1,067	1,182	10.8	Ogema, town	882	911	3.3
Balsam Lake, town	1,384	1,464	5.8	Park Falls, city	2,793	2,617	–6.3
Balsam Lake, village	950	1,075	13.2	Phillips, city	1,675	1,625	–3.0
Beaver, town	753	853	13.3	Prentice, town	479	501	4.6
Black Brook, town	1,208	1,416	17.2	Prentice, village	626	634	1.3
Bone Lake, town	710	807	13.7	Spirit, town	315	360	14.3
Centuria, village	865	939	8.6	Worcester, town	1,711	1,771	3.5
Clam Falls, town	547	593	8.4				
Clayton, town	912	1,048	14.9	RACINE COUNTY	188,831	196,321	4.0
Clayton, village	507	572	12.8	Burlington (part), city	9,936	10,490	5.6
Clear Lake, town	800	887	10.9	Burlington, town	6,384	6,491	1.7
Clear Lake, village	1,051	1,143	8.8	[7]Caledonia, village	23,614	25,110	6.3
Dresser, village	732	875	19.5	Dover, town	3,908	4,105	5.0
Eureka, town	1,338	1,605	20.0	Elmwood Park, village	474	439	–7.4
Farmington, town	1,625	1,902	17.0	Mount Pleasant, village	23,142	26,040	12.5
Frederic, village	1,262	1,239	–1.8	North Bay, village	260	244	–6.2
Garfield, town	1,443	1,678	16.3	Norway, town	7,600	8,061	6.1
Georgetown, town	1,004	1,103	9.9	Racine, city	81,855	80,320	–1.9
Johnstown, town	520	590	13.5	Raymond, town	3,516	3,797	8.0
Laketown, town	918	972	5.9	Rochester, town	2,254	2,539	12.6
Lincoln, town	2,304	2,483	7.8	Rochester, village	1,149	1,192	3.7
Lorain, town	328	332	1.2	Sturtevant, village	5,287	6,354	20.2
Luck, town	881	864	–1.9	Union Grove, village	4,322	4,530	4.8
Luck, village	1,210	1,226	1.3	Waterford, town	5,938	6,566	10.6
McKinley, town	328	358	9.1	Waterford, village	4,048	4,848	19.8
Milltown, town	1,146	1,270	10.8	Wind Point, village	1,853	1,810	–2.3
Milltown, village	888	914	2.9	Yorkville, town	3,291	3,385	2.9
Osceola, town	2,085	2,793	34.0				
Osceola, village	2,421	2,732	12.8	RICHLAND COUNTY	17,924	18,317	2.2
St. Croix Falls, city	2,033	2,184	7.4	Akan, town	444	456	2.7
St. Croix Falls, town	1,119	1,256	12.2	Bloom, town	487	490	0.6
Sterling, town	724	780	7.7	Boaz, village	137	133	–2.9
Turtle Lake (part), village	65	153	135.4	Buena Vista, town	1,575	1,722	9.3
West Sweden, town	731	758	3.7	Cazenovia (part), village	326	332	1.8
				Dayton, town	723	739	2.2
PORTAGE COUNTY	67,182	70,506	4.9	Eagle, town	593	588	–0.8
Alban, town	897	916	2.1	Forest, town	390	403	3.3
Almond, town	679	682	0.4	Henrietta, town	479	489	2.1
Almond, village	459	431	–6.1	Ithaca, town	648	669	3.2
Amherst, town	1,435	1,496	4.3	Lone Rock, village	929	907	–2.4
Amherst, village	964	1,052	9.1	Marshall, town	600	621	3.5
Amherst Junction, village	305	339	11.1	Orion, town	628	650	3.5
Belmont, town	623	644	3.4	Richland, town	1,364	1,388	1.8
Buena Vista, town	1,187	1,201	1.2	Richland Center, city	5,114	5,167	1.0
Carson, town	1,299	1,367	5.2	Richwood, town	618	621	0.5
Dewey, town	975	1,036	6.3	Rockbridge, town	721	774	7.4

WISCONSIN POPULATION
BY COUNTY AND MUNCIPALITY
April 1, 2000 and January 1, 2008–Continued

County and Municipality	2000 Census	2008 Estimate	Percent Change	County and Municipality	2000 Census	2008 Estimate	Percent Change
Sylvan, town	547	564	3.1	Forest, town	590	642	8.8
Viola (part), village	422	414	-1.9	Glenwood, town	755	871	15.4
Westford, town	594	601	1.2	Glenwood City, city	1,183	1,218	3.0
Willow, town	493	504	2.2	Hammond, town	947	1,693	78.8
Yuba, village	92	85	-7.6	Hammond, village	1,153	1,638	42.1
				Hudson, city	8,775	11,865	35.2
ROCK COUNTY	152,307	160,477	5.4	Hudson, town	6,213	7,931	27.7
Avon, town	586	610	4.1	Kinnickinnic, town	1,400	1,688	20.6
Beloit, city	35,775	37,110	3.7	New Richmond, city	6,310	7,981	26.5
Beloit, town	7,038	7,445	5.8	North Hudson, village	3,463	3,700	6.8
Bradford, town	1,007	1,035	2.8	Pleasant Valley, town	430	497	15.6
Brodhead (part), city	0	50	0.0	Richmond, town	1,556	2,883	85.3
Center, town	1,005	1,093	8.8	River Falls (part), city	2,318	2,843	22.6
Clinton, town	893	926	3.7	Roberts, village	969	1,554	60.4
Clinton, village	2,162	2,218	2.6	Rush River, town	498	529	6.2
Edgerton (part), city	4,891	5,286	8.1	St. Joseph, town	3,436	3,884	13.0
Evansville, city	4,039	4,947	22.5	Somerset, town	2,644	3,447	30.4
Footville, village	788	763	-3.2	Somerset, village	1,556	2,300	47.8
Fulton, town	3,158	3,291	4.2	Spring Valley (part), village	2	4	100.0
Harmony, town	2,351	2,469	5.0	Springfield, town	808	930	15.1
Janesville, city	60,200	63,540	5.5	Stanton, town	1,003	1,004	0.1
Janesville, town	3,048	3,416	12.1	Star Prairie, town	2,944	3,544	20.4
Johnstown, town	802	809	0.9	Star Prairie, village	574	645	12.4
La Prairie, town	929	891	-4.1	Troy, town	3,661	4,534	23.8
Lima, town	1,312	1,326	1.1	Warren, town	1,320	1,541	16.7
Magnolia, town	854	840	-1.6	Wilson, town	176	205	16.5
Milton, city	5,132	5,667	10.4	Woodville, village	1,104	1,328	20.3
Milton, town	2,844	3,005	5.7				
Newark, town	1,571	1,582	0.7	SAUK COUNTY	55,225	61,086	10.6
Orfordville, village	1,272	1,407	10.6	Baraboo, city	10,711	11,755	9.7
Plymouth, town	1,270	1,306	2.8	Baraboo, town	1,828	1,966	7.5
Porter, town	925	968	4.6	Bear Creek, town	497	580	16.7
Rock, town	3,338	3,277	-1.8	Cazenovia (part), village	0	24	0.0
Spring Valley, town	813	823	1.2	Dellona, town	1,199	1,536	28.1
Turtle, town	2,444	2,406	-1.6	Delton, town	2,024	2,238	10.6
Union, town	1,860	1,971	6.0	Excelsior, town	1,410	1,578	11.9
				Fairfield, town	1,023	1,071	4.7
RUSK COUNTY	15,347	15,657	2.0	Franklin, town	696	697	0.1
Atlanta, town	627	669	6.7	Freedom, town	416	428	2.9
Big Bend, town	402	429	6.7	Greenfield, town	911	966	6.0
Big Falls, town	107	114	6.5	Honey Creek, town	736	746	1.4
Bruce, village	787	758	-3.7	Ironton, town	650	699	7.5
Cedar Rapids, town	37	36	-2.7	Ironton, village	250	248	-0.8
Conrath, village	98	105	7.1	La Valle, town	1,203	1,413	17.5
Dewey, town	523	600	14.7	La Valle, village	326	324	-0.6
Flambeau, town	1,067	1,135	6.4	Lake Delton, village	1,982	2,770	39.8
Glen Flora, village	93	94	1.1	Lime Ridge, village	169	163	-3.6
Grant, town	767	792	3.3	Loganville, village	276	273	-1.1
Grow, town	473	478	1.1	Merrimac, town	868	948	9.2
Hawkins, town	170	177	4.1	Merrimac, village	416	457	9.9
Hawkins, village	317	333	5.0	North Freedom, village	649	629	-3.1
Hubbard, town	168	179	6.5	Plain, village	792	803	1.4
Ingram, village	76	72	-5.3	Prairie du Sac, town	1,138	1,138	0.0
Ladysmith, city	3,932	3,648	-7.2	Prairie du Sac, village	3,231	3,735	15.6
Lawrence, town	240	276	15.0	Reedsburg, city	7,827	9,118	16.5
Marshall, town	683	714	4.5	Reedsburg, town	1,236	1,256	1.6
Murry, town	275	287	4.4	Rock Springs, village	425	406	-4.5
Richland, town	206	251	21.8	Sauk City, village	3,109	3,300	6.1
Rusk, town	475	525	10.5	Spring Green, town	1,585	1,771	11.7
Sheldon, village	256	245	-4.3	Spring Green, village	1,444	1,513	4.8
South Fork, town	120	118	-1.7	Sumpter, town	1,021	1,060	3.8
Strickland, town	300	304	1.3	Troy, town	773	774	0.1
Stubbs, town	587	624	6.3	Washington, town	904	959	6.1
Thornapple, town	811	834	2.8	West Baraboo, village	1,248	1,288	3.2
Tony, village	105	99	-5.7	Westfield, town	611	606	-0.8
True, town	291	282	-3.1	Winfield, town	752	832	10.6
Washington, town	312	369	18.3	Wisconsin Dells (part), city	106	113	6.6
Weyerhaeuser, village	353	329	-6.8	Woodland, town	783	905	15.6
Wilkinson, town	66	69	4.5				
Willard, town	539	623	15.6	SAWYER COUNTY	16,196	17,753	9.6
Wilson, town	84	89	6.0	Bass Lake, town	2,244	2,447	9.0
				Couderay, town	469	483	3.0
ST. CROIX COUNTY	63,155	79,702	26.2	Couderay, village	96	95	-1.0
Baldwin, town	903	965	6.9	Draper, town	171	200	17.0
Baldwin, village	2,667	3,568	33.8	Edgewater, town	586	641	9.4
Cady, town	710	815	14.8	Exeland, village	212	208	-1.9
Cylon, town	629	672	6.8	Hayward, city	2,129	2,321	9.0
Deer Park, village	227	222	-2.2	Hayward, town	3,279	3,574	9.0
Eau Galle, town	882	1,077	22.1	Hunter, town	765	839	9.7
Emerald, town	691	801	15.9	Lenroot, town	1,165	1,342	15.2
Erin Prairie, town	658	683	3.8	Meadowbrook, town	146	153	4.8

WISCONSIN POPULATION
BY COUNTY AND MUNCIPALITY
April 1, 2000 and January 1, 2008–Continued

County and Municipality	2000 Census	2008 Estimate	Percent Change	County and Municipality	2000 Census	2008 Estimate	Percent Change
Meteor, town	170	185	8.8	TAYLOR COUNTY	19,680	20,065	2.0
Ojibwa, town	267	319	19.5	Aurora, town	386	364	−5.7
Radisson, town	465	476	2.4	Browning, town	850	896	5.4
Radisson, village	222	216	−2.7	Chelsea, town	719	763	6.1
Round Lake, town	962	1,103	14.7	Cleveland, town	262	276	5.3
Sand Lake, town	774	838	8.3	Deer Creek, town	733	759	3.5
Spider Lake, town	391	423	8.2	Ford, town	276	269	−2.5
Weirgor, town	370	431	16.5	Gilman, village	474	454	−4.2
Winter, town	969	1,126	16.2	Goodrich, town	487	500	2.7
Winter, village	344	333	−3.2	Greenwood, town	642	674	5.0
				Grover, town	233	236	1.3
SHAWANO COUNTY	40,664	42,602	4.8	Hammel, town	735	745	1.4
Almon, town	591	595	0.7	Holway, town	854	878	2.8
Angelica, town	1,635	1,762	7.8	Jump River, town	311	316	1.6
Aniwa, town	586	601	2.6	Little Black, town	1,148	1,194	4.0
Aniwa, village	272	268	−1.5	Lublin, village	110	100	−9.1
Bartelme, town	700	791	13.0	Maplehurst, town	359	377	5.0
Belle Plaine, town	1,867	1,921	2.9	McKinley, town	418	439	5.0
Birnamwood, town	711	771	8.4	Medford, city	4,350	4,275	−1.7
Birnamwood (part), village	785	797	1.5	Medford, town	2,216	2,336	5.4
Bonduel, village	1,416	1,436	1.4	Molitor, town	263	281	6.8
Bowler, village	343	341	−0.6	Pershing, town	180	183	1.7
Cecil, village	466	572	22.7	Rib Lake, town	768	778	1.3
Eland, village	251	230	−8.4	Rib Lake, village	878	860	−2.1
Fairbanks, town	687	699	1.7	Roosevelt, town	444	459	3.4
Germania, town	339	355	4.7	Stetsonville, village	563	551	−2.1
Grant, town	974	996	2.3	Taft, town	361	387	7.2
Green Valley, town	1,024	1,048	2.3	Westboro, town	660	715	8.3
Gresham, village	575	593	3.1				
Hartland, town	825	901	9.2	TREMPEALEAU COUNTY	27,010	28,278	4.7
Herman, town	741	765	3.2	Albion, town	595	673	13.1
Hutchins, town	539	581	7.8	Arcadia, city	2,402	2,416	0.6
Lessor, town	1,112	1,243	11.8	Arcadia, town	1,555	1,685	8.4
Maple Grove, town	1,045	1,047	0.2	Blair, city	1,273	1,292	1.5
Marion (part), city	1	11	1000.0	Burnside, town	529	536	1.3
Mattoon, village	466	447	−4.1	Caledonia, town	759	900	18.6
Morris, town	485	521	7.4	Chimney Rock, town	276	286	3.6
Navarino, town	422	408	−3.3	Dodge, town	414	426	2.9
Pella, town	877	914	4.2	Eleva, village	635	658	3.6
Pulaski (part), village	45	152	237.8	Ettrick, town	1,284	1,307	1.8
Red Springs, town	981	1,048	6.8	Ettrick, village	521	516	−1.0
Richmond, town	1,719	1,872	8.9	Gale, town	1,426	1,597	12.0
Seneca, town	567	560	−1.2	Galesville, city	1,427	1,479	3.6
Shawano, city	8,298	8,754	5.5	Hale, town	988	1,056	6.9
Tigerton, village	764	726	−5.0	Independence, city	1,244	1,257	1.0
Washington, town	1,903	2,038	7.1	Lincoln, town	829	815	−1.7
Waukechon, town	928	1,051	13.3	Osseo, city	1,669	1,660	−0.5
Wescott, town	3,653	3,780	3.5	Pigeon, town	894	956	6.9
Wittenberg, town	894	894	0.0	Pigeon Falls, village	388	390	0.5
Wittenberg, village	1,177	1,113	−5.4	Preston, town	951	974	2.4
				Strum, village	1,001	1,045	4.4
SHEBOYGAN COUNTY	112,656	117,472	4.3	Sumner, town	806	854	6.0
Adell, village	517	517	0.0	Trempealeau, town	1,618	1,812	12.0
Cascade, village	681	707	3.8	Trempealeau, village	1,319	1,456	10.4
Cedar Grove, village	1,887	2,052	8.7	Unity, town	556	566	1.8
Elkhart Lake, village	1,021	1,207	18.2	Whitehall, city	1,651	1,666	0.9
Glenbeulah, village	378	438	15.9				
Greenbush, town	2,619	2,616	−0.1	VERNON COUNTY	28,056	29,719	5.9
Herman, town	2,044	2,296	12.3	Bergen, town	1,317	1,385	5.2
Holland, town	2,360	2,365	0.2	Chaseburg, village	306	294	−3.9
Howards Grove, village	2,792	3,095	10.9	Christiana, town	871	900	3.3
Kohler, village	1,926	2,045	6.2	Clinton, town	1,354	1,480	9.3
Lima, town	2,948	2,963	0.5	Coon, town	683	725	6.1
Lyndon, town	1,463	1,500	2.5	Coon Valley, village	714	717	0.4
Mitchell, town	1,286	1,344	4.5	De Soto (part), village	248	258	4.0
Mosel, town	839	803	−4.3	Forest, town	583	604	3.6
Oostburg, village	2,660	2,905	9.2	Franklin, town	923	1,004	8.8
Plymouth, city	7,781	8,420	8.2	Genoa, town	705	719	2.0
Plymouth, town	3,115	3,296	5.8	Genoa, village	263	252	−4.2
Random Lake, village	1,551	1,659	7.0	Greenwood, town	770	848	10.1
Rhine, town	2,244	2,331	3.9	Hamburg, town	848	934	10.1
Russell, town	399	401	0.5	Harmony, town	739	830	12.3
Scott, town	1,804	1,862	3.2	Hillsboro, city	1,302	1,310	0.6
Sheboygan, city	50,792	50,580	−0.4	Hillsboro, town	766	813	6.1
Sheboygan, town	5,874	7,195	22.5	Jefferson, town	974	1,069	9.8
Sheboygan Falls, city	6,772	7,501	10.8	Kickapoo, town	566	612	8.1
Sheboygan Falls, town	1,706	1,787	4.7	La Farge, village	775	783	1.0
Sherman, town	1,520	1,570	3.3	Liberty, town	167	226	35.3
Waldo, village	450	480	6.7	Ontario, village	476	467	−1.9
Wilson, town	3,227	3,537	9.6	Readstown, village	395	391	−1.0
				Stark, town	349	381	9.2

WISCONSIN POPULATION
BY COUNTY AND MUNCIPALITY
April 1, 2000 and January 1, 2008–Continued

County and Municipality	2000 Census	2008 Estimate	Percent Change	County and Municipality	2000 Census	2008 Estimate	Percent Change
Sterling, town	713	717	0.6	Spooner, town	677	744	9.9
Stoddard, village	815	825	1.2	Springbrook, town	536	565	5.4
Union, town	531	614	15.6	Stinnett, town	263	260	−1.1
Viola (part), village	245	280	14.3	Stone Lake, town	544	591	8.6
Viroqua, city	4,335	4,404	1.6	Trego, town	885	1,064	20.2
Viroqua, town	1,560	1,748	12.1				
Webster, town	676	750	10.9	WASHINGTON COUNTY	117,496	130,493	11.1
Westby, city	2,045	2,191	7.1	Addison, town	3,341	3,570	6.9
Wheatland, town	533	631	18.4	Barton, town	2,546	2,651	4.1
Whitestown, town	509	557	9.4	Erin, town	3,664	3,911	6.7
				Farmington, town	3,239	3,560	9.9
VILAS COUNTY	21,033	23,044	9.6	Germantown, town	278	285	2.5
Arbor Vitae, town	3,153	3,371	6.9	Germantown, village	18,260	19,895	9.0
Boulder Junction, town	958	1,021	6.6	Hartford (part), city	10,895	13,700	25.7
Cloverland, town	919	1,054	14.7	Hartford, town	4,031	3,992	−1.0
Conover, town	1,137	1,262	11.0	Jackson, town	3,516	3,910	11.2
Eagle River, city	1,443	1,641	13.7	Jackson, village	4,938	6,309	27.8
Lac du Flambeau, town	3,004	3,299	9.8	Kewaskum, town	1,119	1,130	1.0
Land O'Lakes, town	882	955	8.3	Kewaskum (part), village	3,277	4,209	28.4
Lincoln, town	2,579	2,810	9.0	Milwaukee (part), city	0	0	0.0
Manitowish Waters, town	646	703	8.8	Newburg (part), village	1,027	1,107	7.8
Phelps, town	1,350	1,504	11.4	Polk, town	3,938	4,023	2.2
Plum Lake, town	486	544	11.9	[8]Richfield, village	10,373	11,440	10.3
Presque Isle, town	513	612	19.3	Slinger, village	3,901	4,742	21.6
St. Germain, town	1,932	2,112	9.3	Trenton, town	4,440	4,855	9.3
Washington, town	1,577	1,637	3.8	Wayne, town	1,727	2,009	16.3
Winchester, town	454	519	14.3	West Bend, city	28,152	30,320	7.7
				West Bend, town	4,834	4,875	0.8
WALWORTH COUNTY	92,013	101,315	10.1				
Bloomfield, town	5,537	6,357	14.8	WAUKESHA COUNTY	360,767	382,697	6.1
Burlington (part), city	0	0	0.0	Big Bend, village	1,278	1,313	2.7
Darien, town	1,747	1,971	12.8	Brookfield, city	38,649	39,780	2.9
Darien, village	1,572	1,640	4.3	Brookfield, town	6,390	6,377	−0.2
Delavan, city	7,956	8,440	6.1	Butler, village	1,881	1,799	−4.4
Delavan, town	4,559	4,887	7.2	Chenequa, village	583	592	1.5
East Troy, town	3,830	3,953	3.2	Delafield, city	6,472	6,934	7.1
East Troy, village	3,564	4,172	17.1	Delafield, town	7,820	8,331	6.5
Elkhorn, city	7,305	8,953	22.6	Dousman, village	1,584	1,873	18.2
Fontana on Geneva Lake,				Eagle, town	3,117	3,571	14.6
village	1,754	1,874	6.8	Eagle, village	1,707	1,846	8.1
Geneva, town	4,642	5,159	11.1	Elm Grove, village	6,249	6,146	−1.6
Genoa City (part), village	1,949	2,758	41.5	Genesee, town	7,284	7,556	3.7
Lafayette, town	1,708	2,587	5.9	Hartland, village	7,905	8,486	7.3
La Grange, town	2,444	1,992	16.6	Lac La Belle (part), village	329	336	2.1
Lake Geneva, city	7,148	7,661	7.2	Lannon, village	1,009	1,055	4.6
Linn, town	2,194	2,389	8.9	Lisbon, town	9,359	9,863	5.4
Lyons, town	3,440	3,743	8.8	Menomonee Falls, village	32,647	34,600	6.0
Mukwonago (part), village	0	56	0.0	Merton, town	7,988	8,458	5.9
Richmond, town	1,835	1,973	7.5	Merton, village	1,926	2,618	35.9
Sharon, town	912	927	1.6	Milwaukee (part), city	0	0	0.0
Sharon, village	1,549	1,535	−0.9	Mukwonago, town	6,868	7,558	10.0
Spring Prairie, town	2,089	2,194	5.0	Mukwonago (part), village	6,162	6,897	11.9
Sugar Creek, town	3,331	3,802	14.1	Muskego, city	21,397	23,075	7.8
Troy, town	2,328	2,419	3.9	Nashotah, village	1,266	1,360	7.4
Walworth, town	1,676	1,794	7.0	New Berlin, city	38,220	39,500	3.3
Walworth, village	2,304	2,640	14.6	North Prairie, village	1,571	1,955	24.4
Whitewater (part), city	10,826	11,260	4.0	Oconomowoc, city	12,382	14,300	15.5
Whitewater, town	1,399	1,491	6.6	Oconomowoc, town	7,451	8,217	10.3
Williams Bay, village	2,415	2,688	11.3	Oconomowoc Lake, village	564	633	12.2
				Ottawa, town	3,758	3,807	1.3
WASHBURN COUNTY	16,036	17,646	10.0	Pewaukee, city	11,783	12,645	7.3
Barronett, town	405	440	8.6	Pewaukee, village	8,170	8,934	9.4
Bashaw, town	921	1,184	28.6	Summit, town	4,999	5,162	3.3
Bass Lake, town	535	659	23.2	Sussex, village	8,828	10,045	13.8
Beaver Brook, town	643	745	15.9	Vernon, town	7,227	7,450	3.1
Birchwood, town	453	565	24.7	Wales, village	2,523	2,655	5.2
Birchwood, village	518	561	8.3	Waukesha, city	64,825	68,030	4.9
Brooklyn, town	281	314	11.7	Waukesha, town	8,596	8,940	4.0
Casey, town	466	476	2.1				
Chicog, town	268	304	13.4	WAUPACA COUNTY	51,825	54,157	4.5
Crystal, town	323	351	8.7	Bear Creek, town	838	887	5.8
Evergreen, town	1,076	1,131	5.1	Big Falls, village	85	82	−3.5
Frog Creek, town	160	162	1.3	Caledonia, town	1,466	1,611	9.9
Gull Lake, town	158	178	12.7	Clintonville, city	4,736	4,641	−2.0
Long Lake, town	737	769	4.3	Dayton, town	2,734	2,956	8.1
Madge, town	454	500	10.1	Dupont, town	741	796	7.4
Minong, town	858	1,020	18.9	Embarrass, village	487	467	−4.1
Minong, village	531	566	6.6	Farmington, town	4,148	4,247	2.4
Sarona, town	382	421	10.2	Fremont, town	632	695	10.0
Shell Lake, city	1,309	1,392	6.3	Fremont, village	666	725	8.9
Spooner, city	2,653	2,684	1.2	Harrison, town	509	514	1.0

WISCONSIN POPULATION
BY COUNTY AND MUNCIPALITY
April 1, 2000 and January 1, 2008–Continued

County and Municipality	2000 Census	2008 Estimate	Percent Change	County and Municipality	2000 Census	2008 Estimate	Percent Change
Helvetia, town	649	701	8.0	Neenah, city	24,507	25,560	4.3
Iola, town	818	922	12.7	Neenah, town	2,657	2,917	9.8
Iola, village	1,298	1,352	4.2	Nekimi, town.	1,419	1,457	2.7
Larrabee, town	1,301	1,400	7.6	Nepeuskun, town.	689	713	3.5
Lebanon, town	1,648	1,786	8.4	Omro, city	3,177	3,421	7.7
Lind, town	1,381	1,526	10.5	Omro, town	1,875	2,121	13.1
Little Wolf, town.	1,430	1,559	9.0	Oshkosh, city.	62,916	65,920	4.8
Manawa, city.	1,330	1,313	–1.3	Oshkosh, town	3,234	2,823	–12.7
Marion (part), city	1,296	1,230	–5.1	Poygan, town.	1,037	1,211	16.8
Matteson, town.	956	1,009	5.5	Rushford, town.	1,471	1,607	9.2
Mukwa, town	2,773	3,053	10.1	Utica, town.	1,168	1,224	4.8
New London (part), city . .	5,618	5,713	1.7	Vinland, town	1,849	1,935	4.7
Ogdensburg, village	224	213	–4.9	Winchester, town.	1,676	1,803	7.6
Royalton, town.	1,544	1,540	–0.3	Winneconne, town	2,145	2,304	7.4
St. Lawrence, town	740	756	2.2	Winneconne, village	2,401	2,520	5.0
Scandinavia, town	1,075	1,162	8.1	Wolf River, town.	1,223	1,253	2.5
Scandinavia, village	349	374	7.2				
Union, town	804	833	3.6	WOOD COUNTY	75,555	77,049	2.0
Waupaca, city	5,676	6,028	6.2	Arpin, town	786	834	6.1
Waupaca, town.	1,155	1,236	7.0	Arpin, village	337	332	–1.5
Weyauwega, city.	1,806	1,885	4.4	Auburndale, town	829	859	3.6
Weyauwega, town	627	642	2.4	Auburndale, village. . . .	738	773	4.7
Wyoming, town	285	303	6.3	Biron, village.	915	868	–5.1
				Cameron, town.	510	538	5.5
WAUSHARA COUNTY. . . .	23,066	25,322	9.8	Cary, town	398	414	4.0
Aurora, town.	971	1,057	8.9	Cranmoor, town	175	174	–0.6
Berlin (part), city.	83	75	–9.6	Dexter, town	379	404	6.6
Bloomfield, town.	1,018	1,065	4.6	Grand Rapids, town	7,801	7,998	2.5
Coloma, town	660	753	14.1	Hansen, town.	707	717	1.4
Coloma, village	461	475	3.0	Hewitt, village	670	764	14.0
Dakota, town.	1,259	1,292	2.6	Hiles, town.	188	187	–0.5
Deerfield, town.	629	693	10.2	Lincoln, town	1,554	1,670	7.5
Hancock, town	531	580	9.2	Marshfield (part), city . . .	18,383	18,800	2.3
Hancock, village	463	443	–4.3	Marshfield, town	811	841	3.7
Leon, town	1,281	1,473	15.0	Milladore, town	706	727	3.0
Lohrville, village.	408	413	1.2	Milladore (part), village . .	268	262	–2.2
Marion, town.	2,065	2,226	7.8	Nekoosa, city.	2,590	2,620	1.2
Mount Morris, town	1,092	1,159	6.1	Pittsville, city	866	908	4.8
Oasis, town.	405	394	–2.7	Port Edwards, town	1,446	1,479	2.3
Plainfield, town	533	581	9.0	Port Edwards, village . . .	1,944	1,893	–2.6
Plainfield, village	899	886	–1.4	Remington, town.	305	305	0.0
Poysippi, town	972	970	–0.2	Richfield, town.	1,523	1,686	10.7
Redgranite, village.	1,040	2,087	100.7	Rock, town.	856	905	5.7
Richford, town	588	637	8.3	Rudolph, town	1,161	1,162	0.1
Rose, town	595	647	8.7	Rudolph, village	423	433	2.4
Saxeville, town.	974	1,028	5.5	Saratoga, town	5,383	5,548	3.1
Springwater, town	1,389	1,451	4.5	Seneca, town	1,202	1,172	–2.5
Warren, town.	675	729	8.0	Sherry, town	809	837	3.5
Wautoma, city	1,998	2,101	5.2	Sigel, town.	1,130	1,140	0.9
Wautoma, town	1,312	1,379	5.1	Vesper, village	541	531	–1.8
Wild Rose, village	765	728	–4.8	Wisconsin Rapids, city. . .	18,435	18,480	0.2
				Wood, town	786	788	0.3
WINNEBAGO COUNTY . . .	156,763	165,358	5.5				
Algoma, town	5,702	6,423	12.6				
Appleton (part), city	812	932	14.8				
Black Wolf, town	2,330	2,485	6.7				
Clayton, town	2,974	3,579	20.3				
Menasha (part), city	15,643	15,775	0.8				
Menasha, town.	15,858	17,375	9.6				

[1]The Town of Bellevue became a village on 2/14/2003.
[2]The Town of Hobart became a village on 5/13/2002.
[3]Part of the Town of Hallie became the Village of Lake Hallie on 2/18/2003.
[4]Part of the Town of Ixonia became the Village of Lac La Belle on 3/28/2004.
[5]Part of the Town of Kronenwetter became the Village of Kronenwetter on 11/20/2002.
[6]Part of the Town of Kaukauna was annexed by the Village of Wrightstown on 2/28/2002.
[7]The Town of Caledonia became a village on 11/16/2005.
[8]The Town of Richfield became a village on 2/13/2008.

Sources: Wisconsin Department of Administration, Demographic Services Center, *January 1, 2008 Final Population Estimates, Municipality Population Estimates, Alphabetical List (with rank), Final Population Estimates for Wisconsin Counties,* and *Estimates for Municipalities in Multiple Counties,* March 2009.

HIGHLIGHTS OF MILITARY AND VETERANS AFFAIRS IN WISCONSIN

Military Service — More Wisconsinites served in World War II than in any other conflict, with Vietnam ranking second, but fatalities were heaviest in the Civil War. From the Civil War through the operations in Iraq and Afghanistan, about 26,800 Wisconsinites have lost their lives performing military service during times of conflict. Since September 11, 2001, nearly every unit in the Wisconsin Army and Air National Guard has been ordered to active duty in support of operations in Afghanistan (Operation Enduring Freedom) and Iraq (Operation Iraqi Freedom), as well as homeland defense missions in the United States (Operation Noble Eagle) and continuing operations in the Balkans. In 2009, nearly 4,000 Wisconsin National Guard members will be mobilized, including 3,200 members of the 32nd Infantry Brigade Combat Team who are conducting the largest operational deployment since World War II.

As of June 2009, about 10,000 citizen-soldiers and airmen were serving in Army and Air National Guard units at military facilities located in 66 communities throughout the state.

Veterans' Programs — Since the end of World War II, more than 586,000 grants and loans totaling about $3.2 billion have been provided to Wisconsin veterans. Historically, most of the grants have been for educational purposes, while the overwhelming number of loans were for housing. The grants have also covered subsistence and emergency health care assistance for needy veterans. Veterans may qualify for low-interest home mortgage and home improvement loans. In addition, eligible veterans and, in some instances, spouses and dependent children of deceased veterans may qualify for personal loans to finance expenses, such as education, business start-ups or purchases, medical bills, debt consolidation, and mobile home purchases.

In 2008, Wisconsin veterans and their families received about $43 million in federal educational and vocational rehabilitation assistance. A total of 53,718 Wisconsin veterans received almost $642 million in benefits through the compensation and pension programs.

The Wisconsin Veterans Homes at King and Union Grove had 870 members at the end of 2008. In general, to be eligible for residence, a veteran must have completed certain military service requirements and be a Wisconsin resident on the date of admission to a veterans home. In addition, he or she must have been a resident of Wisconsin at the time of entry into service or a resident of the state for any 5-year period after service and prior to application for admission. Depending on availability of space, spouses and surviving spouses or parents of qualifying veterans may also be admitted.

The following tables present selected data. Consult the footnoted sources for more detailed information about military and veterans affairs.

WISCONSIN'S MILITARY SERVICE

Military Action	Number Served	Number Killed
Civil War.	91,379[1]	12,216
Spanish-American War	5,469	134[2]
Mexican Border Service.	4,168	NA
World War I.	122,215	3,932
World War II.	332,200[3]	8,390
Korean Conflict	132,000[3]	729
Vietnam	165,400[4]	1,239[5]
Lebanon/Grenada	400[6]	1
Panama.	520[7]	1
Operations Desert Shield/Desert Storm	10,400[8]	11
Somalia	426[9]	2
Bosnia/Kosovo.	678[10]	NA
Iraq and Afghanistan Theaters of Operations since September 11, 2001	25,049[11]	99[12]

Note: Includes Wisconsin residents who served on active duty during declared wars and officially designated periods of hostilities.

NA – Not available.

[1]Total includes some who enlisted more than once. The net number of soldiers recruited in Wisconsin was about 80,000.

[2]Casualties only from Wisconsin 1st, 2nd, 3rd and 4th Regiments. No details available for Wisconsin residents serving in federal units.

[3]U.S. Veterans Administration letter, October 17, 1961.

[4]U.S. Veterans Administration report, March 31, 1990.

[5]Total includes 1,131 from U.S. Department of Defense and 108 additional names from Wisconsin Department of Veterans Affairs.

[6]Based on statistics developed for legislation to extend state benefits to veterans who served on active duty in Lebanon or its territorial waters between August 1, 1982, and August 1, 1984, or in Grenada between October 23, 1983, and November 21, 1983.

[7]U.S. Department of Defense statistics on troop involvement.

[8]Based on Wisconsin Department of Veterans Affairs formula for determining number of state residents on active duty who served in the Middle East/Persian Gulf area (beginning August 1990) and Guard and Reserve troops activated for duty in support of Desert Shield/Desert Storm.

[9]Based on Wisconsin Department of Veterans Affairs formula for determining the number of state residents who served during Operation Restore Hope, beginning December 9, 1992.

[10]Based on Wisconsin Department of Veterans Affairs formula for determining the number of state residents who served in Operation Joint Endeavor, Operation Joint Guard, and Operation Joint Forge from November 1995 to present.

[11]Based on CTS Deployment File (Service Members Ever Deployed) as of December 31, 2008.

[12]Based on Wisconsin Department of Veterans Affairs, departmental data, April 15, 2009.

Source: Wisconsin Department of Veterans Affairs, departmental data, April 15, 2009.

DIRECT STATE BENEFITS TO WISCONSIN WAR VETERANS
1943 – 1961

Fiscal Year	Number of Grants and Loans	Total Benefits	Rehabilitation Trust Funds	Housing Fund
8/1/43-1946	6,359	$975,173	$975,173	—
1947	10,701	2,207,914	2,207,914	—
1948	9,578	3,511,527	3,511,527	—
1949	6,086	2,512,517	2,512,517	—
1950	5,867	3,463,058	2,040,658	$1,422,400
1951	6,137	5,178,106	2,104,550	3,073,556
1952	10,442	22,362,081	1,995,116	20,366,965
1953	5,099	8,842,780	1,331,140	7,511,640
1954	4,507	4,420,030	1,502,748	2,917,282
1955	3,482	4,236,298	1,112,173	3,124,125
1956	3,639	5,389,187	787,861	4,601,326
1957	2,890	4,246,004	730,452	3,515,552
1958	2,779	4,912,233	660,994	4,251,239
1959	2,954	5,419,609	670,262	4,749,347
1960	3,345	7,341,922	591,272	6,750,650
1961	3,081	6,654,189	584,426	6,069,763

Note: The 1961 Legislature merged all veterans' funds into the Veterans Trust Fund.

Source: Wisconsin Department of Veterans Affairs, departmental data, March 1995.

VETERANS BENEFITS, 1962 – 2008

Fiscal Year	Number of Grants and Loans	Total Benefits	Grants					Loans		
			Economic	Educational	Full-Time Educational Grants	Economic Assistance	Personal Loan Program	Second Mortgage Housing	Revenue Bond Housing Loans	Gen. Obligation Bond Housing Loans
1962	3,073	$6,681,585	$53,891	$2,100	—	$515,008	—	$6,110,586	—	—
1965	2,384	3,737,259	100,751	13,654	—	359,705	—	3,263,149	—	—
1970	8,296	9,265,183	193,044	289,743	—	3,605,092	—	5,177,305	—	—
1975	32,898	69,554,865	607,279	1,240,917	$1,836,207	9,098,837	—	10,076,963	$46,694,662	—
1980	25,670	197,668,743	362,556	1,099,266	731,672	6,735,632	—	843,433	—	$187,896,184
1981	16,926	90,183,867	424,041	1,092,510	479,232	4,323,114	—	1,345,430	67,130,619	15,388,921
1982	13,333	16,221,058	378,614	1,159,025	469,347	3,656,939	—	1,062,015	8,400,780	1,094,338
1983	11,516	56,700,920	591,351	986,106	391,542	3,073,217	—	762,930	—	50,895,774
1984	11,522	58,137,350	469,314	1,227,239	328,036	3,116,789	—	782,463	—	52,213,509
1985	10,326	47,689,638	453,502	1,483,693	225,043	2,737,544	—	552,106	—	42,237,750
1986	9,648	19,297,133	378,999	1,255,252	157,379	3,678,759	—	243,147	—	13,583,597
1987	7,690	18,883,716	529,634	807,253	127,789	2,802,819	—	141,370	—	14,474,851
1988	6,643	28,134,558	426,595	696,352	91,392	2,405,642	—	289,606	—	24,224,971
1989	6,614	35,412,289	533,929	698,946	77,787	2,459,813	—	832,436	—	30,809,378
1990	6,150	44,837,433	636,434	683,355	62,025	2,776,835	—	327,819	—	40,350,965
1991	6,279	48,562,575	398,706	743,351	50,993	3,945,614	—	62,960	—	43,360,951
1992	4,871	35,155,551	381,312	526,215	137,799	4,192,505	—	18,799	—	29,898,921
1993	4,314	22,446,997	472,302	512,770	167,838	2,673,585	—	—	—	18,620,502
1994	5,314	58,337,813[1]	451,666	716,858	667	2,567,053	—	—	—	33,157,403
1995	6,080	126,009,594[1]	552,893	754,052	—	2,544,584	—	—	—	111,133,109
1996	7,483	80,581,789	601,030	1,609,350	—	3,189,625	—	—	—	75,181,784
1997	7,231	99,984,937	937,294	1,797,649	—	2,401,548	—	—	—	94,848,446
1998	7,767	160,760,389	783,664	1,680,881	—	666,575[2]	$10,215,928[2]	—	—	147,413,341
1999	6,493	139,857,465	2,263,317	1,447,882	—	—	11,837,974	—	—	124,908,352
2000	5,912	143,192,551	3,226,128	1,786,205	—	—	10,802,068	—	—	127,378,150
2001	5,020	73,390,596	1,205,846	1,768,452	—	—	9,034,356	—	—	61,381,942
2002	5,951	88,227,531	1,925,094	2,822,134	—	—	15,780,270	—	—	67,700,033
2003	6,255	83,866,773	1,752,733	2,909,812	—	—	19,792,680	—	—	59,411,548
2004	5,628	95,593,212	1,296,310	4,384,642	—	—	11,808,566	—	—	78,103,694
2005	4,424	37,428,288	413,564	5,698,107	—	—	2,271,942	—	—	29,044,675
2006	4,068	23,935,069	1,052,493	4,751,263	—	—	4,113,262	—	—	14,018,050
2007	4,117	48,026,312	678,109	3,715,648	—	—	5,933,810	—	—	37,698,745
2008	2,595	59,388,230	1,028,788	2,276,489	—	—	5,081,986	—	—	51,000,967

Note: The 1961 Legislature merged all veterans' funds into the Veterans Trust Fund.
[1] Includes $21,444,166 (FY94) and $11,024,956 (FY95) in consumer loans under the Veterans Trust Fund stabilization provision of 1993 Wisconsin Act 16.
[2] Personal loan program replaced economic assistance loans.
Source: Wisconsin Department of Veterans Affairs, departmental data, April 2009.

WISCONSIN NATIONAL GUARD

JOINT UNITS

Joint Force Headquarters Wisconsin
Joint Force Headquarters Detachment – Madison
  54th Civil Support Team (WMD) – Madison

ARMY UNITS

Headquarters, Wisconsin Army National Guard –
  Madison
Joint Force Headquarters Separate Units
  Recruiting and Retention Command – Madison
  Det. 52, Operational Support Airlift Command –
    Madison
  54th Civil Support Team – Madison
32nd Infantry Brigade Combat Team
Headquarters and Headquarters Co. – Camp Douglas
  1st Battalion, 120th Field Artillery
  Headquarters and Headquarters Battery – Wisconsin
    Rapids
    Battery A – Marshfield
    Battery B – Stevens Point
  2nd Battalion, 127th Infantry
  Headquarters and Headquarters Co. (–) – Appleton
    Det. 1, Headquarters Co. – Clintonville
    Company A (–) – Waupun
      Det. 1, Co. A – Ripon
    Company B – Green Bay
    Company C – Fond du Lac
    Company D – Marinette
  1st Battalion, 128th Infantry
  Headquarters and Headquarters Co. (–) – Eau Claire
    Det. 1, Headquarters Co. – Abbotsford
    Company A – Menomonie
    Company B (–) – New Richmond
      Det. 1, Co. B – Rice Lake
    Company C (–) – Arcadia
      Det. 1, Co. C – Onalaska
    Company D – River Falls
  132nd Brigade Support Battalion
  Headquarters and Headquarters Co. – Portage
    Company A (–) (Distribution) – Janesville
      Det. 1, Co. A – Elkhorn
    Company B (Maintenance) – Mauston
    Company C (Medical) – Milwaukee
    Company D (–) (Forward Support) – Baraboo
      Det. 1, Co. D – Madison
    Company E (–) (Forward Support) – Waupaca
      Det. 1, Co. E – Appleton
    Company F (–) (Forward Support) – Neillsville
      Det. 1, Co. F – Eau Claire
    Company G (–) (Forward Support) – Mosinee
      Det. 1, Co. G – Wisconsin Rapids
  Brigade Special Troops Battalion
  Headquarters and Headquarters Co. (–) – Wausau
    Det. 1, Headquarters Co. – Merrill
    Company A (Engineer) – Onalaska
    Company B (Military Intelligence) – Madison
    Company C (Signal) – Antigo
  1st Squadron, 105th Cavalry (Reconnaissance,
    Surveillance and Target Acquisition)
  Headquarters and Headquarters Troop – Madison
    Troop A – Fort Atkinson
    Troop B – Watertown
    Troop C – Reedsburg
64th Troop Command
Headquarters and Headquarters Det. – Madison
  Wisconsin Medical Detachment – Madison
    Det. 1, Wisconsin Medical Detachment – Marshfield

  332nd Rear Operations Center – Berlin
  1967th Contingency Contracting Team – Camp
    Douglas
  64th Rear Operations Center – Monroe
  641st Troop Command Battalion
    Headquarters and Headquarters Detachment –
      Madison
    135th Medical Co. – Waukesha
    832nd Medical Co. (–) (Air Ambulance) – West Bend
      Det. 1, Co. B, 248th Aviation Support Bn. – West Bend
    112th Mobile Public Affairs Det. – Madison
    132 Army Band – Madison
  732nd Combat Sustainment Support Battalion
  Headquarters and Headquarters Det. – Tomah
    107th Maintenance Co. (–) – Sparta
      Det. 1, 107th Maintenance Co. – Viroqua
    1157th Transportation Co. – Oshkosh
    1158th Transportation Co. (–) – Beloit
      Det. 1, 1158th Trans. Co. – Black River Falls
  1st Battalion, 147th Aviation Regiment
  Headquarters and Headquarters Co. – Madison
    Company A – Madison
      Det. 1, Co. C – Madison
    Company D (–) – Madison
    Company E (–) – Madison
157th Maneuver Enhancement Brigade
Headquarters and Headquarters Co. – Milwaukee
  1st Battalion, 121st Field Artillery (HIMARS)
  Headquarters and Headquarters Battery – Milwaukee
    Battery A – Racine
    Battery B – Plymouth
    Battery C – Sussex
    108th Forward Support Company (HIMARS) – Sussex
  257th Brigade Support Battalion
  Headquarters and Headquarters Det. – Oak Creek
    Company A (Distribution) – Whitewater
    Company B (Support Maintenance) – Kenosha
  32nd Military Police Company (–) – Milwaukee
    Det. 1, 32nd MP Company – Oconomowoc
  357th Signal Network Support Co. – Two Rivers
  457th Chemical Co. – Burlington
  724th Engineer Battalion
  Headquarters and Headquarters Co. – Chippewa Falls
    Company A – Hayward
    106th Engineer Det. (Quarry Team) – Tomah
    229th Engineer Co. (–) (Horizontal) – Prairie du Chien
      Det. 1, 229th Engineer Co. – Platteville
    273rd Engineer Co. (Wheeled Sapper) – Medford
    824th Engineer Det. (Concrete) – Richland Center
    829th Engineer Co. (–) (Vertical) – Chippewa Falls
      Det. 1, 829th Engineer Co. – Richland Center
      Det. 2, 829th Engineer Co. – Ashland
    924th Engineer Det. (Facilities) – Chippewa Falls
    949th Engineer Det. (Survey & Design Tm.) –
      Chippewa Falls
    950th Engineer Co. (–) (Clearance) – Superior
      Det. 1, 950th Engineer Co. – Spooner
    951st Engineer Co. (–) (Wheeled Sapper) – Tomahawk
      Det. 1, 951st Engineer Co. – Rhinelander

426th Leadership Regiment (Wisconsin Military Academy)
Headquarters and Headquarters Det. – Fort McCoy
Training Site Command – Fort McCoy

1st Battalion, 426th Rgt. (Field Artillery) – Fort McCoy
2nd Battalion, 426th Rgt. (Modular Training) – Fort McCoy

AIR UNITS

Headquarters, Wisconsin Air National Guard – Madison
115th Fighter Wing – Truax Field, Madison
  115th Operations Group
    176th Fighter Squadron
    115th Operations Support Flight
  115th Maintenance Group
    115th Aircraft Maintenance Squadron
    115th Maintenance Squadron
    115th Maintenance Operations Flight
  115th Mission Support Group
    115th Logistics Readiness Squadron
    115th Security Forces Squadron
    115th Mission Support Flight
    115th Services Flight
    115th Civil Engineer Squadron
    115th Communications Flight
  115th Medical Group

128th Air Refueling Wing – Mitchell Field, Milwaukee
  128th Operations Group
    126th Air Refueling Squadron
    128th Operations Support Flight
  128th Maintenance Group
    128th Aircraft Maintenance Squadron
    128th Maintenance Squadron
    128th Maintenance Operations Flight
  128th Mission Support Group
    128th Logistics Readiness Squadron
    128th Security Forces Squadron
    128th Mission Support Flight
    128th Services Flight
    128th Civil Engineer Squadron
    128th Communications Flight
    126th Weather Flight
  128th Medical Group
Volk Field Combat Readiness Training Center – Camp Douglas
128th Air Control Squadron – Volk Field CRTC, Camp Douglas

Bold Face – Major Command
(–) – Headquarters of a split unit
Abbreviations:
Bn. – Battalion
Co. – Company
CRTC – Combat Readiness Training Center

Det. – Detachment
HIMARS – High-Mobility Artillery Rocket System
MP – Military Police
Rgt. – Regiment
Trans. – Transportation
WMD – Weapons of Mass Destruction

Source: Wisconsin Department of Military Affairs, departmental data, May 2009.

MEMBERSHIP, WISCONSIN VETERANS HOMES
1888 – 2008

	Civil and Indian Wars	Spanish– American	World War I		World War II		Korean Conflict		Total
			Men	Women	Men	Women	Men	Women	
1888	72	—	—	—	—	—	—	—	72
1890	139	—	—	—	—	—	—	—	139
1900	680	—	—	—	—	—	—	—	680
1910	699	—	—	—	—	—	—	—	699
1920	532	—	—	—	—	—	—	—	532
1930	254	108	10	14	—	—	—	—	386
1940	89	196	101	130	—	—	—	—	516
1950	27	156	189	93	5	1	—	—	471
1960	4	74	203	94	40	5	—	—	450
1961	3	66	221	88	39	8	—	—	427
1962	3	66	223	82	52	9	—	—	431
1963	3	67	235	87	57	10	—	—	459
1964	3	63	237	105	61	16	—	—	485
1965	2	62	247	112	77	16	—	—	516
1966	1	56	258	112	86	21	—	—	534
1967	1	46	272	120	93	20	—	—	555
1968	1	48	253	123	93	16	—	—	534
1969	1	43	253	145	101	14	—	—	560
1970	1	35	279	146	153	20	1	0	635
1971	1	39	316	160	184	31	2	0	723
1972	0	28	279	155	199	39	2	0	702
1973	0	25	285	108	199	37	0	1	715
1974	0	21	279	175	185	37	0	2	699

	Spanish– American		World War I		World War II		Korean Conflict		Vietnam		Other Eras[1]		Total
	Vets.	Deps.	Vets.	Deps.	Vets.	Deps.	Vets.	Deps.	Vets.	Deps.	Vets.	Deps.	
1975 . .	1	18	272	171	198	40	3	2	0	0	0	0	705
1976 . .	1	14	254	167	209	40	2	2	0	0	0	0	689
1977 . .	1	13	270	164	205	41	4	2	0	0	0	0	700
1978 . .	1	11	261	158	218	38	3	2	0	0	0	0	692
1979 . .	1	11	244	146	227	37	4	1	0	0	0	0	672
1980 . .	1	8	242	144	241	36	5	1	0	0	0	0	678
1981 . .	0	8	224	139	264	40	8	2	0	0	0	0	685
1982 . .	0	7	189	124	282	43	11	2	0	0	0	0	658
1983 . .	0	5	171	111	297	42	14	2	1	0	0	0	643
1984 . .	0	4	144	97	316	47	21	2	3	0	0	0	634
1985 . .	0	4	129	102	329	54	28	0	5	0	0	0	651
1986 . .	0	4	117	92	348	56	35	5	7	0	0	0	664
1987 . .	0	2	108	84	384	60	36	4	8	0	0	0	686
1988 . .	0	1	84	76	395	55	45	7	8	0	0	0	671
1989 . .	0	2	62	75	399	67	50	7	9	1	0	0	672
1990 . .	0	2	49	65	431	76	62	8	10	1	3	0	707
1991 . .	0	2	43	57	440	74	69	10	10	2	3	0	710
1992 . .	0	1	33	44	442	77	82	10	12	1	2	0	704
1993 . .	0	1	23	41	463	73	94	9	11	1	2	0	718
1994 . .	0	1	14	33	488	83	99	11	12	2	1	0	744
1995 . .	0	1	8	31	484	84	99	12	16	2	1	0	738
1996 . .	0	1	4	24	489	79	103	12	25	1	1	0	739
1997 . .	0	1	3	20	479	82	107	11	38	1	3	0	744
1998 . .	0	0	1	17	460	83	123	12	39	1	9	0	745
1999 . .	0	0	0	12	445	87	128	11	41	3	13	1	741
2000 . .	0	0	0	10	423	94	132	12	47	4	21	2	745
2001[2] . .	0	0	0	9	414	95	133	10	51	3	25	2	742
2002 . .	0	0	0	8	404	103	130	11	54	3	29	2	744
2003 . .	0	0	0	7	433	105	140	13	67	3	35	2	805
2004 . .	0	0	0	3	416	99	148	15	72	3	40	2	798
2005 . .	0	0	0	2	350	103	144	15	71	3	40	2	730
2006 . .	0	0	0	1	407	119	164	17	87	5	50	4	854
2007 . .	0	0	0	1	475	135	173	26	100	8	3	0	921
2008 . .	0	0	0	1	417	123	177	26	115	7	4	0	870

Deps. – Dependents.

[1]Other periods of hostilities for which expeditionary medals were awarded.

[2]The Wisconsin Veterans Home at King was established in 1887, and the home at Union Grove opened in 2001. Numbers starting in 2001 include both homes.

Source: Wisconsin Department of Veterans Affairs, departmental data, April 2009.

FEDERAL EXPENDITURES FOR VETERANS
By State, Federal Fiscal Year 2008

State	Number of Veterans[1]	Education and Vocational Rehabilitation (in thousands)	Compensation and Pension (in thousands)[2]	Number of Veterans Receiving Compensation and Pension
Alabama	413,579	$58,269	$990,466	72,654
Alaska	75,597	10,518	134,191	12,850
Arizona	564,796	86,662	891,943	70,222
Arkansas	260,074	31,299	632,339	40,891
California	2,078,267	310,005	3,158,635	256,712
Colorado	426,162	76,492	712,532	59,703
Connecticut	245,643	42,845	236,036	21,612
Delaware	79,916	6,842	101,717	9,085
District of Columbia	38,589	14,044	103,304	5,109
Florida	1,715,114	225,209	3,067,797	246,753
Georgia.	769,567	169,517	1,389,207	112,461
Hawaii	118,017	19,602	197,498	15,988
Idaho	137,203	16,757	222,034	18,940
ILLINOIS	822,104	95,238	851,369	74,474
Indiana	509,313	41,358	602,184	54,777
IOWA	245,845	23,290	322,473	26,944
Kansas	232,868	27,971	328,384	28,730
Kentucky	343,558	43,229	711,243	50,940
Louisiana.	318,924	36,796	641,160	46,289
Maine	142,316	23,729	342,468	23,749
Maryland.	480,218	59,499	611,915	55,728
Massachusetts	424,765	42,860	657,362	54,986
MICHIGAN	742,221	63,418	918,187	75,712
MINNESOTA	399,496	43,836	652,123	57,724
Mississippi	212,508	21,629	429,787	33,123
Missouri	522,798	58,463	809,602	64,442
Montana	103,730	13,047	204,914	16,909
Nebraska	150,394	22,629	306,510	30,513
Nevada	245,608	28,090	363,097	30,796
New Hampshire	131,027	17,619	177,670	15,885
New Jersey	484,750	61,435	611,039	51,208
New Mexico	178,082	29,471	437,305	30,668
New York	1,026,289	155,920	1,377,655	119,241
North Carolina	772,264	127,301	1,609,268	120,819
North Dakota.	57,703	8,964	99,912	9,331
Ohio	935,440	80,004	1,173,148	102,341
Oklahoma	333,877	57,477	993,453	63,427
Oregon	345,873	46,135	690,566	48,221
Pennsylvania	1,025,770	81,726	1,289,041	107,403
Rhode Island	76,726	7,056	133,689	10,707
South Carolina	409,648	62,739	882,195	63,351
South Dakota.	73,504	11,951	150,856	12,662
Tennessee	507,150	60,403	900,195	74,336
Texas	1,705,311	303,923	3,628,436	272,808
Utah	156,107	21,327	207,249	17,801
Vermont	54,306	17,633	81,194	6,386
Virginia.	813,977	143,256	1,357,031	117,474
Washington.	640,419	95,446	1,131,877	93,669
West Virginia.	174,163	57,531	426,831	27,656
WISCONSIN	436,958	43,302	641,996	53,718
Wyoming.	56,141	5,062	83,180	7,335
UNITED STATES	23,214,672	$3,208,822	$38,674,264	3,095,263

[1]Estimate as of September 30, 2008.

[2]Includes expenditures for the following programs: veterans' compensation for service-connected disability; dependency and indemnity compensation for service-connected deaths; veterans' pension for nonservice-connected disabilities; and burial and other benefits to veterans and their survivors.

Source: Wisconsin Department of Veterans Affairs, departmental data, April 2009.

WISCONSIN NEWSPAPERS
Daily Newspapers

Municipality	Newspaper[1]	Publisher	Web Address
Antigo	Antigo Daily Journal	Marie Berner	www.antigodailyjournal.com
Appleton	The Post-Crescent	Genia Lovett	www.postcrescent.com
Ashland	The Daily Press	Gary Pennington	www.ashlandwi.com
Baraboo	Baraboo News Republic	George Althoff	www.wiscnews.com/bnr
Beaver Dam	Daily Citizen	Jim Kelsh	www.wiscnews.com/bdc
Beloit	Beloit Daily News	Kent Eymann	www.beloitdailynews.com
Chippewa Falls	The Chippewa Herald	Mark Baker	www.chippewa.com
Eau Claire	Leader-Telegram	Pieter Graaskamp	www.leadertelegram.com
Fond du Lac	The Reporter	Bill Hackney	www.fdlreporter.com
Fort Atkinson	Daily Jefferson County Union	Brian Knox	www.dailyunion.com
Green Bay	Green Bay Press-Gazette	Kevin Corrado	www.greenbaypressgazette.com
Janesville	The Janesville Gazette	Skip Bliss	www.gazetteextra.com
Kenosha	Kenosha News	Kenneth Dowdell	www.kenoshanews.com
La Crosse	La Crosse Tribune	Rusty Cunningham	www.lacrossetribune.com
Madison	Wisconsin State Journal	Bill Johnston	www.madison.com/wsj/
Manitowoc	Herald Times Reporter	Kevin Corrado	www.htrnews.com
Marinette	Eagle Herald	Dennis Colling	www.ehextra.com
Marshfield	Marshfield News-Herald	Michael Beck	www.marshfieldnewsherald.com
Milwaukee	The Daily Reporter	Ann Richmond	www.dailyreporter.com
Milwaukee	Milwaukee Journal Sentinel	Elizabeth Brenner	www.jsonline.com
Monroe	Monroe Times	Carl Hearing	www.themonroetimes.com
Oshkosh	The Oshkosh Northwestern	Thomas Cooper	www.thenorthwestern.com
Portage	Portage Daily Register	George Althoff	www.portagedailyregister.com
Racine	The Journal Times	Rick Parrish	www.journaltimes.com
Rhinelander	The Daily News	Greg Mellis	www.rhinelanderdailynews.com
Shawano	Shawano Leader	Paul Seveska	www.shawanoleader.com
Sheboygan	The Sheboygan Press	Richard Roesgen	www.sheboygan-press.com
Stevens Point	Stevens Point Journal	Mark Baldwin	www.stevenspointjournal.com
Watertown	Watertown Daily Times	James Clifford	www.wdtimes.com
Waukesha	The Freeman	Phil Paige	www.gmtoday.com
Wausau	Wausau Daily Herald	Michael Beck	www.wausaudailyherald.com
West Bend	Daily News	Steve Ciccantelli	www.gmtoday.com
Wisconsin Rapids	Daily Tribune	Matthew Wolk	www.wisconsinrapidstribune.com

Other Newspapers

Municipality	Newspaper	Published	Publisher
Abbotsford 54405	The Tribune-Phonograph	Wed.	Carol O'Leary
Adams 53910	Adams-Friendship Times Reporter	Wed.	Dan & Mark Witte
Albany 53502	Hometown Herald	Thurs.	Amy Ross & Lisa Bloedel
Algoma 54201	Kewaunee County News	Wed.	Kevin Corrado
Alma (Cochrane 54622)	Buffalo County Journal	Thurs.	Michael, Gary, Daniel Stumpf
Amery 54401	Amery Free Press	Tues.	Palmer H. & Steve Sondreal
Arcadia 54612	The Arcadia News-Leader	Thurs.	Charles Blaschko
Argyle 53405	Pecatonica Valley Leader	Thurs.	Patrick & Michael Reilly
Ashwaubenon (Green Bay 54304)	The Press	Fri.	Michael Aubinger
Augusta 54722	Augusta Area Times	Thurs.	Chad Nyseth
Baldwin 54002	The Baldwin Bulletin	Tues.	Thomas Hawley
Balsam Lake 54810	County Ledger Press	Thurs.	Tom Miller
Barron 54812	Barron News-Shield	Wed.	James Bell
Bayside[2]	North Shore NOW	Thurs.	Hugh McGarry
Berlin 54923	The Berlin Journal	Thurs.	Ty Gonyo
Birnamwood (Wittenberg 54499)	Birnamwood News	Thurs.	Darlene Block
Black Earth 53515	News-Sickle-Arrow	Thurs.	Dan & Mark Witte
Black River Falls 54615	Banner Journal	Wed.	Dan Witte
Black River Falls 54615	Jackson County Chronicle	Wed.	Chris Hardie
Blair 54616	The Blair Press	Thurs.	Lee Henschel
Bloomer 54724	Bloomer Advance	Wed.	James L. Bell
Boscobel 53805	The Boscobel Dial	Thurs.	John Ingebritsen
Brillion 54110	The Brillion News	Thurs.	Kristine Bastian
Brodhead 53520	The Independent Register	Wed.	Pete Cruger
Brookfield[2]	Brookfield-Elm Grove NOW	Thurs.	Hugh McGarry
Brown Deer[2]	North Shore NOW	Thurs.	Hugh McGarry
Burlington 53105	Burlington Standard Press	Thurs.	Jack Cruger
Cadott 54727	The Cadott Sentinel	Thurs.	Trygg Hansen
Cambridge 53523	The Cambridge News	Thurs.	Brian Knox
Campbellsport 53010	Campbellsport News	Thurs.	Andrew Johnson
Cashton 54619	Cashton Record	Wed.	Paul Fanning
Cedarburg 53012	News Graphic	Tues. & Thurs.	Philip Paige
Chetek 54728	The Chetek Alert	Wed.	Melodee Eckerman
Chilton 53014	Times-Journal	Thurs.	James H. Moran

WISCONSIN NEWSPAPERS
Other Newspapers–Continued

Municipality	Newspaper	Published	Publisher
Clinton 53525	The Clinton Topper	Thurs.	Jack Cruger
Clintonville 54929	Clintonville Tribune-Gazette	Thurs.	John McClure
Cochrane 54622	Cochrane-Fountain City Recorder	Thurs.	Michael & Gary Stumpf
Colfax 54730	The Colfax Messenger	Wed.	Carlton R. DeWitt
Columbus 53925	Columbus Journal	Sat.	Jim Kelsh
Cornell 54732	Cornell & Lake Holcombe Courier	Thurs.	Trygg Hansen
Cottage Grove 53527	The Herald-Independent	Thurs.	Brian Knox
Crandon 54520	The Forest Republican	Wed.	Greg Mellis
Cuba City 53807	Tri-County Press	Thurs.	John Ingebritsen
Cudahy[2]	South Shore NOW	Thurs.	Hugh McGarry
Cumberland 54829	Cumberland Advocate	Wed.	Paul Bucher
Darlington 53530	Republican Journal	Thurs.	Brian Lund
Deerfield 53531	The Independent	Thurs.	Brian Knox
DeForest 53532	DeForest Times-Tribune	Thurs.	Brian Knox
Delavan 53115	The Delavan Enterprise	Thurs.	Jack Cruger
De Pere 54115	De Pere Journal	Thurs.	Kevin Corrado
Dodgeville 53533	The Dodgeville Chronicle	Thurs.	Patrick & Michael Reilly
Dousman (Hartland 53029)	The Kettle Moraine Index	Thurs.	Steve Lyles
Durand 54736	The Courier-Wedge	Thurs.	Michael Stumpf
Eagle River 54521	Vilas County News-Review	Wed.	Byron McNutt
East Troy 53120	East Troy News	Thurs.	Jack Cruger
East Troy 53120	East Troy Times	Wed.	Jack Cruger
Eau Claire 54701	The Country Today	Wed.	Pieter Graaskamp
Edgar (Abbotsford 54405)	The Record-Review	Wed.	Carol O'Leary
Edgerton 53534	The Edgerton Reporter	Wed.	Diane & Helen Everson
Elkhorn 53121	Elkhorn Independent	Thurs.	Jack Cruger
Ellsworth 54011	Pierce County Herald	Wed.	Steve Dzubay
Elm Grove[2]	Brookfield-Elm Grove NOW	Thurs.	Hugh McGarry
Elmwood (Spring Valley 54767)	Sun-Argus	Wed.	Paul Seeling
Elroy 53929	The Messenger of Juneau County	Thurs.	Bill Smith
Evansville 53536	Evansville Review	Wed.	Danley C. Gildner
Fennimore 53809	The Fennimore Times	Thurs.	John Ingebritsen
Florence 54121	The Florence Mining News	Wed.	Hank Murphy
Fox Lake 53933	Fox Lake Representative	Thurs.	Ty Gonyo
Fox Point[2]	North Shore NOW	Thurs.	Hugh McGarry
Franklin (Burlington 53105)	Franklin Citizen	Fri.	Bonnie Seeger
Franklin[2]	Oak Creek-Franklin-Greendale-Hales Corners NOW	Thurs.	Hugh McGarry
Frederic 54837	Inter-County Leader	Wed.	Doug Panek
Freedom 54131	Freedom Pursuit	Thurs.	Angie Griepentrog
Galesville 54630	Galesville Republican	Thurs.	John Ph. Graf
Gays Mills 54631	Crawford County Independent & The Kickapoo Scout	Thurs.	John Ingebritsen
Germantown[2]	Germantown-Menomonee Falls NOW	Thurs.	Hugh McGarry
Glendale[2]	North Shore NOW	Thurs.	Hugh McGarry
Glenwood City 54013	Tribune Press Reporter	Wed.	Carlton DeWitt
Glidden 54527	The Glidden Enterprise	Wed.	Judy Hauschild
Grantsburg 54840	Burnett County Sentinel	Wed.	Carter Johnson
Green Lake (Berlin 54923)	Green Lake Reporter	Thurs.	Ty Gonyo
Greendale[2]	Oak Creek-Franklin-Greendale-Hales Corners NOW	Thurs.	Hugh McGarry
Greenfield[2]	Greenfield-West Allis NOW	Thurs.	Hugh McGarry
Hales Corners[2]	Oak Creek-Franklin-Greendale-Hales Corners NOW	Thurs.	Hugh McGarry
Hammond 54015	Central St. Croix News	Thurs.	Michelle Calcagno
Hartford 53027	Hartford Times Press	Wed.	Phil Hermann
Hartland 53029	Lake Country Reporter	Tues. & Thurs.	Steve Lyles
Hayward 54843	Sawyer County Record	Wed.	Mark Dobie
Hillsboro 54634	Hillsboro Sentry-Enterprise	Thurs.	John Ingebritsen
Holmen (West Salem 54669)	Courier-Life	Fri.	Chris Hardie
Horicon 53032	Horicon Reporter	Thurs.	Andrew Johnson
Hudson 54016	Hudson Star-Observer	Thurs.	Steve Dzubay
Hurley 54534	Iron County Miner	Thurs.	Ernest Moore
Iola 54945	Iola Herald	Thurs.	John McClure
Juneau 53039	Dodge County Independent News	Thurs.	James Clifford
Kaukauna 54130	Times-Villager	Wed. & Sat.	Bart Landsverk
Kenosha 53144	Labor Paper	Fri.	Craig Swanson
Kewaskum 53040	The Statesman	Thurs.	Andrew Kuehl
Kiel 53042	Tri-County News	Thurs.	Mike Mathes
Ladysmith 54848	Ladysmith News	Thurs.	James Bell
La Farge 54639	Epitaph-News	Thurs.	Bonnie Howell-Sherman
La Farge 54639	Episcope	Tues.	Gail Muller
Lake Geneva 53147	Lake Geneva Regional News	Thurs.	Howard Brown
Lake Mills 53551	The Lake Mills Leader	Thurs.	Brian Knox
Lancaster 53813	Grant County Herald Independent	Thurs.	John Ingebritsen

WISCONSIN NEWSPAPERS
Other Newspapers–Continued

Municipality	Newspaper	Published	Publisher
Lodi 53555	Lodi Enterprise	Wed.	Brian Knox
Loyal 54446	Tribune Record Gleaner	Wed.	Dean Lesar
Luck 54853	Enterprise Press	Thurs.	Tom Miller
Madison 53713	The Capital Times[3]	Wed. & Thurs.	Clayton Frink
Madison 53703	Isthmus	Thurs.	Vincent P. O'Hern
Madison 53703	The Madison Times	Thurs.	David Hammonds
Manawa (Iola 54945)	The Manawa Advocate	Thurs.	John McClure
Marion 54950	The Marion Advertiser	Thurs.	Dan Brandenburg
Markesan 53946	Markesan Regional Reporter	Thurs.	Ty Gonyo
Mauston 53948	Juneau County Star-Times	Wed. & Sat.	George Althoff
Mayville 53050	The Mayville News	Thurs.	Andrew Johnson
McFarland 53558	McFarland Thistle & McFarland Community Life	Thurs.	Brian Knox
Medford 54405	The Star News	Thurs.	Carol O'Leary
Mellen 54546	The Mellen Weekly-Record	Wed.	Sandy & James Christl
Menomonee Falls[2]	Germantown-Menomonee Falls NOW	Thurs.	Hugh McGarry
Menomonie 54751	The Dunn County News	Sun. & Wed.	Mark Baker
Mequon[2]	North Shore NOW	Thurs.	Hugh McGarry
Merrill 54452	Merrill Courier	Fri.	Jeff Hovind
Middleton 53562	Middleton Times-Tribune	Thurs.	Dan & Mark Witte
Milton 53563	Milton Courier	Thurs.	Brian Knox
Milwaukee 53204	The Business Journal	Fri.	Mark Sabljak
Milwaukee 53212	Milwaukee Community Journal	Wed. & Fri.	Patricia O'Flynn Pattillo
Milwaukee 53206	Milwaukee Courier	Fri.	Faithe Colas
Milwaukee 53206	Milwaukee Star	Thurs.	Faithe Colas
Milwaukee 53212	The Milwaukee Times	Thurs.	Linda Jackson
Milwaukee 53202	Shepherd Express Metro	Thurs.	Louis Fortis
Mineral Point 53565	The Democrat Tribune	Thurs.	Patrick & Michael Reilly
Minocqua 54548	Lakeland Times	Tues. & Fri.	Gregg Walker
Mondovi 54755	Mondovi Herald News	Thurs.	Perry Nyseth
Montello 53949	The Marquette County Tribune	Thurs.	Dan & Mark Witte
Mosinee 54455	The Mosinee Times	Thurs.	John Durst & James Kress
Mount Horeb 53572	Mount Horeb Mail	Thurs.	Dan & Mark Witte
Mukwonago 53149	Mukwonago Chief	Wed.	Steve Lyles
Muscoda 53573	The Progressive	Thurs.	Wendell Smith
Muskego[2]	Muskego-New Berlin NOW	Thurs.	Hugh McGarry
Neillsville 54456	The Clark County Press	Wed.	Dan & Mark Witte
New Berlin[2]	Muskego-New Berlin NOW	Thurs.	Hugh McGarry
New Glarus 53574	Post Messenger Recorder	Thurs.	Dan & Mark Witte
New London 54961	Press-Star	Thurs.	John McClure
New Richmond 54017	New Richmond News	Thurs.	Steve Dzubay
Oak Creek[2]	Oak Creek-Franklin-Greendale-Hales Corners NOW	Thurs.	Hugh McGarry
Oconomowoc 53066	Oconomowoc Enterprise	Thurs.	Kevin Passon
Oconomowoc (Hartland 53029)	Oconomowoc Focus	Tues. & Thurs.	Steve Lyles
Oconto 54153	Oconto County Reporter	Wed.	Genia Lovett
Oconto Falls 54154	Oconto County Times-Herald	Wed.	Paul Peveska
Omro 54963	Omro Herald	Thurs.	Ty Gonyo
Ontario 54651	The County Line	Thurs.	Karen Parker
Oregon 53575	The Oregon Observer	Thurs.	Judy Shingler
Osceola 54020	The Sun	Wed.	Carter Johnson
Osseo 54758	The Tri-County News	Wed.	Chad Nyseth
Park Falls 54552	The Park Falls Herald	Thurs.	Ken Dischler
Peshtigo 54157	Peshtigo Times	Wed.	Mary Ann Gardon
Phillips 54555	The-Bee	Thurs.	Susan Mergen
Platteville 53818	The Platteville Journal	Wed.	John Ingebritsen
Plymouth 53073	The Review	Tues. & Thurs.	Barry & Christie Johanson
Port Washington 53074	Ozaukee Press	Thurs.	William F. Schanen III
Poynette 53955	Poynette Press	Wed.	Brian Knox
Prairie du Chien 53821	Courier Press	Mon. & Wed.	William H. Howe
Prescott 54021	Prescott Journal	Thurs.	John McLoone
Princeton 54968	Princeton Times-Republic	Thurs.	Ty Gonyo
Random Lake 53075	The Sounder	Thurs.	Gary Feider
Reedsburg 53959	Reedsburg Independent	Thurs.	Dan & Mark Witte
Reedsburg 53959	Reedsburg Times Press	Wed. & Sat.	George Althoff
Rice Lake 54868	The Chronotype	Wed.	Warren Dorrance
Richland Center 53581	The Richland Observer	Thurs.	John Ingebritsen
Ripon 54971	The Ripon Commonwealth Press	Wed.	Tim Lyke
River Falls 54022	River Falls Journal	Thurs.	Steve Dzubay
River Hills[2]	North Shore NOW	Thurs.	Hugh McGarry
St. Croix Falls 54024	Standard Press	Thurs.	Tom Miller
St. Francis[2]	South Shore NOW	Thurs.	Hugh McGarry
Sauk City 53583	The Sauk Prairie Eagle	Wed.	George Althoff
Sauk City 53583	The Sauk Prairie Star	Thurs.	Dan & Mark Witte
Seymour 54165	Times-Press	Thurs.	Ken Hodgden

WISCONSIN NEWSPAPERS
Other Newspapers–Continued

Municipality	Newspaper	Published	Publisher
Sharon (Walworth 53184)	The Sharon Reporter	Thurs.	Pete Cruger
Sheboygan Falls (Plymouth 53073)	The Sheboygan Falls News	Wed.	Barry & Christie Johanson
Shell Lake 54871	Washburn County Register	Wed.	Douglas Panek
Shorewood[2]	North Shore NOW	Thurs.	Hugh McGarry
South Milwaukee[2]	South Shore NOW	Thurs.	Hugh McGarry
Sparta 54656	Monroe County Democrat	Thurs.	William Gleiss
Sparta 54656	The Sparta Herald	Mon.	Theodore C. Radde
Spooner 54801	Spooner Advocate	Thurs.	Janet Krokson
Spring Green 53588	Home News	Wed.	Jim & Linda Schwanke
Spring Valley 54767	Sun-Argus	Wed.	Paul Seeling
Stanley 54768	The Stanley Republican	Thurs.	John E. McLoone
Stevens Point 54481	Portage County Gazette	Fri.	Pete Leahy
Stoughton 53589	The Stoughton Courier Hub	Thurs.	Judy Shingler
Sturgeon Bay 54235	Door County Advocate	Wed. & Sat.	Kevin Corrado
Sun Prairie 53590	The Star	Thurs.	Brian Knox
Superior 54880	Superior Telegram	Wed. & Fri.	Leslee LeRoux
Sussex (Hartland 53029)	Sussex Sun	Wed.	Steve Lyles
Thiensville[2]	North Shore NOW	Thurs.	Hugh McGarry
Thorp 54771	The Thorp Courier	Wed.	Mark LaGasse
Three Lakes (Eagle River 54521)	The Three Lakes News	Wed.	Byron McNutt
Tomah 54660	Monitor Herald	Mon.	Chris Hardie
Tomah 54660	The Tomah Journal	Thurs.	Chris Hardie
Tomahawk 54487	Tomahawk Leader	Tues.	Kathleen & Larry Tobin
Turtle Lake 54889	The Times	Thurs.	David Slack
Twin Lakes 53181	Westosha Report	Sat.	David Slack
Union Grove (Burlington 53105)	Westine Report	Fri.	Cathy Warren
Valders 54245	The Valders Journal	Thurs.	Brian Thomsen
Verona 53593	The Verona Press	Thurs.	Judy Shingler
Viroqua 54665	Vernon County Broadcaster	Thurs.	Chris Hardie
Walworth 53184	Walworth/Fontana Times	Fri.	Cathy Warren
Washburn 54891	The County Journal	Wed.	Gary Pennington
Washington Island 54246	Washington Island Observer	Thurs.	Gail Larson Toerpe
Waterford (Burlington 53105)	The Waterford Post	Fri.	Jack Cruger
Waterloo 53594	The Courier	Thurs.	Brian Knox
Waunakee 53597	The Waunakee Tribune	Thurs.	Brian Knox
Waupaca 54981	Waupaca County Post	Thurs.	John McClure
Wausau 54402	City Pages	Thurs.	Tammy Stezenski
Wautoma 54982	The Waushara Argus	Fri.	Mary Kunasch
Wauwatosa[2]	Wauwatosa NOW	Thurs.	Hugh McGarry
West Allis[2]	Greenfield-West Allis NOW	Thurs.	Hugh McGarry
West Salem 54669	The Coulee News	Thurs.	Chris Hardie
West Salem 54669	Courier Life	Fri.	Stephani Smith
Westby 54667	The Westby Times	Thurs.	Chris Hardie
Weyauwega (Waupaca 54981)	The Chronicle	Thurs.	John McClure
Whitefish Bay[2]	North Shore NOW	Thurs.	Hugh McGarry
Whitehall 54773	Whitehall Times	Thurs.	Charles A. Gauger
Whitewater 53190	Palmyra/Eagle Enterprise	Fri.	Cathy Warren
Whitewater 53190	Whitewater Register	Thurs.	Cathy Warren
Winneconne 54986	The Winneconne News	Wed.	John Rogers
Winter 54896	Sawyer County Gazette	Wed.	Nancy E. Rickert
Wisconsin Dells 53965	Wisconsin Dells Events	Wed. & Sat.	George Althoff
Withee 54498	O-W Enterprise	Wed.	Mark Gorke & Mark Renderman
Wittenberg 54499	The Wittenberg Enterprise	Thurs.	Miriam Nelson
Woodville 54028	The Woodville Leader	Wed.	Paul Seeling

[1]A "newspaper" is defined by Section 985.03 (1) (c), Wisconsin Statutes, as follows: "A newspaper, under this chapter, is a publication appearing at regular intervals and at least once a week, containing reports of happenings of recent occurrence of a varied character, such as political, social, moral and religious subjects, designed to inform the general reader ...".

[2]Combined editorial office in Waukesha 53186.

[3]Also publishes a daily edition on-line.

Sources: Wisconsin Newspaper Association, *2009 Member Directory* and data compiled by Wisconsin Legislative Reference Bureau.

WISCONSIN PERIODICALS

Name	Issued	Publishers
AAA Living/Wisconsin	Bimonthly	AAA Wisconsin, P.O. Box 33, Madison 53701-0033
Action Tracks	1 per year	Byron McNutt, P.O. Box 1929, Eagle River 54521-1929 www.vilascountynewsreview.com
AFSCME Reports	Monthly	AFSCME Int'l Area Office, 8033 Excelsior Dr., Suite A, Madison 53717-1903
Agri-View	Weekly	Capital Newspapers, 2001 Fish Hatchery Rd., Madison 53713 www.agriview.com
Agronomy Journal	Bimonthly	American Society of Agronomy, 677 S. Segoe Rd., Madison 53711-1048 agron.scijournals.org
Airwaves	10 per year	Wisconsin Public Television, R. 1076 Vilas Hall, 821 University Ave., Madison 53706 www.wpt.org
American Orthoptic Journal	1 per year	UW Press, 1930 Monroe St., 3rd Floor, Madison 53711-2059 www.wisc.edu/wisconsinpress/journals
Antique Trader	40/year	Krause Publications, Inc., 700 E. State St., Iola 54990-0001 www.fwpubs.com
Arctic Anthropology	2 per year	UW Press, 1930 Monroe St., 3rd Floor, Madison 53711-2059 www.wisc.edu/wisconsinpress/journals
Astronomy	Monthly	Kalmbach Publishing Co., P.O. Box 1612, Waukesha 53187-1612 www.astronomy.com
At Ease	Quarterly	Wisconsin National Guard, 2400 Wright St., Madison 53704 dma.wi.gov
Backyard Poultry Magazine	Bimonthly	Dave Belanger, 145 Industrial Dr., Medford 54451 www.backyardpoultrymag.com
Badger Common 'Tater	Monthly	Wis. Potato and Vegetable Growers Assn., Inc., P.O. Box 327, Antigo 54409-0327 www.wisconsinpotatoes.com
Badger Herald	Daily (M-F)	Nick Penzenstadler, 326 W. Gorham St., Madison 53703 www.badgerherald.com
Badger Legionnaire	Monthly	Wisconsin American Legion, 2930 American Legion Dr., P.O. Box 388, Portage 53901 www.wilegion.org
Badger Rails	6 per year	Wis. Assn. of Railroad Passengers, 408 Fremont, Lake Mills 53551 www.wisarp.org
Badger Sportsman	Monthly	James Moran, 19 E. Main St., P.O. Box 227, Chilton 53014 www.badgersportsman.com
Bank Note Reporter	Monthly	Krause Publications, Inc., 700 E. State St., Iola 54990-0001 www.fwpubs.com
Beloit College Magazine	3 per year	Beloit College, Office of Public Affairs, 700 College St., Beloit 53511-5595 www.beloit.edu
Beloit Fiction Journal	1 per year	Chris Fink, Beloit College, Box 11,700 College St., Beloit 53511 www.beloit.edu/~english/bfjournal.htm
Benefits & Compensation Digest	Monthly	International Foundation of Employee Benefit Plans, 18700 W. Bluemound Rd., Brookfield 53045 www.ifebp.org/resources/periodicals
Benefits & Compensation Legal & Legislative Reporter	Monthly	International Foundation of Employee Benefit Plans, 18700 W. Bluemound Rd., Brookfield 53045 www.ifebp.org/resources/periodicals
Benefits Quarterly	4 per year	International Soc. of Certified Employee Benefit Specialists, P.O. Box 209, Brookfield 53008-0209 www.iscebs.org
Blade	Monthly	F & W Media, Inc., 700 E. State St., Iola 54990-0001 www.blademag.com
Business Journal, The	Weekly	Mark J. Sabljak, 600 W. Virginia St., Suite 500, Milwaukee 53204 milwaukee.bizjournals.com
Card Trade	Monthly	Krause Publications, Inc., 700 E. State St., Iola 54990-0001 www.fwpubs.com

WISCONSIN PERIODICALS–Continued

Name	Issued	Publishers
Catholic Knight	4 per year	Catholic Knights, 1100 West Wells St., Milwaukee 53223 www.catholicknights.org
Cessna Owner Magazine.	Monthly	Jones Publishing, Inc., N7450 Aanstad Rd., Iola 54945-5000 www.cessnaowner.org
Cheese Reporter	Weekly	Dick Groves, 2810 Crossroads Dr., Suite 3000, Madison 53718 www.cheesereporter.com
Classic Toy Trains	9 per year	Kalmbach Publishing Co., P.O. Box 1612, Waukesha 53187-1612 www.classictoytrains.com
Coin Prices.	Bimonthly	Krause Publications, Inc., 700 E. State St., Iola 54990-0001 www.fwpubs.com
Coins.	Monthly	Krause Publications, Inc., 700 E. State St., Iola 54990-0001 www.fwpubs.com
Columns	Bimonthly	Wisconsin Historical Society, 816 State St., Madison 53706-1482 www.wisconsinhistory.org
Comics Buyer's Guide.	Monthly	F&W Media, 700 E. State St., Iola 54990-0001 www.cbgxtra.com
Connection, The	Semimonthly	Jeanne Gardner, P.O. Box 189, Iron River 54847 theconnectionnewspaper.com
Contemporary Literature.	Quarterly	UW Press, 1930 Monroe St., 3rd Floor, Madison 53711-2059 www.wisc.edu/wisconsinpress/journals
Corporate Report Wisconsin.	Monthly	Dan Newman, 1131 Mills St., P.O. Box 317, Black Earth 53515 crwmag.com
Countryside and Small Stock Journal	Bimonthly	Dave Belanger, 145 Industrial Dr., Medford 54451 www.countrysidemag.com
Courier, The	Monthly	Wisconsin Veterans Home, Wisconsin Veterans Home, N2665 County Rd. QQ, King 54946 dva.state.wi.us/PA_publications.asp
Crafts Report, The	Monthly	Jones Publishing, Inc., N7450 Aanstad Rd., Iola 54945-5000 www.craftsreport.com
Credit Union Executive	Semimonthly	Steve Rodgers, Credit Union National Assn., 5710 Mineral Point Rd., Madison 53705 cu360.cuna.org
Credit Union Magazine	Monthly	Roger Napiwocki, Credit Union National Assn., P.O. Box 431, Madison 53701-0431 creditunionmagazine.com
Crop Science.	Bimonthly	Crop Science Soc. of Amer., 677 S. Segoe Rd., Madison 53711-1048
Crop Weather	Weekly (Apr.-Nov.)	Dept. of Agriculture, Trade and Consumer Protection, P.O. Box 8934, Madison 53708-8934 www.nass.usda.gov
Daily Cardinal	Daily (M-F)	Daily Cardinal Media Corp., 821 University Ave., Madison 53706-1497 www.dailycardinal.com
Dairy Goat Journal.	Bimonthly	Dave Belanger, 145 Industrial Dr., Medford 54451 www.dairygoatjournal.com
Deer and Deer Hunting	10 per year	F & W Media, 700 E. State St., Iola 54990-0001 www.deeranddeerhunting.com
Director, The.	Monthly	NFDA Services, Inc., 13625 Bishop's Dr., Brookfield 53005 www.nfda.org
Doll Crafter and Costuming	Monthly	Jones Publishing, Inc., N7450 Aanstad Rd., Iola 54945-5000 www.dollccmag.com
Dolls	10 per year	Jones Publishing, Inc., N7450 Aanstad Rd., Iola 54945-5000 www.dollsmagazine.com
Drum Corps World.	Monthly	Steve Vickers, 56 Golf Course Rd., Madison 53704-1423 www.drumcorpsworld.com
EAA Sport Aviation	Monthly	Experimental Aircraft Association, EAA Aviation Center, P.O. Box 3086, Oshkosh 54903-3086 www.eaa.org

WISCONSIN PERIODICALS–Continued

Name	Issued	Publishers
EAA Sport Pilot	Monthly	Experimental Aircraft Association, EAA Aviation Center, P.O. Box 3086, Oshkosh 54903-3086 www.sportpilot.org
Easter Seals Network News	2 per year	Easter Seals Wisconsin, Inc., 101 Nob Hill Rd., Suite 301, Madison 53713-3969 eastersealswisconsin.com
Ecological Restoration.	Quarterly	UW Press, 1930 Monroe St., 3rd Floor, Madison 53711-2059 www.wisc.edu/wisconsinpress/journals
Ecquid Novi	2 per year	UW Press, 1930 Monroe St., 3rd Floor, Madison 53711-2059 www.wisc.edu/wisconsinpress/journals
Equipment Today	13 per year	Cygnus Business Media, 1233 Janesville Ave., Fort Atkinson 53538 www.forconstructionpros.com
Exponent.	Weekly	UW-Platteville, 102 Russell Hall,1 University Plz., Platteville 53818-3012
Fantasy Sports	Quarterly	F & W Publications, 700 E. State St., Iola 54490-0001 fantasysportsmag.com
Feminist Collections: A Quarterly of Women's Studies Resources	Quarterly	UW System Women's Studies Librarian, 430 Memorial Library, 728 State St., Madison 53706 womenst.library.wisc.edu
Feminist Periodicals: A Current Listing of Contents	Quarterly/electronic	UW System Women's Studies Librarian, 430 Memorial Library, 728 State St., Madison 53706 womenst.library.wisc.edu/publications/feminist-periodicals.html
FineScale Modeler.	10 per year	Kalmbach Publishing, 21027 Crossroads Cir., Waukesha 53186-4055 www.finescale.com
Fired Arts and Crafts.	Monthly	Jones Publishing, Inc., N7450 Aanstad Rd., Iola 54945-5000 www.firedartsandcrafts.com
Focus.	28 issues per yr.	Wis. Taxpayers Alliance, 401 North Lawn Ave., Madison 53704-5033 www.wistax.org
Forward	4 per year	League of Women Voters of Wis., 122 State St., Suite 201A, Madison 53703-2500 www.lwvwi.org
Forward in Christ	Monthly	Wis. Evangelical Lutheran Synod, 2929 N. Mayfair Rd., Milwaukee 53222-4398 www.forwardinchrist.net
Foto News	Weekly	Tim Schreiber, 807 E. First St., Merrill 54452 www.merrillfotonews.com
Frame Building News	5 per year	F & W Media, 700 E. State St., Iola 54990-0001 www.fwmedia.com
Free Riders Press.	Monthly	Daron Jensen, 4500 State Highway 66, Stevens Point 54481 freeriderspress.us
Freedom Pursuit	Semimonthly	Angie and Roger Griepentrog, P.O. Box 1016, Freedom 54131 www.thefreedompursuit.com
Freethought Today	10 per year	Freedom From Religion Foundation, Inc., P.O. Box 750, Madison 53701-0750 ffrf.org/fttoday
FYI Northwoods	Biweekly	Sarah Johnson, P.O. Box 238, Presque Isle 54557 www.fyinorthwoods.net
Gargoyle, The	2 per year	Wis. Law Alumni Assn., UW Law School, 975 Bascom Mall, Madison 53706 www.law.wisc.edu/alumni/gargoyle
GFWC-WI Clubwoman	Quarterly	Lynn Mickelson, W383 N8633 Blue River Pass, Oconomowoc 53066
Goldmine.	Biweekly	F & W Media, 700 E. State St., Iola 54990-0001 www.goldminemag.com
Great Lakes TPA.	Monthly	Hahn Printing/GLTPA, P.O. Box 1278, Rhinelander 54501 www.timberpa.com

WISCONSIN PERIODICALS–Continued

Name	Issued	Publishers
Grow	3 per year	College of Agricultural and Life Sciences, 136 Agricultural Hall, 1450 Linden Drive, Madison 53706 www.cals.wisc.edu/grow
Guide, The	Quarterly	Equitable Reserve Assn., P.O. Box 448, Neenah 54957-0448 www.equitablereserve.com
Gun and Knife Show Calendar	Quarterly	Krause Publications, Inc., 700 E. State St., Iola 54990-0001 www.fwpubs.com
Gun List	Biweekly	Krause Publications, Inc., 700 E. State St., Iola 54990-0001 www.fwpubs.com
Gwiazda Polarna Polish Biweekly Newspaper	Biweekly	Point Publications, Inc., 2804 Post Rd., Stevens Point 54481-6452 www.gwiazdapolarna.com
Hoard's Dairyman	Semimonthly	W.D. Hoard and Sons Co., 28 Milwaukee Ave., W., Fort Atkinson 53538-2018 www.hoards.com
Home & Family Finance	Quarterly	Credit Union National Assn., P.O. Box 431, Madison 53701-0431
Hummingbird: Magazine of the Short Poem	2 per year	Phyllis Walsh, Harbour Village, #D103, 5600 Mockingbird Ln., Greendale 53219
Impact Magazine	Quarterly	Wis. Park and Recreation Assn., 6601-C Northway, Greendale 53129 www.wpraweb.org
In Business	Monthly	Jody Glynn Patrick, 200 River Place, #250, Madison 53716 www.inbusinessmagazine.com
Inscriptions	3 per year	Don Silldorff, 12116 N. Briarhill Rd., Mequon 53097
Journal of Environmental Quality	Bimonthly	American Society of Agronomy, 677 S. Segoe Rd., Madison 53711-1048 jeq.scijournals.org
Journal of Human Resources	Quarterly	UW Press, 1930 Monroe St., 3rd Floor, Madison 53711-2059 www.wisc.edu/wisconsinpress/journals
Journal of Natural Resources and Life Sciences Education	1 per year	American Society of Agronomy, 677 S. Segoe Rd., Madison 53711-1048 www.jnrlse.org
Journal of the Pharmacy Society of Wisconsin	6 per year	Pharmacy Society of Wisconsin, 701 Heartland Trail, Madison 53717 www.pswi.org
Kalihwisaks	Biweekly	Oneida Tribe of Indians, N7210 Seminary Rd., P.O. Box 365, Oneida 54155 www.oneidanation.org
Labor Press	Monthly	AFL-CIO Milwaukee, 633 S. Hawley Rd., #110, Milwaukee 53214
Land Economics	Quarterly	UW Press, 1930 Monroe St., 3rd Floor, Madison 53711-2059 www.wisc.edu/wisconsinpress/journals
Landscape Journal	2 per year	UW Press, 1930 Monroe St., 3rd Floor, Madison 53711-2059 www.wisc.edu/wisconsinpress/journals
Living Church, The	Weekly	The Living Church Foundation, Inc., P.O. Box 514036, Milwaukee 53203-3436 www.livingchurch.org
Luso-Brazilian Review	2 per year	UW Press, 1930 Monroe St. 3rd Floor, Madison 53711-2059 www.wisc.edu/wisconsinpress/journals
Madison Magazine	Monthly	Jenifer Winiger, 7025 Raymond Rd., Madison 53719
Marketplace Magazine	4 weeks	Leslie Asare, 1486 Kenwood Center, Menasha 54952 www.marketplacemagazine.com
Marquette Law Review	Quarterly	Students and Faculty of Marquette Law School, 1103 W. Wisconsin Ave., Milwaukee 53233 law.marquette.edu/cgi-bin/site.pl?2130&pageID=1561
Marquette Magazine	Quarterly	Marquette University, P.O. Box 1881, Milwaukee 53201-1881 www.marquette.edu/magazine
Maturity Times	Monthly	Action Publications, P.O. Box 1955, Fond du Lac 54936-1955
Menominee Nation News	Weekly	Menominee Indian Tribe, P.O. Box 910, Keshena 54135 www.menominee-nsn.gov

WISCONSIN PERIODICALS–Continued

Name	Issued	Publishers
Metal Roofing	Bimonthly	F & M Media, 700 E. State St., Iola 54990-0001 www.fwmedia.com
Midwest Flyer Magazine	Bimonthly	Dave Weiman, P.O. Box 199, Oregon 53575-0199 www.midwestflyer.com
Military Trader	Monthly	Krause Publications, Inc., 700 E. State St., Iola 54990-0001 www.fwpubs.com
Milwaukee History	Quarterly	Milwaukee County Historical Society, 910 N. Old World 3rd St., Milwaukee 53203-1591 milwaukeecountyhistsoc.org
Milwaukee Magazine	Monthly	Betty Quadracci, 417 E. Chicago St., Milwaukee 53202 www.milwaukeemagazine.com
Model Railroader	Monthly	Kalmbach Publishing Co., 21027 Crossroads Cir., Waukesha 53186-4055 www.modelrailroader.com
Monatshefte	Quarterly	UW Press, 1930 Monroe St., 3rd Floor, Madison 53711-2059 www.wisc.edu/wisconsinpress/journals
N (Nude and Natural)	4 per year	The Naturists, LLC, P.O. Box 132, Oshkosh 54903-0132 www.naturistsociety.com
New Books on Women, Gender and Feminism	2 per year	UW System Women's Studies Librarian, 430 Memorial Library,728 State St., Madison 53706 womenst.library.wisc.edu
North Woods Trader	2 per week	Byron McNutt, P.O. Box 1929, Eagle River 54521-1929 www.vilascountynewsreview.com
Northbound	2 per year	Trees For Tomorrow, Natural Resources Education Center, 19 Sheridan E.P.O. Box 609, Eagle River 54521 www.treesfortomorrow.com
Numismatic News	Weekly	Krause Publications, Inc., 700 E. State St., Iola 54990-0001 www.fwpubs.com
Old Cars Price Guide	Bimonthly	Krause Publications, Inc., 700 E. State St., Iola 54990-0001 www.fwpubs.com
Old Cars Weekly	Weekly	Krause Publications, Inc., 700 E. State St., Iola 54990-0001 www.oldcarsweekly.com
On Premise	Bimonthly	Pete Madland, 2817 Fish Hatchery Rd., Fitchburg 53713 tlw.org
On Wisconsin	Quarterly	Wis. Alumni Assn., 650 N. Lake St., Madison 53706-1476 www.uwalumni.com/onwisconsin
Passenger Pigeon, The	Quarterly	Wisconsin Society for Ornithology, 810 Ganser Dr., Waunakee 53597-1930 www.wsobirds.org
Pharmacy in History	Quarterly	Amer. Institute of the History of Pharmacy, 777 Highland Ave., Madison 53705-2222 www.aihp.org
PhotoDaily	Daily	Rohn-Engh, PhotoSource Internatl., Pine Lake Farm, 1910 35th Rd., Osceola 54020-5602
PhotoLetter	Weekly	Rohn Engh, PhotoSource Internatl., Pine Lake Farm, 1910 35th Rd., Osceola 54020-5602
PhotoStockNOTES	Weekly (on-line)	Rohn Engh, PhotoSource Internatl., Pine Lake Farm, 1910 35th Rd., Osceola 54020-5602
Picture Post	Weekly (15 summer weeks)	John McClure, P.O. Box 609, Waupaca 54981
Pipers Magazine	Monthly	Jones Publishing, Inc., N7450 Aanstad Rd., Iola 54945-5000 www.piperowner.org
Professional, The	Quarterly	AFT-Wisconsin, 6602 Normandy Lane, Madison 53719 www.aft-wisconsin.org
Progressive, The	Monthly	Matthew Rothschild, 409 E. Main St., Madison 53703-2863 www.progressive.org
Quality Progress	Monthly	American Society for Quality, P.O. Box 3005, Milwaukee 53201-3005 www.asq.org

WISCONSIN PERIODICALS–Continued

Name	Issued	Publishers
Renascence: Essays on Values in Literature. .	Quarterly	Marquette University, Raynor Memorial Libraries, M-164,P.O. Box 1881, Milwaukee 53201-1881 www.marquette.edu/renascence
Rethinking Schools	Quarterly	Rethinking Schools, Ltd., 1001 E. Keefe Ave., Milwaukee 53212 www.rethinkingschools.org
Royal Purple	Weekly (during semester)	UW-Whitewater, 66 University Center, Whitewater 53190 www.royalpurplenews.com
Rural Builder.	7 per year	Krause Publications, Inc., 700 E. State St., Iola 54990-0001 www.fwmedia.com
Sabbath Recorder, The.	Monthly	American Sabbath Tract and Comm. Council, P.O. Box 1678, Janesville 53547 www.seventhdaybaptist.org
Safety Zone (E-Newsletter)	Monthly	Wis. Safety Council, 501 E. Washington Ave., Madison 53703-2914 www.wisafetycouncil.org
SCRYE: The Guide to Collectible Games. . .	Monthly	F & W Media, 700 E. State St., Iola 54990-0001 www.gamingreport.com
Sheep!	Bimonthly	Dave Belanger, 145 Industrial Dr., Medford 54451 www.sheepmagazine.com
Silent Sports	Monthly	John McClure, P.O. Box 609, Waupaca 54981 silentsports.net
Soil Science Society of America Journal . . .	Bimonthly	Soil Science Society of America, 677 S. Segoe Rd., Madison 53711-1048
Soo, The	Quarterly	Soo Line Historical and Technical Society, 3410 Kasten Ct., Middleton 53562-1026
Southeastern Wisconsin Regional Planning Commission Newsletter	Irregular	Southeastern Wis. Regional Planning Comn., P.O. Box 1607, Waukesha 53187-1607 www.sewrpc.org
Spanish Journal	Weekly	Rhonda Welch, 719 South 6th St., Milwaukee 53204 www.spanishjournal.com
Spectator	Biweekly	UW-Eau Claire, 108 Hibbard Hall, Eau Claire 54701 www.spectatornews.com
Sports Collectors Digest	Weekly	F & W Publications, 700 E. State St., Iola 54490-0001 sportscollectorsdigest.com
SubStance	3 per year	UW Press, 1930 Monroe St., 3rd Floor, Madison 53711-2059 www.wisc.edu/wisconsinpress/journals
Teddy Bear Review	6 per yr.	Jones Publishing, Inc., N7450 Aanstad Rd., Iola 54945-5000 www.teddybearreview.com
Today's Dads.	6 per yr.	Wisconsin Fathers for Children and Families, P.O. Box 1742, Madison 53701-1742 wisconsinfathers.org
Tourism Business Journal (E-Newsletter) . . .	6 per year	Lisa Marshall, Wis. Dept. of Tourism, P.O. Box 8690, Madison 53708 industry.travelwisconsin.com/
Trains Magazine	Monthly	Kalmbach Publishing Co., 21027 Crossroads Cir., P.O. Box 1612, Waukesha 53187-1612 www.trainsmag.com
Trapper and Predator Caller	10 per year	Krause Publications, Inc., 700 E. State St., Iola 54990-0001 www.fwpubs.com
Tuff Stuff's Sports Collectors Monthly	Monthly	F & W Media, 700 E. State St., Iola 54990-0001 www.tuffstuff.com
Turkey & Turkey Hunting	6 per year	Krause Publications, Inc., 700 E. State St., Iola 54990-0001 www.fwpubs.com
Union Herald, The	Monthly	Union Herald, Inc., 1920 Ward Ave., Suite 12,, La Crosse 54601-6761 www.westernwisconsinaflcio.org
Union Labor News.	Monthly	Union Labor News Publishers, Ltd., 1602 S. Park St., Madison 53715-2159 www.scfl.org

WISCONSIN PERIODICALS–Continued

Name	Issued	Publishers
U.S. Youth Bowler.	4 per year	United States Bowling Congress, 5301 S. 76th St., Greendale 53129 bowl.com
Update	2 per year	Wisconsin School of Business, 975 University Ave., Madison 53706-1323 www.bus.wisc.edu/update
Vacation Week	Weekly (June-Aug.)	Byron McNutt, P.O. Box 1929, Eagle River 54521-1929 www.vilascountynewsreview.com
Voyageur: NE Wisconsin's Historical Review.	2 per year	Bill Meindl, P.O. Box 8085, Green Bay 54308-8085 www.uwgb.edu/voyageur
WEAC in Print.	8 per year	Wis. Education Assn. Council, 33 Nob Hill Dr., Madison 53713-2199 www.weac.org
Western Builder	Weekly	Mike Larson, Editor, 863 N. 10th St., Manitowoc 54220 www.acppubs.com
WFU News.	10 per year	Wis. Farmers Union, 117 W. Spring St., Chippewa Falls 54729-2359 www.wisconsinfarmersunion.com
Wisconservation	Monthly	Wisconsin Wildlife Federation, W7303 Cty Hwy CS & Q, Poynette 53955 www.wiwf.org
Wis. Archeologist	Semiannual	Wis. Archeological Society, 215 Sabin Hall, UW-Milwaukee, 3413 N. Downer Ave., Milwaukee 53211
Wis. Counties	Monthly	Wis. Counties Assn., 22 E. Mifflin St., Suite 900, Madison 53703 www.wicounties.org
Wis. Economic Indicators	Monthly	Wis. Dept. of Workforce Development, P.O. Box 7944, Madison 53707-7944 www.dwd.state.wi.us/oea
Wis. Energy Cooperative News	Monthly	Wis. Federation of Cooperatives, 131 W. Wilson St., Suite 400, Madison 53703 www.wecnmagazine.com
Wis. Farm Reporter	Semimonthly	Dept. of Agriculture, Trade and Consumer Protection, P.O. Box 8934, Madison 53708-8934 www.nass.usda.gov
Wis. Horsemen's News	Monthly	John McClure, P.O. Box 609, Waupaca 54981 wishorse.com
Wis. International Law Journal	4 per year	UW Law School, 975 Bascom Mall, Madison 53706 hosted.law.wisc.edu/wilj
Wis. Jaycee Journal	2 per year	Jaycees of Wis. Foundation, Inc., P.O. Box 1547, Appleton 54912 www.wijaycees.org
Wis. Law Journal	Weekly	Ann Richmond, 225 E. Michigan St., Milwaukee 53203-3433 www.wislawjournal.com
Wis. Law Review	Bimonthly	UW Law School, 2347 Law Building, 975 Bascom Mall, Madison 53706-1399
Wis. Lawyer	Monthly	State Bar of Wisconsin, P.O. Box 7158, Madison 53707-7158 www.wisbar.org
Wis. Lion.	Monthly	Wisconsin Lions, 2809 Post Road, Stevens Point 54481 www.wisconsinlions.org/magazine
Wis. Magazine of History	Quarterly	State Historical Society of Wis., 816 State St., Madison 53706-1488 www.wisconsinhistory.org
Wis. Mapping Bulletin.	Electronic	State Cartographer's Office, 384 Science Hall, UW-Madison, 550 N. Park St., Madison 53706 news.sco.wisc.edu
Wis. Medical Journal	8 per year	Wisconsin Medical Society, 330 E. Lakeside St., Madison 53715 www.wisconsinmedicalsociety.org/wmj
Wis. Natural Resources	Bimonthly	Wisconsin Department of Natural Resources, P.O. Box 7921, Madison 53707-7921 www.wnrmag.com
Wis. People & Ideas	Quarterly	Wis. Academy of Sciences, Arts and Letters, 1922 University Ave., Madison 53726 www.wisconsinacademy.org
Wis. Police Journal.	Quarterly	Wis. Professional Police Assn., 340 Coyier Ln., Madison 53713 www.wppa.com

WISCONSIN PERIODICALS–Continued

Name	Issued	Publishers
Wis. Professional Agent	Monthly	PIA of Wisconsin, 6401 Odana Rd., Madison 53719-1126 www.piaw.org
Wis. Real Estate Magazine	Monthly	Wisconsin Realtors Assn., 4801 Forest Run Rd., Suite 201, Madison 53704 www.wra.org
Wis. Restaurateur	Bimonthly	Wis. Restaurant Assn., 2801 Fish Hatchery Rd., Madison 53713-3120 www.wirestaurant.org/pdf/09WRMediaKit_Full.pdf
Wis. School Musician	3 per year	Robert W. Kase, 1005 Quinn Dr., Waunakee 53597
Wis. School News	Monthly	Wis. Assn. of School Boards, Inc., 122 W. Washington Ave., Suite 400, Madison 53703-2718 www.wasb.org
Wis. State Farmer	Weekly	John McClure, P.O. Box 609, Waupaca 54981 wisfarmer.com
Wis. State Genealogical Society Newsletter	Quarterly	Wis. State Genealogical Soc., P.O. Box 5106, Madison 53705-0106 www.wsgs.org
Wis. Taxpayer, The.	Monthly	Wis. Taxpayers Alliance, 401 North Lawn Ave., Madison 53704-5033 www.wistax.org
Wis. Trails	Bimonthly	Journal Publications, 4101 W. Burnham Street, West Milwaukee 53215 www.wisconsintrails.com
Wis. Waterfowl.	2 per year	Bast and Durbin and Associates, P.O. Box 427, Wales 53183 www.wisducks.org
Wisconsin Week	Biweekly (during school year)	University Communications, 19 Bascom Hall,500 Lincoln Dr., Madison 53706-1380 www.news.wisc.edu/wisweek
Women in Higher Education.	Monthly	The Wenniger Company, 5376 Farmco Dr., Madison 53704 www.wihe.com
Woodland Management	Quarterly	Wisconsin Woodland Owners Assn., Inc., P.O. Box 285, Stevens Point 54481-0285 www.wisconsinwoodlands.org
World Airshow News	9 per year	Jeff Parnau, P.O. Box 975, East Troy 53120-0975 www.airshowmag.com
World Coin News	Monthly	Krause Publications, Inc., 700 E. State St., Iola 54990-0001 www.fwpubs.com

---

NOTE

If you know of any additional permanent Wisconsin publications that are published at periodic intervals, please send the information to the Blue Book Editor, Legislative Reference Bureau, P.O. Box 2037, Madison, Wisconsin 53701-2037.

BROADCASTING STATIONS IN WISCONSIN

Commercial Television Stations

City	Station	Analog Channel	Digital Channel	City	Station	Analog Channel	Digital Channel
Appleton	WACY	32	27	Madison	WMSN-TV	47	11
Eagle River	WYOW	34	28	Madison	WMTV	15	19
Eau Claire	WEAU-TV	13	13	Milwaukee	WBME	49	48
Eau Claire	WEUX	48	49	Milwaukee	WCGV-TV	24	25
Eau Claire	WQOW-TV	18	15	Milwaukee	WDJT-TV	58	46
Fond du Lac	WWAZ	68	44	Milwaukee	WISN-TV	12	34
Green Bay	WBAY-TV	2	23	Milwaukee	WITI	6	33
Green Bay	WFRV-TV	5	39	Milwaukee	WPXE	55	40
Green Bay	WGBA	26	41	Milwaukee	WTMJ-TV	4	—
Green Bay	WIWB	14	21	Milwaukee	WVCY-TV	30	22
Green Bay	WLUK-TV	11	51	Milwaukee	WVTV	18	61
La Crosse	WKBT	8	41	Milwaukee	WWRS-TV	52	43
La Crosse	WLAX	25	17	Oshkosh	WBIJ	4	—
La Crosse	WXOW-TV	19	14	Rhinelander	WJFW-TV	12	16
Madison	WBUW-TV	57	32	Wausau	WAOW-TV	9	29
Madison	WISC-TV	3	50	Wausau	WFXS	55	31
Madison	WKOW-TV	27	26	Wausau	WSAW-TV	7	40

Educational Television Stations

City	Station	Analog Channel	Digital Channel	City	Station	Analog Channel	Digital Channel
Green Bay	WPNE[1]	38	42	Milwaukee	WMVT[3]	36	35
La Crosse	WHLA-TV[1]	31	30	Wausau	WHRM-TV[1]	20	24
Madison	WHA-TV[2]	21	20	Wausau	WLEF-TV[1]	36	47
Menomonie	WHWC-TV	28	—	Wausau	WTPX	0	46
Milwaukee	WMVS	10	8				

Note: All analog broadcasting ended and was replaced by digital broadcasting on June 12, 2009.

Commercial Radio Stations

City	Station	Frequency	City	Station	Frequency
Adams	WDKM-FM	106.1	Eagle River	WERL	950
Algoma	WBDK-FM	96.7	Eagle River	WRJO-FM	94.5
Algoma	WRLU-FM	104.1	Eau Claire	WAXX-FM	104.5
Allouez	WZNN-FM	106.7	Eau Claire	WAYY	790
Altoona	WISM-FM	98.1	Eau Claire	WBIZ	1400
Amery	WXCE	1260	Eau Claire	WBIZ-FM	100.7
Antigo	WACD-FM	106.1	Eau Claire	WIAL-FM	94.1
Antigo	WATK	900	Elk Mound	WECL-FM	92.9
Antigo	WRLO-FM	105.3	Elm Grove	WGLB	1560
Appleton	WAPL-FM	105.7	Evansville	WWHG-FM	105.9
Appleton	WSCO	1570	Fond du Lac	KFIZ	1450
Ashland	WATW	1400	Fond du Lac	WFDL-FM	97.7
Ashland	WBSZ-FM	93.3	Fond du Lac	WFON-FM	107.1
Ashland	WJJH-FM	96.7	Fond du Lac	WRPN	1600
Bailey's Harbor	WLGE-FM	106.9	Fond du Lac	WTCX-FM	96.1
Balsam Lake	WLMX-FM	104.9	Forestville	WRKU-FM	102.1
Baraboo	WRPQ	740	Fort Atkinson	WFAW	940
Barron	WAQE-FM	97.7	Fort Atkinson	WSJY-FM	107.3
Beaver Dam	WBEV	1430	Green Bay	WDUZ	1400
Beaver Dam	WXRO-FM	95.3	Green Bay	WTAQ	1360
Beloit	WGEZ	1490	Green Bay	WIXX-FM	101.1
Beloit	WTJK	1380	Green Bay	WKSZ-FM	95.9
Berlin	WBJZ-FM	104.7	Green Bay	WNFL	1440
Berlin	WISS	1100	Green Bay	WQLH-FM	98.5
Birnamwood	WYNW-FM	92.9	Hallie	WOGO	680
Black River Falls	WWIS	1260	Hallie	WWIB-FM	103.7
Black River Falls	WWIS-FM	99.7	Hartford	WTKM	1540
Bloomer	WQRB-FM	95.1	Hartford	WTKM-FM	104.9
Brillion	WDUZ-FM	107.5	Hayward	WHSM	910
Brookfield	WFMR-FM	106.9	Hayward	WHSM-FM	101.1
Chetek	WATQ-FM	106.7	Hayward	WRLS-FM	92.3
Chilton	WMBE	1530	Holmen	WKBH	1570
Chippewa Falls	WCFW-FM	105.7	Hudson	WDGY	740
Chippewa Falls	WEAQ	1150	Hurley	WHRY	1450
Cleveland	WLKN-FM	98.1	Iron River	WNXR-FM	107.3
Clintonville	WFCL	1380	Jackson	WAUK	540
Clintonville	WJMQ-FM	92.3	Janesville	WCLO	1230
Columbus	WTLX-FM	100.5	Janesville	WJVL-FM	99.9
Cornell	WDRK-FM	99.9	Kaukauna	WJOK	1050
DeForest	WHLK-FM	93.1	Kaukauna	WOGB-FM	103.1
Denmark	WPCK-FM	104.9	Kenosha	WIIL-FM	95.1
Dickeyville	WVRE-FM	101.1	Kenosha	WLIP	1050
Dodgeville	WDMP	810	Kewaunee	WAUN-FM	92.7
Dodgeville	WDMP-FM	99.3	Kimberly	WHBY	1150
Durand	WDMO-FM	95.9	La Crosse	KQEG-FM	102.7
Durand	WQOQ	1430	La Crosse	WIZM	1410

BROADCASTING STATIONS IN WISCONSIN–Continued

City	Station	Frequency	City	Station	Frequency
La Crosse	WIZM-FM	93.3	Plymouth	WJUB	1420
La Crosse	WKBH-FM	100.1	Plymouth	WXER-FM	104.5
La Crosse	WKTY	580	Port Washington	WPJP-FM	100.1
La Crosse	WLFN	1490	Portage	WBKY-FM	95.9
La Crosse	WLXR-FM	104.9	Portage	WDDC-FM	100.1
La Crosse	WQCC-FM	106.3	Portage	WPDR	1350
La Crosse	WRQT-FM	95.7	Poynette	WHFA	1240
Ladysmith	WJBL-FM	93.1	Prairie du Chien	WPRE	980
Ladysmith	WLDY	1340	Prairie du Chien	WQPC-FM	94.3
Lake Geneva	WLKG-FM	96.1	Racine	WJTI	1460
Lake Geneva	WZRK	1550	Racine	WEZY-FM	92.1
Lancaster	WGLR	1280	Racine	WKKV-FM	100.7
Lancaster	WGLR-FM	97.7	Racine	WRJN	1400
Madison	WIBA	1310	Reedsburg	WBDL-FM	102.9
Madison	WIBA-FM	101.5	Reedsburg	WNFM-FM	104.9
Madison	WLMV	1480	Reedsburg	WRDB	1400
Madison	WMAD-FM	96.3	Rhinelander	WHDG-FM	97.5
Madison	WMGN-FM	98.1	Rhinelander	WOBT	1240
Madison	WOLX-FM	94.9	Rhinelander	WRHN-FM	100.1
Madison	WTDY	1670	Rice Lake	WAQE	1090
Madison	WTSO	1070	Rice Lake	WJMC	1240
Madison	WTUX	1550	Rice Lake	WJMC-FM	96.1
Madison	WZEE-FM	104.1	Rice Lake	WKFX-FM	99.1
Manitowoc	WCUB	980	Richland Center	WRCO	1450
Manitowoc	WLTU-FM	92.1	Richland Center	WRCO-FM	100.9
Manitowoc	WOMT	1240	River Falls	WEVR	1550
Manitowoc	WQTC-FM	102.3	River Falls	WEVR-FM	106.3
Marathon	WKQH-FM	104.9	Rudolph	WIZD-FM	99.9
Marinette	WLST-FM	95.1	Schofield	WRIG	1390
Marinette	WMAM	570.0	Seymour	WECB-FM	104.3
Marshfield	WDLB	1450	Shawano	WOWN-FM	99.3
Marshfield	WYTE-FM	106.5	Shawano	WTCH	960
Mauston	WRJC	1270	Sheboygan	WBFM-FM	93.7
Mauston	WRJC-FM	92.1	Sheboygan	WCLB	950
Mayville	WMDC-FM	98.7	Sheboygan	WHBL	1330
Medford	WIGM	1490	Sheboygan Falls	WHBZ-FM	106.5
Medford	WKEB-FM	99.3	Shell Lake	WCSW	940
Menomonee Falls	WJMR-FM	98.3	Shell Lake	WGMO-FM	95.3
Menomonie	WMEQ	880	Siren	WXCX-FM	105.7
Menomonie	WMEQ-FM	92.1	Soldiers Grove	WKAW-FM	105.9
Merrill	WJMT	730.0	Sparta	WCOW-FM	97.1
Merrill	WMZK-FM	104.1	Sparta	WKLJ	1290
Middleton	WWQM-FM	106.3	Spencer	WOSQ-FM	92.3
Milwaukee	WHQG-FM	102.9	Stevens Point	WSPT	1010
Milwaukee	WISN	1130	Stevens Point	WSPT-FM	97.9
Milwaukee	WJYI	1340	Sturgeon Bay	WDOR	910
Milwaukee	WJZI-FM	93.3	Sturgeon Bay	WDOR-FM	93.9
Milwaukee	WKLH-FM	96.5	Sturgeon Bay	WSRG-FM	97.7
Milwaukee	WKTI-FM	94.5	Sturgeon Bay	WZBY-FM	99.7
Milwaukee	WLUM-FM	102.1	Sturtevant	WDDW-FM	104.7
Milwaukee	WMCS	1290	Sun Prairie	WXXM-FM	92.1
Milwaukee	WMYX-FM	99.1	Superior	KHQG-FM	102.5
Milwaukee	WNOV	860	Superior	WDSM	710
Milwaukee	WOKY	920	Superior	WGEE	970
Milwaukee	WQBW-FM	97.3	Sussex	WKSH	1640
Milwaukee	WRIT-FM	95.7	Three Lakes	WCYE-FM	93.7
Milwaukee	WSSP	1250	Tomah	WBOG	1460
Milwaukee	WTMJ	620	Tomah	WTMB-FM	94.5
Minocqua	WLKD	1570	Tomah	WXYM-FM	96.1
Minocqua	WMQA-FM	95.9	Tomahawk	WJJQ	810
Mishicot	WZOR-FM	94.7	Tomahawk	WJJQ-FM	92.5
Monroe	WEKZ	1260	Trempealeau	WFBZ-FM	105.5
Monroe	WEKZ-FM	93.7	Two Rivers	WGBW	1590
Mosinee	WOFM-FM	94.7	Verona	WMMM-FM	105.5
Mount Horeb	WJQM-FM	106.7	Viroqua	WVRQ	1360
Neenah-Menasha	WNAM	1280	Viroqua	WVRQ-FM	102.3
Neenah-Menasha	WNCY-FM	100.3	Watertown	WJJO-FM	94.1
Neenah-Menasha	WROE-FM	94.3	Watertown	WTTN	1580
Neillsville	WCCN	1370	Waukesha	WRRD	1510
Neillsville	WCCN-FM	107.5	Waukesha	WMIL-FM	106.1
Neillsville	WPKG-FM	92.7	Waunakee	WCHY-FM	105.1
Nekoosa	WMMA-FM	93.9	Waupaca	WDUX	800
Nekoosa	WRCW-FM	105.5	Waupaca	WDUX-FM	92.7
New London	WOZZ-FM	93.5	Waupun	WFDL	1170
Oconto	WOCO	1260	Wausau	WBCV-FM	107.9
Oconto	WOCO-FM	107.1	Wausau	WDEZ-FM	101.9
Oshkosh	WOSH	1490	Wausau	WIFC-FM	95.5
Oshkosh	WPKR-FM	99.5	Wausau	WSAU	550
Oshkosh	WVBO-FM	103.9	Wausau	WXCO	1230
Oshkosh	WWWX-FM	96.9	Wautoma	WAUH-FM	102.3
Park Falls	WCQM-FM	98.3	Wauwatosa	WXSS-FM	103.7
Park Falls	WNBI	980	West Bend	WBKV	1470
Peshtigo	WSFQ-FM	96.3	West Bend	WBWI-FM	92.5
Platteville	WPVL	1590	Whitehall	WHTL-FM	102.3
Platteville	WPVL-FM	107.1	Whitewater	WKCH-FM	106.5

BROADCASTING STATIONS IN WISCONSIN–Continued

City	Station	Frequency	City	Station	Frequency
Whitewater	WSLD-FM	104.5	Wisconsin Dells	WNNO-FM	106.9
Whiting	WLJY-FM	96.7	Wisconsin Rapids	WFHR	1320
Wisconsin Dells	WDLS	900	Wisconsin Rapids	WGLX-FM	103.3

Noncommercial Radio Stations

City	Station	Frequency	City	Station	Frequency
Appleton	WEMI-FM	91.9	Milwaukee	WUWM-FM[2]	89.7
Appleton	WOVM-FM	91.1	Milwaukee	WVCY-FM	107.7
Auburndale	WLBL[1]	930.0	Milwaukee	WVFL-FM	89.9
Beloit	WBCR-FM	90.3	Milwaukee	WYMS-FM	88.9
(Beloit College)			(Milwaukee Board of Education)		
Brule	WHSA-FM[1]	89.9	Mukwonago	WKMZ-FM	105.3
Burlington	WBSD-FM	89.1	Oshkosh	WRST-FM[2]	90.3
(Burlington Area School District)			Oshkosh	WVCY	690
Delafield	WHAD-FM[1]	90.7	Park Falls	WHBM-FM	90.3
Eau Claire	WDVM	1050	Platteville	WSSW-FM	89.1
Eau Claire	WHEM-FM	91.3	Platteville	WSUP-FM[2]	90.5
Eau Claire	WUEC-FM[2]	89.7	Reserve	WOJB-FM	88.9
Eau Claire	WVCF-FM	90.5	Rhinelander	WXPR-FM	91.7
Fond du Lac	WDKV-FM	91.7	Ripon	WRPN-FM	90.1
Green Bay	WEMY-FM	91.5	(Ripon College)		
Green Bay	WHID-FM[2]	88.1	River Falls	WRFW-FM[2]	88.7
Green Bay	WORQ-FM	90.1	Sheboygan	WSHS-FM	91.7
Green Bay	WPNE-FM[1]	89.3	(Sheboygan Area School District)		
Highland	WHHI-FM[1]	91.3	Sister Bay	WHDI-FM[1]	91.9
Kenosha	WGTD-FM	91.1	Sister Bay	WHND-FM[1]	89.7
(Gateway Technical College)			Stevens Point	WWSP-FM[2]	89.9
La Crosse	WHLA-FM[1]	90.3	Sturgeon Bay	WPFF-FM	90.5
La Crosse	WLSU-FM[2]	88.9	Sturgeon Bay	WNLI-FM	88.5
Lancaster	WJTY-FM	88.1	Sun Prairie	WNWC	1190
Madison	WERN-FM[1]	88.7	(Northwestern College)		
Madison	WHA[2]	970	Superior	KUWS-FM[2]	91.3
Madison	WNWC-FM	102.5	Suring	WRVM-FM	102.7
(Northwestern College)			Tomah	WVCX-FM	98.9
Madison	WORT-FM	89.9	Washburn	WEGZ-FM	105.9
Madison	WSUM-FM[2]	91.7	Waukesha	WCCX-FM	104.5
Marshall	WJWD-FM	90.3	(Carroll College)		
Menomonie	WHWC-FM[1]	88.3	Wausau	WCLQ-FM	89.5
Menomonie	WVSS-FM[2]	90.7	Wausau	WHRM-FM[1]	90.9
Milladore	WGNV-FM	88.5	Wausau	WLBL-FM[1]	91.9
Milwaukee	WMSE-FM	91.7	Wausau	WXPW-FM	91.9
(Milwaukee School of Engineering)			Whitewater	WSUW-FM[2]	91.7
Milwaukee	WMWK-FM	88.1	Wittenberg	WVRN-FM	88.9

[1]Licensed to the Wisconsin Educational Communications Board.

[2]Licensed to the University of Wisconsin System Board of Regents.

[3]Operated by the Milwaukee Area Technical College Board.

Sources: *Broadcasting and Cable Yearbook 2009*, R.R. Bowker, 2009; Wisconsin Broadcasters Association, *2009-2010 Directory.*.

HIGHLIGHTS OF POPULATION AND VITAL STATISTICS IN WISCONSIN

State and County Population — Wisconsin's 2008 population was estimated to be 5,675,156, a 5.8% increase over the 2000 U.S. Census count of 5,363,715. The state grew 9.6% in the 1990s. By contrast, the growth in the preceding decade from 1980 to 1990 was less than 4% and represented the smallest increase in decennial census counts in state history. The greatest increase occurred between 1840 and 1850, the decade in which Wisconsin became a state, when population jumped 886.9% from 30,945 to 305,391.

Between 1990 and 2000, population increased over 20% in Marquette, St. Croix, Walworth, and Washington Counties. Since 2000, St. Croix County has been the fastest growing county with a population increase of 26.2%, followed by Calumet and Juneau Counties. Dane County had the largest absolute growth, adding an estimated 45,033 people. Waukesha County grew by 21,930 people.

Population by Race and Age — In responding to the 2000 U.S. Census of Population, for the first time individuals were given the opportunity to identify themselves as being of more than one race. About 1.2% of Wisconsin's population selected multiple races. As a result, comparisons between the 2000 Census and earlier censuses must be made with caution. It is not clear whether someone who selected Asian and white, for example, for the 2000 Census would have selected Asian or white in 1990. Only those who selected a single race are used in the following comparisons. Between 1890 and 2000, the nonwhite population in Wisconsin increased from 0.7% to over 11.0%. Native Americans were the largest minority group from 1890 until 1950; Blacks have been the largest since 1950. In 2000, Milwaukee County had the largest Black population at 231,157, followed by Racine County with 19,777, Dane County with 17,069, Kenosha County with 7,600, and Rock County with 7,048. For the first time, more than half of the population of the City of Milwaukee was nonwhite. Wisconsin's Hispanic population more than doubled from 1990 to 2000, reaching 192,921. The Asian population almost doubled to 90,393.

The 2000 Wisconsin Native American population was 47,228, an increase of 21.1% over the 1990 population of 38,986. Wisconsin has 11 Indian reservations.

According to the 2008 estimates, Wisconsin had a voting age population of 4,330,695 or 76.3% of the total population.

Vital Statistics — In 2007, Wisconsin recorded 32,159 marriages and 16,458 divorces and annulments. Both the marriage and divorce rates in Wisconsin have been lower than the national rate for more than 75 years. Total deaths in 2007 numbered 46,117 (8.2 per 1,000 population).

The following tables present selected data. Consult footnoted sources for more detailed information about population and vital statistics.

WISCONSIN POPULATION, 1840 – 2008

Year	Population	Increase	Percent Increase	Rural	Urban	Percent Urban	Density[1]
1840	30,945	---	---	30,945	---	---	0.6
1850	305,391	274,446	886.9%	276,768	28,623	9.4%	5.6
1860	775,881	470,490	154.1	664,007	111,874	14.4	14.1
1870	1,054,670	278,789	35.9	847,471	207,099	19.6	19.2
1880	1,315,497	260,827	24.7	998,293	317,204	24.1	24
1890	1,693,330	377,833	28.7	1,131,044	562,286	33.2	30.9
1900	2,069,042	375,712	22.2	1,278,829	790,213	38.2	37.4
1910	2,333,860	264,818	12.8	1,329,540	1,004,320	43	42.6
1920	2,632,067	298,207	12.8	1,387,209	1,244,858	47.3	47.6
1930	2,939,006	306,939	11.7	1,385,163	1,553,843	52.9	53
1940	3,137,587	198,581	6.7	1,458,443	1,679,144	53.5	57.3
1950	3,434,575	296,988	9.5	1,446,687	1,987,888[2]	57.9	62.7
1960	3,951,777	517,202	15.1	1,429,598	2,522,179	63.8	72.2
1970	4,417,821	466,044	11.8	1,507,313	2,910,418	65.9	81.3
1980	4,705,642	287,821	6.5	1,685,035	3,020,732	64.2	86.6
1990	4,891,769	186,127	4.0	1,679,813	3,211,956	65.7	90.1
2000	5,363,715	471,946	9.6	1,700,032	3,663,643	68.3	98.8
2001	5,400,449	36,734	0.7	NA	NA	NA	NA
2002	5,453,896	53,447	1.0	NA	NA	NA	NA
2003	5,490,718	36,822	0.7	NA	NA	NA	NA
2004	5,532,955	42,237	0.8	NA	NA	NA	NA
2005	5,580,757	47,802	0.9	NA	NA	NA	NA
2006	5,617,744	36,987	0.7	NA	NA	NA	NA
2007	5,648,124	30,380	0.5	NA	NA	NA	NA
2008	5,675,156	27,032	0.5	NA	NA	NA	NA

NA – Not available.

[1]Population per square mile of land area.

[2]The "urban" definition was revised beginning with the 1950 census.

Sources: 2000 Census of Population, *Wisconsin Summary Population Characteristics,* November 2002; Wisconsin Department of Administration, Demographic Services Center, *Official Population Estimates, January 1, 2002,* October 2002, and previous issues; Wisconsin Department of Administration, Demographic Services Center, *Time Series of the Final Official Population Estimates and Census Counts for Wisconsin Counties: 1970-2008;* Wisconsin Department of Administration, Demographic Services Center, *Final Population Estimates for Wisconsin Counties, January 1, 2008,* December 2008, and previous issues.

WISCONSIN POPULATION – 2000 CENSUS
By Sex, Race, and Hispanic Origin

County	Total Population	Sex Male	Sex Female	White	Black	Indian, Eskimo, Aleut	Asian, Pacific Islander	Other	2 or More*	Hispanic Origin (of any race)
Adams	18,643	9,456	9,187	18,201	50	110	65	62	155	268
Ashland . . .	16,866	8,307	8,559	14,690	36	1,745	61	49	285	188
Barron	44,963	22,274	22,689	43,924	63	363	163	142	308	430
Bayfield . . .	15,013	7,590	7,423	13,280	20	1,409	42	39	223	91
Brown	226,778	112,763	114,015	206,688	2,641	5,191	4,999	4,300	2,959	8,698
Buffalo	13,804	6,926	6,878	13,623	16	42	48	11	64	85
Burnett	15,674	7,897	7,777	14,616	56	698	48	33	223	120
Calumet . . .	40,631	20,311	20,320	39,282	124	139	632	154	300	435
Chippewa . . .	55,195	27,468	27,727	54,006	89	176	500	93	331	289
Clark	33,557	16,819	16,738	32,904	43	161	104	188	157	404
Columbia . . .	52,468	26,448	26,020	50,990	460	185	187	232	414	827
Crawford. . .	17,243	8,717	8,526	16,780	233	37	47	29	117	129
Dane	426,526	211,020	215,506	379,447	17,069	1,404	14,868	6,118	7,620	14,387
Dodge	85,897	44,942	40,955	81,843	2,142	345	321	744	502	2,188
Door.	27,961	13,773	14,188	27,356	53	183	84	91	194	267
Douglas . . .	43,287	21,332	21,955	41,273	246	786	285	85	612	315
Dunn	39,858	20,094	19,764	38,294	135	107	854	148	320	335
Eau Claire . .	93,142	45,093	48,049	88,443	482	500	2,375	305	1,037	879
Florence . . .	5,088	2,597	2,491	4,995	8	22	15	7	41	23
Fond du Lac .	97,296	47,477	49,819	93,562	876	371	873	814	800	1,987
Forest.	10,024	5,016	5,008	8,607	118	1,133	21	23	122	108
Grant	49,597	25,164	24,433	48,719	259	64	234	71	250	280
Green.	33,647	16,558	17,089	33,021	86	70	97	120	253	327
Green Lake. .	19,105	9,407	9,698	18,687	29	38	66	170	115	393
Iowa	22,780	11,350	11,430	22,484	38	25	81	26	126	75
Iron.	6,861	3,362	3,499	6,743	6	41	12	4	55	45
Jackson. . . .	19,100	10,198	8,902	17,109	433	1,176	39	193	150	357
Jefferson . . .	74,021	36,712	37,309	71,309	210	249	347	1,220	686	3,031
Juneau	24,316	12,162	12,154	23,491	81	316	110	138	180	347
Kenosha . . .	149,577	74,149	75,428	132,193	7,600	564	1,438	4,924	2,858	10,757
Kewaunee . .	20,187	10,126	10,061	19,897	31	55	28	61	115	153
La Crosse . .	107,120	51,926	55,194	100,883	1,016	440	3,397	286	1,098	990
Lafayette . . .	16,137	8,060	8,077	15,980	17	18	42	23	57	92
Langlade . . .	20,740	10,291	10,449	20,311	31	113	62	42	181	171
Lincoln. . . .	29,641	14,810	14,831	28,977	123	130	124	86	201	243
Manitowoc. .	82,887	41,060	41,827	79,485	245	356	1,678	494	629	1,343
Marathon. . .	125,834	62,774	63,060	118,079	347	435	5,741	324	908	979
Marinette. . .	43,384	21,415	21,969	42,550	100	215	128	91	300	325
Marquette . .	15,832	8,600	7,232	14,828	545	165	58	60	176	421
Menominee . .	4,562	2,250	2,312	528	3	3,981	1	15	34	122
Milwaukee . .	940,164	450,574	489,590	616,973	231,157	6,794	24,567	39,931	20,742	82,406
Monroe. . . .	40,899	20,605	20,294	39,474	188	376	210	347	304	740
Oconto	35,634	17,935	17,699	34,836	48	277	77	84	312	240
Oneida	36,776	18,310	18,466	35,934	121	242	126	77	276	244
Outagamie . .	160,971	80,285	80,686	151,101	867	2,471	3,651	1,311	1,570	3,207
Ozaukee . . .	82,317	40,592	41,725	79,621	765	162	896	276	597	1,073
Pepin.	7,213	3,626	3,587	7,134	6	14	18	6	35	25
Pierce.	36,804	18,151	18,653	36,071	91	105	168	104	265	301
Polk	41,319	20,650	20,669	40,342	63	436	118	82	278	329
Portage. . . .	67,182	33,490	33,692	64,316	215	242	1,540	288	581	967
Price	15,822	7,949	7,873	15,541	16	95	52	23	95	116
Racine	188,831	93,457	95,374	156,796	19,777	687	1,440	6,972	3,159	14,990
Richland . . .	17,924	8,882	9,042	17,636	27	46	43	51	121	167
Rock	152,307	74,980	77,327	138,610	7,048	422	1,252	2,691	2,284	5,953
Rusk	15,347	7,614	7,733	14,992	79	65	55	54	102	116
St. Croix . . .	63,155	31,608	31,547	61,796	177	159	403	141	479	483
Sauk	55,225	27,292	27,933	53,775	142	479	153	324	352	938
Sawyer. . . .	16,196	8,169	8,027	13,236	51	2,603	51	56	199	145
Shawano . . .	40,664	20,311	20,353	37,251	91	2,545	154	128	495	407
Sheboygan . .	112,646	56,503	56,143	104,438	1,224	409	3,726	1,642	1,207	3,789
Taylor	19,680	9,966	9,714	19,427	17	37	46	37	116	127
Trempealeau .	27,010	13,526	13,484	26,688	35	45	39	77	126	240
Vernon	28,056	13,867	14,189	27,723	18	42	62	75	136	186
Vilas	21,033	10,469	10,564	18,865	43	1,909	40	39	137	181
Walworth. . .	93,759	46,626	47,133	88,597	790	219	636	2,452	1,065	6,136
Washburn . .	16,036	8,071	7,965	15,599	27	162	34	19	195	143
Washington. .	117,493	58,608	58,885	114,778	465	296	709	474	771	1,529
Waukesha . .	360,767	177,484	183,283	345,506	2,646	788	5,468	3,128	3,231	9,503
Waupaca . . .	51,731	25,899	25,832	50,660	87	217	146	280	341	714
Waushara . .	23,154	11,669	11,485	22,413	62	72	87	314	206	848
Winnebago . .	156,763	78,149	78,614	148,795	1,756	726	2,924	1,121	1,441	3,065
Wood.	75,555	37,030	38,525	72,855	201	528	1,227	223	521	709
STATE . .	5,363,675	2,649,041	2,714,634	4,769,857	304,460	47,228	90,393	84,842	66,895	192,921

*For the first time in the 2000 Census, individuals were allowed to select more than one race.

Source: U.S. Department of Commerce, U.S. Census Bureau, *Profile of General Demographic Characteristics, 2000 Census of Population and Housing, Wisconsin,* May 2001. For more current state and select county estimates see 2007 American Community Survey, Data Profile Highlights, at: http://factfinder.census.gov/home/saff/main.html?_lang=en.

POPULATION CHANGES BY COUNTY, 2000-2008
State Increase: +5.81%

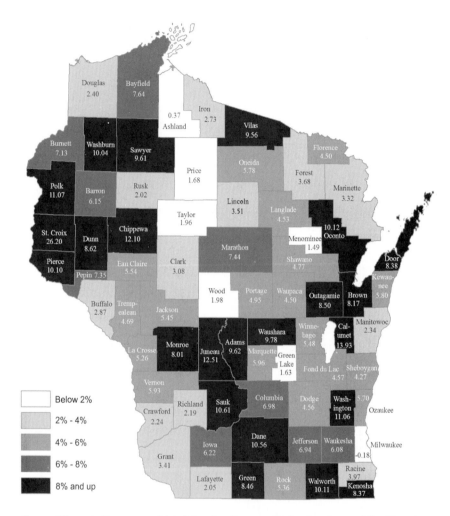

Source: Wisconsin Department of Administration, Demographic Services Center, *Official Population Estimates, January 1, 2008,* March 2009. Map produced by Wisconsin Legislative Technology Services Bureau.

WISCONSIN POPULATION, BY RACE, 1890 – 2007
Population Totals

U.S. Census Year	Total Population	Race						Hispanic or Latino Origin (of any race)[4]
		White	Black	American Indian[1]	Asian[2]	Other Races	2 or More[3]	
1890	1,693,330	1,680,828	2,444	9,930	128	—	—	—
1900	2,069,042	2,057,911	2,542	8,372	217	—	—	—
1910	2,333,860	2,320,555	2,900	10,142	260	3	—	—
1920	2,632,067	2,616,938	5,201	9,611	314	3	—	—
1930	2,939,006	2,916,255	10,739	11,548	451	13	—	—
1940	3,137,587	3,112,752	12,158	12,265	388	24	—	—
1950	3,434,575	3,392,690	28,182	12,196	1,119	388	—	—
1960	3,951,777	3,858,903	74,546	14,297	2,836	1,195	—	—
1970[5]	4,417,933	4,258,959	128,224	18,924	6,557	5,067	—	62,875
1980[5]	4,705,642	4,443,035	182,592	29,320	22,043	41,788	—	62,782
1990	4,891,769	4,512,523	244,539	39,387	53,583	42,538	—	93,194
2000	5,363,675	4,769,857	304,460	47,228	90,393	84,842	66,895	192,921
2007[6]	5,601,640	4,960,052	368,138	72,868	128,301	140,771	76,891	270,179

Population Percentages

U.S. Census Year	Race						Hispanic or Latino Origin (of any race)[4]
	White	Black	American Indian[1]	Asian[2]	Other Races	2 or More[3]	
1890	99.3%	0.1%	0.6%	—	—	—	—
1900	99.5	0.1	0.4	—	—	—	—
1910	99.4	0.1	0.4	—	—	—	—
1920	99.4	0.2	0.4	—	—	—	—
1930	99.2	0.4	0.4	—	—	—	—
1940	99.2	0.4	0.4	—	—	—	—
1950	98.8	0.8	0.4	—	—	—	—
1960	97.6	1.9	0.4	0.1%	—	—	—
1970	96.4	2.9	0.4	0.2	0.1%	—	1.4%
1980	94.4	3.9	0.6	0.3	0.9	—	1.3
1990	92.2	5	0.8	1.2	0.9	—	1.9
2000	88.9	5.7	0.9	1.7	1.6	1.2%	3.6
2007[6]	88.5	6.6	1.3	2.3	2.5	1.4	4.8

[1]Aleut and Eskimo populations included beginning in 1960.
[2]Native Hawaiian and Other Pacific Islanders are grouped with Asian.
[3]For the first time in the 2000 Census, individuals were allowed to select more than one race.
[4]The 1990 data on Hispanic/Spanish origin are generally comparable with those for the 1980 census, but not the 1970 census. In the 2000 Census, "Hispanic or Latino Origin" represents ethnicity and includes people of Cuban, Mexican, Puerto Rican, South or Central American, or other Spanish culture or origin, regardless of race.
[5]Total has been corrected by the U.S. Census Bureau. Details not adjusted to revised total.
[6]American Community Survey (ACS) is conducted every month on independent samples and produces annual or annual average estimates. These estimates consist of totals, proportions, percentages, means, medians, and ratios. The ACS provides annually updated data on demographic, socioeconomic, and housing characteristics.
Sources: U.S. Department of Commerce, Bureau of the Census, 1970 Census of Population, *Characteristics of Population, Wisconsin;* 1980 Census of Population, *Characteristics of Population, General Social and Economic Characteristics;* 1990 Census of Population, *General Population Characteristics, Wisconsin,* Table 3, June 1992; *Profile of General Demographic Characteristics, 2000 Census of Population and Housing, Wisconsin,* May 2001; 2007 American Community Survey 1-Year Estimates, *Wisconsin ACS Demographic and Housing Estimates: 2007.*

WISCONSIN POPULATION BY RACE AND HISPANIC ORIGIN
2007 Estimate[1]

Race	Total	Percent	Race	Total	Percent
		Total Wisconsin Population: 5,571,593			
One race	5,501,311	98.7%	Two or more races	70,282	1.3%
White.	4,876,425	87.5			
Black or African American	331,483	5.9	**Race as selected alone or in**		
American Indian and Alaska Native	46,322	0.8	**combination with other race(s)[4]**		
Asian.	110,531	2.0	White.	4,939,911	88.7
Asian Indian	18,958	0.4	Black or African American . .	359,052	6.4
Chinese.	15,155	0.3	American Indian and		
Filipino.	7,231	0.1	Alaska Native	71,948	1.3
Japanese	3,135	0.0	Asian.	124,043	2.2
Korean	7,595	0.1	Native Hawaiian and Other		
Vietnamese.	5,679	0.1	Pacific Islander.	3,268	0.1
Other Asian[2]	52,778	0.9	Other race	148,294	2.7
Native Hawaiian and Other					
Pacific Islander.	1,835	0.0	**Hispanic or Latino and Race**		
Native Hawaiian	653	0.0	Hispanic or Latino (of any race). .	260,103	4.7
Guamanian or Chamorro.	380	0.0	Mexican	186,605	3.3
Samoan.	75	0.0	Puerto Rican	37,330	0.7
Other Pacific Islander[3]	727	0.0	Cuban	2,197	0.0
Other race	134,715	2.4	Other Hispanic or Latino . . .	33,971	0.6

[1]Information from U.S. Census Bureau American Community Survey. American Community Survey (ACS) provides annually updated data on the characteristics of population and housing. The ACS is conducted every month on independent samples, and produces annual or average estimates. The estimates consist of totals, proportions, percentages, means, medians, and ratios.

[2]Other Asian alone, or two or more Asian categories.

[3]Other Pacific Islander alone, or two or more Native Hawaiian and Other Pacific Islander categories.

[4]The total population of the categories adds to more than 100 percent because individuals may report more than one race.

Source: U.S. Census Bureau, 2007 American Community Survey, *Data Profile Highlights and ACS Demographic and Housing Estimates: 2005-2007.*

WISCONSIN ASIAN POPULATION
1940 – 2007

	Total[1]	Asian Indian	Chinese	Filipino	Hmong	Japanese	Korean	Laotian	Vietnamese
1940	388	NA	290	75	NA	23	NA	NA	NA
1950	1,119	NA	590	NA	NA	529	NA	NA	NA
1960	2,836	NA	1,010	401	NA	1,425	NA	NA	NA
1970	6,557	NA	2,700	1,209	NA	2,648	NA	NA	NA
1980	22,043	3,902	4,835	3,036	NA	2,900	NA	1,699
1990	53,583	6,914	7,354	3,690	16,373	2,765	5,618	3,622	2,494
2000	90,393[2]	12,665	11,184	5,158	33,791	2,868	6,800	4,469	3,891
2007[3]	108,711	19,588	14,598	6,874	NA	2,994	9,997	NA	5,403

NA – Not available.

[1]Includes Native Hawaiian, other Pacific Islanders until 2000, and all other Asians not identified in the detailed categories.

[2]Also includes those listed in two or more Asian categories.

[3]American Community Survey (ACS) is conducted every month on independent samples, and produces annual or annual average estimates. These estimates consist of totals, proportions, percentages, means, medians, and ratios. The ACS provides annually updated data on the characteristics of population and housing.

Sources: U.S. Department of Commerce, Bureau of the Census, 1970 Census of Population, *Characteristics of the Population, Wisconsin;* 1980 Census of Population, *Characteristics of the Population, General Social and Economic Characteristics;* 1990 Census of Population, *General Population Characteristics, Wisconsin,* Table 3, June 1992; *Profiles of General Demographic Characteristics, 2000 Census of Population and Housing, Wisconsin,* 2001; 2007 American Community Survey, *ACS Demographic and Housing Estimates: 2007.*

WISCONSIN INDIANS
Wisconsin Indian Population, 1900 – 2007

Year	Total	Male	Female
1900	8,372	4,321	4,051
1910	10,142	5,231	4,911
1920	9,611	4,950	4,661
1930	11,548	5,951	5,597
1940	12,265	6,354	5,911
1950	12,196	6,274	5,922
1960	14,297	7,195	7,102
1970	18,924	9,251	9,673
1980	29,320	14,489	14,831
1990	38,986	19,240	19,746
2000	47,228*	23,462	23,766
2007	48,673	24,199	24,474

*For the first time in the 2000 Census, individuals were allowed to select more than one race.
Source: U.S. Census Bureau, *Profiles of General Demographic Characteristics, 2000 Census of Population and Housing, Wisconsin,* 2001 and *Annual Estimates of the Resident Population by Sex, Race, and Hispanic Origin for Wisconsin: April 1, 2000 to July 1, 2008,* 2009.

Wisconsin Indian Reservations: Population and Acreage

Reservation Total/ County Detail	Tribe	2000 Reservation Population			October 2008 Acreage Ownership Status[1,3]		
		Total	Indian	% Indian	Total	Tribal	Individual
Bad River	Chippewa	1,411	1,096	77.68%	58,432.93	24,493.03	33,938.90
Ho-Chunk Nation	Ho-Chunk Nation	960	827	86.15	6,178.19	2,952.00	3,226.19
Lac Courte Oreilles	Chippewa	2,900	2,150	74.14	48,043.15	24,390.89	23,652.26
Lac du Flambeau	Chippewa	2,995	1,778	59.37	44,995.37	31,458.42	13,521.89
Menominee[2]	Menominee	3,225	3,070	95.19	238,073.00	235,078.00	2,995.00
Oneida (West)	Oneida	21,321	3,288	15.42	8,253.87	6,216.35	2,037.52
Potawatomi (Wisconsin)	Potawatomi	531	482	90.77	12,280.18	11,560.18	400.00
Red Cliff	Chippewa	1,078	928	86.09	8,112.35	6,330.62	1,767.08
St. Croix	Chippewa	641	561	87.52	2,247.05	2,247.05	0.00
Sokaogon	Chippewa	392	332	84.69	3,072.01	3,072.01	0.00
Stockbridge-Munsee	Mahican/Munsee	1,527	769	50.36	16,560.29	16,404.67	155.62
TOTAL		37,276	15,567	41.73%	446,248.39	364,203.22	81,694.46

[1]Figures do not include off-reservation public domain acreage.
[2]Public Law 93-107, the Menominee Restoration Act, effective on December 22, 1973, repealed the Menominee Termination Act of June 17, 1954 (P.L. 83-399) and acknowledged the Menominee Indian Tribe of Wisconsin as a federally recognized Indian tribe.
[3]Menominee Indian Tribe numbers are from June 2006. Acreage ownership totals reflect this.
Sources: U.S. Census Bureau, *Profiles of General Demographic Characteristics, 2000 Census of Population and Housing, Wisconsin,* 2001; U.S. Bureau of Indian Affairs, departmental data, May 2009; Menominee Indian Tribe of Wisconsin, tribal data, May 2007. Acreage ownership totals calculated by the Wisconsin Legislative Reference Bureau.

Wisconsin Indian Land Holding in Acres, By County, October 2008

County	Total Holdings	Tribal Land	Individual Land
Adams	121.35	0.34	121.01
Ashland	55,963.43	23,810.47	32,151.96
Barron	168.61	168.61	0.00
Bayfield	8,112.35	6,330.62	1,767.08
Brown	2,402.03	1,896.44	505.59
Burnett	1,278.24	1,278.24	0.00
Clark	640.24	42.50	597.74
Crawford	193.20	80.00	113.20
Dane	4.45	4.45	0.00
Douglas	516.27	0.00	516.27
Eau Claire	160.00	160.00	0.00
Forest	15,172.69	14,492.69	360.00
Iron	16,483.34	12,344.89	4,138.45
Jackson	1,302.72	517.40	785.32
Juneau	393.85	83.00	310.85
La Crosse	92.30	0.00	92.30
Marathon	200.00	0.00	200.00
Marinette	40.00	0.00	40.00
Menominee*	238,073.00	235,078.00	2,995.00
Milwaukee	19.50	19.50	0.00
Monroe	445.50	52.50	393.00
Oconto	120.00	120.00	0.00
Oneida	355.41	176.07	179.34
Outagamie	5,710.32	4,656.48	1,053.84
Polk	851.80	851.80	0.00
Sauk	88.27	88.27	0.00
Sawyer	48,043.15	24,390.89	23,652.26
Shawano	17,298.99	16,817.87	481.12
Vilas	30,626.16	19,840.40	10,770.70
Vernon	1,200.00	1,200.00	0.00
Washburn	20.00	20.00	0.00
Wood	537.72	134.05	403.67

Note: Total holdings include government land.
*Tribal data from 2007.
Sources: U.S. Bureau of Indian Affairs, departmental data, May 2009; Menominee Indian Tribe of Wisconsin, tribal data, April 2007.

Tribal Chairpersons, Mailing Addresses, and Web Sites
May 2009

Tribe and Chairperson	Tribal Mailing Address and Web Sites

Bad River Band (Lake Superior Chippewa)
   Eugene Bigboy, Sr.
	P.O. Box 39, Odanah 54861-0039, (715) 682-7111
	   http://www.badriver.com

Forest County Potawatomi Tribe
   Philip Shopodock
	P.O. Box 340, Crandon 54520-0346, (715) 478-7200
	   http://www.fcpotawatomi.com

Ho-Chunk Nation
   Wilfrid Cleveland (President)
	P.O. Box 667, Black River Falls 54615-0667, (715) 284-9343
	   http://www.ho-chunknation.com

Lac Courte Oreilles Band (Lake Superior Chippewa)
   Louis Taylor
	13394 W. Trepania Road, Hayward 54843-2186, (715) 634-8934
	   http://www.lco-nsn.gov

Lac du Flambeau Band (Lake Superior Chippewa)
   Carl Edwards (President)
	P.O. Box 67, Lac du Flambeau 54538-0067, (715) 588-3303
	   http://www.lacduflambeaunation.com/

Menominee Tribe
   Lisa Waukau
	P.O. Box 910, Keshena 54135-0910, (715) 799-5114
	   http://www.menominee-nsn.gov

Oneida Tribe
   Rick Hill
	P.O. Box 365, Oneida 54155-0365, (920) 869-4380
	   http://www.oneidanation.org

Red Cliff Band (Lake Superior Chippewa)
   Rose Soulier
	88385 Pike Road, Red Cliff 54814-0529, (715) 779-3700
	   http://www.redcliff-nsn.gov

St. Croix Band (Lake Superior Chippewa)
   Hazel Hindsley
	24663 Angeline Avenue, Webster 54893, (715) 349-2195
	   http://www.stcciw.com/

Sokaogon Chippewa Community
   Arlyn Ackley
	3051 Sand Lake Road, Crandon 54520, (715) 478-7500
	   http://www.sokaogonchippewa.com

Stockbridge-Munsee Band, Mohican Nation
   Robert Chicks (President)
	P.O. Box 70, Bowler 54416-9801, (715) 793-4111
	   http://www.mohican-nsn.gov

Sources: Wisconsin State Tribal Relations Initiative, http://witribes.wi.gov/; Great Lakes Inter-Tribal Council, www.glitc.org [April 2009]; and individual tribal Web sites.

WISCONSIN VOTING AGE POPULATION BY RACE AND COUNTY
2000 Census and 2008 Estimate

County	2008 Total[1]	2000 Total[1]	White	Black/ African American	American Indian and Alaska Native	Asian	Native Hawaiian and Other Pacific Islander	Other	More Than One	Hispanic or Latino Origin[2]
Adams	17,734	15,761	14,482	34	72	39	3	31	99	148
Ashland	12,932	12,582	11,249	20	1,089	37	8	37	142	110
Barron	36,542	33,583	32,980	39	229	88	11	72	164	229
Bayfield	12,491	11,313	10,307	4	835	20	1	28	118	41
Brown	185,422	167,551	156,000	1,798	3,334	2,498	49	2,727	1,249	5,302
Buffalo	10,899	10,343	10,238	9	25	27	3	7	34	48
Burnett	13,409	12,209	11,560	30	456	25	8	17	113	63
Calumet	33,802	29,014	28,301	72	98	323	3	93	122	248
Chippewa . . .	46,645	40,593	39,980	45	121	236	5	42	164	148
Clark	24,796	23,494	23,148	25	94	65	3	111	73	244
Columbia. . . .	43,019	39,247	38,242	411	135	118	11	140	190	521
Crawford. . . .	13,337	12,731	12,416	173	27	31	2	17	65	69
Dane	373,416	330,269	299,370	10,861	1,041	10,823	112	4,268	3,796	9,871
Dodge	69,278	64,641	61,377	2,051	278	182	19	460	267	1,447
Door	24,246	21,789	21,425	27	124	51	3	57	102	172
Douglas	34,716	33,085	31,814	173	548	162	9	46	333	168
Dunn	33,969	30,553	29,693	92	83	403	4	96	182	212
Eau Claire . . .	77,175	71,322	68,798	291	338	1,211	18	180	486	547
Florence	4,206	3,924	3,863	6	19	10	1	3	22	11
Fond du Lac . .	78,006	72,779	70,520	687	275	418	12	501	394	1,209
Forest.	7,965	7,488	6,679	82	631	13	4	16	63	48
Grant.	40,108	37,829	37,217	205	45	174	4	44	140	187
Green.	27,467	24,739	24,419	41	44	51	—	62	122	190
Green Lake. . .	15,094	14,491	14,254	16	30	30	3	99	59	234
Iowa	18,070	16,609	16,446	19	16	44	1	15	68	49
Iron.	5,824	5,527	5,457	3	25	7	3	1	31	28
Jackson.	15,658	14,497	13,081	417	732	21	8	158	80	273
Jefferson	62,039	56,625	53,639	158	166	239	10	792	360	1,911
Juneau	20,947	18,134	17,648	42	188	64	3	87	102	198
Kenosha	121,132	109,075	98,672	4,583	397	987	37	3,100	1,299	6,391
Kewaunee . . .	16,218	14,970	14,795	18	33	18	1	35	70	101
La Crosse . . .	88,019	81,856	78,623	621	287	1,630	15	186	497	603
Lafayette	12,281	11,748	11,668	11	12	17	3	13	24	54
Langlade	16,811	15,683	15,437	16	75	36	2	23	94	95
Lincoln	23,502	22,100	21,793	27	83	61	2	38	96	109
Manitowoc. . .	64,808	61,790	60,035	149	265	743	19	301	274	776
Marathon. . . .	101,443	92,118	88,632	192	313	2,384	14	187	396	565
Marinette. . . .	35,156	33,181	32,674	44	162	84	8	57	154	193
Marquette . . .	12,316	11,345	11,600	532	149	32	16	41	127	323
Menominee . .	2,899	2,786	487	2	2,263	—	1	14	19	50
Milwaukee. . .	708,667	692,339	496,391	140,938	4,494	15,397	299	24,612	10,228	49,981
Monroe.	32,558	29,398	28,549	118	245	110	12	225	142	448
Oconto	29,838	26,487	26,004	21	185	49	2	44	169	131
Oneida	30,999	28,573	28,050	100	160	74	10	38	141	130
Outagamie . . .	129,458	116,523	110,855	585	1,602	1,764	32	853	753	1,971
Ozaukee	65,323	60,308	58,732	553	103	573	11	164	250	636
Pepin	5,836	5,304	5,250	3	9	10	2	5	25	18
Pierce.	31,372	27,808	27,361	63	63	118	7	67	128	182
Polk	34,646	30,484	29,953	35	263	63	4	42	124	179
Portage.	54,874	51,005	49,449	123	178	784	19	178	274	574
Price	12,554	12,052	11,884	7	61	30	3	10	57	68
Racine	147,161	137,880	118,057	12,718	498	919	46	4,297	1,345	9,042
Richland	14,044	13,412	13,254	14	28	25	—	23	68	81
Rock	120,865	111,913	103,716	4,409	310	836	44	1,671	955	3,663
Rusk	12,060	11,544	11,299	69	41	29	9	31	66	63
St. Croix	58,919	45,538	44,740	141	101	226	12	91	227	277
Sauk	46,378	40,854	40,018	82	289	93	4	202	166	542
Sawyer.	13,829	12,295	10,486	46	1,577	30	3	41	112	77
Shawano	32,447	30,231	28,159	33	1,631	73	10	81	244	211
Sheboygan . . .	89,639	83,877	79,285	990	282	1,723	17	1,008	566	2,300
Taylor	14,979	14,348	14,207	4	23	29	—	18	67	61
Trempealeau . .	21,623	20,166	19,966	21	26	26	2	53	72	149
Vernon	22,071	20,360	20,170	6	29	36	1	42	76	95
Vilas	18,750	16,688	15,416	32	1,120	25	2	23	70	99
Walworth. . . .	78,330	69,548	67,786	599	160	449	21	1,543	547	3,749
Washburn . . .	13,786	12,221	11,969	13	121	16	2	12	88	75
Washington. . .	98,061	86,165	84,568	292	199	444	25	278	357	876
Waukesha . . .	288,979	265,864	256,676	1,505	553	3,686	65	1,927	1,452	5,738
Waupaca	41,246	38,526	37,867	38	141	84	7	164	153	384
Waushara	19,851	17,639	17,280	39	48	45	3	181	114	502
Winnebago. . .	129,059	119,420	114,521	1,408	559	1,540	25	694	673	1,836
Wood.	58,696	56,170	54,804	109	324	578	5	123	227	358
STATE . . .	4,330,695	3,994,314	3,635,741	189,140	30,560	53,286	1,143	52,943	32,106	117,682

Note: The voting age population is 18 and older.
[1]Wisconsin Department of Administration estimate. Race and ethnicity data have not been adjusted.
[2]"Hispanic or Latino Origin" represents ethnicity and includes people of Cuban, Mexican, Puerto Rican, South or Central American, or other Spanish culture or origin, regardless of race.
Sources: U.S. Department of Commerce, Census Bureau, P.L. 94-171 Redistricting File, as processed by the Wisconsin Legislative Technology Services Bureau, March 2001; Wisconsin Department of Administration, Demographic Services Center, *Final Population Estimates for Wisconsin Counties*, January 1, 2008.

WISCONSIN VITAL STATISTICS
1910 – 2007

Year	Marriages Number	Marriages Rate[3]	Divorces, Annulments Number[4]	Divorces, Annulments Rate[3]	Live Births Number	Live Births Rate[3]	Total Deaths[1] Number	Total Deaths[1] Rate[3]	Infant Deaths Number	Infant Deaths Rate[5]	Fetal Deaths[2] Number	Fetal Deaths[2] Rate[6]	Maternal Deaths Number	Maternal Deaths Rate[7]
1910	18,528	7.9	1,189	0.5	51,435	22.0	28,213	12.1	5,621	109.3	1,414	26.8	255	49.6
1915	17,833	7.2	1,721	0.7	58,014	23.3	26,676	10.7	4,520	77.9	1,711	28.6	291	50.2
1920	22,294	8.4	2,425	0.9	59,269	22.4	29,859	11.3	4,566	77.0	1,673	27.5	338	57.0
1925	16,385	5.8	2,467	0.9	58,024	20.7	29,380	10.5	3,861	66.5	1,712	28.7	294	50.7
1930	15,328	5.2	2,553	0.9	56,643	19.2	30,488	10.4	3,149	55.6	1,683	28.9	298	52.6
1935	21,075	6.9	3,543	1.2	52,402	17.2	30,404	10.0	2,413	46.0	1,257	23.4	193	36.8
1940	23,379	7.5	3,599	1.1	56,324	17.9	31,457	10.0	2,030	36.0	1,209	21.0	151	26.8
1945	25,269	8.5	6,393	2.2	61,577	20.9	31,776	10.7	1,890	30.7	1,141	18.2	81	13.2
1950	29,081	8.4	4,845	1.4	82,364	23.9	33,573	9.7	2,098	25.5	1,241	14.8	35	4.3
1955	25,543	7.0	4,720	1.3	92,333	25.2	35,250	9.6	2,175	23.6	1,233	13.2	22	2.4
1960	24,573	6.2	3,672	0.9	99,493	25.1	38,121	9.6	2,173	21.8	1,341	13.3	27	2.7
1965	28,410	6.7	5,232	1.2	82,919	19.7	40,146	9.5	1,829	22.1	1,042	12.4	13	1.6
1970	34,415	7.8	8,930	2.0	77,455	17.5	40,820	9.2	1,308	16.9	817	10.4	6	0.8
1975	35,888	7.8	13,187	2.9	65,145	14.3	39,916	8.8	881	13.5	530	8.1	6	0.5
1980	41,113	8.7	17,589	3.7	74,763	15.9	40,801	8.7	763	10.2	549	7.3	5	0.7
1985	40,014	8.4	16,596	3.5	73,647	15.4	41,434	8.7	674	9.2	471	6.4	4	0.5
1990	38,934	8.0	17,727	3.6	72,636	14.8	42,655	8.7	611	8.4	443	6.1	3	0.4
1995	36,354	7.1	17,313	3.4	67,493	13.2	45,037	8.8	493	7.3	403	5.9	3	0.3
1996	36,186	7.0	17,218	3.3	67,076	13.0	45,107	8.7	492	7.3	416	6.2	2	0.3
1997	35,546	6.8	17,289	3.3	66,490	12.7	44,860	8.6	431	6.5	361	5.4	2	0.3
1998	34,946	6.7	17,484	3.3	67,379	12.8	45,890	8.7	488	7.2	401	5.9	6	0.9
1999	35,754	6.8	17,302	3.3	68,181	12.9	46,571	8.8	456	6.7	353	5.2	6	0.9
2000	36,100	6.7	17,388	3.2	69,289	12.9	46,405	8.7	457	6.6	414	5.9	5	0.7
2001	34,790	6.5	17,457	3.3	69,012	12.7	46,537	8.6	491	7.1	375	5.4	5	0.6
2002	34,241	6.3	17,471	3.2	68,510	12.6	46,893	8.6	471	6.9	379	5.5	4	0.6
2003	34,220	6.3	17,150	3.1	69,999	12.7	46,040	8.4	454	6.5	344	4.9	9	0.1
2004	34,056	6.2	16,802	3.0	70,131	12.7	45,488	8.2	420	6.0	352	5.0	6	0.9
2005	33,876	6.1	16,297	2.9	70,934	12.7	46,544	8.3	469	6.6	363	5.1	15	2.1
2006	33,437	6.0	16,730	3.0	72,302	12.9	46,051	8.2	462	6.4	384	5.3	15	2.1
2007	32,159	5.7	16,458	2.9	72,757	12.9	46,117	8.2	469	6.4	386	5.3	15	2.1

[1]Excludes fetal deaths (20 weeks gestation and over).
[2]A fetal death report is not used for induced abortions.
[3]Per 1,000 population.
[4]Pre-1960 data includes legal separations.
[5]Per 1,000 live births.
[6]Per 1,000 deliveries (live births plus stillbirths of 20 weeks or more gestation).
[7]Per 10,000 live births.

Sources: Wisconsin Department of Health and Family Services, *Vital Statistics 1994*, August 1995, and previous issues; *Wisconsin Births and Infant Deaths, 2007*, November 2008, and previous issues; *Wisconsin Deaths, 2007*, September 2008, and previous issues; *Wisconsin Marriages and Divorces, 2007*, April 2008, and previous issues; departmental data.

RESIDENT LIVE BIRTHS AND DEATHS IN WISCONSIN
By County, 1980 – 2007

County	Live Births						Deaths					
	1980	1985	1990	1995	2000	2007	1980	1985	1990	1995[1]	2000	2007[1]
Adams	179	170	175	167	158	154	136	178	182	185	226	250
Ashland	279	248	202	239	224	214	219	196	214	218	206	203
Barron	654	628	579	550	466	548	411	432	433	450	442	467
Bayfield	219	193	155	135	141	121	146	159	151	152	153	157
Brown	2,802	2,917	3,169	2,962	3,212	3,518	1,181	1,310	1,349	1,482	1,591	1,641
Buffalo	236	227	176	165	163	148	129	147	145	121	123	116
Burnett	167	160	143	171	136	136	168	128	159	179	183	166
Calumet	546	514	491	488	513	679	205	221	242	235	252	288
Chippewa	903	867	704	633	673	786	456	495	498	534	533	507
Clark	641	514	464	448	496	561	316	345	355	323	307	296
Columbia	667	650	610	607	616	679	436	440	450	532	508	502
Crawford	293	239	230	215	183	168	167	176	180	178	178	178
Dane	4,685	4,984	5,305	5,023	5,555	6,198	1,928	2,112	2,078	2,397	2,512	2,777
Dodge	1,186	1,146	985	947	994	962	678	711	765	810	848	871
Door	412	400	325	254	232	248	262	245	311	311	315	286
Douglas	702	590	540	493	513	510	457	422	440	455	454	439
Dunn	537	501	417	444	483	467	240	305	271	289	280	288
Eau Claire	1,117	1,201	1,208	1,118	1,116	1,215	646	618	658	664	639	719
Florence[2]	55	63	26	36	36	32	52	39	44	66	63	46
Fond du Lac	1,512	1,368	1,270	1,119	1,151	1,257	824	807	771	867	908	932
Forest[2]	140	156	132	137	114	118	104	118	122	109	131	120
Grant	867	743	661	561	540	576	454	476	493	465	495	511
Green	483	471	418	390	402	472	311	303	270	316	322	331
Green Lake	262	266	241	192	219	217	208	204	201	248	243	190
Iowa	345	319	318	296	263	308	204	205	195	191	195	185
Iron[2]	84	76	68	63	40	38	93	75	97	87	84	85
Jackson	276	240	217	189	233	257	179	176	187	187	219	202
Jefferson	973	1,004	873	852	931	1,026	605	576	541	579	608	577
Juneau	347	339	277	308	275	307	221	227	230	271	264	277
Kenosha	1,826	1,910	2,043	2,040	2,151	2,142	1,093	1,034	1,131	1,229	1,222	1,306
Kewaunee	323	303	237	218	224	199	166	179	184	193	189	195
La Crosse	1,349	1,394	1,416	1,267	1,234	1,304	768	798	836	869	888	936
Lafayette	289	271	227	176	174	217	139	147	172	147	144	142
Langlade	287	259	232	228	209	217	207	234	220	252	220	242
Lincoln	406	363	343	320	281	318	284	279	281	298	333	286
Manitowoc	1,338	1,228	1,072	898	894	914	779	779	774	819	852	817
Marathon	1,930	1,812	1,685	1,585	1,520	1,760	853	827	875	907	924	1,035
Marinette[2]	662	592	431	454	457	448	446	424	491	478	470	482
Marquette[2]	167	158	148	121	146	167	134	152	149	141	174	159
Menominee[2]	111	132	128	92	93	102	36	37	42	45	36	37
Milwaukee	15,841	16,296	17,013	15,067	14,846	15,318	9,278	9,143	9,282	9,200	9,063	8,151
Monroe	607	600	591	529	602	666	339	376	384	383	414	384
Oconto	469	451	398	388	383	397	300	304	272	331	357	315
Oneida	423	437	371	352	316	304	316	348	363	375	431	422
Outagamie	2,340	2,320	2,273	2,056	2,289	2,281	895	923	993	1,026	1,109	1,190
Ozaukee	992	960	945	934	869	864	437	436	497	541	583	690
Pepin	128	94	90	83	79	91	107	82	93	72	73	76
Pierce	507	492	477	403	412	442	234	225	237	235	244	232
Polk	506	506	529	470	454	521	319	360	352	380	376	406
Portage	927	876	913	788	805	782	360	375	398	438	404	481
Price	242	225	185	184	125	130	211	220	196	198	207	192
Racine	2,980	2,641	2,697	2,512	2,650	2,623	1,393	1,328	1,438	1,534	1,616	1,495
Richland	275	267	219	196	201	220	184	189	186	200	185	183
Rock	2,256	2,189	2,166	1,963	2,075	2,161	1,205	1,204	1,277	1,268	1,335	1,267
Rusk	222	216	213	192	148	179	135	170	157	183	168	147
St. Croix	835	741	840	725	908	1,195	303	334	375	438	444	443
Sauk	654	690	670	670	755	816	433	459	485	484	485	563
Sawyer	219	203	176	196	182	208	155	136	171	194	183	172
Shawano	528	488	525	456	470	510	414	399	418	444	476	413
Sheboygan	1,588	1,507	1,401	1,336	1,437	1,407	954	982	908	957	1,083	991
Taylor	379	354	289	221	247	257	159	143	195	191	176	175
Trempealeau	373	370	369	315	322	385	314	296	300	338	298	331
Vernon	408	409	332	351	390	415	325	289	290	311	330	296
Vilas	228	240	201	205	155	199	204	215	244	254	251	274
Walworth	1,026	1,009	996	952	1,102	1,231	626	662	651	710	826	806
Washburn	226	198	159	168	163	191	136	175	167	194	198	163
Washington	1,442	1,383	1,349	1,440	1,490	1,518	562	583	650	687	795	924
Waukesha	3,841	3,727	4,046	4,120	4,357	4,067	1,648	1,800	1,906	2,316	2,795	2,731
Waupaca	697	656	667	619	567	592	618	610	620	658	634	685
Waushara	243	247	245	240	225	263	214	238	223	242	243	271
Winnebago	1,901	2,028	1,936	1,838	1,926	1,931	1,099	1,095	1,094	1,271	1,194	1,272
Wood	1,198	1,211	1,039	923	878	885	583	599	646	704	695	731
STATE	74,758	73,647	72,661	67,493	69,289	72,757	40,801	41,434	42,655	45,036	46,405	46,117

[1] The totals for 1995 and 2007 include one death with an unknown county of residence.

[2] Since nearly all births and deaths occur in hospitals, the numbers for Florence, Forest, Iron, Marinette, Marquette, and Menominee Counties are small because they have no hospitals. Caution must be used in making inferences based on this data

Sources: Wisconsin Department of Health Services, Division of Public Health, Bureau of Health Information and Policy, *Wisconsin Births and Infant Deaths, 2007,* at: http://dhs.wisconsin.gov/births/pdf/07births.pdf, and previous issues; *Wisconsin Deaths, 2007,* at: http://dhs.wisconsin.gov/deaths/pdf/07deaths.pdf, and previous issues.

MARRIAGES AND DIVORCES, BY STATE OF OCCURRENCE
1970 – 2007
(In Thousands)

State	Marriages[1]						Divorces[2]					
	1970	1980	1990	2000	2006	2007[3]	1970	1980	1990	2000	2006	2007[3]
Alabama	47.0	49.0	43.3	45.0	54.5	41.4	15.1	26.9	25.3	23.5	35.2	32.1
Alaska	3.4	5.3	5.7	5.6	5.7	7.1	1.7	3.4	2.9	2.7	4.1	4.8
Arizona.	18.5	30.2	37.0	38.7	61.2	58.0	12.7	19.9	25.1	21.6	37.7	39.3
Arkansas	23.3	25.2	35.7	41.1	48.1	36.9	9.3	21.8	16.8	17.9	25.9	21.3
California	172.4	218.4	236.7	196.9	295.9	295.6	112.9	134.0	NA	NA	NA	NA
Colorado	25.0	34.1	31.5	35.6	36.9	29.3	10.4	18.1	18.4	20.0	36.6	36.5
Connecticut	25.0	25.9	27.8	19.4	17.5	14.9	5.8	11.9	10.3	6.5	19.2	19.7
Delaware.	4.3	4.4	5.6	5.1	4.3	7.0	1.7	2.3	3.0	3.2	4.6	9.1
District of Columbia	7.3	5.2	4.7	2.8	1.9	1.9	2.3	4.7	3.3	1.5	1.2	0.8
Florida	69.2	110.6	142.3	141.9	223.4	249.5	37.2	71.4	81.7	81.9	127.9	140.8
Georgia.	63.9	69.4	64.4	56.0	75.9	103.5	18.6	33.6	35.7	30.7	NA	NA
Hawaii	10.6	11.7	18.1	25.0	37.7	28.2	2.6	4.4	5.2	4.6	NA	NA
Idaho	10.9	13.1	15.0	14.0	15.1	21.3	3.6	6.6	6.6	6.9	11.6	10.8
ILLINOIS	115.5	110.7	NA	85.5	74.0	70.7	36.5	50.5	NA	39.1	44.1	45.2
Indiana	55.2	57.8	54.3	48.1	70.3	64.1	15.2	NA	NA	NA	NA	NA
IOWA	24.6	27.5	24.8	20.3	15.8	19.0	7.2	11.8	11.1	9.4	12.7	13.2
Kansas	22.4	24.9	23.4	22.2	18.5	23.3	8.8	13.4	12.6	10.6	8.4	15.2
Kentucky.	36.3	34.3	51.3	39.7	39.5	41.8	10.7	17.0	21.8	21.6	32.8	30.5
Louisiana.	35.4	41.7	41.2	40.5	NA	41.1	5.1	NA	NA	NA	NA	NA
Maine	11.0	14.3	11.8	11.3	6.8	4.4	3.9	6.2	5.3	6.4	9.2	1.8
Maryland.	52.2	46.0	46.1	40.0	37.5	26.7	9.3	16.3	16.1	17.0	25.7	29.8
Massachusetts	47.4	49.0	47.8	37.0	32.5	40.5	11.0	16.5	16.8	16.0	27.1	13.6
MICHIGAN	89.7	89.6	76.1	66.4	49.3	58.6	30.0	40.8	40.2	39.4	56.6	58.7
MINNESOTA	31.3	37.8	33.7	33.4	28.7	25.8	8.3	15.1	15.4	14.8	NA	NA
Mississippi	26.3	28.0	24.3	19.7	18.6	23.4	8.2	13.5	14.4	14.4	22.9	23.7
Missouri	50.1	55.5	49.3	43.7	37.3	40.6	17.9	27.8	26.4	26.5	33.1	33.0
Montana	6.9	8.4	7.0	6.6	6.3	5.8	3.0	5.0	4.1	2.1	7.1	4.8
Nebraska.	15.7	14.2	12.5	13.0	11.0	14.1	3.7	6.5	6.5	6.4	9.8	6.6
Nevada.	97.6	115.4	NA	144.3	202.2	185.3	9.1	13.7	13.3	18.1	27.1	25.6
New Hampshire	10.0	9.3	10.6	11.6	7.3	8.3	2.4	5.2	5.3	7.1	8.2	10.9
New Jersey.	56.6	55.0	58.0	50.4	46.6	39.7	10.8	25.9	23.6	25.6	43.7	44.4
New Mexico	12.4	16.3	13.2	14.5	19.4	15.1	4.4	10.4	7.7	9.2	14.2	14.2
New York	161.2	141.3	169.3	133.9	135.4	207.0	26.4	54.2	57.9	62.8	92.0	82.8
North Carolina	48.3	46.3	52.1	65.6	70.1	67.1	13.7	28.2	34.0	36.9	50.3	50.8
North Dakota.	5.3	6.1	4.8	4.6	3.3	3.9	1.0	2.1	2.3	2.0	3.2	2.1
Ohio	90.1	99.5	95.8	88.5	64.7	73.8	39.3	58.2	51.0	49.3	61.7	56.4
Oklahoma	39.0	46.5	33.2	NA	34.6	33.0	16.8	24.2	24.9	NA	29.1	28.6
Oregon	17.3	23.1	25.2	26.0	25.2	47.2	9.6	17.9	15.9	16.7	22.2	23.6
Pennsylvania.	94.5	95.4	86.8	73.2	65.0	69.9	22.6	34.8	40.1	37.9	53.0	53.8
Rhode Island	7.5	7.1	8.1	8.0	5.2	5.0	1.7	3.6	3.8	3.1	5.1	5.1
South Carolina	57.9	53.9	55.8	42.7	24.5	42.0	5.8	13.8	16.1	14.4	12.6	20.0
South Dakota.	11.0	8.9	7.7	7.1	5.3	5.8	1.4	2.8	2.6	2.7	3.9	4.0
Tennessee	45.4	58.8	66.6	88.2	78.8	135.9	16.6	30.1	32.3	33.8	47.5	64.7
Texas.	139.5	187.1	182.8	196.4	248.9	225.6	51.2	97.2	95.1	85.2	118.1	118.1
Utah	11.7	17.1	19.0	24.1	23.7	28.3	3.9	8.0	8.8	9.7	16.8	10.0
Vermont	4.5	5.2	6.1	6.1	3.8	5.0	1.0	2.5	2.6	2.5	3.8	4.4
Virginia.	52.0	60.2	71.3	62.4	67.5	66.4	11.9	23.6	27.3	30.2	43.0	42.4
Washington.	41.3	46.6	48.6	40.9	42.4	47.5	17.9	28.4	28.8	27.2	41.2	69.3
West Virginia.	15.9	17.4	13.2	15.7	13.3	12.4	5.6	9.9	9.7	9.3	15.7	15.3
WISCONSIN	34.4	40.9	41.2	36.1	25.9	29.5	8.9	17.9	17.8	17.6	29.1	27.3
Wyoming.	4.5	6.8	4.8	4.9	4.4	5.2	1.8	4.0	3.1	2.8	4.4	4.3

NA – Not available.

[1]Data represent marriages performed or licenses issued in the state.

[2]Data includes reported annulments.

[3]Figures based on monthly counts and may be underreported.

Sources: National Center for Health Statistics, *National Vital Statistics Reports*, July 21, 2006, and previous issues; *Table 3: Provisional Number of Marriages and Divorces: Each State, December 2001 and 2002 and Cumulative Figures, 2000-2002,* and previous issues; and *Table 2: Provisional Number of Marriages and Divorces: Each State and Puerto Rico, February 2007 and 2008, and Cumulative Figures, 2006-2008,* at: http://www.cdc.gov/nchs [December 2008].

WISCONSIN DEATHS AND DEATH RATES – 2007

	Total		Males		Females	
Age Group	Deaths	Rate*	Deaths	Rate*	Deaths	Rate*
Under 1 year	469	644.6	252	676.7	217	611.0
1-4 years	73	25.5	42	28.7	31	22.2
5-9 years	53	14.9	33	18.2	20	11.5
10-14 years.	60	16.1	41	21.6	19	10.5
15-19 years.	254	63.2	184	88.8	70	35.9
20-24 years.	360	91.0	276	136.5	84	43.4
25-29 years.	323	85.4	228	115.6	95	52.5
30-34 years.	311	91.7	222	128.4	89	53.6
35-39 years.	458	121.9	291	152.4	167	90.3
40-44 years.	771	183.6	474	223.7	297	142.7
45-49 years.	1,279	281.2	816	357.8	463	204.1
50-54 years.	1,664	398.0	1,057	503.4	607	291.6
55-59 years.	2,160	604.4	1,339	746.2	821	461.4
60-64 years.	2,598	954.4	1,553	1,161.3	1,045	754.6
65-69 years.	2,957	1,454.5	1,733	1,787.2	1,224	1,151.1
70-74 years.	3,857	2,347.8	2,213	2,926.5	1,644	1,854.3
75-79 years.	5,355	3,712.8	2,849	4,571.6	2,506	3,059.5
80-84 years.	7,127	6,259.4	3,422	7,676.1	3,705	5,347.9
85-89 years	7,621	9,983.0	3,090	12,165.4	4,531	8,894.8
90-94 years.	5,652	18,132.8	1,795	21,142.5	3,857	17,006.2
95 years and over . . .	2,715	32,554.0	538	29,081.1	2,177	33,543.9
ALL AGES	46,117	817.5	22,448	801.2	23,669	836.0

*Per 100,000 population in that group.
Source: Wisconsin Department of Health and Family Services, Bureau of Health Information and Policy, *Wisconsin Deaths, 2007,* November 2008, at: http://dhs.wisconsin.gov/deaths/pdf/07deaths.pdf.

WISCONSIN POPULATION, BY AGE GROUP, 2000 and 2007

	Population of Group		Male		Female	
Age Group	2000 Census	2007	2000	2007	2000	2007
Under 5 years	342,340	356,287	175,041	182,301	167,299	173,986
5-9 years	379,484	353,480	194,506	180,135	184,978	173,345
10-14 years.	403,074	369,133	206,665	188,793	196,409	180,340
15-19 years.	407,195	399,323	208,785	205,671	198,410	193,652
20-24 years.	357,292	392,849	182,372	200,807	174,920	192,042
25-29 years.	333,913	375,534	170,011	195,852	163,902	179,682
30-34 years.	372,255	336,600	188,414	171,659	183,841	164,941
35-39 years.	435,255	373,035	217,663	189,530	217,592	183,505
40-44 years.	440,267	417,089	221,424	210,455	218,843	206,634
45-49 years.	397,693	451,706	200,621	226,500	197,072	225,206
50-54 years.	334,613	415,153	168,086	208,488	166,527	206,665
55-59 years.	252,742	354,844	124,363	178,156	128,379	176,688
60-64 years.	204,999	270,306	99,580	132,796	105,419	137,510
65-69 years.	182,119	201,849	85,771	96,289	96,348	105,560
70-74 years.	173,188	163,126	78,610	75,083	94,578	88,043
75-79 years.	146,675	143,227	61,121	61,913	85,554	81,314
80-84 years.	104,946	113,063	38,757	44,253	66,189	68,810
85 years and over	95,625	115,036	27,251	35,489	68,374	79,547
STATE	5,363,675	5,601,640	2,649,041	2,784,170	2,714,634	2,817,470
Median age.	36.0	37.9	35.0	36.8	37.1	39.1

Source: U.S. Census Bureau, Population Division, *Annual Estimates of the Population by Sex and Age for Wisconsin: April 1, 2000 to July 1, 2007,* November 2008.

Post Office and County[1]	ZIP Code
Abbotsford, Clark	54405
Abrams, Oconto	54101
Adams, Adams	53910
Adell, Sheboygan	53001
Afton, Rock	53501
Albany, Green	53502
Algoma, Kewaunee	54201
Allenton, Washington	53002
Alma, Buffalo	54610
Alma Center, Jackson	54611
Almena, Barron	54805
Almond, Portage	54909
Altoona, Eau Claire	54720
Alvin, Florence	54542
Amberg, Marinette	54102
Amery, Polk	54001
Amherst, Portage	54406
Amherst Junction, Portage	54407
Aniwa, Shawano	54408
Antigo, Langlade	54409
Appleton, Outagamie	54911[2]
Arbor Vitae, Vilas	54568
Arcadia, Trempealeau	54612
Arena, Iowa	53503
Argonne, Forest	54511
Argyle, Lafayette	53504
Arkansaw, Pepin	54721
Arkdale, Adams	54613
Arlington, Columbia	53911
Armstrong Creek, Forest	54103
Arpin, Wood	54410
Ashippun, Dodge	53003
Ashland, Ashland	54806
Athelstane, Marinette	54104
Athens, Marathon	54411
Auburndale, Wood	54412
Augusta, Eau Claire	54722
Avalon, Rock	53505
Avoca, Iowa	53506
Babcock, Wood	54413
Bagley, Grant	53801
Baileys Harbor, Door	54202
Baldwin, St. Croix	54002
Balsam Lake, Polk	54810
Bancroft, Portage	54921
Bangor, La Crosse	54614
Baraboo, Sauk	53913
Barnes, Douglas	54873
Barneveld, Iowa	53507
Barron, Barron	54812
Barronett, Barron	54813
Bassett, Kenosha	53101
Bay City, Pierce	54723
Bayfield, Bayfield	54814
Bay View, Milwaukee (Milwaukee)[3]	53207
Bear Creek, Outagamie	54922
Beaver, Marinette	54114
Beaver Dam, Dodge	53916
Beetown, Grant	53802
Beldenville, Pierce	54003
Belgium, Ozaukee	53004
Belleville, Dane	53508
Belmont, Grant	53510
Beloit, Rock	53511[2]
Benet Lake, Kenosha	53102
Bennett, Douglas	54873
Benoit, Bayfield	54816
Benton, Lafayette	53803
Berlin, Green Lake	54923
Big Bend, Waukesha	53103
Big Falls, Waupaca	54926
Birchwood, Washburn	54817
Birnamwood, Shawano	54414
Black Creek, Outagamie	54106
Black Earth, Dane	53515
Black River Falls, Jackson	54615

Post Office and County[1]	ZIP Code
Blair, Trempealeau	54616
Blanchardville, Lafayette	53516
Blenker, Wood	54415
Bloom City, Richland	54634
Bloomer, Chippewa	54724
Bloomington, Grant	53804
Blue Mounds, Dane	53517
Blue River, Grant	53518
Bonduel, Shawano	54107
Boscobel, Grant	53805
Boulder Junction, Vilas	54512
Bowler, Shawano	54416
Boyceville, Dunn	54725
Boyd, Chippewa	54726
Branch, Manitowoc	54247
Brandon, Fond du Lac	53919
Brantwood, Price	54513
Briggsville, Marquette	53920
Brill, Barron	54818
Brillion, Calumet	54110
Bristol, Kenosha	53104
Brodhead, Green	53520
Brokaw, Marathon	54417
Brookfield, Waukesha	53045[2]
Brooklyn, Green	53521
Brooks, Adams	53952
Brownsville, Dodge	53006
Browntown, Green	53522
Bruce, Rusk	54819
Brule, Douglas	54820
Brussels, Door	54204
Bryant, Langlade	54418
Buffalo City, Buffalo	54622
Burlington, Racine	53105
Burnett, Dodge	53922
Butler, Waukesha	53007
Butte des Morts, Winnebago	54927
Butternut, Ashland	54514
Cable, Bayfield	54821
Cadott, Chippewa	54727
Caledonia, Racine	53108
Cambria, Columbia	53923
Cambridge, Dane	53523
Cameron, Barron	54822
Campbellsport, Fond du Lac	53010
Camp Douglas, Juneau	54618[4]
Camp Lake, Kenosha	53109
Canton, Barron	54868
Caroline, Shawano	54928
Cascade, Sheboygan	53011
Casco, Kewaunee	54205
Cashton, Monroe	54619
Cassville, Grant	53806
Cataract, Monroe	54620
Catawba, Price	54515
Cato, Manitowoc	54230
Cavour, Forest	54511
Cazenovia, Richland	53924
Cecil, Shawano	54111
Cedarburg, Ozaukee	53012
Cedar Grove, Sheboygan	53013
Centuria, Polk	54824
Chaseburg, Vernon	54621
Chelsea, Taylor	54451
Chetek, Barron	54728
Chili, Clark	54420
Chilton, Calumet	53014
Chippewa Falls, Chippewa	54729[4]
Clam Falls, Polk	54837
Clam Lake, Ashland	54517
Clayton, Polk	54004
Clear Lake, Polk	54005
Cleveland, Manitowoc	53015
Clinton, Rock	53525
Clintonville, Waupaca	54929
Clyman, Dodge	53016
Cobb, Iowa	53526

Post Office and County[1]	ZIP Code	Post Office and County[1]	ZIP Code
Cochrane, Buffalo	54622	Elkhart Lake, Sheboygan	53020
Colby, Clark	54421	Elkhorn, Walworth	53121
Coleman, Marinette	54112	Elk Mound, Dunn	54739
Colfax, Dunn	54730	Ellison Bay, Door	54210
Colgate, Washington	53017	Ellsworth, Pierce	54011[4]
Collins, Manitowoc	54207	Elm Grove, Waukesha	53122
Coloma, Waushara	54930	Elmwood, Pierce	54740
Columbus, Columbia	53925	Elroy, Juneau	53929
Combined Locks, Outagamie	54113	Elton, Langlade	54430
Comstock, Barron	54826	Embarrass, Waupaca	54933
Conover, Vilas	54519	Emerald, St. Croix	54012
Conrath, Rusk	54731	Endeavor, Marquette	53930
Coon Valley, Vernon	54623	Ephraim, Door	54211
Cornell, Chippewa	54732	Ettrick, Trempealeau	54627
Cornucopia, Bayfield	54827	Eureka, Winnebago	54934
Cottage Grove, Dane	53527	Evansville, Rock	53536
Couderay, Sawyer	54828	Exeland, Sawyer	54835
Crandon, Forest	54520		
Crivitz, Marinette	54114	**F**airchild, Eau Claire	54741
Cross Plains, Dane	53528	Fairwater, Fond du Lac	53931
Cuba City, Grant	53807	Fall Creek, Eau Claire	54742
Cudahy, Milwaukee	53110	Fall River, Columbia	53932
Cumberland, Barron	54829	Fence, Florence	54120
Curtiss, Clark	54422	Fennimore, Grant	53809
Cushing, Polk	54006	Fenwood, Marathon	54426
Custer, Portage	54423	Ferryville, Crawford	54628
Cutler, Juneau	54618	Fifield, Price	54524
		Fish Creek, Door	54212
Dairyland, Burnett	54830	Florence, Florence	54121
Dale, Outagamie	54931	Fond du Lac, Fond du Lac	54935[2]
Dallas, Barron	54733	Fontana, Walworth	53125
Dalton, Green Lake	53926	Footville, Rock	53537
Danbury, Burnett	54830	Forest Junction, Calumet	54123
Dane, Dane	53529	Forestville, Door	54213
Darien, Walworth	53114	Fort Atkinson, Jefferson	53538
Darlington, Lafayette	53530	Fountain City, Buffalo	54629
Deerbrook, Langlade	54424	Foxboro, Douglas	54836
Deerfield, Dane	53531	Fox Lake, Dodge	53933
Deer Park, St. Croix	54007	Francis Creek, Manitowoc	54214
DeForest, Dane	53532	Franklin, Milwaukee	53132
Delafield, Waukesha	53018	Franksville, Racine	53126
Delavan, Walworth	53115	Frederic, Polk	54837
Dellwood, Adams	53927	Fredonia, Ozaukee	53021
Delta, Bayfield	54856	Freedom, Outagamie	54131
Denmark, Brown	54208	Fremont, Waupaca	54940
De Pere, Brown	54115	Friendship, Adams	53934
Deronda, Polk	54001	Friesland, Columbia	53935
De Soto, Vernon	54624		
Dickeyville, Grant	53808	**G**alesville, Trempealeau	54630
Dodge, Trempealeau	54625	Galloway, Marathon	54432
Dodgeville, Iowa	53533[4]	Gays Mills, Crawford	54631
Dorchester, Clark	54425	Genesee Depot, Waukesha	53127
Dousman, Waukesha	53118	Genoa, Vernon	54632
Downing, Dunn	54734	Genoa City, Walworth	53128
Downsville, Dunn	54735	Germantown, Washington	53022
Doylestown, Columbia	53928	Gile, Iron	54525
Dresser, Polk	54009	Gillett, Oconto	54124
Drummond, Bayfield	54832	Gilman, Taylor	54433
Dunbar, Marinette	54119	Gilmanton, Buffalo	54743
Durand, Pepin	54736	Gleason, Lincoln	54435
		Glenbeulah, Sheboygan	53023
Eagle, Waukesha	53119	Glen Flora, Rusk	54526
Eagle River, Vilas	54521	Glen Haven, Grant	53810
Earl, Washburn	54833	Glenwood City, St. Croix	54013
Eastman, Crawford	54626	Glidden, Ashland	54527
East Troy, Walworth	53120	Goodman, Marinette	54125
Eau Claire, Eau Claire	54703[2]	Gordon, Douglas	54838
Eau Galle, Dunn	54737	Gotham, Richland	53540
Eden, Fond du Lac	53019	Grafton, Ozaukee	53024
Edgar, Marathon	54426	Grand Chute, Outagamie (Appleton)[3]	54911
Edgerton, Rock	53534	Grand Marsh, Adams	53936
Edgewater, Sawyer	54834	Grand View, Bayfield	54839
Edmund, Iowa	53535	Granton, Clark	54436
Egg Harbor, Door	54209	Grantsburg, Burnett	54840
Eland, Marathon	54427	Gratiot, Lafayette	53541
Elcho, Langlade	54428	Green Bay, Brown	54303[2]
Elderon, Marathon	54429	Greenbush, Sheboygan	53026
Eldorado, Fond du Lac	54932	Greendale, Milwaukee	53129
Eleva, Trempealeau	54738	Greenfield, Milwaukee (Milwaukee)[3]	53220

Post Office and County[1]	ZIP Code
Green Lake, Green Lake	54941
Greenleaf, Brown	54126
Green Valley, Shawano	54127
Greenville, Outagamie	54942
Greenwood, Clark	54437
Gresham, Shawano	54128
Gurney, Iron	54559
Hager City, Pierce	54014
Hales Corners, Milwaukee	53130
Hamburg, Marathon	54411
Hammond, St. Croix	54015
Hancock, Waushara	54943
Hannibal, Taylor	54439
Hanover, Rock	53542
Harshaw, Oneida	54529
Hartford, Washington	53027
Hartland, Waukesha	53029
Hatley, Marathon	54440
Haugen, Barron	54841
Haven, Sheboygan (Sheboygan)[3]	53083
Hawkins, Rusk	54530
Hawthorne, Douglas	54842
Hayward, Sawyer	54843
Hazel Green, Grant	53811
Hazelhurst, Oneida	54531
Heafford Junction, Lincoln	54532
Helenville, Jefferson	53137
Herbster, Bayfield	54844
Hertel, Burnett	54845
Hewitt, Wood	54441
High Bridge, Ashland	54846
Highland, Iowa	53543
Hilbert, Calumet	54129
Hiles, Forest	54511
Hillpoint, Sauk	53937
Hillsboro, Vernon	54634
Hillsdale, Barron	54744
Hingham, Sheboygan	53031
Hixton, Jackson	54635
Holcombe, Chippewa	54745
Hollandale, Iowa	53544
Holmen, La Crosse	54636
Honey Creek, Walworth	53138
Horicon, Dodge	53032
Hortonville, Outagamie	54944
Houlton, St. Croix	54082
Howards Grove, Sheboygan	53083
Hubertus, Washington	53033
Hudson, St. Croix	54016
Humbird, Clark	54746
Hurley, Iron	54534
Hustisford, Dodge	53034
Hustler, Juneau	54637
Independence, Trempealeau	54747
Ingram, Rusk	54526
Iola, Waupaca	54945[4]
Irma, Lincoln	54442
Iron Belt, Iron	54536
Iron Ridge, Dodge	53035
Iron River, Bayfield	54847
Ixonia, Jefferson	53036
Jackson, Washington	53037
Janesville, Rock	53545[2]
Jefferson, Jefferson	53549
Jim Falls, Chippewa	54748
Johnson Creek, Jefferson	53038
Juda, Green	53550
Jump River, Taylor	54434
Junction City, Portage	54443
Juneau, Dodge	53039
Kansasville, Racine	53139
Kaukauna, Outagamie	54130[4]
Kellnersville, Manitowoc	54215
Kempster, Langlade	54424
Kendall, Monroe	54638

Post Office and County[1]	ZIP Code
Kennan, Price	54537
Kenosha, Kenosha	53140[2]
Keshena, Menominee	54135
Kewaskum, Washington	53040
Kewaunee, Kewaunee	54216
Kiel, Manitowoc	53042
Kieler, Grant	53812
Kimberly, Outagamie	54136
King, Waupaca	54946
Kingston, Green Lake	53939
Knapp, Dunn	54749
Knowles, Dodge	53048
Kohler, Sheboygan	53044
Krakow, Shawano	54137
Lac du Flambeau, Vilas	54538
La Crosse, La Crosse	54601[2]
Ladysmith, Rusk	54848
La Farge, Vernon	54639
Lake Delton, Sauk	53940
Lake Geneva, Walworth	53147
Lake Mills, Jefferson	53551
Lake Nebagamon, Douglas	54849
Lake Tomahawk, Oneida	54539
Lakewood, Oconto	54138
Lancaster, Grant	53813
Land O'Lakes, Vilas	54540
Lannon, Waukesha	53046
Laona, Forest	54541
La Pointe, Ashland	54850
Larsen, Winnebago	54947
La Valle, Sauk	53941
Lebanon, Dodge	53047
Lena, Oconto	54139
Leopolis, Shawano	54948
Lewis, Polk	54851
Lily, Langlade	54491
Lime Ridge, Sauk	53942
Linden, Iowa	53553
Little Chute, Outagamie	54140
Little Suamico, Oconto	54141
Livingston, Grant	53554
Lodi, Columbia	53555
Loganville, Sauk	53943
Lomira, Dodge	53048
Lone Rock, Richland	53556
Long Lake, Florence	54542
Loretta, Sawyer	54896
Lowell, Dodge	53557
Loyal, Clark	54446
Lublin, Taylor	54447
Luck, Polk	54853
Luxemburg, Kewaunee	54217
Lyndon Station, Juneau	53944
Lynxville, Crawford	54626
Lyons, Walworth	53148
Madison, Dane	53714[2]
Maiden Rock, Pierce	54750
Malone, Fond du Lac	53049
Manawa, Waupaca	54949
Manchester, Green Lake	53946
Manitowish Waters, Vilas	54545
Manitowoc, Manitowoc	54220[4]
Maple, Douglas	54854
Maplewood, Door	54226
Marathon, Marathon	54448
Marengo, Ashland	54855
Maribel, Manitowoc	54227
Marinette, Marinette	54143
Marion, Waupaca	54950
Markesan, Green Lake	53946
Marquette, Green Lake	53947
Marshall, Dane	53559
Marshfield, Wood	54449[4]
Mason, Bayfield	54856[4]
Mather, Juneau	54641
Mattoon, Shawano	54450
Mauston, Juneau	53948

Post Office and County[1]	ZIP Code
Mayville, Dodge	53050
Mazomanie, Dane	53560
McFarland, Dane	53558
McNaughton, Oneida	54543
Medford, Taylor	54451
Mellen, Ashland	54546
Melrose, Jackson	54642
Menasha, Winnebago	54952
Menomonee Falls, Waukesha	53051[4]
Menomonie, Dunn	54751
Mequon, Ozaukee	53097
Mercer, Iron	54547
Merrill, Lincoln	54452
Merrillan, Jackson	54754
Merrimac, Sauk	53561
Merton, Waukesha	53056
Middle Inlet, Marinette	54114
Middleton, Dane	53562
Mikana, Barron	54857
Milan, Marathon	54411
Milladore, Wood	54454
Millston, Jackson	54643
Milltown, Polk	54858
Milton, Rock	53563
Milwaukee, Milwaukee	53201[2]
Mindoro, La Crosse	54644
Mineral Point, Iowa	53565
Minocqua, Oneida	54548
Minong, Washburn	54859
Mishicot, Manitowoc	54228
Modena, Buffalo	54755
Mondovi, Buffalo	54755[4]
Monico, Oneida	54501
Monona, Dane (Madison)[3]	53716
Monroe, Green	53566
Montello, Marquette	53949
Montfort, Grant	53569
Monticello, Green	53570
Montreal, Iron	54550
Moquah, Ashland	54806
Morrisonville, Dane	53571
Mosinee, Marathon	54455
Mountain, Oconto	54149
Mount Calvary, Fond du Lac	53057
Mount Hope, Grant	53816
Mount Horeb, Dane	53572
Mount Sterling, Crawford	54645
Mukwonago, Waukesha	53149
Muscoda, Grant	53573
Muskego, Waukesha	53150
Nashotah, Waukesha	53058
Navarino, Shawano	54107
Necedah, Juneau	54646
Neenah, Winnebago	54956[4]
Neillsville, Clark	54456
Nekoosa, Wood	54457
Nelma, Forest	54542
Nelson, Buffalo	54756
Nelsonville, Portage	54458
Neopit, Menominee	54150
Neosho, Dodge	53059
Neshkoro, Marquette	54960
Newald, Forest	54511
New Auburn, Chippewa	54757
New Berlin, Waukesha	53186[2]
Newburg, Washington	53060
New Franken, Brown	54229
New Glarus, Green	53574
New Holstein, Calumet	53061[4]
New Lisbon, Juneau	53950
New London, Waupaca	54961
New Munster, Kenosha	53152
New Post, Sawyer	54828
New Richmond, St. Croix	54017
Newton, Manitowoc	53063
Niagara, Marinette	54151
Nichols, Outagamie	54152

Post Office and County[1]	ZIP Code
North Fond du Lac, Fond du Lac (Fond du Lac)[3]	54935
North Freedom, Sauk	53951
North Lake, Waukesha	53064
North Prairie, Waukesha	53153
North Woods Beach, Sawyer	54843
Northfield, Jackson	54635
Norwalk, Monroe	54648
Oak Creek, Milwaukee	53154
Oakdale, Monroe	54649
Oakfield, Fond du Lac	53065
Oconomowoc, Waukesha	53066
Oconto, Oconto	54153
Oconto Falls, Oconto	54154
Odanah, Ashland	54861
Ogdensburg, Waupaca	54962
Ogema, Price	54459
Ojibwa, Sawyer	54862
Okauchee, Waukesha	53069
Omro, Winnebago	54963
Onalaska, La Crosse	54650
Oneida, Outagamie	54155
Ontario, Vernon	54651
Oostburg, Sheboygan	53070
Oregon, Dane	53575
Orfordville, Rock	53576
Osceola, Polk	54020
Oshkosh, Winnebago	54901[2]
Osseo, Trempealeau	54758
Owen, Clark	54460
Oxford, Marquette	53952
Packwaukee, Marquette	53953
Palmyra, Jefferson	53156
Pardeeville, Columbia	53954
Park Falls, Price	54552
Patch Grove, Grant	53817
Pearson, Langlade	54462
Pelican Lake, Oneida	54463
Pell Lake, Walworth	53157
Pembine, Marinette	54156
Pence, Iron	54550
Pepin, Pepin	54759
Peshtigo, Marinette	54157
Pewaukee, Waukesha	53072
Phelps, Vilas	54554
Phillips, Price	54555
Phlox, Langlade	54464
Pickerel, Langlade	54465
Pickett, Winnebago	54964
Pigeon Falls, Trempealeau	54760
Pine River, Waushara	54965
Pittsville, Wood	54466
Plain, Sauk	53577
Plainfield, Waushara	54966
Platteville, Grant	53818
Pleasant Prairie, Kenosha	53158
Plover, Portage	54467
Plum City, Pierce	54761
Plymouth, Sheboygan	53073
Poplar, Douglas	54864
Portage, Columbia	53901
Port Edwards, Wood	54469
Porterfield, Marinette	54159
Port Washington, Ozaukee	53074
Port Wing, Bayfield	54865
Poskin, Barron	54812
Potosi, Grant	53820
Potter, Calumet	54160
Pound, Marinette	54161
Powers Lake, Kenosha	53159
Poynette, Columbia	53955
Poy Sippi, Waushara	54967
Prairie du Chien, Crawford	53821
Prairie du Sac, Sauk	53578
Prairie Farm, Barron	54762
Prentice, Price	54556
Prescott, Pierce	54021

Post Office and County[1]	ZIP Code
Presque Isle, Vilas	54557
Princeton, Green Lake	54968
Pulaski, Brown	54162
Pulcifer, Oconto	54124
Racine, Racine	53401[2]
Radisson, Sawyer	54867
Randolph, Columbia	53956[4]
Random Lake, Sheboygan	53075
Readfield, Waupaca	54969
Readstown, Vernon	54652
Redgranite, Waushara	54970
Reedsburg, Sauk	53959[4]
Reedsville, Manitowoc	54230
Reeseville, Dodge	53579
Rewey, Iowa	53580
Rhinelander, Oneida	54501
Rib Lake, Taylor	54470
Rice Lake, Barron	54868
Richfield, Washington	53076
Richland Center, Richland	53581
Ridgeland, Dunn	54763
Ridgeway, Iowa	53582
Ringle, Marathon	54471
Rio, Columbia	53960
Rio Creek, Kewaunee	54201
Ripon, Fond du Lac	54971
River Falls, Pierce	54022
Roberts, St. Croix	54023
Rochester, Racine	53167
Rock Falls, Dunn	54764
Rockfield, Washington	53022
Rockland, La Crosse	54653
Rock Springs, Sauk	53961
Rosendale, Fond du Lac	54974
Rosholt, Portage	54473
Rothschild, Marathon	54474
Royalton, Waupaca	54961
Rubicon, Dodge	53078
Rudolph, Wood	54475
St. Cloud, Fond du Lac	53079
St. Croix Falls, Polk	54024
St. Francis, Milwaukee	53235
St. Germain, Vilas	54558
St. Nazianz, Manitowoc	54232
Salem, Kenosha	53168
Sanborn, Ashland	54806
Sand Creek, Dunn	54765
Sarona, Washburn	54870
Sauk City, Sauk	53583
Saukville, Ozaukee	53080
Saxeville, Waushara	54976
Saxon, Iron	54559
Sayner, Vilas	54560
Scandinavia, Waupaca	54977
Schofield, Marathon	54476
Seneca, Crawford	54654
Sextonville, Richland	53584
Seymour, Outagamie	54165
Sharon, Walworth	53585
Shawano, Shawano	54166
Sheboygan, Sheboygan	53081[2]
Sheboygan Falls, Sheboygan	53085
Sheldon, Rusk	54766
Shell Lake, Washburn	54871
Sherwood, Calumet	54169
Shiocton, Outagamie	54170
Shorewood, Milwaukee (Milwaukee)[3]	53211
Shullsburg, Lafayette	53586
Silver Cliff, Marinette	54104
Silver Lake, Kenosha	53170[4]
Sinsinawa, Grant	53824
Siren, Burnett	54872
Sister Bay, Door	54234
Slinger, Washington	53086
Sobieski, Oconto	54171
Soldiers Grove, Crawford	54655
Solon Springs, Douglas	54873

Post Office and County[1]	ZIP Code
Somers, Kenosha	53171
Somerset, St. Croix	54025
South Byron, Fond du Lac	53006
South Milwaukee, Milwaukee	53172
South Range, Douglas	54874
South Wayne, Lafayette	53587
Sparta, Monroe	54656
Spencer, Marathon	54479
Spooner, Washburn	54801
Springbrook, Washburn	54875
Springfield, Walworth	53176
Spring Green, Sauk	53588
Spring Valley, Pierce	54767
Stanley, Chippewa	54768
Star Lake, Vilas	54561
Star Prairie, St. Croix	54026
Stetsonville, Taylor	54480
Steuben, Crawford	54657
Stevens Point, Portage	54481[4]
Stiles, Oconto	54139
Stitzer, Grant	53825
Stockbridge, Calumet	53088
Stockholm, Pepin	54769
Stoddard, Vernon	54658
Stone Lake, Sawyer	54876
Stoughton, Dane	53589
Stratford, Marathon	54484
Strum, Trempealeau	54770
Sturgeon Bay, Door	54235
Sturtevant, Racine	53177
Suamico, Brown	54173
Sullivan, Jefferson	53178
Summit Lake, Langlade	54485
Sun Prairie, Dane	53590[4]
Superior, Douglas	54880
Suring, Oconto	54174
Sussex, Waukesha	53089
Taycheedah, Fond du Lac	53090
Taylor, Jackson	54659
Theresa, Dodge	53091
Thiensville, Ozaukee	53092
Thorp, Clark	54771
Three Lakes, Oneida	54562
Tigerton, Shawano	54486
Tiffany, Rock	53592
Tilleda, Shawano	54978
Tipler, Florence	54542
Tisch Mills, Manitowoc	54240
Tomah, Monroe	54660
Tomahawk, Lincoln	54487
Tony, Rusk	54563
Townsend, Oconto	54175
Trego, Washburn	54888
Trempealeau, Trempealeau	54661
Trevor, Kenosha	53179
Tripoli, Oneida	54564
Tunnel City, Monroe	54662
Turtle Lake, Barron	54889
Twin Lakes, Kenosha	53181
Underhill, Oconto	54176
Union Center, Juneau	53962
Two Rivers, Manitowoc	54241
Union Grove, Racine	53182
Unity, Marathon	54488
Upson, Iron	54565
Valders, Manitowoc	54245
Van Dyne, Fond du Lac	54979
Vernon, Waukesha (Waukesha)[3]	53186
Verona, Dane	53593
Vesper, Wood	54489
Victory, Vernon	54624
Viola, Vernon	54664
Viroqua, Vernon	54665
Wabeno, Forest	54566
Waldo, Sheboygan	53093

Post Office and County[1]	ZIP Code	Post Office and County[1]	ZIP Code
Wales, Waukesha.	53183	White Lake, Langlade	54491
Walworth, Walworth.	53184	Whitelaw, Manitowoc	54247
Warrens, Monroe.	54666	Whitewater, Walworth	53190
Wascott, Douglas	54838[4]	Wild Rose, Waushara	54984
Washburn, Bayfield	54891	Willard, Clark	54493
Washington Island, Door.	54246	Williams Bay, Walworth	53191
Waterford, Racine	53185	Wilmot, Kenosha.	53192
Waterloo, Jefferson	53594	Wilson, St. Croix.	54027
Watertown, Jefferson.	53094[2]	Wilton, Monroe	54670
Waubeka, Ozaukee.	53021	Winchester, Vilas.	54557
Waukau, Winnebago.	54980	Wind Lake, Racine.	53185
Waukesha, Waukesha	53186[2]	Windsor, Dane.	53598
Waumandee, Buffalo.	54622	Winnebago, Winnebago	54985
Waunakee, Dane.	53597	Winneconne, Winnebago	54986
Waupaca, Waupaca.	54981	Winter, Sawyer.	54896
Waupun, Dodge	53963	Wisconsin Dells, Columbia	53965
Wausau, Marathon	54403[2]	Wisconsin Rapids, Wood	54494[2]
Wausaukee, Marinette	54177	Withee, Clark	54498
Wautoma, Waushara	54982	Wittenberg, Shawano	54499
Wauwatosa, Milwaukee (Milwaukee)[3]	53210	Wonewoc, Juneau	53968
Wauzeka, Crawford	53826	Woodford, Lafayette.	53599
Webb Lake, Burnett	54830	Woodland, Dodge	53099
Webster, Burnett	54893	Woodman, Grant.	53827
Wentworth, Douglas.	54874	Woodruff, Oneida	54568
West Allis, Milwaukee (Milwaukee)[3]	53214	Woodville, St. Croix.	54028
West Bend, Washington	53095[2]	Woodworth, Kenosha	53194
West Lima, Vernon.	54639	Wrightstown, Brown.	54180
West Milwaukee, Milwaukee (Milwaukee)[3]	53214	Wyeville, Monroe	54671
West Salem, La Crosse.	54669	Wyocena, Columbia	53969
Westboro, Taylor.	54490		
Westby, Vernon	54667	Yellow Lake, Burnett	54830
Westfield, Marquette.	53964	Yuba, Richland.	54634
Weston, Marathon	54476		
Weyauwega, Waupaca	54983	Zachow, Shawano.	54182
Weyerhaeuser, Rusk	54895	Zenda, Walworth.	53195
Wheeler, Dunn.	54772		
Whitehall, Trempealeau	54773		

[1]Many of these locations no longer have post offices but their names may be used for addressing mail. Does not include stations.

[2]Indicates multicoded city. To determine last 2 digits of ZIP code for any specific city street, consult the local post office. The ZIP code given is the general delivery ZIP code for the city.

[3]Post office is located in the city shown in parenthesis. ZIP code is listed as "acceptable" on USPS Web site.

[4]Indicates there is an additional ZIP code that is used for a specific P.O. Box, company or organization, or a military installation.

Source: U.S. Postal Service, at: http://www.usps.com [February 27, 2009].

HIGHLIGHTS OF SOCIAL SERVICES IN WISCONSIN

Welfare — According to the U.S. Census Bureau, during 2005-06, about $370 billion was spent nationally by state and local governments on a variety of public welfare programs. Wisconsin spent about $7.2 billion, or $1,293 per capita, which ranked it 17th among the states and slightly above the national average of $1,241. New York's per capita expenditure was highest at $2,229 and Nevada the lowest at $721. State and local welfare expenditures represented $37.53 per $1,000 of personal income in Wisconsin, ranking it 17th among the states and slightly above the national average ($33.73), while Maine ($58.88), Rhode Island ($53.90), and Alaska ($53.87) ranked highest, with Wisconsin's neighbor Minnesota ($45.81) ranked 9th. Nevada ($18.57) and Colorado ($18.63) were the lowest.

Participation in Wisconsin Works (W-2), a program providing job subsidies to employers and cash and noncash benefits, such as job assistance and subsidized child care, to participants if they meet certain work requirements, has decreased since earlier in the decade. The average monthly caseload for W-2 during 2008 was 6,402 households with a statewide average monthly payment of $541. Average monthly payments show considerably less variation in average benefit payments among the larger counties than had been true earlier in the decade. Total W-2 expenditures fell from $105.5 million in 2007 to $92.0 million in 2008.

Medical Assistance and BadgerCare — Of the total combined Medical Assistance and BadgerCare provider payments of $5.14 billion in fiscal year 2007-08, $1.42 billion (27.7%) was spent on managed care/HMOs. The next highest payment categories were long-term care in nursing homes and state centers (18.6%) and home care (15.8%).

Medical assistance expenditures in Wisconsin in calendar year 2006 fell to $3.86 billion, from about $4.16 billion in 2005. A county breakdown of medical assistance for 2006 shows average expenditures of $3,879 per recipient for 995,494 people, or 17.7% of the population of Wisconsin. The counties with the greatest percentage of recipients were Menominee (42.97%), Ashland (28.04%), Milwaukee (27.33%), and Sawyer (27.28%). The counties with the smallest proportion of recipients were Ozaukee (5.98%), Waukesha (6.16%), and Washington (8.79%). The highest average expenditures per recipient were in Waupaca ($8,240) and Richland ($5,784) counties; Menominee ($2,498) and Marquette ($2,525) counties were lowest.

Institutions — Since 2006, the average daily adult corrections population increased by about 4.4% per year, from 22,071 in 2006 to 23,034 in 2007, and 24,054 in 2008. In 2008, a daily average of 53,681 persons were on probation and 17,726 on parole. Overall, more than 96,000 people were under the control of the Department of Corrections.

A per inmate state expenditure for corrections of $46,047 ranked Wisconsin 19th among the states in FY2007. As of June 30, 2006, Wisconsin had an incarceration rate of 386 persons per 100,000 population, not counting prisoners under local jurisdiction. Louisiana (858), Mississippi (749), Texas (668), Oklahoma (668), and Alabama (619) had the highest rates. Maine (133), Minnesota (191), New Hampshire (213), North Dakota (226), Utah (232), and Nebraska (238) had the lowest rates.

The total average daily number of persons in Wisconsin's care and treatment facilities declined from 1,777 in 2006 to 1,748 in 2007 and to 1,703 in 2008.

The number of youths in the state's juvenile corrections institutions declined from 568 in 2006 to 552 in 2007 and up slightly to 558 in 2008.

The following tables present selected data. Consult footnoted sources for more detailed information about corrections and social services.

STATE AND LOCAL PUBLIC WELFARE EXPENDITURES
State Fiscal Year 2005-06

State	Amount (in thousands)			Per Capita*		Per $1,000 Personal Income*	
	State and Local	State	Local	Amount	Rank	Amount	Rank
Alabama	$5,150,273	$5,093,063	$57,210	$1,122.66	29	$36.36	19
Alaska	1,396,920	1,392,897	4,023	2,065.53	2	53.87	3
Arizona.	6,059,588	5,796,764	262,824	980.79	42	30.38	34
Arkansas	3,443,502	3,425,852	17,650	1,227.98	20	43.13	13
California	44,667,030	30,052,660	14,614,370	1,236.58	19	30.90	31
Colorado	3,507,268	2,935,540	571,728	738.14	49	18.63	49
Connecticut	4,636,259	4,526,010	110,249	1,329.24	14	25.76	46
Delaware.	1,241,647	1,241,330	317	1,460.13	10	37.69	16
District of Columbia	1,840,853	—	1,840,853	3,144.51	—	53.45	—
Florida	17,950,759	16,921,837	1,028,922	996.21	40	26.85	43
Georgia.	8,492,975	8,350,939	142,036	911.39	45	28.22	40
Hawaii	1,444,426	1,423,010	21,416	1,132.65	27	30.52	33
Idaho.	1,465,508	1,431,555	33,953	1,002.96	39	33.02	25
ILLINOIS	13,443,926	12,921,198	522,728	1,053.63	34	27.40	41
Indiana	6,460,373	5,855,177	605,196	1,026.41	38	32.07	27
IOWA	3,529,889	3,426,722	103,167	1,189.61	21	36.33	20
Kansas	2,846,821	2,791,489	55,332	1,032.85	36	29.92	35
Kentucky.	5,681,183	5,635,923	45,260	1,352.84	13	45.79	10
Louisiana.	4,561,496	4,505,127	56,369	1,074.90	32	32.74	26
Maine	2,496,584	2,460,938	35,646	1,900.92	4	58.88	1
Maryland.	6,509,690	6,361,933	147,757	1,161.98	22	26.48	44
Massachusetts	11,449,407	11,384,123	65,284	1,776.91	7	38.37	15
MICHIGAN	9,891,413	9,099,027	792,386	980.91	41	29.74	36
MINNESOTA	9,174,962	7,625,534	1,549,428	1,783.92	6	45.81	9
Mississippi	3,751,720	3,715,911	35,809	1,295.16	16	47.84	7
Missouri	5,997,742	5,902,301	95,441	1,028.25	37	31.62	28
Montana	860,278	823,298	36,980	909.93	47	29.30	38
Nebraska	2,002,501	1,932,846	69,655	1,137.93	26	33.42	24
Nevada	1,792,192	1,533,539	258,653	721.44	50	18.57	50
New Hampshire	1,471,657	1,284,130	187,527	1,124.41	28	28.32	39
New Jersey.	12,438,643	11,469,633	969,010	1,439.62	12	30.75	32
New Mexico	2,865,694	2,782,413	83,281	1,478.75	9	50.39	6
New York	43,176,118	33,259,057	9,917,061	2,229.36	1	50.99	5
North Carolina	9,837,851	8,456,874	1,380,977	1,112.21	30	34.46	23
North Dakota.	728,947	688,370	40,577	1,145.33	23	35.53	21
Ohio	16,646,360	14,027,287	2,619,073	1,452.77	11	44.02	12
Oklahoma	4,069,771	4,035,601	34,170	1,140.59	25	34.82	22
Oregon	3,876,977	3,613,067	263,910	1,053.25	35	31.30	29
Pennsylvania.	20,251,802	16,936,213	3,315,589	1,634.78	8	44.42	11
Rhode Island	2,150,032	2,136,882	13,150	2,030.26	3	53.90	2
South Carolina	4,775,310	4,755,649	19,661	1,104.17	31	36.76	18
South Dakota.	748,503	734,822	13,681	950.62	44	29.44	37
Tennessee	7,592,937	7,436,070	156,867	1,251.24	18	38.90	14
Texas	20,357,232	20,015,439	341,793	871.18	48	24.78	47
Utah	2,355,508	2,270,461	85,047	911.17	46	31.16	30
Vermont	1,122,519	1,121,285	1,234	1,809.94	5	51.47	4
Virginia.	7,270,306	5,945,024	1,325,282	953.06	43	23.69	48
Washington	6,705,827	6,620,779	85,048	1,054.29	33	27.29	42
West Virginia.	2,347,758	2,342,699	5,059	1,299.43	15	46.52	8
WISCONSIN	7,202,720	5,642,184	1,560,536	1,293.47	17	37.53	17
Wyoming.	585,646	573,481	12,165	1,142.56	24	26.34	45
UNITED STATES	$370,325,303	$324,713,963	$45,611,340	$1,241.19		$33.73	

*Rates and rankings calculated by the Wisconsin Legislative Reference Bureau.

Sources: U.S. Department of Commerce, Census Bureau, Governments Division, "State and Local Government Finances: 2005-06", at: 'http://www.census.gov/govs/www/estimate06.html; U.S. Department of Commerce, Bureau of Economic Analysis, "Regional Economic Accounts: State Annual Personal Income (SA1-3)", at: http://www.bea.gov/spi [March 23, 2009] (2006 data used in calculations); and "Population for the United States and States, and for Puerto Rico: April 1, 2000 to July 1, 2008 (NST-EST2008-01)", at: http://www.census.gov/popest/states/NST-ann-est.html [March 18, 2009] (2006 estimates used in calculations).

WISCONSIN WORKS (W-2) EXPENDITURES, BY AGENCY
Calendar Years 2007 and 2008

W-2 Contract Agency	Total Expenditures 2007	2008	Counties Served by Consortia
County W-2 Agencies			
Bayfield	$86,202	$51,774	
Buffalo[1]	11,503	0	
Burnett	47,473	37,100	
Clark	180,429	88,404	
Crawford	77,674	95,204	
Door	151,421	110,033	
Dunn	362,063	354,139	
Eau Claire	741,953	650,970	
Fond du Lac	742,817	541,172	
Green Lake	130,465	96,035	
Iron	70,557	57,578	
Jefferson	197,133	153,295	
Kenosha	3,522,061	3,491,720	
La Crosse	500,667	363,292	
Marathon	1,052,598	715,109	
Marinette	180,834	93,943	
Oconto	155,912	66,091	
Pepin	78,047	32,616	
Polk	153,884	141,936	
Racine	2,335,760	2,238,311	
Rock	1,627,326	1,493,908	
Rusk	64,366	53,226	
Taylor	100,907	66,767	
Vernon	82,049	31,065	
Waupaca	233,250	203,974	
Winnebago	908,032	816,751	
Subtotal	$13,795,383	$12,044,412	
County Agency Consortia			
Ashland Consortium	$233,665	$206,433	Ashland[2], Price
Capitol Consortium	5,782,909	4,380,330	Dane[2], Dodge, Marquette, Sauk
Lakeshore Consortium	729,761	721,635	Manitowoc, Sheboygan[2]
Outagamie Consortium	724,855	683,712	Calumet, Outagamie[2]
PAW Consortium	1,433,917	1,190,015	Adams, Portage, Wood[2]
Sawyer Consortium	172,130	92,187	Sawyer[2], Washburn
Southwest Consortium	305,386	231,634	Grant[2], Green, Iowa, Lafayette, Richland
Subtotal	$9,382,623	$7,505,946	
Private W-2 Agencies			
Forward Service Corporation – Waushara	$191,060	$86,964	
Kaiser Group – Walworth	464,177	379,788	
MAXIMUS – Milwaukee Job Development and Placement Agency (SW)	3,583,228	2,269,641	
Shawano Job Center	223,969	219,015	
United Migrant Opportunity Services – Milwaukee SSI Advocacy Agency	4,187,871	3,967,304	
Workforce Connections, Inc. – Columbia	280,606	207,966	
Workforce Connections, Inc. – Douglas	391,729	388,875	
YWCA GM – Milwaukee Case Management Agency (NE)	7,615,810	7,111,527	
Subtotal	$16,938,451	$14,631,079	
Private Agency Consortia			
Arbor Education and Training	1,659,108	1,378,031	Ozaukee, Washington, Waukesha
Forward Service Corporation – Bay Area	1,528,925	1,327,104	Brown, Florence, Kewaunee, Menominee
Forward Service Corporation – Northern	667,161	471,642	Forest, Langlade, Lincoln, Oneida, Vilas
MAXIMUS – Milwaukee Case Management Agency	22,396,531	20,457,627	Northwest and Southwest Milw.
Policy Studies, Inc. – Milwaukee Job Development and Placement Agency	7,605,555	5,311,040	Northwest and Northeast Milw.
United Migrant Opportunity Services – Milwaukee Case Management Agency	21,535,411	22,341,557	Southeast and Central Milw.
United Migrant Opportunity Services – Milwaukee Job Development and Placement Agency	8,216,859	5,360,409	Southeast and Central Milw.
Workforce Connections, Inc. – Pierce and St. Croix	322,162	202,231	Pierce, St. Croix
Workforce Connections, Inc. – Western Wisconsin[1]	869,677	593,308	Buffalo, Jackson, Juneau, Monroe, Trempealeau
Workforce Resource, Inc. – Barron and Chippewa	538,246	417,874	Barron, Chippewa
Subtotal	$65,339,635	$57,860,823	
TOTAL	$105,456,091	$92,042,260	

[1]Buffalo County administered W-2 for Buffalo County through 03/31/07. Effective 04/01/07 Buffalo County became part of the Workforce Connections, Inc. – Western Wisconsin Consortium.
[2]Lead county.
Source: Wisconsin Department of Children and Families, departmental data, June 2009.

WISCONSIN WORKS (W-2) BENEFITS, BY COUNTY
Calendar Years 2007 and 2008

County	2007 Average Monthly Paid Caseload	2007 Average Monthly Benefit Payment	2008 Average Monthly Paid Caseload	2008 Average Monthly Benefit Payment	County	2007 Average Monthly Paid Caseload	2007 Average Monthly Benefit Payment	2008 Average Monthly Paid Caseload	2008 Average Monthly Benefit Payment
Adams	19	$603	13	$550	Marinette. . .	7	$402	5	$581
Ashland . . .	8	517	10	512	Marquette . .	3	560	4	535
Barron	15	487	18	492	Menominee .	0	—	6	384
Bayfield . . .	5	553	4	512	Milwaukee . .	4,580	569	4,514	555
Brown	84	486	106	507	Monroe. . . .	11	440	12	470
Buffalo	3	587	2	397	Oconto	5	446	4	502
Burnett	2	481	3	484	Oneida	6	532	9	441
Calumet . . .	4	605	8	502	Outagamie . .	36	491	41	503
Chippewa . .	21	560	17	467	Ozaukee . . .	19	587	14	509
Clark	8	482	5	508	Pepin	1	565	0	—
Columbia. . .	10	527	10	453	Pierce.	4	406	4	365
Crawford. . .	5	463	7	565	Polk	8	595	3	516
Dane	297	541	299	540	Portage. . . .	27	580	23	547
Dodge	32	469	29	552	Price	6	518	5	542
Door	8	559	5	487	Racine	157	482	186	471
Douglas . . .	25	518	35	501	Richland . . .	3	549	3	498
Dunn	15	583	20	477	Rock	120	505	110	512
Eau Claire . .	40	527	48	560	Rusk	3	526	3	638
Florence . . .	4	582	2	623	St. Croix . . .	3	497	5	369
Fond du Lac .	25	584	22	520	Sauk	6	576	8	453
Forest.	3	493	3	539	Sawyer. . . .	2	495	2	421
Grant	4	490	4	440	Shawano . . .	19	513	23	498
Green.	4	583	4	435	Sheboygan . .	44	515	60	519
Green Lake. .	3	632	4	435	Taylor	6	574	4	530
Iowa	2	467	1	405	Trempealeau .	8	551	7	438
Iron.	2	622	3	431	Vernon	3	393	2	478
Jackson. . . .	4	415	7	369	Vilas	2	777	1	402
Jefferson . . .	12	489	13	473	Walworth . .	31	570	27	544
Juneau	3	382	4	475	Washburn . .	2	396	1	549
Kenosha . . .	246	524	281	509	Washington. .	25	568	29	457
Kewaunee . .	3	478	3	497	Waukesha . .	79	538	67	518
La Crosse . .	33	483	25	490	Waupaca . . .	14	509	16	487
Lafayette. . .	1	451	2	426	Waushara. . .	8	506	5	505
Langlade . . .	9	490	7	488	Winnebago. .	52	522	69	483
Lincoln. . . .	5	597	5	499	Wood.	42	540	55	484
Manitowoc. .	3	348	7	501	TOTAL. . .	6,354	$556	6,402	$541
Marathon. . .	45	514	40	530					

Source: Wisconsin Department of Children and Families, departmental data, June 2009.

BADGERCARE AND MEDICAL ASSISTANCE IN WISCONSIN
By Type of Service, Fiscal Years 1999-2000 – 2007-08
(In Millions)

| | Long-Term Care | | | | Hospitals | | | | Physicians and Clinics | | Drugs | | Home Care[1] | | Managed Care (HMO)[2] | | Other Non-Institutional Fee-for-Service[3] | | Total Provider Payments[4,5] | |
| | Nursing Homes | | State Centers | | Inpatient | | Outpatient | | | | | | | | | | | | | |
Fiscal Year	Amount	% of Total	Amount	% of Total	Amount	% of Total	Amount	% of Total	Amount	% of Total	Amount	% of Total	Amount	% of Total	Amount	% of Total	Amount	% of Total	Amount	Annual % Change
1999-2000	$906.3	29.8%	$135.9	4.5%	$270.6	8.9%	$55.3	1.8%	$63.2	2.1%	$336.5	11.1%	$498.8	16.4%	$394.4	13.0%	$251.8	8.3%	$3,044.0	—
2000-01	916.2	27.8	115.3	3.5	297.8	9.0	58.7	1.8	72.4	2.2	373.6	11.4	522.2	15.9	523.6	15.9	280.1	8.5	3,291.8	8.1%
2001-02	980.6	26.5	126.9	3.4	333.2	9.0	69.6	1.9	78.7	2.1	432.5	11.7	528.4	14.3	681.8	18.4	319.2	8.6	3,700.9	12.4
2002-03	990.6	25.7	123.9	3.2	332.0	8.6	75.6	2.0	85.2	2.2	494.7	12.9	592.6	15.4	657.9	17.1	334.5	8.7	3,849.2	4.0
2003-04	972.2	21.3	143.0	3.1	338.0	7.4	91.6	2.0	116.9	2.6	700.5	15.4	636.8	14.0	1,013.6	22.2	381.8	8.4	4,558.9	18.4
2004-05	963.8	20.2	117.7	2.5	388.6	8.1	103.7	2.2	133.2	2.8	772.0	16.2	754.9	15.8	873.7	18.3	487.2	10.2	4,777.1	4.8
2005-06	940.1	20.7	111.5	2.5	357.0	7.9	85.8	1.9	104.9	2.3	459.6	10.1	789.2	17.4	1,068.0	23.5	424.2	9.3	4,546.3	-4.8
2006-07	878.2	18.3	111.4	2.3	372.6	7.7	81.6	1.7	111.0	2.3	389.7	8.1	773.6	16.1	1,307.5	27.2	472.3	9.8	4,809.4	5.8
2007-08	837.2	16.3	117.1	2.3	409.7	8.0	85.1	1.7	157.2	3.1	466.3	9.1	812.5	15.8	1,422.3	27.7	599.3	11.7	5,137.5	6.8

Note: Enrollments in BadgerCare began in July 1999, and expenditures for the program are included in the Medical Assistance figures above. Medical Assistance expenditure data prior to BadgerCare can be found in previous *Blue Books*.

[1] Home Care includes HCBS waivers.

[2] Managed Care includes all capitated programs (BC/BS+, HMOs, CCF/WAM, SSI managed care, PACE/Partnership, Family Care).

[3] All non-institutional fee-for-service acute care not otherwise captured plus local government plus Medicare crossovers.

[4] Does not include offsetting recoveries and collections, such as estate recoveries, drug rebates, etc.

[5] Total includes expenditures not listed separately.

Source: Wisconsin Department of Health Services, departmental data, June 2009. Data prior to 2006 is from Wisconsin Legislative Fiscal Bureau. Percentages calculated by Wisconsin Legislative Reference Bureau.

MEDICAL ASSISTANCE IN WISCONSIN
Calendar Years 2005 and 2006

County	Recipients 2005	Recipients 2006	2006 as % of County Population	Expenditures 2005	Expenditures 2006	2006 Per Recipient Amount	Rank
Adams	4,454	4,304	19.97%	$16,031,712	$13,668,338	$3,175.73	63
Ashland	4,796	4,740	28.04	18,463,214	17,519,723	3,696.14	30
Barron	10,432	10,602	22.44	42,428,418	38,139,455	3,597.38	38
Bayfield	2,860	2,854	18.03	11,452,938	9,526,849	3,338.07	55
Brown	34,098	34,814	14.34	124,314,081	109,546,463	3,146.62	65
Buffalo	2,204	2,247	15.89	9,857,152	8,282,750	3,686.14	32
Burnett	3,383	3,414	20.55	13,191,558	12,542,550	3,673.86	33
Calumet	4,197	4,326	9.46	12,979,318	12,435,356	2,874.56	69
Chippewa	11,775	11,911	19.56	49,233,056	46,317,707	3,888.65	23
Clark	6,491	6,440	18.67	27,372,963	23,897,360	3,710.77	29
Columbia	6,732	6,729	12.17	27,725,569	24,561,985	3,650.17	35
Crawford	3,564	3,463	19.83	14,081,610	12,263,903	3,541.41	41
Dane	47,659	49,046	10.56	237,172,326	224,460,434	4,576.53	7
Dodge	10,820	10,869	12.20	49,046,489	43,403,723	3,993.35	20
Door	3,869	3,845	12.94	14,584,435	12,752,131	3,316.55	57
Douglas	9,681	9,319	21.21	40,779,560	35,671,905	3,827.87	24
Dunn	8,504	8,514	19.91	28,694,352	28,173,505	3,309.08	58
Eau Claire	18,801	19,017	19.45	76,639,950	75,300,850	3,959.66	21
Florence	900	857	16.30	3,651,367	2,734,288	3,190.53	61
Fond du Lac	14,349	14,515	14.41	77,263,903	69,000,771	4,753.76	6
Forest	2,150	2,165	21.07	9,551,923	8,256,647	3,813.69	25
Grant	7,631	7,798	15.43	37,501,991	35,254,359	4,520.95	9
Green	4,642	4,754	13.19	20,364,849	18,733,633	3,940.60	22
Green Lake	3,154	3,025	15.63	11,943,661	10,522,760	3,478.60	45
Iowa	2,938	3,035	12.66	12,188,521	12,210,412	4,023.20	17
Iron	1,510	1,485	21.27	6,782,848	5,939,572	3,999.71	19
Jackson	4,208	4,121	20.64	15,014,510	13,091,936	3,176.88	62
Jefferson	9,780	10,138	12.66	55,459,693	49,584,589	4,890.96	5
Juneau	5,317	5,272	19.60	21,148,332	17,346,295	3,290.27	59
Kenosha	30,168	30,909	19.36	115,464,700	105,081,251	3,399.70	50
Kewaunee	2,483	2,463	11.64	11,363,844	10,070,783	4,088.83	16
La Crosse	18,889	18,920	17.08	96,522,896	92,644,922	4,896.67	4
Lafayette	2,451	2,488	15.25	7,812,241	8,271,193	3,324.43	56
Langlade	5,025	4,929	22.96	18,327,182	16,082,396	3,262.81	60
Lincoln	4,843	4,849	15.86	20,579,907	18,446,934	3,804.28	26
Manitowoc	11,503	11,518	13.61	55,793,317	47,932,997	4,161.57	14
Marathon	20,531	20,975	15.81	75,064,880	70,430,918	3,357.85	53
Marinette	7,775	7,841	17.60	38,225,619	33,995,275	4,335.58	10
Marquette	2,765	2,961	19.41	8,319,025	7,476,281	2,524.92	71
Menominee	1,972	1,991	42.97	5,638,995	4,973,197	2,497.84	72
Milwaukee	258,194	256,040	27.33	1,168,418,306	1,076,494,461	4,204.40	13
Monroe	7,745	7,782	17.87	26,822,040	24,110,460	3,098.23	66
Oconto	5,426	5,652	14.61	21,330,556	19,209,862	3,398.77	51
Oneida	7,072	6,890	17.98	30,900,362	25,465,049	3,695.94	31
Outagamie	18,546	19,191	11.12	72,103,376	66,290,387	3,454.24	46
Ozaukee	5,046	5,165	5.98	22,980,100	19,614,556	3,797.59	27
Pepin	1,319	1,303	17.07	6,813,418	6,718,363	5,156.07	3
Pierce	4,537	4,273	10.73	16,668,779	14,987,494	3,507.49	43
Polk	6,879	6,874	15.23	28,972,130	27,521,022	4,003.64	18
Portage	10,467	10,973	15.77	48,254,510	46,951,282	4,278.80	12
Price	3,764	3,863	24.04	15,662,859	13,207,778	3,419.05	48
Racine	32,233	34,731	17.85	124,707,725	121,451,123	3,496.91	44
Richland	3,474	3,475	19.17	20,087,922	20,100,443	5,784.30	2
Rock	30,443	31,513	19.88	105,755,506	94,106,452	2,986.27	68
Rusk	3,852	3,780	24.27	15,337,089	13,853,211	3,664.87	34
St. Croix	7,311	7,501	9.61	32,904,376	30,942,288	4,125.09	15
Sauk	8,078	8,254	13.74	33,285,281	29,339,050	3,554.53	40
Sawyer	4,774	4,749	27.28	16,394,941	14,683,262	3,091.86	67
Shawano	7,082	7,164	16.93	29,513,591	26,089,620	3,641.77	36
Sheboygan	15,437	15,450	13.28	64,435,866	55,970,240	3,622.67	37
Taylor	3,913	3,827	19.21	15,453,447	13,624,303	3,560.05	39
Trempealeau	4,992	4,938	17.56	26,249,947	22,587,545	4,574.23	8
Vernon	4,894	4,877	16.59	20,964,509	18,131,710	3,717.80	28
Vilas	2,991	2,949	13.16	11,266,792	9,934,460	3,368.76	52
Walworth	13,660	13,916	13.95	50,990,376	47,634,747	3,423.02	47
Washburn	4,355	4,411	25.59	15,875,860	13,886,597	3,148.17	64
Washington	11,007	11,245	8.79	48,099,788	39,695,271	3,530.03	42
Waukesha	22,765	23,375	6.16	117,656,486	101,263,097	4,332.11	11
Waupaca	9,000	9,518	17.77	56,936,426	78,431,202	8,240.30	1
Waushara	4,357	4,421	17.63	13,129,071	12,070,620	2,730.29	70
Winnebago	22,101	22,998	14.03	86,041,210	78,613,894	3,418.29	49
Wood	14,022	14,412	18.73	52,839,896	48,311,852	3,352.20	54
STATE	979,827	995,494	17.72%	$4,163,088,237	$3,861,173,055	$3,878.65	

Note: State totals include categories not separately displayed, as well as some duplication of recipients if they resided in more than one county during the year.

Sources: Wisconsin Department of Health and Family Services, Division of Health Care Financing, departmental data; Wisconsin Department of Administration, Division of Intergovernmental Relations, Demographic Services Center, *County Population Estimates, January 1, 2006.* Percentages and rankings calculated by Wisconsin Legislative Reference Bureau.

PRISON POPULATION AND CORRECTIONAL EXPENDITURES
by State, 1970 – 2008

State	Total confined as of Dec. 31[1]				Prison Population (as of 6/30/2008)		State Corrections Expenditures FY2007		
	1980	1990	2000	2007	Total	Rate[2]	Total (in thousands)	per Inmate Amount	Rank
Alabama	6,543	15,665	26,034	28,605	28,844	619	$514,385	$17,982	48
Alaska[3]	822	2,622	2,128	3,072	2,449	357	237,144	77,195	2
Arizona[4]	4,372	14,261	25,412	35,490	36,735	565	946,922	26,681	37
Arkansas	2,911	6,766	11,851	14,310	14,484	507	331,717	23,181	42
California	24,569	97,309	160,412	172,856	173,186	471	8,093,209	46,821	17
Colorado[5]	2,629	7,671	16,833	22,841	23,130	468	895,827	39,220	22
Connecticut[3]	4,308	10,500	13,155	14,397	14,389	411	668,179	46,411	18
Delaware[3]	1,474	3,471	3,937	4,201	4,130	473	265,937	63,303	6
Florida	20,735	44,387	71,318	98,219	100,494	548	2,542,387	25,885	39
Georgia[4]	12,178	22,345	44,141	54,232	52,481	542	1,465,496	27,023	35
Hawaii[3]	985	2,533	3,553	4,367	4,280	332	197,273	45,174	20
Idaho	817	1,961	5,535	7,319	7,338	482	210,533	28,765	34
ILLINOIS[6]	11,899	27,516	45,281	45,215	45,215	—	1,209,228	26,744	36
Indiana	6,683	12,736	19,811	27,114	27,343	429	632,737	23,336	41
IOWA[4,5]	2,481	3,967	7,955	8,732	8,740	291	259,104	29,673	32
Kansas[5]	2,494	5,777	8,344	8,696	8,633	308	317,649	36,528	29
Kentucky	3,588	9,023	14,919	21,823	20,825	488	471,523	21,607	45
Louisiana[5]	8,889	18,599	35,207	37,341	37,830	858	651,468	17,446	49
Maine	814	1,523	1,635	1,950	1,747	133	130,051	66,693	5
Maryland	7,731	17,848	22,490	22,780	22,636	402	1,376,322	60,418	8
Massachusetts[7]	3,185	8,273	9,479	9,872	10,171	252	1,209,443	122,512	1
MICHIGAN	15,124	34,267	47,718	50,233	50,482	505	1,801,658	35,866	30
MINNESOTA	2,001	3,176	6,238	9,468	9,964	191	535,237	56,531	9
Mississippi	3,902	8,375	19,239	21,502	22,009	749	326,751	15,196	50
Missouri	5,726	14,943	27,519	29,844	30,455	515	669,121	22,421	43
Montana	739	1,425	3,105	3,431	3,564	368	146,574	42,720	21
Nebraska	1,446	2,403	3,816	4,329	4,244	238	212,598	49,110	15
Nevada[6]	1,839	5,322	10,063	13,245	12,915	497	294,380	22,226	44
New Hampshire . . .	326	1,342	2,257	2,930	2,798	213	110,297	37,644	27
New Jersey[5]	5,884	21,128	29,784	26,827	26,490	305	1,489,950	55,539	11
New Mexico	1,279	3,187	4,666	6,225	6,096	307	341,179	54,808	12
New York	21,815	54,895	70,199	62,177	61,799	317	3,126,699	50,287	13
North Carolina	15,513	18,411	27,043	33,016	33,775	366	1,271,328	38,506	24
North Dakota	253	483	994	1,416	1,450	226	54,283	38,335	25
Ohio[5]	13,489	31,822	45,833	50,731	51,160	445	1,335,897	26,333	38
Oklahoma	4,796	12,285	23,181	24,197	24,345	668	586,836	24,252	40
Oregon[5]	3,177	6,492	10,553	13,918	14,035	370	697,622	50,124	14
Pennsylvania	8,171	22,290	36,844	45,446	45,770	368	1,720,374	37,855	26
Rhode Island[3]	813	2,392	1,966	2,481	2,534	241	178,364	71,892	3
South Carolina	7,862	17,319	21,017	23,314	24,074	537	470,894	20,198	47
South Dakota	635	1,341	2,613	3,306	3,351	417	103,166	31,206	31
Tennessee	7,022	10,388	22,166	26,267	26,998	434	769,362	29,290	33
Texas	29,892	50,042	158,008	161,695	162,578	668	3,302,304	20,423	46
Utah	932	2,496	5,541	6,415	6,353	232	310,334	48,376	16
Vermont[3]	480	1,049	1,313	1,617	1,555	250	114,748	70,964	4
Virginia	8,920	17,593	29,643	37,984	39,224	505	1,425,372	37,526	28
Washington	4,399	7,995	14,666	17,757	17,398	266	1,090,342	61,404	7
West Virginia	1,257	1,565	3,795	6,049	6,058	334	233,639	38,624	23
WISCONSIN	3,980	7,362	20,336	22,307	21,705	386	1,027,163	46,047	19
Wyoming	534	1,110	1,680	2,084	2,073	389	117,171	56,224	10
UNITED STATES[1] . .	302,313	706,288	1,201,226	1,353,643	1,360,332	450	$46,490,177	$34,344	

[1]Except where noted otherwise, total confined refers to "sentenced prisoners" (serving a term of more than one year) under a state's jurisdiction, whether in the state's custody in its own institutions or in the custody of a local jail, another state's prison, or other correctional facility, including private institutions. Jail inmates under the jurisdiction of local authorities are not included. District of Columbia inmates sentenced to more than one year are under the responsibility of the Federal Bureau of Prisons. U.S. totals do not include federal prisoners for December 31, 2007 (179,204) and June 30, 2008 (180,473). With federal prisoners included, the U.S. incarceration rate is 509.

[2]Number of state prisoners with a sentence of more than one year per 100,000 state residents. Rates for states with integrated systems are likely to be overstated compared to states that do not include jails in total population counts.

[3]Prisons and jails form one integrated system. Data include total jail and prison population.

[4]Population figures are based on custody counts.

[5]Includes some prisoners sentenced to one year or less. Colorado includes 220 inmates in Youthful Offender System. Iowa also includes some nonsentenced prisoners. Louisiana counts include Hurricane Katrina evacuees and other pretrial offenders from Orleans and Jefferson Parish jails.

[6]Includes estimates for Illinois for 2007 and 2008, and Nevada for December 31, 2007. No imprisonment rate available for Illinois.

[7]An estimated 6,200 inmates sentenced to more than one year but held in local jails or houses of correction are excluded from the population count but included in the incarceration rate.

Sources: U.S. Department of Justice, Office of Justice Programs, Bureau of Justice Statistics, "Prison and Jail Inmates at Midyear 2008 – Statistical Tables." [April 8, 2009]; U.S. Department of Commerce, U.S. Census Bureau, Governments Division, "2007 State Government Finance Data" [April 1, 2009]. Per inmate averages and rankings calculated by Wisconsin Legislative Reference Bureau.

STATE CORRECTIONS AND HEALTH SERVICES INSTITUTIONS
Population, 1970 – 2008

Institutions	2008 Avg. Pop.	Rated Cap.[1]	1970	1980	1990	2000	2006	2007
			Average Daily Population (Year ending June 30)					
STATE CORRECTIONS POPULATION								
Maximum Security (Men)								
Assessment and Evaluation[2]	1,249	904	—	—	—	—	1,165	1,216
Columbia Correctional Institution	818	541	—	—	477	808	815	830
Dodge Correctional Institution[2].	358	261	—	88	551	1,377	344	355
Green Bay Correctional Institution	1,086	749	755	658	832	1,002	1,068	1,079
Wisconsin Secure Program Facility	449	487	—	—	—	101	356	391
Waupun Correctional Institution	1,233	882	954	1,087	1,126	1,225	1,227	1,237
	5,954	3,824	1,709	1,833	2,986	4,513	4,975	5,108
Medium Security								
Fox Lake Correctional Institution	1,049	691	553	570	785	1,112	1,033	1,060
Jackson Correctional Institution	981	837	—	—	—	971	975	985
Kettle Moraine Correctional Institution	1,178	783	293	368	542	1,233	1,181	1,181
New Lisbon Correctional Institution	1,001	950	—	—	—	—	991	1,003
Oshkosh Correctional Institution	2,027	1,494	—	—	444	1,859	2,019	2,046
Prairie du Chien Correctional Institution	491	326	—	—	—	297	400	479
Racine Correctional Institution	1,828	1,021	—	—	—	1,414	1,527	1,835
Racine Youthful Offender Correctional Facility . . .	445	400	—	—	—	395	444	446
Red Granite Correctional Institution	1,010	990	—	—	—	—	1,001	1,015
Stanley Correctional Institute.	1,520	1,500	—	—	—	—	1,499	1,529
	11,530	8,992	846	938	1,771	7,281	11,068	11,579
Minimum Security								
Chippewa Valley Correctional Treatment Center. . .	452	450	—	—	—	—	441	451
Fox Lake	279	288	—	—	—	—	274	280
Oakhill Correctional Institution.	694	300	—	198	368	564	625	672
Sturtevant Transitional Facility[3]	279	150	—	—	—	—	277	280
Wisconsin Correctional Center System (WCCS)[4] . .	1,687	1,100	390	276	1,071	1,816	1,618	1,662
	3,391	2,288	390	474	1,439	2,380	3,235	3,345
Detention Facility								
Milwaukee Secure Detention Facility[3]	1,052	326	998	—	—	—	1,018	1,072
Wisconsin Women's Correctional System[4]								
Taycheedah Correctional Institution (medium/. . . . maximum)	761	653	141	123	203	644	707	720
Correctional Centers (minimum)	649	470					563	618
Contract Facilities								
Federal Contract	29	—	—	—	—	—	31	29
In-State	685	—	—	—	—	—	474	564
Corrections Corporation of America	0	—	—	—	—	—	0	0
	717	—	—	—	78	4,665	505	592
Other Adults								
Community Residential Confinement	—	—	—	—	48	—	—	—
Division of Intensive Sanctions.	—	—	—	—	—	412	—	—
Parole and mandatory release[5]	17,726	—	4,329	3,045	4,217	8,951	15,963	16,943
Probation	53,681	—	4,530	16,797	25,907	55,046	56,002	56,267
	71,407	—	8,859	19,842	30,172	64,409	71,965	73,211
Juvenile Corrections[6]								
Ethan Allen School	273	342	365	306	320	438	280	275
Lincoln Hills School	224	298	—	245	252	330	233	220
Southern Oaks Girls School	56	57	—	—	—	87	47	52
Youth Leadership Training Center[7]	—	—	—	—	—	40	—	—
Sprite Program	5	12	—	—	—	9	8	5
Juvenile Correctional Camp System	—	—	81	24	—	—	—	—
	558	709	446	575	572	904	568	552
Juvenile Aftercare.	68	—	—	—	—	—	90	84
Alternate Care.	48	—	—	—	—	174	54	58
Corrective Sanctions	144	—	—	—	—	134	139	135
TOTAL POPULATION	**96,279**		**12,391**	**23,785**	**37,221**	**84,796**	**94,887**	**97,074**
MENTAL HEALTH INSTITUTIONS (MHI)								
Mendota MHI	256	264	522	202	266	238	244	255
Winnebago MHI	224	242	574	310	266	279	253	239
Mendota Juvenile Treatment Center	29	29	—	—	—	43	29	29
Sand Ridge Secure Treatment Center.	272	288	—	—	—	72	267	278
Central State Hospital.	—	—	258	154	—	—	—	—
Wisconsin Resource Center[8]	436	434	—	—	161	421	397	415
CENTERS FOR DEVELOPMENTALLY DISABLED (CDD)								
Central Wisconsin CDD	270	387	1,070	731	606	380	324	292
Northern Wisconsin CDD.	15	30	1,421	676	495	189	22	27
Southern Wisconsin CDD.	201	292	1,207	735	576	274	241	213
TOTAL POPULATION	**1,703**	**1,966**	**5,052**	**2,808**	**2,370**	**1,896**	**1,777**	**1,748**

[1]For DOC, "rated capacity" is the original design capacity of the institution, based on industry standards, plus modifications and expansions. It excludes beds and multiple bunking installed to accommodate crowding. DHS Care and Treatment Facilities' capacity is "staffed capacity" based on staffing and other budgetary resources rather than number of beds. [2]Dodge CI serves as the assessment and evaluation center for sentenced adult felons. Assessment and evaluation for sentenced adult female felons was moved from Dodge CI to Taycheedah CI December 1, 2004. [3]Milwaukee Secure Detention Facility includes capacity of 688 male and 40 female probation and parole holds. [4]In July 2005, DOC designated the institutions housing female offenders as the Wisconsin Women's Correctional System, which includes Taycheedah CI and 3 of the minimum security Correctional Centers. A limited number of female inmates (currently 12) are housed outside WWCS at predominantly male St. Croix CC. WCCS population statistics prior to 2005 include both male and female inmates. [5]Parole data through 1991 included juveniles; figures from 1992 to date do not include juvenile cases. [6]Juvenile incarceration has been administered by the DOC since July 1, 1996. [7]Youth Leadership Training Camp program, formerly at Camp Douglas and closed in February 2002, is now part of the program at Lincoln Hills. [8]Wisconsin Resource Center is administered by DHS in partnership with the Wisconsin DOC as a specialized mental health facility.
Sources: Wisconsin Department of Corrections, *Fiscal Year Summary Report of Population Movement for 1991* and previous issues, and departmental data, July 2009 and prior years; Wisconsin Department of Health Services, departmental data, June 2009 and prior years. Amounts may not sum to totals due to rounding.

HIGHLIGHTS OF STATE AND LOCAL FINANCE IN WISCONSIN

Revenues and Expenditures — In the 2007-08 fiscal year, a loss of $18.3 billion in interest and investment income compared to the prior year caused total Wisconsin state government revenues to fall to $28.7 billion from all sources, and its expenditures totaled $36.3 billion. Of these expenditures, $24.1 billion were general fund and the remaining $12.2 billion were from special funds (such as the conservation and transportation funds), federal funding, pension and retirement funds, and other sources.

Of the total state budget allocations of $57.0 billion for the 2007-09 biennium, state operations accounted for 37.7% ($21.5 billion) and local assistance for 35.4% ($20.2 billion). The remaining 26.9% ($15.3 billion) comprised aids to individuals and organizations.

For the 2007-08 fiscal year, two state agencies accounted for about 37.3% of total state expenditures. The largest expenditure total was $7.3 billion (20.3%) by the Department of Health and Family Services. Expenditures by the Department of Public Instruction, including state aids to local schools, were $6.2 billion (17.1%). Shared revenue and tax relief of $2.0 billion accounted for 5.6%.

Total state tax revenues for 2007-08 were just over $14.3 billion, including about $13.0 billion in general purpose revenue. These collections were about $432 million higher than during fiscal year 2006-07. Revenue from income taxes totaled almost $7.6 billion, about $6.7 billion of which was individual income taxes and almost $838 million in corporation income taxes, while sales and excise taxes were about $4.8 billion.

State-Local Finances — In 2005-06, Wisconsin ranked 28th nationally in total per capita state and local government general revenues ($6,890, or lower than the U.S. average of $7,327). In total direct general state and local government per capita expenditures, Wisconsin ranked 20th ($7,078 compared to the U.S. average of $7,112). In 2007-08, Wisconsin ranked 17th in total state tax revenues at $71.85 per $1,000 personal income, compared to a national average of $64.89.

Wisconsin returned $1.63 billion to local units of government in property tax relief and shared revenue in fiscal year 2009 ($672.4 million as school levy credits and about $957.8 million in shared revenue).

Property Taxes — General property taxes levied in Wisconsin in 2007 totaled almost $9.3 billion for a net amount of almost $8.6 billion after state property tax relief. Lafayette and Milwaukee counties ($21.85 and $21.19, respectively, per $1,000) had the highest effective (full value equalized) net tax rate and Vilas ($8.43) and Sawyer ($9.57) counties the lowest, compared to the state average of $17.23, a 0.4% reduction from 2006. The share of property taxes paid by residential taxpayers (71.4%) continues to increase. Commercial taxpayers pay 18.9%, and the share paid by manufacturing (2.7%) continues to decline.

State-Federal Finances — Federal tax receipts from Wisconsin in fiscal year 2008 totaled almost $45.6 billion, with the largest amount generated by individual income and employment taxes ($38.5 billion). Federal expenditures in Wisconsin – including grants to state and local government, salaries and wages, direct payments to individuals, procurement, and other programs – amounted to $6,815 per resident. This distribution, on a per capita basis, ranked Wisconsin 47th among the states in federal funds received, with only Oregon ($6,736), Utah ($6,486), and Nevada ($6,032) lower. Virginia was the highest at $14,277 per person, followed by Alaska ($13,721) and Maryland ($12,569). Direct federal aid to Wisconsin in 2007-08 totaled $7.6 billion, and about 52% of that applied to health and family services. Local units of government received about $1.24 billion for all functions.

Indebtedness — Total outstanding state government debt in Wisconsin, as of May 31, 2009, amounted to $5.85 billion, of which $4.52 billion was tax-supported and $1.33 billion was revenue-supported. Total state indebtedness at the end of 2007 constituted 1.18% of state-assessed valuation and amounted to $1,052.05 per capita. Local debt in 2007 totaled about $13.1 billion. Among state political subdivisions, school district debt ($5.43 billion) was largest, followed by city debt ($3.87 billion).

The following tables present selected data. Consult footnoted sources for more detailed information about state and local finance.

STATE BUDGET ALLOCATIONS
By Type of Revenue Source
Fiscal Years 2007-08 and 2008-09

Revenue Type and Allocation	2007-08	2008-09	2007-09 Total	% of Total – All Sources
GENERAL PURPOSE REVENUE	**$13,799,410,400**	**$14,117,942,500**	**$27,917,352,900**	**48.99%**
State operations	3,326,640,500	3,586,773,700	6,913,414,200	12.13
Local assistance	7,671,481,600	7,902,398,700	15,573,880,300	27.33
Aids to individuals and organizations	2,801,288,300	2,628,770,100	5,430,058,400	9.53
PROGRAM REVENUE – TOTAL	**$10,260,511,700**	**$10,579,270,500**	**$20,839,782,200**	**36.57%**
State operations	4,936,337,700	4,990,560,700	9,926,898,400	17.42
Local assistance	1,096,621,100	1,096,784,800	2,193,405,900	3.85
Aids to individuals and organizations	4,227,552,900	4,491,925,000	8,719,477,900	15.30
Program Revenue – Federal	**$6,236,807,500**	**$6,440,565,100**	**$12,677,372,600**	**22.25%**
State operations	1,259,269,500	1,257,941,100	2,517,210,600	4.42
Local assistance	1,015,205,000	1,016,724,300	2,031,929,300	3.57
Aids to individuals and organizations	3,962,333,000	4,165,899,700	8,128,232,700	14.26
Program Revenue – Service	**$785,872,200**	**$792,987,100**	**$1,578,859,300**	**2.77%**
State operations	623,111,400	612,586,800	1,235,698,200	2.17
Local assistance	49,000,100	49,000,100	98,000,200	0.17
Aids to individuals and organizations	113,760,700	131,400,200	245,160,900	0.43
Program Revenue – Other	**$3,237,832,000**	**$3,345,718,300**	**$6,583,550,300**	**11.55%**
State operations	3,053,956,800	3,120,032,800	6,173,989,600	10.84
Local assistance	32,416,000	31,060,400	63,476,400	0.11
Aids to individuals and organizations	151,459,200	194,625,100	346,084,300	0.61
SEGREGATED REVENUE – TOTAL	**$4,008,411,000**	**$4,216,063,800**	**$8,224,474,800**	**14.43%**
State operations	2,354,879,200	2,298,521,000	4,653,400,200	8.17
Local assistance	1,204,182,100	1,206,069,700	2,410,251,800	4.23
Aids to individuals and organizations	449,349,700	711,473,100	1,160,822,800	2.04
Segregated Revenue – Federal	**$898,259,200**	**$827,524,100**	**$1,725,783,300**	**3.03%**
State operations	668,563,000	596,477,800	1,265,040,800	2.22
Local assistance	223,815,500	225,165,600	448,981,100	0.79
Aids to individuals and organizations	5,880,700	5,880,700	11,761,400	0.02
Segregated Revenue – Local	**$106,167,600**	**$107,191,700**	**$213,359,300**	**0.37%**
State operations	5,989,700	5,989,700	11,979,400	0.02
Local assistance	91,947,400	92,971,500	184,918,900	0.32
Aids to individuals and organizations	8,230,500	8,230,500	16,461,000	0.03
Segregated Revenue – Service	**$204,037,400**	**$233,694,700**	**$437,732,100**	**0.77%**
State operations	204,037,400	233,694,700	437,732,100	0.77
Segregated Revenue – Other	**$2,799,946,800**	**$3,047,653,300**	**$5,847,600,100**	**10.26%**
State operations	1,476,289,100	1,462,358,800	2,938,647,900	5.16
Local assistance	888,419,200	887,932,600	1,776,351,800	3.12
Aids to individuals and organizations	435,238,500	697,361,900	1,132,600,400	1.99
FEDERAL REVENUE – TOTAL	**$7,135,066,700**	**$7,268,089,200**	**$14,403,155,900**	**25.28%**
State operations	1,927,832,500	1,854,418,900	3,782,251,400	6.64
Local assistance	1,239,020,500	1,241,889,900	2,480,910,400	4.35
Aids to individuals and organizations	3,968,213,700	4,171,780,400	8,139,994,100	14.29
TOTAL – ALL SOURCES	**$28,068,333,100**	**$28,913,276,800**	**$56,981,609,900**	**100.00%**
State operations	10,617,857,400	10,875,855,400	21,493,712,800	37.72
Local assistance	9,972,284,800	10,205,253,200	20,177,538,000	35.41
Aids to individuals and organizations	7,478,190,900	7,832,168,200	15,310,359,100	26.87

General purpose revenue: general taxes, miscellaneous receipts and revenues collected by state agencies that are paid into the general fund, lose their identity, and are available for appropriation by the legislature.

Program revenue: revenues paid into the general fund and credited by law to an appropriation used to finance a specific program or agency.

Segregated fund revenue: revenues deposited, by law, into funds other than the general fund and available only for the purposes for which such funds were created.

Federal revenue: money received from the federal government (may be disbursed either through a segregated fund or through the general fund).

Service revenue: money transferred between or within state agencies for reimbursement for services rendered or materials purchased.

State operations: amounts budgeted to operate programs carried out by state government.

Local assistance: amounts budgeted as state aids to assist programs carried out by local governmental units in Wisconsin.

Source: Wisconsin Department of Administration, State Budget Office, departmental data, February 2009.

WISCONSIN STATE REVENUES – ALL FUNDS
Fiscal Years 2005-06, 2006-07, 2007-08
(In Thousands)

	2005-06	2006-07	2007-08
TOTAL GENERAL FUND TAX REVENUES*	$12,051,460	$12,637,885	$13,065,359
TOTAL GPR TAX REVENUES*	$12,030,086	$12,617,997	$13,042,943
Income Taxes*	6,924,619	7,463,834	7,551,488
Individual	6,144,299	6,573,778	6,713,681
Corporation	780,320	890,056	837,807
Sales and Excise Taxes*	4,496,278	4,524,460	4,808,304
General sales and use	4,127,585	4,158,612	4,268,045
Cigarette	301,490	296,129	455,722
Other tobacco products	16,421	17,515	29,747
Liquor and wine.	41,023	42,674	45,166
Malt beverage (beer)	9,759	9,530	9,624
Public Utility Taxes*	275,147	284,940	297,460
Private light, heat, and power.	189,063	195,429	212,126
Municipal light, heat, and power	2,439	2,335	2,704
Telephone.	62,997	65,255	59,542
Pipeline	10,655	10,668	11,189
Electric cooperative.	8,106	8,826	9,359
Municipal electric.	1,504	2,044	2,238
Conservation and regulation	368	291	264
Utility tax (refunds) interest and penalties	15	92	38
Inheritance and Estate Taxes	108,571	121,114	158,789
Miscellaneous Taxes*.	225,471	223,649	226,902
Insurance companies (premiums).	134,665	141,405	156,606
Real estate transfer fee	80,536	71,731	59,447
Lawsuits (courts)	10,170	10,407	10,736
Other	100	106	113
PROGRAM TAX REVENUES*	21,374	19,888	22,416
Fire dues	16,151	15,362	15,466
Pari-mutuel taxes	1,246	1,017	908
County expo tax administration.	423	450	151
Baseball park administration fee	349	400	322
Business trust regulation fee	2,149	1,886	1,442
Other	1,056	773	4,127
TRANSPORTATION FUND*.	1,001,808	1,028,785	1,035,040
Motor fuel tax.	974,106	994,677	999,949
Air-carrier tax.	4,715	6,690	6,701
Railroad tax	16,449	18,255	19,856
Aviation fuel tax	1,540	1,523	1,391
Other taxes	4,998	7,640	7,143
CONSERVATION FUND*.	84,001	87,405	89,819
2/10 Mill forestry tax	80,262	82,446	84,529
Forest crop taxes	3,739	4,959	5,290
MEDIATION FUND	2	2	2
PETROLEUM INSPECTION TAX.	71,331	52,471	47,013
RECYCLING FUND TEMPORARY SERVICE CHARGES. . .	19,523	23,527	25,091
TOTAL STATE TAX REVENUES	$13,228,125	$13,830,075	$14,262,324
TOTAL DEPARTMENT REVENUES*	25,893,191	31,404,355	13,190,173
Intergovernmental revenue	7,181,218	7,369,155	7,726,329
Licenses and permits	1,020,799	1,046,966	1,068,095
Charges for goods and services.	3,113,814	3,035,751	3,170,633
Contributions	2,672,970	2,540,834	2,672,069
Interest and investment income.	8,542,094	13,879,927	-4,432,460
Gifts and donations	384,897	498,194	414,079
Proceeds from sale of bonds	1,197,761	973,120	524,289
Other revenues	1,504,409	1,804,042	1,769,089
Other transactions.	275,229	256,366	278,050
TRANSFERS	812,004	1,029,551	1,213,609
TOTAL REVENUES	$39,933,320	$46,263,981	$28,666,106

*Total of subsequent detail.
Source: Wisconsin Department of Administration, *2008 Annual Fiscal Report,* October 15, 2008.

WISCONSIN STATE EXPENDITURES BY AGENCY
Fiscal Years 2006-07 and 2007-08

Agency	2006-07 Amount	2006-07 Percent	2007-08 Amount	2007-08 Percent
Administration, Department of	$636,784,563.48	1.86%	$676,414,741.67	1.87%
Aging and Long-Term Care, Board on	2,135,176.94	0.01	2,229,769.98	0.01
Agriculture, Trade and Consumer Protection, Department of	82,062,076.48	0.24	83,965,905.81	0.23
Arts Board	3,863,864.65	0.01	4,028,804.17	0.01
Child Abuse and Neglect Prevention Board	2,942,262.03	0.01	3,389,507.01	0.01
Commerce, Department of.	173,913,787.22	0.51	133,076,357.08	0.37
Corrections, Department of	1,170,342,969.53	3.42	1,217,338,548.89	3.37
Developmental Disabilities, Board for People with . .	—	—	298,577.09	0.00
District Attorneys (DOA)	45,870,391.43	0.13	46,831,854.56	0.13
Educational Communications Board	15,804,774.35	0.05	15,959,937.88	0.04
Elections Board	23,497,957.25	0.07	−1,806,186.11	−0.01
Employee Trust Funds, Department of	4,895,449,535.18	14.29	5,464,869,195.58	15.14
Employment Relations, Office of State	5,351,478.40	0.02	5,220,814.78	0.01
Employment Relations Commission.	2,915,321.69	0.01	3,010,635.67	0.01
Environmental Improvement Program (DOA)	148,034,506.47	0.43	229,577,255.98	0.64
Ethics Board	703,676.95	0.00	−30,000.00	−0.00
Financial Institutions, Department of	15,505,580.69	0.05	15,585,682.26	0.04
Fox River Navigation System Authority.	30,700.00	0.00	126,700.00	0.00
Government Accountability Board	—	—	5,795,727.48	0.02
Governor, Office of the	3,452,507.29	0.01	3,645,344.10	0.01
Health and Family Services, Department of.	7,007,477,434.40	20.46	7,310,658,720.89	20.26
Higher Education Aids Board	100,566,973.00	0.29	120,737,093.94	0.33
Historical Society, State	19,319,885.54	0.06	20,002,789.97	0.06
Insurance, Office of the Commissioner of.	89,132,499.47	0.26	88,883,398.37	0.25
Investment Board	19,546,181.29	0.06	21,052,371.28	0.06
Justice, Department of	90,028,743.91	0.26	95,845,913.69	0.27
Lieutenant Governor, Office of the	369,198.61	0.00	392,844.66	0.00
Lower Wisconsin Riverway Board	171,776.89	0.00	177,688.51	0.00
Medical College of Wisconsin.	6,160,991.25	0.02	6,591,577.46	0.02
Military Affairs, Department of	60,098,454.79	0.18	82,582,429.81	0.23
Natural Resources, Department of.	543,387,072.06	1.59	562,768,711.43	1.56
Public Defender, Office of the	80,577,537.98	0.24	85,108,746.16	0.24
Public Instruction, Department of	6,083,337,037.58	17.76	6,153,686,234.05	17.05
Public Lands, Board of Commissioners of	1,312,107.32	0.00	1,301,588.85	0.00
Public Service Commission	29,173,643.11	0.09	25,258,082.19	0.07
Regulation and Licensing, Department of.	12,661,189.44	0.04	12,847,566.57	0.04
Revenue, Department of.	451,397,556.76	1.32	452,088,544.98	1.25
Secretary of State, Office of the	675,177.05	0.00	647,521.69	0.00
State Fair Park Board	18,465,516.61	0.05	17,371,111.79	0.05
Technical College System Board	175,465,964.87	0.51	175,169,734.27	0.49
Tourism, Department of	16,070,614.37	0.05	15,023,642.13	0.04
Transportation, Department of.	2,277,724,586.77	6.65	2,539,692,078.68	7.04
Treasurer, Office of the State	5,694,042.67	0.02	3,480,257.20	0.01
University of Wisconsin System.	4,203,537,586.51	12.27	4,438,133,526.08	12.30
Veterans Affairs, Department of	163,968,271.16	0.48	194,533,349.71	0.54
Workforce Development, Department of	1,955,968,912.22	5.71	1,971,875,063.87	5.46
TOTAL EXECUTIVE	$30,640,950,085.66	89.46%	$32,305,439,762.01	89.51%
TOTAL JUDICIAL	121,680,627.23	0.36	126,899,676.39	0.35
TOTAL LEGISLATIVE	63,371,990.69	0.19	65,045,988.07	0.18
Budget Stabilization	—	—	57,000,000.00	0.16
Shared Revenue and Tax Relief	1,830,454,679.54	5.34	2,030,208,034.68	5.63
Miscellaneous Appropriations	145,333,186.94	0.42	190,046,983.05	0.53
Program Supplements	−91,235,013.56	−0.27	63,445,320.32	0.18
Public Debt.	631,186,188.26	1.84	617,728,265.12	1.71
Building Commission	13,797,559.66	0.04	9,564,178.42	0.03
BUILDING PROGRAM	897,312,327.79	2.62	624,973,167.21	1.73
GRAND TOTAL.	$34,252,851,632.21	100.00%	$36,090,351,375.37	100.00%

Source: Wisconsin Department of Administration, State Controller's Office, *Appendix to Annual Fiscal Report (Budgetary Basis)*, October 2007 and 2008. Agency percentages calculated by Wisconsin Legislative Reference Bureau.

WISCONSIN STATE REVENUES AND EXPENDITURES
Fiscal Years 1970-71 – 2007-08
(In Thousands)

Fiscal Year	General Fund[1]		Other Funds[2]		Total – All Funds		Net Surplus[3]
Ending 6/30	Revenues	Expenditures	Revenues	Expenditures	Revenues	Expenditures	(or deficit)
1971	$1,790,957	$1,780,703	$929,124	$726,545	$2,720,081	$2,507,247	$34,840
1972	2,096,084	2,031,896	961,970	697,144	3,058,054	2,729,040	116,914
1973	2,480,748	2,296,679	1,112,600	791,657	3,593,347	3,088,337	217,404
1974	2,687,517	2,729,854	1,114,326	865,724	3,801,842	3,595,577	241,359
1975	2,966,532	3,148,968	1,252,422	924,455	4,218,954	4,073,423	78,120
1976	3,476,690	3,439,062	1,677,155	1,283,467	5,153,846	4,722,529	86,473
1977	3,807,748	3,712,595	1,887,150	1,376,726	5,694,898	5,089,322	166,587
1978	4,240,298	3,994,220	1,875,978	1,446,286	6,116,277	5,440,486	407,770
1979	4,622,611	4,696,263	2,200,365	1,620,899	6,822,976	6,317,162	280,561
1980	4,900,275	5,027,130	2,481,324	1,809,840	7,381,599	6,836,970	72,627
1981	5,335,427	5,452,247	2,738,491	1,922,648	8,073,918	7,374,895	14,065
1982	5,564,585	5,520,811	2,757,388	2,021,266	8,321,974	7,542,078	70,811
1983	6,036,016	6,302,575	3,905,944	2,288,804	9,941,961	8,591,379	(182,126)
1984	6,966,282	6,360,657	3,614,895	2,528,273	10,581,177	8,888,930	383,085
1985	7,160,174	7,237,716	4,908,582	2,743,287	12,068,756	9,981,002	314,084
1986	7,798,367	7,757,063	6,380,605	2,774,683	14,178,972	10,531,747	279,744
1987	8,133,265	8,205,100	5,061,597	2,693,737	13,194,863	10,898,836	232,733
1988	8,432,698	8,427,084	3,566,763	2,790,038	11,999,461	11,217,121	216,963
1989	9,030,466	8,809,189	5,778,125	3,094,116	14,808,591	11,903,305	375,016
1990	9,418,918	9,464,483	5,483,442	3,287,809	14,902,360	12,752,292	306,452
1991	10,184,183	10,350,332	5,930,658	3,706,452	16,114,839	14,056,784	113,609
1992	11,033,948	11,082,220	7,786,483	4,218,565	18,820,431	15,300,785	73,681
1993	11,828,599	11,708,360	8,192,793	4,596,981	20,021,392	16,305,341	153,540
1994	12,442,349	12,323,509	5,812,805	4,756,564	18,255,154	17,080,073	234,877
1995	13,259,772	13,094,450	9,823,810	4,963,553	23,083,582	18,058,003	400,881
1996	13,804,399	13,648,601	10,038,961	5,057,062	23,843,360	18,705,663	581,690
1997	14,669,320	14,932,404	12,741,438	5,144,002	27,410,758	20,076,406	386,558
1998	15,701,212	15,509,615	13,896,719	6,071,649	29,597,931	21,581,264	533,240
1999	16,252,539	16,098,587	11,847,678	6,864,567	28,100,217	22,963,154	737,748
2000	18,185,980	18,333,634	14,687,330	8,111,005	32,873,310	26,444,639	574,416
2001	19,285,734	19,448,417	2,990,770	8,719,341	22,276,504	28,167,758	445,999
2002	20,850,074	21,248,608	5,920,241	10,395,514	26,770,315	31,644,122	44,469
2003	20,683,921	20,956,485	10,598,486	11,025,745	31,282,407	31,982,230	(163,608)
2004	22,040,940	21,716,332	19,544,497	12,177,401	41,585,437	33,893,733	127,369
2005	21,191,600	21,488,178	15,827,541	10,772,231	37,019,141	32,260,409	(131,675)
2006	22,321,870	22,148,049	17,611,450	11,636,031	39,933,320	33,784,080	35,014
2007	23,123,424	23,205,243	23,140,557	11,329,591	46,263,981	34,534,834	36,467
2008	23,997,838	24,103,773	4,668,268	12,195,449	28,666,106	36,299,222	110,424

[1]Includes general purpose revenue (GPR), program revenue, and federal funding.
[2]Includes special revenue funds (such as conservation and transportation), federal funding, debt service, capital projects, pension and retirement funds, trust and agency funds, and others.
[3]Unappropriated (unreserved) balance of the general fund for the fiscal year.

Source: Wisconsin Department of Administration, Bureau of Financial Operations, *2008 Annual Fiscal Report,* October 15, 2008, and previous editions.

WISCONSIN CONSERVATION FUND
REVENUES, EXPENDITURES, AND BALANCES
Fiscal Years 2003-04 – 2007-08

	2003-04	2004-05	2005-06	2006-07	2007-08
OPENING CASH BALANCE	$22,913,012	$28,035,654	$26,996,916	$28,864,563	$19,348,420
REVENUES	234,076,587	249,828,803	271,931,119	272,087,852	288,313,532
User fees (licenses, registration)	91,022,359	93,357,473	102,148,707	102,860,900	100,405,430
Forestry mill tax	72,189,588	78,264,206	80,262,338	82,445,975	84,529,264
Federal aids	26,425,275	33,129,983	43,700,138	34,663,462	49,679,136
Motor fuel tax formula	21,147,710	21,721,256	21,694,279	22,942,677	23,055,418
Severance tax	4,610,242	3,475,509	3,738,671	4,959,436	5,289,754
Other revenues (sales, services)	18,681,413	19,880,376	20,386,986	24,215,402	25,354,530
EXPENDITURES	228,896,029	250,835,541	274,318,572	281,600,095	290,829,057
Land management – state	76,923,406	78,597,697	83,491,397	89,490,667	92,208,338
Land management – federal	8,411,268	10,308,186	11,220,590	12,197,778	13,976,944
Enforcement/science – state	20,035,522	21,790,443	21,694,361	23,525,890	24,652,483
Enforcement/science – federal	5,465,792	5,434,434	6,386,785	6,463,300	7,688,614
Water management – state	19,542,407	20,466,726	20,468,123	23,514,258	25,739,492
Water management – federal	4,095,346	4,046,282	4,828,512	4,829,908	5,327,011
Conservation aids – state	24,503,633	34,937,064	36,759,114	34,555,881	31,762,786
Conservation aids – federal	1,820,296	2,282,965	2,748,689	1,216,406	1,585,027
Environmental aids – state	2,736,567	4,399,542	4,190,874	4,087,066	5,101,556
Development/debt service – state	14,117,341	13,540,419	18,775,114	29,015,060	18,984,845
Development/debt service – federal . .	4,646,964	8,237,286	6,900,795	4,150,941	8,313,349
Administrative services – state	15,267,898	13,859,170	11,788,109	14,077,020	14,650,722
Administrative services – federal	5,615,766	7,233,238	4,560,577	3,643,073	5,052,664
CAER management – state*	14,007,620	13,742,279	14,939,676	16,195,788	16,883,471
CAER management – federal*	709,948	1,016,963	1,382,642	507,958	532,502
Other activities – state	10,996,255	10,942,848	24,183,214	14,129,101	18,369,253
TRANSFER TO GENERAL FUND .	57,916	(32,000)	4,255,100	(3,900)	
FUND BALANCE	$28,035,654	$26,996,916	$28,864,563	$19,348,420	$16,832,895

*CAER - Customer Assistance and External Relations.

Note: The Conservation Fund is a segregated fund that provides funding for many activities of the Wisconsin Department of Natural Resources, including fish and wildlife management, forestry, parks and recreation, law enforcement, administrative activities, and a portion of the Wisconsin Conservation Corps program.

Source: Wisconsin Department of Administration, Bureau of Financial Operations, *2008 Annual Fiscal Report (Budgetary Basis) Appendix,* October 15, 2008, and previous issues.

WISCONSIN TRANSPORTATION FUND
REVENUES AND EXPENDITURES[1]
Fiscal Years 2006-07 and 2007-08

	2006-07		2007-08	
	State Funds	Federal, Local, and Agency Funds	State Funds	Federal, Local, and Agency Funds
OPENING BALANCE	$11,788,400	–$809,114,410	$139,949,627	–$837,340,615
REVENUES				
Motor fuel taxes[2]	$1,006,012,679	—	$999,949,122	—
Vehicle registration[3]	335,484,187	—	371,887,497	—
Drivers license fees	30,514,077	—	35,655,772	—
Motor carrier fees	626,389	—	3,744,638	—
Other motor vehicle fees	25,525,484	—	26,047,181	—
Overweight/oversize permits	5,089,784	—	5,341,777	—
Investment earnings	12,913,359	—	12,701,782	—
Aeronautical taxes and fees	8,822,946	—	8,488,466	—
Railroad property taxes	18,255,608	—	19,860,546	—
Dealers' licenses	663,545	—	700,535	—
Miscellaneous	16,262,744	$3,761,535	29,522,028	$4,291,518
Service center operations	—	19,094,597	—	23,682,522
State and local highway facilities – Federal	—	551,273,752	—	602,614,890
State and local highway facilities – Local	—	74,186,831	—	65,409,948
Major highway development – Revenue bonds	—	145,495,713	—	117,077,742
Highway administration and planning – Federal	—	3,913,197	—	3,065,223
Aeronautics – Federal	—	58,224,170	—	47,446,183
Aeronautics – Local	—	7,159,025	—	23,579,017
Railroad assistance – Federal	—	1,938,457	—	6,357,138
Railroad assistance – Local	—	6,269,015	—	7,854,579
Railroad passenger service – Federal	—	8,615,034	—	8,433,411
Railroad passenger service – Local	—	3,042,200	—	4,853,446
Transit assistance – Federal	—	18,740,385	—	20,390,658
Transit assistance – Local	—	835,394	—	1,157,679
Congestion mitigation air quality – Federal	—	11,485,122	—	5,244,522
Congestion mitigation air quality – Local	—	3,618,814	—	2,115,916
Surface transportation grants – Federal	—	189,971	—	31,385
Surface transportation grants – Local	—	25,171	—	35,612
Harbors assistance – Federal	—	—	—	369,849
Harbors assistance – Local	—	—	—	130,017
Safe routes to school – Federal	—	—	—	605,084
Transportation enhancement activities – Federal	—	7,585,279	—	8,168,192
Transportation enhancement activities – Local	—	4,266,204	—	3,843,708
Transportation facilities economic assistance and development – Local	—	1,985	—	—
Transportation planning grants	—	480,059	—	304,200
General administration and planning – Federal	—	23,807,219	—	24,031,236
General administration and planning – Local	—	1,131,249	—	1,080,434
Administrative facilities – Revenue bonds	—	2,478,884	—	3,602,827
Highway safety – Federal	—	2,339,632	—	3,812,709
Gifts and grants	—	279,971	—	437,766
TOTAL REVENUES	$1,460,170,802	$960,238,865	$1,513,899,344	$990,027,411
TOTAL AVAILABLE	$1,471,959,202	$151,124,455	$1,653,848,971	$152,686,796

[1]The Transportation Fund is a multipurpose special revenue fund created to provide resources for transportation-related facilities and modes with revenues derived from users of transportation facilities. Transportation facilities and major highway projects are also funded with revenue bonds and general obligation bonds.

[2]Effective April 1, 2006, motor fuel tax is $0.309 per gallon. 2005 Wisconsin Act 85 amended s. 78.015 to include "after the calculation of the rate that takes effect on April 1, 2006, the department shall make no further calculation under this subsection." This act eliminated motor fuel tax indexing.

[3]Section 84.59, Wisconsin Statutes, provides that vehicle registration revenues derived under s. 341.25 are deposited with a trustee in a fund outside the state treasury. Only those funds not required for the repayment of revenue bond obligations are considered income to the Transportation Fund. During FY 2007-08, $167.4 million was retained by the trustee and in FY 2006-07, $152.7 million was retained by the trustee.

WISCONSIN TRANSPORTATION FUND
REVENUES AND EXPENDITURES[1]
Fiscal Years 2006-07 and 2007-08–Continued

	2006-07		2007-08	
	State Funds	Federal, Local, and Agency Funds	State Funds	Federal, Local, and Agency Funds
EXPENDITURES				
Local Assistance				
Highway aids	$401,423,906	—	$410,575,320	—
Local bridge and highway improvement	39,029,869	$140,819,853	28,635,207	$107,501,101
Mass transit	112,825,272	17,510,868	116,255,102	19,350,222
Railroads.	2,120,459	1,452,789	2,230,373	3,656,734
Aeronautics	9,324,994	61,051,762	11,450,693	79,565,502
Highway safety	—	3,426,380	—	4,449,669
Multimodal transportation studies	—	—	185,114	—
Rail passenger service[4]	615,619	6,001,007	1,269,057	1,574,676
Surface transportation grants	—	55,954	—	−153,254
Harbor	196,041	369,849	1,106,017	132,201
Safe routes to school.	—	—	—	1,557,760
Transportation planning grants to local governmental units.	—	−13,530	—	−78,000
Transportation enhancement activities.	—	12,071,025	—	9,347,432
Total Local Assistance	$565,536,160	$242,745,957	$571,706,883	$226,904,043
Aids to Individuals and Organizations				
Transportation facilities economic assistance and development	8,121,121	−287,547	1,614,143	517,981
Railroad crossings	3,601,772	3,924,684	4,571,321	4,035,614
Elderly and disabled	1,046,531	3,925,886	803,645	2,103,515
Freight rail	−1,100,984	8,735,353	1,219,308	4,060,012
Total Aids to Individuals and Organizations	$11,668,440	$16,298,376	$8,208,417	$10,717,122
State Operations				
Highway improvements[5].	$229,594,790	$504,901,664	$370,529,568	$588,089,028
Major highway development – Revenue bonds . .	—	139,263,849	—	159,054,247
Highway maintenance, repair and traffic operations	184,116,783	17,783,502	199,731,352	27,516,667
Highway administration and planning.	15,106,561	3,658,485	17,317,834	2,753,313
Traffic enforcement and inspection	58,684,867	6,144,613	62,944,459	4,775,366
Transportation safety.	1,036,925	3,939,137	1,359,795	4,179,245
General administration and planning	50,247,171	12,526,945	61,613,209	12,641,700
Administrative facilities – Revenue bonds	—	2,596,194	—	3,845,349
Vehicle registration and drivers' licensing.	73,264,620	761,128	71,145,428	1,112,782
Vehicle inspection and maintenance	13,274,400	—	13,271,767	—
Debt repayment and interest	12,621,425	—	20,092,703	—
Service centers	—	16,954,018	—	22,169,397
Congestion mitigation air quality	—	8,628,685	—	4,681,831
Miscellaneous[4].	3,691,056	12,262,517	3,072,902	11,501,513
Total State Operations	$641,638,598	$729,420,737	$821,079,017	$842,320,438
Transfers				
Conservation fund	19,942,677	—	20,049,174	—
General fund[6]	93,223,700	—	155,208,700	—
Total Transfers	$113,166,377	—	$175,257,874	—
TOTAL EXPENDITURES.	$1,332,009,575	$988,465,070	$1,576,252,191	$1,079,941,603
UNRESERVED FUND BALANCE	$139,949,627	−$837,340,615	$77,596,780	−$927,254,807

[4]The Fiscal Year 2007 amounts have been restated to account for $9,725,316.62 which was recorded in rail passenger service that should have been recorded in State operations – Miscellaneous.

[5]2005 Wisconsin Act 25 (2005-2007 biennial budget act) authorized general obligation bond funding for the Marquette Interchange Reconstruction project and continued general obligation funding authority for state highway rehabilitation projects.

[6]Transfer to the general fund required by 2007 Wisconsin Act 20 (2007-2009 biennial budget act), 2007 Wisconsin Act 226 (budget adjustment act), and 2005 Wisconsin Act 25 (2005-2007 biennial budget act).

Source: Wisconsin Department of Administration, Division of Executive Budget and Finance, *2008 Annual Fiscal Report (Budgetary Basis) Appendix*, October 15, 2008.

WISCONSIN STATE AIDS BY COUNTY
Calendar Year 2007

County	Health and Human Services	Transportation	Recycling and Sanitation	Public Housing	Conservation	Public Safety	Total State Aids
Adams	$4,517,937	$3,572,686	$182,767	$148,500	$330,440	$184,285	$9,637,192
Ashland . . .	6,999,457	3,233,932	111,742	9,200	210,862	199,355	10,980,847
Barron . . .	9,950,773	5,685,004	226,317	—	218,780	274,483	16,878,258
Bayfield . . .	6,660,476	4,379,008	72,353	6,293	272,889	361,593	12,374,649
Brown	66,955,025	20,766,655	1,413,356	—	977,629	1,235,489	97,466,925
Buffalo	4,723,376	2,079,218	181,632	—	205,760	77,914	7,465,102
Burnett	5,590,998	3,087,372	158,265	—	565,604	618,316	10,409,268
Calumet . . .	10,168,856	2,694,294	279,456	—	222,607	270,519	13,912,882
Chippewa . .	16,254,271	5,643,510	497,487	—	496,575	344,413	24,752,494
Clark	11,204,209	5,608,262	126,092	1,227,649	348,330	206,373	19,252,918
Columbia. . .	16,533,104	6,240,491	317,756	174,918	333,094	559,379	24,871,796
Crawford . . .	5,614,206	3,626,390	46,335	620,700	108,171	145,225	10,898,911
Dane	141,085,094	25,827,709	1,990,581	1,466,508	1,667,991	3,387,991	205,462,093
Dodge*	16,677,854	9,311,400	370,394	300,034	202,558	802,120	28,668,435
Door	7,423,387	4,055,304	119,314	2,266,000	1,145,319	186,708	15,750,442
Douglas . . .	17,192,143	6,899,650	196,578	1,231,817	119,929	729,013	32,028,637
Dunn	12,170,248	5,142,217	245,176	—	206,268	206,468	19,391,496
Eau Claire . .	26,029,019	6,194,967	703,053	125,120	269,972	997,862	37,057,450
Florence . . .	2,250,391	988,667	101,377	40	277,461	447,986	4,364,935
Fond du Lac .	15,461,510	8,072,479	482,849	782,977	491,766	370,099	26,480,068
Forest.	2,866,760	2,152,818	112,514	—	203,473	570,202	6,172,589
Grant	12,748,615	6,200,104	288,185	300,896	268,235	603,709	22,690,134
Green.	9,052,058	3,651,304	248,313	—	205,855	202,328	13,488,703
Green Lake. .	5,348,209	2,176,464	83,107	—	197,374	70,704	8,093,574
Iowa	1,725,536	3,307,421	126,177	15,131	197,359	364,310	6,050,275
Iron.	2,883,481	1,563,531	111,797	—	327,967	45,575	5,577,668
Jackson. . . .	7,480,895	3,346,027	158,461	—	521,580	206,954	11,939,018
Jefferson . . .	24,270,242	6,833,448	407,964	75,746	180,981	758,505	33,549,424
Juneau	7,409,066	3,854,906	146,996	1,600,225	222,530	177,276	14,486,698
Kenosha . . .	52,910,843	7,392,541	660,198	524,924	291,660	1,379,852	67,060,868
Kewaunee . .	5,867,109	2,873,828	183,540	81,000	358,645	167,925	9,730,375
La Crosse . .	20,013,818	8,599,931	526,848	391,374	262,335	1,339,833	33,033,878
Lafayette . . .	4,294,721	2,513,056	80,592	539,659	276,896	177,486	8,487,548
Langlade . . .	4,008,176	3,173,185	123,791	1,309	255,404	223,805	8,352,879
Lincoln. . . .	7,722,912	3,840,635	150,083	—	266,980	320,360	12,715,226
Manitowoc . .	28,237,635	7,917,055	625,861	189,949	653,323	504,395	40,688,165
Marathon* . .	17,015,257	14,472,792	624,751	2,334,333	678,862	622,814	41,597,890
Marinette . . .	11,253,788	5,883,003	155,218	—	391,072	303,681	19,895,875
Marquette . .	3,996,085	1,874,692	122,291	—	169,361	133,199	6,472,735
Menominee . .	3,348,144	303,960	102,083	62,203	84,732	124,735	4,721,784
Milwaukee . .	290,140,467	47,772,003	4,532,631	1,139,426	—	8,300,269	433,365,148
Monroe. . . .	11,676,182	4,809,344	277,649	6,000	296,492	161,152	17,672,388
Oconto	10,008,003	4,963,356	328,056	80,000	872,225	273,978	17,238,144
Oneida	5,983,077	4,231,104	218,673	10,110	616,709	697,298	12,883,184
Outagamie . .	34,061,818	11,260,734	866,539	565,975	506,246	693,872	53,725,292
Ozaukee . . .	15,156,308	6,840,206	267,172	—	430,713	187,576	23,954,601
Pepin	4,009,470	1,738,396	102,612	183,353	159,396	222,387	6,521,545
Pierce.	8,652,454	3,742,888	347,900	181,000	357,089	385,482	14,267,504
Polk	8,739,588	4,953,574	207,080	163,304	517,659	1,292,118	16,658,688
Portage. . . .	10,519,855	6,184,988	352,926	209,500	301,976	487,828	20,709,263
Price	6,572,858	3,010,092	54,267	—	289,127	47,357	10,335,392
Racine	39,384,527	11,722,654	808,912	1,380,419	215,696	1,368,196	60,818,450
Richland . . .	4,667,780	2,983,144	218,483	42,919	230,534	80,820	8,931,877
Rock	23,778,469	9,662,962	685,729	229,181	69,928	816,307	38,669,423
Rusk	6,868,219	4,519,423	161,173	238,469	417,497	236,352	12,787,110
St. Croix . . .	29,037,938	9,911,684	429,496	—	286,982	607,728	42,452,470
Sauk	17,457,358	6,290,454	412,212	184,302	211,648	729,351	26,098,630
Sawyer* . . .	18,114,428	7,031,988	174,058	345,708	311,342	1,070,331	28,311,772
Shawano . . .	5,599,658	3,444,421	86,454	222,021	494,665	241,703	10,839,339
Sheboygan . .	11,119,178	4,949,703	215,213	389,101	483,803	359,037	24,877,976
Taylor	6,172,959	3,321,410	169,650	—	510,630	112,540	10,544,396
Trempealeau .	9,319,107	3,568,761	128,542	452,981	363,869	437,979	14,417,832
Vernon	7,955,703	5,314,364	283,693	—	359,090	612,664	14,912,830
Vilas	3,790,279	3,258,182	252,672	—	541,662	493,176	8,859,845
Walworth. . .	14,099,869	7,750,086	378,201	—	293,649	408,007	24,457,369
Washburn . .	6,572,908	2,865,345	131,403	—	427,272	43,387	11,303,084
Washington. .	24,064,460	10,985,134	406,503	2,157,802	257,385	601,758	39,457,952
Waukesha . .	61,012,119	21,556,422	1,752,880	—	246,087	1,296,947	91,985,326
Waupaca . . .	14,951,954	6,040,637	350,877	1,000,187	639,607	258,520	24,298,586
Waushara . . .	7,282,738	2,756,724	133,548	18,796	601,970	414,402	11,446,741
Winnebago . .	48,777,399	11,415,351	938,045	941,520	591,147	1,125,058	67,474,222
Wood	22,795,186	7,434,147	367,919	210,000	364,188	475,100	32,807,173
TOTAL. . .	$1,424,258,000	$471,329,597	$28,902,818	$24,828,579	$26,952,912	$44,441,919	$2,235,993,656

Note: Table includes state aids to municipalities and county governments. Data does not include state school aids distributed to school districts or state property tax relief. Totals include categories not listed separately.

*County totals do not include data for three local governments that did not file reports with the Wisconsin Department of Revenue: Lowell (Dodge County), Unity (Marathon County), and Couderay (Sawyer County).

Source: Wisconsin Department of Revenue, departmental data, June 2009. Categories and county totals computed by Wisconsin Legislative Reference Bureau.

STATE PAYMENTS TO LOCAL UNITS OF GOVERNMENT
Property Tax Relief and Shared Revenue
By County, Fiscal Year 2009

County	School Levy Credits	Shared Revenue Payments	County Total	Per Capita Amount*	Rank
Adams	$2,934,682	$1,334,443	$4,269,125	$195.51	69
Ashland	1,741,449	6,059,989	7,801,438	460.83	1
Barron	5,026,686	7,976,507	13,003,193	272.45	33
Bayfield	2,554,187	1,592,686	4,146,873	256.61	39
Brown	26,444,629	31,165,048	57,609,677	234.98	56
Buffalo	1,258,819	2,920,028	4,178,847	294.29	23
Burnett	3,165,919	1,283,408	4,449,327	264.98	35
Calumet	4,476,232	4,180,845	8,657,077	187.01	71
Chippewa	5,804,689	11,392,215	17,196,904	277.94	30
Clark	2,341,976	8,558,473	10,900,449	315.14	12
Columbia	6,908,613	6,859,290	13,767,903	245.29	50
Crawford	1,561,062	3,877,126	5,438,188	308.48	16
Dane	77,658,991	28,530,002	106,188,993	225.19	63
Dodge	8,252,135	13,990,361	22,242,496	247.66	47
Door	5,234,054	1,645,772	6,879,826	227.03	60
Douglas	4,085,256	12,250,212	16,335,468	368.53	4
Dunn	4,108,111	8,712,706	12,820,817	296.15	22
Eau Claire	10,781,500	14,961,147	25,742,647	261.87	37
Florence	803,437	394,088	1,197,525	225.23	62
Fond du Lac	8,988,518	15,452,428	24,440,946	240.23	54
Forest	1,541,579	1,139,379	2,680,958	257.96	38
Grant	3,627,293	13,020,493	16,647,786	324.58	9
Green	4,034,429	4,470,809	8,505,238	233.06	58
Green Lake	2,738,657	3,295,691	6,034,348	310.79	14
Iowa	2,947,861	2,257,001	5,204,862	215.11	66
Iron	1,092,144	1,428,917	2,521,061	357.70	6
Jackson	1,622,606	3,426,900	5,049,506	250.72	45
Jefferson	8,763,743	10,782,538	19,546,281	241.25	53
Juneau	2,858,594	5,411,597	8,270,191	302.28	19
Kenosha	19,110,146	21,730,820	40,840,966	251.96	44
Kewaunee	1,896,947	4,314,982	6,211,929	290.85	25
La Crosse	11,843,634	20,937,338	32,780,972	290.72	26
Lafayette	1,359,173	4,739,997	6,099,170	370.36	3
Langlade	2,228,187	4,598,806	6,826,993	314.90	13
Lincoln	3,046,791	6,143,606	9,190,397	299.55	20
Manitowoc	7,029,279	17,910,711	24,939,990	294.00	24
Marathon	13,125,562	19,524,888	32,650,450	241.52	52
Marinette	5,130,790	10,060,925	15,191,715	338.93	7
Marquette	1,830,076	1,100,503	2,930,579	190.01	70
Menominee	415,911	729,075	1,144,986	247.30	49
Milwaukee	91,961,873	326,731,907	418,693,780	446.14	2
Monroe	3,187,697	9,121,878	12,309,575	278.69	29
Oconto	4,740,602	4,969,327	9,709,929	247.32	48
Oneida	7,661,911	2,234,813	9,896,724	254.39	40
Outagamie	17,335,035	26,728,013	44,063,048	252.11	43
Ozaukee	16,329,780	5,722,226	22,052,006	253.45	42
Pepin	821,956	1,486,523	2,308,479	298.14	21
Pierce	4,524,778	5,781,740	10,306,518	254.34	41
Polk	6,374,548	4,557,568	10,932,116	238.21	55
Portage	6,339,776	9,298,010	15,637,786	221.79	65
Price	1,815,883	3,150,219	4,966,102	308.68	15
Racine	19,055,356	37,685,579	56,740,935	289.02	27
Richland	1,741,783	4,124,328	5,866,111	320.26	11
Rock	14,156,398	34,735,383	48,891,781	304.67	18
Rusk	1,843,559	3,874,377	5,717,936	365.20	5
St. Croix	11,107,864	4,497,941	15,605,805	195.80	68
Sauk	8,000,068	5,708,978	13,709,046	224.42	64
Sawyer	3,696,990	1,037,807	4,734,797	266.70	34
Shawano	3,723,959	5,923,931	9,647,890	226.47	61
Sheboygan	12,384,924	19,972,195	32,357,119	275.45	32
Taylor	1,632,026	3,943,482	5,575,508	277.87	31
Trempealeau	2,276,208	6,838,233	9,114,441	322.32	10
Vernon	2,393,034	6,027,345	8,420,379	283.33	28
Vilas	6,894,959	608,951	7,503,910	325.63	8
Walworth	17,868,633	7,418,600	25,287,233	249.59	46
Washburn	2,642,058	1,489,244	4,131,302	234.12	57
Washington	17,406,874	6,710,684	24,117,558	184.82	72
Waukesha	74,774,943	13,067,931	87,842,874	229.54	59
Waupaca	5,205,866	9,023,941	14,229,807	262.75	36
Waushara	3,155,059	1,928,635	5,083,694	200.76	67
Winnebago	14,963,718	25,502,839	40,466,557	244.72	51
Wood	6,007,539	17,709,548	23,717,087	307.82	17
STATE	**$672,400,004**	**$957,773,926**	**$1,630,173,930**	**$287.25**	

*Per capita calculations are based on 2008 county population estimates, the most recent available at publication time.

Source: Wisconsin Department of Revenue, Division of State and Local Finance, Bureau of Property Tax, Local Government Services Section, departmental data, May 2009; Wisconsin Department of Administration, Division of Intergovernmental Relations, Demographic Services Center, *January 1, 2008 Final Population Estimates for Wisconsin Counties,* October 2008. Per capita amounts and rankings calculated by Wisconsin Legislative Reference Bureau.

SELECTED STATE TAX REVENUES
By State, Per $1,000 Personal Income
Fiscal Years Ending in 2008

State	Total Taxes[1] Amount	Rank	General Sales	Motor Fuels	Public Utilities	Tobacco	Alcohol	Individual Income	Corporation Net Income	Motor Vehicle	Property
			Sales and Gross Receipts Taxes								
				Selective Sales Taxes							
Alabama	$57.83	39	$14.58	$3.48	$4.99	$0.92	$1.05	$19.62	$3.35	$1.47	$1.92
Alaska	283.37	1	NA	1.41	0.14	2.47	1.32	NA	33.02	1.80	2.74
Arizona.	62.80	33	28.85	3.41	0.18	1.90	0.30	15.91	3.66	1.15	4.21
Arkansas	84.35	7	31.45	5.28	NA	1.65	0.48	26.27	3.84	1.74	7.64
California	74.78	13	20.37	2.18	0.48	0.66	0.21	35.52	7.55	1.87	1.45
Colorado	45.98	48	11.05	3.04	0.06	1.05	0.17	24.21	2.43	1.11	NA
Connecticut	67.88	25	16.14	2.29	0.88	1.61	0.21	35.55	2.71	1.22	NA
Delaware	82.17	8	NA	3.30	1.40	3.51	0.41	28.23	8.65	1.38	NA
Florida	50.06	46	30.05	3.20	4.41	0.62	0.85	NA	3.08	1.84	0.00
Georgia.	55.26	42	17.62	3.07	NA	0.71	0.50	26.88	2.87	1.10	0.25
Hawaii	98.69	3	50.22	1.80	2.44	1.71	0.87	29.62	2.02	2.14	NA
Idaho	74.58	14	27.52	4.90	0.03	1.12	0.15	29.38	3.88	2.69	NA
ILLINOIS	57.71	40	14.51	2.63	3.43	1.12	0.29	20.42	5.70	2.84	0.11
Indiana	68.59	24	26.39	3.94	0.07	2.39	0.21	22.24	4.18	1.91	0.03
IOWA	62.58	34	16.71	4.01	NA	2.30	0.13	25.86	3.15	3.80	NA
Kansas	67.28	26	21.28	4.06	0.01	1.11	1.00	27.67	4.96	1.78	0.74
Kentucky.	74.01	16	21.17	4.55	NA	1.31	0.79	25.64	3.93	1.71	3.70
Louisiana.	68.78	23	21.62	3.78	0.09	0.91	0.34	19.81	4.40	0.62	0.29
Maine	79.04	11	23.01	4.93	0.70	3.23	0.44	31.09	3.96	2.10	0.80
Maryland.	61.29	36	13.84	2.99	0.49	1.39	0.11	28.91	2.71	1.74	2.33
Massachusetts . .	66.24	28	12.43	2.04	NA	1.33	0.22	37.90	6.61	1.15	0.00
MICHIGAN	70.92	20	22.04	2.82	0.06	3.05	0.39	20.34	7.03	2.68	6.41
MINNESOTA . . .	82.05	9	20.38	2.90	0.00	1.88	0.32	34.83	4.66	2.52	3.19
Mississippi	76.17	12	36.08	5.09	0.02	0.67	0.48	17.85	4.43	1.81	0.58
Missouri	52.65	45	15.50	3.54	NA	0.53	0.15	24.58	1.84	1.37	0.14
Montana	74.17	15	NA	6.21	1.47	2.84	0.82	26.25	4.88	4.58	6.65
Nebraska	62.05	35	22.80	4.37	0.05	1.12	0.39	25.65	3.46	1.48	0.03
Nevada	58.29	38	29.33	2.97	0.12	1.28	0.39	NA	NA	1.77	1.83
New Hampshire . .	39.95	50	NA	2.43	1.40	3.01	0.22	2.09	10.91	1.90	6.88
New Jersey.	69.25	22	20.17	1.27	2.10	1.79	0.24	28.51	6.38	1.06	0.01
New Mexico	89.11	5	30.62	3.93	0.56	0.76	0.65	19.05	6.34	2.89	0.91
New York	69.80	21	12.05	0.56	0.85	1.04	0.22	39.02	5.38	1.07	NA
North Carolina . . .	71.73	18	16.59	4.98	1.22	0.78	0.82	34.61	3.80	2.34	NA
North Dakota. . . .	91.66	4	21.01	5.68	1.37	0.96	0.27	12.58	6.42	3.67	0.08
Ohio	66.57	27	21.51	4.57	2.78	2.34	0.23	25.89	2.74	2.18	0.08
Oklahoma	63.13	32	15.60	2.86	0.23	1.88	0.64	20.74	2.68	4.81	NA
Oregon	53.20	44	NA	3.03	0.17	1.87	0.11	36.46	3.50	3.79	0.16
Pennsylvania	64.09	30	17.70	4.19	2.70	2.05	0.55	20.77	4.37	1.75	0.12
Rhode Island	64.08	31	19.65	2.94	2.33	2.65	0.27	25.33	3.39	1.23	0.03
South Carolina . . .	59.20	37	21.36	3.74	0.19	0.22	1.05	23.38	2.24	1.31	0.07
South Dakota. . . .	43.96	49	24.37	4.31	0.11	2.13	0.46	NA	2.32	1.66	NA
Tennessee	54.08	43	32.03	4.09	0.05	1.28	0.54	1.36	4.71	1.47	NA
Texas	47.61	47	23.09	3.31	1.08	1.54	0.84	NA	NA	1.74	NA
Utah	71.72	19	23.70	4.55	0.37	0.75	0.48	31.28	4.76	1.56	0.07
Vermont	105.33	2	14.03	3.79	0.44	2.45	0.82	25.79	3.51	3.48	33.54
Virginia.	55.26	41	10.98	2.76	0.45	0.50	0.53	30.36	2.36	1.20	0.07
Washington.	64.69	29	40.90	4.22	1.69	1.49	0.96	NA	NA	1.98	6.28
West Virginia. . . .	87.22	6	19.84	7.23	2.83	2.05	0.17	27.15	9.63	1.57	0.08
WISCONSIN . . .	71.85	17	20.32	4.77	1.56	2.31	0.26	31.62	4.11	2.11	0.59
Wyoming.	81.86	10	28.11	2.83	0.12	1.03	0.06	NA	NA	2.19	10.53
UNITED STATES[2]	$64.89		$19.97	$3.03	$1.20	$1.33	$0.44	$23.30	$4.30	$1.81	$1.06

NA – Not available or not applicable.

[1]Includes other taxes not listed separately.

[2]United States totals exclude District of Columbia.

Sources: U.S. Census Bureau, Governments Division, "2008 State Government Tax Collections" (April 1, 2009), at: http://www.census.gov/govs/www/statetax08.html [April 28, 2009]; and U.S. Department of Commerce, Bureau of Economic Analysis, Regional Economic Information System, "Regional Economic Accounts: SA1-3 – Personal Income" 2008 preliminary estimates (March 24, 2009), at: http://www.bea.gov/regional/spi/ [May 6, 2009]. Amounts per $1,000 personal income and rankings calculated by Wisconsin Legislative Reference Bureau.

PER CAPITA STATE AND LOCAL REVENUES
Selected Sources, Fiscal Year 2005-06

| | Total State and Local General Revenue Per Capita | | | | | | State and Local Taxes Per Capita | | | |
| | | | Federal Sources | | State/Local Sources | | Total | | | Individual |
State	Amount	Rank	Amount	Percent	Amount¹	Percent	Taxes²	Property	Sales	Income
Alabama	$6,449	39	$1,677	26.0%	$4,772	74.0%	$2,783	$420	$1,336	$627
Alaska	16,300	1	3,558	21.8	12,741	78.2	5,419	1,433	644	—
Arizona.	5,905	50	1,427	24.2	4,478	75.8	3,228	894	1,513	527
Arkansas	6,135	45	1,615	26.3	4,520	73.7	3,119	471	1,655	718
California	8,113	9	1,561	19.2	6,551	80.8	4,533	1,031	1,440	1,418
Colorado	6,868	29	1,122	16.3	5,745	83.7	3,625	1,109	1,308	896
Connecticut	8,298	6	1,318	15.9	6,981	84.1	5,697	2,169	1,425	1,656
Delaware.	8,487	5	1,460	17.2	7,027	82.8	4,255	624	518	1,266
District of Columbia . .	15,665	—	5,227	33.4	10,438	66.6	7,764	2,073	2,148	2,105
Florida	6,861	30	1,314	19.1	5,548	80.9	3,701	1,279	1,795	—
Georgia.	5,989	48	1,224	20.4	4,765	79.6	3,329	960	1,291	863
Hawaii	8,208	8	1,576	19.2	6,632	80.8	4,861	771	2,484	1,216
Idaho	6,061	47	1,343	22.2	4,718	77.8	3,081	848	1,024	837
ILLINOIS	6,855	31	1,250	18.2	5,605	81.8	4,087	1,533	1,402	677
Indiana	7,283	19	1,190	16.3	6,092	83.7	3,646	1,336	1,217	794
IOWA	6,956	26	1,520	21.9	5,436	78.1	3,457	1,143	1,126	837
Kansas	6,652	36	1,264	19.0	5,388	81.0	3,792	1,188	1,385	871
Kentucky.	6,266	41	1,606	25.6	4,660	74.4	3,229	576	1,210	934
Louisiana.	7,904	14	2,365	29.9	5,539	70.1	3,705	582	2,066	589
Maine	8,025	12	2,050	25.5	5,975	74.5	4,420	1,683	1,272	1,042
Maryland.	7,467	17	1,407	18.8	6,060	81.2	4,603	1,064	1,111	1,758
Massachusetts	8,109	10	1,512	18.6	6,597	81.4	4,755	1,681	946	1,627
MICHIGAN	6,768	32	1,385	20.5	5,383	79.5	3,572	1,341	1,176	664
MINNESOTA	7,657	16	1,402	18.3	6,255	81.7	4,373	1,038	1,446	1,334
Mississippi.	6,979	25	2,547	36.5	4,432	63.5	2,824	717	1,377	433
Missouri	6,088	46	1,478	24.3	4,610	75.7	3,139	855	1,213	827
Montana	7,118	21	2,149	30.2	4,969	69.8	3,194	1,120	548	813
Nebraska	7,341	18	1,488	20.3	5,853	79.7	3,906	1,269	1,244	878
Nevada	6,673	35	963	14.4	5,710	85.6	3,930	1,010	2,313	—
New Hampshire	6,182	43	1,262	20.4	4,920	79.6	3,451	2,124	541	62
New Jersey.	8,494	4	1,359	16.0	7,134	84.0	5,475	2,378	1,228	1,216
New Mexico	7,932	13	2,110	26.6	5,822	73.4	3,599	492	1,655	580
New York	10,825	3	2,267	20.9	8,557	79.1	6,385	1,881	1,632	1,994
North Carolina	6,467	38	1,497	23.1	4,970	76.9	3,393	790	1,167	1,070
North Dakota.	7,766	15	2,041	26.3	5,725	73.7	3,720	997	1,313	433
Ohio	7,069	22	1,575	22.3	5,494	77.7	3,774	1,099	1,133	1,201
Oklahoma	6,291	40	1,516	24.1	4,776	75.9	3,155	505	1,186	772
Oregon	6,949	27	1,472	21.2	5,477	78.8	3,369	1,001	293	1,504
Pennsylvania	7,062	23	1,462	20.7	5,600	79.3	3,960	1,147	1,152	995
Rhode Island	8,062	11	2,057	25.5	6,005	74.5	4,419	1,783	1,327	963
South Carolina	6,677	34	1,565	23.4	5,112	76.6	2,877	916	1,037	631
South Dakota.	6,141	44	1,756	28.6	4,385	71.4	2,846	974	1,544	—
Tennessee	5,940	49	1,428	24.0	4,513	76.0	2,841	680	1,663	32
Texas	6,200	42	1,330	21.5	4,870	78.5	3,241	1,390	1,459	0
Utah	6,496	37	1,361	20.9	5,135	79.1	3,204	726	1,282	881
Vermont	8,243	7	2,185	26.5	6,057	73.5	4,439	1,852	1,307	874
Virginia.	6,722	33	935	13.9	5,787	86.1	3,940	1,210	1,061	1,189
Washington.	7,236	20	1,381	19.1	5,855	80.9	3,957	1,087	2,423	—
West Virginia.	7,014	24	1,876	26.7	5,138	73.3	3,256	586	1,243	718
WISCONSIN	6,890	28	1,279	18.6	5,611	81.4	4,005	1,441	1,128	1,061
Wyoming.	13,709	2	3,989	29.1	9,720	70.9	6,118	1,922	1,847	—
UNITED STATES .	$7,327		$1,516	20.7%	$5,811	79.3%	$4,006	$1,204	$1,381	$900

¹Includes taxes, charges, and miscellaneous general revenues.
²Total taxes also include corporate income, motor vehicle license, and other taxes not listed separately.
Source: U.S. Department of Commerce, U.S. Census Bureau, "State and Local Government Finances: 2005-06", at:
http://www.census.gov/govs/www/estimate06.html and "Annual Estimates of the Population for the United States and
States, and for Puerto Rico: April 1, 2000 to July 1, 2008 (NST-EST2006-01)",
at: http://www.census.gov/popest/states/NST-ann-est.html (2006 estimates used in calculations). Per capita figures,
percentages, and rankings calculated by Wisconsin Legislative Reference Bureau.

SELECTED PER CAPITA STATE AND LOCAL
GOVERNMENT EXPENDITURES, BY FUNCTION
Fiscal Year 2005-06

State	Direct General Expenditure* Amount	Rank	Public Welfare	Health and Hospitals	Highways	Police and Fire	Corrections	Parks and Natural Resources	Sewerage and Solid Waste
Alabama	$6,697	26	$1,123	$1,124	$420	$283	$141	$170	$188
Alaska	13,839	1	2,066	512	1,928	480	314	540	218
Arizona.	5,786	48	981	387	399	405	231	295	180
Arkansas	5,914	45	1,228	446	404	245	186	150	152
California	8,125	7	1,237	726	428	534	302	300	250
Colorado	6,478	35	738	522	435	365	211	321	168
Connecticut	7,880	9	1,329	537	366	390	177	102	198
Delaware	8,772	4	1,460	471	729	371	288	220	300
District of Columbia . .	13,672	—	3,145	1,143	164	1,144	351	568	860
Florida	6,805	24	996	556	495	479	225	319	264
Georgia.	5,817	47	911	597	292	304	215	145	208
Hawaii	7,720	11	1,133	725	349	326	141	276	302
Idaho	5,767	49	1,003	594	506	263	179	235	172
ILLINOIS	6,598	30	1,054	386	421	432	136	249	140
Indiana	6,338	36	1,026	603	380	269	148	133	208
IOWA	6,944	22	1,190	795	628	252	121	207	148
Kansas	6,547	33	1,033	410	649	320	137	179	156
Kentucky.	6,029	41	1,353	432	447	241	150	170	135
Louisiana.	7,181	16	1,075	904	496	393	235	269	186
Maine	7,588	13	1,901	469	608	260	139	186	194
Maryland.	7,030	21	1,162	347	434	413	261	278	228
Massachusetts	8,135	6	1,777	338	350	412	177	102	226
MICHIGAN	6,598	31	981	709	359	322	227	125	205
MINNESOTA	7,537	14	1,784	486	594	313	144	270	168
Mississippi	6,645	27	1,295	931	595	270	130	144	114
Missouri	5,921	43	1,028	630	473	302	138	160	129
Montana	6,585	32	910	478	737	270	186	335	151
Nebraska	6,642	28	1,138	573	624	272	167	254	110
Nevada	6,480	34	721	430	590	511	224	318	102
New Hampshire	6,224	39	1,124	137	474	334	126	126	168
New Jersey.	8,238	5	1,440	337	413	442	222	174	259
New Mexico	7,671	12	1,479	632	616	364	246	296	136
New York	10,055	3	2,229	949	450	537	264	138	305
North Carolina	6,320	38	1,112	843	378	298	175	157	226
North Dakota.	7,094	19	1,145	159	901	214	116	454	113
Ohio	7,160	17	1,453	635	405	362	174	116	244
Oklahoma	5,838	46	1,141	397	422	291	177	151	145
Oregon	6,880	23	1,053	610	488	361	250	240	213
Pennsylvania.	7,214	15	1,635	486	544	250	226	122	189
Rhode Island	7,788	10	2,030	262	373	501	184	98	211
South Carolina	6,719	25	1,104	1,088	392	262	143	126	148
South Dakota.	5,925	42	951	264	849	229	179	313	123
Tennessee	5,666	50	1,251	676	360	285	148	125	157
Texas	5,917	44	871	459	472	296	190	125	150
Utah	6,039	40	911	452	425	293	173	231	180
Vermont	7,921	8	1,810	235	612	286	163	207	153
Virginia.	6,606	29	953	564	386	350	230	160	211
Washington	7,102	18	1,054	822	463	348	222	243	243
West Virginia.	6,329	37	1,299	333	610	178	141	163	157
WISCONSIN	7,078	20	1,293	473	586	357	229	237	210
Wyoming	10,474	2	1,143	1,753	1,128	409	351	628	208
UNITED STATES . .	$7,112		$1,241	$609	$454	$380	$210	$202	$207

*Includes amounts for categories not shown separately.

Sources: U.S. Department of Commerce, U.S. Census Bureau, "State and Local Government Finances: 2005-06", at: http://www.census.gov/govs/www/estimate06.html and "National and State Population Estimates", at: http://www.census.gov/popest/states/NST-ann-est.html. Per capita values and rankings calculated by Wisconsin Legislative Reference Bureau.

FEDERAL TAX COLLECTIONS
By State, Fiscal Year 2008
(In Thousands of Dollars)

State[1]	Total	Individual Income and Employment[2]	Corporate Income[3]	Estate and Gift	Excise[4]
Alabama	$24,563,503	$21,938,012	$2,229,203	$270,201	$126,087
Alaska	4,748,628	4,359,791	316,380	24,077	48,379
Arizona	35,813,663	32,008,838	2,200,364	359,402	1,245,059
Arkansas	28,165,013	20,985,443	6,254,333	246,881	678,356
California	318,083,114	268,461,994	40,440,402	5,800,735	3,379,983
Colorado	48,257,249	41,964,442	4,633,621	403,607	1,255,579
Connecticut	54,421,151	46,709,549	6,682,419	601,943	427,240
Delaware	21,589,039	12,761,439	8,705,946	73,051	48,603
District of Columbia	19,432,111	17,581,931	1,505,984	326,942	17,255
Florida	134,337,889	125,089,899	5,977,696	2,515,136	755,158
Georgia	69,069,197	57,924,061	8,715,040	525,523	1,904,574
Hawaii	8,489,937	7,500,971	735,937	127,867	125,161
Idaho	8,600,349	8,083,539	391,321	99,775	25,715
ILLINOIS	134,871,112	110,521,255	18,753,405	1,368,809	4,227,644
Indiana	43,231,402	38,213,422	4,433,185	263,840	320,955
IOWA	19,683,455	17,166,708	2,300,782	109,542	106,424
Kansas	22,177,597	18,629,451	2,095,324	287,061	1,165,761
Kentucky	24,937,707	22,840,375	1,670,372	170,747	256,214
Louisiana	35,234,657	32,375,089	2,344,846	215,405	299,317
Maine	6,736,963	6,040,922	431,929	81,894	182,218
Maryland	54,131,790	48,907,217	4,344,480	747,288	132,806
Massachusetts	81,367,437	72,230,278	7,708,521	865,438	563,199
MICHIGAN	66,618,158	60,809,236	4,895,778	701,755	211,390
MINNESOTA	81,025,159	63,161,450	16,202,949	308,917	1,351,844
Mississippi	12,697,324	10,766,668	1,610,632	71,333	248,692
Missouri	48,298,002	41,038,981	5,665,429	510,179	1,083,413
Montana	4,713,181	4,403,646	212,189	44,966	52,380
Nebraska	21,366,643	13,777,188	7,417,558	97,378	74,518
Nevada	17,753,419	15,847,639	1,608,398	196,616	100,766
New Hampshire	10,640,725	10,303,644	146,722	113,975	76,384
New Jersey	122,535,119	101,060,594	19,649,720	825,659	999,146
New Mexico	9,858,908	8,897,827	817,494	118,208	25,379
New York	229,647,494	192,567,025	32,710,990	3,263,502	1,105,977
North Carolina	73,917,681	60,045,400	13,017,527	623,972	230,782
North Dakota	4,149,764	3,684,185	432,439	13,297	19,844
Ohio	111,029,042	95,002,155	12,535,213	604,558	2,887,116
Oklahoma	30,202,018	19,755,434	6,159,229	177,117	4,110,178
Oregon	26,138,979	23,778,334	1,922,975	263,108	174,562
Pennsylvania	116,554,665	100,087,870	12,901,103	1,165,125	2,400,566
Rhode Island	11,628,434	8,475,354	3,017,092	126,727	9,260
South Carolina	20,379,879	18,850,001	1,118,940	268,992	141,945
South Dakota	4,860,642	4,612,927	179,045	37,650	31,020
Tennessee	49,227,614	43,751,658	4,266,824	276,072	933,059
Texas	235,676,058	178,761,539	39,971,658	1,792,809	15,150,053
Utah	17,124,954	14,199,560	1,997,580	118,735	809,079
Vermont	3,721,718	3,456,136	202,432	44,043	19,107
Virginia	66,865,525	54,324,275	11,631,016	698,562	211,672
Washington	66,887,298	53,831,470	11,794,598	630,944	630,286
West Virginia	6,884,310	6,183,472	505,988	83,814	111,036
WISCONSIN	45,586,757	38,456,081	6,466,352	322,677	341,648
Wyoming	5,129,559	3,939,671	984,343	93,025	112,519
UNITED STATES[5]	$2,745,035,410	$2,309,187,810	$354,315,825	$29,823,935	$51,707,840

[1]Taxes may be collected in one state from residents of another state for a variety of reasons, and some corporations pay taxes from a principal office, although their operations may be located in several states.

[2]Collections of individual income tax are not reported by taxpayers separately from old-age, survivors, disability, and hospital insurance (OASDHI) taxes on salaries and wages under the Federal Insurance Contributions Act (FICA), and on self-employment income under the Self-Employment Insurance Contributions Act (SECA). Includes estate and trust income tax collections of $25.6 billion.

[3]Includes "unrelated business income" business income taxes from tax-exempt organizations and farmers' cooperatives.

[4]Excludes excise taxes paid to the Customs Service and the Alcohol and Tobacco Tax and Trade Bureau.

[5]United States totals include international and undistributed totals not included in state listing for taxes filed by members of armed forces stationed overseas or other U.S. citizens abroad. Also included are returns from residents of Puerto Rico and other territories. Corporation taxes include those paid by domestic and foreign businesses with principal offices outside the United States. Adjustments and credits are not shown by state, but are included in the U.S. totals.

Source: U.S. Department of the Treasury, Internal Revenue Service, "Internal Revenue Service Data Book, 2008," Publication 55B, March 2009.

PER CAPITA FEDERAL EXPENDITURES
by State, Fiscal Year 2007

State	Total Amount	Rank	Retirement and Disability	Grants	Procurement	Salaries and Wages	Other Direct Payments
Alabama	$10,348.06	9	$3,338.60	$1,671.27	$2,289.68	$750.75	$2,297.76
Alaska	13,721.43	2	1,963.01	4,383.96	3,423.66	2,996.94	953.86
Arizona.	7,574.39	33	2,461.51	1,477.89	1,659.52	661.47	1,314.00
Arkansas	7,920.85	30	3,137.26	1,801.79	436.17	625.43	1,920.20
California	7,124.46	44	2,004.55	1,576.77	1,250.79	664.48	1,627.86
Colorado	7,164.00	43	2,204.52	1,264.81	1,386.42	1,048.70	1,259.55
Connecticut	9,244.78	16	2,533.51	1,631.71	2,657.23	529.71	1,892.62
Delaware	7,208.46	41	2,955.17	1,604.04	474.14	674.92	1,500.18
District of Columbia . . .	73,900.38	--	3,920.71	9,996.79	25,024.36	30,158.90	4,799.63
Florida	8,059.22	29	3,044.38	1,173.11	863.36	646.50	2,331.86
Georgia.	7,446.92	35	2,264.85	1,298.24	1,487.44	985.61	1,410.77
Hawaii	10,956.84	5	2,923.81	1,910.86	1,813.68	2,818.57	1,489.93
Idaho	7,300.49	38	2,519.89	1,484.65	1,436.65	710.66	1,148.65
ILLINOIS	6,898.98	46	2,297.50	1,394.70	697.87	585.96	1,922.95
Indiana	7,447.13	34	2,614.01	1,392.01	1,053.88	437.94	1,949.28
IOWA	7,245.24	40	2,706.38	1,418.77	645.41	468.93	2,005.75
Kansas	8,190.46	26	2,656.98	1,352.24	1,215.94	1,018.54	1,946.76
Kentucky.	8,470.32	23	2,966.12	1,624.42	1,120.25	956.48	1,803.04
Louisiana.	10,024.23	11	2,605.78	3,404.70	1,066.17	685.96	2,261.61
Maine	8,996.01	18	3,229.91	2,130.82	1,256.09	773.80	1,605.40
Maryland.	12,568.98	3	2,936.98	1,655.58	3,756.06	2,041.36	2,179.00
Massachusetts	9,462.06	12	2,509.77	2,231.31	1,852.66	619.53	2,248.80
MICHIGAN	7,114.06	45	2,703.82	1,374.89	771.01	409.79	1,854.55
MINNESOTA	7,710.33	32	2,317.60	1,515.09	598.77	518.57	2,760.29
Mississippi	10,489.28	7	2,904.35	2,537.94	2,245.79	755.98	2,045.23
Missouri	9,452.29	13	2,811.39	1,616.85	2,099.54	841.43	2,083.08
Montana	8,871.18	20	3,008.59	2,325.80	594.73	1,076.24	1,865.83
Nebraska	7,881.41	31	2,588.66	1,534.77	586.16	809.33	2,362.49
Nevada	6,031.85	50	2,359.64	1,161.69	831.36	626.80	1,052.35
New Hampshire	7,420.50	36	2,767.32	1,377.56	1,434.32	566.56	1,274.74
New Jersey.	7,365.02	37	2,501.97	1,419.05	983.28	555.89	1,904.83
New Mexico	11,380.00	4	2,829.33	2,533.85	3,438.45	1,163.16	1,415.21
New York	8,176.58	27	2,453.91	2,494.40	608.26	550.85	2,069.17
North Carolina	7,268.81	39	2,727.78	1,563.68	566.52	971.08	1,439.75
North Dakota.	10,576.11	6	2,669.63	2,265.04	1,076.09	1,431.07	3,134.28
Ohio	9,175.41	17	2,643.63	1,523.97	783.49	528.27	3,696.06
Oklahoma	8,483.19	22	3,024.70	1,748.91	788.83	1,061.04	1,859.72
Oregon	6,735.73	48	2,725.02	1,546.06	488.28	563.73	1,412.65
Pennsylvania	9,422.75	14	3,071.97	1,677.46	1,164.88	588.82	2,919.61
Rhode Island	8,580.44	21	2,798.52	2,253.63	622.02	828.38	2,077.90
South Carolina	8,407.13	24	2,999.61	1,466.77	1,508.10	865.48	1,567.17
South Dakota.	10,399.54	8	2,749.08	1,903.39	791.20	1,056.71	3,899.16
Tennessee	8,357.68	25	2,846.49	1,606.03	1,553.08	497.28	1,854.81
Texas	7,185.54	42	2,113.81	1,232.32	1,643.04	760.03	1,436.34
Utah	6,486.29	49	1,895.91	1,283.99	1,495.78	911.27	899.35
Vermont	8,979.73	19	2,735.67	2,398.68	1,500.68	742.02	1,602.68
Virginia.	14,276.91	1	3,154.55	1,192.25	5,885.65	2,239.60	1,804.86
Washington.	8,109.38	28	2,673.78	1,498.44	1,425.25	1,073.19	1,438.72
West Virginia.	9,418.47	15	3,797.87	2,058.28	747.93	872.48	1,941.92
WISCONSIN	6,815.38	47	2,547.92	1,346.52	793.56	396.39	1,730.99
Wyoming.	10,242.45	10	2,688.08	3,824.93	963.68	1,148.34	1,617.42
UNITED STATES* . .	$8,339.19		$2,571.22	$1,624.13	$1,392.57	$824.91	$1,926.36

*Totals include the 50 states and District of Columbia. U.S. Outlying Areas are excluded.

Source: U.S. Department of Commerce, U.S. Census Bureau, *Consolidated Federal Funds Report for Fiscal Year 2007: State and County Areas,* September 2008.

FEDERAL REVENUE DISTRIBUTED
TO STATE AND LOCAL GOVERNMENTS
by State, Fiscal Year 2005-06

State	Per Capita Amount	Per Capita Rank	Intergovernmental Revenue (in thousands) to State Government	Intergovernmental Revenue (in thousands) to Local Government	Total	Percent of all State and Local General Revenue
Alabama	$1,677	14	$6,977,227	$714,866	$7,692,093	26.0%
Alaska	3,558	2	2,152,024	254,415	2,406,439	21.8
Arizona.	1,427	31	7,607,086	1,211,087	8,818,173	24.2
Arkansas	1,615	15	4,267,300	261,688	4,528,988	26.3
California	1,561	20	48,286,650	8,115,817	56,402,467	19.2
Colorado	1,122	48	4,657,421	675,978	5,333,399	16.3
Connecticut	1,318	40	4,160,525	435,674	4,596,199	15.9
Delaware	1,460	29	1,176,604	64,537	1,241,141	17.2
District of Columbia	5,227	—	—	3,060,038	3,060,038	33.4
Florida	1,314	41	19,709,285	3,964,312	23,673,597	19.1
Georgia.	1,224	46	10,335,726	1,069,146	11,404,872	20.4
Hawaii	1,576	17	1,833,188	176,829	2,010,017	19.2
Idaho	1,343	38	1,823,377	139,181	1,962,558	22.2
ILLINOIS	1,250	45	12,848,714	3,097,223	15,945,937	18.2
Indiana	1,190	47	7,059,038	433,616	7,492,654	16.3
IOWA	1,520	21	4,089,091	421,841	4,510,932	21.9
Kansas	1,264	43	3,228,955	254,861	3,483,816	19.0
Kentucky.	1,606	16	6,354,046	391,715	6,745,761	25.6
Louisiana.	2,365	4	9,026,421	1,011,146	10,037,567	29.9
Maine	2,050	10	2,572,822	119,495	2,692,317	25.5
Maryland.	1,407	32	6,737,906	1,144,266	7,882,172	18.8
Massachusetts	1,512	23	8,431,197	1,308,672	9,739,869	18.6
MICHIGAN	1,385	34	12,329,094	1,637,481	13,966,575	20.5
MINNESOTA	1,402	33	6,479,317	729,645	7,208,962	18.3
Mississippi	2,547	3	6,854,953	523,876	7,378,829	36.5
Missouri	1,478	26	7,772,682	846,323	8,619,005	24.3
Montana	2,149	7	1,819,303	212,141	2,031,444	30.2
Nebraska	1,488	25	2,416,906	201,158	2,618,064	20.3
Nevada	963	49	1,826,672	565,668	2,392,340	14.4
New Hampshire	1,262	44	1,522,250	129,653	1,651,903	20.4
New Jersey.	1,359	37	10,828,458	917,843	11,746,301	16.0
New Mexico	2,110	8	3,750,380	339,455	4,089,835	26.6
New York	2,267	5	39,168,076	4,745,427	43,913,503	20.9
North Carolina	1,497	24	12,183,355	1,055,515	13,238,870	23.1
North Dakota.	2,041	11	1,188,223	110,787	1,299,010	26.3
Ohio	1,575	18	16,120,294	1,930,372	18,050,666	22.3
Oklahoma	1,516	22	5,044,898	363,758	5,408,656	24.1
Oregon	1,472	27	4,610,851	807,192	5,418,043	21.2
Pennsylvania.	1,462	28	15,100,157	3,014,093	18,114,250	20.7
Rhode Island	2,057	9	2,027,665	150,997	2,178,662	25.5
South Carolina	1,565	19	6,463,003	306,380	6,769,383	23.4
South Dakota.	1,756	13	1,235,712	146,907	1,382,619	28.6
Tennessee	1,428	30	8,024,312	638,458	8,662,770	24.0
Texas	1,330	39	27,814,334	3,265,703	31,080,037	21.5
Utah	1,361	36	3,157,491	360,205	3,517,696	20.9
Vermont	2,185	6	1,287,546	67,709	1,355,255	26.5
Virginia.	935	50	6,196,362	938,757	7,135,119	13.9
Washington.	1,381	35	7,438,238	1,346,981	8,785,219	19.1
West Virginia.	1,876	12	3,156,821	233,056	3,389,877	26.7
WISCONSIN	1,279	42	6,487,668	637,170	7,124,838	18.6
Wyoming	3,989	1	1,957,575	87,008	2,044,583	29.1
UNITED STATES	$1,516	1	$397,597,199	$54,636,121	$452,233,320	20.7%

Source: U.S. Department of Commerce, U.S. Census Bureau, "State and Local Government Finances: 2005-06", at:
http://www.census.gov/govs/www/estimate06.html [April 1, 2009] and "Annual Estimates of the Resident Population for
the United States, Regions, States, and Puerto Rico: April 1, 2000 to July 1, 2008 (NST-EST2008-01)",
at: http://www.census.gov/popest/states/NST-ann-est.html [March 18, 2009] (2006 estimates used in calculations).
Per capita amounts, percentages, and rankings calculated by Wisconsin Legislative Reference Bureau.

FEDERAL AIDS TO WISCONSIN
Fiscal Years 2006-07 and 2007-08
(In Thousands)

Agency Administering Aid	Federal Aid Received by Wisconsin		Disbursed to Local Governments		Aid to Individuals and Organizations	
	2007-08	2006-07	2007-08	2006-07	2007-08	2006-07
Administration, Department of . .	$159,520	$157,160	$150,918	$122,560	$4,822	$4,498
Agriculture, Trade and Consumer Protection, Department of	16,825	14,875	—	—	—	—
Arts Board	645	730	—	—	207	247
Child Abuse and Neglect Prevention Board	663	572	—	—	739	584
Circuit Courts	—	—	—	—	—	—
Commerce, Department of.	46,156	50,423	26,342	33,242	11,880	23,773
Corrections, Department of	3,207	1,139	—	—	—	—
Government Accountability Board*	4,026	158	—	—	—	—
Clean Water Fund Program	38,690	38,875	38,690	38,875	—	—
Health and Family Services, Department of	3,989,333	3,782,216	165,937	165,196	3,610,149	3,418,652
Higher Educational Aids Board . .	1,464	1,361	—	—	1,454	1,354
Historical Society	1,003	1,287	—	—	—	—
Insurance, Office of the Commissioner of	—	4,423	—	—	—	4,423
Judicial Council	12	—	—	—	—	—
Justice, Department of	13,409	14,293	7,237	7,008	975	1,150
Medical College of Wisconsin. . .	—	—	—	—	—	—
Military Affairs, Department of . .	51,100	38,658	14,381	5,649	717	54
Natural Resources. Department of	76,231	65,052	6,952	6,115	—	—
People with Developmental Disabilities, Board for	197	—	—	—	—	—
Public Instruction, Department of .	687,958	674,653	590,626	581,063	54,425	47,168
Public Lands Board	41	39	41	39	—	—
Public Service Commission	326	300	—	—	—	—
Regulation and Licensing, Department of	—	—	—	—	—	—
Supreme Court.	514	455	—	—	—	—
Technical College System Board .	30,139	32,650	26,271	29,299	1,075	1,021
Tourism, Department of	36	—	—	—	—	—
Transportation, Department of. . .	731,059	689,591	156,089	188,262	4,621	6,175
University of Wisconsin System. .	1,049,341	972,150	—	—	326,104	302,536
Veterans Affairs, Department of . .	1,709	1,421	—	—	892	687
Workforce Development, Department of	700,181	662,139	52,213	61,539	443,934	462,600
TOTAL.	$7,603,785	$7,204,621	$1,235,699	$1,238,847	$4,461,994	$4,274,922

Note: Aid is not necessarily disbursed in the same fiscal year in which it is received by the agency. In some cases, aid is received as reimbursement for previous expenditures.

*Includes former Elections Board.

Source: Wisconsin Department of Administration, State Controller's Office, *Annual Fiscal Report – Appendix,* October 2007 and October 2008.

STATE AND LOCAL PUBLIC DEBT, BY STATE
State Fiscal Years Ending Between July 1, 2005 and June 30, 2006

State	Debt Outstanding at End of Fiscal Year (in thousands)			Per Capita Debt Outstanding		Per Capita Interest on Debt	Interest as % of Debt
	Total	State	Local	Amount	Rank		
Alabama	$22,310,384	$6,372,976	$15,937,408	$4,863.23	42	$175.81	3.62%
Alaska	9,449,065	6,259,951	3,189,114	13,971.69	1	574.17	4.11
Arizona.	34,654,849	8,410,076	26,244,773	5,609.17	33	211.74	3.77
Arkansas	11,814,963	4,534,205	7,280,758	4,213.31	47	154.56	3.67
California	299,534,303	109,416,606	190,117,697	8,292.46	11	322.16	3.88
Colorado	39,931,671	13,267,266	26,664,405	8,404.06	10	365.46	4.35
Connecticut	32,227,955	24,035,678	8,192,277	9,239.94	4	393.42	4.26
Delaware	6,087,469	4,204,365	1,883,104	7,158.65	19	283.17	3.96
District of Columbia . . .	8,020,359	—	8,020,359	13,700.20	—	545.83	3.98
Florida	119,674,087	29,311,808	90,362,279	6,641.52	24	236.79	3.57
Georgia.	42,086,356	10,493,212	31,593,144	4,516.33	45	121.69	2.69
Hawaii	9,503,975	5,791,783	3,712,192	7,452.55	15	435.20	5.84
Idaho	4,441,932	2,455,293	1,986,639	3,039.96	50	132.58	4.36
ILLINOIS	110,788,132	53,655,358	57,132,774	8,682.68	7	372.14	4.29
Indiana	34,346,922	17,322,486	17,024,436	5,456.98	38	229.01	4.20
IOWA	13,805,614	6,598,342	7,207,272	4,652.63	43	180.12	3.87
Kansas	19,906,619	5,743,506	14,163,113	7,222.31	18	301.75	4.18
Kentucky.	32,480,177	9,775,059	22,705,118	7,734.41	13	300.15	3.88
Louisiana.	24,732,619	11,735,410	12,997,209	5,828.17	29	290.80	4.99
Maine	7,473,265	5,000,296	2,472,969	5,690.21	32	249.93	4.39
Maryland.	30,673,327	16,402,542	14,270,785	5,475.17	37	256.48	4.68
Massachusetts	86,940,283	65,310,233	21,630,050	13,492.87	2	575.88	4.27
MICHIGAN	70,825,250	28,985,739	41,839,511	7,023.61	22	257.55	3.67
MINNESOTA	36,618,230	7,434,990	29,183,240	7,119.83	20	314.21	4.41
Mississippi.	11,161,004	4,870,486	6,290,518	3,852.99	48	160.16	4.16
Missouri	33,957,144	17,668,630	16,288,514	5,821.58	30	265.15	4.55
Montana	5,787,224	4,353,768	1,433,456	6,121.27	26	217.59	3.55
Nebraska	9,335,704	1,844,346	7,491,358	5,305.04	39	138.56	2.61
Nevada	20,581,317	4,050,212	16,531,105	8,284.90	12	283.30	3.42
New Hampshire	9,951,943	7,433,238	2,518,705	7,603.73	14	344.87	4.54
New Jersey.	79,280,686	47,800,663	31,480,023	9,175.77	5	318.37	3.47
New Mexico	10,707,401	6,316,043	4,391,358	5,525.21	35	239.46	4.33
New York	241,407,354	105,306,179	136,101,175	12,464.86	3	460.74	3.70
North Carolina	43,937,611	17,749,382	26,188,229	4,967.32	40	161.49	3.25
North Dakota.	3,486,490	1,770,327	1,716,163	5,478.00	36	266.07	4.86
Ohio	63,657,638	24,713,030	38,944,608	5,555.55	34	268.17	4.83
Oklahoma	15,244,309	8,138,043	7,106,266	4,272.35	46	197.12	4.61
Oregon	26,918,679	11,006,762	15,911,917	7,312.93	17	286.18	3.91
Pennsylvania.	106,041,807	32,121,487	73,920,320	8,560.00	8	347.80	4.06
Rhode Island.	8,944,729	6,964,172	1,980,557	8,446.46	9	324.32	3.84
South Carolina	32,158,974	13,737,148	18,421,826	7,435.95	16	240.35	3.23
South Dakota.	4,560,455	3,146,063	1,414,392	5,791.94	31	215.88	3.73
Tennessee	27,930,502	3,821,278	24,109,224	4,602.69	44	166.00	3.61
Texas.	165,571,764	24,501,385	141,070,379	7,085.55	21	258.49	3.65
Utah	15,326,776	5,931,486	9,395,290	5,928.76	28	172.66	2.91
Vermont	3,853,686	2,982,108	871,578	6,213.66	25	278.12	4.48
Virginia.	46,387,625	17,611,111	28,776,514	6,080.95	27	243.02	4.00
Washington.	56,655,485	18,329,181	38,326,304	8,907.35	6	288.95	3.24
West Virginia.	8,937,021	5,406,391	3,530,630	4,946.44	41	198.15	4.01
WISCONSIN	38,833,679	19,866,204	18,967,475	6,973.81	23	303.99	4.36
Wyoming.	1,947,302	982,753	964,549	3,799.07	49	152.07	4.00
UNITED STATES . .	$2,200,892,115	$870,939,056	$1,329,953,059	$7,376.56		$287.10	3.89%

Sources: U.S. Department of Commerce, U.S. Census Bureau, "State and Local Government Finances: 2005-06", at:
http://www.census.gov/govs/www/estimate06.html and "National and State Population Estimates", at:
http://www.census.gov/popest/states/NST-ann-est.html [March 18, 2009] (2006 estimates used in calculations).
Per capita values and rankings calculated by Wisconsin Legislative Reference Bureau.

PUBLIC INDEBTEDNESS IN WISCONSIN
Outstanding State Indebtedness, May 31, 2009
(In Thousands)

| | Tax Supported Debt | | Revenue Supported Debt[2] | | |
| | General | Segregated | Veterans | | |
Type of Debt[1]	Fund	Funds[3]	Housing	Other[4]	Total
General Obligations – State of Wisconsin	$4,111,161	$407,805	$317,110	$1,016,482	$5,852,558

[1]Amendment of the state constitution in April 1969 permitted direct state borrowing. Previously, debt was incurred through public, nonstock, nonprofit building corporations.

[2]Revenue supported debt includes debt that is issued with initial expectation that revenues and other proceeds from the operation of the programs or facilities financed will amortize the debt without recourse to the general fund.

[3]Includes the Transportation Fund and certain administrative facilities for the Wisconsin Department of Natural Resources.

[4]Includes dormitories, food service, and intercollegiate athletic facilities; certain facilities on the State Fair grounds; and capital equipment.

Source: Wisconsin Department of Administration, Division of Executive Budget and Finance, departmental data, July 2009.

Selected Data on State Indebtedness, 1970 – 2007

| | Outstanding State Indebtedness (Dec. 31) | | As Percent of State Assessed | Annual Debt | Actual Debt | Debt as Percent of |
Calendar Year	Total[1]	Per Capita	Value	Limitation[1,2]	Incurred[1]	Limitation
1970	$646,414	$146.31	1.86%	$260,929	$156,810	60.1%
1975	1,078,215	235.47	1.84	439,124	217,600	49.6
1980	1,916,177	407.18	1.77	813,604	123,500	15.2
1985	2,410,628	507.93	1.96	922,661	440,955	47.8
1990	2,781,071	568.49	1.97	1,060,277	484,099	45.7
1991	3,126,390	631.34	2.07	1,131,958	359,716	31.8
1992	3,065,122	612.41	1.92	1,196,903	427,655	35.7
1993	3,104,055	613.93	1.81	1,287,579	129,325	10.0
1994	3,244,079	636.59	1.75	1,387,461	289,810	20.9
1995	3,305,471	643.46	1.64	1,511,536	368,322	24.4
1996	3,468,447	670.36	1.60	1,627,078	353,295	21.7
1997	3,604,798	693.23	1.55	1,748,057	404,310	23.1
1998	3,751,542	718.41	1.51	1,867,462	475,485	25.5
1999	3,942,659	750.92	1.48	1,999,256	482,360	24.1
2000	4,270,718	796.18	1.49	2,147,411	538,795	25.1
2001	4,452,626	824.26	1.42	2,343,628	485,645	20.7
2002	4,682,045	860.67	1.40	2,514,949	481,000	19.1
2003	4,794,398	876.17	1.33	2,705,327	499,030	18.5
2004	5,116,439	929.59	1.31	2,933,909	664,435	22.6
2005	5,445,615	983.67	1.27	3,209,502	571,990	17.8
2006	5,898,647	1,061.48	1.26	3,517,374	891,285	25.3
2007	5,893,590	1,052.05	1.18	3,734,403	483,280	12.9

[1]In thousands.

[2]An aggregate debt limit is derived for each calendar year through a formula specified in Section 18.05, Wisconsin Statutes.

Source: Wisconsin Department of Administration, Division of Executive Budget and Finance, departmental data, July 2009.

State Revenue Bond Indebtedness, May 31, 2009
(In Thousands)

Program Funded	Amount Authorized	Amount Issued	Amount Outstanding
Student loans	$295,000	$215,000	—
Veterans mortgage loans	280,000	90,055	—
Transportation facilities and highway projects	2,708,341	3,722,503[1]	$1,688,753
Health education loans	92,000	129,230[2]	—
Property tax deferral loans	10,000	—	—
Clean water	1,984,100	1,704,595[3]	773,825
Petroleum environmental cleanup	436,000	483,020[4]	252,300
TOTAL	$5,805,441	$6,344,403	$2,714,878

Note: Revenue bonds are issued for purposes and amounts specifically authorized by the legislature. This debt is not a legal obligation of the state and is not subject to existing debt limitations.

[1]Includes $1,230,367,036 par amount of refunding bonds that do not count against the authorization.

[2]Includes $48,002,520 par amount of refunding bonds that do not count against the authorization.

[3]Includes $423,040,000 par amount of refunding bonds that do not count against the authorization.

[4]Includes $95,470,000 par amount of refunding bonds and $550,000 par amount for issuance expenses that do not count against the authorization.

Source: Wisconsin Department of Administration, Division of Executive Budget and Finance, departmental data, July 2009.

PUBLIC INDEBTEDNESS IN WISCONSIN–Continued
State Authority Indebtedness
(In Thousands)

	Total Outstanding Indebtedness of State Authorities	
Wisconsin Health and Educational Facilities Authority	$7,910,904	(6/30/09)
Wisconsin Housing and Economic Development Authority	$3,029,923	(12/31/08)

Source: Data provided by Authorities, June 2009.

Wisconsin Local Governments, 1955 – 2007
(In Millions)

Unit	1955	1965	1975	1985	1995	2000	2006	2007
Counties	$61.7	$192.5	$261.0	$532.5	$1,221.6	$1,449.2	$1,790.1	$1,788.1
Cities.	175.4	548.1	598.7	1,320.4	2,082.8	2,797.8	3,823.1	3,867.2
Villages	6.1	22.5	69.8	227.6	418.7	700.0	1,187.8	1,256.2
Towns	4.0	9.2	26.2	75.2	193.8	281.0	309.9	321.8
School districts.	62.1	336.6	798.7	448.7	2,104.9	4,314.1	5,208.9	5,434.7
Technical College districts[1] . . .	—	—	97.2	64.7	192.8	329.1	462.6	459.2
TOTAL[2]	$309.4	$1,108.8	$1,851.6	$2,669.0	$6,214.5	$9,871.2	$12,782.4	$13,127.1

Note: Long-term indebtedness includes issues maturing more than one year after date of issue that constitute an obligation of the taxable property in the issuing district.
[1]Technical College districts (previously called Vocational, Technical and Adult Education districts) were included within the municipal bonding statute provisions by Chapter 47, Laws of 1967.
[2]Detail may not add to total due to rounding.
Sources: Wisconsin Department of Revenue, Bureau of Local Financial Assistance, *Indebtedness 1981* and previous issues; *County and Municipal Revenues and Expenditures, 2007* and previous issues; departmental data from Wisconsin Department of Revenue, Wisconsin Department of Public Instruction, and the Wisconsin Technical College System Board (June 2009).

ANNUAL APPROPRIATION OBLIGATIONS
Outstanding, May 31, 2009
(In Thousands)

	Amount Issued	Amount Outstanding
General Fund Annual Appropriation Bonds	$3,386,185	$3,379,710
Master Lease Obligations	121,400	67,552
TOTAL.	$3,507,585	$3,447,232

Note: Appropriation obligations are not general obligations of the state, and they do not constitute "public debt" of the state as that term is used in the Wisconsin Constitution and in the Wisconsin Statutes. The payment of the principal of, and interest on appropriation obligations is subject to annual appropriation. The state is not legally obligated to appropriate any amounts for payment of debt service on the appropriation obligations, and if it does not do so, it incurs no liability to the owners of the appropriation obligations.
Source: Wisconsin Department of Administration, Division of Executive Budget and Finance, departmental data, June 2009.

WISCONSIN GENERAL PROPERTY TAX LEVIES
By Type of Property and Municipality, 2007

Type of Property	Towns	Villages	Cities	Total
Real Estate	**$2,884,265,221**	**$1,466,672,701**	**$4,673,129,232**	**$9,024,067,155**
Residential	2,278,725,633	1,122,707,914	3,200,009,277	6,601,442,824
Commercial	164,604,879	280,504,843	1,299,174,485	1,744,284,208
Manufacturing	24,994,789	55,817,622	169,323,311	250,135,724
Forest lands	120,638,127	1,476,552	577,368	122,692,048
Agricultural	39,842,744	626,544	443,736	40,913,025
Ag. forest.	38,243,928	348,628	121,409	38,713,966
Undeveloped.	24,335,561	961,755	368,256	25,665,573
Other land and improvements	192,879,555	4,228,840	3,111,385	200,219,781
Personal Property	**$33,076,138**	**$33,766,016**	**$159,407,192**	**$226,249,347**
Furniture, fixtures, equipment	8,573,352	15,741,878	80,706,008	105,021,239
Machinery, tools, patterns	14,702,086	13,256,671	51,394,080	79,352,838
Boats and other watercraft	109,355	14,860	134,865	259,081
All other personal property	9,691,344	4,752,604	27,172,238	41,616,187
Total General Property Taxes	**$2,917,341,386**	**$1,500,438,735**	**$4,832,536,325**	**$9,250,316,446**
Total State Tax Credit	246,833,263	108,588,511	316,978,239	672,400,013
TOTAL EFFECTIVE TAXES.	**$2,670,508,123**	**$1,391,850,224**	**$4,515,558,086**	**$8,577,916,433**

Note: The sums of some columns and rows may differ slightly from the reported totals because the Department of Revenue truncates (rather than rounds) amounts under $1 for individual units of government.
Source: Wisconsin Department of Revenue, Division of State and Local Finance, Bureau of Property Tax, *Town, Village, and City Taxes – 2007: Taxes Levied 2007 – Collected 2008,* 2008.

WISCONSIN GENERAL PROPERTY ASSESSMENTS
AND TAX LEVIES
1900 – 2007

Calendar Year	Full Value Assessment of All Property Amount (in millions)	Percent Change	Total State and Local Property Taxes Levied Amount (in millions)	Percent Change	State Property Tax Relief Amount (in millions)	Average Full Value Tax Rate Per $1,000 Rate	Percent Change	Average Net Rate Per $1,000 After State Relief Rate	Percent Change
1900	$630	—	$19	—	—	$30.75	—	—	—
1910	2,743	—	31	—	—	11.18	—	—	—
1920	4,571	—	96	—	—	21.06	—	—	—
1930	5,896	—	121	—	—	20.49	—	—	—
1940	4,354	—	110	—	—	25.26	—	—	—
1950	9,201	—	226	—	—	24.52	—	—	—
1960	18,844	—	481	—	—	25.55	—	—	—
1970	34,790	—	1,179	—	$140	33.88	—	—	—
1980	108,480	—	2,210	—	309	20.37	—	—	—
1990	141,370	6.1%	4,388	7.6%	319	31.04	1.4%	$28.78	2.0%
1991	150,928	6.8	4,733	7.9	319	31.35	1.0	29.24	1.6
1992	159,587	5.7	5,169	9.2	319	32.39	3.3	30.39	3.9
1993	171,677	7.6	5,438	5.2	319	31.67	–2.2	29.81	–1.9
1994	184,995	7.8	5,572	2.5	319	30.12	–4.9	28.39	–4.8
1995	201,538	8.9	5,739	3.0	319	28.47	–5.5	26.89	–5.3
1996	216,944	7.6	5,378	–6.3	469	24.78	–13.0	22.62	–15.9
1997	233,074	7.4	5,636	4.8	469	24.18	–2.8	22.16	–2.0
1998	248,995	6.8	5,975	6.0	469	23.99	–0.8	22.11	–0.2
1999	266,568	7.1	6,191	3.6	469	23.22	–3.2	21.46	–2.9
2000	286,321	7.4	6,605	6.7	469	23.07	–0.7	21.43	–0.2
2001	312,484	9.1	7,044	6.7	469	22.54	–2.3	21.04	–1.8
2002	335,326	7.3	7,364	4.5	469	21.96	–2.6	20.56	–2.3
2003	360,710	7.6	7,687	4.4	469	21.31	–3.0	20.01	–2.7
2004	391,188	8.4	8,151	6.0	469	20.83	–2.2	19.64	–1.9
2005	427,934	9.4	8,327	2.2	469	19.46	–6.6	18.36	–6.5
2006	468,983	9.6	8,706	4.6	593	18.56	–4.6	17.30	–5.8
2007	497,920	6.2	9,251	6.3	672	18.58	0.1	17.23	–0.4

Source: Wisconsin Department of Revenue, Division of State and Local Finance, Bureau of Property Tax, *Town, Village, and City Taxes – 2007: Taxes Levied 2007 – Collected 2008,* 2008, and previous issues. Percentages calculated by Wisconsin Legislative Reference Bureau.

TOTAL MUNICIPAL PROPERTY TAXES LEVIED IN WISCONSIN
1960 – 2007

Year Levied	Total Taxes (in millions)	Residential	Commercial	Manufacturing	Agricultural	Personal[1]	Other[2]
1960	$481.4	47.5%	13.5%	10.7%	11.2%	16.5%	0.6%
1965	664.1	48.4	14.4	10.3	10.6	15.8	0.6
1970	1,179.0	47.3	15.2	10.4	9.7	16.9	0.5
1975	1,601.3	50.5	16.8	5.7	10.1	16.2	0.7
1980	2,210.0	57.7	16.2	4.8	12.5	7.5	1.3
1985	3,203.5	58.9	17.7	4.7	12.4	4.8	1.6
1986	3,489.4	59.6	18.3	4.5	11.0	5.1	1.5
1987	3,499.2	60.3	19.0	4.3	9.7	5.2	1.5
1988	3,755.4	60.3	19.9	4.2	9.0	5.3	1.4
1989	4,078.9	60.3	20.1	4.1	8.7	5.4	1.4
1990	4,388.2	60.4	20.2	4.1	8.4	5.5	1.3
1991	4,732.7	60.9	20.2	4.0	8.1	5.5	1.3
1992	5,169.5	61.7	19.8	4.0	7.9	5.4	1.2
1993	5,438.0	62.7	19.5	3.9	7.5	5.2	1.2
1994	5,572.1	63.8	19.2	3.7	7.1	5.0	1.1
1995	5,738.9	64.8	18.8	3.6	6.7	4.9	1.1
1996	5,378.0	65.7	18.9	3.6	3.6	4.6	3.7
1997	5,635.9	66.2	18.7	3.6	3.3	4.5	3.7
1998	5,975.0	66.5	18.7	3.6	2.9	4.5	3.9
1999	6,190.9	67.3	18.8	3.7	2.7	3.5	4.0
2000	6,604.5	67.9	18.9	3.7	1.7	3.4	4.3
2001	7,043.7	68.1	19.0	3.6	1.6	3.4	4.4
2002	7,363.6	69.0	18.9	3.5	0.8	3.2	4.6
2003	7,687.3	69.7	18.8	3.4	0.6	2.9	4.7
2004	8,150.8	70.3	18.8	3.2	0.5	2.7	4.5
2005	8,326.7	71.0	18.7	3.0	0.5	2.6	4.2
2006	8,706.4	71.4	18.7	2.8	0.5	2.5	4.2
2007	9,250.3	71.4	18.9	2.7	0.4	2.4	4.2

[1]An exemption for "Line A" business property was phased in beginning in 1977. "Line A" property was completely exempted by 1981.

[2]Beginning in 1996, "Other" includes agricultural property not considered agricultural land for the purposes of use value assessment.

Sources: Wisconsin Department of Revenue, Division of State and Local Finance, *Town, Village, and City Taxes – 2007: Taxes Levied 2007 – Collected 2008,* 2008 and previous issues. For 1980 and earlier, *Property Tax, 1981* and previous issues. 1960 and 1965 data are from Wisconsin Department of Taxation. Percentages calculated by Wisconsin Legislative Reference Bureau. Row totals may not add to 100.0% due to rounding.

GENERAL PROPERTY ASSESSMENTS, TAXES AND RATES
By County, 2007

County	Full Value Assessment[1]	Total Property Tax[2]	State Property Tax Credit[3]	Average Full Value Tax Rate per $1,000[4] Gross	Net
Adams	$2,825,672,400	$46,476,041	$2,934,684	$16.45	$15.41
Ashland	1,272,194,800	23,652,136	1,741,452	18.59	17.22
Barron	3,935,741,800	68,769,587	5,026,685	17.47	16.20
Bayfield	2,612,673,700	34,209,125	2,554,187	13.09	12.12
Brown	18,388,879,100	370,811,416	26,444,630	20.16	18.73
Buffalo	938,069,200	18,357,372	1,258,822	19.57	18.23
Burnett	2,920,020,900	36,983,766	3,165,917	12.67	11.58
Calumet	3,258,815,600	65,356,230	4,476,231	20.06	18.68
Chippewa	4,297,207,000	70,164,012	5,804,687	16.33	14.98
Clark	1,679,530,800	35,777,812	2,341,979	21.30	19.91
Columbia	5,088,614,700	92,149,006	6,908,611	18.11	16.75
Crawford	1,083,222,500	24,127,143	1,561,063	22.27	20.83
Dane	50,114,197,800	971,850,003	77,658,992	19.39	17.84
Dodge	6,094,768,500	119,880,126	8,252,132	19.67	18.32
Door	7,185,361,600	83,758,197	5,234,054	11.66	10.93
Douglas	3,292,211,900	56,976,370	4,085,258	17.31	16.07
Dunn	2,806,515,000	58,596,573	4,108,114	20.88	19.41
Eau Claire	6,454,280,300	129,494,337	10,781,500	20.06	18.39
Florence	576,640,500	10,708,713	803,437	18.57	17.18
Fond du Lac	6,733,229,200	131,967,950	8,988,519	19.60	18.26
Forest	1,135,240,000	18,038,723	1,541,579	15.89	14.53
Grant	2,598,570,900	52,406,331	3,627,292	20.17	18.77
Green	2,612,647,300	57,441,629	4,034,430	21.99	20.44
Green Lake	2,297,614,200	38,194,511	2,738,657	16.62	15.43
Iowa	1,828,317,900	38,869,596	2,947,863	21.26	19.65
Iron	973,139,300	14,229,137	1,092,144	14.62	13.50
Jackson	1,302,415,000	25,115,368	1,622,605	19.28	18.04
Jefferson	6,676,844,000	117,796,256	8,763,744	17.64	16.33
Juneau	2,052,223,500	39,561,204	2,858,594	19.28	17.88
Kenosha	14,640,280,200	275,866,203	19,110,145	18.84	17.54
Kewaunee	1,410,393,500	26,159,842	1,896,947	18.55	17.20
La Crosse	7,642,785,200	167,768,711	11,843,631	21.95	20.40
Lafayette	886,238,800	20,723,839	1,359,174	23.38	21.85
Langlade	1,677,862,700	28,722,846	2,228,187	17.12	15.79
Lincoln	2,304,073,100	41,837,737	3,046,792	18.16	16.84
Manitowoc	5,079,420,500	101,463,887	7,029,281	19.98	18.59
Marathon	9,495,029,700	201,650,439	13,125,559	21.24	19.86
Marinette	3,701,536,800	60,686,508	5,130,789	16.39	15.01
Marquette	1,533,891,900	25,830,520	1,830,077	16.84	15.65
Menominee	285,550,500	6,412,087	415,911	22.46	21.00
Milwaukee	67,119,283,700	1,514,095,092	91,961,873	22.56	21.19
Monroe	2,469,779,000	53,179,672	3,187,695	21.53	20.24
Oconto	3,528,606,900	59,667,517	4,740,602	16.91	15.57
Oneida	7,285,470,000	87,485,118	7,661,911	12.01	10.96
Outagamie	12,846,626,500	251,807,771	17,335,035	19.60	18.25
Ozaukee	11,298,570,500	186,118,202	16,329,780	16.47	15.03
Pepin	541,884,500	11,467,626	821,956	21.16	19.65
Pierce	3,213,431,800	59,188,611	4,524,781	18.42	17.01
Polk	4,989,035,500	81,464,142	6,374,549	16.33	15.05
Portage	4,738,653,800	93,061,019	6,339,776	19.64	18.30
Price	1,461,100,100	24,999,891	1,815,885	17.11	15.87
Racine	15,659,760,100	290,222,286	19,055,355	18.53	17.32
Richland	1,073,360,000	22,513,975	1,741,782	20.98	19.35
Rock	10,165,219,400	215,961,654	14,156,402	21.25	19.85
Rusk	1,166,267,100	19,886,290	1,843,562	17.05	15.47
St. Croix	8,604,072,400	134,729,187	11,107,863	15.66	14.37
Sauk	6,759,981,800	114,502,834	8,000,066	16.94	15.75
Sawyer	3,827,416,800	40,327,132	3,696,989	10.54	9.57
Shawano	2,899,081,900	50,863,207	3,723,960	17.54	16.26
Sheboygan	8,917,700,600	180,657,128	12,384,922	20.26	18.87
Taylor	1,278,609,100	24,318,175	1,632,026	19.02	17.74
Trempealeau	1,659,035,900	35,307,716	2,276,209	21.28	19.91
Vernon	1,668,824,800	34,425,526	2,393,037	20.63	19.19
Vilas	7,686,161,200	71,690,406	6,894,959	9.33	8.43
Walworth	14,599,872,200	232,039,363	17,868,632	15.89	14.67
Washburn	2,665,557,600	37,993,808	2,642,060	14.25	13.26
Washington	13,661,989,000	223,752,483	17,406,873	16.38	15.10
Waukesha	51,988,144,000	831,893,245	74,774,939	16.00	14.56
Waupaca	3,803,179,600	75,114,270	5,205,868	19.75	18.38
Waushara	2,489,838,400	41,679,585	3,155,058	16.74	15.47
Winnebago	11,601,104,500	246,984,005	14,963,717	21.29	20.00
Wood	4,560,800,700	94,078,221	6,007,536	20.63	19.31
TOTAL	$497,920,348,700	$9,250,316,446	$672,400,013	$18.58	$17.23

[1]Reflects actual market value of all taxable general property, as determined by the Wisconsin Department of Revenue independent of locally assessed values, which vary substantially from full value – from 50.05% (Village of Dousman, Waukesha County) to 116.04% (Town of Ahnapee, Kewaunee County). (The ratio was 234.66% for the Clark County portion of the City of Stanley, population – 7.)

[2]Includes taxes and special charges levied by schools, counties, cities, villages, towns, special purpose districts, and the State of Wisconsin.

[3]Total amount of general property tax credit paid by the state to taxing districts and credited to taxpayers on their tax bills.

[4]A county's average tax rate per $1,000 of assessed valuation (determined by dividing total taxes by equalized value and multiplying by 1,000) is the preferred figure for comparison purposes, rather than the general local property tax rate because the average is based on full market value. Net tax rate per $1,000 reflects the effect of state property tax relief.

Source: Wisconsin Department of Revenue, Division of State and Local Finance, *Town, Village, and City Taxes — 2007: Taxes Levied 2007 — Collected 2008*, 2008.

HIGHLIGHTS OF TRANSPORTATION IN WISCONSIN

Roads — As of January 1, 2008, there were 114,705 miles of roads in Wisconsin. The total included 11,769 miles of state trunk highways, 19,868 miles of county trunk highways, and 81,324 miles of local roads. Over 78% of Wisconsin roads, constituting 89,888 miles, have a bituminous surface.

Motor Vehicles and Drivers — Over the decades, the total number of motor vehicle registrations has increased from 819,718 in 1930 to 5,499,872 in 2008. Of 4,075,764 drivers licensed in 2007, 688,707 (16.9%) were 25-34 years old; 742,130 (18.2%) were 35-44 years old; 829,772 (20.4%) were 45-54 years old; 610,064 (15.0%) were 55-64 years old. Of the drivers age 65 and older, 67,811 (1.7%) were 85 years and above.

In 2007, 125,123 single- or multi-vehicle traffic crashes were reported, including 655 fatal and 36,048 injury crashes. The 16-year-old-age group had the highest percentage of drivers involved in crashes with 15.1%, followed by the 17-year-old group with 11.8%. Of 511 drivers killed in fatal crashes, 456 were tested for blood alcohol content (BAC). Of all drivers involved in fatal crashes, 30 registered a BAC of 0.001 to 0.079 and 188 of them registered a BAC of 0.08% or above. Vehicle miles traveled in 2007 totaled 59.5 billion; the fatality rate for that year was 1.24 per 100 million vehicle miles, and the fatal crash rate was 1.10.

Mass Transit — As of January 2009, there were 24 urban bus systems operating in Wisconsin (22 publicly owned and 2 privately owned). There were 11 rural/intercity systems (5 publicly owned and 6 privately contracted). In 43 municipalities, shared-ride taxi service was available.

Statewide urban bus systems showed an increase in usage in 2007 with 51.8 million revenue miles traveled and 81.2 million revenue passengers.

Air Carriers — In 2008, there were 726 airports operating in Wisconsin. Of these, 98 were publicly owned and 415 privately owned. The remaining 211 specialized facilities included heliports (146), seaplane bases (27), and military/police fields (6). In 2008, certificated air carriers carried 5,739,204 passengers and transported 119,407,691 pounds of cargo.

Railroads — Since 1920, the number of railroads operating in Wisconsin has decreased from 35 to 12. Over the same period, railroad road mileage declined to 3,417 miles. Rail freight traffic rose from 9.1 billion ton-miles in 1920 to 23.0 billion ton-miles in 2008, and revenue rose from $92,826 million in 1920 to $784,264 million in 2008.

Harbors — In 2007, there were 10 active lake harbors on Lake Michigan and Lake Superior, which handled 54.1 million short tons of commodities. The Duluth-Superior harbor reported the greatest amount of commerce at 46.5 million tons.

The following tables present selected data. Consult footnoted sources for more detailed information about transportation.

WISCONSIN AIRPORTS
by Type, 2002 – 2008

Type of Airport	Number of Airports						
	2002	2003	2004	2005	2006	2007	2008
Publicly owned airports	97	99	99	97	97	98	98
Scheduled air carrier airports	(9)	(8)	(8)	(8)	(8)	(8)	(8)
All other publicly owned or operated airports.	(88)	(91)	(91)	(89)	(89)	(90)	(90)
Privately owned airports open to the public	37	35	35	33	34	34	34
Private use airports.	407	403	405	402	403	415	415
Heliports	132	136	139	140	139	141	146
Seaplane bases	27	25	26	26	26	28	27
Military/police fields and helipads.	7	7	7	7	7	7	6
TOTAL.	700	705	711	705	706	723	726

Source: Wisconsin Department of Transportation, *2008 Wisconsin Aviation Activity*, at: http://www.dot.wisconsin.gov/travel/air/activity.htm [April 2009].

WISCONSIN AIRPORT USAGE
BY CERTIFIED AIR CARRIERS, 2006 – 2008*

Airport (location)	2006 Passengers[1]	2006 Cargo (lbs.)[2]	2007 Passengers[1]	2007 Cargo (lbs.)[2]	2008 Passengers[1]	2008 Cargo (lbs.)[2]
General Mitchell International (Milwaukee)	3,641,503	92,585,706	3,868,098	90,088,838	4,000,765	95,203,653
Dane County Regional (Madison) . . .	796,032	11,679,897	785,546	12,067,790	739,729	10,986,951
Austin Straubel International (Green Bay)	455,514	494,552	450,472	373,720	423,504	184,705
Outagamie County Regional (Appleton)	289,116	9,268,397	295,058	9,520,816	258,510	10,433,062
Central Wisconsin (Mosinee)	161,697	1,982,628	160,380	1,580,387	157,850	1,308,437
La Crosse Municipal (La Crosse) . . .	119,897	—	125,476	—	115,014	—
Rhinelander-Oneida County (Rhinelander)	38,820	1,543,978	36,002	1,353,251	25,674	1,117,049
Chippewa Valley Regional (Eau Claire)	22,832	—	22,193	—	18,158	—
Southern Wisconsin Regional (Janesville)	—	504,333	—	1,284,908	—	173,834
TOTAL	5,525,411	118,059,491	5,743,225	116,269,710	5,739,204	119,407,691

*Certified air carrier is an airline that is registered by the Federal Aviation Administration.

[1]Beginning in 1965, the passenger count includes originating, stopover, and transfer revenue passengers. Prior to that, only those revenue passengers boarding aircraft at point of origin were counted.

[2]Cargo loaded at the point of origin or transferred cargo from the point of origin.

Source: Wisconsin Department of Transportation, *2008 Wisconsin Aviation Activity,* at: http://www.dot.wisconsin.gov/travel/air/activity.htm [March 2009].

RAILROAD MILEAGE, USAGE, AND REVENUE IN WISCONSIN
1920 – 2008

Year	No. of Railroads	Mileage Operated in Wisconsin[1] Road[2]	Mileage Operated in Wisconsin[1] Track[3]	Freight Traffic (in thousands) Tons	Freight Traffic (in thousands) Ton-Miles[4]	Freight Traffic (in thousands) Revenue (in thousands)	Passenger Traffic (in thousands) Passengers	Passenger Traffic (in thousands) Miles[5]	Passenger Traffic (in thousands) Revenue (in thousands)
1920	35	7,546	11,615	100,991	9,052,084	$92,826	20,188	960,569	$28,646
1930	27	7,231	11,583	83,672	6,908,656	78,747	4,799	466,154	14,071
1940	22	6,646	10,484	87,980	6,910,647	69,941	3,952	445,938	8,201
1950	20	6,337	10,000	121,576	10,850,178	141,762	5,575	646,353	14,933
1960	18	6,195	9,625	93,475	9,096,855	134,065	3,127	383,457	9,800
1970	15	5,965	9,127	97,130	13,432,055	191,764	1,463	138,572	4,264
1980[6]	21	5,192	7,990	101,008	14,727,522	453,977	174	1,122	54
1990	15	4,415	6,125	116,099	14,436,776	455,541	112	783	63
2000	12	3,548	4,956	151,573	21,321,266	580,678	NA	NA	NA
2001	13	3,699	5,107	158,881	25,922,949	700,258	NA	NA	NA
2002	12	3,688	5,095	NA	21,417,016	704,167	NA	NA	NA
2003	11	3,450	4,643	118,387	26,092,960	667,736	NA	NA	NA
2004	11	3,417	4,610	106,719	27,408,816	713,951	NA	NA	NA
2005	11	3,417	4,614	109,214	27,966,142	715,206	NA	NA	NA
2006	12	3,432	4,634	114,609	28,024,633	717,421	NA	NA	NA
2007	12	3,430	4,585	109,210	22,942,906	737,119	NA	NA	NA
2008	12	3,417	4,560	109,207	22,906,152	784,264	NA	NA	NA

NA – Not available.

[1]In order to avoid duplication, mileage shown is exclusive of trackage rights.

[2]Road mileage is the measurement of stone roadbed in miles.

[3]Track mileage is the measurement of track (2 steel rails) on roadbeds in miles.

[4]A ton-mile is the movement of one ton (2,000 pounds) of cargo over the distance of one mile.

[5]Passenger miles are the combination of the number of passengers carried on Wisconsin trains and the miles traveled by the passengers while within Wisconsin boundaries.

[6]Intercity passenger service operated by Amtrak after May 1, 1971.

Source: Office of the Wisconsin Commissioner of Railroads, departmental data, June 2009.

HIGHWAY MILEAGE, BY COUNTY AND SYSTEM
January 1, 2008

County	Total All Systems	State Trunk System	County Trunk System	Local Roads (City, Village, Town)	Other Roads (Parks, Forests)
Adams	1,451.63	91.46	227.09	1,131.88	1.20
Ashland	1,170.98	120.06	93.82	872.50	84.60
Barron	1,993.56	141.78	290.74	1,559.94	1.10
Bayfield	2,200.80	155.09	172.81	1,777.23	95.67
Brown	2,336.31	184.97	358.68	1,768.86	23.80
Buffalo	1,042.84	147.85	317.98	577.01	—
Burnett	1,574.60	106.39	220.20	1,204.34	43.67
Calumet	860.84	93.70	135.45	631.69	—
Chippewa	2,131.71	210.38	489.61	1,410.28	21.44
Clark	2,195.42	157.37	300.87	1,681.09	56.09
Columbia	1,735.48	278.04	357.29	1,100.15	—
Crawford	1,080.81	180.13	132.93	764.75	3.00
Dane	4,091.07	401.81	538.92	3,149.64	0.70
Dodge	2,047.26	236.92	539.15	1,271.19	—
Door	1,252.66	101.95	279.26	871.45	—
Douglas	2,091.58	161.76	337.09	1,496.35	96.38
Dunn	1,753.96	205.75	425.41	1,122.80	—
Eau Claire	1,585.53	150.41	421.02	995.26	18.84
Florence	529.07	66.84	49.18	376.66	36.39
Fond du Lac	1,782.23	206.15	380.48	1,195.41	0.19
Forest	1,058.46	152.52	109.01	775.73	21.20
Grant	2,121.37	258.85	310.96	1,551.56	—
Green	1,257.68	122.52	278.66	856.50	—
Green Lake	703.24	69.98	228.87	404.39	—
Iowa	1,315.90	169.72	364.72	781.46	—
Iron	753.61	114.00	66.89	553.52	19.20
Jackson	1,527.21	185.98	231.33	1,036.53	73.37
Jefferson	1,432.53	179.56	258.07	984.57	10.33
Juneau	1,527.17	191.87	234.22	1,085.09	15.99
Kenosha	1,092.85	117.20	262.86	712.79	—
Kewaunee	827.14	61.76	217.60	547.60	0.18
La Crosse	1,190.56	159.17	284.81	745.68	0.90
Lafayette	1,157.88	126.92	272.29	758.67	—
Langlade	1,150.71	142.48	271.08	729.48	7.67
Lincoln	1,320.42	155.45	270.18	865.54	29.25
Manitowoc	1,658.84	155.12	285.52	1,218.20	—
Marathon	3,364.61	275.86	613.45	2,463.32	11.98
Marinette	2,344.00	153.78	341.65	1,624.41	224.16
Marquette	859.64	87.13	237.28	535.23	—
Menominee	453.54	40.68	36.51	79.05	297.30
Milwaukee	3,014.74	253.18	145.37	2,613.22	2.97
Monroe	1,648.07	238.22	344.28	1,061.27	4.30
Oconto	2,032.97	149.50	313.42	1,531.97	38.08
Oneida	1,711.26	159.73	172.24	1,342.51	36.78
Outagamie	1,990.82	187.18	347.81	1,452.33	3.50
Ozaukee	937.11	82.28	152.07	702.76	—
Pepin	462.08	48.52	154.80	258.76	—
Pierce	1,302.30	165.00	248.65	888.65	—
Polk	1,984.99	159.15	331.36	1,478.77	15.71
Portage	1,880.74	156.62	426.32	1,297.80	—
Price	1,439.77	154.87	220.04	1,049.74	15.12
Racine	1,324.81	159.95	162.47	1,002.39	—
Richland	1,132.15	150.20	296.50	681.45	4.00
Rock	2,066.03	251.97	213.39	1,600.67	—
Rusk	1,240.57	105.26	255.09	859.42	20.80
St. Croix	1,922.94	204.10	338.64	1,380.20	—
Sauk	1,816.61	220.75	302.60	1,284.96	8.30
Sawyer	1,512.86	161.33	229.01	1,095.03	27.49
Shawano	1,828.92	179.04	293.28	1,250.36	106.24
Sheboygan	1,554.68	166.67	451.02	936.99	—
Taylor	1,455.24	110.21	248.30	1,079.37	17.36
Trempealeau	1,355.42	176.31	292.03	887.08	—
Vernon	1,652.00	214.01	285.26	1,147.53	5.20
Vilas	1,598.69	136.29	204.17	1,131.63	126.60
Walworth	1,518.84	215.59	199.50	1,103.75	—
Washburn	1,410.56	137.10	198.74	979.42	95.30
Washington	1,528.35	187.29	185.63	1,155.43	—
Waukesha	3,033.75	236.10	397.52	2,400.13	—
Waupaca	1,660.33	198.61	335.72	1,126.00	—
Waushara	1,331.35	132.32	333.56	865.47	—
Winnebago	1,553.74	168.82	220.41	1,164.51	—
Wood	1,776.65	183.85	324.60	1,246.98	21.22
STATE	114,705.04	11,769.38	19,867.74	81,324.35	1,743.57

Source: Wisconsin Department of Transportation, Division of Transportation Investment Management, departmental data, March 2009.

WISCONSIN ROAD MILEAGE, BY SYSTEM AND SURFACE TYPE
January 1, 2008

Type of Road System	Miles	Percent	Surface Type	Miles	Percent
State trunk highways.	11,769	10.3%	Bituminous or higher*	89,888	78.4%
County trunk highways	19,868	17.3	Gravel or soil-surfaced.	16,724	14.6
City streets	13,571	11.8	Sealcoat	5,154	4.5
Village streets	5,612	4.9	Graded and drained	2,767	2.4
Town roads.	62,141	54.2	Unimproved	172	0.1
Park, forest, and other roads	1,744	1.5	TOTAL.	114,705	100.0%
TOTAL	114,705	100.0%			

*Bituminous or higher includes 3,210 surface types.

Source: Wisconsin Department of Transportation, Division of Transportation Investment Management, departmental data, March 2009.

MOTOR VEHICLES IN WISCONSIN, BY TYPE
1930 – 2008

Fiscal Year (ending June 30)	Total	Autos	Trucks*	Trailers, Semitrailers	Motor Homes	Buses	Motor-cycles	Mopeds
1930	819,718	700,251	115,883	—	—	554	3,030	—
1935	722,797	597,197	116,912	5,634	—	498	2,556	—
1940	874,652	741,583	123,742	5,144	—	675	3,508	—
1945	828,425	676,978	139,591	6,484	—	1,489	3,883	—
1950	1,157,221	921,194	209,083	14,124	—	2,465	10,355	—
1955	1,369,636	1,108,084	227,367	21,643	—	3,337	9,205	—
1960	1,598,693	1,303,679	246,353	31,502	—	5,184	11,975	—
1965	1,867,223	1,517,397	269,771	44,017	—	7,218	28,820	—
1970	2,205,662	1,762,681	317,096	64,065	—	8,178	53,642	—
1975	2,737,164	2,096,694	425,854	91,609	—	11,897	111,110	—
1980	3,417,748	2,509,904	558,840	102,256	17,071	13,775	205,786	10,116
1985	3,372,029	2,310,024	765,852	72,289	17,195	10,325	176,023	20,321
1990	3,834,608	2,456,175	1,045,583	123,061	21,095	15,081	149,268	24,345
1995	4,285,753	2,464,358	1,391,374	207,042	22,554	15,593	161,762	23,070
2000	4,703,294	2,405,408	1,813,385	214,344	24,427	15,587	160,920	17,977
2003	5,091,716	2,401,816	2,094,464	252,352	25,022	17,555	215,225	24,597
2004	5,170,728	2,387,459	2,167,503	279,843	25,258	14,099	207,586	24,519
2005	5,226,584	2,347,042	2,216,863	342,879	22,598	12,478	249,979	34,745
2006	5,326,157	2,361,853	2,281,988	364,024	22,406	13,174	246,307	36,405
2007	5,428,629	2,357,616	2,333,538	396,229	21,147	13,516	266,036	40,547
2008	5,499,872	2,381,911	2,370,655	410,737	20,209	10,736	260,220	45,404

*"Trucks" includes minivans and sport utility vehicles.

Sources: Wisconsin Secretary of State, *Biennial Report – 1928-30;* Wisconsin Highway Commission, *Biennial Reports – 1933-35, 1938-40;* Wisconsin Motor Vehicle Department, *Wisconsin Motor Vehicle Registrations – Fiscal Years 1944-45 through 1964-65;* Wisconsin Department of Transportation, *Wisconsin Motor Vehicle Registrations – Fiscal Year 1979-80, 1980,* and previous issues, and *Wisconsin Transportation Facts* (periodical); departmental data, March 2009.

WISCONSIN MOTOR VEHICLE CRASHES
Statistical Summary, 1997 – 2007

Year	Total Licensed Drivers	Crashes[1] Total	Fatal	Injury	Persons Killed	Persons Injured	Miles Traveled (in millions)	Fatality Rate[2]	Fatal Crash Rate
1997	3,672,469	129,954	631	41,962	721	63,166	53,729	1.34	1.17
1998	3,709,957	125,831	628	41,594	709	62,236	56,048	1.26	1.12
1999	3,733,077	130,950	674	41,345	744	61,577	56,960	1.31	1.18
2000	3,667,497	139,510	718	43,145	801	63,890	57,266	1.40	1.25
2001	3,835,549	125,403	684	39,358	764	58,279	57,266	1.33	1.19
2002	3,839,930	129,072	723	39,634	805	57,776	58,745	1.37	1.23
2003	3,933,924	131,191	748	39,413	836	56,882	59,617	1.40	1.25
2004	3,993,348	128,308	714	38,451	784	55,258	60,398	1.31	1.18
2005	4,049,450	125,174	700	37,515	801	53,462	60,018	1.33	1.17
2006	4,066,273	117,877	659	35,296	712	50,236	59,401	1.20	1.11
2007	4,075,764	125,123	655	36,048	737	50,676	59,493	1.24	1.10

[1]A motor vehicle crash is defined as an event caused by a single variable or chain of variables. Property damage threshold for a reportable crash was raised from $500 to $1,000, effective January 1, 1996.

[2]Per 100-million vehicle miles traveled.

Source: Wisconsin Department of Transportation, *2007 Wisconsin Traffic Crash Facts,* December 2008, and previous issues.

Fatal Crashes on Wisconsin Highways and Roads, 1997 – 2007

Year	Total	Interstate	State	County	Local
1997	631	32	303	132	164
1998	628	35	297	156	140
1999	674	41	301	164	168
2000	718	39	311	143	225
2001	684	35	286	167	196
2002	723	44	310	171	198
2003	748	46	317	174	211
2004	714	47	298	155	214
2005	700	42	284	163	211
2006	659	34	294	128	203
2007	655	43	259	143	210

Source: Wisconsin Department of Transportation, *2007 Wisconsin Traffic Crash Facts,* December 2008, and previous issues.

Drivers in Fatal Crashes – Age and BAC of Drivers Killed, 2007

Age of Drivers	All Drivers	Drivers Killed	Tests of Drivers Killed[1] Total	Negative	Positive	Blood Alcohol Concentration (BAC) 0.001-0.079	0.08 and over
14 years and under . . .	2	1	0	0	0	0	0
15 years	4	2	2	0	2	2	0
16 years	19	10	10	5	5	2	3
17 years	20	8	8	7	1	0	1
18 years	41	21	20	11	9	2	7
19 years	25	11	10	2	7	2	5
20 years	31	12	9	3	6	0	6
21 years	24	14	12	4	8	0	8
22 years	33	21	19	5	14	1	13
23 years	32	19	17	5	12	0	12
24 years	31	14	13	5	8	0	8
25-34 years.	180	91	83	23	59	7	52
35-44 years.	163	74	69	32	37	4	33
45-54 years.	165	85	79	45	34	5	29
55-64 years.	115	58	54	39	15	4	11
65-74 years.	47	28	20	19	0	0	0
75-84 years.	43	31	23	22	1	1	0
85 and over.	14	11	8	8	0	0	0
TOTAL.	1,023[2]	511	456	235	218	30	188

Note: Drivers include motorcycle and moped drivers.

[1]Blood Alcohol Concentration (BAC) measures the level of alcohol in a person's bloodstream. The prohibited BAC for Operating While Intoxicated (OWI) is 0.08%.

[2]Includes 33 of unknown age.

Source: Wisconsin Department of Transportation, *2007 Wisconsin Traffic Crash Facts,* December 2008.

WISCONSIN MOTOR VEHICLE CRASHES–Continued
Motorcycle Crashes, 1997 – 2007

Year	Total Registered Cycles	Cycle Crashes				Cyclist Fatalities*		
		Total	Fatal	Injury	Property Damage	Total	No Helmet or Unknown	Helmet
1997	167,997	1,760	59	1,487	214	63	52	11
1998	157,230	1,989	63	1,691	235	65	51	14
1999	179,494	2,012	61	1,720	231	65	46	17
2000	175,486	2,078	76	1,760	242	78	57	15
2001	201,143	2,285	69	1,928	288	70	53	14
2002	198,495	2,184	73	1,794	317	78	59	15
2003	225,181	2,512	98	2,099	315	100	74	24
2004	221,982	2,423	81	2,015	327	80	60	18
2005	239,938	2,680	91	2,277	312	92	69	22
2006	291,534	2,441	88	2,065	288	93	69	24
2007	322,505	2,788	102	2,331	355	106	70	26

*Number of cyclists killed includes both drivers and passengers.

Source: Wisconsin Department of Transportation, *2007 Wisconsin Traffic Crash Facts,* December 2008, and previous issues.

Drivers Involved in Crashes, By Age Group, 2007

Age of Drivers	Total Licensed Drivers		Drivers Involved in Crashes*		Drivers by Type of Crash*		
	Number	Age Group as Percent of Total Drivers	Number	Percent of Total Drivers in Crashes	Fatal	Injury	Property Damage
14 years and under . . .	0	0.0%	113	—	2	38	73
15 years	0	0.0	298	—	4	108	186
16 years	36,522	0.9	5,504	15.1%	19	1,762	3,723
17 years	54,868	1.3	6,467	11.8	20	2,123	4,324
18 years	61,489	1.5	6,896	11.2	41	2,275	4,580
19 years	62,001	1.5	6,066	9.8	25	2,069	3,972
20 years	65,886	1.6	5,766	8.8	31	1,911	3,824
21 years	68,961	1.7	5,846	8.5	24	1,916	3,906
22 years	71,728	1.8	5,469	7.6	33	1,793	3,643
23 years	72,442	1.8	5,071	7.0	32	1,604	3,435
24 years	72,842	1.8	4,866	6.7	31	1,600	3,235
25-34 years.	688,707	16.9	36,801	5.3	180	11,873	24,748
35-44 years.	742,130	18.2	33,275	4.5	163	10,635	22,477
45-54 years.	829,772	20.4	31,108	3.7	165	10,002	20,941
55-64 years.	610,064	15.0	18,917	3.1	115	6,006	12,796
65-74 years.	347,973	8.5	8,300	2.4	47	2,689	5,564
75-84 years.	222,568	5.5	5,117	2.3	43	1,685	3,389
85 and over.	67,811	1.7	1,288	1.9	14	430	844
Unknown.	0	0.0	19,414	—	34	2,866	16,514
TOTAL.	4,075,764	100.0%	206,582	NA	1,023	63,385	142,174

NA – Not applicable.

*Figure indicates the number of times a driver in this age group was involved in a crash. If a driver had more than one crash, the driver is counted more than once.

Source: Wisconsin Department of Transportation, *2007 Wisconsin Traffic Crash Facts,* December 2008.

WISCONSIN MOTOR VEHICLE CRASHES–Continued
Possible Contributing Circumstances, 2007

Circumstance by category	All Crashes				Urban Crashes				Rural Crashes			
	Total	Fatal	Injury	Property Damage	Total	Fatal	Injury	Property Damage	Total	Fatal	Injury	Property Damage
DRIVER												
Inattentive driving	24,581	133	8,742	15,706	14,666	31	4,879	9,756	9,915	102	3,863	5,950
Failure to have control	23,025	269	7,996	14,760	9,690	50	2,848	6,792	13,335	219	5,148	7,968
Failure to yield right-of-way	20,853	88	8,284	12,481	15,450	26	5,913	9,511	5,403	62	2,371	2,970
Speed too fast for conditions	17,420	121	5,380	11,919	6,961	23	1,914	5,024	10,459	98	3,466	6,895
Following too close	9,850	10	3,521	6,319	7,167	4	2,557	4,606	2,683	6	964	1,713
Driver condition	8,311	169	4,060	4,082	4,001	49	1,729	2,223	4,310	120	2,331	1,859
Disregarded traffic control	5,991	43	2,792	3,156	4,901	9	2,286	2,606	1,090	34	506	550
Improper turn	3,855	5	800	3,050	2,849	1	516	2,332	1,006	4	284	718
Exceeding speed limit	3,769	144	1,727	1,898	2,117	57	882	1,178	1,652	87	845	720
Unsafe backing	3,273	4	223	3,046	2,135	3	152	1,980	1,138	1	71	1,066
Left of center	2,355	92	1,041	1,222	697	4	264	429	1,658	88	777	793
Improper overtake	1,869	14	441	1,414	1,086	5	223	858	783	9	218	556
Physically disabled	146	2	78	66	92	0	51	41	54	2	27	25
Other	5,745	39	1,693	4,013	4,188	14	1,200	2,974	1,557	25	493	1,039
HIGHWAY												
Snow/ice/wet	32,028	150	8,909	22,969	16,133	24	4,319	11,790	15,895	126	4,590	11,179
Visibility obscured	2,505	17	975	1,513	1,518	6	592	920	987	11	383	593
Constructions zone	1,342	8	394	940	867	0	261	606	475	8	133	334
Loose gravel	596	5	308	283	95	0	47	48	501	5	261	235
Other debris	501	0	122	379	163	0	42	121	338	0	80	258
Narrow shoulder	246	7	86	153	33	0	6	27	213	7	80	126
Soft shoulder	139	0	64	73	14	0	3	11	125	0	61	62
Debris from prior crash	127	2	53	72	41	0	20	21	86	2	33	51
Low shoulder	114	2	46	66	14	0	4	10	100	2	42	56
Sign obscured or missing	80	0	29	51	66	0	25	41	14	0	4	10
Rough pavement	71	1	31	39	35	0	18	17	36	1	13	22
Narrow bridge	40	0	26	14	19	0	16	3	21	0	10	11
Other debris	989	5	352	632	509	1	158	350	480	4	194	282
VEHICLE												
Tires	1,276	18	419	839	433	3	119	311	843	15	300	528
Brakes	1,180	7	409	764	724	1	259	464	456	6	150	300
Steering	333	0	96	237	196	0	50	146	137	0	46	91
Turn signals	96	1	22	73	36	0	7	29	60	1	15	44
Other disabled	114	3	38	73	66	1	23	42	48	2	15	31
Disabled prior to crash	83	0	33	50	39	0	13	26	44	0	20	24
Head lamps	79	2	37	40	45	0	21	24	34	2	16	16
Stop lamps	68	1	24	43	35	0	12	23	33	1	12	20
Suspension	60	0	19	41	26	0	7	19	34	0	12	22
Tail lamps	50	1	24	25	16	0	6	4	34	1	18	21
Mirrors	49	0	10	39	16	0	2	14	33	0	8	25
Other	1,546	5	288	1,253	767	2	150	615	779	3	138	638

Note: Numbers represent the number of times a possible contributing circumstance was cited and not number of accidents.

Source: Wisconsin Department of Transportation, *2007 Wisconsin Traffic Crash Facts*, December 2008.

MASS TRANSIT SYSTEMS IN WISCONSIN, BY TYPE,
January 2009

Urban Bus	Rural/Intercity Bus	Shared-Ride Taxi[1]	
Appleton	Adams County Transit[3]	Baraboo	Plover
Bay Area Transit (Ashland)	Bad River Transit	Beaver Dam	Portage
Beloit	Door County Transit	Berlin	Port Washington
Eau Claire	La Crosse[3]	Black River Falls	Prairie du Chien
Fond du Lac	Marshfield Shuttle[3]	Chippewa Falls	Prairie du Sac
Green Bay[2]	Menominee Indian Reservation	Clintonville	Reedsburg
Janesville	Oneida Indian Reservation	Edgerton	Rhinelander
Kenosha	Ozaukee County Express[3]	Fort Atkinson	Ripon
La Crosse	Racine Commuter[3]	Grant County[1]	River Falls
Ladysmith	Rusk County	Hartford[1]	Shawano
Madison	Sawyer County	Jefferson	Stoughton
Manitowoc	Washington County Express[3]	Lake Mills	Sun Prairie
Merrill	Waukesha County Commuter[3]	Marinette	Viroqua
Milwaukee County[2]		Marshfield	Washington County
Monona[3]		Mauston	Waterloo/Marshall
Oshkosh		Medford	Watertown
Racine[2]		Monroe	Waupaca
Rice Lake		Neillsville	Waupun
Sheboygan		New Richmond	West Bend
Stevens Point		Onalaska	Whitewater
Superior[4]		Ozaukee County	Wisconsin Rapids
Verona		Platteville	
Waukesha			
Wausau			

[1]Taxi services are privately contracted except for the City of Hartford and Grant County, where they are publicly owned and operated.
[2]Privately managed.
[3]Privately contracted. (Note: The private service in Waukesha County is an inter-urban service.)
[4]Contracted with Duluth Transit System.
Source: Wisconsin Department of Transportation, Division of Transportation Investment Management, departmental data, April 2009.

WISCONSIN URBAN TRANSIT SYSTEMS
USAGE AND REVENUE, 1950 – 2007
(In Thousands)

Year	Revenue Miles	Revenue Passengers	Operating Revenue*
1950	53,362	288,996	$22,692
1955	42,807	169,129	23,134
1960	34,950	130,299	20,665
1965	32,330	110,979	20,457
1970	28,371	80,172	22,078
1975	26,119	63,587	22,454
1980	33,943	88,756	29,631
1985	31,829	79,540	39,635
1990	33,685	78,215	39,594
1991	33,820	74,764	45,489
1992	33,941	72,981	45,356
1993	33,954	71,444	46,492
1994	33,996	71,242	48,291
1995	30,734	71,875	50,171
1996	34,306	73,172	54,147
1997	38,222	74,703	55,842
1998	45,064	76,367	57,836
1999	54,585	77,169	58,101
2000	42,447	89,821	58,785
2001	46,755	87,729	60,299
2002	48,322	84,874	64,263
2003	47,753	81,650	61,868
2004	46,696	81,812	65,621
2005	52,163	83,545	67,628
2006	51,700	83,913	72,896
2007	51,751	81,229	pending audit

*As recognized by the Wisconsin Department of Transportation.
Sources: Wisconsin Department of Transportation, Division of Transportation Assistance, Bureau of Transit, *Wisconsin Urban Bus System Annual Report 1989,* and previous issues; departmental data, April 2009.

WISCONSIN HARBOR COMMERCE – 2007
(In Thousands of Short Tons)

Harbors[1]	Total Tonnage[2]	Crude Inedible Materials (except fuels)	Coal and Lignite	Food and Farm Products	Primary Manufactured Goods	Petroleum and Petroleum Products	Manufactured Equipment, Machinery and Products	Chemicals and Related Products	Unknown
LAKE SUPERIOR									
Duluth-Superior	46,498	22,504	20,696	2,877	342	—	34	—	4
Ashland	111	—	111	—	—	1	9	—	—
Bayfield	10	—	—	—	—	1	9	—	—
La Pointe	10	—	—	—	—	—	—	—	—
LAKE MICHIGAN									
Milwaukee	4,019	1,643	884	334	1,033	99	27	—	—
Green Bay	2,610	913	1,182	7	456	51	—	—	—
Manitowoc	381	—	115	88	179	—	—	—	—
Menominee[3]	308	157	16	—	117	—	19	—	—
Racine	154	154	—	—	—	—	—	—	—
Detroit Harbor[4]	10	—	—	—	—	6	—	—	4
TOTAL	54,111	25,371	23,004	3,306	2,127	152	98	0	4

Note: Tonnage reported in short tons. One short ton equals 2,000 lbs.

[1] Zero or no commerce reported for the following harbors: Algoma, Cornucopia, Kenosha, Kewaunee, Oconto, Pensaukee, Port Washington, Port Wing, Sheboygan, Sturgeon Bay, and Two Rivers.

[2] Detail may not add due to rounding.

[3] Includes tonnage handled at Marinette, Wisconsin.

[4] Washington Island.

Source: U.S. Army Corps of Engineers, Navigation Data Center, Water Resources Support Center, *Waterborne Commerce of the United States, Calendar Year 2007*, Part 3, at: http://www.iwr.usace.army.mil/ndc/wcsc/wcsc.htm [June 2009].

Political
Parties

9

Wisconsin political parties: state organizations and current party platforms

Moon Crater

(NASA)

POLITICAL PARTY ORGANIZATION IN WISCONSIN

What Is a Political Party?

A political party is a private, voluntary organization of people with similar political beliefs that vies with other parties for control of government. Political parties help voters select their government officials and create a consensus on the basic principles that direct governmental activities and processes.

Political parties in the United States have traditionally provided an organized framework for the orderly performance of several basic political tasks necessary to representative democracy. Parties act to:

- Provide a stable institution for building coalitions based on shared principles and priorities.
- Recruit and nominate candidates for elective and appointive offices in government.
- Promote the election of the party's slate of candidates.
- Guard the integrity of election procedures and vote canvassing.
- Educate the voters by defining issues, taking policy positions, and formulating programs.

U.S. parties offer a marked contrast to the party apparatus in other nations. In many parts of the world, political parties begin with defined ideologies and programs. Their members are recruited on the basis of these ideas, and there is not much room for disagreement within the ranks. In other cases, parties represent regional interests or ethnic groups. By contrast, parties in the United States are loosely organized groups reflecting a broad spectrum of interests. They are truly populist parties in the sense that they accommodate diversity and are instruments of party activists at the grass roots level. Political ideology, as stated in a party's national platform, is formulated first at the local level and then refined through debate and compromise at meetings representing successively larger geographic areas.

Depending on the time, place, and circumstances, political party labels in the United States may have widely different meanings, and within a single party there may be room for members whose ideologies span a wide political spectrum. Individual Republicans or Democrats, for instance, are often further identified as "liberal", "conservative", "right-wing", "left-wing", or "moderate".

Despite the diversity within a party, specific philosophies are generally associated with the various political parties. In the public's perception, the name of a particular party conjures up a surprisingly distinct set of economic, social, and political principles.

Political Parties in Wisconsin

Throughout its history, the United States has operated with a two-party political structure, rather than single-party or multiparty systems found elsewhere. Although minor parties have always been a part of American politics, few have gained the support necessary to challenge the two dominant parties at the national level. Those that did lasted only briefly, with the predominant exception of the Republican Party, which replaced the Whig Party in the 1850s. The same cannot be said of politics on the state level. In Wisconsin, for example, the Socialist Party regularly sent one or more representatives to the legislature between 1911 and 1937, and the Progressive Party was influential between 1933 and 1947, capturing a plurality of both houses of the 1937 Legislature. Third parties were relatively quiet in Wisconsin in the 1950s, but the last 30 years have seen more activity with more parties officially recognized on the ballot.

Under Wisconsin law, a "recognized political party" is a political party that qualifies for a separate ballot or column on the ballot, based on receiving at least 1% of the votes for a statewide office at the previous November election or through acquiring the required number of petition signatures (10,000 electors, including at least 1,000 electors residing in each of at least three separate congressional districts). At the beginning of 2009, Wisconsin had four recognized political parties: Democratic, Libertarian, Republican, and Wisconsin Green.

The Wisconsin Statutes define a political party in Section 5.02 (13) as a state committee that is legally registered with the Government Accountability Board and "all county, congressional, legislative, local and other affiliated committees authorized to operate under the same name". It must be a body "organized exclusively for political purposes under whose name candidates appear on a ballot at any election".

The delegates from the political party's local units meet in an annual state convention to draft or amend the party's state platform (a statement of its principles and objectives), select national committee members, elect state officers, consider resolutions, and conduct other party business. Every four years, party delegates from throughout the United States meet in a national convention to nominate their candidates for president and vice president and to adopt a national platform for the next four years. In Wisconsin, the slates of national convention delegates are usually based on the April presidential preference primary vote.

Statutory and Voluntary Organizations

Wisconsin law provides that each major political party must have certain local officers and committees, but over the years, these statutory organizations have been merged within the voluntary party organizations that are governed by their own constitutions and bylaws. The actual power is found in the voluntary structures.

In the case of the majority parties, voluntary organizations are composed of dues-paying members, who are affiliated with Wisconsin chapters of the national political parties. Third parties vary in the amount of regional autonomy and/or national control allowed. Given minor organizational differences, voluntary parties operate to tend to their party's interests, collect money to finance campaigns, maintain cooperation between the various county and congressional district organizations, and act as liaison with national parties. (Currently recognized parties and their voluntary organizations are discussed in the party descriptions that follow this introduction.)

The History of Wisconsin's Political Parties

In *How Wisconsin Voted*, Professor James R. Donoghue divided Wisconsin's political history into four eras. From statehood in 1848 until 1855, the Democratic Party was the dominant political party, and the Whig Party provided major opposition. This was a continuation of the party alignment that had prevailed during the state's territorial period.

The second era was one of Republican domination from 1856 to 1900. The birth of the national Republican Party is attributed to a meeting in Ripon, Wisconsin, in 1854. Its founding was based on the conditions and events that eventually led to the Civil War, and within Wisconsin these same circumstances contributed to the rapid growth of the Republican Party and the demise of the Whigs.

The second era ended at the turn of the century with the election of Governor Robert M. La Follette. The third era, from 1900 to 1945, was a time of great stress and change, encompassing the Great Depression and World Wars I and II. Until 1932, the major political battles usually occurred not between two parties, but between two factions of the Republican Party – the conservative "stalwart" Republicans and the "progressive" (La Follette) Republicans. The Democratic Party was in eclipse, and election contests tended to be decided in Republican primary elections.

The third era also saw the high point of third party influence in Wisconsin. The progressive faction formally split from the Republicans to form its own party in 1934. The new Progressive Party won gubernatorial elections in 1936 and 1942 and a plurality in both houses of the legislature in 1936. Declining popularity, however, led to its dissolution in 1946, and Progressive Party leadership urged its members and supporting voters to return to the Republican Party. The period from 1900 to 1937 was also the time of greatest strength for the Socialists.

The fourth era, from 1945 to the present, witnessed a realignment of the major parties. A resurgence of the Democratic Party ended the long Republican domination, turning the state to a more balanced, two-party, competitive system. In the late 1940s, some former Progressives, Socialists, and others began moving into a moribund Democratic Party. This influx both revitalized the party and made it more liberal. In the following decade, the Democrats worked at uniting their party and building their strength at the polls. Meanwhile, the conservative faction solidified its control of the Republican Party with the departure of more liberal-minded Progressives and addition of conservative Democrats fleeing their former party as it became more liberal.

In the years following World War II, the resurgent Democratic Party began seriously challenging the majority Republicans. Steady Democratic growth culminated in the 1957 election of William Proxmire to the U.S. Senate, the first "new" Democrat to win a major statewide election, followed by the election of Gaylord Nelson as governor in 1958. These elections marked the emergence on Wisconsin's political scene of a Democratic Party fully capable of competing successfully with the long dominant Republicans for public office. During this period, third party and independent candidates usually failed to garner any significant support on a statewide level.

The hallmark of contemporary Wisconsin politics is a highly competitive, two-party, issue-oriented system. At the beginning of the 1995 session, Republicans gained control of both houses for the first time since 1969. In 1993, 1995, and 1997, the majority party in the senate shifted during the session. Democrats controlled the senate in 1999 and 2001, while Republicans retained the control of the assembly they had won in the 1994 elections. For the first time since 1982, a Democrat was elected governor in November 2002.

Republicans controlled both the senate and assembly under a Democratic governor from 2003 to 2006. In 2006, Democrats won a majority in the senate. In 2008, they took control of the assembly for the first time since 1994. At the beginning of the 2009 session, Democrats controlled the governor's office, senate, and assembly for the first time since 1986.

Of the state's major elected partisan officers in January 2009, the Democrats held the positions of governor, lieutenant governor, secretary of state, and state treasurer, as well as both U.S. Senate seats, five of the eight congressional seats, and majorities in the state senate and assembly. Republicans filled the position of attorney general and held three congressional seats.

DEMOCRATIC PARTY OF WISCONSIN
June 2009

Headquarters

State Headquarters: 110 King Street, Suite 203, Madison 53703.

Telephone: (608) 255-5172; Fax: (608) 255-8919.

Executive Director: JASON STEPHANY.

Compliance Director: MEGAN BRENGARTH.

Membership Director: JAMIE GUTKOWSKI.

Finance Director: MARY LANG SOLLINGER.

Organizing Director: JACOB HAJDU.

Internet Address: http://www.wisdems.org

State Administrative Committee

Chair: MIKE TATE, Madison.

First Vice Chair: MELISSA SCHROEDER, Merrill.

Second Vice Chair: JEF HALL, Oshkosh.

Secretary: ANGELA SUTKIEWICZ, Sheboygan.

Treasurer: MICHAEL CHILDERS.

National Committee Members: ROLLIE HICKS, Eau Claire; JASON RAE, Rice Lake; TIM SULLIVAN, Verona; PAULA ZELLNER, Porterfield.

Legislative Representatives: SENATOR JUDY ROBSON, Beloit; REPRESENTATIVE GARY SHERMAN, Port Wing.

College Democrats Representative: ANALIESE EICHER, Madison.

County Chairs Association Chair: RICH MANTZ, Fond du Lac.

Milwaukee County Chair: MARTHA LOVE, Milwaukee.

At-Large Members: GWEN CARR, Madison; SPENCER COGGS, Madison; LINDA HONOLD, Milwaukee; DIAN PALMER, Brookfield.

Congressional District Representatives:

1st District	*5th District*
Ray Rivera, chair	Les Nakamoto, chair, Jackson
Mike Nemeth, Racine	Chris Marshall, Mequon
2nd District	*6th District*
Peter Rickman, chair, Fitchburg	Gordon Hintz, chair, Oshkosh
Heather Colburn, Madison	Jan Banicki, Montello
3rd District	*7th District*
Melanie Franklin, chair	Jan Kelton-Wolden, chair, Frederic
Bob Johnson, La Crosse	Gary Hawley, Stevens Point
4th District	*8th District*
Stephanie Findley, chair, Milwaukee	Sid Vineburg, chair, Green Bay
Demond Means	Dottie Leclair, Appleton

Source: Democratic Party of Wisconsin.

County Organization. The county organization is the basic unit of the Democratic Party of Wisconsin. In each county, the membership elects the county officers. They include a chairperson, vice chairperson, secretary, and treasurer (or secretary/treasurer). Their terms of office are usually one year, but some county organizations may provide for 2-year terms.

Congressional District Organization. Congressional district organizations function mainly as a base of support for Democratic congressional candidates. They also select representatives to the state administrative committee. An executive committee directs each congressional district organization.

State Convention. The party holds its annual state convention in June. Each year, the convention considers amendments to the state party constitution and other resolutions and party business.

State party officers are elected in odd-numbered years, and state party platforms are adopted in even-numbered years. State convention delegates elect Democratic National Committee members every four years.

Each county unit elects delegates to the state convention, and all party members are eligible.

The state administrative committee determines the number of delegates that represent each county by using a formula based on the number of party members and the percentage of the vote cast for the Democratic candidate in the most recent U.S. Senate election. In addition to the regular quota, certain Democratic officeholders are automatically delegates to the state convention.

State Officers and Administrative Committee. The Democratic Party of Wisconsin is headed by a state administrative committee, composed of 32 party officials chosen in a variety of ways. Delegates to the state convention elect the 5 party officers and the 4 Democratic National Committee members. The 8 congressional district conventions each select 2 representatives to serve on the state administrative committee in the spring of each odd-numbered year: the district chairperson and an additional representative of the opposite sex. The remaining voting committee members include the County Chairs Association chairperson; the Milwaukee County chairperson; a representative of the College Democrats; 2 state legislative representatives, elected by their house caucuses prior to the beginning of the new legislative term; the immediate past state chairperson; and an at-large administrative committee member.

The party officers are the state chairperson, first vice chairperson, second vice chairperson, treasurer, and secretary. The chairperson and first vice chairperson must be of the opposite sex.

Party officers are elected in the odd-numbered year for 2-year terms. Democratic National Committee members are elected each presidential election year and serve 4-year terms. The state chairperson and the first vice chairperson are also *ex officio* members of the Democratic National Committee.

Whenever a vacancy occurs, the chairperson, with the concurrence of the entire state administrative committee, appoints a successor to serve until the next annual convention, where the delegates elect an individual to fill the position for the remainder of the unexpired term.

National Committee. The Democratic National Committee is composed of the chairperson and the highest ranking officer of the opposite sex in each recognized state Democratic Party. In Wisconsin, these are the chairperson and the first vice chairperson of the state administrative committee.

An additional 200 committee memberships are apportioned to the states on the same basis as delegates to the national convention, and other specified members are appointed. Wisconsin's Democratic National Committee members are selected every 4 years at the annual state conventions held in presidential election years.

WISCONSIN DEMOCRATIC PARTY PLATFORM
As Adopted at State Convention, Stevens Point, June 14, 2008
Preamble

The Democratic Party of Wisconsin strives to build an open, just and strong society where all citizens have equal opportunities to live meaningful, secure lives. We work actively for open, honest and responsive government that is accountable to the needs and the will of the people.

Justice, Human Concerns, and Democracy

Our government must support values common to all people, including freedom, fairness, family, responsibility and community.

One of the primary jobs of government is to ensure that everyone can lead dignified, healthy and fulfilling lives. We value love, commitment, stability and nurturing of all family members. Our Constitution guarantees that we are all equal regardless of race, color, class, religion, actual or perceived gender, sexual orientation, age, occupation, national origin, physical disabilities or appearance, or political beliefs. We support equal legal rights for all individuals in committed, loving relationships. We will work to ensure that basic civil liberties are forever preserved.

It is vital that government respect, support and protect freedom of expression. When government attempts to limit the rights of its citizens, the fundamental philosophy on which our nation was established is destroyed. We hold sacrosanct our civil liberties, including but hardly limited to freedom of speech, the right to privacy, the presumption of innocence and the principle of *habeus corpus*. Nothing less than the humane treatment of our fellow human beings is acceptable. Our government, checked and balanced among its three branches, serves us, and should it fail to protect our civil rights or one branch usurp another, has itself failed.

Our government serves us and protects our constitutional rights. We must fully fund our law enforcement activities and the defense of our nation. The men and women who serve us are our first line of defense, and we must provide for them. Security of our society must be our concern, it cannot be given over to foreign interests nor can it be achieved if the resources of our first responders and military are unavailable here at home when we are in our greatest need.

We will work to ensure that everyone has an equal opportunity to succeed, an equal voice in government and fair and equal treatment under the law. We recognize that minorities, senior citizens, and the poor often face formidable challenges, including obstacles to voting. We will work to eliminate those obstacles. We pursue legislation and cultural change that end racial and ethnic profiling, respect the sovereignty of our indigenous Native American host nations and ensure equality between men and women. We shall work for gender-balanced, qualified representation at all levels of government. Our goal is a government and an electoral process free of the corrupting influences of money and power wielded by some who lobby our representatives.

Empowerment of citizens in all civic affairs strengthens our nation. Government must be an open institution that people trust, complying with open meeting and public record laws and elected through publicly funded state and national elections. Every citizen is guaranteed the right to vote and equal access thereto, including ex-offenders immediately upon release into their communities. We oppose voter ID requirements as discriminatory, equivalent to a poll tax, a voter suppression tactic, and a fraudulent solution to exaggerated voter fraud. We have the right and duty to inspect and count all votes and to have a voter-verified paper ballot that guarantees accurate vote counting.

We expect the swift impeachment and removal from office of officials who commit high crimes and misdemeanors.

Access to accurate information and a diversity of viewpoints are essential to citizen empowerment. The broadcast spectrum belongs to all citizens. Therefore we will work to ensure diverse local ownership of media outlets. We will provide strong support for public broadcasting and other community-owned media outlets. We support free and equal access to news media for all candidates for public office.

We respect the religious liberties of all people and welcome them into the Democratic Party. It is vital that we observe a strict separation between government and religion. It is imperative to the survival of our Democratic Republic that the rights of citizens to choose their own religious and philosophical beliefs remain whole.

We require a fair immigration policy providing a reasonable legal path to residency and citizenship. The policy must include a fair opportunity for current undocumented residents to achieve legal status. All people should be afforded the same basic principles of life, liberty, justice, and fair access to economic security.

It is important to care for all generations. We need affordable, quality, licensed daycare centers and government support to pay for childcare. We cannot neglect our nation's future. We need health education and disease prevention programs concerning smoking, alcohol, and sexually transmitted infections.

Rather than abandoning our elderly and disabled, it is essential that we preserve Social Security programs. Privatizing Social Security threatens the financial security of the most vulnerable. We must enhance programs for the aging and disabled, including subsidized long-term in-home or nursing home care.

We believe access to affordable health care is a right and that the best solution to our national health care crisis is a single-payer system. Such a system must provide universal access for individuals of all ages, promote preventive measures, provide medications and therapy and cover all physical and mental illnesses equally. Until that system is available, we support broader coverage and increased funding for the current health care programs on local, state and national levels, including BadgerCare, Medicaid and Healthy Wisconsin.

Personal moral, religious and medical decisions should be left up to the individual. We believe in complete freedom of reproductive choice, as well as the individual's right to choose death with dignity. Everyone has the right to timely obtain medications, properly and legally prescribed by their physician, from any licensed pharmacy. It is neither the role of the pharmacist nor the government to interfere in private medical decisions. Funding for stem-cell research should not be influenced by religious beliefs. This research, which would benefit all people, should be supported on its scientific merits.

Considering the rising cost of corrections and long-lasting effects of incarceration, we support alternatives to prison.

We oppose the death penalty as an inhumane and ineffective means of punishment. We believe in equitable sentencing standards and increasing the authority of judges to modify sentences. The war on drugs is a colossal failure. We must discourage dangerous drug use without criminalizing the user and provide rehabilitative treatment to addicted persons. Furthermore, the law should be changed immediately to process minor drug offenses as local ordinance violations.

We support reasonable firearms regulations to ensure the safety of citizens and law enforcement officials. We support the right to hunt and bear arms. We support Wisconsin's concealed carry ban.

Education, Labor, and Economics

Quality public education for all is critical to a healthy democracy and economy. Public funding for private schools diverts resources from and adversely impacts public schools. Increased governmental funding and financial aid is essential for all levels of public education. Nobody should be denied a quality education because of a personal lack of financial resources. The benefits of a quality education always outweigh the costs.

We believe that students have the right to receive their education in a safe, respectful, and nurturing environment, free from harassment or discrimination by teachers, staff, parents, or other students. We support fair and equitable funding for all elements of the curriculum, including art, music and physical education. A strong Wisconsin public education system builds a strong Wisconsin.

Wisconsin's current educational funding system has failed. The law allowing a limited qualified economic offer has caused diminishing compensation for teachers. Teacher compensation must keep pace with costs of benefits and inflation. Public school teachers must not be taken for granted. They deserve tremendous respect for their work educating our youth under challenging circumstances.

Revenue caps on school districts and other local governments must be eliminated. State or federal governments must fully fund their mandates.

Public investment in arts and humanities promotes healthy communities and a healthy economy. We support increased local, state, and federal funding of arts and humanities.

A strong and secure nation depends on sound economic policy that promotes and sustains full, meaningful employment. Business, labor and the public must work together to re-establish American jobs on American soil. We must resist outsourcing, thus reinvigorating domestic industries.

Workers have rights to safe and equitable workplaces, living wages including pay equity for women, and secure benefits. Workers' rights to organize, bargain collectively and strike without fear of reprisal must continue and be strengthened. We support public employees' rights to speedy mediation and binding arbitration of labor disputes. Businesses must be held accountable for contracts with their employees. Right-to-work legislation and the hiring of strikebreakers are anathema to a strong, justly-compensated workforce. Pension and other retirement funds must be strictly safeguarded and responsibly managed through regulation. In the event of bankruptcy, workers' unpaid wages must be the first claim on remaining assets.

We support a tax system that is based on ability to pay. It is immoral to increase the tax burden on those less able to pay while reducing it for the wealthy. Doing so fails to spur economic and job development and hurts those with the least income. The Federal budget must be balanced through responsible spending and fair taxation. We call on the State Legislature to make corporate taxes on par with the national average.

State and Federal governments must quickly take measures to protect victims of all forms of fraudulent, unscrupulous, or usurious lending.

America must invest in an healthy economy by supporting worker training, affordable tuition at our state-supported universities and technical colleges and ample funding for research.

American companies have an obligation to our nation to be established here at home, follow our labor and environmental laws and pay taxes for the good of the commons. Furthermore, we must protect our industries from competition by enforcing tariffs against nations that tolerate unfair worker conditions and environmental degradation.

All products sold by vendors at Democratic Party functions must be marked made in America or union made.

Our wealth should be measured not only by the GDP but also by broad measures of well-being, such as the United Nations Human Development Index, that incorporate factors like health, education, literacy, employment and wages and environmental quality.

Agriculture and Environment

We must preserve family farming by creating market systems that assure a fair return to both farmers and processors. True Cooperatives and family farm subsidies are essential to the economic viability and quality of life in rural areas. In addition we support value-added agriculture which includes farming endeavors outside traditional forms of agriculture. Price supports for non-owner operated farms should be eliminated.

We encourage legislators and Democratic Party leaders to support farming systems that are humane to animals, preserve our soil, water and forest resources, and produce wholesome, safe food for consumers. We support agricultural sustainability through growth in "buy fresh buy local" practices which insure markets for local farmers and save fuel by eliminating costly transport. We also support truth in labeling of conventional, organic, and genetically modified food.

Protecting the ecological systems of our planet is essential to the economic and social welfare of our state and nation and to the future of humanity. Our legislators and leaders must pay heed to soil, water, and atmospheric pollution; scientific evidence of global warming; invasive species; and decreasing biodiversity while enacting appropriate legislation to safeguard our environment. We must maintain the integrity of the vast fresh water supply in the Great Lakes.

We must reduce greenhouse gases by developing alternative and sustainable fuels and energy sources; increase production of fuel-efficient vehicles; reduce urban sprawl onto prime agricultural soils; improve and expand local, regional and national mass transportation systems; and increase recycling and waste management, all while maintaining biodiversity. We will restore responsible environmental regulations affecting open space, wilderness areas, soil conservation, forest management, toxic and hazardous waste disposal and cleanup and watershed protection. We call for the use of advanced technology and environmentally-friendly practices to be implemented in industrial settings and mining natural resources and the enforcement and strengthening of safety regulations. To ensure the protection of our state's valuable natural resources, we support the re-establishment of a Public Intervener's Office and an independent Department of Natural Resources.

Foreign Affairs

We stand for human rights, social and economic justice, the rule of law, and popularly adopted democratic government worldwide. Our leaders must honor international law and honor and promote international agreements that provide groundwork for a just, prosperous, environmentally healthy, and peaceful world. Our United Nations dues must be fully paid.

We call on our government to be a cooperative and effective leader, a partner in the pursuit of global accords to improve the human condition and protect the environment. We encourage international efforts to combat poverty, hunger, disease, illiteracy, discrimination, genocide, torture, genital mutilation, human slavery and trafficking, capital punishment, pollution, and global warming. We support expansion of the Peace Corps.

We oppose unfair trade and immigration policies that undermine our economy, harm working people in our country and elsewhere, and harm the environment.

We oppose unfettered international arms trade, nuclear, chemical and biological weapons, land mines, radioactive materials in conventional munitions, ballistic missile defense systems, cluster bombs, militarization of space, American-run internment camps and torture.

We support a strong military as essential to our security and providing amply for the health and well-being of members of the military after their service.

War must always be a last resort. We must address the grievances that foster terrorism rather than fight wars that perpetuate them. All in our Government and military must abide by the Geneva Conventions.

Preemptive war without direct threat to our country and the continued occupation of Iraq are fraudulent, illegal, and disastrous. The occupation diverts our attention from defeating terrorists in Afghanistan and is killing or maiming tens of thousands of our military and millions of innocent Iraqis, contributing to devastation of our economy, encouraging terrorism, and undermining our credibility and standing in the world. We must end our occupation of Iraq. Congressional action to stop funding it is long overdue.

The bulk of today's dangerous misdirection in our foreign affairs and turmoil undermining our military strength is due to individuals at the highest levels of our government who disdain our Constitution and the rule of law. Therefore we call upon Congress to begin impeachment proceedings immediately against President Bush, Vice President Cheney, and former Secretary of Defense Rumsfeld and that they investigate and prosecute all members of the Bush Administration who have exceeded their office.

We support leaders with vision and values who will uphold our Constitution, reverse the failures and illegalities of Bush's administrations, and regain the global community's admiration for our country.

Conclusion

The membership of the Democratic Party of Wisconsin has crafted and adopted this platform. Our state and our country will become stronger and better by following the principles outlined herein. We expect all candidates supported by the Democratic Party to support this Platform and, when elected, to work to implement it.

WISCONSIN GREEN PARTY
June 2009

Headquarters

State Headquarters: P.O. Box 1701, Madison 53701-1701.

Telephone: (608) 204-7336 or (608) 20-GREEN.

Internet Address: www.wisconsingreenparty.org

E-mail: mail@wisconsingreenparty.org

Coordinating Council

Co-Chairs: BRUCE HINKFORTH, Oconomowoc; CYNTHIA STIMMLER, Dresser.

Corresponding Secretary: JEFF SCHIFFMAN, Madison.

Recording Secretary: CLAUDE VANDERVEEN, Cudahy.

Elections Treasurer: ROBIN LUTZ, Oshkosh.

Operations Treasurer: RON HARDY, Oshkosh.

Diversity Caucus Chair: DEAN KATAHIRA, Ripon.

Lavender Caucus Chair: DENNIS BERGREN, Madison.

Women's Caucus Chair: vacancy.

Youth Caucus Chair: vacancy.

Disability Caucus Chair: vacancy.

Council Members:

1st District:
Pete Karas, Racine
vacancy

2nd District:
Larry Dooley, Madison
vacancy

3rd District:
Monte LeTourneau, Necedah
Dennis Boyer, Dodgeville

4th District:
Tommy King, Milwaukee
Leon Todd, Milwaukee

5th District:
vacancy
vacancy

6th District:
Michael Slattery, Maribel
Fred Depies, Oshkosh

7th District:
Nadine Holder, Osceola
vacancy

8th District:
Jill Bussiere, Kewaunee
vacancy

Source: Wisconsin Green Party at wisconsingreenparty.org, June 8, 2009.

Officers. Officers include two co-chairs, a recording secretary, a corresponding secretary, an elections treasurer, and an operations treasurer. The co-chairs serve staggered 2-year terms and may not be reelected for successive terms. The other officers serve one-year terms and may be reelected. Elections are held at the fall convention.

Coordinating Council. The Wisconsin Green Party Coordinating Council includes all of the officers plus two members from each of the eight congressional districts in Wisconsin, as well as a representative from each statewide caucus. The officers and members are elected each year at the fall convention.

State Membership Meetings. Membership meetings are held in the spring and fall of each year. A five state regional membership meeting is held during the summer. Officers are elected at the fall convention.

STATE PLATFORM OF THE WISCONSIN GREEN PARTY
(Amended May 23, 2007)
Preamble

We hold these truths to be self-evident: that we must treat each other with love, respect and fairness, and that we must protect the earth for future generations.

The crises of our times demand a fundamental shift in human values and culture, and in our social, economic and political institutions. The way we live today is based on using things up: our air, our water, our natural resources, and our people. We need a new way of doing things that is sustainable, that will allow our people and our environment to flourish now and in the future. We can't keep spending today what we – and our children and their children – will need tomorrow.

The Wisconsin Greens offer a new vision for change, for a sustainable future. We recognize that one of great obstacles to that change is the fact that government no longer responds to the needs of citizens. Only by building grassroots democracy can we be sure that changes will be real, not just appearances or promises. Since neither the Democratic Party nor the Republican Party has shown a real commitment to running government in the public interest, The Wisconsin Greens believe another political party is needed: one that people can believe in; one that they can trust.

Our vision is of a sustainable society in harmony with the environment, one that meets all people's needs for security, self-respect, freedom, creativity, and community. We recognize that personal, cultural, social, economic, political, and ecological problems are interconnected. We reject the current simplistic solutions to these problems. New, creative solutions are needed which allow us to live well and happily without destroying our environment or our society. We are confronted with the challenge of letting go of old ways and creating a new vision and a new way of life.

Ecological Wisdom

The Wisconsin Green Party believes that Ecological Wisdom has a direct effect on quality of life. Only by practicing sound stewardship and ecological responsibility can we stop the degradation of the life-giving relationships that exist between humankind and the earth. The "public trust doctrine," which holds that public land, water, minerals, forests, and other natural resources are held in trust for the public and used for the common good, must be enforced. The precautionary principle must be applied to public policy decisions, especially those concerning the approval of drugs, pesticides, and genetically modified organisms to protect the public from practices of uncertain consequence.

Agriculture

1. The state government should provide subsidies to make the change from petrochemical-based to organic farming methods economically feasible for small-scale farmers.

2. The state should develop the necessary infrastructure to support the regionalization of food production and distribution systems, such as urban farms, farmers markets, community supported agriculture, and regional food processing facilities.

3. Wisconsin should establish a system of subsidies and tax incentives to protect family farms as an indispensable component of a healthy and sustainable agricultural economy.

4. A state land banking system of prime farmland to prevent diversion to non-farm use through first-option state acquisition of the land should be created.

Chemical use

5. The state will create and maintain a citizen accessible central database of the products used, concentration applied, chemical contents, health effects, and company responsible, for any private or commercial pesticide application.

6. Pesticides will not be used on or in public property, except as a last resort, after the failure of organic alternatives has been demonstrated. Tax incentives will reward the use of organic pest control methods.

7. Communities in the state will have the right to pass stronger controls on pesticides than those specified in state and federal regulations.

Forest, Wetlands, and Water

8. The Department of Natural Resources will maintain forests, wetlands, and all other ecological communities in a manner which will protect biodiversity and will allow future generations to benefit.

9. We support a general moratorium on the draining of wetlands, on road building in public forests.

10. DNR water quality rules will be stiffened to require absolute non-degradation of existing water bodies.

Energy

11. The Public Service Commission should not grant licenses to new nuclear facilities or the renewal of licenses for existing facilities.

12. We support higher average miles per gallon requirements and stricter emission control requirements on new vehicles, as well as "gas guzzler" taxes and renewable fuel and "gas sipper" rebates on new car purchases.

13. As a response to oil production having reached its peak, we support building and promoting mass transit infrastructure for light rail, high-speed rail, commuter rail, as well as intra and intercommunity bicycling and walking trails.

14. Community owned utilities and decentralized, neighborhood networks will receive financial aid for the purchase and installation of renewable energy technology such as wind, solar and biomass. The Public Service

Commission will require that the electric grid be reconfigured to accept power from widely distributed, diverse sources.

15. We will work towards statewide energy independence, and will promote, encourage, and fund energy research that brings Wisconsin closer to a self-sustaining energy system.

16. Under Green Party leadership, the state of Wisconsin will independently implement the terms of the Kyoto Protocol on global warming.

17. Green Party leaders will enact policies that significantly reduce the release of gases that deplete the ozone layer, contribute to global warming and cause acid rain.

Waste

18. The Greens will apply the principles of reduce, reuse and recycle to policies in order to reduce waste streams, reduce demands on natural resources and reduce the generation of pollutants.

19. Regional high level nuclear waste dumps will not be located in Wisconsin.

20. Tipping fees at Wisconsin landfills will be increase for commercial haulers. Commercial haulers will be required to bill their commercial customers on a per weight basis.

21. High-level radioactive and highly toxic waste storage will be only for waste generated in Wisconsin.

22. The history and environmental record of recycling or waste disposal firms will be used as major criteria in considering awarding contracts for municipal services.

23. We will require the DNR and State Attorney General to be more vigorous in prosecuting corporate offenses and will hold individuals accountable when appropriate. Corporations that engage in gross violations will have their corporate charter revoked.

Social and Economic Justice

While the Wisconsin Green party understands and applauds the initiative and ambition shown by people who seek financial security or self-improvement, we believe that it is the role of government to ensure that the financial security and social status of one group does not come via the exploitation and marginalization of another group. Additionally, common methods of measuring the economy view production for its own sake as a positive and low unemployment, a condition that favors the majority, is viewed as a threat to economic health. Clearly, new economic paradigms are needed that regard measurements for quality of life and the environment and the full employment of the population as a positive. Lastly, the Wisconsin Green Party asserts that it is the duty of government to earn the allegiance of its citizens by protecting the public from threats "economic and physical," as well as "foreign and domestic".

Economic Justice

24. Laws regarding Articles of Incorporation will be revised to make executives and board members more accountable for the effects of their decision-making.

25. Under a Green Party government the right of people to form unions, bargain collectively, and strike will be upheld. We oppose "union-busting" tactics. The State should assist management in working more closely and cooperatively with unions.

26. Green Party plans for economic development will focus on jobs that are based in the community and that have a vested interest in the community where their employees live – especially small businesses.

27. The Wisconsin Greens support family leave legislation, paid vacation time, job sharing, and the involvement of workers in decision-making, management, and scheduling.

28. Green elected officials will emphasize and promote regional trade emphasizing stronger ties with our Canadian neighbors who share the Great Lakes basin. State trade missions should promote "fair trade" over "free trade" with specific countries that are moving toward more equitable, sustainable economies.

Education

29. The Green Party will repeal laws that prevent teachers from striking or laws that interfere with collective bargaining such a Qualified Economic Offer or QEO.

30. The Wisconsin Greens oppose the use of 'high stakes' standardized tests as the primary determinant for grade advancement, graduation or teacher pay.

31. The state should redraw district boundaries to promote decentralization of schools and an appropriate scale for school districts. The transportation of students over great distances is already a burden on the budgets in many rural districts.

32. For parents to have a meaningful impact on school board policies, district boundaries should be redrawn taking into account the ratio of electors to school board and reduced to defined, equitable limits.

33. Green Party education policy will foster an understanding of the history of our conflicts and treaties with Wisconsin's tribes and a respect for native cultures.

Health Care System

34. The Green Party will implement a universal, single-payer system that will be funded through state taxes. The system will be designed to allow citizens to select health care providers and treatment.

35. The state shall promote the revitalization of public health care clinics and school nurses to provide necessary health services and counseling, preventative care, and instruction in hygiene, nutrition, contraception and wellness.

36. The state shall promote the chartering of non-profit and not-for-profit hospitals.

37. The state shall establish work rules that abolish mandatory overtime for nurses and other paraprofessionals in hospitals.

38. We will fund the University of Wisconsin system to develop new programs to provide paraprofessionals required to expand the public health service.

39. Drug abuse of all kinds should be treated as a disease, rather than a criminal offense.

40. We defend a woman's right to make reproduction choices affecting their own body. Birth control prescriptions should be covered by all health care plans and/or subsidized by the state.

Rights of Lesbian, Gay, Bisexual, and Transgender Individuals

41. Wisconsin Greens will defend the rights of all individuals to freely choose intimate partners, regardless of their sex, gender or sexual orientation.

42. Wisconsin Greens support the right of gay, lesbian, bisexual and transgender people to be treated equally with all other people, in all areas of life, including in housing, employment, civil marriage, benefits, and child custody.

Grassroots Democracy

Democracy and self-governance are dependent on the public being fully informed and all political parties having access to the ballot and public debate and discourse. Additionally, since the voter is consenting to being governed, the full will of the voter must be expressed and reflected in election results. To this end the Wisconsin Green Party will work to implement policies that result in the public being fully informed about issues and policies that tear down the barriers between the voters and the government that represents them.

Taxation

43. Wisconsin Greens will institute a progressive method of taxation that shifts the tax burden away from those that can least afford it. We will eliminate the income tax for households making less than $20,000.00 a year and reduce the income tax for households making between $20,000.00 and $30,000.00 a year.

44. A portion of funds from an increase in the motor fuel tax will go for development of alternative transportation such as mass transit and bicycle trails.

45. We will eliminate tax loopholes for corporations and the wealthy, including the state capital gains deduction and the exemption of manufacturing machinery and equipment from property tax.

46. Independent businesses that are locally owned and not affiliated with any out-of-state entity will be taxed at a lower rate than franchises that export local dollars out of the community.

47. The Greens oppose state caps on local property tax levies.

Electoral Reforms

48. We support the adoption of Instant Runoff Voting as the ballot counting procedure to ensure the full expression of voter will and to eliminate the cost of primaries in non-partisan local elections.

49. We support the gradual transition to a system of Proportional Representation for legislative offices.

50. Ballot access laws will assure access thresholds that are set low enough to reflect emerging shifts in local voter will.

51. Voters will not be denied access to the views of any political party or candidates. We will insist on the full inclusion of all political parties in all public debates regardless of candidate will.

52. The Wisconsin Green Party opposes term limits, as they are restrictions on the will of the people.

Nonviolence

The problem of violence in society is complex and multifaceted and must be addressed on different fronts. For this reason we regard economic justice, education and programs that create opportunity to have as much potential at decreasing the incidence of crime and violence as traditional punitive measures. Greens emphasize that the solutions to violence, poverty, alienation, anger and political inequality are the key to solving the dilemma of crime and punishment.

Crime & Punishment

53. The Green Party will continue to oppose the death penalty in Wisconsin.

54. Crimes against people and communities must be punished through restitution and/or jail time. Alternative sentencing must be emphasized as much as possible for victimless crimes and nonviolent offenders. Ex-offenders need to come out into a healthy community that both supports them and holds them accountable.

55. We oppose the privatization of the prison system.

56. Our justice system must attach equal importance to justice for white-collar criminals, including environmental violators of our common property. Corporate executives should be held personally responsible for the consequences of their corporate actions.

57. Community members must be involved directly in crime control in their own communities through citizen police boards and neighborhood watch programs.

LIBERTARIAN PARTY OF WISCONSIN
June 2009

Headquarters

State Headquarters: P.O. Box 20815, Greenfield 53220-0815.
Telephone: (800) 236-9236.
Internet Address: www.lpwi.org

State Executive Committee

Chair: Ben Olson, Wisconsin Dells.
Vice-Chair: Jim Maas, Rothschild.
Secretary: John Gatewood, Oconomowoc.
Treasurer: Tim Krenz, Osceola.
Past Chair: vacancy.
At-Large Member: Paul Ehlers, Rhinelander.
At-Large Member: Terry Gray, Madison.
Congressional District Representatives:

1st District: Jim Sewell, Racine	*5th District:* Tim Peterson, Oconomowoc
Alternate: Brad Sponholz, Greenfield	Alternate: Toni Cattani, Oconomowoc
2nd District: Tim Nerenz, Madison	*6th District:* vacancy
Alternate: Tim Szcsykutowicz, Madison	Alternate: vacancy
3rd District: Todd Welch, Eau Claire	*7th District:* Al Arnold, Athens
Alternate: Randy Palmer, Altoona	Alternate: Will Losch, Osceola
4th District: Mike McKenna, Milwaukee	*8th District:* Ralph Klingsporn, Green Bay
Alternate: vacancy	Alternate: Alan Basche, Green Bay

Source: Libertarian Party of Wisconsin at lpwi.org, June 2009.

State Convention. The Libertarian Party of Wisconsin holds its state convention in the spring of each year to conduct party business. In even-numbered years, the convention adopts proposed changes to the party platform and selects delegates to the national convention. It may also endorse candidates for election. In odd-numbered years, it adopts proposed changes to the constitution and/or bylaws and elects party officers and members-at-large to the executive committee. The congressional district representatives and alternates are also elected in odd-numbered years by a caucus of members from the particular district.

State Officers and Executive Committee. The party is headed by an executive committee consisting of the 4 party officers, the immediate past state party chair who is willing to serve, a representative and alternate from each of the 8 congressional districts, and 2 members-at-large. The 4 party officers and the 2 members-at-large serve 2-year terms, which begin at the end of the convention at which they are elected. Party officer or member-at-large vacancies are filled by a vote of the committee.

Congressional district members are elected by a caucus of members from that district and generally serve for 2 years as well. Congressional district conventions may meet annually, although state party members within a congressional district may hold an election at any time. Any vacant congressional district position is filled by a vote of state party members residing within that congressional district. A party member receiving the most votes at a congressional district election becomes a representative when the executive committee accepts his or her credentials. If no congressional district election is held, the executive committee may fill a vacant congressional district position by a majority vote.

National Committee. The Libertarian National Committee is composed of the 4 national officers, the immediate past chair, 5 members-at-large, and 9 regional representatives. A state's affiliation with a region is determined by the convention delegates from that state and is often the subject of negotiations before and during the national convention. Members of the Libertarian National Committee are selected at each biennial national convention and serve for 2 years from one national convention to the next. The Libertarian National Committee addresses national issues and serves, but does not control, the state parties.

LIBERTARIAN PARTY OF WISCONSIN PLATFORM
As Adopted at State Convention, Madison, April 8, 2006
PREAMBLE

As Libertarians, we defend each person's right to engage in any activity that is peaceful and honest and we welcome the diversity that freedom brings. We seek a world of liberty; a world in which all individuals control their own lives and are never forced to compromise their values or sacrifice their property. We believe that no conflict exists between civil order and individual rights and that individuals, groups, or governments should not initiate force against other individuals, groups, or governments.

PRINCIPLES

LIFE: We believe that all individuals have the right to control their own lives and live in whatever manner they choose, as long as they do not interfere with the identical rights of others.

LIBERTY: The only proper functions of government are the protection of the people from actual foreign or domestic threats to their lives and freedoms; and the protection of their individual rights, namely – life, property, and liberty of speech and action.

PROPERTY: The only economic system compatible with the protection of individual human rights is the free market; therefore, the fundamental right of individuals to own property and to enjoy the rewards of their just earnings should not be compromised.

PREFACE:

While members of the Libertarian Party of Wisconsin advocate abolishing laws governing certain voluntary behaviors, this does not necessarily imply endorsement of such behaviors. We only make the statement that in such matters an individual's right to free choice must be recognized and the morality of such choices is not a concern of government. It follows that our silence regarding any other government activity should not be interpreted as implying our approval of such activity.

TAXES:

We advocate phasing out taxes on incomes, personal property, and real property, along with corresponding decreases in the size of government.

TERM LIMITS:

We advocate limits on the time any elected official may serve in office.

ELECTIONS:

We advocate election law reforms that make it easier for the people to nominate and finance the election of the candidates of their choice.

TREATING ADULTS AS CHILDREN:

We believe laws mandating automobile insurance, use of seat belts and helmets, minimum wage, and curfews hamper individual freedom and the responsibility that must go with it. We further believe that laws restricting such things as cruising and tattoos trivialize the law and breed disrespect for it.

STATE MANDATES:

We believe that state mandates, such as the Binding Arbitration Law, are unreasonable burdens on those who must comply with and pay for them. They only represent the desires of special interest groups and their advocates in the legislature. When these mandates are unfunded they become even more unacceptable.

GUN OWNERSHIP:

We believe the right to keep and bear arms should not be infringed. We therefore oppose all laws which tax or otherwise restrict the ownership, open or concealed carry, manufacture, transfer, or sale of firearms or ammunition. We further oppose all laws requiring registration of firearms. We also cannot ignore the clear lessons from history of the suffering which can fall upon a disarmed people.

CHILDREN AND THE FAMILY:

We believe that children are a special group of citizens possessing fundamental rights involving their life and health. However, until they reach the age of legal responsibility, their other rights are limited and their parents or guardians are responsible for their actions and upbringing. Therefore, the rights and authority that parents or guardians need to fulfill their child raising responsibilities must be respected, but never at the expense of the child's life and health.

EDUCATION:

Since private education is today outperforming public education at half the cost, we call for the phase out of all state and federal involvement in education. We therefore endorse "School Choice".

GOVERNMENT WELFARE:

Today's confusion between a person's material needs and that person's rights has led to our current system of taxpayer provided, government welfare programs. These programs often invade privacy and have proven to be demeaning and inefficient. Welfare is not charity. Charity must be freely given. More charity needs to be substituted for welfare. It is also good to remember that for people to be truly free they must become responsible for their own welfare and actions.

FEDERAL "STRINGS":

The federal government often uses the threat of withholding "federal" funds to coerce states into specific actions. We strongly urge elected officials of Wisconsin to resist such pressure and applaud them when they do.

ENVIRONMENT:

A clean environment is in everyone's interest. Our legal system should protect public and private property from pollution. However, a balance must be found between environmental regulation and the long term economic health of a free society. The right of property owners to prosecute any polluter under trespass, nuisance, and negligence laws should be reinstated. It follows that bureaucracies should not be allowed to harass alleged environmental violators or restrict their direct access to just treatment under the judicial system.

TRANSPORTATION:

We support the maximum possible privatization of all publicly owned transportation systems and therefore oppose the creation of any new publicly funded or managed transportation systems.

VICTIMLESS CRIME:

Because only actions that infringe on the rights of others can properly be termed "crimes", we favor the repeal of federal, state, and local laws restricting our fundamental freedom to govern our own lives.

In particular, we advocate: The repeal of laws restricting the production, sale, possession, or use of prohibited drugs and medicines. The repeal of laws regarding a minimum drinking age which are in conflict with the legally recognized age for maturity and responsibility. The repeal of laws restricting consensual sexual relations between adults. The repeal of laws regulating or prohibiting gambling. The decriminalization of assisted suicide.

HEALTH CARE:

We believe the problems with our current health care system are due to government interference and mandates and that any government program to "provide" health care to some at the expense of others will most certainly reduce the overall quality, responsiveness, and individuality of health care for everyone. It would also reduce the influx of the most talented people our society has to offer into the medical profession and diminish the exemplary worldwide progress and leadership our medical system has demonstrated. For these reasons, we advocate the free enterprise system as the only system capable of making quality, affordable, individualized medical care available to all.

PRIVACY:

We believe that free individuals may not be compelled to authorize the assignment, collection or dissemination of personal and private information on themselves; nor may any rights and privileges available to others be denied to them for using such discretion.

REPUBLICAN PARTY OF WISCONSIN
June 2009

Headquarters and Staff

State Headquarters: 148 East Johnson Street, Madison 53703.

Telephone: (608) 257-4765; Fax: (608) 257-4141.

Internet Address: http://www.wisgop.org

Executive Director: MARK JEFFERSON.

Political Director: JUSTON JOHNSON.

Communications Director: KRISTIN RUESCH.

Finance Director: KARI REZIN.

IT Coordinator: BRIAN KIND.

Telemarketing Manager: RICHARD DICKIE.

State Executive Committee

State Chairman: REINCE PRIEBUS, Kenosha.

Finance Chairman: MARK CULLEN, Janesville.

Vice Chairmen: 1st − BILL JOHNSON, Hayward; *2nd* − DARLENE ROSS, Shawano; *3rd* − MICHELLE LITJENS, Oshkosh; *4th* − TROY FULLERTON, Waukesha.

Secretary: DAVID ANDERSON, Malone.

Treasurer: CATHY STEPP, Sturtevant.

National Committeewoman: MARY BUESTRIN, Mequon.

National Committeeman: STEVE KING, Janesville.

Wisconsin African American Council: HATTIE DANIELS-RUSH, Milwaukee.

Republican Heritage Council: PERFECTO RIVERA, Milwaukee.

Wisconsin Labor Council Chairman: vacancy.

Immediate Past Chairman: BRAD COURTNEY, Whitefish Bay.

Congressional District Chairmen and Vice Chairmen:

1st District
Tyler August, Walworth
Bob Geason, Burlington
2nd District
Kim Babler, Madison
Regina Schaar, Lake Mills
3rd District
Maripat Krueger, Menomonie
Steve Brody, Mineral Point
4th District
Bob Spindell, Milwaukee
Doug Haag, Milwaukee

5th District
Crystal Berg, Hartford
Curt David, Brookfield
6th District
Ralph Prescott, Chilton
Dan Feyen, Fond du Lac
7th District
Sean Duffy, Ashland
Mike Monson, Antigo
8th District
Jean Hundertmark, Clintonville
Grant Staszak, Bonduel

Source: Republican Party of Wisconsin at wisgop.org. June 2009.

County Organization. County party organizations are the basic building blocks of the Republican Party of Wisconsin. County party leaders are elected in county caucuses prior to April 1 of the odd-numbered year. Each committee has a chairman, first vice chairman, secretary, and treasurer.

Congressional District Organization. Each congressional district has an organization that coordinates the activities of the county organizations in the district, with special emphasis on the election of Republican congressional candidates. The district organization is directed by a committee consisting of district members of the state executive committee and, at minimum, an elected chairman, vice chairman, secretary, and treasurer. Committee officers are elected in odd-numbered years prior to the state convention.

State Officers and Executive Committee. Party leadership is vested in a 32-member state executive committee, consisting of the 11 party officers (including the chairman of the county chairmen's organization and the chairman of the Young Republicans Professionals, who are designated respectively as the third and fifth vice chairmen of the committee); the immediate past state party chairman; the chairman and vice chairman from each of the state's 8 congressional district organizations; and the Wisconsin Republican African American Council, the Wisconsin Heritage Council, the Wisconsin Senior Citizen Council, and the Wisconsin Labor Council. State committee vacancies are filled by the committee. Five of the 11 party officers – the chairman, first and second vice chairmen, secretary, and treasurer – are selected in odd-numbered years by the state executive committee at an organizational meeting within 30 days following the state convention. Their 2-year terms begin upon adjournment of the organizational meeting. The persons holding those offices and the immediate past state party chairman may not vote in the selection of the new officers. The national committeeman and committeewoman are included among the 11 state executive committee officers and are elected for 4-year terms by state convention delegates in presidential election years. They serve from the adjournment of one national party convention to the end of the next and must be approved by the assembled delegates at the party's national convention. The party finance chairman is also included among the 11 party officers. The finance chairman serves at the pleasure of the newly elected state chairman and is appointed with the consent of the committee to a term that continues until a successor is named.

State Convention. The party holds its state convention in May, June, or July of each year to pass resolutions and conduct other party business. In even-numbered years, the convention adopts a state party platform. A national committeeman and committeewoman are selected in those years in which a national party convention is held.

National Convention and National Committee. The Republican National Committee consists of a committeeman, committeewoman, and a chairman from each state, plus American Samoa, Washington, D.C., Guam, Puerto Rico, and the Virgin Islands. Each state and territory has its own method of electing representatives. National committee members serve from convention to convention. The national committee is led by a chairman and cochairman, who serve 2-year terms.

REPUBLICAN PARTY OF WISCONSIN PLATFORM
As Adopted at the State Convention, Stevens Point, May 2008
PREAMBLE

It's time to Make Wisconsin Great Again.

For six long years the state that led the nation in meaningful reforms and innovation has floundered under a Democrat administration. Sadly, our state motto, *Forward*, has become a symbol of the past instead of the beacon that reflected our people's traditional passion and potential for the future.

As Republicans, we know Wisconsin deserves better. And we will strive to ensure the *Wisconsin Spirit* is no longer held in check, but flourishes to lift the hearts and minds of every Wisconsin family. The soul of that spirit embodies certain principles and values that unite us.

We believe that keeping the reference to "One Nation Under God" in the Pledge of Allegiance is very important.

We will hold true to our values and traditions that strengthen families, builds moral character and protects the innocent.

We believe that English should be the official language of government.

We believe we have an obligation to be good stewards of God's creation for future generations, and we will do so while safeguarding our property rights.

We believe taxpayers should be given the option of a single rate system that will give them the convenience of filing their taxes with just a single sheet of paper.

We believe that The United States should only grant citizenship to those who want to embrace and defend American values and culture.

We believe that every worker should continue to have the right to a federally supervised secret ballot election when deciding whether to organize a union.

We will defend our right to protect family and home while defending America and her allies and defeating America's enemies.

We will demand accountability in all public institutions and at all levels of government.

We will lead our state into a new era of prosperity, innovation and opportunity for all.

The changes we propose in government have to occur in all 513,000 elected offices throughout the country and will start here in Wisconsin.

As Republicans, we *can and will* make Wisconsin and our country better for future generations.

AMERICAN VALUES AND AMERICAN SOLUTIONS

We want to strengthen and revitalize America's core values which unite a large majority of Americans.

Our goal should be to provide long-term solutions instead of short-term fixes.

Government clearly has to change the way it operates by bringing in ideas and systems currently employed in the private sector to increase productivity and effectiveness.

The changes we need in government have to occur in all elected offices throughout the country and cannot be achieved by focusing only on Washington.

ENGLISH AND THE AMERICAN CIVILIZATION

English

English should be the official language of government, and all election ballots and other government documents should be printed in English.

Immigrants should be required to learn English.

Government should make available English language instruction to all who need it.

Businesses should be able to require employees to speak the English language while on the job.

American Civilization

Individuals have basic Constitutional rights to defend themselves, their families and property.

We believe that our basic Constitutional rights begin at conception and continue until death.

It is important to have references to God in the Pledge of Allegiance. As it states in the Declaration of Independence, "we are endowed by our Creator with the right to life, liberty, and the pursuit of happiness" which makes clear that certain rights can't be taken away by government.

Statements regarding religion and morality made by the Founding Fathers are just as important today as they were 200 years ago.

The language in the Pledge of Allegiance and the Declaration of Independence are very important and must be protected. We reject the idea that because the times change so must the meaning of the language in the Pledge and the Declaration.

Public schools should teach more American history and civics.

IMMIGRATION, THE BORDER, AND ASSIMILATION

The United States should grant citizenship only to those who want to embrace and defend American values and culture.

The American people believe border control is a security issue and current laws must be vigorously enforced.

Illegal immigrants who commit felonies should be deported. Allowing illegal immigrants to remain in this country undermines respect for the law.

There should be a worker visa program making it easier for people to work legally in the United States.

When applying for a temporary worker visa each worker should take an oath to obey American law and be deported if they commit a felony while in the United States.

In a worker visa program each worker will receive a secure identification card that will allow the government to locate him or her.

Each worker must go to immigration centers in their home country that will help them find jobs in the United States so they apply for a visa with a job in hand.

There should be heavy monetary fines against employers and businesses who knowingly hire illegal immigrants.

The Internal Revenue Service should conduct audits of companies who hire illegal immigrants to determine if those companies have paid the taxes they owe.

SCIENCE AND TECHNOLOGY

There will be incredible possibilities to meet our country's challenges in a variety of fields because in the next 25 years there will be 4 to 7 times the amount of new science and technology in the world as in the last 25 years.

Therefore we should dramatically increase our investment in math and science education.

We must rely on innovation and new technology if we are going to compete globally.

ENERGY AND THE ENVIRONMENT

We have an obligation to be good stewards of God's creation for future generations.

We can have a healthy economy and a healthy environment.

We can solve our environmental problems faster and cheaper with innovation and new technology than with more litigation and more government regulation.

Entrepreneurs are more likely to solve America's energy and environmental problems than bureaucrats.

If we use technology and innovation we do not need to raise taxes to clean up our environment.

We want to encourage businesses to voluntarily cut pollution.

We should give tax credits to homeowners and builders who incorporate alternative energy systems in their homes including solar, wind, and geothermal energy.

We should hold city governments to the same standards for cleaning waste water as are applied to private industry.

We are prepared to develop public and private partnerships to preserve green space and parks and to protect natural areas from development.

OIL AND NATIONAL SECURITY

Our current dependence on foreign oil threatens our national security and economic prosperity by making us vulnerable.

We should encourage the building of more oil refineries in America to lower the cost of gas and reduce our dependence on foreign oil.

With appropriate safeguards to protect the environment we should drill for oil off America's coasts to reduce our dependence on foreign oil.

TAXES

The federal income tax system is unfair and the death tax should be abolished.

Taxpayers should be given the option of a single income tax rate. Taxpayers would still have the option of filing their taxes in the current system if they choose to do so.

The option of a single rate system should give taxpayers the convenience of filing their taxes with just a single sheet of paper.

We favor the option of a single corporate tax rate of 17% that would lower taxes for some businesses that pay up to 38% while also closing loopholes that some corporations use to pay less in taxes.

The United States has one of the highest corporate tax rates in the industrialized world making it difficult for U.S. corporations to compete internationally which gives incentives for companies to move overseas. This plan will make America a more attractive place for businesses that provide good paying jobs.

SOCIAL SECURITY AND RETIREMENT

It is important for the President and Congress to address the issue of Social Security in the next few years.

The current Social Security systems is broken and if it isn't reformed future generations will no longer have it as a safety net for retirement.

We favor a Social Security proposal in which Personal Social Security Savings Accounts would be optional, with workers given the choice of continuing to depend on the current system with current benefits.

We favor a Social Security proposal in which when a worker retires he or she would use the money in the account to buy an annuity, which is a type of financial benefit. The annuity will pay at least the same amount as traditional Social Security would.

We favor this Social Security proposal because in the current system, workers cannot pass onto their family members the money they paid into Social Security. This would not be the case in this new plan.

We favor a Social Security proposal in which any money in the account left after the purchase of an annuity would be the property of the worker and the extra money can be left to family members at death.

FREEDOM OF RELIGION

Statements regarding religion and morality made by the Founding Fathers are just as important today as they were 200 years ago.

References to the Creator in the Declaration of Independence are very important. We reject the Ninth Federal Circuit Court declaring the Pledge of Allegiance unconstitutional.

The phrase "Under God" in the Pledge of Allegiance is perfectly in line with the United States Constitution.

Separation between Church and State does not mean there can be no references to God in government sanctioned activities or public buildings.

The best way to ensure religious freedom is to protect ALL religious references and symbols; including those on public buildings, lands, or documents.

Children should be allowed a moment of silence to pray for themselves in public school if they desire.

We reject banning all prayer in public schools.

We support the right of high schools students saying thanks to God in a graduation speech.

We approve of nativity scenes, Menorahs or other religious symbols being placed on public property during their appropriate holiday season.

We favor a law to protect city, county, and state lands that have crosses or other religious symbols from being removed.

Many of the problems our country faces are because America is no longer as religious and moral as it once was.

The Founding Fathers understood that religion and morality were important to creating and building this country and talked about it regularly. This was understood throughout American history and is central to America's success today.

We reject that this violates the U.S. Constitution and discriminates against those who are of other faiths or are not religious.

DEFENDING AMERICA

We must help defend America and her allies and defeat our enemies.

America should take the threat of terror by fanatical religious groups seriously.

We have to be prepared to survive an attack by a nuclear, biological, or chemical weapon.

Terrorist organizations pose very serious threats for the United States and it will not be possible to negotiate with these groups.

Iran poses a serious threat to the United States.

There should be a death penalty for someone caught and convicted of carrying out a terrorist attack in the United States.

Congress should make it a crime to advocate acts of terrorism or violent conduct or the killing of innocent people in the United States.

The Department of Homeland Security and other government agencies should develop programs to teach Americans what they can do as individuals to help in the fight against terror.

Terrorist websites at home and abroad should be closed down using technology.

Elections

10

Elections in Wisconsin: September 2008 through June 2009 elections, including U.S. Congress, presidential preference primary, presidential, legislative, and judicial statistics

Flowing Barchan Sand Dunes on Mars

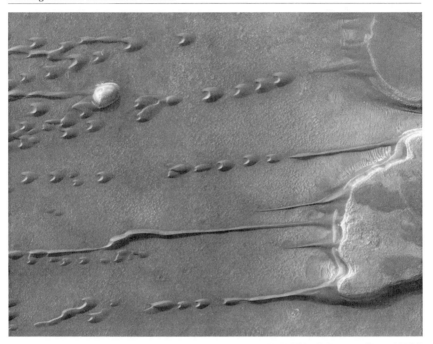

(HiRSI, MRO, LPL (University of Arizona), NASA)

ELECTIONS IN WISCONSIN

I. The Wisconsin Electorate

History of the Suffrage. When Wisconsin became a state in 1848, suffrage (the right to vote) was restricted to white or Indian males who were citizens of the United States or white male immigrants in the process of being naturalized. To be eligible to vote, these men had to be at least 21 years of age and Wisconsin residents for at least one year preceding the election. Wisconsin extended suffrage to male "colored persons" in a constitutional referendum held in November 1849. In 1908, the Wisconsin Constitution was amended to require that voters had to be citizens of the United States. Women's suffrage came with the 19th Amendment to the U.S. Constitution in 1920. (Wisconsin was one of the first states in the nation to ratify this amendment, on June 10, 1919.) The most recent major suffrage change was to lower the voting age from 21 to 18 years of age. This was accomplished by the 26th Amendment to the U.S. Constitution, which was ratified by the states in July 1971.

Size of the Electorate. Based on information from the Department of Administration, it is estimated that in November 2008 there were about 4,331,000 potential voters 18 years of age and older. An estimated 69% of eligible voters cast 2,983,417 ballots in the 2008 presidential election.

Age and Residence Requirements. The right to vote in Wisconsin state and local elections is granted to U.S. citizens who are age 18 or older and have resided in the election district or ward for 10 days prior to the election. Residence for purposes of voting is statutorily defined as "the place where the person's habitation is fixed, without any present intent to move, and to which, when absent, the person intends to return."

Voter Registration. Beginning with the 2006 spring primary, with limited exceptions, voter registration is required for all voters prior to voting. Voters registering in Wisconsin do not have to record a political party affiliation.

State law permits registration on election day at the proper polling place, and it also provides for advance registration by mail or in person with the municipal clerk, the county clerk, or the city board of election commissioners in the case of residents of the City of Milwaukee. Municipal officials may designate other locations, such as fire stations or libraries for registration, or conduct door-to-door registration drives. In addition, high school students and staff may register at public high schools or, in some cases, private high schools designated by the municipal clerk.

II. A Capsule View of Elections

The Wisconsin Statutes, Chapters 5 through 12, provide for four regularly scheduled elections: the spring primary, the spring election, the September primary, and the general election in November.

The spring primary on the third Tuesday in February of each year is followed by the spring election on the first Tuesday in April. The September primary is held on the second Tuesday in September in even-numbered years. It is followed by the general election on the first Tuesday after the first Monday in November.

Nonpartisan officials are chosen in the spring. These include the state superintendent of public instruction, judicial officers, county board members, county executives, and municipal and school district officers.

Partisan officials, chosen in the fall, include all other county administrative officials, members of the legislature, state constitutional officers (except for the state superintendent), and members of the U.S. Congress. Not all of these offices are filled at each election because their terms vary from two to six years.

In presidential election years, the presidential preference primary vote is held at the spring primary in February, and the vote for U.S. President occurs at the general election in November. In some elections, referendum questions allow Wisconsin voters to advise the state legislature or local government on matters of public policy or to ratify a proposed law, ordinance, or amendment to the Wisconsin Constitution.

Primary Elections

Until 1905, Wisconsin candidates for public office were selected through caucuses or conventions composed of delegates, eligible voters, or members of a political party. Since then, candidates have been chosen in primary elections, but the nominating caucus remains an optional method of selecting candidates for town and village offices. Aspirants must file a declaration of candidacy to run in a primary election, and they usually are required to file nomination papers signed by a specified number of persons eligible to vote in the jurisdiction or district in which they seek office.

Nonpartisan February Spring Primary. A nonpartisan primary election must be held in February if three or more candidates run for one of the offices on the April ballot and no caucus is held to nominate candidates. The two persons receiving the highest number of votes for the specific office in the primary are nominated to run as finalists in the nonpartisan election.

Partisan September Primary. The purpose of the September partisan primary is to select a party's nominees for the general election in November. In a partisan primary, the voter may vote on the ballot of only one political party (unlike the general election where it is possible to select any party's candidate for a particular office). Some voters express frustration that their choices are limited because they are not permitted to vote for candidates of more than one party. It is important to remember that the primary is a nominating device for the political parties; its purpose is to nominate the candidates that one political party will support against the nominees of the other parties in the general election.

Most states have a closed primary system that requires voters to publicly declare their party affiliation before they can receive the primary ballot of that party. Wisconsin's "open primary" law does not require voters to make a public declaration of their party preference. Instead, the voter is given the primary ballots of all parties but, once inside the voting booth, may cast only one party's ballot.

Candidates must appear on the primary ballot, even if unopposed, in order to be nominated by their respective parties. The candidate receiving the largest number of party votes for an office becomes the party's nominee in the November election. (In the case of a special election, which is held at a time other than the general election to fill a vacated partisan office, a primary is not held if there is no more than one candidate for a party's nomination.)

Elections

Nonpartisan April Spring Election. The officials chosen in the spring nonpartisan election are the state superintendent of public instruction; judicial officers; county executive (if the county elects one); county supervisor; town, village, and city officers; and school board members. Because the terms of office vary, not all offices are filled each year. The only nonpartisan officers elected on a statewide basis are the state superintendent of public instruction and justices of the supreme court; all others are elected from the county, circuit, district, or municipality represented.

The governor is authorized to fill vacancies that occur in nonpartisan state elective offices by appointment. Gubernatorial appointments strongly influence the composition of the Wisconsin judiciary, because many of the state's justices and judges who are appointed to the bench are later elected to office by the voters.

Partisan November General Election. In November, Wisconsin voters select their federal, state, and county partisan officials on a ballot listing the winners of the September primary election plus "independent" candidates who are either unaffiliated or affiliated with minor parties that are not recognized for separate ballot status. "Write-in" votes may be cast for persons whose names do not appear on the ballot.

The general election ballot includes a broad range of offices. The constitutional offices of governor, lieutenant governor, secretary of state, state treasurer, and attorney general are filled through a statewide vote. These officers are elected for 4-year terms in the even-numbered years that alternate with the U.S. presidential election.

Candidates for congressional representative and for representative to the state assembly are included on every general election ballot, because the terms for these offices are two years. Wisconsin's 33 state senators are elected for 4-year terms, with the odd-numbered senate districts electing their senators in the years when a gubernatorial election is held and even-numbered senate districts electing their senators in the presidential election years. U.S. Senators, who serve 6-year terms, are also chosen at the appropriate general election.

The state's 72 counties elect certain partisan officers for 4-year terms at each general election. Clerks of circuit court, coroners, and sheriffs are elected at the general election in which the governor is also elected, while county clerks, district attorneys, registers of deeds, surveyors, and treasurers are elected at the general election in which the president is elected. State law requires all counties either to elect a coroner or appoint a medical examiner. The post of surveyor may be filled by election or appointment at the county's option. (Milwaukee County is required by law to appoint its medical examiner and surveyor.)

Vacancies in the offices of U.S. Senator, U.S. Congressional representative, state senator, and representative to the assembly may be filled only by special election, but vacancies in state constitutional offices and most county offices are filled through appointment by the governor. The exception is that the lieutenant governor constitutionally succeeds the governor in case of a vacancy in that office.

Presidential Preference Vote

Wisconsin conducts its presidential preference vote on the third Tuesday in February of each presidential election year, in conjunction with the nonpartisan spring primary. 1985 Wisconsin Act 304 gave political parties complete freedom to select delegates for their national conventions on any basis they choose, so the vote has no binding effect. It does, however, indicate voter preferences.

A committee, composed of officials of the recognized political parties, meets on the second Tuesday in December of the year prior to the presidential preference vote in February to certify to the Government Accountability Board (GAB) the list of names to be placed on the ballot. (If a party's candidate for governor received at least 10% of the vote in the previous election, the party is considered a "recognized party".) The committee lists the names of all nationally advocated or recognized candidates of the recognized parties and such other names as it chooses. The committee includes each party's state chairperson (or designee), one national committeeman and one committeewoman (designated by the party's state chairperson), the president and the minority leader of the senate (or designees), and the speaker and minority leader of the assembly (or designees). An additional member is elected by the committee to serve as chairperson.

Any person named by the committee as a potential presidential candidate may withdraw from the ballot by filing a disclaimer with the GAB. Persons not named may have their names placed on the ballot by filing a nomination petition signed by a specified number of qualified electors.

Presidential Elections

Presidential Electors. On the first Tuesday in October in each presidential election year, the five partisan constitutional state officers, all hold-over senators, and the senate and assembly candidates nominated by each political party at the September primary election meet at the State Capitol to select a slate of presidential electors, who will cast Wisconsin's official ballots for the offices of U.S. President and Vice President. A party selects one elector from each of the Wisconsin congressional districts and two electors at large, and then certifies its list of electors to the GAB. After the November presidential election, the party that receives a plurality of the votes statewide sends its electors to the State Capitol on the first Monday after the second Wednesday in December to perform their duties as Wisconsin's electors. They compose Wisconsin's delegation to the Electoral College – the group of 538 electors nationwide who actually cast the votes for president and vice president. Independent candidates for president list their electors on their nomination papers.

Referendum and Recall

Referendum. A "referendum" is simply a question referred to the people for determination through a vote. On the state level, Wisconsin provides for four types of referenda: 1) amendments to the state constitution, 2) measures extending the right of suffrage, 3) ratification of legislation prior to its becoming law, and 4) advisory questions.

The procedure for amending the Wisconsin Constitution requires that two consecutive legislatures must adopt an identically worded amendment proposal and a majority of the voters must ratify the change at a subsequent election.

An advisory referendum gives the legislature a means of asking the voters their opinion on legislative policy. Advisory referenda are usually submitted to the electorate at the April or November elections. Wisconsin county boards may submit advisory or ratifying referenda to county voters. Municipalities also are permitted and sometimes required to submit referendum questions relating to village and city charter ordinances and certain other subjects.

Recall. The Wisconsin Constitution and statutes provide for the removal of elected officers through a process of petition and special election, known as "recall." Officials may be recalled after serving the first year of a term, and no reason need be given for the recall in the case of a state, congressional, legislative, state judicial, or county officer. A petition seeking recall of a city, village, town, or school district official must contain a statement of a reason for the recall. The reason must be related to the official responsibilities of the office, but the petitioners need not provide supporting evidence for the reason.

A petition for the recall of an officer must be signed by electors equal to at least 25% of the vote cast in the district or territory served by the official during the last gubernatorial election. Following the filing of a successful recall petition, an election is held to fill the office. A recall primary is required whenever two or more persons compete for a nonpartisan office or whenever more than one person competes for the nomination of a political party for a partisan office. Unless the official facing recall resigns, he or she is listed on the recall ballot along with the other candidates who have been nominated.

Prior to 1977, the recall was seldom used. In August of that year, five La Crosse school board members were recalled, and in the following month a county judge was recalled for the first time in Wisconsin history. Attempts to recall state legislators are rare, but on June 4, 1996, a state senator became the first state legislator to be recalled. Since 1996 only one other legislator has been recalled, a state senator defeated in a special recall primary on October 21, 2003.

Mechanics of the Election Process

Certifying candidates, registering voters, and recording and reporting millions of votes is a complex process governed by state law. Legislation passed in 2007 created a Government Accountability Board that replaced both the Ethics Board and the Elections Board. The Government Accountability Board, Elections Division took over responsibility for the administration of elections laws in January 2008.

The GAB, Elections Division determines the format for all federal, state, county, municipal and special district ballots, certifies to each county clerk the list of candidates for federal and state office, and performs many other duties pertaining to elections.

County clerks prepare the ballots for federal, state, and county elections and distribute them to the municipal clerks. The law requires every city, village, and town having a population of 7,500 or more to use an electronic voting system, unless otherwise permitted by the Elections Division. If an electronic voting system is used, the equipment must generate a complete, permanent record showing all votes cast by each voter, which can be verified by the voter.

Municipal clerks supervise registration and elections in their municipalities. In cities or counties with more than 500,000 population, election duties are performed by a city board of election commissioners and a county board of election commissioners. (This provision currently applies only to the City of Milwaukee and Milwaukee County.)

Registration and Voting

The first step in casting a Wisconsin ballot usually is to register to vote. The voter must provide information on name; residence; citizenship; date of birth; age; the voter's driver's license number or last 4 digits of the voter's social security number, if any; length of residence in the ward or election district; whether the applicant has been convicted of a felony for which he or she has not been pardoned, and if so, whether the applicant is incarcerated, on parole, probation or extended supervision; and whether the applicant is disqualified on any other ground from voting; or is currently registered to vote at any other location.

Most voter registration information is open to public inspection, but victims of domestic abuse, sexual assault, or stalking can request that their registration information be kept confidential. A voter's registration is considered permanent unless the person changes his or her residence, in which case it is necessary to transfer registration to the new residence. Municipalities, however, must cancel the registration of a person who, though eligible, does not vote during a 4-year period and does not respond to a written request to apply for continued registration.

A voter who is unable or unwilling to come to the polling place on election day may vote by absentee ballot. An absentee ballot may be cast by mail or in person at the municipal clerk's office serving the voter's residence. Every request for an absentee ballot must be made in writing.

On election day, there are usually seven inspectors (election officials) for each polling place. The number may vary, but no polling place may have fewer than three. Any member of the public may be present in any polling place for the purpose of observation and the major parties often designate official polling place observers.

III. Campaign Finance Regulation

Early Reforms. Wisconsin's first attempt to regulate election practices (Chapter 358, Laws of 1897) was passed to stymie the crudest forms of corrupt practices, such as bribery, illegal voting, election fraud, and related corruption. It also required the filing of financial statements that were open to the public.

The current ban on campaign contributions by corporations dates back to 1905 (Chapter 492). Corporations are still prohibited from donating to candidates, political parties, or committees. (Labor organizations were also banned from making such contributions by Chapter 135, Laws of 1935, but the prohibition was repealed by Chapter 429, Laws of 1959.)

The "Corrupt Practices Act" of 1911 (Chapter 650) strengthened and expanded the earlier laws. Central to the act were tightening disclosure provisions. Candidates were required to report all sources of their funding, and they were barred from trading favors, monetary or otherwise, in return for financial support.

1974 Campaign Finance Reforms. The legislature passed sweeping campaign finance reform in Chapter 334, Laws of 1973, which created the current statutory "Chapter 11 – Campaign Finance". The law regulated campaign contributions and expenditures and required central filing of financial reports. It also created the state Elections Board, with representation from the three branches of government and the major political parties, to administer and enforce both election and campaign finance laws. These duties are now performed by the GAB. Candidates, individuals, committees, and groups involved in campaigns for state offices and statewide referenda must file detailed campaign finance reports with the board, which supervises the auditing of the reports. The GAB investigates election law violations and must notify the district attorney, attorney general, or the governor of any facts or evidence that might be grounds for civil action or criminal prosecution.

Regulation of Contributions

Wisconsin regulates campaign finance according to function – contribution or expenditure – with separate dollar limits and reporting requirements.

Contributions are moneys or certain other things of value that are donated directly either to individual candidates or to political committees, with the recipients determining how the money will be spent. The state determines the contribution limits in the case of state or local offices, but candidates running for federal office are subject to the limits set by federal campaign finance laws.

Contributions by candidates from their own personal funds or by individuals and committees acting independently of the candidate cannot be limited because they are considered to be free expression and are protected by the First Amendment. However, independent individuals and committees are required to file reports disclosing the contributions they receive and the expenditures they make.

Individuals. States are free to set their own limits on contributions to candidates for state or local office. Limitations usually pertain to the type of office. Wisconsin also limits the overall amount a single individual is allowed to contribute to all candidates in a calendar year.

Other than a candidate's own contributions to the campaign, no individual may contribute more than the amounts specified to the following candidates or any individuals or independent groups supporting them: constitutional officer (governor, lieutenant governor, secretary of state, state treasurer, attorney general, or superintendent of public instruction) or supreme court justice

– $10,000; state senator – $1,000; representative to the assembly – $500; and all other state and local candidates – a maximum of $250 to $3,000 depending upon the office. Furthermore, no individual may make contributions to a combination of candidates or registered committees that exceed a total of $10,000 in any calendar year.

Committees. Wisconsin limits campaign contributions made by political committees. Different limits apply in terms of the amounts a particular type of committee may donate and the amounts a candidate may receive from committees. Committees subject to contribution limits include: 1) the *political action committee (PAC),* which may be created by but operate separately from a private interest group (such as a trade association or a union) to raise and spend money to elect or defeat particular candidates; 2) the *political party committee,* organized by a formal political party; 3) the *legislative campaign committees,* organized by the respective political parties within the State Senate or the State Assembly; and 4) the candidate's *personal campaign committee.* Any committee that contributes directly to a particular candidate's campaign is subject to specific contribution limits, which vary according to the type of committee and the type of elective office. However, legislative campaign committees and political party committees are allowed to use contributions for party building activities or administrative expenses. PACs may contribute to the political parties and legislative campaign committees in which case the PAC per-candidate limitations do not apply (although other limitations remain applicable).

No committee, other than a political party or legislative campaign committee, may make contributions to a candidate for statewide constitutional office or justice of the supreme court that exceed 4% of the candidate's statutory expenditure level. (Similar limits on contributions apply to candidates for other state and local offices.)

Regulation of Expenditures

Expenditures by the Candidate. Candidates may make campaign expenditures from their own personal funds and the moneys received as contributions from individuals and registered committees, plus any public funding they are awarded. There are no limits on the amount the candidates can spend on their own campaigns, unless they voluntarily accept public funding. There were attempts at the federal and state level in the early 1970s to limit candidates' personal expenditures, but the U.S. Supreme Court in *Buckley v. Valeo* held that this type of financing was protected by the U.S. Constitution as an exercise of free speech.

Expenditures by Independent Committees. Committees are considered to be making independent expenditures if they do not coordinate their efforts with a candidate. Independent committees are permitted to spend unlimited amounts promoting or opposing a candidate, but in Wisconsin they are required to file a statement declaring that the expenditures will be made without consultation or coordination with any candidate. (If the candidate is knowingly involved in the expenditure, the expenditure is viewed as a contribution, and the contributor must adhere to contribution limits.)

Expenditures by Political Party Committees. When a political party makes an expenditure to support its candidate, the expenditure is normally counted as a contribution to that candidate. Candidates are subject to aggregate limitations on the amount they may receive from parties and other committees. In *Colorado Republican Federal Campaign Committee et al. v. Federal Election Commission,* 518 U.S. 604 (1996), the U.S. Supreme Court held, however, that political party committees may make unlimited independent expenditures as long as they are not acting in consultation or coordination with a candidate.

Reporting Requirements

Registration and Reporting. Campaign finance laws are designed to track the flow of dollars received and spent by the candidates. Expenditures from the campaign depository may not be made anonymously, nor may contributions or expenditures be made in a fictitious name. Any anonymous contribution of more than $10 must be donated to a charity or the common school fund.

Generally, all candidates for state office, the four types of committees listed above, and other committees that make contributions or expenditures expressly supporting or opposing state candidates must register and file campaign finance reports with the GAB. These reports must include the name, address, and total contributions of each contributor who donates more than $20 in a calendar year and must give the occupation and principal place of employment of each contributor who makes cumulative contributions of over $100 in a calendar year. Reports must also itemize all contributions, loans, expenditures, or obligations in excess of $20. Registrants with limited financial activity may be exempted from reporting.

Each candidate must appoint one campaign treasurer and designate one campaign depository, such as a numbered bank account, before receiving any contributions or making any expenditures. The candidate and campaign treasurer are then required to file a registration statement regardless of the amount of money they expect to receive or dispense. Unless exempted from reporting, the candidate, or the treasurer acting on the candidate's behalf, must file periodic financial reports. The candidate is considered personally responsible for the accuracy of these reports.

Political party committees or other committees that make or accept contributions or make expenditures amounting to more than $25 per year, and individuals (other than candidates) who accept contributions or make expenditures amounting to more than $25 per year must file registration statements. These statements include such information as the name and address of the registrant, the officers, the campaign depository, and the candidate or referendum question they support or oppose.

Since July 1, 1999, registrants with the Government Accountability Board, Ethics and Accountability Division who have accepted contributions totaling more than $20,000 within a campaign or biennial period have been required to file their reports electronically. These reports may be viewed on the GAB Web site.

Nonresident committees, groups, or individuals making contributions or expenditures in this state must also file their names and addresses and those of a designated agent in the state with the secretary of state and must also file regular reports, unless a reporting exemption applies.

Disclosure. Candidates and political committees that are subject to state reporting requirements must identify themselves on any mass media communications, such as billboards, handbills, and radio or TV advertisements. This disclosure must contain the words "paid for" followed by the name of the organization responsible for the communication.

IV. Public Campaign Financing

Chapter 107, Laws of 1977, created the Wisconsin Election Campaign Fund in the state treasury as a mechanism for publicly funding campaigns. Under the state's public financing law, each individual who files a state income tax return may specify that $1 shall be set aside for the election fund without increasing the person's tax liability or reducing any refund due. (The $1 contributions are derived from an appropriation created by the legislature to support the campaign fund.)

The public campaign fund is available to candidates for statewide executive and judicial offices, as well as legislative candidates, for use after the primary, provided, in the case of candidates for partisan office, that they obtain a specified number of primary votes and raise a specified amount of private contributions from individuals in amounts limited to $100 or less per individual.

To receive public funding, candidates must agree to accept spending limits and limit personal contributions to their own campaigns. These restrictions are lifted if the candidate's opponent qualifies for a grant but does not accept it and refuses to file a sworn statement affirming adherence to the limits. Money from the campaign fund can be used only for media advertising, printing, graphic arts or advertising services, office supplies, or postage. Other campaign expenses must be financed with contributions from individuals, political parties, PACs, or other committees. Because the spending limits imposed as a condition of acceptance of public funding are low and the amount of money generated for distribution from the fund at any given election is limited, participation in public funding has become rare in competitive races.

U.S. Senator Barack Obama spoke at the Brown County Arena in Green Bay on September 21, 2008, during his presidential campaign. (Timothy Ditzman)

PROHIBIT PARTIAL VETO AUTHORITY

Creating Article V, Section 10 (1) (c); 2005 SJR 33 (JR 46); 2007 SJR 5 (JR 26); Adopted.

Ballot Question: *"Partial Veto.* Shall section 10 (1) (c) of article V of the constitution be amended to prohibit the governor, in exercising his or her partial veto authority, from creating a new sentence by combining parts of two or more sentences of the enrolled bill?"

Text of Section:

[Article V] Section 10 (1) (c). In approving an appropriation bill in part, the governor may not create a new word by rejecting individual letters in the words of the enrolled bill, and may not create a new sentence by combining parts of 2 or more sentences of the enrolled bill.

County Vote for Constitutional Amendment
April 1, 2008 Spring Election

County	Yes	No	County	Yes	No
Adams	1,775	792	Marinette	3,155	1,626
Ashland	1,475	863	Marquette	2,238	799
Barron	5,748	3,880	Menominee	80	61
Bayfield	2,129	1,286	Milwaukee	96,438	49,918
Brown	19,596	9,310	Monroe.	3,265	1,427
Buffalo	1,124	758	Oconto	2,950	1,391
Burnett	1,592	634	Oneida	5,554	3,220
Calumet	4,926	2,142	Outagamie	16,932	7,279
Chippewa	5,369	2,538	Ozaukee	10,185	2,873
Clark	3,076	1,707	Pepin	1,036	811
Columbia.	6,478	1,833	Pierce.	2,976	1,607
Crawford	2,053	952	Polk	3,787	1,600
Dane	55,191	15,752	Portage	4,752	2,376
Dodge	11,389	4,140	Price	1,837	924
Door	3,586	1,996	Racine	20,398	8,101
Douglas	2,814	1,618	Richland	2,013	597
Dunn	3,086	1,427	Rock	12,931	4,463
Eau Claire	7,492	3,287	Rusk	1,824	1,111
Florence	451	293	St. Croix	6,326	3,315
Fond du Lac	9,147	3,482	Sauk	7,448	2,056
Forest.	1,382	808	Sawyer	1,284	723
Grant	5,667	2,245	Shawano	3,760	1,761
Green	3,720	946	Sheboygan	13,625	3,784
Green Lake.	2,377	849	Taylor	1,511	682
Iowa	2,987	1,017	Trempealeau	2,119	1,151
Iron.	845	515	Vernon	2,737	1,202
Jackson.	1,454	795	Vilas	2,425	854
Jefferson	9,324	2,815	Walworth	9,633	4,407
Juneau	2,942	1,110	Washburn	1,781	1,105
Kenosha	13,549	6,771	Washington.	17,083	5,294
Kewaunee	2,345	1,515	Waukesha	48,741	13,521
La Crosse	10,829	5,303	Waupaca	4,719	2,017
Lafayette	2,309	921	Waushara	2,525	1,010
Langlade	2,583	1,678	Winnebago	14,332	6,082
Lincoln	3,472	1,512	Wood.	9,192	5,331
Manitowoc	7,912	2,261	TOTAL.	575,582	239,613
Marathon	11,796	5,383			

Source: Official records of the Government Accountability Board, Elections Division. Scattered votes omitted.

COUNTY VOTE FOR SUPREME COURT JUSTICE
April 1, 2008 Spring Election

County	Louis Butler*	Mike Gableman	County Total
Adams	1,197	1,329	2,526
Ashland	1,296	1,178	2,484
Barron	3,779	5,324	9,118
Bayfield	1,884	1,589	3,482
Brown	13,666	15,603	29,423
Buffalo	767	1,109	1,882
Burnett	540	1,851	2,394
Calumet	2,859	4,110	6,978
Chippewa	3,781	4,268	8,065
Clark	1,999	2,978	4,992
Columbia	4,274	3,840	8,131
Crawford	1,380	1,541	2,923
Dane	51,484	19,783	71,405
Dodge	6,360	8,923	15,304
Door	2,647	2,857	5,548
Douglas	2,069	2,381	4,455
Dunn	2,091	2,430	4,527
Eau Claire	6,005	5,030	11,065
Florence	226	421	647
Fond du Lac	4,524	8,338	12,882
Forest	847	1,213	2,061
Grant	3,613	4,120	7,741
Green	2,433	2,035	4,520
Green Lake	1,079	2,124	3,210
Iowa	2,251	1,598	3,857
Iron	642	749	1,391
Jackson	961	1,245	2,208
Jefferson	5,233	6,826	12,100
Juneau	1,741	2,134	3,883
Kenosha	10,396	9,851	20,318
Kewaunee	1,541	2,453	4,014
La Crosse	8,774	7,224	16,083
Lafayette	1,549	1,494	3,061
Langlade	1,654	2,471	4,140
Lincoln	2,376	2,588	4,991
Manitowoc	4,056	6,105	10,179
Marathon	8,816	8,965	17,834
Marinette	1,811	2,892	4,713
Marquette	1,636	1,273	2,911
Menominee	102	49	151
Milwaukee	91,627	67,203	159,645
Monroe	2,088	2,616	4,716
Oconto	1,747	2,658	4,418
Oneida	4,041	4,387	8,482
Outagamie	11,559	12,567	24,174
Ozaukee	4,268	8,993	13,281
Pepin	778	1,047	1,829
Pierce	1,746	2,575	4,324
Polk	1,913	3,445	5,361
Portage	3,929	3,351	7,317
Price	1,170	1,551	2,728
Racine	13,016	15,383	28,440
Richland	1,350	1,348	2,703
Rock	10,026	7,425	17,479
Rusk	1,204	1,643	2,849
St. Croix	3,321	5,472	8,809
Sauk	5,172	4,064	9,291
Sawyer	728	1,217	1,945
Shawano	2,020	3,413	5,449
Sheboygan	6,634	10,783	17,437
Taylor	792	1,400	2,208
Trempealeau	1,548	1,733	3,290
Vernon	1,901	2,020	3,921
Vilas	1,460	1,721	3,201
Walworth	5,655	8,122	13,840
Washburn	980	1,849	2,831
Washington	6,716	15,600	22,343
Waukesha	21,649	43,637	65,378
Waupaca	2,502	4,193	6,704
Waushara	1,256	2,208	3,478
Winnebago	9,002	11,346	20,429
Wood	6,661	7,839	14,553
TOTAL	402,798	425,101	830,450

*Incumbent.

Source: Official records of the Government Accountability Board, Elections Division. County totals include scattered votes.

COUNTY VOTE FOR SUPREME COURT JUSTICE
April 7, 2009 Spring Election

County	Shirley S. Abrahamson*	Randy R. Koschnick	County Total
Adams	2,029	1,210	3,245
Ashland	1,984	1,073	3,064
Barron	2,500	2,160	4,661
Bayfield	3,079	1,465	4,547
Brown	14,754	9,214	23,983
Buffalo	1,118	683	1,801
Burnett	1,737	1,434	3,173
Calumet	3,354	2,094	5,448
Chippewa	5,466	3,801	9,268
Clark	3,469	2,543	6,016
Columbia	5,025	3,293	8,322
Crawford	1,738	1,088	2,827
Dane	71,839	26,106	97,978
Dodge	5,687	5,646	11,335
Door	3,925	1,515	5,441
Douglas	5,289	2,711	8,010
Dunn	3,593	2,237	5,832
Eau Claire	6,485	4,079	10,577
Florence	372	328	701
Fond du Lac	7,779	6,170	13,951
Forest	1,018	654	1,673
Grant	6,050	3,824	9,879
Green	3,799	2,090	5,892
Green Lake	1,889	1,403	3,294
Iowa	2,860	1,346	4,207
Iron	789	607	1,396
Jackson	1,615	1,160	2,775
Jefferson	6,352	7,455	13,817
Juneau	2,247	1,569	3,818
Kenosha	11,085	6,016	17,128
Kewaunee	1,614	969	2,583
La Crosse	12,531	7,569	20,120
Lafayette	2,030	1,136	3,166
Langlade	2,497	1,662	4,159
Lincoln	3,793	2,184	5,980
Manitowoc	10,733	6,138	16,876
Marathon	12,017	7,846	19,879
Marinette	4,204	2,539	6,746
Marquette	1,238	1,131	2,369
Menominee	186	55	241
Milwaukee	51,544	34,400	86,026
Monroe	3,329	2,398	5,735
Oconto	3,434	2,095	5,532
Oneida	4,019	2,214	6,237
Outagamie	11,710	6,423	18,139
Ozaukee	6,745	8,624	15,373
Pepin	667	471	1,138
Pierce	1,996	1,596	3,593
Polk	2,913	2,275	5,190
Portage	4,867	2,418	7,287
Price	1,871	1,152	3,023
Racine	13,648	11,149	24,816
Richland	1,655	1,049	2,705
Rock	11,398	5,778	17,190
Rusk	1,368	1,079	2,447
St. Croix	3,894	3,452	7,355
Sauk	7,077	3,769	10,854
Sawyer	2,785	1,820	4,605
Shawano	3,497	2,405	5,902
Sheboygan	13,039	8,999	22,052
Taylor	2,971	1,799	4,773
Trempealeau	2,477	1,491	3,968
Vernon	2,561	1,900	4,461
Vilas	3,820	2,255	6,083
Walworth	6,735	5,464	12,212
Washburn	1,684	1,108	2,794
Washington	9,642	13,461	23,112
Waukesha	23,844	35,619	59,469
Waupaca	4,965	2,501	7,466
Waushara	1,818	1,300	3,119
Winnebago	15,124	8,475	23,618
Wood	6,846	4,564	11,412
TOTAL	**473,712**	**319,706**	**793,864**

*Incumbent.

Source: Official records of the Government Accountability Board, Elections Division. County totals include scattered votes.

DISTRICT VOTE FOR COURT OF APPEALS
April 1, 2008 Spring Election

District I

County	Patricia S. Curley*	County Total
Milwaukee	110,916	112,274
TOTAL.	110,916	112,274

District II

County	William Gleisner	Lisa S. Neubauer	County Total
Calumet	2,075	4,475	6,558
Fond du Lac	4,376	7,554	11,943
Green Lake	959	2,004	2,967
Kenosha	4,499	14,866	19,409
Manitowoc	3,138	6,625	9,776
Ozaukee	5,291	6,795	12,101
Racine	7,611	19,846	27,490
Sheboygan	6,378	10,338	16,729
Walworth.	4,251	8,633	12,917
Washington.	9,549	11,235	20,797
Waukesha	28,031	33,097	61,182
Winnebago.	6,144	12,773	18,960
TOTAL.	82,302	138,241	220,829

District IV

County	Burneatta L. Bridge*	County Total	County	Burneatta L. Bridge*	County Total
Adams	1,864	1,864	Lafayette.	2,381	2,382
Clark	3,628	3,642	Marquette	2,185	2,190
Columbia.	6,056	6,081	Monroe.	3,662	3,675
Crawford.	2,211	2,218	Portage.	4,711	4,734
Dane	45,962	46,260	Richland	1,996	1,998
Dodge	11,460	11,489	Rock	12,891	12,933
Grant	5,853	5,868	Sauk	6,614	6,648
Green.	3,251	3,265	Vernon	2,891	2,900
Iowa	2,921	2,923	Waupaca	5,267	5,284
Jackson.	1,672	1,672	Waushara.	2,695	2,705
Jefferson	8,560	8,613	Wood.	11,264	11,284
Juneau	2,954	2,964	TOTAL.	164,795	165,526
La Crosse	11,846	11,934			

*Incumbent.

Source: Official records of the Government Accountability Board, Elections Division. County totals include scattered votes.

DISTRICT VOTE FOR COURT OF APPEALS
April 7, 2009 Spring Election
District I

County	Kitty K. Brennan*	County Total
Milwaukee	53,710	54,274
TOTAL	53,710	54,274

District III

County	Michael W. Hoover*	County Total
Ashland	1,962	1,979
Barron	3,563	3,568
Bayfield	3,199	3,209
Brown	16,845	16,895
Buffalo	1,424	1,425
Burnett	2,435	2,438
Chippewa	6,588	6,604
Door	3,700	3,711
Douglas	6,149	6,170
Dunn	4,470	4,483
Eau Claire	7,280	7,350
Florence	489	489
Forest	1,197	1,197
Iron	1,014	1,015
Kewaunee	1,768	1,770
Langlade	3,156	3,159
Lincoln	4,309	4,336
Marathon	15,546	15,611
Marinette	4,939	4,948
Menominee	134	134
Oconto	4,257	4,263
Oneida	4,434	4,454
Outagamie	13,093	13,134
Pepin	876	879
Pierce	2,761	2,774
Polk	4,184	4,195
Price	1,928	1,929
Rusk	1,849	1,851
St. Croix	5,656	5,683
Sawyer	3,598	3,602
Shawano	4,561	4,571
Taylor	3,302	3,312
Trempealeau	3,210	3,211
Vilas	4,413	4,422
Washburn	2,124	2,126
TOTAL	150,413	150,897

*Incumbent.

Source: Official records of the Government Accountability Board, Elections Division. County totals include scattered votes.

VOTE FOR CIRCUIT JUDGES
February 19, 2008 Spring Primary

Circuit Court	Vote
Chippewa County, Branch 3	
Julie Anderl	6,538
Steven R. Cray	4,208
Robert A. Ferg	2,918
Florence-Forest County	
Douglas J. Drexler	1,003
Robert A. Kennedy, Jr.*	1,859
Leon D. Stenz	1,478
Outagamie County, Branch 2	
Maureen Roberts Budiac	6,366
Dan Hoff	10,626
Nancy J. Krueger*	21,030
St. Croix County, Branch 4	
Howard Cameron	3,077
Mark J. Gherty	4,593
Charles B. Harris	2,107
Carol L. Law	2,395
Ken Sortedahl	1,502

*Incumbent.
Source: Official records of the Government Accountability Board, Elections Division. Scattered votes omitted.

February 17, 2009 Spring Primary

Circuit Court	Vote
Chippewa County, Branch 2	
Robert A. Ferg	1,197
Steve Gibbs	1,495
James Isaacson	1,668
Dane County, Branch 13	
Stephen Ehlke	5,032
Julie Genovese	15,104
Charlie Schutze	3,835
Green County, Branch 2	
Timothy J. Burns	874
Dan Gartzke	982
Thomas J. Vale	1,401
Jefferson County, Branch 1	
Steven J. Luchsinger	1,137
Jennifer L. Weber	678
Jennifer L. Weston	2,155
Kenosha County, Branch 8	
Gregg Norman Guttormsen	1,543
Chad G. Kerkman	2,971
David P. Wilk	2,512
Frederick L. Zievers	3,547
Marathon County, Branch 1	
Douglas Bauman	452
Jill N. Falstad	4,186
Alan E. Grischke	582
Sandra J. Marcus	1,485
Peter C. Rotter	1,619
Milwaukee County, Branch 15	
Ronald Dague	6,325
Daniel J. Gabler	16,356
J.D. Watts	13,830
Ozaukee County, Branch 3	
Steven H. Glamm	1,653
Darcy McManus	2,152
Sandy A. Williams	3,728
Wood County, Branch 3	
John P. Henkelmann	434
John Adam Kruse	1,770
Richard D. Weymouth	1,535
Todd P. Wolf	2,544

Source: Official records of the Government Accountability Board, Elections Division. Scattered votes omitted.

VOTE FOR CIRCUIT JUDGES
April 1, 2008 Spring Election

Circuit Court	Vote	Circuit Court	Vote
Barron County		Branch 21	
Branch 2		Bill Brash*	104,299
Timothy M. Doyle	8,423	Branch 27	
Branch 3		Kevin E. Martens*	105,520
James D. Babbitt	6,857	Branch 31	
Jim McLaughlin	3,231	Daniel A. Noonan*	105,413
Chippewa County		Branch 32	
Branch 1		Michael D. Guolee*	105,561
Roderick A. Cameron*	6,736	Branch 40	
Branch 3		Rebecca Dallet	90,029
Julie Anderl	3,994	Jeffrey Norman	44,034
Steven R. Cray	4,496	Branch 41	
Dane County		John J. DiMotto*	106,359
Branch 1		Oneida County	
John W. Markson	45,929	Branch 1	
Branch 7		Patrick F. O'Melia	7,926
William E. Hanrahan	45,847	Outagamie County	
Dodge County		Branch 2	
Branch 1		Dan Hoff	8,106
William H. Gergen	7,236	Nancy J. Krueger	16,464
Brian A. Pfitzinger	8,380	Branch 3	
Branch 4		Mitchell J. Metropulos	12,888
Steven Bauer	12,803	Carrie Schneider	11,790
Eau Claire County		Polk County	
Branch 2		Branch 1	
Michael Schumacher	7,969	Molly E. GaleWyrick*	4,896
Florence-Forest County		Price County	
Robert A. Kennedy, Jr.*	1,555	Douglas T. Fox*	2,408
Leon D. Stenz	1,629	Racine County	
Fond du Lac County		Branch 7	
Branch 1		Charles H. Constantine*	21,678
Dale L. English*	10,925	Rock County	
Jackson County		Branch 1	
Eric F. Stutz	1,943	James P. Daley*	14,227
Juneau County		St. Croix County	
Branch 2		Branch 1	
Paul S. Curran	2,364	Eric J. Lundell*	8,306
Stacy A. Smith	1,770	Branch 4	
Kenosha County		Howard Cameron	4,949
Branch 3		Mark J. Gherty	4,751
Bruce E. Schroeder*	16,926	Washington County	
Marathon County		Branch 2	
Branch 3		James K. Muehlbauer	16,265
Vincent K. Howard*	14,763	Waukesha County	
Marinette County		Branch 2	
Branch 1		Mark S. Gempeler*	47,839
David G. Miron*	4,253	Branch 5	
Branch 2		Lee S. Dreyfus, Jr.*	49,635
Tim A. Duket*	4,198	Branch 6	
Menominee-Shawano County		Patrick C. Haughney*	46,690
Branch 1		Wood County	
James R. Habeck*	5,045	Branch 1	
Milwaukee County		Gregory J. Potter*	12,607
Branch 17			
Francis T. Wasielewski*	107,208		

*Incumbent.

Source: Official records of the Government Accountability Board, Elections Division. Scattered votes omitted.

VOTE FOR CIRCUIT JUDGES
April 7, 2009 Spring Election

Circuit Court	Vote	Circuit Court	Vote
Adams County		Branch 3	
Charles A. Pollex*	2,742	Clare L. Fiorenza*	50,560
Bayfield County		Branch 6	
John P. Anderson*	3,222	Ellen Brostrom	37,392
Gene D. Linehan	1,560	Christopher R. Lipscomb, Sr.	35,196
Brown County		Branch 7	
Branch 1		Jean W. DiMotto*	51,244
Donald R. Zuidmulder*	18,649	Branch 12	
Branch 4		David L. Borowski*	50,160
Kendall M. Kelley*	17,473	Branch 15	
Branch 5		Daniel J. Gabler	35,829
Marc A. Hammer*	17,441	J.D. Watts	38,933
Branch 6		Branch 16	
J.D. McKay*	17,542	Michael J. Dwyer*	50,420
Branch 8		Branch 22	
William M. Atkinson*	17,733	Timothy M. Witkowiak*	50,202
Burnett County		Branch 29	
Paul W. Baxter	1,073	Richard J. Sankovitz*	49,964
Kenneth L. Kutz*	2,349	Branch 30	
Chippewa County		Jeffrey Conen*	49,786
Branch 2		Branch 42	
Steve Gibbs	4,612	David A. Hansher*	50,314
James Isaacson	4,906	Outagamie County	
Columbia County		Branch 5	
Branch 1		Michael Gage*	13,997
Daniel S. George*	6,681	Ozaukee County	
Dane County		Branch 1	
Branch 6		Paul V. Malloy*	10,841
Shelley J. Gaylord*	63,743	Branch 3	
Branch 10		Darcy McManus	6,606
Juan B. Colas*	61,916	Sandy A. Williams	8,402
Branch 11		Polk County	
Dan Moeser*	65,431	Branch 2	
Branch 13		Robert H. Rasmussen*	4,577
Stephen Ehlke	27,251	Racine County	
Julie Genovese	56,673	Branch 6	
Douglas County		Wayne J. Marik*	16,730
Branch 1		Branch 8	
Daniel W. Blank	4,390	Faye M. Flancher*	16,842
Kelly J. Thimm	4,690	Branch 9	
Branch 2		Allan B. Torhorst*	16,787
George L. Glonek*	7,312	Richland County	
Dunn County		Edward E. Leineweber*	2,266
Branch 2		Rock County	
Rod W. Smeltzer*	5,191	Branch 3	
Fond du Lac County		Michael R. Fitzpatrick*	13,005
Branch 3		Branch 5	
Richard J. Nuss*	10,552	Kenneth Forbeck*	13,049
Grant County		Branch 6	
Branch 2		Richard T. Werner*	13,079
George S. Curry*	4,314	Sawyer County	
Craig R. Day	6,236	Thomas J. Duffy	2,371
Green County		Jerry Wright	2,741
Branch 1		Sheboygan County	
Jim Beer*	4,722	Branch 1	
Branch 2		L. Edward Stengel*	18,110
Dan Gartzke	2,800	Branch 4	
Thomas J. Vale	3,012	Terence T. Bourke*	17,768
Jackson County		Taylor County	
Thomas E. Lister*	2,419	Bill Grunewald	1,587
Jefferson County		Ann N. Knox-Bauer*	3,483
Branch 1		Walworth County	
Steven J. Luchsinger	4,294	Branch 3	
Jennifer L. Weston	8,240	John R. Race*	9,678
Branch 3		Washburn County	
Jacqueline R. Erwin*	10,331	Eugene D. Harrington*	2,468
Kenosha County		Waukesha County	
Branch 1		Branch 4	
David Mark Bastianelli*	12,732	Paul F. Reilly*	39,907
Branch 5		Branch 7	
Wilbur W. Warren, III*	12,613	J. Mac Davis*	39,900
Branch 6		Branch 8	
Mary K. Wagner*	13,524	James R. Kieffer*	39,643
Branch 8		Branch 10	
Chad G. Kerkman	8,910	Linda M. Van De Water*	38,870
Frederick L. Zievers	8,397	Winnebago County	
Lafayette County		Branch 6	
William D. Johnston*	2,830	Bruce K. Schmidt*	17,978
Marathon County		Wood County	
Branch 1		Branch 3	
Jill N. Falstad	11,492	John Adam Kruse	4,875
Peter C. Rotter	8,423	Todd P. Wolf	6,633
Milwaukee County			
Branch 2			
Joe Donald*	50,774		

*Incumbent.

Source: Official Records of Government Accountability Board, Elections Division. Scattered votes omitted.

COUNTY VOTE FOR SUPERINTENDENT OF PUBLIC INSTRUCTION
February 17, 2009 Primary

County	Tony Evers	Rose Fernandez	Lowell E. Holtz	Van Mobley	Todd Price
Adams	192	139	45	110	74
Ashland	406	169	92	137	94
Barron	275	260	97	173	129
Bayfield	448	190	82	100	126
Brown	3,351	2,768	771	1,004	733
Buffalo	113	90	27	32	70
Burnett	178	148	58	131	106
Calumet	1,043	564	168	308	231
Chippewa	791	997	589	545	629
Clark	326	333	107	145	152
Columbia	1,035	470	185	340	297
Crawford	160	118	51	72	62
Dane	12,499	4,948	1,484	2,650	2,989
Dodge	1,337	1,279	434	553	559
Door	714	336	106	164	158
Douglas	413	383	186	201	242
Dunn	315	219	58	154	90
Eau Claire	854	794	368	481	361
Florence	72	36	13	21	16
Fond du Lac	1,838	1,572	416	625	527
Forest	148	209	47	60	130
Grant	590	279	84	224	188
Green	1,152	706	288	238	389
Green Lake	273	205	65	82	81
Iowa	416	249	59	141	152
Iron	127	72	35	41	38
Jackson	164	110	47	68	72
Jefferson	1,316	1,079	454	620	407
Juneau	294	155	66	116	87
Kenosha	2,921	2,299	1,035	947	1,811
Kewaunee	371	218	93	97	99
La Crosse	2,244	2,249	675	816	1,053
Lafayette	223	107	43	74	54
Langlade	200	130	64	87	75
Lincoln	263	182	115	145	119
Manitowoc	3,051	2,165	796	1,012	1,052
Marathon	1,979	2,165	897	1,143	1,140
Marinette	737	519	254	170	252
Marquette	296	210	63	133	76
Menominee	22	8	0	3	2
Milwaukee	11,864	14,624	2,884	4,799	3,270
Monroe	463	146	36	137	94
Oconto	605	427	120	89	140
Oneida	451	195	91	194	124
Outagamie	5,822	2,636	982	1,627	1,278
Ozaukee	1,614	2,684	408	1,772	502
Pepin	73	66	20	13	16
Pierce	244	191	64	149	92
Polk	313	218	75	149	172
Portage	771	398	183	270	193
Price	306	178	81	147	161
Racine	1,909	2,859	416	955	647
Richland	254	87	59	89	60
Rock	1,992	877	948	552	521
Rusk	158	126	58	128	76
St. Croix	337	267	138	280	142
Sauk	1,227	461	232	570	272
Sawyer	182	143	53	114	102
Shawano	709	435	206	295	224
Sheboygan	3,579	3,001	978	1,840	1,247
Taylor	150	152	67	131	76
Trempealeau	223	170	61	79	114
Vernon	239	255	60	113	114
Vilas	295	338	128	197	179
Walworth	982	1,018	323	396	330
Washburn	220	93	48	79	39
Washington	1,549	3,531	410	788	466
Waukesha	5,157	11,609	1,263	2,769	1,395
Waupaca	695	400	139	197	171
Waushara	251	145	56	122	58
Winnebago	2,623	1,612	670	909	720
Wood	1,479	1,286	599	828	1,010
TOTAL	89,883	79,757	22,373	34,940	28,927

Source: Official records of the Government Accountability Board, Elections Division. Scattered votes omitted.

COUNTY VOTE FOR SUPERINTENDENT OF PUBLIC INSTRUCTION
April 7, 2009 Spring Election

County	Tony Evers	Rose Fernandez	County Total
Adams	1,916	1,182	3,104
Ashland	1,799	1,081	2,896
Barron	2,620	1,848	4,472
Bayfield	2,496	1,686	4,192
Brown	13,518	10,099	23,655
Buffalo	1,074	684	1,760
Burnett	1,548	1,445	2,997
Calumet	3,238	2,141	5,385
Chippewa	5,161	3,658	8,827
Clark	3,481	2,301	5,790
Columbia	5,172	2,905	8,083
Crawford	1,748	1,078	2,829
Dane	61,197	30,379	91,676
Dodge	6,004	5,111	11,127
Door	3,413	1,828	5,250
Douglas	4,093	3,490	7,593
Dunn	3,222	2,313	5,546
Eau Claire	6,262	3,903	10,183
Florence	399	297	697
Fond du Lac	7,287	6,434	13,727
Forest	993	614	1,607
Grant	5,955	3,617	9,579
Green	3,485	2,117	5,614
Green Lake	1,871	1,352	3,224
Iowa	2,625	1,529	4,158
Iron	804	511	1,315
Jackson	1,685	1,026	2,711
Jefferson	7,128	5,901	13,061
Juneau	2,311	1,435	3,752
Kenosha	9,611	6,817	16,464
Kewaunee	1,521	1,046	2,567
La Crosse	12,245	7,040	19,322
Lafayette	1,956	1,128	3,085
Langlade	2,294	1,706	4,000
Lincoln	3,555	2,108	5,668
Manitowoc	9,791	6,789	16,595
Marathon	11,376	7,694	19,097
Marinette	4,073	2,585	6,663
Marquette	1,300	1,055	2,356
Menominee	146	90	236
Milwaukee	45,865	38,370	84,360
Monroe	3,627	2,018	5,659
Oconto	3,217	2,297	5,519
Oneida	3,822	2,148	5,980
Outagamie	11,311	6,543	17,863
Ozaukee	6,086	8,956	15,059
Pepin	643	459	1,102
Pierce	1,894	1,543	3,440
Polk	2,750	2,225	4,984
Portage	4,474	2,508	6,986
Price	1,750	1,107	2,858
Racine	12,415	11,772	24,207
Richland	1,642	1,011	2,653
Rock	10,488	6,082	16,596
Rusk	1,459	934	2,397
St. Croix	3,781	3,096	6,900
Sauk	6,565	3,900	10,471
Sawyer	2,463	1,974	4,442
Shawano	3,625	2,199	5,827
Sheboygan	12,334	9,463	21,809
Taylor	2,741	1,775	4,524
Trempealeau	2,392	1,514	3,911
Vernon	2,647	1,735	4,383
Vilas	3,499	2,335	5,848
Walworth	6,398	5,380	11,806
Washburn	1,661	1,024	2,689
Washington	9,226	13,453	22,703
Waukesha	22,162	36,225	58,401
Waupaca	4,575	2,806	7,382
Waushara	1,912	1,168	3,081
Winnebago	14,550	8,408	22,996
Wood	6,901	4,060	10,965
TOTAL	439,248	328,511	768,664

Source: Official records of the Government Accountability Board, Elections Division. County totals include scattered votes.

DISTRICT VOTE FOR MEMBERS OF THE 111TH U.S. CONGRESS
September 9, 2008 Primary

First Congressional District

County	Paulette Garin (Dem.)	Mike Hebert (Dem.)	Marge Krupp (Dem.)	John Mogk (Dem.)	Joseph Kexel (Lib.)	Paul Ryan* (Rep.)
Kenosha	2,399	2,485	2,309	322	35	1,796
Milwaukee (part). . . .	537	548	1,006	129	18	2,637
Racine	1,257	941	1,492	133	56	3,095
Rock (part).	606	238	686	51	8	623
Walworth (part)	262	197	329	25	13	1,337
Waukesha (part)	160	102	193	29	11	2,230
TOTAL.	5,221	4,511	6,015	689	141	11,718

Second Congressional District

County	Tammy Baldwin* (Dem.)	Peter Theron (Rep.)
Columbia.	1,821	1,276
Dane	13,085	3,342
Green.	1,218	359
Jefferson (part).	651	1,400
Rock (part).	925	462
Sauk (part).	515	435
Walworth (part)	199	133
TOTAL.	18,414	7,407

Third Congressional District

County	Ron Kind* (Dem.)	Kevin Barrett (Lib.)	Ben Olson III (Lib.)	Paul Stark (Rep.)
Buffalo.	1,090	5	4	663
Clark (part).	471	8	7	351
Crawford.	374	13	8	254
Dunn	731	12	7	566
Eau Claire	1,784	48	33	1,649
Grant.	973	18	4	3,716
Iowa	743	27	20	530
Jackson.	1,213	2	4	252
Juneau	661	12	11	1,328
La Crosse	1,264	71	68	795
Lafayette.	265	13	2	754
Monroe.	740	15	9	586
Pepin.	531	1	0	170
Pierce.	974	7	7	1,180
Richland	637	10	6	875
St. Croix	2,465	12	5	1,892
Sauk (part)	569	15	13	1,018
Trempealeau	2,210	14	4	865
Vernon	344	42	13	397
TOTAL.	18,039	345	225	17,841

DISTRICT VOTE FOR MEMBERS OF THE 111TH U.S. CONGRESS
September 9, 2008 Primary–Continued

Fourth Congressional District

County	Gwen Moore* (Dem.)
Milwaukee (part).	18,342
TOTAL.	18,342

Fifth Congressional District

County	Jim Burkee (Rep.)	F. James Sensenbrenner, Jr.* (Rep.)
Jefferson (part).	101	517
Milwaukee (part).	2,047	7,333
Ozaukee	3,043	7,338
Washington.	2,484	9,039
Waukesha (part)	5,403	22,917
TOTAL.	13,078	47,144

Sixth Congressional District

County	Roger A. Kittelson (Dem.)	Mark Wollum (Dem.)	Tom Petri* (Rep.)
Adams	746	272	485
Calumet (part)	156	79	413
Dodge	628	310	1,819
Fond du Lac	680	337	5,438
Green Lake.	100	64	2,139
Jefferson (part).	118	85	564
Manitowoc.	1,837	1,245	656
Marquette	491	208	1,089
Outagamie (part).	84	59	143
Sheboygan.	1,546	1,003	4,814
Waushara.	173	82	1,031
Winnebago.	882	804	3,248
TOTAL.	7,441	4,548	21,839

DISTRICT VOTE FOR MEMBERS OF THE 111TH U.S. CONGRESS
September 9, 2008 Primary–Continued

Seventh Congressional District

County	David R. Obey* (Dem.)	Dan Mielke (Rep.)
Ashland	882	94
Barron	518	303
Bayfield	1,431	163
Burnett	573	317
Chippewa	644	959
Clark (part)	216	178
Douglas	4,743	209
Iron	1,564	95
Langlade (part)	1,662	228
Lincoln	366	302
Marathon	1,346	954
Oneida (part)	2,443	975
Polk	1,640	669
Portage	1,357	416
Price	1,046	206
Rusk	619	178
Sawyer	469	241
Taylor	388	850
Washburn	557	209
Wood	2,636	662
TOTAL	25,100	8,208

Eighth Congressional District

County	Steve Kagen* (Dem.)	John Gard (Rep.)
Brown	3,904	3,013
Calumet (part)	124	120
Door	1,899	588
Florence	82	380
Forest	262	166
Kewaunee	790	215
Langlade (part)	495	112
Marinette	826	1,639
Menominee	146	20
Oconto	747	2,217
Oneida (part)	674	396
Outagamie (part)	2,291	3,254
Shawano	1,241	3,073
Vilas	296	413
Waupaca	723	963
TOTAL	14,500	16,569

Dem. – Democratic Party; Lib. – Libertarian Party; Rep. – Republican Party.
*Incumbent.
Source: Official records of the Government Accountability Board, Elections Division. Scattered votes omitted.

DISTRICT VOTE FOR MEMBERS OF THE 111TH U.S. CONGRESS
November 4, 2008 General Election
First Congressional District

County	Marge Krupp (Dem.)	Joseph Kexel (Lib.)	Paul Ryan* (Rep.)
Kenosha	31,372	1,372	43,647
Milwaukee (part).	21,871	681	43,961
Racine	36,307	1,038	59,666
Rock (part).	15,731	504	24,791
Walworth (part)	12,098	699	30,400
Waukesha (part)	7,889	312	28,544
TOTAL	125,268	4,606	231,009
Percent of Total Vote†	34.69%	1.28%	63.97%

Second Congressional District

County	Tammy Baldwin* (Dem.)	Peter Theron (Rep.)
Columbia.	16,512	11,696
Dane	196,948	75,859
Green.	11,513	6,570
Jefferson (part).	14,472	9,957
Rock (part).	24,792	10,990
Sauk (part)	9,899	5,531
Walworth (part)	3,778	1,910
TOTAL.	277,914	122,513
Percent of Total Vote†	69.33%	30.56%

Third Congressional District

County	Ron Kind* (Dem.)	Kevin Barrett (Lib.)	Paul Stark (Rep.)
Buffalo.	4,529	119	2,129
Clark (part).	5,179	150	2,969
Crawford.	5,502	109	2,020
Dunn	13,578	572	8,023
Eau Claire	34,254	1,187	17,360
Grant	15,055	389	7,566
Iowa	7,758	198	3,483
Jackson.	6,200	160	2,667
Juneau	6,291	224	4,393
La Crosse	41,624	1,540	18,374
Lafayette.	4,444	130	2,716
Monroe.	11,440	399	6,757
Pepin.	2,352	46	1,261
Pierce.	12,617	584	7,997
Richland	4,670	117	3,079
St. Croix	23,251	1,287	18,806
Sauk (part)	8,554	426	5,079
Trempealeau	8,926	248	3,773
Vernon	8,984	351	4,308
TOTAL.	225,208	8,236	122,760
Percent of Total Vote†	63.19%	2.31%	34.44%

DISTRICT VOTE FOR MEMBERS OF THE 111TH U.S. CONGRESS
November 4, 2008 General Election–Continued

Fourth Congressional District

County	Gwen Moore* (Dem.)	Michael D. LaForest (Ind.)
Milwaukee (part)...................	222,728	29,282
TOTAL....................	222,728	29,282
Percent of Total Vote†...............	87.63%	11.52%

Fifth Congressional District

County	F. James Sensenbrenner, Jr.* (Rep.)	Robert R. Raymond (Ind.)
Jefferson (part).....................	4,679	1,070
Milwaukee (part).....................	46,352	19,960
Ozaukee	36,454	10,018
Washington.........................	53,726	11,215
Waukesha (part)....................	134,060	27,452
TOTAL........................	275,271	69,715
Percent of Total Vote†...............	79.58%	20.15%

Sixth Congressional District

County	Roger A. Kittelson (Dem.)	Tom Petri* (Rep.)
Adams	4,636	4,840
Calumet (part)......................	6,218	13,938
Dodge	15,529	25,509
Fond du Lac	14,854	34,219
Green Lake........................	2,587	6,617
Jefferson (part).....................	3,241	6,531
Manitowoc.........................	15,973	24,702
Marquette	3,189	4,342
Outagamie (part)....................	2,223	3,421
Sheboygan.........................	21,848	38,095
Waushara..........................	4,235	7,307
Winnebago.........................	31,557	52,354
TOTAL........................	126,090	221,875
Percent of Total Vote†...............	36.21%	63.71%

DISTRICT VOTE FOR MEMBERS OF THE 111TH U.S. CONGRESS
November 4, 2008 General Election–Continued

Seventh Congressional District

County	David R. Obey* (Dem.)	Dan Mielke (Rep.)
Ashland	6,009	2,272
Barron	13,114	9,132
Bayfield	6,258	3,026
Burnett	4,735	3,658
Chippewa	18,589	10,812
Clark (part)	3,293	2,271
Douglas	16,687	6,746
Iron	2,055	1,194
Langlade (part)	4,266	3,126
Lincoln	8,578	6,490
Marathon	37,093	29,779
Oneida (part)	7,411	3,760
Polk	11,929	9,845
Portage	25,426	12,247
Price	5,116	2,894
Rusk	4,478	2,578
Sawyer	4,936	3,647
Taylor	4,991	4,157
Washburn	4,907	3,851
Wood	22,795	15,453
TOTAL	212,666	136,938
Percent of Total Vote†	60.79%	39.14%

Eighth Congressional District

County	Steve Kagen* (Dem.)	John Gard (Rep.)
Brown	66,069	56,184
Calumet (part)	3,141	2,337
Door	9,936	7,261
Florence	1,216	1,344
Forest	2,601	1,800
Kewaunee	5,770	4,918
Langlade (part)	1,343	1,257
Marinette	11,505	9,445
Menominee	1,166	227
Oconto	9,686	9,087
Oneida (part)	4,757	5,308
Outagamie (part)	47,193	36,688
Shawano	10,336	9,374
Vilas	6,094	7,292
Waupaca	12,849	12,099
TOTAL	193,662	164,621
Percent of Total Vote†	54.00%	45.90%

Dem. – Democratic Party; Lib. – Libertarian Party; Rep. – Republican Party; Ind. – Independent.
*Incumbent.
†Percentages do not sum to 100%, as scattered votes are included in total vote.
Source: Official records of the Government Accountability Board, Elections Division.

COUNTY VOTE FOR STATE SENATORS
September 9, 2008 Primary

County or Part	Senate District	Democratic	Vote	Republican	Vote
Adams (part)	14	No candidate		Olsen*	33
(part)	24	Lassa*	981	Kimmet	372
Brown (part)	2	No candidate		Cowles*	941
(part)	30	Hansen*	2,227	Fradette	1,381
Burnett	10	Page	225	Harsdorf*	247
Columbia (part)	14	No candidate		Olsen*	351
(part)	16	Miller*	1,250	No candidate	
Crawford	32	Johnson	321	Kapanke*	303
Dane (part)	16	Miller*	2,987	No candidate	
(part)	26	Risser*	3,185	No candidate	
Dodge (part)	18	King	38	Hopper	165
(part)†	20	No candidate		Grothman*	111
Dunn (part)	10	Page	378	Harsdorf*	162
Florence	12	Holperin	69	Tiffany	336
Fond du Lac (part)	14	No candidate		Olsen*	274
(part)	18	King	767	Hopper	3,641
(part)†	20	No candidate		Grothman*	839
Forest	12	Holperin	242	Tiffany	159
Green Lake	14	No candidate		Olsen*	2,046
Kenosha	22	Wirch*	7,443	Bakke	1,442
La Crosse	32	Johnson	1,176	Kapanke*	903
Langlade	12	Holperin	1,941	Tiffany	325
Lincoln	12	Holperin	359	Tiffany	318
Marathon (part)	12	Holperin	41	Tiffany	25
(part)	24	Lassa*	4	Kimmet	3
Marinette (part)	12	Holperin	274	Tiffany	574
(part)	30	Hansen*	405	Fradette	785
Marquette (part)	14	No candidate		Olsen*	920
(part)	24	Lassa*	49	Kimmet	52
Menominee	12	Holperin	98	Tiffany	22
Milwaukee (part)	4	Taylor*	4,098	No candidate	
(part)	6	Coggs*	4,730	No candidate	
(part)	8	Wasserman	7,341	Darling*	3,108
(part)	28	No candidate		Lazich*	1,458
Monroe (part)	32	Johnson	86	Kapanke*	117
Oconto (part)	2	No candidate		Cowles*	1,017
(part)	12	Holperin	118	Tiffany	187
(part)	30	Hansen*	313	Fradette	854
Oneida	12	Holperin	3,129	Tiffany	1,422
Outagamie (part)	2	No candidate		Cowles*	563
(part)	14	No candidate		Olsen*	118
Ozaukee (part)	8	Wasserman	602	Darling*	3,036
(part)†	20	No candidate		Grothman*	4,744
Pierce	10	Page	555	Harsdorf*	1,004
Polk (part)	10	Page	1,393	Harsdorf*	672
Portage (part)	24	Lassa*	1,350	Kimmet	395
Racine (part)	22	Wirch*	165	Bakke	256
(part)	28	No candidate		Lazich*	197
Richland (part)	32	Johnson	80	Kapanke*	81
St. Croix	10	Page	2,238	Harsdorf*	2,105
Sauk (part)	14	No candidate		Olsen*	250
(part)	16	Miller*	69	No candidate	
Shawano (part)	2	No candidate		Cowles*	2,798
(part)	12	Holperin	101	Tiffany	203
(part)	14	No candidate		Olsen*	0
(part)	30	Hansen*	0	Fradette	2
Sheboygan (part)†	20	No candidate		Grothman*	2,746
Vernon	32	Johnson	313	Kapanke*	468
Vilas	12	Holperin	311	Tiffany	403
Walworth (part)	22	Wirch*	0	Bakke	0
(part)	28	No candidate		Lazich*	176
Washington (part)	8	Wasserman	332	Darling*	2,686
(part)†	20	No candidate		Grothman*	5,210
Waukesha (part)	4	Taylor*	0	No candidate	
(part)	8	Wasserman	436	Darling*	3,663
(part)	28	No candidate		Lazich*	4,048
Waupaca (part)	2	No candidate		Cowles*	32
(part)	14	No candidate		Olsen*	872
Waushara (part)	14	No candidate		Olsen*	843
(part)	24	Lassa*	44	Kimmet	114
Winnebago (part)	18	King	1,033	Hopper	1,977
Wood	24	Lassa*	2,399	Kimmet	619

*Incumbent.

†Votes for Independent candidate Clyde Winter in 20th SD: Dodge – 0, Fond du Lac – 1, Ozaukee – 44, Sheboygan – 9, Washington – 38.

Source: Official records of the Government Accountability Board, Elections Division. Scattered votes omitted.

COUNTY VOTE FOR STATE SENATORS
November 4, 2008 General Election

County or Part	Senate District	Democratic	Vote	Republican	Vote
Adams (part)	14	No candidate		Olsen*	648
(part)	24	Lassa*	5,516	Kimmet	2,923
Brown (part)	2	No candidate		Cowles*	28,102
(part)	30	Hansen*	38,506	Fradette	19,565
Burnett	10	Page	2,300	Harsdorf*	3,208
Columbia (part)	14	No candidate		Olsen*	6,301
(part)	16	Miller*	10,063	No candidate	
Crawford	32	Johnson	3,410	Kapanke*	4,364
Dane (part)	16	Miller*	63,083	No candidate	
(part)	26	Risser*	80,923	No candidate	
Dodge (part)	18	King	982[2]	Hopper	1,304[2]
(part)[1]	20	No candidate		Grothman*	850
Dunn (part)	10	Page	5,972	Harsdorf*	4,863
Florence	12	Holperin	1,085	Tiffany	1,432
Fond du Lac (part)	14	No candidate		Olsen*	4,512
(part)	18	King	16,242[2]	Hopper	20,336[2]
(part)[1]	20	No candidate		Grothman*	3,776
Forest	12	Holperin	2,521	Tiffany	1,978
Green Lake	14	No candidate		Olsen*	7,267
Kenosha	22	Wirch*	50,876	Bakke	23,184
La Crosse	32	Johnson	31,000	Kapanke*	30,584
Langlade	12	Holperin	4,622	Tiffany	5,483
Lincoln	12	Holperin	7,357	Tiffany	7,604
Marathon (part)	12	Holperin	1,031	Tiffany	1,070
(part)	24	Lassa*	159	Kimmet	78
Marinette (part)	12	Holperin	4,436	Tiffany	4,728
(part)	30	Hansen*	7,348	Fradette	3,728
Marquette (part)	14	No candidate		Olsen*	4,254
(part)	24	Lassa*	526	Kimmet	404
Menominee	12	Holperin	1,103	Tiffany	177
Milwaukee (part)	4	Taylor*	66,751	No candidate	
(part)	6	Coggs*	60,606	No candidate	
(part)	8	Wasserman	31,337	Darling*	17,704
(part)	28	No candidate		Lazich*	26,342
Monroe (part)	32	Johnson	1,327	Kapanke*	1,939
Oconto (part)	2	No candidate		Cowles*	5,286
(part)	12	Holperin	1,178	Tiffany	1,018
(part)	30	Hansen*	5,756	Fradette	3,155
Oneida	12	Holperin	11,672	Tiffany	9,812
Outagamie (part)	2	No candidate		Cowles*	16,271
(part)	14	No candidate		Olsen*	1,814
Ozaukee (part)	8	Wasserman	6,176	Darling*	10,055
(part)[1]	20	No candidate		Grothman*	24,611
Pierce	10	Page	8,288	Harsdorf*	9,243
Polk (part)	10	Page	8,992	Harsdorf*	12,296
Portage (part)	24	Lassa*	26,224	Kimmet	10,570
Racine (part)	22	Wirch*	4,070	Bakke	4,199
(part)	28	No candidate		Lazich*	4,944
Richland (part)	32	Johnson	607	Kapanke*	684
St. Croix	10	Page	17,489	Harsdorf*	26,206
Sauk (part)	14	No candidate		Olsen*	6,677
(part)	16	Miller*	526	No candidate	
Shawano (part)	2	No candidate		Cowles*	10,417
(part)	12	Holperin	1,814	Tiffany	1,425
(part)	14	No candidate		Olsen*	4
(part)	30	Hansen*	33	Fradette	35
Sheboygan (part)[1]	20	No candidate		Grothman*	9,995
Vernon	32	Johnson	6,303	Kapanke*	7,583
Vilas	12	Holperin	6,676	Tiffany	6,753
Walworth (part)	22	Wirch*	0	Bakke	0
(part)	28	No candidate		Lazich*	3,653
Washington (part)	8	Wasserman	4,734	Darling*	10,312
(part)[1]	20	No candidate		Grothman*	30,710
Waukesha (part)	4	Taylor*	0	No candidate	
(part)	8	Wasserman	6,871	Darling*	12,054
(part)	28	No candidate		Lazich*	40,012
Waupaca (part)	2	No candidate		Cowles*	431
(part)	14	No candidate		Olsen*	15,953
Waushara (part)	14	No candidate		Olsen*	6,708
(part)	24	Lassa*	1,296	Kimmet	783
Winnebago (part)	18	King	24,517[2]	Hopper	20,264[2]
Wood	24	Lassa*	24,264	Kimmet	12,902

*Incumbent.

[1]Votes for Independent candidate Clyde Winter in 20th SD: Dodge – 207, Fond du Lac – 717, Ozaukee – 7,239, Sheboygan – 1,892, Washington – 7,058.

[2]Recount vote totals.

Source: Official records of the Government Accountability Board, Elections Division. Scattered votes omitted.

DISTRICT VOTE FOR STATE SENATORS
September 9, 2008 Primary

Senate District	Composed of Assembly Districts	Political Party	Candidates	Vote
2	4, 5, 6.	.Rep.	Robert L. Cowles*	5,351
4	10, 11, 12.	.Dem.	Lena C. Taylor*	4,098
6	16, 17, 18.	.Dem.	Spencer Coggs*	4,730
8	22, 23, 24.	.Dem.	Sheldon A. Wasserman.	8,711
		Rep.	Alberta Darling*	12,493
10.	28, 29, 30.	.Dem.	Alison H. Page	4,789
		Rep.	Shelia Harsdorf*	4,190
12.	34, 35, 36.	.Dem.	Jim Holperin	6,683
		Rep.	Tom Tiffany	3,974
14.	40, 41, 42.	.Rep.	Luther S. Olsen*	5,707
16.	46, 47, 48.	.Dem.	Mark Miller*	4,306
18.	52, 53, 54.	.Dem.	Jessica King	1,838
		Rep.	Randy Hopper	5,783
20.	58, 59, 60.	.Rep.	Glenn Grothman*	13,650
		Ind.	Clyde Winter	92
22.	64, 65, 66.	.Dem.	Robert W. Wirch*	7,608
		Rep.	Benjamin Lee Bakke.	1,698
24.	70, 71, 72.	.Dem.	Julie M. Lassa*	4,827
		Rep.	Tom Kimmet	1,555
26.	76, 77, 78.	.Dem.	Fred A. Risser*	3,185
28.	82, 83, 84.	.Rep.	Mary Lazich*	5,879
30.	88, 89, 90.	.Dem.	Dave Hansen*	2,945
		Rep.	Chad Fradette	3,022
32.	94, 95, 96.	.Dem.	Tara Johnson	1,976
		Rep.	Dan Kapanke*	1,872

Dem. – Democratic Party; Rep. – Republican Party; Ind. – Independent.
*Incumbent.
Source: Official records of the Government Accountability Board, Elections Division. Scattered votes omitted.

DISTRICT VOTE FOR STATE SENATORS
General Elections

Senate District	Composed of Assembly Districts	Political Party	Candidates	Vote	Percent of Total Vote[1]
		November 7, 2006 General Election			
1	1, 2, 3.	Dem.	Charlie Most.	29,066	39.72%
		Rep.	Alan J. Lasee*.	40,341	55.12
		WG	Jill Bussiere	3,712	5.07
3	7, 8, 9.	Dem.	Tim Carpenter*.	30,768	98.51
5	13, 14, 15.	Dem.	Jim Sullivan.	36,148	51.68
		Rep.	Tom Reynolds*.	33,686	48.16
7	19, 20, 21.	Dem.	Jeff Plale*.	41,502	62.61
		Rep.	Dimity Grabowski.	21,104	31.84
		WG	Claude VanderVeen	3,564	5.38
9	25, 26, 27.	Dem.	Jamie John Aulik.	26,224	40.60
		Rep.	Joseph Leibham*.	38,335	59.36
11.	31, 32, 33.	Dem.	L.D. Rockwell.	22,038	32.54
		Rep.	Neal Kedzie*.	45,643	67.40
13.	37, 38, 39.	Rep.	Scott Fitzgerald*.	47,351	96.87
15.	43, 44, 45.	Dem.	Judy Robson*.	39,165	68.18
		Rep.	Gregory Addie.	18,187	31.66
17.	49, 50, 51.	Dem.	John C. Simonson.	26,688	45.78
		Rep.	Dale W. Schultz*.	31,590	54.19
19.	55, 56, 57.	Rep.	Michael G. Ellis*.	51,162	98.66
21.	61, 62, 63.	Dem.	John W. Lehman.	31,737	53.03
		Rep.	William L. McReynolds.	28,069	46.90
23.	67, 68, 69.	Dem.	Pat Kreitlow.	31,590	50.84
		Rep.	Dave Zien*.	30,505	49.09
25.	73, 74, 75.	Dem.	Robert Jauch*.	38,721	62.24
		Rep.	Shirley J. Riedmann.	23,454	37.70
27.	79, 80, 81.	Dem.	Jon B. Erpenbach*.	60,974	99.32
29.	85, 86, 87.	Dem.	Russ Decker*.	42,139	67.68
		Rep.	Jimmy Boy Edming.	20,101	32.28
31.	91, 92, 93.	Dem.	Kathleen Vinehout.	31,895	51.58
		Rep.	Ron Brown*.	29,890	48.33
33.	97, 98, 99	Dem.	Andrew Stiffler.	23,413	32.66
		Rep.	Theodore J. Kanavas*.	48,241	67.29
		November 4, 2008 General Election			
2	4, 5, 6.	Rep.	Robert L. Cowles*.	60,507	99.35
4	10, 11, 12.	Dem.	Lena C. Taylor*.	66,751	98.82
6	16, 17, 18.	Dem.	Spencer Coggs*.	60,606	98.85
8	22, 23, 24.	Dem.	Sheldon A. Wasserman.	49,118	49.45
		Rep.	Alberta Darling*.	50,125	50.46
10.	28, 29, 30.	Dem.	Alison H. Page.	43,041	43.49
		Rep.	Shelia Harsdorf*.	55,816	56.40
12.	34, 35, 36.	Dem.	Jim Holperin.	43,595	51.21
		Rep.	Tom Tiffany.	41,480	48.73
14.	40, 41, 42.	Rep.	Luther S. Olsen*.	54,138	99.36
16.	46, 47, 48.	Dem.	Mark Miller*.	73,672	99.29
18.	52, 53, 54.	Dem.	Jessica King.	41,741[2]	49.86
		Rep.	Randy Hopper*.	41,904[2]	50.05
20.	58, 59, 60.	Rep.	Glenn Grothman*.	69,942	80.26
		Ind.	Clyde Winter.	17,113	19.64
22.	64, 65, 66.	Dem.	Robert W. Wirch*.	54,946	66.65
		Rep.	Benjamin Lee Bakke.	27,383	33.21
24.	70, 71, 72.	Dem.	Julie M. Lassa*.	57,985	67.67
		Rep.	Tom Kimmet.	27,660	32.28
26.	76, 77, 78.	Dem.	Fred A. Risser*.	80,923	99.13
28.	82, 83, 84.	Rep.	Mary Lazich*.	74,951	99.24
30.	88, 89, 90.	Dem.	Dave Hansen*.	51,643	66.06
		Rep.	Chad Fradette.	26,483	33.88
32.	94, 95, 96.	Dem.	Tara Johnson.	42,647	48.53
		Rep.	Dan Kapanke*.	45,154	51.38

Dem. – Democratic Party; Rep. – Republican Party; WG – Wisconsin Green Party; Ind. – Independent.
*Incumbent.
[1]Percentages do not sum to 100%, as scattered votes have been omitted.
[2]Recount vote total.
Source: Official records of the Government Accountability Board, Elections Division. Scattered votes omitted.

COUNTY VOTE FOR REPRESENTATIVES TO THE ASSEMBLY
September 9, 2008 Primary Election

County or Part	Assembly District	Democratic	Vote	Republican	Vote
Adams (part)	42	Clark	47	Hines*	43
(part)	72	Kubisiak	505	Tyberg	371
		Schneider*	697		
Ashland	74	Ralph	339	LaBarre	96
		Sherman*	852		
Barron (part)[1]	67	No candidate		No candidate	
(part)	75	Hubler*	477	No candidate	
Bayfield	74	Ralph	482	LaBarre	165
		Sherman*	1,460		
Brown (part)	1	Baeb	119	Bies*	96
		Skare	75		
(part)	2	Brocher	144	Lasee*	357
		Garthwaite	212		
		Zigmunt	158		
(part)	3	Krueger	22	Ott, A.*	34
(part)	4	Dunlop	647	Montgomery*	765
(part)	5	Nelson*	142	Steineke	163
(part)	88	Soletski*	912	Theisen	539
(part)	89	Koehn	124	Nygren*	138
(part)	90	Weix	972	Van Roy*	770
Buffalo[1,2]	91	Baecker	313	Anderson	304
		Boe	85	Hegenbarth	466
		Ceci	48		
		Danou	476		
		Kimmel	101		
		Kraft	136		
Burnett (part)	28	Hraychuck*	268	Muschinske	218
(part)[1]	73	Johnson, V.	41	No candidate	
		Meyers	6		
		Milroy	210		
		Tripp	94		
Calumet (part)	3	Krueger	233	Ott, A.*	381
(part)	25	Ziegelbauer*	17		
(part)	27	Cox	41	Kestell*	90
Chippewa (part)[1]	67	No candidate		No candidate	
(part)	68	Dexter	131	Moulton*	159
(part)	69	Swiggum	46	Suder*	62
Clark (part)	69	Swiggum	620	Suder*	622
(part)	92	Miller	13	Hellman	25
		Radcliffe	28		
Columbia (part)	38	Pas	69	Kleefisch*	67
(part)	39	Onsrud	7	Fitzgerald*	9
(part)	42	Clark	355	Hines*	352
(part)[1]	47	Fisk	692	McCumber	266
		O'Neil	861	Pate	275
				Ripp	991
				Ruth	189
Crawford	96	Klemme	336	Nerison*	277
Dane (part)	37	Jorgensen*	296	Koebke	99
				Luetzow	64
				Peters	89
(part)	43	Hixson*	0	Towns	0
(part)	46	Hebl*	900	Maves	405
				Zimmerman	312
(part)[1]	47	Fisk	374	McCumber	170
		O'Neil	829	Pate	75
				Ripp	683
				Ruth	375
(part)	48	Parisi*	1,122	No candidate	
(part)	76	Berceau*	960	No candidate	
(part)	77	Black*	1,151	No candidate	
(part)	78	Pocan*	1,099	No candidate	
(part)	79	Pope-Roberts*	1,205	Skalitzky	494
(part)	80	Waelti	264	Davis*	126
		Wisnefske	294		
(part)	81	Englund	904	No candidate	
		Her	337		
		Kiefer	410		
		Laubmeier	1,001		
		Roys	1,960		
		Sargent	1,683		
Dodge (part)	38	Pas	163	Kleefisch*	538
(part)	39	Onsrud	535	Fitzgerald*	986
(part)	53	Mann	38	Burns	2
				Christianson	20
				Hatch	103
				Spanbauer	52
				Streeter	38
(part)	59	No candidate		LeMahieu*	42
				McCarty	86
(part)	99	No candidate		Pridemore*	0
Door	1	Baeb	400	Bies*	593
		Skare	1,863		

COUNTY VOTE FOR REPRESENTATIVES TO THE ASSEMBLY
September 9, 2008 Primary Election–Continued

County or Part	Assembly District	Democratic	Vote	Republican	Vote
Douglas[1]	73	Johnson, V.	1,440	No candidate	
		Meyers	64		
		Milroy	3,158		
		Tripp	2,429		
Dunn (part)[2]	29	Buckel	256	Murtha*	160
		Peters	184		
(part)[1]	67	No candidate		No candidate	
(part)	93	Smith*	65	Fields, D.	60
				Schiess	14
Eau Claire (part)	68	Dexter	645	Moulton*	505
(part)	69	Swiggum	8	Suder*	5
(part)	92	Miller	39	Hellman	42
		Radcliffe	48		
(part)	93	Smith*	1,004	Fields, D.	1,204
				Schiess	241
Florence	36	Gruszynski	61	Mursau*	365
Fond du Lac (part)	27	Cox	34	Kestell*	291
(part)	41	Milheiser	90	Ballweg*	274
(part)	52	Keifenheim	604	Matthew	972
				Townsend*	2,311
(part)	53	Mann	151	Burns	12
				Christianson	116
				Hatch	589
				Spanbauer	432
				Streeter	115
(part)	59	No candidate		LeMahieu*	326
				McCarty	823
Forest	36	Gruszynski	215	Mursau*	159
Grant	49	Garthwaite*	954	Kuhle	1,467
				Lundell	1,527
				Tranel	2,063
Green	80	Waelti	947	Davis*	429
		Wisnefske	745		
Green Lake	41	Milheiser	149	Ballweg*	2,071
Iowa (part)	49	Garthwaite*	3	Kuhle	1
				Lundell	4
				Tranel	4
(part)	51	Hilgenberg*	727	Russell	553
Iron (part)	74	Ralph	408	LaBarre	85
		Sherman*	1,363		
Jackson (part)[1,2]	91	Baecker	4	Anderson	4
		Boe	124	Hegenbarth	7
		Ceci	2		
		Danou	22		
		Kimmel	2		
		Kraft	2		
(part)	92	Miller	389	Hellman	256
		Radcliffe	844		
Jefferson (part)	31	Urban	97	Nass*	481
(part)	37	Jorgensen*	725	Koebke	1,130
				Luetzow	877
				Peters	418
(part)	38	Pas	89	Kleefisch*	244
(part)	43	Hixson*	6	Towns	4
Juneau	50	Crofton	227	Allbaugh	387
		Teske	477	Brooks	580
				Buswell	115
				Carver	623
Kenosha (part)[1]	32	Harrod	41	Lothian*	45
(part)	64	Barca	3,134	No candidate	
		Huff	928		
		Orth	122		
(part)	65	Steinbrink*	2,466	Tiahnybok	494
(part)	66	Orr	431	Kerkman*	682
		Zamba	910		
Kewaunee (part)	1	Baeb	535	Bies*	210
		Skare	415		
(part)	2	Brocher	10	Lasee*	11
		Garthwaite	7		
		Zigmunt	5		
La Crosse (part)	94	Hancock	402	Huebsch*	433
(part)	95	Shilling*	824	No candidate	
Lafayette (part)	49	Garthwaite*	40	Kuhle	37
				Lundell	38
				Tranel	50
(part)	51	Hilgenberg*	189	Russell	731
(part)	80	Waelti	9	Davis*	429
		Wisnefske	14		
Langlade (part)	35	Schmelling	1,538	Friske*	257
(part)	36	Gruszynski	284	Mursau*	75
Lincoln	35	Schmelling	358	Friske*	337
Manitowoc (part)	2	Brocher	489	Lasee*	0
		Garthwaite	247		
		Zigmunt	484		

COUNTY VOTE FOR REPRESENTATIVES TO THE ASSEMBLY
September 9, 2008 Primary Election–Continued

County or Part	Assembly District	Democratic	Vote	Republican	Vote
(part)	25	Ziegelbauer*	2,054	No candidate	
(part)	27	Cox	70	Kestell*	61
Marathon (part)	35	Schmelling	28	Friske*	24
(part)	36	Gruszynski	10	Mursau*	5
(part)	69	Swiggum	176	Suder*	171
(part)	70	Vruwink*	4	Seevers	3
(part)	85	Seidel*	692	Kufahl	427
(part)	86	Myszka	392	Petrowski*	336
(part)	87	Murphy	14	Williams, M.*	22
		Reas	30		
Marinette (part)	36	Gruszynski	308	Mursau*	661
(part)	89	Koehn	378	Nygren*	956
Marquette (part)	41	Milheiser	92	Ballweg*	140
(part)	42	Clark	488	Hines*	817
(part)	72	Kubisiak	20	Tyberg	50
		Schneider*	38		
Menominee	36	Gruszynski	97	Mursau*	23
Milwaukee (part)[2]	7	Krusick*	1,728	Wiesmueller	708
(part)	8	Colón*	571	No candidate	
		Guzman	206		
		Manriquez	284		
(part)	9	Zepnick*	991	No candidate	
(part)	10	Allen	244	No candidate	
		Williams, A.*	1,775		
(part)	11	Fields, J.*	974	No candidate	
(part)	12	Kessler*	1,106	No candidate	
(part)	13	Cullen*	1,530	No candidate	
(part)	14	Hucke	608	Vukmir*	1,712
(part)	15	Hoisington	509	Nickel	751
		Staskunas*	1,590		
(part)	16	Badger*	205	No candidate	
		King	290		
		Parker	362		
		Young*	985		
(part)	17	Bady	252	No candidate	
		Toles*	2,115		
(part)	18	Grigsby*	965	No candidate	
(part)	19	Richards*	1,618	No candidate	
(part)	20	Landowski	807	No candidate	
		Sinicki*	2,113		
		Sutherland	487		
(part)	21	Brower	1,005	Honadel*	1,084
(part)	22	Feldman	2,852	Wadhwa	1,664
		Johnson, G.	329		
		Kohl	1,802		
		Pasch	2,930		
(part)	23	Settle-Robinson	598	Ott, J.*	1,055
(part)	82	No candidate		Stone*	1,234
(part)	84	No candidate		Gundrum*	212
Monroe (part)	50	Crofton	22	Allbaugh	14
		Teske	20	Brooks	31
				Buswell	36
				Carver	13
(part)	92	Miller	486	Hellman	415
		Radcliffe	276		
(part)	94	Hancock	14	Huebsch*	26
(part)	96	Klemme	69	Nerison*	84
Oconto (part)	6	Powers	238	Tauchen*	982
(part)	36	Gruszynski	112	Mursau*	204
(part)	89	Koehn	264	Nygren*	961
Oneida (part)	34	Tubbs	2,670	Meyer*	1,192
(part)	35	Schmelling	304	Friske*	204
Outagamie (part)	3	Krueger	277	Ott, A.*	238
(part)	5	Nelson*	628	Steineke	414
(part)	6	Powers	74	Tauchen*	124
(part)	40	Kuehl	66	Petersen*	124
(part)	56	Franz	368	Roth*	681
(part)	57	Bernard Schaber	738	Egelhoff	2,051
				Stueck	464
Ozaukee (part)	23	Settle-Robinson	440	Ott, J.*	3,093
(part)	59	No candidate		LeMahieu*	622
				McCarty	275
(part)	60	Duman	180	Gottlieb*	3,962
Pepin (part)[1,2]	91	Baecker	34	Anderson	69
		Boe	13	Hegenbarth	88
		Ceci	107		
		Danou	188		
		Kimmel	4		
		Kraft	219		
(part)	93	Smith*	33	Fields, D.	20
				Schiess	12
Pierce (part)[2]	29	Buckel	79	Murtha*	66
		Peters	38		

COUNTY VOTE FOR REPRESENTATIVES TO THE ASSEMBLY
September 9, 2008 Primary Election–Continued

County or Part	Assembly District	Democratic	Vote	Republican	Vote
(part)	30	Bruch.	459	Hughes.	211
				Rhoades*.	901
(part)[1,2]	91	Baecker	39	Anderson.	155
		Boe.	32	Hegenbarth.	119
		Ceci	69		
		Danou	133		
		Kimmel	9		
		Kraft*	68		
(part)	93	Smith*	15	Fields, D.	6
				Schiess.	5
Polk (part)	28	Hraychuck*	1,577	Muschinske	610
(part)	75	Hubler*	73	No candidate	
Portage (part)	70	Vruwink*.	247	Seevers.	81
(part)	71	Molepske*	1,021	Jensen	270
(part)	72	Kubisiak	28	Tyberg	4
		Schneider*	38		
(part)	86	Myszka.	40	Petrowski*.	23
Price	87	Murphy.	223	Williams, M.*	222
		Reas	1,007		
Racine (part)[2]	61	Turner*.	1,213	No candidate	
(part)[2]	62	Mason*.	1,118	No candidate	
(part)	63	Flashinski	959	Vos*	1,253
(part)	66	Orr	85	Kerkman*	271
		Zamba	99		
(part)	83	Robertson	62	Gunderson*	199
Richland (part).	49	Garthwaite*	53	Kuhle.	66
				Lundell.	30
				Tranel	33
(part)	50	Crofton.	369	Allbaugh	537
		Teske.	98	Brooks.	199
				Buswell	6
				Carver	79
(part)	51	Hilgenberg*	42	Russell	65
(part)	96	Klemme	78	Nerison*	83
Rock (part)	43	Hixson*	558	Towns	399
(part)	44	Sheridan*	957	No candidate	
(part)	45	Benedict*	531	Hahn	302
(part)	80	Waelti	144	Davis*	83
		Wisnefske	99		
Rusk	87	Murphy.	119	Williams, M.*	197
		Reas	520		
St. Croix (part).	28	Hraychuck*	80	Muschinske	45
(part)[2]	29	Buckel	1,258	Murtha*	573
		Peters.	345		
(part)	30	Bruch.	887	Hughes	161
				Rhoades*.	1,531
Sauk (part)	42	Clark	325	Hines*	251
(part)[1]	47	Fisk.	16	McCumber.	131
		O'Neil	69	Pate.	3
				Ripp	46
				Ruth	1
(part)	50	Crofton.	266	Allbaugh	223
		Teske.	211	Brooks.	1,060
				Buswell	17
				Carver	134
(part)	51	Hilgenberg*	211	Russell	150
Sawyer (part).	74	Ralph.	94	LaBarre	216
		Sherman*	398		
(part)	87	Murphy.	6	Williams, M.*	26
		Reas	24		
Shawano (part).	5	Nelson*	6	Steineke	16
(part)	6	Powers	771	Tauchen*.	2,845
(part)	36	Gruszynski.	93	Mursau*	210
(part)	40	Kuehl.	0	Petersen*.	0
(part)	85	Seidel*	22	Kufahl	19
(part)	86	Myszka.	32	Petrowski*.	60
(part)	89	Koehn	0	Nygren*	2
Sheboygan (part).	26	Van Akkeren*	1,473	Hou-Seye.	563
				Pieper	810
(part)	27	Cox.	653	Kestell*	810
(part)	59	No candidate		LeMahieu*.	2,871
				McCarty	354
Taylor (part)	69	Swiggum.	4	Suder*	5
(part)	87	Murphy.	127	Williams, M*.	1,056
		Reas	277		
Trempealeau[1,2]	91	Baecker	812	Anderson.	325
		Boe.	297	Hegenbarth.	848
		Ceci	23		
		Danou	836		
		Kimmel	463		
		Kraft	102		
Vernon	96	Klemme	297	Nerison*	456
Vilas	34	Tubbs.	272	Meyer*.	394

COUNTY VOTE FOR REPRESENTATIVES TO THE ASSEMBLY
September 9, 2008 Primary Election–Continued

County or Part	Assembly District	Democratic	Vote	Republican	Vote
Walworth (part)	31	Urban	170	Nass*	399
(part)[1]	32	Harrod	401	Lothian*	636
(part)	43	Hixson*	218	Towns	168
(part)	45	Benedict*	19	Hahn	26
(part)	66	Orr	0	Kerkman*	0
		Zamba	0		
(part)	83	Robertson	60	Gunderson*	181
Washburn (part)[1]	73	Johnson, V.	39	No candidate	
		Meyers	6		
		Milroy	228		
		Tripp	135		
(part)	75	Hubler*	206	No candidate	
Washington (part)	23	Settle-Robinson	0	Ott, J.*	0
(part)	24	Brady	270	Knodl	1,174
		Lauer	141	LaSage	1,061
				Melchert	654
				Moscicke	71
(part)[1]	58	No candidate		Strachota*	3,617
(part)	59	No candidate		LeMahieu*	955
				McCarty	416
(part)	60	Duman	5	Gottlieb*	315
(part)	99	No candidate		Pridemore*	1,614
Waukesha (part)	12	Kessler*	0	No candidate	
(part)	14	Hucke	109	Vukmir*	1,859
(part)	24	Brady	294	Knodl	1,532
		Lauer	245	LaSage	1,251
				Melchert	1,341
				Moscicke	144
(part)	31	Urban	159	Nass*	1,395
(part)	33	No candidate		Newcomer*	3,558
(part)	38	Pas	58	Kleefisch*	996
(part)	83	Robertson	236	Gunderson*	1,310
(part)	84	No candidate		Gundrum*	2,783
(part)	97	Jones	645	Kramer*	2,200
		Schmuki	637		
(part)	98	Weers	210	Zipperer*	4,136
(part)	99	No candidate		Pridemore*	1,937
Waupaca (part)	6	Powers	10	Tauchen*	32
(part)	40	Kuehl	561	Petersen*	907
(part)	41	Milheiser	21	Ballweg*	27
Waushara (part)	41	Milheiser	186	Ballweg*	838
(part)	71	Molepske*	43	Jensen	110
Winnebago (part)	53	Mann	313	Burns	11
				Christianson	468
				Hatch	302
				Spanbauer	631
				Streeter	316
(part)	54	Hintz*	745	Reiff	706
(part)	55	Westphal	488	Kaufert*	674
(part)	56	Franz	131	Roth*	329
Wood (part)	69	Swiggum	7	Suder*	18
(part)	70	Vruwink*	799	Seevers	356
(part)	72	Kubisiak	919	Tyberg	267
		Schneider*	1,369		

*Incumbent.

[1]Votes for Independent candidates: 32nd AD: John K. Finley: Kenosha – 1; Walworth – 14; 47th AD: Dennis E. Hruby: Columbia – 16, Dane – 12, Sauk – 3; 58th AD: Greg Dombro: Washington – 30; 67th AD: Jeff Wood*: Barron – 7, Chippewa – 234, Dunn – 37; 73rd AD: Jeffery Lawrence Monaghan: Burnett – 6, Douglas – 37, Washburn – 8; 91st AD: Paul A. Beseler: Buffalo – 15, Pepin – 1, Pierce – 6, Trempealeau – 44.

[2]Votes for Libertarian Party candidates: 7th AD: Brad Sponholz: Milwaukee – 13; 29th AD: Craig Mohn: Dunn – 3, Pierce – 0, St. Croix – 10; 61st AD: George Meyers: Racine – 17; 62nd AD: Keith R. Deschler: Racine – 11; 91st AD: Ted Burleson: Buffalo – 8, Jackson – 0, Pepin – 1, Pierce – 5, Trempealeau – 11.

Source: Official records of the Government Accountability Board, Elections Division. Scattered votes omitted.

COUNTY VOTE FOR REPRESENTATIVES TO THE ASSEMBLY
November 4, 2008 General Election

County or Part	Assembly District	Democratic	Vote	Republican	Vote
Adams (part)	42	Clark	622	Hines*	558
(part)	72	Schneider*	5,355	Tyberg	3,007
Ashland	74	Sherman*	5,769	LaBarre	2,536
Barron (part)[1]	67	No candidate		Moga	524
(part)	75	Hubler*	15,821	No candidate	
Bayfield	74	Sherman*	5,970	LaBarre	3,311
Brown (part)	1	Skare	1,584	Bies*	2,169
(part)	2	Zigmunt	8,395	Lasee*	8,741
(part)	3	Krueger	550	Ott, A.*	1,093
(part)	4	Dunlop	13,520	Montgomery*	15,106
(part)	5	Nelson*	4,984	Steineke	4,279
(part)	88	Soletski*	13,155	Theisen	10,368
(part)	89	Koehn	3,364	Nygren*	4,456
(part)	90	Weix	12,016	Van Roy*	13,959
Buffalo[1, 2]	91	Danou	3,660	Hegenbarth	2,914
Burnett (part)	28	Hraychuck*	3,073	Muschinske	2,429
(part)[1]	73	Milroy	1,850	No candidate	
Calumet (part)	3	Krueger	7,753	Ott, A.*	12,712
(part)	25	Ziegelbauer*	780	No candidate	
(part)	27	Cox	1,417	Kestell*	2,331
Chippewa (part)[1]	67	No candidate		Moga	7,775
(part)	68	Dexter	3,870	Moulton*	4,955
(part)	69	Swiggum	1,054	Suder*	1,445
Clark (part)	69	Swiggum	5,572	Suder*	8,020
(part)	92	Radcliffe	214	Hellman	190
Columbia (part)	38	Pas	1,319	Kleefisch*	1,090
(part)	39	Onsrud	73	Fitzgerald*	148
(part)	42	Clark	6,101	Hines*	4,259
(part)[1, 3]	47	O'Neil	7,072	Ripp	7,662
Crawford	96	Klemme	3,845	Nerison*	3,816
Dane (part)	37	Jorgensen*	3,086	Koebke	1,432
(part)	43	Hixson*	10	Towns	12
(part)	46	Hebl*	22,350	Maves	11,365
(part)[1, 3]	47	O'Neil	7,992	Ripp	7,397
(part)	48	Parisi*	27,640	No candidate	
(part)	76	Berceau*	27,218	No candidate	
(part)	77	Black*	25,798	No candidate	
(part)	78	Pocan*	27,273	No candidate	
(part)	79	Pope-Roberts*	26,835	Skalitzky	13,361
(part)	80	Waelti	4,172	Davis*	4,050
(part)	81	Roys	23,984	No candidate	
Dodge (part)	38	Pas	3,843	Kleefisch*	7,832
(part)	39	Onsrud	10,534	Fitzgerald*	15,424
(part)	53	Mann	845	Spanbauer	1,424
(part)	59	No candidate		LeMahieu*	971
(part)	99	No candidate		Pridemore*	0
Door	1	Skare	8,755	Bies*	8,457
Douglas[1]	73	Milroy	16,888	No candidate	
Dunn (part)[2]	29	Buckel	5,485	Murtha*	4,690
(part)[1]	67	No candidate		Moga	3,916
(part)	93	Smith*	1,158	Fields, D.	951
Eau Claire (part)	68	Dexter	11,567	Moulton*	10,210
(part)	69	Swiggum	100	Suder*	100
(part)	92	Radcliffe	937	Hellman	622
(part)	93	Smith*	17,654	Fields, D.	11,844
Florence	36	Gruszynski	1,001	Mursau*	1,534
Fond du Lac (part)	27	Cox	796	Kestell*	1,802
(part)	41	Milheiser	2,031	Ballweg*	3,824
(part)	52	Keifenheim	10,966	Townsend*	15,116
(part)	53	Mann	2,950	Spanbauer	6,784
(part)	59	No candidate		LeMahieu*	4,095
Forest	36	Gruszynski	2,299	Mursau*	2,079
Grant	49	Garthwaite*	12,775	Tranel	10,897
Green	80	Waelti	7,324	Davis*	10,886
Green Lake	41	Milheiser	2,862	Ballweg*	6,296
Iowa (part)	49	Garthwaite*	39	Tranel	40
(part)	51	Hilgenberg*	7,219	Russell	4,374
Iron (part)	74	Sherman*	2,053	LaBarre	1,176
Jackson (part)[1, 2]	91	Danou	266	Hegenbarth	134
(part)	92	Radcliffe	5,468	Hellman	3,170
Jefferson (part)	31	Urban	2,605	Nass*	4,676
(part)	37	Jorgensen*	14,638	Koebke	10,729
(part)	38	Pas	2,384	Kleefisch*	4,812
(part)	43	Hixson*	1,017	Towns	595
Juneau	50	Crofton	5,058	Brooks	5,825
Kenosha (part)[1]	32	Harrod	619	Lothian*	930
(part)	64	Barca	19,739	No candidate	
(part)	65	Steinbrink*	18,093	Tiahnybok	10,994
(part)	66	Zamba	8,717	Kerkman*	12,435
Kewaunee (part)	1	Skare	4,716	Bies*	5,279
(part)	2	Zigmunt	298	Lasee*	243
La Crosse (part)	94	Hancock	14,600	Huebsch*	17,248
(part)	95	Shilling*	22,341	No candidate	

COUNTY VOTE FOR REPRESENTATIVES TO THE ASSEMBLY
November 4, 2008 General Election–Continued

County or Part	Assembly District	Democratic	Vote	Republican	Vote
Lafayette (part)	49	Garthwaite*	462	Tranel	335
(part)	51	Hilgenberg*	2,845	Russell	3,524
(part)	80	Waelti	145	Davis*	262
(part)	36	Gruszynski	817	Mursau*	956
Langlade (part)	35	Schmelling	3,243	Friske*	4,907
(part)	36	Gruszynski	817	Mursau*	956
Lincoln	35	Schmelling	6,738	Friske*	8,291
Manitowoc (part)	2	Zigmunt	7,315	Lasee	5,703
(part)	25	Ziegelbauer*	18,910	No candidate	
(part)	27	Cox	1,073	Kestell*	1,898
Marathon (part)	35	Schmelling	762	Friske*	935
(part)	36	Gruszynski	215	Mursau*	168
(part)	69	Swiggum	2,764	Suder*	4,369
(part)	70	Vruwink*	177	Seevers	62
(part)	85	Seidel*	16,817	Kufahl	9,407
(part)	86	Myszka	13,001	Petrowski*	16,627
(part)	87	Reas	423	Williams, M.*	527
Marinette (part)	36	Gruszynski	3,924	Mursau*	5,577
(part)	89	Koehn	5,331	Nygren*	5,760
Marquette (part)	41	Milheiser	634	Ballweg*	834
(part)	42	Clark	2,663	Hines*	2,508
(part)	72	Schneider*	515	Tyberg	392
Menominee	36	Gruszynski	997	Mursau*	251
Milwaukee (part)[2]	7	Krusick*	16,568	Wiesmueller	10,578
(part)	8	Colón*	8,743	No candidate	
(part)	9	Zepnick*	14,070	No candidate	
(part)	10	Williams, A.*	22,952	No candidate	
(part)	11	Fields, J.*	21,083	No candidate	
(part)	12	Kessler*	20,399	No candidate	
(part)	13	Cullen*	21,963	No candidate	
(part)	14	Hucke	8,293	Vukmir*	11,126
(part)	15	Staskunas*	15,652	Nickel	10,200
(part)	16	Young*	19,200	No candidate	
(part)	17	Toles*	23,041	No candidate	
(part)	18	Grigsby*	17,377	No candidate	
(part)	19	Richards*	25,281	No candidate	
(part)	20	Sinicki*	19,917	No candidate	
(part)	21	Brower	14,184	Honadel*	15,679
Pasch	22	Pasch	21,938	Wadhwa	10,720
(part)	23	Settle-Robinson	8,671	Ott, J.*	6,077
(part)	82	No candidate		Stone*	22,773
(part)	84	No candidate		Gundrum*	3,276
Monroe (part)	50	Crofton	313	Brooks	371
(part)	92	Radcliffe	6,880	Hellman	7,862
(part)	94	Hancock	454	Huebsch*	471
(part)	96	Klemme	1,067	Nerison*	1,240
Oconto (part)	6	Powers	3,276	Tauchen*	3,748
(part)	36	Gruszynski	1,098	Mursau*	1,113
(part)	89	Koehn	4,116	Nygren*	4,563
Oneida (part)	34	Tubbs	10,363	Meyer*	8,602
(part)	35	Schmelling	1,008	Friske*	1,283
Outagamie (part)	3	Krueger	5,778	Ott, A.*	5,884
(part)	5	Nelson*	14,131	Steineke	6,215
(part)	6	Powers	1,854	Tauchen*	1,996
(part)	40	Kuehl	1,122	Petersen*	1,405
(part)	56	Franz	8,736	Roth*	12,948
(part)	57	Bernard Schaber	15,383	Egelhoff	11,560
Ozaukee (part)	23	Settle-Robinson	4,289	Ott, J.*	11,727
(part)	59	No candidate		LeMahieu*	3,833
(part)	60	Duman	9,125	Gottlieb*	21,321
Pepin (part)[1,2]	91	Danou	1,546	Hegenbarth	1,440
(part)	93	Smith*	324	Fields, D.	264
Pierce (part)[2]	29	Buckel	824	Murtha*	952
(part)	30	Bruch	7,672	Rhoades*	7,882
(part)[1,2]	91	Danou	1,788	Hegenbarth	1,746
(part)	93	Smith*	140	Fields, D.	102
Polk (part)	28	Hraychuck*	11,901	Muschinske	9,504
(part)	75	Hubler*	645	No candidate	
Portage (part)	70	Vruwink*	5,514	Seevers	2,196
(part)	71	Molepske*	19,248	Jensen	8,359
(part)	72	Schneider*	479	Tyberg	277
(part)	86	Myszka	379	Petrowski*	303
Price	87	Reas	4,704	Williams, M.*	3,373
Racine (part)[2]	61	Turner*	16,267	No candidate	
(part)[2]	62	Mason*	17,892	No candidate	
(part)	63	Flashinski	12,609	Vos*	20,172
(part)	66	Zamba	3,082	Kerkman*	5,224
(part)	83	Robertson	1,528	Gunderson*	4,731
Richland (part)	49	Garthwaite*	589	Tranel	521
(part)	50	Crofton	2,055	Brooks	2,159
(part)	51	Hilgenberg*	811	Russell	588
(part)	96	Klemme	614	Nerison*	669
Rock (part)	43	Hixson*	10,394	Towns	11,155
(part)	44	Sheridan*	19,531	No candidate	

COUNTY VOTE FOR REPRESENTATIVES TO THE ASSEMBLY
November 4, 2008 General Election–Continued

County or Part	Assembly District	Democratic	Vote	Republican	Vote
(part)	45	Benedict*	15,612	Hahn	10,006
(part)	80	Waelti	1,876	Davis*	2,093
Rusk	87	Reas	3,686	Williams, M.*	3,355
St. Croix (part)	28	Hraychuck*	1,433	Muschinske	1,281
(part)[2]	29	Buckel	7,806	Murtha*	11,991
(part)	30	Bruch	8,606	Rhoades*.	11,847
Sauk (part)	42	Clark	6,550	Hines*	3,979
(part)[1, 3]	47	O'Neil	379	Ripp	407
(part)	50	Crofton	3,768	Brooks	6,032
(part)	51	Hilgenberg*	4,980	Russell	3,540
Sawyer (part)	74	Sherman*	4,259	LaBarre	3,851
(part)	87	Reas	253	Williams, M.*	301
Shawano (part)	5	Nelson*	269	Steineke	190
(part)	6	Powers	6,255	Tauchen*	8,139
(part)	36	Gruszynski	1,808	Mursau*	1,386
(part)	40	Kuehl	6	Petersen*	4
(part)	85	Seidel*	158	Kufahl	80
(part)	86	Myszka	336	Petrowski*	472
(part)	89	Koehn	28	Nygren*	35
Sheboygan (part)	26	Van Akkeren*	16,046	Pieper	8,463
(part)	27	Cox	7,386	Kestell*	14,673
(part)	59	No candidate		LeMahieu*	11,204
Taylor (part)	69	Swiggum	74	Suder*	94
(part)	87	Reas	3,619	Williams. M.*	5,361
Trempealeau[1, 2]	91	Danou	7,117	Hegenbarth	5,349
Vernon	96	Klemme	6,528	Nerison*	7,194
Vilas	34	Tubbs	5,729	Meyer*	7,698
Walworth (part)	31	Urban	4,025	Nass*.	7,400
(part)[1]	32	Harrod	10,309	Lothian*	12,762
(part)	43	Hixson*	3,882	Towns	2,819
(part)	45	Benedict*	441	Hahn	518
(part)	66	Zamba	0	Kerkman*	0
(part)	83	Robertson	1,321	Gunderson*	3,253
Washburn (part)[1]	73	Milroy	1,946	No candidate	
(part)	75	Hubler*	3,788	No candidate	
Washington (part)	23	Settle-Robinson	0	Ott, J.*	0
(part)	24	Brady	5,176	Knodl	9,569
(part)[1]	58	No candidate		Strachota*	23,603
(part)	59	No candidate		LeMahieu*	6,151
(part)	60	Duman	696	Gottlieb*	1,961
(part)	99	No candidate		Pridemore*	11,981
Waukesha (part)	12	Kessler*	0	No candidate	
(part)	14	Hucke	3,415	Vukmir*	8,293
(part)	24	Brady	7,385	Knodl	10,941
(part)	31	Urban	4,223	Nass*.	9,704
(part)	33	No candidate		Newcomer*	27,746
(part)	38	Pas	2,749	Kleefisch*	6,560
(part)	83	Robertson	6,333	Gunderson*	16,850
(part)	84	No candidate		Gundrum*	21,860
(part)	97	Jones	12,268	Kramer*	14,801
(part)	98	Weers	9,498	Zipperer*	24,325
(part)	99	No candidate		Pridemore*	15,925
Waupaca (part)	6	Powers	246	Tauchen*	354
(part)	40	Kuehl	9,409	Petersen*	13,332
(part)	41	Milheiser	302	Ballweg*	431
Waushara (part)	41	Milheiser	4,024	Ballweg*	5,273
(part)	71	Molepske*	1,111	Jensen	912
Winnebago (part)	53	Mann	6,321	Spanbauer	9,664
(part)	54	Hintz*	18,758	Reiff	9,531
(part)	55	Westphal	12,179	Kaufert*	14,259
(part)	56	Franz	5,408	Roth*	8,023
Wood (part)	69	Swiggum	341	Suder*	509
(part)	70	Vruwink*	13,799	Seevers	6,237
(part)	72	Schneider*	10,543	Tyberg	6,554

*Incumbent

[1]Votes for Independent candidates: 32nd AD: John K. Finley: Kenosha – 101, Walworth – 1,764; 47th AD: Dennis E. Hruby: Columbia – 690, Dane – 651, Sauk – 47; 58th AD: Greg Dombro: Washington – 4,891; 67th AD: Jeff Wood*: Barron – 437, Chippewa – 8,233, Dunn – 3,723;73rd AD: Jeffery Lawrence Monaghan: Burnett – 388, Douglas – 4,000, Washburn – 400; 91st AD: Paul A. Beseler: Buffalo – 122, Jackson – 16, Pepin – 32, Pierce – 119, Trempealeau – 423.

[2]Votes for Libertarian Party candidates: 7th AD: Brad Sponholz: Milwaukee – 655; 29th AD: Craig Mohn: Dunn – 521, Pierce – 72, St. Croix – 664; 61st AD: George Meyers: Racine – 2,242; 62nd AD: Keith R. Deschler: Racine – 3,217; 91st AD: Ted Burleson: Buffalo – 65, Jackson – 1, Pepin – 16, Pierce – 48, Trempealeau – 126.

[3]Recount results.

Source: Official records of the Government Accountability Board, Elections Division. Scattered votes omitted.

DISTRICT VOTE FOR REPRESENTATIVES TO THE ASSEMBLY
September 9, 2008 Primary Election

Assembly District	Political Party	Candidates	Vote
1	Dem.	Christopher Baeb	1,054
	Dem.	Dick Skare	2,353
	Rep.	Garey Bies*	899
2	Dem.	Lee Brocher	642
	Dem.	Kevin R. Garthwaite	464
	Dem.	Ted Zigmunt	649
	Rep.	Frank Lasee*	368
3	Dem.	Justin Krueger	532
	Rep.	Al Ott*	653
4	Dem.	Sam Dunlop	647
	Rep.	Phil Montgomery*	765
5	Dem.	Tom Nelson*	776
	Rep.	Jim Steineke	593
6	Dem.	John Powers	1,093
	Rep.	Gary Tauchen*	3,983
7	Dem.	Peggy Krusick*	1,728
	Lib.	Brad Sponholz	13
	Rep.	Corrine Wiesmueller	708
8	Dem.	Pedro Colón*	571
	Dem.	Jose Guzman	206
	Dem.	Laura L. Manriquez	284
9	Dem.	Josh Zepnick*	991
10.	Dem.	Charisha Allen	244
	Dem.	Annette Polly Williams*	1,775
11.	Dem.	Jason Fields*	974
12.	Dem.	Frederick P. Kessler*	1,106
13.	Dem.	David Cullen*	1,530
14.	Dem.	Dave Hucke	717
	Rep.	Leah Vukmir*	3,571
15.	Dem.	Josh Hoisington	509
	Dem.	Tony Staskunas*	1,590
	Rep.	David Nickel	751
16.	Dem.	Richard M. Badger	205
	Dem.	David D. King	290
	Dem.	Andy Parker	362
	Dem.	Leon D. Young*	985
17.	Dem.	Samantha H. Bady	252
	Dem.	Barbara L. Toles*	2,115
18.	Dem.	Tamara D. Grigsby*	965
19.	Dem.	Jon Richards*	1,618
20.	Dem.	Philip Landowski	807
	Dem.	Christine M. Sinicki*	2,113
	Dem.	Steven Sutherland	487
21.	Dem.	Glen Brower	1,005
	Rep.	Mark Honadel*	1,084
22.	Dem.	Andy Feldman	2,852
	Dem.	Guy Johnson	329
	Dem.	Dan Kohl	1,802
	Dem.	Sandy Pasch	2,930
	Rep.	Yash P. Wadhwa	1,664
23.	Dem.	Rene Settle-Robinson	1,038
	Rep.	Jim Ott*	4,148
24.	Dem.	Charlene S. Brady	564
	Dem.	Torrey Lauer	386
	Rep.	Dan Knodl	2,706
	Rep.	Jason LaSage	2,312
	Rep.	Randall Ryan Melchert	1,995
	Rep.	Michael Moscicke	215
25.	Dem.	Bob Ziegelbauer*	2,071
26.	Dem.	Terry Van Akkeren*	1,473
	Rep.	Job Hou-Seye	563
	Rep.	Alex Pieper	810
27.	Dem.	Bob Cox	798
	Rep.	Steve Kestell*	1,252
28.	Dem.	Ann Hraychuck*	1,925
	Rep.	Kent Muschinske	873
29.	Dem.	Chris Buckel	1,593
	Dem.	L. John Peters	567
	Lib.	Craig Mohn	13
	Rep.	John Murtha*	799
30.	Dem.	Sarah A. Bruch	1,346
	Rep.	Bob Hughes	372
	Rep.	Kitty Rhoades*	2,432
31.	Dem.	Frank E. Urban	426
	Rep.	Steve Nass*	2,275
32.	Dem.	Doug A. Harrod	442
	Rep.	Thomas A. Lothian*	681
	Ind.	John K. Finley	15
33.	Rep.	Scott Newcomer*	3,558
34.	Dem.	Paul Tubbs	2,942
	Rep.	Dan Meyer*	1,586
35.	Dem.	Jay Schmelling	2,228
	Rep.	Don Friske*	822

DISTRICT VOTE FOR REPRESENTATIVES TO THE ASSEMBLY
September 9, 2008 Primary Election–Continued

Assembly District	Political Party	Candidates	Vote
36.	Dem.	Stan Gruszynski	1,180
	Rep.	Jeffrey L. Mursau*	1,702
37.	Dem.	Andy Jorgensen*	1,021
	Rep.	Kent Koebke	1,229
	Rep.	Tom Luetzow	941
	Rep.	Brian A. Peters	507
38.	Dem.	Dick Pas	379
	Rep.	Joel Kleefisch*	1,845
39.	Dem.	Aaron E. Onsrud	542
	Rep.	Jeff Fitzgerald*	995
40.	Dem.	Kevin M. Kuehl	627
	Rep.	Kevin David Petersen*	1,031
41.	Dem.	Scott Milheiser	538
	Rep.	Joan A. Ballweg*	3,350
42.	Dem.	Fred Clark	1,215
	Rep.	J.A. Hines*	1,463
43.	Dem.	Kim Hixson*	782
	Rep.	Debi Towns	571
44.	Dem.	Mike Sheridan*	957
45.	Dem.	Chuck Benedict*	550
	Rep.	Mike Hahn	328
46.	Dem.	Gary Hebl*	900
	Rep.	Kathy Maves	405
	Rep.	Spencer Zimmerman	312
47.	Dem.	Paul Fisk	1,082
	Dem.	Trish O'Neil	1,759
	Rep.	Tim McCumber	567
	Rep.	Steven Pate	353
	Rep.	Keith Ripp	1,720
	Rep.	Erich Ruth	565
	Ind.	Dennis E. Hruby	31
48.	Dem.	Joseph T. Parisi*	1,122
49.	Dem.	Phil Garthwaite*	1,050
	Rep.	David E. Kuhle	1,571
	Rep.	Dennis Lundell	1,599
	Rep.	Travis Tranel	2,150
50.	Dem.	Tom Crofton	884
	Dem.	Darryl Teske	806
	Rep.	Todd R. Allbaugh	1,161
	Rep.	Ed Brooks	1,870
	Rep.	Craig Buswell	174
	Rep.	Anthony Carver	849
51.	Dem.	Steve Hilgenberg*	1,169
	Rep.	Nathan R. Russell	1,499
52.	Dem.	Jerry Keifenheim	604
	Rep.	Scott Matthew	972
	Rep.	John Townsend*	2,311
53.	Dem.	Jeff Mann	502
	Rep.	Jacob Burns	25
	Rep.	Mike Christianson	604
	Rep.	Mike Hatch	994
	Rep.	Richard J. Spanbauer	1,115
	Rep.	Cecil Streeter	469
54.	Dem.	Gordon Hintz*	745
	Rep.	Mark Reiff	706
55.	Dem.	Mark Westphal	488
	Rep.	Dean R. Kaufert*	674
56.	Dem.	Susan Garcia Franz	499
	Rep.	Roger J. Roth, Jr.*	1,010
57.	Dem.	Penny Bernard Schaber	738
	Rep.	Jo Egelhoff	2,051
	Rep.	Peter Stueck	464
58.	Rep.	Pat Strachota*	3,617
	Ind.	Greg Dombro	30
59.	Rep.	Daniel R. LeMahieu*	4,816
	Rep.	Karl McCarty	1,954
60.	Dem.	Perry Duman	185
	Rep.	Mark Gottlieb*	4,277
61.	Dem.	Robert Turner*	1,213
	Lib.	George Meyers	17
62.	Dem.	Cory Mason*	1,118
	Lib.	Keith R. Deschler	11
63.	Dem.	Linda Flashinski	959
	Rep.	Robin J. Vos*	1,253
64.	Dem.	Peter W. Barca	3,134
	Dem.	Jim Huff	928
	Dem.	Michael J. Orth	122
65.	Dem.	John P. Steinbrink*	2,466
	Rep.	Alex Tiahnybok	494
66.	Dem.	Mike Orr	516
	Dem.	Larry Zamba	1,009
	Rep.	Samantha Kerkman*	953
67.	Ind.	Jeff Wood*	278

DISTRICT VOTE FOR REPRESENTATIVES TO THE ASSEMBLY
September 9, 2008 Primary Election–Continued

Assembly District	Political Party	Candidates	Vote
68.	Dem.	Kristen Dexter	776
	Rep.	Terry Moulton*	664
69.	Dem.	Tim Swiggum	861
	Rep.	Scott Suder*	883
70.	Dem.	Amy Sue Vruwink*	1,050
	Rep.	Dennis Seevers	440
71.	Dem.	Louis John Molepske, Jr.*	1,064
	Rep.	Daron L. Jensen	380
72.	Dem.	Thad Kubisiak	1,472
	Dem.	Marlin D. Schneider*	2,142
	Rep.	Jeff Tyberg	692
73.	Dem.	Vern Johnson	1,520
	Dem.	Bruce Meyers	76
	Dem.	Nick Milroy	3,596
	Dem.	Mary Tripp	2,658
	Ind.	Jeffery Lawrence Monaghan	51
74.	Dem.	Alan E. Ralph	1,323
	Dem.	Gary E. Sherman*	4,073
	Rep.	Shirl LaBarre	562
75.	Dem.	Mary Hubler*	756
76.	Dem.	Terese Berceau*	960
77.	Dem.	Spencer Black*	1,151
78.	Dem.	Mark Pocan*	1,099
79.	Dem.	Sondy Pope-Roberts*	1,205
	Rep.	Carl Skalitzky	494
80.	Dem.	John Waelti	1,364
	Dem.	Kristin Wisnefske	1,152
	Rep.	Brett Davis*	667
81.	Dem.	Eric Englund	904
	Dem.	Peng Her	337
	Dem.	Tim Kiefer	410
	Dem.	John W. Laubmeier	1,001
	Dem.	Kelda Helen Roys	1,960
	Dem.	Justin Sargent	1,683
82.	Rep.	Jeff Stone*	1,234
83.	Dem.	Aaron Robertson	358
	Rep.	Scott L. Gunderson*	1,690
84.	Rep.	Mark Gundrum*	2,995
85.	Dem.	Donna Seidel*	714
	Rep.	Jess F. Kufahl	446
86.	Dem.	Nate Myszka	464
	Rep.	Jerry J. Petrowski*	419
87.	Dem.	J. Suzanne Murphy	489
	Dem.	Judy Reas	1,858
	Rep.	Mary Williams*	1,523
88.	Dem.	Jim Soletski*	912
	Rep.	Tony Theisen	539
89.	Dem.	Randy Koehn	766
	Rep.	John Nygren*	2,057
90.	Dem.	Lou Ann Weix	972
	Rep.	Karl Van Roy*	770
91.	Dem.	Marge Baecker	1,202
	Dem.	Steve Boe	551
	Dem.	Remy Ceci	249
	Dem.	Chris Danou	1,655
	Dem.	John Kimmel	579
	Dem.	James K. Kraft	527
	Lib.	Ted Burleson	25
	Rep.	David Anderson	857
	Rep.	Dave Hegenbarth	1,528
	Ind.	Paul A. Beseler	66
92.	Dem.	Curtis Miller	927
	Dem.	Mark A. Radcliffe	1,196
	Rep.	Dan Hellman	738
93.	Dem.	Jeff Smith*	1,117
	Rep.	Darcy Fields	1,290
	Rep.	John Schiess	272
94.	Dem.	Cheryl Hancock	416
	Rep.	Mike Huebsch*	459
95.	Dem.	Jennifer Shilling*	824
96.	Dem.	Dale Klemme	780
	Rep	Lee Nerison*	900
97.	Dem.	Ruth Page Jones	645
	Dem.	Steve Schmuki	637
	Rep.	Bill Kramer*	2,200
98.	Dem.	Victor Weers	210
	Rep.	Rich Zipperer*	4,136
99.	Rep.	Don Pridemore*	3,551

Dem. – Democratic Party; Lib. – Libertarian Party; Rep. – Republican Party; Ind. – Independent
*Incumbent.
Source: Official records of the Government Accountability Board, Elections Division. Scattered votes omitted.

DISTRICT VOTE FOR REPRESENTATIVES TO THE ASSEMBLY
November 4, 2008 General Election

Assembly District	Political Party	Candidates	Vote	Percent of Total Vote[1]
1	Dem.	Dick Skare	15,055	48.59%
	Rep.	Garey Bies*	15,905	51.33
2	Dem.	Ted Zigmunt	16,008	52.12
	Rep.	Frank Lasee*	14,687	47.82
3	Dem.	Justin Krueger	14,081	41.67
	Rep.	Al Ott*	19,689	58.26
4	Dem.	Sam Dunlop	13,520	47.20
	Rep.	Phil Montgomery*	15,106	52.73
5	Dem.	Tom Nelson*	19,384	64.44
	Rep.	Jim Steineke	10,684	35.52
6	Dem.	John Powers	11,631	44.95
	Rep.	Gary Tauchen*	14,237	55.02
7	Dem.	Peggy Krusick*	16,568	59.53
	Lib.	Brad Sponholz	655	2.35
	Rep.	Corrine Wiesmueller	10,578	38.01
8	Dem.	Pedro Colón*	8,743	98.26
9	Dem.	Josh Zepnick*	14,070	98.53
10	Dem.	Annette Polly Williams*	22,952	99.19
11	Dem.	Jason Fields*	21,083	99.24
12	Dem.	Frederick P. Kessler*	20,399	98.92
13	Dem.	David Cullen*	21,963	98.42
14	Dem.	Dave Hucke	11,708	37.55
	Rep.	Leah Vukmir*	19,419	62.28
15	Dem.	Tony Staskunas*	15,652	60.45
	Rep.	David Nickel	10,200	39.40
16	Dem.	Leon D. Young*	19,200	98.81
17	Dem.	Barbara L. Toles*	23,041	99.20
18	Dem.	Tamara D. Grigsby*	17,377	98.96
19	Dem.	Jon Richards*	25,281	98.52
20	Dem.	Christine M. Sinicki*	19,917	98.22
21	Dem.	Glen Brower	14,184	47.43
	Rep.	Mark Honadel*	15,679	52.43
22	Dem.	Sandy Pasch	21,938	67.06
	Rep.	Yash P. Wadhwa	10,720	32.77
23	Dem.	Rene Settle-Robinson	12,960	42.10
	Rep.	Jim Ott*	17,804	57.83
24	Dem.	Charlene S. Brady	12,561	37.90
	Rep.	Dan Knodl	20,510	61.88
25	Dem.	Bob Ziegelbauer*	19,690	98.85
26	Dem.	Terry Van Akkeren*	16,046	65.43
	Rep.	Alex Pieper	8,463	34.51
27	Dem.	Bob Cox	10,672	33.99
	Rep.	Steve Kestell*	20,704	65.95
28	Dem.	Ann Hraychuck*	16,407	55.37
	Rep.	Kent Muschinske	13,214	44.59
29	Dem.	Chris Buckel	14,115	42.73
	Lib.	Craig Mohn	1,257	3.80
	Rep.	John Murtha*	17,633	53.38
30	Dem.	Sarah A. Bruch	16,278	45.17
	Rep.	Kitty Rhoades*	19,729	54.74
31	Dem.	Frank E. Urban	10,853	33.22
	Rep.	Steve Nass*	21,780	66.66
32	Dem.	Doug A. Harrod	10,928	41.23
	Rep.	Thomas A. Lothian*	13,692	51.65
	Ind.	John K. Finley	1,865	7.04
33	Rep.	Scott Newcomer*	27,746	99.77
34	Dem.	Paul Tubbs	16,092	49.64
	Rep.	Dan Meyer*	16,300	50.28
35	Dem.	Jay Schmelling	11,751	43.23
	Rep.	Don Friske*	15,416	56.72
36	Dem.	Stan Gruszynski	12,159	48.19
	Rep.	Jeffrey L. Mursau*	13,064	51.78
37	Dem.	Andy Jorgensen*	17,724	59.23
	Rep.	Kent Koebke	12,161	40.64
38	Dem.	Dick Pas	10,295	33.62
	Rep.	Joel Kleefisch*	20,294	66.27
39	Dem.	Aaron E. Onsrud	10,607	39.89
	Rep.	Jeff Fitzgerald*	15,974	60.08
40	Dem.	Kevin M. Kuehl	10,537	41.67
	Rep.	Kevin David Petersen*	14,741	58.29
41	Dem.	Scott Milheiser	9,853	37.14
	Rep.	Joan A. Ballweg*	16,658	62.78
42	Dem.	Fred Clark	15,936	58.47
	Rep.	J.A. Hines*	11,304	41.47
43	Dem.	Kim Hixson*	15,303	51.16
	Rep.	Debi Towns	14,581	48.74
44	Dem.	Mike Sheridan*	19,531	99.15

DISTRICT VOTE FOR REPRESENTATIVES TO THE ASSEMBLY
November 4, 2008 General Election–Continued

Assembly District	Political Party	Candidates	Vote	Percent of Total Vote[1]
45.	Dem.	Chuck Benedict*	16,053	60.37
	Rep.	Mike Hahn	10,524	39.58
46.	Dem.	Gary Hebl*	22,350	66.28
	Rep.	Kathy Maves	11,365	33.70
47.	Dem.	Trish O'Neil	15,443[2]	47.80
	Rep.	Keith Ripp	15,466[2]	47.87
	Ind.	Dennis E. Hruby	1,388	4.30
48.	Dem.	Joseph T. Parisi*	27,640	99.51
49.	Dem.	Phil Garthwaite*	13,865	53.96
	Rep.	Travis Tranel	11,793	45.90
50.	Dem.	Tom Crofton	11,194	43.73
	Rep.	Ed Brooks	14,387	56.20
51.	Dem.	Steve Hilgenberg*	15,855	56.84
	Rep.	Nathan R. Russell	12,026	43.12
52.	Dem.	Jerry Keifenheim	10,966	42.02
	Rep.	John Townsend*	15,116	57.92
53.	Dem.	Jeff Mann	10,116	36.11
	Rep.	Richard J. Spanbauer	17,872	63.80
54.	Dem.	Gordon Hintz*	18,758	66.21
	Rep.	Mark Reiff	9,531	33.64
55.	Dem.	Mark Westphal	12,179	46.02
	Rep.	Dean R. Kaufert*	14,259	53.88
56.	Dem.	Susan Garcia Franz	14,144	40.24
	Rep.	Roger J. Roth, Jr.*	20,971	59.66
57.	Dem.	Penny Bernard Schaber	15,383	56.98
	Rep.	Jo Egelhoff	11,560	42.82
58.	Rep.	Pat Strachota*	23,603	82.77
	Ind.	Greg Dombro	4,891	17.15
59.	Rep.	Daniel R. LeMahieu*	26,254	99.32
60.	Dem.	Perry Duman	9,821	29.65
	Rep.	Mark Gottlieb*	23,282	70.29
61.	Dem.	Robert Turner*	16,267	87.71
	Lib.	George Meyers	2,242	12.09
62.	Dem.	Cory Mason*	17,892	84.54
	Lib.	Keith R. Deschler	3,217	15.20
63.	Dem.	Linda Flashinski	12,609	38.45
	Rep.	Robin J. Vos*	20,172	61.51
64.	Dem.	Peter W. Barca*	19,739	98.71
65.	Dem.	John P. Steinbrink*	18,093	62.12
	Rep.	Alex Tiahnybok	10,994	37.75
66.	Dem.	Larry Zamba	11,799	40.03
	Rep.	Samantha Kerkman*	17,659	59.91
67.	Rep.	Don Moga	12,215	49.55
	Ind.	Jeff Wood*	12,393	50.28
68.	Dem.	Kristen Dexter	15,437	50.35
	Rep.	Terry Moulton*	15,165	49.47
69.	Dem.	Tim Swiggum	9,905	40.51
	Rep.	Scott Suder*	14,537	59.46
70.	Dem.	Amy Sue Vruwink*	19,490	69.62
	Rep.	Dennis Seevers	8,495	30.34
71.	Dem.	Louis John Molepske, Jr.*	20,359	68.61
	Rep.	Daron L. Jensen	9,271	31.24
72.	Dem.	Marlin D. Schneider*	16,892	62.23
	Rep.	Jeff Tyberg	10,230	37.69
73.	Dem.	Nick Milroy	20,684	80.76
	Ind.	Jeffery Lawrence Monaghan	4,788	18.69
74.	Dem.	Gary E. Sherman*	18,051	62.38
	Rep.	Shirl LaBarre	10,874	37.58
75.	Dem.	Mary Hubler*	20,254	99.03
76.	Dem.	Terese Berceau*	27,218	99.39
77.	Dem.	Spencer Black*	25,798	99.40
78.	Dem.	Mark Pocan*	27,273	99.38
79.	Dem.	Sondy Pope-Roberts*	26,835	66.71
	Rep.	Carl Skalitzky	13,361	33.22
80.	Dem.	John Waelti	13,517	43.86
	Rep.	Brett Davis*	17,291	56.10
81.	Dem.	Kelda Helen Roys	23,984	98.89
82.	Rep.	Jeff Stone*	22,773	99.02
83.	Dem.	Aaron Robertson	9,182	26.98
	Rep.	Scott L. Gunderson*	24,834	72.97
84.	Rep.	Mark Gundrum*	25,136	99.46
85.	Dem.	Donna Seidel*	16,975	64.08
	Rep.	Jess F. Kufahl	9,487	35.81
86.	Dem.	Nate Myszka	13,716	44.06
	Rep.	Jerry J. Petrowski*	17,402	55.90
87.	Dem.	Judy Reas	12,685	49.52
	Rep.	Mary Williams*	12,917	50.42
88.	Dem.	Jim Soletski*	13,155	55.86
	Rep.	Tony Theisen	10,368	44.03

DISTRICT VOTE FOR REPRESENTATIVES TO THE ASSEMBLY
November 4, 2008 General Election–Continued

Assembly District	Political Party	Candidates	Vote	Percent of Total Vote[1]
89.	Dem.	Randy Koehn	12,839	46.40
	Rep.	John Nygren*	14,814	53.54
90.	Dem.	Lou Ann Weix	12,016	46.23
	Rep.	Karl Van Roy*	13,959	53.70
91.	Dem.	Chris Danou	14,377	53.34
	Lib.	Ted Burleson	256	0.95
	Rep.	Dave Hegenbarth	11,583	42.97
	Ind.	Paul A. Beseler	712	2.64
92.	Dem.	Mark A. Radcliffe	13,499	53.17
	Rep.	Dan Hellman	11,844	46.66
93.	Dem.	Jeff Smith*	19,276	59.35
	Rep.	Darcy Fields	13,161	40.52
94.	Dem.	Cheryl Hancock	15,054	45.91
	Rep.	Mike Huebsch*	17,719	54.04
95.	Dem.	Jennifer Shilling*	22,341	97.29
96.	Dem.	Dale Klemme	12,054	48.26
	Rep	Lee Nerison*	12,919	51.72
97.	Dem.	Ruth Page Jones	12,268	45.27
	Rep.	Bill Kramer*	14,801	54.62
98.	Dem.	Victor Weers	9,498	28.07
	Rep.	Rich Zipperer*	24,325	71.88
99.	Rep.	Don Pridemore*	27,906	99.40

Dem. – Democratic Party; Lib. – Libertarian Party; Rep. – Republican Party; Ind. – Independent.

*Incumbent.

[1]Percentages do not equal 100%, as scattered votes have been omitted.

[2]Recount vote total.

Source: Official records of the Government Accountability Board, Elections Division. Scattered votes omitted.

DEMOCRATIC PRESIDENTIAL PREFERENCE VOTE, BY COUNTY
February 19, 2008

County	Total*	Joe Biden	Hillary Clinton	Chris Dodd	John Edwards
Adams	3,955	3	2,104	1	48
Ashland	3,449	6	1,583	1	30
Barron	7,483	6	3,398	2	63
Bayfield	3,898	6	1,675	2	33
Brown	43,798	24	18,608	23	249
Buffalo	2,287	1	1,091	3	15
Burnett	2,390	2	1,266	2	29
Calumet	8,186	3	3,460	2	46
Chippewa	10,353	8	4,743	1	60
Clark	5,189	5	2,354	3	56
Columbia	10,874	8	4,630	3	78
Crawford	2,963	2	1,349	0	28
Dane	141,350	74	44,187	73	755
Dodge	13,077	14	6,055	8	83
Door	7,047	5	2,767	0	49
Douglas	8,444	14	4,756	5	77
Dunn	6,960	3	2,716	1	41
Eau Claire	20,311	9	7,099	15	88
Florence	828	1	385	1	7
Fond du Lac	15,287	10	6,790	4	88
Forest	2,036	0	1,130	1	25
Grant	7,827	5	3,163	5	66
Green	7,289	5	2,898	4	39
Green Lake	2,871	4	1,265	1	20
Iowa	5,027	0	2,126	1	29
Iron	1,313	3	651	1	14
Jackson	3,508	3	1,651	4	24
Jefferson	14,599	9	6,021	4	111
Juneau	3,765	1	1,910	0	27
Kenosha	30,388	28	14,552	11	218
Kewaunee	3,962	2	1,887	4	29
La Crosse	22,759	17	9,312	7	141
Lafayette	3,059	0	1,347	3	30
Langlade	3,853	2	1,879	0	23
Lincoln	6,574	4	2,995	2	66
Manitowoc	15,475	7	6,886	14	137
Marathon	24,728	17	11,090	6	168
Marinette	7,396	8	3,797	4	43
Marquette	2,849	1	1,353	1	14
Menominee	400	0	190	0	3
Milwaukee	208,042	143	73,430	109	910
Monroe	6,282	3	2,965	4	57
Oconto	7,096	6	3,532	4	56
Oneida	8,083	6	3,383	7	72
Outagamie	30,968	20	12,317	7	160
Ozaukee	17,592	7	7,606	6	89
Pepin	1,245	1	590	0	11
Pierce	5,738	6	2,583	3	42
Polk	6,898	11	3,504	3	88
Portage	15,926	11	6,708	8	115
Price	3,333	5	1,468	1	29
Racine	37,324	16	16,294	17	227
Richland	3,170	1	1,411	0	17
Rock	31,004	16	13,134	16	206
Rusk	2,684	2	1,273	1	20
St. Croix	10,566	15	4,930	6	79
Sauk	11,850	7	4,821	4	86
Sawyer	2,714	3	1,196	1	24
Shawano	6,458	3	3,004	1	39
Sheboygan	20,660	23	9,492	5	129
Taylor	3,115	2	1,394	0	35
Trempealeau	5,394	5	2,690	5	39
Vernon	5,098	3	2,225	5	27
Vilas	4,784	7	1,991	1	36
Walworth	16,437	8	6,462	9	103
Washburn	3,021	5	1,424	1	34
Washington	20,409	19	9,676	8	108
Waukesha	72,250	41	34,009	23	308
Waupaca	8,005	7	3,344	4	36
Waushara	3,634	3	1,743	0	29
Winnebago	30,508	24	11,909	9	173
Wood	15,658	6	6,327	10	159
TOTAL	1,113,753	755	453,954	501	6,693

*Scattered vote included in county total.

Source: Official records of the Government Accountability Board, Elections Division.

DEMOCRATIC PRESIDENTIAL PREFERENCE VOTE, BY COUNTY
February 19, 2008–Continued

Mike Gravel	Dennis Kucinich	Barack Obama	Bill Richardson	Uninstructed Delegation	County
3	7	1,782	2	2	Adams
4	13	1,800	2	6	Ashland
2	26	3,970	1	10	Barron
3	15	2,157	1	6	Bayfield
21	70	24,737	18	31	Brown
3	7	1,163	1	2	Buffalo
1	11	1,073	1	5	Burnett
3	13	4,648	4	7	Calumet
3	11	5,519	4	4	Chippewa
3	10	2,751	2	3	Clark
6	32	6,098	6	11	Columbia
1	20	1,559	1	1	Crawford
95	528	95,416	78	92	Dane
2	32	6,867	6	6	Dodge
4	14	4,196	3	5	Door
2	15	3,549	3	14	Douglas
6	22	4,156	4	5	Dunn
11	47	13,008	12	13	Eau Claire
0	3	429	0	1	Florence
6	33	8,335	7	10	Fond du Lac
4	6	867	3	0	Forest
8	17	4,544	10	7	Grant
2	12	4,322	2	4	Green
2	1	1,577	1	0	Green Lake
0	16	2,848	3	4	Iowa
0	4	635	1	4	Iron
2	17	1,804	0	1	Jackson
4	31	8,382	9	17	Jefferson
1	12	1,810	0	3	Juneau
12	44	15,467	8	30	Kenosha
0	4	2,031	3	2	Kewaunee
19	45	13,180	12	14	La Crosse
0	10	1,662	3	4	Lafayette
0	14	1,913	6	14	Langlade
0	5	3,493	3	5	Lincoln
9	26	8,375	5	10	Manitowoc
4	38	13,363	10	23	Marathon
3	19	3,504	4	12	Marinette
4	14	1,458	2	1	Marquette
0	1	206	0	0	Menominee
86	514	132,501	75	156	Milwaukee
1	11	3,232	2	3	Monroe
3	19	3,463	7	4	Oconto
3	15	4,578	5	10	Oneida
10	50	18,359	12	25	Outagamie
10	26	9,816	9	16	Ozaukee
1	9	629	1	3	Pepin
4	15	3,076	3	5	Pierce
5	36	3,233	5	10	Polk
13	44	8,993	9	10	Portage
0	12	1,813	1	3	Price
13	75	20,625	20	24	Racine
0	4	1,730	3	2	Richland
11	53	17,525	13	18	Rock
1	14	1,369	3	0	Rusk
4	27	5,467	5	25	St. Croix
5	21	6,890	7	6	Sauk
4	5	1,468	4	5	Sawyer
3	12	3,386	8	2	Shawano
13	44	10,916	13	19	Sheboygan
2	8	1,673	1	0	Taylor
4	17	2,629	2	2	Trempealeau
2	25	2,805	2	1	Vernon
3	8	2,733	1	3	Vilas
12	35	9,766	11	21	Walworth
1	17	1,533	1	3	Washburn
8	36	10,530	9	10	Washington
21	104	37,662	30	33	Waukesha
4	16	4,577	4	10	Waupaca
1	13	1,835	2	6	Waushara
11	43	18,303	8	19	Winnebago
5	32	9,082	11	18	Wood
517	2,625	646,851	528	861	TOTAL

REPUBLICAN PRESIDENTIAL PREFERENCE VOTE, BY COUNTY
February 19, 2008

County	Total*	Rudy Giuliani	Mike Huckabee	Duncan Hunter	John McCain
Adams	1,479	5	605	4	725
Ashland	832	14	298	2	459
Barron	3,057	16	1,370	11	1,422
Bayfield	1,150	3	379	1	663
Brown	17,659	81	6,400	33	9,862
Buffalo	893	4	407	5	427
Burnett	1,105	5	401	3	575
Calumet	3,855	15	1,442	4	2,103
Chippewa	4,720	20	2,710	4	1,733
Clark	2,736	10	1,544	5	1,040
Columbia	4,073	13	1,708	11	2,114
Crawford	935	6	386	4	401
Dane	24,609	116	8,229	31	13,818
Dodge	7,198	30	2,859	5	3,892
Door	2,728	10	955	2	1,591
Douglas	2,111	3	776	6	1,099
Dunn	2,601	14	1,388	5	968
Eau Claire	7,349	15	4,156	8	2,684
Florence	577	5	200	2	323
Fond du Lac	8,423	36	3,090	12	4,828
Forest	868	6	313	5	490
Grant	2,672	11	1,108	10	1,330
Green	2,269	12	990	6	1,113
Green Lake	1,848	4	649	3	1,093
Iowa	1,312	7	591	3	633
Iron	478	2	137	1	284
Jackson	1,364	6	716	4	553
Jefferson	6,690	19	2,719	11	3,481
Juneau	1,935	5	826	7	853
Kenosha	10,495	74	3,649	13	5,935
Kewaunee	1,539	5	596	2	858
La Crosse	8,005	37	3,293	9	3,911
Lafayette	1,045	8	463	3	502
Langlade	1,761	16	834	5	793
Lincoln	2,924	15	1,265	4	1,407
Manitowoc	6,171	26	2,306	22	3,256
Marathon	10,078	32	5,175	26	4,121
Marinette	3,628	16	1,511	12	1,843
Marquette	1,285	1	548	5	645
Menominee	40	0	18	0	21
Milwaukee	48,004	294	13,885	92	29,849
Monroe	3,173	8	1,509	8	1,434
Oconto	3,320	20	1,269	18	1,779
Oneida	3,562	20	1,246	9	1,971
Outagamie	13,557	40	5,183	19	7,198
Ozaukee	10,310	62	2,602	11	6,971
Pepin	472	34	218	1	175
Pierce	1,809	9	641	2	911
Polk	3,405	20	1,161	29	1,698
Portage	4,524	16	2,187	6	1,867
Price	1,432	6	597	10	734
Racine	14,438	49	4,986	27	8,338
Richland	1,143	4	559	3	445
Rock	8,494	32	3,169	16	4,535
Rusk	1,338	3	724	5	507
St. Croix	4,739	19	1,597	14	2,459
Sauk	4,137	19	1,814	1	2,061
Sawyer	1,339	7	532	4	684
Shawano	3,128	14	1,275	9	1,635
Sheboygan	10,744	46	4,371	32	5,489
Taylor	1,587	7	796	2	660
Trempealeau	1,742	4	898	6	729
Vernon	2,031	10	1,049	4	745
Vilas	2,757	16	933	3	1,604
Walworth	8,405	43	2,835	9	4,858
Washburn	1,273	7	530	6	620
Washington	13,845	66	4,487	24	8,403
Waukesha	45,082	211	13,926	77	28,160
Waupaca	4,172	17	1,671	15	2,215
Waushara	1,938	12	739	3	1,069
Winnebago	13,079	64	4,119	18	7,746
Wood	7,131	33	3,189	8	3,357
TOTAL	**410,607**	**1,935**	**151,707**	**799**	**224,755**

*Scattered vote included in county total.

Source: Official records of the Government Accountability Board, Elections Division.

REPUBLICAN PRESIDENTIAL PREFERENCE VOTE, BY COUNTY
February 19, 2008–Continued

		Choices on Ballot			
Ron Paul	Mitt Romney	Tom Tancredo	Fred Thompson	Uninstructed Delegation	County
97	26	0	12	5	. . . . Adams
31	22	0	4	2	. . . . Ashland
134	61	2	23	14	. . . . Barron
66	21	2	11	3	. . . . Bayfield
700	421	8	95	30	. . . . Brown
36	9	0	3	2	. . . . Buffalo
83	16	1	14	3	. . . . Burnett
229	38	3	11	8	. . . . Calumet
162	66	1	17	7	. . . . Chippewa
84	32	4	8	4	. . . . Clark
138	57	2	19	8	. . . . .Columbia
110	21	0	5	1	. . . . Crawford
1,616	533	23	164	55	. . . . Dane
233	113	1	49	10	. . . . Dodge
101	44	2	12	7	. . . . Door
144	57	1	11	9	. . . . Douglas
139	57	0	24	3	. . . . Dunn
327	119	1	25	6	. . . . Eau Claire
24	14	1	6	2	. . . . Florence
262	130	0	50	8	. . . . Fond du Lac
32	16	0	3	3	. . . . .Forest
133	52	2	19	4	. . . . .Grant
87	28	3	20	2	. . . . .Green
65	22	0	8	3	. . . . .Green Lake
53	13	0	6	4	. . . . Iowa
38	13	0	0	2	. . . . .Iron
52	17	1	12	1	. . . . .Jackson
278	105	4	44	24	. . . . Jefferson
201	19	1	13	3	. . . . Juneau
487	239	6	64	14	. . . . Kenosha
51	19	0	8	0	. . . . Kewaunee
504	185	2	45	14	. . . . La Crosse
39	18	1	7	4	. . . . Lafayette
75	19	0	8	10	. . . . Langlade
143	64	0	17	7	. . . . .Lincoln
381	130	2	32	2	. . . . .Manitowoc
463	172	5	52	21	. . . . .Marathon
180	42	4	11	3	. . . . .Marinette
58	15	1	7	4	. . . . Marquette
1	0	0	0	0	. . . . Menominee
2,155	1,101	21	404	122	. . . . .Milwaukee
147	42	0	19	2	. . . . .Monroe
156	51	3	16	6	. . . . Oconto
210	75	4	13	11	. . . . Oneida
785	220	6	61	27	. . . . Outagamie
290	271	4	60	29	. . . . Ozaukee
23	4	1	5	4	. . . . .Pepin
154	46	3	32	2	. . . . .Pierce
313	84	1	70	22	. . . . Polk
330	69	2	21	11	. . . . Portage
55	20	1	5	3	. . . . Price
618	269	9	103	28	. . . . Racine
113	8	0	7	3	. . . . Richland
481	188	6	40	14	. . . . Rock
73	15	1	9	1	. . . . Rusk
381	135	3	94	30	. . . . St. Croix
170	54	1	10	7	. . . . Sauk
59	30	1	12	6	. . . . Sawyer
114	55	4	15	4	. . . . Shawano
447	226	4	96	25	. . . . Sheboygan
91	17	0	8	6	. . . . Taylor
60	23	1	13	3	. . . . Trempealeau
189	19	1	6	4	. . . . Vernon
107	77	1	9	7	. . . . Vilas
387	163	3	64	27	. . . . .Walworth
58	33	3	12	2	. . . . Washburn
441	280	3	109	24	. . . . .Washington
1,259	1,035	7	308	54	. . . . Waukesha
158	48	1	32	12	. . . . Waupaca
78	21	1	10	4	. . . . .Waushara
798	226	3	69	26	. . . . .Winnebago
353	130	2	38	12	. . . . .Wood
19,090	8,080	185	2,709	850	. . . . TOTAL

2008 DEMOCRATIC NATIONAL CONVENTION DELEGATES
August 25-28, 2008 – Denver

Delegate	Address	Delegate	Address
For Hillary Clinton			
Pledged Leaders and Elected Officials		**Fourth Congressional District**	
Jan Banicki	Montello	Patrick Kehoe	Milwaukee
Heather Colburn	Madison	Candice Owley	Milwaukee
Pedro Colón	Milwaukee	**Fifth Congressional District**	
Kathleen Falk	Madison	Charlene Brady	Germantown
Barbara Lawton	Madison	Shah Haqqi	Brookfield
At-Large		**Sixth Congressional District**	
Nabeela Baig	Madison	Jennifer Giedd	Beaver Dam
Mark Boswell (alternate)	Waukesha	Ron Gruett	Chilton
Kira Brenner (alternate)	Madison	**Seventh Congressional District**	
Paula Dorsey	Milwaukee	Virginia Bosse	Park Falls
Jack Krueger	Green Bay	Denise Haughian	Chippewa Falls
Nancy Nusbaum	De Pere	Gerald Ugland	Plover
Shawn Pfaff	Fitchburg	**Eighth Congressional District**	
Cris Selin	Middleton	Mary Goulding	Green Bay
Gloria Villanueva	Racine	Robert Yingst	Abrams
First Congressional District		Tony Vanderbloemen	Green Bay
William Cobb	Kenosha	**Standing Committee**	
Marilyn Nemeth	Racine	James Sullivan, Jr.	Wauwatosa
Marlene Ott	Greendale	Dawn Sass	Belleville
Second Congressional District		Lisa Goldman	Madison
Anne Boley	Madison	Pamela Campbell	Chippewa Falls
Brett Hulsey	Madison		
Richard Loeper	Madison		
Third Congressional District			
Merna Fremstad	Westby		
Kurt Randorf	Tomah		
Lori Scott	Eau Claire		
For Barack Obama			
Pledged Leaders and Elected Officials		**Sixth Congressional District**	
Tom Barrett	Milwaukee	Gordon Hintz	Oshkosh
David Cieslewicz	Madison	Peg Lautenschlager	Fond du Lac
Russ Decker	Schofield	Angela Sutkiewicz	Sheboygan
Martha Love	Milwaukee	Wendy Volz-Daniels (alternate)	Campbellsport
Mark Pocan	Madison	**Seventh Congressional District**	
At-Large		Christine Bremer-Muggli	Wausau
Ingrid Ankerson (alternate)	Madison	Daniel Hannula (alternate)	Superior
Katie Boyce	Cross Plains	Gary Hawley	Stevens Point
Guy Costello	South Milwaukee	Patrick Kreitlow	Chippewa Falls
Jessica Doyle	Madison	**Eighth Congressional District**	
Harold Jackson (alternate)	Lac du Flambeau	Margaret Lardinois	Green Bay
Beverly Jenkins	Milwaukee	Jane Rufe (alternate)	Appleton
Bethany Ordaz	Madison	Jamie Stark	Green Bay
Molly Rivera	Pleasant Prairie	Jennie Sykes-Schwenk	Green Bay
Sara Rogers	Milwaukee	**Standing Committee**	
Marwill Santiago	Milwaukee	Dian Palmer	Brookfield
Martin Schreiber	Milwaukee	Marc Marotta	Mequon
First Congressional District		Susan Goodwin	Madison
Margaret Andrietsch	Racine	Scott Tyre	Madison
Cory Mason	Racine	Ed Matuszak	Wausau
Jason Smith (alternate)	Racine	**Unpledged Delegates**	
Michael Underhill	Salem	Tammy Baldwin	Washington, D.C.
Second Congressional District		Jim Doyle	Madison
Stan Davis	Sun Prairie	Russell Feingold	Washington, D.C.
Bryon Eagon	Madison	Stan Gruszynski	Porterfield
Roberta Gassman	Madison	Linda Honold	Milwaukee
Frances Huntley-Cooper	Fitchburg	Steve Kagen	Washington, D.C.
Celia Jackson (alternate)	Madison	Awais Khaleel	Madison
Mary Lang Sollinger	Madison	Ron Kind	La Crosse
Third Congressional District		Herb Kohl	Washington, D.C.
Graham Clumpner	La Crosse	Walter Kunicki	Milwaukee
Steve Mercaitis (alternate)	Mount Hope	Gwen Moore	Milwaukee
Mary Rasmussen	Boyceville	David Obey	Washington, D.C.
James Wine	Onalaska	Jason Rae	Rice Lake
Fourth Congressional District		Melissa Schroeder	Merrill
Milton Bond, Jr.	Milwaukee	Tim Sullivan	Verona
Stephanie Findley	Milwaukee	Lena Taylor	Milwaukee
Michael Rosen	Milwaukee	Joe Wineke	Madison
Thelma Sias	Milwaukee	Paula Zellner	Porterfield
Martha Toran (alternate)	Milwaukee		
Fifth Congressional District			
Mushir Hassan (alternate)	Brookfield		
Leslie Jorgensen	Wauwatosa		
Larry Nelson	Waukesha		
Frank Shansky	Wauwatosa		

Source: Democratic Party of Wisconsin.

2008 REPUBLICAN NATIONAL CONVENTION DELEGATES
September 1-4, 2008 – Minneapolis, St. Paul

Delegate	Address	Delegate	Address
		For John McCain	

Delegates At Large

Molly Ahlborn (alternate)	St. Germain		
Dave Anderson	Malone		
Candee Arndt (alternate)	Brookfield		
Mark Block (alternate)	New Berlin		
Tom Bode (alternate)	Racine		
Brad Courtney	Whitefish Bay		
Mark Cullen	Janesville		
Dan Feyen (alternate)	Fond du Lac		
Laurie Forcier (alternate)	Eau Claire		
Jon Hammes	Mequon		
Mary Hildebrandt (alternate)	Eau Claire		
John Hiller (alternate)	Mequon		
Bill Johnson	Hayward		
Dean Knudson (alternate)	Hudson		
John Knuteson (alternate)	Racine		
Craig Leipold	Racine		
Virginia Marschman	Waukesha		
Tim Michels	Oconomowoc		
Sandra Mills (alternate)	Menasha		
Phil Prange (alternate)	Madison		
Char Rassmussen (alternate)	Stanley		
Darlene Ross	Shawano		
Bill Stone	Burlington		
Tommy Thompson	Madison		
J.B. Van Hollen	Waunakee		
Scott Walker	Wauwatosa		

First Congressional District

Erin Decker (alternate)	Silver Lake
Jan Deters (alternate)	Janesville
RoseAnn Dieck (alternate)	Greendale
Robert Geason	Burlington
David Karst	Greenfield
Reince Priebus	Kenosha
Kim Travis	Williams Bay

Second Congressional District

Kim Babler	Madison
Connie Blau (alternate)	Waunakee
Steve King	Janesville
Andrew Kolberg (alternate)	Marshall
Regina Schaar	Lake Mills
Patty Shabaz (alternate)	Madison
Jeff Waksman	Madison

Third Congressional District

Becky Balts (alternate)	Eau Claire
Steve Brody (alternate)	Mineral Point
Linda Hansen	Prairie du Chien
Maripat Krueger	Menomonie
Tom Lynch (alternate)	West Salem
Scott Southworth	Mauston

Fourth Congressional District

Rick Baas	Milwaukee
Douglas Haag	Milwaukee
James McFarland (alternate)	Milwaukee
Gerard Randall (alternate)	Milwaukee
Perfecto Rivera (alternate)	Milwaukee
Robert Spindell	Milwaukee

Fifth Congressional District

Mary Buestrin	Mequon
Jennie Frederick	Jackson
Jay Hintze (alternate)	Glendale
Van Mobley (alternate)	Thiensville
Robin Moore	Brookfield
Mark Neumann (alternate)	Nashotah
Patty Reiman	Whitefish Bay

Sixth Congressional District

Michelle Litjens	Oshkosh
Margaret Mueller	Newton
Ralph Prescott (alternate)	Chilton
Pat Schutt (alternate)	Sheboygan
Ruth Streck (alternate)	Neenah
Carl Toepel	Sheboygan

Seventh Congressional District

Sean Duffy	Ashland
Sandra Ermeling	Wausau
Michelle Farrow	Chippewa Falls
Ashely King (alternate)	Chippewa Falls
Hank Martenson (alternate)	Ashland
Jeanie Moore (alternate)	Marshfield

Eighth Congressional District

Sol Grosskopf (alternate)	Shawano
Virginia Jesse	Shawano
William Ross	Shawano
Grant Staszak (alternate)	Bonduel
Thomas Van Drasek (alternate)	Green Bay
Jack Voight	Appleton

Source: Republican Party of Wisconsin.

COUNTY VOTE FOR PRESIDENT AND VICE PRESIDENT
November 4, 2008 General Election

County	Barack Obama Joe Biden (Dem.)	Bob Barr Wayne A. Root (Lib.)	John McCain Sarah Palin (Rep.)	Cynthia McKinney Rosa Clemente (WG)	Chuck Baldwin Darrell L. Castle (Ind.)[1]	Gloria LaRiva Robert Moses (Ind.)[2]	Brian Moore Stewart A. Alexander (Ind.)[3]	Ralph Nader Matt Gonzalez (Ind.)	Jeffrey J. Wamboldt David J. Klimisch (Ind.)[4]
Adams	5,806	27	3,974	16	43	0	0	76	6
Ashland	5,818	15	2,634	15	11	0	1	59	2
Barron	12,078	72	10,457	34	46	3	3	140	4
Bayfield	5,972	15	3,365	11	13	1	0	65	4
Brown	67,269	426	55,854	132	174	16	11	638	15
Buffalo	3,949	25	2,923	14	17	2	0	64	1
Burnett	4,337	36	4,200	24	19	2	3	42	5
Calumet	13,295	83	12,722	38	76	0	3	196	11
Chippewa	16,239	55	13,492	26	67	2	4	283	5
Clark	7,454	45	6,383	31	48	3	3	151	11
Columbia.	16,661	78	12,193	27	54	1	2	177	4
Crawford.	4,987	32	2,830	27	28	0	3	46	1
Dane	205,984	983	73,065	435	316	20	103	1,491	31
Dodge	19,183	85	23,015	52	81	1	1	303	20
Door	10,142	35	7,112	28	27	0	1	97	2
Douglas	15,830	63	7,835	37	39	8	4	188	8
Dunn	13,002	98	9,566	52	30	3	6	160	6
Eau Claire	33,146	192	20,959	75	89	3	11	413	10
Florence	1,134	10	1,512	3	5	0	2	12	1
Fond du Lac	23,463	132	28,164	74	89	1	9	283	13
Forest.	2,673	12	1,963	6	3	0	2	20	0
Grant.	14,875	79	9,068	39	51	4	8	144	2
Green.	11,502	61	6,730	27	36	3	1	113	9
Green Lake.	4,000	19	5,393	19	15	0	2	70	3
Iowa	7,987	28	3,829	33	21	1	0	46	3
Iron.	1,914	12	1,464	7	6	0	2	22	1
Jackson.	5,572	22	3,552	17	23	1	0	62	0
Jefferson	21,448	140	21,096	61	78	1	10	231	5
Juneau	6,186	31	5,148	22	36	1	1	69	5
Kenosha	45,836	251	31,609	103	113	3	13	511	79
Kewaunee	5,902	23	4,711	13	26	1	2	88	2
La Crosse	38,524	191	23,701	70	104	5	10	404	14
Lafayette.	4,732	14	2,984	16	12	1	1	59	4
Langlade	5,182	25	5,081	24	18	0	2	47	1
Lincoln.	8,424	60	6,519	21	38	1	0	134	8
Manitowoc	22,428	125	19,234	71	65	1	7	375	12
Marathon.	36,367	323	30,345	96	152	1	11	462	26
Marinette.	11,195	63	9,726	40	49	2	9	123	8
Marquette	4,068	19	3,654	13	29	3	1	46	2
Menominee	1,257	0	185	2	0	0	0	4	0
Milwaukee	319,819	1,105	149,445	589	540	56	120	2,360	69
Monroe.	10,198	66	8,666	37	26	0	8	112	8
Oconto.	9,927	50	8,755	37	32	1	2	130	2
Oneida	11,907	110	9,630	34	52	3	2	123	7
Outagamie	50,294	399	39,677	134	228	11	11	611	20
Ozaukee	20,579	140	32,172	57	63	2	6	238	8
Pepin	2,102	10	1,616	8	8	0	0	26	1
Pierce.	11,803	85	9,812	52	43	2	4	217	8
Polk	10,876	97	11,282	66	58	2	6	180	5
Portage.	24,817	134	13,810	102	76	8	11	329	9
Price	4,559	42	3,461	15	21	0	0	73	5
Racine	53,408	240	45,954	145	170	10	8	496	19
Richland	5,041	24	3,298	14	23	1	3	29	1
Rock	50,529	187	27,364	111	230	4	16	529	22
Rusk	3,855	36	3,253	12	22	1	1	69	5
St. Croix	21,177	182	22,837	61	82	2	3	339	17
Sauk	18,617	77	11,562	47	44	1	3	202	6
Sawyer.	4,765	24	4,199	21	18	0	1	43	1
Shawano	10,259	66	9,538	32	33	3	4	119	5
Sheboygan.	30,395	142	30,801	89	127	3	14	382	21
Taylor.	4,563	29	4,586	14	21	1	4	96	9
Trempealeau	8,321	44	4,808	23	19	1	2	75	2
Vernon	8,463	43	5,367	34	48	2	2	93	1
Vilas	6,491	40	7,055	19	25	1	0	82	4
Walworth.	24,177	138	25,485	63	94	4	7	288	24
Washburn	4,693	27	4,303	10	19	1	6	40	3
Washington.	25,719	193	47,729	98	90	7	11	393	24
Waukesha	85,339	565	145,152	209	311	6	14	908	47
Waupaca	12,952	62	12,232	31	60	2	2	128	4
Waushara	5,868	38	5,770	16	37	1	1	80	9
Winnebago	48,167	323	37,946	132	209	4	12	567	33
Wood.	21,710	135	16,581	53	96	2	5	334	21
TOTAL.	1,677,211	8,858	1,262,393	4,216	5,072	237	540	17,605	764
Percent of Total[5] .	56.22%	0.30%	42.31%	0.14%	0.17%	0.01%	0.02%	0.59%	0.03%

Dem. – Democratic Party; Lib. – Libertarian Party; Rep. – Republican Party; WG – Wisconsin Green Party; Ind. – Independent.

Note: Only 4 parties qualified for ballot status according to Section 5.62, Wisconsin Statutes. Other candidates were listed as "independent" although they indicated a name of party or statement of principle to the Government Accountability Board as footnoted.

[1]Constitution Party. [2]Party for Socialism and Liberation. [3]Socialist Party USA. [4]We, the People. [5]Percentages do not equal 100%, as scattered votes have been omitted.

Source: Official records of the Government Accountability Board, Elections Division.

VOTE FOR PRESIDENT AND VICE PRESIDENT BY WARD
November 4, 2008 General Election

District	Barack Obama Joe Biden (Dem.)	John McCain Sarah Palin (Rep.)
ADAMS COUNTY		
Adams		
Wards 1 & 2	405	235
Adams, city		
Wards 1 – 5	539	229
Big Flats	314	169
Colburn	67	54
Dell Prairie		
Wards 1 & 2	446	345
Easton		
Wards 1 & 2	269	184
Friendship, vil.	192	103
Jackson	293	220
Leola	51	95
Lincoln	86	73
Monroe	149	107
New Chester		
Wards 1 & 2	268	132
New Haven	238	142
Preston		
Wards 1 – 3	421	233
Quincy		
Wards 1 & 2	428	205
Richfield	50	26
Rome		
Wards 1 – 5	903	920
Springville		
Wards 1 & 2	308	240
Strongs Prairie		
Wards 1 & 2	372	250
Wisconsin Dells, city		
Ward 5	7	12
TOTAL	5,806	3,974
ASHLAND COUNTY		
Agenda	120	127
Ashland	200	91
Ashland, city		
Ward 1	278	199
Ward 2	236	76
Ward 3	265	104
Ward 4	276	152
Ward 5	300	101
Ward 6	254	79
Ward 7	386	87
Ward 8	252	96
Ward 9	252	63
Ward 10	261	112
Ward 11	311	108
Butternut, vil.		
Wards 1 & 2	128	57
Chippewa	116	83
Gingles		
Wards 1 & 2	279	131
Gordon	129	76
Jacobs	244	174
La Pointe	190	57
Marengo		
Wards 1 & 2	143	62
Mellen, city		
Wards 1 – 3	266	98
Morse		
Wards 1 & 2	174	112
Peeksville	47	48
Sanborn		
Wards 1 & 2	447	57
Shanagolden	44	41
White River		
Wards 1 – 3	220	243
TOTAL	5,818	2,634
BARRON COUNTY		
Almena		
Wards 1 – 3	218	202
Almena, vil.	157	137
Arland	154	131
Barron		
Wards 1 & 2	166	257
Barron, city		
Wards 1 – 7	780	649
Bear Lake	202	157
Cameron, vil.		
Wards 1 & 2	402	343
Cedar Lake	292	315
Chetek		
Wards 1 – 3	505	491
Chetek, city		
Wards 1 – 4	598	468
Clinton		
Wards 1 & 2	147	187
Crystal Lake	231	187
Cumberland	228	204
Cumberland, city		
Wards 1 – 5	708	416
Dallas		
Wards 1 & 2	138	150
Dallas, vil.	86	88
Dovre	222	167
Doyle	134	141
Haugen, vil.	94	60
Lakeland		
Wards 1 & 2	296	241
Maple Grove		
Wards 1 – 3	200	270
Maple Plain	258	213
New Auburn, vil.		
Ward 2	2	5
Oak Grove		
Wards 1 & 2	285	202
Prairie Farm		
Wards 1 & 2	150	124
Prairie Farm, vil.	120	88
Prairie Lake		
Wards 1 & 2	387	408
Rice Lake		
Wards 1 – 4	821	778
Rice Lake, city		
Wards 1 – 17	2,321	1,775
Sioux Creek	155	168
Stanfold	177	170
Stanley		
Wards 1 – 3	633	674
Sumner		
Wards 1 & 2	210	184
Turtle Lake	160	125
Turtle Lake, vil.		
Ward 1	258	141
Vance Creek	183	141
TOTAL	12,078	10,457
BAYFIELD COUNTY		
Ashland, city		
Ward 12	0	0
Barksdale	274	194
Barnes	315	262
Bayfield	318	151
Bayfield, city		
Wards 1 – 4	251	85
Bayview	207	134
Bell	119	72
Cable	257	243
Clover	95	72
Delta	113	94
Drummond	223	118
Eileen		
Wards 1 & 2	257	162
Grand View	189	103
Hughes	152	106
Iron River		
Wards 1 & 2	426	285
Kelly	134	105
Keystone	130	80
Lincoln	110	66
Mason	90	85
Mason, vil.	36	15
Namakagon	99	127
Orienta	48	32
Oulu	173	128
Pilsen	110	40
Port Wing	177	96
Russell		
Wards 1 & 2	499	58
Tripp	52	51
Washburn	250	90
Washburn, city		
Wards 1 – 4	868	311
TOTAL	5,972	3,365
BROWN COUNTY		
Allouez, vil.		
Wards 1 & 2	1,021	626
Wards 3 & 4	1,205	947
Wards 5 & 6	1,071	1,197
Wards 7 – 9	926	865
Ashwaubenon, vil.		
Wards 1 & 2	741	483
Wards 3 & 4	762	571
Wards 5 & 6	795	690
Wards 7 & 8	754	776
Ward 9	298	299

VOTE FOR PRESIDENT AND VICE PRESIDENT BY WARD
November 4, 2008 General Election–Continued

District	Barack Obama Joe Biden (Dem.)	John McCain Sarah Palin (Rep.)
Ward 10	564	538
Wards 11 & 12	891	908
Bellevue		
Wards 1 – 6	1,923	1,606
Wards 7 – 10	1,946	1,887
Denmark, vil.		
Wards 1 – 3	630	441
De Pere, city		
Wards 1 – 3	1,740	1,596
Wards 4 – 7	1,684	1,328
Wards 8 – 10	1,567	1,083
Wards 11 – 14	1,842	1,662
Wards 15 – 17	60	51
Eaton		
Wards 1 & 2	483	379
Glenmore		
Wards 1 & 2	301	335
Green Bay		
Wards 1 & 2	557	569
Green Bay, city		
Ward 1	712	625
Ward 2	876	412
Ward 3	583	588
Ward 4	642	405
Ward 5	878	744
Ward 6	560	254
Ward 7	814	665
Ward 8	713	605
Ward 9	507	462
Ward 10	576	572
Ward 11	631	361
Ward 12	408	206
Ward 13	482	250
Ward 14	590	330
Ward 15	706	365
Ward 16	621	291
Ward 17	470	205
Ward 18	401	102
Ward 19	442	117
Ward 20	490	223
Ward 21	625	297
Ward 22	487	237
Ward 23	442	216
Ward 24	430	183
Ward 25	395	118
Ward 26	239	107
Ward 27	609	249
Ward 28	764	529
Ward 29	648	333
Ward 30	681	408
Ward 31	392	175
Ward 32	825	497
Ward 33	752	530
Ward 34	611	312
Ward 35	500	292
Ward 36	450	170
Ward 37	538	190
Ward 38	555	403
Ward 39	455	230
Ward 40	508	321
Ward 41	568	335
Ward 42	575	491
Ward 43	594	519
Ward 44	632	452
Ward 45	684	439
Ward 46	602	634
Ward 47	604	309
Ward 48	618	811
Ward 49	446	625
Ward 50	3	12
Hobart, vil.		
Wards 1 – 7	1,619	1,897
Holland		
Wards 1 & 2	408	419
Howard, vil.		
Wards 1 – 4, 11 & 12	1,378	1,177
Wards 5 – 10	1,580	1,634
Wards 13 – 16	1,448	1,590
Humboldt		
Wards 1 & 2	364	336
Lawrence		
Wards 1 – 3	1,046	1,216
Ledgeview		
Wards 1 – 4	1,548	1,877
Morrison		
Wards 1 & 2	354	521
New Denmark		
Wards 1 – 3	438	468
Pittsfield		

District	Barack Obama Joe Biden (Dem.)	John McCain Sarah Palin (Rep.)
Wards 1 – 4	670	836
Pulaski, vil.		
Wards 1 – 3 & 6	787	681
Rockland		
Wards 1 & 2	443	556
Scott		
Wards 1 – 4	1,113	958
Ward 5	35	28
Suamico, vil.		
Wards 1 – 3 & 10	953	1,248
Ward 7	281	514
Wards 4 – 6, 8 & 9	1,514	1,696
Wrightstown		
Wards 1 – 3	583	561
Wrightstown, vil.		
Wards 1 & 2	612	598
TOTAL	**67,269**	**55,854**
BUFFALO COUNTY		
Alma	94	64
Alma, city		
Wards 1 & 2	252	189
Belvidere	147	101
Buffalo	247	168
Buffalo, city	361	260
Canton	89	55
Cochrane, vil.	122	104
Cross	111	82
Dover	148	78
Fountain City, city		
Wards 1 & 2	278	195
Gilmanton	130	67
Glencoe	122	102
Lincoln	60	56
Maxville	77	81
Milton	182	108
Modena	98	85
Mondovi		
Wards 1 & 2	129	114
Mondovi, city		
Wards 1 – 3	656	498
Montana	78	61
Naples	177	155
Nelson	163	131
Nelson, vil.	104	66
Waumandee	124	103
TOTAL	**3,949**	**2,923**
BURNETT COUNTY		
Anderson	92	114
Blaine	70	41
Daniels	169	207
Dewey	152	131
Grantsburg		
Wards 1 – 3	236	303
Grantsburg, vil.		
Wards 1 & 2	305	355
Jackson	308	245
La Follette		
Wards 1 & 2	153	125
Lincoln	80	74
Meenon		
Wards 1 – 3	262	277
Oakland		
Wards 1 & 2	317	233
Roosevelt	64	50
Rusk		
Wards 1 & 2	120	104
Sand Lake	157	91
Scott		
Wards 1 & 2	192	210
Siren		
Wards 1 – 3	260	238
Siren		
Wards 1 & 2	225	165
Swiss		
Wards 1 & 2	270	156
Trade Lake		
Wards 1 & 2	212	299
Union	104	88
Webb Lake	123	140
Webster, vil.	185	131
West Marshland		
Wards 1 & 2	66	104
Wood River		
Wards 1 & 2	215	319
TOTAL	**4,337**	**4,200**
CALUMET COUNTY		
Appleton, city		
Ward 12	76	53

VOTE FOR PRESIDENT AND VICE PRESIDENT BY WARD
November 4, 2008 General Election–Continued

District	Barack Obama Joe Biden (Dem.)	John McCain Sarah Palin (Rep.)
Ward 13	298	245
Ward 14	398	336
Ward 40	535	402
Ward 42	528	509
Ward 43	563	361
Ward 44	499	316
Ward 45	248	105
Ward 46	31	44
Ward 47	7	10
Ward 48	0	0
Brillion, city		
Wards 1 – 6	797	751
Brillion		
Wards 1 & 2	358	433
Brothertown		
Wards 1 & 2	326	397
Charlestown		
Wards 1 & 2	203	236
Chilton		
Wards 1 & 2	225	356
Chilton, city		
Wards 1 – 4	1,004	773
Harrison		
Wards 1 – 3, 6 & 8	1,490	1,391
Wards 4, 5 & 7	1,568	1,957
Ward 9	1	0
Hilbert, vil.		
Wards 1 & 2	263	295
Ward 3	0	0
Kiel, city		
Wards 7 & 8	95	49
Menasha, city		
Wards 11, 15 – 17, 19 – 21 & 23	571	538
New Holstein		
Wards 1 & 2	316	295
Ward 3	74	81
New Holstein, city		
Wards 1 – 7	1,028	722
Potter, vil.	59	81
Rantoul		
Wards 1 & 2	184	246
Sherwood, vil.		
Wards 1 – 8	745	842
Stockbridge		
Wards 1 – 3	388	437
Stockbridge, vil.	197	176
Woodville		
Wards 1 & 2	220	285
TOTAL	13,295	12,722
CHIPPEWA COUNTY		
Anson		
Wards 1 – 3	517	615
Arthur	178	167
Auburn	214	139
Birch Creek	145	151
Bloomer	237	248
Bloomer, city		
Wards 1 – 4	924	773
Boyd	195	113
Cadott, vil.		
Wards 1 & 2	349	282
Chippewa Falls, city		
Ward 1	545	343
Ward 2	495	410
Ward 3	569	481
Ward 4	477	332
Ward 5	482	243
Ward 6	533	347
Ward 7	484	336
Cleveland	181	230
Colburn	190	199
Cooks Valley	163	169
Cornell, city		
Wards 1 – 4	345	325
Delmar	199	228
Eagle Point		
Wards 1 – 4	897	906
Eau Claire, city		
Ward 16	597	317
Ward 40	0	0
Ward 41	15	9
Edson	200	174
Estella	109	111
Goetz		
Wards 1 & 2	216	159
Hallie		
Wards 1 & 2	47	44
Howard	233	155

District	Barack Obama Joe Biden (Dem.)	John McCain Sarah Palin (Rep.)
Lafayette		
Wards 1 – 7	1,756	1,495
Lake Hallie, vil.		
Wards 1 – 5	1,793	1,292
Lake Holcombe		
Wards 1 & 2	296	271
New Auburn, vil.		
Ward 1	119	92
Ruby	117	81
Sampson	220	246
Sigel		
Wards 1 & 2	270	215
Stanley, city		
Wards 1 – 4	470	468
Tilden		
Wards 1 – 3	394	386
Wheaton		
Wards 1 – 3	814	721
Woodmohr		
Wards 1 – 3	254	219
TOTAL	16,239	13,492
CLARK COUNTY		
Abbotsford, city		
Wards 2 – 4	330	341
Beaver		
Wards 1 & 2	150	117
Butler	25	28
Colby	155	125
Colby, city		
Wards 2 – 4	283	267
Curtiss, vil.	33	29
Dewhurst	88	90
Dorchester, vil.		
Ward 1	173	136
Eaton		
Wards 1 & 2	112	123
Foster	30	26
Fremont		
Wards 1 & 2	234	239
Grant		
Wards 1 & 2	205	185
Granton, vil.	127	45
Green Grove	131	111
Greenwood, city		
Wards 1 & 2	290	217
Hendren	123	84
Hewett		
Wards 1 & 2	107	62
Hixon		
Wards 1 & 2	126	86
Hoard		
Wards 1 & 2	125	134
Levis		
Wards 1 & 2	92	132
Longwood		
Wards 1 & 2	125	107
Loyal		
Wards 1 & 2	133	139
Loyal, city		
Wards 1 – 3	344	267
Lynn		
Wards 1 & 2	134	142
Mayville		
Wards 1 & 2	167	176
Mead	70	44
Mentor	138	120
Neillsville, city		
Ward 1	146	115
Ward 2	135	116
Ward 3	138	99
Ward 4	91	87
Ward 5	114	102
Owen		
Wards 1 – 3	271	180
Pine Valley		
Wards 1 & 2	297	290
Reseburg		
Wards 1 & 2	119	72
Seif	64	38
Sherman	164	148
Sherwood	87	47
Stanley, city		
Ward 5	1	1
Thorp	170	117
Thorp, city		
Wards 1 – 6	434	323
Unity	161	147
Unity, vil.		
Ward 2	29	41

VOTE FOR PRESIDENT AND VICE PRESIDENT BY WARD
November 4, 2008 General Election–Continued

District	Barack Obama Joe Biden (Dem.)	John McCain Sarah Palin (Rep.)	District	Barack Obama Joe Biden (Dem.)	John McCain Sarah Palin (Rep.)
Warner			Lynxville, vil.	47	35
Wards 1 & 2	133	119	Marietta	138	109
Washburn			Mount Sterling, vil.	67	34
Wards 1 & 2	75	77	Prairie du Chien	270	186
Weston			Prairie du Chien, city		
Wards 1 & 2	172	149	Ward 1	262	184
Withee	141	163	Wards 2 & 3	227	136
Withee, vil.	157	88	Wards 4 & 5	266	151
Worden			Ward 6	291	124
Ward 1	69	110	Wards 7 & 8	312	159
Ward 2	41	20	Ward 9	314	154
York	195	162	Scott	184	72
TOTAL	7,454	6,383	Seneca	259	167
COLUMBIA COUNTY			Soldiers Grove, vil.	173	92
Arlington			Steuben, vil.	32	16
Wards 1 & 2	285	178	Utica	240	118
Arlington, vil.	273	177	Wauzeka		
Caledonia			Wards 1 & 2	114	68
Wards 1 & 2	450	350	Wauzeka, vil.	202	79
Cambria, vil.	204	167	TOTAL	4,987	2,830
Columbus	155	174	DANE COUNTY		
Columbus, city			Albion		
Wards 1 – 8	1,542	1,000	Wards 1 & 2	753	315
Courtland			Belleville, vil.		
Wards 1 & 2	91	163	Wards 1, 2, 4 – 6	723	274
Dekorra			Berry		
Wards 1 – 4	770	621	Wards 1 & 2	478	276
Doylestown, vil.	77	70	Black Earth	184	107
Fall River, vil.			Black Earth, vil.		
Wards 1 & 2	430	264	Wards 1 & 2	516	227
Fort Winnebago			Blooming Grove		
Wards 1 & 2	272	230	Wards 1 – 3	739	298
Fountain Prairie			Blue Mounds	343	210
Wards 1 & 2	304	197	Blue Mounds, vil.	294	157
Friesland, vil.	56	127	Bristol		
Hampden	163	164	Wards 1 – 3	1,164	878
Leeds			Brooklyn, vil.		
Wards 1 & 2	266	212	Ward 1	342	120
Lewiston			Burke		
Wards 1 & 2	346	312	Wards 1 – 4	1,105	756
Lodi			Cambridge, vil.		
Wards 1 – 5	1,020	810	Wards 2 & 3	494	290
Lodi, city			Christiana		
Wards 1 – 4	1,027	554	Wards 1 & 2	441	244
Lowville			Cottage Grove		
Wards 1 & 2	354	270	Wards 1 – 5	1,430	856
Marcellon			Cottage Grove, vil.		
Wards 1 & 2	275	265	Wards 1 – 9	2,206	1,201
Newport	212	144	Cross Plains		
Otsego	207	153	Wards 1 & 2	586	349
Pacific			Cross Plains, vil.		
Wards 1 – 3	867	732	Wards 1 – 4	1,368	722
Pardeeville, vil.			Dane	293	234
Wards 1 – 3	628	447	Dane, vil.	309	166
Portage, city			Deerfield		
Wards 1 – 6	953	591	Wards 1 & 2	552	297
Wards 7 – 12	955	561	Deerfield, vil.		
Wards 13 – 18	711	395	Wards 1 – 4	772	378
Poynette, vil.			De Forest, vil.		
Wards 1 – 3	813	450	Wards 1, 2, 4, 7 & 10	1,484	768
Randolph	91	319	Wards 3, 5, 6, 8 & 9	1,441	810
Randolph, vil.			Dunkirk		
Ward 3	90	138	Wards 1 – 3	802	398
Rio, vil.	369	150	Dunn		
Scott	174	176	Wards 1 & 7	515	351
Springvale	147	144	Wards 2 – 6	1,493	796
West Point			Edgerton, city		
Wards 1 & 2	669	503	Ward 7	11	11
Wisconsin Dells, city			Fitchburg, city		
Wards 1 – 3 & 6	700	453	Wards 1 – 3	1,902	511
Wyocena			Wards 4 & 6	1,269	570
Wards 1 – 3	506	393	Ward 5	677	128
Wyocena, vil.	209	139	Wards 7 – 9	2,332	1,029
TOTAL	16,661	12,193	Wards 10 – 12 & 14	2,591	1,080
CRAWFORD COUNTY			Ward 13	0	0
Bell Center, vil.	34	14	Madison		
Bridgeport	298	236	Ward 1	318	32
Clayton			Wards 2 – 4 & 6	693	111
Wards 1 – 3	305	157	Wards 5, 7 – 11	1,123	139
De Soto, vil.			Madison, city		
Ward 2	35	14	Ward 1	1,841	563
Eastman			Ward 2	1,576	647
Wards 1 & 2	195	150	Ward 3	837	322
Eastman, vil.	109	77	Ward 4	1,004	385
Ferryville, vil.	82	35	Ward 5	1,833	657
Freeman	215	143	Ward 6	998	403
Gays Mills, vil.	206	70	Ward 7	1,263	368
Haney	110	50	Ward 8	1,133	314
			Ward 9	605	108

VOTE FOR PRESIDENT AND VICE PRESIDENT BY WARD
November 4, 2008 General Election–Continued

District	Barack Obama Joe Biden (Dem.)	John McCain Sarah Palin (Rep.)	District	Barack Obama Joe Biden (Dem.)	John McCain Sarah Palin (Rep.)
Ward 10	1,169	258	Ward 99	2,410	1,145
Ward 11	1,730	370	Ward 100	0	1
Ward 12	910	76	Ward 101	0	0
Ward 13	373	39	Ward 102	280	93
Ward 14	954	142	Ward 103	0	0
Ward 15	523	111	Ward 104	0	0
Ward 16	508	135	Ward 105	0	2
Ward 17	1,161	320	Ward 106	0	0
Ward 18	764	273	Ward 107	73	28
Ward 19	1,375	351	Ward 108	116	22
Ward 20	368	115	Ward 109	23	7
Ward 21	316	36	Ward 110	125	71
Ward 22	784	256	Ward 111	0	0
Ward 23	700	111	Ward 112	30	9
Ward 24	1,037	237	Ward 113	1	8
Ward 25	1,899	722	Ward 114	33	18
Ward 26	231	45	Ward 115	0	0
Ward 27	1,171	245	Ward 116	0	0
Ward 28	217	29	Ward 117	1	0
Ward 29	213	76	Ward 118	0	0
Ward 30	847	172	Ward 119	0	0
Ward 31	787	116	Ward 120	0	0
Ward 32	1,594	129	Ward 121	0	0
Ward 33	2,325	133	Ward 122	16	4
Ward 34	2,594	117	Ward 123	0	0
Ward 35	1,639	75	Ward 124	0	0
Ward 36	474	51	Ward 125	2	0
Ward 37	1,386	117	Ward 126	0	0
Ward 38	1,199	78	Ward 127	0	0
Ward 39	1,927	173	Ward 128	0	0
Ward 40	1,287	250	Ward 129	0	0
Ward 41	1,189	204	Ward 130	0	0
Ward 42	2,074	469	Ward 131	1	0
Ward 43	1,517	283	Ward 132	1	0
Ward 44	2,856	652	Ward 133	0	2
Ward 45	1,601	600	Ward 134	0	0
Ward 46	1,657	327	Ward 135	7	3
Ward 47	1,029	296	Ward 136	0	0
Ward 48	1,471	497	Ward 137	11	3
Ward 49	744	122	Ward 138	3	0
Ward 50	1,981	415	Ward 139	0	0
Ward 51	914	97	Ward 140	0	0
Ward 52	1,496	166	Ward 141	1	0
Ward 53	545	24	Ward 142	11	3
Ward 54	822	194	Ward 143	0	0
Ward 55	93	4	Ward 144	0	0
Ward 56	1,047	236	Ward 145	0	0
Ward 57	514	51	Maple Bluff, vil.		
Ward 58	375	53	Wards 1 & 2	593	386
Ward 59	924	220	Ward 3	21	3
Ward 60	382	129	Marshall, vil.		
Ward 61	1,789	456	Wards 1 – 7	1,170	567
Ward 62	789	252	Mazomanie		
Ward 63	491	99	Wards 1 & 2	408	219
Ward 64	1,499	196	Mazomanie, vil.		
Ward 65	1,303	166	Wards 1 & 2	647	228
Ward 66	1,541	178	Wards 3 & 4	34	8
Ward 67	1,846	340	McFarland, vil.		
Ward 68	711	78	Wards 1 – 7	3,043	1,490
Ward 69	1,207	272	Medina		
Ward 70	1,468	198	Wards 1 & 2	431	303
Ward 71	827	86	Middleton		
Ward 72	1,169	233	Wards 1 – 5	2,076	1,529
Ward 73	1,270	292	Middleton, city		
Ward 74	1,483	293	Wards 1 & 9	1,069	349
Ward 75	1,751	458	Wards 2 – 4	2,609	954
Ward 76	786	239	Wards 5 – 7, 10, 12 & 13	3,219	1,003
Ward 77	503	157	Wards 8, 11 & 14	724	417
Ward 78	1,058	334	Monona, city		
Ward 79	758	177	Wards 1 – 5	2,070	683
Ward 80	511	123	Wards 6 – 10	1,750	544
Ward 81	1,277	413	Montrose		
Ward 82	1,297	524	Wards 1 & 2	488	196
Ward 83	1,736	1,000	Mount Horeb, vil.		
Ward 84	887	188	Wards 1, 5 & 6	1,314	633
Ward 85	1,059	256	Wards 2 – 4	1,211	590
Ward 86	1,411	486	Oregon		
Ward 87	1,226	388	Wards 1 – 4	1,259	702
Ward 88	425	86	Oregon, vil.		
Ward 89	524	177	Wards 1, 5 & 6	1,238	544
Ward 90	793	242	Wards 2 – 4	1,127	560
Ward 91	1,270	471	Wards 7 – 10	1,102	567
Ward 92	1,694	596	Perry	322	132
Ward 93	1,618	455	Pleasant Springs		
Ward 94	600	168	Wards 1 – 4	1,100	745
Ward 95	592	127	Primrose	313	124
Ward 96	1,478	335	Rockdale, vil.	78	29
Ward 97	289	107	Roxbury		
Ward 98	1,568	410	Wards 1 & 2	562	430

VOTE FOR PRESIDENT AND VICE PRESIDENT BY WARD
November 4, 2008 General Election–Continued

District	Barack Obama Joe Biden (Dem.)	John McCain Sarah Palin (Rep.)	District	Barack Obama Joe Biden (Dem.)	John McCain Sarah Palin (Rep.)
Rutland			Kekoskee, vil.	37	63
Wards 1 & 2	787	398	Lebanon		
Shorewood Hills, vil.			Wards 1 & 2	368	539
Wards 1 & 2	1,032	157	Leroy		
Springdale			Wards 1 & 2	187	334
Wards 1 & 2	737	430	Lomira		
Wards 1 – 3	960	585	Wards 1 & 2	182	428
Stoughton, city			Lomira, vil.		
Wards 1 – 3	1,150	444	Wards 1 – 3	456	681
Wards 4 & 5	1,198	412	Lowell		
Wards 6 – 8	1,174	467	Wards 1 & 2	234	333
Wards 9 & 10	1,191	660	Lowell, vil.	66	92
Sun Prairie			Mayville, city		
Wards 1 – 3	735	495	Wards 1 – 7	1,223	1,309
Sun Prairie, city			Neosho, vil.	125	203
Wards 1 – 4, 18, 19, 22 & 25	2,410	1,185	Oak Grove		
Wards 5 – 9	2,294	1,230	Wards 1 – 3	273	311
Wards 10 – 13, 20, 29, 30 & 33	1,963	803	Portland		
Wards 14 – 17	2,831	1,873	Wards 1 & 2	302	277
Wards 21, 23, 26 – 28	2	0	Randolph, vil.		
Wards 24, 31 & 34	2	2	Wards 1 & 2	228	405
Ward 32	0	0	Reeseville, vil.	173	141
Vermont	410	152	Rubicon		
Verona			Wards 1 – 3	353	906
Wards 1 – 3	760	486	Shields	123	181
Verona, city			Theresa		
Wards 1 – 4	1,857	969	Wards 1 & 2	187	422
Wards 5 – 8	2,123	970	Theresa, vil.		
Vienna			Wards 1 – 3	270	380
Wards 1 & 2	461	392	Trenton		
Waunakee, vil.			Wards 1 – 3	248	448
Wards 1 – 7	1,626	1,060	Watertown, city		
Wards 8 – 14	2,254	1,591	Wards 1 & 2	708	825
Westport			Wards 3 & 4	538	642
Wards 1 – 4	1,604	1,124	Wards 5 & 6	482	595
Windsor			Ward 7	258	301
Wards 1 – 7	2,073	1,359	Waupun, city		
York	217	158	Wards 1 – 3 & 8	583	646
TOTAL	205,984	73,065	Wards 4 – 7	448	625
DODGE COUNTY			Westford		
Ashippun			Wards 1 & 2	330	367
Wards 1 – 3	440	1,045	Williamstown	138	290
Beaver Dam			TOTAL	19,183	23,015
Wards 1 – 5	996	953	**DOOR COUNTY**		
Beaver Dam, city			Baileys Harbor		
Wards 1, 3 & 5	927	556	Wards 1 & 2	496	277
Wards 2 & 6	690	472	Brussels		
Wards 4 & 10	548	313	Wards 1 & 2	305	261
Wards 7, 12 & 13	970	544	Claybanks	144	119
Wards 8 & 14	570	393	Egg Harbor		
Wards 9 & 11	684	546	Ward 1	362	241
Brownsville, vil.	114	210	Wards 2 & 3	189	124
Burnett			Egg Harbor, vil.	116	73
Wards 1 & 2	225	309	Ephraim, vil.	123	121
Calamus			Forestville		
Wards 1 & 2	240	250	Wards 1 & 2	378	229
Chester			Forestville, vil.	151	95
Wards 1 & 2	122	263	Gardner	399	289
Clyman			Gibraltar		
Wards 1 & 2	138	274	Wards 1 & 2	512	288
Clyman, vil.	112	88	Jacksonport	282	226
Columbus, city			Liberty Grove		
Ward 9	0	0	Wards 1 – 3	862	555
Elba			Nasewaupee		
Wards 1 & 2	301	292	Wards 1 – 3	665	536
Emmet			Sevastopol		
Wards 1 & 2	260	454	Wards 1 – 3	921	820
Fox Lake			Sister Bay, vil.	338	280
Wards 1 – 4	288	393	Sturgeon Bay		
Fox Lake, city			Wards 1 & 2	283	243
Wards 1 – 3	370	341	Sturgeon Bay, city		
Hartford, city			Wards 1 & 2	425	167
Ward 16	0	0	Wards 3 & 4	405	207
Ward 39	0	0	Wards 5 & 6	460	337
Herman			Wards 7 & 8	435	275
Wards 1 & 2	159	490	Wards 9 & 10	428	270
Horicon, city			Wards 11 & 12	401	205
Wards 1 – 6	944	836	Wards 13 & 14	339	257
Hubbard			Wards 15 – 17	28	19
Wards 1 – 3	390	589	Wards 18, 19 & 25	36	21
Hustisford			Wards 20, 21 & 24	27	19
Wards 1 – 3	269	527	Wards 22 & 23	5	1
Hustisford, vil.			Ward 26	1	3
Wards 1 & 2	237	324	Ward 27	20	6
Iron Ridge, vil.	191	279	Ward 28	1	1
Juneau, city			Union	328	254
Wards 1 – 3	478	530	Washington	277	293
			TOTAL	10,142	7,112

VOTE FOR PRESIDENT AND VICE PRESIDENT BY WARD
November 4, 2008 General Election–Continued

District	Barack Obama / Joe Biden (Dem.)	John McCain / Sarah Palin (Rep.)
DOUGLAS COUNTY		
Amnicon		
Wards 1 & 2	383	208
Bennett	194	161
Brule	256	120
Cloverland	74	56
Dairyland	63	51
Gordon	233	190
Hawthorne		
Wards 1 & 2	334	254
Highland	109	83
Lake Nebagamon, vil.		
Wards 1 & 2	389	342
Lakeside	215	156
Maple		
Wards 1 & 2	278	120
Oakland		
Wards 1 & 2	465	202
Oliver, vil.	177	53
Parkland		
Wards 1 & 2	472	182
Poplar, vil.	170	169
Solon Springs	297	237
Solon Springs, vil.	215	118
Summit		
Wards 1 & 2	430	178
Superior		
Wards 1 – 3	792	474
Superior, vil.	278	116
Superior, city		
Wards 1 – 5	1,069	485
Wards 6 – 8	1,057	404
Wards 9 – 12	939	427
Wards 13 – 19	1,006	476
Wards 20 – 24	1,133	528
Wards 25 – 27	750	261
Wards 28 – 31	952	360
Wards 32 – 37	950	386
Wards 38 – 43	980	570
Wards 44 – 47	875	257
Wascott	295	211
TOTAL	15,830	7,835
DUNN COUNTY		
Boyceville, vil.	282	207
Colfax		
Wards 1 – 3	323	239
Colfax, vil.		
Wards 1 & 2	318	201
Downing, vil.	55	46
Dunn		
Wards 1 – 3	451	293
Eau Galle	229	213
Elk Mound		
Wards 1 – 3	404	397
Elk Mound, vil.	243	162
Grant	125	108
Hay River		
Wards 1 & 2	177	102
Knapp, vil.	92	137
Lucas	192	178
Menomonie		
Wards 1 – 4	952	749
Menomonie, city		
Wards 1 & 2	1,017	665
Wards 3 & 4	1,139	558
Wards 5 & 7	1,104	546
Ward 6	487	280
Wards 8 & 9	836	421
Wards 10 & 11	885	582
New Haven	154	156
Otter Creek	138	123
Peru	55	67
Red Cedar		
Wards 1 – 3	567	606
Ridgeland, vil.	74	39
Rock Creek	285	234
Sand Creek	150	155
Sheridan	135	119
Sherman	241	244
Spring Brook		
Wards 1 – 3	408	441
Stanton	190	199
Tainter		
Wards 1 – 3	724	635
Tiffany		
Wards 1 – 3	164	186
Weston		
Wards 1 & 2	175	125
Wheeler, vil.	69	46
Wilson	162	107
TOTAL	13,002	9,566
EAU CLAIRE COUNTY		
Altoona, city		
Wards 1 – 7, 9 – 11	1,590	1,048
Wards 8, 12 & 13	477	317
Augusta, city		
Wards 1 – 5	362	312
Bridge Creek		
Wards 1 & 2	311	266
Brunswick		
Wards 1 & 2	522	434
Clear Creek		
Wards 1 & 2	223	188
Drammen	251	177
Eau Claire, city		
Ward 1	778	299
Ward 2	777	261
Ward 3	1,303	414
Ward 4	551	372
Ward 5	852	314
Ward 6	559	176
Ward 7	396	271
Ward 8	665	416
Ward 9	40	7
Ward 10	349	200
Ward 11	741	556
Ward 12	727	445
Ward 13	393	325
Ward 14	773	434
Ward 15	799	549
Ward 17	821	684
Ward 18	1,043	790
Ward 19	377	136
Ward 20	1,746	842
Ward 21	560	265
Ward 22	427	278
Ward 23	1,140	599
Ward 24	188	59
Ward 25	692	513
Ward 26	317	241
Ward 27	338	223
Ward 28	491	340
Ward 29	717	310
Ward 30	887	441
Ward 31	1,223	428
Ward 32	159	94
Ward 33	99	88
Ward 34	473	215
Ward 35	74	26
Ward 36	450	231
Ward 37	317	217
Ward 38	369	308
Ward 39	478	287
Fairchild	86	54
Fairchild, vil.	150	56
Fall Creek, vil.		
Wards 1 & 2	396	310
Lincoln		
Wards 1 & 2	302	274
Ludington	258	267
Otter Creek	102	119
Pleasant Valley		
Wards 1 – 4	940	964
Seymour		
Wards 1 – 4	1,014	808
Union		
Wards 1 – 3	807	609
Washington		
Wards 1 – 8, 10 – 12	1,766	1,613
Wards 9 & 13	398	396
Wilson	102	93
TOTAL	33,146	20,959
FLORENCE COUNTY		
Aurora		
Wards 1 – 3	250	289
Commonwealth		
Wards 1 – 3	103	141
Fence	65	69
Fern	46	60
Florence		
Wards 1 – 7	505	685
Homestead	93	124
Long Lake	41	77
Tipler	31	67
TOTAL	1,134	1,512

VOTE FOR PRESIDENT AND VICE PRESIDENT BY WARD
November 4, 2008 General Election–Continued

District	Barack Obama Joe Biden (Dem.)	John McCain Sarah Palin (Rep.)	District	Barack Obama Joe Biden (Dem.)	John McCain Sarah Palin (Rep.)
FOND DU LAC COUNTY			Rosendale	133	256
Alto			Rosendale, vil.	206	352
Wards 1 & 2	134	452	St. Cloud, vil.	116	181
Ashford			Springvale.	139	228
Wards 1 – 3	350	605	**Taycheedah**		
Auburn			Wards 1 – 5	1,021	1,568
Wards 1 – 3	440	923	**Waupun**		
Brandon, vil.	171	281	Wards 1 & 2	244	536
Byron			**Waupun, city**		
Wards 1 & 2	333	637	Wards 9 – 12	664	1,086
Calumet			TOTAL	23,463	28,164
Wards 1 & 2	372	458	**FOREST COUNTY**		
Campbellsport, vil.			**Alvin**		
Wards 1 – 4	470	586	Wards 1 & 2	55	55
Eden.	202	398	**Argonne**		
Eden, vil.	177	213	Wards 1 & 2	161	95
Eldorado			Armstrong Creek	128	103
Wards 1 – 3	288	500	Blackwell	100	36
Empire			Caswell	19	30
Wards 1 – 3	636	1,107	**Crandon**		
Fairwater, vil.	75	103	Wards 1 & 2	212	116
Fond du Lac			**Crandon, city**		
Wards 1 – 3	637	1,023	Wards 1 – 4	450	359
Fond du Lac, city			Freedom.	105	113
Ward 1	591	371	Hiles.	141	102
Ward 2	795	681	**Laona**		
Ward 3	618	425	Wards 1 – 3	355	256
Ward 4	790	425	**Lincoln**		
Ward 5	596	415	Wards 1 – 3	286	197
Ward 6	507	353	**Nashville**		
Ward 7	585	446	Ward 1	50	70
Ward 8	661	601	Ward 2	94	129
Ward 9	836	989	Ward 3	175	40
Ward 10	888	836	Ward 4	3	3
Ward 11	639	627	Popple River	18	13
Ward 12	915	855	Ross	35	34
Ward 13	846	819	**Wabeno**		
Ward 14	563	798	Wards 1 – 5	286	212
Ward 15	535	682	TOTAL	2,673	1,963
Ward 16	174	152	**GRANT COUNTY**		
Ward 17	0	0	Bagley, vil.	143	54
Ward 18	0	0	Beetown.	170	126
Ward 19	7	9	**Bloomington**		
Ward 20	0	0	Wards 1 & 2	96	69
Ward 21	0	0	Bloomington, vil	198	122
Ward 22	12	4	Blue River, vil.	127	70
Ward 23	6	2	**Boscobel**		
Ward 24	0	5	Wards 1 & 2	125	67
Ward 25	0	1	**Boscobel, city**		
Ward 26	7	1	Wards 1 – 4	759	401
Ward 27	2	7	**Cassville**		
Ward 28	0	1	Wards 1 & 2	108	75
Ward 29	2	0	**Cassville, vil.**		
Ward 30	0	1	Wards 1 & 2	239	151
Ward 31	0	0	Castle Rock	74	54
Ward 32	0	2	Clifton.	80	59
Ward 33	0	1	**Cuba City, city**		
Ward 34	0	0	Wards 1 – 5	640	307
Ward 35	0	0	**Dickeyville, vil.**		
Ward 36	0	0	Wards 1 & 2	302	240
Ward 37	0	0	**Ellenboro**		
Ward 38	0	0	Wards 1 & 2	129	118
Ward 39	0	2	**Fennimore**		
Forest			Wards 1 & 2	121	93
Wards 1 & 2	218	421	**Fennimore, city**		
Friendship			Wards 1 – 6	647	415
Wards 1 – 4	571	764	Glen Haven	107	80
Kewaskum, vil.			Harrison.	118	116
Ward 5	0	0	**Hazel Green**		
Lamartine			Wards 1 & 2	436	220
Wards 1 – 3	369	623	**Hazel Green, vil.**		
Marshfield			Wards 1 & 2	385	179
Wards 1 & 2	229	404	**Hickory Grove**		
Metomen	155	234	Wards 1 & 2	77	87
Mount Calvary, vil.	171	169	**Jamestown**		
North Fond du Lac, vil.			Wards 1 – 3	591	482
Wards 1 – 7	1,262	1,119	**Lancaster, city**		
Oakfield	157	216	Wards 1 – 8	1,104	712
Oakfield, vil.			Liberty	101	121
Wards 1 & 2	248	311	Lima.	218	128
Osceola			Little Grant	71	50
Wards 1 & 2	341	770	**Livingston, vil.**		
Ripon			Ward 1	192	101
Wards 1 & 2	317	415	Marion	138	77
Ripon, city			Millville	55	29
Wards 1 – 3	408	443	**Montfort, vil.**		
Wards 4 – 6	676	469	Ward 1	199	77
Wards 7 & 8	471	404			
Wards 9 – 11	487	399			

VOTE FOR PRESIDENT AND VICE PRESIDENT BY WARD
November 4, 2008 General Election–Continued

District	Barack Obama Joe Biden (Dem.)	John McCain Sarah Palin (Rep.)
Mount Hope		
Wards 1 & 2	53	36
Mount Hope, vil.		
Wards 1 & 2	38	22
Mount Ida	126	115
Muscoda		
Wards 1 & 2	192	113
Muscoda, vil.		
Wards 1 & 2	394	159
North Lancaster	141	112
Paris		
Wards 1 & 2	216	156
Patch Grove		
Wards 1 & 2	89	58
Patch Grove, vil.		
Wards 1 & 2	52	23
Platteville		
Wards 1 & 2	393	350
Platteville, city		
Wards 1 – 4	924	525
Wards 5 – 7	909	425
Wards 8 – 10	1,045	577
Wards 11 – 13	1,043	524
Potosi		
Wards 1 & 2	234	154
Potosi, vil..	217	130
Smelser		
Wards 1 & 2	256	175
South Lancaster		
Wards 1 – 3	193	129
Tennyson, vil..	109	70
Waterloo.	128	105
Watterstown.	99	57
Wingville	91	45
Woodman .	41	45
Woodman, vil.	27	18
Wyalusing..	115	65
TOTAL	14,875	9,068
GREEN COUNTY		
Adams.	163	98
Albany		
Wards 1 & 2	330	222
Albany, vil.		
Wards 1 & 2	322	130
Belleville, vil.		
Ward 3	177	64
Brodhead, city		
Wards 1 – 6	926	490
Brooklyn		
Wards 1 & 2	380	221
Brooklyn, vil.		
Ward 2	165	67
Browntown, vil..	70	58
Cadiz	255	168
Clarno		
Wards 1 & 2	323	257
Decatur		
Wards 1 – 3	537	379
Exeter		
Wards 1 & 2	757	311
Jefferson		
Wards 1 – 3	297	281
Jordan.	175	154
Monroe		
Wards 1 & 2	365	272
Monroe, city		
Wards 1 – 10	3,160	1,844
Monticello, vil.		
Wards 1 & 2	429	181
Mount Pleasant		
Wards 1 & 2	192	128
New Glarus		
Wards 1 & 2	479	296
New Glarus, vil.		
Wards 1 – 4	843	335
Spring Grove	231	217
Sylvester	281	247
Washington	303	130
York.	342	180
TOTAL	11,502	6,730
GREEN LAKE COUNTY		
Berlin		
Wards 1 & 2	213	420
Berlin, city		
Wards 1 – 6, 8 – 10	1,145	1,143
Brooklyn		
Wards 1 – 3	483	692

District	Barack Obama Joe Biden (Dem.)	John McCain Sarah Palin (Rep.)
Green Lake		
Wards 1 – 3	225	486
Green Lake, city		
Wards 1 – 6	249	326
Kingston		
Wards 1 & 2	113	190
Kingston, vil	61	114
Mackford	74	201
Manchester	135	225
Markesan, city		
Wards 1 – 3	278	422
Marquette		
Wards 1 & 2	95	177
Marquette, vil.	34	35
Princeton		
Wards 1 – 4	362	437
Princeton, city		
Wards 1 – 4	325	290
St. Marie	107	122
Seneca	101	113
TOTAL	4,000	5,393
IOWA COUNTY		
Arena		
Wards 1 & 2	540	255
Arena, vil.	284	105
Avoca, vil..	158	61
Barneveld, vil.		
Wards 1 & 2	425	152
Blanchardville, vil.		
Ward 2	75	29
Brigham		
Wards 1 – 3	429	180
Clyde		
Wards 1 – 3	129	57
Cobb, vil.	173	72
Dodgeville		
Wards 1 – 3	594	333
Dodgeville, city		
Wards 1 & 2	389	231
Wards 3 & 4	359	141
Wards 5 & 6	295	152
Wards 7 & 8	376	222
Eden.	119	75
Highland		
Wards 1 & 2	235	143
Highland, vil.	288	119
Hollandale, vil.	124	23
Linden		
Wards 1 – 3	224	165
Linden, vil..	188	53
Livingston, vil.		
Ward 2	4	0
Mifflin		
Wards 1 & 2	149	124
Mineral Point		
Wards 1 & 2	250	200
Mineral Point, city		
Ward 1	237	90
Ward 2	230	106
Wards 3 & 4	286	99
Wards 5 & 6	218	69
Montfort, vil.		
Ward 2	30	18
Moscow		
Wards 1 & 2	241	123
Muscoda, vil.		
Ward 3	14	13
Pulaski	106	66
Rewey, vil.	71	42
Ridgeway		
Wards 1 & 2	229	101
Ridgeway, vil..	203	73
Waldwick	166	88
Wyoming	149	49
TOTAL	7,987	3,829
IRON COUNTY		
Anderson	29	12
Carey	53	45
Gurney	61	25
Hurley, city		
Ward 1	119	67
Ward 2	138	74
Ward 3	105	57
Ward 4	134	54
Kimball	160	117
Knight.	88	53
Mercer		
Ward 1	133	112
Ward 2	139	156

VOTE FOR PRESIDENT AND VICE PRESIDENT BY WARD
November 4, 2008 General Election–Continued

District	Barack Obama Joe Biden (Dem.)	John McCain Sarah Palin (Rep.)	District	Barack Obama Joe Biden (Dem.)	John McCain Sarah Palin (Rep.)
Ward 3	115	116	Oakland		
Ward 4	108	112	Wards 1 – 4	1,046	798
Montreal, city			Palmyra		
Ward 1	67	88	Wards 1 & 2	254	507
Ward 2	62	40	Palmyra, vil.		
Oma.	114	100	Wards 1 & 2	402	503
Pence	65	41	Sullivan		
Saxon	118	81	Wards 1 – 3	466	750
Sherman.	106	114	Sullivan, vil.	137	191
TOTAL	1,914	1,464	Sumner	263	210
JACKSON COUNTY			Waterloo.	253	241
Adams			Waterloo, city		
Wards 1 – 4	449	308	Wards 1 – 5	963	589
Albion			Watertown		
Wards 1 – 4	349	231	Wards 1 & 2	465	646
Alma			Watertown, city		
Wards 1 & 2	232	243	Ward 8	236	219
Alma Center, vil.	141	89	Wards 9 & 10	396	811
Bear Bluff.	20	52	Wards 11 & 12	452	499
Black River Falls, city			Wards 13 & 14	547	619
Wards 1 – 4	1,052	633	Wards 15 & 16	699	764
Brockway			Wards 17 & 18	651	879
Wards 1 – 6	519	196	Wards 19 – 21	1	2
City Point	56	53	Whitewater, city		
Cleveland	116	122	Wards 9 – 11	1,090	634
Curran.	104	69	Wards 14, 15, 20 – 22 . . .	9	14
Franklin	130	56	TOTAL	21,448	21,096
Garden Valley.	106	115	JUNEAU COUNTY		
Garfield	173	123	Armenia.	165	162
Hixton			Camp Douglas, vil.	114	130
Wards 1 & 2	175	135	Clearfield		
Hixton, vil.	143	74	Wards 1 & 2	189	183
Irving			Cutler	100	88
Wards 1 & 2	239	123	Elroy, city		
Knapp.	81	82	Wards 1 – 5	392	223
Komensky.	125	17	Finley	17	29
Manchester	209	175	Fountain.	130	147
Melrose			Germantown		
Wards 1 & 2	113	100	Wards 1 & 2	380	355
Melrose, vil.	184	106	Hustler, vil.	61	38
Merrillan, vil.	177	75	Kildare	180	123
Millston	54	47	Kingston	7	14
North Bend	168	80	Lemonweir		
Northfield	170	118	Wards 1 – 4	465	295
Springfield			Lindina		
Wards 1 & 2	146	80	Wards 1 & 2	206	161
Taylor, vil.	141	50	Lisbon		
TOTAL	5,572	3,552	Wards 1 & 2	237	196
JEFFERSON COUNTY			Lyndon		
Aztalan			Wards 1 & 2	424	213
Wards 1 & 2	378	418	Lyndon Station, vil.	163	56
Cambridge, vil.			Marion	114	105
Ward 1	34	16	Mauston, city		
Cold Spring			Wards 1 – 10	894	704
Wards 1 & 2	201	247	Necedah		
Concord			Wards 1 – 3	434	617
Wards 1, 2 & 4	393	709	Necedah, vil.	213	194
Ward 3	45	73	New Lisbon, city		
Farmington			Wards 1 – 6	292	299
Wards 1 & 2	340	486	Orange	142	130
Fort Atkinson, city			Plymouth		
Wards 1 – 3	1,277	955	Wards 1 & 2	170	149
Wards 4 – 6	1,154	711	Seven Mile Creek		
Wards 7 – 9	1,207	787	Wards 1 & 2	105	65
Hebron			Summit	145	153
Wards 1 & 2	257	331	Union Center, vil.	68	36
Ixonia			Wisconsin Dells, city		
Wards 1, 3 & 4	573	1,159	Ward 7	0	0
Ward 2	218	396	Wonewoc		
Jefferson			Wards 1 & 2	165	145
Wards 1 & 2	176	304	Wonewoc, vil.	214	138
Wards 3 – 5	346	323	TOTAL	6,186	5,148
Jefferson, city			KENOSHA COUNTY		
Wards 1 – 8	2,112	1,452	Brighton		
Ward 9	0	0	Wards 1 – 3	333	509
Johnson Creek, vil.			Bristol		
Wards 1 & 2	647	631	Wards 1 – 4 & 8	624	879
Wards 3 & 4	5	4	Wards 5 & 7	300	319
Koshkonong			Ward 6	212	366
Wards 1 – 5	1,033	1,005	Genoa City, vil.		
Lac la Belle, vil.			Wards 4 & 5	0	2
Ward 2	0	0	Kenosha, city		
Lake Mills			Ward 1	729	328
Wards 1 & 2	647	565	Ward 2	1,106	505
Lake Mills, city			Ward 3	741	357
Wards 1 – 4	1,779	1,341	Ward 4	846	339
Milford			Ward 5	902	566
Wards 1 & 2	296	307	Ward 6	823	418

VOTE FOR PRESIDENT AND VICE PRESIDENT BY WARD
November 4, 2008 General Election–Continued

District	Barack Obama Joe Biden (Dem.)	John McCain Sarah Palin (Rep.)	District	Barack Obama Joe Biden (Dem.)	John McCain Sarah Palin (Rep.)
Ward 7	987	534	Twin Lakes, vil.		
Ward 8	1,058	427	Wards 1 – 12	1,301	1,287
Ward 9	1,218	650	Wheatland		
Ward 10	874	577	Wards 1 – 5	774	962
Ward 11	771	366	TOTAL	45,836	31,609
Ward 12	762	298	KEWAUNEE COUNTY		
Ward 13	658	163	Ahnapee	292	222
Ward 14	427	77	Algoma, city		
Ward 15	539	97	Wards 1 – 7	965	581
Ward 16	642	128	Carlton		
Ward 17	918	424	Wards 1 & 2	315	273
Ward 18	647	307	Casco		
Ward 19	752	185	Wards 1 & 2	296	312
Ward 20	749	183	Casco, vil.	155	136
Ward 21	866	467	Franklin	309	233
Ward 22	615	222	Kewaunee		
Ward 23	677	219	Wards 1 – 5	856	573
Ward 24	903	402	Lincoln	278	183
Ward 25	911	525	Luxemburg		
Ward 26	875	538	Wards 1 & 2	385	411
Ward 27	954	575	Luxemburg, vil.		
Ward 28	823	662	Wards 1 & 2	639	555
Ward 29	1,063	668	Montpelier		
Ward 30	723	515	Wards 1 – 3	395	383
Ward 31	941	483	Pierce		
Ward 32	770	412	Wards 1 & 2	248	197
Ward 33	796	506	Red River		
Ward 34	1,478	1,117	Wards 1 – 3	416	331
Ward 35	85	111	West Kewaunee		
Ward 36	40	44	Wards 1 – 3	353	321
Ward 37	0	0	TOTAL	5,902	4,711
Ward 38	1	1	LA CROSSE COUNTY		
Ward 39	14	27	Bangor	159	162
Ward 40	31	26	Bangor, vil.		
Ward 41	175	108	Wards 1 & 2	429	283
Ward 42	0	0	Barre		
Ward 43	45	41	Wards 1 & 2	303	360
Ward 44	26	21	Burns	269	236
Ward 45	12	14	Campbell		
Ward 46	2	0	Wards 1 – 6	1,601	932
Ward 47	2	0	Ward 7	26	1
Ward 48	1	5	Farmington		
Ward 49	10	8	Wards 1 – 3	613	400
Ward 50	1	0	Greenfield		
Ward 51	0	0	Wards 1 – 3	617	477
Ward 52	11	15	Hamilton		
Ward 53	11	16	Wards 1 – 3	679	709
Ward 54	0	0	Holland		
Ward 55	0	0	Wards 1 – 4	1,020	980
Ward 56	0	0	Holmen, vil.		
Ward 57	0	0	Wards 1 – 10	2,509	1,694
Ward 58	2	0	La Crosse, city		
Ward 59	0	1	Ward 1	1,041	518
Ward 60	0	0	Ward 2	928	468
Ward 61	1	0	Ward 3	888	312
Ward 62	0	0	Ward 4	1,071	416
Ward 63	0	0	Ward 5	1,633	707
Ward 64	0	0	Ward 6	1,503	686
Ward 65	0	0	Ward 7	1,189	363
Ward 66	2	0	Ward 8	1,319	637
Ward 67	14	13	Ward 9	1,141	648
Ward 68	0	0	Ward 10	1,170	526
Ward 69	0	0	Ward 11	1,041	356
Ward 70	0	0	Ward 12	1,010	352
Ward 72	0	0	Ward 13	987	419
Paddock Lake, vil.			Ward 14	1,184	578
Wards 1 – 5	774	703	Ward 15	1,020	574
Paris			Ward 16	985	518
Wards 1 & 2	389	495	Ward 17	1,274	695
Pleasant Prairie, vil.			Ward 18	1	8
Wards 1 – 3	1,066	842	Ward 19	23	13
Wards 4 & 5	694	700	Ward 20	1	0
Wards 6 & 7	916	799	Ward 21	0	1
Wards 8 – 11	1,543	1,556	Medary		
Wards 12 & 13	1,086	1,004	Wards 1 & 2	456	433
Randall			Onalaska		
Wards 1 – 5	763	901	Wards 1 – 7	1,683	1,560
Salem			Onalaska, city		
Wards 1 – 3, 5 – 7, 11 – 15	1,530	1,778	Wards 1 – 4	2,090	1,796
Wards 4, 8 – 10	934	976	Wards 5 & 8 & 13	1,539	952
Silver Lake, vil.			Wards 9 – 12	1,688	1,389
Wards 1 – 3	549	571	Rockland, vil.	159	120
Somers			Shelby		
Wards 1 – 4	882	843	Wards 1, 4 – 6	1,085	777
Wards 5, 6 & 12	987	584	Wards 2 & 3	619	489
Ward 7	260	158	Washington	209	113
Ward 8	274	146	West Salem, vil.		
Wards 9 – 11	615	538	Wards 1 – 6	1,362	1,043
			TOTAL	38,524	23,701

VOTE FOR PRESIDENT AND VICE PRESIDENT BY WARD
November 4, 2008 General Election–Continued

District	Barack Obama Joe Biden (Dem.)	John McCain Sarah Palin (Rep.)	District	Barack Obama Joe Biden (Dem.)	John McCain Sarah Palin (Rep.)
LAFAYETTE COUNTY			Merrill		
Argyle			Wards 1 – 5	852	751
Wards 1 & 2	132	92	Merrill, city		
Argyle, vil.	259	124	Ward 1	329	266
Belmont			Ward 2	337	269
Wards 1 & 2	144	129	Ward 3	287	192
Belmont, vil.	288	187	Ward 4	338	208
Benton			Ward 5	351	191
Wards 1 & 2	136	95	Ward 6	408	236
Benton, vil.	327	117	Ward 7	318	241
Blanchard	105	54	Ward 8	302	175
Blanchardville			Pine River		
Ward 1	254	84	Wards 1 – 3	558	514
Cuba City, city			Rock Falls		
Wards 6 & 7	79	37	Wards 1 & 2	182	191
Darlington			Russell	198	146
Wards 1 & 2	238	175	Schley		
Darlington, city			Wards 1 & 2	261	221
Wards 1 – 7	679	383	Scott		
Elk Grove	111	95	Wards 1 & 2	395	357
Fayette	96	85	Skanawan	147	92
Gratiot	137	145	Somo	39	30
Gratiot, vil.	90	37	Tomahawk		
Hazel Green, vil.			Wards 1 & 2	139	91
Ward 3	8	3	Tomahawk, city		
Kendall	85	93	Wards 1 & 2	317	172
Lamont	88	61	Wards 3 & 4	349	259
Monticello	31	31	Wards 5 & 6	317	248
New Diggings	145	105	Wilson	102	81
Seymour	95	72	TOTAL	8,424	6,519
Shullsburg	100	54	**MANITOWOC COUNTY**		
Shullsburg, city			Cato		
Wards 1 – 3	390	171	Wards 1 & 2	380	502
South Wayne, vil.	118	76	Centerville	164	212
Wayne	108	114	Cleveland, vil.		
White Oak Springs	24	29	Wards 1 & 2	388	391
Willow Springs	202	147	Cooperstown		
Wiota	263	189	Wards 1 & 2	353	365
TOTAL	4,732	2,984	Eaton	195	253
LANGLADE COUNTY			Francis Creek, vil.	188	171
Ackley	138	139	Franklin		
Ainsworth	182	130	Wards 1 & 2	290	396
Antigo			Gibson		
Wards 1 & 2	368	420	Wards 1 & 2	371	345
Antigo, city			Kellnersville, vil.	108	78
Ward 1	225	173	Kiel, city		
Ward 2	217	207	Wards 1 – 6	949	895
Ward 3	222	156	Kossuth		
Ward 4	234	167	Wards 1 – 3	590	572
Ward 5	213	140	Liberty		
Ward 6	174	173	Wards 1 & 2	276	452
Ward 7	235	233	Manitowoc		
Ward 8	201	182	Wards 1 – 3	309	309
Ward 9	234	178	Manitowoc, city		
Elcho			Wards 1 & 2	877	555
Wards 1 – 3	366	369	Wards 3, 4, 21 & 35	997	737
Evergreen	132	137	Wards 5 & 6	833	455
Langlade			Wards 7 & 8	671	308
Wards 1 & 2	154	120	Wards 9 & 10	912	565
Neva	239	269	Wards 11 & 12	967	842
Norwood			Wards 13, 14, 23, 27 & 37	956	581
Wards 1 & 2	202	294	Wards 15 & 16	1,020	960
Parrish	33	26	Wards 17, 18, 22, 24 – 26, 28 – 30, 32, 34 & 36	894	665
Peck	99	112	Wards 19, 20, 31 & 33	984	1,130
Polar			Manitowoc Rapids		
Wards 1 & 2	247	316	Wards 1 – 5	603	840
Price			Maple Grove	182	240
Wards 1 & 2	63	63	Maribel, vil.	99	80
Rolling			Meeme		
Wards 1 & 2	363	376	Wards 1 & 2	403	425
Summit	56	50	Mishicot		
Upham	204	269	Wards 1 – 4	333	350
Vilas	59	57	Mishicot, vil.		
White Lake, vil.	85	79	Wards 1 & 2	428	351
Wolf River			Newton		
Wards 1 & 2	237	246	Wards 1 – 4	543	736
TOTAL	5,182	5,081	Reedsville, vil.		
LINCOLN COUNTY			Wards 1 & 2	345	220
Birch			Rockland		
Wards 1 & 2	144	106	Wards 1 & 2	215	257
Bradley			St. Nazianz, vil.	208	159
Wards 1 – 4	783	682	Schleswig		
Corning	251	198	Wards 1 – 3	565	580
Harding	118	102	Two Creeks	111	128
Harrison			Two Rivers		
Wards 1 – 4	280	250	Wards 1 – 4	525	491
King	322	250	Two Rivers, city		
			Wards 1 – 3	923	583

VOTE FOR PRESIDENT AND VICE PRESIDENT BY WARD
November 4, 2008 General Election–Continued

District	Barack Obama Joe Biden (Dem.)	John McCain Sarah Palin (Rep.)	District	Barack Obama Joe Biden (Dem.)	John McCain Sarah Palin (Rep.)
Wards 4, 5, 10 & 11	1,045	754	Schofield, city		
Wards 6 & 7	843	501	Wards 1 – 4	635	453
Wards 8 & 9	935	376	Spencer		
Valders, vil.	231	247	Wards 1 & 2	382	312
Whitelaw, vil.	219	177	Spencer, vil.		
TOTAL	22,428	19,234	Wards 1 – 3	500	381
MARATHON COUNTY			Stettin		
Abbotsford, city			Wards 1 & 2	382	442
Ward 1	82	74	Wards 3 & 4	274	389
Athens, vil.			Stratford, vil.		
Wards 1 & 2	300	230	Wards 1 & 2	340	374
Bergen.	252	168	Texas		
Berlin	207	298	Wards 1 & 2	493	468
Bern	135	82	Unity, vil.		
Bevent			Ward 1	53	40
Wards 1 & 2	411	194	Wausau		
Birnamwood, vil.			Wards 1 – 3	608	651
Ward 2	9	0	Wausau, city		
Brighton.	119	120	Ward 1	520	322
Brokaw, vil.	87	53	Ward 2	501	338
Cassel	260	223	Ward 3	301	178
Cleveland	345	328	Ward 4	413	230
Colby, city			Ward 5	60	45
Ward 1	152	85	Ward 6	96	101
Day			Ward 7	66	63
Wards 1 & 2	278	262	Ward 8	366	145
Dorchester, vil.			Ward 9	408	192
Ward 2	0	0	Ward 10	375	169
Ward 3	0	0	Ward 11	479	328
Easton			Ward 12	422	218
Wards 1 & 2	276	356	Ward 13	401	269
Eau Pleine.	182	197	Ward 14	515	476
Edgar, vil.			Ward 15	499	493
Wards 1 & 2	403	319	Ward 16	494	304
Ward 3	0	2	Ward 17	532	325
Elderon	163	132	Ward 18	472	257
Elderon, vil.	45	39	Ward 19	418	303
Emmet.	289	196	Ward 20	625	477
Fenwood, vil.	54	37	Ward 21	527	503
Frankfort	159	145	Ward 22	54	40
Franzen	140	135	Ward 23	327	155
Green Valley	160	152	Ward 24	356	206
Guenther	102	91	Ward 25	409	200
Halsey.	146	123	Ward 26	366	158
Hamburg	227	206	Ward 27	470	305
Harrison	81	98	Ward 28	354	184
Hatley, vil.			Ward 29	58	26
Ward 1	135	137	Ward 30	0	0
Ward 2	2	1	Ward 31	2	0
Hewitt.	166	152	Ward 32	0	0
Holton			Ward 33	0	1
Wards 1 & 2	193	177	Ward 34	3	7
Hull	153	164	Ward 35	36	56
Johnson	206	175	Ward 36	2	4
Knowlton			Ward 37	0	0
Wards 1 – 3	543	558	Ward 38	0	0
Kronenwetter, vil.			Ward 39	0	0
Wards 1 – 4	1,008	843	Ward 40	2	0
Wards 5 – 8	939	788	Ward 41	0	1
Maine			Ward 42	0	0
Wards 1 – 4	639	714	Ward 43	0	2
Marathon			Ward 44	8	6
Wards 1 & 2	269	376	Ward 45	0	10
Marathon City, vil.			Ward 46	0	2
Wards 1 – 3	476	398	Ward 47	0	0
Marshfield, city			Ward 48	0	0
Wards 21, 22 & 26.	147	91	Ward 49	0	0
Wards 28 – 34	77	56	Ward 50	0	0
McMillan			Ward 51	4	0
Wards 1 – 3	567	553	Ward 52	0	0
Mosinee			Ward 53	0	0
Wards 1 – 3	593	598	Ward 54	0	0
Mosinee, city			Ward 55	0	0
Wards 1, 2 & 6	522	429	Ward 56	0	0
Wards 3 – 5	691	517	Ward 57	0	0
Norrie	270	212	Ward 58	0	0
Plover	177	152	Ward 59	0	0
Reid			Ward 60	0	0
Wards 1 & 2	407	252	Ward 61	0	0
Rib Falls.	232	293	Ward 62	0	0
Rib Mountain			Ward 63	0	0
Wards 1 – 10	2,026	2,315	Ward 64	0	0
Rietbrock	247	216	Ward 65	0	0
Ringle			Ward 66	0	0
Wards 1 & 2	450	475	Ward 67	0	1
Rothschild, vil.			Ward 68	0	0
Wards 1 & 2	513	381	Weston	139	170
Wards 3 & 4	518	400	Weston, vil.		
Wards 5 & 6	656	537	Wards 1, 2 & 4	1,148	882

VOTE FOR PRESIDENT AND VICE PRESIDENT BY WARD
November 4, 2008 General Election–Continued

District	Barack Obama Joe Biden (Dem.)	John McCain Sarah Palin (Rep.)
Wards 3 & 6	804	647
Ward 5	463	512
Wards 7 – 11	1,118	1,030
Wien	201	189
TOTAL	36,367	30,345
MARINETTE COUNTY		
Amberg	203	208
Athelstane		
Wards 1 & 2	163	161
Beaver		
Wards 1 – 3	273	351
Beecher		
Wards 1 – 3	179	181
Coleman, vil.	155	181
Crivitz, vil.	278	225
Dunbar		
Wards 1 & 2	108	594
Goodman	190	130
Grover		
Wards 1 – 3	436	394
Lake		
Wards 1 & 2	329	278
Marinette, city		
Ward 1	405	232
Wards 2 & 4	818	452
Wards 3 & 5	740	500
Ward 6	390	165
Wards 7 & 8	799	487
Middle Inlet		
Wards 1 & 2	236	193
Niagara	246	226
Niagara, city		
Wards 1 – 3	408	326
Pembine		
Wards 1 & 2	245	251
Peshtigo		
Wards 1 – 5	1,149	981
Peshtigo, city		
Wards 1 – 8	806	667
Porterfield		
Wards 1 – 3	529	459
Pound		
Wards 1 – 4	281	416
Pound, vil.	68	91
Silver Cliff		
Wards 1 & 2	140	167
Stephenson		
Wards 1 – 3	525	397
Wards 4 – 6	427	384
Wagner	195	195
Wausaukee		
Wards 1 – 4	321	335
Wausaukee, vil.	153	99
TOTAL	11,195	9,726
MARQUETTE COUNTY		
Buffalo		
Wards 1 & 2	321	234
Crystal Lake	171	149
Douglas	224	215
Endeavor, vil.	105	105
Harris	225	244
Mecan	202	187
Montello		
Wards 1 – 3	319	277
Montello, city		
Wards 1 – 4	254	210
Moundville		
Wards 1 & 2	136	115
Neshkoro		
Wards 1 & 2	158	183
Neshkoro, vil.	108	104
Newton		
Wards 1 & 2	118	130
Oxford		
Wards 1 & 2	248	241
Oxford, vil.	144	102
Packwaukee		
Wards 1 – 3	451	320
Shields	147	175
Springfield	224	211
Westfield		
Wards 1 & 2	211	226
Westfield, vil.		
Wards 1 & 2	302	226
TOTAL	4,068	3,654
MENOMINEE COUNTY		
Menominee		
Wards 1, 3 – 5	992	174

District	Barack Obama Joe Biden (Dem.)	John McCain Sarah Palin (Rep.)
Ward 2	265	11
TOTAL	1,257	185
MILWAUKEE COUNTY		
Bayside, vil.		
Wards 1 & 4	461	288
Wards 2 & 5	705	390
Wards 3 & 7	581	422
Brown Deer, vil.		
Wards 1 – 3	1,945	920
Wards 4, 5 & 7	1,313	976
Wards 6, 8 & 9	1,179	793
Cudahy, city		
Wards 1 – 3	1,165	842
Wards 4 – 6	1,110	712
Wards 7 – 9	806	510
Ward 10	458	349
Wards 11 & 12	529	422
Wards 13 & 14	514	376
Ward 15	832	745
Fox Point, vil.		
Wards 1 – 4	1,107	989
Wards 5 – 9	1,466	956
Franklin, city		
Wards 1 – 4	1,188	1,526
Wards 5 – 8	1,248	1,807
Wards 9 – 12	1,522	1,518
Wards 13 – 16	1,466	2,043
Wards 17 – 20	1,435	2,050
Wards 21 – 24	1,488	1,747
Glendale, city		
Ward 1	470	247
Wards 2 & 8	1,035	489
Wards 3 & 9	820	594
Wards 4 & 10	859	497
Wards 5 & 11	933	544
Wards 6 & 12	941	459
Ward 7	338	223
Greendale, vil.		
Wards 1 & 2	589	1,015
Wards 3 & 4	1,003	973
Wards 5 & 6	818	868
Wards 7 & 8	805	907
Wards 9 & 10	848	1,005
Greenfield, city		
Ward 1	568	486
Ward 2	568	453
Ward 3	510	366
Ward 4	479	341
Ward 5	487	433
Ward 6	398	498
Ward 7	509	589
Ward 8	611	481
Ward 9	497	607
Ward 10	452	518
Ward 11	472	688
Ward 12	383	562
Ward 13	326	315
Ward 14	478	406
Ward 15	309	242
Ward 16	342	332
Ward 17	448	323
Ward 18	500	498
Ward 19	643	643
Ward 20	561	594
Ward 21	471	348
Hales Corners, vil.		
Wards 1 – 3	639	963
Wards 4 – 6	595	803
Wards 7 – 9	659	848
Milwaukee, city		
Ward 1	940	192
Ward 2	691	12
Ward 3	937	18
Ward 4	495	18
Ward 5	660	20
Ward 6	680	41
Ward 7	713	35
Ward 8	739	81
Ward 9	690	50
Ward 10	870	105
Ward 11	720	5
Ward 12	860	13
Ward 13	730	7
Ward 14	722	6
Ward 15	1,511	50
Ward 16	835	11
Ward 17	1,469	27
Ward 18	1,024	13
Ward 19	929	13

VOTE FOR PRESIDENT AND VICE PRESIDENT BY WARD
November 4, 2008 General Election–Continued

District	Barack Obama Joe Biden (Dem.)	John McCain Sarah Palin (Rep.)	District	Barack Obama Joe Biden (Dem.)	John McCain Sarah Palin (Rep.)
Ward 20	703	83	Ward 109	1,050	3
Ward 21	753	83	Ward 110	1,220	384
Ward 22	686	34	Ward 111	568	41
Ward 23	644	80	Ward 112	769	23
Ward 24	622	68	Ward 113	1,083	90
Ward 25	760	100	Ward 114	656	40
Ward 26	1,112	124	Ward 115	1,140	36
Ward 27	1,136	192	Ward 116	744	14
Ward 28	631	78	Ward 117	1,114	41
Ward 29	672	44	Ward 118	713	87
Ward 30	854	91	Ward 119	471	165
Ward 31	929	131	Ward 120	870	138
Ward 32	923	58	Ward 121	491	36
Ward 33	970	73	Ward 122	665	14
Ward 34	608	81	Ward 123	784	87
Ward 35	859	59	Ward 124	815	72
Ward 36	1,140	176	Ward 125	761	138
Ward 37	1,329	590	Ward 126	686	178
Ward 38	817	423	Ward 127	842	40
Ward 39	1,356	582	Ward 128	1,202	39
Ward 40	1,269	367	Ward 129	434	17
Ward 41	1,177	175	Ward 130	365	5
Ward 42	1,063	496	Ward 131	888	14
Ward 43	808	289	Ward 132	375	56
Ward 44	1,332	485	Ward 133	292	50
Ward 45	742	224	Ward 134	426	88
Ward 46	812	223	Ward 135	578	181
Ward 47	726	157	Ward 136	628	125
Ward 48	1,024	164	Ward 137	502	155
Ward 49	869	222	Ward 138	607	190
Ward 50	728	227	Ward 139	263	39
Ward 51	1,324	280	Ward 140	516	133
Ward 52	1,113	365	Ward 141	394	98
Ward 53	941	277	Ward 142	630	164
Ward 54	1,740	580	Ward 143	307	134
Ward 55	648	360	Ward 144	496	286
Ward 56	957	521	Ward 145	533	369
Ward 57	732	214	Ward 146	456	375
Ward 58	1,509	751	Ward 147	855	171
Ward 59	1,018	484	Ward 148	635	304
Ward 60	1,017	400	Ward 149	1,227	213
Ward 61	487	174	Ward 150	715	111
Ward 62	640	428	Ward 151	533	141
Ward 63	240	46	Ward 152	1,406	196
Ward 64	638	113	Ward 153	346	120
Ward 65	537	94	Ward 154	853	144
Ward 66	439	28	Ward 155	849	144
Ward 67	616	26	Ward 156	949	72
Ward 68	333	32	Ward 157	1,004	143
Ward 69	326	19	Ward 158	834	89
Ward 70	607	48	Ward 159	1,108	99
Ward 71	692	49	Ward 160	600	22
Ward 72	645	46	Ward 161	676	51
Ward 73	474	33	Ward 162	972	62
Ward 74	807	72	Ward 163	712	48
Ward 75	799	113	Ward 164	613	1
Ward 76	604	325	Ward 165	856	10
Ward 77	891	342	Ward 166	767	5
Ward 78	639	104	Ward 167	691	5
Ward 79	589	134	Ward 168	782	3
Ward 80	664	123	Ward 169	880	8
Ward 81	498	191	Ward 170	999	24
Ward 82	635	215	Ward 171	1,152	38
Ward 83	615	116	Ward 172	1,417	26
Ward 84	665	311	Ward 173	683	10
Ward 85	440	280	Ward 174	545	3
Ward 86	406	406	Ward 175	442	3
Ward 87	353	369	Ward 176	605	4
Ward 88	625	303	Ward 177	707	6
Ward 89	577	328	Ward 178	523	1
Ward 90	459	365	Ward 179	938	5
Ward 91	376	411	Ward 180	1,053	15
Ward 92	903	538	Ward 181	606	9
Ward 93	454	407	Ward 182	249	91
Ward 94	502	457	Ward 183	309	182
Ward 95	912	73	Ward 184	606	536
Ward 96	629	65	Ward 185	385	258
Ward 97	768	11	Ward 186	346	374
Ward 98	703	4	Ward 187	341	270
Ward 99	919	6	Ward 188	589	511
Ward 100	846	9	Ward 189	667	488
Ward 101	933	19	Ward 190	596	544
Ward 102	559	103	Ward 191	407	429
Ward 103	1,174	125	Ward 192	751	698
Ward 104	523	18	Ward 193	471	557
Ward 105	999	90	Ward 194	288	322
Ward 106	661	34	Ward 195	316	315
Ward 107	687	7	Ward 196	795	597
Ward 108	801	1	Ward 197	619	660

VOTE FOR PRESIDENT AND VICE PRESIDENT BY WARD
November 4, 2008 General Election–Continued

District	Barack Obama Joe Biden (Dem.)	John McCain Sarah Palin (Rep.)	District	Barack Obama Joe Biden (Dem.)	John McCain Sarah Palin (Rep.)
Ward 198	632	515	Ward 289	742	344
Ward 199	459	413	Ward 290	293	67
Ward 200	1,005	657	Ward 291	253	57
Ward 201	659	179	Ward 292	425	93
Ward 202	381	63	Ward 293	194	63
Ward 203	327	65	Ward 294	250	52
Ward 204	279	34	Ward 295	475	136
Ward 205	248	41	Ward 296	556	164
Ward 206	350	51	Ward 297	480	8
Ward 207	353	50	Ward 298	832	12
Ward 208	292	50	Ward 299	880	9
Ward 209	490	62	Ward 300	709	21
Ward 210	380	66	Ward 301	642	11
Ward 211	386	84	Ward 302	765	16
Ward 212	428	82	Ward 303	766	34
Ward 213	320	62	Ward 304	616	18
Ward 214	208	67	Ward 305	654	37
Ward 215	366	91	Ward 306	632	18
Ward 216	474	338	Ward 307	558	57
Ward 217	463	363	Ward 308	443	15
Ward 218	494	329	Ward 309	754	12
Ward 219	396	255	Ward 310	730	22
Ward 220	680	372	Ward 311	918	367
Ward 221	579	320	Ward 312	740	511
Ward 222	489	322	Ward 313	729	31
Ward 223	447	349	Ward 314	760	15
Ward 224	483	437	Oak Creek, city		
Ward 225	530	361	Wards 1 – 3	1,184	1,222
Ward 226	566	195	Wards 4 – 6	1,341	1,308
Ward 227	223	127	Wards 7 – 9	1,524	1,570
Ward 228	586	495	Wards 10 – 12	1,270	1,292
Ward 229	644	454	Wards 13 – 15	1,600	2,051
Ward 230	545	668	Wards 16 – 18	1,594	1,388
Ward 231	986	794	River Hills, vil.		
Ward 232	665	611	Ward 1	117	78
Ward 233	373	381	Wards 2 & 3	419	539
Ward 234	482	348	St. Francis, city		
Ward 235	620	175	Wards 1 – 4	722	600
Ward 236	826	253	Wards 5 – 8	920	644
Ward 237	659	211	Wards 9 – 12	1,221	880
Ward 238	695	345	Shorewood, vil.		
Ward 239	574	238	Wards 1 & 2	1,026	427
Ward 240	621	216	Wards 3 & 4	1,449	478
Ward 241	414	186	Wards 5 & 6	980	349
Ward 242	403	217	Wards 7 & 8	1,059	325
Ward 243	378	169	Wards 9 & 10	1,017	315
Ward 244	382	151	Wards 11 & 12	904	360
Ward 245	427	174	South Milwaukee, city		
Ward 246	321	87	Wards 1 & 2	834	680
Ward 247	348	206	Wards 3 & 4	710	489
Ward 248	363	198	Wards 5 & 6	771	538
Ward 249	507	203	Wards 7 & 8	617	531
Ward 250	633	291	Wards 9 & 10	848	803
Ward 251	694	277	Wards 11 & 12	694	586
Ward 252	703	265	Wards 13 & 14	745	621
Ward 253	690	293	Wards 15 & 16	820	653
Ward 254	457	239	Wauwatosa, city		
Ward 255	641	439	Ward 1	678	399
Ward 256	595	343	Ward 2	727	465
Ward 257	410	294	Ward 3	709	490
Ward 258	992	138	Ward 4	838	653
Ward 259	819	246	Ward 5	965	908
Ward 260	424	31	Ward 6	290	287
Ward 261	1,015	315	Ward 7	664	625
Ward 263	461	192	Ward 8	332	366
Ward 264	1,363	421	Ward 9	688	737
Ward 265	747	148	Ward 10	872	631
Ward 266	661	199	Ward 11	758	500
Ward 267	972	334	Ward 12	581	633
Ward 268	508	294	Ward 13	366	287
Ward 269	1,165	264	Ward 14	826	517
Ward 270	690	79	Ward 15	851	542
Ward 271	1,134	211	Ward 16	773	747
Ward 272	728	72	Ward 17	615	745
Ward 273	1,017	709	Ward 18	444	466
Ward 275	975	266	Ward 19	720	692
Ward 276	1,157	414	Ward 20	718	908
Ward 277	547	264	Ward 21	268	272
Ward 278	657	246	Ward 22	646	634
Ward 279	671	137	Ward 23	557	642
Ward 280	434	245	Ward 24	687	582
Ward 281	340	107	West Allis, city		
Ward 282	481	285	Ward 1	565	394
Ward 283	431	302	Ward 2	556	308
Ward 284	475	350	Ward 3	551	353
Ward 285	367	399	Ward 4	430	275
Ward 286	407	321	Ward 5	471	371
Ward 287	363	528	Ward 6	402	379
Ward 288	482	337	Ward 7	398	334

VOTE FOR PRESIDENT AND VICE PRESIDENT BY WARD
November 4, 2008 General Election–Continued

District	Barack Obama / Joe Biden (Dem.)	John McCain / Sarah Palin (Rep.)
Ward 8	547	468
Ward 9	444	334
Ward 10	448	333
Ward 11	575	412
Ward 12	525	444
Ward 13	588	497
Ward 14	514	487
Ward 15	465	432
Ward 16	390	429
Ward 17	500	457
Ward 18	455	479
Ward 19	665	507
Ward 20	421	332
Ward 21	480	478
Ward 22	511	470
Ward 23	458	457
Ward 24	365	387
Ward 25	484	530
Ward 26	442	500
Ward 27	455	341
Ward 28	505	456
Ward 29	593	480
Ward 30	635	737
Ward 31	516	519
Ward 32	467	310
Ward 33	385	446
Ward 34	0	0
Ward 35	105	120
West Milwaukee, vil.		
Wards 1, 2 & 5	513	276
Wards 3, 4 & 6	599	312
Whitefish Bay, vil.		
Wards 1 & 2	734	745
Wards 3 & 4	682	579
Wards 5 & 6	795	642
Wards 7 & 8	832	621
Ward 9	492	309
Ward 10	594	385
Wards 11 & 12	959	639
TOTAL	319,819	149,445
MONROE COUNTY		
Adrian	179	165
Angelo		
Wards 1 – 3	321	272
Byron		
Wards 1 & 2	304	256
Cashton, vil.		
Wards 1 & 2	316	164
Clifton	109	94
Glendale	135	160
Grant	81	143
Greenfield	166	220
Jefferson	139	110
Kendall, vil.	130	57
Lafayette		
Wards 1 & 2	79	101
La Grange		
Wards 1 – 3	452	516
Leon	269	286
Lincoln	146	256
Little Falls		
Wards 1 & 2	363	294
Melvina, vil.	26	6
New Lyme	35	40
Norwalk, vil.	135	78
Oakdale	174	173
Oakdale, vil.	73	54
Portland	192	146
Ridgeville	133	108
Scott	10	37
Sheldon	93	106
Sparta		
Wards 1 – 4	780	703
Sparta, city		
Wards 1 – 17	2,251	1,602
Tomah		
Wards 1 & 2	315	360
Tomah, city		
Wards 1 – 16	2,143	1,635
Warrens, vil.	62	79
Wellington		
Wards 1 & 2	162	94
Wells	145	107
Wilton		
Wards 1 – 3	131	112
Wilton, vil.	127	89
Wyeville, vil.	22	43
TOTAL	10,198	8,666
OCONTO COUNTY		
Abrams		
Wards 1 – 4	512	479
Bagley	80	82
Brazeau		
Wards 1 – 3	375	352
Breed	169	153
Chase		
Wards 1 – 4	750	690
Doty		
Wards 1 & 2	77	102
Gillett		
Wards 1 & 2	193	305
Gillett, city		
Wards 1 – 4	317	259
How		
Wards 1 – 3	126	178
Lakewood	237	254
Lena		
Wards 1 & 2	166	159
Lena, vil.	145	94
Little River		
Wards 1 & 2	326	221
Little Suamico		
Wards 1 – 7	1,118	1,171
Maple Valley		
Wards 1 & 2	171	201
Morgan	264	259
Mountain		
Wards 1 & 2	266	187
Oconto		
Wards 1 – 3	402	317
Oconto, city		
Wards 1 – 8	1,243	756
Oconto Falls		
Wards 1 & 2	323	335
Oconto Falls, city		
Wards 1 – 5	643	562
Pensaukee		
Wards 1 – 3	390	346
Pulaski, vil.		
Ward 5	0	0
Riverview		
Wards 1 & 2	305	201
Spruce		
Wards 1 & 2	244	192
Stiles		
Wards 1 – 3	407	360
Suring, vil.	139	115
Townsend	350	283
Underhill	189	142
TOTAL	9,927	8,755
ONEIDA COUNTY		
Cassian		
Wards 1 & 2	341	325
Crescent		
Wards 1 – 3	786	525
Enterprise	97	120
Hazelhurst		
Wards 1 & 2	403	396
Lake Tomahawk		
Wards 1 & 2	316	334
Little Rice	106	106
Lynne	46	46
Minocqua		
Wards 1 – 6	1,391	1,560
Monico	69	83
Newbold		
Wards 1 – 4	868	754
Ward 5	55	41
Nokomis		
Wards 1 & 2	475	341
Pelican		
Wards 1 – 5	926	647
Piehl	37	18
Pine Lake		
Wards 1 – 4	950	708
Rhinelander, city		
Wards 1 & 2	321	134
Wards 3 & 4	286	132
Wards 5 – 7	390	156
Wards 8 & 9	298	124
Wards 10 & 11	356	230
Wards 12 – 14	220	143
Wards 15 – 17	313	134
Wards 18 – 20	370	189
Schoepke	123	103
Stella	223	145

VOTE FOR PRESIDENT AND VICE PRESIDENT BY WARD
November 4, 2008 General Election–Continued

District	Barack Obama Joe Biden (Dem.)	John McCain Sarah Palin (Rep.)	District	Barack Obama Joe Biden (Dem.)	John McCain Sarah Palin (Rep.)
Sugar Camp			Hortonia		
Wards 1 & 2	524	546	Wards 1 & 2	280	343
Three Lakes			Hortonville, vil.		
Wards 1 – 3	666	785	Wards 1 – 3	708	696
Woodboro	326	221	Howard, vil.		
Woodruff			Ward 17	0	0
Wards 1 – 3	625	584	Kaukauna		
TOTAL	11,907	9,630	Wards 1 & 2	317	332
OUTAGAMIE COUNTY			Kaukauna, city		
Appleton, city			Wards 1 – 3	1,200	590
Ward 1	786	357	Wards 4 – 6	1,185	765
Ward 2	267	110	Wards 7 & 8	1,049	552
Ward 3	1,156	386	Wards 9 – 11	1,104	593
Ward 4	266	162	Wards 12, 17 & 18	80	45
Ward 5	247	196	Ward 13	136	63
Ward 6	530	430	Wards 14 – 16, 19 & 20	117	98
Ward 7	829	566	Kimberly, vil.		
Ward 8	435	228	Wards 1 – 4	1,278	722
Ward 9	571	374	Wards 5 – 8	888	564
Ward 10	434	394	Liberty	200	245
Ward 11	394	222	Little Chute, vil.		
Ward 15	417	215	Wards 1, 4, 9, 10 & 15	1,197	777
Ward 16	925	597	Wards 2, 8, 12, 13, 16 – 19	328	190
Ward 17	367	456	Ward 3	45	42
Ward 18	690	509	Wards 5 & 11	490	357
Ward 19	645	454	Wards 6 & 7	1,114	739
Ward 20	366	220	Ward 14	2	0
Ward 21	500	89	Maine	224	185
Ward 22	753	520	Maple Creek	157	149
Ward 23	554	385	New London, city		
Ward 24	838	490	Wards 1 & 2	390	260
Ward 25	487	244	Nichols, vil.	54	60
Ward 26	460	177	Oneida		
Ward 27	302	192	Wards 1 – 5	1,201	740
Ward 28	621	385	Osborn		
Ward 29	837	569	Wards 1 & 2	308	284
Ward 30	424	372	Seymour		
Ward 31	521	749	Wards 1 & 2	251	318
Ward 32	475	595	Seymour, city		
Ward 33	728	854	Wards 1 – 6	894	744
Ward 34	155	109	Shiocton, vil.	278	124
Ward 35	385	316	Vandenbroek		
Ward 36	435	351	Wards 1 & 2	425	385
Ward 37	235	178	Wrightstown, vil.		
Ward 50	0	0	Ward 3	47	49
Ward 51	0	0	TOTAL	50,294	39,677
Ward 52	2	2	**OZAUKEE COUNTY**		
Ward 53	0	3	Bayside, vil.		
Ward 54	12	17	Ward 6	53	26
Ward 55	24	37	Belgium		
Ward 56	0	0	Wards 1 – 3	287	563
Ward 57	2	6	Belgium, vil.		
Ward 58	0	2	Wards 1 & 2	459	730
Ward 59	0	0	Cedarburg		
Ward 60	0	0	Wards 1, 2 & 10	260	591
Ward 61	0	0	Wards 3 & 4	304	597
Ward 62	0	0	Wards 5 & 6	311	794
Ward 63	0	0	Wards 7 – 9	329	693
Bear Creek, vil.	96	48	Cedarburg, city		
Black Creek			Wards 1 & 2	337	610
Wards 1 & 2	291	321	Wards 3 & 4	378	743
Black Creek, vil.			Wards 5 & 6	487	532
Wards 1 & 2	327	256	Wards 7 & 8	365	466
Bovina			Wards 9 & 10	459	593
Wards 1 & 2	339	253	Wards 11 & 12	400	586
Buchanan			Wards 13 & 14	388	633
Wards 1 – 5 & 10	1,222	1,172	Fredonia		
Wards 6 – 9	676	588	Wards 1 – 3	383	872
Center			Fredonia, vil.		
Wards 1 – 5	839	1128	Wards 1 – 4	413	799
Cicero			Grafton		
Wards 1 & 2	277	234	Wards 1, 2 & 6	418	921
Combined Locks, vil.			Wards 3 – 5 & 7	491	861
Wards 1 – 4	1,025	781	Grafton, vil.		
Dale			Ward 1	200	245
Wards 1 – 4	687	790	Ward 2	134	284
Deer Creek			Ward 3	160	239
Wards 1 & 2	154	143	Ward 4	208	301
Ellington			Ward 5	453	607
Wards 1 – 4	655	801	Ward 6	191	334
Freedom			Ward 7	181	254
Wards 1 – 7	1,632	1,408	Ward 8	249	419
Grand Chute			Ward 9	127	231
Wards 1, 6 – 8	1,857	1,780	Ward 10 & 11	371	532
Wards 2 – 5	1,679	1,478	Ward 12	195	351
Wards 9 & 11	1,060	811	Ward 13	248	387
Wards 10, 12 & 13	1,070	1,233	Mequon, city		
Greenville			Wards 1, 6 & 20	754	953
Wards 1 – 8	2,386	2,923	Ward 2	183	454

VOTE FOR PRESIDENT AND VICE PRESIDENT BY WARD
November 4, 2008 General Election–Continued

District	Barack Obama Joe Biden (Dem.)	John McCain Sarah Palin (Rep.)
Wards 3 – 5	685	1,341
Ward 7	354	553
Wards 8, 9, 18 & 21	989	1,541
Wards 10 & 11	678	1,051
Wards 12 & 13	744	1,022
Wards 14 & 15	772	1,066
Wards 16, 17 & 19	637	998
Newburg, vil.		
Ward 3	10	32
Port Washington		
Wards 1 & 2	353	558
Port Washington, city		
Ward 1	396	521
Wards 2 & 3	391	408
Wards 4 & 5	404	447
Ward 6	370	452
Wards 7 & 8	537	664
Wards 9 & 10	403	457
Ward 11	442	448
Saukville		
Ward 1	113	228
Wards 2 – 5	260	592
Saukville, vil.		
Wards 1, 6 & 7	385	623
Wards 2 & 5	293	378
Wards 3, 4 & 8	286	368
Thiensville, vil.		
Wards 1 & 2	385	681
Wards 3 & 4	516	542
TOTAL	20,579	32,172
PEPIN COUNTY		
Albany	175	122
Durand		
Wards 1 & 2	168	187
Durand, city		
Wards 1 – 3	486	455
Frankfort		
Wards 1 & 2	119	62
Lima		
Wards 1 & 2	168	135
Pepin		
Wards 1 & 2	222	143
Pepin, vil.		
Wards 1 & 2	331	152
Stockholm	66	64
Stockholm, vil.	35	14
Waterville		
Wards 1 & 2	226	170
Waubeek	106	112
TOTAL	2,102	1,616
PIERCE COUNTY		
Bay City, vil.	114	77
Clifton		
Wards 1 & 2	564	627
Diamond Bluff	136	142
Ellsworth		
Wards 1 & 2	311	341
Ellsworth, vil.		
Wards 1 – 4	794	669
Elmwood, vil.	258	157
El Paso		
Wards 1 & 2	203	166
Gilman	281	235
Hartland	182	272
Isabelle	68	75
Maiden Rock	160	164
Maiden Rock, vil.	40	21
Martell		
Wards 1 & 2	326	345
Oak Grove		
Wards 1 & 2	507	640
Plum City, vil.	148	142
Prescott, city		
Wards 1 – 4	1,113	1,005
River Falls		
Wards 1 – 3	796	666
River Falls, city		
Wards 3 & 4	423	267
Wards 5 – 7	1,033	590
Wards 8 – 10	1,336	752
Wards 11 & 12	1,110	679
Rock Elm	137	114
Salem		
Wards 1 & 2	142	132
Spring Lake		
Wards 1 & 2	171	133
Spring Valley, vil.		
Wards 1 & 2	376	251

District	Barack Obama Joe Biden (Dem.)	John McCain Sarah Palin (Rep.)
Trenton		
Wards 1 & 2	491	490
Trimbelle		
Wards 1 & 2	442	492
Union	141	168
TOTAL	11,803	9,812
POLK COUNTY		
Alden		
Wards 1 – 3	675	820
Amery, city		
Wards 1 – 5	737	676
Apple River		
Wards 1 & 2	282	332
Balsam Lake		
Wards 1 & 2	342	436
Balsam Lake, vil.	280	223
Beaver	201	189
Black Brook		
Wards 1 & 2	288	379
Bone Lake	207	178
Centuria, vil.	169	172
Clam Falls	151	122
Clayton	264	231
Clayton, vil.	97	94
Clear Lake		
Wards 1 & 2	197	214
Clear Lake, vil.		
Wards 1 – 3	263	219
Dresser, vil.	179	224
Eureka		
Wards 1 & 2	371	464
Farmington		
Wards 1 & 2	409	547
Frederic, vil.		
Wards 1 & 2	307	237
Garfield		
Wards 1 – 3	402	454
Georgetown		
Wards 1 & 2	338	217
Johnstown	155	108
Laketown	258	246
Lincoln		
Wards 1 – 4	571	670
Lorain	71	78
Luck		
Wards 1 & 2	255	225
Luck, vil.		
Wards 1 & 2	295	242
McKinley	80	113
Milltown		
Wards 1 & 2	315	293
Milltown, vil.	214	157
Osceola		
Wards 1 – 4	658	864
Osceola, vil.		
Wards 1 – 4	587	563
St. Croix Falls		
Wards 1 & 2	293	373
St. Croix Falls, city		
Wards 1 – 3	619	542
Sterling	158	184
Turtle Lake, vil.		
Ward 2	22	9
West Sweden		
Wards 1 & 2	166	187
TOTAL	10,876	11,282
PORTAGE COUNTY		
Alban	302	155
Almond	193	182
Almond, vil.	113	81
Amherst		
Wards 1 & 2	450	333
Amherst, vil.	351	187
Amherst Junction, vil.	128	67
Belmont	188	150
Buena Vista		
Wards 1 & 2	369	264
Carson		
Wards 1 & 2	444	327
Dewey	343	208
Eau Pleine	289	197
Grant		
Wards 1 & 2	431	341
Ward 3	188	168
Hull		
Wards 1 – 8	1,921	1,242
Junction City, vil.	147	58
Lanark		
Wards 1 & 2	472	347

VOTE FOR PRESIDENT AND VICE PRESIDENT BY WARD
November 4, 2008 General Election–Continued

District	Barack Obama Joe Biden (Dem.)	John McCain Sarah Palin (Rep.)
Linwood		
Wards 1 & 2	432	223
Milladore, vil.		
Ward 2	3	1
Nelsonville, vil.	59	30
New Hope	335	139
Park Ridge, vil.	194	133
Pine Grove		
Wards 1 & 2	240	161
Plover		
Wards 1 & 4	270	263
Ward 2	155	127
Plover, vil.		
Wards 1 – 9	3,707	2,398
Ward 10	9	0
Rosholt, vil.	149	79
Sharon		
Wards 1 – 3	740	424
Stevens Point, city		
Wards 1 & 2	886	330
Wards 3 & 4	970	464
Wards 5 & 6	1,120	452
Wards 7 & 8	818	273
Wards 9 & 10	784	272
Wards 11 & 12	1,138	709
Wards 13 & 14	1,075	465
Wards 15 & 16	963	500
Wards 17 & 18	824	316
Wards 19 & 20	846	345
Wards 21 & 22	1,000	437
Wards 23 – 25	3	1
Wards 26 – 30	7	3
Wards 31 – 36	9	6
Wards 37 – 40	40	29
Stockton		
Wards 1 – 4	1,035	634
Whiting, vil.		
Wards 1 – 4	677	289
TOTAL	24,817	13,810
PRICE COUNTY		
Catawba	82	52
Catawba, vil.	40	11
Eisenstein		
Wards 1 & 2	233	176
Elk		
Wards 1 – 3	348	305
Emery	110	58
Fifield		
Ward 1	170	104
Ward 2	175	142
Flambeau	163	122
Georgetown	50	40
Hackett		
Wards 1 & 2	59	49
Harmony	75	54
Hill	85	107
Kennan	122	54
Kennan, vil.	46	23
Knox		
Wards 1 & 2	108	81
Lake		
Wards 1 & 2	440	257
Ogema		
Wards 1 & 2	191	177
Park Falls, city		
Wards 1 – 7	785	505
Phillips, city		
Wards 1 – 5	416	266
Prentice		
Wards 1 & 2	104	147
Prentice, vil.	160	137
Spirit	79	88
Worcester		
Wards 1, 3 & 4	338	322
Ward 2	180	184
TOTAL	4,559	3,461
RACINE COUNTY		
Burlington		
Wards 1 – 8	753	1,277
Wards 9 – 12	659	785
Burlington, city		
Wards 1 – 8	1,157	1,071
Wards 9 – 16	1,267	1,596
Caledonia, vil.		
Wards 1 – 3	924	1,396
Wards 4, 20 & 21	695	1,035
Wards 5, 6 & 18	1,010	1,158
Wards 7 – 9 & 19	1,369	1,075

District	Barack Obama Joe Biden (Dem.)	John McCain Sarah Palin (Rep.)
Wards 10 – 12, 16 & 17	1,839	2,113
Wards 13 – 15	992	1,060
Dover		
Wards 1 – 8	787	1,163
Elmwood Park, vil.	157	171
Mount Pleasant, vil.		
Wards 1, 2 & 16	1,176	862
Wards 3 – 5 & 7	1,247	1,043
Ward 6	446	362
Wards 8 & 9	871	1,083
Wards 10 – 12	1,380	1,230
Wards 13 & 15	511	595
Ward 14	272	323
Wards 17, 18 & 20	980	873
Wards 19, 21 & 23	907	832
Ward 22	284	159
North Bay, vil.	83	93
Norway		
Wards 1 – 11	1,519	3,073
Racine, city		
Ward 1	166	80
Ward 2	834	135
Ward 3	582	52
Ward 4	592	17
Ward 5	335	79
Ward 6	758	278
Ward 7	732	105
Ward 8	908	164
Ward 9	592	133
Ward 10	409	134
Ward 11	487	18
Ward 12	306	143
Ward 13	332	180
Ward 14	896	479
Ward 15	847	429
Ward 16	769	367
Ward 17	732	251
Ward 18	880	594
Ward 19	623	78
Ward 20	712	38
Ward 21	846	341
Ward 22	825	485
Ward 23	979	493
Ward 24	966	448
Ward 25	813	504
Ward 26	877	273
Ward 27	975	682
Ward 28	811	654
Ward 29	818	468
Ward 30	815	307
Ward 31	790	405
Ward 32	886	312
Ward 33	836	416
Ward 34	851	630
Raymond		
Wards 1 – 5	875	1,445
Rochester		
Wards 1 – 5	547	963
Rochester, vil.		
Wards 1 & 2	204	365
Sturtevant, vil.		
Wards 1 – 6	1,447	1,260
Union Grove, vil.		
Wards 1 – 7	956	1,458
Waterford		
Wards 1 – 10	1,156	2,440
Waterford, vil.		
Wards 1 – 7	1,136	1,649
Wind Point, vil.		
Wards 1 – 3	557	736
Yorkville		
Wards 1 – 5	665	1,038
TOTAL	53,408	45,954
RICHLAND COUNTY		
Akan	125	96
Bloom	125	99
Boaz, vil.	57	5
Buena Vista		
Wards 1 & 2	483	262
Cazenovia, vil.		
Ward 1	116	35
Dayton	176	155
Eagle	118	113
Forest	99	72
Henrietta	178	88
Ithaca	214	127
Lone Rock, vil.		
Wards 1 & 2	245	113

VOTE FOR PRESIDENT AND VICE PRESIDENT BY WARD
November 4, 2008 General Election–Continued

District	Barack Obama Joe Biden (Dem.)	John McCain Sarah Palin (Rep.)
Marshall	134	157
Orion	171	108
Richland		
Wards 1 – 4	338	336
Richland Center, city		
Ward 1	148	80
Ward 2	128	68
Ward 3	115	82
Ward 4	87	45
Ward 5	117	99
Ward 6	124	83
Ward 7	119	68
Ward 8	125	78
Ward 9	108	92
Ward 10	169	84
Ward 11	111	72
Ward 12	128	79
Richwood		
Wards 1 & 2	157	77
Rockbridge		
Wards 1 – 3	241	149
Sylvan		
Wards 1 – 4	118	95
Viola, vil.		
Ward 2	128	62
Westford		
Wards 1 & 2	162	96
Willow	147	110
Yuba, vil.	30	13
TOTAL	5,041	3,298
ROCK COUNTY		
Avon	169	150
Beloit		
Wards 1 – 3	682	587
Wards 4 & 5	557	262
Wards 6 – 9	1,014	1,030
Beloit, city		
Ward 1	366	166
Ward 2	424	299
Ward 3	481	270
Ward 4	475	272
Ward 5	546	314
Ward 6	383	151
Ward 7	467	185
Ward 8	329	178
Ward 9	361	103
Ward 10	451	150
Ward 11	221	37
Ward 12	414	78
Ward 13	583	123
Ward 14	460	33
Ward 15	902	99
Ward 16	473	155
Ward 17	272	104
Ward 18	285	135
Ward 19	525	214
Ward 20	496	274
Ward 21	461	277
Ward 22	393	350
Ward 23	511	448
Ward 24	259	196
Bradford	242	284
Brodhead, city		
Ward 7	16	13
Ward 8	0	0
Center	417	210
Clinton	202	285
Clinton, vil.		
Wards 1 – 3	548	455
Edgerton, city		
Wards 1 – 6	1,877	741
Evansville, city		
Wards 1 – 8	1,763	755
Footville, vil.	257	118
Fulton		
Wards 1 – 4	1,186	740
Harmony		
Wards 1 – 5	784	630
Janesville		
Wards 1 – 5	1,227	833
Ward 6	8	3
Janesville, city		
Ward 1	863	496
Ward 2	854	328
Ward 3	763	353
Ward 4	807	344
Ward 5	1,661	1,195
Ward 6	717	447
Ward 7	1,026	514

District	Barack Obama Joe Biden (Dem.)	John McCain Sarah Palin (Rep.)
Ward 8	844	413
Ward 9	752	299
Ward 10	893	554
Ward 11	843	604
Ward 12	891	559
Ward 13	973	465
Ward 14	743	311
Ward 15	684	187
Ward 16	641	203
Ward 17	882	333
Ward 18	917	440
Ward 19	824	389
Ward 20	951	348
Ward 21	944	318
Ward 22	755	237
Ward 23	753	325
Ward 24	820	534
Ward 25	7	3
Ward 26	78	38
Ward 27	37	14
Ward 28	1	0
Ward 29	5	4
Ward 30	1	3
Ward 31	8	3
Ward 32	0	0
Johnstown	275	167
La Prairie		
Ward 1	260	212
Lima		
Wards 1 & 2	341	254
Magnolia	260	140
Milton		
Wards 1 – 5	932	638
Milton, city		
Wards 1 – 8	1,828	1,006
Newark		
Wards 1 & 2	440	450
Orfordville, vil.		
Wards 1 & 2	424	239
Plymouth		
Wards 1 & 2	448	260
Porter	378	205
Rock		
Wards 1 – 7	888	519
Spring Valley	232	164
Turtle		
Wards 1 & 4	194	204
Wards 2 & 3	476	569
Union		
Wards 1 & 2	728	369
TOTAL	50,529	27,364
RUSK COUNTY		
Atlanta	161	156
Big Bend	151	112
Big Falls	44	43
Bruce, vil.		
Wards 1 & 2	170	173
Cedar Rapids	12	14
Conrath, vil.	23	16
Dewey	149	155
Flambeau		
Wards 1 – 3	258	253
Glen Flora, vil.	15	12
Grant		
Wards 1 & 2	191	154
Grow	79	128
Hawkins	54	40
Hawkins, vil.	109	48
Hubbard	59	47
Ingram, vil.	32	7
Ladysmith, city		
Wards 1 – 14	883	592
Lawrence	41	80
Marshall		
Wards 1 & 2	93	127
Murry	71	63
Richland		
Wards 1 & 2	66	38
Rusk		
Wards 1 & 2	186	150
Sheldon, vil.	61	49
South Fork	41	31
Strickland	94	68
Stubbs	199	122
Thornapple		
Wards 1 & 2	166	215
Tony, vil.	33	15
True	69	74
Washington	88	89

VOTE FOR PRESIDENT AND VICE PRESIDENT BY WARD
November 4, 2008 General Election–Continued

District	Barack Obama Joe Biden (Dem.)	John McCain Sarah Palin (Rep.)
Weyerhaeuser, vil.		
Wards 1 & 2	98	34
Wilkinson	17	17
Willard	109	107
Wilson	33	24
TOTAL	3,855	3,253
ST. CROIX COUNTY		
Baldwin	226	327
Baldwin, vil.		
Wards 1 – 5	917	877
Cady	190	251
Cylon	165	176
Deer Park, vil.	46	65
Eau Galle		
Wards 1 & 2	278	353
Emerald		
Wards 1 & 2	197	183
Erin Prairie	157	220
Forest	134	171
Glenwood	183	227
Glenwood City, city		
Wards 1 & 2	297	256
Hammond	426	668
Hammond, vil.		
Wards 1 & 2	501	421
Hudson		
Wards 1 – 11	1,982	2,700
Hudson, city		
Wards 1 – 3, 11 & 12	935	735
Wards 4, 5, 13 & 14	1,635	1,501
Wards 6 – 10	1,137	998
Kinnickinnic		
Wards 1 – 3	480	521
New Richmond, city		
Wards 1 – 6	944	793
Wards 7 – 13	1,122	1,061
North Hudson, city		
Wards 1 – 6	1,078	1,077
Pleasant Valley	125	146
Richmond		
Wards 1 – 3	732	880
River Falls, city		
Wards 1 & 2	912	684
Ward 13	76	74
Roberts, vil.		
Wards 1 – 3	447	394
Rush River	121	123
St. Joseph		
Wards 1 – 7	1,045	1,261
Somerset		
Wards 1, 3 – 5	713	985
Ward 2	99	184
Somerset, vil.		
Wards 1 – 3	515	564
Spring Valley, vil.		
Ward 3	2	2
Springfield	253	220
Stanton		
Wards 1 & 2	252	282
Star Prairie		
Wards 1 – 5	775	907
Star Prairie, vil.	151	154
Troy		
Wards 1 – 7	1,202	1,521
Warren		
Wards 1 & 2	381	511
Wilson, vil.	55	53
Woodville, vil.		
Wards 1 & 2	291	311
TOTAL	21,177	22,837
SAUK COUNTY		
Baraboo		
Wards 1 – 4	579	464
Baraboo, city		
Ward 1	187	79
Ward 2	226	117
Ward 3	403	166
Ward 4	182	96
Ward 5	324	155
Ward 6	325	158
Ward 7	324	145
Ward 8	154	101
Ward 9	170	92
Ward 10	374	254
Ward 11	237	160
Ward 12	286	231
Ward 13	172	128
Ward 14	185	97

District	Barack Obama Joe Biden (Dem.)	John McCain Sarah Palin (Rep.)
Bear Creek	243	104
Cazenovia, vil.		
Ward 2	5	4
Dellona		
Wards 1 & 2	459	322
Delton		
Wards 1 – 4	672	430
Excelsior		
Wards 1 – 3	510	371
Fairfield		
Wards 1 & 2	404	232
Franklin		
Wards 1 – 3	213	148
Freedom	125	137
Greenfield	361	232
Honey Creek	241	163
Ironton	153	131
Ironton, vil.	67	28
Lake Delton, vil.		
Wards 1 – 3	678	424
La Valle		
Wards 1 & 2	373	323
La Valle, vil.	124	66
Lime Ridge, vil.	65	22
Loganville, vil.	89	52
Merrimac	337	258
Merrimac, vil.	139	107
North Freedom, vil.	192	131
Plain, vil.	245	178
Prairie du Sac		
Wards 1 – 3	391	279
Prairie du Sac, vil.		
Wards 1 – 5	1,327	725
Reedsburg		
Wards 1 – 4	322	270
Reedsburg, city		
Wards 1 – 3 & 13	555	333
Wards 4, 6, 11 & 14	680	507
Wards 5, 9, 12 & 16	431	262
Wards 7, 8, 10 & 15	714	483
Rock Springs	84	72
Sauk City, vil.		
Wards 1 – 4	1,181	539
Spring Green		
Wards 1 – 4	692	339
Spring Green, vil.		
Wards 1 & 2	628	259
Sumpter		
Wards 1 – 3	241	138
Troy	276	157
Washington	226	179
West Baraboo, vil.		
Wards 1 & 2	410	221
Westfield		
Wards 1 & 2	167	134
Winfield		
Wards 1 & 2	251	179
Wisconsin Dells, city		
Ward 4	36	25
Woodland	182	155
TOTAL	18,617	11,562
SAWYER COUNTY		
Bass Lake		
Wards 1 – 4	764	455
Couderay		
Wards 1 & 2	108	47
Couderay, vil.	33	17
Draper	72	57
Edgewater	165	212
Exeland, vil.	50	37
Hayward		
Wards 1 – 6	883	813
Hayward, city		
Wards 1 – 4	592	438
Hunter		
Wards 1 & 2	229	195
Lenroot		
Wards 1 – 3	371	416
Meadowbrook	32	40
Meteor	38	41
Ojibwa	69	76
Radisson		
Wards 1 & 2	96	115
Radisson, vil.	54	37
Round Lake		
Wards 1 & 2	320	346
Sand Lake	272	238
Spider Lake	127	160
Weirgor	70	113

VOTE FOR PRESIDENT AND VICE PRESIDENT BY WARD
November 4, 2008 General Election–Continued

District	Barack Obama Joe Biden (Dem.)	John McCain Sarah Palin (Rep.)
Winter		
Wards 1 & 2	321	300
Winter, vil.	99	46
TOTAL	4,765	4,199
SHAWANO COUNTY		
Almon		
Wards 1 & 2	140	121
Angelica		
Wards 1 – 3	414	451
Aniwa	94	143
Aniwa, vil.	60	51
Bartelme	310	60
Belle Plaine		
Wards 1 – 3	420	511
Birnamwood		
Wards 1 & 2	188	161
Birnamwood, vil.		
Ward 1	207	130
Bonduel, vil.		
Wards 1 & 2	285	388
Bowler, vil.	86	36
Cecil, vil.	150	137
Eland, vil.	98	41
Fairbanks		
Wards 1 & 2	130	183
Germania	117	65
Grant		
Wards 1 & 2	208	265
Green Valley		
Wards 1 & 2	258	250
Gresham, vil.	122	126
Hartland	151	247
Herman		
Wards 1 & 2	170	221
Hutchins	113	175
Lessor		
Wards 1 & 2	306	304
Maple Grove		
Wards 1 & 2	231	239
Marion, city		
Wards 4 – 6	6	4
Mattoon, vil.	92	77
Morris		
Wards 1 & 2	122	109
Navarino	124	115
Pella	217	249
Pulaski, vil.		
Wards 4 & 7	32	40
Red Springs	316	146
Richmond		
Wards 1 – 3	455	577
Seneca	145	136
Shawano, city		
Wards 1 & 2	363	325
Wards 3 & 4	308	267
Wards 5 & 6	316	238
Wards 7 & 8	318	204
Wards 9 & 10	470	375
Wards 11 & 12	410	323
Tigerton, vil.	175	147
Washington		
Wards 1 & 2	513	515
Waukechon		
Wards 1 & 2	217	251
Wescott		
Wards 1 – 5	927	764
Wittenberg		
Wards 1 & 2	217	205
Wittenberg, vil.		
Wards 1 & 2	258	166
TOTAL	10,259	9,538
SHEBOYGAN COUNTY		
Adell, vil.	94	183
Cascade, vil..	192	198
Cedar Grove, vil.		
Wards 1 & 2	277	910
Elkhart Lake, vil.		
Wards 1 – 3	316	340
Glenbeulah, vil.	175	108
Greenbush		
Wards 1 – 4	422	491
Herman		
Wards 1 – 3	580	598
Holland		
Wards 1 – 4	368	1,063
Howards Grove, vil.		
Wards 1 – 3	905	958
Kohler, vil.		
Wards 1 – 3	546	781
Lima		
Wards 1 – 4	534	1,200
Lyndon		
Wards 1 & 2	310	558
Mitchell		
Wards 1 & 2	265	420
Mosel	220	257
Oostburg, vil.		
Wards 1 – 4	345	1,456
Plymouth		
Wards 1 – 4	809	1,061
Plymouth, city		
Wards 1 – 3	518	456
Wards 4 & 5	536	489
Wards 6 – 8	773	779
Wards 9 & 10	496	553
Random Lake, vil.		
Wards 1 & 2	332	561
Rhine		
Wards 1 – 3	643	724
Russell	80	146
Scott		
Wards 1 & 2	319	689
Sheboygan		
Wards 1, 3 & 4	822	990
Ward 2	341	259
Wards 5 – 7	1,011	1,058
Sheboygan, city		
Ward 1	875	625
Ward 2	881	724
Ward 3	710	396
Ward 4	816	382
Ward 5	686	243
Ward 6	824	665
Ward 7	804	464
Ward 8	1,060	710
Ward 9	930	700
Ward 10	947	536
Ward 11	957	498
Ward 12	795	500
Ward 13	1,127	847
Ward 14	1,012	695
Ward 15	904	484
Ward 16	717	299
Ward 17	0	0
Ward 18	2	2
Ward 19	0	1
Ward 20	2	4
Ward 21	10	7
Ward 22	0	2
Ward 23	0	0
Ward 25	0	0
Sheboygan Falls		
Wards 1 & 2	416	583
Sheboygan Falls, city		
Wards 1, 2 & 9	970	1,007
Wards 3 & 4	590	495
Wards 5 – 8	673	518
Ward 10	97	90
Sherman		
Wards 1 & 2	295	596
Waldo, vil.	99	175
Wilson		
Wards 1 – 4	965	1,267
TOTAL	30,395	30,801
TAYLOR COUNTY		
Aurora	80	79
Browning		
Wards 1 & 2	169	216
Chelsea	158	174
Cleveland	44	81
Deer Creek		
Wards 1 & 2	129	202
Ford	68	66
Gilman, vil.	104	99
Goodrich	91	144
Greenwood	169	139
Grover	47	69
Hammel		
Wards 1 & 2	176	184
Holway	125	107
Jump River	69	59
Little Black		
Wards 1 & 2	290	248
Lublin, vil.	40	28
Maplehurst		
Wards 1 & 2	84	75
McKinley	64	99

VOTE FOR PRESIDENT AND VICE PRESIDENT BY WARD
November 4, 2008 General Election–Continued

District	Barack Obama Joe Biden (Dem.)	John McCain Sarah Palin (Rep.)
Medford		
Wards 1 – 3	508	663
Medford, city		
Wards 1 – 8	1,065	920
Molitor	80	85
Pershing	63	16
Rib Lake		
Wards 1 & 2	193	227
Rib Lake, vil.	213	154
Roosevelt	112	60
Stetsonville, vil.	146	112
Taft	86	82
Westboro	190	198
TOTAL	4,563	4,586
TREMPEALEAU COUNTY		
Albion		
Wards 1 & 2	187	94
Arcadia		
Wards 1 – 3	461	315
Arcadia, city		
Wards 1 – 3	567	299
Blair, city		
Wards 1 – 3	352	135
Burnside		
Wards 1 & 2	168	52
Caledonia	288	206
Chimney Rock	82	44
Dodge	155	88
Eleva, vil.	213	89
Ettrick		
Wards 1 & 2	436	232
Ettrick, vil.	148	91
Gale		
Wards 1 & 2	475	379
Galesville, city		
Wards 1 – 4	449	302
Hale		
Wards 1 – 3	302	185
Independence, city		
Wards 1 – 3	374	160
Lincoln		
Wards 1 & 2	216	105
Osseo, city		
Wards 1 – 4	509	290
Pigeon		
Wards 1 & 2	223	135
Pigeon Falls, vil.	155	61
Preston		
Wards 1 – 3	252	154
Strum, vil.		
Wards 1 & 2	400	153
Sumner	246	196
Trempealeau		
Wards 1 – 3	540	384
Trempealeau, vil.		
Wards 1 & 2	501	313
Unity		
Wards 1 & 2	172	96
Whitehall, city		
Wards 1 – 4	450	250
TOTAL	8,321	4,808
VERNON COUNTY		
Bergen		
Wards 1 – 3	433	316
Chaseburg, vil.	75	66
Christiana		
Wards 1 & 2	274	175
Clinton		
Wards 1 & 2	148	111
Coon		
Wards 1 & 2	262	160
Coon Valley, vil.	257	160
De Soto, vil.		
Ward 1	66	60
Forest	144	104
Franklin	224	284
Genoa		
Wards 1 & 2	259	129
Genoa, vil.	97	50
Greenwood	100	81
Hamburg		
Wards 1 & 2	287	218
Harmony	178	135
Hillsboro		
Wards 1 & 2	196	141
Hillsboro, city		
Wards 1 – 4	362	233

District	Barack Obama Joe Biden (Dem.)	John McCain Sarah Palin (Rep.)
Jefferson		
Wards 1 – 4	367	216
Kickapoo	194	81
La Farge, vil.	257	106
Liberty	76	55
Ontario, vil.	111	76
Readstown, vil.	130	66
Stark		
Wards 1 & 2	115	73
Sterling	152	163
Stoddard, vil.	299	129
Union		
Wards 1 & 2	117	92
Viola, vil.		
Ward 1	52	45
Viroqua		
Wards 1 – 4	525	363
Viroqua, city		
Wards 1 – 9	1,452	830
Webster	209	116
Westby, city		
Wards 1 – 5	761	349
Wheatland	169	92
Whitestown	115	92
TOTAL	8,463	5,367
VILAS COUNTY		
Arbor Vitae		
Wards 1 – 4	954	1,046
Boulder Junction		
Wards 1 & 2	315	416
Cloverland	289	401
Conover		
Wards 1 – 3	372	425
Eagle River, city		
Wards 1 – 5	314	333
Lac du Flambeau		
Wards 1 – 3	1,044	501
Land O'Lakes	262	338
Lincoln		
Wards 1 – 4	728	829
Manitowish Waters	212	297
Phelps		
Wards 1 & 2	361	443
Plum Lake		
Wards 1 & 2	176	189
Presque Isle	246	320
St. Germain		
Wards 1 & 2	599	794
Washington		
Wards 1 – 3	486	531
Winchester	133	192
TOTAL	6,491	7,055
WALWORTH COUNTY		
Bloomfield		
Wards 1 – 7	1,262	1,172
Burlington, city		
Ward 17	0	0
Darien		
Wards 1 – 6	368	460
Darien, vil.		
Wards 1 & 2	338	287
Delavan		
Wards 1 – 6	1,200	1,412
Delavan, city		
Wards 1 – 12	1,868	1,459
East Troy		
Wards 1 – 7	835	1,613
East Troy, vil.		
Wards 1 – 7	893	1,340
Elkhorn, city		
Wards 1 & 6	303	303
Wards 2 & 3	265	177
Wards 4, 5 & 15	429	421
Wards 7 & 8	374	408
Wards 9 & 11	418	439
Wards 10, 12 & 13	425	387
Wards 14, 16 – 18	15	6
Fontana, vil.		
Wards 1 – 4	397	554
Geneva		
Wards 1 – 8	1,136	1,288
Geneva City, vil.		
Wards 1 – 3	646	595
Lafayette		
Wards 1 – 4	439	759
La Grange		
Wards 1 – 3	554	796

VOTE FOR PRESIDENT AND VICE PRESIDENT BY WARD
November 4, 2008 General Election–Continued

District	Barack Obama Joe Biden (Dem.)	John McCain Sarah Palin (Rep.)
Lake Geneva, city		
Wards 1, 2, 12 & 18	507	350
Wards 3, 4, 11, 16 & 24 . .	357	311
Wards 5, 6, 9, 10, 13, 14,		
17, 19 – 23	589	444
Wards 7, 8 & 15	360	297
Linn		
Wards 1, 2 & 4	423	548
Wards 3 & 5	115	136
Lyons		
Wards 1 – 6	826	1,066
Mukwonago, vil.		
Ward 9	25	23
Richmond		
Wards 1 – 3	497	490
Sharon.	202	260
Sharon, vil.		
Wards 1 & 2	362	294
Spring Prairie		
Wards 1 – 4	442	801
Sugar Creek		
Wards 1 – 5	997	1,166
Troy		
Wards 1 – 3	566	876
Walworth		
Wards 1 – 4	350	539
Walworth, vil.		
Wards 1 – 3	559	627
Whitewater		
Wards 1 – 4	384	442
Whitewater, city		
Wards 1 & 2	999	625
Wards 3 & 4	804	451
Wards 5 & 6	954	548
Wards 7 & 8	1,097	499
Wards 12, 16 & 18.	5	3
Wards 13, 17 & 19. . . .	0	0
Williams Bay, vil.		
Wards 1 – 4	592	813
TOTAL	24,177	25,485
WASHBURN COUNTY		
Barronett		
Wards 1 & 2	131	103
Bashaw		
Wards 1 – 3	273	307
Bass Lake	103	159
Beaver Brook		
Wards 1 – 3	192	192
Birchwood		
Wards 1 & 2	143	199
Birchwood, vil.	137	108
Brooklyn	93	74
Casey	144	166
Chicog		
Wards 1 & 2	108	66
Crystal		
Wards 1 & 2	74	88
Evergreen		
Wards 1 & 2	322	302
Frog Creek	47	33
Gull Lake	63	47
Long Lake.	249	183
Madge		
Wards 1 – 3	188	156
Minong		
Wards 1 & 2	290	255
Minong, vil.	142	80
Sarona.	103	99
Shell Lake, city		
Wards 1 & 2	425	326
Spooner		
Wards 1 – 3	199	214
Spooner, city		
Wards 1 – 4	692	546
Springbrook.	126	126
Stinnett	52	67
Stone Lake	126	152
Trego		
Wards 1 – 3	271	255
TOTAL	4,693	4,303
WASHINGTON COUNTY		
Addison		
Wards 1 – 6	561	1,414
Barton		
Wards 1 – 4	541	1,071
Erin		
Wards 1 – 4	713	1,706
Farmington		
Wards 1 – 4	614	1,513

District	Barack Obama Joe Biden (Dem.)	John McCain Sarah Palin (Rep.)
Germantown	41	111
Germantown, vil.		
Wards 1, 7, 15 – 17	1,157	2,493
Wards 2, 4 – 6	1,126	1,477
Wards 3, 8 – 10 & 18 . . .	1,032	1,758
Wards 11 – 14	919	1,782
Hartford		
Wards 1 – 4 & 6	521	1,061
Ward 5	175	334
Hartford, city		
Wards 1 – 8, 18, 24, 25,		
29, 32, 36 & 37	1,121	1,687
Wards 9 – 11, 23, 31,		
38 & 42	796	1,154
Wards 12 – 15, 17, 19 – 22,		
26 – 28, 30, 33 – 35,		
40 & 41	910	1,242
Jackson		
Wards 1 – 5	638	1,918
Jackson, vil.		
Wards 1 – 12.	1,205	2,300
Kewaskum		
Wards 1 & 2	193	459
Kewaskum, vil.		
Wards 1 – 4 & 6	762	1,276
Milwaukee, city		
Ward 262.	0	0
Newburg, vil.		
Wards 1 & 2	191	387
Polk		
Wards 1 – 4, 6 & 7.	586	1,408
Ward 5	104	331
Richfield, vil.		
Ward 1	271	705
Wards 2 – 4	468	1,137
Ward 5	143	310
Wards 6, 12 & 13	446	1,104
Ward 7 & 11	289	692
Ward 8	180	556
Wards 9 & 10	292	662
Slinger		
Wards 1 – 8 & 10	936	1,539
Ward 9	10	95
Trenton		
Wards 1, 2, 5 – 7	668	1,520
Wards 3 & 4	197	425
Wayne		
Wards 1 – 3	332	834
West Bend		
Wards 1 – 9	926	2,091
West Bend, city		
Wards 1 & 12	874	1,216
Wards 2, 3 & 5.	802	923
Wards 4, 11, 22 & 29 . . .	754	919
Wards 6, 7, 24, 31 & 35 . .	865	1,395
Wards 8 – 10	981	1,410
Wards 13 – 15	825	1,130
Wards 16, 18 & 21.	678	938
Wards 17, 19, 20, 23,		
25 & 26	872	1,243
Ward 27	0	0
Wards 28 & 34.	0	0
Ward 30	4	2
Ward 32	0	1
Wards 33 & 36	0	0
TOTAL	25,719	47,729
WAUKESHA COUNTY		
Big Bend, vil.		
Wards 1 – 3	256	460
Brookfield		
Wards 1 & 4	360	529
Wards 2 & 8	231	292
Wards 3 & 6	439	761
Wards 5 & 7	305	571
Wards 9 & 10	247	412
Brookfield, city		
Ward 1	404	647
Ward 2	442	749
Ward 3	444	798
Ward 4	448	762
Ward 5	403	829
Ward 6	348	826
Ward 7	289	593
Ward 8	307	573
Ward 9	350	662
Ward 10	237	561
Ward 11	415	921
Ward 12	398	774
Ward 13	325	677

VOTE FOR PRESIDENT AND VICE PRESIDENT BY WARD
November 4, 2008 General Election–Continued

District	Barack Obama Joe Biden (Dem.)	John McCain Sarah Palin (Rep.)
Ward 14	263	399
Ward 15	280	488
Ward 16	252	566
Ward 17	427	991
Ward 18	334	656
Ward 19	520	834
Ward 20	432	863
Ward 21	333	398
Ward 22	308	508
Ward 23	268	477
Ward 24	476	681
Butler, vil.		
Wards 1 – 3	441	569
Chenequa, vil..	71	307
Delafield		
Wards 1, 2, 5 & 6	521	1,307
Wards 3 & 4	263	948
Wards 7 & 8	249	651
Wards 9 – 11	421	861
Delafield, city		
Wards 1 – 7	1,519	2,638
Dousman, vil.		
Wards 1 & 2	433	773
Eagle		
Wards 1 – 4	666	1,343
Eagle, vil.		
Wards 1 & 2	347	716
Elm Grove, vil.		
Wards 1 – 4	748	1,487
Wards 5 – 8	741	1,234
Genesee		
Wards 1, 2 & 5	426	952
Wards 3 & 4	363	763
Wards 6, 9 & 10	411	885
Wards 7 & 8	356	677
Hartland, vil.		
Wards 1 – 7	1,106	1,589
Wards 8 – 13	840	1,494
Lac la Belle, vil.		
Ward 1	48	157
Lannon, vil.		
Wards 1 & 2	257	389
Lisbon		
Wards 1, 9, 10 & 12	699	1,403
Wards 2, 3 & 11	506	967
Ward 4	114	228
Wards 5 – 7	518	1,118
Ward 8	165	452
Menomonee Falls, vil.		
Wards 1 & 2	534	854
Wards 3, 9 & 10	919	1,337
Wards 4, 8 & 11	762	1,010
Wards 5, 6 & 13	782	965
Wards 7 & 12	634	971
Wards 14, 15 & 21	997	1,618
Wards 16 & 17	517	880
Wards 18, 25 & 26	671	1,295
Ward 19	264	419
Wards 20 & 22	869	1,488
Wards 23 & 29	693	980
Ward 24	183	337
Ward 27	253	391
Ward 28	288	463
Merton		
Wards 1 – 3	523	1,351
Wards 4 – 6	472	1,133
Wards 7 – 9	439	1,357
Merton, vil.		
Wards 1 – 3	425	1,295
Milwaukee, city		
Ward 274	0	0
Mukwonago		
Wards 1, 2, 4 – 10	1,259	3,040
Ward 3	141	321
Mukwonago, vil.		
Wards 1 – 8	1,417	2,458
Ward 10	0	0
Muskego, city		
Wards 1 – 3	687	1,193
Wards 4 – 6	862	1,433
Wards 7 – 9	760	1,349
Wards 10 & 11	647	1,063
Wards 12 & 13	692	1,366
Wards 14 & 15	656	1,384
Wards 16 & 17	753	1,544
Nashotah, vil.		
Wards 1 & 2	275	617
New Berlin, city		
Ward 1	388	545
Ward 2	521	784
Ward 3	454	674
Ward 4	327	292
Ward 5	561	806
Ward 6	327	343
Ward 7	249	405
Ward 8	165	267
Ward 9	404	525
Ward 10	489	671
Ward 11	223	363
Ward 12	186	365
Ward 13	378	613
Ward 14	447	928
Ward 15	376	689
Ward 16	274	444
Ward 17	245	503
Ward 18	518	743
Ward 19	408	608
Ward 20	396	733
Ward 21	399	604
Ward 22	586	780
Ward 23	318	741
Ward 24	431	693
Ward 25	231	436
Ward 26	274	451
Ward 27	5	27
Ward 28	5	8
North Prairie, vil.		
Wards 1 – 3	407	898
Oconomowoc		
Wards 1, 2 & 4	623	1,351
Wards 3, 6 & 7	582	1,100
Wards 5, 8 & 9	494	1,101
Oconomowoc, city		
Wards 1 – 3 & 21	994	1,399
Wards 4 – 6, 14 & 22	663	1,022
Wards 7 – 9, 17 – 19	756	1,137
Wards 10 – 13, 15, 16, 23 – 25	985	1,580
Ward 20	0	0
Oconomowoc Lake, vil.	94	303
Ottawa		
Wards 1 – 5	838	1,565
Pewaukee, vil.		
Wards 1 – 5	1,057	1,709
Wards 6 – 10	792	1,056
Pewaukee, city		
Wards 1 – 3	777	1,595
Wards 4 – 6	887	1,841
Ward 7	173	404
Wards 8 – 10	985	1,963
Summit		
Wards 1 – 3	487	945
Wards 4 – 6	510	1,124
Sussex, vil.		
Wards 1, 2 & 10	599	884
Wards 3, 4 & 11	622	1,031
Wards 5 – 7	472	866
Wards 8, 9, 13, 18 & 19	428	936
Wards 12, 14 – 17, 20 & 21	15	26
Vernon		
Wards 1, 6 – 10	998	2,034
Wards 2 – 5	592	1,267
Wales, vil.		
Wards 1 – 3	588	1,060
Waukesha		
Wards 1 & 4	272	534
Wards 2 & 5	334	577
Ward 3	204	395
Ward 6	210	267
Wards 7 & 8	257	644
Wards 9 & 10	336	664
Wards 11 & 12	277	639
Waukesha, city		
Ward 1	504	598
Ward 2	526	718
Ward 3	511	481
Ward 4	424	580
Ward 5	397	359
Ward 6	388	323
Ward 7	352	487
Ward 8	422	530
Ward 9	286	410
Ward 10	318	299
Ward 11	357	584
Ward 12	421	685
Ward 13	391	720
Ward 14	36	37
Ward 15	359	474

VOTE FOR PRESIDENT AND VICE PRESIDENT BY WARD
November 4, 2008 General Election–Continued

District	Barack Obama Joe Biden (Dem.)	John McCain Sarah Palin (Rep.)
Ward 16	360	366
Ward 17	459	437
Ward 18	167	201
Ward 19	392	428
Ward 20	732	446
Ward 21	489	335
Ward 22	486	316
Ward 23	218	251
Ward 24	428	458
Ward 25	523	693
Ward 26	610	801
Ward 27	490	656
Ward 28	327	360
Ward 29	323	281
Ward 30	349	278
Ward 31	383	368
Ward 32	540	728
Ward 33	530	803
Ward 34	301	382
Ward 35	291	309
Ward 36	975	1,473
Ward 37	453	519
Ward 38	505	513
Ward 39	172	318
Ward 40	0	2
Ward 41	1	0
Ward 42	4	6
Ward 43	2	5
Ward 44	2	9
Ward 45	0	0
Ward 46	35	13
Ward 47	41	48
Ward 48	4	0
Ward 49	2	7
Ward 50	0	0
Ward 51	5	3
Ward 52	1	1
Ward 53	0	0
Ward 54	0	0
Ward 55	8	2
Ward 56	2	0
Ward 57	0	0
Ward 58	0	0
Ward 59	0	10
Ward 60	0	5
Ward 61	0	0
TOTAL	85,339	145,152
WAUPACA COUNTY		
Bear Creek	175	211
Big Falls, vil.	23	20
Caledonia		
Wards 1 & 2	397	512
Clintonville, city		
Wards 1 – 7	1,067	878
Dayton		
Wards 1 – 4	720	829
Dupont		
Wards 1 & 2	145	159
Embarrass, vil.	70	95
Farmington		
Wards 1 – 6	992	1,027
Fremont	160	200
Fremont, vil.	162	247
Harrison	154	107
Helvetia		
Wards 1 & 2	193	258
Iola		
Wards 1 & 2	277	256
Iola, vil.		
Wards 1 – 5	357	281
Larrabee		
Wards 1 & 2	305	356
Lebanon		
Wards 1 & 2	412	375
Lind		
Wards 1 & 2	341	417
Little Wolf		
Wards 1 – 3	294	395
Manawa, city		
Wards 1 – 3	249	249
Marion, city		
Wards 1 – 3	259	276
Matteson	229	247
Mukwa		
Wards 1 & 4	355	248
Wards 2, 3 & 5	500	428
New London, city		
Wards 3, 4 & 8	447	349
Wards 5, 9 & 10	318	238

District	Barack Obama Joe Biden (Dem.)	John McCain Sarah Palin (Rep.)
Wards 6 & 7	435	250
Wards 11 & 12	351	154
Ogdensburg, vil.	47	40
Royalton		
Wards 1 – 3	362	484
St. Lawrence		
Wards 1 & 2	194	136
Scandinavia		
Wards 1 & 2	321	280
Scandinavia, vil.	117	80
Union	177	187
Waupaca		
Wards 1 & 2	288	348
Waupaca, city		
Wards 1 – 13	1,470	1,076
Weyauwega	110	170
Weyauwega,city		
Wards 1 – 3	402	309
Wyoming	77	60
TOTAL	12,952	12,232
WAUSHARA COUNTY		
Aurora	230	269
Berlin, city		
Ward 7	17	33
Bloomfield		
Wards 1 & 2	199	285
Coloma		
Wards 1 & 2	177	192
Coloma, vil.	114	96
Dakota		
Wards 1 – 3	212	297
Deerfield		
Wards 1 & 2	199	213
Hancock	141	126
Hancock, vil.	138	70
Leon		
Wards 1 – 3	380	410
Lohrville, vil.	123	77
Marion		
Wards 1 – 4	548	619
Mount Morris		
Wards 1 & 2	343	344
Oasis	118	152
Plainfield	123	129
Plainfield, vil.		
Wards 1 & 2	202	150
Poysippi	189	280
Redgranite, vil.		
Wards 1 & 2	282	142
Richford		
Wards 1 & 2	85	130
Rose	211	142
Saxeville		
Wards 1 & 2	286	271
Springwater		
Wards 1 – 3	438	381
Warren	167	147
Wautoma		
Wards 1 & 2	325	360
Wautoma, city		
Wards 1 – 4	389	316
Wild Rose, vil.		
Wards 1 & 2	232	139
TOTAL	5,868	5,770
WINNEBAGO COUNTY		
Algoma		
Wards 1 – 10 & 12	1,835	2,255
Appleton, city		
Ward 38	193	124
Ward 49	69	24
Black Wolf	0	2
Wards 1 – 3	710	890
Clayton		
Wards 1 – 4	965	1,256
Menasha		
Ward 1	494	449
Ward 2	958	924
Wards 3 & 4	609	460
Wards 5 & 6	840	952
Wards 7, 8, 10 & 13	1,212	877
Wards 9, 11 & 12	989	585
Menasha, city		
Wards 1 & 2	1,090	619
Wards 3, 4, 7, 12 & 13	1,273	701
Wards 5 & 6	1,236	582
Wards 8 – 10, 14 & 18	1,056	611
Neenah		
Wards 1 – 5	956	972

VOTE FOR PRESIDENT AND VICE PRESIDENT BY WARD
November 4, 2008 General Election–Continued

District	Barack Obama Joe Biden (Dem.)	John McCain Sarah Palin (Rep.)	District	Barack Obama Joe Biden (Dem.)	John McCain Sarah Palin (Rep.)
Neenah, city			Winneconne		
Wards 1 – 4	1,155	759	Wards 1 – 3	614	869
Wards 5 – 8	1,153	671	Winneconne, vil.		
Wards 9 – 12	1,195	1,179	Wards 1 – 4	597	772
Wards 13 – 16	1,318	942	Wolf River		
Wards 17 – 20	1,144	705	Wards 1 & 2	328	423
Wards 21 – 24	1,333	976	TOTAL	48,167	37,946
Wards 25, 26, 31 & 34	145	188	WOOD COUNTY		
Wards 27, 28, 33 & 35	44	33	Arpin		
Wards 29 & 32	1	0	Wards 1 – 3	236	202
Ward 30	0	0	Arpin, vil.	94	42
Nekimi			Auburndale	230	192
Wards 1 & 2	358	501	Auburndale, vil.	190	172
Nepeuskun	173	222	Biron, vil.	271	201
Omro			Cameron	134	146
Wards 1 – 3	583	689	Cary	108	128
Omro, city			Cranmoor	40	57
Wards 1 – 7	878	739	Dexter	128	74
Oshkosh			Grand Rapids		
Wards 1 – 6	687	866	Wards 1 – 13	2,381	2,105
Oshkosh, city			Hansen	187	205
Ward 1	557	449	Hewitt, vil.	246	203
Ward 2	758	519	Hiles	47	54
Ward 3	552	401	Lincoln		
Ward 4	361	245	Wards 1 & 2	461	439
Ward 5	85	68	Marshfield	228	190
Ward 6	65	53	Marshfield, city		
Ward 7	476	397	Wards 1 – 4, 10, 11, 13, 14, 20, 23 & 24	2,577	2,091
Ward 8	584	526	Wards 5 – 7, 15 – 17 & 27	1,644	1,195
Ward 9	484	273	Wards 8, 9, 12, 18, 19 & 25	1,088	697
Ward 10	772	343	Milladore	239	118
Ward 11	728	388	Milladore, vil.		
Ward 12	673	354	Ward 1	79	53
Ward 13	1,022	466	Nekoosa, city		
Ward 14	790	376	Ward 1	173	101
Ward 15	993	385	Ward 2	117	88
Ward 16	459	168	Wards 3 & 5	211	163
Ward 17	840	491	Wards 4 & 6	160	99
Ward 18	430	219	Pittsville, city		
Ward 19	614	275	Wards 1 – 3	231	199
Ward 20	644	314	Port Edwards		
Ward 21	369	231	Wards 1 – 3	403	279
Ward 22	678	339	Port Edwards, vil.		
Ward 23	517	445	Wards 1 – 3	524	453
Ward 24	670	497	Remington	66	67
Ward 25	317	226	Richfield		
Ward 26	642	504	Wards 1 & 2	414	360
Ward 27	626	395	Rock	237	224
Ward 28	659	733	Rudolph		
Ward 29	721	697	Wards 1 & 2	362	221
Ward 30	514	409	Rudolph, vil.	160	84
Ward 31	710	499	Saratoga		
Ward 32	872	454	Wards 1 – 6	1,551	1,103
Ward 33	618	525	Seneca		
Ward 34	4	5	Wards 1 – 3	345	289
Ward 35	46	41	Sherry	247	177
Ward 36	0	0	Sigel		
Ward 37	0	0	Wards 1 – 4	327	261
Ward 38	0	0	Vesper, vil.	137	147
Ward 39	0	0	Wisconsin Rapids, city		
Ward 40	0	0	Wards 1 – 3	699	391
Poygan			Wards 4 – 6	723	472
Wards 1 & 2	336	373	Wards 7 – 11	932	602
Rushford			Wards 12 – 15	1,330	888
Wards 1 & 2	384	440	Wards 16 – 20	758	586
Utica			Wards 21 – 23	752	555
Wards 1 & 2	334	435	Wood	243	208
Vinland			TOTAL	21,710	16,581
Wards 1 – 3	590	604			
Winchester					
Wards 1 & 2	482	567			

Note: Other presidential and vice presidential candidates received the following votes: Bob Barr and Wayne A. Root (Libertarian Party) – 8,858; Cynthia McKinney and Rosa Clemente (Wisconsin Green Party) – 4,216; Chuck Baldwin and Darrell L. Castle (Independent) – 5,072; Gloria LaRiva and Robert Moses (Independent) – 237; Brian Moore and Stewart A. Alexander (Independent) – 540; Ralph Nader and Matt Gonzalez (Independent) – 17,605; Jeffrey J. Wamboldt and David J. Klimisch (Independent) – 764.

All municipalities are towns, unless noted as a village (vil.) or city.

Source: Official records of the Government Accountability Board, Elections Division. Scattered votes omitted.

Wisconsin
State Symbols

11

Wisconsin state symbols: origin and descriptions of the official state symbols as specified by law

Closeup Image of Saturn Moon Phoebe by the Cassini Spacecraft

(NASA/JPL/Space Science Institute)

WISCONSIN STATE SYMBOLS

(See front and back endpapers)

Over the years, the Wisconsin Legislature has officially recognized a wide variety of state symbols. In order of adoption, Wisconsin has designated an official seal, coat of arms, motto, flag, song, flower, bird, tree, fish, state animal, wildlife animal, domestic animal, mineral, rock, symbol of peace, insect, soil, fossil, dog, beverage, grain, dance, ballad, waltz, fruit, and tartan. (The "Badger State" nickname, however, remains unofficial.) These symbols provide a focus for expanding public awareness of Wisconsin's history and diversity. They are listed and described in Section 1.10 of the Wisconsin Statutes.

The Coat of Arms   *The Great Seal*

Seal and coat of arms. Article XIII, Section 4, of the Wisconsin Constitution requires the legislature to provide a "great seal" to be used by the secretary of state to authenticate all of the governor's official acts except laws. The seal consists of the coat of arms, described below, with the words "Great Seal of the State of Wisconsin" centered above and a curved line of 13 stars, representing the 13 original United States, centered below, surrounded by an ornamental border. A modified "lesser seal" serves as the seal of the secretary of state.

The coat of arms is an integral part of the state seal and also appears on the state flag. It contains a sailor with a coil of rope and a "yeoman" (usually considered a miner) with a pick, who jointly represent labor on water and land. These two figures support a quartered shield with symbols for agriculture (plow), mining (pick and shovel), manufacturing (arm and hammer), and navigation (anchor). Centered on the shield is a small U.S. coat of arms and the U.S. motto, "E pluribus unum" ("out of many, one"), referring to the union of U.S. states, to symbolize Wisconsin's loyalty to the Union. At the base, a cornucopia, or horn of plenty, stands for prosperity and abundance, while a pyramid of 13 lead ingots represents mineral wealth and the 13 original United States. Centered over the shield is a badger, the state animal, and the state motto "Forward" appears on a banner above the badger.

The history of the seal is inextricably entwined with that of the coat of arms. An official seal was created in 1836, when Wisconsin became a territory, and was revised in 1839. When Wisconsin achieved statehood in 1848, a new seal was prepared. This seal was changed in 1851 at the instigation of Governor Nelson Dewey and slightly modified to its current design in 1881 when Dewey's seal wore out and had to be recast. (See "Motto" below.) Chapter 280, Laws of 1881, provided the first precise statutory description of the great seal and coat of arms.

Motto: "Forward". The motto, "Forward", was introduced in the 1851 revision of the state seal and coat of arms. Governor Dewey had asked University of Wisconsin Chancellor John H. Lathrop to design a new seal. It is alleged the motto was selected during a chance meeting between Governor Dewey and Edward Ryan (later chief justice of the Wisconsin Supreme

Court) when the governor went to New York City, carrying the Lathrop design to the engraver. Ryan objected to the Latin motto, "Excelsior", which Lathrop proposed. According to tradition, Dewey and Ryan sat down on the steps of a Wall Street bank, designed a new seal and chose "Forward" on the spot.

Flag. An official design for Wisconsin's state flag was initially provided by the legislature in 1863. Noting that a flag had not been adopted and that Civil War regiments in the field were requesting flags, the legislature formed a 5-member joint select committee to report "a description for a proper state flag." This action resulted in the adoption of 1863 Joint Resolution 4, which provided a design for a state flag that was substantially the same as the regimental flags already in use by Wisconsin troops.

It was not until 1913, however, that language concerning flag specifications was added to the Wisconsin Statutes. Chapter 111, Laws of 1913, created a state flag provision, specifying a dark blue flag with the state coat of arms centered on each side.

The 1913 design remained unchanged until the enactment of Chapter 286, Laws of 1979, which culminated years of legislative efforts to alter or replace Wisconsin's flag so it would be more distinctive and recognizable. The most significant changes made by the 1979 act were adding the word "Wisconsin" and the statehood date "1848" in white letters, centered respectively above and below the coat of arms.

Song: "On, Wisconsin!" The music for "On, Wisconsin!" was composed in 1909 by William T. Purdy with the idea of entering it in a contest for the creation of a new University of Minnesota football song. ("Minnesota" would have replaced "On, Wisconsin" in the opening lines.) Carl Beck persuaded Purdy to dedicate the song to the University of Wisconsin football team instead, and Beck collaborated with the composer by writing the lyrics. The song was introduced at the Madison campus in November 1909. It was later acclaimed by world-famous composer and bandmaster John Philip Sousa as the best college song he had ever heard.

Lyrics more in keeping with the purposes of a state song were subsequently written in 1913 by Judge Charles D. Rosa and J. S. Hubbard, editor of the *Beloit Free Press*. Rosa and Hubbard were among the delegates from many states convened in 1913 to commemorate the centennial of the Battle of Lake Erie. Inspired by the occasion, they provided new, more solemn words to the already well-known football song.

Although "On, Wisconsin!" was widely recognized as Wisconsin's song, the state did not officially adopt it until 1959. Representative Harold W. Clemens discovered that Wisconsin was one of only 10 states without an official song. He introduced a bill to give the song the status he thought it deserved. On discovering that many different lyrics existed, an official text for the first verse was incorporated in Chapter 170, Laws of 1959:

On, Wisconsin! On, Wisconsin! Grand old badger state!
We, thy loyal sons and daughters, Hail thee, good and great.
On, Wisconsin! On, Wisconsin! Champion of the right,
'Forward', our motto — God will give thee might!

Flower: wood violet *(Viola papilionacea).* In 1908, Wisconsin school children nominated four candidates for state flower: the violet, wild rose, trailing arbutus, and white water lily. On Arbor Day 1909, the final vote was taken, and the violet won. Chapter 218, Laws of 1949, named the wood violet Wisconsin's official flower.

Bird: robin *(Turdus migratorius).* In 1926-27, Wisconsin school children voted to select a state bird. The robin received twice as many votes as those given any other bird. Chapter 218, Laws of 1949, officially made the robin the state bird.

Tree: sugar maple *(Acer saccharum).* A favorite state tree was first selected by a vote of Wisconsin school children in 1893. The maple tree won, followed by oak, pine, and elm. Another vote was conducted in 1948 among school children by the Youth Centennial Committee. In that election, the sugar maple again received the most votes, followed by white pine and birch. The 1949 Legislature, in spite of efforts by white pine advocates, named the sugar maple the official state tree by enacting Chapter 218, Laws of 1949.

Fish: muskellunge *(Esox masquinongy).* Members of the legislature attempted to adopt the muskellunge as the state fish as early as 1939. The trout was a very distant alternative suggestion. In 1955, the legislature unanimously passed legislation which became Chapter 18, Laws of 1955, to designate the muskellunge as Wisconsin's official fish.

Animals: badger *(Taxidea taxus),* **white-tailed deer** *(Odocoileus virginianus),* **dairy cow** *(Bos taurus).* Although the *badger* has been closely associated with Wisconsin since territorial days, it was not declared the official state animal until 1957. Over the years, its likeness had been incorporated in the state coat of arms, the seal, the flag, and even State Capitol architecture, as well as being immortalized in the song, "On, Wisconsin!" ("Grand old badger state!"). "Bucky Badger" has long been the mascot of the UW-Madison. In 1957, a bill to establish the badger as state animal was introduced at the request of four Jefferson County elementary school students who discovered from a historical society publication that the badger had not been given the official status most people assumed. Serious opposition developed, however, when a faction from Wisconsin's northern counties introduced a bill to make the *white-tailed deer* the official animal, citing the state's large native deer population, the animal's physical attributes, and the considerable economic benefits derived from the annual deer hunt. The legislature reached a compromise by adding two official animals. In Chapter 209, Laws of 1957, it named the badger the "state animal", and Chapter 147 designated the white-tailed deer as the state "wildlife animal".

The *dairy cow* was added as Wisconsin's official "domestic animal" by Chapter 167, Laws of 1971, in recognition of the animal's many contributions to the state. This action was termed a logical and long overdue step, consistent with the state's promoting itself as *America's Dairyland,* the slogan placed on state automobile license plates by Chapter 115, Laws of 1939. 1972 Executive Order 32 designated Wisconsin's first official dairy cow, but the Secretary of the Department of Agriculture, Trade and Consumer Protection is now required to establish an annual rotation among Wisconsin's remaining purebreds. The Holstein was selected for 2009, followed by the Milking Shorthorn in 2010.

Badger nickname. History, rather than the law, explains Wisconsin's unofficial nickname as the "Badger State". During the lead-mining boom that began just prior to 1830 in southwestern Wisconsin, the name was first applied to miners who were too busy digging the "gray gold" to build houses. Like badgers, they moved into abandoned mine shafts and makeshift burrows for shelter. Although "badgers" had a somewhat derogatory connotation at first, it gradually gained acceptance as an apt description of the hardworking and energetic settlers of the Wisconsin Territory.

Mineral and rock: galena (lead sulphide) and **red granite.** Galena was made the official state mineral and red granite the state rock by Chapter 14, Laws of 1971. The proposal was introduced at the request of the Kenosha Gem and Mineral Society to promote geological awareness. Galena met the criteria for selection, as set by the Wisconsin Geological Society, including abundance, uniqueness, economic value, historical significance, and native nature. Red granite is an igneous rock composed of quartz and feldspar. It is mined in several sections of the state and was selected as the state rock because of its economic importance.

Symbol of peace: mourning dove *(Zenaidura macroura).* Various individuals and organizations concerned with conservation and wildlife long sought a protected status for the dove. Concluding an effort that stretched over a decade, the mourning dove was added as Wisconsin's official symbol of peace and removed from the statutory definition of game birds by Chapter 129, Laws of 1971. However, an increase in the mourning dove population led to its reinstatement as a game bird in 2001 and loss of its protected status.

Insect: honey bee *(Apis mellifera).* The honey bee was designated the official state insect by Chapter 326, Laws of 1977. The bill was introduced at the request of the third grade class of Holy Family School of Marinette and the Wisconsin Honey Producers Association. Attempts to allow all elementary school pupils in the state to decide the selection by popular ballot were unsuccessful. Other contenders for the title were the monarch butterfly, dragonfly, ladybug, and mosquito.

Soil: Antigo Silt Loam *(Typic glossoboralf).* An official state soil was created by 1983 Wisconsin Act 33 to remind Wisconsinites of their soil stewardship responsibilities. Advocates argued that soil, a natural resource that took 10,000 years to produce, is essential to Wisconsin's economy and is also the foundation of life. Selected to represent the more than 500 major soil types in Wisconsin, Antigo Silt Loam is a productive, level, silty soil of glacial origin, subsequently enriched by organic matter from prehistoric forests. The soil, named after a Wisconsin city, is found chiefly in Wisconsin and stretches in patches across the north central part of the state. It is a versatile soil that supports dairying, potato growing, and timber. The addition of the state soil was the result of a successful drive led by Professor Francis D. Hole, a UW-Madison soil scientist.

Fossil: trilobite *(Calymene celebra)*. The trilobite was designated the official state fossil by 1985 Wisconsin Act 162. Pronounced "TRY-loh-bite", the Latin term describes the 3-lobed anatomy of this small invertebrate body divided by furrows into segments. The trilobite is an extinct marine arthropod with multiple sets of paired, jointed legs. Its head and tapering body were armored in an exoskeleton that was repeatedly molted as the animal grew. Trilobites flourished in the warm, shallow saltwater sea that periodically covered Wisconsin territory hundreds of millions of years ago. Their fossil remains average 1 to 2 inches in length. The largest complete specimen is 14 inches, while incomplete parts indicate some were possibly much longer (over 30 inches). Trilobite fossils are abundant and distinctive enough to be easily recognized. Good specimens are preserved in rock formations throughout most of Wisconsin.

The Wisconsin Geological Society proposed the fossil to symbolize Wisconsin's ancient past and encourage interest in the state's rich geological heritage. A major rival for recognition as state fossil was the mastodon, a large prehistoric, elephant-like creature.

Dog: American water spaniel. The American water spaniel was named Wisconsin's official state dog by 1985 Wisconsin Act 295. Enactment of the law was the culmination of years of effort by eighth grade students of Lyle Brumm at Washington Junior High School in New London. The American water spaniel is said to be one of only five dog breeds indigenous to the United States and the only one native to Wisconsin. A New London area physician, Dr. Fred J. Pfeifer, is generally credited with developing and standardizing the breed and working to secure United Kennel Club registration for it in 1920. American Kennel Club recognition followed in 1940. The American water spaniel was developed as a practical, versatile hunting dog that combined certain physical attributes with intelligence and a good disposition. No flashy show animal, the American water spaniel is described as an unadorned, utilitarian dog that earns its keep as an outstanding hunter, watchdog, and family pet.

Beverage: milk. The Wisconsin Legislature designated milk as the official state beverage by 1987 Wisconsin Act 279. This action recognized Wisconsin's position as the nation's leading milk-producing state and the contribution of milk to the state's economy. The World Dairy Expo and various Wisconsin dairy production and dairy cattle associations supported the legislation.

Grain: corn *(Zea mays)*. Corn was designated the official state grain by 1989 Wisconsin Act 162. During legislative debate, sponsors claimed designating corn as the state grain would draw attention to its importance as a cash crop in Wisconsin and make people more aware of corn's many uses, including livestock feed, sweeteners, ethanol fuel, and biodegradable plastics.

Dance: polka. The polka was designated the state dance by 1993 Wisconsin Act 411. The legislation was introduced at the request of a second grade class from Charles Lindbergh Elementary School in Madison and supported by several groups, including the Wisconsin Polka Boosters, Inc., and the Wisconsin Folk Museum. Supporters documented the polka heritage of Wisconsin and provided evidence that the polka is deeply ingrained in Wisconsin cultural traditions.

Ballad: "Oh Wisconsin, Land of My Dreams". "Oh Wisconsin, Land of My Dreams" was designated the Wisconsin state ballad by 2001 Wisconsin Act 16. The ballad was the work of Shari Sarazin of Mauston, who set to music a poem written in the 1920s by her grandmother, Erma Barrett of Juneau County. The words to this ballad are:

Oh Wisconsin, land of beauty, with your hillsides and your plains, with your jackpine and your birch tree, and your oak of mighty frame.

Land of rivers, lakes and valleys, land of warmth and winter snows, land of birds and beasts and humanity, Oh Wisconsin, I love you so.

Oh Wisconsin, land of my dreams. Oh Wisconsin, you're all I'll ever need. A little heaven here on earth could you be? Oh Wisconsin, land of my dreams.

In the summer, golden grain fields; in the winter, drift of white snow; in the springtime, robins singing; in the autumn, flaming colors show.

Oh I wonder who could wander, or who could want to drift for long, away from all your beauty, all your sunshine, all your sweet song?

Oh Wisconsin, land of my dreams. Oh Wisconsin, you're all I'll ever need. A little heaven here on earth could you be? Oh Wisconsin, land of my dreams.

Oh Wisconsin, land of my dreams. And when it's time, let my spirit run free in Wisconsin, land of my dreams.

Waltz: "The Wisconsin Waltz". "The Wisconsin Waltz" was designated the state waltz by 2001 Wisconsin Act 16. The music and lyrics were written by Eddie Hansen, a Waupaca native and one-time theater organist. The words to this waltz are:

Music from heaven throughout the years; the beautiful Wisconsin Waltz.

Favorite song of the pioneers; the beautiful Wisconsin Waltz.

Song of my heart on that last final day, when it is time to lay me away. One thing I ask is to let them play the beautiful Wisconsin Waltz.

My sweetheart, my complete heart, it's for you when we dance together; the beautiful Wisconsin Waltz.

I remember that September, before love turned into an ember, we danced to the Wisconsin Waltz.

Summer ended, we intended that our lives then would both be blended, but somehow our planning got lost.

Memory now sings a dream song, a faded love theme song; the beautiful Wisconsin Waltz.

Fruit: cranberry *(vaccinium macrocarpon)*. The cranberry was designated the state fruit by 2003 Wisconsin Act 174. The legislation was the culmination of a class project by fifth grade students from Trevor Grade School in Kenosha County, who decided that the cranberry, rather than the cherry, was the best candidate for Wisconsin's state fruit. Wisconsin leads the nation in cranberry production, accounting for over half of the nation's output. Cranberries are grown in 20 of Wisconsin's 72 counties, primarily in the central part of the state.

Tartan. The newest state symbol is the state tartan, created by 2007 Wisconsin Act 217. Legislation was introduced at the request of Saint Andrew's Society of Milwaukee, which had formed a committee to recommend an appropriate design. The design selected was chosen to reflect the diversity and uniqueness of the state. Historically, tartans served to identify Scottish highland clans and families.

Wisconsin's tartan is a hunting tartan with a blue green background and multiple stripes of various colors. The color scheme reflects the tartans of many notable Wisconsin families of Scottish ancestry and the natural resources and industries of Wisconsin. The color brown represents the fur trade; grey represents lead mining; green represents the lumber industry; blue reflects the two Great Lakes bordering Wisconsin, commercial and recreational fishing, and the resort industry; yellow signifies the dairy and brewing industries; red represents the University of Wisconsin System; and, where yellow and green stripes intersect, it represents Wisconsin's professional sports teams, exemplified by the Green Bay Packers.

Alphabetical
Index

12

M45: The Pleiades Star Cluster

(Robert Gendler)

ALPHABETICAL INDEX

M

T

Honey Bee

STATE INSECT

Antigo Silt Loam

STATE SOIL

Red Granite

STATE ROCK

Galena

STATE MINERAL

Trilobite

STATE FOSSIL

American Water Spaniel

STATE DOG

Cranberry

STATE FRUIT